International *Directory of*
COMPANY
HISTORIES

INTERNATIONAL DIRECTORY OF COMPANY HISTORIES

International Directory of

COMPANY HISTORIES

VOLUME V

Editor-in-Chief
Adele Hast

Editors
Diane B. Pascal (Chicago)

Philippe A. Barbour (London)
Jessica Griffin (London)

StJ

St James Press

Detroit and London

Copyright © 1992 by St. James Press
835 Penobscot Building
Detroit, MI 48226

2-6 Boundary Row
London SE1 8HP
England

Library of Congress Catalog Number: 89-190943

British Library Cataloguing in Publication Data

International directory of company histories. Vol. 5
I. Hast, Adele
338.7409

ISBN 1-55862-061-3

Printed in the United States of America
Published simultaneously in the United Kingdom

Cover photograph of the Midwest Stock Exchange courtesy of the Midwest Stock Exchange, Chicago.

INDUSTRIES COVERED IN THE DIRECTORY

CONTENTS _____

PREFACE

The *International Directory of Company Histories* provides detailed information on the development of the world's largest and most influential companies. To date, the *Directory* covers approximately 1,200 companies in five volumes.

Inclusion Criteria

Most companies chosen for inclusion in the *Directory* have achieved a minimum of two billion U.S. dollars in annual sales. Some smaller companies are included if they are leading influences in their respective industries or geographical locations. State-owned companies that are important in their industries and that may operate much like public or private companies also are included. Wholly owned subsidiaries of other companies are entries if they meet the requirements for inclusion, provided they were independent within the past five years or are still highly visible and important in their respective industries.

St. James Press does not endorse any of the companies or products mentioned in this book. Companies that appear in the *Directory* were selected without reference to their wishes and have in no way endorsed their entries. The companies were given the opportunity to read their entries for factual inaccuracies, and we are indebted to many of them for their comments and corrections. We thank them for allowing the use of their logos for identification purposes.

Entry Format

Each entry begins with a company's legal name, the address of its headquarters, its telephone number and fax number, and a statement of public, private, or state ownership. A company with a legal name in both English and the language of its headquarters country is listed by the English name, with the native-language name in parentheses.

Also provided are the company's earliest incorporation date, the number of employees, and the most recent sales or assets figures available, for fiscal year 1990 or 1991 unless otherwise noted. Sales figures are given in local currencies with equivalents in U.S. dollars at the exchange rate on December 31, 1991, the last trading day of the year. For some private companies, sales figures are estimates. Finally, the entry lists the cities where a company's stock is traded. Throughout the *Directory* spelling is according to American style, and the word "billion" is used in its American sense of a thousand million.

Sources

The histories were compiled from publicly accessible sources such as magazines, general and academic periodicals, books, and annual reports, as well as from material supplied by the companies themselves. The *Directory* is intended for reference use and research, for students, business people, librarians, historians, economists, investors, job candidates, and others who want to learn more about the historical development of the world's most important companies.

Acknowledgments

St. James Press would like to thank the staffs of the following institutions for their courteous assistance and invaluable guidance: in Chicago, The Chicago Public Library, the University of Chicago Library, the Paul V. Galvin Library at the Illinois Institute of Technology, The Newberry Library, the Japan Information Service, and the Japan External Trade Organization; Northwestern University Library in Evanston, Illinois; and in London, The British Library, Business Archives Council, The City Business Library, The Financial Times Editorial Library, The London School of Economics and Political Science Business History Unit, and Westminster Reference Library.

The editors wish to thank the advisers, whose counsel assisted us in the organization of industries and the selection of companies. In particular, we would like to thank John Dawson, Professor of Marketing, University of Edinburgh; James Jefferys, formerly General Secretary of the International Association of Department Stores, Paris; and Stephen Kromer of the Anglo-Japanese Economic Institute, London, for their advice. In addition, we thank Jackie Griffin, Trudy Ring, and Naomi S. Suloway for their editorial assistance.

ADVISERS AND CONTRIBUTORS

Linda Anderson
Kenji Arima
Claire Badarraco
William Baranès
Philippe A. Barbour
T. C. Barker
Ingrid Bauert-Keetman
Elaine Belsito
Bernard A. Block
Martin Bloom
Michael Robert Bonavia
Jim Bowman
Richard Brass
Asa Briggs
Beate Brüninghaus
Berthold Busch
Noel Peter Byde
Cristina Caffarra
Alfred D. Chandler, Jr.
Ron Chepesiuk
Tomohei Chida
Alison Classe
Olive Classe
D. C. Coleman
Lisa Collins
Gerald W. Crompton
Martin James Daunton
Clare Doran
Marc Du Ry
Sina Dubovoj
Michael John French
Konrad Fuchs
Anne-Laure Gaudillat
Steven P. Gietschier
Lois Glass
Francis Goodall
Rowland G. Gould

Jessica Griffin
Daniel Gross
William R. Grossman
Judith Gurney
Richard Hawkins
Charles C. Hay III
Carole Healy
Patrick Heenan
Caroline Hinton
Theo Horstmann
Robert R. Jacobson
James B. Jefferys
Debra Johnson
Lynn M. Kalanik
Carol I. Keeley
Patrick Keeley
Julian James Kinsley
Stephen Christopher Kremer
Monique Lamontagne
Roy Larke
Joseph V. Leunis
Scott M. Lewis
Wilson B. Lindauer
Jonathan Lloyd-Owen
Andreas Loizou
Rachel Loos
Catriona Luke
Susan Mackervoy
Kim M. Magon
Jonathan Martin
Mary Sue Mohnke
Alejandro Molla Descals
Bruce P. Montgomery
Betty T. Moore
Eva Moser
Kota Nagashima
Frances E. Norton

D. H. O'Leary
John Parry
Florence Protat
Trudy Ring
Lionel Alexander Ritchie
Julia Roberts
Mark Roseman
Roger W. Rouland
Elizabeth Rourke
Maya Sahafi
Norimasa Satoh
Sandy Schusteff
Timothy J. Shannon
Clark Siewert
Eric Milton Sigsworth
Judy Slinn
Donald R. Stabile
Paul Stevens
Douglas Sun
John Swan
Mary F. Sworsky
Dylan Tanner
Mariko Tatsuki
Susan Telingator
Yoko Togawa
Thomas M. Tucker
Bruce Vernyi
Lynn M. Voskuil
Ray Walsh
Jordan Wankoff
Gillian Wolf
Angela Woodward
William D. Wray
Hiroaki Yamazaki
Tsunehiko Yui
Takeshi Yuzawa
Stephanie Zarach

A.B.	Aktiebolaget (Sweden)
A.G.	Aktiengesellschaft (Germany, Switzerland)
A.S.	Atieselskab (Denmark)
A.S.	Aksjeselskap (Denmark, Norway)
A.Ş.	Anonim Şirket (Turkey)
B.V.	Besloten Vennootschap met beperkte, Aansprakelijkheid (The Netherlands)
Co.	Company (United Kingdom, United States)
Corp.	Corporation (United States)
G.I.E.	Groupement d'Intérêt Economique (France)
GmbH	Gesellschaft mit beschränkter Haftung (Germany)
H.B.	Handelsbolaget (Sweden)
Inc.	Incorporated (United States)
KGaA	Kommanditgesellschaft auf Aktien (Germany)
K.K.	Kabushiki Kaisha (Japan)
LLC	Limited Liability Company (Middle East)
Ltd.	Limited (Canada, Japan, United Kingdom, United States)
N.V.	Naamloze Vennootschap (The Netherlands)
OY	Osakeyhtiöt (Finland)
PLC	Public Limited Company (United Kingdom)
PTY.	Proprietary (Australia, Hong Kong, South Africa)
S.A.	Société Anonyme (Belgium, France, Switzerland)
SpA	Società per Azioni (Italy)

DA	Algerian dinar	LuxFr	Luxembourgian franc
A$	Australian dollar	M$	Malaysian ringgit
Sch	Austrian shilling	Dfl	Netherlands florin
BFr	Belgian franc	NZ$	New Zealand dollar
Cr	Brazilian cruzado	N	Nigerian naira
C$	Canadian dollar	NKr	Norwegian krone
DKr	Danish krone	RO	Omani rial
E£	Egyptian pound	Esc	Portuguese escudo
Fmk	Finnish markka	R	South African rand
FFr	French frac	Pta	Spanish peseta
DM	German mark	SKr	Swedish krona
HK$	Hong Kong dollar	SFr	Swiss franc
Rs	Indian rupee	NT$	Taiwanese dollar
IR£	Irish pound	TL	Turkish lira
L	Italian lira	£	United Kingdom pound
¥	Japanese yen	$	United States dollar
W	Korean won	B	Venezuelan bolivar
KD	Kuwaiti dinar	K	Zambian kwacha

International Directory of
COMPANY
HISTORIES

RETAIL & WHOLESALE

Au Printemps S.A.
Belk Stores Services, Inc.
Bergen Brunswig Corporation
The Boots Company PLC
The Burton Group plc
C&A Brenninkmeyer KG
Campeau Corporation
Carter Hawley Hale Stores, Inc.
Coles Myer Ltd.
Costco Wholesale Corporation
Cotter & Company
The Daiei, Inc.
The Daimaru, Inc.
Dayton Hudson Corporation
Dillard Department Stores, Inc.
Dixons Group plc
El Corte Inglés Group
Fred Meyer, Inc.
Galeries Lafayette S.A.
The Gap, Inc.
GIB Group
The Great Universal Stores P.L.C.
Hankyu Department Stores, Inc.
Hertie Waren- und Kaufhaus GmbH
The Home Depot, Inc.
Home Shopping Network, Inc.
Hudson's Bay Company
The IKEA Group
Isetan Company Limited
Ito-Yokado Co., Ltd.
J.C. Penney Company, Inc.
John Lewis Partnership plc
Jusco Co., Ltd.
Karstadt Aktiengesellschaft
Kaufhof Holding AG
Kingfisher plc
Kmart Corporation
Kotobukiya Co., Ltd.
The Limited, Inc.
The Littlewoods Organisation PLC
Longs Drug Stores Corporation
Lowe's Companies, Inc.
Marks and Spencer p.l.c.
Marui Co., Ltd.
Matsuzakaya Company Limited
The May Department Stores Company

Melville Corporation
Mercantile Stores Company, Inc.
Mitsukoshi Ltd.
Montgomery Ward & Co., Incorporated
Nagasakiya Co., Ltd.
National Intergroup, Inc.
Nichii Co., Ltd.
Nordstrom, Inc.
Otto-Versand (GmbH & Co.)
The Price Company
Quelle Group
R.H. Macy & Co., Inc.
Revco D.S., Inc.
Rite Aid Corporation
Sears plc
Sears, Roebuck and Co.
Seibu Department Stores, Ltd.
The Seiyu, Ltd.
Service Merchandise Company, Inc.
Takashimaya Co., Limited
The TJX Companies, Inc.
Tokyu Department Store Co., Ltd.
Toys "R" Us, Inc.
The United States Shoe Corporation
Uny Co., Ltd.
W H Smith Group PLC
W.W. Grainger, Inc.
Wal-Mart Stores, Inc.
Walgreen Co.
Wickes Companies, Inc.
Woolworth Corporation

RUBBER & TIRE

The BFGoodrich Company
Bridgestone Corporation
Compagnie Générale des Établissements Michelin
Continental Aktiengesellschaft
The Goodyear Tire & Rubber Company
Pirelli S.p.A.
Sumitomo Rubber Industries, Ltd.
The Yokohama Rubber Co., Ltd.

TELECOMMUNICATIONS

American Telephone and Telegraph Company
Ameritech
BCE Inc.

Bell Atlantic Corporation
BellSouth Corporation
British Telecommunications plc
Cable and Wireless plc
Deutsche Bundespost TELEKOM
France Télécom Group
GTE Corporation
Koninklijke PTT Nederland NV
MCI Communications Corporation
Nippon Telegraph and Telephone Corporation
Northern Telecom Limited
NYNEX Corporation
Österreichische Post-und Telegraphenverwaltung
Pacific Telesis Group
Schweizerische Post-, Telefon-und
    Telegrafen-Betriebe
Società Finanziaria Telefonica per Azioni
Southwestern Bell Corporation
Swedish Telecom
Telefonaktiebolaget LM Ericsson
Telefónica de España, S.A.
U S West, Inc.
United Telecommunications, Inc.

TEXTILES & APPAREL

Brown Group, Inc.
Burlington Industries, Inc.
Coats Viyella Plc
Courtaulds plc
Levi Strauss & Co.
Milliken & Co.
Mitsubishi Rayon Co., Ltd.
Nike, Inc.
Reebok International Ltd.
Springs Industries, Inc.
Teijin Limited
Toray Industries, Inc.
Unitika Ltd.
VF Corporation

TOBACCO

American Brands, Inc.
Gallaher Limited
Imasco Limited
Japan Tobacco Incorporated
Philip Morris Companies Inc.

RJR Nabisco Holdings Corp.
Rothmans International p.l.c.
Tabacalera, S.A.
Universal Corporation

TRANSPORT SERVICES

British Railways Board
Burlington Northern Inc.
Canadian Pacific Limited
Consolidated Freightways, Inc.
Consolidated Rail Corporation
CSX Corporation
Danzas Group
Deutsche Bundesbahn
East Japan Railway Company
Federal Express Corporation
Hankyu Corporation
Kawasaki Kisen Kaisha, Ltd.
Keio Teito Electric Railway Company
Kinki Nippon Railway Company Ltd.
Kühne & Nagel International AG
La Poste
Mitsui O.S.K. Lines, Ltd.
Nippon Express Co., Ltd.
Nippon Yusen Kabushiki Kaisha
Norfolk Southern Corporation
Odakyu Electric Railway Company Limited
The Peninsular and Oriental Steam Navigation
    Company
Penske Corporation
PHH Corporation
Post Office Group
Roadway Services, Inc.
Ryder System, Inc.
Santa Fe Pacific Corporation
Seibu Railway Co. Ltd.
Société Nationale des Chemins de Fer Français
Southern Pacific Transportation Company
The Swiss Federal Railways (Schweizerische
    Bundesbahnen)
TNT Limited
Tokyu Corporation
Union Pacific Corporation
United Parcel Service of America Inc.
Yamato Transport Co. Ltd.
Yellow Freight System, Inc. of Delaware

UTILITIES

Allegheny Power System, Inc.
American Electric Power Company, Inc.
Arkla, Inc.
Baltimore Gas and Electric Company
Bayernwerk AG
British Gas plc
Carolina Power & Light Company
Centerior Energy Corporation
Central and South West Corporation
Chubu Electric Power Company, Incorporated
Chugoku Electric Power Company Inc.
CMS Energy Corporation
The Columbia Gas System, Inc.
Commonwealth Edison Company
Consolidated Edison Company of New York, Inc.
Consolidated Natural Gas Company
The Detroit Edison Company
Dominion Resources, Inc.
Duke Power Company
Electricité de France
ENDESA Group
Enron Corp.
Enserch Corporation
Ente Nazionale per L'Energia Elettrica
Entergy Corporation
Florida Progress Corporation
FPL Group, Inc.
Gaz de France
General Public Utilities Corporation
Générale des Eaux Group
Hokkaido Electric Power Company Inc.
Hokuriku Electric Power Company
Houston Industries Incorporated
The Kansai Electric Power Co., Inc.
Kyushu Electric Power Company Inc.

Long Island Lighting Company
Lyonnaise des Eaux-Dumez
N.V. Nederlandse Gasunie
New England Electric System
Niagara Mohawk Power Corporation
Northeast Utilities
Northern States Power Company
Nova Corporation of Alberta
Ohio Edison Company
Osaka Gas Co., Ltd.
Pacific Enterprises
Pacific Gas and Electric Company
PacifiCorp
Panhandle Eastern Corporation
Pennsylvania Power & Light Company
Philadelphia Electric Company
PreussenElektra Aktiengesellschaft
Public Service Enterprise Group Incorporated
Ruhrgas AG
RWE Group
San Diego Gas & Electric Company
SCEcorp
Shikoku Electric Power Company, Inc.
The Southern Company
Texas Utilities Company
Tohoku Electric Power Company, Inc.
The Tokyo Electric Power Company, Incorporated
Tokyo Gas Co., Ltd.
TransCanada PipeLines Limited
Transco Energy Company
Union Electric Company
Vereinigte Elektrizitätswerke Westfalen AG

WASTE SERVICES

Browning-Ferris Industries, Inc.
Waste Management, Inc.

RETAIL & WHOLESALE

Au Printemps S.A.
Belk Stores Services, Inc.
Bergen Brunswig Corporation
The Boots Company PLC
The Burton Group plc
C&A Brenninkmeyer KG
Campeau Corporation
Carter Hawley Hale Stores, Inc.
Coles Myer Ltd.
Costco Wholesale Corporation
Cotter & Company
The Daiei, Inc.
The Daimaru, Inc.
Dayton Hudson Corporation
Dillard Department Stores, Inc.
Dixons Group plc
El Corte Inglés Group
Fred Meyer, Inc.
Galeries Lafayette S.A.
The Gap, Inc.
GIB Group
The Great Universal Stores P.L.C.
Hankyu Department Stores, Inc.
Hertie Waren- und Kaufhaus GmbH
The Home Depot, Inc.
Home Shopping Network, Inc.
Hudson's Bay Company
The IKEA Group
Isetan Company Limited
Ito-Yokado Co., Ltd.
J.C. Penney Company, Inc.
John Lewis Partnership plc
Jusco Co., Ltd.
Karstadt Aktiengesellschaft
Kaufhof Holding AG
Kingfisher plc
Kmart Corporation
Kotobukiya Co., Ltd.
The Limited, Inc.

The Littlewoods Organisation PLC
Longs Drug Stores Corporation
Lowe's Companies, Inc.
Marks and Spencer p.l.c.
Marui Co., Ltd.
Matsuzakaya Company Limited
The May Department Stores Company
Melville Corporation
Mercantile Stores Company, Inc.
Mitsukoshi Ltd.
Montgomery Ward & Co., Incorporated
Nagasakiya Co., Ltd.
National Intergroup, Inc.
Nichii Co., Ltd.
Nordstrom, Inc.
Otto-Versand (GmbH & Co.)
The Price Company
Quelle Group
R.H. Macy & Co., Inc.
Revco D.S., Inc.
Rite Aid Corporation
Sears plc
Sears, Roebuck and Co.
Seibu Department Stores, Ltd.
The Seiyu, Ltd.
Service Merchandise Company, Inc.
Takashimaya Co., Limited
The TJX Companies, Inc.
Tokyu Department Store Co., Ltd.
Toys "R" Us, Inc.
The United States Shoe Corporation
Uny Co., Ltd.
W H Smith Group PLC
W.W. Grainger, Inc.
Wal-Mart Stores, Inc.
Walgreen Co.
Wickes Companies, Inc.
Woolworth Corporation

AU PRINTEMPS S.A.

102, rue de Provençe
75451 Paris
Cedex 09
France
(1) 42 82 40 00
Fax: (1) 42 82 49 81

Public Company
Incorporated: 1972
Employees: 29,000
Sales: FFr29.40 billion (US$5.67 billion)
Stock Exchange: Paris

Au Printemps S.A. is a diversified retailer with operations ranging from department stores to variety stores, from specialty chain stores to mail order and a wholesaling business. Through its subsidiaries and affiliates, the group has retail operations in nearly 20 countries as well as in France.

In 1865, 31-year-old Jules Jaluzot, who had been a department head at Bon Marché, France's oldest department store, opened Au Printemps, a small store on the corner of boulevard Haussmann and rue du Havre in Paris. The store consisted of a basement for stock, a ground floor, and the mezzanine of a residential building, some 200 square meters in all. Au Printemps was a rapid success and Jaluzot purchased the upper floors of the building. By 1870 the staff had grown from 30 to 250. The acquisition of adjacent buildings followed, and the store soon occupied a whole block on boulevard Haussmann, between rue du Havre and rue Caumartin. As its reputation grew, Jaluzot began mail-order operations in France and other European countries, with catalogs in different languages.

In 1881 a fire destroyed two-thirds of the somewhat ramshackle store, which by then employed more than 700 people. Jaluzot decided to rebuild immediately, turning the business into a *société en commandite par actions*—limited partnership—called Jaluzot & Cie. This form of company was common in France at the time, consisting of a managing partner—or partners—and shareholders who played no part in the management of the business. The managing partner, appointed for life, named his co-partners and successors and was guaranteed a fixed percentage of the profits—in this case 18%. He was also entirely responsible for any debts incurred by the company. Jules Jaluzot provided about 35% of the capital of the new company, and the shareholders provided the rest. In 1882 the new department store was opened. It occupied a

ground area of 2,900 square meters and had six floors, occupying the entire area between rue de Provençe and rue Caumartin. Further commercial success followed, but Jaluzot, a Member of Parliament for his native Nièvre and a prominent figure in Paris society, became involved in financial speculation of various sorts. In 1905 he speculated in sugar, using his own money and also in the name of and with capital from Au Printemps (Printemps), but this venture failed and he had to resign. His initials, JJ, can still be seen in the ceramic tiles on the facade of his 1882 store. His place as managing partner was taken by Gustave Laguionie, who had worked alongside Jaluzot at Au Printemps from 1867 to 1882, before leaving to become director of a wholesale business in piece goods. In 1907 Laguionie, then age 64, named his 23-year-old son Pierre as joint managing partner, and in the same year the foundation stone was laid for an adjacent store between rue Caumartin and rue Charras. The new building was opened in 1910. It was larger than the first store, occupying six floors, with a ground floor of 5,000 square meters.

Gustave Laguionie died in 1920, leaving the business under the control of his son Pierre, alongside Alcide Poulet, named partner in 1920. In 1921 there was another disaster when the 1910 store partially burned down; rebuilding began immediately and the store was reopened in 1924. Adjacent buildings were acquired in rue du Havre and used for mail-order operations—then about 20% of total sales—and small stores were purchased in Le Havre, Rouen, and Lille in 1928 and 1929. Furthermore, some independent retailers became affiliated with Printemps for the purchase of merchandise. More important were the changes in management methods. Between 1926 and 1930 a number of innovations were introduced. Advertising and sales promotion formed an integral part of the selling activities of the firm which adopted a strict budget. A house magazine was started in addition to training and research departments. In 1929 the functions of buying and selling were separated instead of being the responsibility of a single department head, and a separate buying company, the Société Parisienne d'Achats en Commun (SAPAC), was founded. In 1930 a system of budgetary control was introduced, by which each major activity had a planned budget of expenditure and results. In 1928 Pierre Laguionie became a founding member of the International Association of Department Stores, a society for management research.

The year 1931 saw Printemps involved in an entirely new form of retailing, the limited-price variety store. In that year the first Prisunic store opened in Paris, operated by Prisunic SA, a wholly controlled subsidiary. A central buying company, SAPAC-Prisunic, was created in 1932, and by 1935 there were eight Prisunic stores in operation, four in Paris and four in the provinces, with another 30 stores operated by retailers affiliated with SAPAC. In 1932 one of the first groups to become a Prisunic affiliate was Maus Frères of Geneva, which opened Prisunic stores in eastern France with French associates, including Pierre Lévy, the textile manufacturer. In 1936, however, a law was passed forbidding companies to open further one-price stores. This virtually brought to an end the expansion of Prisunic through new stores, but progress was made with affiliated stores, as in most cases these were establishments that did not necessarily carry the Prisunic name.

At the outbreak of World War II the Printemps group consisted of the Paris store and seven stores elsewhere in France, plus 20 stores affiliated with the SAPAC buying organization. The Prisunic division had 10 stores of its own and 60 affiliated stores, which employed about 5,500 workers. The group was still a limited partnership, and after the death of Alcide Poulet in 1928, Pierre Laguionie appointed his two brothers-in-law, Georges Marindaz—who died in 1931—and Charles Vignéras, as co-partners. Both were married to daughters of Gustave Laguionie.

The war, the German occupation, and the postwar shortages of merchandise meant a period of survival rather than of growth. But with the economic recovery starting in the early 1950s expansion again gathered pace, in two overlapping phases. The first was vigorous growth of the Prisunic variety store chain from 1950 to 1965. The number of Prisunic stores owned by the group rose from 13 in 1950 to more than 80 in 1965, and in the same period the number of affiliated stores rose from 80 to more than 230. Affiliated stores were a very effective way of earning commission on sales and increasing the purchasing power of the central buying organization with virtually no investment in land, buildings, or stock. Furthermore, it was no secret that, for the Printemps group, the Prisunic operation was extremely profitable and provided capital for the subsequent growth of the department store division.

Starting in 1954, the buildings of the Paris department store were completely transformed. While the facades were untouched, the interiors were changed beyond recognition. All nonselling activities were transferred to the outskirts of the city, the enormous lightwells were filled in to provide selling space, the buildings on the north side of rue du Havre became the large Brummell menswear and sporting goods store, new banks of escalators were installed, and in 1963 two additional sales floors were built on top of the 1882 building. Selling space in these units was increased from 32,000 square meters in 1950 to 45,000 in 1970. Apart from the main store, heavy investments were made in rebuilding, enlarging, and modernizing seven provincial stores between 1956 and 1964. In the latter years a completely new store was built in Paris at the Nation, and in 1969 the Printemps opened its first store in the Parly-2 regional shopping center near Paris.

The various activities of the group during these years were mostly handled by separate limited partnerships, which by the early 1970s numbered more than 120, including 50 separate Prisunic companies. This structure was adopted partly because the managing partners did not want to risk their personal wealth in other activities but also because of the effects of the La Patente tax, which, until it was reformed, increased in proportion to the number of people employed by each company. The slowing of Prisunic's profitable expansion from 1965 onward and the heavy capital expenditure by the department store division, which did not lead to immediate returns, led shareholders and the managing partners to realize that the limited partnership system was no longer an effective way of running a diversified business employing more than 13,000 people. Furthermore, Pierre Laguionie was by this time 87 years old and wanted to retire from active management. In 1971 the managing partners, Pierre Laguionie and his nephew Jean Vignéras, son of Charles Vignéras, who had died in 1970, agreed with the share-holders to consolidate the partnerships into a limited company, or *société anonyme*.

The process was not a simple one. Capital had to be found for the managing partners, and some interested parties were more concerned with the group's real estate value than its commercial activities. Eventually an agreement was reached with the Swiss retail group Maus-Nordmann of Geneva. Maus-Nordmann, a private family company, operated a chain of more than 60 department stores in Switzerland and owned a store chain, P.A. Bergner, in the United States. They were also familiar with the French retail industry since they had important shareholdings in the department store groups Nouvelles Galeries Réunies (SFNGR) and Bazar de l'Hotel de Ville (BHV). Perhaps most important, the Maus group had become an affiliate of Prisunic as early as 1932. By 1970 its company, Société Alsacienne de Magasins SA (SAMAG), had 45 affiliated Prisunic stores in eastern France. In a series of complicated transactions that involved the transfer of the assets of SAMAG to Printemps, the withdrawal of Maus-Nordmann from its holdings in SFNGR and BHV, and the compensation of the managing partners, a new company—Au Printemps S.A.—came into being in 1972. The Maus-Nordmann group owned 34% of the share capital, a figure that increased to 42.7% 20 years later, while the next largest shareholder held 6%. Pierre Laguionie was made honorary president, and Jean Vignéras continued for a while as president director general. But Laguionie died in 1978, and Vignéras withdrew in the same year, thus ending some 70 years of control and management by the Laguionie family.

The first five years of the new company were not easy. The French economy was in recession following the oil crisis, the profits of the company fell, and the new management was faced with commitments that had been entered into by the previous management, such as opening new stores in shopping centers in the Paris area. These included stores in Vélizy, opened in 1972; Créteil, opened in 1974; and Galaxie in Paris, opened in 1976, but they were not very profitable. Eventually the Créteil store was closed, and a contract to open a store in the Défense shopping center was canceled.

The Prisunic variety store division, while profitable, was no longer expanding. Competition from hypermarkets—combined grocery and general merchandise stores—and specialty shops had reduced the general appeal of variety stores, and emphasis was placed on the development of supermarkets and increasing food sales in the downtown locations of most of the stores. As a result of the stagnation of the variety stores, an attempt was made to develop the Escale chain of hypermarkets. The first of these opened in 1969, and by 1972 there were five in operation. Printemps realized that it did not have the expertise to start up a new hypermarket chain, and by 1976 its Escale stores had been transferred to the established Euromarché group of hypermarkets, with Printemps acquiring a 26% share in Euromarché SA.

The years from 1977, however, were to see the beginning of a transformation in the activities of the Printemps group that was possibly more important than the opening of the Prisunic variety stores in the 1930s. Responsible for this change were Jean-Jacques Delort, who was appointed managing director in 1978 and had joined the group 18 months earlier, and his president, Bertrand Maus. Commercial strategy consisted of four main policies. First was the recognition that well-managed department stores and variety stores could, provided with the necessary investments, continue to be profitable. However, these methods of retailing did not constitute important areas of expansion and growth. Second, commercial activities in the food sector offered growth prospects, particularly in more modern forms such as supermarkets, hypermarkets, and affiliated food stores. Third, specialty stores and home shopping—including mail order and shopping by telephone—were growing retail sectors. Fourth, when opportunities occurred or could be created, the export of know-how and merchandise were to be pursued vigorously. These policies dominated the activities of Printemps beginning in 1978.

No great change took place in the number of owned department and variety stores. Some smaller stores were closed, a few new stores were acquired or built, and investments continued to be made in existing stores. In the case of Prisunic, emphasis continued to be placed on increasing food sales and by 1990 food accounted for 58% of Prisunic's total sales. At the same time the concept of exporting department and variety store expertise and merchandise gathered strength. In 1979 an important agreement was made with Japan's Daiei retailing group to open Printemps department stores in Japan. Printemps provided the expertise and Daiei the building, so Printemps's capital investment was negligible. Daiei opened several such stores in Japan and similar agreements were made in other countries, including Portugal. In the early 1990s there were 11 stores outside France carrying the Printemps name, and a larger number affiliated with Printemps for supplies of merchandise. Prisunic has followed a similar policy, and there are Prisunic or Escale—large supermarket—stores in French territories overseas and in Greece and Portugal: 44 Prisunic and 11 Escale. Specialty non-food retailing was developed in the menswear market. In 1974 the Printemps group had opened a specialty menswear store called Brummell in Toulouse. But perhaps the most important step forward took place in 1980 when Printemps bought a 40% share in Magasins Armand Thiéry et Sigrand (ATS), an existing menswear chain. This shareholding was increased to 80% in 1981 and is now 87.4%. The subsidiary now has 65 stores trading under the names of Armand Thiéry and Brummell.

In 1984 an entirely different type of move was made with the purchase of 51% of Disco SA, a food wholesaling group, and 99% of a related company called Discol SA. In association with seven other wholesalers, Disco, the second-largest food wholesaler in France, supplies more than 1,500 affiliated food retailers. Discol acts as a food wholesaler to restaurants, schools, and hospitals, and is France's second-largest firm in this sector. Together Disco and Discol own and operate 18 food distribution centers and their associated firms have a further 38. These acquisitions, along with the significant food sales of Prisunic stores, afforded Printemps a strong presence in France's food industry.

The most dramatic acquisition of the Printemps company took place in 1987-1988, when first 15%, then 20%, then 32%, and finally, on an agreed bid, 54.7% of the shares of La Redoute S.A., the largest mail-order company in France,

passed to its control. La Redoute owned not only two smaller mail-order firms in France, Vert Baudet and Maison de Valérie, but also controlled Vestro, the second largest mail-order company in Italy, and the Prénatal chain of stores which boasted 330 branches in Italy, Spain, Austria, Germany, and Portugal. Since Printemps took control, mail-order selling has been developed in the Benelux countries and Portugal and an agreement has been made with Sears Canada. The 25% share of La Redoute in Empire Stores, the fifth largest mail-order firm in the United Kingdom, was increased in 1991 to complete control at 98.9%. In the hypermarket retail sector, the Printemps group had acquired a 25% interest in the Euromarché hypermarket company in 1975. Through cross-holdings in Viniprix SA, this share rose to 43.5% by 1986. The profits of Euromarché fell, however, in 1987 and 1988, and in 1989 the firm incurred a heavy loss with only a marginal improvement in 1990. Unable to control the management of Euromarché, Printemps disposed of its share in 1991, selling it at a profit to the hypermarket group Carrefour.

Another, but less important, change occurred in 1991 when the Printemps group sold the Disco food wholesale company. In effect, however, this made little difference to the commitment of the Printemps group to food wholesaling. While giving up the day-to-day operation of wholesale depots, Printemps, through its Prisunic buying organization, remained the chief source of supply for the 1,775 franchised retailers of Disco.

Printemps appears well placed to face the future. Total sales doubled between fiscal years 1987 and 1990. Department stores and variety stores will see limited growth, but they should continue to be profitable during the 1990s. Mail order, which in the early 1990s represented more than one-third of sales, is a growth sector in Europe, and La Redoute is active in four European countries. Specialty chains have found their place and should continue to develop. The extensive interests of Printemps in food wholesaling and retailing should enable it to offset any temporary downturn in consumer demand for department store and mail-order merchandise. By their nature, however, these diversified activities will require a strong management team to ensure effective coordination.

Principal Subsidiary: La Redoute S.A. (54.7%).

Further Reading: Mac Orlan, Pierre, *Le Printemps,* Paris, Ed. Gallimard, 1930; Rives, Marcel, *Traité d'Economie Commercial,* Paris, Presses Universitaires de France, 1958; Dumas, Solange, *Cent ans de Jeunesse,* Paris, Printania, 1965; Carracalla, Jean-Paul, *Le Roman du Printemps, Histoire d'un Grand Magasin,* Paris, Denoël, 1989.

—James B. Jefferys

BELK STORES SERVICES, INC.

2801 West Tyvola Road
Charlotte, North Carolina 28217
U.S.A.
(704) 357-1000
Fax: (704) 357-1876

Private Company
Incorporated: 1955
Employees: 35,000
Sales: $2.98 billion

Belk Stores Services, Inc. (BSS) dates back to a small bargain store opened in 1888 that grew to be the U.S.'s largest family- and management-owned department store organization. BSS provides centralized buying, data processing, market research, legal planning, training, and development for about 300 Belk and Leggett stores, which are primarily fashion department stores and are located in 14 states, largely in the southern United States. The stores are not a chain; various numbers of the stores are owned by several different corporations.

In 1888 William Henry Belk opened a small bargain store in Monroe, North Carolina. The store, New York Racket, was financed with a loan from a local widow, Belk's savings, and goods on consignment. The goods' prices were clearly marked and not negotiated with customers, an idea that was just becoming accepted in retailing. Seven months later, Belk's books showed significant profits.

The founder approached his brother, John Belk, in 1891, to become a partner in the prospering store. Thus the Belk Brothers Company was formed. A second store was opened in 1893 in Chester, South Carolina. A third opened in Union, South Carolina, in 1894, and the following year, William Belk moved to Charlotte, North Carolina, to open the company's fourth store. His brother John remained to manage the Monroe store until his death in 1928. The brothers' stores were doing so well by 1895 that other merchants began to copy even their slogans.

William Belk's success resulted from some retailing ideas that were innovative for the time. In 1897 he combined the purchasing power of the four stores, plus two others in which the brothers had no financial interest, and formed a loose co-operative buying network. This allowed them to purchase goods in bulk quantity at favorable prices. All purchases and sales were cash. Belk also made extensive use of advertising.

The brothers opened a store in Greensboro, North Carolina, in 1899.

In the early 1900s, Charlotte was a boom town, expanding along with the textile industry and was the state's largest city by 1910. That year, Belk sales approached $1 million, and a new five-story building was unveiled to house the Charlotte store. The company's greatest expansion followed World War I, as the southern economy received a boost. Cotton prices went up, and soldiers came home. Between 1918 and 1920, Belk stores' total sales more than doubled, to $12 million a year. In 1920 Will Leggett—John Belk's nephew by marriage—opened a store with the Belks in Burlington, North Carolina. His brother Fred Leggett opened a store in Danville, Virginia, that same year—the Belk-Leggett. The Belk brothers often added managers' names to their own on new stores.

Boom days and postwar prosperity gave way to recession, however, and the Belks retrenched, not opening any stores between 1922 and 1925. In 1925, however, they opened three more stores and three again in 1926. In 1927 the Belks and the Leggett brothers agreed that the Leggetts would own 80% of the stores they opened, with Belk Brothers Company owning the remaining 20%. In the past, the Belks had always owned the majority of their stores.

The years between 1910 and 1930 were prosperous for retailing. Competition, however, began to creep up on the Belks. Then the stock market crash of 1929 slowed Belk's sales growth, but stores stayed open. While other companies' stores closed, Belk acquired 22 stores in 1930 and 1931. In 1934 Belk opened 27 stores, the most it had ever opened in a single year. These included locations in Tennessee and Georgia. By 1938 Charlotte was again a booming southern city, and the Belks's headquarters store there expanded. Through this store, consolidated purchasing services, assistance with taxes and merchandise distribution, and other services were offered to all stores. In 1938 Belk was doing business in 162 locations in seven states. The stores, however, faced competitive challenges from national chains such as J.C. Penney, Montgomery Ward, and Sears Roebuck, which were thriving in larger cities.

In response, Belk stores were remodeled and expanded. Belk Stores Association had formed in the 1920s, gathering the new store managers for quarterly meetings. By the late 1930s, the group was too large feasibly organize meetings four times a year, so it gathered at annual conventions. Belk Buying Service was formally set up in 1940. World War II defense spending enhanced the economy, and by the war's end, sales were two-and-one-half times what they had been in 1941. This helped pay off Depression debts and feed expansion. In 1946 the Belks opened 25 stores. Altogether they opened more than 60 stores between the end of World War II and the close of the decade. In 1952 founder William Belk died at the age of 89. He had worked as the head of the company right up to his death.

After Belk's death, his son Henry took his place. The founder's other sons, John and Tom, were also active in the company. Six months after his father's death, Henry opened the company's first shopping center store, in Florida. This store marked a dramatic break from Belk traditions: a New York design firm created a fancy interior, music was played, and merchandise was displayed for self-service. This contrasted sharply with the Belk stores' trademark features of spare, no-nonsense decor, and an army of well-trained sales clerks.

Henry opened several more stores afterward without consulting his family, and by 1955 legal disputes were brewing among family members and other shareholders. Although law suits were filed, they eventually were dropped. Later that year, Belk Stores Services, Inc., was established to make a formal organization out of what had long been an operating entity. The BSS board then elected John Belk as president, leaving Henry to his Florida pursuit, the Belk-Lindsey Company. In November 1955 BSS cut all ties with Henry's company. John eventually become chairman of BSS, with Tom as president.

The Belks' private-label business was thriving by 1954. By 1959 it accounted for a major share of the buying office's inventory. In the late 1950s, the Belks department stores had nearly peaked in the South, with 325 stores in 16 states. In 1956 Belk acquired its only real competitor in the region, the Efird department stores.

During the 1960s, the company had to adjust to the changing South. Stores that were once local institutions found themselves in the midst of a highly mobile population that was attracted to the offerings of big-city stores. The largely autonomous and divergent stores making up the Belk group were not prepared to compete. A more mobile society, newly popular shopping centers, and the south's expanding economy presented BSS with the task of uniting its network of stores.

In 1958 there were 380 stores in 17 states. By 1963 the stores were, for the first time, presented to the public as a unit, instead of the string of independent operations they had been. Change was still slow, however. At a time when more buyers were using credit, 87% of Belk's sales were still cash. In 1967 extensive meetings were held by BSS and its long-range planning committees to chart the company's future.

Meanwhile, more stores were added to the fold: 14 opened in 1969 and 16 in 1970. The new stores were larger and used modern management techniques, such as computerized payrolls and centralized personnel departments. As planning and coordination gained in importance, so did BSS's role. By as-suming more leadership, it accelerated the changes as the stores moved from budget to fashion merchandise. Expansion continued—between 1972 and 1975, more than 50 stores were opened. Several of the company's signature downtown stores were closed in favor of stores in the prospering outlying malls. Credit and data processing systems were centralized and upgraded. Another change was Belk's pursuit of upscale brand names. Estee Lauder, a brand of cosmetics, was aggressively wooed until it was added to product lines in 1975. Even Belk stores in smaller towns upgraded their look and merchandise. This served to add new customers to an already loyal clientele.

Belk had had a buying office in New York since 1924, but it was not until 1983 that it had its first fashion buying show in the city. Four years later, representatives from the nation's top fashion lines were competing for sites in the show. This further consolidated buying and proved Belk's place in the fashion retail market. Marking the change from bargain chain to fashion stores was top designer Oscar de la Renta's appearance at a grand reopening of a Belk store in 1986. The company celebrated its 100th birthday in 1988 while opening a huge new BSS office complex in Charlotte.

BSS stores succeeded in meeting the demand of style-conscious shoppers in the 1970s and 1980s, as opposed to the previous demand for thrift, durability, and value. Belk also succeeded in transplanting itself from downtown areas to outlying malls. The 1990s constellation of stores reflected variation; some stores retained the bargain-budget flavor of Belk's founder's vision. The consolidated planning, distribution, buying power, and administrative legal resources of BSS, however, rendered even the smallest Belk store competitive.

Further Reading: Covington, Howard, *Belk: A Century of Retail Leadership,* Chapel Hill, University of North Carolina Press, 1988.

—Carol I. Keeley

BERGEN BRUNSWIG CORPORATION

4000 Metropolitan Drive
Orange, California 92668
U.S.A.
(714) 385-4000
Fax: (714) 978-7415

Public Company
Incorporated: 1969
Employees: 3,8000
Sales: $4.84 billion
Stock Exchange: American

Bergen Brunswig Corporation—consisting of two subsidiaries, Bergen Brunswig Drug Company, a wholesale drug distribution firm, and Commtron, which warehouses and distributes home videos and electronic products—is one of the fastest growing corporations in the United States. Over the past decade, the corporation's sales have increased sevenfold. Bergen Brunswig is the second largest pharmaceutical wholesaler nationwide, and since its incorporation in 1969, it has been on the leading edge of technological advances in accounting and marketing. It is the largest distributor of pharmaceuticals and health aids to hospitals in the United States. Commtron, with headquarters in Des Moines, Iowa, is the country's largest home video warehouser and distributor. In the three years between 1987 and 1990, Bergen Brunswig Corporation has seen its earnings grow an extraordinary 300%.

The founder of Bergen Brunswig was born in 1854, in France: Lucien Napoleon Brunswig, the son of a country doctor. The youthful Lucien felt little inclination to pursue the healing art of his father; instead, his ambition lay in some day providing the drugs that were vital to patients' treatment. Political turmoil in France, starting with the proclamation of the Paris Commune by radicals in 1870 and the Prussian invasion of 1871, which marked the onset of the Franco-Prussian War, propelled Lucien, as it did many other young Frenchmen, to emigrate to the United States.

Arriving unemployed and nearly penniless in 1871, 17-year-old Lucien was accepted as an apprentice to a U.S. druggist. Apprenticeship meant more than learning the drug trade; it also entailed sweeping floors, cleaning out the cages of the druggist's pets, and other menial tasks. Despite his meager income, Lucien Brunswig's hard work and self-denial led to his saving enough to open a retail drug store in Atchison,

Kansas, when he was 21 years old. His drugstore was such a success that he sold it profitably and took the train as far southwest as it would go, to a few miles outside of Fort Worth, Texas—a dusty, crude town of a few hundred people.

His Fort Worth drugstore, serving both retail and wholesale, flourished. By 1883, less than five years after he had opened the store, his business did $350,000 in annual sales. In 1882, George R. Finlay, the owner of a well-established wholesale drug firm in New Orleans, invited Brunswig to join him as a partner. Lucien Brunswig, who had spent most of his life in France, readily agreed to sell his own drug business, head down to the United States's "little France," and became Finlay's business partner. Finlay's firm, Wheelock-Finlay, became Finlay and Brunswig. Upon Finlay's death in 1885, Lucien Brunswig took over the entire wholesale drug operation, remaining, however, in New Orleans until 1903. His devotion to New Orleans is shown by the fact that he served as a police commissioner of the city for four years. In 1887 Brunswig took on a partner, F.W. Braun.

Although Brunswig was thoroughly acclimated and at home in New Orleans, he turned his ambition to faraway Los Angeles, California, a growing town of 30,000. Its future, he guessed, promised more than the South's, and in 1888, Brunswig dispatched Braun to Los Angeles to open one of the few wholesale drug companies in the area, the F.W. Braun Company. Brunswig remained in New Orleans.

Business opened in Los Angeles in a two-story adobe house, conducted in one or two rooms on the first floor. Pharmaceuticals were not only sold over the counter, but a few salesmen also ventured out to visit druggists and procure their orders, which could be filled within two or three weeks. After a year, F.W. Braun Company was flourishing and moved into the Old Post Office Building next door, the first of a series of major expansions.

In 1890, Lucien Brunswig was still unwilling to uproot himself from New Orleans. He ordered, nevertheless, the opening of what would become a prosperous branch of F.W. Braun in San Diego, California, a city even smaller, dustier, and with fewer drugstores than Los Angeles. The coming of the Spanish-American War was a boost for the drug business nationwide, and Lucien Brunswig's profits continued to soar. In 1903, deciding that the future of his company lay in the West, Brunswig finally sold his profitable New Orleans establishment and moved with his family to Los Angeles, to preside over the continued expansion of his business. In 1907, he bought out Braun, and henceforth, his business was named Brunswig Drug Company. It would be headquartered in Los Angeles. Lucien Brunswig steadily expanded his wholesale drug enterprise, opening branches in Phoenix and Tucson, Arizona, and a short-lived one in Guaymas, Mexico. As a result of World War I, Pacific Coast business boomed, far beyond Brunswig's wildest dreams. In 1922 when other U.S. businesses were experiencing a slump, Brunswig's sale of drugs as well as cosmetics, a recent and lucrative addition to the drug line, reached a record high level. In that same year, Brunswig decided that a manufacturing plant was in order that would eventually house a laboratory and would produce cosmetics. Goods that were manufactured in the Brunswig labs eventually made their way to the Philippines, Japan, and the Hawaiian Islands. Wealth had made of Brunswig an ardent bibliophile and art collector. In 1927 he presented to the University of

California at Los Angeles more than 1,000 books for its library of French language and literature. With the onset of the Depression, Brunswig's company opened soup kitchens to feed the desperately poor, since his own business did not suffer significantly. Brunswig died in 1943, two years after his retirement; he did not live to see his kingdom expand tremendously, as it did in the years following World War II.

Roy V. Schwab succeeded Lucien Brunswig as president of the Brunswig Drug Corporation, moving the company's headquarters in 1947 to Vernon, California. By then, the Brunswig Drug Corporation had divested itself of its manufacturing plant and laboratories, concentrating solely on the wholesale distribution of pharmaceuticals. Brunswig was considered to be the most advanced wholesale drug operation in the United States, although by no means the largest. It was the first wholesale drug company in the United States to introduce computerized punch-cards for keeping track of inventories. In 1949, the 61-year-old Brunswig Drug Corporation merged with the Coffin Redington Company of San Francisco, the first of numerous significant mergers. The company expanded rapidly in California. In 1950 it opened its San Jose division; in 1951, its Sacramento division; and in 1954, its San Bernardino division. In 1952, it acquired the Smith-Faus Drug Company, and by 1960, had 14 divisions in the southwestern United States.

In the eastern United States, another drug company benefited from the postwar economic boom. In 1947 Emil P. Martini founded and became the first president of the Bergen Drug Company based in Hackensack, New Jersey. A graduate of the New Jersey College of Pharmacy in 1923, Martini opened his first retail pharmacy in Hackensack five years later. A second one was acquired at the height of the Depression, and a third was acquired in 1937. A well-established member of the community and president of the New Jersey State Board of Pharmacy, Martini, along with a group of business associates, established a wholesale drug distribution company in 1947 named after the county of Bergen in which they lived. The success of the Bergen Drug Company was phenomenal, in part because of the insatiable demand for the wonder drugs of World War II, including such antibiotics as penicillin. Despite its growth, the company continued to offer same-day service.

With the 1955 death of Emil P. Martini Sr., his son, Emil P. Martini Jr., took over the helm in 1956. From then on, the Bergen Drug Company rapidly expanded and acquired other wholesale drug companies. In 1956, Bergen acquired Drug Service Inc. of Bridgeport, Connecticut. Between 1957 and 1958, Bergen operations were started in three California cities, Fresno, San Francisco, and Covina. In 1959, it became the first company in the nation to use computers for inventory control and accounting purposes. It continued to be on the leading edge of that technology thereafter. By the 1960s, Bergen Drug Company was among the largest wholesale drug distributors in the United States, supplying 5,000 pharmacists and hospitals. In May 1969 Martini successfully negotiated the purchase of Brunswig Drug Corporation. The latter had sought to buy the former until Brunswig Drug managers realized that financially it made more sense to have Bergen buy their company, as the price-earnings figures of Bergen's stocks were more advantageous. The name of the new company would be the Bergen Brunswig Corporation.

Innumerable acquisitions followed. In 1970 alone, the Bergen Brunswig Corporation added 12 drug companies and laboratories, and transformed itself into a truly national drug distribution business. Head of the Bergen Drug Company since 1956, Martini, who had graduated with a degree in pharmacy from Purdue University, was given his original job in his father's firm with the understanding that he was to learn the drug distribution business from the bottom up, which he did. Under his direction and that of his younger brother, Robert E. Martini, also a pharmacist and vice president of the company, the Bergen Brunswig Corporation became in the 1970s one of the most modern drug distribution companies in the United States. Bergen Brunswig revolutionized the trade in 1971 when it pioneered the electronic transmission of purchase orders to Eli Lilly & Co. In the early 1970s, Bergen Brunswig introduced the hand-held computer scanner, with which pharmacists could scan the bar-codes on merchandise. Stock was then reordered on the basis of the information collected by the scanner. The inauguration in the late 1970s of an advanced computer system automated the prescription department still further, connecting hospitals and chain pharmacies electronically to Bergen Brunswig's distribution centers. Soon the majority of orders could be transmitted to Bergen Brunswig via telephone lines, and in the 1980s, satellite communication replaced conventional telephone lines. One hundred years after the opening of the F.W. Braun Company wholesale drug store in Los Angeles, the distribution time of drug orders was down from two to three weeks to less than 24 hours.

The 1980s saw the explosion of pharmaceutical and health care needs that in part explained Bergen Brunswig's phenomenal growth. In 1981 the president of the National Wholesale Drug Association noted a 17% increase in the sales of pharmaceuticals in the first half of that year. The stock value of Bergen Brunswig Corporation increased between 1977 and 1981 by 50%, while its net earnings in the three-year period of 1987 to 1990 increased 316%, with an average annual growth rate of 25%. The aging of the U.S. population had something to do with this success, as did the popularity of its two biggest selling drugs, Zantac, for the treatment of ulcers, and Epogen, used in kidney dialysis treatment.

Despite the considerable increase in the number of its customers—10,000 by 1990—Bergen Brunswig could still guarantee next day service by means of its computer system. Bergen Brunswig supplies software to some 300 hospitals, thereby linking them to the company's computer-driven distribution and pricing system. This equipment has helped Bergen Brunswig become over the years the largest supplier in the United States of pharmaceuticals to hospitals. In addition, the company has managed to attract customers through its Good Neighbor Pharmacy plan, which especially caters to the needs of independent pharmacies. The development in the 1980s of a new generation of automated distribution centers has speeded up service and delivery to the point where Bergen Brunswig has become the model for drug distribution companies nationwide, although it is second-largest in the drug distribution industry. The corporation's new distribution facility in Corona, California, can process an order every three seconds—with 100% accuracy—of any of the 2,500 most popular pharmaceuticals or health care products. The goal of Bergen Brunswig is to get closer to the customer—the pharmacist or store manager—and anticipate needs to the point where the customer would never have to place an order. In this system Bergen Brunswig would monitor the customer's stocks and automatically replenish supplies. The automated distribution system enables Bergen Brunswig and all other wholesale drug companies to process three times as many orders as previously.

The 1980s also saw the development of another line of products, the result of Bergen Brunswig's acquisition in 1982 of Commtron, Inc., a national distributor of home videos as well as 4,000 consumer electronic products. By 1990 Commtron, a 79%-owned subsidiary of the Bergen Brunswig Corporation, became the nation's number-one distributor of videos, with distribution centers and headquarters in Des Moines, Iowa; Salt Lake City, Utah; and Chicago. With 1,000 employees, Commtron's sales in 1990 increased 17% over the previous year. Also in 1990 Robert Martini became president and CEO, and Emil Martini Jr. took the post of chairman of the board.

The Bergen Brunswig Drug Company, the 100%-owned subsidiary of the Bergen Brunswig Corporation (BBC), which generates more than 87% of the business of BBC, was converting to paperless billing, and constantly refining its funds transfer and information management systems in the 1990s. Pharmacists occupy many of the company's top management positions, a trend that will continue well into the next century. CQI, a "continuous quality improvement" program, inaugurated in 1990, should also produce results in terms of in-

creased customer satisfaction. With CQI, volunteer employees attend team leadership workshops, consisting of 80 teams of 5 to 8 members, to analyze problem areas. An example of the results of CQI is the case of truck drivers who find better routes to hospital pharmacies, and who devise quicker means of processing returnables. The future of Bergen Brunswig Corporation undoubtedly anticipates greater growth and a stronger emphasis on pharmaceuticals rather than on videos and electronic goods, plus a continuing application of technology and streamlined customer service.

Principal Subsidiaries: Bergen Brunswig Drug Company; Commtron, Inc. (79%).

Further Reading: Fay, John T., *NWDA 1876–1986: Centennial Plus Ten,* Alexandria, Virginia, National Wholesale Druggists' Association, 1987; Wiley, Karen, ed., *Centennial Sampler: 1888–1988,* Orange, California, Bergen Brunswig Corporation, [1988].

—Sina Dubovoj

THE BOOTS COMPANY

THE BOOTS COMPANY PLC

Nottingham NG2 3AA
United Kingdom
(0602) 506111
Fax: (0602) 592727

Public Company
Incorporated: 1883 as Boot and Company Ltd.
Employees: 78,648
Sales: £3.38 billion (US$6.32 billion)
Stock Exchange: London

The Boots Company PLC's business is the manufacture, marketing, and distribution of pharmaceutical and consumer products in its own retail stores, in Britain and overseas. Manufacturing takes place at four sites in the United Kingdom and the group's subsidiary companies have manufacturing units in Australia, France, Kenya, Pakistan, South Africa, Spain, and the United States, while its associated and joint-venture companies manufacture in India, West Germany, and Yugoslavia. Despite this geographical spread, the company's business remains principally in the United Kingdom, which provided more than 80% of total turnover in 1990; business in the United States accounted for 8% of turnover in that year and in Europe for between 5% and 6%. The company's activities are carried on through four operating divisions, a structure adopted in 1989.

Boots The Chemists is the largest division, in 1990 contributing 67% of the company's total turnover and 53% of its profit before tax, and is responsible for the 1,051 retail stores that offer a wide range of health and beauty products, toiletries, baby products, film, and film processing services—areas in which Boots is a market leader. The 220 larger stores also sell audiovisual equipment, kitchen equipment, leisure products, and other home merchandise.

The retail division, which in 1990 accounted for 16% of the company's turnover and 7% of its profit before tax, is composed of a number of separate retail businesses owned by the parent company—Boots Opticians, Children's World, Halfords, A.G. Stanley, and the Payless do-it-yourself (DIY) home improvements chain, the latter merged in 1990 into a jointly owned operation with W H Smith's Do It All DIY business. Two small overseas retailing operations—Sephora in France and Boots The Chemists in New Zealand—are also part of the retail division.

The pharmaceutical division, which in 1990 contributed 17% of total turnover and 31% of profit before tax, carries out research and development on prescriptions drugs; its major products are ibuprofen, flurbiprofen, dothiepin, and levithyroxine. It also manufactures and markets over-the-counter pharmaceutical products, such as Strepsils throat lozenges, Sweetex artificial sweetener, and Optrex eye drops. The property division was established to manage the company's property portfolio in the United Kingdom.

Jesse Boot, the founder of the company, was born in Nottingham in 1850, the first child and only son of John Boot and his second wife, Mary. An agricultural laborer by trade, John Boot was much influenced by the ideas of popular medicine then current among nonconformists, particularly those of the disciples of the American Samuel Thompson, whose remedies, based on medical botany, were then enjoying considerable success in Britain. After John Boot's health broke down, he opened a small shop in 1849 in Goosegate, Nottingham, selling his own herbal and botanical medicines. His death in 1860 left his widow and her two children dependent on the shop for their livelihood, and Mary Boot continued to run the business with the help of her 10-year-old son. Three years later Jesse Boot left school to work full time in the business, and over the next few years he took charge of it.

In the 1870s, rising real incomes allowed the working class to purchase the patent and proprietary medicines of the kind manufactured and sold by Thomas Holloway and Thomas Beecham, displacing the remedies of medical botany. Although the shop in Goosegate continued to sell herbal medicines, young Jesse Boot started to expand the business, first by adding a range of household goods, including groceries, sold at cut prices; an advertisement of the early 1870s claimed more than 2,000 articles in stock. He decided in 1874 to enter the business of retailing proprietary medicines; as he recalled in 1904, he thought that "if he could afford to sell proprietary articles at prices lower than were being charged by the ordinary chemists, there would be a large future before him." Jesse Boot's commercial strategy, the basis on which he built his large and successful business, was to buy in large quantities from wholesalers and to sell at prices well below those prevailing in the town. It won for him the enduring hostility of the established chemists, first in Nottingham, and later in other towns and cities where he opened branches.

Although at first Boot had difficulties both in persuading the wholesalers to supply him with such large quantities and in finding the money to pay them, he secured the support of a number of influential businessmen and professional men in Nottingham, and, following an extensive advertising campaign in the local press, his business grew rapidly. By the autumn of 1877 his turnover had reached £100 a week, far surpassing his own original target of £20 a week. In the following year he opened a new and larger shop, also in Goosegate, and five years later he extended, refurbished, and refitted it.

In July 1883 Boot incorporated his business as Boot & Company Ltd., with a nominal capital of £10,000 of which almost a half was fully subscribed, most of it by Boot himself. Incorporation with limited liability could have opened the way for external investment in the business, but Boot chose to keep control in his own hands, offering shares only to a few close friends and associates in the 1880s; for the time being, he continued to rely on the banks for financial backing, and a decade later, when he started to encourage investors, he sold only preference, nonvoting shares. Some of these shares were offered to customers, through the shops, and some to employees, for the cooperative ideal attracted the nonconformist and liberal side of Jesse Boot's character, although at the same time he was determined to keep control of his business.

More significantly at the time, incorporation opened up a new area of business for Boot's shop, that of dispensing prescriptions. In a test case brought by the Pharmaceutical Society in 1880 against the London and Provincial Supply Association, the House of Lords decided, much to the chagrin of the society, that limited liability companies had the right to employ qualified pharmacists or chemists to dispense prescriptions. Boot recruited Edward Waring as the company's first pharmacist in the Nottingham store and, with dispensing at half-price, the prescription section was off to a good start.

Expansion of the business continued with the opening in 1884 of branches in Lincoln and Sheffield and the start of small-scale manufacturing behind the shop in Goosegate. By 1885 Boot's annual turnover had reached £40,000, but in that year his health deteriorated, and he briefly contemplated selling the business. He recovered, and while recuperating on holiday in Jersey he met Florence Rowe. In August 1886 they were married.

The 1890s saw an ambitious plan of expansion implemented. New shops were opened to extend the company's coverage of England and Wales, and Boot also bought, where he could, small chains of chemists' shops. By the end of 1893, according to *The Chemist and Druggist*, Boots was then the largest of the company-chemist chains.

Boots and Company was reconstituted in 1888 as Boots Pure Drug Company, which became the holding company for a number of subsidiary companies such as Boots Cash Chemists (Lancs) Ltd., 1899. The size of the company—there were 180 shops by the end of the century—was enhanced when in 1901 Boot bought the Southern Drug Company and the Metropolitan Drug Company, which together formed a chain of more than 60 shops, the largest in the metropolitan area. Between 1901 and 1914 more new shops were opened, bringing the total to 560 in 1914, including prestigious sites in Princes Street, Edinburgh, in 1911 and Regent Street, London, in 1912.

While pharmaceuticals and dispensing remained the core of the business, the range of merchandise retailed also widened, particularly in the larger shops, which were closer to department stores, and as the company tried to widen its appeal to attract middle-class customers. Florence Boot's experience of retailing in her father's bookshop gave her a direct interest in the business, resulting in the introduction of departments offering stationery, books, artists' materials, and gifts that proved popular and successful and remained in her charge. Around the turn of the century, Boots Booklovers Libraries were established and cafés or tea-rooms were installed in some of the larger stores; both these innovations proved a success in terms of customer appeal.

By 1892 manufacturing, which had started in a small way behind the shop, occupied the whole of a former cotton mill in Nottingham, and the interest always taken by Jesse Boot in the design, fitting, and appearance of the shops led to the establishment and growth of a building and shopfitting department. A printing department to serve the company's needs opened in 1890. The continued growth of the business was reflected in its

rising sales, which passed the £2 million mark in 1911 and reached £2.5 million in 1913.

World War I brought new opportunities that Sir Jesse Boot—knighted in 1909—was quick to sieze. Despite being increasingly disabled by arthritis, he continued to control the company. In the last two decades of the 19th century, the German fine-chemical industry had discovered, developed, and patented a number of pharmaceuticals—aspirin and phenacetin for example—that it exported to the United Kingdom. The outbreak of war left Boots and the country without a supply of these and other essential fine chemicals, and Boot soon decided to start to manufacture them. He recruited research chemists from Burroughs Wellcome, and production at the new plant started in 1915. In addition to fine chemicals, the company also started to manufacture saccharin during the war. Sales increased at this time, reaching £5 million in 1918.

Sir Jesse Boot, who was awarded baronetcy in 1916 as a reward for contributions to the Liberal Party, was 70 in 1920. Fearing the effects of the post-war slump on business, which was becoming increasingly burdensome to him to run but which he did not want to hand over to his son John, Boot negotiated privately the sale of his controlling interest to American Louis K. Liggett and his Rexall group of U.S. drugstores. Liggett paid £2.27 million for Boots. Sir Jesse, who remained titular chairman of Boots until 1926 and was made Lord Trent in 1928, gave large amounts of the money to his home city, particularly to University College, Nottingham, which used the money to fund the construction of buildings on the city's outskirts. After the sale of the business, he retired to Jersey where he died in 1931.

Boots was part of the Liggett group from 1920 to 1933, although in 1923 John Boot, vice chairman of the company, who had disliked his father's transaction with Liggett, persuaded Liggett to sell 25% of its shareholding in Britain; thus, for the first time, Boots shares became publicly held, and the company was quoted on the London Stock Exchange. In 1928 the L.K. Liggett Company became part of a much larger U.S. combine, Drug Inc., which, faced with the effects of the American Depression, decided to sell Boots. The money required for the purchase, between £6 million and £7 million, was raised by a group led by Sir Hugo Cunliffe-Owen and Reginald McKenna.

During the 13 years of U.S. ownership there were some major organizational changes, which lasted beyond that time. Two committees—later merged into one—composed of Boots's senior managers and American representatives, were designated in 1920 to run the company. Nine territorial general managers were appointed to control the 600 shops, and senior managers were sent to the United States to be trained. Stricter control of stock and better accounting systems were introduced, for although sales had continued to rise, profitability had slipped.

As Britain emerged from the worst of the postwar slump, Boots became prosperous again. John Boot, joint managing director, gradually asserted his control over the business, and in 1927 work started on a long-planned new factory at Beeston, just outside Nottingham, which opened in 1933.

From 1933 until 1953 John Boot, now the second Lord Trent and chairman and managing director as his father had been before him, ruled Boots as autocratically as his predecessor. In the years immediately before World War II, expansion was steady—the 1,000th shop opened in Scotland, at Galashiels in 1933, and in 1936 the first shop in New Zealand was opened.

Between 1939 and 1945, like most of the British industry, Boots's manufacturing capacity was directed to the war effort, and the production of pharmaceuticals such as mepacrine, for the treatment of malaria, took priority. Many of the company's shops and some of its manufacturing sites were destroyed or severely damaged by the bombing. Recovery after the war was slow, not least because of the shortage of building materials and skills. The manufacture of new pharmaceutical products increased as Boots started to make antibiotics and, in 1953, cortisone products. The immediate postwar years also saw the start of businesses in Kenya, South Africa, Singapore, Australia, and Pakistan. At home, however, the company had an increasingly old-fashioned image as consumer tastes started to change and shoppers expected a wider range of products.

The second Lord Trent retired in 1954 and died in 1956; his successor as chairman was his former chief assistant, J.P. Savage, who had then been with the company for more than 40 years. When Savage retired in 1961, the offices of chairman and managing director were separated, with W.R. Norman, the second Lord Trent's son-in-law, becoming chairman and F.A. Cockfield, who had joined the company in 1952 from the Board of the Inland Revenue in order to introduce cost accounting methods, being named managing director.

A reorganization of the company took place in 1967 and included establishment of a divisional structure. In 1968 Boots bought—it was described at the time as a merger, a face-saving formula to preserve corporate pride—the business of Timothy Whites, a long-standing competitor holding more than 600 retail branches, most of them drugstores selling other consumer goods, and more than 100 shops selling housewares merchandise only. The Timothy Whites business had been founded in Portsmouth in 1848 and had followed a pattern of growth similiar to that of Boots. In 1935 it had merged with Taylors Drug Company Ltd., a long-time competitor of Boots. The drugstores were integrated immediately with Boots, but the Timothy Whites Houseware branches continued to operate as such until 1983.

In 1971 the purchase of Crookes Laboratories Ltd. and Crookes Anestan Ltd. brought more pharmaceutical business to Boots, and a merger proposed in the following year would have given Boots greater presence in that field. In 1972 the Beecham Company made an unwelcome bid for Glaxo, which instead turned to Boots and a hastily arranged defensive merger. Both arrangements, however, were reported to the Monopolies Commission and in July of that year the commission ruled that neither should take place.

Anxious for expansion in Europe, Boots tried in 1973 to take over the House of Fraser, which already had some department stores in Europe. The bid was referred to the Monopolies Commission again, but even before their adverse recommendation was made, the oil crisis of that year and its effect on stock market prices made it impossible for the two to agree on price.

Instead Boots turned its attention to the United States, where in 1977 it acquired Rucker Pharmacol, and in 1986 it added to the company's United States operations with the £377 million purchase of the Flint Division of Baxter Travenol. Also across the Atlantic, Boots bought in 1977 and 1978 two chains of drugstores in Canada, and in 1978 it also bought 60% of Hercules Agrochemical in the United States. This was merged with Fisons agrochemical interests in 1980, and the joint venture was sold to Schering in 1983. In Europe Boots acquired 50% of the Spanish company Laboratorios Liade S.A. in 1979, and 95% of the West German company Kanoldt in 1984. New branches of the Sephora shops in France were opened. In 1985 the parent company was renamed The Boots Company PLC.

The acquisition of consumer eye products manufacturer Optrex in 1983, for £9 million, led to the opening of optical services departments, and sometimes separate shops, augmented by the purchase of opticians' chains, including Clement Clarke in 1986, Curry & Paxton in 1987, and Miller and Santhouse in 1989. Boots bought Farleys Health Products in 1986 to add to its manufacturing base. Drugstore operations were increased with the acquisition of Underwoods in 1989, and in the same year the purchase of the Ward White group brought Halfords and DIY retailing into Boots. Ward White's U.S. operations were eventually sold off.

The strength of the Boots the Chemists retailing chain is largely unchallenged; the synergy with Halfords and DIY retailing, however, could well be questioned. Despite its acquisitions and diversifications of the last ten years, Boots remains, in an age of global business, predominantly a U.K. operation.

Principal Subsidiaries: A.G. Stanley Ltd.; Boots Development Properties Ltd.; Boots Opticians Ltd.; Boots Print Ltd.; Boots Properties plc; Boots the Chemists Ltd.; Children's World Ltd.; Crookes Healthcare Ltd.; Farley Health Products Ltd.; Halfords Ltd.; LCP Holdings PLC; Lowpine Properties Ltd.; Miller and Santhouse PLC; Optrex Ltd.; Payless DIY Ltd.; Underwoods (Cash Chemists) Ltd.; Ward White Group plc; Ward White Developments Ltd.; Whites Property Co. Ltd.; The Boots Company (Australia) Pty. Ltd.; The Boots Company (Belgium) S.A.; Flint Laboratories (Canada) Ltd.; Laboratories Boots-Dacour S.A. (France); Beauté, Hygiène et Soins, S.A. (France); The Boots Company (Holland) B.V.; The Boots Company (Ireland) Ltd.; Boots Italia S.p.A.; Boots Finance Ltd. (Jersey); The Boots Company (Kenya) Ltd.; Optrex (Malaya) Sdn. Bhd.; Boots the Chemists (New Zealand) Ltd.; The Boots Company (Pakistan) Ltd. (56.5%); The Boots Company (Philippines) Inc.; The Boots Company (Far East) Pte. Ltd. (Singapore); The Boots Company (South Africa) Pty. Ltd.; Laboratorios Liade S.A. (Spain); The Boots Company (Thailand) Ltd.; The Boots Company (USA) Inc.; Boots Pharmaceuticals PR. Inc. (U.S.A.); Kanoldt Arzeneimittel GmbH (Germany).

Further Reading: Chapman, S., *Jesse Boot of Boots the Chemists,* London, Hodder & Stoughton, 1974; Chapman, S., "Strategy and Structure at Boots the Chemists," in Hannah, L., ed., *Management Strategy and Business Development,* London, Macmillan, 1976.

—Judy Slinn

THE BURTON GROUP PLC

THE BURTON GROUP PLC

214 Oxford Street
London W1N 9DF
United Kingdom
(071) 636 8040

Public Company
Incorporated: 1917 as Montague Burton Limited
Employees: 38,054
Sales: £1.80 billion (US$3.37 billion)
Stock Exchange: London

The Burton Group consists of 12 companies. In 1990 the group owned 450 shops carrying clothing for both sexes. Different component firms in the group target various sectors within the market. Debenhams, for example, of which there are now 85 stores, offers clothing and housewares for the whole family.

It was at the beginning of the 20th century that the foundations of the Burton Group were laid. In 1900 the 15-year-old Meshe David Osinsky joined the thousands of Jews fleeing westward from Russian persecution. Osinsky evidently opened his first store in Holywell Street, Chesterfield, England, in 1904. The merchandise offered for sale consisted of cheap ready-made suits for men and boys' wear under the name Burton. Men's suits "noted for hard wear and perfect fit," to quote a contemporary advertisement, were offered from eleven shillings and ninepence, boys' suits "in endless variety" for one shilling and ninepence, caps at one penny, and shirts of emerald green flannel with yellow stripes were sold to Irish farm workers. Advertisements also solicited orders for bespoke—made to order—suits. In 1908 a second Burton shop was opened in Mansfield and in 1909 a third in Sheffield. Also in 1909 Osinsky, who was to change his name to Montague Burton, married Sophia Marks, daughter of a furniture dealer.

In the same year Osinsky also established the Progress Mills works in Leeds, setting up Elmwood Mills and the headquarters of the firm there in 1910. Between 1910 and the outbreak of World War I, 14 branches of the firm were created, mainly in the industrial towns of the Midlands and the North East. The number of branches had grown to 40 by 1919, including eight shops in Ireland. These were all to be stocked with clothing. There was also the mounting task of meeting the demand for uniforms, which the firm was under contract to supply, all this with a constantly changing labor force as men joined the war effort and were replaced by women. By the end of the war

Elmwood Mills occupied five premises in Leeds, and the labor force had grown from 56 in 1914 to 500. Production was divided between civilian needs and contract requirements, which posed a problem. The firm had either to shelve half its productive capacity or expand the number of retail outlets. It chose the latter, and the number of shops grew from 40 in 1919 to 140 by 1922.

Rapidity of growth was accompanied by change in status: the company, Montague Burton Ltd., adopted limited liability in 1917 with a share capital of £5,002 increasing to £47,002 by 1924, all the shares but one—which belonged to Mrs. Burton—being held by Montague Burton. The firm by this time made almost entirely wholesale bespoke clothing, with the customer being measured in the branch shop and his requirements sent for translation into the appropriate garment. The advantage of the wholesale bespoke system to the customer was that he got exactly what he had ordered to suit his size and personal preferences, instead of the approximation he would be likely to get by buying ready-made. The benefits to the producer were not having to finance stocks of ready-made clothing for his customers to choose from and cutting out intermediaries. The success of the system lay in the speed with which the customer's order could be processed. This required organizational ability of a high degree and was of crucial importance in this highly competitive business. To this end, production was centralized at Hudson Road Mills, on a site offering plenty of scope for expansion, the first stage being opened in 1921.

The main force behind the move to the new factory was the growth in retail trade. Whatever the state of the national economy, there was no year between the wars in which the number of Burton shops failed to grow. From 140 in 1922, the number had more than doubled to reach 291 by 1929 and doubled again by 1939. The early increase in the number of shops was in the older industrial areas of the country such as the West Riding of Yorkshire, Lancashire, the Midlands, and North East, accounting for 80% in 1919, but this had fallen by 1939 to 50%. This diversification of outlets was behind the firm's remarkable record. The shops themselves set new standards of excellence, reflected in the expenditure on fixtures and fittings. From 1917 to 1939 the average amount spent on these items rose from £123 to £1,834. The 1925 publication *Goodwill in Industry*, by J. Foster Fraser, produced to mark the years that the firm had been in business, contained the following description: "Every Montague Burton shop has the same outward appearance, both in its window dressing and in the name of the firm uniformly presented in bronze lettering on the marble. The exterior stonework is always of emerald pearl granite with shafts of Scotch grey granite. The interior fittings of oak and gun-metal quiet and dignified are the same at every branch." This impression of quiet dignity was emphasized by the reception accorded to the customer. Each Burton shop received an instruction manual containing the following advice: "Impress on staff (a) to offer customer a chair and an invitation to be seated (b) to greet customer with a cheerful 'Good morning' entering (or Good evening) (c) to wish the customer a pleasant 'Good day' when departing. The prefix 'Sir' after 'Good morning' or similar conversational courtesies appeals to the average man whether your intellectual, social, economical superior or inferior. Make your customer feel he is welcome and that you are anxious to please him. Avoid the severe style of the income tax collector and the smooth tongue of the fortune teller. Cultivate the dignified style of the 'Quaker tea blender' which is the happy medium."

The care and attention paid to the running of the branches was matched by that shown to the work force, and the new factory building at Hudson Road facilitated this. Here it was possible to provide a fully equipped canteen for two thousand, serving a midday meal costing between four and ten pence, together with comprehensive welfare services. The motivation behind this provision was rooted in the belief that productivity and contentment of the work force were positively related.

When the new canteen was opened by the Princess Royal in 1934 it seated 8,000 workers, indicating the firm's growth. In 1929 the company became a public limited liability company with a capital of £4 million, having been a limited liability company since 1917. Montague Burton was knighted in 1931. For the rest of the 1930s the story was one of uninterrupted expansion. The number of shops had reached 595 by the outbreak of World War II. The success of retailing brought pressure on the making-up departments at Hudson Road, which produced the ready-to-wear suits, and there was a shortage of female labor, which Burton's own success had helped to create. At first the labor surpluses of the Yorkshire coalfield area were tapped and female workers were bused in from places such as Castleford and Normanton. This source of labor proved inadequate, however, and the firm sought relief in the blighted cotton towns of Lancashire. Three factories were opened in the 1930s, including a custom-built one at Burtonville on the East Lancashire highway. Between them they employed 6,000 workers in addition to the 10,600 employed at Hudson Road.

The decade witnessed the beginnings of a move away from wholesale bespoke tailoring, which had been the mainstay of the firm's output, to the ready-made suit. According to *The Outfitter*, March 26, 1938: "Montague Burton's are to make a definite and strenuous effort to popularise the ready to wear lounge suits throughout the British Isles. Some of the larger branches have always carried made-up suits, now a ready-to-wear department is to be part of every shop. For the first time a ready-made lounge suit is illustrated in the general spring catalogue issued from all branches. . . . the main branch in Tottenham Court Road, London W1 is the largest of its kind in Britain. Over 2,000 garments are always in stock in 250 different fittings."

Change of this kind carried revolutionary implications that were far from complete by the outbreak of World War II. The firm threw itself wholeheartedly into the war effort. The float representing Burton at the London victory parade of June 6, 1946, bore the proud inscription "13,642,169 Garments For The Fighting Services," and the importance attached to the factory by the Germans is illustrated by a map discovered in German archives, pinpointing it as a Luftwaffe target. War-time shortages of materials, the disruption of the labor force in response to the demands of the armed forces, and clothes rationing continued into peacetime. Not until 1950 did the chairman's annual report to the shareholders refer to improved stocks commensurate with prewar standards. The unfortunate outcome of a policy of buying in stocks of raw material on such a scale in a rising market due to extraneous circumstances was revealed when those prices suddenly fell. In Burton's case it meant writing off stocks to the value of £1

million. This was followed in September 1952 by the sudden death of Sir Montague Burton.

Measured in terms of turnover the £19.5 million that the firm achieved in 1953 had grown to almost £42 million by 1964. By 1990 this figure had been eclipsed by a turnover just short of £2 billion. Growth statistics, however impressive, conceal fundamental changes in the structure, organization, and purpose of the firm. By 1991 it had shed all its cloth and clothing manufacturing activities. The Hudson Road factory, which once housed thousands of workers, became a distribution center with the vast floor spaces carved up into smaller rooms. The Lancashire factories are gone, the one at Burtonville was demolished, and the two at Goole and Doncaster, acquired since the war, were vacated. The business has become more diversified, ceasing to serve men only, with more than half its sales to women. The shops cater to different sectors of the market and carry a comprehensive stock of clothing. They consist of Burton Retail, Dorothy Perkins, Top Man, Top Shop, Evans, Debenhams, Principles for Men, and Principles for Women. All stores comprise The Burton Group.

The long march to achieve this position started in 1953 when Burton acquired the firm Jackson the Tailor, thereby seeking to strengthen the management by acquiring the services of Sidney and Lionel Jacobson, directors of the company Weaver to Wearer Ltd., who had built a reputation of successful trading and who became directors of Burton in 1953. It was due to them that the firm divested itself of its clothmaking activities. The acquisition of the Peter Robinson shops, which by 1967 had grown in number to 39, predated the arrival of the Jacobsons by six years and heralded the movement of the firm into the women's side of the market. A new departure was the introduction of credit facilities for customers in November 1958 to make the firm more competitive. In 1963 Burton set up in business in France, anticipating Britain's entry into the European Common Market by ten years. This was one strategy open to a firm that had saturated the home market. Ultimately it was a failure, notwithstanding the acquisition of the St. Remy company with 35 shops, which made Burtons one of the largest specialty clothing firms in France and which was finally sold in 1981.

Another venture that the firm tried was mail order. It was announced in 1964 that after much detailed organization and planning, the firm was ready to go ahead with the newly created Burton-by-Post venture. This was unprofitable and was sold in 1970. In spite of these schemes, aimed at diversifying the company's outlets and products, it remained dependent on sales of men's tailored clothing. With the exception of the small chain of women's shops doing business as Peter Robinson and the prestigious general outfitters Browns of Chester, the only women's clothing outlets were the Burton shops, hence the move into the women's trade with the purchase of Evans Outsizes in 1971. Sometimes the search for diversity could lead the firm in unaccustomed directions, as with the acquisition of Ryman's chain of shops specializing in office equipment, with a separate drawing office. This venture ended in 1981.

Another example of the search for diversity, announced by Ladislas Rice on joining the firm in 1969, was the purchase of Greens Leisure Centre with 41 branches specializing in photographic equipment. This was never a profitable enterprise and was disposed of in 1976. A venture more closely related to

Burton's primary business was an attempt to break into the children's market with the establishment of the Orange Hand Shops. This development lasted just four years, and in 1976 the company decided that it could no longer justify further investment in the endeavor as it was unprofitable.

In January 1972 the chairman's report, having declared its intentions to become known as a group in 1969, announced: "Our company is now on the way to becoming a group of specialist retail chains each with a clearly defined market and a distinctive face to the public . . . . We intend to maintain and develop our dominant position in the menswear market. However, we shall become less completely dependent on it as our newer retailing activities grow."

In conjunction with this strategy, Burton discontinued manufacturing on grounds of cost. The rationale of the process—probably the most important in its history—was outlined by Ralph Halpern (later Sir Ralph) in his chairman's report of December 1981. After detailing the reasons why Burton had fallen behind the British clothing retailers in general, he outlined measures to retrieve the situation. First was the curtailing of the company's manufacturing activity. Second was the application to other company chains of retailing methods evolved by the Top Shop sector, and third was the shedding of all the loss-making activities.

Draconian measures saw Burton emerge with its sights set on retail selling with different divisions specializing in differ-ent market areas. Two new chains of shops were added, Principles for Women in 1984 and Principles for Men in 1985, specializing in high-quality clothing, and Debenhams's chain of 67 stores and the shops of John Collier were acquired. The parent company changed its name to The Burton Group plc in 1985. Principles for Women and Principles for Men merged to become Principles in 1990. November 1990 saw the retirement of Sir Ralph Halpern, the man who had transformed the firm of Burton almost beyond recognition. The company continues to develop new retailing initiatives.

Principal Subsidiaries: Burton BV (Netherlands); Burton Capital BV (Netherlands); Burton Fashion Holdings Ltd.; Collier Holdings Ltd.; Debenhams plc; Montague Burton Property Investments Ltd.

Further Reading: Fraser, J. Foster, *Goodwill in Industry*, Leeds, Burton, 1925; Redmayne, Ronald, *Ideals in Industry*, Leeds, Burton, 1951; Sigsworth, Eric M., *Montague Burton the Tailor of Taste*, Manchester, Manchester University Press, 1990.

—Eric Milton Sigsworth

C&A BRENNINKMEYER KG

Bleichstrasse 20
4000 Düsseldorf 1
Federal Republic of Germany
(0211) 35591

Private Company
Incorporated: 1841
Sales: DM7.04 billion (US$4.65 billion)

C&A Brenninkmeyer KG is a paradox. It operates highly visible stores in Germany, but is a secretive, privately-owned company. Little has been published on the organization and it is hard to get information from the company on its operations beyond its publicity for its fashions.

Large clothing stores of similar appearance to the German ones operate under the name C&A in other Western European countries, for example in the United Kingdom and the Netherlands. They are described as being operated by entirely autonomous and independent companies. Any links that might exist are unclear and ambiguous, and company sources are unwilling to qualify them. Confusion exists among the general public about the various C&A companies. In the United Kingdom, for example, some people believe C&A to be a Dutch company. In fact, both C&A and the large family that controls it have a long history of keeping a foot in both Germany and the Netherlands.

The Brenninkmeyer family has its roots in Mettingen, a small community in the Tecklenburg area of today's northwest Germany, not far from the present border with the Netherlands, a country with which the area has strong links. Originally, Tecklenburg natives spoke a dialect of Low German with some resemblances to Dutch. Especially in the 17th century, Holland's golden age, much of the area's commerce focused on Holland's international ports and rich trading markets. Even today, the Rhine River and canals link much of northwest Germany to the ports of Rotterdam and Amsterdam.

The first trading Brenninkmeyers left the family farm in Mettingen in 1671 to become traveling linen sellers in Holland. It is said that even then they were secretive about their business. At this time, secrecy gave them a commercial advantage and permitted the avoidance of customs charges.

In 1841, the brothers Clemens and August Brenninkmeyer abandoned the itinerant life and laid the groundwork for the C&A chain when they opened their first store in the small Dutch town of Snook. The small firm of textile sellers was

very successful, and within the next few years further stores were opened in the Dutch cities of Leuuwarden, Amsterdam, Utrecht, Rotterdam, Groningen, Leiden, Haarlem, and Enschede. Many of Clemens and August Brenninkmeyer's descendants have been active in the company throughout its history.

The second Clemens Brenninkmeyer became the driving force behind the family's expansion into Germany. In 1911 he opened C&A, the family's first large German department store, in Berlin. In the next year he opened another Berlin clothing store. In 1913 new branches were opened in Hamburg and Cologne and in 1914 another store was established in Essen. World War I presented the family with few international problems, because Holland remained neutral throughout the conflict.

After World War I, Germany became the major focus of expansion, despite its inflation and other economic problems. By hard work and constant travel between branches, Clemens Brenninkmeyer made a success of the German operation. By 1928, C&A had eight stores, and at the outbreak of World War II, there were 17.

Clemens Brenninkmeyer's efforts at further international expansion were only partially successful. The first British store was opened in London's Oxford Street in 1922. Later in the decade, other British stores were opened in Birmingham and Liverpool.

In contrast, C&A's most successful field of operations, Germany, was coming under the control of the strongly nationalist and anti-Semitic Nazi regime. The Dutch Catholic family had to come to terms with this new German government. C&A's Dutch background put its German expansion plans at risk. Nazi laws required the firm to gain government permission to open new branches. Some Nazis were also suspicious of the firm's church connections.

The firm emphasized its pre-Nazi, anti-Jewish hiring policies and the family's distant German origins. In a 1937 application to open a store in Leipzig, the board asked for assistance from Hermann Göring, the author of the state economic plan, and successfully argued that it had struggled against Jewish-owned business and prohibited the employment of Jews in the past.

Against further 1938 allegations by influential Nazi party members that C&A was Dutch, the firm's Berlin representatives stressed the Brenninkmeyer family's German roots in Mettingen. They claimed the family had been forced to take Dutch citizenship by a 1787 law.

World War II brought hardship as the officially neutral firm was cut off from its stores in England by the German invasion of Holland in 1940, and merchandise supplies became harder to obtain because of rationing. As the tide of the war began to turn in favor of the Allies, the Brenninkmeyers began to return to the Netherlands. By the end of the war, only two of the firm's 17 German locations remained relatively unscathed by bombing and fighting.

As the West German *Wirtschaftswunder*—economic miracle—proved to be a powerhouse in the rebuilding of the wider European economy, the Brenninkmeyers returned to make Germany the focal point of their business empire again. The 1950s and 1960s were boom years for C&A in Germany. From 1952 to 1971, the number of C&A clothing and textile stores rose from 17 to 72. By 1982 there were 116 branches worldwide.

This success was based on an ability to spot trends in clothing fashions and sell inexpensive versions to an increasingly affluent and style-conscious public. Unlike some competitors, C&A's buying was centralized in specialized teams at an early date to achieve volume discounts.

Constant review of stocks and demand by buyers and managers has long been another policy of C&A. Heavy advertising is then concentrated on the appropriate merchandise. Small manufacturers with C&A contracts, considered lucrative in Germany, had to be willing to change specifications at short notice. C&A also produces confectionery and a small minority of its clothing merchandise in its own factories.

The organization has also been characterized by very tight cost controls. Brenninkmeyer family managers always carried little books, constantly updated with the details of every business for quick review.

In the 1960s stores under the name C&A were opened in Belgium, France, and Switzerland. By 1963, C&A fulfilled a long-cherished dream by gaining a foothold in the U.S. market with the acquisition of the seven Nathan Ohrbach retail stores.

Throughout the postwar period, secrecy has remained a pillar of C&A corporate policy. Important members of the Brenninkmeyer family on the governing board are hardly known outside German financial circles. When C&A's management is quoted in the press, it tends to be in the form of positive statements of company sales policy, such as "No store sells cheaper" or—the most famous statement—"We let our merchandise speak for us."

The desire for secrecy is so important that it even led the firm to change its legal status. After the German Bundestag passed new disclosure rules for the GmbH (Gesellschaften mit beschränkter Haftung), C&A Brenninkmeyer became a KG (Kommanditgesellschaft), or limited partnership, in September 1969. The move allowed the family to withhold much of the company's financial information from the public.

Secrecy seemed to insulate the company from change and criticism of other policies that appeared anachronistic. The company's paternalism and preference for hiring Catholics have attracted particular criticism from the media. An article published in *Manager Magazine* in 1982 described how the Brenninkmeyers expected their recruits in Germany to live an austere existence in company-run hostels during a four-year training period. Recruits were required to be devout Catholics and attend mass. The rest of the week was devoted to work training and study for compulsory examinations. If managers became engaged, they were required to give the company details on the betrothed's parents and religion. Non-Catholic affianced partners were expected to convert, or at least agree to a Catholic ceremony and Catholic religious education for the couple's children. A fiancé or fiancée who worked for C&A was expected to resign.

The company's governing board and top management positions have been dominated by members of the Brenninkmeyer family and those related to them through marriage. There are some indications that these policies are changing.

C&A was slower than some other firms in reacting to the collapse of the East German regime in November 1989 and to subsequent German unification. This initial reluctance was partly its usual caution, but was also due to the need to settle property questions over prewar store sites in Leipzig and elsewhere. After C&A's inexpensive fashions proved popular with East Germans living near the border, making a strong contribution to 1990 profits, the company required no more convincing to expand into the former East Germany.

By autumn 1991, new C&A stores had opened in Guntherstadt, Chemnitz, formerly Karl Marx Stadt, and Magdeburg. There were plans to reopen a C&A on a prewar site in Leipzig. West German expansion continued, however, with new stores planned in Lunen, Ingolstadt, Ravensburg, and Regensburg. Some expenditures and expansion plans elsewhere were reduced in order to concentrate on investment in a unified Germany.

Many Brenninkmeyer family members have retained Dutch citizenship and strong ties to Holland, but others have taken on German or other citizenships.

Düsseldorf became the company's center of operations in the early 1950s. Nearly two-thirds of the stores operating under the name C&A are in Germany. Like the company's tradition of secrecy, strict family control, and Catholic paternalism over management and employees, C&A's national focus seems anachronistic in a competitive, multinational European Community. C&A is, however, a successful company, with consistent profits and growth.

Principal Subsidiaries: C&A Unterstutzugskasse GmbH; C&A Nederland CV; C&A Mode AG (Switzerland).

—Clark Siewert

CAMPEAU CORPORATION

40 King Street West, Suite 5800
Toronto, Ontario M5H 3Y8
Canada
(416) 868-6460

Public Company
Incorporated: 1968
Employees: 91,800
Sales: C$12.13 billion (US$10.46 billion)
Stock Exchanges: Toronto Montreal NASDAQ

Once a successful Canadian real estate development company, Campeau Corporation struggled in the late 1980s and early 1990s under the burden of debt incurred in its ambitious, some have said ill-advised, leveraged buyouts of U.S. retailers Allied Stores Corporation and Federated Department Stores, Inc. Retained as subsidiaries, both Allied and Federated filed for Chapter 11 bankruptcy protection soon after they were acquired, developments that would seem to threaten their parent company's long-term welfare. In 1991 Campeau Corporation planned a restructuring that would take it back to being primarily a real estate developer and manager.

The story of Campeau Corporation is inseparable from that of its founder and longtime guiding light, Robert Campeau. Born in 1924 to a poor French-Canadian family in the Ontario mining town of Sudbury, Campeau dropped out of school at the age of 14 to help support his siblings. He started out as a factory laborer, but ventured into real estate at the age of 25 after building a house for his family. Instead of moving in to it, he sold it for a hefty profit, and from then on construction and development were his life. During the 1950s and 1960s he would make a successful career by building houses in the Ottowa area and developing several prominent commercial real estate projects on Toronto's lakefront. His residential developments proved quite popular, and the term "Campeau-built house" became synonymous in Canada with high quality. In 1968 he consolidated seven of his companies into Campeau Corporation.

Campeau confined his activities to real estate through the 1970s, except when he tried to acquire Bushnell Communications from Vancouver-based Western Broadcasting Company in 1974. The Canadian Radio-Television Commission voided the deal, ruling that Campeau had insufficient expertise and interest in operating television stations to make a suitable owner of Bushnell.

Campeau reached something of a turning point in 1980 when he tried to acquire Royal Trustco, Canada's largest real estate trust company and a stalwart member of the country's English-speaking banking establishment. He already owned 5.4% of the company and wanted to gain access to its considerable real estate holdings. Royal Trustco's directors vetoed the offer on the grounds that Campeau did not yet have approval from the U.S. Securities and Exchange Commission, which was required because of the trust company's 17 branch banks in Florida. When this did not deter him, Royal Trustco management, appalled at the prospect of being controlled by an outsider, secretly persuaded some of the nation's largest corporations to buy up the majority of its stock and keep it out of Campeau's hands. Campeau professed no bitterness, but likely harbored some resentment over the Royal Trustco affair, which convinced him that Canada's business establishment would always be closed to him.

To a substantial extent Robert Campeau's quest for respectability had influenced the course of his career. As a French-Canadian, Campeau is likely to have seen himself as a representative of a minority group that believes itself to be an underdog in a nation dominated by its English majority. "There aren't enough French-Canadian businesses," he once said. "It's very much my plan that my business should stay in the hands of my children and that it represent part of the French-Canadian business world."

Campeau's ambition soon took him south of the U.S.-Canadian border. He saw U.S. society as free and open, unlike what he saw as the closed and snobbish Canadian establishment that he had just tried to join. He also viewed an acquisition in retailing as a way of building a U.S. commercial real estate empire—Campeau-owned stores would provide ready-made tenants for Campeau-developed shopping centers. He spent five years casting about for a suitable target before settling on Allied, then the sixth-largest department store company in the United States.

Allied was founded in 1929, when 27 department store companies—including Boston, Massachusetts's Jordan Marsh Co. and Seattle, Washington's The Bon Marche—merged to form Hahn Department Stores, Inc. The next year, Hahn added Joske Bros. Co. of San Antonio, Texas, and Tampa, Florida's Maas Bros. The early years of the Great Depression inflicted such hardship, however, that the company soon felt that it ought to look outside its ranks for financial guidance. It brought in real estate baron B. Earl Puckett, who would run the company for 25 years. In 1935, Hahn Department Stores changed its name to Allied Stores Corporation.

Under Puckett, Allied pursued a policy of opportunistic expansion. From the mid-1930s through the 1940s, the company accumulated retailers and real estate from coast to coast as good bargains became available. By the end of World War II Allied had become the largest department store holding company in the United States, as well as the most profitable. Puckett also foresaw many of the most important developments to affect retailing in the postwar period, like the flight of the U.S. middle class to the suburbs and the decay of downtown areas, and positioned Allied to take advantage of them. In 1950 the company opened one of the first suburban shopping malls—the Northgate shopping center in Tacoma, Washington, just outside Seattle, with a Bon Marche branch as its centerpiece.

Allied continued to expand in the early 1950s. In 1951 it acquired New York–based Stern Bros., through which it hoped to establish a substantial presence in the New Jersey suburban market. At the same time, the company began to show the ill effects of its lack of coherent planning. Puckett had acquired properties haphazardly, more or less without giving thought to how they would integrate into the company or affect Allied's long-term position in a given market. They were simply bargains too good to miss. As a result Allied wound up with many stores in small towns, away from the lucrative metropolitan areas. Although it dominated Boston through Jordan Marsh, Florida through Maas Brothers, and the Pacific Northwest through Bon Marche, it was unrepresented in fast-growing markets like Chicago, Washington, D.C., and Los Angeles and San Francisco, California. In many cities in which it was present, its position was weak or its growth potential was limited. So while its rivals boomed amid the general prosperity of the decade, Allied suffered, its return on sales in 1960 being only half of what it had been ten years earlier. In 1957 the company lost its position as the leading U.S. department store company to its future companion in the Campeau fold, Federated Department Stores, Inc.

Puckett retired in 1959 and was succeeded as CEO by Theodore Schlesinger, an Allied executive who had already logged 30 years with the company. Schlesinger tried to revitalize Allied by decentralizing authority, giving more autonomy to its units in big cities, while grouping its stores in small cities under regional managers. He also tried to attract customers by giving some units, like Stern Brothers and Joske, a more upscale image, and turning others into discounters. In 1960 Allied also acquired Cincinnati-based Mabley & Carew Co. and merged it with its own struggling Rollman subsidiary, formerly Rollman & Sons Co. Discounting proved to be an unsuccessful strategy at first, but the company learned from those early mistakes and opened a chain of stores called Almart in the mid-1960s.

Allied showed considerable financial improvement under Schlesinger, but the retail slump of the late 1960s practically wiped out those gains. To make matters even worse, recessions in the aerospace and paper industries slowed the economy in the Northwest and hurt Bon Marche's sales. Thomas Macioce succeeded Schlesinger in 1971 and immediately revived Allied by reducing store size and changing the merchandise mix to include more high-margin, high-turnover soft goods like clothes and less low-turnover hard goods, like housewares and furniture. Believing that discounting would soon become a thing of the past, he also began to close down Almart stores, selling the last of them to Montgomery Ward in 1979.

Macioce wanted to upgrade Allied's image. In 1979 the company purchased several fashion chains: the stores of the Bonwit Teller Division and Plymouth Shops Division of Genesco. In 1981 it acquired Garfinckel, Brooks Brothers, and Miller & Rhoads, which also owned the AnnTaylor chain of women's clothing shops. Allied's profitability continued to improve as it terminated unprofitable subsidiaries; in 1982 it merged Gertz's, formerly B. Gertz, Inc., into Stern's, and in 1984 it closed down its Pennsylvania-based Troutman's division, formerly A.E. Troutman Co. Under Macioce, Allied regained its footing—although its most recent acquisitions had saddled it with a debt slightly higher than normal—and anchored itself in a handful of upscale, high-profile department and speciality stores. This, in short, was the state of the company when Robert Campeau set his sights on it.

In the spring of 1986, Campeau began friendly merger talks with Allied, but got no further than a proposal that Allied would sell him five shopping centers. By the end of the summer it became apparent that to acquire Allied, a hostile takeover would be necessary. To the naked eye, the prospect of Campeau buying out Allied seemed like a herring trying to swallow a whale; Campeau Corporation posted revenues of only $153 million in 1985, compared to Allied's $4.1 billion in sales. With Wall Street feverish and wild-eyed over leveraged buyouts, however, Campeau assumed that he could borrow as much as he needed to do the job. He was right. Help came from First Boston and a Citibank-led syndicate, promising more than $3 billion in credit, and Campeau commenced hostilities in September. Allied tried to escape by making a deal that would allow shopping center magnate Edward DeBartolo Sr. to acquire it. Campeau responded with a tender offer worth $66 a share, more than $20 above Allied's share price two months earlier. Then, on October 24, Campeau suddenly dropped his offer and took Allied by force, buying huge blocks of stock on the open market at $67 a share. Within 30 minutes, he accumulated a 53% stake.

For tax reasons, the deal had to be completed before the end of the year, and would require an extra $300 million in financing. Citibank and DeBartolo, the latter of whom wanted to ensure his own long-term relationship with Allied's real estate operations, obliged, each supplying half. When Campeau's and Allied's debts were figured together—along with $210 million in advising fees—the acquisition was estimated to cost more than $5 billion. In order to pay for it, Campeau announced that he would sell off most of Allied's units, retaining only choice morsels like Brooks Brothers, Jordan Marsh, and AnnTaylor. In March 1987, he launched a $1.2 billion junk bond and preferred stock offering to pay off First Boston. By the end of 1987, Campeau had sold off $1 billion worth of Allied property and paid off much of his debt ahead of schedule.

All was not well at Allied. Thomas Macioce resigned in January, even though Campeau had made him chairman of the new parent company. Campeau succeeded him at Allied on an interim basis, then hired Howard Morosky, a former executive at rival retailer The Limited, as a replacement later that year. Allied's financial results were not encouraging. The company earned just $44 million in the first three quarters of 1987, while interest payments for that period totaled $244 million.

Casting aside whatever doubts this might have raised, however, Campeau soon made plans to grab Federated. True to its name, Federated Department Stores began as a loose federation of three department store companies. It was formed in 1929 when Walter Rothschild of New York City–based Abraham & Straus, Inc.; Louis Kirstein of Boston-based William Filene's Sons Co.; and Fred Lazarus of Cincinnati-based F. & R. Lazarus & Co. met on Rothschild's yacht and decided to band together to spread the risks of the retail trade among themselves. They were joined the next year by New York's Bloomingdale Bros. Inc.

The arrangement worked so well that it eventually outlived its usefulness. By the end of World War II all of the stores were so profitable that it bred some resentment among those who were contributing the most profits to the group—specifically F. & R. Lazarus. Instead of disbanding, however, Federated took the opposite approach and established a central management group in 1945, headed by Fred Lazarus. Thus,

Federated evolved from a loose tribal alliance into a genuine department store holding company.

After three months at the helm, Lazarus acquired Foley Brothers Dry Goods Co., a Houston department store. Foreseeing that the Sun Belt would attract more and more of the U.S. population in the postwar period, he was anxious to enter the Texas market. Changes were also taking place in New York, where Bloomingdale's was shedding its image as "the poor man's Macy's" to become an upscale fashion store. In 1948 Federated acquired the Milwaukee Boston Store, Inc., and three years later it returned to Texas to purchase Dallas-based Sanger Bros., Inc. Also in 1951, the company began building a chain of department stores in small and medium-sized cities. The Fedway stores, as they were called, never proved to be very profitable, however, and the division was sold off 20 years later. Federated, however, continued to grow and prosper; in 1956 it acquired Miami-based Burdine's, Inc., and the next year it overtook Allied.

Federated did not stop there. In 1959 it acquired Gold-smith's of Memphis, Tennessee, and Dayton's Rike-Kumler Co. In 1961 it purchased Dallas-based A. Harris & Co., later merging it with Sanger Brothers to form Sanger-Harris & Co. In 1964 Federated entered the Los Angeles market when it acquired Bullock's, Inc., the city's fourth-largest department store, despite bitter opposition from Bullock's chief executive and founder, Percy G. Winnett. Bullock's later formed two divisions: Bullock's and I. Magnin. What made Federated's continuous growth by acquisition all the more remarkable was that it had always operated with relatively little direction from central management; divisions were granted a high degree of autonomy and had the freedom to develop individual identities. In fact, Abraham & Straus Chairman Sidney Solomon liked to refer to the company as a "states' rights organization."

Fred Lazarus's son Ralph succeeded him as chairman and CEO of Federated in 1967. Under Ralph Lazarus, Federated pushed the limits of its diversity even further. In 1967 the company opened a chain of discount stores called Gold Circle to sell clothing and other soft goods. The next year, it plunged into the supermarket business when it acquired Los Angeles–based Ralphs Industries, subsequently renamed Ralphs Grocery Company. Also in 1968, Federated formed another discount chain, Gold Triangle, which specialized in housewares and other hard goods, and in 1971 it launched a discounting venture, Gold Key, that sold furniture.

Federated rode high during the 1970s, despite the economic stagnation that seemed to mark the entire decade. The company's sales reached $3.3 billion in 1975, and it solidified its place as the kingpin of the department store industry. All of its units occupied strong or dominant positions in their local markets, and the autonomy that they had under Federated's management scheme allowed them to stock merchandise independently, according to local customer taste, and adjust inventory levels as justified by the strength or weakness of local economies. The company continued to expand; in 1976 it acquired the Atlanta-based department store Rich's Inc.

Federated's prosperity was beginning to sour even as Howard Goldfeder succeeded Ralph Lazarus in 1981. Discounting had failed as a valid concept for department stores, but Federated was slow to catch on to that idea. Finally, in 1981, it closed its Gold Circle stores in California and six Gold Triangle stores. In 1985 it closed its Gold Circle stores in Pitts-burgh and sold the properties to Kimco Development, a Roslyn, New York–based strip-mall developer. Poor financial results from several other units also hurt the company, as did Federated's inability to centralize billing and inventory control because division presidents could not agree on what computer system to use. The company's celebrated autonomy, it seemed, had finally become a hindrance.

Despite its travails, Federated was still a daunting objective for Campeau, three times as large as Allied; but Campeau would not be denied. On January 25, 1988, he launched a takeover bid valued at $4.2 billion, or $47 a share; Federated had sold at $33 a month earlier. Two weeks later, Federated announced its refusal, after which Campeau sweetened his offer to $66 a share. Then, on February 29, R.H. Macy & Co., Inc., jumped into the fray with a surprise bid worth $73.80 a share. Proposals and counterproposals followed throughout March. Finally, on April 1, all three sides announced a deal in which Campeau would acquire Federated for $73.50 a share—total cost, $6.6 billion—and give Macy a commitment to sell it Bullock's, Bullock's Wilshire, and I. Magnin, the units it had wanted all along, for $1.1 billion.

Campeau's backing for the Federated deal included more than $4 billion in loans from First Boston, Dillon Read, and Paine Webber as well as loan commitments from a syndicate led by Citibank and the Japanese Sumitomo group. For its part, Campeau had to pony up $1.4 billion in equity, most of which was actually disguised debt. The Reichmann brothers, who owned Toronto-based real estate developer Olympia & York, bought $260 million worth of Campeau convertible debentures, and most of their money went into the Federated deal. Edward DeBartolo loaned Campeau $480 million in exchange for a minority stake in Federated. Bank of Montreal and Banque Paribas also made a $500 million, steep-interest loan that had to be repaid in one year. The remaining cash appeared when Campeau sold high-toned, high-income Brooks Brothers to British department store company Marks & Spencer PLC in April for a whopping $750 million. He used most of the cash to pay off bank debt, but sank the remaining $193 million into Federated stock. The move infuriated Allied bondholders, who felt that the money should have been used to satisfy his debt to them.

It got no easier for Campeau once the deal was done. In May 1988 Howard Morosky resigned after it became apparent that his boss had lost confidence in him. He was replaced as Campeau's retail chief by Federated executive John Burden III. Both Allied and Federated posted huge losses in the third quarter, due entirely to enormous interest costs. Layoffs and consolidations between the two subsidiaries only lowered employee morale even further and failed to yield significant savings. Before the year was out, Campeau sold Gold Circle to Kimco Development, AnnTaylor to former Lord & Taylor chairman Joseph E. Brooks, and Federated's MainStreet division to Kohl's Department Stores, but none fetched the prices expected of them. Even junk bond investors were becoming skeptical. In October 1988, a $1.2 billion Federated offering at 14% had to be cut back to $723 million at 16% and 17.75% because of lack of demand.

Campeau's inexperience in the retail trade had led him to grossly overestimate the revenues he could expect from Allied and Federated. In early 1989 a retail recession, the consequence of all-time high levels of consumer debt, proved crippling.

Sales for the two units were only a fraction of what had been projected, and with interest costs, they posted a combined $306.3 million loss in the first half of the year. In September the Reichmanns, who had agreed to loan $250 million to the retail operations, persuaded Campeau to accept a plan under which he would sell Bloomingdale's and negotiate with his bondholders to buy back 75% of his junk debt at reduced rates. When the plan was made public and the depth of Campeau's predicament became clear, the value of his bonds plummeted, and they took the rest of the junk-bond market with them. Still desperate for cash at the end of the year, Allied and Federated stores started a brutal and costly price war with their competitors during the Christmas shopping season.

As 1990 began, no buyer for Bloomingdale's could be found. The Reichmanns were wielding significant influence in the company by now, and in January Campeau's board of directors pulled the retail operations out from under him and placed them under independent control. The board then put Allied and Federated into Chapter 11 and later reorganized them as Federated Stores, with former Treasury Secretary and Federated director G. William Miller at its head. In February Campeau Corporation dismantled its Campeau Development subsidiary and began selling off its Canadian real estate assets to raise cash.

The trouble did not end even there. The real estate market in Canada had gone soft, and there was little money to be raised there. In March 1990 Campeau Corporation defaulted on $225 million owed to Olympia & York, as well as the $480 million Edward DeBartolo had loaned for the Federated takeover. In August, the final blow fell as Robert Campeau's own board of directors voted to remove him as chairman and CEO of the company that he had founded. He was succeeded on an interim basis by James Raymond, a representative of National Bank of Canada, one of Campeau's personal creditors, and Gary Goodman, an Olympia & York executive, both serving as co-CEOs. Three months later, the board appointed Stanley Hartt, a former chief of staff to Canadian Prime Minister Brian Mulroney, as permanent president and CEO. Observers considered Hartt to be a fortunate choice, not only because of his status as a public figure, but because he had no past associations with the company.

Hartt engineered a restructuring designed to make Campeau a smaller and vastly different company. In 1990 and 1991 it sold 22 office buildings, shopping centers, and development properties for $1.2 billion, which went to pay off debts. It reached settlements with DeBartolo and the Reichmanns, and set up a new subsidiary, Camdev Properties Inc., to operate Campeau's real estate business. It made plans to sell off its U.S. subsidiaries to their creditors and to create a new parent company, Camdev Corporation, which would be involved primarily in real estate development and management, with its only interest in retailing being a 13% share in Ralphs. U.S. and Canadian courts were scheduled to act on this plan early in 1992. If the plan were approved, the new company would have only 180 employees, thus marking the end of Campeau Corporation's era as a retailing giant.

Principal Subsidiaries: Allied Stores Corp. (U.S.A.); Federated Department Stores, Inc. (U.S.A.); Campeau Canada; Ralphs Grocery Company; Federated Stores, Inc. (U.S.A.).

Further Reading: "The First Family of Retailing," *Forbes,* March 15, 1961; "Renaissance at Allied Stores," *Forbes,* August 1, 1966; Carruth, Eleanore, "Federated Department Stores: Growing Pains at Forty," *Fortune,* June 1969; "This Peacock Won't Be Tomorrow's Feather Duster," *Forbes,* June 15, 1975; McNish, Jacquie, "Campeau's Bid to Acquire Allied Stores Is Its Chairman's Boldest Endeavor Yet," *The Wall Street Journal,* September 8, 1986; Barmash, Isadore, "Canadian Bidder Beats Macy in Fight for Federated Stores," *The New York Times,* April 2, 1988; "Campeau Retail Chains are Heavily in Debt, Face Rising Troubles," *The Wall Street Journal,* December 14, 1988; Loomis, Carol J., "The Biggest, Looniest Deal Ever," *Fortune,* June 18, 1990.

—Douglas Sun

CARTER HAWLEY HALE STORES, INC.

444 South Flower Street
Los Angeles, California 90071
U.S.A.
(213) 620-0150
Fax: (213) 620-0555

Public Company
Incorporated: 1919 as The Broadway Department Store
Employees: 29,000
Sales: $2.86 billion
Stock Exchanges: New York Pacific London

Carter Hawley Hale Stores, Inc. is one of the largest department store retailers in the United States. Headquartered in Los Angeles and concentrated in California, it operates 89 stores through four divisions: The Broadway-Southern California, The Broadway-Southwest, The Emporium, and Weinstocks. In 1991 the company was in reorganization under Chapter 11 of the U.S. Bankruptcy Code, a situation brought about by high debt levels and a downturn in the retail industry.

Carter Hawley Hale traces its origins back to 1896, when Arthur Letts opened the first Broadway department store at 4th and Broadway in downtown Los Angeles. Letts's Broadway store was among the first wave of indigenous California department stores, a wave that included The Emporium in San Francisco, The H.C. Capwell Company in Oakland, and O.A. Hall & Co. in northern California, among others.

With more than 600,000 square feet of selling space, Letts's store was successful in selling men's and women's clothing, crockery, and a variety of other items. In 1919 the Broadway Department Store of Los Angeles incorporated in the state of California. Business remained good through the 1920s, and in 1926 the Broadway reincorporated under the more favorable laws of Delaware.

By 1931 Malcom McNaghten had become The Broadway's president. McNaghten made his first move toward expansion in March 1931 when he acquired the Hollywood store of the B.H. Dyas Corporation. McNaghten quickly converted the 230,000-square-foot facility to Broadway standards and began operating it as the Broadway-Hollywood the same year. Sales increased yearly during the 1930s, reaching $16.2 million in 1939. Earnings, however, were erratic. In 1934 the company lost $5,000. Net income hit $539,000 in 1937 but fell to $160,000 the following year.

In 1940 McNaghten returned to expansion, opening The Broadway-Pasadena on November 15. With 95,000 square feet of floor space, the new store contained three stories for selling and a partial basement for service departments. At year's end, sales reached $15.9 million, while income topped $231,000. During World War II, both sales and profits boomed; 1945 sales reached $31.7 million, and that year's profits topped $1 million for the first time.

With McNaghten's retirement imminent, the directors hired Edward W. Carter as vice president in 1945. Promoted to president the following year, he took charge of an outfit not yet at the top of the southern California market. In fact Carter later ranked Broadway stores as "last among Los Angeles department stores both in size and in stature." Carter was a scholarly Harvard graduate with sparkling retail credentials. Within months of his accession to the presidency, he pioneered the suburban shopping center, building one of the nation's first, The Crenshaw Center, on a former golf course outside Los Angeles. In succeeding years, he built a series of Broadway stores along the freeways of suburban Los Angeles.

Carter's plans were ambitious, and he needed capital to fund them. He sought outside investors and in May 1949, sold 195,348 shares of newly issued Broadway Department Stores stock to Hale Brothers Stores, Inc. of San Francisco. First established in 1876, Hale was a family-owned business that operated a women's specialty shop, several radio and appliance stores, Weinstock Lubin & Co., and four other department stores in San Francisco, Sacramento, Oakland, and San Jose. Although Hale had 12 stores, compared to Broadway's four, they were smaller than Broadway's, and Hale's 1948 sales of $38.5 million were almost $10 million less than Broadway's $47.9 million.

Hale operated as a Broadway affiliate until 1951, when Edward Carter and Prentis Hale merged the two companies into Broadway-Hale Stores, Inc. Carter became president of the new company, while Prentis Hale took the new position of chairman of the board. The chains retained their respective names and operated as separate divisions, an arrangement that set the pattern for Broadway-Hale's many future acquisitions.

In the 1950s Carter upgraded the look of Broadway stores, adding carpeting and new, more expensive fixtures. His approach to expansion was regional. He created clusters of stores around metropolitan areas and serviced these stores through centralized local headquarters. All stores had to be within 35 miles or a one-hour drive of a local headquarters that handled buying.

In 1956 Carter and Prentis Hale made their first joint acquisition, paying about $10 million for 99.2% of Dohrmann Commercial Co. First incorporated in 1904, Dohrmann offered diverse operations in retailing and service. Dohrmann Commercial distributed china, glassware, silverware, furniture, appliances, and kitchen equipment through specialty stores in San Francisco and leased departments on the West Coast. Dohrmann Hotel Supply operated 19 hotel supply branches and ran sheet metal plants in California, Washington, Oregon, Nevada, Arizona, and Hawaii. Dohrmann also owned 16% of the Emporium Capwell Company, which in turn owned the largest department stores in San Francisco and Oakland. At the end of 1956, sales topped $106 million, while profits reached $2.7 million. Between 1951 and 1960, sales increased 96%, and earnings tripled, rising from $2.1 million to $6.3 million.

Carter made numerous acquisitions in the 1960s. In March of 1960, Broadway-Hale paid $1.55 million and 60,225 shares of common stock for Coulter's of Los Angeles. The following year Carter forked over 214,857 shares of Broadway-Hale stock for Marston Co. of San Diego, and in June of 1962, Broadway-Hale acquired the entire common stock of Korrick's Inc., an Arizona department store, for 100,000 shares worth an estimated $4.15 million.

Because retailing was Broadway-Hale's concentration, Carter sold Dohrmann Commercial Co. and Dohrmann Hotel Supply for $11.3 million in January of 1962. Broadway-Hale retained the important stock in the Emporium Capwell Corporation and was growing quickly; in 1964, it listed its stock on the New York Stock Exchange.

In 1966 Carter and Hale began making moves toward acquiring a controlling interest in Emporium Capwell. In the mid-1960s the Federal Trade Commission (FTC) was actively involved in approving or disapproving mergers that it felt might impair competition. After consideration, the FTC approved the Emporium merger, but banned Broadway-Hale from further mergers without FTC approval. Broadway-Hale achieved 50.3% ownership of Emporium Capwell in two installments, one in 1967 and another in 1968. At a total cost of more than $72 million, the actual merger of Emporium Capwell into Broadway-Hale did not occur until 1970.

Emporium Capwell was as old as the Broadway and traced its roots to two San Francisco stores, the Golden Rule Bazaar, founded in 1871, and The Emporium, founded in 1886. At the time that Broadway-Hale was seeking a controlling interest, Emporium Capwell consisted of The Emporium, the largest department store in San Francisco; H.C. Capwell Co., the largest department store in Oakland; and 11 other department stores in northern California. The Emporium Capwell acquisition was part of a buying spree that tripled sales between 1968 and 1973. It was a time of voracious acquisitions, one occurring on the heels of another.

On January 15, 1969, Broadway-Hale acquired Sunset House, a leading mail-order chain, for approximately 300,000 convertible $2 preferred shares. On April 16 of the same year, Carter paid $40 million for Dallas-based Neiman Marcus Company. Stanley Marcus's high fashion specialty stores were the darlings of the media, and their acquisition gave Broadway-Hale a caché it had never attained previously. The actual Neiman Marcus stores, however, all three of which were in Texas, had low profit margins. After approving the deal, the FTC ordered Broadway-Hale to refrain from further retailing mergers until 1974. Despite FTC warnings, Edward Carter capped 1969 on November 13, by acquiring Walden Book Company, Inc., the country's largest bookstore chain, for 105,000 convertible common shares.

At the close of 1969, Broadway-Hale Stores was the nation's 13th-largest department store chain—boasting 45 stores—and the biggest retailer in the West. In 1970 Carter finally merged Emporium Capwell and Broadway-Hale, giving Broadway-Hale a network of stores in the major cities of California and parts of the Southwest.

In March 1971 Carter agreed to acquire Bergdorf Goodman Company, one of New York City's most respected retailers. At the time, Bergdorf Goodman had a single store on New York's Fifth Avenue, but as part of the deal, Carter and Andrew Goodman agreed that Broadway-Hale would finance Goodman's move into the suburban markets adjacent to Manhattan. By the end of 1971 sales were up 11%, hitting a record $755.4 million. Earnings, too, soared 24% to $28.6 million.

As a result of Carter's many business achievements, other retailers respected him as a good merchant and a man on top of consumer trends. His approach was decentralized: rather than molding diverse stores into a single coherent chain, as Nordstrom's or Dillard's did, he organized Broadway-Hale into divisions in which each chain had substantial autonomy over its own operations. For their part, Carter and his staff kept close watch on financial reports.

Carter had been president for 25 years and realized it was time to groom a successor. In 1972 he appointed Philip M. Hawley, a Phi Beta Kappa graduate with a degree in economics from the University of California at Berkeley. After a stint at Merrill Lynch, Hawley started a chain of ice cream parlors, one of which was called Broadway Ice Cream Bowl. He began his retail career at Lipman Wolfe Co. in 1952, and in 1958 joined Broadway-Hale as a buyer. In ten years he worked his way up to the presidency of Broadway, completing Harvard's advanced business management program along the way.

With Hawley president, Carter became chief executive officer and Prentis Hale remained chairman of the board. Despite the corporate changes, expansion continued as planned. The acquisition of Bergdorf Goodman was completed, and the Neiman Marcus division opened its first store outside Texas in fashionable Bal Harbour, Florida. Broadway-Hale then acquired Holt Renfrew & Co., a 19-store upscale specialty group based in Montreal.

In May 1973, Carter announced a huge new expansion plan. Broadway-Hale would open 40 stores in a five-year period at a total cost of $350 million. There would be 15 new specialty stores for Bergdorf Goodman, Holt Renfrew, and Neiman Marcus, and 25 new department stores for Broadway, Emporium, Capwell, and Weinstocks. The goal of the expansion program was $1.5 billion in sales by 1977.

While Carter and Hawley were pursuing their expansion plans, they continued on the acquisitions trail. In 1974, they paid more than $78 million for a 20% stake in House of Fraser Ltd., which operated Harrods of London, 135 other retail stores in Britain, and Illium's of Copenhagen. Although European merchandising was not the company's grand ambition, the deal seemed too good to pass up. In 1975, management changed the company's name from Broadway-Hale to Carter Hawley Hale Stores, Inc.

In 1977 Philip Hawley succeeded Edward Carter as chief executive officer. In an interview with *The Wall Street Journal*, June 19, 1984, Hawley said the company he now took charge of was a "confederation of retailers under a common owner that hadn't made any effort at melding the various businesses." With this in mind, Hawley saw his main goal as melding Carter Hawley Hale's diverse retailing businesses into a single well-run company. He convened a six-member corporate planning committee that over a period of 18 months created a plan for the future.

While Hawley saw the need for better management of existing holdings, he continued shuffling divisions, first selling the House of Fraser holdings for $76 million and then unsuccessfully bidding for Chicago-based Marshall Field & Company. In fiscal year 1977, the company earned $42 million, or $1.97 a share, on sales of $1.4 billion. Earnings as a percentage of total revenue were lower than in the early 1970s, and the company fell short of its goal of $1.7 billion for 1977 sales.

One of Carter Hawley Hale's biggest years for acquisitions was 1978. In February, the trustees of John Wanamaker, the venerable but shaky Philadelphia chain, asked Hawley to acquire the concern. In May a deal was completed for the 15-store, $280 million–in-sales retailer. In June of the same year, Carter Hawley Hale acquired Thalhimer Brothers of Richmond, Virginia. With 26 outlets and sales of $140 million, Thalhimer was one of the largest independent department stores in the Southeast.

Despite the massive growth, many were dissatisfied with Carter Hawley Hale's earnings. In 1978, Carter Hawley ranked 13th in return on sales with a 3.3% profit margin. In April 1980 *Forbes* complained that "Carter Hawley Hale's weak per share-earnings progress stems not from management bumbling but rather from the company's almost limitless fascination with buying up great old retailing names and trying to convert them into profitable businesses."

To improve profits, Philip Hawley centralized and standardized store planning and design, security, budget reviews, and personnel policies. He instituted a corporate marketing services department that centralized buying and began working on higher-margin house brands. Despite these moves, which expanded the staff from 65 to 275—not huge for a company with annual sales of $3.63 billion—earnings dropped 17% in 1981.

By 1983, Carter Hawley Hale's portfolio of stores made it the nation's sixth-largest retailer. Department stores accounted for 66% of sales, including 40 Broadway stores in Southern California; 10 Broadway-Southwest stores in Arizona, Nevada, and New Mexico; 21 Emporium Capwell stores in northern California; 25 Thalhimers stores in southern Virginia, North Carolina, and South Carolina; 16 John Wanamakers in Pennsylvania, New Jersey, Delaware, and New York; and 12 Weinstocks in California, Nevada, and Utah.

High-fashion specialty stores accounted for 21% of sales, including Bergdorf Goodman in New York City, 19 Neiman-Marcus stores around the country, and 17 assorted stores in Canada. Specialized merchandising operations produced the 13% balance of sales, including 71 Contempo Casuals and 810 Waldenbooks owned by Walden Book Company.

While sales and operations continued to grow, profits declined in 1981 and 1982 and were stagnant in 1983. Some suggested that earnings had been depressed because of Hawley's long-term centralization and modernization strategy, which included building a $75 million computer center. Others were merely dissatisfied with low earnings. When Edward Carter retired in 1983 and Philip Hawley was named chairman, critics further complained that Carter Hawley Hale was too much a one-man show.

Low earnings made Carter Hawley vulnerable to a takeover attempt, which is exactly what happened early in 1984, when Ohio-based retailer The Limited, Inc. offered to buy Carter Hawley for $1.1 billion. Hawley was against selling the company and responded to The Limited's offer by selling 38.6% of voting securities to General Cinema Corporation, a Newton, Massachusetts, soft drink bottler and theater owner that had promised to support Carter Hawley's management. Fearing institutional investors would sell the company out from under it, Carter Hawley also bought 51% of its shares on the open market for $470 million, much of it borrowed. To pay the debt,

Hawley sold Waldenbooks to Kmart Corporation for $295 million.

At the company's June 1985 annual meeting, an optimistic Philip Hawley predicted "substantial profit growth every quarter" and announced plans to spend $650 million renovating stores. At the same time, the more critical press characterized the company as "laggard" and "frequently saddled with stale inventories and a murky merchandising strategy."

Low profits, high interest rates, and substantial debts taken on during the takeover fight proved to by a volatile combination in March 1986, when Standard & Poor's (S&P) placed about $545 million in Carter Hawley Hale Stores debt securities on its Creditwatch list, with negative implications. S&P said, "it now appears that Carter's various retail businesses do not have the fundamental strengths necessary to achieve this turnaround, especially in a competitive retailing environment."

Sensing weakness, The Limited, Inc., in partnership with shopping-mall builder Edward J. DeBartolo Corporation, renewed the takeover fight, offering $55 and then $60 per share for Carter Hawley Hale's assets. Hawley again rejected the takeover bid. As with the first takeover attempt, it bought back shares and turned to General Cinema as its white knight. General Cinema bought 3.56 million shares for a total of $177.9 million.

Once Carter Hawley made the second sale to General Cinema, The Limited withdrew its offer. Hawley had won the takeover battle, but he may have lost the corporate war. Debts were reaching crushing levels, and Carter Hawley Hale now had neither the cash nor the credit for renovation, which was desperately needed if it was to raise earnings.

Hawley's first move was to sell the John Wanamaker stores to Woodward & Lothrop Inc. in January 1987. Next he split the company into two entities: department stores, that would continue to be called Carter Hawley Hale Stores, Inc., and specialty stores that would be controlled by General Cinema. General Cinema would no longer have a significant interest in Carter Hawley Hale. Each of half of Carter Hawley 32.7 million shares was converted into one share in the surviving department store company, one share in the specialty store spin-off, and $17 in cash.

At deal's end, General Cinema controlled Neiman Marcus, Contempo Casuals, and Bergdorf Goodman. These once classy stores were in bad shape and in need of refurbishing. Carter Hawley Hale was left with The Broadway, Broadway-Southwest, Emporium Capwell, Thalhimers, and Weinstocks. Often neglected, these surviving department stores would need much remodeling and remerchandising if they were to provide substantial profits. With huge debts, it was doubtful that Carter Hawley Hale could meet those capital needs.

Disaster struck again in 1989 when the San Francisco earthquake damaged twelve Emporium stores. All closed temporarily, and Emporium's downtown Oakland store remained closed for most of the fiscal year. At year's end the company reported a net loss of $26 million, or $1.03 a share, on sales of $2.86 billion.

Awash in debt, Carter Hawley Hale found it could not finance the store remodeling programs at its four West Coast Divisions—Broadway-California, Broadway-Southwest, Weinstocks, and Emporium—while taking care of Thalhimer in the Southeast. In October 1990 it agreed to sell Thalhimer to May Department Stores for $325 million. Much of the money was used to cut losses and pare debt by about 20% of $1.32 billion. Some money, however, was earmarked for a $110 million remodeling program for 16 to 20 California stores.

Circumstances continued to deteriorate in the winter months. Hawley cut staff by more than 1,000. Stock prices fell to 1⅞ from 14. On February 5, 1991, the major rating agencies downgraded Carter Hawley's $350 million in junk bonds. A plan to sell credit card operations to General Electric Capital Corporation fell through, and a $100 million credit line from the Bank of America collapsed.

On February 11, 1991, the company sought protection from creditiors under Chapter 11 of the U.S. Bankrupcy Code. In hopes of accelerating its emergence from Chapter 11, Carter Hawley Hale sold about 80% of its debt to an investor group, Z/C Subsidiary Corporation, a subsidiary of Zell/Chilmark Fund L.P. In the first six months of its 1991 fiscal year, Carter Hawley Hale reported a slight decrease from the previous year, although revenues began to recover toward the end of the period.

Principal Subsidiaries: Carter Hawley Hale Credit Corp.; Carter Hawley Hale Properties; CHH Holdings, Inc.; Private Business Airservice, Inc.

Further Reading: Barmash, Isadore, "Merchant From the West: E.W. Carter Heads Retail Chain That Bought Bergdorf's," *The New York Times,* June 1971; "Broadway-Hale's Elegant Growth Plan," *Business Week,* April 15, 1972; Merwin, John, "Promises to Keep," *Forbes,* April 28, 1980; Sansweet, Stephen J., "Carter Hawley Trails Show Risk in Adopting Long-Range Strategy," *The Wall Street Journal,* June 19, 1984.

—Jordan Wankoff

Coles Myer Ltd.

COLES MYER LTD.

800 Toorak Road
Tooronga
Victoria 3146
Australia
(03) 829 3111
Fax: (03) 829 6787

Public Company
Incorporated: 1921 as G.J. Coles and Coy. Pty. Ltd.
Employees: 143,000
Sales: A$14.94 billion (US$11.35 billion)
Stock Exchanges: London New York Australia New Zealand

Coles Myer Ltd. is Australia's leading retailer in terms of number of stores—1,650—and selling area. The company owns and operates stores in most sectors of the Australian and New Zealand retail markets. Coles Myer operates a wide range of supermarkets, discount department stores, department stores, clothing stores, liquor stores, take-away food outlets, and automotive service centers. The company claims almost a 16% share of Australian retail sales and is Australia's largest private employer. Coles Myer is one of Australia's leading owners and managers of retail property, with real estate assets estimated at A$1.43 billion in 1991.

The origins of Coles Myer can be traced to the first G.J. Coles & Coy. Ltd. (Coles) discount store, opened in the working-class suburb of Collingwood, Victoria, on April 9, 1914. The "3d., 6d., and 1/-" variety store was founded by George James Coles, who had studied U.S. and U.K. chain-store retailing methods.

In 1919 a much larger store was opened, again in Collingwood, with the slogan "Nothing over 2/6d." In 1921 the proprietary company G.J. Coles & Coy. Pty. Ltd. was formed, and in 1924 the company opened its first city store in Bourke Street, Melbourne. With eight stores to its name, a public company, G.J. Coles & Coy. Ltd. was floated on the Melbourne Stock Exchange in 1927. One year later the first out-of-state store was opened in Pitt Street, Sydney.

The 1930s were years of rapid expansion for the company, with Coles's variety stores being represented in all states of Australia by 1933. A strong commitment to offering affordable goods to all sectors of the community meant that Coles continued to expand despite the Great Depression. The managing director A.W. Coles wrote at this time, "A store has no right to success just because it is open for business and has a bright

display. The goods must reflect the wishes of the community in which the store is located." In 1938 inflation forced the "Nothing over 2/6" policy to be abandoned. A promise of "Satisfaction Guaranteed or Money Cheerfully Refunded" was instituted and continues today.

The outbreak of war in 1939 led to severe merchandise shortages, and 95% of Coles's male staff enlisted. Despite problems, the company survived with the assistance of newly-promoted female managers under the leadership of A.W. Coles, who acted as managing director until 1944. His successor and brother, E.B. Coles, then led the company into another period of expansion that would earn him the title "The Takeover King." Major retailers acquired in this phase included Selfridges (A'asia) Ltd. in New South Wales in 1950, F&G Stores Ltd. in Victoria in 1951, and the Queensland chain of Penneys Ltd. in 1956.

Food retailing was the next significant area to be explored by the company. This began in 1958 with the acquisition of the John Connell Dickins Pty. Ltd. group of 54 grocery stores. The link with supermarket retailing was reinforced in 1959 by the purchase of Beilby's in South Australia and again in 1960 by the acquisition of the Matthews Thompson chain of 265 grocery stores in New South Wales.

In 1962 customers were treated to a "New World of Shopping" with the opening of the first New World supermarket in Frankston, Victoria. This was a new concept in food retailing for Australia—selling groceries, fresh meat, fruit and vegetables, dairy goods, produce, and frozen foods all within one store. Coles New World Supermarkets offered customers more choice, greater savings, and a consistently higher standard of quality than ever before. Coles, in fact, was one of the first Australian retailers to take advantage of the customer trend toward supermarkets—a move that would earn the company a net profit increase of 30.7% and a jump in annual sales of £83 million in the first year.

Following this success, the company then ventured into discount stores. This began in 1967 with the opening of Colmart in Whyalla, South Australia—Coles's first major discount store. In 1968 the company entered a joint venture with U.S. company S.S. Krege—now K mart Corporation—to open K mart discount stores in Australia, giving Coles a 49% interest. The first K mart store was opened in April 1969 at East Burwood, Victoria, introducing the concept of U.S. discount department stores to Australia. The sales performance of these stores surpassed those of many established retailers and K mart soon became a significant force in Australian retailing. In the same year as K mart's launch, the Coles New World Supermarket chain opened its 100th store and became Australia-wide with the unveiling of a store in Freemantle, Western Australia.

In 1977 Sir George Coles, the company's founder, died at the age of 92, having served the company for over 62 years. Continuing a long tradition of positive employee relations, Coles introduced equal benefits for male and female staff in the company's medical scheme and staff superannuation fund. The retirement age for females was extended to 60 years, and the number of staff members who had served the company for more than 25 years exceeded 1,000. The balance of the K mart joint venture was acquired by the company in December 1978, making it a wholly owned subsidiary of Coles and making the company the second-largest employer in Australia, with more than 50,000 employees.

The 1980s saw Coles diversify still further. In July 1981, 54 liquor stores operating as Claude Fay Cellars were acquired for cash. In August of the same year, 14 Liquorland stores and the Mac the Slasher liquor chain were purchased. The following year the name Liquorland was extended to cover all company liquor stores around Australia. These comprised Australia's largest nonbrewery chain. Coles entered the footwear business when Edward Fay Pty. Ltd. and Ezywalkin were purchased in 1981. Due to unsatisfactory results, however, the company divested itself of these in 1988.

In 1982 Coles opened Australia's first hypermarket, Super K mart, the name used for combined K mart and grocery stores until 1989, using the pooled resources and skills of the established K mart business and Coles supermarkets. Many of the Super K marts that opened included automotive sections under the name K Auto, which were first established in 1961. They sold an extensive range of automotive accessories and parts, and offered full servicing and maintenance to fleet and private vehicle operators.

Women's clothing retailing was the next area of investment for Coles with the acquisition of the Katies Fashion (Australia) Pty. Ltd. (Katies) national chain of 117 specialty stores in November 1984 for A$47 million. At the time of purchase, Katies had an established reputation for quality women's fashions at competitive prices. Contrary to the usually high level of imported merchandise in the Australian clothing and textile area, Katies consistently offered a large proportion of domestically-produced goods, with over 90% of garments for the 1987 summer season being made in Australia. In the same year, the 100th K mart store opened in Campbelltown, New South Wales, and net profit for the company exceeded A$100 million for the first time.

In 1985 the Coles Myer Ltd. organization was born, after a merger proposal was accepted by Myer Emporium Ltd. (Myer), a Melbourne-based retailer. Myer, the third-largest retail group in Australia, was acquired through an agreed bid for a total cash offer of A$918 million.

Myer Emporium Ltd., which had been operating since 1901, strengthened its position in 1983 as the major department store retailer in Australia by purchasing Grace Bros, the largest department store retailer in New South Wales, for A$213 million. This was bought along with Boans, the largest Western Australian department store operator, for A$39.2 million.

The 1985 Myer merger brought in 56 department stores, 68 Target discount stores, 122 Fosseys discount variety stores, the Country Road chain of 45 stores which was subsequently sold for a profit of A$33.27 million, and the Red Rooster chain of fast food chicken outlets. The name of the company was changed to Coles Myer Ltd. on January 27, 1986, and a new corporate symbol was adopted. In addition, a new company structure consisting of five divisions—discount stores and supermarkets; food and liquor; Grace Bros; Myer Stores; and specialty stores—was introduced at this time.

Coles Myer continued to grow and consolidate existing interests. In May 1986, 52 stores were added to the Red Rooster chain, making it the second largest take-out chicken restaurant chain and the largest Australian-owned fast food group. In the same year the administrative structures of Coles and Fosseys amalgamated into a single business to become a market leader in the discount variety store segment. The ranges in both stores were rationalized to concentrate on their strong positions in budget clothing, toiletries, toys, fancy goods, and confectionery.

In 1987 the company's shares were listed on the London Stock Exchange, and a new corporate headquarters was officially opened at Tooronga, Victoria, by Prime Minister R.J.L. Hawke. A revised management structure requiring group managers to report to the managing director of retail operations led to strong growth during the year. Also in 1987 the company entered the discount food retailing field with the purchase of the Bi-Lo Supermarket chain. Originally from South Australia, Bi-Lo stores were known for doing business in relatively small sites with discount prices and cut-case displays, whereby goods are stacked in supermarket aisles in cardboard boxes that can be cut open for customers to help themselves directly. This keeps store overheads to a minimum. The company's expansion into discount food retailing continued the following year with the A$31.55 million acquisition of the Shoey's chain of budget food markets in New South Wales, adding 40 stores to the group. The company's discount food division, which was managed independently from the New World chain, now included both the Bi-Lo chain and the Shoey's group as well as a number of converted former New World stores.

In July 1987 Coles Myer acquired Charlton Feedlot Pty Ltd., a dairy and beef producing operation that supplies premium produce to Coles Myer's supermarket business.

Coles Myer made its first move overseas with the acquisition of Progressive Enterprises Limited in New Zealand in May 1988. This included 29 Foodtown premium supermarkets, 23 3 Guys discount supermarkets, and Georgie Pie family restaurants. The first K mart discount store opened in New Zealand in October of the same year.

In October 1988 Coles Myer was listed on the New York Stock Exchange. During 1987–1988, the company established Coles Myer Ansett Travel Pty. Ltd. (CMAT), a joint venture with Ansett Transport Industries Ltd., to manage retail travel centers located in company stores. In 1990 CMAT acquired the travel business of the ANZ Bank Ltd. Electronic funds transfer at the point of sale was introduced to all Coles Myer stores as part of the development of electronic scanning cash registers and other point-of-sale register systems to improve efficiency in 1989. In mid-1989, as part of a decision to concentrate on core businesses, the company sold its 25% minority stake in Bank of America Australia Ltd. to the bank's U.S. parent, BankAmerica Corporation.

As of August 1, 1990, the administrative and buying functions of the Myer Stores and Grace Bros businesses were merged to form the Department Stores Group. While each group continued to operate under the separate Myer and Grace Bros names, the move resulted in significant gains from overhead reductions and economies in buying and sales promotion.

In April 1991 Coles New World Supermarkets changed their name to Coles Supermarkets, together with the launch of a new visual identity and customer service programs. Later that year Coles reduced the prices of 6,000 product lines as part of a new pricing and advertising policy.

In November 1991 Solomon Lew was elected chairman of the board, following Brian Quinn's decision to relinquish the chairmanship and concentrate on his role as chief executive officer.

Coles Myer's retail operations in the early 1990s comprised Coles and Bi-Lo supermarkets, department stores, K mart, Target, Coles.Fossey, Liquorland, Katies, Red Rooster, 3 Guys and Foodtown supermarkets in New Zealand, and Georgie Pie fast food outlets in New Zealand.

In the future, Coles Myer is set to continue a long-term plan for overseas expansion, and can be expected to take advantage of the many highly profitable opportunities that exist in Australia and New Zealand. Capital expenditure will continue to be focused on store refurbishment and the installation of the latest technology. This policy places Coles Myer in a strong position to benefit from recovery in the Australian and New Zealand economies.

Principal Subsidiaries: S.E. Dickins Pty. Ltd.; Katies Fashions (Aust.) Pty. Ltd; Myer Stores Ltd.; Coles Myer Properties Ltd.; Target Australia Pty. Ltd.; Coles Myer Finance Ltd.; Progressive Enterprises Ltd.; Barkly Square Shopping Centre Pty. Ltd.; Amalgamated Food and Poultry Pty. Ltd.; Liquorland (Australia) Pty. Ltd.; Bi-Lo Pty. Ltd.

Further Reading: "The Story So Far—Coles Myer Ltd.," Victoria, Coles Myer Ltd., 1989; "Coles Myer Ltd.—A Brief History of the Company," Victoria, Coles Myer Ltd., 1991.

—Julia Roberts

COSTCO WHOLESALE CORPORATION

10809 120th Avenue N.E.
Kirkland, Washington 98033
U.S.A.
(206) 828-8100

Public Company
Incorporated: 1983
Employees: 15,000
Sales: $5.20 billion
Stock Exchange: NASDAQ

Costco Wholesale Corporation operates a chain of membership warehouses that sell a wide variety of name-brand products at discount prices to businesses and individuals who are members of selected employee groups. The membership warehouse-club concept emerged in the early 1980s and has become a $30 billion industry. Costco is the third largest of such companies; the top four account for 85% of industry sales. With 82 warehouses, located mostly in the Pacific Northwest, California, Florida, and Canada, it was, in the early 1990s, the fastest growing chain in the industry.

In September 1983 Costco's first warehouse opened in Seattle, Washington. At this time, warehouse outlets had long existed, but the concept of a wholesale club was relatively new and promising. Dubbed "buyers' clubs" and begun in 1976, these warehouses were wholesalers that required shoppers to become members and pay an annual membership fee. The membership fee helps reduce already-low overhead, so that items can be sold at an average of 9% over cost from the manufacturer. At the time Costco was formed, membership warehouses were primarily a west-coast phenomenon. Their popularity has since spread throughout the United States and Canada.

From the company's inception, Jeffrey H. Brotman has served as chairman, and James D. Sinegal has been president. While Sinegal had a background in membership warehouses and retail chains, Brotman was an executive of an oil exploration company and co-founder of a group that operated a chain of apparel stores. In 1985 Costco became a publicly owned company.

The economic slowdown of the late 1980s gave a further boost to membership warehouses. Where most retailers suffered during this period, Costco thrived. Roughly one-third of its sales being food and one-third vending-machine sundries such as candy, tobacco, and soft drinks, the majority of Costco's primary sales are recession-proof basics. In the fiscal year ending September 1, 1991, Costco's net income rose 72%. At this time, 60% to 65% of industry-wide club members were small-business owners, for whom cost-cutting was imperative.

Costco closed three units in west Florida in 1990. They were still performing poorly after several years. Stores in central and south Florida, however, had done well. In the fall of 1990 Costco opened its first two units in the Northeast, both in Massachusetts. In 1991 a third Massachusetts location opened. These stores have been successful, and the company continued an ambitious expansion program. During the 1992 fiscal year, Costco planned to open 18 new warehouses.

A factor in Costco's strong growth was its creative merchandising. Most of Costco's warehouses offer a complete fresh food section—including a bakery, refrigerated produce area, fresh meats, and seafood. It was the first membership warehouse to offer such a selection.

Costco has two basic memberships, business and individual. Any business or store with a retail sales license is qualified for a business membership. Business members can also buy goods for private use. Gold Card memberships are available to individuals in selected occupations or groups. These memberships include the same wholesale prices offered to business members. Annual fees are refunded fully if members are not satisfied.

Costco's strategy is to offer high-quality, brand-name merchandise at prices below those of traditional wholesalers, discount retailers, and supermarkets. To achieve this, Costco buys nearly all of its merchandise at volume discounts from manufacturers, rather than distributors, and stock is usually shipped directly to selling warehouses to minimize freight costs. Warehouses are often on industrial sites or in other areas where property costs are at a minimum, and stocked items are placed directly onto the selling floor, reducing handling and stocking labor. The number of sales and service employees is also minimal. Half of the company's employees in 1990 held part-time status. Warehouses are almost entirely self-service, from finding and buying items, to loading them into a customer's vehicle.

Another key to Costco's low overhead is its advertising policy, which limits expenditures to new warehouse openings. Word of mouth and savings do the rest. The entire operation is cash and carry, eliminating the expense of credit card administration. Bad checks are rare since qualifications for membership minimize them.

In March 1991 the company completed a public offering of 3.45 million shares of common stocks. Proceeds of approximately $200 million were used to fund expansion and to reduce the company's debt.

—Carol I. Keeley

Cotter & Company

100% RETAILER-OWNED

COTTER & COMPANY

2740 North Clybourn Avenue
Chicago, Illinois 60614
U.S.A.
(312) 975-2700
Fax: (312) 975-1712

Private Company
Incorporated: 1948
Employees: 3,500
Sales: $2.20 billion

Cotter & Company is the largest wholesaler of hardware in the world. It is a member-owned company that supplies more than 8,000 stores from 15 distribution centers throughout the United States. The company's retail outlets include more than 7,000 True Value Hardware Stores and more than 1,000 V&S Variety Stores. Cotter manufactures many of its own products such as paint and paint brushes, lawn mowers, lawn tractors, and snow shovels. The company also operates an insurance company, real estate office, and travel agency.

Cotter was incorporated in Chicago on January 15, 1948. Twenty years earlier, John Cotter, at the time a young hardware clerk, came up with the idea for the enterprise. He believed the way to prosperity for independent hardware retailers was through ownership of their own professionally run, low-cost distribution and merchandising organization. After a long career in hardware, Cotter was able to implement his idea. In July 1947 Cotter and Ed Lanctot, an associate who would remain with the company for many years, met with 12 local hardware merchants in a small hotel in Sycamore, Illinois. At the meeting, Cotter proposed the organization of a wholesale company that would be owned by its member merchants. The dealers in attendance liked his idea but were cautious about making any commitments. Cotter estimated that it would take 25 retailers, each contributing $1,500 to capitalize the new business. Having gotten a positive response from the retailers who had attended the meeting, Cotter set out to raise the required $37,500. The initial capitalization of Cotter & Company took six months. The company began with 25 participating dealers; by the end of 1948, the dealer roster had grown to 84, and Cotter had shipped $385,000 worth of goods.

Cotter's early years were tenuous. The traditional hardware retailer faced competition from an onslaught of mass merchandisers. Discount stores, department store chains, mail-order

catalog houses, drugstores, and even supermarket chains got into the battle for their share of the postwar boom in home improvement products and hardware. World War II veterans had come home, gotten married, and bought houses. Businesses at the wholesale level of the hardware market reported increasing sales volume but declining profits. During these times, Cotter & Company blossomed into a major force in the hardware business. In such a mutually held operation, the dealers and store owners own the central organization. Profits made at the wholesale level are rebated back to the members at the end of each year. This allows the dealers to take advantage of the middleman's distribution and merchandising methods without having to pay the middleman's fee, thus permitting the retailer to sell merchandise at a lower cost. This technique enabled the independent True Value dealers to compete with the large cost-cutting retail giants and still offer personal service, something not always available in huge retail locations.

By 1956 the company was selling more than $1 million worth of merchandise a month. Direct-mail advertising was the key to the company's growth and the main thrust of its merchandising effort. By the mid-1950s the True Value circular was reaching more than 700,000 customers. In the early 1990s, 200 million copies of the direct-mail circulars reached an estimated 592 million readers annually.

Cotter was one of the first companies to tap into the pool of cooperative advertising funds that many of the manufacturers from which it bought merchandise made available to help promote retail sales of their product lines. The money was spent on local print advertising, allowing independent neighborhood dealers to run advertisements in local newspapers and do regional advertising in consumer publications like *Better Homes and Gardens* and *Sports Illustrated*.

In 1959 Cotter moved into its longtime headquarters, a 200,000-square-foot warehouse and office on the northwest side of Chicago. Later that year, the company purchased an adjacent building, adding 88,000 square feet to the warehouse's already huge storage capacity.

In the 1960s and early 1970s Cotter began major moves that would make it a national giant in the hardware business. The company expanded its markets nationally and in the process diversified its activities into several other areas of business. Cotter bought its own fleet of trucks, got into the real estate business, and developed a member insurance program. A complete retail member organization was formed to perform services ranging from store fixtures sales to computerized accounting.

In 1962 the company opened its first regional distribution center in Cleveland, Ohio. The following year, Cotter acquired 400 new members and the True Value trademark through consolidation with Chicago-based wholesaler Hibbard, Spencer, Bartlett & Company. This acquisition necessitated the purchase of a 175,000-square-foot building next to Cotter headquarters in Chicago. Two years later Cotter acquired another 320 members through a consolidation with the Dallas, Texas-based Walter H. Allen Company and opened a third distribution facility, in Philadelphia, Pennsylvania. In 1966 Cotter broke the $100 million mark in total shipments.

Traditionally hardware distributors sold only items that they purchased from manufacturers. Cotter broke with tradition when it began to manufacture many of the products it supplied to its member merchants. In 1967 the company bought the

General Paint & Chemical Company and began to market its own paint and related products under the Tru-Test name. Three years later, Cotter opened its own power lawn mower factory in Carpentersville, Illinois. By 1970 the company was shipping more than $1 million worth of goods each business day.

In 1978 John Cotter assumed the post of chairman of the board, and his son, Dan, took over the presidency. By then, the company had more than 5,000 members, and in 1979 it broke the $1 billion level for annual sales. The company acquired the Warner Hardware Company of Minneapolis, Minnesota, in 1979, constructed a 1.3-million-square-foot factory and warehouse in Harvard, Illinois, in 1980, and purchased the Atlas Tool Company in 1983. Also in 1983, Cotter introduced the True Value charge card program and the company's line of Green Thumb lawn care products. By the late 1980s, Cotter & Company had more than 7,000 members, and sales were approaching $2 billion per year.

Cotter entered the 1990s selling ten different lines of merchandise that it manufactured under nationally recognized brand names such as Master Mechanic Hand Tools, Master Plumber plumbing supplies, Master Electrician electrical products, Green Thumb Lawn products, Tru Bond household adhesives, and Tru Guard Electric Garage Door Openers. The company was operating 15 materials distribution centers nationally, occupying more than 5.3 million square feet.

As a result of a comprehensive nationwide advertising program, Cotter estimated that the True Value name is recognized by more than 90% of U.S. consumers. True Value hardware stores rate among the top three radio advertisers in the United States, and the company's print advertising can be seen in almost every major national publications.

In the early 1990s the company experienced many upper-level management changes as a result of the retirement of many members of its original management team. On the whole, however, it appeared that the methods and practices initiated by the company's founders would continue to be followed.

Principal Subsidiaries: Tru-Test Manufacturing Co., Inc.; General Power Equipment Co.; Baltimore Brush & Roller Co., Inc.

Further Reading: ''The Man Behind The Company,'' Chicago, Cotter & Company, 1985; Kantowicz, Edward R., *True Value, John Cotter: 70 Years of Hardware,* Chicago, Regnery Gateway, 1986; ''Where is Cotter Going?'' *Hardware Age,* November 1988.

—William R. Grossman

THE DAIEI, INC.

4-1-1, Minatojima Nakamachi
Chuo-ku, Kobe 650
Japan
(078) 302-5001
Fax: (078) 302-5572

Public Company
Incorporated: 1957
Employees: 16,797
Sales: ¥2.19 trillion (US$16.12 billion)
Stock Exchanges: Tokyo Osaka NASDAQ

The Daiei, Inc. is Japan's largest retailer in terms of sales. Although most often described as a supermarket chain, its merchandise is not limited to food; it operates more than 200 superstores under its own name. Daiei sells a broad range of products at low prices and operates thousands of specialty and convenience stores, ranging from fast-food restaurants to department stores, bearing Western names like Wendy's, Big Boy, Au Printemps, and Joseph Magnin. Daiei Chairman and CEO Isao Nakauchi once boasted that his company sells "everything except ladies and opium."

Nakauchi founded Daiei in his hometown of Osaka in 1957; the company's name is a complicated play on words that means both prosperity of Osaka and big prosperity. A pharmacist's son, Nakauchi had made a small fortune in the years after World War II by participating in a venture that sold penicillin at above the legal price. His brother and some associates were arrested for their roles in the scheme, but the experience taught Nakauchi that risk-taking and making money were inseparable. His first Daiei store was a pharmacy called Housewives' Store Daiei. He gave its parent company the name Daiei Pharmaceutical Company. Japan's post-Korean-War depression was then reaching its lowest point, and Osaka shoppers appreciated Daiei's discount pricing policy. Its initial success soon inspired him to open more stores in the Osaka area.

The depression also proved fortuitous for Daiei at the wholesale level. Manufacturers were grateful for the fact that Nakauchi always paid cash for their goods. He also bought up whatever surpluses overextended manufacturers may have accumulated and passed on the savings to consumers. Thus, Daiei quickly ceased to be merely a drug store chain; as Nakauchi would recall years later, "We soon moved from drugs into candies and other foods and from cosmetics and toiletries

into hard goods." In 1970 the company dropped the focus on specialized retailing and shortened its name to its current form.

Daiei expanded to become a nationwide chain. By the time it celebrated its fifteenth anniversary in 1972, the company was operating 75 superstores and had become Japan's largest supermarket operator and second-largest retailer. It had achieved such rapid and overwhelming success by breaking many of Japanese retailing's time-honored rules. In a nation where small shops often banded together in cartels to keep prices artificially high, Daiei was a high-volume, low-price retailer. "Even our barbers and laundries have self-protective cartels," Nakauchi once complained. Nakauchi, an unlikely but open admirer of Mao Tse-tung's strategic wisdom, cast Daiei in such a mold in order to draw on the strength of "the masses," offering quality goods at the lowest possible prices. In 1970, when outraged consumers realized that Japanese television sets were being sold for less in the United States than at home, Daiei leapt into the breach, signing a marketing deal with Crown Radio and selling Crown sets under their own name for less than half the going rate. Daiei was a pioneer in introducing the concept of house brands to Japanese consumers, who were used to paying higher prices for recognized brand names. The following year, Daiei acquired Crown and added more electronics goods and household appliances to the Daiei name. Nakauchi kept his overhead low by opening stores in the suburbs, rather than the densely-populated, high-rent urban areas favored by Japanese department stores. For his iconoclasm in a consensus-oriented society, he was reviled by ex-friends, threatened by irate competitors, and ostracized by the business establishment, but this treatment did not deter him from his vision of revolutionizing Japanese retailing, an arduous process he once compared to Mao's travails.

In the 1970s the company began to internationalize, diversifying its range of goods and services even further. In 1972 it created Daiei U.S.A. as a wholly owned subsidiary and opened a branch in a Honolulu shopping center. Taking advantage of the liberalization of Japanese laws regarding the presence of foreign retailers, Daiei entered into joint ventures to open branches of U.S. department store Joseph Magnin and Swift & Company's Dipper Dan Ice Cream Shoppe chain in Japan.

In 1974 Daiei surpassed the sales of department store giant Mitsukoshi to become Japan's largest retailer. Once again, Nakauchi's ambitions were scarcely satisfied. In the spring of that year, Daiei began selling J.C. Penney merchandise as part of an arrangement with the U.S. retailer to test its popularity in Japan. The venture proved successful, and several months later, Daiei and J.C. Penney entered into a joint venture to open stores in Japan under the Penney name, beginning in 1976. Under the agreement, Daiei and Penney each owned 47.5%, with the remaining 5% going to trading company C. Itoh.

In 1978 Daiei continued to capitalize on the popularity of Western goods in Japan when it became the sole Japanese agent for British department store Marks & Spencer. Daiei chose Marks & Spencer merchandise because of its reputation for price competitiveness, especially in food and clothing. For its part, Marks & Spencer, which already had a substantial presence in Hong Kong, saw Japan as its largest remaining potential export market. The next year Daiei joined with Wendy's International to open Wendy's fast-food restaurants and Victoria Station steak houses in Japan. In 1980 Daiei made its first serious incursion into the U.S. market when it acquired in its entirety Holiday Mart, a three-store discount chain in Honolulu, Hawaii. It also opened its first U.S. purchasing office. Not least of all, it joined with Au Printemps to open branches of that venerable French department store in Japan; the first Au Printemps Japan opened in Kobe in 1981, followed by stores in Sapporo in 1982 and in Tokyo the year after that.

Daiei's supermarket operations continued to flourish. As the decade turned, Daiei controlled one-fifth of the entire Japanese food retail market. In 1981 it reorganized that side of its business somewhat when it merged its Sanko affiliate with food store chain Maruetsu. Daiei and Maruetsu each owned 50% of the new company, which immediately became the nation's ninth-largest retailer, boasting 140 branches. Also in 1981, Daiei acquired a 10.5% stake in Takashimaya, another department store chain, making it that company's principal shareholder.

In 1984 Daiei's sales reached ¥1.4 trillion, and its chain of superstores had grown to 160. Daiei continued to expand at a breakneck pace. The company opened a branch in Tokyo's expensive Ginza district. Daiei financed this continuous augmentation with heavy borrowing, and the cost of financing its debt forced the company to post a ¥11.9 billion loss in 1984, despite its massive sales. The next year, it lost ¥8.8 billion.

Nakauchi insisted all along that these deficits were part of his plan, and that continued expansion would pay off in the long run. Daiei had cleverly spread its borrowing among four different banks—contrary to the usual Japanese corporate practice of borrowing from one bank, which then allowed that bank to become a company's principal stockholder. This wise move enabled Daiei to preserve its independence; indeed, Nakauchi has always been Daiei's principal shareholder. In 1986 the company returned to profitability, earning ¥1.1 billion. In 1987 it was healthy enough to acquire bankrupt sewing machine manufacturer Riccar at the request of the Ministry of International Trade and Industry. In that same year, it announced a five-year plan to install an electronic information network to link all of its branches, offices, and affiliates, starting with an ¥11 billion point-of-sale (POS) system for its superstores. POS systems give retailers quick and accurate information on sales and inventories, information that can be used to improve inventory control. In 1988, Daiei announced plans to enter the hotel business by building a recreation complex in Fukuoka City.

Daiei continued to expand and thrive under the guidance of its founder and only chief executive. Sales and profits have both increased steadily in recent years. The revolution that Isao Nakauchi had preached and sought to bring about shows some signs of getting underway; the Japanese retail market is reaching the limits of its growth, forcing retailers to fight for market share by cutting prices. Some have followed Daiei's lead in buying foreign goods directly from manufacturers instead of going through Japanese trading companies. As he nears retirement age, this singular man—an aggressive capitalist who quotes Chairman Mao and a blunt, outspoken iconoclast in a society that discourages dissension and requires politeness—should, despite his restless ambition, take some measure of satisfaction in the success that his company has achieved.

Principal Subsidiaries: Robelt Co., Ltd.; Daiei Convenience Systems; Pacific Sports Co., Ltd.; Lobelia Co., Ltd.; Daichu, Inc.; The Deiei (U.S.A.), Inc.; Cordoba, Inc. (85%); Joseph Magnin; Japan Ltd.; Riccar Co., Ltd.

Further Reading: "Japan: Mao in the Supermarket," *Time,* June 28, 1971; Butterfield, Fox, "Japan's Retailing Colossus," *The New York Times,* November 3, 1974; "Retailers Get Ready to Move into the U.S.," *Business Week,* August 4, 1980; "Daiei's Discount Empire Prospers," *World Business Weekly,* January 12, 1981.

—Douglas Sun

THE DAIMARU, INC.

7-1, Shinsaibashisuji 1-chome
Chuo-ku, Osaka 542
Japan
(06) 271-1231
Fax: (06) 245-1343

Public Company
Incorporated: 1920 as The Daimaru Drapery Store,
 Inc.
Employees: 6,899
Sales: ¥868.68 billion (US$6.96 billion)
Stock Exchanges: Osaka Tokyo Kyoto

At the center of the vast international marketing complex known as The Daimaru, Inc. is a network of department stores that ranks among the five largest department store companies in Japan. In addition to its department stores, located in Japan and overseas, and its closely associated credit card, data center, and mail-order businesses, the Daimaru encompasses chains of supermarkets, restaurants, and specialty stores that help make it one of the top retailers in the world. Daimaru operations extend to advertising and printing; freight shipment; fitness and sports; and the manufacture, import, and export of a variety of merchandise. The company also operates its own research center, where it develops and tests merchandise.

From the opening of the Daimaru's first store, a drapery shop in Kyoto, in 1717, the company has been known for the close ties it cultivates with the communities in which its stores are situated, and for its upscale, high-quality goods and services. These characteristics evoke comparison with another pioneering retailer, the top-ranking Mitsukoshi department store company.

Aside from the few stores opened by Mitsukoshi's predecessor in other areas in the 30-some years preceding 1717, the purchasing process in most of Japan was inconvenient and costly for both consumer and merchant. Only wealthy persons could afford to patronize the drapery purveyors, who, as traveling salesmen, had to haul their samples over rough terrain in all kinds of weather in order to show the fabric to customers in their homes. The costs involved in this time-consuming process ran up the prices of the goods. Earnings were meager, for few sales could be made relative to the number of hours worked.

Locating the business in a shop increased the pace of sales, lowered overhead, and provided customers with a greater selection of samples than could be carried in a salesman's backpack. The stores also became meeting places where customers could relax with a cup of tea and exchange ideas.

Hikoemon Shimomura chose a propitious place to open his drapery business. Kyoto in 1717 was the home of the imperial family and the nobles of the court. Although long bereft of political power, they were supported in style by Japan's ruler, the Tokugawa shogun. Far removed though they were from the new capital, Edo, later to be known as Tokyo, they had an ardent desire for traditional garments and fine fabrics. This provided a willing and able customer base at a time when purchasing power was largely held in a few widely scattered clusters of wealthy families.

Service before profit was a principle Hikoemon Shimomura announced to his customers. The Daimaru's president, Shotaro Shimomura, in the early 1990s explained that it is still the stores' guiding principle to consider service to the customer first, in the belief that profits will follow. In 1726 the Daimaru's founder opened a shop in Osaka, a busy trade center. Purchasing power was beginning to spread into the hands of a rising merchant class. This meant that the new business, given its start among titled and wealthy patrons, could continue to grow. The shogun's political power and isolationist policies had created a kind of stability that allowed Japan's economy time to recover from the drain imposed on it by centuries of civil strife. The country's stability and unity under the shogun also made it possible to establish a standard currency that helped accelerate the pace at which transactions could be made.

By 1728 Hikoemon Shimomura was able to open a third shop, locating it in Nagoya, another busy trade center. The name Daimaru-ya came into use for the first time.

During the Daimaru stores' first 150 years, the shogunate's intricate web of restrictions held Japanese lifestyles in a fairly rigid pattern, but below the change-resistant surface of life in a feudal state, the nation's commercial economy was racing toward modernization. That became apparent in the mid-19th century, when the weakened shogunate government had to yield to foreign pressures to open its ports to international trade. By 1868, when the progressive Meiji emperor replaced the shogun, Japan had a number of commercial entities that were ready to compete in international markets.

Western nations' styles at first repelled some segments of the Japanese populace, but increasingly the majority of purchasers of goods were attracted to imports. At the same time, just before and after the turn of the century, brief wars with China and Russia had brought increasing numbers of workers from rural Japan to urban centers for the manufacture of essential materials. Responding to their needs and to a new demand for variety in consumer goods, Daimaru transformed its shops.

Little by little, the transformation was reflected in the Daimaru's organizational structure and, eventually, in its official name and written policies. In 1907, with ¥500,000 in capital, the Daimaru became a partnership, and took the name The Partnership Daimaru Drapery Store. The store management took some steps forward, hiring women as sales clerks for the first time in 1913 and accelerating the pace of business as Japan's victorious participation in World War I expanded the economy. By 1920 the Daimaru was ready for another reorganization, this time as a corporation, with ¥12 million in capital.

The new corporation also had a new name: Daimaru Drapery Store, Inc. Although the name did not hint at the widened variety of goods and services Daimaru offered, it conveyed continuity with the company's centuries of service.

The Great Kanto Earthquake of 1923 destroyed the Tokyo store. In 1925, when the rebuilding process was completed, the modernized premises, constructed to accommodate the Daimaru's many types of merchandise, were obviously those of a department store. Three years later, the name was officially changed to The Daimaru, Inc.

Japan's rapid military-based expansion in the 1930s brought an influx of workers into urban and manufacturing centers, creating new customer bases. The company formed an affiliate, Daimaru Kogyo Co., Ltd. which started wholesale import and export operations in 1933. Japan's devastation and defeat in World War II, however, brought the nation's economy to a virtual standstill.

The nation's new constitution provided for the dissolution of the monopolistic *zaibatsu* and supported the development of individual enterprises. During the seven years of occupation by the Allied forces under U.S. General Douglas MacArthur, the Daimaru reorganized, starting several new businesses and acquiring affiliates. In July 1947 the Daimaru Creation Co., Ltd., was established as a subsidiary, to plan marketing strategies and provide printing and advertising services. A facility for leasing real estate and vehicles was added to the Daimaru group in October 1949. The following year, the Daimaru began a furniture manufacturing and construction contracting business under the name of Daimaru Mokko Co., Ltd.

All the new businesses were centered in Osaka and began to expand their operations as the nation's economy recovered from the ravages of war. Postwar construction and repair of highways and the building of shopping malls through the countryside helped make a greater variety of merchandise accessible.

Interest in foreign fashions and accessories reached a new height in Japan's post–World War II period. With the economy's rapid recovery came expanded buying power. In 1953 The Daimaru, with stores in Osaka, Kyoto, Tottori, Shimonoseki, Hakata, and Nihama, became the first retailer in Japan to sign an exclusive agreement with Christian Dior. The following year, a new multi-story Tokyo store was opened. The Daimaru began selling its own ready-made men's wear in 1959.

At the requests of local business communities, Daimaru opened stores in Hong Kong in 1960 and Bangkok four years later. In 1960, in Japan, The Daimaru opened the first of a chain of supermarkets. In 1974 the Peacock Sangyo, with 24 shops, became Daimaru Peacock Co., Ltd., a subsidiary of Daimaru. By 1991 this company had 50 outlets. The Daimaru formed an exclusive agreement with the fashion designer Givenchy and also began manufacturing its own line of women's fashions. With the opening of stores in Paris and Lyon and the addition of specialty stores and restaurants, The Daimaru was well established by 1975 as one of Japan's top five department store companies. The company sustained its position within the top five department store companies and among the top retailers in the world through the ensuing years, despite such woes as the late 1980s' stock market crash and some fluctuations in the value of the yen. Daimaru began the 1990s in third place.

Close attention to changes in consumers' buying habits has led to the remodeling and expansion of some of the stores and to the creation of new businesses. The increase in dual-career families with little time to visit department stores, for example, led to the organization of the Home Shopping Division, a mail-order facility, in 1983. In a sense, for these shoppers, the purchasing process had come full circle since Hikoemon Shimomura had set up his first drapery store in 1717. The popularity of the mail-order service soon exceeded the volume a division could handle, and the service became the Daimaru Home-Shopping Co., Ltd., in 1988.

In 1987 The Daimaru transformed its store in Machida, a depressed area in Tokyo, from a fiscally ailing outlet to a profit-making venture by reorganizing it and creating a separate corporation, Machida Daimaru Co. Ltd., to operate it. The reduced costs to Daimaru, resulting from its separation from the Machida store, have also to some degree offset the company's huge investment in the 1983 opening of its highrise, ultramodern Osaka Umeda store.

During the 1980s, The Daimaru stepped up its activities in Southeast Asia. The company opened its second store in Bangkok in 1980 and a store in Singapore in 1983. The same year, it added an annex to the Hong Kong Daimaru, doubling its space.

In October 1991 Daimaru Australia was opened in Melbourne. Large-scale expansions were scheduled for Daimaru's Kobe and Kyoto stores for 1992 and 1994, respectively.

Principal Subsidiaries: Daimaru Home-Shopping Co., Ltd.; Daimaru Credit Service Co., Ltd.; Daimaru Information Center Co., Ltd.; Daimaru Peacock Co., Ltd.; Restaurant Peacock Co., Ltd.; Daimaru Mariepaul Co., Ltd.; Daimaru Kogyo Co., Ltd.; Daimaru Sports Co., Ltd.; Daimaru Creation Co., Ltd.; Daimaru Mode Atelier Co., Ltd.; Alembic Co., Ltd.; Mich International Co., Ltd.; Daimaru Mokko Co., Ltd.; Consumer Product End-Use Research Institute Co., Ltd.; Daimaru Transportation Co., Ltd.; Rakuto Transportation Co., Ltd.; Chuo Kogyo Co., Ltd.; Daimaru Plan & Development Co., Ltd.; Daimaru Realty Co., Ltd.; Daito Realty Co., Ltd.; Roots Japan Inc.

Further Reading: Daimaru Now: 1989, Osaka, The Daimaru, Inc., 1989.

—Betty T. Moore

DAYTON HUDSON CORPORATION

777 Nicollet Mall
Minneapolis, Minnesota 55402
U.S.A.
(612) 370-6948
Fax: (612) 370-5521

Public Company
Incorporated: 1969
Employees: 161,215
Sales: $14.74 billion
Stock Exchanges: New York Pacific

Dayton Hudson Corporation operates the well-known Target discount stores, Mervyn's moderately priced retail stores, and the Dayton's, Hudson's, and Marshall Field department stores in the Midwest. From its impecunious beginnings in 1902 on a small plot of land in Minneapolis, the Dayton Hudson Corporation grew by the 1990s into one of the five largest retailers in the United States, with stores in 33 states and annual sales of more than $13 billion. Its philanthropy has been and still is legendary. In 1989 Dayton Hudson received the America's Corporate Conscience Award for its magnanimity, and in the same year, U.S. President George Bush presented the chairman and chief executive officer, Kenneth A. Macke, with the National Medal of Arts Award in recognition of the corporation's generous financial support of the arts. Dayton Hudson also has been recognized for its efficiency. In 1984 the University of California's School of Business Administration named it "best managed company in the U.S.A."

Dayton Hudson bears the strong imprint of its founder, George Draper Dayton. Dayton's father, a physician in New York state, could not afford to send him to college, in part because the doctor freely gave his services to the poor. Hence Dayton set off on his own in 1873 at age 16 to work in a coal and lumberyard. A workaholic, he undermined his health and a year later had to return to the family home to recuperate. Undeterred, he went on to become a banker. Less than ten years later, in 1883, he was rich enough to buy the Bank of Worthington in Minnesota. Meanwhile he had married and had become active in the Presbyterian Church.

Dayton's connection with religion and the Presbyterian Church explains the rise of his Dayton Company. In 1893, the year of a recession that sent real estate prices tumbling, the Westminster Presbyterian Church in Minneapolis burned down.

The insurance did not cover the cost of a new building, and the only other source of income, a corner lot next to the demolished church, was unsalable because the real estate market was doing poorly. The congregation prevailed on the Dayton family, who were faithful members of the church, to purchase it so the building of a new church could proceed. George Draper Dayton bought it and eventually erected a six-story building on the lot. Casting about for tenants, he decided to buy the nearby Goodfellow Dry Goods store and set it up in the new building. In the spring of 1902 the store was known as the Goodfellow Dry Goods store; it was then named the Dayton Dry Goods store, then simply the Dayton Company, the forerunner of Dayton Hudson Corporation.

Eventually the store would expand into the six-story edifice. George Draper Dayton, with no experience in the retail trade, wielded tight control of the company until his death in 1938. His principles of thrift and sobriety and his connections as a banker enabled the company to grow. As long as he was at the helm, the store was run as a family enterprise. Every Christmas Eve he would hand out candy to each employee of the store. Obsessed with punctuality, he was known to lock the doors at the onset of a meeting, forcing latecomers to wait and apologize to him in person afterwards. The store was run on strict Presbyterian guidelines: no liquor was sold, the store was closed on Sunday, no business travel or advertising was permitted on the Sabbath, and the Dayton Company refused to advertise in a newspaper that sponsored liquor ads.

This approach did not stifle business; the Dayton Company became extremely successful. A multi-million dollar business by the 1920s, the Dayton Company decided it was ready to expand, purchasing J.B. Hudson & Son, Minneapolis jewelers, in 1929, just two months before the stock market crash.

The Dayton Company managed to weather the Great Depression, although throughout it, the jewelry company operated in the red. George Draper Dayton's son David had died in 1923 at age 43, and George turned more and more of the company business over to another son, Nelson. George Draper Dayton died in 1938. He left only a modest personal fortune, having given away millions of dollars to charity. In 1918 the Dayton Foundation had been established with $1 million.

Nelson Dayton took over the presidency of the Dayton Company in 1938, when it was already a $14 million business, and saw it grow to a $50 million enterprise. World War II did not hamper business; rather, Dayton's turned the war into an asset. Consumer goods were so scarce that it was no longer necessary to persuade shoppers to buy what merchandise was available. Sales volume increased dramatically thanks to Dayton's managers, who obtained goods to keep the store full. Nelson Dayton was scrupulous about complying with the government's wartime control of business and when, for instance, the government carried out its drive for scrap metal, he ordered the store's electric sign dismantled and added to the scrap heap. Until Nelson Dayton's death in 1950, the company was run along the strict moral lines of its founder. In January 1944 Dayton's became one of the first stores in the nation to offer to its workers a retirement policy, followed in 1950 by a comprehensive insurance policy.

With Nelson Dayton's death in 1950, the Dayton Company embarked on a new era. Instead of one-man rule, the company was led by a team of five Dayton cousins, although one of them, Nelson's son Donald Dayton, assumed the title of president.

The prohibition of liquor in the store's dining rooms was dropped, and soon the Dayton Company would be completely secularized, advertising and doing business on Sunday.

The new management of the Dayton Company undertook radical and costly innovations. In 1954 the J.L. Hudson Company, which would eventually merge with Dayton, opened the world's largest shopping mall in Detroit. It was a great success, and two years later the Dayton Company decided to build a mall on a 500-acre plot of land outside of Minneapolis. Horrified to learn that Minneapolis had only 113 good shopping days a year, the architect decided to build a mall under cover, and the first enclosed shopping mall in history made its appearance.

The safe, conservative management style favored by George Draper Dayton and his son Nelson was history, and a younger, more aggressive management pushed for radical expansion and innovation. The company established the large discount chain Target in 1962, and in 1966 decided to enter the highly competitive market of retail bookselling, opening B. Dalton bookstores.

In 1967 the company, by then known as Dayton Corporation, made its first public stock offering. That year, it acquired San Francisco's Shreve and Company, which merged with J.B. Hudson to form Dayton Jewelers. In 1968 it bought the Pickwick Book Shops in Los Angeles and later merged them with B. Dalton. Also in 1968 the company acquired department stores in Oregon and Arizona. The following year brought the acquisition of J.E. Caldwell, a Philadelphia-based chain of jewelry stores, and Lechmere, a Boston retailer.

The year 1969 also saw a major acquisition, of the Detroit-based J.L. Hudson Company, a department store chain that had been in existence since 1881. The merger resulted in Dayton Hudson Corporation, the 14th-largest retailer in the United States. Dayton Hudson stock was listed on the New York Stock Exchange.

With the merger, the Dayton Foundation changed its name to the Dayton Hudson Foundation. Since 1946, 5% of the Dayton Company's taxable income was donated to the foundation, which continued to be the case after the merger. The foundation inspired the Minneapolis Chamber of Commerce in 1976 to establish the Minneapolis 5% Club, which eventually included 23 companies, each donating 5% of their respective taxable incomes to charities.

Dayton Hudson bought two more jewelers in 1970—C.D. Peacock, Inc., of Chicago, and J. Jessop and Sons of San Diego. Company revenues surpassed $1 billion in 1971.

Mervyn's, a line of moderate-price department stores, merged with Dayton Hudson in 1978. That year, Dayton Hudson became the seventh-largest general merchandise retailer in the U.S., its revenues topping $3 billion in 1979.

Dayton Hudson bought Ayr-Way, an Indianapolis-based chain of 50 discount stores, in 1980, and converted those units to Target stores. In 1982 the company sold Dayton Hudson Jewelers, and in 1986 it divested itself of B. Dalton.

The year 1987 brought an unsolicited takeover bid from Dart Group, a company controlled by the acquisition-minded Haft family. The struggle that ensued featured lawsuits by both parties as well as a bogus counteroffer by a small investor who, as it turned out, had no financing. The October stock market crash further complicated the matter, and Dart withdrew its bid. In 1990 Dayton Hudson bought the Marshall Field stores from BATUS Inc. for about $1 billion. The acquisition added 24 department stores to the Dayton Hudson group and doubled its department store retail space. The venerable Marshall Field's was as much a landmark in the Chicago area as Dayton's was in Minneapolis and the Hudson stores were in Detroit.

By 1991 the Dayton Hudson Corporation consisted of three major operating units: Target, with 420 discount stores in 32 states; Mervyn's, with 227 stores in 15 states, and the Department Store Company, operating 20 Hudson's, 17 Dayton's, and 24 Marshall Field's stores. Such vast expansion from the one building in which Dayton was housed for so long no doubt would have stunned the company's founder. Capital expansion as well as more varied retailing had become the new mottos added to the old policies of thrift and sobriety. Hence while Dayton, Hudson, and Marshall Field department stores offer the monied customer more costly and sophisticated merchandise, the popular Target and Mervyn's cater to the budget-conscious customer, offering apparel and recreational items on a self-service basis. With the onset of the 1990s, Target continued to be Dayton Hudson Corporation's biggest money maker. The company opened its first Target Greatland, larger than typical Target stores, in 1990, and planned additional ones in 1991.

Dayton Hudson's three units operate autonomously. Significant investment is made for the long term; in 1990 alone the company's capital spending program amounted to $1 billion. Target and Mervyn stores will likely continue to be the fastest growing and most profitable for the corporation.

Operating Divisions: Department Store Division; Mervyn's; Target.

Further Reading: Dayton, George Draper, II, *Our Story: With Histories of the Dayton, McDonald and Winchell Families,* Wyzata, Minnesota [n.p.], 1987.

—Sina Dubovoj

DILLARD DEPARTMENT STORES, INC.

1600 Cantrell Road
Little Rock, Arkansas 72201
U.S.A.
(501) 376-5200
Fax: (501) 376-5917

Public Company
Incorporated: 1964 as Mayer & Schmidt
Employees: 31,786
Sales: $3.60 billion
Stock Exchange: New York

Based in Little Rock, Arkansas, and located throughout suburbs and secondary markets in the South, Southwest, and Midwest, Dillard Department Stores, Inc., operates 186 stores selling brand-name goods in the middle to upper-middle price ranges. Key product lines are home furnishings and fashionable clothing. Stores rarely run discount promotions, preferring a constant supply of reasonably priced goods.

The company was founded—and in the early 1990s was still run—by William Dillard. Born in 1914 Dillard was raised in a merchandising family in tiny Mineral Springs, Arkansas. He worked in his father's hardware store and later studied at the University of Arkansas and the Columbia University School of Business. After earning his master's degree at Columbia and completing a Sears training program, Dillard borrowed $8,000 from his father and in February 1938 opened T.J. Dillard's in Nashville, Arkansas, near his home town. His father's wholesalers extended him credit, and customers reacted positively to his well-known father's name, "T.J."

From the first, business was good. Dillard and his wife, Alexa, stocked the store with name-brand merchandise they had bought at low prices. With heavy advertising, first-year sales reached $42,000.

Dillard volunteered for the Navy in 1942, during World War II. He sold his merchandise to another store, but kept his store open to collect on credit accounts. While Dillard was waiting for his naval commission, his father died. Family responsibilities called him home, and when the commission came through, he declined it.

In 1944 Dillard and his wife reopened their store. Despite the war, retail sales hit $300,000 in 1945. Business was so good that in 1946, Dillard added an 80-foot-long addition.

Considering the following year's $340,000 in sales an absolute maximum, Dillard sought new opportunities elsewhere. He invested $50,000 in the proposed expansion of Wooten's Department Store in Texarkana, a town split down the middle by the Texas-Arkansas border. After commuting between Nashville and Texarkana for six months he decided to settle in Texarkana. In March 1948, Dillard sold T.J. Dillard's and upped his stake in Wooten's to 40%, changing its name to Wooten & Dillard Inc.

With Wooten's consent, Dillard decided that, instead of expanding the existing store, Wooten & Dillard should open a new store featuring name brands and revolving credit. Despite strong sales, Wooten & Dillard lost money during its first six months, and Wooten asked Dillard to buy him out. To assemble the needed $100,000 in capital, Dillard collected investors and obtained a loan from the Federal Reconstruction Finance Corporation. By March 1949, he controlled the company. Dillard then began a massive newspaper advertising campaign, developing a relationship with the media that was to become his trademark. Within three months the store was profitable.

Ready to expand again in 1955, Dillard bought a 7,500-square-foot Magnolia, Arkansas, store from a family friend. Magnolia, a town of 7,000 located 55 miles from Texarkana, proved to be a lucrative market. The following February Dillard added appliances and furniture to his line of products.

His next opportunity came in 1956. Mayer & Schmidt had long been Tyler, Texas's most successful store. A failed attempt at expansion, however, had left it financially vulnerable. In April 1956 Dillard and a group of investors bought it. Dillard completely remodeled the place, expanding into the basement and leasing some departments. When he reopened in September, he advertised heavily in the local papers; the store soon set records for one-day sales.

Dillard's astute financing and smooth turnarounds caught the attention of the region's bankers. In 1959 Fred Eisman, a director of the First National Bank of St. Louis, asked Dillard to buy a failing Tulsa, Oklahoma, department store, Brown-Dunkin. Dillard jumped at the idea. Tulsa was bigger than Tyler, and Brown-Dunkin was bigger than Mayer & Schmidt. With the help of friends, bankers, and other investors, Dillard raised $325,000 and in February of 1960 bought the store.

Turning Brown-Dunkin around was difficult. Within 24 hours of the purchase, disgruntled union members began picketing the store, protesting a previous dismissal of maids and elevator operators. A week later Dillard discovered a cigar box filled with $150,000 in unpaid bills. Struggling with the situation, Dillard sold his Texarkana and Magnolia stores to Alden's for $775,000. In three months, the union gave up picketing, and with a loan from the National Bank of Tulsa, he paid off Brown-Dunkin's debts. Finally he launched a newspaper campaign and got the store into the black.

In 1961, as Dillard was consolidating Brown-Dunkin, he formed Dillard Investment Company, Inc. With bank loans, Dillard Investment bought Dillard's credit accounts. As customers paid their bills, the subsidiary repaid the banks. This gave Dillard stores the benefit of credit sales while remaining free of debts.

In 1962 Dillard wanted to return with his family to Arkansas. At the time, there were two leading stores in Little Rock, the Gus Blass Department Store and the Joseph Pfeifer Department Store. Rebuffed in his bid for Blass, Dillard turned to

Pfeifer. After extensive negotiations, Pfeifer president Sam Strauss accepted Dillard's bid of more than $3 million.

Dillard was again creative with capital. He collected investors, sold $325,000 worth of stock to Mayer & Schmidt shareholders, and convinced Sperry & Hutchinson, makers of S & H Green Stamps, to invest $1.5 million in exchange for issuing its stamps in his stores. In the fall of 1963, the Mayer & Schmidt store bought the Pfeifer store.

In January of 1964, shareholders reincorporated Mayer & Schmidt in Delaware, where laws were more favorable. They changed the name of the company to Dillard Department Stores, Inc., but retained the names of the individual stores until 1974.

In February of 1964, Gus Blass Co. allowed Dillard to buy the 192,000-square-foot Little Rock store and a 61,000-square-foot store at Pine Bluff, Arkansas. Since the main Blass store was just two blocks from Pfeifer, Dillard concentrated on remodeling the Pine Bluff store. By year's end, total corporate sales reached $41.2 million.

Two other key events occurred in 1964: the company installed its first computer system and opened its first mall store. The computers were the start of one of the industry's most advanced tracking systems. The mall store, on the west edge of Little Rock, marked the beginning of a move to the suburbs. Under various names, Dillard opened six more mall stores during the years from 1964 to 1968.

The year 1968 also marked the next turning point in corporate organization. For better administration, Dillard divided his 15 stores into three divisions: Arkansas, Oklahoma, and Texas. He also formed Construction Developers, Inc., a wholly owned subsidiary that manages the company's real estate holdings.

In 1969 Dillard turned to the stock market. He divided the stock into two classes. Class A would raise money. Class B, the voting stock, would remain under Dillard's control. Listed on the American Stock Exchange, the first offering sold 242,430 shares worth $4 million.

Dillard opened three mall stores in 1970, and in August 1971, he purchased five Fedway stores from Federated Department Stores. Though not unprofitable, Federated considered the Fedway stores less than successful. After re-stocking the stores with name brands, Dillard made them Dillard's in 1972.

By the end of 1972, Dillard had 22 stores and sales of more than $100 million. Three of that year's four new stores had a regional rather than metropolitan focus. As such, they were placed at the convergence of major highways.

The year 1973 marked the beginning of Dillard's border operations. To attract the inhabitants of nearby Matamoros, Mexico, the recently opened Brownsville store accepted the peso and extended credit to Mexican citizens.

In 1974 Dillard bought five Leonard's stores from the Tandy Corporation for stock and cash. Leonard's provided an instant saturation of the Dallas-Fort Worth, Texas, market. Saturation is an important factor as it allows a company to spread advertising costs over many stores. By year's end, company-wide sales reached $173.4 million.

More mall stores opened through the mid-1970s. Two stores came on line in 1975, including the first in Kansas, and in 1976 Dillard opened a record six stores in Texas, Oklahoma, and Louisiana.

In 1977 William (Bill) Dillard II, William Dillard's son, was named president and chief operating officer. William Dillard remained chief executive officer and chairman of the board, while E. Ray Kemp was named vice chairman of the board and chief administrative officer. By year's end, there were 38 Dillard's with sales of $269 million.

Sales had doubled from 1973 to 1977, but debts had also doubled. By the end of 1977, the company lacked expansion capital. Searching for money, William Dillard met A.C.R. Dreesmann, chief executive officer of Vroom en Dreesmann B.V., the Netherlands largest retail company. Dreesmann agreed to become Dillard's largest stockholder and to stay out of management. In February 1978, the board approved the sale of $24 million worth of Class A stock to Vroom en Dreesmann's subsidiary, Vendamerica B.V. The sale took place in three annual installments and gave Vendamerica 55% of the Class A shares. In 1979 Dillard used Vendamerica's first installment to build four new stores and remodel several older ones.

In 1980 rising interest rates checked Dillard's profits growth. Higher rates meant bigger payments on borrowed money and also hurt Dillard's own credit sales. Nevertheless, in 1980, Dillard added six stores in Texas and Oklahoma.

By contrast, 1981 was a banner year. The booming oil industry fueled sales growth, and management shifted its emphasis toward fast moving soft goods and away from less profitable home furnishings. Sales increased 26% to $470.7 million, profits vaulted 91% to $16.3 million, and earnings per share surged 85% to $5.35.

New Dillard's stores opened in Dallas, Texas, and Memphis, Tennessee. The success of the Memphis store prompted Dillard to lease three former Lowenstein stores and saturate the Memphis market. The three Memphis stores were a part of the record eleven new Dillard's opened in 1982. In the early 1980s, Dillard's grew at twice the department store average. Although the devaluation of the peso had a negative effect on border operations, 1982 profits still rose to $21.95 million.

As profits skyrocketed, so did stock prices. High stock prices reduced the company's financial flexibility, and in 1983 it embarked on a series of stock splits.

With new capital available, Dillard acquired 12 St. Louis, Missouri-area Stix, Baer & Fuller stores from Associated Dry Goods. The purchase came about through a chance meeting. While waiting for a flight at New York's LaGuardia Airport, William and Bill Dillard spotted mall developer Ed DeBartolo's corporate jet. They stopped for a visit and by chance met Bill Arnold, Associated's chairman. Arnold mentioned the possibility of selling Stix, Baer & Fuller, and months later, when new mall space became difficult to find, Dillard bought the stores.

The company had yet another year of massive expansion in 1984. In August Dillard agreed to pay the Dayton Hudson Corporation $140 million for 18 John A. Brown stores and 12 Diamond stores in the southwestern United States. Though not unprofitable, the stores performed below the Dayton Hudson average. Dillard immediately changed the John A. Brown stores to Dillard's. The Diamond stores went through a longer process in order to acquire the Dillard's name. In response to the needs of these western stores, Dillard added a new division based in Phoenix, Arizona.

By the end of 1984, Dillard's sales had increased 50.7% to $1.27 billion. Net profit jumped $15 million to $49.5 million, and the number of stores increased from 66 to 93.

The only stain in 1984 was Dillard's failure to feature any minority models in a major advertising supplement, and the

National Association for the Advancement of Colored People (NAACP) complained. The next year the NAACP protested the company's treatment of minorities and announced a boycott of the stores. In 1986 William Dillard agreed to hire more blacks and include more of them in management, a move that resolved the dispute.

The middle and late 1980s were marked by a shrewd reading of other department stores' finances. In 1985, after a management-led buyout of the R.H. Macy Company, Dillard went to New York, hoping that Macy's management would sell stores for needed capital. Within three months he closed a $100 million deal for 12 Macy's stores in Kansas City, Missouri, and Topeka and Wichita, Kansas.

Campeau Corp., a Canadian company, had bought Allied Stores Corp. and in 1987 needed cash to defray expenses. For $225 million, Campeau sold Dillard's 27 Joske's department stores and three Cain-Sloan department stores. Joske's gave Dillard what some described as a monopoly in Texas and pushed the retailer into the Houston market. Cain-Sloan gave Dillard's a presence in Nashville, Tennessee. In 1989, in a joint venture with The Edward J. DeBartolo Corporation, Dillard's acquired the Higbee Company, a chain of 12 Ohio department and specialty stores.

While continuing to open new stores in Missouri, Oklahoma, and Texas, Dillard's 1989 focus was again on acquisitions. Dillard acquired New Orleans, Louisiana-based D.H. Holmes Company, a chain of 17 stores located in Louisiana, Mississippi, Alabama, and Florida. Although Holmes was a consistent money-loser, Dillard was confident of a turnaround and was hungry for Holmes's New Orleans and Baton Rouge properties. In 1989 Dillard also moved its stock listing to the New York Stock Exchange and offered 2,000,000 shares of Class A common stock as well as two sets of debentures.

Dillard continued its acquisition campaign in 1990, paying BAT Industries $110 million for J.B. Ivey & Company's 23 stores in the Carolinas and Florida. The price of $110 million, or one-third of annual sales, compared favorably with rates others were paying for BAT assets.

For many retailers, 1990 was a disastrous year, but not for Dillard. Some estimated that Dillard enjoyed an 18% same-store sales gain over 1989. In 1990 every expense item on the company's income statement dropped as a percentage of sales. Because the company's ratio of debt to capital is lower than that of competitors, interest is less of a problem than for the competition.

From a small department store in Nashville, Arkansas, William Dillard built one of the fastest growing department store chains in the United States. Expanding first by acquisition and later by placing stores in suburban malls and buying underperforming assets from debt-burdened competitors, Dillard's has grown without burdening itself with crushing debt. With all of William Dillard's five children involved in management and holding a secure control of voting stock, the horizons seem bright for this growing company.

Principal Subsidiaries: Construction Developers, Inc.; Dillard Investment Company.

Further Reading: Rosenberg, Leon Joseph, *Dillard's: The First Fifty Years,* Fayetteville, The University of Arkansas Press, 1988.

—Jordan Wankoff

Dixons Group plc

DIXONS GROUP PLC

29 Farm Street
London W1X 7RD
United Kingdom
(071) 499 3494
Fax: (071) 629 1402

Public Company
Incorporated: 1937 as Dixon Studios Ltd.
Employees: 14,225
Sales: £1.69 billion (US$3.16 billion)
Stock Exchanges: London Tokyo

Dixons Group plc is one of the world's leading specialty retailers of consumer electronics, has a strong presence in photographic goods, and sells most kinds of domestic electric appliances. In the United Kingdom it operates under the names Dixons, Currys, and Supasnaps, and in the United States as Silo.

From one small shop in London in 1937, Dixons grew by 1991 to 1,450 stores spread across the United Kingdom and United States. It achieved this rapid growth by entering two fast-growing markets at an early stage in their development: photographic goods in the 1950s and consumer electronics in the 1970s. In both cases, Dixons helped to build these markets in the United Kingdom and grew with them.

The driving force behind the company's growth since the 1950s has been the man who continued to head it in the early 1990s, Stanley Kalms. It was his father, Charles Kalms, however, who started the business. He began as a portrait photographer in London and later acquired interests in several small businesses. In 1937 he and a friend decided to set up a photographic studio at Southend-on-Sea, not far from London. They incorporated the business as Dixon Studios Ltd., choosing the name Dixon out of a telephone directory in preference to their own. Kalms's friend gave up his share in the business within two years, and Kalms took full control, while continuing to run another business at the same time.

During World War II, when so many men and women were separated from their families, there was a great demand for portrait photographs, and the business flourished. By the end of the war the company had expanded to a chain of seven studios in the London area. After 1945, however, the market contracted as fast as it had grown, and Dixon was reduced to a single studio in the North London suburb of Edgware.

In an effort to boost sales, Charles Kalms began to sell cameras and other photographic equipment, and the studio gradually turned into a shop. This changeover gathered pace when Charles Kalms's son Stanley joined the business in 1948. Although only 17, he proved to be a natural salesman. A one-time colleague recalled that Stanley Kalms sold some cameras with great success even before he had discovered how to load the film. The retail side of the business grew quickly, and father and son agreed to concentrate on developing it. By 1953 the company was able to start opening branches again, this time under the name Dixon Camera Centres.

In those early postwar years, few people in Britain could afford to spend much on their hobbies, but interest in photography was growing fast. Dixon met this situation by selling new and used goods at attractive prices and by offering credit terms. At an early stage it started advertising, at first in photographic magazines and local papers, then in national newspapers. In this way it built up a large mail-order business as well as shop sales. By 1958 it had 60,000 mail-order customers, and the shop business had grown to six branches. In that year Dixon moved its head office to larger premises, still in Edgware. The company then employed almost 100 people.

The company showed unusual enterprise in buying as well as selling. In the 1950s the photographic market in the United Kingdom was dominated by U.K., U.S., and German manufacturers, and the law at that time allowed manufacturers to dictate the prices at which their products were retailed. This did not suit Dixon's competitive style, and Stanley Kalms began to look elsewhere for manufacturers who would supply him directly at low prices. He began regular buying trips to the Far East and by hard bargaining and bulk buying was able to import goods at prices which enabled Dixon to offer unbeatable value to its customers. In Japan he found manufacturers willing to supply products made to Dixon's specification. At that time Japanese goods were not highly regarded in Europe, so Dixon marketed the goods under the German-sounding name of Prinz.

By the end of the 1950s incomes in Britain were rising sharply, and the market for photographic goods doubled in value between 1958 and 1963. Camera design was improving, color film prices were falling, and a craze for home-movie kits—camera, projector, and screen—swelled demand. Dixon, having established a reputation for good value and quality, was one of the chief beneficiaries. Its profits rocketed from £6,800 in 1958 to £160,000 in 1962, and in that year the company went public under the new name of Dixons Photographic Ltd. The Kalms family retained voting control, with more than three-quarters of the shares in their hands at this time, but the shares released to the market proved highly popular. Stanley Kalms was chairman until 1971, and another member of the family, Peter Kalms, was financial director until 1980.

At the time of the stock offering Dixons had only 16 shops, five of them in London, and with the help of the offering it acquired more. Two chains of camera shops, Ascotts, with 13 stores, and Bennetts, Dixons's largest specialty competitor, with 29 branches, were bought in the next two years. Dixons also opened more shops from scratch, including one on a prime site near Marble Arch, London. By the end of 1964 the company had 70 shops and by 1969 it had more than 100.

Growth in profits was more erratic. Retail sales were depressed in some years by government action to restrict credit, and some of the company's expansionary moves lost money in the short term. In 1967 a large color film processing plant at Stevenage was purchased, the most up-to-date one in Europe at the time; it operated at a loss for a while before making a profit. Dixons also began to manufacture photographic accessories and display material and made substantial losses on this business before abandoning it in 1970.

The key to Dixons's next leap in profits, in the early 1970s, was its move into electronics retailing. This began very cautiously in 1967, when some audio and hi-fidelity units were put on sale in six branches as an experiment. They sold well and were soon introduced into all branches. By 1970 Dixons had introduced its own Prinzsound brand. The next year, television sets were sold experimentally in 25 stores. They too were a great success, partly because the recent arrival of color television had created a large television replacement market. After that, Dixons introduced a host of new products in quick succession, including electronic calculators, radio/cassette recorders, music centers, and digital clock/radios. To make room for all these new products, the company had to enlarge its stores. In two consecutive years its total selling space was increased by 30% or more.

The effect of these developments on profits was dramatic. From £226,000 in 1970—a bad year—profits soared £828,000 in 1971, £2.3 million in 1972, and to £4.9 million in 1973. The company had established itself in a new market with tremendous growth potential, and its reputation with the investing public, who by this time held the majority of its shares, stood high.

In fact, its next few years proved to be an unhappy period. This was partly because the economic climate changed for the worse in 1974, but chiefly because the company tried to buy its way into other new markets with less positive results.

Dixons started to expand abroad in the early 1970s, at first with success. Through small marketing companies in Sweden and Switzerland, it found valuable new outlets for its own brand of products throughout Europe. In 1972 it bought a large Dutch photographic and optical retail business, G.H. Rinck NV, a company with nearly 60 stores in the Netherlands, compared with Dixons's 150 stores in the United Kingdom at that time. As in Britain, Dixons opened more branches and introduced more products, but the Dutch business never approached the U.K. stores in profitability and for two consecutive years incurred losses.

This experience deterred Dixons from further expansion overseas for some years. Instead, it embarked in 1976 on a new form of expansion in the United Kingdom. With the hope of achieving a large increase in outlets for its goods at one stroke, it bought Weston Pharmaceuticals, a chain of 200 drugstores, for £11 million, together with a wholesale business supplying independent druggists. The idea was to widen Weston's range to include Dixons products, in the same way that Boots—originally a pharmaceutical company—had so successfully broadened its range to include other consumer goods. "Boots must be our model," said Peter Kalms in the *Investors Chronicle* of January 30, 1976, soon after the takeover.

These hopes were never realized. It became apparent within a short time that Weston had serious problems within its existing business and that any major expansion was out of the question. Its profits declined, then turned to losses. Dixons wrestled with Weston's financial problems for four years in an effort to turn it around, but in 1980 decided to recoup what it could of its investment by selling all the drugstores. The wholesale business was kept for some years longer, but seldom produced a substantial profit.

Meanwhile, the struggle to save Weston's retail business had left Dixons with a shortage of working capital, and this had led the company to sell G.H. Rinck in 1978. Thus by 1980 two major investments had come to nothing, and the company's reputation as a growth stock was tarnished. The recession of 1981–1982 delayed Dixons's recovery, with the result that its profits, after discounting inflation, showed no real growth for six years.

Dixons's main electronics retailing business, however, continued to expand throughout this period. By 1982 the company had raised the number of its stores to 260 and increased their average size. New electronic products were introduced as they were manufactured, including home computers, video recorders, and digital watches. By competitive pricing policies, Dixons won a sizable share of all these new markets. It launched a new house brand, this time with a Japanese name, Saisho. The photographic side of the business also continued to grow; its processing capacity was increased, and a property development unit was established successfully.

All these investments paid off handsomely once Weston's problems had been left behind and the recession ended. In 1984 Dixons's profits jumped by 46%. On the strength of this fresh spurt of growth, the company made its biggest-ever takeover in December of that year. This time it chose a British company with a business closely complementary to its own. Currys Group PLC (Currys) was a chain of 570 shops, selling refrigerators, freezers, washing machines, and electronics, including a television rental business. Although it owned twice as many shops as Dixons, Currys's turnover was no greater, and its recent performance had been less dynamic. Nevertheless, it was a very sound business with a good name, and Dixons had to pay £248 million for it.

Currys was a much older business than Dixons. It began in Leicester in 1888 as a bicycle shop and, in the cycling boom of the 1890s, manufactured and sold bicycles. When its founder, Henry Curry, retired in 1910, his sons carried on the business—a partnership formed in 1897 as H Curry & Sons—and expanded it greatly. It ceased to manufacture, but developed into a nationwide chain of shops selling cycles, radios, baby carriages, toys, and sporting goods, and became a public company in 1927. The second and third generations of the Curry family continued to manage it, however, until the Dixons takeover. By that time the company had ceased to deal in cycles and sporting goods, but had become one of the leading retailers of domestic electric appliances of all kinds.

The merger of Dixons and Currys, under the name of Dixons Group, put the company into the top echelon of British retailers. Even after selling the television rental shops, the new company had more than 800 stores in the United Kingdom and its staff had grown to 11,000. Currys retained its separate identity within the company, but its business methods were brought more into line with Dixons's. In the boom conditions of the mid–1980s, the combination brought further large increases in profits.

Stanley Kalms, however, was not content even with this empire. In 1986 he launched a bid for Woolworth Holdings, the British branch of Woolworth. The U.S. parent had sold its

52% controlling stake in this to a consortium of British investors in 1982, and Woolworth Holdings was still struggling to raise its profits after a long period of stagnation. Kalms believed that Dixons could do the job better, as well as obtain new outlets for its own merchandise. In the end, Dixons's £1.8 billion bid was turned down by the institutional investors who controlled most of Woolworth Holdings' shares.

Thwarted in this plan, Dixons looked around for other investment opportunities. In 1986 it acquired the 340-shop Supasnaps chain, the leading U.K. specialist in retail film processing. Then, in 1987, it made two major acquisitions in the United States, the Silo and Tipton electrical and appliance retailing chains. Silo Inc., with 119 stores and 2,000 employees, was the third largest electrical retailer in the United States and was strong in the East and Midwest. Tipton Centers Inc. was based in St. Louis and had 24 other stores.

With these acquisitions Dixons controlled more than 1,300 stores worldwide, with 3.5 million square feet of selling space. By 1991 it doubled the number of its U.S. outlets, gaining a presence on the West Coast too, and the worldwide store total had risen to nearly 1,450.

Dixons's profits reached a peak of £103 million in 1988. Since then business conditions have become considerably tougher and profits have declined. As a result, Dixons found itself at the receiving end of a takeover bid in 1989. The bidder was none other than Woolworth, by then renamed Kingfisher, a company that had made a strong recovery since its 1986 financial difficulties. Dixons was saved from this threat by the Monopolies and Mergers Commission, which ruled that Dixons and Kingfisher as a unit would have an excessive share of the electrical goods market.

In the face of these pressures Dixons made some cutbacks in 1989 and 1990, although it continued to invest in its mainstream activities. If the company's history is any guide, further growth can be expected when the recession of the early 1990s ends.

Principal Subsidiaries: Dixons Stores Group Limited; Mastercare Limited; Supasnaps Limited; Silo Inc. (USA); Dixons Commercial Properties International Limited.

—John Swan

EL CORTE INGLÉS GROUP

Hermosilla, 112
28009 Madrid
Spain
(91) 402 8112
Fax: (91) 402 5821

Private Company
Incorporated: 1940 as El Corte Inglés, S.L.
Employees: 48,903
Sales: Pta 805.89 billion (US$8.34 billion)

El Corte Inglés, S.A. is a joint-stock company that forms the core of the El Corte Inglés Group and was incorporated on January 2, 1952, from the limited liability company El Corte Inglés S.L., itself incorporated on June 28, 1940. The company runs Spain's largest chain of department stores, and operates through its subsidiaries, a wide range of services, such as travel agencies, insurance brokerage, and computer services.

The company has become a model for the Spanish business world, owing to the efforts of its founder, Ramón Areces Rodriguez, and the firm's directors. The history of El Corte Inglés is closely linked with the life of Areces. Born in 1905 in Asturias, he emigrated to Cuba in 1919 aboard the ship *Alfonso XII,* following his brother, who had emigrated a few years earlier. With help from his uncle, César Rodríguez, Areces was able to find work in the department store El Encanto, owned by a Spanish family. At El Encanto he worked alongside José (Pepín) Fernández Rodríguez, his uncle's cousin, who would later become Areces' business rival in Spain.

El Encanto employed some of the retail management techniques that had been developed in the United States, based in particular on diversification and aggressiveness. Wishing to improve his understanding of business administration, Areces left Cuba in 1924 to go to New York and Montreal with César Rodriquez. For a year and a half he worked in a New York export firm, learning about international trade.

In 1928 at the age of 23, Areces returned to work in Cuba for six years before deciding to return to Spain to set up his own business. Spain was on the verge of civil war, but Areces launched directly into business nonetheless. He established himself in Madrid and invested his Cuban savings in the acquisition of a tailor's shop. This shop was strategically located in the center of Madrid, and had exits onto three streets, Pre-

ciados, Rompelanzas, and Carmen. Areces paid Pta 150,000 for the tailor's shop and changed everything except the store's name, El Corte Inglés.

The business started out with seven employees and was an immediate success, causing the company to expand quickly. In 1940, shortly after the end of the Spanish civil war, the business was moved to a location on Preciados Street, where Areces bought the department store El Aguila. The store would be converted, after several extensions, into the firm's first commercial shopping center. Areces's cousin, José Fernández, bought the original shop on Rompelanzas Street from him; it became the first store of the Galerías Preciados after it had been expanded several times.

On June 28, 1940, Ramón Areces Rodriguez formed El Corte Inglés, S.L., a limited liability company with a capital of Pta 1 million, with his younger brothers Luis and Celestino. In July 1949 the company formed Industrias y Confecciones, S.A. (Induyco) as an independent company. It became a joint stock company in December 1955. Induyco was established to make clothes, as part of the founder's clear vision of vertical expansion and integration for El Corte Inglés. The aim of the new company was to ensure the supply of manufactured clothes to meet the demand at the shop in Preciados Street. This decision was made because during the civil war the Spanish clothing industry found itself facing great difficulties owing to the shortage of raw materials and capital to buy machinery and other basic items.

To ensure the company's continued development, it was changed into a joint-stock venture, being incorporated as El Corte Inglés, S.A. on January 2, 1952. At first Induyco manufactured clothes exclusively for El Corte Inglés, but later it began trading with clients outside the group. Induyco is not part of the El Corte Inglés Group, although El Corte Inglés S.A.'s president is also president of Induyco.

Ramón Areces Rodriguez did not have any children. He brought his 18-year-old nephew, Isidoro Alvarez, onto the staff of El Corte Inglés in 1953. Alvarez continued to study economics and business at the Complutense University, and in 1957 graduated with special distinction. Areces dedicated his time to training Alvarez. Alvarez was made a member of the board of directors of El Corte Inglés in 1959, having started in the company's warehouse and then worked in many of the firm's departments.

Ramón Areces Rodriguez's rival, Pepín Fernández, managing Galerías Preciados, had taken a great lead over him, with Galerías Preciados having a merchandise turnover 20 times greater than El Corte Inglés in 1960. Ramón Areces Rodriguez had to develop a strategy that would distinguish him from his competitor. He decided to change his shop's image to that of a store offering luxury goods. If Galerías Preciados worked on the principle of making huge sales of a wide range of products at cheap prices, El Corte Inglés would concentrate on offering personalized service and specialized articles. Areces's business strategy and his decision to start up business in Barcelona in 1962 were prompted by an external factor, a managerial crisis at Galerías Preciados, which affected that company's image and permitted Areces to achieve supremacy in the large department store sector.

The time from 1965 to 1975 was a boom period for El Corte Inglés. The opening of the El Corte Inglés department store in Barcelona was the first step in a policy of expansion that led to the opening of 20 shopping centers that were still open in 1991. This evolution was the result not only of the particular activities El Corte Inglés had developed in its department stores, but also of its strategy of vertical expansion and integration and its development of diversified services and activities.

In May 1966 El Corte Inglés shareholders formed the company Móstoles Industrial S.A. This company, with a capitalization of Pta 4 million, arose from the consolidation of the group's divisions dealing with window displays and wooden kitchen furniture. (Móstoles Industrial is not included in the El Corte Inglés Group.) In November 1969 the travel agency company Viajes El Corte Inglés, S.A. was formed as a fully owned subsidiary of El Corte Inglés. With initial capital of Pta 5 million, it grew out of the company department that had previously organized staff vacations. At the beginning of the 1990s it was the second-largest of El Corte Inglés's subsidiaries by turnover, having established itself as one of the leaders in its field. Its turnover for the fiscal year 1990 was Pta 41.11 billion.

To help ensure the growth of the group, Induyco was strengthened by the creation of two additional companies, Confecciónes Teruel, S.A., incorporated in May 1975, and Industrias del Vestido, S.A., incorporated in June 1976. Both are fully owned subsidiaries of El Corte Inglés. A further fully owned subsidiary, Construcción, Promociones a Instalaciones, S.A., was formed in May 1976. It is concerned with the construction needs of the firms within the group.

The Ramón Areces Foundation was formed in 1976. Its purpose, apart from arranging a secure future for the company in the case of Ramón Areces Rodriguez's death, was to encourage scientific research, award grants, and support training programs, publications, and cultural activities in general. Its projects include the computerization of the Archivo de Indias in Seville, in collaboration with IBM and the Ministry of Culture, assisting with grants for overseas studies, and the support of organizaitions such as the Centro de Biología Molecular and the University of Navarra.

Hipercor, S.A., another of El Corte Inglés's fully owned subsidiaries, was founded in 1979 with a capital of Pta 1 million, which increased to Pta 1 billion the following year. Hipercor, operating in the hypermarket sector, bases its strategy on combining the traditional hypermarket concept of low prices with the range of products and the customer care of a large department store. Hypermarkets typically combine grocery stores, nonfood retailing, and service businesses. The Hipercor centers cover a large surface area like a hypermarket. Within Tiendas Cortty, little shops give the impression of independent franchise operations and sell products exclusive to El Corte Inglés under the Cortty trademark. Hipercor grew spectacularly during the 1980s. Its sales figure rose to Pta 121.77 billion in 1990, making it the group's largest subsidiary.

Induyco created two important new companies in the 1980s. Investrónica S.A. was incorporated in 1980 and is involved in the electronics and computer sector, in particular in the manufacture of microcomputers and hi-fi equipment and the design of software. The second, Invesgen S.A., was incorporated in 1985 and is geared toward the use of advanced technologies in biochemistry and genetics.

El Corte Inglés also created two new subsidiaries in the early 1980s. In 1982, it created Centro de Seguros, Corre-duría de Seguros, S.A., an insurance broker and assessor also offering family policies. In 1984, it created Videcor S.A., dedicated to the development of video clubs in El Corte Inglés's and Hipercor's shopping centers. Centro de Seguros developed successfully, collecting Pta 7.094 billion in premiums in 1990. Videcor ceased to exist as a public limited company in August 1988 and its activities were transferred to El Corte Inglés.

In 1983, branching out onto the international market, El Corte Inglés bought The Harris Company in the United States, which runs a chain of medium-sized stores in California and also owns various shopping centers.

In February 1988 Informática El Corte Inglés was formed to sell computer products and services to large firms and public institutions using computer centers and data processing. The subsidiary's turnover for the fiscal year 1990 was Pta 12.40 billion.

The year 1988 also saw the foundation of the publishing company Editorial Centro de Estudios Ramón Areces, S.A. Its aim was to become a publisher of texts for universities, and in particular of works needed for courses at the Ramón Areces Center for University Studies. In 1990 sales totaled Pta 295 million.

In December 1989 El Corte Inglés formed two insurance companies. The first, Seguros El Corte Inglés, Vida, Pensiones y Reaseguros S.A., covers life assurance and underwriting. The second, Seguros El Corte Inglés, Ramos Generales y Reaseguros S.A., covers accident, health, and travel insurance, as well as damages. El Corte Inglés has a 99.9% holding in these two companies; their accounts are separate from El Corte Inglés since their activities differ from those of other firms in the group.

Ramón Areces Rodriguez died on July 30, 1989, leaving all his capital inheritance to the Ramón Areces Foundation. As a result, the foundation received Pta 36.5 billion. This effectively means that the Ramón Areces Foundation controls the business group, holding practically all the shares in the group's companies except for the insignificant number owned by the administrative board.

After Ramón Areces Rodriguez's death, the administrative board agreed unanimously to appoint Isidoro Alvarez as the new president of El Corte Inglés on August 1, 1989. Thus Alvarez took the position of patron and president for life of the Ramón Areces Foundation board of patrons.

Alvarez inherited a paternalistic style of management from Areces and rigorously follows the latter's stated principles of prudent investment, careful reinvestment of profits, and the avoidance of incurring unnecessary debts with banks. His aims are to compete successfully with the great retail multinationals, to increase the group's international ventures, and to raise profit margins. From his numerous trips and connections abroad he has an excellent knowledge of retailing outside of Spain. He was also intimately involved with Areces in El Corte Inglés's expansion, including the development of the Hipercor network and its expansion into new areas of business. In the fiscal year 1990, El Corte Inglés, S.A.'s sales rose to Pta 646.54 billion, representing an increase of 16.7% over the previous year.

El Corte Inglés is also a major competitor of the Spanish banks. It offers consumer credit in the manner of a bank or savings society. It holds accounts for its employees, where they can cash or deposit their paychecks and take care of the expenses and purchases that they make within the company. El Corte Inglés introduced personal credit cards for its stores in 1967, and in 1991 it was the largest issuer of personal credit cards in Spain, with around 1.8 million in issue.

The company's ability to adapt will be particularly important at a time when competition is increasing both from national and international groups. El Corle Inglés had commercial offices in Paris, London, Frankfurt, Lisbon, and Milan. It had 31 external buyers who cover practically all of the world markets. In 1990 purchases from abroad by El Corte Inglés and Hipercor exceeded Pta 45 billion in value. El Corte Inglés was set on meeting customers' needs of the future, continuously working to update and improve the quality and variety of its products and services, developing new systems of management and personnel training, and continuing on its path of expansion.

Principal Subsidiaries: Hipercor, S.A.; Viajes El Corte Inglés, S.A.; Informática El Corte Inglés, S.A.; Construcción, Promociones e Instalaciones, S.A.; Centro de Seguros, Correduría de Seguros, S.A.; Editorial Centro de Estudios Ramón Areces, S.A.; The Harris Company (U.S.A).

Further Reading: Dauder, E., *Los empresarios,* Barcelona, Editorial Dopesa, 1974; Areces, Ramón, "Discurso de investidura de Doctor Honoris Causa por la Universidad de Oviedo," 1987; Bueno Campos, E., "El caso El Corte Inglés" in *Dirección estratégica de la empresa, Metodología, técnicas y casos,* Madrid, Ediciones Pirámide S.A., 1987; Cuervo, Alvaro, "Ramón Areces: empresa y cultura," *Revista de Económica,* No. 1, 1989; Bueno Campos, E., and Morcillo, P., "El Corte Inglés-Hipercor" in *La dirreción eficiente,* Madrid, Ediciones Pirámide S.A., 1990; Celma, J. "El misterio de El Corte Inglés" in *Anuario de la Distribución,* 1990; "El Corte Inglés. Una herencia bien aprovechada," *Actualidad Económica,* May 1991.

—Alejandro Molla Descals

FRED MEYER, INC.

3800 Southeast 22nd Avenue
Portland, Oregon 97202
U.S.A.
(503) 232-8844
Fax: (503) 233-4535

Public Company
Incorporated: 1923
Employees: 24,000
Sales: $2.48 billion
Stock Exchange: NASDAQ

Fred Meyer, Inc. is a major retailer in the western United States, featuring large, one-stop shopping stores that range in size up to 200,000 square feet and offer hundreds of thousands of food and nonfood products. A full-size Fred Meyer store features full-service grocery, pharmacy, nutrition, restaurant, housewares, building materials and hardware, gardening and floral, sporting goods, automotive, stationery, book, toy, clothes, fine jewelery, and home electronics areas.

Fred Meyer, Inc. traces its history to 1922, when its first store opened in downtown Portland, Oregon. At the end of 1991, the company had 122 stores in such states as Oregon, Utah, Washington, Idaho, Alaska, Montana, and California, 94 of which were large department stores. The remainder were smaller, specialty stores. Fred Meyer's department stores contain up to 21 smaller specialty "stores" or departments.

The history of Fred Meyer, Inc. revolves around its founder, Fred G. Meyer, who guided the company until his death in 1978. In 1908, 22-year-old Frederick Grubmeyer, son of a Brooklyn grocer, moved to Portland and began selling coffee to workers at the farms and lumber camps that surrounded the burgeoning town of Portland. The horse-drawn route prospered, but young Grubmeyer, who eventually changed his name to Fred G. Meyer, wanted more. In a few years he moved to Alaska to seek other business opportunities. Alaska was overrun with would-be entrepreneurs, however, and Meyer returned to Portland and founded the Java Coffee Company, selling coffee, tea, and spices from a storefront in the market district.

The Java Coffee Company, later renamed the Mission Tea Company, prospered, but many neighboring businesses succumbed to the uncertain economics of the time. Meyer snapped up their properties and soon was landlord and sometimes operator of several specialty food operations.

In the early 1920s, the center of commercial activity moved uptown, and Meyer moved with it, consolidating his several specialty businesses into a single location that became the flagship store for the Fred Meyer chain. The store, which opened in 1922, had 20 employees, with Meyer serving as buyer and manager. Its seven departments included meat, delicatessen, coffee, lunch, homemade mayonnaise, grocery, and tobacco.

The next year Fred Meyer, Inc. was incorporated in Oregon, and a second store was opened that featured grocery and dairy products.

Fred Meyer continued expanding throughout the 1920s. Across the street from the parent store, he opened a packaged food store selling sugar, dry beans, rice, macaroni, spaghetti, coffee, and dried fruits. Then in 1928, he opened what many regard as the world's first self-service drugstore. The store's lower labor costs meant lower prices, and Meyer's reputation as a value merchandiser was established.

The company prospered despite the stock market crash of 1929 and the ensuing Great Depression. Meyer opened four new stores between 1929 and 1932: a toiletry store, a department store in the outlying Portland neighborhood of Hollywood, and his first stores outside Portland, in the towns of Salem and Astoria, Oregon.

The Hollywood, Oregon, store marked Meyer's recognition of the growing importance of the car in retailing. Finding that customers were often double-parking in front of his downtown stores and getting ticketed in the process—Meyer would pay the tickets—Meyer did an informal survey and found that many customers lived in the Hollywood section of Portland, about five miles from downtown. This led to the opening of the Hollywood store, which included an automobile lubrication and oil service and an off-street parking lot.

Throughout the 1930s, Meyer ran a series of aggressive promotions that highlighted the company's low prices. Meyer saw these entertaining promotions as ways of getting customers into stores during cash-starved times. He rented movie theaters and gave children free admission if they brought three My-Te-Fine store-brand labels. He had newspapers add peppermint to their ink, giving his candy ads a special sweet smell.

These and other promotions helped make Fred Meyer a major player in Portland, but the company was not without competition. Drugstores banded together to stop the company from obtaining a prescription license. Retailers threatened to drop lines if manufacturers sold to Fred Meyer. An anonymously sponsored radio show spent all its time lambasting the quality of Fred Meyer goods—all to no avail.

Fred Meyer began adding new products in the early 1930s, and the stores began selling men's and women's wear in 1933. Automotive departments, housewares, and other nonfood products followed in succeeding years. The middle of the decade saw the opening of a central bakery, a candy kitchen, an ice cream plant, and a photo-finishing plant. These facilities paved the way for house brands such as Vita Bee bread, Hocus Pocus desserts, and Fifth Avenue candies. Fred Meyer capped the decade with large new stores in northeast and southeast Portland.

As with other retailers, Fred Meyer was challenged by World War II. Demand was high but supplies were low, and many employees were called to service. After the war, a more modern Fred Meyer began to emerge. Old stores were renovated and standardized, and new Fred Meyer stores were built from the ground up—instead of being housed in existing space. A new management team still working under Meyer himself, began adding departments such as home improvement, nutrition centers, fine jewelry, and photo and audio. Some experiments, such as carpet and draperies, major appliances, furniture, and automotive service did not meet expectations and were eventually dropped.

The 1950s saw Fred Meyer opening a stream of successful outlets in suburban Portland. These stores were larger than previous Fred Meyer outlets, at 45,000 to 70,000 square feet. Meyer often led or kept pace with developers and was able to spot prime retail space on major suburban thoroughfares before suburban traffic patterns were apparent.

The mid-1950s also saw the construction of Fred Meyer's first modern distribution facility at Swan Island, Oregon. Also to be located at Swan Island was a new dairy plant and a central kitchen for the company's in-house food operation, Eve's Buffet Restaurant. In 1959 the company made its first major acquisition. For stock worth close to $1 million, Fred Meyer acquired four Marketime drug stores in Seattle, Washington.

In 1960, when there were 20 Fred Meyer stores with combined annual sales of $56 million, the company went public. Meyer then made a series of large acquisitions. In 1964 the company acquired Roundup Wholesale Grocery Company of Spokane, Washington, including 14 Sigman supermarkets in Washington and Oregon and three B & B Stores in Montana. The following year Fred Meyer purchased seven Market Basket stores in Seattle and one in Yakima, Washington.

In 1966 management again upgraded the look of Fred Meyer stores. Tiled aisles and carpeted apparel departments replaced concrete floors. Displays were made more colorful, and new marketing ideas were introduced throughout the store. By year's end, earnings had reached $1.56 million on sales of $170.8 million.

Fred Meyer also continued to develop a vertical management organization. The heads of each of up to 11 departments in each store would eventually report to corporate vice presidents in charge of those departments rather than to an individual store manager. Individual departments became as strong as specialty stores and operated as such, complete with their own check-outs.

Although business was booming, not every venture went as planned. In 1968 Fred Meyer sold the Market Basket stores it had bought three years earlier, as the small stores did not fit in with other operations. This move meant a $225,000 write-off against 1968 profits. Nevertheless, sales and income continued to grow.

Meyer, by now in his early 80s, continued to rule the company. A younger management team was beginning to take at least some of the reins of power, however. In 1969 Jack Crocker, a 20-year employee of the company, became president of Fred Meyer, Inc., with Meyer as chairman. Crocker's presidency coincided with Fred Meyer's opening of its Levi jeans centers.

While profits continued to increase, the early 1970s were a difficult time for Fred Meyer's management. In 1971 Meyer suffered a stroke that left him weakened but still alert. In November of the same year President Crocker tendered his resignation, effective January 1, 1972. In March of 1972, the Fred Meyer board elected Cyril K. Green to replace Crocker as

president and Oran W. Robertson as first vice president of the company.

The new management team continued relentless expansion. The main focus was on additions to existing stores, but plans also called for three new stores in 1972 and one in 1973. Acquisitions were also part of the plan. In 1973, Fred Meyer acquired five Valu-Mart stores in Oregon from Seattle-based Weisfield's Inc., ending the year with 52 stores and a thriving business in the Pacific Northwest.

In 1975 the company ventured into finance, buying a local savings and loan with deposits of $3.8 million. The idea was to install S&Ls in each of his full-service stores. The S&Ls would make money through banking and by bringing more customers and money into the stores. Although many in the banking industry were skeptical, Fred Meyer Savings and Loan Association grew rapidly, bringing in small depositors who probably had not saved at all before opening their Fred Meyer accounts. The company drew on its retailing experience to build the bank, offering free loaves of bread and steaks for customers opening accounts. The Fred Meyer Savings and Loans also stayed open longer hours than their competitors.

In 1975 Fred Meyer bought three Baza'r outlets and nine more department stores from Weisfield's Inc. of Seattle, including two Valu-Mart stores and six Leslie's stores located in Seattle, Spokane, and Yakima, Washington and Anchorage, Alaska. All were to be merged into Fred Meyer operations.

In 1976 Fred Meyer retired from the day-to-day affairs of the company and became chairman of the executive committee. Oran B. Robertson was named chairman of the board and chief executive officer. Cyril K. Green remained president, and Virgil Campbell became executive vice president.

In 1978 Meyer died. The success of Fred Meyer, Inc. was a testament to his hard work, intuition, and intelligence. His stores dominated the Northwest and continued to expand. Their net profit margin of 1.9% was better than those of big national chains like Winn-Dixie Stores (1.7%), Lucky Stores (1.5%), and Safeway (0.9%).

Meyer's death inspired many testimonials, but it also set the stage for a power struggle among the four executors of his will; Meyer owned 29.1% of the company's outstanding stock. On one side was Oran B. Robertson, chairman and CEO. Opposing him was G. Gerry Pratt, a Meyer protege, and chairman and chief executive of Fred Meyer Savings and Loan. Other executors included a Fred Meyer vice president, and Warne H. Nunn, Pratt's friend and longtime local power company executive.

The struggle over the will was further complicated by Pratt's troubles at Fred Meyer S&L. Pratt, a former journalist and talk-show host, was hired by Meyer in 1972. Two years later he was made head of Fred Meyer S&L. With Pratt's innovative flair, the Fred Meyer S&L grew fast, but when the cost of money skyrocketed in 1979, the S&L was overextended and lost $1 million. The savings and loan's loss ended nearly 20 years of quarterly profit increases. In May 1980 chairman and CEO Oran B. Robertson fired Pratt and replaced the Fred Meyer S&L board with Fred Meyer executives. Pratt responded with a lawsuit that was later settled. Fred Meyer sold its savings and loan.

With the death of Meyer, outside investors began showing an interest in the company. In September 1980, the investment firm of Kohlberg Kravis Roberts & Co. (KKR) offered to buy the entire organization for $45 a share—more than $300 million. Ultimately KKR successfully negotiated a leveraged buyout in December 1981 with the Fred Meyer management as equity participants for $55 per share, or $435 million. This took Fred Meyer stock out of circulation and made the company private once again. In the meantime, the company had sold Roundup Wholesale to West Coast Grocery. The leveraged buyout split Fred Meyer into two companies. The retail operations continued as Fred Meyer, Inc., and the real estate assets were transferred to a separate partnership, Fred Meyer Real Estate Properties Ltd., which leased properties back to Fred Meyer, Inc. Occupancy expenses rose dramatically due to the spin-off of real estate holdings, and initially the company operated in the red.

Despite higher occupancy expenses and the cost of debt normally associated with leveraged buyouts, Fred Meyer continued to expand aggressively. Over the next five years it built 11 new stores and acquired the Grand Central chain, which had stores in several Rocky Mountain states. The company sold Grand Central's New Mexico and Nevada stores but kept its 21 stores in Utah and Idaho, remodeling 15 of them. Furthermore, it cut costs by consolidating departmental checkouts.

Overall, during the time the company was private, Fred Meyer grew from 64 to 93 stores. Net income increased from $5.2 million in fiscal 1982 to $22.5 million in fiscal 1986. Sales jumped from $1.1 billion to $1.7 billion over the same period.

Management attempted and failed to bring Fred Meyer public again in 1983. By 1986 management felt investors were ready to buy Fred Meyer stock. In the fall of 1986, the company issued 6.75 million shares of common stock, 4.5 million new shares and 2.25 million from existing shareholders, at $14.25 per share.

Through the late 1980s and early 1990s, Fred Meyer continued its expansion, adding several new stores yearly as well as replacing and expanding existing stores. The Pacific Northwest had become a more competitive market with the entrance of discounters like Dayton Hudson's Target stores and the grocery chains Food 4 Less and Cub Foods, but most analysts believed Fred Meyer's one-stop shopping centers gave it a unique niche in the market.

In the early 1990s, Fred Meyer executives began a major overhaul of their stores and management organization. The company created the Fred Meyer Institute to improve training of employees.

Fred Meyer also unveiled a new prototype store with a flexible design to facilitate layout changes without expensive remodeling; the first store in the new format opened in 1989. In 1990 and 1991 the company opened eight large new stores, closed ten small stores, and remodeled several other stores.

—Jordan Wankoff

GALERIES LAFAYETTE S.A.

40, boulevard Haussmann
75009 Paris
France
(1) 42 82 34 56
Fax: (1) 48 78 25 19

Public Company
Incorporated: 1905 as Société anonyme des Galeries Lafayette
Employees: 18,000
Sales: FFr16.5 billion (US$3.19 billion)
Stock Exchange: Paris

Galeries Lafayette S.A. is a holding company for 55 subsidiary companies, which include department stores, variety stores, and hypermarkets. In the early 1990s the company controlled 80 department stores, 175 variety stores and 90 specialty chain stores.

The company began in 1895, when Albert Kahn rented a shop in Paris at the corner of Chaussée-d'Antin and rue Lafayette to sell gloves, ribbons, veils, and other goods. The shop was small, but sales were good. It was eventually enlarged, and in 1898 Kahn was joined by his cousin, 34-year-old Théophile Bader. The partnership flourished and soon purchased the entire building along with adjacent buildings on the Chaussée-d'Antin. In 1905 a limited company was created, Société anonyme des Galeries Lafayette, with Bader as president. Kahn retired from active management and in 1912 sold his shares to Bader.

The company bought buildings on the other side of the Chaussée-d'Antin, on the corner of the boulevard Haussmann, and in 1906 it built a store bearing the name Aux Galeries Lafayette. By then, some 350 persons were employed in the various buildings. The company purchased more property along the boulevard Haussmann near rue Mogador, and Bader planned a completely new department store, which opened in 1912. The five-story building occupied around 3,000 square meters. The store had a giant glass dome, a sweeping monumental staircase rising up in the light well, and wrought-iron curved balconies overlooking the light well. By 1914 Galeries Lafayette employed over 1,000 people, and mail-order operations, begun in 1905, represented about a quarter of the sales. In the Paris market, Galeries Lafayette was of equal importance to its near neighbor and competitor, the Printemps department store, which was some 30 years older. Both stores, however, lagged behind the Bon Marché and La Samaritaine stores.

In 1919 Bader brought Raoul Meyer, his 27-year-old son-in-law, into the management of the company. This was followed in 1926 by the appointment of Max Heilbronn, another son-in-law, aged 23. The three managed the group until 1935 when Bader became seriously ill, after which Meyer and Heilbronn directed the firm for another 35 years. During the 1920s the main store expanded gradually toward rue Mogador and rue de Provençe. Expansion also took place outside Paris: in 1916 a store had been opened in Nice, followed by the purchase in 1919 of Les Grands Magasins des Cordeliers in Lyons. A store opened in Nantes in 1923 and another in Montpellier in 1926, and at the same time the mail-order operations were consolidated, with a network of agents throughout France. By 1930 Galeries Lafayette had become the second-largest department store group in France, overtaken only by La Samaritaine, but ahead of Printemps. Bon Marché, Paris's oldest department store, was now in fourth position.

An important development in Galeries Lafayette's commercial policy took place in 1931 and 1932, when variety-store operations started. At the end of 1931 a subsidiary company, La Nouvelle Maison, was formed, and two variety stores called Lanoma were opened in Paris, followed in 1932 by two others, called Monoprix and located in the provinces. The name Lanoma was quickly abandoned, and all stores became Monoprix, with the subsidiary company changing its name to Société anonyme des Monoprix. To buy merchandise for the new variety stores, Société Centrale d'Achats (SCA) was formed in 1932.

The early years of the Monoprix variety stores were difficult, and they operated at a loss. Max Heilbronn traveled fortnightly to London to get inspiration from two well-established variety store groups, Woolworth and Marks & Spencer; he eventually received advice from Simon Marks himself. By 1935 the situation improved, and Monoprix continued to expand up to 1938, when a French law banning the opening of new one-price stores slowed down the development of owned stores; other retailers, though, were encouraged to join the SCA central buying organization. In 1938 there were 38 Monoprix stores—12 were owned stores and the rest were affiliates.

World War II was a troubled period for the Galeries Lafayette, and, being under Jewish management, it suffered severely during German occupation of France. The leadership was disbanded, and the business landed in the hands of French *collaborateurs*—those who collaborated with the Germans. Raoul Meyer went into hiding in unoccupied territory. Max Heilbronn, after serving in the French army, took part in the *Résistance* and was caught in 1943 and sent to Buchenwald concentration camp. Bader, the company's founder, died in 1942.

At the end of the war Meyer and Heilbronn, who together owned 80% of Galeries Lafayette, began to rebuild the company. In 1947 they were joined by Etienne Moulin, aged 35, who had helped to save Max Heilbronn's life in Buchenwald and had subsequently married his daughter.

Their main efforts in the postwar years were directed toward the expansion of the Monoprix variety stores. By 1950 there were 60 Monoprix stores in France, half of which were owned and half of which were affiliates. Ten years later there were

200 Monoprix stores and by 1965, there were 235—85 owned and 150 affiliated—with 200,000 square meters of selling space. Of the affiliated stores, 44 were linked directly or indirectly with the department store group Nouvelles Galeries Réunies. These affiliated stores had joined the SCA in 1952, when Galeries Lafayette, through Monoprix, acquired a 14% share in the company.

For Monoprix and Galeries Lafayette, the early 1960s were marked by what can be called the Inno-France interlude. In 1960 Innovation S.A., a Belgian department store group, created in France a company called the Société des Grandes Entreprises de Distribution, Inno-France. The aim of this company was to establish large self-service units in France, selling food and other merchandise. These were similar to hypermarkets, but were situated in downtown locations without parking facilities rather than in outlying areas. Before the first Inno-France store opened, Galeries Lafayette reacted vigorously, buying shares in the La Bourse department store group in Belgium, a competitor of Innovation.

The first Inno-France store opened in Paris in 1962, followed by five more by 1964. All the Inno-France stores made losses, and in 1964 Galeries Lafayette made an agreement with Innovation to buy a stake—first 25%, then 33%—in Inno-France and to manage non-food buying for the group. The following year all six Inno-France stores, with 2,200 employees, came under the direct management of the Monoprix organization and within four years became profitable. In 1971 Galeries Lafayette acquired the outstanding shares of Inno-France for a symbolic one franc. The company became part of the Monoprix organization, and the investment made by Galeries Lafayette in La Bourse of Belgium was written off.

Two other developments marked the Galeries Lafayette group in the 1960s: one a failure, the other a success. The former were related to the mail-order operations, which had continued somewhat sleepily since Bader had started them in 1905. Mailorder was beginning to be a growing business in France, and Galeries Lafayette decided to revitalize and modernize its operations. In 1966 an entirely new, mechanized and computerized distribution center, with more than 300 employees, was opened at Châlons-sur-Marne near Paris. It was not a success, due to troubles with the new systems and an inadequate network of agents throughout France, composed mainly of local drapers. The main competitors, Les Trois Suisses and La Redoute, were highly professional, specialized mailorder organizations. It was decided therefore to cut the losses, and in 1970 Galeries Lafayette's mail-order operations were closed.

The success of the 1960s was a major increase in the size of the flagship store on the boulevard Haussmann, no mean feat in the crowded center of Paris. Two additional floors were constructed on top of the original 1912 building. In 1961 an important extension to the store was made on the rue Mogador and boulevard Haussmann, and in 1969 a new store, Galeries Lafayette 2, was opened on the other side of the rue Mogador, linked by a bridge to the older store. A new Monoprix store was also opened in the new complex and, important in a period of growing automobile use, an underground car park was added. At the end of 1969 a do-it-yourself (DIY) store of some 1,000 square meters was opened on the corner of rue Lafayette and Chaussée d'Antin, where Kahn and Bader had opened their little shop nearly 75 years earlier. The DIY merchandise did not, however, sell as well as the ribbons and veils of the original store. In some ten years, the size of the flagship store had been increased by one-third to more than 44,000 square meters, making it one of the five largest department stores in Europe.

In 1971 a change in management took place. Raoul Meyer had died in 1970, and in 1971 Max Heilbronn became honorary president, while Etienne Moulin became president and Georges Meyer was named vice president. Georges Meyer had married the daughter of Raoul Meyer and had joined the management staff in 1965 at the age of 35. The business was still controlled by the family.

With the completion of the extension to the flagship store, the next phase of expansion was the opening of department stores in regional shopping centers. Stores were opened in the Belle-Epine center near Paris in 1971; the Maine-Montparnasse center in Paris in 1973; the Part-Dieu center in Lyons in 1975; and the Polygone center in Montpellier in 1975. The stores in shopping centers were not all an immediate success, but after many changes and improvements, they finally became profitable. After 1975, however, Galeries Lafayette stopped opening stores in shopping centers, and the Belle-Epine store closed in 1985.

The oil crisis of the early 1970s, heavy capital expenditures on enlarging the main store, expansion into shopping centers, and losses on the mail-order operations led to difficult years for the company. No dividends were paid between 1974 and 1979, but by 1980 most of the investments were beginning to show good returns.

The other main subsidiary of the Galeries Lafayette group, the Monoprix variety stores, continued to be profitable, but expansion in terms of number of stores was limited. New forms of retailing—for example 200 new hypermarkets—were opened in France between 1970 and 1980, and changes in the shopping habits of customers had altered variety stores' growth prospects. On the other hand, by doubling the average size of Monoprix stores and achieving very strong food sales in the supermarkets—food accounted for more than 50% of sales—the Monoprix management made the stores attractive in their given, local, markets. At the same time, cautious moves were made into the hypermarket sector by opening a small chain of Super M stores.

In the 1980s, many observers were beginning to question the viability of the department store and the variety store as modern forms of retailing. Department stores had first emerged more than a century earlier in France, and large department stores were seen by some as a rather inefficient relic of the past. Executives of the Galeries Lafayette were, however, convinced of the future of such stores. They argued that a store big enough to carry under one roof a very large assortment of attractive merchandise, including textiles and clothing, leisure goods, and decoration for the home, was appealing to customers. Furthermore, rapidly emerging techniques in stock control, logistics, and credit would resolve many of the past inefficiencies.

Galeries Lafayette's belief in the future of department stores was reflected in the 1980s by heavy investments in remodeling and the enhanced presentation of merchandise in all stores. These investments were accompanied by expenditure on computers, point-of-sale terminals, and customer credit promotion.

This policy of developing department stores received a boost when in 1985 Galeries Lafayette took over stores of the

Paris-France group. Paris-France had been founded in 1898 and had slowly built up a chain of department stores in the French provinces. Most of the stores were called Dames de France. Paris-France was a family business, the stores were somewhat old-fashioned, and the group ran into financial difficulties when faced with competition from specialty boutiques and hypermarkets. The Galeries Lafayette took over 12 well-located Paris-France stores with more than 2,000 employees, and thus more than doubled the number of its stores in the French provinces. Nineteen of Paris-France's Parunis variety stores were acquired at the same time and were integrated into the Monoprix variety store organization.

Also in 1985 a change was made in the top management. Etienne Moulin stepped down as president of the company, while Georges Meyer rose to the helm. This change did not affect the founding family's 61.9% holding in the company.

Further investments were made in the Paris-France stores to bring them up to Galeries Lafayette's standards. In 1989 a 50.1% majority shareholding was taken in Télemarket, the small but successful home-shopping operation in the greater Paris area, which is supported by Monoprix expertise. In the future, this could well be a popular means of shopping for food and household goods. A lease was signed to open a Galeries Lafayette store in New York late in 1991. Galeries Lafayette also was involved in a major reconstruction project in former East Berlin and was considering opening a store in that city in 1993.

A landmark in the development of Galeries Lafayette, and evidence of the management's belief in department stores, was the decision in the early part of 1991 to bid for majority control of the department store group Société Française des Nouvelles Galeries Réunies (Nouvelles Galeries). Since 1952 Galeries Lafayette had held shares in the Nouvelles Galeries through its subsidiary Monoprix, at first 14%, gradually rising to 22%. Early in 1991 a Swedish investment group, Proventus, which had built up a shareholding of 25.6% in Nouvelles Galeries, decided to sell its holding. Galeries Lafayette bought some of the shares, increasing its stake to 39.2%, but at the same time stressing that it did not wish to change control or management of Nouvelles Galeries. The French stock exchange commission, however, ruled that once the Galeries Lafayette had a share of more than one-third of Nouvelles Galeries, it must bid for control. Galeries Lafayette could have sold part of its stake and withdrawn, but it went ahead and gained 72.5% of Nouvelles Galeries.

The well-managed and profitable Nouvelles Galeries group owns the largest chain of provincial department stores in France, with 56 stores, two diversified chains, 31 Home and Garden Centers, and 43 Vetland discount clothing stores. It also controls Cofinoga, one of the most important private consumer-credit organizations in France. Nouvelles Galeries also has an 85% majority shareholding in the Uniprix variety store chain and a 50.04% majority holding in the Bazar de l'Hotel de Ville department store group. Nouvelles Galeries and its subsidiaries have nearly 18,500 employees.

Once the integration of the Nouvelles Galeries group has been achieved, the new group will be soundly based and profitable. Longer-term prospects are linked directly with the future of the department store and variety store method of retailing.

Principal Subsidiaries: Société Anonyme des Monoprix (54.96%); Société Française des Nouvelles Galeries Réunies (72.47%).

Further Reading: du Closel, Jacques, *Les Grands Magasins Français. Cent Ans Aprés,* Paris, Clotard et Associés, 1989; Heilbronn, Max, *Galeries Lafayette, Buchenwald, Galeries Lafayette,* Paris, Éditions Economica, 1989.

—James B. Jefferys

THE GAP, INC.

One Harrison
San Francisco, California 94105
U.S.A.
(415) 952-4400
Fax: (415) 512-1830

Public Company
Incorporated: 1969 as The Gap Stores, Inc.
Employees: 26,000
Sales: $1.93 billion
Stock Exchanges: New York   Pacific

The Gap, Inc. has remained one of the top retailers in the United States since 1969 by tailoring its clothes to the evolving tastes of the baby-boom generation. As the members of that demographic group have shifted from the wearing of jeans as an expression of rebellion to the more general preference for informality in all modes of dress, The Gap has expanded beyond its original Levi's-only format to the creation of a complete line of casual wear suitable for all ages. This successful corporate transformation was due largely to the ingenuity of Millard Mickey Drexler, president since 1983. The company was founded and remains under the overall control of Donald G. Fisher and his wife Doris F. Fisher.

Donald Fisher is not of the generation to whom The Gap owes its popularity. A member of a family that has made its home in California for generations, Fisher was 40 years old and a successful real estate developer in 1969 when he took note of a new trend among the city's increasingly disaffected youth. Blue jeans, for years made chiefly by Levi Strauss & Co. for laborers and outdoorsmen, were suddenly becoming a part of the counterculture's standard costume. Durable, cheap, comfortable, and acceptably offbeat, jeans were the perfect uniform for a generation of young people anxious to demonstrate its antipathy to corporate America.

Donald Fisher is said to have conceived of The Gap when he was unable to find the right size of Levi's in a department store in Sacramento, California. He realized that jeans had become more popular than the current merchandising outlets could accommodate, and that like hamburgers, stereo equipment, and gasoline, they were ready to be sold through a chain of small stores devoted solely to that product. With the help of his wife, Doris, Fisher opened a shop near San Francisco State University in one of his own buildings, offering a combination of records and jeans. Their intention was to attract jeans cus-

tomers by means of the records, but at first no one noticed the jeans, and Fisher was driven close to bankruptcy. In desperation, he placed ads in local newspapers announcing the sale of "four tons" of jeans at rock-bottom prices, and the clothes were soon gone. To emphasize the youthful ambiance of his new store, Fisher named it The Gap, an allusion to a currently hot topic, the "generation gap."

He incorporated his business as The Gap Stores, Inc., an immediate success. Although the Fishers had no experience in retailing, their stores' combination of jeans low prices, and wide selection proved irresistible to the huge market of 14- to 25-year-olds. Fisher added new outlets in San Francisco and was soon enjoying the benefits of chain store merchandising: centralized buying and advertising, excellent name recognition, and uniform pricing. Initially, The Gap Stores's buying program was singularly uncomplicated, as the stores carried only one product, jeans by Levi Strauss & Co. The stores were brightly painted, often orange; filled with circular metal display racks known as rounders; and usually enlivened by rock and roll music. To keep rents low, the Fishers kept stores small—about 3,000 to 4,000 square feet. They located most of their stores in shopping centers, many of them enclosed in malls.

Two years after opening its first stores, The Gap Stores's sales were running at $2.5 million annually, and the Fishers converted the company into a public corporation, although retaining the great majority of stock. With extraordinary celerity, they opened stores across the United States while maintaining tight control over the critical accounting, purchasing, and marketing functions of what was soon a sizable corporation. In five years, sales had increased almost 50-fold, to $97 million, and the number of stores had grown to 186, spread over 21 states. Analysts credited the company's success to the Fishers's observance of a few cardinal rules of retailing: The Gap Stores replaced its stock with maximum speed; its prices were low and stayed that way; big sellers were kept on the rack until they stopped moving, rather than being retired in favor of new styles simply for the sake of novelty; and few items were stocked—jeans, a few shirts, light jackets—each offered in its complete range of colors and sizes, ensuring a minimum of disappointed customers. The company's growth was also made possible by the extensive national advertising of Levi Strauss, which provided 100% of the The Gap Stores's merchandise during its early years. Such dependence on a single supplier has obvious dangers, however, and around 1973 The Gap Stores began marketing several labels of its own, as well as national brands other than Levi's. These proved crucial to the company's permanent health.

By 1976 the Fishers were ready to make The Gap Stores's first substantial public stock offering. The company's spectacular growth had attracted widespread interest, and its offering of 1.2 million shares sold quickly at $18 per share in May of 1976. Coincidentally, however, the retail industry went into a steep slide, which, when combined with The Gap Stores's large expenditures for new stores, pushed the company into the red for the final quarter of its fiscal year, ending July 31. The value of the newly issued stock fell to $7.25, prompting nine separate class-action suits from outraged stock purchasers who alleged that the Fishers had tried to dump their holdings before The Gap Stores announced its bad news. These charges came despite the fact that the Fishers sold only about 10% of their holdings during the period in question. Rather than wage endless litigation, The Gap Stores settled the suits in 1979 for a total of $5.8 million, or 40¢ per share and did its best to mend its frayed relations with Wall Street.

By that time the company could pay such a figure without undue strain. Adding between 50 and 80 stores annually, The Gap Stores pushed its sales to $307 million in 1980 and was close to achieving nationwide representation. The jeans market was no longer quite so straightforward, however. Members of the great wave of youngsters who had come of age wearing blue jeans in the 1970s, were now older, wealthier, and more conservative, and the Fishers were busily attempting to break out of the jeans niche by expanding The Gap's selection of clothing. Several experimental chains featuring upscale fashions were essayed, brought together under the Taggs name, but were eventually liquidated because they were unprofitable. Gap stores were enlarged to handle increasing amounts of what became known as casual wear and were frequently moved outside of shopping centers to free standing locations, where space was plentiful and rent lower per square foot.

Along with the search for a line of clothes that would appeal to an older clientele, the Fishers also faced Levi Strauss & Co.'s decision to supply big mass-marketers such as Sears and J.C. Penney with its jeans. Levi's were now sold everywhere, underscoring The Gap Stores's need to develop a label and look of its own. The company's own brands, created during the 1970s, generated about 45% of Gap sales in 1980, with Levi's adding an equal amount and other national brands making up the balance. Considering that ten years earlier essentially all of the Gap's sales were Levi Strauss & Co. products, the 1980 figures represented an achievement, but it was clear that if the company were to avoid inundation by the rising tide of jeans discounters it would have to fashion a new, exclusively Gap image.

To accomplish this task, Donald Fisher hired Mickey Drexler as president in 1983. Drexler, then 40, had just solved a similar problem with AnnTaylor, creating for that chain a new, more chic image and quadrupling sales in the bargain. Drexler was born in the Bronx to a family with roots in the garment business and by age 23 was a buyer for Bloomingdale's. After a stint at Macy's, he became president of AnnTaylor in 1980, where his work caught the eye of Donald Fisher, who was contemplating the future of The Gap. Drexler accepted the job as president at the end of 1983 and was given a block of stock that has made him one of the country's wealthiest retail executives. He immediately began designing The Gap wholesale transformation, in spite of the company's currently excellent financial status. The new president found little that he liked; proliferating competition in jeans and The Gap's youthful marketing image had forced the company into a price-driven volume business. Its orange-painted stores were cluttered with rounders displaying merchandise of many labels that Drexler would later describe to *The New York Times* as "trendy but not tasteful. . . well, just plain ugly." Worst of all, most consumers perceived The Gap as strictly for teenagers, at a time when people who grew up in the 1960s were developing more upmarket tastes. It would be difficult to overcome The Gap's 15-year tradition as the place where kids went to pick up a pair of Levi's.

Drexler began by eliminating all private label brands but one: Gap. Levi Strauss products were kept but relegated to the background; henceforth, The Gap would be known not only as a store, but as a line of clothes as well. Drexler created a large in-house design staff to develop clothes that would be casual, simple, made of natural fibers, and more clearly differentiated by gender than were jeans. The look was informal but classic—still denim-based but including a variety of shirts, skirts, blouses, and sweaters in assorted colors and weaves. It was clothing for people who wanted to look and feel young without appearing slovenly or rebellious, a description that fit a vast number of U.S. consumers in the 1980s.

Gap stores were substantially revamped. Neutral grays and white replaced the garish orange, and the ubiquitous rounders gave way to shelves of neatly folded clothing under soft lighting. The company's advertising, as devised by Drexler's long-time colleague, Maggie Gross, shifted from radio and television to upscale magazines and newspapers and featured older models engaged in familiar, outdoor activities that were not necessarily connected with the youth culture. A few years later, Gross launched the "Individuals of Style" campaign, a series of black and white portraits of both famous and unknown subjects by a team of celebrated photographers. The ads stressed style, not The Gap, whose clothes did not even appear in all of the photos, and they were enormously successful in helping to change the public's perception of the company. The Gap came to mean good taste of an informal variety, and the brand name Gap soon acquired the cachet needed if the company were to compete with other retailers of casual wear such as Benetton and The Limited. In addition the word "stores" was dropped from the company's name.

Drexler's revolution at The Gap cost a good deal of money, and financial results for 1984 were poor, with profits down 43% to $12.2 million. By the middle of the following year, however, it was clear that he had pulled off something of a miracle. Gross revenue, profits, and same-store sales were all up; more importantly, the company had fresh energy and a merchandising focus that could carry it for years to come. In the meantime, The Gap had acquired a number of other retail chains, for better and worse. Foremost among these was Banana Republic, founded in 1979 by another California husband and wife team, Melvyn and Patricia Ziegler. The chain of safari and travel clothing stores was bought by The Gap in 1983 and its sales were doubled each year through the mid-1980s, slowing quickly thereafter. At its peak in the late 1980s, Banana Republic achieved highly profitable revenue of more than $250 million a year and figured largely in The Gap's long-range planning. However, the bubble eventually burst for safari gear, and Banana Republic soon became a money-losing liability. In 1988 Mickey Drexler took over direct control of the division, shifting it from jungle attire toward gentler species of outdoor wear. In the early 1990s, Banana Republic was continuing to tread water.

Two other chain store acquisitions were not as profitable for The Gap. Pottery Barn was a housewares chain of about 30 stores in New York and California that had problems for several years before it was liquidated in 1986. The Gap also tested the higher end of the clothing market with Hemisphere, a nine-store chain of upscale U.S. sportswear with European styling. Created in 1987, Hemisphere offered elegant fashions, but soon ran afoul of a severe recession; the chain was disposed of only two years later. Neither mistake was serious enough to cause more than a few tremors at the parent company, which had a spectacular rebirth in the Drexler era that left ample room for such experimentation.

Revenue, net income, and return on equity have all been outstanding since Drexler's program took effect in 1985. The Gap's transition from a discount jeans warehouse to a sleek fashion arbiter was not altogether painless, yet the result had been more successful than Donald Fisher and his wife could have imagined. In 1991 the Fisher family still held more than 40% of the company, which operated more than 1100 stores in the United States, Canada, and the United Kingdom and had plans to expand total sales area by 15% annually. Not only had The Gap followed its baby-boom clientele as they grew older and wealthier, it provided for their children, too. GapKids in the early 1990s was the fastest growing segment of The Gap as a whole, offering a modified selection of Gap clothing in children's sizes. One-third of the more than 170 GapKids stores included a babyGap department for toddlers. Banana Republic remained something of a blemish on the otherwise perfect Gap picture, but it was at least able to pay its bills.

Further Reading: Abend, Jules, "Widening the Gap," *Stores,* November 1985; Van Meter, Jonathan, "Fast fashion. Americans want clothing that is quick and easy. The Gap made a billion giving it to them," *Vogue,* May 1990; Barmash, Isidore, "Gap Finds Middle Road to Success," *The New York Times,* June 24, 1991.

—Jonathan Martin

GIB GROUP

111, rue Neuve
1000 Brussels
Belgium
(02) 729 21 11
Fax: (02) 729 20 96

Public Company
Incorporated: 1974 as s.a. GB-Inno-BM n.v.
Employees: 70,862
Sales: BFr278.32 billion (US$8.89 billion)
Stock Exchange: Brussels

The GIB Group, Belgium's top retailer, is active in four sectors: supermarkets and hypermarkets; do-it-yourself (DIY) home improvement and auto care stores; self-service and fast food restaurants; and specialty retailing. The group's parent company is s.a. GB-Inno-BM n.v. Total group sales increased from BFr178.19 billion in 1986 to BFr278.32 billion in 1990. If any single company is emblematic of the trend toward internationalization in Belgium's retail sector, it is the GIB Group.

The GIB Group's supermarkets and hypermarkets operate under such diverse names as GB, with 56 stores trading under the name "Maxi" and 88 as "Super"; Sarma Star, with 14 stores; Rob, with 3 stores; Unic, with 352 stores; and Nopri, with 203 stores. The supermarket and hypermarket sector is by far the most important division for the GIB Group, accounting for 64% of its total sales.

The DIY sector accounts for almost a quarter of the GIB Group's total sales and seems to offer major growth potential both in Belgium and abroad. Within Belgium, Brico, with its 95 outlets, is the undisputed leader in the country's DIY market. In addition, Auto 5 sells car accessories through its 48 outlets. The DIY division also has a large international presence. Three companies operate in the United States: Scotty's, with 163 stores in Florida; Handy Andy, with 50 stores in the Great Lakes region; and Central Hardware, operating 38 stores in the Midwest. DIY stores are operating in France (51 Obi stores), Portugal and Spain (7 Aki stores), and the United Kingdom (63 Homebase stores) as well.

The success of fast food restaurants is a phenomenon of our time, and the GIB Group continues to expand in this high-growth market. In Belgium and Luxembourg, 49 Quick restaurants account for 78% of the hamburger restaurant market, and their market share is still rising. In France, 132 Quick restaurants account for 25% of sales in the market. Excellent

opportunities for expansion exist in Belgium and France, in particular through franchise operations. Under a franchise agreement with Pepsico, the GIB Group also operates 18 pizza restaurants under the trade name Pizza Hut. In addition, the GIB Group operates two self-service restaurant chains, including 53 Resto GB restaurants and 20 Lunch Garden restaurants.

The specialty sector of the GIB Group includes department stores and some smaller retail chains. Inno, Belgium's only modern department store chain, operates 16 stores in major urban centers and shopping centers. The GIB Group also operates a specialty clothing chain, consisting of 6 Sarma Lux shops and 26 Sarma Shop boutiques. In addition there are 4 Fnac stores and 14 Fnac Services boutiques, specializing in books, hi-fi, and photographic equipment, and 16 Club shops, selling books, newspapers, and stationery. The GIB Group also operates a major travel agency, Transcontinental, with 38 agencies; a chain of toys and games specialist stores called Christiaensen, with 68 shops in Belgium and 19 shops in France; 21 Disport stores, 12 of which are in France; and 35 Pearle Vision Center shops, selling glasses and other optical goods.

S.A. GB-Inno-BM—from 1987, the name "GIB Group" has generally been used to refer to all the activities of S.A. GB-Inno-BM and its subsidiaries—is the result of several mergers that took place in the 1960s and 1970s. In 1969, Innovation and Bon Marché, operating major department stores in Belgium, merged to form Inno-BM. Two years later, Inno-BM also incorporated its subsidiary, Priba, which the two merged companies had jointly set up to operate variety stores. Finally, GB Enterprises merged with Inno-BM to form GB-Inno-BM on February 1, 1974.

In 1861 François Vaxelaire, a 21-year-old native of the Vosges region of France, became manager of a small textile store, Au Bon Marché, at the rue Neuve in Brussels. During the following 30 years, Vaxelaire and his wife, Jeanne Claes, succeeded in expanding the company through the opening of new stores in Belgium and France. In 1894 upon the death of their mother, Raymond and Georges Vaxelaire joined their father as partners in the family business. Under their dynamic leadership, the company was gradually transformed into a full-fledged department store operator. A new department store, Au Bon Marché, was opened at the boulevard du Jardin Botanique in Brussels.

The company, from 1927 named Les Grands Magasins Au Bon Marché: Etablissements Vaxelaire-Claes, continued to grow with the founding of the Société Congolaise des Grands Magasins Au Bon Marché (Coboma) in 1928 and the Société Anonyme Belge des Immeubles Commerciaux in 1928, in 1933 renamed Société Anonyme Belge des Magasins Prisunic-Uniprix. Whereas the purpose of the first company was to enter the market of the then Belgian Congo, the goal of the second company was essentially a move to compete with variety stores, a new retail formula introduced by Sarma in 1928.

World War II and its aftermath—especially the Loi de Cadenas, or Padlock Law, which forbade the opening of new large diversified stores—slowed down the growth of the company considerably. However, the withdrawal of the Padlock Law in 1959 and the advent of the 1960s resulted in a new wave of expansion with the opening of new department stores in Belgium's first shopping center.

In 1882 another Frenchman, Adolphe Kileman, opened his first store in Ghent, Belgium, under the name La Maison Universelle. He entrusted the running of this store to Mr. and Mrs. A. Martin. However, 1885, the year of his acquisition of the Grand Bazar du Bon Marché in Antwerp, is generally considered to be the founding date of the Grand Bazar d'Anvers, which would merge with Supermarchés GB in 1968 to become GB Enterprises. Kileman summoned Mr. and Mrs. Martin to Antwerp to run the newly acquired store, and in 1888 Mrs. Martin's sister and the latter's husband, Alfred Deslandes, were put in charge of the Ghent store.

World War I left the young company in a shambles. Upon his return from the French army in 1919, Auguste-Pierre Deslandes, nephew of Eugenie Martin—since 1890, a partner of Adolphe Kileman, and subsequently his heir—set up a new company, Les Grands Magasins d'Anvers Réunis S.A., with the aid of Emile Chaumont, an industrialist from Liège. The opening of new department stores in Antwerp in 1920 and in Ghent in 1921 were important events for the new company.

The Depression of the 1930s was almost fatal to Deslandes's company. Although the company had expanded its traditional range of merchandise through the introduction of novelties and had changed its name to the more stylish Galeries du Bon Marché, its financial situation deteriorated.

In 1932 Maurice Cauwe, previously employed by Innovation, was hired as administrative manager. After further difficult years and a reversion to the store's original and more popular name Grand Bazar du Bon Marché, the new management was able to accomplish a gradual improvement over the period 1935–1939. Despite World War II, the company was able to continue its expansion.

Cauwe was one of the first Belgian retailers to discover the United States and its modern distribution system. In 1956 he and Baron François Vaxelaire—son of Raymond Vaxelaire and later Cauwe's major negotiator in the merger of Inno-BM and GB Enterprises—attended a seminar held by the National Cash Register Company and led by Bernard Trujillo, in which they became acquainted with new retail formulas, such as shopping centers, supermarkets, and self-service discount department stores. Supermarkets and hypermarkets would become the keystones of GB Enterprises's fast growth during the 1960s.

The end of the Padlock Law in 1959 offered new opportunities for the company through the opening of a series of new department stores. Further growth was realized, however, with the introduction of supermarkets in 1958 and hypermarkets in 1961. Two separate companies were set up by the parent company: Supermarchés GB in 1960, and Super Bazars in 1961, in charge of the expansion process of a network of supermarkets and hypermarkets respectively.

The opening of supermarkets and hypermarkets was pursued at a fast rate over the next ten years, partially in anticipation of the second Padlock Law. Soon the hypermarkets were joined by specialty stores such as Auto Centers in 1966, Garden Centers in 1968, and Brico Centers from 1973 onward. Initiatives to pursue expansion abroad were generally unsuccessful at the time. In 1967 Grand Bazar d'Anvers merged with Supermarchés GB to become GB Enterprises. A year later, Super Bazars also merged with GB Enterprises.

In 1897 the third company, Bernheim-Meyer: A l'Innovation, established by Julien Bernheim and three brothers Meyer, all natives of the Alsace region, opened its first store in the rue Neuve in Brussels. The store proved highly successful, and additional stores were opened in Liège, Ghent, and Verviers.

After World War I the Tietz stores in Brussels, Bruges, and Antwerp, under sequester after the German defeat, were bought and gradually transformed into A l'Innovation department stores. Late in 1919 the company was renamed Les Grands Magasins à l'Innovation (Innovation).

In 1934 Priba, a subsidiary of Innovation, which had been set up in 1930 to develop a chain of variety stores, merged with Prisunic-Uniprix, a subsidiary of Au Bon Marché. For the first time a major link was established between two companies which would later participate in the GIB Group. During the 1930s the variety stores did extremely well: by 1938 Sarma had become the first and Uniprix-Priba the fourth largest retailers in Belgium.

From 1959 onward, Innovation also pursued renewed growth through the opening of new department stores in several Belgian towns as well as in the Westland shopping center in Brussels. The great fire of May 22, 1967 in its Brussels department store, in which 251 people died, still casts a major shadow upon the success of Innovation in the 1960s. Growth was also pursued abroad through companies such as Inno-France, but with very little success. The time did not seem right yet for Belgian retailers to pursue expansion abroad.

Initiatives for cooperation or outright merger had been taken by several Belgian retail companies in the late 1920s, for example, by Emile Bernheim, but the first serious attempt at cooperation between Bon Marché and Grand Bazar d'Anvers did not happen until the early 1960s. The negotiations between the two department stores Innovation and Bon Marché were more fruitful, however. The companies decided to merge in October 1969 to form S.A. Innovation—Bon Marché N.V. (Inno-BM).

New initiatives for cooperation were taken in the early 1970s between GB Enterprises under Maurice Cauwe, and Inno-BM under Emile Bernheim and François Vaxelaire. By the end of 1973 the two companies decided that the GM-Inno-BM merger would take place on February 1, 1974.

Maurice Cauwe became the first chairman of the board of directors of the new company, with Baron François Vaxelaire and Jacques Dopchie as managing directors. Upon Cauwe's retirement in 1977, Baron François Vaxelaire became chairman and Dopchie vice-chairman: both continued to act as managing directors.

The first two years after the merger were largely spent in streamlining the organization and its operations, and consolidating the selling and merchandising activities. Apart from the usual difficulties which follow any merger, the group was confronted with a series of problems arising from its economic and legal environment.

Firstly, the Business Premises Act, the so-called second Padlock Law, made it virtually impossible to open new large stores or to enlarge existing ones. Expansion through the opening of supermarkets and hypermarkets all but stopped. Secondly, Belgium's small territory, already covered by an intensive distribution network, necessitated that further growth be pursued abroad. A third problem was related to the internal competition with which the department store division was confronted. In several major towns two or even three department stores, originally operated by GB-Inno-BM's constituent companies, fought for market share.

In the following years, GB-Inno-BM pursued expansion primarily through diversification. Important changes in structure were introduced in order to make this strategy possible. At the same time the group sought to rationalize its systems and to achieve economies of scale by integrating operations and merging production and service activities.

The department store division constituted a particular problem for the group. A special effort was made to assure its profitability, resulting in a "modularization" in the merchandising of the division, a revolutionary technique in department stores. Other measures included closing or modernizing older stores as well as opening new department stores in the newly developed shopping centers. In this context Fnac, the well-known French leisure goods retailer, was offered an opportunity to enter the Belgian market via the renovated Bon Marché store in the middle of Brussels (the New BM). GB-Inno-BM also decided to use the trade name Inno for all the department stores of the groups, with some minor exceptions. In 1975 GB-Inno-BM had already decided to close or convert the Priba variety stores as soon as possible, owing to reduced profitability and the need to reduce competition between the group's stores.

The strategy of diversification into new products and markets was maintained during the 1970s. Managers who were surplus to requirements after the merger were encouraged to study the opportunities for small specialty shops in Belgium. Benefiting from the growing success of the franchise formula in European retailing, this resulted in such new companies as Santal (perfumery shops, 1975); Club (books, stationery, and toys, 1975) and Sportland (sporting goods and sportswear, 1976). In 1982 the group acquired Christiaensen, the toys and games specialist.

In 1978 in response to an economic situation characterized by stagnation, inflation, and reduced consumer buying power, and in a further move to become even more diversified, GB-Inno-BM successfully introduced its own brand of goods (*produits blancs*) to offer consumers a low-cost alternative to branded goods. A diversification strategy was also actively pursued in 1979, where partnerships were established with other retailers abroad. Two activities stand out in this international expansion: DIY retailing and fast food restaurants. New DIY ventures have included Homebase in Great Britain (with Sainsbury), Somabri in France (with Casino), and Superdoe (with Vendex International) in the Netherlands. In the United States the group took a share in Scotty's, a DIY retailer in Florida. In the fast food business the group established France Quick, a joint venture with Casino in France. GB-Inno-BM supplied the expertise and took a minority share in these new companies.

In the 1980s the GB-Inno-BM merger had reached a certain level of maturity. After a very active period of diversification, the group concentrated on improvements and standardization of image, design, and equipment in its hypermarkets and supermarkets, cost reductions, and better merchandising, ranges, and pricing.

In October 1982 GB-Inno-BM introduced its new hypermarket formula. The group's hypermarkets, whose image would be determined largely by a permanent offer of discounts on products, became Maxi stores.

In an attempt to improve the performance of the unsuccessful GB Home-Stocks, established in 1974, IKEA-Belgium was set up as a 50–50 joint venture with IKEA, a furniture specialist, in 1983. In 1989, however, the GIB Group withdrew from this sector.

After a thorough study of GB-Inno-BM by U.S. management consultants McKinsey, a restructuring plan was developed, focusing in particular on the decentralization of the group's commercial activities, and was gradually implemented during the next few years. The plan proved to be very effective in terms of sales, cash flow, and net profit.

In 1987 GB-Inno-BM took over the activities of Sarma-Nopri, a J.C. Penney subsidiary. After major reorganization and rationalization, a new company, Sarmag, began to operate 14 Sarma-Star hypermarkets, 6 department stores, and 26 Sarma Shop boutiques.

Since 1987, GB-Inno-BM or GIB Group also has been the largest franchiser in Belgium. In addition to Unic, the leading chain of independent supermarkets in Belgium, it operates the Nopri chain of supermarkets, Nopri being the trade name for the former Sarma affiliates.

The favorable results of 1990, confirming the positive developments of the previous years, were overshadowed by the unexpected death of François Vaxelaire, chairman of GIB Group since 1977. Baron Vaxelaire was an early advocate of closer cooperation among major Belgian retailers. As managing director of Inno-BM, he carried out the negotiations with Maurice Cauwe that finally led to the merger of Inno-BM and GB Enterprises. Vaxelaire, as chairman essentially responsible for the internal activities, left behind a highly diversified and successful company.

On March 19, 1991, Pierre Schohier, a banker and—as a major shareholder of GIB Group—a member of the board of directors for many years, became the new chairman of GIB Group. A new executive structure in which a clear distinction is made between the responsibilities of the board of directors and those of the executive board was implemented in June 1991.

As he reached the age limit for senior executives, Jacques Dopchie, who for years had been largely responsible for all operations and more recently for the external relations and the international activities of GIB Group, relinquished his position as managing director on this occasion: he remains, however, a vice-chairman of the board of directors. He has also been very active in several professional organizations, including the Fédération Belge des Entreprises de Distribution (FEDIS) of which he was chairman from 1987 to 1990, and the Institut de l'Entreprises, of which he was chairman from its beginning in 1980. Also in 1991 the board of directors appointed Count Diego du Monçeau de Bergendal, already managing director, as chairman of the executive board.

The GIB Group, ranked among the 40 largest European retailers, was in the early 1990s preparing to operate in the Unified European market, which was set to become a reality by the end of 1992. As the single European market approaches, retailers are reassessing their buying position on a continental scale. In 1988 the GIB Group joined Eurogroup, with Rewe of Germany and the Vendex Food Group of the Netherlands.

Principal Subsidiaries: Sarmag s.a. (Belgium, 45%); Lunch Garden s.a. (Belgium, 45%); Nopri s.a. (Belgium, 97%); Rob s.a. (Belgium, 93%); Motorest s.a. (Belgium); France Quick s.a. (France, 50%); Pizza Belgium s.a. (Belgium, 50%); Obi s.a. (France); Homebase Ltd. (Great Britain, 25%); Bricobi s.a. (Spain, 51%); Bricogal s.a. (Portugal, 55%); Scotty's Inc. (U.S.A.); A-OK of Delaware Inc. (U.S.A., 65%); Spirit Holding Cy Inc. (U.S.A., 29%); Club s.a. (Belgium); Sodal s.a. (Belgium, 60%); Christiaensen Int. s.a. (Belgium); Christiaensen s.a. (France); Disport Int. s.a. (Belgium, 96%); Disport s.a. (France, 95%); Vision Center s.a. (Belgium); Transcontinental s.a. (Belgium, 88%).

Further Reading: Beenkens, A., *Historique du Grand Bazar d'Anvers: 1965–1968,* Antwerp, Imprimeries Générales Anversoises, 1972; Knee, D., and D. Walters, *Strategy in Retailing: Theory and Application,* Oxford, Philip Allan Publishers Limited, 1985; De Coster, P., *GB-INNO-BM—Het nederige begin en de groei,* Brussels, [n.p.], 1989.

—Joseph V. Leunis

THE GREAT UNIVERSAL STORES P.L.C.

Universal House
251-256 Tottenham Court Road
London W1A 1BZ
United Kingdom
(071) 636-4080
Fax: (071) 631-3641

Public Company:
Incorporated: 1917 as Universal Stores (Manchester) Ltd.
Employees: 32,000
Sales: £2.69 billion (US$5.03 billion)
Stock Exchange: London

The Great Universal Stores P.L.C. (GUS) is the leading mail-order company in the United Kingdom with the mail-order brand Kays and a 40% share of a market worth £3.6 billion. It is one of the two largest operators in this field outside the United States, the other being Otto Versand of Germany. In addition to its mail-order core, the group derives around a third of its profits from property and finance. Property assets exceed £1 billion and yield substantial rentals. GUS is the largest nonbank provider of consumer and industrial finance in the United Kingdom, mainly through its Whiteaway Laidlaw and General Guarantee subsidiaries. Retail clothing, represented by Burberry's Ltd. and Scotch House Ltd., is an important part of the company, although much reduced in scale and more upmarket than in the past. There is a continuing small interest in manufacturing, especially clothing, bedding, and printing. Overseas interests, both mail-order and conventional retailing, contribute around one-fifth of total profits. GUS has low leverage, large cash reserves, and a strong balance sheet. Annual profits have risen every year since the mid-1930s, and have reached a total of over £400 million by 1990.

The company's history began in Manchester in 1900. Three brothers, George, Jack, and Abraham Rose, started a general dealing and merchanting business. By 1917, when Universal Stores was registered as a limited, or incorporated, company, it supplied a wide range of consumer goods. Increased success accompanied a move into mail order in the 1920s. The Roses, who had previously relied on newspaper advertising of single items, began to draw up catalogs instead. Early versions were small in format but bulky, containing about 100 pages, with one product illustrated on each page. Agents were recruited to promote sales via the catalog and were allowed discounts on

their own purchases. Customers paid by installment, usually over a period of up to 20 weeks. Sometimes the credit club method was employed, by which members paid a weekly sum and drew lots to determine the order in which they would receive their chosen goods. The catalog, the commissioned agent, and installment credit have remained the characteristic institutions of mail-order operations. Another form of direct selling by credit had been established earlier. This was the tallyman—or salesman collector—system, which was later used by some GUS subsidiaries. The salesman made regular home visits to collect installments and deliver goods.

Universal Stores grew rapidly toward the end of the 1920s. Profits averaged £244,000 over the three years 1929 to 1931, reaching a peak of £411,000 in 1931. The company added the word "Great" to its title in 1930, and successfully went public in 1931. A combination of falling demand—induced by the Great Depression—and poor stock control reduced profits by half in 1932 and resulted in a small loss in 1933. The Roses, who had benefited considerably from the public issue, felt obliged to pay nearly £100,000 out of their own pockets in order to maintain the dividend at its previously anticipated level. Several members resigned from the board in late 1932, and three new directors, including Sir Philip Nash as chairman, were appointed to represent the interests of the U.K. securities firm Cazenove's clients. The most significant change precipitated by this crisis was the appointment of a new joint managing director, Isaac Wolfson, along with George Rose, who resigned two years later. Under Wolfson's leadership, GUS was to make the lengthy transition from the unpromising circumstances of 1932 to its present financial strength.

Wolfson was born in Glasgow in the late 1890s, starting his career as a salesman for his father's modest furniture business. Moving to London in 1920, he traded on his own account, selling such items as clocks and mirrors and also building up an informal private banking practice. By 1932 Wolfson had become merchandise controller of GUS, having first met and impressed George Rose at a trade exhibition in Manchester. Wolfson specified that not all his time would be devoted to his employer, and his remuneration consisted at least in part of an option to buy GUS shares from the Roses. The option was exercised when the share price fell heavily in 1932, with the assistance of both his father-in-law, Ralph Specterman, and of his stockbroker friend, Sir Archibald Mitchelson, who later succeeded Nash as chairman of the company.

GUS soon recovered. Despite heavy unemployment, the majority of working-class consumers enjoyed rising real incomes, and the company had prospects of increased sales once the internal problems were under control. By 1934 the new 150-page catalog claimed to be the largest of any mail-order house in Europe. A few years later GUS took over the similar business of its Manchester neighbor Samuel Driver. However, acquisitions were not confined to mail order. A Wembley-based furniture concern, with large factory and warehouse capacity, had already been added to the company. Midland and Hackney, a recent amalgamation of two of the oldest established installment-purchase furniture businesses in the country, joined GUS in 1934. A feature of this firm that made it an attractive proposition was its substantial debts in installment purchases. Collection of outstanding debt and mortgaging of properties—wholly owned properties were mortgaged, then rented back—could unlock valuable cash resources. In 1938 Alexander Sloan of Glasgow, with 20 shops and a tallyman—an installment selling business—and two other similar Scottish concerns, were brought into the group. These 1930s acquisitions were on a cash basis and were financed by a combination of retained profit and debenture issues. Altogether, more than £2 million was raised in this way in 1936 and 1938. Expansion into the retail trade in the prewar years was not very successful in the short run, however. Profits fell in 1935, and thereafter grew more slowly than assets until after the outbreak of World War II.

GUS's profits were maintained during the war. By the late 1940s it had emerged as the owner of a large chain of furniture shops, while the mail-order base had been strengthened further by the purchase of Kays of Worcester in 1943. Jays and Campbells, with nearly 200 furniture outlets, was bought in 1943 for £1.2 million, after the previous owners had run into trouble with wartime price control legislation. In 1945 the British and Colonial Furniture Company sold a controlling interest to GUS for around £1 million. This included some 75 Cavendish and Woodhouse stores in the United Kingdom and a larger number in Canada. Another important furniture business, Smarts, was taken over in 1949, again for about £1 million. Jackson's followed soon after. By fiscal 1953–1954 furniture sales, mainly by installment buying, accounted for about a third of the company's expanded profits of some £15 million.

The major acquisitions of the 1940s owed much to three major factors. One was that wartime trading restrictions, regulating allocation and use of raw materials, plus controls on capital and on profit margins in distribution, were a less severe constraint for GUS—which was accustomed to working on lower margins—than for retail concerns with weaker and more traditional management. Another was that Wolfson was sufficiently confident and farsighted to anticipate a postwar housing boom and a strong demand for furniture on credit. A final consideration was that after the war many retailers continued to hold properties at prewar valuations. Current values understated the potential for a buyer aware of the possibilities of property sales, or mortgage-and-lease-back deals with insurance companies. Property revaluation strengthened the balance sheet of the buyer and lifted the price of its shares.

In the postwar years GUS and Wolfson, who had become chairman in 1945 on the death of Mitchelson, quickly gained a higher public profile. Wolfson's growing reputation rested on the rapid growth of the firm and especially on his success as a practitioner of the takeover bid. Some of the techniques employed in the acquisitions of the 1950s were already familiar—notably the targeting of companies with undervalued properties, and the sale, with or without lease-back, of selected properties. A major new element was the use of the buyer's own shares, in particular of the nonvoting variety. GUS created more than five million five-shilling "A" ordinary shares in the form of a stock split in 1952. Eventually the "A" shares vastly outnumbered the ordinary, allowing the Wolfson family, and from 1955 the trustees of the Wolfson Foundation, to maintain control with a minority of the total stock. For the larger takeovers of the 1950s GUS offered a combination of cash and "A" shares. Bids on this basis were frequently acceptable, and recipients, like the directors of the women's clothing group Morrison's in 1957, announced their willingness to hold GUS "A" shares as a long-term investment. Similar offers succeeded in some cases where the bid was resisted or contested, as in 1954 with Jones and Higgins, the drapers and house furnishers. Probably the most publicized disputed takeover was for control of Hope Brothers in late 1957, for which Debenhams was also competing. As GUS grew and flourished, the "A" shares were a highly marketable security. As the *Economist* observed, on July 26, 1958, their holders were generally "content with bigger dividends, scrip issues and high market values."

Acquisitions promoted the company's growth in the 1950s, and at times did so at a hectic pace. During fiscal 1953–1954, 350 retail outlets were added to the existing 870. In the fiscal year 1957–1958, the contribution of new subsidiaries exceeded the total increase in profits. Takeovers preserved the record of unbroken profit growth. Expansion of this kind resulted in diversification of trading interests. By the early 1960s the established base in mail order and furniture had been broadened not only by large investments in drapery and men's and women's clothing, but also by stakes in footwear, hotels, electrical goods, builder's merchants, food retailing, and a travel agency. Two of the less predictable of these purchases were perhaps most significant for the future of GUS. The arrival in the group of Burberry's in 1956 signaled a move into more specialized and upmarket areas of the clothing trade, and the absorption in 1957 of Whiteaway Laidlaw, an export drapery and finance company, pointed in some new directions. By the beginning of the 1960s the board had indicated its awareness of reduced opportunities for growth by takeover, and of the need for expansion within the existing structure.

Since the 1960s the company has experienced major acquisitions, more disposals, and increasing concentration on a reduced number of principal sectors. However, the high degree of diversification was a factor in spreading risk and in enabling the group to avoid any setback to the growth of profits. The chairman complained in 1974 of 18 changes in hire-purchase—or installment buying—regulations over the previous 19 years. A further contribution toward smoothing the retail cycle came from GUS's own accounting practice, by which revenue from hire-purchase sales was not credited to profit until after the final installment was paid. Thus, when such sales were rising, debt provision rose faster than profit, but when they were falling, profits were boosted by sales made before the downturn. An additional factor in the stability of GUS's profit growth was the rising share from overseas, which reduced dependence on the performance of the U.K. economy. Until the early 1960s there were only modest earnings abroad, mainly from stores in the U.K. Commonwealth markets of Canada and South Africa. Then entry into both the United States and continental Europe helped to lift the overseas contribution of total profits to around 10% by the end of the 1960s and to 12.5% ten years later.

Much of GUS's postwar growth had been in the sector in which it achieved early market leadership—mail order. Even here, some expansion has been bought by absorbing smaller competitors, although the last occasion was the acquisition of John Myers in 1981. A proposed deal with Empire Stores was blocked on antimonopoly grounds in 1982. By then GUS held a position of strength in a market that had expanded since the war to a point where mail order represented perhaps 8% of nonfood retail sales in the late 1970s. Before the war, mail order had been popular mainly in northern England and Scotland, in rural areas, and among low-income groups. Since the early 1950s it has expanded both geographically and socially. The fastest phase of growth occurred in the late 1950s and 1960s before alternative sources of credit became more readily available in shops. The worst setback to the mail-order market was felt in the early 1980s, when recession and unemployment had a negative impact on installment buying. Some of GUS's techniques were unchanged—for example, the reliance on commissioned agents. The major catalogs were transformed into color-printed, 1,000-page, 26,000-item publications. Computerized stock control was introduced, along with automated storage buildings. The stock itself was to a large extent designed and manufactured to the company's own specifications. Deliveries were handled increasingly by GUS's own national distribution network, which included the White Arrow fleet.

Apart from its home-shopping division, GUS was also expanding vigorously in the 1970s and 1980s in property and finance and was disposing of its less successful retail interests. Two important milestones were passed in 1977, when turnover first reached £1 billion and profits £100 million. A new orientation towards property became apparent in the growing tendency to retain the owned property and longer leaseholds when a subsidiary was sold, as in the cases of the Paige clothing shops and Times Furnishing in 1986. By then, the company had long since discarded the image it had sported during earlier phases of growth. Its shares had once been regarded as volatile and speculative, and concern was sometimes expressed about the size of borrowings. More recently, criticism

had come from a different angle. The group made appearances on lists of British firms with "cash mountains." Some well-known GUS characteristics did not change at all—the relatively conservative accounting policies and the ungenerous rationing of public information about its activities. Shareholders had to wait a long time for full lists of subsidiaries and even longer for breakdowns of turnover or profit by sector.

Sir Isaac Wolfson, made a baronet in 1962 for his charitable activities, stepped down as cochairman in 1986 in favor of his son Leonard, Lord Wolfson of Marylebone, who had become joint managing director in 1963 and later co-chairman. There has been some speculation as to the identity of his eventual successor and as to whether family control will itself survive the impact of the European Economic Community on company law.

Principal Subsidiaries: GUS Catalogue Order Ltd,; Kay & Co., Ltd.; Wehkamp B.V. (Netherlands); Halens Postorder A.B. (Sweden); Burberry's Ltd.; The Scotch House Ltd.; Whiteway Laidlaw Bank Ltd.; C.C.N. Systems Ltd.; General Guarantee Corporation Ltd.; G.U.S. Property Management Ltd.

Further Reading: Bull, George, and Anthony Vice, *Bid for Power,* London, Elek Books, 1958; Aris, Stephen, *The Jews in Business,* London, Jonathan Cape, 1970.

—Gerald W. Crompton

HANKYU DEPARTMENT STORES, INC.

8-7 Kakuda-cho
Kita-ku
Osaka 530
Japan
(06) 361 1381
Fax: (06) 367 8145

Public Company
Incorporated: 1947
Employees: 5,185
Sales: ¥384.77 billion (US$3.08 billion)
Stock Exchange: Tokyo

Hankyu Department Stores, Inc. is one of Japan's ten largest department store organizations and one of the three main companies of the Hankyu and Toho Group, whose nucleus is the Hankyu Corporation, a traffic and transportation company. Its primary bases of operation are found in the Kansai region and the Tokyo metropolitan area, where, together, the company has eight department stores and a smaller boutique.

Although the first Hankyu Department Store did not open until 1929, the history of the company dates back to 1907 when the Japanese entrepreneur Ichizo Kobayashi helped found the Mino-Arima Electric Railway Company, the forerunner to the Hankyu Corporation. To promote the use of the railway, Kobayashi developed a number of leisure facilities at sites along the track. The foremost of these was the Takarazuka Resort, famous for its Girl's Revue, an all-women theater group, whose international reputation gained the group much valuable publicity. In 1918 Kobayashi attempted to expand the Mino-Arima railway company to run trains from Mino-Arima to Kobe. Unable to acquire permission to do so, he had to settle for a line from Osaka to Kobe. It was at this time that the company changed its name to Hankyu Corporation. The name Hankyu derived from a combination of the Chinese characters for Osaka, which can be read as "Han," and the word "Kyu" which means express.

To promote the use of the railway further, Kobayashi opened the first Hankyu department store at Umeda railway station in the city of Osaka in 1929. It became the first railway terminal department store, designed to serve several hundred thousand daily commuters, and as such heralded a new wave of Japanese retailers. This wave was characterized by the opening of department stores by railroad companies on prime sites along the railway lines, in particular at important terminals and main interchange stations, and using capital from their parent companies. The railway lines often originated within the stores themselves.

Hankyu Department Stores opened its second store in 1936 in Kobe, but growth soon came to a virtual standstill because of World War II. During the war, the company was enlisted to help the cause of the Japanese army. It donated money, and the escalators and lifts of the stores were stripped to provide the army with much-needed metal. During World War II the department stores also became focal points for control and distribution of all consumer goods by the government. The store in Osaka was damaged by an Allied bombing raid.

After the war the American forces who were now occupying Japan also used Hankyu and other department stores as distribution points for food and clothing, which were in short supply. In 1947 the Hankyu Corporation was reorganized into two smaller companies on the instructions of the U.S. occupying forces who were looking to reduce the power of Japan's big conglomerates in the wake of the war. The transport group became Hankyu Corporation and the retail business became Hankyu Department Stores, Inc. This breakup was seen to be in Hankyu Department Stores' favor, as the transport side of the company was facing a series of strikes by railwaymen demanding better conditions. This industrial action might have affected the department stores had they remained within the same group.

It was not until Japan's postwar boom years that Hankyu Department Stores really began to prosper, at a time when Japan was experiencing rapid growth in income levels, personal consumption, and the general standard of living. Together with the system of floating exchange rates and the resultant appreciation of the yen which made imported goods cheaper and therefore more competitive, Japan's retail industry expanded, opening it to a wider variety of consumer goods, including imports. Between 1953 and 1959 Hankyu Department Stores opened three more stores: Tokyo Oi in 1953; Sukiyabashi Hankyu in 1956; and, in the United States, Los Angeles Hankyu in 1967.

The Tokyo Oi store was a landmark in the company's development, taking the reputation of Hankyu Department Stores out of the suburbs and placing it firmly in the city and in the national consideration. This standing was enhanced by the opening of the second Tokyo store in 1956.

Los Angeles Hankyu was originally a retail store but because of the appreciation of the yen it became too expensive to maintain import goods from Japan. Los Angeles Hankyu therefore became a buying center for the Japanese stores and has remained as such.

The next boom in Hankyu Department Stores' history took place in the 1970s when additional stores were opened: Senri Hankyu in Senri, a satellite town of Osaka, in 1970 and Shijo-Kawaramachi Hankyu in Kyoto in 1976.

Each store Hankyu Department Stores opened exploited its strategic location. The Umeda Main Store is situated in the commercial area which surrounds Umeda, in the city of Osaka. Umeda is one of the largest railway terminals in Japan, and Hankyu Department Stores expects good sales growth from this store as Osaka becomes one of the nation's major international cities with the completion of Kansai International Airport.

Senri Hankyu was created to cater to families in the nearby housing development district, providing locally oriented goods and services. It was also the pioneer store in the metropolitan suburbs. The store in the international port of Kobe was conveniently located for the users of Sannomiya terminal station. The Kyoto and Sukiyabashi stores both targeted young Japanese women who were starting to enjoy an increase in status and jobs. The early 1980s, however, saw a downturn in sales due to the worldwide recession, and in fiscal year 1983 the *Japan Economic Journal* reported that sales by Japan's 200 leading retailers rose by only 5.3%. The department stores' slowed growth was also due in part to changing lifestyles in Japan. Despite Japanese women's greater disposable income they began to look more toward convenience stores and supermarkets, which grew rapidly. Department stores responded to this switch in allegiance with a range of measures designed to woo consumers back to their stores. They commissioned market research to discover what consumers wanted, and they extended shopping hours so that working women could shop after work. Hankyu Department Stores and other department store retailers transformed their shops, making them not only places to shop, but also entertainment and cultural centers encompassing restaurants, recreational areas for children, golf ranges and tennis courts, educational facilities, theaters, and art exhibitions. They also invested in sponsoring events. Hankyu Department Stores regularly sponsors cultural events. The company puts particular emphasis on introducing the traditional crafts and cultures of foreign countries, illustrated by its "British Fair" and "French Fair," as well as its "Wonders of China" and "9,000 year-old Art and Culture of Jordan" exhibitions. Hankyu Department Stores also supports Japanese baseball and is one of the many major retailers that owns a team, Hankyu's being the Hankyu Braves.

Hankyu Department Stores continued to expand, opening another two stores, Yurakucho in 1984 and Kawanishi Hankyu in 1989. Meanwhile, the company responded to the increasing popularity of the Western-style department store by adopting the decoration, fittings, and look of the modern department stores of America and Europe. In the Ginza shopping area, which caters for 200,000 shoppers per day, the company has used this theme in its Yurakucho store, complementing the more traditional-style store, Sukibayashi Hankyu.

In 1988 the company's pretax profits rose by 14.3% thanks to the longer shopping hours and increased sales in high-profit items, including accessories, handbags, and imported clothes such as American jeans. Imported products, or those seen to have a Western flavor, are particularly popular with Japanese consumers, and Hankyu Department Stores has responded to this by developing its own brand of children's clothing, Potato Chips, which has been highly successful and is even sold in other major department stores. In its Yurakucho store in central Tokyo the company only stocks exclusive overseas labels.

The company is also known for its high quality foodstuffs and has responded to changes in eating habits, especially the trend toward gourmet food, by introducing a wide assortment of value-added products and more ready-to-serve products.

In 1989 the success of Hankyu Department Stores attracted the interest of the American retailer Bloomingdales, and in November of that year the company approached Hankyu Department Stores with an invitation to participate in a buy-out of the chain. Hankyu Department Stores' president Shoji Fu-kumitsu met with Bloomingdale's chairman Marvin Traub but turned down a reported financing of US$250 million out of the $1.2 billion to $1.3 billion needed for the buy-out.

Profitability of department stores throughout Japan and for Hankyu Department Store fell as a result of the Japanese government's introduction of consumption tax on April 1, 1989. A large increase in sales volume in March 1989, just prior to the introduction of the tax, was followed by a slump in April. The slump was shortlived, however, mainly due to the fact that the tax only had a slight impact on commodity prices. Consumer spending recovered soon after, but greater emphasis was placed on better quality.

Hankyu Department Stores seems to be entering one of its strongest periods of growth, with a large number of developments planned for the next few years. However, Hankyu, like other Japanese department stores, faces a challenge from the relaxation of legal limitations on large-scale retail stores, triggered by Japan-U.S. Structural Impediments Initiative talks. This will inevitably lead to intensified competition in Japan's distribution and retail industries in the coming years.

In preparation, the company is looking to develop a variety of management measures including entering new markets and expanding its business base. The company plans to open a store in Kobe Harbor Land, one of Japan's largest waterfront development projects. The new store will have a sales floor of approximately 30,000 square meters and its opening is scheduled for fiscal year 1992. Adjoining the store will be a restaurant of a similar size.

Further expansion includes a plan to open a new store in Takarazuka, a place of symbolic significance for the Hankyu and Toho Group because of its associations with the first store. In this the company hopes to deepen its market through the formation of a store network encompassing a large part of the commercial sphere in northern Hanshin (Osaka-Kobe) area at sites centered on the Hankyu Railways' service area.

A new affiliated merchandising company, Hankyu Ings Co., Ltd., will be established, separate from the merchandising function of Hankyu Main Store (Umeda). There will also be further product development of attractive, economical overseas brands and materials which the company sees as essential if it is to survive the retail wars of the future.

The company also plans to expand overseas with the development of a food business in Bangkok, Thailand, through a joint venture with Central Department Store, the leading local operator. The new company, Central Hankyu Ltd., will have capital of 20 million bahts, 51% provided by Central and 49% by Hankyu.

Hankyu will occupy one floor of the Thai store, selling foodstuffs. The company's policy states that its stores are to exist mainly for the people of that country, not as souvenir stores for Japanese tourists. Combined with the fact that the company has started expanding overseas, Hankyu Department Stores is set to continue as one of Japan's major retailers.

Principal Subsidiaries: Hankyu Kyoei Bussan Inc; Hankyu Foods Industry Co., Ltd.; Hankyu Oasis Inc.; Kyoei Seicha Co. Ltd; Able Co., Ltd; Hankyu Seisakusho Co., Ltd; Kitano Shokuhin Co., Ltd; Esaka Transportation Co., Ltd.

—Rachel Loos

HERTIE WAREN- UND KAUFHAUS GMBH

Herriotstrasse 4
D-6000 Frankfurt am Main 71
Federal Republic of Germany
(69) 6681-1
Fax: (69) 6681-545

Private Company
Incorporated: 1882 as Garn-, Knopf, Posamentier, Weiss- und
Wollwarengeschäft en gros und en detail Hermann Tietz
Employees: 32,050
Sales: DM6.67 billion (US$4.40 billion)

Hertie Waren- und Kaufhaus GmbH (HWK) heads one of Germany's largest department store groups. The history of HWK can be traced back to the firm of Garn-, Knopf, Posamentier, Weiss- und Wollwarengeschäft en gros und en detail Hermann Tietz, founded in March 1882 in Gera, Thuringia, by Hermann Tietz and his nephew Oskar Tietz, who was 24 years old at the time. Hermann Tietz provided the necessary capital for Oskar's venture as a linen and wool draper. It is also from Herman Tietz's name that the popular name for the stores, Hertie, derives. The first day's sales totaled 34.5 marks. Hermann Tietz had become familiar with new business methods in the United States and passed on what he had learnt to his nephew.

The basic concept gleaned from Hermann Tietz's observations and experience in the United States was to win the customer's long-term confidence by offering a range of goods that was both inexpensive and of high quality. In contrast to the prevailing principle of making large profits on a small turnover, the Tietzes aimed to make a small profit on a large turnover. To achieve this goal, new methods were required. Of particular importance among these was the system of selling at fixed prices. Since a department store had a high turnover compared with the low turnover of the traditional retail store, the department store owner could afford to sell goods at a relatively low profit margin. The Tietzes' business methods were remarkably successful, and by the second half of the 1890s it became necessary to expand the Gera department store.

The company grew rapidly, having opened 11 branches by the end of the 19th century in Gera, Weimar, Karlsruhe, Munich, Strasbourg (under German rule from 1870 until 1918), Munich, and Hamburg. It was, however, badly affected by an

economic depression in 1901. Another store was opened in Munich in 1905, opposite the main railroad station. It was the first building in Germany to be specifically designed as a department store.

The company's successes in central, southern, and southwest Germany led it to establish further stores in Berlin as well. Three imposing department stores were constructed in the center of the imperial capital, one in Leipziger Strasse in 1900, another on the Alexanderplatz in 1905, and a third on the Frankfurter Allee in 1911.

During World War I Hertie became a war supplier on a very large scale. At first the company supplied blankets, campbeds, clothing, and provisions. Leather goods were transformed into army gear, and a printing works in one of the Berlin stores was converted into a saddlery. The company invested money from its deliveries to the army in specialist machinery to cater for military needs, and the stores themselves mounted extravagantly patriotic displays.

Throughout the war the company suffered from a lack of demand, from high levels of debt on loans it had recently taken out to build its new Leipziger Strasse store in Berlin, and from the collapse of the Pommersche Hypotheken-Aktienbank, which had given the company a 3 million mark mortgage. Goods became increasingly hard to find. Georg Tietz, one of Oskar's sons, traveled to Holland and to Switzerland to buy what he could, but supplies became scarcer and the bureaucratic channels he had to pass through increasingly difficult.

Oskar Tietz, as chairman of the German association of department stores, was involved with the German war companies and given the title of delegate for the acquisition of woolen wares and clothing by the Red Cross, a civilian post with a rank equivalent to major general and its own special uniform.

After 1918 Oskar Tietz succeeded in rapidly reestablishing the company's prewar position as the second largest department store in Germany after Karstadt. By the time he died in 1923, the group had 40 stores. It had a buying concern based in Berlin, with branches in Plauen, Chemnitz, Offenbach, and Elberfeld. It had formed a joint buying venture with the provincial stores of the firm Conitzer. The Tietz group also owned seven textile factories of its own, helping it to reduce costs in textile manufacturing. Its production operations in the manufacturing of linen, as well as clothing, were separated.

After the death of Oskar Tietz, the company acquired A. Jarndorf in Berlin, which had six department stores, including Kaufhaus des Westens, the so-called KaDeWe, in existence since 1907 and situated on the Tauentzeinstrasse, and to this day the flagship of the Hertie group. With a turnover of 128 million marks in December 1926 and 18,000 employees, the company had become the largest department store group in Europe. By 1932, the year of Hertie's 50th anniversary, the company had 19 of its own branches and 20 annexes, with 20,000 employees.

Despite the group's powerful growth, the worldwide Depression that began in 1929 coupled with the mass unemployment that followed in its wake led to a decline in the group's turnover of 46.6% between 1930 and 1933. This caused the company considerable financial difficulties.

Following the National Socialists' putsch on January 30, 1933, the situation worsened dramatically for the company, since Hertie, as a Jewish-owned company, was at the mercy of the new dictatorship's boycott measures from March 5, 1933. The banks refused to secure any more loans for the company. By the end of June, 1933, the group was on the point of bankruptcy, the banks demanding either the liquidation of the company or a complete restructuring. Fourteen thousand jobs, together with the numerous suppliers, were under threat. The Reich's minister for trade and commerce, Dr. Kurt Schmidt, was able to persuade Hitler of the necessity of setting Hertie back on its feet. Eleven million marks of credit were made available by the banking consortium which, via the Hertie Kaufhaus-Beteiligungs-GmbH, took a 60% share in the company. The banks appointed Georg Karg, Dr. Trabant von und zu der Tamm, and Wilhelm Hermsdorf to direct the company. In 1934 the Tietz family sold the shares it still held.

The banking consortium soon proposed to Georg Karg that he should take on the company as sole owner. Georg Karg had become a manager of the Charlottenburg branch of Jarndorf before it was acquired by the group, and since the time of the takeover he had risen rapidly through Hertie's ranks. In spite of three loss-making years for the company and debts of 129 million marks, from 1937 to 1938 Georg Karg gradually began to acquire two-thirds of the shares in the company from the banks, acquiring the remaining third at the beginning of World War II. The Tietz family, in the meantime, had left Germany.

During World War II the stores continued operating. Many of them, located in the center of large cities, were badly damaged by bombs. Some of the stores were taken over in part for use as military hospitals.

By the end of the war in 1945 only three of the ten Berlin stores still existed. Four-fifths of the group's real estate had either been destroyed or now lay in East Germany, outside the company's hands. Apart from the Berlin stores that remained, only the so-called Alsterhaus store in Hamburg and the stores in Munich, Stuttgart, and Karlsruhe remained for the company to control.

Georg Karg swiftly set about rebuilding his business. He began selling what goods he could acquire in provisionally reconstructed ground-floor stores and in rented shops. In 1948 he moved his headquarters from Berlin to Hamburg. His son Hans-Georg joined him in 1950 to help revive the Hertie business empire. Georg Karg's determination led to the company's recovery, and Hertie was restored as one of Germany's leading companies. Georg Karg kept his group's independence secure, in particular through remaining independent of any large banks. He also remained secretive about the company's activities.

In 1949 the Tietz heirs regained ownership of the stores in Munich, Stuttgart, and Karlsruhe in a private restitution settlement. The settlement also contained a rent based on the turnover of the three aforementioned stores as well as a provision for reinvestment until 1970.

Hertie then embarked upon a period of great expansion. In 1949 Hertie took over three stores, in Stuttgart, Wiesbaden, and Hamburg-Bergedorf, and in 1950 KaDeWe was reopened, on two stories only. By 1990 KaDeWe, with 43,000 square meters of sales area, 2,811 employees, and turnover of DM508 million, was the largest Hertie department store. In 1951 an opening and two takeovers of stores in Neumünster, Landshut, and Frankfurt-Höchst took place. Nineteen fifty-two saw the acquisition of a majority shareholding in Wertheim (department store founded in Stralsund in 1877); the

founding of Bilka; the takeover of Hansa-AG (originally the Grand Bazar founded in 1900 in Frankfurt) with branches in Frankfurt-Zeil, Hanau, and Mannheim; and the takeover of two department stores in Berlin-Neuköln, as well as a new opening in Wuppertal.

The group underwent an important reconstruction in 1953. Georg Karg set up the Karg'sche Familienstiftung (Hertie Family Foundation). Its primary purpose was to protect the group's independence and to make it secure from outside shareholders. Its founder felt that all members of the family should earn their own living and be paid according to individual performance. He made the condition that the trustees should only receive allowances from the foundation, if they found in difficult circumstances not of their own making that prevented them from maintaining a standard of living appropriate to their station. Such allowances have never had to be granted. Ninety-eight percent of the shares of the Hertie parent company, HWK, were transferred to the family foundation. At the same time the foundation was tied to the company, both as the major shareholder in the Hertie Group and in terms of management of the group; it was stipulated that two family members must have seats on the seven-man board and that at least one family member must agree to all decisions of the board for them to be legally binding. Hans-Georg Karg was made chairman of the board for life.

Forty-two more department stores were opened before Georg Karg's death in 1972. The company's turnover, which had grown at an annual rate of more than 10%, reached more than DM5 billion in 1972 from the combined sales in the total of 101 branches.

During the four decades before Georg Karg's death, the Hertie Group had come to be nicknamed "the silent giant" because of Karg's discreet business manner. Georg Karg remained secretive about his business and out of the public eye.

In 1972 the Karg Family Foundation was renamed the Hertie Stiftung. The management of the company was passed on to Georg Karg's son Hans-Georg, who saw to the company's restructuring, bringing younger persons into the management. Faced with huge problems of inheritance tax that might have made it necessary to introduce outside shareholders into the group, in 1974 Hans-Georg Karg and his sister, Brigitte, Countess of Norman, decided to establish the Gemeinnützige Stiftung zur Förderung von Wissenschaft, Erziehung, Volks- und Berufsbildung, known as the Gemeinnützige Hertie-Stiftung or Public Benefit Hertie Foundation. Of the 98% of shares held by the Hertie Stiftung in the Hertie Group parent company, HWK, 97.5% were transferred to the Gemeinnützige Hertie-Stiftung. It was stipulated that the chairman of both entities should be the same person; Hans-Georg Karg became chairman of the two. The Hertie-Stiftung kept only 0.5% of the share capital of HWK, but the family foundation retained the majority voting rights, maintaining its controlling influence over all group decisions. The Gemeinnützige Hertie-Stiftung is limited to receiving and distributing company profits for charitable purposes. It sponsors scientific and social research and educational and vocational training. It is particularly committed to supporting research into multiple sclerosis.

In 1977 there was a further expansion in the management structure of the Hertie Group. Since 1981 a board consisting of several members has existed alongside the chairman of the board, bringing the company's structure closer in line with the other main German department store companies. The group's turnover amounted to DM6.1 billion in 1981.

Despite the difficulties suffered by department store groups in the 1980s, caused primarily by the increasing popularity of big supermarkets on the edges of towns, Hertie managed to maintain its prominent position. After turnover had declined to DM5.90 billion in 1985, DM5.62 billion in 1986, and DM5.57 billion in 1987, it began to rise again, to DM6.01 billion in 1988, and DM6.18 billion in 1989.

In the second half of the 1980s Hertie created or acquired a variety of subsidiaries in specialist areas, in particular in restaurants, groceries, electronics, and music. Le Buffet System-Gastronomie, founded by the Hertie group in 1986, had 72 restaurant outlets in 1990, 57 of them operating within Hertie stores. The company employed 2,281 employees in 1990 and had a turnover of DM191.7 million. In 1987 the group branched out into electronics, acquiring Schaulandt GmbH and Schürmann Elektrohandelsgesellschaft mbH. Schaulandt GmbH specialized in entertainments electronics and had eight retail outlets in addition to its wholesale company in 1990. It employed 348 people and its turnover for that year was DM202.1 million. Schürmann Elektrohandelsgesellschaft, with a network of 28 outlets in 1990, had a turnover of DM322.7 and employed 691 people. The year 1987 also saw the acquisition of 50% of WOM World of Music Produktions- und Verlags-GmbH, a music specialist. In 1990 it had 11 branches and a turnover of DM136.2 million. Hertie also established WOM World of Music Musikhandelsgesellschaft mbH in 1988 to establish specialist music shops within its stores.

NUG Optimus Lebensmittel-Einzelhandelsgesellschaft mbH was founded in 1988 by Hertie to sell groceries and confectionery within its department stores. In 1990 there were 62 grocery and 11 confectionery outlets. Employing 3,855 people, it had a turnover of DM704 million. The textile company Wehmeyer GmbH & Co. KG was acquired by Hertie in 1988. In 1990 it had 19 outlets, employed 1,313 people, and recorded a turnover of DM258.8 million. By 1989 Hertie took a one-third share in Sono Centra Trading Limited, a joint buying company in Asia that it founded with Horten and Kaufring.

The reunification of East and West Germany brought a dramatic upsurge in sales for Hertie. By the end of 1991 Hertie had opened 11 stores in former East Germany employing 3,000 people with a turnover of DM400 million. The group's whole network comprised 267 branches, with 32,050 employees. With an increase in turnover of 9.6% in the first half of 1991, the Hertie group was set to continue the successful development of the previous year.

Principal Subsidiaries: Le Buffet System-Gastronomie und Dienstleistungs-GmbH; NUG Optimus Lebensmittel-Einzelhandelsgesellschaft mbH; Optimus Bank für Finanz-Service GmbH; Schaulandt GmbH; Schürmann Elektrohandelsgesellschaft mbH; Sono Centra Trading Limited; Wehmeyer GmbH & Co. KG (75%); WOM World of Music Musikhandelsgesellschaft mbH; WOM World of Music Produktions- und Verlags-GmbH (50%); Autoreparaturwerkstatt Hahnstrasse-Niederrad GmbH; Bilka Verwaltungsgesellschaft mbH (98%); CBG Center-Betriebsgesellschaft mbH; Funny Paper Papier- und Bürobedarfs-Vertriebsgesellschaft mbH; Hertie Center Verwaltungsgesellschaft mbH; Optimus Finanzdienstleistungs-Center GmbH; Optimus Versicherungs-Vermittlung GmbH; Optimus Waren-Vertriebsgesellschaft mbH; Sports World Sport and Freizeit Handelsgesellschaft mbH; Warenhaus Wertheim GmbH (99%); Wir Kinder Optimus Spielwaren-Vertriebsgesellschaft mbH.

—Philippe A. Barbour and Konrad Fuchs

THE HOME DEPOT, INC.

2727 Paces Ferry Road
Atlanta, Georgia 30339
U.S.A.
(404) 433-8211
Fax: (404) 431-2739

Public Company
Incorporated: 1978
Employees: 21,500
Sales: $3.82 billion
Stock Exchange: New York

The Home Depot, Inc. (HD), the largest home center retailer in the United States, operates 165 warehouse stores and sells more than 30,000 items to the rapidly growing do-it-yourself home improvement market. The company's stores are located on the West Coast and in the southwestern, northeastern, and southeastern regions of the United States. A typical HD warehouse stocks building materials, wall and floor coverings, paint, plumbing supplies, hardware, tools, electrical supplies, and supplies for landscaping and gardening.

The company was incorporated in June of 1978 as a result of a corporate management shake-up by new ownership of the Handy Dan home center chain. As a result of the managerial shuffle, Bernard Marcus, Arthur Blank, and Ronald Brill found themselves out of work. With backing from a New York venture capital firm, Marcus and his two associates formed The Home Depot and opened the company's first outlets in the Atlanta, Georgia, area. The concept that had helped secure financing for the project was that when the price of merchandise was marked down, sales increased while the cost of making those sales decreased. The major problem that had plagued most cut-rate retail operations, however, was poor service at the operations level, which hired unskilled, low-paid employees to keep costs down.

Marcus and his partners realized that recognizing customers' needs was one of the most important elements in a company's growth. They were aware that at the time do-it-yourselfers made up more than 60% of the building supply industry's sales volume, but the majority of them did not have the technical knowledge or expertise to accomplish most home repair or improvement projects.

The HD management team set about to solve this problem in two ways. First, they made sure that all HD stores were large enough to stock at least 25,000 different items. Their competi-

tor locations normally had room for only 10,000. The second solution was to train the sales staff in each store to help remove much of the mystery attached to home improvement projects. The educated salespeople helped to create an increasing customer base in this fashion. Marcus and his partners believed an educated customer would take on more projects at home and would come back to HD outlets to purchase what was needed and get advice from a knowledgeable sales staffer.

HD composed its sales staff of dedicated do-it-yourselfers and professional tradespeople, in full-time capacities. Only 10% of HD's sales personnel were part-time. Whenever possible, each store had a licensed plumber and electrician on staff, and customers were urged to call the HD store in their area if they had any problem or questions while they were doing their home repair or improvement projects. The company also scheduled in-store instructional workshops for its customers and in some cases brought in local contractors to teach.

This approach paid off. By 1984 the company was operating 19 stores and reported sales of $256 million, a 118% increase over 1983. In 1986 HD's sales reached the $1 billion mark, and the company was operating 50 retail outlets.

The company's growth was not without its problems. In 1984 HD paid $38.4 million for the nine-store Bowater warehouse chain with outlets in Texas, Louisiana, and Alabama. The acquisition created immediate difficulties. Bowater's reputation with consumers was shoddy, and the merchandise in its stores did not match what HD carried in its other outlets. In addition, Bowater's employees did not meet HD's standards and, eventually, HD dismissed almost all of them.

During these years HD's sales continued to climb, but for the first time in the company's history, the cost of sales increased. In 1985 the company's earnings fell 42%, and with the ever-increasing costs of opening new outlets—at that time it was more than $8 million per store—the company's long-term debt rose from $4 million to $200 million in just two years. By the end of 1985, the company's stock price had plummeted, and changes were needed if the company was to continue to grow and prosper.

The company slowed down its expansion. In 1986 it only opened ten new stores, all in existing, established markets. A stock offering of 2.99 million shares at $17 helped reduce and restructure the company debt. Marcus also installed a computerized inventory control system and upgraded the company's management training programs. In keeping with Marcus's commitment to slower, more conservative growth, the company continued opening new stores to completely capture existing markets instead of striking out into new regions of the country.

In 1989 HD surpassed Lowe's Companies in sales to become the largest home-repair chain in the United States. The company began the 1990s with a goal of becoming a national retail chain doing more than $10 billion in sales from 350 locations by 1995. Part of this plan included an expansion into the northeastern United States by the addition of 75 stores. Company officials believed the area's dense population and large number of older homes would generate impressive results. Expansion plans also included the state of Washington.

By the end of 1989, almost all outlets were using the company's new satellite data communications network. The fast and accurate exchange of information between stores was designed to permit continued growth with responsiveness to market changes. The satellite is also the foundation of the company's new Home Depot television network, a system that produces and transmits live programming by top management to each outlet. The company's net earnings increased 46% in 1990, and HD effected a three-for-two stock split that same year. Sales increased 38% over 1989. With the trend for continued growth in the do-it-yourself market shown by a 33% increase in the number of customer transactions logged by the company in 1990, along with an increase of 4% for the average cus-

tomer sale, HD seems to be an emerging giant in the U.S. retail marketplace.

Further Reading: Zemke, Ron, *The Service Edge,* New York, NAL Books, 1986; "Will Home Depot Be 'The Wal-Mart of the '90s?' " *Business Week,* March 19, 1990; "The Home Depot," *Management Horizons,* July 1990.

—William R. Grossman

HOME SHOPPING NETWORK, INC.

12000 25th Court North
St. Petersburg, Florida 33716
U.S.A.
(813) 572-8585
Fax: (813) 572-8585, extension 7356

Public Company
Incorporated: 1985
Employees: 5,341
Sales: $1.01 billion
Stock Exchange: New York

The Home Shopping Network (HSN) is most well known as a live television shop-at-home service. It is, however, a holding company that participates in an array of direct marketing activities through its subsidiaries, which include electronic retail sales, catalog and mail order sales, and telemarketing sales for products and services offered by HSN, as well as by other companies on a contractual basis. HSN's inventory includes electronics, housewares, jewelry, cosmetics and beauty products, soft goods, and home entertainment items. All of HSN's merchandise is reportedly sold at a deep discount. In the early 1990s, HSN was in the process of diversifying both the products and services offered, making available additional lines of products to include prescription drugs, vitamins, over-the-counter health care items, ticketing and reservation services, insurance, and financial services.

The idea for HSN originated in the 1970s, when Lowell W. Paxson, now the company's president, owned an AM radio station in Clearwater, Florida, that began to lose listeners to FM alternatives. Paxson also lost advertisers. He decided to try selling merchandise directly over the air, switching from a beautiful-music format to an at-home radio shopping service called The Bargaineers. To finance the new format, Paxson turned to Roy M. Speer, a lawyer and real estate developer. Speer later became HSN's chairman.

Almost immediately after the switch in format the station's revenues swelled so much that Paxson was eager to try out his home shopping idea on television. Speer liked the idea of expanding to TV but wanted to proceed slowly. Speer invested $500,000 for a 60% stake and set out to make sure that viewers would not be disappointed before he gave the go-ahead in July of 1982.

Speer and Paxson called their local TV program the Home Shopping Club (HSC). Within three months it was turning a profit. After two more Tampa Bay–area cable companies decided to carry HSC, Speer and Paxson began to explore markets in Fort Lauderdale and Miami. By 1985 HSC was so successful that it went national, calling itself the Home Shopping Network (HSN). Speer based his decision to expand on the belief that the profiles of Tampa Bay customers would be the same for people all over the United States.

Speer commissioned the development of a computer system that would have the capacity to respond to customers' needs immediately. He acquired a large number of phone lines and hired many operators, all in an effort to make a return customer of that first-time buyer. Within three months HSN had become the world's first network to broadcast live 24 hours a day, and its number of employees had grown from 300 to 1,280. Speer's approach was successful; in just one year he was able to take the company public.

In February of 1986 Merrill Lynch underwrote the initial public offering at $18 a share. An investment banker who helped with the offering commented on Speer's wisdom in pricing HSN's stock so low, because it was still perceived as a risky company in an untried industry. At that time HSN was still in the process of trying to convince cable operators to carry its show over other alternative programming. Speer's move assured interested stock buyers at the specialist-broker's stand. HSN stock became the fastest rising new issue of 1986, registering a 137% gain by the end of the day. Since the initial offering, HSN stock went on to split twice, the first time at three for one, and the second time at two for one.

The Home Shopping Club had developed three formats: Home Shopping Network 1 (HSN 1), Home Shopping Network 2 (HSN 2), and Home Shopping Spree. HSN 1 is available live, 24 hours a day, 7 days a week, and is produced exclusively for cable. HSN 2, which offers upscale merchandise, is also available live, 24 hours a day, 7 days a week, but is marketed to both broadcast and cable television. Home Shopping Spree offers limited-time or 24-hour programming to broadcast stations.

There are many different opinions on what initially generated the cult-like following of Home Shopping Club, both HSN 1 and HSN 2. One reason could be that viewers automatically become members the first time they place an order, and that they receive a $5 credit applicable to the next purchase. Another reason could be that HSN gives no warning as to what items will appear on the TV screen and when. As viewers may only purchase items for as long as the products appear on their screens, anywhere from two to ten minutes, the typical member will watch the program for several hours each day.

The hosts, almost all of whom have a background in retail sales, develop personas, complete with nicknames and a fan following. As HSN's success grew, competing stations began popping up, causing host as well as viewer defections. As competition continued to grow, many stations in the industry, including HSN, turned to celebrity endorsements and hosts.

Another more conventional way that HSN ensures that customers keep coming back is by allowing the return of any purchase if for any reason a member is not satisfied. Credit card purchases will be credited, or for a cash sale a refund check will be issued for the whole purchase cost, including shipping and handling. HSN also assures shipment within 48 hours after an order is placed with a credit card, or within 48 hours after a check for payment has been received.

In 1987 HSN acquired Sky Merchant, Inc., a TV shopping service viewed by at least one million subscribers of Jones Intercable, Inc. As HSN grew, so did the companies that supported it. HSN is one of United Parcel Service's largest accounts. And Many suppliers owe their success to HSN. A new product can be introduced to the nation on the network and within minutes, thousands of items can be sold. While some of the merchandise sold over HSN comes from closeouts, overstocks, or overruns, HSN's purchasing clout is evident in the fact that at least 60% of the company's sales in 1987 consisted of products made specifically for HSN and sold to HSN for rock-bottom prices.

Not everything, however, was on the upswing in 1987. In that year alone more than 15 television shop-at-home programs went off the air. Stock market analysts began to question how long HSN could sustain its rapid growth rate. Sales in the period between February and May of 1985, for example, were $3.6 million; for the same period in 1986, sales were $42.6 million. Some believed that members would eventually reach their credit card limits. Some thought HSN was paying too much for its acquisitions of UHF television stations and burdening itself with excessive debt. Some believed HSN would lose market share to its ever growing number of competitors who offered improvements on HSN's unpredictable format, such as the plan J.C. Penney and Sears announced for Telaction, which would allow customers to use their phone to select items from their screens.

In one year, between March of 1987 and March of 1988, HSN stock had experienced a market slip of 18.95%, compared to a 6.76% drop in the Dow Jones Industrial Average. HSN lost no time in reacting, however; as early as 1987 it was looking around for better ways to harness its market. In January 1987 HSN announced plans to build a new telecommunications center and corporate headquarters in St. Petersburg, Florida. By September HSN had started using the UHF televi-

sion stations it had been acquiring, and the network began broadcasting from its new 180,000 square-foot telecommunications facility, hoping to beat down its competitors with better reception. In September 1987 HSN announced its plans for a major corporate restructuring with HSN becoming a holding company for the various subsidiaries conducting its businesses.

Distinctions such as fast delivery and guaranteed products, the ability to process orders rapidly and reduce labor costs, and the higher quality of television reception provided by its own TV stations enabled HSN to preserve its market share, as well as distance itself from all but one of its competitors. It also reported good annual sales gains, passing the $1 billion mark in 1990. These distinctions by 1990, however, still had not succeeded in reinteresting wary investors. There was worry about the stability of the home shopping industry in the face of recession years, as statistics suggest that a great many of its customers are blue-collar workers who face cutbacks during such times. HSN stock, however, moved to the New York Stock Exchange from the smaller American Stock Exchange in 1990, and the company began a stock repurchase program.

Principal Subsidiaries: Home Shopping Club, Inc.; HSN Communications, Inc.; HSN Mistix Corporation; Precision Software, Inc.; HSN Lifeway Health Products, Inc.; HSN Telemation, Inc.; HSN Mail Order, Inc.; HSN Insurance, Inc.; HSN Entertainment, Inc.; HSN Travel, Inc.; HSN Fulfillment, Inc.; Home Shopping Club Outlets, Inc.

Further Reading: James, Ellen L., "So What's a Billion to Roy Speer?" *Venture,* May 1987; "Home Shopping Network, Inc.: A History of Growth," Home Shopping Network, Inc. corporate typescript, [1988].

—Maya Sahafi

INCORPORATED 2ND MAY 1670

HUDSON'S BAY COMPANY

401 Bay Street
Toronto, Ontario M5H 2Y4
Canada
(416) 861-6112
Fax: (416) 861-4720

Public Company
Incorporated: 1670
Employees: 60,000
Sales: C$4.97 billion (US$4.28 billion)
Stock Exchanges: Montreal Toronto

Hudson's Bay Company is Canada's oldest corporation. On May 2, 1670, King Charles II granted 18 investors a charter incorporating them as the Governor and Company of Adventurers of England. In its first century, the company traded with the North American Indians, established forts on Hudson Bay, and successfully fought with U.S. and Canadian competitors to build its fur trade. By the early 1990s, in a coast-to-coast operation accounting for 7% of Canadian retail sales, excluding food and automobiles, the company owned and managed 483 stores in three retail divisions: the Bay, Zellers, and Fields. At the end of the 1980s, retailing assets generated net annual earnings of approximately C$168 million on revenue of C$4.59 billion.

The development of the company is tied to the growth of Canada and settlement of its western region. Those who were important to the development of the company were also important politically and historically to the economic and political growth of the New World. The list of well-known people associated with the company is long and includes Peter Skene Ogden, Solomon Juneau, Henry Kelsey, James Knight, Samuel Hearne, Peter Pond, Alexander Mackenzie, Sir George Simpson, Sir James Douglas, John McLoughlin, and others. The chartering of the company on May 2, 1670, with Prince Rupert—a cousin of Charles II—as the company's first governor, followed the successful fur trading voyage of the ketch *Nonsuch* that brought back beaver pelts for the English market, used by felters and hatters to make the beaver hats that were fashionable at the time.

The Adventurers' charter of 1670 gave it 1.49 million square miles of virgin territory, or nearly 40% of today's Canadian provinces, including what would become Ontario, Quebec north of the Laurentian watershed and west of the Labrador boundary, Manitoba, the better part of Sakatchewan, southern

Alberta, and much of the northwest territories. The group's rights to the lucrative fur trade did not go uncontested, and it was not until 20 years later that the company made its first inland expedition. Henry Kelsey, an apprentice who joined the company in 1677 and who later became a company governor, made the first journey into the prairie in 1690, learning the Cree language, and adapting to Indian life. He wished to encourage peace among the Indian tribes so that they could bring beaver pelts to the forts without being attacked. Three forts on James Bay—Rupert's House, Moose, and Albany in the east—and a fourth, York Factory, on the west coast of Hudson Bay were the sites of battles for nearly 30 years between the French and English contesting the territory and the right to conduct trade. The Treaty of Ryswick in 1697 brought peace, but by then the company was near ruin. Most of the company's first century of business was devoted to establishing forts and territorial rights and making peace with the Indians and the French merchants who wanted to be a part of the fur trade in the New World.

One of the Hudson's Bay Company's fiercest early competitors was North West Company, established in 1779 by a Scottish-Canadian group of nine traders that moved into the Canadian interior around 1780 and claimed to be the rightful successor to the early French traders who had opened up the land. North West Company had two types of shareholders: the eastern partners, merchants in Montreal and Quebec who supplied the venture capital, and the "wintering" partners, who became responsible for exploratory and sales operations. By 1800 North West became a serious competitor, forcing Hudson's Bay Company to become increasingly more adventurous, pushing the trade boundaries westward from the Hudson Bay, in fear of losing trade with the western Indians. Each company drove the other toward new expeditions, so that by the turn of the century, they each had men trading on the upper Missouri River.

North West's Alexander Mackenzie, who later was knighted, was the most famous fur trader of his day. Mackenzie pushed the trade boundaries farther westward. Several of his trade expeditions were historical achievements: in 1789 he covered 1,600 miles and back in 102 days, and in 1793, he crossed the Rocky Mountains to reach the Pacific Ocean.

Other companies also envied the apparent monopoly of Hudson's Bay Company. U.S. traders wanted a share in the fur trade following the Lewis and Clark expedition of 1804 to 1806. In 1808 Pierre Chouteau, William Clark, and five others established the Missouri Fur Company, and in New York John Jacob Astor, the leading fur dealer in the United States, started the American Fur Company, capitalized at US$300,000, of which he owned all but a few shares.

Peter Skene Ogden, who worked for a time for the American Fur Company, moved to Quebec after being appointed judge of the Admiralty Court in 1788. Ogden wanted to be among the first white men to see the great wilderness. After living in Quebec for six years with his wife and children, he was sent by North West Company into the interior of North America to clerk at the company's post in what is today Saskatchewan Province. Ogden wintered on the prairies for the first time in September 1810, where he met Samuel Black, a Scotsman and also a clerk, who would become a lifelong friend. The two men made a sport of harassing Hudson's Bay men. Among the tales cited by Gloria Cline, author of *Peter Skene Odgen and the Hudson's Bay Company*, was that of the harassment of Peter Fidler of Hudson's Bay Company. Fidler departed in 3 boats with 16 men for Churchill Factory on Hudson Bay, an important post, and Ogden, with two canoes-full of Canadians, taunted the British traders for six days by keeping just ahead of them in order "to get everything from Indians that may be on the road, as they can go much faster than us," according to Fidler. Ogden was a much valued employee of North West and was promoted as a result of his antics with Black.

Along with Ogden, the North West company entrusted its goal of westward expansion to David Thompson. In 1807 Thompson had crossed the Rockies and reached the headwaters of the Columbia. In 1809 he again crossed the Rockies and established an outpost in what is now northern Idaho; from there he proceeded into Montana. Directly ahead of Thompson's trading party was the first far-western expedition of John Jacob Astor's Pacific Fur Company, the west coast subsidiary of American Fur Company. Although a U.S. company, it was managed by three Canadians, former Nor'westers—employees of North West. The War of 1812 altered hopes for Astor's company, and the following year Pacific Fur Company sold all of its interests in the region to North West Company.

During the fall of 1818, Ogden took charge of David Thompson's old post, near what is now Spokane, Washington. The following year, Ogden returned east. In 1821 the two companies merged under the name of the Hudson's Bay Company after the Nor'westers learned that their company was in poor financial condition. Ogden was excluded from the merger by the company because he had fought so fiercely, although he continued for the new firm as an explorer and trapper.

The next phase of the company's growth was shaped by the 1849 gold fever that caused a great rush westward; almost 40,000 '49ers came west that year. The Bay Company suffered as a result. Demand made the cost of basic goods skyrocket. Lumber rose from $16 to $65 per thousand feet; unskilled labor received $5 to $10 a day; sailors were paid $150 a month. The steady flow of gold, however, created a favorable balance of trade. With settlement, though, came new tax laws. In 1850, the Treasury Department prohibited trade between Fort Victoria and the English Vancouver Island and Fort Nisqually on the U.S. Puget Sound. This hurt Hudson's Bay Company considerably because it legally tied up all vessels for custom inspection, which took them 350 miles off course, subjected them to twice crossing the hazardous Columbia sandbar, and made them pay heavy piloting fees at the custom house port. To add to Ogden's troubles in the western outposts of the company, the gold fever created labor difficulties, with many crewmen deserting to seek the possibility of finding gold. After several years of health problems, Ogden returned east for 18 months. Upon returning to his post in the western provinces, the strenuous trip and his advancing age took their toll; Ogden died in 1854.

Equal in importance to the growth of the company was Sir George Simpson, who served as administrator of the company for 40 years following the merger with North West. John McLoughlin, called the Father of Oregon, governed the district under Simpson with wide powers. Sir James Douglas assisted McLoughlin; he later became Governor of the Crown Colonies of Vancouver and British Columbia.

When the westward settlement reached St. Paul, the British government tried to break the Bay Company monopoly by charging it with poor administration. A select committee of the House of the Commons investigated the charges, and with Sir George Simpson as one of the principal witnesses, the charges were dismissed. The company's territory and the North West territories became part of the Canadian Confederation through the British North America Act of 1867. The government of Canada transferred to itself the company's chartered territory, Rupertsland, in 1870, in return for farm lands in the prairie provinces, which were sold to settlers over the following 85 years.

Demand for general merchandise increased, and shops were established on the outskirts of the forts. In 1912 a major remodeling and reconstruction of retail trade shops was interrupted by World War I. Following the war, the company diversified, incorporating elements of oil exploration in Alberta, revitalizing its Fur Trade Department, and venturing into the oil business as a favored partner of Hudson's Bay Oil and Gas. After the 1929 stock market crash and Great Depression, the fur department revitalized itself, improving working conditions, and in some areas acted as an agent for Inuit Indian carvings.

Early in the 20th century, the company made retail stores its first priority, building downtown department stores in each of the major cities of western Canada, moving east through acquisitions, and expanding into the suburbs of major Canadian cities beginning in the 1960s. Hudson's Bay Company acquired Markborough Properties, a real estate company, in 1973; Zellers, a chain of discount stores, in 1978; and Simpsons, a group of Toronto-area department stores, the following year. Kenneth Thomson, representing the family of the late Lord Thomson of Fleet, acquired a 75% controlling interest in the company in 1979.

In the 1970s, the company's governor was Donald McGiverin, and George Kosich was chief operating officer. In that decade and into the 1980s, sales and oil prices slipped, while debt from acquisitions piled up. By 1985 the company owed C$2.5 billion and with feeble operating profits wiped out by C$250 million in interest payments, the company suffered its fourth consecutive yearly loss. In response, management shed assets, including the Bay's 179 northernmost stores, some of which could be traced back to the fur-trading days of Ogden. In a strong attempt to survive, Thomson shook up top management, eventually appointing George Kosich, a career merchandiser, president. Thomson revamped retail operations. The combined market share of the three department store chains rose to 33% from 29% in two years.

Kosich refocused Simpsons to the upscale market and the Bay toward the middle-to-lower-priced market. In repositioning the Bay, Kosich put the 300-year-old Canadian giant up against its closest U.S. counterpart, Sears. In 1985 the Bay had 10% of the market, Sears 27%. Employing an intensive advertising campaign—C$75 million—the Bay produced a bold and aggressive image before Canadians. In the first half of 1986, sales rose 13.2% over that of 1985. Operating profit rose to C$31 million in 1985, and to C$83 million on C$1.8 billion in total sales in 1986. Sears was feeling the results, reporting barely a 3% rise in 1986 and a continuous downturn ever since. Zellers was positioned to appeal to the budget shopper as a "junior" department store. Club Z, a frequent-buyer program that allowed customers to accumulate points for prizes, boasts three million members. Hudson's Bay Company reversed a formidable debt picture in 1987 by shedding non-strategic assets such as its wholesale division and getting out of the oil and gas business. In 1990 it spun off its real estate subsidiary, Markborough Properties, as a separate, public company. Shareholders received one share of Markborough for each share they held of Hudson's Bay, with the Thomson family retaining a majority interest in Markborough. Also in 1990, the company bought 51 Towers Department Stores and merged them with Zellers.

In January 1991 Hudson's Bay Company permanently left the Canadian fur trade, an estimated C$350 million market, because its own share of that had degenerated to a paltry C$7 million in 1990. The company had been targeted by increasingly vocal antifur groups. Early in 1991, the company sold three million new common shares, with net proceeds of $72.5 million. It also repurchased slightly more than two million Series A preferred shares for $42.5 million. Company officials said these transactions would result in a stronger financial position. Because of declines in interest rates in the early 1990s, the Series A shares, with an 8% dividend, had become more expensive to service than debt. Later in 1991 the company broke up its Simpsons division, when it sold eight Simpsons stores to Sears Canada Inc., and moved the remaining 6 stores into the Bay division.

The company entered the 1990s expecting a recession to adversely affect retail sales. Hudson's Bay continued, however, to expect growth in earnings. The company planned to divest itself of under-performing stores, expand stores in promising locations, and increase overall productivity and flexibility.

Further Reading: Rich, Edwin Ernest, ed., *Minutes of the Hudson's Bay Company, 1671–1674,* London, Ontario, Hudson's Bay Record Society Publications, 1942; Innis, Harold, *The Fur Trade in Canada,* Toronto, University of Toronto Press, 1967; Cline, Gloria G., *Peter Skene Odgen and the Hudson's Bay Company,* Norman, Oklahoma, University of Oklahoma Press, 1974; Ray, Auther J., and Donald B. Freeman, *Give Us Good Measure: An Economic Analysis of Relations between the Indians and the Hudson's Bay Company before 1763,* Toronto, University of Toronto Press, 1978; Newman, Peter C., "The Hudson's Bay Company: Canada's Fur-Trading Empire," *National Geographic,* August 1987.

—Claire Badaracco

THE IKEA GROUP

IKEA International A/S
Ny Strandvej 21
3050 Humlebaek
Denmark
(45) 42 19 22 11
Fax: (45) 42 19 44 38

Private Company
Incorporated: 1943 as IKEA, Ingvar Kamprad
Employees: 19,000
Sales: SKr22.3 billion (US$4.03 billion)

The IKEA group belongs to a charitable foundation established in the Netherlands, whose aim is to promote "outstanding achievements within the area of architecture and interior decoration." Each IKEA store in the group, as well as IKEA stores outside the group, is operated under franchise from Inter IKEA Systems B.V., a company outside the IKEA Group, also based in the Netherlands. IKEA International A/S of Denmark is the advisory management company of the IKEA Group.

In 1991, the IKEA group had 79 outlets selling specially designed furniture and home furnishings in 16 countries throughout the world. Outside the IKEA Group there were 17 outlets in another 8 countries. The selling system is that of self-selection and self-service by the customers. IKEA was founded in Sweden by Ingvar Kamprad. Kamprad, born in 1926, was the son of a farmer in Småland in southern Sweden.

In 1943, at the age of 17 he created a commercial company, IKEA, Ingvar Kamprad. The word IKEA was an acronym of his name and address: *I*ngvar *K*amprad and *E*lmtaryd, the name of the farm and *A*gunnaryd, the name of the village. The company—in effect it was a one-man band—sold fish, vegetable seeds, and magazines, delivery being made by bicycle and later using the milk round. In 1947 IKEA issued its first primitive mail-order catalog and the newly-invented ballpoint pen was added to the assortment.

In 1950, Kamprad added furniture and home furnishings to the mail-order range. In 1953 Kamprad bought a small furniture factory and the headquarters of the firm were moved from the village Agunnaryd to Älmhult. A small furniture and home-furnishing showroom was opened in Älmhult employing 15 persons. Success followed, and in 1958 the tiny showroom was replaced by a giant store, by contemporary standards, of 13,000 square meters in the same town. The mail-order business continued to flourish and in 1963 the first IKEA store outside Sweden was opened in Norway near Oslo.

The event that marked the turning point of the business, however, was in 1965 when Kamprad opened a store just outside the major city of Stockholm, to show what could be done in the way of designing and selling modern low-priced furniture. The store, on a greenfield site at Kungens Kurva just ten kilometers southwest of Stockholm, was extraordinary for two reasons. First, it was very large, with some 33,000 square meters of total space and 15,000 square meters of selling space, and it consisted of two connected buildings. One building, circular in shape, had four floors connected ingeniously so that customers could move easily from floor to floor. This building was the main display area for furniture. The second building, consisting of three floors and a basement, was the stockroom and service unit and there was also a selling area for smaller pieces of furniture and home furnishings. Customer services ranged from a baby carriage hire service, a children's nursery, and a restaurant with 350 places, to cloakrooms, toilets, a bank, and parking for 1,000 cars.

More important than the physical characteristics of the IKEA store was the manner in which it revolutionized furniture manufacturing and selling. Some of the new ideas that Kamprad put into practice included selling most furniture in flat-pack form in order, as Kamprad said, "to avoid transporting and storing air". To make this possible, the furniture had to be specially designed by IKEA staff in workshops in the Älmhult headquarters and warehouse. For the mass production of the component parts of the flat-pack furniture, Kamprad had to bypass traditional furniture manufacturers and instead use specialist factories. Unfinished pine shelving, for example, came directly from saw mills, cabinet doors were made in door factories, metal frames came from machine shops, and upholstery materials came directly from textile mills. Almost all the components of each piece of furniture could be put together by the customers themselves but in some cases IKEA staff could help the customer to assemble the furniture at home. IKEA's innovations ranged from table legs which fixed into place with snap locks to kitchen chairs that were assembled with one screw. A large number of IKEA products carried the label of the Swedish Furniture Research Institute, a byword for good quality and design.

The IKEA self-service method of selling was largely unknown in the furniture and home furnishing retail trades at the time. Customers were invited to walk around the whole store and select items by themselves. There were information desks, but no sales assistants to persuade customers to buy. In IKEA's early days, customers had to pay for their purchases in cash to improve the finances of the firm. The customer was given a docket and collected the flat-pack, pre-packed merchandise at the delivery dock. There was no home delivery service; the customer had to provide his or her own transport. Car racks could be bought, and later self-drive vans could be rented.

The IKEA formula was an instant success, particularly for kitchen and children's furniture. Further stores were opened in Sweden in 1966 and 1967. In 1969 a store was opened in Denmark, followed by a store in Switzerland in 1973, to test the European market, and another in Germany in 1974. By 1974 there were ten IKEA stores in five European countries. The stores employed a total of 1,500 persons, and sales in 1974 were SKr616 million. Sweden was the main market, with 75% of total sales.

The years 1975–1990 saw a remarkable establishment of IKEA stores beyond Sweden. In 1973 Kamprad moved to Copenhagen, Denmark, a more central location for European expansion. The first major expansion was in Germany. After the first store in 1974, ten more were opened by 1980, more than were in operation in Sweden, and by 1990 there were 17 stores in Western Germany. Elsewhere in Europe, stores were opened in Austria in 1977, the Netherlands in 1979, France in 1981, Belgium in 1984, the United Kingdom in 1987, and Italy in 1989. By 1990 there were 60 IKEA stores in western European countries compared with the 10 stores in 5 countries in 1974–1975.

This rapid expansion was not confined to Europe. A first store was opened in Canada in 1976, followed by six further stores up to 1982. These stores were initially operated by companies outside the IKEA Group. Later the IKEA group bought the Canadian operations. In IKEA stores operated by outside companies, capital investment and management were the responsibility of local entrepreneurs. Such stores were opened in Australia in 1975, Hong Kong in 1975, Singapore in 1978, the Canary Islands in 1980, Iceland in 1981, Saudi Arabia in 1983, Kuwait in 1984, and the United Arab Emirates in 1991.

The IKEA Group's most challenging expansion, however, started in 1985 when a store of 15,700 square meters was opened in the United States in Philadelphia, Pennsylvania. Could a European retail concept, however enterprising in its methods and outlook, succeed in the U.S. market? The answer was yes. If anything, the American consumer was more receptive to innovative ideas and merchandise than many of the more conservative European customers. The experience of the Canadian stores was useful. By 1991 there were seven stores operating in the United States, including one in California and two in New York.

A second challenge was taken up in 1990 when IKEA stores were opened in eastern Europe. A store was opened in Budapest in a joint venture with a Hungarian firm, Butorker, and in the same year a small store was opened in Warsaw, Poland. The opening of a store in the former Soviet Union, now known as the Commonwealth of Independent States, is under discussion. These exploratory moves into eastern Europe are, however, still at a very early stage. This rapid expansion in a decade and a half changed the pattern of sales. Whereas in 1975 the Scandinavian markets represented around 85% of total sales, by 1990 this proportion had dropped to just over 26%. Sales in Germany had risen to more than 27% of the total. The rest of Europe contributed 34% of sales, and the rest of the world just over 12%.

Expansion also presented supply problems. The component parts had to be made to strict specifications. The originality of the Kamprad approach was to replace the craftsman philosophy with an engineering philosophy. In the early years of growth, while using Sweden, Denmark, and Finland as the main sources of supply (70%), the IKEA group saw the advantages of supplies from eastern European countries. Contracts were signed with state-controlled and other factories in East Germany, Poland, and Yugoslavia for the supply of furniture components. Since payment was made in "hard" currency, strict specifications could be enforced and the dates of payment could be flexible, thus improving IKEA's cash flow. In the 1970s, some 20 to 25% of total supplies came from eastern Europe. By 1990 the proportion had fallen to around 15%, but

it was part of a much larger total. With the geographical expansion of IKEA stores, other sources of supply were found. By 1990 the share of Scandinavian manufacturers in the total purchases of IKEA products had fallen to 45%, while the share of the rest of western Europe was 30%. The share of the Far East and other areas, 10%, had become more important. In 1990, there were around 1,500 suppliers in 45 different countries, presenting a formidable problem of planning and logistics.

In the IKEA group there are four main interlocking functions. The first, Product Range and Development, is primarily carried out by IKEA of Sweden AB. New or improved products are an essential part of the success of the firm. This work is undertaken by separate product groups within IKEA of Sweden: for example, living-room furniture, kitchen and bathroom furniture, carpets and textiles, lighting, and glassware and ceramics. Second, Purchasing is conducted by agents who are responsible for placing orders to the specifications laid down by IKEA of Sweden. Third, the Distribution Service, undertakes the transport and distribution of the finished products to twelve regional distribution centers and stores throughout the world. Finally, Retailing, carried out by retailing companies operating under the same retail concept, ensures that selling methods and customer service are of the same standards in all stores. In addition there are financial, real estate, legal, and personnel operations.

The IKEA concept of specialized component production and selling its flat-pack finished products in large out-of-town locations with low occupancy costs, at 3–4% of sales, as well as self-selection and practically no delivery, leading to low personnel costs of 7 to 8%, combine, in the words of Ingvar Kamprad, "to offer a wide range of home furnishing items of good design and function at prices so low that the majority of people can afford to buy them."

Another factor in the Group's success has been its effective, and at times unusual, advertising and sales promotion campaigns in all countries of operation. The 20 to 35-year-old customers are targeted, and the high quality of modern Swedish design is emphasized. The IKEA catalogues have played a primary role in advertising success. The catalogues are attractive and easy to use, emphasizing quality of design and the efficiency of IKEA products. Before the opening of a new store, every household in a wide area receives a copy. Although direct mail-order sales represent less than 10% of total sales and the catalogs do not offer the whole IKEA range, they are a key factor in attracting customers to the stores.

The IKEA advertisements are unusual in their contradiction of the traditional image of the Swedish as conservative and rather serious. In France, for example, one slogan used was "Ils sont fous ces Suédois"; in Germany, the "unmögliche Möbelhaus aus Schweden"; in the United Kingdom "the mad Swedes are coming". In the United States, advertising campaigns have been even more outrageous. Almost every advertisement includes a reindeer, leaving no doubt as to the origin of the campaign. This combination of off-beat advertising and well-designed merchandise has had a very effective impact on the target group of customers.

In 1990 there were 86 IKEA stores in 21 different countries. The total selling space, excluding central and regional warehouses, was around 1,220,000 square meters. The group estimated that the stores were visited by around 78 million persons in 1990. In the last decade, the number of stores has more than doubled and employment has risen from 4,500 to nearly 17,000 in 1990.

There are two possible causes for concern in the future. The first concerns the market. Saturation point in the number of stores may have been reached already in some countries, for example Sweden, Germany, Belgium, and the Netherlands. In other developed countries, expansion is still possible, but demand is linked to trends in the birth rate, in new housing starts, and in the age structure of the population. These factors are less important in other parts of the world, but testing of those markets has hardly begun.

Secondly, there is the complex question of the group's future finances. Ingvar Kamprad has said that he will be satisfied if his idea is sufficiently successful to provide him with "bread, schnapps and crayfish." So far, all profits—new investments are reported to have been some 15% of sales—have been ploughed back into the firm. To avoid problems of outside shareholders and succession, in the 1970s Kamprad donated the IKEA Group to a charitable foundation in the Netherlands. If expansion is to continue and IKEA is to keep ahead of the growing number of direct competitors, such as Habitat in the United Kingdom and France and Interio in Switzerland, other methods of finance will have to be found in the future.

—James B. Jefferys

ISETAN

ISETAN COMPANY LIMITED

14-1, Shinjuku 3-chome
Shinjuku-ku, Tokyo 160
Japan
(03) 3352-1111
Fax: (03) 3225-2464

Public Company
Incorporated: 1930
Employees: 5,602
Sales: ¥430.95 billion (US$3.45 billion)
Stock Exchange: Tokyo Niigata

Isetan is one of Japan's leading department store companies, particularly noted for its merchandising strength in the area of men's and women's high-fashion apparel. It has compensated for its comparatively late entry into the field by innovation and niche-building, establishing itself as a fashion leader through sophisticated consumer research and extensive introduction of merchandise from abroad, both well-known designer labels and brands developed exclusively for Isetan. While its department store operations in Japan remain the nucleus of its business, the company is rapidly diversifying its interests and steadily building up its overseas presence.

In common with other top Japanese department stores, Isetan traces its origins back to a kimono shop. Whereas the likes of Mitsukoshi, Daimaru, and Takashimaya have histories going back hundreds of years, Isetan's story began in 1886, with the opening of the Iseya Tanji Drapery in Tokyo's Kanda district, then a bustling center of commerce located near the Kanda river. Its founder, Tanji Kosuge, was born Tanji Nowatari in 1859. At the age of 12 he was apprenticed to the Isesho Drapery in Kanda. By the age of 20 Tanji had risen to the position of *banto,* or head clerk. In 1881 he married Hanako Kosuge, the daughter of one of Isesho's best customers, a local rice merchant, and took the surname Kosuge. Five years later, with the blessing of his employer, Tanji Kosuge went into business for himself.

Kanda was one of the most densely populated areas of the city, and the new shop's location near a busy intersection guaranteed it a steady stream of business. Because of the shop's proximity to several well-known geisha districts, Kosuge's customers included many geisha who needed to maintain a well-stocked wardrobe of fine kimonos. He created his own range of original products, and the Iseya Tanji Drapery came to be associated with exquisite obi—the belt used to tie the kimono—and quality design.

Tanji Kosuge began expanding the business in various ways. He experimented with staying open at night, he sent out salesmen with samples of the stores' original designs to visit the homes of customers, he introduced seasonal bargain sales, he began buying out other kimono stores, and in 1899, as business prospered, he enlarged the Kanda store. So successful had he been that by the turn of the century, the Iseya Tanji Drapery had entered the ranks of Tokyo's top five dry-goods stores.

Nevertheless, there was still a big gap between Kosuge's store and those of its long-established rivals. While the older stores were already thinking of moving to a department store format, complete with display cabinets for their products and a wider variety of merchandise, Kosuge was still concentrating on building up the kimono business.

In an effort to bring the store's image more in line with those of its rivals, in 1907 he simplified the store's name to Isetan Drapery, combining the first two syllables of Iseya with the first syllable of Tanji. Three years later he considered building a department store in Tokyo's Hibiya district but shelved the idea as premature. At his death in 1916, Isetan was well-established as a kimono store, but had yet to make the switch to a department store.

Kosuge was succeeded by his son-in-law, Gihei Takahashi. Takahashi had married Tanji Kosuge's eldest daughter in 1908, taking the family name of Kosuge. Upon his father-in-law's death, he took the name Tanji as well.

Takahashi had been working for another kimono store when he first came to the attention of Isetan in 1908. One day he bought 20 obi for his store at a 10% discount from an Isetan salesman, who assured him that the obi were not being sold at the Isetan store. Walking past Isetan some days later, he discovered that the same obi were being sold, and for a 20% discount. Going in to complain, he handled himself so well that he got a further discount. He impressed the man he dealt with—Tanji Kosuge's younger brother—as both a good businessman and a potential husband for Tanji's eldest daughter. Takahashi joined Isetan shortly afterward and was married within six months.

A man who read widely, Takahashi had many ideas about retailing. As Tanji Kosuge II, he began to lay the groundwork for Isetan's transformation from a kimono shop to a department store. His first move was to place Isetan on a more businesslike footing by creating the Isetan Partnership to run the store in 1917. It was, however, a catastrophic event six years later that would really move Isetan's plans forward.

The Great Kanto Earthquake of September 1, 1923, killed some 130,000 people. The Kanda store burned to the ground, along with much of the rest of Kanda. The necessity of rebuilding the Kanda store provided Kosuge with the opportunity to introduce a department store format. When Isetan reopened in 1924 it was selling not only kimono but also children's clothes, toys, umbrellas, cosmetics, stationery, household goods, and food. If the store had changed, so had Kanda, and it gradually became apparent that Kanda was no longer the prime site it once had been.

There were three reasons for this. First, within Kanda, the devastation caused by the earthquake and subsequent conflagration resulted in a changed street configuration, and Isetan no longer was situated near the corner of a busy intersection. Second, transportation was improving steadily, making the public more mobile. As the subway system was extended, Ginza and Nihonbashi, where Tokyo's leading department stores were located, became more accessible. With the completion of the Yamanote Line, a surface railway that circles Tokyo, new shopping and recreational areas grew up around stations such as Shibuya, Shinjuku, and Ikebukuro. Third, and in many ways most far-reaching, as a result of the Great Kanto Earthquake the center of the population moved away from the devastated areas in central and eastern Tokyo to the suburbs in the west.

By 1928 it was clear that there was no future for Isetan in Kanda. It abandoned a project to build a new eight-story department store there, although four stories of the building had been completed, and began looking for an alternative site. Hibiya, in downtown Tokyo, was considered once more, but after Tanji Kosuge had spent three days looking at the proposed site, he decided that there would not be enough customers and continued the search elsewhere. His eventual choice was Shinjuku, in the west of Tokyo, an area that had begun to develop after the opening of Shinjuku Station in 1875, but which had really taken off after the Great Kanto Earthquake. It was a decision that was to be as important for Shinjuku as it was for Isetan, and the two have grown in tandem ever since.

In 1930, in preparation for its move into the department store business proper, Isetan formed itself into a limited company, Isetan Company Limited, capitalized at ¥500,000. In 1931 it purchased the land on which its new flagship store would stand, adjacent to an existing department store called Hoteiya. Work began on the Isetan building in 1932, and the main building was completed in 1933. It consisted of two floors below ground and seven above, including an auditorium. On its first day of business, it attracted 130,000 customers. Three months later, the old store in Kanda closed.

In 1935 Isetan bought the ailing Hoteiya department store for ¥2 million. This included the building, the land it stood on, and the entire contents of the store. It borrowed ¥3.3 million from the Bank of Japan to pay for the purchase and redevelopment of the store as part of Isetan. A year later, this new addition to Isetan was open for business.

Shinjuku was by then established as one of Tokyo's new city subcenters. It was frequented by middle-class salaried workers and their families, attracted to its shops, cafes, and cinemas. As a new, up-and-coming department store, Isetan fitted in perfectly. A play on a popular catch phrase of the day captures the mood of those times. "Today the Imperial Theatre, tomorrow Mitsukoshi" went the original, linking together these bastions of tradition in the heart of downtown Tokyo. "Today the Moulin Rouge [a new Shinjuku theatre that opened in 1931], tomorrow Isetan," went the other, clearly identifying Isetan as something of a trendsetter, appealing to those who preferred black comedy to traditional Kabuki.

During World War II Isetan remained open for business almost until the end of the war, although its displays grew barer and its sales area gradually shrank to 50% of prewar levels. Escalators and elevators were removed and melted down for the war effort in 1943. That year, Isetan was asked by the Imperial Japanese Army to manage a hotel and store taken over by the Japanese in Sumatra, which it did until the end of the war. The Allied fire bomb raids on the night of March 10, 1945 devastated large areas of Tokyo, reducing the old Kanda

store to ashes, but Isetan's flagship store remained standing. Quick action that night on the part of employees put out a fire that threatened to rage out of control; neighboring buildings, however, were not so lucky.

According to one of his sons, Tanji Kosuge shrugged off the despondent comments of his employees on August 15, 1945, the day the Japanese emperor announced Japan's surrender. "What are you saying? The store's still standing, isn't it? You've got nothing to worry about. I'm going back to work tomorrow." Kosuge's wish for a quick return to business as usual was not fulfilled for several years, however. Apart from the problem of the lack of merchandise, the Allied occupation authorities had taken a liking to the building, and in 1945 requisitioned it for Allied use from the third floor up. Not until the end of the occupation, in 1952, would Isetan have the building to itself again.

The department store business after World War II saw a much greater emphasis on Western-style clothing. In the years immediately following the war, women made do with what they had—blouses and Japanese-style pantaloons called *monpei*—but from the late 1940s there was a growing fashion-consciousness, initially inspired by the "military look" sported by women in the Allied occupation forces. In 1951 Isetan sponsored Tokyo's first postwar fashion show—Tokyo Fashion 51—which presaged a boom in fashion shows, modeling, and modeling schools.

In 1956 Isetan underwent its first major postwar extension. Three new buildings were added, increasing the sales area by 25%. The purpose was not simply to increase Isetan's size; it was to reaffirm Isetan's image as a fashion leader. From this period Isetan introduced modern merchandising techniques, dividing up customers very specifically on the basis of age, sex, taste, and spending power. The new-look Isetan—it also changed its logo—celebrated the completion of its refurbishment with a grand opening in October 1957.

In 1960 Tanji Kosuge II stepped down as president and was succeeded by his eldest son, Toshio, who took the name Tanji upon his father's death two years later. The new president was a graduate of Keio University who had joined Mitsui Trading Company in 1941, before being drafted into the Imperial Japanese Army in 1942. After the war he had spent three years at Showa Textile Company before joining Isetan as a director in 1948.

Under Tanji Kosuge III, Isetan maintained its reputation for innovation during the 1960s. Anticipating the growth in private car ownership, it opened a parking garage adjacent to the store in 1960, becoming the first Japanese department store to have its own car park. In 1963 it introduced designer brands to the store with a Pierre Balmain haute couture salon, and in 1964 took the initiative in rationalizing women's clothing sizes, developing a system that has since been utilized by all Japanese department stores. In 1968 it opened a new annex devoted entirely to menswear. Many were opposed to the move, but Kosuge believed that by removing all men's clothes from the main building he could both create space for more women's and children's clothing and target the different categories of male shoppers more effectively in a building designed for that purpose. "Bring him along, too," said the publicity as Isetan sought to reach out to male shoppers through wives, girlfriends, sisters, and daughters who already shopped regularly at Isetan.

By the late 1960s Isetan had established itself as the number-one fashion merchandiser in Japan and recorded Japan's highest sales per month for a single store. In a move to strengthen its fashion merchandising capability further, in 1967 it established the Isetan Research Institute Company, Ltd., a think tank for collecting and analyzing information about the latest fashion, industrial, and consumer trends. The institute is an important source of ideas for Isetan's new-product development. A year later, it opened its first overseas representative office, in Paris, which, along with other offices opened subsequently, has also acted as a source of information on fashion trends.

From the 1970s Isetan began a period of expansion, opening new stores both at home and overseas. Isetan's first overseas store opened in Singapore in 1972, followed by a store in Hong Kong a year later. The increase in stores continued in the 1980s, accompanied by the growing diversification of Isetan's business activities in the areas of fashion, food, leisure, and finance.

Subsidiaries set up in these areas in the 1980s include J.F. Corporation, which supplies Isetan with originally developed brands and also creates brands for specialty stores around the country; Prio Company, Ltd., an importer-wholesaler of quality women's wear; Queens Isetan Co., Ltd., a gourmet foods store; Isetan Travel Service Company, Ltd., which arranges package tours to domestic and overseas destinations; and Isetan Finance Company, Ltd., which is responsible for a wide range of nonbanking financial operations including the credit management of Isetan's charge card, the I-Card, the use of which was extended in 1988 to all shoppers at Isetan, as well as cashing, leasing, and loan services.

Isetan also runs a chain of supermarkets through Queens Isetan Co., Ltd.; operates a nationwide restaurant chain of approximately 100 outlets through Isetan Petit Monde Company, Ltd., started in 1957; and imports and sells cars through Isetan Motors Company, Ltd., started in 1970.

Under Kuniyasu Kosuge, who succeeded his father, Tanji Kosuge III, in 1984, the company has continued to grow. A graduate of Keio University who subsequently studied in the United States, Kosuge worked for Mitsubishi Bank for seven years, including a stint in London, before joining Isetan as a director in 1979. His overseas experience is useful as he presides over a growing international network of companies.

In Europe, Isetan operates stores in London, established in 1988, and Vienna, opened in 1990, which together with the company's representative offices in Paris, Milan, and Barcelona have been strengthening their business capabilities, including the procurement of merchandise through licensing agreements, product development projects, and information gathering. In 1988 Isetan established an international finance company in Amsterdam to support its overseas business activities. It opened a store in Barcelona in October 1991.

In Asia, with existing stores in Singapore, Hong Kong, and Malaysia, Isetan is set to add to its network of stores in Associ-ation of South East Asian Nations (ASEAN) countries with the opening of a store in Bangkok, Thailand, at the beginning of 1992. The Bangkok store will be Isetan's biggest in the region.

Active in the United States since the opening of a representative office in New York in 1979, Isetan is moving into the U.S. market with more purpose since it entered into a joint venture with Barneys, Inc. of New York, an upscale retailer of clothing and sundry goods, in 1989. Isetan is looking to strengthen its merchandising and increase its expertise in specialty-store management through the joint venture, while helping Barneys to open new stores across the United States. The tie-up has also resulted in the opening of a branch of Barneys in Tokyo in November 1990. The Shinjuku store became the largest joint venture between a Japanese and a U.S. retailer, and Isetan has plans to open Barneys outlets in other Japanese cities.

Other plans for Japan included the opening of a department store at Kyoto Station as part of the redevelopment of the station area. A joint venture between Isetan and the West Japan Railway Corporation, it would be Isetan's first department store in western Japan and one of the largest department stores in the region. Isetan was also looking to open a store after 1995 in the Odaiba area of Tokyo as part of the Tokyo Bay development scheme. This will also be a joint venture, with the Sumitomo group.

Apart from joint ventures, Isetan is planning to open several new stores on its own, based on the store it opened in 1990 as part of the urban redevelopment project carried out in Sagamihara City in the outskirts of Tokyo, where the store is designed to be an integral part of the community. Shinjuku, however, remains the hub of operations, and the faith of Tanji Kosuge in its potential has been rewarded by the relocation to Shinjuku of the massive apparatus of the Tokyo metropolitan government.

Principal Subsidiaries: Isetan Petit Monde Company, Ltd.; Queens Isetan Co., Ltd.; Mammina Company, Ltd. (90%); Century Trading Company (80%); Isetan Clean System; Atelier Francais; Isetan Research Institute; Isetan Data Center; Isetan Motors; Isetan Clover Circle; Isetan Sports Club; J.F. Corporation; Isetan Travel Service, Inc.; Isetan Finance Company, Ltd.; The Box; Barneys Japan; Niigata Isetan (80%); Prio (80%); Shizuoka Isetan (77%); Isetan International Finance B.V. (Netherlands); Isetan of Japan Ltd. (Hong Kong); Isetan (Thailand) Company, Ltd. (49%); Isetan (United Kingdom) Ltd.; Isetan of America Inc.; Isetan (Singapore) Ltd. (58.7%); Superio Company, Ltd. (Hong Kong); Barneys America Inc. (35%).

Further Reading: Katayama, Mataichiro, *Isetan 100 nen no shoho,* Tokyo, Hyogensha, 1983; *Isetan hyakunenshi,* Tokyo, Isetan, 1990.

—Jonathan Lloyd-Owen

ITO-YOKADO CO., LTD.

4-1-4 Shiba-Koen
Minato-ku
Tokyo 105
Japan
(3) 459 2111
Fax: (3) 434 8375

Public Company
Incorporated: 1958 as Yokado Co., Ltd.
Employees: 31,110
Sales: ¥1.83 trillion (US$14.66 billion)
Stock Exchanges: Tokyo Luxembourg Paris

Ito-Yokado Co., Ltd. (Ito-Yokado) and its subsidiaries represent the second-largest supermarket chain in Japan in terms of sales. The company is, however, by far the largest in terms of earnings, ahead of its closest rivals The Daiei, Inc. and The Seiyu, Ltd. The stores are concentrated in the Kanto region of Japan which includes the cities of Tokyo, Yokohama, and Kawasaki. Ito-Yokado holds a majority stake in 7-Eleven Japan, Japan's largest convenience store chain, and the restaurant chain Denny's Japan. These two companies, along with 26 other subsidiaries and affiliated companies, are known as the Ito-Yokado Group, with activities ranging from the core business of supermarket retailing to real estate and food processing. The group has strong connections with Western retailers; both Denny's Japan and 7-Eleven Japan are Japanese versions of major U.S. chains. In March 1991, Ito-Yokado acquired a majority stake in Southland Corporation, the U.S.-based operator of the worldwide 7-Eleven convenience store chain.

Ito-Yokado developed from a subsidiary of Yokado Clothing Store—Yokado Yohin-ten in Japanese—established by Binyu Yoshikawa in 1920. The store was located in the Asakusa area of Tokyo and its main customers were prosperous members of the emerging Japanese middle class. Japan was in a period of high economic growth following its military defeat of China and Russia in conflicts in 1897 and 1904. Western goods such as home appliances and suits were in high demand, and stores specializing in such goods flourished. By 1930, Yoshikawa's business had expanded to include four stores in the Asakusa area, but sales suffered in the late stages of World War II, as rationing of basic goods was introduced by Japan's military government. The public had very little money to spend on nonessential goods and the stores were forced to close due to bombing raids by the U.S. air force in the first half of 1945.

The original store in Asakusa was destroyed in the air raids, and the other stores were badly damaged. Yoshikawa's situation was similar to that of numerous small retailers in postwar Tokyo and, like them, he began the painful task of rebuilding his business. He chose to relocate to the Kitasenju part of Tokyo, not far from Asakusa. Like his old stores, the new store sold goods imported from the West, such as clothes and cosmetics, but it also stocked household goods.

During the 1950s the Japanese economy was growing rapidly, fueled by exports and growing consumer demand. Yoshikawa gave his nephew Masatoshi Ito's parents control of the Yokado store in 1958, and they established Yokado Co., Ltd. It was here that the history of Ito–Yokado really began. Ito was determined to make his mark on the company. In 1961, at the age of 39, Ito traveled to the United States and Europe to gather information on Western retailing methods. This flow of information from the West to Japan was occurring in most sectors of the Japanese business world at the time. Ito studied the major U.S. retailing chains and was convinced that the future of consumer goods retailing in Japan lay in the establishment of such chains. Following his return to Japan, Ito began to take an active role in the family business. In October of 1961 a second Yokado store was opened in the Tokyo region of Akabane, and this came about largely as a result of Ito's efforts. He succeeded in raising the capital to open another store in 1963 and two more in 1964. The stores were based on large U.S. retail outlets, and stocked food as well as clothes and household goods. In 1965, to avoid confusion with the original Yokado stores, the name was changed from Yokado Co., Ltd. to Ito-Yokado Co., Ltd., with Ito as president. He continued his policy of making the company a major supermarket chain by opening nine new Ito-Yokado stores between 1965 and 1970. They included a supermarket in Noda, Chiba prefecture, the first store outside Tokyo.

By the early 1970s Ito-Yokado was a medium-sized but fast-growing supermarket chain in Tokyo, and in 1972 it obtained a listing on the Second Section of the Tokyo Stock Exchange. Also in this year the corporate logo, which became a familiar sight all over Japan, was conceived. It consists of a white dove on a background of red and blue. Japan's economy, led by consumer spending, was booming, and Ito wished to expand his company's business into other areas. In 1972 the restaurant chain Famil was established with the opening of a family diner in Tokyo. Like the Ito-Yokado supermarkets, the Famil chain was aimed at the middle-class family market. The company's diversification into the restaurant business continued in the following year when, under license from the U.S. chain Denny's, Denny's Japan Co. Ltd. was formed. The plan was to open restaurants with a visible Western brand name in the Tokyo suburbs by the side of major roads. The first store, in Tokyo, was highly successful, and Denny's restaurants were soon opening up all over Japan. In 1973 Ito-Yokado was listed on the First Section of the Tokyo Stock Exchange, and the company acquired a stake in the Fukushima-based supermarket chain Benimaru Co. Ltd. A joint-venture company, York-Benimaru, was established. Ito-Yokado contributed its knowledge of chain retailing as well as the familiar Ito-Yokado company logo. Established in 1948, the Benimaru chain of supermarkets thus became an affiliate of Ito-Yokado, and aided in the latter company's plans for nationwide expansion.

In 1973 under license from the Dallas-based Southland Corporation, Ito-Yokado established 7-Eleven Japan, with a majority shareholding retained by Ito-Yokado. At the time 7-Eleven was the leading convenience-store franchise in the United States, and Ito was determined to establish his company's dominance in the Japanese market with the aid of the 7-Eleven brand name. The stores were extremely successful and were opened at the rate of about a hundred a year, initially in the Kanto region and subsequently all over Japan. Like the Denny's restaurants, Ito-Yokado's 7-Eleven stores were mainly located in suburban regions near major roads.

In the middle to late 1970s Japanese consumers were becoming increasingly concerned about the quality of the goods they bought, as well as the cost. Young Japanese consumers, notably women, were becoming increasingly fashion-conscious and discerning in shopping. In 1978 Ito-Yokado established Mary Ann Co. Ltd., a chain store specializing in fashionable women's clothing, and the stores became boutiques within shopping centers. The expansion of the Ito-Yokado stores continued. The stores became known as "superstores" because of their large size and abundant floor space. They began to stock such goods as electrical appliances and furniture, and many of them were multilevel. In the 1970s Ito-Yokado opened more than 70 new flagship (Ito-Yokado) stores, with the expansion mainly occurring in the prefectures of Tokyo, Kanagawa, and Chiba.

In 1978 Ito-Yokado increased its penetration of the retail sector in Kanagawa by its purchase of Daikuma Co. Ltd., a Kanagawa-based chain specializing in discount retailing. The stores sold everything from clothes to television sets in warehouse-like buildings. The Ito-Yokado logo was not incorporated into these stores. In 1978 Ito-Yokado joined forces with Japan's most prestigious department-store chain, Matsuzakaya Co. Ltd., to establish a department store in Hokkaido, Japan's northernmost island. The store is 90%-owned by Ito-Yokado and is called York-Matsuzakaya. This venture highlighted the company's aim to expand into every sector of retailing in Japan. In 1981 Steps Co. Ltd., a chain of menswear stores, was established to complement the existing Mary Ann chain. That same year, 7-Eleven Japan was listed on the First Section of the Tokyo Stock Exchange. By 1982 a computerized point-of-sale (POS) stock monitoring system was introduced throughout the chain. The system speeds up the checkout process and also enables information such as the time of purchase and type of customer to be recorded. The information is sent to the mainframe computer at 7-Eleven Japan's headquarters, which then returns information to the individual store to aid in ordering decisions. The presence of a bar code on all products sold and a scanner capable of identifying the code made the system possible. With the high rate of stock turnover and slim profit margins on sales, this became a vital ingredient in the chain's success. POS systems were introduced into all Ito-Yokado stores by 1985.

In 1984 Ito-Yokado made further inroads into the department-store business in Japan with the establishment of Robinson's Japan Co. Ltd., a wholly owned subsidiary of Ito-Yokado. Although the name suggests foreign influence, the concept was conceived by Ito-Yokado. The first store opened in 1985 in Kasukabe, Saitama prefecture, near Tokyo, and sold a range of luxury goods in a relaxed atmosphere, contrasting with the more frantic pace of the Ito-Yokado superstores. In 1990 a second Robinson's store was opened in Utsunomiya, Tochigi prefecture. Ito-Yokado entered the sporting goods market with the establishment of Oshman's Japan Co. Ltd. This venture has only opened two stores, both of them in Tokyo. By 1986 the Ito-Yokado chain was well established in the Kanto region as one of the leading retail chains. This was also true in the northern Japanese island of Hokkaido, and northern Honshu. However, the company had yet to open a store in Japan's second-largest metropolitan area, the Kansai plain. In 1986 Ito-Yokado's first store in Kansai opened in Osaka, but as of 1991 it was the only Ito-Yokado store in the region. This market represents a challenge for Ito-Yokado for the 1990s.

The company, with Masatoshi Ito still at the helm, began expansion overseas in 1989 with the opening of a liaison office in Seattle, Washington. In the same year 7-Eleven Japan acquired the 58 branches of 7-Eleven in Hawaii, at the request of owners Southland Corporation. It was apparent that Southland was in financial difficulty, and—according to 7-Eleven Japan's president, Toshifumi Suzuki—was not responding to the changing U.S. retail market. In reorganizing the stores in Hawaii, Suzuki noticed that the amount of inventory present at a given time was three times the average for his stores in Japan. In addition the stores in Japan had an average floor space of 100 square meters and daily sales of ¥650,000. The equivalent figures for the stores in Hawaii were 170 square meters and ¥400,000. Suzuki realized that tight inventory control was the key to success, and in 1991 Ito-Yokado acquired a 70% stake in Southland Corporation, with the full cooperation of the latter firm's management. One of the prerequisites put forward by Ito-Yokado before the purchase was that Southland's management would have to be prepared to listen and learn from 7-Eleven Japan. This represents a major purchase for Ito-Yokado and will push the group's annual sales past the ¥4 trillion mark, the largest for a Japanese-owned retail group.

Ito-Yokado's future plans include expansion of all the retail chains, notably in the Kansai region, and the increased use of computer systems in the control and monitoring of sales. This is an area in which Ito-Yokado has gained a competitive advantage. Yasuhisa Ito is currently a director in Ito-Yokado, but it remains to be seen whether or not he will follow in his father's footsteps at the helm of the company.

Principal Subsidiaries: Marudai Co. Ltd. (80%); Maruki Tobishima Co. Ltd. (80%); Robinson's Japan Co. Ltd.; York Matsuzakaya Co. Ltd. (90%); York Mart Co. Ltd.; York Benimaru Co. Ltd. (28%); Daikuma Co. Ltd. (82%); Mary Ann Co. Ltd.; Oshman's Japan Co. Ltd. (90%); Steps Co. Ltd. (15%); 7-Eleven Japan (50.3%); Denny's Japan Co. Ltd. (51%); Famil Co. Ltd. (96%); York Bussan Co. Ltd.; Union Lease Co. Ltd. (97%); York Keibi Co. Ltd.; Southland Corporation (U.S.A., 70%).

—Dylan Tanner

JCPenney

J.C. PENNEY COMPANY, INC.

14841 North Dallas Parkway
Dallas, Texas 75240
U.S.A.
(214) 591-1000
Fax: (214) 591-1455

Public Company
Incorporated: 1913
Employees: 190,000
Sales: $17.40 billion
Stock Exchanges: New York Brussels Antwerp

J.C. Penney is the fourth-largest retailer in the United States. The company boomed in its early days in western mining towns because it offered all goods at "one fair price" and brought fashionable goods from the East to remote towns. The company struggled through the 1970s, as upstart companies like Wal-Mart Inc. began selling goods at discount prices and long-time rivals like Sears, Roebuck and Co. gave Penney tough competition in the hardware and appliance departments. A massive reorganization of the company from a mass marketer into a fashion-oriented national department store during the 1980s, along with the relocation of its corporate headquarters from New York to less expensive Dallas, Texas, put Penney in a strong position to compete in the tough retailing climate of the 1990s.

James Cash Penney started his first retail store in 1902 in Kemmerer, Wyoming, a small mining town. He was 26 years old and had grown up on a farm near Hamilton, Missouri. Two years after graduating from high school, Penney went to work for a Hamilton retailer, J.M. Hale. Penney's health suffered while he was in the Midwest, and his doctor advised him to move to the cooler climate of Colorado. After several ups and down in Longmont, Colorado, Penney started working for the Golden Rule Mercantile Company, a dry-goods retailer founded by T.M. Callahan. Callahan soon promoted young Penney to his Evanston, Wyoming, store to work with one of his partners, Guy Johnson. Penney put in three years as a salesman, and Callahan and Johnson decided to make him a manager and partner. Penney chose to open a store in Kemmerer because many of his Evanston customers lived in that mining town.

The local banker cautioned Penney against opening a "cash only" store, as three others had failed in Kemmerer, but Penney did not want to accept mining company scrip or credit.

Penney invested his whole savings—$500—and had to borrow $1,500 to be the third partner, with Callahan and Johnson, in the Kemmerer store.

Penney's instinct proved correct; the store had $28,898 in sales its first year. In 1907 Callahan and Johnson dissolved their partnership, and Penney bought them out, taking over three stores. He implemented the principles of his former partners, as he expanded the chain throughout the Rocky Mountains by allowing his store managers to buy a one-third partnership in new stores provided they had trained a salesperson to take their place as manager at the old store. He established a central buying and accounting office in Salt Lake City, Utah, in 1909, and had 34 stores with more than $2 million in sales by 1912. In 1913, he incorporated the company as J.C. Penney Company, Inc. and moved the corporate headquarters to New York City to be closer to manufacturers and suppliers. By 1915 the company had 83 stores, and the next year ventured east of the Mississippi River for the first time with stores in Wausau and Watertown, Wisconsin.

Penney became chairman of the board in 1917, when the company had 175 stores, and Earl Sams became president. The company continued to open stores at a fast clip. Private label brands were a major reason for the success of the company. Customers liked them because Penney could control quality and offer the goods at a cheaper price than brand names. They also were good for the company because Penney could control the price better and make a higher profit margin. Belle Isle, Ramona, Honor Brand, and Nation Wide were private label names for piece goods, and Big Mac, Waverly, and Lady Lyke were labels on work shirts, men's caps, and lingerie, respectively.

During the next six years, the company's growth was explosive. In 1925 there were 674 stores boasting sales of $91 million. By 1930 the company 1,452 stores with 25,000 employees. In 1926 the company opened an 18-story office and warehouse building in New York. The 25th anniversary was celebrated in 1927, and founder James Cash Penney declared that the company had a good shot at achieving sales of $1 billion by its 50th anniversary in 1952. The company's managers and executives, who had equity in individual stores they ran or oversaw, traded their ownership for a stake in the company as a whole.

In 1929 the company was listed on the New York Stock Exchange. When the Great Depression hit, the company coped by cutting back its inventory and trying to purchase goods at lower prices so it could pass the price cuts on to customers. The company survived these hard times largely because it had become known for its high quality goods and service, and people turned to J.C. Penney for the basic items they needed. The company's profits even increased during the Depression, and by 1936 sales rose to $250 million, and the number of stores grew to 1,496.

During World War II, the company sold a record number of war bonds through its stores. Materials and merchandise were scarce, yet the company increased its sales to $500 million in 1945. In 1946 Earl Sams was promoted to chairman, with Penney as honorary chairman, and Albert Hughes, a former Utah store manager, was elevated to the presidency. The company—now with 1,602 stores—opened a store in Hampton Village, Missouri, in 1949 in a "drive-in shopping district," a precursor to suburban malls. After only four years as chairman,

Earl Sams died in 1950. In an unusual corporate move, J.C. Penney resumed the chairmanship instead of promoting Albert Hughes. A year before its 50th anniversary, the company reached its goal of $1 billion in sales.

Vice President William Batten conducted a study in 1957; the results indicated the company should adapt to changing consumer spending habits, especially by beginning to sell on credit instead of for cash only. The next year, Hughes became chairman and Batten became president. The company instituted a credit policy and other changes as a result of the study, including the introduction of major appliances, home electronics, furniture, and sporting goods.

In 1962 J.C. Penney, Inc. got into the mail-order business for the first time by buying General Merchandise Company, a Wisconsin firm with a discount store operation as well. J.C. Penney was different from many of its competitors with its late entry into the catalog mail-order business. Other big retailers started in mail-order and then launched into retail stores. J.C. Penney created the Treasury discount stores from the General Merchandise discount operation. The next year, it mailed its first J.C. Penney catalog. In eight states, customers could order from the catalog from inside J.C. Penney stores. A Milwaukee distribution center supplied the catalog goods. The company's first full-line stores, with all the new merchandise lines instituted by President Batten, opened in 1963 in Audubon, New Jersey, and King of Prussia, Pennsylvania. They were prototypes for the Penney stores of the 1960s and 1970s.

The company needed bigger headquarters because it had grown significantly in 38 years; it built a 45-story office in New York in 1964, where the company stayed until its later move to Dallas. Batten became chairman that year, and Ray Jordan became president. Beauty salons, portrait studios, food facilities, and auto service centers were added to full-line stores. Sales topped $3 billion in 1968, and Cecil Wright became president. The company added an Atlanta, Georgia, catalog distribution center in 1969 and purchased Thrift Drug Company.

James Cash Penney died in 1971 at age 95. The same year, the catalog business made a profit for the first time. Jack Jackson became president in 1972, and sales hit $5 billion. The company was able to profit from the fact that disposable income in the U.S. was rising faster than inflation.

The company reached its highest number of stores in 1973, with 2,053 stores, 300 of which were full-line establishments. Donald Seibert was elected chairman of the board and chief executive officer in 1974, and Jackson continued as president. A third catalog distribution center was opened, in Columbus, Ohio, that year. The company offered, and sold, three million shares of common stock in 1975, and Sesame Street joined the Penney's fold by signing an exclusive licensing agreement for children's wear. While the company was riding high on these achievements, the recession of 1974 took its toll. Penney's stock plunged from a high of $51 a share to $17. Earnings dropped from $185.8 million to $125.1 million. Investors saw that low-margin items like appliances were squeezing profits, and that discount and self-service home-center stores were doing a better job than Penney in the hardware business. The advent and strong growth of the specialty apparel store also meant tough competition for Penney. Like other businesses, Penney rebounded and had good growth in 1975, but its executives began to suspect the company needed to be restructured.

Walter Neppl became president in 1976, and the company launched its women's fashion program in five markets, designed to help the company compete against the specialty stores cropping up in all the malls. A fourth catalog distribution center, in Lenexa, Kansas, was added in 1978. By then, sales had grown to $10.8 billion, the women's fashion program was introduced in new markets, and a home furnishings line was added.

As a fifth distribution center was added in 1979, in Reno, Nevada, the catalog service went nationwide. Sales of the service surpassed $1 billion, making the company the second-largest catalog merchandiser in the United States. To continue expanding the credit policies of the company, J.C. Penney began accepting Visa in stores in 1979. The next year, Master-Card was accepted. The company closed the Treasury discount stores in 1980 because they were unprofitable and because the company wanted to focus resources on its Penney stores.

In 1981 when the company's sales totaled $11.9 billion, Penney was the first to sell zero-coupon bonds in domestic public markets. It also reorganized its executive structure around an office of the chairman. Seibert continued as chairman, and Neppl moved to the new vice chairmanship. Kenneth Axelson and William Howell were made executive vice presidents.

With these officers in place, the company launched a massive reorganization, which would transform the company into a national department store from a mass merchant. It would take almost a decade to achieve the goals outlined in the J.C. Penney stores positioning statement, issued in 1982. The company's first order of business was to expand the fashion programs in men's, women's and children's departments, and the company divided its stores into two categories, metropolitan—based in regional shopping centers—and geographic—in smaller communities. Seibert, the chairman, continued to oversee the beginning of the process, and Robert Gill and Howell were made vice chairmen. A sixth catalog distribution center was also opened in 1982, in Manchester, Connecticut. With the $14 million remodeling of its key store in Atlanta, Penney rolled out the prototype of its new store design.

Atlanta was only the beginning. In 1983 Penney announced a $1 billion program for giving its stores facelifts and for rearranging merchandise. Apparel, home furnishings, and leisure lines would be emphasized, and auto service, hard line appliances, paint, hardware, lawn and garden merchandise, and fabrics were all phased out in 1983. Its big mass merchant competitors, Montgomery Ward and Sears, Roebuck and Co., continued in these lines. Retail analysts who followed J.C. Penney called the company's decision difficult but necessary. These lines provided $1.5 billion in annual sales, but were keeping the company from positioning itself as a true department store. In addition low-margin goods were preventing it from making its profit potential. Howell was elected the sixth chairman of the board, a position he held as the 1990s began. Gill stayed on as vice chairman, and David Miller became president of J.C. Penney stores and catalog. Ralph Henderson and Thomas Lyons were named executive vice presidents.

The company also introduced a communications system for broadcasting live and direct to its stores, using satellite transmission, from headquarters. Merchandise buyers from the home office could show store managers, salespeople, and local buyers what merchandise was available, and the local employees could help select what goods would likely sell in their stores. This gave the company the cost-saving advantages of being centralized, but also allowed it to be sensitive to fashion and seasonal preferences in local markets.

Thrift Drug, long dormant since Penney purchased it, scored some big points in 1984, when several major industrial companies became mail-order pharmacy customers. Also in 1984, Penney purchased the First National Bank of Harrington, Delaware and renamed it J.C. Penney National Bank, to assist in credit and financial services. The company began accepting American Express cards as well as Visa, Master-Card, and J.C. Penney credit cards, and the bank was issuing Visa and MasterCards. In 1986, Penney acquired Units, a chain of stores selling contemporary knitwear.

In 1987 the company was well on its way to achieving the goals it set forth in 1982. The company decided to move its corporate headquarters to Dallas, Texas. It was able to cut $60 million from its annual budget because of the move, which cost about 1,250 New Yorkers their jobs. David Miller was elected vice chairman and chief operating officer, and the company began focusing on four major merchandising groups by dividing them into separate business divisions: women's, men's, children's, and home and leisure. The company made itself leaner by discontinuing sales of home electronics, hard sporting goods, and photo equipment in 1987. The space that became available was then used for women's apparel. Also in the late 1980s, Penney opened freestanding furniture stores, called Portfolio, on an experimental basis.

The company's five regional operations were narrowed to four in 1988 to make communication between merchandising divisions and stores easier. The company also launched a leveraged employee stock ownership plan in 1988. With its new emphasis on being a national department store with leaner merchandise lines focusing on apparel, the company had benefited from its prime regional shopping center space, the most such space of all U.S. retailers. Shoppers at regional malls were there to buy clothes and accessories, not washing machines and paint, and Penney was poised to take better advantage of these spending habits. Earnings rebounded as a result, rising from $4.11 per share in 1987 to $5.92 in 1988. Penney was not immune to the intense competition and promotional atmosphere in retailing in late 1989 and early 1990, and earnings slipped slightly to $5.86 per share in 1989 and further to $4.33 in 1990. Lower earnings in the catalog business were dragging down the company's profit margins as a whole during 1990 and 1991.

During the 1980s, the company winnowed the number of stores down to 693 metropolitan and 635 geographic stores. The company closed its unproductive stores or locations that did not perform well as department stores, but continued to open stores in new markets, albeit at a much slower pace than a few decades earlier. Major brand names had become the company's focus, lessening the importance of private labels. Penney had been successful in winning over some big names, such as Levi Strauss & Company, Maidenform Inc., Van Heusen, and Henry Grethel. In the catagory of women's dresses, the company eliminated all private labels. Retail experts called the company's turnaround dramatic and cited Penney as one of a handful of retailers that would grow and prosper in the 1990s.

Principal Subsidiaries: Thrift Drug Stores; J.C. Penney Financial Services; J.C. Penney National Bank; J.C. Penney Realty Inc.; Units; Portfolio.

Further Reading: "J.C. Penney Co.: Background on the J.C. Penney Company, Inc.," J.C. Penney Company corporate typescript, [1988]; "JC Penney Milestones," J.C. Penney Company corporate typescript, [1988].

—Lisa Collins

JOHN LEWIS PARTNERSHIP

JOHN LEWIS PARTNERSHIP PLC

171 Victoria Street
London SW1E 5NN
United Kingdom
(071) 828 1000
Fax: (071) 828 6931

Public Company
Incorporated: 1929 as John Lewis Partnership Ltd.
Employees: 39,800
Sales: £2.16 billion (US $4.04 billion)
Stock Exchange: London

John Lewis Partnership plc is unique among large companies in Britain in that it is run for the benefit of its employees, as the majority of its profits are shared among them. Because of the independence this affords, it is perhaps less hungry for publicity than most companies of its size, and outsiders are often surprised to realize how large and successful it is. The company has two main arms, of almost equal size in turnover. The original business was department stores, of which it has 22, about half named John Lewis and the rest under a variety of local monikers. The other arm is supermarkets, of which it has 94, all trading as Waitrose. That these 116 outlets can generate total sales of over £2 billion is an indication of the size and efficiency of each unit. The group also includes some factories, which supply the stores with textiles and furniture. It has no overseas operations, and within the United Kingdom its business is mainly concentrated in the south of England.

The business is essentially the creation of two men, John Lewis and his son John Spedan Lewis. The former created the first store and laid down its trading policy, the latter expanded it into a group of stores and gave the company its unique constitution. Since then the business has continued to thrive under non-family management, but a grandson of the first John Lewis is currently its chairman, and the ideas of John Spedan Lewis still permeate the whole enterprise.

The company's first small shop opened in 1864, on part of the site that its main store still occupies in Oxford Street, London. This street was already well known for its shops, especially those supplying dresses and dress fabrics to the more prosperous classes. Other shops of this kind which were to become very successful; they included the already well-established Debenham and Freebody and Marshall & Snelgrove.

John Lewis was 28 years old when he opened his first shop. He had come to London from Somerset eight years earlier, having served an apprenticeship in the drapery trade. In London he took a job with another Oxford Street drapery shop, Peter Robinson, and became its silk buyer.

The early days were hard and dreary, as John Lewis told his son, but the shop gradually became a success. At first his store specialized in dress fabrics, sewing threads, ribbons, and other trimmings, but then diversified into readymade clothes, hat, and shoes. He did not advertise, but had a policy of displaying prices clearly, which was not common at that time. He offered a wide assortment, fair dealing, and retained low margins. These principles are still followed in the group's stores today.

By 1875 Lewis was doing well enough to need more space, and he began to take over neighboring properties. With the extra space, he was able to stock more merchandise. From clothing, the store's range broadened to include furniture, carpets, china, and most household goods. During the 1870s Lewis's turnover almost tripled, and it continued growing throughout the 1880s.

By 1895 he was able to rebuild the whole store, which by then had a large corner site with fronts on Oxford Street and Holles Street. The new building occupied six floors, with impressive facades in Renaissance style, and the staff by this time numbered about 150.

In slightly more than 30 years Lewis had created a major department store in one of London's best shopping streets. Even more remarkably, he had done so entirely out of retained profits. In the early years he lived frugally and saved enough of the profits to finance each new step without the need to bring in partners or to turn the business into a joint stock company. The whole store belonged to him alone, and he ran it in a totally autocratic way.

Not until he was 48 did Lewis marry and start to raise a family. His wife was a teacher, 18 years younger than himself, and one of the first women to go to university. She bore him two sons and had a strong influence on them. They received an excellent education and grew up with very different attitudes from those of their father. John Lewis had little education but had strongly individual views; he was an atheist and a liberal and once went to prison for defying a court order in a dispute with his landlord. There was little generosity in his character, and he was a harsh employer. Both sons reacted against this hardness in different ways.

Lewis's sons both entered the business on leaving school and were given a quarter share in it on reaching the age of 21. The younger son, Oswald, soon left the business to study law, provoking a long quarrel with his father, while Spedan became very interested in the business but increasingly critical of his father's methods.

The main issue of contention was staff wages. Spedan was shocked to find that the entire wage bill for 300 employees was a good deal less than the three partners were receiving in interest and profit. To him this was plainly unjust and probably bad for business too. He also discovered inefficiencies in the operation of the store; some departments were trading at a loss, and much of the upper floor space was being wasted. His father, however, angrily rejected all suggestions for change.

John Lewis was over 70 when his sons became partners, but was still full of vigor. Satisfied with the profits the rebuilt store was making, he turned his attention to other things, becoming a member of the London County Council and investing some of his growing fortune in buying a second department store.

The opportunity to do this arose in 1905, when one of his business rivals, Peter Jones, died. Jones had founded another successful store in Sloane Square. Some two miles away from John Lewis's store, it served a different clientele. The business, started in 1877, had grown rapidly and was by this time a limited company. Lewis bought Jones's controlling shareholding and became chairman, but seems not to have taken a close interest in the management of the business.

It proved to be an unrewarding investment. Without the flair of its founder, the store quickly went downhill. Sales dropped by a third, and for six years the company paid no dividends. Eventually, in 1914, Lewis decided to see what his son could do with it. He transferred his shares in the store to Spedan and made him chairman on the condition that he continue working at the Oxford Street store until 5.00 p.m. each day. Spedan jumped at the chance to try out his ideas, even though it meant giving up most of his evenings to the job.

Following a riding accident a few years earlier, Spedan had spent much time either in hospital or at home, using this time to work out his ideas in detail. At Peter Jones he immediately began to implement them. Pay and working conditions were improved, and sales incentives were introduced. In addition committees were set up to encourage new ideas, management functions were redefined, and new managers were hired. John Lewis became alarmed and demanded his shares back, but Spedan refused to relinquish them. As punishment, his father canceled Spedan's share in the partnership, banished him from Oxford Street, and reinstated Oswald there.

This at least enabled Spedan to give all his time to Peter Jones, and business there improved rapidly under his management. By 1919 the company was making a handsome profit, and John Lewis paid a visit of inspection. He said little to his son, relations between them still being cool, but afterwards told his wife, "That place is a great credit to the boy—a very great credit."

Spedan took his reforms a stage further by introducing a profit-sharing scheme. Employees became known as partners and received weekly reports on sales and profits through a new house magazine, which also provided a forum for ideas and complaints. Today, all these practices are standard throughout the group. At the time, they were revolutionary and contrasted sharply with events at Oxford Street, where the employees went on strike for five weeks in 1920, earning the store much bad publicity. Over the next few years, however, there was a general slump in trade, which John Lewis withstood better than Peter Jones. This change in fortunes at last healed the rift between Spedan and his father, who advanced some much-needed money to Peter Jones and restored Spedan's share in the Oxford Street business.

By this time John Lewis was 88 and more or less content to let his sons manage the business. Oswald, however, did not agree with Spedan's radical views, and after two years Spedan persuaded him to give up his share in return for a cash settlement. Oswald was more interested in politics and soon afterwards became a Conservative member of Parliament. From 1926, therefore, Spedan was effectively in control of both businesses and could begin to reorganize the Oxford Street store on the principles established at Peter Jones. All these

were swiftly applied except that the transfer of profits had to be delayed until after John Lewis's death, which occurred in 1928. Spedan was left sole owner of the Oxford Street store as well as majority shareholder in Peter Jones. He immediately converted the former into a public company, John Lewis and Company Ltd. To raise capital for expansion he offered preference shares to the public, but kept all the ordinary shares in his hands. Then he transferred these and his shares in Peter Jones to another company, John Lewis Partnership Ltd., which was to hold them in trust for the employees. The transfer was not a gift, but was made on very generous terms and was irrevocable. Spedan retained control of the trust for an experimental period.

From then on all employees were considered partners in the business. Spedan worked out an elaborate constitution for the partnership to ensure that all partners were represented in the decision-making process, while at the same time giving the board full powers to manage the business on their behalf. It was a unique structure for a business, devised by a very practical idealist. Having laid these foundations, Spedan and his colleagues turned their energies to building up the business. They proved to be a very able team. In the 1920s Spedan had begun to recruit men and women from the universities, the best of whom were given quick promotions to important jobs.

The capital raised by the public offer of 1928—and another in 1935—was used to enlarge and modernize the stores. John Lewis acquired two new buildings in seven years, one on the other side of Holles Street, followed by another part of the island site, which the John Lewis store now fills. At the same time Peter Jones was completely rebuilt in stages so that trading could continue. The new building was ultramodern in style, the first in Britain to make full use of curtain walling of steel and glass.

The company next began to broaden its base by acquiring some provincial stores: two in 1933 and two more the following year. All were in a rundown state, but were gradually made profitable. With six stores in the group there was opportunity for more centralized buying, and a single warehouse was set up in London to service them all.

Most significantly for the future, although the move was not seen that way at the time, the company entered the food trade by buying a chain of ten grocery shops. The business traded as Waitrose, because its first partners were called Waite and Rose, and grew from a single shop in Acton in 1904 to 10 in various parts of London by 1937. Like Sainsbury's, Waitrose was at the quality end of the grocery trade and was a well run business, albeit a small one. As a result of this expansion, the turnover of the John Lewis Partnership grew from £1.25 million in 1928 to £3 million in 1939, and by then the company had some 6,000 partners. In 1940 the business again doubled in size by acquiring 15 more department stores and 4,000 more staff at one stroke.

Encouraged by its success in reviving the four provincial stores it already had, the John Lewis Partnership seized an opportunity to buy all the provincial stores in the Selfridge group. They had never been successful under Selfridge's ownership and were still losing money. Consequently, the John Lewis Partnership was able to buy control of these 15 stores, which had a combined turnover of £3.3 million, for a mere £30,000.

The stores had never traded under Selfridge's name, but had kept their various founders' names and continued to do so when they joined the John Lewis Partnership. Examples are Cole Brothers of Sheffield, Trewin Brothers of Watford and Caleys of Windsor, all still members of the group.

Their purchase, and the extensions to the Oxford Street store, were to prove a life-saver over the next few years. By this time Britain was at war, and later in 1940 the main John Lewis building was almost completely destroyed by fire bombs. Four of the John Lewis Partnership's other stores were also destroyed. Had the business not been as widely scattered as it was, this would have been a calamity; as it was, it was just a bad setback. The loss of selling space was matched by shortages of staff and merchandise, which continued for some years after World War II. These shortages, and tight controls on building supplies, delayed further expansion of the John Lewis Partnership until the 1950s.

Spedan was by then approaching retirement age, and management had largely passed into the hands of the people he had brought into the business. Unlike his father, who never formally retired, Spedan decided to do so at the age of 70, which he reached in 1955. Before retiring he signed over the last of his rights in the business to a corporate trustee. He also wrote two books about the John Lewis Partnership in the hope that its principles would be copied in other businesses. In fact, this has not happened. By 1955 the John Lewis Partnership had acquired the whole of its island site in Oxford Street and began to rebuild its store there. The work had to be done in stages and was finished not until 1960. The new building, still in use, gave the group a bigger selling area in central London than it had ever had before. The other war-damaged stores were also rebuilt at this time, and several more stores were acquired.

The biggest development in the business in the 1950s and 1960s, however, was the rapid expansion of the Waitrose chain. It had more shops than in 1937, but they were all small shops operated on the prewar pattern. In the United States self-service had largely superseded counter service in the 1940s, but retailers in Britain had been unable to experiment with this due to food rationing.

When rationing ended in the early 1950s, Waitrose was among the first British chains to try out self-service. It was also among the first to realize that self-service called for much larger shops. By 1959 it had built seven new-style supermarkets and owned 20 smaller shops. In the 1960s all the smaller shops were replaced by supermarkets. The total reached 50 in 1974 and 70 five years later. The John Lewis Partnership was quicker to embrace the new concept than many traditional food retailers and was rewarded with an increasing share of the retail food trade.

Waitrose became a far more important constituent of the John Lewis Partnership than it had been previously. Its contribution to group turnover jumped from under 15% in the early 1960s to over 40% by 1979. It developed its own trading style and own label products as well as its own distribution network and management hierarchy within the group.

Department stores, however, remained by far the more profitable part of the business, and investment in these continued. In the 1970s three new stores were started under the John Lewis name (in Edinburgh, Milton Keynes, and Brent Cross, London), and since 1980 another seven have been built or acquired from other owners. These new stores are much bigger than was the norm outside London. Some of the older stores have been closed and others rebuilt or enlarged. As a result, the combined turnover of department stores has risen almost as fast in the last decade as that of the Waitrose food shops.

Almost 40,000 people now share the fruits of this business. Profits reached a peak in 1988 and 1989 of £131 million before taxes, of which £47 million were distributed among the employees.

Principal Subsidiaries: John Lewis plc; John Lewis Properties plc; Waitrose Ltd.; Cavendish Textiles Ltd.; Stead McAlpin and Company Ltd.; Herbert Parkinson Ltd.; J.H. Birtwistle and Company Ltd.; John Lewis Overseas Ltd.; Leckford Estate Ltd.

Further Reading: Lewis, John Spedan, *Partnership for All,* London, John Lewis Partnership, 1948; Lewis, John Spedan, *Fairer Shares,* London, Staples Press, 1954; Macpherson, Hugh, ed., *John Spedan Lewis, 1885–1963, Remembered by some of his contemporaries in the centenary year of his birth,* London, John Lewis Partnership, 1985.

—John Swan

JUSCO

JUSCO CO., LTD

1-1 Kandanishiki-cho
Chiyoda-ku
Tokyo 101
Japan
(03) 3296 7894
Fax: (03) 3292 2745

Public Company
Incorporated: 1969
Employees: 11,700
Sales: ¥1.53 trillion (US$2.26 billion)
Stock Exchanges: Tokyo Osaka Nagoya Kyoto Hiroshima
   Fukuoka Niigata Luxembourg Düsseldorf Frankfurt

Since its foundation in 1969, JUSCO has established itself as one of the largest and most profitable retail chains in Japan. JUSCO's sensitivity to the varying needs of its local customer bases, its agility in adapting to changes in the business environment, and its attentiveness to quality of service have helped it to succeed in a highly competitive and strongly regulated market sector. The company's attitude to its customers is expressed in the corporate slogan "Serving the local community through commerce".

The AEON group, as JUSCO and its affiliates have been called since 1989, comprises around 160 companies. In Japan, the group has nearly 170 superstores under its direct control and nearly 560 more superstores and supermarkets managed by regional chains that it owns. At the same time the group has diversified from supermarkets into other retail businesses, including department stores, a wide range of smaller convenience and specialty stores, and a number of restaurant chains. It is also becoming increasingly involved in the provision of leisure, financial, and other services and in commercial property development.

AEON has global ambitions and is known as one of the most internationally-orientated of the Japanese retail groups. The group already has extensive interests outside Japan, including a variety of overseas retail outlets opened through subsidiaries and joint ventures, as well as overseas buying operations in both developed and newly-industrialized countries.

The first self-service stores in Japan opened in the 1950s, and the sector grew rapidly despite the hostility of small shopkeepers. Early supermarkets operated on a local rather than a national scale, however, and were ill-equipped to withstand recessions. Many went out of business during the recession of 1964–1965, and in consequence, the late 1960s were a period of consolidation among the survivors, many of which decided to form alliances or merge. It was against this background that JUSCO was formed in 1969 through the business tie-up of three companies—Okadaya, Futagi, and Shiro—in the Chubu and Kansai areas.

Okadaya Co., Ltd. had the longest pedigree of the three, having been founded in 1758. Up until World War II it was a store trading in clothing, including kimonos. After the war it was restarted by Takuya Okada in a single building, built on a devastated site and staffed by five employees. It grew into a chain of 14 department stores in the Mie prefecture, but was still very much a regional enterprise in the late 1960s, when Okada, in the light of his observations in both Japan and the United States, decided that, for chain stores, size was becoming a critical issue. Larger chains, he realized, could achieve vital economies of scale in both buying and selling, as well as greater administrative efficiency.

Takuya Okada first broached the subject of a merger to Kazuichi Futagi, the president of Futagi Co., Ltd. This company had been established in 1937 as a clothing store. Although the store was destroyed in the war, its proprietor had reopened for business in 1945 with a stock of second-hand clothes. So successful was Futagi in rebuilding his business that by 1968, when the foundation of JUSCO was conceived, he had a chain of 26 stores in the Hyogo prefecture.

Shiro Co., Ltd, was a relative newcomer, a chain of 15 stores in the Osaka prefecture dating back to 1955. Its head, Jiro Inoue, learned of the proposed merger between Okadaya and Futagi and let it be known that he, too, would like to participate.

Headquarters for the new company was set up in February 1969, with capital of ¥150 million provided by the three participants in three equal parts. The actual merger was to follow slightly later, in 1970. The infant company was given the name Japan United Stores Company—soon abbreviated to JUSCO, which became the official name. Futagi was to be chairman and Okada president.

Sadly, the vice-president designate, Inoue, died at the early age of 41, shortly after the establishment of JUSCO. Inoue's firm of Shiro was heavily indebted, so in the first instance only Okadaya and Futagi merged, keeping Shiro as a separate company called Keihan JUSCO. Okada used Okadaya's profits to help put Keihan JUSCO back on its feet, and it became part of JUSCO proper a couple of years later.

The foundation of JUSCO coincided with a retail boom, but that did not mean the climate was entirely hospitable to the new enterprise. Along with the economic effects of the oil crises of the 1970s, the company had to contend with stringent building restrictions. In 1973 the persistent lobbying of smaller retailers culminated in the enactment of the Large-Scale Retail Law by the Japanese National Assembly. As a result of the law, further strengthened in the late 1970s, the development of new supermarkets, especially those with floor areas of more than 500 square meters, was made subject to a lengthy planning application process that some said amounted to a veto by the smaller retailers. This legislation naturally put a damper on the internal growth of a company like JUSCO, which nonetheless continued to construct new stores, and made expansion by acquisition the natural course to take.

Throughout the 1970s more and more local chains came under the JUSCO umbrella. The company acquired a reputation for harmonious cooperation with local businesses and communities, as Takuya Odaka illustrates in his memoirs with the story of the Ezuriko PAL Shopping Center. The citizens of Ezuriko, he recounts, actually sent a deputation to JUSCO's head office to ask for help in constructing a new shopping center.

The internationalization of JUSCO began during the 1970s, particularly with respect to the development of overseas buying operations. In 1973 JUSCO established the Miwon Fishery Co., Ltd., in South Korea, jointly with the local Miwon Co., Ltd. The following year saw the opening of agricultural ventures in Australia and Brazil.

There was a general trend during the 1970s for Japanese retailers to import. To gain leverage, JUSCO's largest competitor, Daiei formed a buying group with 150 other companies for collective purchasing of overseas merchandise. In 1979 JUSCO, together with other leading retailers, formed a similar retail consortium, the Allied Import Company (AIC). In 1981 AIC would gain exclusive distribution rights in Japan over the products of the world's largest supermarket chain, Safeway of the United States.

In 1980 JUSCO's own-label products, known as White Brand, were launched. White Brand denoted a basic but high-quality product sold in plain packaging at the lowest possible price.

The 1980s were a period of rapid growth for chain stores. JUSCO was in the forefront of this movement and was usually ranked fourth among the supermarket chains in terms of turnover and second in profitability. Many of JUSCO's acquisitions were allowed to retain their identity as regional chains rather than being absorbed by the parent company. This afforded JUSCO a number of advantages, including cheaper advertising in local media and better levels of cooperation with suppliers.

Increasingly during the 1980s, JUSCO's strategy extended beyond the pursuit of market share in the supermarket sector. The company sought to compensate for government restrictions on the opening of new supermarkets and to cater to an ever more sophisticated Japanese consumer via diversification. It spawned an imaginative range of retail outlets, such as Nihon Direct, a mail-order business; discount store Big Barn; Blue Grass shops for teenagers; and Nishiki, a kimono store. There were also Autorama Life, a car sales company started in 1982, and JUSCO Car Life, which opened five years later to provide automobile maintenance services.

Another JUSCO venture, Mini Stop, was a chain of convenience stores providing not only 24-hour neighborhood shopping facilities, but also fast food and some financial services for public utility charges. Appealing particularly to Japan's growing body of working women, Mini Stop, founded in 1980, had 340 stores by 1990.

JUSCO was also beginning to develop a variety of restaurant and fast-food operations to enable it to profit from the growing popularity of eating out in Japan. The first of the Gourmet D'Or Co., Ltd. restaurants, which were to form the most important chain, began appearing in 1979 and were originally known as Coq D'Or JUSCO Co., Ltd. These were family restaurants in the Japanese idiom, catering to travelers and shoppers alike.

The 1980s also saw the continued expansion of JUSCO's overseas business. In 1988 the *Financial Times* called it "one of Japan's most internationally-minded retailers." It opened outlets in various parts of Southeast Asia, formed joint ventures with overseas companies to trade both in Japan and elsewhere, and systematically developed foreign lines of supply. It also raised capital abroad, issuing its first Eurobonds in 1976.

JUSCO had opened its first overseas store in Malaysia in 1985. This was operated by Jaya JUSCO Stores SDN. BHD., a company originally jointly owned with Cold Storage (Malaysia) and three other local companies. It was the first time that a Japanese company had entered into a significant joint venture in the Malaysian retail industry. JUSCO assumed operational control of Jaya JUSCO in 1988.

Since the latter part of the 1980s JUSCO's retail operations in Asia have grown to include another Malaysian superstore, four in Hong Kong—including Hong Kong's biggest store, opened in the Kornhill Complex in 1987—and five in Thailand. In 1990 a chain of Mini Stop convenience stores was launched in South Korea under an agreement with the Korean Miwon Group.

One of JUSCO's best-known European joint ventures, formed during the 1980s, was its partnership with British fashion manufacturer and retailer Laura Ashley. Laura Ashley was Japan's first store opened in Tokyo's Ginza district in 1986. The appeal of the brand's "traditionally English" style to Japanese consumers was so strong that by the end of 1990 there were 36 shops, two-thirds of them existing within department stores such as Mitsukoshi, and there were plans to open a further 11 stores in 1991. During 1990, JUSCO increased its share in Laura Ashley Japan from 50% to 60%, giving it overall control, and also announced the purchase of a 15% stake in Laura Ashley UK for £29.9 million, a deal that rescued the British company from a heavily indebted state.

In the United States, JUSCO had made an important acquisition in 1988. The Talbots Inc. was a chain of fashion stores belonging to General Mills Inc., a Minneapolis-based corporation that had decided to focus on its core business in the food industry. JUSCO's purchase of The Talbots for $325 million was the first noteworthy foray by any Japanese firm into the U.S. retail business. JUSCO made a point of leaving the existing management in place and said that it hoped to apply the retailing expertise of its new subsidiary to its domestic operations.

The chain grew rapidly in the United States after the takeover. The Talbots stores were also introduced in Japan: the first six establishments opened in 1990, against a five-year plan to open 50.

JUSCO and General Mills's relationship predated the Talbot deal. Since 1982 they had been running a joint venture in Japan that proved to be one of JUSCO's most popular catering operations. The chain of Red Lobster seafood restaurants was created around the supply of Maine lobster, obtained "jet-fresh" through an agreement with U.S. food conglomerate General Mills Inc.

In 1990 a wholly owned JUSCO subsidiary, the AEON Forest Co. Ltd., was created to become head franchisee within Japan of The Body Shop. This U.K. company specializing in "environmentally friendly" toiletries was an ideal partner for JUSCO, which was increasingly seeking to be seen as a "green" enterprise. Japanese consumers had been becoming increasingly environmentally aware during the late 1980s, and the popularity of the first Body Shop in Tokyo solidified JUSCO's plan to open 50 stores in five years.

Here JUSCO was not just jumping on a "green" bandwagon. Co-founder Takuya Okada had always been interested in conservation and had encouraged a range of conservation projects such as tree-planting. The "JUSCO: in tune with the Earth" conservation project was launched shortly after the Body Shop tie-up, and JUSCO would soon begin experimenting with recycling of packaging in its own stores.

Throughout the 1980s JUSCO was expanding its buying activities in the so-called Newly Industrializing Economies (NIEs), following a "develop and import" strategy whereby JUSCO would establish links with NIE companies—for example, City Knitting, a knitwear manufacturer in India, in 1988—with the aim of developing products suitable for the quality-sensitive Japanese consumer.

In 1987 *The Economist* noted that although 15 years earlier the top Japanese retailers had been department stores, the five biggest were now supermarket chains, with JUSCO in fourth place. The writer attributed the supermarkets' success in large part to their rapid adoption of Information Technology. For JUSCO, the second half of the 1980s in particular saw a sustained drive to harness the power of Information Technology to all aspects of the business. TOMM (Total On-Line Merchandising and Management) was an in-store system implemented in 1986 as part of a corporate information system due to be completed in 1989.

Jusco made great progress in the area of Point of Sale (POS) systems. POS systems automate the management of inventory, making it possible to fine-tune the reordering process and minimize the amount of money tied up in stock. POS also allows detailed analysis of turnover at each outlet, so that stocking policy can be attuned to local tastes. JUSCO had Fashion POS installed at all its outlets by 1990 and showed a marked improvement in turnover rates and profitability as a result. It was rapidly extending POS coverage to non-fashion lines.

On its 20th birthday in 1989 the JUSCO group adopted a new corporate identity. The parent company is still called JUSCO, and the directly-owned superstores continue to bear that name; the group is collectively known as the AEON Group.

In the late 1980s the group was becoming increasingly eager to propagate its image of a socially responsible "corporate citizen" on a global level. The AEON Group 1% Club is one manifestation of this concern. Formed in 1989, the Club collects 1% of the pretax profits of 31 member companies and uses these funds to promote cultural activities and exchanges. In 1990 the Club funded an expedition to Japan for a group of "young ambassadors" from Malaysia. In 1991 Takuya Okada—who was now chairman and chief executive officer, having been succeeded by Hidenori Futagi as president in 1984—visited London at the time of the Japan Festival, to promote a similar scheme for 30 U.K. high-school students.

In 1991 the group created its Environmental Foundation to sponsor academic research on conservation issues as well as such practical work as reforestation in Thailand. Group employees were also being encouraged to undertake environmental work in their local communities through a "Clean and Green" campaign.

In its third decade, the AEON group shows every sign of continued profitable growth, inside and outside Japan. AEON has structured itself in such a way as to be able to grow without impeding its ability to respond to change. It has always had

a policy of "federated" management, whereby it employs and develops local management talent rather than imposing managers from group headquarters. The group considers that this policy enhances its ability to understand its customer base and adapt to local needs.

As well as seeking local stock exchange listings, it sponsors local community projects such as playground building and generally establishes itself as a benign local presence. The federated approach allows the group to combine the flexibility of the small- to medium-size unit with the buying power of a giant conglomerate.

In the early 1990s the Japanese retail sector was being deregulated, partly in response to U.S. pressure to lower the barriers to entry that faced would-be overseas entrants. Legislation like the Large Scale Retail Law was beginning to be relaxed under the Structural Impediments Initiative. As a consequence of the liberalization, the AEON group was likely to have a freer rein in opening new large outlets, as well as in expanding its discount-store activities.

Superstores, however, were becoming less central to the group's plans, since its research found, according to a 1991 company report, that "Japanese consumers, with more time and money than ever to spend on shopping, are starting to view the generalized superstore as inadequate." In response, AEON is establishing what it calls "new retail formats with specific consumer targets and product categories," such as its FORUS fashion centers aimed at the youth market.

AEON also expects that it will increasingly become a developer of shopping centers containing a variety of specialized retail outlets under a single roof. AEON's NOA shopping center was one of the earliest centers of this kind. In 1991 its main development arm, AEON Kosan Co., Ltd., was engaged in the construction of another center. Another development company, Diamond City Co., Ltd., had been started as a joint venture with Mitsubishi Corporation in the year of JUSCO's foundation; it, too, was expected to receive a new lease of life after the deregulation. As a retailer AEON is evolving its specialty chains and restaurants looking forward to inclusion in the envisaged large-scale shopping complexes.

Other candidates for inclusion in the complexes include AEON's remarkably wide range of service companies. Nihon Credit Service Co., Ltd. was set up in 1981 to issue credit cards and provide other financial services, including automated teller machines, and insurance. In 1990 it began to operate in Hong Kong as well as Japan. AEON also has a marriage bureau, a travel agency, a tailoring service, and a series of sports and leisure centers.

Interviewed by the *Financial Times* in October 1991, chairman Okada said, "Now Japanese retailing companies have the opportunity to grow very significantly because the government's policies have shifted from encouraging manufacturing to encouraging consumer activities. I believe that the changes in retailing in the next 20 to 30 years will be far greater than those in the past 20 to 30 years." If anyone has the versatility to turn the expected changes to its advantage, it must be the AEON group.

Principal Subsidiaries: Shinshu JUSCO Co., Ltd.; Higashi Nihon Iryo Co., Ltd.; Isejin JUSCO Co., Ltd.; Gumma JUSCO Co., Ltd.; Ogiya JUSCO Co., Ltd.; Hokuriku

JUSCO Co., Ltd.; JUSCO Okuwa Co., Ltd.; Sanyo JUSCO Co., Ltd.; Midori Co., Ltd.; San-in JUSCO Co., Ltd.; Kyushu JUSCO Co., Ltd.; Oita JUSCO Co., Ltd.; Saga JUSCO Co., Ltd.; Okinawa JUSCO Co., Ltd.; Big Barn Shinshu Co., Ltd.; Bon Belta Isejin Co., Ltd.; Bon Belta Ageo Co., Ltd.; Tachibana Department Store Co., Ltd.; Bon Belta Co., Ltd.; Cox Co., Ltd.; Abilities JUSCO Co., Ltd.; AEON Forest Co., Ltd.; Book Bahn Co., Ltd.; Blue Grass Co., Ltd.; Laura Ashley Japan Co., Ltd.; Myland Shoes Co., Ltd.; Nicolo Polo Co., Ltd.; Nishiki Co., Ltd.; Sun-sun Land Co., Ltd.; Talbots Japan Co., Ltd.; Wellmart Co., Ltd.; Aomori Wellmart, Ugo Shopping Co., Ltd.; Kakudai Wellmart Co., Ltd.; Yamagata Wellmart Co., Ltd.; Apple Co., Ltd.; Nishina Co., Ltd.; Tokai Wellmart Co., Ltd.; Mie Wellmart Co., Ltd.; Hokuriku Wellmart Co., Ltd.; Nara Wellmart Co., Ltd.; Sanyo Wellmart Co., Ltd.; Oita Wellmart Co., Ltd.; Masuya Co., Ltd.; Tachibana Store Co., Ltd.; Mini Stop Co., Ltd.; Autorama Life Miyagi Co., Ltd.; Autorama Life Kitakanto Co., Ltd.; Autorama Life Chiba Co., Ltd.; Autorama Life Tokyo Co., Ltd.; Autorama Life Tokai Co., Ltd.; Autorama Life Chubu Co., Ltd.; Autorama Life Shinshu Co., Ltd.; Autorama Life Kinki Co., Ltd.; Autorama Life Hyogo Co., Ltd.; Autorama Life Okayama Co., Ltd.; Autorama Life Kyushu Co., Ltd.; JUSCO Car Life Co., Ltd.; Nihon Direct Co., Ltd.; Food Supply JUSCO Co., Ltd.; AEON Kosan Co., Ltd.; Diamond City Co., Ltd.; Diamond Family Co., Ltd.; JUSCO Maintenance Co., Ltd.; JUS-Photo Co., Ltd.; Jusvel Co., Ltd.; Reform Studio Co., Ltd.; Zwei Co., Ltd.; Chimney Co., Ltd.; Gourmet D'Or Co., Ltd.; Jack Co., Ltd.; Red Lobster Japan Co., Ltd.; Toku Toku Co., Ltd.; Aizu Royal Plaza Co., Ltd.; Nihon Credit Service Co., Ltd.; Brajusco Agro-Pastoril S.A. (Brazil); Jaya JUSCO Stores SDN. BHD. (Malaysia); JUSCO Stores (Hong Kong) Co., Ltd.; Siam JUSCO Co., Ltd. (Thailand); JUSCO (U.S.A.); Inc.; JUSCO (Europe), B.V. (Netherlands); Miwon Fishery Co., Ltd. (South Korea); Tasmania Feedlot Pty, Ltd. (Australia); The Talbots, Inc. (U.S.A.)

Further Reading: AEON Group Magazine, JUSCO, Tokyo, [n/d] (based on Okada, Takuya, *Daikokubashira ni kuruma o tsukeyo,* 1983); Pratley, Nils, "Eternally Yours," *Retail Week,* November 1, 1991.

—Alison Classe and John Parry

KARSTADT AKTIENGESELLSCHAFT

Theodor-Althoff-Strasse 2
Postfach 10 21 64
4300 Essen 1
Federal Republic of Germany
(201) 72 71
Fax: (202) 72 75 216

Public Company
Incorporated: 1920 as Rudolph Karstadt AG
Employees: 70,990
Sales: DM16.8 billion (US$11.09 billion)
Stock Exchanges: Berlin Bremen Düsseldorf Frankfurt
   Hamburg Hanover Munich Stuttgart

Karstadt Aktiengesellschaft is Germany's largest publicly traded retailer, with 155 stores in western Germany, covering 1.4 million square meters of sales area. The company also has nine stores in the eastern federal states, acquired in 1991. Karstadt is principally known for its department stores, and this sector accounted for 70% of its annual sales in 1990. Yet Karstadt, through its subsidiaries Neckermann Versand AG and NUR Touristic GmbH, is also active in the mail-order and travel businesses, which accounted for 14% and 11% of 1990 sales respectively. The company originated in northern Germany toward the end of the 19th century; its development since then has been determined largely by changes both in the economic climate and in attitudes toward retailing in Germany. Phases of expansion and diversification have alternated with periods of crisis, cutbacks, or consolidation. Major shareholders in the group are Commerzbank and Deutsche Bank, each holding more than 25%.

Rudolph Karstadt, founder of the company and a pioneer of the department store in Germany, was born near Lübeck on February 16, 1856. He completed his commercial apprenticeship in Rostock and then worked in his father's textiles shop in Schwerin. Rudolph soon became impatient with the business customs of the time, whereby customers generally bought items on credit, forcing merchants to set prices high as protection against nonpayment, and hindering flexibility in terms of stock changes. He saw the secrets of successful retailing as low prices, cash payment, and rapid stock turnover—a revolutionary concept that caused some disagreements within the family. Finally in 1881 Rudolph's father lent him 3,000 marks to put his ideas into practice. On May 14, 1881, Rudolph,

with his brother Ernst and sister Sophie, opened a shop, Rudolph Karstadt—selling dress materials and ready-to-wear clothes—in the harbor town of Wismar. Newspaper advertisements excited local interest and ensured large crowds on the opening day. Despite the low prices, however, customers were unused to the idea of immediate payment, and monthly sales in the first year were modest. Rudolph Karstadt's brother and sister withdrew from the business at this stage, leaving him as the sole owner.

Karstadt stuck to his convictions and was soon proved right—in the second year of business monthly sales rose to 20,000 marks, and in 1884 another shop was opened in Lübeck, with a range of goods extending to household items, leather goods, and toys. Further branches were opened in Neumünster in 1888 and in Braunschweig in 1890. The business grew rapidly: the balance sheet total in 1882 was 49,000 marks, which rose to 613,000 marks in 1890, and to 1.8 million marks in 1894. Rudolph Karstadt's conception of the modern department store was perfectly in tune with the times: the increasing economic power of the middle and working classes meant that consumer goods were demanded in ever larger quantities. In founding his business, Karstadt was also in line with the broader European trend: department stores had already been successfully established in France—notably with Bon Marché, Magasins du Louvre, Samaritaine, Printemps, and Galeries Lafayette—and in England, with Whiteleys, Harrods, and Selfridges.

A new branch was opened in Kiel in 1893 and Karstadt, who had previously moved from Lübeck to Berlin, now moved from the capital to this rapidly growing town, a focus of imperial military expansionism. During the 1890s and the first decade of this century the business continued to expand at a considerable rate: new branches were opened, established branches were extended, and in 1900 Rudolph Karstadt took over 13 stores owned by his brother Ernst, who had gotten into financial difficulties. By 1906, the 25th anniversary of the company, Rudolph Karstadt owned 24 department stores in northern Germany. In 1912 a prestigious new store was opened in Hamburg, with 10,000 square meters of sales area and a turnover of nearly 7 million marks in the first year, and in 1913 Rudolph Karstadt reestablished the headquarters of the company in that city.

While Karstadt was establishing his chain of stores in northern Germany, a business run by Theodor Althoff in the western part of Germany was following a very similar course. Althoff, born in 1858, had taken over a millinery and linen shop from his mother in 1885 and had soon succeeded in expanding the business considerably, following similar principles to those espoused by Karstadt—cash payment and low prices. In 1904 Althoff opened his first department store, in Dortmund, with a sales area of 5,000 square meters, and in 1910, the 25th anniversary of the business, the enterprise consisted of 11 stores in all. The year 1912 saw the establishment of Althoff's largest store yet, in Essen, with 10,000 square meters of selling space and 53 departments.

World War I put an end to the years of prosperity and expansion for both Karstadt and Althoff. People hoarded their money and goods became increasingly scarce. The similarity of the two businesses and the need to concentrate resources during this crisis brought the two department store pioneers together for the first time, in 1917. In 1919 the firms agreed on a common purchasing arrangement. In 1920 Rudolph Karstadt KG was converted into an *Aktiengesellschaft*—joint stock company—with founding capital of 40 million marks, based in Hamburg. Theodor Althoff was chairman of the supervisory board. A complete merger of Karstadt AG and Theodor Althoff KG followed in May of the same year, and the share capital was raised to 80 million marks; at this time Karstadt had 31 stores and Althoff 13.

The decade which followed the merger was one of rapid expansion, funded by numerous capital-raising measures. The company opened new branches and extended existing ones, as well as acquiring a number of manufacturing businesses in the furniture, textiles, and grocery sectors. EPA Einheitspreis AG, a subsidiary enterprise started by Theodor Althoff's son Heinrich, was established in 1926 following the American model of 5¢ and 10¢ stores, with goods sold at four prices: 10, 25, 50, and 100 pfennigs. This business was tremendously successful, with 52 branches in Germany and a turnover of around 100 million Reichsmarks (RM) in 1932. In 1927 Karstadt acquired the 19 stores owned by M.J. Emden Söhne KG, and in 1929 a new store was opened in Berlin, one of the largest and most modern in Europe at the time, with a sales area of 37,000 square meters. Another 15 stores were added by the merger with Lindemann & Co KG in the same year. By the time of the company's 50th anniversary, in 1931, Rudolph Karstadt AG and its subsidiaries had 89 branches and around 30,000 employees—compared with 11,500 in 1924—and a turnover of around RM200 million.

This phase of growth—conceived and carried through, it appears, on the initiative of Hermann Schöndorff, a dominant member of the company's management board at the time—reached its climax with the construction of an impressive new headquarters in Berlin, covering 70,000 square meters. Employees in the former headquarters in Hamburg were transported to Berlin in a specially commissioned train on January 1, 1932. The plans for expansion ended in crisis, however. The national and international economic difficulties of the early 1930s, combined with debts incurred during the previous decade, brought the company into severe financial troubles. In 1931 only five of Karstadt's stores were showing any profit. Theodor Althoff died in August 1931, when the business he had helped to found was approaching collapse. In April 1933 a consortium of banks assisted in drawing up a program of reorganization in order to ensure the company's survival. All the production subsidiaries were to be divested, share capital was to be reduced from RM80 million to RM7.6 million, the branch network was to be reduced, and EPA Einheitspreis was to be sold. The newly built headquarters was sold in 1934 and the company's administration moved into smaller premises in Berlin.

The restructuring effected a recovery in financial terms. Karstadt then, however, had to contend with difficulties arising from the National Socialists's (Nazi) campaign against department stores, involving boycotts and restrictive legislation, as some department stores had Jewish owners and were seen as representing a threat to the specialty German retail tradition. Despite these obstacles the company reached an economic high point before World War II: in 1939 it had 67 branches, a total sales area of around 260,000 square meters, and a work force of 21,000. Annual sales rose from RM190 million in 1933 to RM300 million in 1939.

Business conditions during and immediately after World War II became increasingly primitive, determined by rationing and the scarcity of goods, by changes of staff as women replaced the men who were called for military service, and—especially in the later years—by the damage to or destruction of stores by Allied bombing. In 1944 Rudolph Karstadt died at the age of 88. The end of the war saw the expropriation of 22 stores in the Soviet occupation zones and the destruction of more than 30 of the 45 branches in the western zones.

The currency reform of 1948 marked the beginning of West Germany's economic recovery. In this year Karstadt had 6,700 employees, 55,000 square meters of sales area, and an annual turnover of DM172 million. During the years that followed, rising incomes and consumer confidence fueled the reestablishment and renewed growth of Karstadt's retail business. In 1952 Karstadt reacquired 75% of the former EPA Einheitspreis AG, now called Kepa Kaufhaus GmbH (Kepa); the remaining 25% was acquired in 1958. In 1956 the year of the company's 75th anniversary, the turnover of Rudolph Karstadt AG exceeded DM1 billion for the first time. By this stage Karstadt had 49 branches and Kepa 51, with a total sales area of 222,000 square meters and 31,000 employees. The company name was changed to Karstadt AG in 1963, and a new administrative headquarters was opened in Essen in 1969.

The 1970s saw another important phase of expansion for the group, accompanied, as in the 1920s, by a diversification of interests. A travel company, TransEuropa Reisen GmbH, was jointly founded by Karstadt and mail-order company Quelle Gustav Schickedanz KG in 1971. The following year the company was renamed KS-Touristik-Beteiligungs GmbH. KS-Touristik itself held 25% of Touristik-Union International GmbH KG. In 1976 Karstadt agreed to buy a stake in mail-order company Neckermann Versand, which was experiencing financial difficulties. As Neckermann itself had a travel subsidiary, the Federal Monopolies Commission required Karstadt to sell its share in KS-Touristik. In 1977 Karstadt raised its share in Neckermann to a controlling 51.2%. Neckermann was converted to a joint-stock company in the same year.

As well as moving into the mail-order and travel businesses, Karstadt diversified its retailing interests during this decade. The group's first furniture and home decoration store was opened in Munich in 1972. By 1980 the group had nine such furniture outlets. Seven self-service department stores began operation with the foundation of Karstadt SB Warenhaus GmbH, a subsidiary of Kepa, in 1974. The first specialized sports equipment store was opened in 1976: nine of these outlets were in operation in 1980. Further specialty outlets for fashion, music, books, and leisure activities were opened between 1977 and 1980.

The second half of the decade also saw the rationalization of Karstadt's retailing businesses. In 1977 it was decided that the concept behind the Kepa outlets would not be successful in the long run, and 25 of Kepa's outlets were reintegrated into the Karstadt chain; the remaining 42 branches were sold or leased. The self-service department stores—by then numbering 18—were also brought into the main Karstadt network. Between 1977 and 1979, 17 of Neckermann's stores were turned into Karstadt outlets and 17 new Karstadt stores were established.

By 1981, the centennial of Karstadt's foundation, the structure of the company was much as it would be in the early 1990s. The department store business had 155 branches and

71,000 employees, and accounted for 77% of turnover. Neckermann Versand AG, the mail-order subsidiary, had a work force of 6,600 and accounted for 13% of the group's annual sales. NUR Touristic GmbH, Neckermann's travel subsidiary, had 1,500 employees and a 10% share of sales. The restructuring at the end of the 1970s indicated a shift in strategy from expansion in store numbers to increasing the productivity of each store. This policy was pursued through the 1980s. Karstadt, in 1991, had 155 stores—the same number as in 1981. However, sales area during the decade increased from 1.3 million square meters to 1.4 million square meters. Work force numbers have tended to decline—from 79,500 in 1981 to 71,000 in 1990. Annual turnover was DM12.7 billion in 1981; after a decline in the first half of the 1980s, this had risen to DM16.8 billion in 1990.

Facing increasing competition from self-service and out-of-town stores, Karstadt's strategy in the 1980s was to maintain its traditional emphasis on department stores carrying a full range of goods in town centers. Since the end of 1984, however, the company has implemented a refurbishment andrealignment program by which individual stores have been modernized and adapted to the nature of their localities. Furthermore, a distribution center has been established at Unna, near Dortmund. The project was started in 1987 and was fully operational for the first time in 1990, costing DM210 million. This center replaced regional warehouses and has enabled Karstadt AG to make efficiency and cost improvements in the area of logistics, the distribution of goods between warehouses and stores. Diversification, which was at the core of Karstadt's development in the 1970s, was not part of the company's strategy during the 1980s. Although the company retained specialty outlets for sports equipment and furniture, accounting for around 9% of annual turnover, all other ventures into specialty areas, except Runners Point, had ceased operations by 1987.

In 1981 Karstadt raised its stake in Neckermann Versand AG to more than 94%, and in 1984 the group acquired all remaining shares in this subsidiary. Both Neckermann Versand AG and its travel subsidiary NUR Touristic GmbH continued to take losses during the first half of the 1980s, returning profits only since 1986 and 1987 respectively. Improvements at Neckermann have been due largely to its abandonment of specialty catalogs, returning to one main catalog targeting families in the medium- to lower-income groups. Staff reductions have also played a part. Neckermann, which produces around three million catalogues each season, is now the third-largest mail-order company in Germany, behind Otto and Quelle, and has subsidiaries in the Netherlands, Belgium, France, and joint ventures in Greece and Poland. NUR Touristic, which has subsidiaries in the Netherlands and Belgium, has also reduced its work force, from 1,445 in 1981 to 937 in 1989. Despite these improvements at Neckermann and NUR, the problems have not been entirely eradicated: while both businesses have shown increases in turnover, their profits have declined since 1988.

The reunification of Germany, along with tax reforms that increased consumer spending power, brought Karstadt and its subsidiaries a significant boost in sales in 1990. Department stores along the border with the former German Democratic Republic benefited from visiting customers from the new federal states, while the mail-order business was able to penetrate into the eastern territories and take advantage of the rise in consumer demand without having to establish retail outlets. Karstadt had believed its coverage of western Germany to have reached saturation point, but the new *Länder,* or federal regions, presented the group with an opportunity for further expansion. In 1990 a cooperation agreement was reached with the Centrum department stores in eastern Germany; in March 1991 Karstadt acquired seven of these stores—in Dresden, Görlitz, Halle, Hoyerswerda, Leipzig-Lindenau, and Magdeburg—as well as leasing two former Magnet stores in Brandenburg and Wismar. Conversion of these stores to western standards will require considerable investment. Neckermann and NUR have also begun to develop mail-order and tourism infrastructures in the east.

Karstadt has become one of the largest department-store groups in Europe. A connection with its origins remains: a grandson of Theodor Althoff was on the supervisory board in the early 1990s. It has always seemed unlikely that Karstadt would expand its core business outside Germany, given the widely held belief that retail concepts cannot be transferred across cultural boundaries, but the group faces the challenge and opportunity of growth. However, for Karstadt as for other German companies the benefits of unification may not be immediate: after the initial boom of 1990 the longer-term economic consequences in terms of investment requirements and reduced consumer spending may prove difficult obstacles to overcome.

Principal Subsidiaries: Neckermann Versand AG; NUR Touristic GmbH; Kepa Kaufhaus GmbH; Runners Point Warenhandelsgesellschaft mbH; Versandhaus Walz GmbH; Neckermann Postorders B.V. (Netherlands); Neckermann Postorders N.V. (Belgium); Neckermann S.ar.l. (France); Neckermann Vliegreizen Nederland B.V. (Netherlands); Neckermann Reizen België N.V. (Belgium).

Further Reading: Karstadt Magazin: Jubiläumsausgabe, 1881–1981, Essen, Karstadt AG, 1981.

—Susan Mackervoy

KAUFhOF

HOLDING AG, KÖLN

KAUFHOF HOLDING AG

Leonhard-Tietz-Strasse 1
5000 Cologne 1
Federal Republic of Germany
(0221) 223-01
Fax: (0221) 223 2800

Public Company
Incorporated: 1879 as Firma Leonhard Tietz
Employees: 46,726
Sales: DM14.69 billion (US$9.69 billion)
Stock Exchanges: Frankfurt Düsseldorf Munich Hamburg
Basel Zurich Geneva Berlin Stuttgart Hanover Bremen

Kaufhof Holding AG heads a group of retailing and service companies. It is best known for its highly competitive chain of department stores. This traditional field of activity is still the most important for the group, but the group's operations outside department stores have grown vigorously through diversification. Kaufhof has extended its activities into specialist markets, mail order, tourism, and specialty services, for instance in travel, food, banking, and insurance. Kaufhof's department stores account for around 61% of the group's turnover. At the same time as the incorporation of Kaufhof Holding AG in 1989, 73 department store operations were transferred to the newly created Kaufhof Warenhaus AG, a fully owned subsidiary of Kaufhof Holding AG.

From the middle of the 19th century, large, elegant department stores called *grands magasins* sprang up in Paris, offering luxury goods. The founding of the German department stores a few decades later was in direct contrast to the rise of France's "cathedrals of commerce," as Emile Zola called them. In Germany all of the great trading houses developed from small retail stores in the eastern provinces of what was then Imperial Germany.

Leonhard Tietz's case is typical. In 1879 the 30-year-old from Birnbaum, Warthe, opened a tiny textile shop in Stralsund with a start-up capital of 3,000 thalers. The shop had only 25 square meters of sales space. It sold thread, buttons, trimmings, woolen wares, and all the articles needed for men's and women's tailoring.

What differentiated Tietz's business was the new retailing methods employed. He ran his business according to the principle of high turnover on a small profit, based on fixed prices and cash payment. This method had, in fact, been put into practice before in the large Parisian department stores. This was, however, a surprising innovation in eastern Germany, where people still haggled over prices and put their purchases on credit. As the extent of the company's purchasing power was a decisive factor in its ability to offer low prices, Tietz formed a buying cooperative with other members of his large, extended family, which included the founders of Hertie. Articles that could be sold in bulk were ordered by the cooperative, prompting the development of new, cheap articles. The manufacturers welcomed the chance to sell to such big purchasers.

Tietz also expanded his field of business through the opening of numerous branches. This took him into the Rhineland, with is expanding economic centers promising good bulk sales with their growing number of inhabitants and their increasing purchasing power. Tietz set up 11 branches between 1889 and 1909 in western Germany and in 1891 moved the headquarters of his company to Cologne.

Leonard Tietz used the same business methods wherever he founded his branches. He rented small shops in the best areas to sell haberdashery and linen. The public would come in droves to these shops on their opening, following which the complete range of goods offered would have to be introduced. Wherever necessary, Tietz would move the stores into bigger premises and eventually acquired his own real estate. It soon became an experience in itself to shop at Tietz. When the Cologne store opened in 1895, its own small electricity works enabled arc lights and electric light bulbs to light the store brightly. Elevators transported the customers to all floors, free of charge. The saleswomen—few salesmen were employed—wore black dresses as their uniform. On a trip to Milan, Tietz admired the Galeria and decided he wanted to own a similar building with a glass cupola and gigantic windows. He fulfilled his dream by having a *Jugendstil*—the German equivalent of art nouveau—building with an arcade constructed on Cologne's main street. This was his first real department store and with its luxurious furnishings it was considered one of the most important landmarks in the town. It was torn down just ten years later to make way for an even larger department store. By this time Leonhard Tietz had his stores built by the most renowned architects of his time.

For the Düsseldorf store, the management approached all German-based architects with an invitation to participate in a prize competition to create a work of great artistic merit without regard to cost. Joseph M. Olbrich, the most famous exponent of *Jugendstil* architecture, was chosen to design the building. The new department stores in Cologne and Wuppertal-Elberfeld were built by Wilhelm Kreis. These large buildings are now classified as historical monuments. Further branches, under the fully owned subsidiary Grands Magasins L. Tietz, founded in 1900, were opened in Belgium, where a huge department store employing 1,000 people was built on the occasion of the World's Fair in Brussels in 1910.

The range of merchandise expanded. Tietz began to offer all-inclusive packages, for instance a set including kitchen furniture, a range, and 323 pieces of kitchen and household equipment. With the introduction of various articles, including bicycles, tinned food, and ready-to-wear clothing, the department store offered new services to its customers. Tietz imported the latest hat and clothing fashions from Paris, where he owned his own buying house. He imported Oriental rugs, majolica and fancy goods from Japan, and precious glassware from Italy.

Influenced by the efforts of the *Deutscher Werkbund,* founded in 1907 to organize avant-garde art exhibitions, "beauty and quality" became the company's catchphrase. Kaufhof was the first retailer to organize avant-garde art exhibitions in its stores. Leonhard Tietz had his portrait painted by Max Liebermann. Tietz looked after his employees' interests by offering benefits, including health care, that were by no means taken for granted at that time. The company's extensive social program developed gradually from this time onward.

In 1905 the firm Leonhard Tietz became a public limited company with a capital of 1 million marks, but remained a family company as the shares were taken up by the Tietz family. At this time the company employed 2,400 employees and had a turnover of 24 million marks. In 1909 the Tietz shares were introduced onto the Berlin stock exchange as the first publicly traded German department store shares.

Leonhard Tietz died on November 14, 1914. His eldest son, Alfred Leonhard Tietz, had been well prepared for his future responsibilities. After studying at the University of Commerce in Cologne under Eugen Schmalenbach, the pioneer of modern business management education, Alfred Tietz then went on to be trained in various large U.S. department stores.

The period following World War I was marked by unrest, hyperinflation, and economic crises. Nevertheless, the network of branches was continuously extended. In 1925 Tietz traveled with a team to the United States and came back with many fresh ideas. The already common practice in the United States of training employees for their jobs was adopted, and Tietz's sales personnel and executives were carefully trained for their tasks. Business and sales training, knowledge of the merchandise, economic geography, and the importance of good taste were impressed upon the company employees. The team also studied fixed-price retailers, such as F. W. Woolworth on their trip, and the EHAPE Einheitspreis Handels Gesellschaft mbH, a fixed-price bazaar, was established in Cologne. It is a successful subsidiary of Kaufhof and now trades under the name of Kaufhalle AG.

When the National Socialists (Nazis) forced Jewish businesses to give up their property in 1933, the owners of Firma Leonhard Tietz engaged Abraham Frowein,president of the International Chamber of Commerce, to represent their interests. The latter stood up for their interests at great personal risk, made it possible for Tietz's heirs to emigrate, helped establish them on a sound financial footing abroad, and later helped them to gain compensation. After 1933, Kaufhof's shares were held by Deutsche Bank, Commerzbank, Dresdner Bank, the Frowein family, and many other private shareholders. During World War II, bombs destroyed most of the company's 40 department stores. Only five survived intact. The branches in the east were lost.

Following the 1948 currency reform, the company, which began calling itself Westdeutsche Kaufhof AG in 1933 and, from 1953, Kaufhof AG, expanded into towns in the north and south of the Federal Republic of Germany. After the years of deprivation and lack of goods, customers came in droves to the rebuilt and newly opened stores.

The well-stocked department stores were as appealing as they had been before the war. "Kaufhof offers everything a thousand times over under one roof" ran the company slogan. Special events such as French, American, and Italian weeks; art exhibitions; and autograph sessions with famous artists attracted many into the stores. Above all, the large grocery departments with their wide variety of cheeses, sausages, breads, fresh meat, fish, and delicatessen products, and the increasingly elegant restaurants and cafes, enjoyed great popularity.

A very important factor in the company's success was imports, especially from the Far East, which allowed the company on the one hand to supply goods at low prices and on the other hand to aid, through its large orders, the development of the manufacturers and factories in these countries.

In 1979, the company's centenary year, Kaufhof AG owned 86 branches and its turnover reached DM8 billion. The business climate for the department stores, however, became less favorable at the beginning of the 1980s and forced Kaufhof to follow a new strategic direction. During this time of great change Kaufhof acquired two new large shareholders—Metro Vermögensverwaltung GmbH & Co. of Düsseldorf (Metro) and its bank, the Schweizerische Bankgesellschaft AG. Metro in the early 1990s owned more than 50% of Kaufhof Holding.

The department store crisis was based on the emergence in the retail trade of competitive new types of businesses. Specialty businesses managed to gain a stronger foothold than before. Self-service markets offering cut-price goods rather than comfortable surroundings and service sprang up on greenfield—out-of-town—sites and on the edges of towns. The increase in automobile use brought a new attitude toward shopping. While parking space in cities became more limited, businesses on the edges of towns allowed customers to take their purchases directly from the check-out to their cars.

As a result of this development, Kaufhof began to diversify into other areas of trading and into the services sector. At the same time, new concepts were developed in the department stores. The stores no longer aimed to sell everything under one roof, but concentrated on selected profit-making ranges that were in strong demand. The grocery departments, which previously had yielded high returns and had been very popular, became to some extent simply departments to attract regular customers rather than yielding satisfactory returns. In many department stores space is rented to outside grocery retailers. In the course of the restructuring, nine of the company's previously traditional department stores selling the whole range of goods became independent in 1987–1988 under the name Kaufhof Mode und Sport GmbH. They now offer a selective range, concentrating predominantly on fashion and sports goods.

The elaboration of a modern electronic system of selling goods, the improvement of merchandise, and the motivating of the work force to become more customer-oriented show the great importance still attached to the activities of the Kaufhof-Warenhaus AG, with its 73 branches in western Germany and further branches to open in eastern Germany from 1991. Banks, travel bureaus, theater ticket booths, insurance, and many other services are making the department stores into multi-functional service centers.

With its total of 636 stores, Kaufhof Holding AG was in the early 1990s set on a course of further expansion. The Kaufhalle subsidiary offered a range of goods geared towards more sophisticated customers. In 1989 Kaufhalle became a joint-stock company and in 1990 25% of its shares were offered on the stock market in order to strengthen the company's financial position for embarking on new projects. The company owns 127 branches in the former West Germany and many more in the new federal states, including one in

Stralsund, the town in which Leonhard Tictz began his business in 1879. Particular areas on which the company is concentrating include electronics, computers, and photographic goods. Kaufhof Holding AG has a 62.3% shareholding in Media-Markt-Gruppe, based in Ingolstadt, which has 37 sites at home and abroad. In 1990 Kaufhof Holding AG merged its subsidiary Saturn-Hansa Handelsgesellschaft für technischen Freizeit-und Haushaltbedarf mbH, a leading company in these specialty areas, with the Media-Markt-Gruppe.

Kaufhof also owns 50% of Vobis-Mikrocomputergruppe, of Aachen, a dynamic specialty market group with 56 branches at home and abroad. "Mac Fash" Textilhandels GmbH, of Cologne, is a fully owned subsidiary that sells fashionable clothing in its 21 branches.

Buying in department stores and buying by mail-order were originally considered the two opposite extremes of retail trading. Once it became evident, however, that mail-order was becoming more popular, Kaufhof Holding also took shareholdings in mail-order companies in the most diverse areas. It acquired a 76% holding in Friedrich Wenz GmbH & Co., which had been selling jewelry, gifts, fashion, and furnishings of high quality by catalog from the jewelers' town of Pforzheim since 1925. Kaufhof also acquired a 50% stake in Reno Versandhandel GmbH, of Thalweiler-Fröschen, a mail-order shoe firm with strong sales operating from close to the shoe metropolis of Pirmasens, which also owns a specialty store chain with 188 branches, 34 of which are abroad.

Since 1989 Kaufhof has owned 61.5% of the capital of Oppermann Versand AG, Neumünster, a mail-order house specializing in promotional goods and advertising gifts for trade and private customers, with numerous subsidiary companies and franchise partners abroad. Kaufhof Holding AG also acquired holdings of 60% and 70% in two companies in the Haweske-Gruppe, of Hamburg, which import, export, and send champagne and high-quality wines and spirits by mail.

One of the factors in Leonhard Tietz's success was the elimination of the then-all-powerful wholesalers through mass purchasing at advantageous prices direct from the manufacturer. By the early 1990s Kaufhof had entered the sphere of wholesaling as part of its strategy of diversification and has taken shareholdings in the wholesalers for its various areas of business. A commitment in this area is the company's 80% shareholding in Rungis Express Gesellschaft für Frischimporte mbH, of Meckenheim, which delivers freshly caught seafood and high-quality fish, exotic fruit, vegetables, meat, cheese, and top-quality champagne several times a week to exclusive restaurants and delicatessens.

Services represent another important new sector for this traditional trading company. As early as 1970 Kaufhof took a shareholding in ITS International Tourist Services Länderdienst GmbH, of Köln, which offers an extensive, worldwide travel program. ITS itself is set on expansion and has acquired shareholdings in various tourist companies both at home and abroad. The company is joining forces with business partners to build hotels in popular vacation areas and vacation sites in subtropical-type aqua parks.

As part of the reorganization of Kaufhof, the existing restaurants and cafes in the Kaufhof and Kaufhalle stores were changed into self-service restaurants and then in 1983 and 1984 transferred to the Kaufhof Gastronomie Service-Gesellschaft mbH (KGSG), of Cologne, a fully owned subsidiary of Kaufhof. There are KGSG restaurants not only in the 118 stores belonging to the group, but also in four other locations.

The structure of Kaufhof with its various sales divisions—department stores, specialty stores, mail order, wholesaling, tourism, and other services—seems well positioned to operate successfully in the five new states of the Federal Republic of Germany. Kaufhof, which already has 48 branches in Europe outside Germany, is also set to be well represented with the merging of sales areas within the European community's internal market through making attractive tenders.

Training for the Kaufhof Group's employees is assuming greater importance, as they must be trained to use new forms of technology and customer care must be improved. Ties are being strengthened between the different companies within the group.

Principal Subsidiaries: Kaufhof Warenhaus AG; Kaufhof Mode und Sport GmbH; Kaufhalle AG; Media Markt Group; Vobis Microcomputer GmbH; Friedrich Wenz GmbH & Co.; Oppermann Versand AG; Reno Group; "Mac Fash" Textilhandels GmbH; Haweske-Gruppe; Kaufhof Gastronomie Service-Gesellschaft mbH; Rungis Express Gesellschaft für Frischimporte mbH; ITS International Tourist Services Ländereisedienste GmbH.

Further Reading: Schwann, Mathieu, *Leonhard Tietz. Ein Wort über ihn und sein persönliches Werden*, Cologne, M. DuMont Schauberg, C. 1914; *50 Jahre Leonard Tietz 1879–1929*, Cologne, Leonhard Tietz AG, 1929.

—Ingrid Bauert-Keetman
Translated from the German by Philippe A. Barbour

KINGFISHER PLC

North West House
119 Marylebone Road
London NW1 5PX
United Kingdom
(071) 724 7749
Fax: (071) 724 1160

Public Company
Incorporated: 1909 as F.W. Woolworth & Co. Ltd.
Employees: 61,497
Sales: £3.1 billion (US$5.79 billion)
Stock Exchange: London

Kingfisher plc is a major British retailing and property group consisting of several retail chains, including Woolworths, a variety chain of 796 shops; B&Q, a chain of 280 do-it-yourself (DIY) centers; Superdrug, a chain of 660 drug stores; Comet, a chain of 270 electrical stores; and Chartwell Land, a property company that started by redeveloping the Woolworth properties and has diversified into redeveloping properties of other companies both in and outside of the group, and also manages an investment portfolio.

Kingfisher originated as a subsidiary of F.W. Woolworth & Co. of the United States. The American company was founded in 1879. The company's founder, Frank Winfield Woolworth, identified the potential for a walk-around open display type of shop in Britain during his first visit to Europe in 1890. He observed that "the [London] stores . . . are very small and are called "shops" and not much like our fine stores. I think a good [threepenny and sixpenny] store run by a live Yankee would create a sensation here, but perhaps not." In 1909 he decided to found a subsidiary in Britain even though his chief executives thought that it would be unsuccessful. On July 23, 1909, the subsidiary was incorporated in England as a private limited company with a share capital of £50,250. In 1912 the share capital was increased to £100,000. After this time the entire increase in assets was built up from earnings, and there was no further increase in capitalization. Between 1909 and 1919 the American shareholders received no dividends at all and for the following six years dividends were paltry. This was not for lack of profits but because the shareholders wanted to build up the reserves of the company so that it was always in a position to expand without recourse to borrowing.

The first shop opened at 25 and 25a Church Street, Liverpool, on November 5, 1909. The *Draper* described it as "a penny, threepenny, and sixpenny bazaar on a large scale. In each of the four large salesrooms there are wide counters, extending the full length of the hall, and on these are placed mahogany trays containing the articles for disposal. . . . The public, we are told, are privileged 'to wander round the immense establishment without being importuned to buy.' " During the first two days of business 60,000 people visited the shop. Following steady business improvement, Woolworth opened a second shop in Preston and properties were also obtained in Manchester, Leeds, and Hull. In 1910 a third shop was opened, on London Road, Liverpool. The premises were obtained from Owen Owen, a department store owner, who told Woolworth that he had no idea that the "bazaar business could be elevated to such a high standard." On the opening of the third shop there was a riot. The riot made the management wary. When the sixth shop opened in Hull later in 1910, crowd barriers were put in place to stem the anticipated rush of customers. By the end of 1910 the company was operating ten shops with another two in preparation.

The same business methods that had worked so well in the United States were adopted in Britain. Everything carried a plain price tag, and the prices were one old penny (£0.004), three old pence (£0.0125), and six old pence (£0.025). Supplies were bought directly from manufacturers. As in the United States, Woolworth had difficulty at first in Britain in persuading manufacturers to deal with him directly. Like the U.S. manufacturers, however, the British manufacturers who agreed to supply Woolworth directly soon found they had made the correct decision. Many of these suppliers also grew with Woolworth from small beginnings. A notable example was Duttons Ltd.. When the first shop was opened in Liverpool, Duttons received its first Woolworth order. Subsequently Duttons set out solely to service Woolworth with all types of price tickets, advertising, and printed matter. By the early 1960s Duttons was also responsible for the supply of many items of stationery to the majority of Woolworth's suppliers.

The Woolworth method of retailing moved from strength to strength. By 1912 the chain had expanded to 28 shops, 26 of which were managed by Britons. The year's net profits were more than US$100,000. In 1914 Woolworth opened its 31st shop, in Grafton Street, Dublin. This was the first Woolworth shop in Ireland. After the creation of the Irish Republic, Woolworth established a separate Irish subsidiary, F.W. Woolworth Company of Ireland, Ltd.. When World War I began, women store managers took the places of the men who joined the armed forces, and when suitable women could not be found, men were drafted from the parent company in the United States. After the war, the British subsidiary was ready for major expansion. The man who was to be principally responsible for the expansion was William L. Stephenson.

Frank Woolworth met Stephenson through Edward Owen of Birmingham, a buyer for Wanamaker and other American shops. Stephenson was Owen's assistant. Stephenson started work at the company in September 1909, at the express invitation of Frank Woolworth, even before the first shop had been opened. Stephenson succeeded Fred M. Woolworth, a cousin of Frank, as managing director of the British subsidiary when Fred died in 1923, becoming chairman in 1931 when Woolworth was floated as a British public company and the U.S. parent corporation's interest in its subsidiary was reduced from 62% to 52.7% of the ordinary shares. Shortly before the flotation, F.W. Woolworth Company of Ireland, Ltd. was voluntarily liquidated and its two shops in Dublin and one each in Cork, Belfast, Limerick, and Kilkenny were incorporated into the British company. The flotation of the chain of 444 shops was underwritten by N.M. Rothschild & Sons. As a result of the company's excellent track record, the Woolworth flotation was a success, despite taking place in the depths of the Great Depression. Since its foundation in 1909 its turnover and profits had never failed to rise from one year to the next, and continued to do so each year until the early part of World War II.

An important change made by Stephenson was to buy freehold properties for his shops instead of taking leases. Stephenson's property investments made a major contribution to the revival of Woolworth's successor, Kingfisher, during the 1980s. Under Stephenson's management Woolworth was soon opening shops in Britain at the rate of at least one every fortnight. This remarkable rate of growth was maintained until the early part of World War II. By the late 1930s each shop returned an operating profit two or three times as large as its U.S. counterpart. In 1939, when World War II began, there were 759 British Woolworth shops and nine more under construction.

World War I had brought difficulties to Woolworth but they had been surmounted. During 1914-18 the number of British shops rose from 44 to 81. World War II was very different. The expansion program ceased. Furthermore, 23 shops were destroyed and 352 damaged by enemy action. The company's Channel Island shops in Guernsey and Jersey were placed under German administration from July 1940. In both wars, many of Woolworth's staff joined the armed forces and many did not return. In World War II, however, many who stayed in Woolworth's service were also killed by enemy action. In November 1944, a single V2 rocket destroyed the shop at New Cross, London. In this second worst air raid of the war, 160 people in the shop were killed, including the manager and 18 members of her staff, and an additional 108 people were seriously injured.

In 1948 Stephenson retired as chairman of Woolworth. In the early postwar period, it was some time before material losses could be made good. It was not until the latter part of 1956 that the last blitzed shop was reopened. There had been 768 shops in operation in 1940. By 1950 there were still only 762, but from the end of 1951 the expansion program was resumed.

In 1954 Woolworth began a new program of expansion into the British Commonwealth with the establishment of a subsidiary in the British West Indies. On November 4, 1954, the company's first store in the West Indies was opened in Kingston, Jamaica. In November 1955 a second West Indian store was opened in Port of Spain, Trinidad. In October 1956 a third shop was opened in Bridgetown, Barbados. Between mid-1958 and the end of 1973 the West Indian subsidiary was expanded to more than a dozen shops located in Jamaica, Trinidad, and Barbados. Woolworth also established a subsidiary in Southern Rhodesia, now Zimbabwe, at the end of the 1950s. A shop was opened on March 18, 1959, in the capital, Salisbury. On November 10, 1960, a second shop was opened in Bulawayo. In early 1974 a subsidiary was established in Cyprus and a shop was opened in Nicosia.

Meanwhile, the number of shops in the British Isles also expanded rapidly. The 1,000th shop was opened in Portslade,

Hove, Sussex, in May 1958. A peak of 1,141 shops was reached in the late 1960s. With the widening range of merchandise stocked by Woolworth there had to be a wider range of prices. Inflation resulted in the end of the three old pence and six old pence price limits during World War II. In the early postwar period Woolworth pioneered the development of self-service in the variety part of the retail sector. In 1955 Woolworth opened its first British self-service shop in the small village of Cobham, Surrey, modeled on the experience in America. Customers could, if they so desired, collect a wire basket at the shop entrance in which to place their purchases, and payment was made at one of three or four cash desks at the exit, eliminating the need to pay separately at each department visited, as in the traditional shops. The first completely self-service Woolworth shop was opened at Didcot near Oxford in September 1956. By the early 1970s Woolworth had more than 190 purely self-service shops in operation, some of them large by British standards, selling a full variety shop range.

In October 1966 Woolworth founded a new division, the Woolco Department Stores. The division was to oversee the creation of a national chain of up to 20 out-of-town department stores which were to operate independently and in addition to the traditional shops. The stores contained a full range of quality merchandise at competitive prices, including clothes, domestic appliances, toys, groceries, confectionery, car service, and restaurants. The new stores were modeled on the parent company's Woolco stores in U.S. and Canadian suburban shopping centers, which had been in operation since 1962. The first British Woolco was opened in October 1967 at Oadby, Leicester. Oadby provided free parking for about 750 cars away from the congestion of the city center. Between 1969 and 1977 a further 13 Woolco stores were opened. In 1977, however, Woolworth began to reassess the value of the Woolco division to the company. In December it sold its Woolco store at Kirkby and a hypermarket site with planning permission in Blackpool.

In the late 1960s profits began to fall at Woolworth. A visible sign of trouble came in 1968, when Woolworth lost its place as Britain's leading retailer and Marks & Spencer overtook it in both sales and profits. Despite a modernization program, Woolworth still possessed a number of small and poorly located branches with an extremely low rate of turnover and profitability. These branches detracted from the improved performance of the larger units. Furthermore, the Woolco stores were still in the development stage. The results announced in January 1970 were the worst since 1962.

During the late 1960s the company's modernization program had been extended to include the enlargement of the company's shops in the major British towns and cities. Two that were opened after extensions in 1968, in Wolverhampton and Ipswich, became the largest in area in Britain. The largest of all, in Wolverhampton, had a shopping area of 70,000 square feet with 1.25 miles of counters. The Aylesbury store, which opened in the jubilee week of the company, on November 7, 1969, became the second largest shop with an area of 69,000 square feet. In the early 1970s major extensions and modernizations took place at Basingstoke, Brentwood, Hartlepool, Brighton, Leith, Liverpool, Manchester, and Wrexham. These shops included extended male, female, and children's clothing departments; fitting rooms; sports departments; music and record departments; and extended hardware and household departments. They also had extensive food departments and restaurants.

In 1971, with profits still falling, Woolworth began a new cash-and-wrap policy and began to convert 777 shops from conventional behind-the-counter service to a system of centralized payment points in each shop where goods could be paid for and wrapped, thus increasing the speed of service. At the same time the company closed 23 of its unprofitable shops and attempted to trade up and lose its reputation as a purveyor of cheap goods. Nonetheless, the consumer boom of the early 1970s appears to have passed Woolworth by. Woolworth's profits failed to recover very strongly, partly as a result of the heavy costs of its shop modernization program in the early 1970s and prolonged start-up problems with a new distribution center at Swindon that had been opened in July 1972.

Despite its stated intention to stop selling cheap goods, in 1973 Woolworth decided to open a chain of catalogue discount shops. The new chain, Shoppers World, was launched in Leeds in September 1974 and initially consisted of 15 shops in Birmingham, Liverpool, Manchester, and Leeds. After considerable initial success, the chain also opened an outlet in London in September 1975. Nonetheless, profits continued to stagnate in the mid-1970s. Although the company showed a determination to change with the times, one of its weaknesses was the poor quality of its customer service. Staff turnover was high and this led to consumer dissatisfaction. Another weakness derived from the expansion in the British Isles during the 1950s. Many of the sites chosen were in secondary locations unsuitable for chain stores. An even more serious weakness was that it launched itself into new products in the wrong way. The success of the new products depended on a well-trained staff, first-rate service, and a more polished consumer image than Woolworth had acquired by the mid-1970s. In the late 1970s, however, the performance of the company began to improve. In 1978 the company lifted itself clear of a ten-year profit trough.

During the late 1970s there was a major change of emphasis in Woolworth away from food into furniture, clothing, DIY, and other durable items. In August 1980, in its first ever takeover bid, Woolworth paid £16.7 million for a Southhampton-based chain of over 40 DIY centers, B&Q (Retail). In October 1981 Woolworth acquired the Dodge City chain of 32 DIY centers for £20.1 million. The centers were complementary to B&Q's 49 existing centers.

Despite the recovery in profits in the late 1970s, Woolworth had still not solved its problems. In 1981, having supposedly repositioned itself upmarket, Woolworth cut prices on 800 of its lines. In addition, Woolworth began to sell off some of its valuable prime freehold town center properties in order to stem the losses these large shops were making. On balance this made sense, as although these properties were valuable, they were also leviathans. The 1981 results, excluding property sales, showed after-tax profits down from £30.3 million to £22.5 million. The company's dividend was cut for the first time in its history. Not only were the shareholders dissatisfied, but also the customers and employees.

In September 1982 a syndicate of institutional investors led by the merchant bank Charterhouse Japhet launched a £310 million takeover bid for the British Woolworth through the specially-created Paternoster Stores plc. Paternoster was led by Wolverhampton-born chairman John Beckett. By November,

more than 90% of the shareholders had accepted the syndicate's bid and Paternoster's name was changed to Woolworth Holdings plc. As Paternoster did not have enough money to cover the whole of the bid, U.S. Woolworth temporarily retained a 12.7% share in the new company. The holding was sold almost immediately afterward.

Woolworth Holdings began to reorganize by removing the unprofitable parts of the business. Between late 1982 and 1991 the group sold about 200 of its unprofitable Woolworth shops in the United Kingdom, reducing the number to around 790. The group also sold all 18 of its shops in the Irish Republic in 1984. In April 1983 the Shoppers World chain of 45 shops was closed down. Later in 1985 the Woolworth shops in Cyprus were sold and between 1987 and 1990 all of the shops in the West Indies and Zimbabwe were also sold. On the other hand B&Q, a profitable part of the business, was expanded, mostly through organic growth, with as many as 30 new stores a year. By January 1984 the company's pretax profits had risen from £6.1 million to £29.4 million. To emphasize that the change in the group's Woolworth shops was fundamental, their trading name was changed from F.W. Woolworth to Woolworths in March 1986. In May 1984 the company launched a successful agreed bid for Comet, the electrical goods discount chain, for £128.9 million. During 1984 Woolworths Holdings profits nearly doubled. Profits came from the still-expanding B&Q, now with 153 centers; the newly-acquired Comet; and the Woolworth shops disposal program.

In early 1986 Beckett retired as chairman of Woolworth Holdings, having successfully overseen the revival of the group. During 1986 the company was subject to an unsuccessful £1.75 billion hostile takeover bid from Dixons Group plc, the electronics retailer. During the takeover battle, the group sold its 12 Woolco superstores to Dee Corporation plc for £26 million. The Woolco sale fitted in with the group's "Focus" program of concentrating on a narrower range of merchandise; toys, gifts, and confectionery, entertainment (including records and cassettes), home and garden accessories, kitchen accessories, kids clothes and cosmetics. Food and adult clothing, which contributed 30% of sales, were completely abandoned. The Woolco stores, which had specialized in groceries and clothing, had been the first out-of-town food stores and could have become as successful as the Sainsbury superstores later became. However, the buyers in the old Woolworth were jealous of Woolco's initial success and started cramming them with old-fashioned variety merchandise.

As part of "Focus" the company formed a joint venture with the Rosehaugh property group to redevelop five of its Woolworth shops by reducing the amount of space occupied by the shops. For example, the Wolverhampton shop was shrunk from three floors to one floor. In the opinion of the *Financial Times,* while it made good sense it was a "humiliating climb-down."

In April 1987 the group was approached by Underwoods, a chain of 40 chemist and consumer goods shops in London. Underwoods suggested the group might like to acquire it, but the chain's profit forecast proved unsatisfactory and the proposal was rejected. However, the group acquired Charlie Browns, a chain of 42 car parts sales and fitting centers in northern England, for £19.2 million. At the end of March, the group made a successful agreed bid of £256.9 million for Superdrug plc, a discount chain of 297 drugstores. The company had been established in 1966 by brothers Peter and Ronald Goldstein. In January 1988 the group acquired Ultimate, a chain of 94 electrical retailing outlets, from Harris Queensway for £6.3 million. Ultimate was integrated into Comet. In January 1988 the group launched a successful agreed takeover bid of £13 million for Tip Top Drugstores plc, a chain of 110 drugstores. These were integrated into the 339-store Superdrug chain. Tip Top's strength lay in northern England and Scotland, while Superdrug's lay in southeast England. In February the group launched another successful agreed bid of £32 million for Share Drug plc, a chain of 145 drugstores that was also integrated into Superdrug, strengthening its position in southern England.

On March 17, 1989, the group was renamed Kingfisher plc. The purpose of the new name was to emphasize how much the group had changed since it was purchased from its U.S. parent in 1982. In October Kingfisher acquired the Laskys chain of 58 electrical goods shops for £3.6 million. Kingfisher claimed that by taking on £5.3 million of bank debt from Granada Plc., the shops would be integrated with Comet's 308 shops. In fact, most of them were closed after they had been operating under the Comet name for only a few months. In November 1989 Kingfisher acquired the Medicare chain of 86 drug stores from Isosceles for about £5 million. About a third were closed and the remainder were integrated with Superdrug.

In December 1989 Kingfisher launched a hostile £568 million takeover bid for Dixons. In January 1990 the bid was referred by the British government to the Monopolies and Mergers Commission (MMC) because "there are possible effects on competition in the UK market for the retail of electrical goods. . . . " The bid was blocked by the Trade and Industry Secretary at the end of May following the publication of the MMC's report, which had recommended that the merger should not be permitted.

Since 1982 Kingfisher's profits have risen sharply, efficiency has improved, and the merchandise range has been focused. Profit before tax has risen from £29.4 million in 1983–1984 to £215.3 million in 1990–1991.

Principal Subsidiaries: Woolworths plc; B&Q plc; Comet Group PLC; Superdrug Stores PLC; Chartwell Land plc.

Further Reading: Winkler, John K., *Five and Ten: The Fabulous Life of F.W. Woolworth,* London, Hale, 1941; "Woolworth: The Story of a Great Achievement," *New Bond,* Vol. 18, No. 1, March 1959; Kirkwood, Robert C., *The Woolworth Story At Home and Abroad,* New York, Newcomen Society in North America, 1960; Mulcahy, Geoffrey, "Woolworth Holdings" in Nelson, Rebecca and David Clutterbuck, eds., *Turnaround: How Twenty Well-Known Companies Came Back From The Brink,* London, Mercury, 1988; The Monopolies and Mergers Commission, "Kingfisher Plc and Dixons Group Plc: A Report On The Proposed Merger," London, HMSO, 1990.

—Richard Hawkins

SM

KMART CORPORATION

3100 West Big Beaver Road
Troy, Michigan 48084
U.S.A.
(313) 643-1000
Fax: (313) 643-5398

Public Company
Incorporated: 1912 as the S.S. Kresge Company
Employees: 373,000
Sales: $32.07 billion
Stock Exchanges: New York Boston Cincinnati Midwest
   Pacific Philadelphia

Kmart Corporation is a discount retailer operating in the United States, Canada, and Puerto Rico. The company has two groups: the general merchandise group, which in 1990 included 2,350 discount department stores and membership warehouse clubs; and the specialty retailing group, with 1,830 retail outlets offering drugs, books, and products for home improvement.

The giant Kmart Corporation grew from a Detroit five-and-dime store that opened in 1899. Its proprietor was Sebastian Spering Kresge, a former Pennsylvania tinware salesman who adopted the chain-store idea first used by Frank W. Woolworth. Kresge's store sold costume jewelry, housewares, and personal grooming aids, and its success encouraged him to open a second store in Port Huron, Michigan, the same year. Others followed in rapid succession; by 1912, when Kresge incorporated his company in Delaware with a capitalization of $7 million, there were 85 stores producing annual sales of $10.3 million. Four years later he reincorporated in Michigan, this time with a $12 million capitalization.

Always in high-traffic, convenient locations, Kresge Red Front stores featured open displays of merchandise with items systematically associated. Following their founder's abhorrence of credit, they kept their prices to thrifty nickel and dime limits, until inflation after World War I made the cost of many items too high. Undaunted, Kresge opened a chain of Green Front units in 1920, all selling merchandise at prices ranging between 25¢ and $1. He also acquired Mount Clemens Pottery, to supply the stores with ever-popular inexpensive dinnerware.

In 1924 the company's 257 stores generated annual sales of $90 million. Convinced that this success should go hand in hand with corporate responsibility toward the less fortunate, the company founder established the Kresge Foundation, making an initial contribution of $1.3 million plus securities worth $65 million.

The following year Kresge resigned the presidency he had held since 1907 to concentrate on long-range goal-setting as company chairman. His planning bore fruit in January 1929, when a Kresge store opened in the United States' first suburban shopping center, Country Club Plaza, in Kansas City, Missouri, thereby anticipating a shift in shopping patterns by some 15 years.

Another long-range goal crystallized in September 1928, with the formation of a Canadian subsidiary that opened the country's first Kresge store the following May. Based in Kitchener, Ontario, the initial venture was so successful that the company's $5 million investment financed another 18 stores in locations from Winnipeg to Montreal by the end of 1929. These brought the total number of Kresge stores to 597, together yielding earnings of $55.1 million on total sales of $156.3 million.

The company's orderly expansion changed after 1929, when the Depression-era stock market plunged the price of Kresge stock from $57.50 per share to an eventual low of $5.50. This was a severe blow to company management, which had pledged its support by taking turns to buy the deflated stock, gambling on its bottoming out at $26. Kresge found himself at a loss, having promised to buy 100,000 shares he could no longer afford, and the company took them off his hands. By 1936, however, the chairman had bought back at cost his own shares plus the 251,306 others owned by the management.

The Depression also brought falling sales as well as inventory losses through the failure of suppliers' businesses. Competition also increased; the scramble for the retail dollar fueled rivalry from Sears, Roebuck and prompted other chains to open department store "bargain basements." Forced to broaden its inventory to meet this threat, Kresge had to raise its prices, so that Green Front stores had many items selling for up to $3 despite their former $1 ceiling.

With the Depression over by 1940, there were 682 stores in 27 U.S. states, plus 61 in Canada. Together, the stores produced 1940 sales figures of $158.7 million. As the decade advanced, many homeowners moved out to the suburbs from inner-city locations. The retailers followed. Kresge management cautiously opened one suburban shopping center store in 1947, adding to the first one that had opened in 1929. Three more followed in 1948. By 1953 there were about 40 suburban stores in the United States, plus one in Canada.

By the mid-1950s chairman Sebastian Kresge was long retired from active company management. An operating committee of 16 executives appointed by the board of directors steered the corporate strategy. Among them was a vice-president in charge of store management, whose chief responsibility was to train and guide all store managers, partly through the district office supervisors who interpreted company policies, improving the performance of individual units. Another committee member, the vice-president in charge of merchandising, handled all merchandise for the U.S. stores, through a department consisting of the buyers who chose all wares from the product lines of the company's 4,600 suppliers, purchased them, and set pricing policies. The sales manager, in charge of public relations, merchandise delivery, advertising, and displays also sat on the committee, along with the vice-president in charge of real estate, store locations, leasing, and modernization programs.

Although the committee frequently combined smaller stores in high-volume areas to provide better selection and more efficient service, there were 616 U.S. stores by 1954, plus 74 in Canada. Many of the units featured modern conveniences like air-conditioning, self-service displays, and shopping baskets. All these operations combined to reach sales figures totaling $337.9 million in 1954—up from $223.2 million in 1945.

Although the variety store image still guided company activities during the 1950s, pricing limits were fading away, with the concept of discount retailing coming to the fore in its stead. Kresge offered economical private-label products ranging from clothing to house paint. The variety of brand-name offerings also broadened to include electric appliances, radios, and power lawn mowers.

In the late 1950s food grew into the largest single department, warranting training in food management for all store managers. Many stores had delicatessens, and Kresge in-store luncheonettes provided shoppers with a large assortment of snacks, lunches, and dinners devised by the test kitchen at the company's Detroit headquarters. By 1958 these mini-restaurants were so popular that at least one new or remodeled facility opened alongside a delicatessen counter in some Kresge store each week.

A wider variety of merchandise plus higher pricing brought a need for a layaway plan allowing customers to save for expensive items. It was, however, still against company policy to offer credit, although competitors were luring customers in this way.

In 1959, coinciding with the opening of the first Kresge store in Puerto Rico, Harry Blair Cunningham succeeded to the presidency of S.S. Kresge Company. Cunningham, aged 58, had been with Kresge since 1928. A former newspaper reporter, he had worked his way up from trainee status through the store manager ranks, eventually becoming general vice-president. Twin assignments went with this position: one was to tour all of Kresge's U.S. stores, assessing the future position of the company and its competitors in the variety store industry; the other was to prepare himself for the company presidency, when Franklin Williams would retire in two years' time.

Cunningham's travels convinced him that Kresge's competitors were not other variety chains, but the new discounters aiming for fast inventory turnover, which they could achieve by lower markups on a large assortment of small items. Discounting, in fact, was a return to Sebastian Kresge's basic merchandising philosophy, which would be a bulwark against competition in the future, just as it had been in the past. Cunningham, after a period of testing, concluded that higher sales volume, rather than higher markups, would boost the company's profits, which had dropped during the 1950s.

In 1962 the company opened its first discount store in a suburb of Detroit, calling it K mart. Within a year, there were 17 others. Unlike Kresge stores, K marts were not placed in shopping centers but were built in plazas by themselves, to avoid internal competition and also to provide ample parking. To ensure a 25% annual pretax return on investment, each store featured decor that was pleasant, if not extravagant, and each aimed for eight inventory turnovers per year. The K mart stores were an instant success; by 1963, there were 63 facili-

ties, 51 of which provided repair and maintenance service for automobiles. Three years later, the number of K marts had swelled to 122.

The K mart introduction still left the company with a number of older Kresge stores, still on long leases, which were too small to display K mart's expanded merchandise lines. Numerous Kresge stores, mostly in deteriorating business areas, were renamed Jupiter Discount Stores and were converted to facilities offering a limited variety of low markup, fast-moving merchandise like clothes, drugstore items, and housewares. By 1966 there were almost 100 Jupiter stores in operation.

In 1965 the company underwent several changes. One involved the sale of long-time subsidiary Mount Clemens Pottery. Another was the acquisition of Holly Stores, a retailer of women's and children's clothing that had been a K mart licensee since 1962, and was operating clothing departments in 124 K marts, Kresges, and Jupiters at the time of the acquisition. The same year, the company acquired Dunhams Stores Corporation, a sporting goods supplier already operating under license in 42 K marts. Dunhams then became K mart Sporting Goods, Inc.

S.S. Kresge Company's sales for 1965 reached a record $851 million, representing a 23.6% gain from 1964. There were 895 stores, of which 108 were in Canada. Although discount retailing had gained momentum somewhat later in Canada than in the United States, the Canadian subsidiary had opened its first K mart in London, Ontario, in 1963. At the same time, while inner-city deterioration in Canada had not reached the same level as in U.S. cities, the company turned some of its smaller, older Canadian stores into Jupiters.

The successful Canadian operations made a large contribution to the total sales figures for 1966, which topped $1 billion for the first time, reflecting a 28% rise over 1965. Company founder Sebastian Kresge did not live to see this triumph. Aged 99, he died in September 1966, having retired from the company chairmanship only three months earlier.

Spurred by its Canadian success, the company found another international opportunity in Australia, via a joint venture: K mart (Australia) Limited, with retailer G.J. Coles & Coy, Limited. The 1968 undertaking, in which K mart held 51% of the shares, produced five Australian K marts by 1970.

By 1969 S.S. Kresge Company had decided against purchasing of the licensee of its automotive departments, instead opening another subsidiary called K mart Enterprises, Inc., to operate the departments, now so popular that 56 had opened in that year alone. That year the number of company stores stood at 1,022; sales at $4.6 billion, and average profit per store at $42,358.

As the 1960s ended, an economic slowdown posed challenges for S.S. Kresge. The company resorted to heavier-than-usual promotional markdowns in December 1969 and January 1970 that shaved profit margins. Other problems were the difficulty of keeping to a 25% annual rate of sales gain for an ever-expanding number of stores; the fact that the rate of sales growth in a store slowed as the store aged; and the increase in inventory that came from formerly licensed in-store departments. All these factors led to an earnings slowdown in 1970's first quarter, bringing its stock down 11.5 points in one day. Still, sales for 1970 reached almost $2.2 billion.

In 1972 Cunningham was succeeded as chief executive by Robert E. Dewar, a former company lawyer and president since 1970. The presidency was filled by Ervin Wardlow, whose forte was merchandising, while Walter Teninga, the new vice-chairman, had been the company's chief financial and development officer.

These three hurdled these challenges with strategies forged under Cunningham's tenure, like the centralized buying for both Kresge and K mart stores that reduced possible in-house conflict between variety store and discount divisions. The company also expanded its management training program, so that variety store managers could switch to discount facilities with ease. Meticulous crafting of the training program guaranteed that each store manager could make decisions about products, promotions, pricing, and locations that would ensure the store's competitiveness. Other policies included limiting each store to one entrance and exit, thus reducing staff needs and escalating sales per employee, and designing smaller stores of 65,000 to 70,000 square feet, adequate for smaller, more affluent shopping communities. All these changes gave the company a chance to upgrade merchandise while phasing out leased departments on all items except shoes.

The course charted for the 1970s brought Kresge an annual sales growth of 22% from 1972 to 1976, with 1976 sales totaling $8.4 billion. The company, however, was not without its failures. A fast-food drive-in chain called K mart Chef, set up in 1967, closed in 1974 after having peaked at just 11 units. The costly credit card operation, used by only 9% of K mart customers, was withdrawn the same year, while a $65 million purchase of Planned Marketing Associates, an insurance company renamed K mart Insurance Services Inc., brought a loss of $8 million in 1975, although a modest profit of $344,000 was recorded for 1976.

By this time the company's 1,206 K marts were accounting for almost 95% of sales. For this reason, shareholders changed the company name to K mart Corporation in 1977.

The late 1970s saw changes in K mart's seemingly impregnable position. New competitors with more inviting stores made company facilities seem shoddy, and specialty stores began to stock K mart staples like sports equipment, drugs, and personal grooming aids. Changes in public taste showed up in lagging profits, which sank 27% in 1980 on record sales reaching $14.2 billion. Other warning signals showed in plunging inventory turnover, which dropped from the 8-times-annually level of the 1960s to 3.8 times by 1979. Utility bills, wages, and other overhead costs soared because of inflation, but fierce competition prevented the company from raising its discount prices.

K mart responded by cutting the number of scheduled new stores in favor of remodeling existing units and restocking them with more fashionable merchandise. It also installed a computer system to handle inventories, orders, shipments and other procedures that could speed up delivery times to each store. Other changes included the 1978 sale of the company's 51% interest in K mart (Australia) Limited to Coles Myer for new Coles Myer shares, thus closing out K mart's ownership of the Australian K mart stores.

Bernard M. Fauber succeeded Dewar as chairman and chief executive in 1980. Fauber steered the company through an economic slowdown and into diversification that year, with purchase of a 44% interest in a Mexican discount chain, as well as a joint venture into Japanese mass-merchandising with Japan's biggest retailer, The Daiei, Inc. K mart also bought Texas-based Furr's Cafeterias Inc., a 76-unit chain that was a natural outgrowth of the cafeterias in K mart stores.

In 1984 K mart expanded its acquisition program and diversified into specialty markets. Because K mart already had been experimenting with its home improvement departments, a logical move was the $88.2 million purchase of a nine-unit Texas chain called Home Centers of America, Inc. K mart made Home Centers's operations into warehouse-type stores, changing the name to Builders Square. Next came Waldenbooks, costing $300 million for 845 stores that had produced sales of $417 million in 1983. An Oregon-based chain of 164 drugstores called Pay Less joined the growing lineup in 1985.

In 1984 there was another change in K mart strategy when apparel division president Joseph Antonini launched a new line of clothes named for actress Jaclyn Smith that helped to turn apparel into the company's fastest-growing business. By the time he succeeded to the company chairmanship in 1987, Antonini's strategy had added both racing driver Mario Andretti to the list for automotive accessories promotions, and caterer Martha Stewart for kitchen and housewares support.

The celebrities helped the bottom line—profits for 1987 rose 19%, to reach $692 million on total sales of $25.6 billion. Other factors in year-end figures were the sale of all U.S. Kresge and Jupiter stores, the $238 million sale of Furr's Cafeterias and another cafeteria chain called Bishop Buffets, Inc., to Cavalcade Foods, Inc., and the disposal of Mexican interests.

New ventures in 1988 included a partnership with Bruno's, Inc., a food retailer, which generated the American Fare hypermarket near Atlanta in 1989; purchase of a 51% ownership interest in Makro Inc., which operated membership warehouses; and launch of Office Square, a discount office supply chain. In 1989 K mart acquired PACE Membership Warehouse, Inc. and the remaining 49% of Makro, converting Makro stores to PACE formats. It also opened Sports Giant, a group of sporting goods stores. The company dropped the space in its name between "K" and "mart" in 1990. In 1990 it bought The Sports Authority and converted the Sports Giant stores into Sports Authority. It also bought a 21.6% interest in OfficeMax, Inc., an office-supply chain. Kmart announced it would acquire the remainder of OfficeMax in October 1991. Also in 1990, the company began a six-year overhaul of all Kmart stores; including some openings, closings, enlargements, and refurbishings.

Principal Subsidiaries: Builders Square, Inc.; Kmart Canada Limited; PACE Membership Warehouse, Inc.; Pay Less Drug Stores Northwest, Inc.; The Sports Authority, Inc.; Walden Book Company, Inc.

Further Reading: "S.S. Kresge Expansion is Costly," *Barron's,* September 7, 1936; "Kresge's," *Fortune,* June 1, 1940; "Kresge's Triple-Threat Retailing," *Business Week,* January 29, 1966; "When 2 Cents = $380 Million," *Forbes,* April 1, 1970; Main, Jeremy, "K mart's Plan to be Born Again, Again," *Fortune,* September 21, 1981; Sellers, Patricia, "Attention, K mart Shoppers," *Fortune,* January 2, 1989.

—Gillian Wolf

KOTOBUKIYA CO., LTD.

3-3-3 Honjo
Kumamoto City 860
Japan
(96) 366 3111
Fax: (96) 372 7470

Public Company
Incorporated: 1949
Employees: 6,091
Sales: ¥285.17 billion (US$2.29 billion)
Stock Exchange: Osaka

Founded shortly after the end of World War II, Kotobukiya has grown to become the leading retailer in Japan's southern island of Kyushu. With 121 major department stores operating under the name Kotobukiya and almost 300 other specialty boutiques, the company sells everything from fashion to food and electric appliances. Like many Japanese retail chains, Kotobukiya provides the full range of shopping-related services, and is actively involved in the credit, travel, property leasing, and restaurant businesses. Although in 1991 Japan is in the midst of its longest consumer spending boom since the end of World War II, the management of the company remains cautious about future expansion plans.

Kotobukiya originated in Kyushu, Japan's second-most populated and industrialized island. The island is divided into seven provinces and contains the major industrial cities of Nagasaki and Fukuoka. It was in Nagasaki that Japan first had contact with the western world in the 16th century and until 1868 it remained the only port open to foreign vessels.

Kotobukiya's founder, Sueko Suzaki, was born in 1904 in Saiki, a small town on the east coast of Kyushu where she lived with her husband and family. After her husband was killed in World War II, she had to raise her family on her own. In postwar Japan there was limited opportunity for women to obtain employment, so in 1947, using her savings, she opened a small store of only 12 square meters selling handbags and cosmetics bags that she made herself. Suzaki named the shop Kotobukiya, which is another reading of the first Japanese character in the name Suzaki. Through her hard work, the shop flourished and Suzaki began selling decorative scrolls and other trinkets. Japan's defeat in World War II meant that in the early postwar years its economy was largely dominated by the United States and to some extent this also applied to consumer fashions. Realizing this, Suzaki began to stock items imported from the United States and gave her shop an American atmosphere. This expansion of the business caused Suzaki's eldest son Hajime to leave his job in a Tokyo tax office and return home in 1953 to help with the family business. The following year, in order to combat inflation and stabilize the economy, which was still fairly weak, the local authorities initiated controls that dictated prices for certain goods, making it easier for retailers and consumers to plan their finances. At the first company meeting in 1955, Sueko and Hajime Suzaki, and the store's ten employees formulated their strategy for expansion. Novel promotional ideas were used to advertise the store; five female models were brought from Kyoto to promote the goods and free samples were handed out. Then Kotobukiya began staff training, which was to become an important factor in the company's success. Employees were taught how to present the souvenirs sold in the store and how to serve the customer with respect. In 1957, ten years after opening her first store, Suzaki opened another in the city of Miyazaki, south of Saiki. To raise money, half of the company's shares were sold to the employees. At the time the firm's capitalization was only ¥1.25 million—slightly less than $3,700. The two stores' combined shop floor area had increased to 1,800 square meters and a management system encouraging employee participation was introduced. The Miyazaki branch, located in a far more prosperous and populated area than Saiki, flourished. A Western products division was formed in 1960, and in the same year Kotobukiya Company was formed as a holding company. The year 1961 saw the opening of the company's first food supermarket in Saiki. The range of products sold in all the stores was enlarged to include processed foods and household items. In 1962 and 1963 several new stores—referred to as compact department stores—were opened, not as large as some of the bigger stores, but still selling a wide range of goods.

As president of the firm, Hajime Suzaki took the leading role in expanding the company and in 1963 visited the United States to observe retailing operations and methods. He studied inventory control and supermarket promotion and picked out aspects of U.S. retailing methods that he thought applicable to his own operation. One was the development of a strong brand image associated with the store, and he sought to apply uniform standards to all Kotobukiya stores so that customers could expect similar service in each branch. By 1966 capitalization had reached ¥40 million and, as a result of growing consumer demand, Kotobukiya continued to open new stores at the rate of about ten a year while closing down or moving smaller and less productive premises. That year, the original store in Saiki was closed and moved to a new location nearby. The company also began sending its store managers on overseas training courses and in the following year a formalized management training program was organized, with 13 new university graduates joining the company.

With 400 employees, Kotobukiya was a medium-sized company and Hajime Suzaki decided to move it to the city of Kumamoto on Kyushu's west coast. The four-story headquarters also contained a department store. With the large amount of real estate that the company owned or rented, Suzaki diversified successfully into property leasing. In 1970 a training program was set up for the sales staff—Japanese department stores provided, and the customers expected, excellent service and Suzaki strove to provide this by comprehensive staff training. In 1971 Kotobukiya opened Bouquet, its first specialty store in Kagoshima, which aimed to be the most modern in the region. The chain grew quickly, selling fashion goods aimed at the youth market. Frequent overseas trips to the United States and Europe by store managers meant that the company was well versed in the latest western fashion trends, many of which were copied in Japan. In 1972 Kotobukiya formed a partnership with the Southern Japan Trust Bank to provide customers with credit services. The following year Kotobukiya became a listed company with its shares traded on the Fukuoka Exchange, moving to the Osaka Exchange in 1976. The range of goods sold at Kotobukiya's stores by than included electrical goods, leisure equipment, and imported liquor. The year 1977 marked the 30th anniversary of the company, and to celebrate the occasion Kotobukiya donated ¥100 million to local charities in Kyushu. In this year, sales reached the ¥100 billion mark—about $500 million—and new stores continued to be opened at the rate of about 12 per year. To cope with the necessary staffing requirements a training center was opened, and in 1979 alone 1,400 people joined the company. The 100th Kotobukiya store was opened in Kumamoto and in 1980 two new companies were formed: Kyushu Consultants, providing leasing and finance services, and Kotobukiya Land, dealing in real estate. To remain competitive, the chain cut prices on groceries at its supermarkets. A new computer system allowed management to control stock more tightly and undercut smaller retailers. By 1981 the chain was ranked 19th among Japanese retailers and employed more than 10,000. Twenty-four-hour convenience stores were launched and an overseas trading company was set up to supply the stores with selected imported goods. For this purpose, a representative office was set up in Korea. Meanwhile Kotobukiya entered two new areas of retailing, fresh fruits and marine products.

In 1983 the company implemented a system subsequently used throughout Japanese business—total quality control. Store managers were introduced to the system, the aim of which was to ensure that there was no price, stock, or quality variation across the chain and a computer system was used to verify this. At the frequent store managers' meetings, exchanges of ideas and information were encouraged. In 1984 Kotobukiya opened its first Sunpark leisure center and in the same year began issuing credit cards that could be used at Kotobukiya stores: there were 23,000 subscribers in the first year. In that year, the Japanese government promoted the industrial development of Kyushu and Shikoku, Japan's smallest island, under the Technopolis scheme and Kotobukiya donated ¥100 million to the project. The year 1985 marked the appointment of the first woman in charge of a Kotobukiya store—well overdue considering that in addition to having a woman as founder, over half of the company's staff were women. Partly in response to overexpansion in the late 1970s and early 1980s and partly due to management plans to concentrate on larger stores, 19 branches were closed in 1985 resulting in job cuts—the work force fell from 10,000 in 1982 to 6,000 by early 1986—and decreased revenues. Profits, however, remained steady. Hajime Suzaki was concerned that the bureaucracy of the company had become too large, and there was a management shakeup in 1986. The headquarters was reorganized into 3 divisions with 11 subdivisions. Early retirement was sought for some, and younger key staff were promoted. Responding to changing times, the company entered the video rental business

and began importing directly from mainland China via a trading department set up within the company.

In response to the growing use of credit cards in Japan, Kotobukiya began accepting various cards and formed a partnership with Visa to issue a new card. The company began to consider permitting shopping by telephone, allowing customers at selected stores to arrange purchase and delivery from home or office. Kotobukiya, like most large Japanese companies at this time, took advantage of the booming Japanese stock market and engaged in *zaitech*—financial engineering—to generate profits. The company also looked to the European warrant market to raise capital, with a $100 million issue in the United Kingdom in 1988. Further consolidation occurred in 1988 and 1989 when 24 Kotobukiya stores were closed. This resulted in a less than 1% drop in sales during that period, indicating the soundness of management decisions. The management relied on its up-to-date computer system to identify the most inefficient stores. In 1990 the company's founder Sueko Suzaki died at the age of 86, having long since retired from active management within the company she started. Following her death, her son Hajime took over as chairman of Kotobukiya, leaving the post of president open to a nonfamily member, Yutaka Yonekawa. Hajime's son Shigeru is a managing director in the company.

Although the collapse of the Japanese stock market in 1990 and 1991 did not greatly weaken Japan's consumer spending boom, which had begun in the late 1980s, it affected corporate earnings considerably. Companies that had engaged in stock and real estate speculation were hit hard, although Kotobukiya was not as exposed as some companies. With the credit squeeze and raising of interest rates imposed by the Bank of Japan, funds for expansion and investment became scarcer. In the wake of this, net operating profits decreased slightly in 1990 to ¥5.6 billion or $39 million. In 1990 the company pursued its policy of careful investment in training and facilities, concentrating on the expansion of point-of-sales information control systems and the refurbishing of stores to meet customer demand. Current trade negotiations between Japan and the United States emphasize the large-scale retail stores. The United States would like to see certain retailing and distribution restrictions for foreign companies lifted, which could result in increased competition in this sector. The management concedes that retailing trends are hard to predict and it therefore responds to what it sees as current trends. It is uncertain how long the consumer boom will continue. This means that Hajime Suzaki and the management of Kotobukiya are content to adopt a cautious approach to expansion in the first half of the 1990s.

Principal Subsidiaries: Gruppe Co. Ltd.; Kyushu Consultants Co. Ltd.; Kotobukiya Bakery Co. Ltd.; Kyushu Region Spar Honbu Co. Ltd; Bouquet Co. Ltd; (90%) Tohya Department Store Co. Ltd.; (50%) Tohya Shoji Co. Ltd (50%); Sakura Department Store Co. Ltd., (55%).

Further Reading: Retail Distribution in Japan, Dodwell Marketing Consultants, 1988 Kotobukiya Company Guide 1991.

—Dylan Tanner

THE LIMITED, INC.

Two Limited Parkway
Columbus, Ohio 43216
U.S.A.
(614) 479-7000
Fax: (614) 479-7080

Public Company
Incorporated: 1963
Employees: 72,500
Sales: $5.25 billion
Stock Exchanges: New York London Tokyo

The Limited, Inc. is one of the largest specialty apparel retailers in the United States. It has more than 3,800 stores, including the Limited and Express stores, selling young women's clothing; Henri Bendel, upscale women's fashion stores; Lane Bryant, focusing on larger sizes; and Victoria's Secret, a group of lingerie shops. The company is largely the vision of its founder and chairman, Leslie Wexner.

In 1961 Leslie Wexner dropped out of law school and went to work in his father's women's wear store in Columbus, Ohio. Wexner suggested business would improve if the store concentrated on sportswear, but his father, Harry Wexner, said a full product line was necessary to attract customers. He encouraged his son to try out this idea, which Leslie Wexner eventually did.

In 1963, with a $5,000 loan from his aunt, Wexner opened a 2,000-square-foot store in Columbus's Kingsdale shopping center. Wexner christened it The Limited for the limited merchandise it carried. Wexner's goal was to gross $100,000 the first year. He surpassed this with sales of $162,000, and opened a second store.

By 1965 The Limited was so successful that Wexner's parents, Harry and Bella, closed their own store and joined him at The Limited. Harry Wexner served as chairman until his death in 1975. As of 1991 Bella was still on the board as corporate secretary, providing her son with advice on his business moves.

One year after his parents closed up shop and joined him, The Limited opened its first corporate headquarters above its Eastland mall store in Columbus. That year its number of employees reached 100. By 1968 The Limited's sales had surpassed the $1 million mark.

In 1969, with five stores operating, Wexner issued The Limited's first public stock, traded over the counter. After going public, the company began to expand rapidly—too rapidly,

causing earnings to collapse. Wexner responded by improving the efficiency of the company's manufacturing and distribution systems. In a brief period, what The Limited had done in order to survive became the company's distinctive strength.

After identifying The Limited's trouble spots, Wexner implemented a system of financial controls supported by electronic point-of-purchase terminals. These terminals allowed the company's Columbus headquarters to monitor inventory levels to see what is selling and where it is selling, which helps The Limited to aggressively mark down slow-selling items, clearing shelf space for hot new items to be brought in. Although marking down slow sellers is not a fresh idea, the speed at which headquarters can evaluate and authorize these markdowns is. The computer lines that link The Limited's shops to corporate headquarters bring the company the flexibility and speed of a small privately run boutique, giving The Limited a competitive edge over department stores that are forced to stick to price adjustment budgets planned months in advance.

The Limited's 1970 annual report, produced with a common copy machine, was so bold as to predict The Limited would become the largest and most profitable retailer of woman's specialty clothing in the nation, although, at the time, there were only six Limited stores in existence. The company's confidence certainly paid off. By 1974 The Limited had more than 1,000 employees, and by 1976 The Limited had opened its 100th store. It had carved out a niche selling to young, fashion-conscious women who could coordinate an entire wardrobe with one stop at The Limited.

The Limited's purchase of Mast Industries in 1978 added to the company's efficiency and flexibility. Mast Industries, a supplier that contracted with more than 150 production facilities around the world, became The Limited's merchandise procurement arm. This acquisition, coupled with the electronic point-of-purchase terminals on line to headquarters, allowed The Limited to place orders and purchase and restock shelves with its most popular merchandise within two to three weeks, compared to the months required by competing department stores. The Limited had also opened its first distribution center, 525,000 square feet on Morse Road in Columbus.

The Limited did more than concentrate on a specific market segment; it segmented the segment. In 1980 it opened its first Limited Express store, which focuses on the youngest of fashion-conscious women, teenagers, putting more trendiness into its designs than would go into women's sportswear. In 1982 The Limited Express, with eight successful stores, became a separate business and was later renamed simply Express. The Limited's expansion and market segmentation did not stop there.

In 1982 alone The Limited acquired Lane Bryant, Victoria's Secret, and Roaman's, merging the latter with Sizes Unlimited. That year The Limited was also listed on the New York Stock Exchange, and its number of employees reached 10,000.

Each acquisition focused on a specific segment of the market. During the restructuring of Lane Bryant, which sells clothing for larger women, The Limited dropped its very largest sizes and restocked shelves with lower-priced, more fashionable sportswear aimed at younger women. It signed a contract with Bonjour to produce jeans and other stylish sportswear in large sizes, giving the chain a new image. When The Limited purchased Victoria's Secret, stores and catalog, it legitimized women's purchase of sexy lingerie on a national scale. Victoria's Secret stores, full of floral and lace pillows, old English furniture, and classical music, projected a respectable image.

The Limited's procurement arm, Mast Industries, helped supply all of the Limited's subsidiaries. In 1984, when Limited buyers stocked stores with career clothes that no one would buy, the Limited was able to develop, place orders for, and receive the completely new, private Forenza line, all within a matter of months, managing to reverse a slump that could have been catastrophic.

These private-label goods, which The Limited manufactures specifically for its stores, are produced at low cost in Third World country and sold for whatever price the market will support. The private labels can support large markups because The Limited creates a desirable image for each line. The Forenza line sported a romantic Italian name, although most of it was produced in the Far East; garment tags bore the name of a fictitious designer, Maria Pia, a production consultant whose name had appealed to Wexner.

By 1984 The Limited's sales had surpassed the $1 billion mark. That same year it was listed on the London Stock Exchange. The Limited's growth showed little sign of slowing. In 1984 The Limited offered to buy the financially troubled Los Angeles–based retailer Carter Hawley Hale Stores for $1.1 billion. The offer was rejected. In 1985 The Limited acquired Lerner Stores, a chain of moderate-price shops that it made profitable within the year, as well as Henri Bendel, which caters to upscale, fashion-conscious women. That year it also opened its second distribution center, a 1.07 million–square-foot facility, and The Limited's number of employees climbed past 25,000.

Net sales rose past $3 billion in 1986. The first Lerner Woman store, carrying large sizes, was opened, and Limited Credit Services was formed. In 1986 The Limited, in partnership with Edward J. DeBartolo Corporation, again attempted to buy Carter Hawley Hale, offering as much as $60 per share. Carter Hawley Hale rejected the bid, selling more than 3.5 billion shares to White Knight General Cinema Corporation.

In 1987 the company opened two Limited International Fashion "superstores." It introduced Limited Too, targeting children. It merged Sizes Unlimited and Lerner Woman. Express unveiled its men's collection, and the number of employees reached 50,000.

The Limited in 1988 acquired Abercrombie & Fitch. The company debuted its own private-label intimate apparel business, Lingerie Cacique. It also opened The Limited Building, a one millions–square-foot distribution center and office. During the fashion slump that year it enlarged its specialty stores, giving them more expansive window displays, attempting to attract women with their look and size. In 1988 sales topped $4 billion.

The Limited sold Lerner Woman in 1989 to United Retail Group, Inc. It also obtained a charter for Limited Credit Services to become the World Financial Network National Bank, making it the first U.S. retailer to transform its credit division in that fashion. The company was ranked first in growth and profitability among specialty apparel by *Forbes* in January 1989.

Some industry experts question how long The Limited can grow at its current pace. They wonder if by leaving its original niche of small stores with limited merchandise for the fashionable yet cost-conscious woman, and by moving to larger stores or groups of stores that carry everything from underwear to clothes for children and men, The Limited might be losing its market advantage. Also, many U.S. manufacturers refuse to produce The Limited's private labels or operate at the company's breakneck pace. Still, the company forecast continued growth, with the expectation of adding $1 billion in sales per year during the early 1990s, toward a goal of $10 billion by mid-decade.

Principal Subsidiaries: The Limited; The Limited Express; Victoria's Secret; Victoria's Secret Catalogue; Henri Bendel; Lerner; Abercrombie & Fitch; Brylane; Mast Industries, Inc.; Limited Credit Services.

Further Reading: "The Unlimited Limited," *Forbes,* November 15, 1977; Baumgold, Julie, "The Bachelor Billionaire: On Pins and Needles with Leslie Wexner," *New York,* August 5, 1985; Weiner, Steven B., "The Unlimited?" *Forbes,* April 6, 1987; *The Limited, Inc.: Fact Book: 1989–1990,* [1989]; Trachtenberg, Jeffrey A., "Merchant in a Rush: Leslie Wexner Pushes Limited's Fast Growth Despite Retailing's Ills," *The Wall Street Journal,* August 15, 1990.

—Maya Sahafi

THE LITTLEWOODS ORGANISATION PLC

JM Centre
Old Hall Street
Liverpool L70 1AB
United Kingdom
(051) 235 2222
Fax: (051) 235 2670

Private Company
Incorporated: 1923 as Littlewoods Pools
Employees: 30,000
Sales: £2.37 billion (US $4.57 billion)

The Littlewoods Organisation PLC (Littlewoods) is the largest privately-owned family company in the United Kingdom, with shareholders' investment valued at £753 million. It was started in Liverpool in 1923 as a football (soccer) pool business by John Moores and two partners, all of them then full-time employees of a telegraph company in that city. The name Littlewoods Pools was chosen to conceal their involvement from their employers. After a loss-making first season the other two withdrew, but Moores held on, assisted by other members of his family and, in particular, by his brother Cecil, who joined the business. John Moores entered retailing in 1932 with a mail-order business and in 1937 opened the first Littlewoods chain store. The three businesses prospered. Two more were started in 1985, as we shall see, after Sir John Moores—he was knighted in 1972—had called in non-family executives to take over the day-to-day management of the Organisation. By 1990 the group's turnover had reached £2.37 billion. At the end of 1991, the whole concern was still owned by the president, Sir John Moores, aged 95, thirty-two other members of the Moores family, and related family trusts.

In and after the 1920s, with large corporations already starting to dominate the British economy, promising niches offering opportunities for rapid growth from ploughed-back profit were relatively rare for those lacking capital. That John Moores hit upon football pools at the beginning of the 1923–1924 playing season was a most timely stroke of good fortune. The Cup Final, held at Wembley for the first time earlier that year, had drawn much attention to Association Football, which soon developed into a well-supported working-class spectator sport on Saturdays and a topic of conversation for the rest of the week. Wage earners' disposable incomes, though still small, grew rapidly in those years, and a business which gave them an opportunity to place small bets did not have difficulty in attracting some of this surplus. Sales of sixpenny postal orders reached unprecedented heights as a normally weekend sport became an even more popular weekday pastime offering the chance of winning more than even the most thrifty wage earner could ever hope to save in a lifetime: £13,000 was laid out on a penny bet in one instance during the 1930s.

John Moores was born at Eccles near Manchester in January 1896, the eldest of four sons in a family eventually to number eight children. He left school at 14 to work as a messenger boy at the Manchester Post Office but was soon accepted in a course at the Post Office School of Telegraphy. This enabled him, in 1912, at 16 years of age, to join the Commercial Cable Company as a junior operator. After World War I, in which he served as a wireless operator in the Royal Navy, he rejoined Commercial Cable and in 1921 was posted from Liverpool to Waterville, the company's base near the southwest tip of Ireland, where he started a private business on the side supplying goods to company colleagues and to the local golf club. Posted back to Liverpool, his keenness to start his own business as great as ever, he tried again, this time with two partners and with a football pool.

How this came about, and the extent to which John Moores was himself an innovator, it is impossible to say, as no biography or any serious history of Littlewoods has been written. It is quite clear, however, that he and his two partners, Colin Askham and Bill Hughes, entered the business when there was only one small, struggling competitor and little capital was needed—each partner put in £50 originally and later another £50. Having weathered unprofitable beginnings, Littlewoods Pools emerged as clear market leader because of its organizational skill and attention to detail in the regular dispatch of coupons early each week, careful checking of the results after the Saturday matches, the handling of an increasing number of small payments—and the larger number of winnings. Growth needed to be at a pace to fund the all-important promotional expenditure required, but overhead was relatively cheap: no prestigious high-street premises were required for a postal business.

Football pools appealed mainly to men. To appeal to women, Littlewoods Mail Order Stores were begun in January 1932 when Great Universal Stores (GUS), an established mail-order business in nearby Manchester, was in trouble. Britain was soon to start climbing out of the deepest trough of depression—again the timing was right—and Moores offered an element of chance in a venture aimed mainly at working-class women who were prepared to lay out a small cash sum each week to buy goods for themselves or their families. This was a logical diversification of the existing business. Besides taking advantage of Littlewoods' already familiar household name, it also built upon the organization and experience gained in postal pools and on John Moores's earlier experience of direct selling in Ireland. Again, nothing was spent on retail outlets, for the business, like GUS, operated on the club principle whereby the many local organizers, working from their own homes, recruited others nearby who paid a small weekly instalment in cash for goods shown in a catalog. A £1 club, for instance, consisted of 20 members who each paid a shilling a week. A weekly draw provided the element of luck, the first winner securing her purchases at once and the others in their turn. There were also £2 and £3 clubs on the same principle. The first catalog ran to 167 pages. The initial cost of launching what was to become an extremely successful enterprise was £20,000.

Moores's venture into chain-store retailing in the mid-1930s was well-timed, too, for the British economy was moving up to a prosperous peak in 1937. Real earnings were growing fast and unemployment was falling. Entering chain-store retailing was a further logical step that took advantage of buying experience and contacts gained in the the mail-order business; but this time it did involve costly high-street premises and competition with well-established chain stores which also offered competitively-priced goods, notably Woolworth and Marks & Spencer. It was altogether a much more costly operation than the two previous postal businesses. The new stores, however, could depend not only upon the familiar Littlewoods name but also on providing basic and serviceable goods at keen prices without undue regard for passing fashion. The first store was opened in Blackpool, Britain's most popular working-class holiday resort, in 1937. By 1939, 24 stores had been opened in various parts of the country.

By then the Moores family had already amassed considerable financial strength. A fine new building, put up on the outskirts of Liverpool as its Pools headquarters, became the postal censorship center during World War II. Other premises—there were 16 by 1944—produced barrage balloons, parachutes, rubber dinghies, and Wellington bomber fuselages, as well as 12 million shells and 6 million fuses.

Immediately after the war the renovation of the stores and the building of new ones were made difficult by building controls. Soon, however, shoppers' habits and tastes were changed by what has come to be called the Retailing Revolution: vastly increased purchasing power and the spread of consumer durables, including motor cars. There were nevertheless 52 Littlewoods stores in operation by 1952, more than twice as many as there had been in 1939, 70 by the mid-1960s, 108 in 1984 and 122 in 1990. They are located throughout the United Kingdom, from Belfast to Norwich and from Inverness to Truro and sell hard-wearing clothing, household goods, food, wines, and spirits; most also have restaurants. Over a third of mothers with young children are said to shop there at least once a month.

In 1953 John Moores, quick to recognize the advent of the credit-buying society, launched Brian Mills, a company based in Sunderland, which supplied goods to customers before any payment was made. Not surprisingly, this made the older club method of mail-order less popular. A second credit mail-order firm, Burlington, also based in Sunderland, was added in 1958 and a third, Littlewoods Warehouses, Liverpool, in 1960, the year after the original business had been renamed the John Moores Home Shopping Service. A fifth credit company, Janet Frazer, was opened in Sunderland in 1964 and a sixth, Peter Craig, followed in 1968.

When he retired from the chairmanship in 1982, Sir John Moores brought in as his successor the first non-family chairman, John Clement, from the dairy business Unigate. Clement, in his turn, recruited as group chief executive Desmond Pitcher, a Liverpudlian and high-technology communications expert, a former employee of Plessey. The Group Board in 1990 was comprised of Sir John, president, his four children, and other non-family members. Some of Sir John Moore's and Cecil Moores's grandchildren sat on the divisional boards. The new regime reorganized Littlewoods' finances and in 1985

started Index, a catalog shop operation which later became a separate division. By 1990 there were already 50 of these shops within existing Littlewoods chain stores and a further 46 on their own sites. The second new venture, also started in 1985, was Credit and Data Marketing Services (CDMS), a credit and information business that operated in retail finance, financial services—mainly general insurance—and marketing. A property company, Centreville Estates, formed jointly with P&O Property Holdings, was added in 1990, to which each concern transferred a small number of its premises of equivalent value.

By opening two shops in St. Petersburg's main shopping street in October 1991, Littlewoods became the first major Western retailer to operate in the Soviet Union. These shops were Anglo-Russian ventures, the first selling (for Russian currency) men's and women's clothing to Western standards and the second a hard-currency business dealing in electrical and photographic goods, beauty products, clothing, wines and spirits, and food.

The relative importance of the different parts of Littlewoods's extensive business—still located in Liverpool and more dominant there not only because of its own development but also because of the disappearance of most of the city's port activity—can best be seen from a glance at its trading results for 1990. The Home Shopping Division, no longer a club enterprise but a sophisticated and highly automated credit system depending increasingly on telephone orders, produced the largest turnover, £933 million, and profit, £53.5 million. Only GUS, with 40% of the U.K. market, was ahead of it. Next came the chain stores, with £623 million turnover and £29.4 million profit. Of the new ventures, Index had the larger turnover, £153 million, but was not yet in profit. CDMS, on an income of £18.6 million, had a profit of £1.8 million. The combined retail sales for all divisions was £1,731 million, with profits of £83.6 million. Much less financial information is known about Littlewoods Pools, the foundation upon which the whole Littlewoods Organisation had been built. It could still claim 77% of the U.K. pools business. The largest prize—or dividend as the company prefers to call it—which had been paid out at the beginning, in 1923, was £2 and 12 shillings. In 1991 Littlewoods paid out over £2 million for a prize, far more than its other U.K. competitors. It distributed £170 million in prize money altogether in the season ended July 1990.

Littlewoods's football pools operations were threatened at the beginning of the 1990s by a campaign to introduce a national lottery. With over three-quarters of the British pools market, the company responded by proposing an arts and sports foundation to which it would contribute, alongside two other U.K. pools companies, Vernons and Zetters. The foundation was launched at the end of July 1991 for the start of the football season in August. The Chancellor of the Exchequer reduced pools betting duty from 40% to 37.5% for an initial period of four years with the 2.5% difference being made available to the foundation and expected to be worth around £20 million a year. In addition, the pools companies will contribute roughly £40 million annually.

In the recession that marked the beginning of the 1990s, Littlewoods proved the resilience of its retailing methods by producing a 46% increase in pre-tax profits in 1990, in contrast to the downward trend of most of the major U.K. retailers.

Principal Subsidiaries: Littlewoods Home Shopping Division; Littlewoods Warehouses Ltd.; John Moores Home Shopping Service Ltd.; Brian Mills Ltd.; Janet Frazer Ltd.; Burlington Warehouses Ltd.; Peter Craig Ltd.; Imagination Homeshop Ltd.; M.C. Hitchen & Sons Ltd.; The International Import & Export Company Ltd.; Peter Harris Ltd. (Hong Kong); The Littlewoods Organisation (Far East) Ltd. (Hong Kong); Littlewoods Chain Store Division; J & C Moores Limited; Credit & Data Marketing Services Ltd.; Index Limited; Littlewoods Pools Partnership.

—T. C. Barker

Longs Drugs

LONGS DRUG STORES CORPORATION

141 North Civic Drive
Walnut Creek, California 94596
U.S.A.
(415) 937-1170
Fax: (415) 944-8335

Public Company
Incorporated: 1946 as Longs Stores
Employees: 15,100
Sales: $2.33 billion
Stock Exchange: New York

Longs Drug Stores Corporation is a retail drug store operation located exclusively in the western United States, including Hawaii and Alaska. The company acquired at least 10 stores in each year from 1986 to 1990, and by early 1990 operated 248 stores.

Longs Drug Stores was incorporated in Maryland on May 24, 1985, as a successor to Longs Stores, incorporated in 1946 in California. The company had specialized in the retail drugstore industry since its founding in 1938 by brothers Joseph and Thomas Long, and changed its name from the general Longs Stores to the more specific Longs Drug Stores in 1961. In 1975, at age 62, Joseph Long credited the company's practice of spreading its wealth among its employees for much of its success. Indeed, a marked decentralization of power has not only brought riches to the company's investors but a sense of purpose and handsome financial rewards to its employees. Store managers are paid quarterly bonuses proportional to their unit's profits, and the bonus system extends down through the half dozen assistant department managers that any specific store might employ. By one estimate, a Longs store manager in the late 1980s might have made $80,000 per year.

Managers have a high degree of autonomy in selecting the merchandise that their stores carry, as well as control over prices and advertising. Longs stores in the same city may sell vastly different products. In this way store managers are able to customize their stock according to their customer base. This autonomy, along with the handsome compensation offered, produces longevity among store managers, who stay in those positions an average of 16 years.

Longs' expansion began in the late 1960s, when the role of the drugstore began shifting in the U.S. retail market. Its stores, located throughout northern California, with one opened in Hawaii in the 1950s, were typical of the old-fashioned drugstore. Ranging from about 4,000 to 8,000 square feet, they included a pharmacist, soda fountain, and sundry health and beauty products. The drugstores appearing during the late 1960s were often triple that size, dispensed with the soda fountain, and added an array of specialty foods, auto maintenance products, toys, liquor, and stationery, among other products. Many stores set prices below the manufacturer's suggested retail price, pushing them into competition with discount retail department stores. Rather than functioning as the traditional specialty shops, drugstores became discount operations concentrating on health products, and retaining a pharmacist.

In 1967 the industry gained 12.2% in revenues, and about 50% was estimated to have come from discount chains. In the late 1960s increased prescription drug sales could be traced to an increasing tendency for government subsidy and private insurance to cover the cost of prescription medicines. Longs' 40 stores, located in the center of discount drugstore retailing on the West Coast, saw revenues rise from $78.3 million in 1967 to $95.7 million in 1968.

By the early 1970s chains of 10 or more stores had numbered 180, accounting for more than half of U.S. drugstores. Two- or three-store operations decreased in number, and big supermarkets opened their own drugstore chains. Longs opened its 50th store in 1970, one of eight it opened that year. From 1970 to 1971, sales rose for the first six months from $77.4 million to $90.5 million. Earnings went from 51¢ per share to 72¢ per share. Its stock split two for one following its annual meeting in May 1971.

Longs increased its sales and earnings every quarter since its founding through 1975, at which time it operated 82 stores. For 1965 through 1975, it showed compounded sales growth of 22%, and earnings per share growth of 25%. With no leverage, Longs earned from 23% to 25% on equity from 1970 to 1975.

Longs expanded conservatively, not only because it thoroughly investigated potential sites but because it preferred to buy the land beneath its stores, and did no business on credit. In the early 1970s Longs opened about six stores a year. Most were located in upper-middle-income areas where retail sales are high. It opened outlets mostly in northern California where competition is less keen. In the tougher retail market of southern California, Longs eschewed highly competitive Los Angeles for its affluent suburbs. Despite the tightening economy, Longs increased expansion to about ten stores annually in the mid-1970s. At that time the company's high earnings allowed it to expand from within rather than by acquisition, like most competitors. Longs carried no debt and took out no loans, so rising interest rates did not affect its growth rate. The Long brothers started the company on $15,000 borrowed from Joseph Long's father-in-law, Safeway founder Marion Skaggs. They had seen their father, a general storekeeper in Mendocino County, California, go under in the credit squeeze right before the Depression. Vowing to avoid that fate, they operated strictly on cash after their initial loan.

Longs was not affected by 1974's retailing slump. Sales for 1974 were up 22% with earnings up 19% for the fiscal nine months ended October 1975. Of that rise, 21% in sales growth in actual volume, not price increases, accounted for 15%. In 1975 each Longs store averaged $4 million in annual sales, versus $500,000 for the industry. Its $250-per-square-foot sales led the industry, where the average was $100. Its gross margin was less than 25% in an industry where it was typically 33% at that time. Longs stores did about as much business as competing stores twice the size. Decentralized pricing gave Longs an advantage in the inflationary ecomomy of the 1970s, allowing managers to raise prices according to their local costs, instead of waiting for the word from the central office. Its decentralized acquisition of store stock also aided their ability to negotiate in the tough economy. Warehousing costs were nil because it did not maintain a central warehousing system. Most stock was purchased at store level from direct manufacturers or local wholesalers and jobbers. Merchandise was stored in the retail unit, but just briefly, as Longs turns over its inventory eight times a year, about twice the industry standard. The stores in general shied away from costly items such as console TVs. A store might sell such an item, but only stock a few until it proves to be a big seller. This way a unit avoided becoming saddled with unsalable merchandise in an economic downturn.

Longs entered Anchorage, Alaska, in 1977, Arizona and Oregon in 1978, and Nevada in 1979. By 1980 it operated 113 outlets in California, 12 in Hawaii, 4 in Arizona and 1 each in Alaska, Nevada, and Oregon. The company's rate of expansion increased to 14 to 17 units annually, and over the next decade it would double its total number of stores. Sales per square foot rose to $381 in 1979 from $351 the previous year. In June 1987 the company acquired 11 Osco drugstores in California and 1 in Colorado, and sold to the Osco chain 15 of its own Arizona stores. Longs typically closed very few stores.

In addition to its lucrative incentive program, Longs had had profit sharing since 1956. The company sold $25 million of its stock to the profit-sharing plan in March 1989. The sale provided liquidity and tax benefits, and significantly increased the plan's holding of company stock. In the late 1980s, Longs bought back 2.5 million shares that had been held by outside investors. Of the outstanding 20 million shares, employees owned 12%, and the Long family owned about 26%. It was speculated that the company was going private, although it announced no such plans, and remained a publicly held company in 1991. The family influence remained great; in 1991 Joseph Long was still chairman, his son Robert president and chief executive officer, and Thomas Long a director.

Long's outlook was bright as it entered the 1990s, carrying no long-term debt and owning the property housing more than half of its stores. The chain's net income had grown 10% a year from 1978 to 1988, and a 28% increase in fiscal 1988 put it at $49 million, on sales of $1.8 billion. For 1988 it was still outperforming all large drugstore chains in sales per employee, $147,000; sales per store, $7.8 million; and sales per square foot, $455. In the early 1990s Longs focused on increasing its pharmacy business. In 1989 and 1990 it remodeled 24 pharmacies and promoted its mail-order prescription business. Fiscal 1990 was the fifth consecutive year that pharmacy sales grew more than 20%.

Company-wide sales surpassed $2 billion for the first time in 1990. Net income grew 10% from the previous year, to $61.3 million. Per-store sales averaged $8.8 million in 1990. While retaining store autonomy for purchasing of most items, Longs was increasing combined purchasing of certain ones to provide economics of scale. With its excellent sales history, conservative finances, and employee loyalty, Longs' outlook appeared to be highly positive.

Principal Subsidiary: Longs Drug Stores California, Inc.

Further Reading: Campanella, Frank W., "Longs' Way Up," *Barron's,* February 11, 1980.

—Elaine Belsito

LOWE'S

LOWE'S COMPANIES, INC.

Post Office Box 1111
North Wilkesboro, North Carolina 28656
U.S.A.
(919) 651-4000
Fax: (919) 651-4766

Public Company
Incorporated: 1952 as Lowe's North Wilkesboro
　Hardware, Inc.
Employees: 15,556
Sales: $2.83 billion
Stock Exchanges: New York Pacific London

Lowe's Companies, Inc., operates a chain of retail stores that sells building materials and related products to the do-it-yourself home improvement and home construction markets. At the end of 1990, the company operated 309 stores, primarily in the southern United States.

In 1921 L.S. Lowe opened a hardware store in the small town of North Wilkesboro, North Carolina. Following his death, his son, James Lowe, took over the business. James Lowe and his brother-in-law, Carl Buchan, served in the U.S. Army during World War II, and during this period Lowe's sister and mother ran the business.

When Buchan was wounded and discharged from the army in 1943, he returned to North Wilkesboro to help operate Lowe's hardware business. In 1946 Buchan took a 50% interest in the store. Buchan quickly sold out much of the store's inventory. He then reorganized the store, which became a wholesale-style seller of hardware and building supplies.

When Lowe was discharged from the army, he returned to aid Buchan in operating the business. The two opened a second store and used profits to buy an automobile dealership and a cattle farm. In 1952 Buchan traded his interests in these two businesses for Lowe's interest in their two stores. Three months later, Buchan opened a third store, in Asheville, North Carolina. From 1952 to 1959, Buchan expanded operations, and sales increased from $4.1 million to $27 million. The post–World War II construction boom made the hardware business very profitable. The frenzied demand for supplies meant that sales often were made directly from a freight car on the railway siding that ran by the store. By purchasing stock directly from the manufacturer, Lowe's was able to avoid paying the higher prices set by wholesalers, which meant lower prices for customers. By 1955 Buchan had six stores.

The big push to become a major force in the home-building market came in 1960 when Buchan died and an office of the president was created. The company went public in 1961. Even though the company grew and new locations were added, the layout of the stores remained basically the same: a small retail floor with limited inventory and a lumberyard out back near the railroad tracks. The bulk of Lowe's customers were contractors and construction companies. By the late 1960s, Lowe's had more than 50 stores, and sales figures hovered around the $100 million mark.

About this time, the burgeoning do-it-yourself market was beginning to change the face of the construction industry. The rising cost of buying a home or having one remodeled by a professional led more homeowners to take on construction projects themselves. Home centers were becoming the modern version of the neighborhood hardware store. At the same time, the home building market was experiencing periodic slumps, and Lowe's management began to notice that their sales figures were moving up and down in tandem with housing trends.

In spite of the fluctuations in the housing market, however, Lowe's revenues rose from $170 million in 1971 to more than $900 million by 1979. This was due in large part to Lowe's financing program that helped local builders get loans, coordinated building plans with the Federal Housing Administration (FHA), and then helped contractors fill out the government forms and trained construction companies to build FHA-approved homes.

When new home construction virtually came to a standstill in the later part of the 1970s, Lowe's made the decision to target consumers. The management team believed that increasing consumer sales would reduce the company's vulnerability during economic and seasonal downswings. In 1980 housing starts decreased, and Lowe's net income fell 24%. While studying the track records of do-it-yourself stores that sold solely to consumers, Lowe's found that these stores were recording strong sales even during the home-building slumps.

Robert Strickland came to Lowe's fresh from the Harvard Business School. Rising steadily through the ranks, Strickland had reached the position of chairman of the board in 1978 and, with newly appointed Lowe's President Leonard Herring, spearheaded the decision to attract consumers in a big way. Using the easily recognizable acronym RSVP (standing for retail sales, volume, and profit), Lowe's embarked on the new marketing strategy. A consultant was hired to remodel the showrooms, and the resulting layout was similar to that of a supermarket. Seasonal items, such as lawn mowers, were placed in the front of the store. The traffic pattern drew customers to the interior decorating section, then moved on to the back of the store where traditional hardware materials were displayed. The theory behind this traffic pattern said that most consumers may come for the basics but, by walking through the other departments, end up purchasing more. The store in Morganton, North Carolina, was the first location remodeled under the RVSP plan.

In another aspect of the redesign, poster-sized photographs depicting Lowe's merchandise as it would look in the consumer's home were used to identify departments rather than lettered signs. Product lines were updated, hours were extended, and advertising was increased. The strategy worked; by 1982 sales had reached $1 billion, and when the figure reached

$1.43 billion in 1983, it marked the first time that Lowe's had made more money selling to consumers than to contractors.

One aspect of the RSVP plan that did not work was Wood World, an extension of the retail floor into one long bay of the lumber warehouse. Fire code regulations required the installation of expensive fire walls and doors, and the idea was soon scrapped. Paneling and other wood products were then put out on the sales floor with the rest of the merchandise.

In the later years of the 1980s, Lowe's began increasing the size of its stores. Prior to that time the stores were approximately 20,000 square feet. In 1988 the company opened a 60,000-square-foot store in Knoxville, Tennessee, a 40,320-square-foot unit in Boone, North Carolina, and a 60,480-square-foot store in North Chattanooga, Tennessee. Lowe's planned for all future units to be either 45,000 or 65,000 square feet. To accommodate the expansion, the company began to lease more of its own space. In 1989 Lowe's owned 89% of the buildings that housed their stores. By the end of 1991, Lowe's expected to add one million square feet of space, bringing the total to eight million.

Future plans also called for the expansion of the core consumer goods: hardware, tools, paint, plumbing, home decor, and stereo equipment. Fringe items that had crept in over the past decade, including exercise equipment, bicycles, and bath linens were to be phased out.

Traditionally, Lowe's preferred to move into small- to medium-sized towns where they did not have to compete with a large local wholesaler. This may change in the 1990s. Industry analysts predicted Lowe's desire to increase its market share would require moves into more heavily populated geographical areas and larger stores.

Further Reading: Korn, Don, "Lowe's Gets Ready to Raise the Roof," *Sales Management,* July 7, 1975; "Lowe's zeroes in on customers," *Chain Store Age Executive,* August 1979; Cochran, Thomas, "Handyman's Special," *Barron's,* June 18, 1980; Auchmutey, Jim, "Warehouses stack the deck," *Hardware Age,* March 1981; Curtis, Carol E., "How much sheetrock, ma'am?," *Forbes,* August 30, 1982; "Lowe's Vision—The Wal-Mart of Home Centers," *Chain Store Age Executive,* May 1989.

—Mary F. Sworsky

St Michael

MARKS AND SPENCER P.L.C.

Michael House
37-67 Baker Street
London W1A 1DN
United Kingdom
(071) 935 4422
Fax: (071) 487 2679

Public Company
Incorporated: 1894
Employees: 75,000
Sales: £5.77 billion (US$10.79 billion)
Stock Exchanges: London Brussels Paris Amsterdam

The large-scale retail business of Marks and Spencer p.l.c. has much publicized small-scale beginnings. It also has a much publicized philosophy and reputation. Over the years it has established a distinctive, if always developing, strategy and image. Indeed, in the process it has become a household name.

In 1894 Michael Marks, born in 1859 in a Jewish ghetto at Slonim in the Russian Polish province of Grodno, entered into a partnership with Tom Spencer, born at Skipton, Yorkshire, in 1851, with Spencer paying £300 for his half-share. Ten years earlier, Marks, a pedlar, had opened his first stall on a trestle table in Leeds market, selling a range of cheap goods all priced at one penny, including hair pins, dolly dyes, and black lead; he is said to have paid 18 pence for the privilege. Tom Spencer, cashier for Leeds textile wholesaler Isaac Jowitt Dewhirst, was an experienced bookkeeper, and Dewhirst had helped Marks by teaching him English and providing him with small loans.

By 1894 Marks had moved house from Leeds and after living in Wigan had settled in Manchester, where he acquired a shop and a home. He had also opened market stalls—bazaars he called them—in several towns, including Warrington, Bolton, and Birkenhead. The new partnership immediately looked further afield to Birmingham and Newcastle and in 1899 to London. Manchester, however, remained the headquarters, and the first Marks and Spencer warehouse was opened there in 1897. In 1903 the partnership was converted into a limited company with £30,000 in £1 ordinary shares of which 14,996 each were allotted to Marks and to Spencer, the latter retiring in 1905. Upon Marks's sudden death in 1907, his executor, William Chapman, a self-made handkerchief manufacturer, became the dominating force in the business.

In each of the first Marks and Spencer bazaars the slogan had been "Don't ask the price, it's a penny," but this selling policy soon changed. It had been a landmark date in 1904 when a new store in a shopping arcade was opened in Leeds not far from Marks's first market trestle table. Two years later, the most successful store was Liverpool with yearly takings of £9,857. Brixton was second with £9,766. Leeds came third with £8,701 and Manchester fourth with £8,459. In 1907 profits reached a new peak of £8,668 and the dividend paid was 20%.

Marks's son Simon acquired his first allocation of shares in April 1907, eight months before his father's death, and from the start he was determined to acquire full control over what he conceived of as a family business. It was not until 1916, however, that he ousted Chapman and became chairman. By then the company had expanded significantly: its turnover in 1913 was already £355,000. It had also successfully braved World War I. In 1915, a year of bitter boardroom battles—concerned not with management policy but with financial control—its turnover was over £400,000, and a dividend of 50% was paid. By then there were 145 branch stores, only ten of them in market halls. No fewer than 56 were in the London area. Some of them had been bought in clusters from existing chains.

Simon Marks, a man of intelligence and drive, in effect entered into his own partnership in 1915 when his close friend Israel Sieff, intellectually able and keenly aware of world trends both in politics and in science, joined the board after having been previously blocked by Chapman. In 1916 Marks won a lawsuit against Chapman, and in June 1917 Chapman resigned. The firm's initials M and S now stood symbolically for Marks and Sieff. The two friends had first met in Manchester, and each was to marry the other's sister. If their talents were complementary, their vision was shared, and it was a vision that extended far beyond the confines of the business. Succession seemed natural in 1964, when on Simon's death, Israel became chairman, to be succeeded in 1967 by his son Marcus, who like Simon Marks and Israel, became a peer.

In 1926 the company, needing an injection of cash, had been converted into a public company in order to raise new capital, fully supported by the Prudential Assurance Company, which played a key role in the negotiations. The capital consisted initially of one million ordinary shares of ten shillings each, £330,000 of which were issued, and 350,000 cumulative participating preference shares at £1. There were to be further appeals to the public in 1929 and 1934, when the nominal value of the capital of the company was raised to £3.05 million. The new A shares issued then carried no voting rights. Indeed, there was to be a sharp distinction between management and ownership until 1966, when Israel Sieff concluded that the granting of voting rights was by then "in line with the enlightened policy which governs our business."

Marks hoped in 1934 that in the future there would be "an ample margin of working capital" for management to promote a substantial development program which included the purchase of properties as well as store building, and the hope was fulfilled. Already by 1930 approximately four-fifths of the new company's assets had consisted of freehold and leasehold properties, and between 1931—a year of international depression—and 1939 no fewer than 162 new stores were built or rebuilt, all on inner–city sites. On the eve of World War II, Marks laid more emphasis on replacement of old premises by new than on an increase in the number of stores in itself. Store design had been transformed. Customers were to be attracted into them, to look around even when they did not buy.

The business philosophy that Marks and Sieff shared was associated with social change even in years of economic depression. As Marks put it in 1936, "Goods and services once regarded as luxuries have become conventional comforts and are now almost decreed necessities. A fundamental change in people's habits has been brought about. Millions are enjoying a substantially higher standard of living. To this substantial rise in the standard of living our company claims to have made a definite contribution.

"Efficient distribution," he went on, "is not a static conception. It involves constant alertness and study of the changing habits, desires and tastes of the consumer." Sieff, who has given his own account of the ten years from 1926 to 1936, has described his "mission" in practical terms. "We saw not through visionary idealists' clouds but from practical results in days of high competition that production and distribution could become a co-operative process making a positive contribution to the common good." Neither he nor Marks wanted to be involved in production, but through bulk buying they were able to influence the policies of those who were producing for them.

In the first postwar year, 1919, turnover had been £550,000; in 1939, when World War II broke out, it was £23.45 million. In the latter year there were 234 stores and over 17,000 employees. In 1924 the head office of the company moved from Manchester to Friendly House, Chiswell Street, London EC1. In 1928 it was moved to a new building, named Michael House, in the same street. Three years later, there was a further move to Baker Street, the present headquarters. Meanwhile, the now-familiar trade mark, St Michael, had first been applied in 1928 to products sold in Marks and Spencer stores, and its use was gradually extended until Marks referred to it for the first time in a chairman's speech in 1949.

The Marks and Spencer stores of the interwar years had represented a new form of business, challenging the role of older department stores. Yet such interwar stores had been simple and unpretentious when compared with the superstores of the late 20th century which were to be visited by prime ministers and royal families. Indeed, the total cost of a new store in the 1920s was exceeded by the costs of electrical installation in the stores of the 1960s.

The prewar stores owed something to American experience, for it was after Marks first visited the United States in 1924 that he decided to follow, if not to copy, American developments. In 1927 a price limit of five shillings per item was set and there was a continuing emphasis on value for money, but there was an increasingly wide range of goods on sale. By 1932 there were more than 20 departments in the biggest stores, including ladies' and children's drapery; men's and boys' wear; footwear; fancy goods; household linens; gramophone records; confectionery; toiletries; lighting; toys; haberdashery; millinery; china, enamel and aluminum ware; stationery; gifts; and food, recently introduced into a number of stores. Along with textiles, sales of which increased three times between then and 1939, food was to be a Marks and Spencer staple of the future.

Marks was right to emphasize how in relation to textiles, in particular, his business within a changing society was to both respond to consumer tastes and to develop them; in an address to shareholders he stated that "it is the function of the modern distributor to purchase healthier and more attractive clothing." The revolution in food followed a generation later with the introduction of such items as iceberg lettuce, smoked salmon, Indian and Chinese foods, avocados, kiwi fruit, and wine. By then Marks and Spencer stores were also selling toiletries of all kinds, travel and holiday ware, and fashion clothes for men as well as women.

Wartime and immediate postwar austerity had been bound to influence both consumer tastes and company profits, although even then the company benefited from the standardizing element in the government's Utility Scheme that regulated the design of a range of consumer goods and favored bulk buyers; the scheme remained in operation until 1952 and in modified form until 1955. The company was also well poised to establish an overseas presence. A Marks and Spencer Export Corporation had been founded in 1940, and in 1955 it was exporting goods to the value of £703,000 to other overseas retailers. It was in 1954 that one of the first editions of a new in-house journal, *St Michael's News,* claimed rightly that by then Marks and Spencer was "news to the general public." This was the year when the Chancellor of the Exchequer, R.A. Butler, claimed that the country would double its standard of living during the next quarter of a century, and the company was well positioned to move into the unprecedented consumer boom of the late 1950s and 1960s.

Turnover rose from £95 million in 1954 to £148 million in 1960, and profit before tax from £7.87 million to £12.81 million. It was in 1960 too that a ten-year progress record became a convenient and impressive feature of the published accounts. The ten-year progress record for the years 1972–1973 to 1983–1984 was to be even more striking in terms of sales and profits, although economic conditions during that period were to be far more difficult. By 1972–1973 turnover had reached £496 million (excluding new sales taxes); in 1983–1984 it was £2.9 billion. Meanwhile profit before tax had leapt from £70 million to £265 million. More sophisticated statistics revealed that sales per employee had risen during the same ten years from £18,651 to £73,099 and per square foot of floor space from £96 to £372. Profit per square foot had risen from £14 to £38.

By 1973–1974 there were 17 overseas stores—the first of them opened in Canada in 1972. A Paris store was opened in 1975. Between 1974 and 1977 exports trebled to over £40 million and the company won the Queen's Award for Export Achievement. It was deeply committed also to another national achievement—supporting British producers whenever it could and encouraging them to develop efficient new lines of business. In the process it established close connections with a number of suppliers that placed it in a virtually monopsonistic position. Relationships with the firms from which it was buying were handled as carefully as relationships with customers.

Before 1939 the main emphasis had been on the price-reducing advantages of bulk buying; during the 1960s and 1970s the main emphasis was on quality control, not least in textiles and in food, then the company's two biggest lines of business. There was continuity, however, rather than a basic shift. As early as 1933 a merchandising committee had been formed to coordinate the work of the various buying departments; a small textiles laboratory had been created in 1935, and a merchandising development department had followed a year later. In 1946 a factory organization section, later called the production engineering department, had been opened "to assist manufacturers in the progressive modernisation of their plant and to adapt themselves to the latest technical advances," and two years later a food development department was created. The department dealt both with British and with foreign suppliers, including suppliers of Israeli oranges; there were visits to Israel, a country especially favored as a supplier as it was close to the hearts of Marks and Sieff, to deal with storage and packing.

Apart from research development and publicity, the company had devised its own approach to the buying process through the training of specified "selectors," so described for the first time during the 1930s, and merchandisers, who meticulously studied store demand and turnover before placing orders with producers. The system was integrated, and there was feedback from store to factory.

Quality control, encouraging suppliers in the interests of quality to use the most modern and efficient techniques of production provided by the latest discoveries in science and technology, was a "principle" that Marks and Sieff insisted upon. Unlike most retailers, Marks and Spencer had its own laboratories and employed its own scientists. Other "principles"—and they were formulated and listed as such by Israel Sieff in 1967 after Marks's death—were to guarantee customers high quality when they bought products using the St Michael's brand name, "to plan the extension of stores for the better display of a widening range of goods and for the convenience of our customers," "to simplify operating procedures so that the business is carried on in an efficient manner," and "to foster good relations with customers, suppliers and staff." "Operation Simplification," introduced in 1956, led to the saving of huge amounts of paper and electricity. The lessons were never lost.

Staffing matters had been taken seriously even before the 1930s, when a personnel department was set up in 1934, a year when the word "welfare" began to be used inside the business. Thereafter a wide enough range of "welfare activities" was organized to make Marks and Spencer a kind of welfare state in itself. They were appreciated by most employees, although a small minority found them somewhat stifling.

Meanwhile, great attention was paid to breaking down what Marcus Sieff called the "fear, suspicion and insecurity that threatened human relations in industry." The familiar term "industrial relations" was taboo at Baker Street; it seemed to imply that there were two sides. In consequence, there was some trade-union criticism of the approach. "We are human beings at work, not industrial beings," Sieff emphasized in 1980. In the same year he stressed that training was not mostly a matter for workers on the shop floor whose talents needed to be mobilized. It began at the top. The first task of the chairman was "to impart the philosophy of our evolving business to our executives." The philosophy extended from employees to pensioners and to schemes for neighboring communities as well as for inner-city stores.

In 1965 Israel Sieff became chairman of the company and Marcus, who had joined the company in 1935 and became a director in 1954, was made vice-chairman. He became chairman in 1972 after J. Edward Sieff, Israel's brother, who had joined the company at Simon Marks's invitation in 1933, had

had five years in the chair. There was thus a strong family thrust behind the company and Marcus (Lord) Sieff remained chairman until 1984, when a man born outside the family circles, Derek (Lord) Rayner, took over and rigorously developed the group's activities overseas. Spotted by Marcus Sieff as a young manager, he had joined the company in 1953 and became a director in 1967 and joint managing director in 1973. In 1979 he was seconded to Prime Minister Margaret Thatcher's newly elected government in an effort to streamline the civil service, returning to the company in 1982. He retired in 1991 and was succeeded by Richard Greenbury, knighted in the 1992 New Year's Honours List. Keith Oates had joined the business at a high level as finance director from outside—a rare kind of appointment—in 1988.

Group turnover (£5.8 billion) increased in difficult trading conditions in 1990–1991, as did group operating profit (£634 million). In Continental Europe profits of £20.4 million were recorded on sales of £148.7 million in 1990–1991. All the French and Belgian stores operating by this time were profitable, and a new store opened in Madrid in March 1991. The five stores Marks and Spencer had opened in Hong Kong from 1988 onwards also performed well in 1990–1991. Due mainly to the recession in the United States, operations were not so smooth for the group's recent acquisitions there, which included the American clothing business Brooks Brothers Inc. and Kings Super Markets Inc., both acquired in 1988–1989, although these two companies were able to show a profit by the end of the financial year. There were business losses in Canada and a senior board of Marks and Spencer directors was given the task of resolving the situation there. Marks and Spencer's flagship store in Continental Europe is in Paris, which was the scene of the great 19th-century department stores at the time when Michael Marks set up his market stall in Leeds.

Principal Subsidiaries: Marks and Spencer (Nederland) BV; Marks and Spencer (France) SA; Marks and Spencer (Ireland) Limited; M&S Export (Ireland) Limited; SA Marks and Spencer (Belgium) NV; M&S (Spain) SA; Marks and Spencer (España) SA (67%); Marks & Spencer Holdings Canada Inc.; Marks & Spencer Canada Inc.; Marks and Spencer Finance (Nederland) BV; MS Insurance Limited (Guernsey); Marks and Spencer US Holdings Inc.; Brooks Brothers Inc. (U.S.A.); Brooks Brothers (Japan) Limited (51%); Kings Super Markets Inc. (U.S.A.); Marks & Spencer Services Inc. (U.S.A.); Marks & Spencer Finance Inc. (U.S.A.); Marks and Spencer Retail Financial Services Holdings Limited; Marks and Spencer Unit Trust Management Limited; St Michael Finance Limited; Marks and Spencer Property Holdings Limited; Marks and Spencer Property Developments Limited; Marks and Spencer Finance plc; Marks and Spencer Export Corporation Limited.

Further Reading: Rees, G., *St. Michael, A History of Marks and Spencer,* 1969; Briggs, Asa, *Marks and Spencer 1884–1984,* Octopus Books Limited, 1984; Bookbinder, Paul, *Marks & Spencer: The War Years, 1939–1945,* Century Benham Limited, 1989.

—Asa Briggs

Ｏ|Ｏ| *MARUI CO., LTD.*

MARUI CO., LTD.

3-7-18 Nakano
Nakano-ku
Tokyo 164-01
Japan
(03) 3384 0101
Fax: (03) 3380 8081

Public Company
Incorporated: 1937
Employees: 10,441
Sales: ¥556.35 billion (US$4.46 billion)
Stock Exchange: Tokyo

Marui Company is one of the largest department store chains in the Tokyo area, operating 33 large stores near major railroad stations. In fiscal year ending February 1991, Marui was by far the most profitable retailing chain in Japan, with profits of ¥58 billion, or 10% of sales. The chain's customers are predominantly fashion-conscious and wealthy young Japanese in their late teens to early 30s. Marui has pioneered the use of credit shopping in Japan, and the credit business provides a large share of the company's revenues. Marui has concentrated on new stores in prime downtown locations but plans to develop large stores in the potentially lucrative suburban areas and also to increase the specialty content of its branches.

Marui's history dates back to 1931 when founder Chuji Aoi opened a store selling household utensils and furniture in the downtown Tokyo district of Nakano. Aoi was an energetic young retailer, who saw a market opportunity and acted on it. Born in Toyama prefecture on the west coast of Japan in 1904, he graduated from the Takaoka Technological High School at the age of 18 and joined a Tokyo trading and retailing company, Maruni. The company was part of Zenshiro Tasaka's Maruzen group which, as a retailing chain, still existed in the early 1990s. The stores within the group were the first in Japan to allow customers to buy goods on monthly installment plans. Tasaka had pioneered credit sales in Japan on the southern island of Kyushu in 1895 by selling lacquerware to customers on monthly installment plans. Chuji Aoi stayed with Maruni in Tokyo for nine years. Using savings and borrowed money, he then used his credit retailing experience to open his own store. The time seemed right for such an operation. The Tokyo region had been devastated in 1923 in the Great Kanto Earthquake. Although the city had largely been rebuilt, there was a high demand for furniture and the prospect of credit

sales was attractive to customers. The store was initially called Maruni, reflecting the initial capital provided by his old company. Aoi's venture flourished and he increased his stock range to include clothes, shoes, electrical goods, and suitcases. By 1935 he had opened another store in nearby Asagaya. At the same time, the company name changed to Marui. In 1936 the business had expanded to such an extent that an adjacent building was acquired and the entire Nakano store renovated. The following year, in order to open a third store in the Tokyo district of Shimokitazawa, Aoi sold part of his share in the stores and formed Marui Co., Ltd., raising ¥50,000.

By 1939 Aoi had opened two more Marui stores in Tokyo. Although Japan's wartime economy boomed, it was not geared toward consumers. During the period 1941 to 1946 all Marui stores ceased business and were destroyed in the subsequent saturation bombing of Tokyo by the Allies. In August 1946, however, Aoi began selling furniture from the site of his old Nakano store. He was in effect starting again, and by 1947 he had rebuilt and reopened the store, with 1,190 square meters of sales space. Aoi had raised ¥200,000 in capital. Furniture was in high demand again in postwar Japan and the store flourished. By 1950 the number of stores had risen to five and in that year four high school graduates joined the company as management trainees. The monthly payment schemes being offered by the company to customers were used to advertise Marui and differentiate it from its competitors. In 1951 many new products were stocked, such as baby clothes and bedding. A fleet of trucks was purchased for supplying and distributing goods to the stores, which by 1952 numbered eight. The first neon sign appeared over Marui's Shinjuku store in this year. In 1953 Japan's economic recovery began. Marui began advertising on the radio and selling gift vouchers that were valid in all eight stores. The company had become a chain with annual sales of more than ¥1 billion and 260 employees who had their own union. In 1955 customers were offered a ten-month payment scheme for selected goods. Opening hours were extended by instituting a shift system among the women counter sales staff—men counter staff did not participate.

Tadao Aoi, the son of the founder, joined the company in 1956 and was anxious to observe how credit sales chains operated in the United States. In 1957 he went on an inspection tour to look for new ideas. In 1959 Marui Advertising—now AIM Create Co., Ltd.—was formed, to attend to the company's promotional needs. In the same year Aoi established Maruishinpan to provide credit services to consumers. The following year saw the issue of the first Marui credit card and the establishment of Marui Transport—now Moving Co., Ltd.—which provided house-moving services.

The year 1961 was the 30th anniversary of the opening of Aoi's first store. There were by then 18 branches around Tokyo and sales totaled ¥5.7 billion. In 1962 the largest Marui branch was established by the renovation of the Shinjuku store. More than 2,000 square meters were added to the site, and the nine-story structure became one of the largest stores in the installment retail industry. The early 1960s marked a consumer boom in Japan and a time of expansion for Marui. In the period 1960 to 1967 sales floor space trebled to 35,000 square meters. A listing of Marui on the Tokyo Stock Exchange followed in 1963. In 1965 Aoi's son Tadao Aoi was promoted to vice president in preparation for his eventual succession to the helm of Marui. The year 1966 was important for Marui, as the company implemented its "scrap and build" policy of redeveloping its sites into large-scale stores that were cost-efficient and comfortable for customers. Most stores were affected.

Major capital investments were made in the operation of the stores with the introduction of an IBM 360 mainframe computer to handle the company's accounts and customers. To organize Marui's work force of 2,900, training schemes were introduced primarily for sales staff. By 1969 Japan had the second-largest gross national product figure in the world. A key part of this success lay in the high percentage of earnings that the average Japanese saved. The Japanese consumer at the time did not generally buy on credit. Marui's slogan at the time, "Play now, pay later," seemed to contradict this trend but Marui provided for the young and not so cautious consumer who expected to be fairly well off in the near future. In 1971 the Marui Computer Centre was founded to centralize computer operations. Real estate and travel services began to be sold through Marui stores. An overseas trade department was set up within the company to handle imports of goods.

An organizational change occurred in the company in 1972 with Chuji Aoi becoming chairman, allowing his son Tadao to take over the running of Marui as president. Tadao's brother Chuzaburo remained on the board of directors. In a 1974 cover story on world leaders, *Time* magazine featured Tadao Aoi along with the crown prince of Japan as representative of the country's rising leaders. In 1975 the Red Card, a house credit card, was offered to all Marui customers. The new cards had an initial interest rate charge of 9%, substantially higher than base rates, but the difficulty in arranging small consumer loans in Japan at the time attracted customers to Marui. In 1974 the company introduced on a trial basis point–of–sales computer system to monitor transactions. The system was installed in all stores in 1977, linking them together and speeding up transaction time. This system greatly increased the number of Marui card holders. During this time the number of Marui stores remained constant at 33, while the floor space was increased annually to reach 183,000 square meters in 1978. Constant renovation and the opening of specialty stores within existing stores accounted for the increase. Marui began to advertise its Red Card heavily and this, as well as the card's innovative nature, accounted for its success. The television and press advertisements were aimed primarily at the youth market and often won awards for their wit and originality. By the end of 1980 the number of card holders had reached four million. In the following year Marui began offering consumer loans in the form of cash-dispensing services to customers.

At the company's 50th anniversary in 1981, it had annual sales of ¥260 billion and almost 7,000 employees. The company had by now developed expertise in the development of retail and credit control software. In 1984 Marui established the company M&C Systems to sell this knowledge to other retailers. Card holders could now withdraw money from all branches of Marui. Within a year this feature had increased the number of holders to six million. Branches of Marui also had online information on exchange rates and other financial indicators.

In 1985 a new management division was added to the company to cope with the expanding work force. On the retail side, Marui continued the policy of expansion within existing sites and the opening of specialty boutiques within the stores. This strategy continued to be successful. By 1988 the combined membership figure for all card holders exceeded ten million. In 1990 Marui formed a joint venture with Richard Branson's Virgin Group in the United Kingdom in the establishment of Virgin Megastores Japan. The ownership of the company was split equally between Virgin and Marui, and the pilot plan was the opening of a small version of Virgin's UK megastores in Marui's Shinjuku branch. The deal gave Marui excellent international publicity and increased its prestige among young Japanese consumers. For Virgin it provided a foothold in the lucrative Japanese retail market while avoiding the excessive costs of renting or buying prime floor space in Tokyo.

Financially Marui has continued to grow steadily, increasing profits even in fiscal year 1990, in the wake of Japan's market crash. Marui has 464 cash-dispensing machines in operation, 69 of them outside Marui stores. Recently established service centers, separate from the stores, offer a wide range of financial services. The policy of developing specialty boutiques, such as the "In The Room" store in the Shibuya branch of Marui, has been successful. In 1991 the company was continuing its slow but steady opening of new stores and expanding to the residential areas around Tokyo and possibly Osaka. Tadao Aoi has remained in charge of Marui, although his son Hiroshi is already on the main Marui board and looks set, some time in the future, to take control of the company his grandfather founded.

Principal Subsidiaries: AIM Create Co. Ltd.; Moving Co. Ltd. (87%); Marui Zero One Net Co. Ltd; M&C Systems Co. Ltd.; CSC Service Co. Ltd. (70%); Virgin Megastores Japan (50%); M-One Card Co. Ltd. (68%).

—Dylan Tanner

MATSUZAKAYA COMPANY LIMITED

3-16-1 Sakae
Naka-ku
Nagoya 460
Japan
052 251 1111
Fax: 052 262 4732

Public Company
Incorporated: 1910 as Ito Gofuku Company Limited
Employees: 6,807
Sales: ¥533.58 billion (US$4.28 billion)
Stock Exchanges: Tokyo Osaka Nagoya

Matsuzakaya is Japan's oldest department store with roots that can be traced back to the 17th century. The Nagoya-based chain operates large stores in most of Japan's major cities, its largest store being in Nagoya. Matsuzakaya ranks sixth among Japanese department stores in terms of sales, and its business centers around the retailing of clothes, accessories, and luxury foodstuffs. Matsuzakaya has a reputation for quality and sound management.

In 1611 Yudo Ito opened a kimono and clothing store in Nagoya in central Japan. Its family were members of the samurai or warrior class in feudal Japan, and it was taken for granted that Yudo would carry on the family name and tradition. Instead, he chose the life of a merchant and used part of the family estate to go into business. The store was moderately successful and was renowned in Nagoya and the surrounding areas for its high-quality clothes. It stayed in the Ito family for many generations.

In 1768 the Ito family decided to expand further afield. It purchased a clothing store called Matsuzakaya—meaning "pine hill store"—in the Ueno district of Tokyo, which was known as a busy shopping area. At the time, Tokyo—then known as Edo—was Japan's most important city and one of the world's major metropolitan areas, with a population exceeding one million. The Ueno store was destroyed in 1858 in a fire that swept through Tokyo, but was subsequently rebuilt.

New stores were opened and continued to be operated and owned by the Itos as a family business. In 1910 the 33-year-old Morimatsu Ito, a fifteenth-generation descendant of Yudo Ito, decided that the time was ripe for expansion. He formed a company called Ito Gofuku Co. Ltd.—"Gofuku" can be translated as drapery or clothing—with capital of ¥500,000. Lead-ing up to the establishment of this company, the Nagoya and Tokyo stores had been expanded and a new store built in Kyoto. A large advertising campaign in major newspapers preceded their opening. An inauguration sale was held in the Nagoya store, with 40,000 people passing through the store's gates during the sale. The store was the largest in Nagoya at the time and flourished in the rapidly growing economy. Japan had defeated China and Russia in 1896 and 1904 respectively and was reaping the benefits of these victories. An affluent upper middle class was appearing in Japanese society as new businesses flourished. The Ito Gofuku store in Nagoya catered to these customers, selling Western clothes, tobacco, jewelry, and footwear as well as the traditional Japanese clothing that had been the foundation of the family's business for many years. In 1914 the Nagoya store established a food department specializing in imported items and delicacies. In 1913 a restaurant was introduced in the Ueno store and in 1917 the store was illuminated by electric lighting, as was the Nagoya store shortly afterwards. In 1916 senior managers of the company traveled to the United States to view the country's prestigious department stores and the current fashion trends. The following year saw the further expansion of the Ueno Matsuzakaya store to a floor space of 5,940 square meters and the addition of elevators. By 1920 the company's capital exceeded ¥5 million, a tenfold increase in ten years. The company's store in Kyoto was expanded further in 1922 and new items, such as imported glassware, were sold at all three stores.

In 1923 the Kanto region of Tokyo suffered its worst earthquake in recent memory, and the resultant fire destroyed or damaged large areas of the city. The destruction was compounded by the fact that most houses were constructed from wood, and that most households used gas lamps, which were easily upset in an earthquake. The Matsuzakaya store in Ueno was totally destroyed and its staff of 150 temporarily relocated to the company's other stores. Within months, however, a new store had been constructed and was open for business by early 1924.

In the same year Ito Gofuku acquired a building in the Ginza, a shopping and entertainment district in Tokyo, and opened a second Matsuzakaya store for the Japanese capital. A store had also been opened in Japan's second largest city, Osaka, in 1923. The opening was preceded by extensive publicity and canvassing by company employees. In 1924 the company's Nagoya flagship store was renovated to become a six-story structure illuminated by neon lighting at night. To unite the company's stores under a brand name, all Ito Gofuku stores became known as Matsuzakaya, and the company changed its name to Matsuzakaya Company Limited in 1925. Company revenues increased rapidly as the stores were expanded and demand for imported Western items boomed.

In 1929 Matsuzakaya's Ueno store was rebuilt and opened to the public with much fanfare. The store was spectacular for its time, with 26,000 square meters of floorspace, eight elevators, heating and air conditioning, and its own post office and hairdresser. The store also contained a zoo on the roof of the six-story building and was hailed as the most prestigious department store in Japan at the time. Fashion shows were regularly held at the store, and it was known as the best place to shop for the latest fashions. The expansion and investment in all Matsuzakaya stores continued in the 1930s as the Japanese economy grew at a fast pace. A new store was opened in the city of Shizuoka in 1932, and in 1937 the Nagoya store was expanded to 30,000 square meters, surpassing the Ueno store. In the same year Matsuzakaya's Nagoya store hosted the New Japan Cultural Exhibition.

With the start of World War II, Matsuzakaya's fortunes declined. The supply of luxury consumer goods from the West slowed greatly after 1940, and the military government's policy was to stimulate the economy and labor force to help the war effort. This led to falling sales for the company, and the military government asked the store to help publicize and take part in energy-saving and recycling initiatives. By 1944 it was clear to many Japanese that the country would lose the war. In this atmosphere, Matsuzakaya began the retailing of gold, silver, platinum, and jewels to nervous investors. By 1945 Japan had lost the war and the U.S. air force had inflicted destruction on major Japanese cities with its nightly B-29 attacks. Matsuzakaya's Ginza and Nagoya stores were destroyed in air raids in March and the Osaka and Ueno stores were damaged. During the war Matsuzakaya had optimistically invested in various parts of South-east Asia occupied by Japanese forces. These investments included a hotel in Kuala Lumpur and a store in Peking. These were confiscated after Japan's defeat and the cost to the company totalled ¥8 million.

Thus Matsuzakaya, along with most other postwar Japanese businesses, was in a state of disarray. The Japanese were, however, quick to rebuild their country and corporate Japan was also quick to reorganize itself, aided greatly by subsidies from the U.S. government, which effectively controlled Japan until 1951. The occupying forces asked most large Japanese companies to aid in the relief effort. Matsuzakaya's contribution was the conversion of its Osaka store, which had escaped the air raids largely undamaged, into a Red Cross center to tend to the sick and wounded. In early 1946 the first postwar shareholders' meeting was held and plans to rebuild the company's stores were announced. This was followed by the reopening later in the year of the Ginza, Nagoya, and Shizuoka stores. The Ueno store was refurbished, with a cinema built on the top floor of the seven-story structure. In 1948 the company launched a promotion campaign in which it claimed to be "binding together lifestyle and culture" in Japan. The late 1940s, however, were a time of rationing in Japan and it was not until 1949 that Matsuzakaya's sales reached the level of prewar years. The year 1949 also marked a turning point in the Japanese economy, with living standards also reaching prewar levels.

In 1950 Matsuzakaya celebrated its 40th anniversary of incorporation and in the following year the 340th anniversary of Yudo Ito's first store. The year 1952 saw the expansion and refurbishment of Matsuzakaya's Ginza store and the following year that of the Nagoya store. The Ueno store followed in 1957. The work on these stores laid the foundation for their present-day position as landmark department stores in Tokyo and Nagoya.

By 1960 the world economy, and Japan's in particular, were booming. The 1960s were years of strong growth for Matsuzakaya at a time when new retail empires such as Ito-Yokado and Daiei were building up large chains of supermarkets. These were hugely successful in catering to the day-to-day shopping needs of the consumer, while Matsuzakaya offered upmarket goods. There was now less emphasis on food and more on luxury goods. In 1964 Japan's economic recovery was in full swing and the country played host to the Olympic Games. The

Matsuzakaya Ginza store mounted several exhibitions connected with the games, and a salon, a pool hall, and a boutique devoted to Nina Ricci clothes were added to the store. This was complemented by the addition of a Henry Poole men's suit boutique in each store in 1964. The boutiques were staffed by tailors hired from the United Kingdom to cut suits in the style worn by the English gentleman. In 1965 the accounting operations of the company were computerized with the introduction of an IBM mainframe. The following year saw investment in staff training with the establishment of a training scheme for all employees and a training school in Nagoya for the company's managers. In 1966 a new store was completed in Osaka with a floor space of 67,000 square meters. The store was built on Osaka Bay and attracted 30,000 customers on its opening day. In 1968 Matsuzakaya set itself a sales target of ¥100 billion to be achieved by the company's sixtieth anniversary in 1970. The company exceeded this figure with sales of ¥103 billion in that year.

By 1971 Matsuzakaya, along with Daimaru Co. Ltd., had become the leading department store in Japan in terms of reputation and prestige. The company completely refurbished its Nagoya store in 1971, and once again this became Matsuzakaya's largest store. With floor space of 71,000 square meters and ten floors above ground and two underground, it was one of the largest department stores in the country. In addition a new store was opened in Nagoya, located near the main railway station. The 1970s saw the continued expansion of the Matsuzakaya chain into other Japanese cities such as Okasaki in 1971 and Kuzuka in 1972. A Paris branch was added in 1978. The original customer base of Matsuzakaya's first overseas department store was the Japanese expatriate community in Paris, but the store soon became popular with native Parisians. In 1980 Mayor Bradley of Los Angeles officially opened the first Matsuzakaya in the United States. Again the targeted customer base was the large Japanese community in Los Angeles.

The 1980s saw Japanese consumers spending more and more on luxury items as the huge and wealthy middle-class reaped the rewards of Japan's booming economy. Women's fashions from France and Italy became especially popular, with an extremely lucrative and competitive market. Matsuzakaya and the other big department stores such as Mitsukoshi Co. Ltd. and Isetan Co. Ltd. devoted several floors of their large city stores to women's fashion and saw large profits from the sales in this department.

A seventeenth-generation Ito, Jirozaemon Ito, currently heads the company, although the Ito family no longer holds a significant number of shares. A recent development for the company was the establishment of retailing via communications satellite tie-ups with Prestel of the United Kingdom and Teletel of France. Although Japanese department stores had a record year in 1991 in terms of earnings, Matsuzakaya included, the current slowing of growth in the Japanese economy has made the company more cautious about future investment plans. However, Matsuzakaya's excellent name and customer base mean that the company is well-positioned to continue enjoying steady, if slower growth.

Principal Subsidiaries: Yamagata Matsuzakaya Co Ltd; Yokohama Matsuzakaya Co Ltd; Boutique Palte Co Ltd; Kanto

Matsuzakaya Store Co Ltd; Chubu Matsuzakaya Store Co Ltd; Sunmen Commerce Co Ltd; Rubisu Store Co Ltd; Matsuei Food Co Ltd; Matsuzaka Trading Company Co Ltd.

—Dylan Tanner

THE MAY DEPARTMENT STORES COMPANY

611 Olive Street
St. Louis, Missouri 63101
U.S.A.
(314) 342-6300
Fax: (314) 342-6584

Public Company
Incorporated: 1910
Employees: 116,000
Sales: $10.04 billion
Stock Exchanges: New York   Pacific

Lord & Taylor of New York City; Filene's in Boston, Massachusetts; and Pittsburgh, Pennsylvania–based Kaufmann's are 3 of the 12 department store chains owned by the May Department Stores Company. At the end of 1991 May's full lineup included more than 335 department stores in 31 states and the District of Columbia. A subsidiary, Payless ShoeSource, Inc., operated about 3,160 self-service shoe stores in 46 states and the District of Columbia.

Company founder David May opened his first store in 1877, in the mining town of Leadville, Colorado when he was 29. An immigrant from Germany, May hadsettled in Indiana during his teen years, where he earned his living as asalesman in a small men's clothing store. Diligence and marketing flair won him a quarter-interest in the business, but ill health forced him to sell his stake and seek a drier, healthier climate in the West, where he tried prospecting. Inexperience brought swift failure, whereupon he returned to the field he knew and opened a men's clothing store with two partners.

The firm of May, Holcomb & Dean supplied the miners with red woolen underwear and copper-riveted overalls. The store was an instant success, but a real estate disagreement dissolved the partnership, leaving May to put up a building on newly purchased ground. This second venture was called The Great Western Auction House & Clothing Store, and was soon large enough to welcome a partner, Moses Shoenberg, whose family owned the local opera house. By 1883 the new partnership was flourishing, for the town's population had become sophisticated enough to demand clothing for many purposes. May and Shoenberg kept pace with demand, ensuring success with aggressive advertising methods and conservative fiscal management. Before long, they were financially able to expand their merchandise to include women's apparel, after testing the

market with a huge stock of expensive dresses bought from an overstocked Chicago store. Despite a post-boom depression that would doom Leadville's prosperity by the end of the decade, May bought out Moses Shoenberg's interest in 1885, adding first one branch store in Aspen, Colorado, then another called the Manhattan Clothing Company in Glenwood Springs, Colorado.

Corporate strategy was already firmly established by this time. Print advertising that trumpeted genuine bargain prices lured an ever-escalating, middle-class clientele, while frequent sales kept the merchandise moving. Fast stock turnover kept the customers in the height of fashion. Energy and swift management decisions were David May trademarks. A frequently quoted story tells that he paid $31,000 for the stock of a bankrupt clothing store he spied during an 1888 visit to Denver, Colorado. Before the day was out, he installed a brass band out front to help sell out the existing stock. It took him just one week to clear the inventory, remodel the store, and establish the property anew as The May Shoe & Clothing Company.

May's expansion efforts continued through the 1890s. First came the 1892 purchase of the Famous Department Store in St. Louis, Missouri, for which he and two Shoenberg brothers-in-law paid $150,000. Then, spreading his interests to Cleveland, Ohio, in 1898, he spent $300,000 to buy the aging Hull & Dutton store.

In 1911, one year after The May Department Stores Company was incorporated in New York, it bought a second St. Louis chain, William Barr Dry Goods Company. To consolidate the firm's Missouri holdings, they merged the two St. Louis chains, forming the Famous-Barr Company. In spite of the investment, sales for the year reached $14.8 million, with net profits of $1.5 million.

By 1917 David May was ready to hand the company presidency to his son Morton. Becoming chairman of the board did not reduce his active interest in business affairs; although he was 75 years old in 1923, he bought a Los Angeles department store, A. Hamburger & Sons, for $4.2 million cash, personally supervising its renovation and its energetic promotion. Renamed The May Company, the new store opened new avenues in California and helped to produce 1926 sales figures that surpassed the $100 million mark for the first time. It was a final triumph for David May, who died in 1927 at the age of 79.

The same year, the company acquired Bernheimer-Leader Stores, Inc. in Baltimore, Maryland. Costing $2.3 million, the new acquisition was also renamed The May Company and by newly established company policy, was the last acquisition for some time. Top priorities then were consolidation, improvement in performance, and store remodeling. Systematic modernization to update delivery systems and to provide customer parking began in 1928, and was completed in 1932.

Still unaffected by the Great Depression, May's sales reached $106.7 million in 1929. During the bleak years that followed, the company maintained its stability with tried-and-true strategy and rigorous financial planning. One important practice focused on inventory. Buyers had always maintained large stocks of merchandise, regardless of the external economic climate. This policy now proved profitable, for higher purchase costs were not a problem; the company simply added the old and the new prices of an item, averaged the two, and held one of its famous sales. Large inventories thus became an asset, leaving the stores unaffected by the Depression-era foundering of distressed suppliers.

A distinct advantage to the company lay in the wide geographical spread of May's subsidiaries. Each store had its own buying department, allowing it to cater to its individual needs. Since the Depression's depth likewise varied from area to area, buyers could gauge their stock requirements with accuracy. Additional centralized buying facilities, however, allowed buyers to take advantage of mass–purchasing practices to keep their costs down. Careful planning paid off—although sales dipped to $72.5 million by 1932, they slowly recovered, rising to $89.2 million by the end of 1935.

A downside of the 1930s came from new competitors. The automobile's increasing popularity made cheaper locations on city outskirts more accessible to customers. These locations became more attractive to specialty stores wanting to keep overheads down, as well as to the new mail-order houses that offered a huge selection at reasonable prices, while catering to an infinitely larger market than any department store had.

Labor disputes were a problem for most department stores during the late 1930s. May's turn came in 1937, when one disturbance resulted in the arrest of a New York May store manager, and another caused panic among customers after strike organizers from the local chapter of the Retail Women's Apparel Salespeople raised false fire alarms at the same store. Sales figures, unaffected by union complaints of low wages and long hours, reached $98.4 million in 1938, yielding a net profit of $3.8 million.

By 1939 the company was ready to expand once again. Foreshadowing a 1940s trend toward suburban shopping centers, it opened a Wilshire Boulevard branch of its Los Angeles store, stocking it with merchandise for the upper-income customer.

In 1946 May organized a merger with Kaufmann Department Stores, Inc., of Pittsburgh. With a history stretching back to 1871, Kaufmann's was western Pennsylvania's largest department store, and had cordially shared several May buying offices for many years. Together, the two operations were large enough to produce combined 1945 sales of $246.4 million. Kaufmann's brought to the partnership a higher-income clientele, seven new units, and its own brand of paint, linens, and toiletries. Terms of the agreement were complex; 0.20 share of new $3.40 dividend preferred stock and 0.45 share of May Department Stores common stock were issued for each outstanding common share of Kaufmann stock. This involved the issuance of 110,532 preferred and 248,697 common shares. May made no changes in Kaufmann's management; instead, it gave the new officers representation in May affairs.

In 1948 there was another important acquisition: the Strouss-Hirshberg Company of Youngstown, Ohio. This gave the company stores in Youngstown and Warren, Ohio, and New Castle, Pennsylvania. These stores had produced a 1947 turnover of $22 million. The price tag was reasonable—approximately 148,000 shares of May common stock, worth $5 each.

By this time May had stores in several cities in Ohio; Los Angeles, California; Denver, Colorado; Baltimore, Maryland; and St. Louis, Missouri. Yet company policy in the 1940s showed little change. Each unit was still independent, each management team autonomous. A loosely knit central organization with auxiliary offices in Chicago, Boston, St. Louis, and Los Angeles provided the financial benefits of combined

purchasing, augmenting the store-buyers' efforts. The founder's formula of aggressive promotion, competitive pricing, and wide selection gave the company dominance in five of the eight cities that were home to May stores. Liberal salaries and incentive plans ensured loyalty, as exemplified by several department store heads who had been with the company for many years. The different elements made a successful mix, resulting in 1949 sales that reached $392.9 million, despite population shifts to the suburbs, competition from discount houses, and increases in customer spending for food and gasoline.

In 1951 Morton D. May succeeded his father as company president, Morton J. May moving on to the company chairmanship. Continuing in his father's expansion and consolidation footsteps, the younger May held the reins of 25 stores by the end of 1953; the lineup now consisted of 10 large downtown stores, 5 large branch stores, and 10 smaller branch stores. Sales for that year topped $447.5 million, and the company could well afford the $10 million it spent over the 1954–1955 period to remodel, modernize, and enlarge suburban stores. Additional potential for suburban expansion spurred construction of the firm's first shopping plaza, The Center of Sheffield. Covering 55 acres near Lorain, Ohio, the development contained about 40 retail stores as well as parking for 3,000 cars. It proved so popular that another center was constructed in Los Angeles within the next two years.

Other new ventures of the 1950s included the 1957 purchase of Denver's Daniels & Fischer Stores Company, which was subsequently merged with existing Denver operations and renamed May D&F. Hecht Company of Washington, D.C., in 1959 was a new subsidiary with branch operations in Baltimore. Secured in 1959 for 42,560 preferred shares issued in exchange for a similar number of Hecht preferred and 827,623 common shares, Hecht welcomed the merger of its Baltimore outlets with existing May operations. Though start-up costs and refurbishing usually curbed earnings in an acquisition's first year, Hecht's merger did not affect profits. May finished the decade with sales reaching $645.1 million, soaring past the 1948 year-end total of $540.9 million.

Operations centralized during this period included real estate, legal, and promotional planning. Demographic research, used to track present and future buying patterns, showed two new trends as the 1960s began. At the one end of the scale, there was a shift to discount merchandising, bringing the company into competition with drugstores, supermarkets, and discount houses. On the other hand, the more expensive end of the spectrum was now showing an increased emphasis on fashion in clothes, linens, and other May staples. To move inexpensive staples more efficiently, the company increased automation in most units. At the specialty merchandise end, the company upgraded its merchandise and exclusive brands.

Two important acquisitions were negotiated in 1965, both of which were finalized in 1966. One was the merger of Meier & Frank Co., Inc., a Portland, Oregon, company. The other, G. Fox & Company, brought May into Hartford, Connecticut. Founded in 1847, G. Fox was now headed by the founder's granddaughter, Beatrice Fox Auerbach, who continued as the store president after the merger, assuming a directorship of the May Company. Terms of the agreement included an exchange of 720,000 May shares. Both these mergers were scrutinized by the Federal Trade Commission (FTC), whose restrictive powers were broadened early in 1966. As both transactions had been initiated before the new restrictions came into force, both acquisitions were allowed, although the company had to agree to make no further acquisitions for 10 years, unless specifically permitted by the FTC.

When Morton D. May became chairman of the board in 1967, to be succeeded as president by Stanley J. Goodman, a disturbing new trend appeared—the vigorous acquisitions program and its concomitant store renovations and expansions began to eat into profits. Downtown stores were waning in popularity, and customer demand at the new suburban branches was not yet enough to compensate, because of a slowdown in the economy. Labor costs also rose significantly. Year-end figures told their own story; in 1966 total sales reached $869.1 million, yielding a profit of $45.9 million, while 1967 total sales, reaching $979 million, brought a profit of just $38.4 million. The following year, although total sales passed the $1 billion mark for the first time, profit sank to $36.2 million.

Plans went ahead, nevertheless, for the discount end of the market. In 1968 the company hired John F. Geisse, an experienced discount merchandiser, to head its new discount subsidiary; he became a vice-president. The new enterprise, called Venture, started in St. Louis in 1970. Achieving quick success, it burgeoned to a 12-unit chain by 1972. Three years later there were 20 stores, serving a population of 11,200,000.

In 1975 the Venture subsidiary contributed an estimated 9% of May's $1.75 billion in sales. Focusing on the Midwest market, the company had eight Chicago-area Venture stores, a number too small to give the advantages of increased productivity or warehousing and distribution savings. To remedy this problem, in 1978 the subsidiary purchased 19 Turn-Style stores with a combined annual sales figure of about $180 million from Jewel Companies. The units were then redesigned and restocked, at a cost of $27 million. Further expansion had to be temporarily shelved, however, because existing distribution and inventory monitoring systems were unable to cope with the sudden increase in the Chicago-area activities.

Catalog shopping, accommodating the ever-swelling numbers of working women, was another new enterprise of the 1970s. In a 50-50 partnership with Canadian Consumers Distributing Company, Ltd., May opened 18 catalog showrooms in 1973, planning an eventual 150 more. Unlike other catalog stores that offered merchandise that was dispatched from separate warehouses, these supplied catalog-ordered items from storage facilities on the premises. The goal was to have many such stores in a given area, to meet competition and also to utilize the efficiency of a central distribution point. Although hopeful that the new enterprise would at least break even by the end of 1976, this was not the case, and May sold its 70 U.S. showrooms to Consumers Distributing Company (CDC) in 1978, in exchange for 24% of CDC stock, valued at $26 million.

In November 1979 the company bought Volume Shoe Corporation for about $150 million in stock. A Topeka, Kansas, family-owned chain of more than 800 self-service stores, Volume was then enjoying annual sales totaling more than $200 million. The following year a recession, coupled with start-up costs for an enlarged shoe distribution center, cut deeply into profits, which rose only 3.6% in 1980. Between 1979 and 1983, however, the chain's compound growth reached 23.4%, producing $58.8 million in 1983 operating earnings, and

showing the biggest jump of any May Department Store Division. Moving purposefully toward its goal of establishing Payless Shoe outlets nationally, Volume purchased 83 stores from HRT Industries as well as 38 from Craddock-Terry Shoe, and was eyeing possibilities in east coast cities by year's end.

At the same time, the new May president, David Farrell, instituted a program of refurbishments to renovate some of the company's more outdated units and rejuvenate their image as trendy fashion outlets. The company spent $117 million on the Famous-Barr chain alone, although other stores were also remodeled.

This substantial amount of money came principally from the company's real estate holdings, among which were 11 shopping centers plus interest in 8 more, along with a 27% interest in a Los Angeles housing complex. Total value of the real estate holdings was $242 million in 1979, an amount enhanced considerably by a 1980 partnership with Prudential Insurance Company of America. Terms of agreement included joint ownership and operation of six of May's regional shopping centers, for which equity and appreciation were shared. Benefits to May from this deal specified a $75 million 20-year loan at only 9% interest, with no principal payments until the loan matured.

Several department store chains noted an earnings slowdown at the beginning of the 1980s. May's annual figures reflected only a 3.3% rise to $117 million, on a total sales rise of 6.6%. Farrell instituted stringent cost-cutting, which included the installation of new telephone and energy-management systems for all 138 department stores. Some units were made smaller for profitability, the extra space being leased to tenants often providing further sales potential with their own business traffic. Merchandise was upgraded to tempt the upscale customer, for the company was competing against specialty stores whose fashion reputations were already established.

A significant threat to market share appeared in the mid-1980s, however, in the form of warehouse stores and off-price outlets. Offering brand-name merchandise at discount prices, they forced retailers to rethink their customary strategy. May's answer, to fulfill its requirements of upgrading merchandise at one end of their market niche and meeting the off-price challenge at the other, was the 1986 acquisition of Associated Dry Goods (ADG), at a cost of $2.5 billion. This steep purchase price brought the company the quality Lord & Taylor chain, J.W. Robinson department stores, L.S. Ayres units, Caldor discount operations, and Loehmann's off-price apparel shops. As was the case with the other May subsidiaries, each chain continued to operate independently.

In 1987 May formed a 50–50 partnership with PruSimon, May Centers Associates (MCA). May transferred its shopping center operations to MCA. Two partners owned PruSimon: Melvin Simon & Associates, Inc., an Indianapolis, Indiana, company, and New York–based Prudential Insurance Company of America. PruSimon paid $550 million in cash for its share of the partnership. May's chief benefit was to disengage from management functions unrelated to the stores, whose number once again increased with the $1.5 billion acquisition of Filene's of Boston and Foley's of Houston in 1988.

To narrow its focus on retailing further, the company decided to discontinue its discount operations. Loehmann's was sold in 1988. Offered next were Venture and the Caldor chain that had been part of the ADG acquisition. There were, however, a large number of retail operations for sale at the end of the 1980s, and the company was unable to reach its asking price of about $600 million for Caldor. It therefore in 1989 sold this unit to an investor group, which formed a company called Odyssey Partners L.P., to buy an 80% share. In 1990 Venture was spun off to shareholders, in a tax-free distribution of 0.13 shares of Venture stock for each share of May stock.

In 1990 May acquired Thalhimers, a 26-store group based in Richmond, Virginia. That year May's sales surpassed $10 billion. From 1991 to 1995, the company planned to open 90 department stores and 1,200 Payless Shoe stores; Volume Shoe Corporation changed its name to Payless ShoeSource, Inc. in 1990. Among the company's existing department stores, 11 were earmarked for remodeling, with an increase in size planned for 6 of these. While May stores continued to face keen competition, they had the strength of their stellar reputations. The company went into the 1990s planning to build on this strength with innovative merchandising ideas, while reducing expenses wherever possible.

Principal Subsidiaries: Lord & Taylor; Foley's; May Company (California); Hecht's; Robinson's; Kaufmann's; Famous-Barr; Filene's; May Company (Ohio); G. Fox; May D&F; Meier & Frank; Payless Shoe-Source, Inc.; May Merchandising Corporation.

Further Reading: "May Stores: Watch Them Grow," *Fortune,* December 1948; "May Department Stores," *Barron's,* March 29, 1954; "A Discounter Bids for Power in Chicago," *Business Week,* August 28, 1978; "Retailers Discover Their Real Estate Riches," *Business Week,* January 19, 1981; "ADG Acquisition Turns May into Super Power," *Chain Store Age Executive,* September 1986; Parkhill, Forbes, "The May Story," The May Department Stores Company corporate typescript, [n.d.].

—Gillian Wolf

MELVILLE CORPORATION

One Theall Road
Rye, New York 10580
U.S.A.
(914) 925-4000
Fax: (914) 925-4026

Public Company
Incorporated: 1922 as Melville Shoe Corporation
Employees: 119,000
Sales: $8.69 billion
Stock Exchange: New York

Melville Corporation, which started as a small string of shoe stores, has become one of the largest U.S. retailing conglomerates. For much of its life, Melville was known chiefly for its chain of discount footwear stores, Thom McAn. During the late 20th century, however, Melville acquired more than a dozen other retailing operations. By the 1990s Melville had diversified to such a degree that shoes accounted for less than a quarter of the company's sales. Melville's apparel, drug, and home furnishing divisions include such chains as Consumer Value Stores, People's Drug, and Marshall's.

The company originated in 1892, when Frank Melville, a shoe jobber, took over the three stores owned by his employer, who had left town under a cloud of debt. Melville parlayed the three New York shops into a small but thriving chain. In 1909 he brought his son, John Ward Melville, into the family business. The younger Melville, who dropped the "John" and was known by "Ward," was named vice-president in 1916 and became the driving force behind much of the company's growth. He ran the corporation for nearly half a century, and served as chairman of the board until the day he died in 1977 at the age of 90.

While serving in the army during World War I, Ward Melville struck up a profitable friendship with J. Franklin McElwain, a New Hampshire shoe manufacturer. Together they devised a method to mass-produce shoes and distribute them at low prices though a chain of stores, which they decided to name after a Scottish golfer, Thomas McCann, which they shortened to Thom McAn. They opened the first Thom McAn store in New York in 1922, offering a few simple styles of men's shoes at the fixed price of $3.99.

Despite the lack of variety, the discounting scheme was an immediate success, and new stores were opened all over the Northeast. By 1927 when the Thom McAn chain had grown to more than 300 stores, demand outstripped the capacity of McElwain's Nashua, New Hampshire, plant, which produced 20,000 pairs a day. Consequently McElwain acquired a new plant in Worcester, Massachusetts.

Melville Shoe, like other businesses, suffered during the Great Depression. In 1932, for example, sales dropped more than 21% from 1931 levels, from $26.2 million to $20.5 million. Despite rumors of bankruptcy that circulated in 1933, Melville Shoe weathered the storm with careful management, prudent expansion, and financial innovation. Melville made a public stock offering in 1936, taking its place on the New York Stock Exchange. Throughout the 1930s, Melville continued to open more outlets. By 1939 Melville operated 650 Thom McAn stores and also marketed its products through its smaller John Ward and Frank Tod shoe-store chains.

In 1939 Ward Melville moved to centralize and unify the entire production and marketing operation under one corporate head. He proposed that Melville merge with McElwain's manufacturing company, J. F. McElwain Company, which then produced about 11 million shoes annually for Melville. The stockholders of both companies approved the merger in December 1939. The following year, J. Franklin McElwain and Ward Melville participated in a ceremony to commemorate the production of their 100 millionth pair of shoes.

In 1940 as the economy started climbing out of the Depression, Melville posted sales topping $40 million for the first time. Sales continued to climb through the war years. The growth continued unabated until 1952, when total sales actually fell for the first time since the Depression. The decline from $92 million to $90 million signified the first inkling of a weakness in Melville's time-tested strategy of producing a few styles of relatively cheap shoes. In an expanding and competitive economy, diversity and specialization became increasingly necessary. Accordingly Melville began to add more women's and children's shoes in an effort to diversify.

In 1952 Melville acquired Miles Shoes, a chain of 151 stores. With this acquisition, better results were realized immediately: sales for 1953 increased about 20%, topping $108 million. By 1955 Melville had grown to include 12 factories and 850 stores. The following year, Ward Melville, then 69, was named chairman of the board, although he retained his post of chief executive officer. Robert C. Erb assumed the post of president that Melville had vacated.

As part of a sustained effort to increase market penetration, Melville created a new division in 1960. The new unit, Meldisco, was dedicated to leasing and supplying family shoe departments in self-service discount department stores. That year, however, earnings declined slightly from the 1959 totals—to $6 million profits on sales of $151 million. The trend continued in 1962, as sales climbed to $176 million while net income dropped to about $5 million.

In 1964 Francis C. Rooney, a vice-president, succeeded Robert Erb as president. Over the next two decades, Rooney oversaw tremendous growth at Melville that transformed the nature, breadth, and scope of Melville's operations.

Rooney helped the company to tremendous growth. Between 1962 and 1967, sales jumped 50% and net profits tripled. By 1967 sales topped $260 million. At the end of the 1960s, Melville was the nation's largest shoe retailer, operating 1,400 Thom McAn, Miles, and Meldisco outlets. The growth also brought increasing differentiation and specialization, as Thom

McAn turned into a suburban-based family chain, while Miles specialized in women's and girls' shoes.

In 1968 Melville made its most important move of the decade, opening the first of its Chess King stores, a clothing chain geared toward fashion-conscious teens and youth. This was Melville's first venture into the fashion industry, but it was not to be its last. In 1968 Melville also acquired Foxwood, renamed Foxmoor, a 16-store apparel chain that catered to young women.

The following year brought even more expansion. Melville bought three companies: the Consumer Value Stores (CVS) chain of drug retail outlets; Mark Steven, Inc., a firm that distributed products to CVS; and Retail Store Management, Inc. Buoyed by these acquisitions, Rooney boldly predicted in 1969 that Melville would attain total sales of $1 billion by 1975.

In 1970 Melville, the fifth-largest and most profitable U.S. shoemaker, operated 1,644 total retail outlets. In 1972 Melville was ranked as the 43rd-largest retailing company in the United States, with sales of $512 million, and more than 15,000 employees.

Not satisfied with this accretion, Melville continued to expand. In 1972 Melville acquired Clinton Merchandising, Inc., which operated 80 stores in the Midwest and Northeast, as well as Metro Pants Co. and Spotwood Apparel, Inc., both manufacturers of men's and boys' clothing. That year Melville left its long-time midtown Manhattan headquarters for a larger building in Westchester County, New York.

Melville's expansion took on an international character in the 1970s as well. In 1971 Melville entered into a joint venture with C. F. Bally of Switzerland, contracting to sell the upscale Bally shoe line in the United States. The same year, Melville formed a European buying company. In 1973 Melville initiated a venture to market Thom McAn shoes in Japan.

Despite the diversification, shoes still accounted for 71% of Melville's $765 million in sales in 1974. In 1975 Melville branched out further into non-shoe retailing when it bought Marshall's Inc., then a chain of 32 retail apparel stores. Expansion continued apace in 1977, when Melville bought the Mack Drug Co. chain, and merged it into the CVS unit.

In 1976 Melville, then the nation's 32nd-largest retailing company, belatedly reached Rooney's vaunted goal of $1 billion in sales, due to the combination of acquiring new chains and expanding existing units. In 1976 total receipts from the firm's 3,300 outlets totaled $1.2 billion. As part of a continuing trend, the footwear sales portion declined to 60%.

After Ward Melville died in June 1977, Francis Rooney, who already held the posts of president and chief executive officer, was named chairman of the board. Ward Melville's death marked the end of an era and the beginning of a new one in which shoes would play an increasingly smaller role in the Melville scheme. By 1978 Melville operated 3,812 stores, and had sales of $1.75 billion. Shoes accounted for about 53% of the total.

As the 1970s came to a close, Melville continued to boom. In 1980, Melville, with 48,000 employees and more than 4,500 stores, saw its 26th straight year of increased sales. That year, Kenneth Berland was named to the post of president.

The following year, in which sales soared to $2.8 billion, Melville acquired the Kay-Bee Toy and Hobby Shops Inc. By 1982 Melville, the largest U.S. shoe retailer, operated nearly 5,200 total stores. These included 470 Chess King, 588 Fox-

moor, 433 CVS, and 1,200 Thom McAn outlets. In 1982 Melville added Wilson's House of Leather and Linens 'N Things to its roster.

Despite the recession of the early 1980s, sales rose to $3.3 billion in 1983; nevertheless, Melville suffered some retrenchment during the 1980s. The firm began to phase out six of its seven shoe factories in late 1983, eventually terminating about 2,000 jobs. In 1985 Melville sold the 614-store Foxmoor chain, whose sales were declining. The same year, Melville shut down 72 Thom McAn outlets. Despite the closures or sales of various stores, 1985 receipts rose to $4.7 billion, and profits surged to $219 million.

In 1985 Stanley Goldstein, a CVS founder who joined Melville when his corporation was acquired by the shoe giant, succeeded Berland as president, and took his place as heir apparent. The following year, Goldstein was named chairman and chief executive officer, replacing the retiring Francis Rooney. To Goldstein fell the task of building on Rooney's phenomenal record. Rooney had transformed the firm from a successful shoe company into a diversified retailing giant.

Melville's expansion continued under Goldstein. In 1987, while amassing $5.9 billion in sales, Melville acquired 25 Heartland and Pharmacity drug stores and 36 Leather Loft stores. In 1988 Melville bought Finish Line, a chain of athletic footwear stores and Bermans Specialty Stores.

In 1989 Melville underwent some structural renovation. The firm created a profit-sharing plan and an employee stock ownership plan, under which about 6% of the company's common stock was distributed among its employees.

The year 1989 brought to a close a remarkably successful decade, one in which sales and earnings both increased more than threefold. The Melville that left the 1980s was vastly different from the one that entered that decade. In 1989 shoes, once the firm's mainstay, accounted for only 22.5% of the total sales; the apparel sections accounted for 36%; and the drug store business accounted for 28%. The toys and household furnishing division accounted for the remainder of sales.

This trend continued in 1990, as Melville acquired more non-footwear retail outlets. Melville bought both Circus World Toy Stores Inc., which it folded into the Kay-Bee division, and Peoples Drug Stores, a 490-store chain. By the end of 1990, Melville operated 7,754 stores and listed 119,000 employees on its payroll. Sales for 1990 totaled $8.68 billion.

Ward Melville's shoe company had come a long way. The process of diversification that began in the last years of Ward Melville's life picked up momentum throughout the 1970s and 1980s. With its vast, diverse holdings and sound financial condition, the Melville Corporation is looking forward to a second century of profits and growth.

Principal Subsidiaries: Melville Realty Co.; Marshalls Inc.; Wilson's Suede & Leather Inc.; Meldisco; Thom McAn Shoe Co.; Kay-Bee Toy Stores; Fan Club Stores; This End Up Furniture Co.

Further Reading: "Grooving shoe sales to a young market," *Business Week,* April 27, 1968; "Melville steps into the billion-dollar class," *Business Week,* April 11, 1977; Sloane,

Leonard, "Ward Melville, 90s Shoe Magnate, Dies," *The New York Times,* June 6, 1977; Rudnitsky, Howard, "Fancy footwork," *Forbes,* March 29, 1982; Barmash, Isadore, "Retailing: The Special Case of Melville Corp.," *The New York Times,* April 4, 1982; Chakravarty, Subrata N., "Reshaping the last," *Forbes,* September 17, 1990.

—Daniel Gross

MERCANTILE STORES COMPANY, INC.

1100 North Market Street
Wilmington, Delaware 19801
U.S.A.
(513) 860-8000
Fax: (513) 860-8251

Public Company
Incorporated: 1914 as Mercantile Stores Corporation
Employees: 27,500
Sales: $2.37 billion
Stock Exchange: New York

Mercantile Stores is a chain of upscale department stores that primarily sell apparel in small cities in the southern and midwestern United States. Owned in large part by one family, the company has made its mark through steady, conservative business practices and through successful interpretation of social trends in the course of its history. Mercantile Stores has aggressively relocated the bulk of its stores from downtown areas to suburban malls since the end of World War II and consistently courted the affluent customer, who has rewarded the chain with continuing, though unspectacular, growth and profits.

The company got its start in 1914 in the wake of the failure of another chain of dry goods stores, H.B. Claflin Company. One of Claflin's largest creditors was the Milliken family, which owned a textiles firm in the South. Claflin's assets were divided into two groups, and the group of less valuable stores was taken over by a committee of creditors that included the Millikens. This new entity, named Mercantile Stores Corporation, assumed ownership of 22 stores on December 14, 1914. Although the company established headquarters in New York City, its stores were located from Washington state to New York and Pennsylvania, as far north as Canada and as far south as Alabama. In its early years, the main preoccupation of the company's leaders was to overcome the Claflin company's heritage of debt and stay in business, so that creditors could receive a portion of what they were owed. At the end of 1917, eight months after the United States entered World War I, the company found itself unable to sell enough assets to pay off the $33 million in notes it had issued three years earlier to old creditors, and the notes were extended two years.

As this new deadline drew near, however, the uncertainty of the postwar U.S. economy, with large-scale unemployment and a spiraling cost of living, made it less likely that the com-

pany would be able to meet it obligations. Mercantile's leaders again decided to start anew, and the company was reorganized at the start of 1919 under a new name, Mercantile Stores Company. The old company's outstanding notes were replaced with newly issued stocks and bonds. Mercantile Stores Company was incorporated in Delaware, under the state's favorable corporate statutes, and a new president, Alexander New, was elected shortly thereafter. New, the son of a dry-goods merchant, brought legal training and a life-long familiarity with retailing to his position.

As the United States entered the turbulent postwar years of the 1920s, Mercantile Stores set about solidifying its shaky financial position. Although the company issued additional stock, both common and preferred, Mercantile Stores continued to struggle. As a later company president commented in *Barron's*, December 28, 1987, the individual stores "were then mostly third and fourth rate." In 1925 Mercantile Stores's many diverse parts were linked more closely when the company discontinued its practice of allowing each store to purchase wholesale goods separately. Instead, the company centralized its purchasing by taking over a New York dry-goods buying office in 1925.

By 1929 the company had experienced some modest growth, as its assets increased 25% from the start of the decade. Late that year, however, the stock market crash of October 29 plunged the country into the Great Depression. Mercantile Stores, entirely dependent upon strong consumer spending, found itself in a perilous position as bank failures, widespread unemployment, and wage cuts reduced the buying power of most U.S. consumers. In 1930 the company was set further adrift when its president for the last decade, Alexander New, resigned due to ill health. He died shortly thereafter. For the next several years, Mercantile Stores was led by an executive committee of four vice presidents, with a member of the Milliken family as the fifth member and chairman of the committee. Under this joint management, the company retrenched. Stores losing in money were sold, and only those properties turning a profit were buttressed by further investment. At one point, fearing the spread of rumors that would set off a frenzy of stock selling and ruin the company's worth, Mercantile Stores's chief executive bypassed the telephone in favor of traveling personally to each store in the chain to tell the manager to sell everything, so that desperately needed cash could be raised to pay off debts. With these measures, the company narrowly staved off collapse, but this close call helped to instill cautious and conservative business principles in the company's leaders.

In 1934, after the resignation of one short-term president, Mercantile Stores emerged from its leaderless limbo: Francis G. Kingsley, who would become a close associate of the Milliken family, assumed the company's top spot. Under Kingsley the company further centralized its operations in New York. Since ready-to-wear clothing purchased off the rack was rapidly replacing clothing made at home, Mercantile also began to devote more of its energy to marketing fashionable clothes. The company farmed out its purchasing in other areas, but kept decisions about coats, dresses, and other manufactured clothing in-house, under a top Mercantile buyer, Rosalie Lavain. By the end of the decade, Mercantile Stores had brought all its purchasing under its own roof to ensure greater control of the merchandise sent to its stores. In 1941 Kingsley was elevated to chairman, and Harold Jockers, who would also develop close ties to the Millikens, became the fourth president of Mercantile Stores. At the end of that year, the United States entered into World War II, after the bombing of Pearl Harbor. The war brought further changes in U.S. society and consumer needs. As men entered the armed forces, women entered the work force in large numbers for the first time and found themselves with increased spending power. The company, whose fashionable goods were sold primarily to women customers, profited from this development, despite the difficulty of obtaining merchandise during times of wartime shortage. By 1945 at the war's end, Mercantile's profits had nearly tripled their 1941 level.

In the second half of the 1940s, the U.S. economy enjoyed a postwar boom, and Mercantile Stores grew along with the vast overall demand for consumer goods. The company began a strong expansion. It acquired additional stores—Duluth Glass Block Store Company, in Minnesota, in 1944, and J.B. White & Company, of Greenville, South Carolina, the following year. In 1946 the company's stock was listed on the New York Stock Exchange for the first time, and expansion continued. Stores in Colorado, North Dakota, and Alabama were soon added to the fold.

In addition to expanding the number of stores it owned, the company also began to change its focus within each separate market. Realizing that the greatest population growth in the postwar years would take place not in the inner city, where previous waves of immigrants from abroad had concentrated large numbers of people, but on the outskirts of urban areas, where internal migration of young city dwellers filled vast new suburban housing tracts, Mercantile Stores began to open branch versions of its downtown stores on the outskirts of metropolitan areas to reach this new breed of customer. The company sought to tap into the vast demand for home furnishings and appliances to fill the new homes of the baby-boom generation.

Throughout the late 1940s and early 1950s, the company continued its strong trend toward centralizing operations for all of its stores to maximize efficiency. Under Kingsley and Jockers, Mercantile Stores embarked on a strategy to compete with the largest national retailing chains, such as Sears, on an equal footing by keeping costs and therefore, prices, down. The resulting policy of maintaining a small profit margin through conservative business practices was based on the company's large degree of centralization for economies of scale and strict limitations on operating expenses. In addition, the introduction of merchandise sold under its own labels allowed Mercantile Stores to market high-quality goods without incurring the expenses of buying through an intermediary. By the end of 1955, these policies started to pay off, enabling Mercantile Stores to solidify its strong position in the postwar department store industry, and sales had more than doubled from their level of ten years earlier. In the second half of the 1950s, sales continued to rise, reaching $170 million by the end of 1960.

The presidency of Mercantile Stores was taken over by F.K. Bradley in 1960, and the company continued on its postwar path of steady expansion into the suburbs. This effort was headed by the Mercantile Stores Real Estate Division, which grew eventually to encompass all aspects of store construction, from property acquisition to architectural design to interior decoration.

In addition, the company began to shift its emphasis in marketing away from appliances, a growth area of the 1950s, to clothing and accessories. To do this more effectively and to garner the business of a more affluent clientele, Mercantile Stores began to supplement its own private-label merchandise with the brand name wares of other manufacturers and to feature products imported from other countries.

In 1964 the company presidency passed to R. Nelson Shaw. By the mid-1960s, its annual sales were nearing $200 million, as Mercantile Stores continued its efforts to maintain its market share by staying abreast of latest fashions. In 1965, for instance, the Mercantile Stores Wig Division was inaugurated, as a result of a fad for hairpieces, and soon shops to make and style wigs of imported human hair and other materials had been set up in all major stores throughout the company's chain.

During the late 1960s and the 1970s, Mercantile continued its steady growth. The number of restaurants within its stores was increased, and its successful beauty salon sideline, which was begun before World War II, was expanded to include freestanding stores. The installation of electronic cash registers in many stores enabled Mercantile Stores to fine-tune inventory control, and plans were made to expand this capability.

In 1974 the chain's 72 stores were generating more than $500 million in sales, although profits had gone flat because of the poor economy. Nevertheless, the company continued its plans to build new stores, primarily in suburban locations, and to renovate its older facilities. Mercantile's fortunes overall picked up in the years following 1974, and demand for apparel and the company's growth continued throughout the late 1970s.

By the early 1980s, the chain encompassed 84 stores, and sales had reached $1.4 billion, despite a recession of the U.S. economy. Mercantile Stores had a year of flat revenues in 1980, but overall they continued to do well, placing its emphasis on flexibility in the mix of products it sold.

In 1987 Mercantile sold its Canadian operations. The late 1980s were a period of consolidation in the department store business, as healthy chains borrowed heavily to finance large mergers and takeovers, and venerable names closed their doors forever. The large-scale discounting and heavy advertising undertaken by competitors softened profits for the company, and Mercantile concentrated on enlarging and renovating existing stores rather than on purchasing or opening new ones. The company continued to de-emphasize goods such as housewares, in favor of higher-profit items like fashionable clothing and accessories, and also phased out less profitable downtown stores for newer, suburban mall stores. Sales and profits in the late 1980s, dampened by in-store construction, fell flat.

In 1990 the company relocated its headquarters from New York City to a suburb of Cincinnati, Ohio, and undertook a program of brisk expansion, laying plans to open two or three new stores a year for five years in hopes of reversing its sluggish sales growth, which resulted in lowered earnings for 1990. In addition, the company made plans to implement advanced computerized inventory control procedures, called Quick Response. The rest of the industry had adopted these money-saving measures much earlier.

As Mercantile Stores entered the 1990s, the company seemed poised to continue its traditionally strong and steady progress. Over the course of the 20th century, Mercantile Stores had refined a retail philosophy that was successful, and, in the careful and conservative stewardship of its leaders, dominated by the presence of the Milliken family, the company is likely to continue to prosper.

Principal Subsidiaries: Hennessy Company; Duluth Glass Block Store Company; DeLendrecie Company; J.B. White & Company; The McAlpin Company; The Joslin Dry Goods Company; Castner-Knott Dry Goods Company; The Jones Store Company; C.J. Gayfer & Company, Inc.; J. Bacon & Sons; Root Dry Goods Company; The Lion Dry Goods Company; Jones Store Company Hairstyling School.

Further Reading: Cochran, Thomas N., "Merchandising Genius: In Good Times or Bad, Mercantile Stores Prosper," *Barron's,* December 28, 1987; Byrne, Harlan S., "Mercantile Stores Co.: It survives in a battered industry, resumes expansion," *Barron's,* June 11, 1990.

—Elizabeth Rourke

MITSUKOSHI

MITSUKOSHI LTD.

4-1, Nihombashi Muromachi 1-chome
Chuo-ku, Tokyo 103-01
Japan
(03) 3241-3311
Fax: (03) 3245-0949

Public Company
Incorporated: 1904 as Mitsukoshi Dry-Goods Store Company
    Limited
Employees: 11,457
Sales: ¥866.68 billion (US$6.94 billion)
Stock Exchanges: Tokyo Osaka Nagoya Luxembourg

Mitsukoshi Ltd., Japan's largest department store company, is
a leader of the Mitsui group, which is second only to Mitsubishi among Japan's powerful financial-commercial-industrial
combines. Mitsui group companies maintain a minority share
in Mitsukoshi, an independent company with its own network
of stores, restaurants, travel agencies, factories, financial and
management services, and related enterprises.

Mitsukoshi's origins date back past its establishment in 1904
as Japan's first modern department store to the nation's feudal
days in the 17th century. The Lord of Echigo, head of the
noble House of Mitsui, fled from the forces of a samurai who
eventually unified Japan by subduing the protectors of the he-
reditary estates. Because Matsusaka, the place of refuge, was a
busy market center near a popular port in a fertile province,
the Lord of Echigo, no longer in a position to collect income
from his estates, renounced his title in order to become a merchant. After an inauspicious effort at a brewery of sake and
soy sauce, a merchandising dynasty was launched through the
work of the former lord's eldest son, Mitsui Sokubei Takatoshi, and his wife, Shuho, daughter of a successful merchant.

The drapery business they opened in 1673 was called
Echigo-ya in recognition of the family's noble heritage, differ-
entiating it from other businesses and attaching some prestige
to its wares. A luxurious ambiance, in which transactions were
discussed secondarily to elaborate social amenities, quickly
attracted a loyal clientele, but the couple soon introduced some
business practices that greatly broadened their customer base.

First, they maneuvered to become purveyors of textiles to
the new government, which by that time had settled down under the thumb of the Tokugawa shogun to a lengthy period of
peace and isolation from the outside world. Second, the couple opened a store where customers could view the merchan-

dise and make cash transactions. This was a drastic departure
from the practices of the late 17th century, when merchants
made house calls on wealthy families—the only persons who
could afford to buy—and would have to wait for payment until
the lord of the manor collected the annual or semiannual
rentals from tenants, who paid in rice rather than currency.
That, in turn, would have to be converted into negotiable instruments by professional moneychangeers or bartered for
other goods.

Centralizing the purchase process in a store eliminated the
transportation costs of making house calls—a saving that
Echigo-ya could pass on to customers in the form of reduced
prices. The couple also introduced fixed prices. This eliminated the uncertainty on both sides that had accompanied the
traditional haggling and speeded the purchase process, making
it possible to handle more transactions.

The success of the first store led to the opening of a second,
in Edo, which became modern Tokyo. It also led to the establishment of a second business—a financial arm. Customers
found it convenient to have a moneychanger on the premises,
and the financial service eventually grew to gigantic proportions. Today it is the powerful Mitsui Bank, another independent member of the Mitsui group.

In pioneering consumer-oriented business practices, the
change that had the greatest effect on attracting new customers
was to make merchandise available in small enough quantities
to be affordable for the common people. Previously, fabric had
to be purchased by the bolt. Echigo-ya was the first store to
allow the customer to limit the purchase to the amount needed.
This resulted in an unprecedented volume of sales, and the
couple was able to open additional stores in other urban centers during the following decades. It was not until the Bon
Marche store was opened in Paris in 1852 that such practices
became known throughout the occidental world.

Another legacy of the founders was the Mitsui House Code,
derived from Takatoshi Mitsui's will in 1722. This was a guide
for the Mitsui heirs for management of the family's companies, which were already proliferating through the country. It
was also a code of ethics, intended to ensure that the founders'
principles and traditions of service would be followed by future generations. For example, Echigo-ya was so accommodating that an early patron wrote, "When ceremonial costumes
are required in a hurry, the shop lets the servants wait and has
the regalia made up immediately by several dozens of their
own tailors. . . . This is an example of a really big merchant."

In the ensuing 150 years, trust in the Mitsui name grew to
be so entrenched that, when the Tokugawa shogunate was succeeded in 1868 by the restoration of the imperial government,
Mitsui's financial arm became, for all practical purposes, its
banker. The management system that the Mitsui House Code
had established was no longer adequate, however, to handle the
rambling empire of businesses and industrial enterprises that
the Mitsui heirs were struggling to keep in order in the late
19th century. Japan's business climate had changed drastically
with the opening of the nation to foreign trade and the new
Meiji emperor actively encouraging openness to Western concepts. Moreover, the various Mitsui enterprises often did not
work in harmony with one another, and each was bound by its
own traditional ways of doing business.

Rizaemon Minomura, a talented manager, was recruited by
the Mitsuis and given power of attorney to make any changes

needed to solve the internal problems of the businesses, which by then represented almost all types of commercial, financial, and industrial enterprises. He was eminently successful. One of his methods was to release certain companies from direct control of Mitsui, but to retain a small share in businesses that were foundering as a result of mismanagement. One of these was the Tokyo Echigo-ya store.

The Tokyo Echigo-ya gained its independence in 1872, under the management of a related family named Mitsukoshi. The store prospered under its new management. Known first as the Mitsui Clothing Store, it became the Mitsui Dry-Goods Store in 1896, to reflect its expansion into additional lines of merchandise. Capitalizing on the Mitsui reputation for high quality and the growing popular fancy for Western-style fashions, the store brought in a designer from France to develop a new apparel department. The designs caught on, along with other innovations, including a display of merchandise in the open, life-size poster displays at railway stations, and a catalog sales department. Home delivery by auto was instituted in 1903. Stocking foreign-made goods also attracted customers.

The following year, under new director Osuke Hibi, the store was reorganized as Mitsukoshi Dry-Goods Store Company and announced its metamorphosis into Japan's first modern department store, with newspaper advertisements emphasizing the convenience of one-stop shopping for an ever-increasing variety of merchandise, simulating "in part, the department stores of the United States." As well as adding items such as jewelry, luggage, food, and photography to its wares, Mitsukoshi also held events such as expositions and exhibitions to contribute to the cultural life of the area. This had the effect of elevating the status of the store and attracted so many new customers that additional Mitsukoshi stores were opened.

By 1914 the Mitsukoshi stores were firmly established as sources of high-quality merchandise that were accessible and affordable for most shoppers, and other stores had begun to copy their innovations. The new Renaissance-style building constructed to house the flagship store that year sported Japan's first escalator. Mitsukoshi was also firmly associated with cultural activities, having participated in the refurbishing of the Imperial Theater, among many community projects.

Japan's eventual entry into World War I did not slow Mitsukoshi's growth. If anything, wartime industries furnished employment that enabled many more persons to become customers. Reduced-price special sale days and the introduction of gift coupons also stimulated sales.

The Great Kanto Earthquake of September 1, 1923, marked a turning point for all Japanese department stores. Along with many other buildings in Tokyo, they were all burned to the ground. Small mobile units were quickly set up throughout the city to supply essentials to the people, many of whom had never before been customers. A large number of customers acquired in this way continued to shop at Mitsukoshi throughout the rebuilding process and remained loyal patrons. The new stores, built as high-rises with many architectural innovations, offered further convenience. They ended the practice of having customers remove their shoes at the entrance and pad through the stores in cotton slippers. Fashion shows were held and beauty salons added. Business burgeoned. In 1928, to reflect the great variety of goods and services offered, Mitsukoshi dropped the Dry-Goods part of its name and became Mitsukoshi Ltd.

In the 1930s, mobilization for war again created industrial activity that increased the number of workers who could become part of Mitsukoshi's customer base. The Mitsukoshi name had begun to be recognized overseas as a result of participation in world's fairs and other expositions in Europe and the United States, increasing the number of foreign customers. As part of the Mitsui group, Mitsukoshi profited from its association with Japan's top business-industrial conglomerate, or *zaibatsu.* However, government constraints on the business, instituted in 1938 and continuing throughout World War II, along with the wartime damage resulting from direct bombing, left Mitsukoshi in a greatly weakened state.

The trust in the company's integrity that had been built up over many generations enabled Mitshkoshi to begin the recovery period by successfully combating the black market with fixed prices. Working with the new government established during the Allied occupation of Japan, Mitsukoshi was able to make rapid progress in rebuilding its business. Reaching out to customers through its continuing involvement in cultural events, as well as adopting Western-style products and retail techniques, Mitsukoshi had recovered enough by 1954 to celebrate its 50th anniversary with exhibitions of fine art and the introduction of new fashions that quickly became popular.

The phenomenal recovery and growth of Japanese business and industry in general brought Mitsukoshi a host of new customers. As Mitsukoshi added new products made possible by Japanese technological advancement, a consumer boom resulted that carried through the 1960s and made it possible for Mitsukoshi to open overseas stores in such locations as Paris and Hong Kong, beginning in 1971. By 1974 Mitsukoshi's flagship store was importing Rolls Royces for purchase. During the 1970s Mitsukoshi stores opened in London, New York, and Rome.

Mitsukoshi's profits dropped in the early 1980s. In September 1982 Mitsukoshi's directors dismissed Shigeru Okada from the presidency, and Akira Ichihara became president; in 1986 he became chairman of the board.

By 1985 the catalog sales, travel and construction, and decorating departments had become so large that they were reorganized as independent business divisions. Mitsukoshi continued opening new department stores, expanding existing ones, and establishing numerous specialty shops. In 1989 Mitsukoshi purchased 1.5 million shares of stock in Tiffany and Co. Mitsukoshi's president, Yoshiaki Sakakura, was appointed a director of Tiffany later that year.

Mitsukoshi is still tied to the Mitsui group through the shares Mitsui holds and through its own participation in the Mitsui group's leadership conferences. Like the rest of the Mitsui group, Mitsukoshi has expanded through takeovers and joint ventures as well as through self-developed businesses. Mitsubishi recovered from World War II somewhat faster than the Mitsui group because all of its businesses were self-developed and therefore closer-knit and easier to control. That is why the Mitsui group had not regained its prewar *zaibatsu* number-one position; however, its number-two position, under the postwar *keiretsu* system, is not seriously threatened. Along with the Mitsui group, Mitsukoshi, too, appears to be securely established as a front runner, both internally in Japan, and worldwide. A sign of the ever-widening circle of Mitsukoshi activities is its joint venture with Marubeni Corporation in 1990 to set up cable television services in Europe. This, plus its stable management and high profitability, promises continuing pre-eminence for Mitsukoshi throughout the 1990s and into the twenty-first century.

Principal Subsidiaries: Niko Co., Ltd.; Mitsukoshi Furniture Co., Ltd.; Mitsukoshi Sewing Co., Ltd.; Sanbi Co., Ltd.; Mitsukoshi Building Services Co., Ltd.; Mitsukoshi Real Estate Co., Ltd.; Muromachi Fine Art Co., Ltd.; Studio Alta Co., Ltd.; Mitsukoshi Housing Co., Ltd.; U.B., Inc.; Mitsukoshi Bridal Excellence Co., Ltd.; Mitsukoshi Restaurant Services Co., Ltd.; Sapporo Operation Services Co., Ltd.; Kansai Operation Services Co., Ltd.; Mitsukoshi Sports Co., Ltd.; Mitsukoshi Cafe Systems Co., Ltd.; Mitsukoshi World Motors, Inc.; Pronet Co., Ltd.; Leo D'Or Trading Co., Ltd.; Mitsukoshi Resort Management Co., Ltd.; PLC Japan, Ltd.; Sansho Credit Co., Ltd.; Mitsukoshi Club Ltd.; P.D.C. Ltd.

Further Reading: Roberts, John G., *Mitsui: Three Centuries of Japanese Business,* New York, Weatherhill, 1989; *About Ourselves,* Tokyo, Mitsukoshi, Ltd., [1990].

—Betty T. Moore

Montgomery Ward

MONTGOMERY WARD & CO., INCORPORATED

Montgomery Ward Plaza
Chicago, Illinois 60671
U.S.A.
(312) 467-2000
Fax: (312) 467-3975

Private Company
Incorporated: 1889
Employees: 67,200
Sales: $5.40 billion

Montgomery Ward is a national retailer with more than 350 stores in 39 states. Each Montgomery Ward Store contains up to four specialty departments: Electric Avenue, major appliances and electronics; Home Ideas, home furnishings and accessories; Auto Express, tires, batteries, parts and service; and The Apparel Store, which includes The Kids Store and Gold 'N Gems fine jewelry. Ward's subsidiary, The Signature Group, provides financial services and operates one of the largest auto clubs in the United States.

Montgomery Ward had its origins in the 1860s when young Chicagoan Aaron Montgomery Ward saw that he could undercut rural retailers by selling directly to farmers via mail order without intermediaries and by delivering via the railroad. After a false start in October 1871—when the Great Chicago Fire destroyed his inventory—Ward and two minority partners sent out their first mailing in the spring of 1872.

Orders trickled in, and soon he bought out his partners, who were discouraged by the slow pace of business. Late in 1872 he got a break. The Illinois Grange, a farmers' organization, named Ward its purchasing agent. He began subtitling Montgomery Ward price lists with the phrase Original Grange Supply House. This gave Ward access to Grange mailing lists and meetings.

As the business grew, Ward needed more capital and more help. Late in 1873, his brother-in-law, George Thorne, put $500 into the firm and became an equal partner. While Ward had the inspiration for the business, George Thorne was a practical day-to-day manager.

Postal rates fell and Ward stepped up advertising in newly popular magazines. Through publications such as the *Prairie Farmer* he told farmers to query him for catalogs with penny postcards. His spring catalog for 1874 had 32 pages. That fall he expanded to 100 pages. By the end of 1874, sales topped $100,000.

Ward's primary customer was the farmer. City orders were a nuisance. His bestseller was the sewing machine, and the catalog was filled with pumps, feed cutters, cane mills, corn shellers, threshers, saws, grinders, and engines.

Ward used buying power to cut prices, sometimes halving retail, but manufacturers formed trusts to keep prices high. Ward, in turn, found bargains in foreign markets and searched out small manufacturers willing to sell for less.

Increased sales—$300,000 in 1875—allowed Ward to increase service. He instituted a satisfaction-guaranteed-or-your-money-back policy; he carried three grades of merchandise, good, better and best; and he counseled customers to band together and split fixed freight costs.

During the 1880s, competition in the form of major department stores began to enter the catalog field. Jordan Marsh & Co., John Wanamaker, Sears, and Carson, Pirie, Scott & Co. all began or resumed mail order operations.

Still the biggest and most popular, Ward's 240-page 1883 catalog listed 10,000 items. In 1884 Ward bought the *Farmer's Voice* weekly newspaper to use as an advertising vehicle. In 1886 William C. Thorne, George Thorne's eldest son, increased the size and circulation of the catalog, leading to a boom in orders. By 1888 Ward's sales had reached $1.8 million. To cap off the decade, Ward and George Thorne turned their partnership into a corporation in 1889.

In 1891 a depression hit. Aaron Ward and George Thorne responded by emphasizing value and quality. Their prices were low but not low enough for the poorest. Into that breach Richard Sears, founder of Sears, Roebuck & Co., walked with the slogan "we always undersell."

By 1892, the Ward catalog contained 568 pages and 8,000 illustrations. Management had sold the *Farmer's Voice,* but kept advertising in it, and worked hard to beat trusts in twine, agricultural implements, sugar, and barbed wire.

In 1893 Aaron Ward and George Thorne turned managing control over to Thorne's four sons. In the deal, the Thornes gained majority control of stock, but Ward remained president.

Thorne's sons believed that Montgomery Ward represented quality and Sears merchandise was inferior. Unwilling to compete for the bottom, they tried to convince the public that cheaply made goods were no bargain. As Sears grew, however, the Thornes began making exaggerated claims for Ward.

Even with competition, Ward's sales were growing, and profits were good. In 1900 Ward built a new headquarters at Michigan Boulevard and Madison Street in Chicago. Sales that year, however, were $8.7 million, trailing Sears's $10 million.

The Thornes's marketing approach was mixed. They did not copy Richard Sears's outrageous copywriting, but they did compete on price. Like Sears they offered premiums as incentives for customers to buy more, and in 1906 they mailed out three million free catalogs, after having charged 15¢ per catalog for many years. Sales for 1906 were $18 million.

The Thornes wanted to increase profit margins by increasing quality and price. To sell higher-priced goods, James Thorne used advertising that compared Ward's and competing goods, and point for point explained why Ward's merchandise was better.

The business situation began to change. The U.S. Postal Service's initiation of a parcel post system in 1913 gave mail-order business a boost. Both Ward and Sears benefited, but the

Thornes had trouble keeping profit levels high. In 1912 Ward made a 6.7% profit, and the following year it made 4.1%, while Sears made 9.1%. Ward, with fewer customers, spent proportionately more on advertising, was building branch warehouses, and made few of its own goods. Both Ward and Sears had become public companies but remained family-controlled.

Montgomery Ward made $3.4 million on 1915 sales of $49 million, as a boom period began. Already ahead in exports, the following year, it created a Spanish-language catalog for Latin America. However, even with record profits—$6.4 million on 1918 sales of $76.2 million—the Thornes could see Montgomery Ward had fallen behind Sears. With the death of co-founder George Thorne in September—Aaron Ward had died in 1913—they sought new capital and new thinking. They sold a majority stake to a group fronted by United Cigar Stores's George Whelan and tobacco magnate James B. Duke and backed by financier J.P. Morgan. The Thorne brothers continued to run the business.

Post-World War I inflation pushed 1919 sales to $99.33 million, but profits were just $4.1 million. Former Quartermaster General of the Army Robert E. Wood was recruited to increase margins. In obtaining materials for the Panama Canal, Wood had instituted a bottom-up plan of buying. Bottom-up buying entailed working with manufacturers to lower prices while ensuring profits for both parties.

In September of 1920 a financial panic hit, and prices began to fall. Caught with a high-priced inventory and a high-priced catalog, Ward sent out new circulars. Sales dropped to two-thirds of their 1919 level. Whelan and Duke sold their stock to J.P. Morgan and the First National Bank of New York. Losses for 1920 totaled $10 million.

To unload inventory, the Thornes set up retail outlets in big cities. As conditions worsened, Robert Thorne resigned from the presidency, and Silas Strawn became interim president. Ward's bankers then brought in their own president, Theodore Merseles, an engineer who had been vice president of the National Cloak and Suit Company.

In 1922 the economy rebounded. Merseles got back into contact with farmers and found a demand for medium-priced, quality goods. Wood used bottom-up pricing to acquire raw materials and get good deals on automotive supplies and radio kits, and Merseles, who had a feel for fashion, got bargains from cash-starved European manufacturers.

Even though 1922 marked a return to profitability, Wood sensed that the automobile would eventually render mail order obsolete. He pushed Merseles to get into retailing but Merseles refused. Ironically, car tires and batteries were then two of Ward's most profitable lines.

Frustrated by his inability to implement retailing, General Wood began negotiating with Sears. In 1924 Merseles heard of the negotiations and fired Wood. Wood soon joined Sears, which embraced his store program.

Through 1925, Merseles stuck with mail order but in 1926 he began to open catalog stores that exhibited merchandise. In the wake of a softening mail-order market, and after these exhibit stores began spontaneously selling merchandise, Merseles announced that Montgomery Ward would open stores in towns with populations of 10,000 to 15,000.

In 1927 Merseles left Montgomery Ward to run Johns-Manville. To replace him, the board picked George Everitt,

Merceles's assistant. Everitt announced a crash plan for 1,500 rural stores by the end of 1929. Ward issued new stock in November of 1928 and opened 208 stores that year. By early 1929 the economy and competition were heating up. Ward's sales for the first eight months of the year were up 31%. Sears began prepaying shipping. After many customers switched, Ward reluctantly followed suit in July.

The stock market crash came in October, but overall 1929 was not a bad year. Profits reached $13 million, and Ward had 531 stores operating. As the Great Depression began to set in, things disintegrated. The retailing business, which had expanded too fast, became unprofitable and disorganized. Executives resigned, catalog sales fell, and profits for 1930 were less than $500,000. Ward received a merger proposal from Sears.

Ward's situation worsened in 1931 with losses of $8.7 million on $198 million in sales. To save Ward, J.P. Morgan & Company representative Harry P. Davison recruited Sewell Avery. Avery was known for leading United States Gypsum (USG) to Depression-era profits.

Avery found cash-starved manufacturers to sell him goods cheaper than Sears could make them. He paid employees less than Sears was paying those it had hired before the crash. He recruited dissatisfied Sears people, who felt blocked from promotions, and talented executives who had lost their jobs with other retailers. Avery and Edwin G. Booz from USG evaluated Ward managers, promoted the good ones, and fired the bad ones. After closing 147 poorly performing stores, Montgomery Ward lost $5.7 million on 1932 sales of $176.4 million.

U.S. President Franklin D. Roosevelt's interventionist policy helped jump-start the economy and gave Ward and Sears an unintended benefit. Through the National Industrial Recovery Act he propped up prices, but Ward and Sears refused to cooperate and kept their prices low. Montgomery Ward returned to the black in 1933, making $2.9 million from store sales, but losing $630,000 on the catalog operation.

Avery continued to expand. Ward initiated telephone orders in 1934. Profits topped $13.5 million in 1935 and broke the $20 million mark in 1936. Credit terms became more generous, and stores were divided into classes ranging from department stores in cities to hard-goods stores in rural areas.

By 1937 Ward's sales were 76% of Sears's and well ahead of J.C. Penney's, but there were also problems. The federal Robinson-Patman Act, passed in 1936, prevented big stores like Wards from getting better deals than small stores. Fair trade laws stated that manufacturers could name retail prices. Ward tried to get around this by selling house brands.

Ward made a public relations coup in 1939, when a Ward copywriter wrote a booklet about a little red-nosed reindeer named Rudolph, which became a Christmas classic. The booklet was included in millions of catalogs.

With talk of war, Sewell Avery, who was not convinced that the Great Depression of the 1930s had run its course, was pessimistic. Profits for 1940 were a disappointing 4.5% of sales. As the United States entered World War II, imports from Europe virtually stopped. Shortages and substitutions became the rule. The government took even closer control of industry.

Avery, who detested interference, fought the government and the unions. In November 1942 he argued with President Roosevelt and the National War Labor Board over a closed shop for the United Mail Order, Warehouse, and Retail Employees' Union. Early in 1944, he refused to sign contracts with store employees. The War Labor Board ordered Avery to extend old contracts. Avery refused. On April 24 Roosevelt sent the National Guard to Montgomery Ward. They removed Avery bodily, got rid of several other top executives, and ran the company.

On May 9, 1944, the government returned Montgomery Ward to the management, but in December, labor problems struck again. The Congress of Industrial Organization (CIO) won an election in Ward's Chicago plant. Avery again refused a union shop. On December 28, 1944, the army seized Ward's Chicago catalog operations. The situation caused orders to pile up at the rate of 10,000 a day.

By 1944 Montgomery Ward's sales were just 62% of Sears's. As the war drew to a close Avery conserved cash for what he saw as an upcoming depression. The postwar boom—profits were $52 million in 1946—did little to change his mind as Sears and others expanded.

Three years later, Avery seemed increasingly out of touch. Disgruntled executives resigned, and others were fired in moments of pique. In 1950 Avery came down with pneumonia, but even on his sickbed he insisted on making decisions.

In 1954 dissident stockholder Louis E. Wolfson began a proxy fight to unseat Avery and take over Ward. The 42-year-old Florida financier had made a fortune during the war, first by selling odd lots to the army and then in movie houses and real estate. The proxy fight culminated at the April meeting, during which the 81-year-old Avery gave disjointed answers to Wolfson and his group. Although Wolfson's bid failed, days after the meeting Avery resigned as chairman, and Edmund Krider, who led the counterattack against Wolfson, resigned as president. Three weeks later the board named John Barr president and chairman.

The Montgomery Ward that Avery left had fallen behind the times. Its 600 stores were smaller and located in less populous areas than Sears's 702 stores. It had 250 catalog offices compared to Sears's 605. Sales were one-third of Sears's $3 billion, and profits were just $35.4 million. Inflation had eroded Ward's cash position. J.C. Penney was moving up fast. Discount chains were undercutting traditional retailers.

Barr tried to re-infuse a positive spirit. He brought back Ward alumni, closed unsuccessful stores, and concentrated on modernizing existing ones. His program was basically the one Wolfson had originally proposed.

In 1957 Barr established a store research and development department that used demographic information to locate the first new stores since before the war. The following year, Barr began opening clusters of stores in key cities. He upgraded packaging, increased private brands, and announced an expansion plan. Ward opened 30 new full-line stores between 1958 and 1960.

The new stores did well, but by 1960, the old ones were doing poorly. Mail order was just a shadow of its former self. Sales for 1960 reached $1.2 billion, but profits were just $15 million, a trend that continued into 1961. Poor results at old downtown and rural stores were balanced to some degree by shiny new suburban and mall outlets. Strapped for cash, Barr stopped building new stores.

In his search for new management, Barr consulted Ward and Sears alumnus Theodore Houser, who recommended two other former Sears executives, Robert E. Brooker, president of Whirlpool Corporation, and Ed Gudeman, undersecretary of commerce in U.S. President John F. Kennedy's administration.

Brooker became president in November 1961 and by 1962 had brought in nearly 200 new executives. He conceived a strategy of encircling growing metropolitan areas, thereby cutting down on per-store costs for advertising. The strategy worked in growing cities like San Diego and Dallas-Fort Worth, but was limited because of high start-up costs.

Working on the Sears model, Brooker cut the number of suppliers and increased private brands. He centralized management for procurement and promotion but decentralized it for retail operations. Like Wood, he established relationships with suppliers. He also increased loyal and profitable credit customers.

Throughout the 1960s Brooker and Gudeman—who became a director in 1963—pushed Montgomery Ward to greater sales and more efficient procurement. By 1966 long-term contracts with suppliers had increased to 75% from 30% in 1960. Profits still did not catch up to Sears's, however. In 1965 Barr retired and Brooker became chairman.

Ed Donnell, who became president in 1966, continued the expansion plans. Montgomery Ward, however, often had too few trained people to run the new stores properly. Profits for 1966 were just $16.5 million on sales of $1.7 billion.

In the late 1960s Brooker began to worry about hostile takeovers. To avoid this, Ward found a friendly acquirer, Container Corporation of America. To its advantage, Container Corporation could defer taxes on its profits because of Ward's tax-advantaged credit sales. The merger was announced in July 1968. Ward stockholders owned two-thirds of Marcor, the new holding company, but Container Corporation President Leo Schoenhofen was the largest stockholder and became chief executive officer of Marcor.

The joined companies retained separate offices. In May 1970 Robert Brooker retired. Leo Schoenhofen became chairman, and Ed Donnell was renamed president and CEO of Montgomery Ward. New stores continued to open at the rate of 25 a year, while old ones closed one by one. By 1972, Ward's 100th anniversary, the big retailer was adding a million square feet of store space a year, primarily in shopping centers.

While Montgomery Ward had been concentrating on its stores and catalogs, Ward executive Dick Cremer had been building a profitable direct-mail business within the company's billing operation. In the late 1960s he began by inserting merchandise offers within bills sent to customers. In 1973 he began offering credit insurance through the mail, and in 1974 he started the hugely successful Montgomery Ward Auto Club, which became a Signature Group subsidiary.

Mobil Corporation secretly bought 4.5% of Marcor in 1973. Although Ward's profits remained low—just 2¢ on the dollar—the following summer Mobil paid $35 a share for 51% of Marcor. In 1975 Mobil bought the rest of Marcor and separated Ward and Container Corporation.

Montgomery Ward's new president under the Mobil regime, Sidney A. McKnight, continued to face disappointing profit levels. In an effort to cut catalog losses Ward began selling advertising space in the company's catalog in 1976.

McKnight's efforts and Mobil's money seemed to pay off at first. In 1978 sales reached $5.47 billion, and pre-tax profits hit $224 million. The following year was a disaster, however; Ward lost $133 million from operations and $30 million from closing old stores. Mobil, whose hopes had been high, lent the retailer $350 million interest-free and was trying to keep from lending more.

Since the end of the Avery regime Ward had been trying to remake itself. According to some analysts it was simultaneously bleeding cash and becoming extremely competitive with its new, modern stores. As losses mounted, Mobil lent Ward another $100 million. By the end of 1980, Montgomery Ward had lost $233 million on sales of $5.92 billion. On the bright side, both the Signature Group and the new Jefferson Ward discount chain made money.

Searching for another savior, Mobil recruited Stephen Pistner, who had turned around Dayton Hudson's B. Dalton and Target chains. Pistner took another $50 million loan from Mobil and offered early retirement to hundreds of executives. He also squelched a plan to convert more than 100 Montgomery Wards to Jefferson Ward stores. He convinced Ward to accept more name brands, closed unprofitable stores, and eliminated unprofitable lines. Further, he experimented with the stores-within-a-store concepts. Yet the losses continued. In 1981 Montgomery Ward lost $217 million on sales of $5.64 billion. The catalog was losing more than the stores.

Ward had another bad year in 1982, but in 1983 finally hit the black again with profits of $56 million. The same year Pistner centralized advertising and buying authority in Chicago and absorbed the fast-growing but sometimes chaotic Signature Group into the catalog and insurance division.

In 1984, after three years of experimentation, Pistner unveiled his seven-stores-within-a-store concept. In Pistner's vision, large stores might contain several smaller specialty stores. Those specialty stores also might stand alone. Before Pistner could implement his plans, however, he had a falling out with Mobil and left the company. Richard F. Tucker, president of Mobil Diversified Business, acted as president of Ward. In January 1985, Ward closed 300 catalog stores. What remained were 322 Montgomery Ward Stores, 44 Jefferson Ward stores, the catalog, and the Signature Group. A few months later the company sold 18 Jefferson Ward stores. Montgomery Ward was the sixth-largest retailer and the third-largest catalog house in the United States.

By then Mobil definitely wanted to sell Montgomery Ward. It also considered spinning Ward off as a dividend to stockholders. To make Ward more attractive it forgave $500 million in loans to Ward.

In June 1985 Mobil persuaded former Ward executive Bernard Brennan to return as president and chief executive officer. Brennan had been co-architect of the stores-within-a-store concept. Brennan closed the unprofitable catalog business and shuttered Jefferson Ward. He refined the seven-stores-within-a-store plan to four types of stores-within-a-store: apparel; home furnishings and accessories; electronics and appliances; and automotive goods. He experimented with stores with all four departments and some with fewer and leased store space to Toys "R" Us, Inc. and small specialty retailers. In another key move he bought 52% of the Clayton Bank and Trust of Clayton, Delaware. Through Clayton, which was later sold, Signature began offering credit cards, loans, and other financial services.

After another year of improved profits in 1987, Brennan oversaw the largest management-led leveraged buyout in U.S. history, paying $1.5 billion for Ward in 1988. Ward became the tenth-largest privately held company in the United States. The ninth-largest U.S. retailer in the early 1990s, Ward continued to expand on its specialty formats, opening some stores with a single specialty. A total of 53 new stores were scheduled to open in 1990 and 1991. Continuing to expand in specialty markets, Montgomery Ward formed a 50–50 joint venture in October 1991 with Fingerhut Companies, Inc., the fourth-largest U.S. catalog marketing company. To be known as Montgomery Ward Direct, the partnership was to pursue the same specialty marketing strategy in its catalogs that Montgomery Ward employed in its stores.

Principal Subsidiaries: The Signature Group; Standard T Chemical.

Further Reading: 1872–1972 A Century of Serving Consumers: The Story of Montgomery Ward, Chicago, Montgomery Ward & Co., Incorporated, 1972; Hoge, Cecil C., Sr., *The First Hundred Years Are the Toughest,* Berkeley, California, Ten Speed Press, 1988.

—Jordan Wankoff

NAGASAKIYA CO., LTD.

3-7-14 Higashi-Nihonbashi
Chuo-ku
Tokyo 103
Japan
(03) 3661 3810
Fax: (03) 3664 3843

Public Company
Incorporated: 1948
Employees: 4,600
Sales: ¥480 billion (US$3.85 billion)
Stock Exchanges: Tokyo Osaka

Nagasakiya Co., Ltd. (Nagasakiya) is one of Japan's leading retail chains, with a nationwide network of large supermarkets. The main line of retail is apparel, but the Nagasakiya group, which includes all the subsidiaries of Nagasakiya, covers a wide range of retail activities, including home appliances, restaurants, and convenience stores. The Nagasakiya group is also involved in leisure development, finance, and import/export.

Nagasakiya was founded early in 1948 by Kohachi Iwata. The original store consisted of a small refreshment stand in Hiratsuka in Kanagawa Prefecture, near Tokyo. Kohachi Iwata was the son of a local retailer, Chohachi Iwata, who in 1919, at the age of 22, opened a small Japanese bedding or *futon* store in Chigasaki. The store was moderately successful, and Chohachi hoped his son Kohachi would join him in the family business after graduating from university. The young Kohachi Iwata failed his entrance exams, however, and left school in 1940 at the age of 19 to work in his father's store. His first job was to stand in front of the store and try to attract customers, and for the next five years he worked extremely hard at this.

The store was destroyed in the bombing of the Kanto area in air raids in the summer of 1945, leaving the Iwata family with nothing but the land on which their store had stood. The young and ambitious Kohachi Iwata decided to start a venture of his own on a small plot of land owned by his family in Hiratsuka, near Chigasaki. The plot was in the ruins of Hiratsuka railway station in the town center, and it was here in 1946 that Kohachi Iwata and his new bride set about making a living. The initial venture, called Nagasakiya, was a small refreshment store of about 20 square meters, and the main product sold was crushed ice flavored with fruit juice. In the summer heat it was

a cheap refreshment for the city dwellers, many of whom were still poverty-stricken and were rebuilding their homes following the end of World War II.

Iwata worked frantically to make ends meet and build a successful business. In the winter, when the demand for iced refreshments had fallen, Iwata expanded his store to offer cotton clothes as well as the bedding that was his family's traditional business. In Hiratsuka, a relatively depressed city in the Kanto plain, Iwata's store offered basic necessities at a cheap price. Business grew to such an extent that by 1948 Iwata formed a company called Nagasakiya Co., Ltd.; its sole purpose at that time was the operation of the store.

Japan was rapidly changing for the better, however, and in the early 1950s the economy experienced very rapid growth. The city of Hiratsuka became a shopping center for consumers in the surrounding suburban areas. Iwata noted that people were coming from Odawara and Isogo to shop at his store, rather than traveling into the city of Yokohama. By 1950 Iwata had accumulated enough savings to open a second store in nearby Machida, it was also called Nagasakiya. Apparel was now the main product line of both stores. In 1953 Iwata bought the building containing his original Hiratsuka store and converted the complex into a larger store.

The success of Iwata's stores in the early 1950s can be attributed to the booming consumer demand for essential household items and also to Iwata's constant hard work. During this time, several of the largest retailing chains in Japan today were emerging. Iwata saw Daiei Co., Ltd. and Ito-Yokado Co., Ltd. as his main competitors. In 1954 he envisaged a ten-year plan to set up a national chain of large supermarkets. He pinpointed the 40 largest metropolitan areas as targets for his stores. In 1957 Iwata was one of 16 entrepreneurial retailers traveling to North America on a month-long fact-finding mission. The group traveled to Hawaii and Los Angeles and then on to New York. Iwata was fascinated by the U.S. retail market and the use of a single brand name, such as J.C. Penney, to cater to mass consumer shopping nationwide. He also noted the use of vending machines, a phenomenon that had yet to reach Japan. These observations helped form Iwata's vision of a retailing empire in Japan. On his return to Japan, Iwata arrived at the port of Ichikawa in Chiba Prefecture, where he happened to notice a restaurant catering to the servicemen of a nearby U.S. Navy base. Iwata thought that the westernized aspects of the restaurant could be applied throughout Japan. He promptly hired the manager of the restaurant and set up a subsidiary called Choeisha, which would eventually become the restaurant chain Oasis, a subsidiary of Nagasakiya.

As the first step in the creation of what he termed "superstores," Iwata decided to construct a seven-story building on the Hiratsuka site. His main problem at the time was the lack of finance for the project, and he succeeded in obtaining not only planning permission but also loans from a wealthy bureaucrat in the Kanagawa Prefectural government in charge of new construction, who was anxious to promote development in the area. Construction began in mid-1959 and was completed by the end of the year. It was the first Nagasakiya superstore, with elevators, escalators, and refrigerated food display cabinets. In order to repay the loans, Iwata announced cut-price sales at his other stores in nearby Hachioji, Kamakura, and Machida.

During this time Iwata opened stores at the rate of about one a year, and by 1961 there were ten Nagasakiya stores in

Kanagawa Prefecture. Nagasakiya was at this time still privately owned by Iwata. He was advised that, in order to achieve the kind of expansion he envisaged, it would be necessary to float the company. Iwata was initially reluctant, being fairly ignorant of the financial world. After looking into the advantages and workings of the stock market he agreed to float his company on the First Section of the Tokyo Stock Exchange. The company was initially capitalized at ¥480 million. Nagasakiya now possessed the foundations for building a nationwide retail empire. It had the capital in the form of publicly traded shares, the market in the form of a booming Japanese consumer market, and leadership in the form of Iwata and his team of able managers.

The 1960s were a dynamic time in Japanese retailing. Supermarket chains Daiei and Ito-Yokado were setting up their nationwide networks at a furious pace. These chains provided a full range of household items. Nagasakiya, on the other hand, concentrated on clothing retailing, although in 1960 food retailing commenced on the ground floor of many Nagasakiya stores.

By 1967 Nagasakiya consisted of 30 superstores, compared with 20 stores 5 years earlier, with combined sales of over ¥3 billion. The period 1967 to 1968 saw massive expansion in the Nagasakiya chain, with over ten new superstores added during this year. These included stores in Shizuoka and Omiya, both in the Kanto region, with floor space of more than 2,500 square meters. The policy was to concentrate on opening large stores in the key areas identified by Iwata ten years earlier. In 1967 Nagasakiya launched its in-house brand of clothing—Sunbird—to be sold exclusively in the stores. The Sunbird line was costlier than Nagasakiya's other clothing, and by 1980 the brand was a well-established name in the Japanese fashion world.

In the period 1970 to 1974 Nagasakiya continued to thrive, with sales and floor space doubling during this time. Nagasakiya achieved sales of ¥100 billion in 1973. In the same year Nagasakiya felt that specialty stores were going to be profitable in the future and established a subsidiary, Babybird Co., Ltd., which sold babies' and children's clothing. In 1974 Nagasakiya established Sunbird Finance Company to engage in corporate and personal loans for customers of Nagasakiya. Sunbird Finance Company sold its services through outlets at Nagasakiya stores, and by 1980 these outlets numbered 200.

Nagasakiya's rapid growth was slowed somewhat by the oil shock of 1973, when the OPEC member nations increased the price of crude oil threefold overnight. This had a devastating effect on the Japanese economy, which relied on Middle Eastern oil for 70% of its energy needs. For the first time in ten years the Japanese economy experienced negative monthly gross domestic product (GDP) growth. The effects were not as severe for Nagasakiya as they were for retailers selling high-class and luxury goods, and the chain continued to grow, albeit at a slower pace. By 1978 sales had reached ¥200 billion, with a total of 90 Nagasakiya stores. By 1981 there were 100 stores. Nagasakiya entered the convenience store market in 1980 with the establishment of Sunkus Co., Ltd. With 630 branches, Sunkus is a fairly large player in this market but does not compare with Seven Eleven Japan and Circle K Japan, which own thousands of stores. The establishment of specialty stores was a policy of all the major retailing groups at this time. Nagasakiya started Sun Men's Shop Co., Ltd., sell-

ing men's clothes, and Sun Optical Co., Ltd., selling eye glasses and watches, in 1981. Cymbal Co., Ltd., started in 1983, specializes in clothes for the 12 to 18 age group, and Sun Techno Services Co., Ltd. was established in 1984 to provide building services for the Nagasakiya stores and other clients. In 1985 Kanoko Co., Ltd. was established to sell woolen goods, Sun Kaden to sell electrical home appliances, and L & B Co., Ltd. to sell high-fashion women's wear. Sun Systems Development was begun in 1986 to provide computer services for Nagasakiya and other customers.

In 1987, with well over 100 Nagasakiya stores open throughout Japan and over a thousand stores operated by Nagasakiya subsidiary companies, the company had become one of the top ten retailing groups in Japan. Like most markets in Japan, the retail market was extremely competitive. Nagasakiya embarked on a large-scale store renewal program in 1987. Old, inefficient stores were rebuilt under the "scrap and build" policy. Maximum use was made of floor space, and extensive market research was undertaken to plan store layout and stock levels. In 1988 the company's founder, Kohachi Iwata, retired as president of Nagasakiya to allow his son Fumiaki to take over the day-to-day operations of the company. Kohachi assumed the position of chairman and remains the inspiration behind the company.

At the beginning of the 1990s the Nagasakiya group of companies comprised 115 Nagasakiya superstores and 53 subsidiaries operating mainly in the retail sector. Other business areas in which group companies are involved include real estate development, leisure centers, import/export, advertising, and an overseas restaurant in Singapore.

A recent major development was the opening in September 1990 of Fantasy Dome near a Nagasakiya store in Tomakomai in Hokkaido. With 30,000 square meters of floor space, it is one of the busiest amusement parks in Japan and, being completely enclosed, it is the first all-weather leisure center in Japan. Nagasakiya's growth was hampered by a fire in its Nagasakiya store in May 1990, in which there were a number of casualties. As a result of the ensuing negative publicity, the company was forced to initiate a costly safety assessment program in all of its stores. Compensation to the victims and their families also tied up capital intended for expansion. The company may even be forced to sell assets, depending on the total cost of the disaster. In the long term, however, this will not affect the company significantly, and steady growth is predicted in the 1990s with slower growth in the mature clothing retail markets contrasting with the high growth of the convenience stores and restaurants.

Principal Subsidiaries: Sun Denka Co., Ltd.; Sun Bird Tour Co., Ltd. (88%); Kanoko Co., Ltd.; Nagasakiya Photo Service Co., Ltd.; L & B Co., Ltd.; Sun Advertising Co., Ltd.; Be Gol Co., Ltd.; Sun Planning Centre Co., Ltd.; Cymbal Co., Ltd. (60%); Sun Systems Development Co., Ltd. (70%); Hiroya Co., Ltd.; Sun Assort Co., Ltd.; Baby Bird Co., Ltd.; Sun East International Co., Ltd. (67%); Sun Men's Shop Co., Ltd.; Sunland Co., Ltd. (98%); Sun Optical Co., Ltd.; Sun-Bird Finance Co., Ltd. (39%); Nagasakiya Home Centre Co.,

Ltd.; Sun Techno Services Co., Ltd.; Sunkus Co., Ltd. (95%); ODS Nagasakiya Co., Ltd. (Singapore, 75%); Oasis Co., Ltd. (80%); Sun Leisure Co., Ltd. (83%); Sun Fantasy Co., Ltd. (90%).

Further Reading: Seiki, Ikai, *Shorai no Gotoshi—Ino no Shonin, Kohachi Iwata,* Tokyo, T and T Co., Ltd., 1988.

—Dylan Tanner

NATIONAL INTERGROUP, INC.

1220 Senlac Drive
Carrollton, Texas 75006
U.S.A.
(214) 446-9090
Fax: (214) 446-4221

Public Company
Incorporated: 1929 as National Steel Corporation
Employees: 4,700
Sales: $2.88 billion
Stock Exchange: New York

National Intergroup, Inc. (NII) is one of the largest drug wholesalers in the United States, through its principal operating unit, FoxMeyer Corporation. It is also a wholesaler to a franchiser of variety stores through its Ben Franklin unit.

The company has made a significant transition from steel-making to merchandising. It was originally incorporated in 1929 as the National Steel Company, a business that was the result of the merging of the Great Lakes Steel Company, Hanna Iron Ore Company, and the Weirton Steel Company. As a result of the slump in the steel industry in the late 1970s and the unpredictability of the steel and metals business in general, a diversification plan was developed by Howard M. (Pete) Love, National Steel's chairman and son of long-time company executive George Love. The program called for the creation of NII as an umbrella holding company that would control various operating companies formed in the wake of National Steel's restructuring. In September 1983, National Steel's stockholders approved a plan under which they received one share in NII for each share of National Steel they held, and National Steel became a wholly owned subsidiary of NII.

In 1984 NII sold Weirton Steel to Weirton's employees and sold 50% of National Steel to Nippon Kokan K.K., now NKK Corporation. Also that year, NII formed a new subsidiary, GENIX, which offered software and computer consulting services. NII also purchased the Permian Corporation, a crude-oil gathering and shipping concern for $88 million in cash and three million shares of common stock.

The main thrust of Howard Love's diversification plan was for NII to move into the wholesale pharmaceuticals business. He reasoned that wholesale pharmaceuticals had none of the problems of the steel business. Large numbers of workers were not necessary, the business was not vulnerable to foreign competition, and it did not require large amounts of capital investment that the steel business did.

In 1985 Love proposed a merger with the Bergen Brunswig Corporation, the second-largest distributor of health-care products and other drugstore-related items in the United States. The Bergen Brunswig merger never came to fruition. While the deal was pending, NII suffered major losses from its speculation in aluminum futures. Bergen Brunswig, perhaps fearing there were other problems at NII, called the deal off.

Love remained undaunted in his diversification plans, and in 1986, after borrowing heavily to fund new acquisitions, NII purchased the United States's third-largest drug distributor, FoxMeyer Corporation. With sales in excess of $1.5 billion, FoxMeyer controlled 400 Health Mart drugstores and was growing rapidly. FoxMeyer in turn acquired the Ben Franklin Stores Inc., a chain of 1,300 5¢-and-10¢ stores, and Lawrence Pharmaceuticals Inc., a regional drug distributor. In total, the deals cost NII $654 million.

The acquisitions of Permian Corporation, FoxMeyer, and Ben Franklin Stores created immediate problems for NII. Oil prices plummeted, causing major difficulties for Permian. FoxMeyer went through a price-cutting war in the pharmaceutical business and was also burdened with large start-up costs in a new hospital-supply venture; it also abandoned a plan to sell computers to pharmacists for handling prescriptions. In 1986 FoxMeyer profits sagged 50% to only $10 million. Ben Franklin Stores were plagued with major problems as attempts to convert the chain's computers to FoxMeyer's systems cost huge amounts of money and created confusion. Ben Franklin's sales fell when orders from the retail stores went unfilled. In the process, the company closed 43 Ben Franklin stores.

By early 1987, NII found itself in serious financial straits. Falling oil prices continued to take their toll on NII's oil transportation and acquisition unit, the Permian Corporation. The company's steel units were experiencing operating problems, made worse by expensive labor contracts and cultural clashes with NKK. The company was technically in default, with $600 million in debt and annual interest payments of $90 million. Seeking financial relief, the company's board voted to sell half of the Permian Corporation to the public. Howard Love cut corporate overhead by 25%. NII's bankers, however, pulled out of a loan agreement due to the failed predictions FoxMeyer's performance. Love had to find new loans; they had much stricter covenants.

The financial debacle was compounded by personnel problems. Howard Love's heir apparent, James Haas, indicated he wished to leave the company. After an extensive search, NII chose Laurence Farley to succeed Haas as president at the end of 1988. Haas remained chief executive officer of the Permian Corporation. Farley, as chief executive officer of Black & Decker, led that company's recovery. He had joined NII as chief financial officer in February 1988 and took responsibility for FoxMeyer the following July.

Farley's first year at the helm of NII brought about some positive results. He organized a new group of bankers, pushed through a write-down of one of NII's European aluminum mills, and began to focus his attention on FoxMeyer, which at the time represented 85% of NII's $3 billion in annual sales, but had profit margins that were half the industry average. Farley, however, did not remain president for long, resigning in April 1989. NII was in its fifth year of operating in the red. There were reports of conflicts between Farley and Love.

James S. Pasman Jr., a former Aluminum Company of America vice chairman, replaced Farley. Pasman had also assisted in the restructuring of Kaiser Aluminum & Chemical Corporation. At the time of Pasman's hiring, the drug wholesaling industry was showing a 15% increase in revenues. FoxMeyer had experienced a 20% increase in annual revenues. Pasman's focus became obvious. While not ignoring Permian Corporation or Ben Franklin, Pasman upgraded FoxMeyer. At the same time he began to explore the possible sale of NII's steel and aluminum subsidiaries.

Further pressure was on NII to begin to show profits, as its five-year-old agreement with NKK, NII's partner in National Steel, was close to expiration. In the agreement with NKK, NII was prohibited from selling its half interest in National Steel to a third party. The agreement also stipulated that NKK could buy NII's share of National Steel at a very low price if an attempt at a hostile takeover ever occurred. With the agreement time coming to an end, it was one of Pasman's major challenges to put National Steel back into a profit mode before an unfriendly takeover attempt could occur by one of the company's disgruntled shareholders. After seven years of losing money, there were many unhappy NII shareholders, some calling for Love's ouster.

Late in 1989, NII sold its aluminum rolling and extrusion divisions. Early in 1990, it sold its 54.5% share of an aluminum smelter. Also in 1990, it reduced its holding in National Steel to 13.33%, with NKK increasing its share. FoxMeyer's wholesale drug sales increased 21% to $2.4 billion, and with a new emphasis of selling arts-and-crafts items, and the company's Ben Franklin unit showed a modest operating profit. In the fiscal year ended March 31, 1990, NII reported profits of $55.7 million compared to a net operating loss of $15.7 million in the previous year.

In 1990 Centaur Partners Group, a dissident shareholder group that held 16.5% of NII, won several important board seats, with Howard Love among the losers. The new board sold Permian Corporation to Ashland Oil and explored the possibility of selling FoxMeyer. NII, however, was not satisfied with the bids it received for FoxMeyer, which had improving sales and profits. Instead of selling the entire company, in late 1991 NII put 30% of FoxMeyer's common shares up for sale to the public. NII also moved its headquarters from Pittsburgh to Carrollton, Texas, a Dallas suburb.

Principal Subsidiary: FoxMeyer Corporation (70%).

Further Reading: Beazley, J. Ernest, "Steelmaker Suffers Diversification Blues," *The Wall Street Journal,* June 30, 1988; Miles, Gregory, "National Intergroup: How Pete Love Went Wrong," *Business Week,* March 6, 1989.

—William R. Grossman

NICHII CO., LTD.

2-9, Awajimachi 2-chome
Chuo-ku, Osaka 541
Japan
(06) 203-5072
Fax: (06) 223-1404

Public Company
Incorporated: 1963
Employees: 16,161
Sales: ¥1.19 trillion (US $8.76 billion)
Stock Exchanges: Tokyo Osaka Fukuoka Hiroshima Kyoto
   Niigata Sapporo Frankfurt Luxembourg

Nichii Co., Ltd. is one of Japan's largest retailers. Although often described as a supermarket chain, Nichii has been in fact more like a low-price general retailer; in Japan, the designation "supermarket" applies to any self-service store that employs more than 50 people. The company in the early 1990s has shifted its strategy to opening large-scale stores with more upscale merchandise. The company operates more than 250 stores in Japan, offering a broad range of merchandise from food to clothing. Nichii stores in Kansai have even sold tombstones at one time. Nichii also operates a five-acre shopping mall just south of downtown Yokohama, around which it plans to develop a self-contained residential community.

Nichii was founded in 1963 when three clothing retailers and a wholesaler in the Kansai area merged. The timing of this amalgamation was fortuitous. At that time the Japanese government had not yet seen supermarkets as a threat to the small, family-run shops whose market share it had protected so strenuously over the years, so supermarket chains had no government restrictions to impede their expansion. Nichii grew by opening new stores and merging with other retailers throughout Japan, a strategy that proved successful. Supermarkets doubled their percentage of total retail sales in Japan during the 1970s, but Nichii's growth outstripped that of its peers. By 1983 it had become the fifth-largest retail chain in the nation.

In 1979, however, the government imposed restrictions on supermarket expansion. Chains would have to gain clearance from the Ministry of International Trade and Industry (MITI) and local officials before building new stores, and those officials would often protect the small merchants in their areas by refusing to grant the necessary construction permits. In 1983 a former Nichii employee was convicted of trying to bribe municipal officials on behalf of his former employers. As a result,

MITI decided to suspend all of the company's applications to open new stores for three months. The scandal, although embarrassing to Nichii, was widely regarded as a symbol of industry-wide frustration over the restrictions on expansion.

This frustration, combined with a decrease in profits for most Japanese retailers in 1982, led Nichii to consider merging with Uny, the nation's sixth-largest supermarket chain. To both companies, it seemed like a chance to expand despite the constrictive control of the government, although Uny, which was slated to become the surviving company, was more sanguine about the prospect of amalgamation than Nichii. The proposed merger, however, fell through in March of 1983 and both remained independent.

In the mid-1980s Nichii began to emphasize imported goods in its merchandise lines and to target young adults as its primary customers. In 1986 it opened a representative office in London. The next year, it merged its import operations into a single subsidiary, Nichii International. Between 1986 and 1990 Nichii's purchases of imported goods rose from ¥2.3 billion to ¥100 billion. In 1988 it officially adopted the name MYCAL Group to cover the parent company and all its subsidiaries. MYCAL is an acronym formed from the English words *m*ind, *y*oung, *c*asual, *a*menities, and *l*ife; it was adapted from the company's slogan for its new, youth-oriented retailing strategy: "Amenities for the casual lifestyle of the young and young-minded."

In 1988 Nichii acquired a substantial minority interest in Nissan Construction for ¥16.9 billion in cash. It was an unusually large deal as Japanese corporate acquisitions go, but Nichii needed Nissan Construction for large projects including its MYCAL Honmoku project. MYCAL Honmoku is located on the site of a former 30-acre U. S. military installation in the Shinhonmoku area of Yokohama, and the 5-acre shopping mall that forms its heart opened in 1989. The mall features more than 200 general retailers and service businesses, 38 restaurants, a sports club, 2 movie theaters, and a theater for live entertainment that is run as a joint venture with Harlem's famous Apollo Theater.

MYCAL Honmoku helped Nichii ride the crest of a new wave of consumerism in Japan. Price competition from discounters and eased government restrictions on imports and retail expansion combined with a growing sense among the Japanese of their own prosperity. The result was a buying power that produced a consumer boom in the late 1980s. As Nichii President and CEO Toshimine Kobayashi put it, "Our economy and our society are making dramatic changes, and we in the retail industry are right in the middle of it."

Nichii smartly combined this new consumerism with the longtime Japanese fascination with U.S. popular culture to produce a retail strategy, and aggressively imported U.S. goods to implement it. In December of 1990 the company sponsored a U.S. sporting event, a post-season college football all-star game played in Yokohama and televised in the United States on cable. During the broadcast, it ran commercials targeted to U.S. companies that might be interested in exporting their products to Japan through Nichii. For Kobayashi, marketing U.S. imports is not just a matter of selling individual products, but of selling a whole way of living. As he told a U.S. journalist: "We want to import your lifestyle. Not just jogging shoes but also your jogging T-shirts, jogging drinks—the whole concept has to come, not just the products. We aspire to your pleasant way of life. We want to buy it, so come sell it to us."

Nichii's ultimate goal had been to sell imported goods at prices competitive with domestically produced merchandise. This would not be an easy task, considering the cost of transporting goods to Japan, as well as the effect of tariffs and import restrictions. As of late 1989, Nichii had succeeded only with the Motta brand Italian cookies and candy. In the case of U.S. meat products imported from Cincinnati-based packer John Morrell, Nichii was charging more than double what U.S. consumers would pay for the same merchandise. For the long term, it remained to be seen whether or not Nichii would succeed in this goal, as well as whether or not its commitment to real estate development would produce a good return. For the near future, however, it will probably continue to benefit from a trend that seems more likely to strengthen than to weaken.

Principal Subsidiaries: Kyushu Nichii Co., Ltd. (97%); Hokkaido Nichii Co., Ltd. (76%); Tohoku Nichii Co., Ltd.; Sunhoyu Co., Ltd. (68%); Hokuho Co., Ltd. (62%); SUN- MELT Co., Ltd. (65%); Allied Shinshu Co., Ltd. (83%); Muroran Family Department Co., Ltd. (70%); Aki Nichii Co., Ltd. (80%); Nichii Yokosan Co., Ltd. (60%); Niigata Nichii Co., Ltd.; Hamada Family Department Co., Ltd. (65%); Edoya Family Department Co., Ltd. (75%); Nippon Allied Chain Co., Ltd. (60%); Nichii International Corp.; DAC City Co., Ltd. (93%); Elleme Co., Ltd. (51%); Friend Co., Ltd.; McLord Co., Ltd. (60%); Sporsium Co., Ltd.; Athlete's Foot Japan Co., Ltd.; Japan Maintenance Co., Ltd. (75%); People Co., Ltd. (83%); Calos Co., Ltd.; Cohms Co., Ltd.; Nichii Financial Service Co., Ltd. (93%); Nichii Credit Service Co., Ltd. (93%); Automacsales Co., Ltd.; MYCAL Tours Co., Ltd.; Travel Joy Co., Ltd.; Nippon Insurance Agency Co., Ltd.; Nichii Co., of America, Inc. (U.S.A.); Nichii Enterprises Co., Ltd. (Hong Kong); Ibis Co., Ltd. (79%).

Further Reading: "Protection Racket," *The Economist,* February 26, 1983; Rapoport, Carla, "Ready, Set, Sell—Japan is Buying," *Fortune,* September 11, 1989.

—Douglas Sun

nordstrom

NORDSTROM, INC.

1501 Fifth Avenue
Seattle, Washington 98101
U.S.A.
(206) 628-2111

Public Company
Incorporated: 1901 as Wallin & Nordstrom
Employees: 30,000
Sales: $2.89 billion
Stock Exchange: NASDAQ

Nordstrom, Inc., was started in 1901 as a single shoe store in Seattle, Washington, that was opened by two Swedish immigrants. From those origins, the family-owned enterprise has expanded into a 68-outlet chain, which tallied $2.89 billion in sales in 1990. Carefully supervised expansion, tight family management, wide selection, and attentive customer service have long been the hallmarks of Seattle-based Nordstrom.

John Nordstrom, a 16-year-old Swede, arrived in Minnesota in 1887 with $5 to his name and, after working his way across the United States, settled briefly in Seattle. In 1897 he headed north to Alaska in search of gold. He found it. In 1899, $13,000 richer, Nordstrom moved back to Seattle, where he opened a shoe store with Carl Wallin, a shoemaker he had met in Alaska. On its first day of business in 1901, their store, Wallin & Nordstrom, sold $12.50 in shoes.

Business quickly picked up. By 1905 sales increased to $80,000. The business continued to grow, and in 1923 the partners opened a second store in Seattle. By 1928, however, 57-year-old John Nordstrom had decided to retire from the shoe business, and passed on his share to his sons Everett and Elmer. Carl Wallin retired soon after and likewise sold his share to the next generation of Nordstroms. In 1933 John Nordstrom's youngest son, Lloyd, joined the partnership.

The business that John Nordstrom left was substantially larger than the one he started back in 1901. It was up to the next generation of Nordstroms, however, to build on their father's success. In 1929 the Nordstrom brothers doubled the size of their downtown Seattle store. In 1930, despite the onset of the Great Depression, the two stores made $250,000 in sales. The shoe stores survived the depression, but faced another severe threat during World War II, when leather rationing prohibited U.S. consumers from buying more than three pairs of shoes per year. The Nordstrom brothers had to search nationwide for supplies of shoes.

In the postwar decades, the Nordstrom brothers built the company into the largest independent shoe chain in the United States. In 1950 the Nordstroms opened two new shoe stores: one in Portland, Oregon, and one in a Seattle suburb. Nine years later, Nordstrom remodeled its Seattle flagship store, and stocked it with 100,000 pairs of shoes—the biggest inventory in the country. By 1961 Nordstrom operated 8 shoe stores and 13 leased shoe departments in Washington, Oregon, and California. That year, the firm grossed $12 million in sales and had 600 employees on its payroll.

In the early 1960s, the Nordstrom brothers came to a crossroads of sorts. Spurred by their success, they were convinced that their business could expand. The brothers were unsure whether they should simply expand their shoe business to the East and South or branch out into other areas of retailing. The brothers chose to diversify, and purchased Best Apparel, a Seattle-based women's clothing store. With the addition of apparel outlets, the company expanded rapidly. In 1965 the Nordstroms opened a new Best Apparel store adjacent to a Nordstrom shoe store in suburban Seattle. In 1966 the company acquired a Portland retail fashion outlet, Nicholas Ungar, and merged it with the Nordstrom shoe store in Portland.

In the late 1960s, the modern Nordstrom department store began to take shape. Between 1965 and 1968, the company opened five stores that combined apparel and shoes. In 1967, when annual sales had reached $40 million, the chain's name was changed to Nordstrom Best. The firm diversified further in these years, as Nordstrom Best began to sell men's and children's clothing as well.

In 1968 Everett Nordstrom turned 65, and he and his two brothers decided to turn over the reins of the company to the next generation of Nordstroms. Five men—Everett's son Bruce, Elmer's sons James and John, Lloyd's son-in-law John A. McMillan, and family friend Robert E. Bender—took control of the company in 1970.

In August 1971 the company went public, offering Nordstrom Best stock on the over-the-counter market. Family members retained a majority of the stock, however, and as of the early 1990s they continued to hold a significant interest. In 1971 Nordstrom earned $3.5 million on sales of $80 million. In 1973 when sales first topped $100 million, the company changed its name to Nordstrom, Inc.

The firm continued to grow steadily throughout the 1970s by opening new stores and increasing volume in existing stores, and diversifying. In 1974 annual sales hit $130 million. The following year, Nordstrom bought three stores in Alaska. In 1976 the firm launched a new division, Place Two, which features, in smaller stores, a selected offering of men's and women's apparel and shoes. By 1977 Nordstrom operated 24 stores, which generated sales of $246 million.

In 1978 Nordstrom expanded into the southern California market, opening an outlet in Orange County. That year, the firm reaped $13.5 million in earnings on nearly $300 million in sales. Buoyed by the success, Nordstrom's executives charted an aggressive expansion program, and began to open bigger stores in California. Their late-1970s confidence presaged a decade of phenomenal, but controlled, growth.

By 1980 Nordstrom was the third-largest specialty retailer in the country, ranking behind only Saks Fifth Avenue and Lord & Taylor. That year, the firm operated 31 stores in California, Washington, Oregon, Utah, Montana, and Alaska. In 1980 a new expansion plan called for 25 new stores to be added in the 1980s, and the Nordstroms projected that both earnings and total square footage would double by 1985.

The projection was not sufficiently optimistic. In 1980 sales hit $407 million, and in the next few years, sales and earnings continued to rise substantially. Between 1980 and 1983, when sales jumped to $787 million, earnings more than doubled, going from $19.7 million to $40.2 million. In 1982 Nordstrom launched a third division, Nordstrom Rack—a string of outlet stores that the firm used to move old inventories at discount prices. The chain's biggest growth area, however, was in the huge California market. By 1984 there were seven Nordstrom stores in that state. Five years later, Nordstrom had 22 full-size stores in California.

Nordstrom increasingly came to be recognized as an efficient, upscale, full-service department store. Its aggressive customer service plainly brought results. The firm has consistently maintained the highest sales per square foot of retail space ratios in the industry, nearly twice those of other department stores.

Nordstrom's success has been due to a variety of factors. Throughout its existence, shoes have accounted for a good deal of the firm's sales—about 18% in 1989. In most fashion and apparel stores, shoes constitute a smaller percentage of sales. In addition Nordstrom has consistently maintained huge inventories and selection, which were usually twice the size those of other department stores. In the mid-1980s, a typical outlet stocked 75,000 pairs of shoes, 5,000 men's dress shirts, and 7,000 ties. Moreover, a decentralized corporate structure has allowed local buyers, who knew their customers' needs, to make inventory selections.

Most significantly, though, Nordstrom's management has encouraged the development of an aggressive sales force. The vast majority of Nordstrom clerks work on commission, and the average salesperson earns $24,000 annually. Managers are generally promoted from within the ranks of salespeople, which intensifies the desire to sell.

In the 1980s the firm's customer service became legendary, as tales of heroic efforts by salespeople became legion: clerks were known to pay shoppers' parking tickets, rush deliveries to offices, unquestioningly accept returns, lend cash to strapped customers, and to send tailors to customers' homes. Salespeople receive constant pep talks from management, and motivational exercises are a routine part of life at Nordstrom. Nordstrom also has created an environment that is extremely customer-friendly. Many stores have free coat check service, concierges, and piano players who serenade shoppers.

As the economy boomed in the 1980s, Nordstrom's figures climbed apace. In 1985 sales first topped $1 billion, as they jumped to $1.3 billion. In 1987 the firm reaped profits of $92.7 million on sales of $1.92 billion.

Nordstrom's growth in the latter half of the 1980s stemmed from a combination of expansion into new territories and the creation of larger stores in existing Nordstrom territory. In 1986, when the firm operated 53 stores in six western states, Nordstrom began to turn its sights to the East. In March of 1988, Nordstrom opened its first store on the East Coast, a 238,000-square-foot facility in McLean, Virginia, just outside Washington, D.C. On its first day, the store racked up more than $1 million in sales. Over the first year, the store brought in $100 million in sales.

The same year, Nordstrom expanded on the West Coast as well, opening its biggest store, a 350,000-square-foot facility, in downtown San Francisco. The lavish San Francisco store featured 103 different brands of champagne, 16 varieties of chilled vodka, and a health spa, among other luxurious amenities.

By the end of 1988, Nordstrom had 21,000 employees toiling in its 58 stores. Together they convinced customers to buy $2.3 billion worth of goods in 1988, and earned profits of $123 million for the corporation.

Expansion in other areas of the East continued in the late 1980s. In 1989 Nordstrom opened a second store in the Washington, D.C., area—in the Pentagon City Mall. The firm also opened outlets in Sacramento and Brea, California, in 1989.

In 1989, when the company won the National Retail Merchants Association's Gold Medal, Nordstrom had become a paragon of retailing success. Envious of its market share and sales figures, many competitors began to imitate its strategies of large inventory and lavish customer service.

Nordstrom continues to rely on its aggressive sales staff, but, the corporate policy of encouraging clerks to go out of their way to make sales has caused the company some grief. The employees' union has complained about the pressure on employees to sell. In late 1989 a group of unionized employees charged that they were not being paid for performing extra services to customers.

In February of 1990, after a three-month investigation, the Washington State Department of Labor & Industries alleged that the company had systematically violated state laws by failing to pay employees for a variety of duties, such as delivering merchandise and doing inventory work. The agency ordered Nordstrom to change its compensation and record-keeping procedures, and to pay back wages to some of Nordstrom's 30,000 employees. Soon after, the firm created a $15-million reserve to pay back-wage claims. The company, however, remained a target of class-action lawsuits on these matters, still pending in the early 1990s.

Other unforeseen events in 1989 and 1990 hit the company as well. The San Francisco earthquake of 1989 took a significant bite out of retail sales in the San Francisco Bay area. The general nationwide downturn in retailing hurt the company more, however. In September of 1990, Nordstrom, then a 61-store company, announced it would cut costs by 3% to 12% and laid off some personnel. In the fourth quarter of 1989, Nordstrom's earnings dropped 34% from the previous year. Earnings fell about 7% for the entire year, falling from $123.3 million in 1988 to $115 million in 1989; however, sales increased nearly 15% in that year, from $2.33 billion to $2.67 billion.

Although Nordstrom suffered from the recession of the early 1990s, it continued to expand and open new stores in the East and Midwest. In September of 1990, Nordstrom opened its first store in the metropolitan New York area, in Paramus, New Jersey. In April of 1991 Nordstrom opened its 64th store—and first Midwest store—in Oak Brook, Illinois, a Chicago suburb. In typical Nordstrom style, the store opened featuring 125,000 pairs of shoes, a concierge, an espresso bar, and a wood-paneled English-style pub. In 1991 the company also opened stores in Riverside, California; Edison, New Jersey; and Bethesda, Maryland.

Sales and earnings rebounded a fraction in 1990. Sales rose 8% to $2.89 billion, and profits rose a miniscule 0.7% to $115.8 million. In 1990 women's apparel and accessories accounted for 59% of Nordstrom's total sales; men's apparel accounted for 16%; and shoes—still a company mainstay—constituted 19% of all sales.

Bruce, James, and John Nordstrom; John McMillian; and Robert Bender continued to maintain tight control of the company, and still owned a 40% stock interest in the early 1990s. As of late 1991, Nordstrom operated 50 large specialty stores, 5 smaller stores, 13 clearance stores, and leased shoe departments in 11 department stores in Hawaii. Unburdened by debt, Nordstrom expected to continue to grow in the 1990s, although the firm will be hard-pressed to reproduce the huge gains it achieved in the 1980s.

Long-term corporate strategy called for several stores to be opened in the next few years in New Jersey, Minnesota, Colorado, Maryland, and New York. Chastened somewhat by labor difficulties and sluggish sales, this self-proclaimed "company of entrepreneurs" should continue to spread its brand of upscale, customer-oriented retailing.

Principal Subsidiaries: Place Two; Nordstrom Rack.

Further Reading: Schwadel, Francine, "Nordstrom's Push East Will Test Its Renown for the Best in Service," *The Wall Street Journal,* August 1, 1989; Stevenson, Richard W., "Watch Out Macy's, Here Comes Nordstrom," *The New York Times Magazine,* August 27, 1989; De Voss, David, "The Rise and Rise of Nordstrom," *Lear's,* October 1989; Bergmann, Joan, "Nordstrom Gets the Gold," *Stores,* January, 1990; Falum, Susan C., "At Nordstrom Stores, Service Comes First—But at a Big Price," *The Wall Street Journal,* February 20, 1990; Solomon, Charlene Marmer, "Nightmare at Nordstrom," *Personnel Journal,* September 1990; "Nordstrom History," Nordstrom corporate typescript, 1990.

—Daniel Gross

**OTTO VERSAND
2000 HAMBURG 400**

OTTO-VERSAND (GMBH & CO.)

Wandsbecker Strasse, 3-7
Hamburg 71
D-2000
Germany
(40) 6461-0
Fax: (40) 6461 8571

Private Company
Incorporated: 1949
Employees: 14,683
Sales: DM6.59 billion (US$4.35 billion)

Otto-Versand (GmbH & Co.) is the world's largest mail-order company with subsidiaries and affiliates in Europe, Japan, and the United States, but it remains very much a family concern, with 65% owned by the Otto family. Founded in 1949, the same year as the creation of the West German nation, it has followed the country's rising fortunes from occupied state to reunification. In March of 1990 after 40 years of steady growth, Otto became the first mail-order company to open an order center in the former East Germany.

The company was founded in Hamburg by Werner Otto, father of the head in the early 1990s, Michael Otto. Werner Otto was one of a generation of extremely successful German entrepreneurs after World War II that included such famous names as Max Grundig, Axel Springer, and Heinx Nixdorf. These men seemed to appear from nowhere after the currency reforms of June of 1948 that restored confidence to consumers in the U.S., British, and French zones of occupied Germany. After three years of severe shortages, Germans had no faith in the money issued by the occupation powers. Cigarettes were a more popular parallel currency and the black market ruled supreme. However, Ludwig Erhard, director of the economic council for the joint Anglo-U.S. occupation zone, persuaded the Western Allies to accept his currency reform plan, which required the population to exchange a limited amount of the old currency for the new Deutsche Mark. Goods suddenly appeared as if by magic and Germans went on a buying spree, first for food, then household goods, and finally clothes, which were to become the mainstay of the Otto mail-order empire. In this new market, Otto's formula was to offer low-cost fashion garments and cheap credit. For the first time, German customers were invoiced, rather than required to pay upon delivery. Later, Otto acquired its own Hanseatic Bank and offered 3-, 6-, and 9-month payment plans.

In retrospect, the mail-order market was ripe for development when 300 copies of Otto's first, 14-page catalog were distributed in 1950. In the then-new West Germany, retail distribution was still badly dislocated by World War II. Rationing and shortages meant that many goods had been unavailable for years in local shops and the range of choice was poor. City commercial centers had been heavily bombed, and the absence of Jews left a noticeable gap in retail distribution, as in many other fields where Jews had been successful and innovative before the rise of the Nazis. By 1950, however, West Germany had restored most of its postal and telephone systems, which were a relatively low-cost way to facilitate the distribution of goods in a country in which many store locations were still in ruins. German shop hours were restrictive, giving working people little opportunity to shop. Even in the early 1990s, all shops must close at 6:30 PM on weekdays. Shops have to shut at 2 PM on Saturday afternoons, except on the first Saturday of the month, and are closed all day on Sundays. These hours are zealously protected by the shopworkers' union.

In 1949 Ludwig Erhard became economics minister of the new Federal Republic of Germany and pushed through further reforms that, along with Marshall Plan aid, helped create the famous *Wirtschaftswunder*, or German economic miracle. Rationing and price controls were ended, duties on imports were lowered, and tax on overtime work was abolished. Erhard encouraged production of consumer goods to stimulate employment and economic revival. The boom has lasted until the early 1990s and the wealth spread downward to lower-paid workers. By 1953 living standards were higher than in 1938, by 1961 Germany was one of the world's largest industrial powers, and German incomes tripled between 1950 and 1965. In this rising tide of prosperity, mail order bridged gaps between supply and demand. Today, Germany remains by far Europe's largest annual per capita spender on mail order with 40% of the total European Community market. Seventy percent of all German households receive at least one catalog, and mail order accounts for 5% of all retail sales.

By 1951, Otto sales had already reached DM1 million, generated by 1,500 catalogues of 20 pages each. In 1952, Werner Otto's next major innovation was to introduce a system whereby customers ordered through agents or representatives who forwarded the orders to the company's main office in Hamburg.

Werner Otto believes that his company owes its early success to this form of personal contact. It also enabled the company to keep costs and prices low through lower catalog numbers. By 1953, Otto had more than 100 employees. Otto's catalog had grown to 82 pages. A total of 37,000 copies were distributed, and sales reached DM5 million.

Unlike Werner Otto's archrival, Quelle, whose market strategy included a safety net of retail stores as well as a mail-order empire, Werner Otto concentrated on mail-order catalogs and representatives throughout the 1950s. From the 1960s telephone ordering to Otto's regional centers began to replace representatives. In the early 1990s, three-quarters of Otto's orders were placed by telephone.

In the United States, the United Kingdom, and a number of other countries, mail order has in the past suffered from a very downmarket image as many of its customers have been low-income bargain hunters or people living in remote rural areas, far from centers of population. By the mid-1950s, however,

German consumers began to demand higher-quality goods, and Otto discovered that all kinds of potential customer groups could be successfully targeted. The company became most successful by going against the grain of conventional mail order wisdom. Otto developed a methodical, computerized approach and gained knowledge of preferred customers in highly concentrated urban areas. Catalogs such as "Otto Heimwerker" targeted specific groups such as home enthusiasts, while "Post Shop" offered the latest styles to fashioned-oriented youth. When the company later began its overseas expansion, areas such as Scandinavia, with its widely dispersed population, were ignored in favor of more urbanized, densely populated countries such as Holland and Belgium.

By the end of Otto's first decade in business, the company had more than 1,000 employees and sales of DM150 million. In the early 1960s, Otto became one of the first German companies to install integrated data-processing equipment. Otto used this equipment to become the first mail-order company to offer telephone ordering.

The 1966 Otto catalog had 828 pages and was now the largest in Germany. It had moved upmarket, featuring designers like Pierre Balmain, Jean Patou, Nina Ricci, and Christian Dior. In 1972 Otto started Hermes, its own delivery service, and by the year's end, only 50% of all Otto shipments were being handled by the German Federal Post Office.

By 1974, the year of the company's 25th anniversary, Otto felt strong enough to begin a period of overseas expansion, which intensified in the 1980s. The company's first move was into France, where it acquired 50% of Trois Suisses, the second-largest mail-order firm in France. In 1979, Otto founded Otto BV, which has grown to become one of the largest mail-order companies in the Netherlands. Otto formed partnerships with Venca, the largest Spanish mail-order company, and Austria's 3 Pagen. In 1974 Otto acquired an interest in Heine, a company specializing in luxury clothing and household goods. At the same time Otto continued to expand within Germany, acquiring Schwab in 1976, Alba Moda in 1982, the linen and home textiles company Witt Weiden in 1987, and a holding in Sport-Scheck in 1988.

In 1981 Michael Otto succeeded his father as chairman, and the company undertook its riskiest venture to date when it seized an opportunity to buy the Spiegel catalog-sales company in the United States. Although Spiegel was still a U.S. household name, its fortunes had been declining for years. Like the early Otto company, it had concentrated on low-cost women's fashions. Otto realized that the U.S. mail-order market had changed and gambled by taking the entire operation upmarket. Four years later, Spiegel had tripled its sales and become the United States' biggest mail-order company. The Spiegel venture was so successful that in 1988 Otto extended its interests in the United States by buying Eddie Bauer Ltd. This company had started as an Alaska expedition outfitter based in Seattle, Washington, but had grown into a national network of stores and mail order. Less well known than the famous Maine outdoor clothing company L.L. Bean, it rode some similar trends to prosperity in the 1970s and 1980s, such as the desire of many affluent young Americans to participate in outdoor activities or, at least, to affect a healthy outdoor image.

The Otto company bought Bauer, with its predominantly male market, ostensibly to complement Spiegel, which spe-

cialized in women's clothing. Through those two companies and also Honeybee, a high-fashion catalog and retail store chain, Otto was appealing to the upwardly mobile young, thought to be an easy target because they had high incomes and little time to shop in retail outlets. With the widely publicized decline in this group's fortunes in the recession of the early 1990s, it remains to be seen whether Otto will continue to be as successful in the U.S. market as it was initially.

Otto did not want to be outdone by its rivals in the former East Germany. By March of 1990, three months before formal economic unification, Otto had opened mail-order centers in Leipzig, Dresden, and the former East Berlin. By July, Otto was the only mail-order house to boast a comprehensive distribution network in all five of the new federal states, the result of an earlier agreement with an East German association of consumer cooperatives. Sales in these new states exceeded DM1.1 billion, more than double the company's original forecast, and more than 1,000 order centers are being established throughout the former East Germany.

Initially the company was less interested in the other former communist countries in Eastern Europe, but moves by Quelle and other competitors rapidly changed Otto's outlook. With the formation of Otto-Epoka mbH, Warsaw, a joint venture, Otto entered the Polish market in May of 1990. Order centers were established in Czechoslovakia, Hungary, and the Soviet Union. At the same time, Otto has been trying to strengthen its presence in Western Europe in anticipation of the 1993 single European market. In 1988 Otto acquired a 75% stake in Euronova S.R.L., the third-largest Italian mail-order house.

Otto had wanted to expand into the United Kingdom for many years before its well publicized £165 million bid for Grattan, the mail-order arm of the troubled Next retailer, finally succeeded in March of 1991. In 1986, it had been outbid by Next, which paid £300 million, but in 1991 it was prepared to pay a premium of £15 million above a rival £150 million bid by Sears plc, which controls the Freemans mail-order house, to secure this U.K. base. Grattan has a computerized warehouse system, a huge customer base, and 13% of the U.K. mail-order market, but it had been devastated by the recession of the early 1990s and a postal strike. Its parent company, Next, desperately needed to refinance a convertible bond issue. Otto had already begun to enter the U.K. market in a joint venture with Fine Art Developments Ltd., a greeting card company. In December of 1988 Otto launched Rainbow Home Shopping Ltd., a Bradford mail-order firm, and announced that Rainbow would join forces with Grattan, also Bradford-based.

Retail industry analysts are divided about the impact of the 1993 single European market on the prospects for mail-order firms. Companies like Otto Versand will undoubtedly achieve economies of scale with pan-European operations, and the development of satellite networks such as Sky will increase opportunities for home shopping, but mail-order firms will still have to cope with problems of distance and national distribution networks. Proposed European Community directives may also threaten the use of mailing lists. With 25% of the European Community market, Otto is concerned not to breach competition laws. In recognition of this situation, Otto announced that it would continue its policy of operating through national subsidiaries and allowing a degree of freedom to local subsidiaries familiar with local customs and markets. In 1990 it also called attention to its environment-friendly policies, including a reduction in energy consumption and careful product selection. In 1988, Otto introduced employee equity ownership through participation rights. By 1990 participation rights capital increased by DM4 million to DM10 million, and a third of employees were participating in the profit-sharing scheme.

Otto is placing its greatest hopes, however, on the development of the Japanese market in a joint venture with Sumitomo Corporation, Otto Sumisho Inc., begun in 1988. Ten years ago, mail order scarcely existed in Japan, but Otto hopes to develop this untapped market with many of the characteristics of markets in which it has been successful elsewhere, namely urban concentrations of the newly affluent and fashion-conscious. From the Japanese base, the company hopes to develop similar markets on the Pacific Rim. Initial results were encouraging. In its third year of operations, the company was able to increase its sales by 30% compared with the previous year, to DM119 million.

In the early 1990s Otto was represented by 28 mail-order firms on three continents and in a total of 13 countries. No firm currently has a wider global reach.

Principal Subsidiaries: Schwab Versand A.G. (94%); Josef Witt GmbH (94%); Corso; Handelsgesellschaft Heinrich Heine GmbH & Co. (99%); KG Hermes Versand Service; Alba Moda GmbH (90%); Fegro-Markt; Trois Suisses (France, 50%); Euronova S.R.L. (Italy, 75%); Modenmuller Versandhandelsgesellschaft (Austria); Heinrich Heine Handelsgesellschaft AG; Otto Sumisho Inc. (Japan); Otto Investments Ltd. (U.K.); Rainbow Home Shopping Ltd. (U.K.).

—Clark Siewert

THE PRICE COMPANY

4649 Morena Boulevard
San Diego, California 92186
U.S.A.
(619) 581-4600

Public Company
Incorporated: 1976
Employees: 13,336
Sales: $2.65 billion
Stock Exchange: NASDAQ

The Price Company operates cash-and-carry membership-only merchandising warehouses in California, Arizona, New Mexico, Colorado, Virginia, Maryland, New York, Connecticut, New Jersey, and in three provinces of Canada: Quebec, Ontario, and British Columbia, all called Price Club. Membership card holders pay a fee of $25 for the privilege of buying any of a variety of about 3,000 different products marked up at generally less than 10% over cost. They each spend an average of $125 every time they shop. The first of the members-only discount warehouses, Price Clubs had to deal with increasing competition in the 1980s. Once the leader in sales for the industry, it had dropped behind Sam's Clubs, a division of Wal-Mart. In the early 1990s, despite the competition, a slowing economy, and a drop in consumer confidence, Price Company had expanded aggressively, continuing to open new stores in the United States and Canada while examining prospects for penetrating other foreign markets. Early in 1991 there were 66 Price Club warehouses in operation.

In 1954 Sol Price started Fedmart, a mass-merchandise supermarket that helped to introduce the concept of one-stop discount shopping. Its customers were government employees, who paid a membership fee of $2 per family.

Beginning with sales of $4.5 million in 1954—four times greater than expected—by 1974 Fedmart was a 45-store chain with sales exceeding $300 million. Price saw golden times ahead for Fedmart, but less than two years later he was ousted from the company, and his two sons resigned. Without Price, the company continued for seven more years until, after heavy losses, it was liquidated.

Out of a job, Sol and his son Robert walked around San Diego, California, talking to retail merchants in the area, such as restaurant owners and newstand operators. At that time small-business operators could acquire their products either

from three or four regional wholesalers or high-priced cash-and-carry operations. This was the section of the marketplace that Price decided to cater to.

Price used $800,000 of his own money, $1 million invested by local business owners, and $500,000 he raised by selling stock to Fedmart employees to start the Price Company along with his two sons. When the first Price Club opened in 1976 on the outskirts of San Diego, the first members were limited to small-business operators or professionals who, while able to buy such items as office stationery, cigarettes, or toilet paper for their business, could also buy items for their personal use. Offsetting the membership fee was the prospect of finding bargains they could get nowhere else.

In its first year of operation, the Price Company lost $750,000 on sales of $16 million. While this may have been partially due to Price's refusal to advertise, he was unable to explain the lack of success. A Price Club member suggested that they expand their membership base by allowing government employees to join. Price sold more stock to friends to keep the company afloat and also invited members of selected credit unions, savings and loan institutions, and employees of utility companies and hospitals to join the club. By restricting membership to these groups, financially secure and screened for the most part, Price minimized the risk of bad checks and reduced losses from shoplifting. This was also important because Price refused to accept credit cards in order to avoid encouraging customers into debt and because in this way he would not have to pay a credit card company 1.5% or more on each sale.

By 1978 the Price Company's financial situation had improved enough to open a warehouse in Phoenix, Arizona. Price's son Larry formed a new association with the company; using money borrowed from the Price Company, he bought leases from it to start up tire-mounting and battery installation centers next to the warehouses. Expansion continued in 1979 with two warehouses in Arizona and California, for a total of four.

In terms of its facilities, the typical Price Club outlet had little consumer appeal. Usually located in an out-of-the-way area on the fringe of a city, its nearest neighbors were body shops and small factories. Small red-lettered signs indicated the low warehouse buildings with an interior space of around 100,000 square feet, about the size of two football fields. Inside, fluorescent lighting illuminated 18-foot-high industrial steel shelves stocked by fork lifts with everything from tires to television sets to snowblowers. In 1988 the Burbank, California, Price Club had 35 check-out counters at which discarded cartons were loaded with purchases. Members paid a $25 annual fee.

Some observers were surprised that customers would pay for the privilege of shopping, but Price Clubs still succeeded, for two primary reasons. First, rising inflation in the late 1970s made consumers more value-conscious. With the growing influence of mass-marketing in the 1970s, people became more aware of what product they wanted to buy and no longer needed trained salespeople to help them make a decision; instead they wanted the lowest possible purchase price. Second, regular discounters were no longer the bargain centers they had been. Competing more directly with department stores, they had increased their advertising budgets and spent more on making their stores more attractive. As their costs went up, the markups on merchandise increased to the 15% to 35% range.

In contrast, the Price Clubs maintained markups of generally less than 10% by keeping their costs down, not only by using discarded boxes at the check-out counters, but also by refusing to take credit cards, to offer free delivery, to advertise in any way except to announce new warehouse openings, or to use direct marketing campaigns. At the stores there is just one worker shift to pay, since they stay open just eight and a half hours a day. Customers seemed to like the Price Club's frugal image and they compensated for the lack of advertising by telling friends about available bargains.

In terms of selection, a Price Club outlet offers only 3,000 different products while the average discount store offers approximately 50,000. The goods offered at a Price Club include items with upscale appeal, such as Baccarat crystal and Courvoisier cognac. The company buys in large quantities, and it packages its lower-priced items in the same way. Rice is sold by the ten-pound bag and peanut butter by the 32-ounce jar. Items that come in smaller sizes are wrapped in groups whenever possible, such as 12 bottles of juice. Thus, the lowest-priced item in a Price Club store sells for $2. Inventory also turns over fast, around 20 times a year, roughly seven times the rate as at a Kmart outlet. This allows the stores to sell their inventory before having to pay for it in the 30 days usually allotted.

Having established a successful market strategy in the late 1970s, the Price Company entered a period of growth in the 1980s as it faced competition from other warehouse clubs. The company went public in 1980, and several stock splits followed. Four new stores opened in 1981 and 1982, three in California and one in Arizona.

The Price Company faced two major challenges in 1983, one from without and one from within. The external challenge was mounted by two new players in the membership warehouse industry. Costco, founded in Seattle, Washington, offered a challenge to the Price Company on the West Coast. Another competitor established that year was Sam's Wholesale Clubs, later renamed Sam's Clubs, spearheaded by Wal-Mart. The internal challenge was one that the Price Company set itself: the expansion of its operations into the eastern United States with the formation of a majority-owned subsidiary, Price Club East, Inc.

While in 1983 the Price Company had opened four stores, all in California, in 1984 it opened twice as many, five in California, one in New Mexico, and two in Richmond and Norfolk, Virginia. The eastern market presented the Price Company with problems both in finding suitably priced land zoned for commercial development as well as in appealing to consumers with less spacious homes and who might be reluctant to brave heavy traffic for substantial distances. To adequately capitalize itself for expansion, the Price Company sold $75 million of debentures in 1984.

Real estate acquisition has always been an important part of the Price Company's corporate strategy, a wholly owned subsidiary, TPCR Corporation, having been formed to develop and operate any land bought in excess of Price Club needs. As Sol Price expanded operations he bought buildings or land in fringe locations on the outskirts of cities rather than in more desirable areas that would be more expensive. When purchasing land on which to construct new warehouses, the Price Company went into partnerships with land developers who would construct retail buildings on the excess land, lease it to other merchants, and split the rental income with the Price Company. As for the competition that these other retailers might pose for their own outlets, Price calculated that the traffic thus attracted would make up for any losses. In addition, the company garnered additional revenues from such rentals, $11.3 million in 1990.

On its sales of $1.9 billion in 1985, the Price Company made $46 million, giving it the leading position in what was then a $4.4 billion-a-year industry. Not only did the company continue to expand both in California, with three stores, and in Maryland, with one store, but it also went into a joint venture, Price Club Canada, with the Steinberg Corporation of Canada to operate Price Clubs in that country. That same year, through a stock-swapping arrangement, Price Club East was merged with its parent company.

As the Price Company opened new stores, Larry Price expanded his tire-mounting and battery installation business, doing $5.2 million in sales in 1985 at 20 centers. At this time, over Larry's objections, the Price Company exercised its option to buy out the business. Larry Price filed for arbitration and received $3.7 million in 1986. After this decision he filed a $100 million lawsuit against the company.

Despite this family dispute, 1986 was a banner year for the Price Company. The company opened its first Canadian warehouse in Montreal, along with two more in California and a third in Virginia. Reflecting the increased confidence of financial analysts in the warehouse industry in general and the Price Company in particular, the company's stock rose to an all-time high of $55.75 per share. Nevertheless, the business press predicted a shakeout in the industry, which was becoming crowded.

By 1986 Sam's Wholesale Clubs had taken the number-one spot away from the Price Company, despite the earnings it had posted of about $95 million on sales of more than $4 billion. Another disappointment that same year was the company's failure to acquire 12 TSS-Seedman stores in New York. Although the Price Company continued to expand, with five new stores in California and one in Arizona as well as one store each in Connecticut, Maryland, New Jersey, New York, and Montreal, its stock price suffered in the crash of 1987, falling to $23.50 per share. Strengthening its cash position, the Price Company made a $200 million debenture offering.

By 1988 the Price Company had grown sufficiently to necessitate some corporate restructuring. Having added photo processing services, packaging of ground meat, eyeglass dispensing, automotive servicing, and pharmacy sales, the Price Company established a new division, Price Club Industries, to manage its growth. For this division, the company made use of part of its latest acquisition, A.M. Lewis, Inc., a wholesale grocer operating in Arizona and southern California, which had been purchased for $52 million. This purchase meshed well with food operations, a part of the business that had grown to contribute 25% of revenues by the late 1980s. After selling the cash-and-carry operations of A.M. Lewis, the Price Company converted one of its facilities to a Price Club warehouse, using another center for its manufacturing business.

The company opened six new stores in 1988, a slower rate of expansion than in previous years. For the first time, however, this number represented fewer stores being opened in the western United States than in the East and Quebec. In a move to create a corporate structure that could manage a business increasingly located on two coasts, the company created two new positions, chief operating officers for each coast, both of whom would report to a three-person committee made up of President Robert Price, Vice Chairman Richard M. Libenson, and Chief Financial Officer Giles H. Bateman.

In 1988 Sol Price resigned as chairman of the board. The company he had founded posted sales that year of more than $4 billion with revenues of $110 million per store. Earnings had grown at 32% annually over the past four years. With Sol Price's departure, his son Robert became chairman of the board in 1989. As chairman, Robert Price authorized in 1989 the first cash dividend in the company's history, a special one-time payment of $1.50 per common share, for a total outlay of $75 million. Along with eight new warehouses, two in Arizona, three in California, one in New York, and two in Quebec, the Price Company launched two new pilot operations in southern California, stand-alone businesses offering home and office furniture. Both of these, however, were closed in 1990. This disappointment along with the shuffling of personnel out of and into the position of the chief of operations for the West Coast were problems for the company.

In the first two years of the 1990s, the Price Company had grown with 13 stores launched in 1990 and 10 projected for 1991, with plans to continue growth in the eastern United States and Canada and to explore opportunities in other countries. The Price Company's interest in foreign investment is shown by the company's purchase in 1990 of the remaining 50% of Price Club Canada for about $54 million. The company also picked up an independent distribution system, allowing it to move supplies for its own stores for the first time. Its venture into food retailing made it the fifth-largest grocer in the United States, by sales, in 1990. Moving into a new field in 1990, the company entered into a joint venture with Atlas Hotels, Inc., enabling it to design and market exclusive travel packages to Price Club members. The Price Company also had an option to purchase a 50% interest in certain hotel properties while guaranteeing a $41 million line of credit for Atlas. On this guarantee, which ran for four years, Atlas had already

drawn $39 million by August 31, 1990. Also that year, Mitchell Lynn, an 11-year veteran of the Price Company, was appointed president.

For the first time in its history, the company announced in 1991 that it would close a warehouse, founded in 1990 in Cheektowaga, New York, near Buffalo, but expressions of support from its members influenced the Price Company to reverse the decision. The warehouse remained while the company kept close track of its sales.

During the early 1990s the Price Company's real estate holdings, worth roughly $400 million, gave it a strong financial standing, and analysts continued to cite the company as a good investment prospect. The Price Company in 1991 made a $250 million debenture offering to buy up land for expansion as well as to ward off a possible takeover. Sol Price, still very much involved in his company's future, planned to buy approximately $15 million of the debentures. Meanwhile the company had bought back its own shares for the first time, buying 500,000 of the 49.9 million outstanding shares at $39 per share. Holding the number-two spot in a $22 billion industry, the Price Company continued to grow, ready to seek profits in good times and bad.

Principal Subsidiaries: Alfred M. Lewis, Inc.; Alfred M. Lewis Properties, Inc.; TPRC Corporation; Price Club Canada, Inc.; Priceus Holdings, Inc.; Price Club Properties, Inc.; Club Distribution, Inc.; Lewis Retail Food, Inc.; Orange Empire Finance, Inc.; Price Club Canada Holdings, Inc.; Price Club Distribution, Inc.; Price Sub, Inc.; Number Company (148623 Canada, Inc.); Club Price St. Laurent, Inc.; Club Price Laval, Inc.; Club Price Quebec, Inc.; Club Price St. Hebert, Inc.; Club Price Anjou, Inc.

Further Reading: Jakobson, Catheryn, "They Get It for You Wholesale," *The New York Times Magazine: Part 2,* December 4, 1988.

—Wilson B. Lindauer

QUELLE GROUP

Nürnberger Strasse 91-95
8510 Fürth
Germany
(911) 742 3157
Fax: (911) 626 224

Private Company
Incorporated: 1927 as Gustav Schickedanz
Employees: 39,300
Sales: DM12.59 billion (US$8.31 billion)

The Quelle Group, headed by Gustav Schickedanz KG, is one of Germany's largest retail and mail-order organizations. The mail-order business in Germany and adjacent countries is at the core of Quelle's success. Quelle is the country's second largest supplier of fashions and textiles, with its own trademarks and household catalog names: Shöpflin, Madeleine, Elégance, Peter Hahn, Euroval, and others. It makes its own Mars bicycles. Its own electrical goods are sold under the Matura, Universum, and Privileg trademarks. Quelle also operates 21 department stores, 151 technical speciality shops, 100 Apollo optical shops, 169 travel bureaus, 14 garden centers and is the franchiser of 1,103 partners in Foto-Quelle film and development shops. In the fiscal year ended January 1991, sales were up 23% from the previous year.

Gustav Schickedanz, Quelle's founder, was born in 1895, the son of a craft factory employee in Fürth, a small city adjacent to Nuremburg. He left school at the age of 15 to work at Speed and Son, the local branch of a sportswear firm. He soon was due to be appointed as a company representative in South America, but he decided to complete his army-service obligation first. World War I broke out and an expected service period of one year turned into seven. He was wounded and discharged in 1919. Schickedanz returned to Fürth where he worked as a salesman and married Anna Zehnder, a local master baker's daughter, in September 1919. In 1922, he opened a small haberdashery business and struggled to keep the firm going in the midst of Germany's period of hyperinflation. His employees were his father, wife, and sister.

Economic reforms led to a degree of stabilization and a short period of improvement. Schickedanz's observations of customer behavior led him to believe that he could sell to a larger market through the mail. With the resulting low overheads and greater volume, he could offer lower prices. These ideas were not new, but hyperinflation presented great difficul-

ties to mail-order firms. The new stabilization convinced him that mailorder could work. The mail-order venture opened in November 1927. The name chosen for the company, Quelle, means "source" in German. Schickedanz hired 15 new workers. One, Grete Lachner, would one day become his second wife and play an essential role in the company's future.

His first catalogs emphasized wool, thread, and materials for home sewing, rather than ready-to-wear clothes. The company enjoyed a modest success in its first 18 months of operation. Schickedanz's 33-year-old wife Anna and their 5-year-old son were killed in an auto accident in July 1929; his 72-year-old father died shortly afterward. His problems were compounded by the Wall Street crash, which halted the German economy's faltering recovery and threw millions out of work. Schickedanz's sister, Liesl Kiesling, stepped into Anna's position in the company.

By the end of 1930, five million Germans were unemployed. Schickedanz's new business survived, however, and, especially by the standards of the Great Depression, prospered. Quelle was able to offer lower prices than many shops, and quickly developed a reputation for reliability and good value. Soon Schickedanz began to offer more clothes and accessories. By 1934 Quelle had 250,000 customers. By 1936 this number had grown to a million, the majority of whom were women.

This success came about despite the restrictions on trade introduced by Adolf Hitler's new Nazi regime, which came to power in January 1933. As Jews began to leave or face imprisonment, they disappeared as competitors in the clothing trade. In 1935 Schickedanz bought VP, a paper factory, to publish catalogs and make cartons. This factory had been Jewish property. Some suspected him of having an invisible Jewish partner, but this was never proved. World War II began on September 1, 1939, and the Nazis required that the paper factory be turned over to war work. Schickedanz continued to operate under severe restrictions and clothing rationing, but the dislocations of the war meant that mailorder provided an alternative source of supply to people in bombed-out cities. Schickedanz was offered several positions as an economic administrator, but he preferred to remain with the business.

In 1942 Schickedanz married Grete Lachner. One year later their only child was born in a bomb-proof bunker. As Allied bombers began to attack the Nuremburg-Fürth area, the Schickedanz family moved out to quarters in the nearby forest village of Hersbruck. In August 1943 Quelle was virtually put out of business when an Allied bombing raid destroyed 90% of the company's warehouse in Fürth. On April 19, 1945, American troops occupied the ruins of Fürth and Nuremburg. Three weeks later, Germany surrendered. Although the Schickedanzes were fortunate to find themselves in the U.S. zone of occupation, their enterprise was not initially encouraged. Schickedanz was classified as a Nazi by the occupation authorities and prohibited from reopening his business. Buildings were in ruins or requisitioned by the occupation authorities and customer records had been lost.

Grete Schickedanz opened a small clothing shop in Hersbruck to support the family. It was a success, but was closed by the military authorities. Eventually, the Schickedanzes were able to use the influence of the anti-Nazi politician and economist Ludwig Erhard, a family friend who was also from Fürth, to gain permission to reopen. The Hersbruck shop remains open as one of Quelle's smallest retail outlets.

Gustav Schickedanz remained under a prohibition and, in theory, could not even discuss business with former employees. The ban was removed in 1949. Former employees were found and Quelle was off to a fresh start. It was just in time to benefit from Ludwig Erhard's currency reforms of the previous year. Following the founding of West Germany in 1949, Erhard moved as quickly as possible to remove restrictions and rationing and to encourage competition. He believed that sales of consumer goods would encourage production and jobs.

After many years of hardship, Germans responded by going on a buying spree. The Quelle name was remembered and respected by many former customers. By utilizing previous contacts, Grete Schickedanz was able to obtain superior but inexpensive goods for sale. It was on this foundation that the new Quelle was built. By the end of 1949 Quelle had a turnover of DM12 million and mailing list of 100,000 addresses, but the couple had also opened their first department store.

Germany, especially, benefited from the economic expansion stimulated by the Korean War in the early 1950s. Between 1949 and 1952 the company's turnover rose by 900%. By 1952 Quelle had one million credit customers and sales of DM103 million. The company now faced the classic problems of a successful business: how to expand without overextending and damaging a reputation for quality. The answer was to invest in new computer and data processing technology that was just appearing in the United States and barely known in Europe.

Schickedanz hired the best experts and gave them a free hand to design systems that would enable Quelle to handle millions of mail-order and credit transactions per year. Thirty-five engineers from the firm SEL in Stuttgart worked for two years to develop and set up a system appropriate for Quelle's needs. In 1955 the first phase of the company's new mail-order center was finished. By 1957 SEL had completed the building of the new system. It was one of the most sophisticated mail-order computer information systems and attracted worldwide interest. Quelle was able to rationalize its operations and achieve even greater efficiency. The company has continued to give high priority to updating its computer and data information systems. In 1990 it maintained information on some 32 million customers.

A new emphasis was placed on quality control. In 1953 Schickedanz set up an institute for testing products to be sold through Quelle. It became known as the Quelle Institute für Warenprufung and is the largest institute of its kind in German commerce. At first only textiles were tested, but gradually it began to examine other product types. In 1990 it had made more than 25,000 annual tests. The institute also attracted international interest.

Grete Schickedanz was increasingly responsible for buying. She also directed careful attention to new catalogs and added more color pages. By 1954 more than half the pages of the spring-summer catalog were in color. She carefully monitored fashion trends. Later, the company hired prominent German designers such as Heinz Oestergard as advisers.

The range of mail-order products was continually expanding. In 1954 the company bought a bicycle factory and began to sell bicycles. The next year, a favorable response to a line of small electronic appliances led to the introduction of washing machines and large appliances, which Quelle was able to offer at very competitive prices. In 1957 one of its most successful

ventures was into photographic equipment, where it was able to offer large mail-order discounts. By the early 1960s it was even offering travel services.

Quelle learned how to target special-interest groups and to develop special catalogs alongside its main catalog to spotlight lifestyle groups and hobbies such as gardening. A bank, NORIS Bank GmbH (later Quelle Bank) was started in 1956 and developed to help customers with credit. By 1958 Quelle had a turnover of DM406 million. It had become the largest mail-order firm in West Germany.

From the early 1960s, Grete Schickedanz traveled to the Far East on buying trips. In 1962 Quelle opened an office in Hong Kong. Eventually, the region became one of the company's most important sources of supply. Later, Grete Schickedanz established important business contacts in the People's Republic of China and opened an office in Shanghai.

In 1964 Quelle had a turnover of DM1.64 billion and called itself "the largest mail-order house in Europe." The 1960s and 1970s were a period of continued growth for Quelle in Germany, but unlike its competitor, Otto Versand, which made a very successful investment in Spiegel in the United States, Quelle has been more cautious about foreign expansion. The process has been slow, mainly into neighboring countries. It began in 1959 with Austria, where results were so encouraging that the company decided in 1966 to make a much more risky move into France, opening a new mail-order facility in Orleans.

Gustav Schickedanz died on March 27, 1977, in the 50th anniversary year of the company. He was succeeded as chairperson by Grete Schickedanz. Because the two had worked as partners for many years, Gustav's death did not disrupt the company or bring about any major policy changes. Grete continued her worldwide buying trips. By 1981, Quelle had a turnover of DM10 billion.

In May 1985 Grete Schickedanz broke new ground in West German-East European trade politics by signing an agreement with Hungarotex, the Hungarian foreign trade organization. The agreement allowed Quelle to sell by mail in Hungary and included plans for a new chain of jointly owned department stores. In 1990 Quelle started Intermoda, a joint-venture catalog operation in the Soviet Union. In 1987 Grete Schickedanz relinquished her position as chairperson of the board of Quelle, but she remained as head of its supervisory board. Into the 1990s she still traveled widely on behalf of the company.

The speedy German reunification process, which began with the collapse of the East German regime in November 1989 and culminated a year later, presented both new markets and challenges from Otto and other German competitors. Quelle moved quickly to distribute its catalog to nine out of ten households in the former East Germany. New stores and facilities were opened in Gera, Jena, and Erfurt. A huge new regional mail-order complex was opened in Leipzig, creating 3,000 new jobs. Quelle described its investment in the new Germany as the largest in its history, creating a total of 7,000 new jobs.

At the end of 1990, Quelle surprised many German financial institutions by entering into a new agreement, through its subsidiary Quelle Bank, with the Bank of Scotland to enter the undeveloped German credit card market. The German market had been thought to be resistant to credit cards. According to the plan, Quelle was to offer direct banking and credit card services using its mail-order data base, with more than 30 million customers in Germany, France, and Austria. Bank of Scotland would handle the processing in its facilities in Dunfermline, Fife, Scotland. Quelle expected to issue about one million cards in its first five years. With the 1992 European economic unification approaching, Quelle sought to acquire a foothold in the United Kingdom and began negotiations with Littlewoods for its mail-order division.

Principal Subsidiaries: Quelle Beteiligungs GmbH; Quelle AG; Foto Quelle; Apollo-Optik GmbH; Mobel Hess GmbH; Quelle Bank GmbH (25%); Sinn AG (51%); Grossversandhaus Schöpflin GmbH (99%); Peter Hahn GmbH; Elégance; Madeleine Mode GmbH; UTS Universal Technik-Service GmbH; Quelle S.A. (France, 99%); Distribucion Quelle S.A. (Spain, 51%); Peter Hahn AG (Switzerland).

Further Reading: Grete Schickedanz: Ein Leben für die Quelle, Fürth, Quelle, 1986.

—Clark Siewert

R. H. MACY & CO., INC.

151 West 34th Street
New York, New York 10001
U.S.A.
(212) 560-3600
Fax: (212) 629-6814

Private Company
Incorporated: 1919
Employees: 78,000
Sales: $6.97 billion

R. H. Macy & Co., Inc. operates through four department store groups: Macy's of New York, Inc., Macy's New Jersey, Macy's California, and Macy's Atlanta. The groups in turn operate approximately 90 stores that collectively occupy some 23 million square feet in 13 states. The corporation owns several shopping centers and has an interest in several others. The Macy's stores target the middle-to-higher-priced market, offering women's, men's, and children's clothing and accessories; housewares; home furnishings; and furniture.

Rowland H. Macy made his fifth attempt at opening a retail store in Manhattan in 1858. His previous four attempts with similar stores had failed resoundingly, culminating, with the demise of his shop of Haverhill, Massachusetts, in his bankruptcy. Although Macy's store was situated far north of the traditional retail market, the store on Sixth Avenue near Fourteenth Street sold a healthy $85,000 worth of merchandise within one year.

Macy instituted a cash-only policy not only for customers but for himself as well. No Macy's inventory was purchased on credit, and no Macy's credit account was issued until well into the 1950s. This was unusual in a day when most stores routinely sold on credit. He maintained each product's assigned price, so customers could routinely estimate how wide to draw the pursestrings. The new store benefited from his advertising and promotion skills as well as his product line instincts. By 1870, when sales broke $1 million, a stable clientele could purchase not only dry goods, but items like men's hosiery and ties, linens and towels, fancy imported goods, costume jewelry, silver, and clocks.

Macy's son was not interested in the retail business, so Macy passed ownership into other hands. In 1860 he hired his cousin Margaret Getchell to do bookkeeping at the store, and she subsequently married a young Macy's salesman, Abiel T. LaForge. Macy increased LaForge's responsibilities, and

eventually chose him as heir to half his store. The other half went to Macy's nephew, Robert M. Valentine.

Valentine and LaForge became the proprietors when the founder died unexpectedly in 1877 on a buying trip in France. LaForge died soon after. Valentine bought LaForge's share, and attempted to continue the family succession by bringing in LaForge's relative, Charles Webster. When Valentine died, Webster married his widow, and brought in his brother-in-law, Jerome B. Wheeler. In 1887, however, Webster bought Wheeler out, becoming the sole proprietor of a thriving business, which he felt he could not perpetuate single-handedly.

Searching for a partner, Webster approached the Straus family, who for 13 years had leased space in Macy's to operate a chinaware department, the store's most profitable section. In 1887 it generated almost 20% of the store's sales. The Strauses eagerly accepted Webster's offer, the partnership culminating many years' work and launching the family into a social role comparable to that of the Rothschilds in Europe. Lazarus Straus, the family's patriarch, emigrated in 1852 from Germany to the United States, dissatisfied with Germany's collapsed 1848 revolution. After several years as a peddler, he was able to send for his wife and four children. The family developed a successful general store in Talbotton, Georgia, then moved to New York City in 1867 after the end of the Civil War. Lazarus Straus bought a wholesale chinaware-importing firm and brought his sons Isidor, Nathan, and Oscar into the business, renaming the company L. Straus and Sons. Lazarus Straus died only a year after buying into Macy's but his sons carried on the business. Under the new partnership, Macy's matched and outpriced its rivals, such as A. T. Stewarts, Hearn's, and Siegel & Cooper. Macy's sales rose to $5 million within a year, and subsequently continued to grow by 10% annually. The Straus brothers introduced their odd-price policy, now used virtually everywhere in U.S. retailing. Charging $4.98 instead of $5.00, the store motivated consumers to buy in quantity in order to accumulate substantial savings. Following in Macy's footsteps, the Strauses brought in line after line of new merchandise—Oriental rugs, ornate furniture, lavish stationery, new-style bicycles, even pianos. They also instituted the store's depositor's accounts, in which shoppers could make deposits with the store and then charge purchases against them. This, in effect, provided Macy's with interest-free loans, and was a forerunner of installment buying and layaway plans.

In 1896 Charles Webster sold his half interest in Macy's to the Strauses, ending the founding family's line of ownership. Jesse, Percy, and Herbert Straus, Isidor's sons, urged their father to relocate the store to its Herald Square location at 34th Street and Broadway in 1902. The giant new store cost $4.5 million, but funds were easily raised on the Straus family's good name, built upon the success of Macy's and the independently operated Abraham & Straus, acquired in Brooklyn in 1893.

No modern convenience was lacking in the Herald Square store. It was equipped with newly designed escalators, pneumatic tubes to move cash or messages, and an air exhaust system that provided the store with a constant supply of fresh air. Macy's spacious building had ample fitting rooms, accommodation desks, an information counter, and comfortable rest rooms. Macy's had a fleet of comparison shoppers who checked out other stores' prices to be sure Macy's merchandise was competitively priced. Sales pushed to $11 million within a year of the move. Called the world's largest store, Macy's Herald Square thrilled tourists and locals alike.

After his father's death, Isidor Straus had emerged as the family patriarch, and remained, among the sons, the most interested in the store. Nathan gradually developed more as a philanthropist than a businessman, and Oscar, after taking a law degree, disregarded the business in favor of politics. Isidor and his wife, Ida, were among the passengers on the ill-fated voyage of the *Titanic.* After their deaths in 1912, Isidor's sons Jesse, Percy, and Herbert bought out Nathan's interest in Macy's and ceded their interests in Abraham & Straus to Nathan. Nathan, thus, became the sole owner of Abraham & Straus.

As it did most of its products, Macy's sold books at substantially below their wholesale price—25% below. In 1909 a book publishers' association sued Macy, charging that the price-cutting hurt their copyright value. The Strauses countersued, claiming that the group constituted an illegal trust under the Sherman Antitrust Act. The publishers responded by cutting Macy off completely. The Strauses, however, obtained stock through other channels—wholesalers, transshippers, or other retailers who had overstocked; they even cut deals directly with authors. The U.S. Supreme Court decided in Macy's favor in 1913, but the controversy made it even tougher for the store to acquire well-known brands in any product line, prompting Macy's to develop its own private labels.

When World War I ended in 1918, sales were up to $36 million, twice that of 1914. Macy's began its expansion into other cities, acquiring substantial interests in LaSalles & Koch Co. in Toledo, Ohio, in 1923 and Davison-Paxon-Stokes Co. in Atlanta, Georgia, in 1925. In subsequent years the balance of stock in both companies was acquired. In the 1920s Macy's began the tradition of sponsoring New York City's Thanksgiving Day parade. The public relations impact of the event went national when two major television networks began to cover the parade in 1952. Just before the Great Depression, Macy's bought L. Bamberger & Co. of Newark, New Jersey, a division that would later lead a renaissance for Macy's. In the 1940s, it added stores in San Francisco, California, and Kansas City, Missouri. By the late 1940s, Macy's was not only the world's largest store but the United States's largest department store chain.

Jack I. Straus, Jesse's son, became chairman of Macy's in 1940. He had grown up with the store, having been present at age two at the Herald Square opening. He realized that the family line was thinning, and began training and promoting outsiders into the top executive positions in the firm. Over the years the Strauses would gradually lessen their holding in the company, but the family remained at the helm of Macy's until the 1980s, when Edward S. Finkelstein, a manager hired by Macy's in 1948, led the company into an entirely new phase.

Straus passed the chairmanship of Macy's on to Robert (Bobby) Weil, his sister's son, as the 1940s ended. Weil beefed up Macy's advertising campaign, billing the store as the "community" store. Nevertheless, as the postwar economy picked up, New Yorkers no longer craved the bargains that were Macy's stock in trade, and did more shopping at other stores. Macy's stock fell from $3.35 per common share in fiscal 1950 to $2.51 in fiscal 1951. Further problems lay ahead.

In 1931 the Federal Fair Trade Law had allowed suppliers of certain products to specify a minimum retail price in order to stabilize the depression–era economy. With the exception of Korvettes, Macy's competitors—Abraham & Straus, Gimbel Brothers, Bloomingdale's, and B. Altman—abided by these minimums. In 1952, however, Schwegmann Brothers, a New Orleans, Louisiana, drugstore chain, contested the law and won its case. The reversal of the 20-year-old practice of price fixing undercut Macy's strategy. Macy's had undersold its competitors with its 6%-less-for-cash policy, but now that fixed minimum prices were not protected by law, all retailers could lower their prices without fear of being sued by suppliers.

Weil decided to combat this by cutting Macy's prices even further. The huge Herald Square store proved to have several weaknesses—while no one could match the giant's prices across the board, Gimbel could undersell Macy's in pharmaceuticals; Gertz of Long Island, New York, in books; and Bloomingdale's in stationery and menswear. In 1952 Macy's posted the first year of loss in its history. Its battle plan was outmoded; Macy's fumbled in directions it had previously ignored, instituting charge accounts and catering more to its suppliers.

While the flagship store struggled with image problems, a renaissance began in another division: Bamberger's of New Jersey. David L. Yunich took the helm of the decaying urban store in Newark in 1955. During his eight years of guidance, Bamberger's mushroomed, opening in suburbs all over New Jersey. The chain's annual sales rose from $82 million to $500 million, its profits being among the highest in the nation and topping even those of the mammoth New York division. Herbert L. Seegal and his protege Finkelstein came to Bamberger's in 1962 to step up its growth, using new customer-oriented merchandising. Instead of buying whatever suppliers offered, Bamberger's bought the top of the line in any new group of goods, and featured that in the most glamorous displays Bamberger's customers had ever seen. The technique garnered notice not only within Macy's but from top executives of other chains as well. The store began its push out of New Jersey to the south and west in 1968, and by the 1980s had three times as many stores as in the late 1960s. Bamberger's of New Jersey's sales for the fiscal year ending July 31, 1981, were $799 million; with Macy's California and New York divisions, it formed a powerful triad generating 86% of Macy's sales.

Macy's had acquired the old O'Connor, Moffat Co. store as its first California outpost in 1945. It was renamed and made Macy's flagship in San Francisco's then-posh Union Square. Like other urban retail centers, however, Union Square and its surrounding complement of chic shops, including I. Magnin, Liberty House, the Emporium, Bonwit Teller, Gumps, and a host of others, fell victim to urban decay in the 1960s. Finkelstein was sent to bail out Macy's California in 1969. Macy's upgraded its image, aiming its product lines at a more well-heeled buyer. The transformation of California's 12 stores helped Macy's surpass most of its competitors, leaving it as one of the top three retailers, along with the Emporium and I. Magnin.

Finkelstein was brought back to the East in 1974 to work on the Herald Square store. He trimmed off departments in which the store could not compete, like pharmaceuticals, major appliances, sporting goods, and toys. Macy's put an end to its concentration on household durables, departments that got heavy competition from Korvettes and Sears as well as local department stores. In place of the discontinued departments, inventories were increased and presentations were refined in certain departments, including linens and domestics, furniture, menswear, and jewelry.

Finkelstein remodeled about 35% of the space in New York's 16 stores, including the Herald Square store, which benefitted from the installation of the Cellar in 1976. Macy's basement, which had been a no-frills depository for bargain merchandise, was transformed into a sparkling esplanade of airy specialty shops offering gourmet foods, yard goods, stationery, baskets, and contemporary housewares. Geared to a trend-conscious consumer, the cross between a European boulevard and a chic suburban mall also offered frequent cooking demonstrations, an old-fashioned apothecary, and a pottery shop complete with a working potter at the wheel. The Cellar caused such a stir that Bloomingdale's hastily installed a similiar group of boutiques, although Bloomingdale's management claimed its conception predated the Cellar's opening. The revitalized Macy's had its biggest Christmas season ever in 1976, and increased its annual earnings greatly from the previous year.

The chinks in Macy's formidable front were minor; competitors claimed that Macy's modern image was tarnished by its refusal to accept major credit cards. In addition, Macy's as a corporation lacked diversity. It operated only department stores, while most other similarly sized operations had diversified into specialty stores. Macy's eventually began development of such stores in the early 1980s.

In 1978 Finkelstein was promoted from president to chairman of Macy's New York division. The Macy Miracle, as it was called, gained momentum as annual sales soared between the years 1979 and 1982. In 1982 corporate sales gains of 20.1% topped the industry, and Macy's supassed its major competitors in operating profit per square foot.

While other stores were consolidating departments under fewer buyers, Macy's added more buyers, encouraging them to find unique products. Stores were overstocked by 10% to 20%, so that unpredicted buying surges could be accommodated. It hired many executives for its training program, up to 300 per year in larger divisions. In 1984 Macy's had its best year ever. Sales rose 17.2% to $4.07 billion from 1983's $3.47 billion, which was up 16.4% from the previous year. At each of its 96 stores, Macy's averaged after-tax profits of $2.31 million. During 1984 Macy's common stock soared in value.

The year 1985 was tough for most retailers, including Macy's. For the year, sales were $4.37 billion, up 6.4% from the previous year, but net income dropped almost 15% from $221.8 million to $189.3 million. The increase in sales was small compared to steady gains of 12% to 17% in the previous four years. Sales costs had risen, due to an increased advertising push, and to new staff training programs.

By 1984 Macy's bulky inventories had gotten out of hand. Inventories were 35% larger than in 1983. Prices were slashed, but the store could not seem to get rid of its excess. The store continued to build stock instead of eliminating it,

miscalculating the buying force of the public; other stores were reducing their inventories. Finkelstein had attempted to expand his private-label lines; he kept the prices too high, however, to attract buyers. Finkelstein's vigilant management had never slipped before; the uncharacteristic miscalculation worried analysts. Wall Street began to waver in its praise. Macy's in 1985 had the second-best year in its history, but the radical drops were not taken kindly in an institution that had been on a steady upward incline for over a decade.

Mergers and acquisitions abounded in the retail industry in 1985. A company with a weak profit record was a likely target because that performance pushed its stock value down, and a change in management could improve it. Although Macy's ten-year profit history was phenomenal, the recent questions from analysts were pushing Macy's stock prices down, and Finkelstein worried about a hostile takeover. In addition, he felt that his best executives were being lured to other stores. Rapid growth and subsequent compensation had satisfied his players over the past ten years, but now the store approached a plateau. Finkelstein had to do something to restore the company's vitality.

Finkelstein's solution was to lead the top 350 executives in a leveraged buyout of Macy's, at $70 per share, not much above a recent market high. He saw ownership and the subsequent share in profits as a way to motivate employees. Some shareholders objected, and one even filed suit, but the offer was sufficiently attractive that they eventually agreed. As for the Straus family, patriarch Jack was outraged, but in effect he had relinquished ownership long ago. In 1924 the Straus family had total ownership; by the 1960s, it was down to 20%; and by the 1980s, the family held only about a 2% interest in the chain. Its attachment to the store could not stop management from executing the biggest takeover of a retailer at that time and the first leveraged buyout of a major retail chain.

The year after the buyout, Macy's stores did so well that the chain could almost report a net profit, despite the debt service on the heavy borrowing needed to fund the buyout. In 1988 Macy's added further to its debt, however, by purchasing Federated's Bullocks and Bullocks-Wilshire and the I. Magnin chains. The $1 billion expenditure weighed heavily on company finance, as did a mediocre 1989 Christmas season. The company's outlook remained marred by its onerous debt. Bankruptcy was a threat, and Macy's needed to tighten management control in the early 1990s.

Principal Subsidiaries: Bay Fair Shopping Center; Brunswick Square (50%); Columbia Mall; The Garden State Plaza Corp.; King's Plaza Shopping Center & Marina (50%); Macy Credit Corp.; I. Magnin & Co.; Mission Shopping Center; New Park Mall (50%); Quaker Bridge Mall (50%); Sunnyvale Towncenter (50%); South Shore Mall; Valley Fair Shopping Center.

Further Reading: Macy's New York 125th Anniversary: 1858–1983, New York, R. H. Macy & Co., 1983; Barmash, Isadore, *Macy's for Sale,* New York, Weidenfeld & Nicolson, 1989.

—Elaine Belsito

REVCO D.S., INC.

1925 Enterprise Parkway
Twinsburg, Ohio 44087
U.S.A.
(216) 425-9811
Fax: (216) 425-3432

Private Company
Incorporated: 1956
Employees: 16,000
Sales: $1.90 billion

The rapid growth and fall in number of stores of Revco D.S., Inc., once the United States's largest drugstore chain, offers a cautionary tale from the 1980s. Through 30 years of innovative marketing, aggressive acquisition, and perpetual expansion, Revco had grown from a single drugstore in Detroit to a 2,000-store nationwide chain with sales in the billions. In the mid-1980s, however, Revco collapsed under the weight of its own expansion. An ill-fated acquisition and the ensuing executive infighting led Revco's top managers to engineer a leveraged buyout in 1986. Saddled with a burdensome debt, and further crippled by stagnant sales and shrinking profits, Revco was forced into Chapter 11 bankruptcy in 1988. Revco subsequently reorganized, retrenched, and downsized as part of an ongoing effort to regain fiscal viability. In 1991 Revco operated 1,100 drugstores, primarily in the Southeast and mid-Atlantic states.

In 1945 Detroit druggist Bernard Shulman hired a 33-year-old accountant to balance the books for his store, Regal Drugs. Shulman could hardly have known that the accountant, Sidney Dworkin, would become, as a trade paper labeled him, "the architect of modern drugstoring." 20 years later, Dworkin would take the reins of Shulman's drug business, and lead Revco to impressive growth through the 1980s.

In 1956 Shulman decided to transform his single store into a discount chain. At that time Regal Drugs had a subsidiary, the Registered Vitamin Company, which sold vitamins door-to-door. Shulman shortened the subsidiary's name to Revco and added the initials D.S., signifying drugstore.

The guiding philosophy behind discounting was to turn over a high volume of low-profit merchandise in a self-service, consumer-oriented environment. To implement this philosophy, Revco used a computer to determine the fast-moving items, and advertised comparative prices for similar products. These early innovations helped transform Revco from a single

store into a large chain. Revco's innovative marketing tactics, however, encountered some resistance from established producers. In 1963, for example, the pharmaceutical giant Eli Lilly successfully sued Revco for selling its products at a discount. Within four years of its incorporation, Revco had grown to 20 stores in Michigan, Ohio, and West Virginia.

Shulman's firm took a giant leap in 1961 when it acquired Cleveland-based Standard Drug Co., a traditional chain that owned 41 stores in Ohio, for $2 million. Revco rapidly transformed the Standard stores into its discount format, folding the entire chain into its prefabricated system. Revco repeated this process time and again in the next several years, growing by leaps and bounds.

In 1964 when Revco reaped $29 million of sales from its 63 stores, Shulman decided to take his company public; in October 1964 Revco issued its first stock offering. Fortified by this influx of capital, Revco was prepared to expand. In 1965 Revco opened six new stores, and purchased Gallaher Drug Co., a 52-store chain. The same year, Revco introduced a new wrinkle into its marketing strategy, and began displaying per-unit prices for competing brands of merchandise, a practice that soon became prevalent in most sectors of retailing.

Despite the company's success and promising future, Bernard Shulman had decided to extricate himself from the company he had founded and nurtured. When he resigned in 1966, Revco owned 117 stores in five states. Shulman was replaced as president and director by Sidney Amster, who had been president of Lane Drug. Amster lasted only four months at these top posts, and was quickly replaced by Sidney Dworkin, who had been an executive vice president. In 1966 sales topped $50 million, spurred in part by the acquisition of Waco Scaffolding Co.

Growth in both profits and number of stores continued apace for the rest of the decade. In 1967 Revco acquired Patterson Drug Co., and in 1968 Revco moved into the Southwest by acquiring Ryan-Evans, a 47-store chain based in Arizona. Sales in 1968 topped $70 million, and in 1969, fueled by the acquisitions, jumped to $98 million.

Consumers and investors alike flocked to Revco. A stock offering issued in 1970 was immediately oversubscribed. That year Revco acquired Cole Drug Co., a 28-store chain operating in Alabama and Georgia. The acquisitions helped the corporation reap profits of $4.3 million from sales of $131 million in 1970. By 1971 Revco was operating 294 stores.

Revco began the 1970s with a spurt of growth. In 1972 the firm acquired vitamin manufacturer Private Formulations Inc., and yet another chain of drugstores. In a stock trade valued at $81 million, Revco acquired the 163-store White Cross chain, and imposed on the stores the parent's name and format. The same year, Revco made another public offering of 675,000 common shares.

Every time Revco acquired a new chain, it instantly converted the new stores to the Revco format. Structure was a key component of Revco's success. Revco's stores were generally smaller than drugstores run by other chains. The size helped maintain a more secure, customer-oriented environment, in which the main products remained drugs and cosmetics. This formula clearly worked. By 1973 Revco, with 527 stores, ranked second only to Walgreen in number of stores, and ranked third in sales volume, behind only the Walgreen and Thrifty chains. Bolstered by the acquisitions, Revco's net income soared in 1973 to $10 million on sales of $300 million.

In the 1970s Revco expanded into different service areas. In 1974 the firm opened the first Revco Optical Center, which was run independently within a drugstore. By 1978, the company operated 48 optical centers.

Revco continued to expand traditional stores in the 1970s. In 1974 Revco purchased Jacobs, a 25-store chain from Read's Inc. In 1976 when Revco tried to buy 11 drugstores from Cook United, a Cleveland-based chain, the federal government tried to block the sale on antitrust grounds because Revco already owned 48 discount drugstores in the Cleveland area. A court ultimately allowed the sale, but only after Revco had revised the terms of the purchase to ensure continued competition.

The following year, Revco encountered more serious difficulties with the law. State and local officials investigated Revco for fraudulent billings of Medicaid prescriptions. Two company officials were ultimately convicted of instituting a false billing scheme. Revco paid a $50,000 fine and was forced to make restitution for more than $500,000 in false billings.

Despite the legal difficulties, Revco continued to grow. In 1975 Revco tallied $461 million in sales. In 1977 Revco's 900 stores sold about $650 million of products. That year Revco initiated a drive to further solidify its image as a discounter by comprehensively introducing generic drugs. Revco was again on the leading edge of a profitable trend, for generic drugs soon became a staple throughout the industry. Revco's expansion was abetted by the acquisition of the 16-unit Elliot's drug chain, which operated in Georgia.

In 1978 when the firm opened a new store on Madison Avenue in Cleveland, Revco became the first drug chain in the United States to operate 1,000 stores. Because it maintained smaller stores, however, Revco lagged behind Walgreen and Eckerd in sales. To produce larger sales, Revco increased the average size of its stores in the late 1970s, from 6,000 square feet to 8,000 square feet.

Sidney Dworkin was not satisfied with 1,000 stores. In 1977 Revco announced that it planned to open a new store every four days for the next several years. In 1978, Revco began developing freestanding film processing centers called Foto-Stops, 14 of which were in operation by the end of the year. In 1978 Revco reaped profits of $29 million on sales of $792 million—both figures were company records. Sidney Dworkin was not satisfied with these impressive figures either. In April 1979 Dworkin predicted that Revco would compound net sales and net earnings at an annual rate of 15%.

The high sales and profit figures greatly enhanced Revco's financial and industrial standing; so much so that in 1979, retailing giant Woolworth, in an effort to stave off a hostile takeover bid, engaged Revco in talks about a possible acquisition. Woolworth was prepared to offer more than $40 a share, three times the chain's book value, for Revco's 1,083 stores.

Although the discussions ended without action, they presaged the events of the coming decade. The 1980s brought with them a whirlwind of mergers, buyouts, and acquisitions that would engulf and ultimately cripple Revco. In 1980, however, Revco was still going strong and seeking to maintain its projected 15% growth rate. With 1,200 drugstores, sales in 1979 had hit $928 million. Although one-quarter of the drugstores' sales came from prescriptions, Revco had diversified and ex-panded. Alone among the major chains, Revco produced its own generic drugs, vitamins, and health products. In all Revco stocked some 385 private-label brands on its shelves.

In 1980 Revco purchased three companies: the 20-store May's chain; the 8-store Sav-Rite chain, and the 145-store Skillern Drug chain. The U.S. Justice Department resisted the acquisition of the huge Texas-based Skillern chain, which itself had tallied sales of $142.2 million in fiscal 1980. Revco and the Justice Department reached an agreement, however, under which the firm would sell a number of existing Revco stores in Texas. These acquisitions raised Revco's store total to nearly 1,300 in 26 states. In 1980 Revco finally topped the $1 billion sales mark, with sales of $1.09 billion.

Revco was generally untouched by the recession of the early 1980s, the firm's wide range of basic goods and general merchandise having rendered it recession-resistant. As the economy contracted, Revco continued to experience significant growth. By the end of 1981 Revco had 1,514 stores in operation. In December 1981 Revco unveiled a five-year growth program, under which the number of stores was slated to rise to 2,300 and sales would rise to $3 billion.

At the end of 1981, then, Revco was a healthy company, sporting high sales, high profit margins, low prices, and long-standing family management; Both of Sidney Dworkin's sons, Marc and Elliot, were Revco executives. In 1981 alone, Revco increased its store count by 21%, raised its sales by nearly 20%, and hiked its earnings by 16%. In 1983 Sidney Dworkin consolidated his hold on the company, assuming the post of chairman. Sales for 1983 totaled $1.8 billion, and they rose to $2.2 billion in 1984.

Behind the veneer of growths and profits, however, developments in 1983 and 1984 would ultimately help push the company into bankruptcy. In 1984 the U.S. Food and Drug Administration investigated the unauthorized distribution of a vitamin supplement called E-Ferol, which was manufactured by Carter-Glogau Laboratories, a Revco unit, and had been linked to 38 infant deaths. In 1988 Revco settled major lawsuits stemming from the ensuing claims. Revco stock slumped in the wake of the initial disclosures in 1984, and Dworkin feared rumblings of an executive coup.

Dworkin and his sons owned only 2% of Revco's stock. In 1984 Dworkin thought he could place more stock in friendly hands by acquiring the Odd Lot Trading Company, a 66-store supplier of close-out consumer products that was run by Chairman Bernard Marden and President Isaac Perlmutter, two longtime business associates and friends. In May 1984 Revco purchased Odd Lot for $113 million in stock, so Perlmutter and Marden held 12% of Revco's stock.

Soon after the acquisition, however, Marden and Perlmutter charged that Revco's purchasing department, which was run by Elliot Dworkin, had overpaid for merchandise. Revco quickly relieved the younger Dworkin of his responsibilities and formed a special committee to investigate the charges. The committee of outside directors later reported that none of the business decisions that Marden and Perlmutter had questioned had a significant financial impact on the company. The dissident shareholders also began talking about engineering a proxy takeover of the company, and demanded six seats on Revco's board.

Sidney Dworkin could no longer tolerate the presence of Marden and Perlmutter in the Revco family; they had accused his son of incompetence and threatened to take over the firm he had run for nearly 20 years. To make matters worse, Odd Lot itself had been a consistent drag on Revco's earnings. In September 1984 Revco dismissed the two dissident shareholders from their posts at Odd Lot. In 1985 Revco bought back their large stake for the hefty price of $98 million. Revco further suffered in 1985 when it took a write-down of $35 million for obsolete Odd Lot inventory. Because of Revco's higher debt, greater operating risks, and general difficulties, Standard & Poor's lowered Revco's commercial paper credit rating to A-2 from A-1 in 1985. Under the financial pressure, Sidney Dworkin stepped down from his posts of president and chief executive officer, although he remained chairman. William Edwards, a former CEO at F&M Distributors, moved into the posts that Dworkin vacated.

Despite these difficulties, Revco continued to grow. In 1985 Revco acquired Carls Drug Co., a 42-store drug chain operating in New Hampshire, Vermont, and upstate New York. Revco added a total of 185 new stores in the year, increasing its total to 2,041. That year, sales totaled $2.4 billion, although net profits slumped from $93 million to $39 million.

Traumatized by the threat of a takeover from within and the dictations of outside directors, Dworkin tried to eliminate threats to his control by taking the company private. In early 1986, Dworkin and several other Revco executives, with the help of Wall Street firm Salomon Brothers, offered Revco's shareholders a $1.16 billion buyout. In August 1986, Revco's board accepted an offer or $38.50 per share, or $1.25 billion. A few months later, the company's shareholders approved the deal.

In the following year, however, Revco's financial health worsened. Sales declined in 1986 to $2.2 billion, and the firm tallied a loss of nearly $60 million that year. In 1986, less than a year after the buyout, Sidney Dworkin and his son, Marc, who together owned 11.6% of the company's stock, severed their connection to Revco. The Dworkins were apparently pushed out by Salomon Brothers and TSG Holdings, the key lenders in the takeover, after Dworkin had resisted their recommendations and policies. The elder Dworkin was replaced by Boake Sells, a former president of the Dayton Hudson Corporation.

In 1988 Revco, saddled with $1.3 billion in long-term debt from the takeover, paid the price for its expensive buyout. In June 1988 the company failed to make a $46 million interest payment on a set of junk bonds, which had provided the bulk of the financing for the buyout. In July 1988, when the firm filed for Chapter 11 bankruptcy, Revco earned the ignominious distinction of becoming the largest leveraged buyout ever to fail. Soon after the filing, Revco abandoned Salomon Brothers, which still owned one-tenth of Revco's stock, and hired Wall Street firm Drexel Burnham Lambert to help restructure its debt.

Revco had been a victim of its own expansion and had scheduled its debt payments based on rosy expectations. In 1986, for example, Revco had estimated that sales for fiscal 1988 would reach $3.37 billion, but they turned out to total only $2.44 billion. Moreover, in 1987, when interest payments

alone were to top $150 million, the firm showed a loss of $60 million; thus no cash was available to make the payments. Burdensome debts, a brief recession, and mismanagement of inventory and products had combined to bring Revco to its knees. In 1987 Revco enacted an inventory-reduction program, which cleared $100 million of products from Revco's shelves. Somehow, however, management failed to replenish shelves for the Christmas season.

Soon after the bankruptcy filing, Boake Sells, the new chairman and CEO, began working to put Revco, which then employed 28,000 people, back on its feet. Sells urged Revco to return to its roots as an operator of discount drugstores and to capitalize on increased concerns about health and fitness. In addition, Revco began to close unprofitable stores, and sold off entire units like the Insta-Care Pharmacy Services Corp. Revco improved its cash flow by closing more than 100 unprofitable stores and selling off Odd Lot Trading.

In 1989 Revco again gained headlines as the Securities and Exchange Commission unraveled an insider-trading scheme stemming from the Revco buyout. Glenn Golenberg, a Cleveland investment banker who played a key role in the buyout, had tipped off several friends and associates about the impending deal. In May 1989 Golenberg was fined $470,000 for his role in the scandal. In 1990 the other seven men charged all reached civil settlements.

Revco continued to languish in Chapter 11, all the while attempting to devise means to become viable. In late 1989 Revco received a $925 million buyout offer from Texas industrialist Robert Bass, but Revco's management, fearing this plan would only heap more debt on the company, refused the offer.

In January 1990 Revco announced it would seek buyers for 712 of its 1,873 stores as part of a comprehensive reorganization plan. The cash raised from these sales would be used to cover debts and reimburse creditors. Over the year, in a process that reflected a mirror image of the means by which Revco had grown, Revco sold off huge chunks of its holdings. In June 1990 Revco sold 221 stores to Reliable Drug Stores, a Texas-based group. A few months later, Revco sold 146 stores to a Maryland company, the RDS Acquisition Corporation. Revco also unloaded 223 stores to the Jack Eckerd chain. In addition, groups of Revco stores in Alabama and Arkansas were sold to other holding groups, and 36 Revco stores in the south were closed. This succession of deals completed the 712-store divestiture program. In October 1990 Revco's creditors filed a reorganization plan, converting debt into common stock.

By 1991 Revco had slimmed down. The firm employed about 16,000 people, and operated 1,100 stores in 10 states, mostly in Ohio, Pennsylvania, New York, and a few southern states. Sales in the fiscal year ended June 30, 1990, had shrunk to $1.9 billion. In the early 1990s the company was still operating under Chapter 11. It could be years before Revco emerges from bankruptcy.

Further Reading: Chain Drug News, December 17, 1984.

—Daniel Gross

RITE AID CORPORATION

431 Railroad Avenue
Shiremanstown, Pennsylvania 17011
U.S.A.
(717) 761-2633

Public Company
Incorporated: 1968
Employees: 29,900
Sales: $3.45 billion
Stock Exchanges: New York Pacific Boston Midwest
Philadelphia

Rite Aid Corporation operates one of the largest retail drugstore chains in the United States. Its stores sell health and beauty aids, housewares, tobaccos, and sundries—a large portion of which are sold under the Rite Aid private label; most stores also sell proprietary and prescription drugs, which represent 45% of the stores' revenues. All of the company's merchandise is sold at a discount. Its stores average about 6,700 square feet in area. In the early 1990s with 2,436 Rite Aid stores in 22 eastern states and the District of Columbia, the company's drugstore operations accounted for roughly 95% of the company's sales. In addition to its retail drug operations, the company operates specialty retailing, including auto parts stores, book stores, dry cleaning outlets, and medical services.

Although Rite Aid was not formally incorporated until 1968, it got its start years earlier through Rack Rite Distributors, developed by Alex Grass, Rite Aid's founder and later chairman and chief executive officer, in 1958. Since then Rack Rite has been providing grocery stores with health and beauty aids, and other nonfood merchandise.

In 1962 U.S. federal legislation repealed the fair trade laws that fixed minimum retail prices on most products, opening up the door to discount stores, price wars, and vigorous competition. Quick to take advantage of the situation, in 1962 in Scranton, Pennsylvania, Rite Aid opened its first discount drugstore, calling it the Thrif D Discount Center, the forerunner of the modern Rite Aid drugstores.

By Christmas 1962 Thrif D was taking in $25,000 each week. It tripled its first-year projected sales of $250,000, pulling in $750,000. While the company continued to develop Rack Rite distributors, Thrif D's sales results proved that discount drugstores were truly profitable. In 1963 Rite Aid opened five more drugstores, extending its market area to New York.

By 1964 Rite Aid's market territory had grown to include New Jersey and Virginia. Its store count had doubled, bringing the total to 12. Its number of employees had climbed to 200. Its expansion did not stop there; in 1965, Rite Aid penetrated Connecticut and its store count rose to 25.

In 1966 Rite Aid continued to expand. Its number of stores reached 36. The growth of both the retail chain and the rack-jobbing portion of the business, Rack Rite Distributors, generated the need for more space, and Rite Aid began to construct a new corporate headquarters and distribution center. It also opened its first Rite Aid pharmacy in one of its drugstores in New Rochelle, New York. The following year Rite Aid introduced 70 of its own private-label products. The results of the Rite Aid pharmacy's first year were so positive that the company planned to continue installing pharmacies throughout its drugstore chain.

The following years were full of changes and firsts for the company. Rite Aid made its first acquisition when it bought the Philadelphia-centered 11-store Martin's chain. Its store count rose to 60, and its market share began to grow in Baltimore, Maryland; Newark, New Jersey; and Rochester and Buffalo, New York. Also, Rite Aid made its first public stock offering, issuing 350,000 shares at $25 per share, as well as formally changing its name to Rite Aid Corporation.

In 1969 Rite Aid acquired the 47-store Daw Drug Co. of Rochester, New York, bringing Rite Aid's store count to 117. The company also acquired Blue Ridge Nursing Homes along with Immuno Serums, Inc., and Sero-Genics, Inc., incorporating them into the company's medical services division. Acquisitions, however, were not the only vehicle with which Rite Aid grew in 1969. That year it was offering more than 260 of its own private label products. Rite Aid also increased its mechanical efficiency, installing material-handling equipment, such as conveyers, in its drug warehouse. It hooked up a telephone order transmission-system between the warehouse and drugstores, so that orders would move swiftly. In addition, Rite Aid installed electronic data processing equipment to produce price tags. That year expansion was so outwardly visible that Rite Aid declared a two-for-one stock split.

The next year, on January 20, 1970, Rite Aid was admitted to the New York Stock Exchange and began trading on the big board at $25 per share with 2.8 million shares outstanding. Although the U.S. economy began to spin into a recession, Rite Aid was among discount stores that flourished during this period. That year Rite Aid acquired the 16-store Fountain Chain in Clarksburg, Virginia. By that time the company offered more than 300 of its own products bearing the Rite Aid logo. Rite Aid added 100,000 square feet to its main distribution center in Shiremanstown, Pennsylvania. In November 1971, Rite Aid sold 250,000 new shares of common stock to the public.

In 1971 the company acquired Sera-Tec Biologicals, Inc., of New Jersey, which combined with the company's prior acquisition of Immuno Serums and Sero-Genics to make up Rite Aid's medical services division. It also purchased a 50% equity in Superdrug Stores Ltd., of the United Kingdom. The year 1971 was a period of rapid growth. Rite Aid pharmacies filled more than five million prescriptions that year alone. To consolidate management and increase efficiency of the rapidly growing number of stores, Rite Aid separated its market area into 5 divisions and 20 supervisory districts.

In 1972 Rite Aid focused on internal efficiency in preparation for additional expansion. Also in 1972, Sera-Tec Biologicals, Biogenics, Inc., and Immuno Blood Services, Inc., were merged to form what in the early 1990s was known as Sera-Tec. That year Hurricane Agnes wrought severe damage on the company's stores in Wilkes-Barre, Pennsylvania, and Elmira, New York, and it also damaged the corporate headquarters's phone and water service. Teams worked around the clock to make the necessary repairs, and stores were reopened fairly rapidly. Rite Aid handled the disaster so well that it filled more than 6.25 million prescriptions that year.

In 1973, through the Middle East oil embargo and ensuing recession, Rite Aid again began making acquisitions. It acquired the 49-store Thomas Holmes Corp. chain and the 50-store Warner chain, both in greater Philadelphia. The company also set about creating distribution centers that could handle the rapidly multiplying number of Rite Aid stores. It expanded its Shiremanstown distribution center by 71,000 square feet, enabling the facility to supply up to 500 stores. The company also built an automated distribution center in Rome, New York, to handle the growing northeastern market. Rite Aid's accounting and data processing departments moved to a separate building in Shiremanstown, Pennsylvania, that is now the hub of the Rite Aid complex. Rite Aid's actions that year did not end there, however. Rite Aid reduced its holdings in Superdrug PLC, the successor to Superdrug Stores, Ltd., to 42.5%, selling a 7.5% interest. The number of private label products that appeared bearing the Rite Aid logo climbed to 700. In addition, that year Rite Aid was one of the first drugstore chains in the United States to implement a senior citizen discount card-holder program.

In one year, by 1974, the Rome distribution center had begun supplying 131 Rite Aid stores. Rite Aid also created a fifth Sera-Tec center in Pittsburgh, just as the Dow Jones Industrial Average was falling to 663—the lowest since 1970—and the sparks of worldwide inflation began to ignite. Over the next year Rite Aid focused on internal organization and increased its security department in an effort to reduce shoplifting.

By 1976 Rite Aid was back on the acquisition track, purchasing the 52-store Keystone Centers, Inc., of Pennsylvania and New Jersey. The following year, it went on to acquire 99 more stores when it bought the Read's Inc. drug chain in Baltimore, paving the way for Rite Aid to garner Baltimore's largest market share. In 1977 Rite Aid's private label products, with almost 900 different items, accounted for 9% of its retail sales.

Although the value of the dollar plunged in 1978, Rite Aid's momentum did not. Rite Aid acquired 11 stores from Red Shield in Pittsburgh and the four-store Quality Drugs chain of greater Philadelphia. By focusing on providing value in the most efficient manner possible, Rite Aid gained substantial market share in the major metropolitan markets of Buffalo, Rochester, and Syracuse, New York; Charleston, South Carolina; Baltimore; and Philadelphia. It added 11,500 square feet to its executive space in Shiremanstown, and it bought a 79,000-square-foot building in Shiremanstown to house the growing finance, advertising, store engineering, and construction departments. Then, focusing its energy on its central businesses, Rite Aid sold the Blue Ridge Nursing Homes in Camp Hill and Harrisburg, Pennsylvania, for an after-tax profit of $1.8 million.

In 1979 Rite Aid acquired six U-Save stores in North Carolina and eastern Tennessee as well as nine Shop Rite stores in the Hudson Valley. It redesigned its company logo. It updated its store interiors, using mirrored canopies and bright colors throughout, streamlining checkout counters in the process. In order to save time and money on West Virginia store openings and transportation costs to 140 of its existing stores, Rite Aid started up a 210,000-square-foot distribution center in Nitro, West Virginia. The company set goals such as increasing store count by 10% every year, and continuing to open higher-margin pharmacies throughout its drugstore chain.

In 1980 Rite Aid adopted some new tactics in its growth plan. Its board of directors agreed tentatively to buy back as many as one million shares of Rite Aid common stock. These shares would be retained as treasury shares to provide liquid assets that could be quickly translated into cash for acquisitions, funds for the employees' stock option plan, or any other corporate purposes. That year Rite Aid acquired the six-store Schuman Drug of Landsdale, Pennsylvania, and the four-store Lane drugstores in Youngstown, Ohio, establishing a new prescription division for Ohio and western Pennsylvania. To expedite the processing of third-party claims, Rite Aid installed a scanning system in its data processing department. The company opened a 43,000-square foot addition to its finance and accounting building, and that year, Rite Aid became one of the nation's largest suppliers of plasma with the opening of its ninth plasmapheresis center.

By 1981 Rite Aid had become the third-largest retail drug chain. It acquired the 31-store South Carolina division of Fays Drug. It made its third stock split since its initial public offering in 1968, and issued additional common stock contingent on the four-for-three stock split. The company also set up a new division to handle its business in West Virginia and western Pennsylvania.

In 1982 Rite Aid became the largest U.S. drug chain as measured by the number of stores and market share in New York, Pennsylvania, New Jersey, Maryland, and West Virginia. Rite Aid continued to expand its market area west. It acquired the 4-store Cochran Drugs in Columbus, Ohio; the 16-store Lomark Discount Drug Stores Inc., in Cincinnati, Ohio; and the 26-store Mann Drugs of Highpoint, North Carolina. In addition to these drugstores, Rite Aid acquired the fifth-largest toy store in the nation, the 128-store Circus World Toy Stores, Inc. Rite Aid also expanded its Nitro, West Virginia, distribution center, bringing the company's total distribution capacity up to 1,200 stores, which was necessary as that year in Durham, North Carolina, Rite Aid opened its 1,000th store.

Rite Aid's sales exceeded $1 billion in 1983. It was listed among Forbes's top 500 companies in both sales volume and number of employees. It issued a three-for-two stock split, its fourth stock split since it became listed and its second in two years. The value of Rite Aid's holdings in Superdrug PLC increased when that company went public and began trading its shares on the London Stock Exchange, at which point Rite Aid sold one-third of its interest in Superdrug, bringing its holdings down to 28.2% of the company's outstanding shares. Partially because of this, Rite Aid was able to offer a new employee stock purchase plan as well as to acquire the four-store Beagle in West Virginia and Ohio, to open its first Heaven novelty shop, and to integrate a point-of-purchase and pharmacy computer system. All of this helped to establish Rite Aid as the largest drugstore chain in the Northeast.

By 1984 Rite Aid started seriously expanding beyond its core business. It bought American Discount Auto Parts (ADAP), a 32-store chain based in Avon, Massachusetts. It also purchased Encore Books, Inc., a 19-store deep discount bookstore chain in Philadelphia. In addition to these departures from the company's core business, Rite Aid acquired the 3-store Nifty Norm's, Inc., of Philadelphia, the 24-store Muir Drug, the 6-store Herrlich Drugstores, the 5-store Remes Drug Stores, the 13-store Lippert Pharmacies, 3 State Vitamin stores of Michigan, and the 3-store Jay's Drugstores in western New York. In 1984 Rite Aid also spun off its subsidiary wholesale and grocery division, Super Rite, as an autonomous public company, selling a partial interest in its holdings for $22 million.

In 1985 Rite Aid focused less on acquisitions than on internally generated growth. While Rite Aid that year acquired four Midland Valley Drug stores in Midland, Michigan, and eight State Vitamin discount stores in Lansing, Michigan, it opened five stores of its own, moving into the deep discount drug market with the company's Drug Palace. Rite Aid further penetrated new markets by opening video rental departments in more that 160 of its drugstores. It also installed point-of-purchase scanning registers and more computerized pharmacy equipment. The newly spun-off Super Rite took its first step into retail grocery with its purchase of the 47-store Food-A-Rama supermarket chain in Baltimore and Washington, D.C. Rite Aid's subsidiary, Sera-Tec, opened two new plasma centers, bringing the count to 11. That year, Rite Aid sold Circus World Toy Stores, Inc., for $35 million cash and 185,000 common shares. In addition to all this, Rite Aid bought 1.1 million shares of its own common stock at $19 per share.

The year 1986 was not a period of major expansion for Rite Aid. It acquired only two Revco stores in Buffalo and opened six more Drug Palaces, bringing Rite Aid's deep discount drugstore total to 11. Rite Aid also installed new computer systems to handle buying and accounting for ADAP. In 1986 two of Rite Aid's corporate officers received prestigious positions. Preston Robert Tisch of Rite Aid's board of directors was appointed Postmaster General of the United States, and company President Alex Grass was named chairman of the board and president of the National Association of Chain Drug Stores.

In 1987 Rite Aid acquired the 9-store Harris Drug in Charleston, South Carolina; 113 SuperRx stores in Florida, Georgia, and Alabama as well as a 200,00 square-foot distribution center in Florida from the Kroger Co.; and 94 Gray Drug Fair, Inc., stores in Florida and Maryland, from the Sherwin-Williams Company. These acquisitions substantially expanded Rite Aid's southern market area. Because of the success of their pilot video departments in 1986, in 1987 Rite Aid added 429 more video departments to its drugstores, bringing the total to 971. Rite Aid also continued to install pharmacy and point-of-purchase automated systems throughout the chain.

That year *Dun's Business Month* ranked Rite Aid 25th among all publicly traded companies for consistent dividend advances. In 1987 Rite Aid was the largest employer in the retail drug industry.

The following year, 1988, Rite Aid purchased from Sherwin-Williams the balance of Gray Drug Fair, consisting of 356 stores in Delaware, District of Columbia, Indiana, Maryland, New York, Ohio, Virginia, West Virginia, North Carolina, and Pennsylvania. This purchase brought Rite Aid's store count to more than 2,100 and greatly expanded the company's market penetration in these states. That year, in Winnsboro, South Carolina, Rite Aid opened its fifth distribution center. This 265,000 square-foot distribution center enabled Rite Aid to supply up to 450 more store in the Southeast. In April of 1988 Rite Aid acquired the Begley Company, consisting of 39 drugstores in Kentucky and 140 dry cleaners in 10 states.

In 1989 the company continued to expand and enhance the technology it provided to its stores. It took steps to increase pharmacy profitability, such as publicly coming out against decreasing third-party reimbursements and cancelling those third-party contracts that became unprofitable. Rite Aid finalized a deal with Super Rite Foods Holding Corporation in March of 1989 to sell its 46% interest in Super Rite Foods, Inc. Also in 1989, Rite Aid acquired 99 People's Drug Stores and 18 Lane Drug units. In September of 1989, it disposed of its 46.8% equity in Super Rite Foods for $18.37 million with a positive cash flow in excess of $40 million. That same year showed record sales for Rite Aid; its revenues of $2.87 billion for this 53-week fiscal year represented a 15.4% increase from the previous 52-week year. Company earnings, however, continued to absorb the cost of the enormous acquisitions the company made in 1987.

The company in 1990 continued to focus on the integration of both its past and present acquisitions. Rite Aid added 1,754 store computer systems, and it enhanced 2,279 pharmacy terminals. The pharmacy terminals enabled drug interaction analysis and cumulative tax information, all of which resulted in speedier prescription service. Prescription sales for 1990 advanced 17.8% from the previous year, and then represented a full 43% of store revenues. Rite Aid's computerization also propelled the company toward greater efficiency, enabling it to cut back on unnecessary corporate staffing in spite of the fact that the company's store count had continued to grow.

From 1987 to 1991, Rite Aid acquired more than 800 drugstores and opened 276 new stores, closing only 103 units. Within this period, Rite Aid's store count has grown by nearly 60%. It is likely that the 1990s will be profitable years for discount stores in general and more than likely for Rite Aid.

Principal Subsidiaries: Encore Books; Rack Rite Distributors, Inc.; Sera-Tec Biologicals, Inc.; ADAP, Inc.

Further Reading: Rite Aid Spectrum, June, 1987.

—Maya Sahafi

Sears plc

SEARS PLC

40 Duke Street
London W1A 2HP
United Kingdom
(071) 408 1180
Fax: (071) 408 1027

Public Company
Incorporated: 1912 as J. Sears & Company (True-Form Boot
   Company) Ltd.
Employees: 51,000
Sales: £2.16 billion (US$4.04 billion)
Stock Exchange: London

No chain of shops in Great Britain bears the name of Sears, but the company operates 3,800 shops under other names, making it one of the country's largest retailers. Its most famous single store is Selfridges in London, but its main strength is in nationwide chains of shops specializing in shoes and clothing. Its 2,000 shoe shops, operating mainly as Freeman Hardy Willis, Curtess, and Saxone, account for one in five pairs of shoes bought in Great Britain. Other chains owned by Sears include Miss Selfridge and Wallis in women's wear, Fosters and Horne Brothers in menswear, Adams Childrenswear in children's clothing, and Olympus Sport and Millet's Leisure in sporting goods. Through Freemans, Sears also owns the third-largest mail order business in Britain.

The reason for this multiplicity of business names lies in Sears's history. The company has no connection with Sears, Roebuck, as Americans might assume, but grew out of a shoe manufacturing and retailing business based in the English Midlands. For some 60 years this was its only business. Then, in 1953, the company was taken over by Charles Clore, one of the new breed of entrepreneurs who revolutionized British business in the 1950s and 1960s. He turned Sears into a conglomerate, adding to its footwear business a host of other interests ranging from ships to silverware; in two decades the company's profits increased 50-fold. Later, the mixture proved less successful, and Clore's successors have concentrated the company's resources on retailing.

The original shoe business was founded in Northampton by two brothers. In 1891 John Sears set up as a shoe and boot manufacturer, selling to other companies in the trade. Then he was joined by his brother William, who had some experience in retailing, and they began to sell directly to the public, opening their own shops and using the trade name of True-Form.

The business mushroomed: within 15 years of opening their first shop, the brothers had a chain of 80, all supplied by their own factory. In 1912 they turned the business into a limited company. John Sears died a few years later, but the business continued to thrive under William, and by the end of the 1920s it was one of the largest companies in the trade.

One of its main competitors was the Leicester-based company of Freeman Hardy & Willis, and in 1929 the two companies decided to merge. Freeman Hardy & Willis had four times as many shops as Sears but made only marginally more profit, which explains perhaps why Sears was the dominant force in the partnership. Together the two companies had more than 700 shops and several factories, and they formed the largest unit in the British footwear industry. The two retail chains continued to trade separately under their old names and by the 1950s had over 900 shops between them.

At this point the business attracted the attention of Charles Clore. He was then 48 and already a very successful entrepreneur, although hardly known to the public. His first big success had been as proprietor and manager of a London theater, which he had made highly profitable. During and after World War II Clore expanded in many directions, buying commercial property and shares in all kinds of companies. Usually he would find a way to increase the value of these assets, sell them at a good profit, and then reinvest the proceeds in his next project. By 1953 the fortune he had amassed in this way was such that, with the help of a bank loan, he was able to offer more than £4 million to acquire Sears.

The Sears directors strongly opposed the bid, but the majority of shareholders accepted Clore's offer, and control passed to him. It was highly unusual at that time for a board of directors to be ousted in this way, and the episode aroused much controversy. Indeed, it introduced the word "takeover" to Britain and made Clore a much feared figure in the financial world.

The reason Clore wanted Sears had more to do with shops than shoes. From his property dealing experience he could see that the company's shop sites were worth far more than its directors realized. He proceeded to prove this when he won control by selling many of the sites to an insurance company, leasing back the shops and using the capital raised—more than £4 million in the first year—to invest in other businesses.

From then onward Sears became the holding company for most of Clore's business interests other than property. His first move was to sell to Sears his controlling stake in two other companies, Furness Shipbuilding and Bentley Engineering. Both were important companies in their own fields. The Furness shipyard on the River Tees was one of the largest in Great Britain, with berths for eight ships, while Bentley was the country's leading producer of hosiery knitting machinery, based at Leicester and selling its goods worldwide. The acquisition of these companies immediately trebled Sears's profits, and footwear became just one of three main subsidiaries. To reflect this change, the company was renamed Sears Holdings Ltd. in 1955. Over the next few years Clore acquired more companies in the footwear and engineering fields, and took Sears into another business, motor sales and servicing. However strange the mixture, it brought rapid growth in profits, and by 1959 Clore was in a position to mount a £20 million bid for one of the major brewery groups, Watney Mann. Had this bid succeeded, Sears might have developed along quite different lines, but Clore was rebuffed.

Meanwhile, the shoe business had become the fastest growing area of Sears's existing divisions. Within a year of taking over Sears, Clore had acquired two small shoe companies that added some 80 shops to his collection. Then, in 1956, he took over two much larger companies of the same kind. The first was Manfield, another Northampton firm, with some 200 shops and a history going back to 1844. The second was Dolcis, a more recently created chain with 250 shops. These purchases increased Sears's total of shops to nearly 1,500 and gave the company almost a quarter of the retail footwear market in Great Britain. Clore then integrated all the group's shoe companies into one, British Shoe Corporation (BSC). A huge new warehouse was built at Leicester to service all its outlets, the factories were rationalized, and large cost savings began to swell BSC's profits.

The success of this operation, in contrast to growing problems in shipbuilding, led Clore to invest increasingly in retailing. In the same year that he failed to win Watney Mann, he gained a new retail arm in Mappin & Webb, a jewelry and silverware business. Three years later he made a major addition to BSC by buying its largest remaining competitor, Saxone Lilley & Skinner. This was a recent union of two formerly independent businesses and had around 500 shops, taking BSC's total of 2,000 and its share of retail sales to almost one-third of the British market.

In 1965 Sears made its largest single acquisition, the Lewis's department store group. It included Selfridges and 10 other department stores in provincial cities, and cost Sears £63 million. Its recent profits had been poor and Clore lost no time in remedying this. Stores were modernized and in some cases enlarged, and buying was centralized. Another very successful innovation was the launch of Miss Selfridge. This began as a young women's fashion department in the main store, but the concept proved so popular that it was soon extended to the other stores and eventually became an independent chain of shops.

The takeover of Lewis's put Sears Holdings for a time among the top 30 industrial companies in Great Britain, and increased its workforce to 65,000 people. From this point onward it was predominantly a retailing business, but for another 20 years it had many other interests which, on the whole, were less successful.

The first to crumble was the engineering subsidiary, which had come to include shipbuilding. Furness Shipbuilding ceased to be profitable from about 1960, and ran into heavy losses over the next few years. Clore tried to reverse its decline by modernizing the yard at great expense, but to no avail, and in 1968 he decided to cut his losses and sell it. The Bentley textile machinery business continued to do well throughout the 1960s, but eventually demand for its products tailed off, and from 1974 onward Sears's engineering division produced more losses than profits. Clore was reluctant to let it go, but his successors disposed of it in the early 1980s.

Another diversification that had patchy results was Sears's attempt to build a small conglomerate in the United States. This began in 1964 with the purchase of a laundry and linen hire business called Consolidated Laundries. This company, renamed Sears Industries Inc., then bought a knitwear manufacturing business which faired poorly, and a retail jewelry chain which was never a great success. In 1981, more hope-

fully, Sears acquired a 500-branch chain of shoe shops, Butler Shoe Corporation, but this also brought more problems than profits and was sold in 1988.

Footwear manufacturing was another field in which Sears was forced to retreat. In the 1950s the company's own factories supplied roughly half the shoes sold in its shops, but with the coming of cheaper products from countries with lower labor costs, this proportion diminished to around 20% in the 1970s. Sears reduced its output by stages until in 1988 the last of its factories was sold. The company's share of the retail market was also eroded by new competition in the mid-1970s.

Against these setbacks Clore could claim some successful new ventures, even in his last years at Sears. The most important of these were betting and property. In 1971 Sears took over the William Hill chain of betting shops and although profits were somewhat erratic, it contributed as much as 10% of Sears's profits in its better years. Sears's involvement in property development began in 1975 with the purchase of a company called Galliford Estates. It specialized in house building in Great Britain, but also had a stake in some commercial developments in the Netherlands, and became the nucleus of what is still a thriving property development unit within Sears.

Charles Clore—by then Sir Charles—retired from the chairmanship of Sears in 1976, and died three years later. He was succeeded by Leonard Sainer, the lawyer who had been his closest colleague for 40 years. Under Sainer, a gradual rationalization of the group began. A number of troublesome subsidiaries were sold, and acquisitions were mainly concentrated in retailing, the area in which the company had always been most successful. Under Geoffrey Maitland Smith, who succeeded Sainer in May 1985, this rationalization was taken much further, to the point where the company's interests are now confined to retailing and property development. The parent company became Sears plc in 1985.

The positive side of this process was the acquisition of new retail businesses with good growth prospects. An early find was Olympus Sportswear, which had about two dozen outlets when Sears bought it in 1978 but has since been expanded into the leading chain of its kind in Great Britain. In 1980 the Wallis fashion group was acquired. In 1985 came Foster Brothers Clothing, with over 700 shops selling menswear, children's clothing—Adams—and outdoor pursuits gear—Millet's. Then, in 1987, Sears added further to its menswear business by buying the more upmarket chain of Horne Brothers.

Besides acquiring and developing these new outlets in the United Kingdom, Sears has made two more far-reaching changes in its retailing strategy. First, it has expanded into continental Europe on a large scale. This development began in the late 1970s with the acquisition of a chain of shoe shops in the Netherlands, and the company subsequently developed large retail interests—some jointly owned with Groupe André of France—in the Netherlands, Germany, and Spain. Second, the purchase of Freemans in 1988, Sears's largest acquisition of the late 1980s, has given the company a major share of the mail-order market in Great Britain, an important sector of retailing in which it was not previously represented. With these developments, Sears has transformed itself from a largely illogical collection of businesses into a wide-ranging but integrated retailing group.

Principal Subsidiaries: Adams Childrenswear Ltd.; British Shoe Corporation Holdings plc; Freemans plc; Galliford Estates Ltd.; Hoogenbosch Beheer B.V. (Netherlands); Millets Leisure Ltd.; Miss Erika Inc. (U.S.A.); Miss Selfridge Ltd.; Olympus Sport International Ltd.; Sears Financial Services Ltd.; Sears Menswear plc; Sears Property Investments Ltd.; Selfridges Ltd.; Wallis Fashion Group Ltd.; The Warehouse Group plc.

Further Reading: Clutterbuck, David, and Marion Devine, *Clore: The Man and His Millions*, London, Weidenfeld & Nicolson, 1987.

—John Swan

SEARS, ROEBUCK AND CO.

Sears Tower
Chicago, Illinois 60684
U.S.A.
(312) 875-2500

Public Company
Incorporated: 1906
Employees: 460,000
Sales: $55.97 billion
Stock Exchanges: New York Midwest Pacific London Basel
   Geneva Lausanne Zürich Amsterdam Tokyo Paris Frankfurt

Sears, Roebuck and Co. is one of the few U.S. corporations whose name is virtually synonymous with an entire business: retail. Sears sells insurance, residential real estate, and financial services through its Allstate, Coldwell Banker, and Dean Witter subsidiaries, respectively, but retailing has always been the source of its fame. For decades, Sears has prided itself on being the U.S. middle class's primary general goods merchant, the place where average people could get everything from clothes to auto supplies, sporting goods to refrigerators, at an affordable price.

Sears bears the name of Richard W. Sears, who was working as the North Redwood, Minnesota, freight agent for the Minneapolis and St. Louis Railroad in 1886 when a local jeweler gave him an unwanted shipment of pocket watches rather than return them to the manufacturer. Sears sold them to agents down the line, who resold them at the retail level. He ordered and sold more watches, and within six months, he had made $5,000. He quit the railroad and founded the R.W. Sears Watch Company in Minneapolis.

Sears's business expanded so quickly that he moved to Chicago in 1887 to locate himself in a more convenient communications and shipping center. Soon customers began to bring in watches for repairs. Since he knew nothing about fixing them, Sears hired Alvah Roebuck, a watch repairman from Indiana, in 1887. A shrewd and aggressive salesman—a colleague once said of him, "He could probably sell a breath of air"—Sears undersold his competition by buying up discontinued lines from manufacturers and passing on his discounts to customers. At various times from 1888 to 1891, thinking himself bored with the business, he sold out to Roebuck, but came back each time.

In 1888 Sears published the first of its famous mail-order catalogs. It was 80 pages long and advertised watches and jew-

elery. Thanks to Richard Sears's restless search for new merchandise, within two years the catalog had grown to 322 pages, selling clothes, jewelry, and durable goods like sewing machines, bicycles, and even keyboard instruments. In 1894 the catalog cover proclaimed that Sears was the "Cheapest Supply House on Earth."

The company changed its name to its current form in 1893, but Alvah Roebuck, uncomfortable with Sears's financial gambles, sold out his share two years later and remained with the firm as a repairman. Sears promptly found two partners to replace him: local entrepreneur Aaron Nusbaum and Nusbaum's brother-in-law, haberdasher Julius Rosenwald. The company recapitalized at $150,000, with each man taking a one-third share. It continued to prosper, so much so that when the cantankerous Nusbaum was forced to sell out in 1901 after clashing with Sears, his interest was worth $1.25 million.

There was little harmony between the two remaining partners, however. Sears believed in continuous expansion and risk-taking, while Rosenwald advocated consolidation and caution. He also objected to Sears's fondness for the hard sell in his catalog and advertising copy. Had the Federal Trade Commission existed then, some of Sears's advertising practices would probably not have passed muster, and Rosenwald preferred a reputation of trustworthiness; it should be said in Sears's defense, though, that he invented the unconditional money-back guarantee and stood by it.

In 1905 construction began on a new headquarters plant on Chicago's west side that would consolidate all of the company's functions. To help raise the necessary capital, Sears went public in 1906. Wall Street was leery of the incautious Richard Sears, however, and he resigned as president in 1908 when it became clear that he was obstructing the company's way in the capital markets. He was appointed chairman, but his heart was never in that job. He retired in 1913 without ever having presided over a board meeting and died the following year at the age of 50. Near the end of his life, he summarized his career as a merchant thus: "Honesty is the best policy. I know, I've tried it both ways."

Sears was now Julius Rosenwald's company to run, and he did it with such skill and success as to make himself one of the richest men in the world. Sales rose sixfold between 1908 and 1920, and in 1911 Sears began offering credit to its customers at a time when banks would not even consider lending to consumers. During this time the company grew to the point where its network of suppliers, combined with its own financing and distribution operations, constituted a full-fledged economic system in itself. Rosenwald's personal fortune allowed him to become a noted philanthropist; he gave away $63 million over the course of his life, much of it to Jewish causes and to improve the education of southern blacks. As a result of the latter, he became a trustee of the Tuskegee Institute and a good friend of its founder, Booker T. Washington.

The depression of the early 1920s dealt Sears a sharp blow. In 1921 the company posted a loss of $16.4 million and omitted its quarterly dividend for the first time. Rosenwald responded by slashing executive salaries and even eliminated his own. He also was persuaded to donate 50,000 shares from his personal holdings to the company treasury to reduce outstanding capital stock and restore Sears's standing with its creditors. Sears thus weathered the crisis and benefited from the general prosperity that followed.

Rosenwald retired as president in 1924, retaining the chairmanship he had inherited from Richard Sears. He was succeeded by Charles Kittle, a former Illinois Central Railroad executive. In 1925 Sears began to take on its current shape when it opened its first retail outlet in Chicago. Seven more new stores followed that year, and by the end of the decade 324 outlets were in operation. Retailing would become so successful for Sears so quickly that by 1931, the stores would top the catalog in sales.

Sears's entry into retailing was the brainchild of vice president Robert Wood, who was an executive at archrival Montgomery Ward before Rosenwald hired him in 1924. Wood would always be known as "the General" for having been the U.S. Army's Quartermaster General during World War I. He had also been chief quartermaster for the construction of the Panama Canal. He much preferred business to the military, however, and his long career in merchandising would earn him a reputation for genius. For its first 40 years, Sears had targeted the U.S. farmer as its main customer, luring him with a combination of down–home earthiness and the tantalizing prospect of material luxury. Two postal service innovations—the rural free delivery system in 1891 and the parcel post rate in 1913—helped target this consumer by making it affordable to reach remote locations by mail; Sears quickly became parcel post's largest single customer. Then Wood saw that the automobile would soon make urban centers more accessible to outlying areas, broadening the customer base for retail outlets. Thwarted by conservative top management at Ward's, he wasted no time in implementing his vision at Sears. At first, the stores simply absorbed surpluses from the catalog, but they soon began to offer a full range of goods. Sears also became the first chain to put free parking lots next to their stores. More than anyone else, it was Robert Wood who turned Sears into a leviathan.

Charles Kittle died suddenly in 1928, and Wood succeeded him. In 1929 Sears arranged a merger between two of its suppliers, Upton Machine and Nineteen Hundred Washer Company, to form Nineteen Hundred Corporation, which would change its name to Whirlpool in 1950. Somewhat against its intentions, Sears was becoming increasingly involved in the affairs of its suppliers, many of which were small companies whose outputs were almost entirely geared to its needs. Another leadership change occurred in 1932, when Julius Rosenwald died at the age of 69 and was succeeded as chairman by his son Lessing.

The onset of the Great Depression hurt sales badly from 1930 to 1934, but thanks to cost-cutting measures, Sears posted a loss only in 1932. The company, in fact, diversified in 1931 when it created its Allstate subsidiary to sell auto insurance. Wood saw it as another way to capitalize on the growing popularity of the automobile. He installed as general manager insurance agent Carl Odell, an acquaintance who had suggested the idea as they commuted to work one day.

Lessing Rosenwald retired in 1939. Preoccupied with running his father's estate, he never attended a board meeting. Wood succeeded him, and the power of chief executive passed from the presidency to the chairmanship. At about this time, however, Wood also became controversial because of his prominent support for America First, an isolationist organization that was the vehicle through which Charles Lindbergh made his notorious anti-Semitic speeches. Wood dropped his

backing once the United States entered World War II and publicly supported the war effort, but remained a strong critic in private ever after.

As war loomed, Sears benefited from increases in military spending and a consumer buying panic. In 1941 sales reached an all-time high of $975 million, a 30% increase over the previous year. Sales then leveled off, however, and raw material shortages made durable goods hard to come by. Even as late as 1946, it had to refund $250 million in orders that could not be filled. Military procurement helped make up for the shortfall. During the war, Sears supplied the armed forces with just about everything that did not need gunpowder to make it work, and even a few things that did; some factories belonging to Sears suppliers were converted into munitions plants by the War Department. Sears also began its first foreign ventures during and immediately after the war. In 1942 it opened a store in Havana, nationalized by the Castro government in 1960, and in 1947 it opened stores in Mexico.

Once the war ended, Sears flourished. Sales edged up to $1 billion in 1945, and doubled the next year. Anticipating an economic boom, Wood launched the company on an aggressive expansion program. Concentrating on the Sun Belt states, in which the most population growth would occur, he located many of the new stores in the path of suburban expansion before the areas built up. One store in California was built on a dairy farm and had cows roaming around the parking lot when it opened. Thanks to the General's prescience, Sears left its rivals in its wake. In 1946 it held a small sales advantage over Montgomery Ward, but in 1954 it posted sales of $3 billion while Ward, which had been slower to anticipate postwar trends, could muster only $1 billion. Sears also became a symbol of U.S. prosperity. In the late 1940s, the Associated Press's Moscow bureau chief reported that the most effective piece of foreign propaganda in the Soviet Union was the Sears catalog.

At the same time, Sears was becoming a widely hailed living experiment in corporate management. Wood had long had it in mind to decentralize the company, and its postwar success gave him the luxury to remold it in his image of "corporate democracy." The merchandising operations were carved up into five regional "territories," with each given a high degree of autonomy. Although buying operations remained centralized in theory, in fact buyers were allowed substantial independence. To its employees, many of them returned veterans—the company hired 50,000 people between 1946 and 1949 alone— Sears became, as author Donald Katz put it in *The Big Store,* "a place where country boys and infantrymen could speak their minds and still roam free."

During the early 1950s, Sears began to stock more clothing as durable goods sales slackened. The new postwar suburbanites who had bought their first homes had already filled them with all the Sears appliances they needed. At about this time, the company also strengthened its ties with its suppliers even further. Between 1951 and 1960, it acquired virtually complete control of Warwick Electronics, which made Sears televisions, radios, phonographs, and tape players. In 1961 it effected a merger between 15 of its soft goods suppliers and created Kellwood Company.

Robert Wood retired in 1954 at the age of 75, but retained power over appointment of his successors until shortly before his death in 1969. A series of caretaker chairmen followed him, all of whom were favorites of his. None of them served more than six years. The first was Theodore Houser, who retired in 1958 and was succeeded by Fowler McConnell. McConnell was followed in 1960 by Charles Kellstadt, who served for two years and after whom the Kellwood Company was named. Austin Cushman succeeded Kellstadt and served until 1967.

In 1963 the company posted sales of $5.1 billion, and an executive with the discount chain Korvette quipped that Sears was not only the number-one retailer in the United States, but also numbers two, three, four, and five. Surveys showed that one in five U.S. consumers shopped at Sears regularly; its sales volume was greater than that of some entire industries. The company had become big enough to justify its own shopping center development subsidiary, Homart Development, which it had formed in 1960.

In 1967 Sears posted $1 billion in monthly sales for the first time. Gordon Metcalf succeeded Cushman as chairman that year. In 1970 Allstate Enterprises, a subsidiary that had been formed in 1960, acquired Metropolitan Savings and Loan Association, the first of several savings and loans it would purchase over the next two decades. Also in 1970, construction began in Chicago on the 110-story Sears Tower. Completed in 1974, the Sears Tower is the tallest building in the world and a symbol of corporate pride at a time when Sears's dominance of U.S. retailing was unchallenged.

That era was fading, however, even as its monument rose above the Chicago skyline. Arthur Wood (no relation to Robert Wood) succeeded Metcalf in 1973, and he would be the last of the General's proteges to serve as chairman. Recession caused by skyrocketing oil prices led to a $170 million drop in profits in 1974 on only a modest sales increase, and financial performance remained flat through the middle of the decade. It became apparent to Wood and others that success had made Sears complacent and that it was ignoring some real problems.

The competition was getting serious. The specialty shops that filled the very malls anchored by Sears stores were cutting into market share, as were discounters like the resurgent S. S. Kresge Co., which changed its name to K mart Corporation in 1977. Robert Wood's vaunted corporate democracy had turned into an ungainly feudal state. The buyers, given complete freedom, operated an internal economy of their own. Terrible inefficiencies and intramural rivalries resulted. Yet this system had become enshrined as the Sears way, and those who had flocked to the General's banner believed in it. Decentralization peaked under Gordon Metcalf; he was known to consult with his territorial chiefs on problems, then leave the solution to them, saying, "You boys just work it out."

Hard times meant that these shortcomings could no longer be obscured by success or justified in the name of tradition. Sears had to be shaken up, and it fell to Edward Telling, a company veteran who succeeded Arthur Wood in 1978, to do it. As head of the eastern territory, Telling had smashed local concentrations of power in the name of efficiency, and he proceeded to do the same for the parent company, centralizing all buying and merchandising operations. The territorial bureaucracies were slowly eliminated.

The General's ghost took a while to exorcise. Income declined from 1978 to 1980 and was subjected to intense scrutiny by Wall Street. Outsiders were not always impressed by Telling, a downstate Illinois native whose homespun manner

tended to conceal—often by choice—his erudition and keen intellect. It was through his guidance that Sears undertook a major corporate reorganization in 1981. This involved the formation of an overall holding company for its three business groups; the buying and merchandising operations; Allstate; and Seraco Group, which included Homart and other commercial real estate and residential real estate finance units.

Telling also saw the burgeoning financial services industry as one in which Sears should get involved. In 1981 Sears acquired Los Angeles–based Coldwell Banker Company, the nation's largest real estate brokerage, and securities firm Dean Witter Reynolds Inc. When he retired at the end of 1985, Telling left Sears a radically different company from the one he had inherited. He had reined in Sears's sprawling bureaucracy and taken the first steps toward complementing the company's store with a diversified financial services company with the size and capital to take on the industry's leaders.

He was succeeded by Edward Brennan, who, as chairman of the Merchandise Group under Telling, liked to preach that Sears was "one big store" and had labored tirelessly to centralize merchandising operations. In 1985 Sears unveiled its Discover Card, a combined credit and financial services card that would also offer savings accounts through Greenwood Trust Company, a bank that Allstate Enterprises, Inc., a Sears subsidiary, had acquired earlier that year. In 1987, perhaps conceding that the era of the big general merchant was over, the Merchandise Group launched a new strategy to turn Sears into a collection of specialty superstores. Sears acquired Eye Care Centers of America, and added Pinstripes Petites and Western Auto Supply the next year.

The company's financial performance was disappointing. Dean Witter and Coldwell Banker failed to show immediate benefits from their relationship with Sears. As Sears's stock price lagged, takeover rumors circulated and the company pondered ways to increase shareholder value and stave off any possible attempt. In October 1988 Sears announced that it would sell Coldwell Banker's commercial real estate unit, buy back 10% of its own stock, and put the Sears Tower up for sale. Brennan, who had become company chairman in 1986, also announced a new, everyday low prices retail strategy that would reduce the number of sales and promotions, slashing everyday prices across the board instead.

These new moves, however, provided unsatisfactory solutions. The Sears Tower went on the block during a commercial real estate glut in downtown Chicago and no buyer could be found. Everyday low prices squeezed profit margins because of the company's still-bloated cost structure. Merchandise Group profits fell from more than $700 million in 1986 to $257 million in 1990. That year, the resurgent financial services divisions contributed the bulk of earnings, with Dean Witter posting its best year ever. In July 1990 Brennan added his old job as Merchandise Group chairman to his responsibilities. By the first quarter of 1991, however, layoffs and other cost-cutting measures had begun to take hold. Sears posted a $202.7 million profit, which included improved earnings for the Merchandise Group despite sluggish sales.

Whether or not Sears could sustain financial improvement through growing sales remained to be seen in the early 1990s. Brennan, representing the third generation of his family to work for Sears, was under considerable pressure from investors and the financial press to turn the company around and increase outsider representation on the board of directors. It is also true that the outcry over Sears's decline had been so sharp only because Sears started from such a great height. For decades, Sears has carved out its place in U.S. life. In the mid-1980s it was estimated that one in 30 living Americans had worked for the company in some way at some time. It had made many of those members of the U.S. work force comfortable retirees through its profit-sharing plan. It was their return for their service and belief in a cause that the company had embodied since the days of Richard Sears: the material prosperity of working people.

Principal Subsidiaries: Sears Roebuck Acceptance Corp.; Sears Overseas Finance N.V. (Netherlands Antilles); Allstate Insurance Company; Sears Consumer Financial Corporation; Coldwell, Banker & Company; Coldwell Banker Real Estate Group, Inc.; Dean Witter Financial Services Group Inc.; Sears Consumer Financial Corporation; Sears Canada Inc.

Further Reading: "Sears's War," *Fortune,* September, 1942; McDonald, John, "Sears Makes It Look Easy," *Fortune,* May, 1964; Emmet, Boris, and John E. Jeuck, *Catalogues & Counters: A History of Sears, Roebuck & Company,* Chicago, University of Chicago Press, 1965; Weil, Gordon L., *Sears, Roebuck, U.S.A.,* New York, Stein and Day, 1977; Loomis, Carol J., "The Leaning Tower of Sears," *Fortune,* July 2, 1979; Katz, Donald R., *The Big Store,* New York, Viking, 1987; Oneal, Michael, "Sears Faces a Tall Task," *Business Week,* November 14, 1988; Bremner, Brian, and Michael Oneal, "The Big Store's Big Trauma," *Business Week,* July 10, 1989; Siler, Julia Flynn, Laura Zinn, and John Finotti, "Are the Lights Dimming for Ed Brennan?" *Business Week,* February 11, 1991.

—Douglas Sun

SEIBU DEPARTMENT STORES, LTD.

1-28-1 Minami-Ikebukuro
Toshima-ku
Tokyo 170
Japan
(03) 3981 0111

Private Company
Incorporated: 1940 as Musashino Department Store
Employees: 20,000
Sales: ¥985.39 billion (US$7.89 billion)

Seibu Department Stores, Ltd., the parent company of Seibu Department Stores Group, operates retail businesses such as department stores, specialty stores, shopping centers, and direct marketing, as well as sports clubs and merchandise development. Seibu Department Stores, Ltd., is also one of the major companies which form the Saison Group. The Saison Group participates in various areas from retail and wholesale to financial, real estate, hotel and leisure, food and information services, and manufacturing. The group also includes several research institutes, covering areas such as the retail industry, consumer goods, biotechnology, and agrobiology.

In fiscal year 1990, Seibu Department Stores contributed 25% of the sales of the Saison Group. The sales of Seibu Department Stores Group, comprising 49 companies, reached about ¥1.4 trillion, 35% of the Saison Group's sales.

Seibu Department Stores, Ltd., has 33 stores throughout Japan, including the Ikebukuro store in Tokyo, one of the biggest department stores in Japan, with a selling space of 65,647 square meters. In 1990 the company also opened a department store in Hong Kong.

The founder of Seibu Department Stores is Yasujiro Tsutsumi, father of the group's former chairman, Seiji Tsutsumi. Yasujiro was not only an entrepreneur but also a member of the House of Representatives. He achieved success in residential development and the leisure industry between 1920 and 1950. Yasujiro Tsutsumi also launched a private railway business.

In 1935 a small-scale department store, Kikuya Department Store, was opened near Ikebukuro Station, the terminal of a private railway in Tokyo. In 1940 Yasujiro Tsutsumi bought the Kikuya Department Store and changed its name to Musashino Department Store, thereby establishing the department store business. Ikebukuro is now one of Tokyo's large shopping districts. When Musashino Department Store was founded, Ikebukuro was a small town undergoing development. Soon afterward, Japan became involved in World War II. Under the controlled wartime economy, the department store was almost forced to stop doing business, and the store building was destroyed in an air raid. After the war, however, business was resumed in a temporary shelter.

During Japan's postwar rehabilitation, Yasujiro Tsutsumi expanded the business and reopened the department store, under the name of Seibu Department Store, in a two-story building with a selling area of about 1,500 square meters. It sold daily necessities such as food, clothes, and sundry goods. Seibu Department Store expanded, taking advantage of Japan's strong economic growth.

Between the 1950s and 1970s, people in Tokyo and other large Japanese cities increasingly moved to the suburbs. The population in the areas along the railway line from Ikebukuro increased rapidly. Seibu Department Store's profits grew steadily in conjunction with this shift in population. Seiji Tsutsumi began to work for Seibu Department Store in 1954. In 1956 Seibu Department Store extended its selling space for the fourth time, to 43,000 square meters, and ranked top in business performance among department stores based near railway terminals in the Ikebukuro district.

Between the late 1950s and early 1960s, the company opened four small-scale stores and expanded the range of merchandise, introduced credit sales, formed customer clubs, and installed information systems. It also diversified into car sales, petroleum and liquid petroleum gas sales, and helicopter services, and launched leisure and real estate businesses. The car sales, helicopter, and real estate businesses were later separated from the department store operations to become one of the Saison Group's core company groups. This attempt became the base for further diversification, and paved the way to a mass market business with a wide range of activities.

In 1967 a department store of about 10,000 square meters was opened in Funabashi in the suburbs of Tokyo. In 1968 a store of about 24,000 square meters was opened in Shibuya, another large shopping area of Tokyo. For the next few years until the early 1970s, Seibu Department Stores endeavored to open more stores in Tokyo's satellite cities and towns, and in the Tokai district. The Ikebukuro store continues to occupy an important strategic position as the flagship store.

In 1971 Seibu Department Stores Kansai Co., Ltd., was founded as a stepping-stone for expansion into the Kansai district, another important Japanese economic center. In the same year, a shopping complex called PARCO was opened in Shinsaibashi, Osaka. The company planned to construct a large-scale department store in Takatsuki, Osaka Prefecture and in Otsu, Shiga Prefecture. These stores were opened in 1974 and 1976 respectively. Between the 1960s and the early 1970s new stores were opened consecutively; Itohan and Darumaya in the Hokuriku district, Matsukiya and Honkin in the Tohoku district, Tabata Department Store in Chiba Prefecture, and Toden Kaikan in the Shikoku district, while other local department stores became affiliates of Seibu Department Stores; all except Matsukiya were bought by Seibu Department Stores.

After the oil crisis in the autumn of 1973, the Japanese economy's rate of growth slowed. In the late 1970s, consumer consumption decreased and many retailers were faced with stagnant sales. The business results of department stores were poor. In response, Seibu Department Stores adopted an aggressive store improvement strategy.

In 1974 Seibu Takatsuki Shopping Center, with a selling area of about 58,000 square meters, was opened in Takatsukishi, Osaka Prefecture. The center was scheduled to open in 1973, but shortly before opening a fire broke out, postponing the opening for about one year.

In 1975 the Ikebukuro store was extended and refurbished for the ninth time, and reappeared as a sophisticated department store, offering a wide range of products. The interior of the store and its advertisement campaign reflected its new sophistication. A museum and a park were constructed within the store, which was intended to be seen as a cultural and social center rather than an ordinary retail store. This innovative concept was later adopted as other stores were remodeled.

PARCO, at that time a subsidiary of Seibu Department Stores, accelerated the trend of developing retail stores as social and cultural centers. PARCO was formerly the Marubutsu Department Store, which, located in Ikebukuro, was on the verge of bankruptcy. Seibu Department Stores bought out Marubutsu in 1969 and reconstructed it as an urban shopping center. In 1969, PARCO Co., Ltd., was established. In 1973 Shibuya PARCO was opened. Five PARCOs have opened in the Hokkaido, Chiba, and Oita prefectures since 1975. In 1976 Seibu Otsu Shopping Center, with a selling area of about 40,000 square meters, was opened.

In the early 1980s consumption slackened and retail sales were low. In addition, the restrictions of the Large Store Law of 1974 were enforced to prohibit large retailers from opening stores and to protect small retailers.

At this time, Seibu Department Stores developed the second multistore project (the first had occurred in the 1970s), remodeled the existing stores, including those at Ikebukuro and Shibuya, and promoted businesses other than department stores. As a result, Seibu Department Stores ranked top in sales in the Japanese department store industry in 1987.

As part of the multistore project of the 1980s, five department stores opened: Yurakucho Seibu (1984); Tsukuba Store and Tsukashin Store (1985); Tokorozawa Seibu (1986); and Kawasaki Seibu (1988). These stores were innovative in terms of merchandising, layout, and interior design.

Yurakucho Seibu is located in an area adjacent to the Ginza, Tokyo's most popular downtown area. It was constructed on the former site of the Asahi Shimbun newspaper offices and the Nippon Theater. Yurakucho Seibu and Hankyu Department Store completed a twin tower, of which they are cotenants. Yurakucho Seibu is an up-to-date store providing modern commodities and services, and acts as a showcase for the merchandise and services of the entire Saison Group. Yurakucho Seibu has advanced beyond the conception of conventional department stores.

The Tsukuba store is located in the center of the Tsukuba Academic City and incorporates advanced distribution information technology. For this reason the store attracted considerable publicity in the new high-technology city as an experimental store.

The Tsukashin store is a town-like shopping center which was developed with the support of the entire Saison Group, including Seibu Department Stores. The store was constructed as part of a redevelopment project on the grounds of a spinning factory. In an area of about 66,000 square meters, a mall of

specialty shops, an eating and drinking zone including various restaurants and bars, a multipurpose hall, and sporting facilities were constructed, in addition to a department store with a selling area of about 30,000 square meters. Moreover, a park, a river, a sports center, and even a church were added. This big urban development project took 12 years to complete, and greatly contributed to the efforts of Seibu Department Stores and the Saison Group to penetrate the Kansai market.

The Tokorozawa Seibu, located in the residential area of a satellite town along a railway line from Ikebukuro, is a suburban-type large-scale department store of about 23,000 square meters. Kawasaki Seibu, covering about 22,000 square meters, is located in Kawasaki, a town next to Tokyo which is changing from an industrial to a more culturally-oriented city. Thus Kawasaki Seibu has tried to offer not only merchandise but also various services and information, including financial information and information on leisure activities.

While department stores were being created along these new lines, large-scale specialty stores were also established, such as WAVE, offering audio-visual goods; THE PRIME, a restaurant complex; SEED, accommodating fashion boutiques; and LOFT, carrying miscellaneous modern goods.

Several other businesses were actively promoted and are still being developed, including marketing to corporations, import/export and other trading activities; direct marketing; new media; fitness; and wholesale, handling mainly Japanese and well-known foreign fashion goods brands such as Hermès, Ralph Lauren, Yves Saint Laurent, and Benetton.

In 1989 Seibu Department Stores Co., Ltd., and Seibu Department Stores Kansai Co., Ltd., which had been separate companies, were merged to form Seibu Department Stores, Ltd. This enterprise ranks fifth among Japanese retail companies, following Daiei, Ito-Yokado, Seiyu, and Jusco.

The Seibu Department Stores Group consists of 11 department store companies and 38 miscellaneous companies. The 11 department store companies are: The Seibu Department Stores, Ltd., Yurakucho Seibu Co., Ltd., Kawasaki Seibu Department Store Co., Ltd., Seibu Hokuriku, Co., Ltd., Seibu Hokkaido, Ltd., Daikokuya, Ltd., Matsukiya, Ltd., Honkin Seibu, Ltd., Seibu Chu-Shikoku, Ltd., Hong Kong Seibu Enterprise Co., Ltd., and Seibu Tohuku, Ltd. The 38 companies include a shopping center, Ikebukuro Shopping Park Co., Ltd.; companies that import and sell foreign goods, Hermès Japon Co., Ltd., Yves Saint-Laurent-Seibu S.A., and Ellebis, Ltd.; and a direct marketing company, Saison Direct Marketing Co., Ltd.

The Seibu Department Stores Group and Saison Group have introduced various innovations to their stores, including importing and selling Euro-American high-grade brand goods, offering life and other insurance, participating in non-bank banking, and issuing international credit cards.

Not all businesses launched by the Seibu Department Stores Group and Saison Group have been successful. A department store of 10,000 square meters opened in Los Angeles in 1962, but was closed in 1968 because of poor business performance. When the group collaborated with U.S. retailer Sears, Roebuck and Co., catalog sales of Sears, Roebuck products were unsuccessful in Japan; the failure, though, taught the group lessons which it has put to use in its own two catalog sales companies. Other new businesses have failed, including sports centers and home furnishing stores. However, the group has learned from these failures and continues to impress its competitors.

Principal Subsidiaries: Seibu Department Stores, Ltd.; Asahi Foods, Ltd.; Yves Saint-Laurent-Seibu S.A.; Ikebukuro Shopping Park Co., Ltd.; Var Co., Ltd.; Van Cleef & Arpels Japan, Ltd.; S. N. Information Systems Co., Ltd.; F Co., Ltd.; MSI Co., Ltd.; Ellebis, Ltd.; Hermès Japon Co., Ltd.; Kawasaki Seibu Department Store Co., Ltd.; Gold House International, Ltd.; Seed International Products Co., Ltd.; Shell Garden Co., Ltd.; JS Associates Co., Ltd.; Giorgio Armani Japan Co., Ltd.; SKIP, Ltd.; Studio CASA Co., Ltd.; Seishin Sangyo Co., Ltd.; Seidenko Co., Ltd.; Seibu Corporation of America, Inc. (U.S.A.); Seibu International Trading, Ltd.; Seibu Chu-Shikoku, Ltd.; Seibu Tohoku, Ltd.; Seibu Fabricant Co., Ltd.; Seibu France S.A.R.L. (France); Seibu Hokuriku, Ltd.; Seibu Hokkaido, Ltd.; Seiwa Interiors Co., Ltd.; Saison Direct Marketing Co., Ltd.; Takanawa Art Co., Ltd.; Daikokuya, Ltd.; Daikokuya, Ltd.; De Griff Club Co., Ltd.; Towada Matsukiya, Ltd.; Nest International Co., Ltd.; Knoll International Japan; Family Seibu Co., Ltd.; Belfe Japan, Ltd.; Beijing Seibu Co., Ltd.; Honkin Seibu, Ltd.; Hong Kong Seibu Enterprise Co., Ltd.; Polo Ralph Lauren Japan Co., Ltd.; Matsukiya, Ltd.; Mutsu Matsukiya, Ltd.; Yanes Japan Co., Ltd.; Yurakucho Seibu Co., Ltd.; Liberty Japan Co., Ltd.; Le Cordon Bleu Japon, Ltd.

Further Reading: Yui, Tsunehiko, *The History of Saison,* Tokyo, Libroport, 1991.

—Yoko Togawa

THE SEIYU, LTD.

3-1-1 Higashi Ikebukuro
Toshima-ku
Tokyo 170
Japan
(03) 989-5111
Fax: (03) 982-3221

Public Company
Incorporated: 1956 as Seibu Stores
Employees: 11,349
Sales: ¥1.05 trillion (US$8.41 billion)
Stock Exchanges: Tokyo Paris Frankfurt Düsseldorf

The Seiyu, Ltd. (Seiyu) leads the Seiyu Group, a subgroup of the Saison Group retail conglomerate. Saison Group is one of Japan's largest retail concerns with annual sales of more than ¥4 trillion, of which Seiyu accounts for almost 30%. The Seiyu Group consists of 22 companies, within which the Seiyu, Ltd. represents the group's main business of superstore retailing and operates 264 stores throughout Japan. In 1991 the Daiei, Inc., was the only other Japanese retailer to have such truly national coverage. Seiyu maintains a wide range of store formats, including large general merchandise stores, which are centrally operated and predominantly self-service department stores; supermarkets; and specialty stores. The stores offer their customers a complete range of services, usually provided by group member companies, covering everything from credit to real estate. Seiyu was originally founded in 1956 to become the supermarket arm of the privately owned Seibu Distribution Companies—now the Saison Group. At the time, the company took the name of its parent, Seibu Stores, and is the oldest of Japan's major superstore chains by one year, although its competitor Ito-Yokado Co. Ltd. had been operating in another form since the early 20th century.

The key personality in the history of Seiyu is Seiji Tsutsumi. Until 1991 Tsutsumi was the head of the then Seibu Saison Group before stepping down to become chairman of the Saison Corporation within the same group. He has been the driving force behind Seibu's successful retailing operations for the past 40 years. His half-brother, Yoshiaki Tsutsumi, is head of the independent Seibu Railways Group. Competition between the brothers contributed to the respective buildup of their companies after the original Seibu companies were split between the two brothers by their father. The early years were difficult for the company. Seiyu was established as a three-store chain with supermarkets in Odawara, Taira, and Shizuoka; however, all three original stores soon failed. The first successful store opened in Tsuchiura in 1958. Others followed but the pace of store openings remained slow, and by 1962 there were only five stores with less than 5,000 square meters in sales space. The main reason for the slow opening of new stores was Seiyu's dependence on its parent company Seibu Distribution. At the time, Seibu was conducting an ill-fated and costly experiment with a department store in Los Angeles. With Tsutsumi's tight overall control of the group's operations and a lack of funds due to losses from department stores, growth was restricted. In many respects, Seibu stores operated as small department stores. Each store sourced and sold goods independently, and did not practice self-service selling.

In November 1962 Tsutsumi decided that it was time to extend the supermarket side of the business. This was a period when Tokyo was growing rapidly, and large housing developments were springing up around the city. Following Tsutsumi's directive, the company began to search for new store sites close to this new housing. These estates represented a totally new market for Japanese retailers, with younger families from all over Japan beginning to move to the capital.

In addition, the company made a positive move toward becoming a chain store business and developed the retail strategy of self-service discount department stores whereby the company would open self-service outlets similar to department stores offering household and food items at a discount. This was the first step in the development of Seiyu's modern superstores.

Five months later, in April 1963, the company changed its name to Seiyu Stores Ltd., a move that emphasized the distinction between Seiyu and Seibu, and indicated a move to greater independence from the Seibu Group. The decision was not entirely voluntary. Complaints from small businesses led the Ministry of International Trade and Industry (MITI) to instruct the company not to operate under the same name as its sister department stores.

Following this change Seiyu rapidly expanded its chain of stores. To achieve this it took advantage of its connection with the Seibu Railway Company, locating stores along major rail arteries to the west of Tokyo. This land was not only cheap, but the sites had several other advantages. Stores at railway terminals provide a guaranteed flow of customers by catching commuters as well as local residents. In urban Japan, unlike most Western nations, shopping by car is seriously restricted because of road congestion and even in the early 1990s railway terminals are employed as prime retail sales.

Throughout the 1960s, Seiyu expanded first along the two main Seibu railway lines, and after 1965 stores were opened along lines operated by Japan National Railways and Keio Railways to the west of Tokyo, and along Sobu railway lines to the north. Store sizes ranged between 900 and 3,000 square meters depending on the site. On the whole, medium-sized stores of slightly more than 1,000 square meters of sales space were employed, with the emphasis on food and household products. The larger superstore outlets also carried a few clothing lines.

In 1969 Seiyu opened its first major distribution depot at Fuchu. In the same year production capacity for private brands was expanded with the founding of the Seiyu Stockbreeding Company and the Seiyu Meat Company. Seiyu Shoes Ltd. and Seiyu Marine Products Ltd. were established in 1970.

By this time the Seiyu chain had grown to more than 80 stores, all within Tokyo and neighboring regions. The early 1970s saw further expansion and diversification. Through the takeover of Koma Stores Ltd., a Kyoto chain of 12 outlets, Seiyu Stores Kansai Ltd. was founded. At the center of the Kansai region is Osaka, Japan's second-largest city and the country's second-largest market. It is also the home base for the major superstore chains of Daiei Inc., Nichii, and Izumiya. Seiyu's entry in 1970 was part of a strategy to open stores throughout the country. The Kansai company acted as a gateway to Nagoya and the southern island of Kyushu, leaving the Tokyo headquarters responsible for the north of Japan.

In 1971, Seiyu acquired a majority shareholding in the regional Uoriki chain in the Central Japan Alps. Unlike the takeover of Koma in Kyoto, this was not simply a market entry strategy. Although Uoriki was a small local chain, it dominated food retailing in the area, and Seiyu has maintained this strong position, becoming highly successful in the region. The company was renamed Seiyu Stores Nagano Ltd. in 1971.

In 1972 the Seibu Group established links with Sears, Roebuck & Co., giving Seibu access to the Sears catalog. Catalog corners were set up in some large Seiyu stores as well as in department stores, and Seiyu gained access to Sears retail experience. Sears maintains a 2.24% stake in Seiyu and was the company's ninth-largest shareholder in 1991.

In the same year, experiments were set up in small store retailing. This was the beginning of the highly successful Family Mart convenience store chain. Seiyu opened a small number of experimental stores during the mid-1970s, eventually establishing Family Mart Company as a viable chain in 1978. Family Mart is the third-largest convenience store chain in Japan and became independent from Seiyu Group in 1981. The Family Mart Group now forms a separate, autonomous part of the Saison Group.

Throughout the mid-1970s Seiyu continued a strategy of store expansion and business diversification and in 1974 expanded production of its own name brands to more than 500 items. These early brands were designed chiefly as discount goods to attract price-conscious consumers.

Ties with Sears, Roebuck were strengthened when the companies exchanged research teams between 1974 and 1978. Sears's chief objective was to gather information on the Japanese market, while Seiyu was interested in learning more about the Sears system of retailing. In 1978 Seiyu established an office in Chicago for the purpose of gathering information and sourcing new products suitable for its business in Japan. Further offices were established in Peking in 1979 and in Paris in 1982.

Although the implementation of a new Large Store Law in 1974, restricting the opening of large stores, did not hinder the opening of stores of less than 1,500 square meters, problems with small local retailers made new large store developments increasingly difficult toward the end of the 1970s. In 1979 MITI tightened the law further, making all new stores of more than 500 square meters subject to official approval. The consequence of this new legislation was that large companies such as Seiyu found it no easier to open medium-sized stores than to open large ones. A new strategy of opening large stores, usually more than 5,000 square meters, emerged and many stores exceeded 10,000 square meters in sales space. This trend continued in the early 1990s, with small and medium supermarkets being opened only in rare cases.

In 1979, Seiyu moved its headquarters to Tokyo's tallest building, the Sunshine 60 in Ikebukuro. The building was constructed to let, and the Saison Group is the main tenant. The building's spectacular size is similar to that of Sears, Roebuck headquarters in Chicago. The complex includes a Seiyu superstore, one of the few in central Tokyo.

By the beginning of the 1980s Seiyu was operating retail outlets that ranged from small convenience stores and medium-sized supermarkets to large-scale department stores. The company was also involved in producing a wide range of own-name brands, notably fresh and processed food products and household goods. The type of low-price, low-quality own-name brands previously available were no longer acceptable to Japanese consumers, and Seiyu responded to this problem in two ways, improving the quality of its supermarket brands and introducing the Shoku no Sachi own-name foodstuffs brand in 1984. In 1980 Seiyu had introduced the famous Mujirushi Ryohin brand. Mujirushi Ryohin means "good unbranded products"; these high-quality basic goods soon became very popular and Mujirushi Ryohin is now a famous brand. Sold initially in special areas of Seiyu stores, against a background of plain stone floors and unpolished wooden shelving, goods are packaged in plain wrappers and sold without the elaborate designs found on much Japanese packing. In doing this, Seiyu created a unique brand image. Large sales within larger Seiyu stores and Seibu department stores led to the opening of independently-sited specialty stores under the Mujirushi Ryohin name, including in 1983 the opening of a store in the highly fashionable Aoyama district of Tokyo. Eventually Daiei Inc., Jusco Ltd., and Uny Ltd. all created their own versions of Mujirushi Ryohin. In 1991 there were 217 Mujirushi Ryohin specialty stores in Japan, stocking a range of over 1,800 items. In 1991 Seiyu opened a Mujirushi Ryohin store in London.

By 1983 the Seiyu name was widely known in all parts of Japan and the group responded by changing the name of its main subsidiaries. Seiyu Stores Ltd. became the Seiyu, Ltd., and the main regional companies also simplified their names to Kansai Seiyu Ltd. and Nagano Seiyu Ltd. Kansai Seiyu was merged with the head company in 1988.

Building on the success of the Mujirushi Ryohin specialty stores, Seiyu continued to expand beyond its traditional core of food retailing. In 1983 links were formalized with Time Ltd. in the United States, and Seibu Time Ltd. was established. Seibu Time Ltd. produces a number of magazines including *Money Japan*, launched in 1985; *Lettuce Club*, launched in 1987; and *any*, launched in 1989.

In the areas of information and culture marketing, further developments included the production and distribution of films. The group's chairman and founder, Seiji Tsutsumi, has always encouraged all forms of art, and his retail stores are the venue for art exhibitions and performances. Cine Saison Ltd. was established in 1984 within the main Seiyu Group structure, and has been responsible for the production of a Japanese movie each year since 1985. Twelve Seiyu stores and shopping centers operate cinemas, and eight more have facilities to run regular drive-in movies.

Since 1987, Seiyu has also operated the 774-seat Ginza Saison Theater in central Tokyo and has been responsible for organizing a large number of cultural events throughout the latter half of the 1980s. In 1988 the Soviet Ballet Institute

School was opened in Tokyo, and in the same year a cultural exchange agreement was established with Robert Redford's Sundance Institute, a film school in the United States.

To strengthen the company's image at the upper end of the retail market, Seiyu began to remodel its larger stores as department stores in the 1980s, increasing the ratio of nonfood products and introducing more concessions within stores. The company also began to use the Seibu name on these larger stores to emphasize the department store image. Kasugai Seibu, Koriyama Seibu, and Maebashi Seibu are all examples of department stores run by Seiyu, with sales that are among the highest for individual outlets in Japan.

Seiyu also operates two large shopping complexes. The Hikari-ga-Oka complex in northwest Tokyo was completed in 1987. Part of a major housing development, it includes a Seiyu-operated Seibu department store, a separate supermarket, many specialty stores, restaurants, and a cinema. Seiyu aims to operate the complex as a community center, providing evening classes and various family events on weekends. The Hikari-ga-Oka complex is one of Seiyu's most successful projects of the late 1980s.

In 1988, Seiyu opened the Rakuichi complex at Nagahama in Shiga prefecture, its second and more ambitious shopping center development. Rakuichi is a shopping center and entertainment complex that includes a superstore, specialty stores, a conference center, and an amusement park. It is designed to cater to a wide geographical area. This kind of development has been emulated by other Japanese retailers and represents the desire to offer complete one-stop shopping and entertainment. Rakuichi is located far from any large urban area, however, and as of the early 1990s had shown only limited success.

Towards the end of the 1980s Seiyu consolidated various arms of its business. Seiyu Finance Ltd., originally established in 1982, was merged with Tokyo City Finance in 1989. The new company offers a wide range of financial services to Seiyu customers, including consumer credit, mortgages, life and other insurance, securities, and some business finance services. These services are offered both independently and at special counters within major stores.

Seiyu expanded its international operations during the latter half of the 1980s, establishing links with companies in South Korea, Indonesia, Thailand, and Hong Kong. These links were formed to promote development imports—whereby Japanese companies contract production in the poorer Southeast Asian countries—of cheap consumer goods. In addition, food products are imported from the western United States. Seiyu now has five buying and representative offices in South-east Asia, and three more in the United States.

In 1990 Seiyu was Japan's third largest retailer, behind Daiei and Ito-Yokado Co.; the three were the only retailers to have sales in excess of ¥1 trillion per annum. The group appears solid, with a wide range of business activities and a national network of stores, yet in 1991 it was experiencing problems. The Saison Group is known for showing only small net profits even by the standards of Japanese retailing as a whole, owing to overinvestment in areas which currently are not not performing well, such as hotels. Seiyu's annual sales growth was falling well behind that of other leading companies in the late 1980s and early 1990s. This will continue to be a problem for the group, but the strategy of diversification into a wide range of retail formats is an important and progressive one, and should support the company in the long term. The company's activities in the fields of culture and entertainment and the emphasis on community services make Seiyu stores popular with consumers. As the government moves progressively to allow greater domestic competition in large store retailing, Seiyu's strategy of department store development and its popularity should keep the firm on solid ground throughout the 1990s.

Principal Subsidiaries: Nagano Seiyu; Seiyu Foods (77.4%); Seibu Time; Super Maruzen (79.8%); Seibu Sekiyu Shoji (80%); Nikoh (26.6%); Kureru; Seiyu Photo Service; Asahi Mediko (80%); Chepo (85.7%); Rolly Doll (69.3%); Tokyo City Finance (50.5%); Seiyu Toshi Komon (65%); S. S. Communications (54.1%); Cine Saison; SMIS (80%); Ryohin Keikaku.

Further Reading: Tominaga, Masabumi, *Seiyu Sutoa no Keiei,* Tokyo, Nihon Jitsugyo Shuppansha, 1978; Asao, Kunio, *Seibu Sezon Gurupu,* Tokyo, Nihon Jitsugyo Shuppansha, 1985; Dodwell Marketing Consultants, *Retail Distribution in Japan,* Tokyo, 1988.

—Roy Larke and Kenji Arima

SERVICE MERCHANDISE COMPANY, INC.

7100 Service Merchandise Drive
Brentwood, Tennessee 37027
U.S.A.
(615) 660-6000
Fax: (615) 660-7912

Public Company
Incorporated: 1970
Employees: 22,765
Sales: $3.44 billion
Stock Exchange: New York

Service Merchandise is the largest U.S. retail catalog store chain. Most of the company's income is generated by its 361 catalog showrooms in 36 states selling jewelry and a variety of hard goods including home furnishings, electronics, sporting goods, toys, and luggage. It also operates one Service Jewelry store. Unlike some of its competitors, Service has remained true to the catalog concept, publishing spring, fall, and Christmas catalogs, seasonal flyers, and newspaper inserts. The catalog showrooms average 50,000 square feet. The company tailors to particular markets the size of each store and the items offered beyond the catalog selection. While many catalog showroom businesses have collapsed, Service has continued to expand, both by opening new stores and by acquiring smaller catalog chains.

Founded in 1960, the company's beginnings can be traced to the variety store that Harry and Mary Zimmerman opened in 1934 in Pulaski, Tennessee. That enterprise grew into a chain of dime stores located in small Tennessee towns. The Zimmermans's son, Raymond, virtually grew up in the stores and began to work in one of them after attending the University of Miami and Memphis State University. After the family sold most of the stores to Kuhn's, a variety store chain, the Zimmermans became variety store jobbers, a business in which they were still involved when they opened their catalog business in 1960. Their warehouse in downtown Nashville, Tennessee, became their first store.

For ten years, the Zimmermans operated this single outlet before entering two additional markets: Memphis and Chattanooga, Tennessee. During those years of limited growth, the company developed its business strategy and management team.

The company incorporated in Tennessee in 1970. Prior to that year, most catalog showroom businesses were privately held and often family-owned companies operating locally. In 1971 Service began to keep its stock in a warehouse connected to each store and to sell merchandise from samples only. By January 1972 Service was operating six showrooms. Later that year, it acquired Warco Supply Company in Indianapolis, Indiana, which operated a showroom, and it assumed the lease of an 80,000-square-foot discount store that it converted into a showroom. In all, Service opened eight new showrooms in 1972 and an additional nine in 1973, expanding into 12 new markets. In April 1974 the company acquired seven showrooms from Malone & Hyde Inc., gaining access to that company's markets in Jackson, Tennessee; Little Rock, Arkansas; and Springfield, Missouri. By mid-1974, Service had 27 showrooms in 11 states in the South and Midwest and was the nation's third–largest catalog showroom company. With most of its marketing dollars sunk into its catalog, Service distributed 1.9 million copies of the annual book in 1974.

The early 1970s saw a shakeout in the catalog industry, with many operators, especially those new to the industry, expanding too quickly and finding themselves unable to pay their debts. The recession of 1973 and 1974 aggravated the situation, but the major catalog operators continued to fare well.

In 1973 Raymond Zimmerman became Service's president and his father Harry assumed the post of chairman. Most Service showrooms converted to point-of-sale electronic cash registers in the summer of 1973. The information recorded on each showroom's mini-computer could be transmitted via telephone wires to Service's headquarters. Greater inventory control was the most important benefit of the new system.

With each expansion, Service sought to achieve maximum visibility by locating in high traffic locations, often near regional shopping centers. In 1974 Service gained entry as an anchor tenant in two shopping malls. Each showroom's layout was similar, reflecting Service's experience with the most profitable floor plan.

In 1975 Raymond Zimmerman told *Discount Merchandiser* that in Service showrooms, while jewelry accounted for only 3% of the total square footage, it represented 25% of the sales volume. By that year the company had reduced the size of its prototype store from 60,000 to 50,000 square feet, which allowed it to enter smaller markets.

By mid-1975 Service had 38 catalog showrooms, and by 1978 it had 51. Service acquired 22 Value House showrooms in 1978, giving the company a foothold in several New England markets.

The tremendous increase in gold prices in 1978 and 1979 wreaked havoc on the catalog showroom business. Since catalogs are printed as much as a year in advance, merchants were left with the dilemma of whether to raise prices or honor an advertised price and lose money. In one instance in 1978, Service had printed flyers for the important months of November and December and chose to honor the stated prices rather than raise them.

The catalog showroom industry began to mature in the late 1970s. The three largest operators, Best Products Company, Modern Merchandising Inc., and Service, had always avoided any direct competition in a single market, but this began to change in 1979 in major markets such as Miami and San Francisco.

Part of what precipitated this change was Service's 1980 withdrawal from Creative Merchandising and Publishing, a

Modern Merchandising subsidiary that published the catalogs for the three largest chains and for several smaller houses. By this time the largest of the three chains, Service had sought the flexibility of being able to tailor its catalog to its own special needs. The move also saved money. From 1979 to 1982, the number of catalogs that Service mailed to customers remained constant at 6.5 million, thanks to Service's tracking of its customers by zip code and by telling those customers in the least productive zip codes that if they wished to receive the Service catalog, they would have to inform the company. By 1982 sales per catalog were $150, compared to $80 just a few years earlier.

Service continued seeking new merchandising ideas. In 1980 and 1981 Service was one of five retailers to experiment with allowing customers to order their wares via specially equipped color television sets. In 1981 Service developed a new computer program using information about demographics and an outlet's competitive characteristics to predict the market. Originally set up in 23 existing stores and in three new units, the program proved very accurate. By 1982 Service had begun to experiment with "Silent Sam," an on-line cash register placed in the middle of the sales floor that allowed customers to check on product availability and to order their merchandise.

In the early 1980s the company diversified its operations with The Toy Store, opening four outlets in 1981 alone, for a total of six. Service, however, closed these stores just a few years later.

Despite a recession, Service managed to top the $1 billion mark in revenues in 1981. That year also marked the retirement of Harry Zimmerman as company chairman. He continued as honorary chairman and a company director, and son Raymond then began to serve as both chairman and president. By that time, Service had 116 outlets.

Service purchased the bankrupt Sam Solomon Company in 1982, adding the company's seven additional outlets in Charlotte, North Carolina, to its 118 units. The company also installed a computer system that allowed for checking current stock levels and making suggestions about alternatives for out-of-stock items.

As the catalog showroom industry matured, industry analysts criticized operators for getting away from the original concept that had made them so successful. Showrooms were often the size of more traditional mass marketers such as K-mart and J. C. Penney, and the leading catalog showroom operators had begun advertising on television. Industry analysts' prediction of a shakeout in the industry proved on target. Many of the smaller operators sold out or declared bankruptcy, and the larger showroom companies were forced to rethink their merchandising approach by making their stores more attractive, offering more upscale and trendy goods, and providing more customer service. The buying power of the large catalog showroom companies allowed them to operate on a lower margin than the smaller companies. Less than a third of the catalog companies operating in 1971 remained in business just a dozen years later.

Service's response to the changing market was aggressive. In 1981 it opened an upscale prototype unit in Novi, Michigan, and a jewelry store in Nashville and also began to plan mini-showrooms of 30,000 square feet.

Attempting to diversify in 1983, Service purchased Home-Owners Warehouse Inc., a company with a retail store in southern Florida that sold construction and home improvement products. It changed the company's name to Mr. How and added outlets. That same year, it also acquired a small chain called The Computer Shoppe.

Although he retained his position as chairman and chief executive officer, Raymond Zimmerman relinquished the company's presidency in late 1983 to James E. Poole, a career cement executive. Poole's tenure was short-lived, however, as he resigned suddenly just seven months later, with Zimmerman assuming the post again.

Service began to move its corporate headquarters in 1983 from four main facilities in metropolitan Nashville to Brentwood, Tennessee, just outside of Nashville. It was not until 1990 that all corporate headquarters employees were under one roof in Brentwood.

Service added 25 new units in 1984, with Chicago receiving its 17th Service outlet. At year's end it had 183 showrooms in 35 states. That year Service remained the second-largest catalog showroom operator, behind Best Products Company, but it was far more profitable than the leader.

Two 1985 acquisitions added significant markets to the Service fold, making it the industry leader in store units. It acquired H. J. Wilson Company, which included apparel in its product mix in many of its 80 showrooms in 12 states, and Ellman's Inc., which offered jewelry and giftware in its seven units in two states. "We never wanted to be the largest, we just wanted to be the most profitable," Zimmerman told the *Atlanta Journal/Constitution* (August 18, 1985), "but of course, we don't mind having the most number of stores in operation, either."

By the mid-1980s catalog showroom operators were being faced with increased price competition from department stores, mass merchants, and warehouse clubs. Service experimented with new approaches and concepts to meet the competition. The company used in-store video promotions, a drive-through pick up window, and a gift-wrapping department. "We'll try anything," Zimmerman told *Business Week* (June 10, 1985).

Service had expanded The Computer Shoppe to 10 units, had opened 2 jewelry stores under the Zimm's name, and had opened a single outlet called The Lingerie Store. The most expansion activity was on the Mr. How stores, with 7 planned for 1985 and 18 for the following year.

In 1985 Service installed a computerized inventory replenishment system that was designed to help reduce inventory costs, react immediately to marketplace demands, and avoid out-of-stock items. Company sales hit the $2 billion mark that year. In line with Service's efforts to operate smarter was the 1986 opening of an automated, 752,000-square-foot warehouse in Montgomery, New York.

The mid-1980s were difficult years for Service. Both Harry and Mary Zimmerman died in 1986. The Mr. How stores proved to be a drain on the company, and after attempts to build the chain at a rapid pace failed, the line of stores was dismantled. Service had discovered that the hardware business was tricky, with the warehouse format needing to turn over its inventory five or six times a year to maximize the profit margin. Such a turnover is approximately twice that of the average small hardware store. The product mix that had worked in

Florida was a failure in Chicago, one of the markets in which Service had opened five Mr. How stores.

The acquisition of H. J. Wilson and Ellman's had also been troublesome, with 60% of Wilson's inventory incompatible with that of Service. The inventory had to be sold at a substantial loss.

These two problem areas seemed to divert management's attention from its main business. Sales per store had stopped growing and operating expenses began eating away at the company's narrow profit margin. Maximizing the number of in-stock items had always been one of Service's foremost priorities, but the company found itself with a growing number of out-of-stock items, which sent customers shopping elsewhere.

Service lost $47 million on sales of $2.5 billion in 1986, a rude dose of reality for a company accustomed to turning a respectable profit, no matter what the economic climate. That same year, Best Products Inc., the second-largest catalog showroom chain, lost $25 million. Industry analysts credited the discount store chains with offering customers wider selection of goods at the same low prices as the catalog showrooms and more amenities such as having to wait in line only to pay for goods, not to pick them up. The discounters also had more price flexibility, since they were not locked in on prices for an entire year, as are the catalog showrooms that publish annual catalogs.

Service responded successfully by discontinuing some apparel lines, moving into selling more jewelry, and improving its inventory techniques. Efforts were also made to entice each customer to buy more, thus making each sales transaction more profitable.

Many catalog showroom operators were unable to adjust to the changes in the market. McDade & Company filed for bankruptcy in late 1987, and Allied Wholesale Distributors and Wilkor Jewelry & Showroom closed in mid-1988.

In September 1988 several members of Service's senior management, headed by Raymond Zimmerman, who held the posts of chairman, president, and chief executive officer, announced they were considering taking the company private through a leveraged buyout. There was speculation that the move was announced simply to put the company into play, with the hope that other bidders would materialize. Four lawsuits, however, were brought by shareholders who felt Service's management was failing to put shareholders' interests first, and this action stopped talk of a management buyout.

Also in September 1988 an unidentified party made an offer to buy Best Products Company. Securities analysts speculated that the offer, which Best rejected, might have been made by Service, since there would have been only minimal duplication of the two stores' territories. This speculation was never confirmed.

Service's 1988 sales surpassed the $3 billion mark. The company sold The Computer Shoppe chain in mid-1989. That same year, following two years of impressive growth and profits, Service announced a $975 million recapitalization plan. Although the company denied it feared a takeover, such fears would not have been unwarranted, since three firms were said to have been interested in Service. To avoid a hostile takeover, Best Products had gone private in 1988 after accepting a leveraged buyout led by New York-based investment firm Adler & Shaykin. The recapitalization plan provided for one-time cash dividend of $10 per share and a discontinuation of quarterly dividends.

In early 1990 Service announced that two of its senior officers were targets of an Internal Revenue Service investigation. The two executives soon stepped aside. Less than a month later, a federal grand jury began to investigate the company for improper or illegal use of funds. Zimmerman appointed four of the company's five outside directors to conduct their own internal investigation. Unidentified sources told *Business Week* (May 28, 1990) that the investigation centered around whether improper payments had been made to judges and politicians.

The late 1980s and early 1990s were very difficult years for retailers. In January 1991 Best Products sought protection from its creditors under Chapter 11 of the federal bankruptcy code.

Service was well suited to weather the recession of the early 1990s. The company had consistently demonstrated an almost exuberant willingness to try any concept or technology that might further streamline its operation and maximize sales and customer satisfaction. For instance, the company uses satellites for its internal communications. The coming years will likely be difficult for retailers as further lean times squeeze out all but the strongest, but it is difficult not to envision Service Merchandise as one of the survivors.

Further Reading: "Flying High with Catalog Showrooms," *Discount Merchandiser,* April, 1975; Kuntz, Mary, "Catalog of Woes," *Forbes,* May 4, 1987; Pellet, Jennifer, "Staying True to a $3 Billion Concept," *Discount Merchandiser,* March, 1990; Konrad, Walecia, and Dean Foust, "Ray Zimmerman, Tightwad in a Tight Spot," *Business Week,* May 28, 1990.

—Mary Sue Mohnke

TAKASHIMAYA CO., LIMITED

5-1-5 Nanba
Chuo-ku
Osaka 542
Japan
(6) 631-1101
Fax: (6) 632-3212

Public Company
Incorporated: 1920 as Takashimaya Gofuku Store Co., Ltd.
Employees: 14,091
Sales: ¥1.18 trillion (US$9.45 million)
Stock Exchanges: Tokyo Osaka Kyoto

Takashimaya Co., Limited is the third-largest department store retailer in Japan in terms of sales, and Japan's seventh-largest retail company. As a retail group, Takashimaya is the sixth-largest retail conglomerate—this includes nonretail companies as well. This is by far the largest group among the traditional department store retailers who have business histories stretching back over 150 years. Takashimaya is one of the most progressive of these traditional stores, with greater international links and more modern stores than its competitors and, along with Mitsukoshi, is alone in maintaining significant success in more than one of Japan's major urban markets. The chain includes some of Japan's premier retail sites with major stores at Nihonbashi in Tokyo, at Yokohama central railway station, and at Nanba in Osaka. Group activities extend beyond retailing to cover all areas of distribution, and Takashimaya is famous for its interior design and direct mail-order businesses, in addition to department store retailing. Group sales exceeded ¥1.18 trillion in 1991, contributed by 40 subsidiary companies and 26 allied businesses.

Takashimaya began in 1831. Like a number of Japan's leading department store retailers, the company originated as a small, specialty retailer of kimono, with the founder, Shinshichi Iida, opening the first store in Kyoto at the age of 27. The store had a sales space of only 3.6 square meters and specialized in Japanese formal wear—*gofuku*—supplying both kimono and related accessories. At the time, Japan was in the final 30 years of the feudal Edo period, and its economy was weak and in some confusion. In order to build a successful business, Iida laid down four principles which Takashimaya's management maintains to this day: high-quality goods, fair prices, honesty in sales, and care and courtesy to all customers.

In 1855 the store was expanded to include more cotton goods and a wider range of formal wear accessories. At this time the company employed 21 people. Japan was finally opened to Western influence in 1867 with the restoration of the Meiji Emperor and Takashimaya began to stock a wider range of goods, including many household products. In 1876 links were formed with U.S. businesses that had come to Japan with the opening of the feudal society, and the company began to import goods from abroad, even targeting the small but growing foreign community in Kyoto. Toward the end of the 1880s Takashimaya moved to expand its overseas trading. Dealing chiefly in fabrics, the company began to export to Europe, with considerable success. Around the turn of the century Takashimaya took part in various European expositions, displaying fine silks and dyed fabrics, and won prizes for its displays in London, Barcelona, and Paris. In 1899 a sales office was established in Lyons, and a direct export business was founded. An office was opened in London in 1903.

The second Takashimaya store opened in eastern Kyoto in 1893, and a further store was opened in Osaka in 1898. The company established a small office in Tokyo in 1890, which became a full store in 1897. With the opening of an export office in Yokohama in 1900, Takashimaya's business extended into the two major commercial areas of Japan, the Kansai area around Kyoto and Osaka, and the Kanto area centered in Tokyo. By the turn of the century Takashimaya employed more than 500 people. Traditional stores like Takashimaya began to expand their businesses as a precursor to becoming general merchandise department stores. Takashimaya, however, maintained a strong emphasis on its original fabrics and clothing business, and the company became famous for the quality of its dyeing and weaving. By importing European expertise in weaving and design, Takashimaya introduced new designs and its own clothing brands, while at the same time keeping full control of costs and the final retail price. To display these new designs, in 1909 Takashimaya opened an art exhibition area within its stores. This later became common practice among Japanese department stores, with many, including some Takashimaya outlets, maintaining permanent art exhibition areas.

In 1909 Takashimaya became an unlimited partnership and at the same time began to operate its stores as departmentalized general merchandise stores. The company expanded and modernized all its outlets to keep pace with other new department stores. The number and range of goods sold was greatly expanded, and by the end of World War I, Takashimaya had six major stores and nine nonretail offices in Japan and overseas. In 1916 the new Tokyo store was opened and Takashimaya introduced a full home-shopping service to its wealthier customers. These customers were given their own accounts and were visited regularly by Takashimaya salespeople. The main items sold in this way were kimono, interior decorations, and furniture. Customers could order by mail, a telephone order service was established, and along with the other major department stores, Takashimaya provided a home-sales service to customers living in the northern and southern regions of Japan. Salespeople would visit wealthy customers living hundreds of miles away from the stores, thus providing a national sales coverage for the Takashimaya stores. Takashimaya Iida Limited was established in 1916 as a separate company, operating as an independent overseas trading arm for the Takashimaya group.

Takashimaya became a private stock company following the end of World War I, with the company taking the name Takashimaya Gofuku Store Co. Ltd. By this time the number of employees had reached 891, and Takashimaya stores had become full department stores. The small restaurant businesses that had operated in the stores since 1912 were formally incorporated and expanded, establishing an independent restaurant business in 1922 based in the newly opened Osaka Takashimaya Store. Immediately after World War I, all stores were equipped with elevators and escalators for the first time. Many of these new facilities were leased from major insurance firms, increasing the level of outside capital involved in the business.

In the Great Kanto Earthquake of 1923, Takashimaya's store in Tokyo was destroyed by fire, and a similar fate befell most other major department stores in the city. Out of the ashes, new department stores were built which were larger and carried a far wider range of merchandise, making department stores available to a wider clientele and not only the most wealthy. Department stores became the general retail stores of Japan. Takashimaya's image was one of privilege, and to introduce its stores to a wider clientele, in 1926 the company began 10 Sen Kinitsu Markets, translated as "Everything for 10 sen," *sen* being a unit of a yen. The markets were opened in existing Takashimaya stores and were highly successful, selling simple household goods.

Takashimaya also expanded its nonstore retailing business, sending salespeople to a greater number of customers and increasing the availability of goods by mail order. Department stores also began to provide free home delivery services and bus services to transport customers to and from major rail stations. As the leading retailers in Japan at the time, department stores engaged in fierce competition as each one fought to establish a strong niche in the market. This competition was heightened by the entrance into the department store business of major railroad companies like Tokyu and Hankyu that opened stores at major rail terminals known as "terminal department stores." The advantages of these sites were clear and Takashimaya followed suit, opening a terminal store in Osaka in 1930. In the same year, Takashimaya changed its legal name to Takashimaya Co., Limited, dropping Gofuku Store which indicated its roots in garment retailing. Takashimaya appointed its first outside director and became a public limited company in 1933, at the height of competition between Japanese department stores. This fierce competition affected many small retailers, not only in the major urban areas but also throughout the regions in which stores sent their traveling salespeople to people's homes. Takashimaya maintained an advantage through its upmarket image and through the development of a new cheap retailing business. The 10 Sen Kinitsu Markets within existing Takashimaya stores proved so successful as a low-price retail strategy that the company began a chain of stores selling low-price household goods in 1931. Within a year, some 51 new outlets were opened.

Eventually public groups began to see the competition between department stores and their rapid expansion as being detrimental to Japanese retailing overall. In 1932 the Japan Department Store Association—founded in 1924—called for self-restraint in new store openings and the restriction of home visit sales, especially in the provinces. Even so, small retailers continued to complain, and in 1937 the Department Store Law, the original forerunner of the modern Large Store Law

(1974) was promulgated to restrict the operations of large stores. As the law was aimed at department stores, the only large-scale retailers in existence at the time, Takashimaya made its new chain of low-price stores into a separate company, calling it Marutaka Kinitsu Store Ltd., and the new company continued to expand the chain store under the name Kinitsu. To get around restrictions on home selling, Takashimaya moved to expand its mail-order business, producing catalogs and advertising widely in national newspapers.

The Department Store Law effectively stopped the expansion of the department store chains, but capital became increasingly scarce as Japan reached the height of its military power during the late 1930s. From 1939 restrictions were placed on the supply of consumer goods, and a black market soon arose. Throughout this period, Takashimaya, along with some other department stores, maintained a policy of setting fair prices, establishing an image of trustworthiness that still exists today. Takashimaya continued to expand its Kinitsu chain of stores and operated 106 outlets covering 39,000 square meters of sales space and employing more than 2,000 people by 1941. However, the ravages of war took their toll, and Takashimaya had lost all but 21 stores by the time the war ended in 1945. Of these, 3 were department stores and 18 were Kinitsu stores.

Takashimaya's outlets in both Osaka and Tokyo were badly damaged in air raids in March 1945, although enough remained for the company to continue trading. These stores were rebuilt and refurbished between 1945 and 1948, and small offices were opened in various parts of Japan including Shikoku, Hiroshima, Kyushu, and Hokkaido. In 1948 the Allied occupation authorities abolished the original Department Store Law and department stores were finally free to consider opening new stores.

Takashimaya, however, chose to expand and improve its existing main stores in Osaka, Kyoto, and Tokyo, and even closed smaller stores in Kyoto and Wakayama in the early 1950s. In 1956 the Department Store Law was reintroduced by the new Japanese government. The 1956 law restricted the opening of new retail businesses over 1,500 square meters, regulated opening hours, and laid down minimum numbers of closing days. The expansion of all department stores was held back by this law, but by careful acquisition of sites and long term negotiations with local retailers Takashimaya opened three major new stores up to 1965, including Yokohama Takashimaya, which was established in 1959 at the west exit of Yokohama Station. The company already owned the site, and the new store was established as a separate company from Takashimaya. Further stores were opened in Sakai and Yonago, with the latter store also operating as a separate company.

During the 1950s and 1960s, Takashimaya began to expand its range of businesses. In 1956 Takashimaya became the Japanese member of the Intercontinental Group of Department Stores, an international body covering stores throughout the world. In the same year, this new contact enabled Takashimaya to become the first Japanese department store to hold an international fair for imported goods, the theme on this occasion being Italian. The company later exhibited the famous collection of anthropological photographs, "The Family of Man," in all its stores, followed by other world-famous art collections. In 1958 Takashimaya opened a store on New York's Fifth Avenue, the first of a number of overseas boutiques and restaurants which later included stores in New York, Paris, Milan, and London.

Takashimaya Shoji Limited was established in 1959 to manufacture a range of exclusive brand-name products. Between 1960 and 1989, 34 of these brands were introduced, including formal wear, food products, cut diamond jewelry, and tableware, designed to be sold at the high-price, high-quality end of the retail market. Other subsidiaries were opened during the 1960s including real estate—Koei Real Estate Ltd.—and a housing and shopping development company, Toshin Kaihatsu Ltd. The latter company was responsible for the development of the Tamagawa Shopping Centre that opened to the southwest of Tokyo in 1969. This was Japan's first major suburban shopping center development and has a Takashimaya Department Store at its center, with some 48,800 square meters of sales floor space, accounting for a little over 50% of the total shopping center.

In 1971, Takashimaya formed the Highland Group, a buying and development organization that allows its members to source and buy products collectively and provides professional consultancy and advice, physical distribution facilities, and some financial support. All Takashimaya stores became members, and the group subsequently expanded to include many independent regional department stores. In 1990 the group included 40 member stores from all over Japan.

Takashimaya is the only company to successfully span the two major markets of Kanto and Kansai, although in each case the company has often found its retail sales falling below that of the local stores, Daimaru in Osaka and Kyoto and Mitsukoshi in Tokyo. Seibu dominates the Tokyo department store market, but is competing at a slightly different level because of its shorter, less prestigious history. Takashimaya, Mitsukoshi, and Daimaru are the prestige stores in Japan and compete with each other on this basis.

Takashimaya maintains a significant advantage in its diversification strategies. In addition to operating a number of overseas boutiques and restaurants, it has introduced many overseas brands into the Japanese market. In 1959, the company acquired a license to manufacture and sell Pierre Cardin goods and in 1990 maintained exclusive licenses to manufacture 15 overseas brands, including Fauchon and Emanuel Ungaro. The store is also the exclusive importer of 12 major brands, including James Martin whiskey and Rosenthal tableware.

After its department store business, Takashimaya's second main activity is nonstore retailing. The company first began mail-order retailing as long ago as 1899 and, following a curtailment of business during World War II, reintroduced a mail-order service in 1953 from the company's main Osaka store. In the 1980s Takashimaya began to expand its catalog sales, introducing a cable television shopping service and a number of multimedia catalogs, including videotapes and floppy disks. Takashimaya is the 14th-largest nonstore retailer in Japan—this category includes direct mail-order or catalog sales as well as home sales—and is far ahead of any other store retailers also competing in the market. The second-largest nonstore retailer is Mitsukoshi. Takashimaya has the third-largest mail-order business in Japan and in 1990 produced 1.45 million catalogs of various kinds, achieving sales of more than ¥65 billion.

Less widely known is Takashimaya's involvement in the interior design business. Based on the company's original fabrics business, Takashimaya has offered high-quality interior design services since 1878 and especially since the early 1970s has been involved in the design of numerous hotels and office and state buildings throughout the world. Some of Takashimaya's most famous projects include the New Showa Palace in Tokyo and the Jeddah State Palace in Saudi Arabia.

For a period at the end of the 1970s and beginning of the 1980s Takashimaya's business benefited from a scandal at the Mitsukoshi Department Store, the company's leading rival in Tokyo, involving the selling of fake antiques and a rumored affair between the chairman and a younger woman. The scandal served to emphasize Takashimaya's reputation for trustworthiness and honesty, and Takashimaya briefly overtook Mitsukoshi as the most popular store at which to buy the obligatory, biannual gifts that are so important in Japanese society. For many consumers this was the first time they had considered using a store other than Mitsukoshi for such socially important purchases. Mitsukoshi has since recovered its position as Tokyo's most prestigious store, but Takashimaya has maintained a more modern image since this incident.

In 1990 Takashimaya formed High Retail System Co., Ltd. to open upscale convenience stores in major urban areas. Using a telephone-ordering system, customers are able to phone their shopping lists to the local store and receive delivery a few minutes later. The stores are geared to serve office areas and include various services such as color copying, in additon to offering basic convenience foods, drinks, and packaged meals. Gifts can also be ordered by catalog from the main department store's full range.

In 1991, despite moves to encourage the development of new large retail stores in Japan with major easing of restrictions under the Large Store Law, it is unlikely that there will be any significant growth in the number of department stores. The department store business will continue to compete on the basis of differentiation between stores and companies. Unlike some of the newer department stores, Takashimaya has not moved downmarket into the supermarket business, preferring to maintain a high-quality image. The number of department stores is limited and each group retains its own identity. Any significant increase in competition from within the same area of retailing seems unlikely in the coming years. The only danger to Takashimaya and other department stores that limit their business to the top end of the consumer market is competition from the leading superstore retailers, notably Ito-Yokado and Seiyu, which are improving quality. These firms are larger, more diverse, and arguably more efficient than the traditional department stores and lack only those stores' long tradition.

Takashimaya continues to expand and modernize its mail-order business and in 1993 plans to open the largest shopping center development in Southeast Asia, in the center of Singapore, and invest directly in other parts of the world. At home, the company is likely to continue as one of Japan's largest and most successful retailers.

Principal Subsidiaries: Yokohama Takashimaya (58.3%); Kanto Takashimaya (50%); Yonago Takashimaya (88.3%); Okayama Takashimaya (45%); Senboku Takashimaya (45%); Gifu Takashimaya (45%); T.F.C.; Takashimaya Kosakujo (38.1%); Takashimaya Nippatsu Kogyo (40%); Koei Real Estate Ltd. (49.4%); Toshin Kaihatsu Ltd. (23.1%).

Further Reading: Takaoka, Sueaki, and Shuzo Koyama, *Gendai no Hyakkaten,* Tokyo, Nihon Keizai Shinbunsha, 1970; Nishiyama, Nobuo, *Takashimaya Foshon: Sekai no Tokusen Gurume wo Uru Butikku,* Buren (ed), *Sutoa Aidentiti Senryaku,* Tokyo, Seibundo Shinkosha, 1987; Okada, Yasushi, *Hyakkaten Gyokai,* Tokyo, Kyoikusha, 1988; Nikkei Ryutsu Shinbun, *Kourigyo: Seme no Jidai,* Tokyo, Nihon Keizai Shinbun 1989; Larke, Roy, "Consumer Perceptions of Large Stores in Japan," unpublished Ph.D. thesis, University of Stirling, 1991.

—Roy Larke and Kota Nagashima

THE TJX COMPANIES, INC.

770 Cochituate Road
Framingham, Massachusetts 01701
U.S.A.
(508) 390-1000
Fax: (508) 390-2091

Public Company
Incorporated: 1962 as Zayre Corp.
Employees: 28,000
Sales: $2.46 billion
Stock Exchange: New York

Composed of T.J. Maxx, Hit or Miss, Chadwick's of Boston, and Winners Apparel Ltd., The TJX Companies, Inc. is the largest off-price apparel retailer in North America. Each of its operating divisions approaches off-price apparel retailing from a different perspective. T.J. Maxx offers discounts on a continually changing inventory of brand-name family apparel, in addition to off-priced jewelry, giftware, shoes, and household goods. Hit or Miss, a chain of women's apparel specialty stores, carries both private label and brand name career and casual fashions at substantial savings. Chadwick's of Boston sells off-price women's apparel through mail-order catalogs. Winners Apparel Ltd. is a small but growing off-price family apparel chain in Canada, acquired in 1990.

The TJX Companies, Inc. was not organized as a separate subsidiary from Zayre until 1987 and did not assume its present form until 1989. Its member companies were part of Zayre Corp., parent of the Zayre Store chain of discount department stores incorporated in 1962. T.J. Maxx, Hit or Miss, and Chadwick's of Boston each got their start several years later.

The first Zayre—Yiddish for "very good"—store had opened in Hyannis, Massachusetts, in 1956. Its founders were two cousins, Stanley and Sumner Feldberg. With sales doubling every second or third year, the Feldbergs were quick to add stores, which numbered more than 200 by the early 1970s. By then, the company had diversified into specialty retailing.

Hit or Miss opened its first store in Natick, Massachusetts, in 1965. The store flourished and grew into a chain so quickly that within four years it attracted the attention of a giant by comparison, Zayre. In 1969 Zayre bought the Hit or Miss chain, and began its exploration of the upscale off-priced fashion market. Zayre's timing could not have been better. During the recession of the 1970s, Hit or Miss's results climbed so rapidly that Zayre began to think of expanding its off-priced upscale apparel merchandising.

T.J. Maxx was definitely a product of this recession. Bernard Cammarata, once a buyer himself, was hired by Zayre Corp. to capitalize on the potential for a chain offering off-priced upscale apparel for the whole family. In Auburn, Massachusetts, in March 1977, he opened the first T.J. Maxx.

Within six years of the opening of the first T.J. Maxx store, Zayre had found yet another avenue of approach to the off-priced fashion market. In 1983 Chadwick's of Boston began to sell selected Hit or Miss items through mail order catalogs. Hit or Miss and Chadwick's crossover operations allowed customers to handle products before ordering, and brought the frequent buyer the convenience of home shopping.

By the mid-1980s, off-priced specialty retailing was becoming more important to Zayre. Hit or Miss and T.J. Maxx had brought in just 14% of the company's operating income in 1980; by the first half of 1983, they were producing nearly 45%. At the same time, however, Zayre was renovating its discount department stores and expanding its product mix. In 1984 Zayre entered the membership warehouse-club market, launching B.J.'s Wholesale Club. It bought Home Club Inc., a chain of home improvement stores, the following year. Neither of those ventures were immediately profitable, but Hit or Miss and T.J. Maxx continued to surge.

By 1986 Hit or Miss's number of stores reached 420 and sales climbed to $300 million. Some 70% of its inventory was made up of nationally known brands. The remaining 30% consisted of standard products such as turtlenecks and corduroy pants, and were produced by Hit or Miss under its own private label. With such a merchandise mix, Hit or Miss was able to sell current fashion at 20% to 50% less than most specialty stores.

In 1986 profits of the Zayre chain, targeting low-to-middle income customers, dropped, although T.J. Maxx, Hit or Miss, and Chadwick's of Boston, targeting mid- to higher-income customers, continued to grow. That year alone, Zayre Corp. opened 35 more T.J. Maxx stores and 31 new Hit or Miss stores. In fact, Zayre Corp.'s off-priced retailing chains were so successful, that by 1987 Zayre thought it prudent to organize them under one name and grant them autonomy from the decreasingly prosperous parent company.

In June 1987, just ten years after its flagship chain, T.J. Maxx, opened its first store, The TJX Companies, Inc. was established as a subsidiary of Zayre, selling 9.35 million shares of common stock in its initial public offering. Zayre owned 83% of the subsidiary.

Zayre was experiencing problems. In the first half of 1988, Zayre had operating losses of $69 million on sales of $1.4 billion. Observers blamed technological inferiority, poor maintenance, inappropriate pricing, and inventory pileups, and speculated Zayre was ripe for takeover. Throughout all this, The TJX Companies continued to yield a profit.

In October 1988, the company decided to concentrate on TJX. It sold the entire chain of over 400 Zayre Stores to Ames Department Stores, Inc. In exchange, the company received $431.4 million in cash, a receivable note, and what was then valued at $140 million of Ames cumulative senior convertible preferred stock.

The company continued to hone in on its profitable new core business, selling unrelated operations. In June 1989 it spun off its warehouse club division, Waban Inc., which owned B.J.'s and Home Club. Zayre gave shareholders one share of Waban for each two shares of Zayre they owned as well as a $3.50 per share cash payment. The same month, the company acquired an outstanding minority interest in TJX. On the day it acquired the minority interest, the company merged with TJX. Later that month, the company changed its name from Zayre Corp. to The TJX Companies, Inc. The newly named company began trading on the New York Stock Exchange.

The company's transition into an off-priced fashion business was relatively smooth, but the Ames preferred stock it received in the Zayre transaction had been a problem. This preferred stock was not registered and had no active market. While the stock is entitled to 6% annual dividends, Ames had the option of paying the first four semi-annual dividends with more Ames preferred stock rather than cash, an option that Ames exercised for each of the payments it had met. However, the value of Ames preferred stock had been in question because Ames had been closing stores and experiencing losses.

In April 1990 TJX established a $185 million reserve against its Ames preferred stock and contingent lease liabilities on former Zayre stores as a result of Ames's announcement of continued poor performance. That same month, Ames filed for protection from creditors under Chapter 11 of the U.S. Bankruptcy Code. Late in 1990, Ames began to show a modest profit, but it was uncertain as to when Ames would emerge from Chapter 11.

TJX's operations remained solid. In 1991 T.J. Maxx, by far the company's largest division, posted record results for the 15th consecutive year since it opened. Hit or Miss had a diffi-cult year, transitioning its business in a recessionary economy. Chadwick's of Boston finished strong in both sales and profitability and Winners Apparel exceeded sales expectations. These results came despite heavy markdown activity among competitors and a weak economy.

At the end of 1991, T.J. Maxx had 437 stores in 46 states. It planned to open many more stores, focusing primarily on the only scantily penetrated southwestern United States, as well as expanding several existing stores. T.J. Maxx also planned to follow up on its success in jewelry and shoes by opening up these respective departments at locations that do not carry these items. It also planned to expand high-performance nonapparel categories such as giftware and domestic items.

Hit or Miss planned to hone in on areas that needed improvement and to close approximately 75 nonperforming stores. After renovating 175 stores in 1991, it planned to upgrade systems for administration and merchandise planning.

Chadwick's of Boston planned to expand its business through aggressive and carefully planned growth. Winners Apparel Ltd. planned to continue to build the off-price concept in Canada.

Principal Subsidiaries: Hit or Miss, Inc.; NBC First Realty Corp.; NBC Second Realty Corp.; Newton Buying Corp.; Chadwicks of Boston, Ltd.; Commonwealth Direct Marketing, Inc.; West Bridgewater Realty, Inc.; Avon Trading Corp.; Winners Apparel Ltd.

—Maya Sahafi

TOKYU DEPARTMENT STORE CO., LTD.

2-24-1, Dogenzaka
Shibuya-ku
Tokyo 150
Japan
(03) 3477-3111
Fax: (03) 3496-7200

Public Company
Incorporated: 1919 as Shirokiya Drapery Shop Co., Ltd.
Employees: 5,738
Sales: ¥393.22 billion (US$3.15 billion)
Stock Exchanges: Tokyo Sapporo

Tokyu Department Store Co., Ltd. is Japan's eighth–largest department store chain, operating ten major stores in Japan. Five of the stores are in the Tokyo area, and the two most important are in the city's busy Shibuya district. Tokyu Department Store also has extensive international links, including seven major overseas outlets in Hawaii and Southeast Asia.

The company is an innovator in its industry; it was the first retailer in Japan to open a department store at a railway station, the first to open a shopping arcade, and the first to introduce door-to-door sales. Perhaps as a consequence of this type of innovation, it tends to show above-average profitability.

Tokyu Department Store is one of the most important of the Tokyu Companies, a complex group of businesses of which Tokyu Corporation is the nucleus. These companies, of which there are nearly 400, are divided into four main groups: retailing and distribution; development; transportation; and recreation and leisure. Tokyu Department Store is the nucleus of the retailing and distribution group, which represented almost 40% of the Tokyu Companies' total sales in 1990. The company works closely with other Tokyu enterprises; for example, its stores are usually sited at Tokyu Corporation railway stations, Tokyu's air and land transportation operations carry its merchandise, and its new shopping facilities are often constructed in conjunction with Tokyu property development companies.

Tokyu Department Store's most venerable antecedent dates back to the 17th century. This ancestor was a drapers' shop, Shirokiya, founded in 1662 by Hikotaro Omura in the Nihonbashi area of Tokyo, or Edo as the city was then called. In 1919 this business was incorporated as the Shirokiya Drapery Shop Co., Ltd. Four years later, the store, like most others in Tokyo, was devastated by fire following the Great Kanto Earth-

quake. Operating under the new trading name of Shirokiya Co., Ltd., the company redeveloped the old site to create a new and more up-to-date store, which opened in June 1933.

The evolution of Shirokiya constitutes one strand of the Tokyu Department Store's history. The other principal strand begins in the 1930s, a boom period for Japanese department stores. At this time Tokyo's suburbs were growing rapidly, and railway lines were stretching out from the center to serve them. The railway companies often used the land adjacent to their commuter stations to build department stores, which they financed with money from their transport activities. One of the earliest railway companies to spot this opportunity was the Tokyo Yokohama Electric Railways Co., Ltd., owned by entrepreneur Keita Gotoh's Tokyo Corporation. In 1934 the Tokyo Yokohama Electric Railways Co. opened Toyoko Department Store, the first department store to be sited at a railway station—"Toyoko" is a portmanteau word formed from "Tokyo" and "Yokohama".

After World War II the Allied occupying forces pursued a policy of dismantling the large combines or *zaibatsu,* which in the Allies' opinion had contributed to Japan's entry into the war. Many Tokyu operations were reconstituted as semi-independent companies. One such company, Toyoko Kogyo, assumed control of Tokyu's department-store business in 1948, shortly afterwards becoming known as Toyoko Department Store Co., Ltd.

Another company originating in 1948, and today affiliated with Tokyu Department Store, is Tokyu Foods. 40 years after its foundation, Tokyu Foods was to become a significant manufacturer and retailer of bakery goods, operating 140 bakeries in Japan and elsewhere under the name "St-Germain," also selling delicatessen-style meats. Tokyu Foods would also build up several restaurant chains. Tokyu Department Store's other important food-manufacturing affiliate, Gold Pak, whose award-winning products are all based on fresh fruit and vegetable juices, would begin trading in 1966.

Meanwhile, after the immediate postwar hardships, Japan's prosperity grew rapidly. Department stores flourished because they offered convenient one-stop shopping; from being primarily dry-goods suppliers before the war, they now came to supply everything from food to consumer durables. They also catered to the Westernization of Japanese tastes by bringing in imports in a way that smaller retailers could not afford to do. Department stores were typically situated at railway stations, as were Toyoko's stores.

It was against this promising background that Toyoko Department Store opened its Ikebukuro store in 1950, which was to close after only 14 years' trading. In 1951 the company inaugurated Tokyo's first shopping arcade under the name Toyoko Norengai. The west wing of the main Toyoko store was also extended during the early 1950s.

The two strands of Tokyu Department Store's history come together in the late 1950s. Shirokiya Co. joined the Tokyu group of companies in 1956. Two years later, after a period of intensive modernization and expansion of the Shirokiya main store, Shirokiya and Toyoko Department Store merged, adopting the name Toyoko Co., Ltd.

The company took an initial step towards globalization with the creation of Shirokiya Incorporated in 1959. In the same year, this new affiliate opened Tokyu's first overseas store, the Hawaii Shirokiya in the Ala Moana Shopping Center.

Over the years Shirokiya Incorporated would open another three stores in Hawaii, two of them in shopping centers and one in a hotel. That Shirokiya became a valued part of Hawaiian life is indicated by the fact that the city of Honolulu designated October 15, 1989, as "Shirokiya Day" in honor of the first store's 30th anniversary.

On the domestic front, the early 1960s found department stores facing unprecedented demand for household goods such as televisions and washing machines. However, the stores were also presented with growing competition from the newly-arrived supermarkets and superstores which, sited away from town centers as they tended to be, could often provide shoppers with a more pleasant environment and lower-priced goods. Despite this competition, Toyoko continued to grow, both through acquisition and through construction of attractive new stores. In 1966 Toyoko formed a tie-up with Nagano Maruzen, which in 1970 would change its name to the Nagano Tokyu Department Store Ltd.

The company adopted its current name of Tokyu Department Store Co., Ltd. in 1967, the year in which it opened a new main store in Shibuya at one of Tokyo's largest railway stations. Both this and the original Toyoko Store nearby were to undergo an important expansion program in the late 1960s.

Also in 1967, the 300-year old Shirokiya shop changed its name to the Nihonbashi Tokyu Department Store. Its advantageous site, adjacent to the intersection of three subway lines and in an important shopping and business district, continued to make it one of Tokyu's busiest enterprises.

The 1973 oil shock precipitated a period of stagnation in the department-store sector. In spite of this, the 1970s were notable for the opening of several new Tokyu stores. In 1973 came the new Sapporo Tokyu Department Store, situated across the road from Sapporo Station in Hokkaido. This was the first Tokyu store to open outside the capital, and Tokyu made a point of staffing it locally to ensure a strong rapport with shoppers and a thorough understanding of their preferences. Initially a company in its own right, Sapporo Tokyu Department Store was to merge with Tokyu Department Store in 1978.

The Kichijoji store opened in 1974 at the Japan Railways Kichijoji Station in Musashino City, Tokyo. In 1980 the Machida Tokyu Department Store Co. began trading; it would become part of the Tokyu Department Store Co. in 1989. Machida is one of Tokyo's most rapidly-growing residential suburbs, and the store offers mainly sporting and leisure equipment to local shoppers.

During the 1970s and 1980s there was a trend toward specialization among Japanese department stores. A store would cater to specific groups of customers, such as newly-married women or teenagers. In 1979 Tokyu Department Store affiliate T.M.D. opened Shibuyu 109, a center aimed at the fashion-conscious woman and by the 1990s containing 93 separate shops. Its success sparked off a series of similar enterprises, including the KOHRINBO 109 in Kanazawa, opened in 1985; One-Oh-Nine, opened in 1986; and 109-2, opened in 1987.

In 1990 Tokyu launched the first of a new style of fashion store, 1 2 3 (pronounced "un deux trois") in Shibuya. Among the boutiques it comprised was Trans Continents, an outlet for Tokyu affiliate Millenium Japan Ltd., also founded in 1990 as a retailer of fashion clothing and accessories. This exemplifies Tokyu's participation in the trend for Japanese retailers to develop own-brand fashion products, appealing to consumers in the way that designer-labeled goods do, but undercutting designer-label prices.

In the 1980s Tokyu added energetically to its overseas interests, starting with the opening of the Hong Kong Tokyu store in 1980 when it became the principal tenant of the then recently-completed New World Center in Kowloon on the Chinese mainland. Then came stores in Bangkok and Thailand in 1985, and in Singapore in 1987. In each case Tokyu made a point of integrating itself into the local community—the slogan of the Singapore store is "Born and Raised in Singapore"—while offering shoppers a taste of Japanese courtesy and quality. Outside Asia, the OK Gift Shop 109 opened in Auckland, New Zealand, in 1990.

As well as opening new stores, Tokyu expanded overseas through acquisition. It bought the Dragon Seed Co. Ltd., a Hong Kong department store company, in 1988 from investment company First Pacific. With Dragon Seed, Tokyu gained a valuable building in the Central area of Hong Kong Island, as well as a ten-store chain. Tokyu bought an equity participation in the Ever Green Department Store Corporation of Taiwan in 1990.

Tokyu's overseas operations were not confined to its retail outlets. International buying operations and tie-ups were becoming increasingly important. Tokyu acquired the monopoly for Jim Thompson Thai silk in 1985, opening a Jim Thompson boutique in its main store. In 1988 it formed an alliance with Williams-Sonoma, a U.S. catalog-sales company, to establish Williams-Sonoma Japan. Williams-Sonoma specialties include household goods and furnishings.

Overseas buying was not exclusively a quest for exotica. Like many of its competitors, Tokyu Department Store sought to reduce its unit costs through imports, and adopted a "develop and import" system whereby it joined forces with local interests to produce goods for sale initially in the local marketplace and, when a sufficiently high standard had been attained, for import to Japan. Goods imported in this way included knitwear from China, clothing from Hong Kong, and fruit from Thailand.

The 1980s was a period of recovery in the Japanese consumer market. Tokyu's expansion in the 1970s had left it well placed to benefit despite continued fierce competition from supermarkets. New Tokyu department stores continued to open. The Kitami Tokyu began trading in 1982 and the Komoro Tokyu store in Nagano prefecture, part of the Nagano Tokyu Department Store Co., began trading the following year, as did the Tama Plaza Tokyu department store. The Tama Plaza Shopping Center, constructed by Tokyu Corporation, was adjacent to Tama Plaza station in Yokohama, and the department store was its principal occupant. The Tama Plaza Tokyu Department Store Co. became the Seinan Tokyu Department Store Co. in 1989, though the store itself continued to be known as Tama Plaza.

Japanese department stores appear to be more successful if they frequently remodel their premises to refresh their appeal to their customers. Interior redesigns of existing outlets have also been a response to government planning restrictions on the building of new stores.

Remodeling of stores was a keynote of Tokyu's activities throughout the 1980s. In 1984 it celebrated the 50th anniversary of the opening of Toyoko Department Store with a radical remodeling of the main store in Shibuya. This flagship store now contains a range of specialty shops under one roof. The Shibuya store's food department in the basement was greatly extended in 1990. The Toyoko store was refitted in 1985 and 1986. This, too, houses a mall of specialty shops, including concessions such as Benetton, and the first Williams-Sonoma Japan retail outlet, which opened in 1988 with a view to enhancing Williams-Sonoma's understanding of local consumer preferences for the benefit of the mail-order side of its business. The store's exterior was renovated in 1989.

Outside Tokyo, too, shops were constantly being restyled to keep abreast of consumer preferences. The Nagano Tokyu store was extended in 1986 and a new annex called Cherchez was added, making this the largest urban department store in the Nagano prefecture.

In 1988 the Kichijoji store was redecorated, and the Sapporo store embarked on an extension and renewal program. Thanks to the opening of a new subway line, the store's food floor in the basement was now directly connected to Sapporo station. The Nihonbashi store, too, underwent a dramatic transformation, reopening complete with La Plasis, a huge customer service mall offering postal, travel, and other facilities. The renovated store also boasted a greatly expanded women's clothing department. A couple of years later the Nihonbashi store was crowned with the imaginative addition of a rooftop golf school.

During the 1970s and 1980s the Japanese department store sector, which had previously dominated the retail industry in terms of both sales and profitability, began to lag behind the supermarket companies with their out-of-town superstores. This tendency was attributed partly to the supermarkets' faster conversion to information technology. In 1988, however, Tokyu introduced a Point of Sale (POS) system to all its department stores to automate stock control and keep track of local customer preferences.

Tokyu was also innovative in finding ways to woo the shopper back from the superstores. In February 1987, for instance, *The Economist* reported that four Tokyu stores had introduced door-to-door sales teams of housewives selling on commission. This personal approach was so successful that several other department stores quickly followed suit.

Japanese stores try to lure shoppers through their own doors by helping to improve the area of the city in which they operate; for example, an adjunct of the Toyoko Store renovation in 1985 was a project to improve and promote the whole street in cooperation with local government. This form of competition has become known as the "Commercial Block War."

Tokyu has played a major role in the revitalization of the Shibuya area, where its headquarters and largest stores are situated. Tokyu's most spectacular contribution to date has been the Bunkamura or Tokyu Culture Village. A cooperative venture between a number of Tokyu companies, it involved the construction of a large complex including art gallery, concert hall, and theatre. It opened in 1989 on a site adjacent to Tokyu's main store, and the *Japan Company Handbook* soon reported that takings at the main store were shooting up under the influence of the Bunkamura.

In the early 1990s, investments such as this should continue to pay dividends. Healthy turnover of goods such as jewelry and fine art reflects the luxurious ambience which Tokyu strives to project in its stores and malls. New stores continue to open, usually in the proximity of stations. In 1990, for instance, Nagano Tokyu Department Store Co., Ltd. opened its Nagano Tokyu Life Store at the Japan Railways Kita-Nagano Station. A new store, provisionally named the Aobadai Tokyu Department Store, is scheduled to open at Aobadai Station in Tokyo in 1993. Refurbishment also continues apace with the expansion of the Machida store, due for completion in 1992.

Tokyu is pursuing an active policy of expansion in and beyond the Pacific Rim area. There are now four Hawaii stores and one each in Hong Kong, Bangkok, and Singapore, as well as a further six representative offices worldwide. A second Thai store is preparing to open in 1993.

Synergy with other companies in the group is an important factor in the success of Tokyu Department Store; for instance, the retailing and distribution group also comprises a supermarket chain, the Tokyu Store Chain, with over 100 stores in the greater Tokyo area. Like the department stores, most of these adjoin the Tokyu Corporation's railway lines. Tokyu Department Store and Tokyu Store Chain can combine to achieve economies of scale in buying and distribution.

Tokyu also operates specialty stores such as Tokyu Time Co., started in 1965 to sell and repair watches, and Sports Tokyu Co., started in 1970. Both of these are affiliates of Tokyu Department Store Co., while a number of other specialty stores, such as Top Shoes, are more closely linked with the Tokyu Store Chain Co. All these specialty stores are available for inclusion in Tokyu Department Store's shopping malls.

The slogan of the Tokyu Companies is "Creating a well-balanced life for the 21st century." This aspiration is reflected in Tokyu Department Store's community- and lifestyle-oriented approach to its customers. The stores do not simply try to sell individual products and services; they offer lectures, cultural events, and educational programs to the public to reinforce the sales message and at the same time improve the quality of life. The stores use local staff to emphasise that the business is rooted in the customer community.

In the 1990s the competitive environment in which Tokyu Department Store operates is undergoing a dramatic transformation. The Large Store Law which restricted the construction of new stores is being relaxed in response to the Japanese-American Structural Impediments Initiative. This liberalization will make it easier for Tokyu to expand, but equally it will throw its market open to foreign competitors.

Writing in *Business JAPAN* (August, 1990) in his capacity as chairman of the Japan Department Stores Association, Tokyu Department Store's president Mamoru Miura discussed the legislative changes and warned that Japan was about to encounter an "increasingly sinister" economic environment with labor shortages, rising interest rates, and unstable stock and foreign exchange markets. He identified the internationalization of the marketplace and the need for better information management as the two main challenges facing the department store industry in the coming decade. With its experience of overseas link-ups and its well-established computer systems—it even owns its own software development company, Tokyu Information Systems—Tokyu Department Store looks well positioned to face both of these challenges.

Principal Subsidiaries: Nagano Tokyu Department Store Co., Ltd.; Seinan Tokyu Department Store Co., Ltd.; Kitami

Tokyu Department Store Co., Ltd.; T.M.D. Co., Ltd.; Tokyu Time Co., Ltd.; Sports Tokyu Co., Ltd.; Shibuya Underground Shopping Center Co., Ltd.; UN International Co., Ltd.; Tokyu Information Systems Co., Ltd.; Williams-Sonoma Japan Co., Ltd.; Millennium Japan Ltd.; Shirokiya, Inc.; Hong Kong Tokyu Department Store Co., Ltd.; Tokyu Department Store (Singapore) Pte. Ltd.; Tokyu Foods Co., Ltd.; Gold Pak Co., Ltd.; Tokyu Department Store Service Co., Ltd.; Sapporo Plaza Co., Ltd.

Further Reading: "Doorsteps, the New Point of Sale," *The Economist,* February 28, 1987; *Retail Distribution in Japan,* Tokyo, Dodwell Marketing Consultants, 1988; Miura, Mamoru, "Department Stores Must Act as Integrated Life Industries, *Business Japan*, August, 1990; *Diamond's Japan Business Directory 1991,* Tokyo, Diamond Lead Co., Ltd., 1991.

—Alison Classe

TOYS "R" US, INC.

461 From Road
Paramus, New Jersey 07652
U.S.A.
(201) 262-7800
Fax: (201) 262-8919

Public Company
Incorporated: 1978
Employees: 40,000
Sales: $5.51 billion
Stock Exchange: New York

With sales of more than $5 billion, Toys "R" Us operates the world's largest toy store chain, with 497 stores in the United States and 126 in Canada, France, Hong Kong, Malaysia, Singapore, Taiwan, the United Kingdom, Germany, Spain, and Japan. The company also operates the 189–store Kids "R" Us children's apparel chain. Industry analysts laud Toys "R" Us for its streamlined operations, ability to respond quickly to its customers' ever-changing demands, and its success in making the toy retail business less seasonal. The company has long been a leader in using sophisticated computer systems to track what is selling in each store, to predict the items that will be popular in coming weeks, and to cut check-out time. All major administrative and buying decisions are made at company head-quarters, and as Chairman and Chief Executive Officer Charles Lazarus often puts it, only the selling is done in the stores.

Identical in design, each supermarket-style Toys "R" Us store is 46,000 square feet and stocks a minimum of 18,000 items on shelves that reach to the ceiling. The stores offer large selections of toys and baby furnishings at discount prices and feature a "no questions asked" return policy. Items such as diapers are sold at little or no profit, serving as a means to entice new parents into the store. The fast-growing Kids "R" Us chain uses many of the same operating principles as its parent company. Also set up as a supermarket, each 20,000-square-foot store offers children's clothing, shoes, and accessories. Although not completely insulated from downturns in the economy, Toys "R" Us consistently succeeds in improving same-store sales and in boosting its market share.

Toys "R" Us founder Charles Lazarus was born above the shop in Washington, D.C., where his father repaired and sold used bicycles. After a stint in the army, Lazarus opened the National Baby Shop, a children's furniture store, in 1948, just two years after the beginning of the baby boom.

Lazarus noted that customers often asked if he sold toys, so just a year after he opened shop, he began adding rattles and stuffed animals to his stock. In 1952 he opened Baby Furniture and Toy Supermarket in Washington, D.C. Five years later, he opened a discount toy supermarket in Rockville, Maryland, a Washington suburb. It was the first to bear the Toys "R" Us name. The store's original name was too long to fit on its sign, so Lazarus changed it to the descriptive Toys "R" Us. By 1965 he was operating four such outlets in the Washington, D.C., area. In 1966 Lazarus sold his four profitable toy super-markets to Interstate Stores Inc., but continued to serve as president of the company he had founded.

Interstate was founded in 1916 and became publicly owned in 1927. In 1957 the company had 46 small department stores in its fold, but it sales growth had dwindled to almost nothing, and its profit margins were shrinking. The company sought relief for its financial woes in the burgeoning discount store arena. It experimented with a discount store in Allentown, Pennsylvania, and by 1960 had acquired two discount chains: the White Front Stores in southern California and the Topps chain, located mainly in New England.

Interstate undertook an aggressive but ill-fated expansion of its discount stores. The company overextended itself in the discount business, and the 1973–1974 recession aggravated its problems. In 1974 Interstate declared bankruptcy, its debt at the time the largest accumulation of liabilities in retail history. By that year Interstate had 51 Toys "R" Us stores, and it continued to open new ones during its court-ordered reorganization.

Before 1974 Toys "R" Us was still ordering and counting stock manually, but that year the company streamlined its ordering and inventory system by installing its first computer mainframe. In years to come the company would upgrade its computer system many times to keep pace with its ever-growing sales volume and inventory level.

In 1978 Interstate emerged from its reorganization a vastly different company. It had closed or sold all its discount store operations; only the 63–store toy chain and 10 traditional department stores remained. To reflect its principal business, the company had changed its name to Toys "R" Us, with Lazarus serving as its president and chief executive officer.

Beginning in 1978 Milton Petrie, owner of Petrie Stores, a women's clothing chain, began to acquire Toys "R" Us stock, owning approximately 25% by 1984. That year Lazarus told Toys "R" Us shareholders that he had received Petrie's assurance that he would not attempt to acquire the company. By the late 1980s, Petrie reduced the amount of stock he owned in the company to 14%.

By the end of 1980 Toys "R" Us was a 101–store chain. The Christmas season that year was a troubled one for many toy retailers, but thanks to its computerized inventory system, Toys "R" Us noted a glut of slow-moving electronics items on its shelves and cut prices on those toys long before the Christmas buying season. This cost-cutting allowed the retailer to make room on its shelves for other, more desired items that were not discounted, while other toy retailers were selling their slow-moving toys at lower prices that holiday season.

Lazarus's approach to pricing was vastly different than that of his competitors. He sold the items shoppers wanted most at little or no profit. Customers would then automatically assume that all of the items in the store were equally well priced and do the rest of their toy shopping there. The company's market share climbed steadily each year, rising from 5% in 1978 to 9% in 1981.

By 1980 Toys "R" Us had earned a solid reputation as a retailer of great efficiency. Since its reorganization three years earlier, Toys "R" Us's sales had more than doubled to nearly 750 million dollars in fiscal 1981. With its 120 stores, there seemed to be no serious threats to the company's growing dominance of the retail toy market, and company executives were often quoted as saying they sought not so much to boost sales as to increase market share. In 1982 Lionel Corporation's Lionel Leisure, a chain of 98 toy stores, filed for bankruptcy.

In a 1982 article in *Advertising Age,* Toys "R" Us Vice President of Real Estate Michael Miller explained that his company was seeking markets of at least 250,000 people, of which 25% must be children. To assure that advertising and distribution dollars are spent cost effectively, Miller explained, each market had to be big enough to support four of the toy stores.

Toys "R" Us announced in 1982 the formation of a new division to sell name-brand children's apparel at discount prices. The company had first-hand experience with the baby-boom generation's willingness to spend money on their children. Social changes such as increasing numbers of divorces, single working mothers, and more two-paycheck families meant more sales for purveyors of children's toys, apparel, and accessories. Divorced parents often spend more money on their children than do married parents. Two-paycheck families, who have often put off having children while they developed careers, were also known to be willing and able to spend more on their children than previous generations.

The company opened two pilot Kids "R" Us stores in the New York metropolitan area during the summer of 1983. The 15,000-square-foot, exuberantly decorated stores featured electronic games and clearly marked departments. From the day the first pilot store opened its doors, the new chain was recognized by owners of department and specialty stores as a major threat to their survival.

All was not easy for Kids "R" Us, however. In the 1980s traditional department stores and small children's shops complained that makers of name-brand apparel were selling their goods to discounters. The new competition from Kids "R" Us further raised the stakes. Just a few months after Kids "R" Us opened its first two stores, Toys "R" Us filed suit in September 1983 against Federated Department Stores Inc. and General Mills Inc., charging the companies with price-fixing. The following month, the company brought a similar suit against Absorba, which had agreed to supply the new stores, but later allegedly refused to fill the order. Toys "R" Us dropped the suits in January 1984, noting only that circumstances had made it prudent to terminate the litigation.

The Kids "R" Us concept successfully implemented many of the policies Toys "R" Us had, such as discount pricing, tight inventory control, purchasing in large volume, and opening stores in low-rent strip malls along major thoroughfares. In 1983 the company surpassed the $1 billion milestone, with sales of $1.3 billion. Two more Kids "R" Us stores opened in New Jersey in the summer of 1984. The new stores added more than 5,000 additional square feet to the prototype's original 15,000. The roomier layout included a "race track" design that wended its way through the store. By spring 1985 there

were 10 Kids "R" Us units in New York and New Jersey, with an additional 15 to be opened by year's end.

The company opened its first toy stores outside the United States in 1984, with four in Canada and one in Singapore. It opened five stores in the United Kingdom the following year.

An article in *Dun's Business Month* in December 1985 cited Toys "R" Us as one of the nation's best-managed companies and credited Lazarus with developing an extraordinary management team. With few exceptions the company promoted from within, the article noted. In 1984 Toys "R" Us stockholders approved a generous stock option plan open to all full-time employees. Lazarus told *Dun's* that salaries alone were no longer enough to make people feel they have a stake in a company's success.

Between 1980 and 1985, the toy retailing industry grew 37%, while Toys "R" Us's sales increased 185%. The company estimated in 1985 that it had 14% of all U.S. retail toy sales, an increase of 9% from the share it had in 1978, the year the company emerged from its reorganization.

Charles Lazarus told *Dun's Business Month* in 1985 that market share was his company's number one priority. To keep increasing market share, he explained, the company was willing to cut prices, even if earnings suffered. Lazarus called Toys "R" Us's highly computerized merchandising system the ultimate market research tool. He explained that it helps the company project sales for each item it sells and to know not only when to order particular toys but also when to drop them.

Toys "R" Us has always been willing to try new tools to increase its market share. During the 1985 Christmas season, the company launched *Toys "R" Us Magazine,* which was sold in its stores for 79¢. Aimed at slightly older children, the well-received magazine contained feature stories on animals, celebrities, adventure, and travel and included ads for television shows, clothes, and toys. A second issue was offered during the summer of 1986, but the magazine was eventually phased out.

By January 1986 Toys "R" Us had 233 toy stores in the United States, 13 international toy stores, 23 Kids "R" Us outlets, and 4 traditional department stores. A little more than a year later, the company opened 37 additional Toys "R" Us stores in the United States, 11 new overseas stores, and 14 new Kids "R" Us stores. The company's market share stood at 15% of the $12 billion toy industry.

During the summer of 1986 Toys "R" Us and Montgomery Ward announced that they would open a store jointly that fall in Gaithersburg, Maryland. Each store would operate independently, but would share an entrance and exterior sign. The arrangement was a boon to Ward, which had restructured its business and had surplus floor space in many of its locations. Toys "R" Us found the arrangement beneficial since many of the Ward stores were in excellent locations, and rental rates were often quite reasonable. Five years later, the companies were sharing six locations and were considering additional sites.

As it grew into a national chain, Toys "R" Us aggressively fought other companies that used the "R" that is such a distinctive part of its name. Tots "R" Us, Lamps "R" Us, and Films "R" Us were among the companies sued by Toys "R" Us for name infringement. Michael Goldstein, the company's executive vice president, told *The Wall Street Journal* in January 1986 that the company had never lost a name-infringement suit.

Even when toy sales were sluggish, Toys "R" Us managed to perform well. During the 1986 Christmas season, the company's sales far exceeded many analysts' grim forecasts. Its success was attributed to its ability to offer the toys that shoppers were interested in buying.

In a bid to further increase its market share, the company surprised the retailing industry in 1987 by announcing that it would pass on to customers the savings it expected to receive from lower tax rates. Two additional retailers, Wal-Mart and Target quickly followed Toys "R" Us's lead.

During 1987, the year in which the Toys "R" Us international division moved into the black, the company opened four stores in as many German cities. The company had planned to open even more stores during the year, but found it difficult to secure the required permits from local bodies for a retail outlet larger than 18,000 square feet. Competing German retailers had good reason for concern. In the United Kingdom Toys "R" Us had captured 9% of the $1.8 billion toy market in just three years.

The products of two prestigious German toy manufacturers, Steiff and Maerklin, were not sold in the new German Toys "R" Us stores. Steiff, maker of high-quality stuffed animals and dolls, chose not to do business with the toy giant out of loyalty to smaller-scale German retailers. Maerklin's electric trains, sold without packaging, could not be offered in a toy supermarket setting.

From the very start, the Toys "R" Us overseas stores had been strikingly similar to those in the United States. Most were freestanding buildings, and all were bulging with many of the 18,000 items for which Toys "R" Us is famous. Approximately 80% of the items offered were the same as those found in U.S. stores, with the remaining 20% chosen to reflect local interests.

Sales for the 1987 fiscal year, the first in which Kids "R" Us earned a profit, surpassed the $3 billion mark. The company attributed part of its success during the 1987 holiday season to its upgraded universal product code (UPC) scanning system, which had been installed in all the Toys "R" Us stores shortly before Thanksgiving. The benefits of product scanning include having up-to-the-minute data about every product the company sells, shorter transaction time, fewer cashier errors, and a reduction in marking costs in those stores that use only shelf tagging.

During the 1987 Christmas season, a Florida newspaper published a cartoon showing a couple burdened with many gifts leaving a Toys "R" Us store. The caption beneath read, "Broke 'R' Us." Company executives thought it was so funny that copies were posted around their offices.

By January 1988 the company had 313 U.S. toy stores, 74 Kids "R" Us outlets and 37 international toy stores. Plans to open stores in Italy and France were also in the offing.

Charles Lazarus told *The Wall Street Journal* in August 1988 that his goal was to sell half of all toys sold in the United States. While that might have sounded overly ambitious, signs abounded that Lazarus was well on the way to meeting his goal. Even though toy sales in 1986 and 1987 grew an average of 2%, sales at Toys "R" Us grew 27% during each of those years.

The toy chain consistently proved itself capable of turning away all pretenders to the throne of top toy retailer. Its two nearest rivals, Child World Inc., with 152 stores and Lionel, with 78, offered similarly large toy selections in equally cav-

ernous structures, but neither had been able to equal the success of the originator of the toy supermarket concept.

The company's success can be attributed to many factors, including its buying clout, great selection, deep inventories, and ability to identify the latest hot items and get them on the sales floor fast. When some companies' stores were finding it difficult to get sufficient quantities of Nintendo games in early 1988, for instance, Toys "R" Us was able to get the number of Nintendo games it wanted.

The Wall Street Journal noted in 1988 that Toys "R" Us sold $330.80 worth of merchandise per square foot annually, with Child World selling only $221.70, and Lionel just $193.10. Average sales for a Toys "R" Us store were $8.4 million; for Child World, $4.9 million; and for Lionel, $4.4 million.

In fall 1988 Toys "R" Us shed the last reminder of its connection to Interstate Stores when it sold its remaining department stores in Albany and Schenectady, New York, and Flint, Michigan, to that division's management. Between 1987 and 1989, Toys "R" Us opened 133 new U.S. toy stores, 50 international toy stores, and 94 children's clothing stores. Company sales hit the $4 billion mark in fiscal year 1988, and the following year, total sales were more than $4.8 billion, with a 25% market share of the $13 billion U.S. retail toy market.

In fall 1989 Toys "R" Us joined McDonald's Company (Japan) Ltd. in announcing a joint venture to open several toy stores in Japan. Toys "R" Us would have an 80% interest in the venture and McDonald's a 20% interest with an option to open restaurants at the store sites. Although difficulties in finding store sites and in circumventing the large-scale retail law still loomed before them, the joint-venture company planned to eventually open 100 stores in Japan.

For many other U.S. retailers interested in opening outlets in Japan, Toys "R" Us was to become a test case in how to overcome local Japanese retailers' resistance to their entry into a particular market. Japanese retailers had already felt the pinch of a birth rate that had been in decline since 1973 and did not relish a further erosion of their market share. U.S. officials, however, persuaded Japanese governmental bodies to speed up their approval process on applications for large retail stores, and the first Toys "R" Us in Japan opened late in 1991 in Ami Town, on the outskirts of Tokyo.

Toys "R" Us launched Geoffrey's Fun Club during the 1989 holiday season. The company said the club was to be low-key and noncommercial, offering club members quarterly mailings featuring items such as an activity booklet with the child's name or a storybook that presented the child as the main character, with his or her name repeated throughout the book. The club, designed to boost Toys "R" Us's profile in the homes of members, more than doubled the company's membership projections.

Toys "R" Us had some difficulties with importing toys deemed dangerous by the Consumer Product Safety Commission. In spring 1990 it had to recall 38,000 "Press N Roll" Toy boats with small parts that, if broken off, could choke a child. That summer Toys "R" Us was one of seven distributors sued by the Justice Department on charges of selling hazardous toys, such as a xylophone painted with lead-based paint, and toys with unsafe, small parts on which children could choke. Toys "R" Us successfully defended itself on the grounds that its safety record was excellent, and a federal judge dismissed the charges.

Toys "R" Us is likely to remain the leading toy retailer for many years to come. It consistently makes innovative, long-term investments that ensure its continued toy retailing preeminence by offering, in Lazarus's words, "selection, stock and price." As Lazarus told *Forbes* magazine in 1988 when describing his company's entry into the U.K. market, "Some very bright people said: 'Your prices could be 20% higher and you'd still undersell everybody in the marketplace.' No. That's not Toys "R" Us. The idea is to be preemptive, to sell at such low prices that no one will even try to compete." There is always room in this tightly controlled company for innovations to further decrease operating costs. For instance, in 1989 Toys "R" Us completed installation of gravity-feed-flow racks in most of its U.S. toy stores to reduce the costs involved in restocking fast-moving diapers and formula. In mid-1990 the company opened a $40 million distribution center in Rialto, California, that holds 45% more merchandise than the company's other warehouses, but takes up one-third less land. As an industry analyst told *The Wall Street Transcript* in 1989, "I can look at a slowing economy and still feel comfortable that Toys "R" Us is going to grow."

Principal Subsidiaries: Toys "R" Us International; Kids "R" Us.

Further Reading: Barmash, Isadore, "Gains in Retail Discounting: Interstate's Story of Growth," *The New York Times,* July 23, 1967; Solomon, Goody L., "Discount Toy Stores Gladden the Hearts of Toddlers and Merchants," *Barron's,* August 11, 1969; Gilman, Hank, "Retail Genius: Founder Lazarus Is a Reason Toys 'R' Us Dominates Its Industry," *The Wall Street Journal,* November 21, 1985; Rosen, M. Daniel, "Toys 'R' Us: Taking Toys to the Top," *Solutions,* March/April 1988.

—Mary Sue Mohnke

U.S. Shoe

THE UNITED STATES SHOE CORPORATION

One Eastwood Drive
Cincinnati, Ohio 45227
U.S.A.
(513) 527-7000
Fax: (513) 561-2007

Public Company
Incorporated: 1931
Employees: 49,000
Sales: $2.72 billion
Stock Exchanges: New York Pacific

The United States Shoe Corporation not only manufactures, imports and sells 25 of the most popular brands of shoes in the United States, but also operates 56 Lens Crafters optical stores as well as 1,763 women's retail clothing stores, among them Casual Corner, Petite Sophisticate, and August Max Woman speciality shops. The company has become the United States's second-largest operator of women's specialty retail stores, while Lens Crafters is the largest optical chain in the United States and Canada.

The origins of the multibillion–dollar United States Shoe Corporation lie in Cincinnati, Ohio, in the 1870s, at a time when there were virtually no brand names for shoes, nor any difference between left and right shoe, and all shoes were of the same width. Nonetheless, the shoe business in those days was intensely competitive and concentrated in New England. Cincinnati, however, was a prosperous, booming area that attracted numerous industrious immigrants, among them German immigrants. Their descendants founded the Stern-Auer Shoe Company in 1879 with a small factory in the heart of Cincinnati. In 1896 two other residents of the city, Irwin Krohn and Samuel Fechheimer, founded the Krohn-Fechheimer Shoe Company, which produced Red Cross shoes. Irwin Krohn was a believer in brand names, with which customers could identify and that were easy to advertise. By the mid-1890s the name Red Cross was a well-known brand. It originated with a red-haired merchant named Cross, who christened his tomato ketchup Red Cross. This name caught on rapidly and was soon used on other products.

Red Cross women's shoes, advertised as the "noiseless" shoe, caught on as quickly as had Red Cross ketchup and brought the firm of Krohn-Fechheimer much prosperity. However, the modest but growing companies of Stern-Auer and

Krohn-Fechheimer suffered setbacks in the aftermath of World War I. The boom years of the war quickly gave way to economic recession and inflation, and high-topped women's shoes, in vogue for generations, had gone out of style. This brought a need for serious adjustments, which were stymied by a six-month strike in the Cincinnati shoe industry in 1921. A local industrialist, Lewis S. Rosenthal, initiated a proposal to merge eight Cincinnati-area shoe firms, including Krohn-Fechheimer, into the United States Shoe Company. The future looked good, as the Red Cross shoe brand was still popular, and the economy had begun to recover.

The new United States Shoe Company foundered, however, the fault lying not in the product as much as in the marketing arena. By 1929 the firm had virtually collapsed and might have expired had not Stern-Auer come to the rescue. In 1913 Joseph S. Stern, Sr., had joined Stern-Auer, and he turned out to have a talent for marketing. Sensing the possibilities of the Krohn-Fechheimer Red Cross shoe brand, Stern-Auer proposed a merger with the United States Shoe Company, but only if Stern-Auer could be in charge of marketing the famous brand. Negotiations dragged on for the formation of the new United States Shoe Corporation, of which Joseph S. Stern, Sr., would become president.

The time for the establishment of a new corporation could not have been less auspicious—the depths of the Great Depression. Critics scoffed when the newly minted United States Shoe Corporation (U.S. Shoe), incorporated in the fall of 1931, announced that henceforth it would produce for $6 retail the same Red Cross shoe that had been selling at $10. Production skyrocketed, however, from 600 pairs per day to 3,000 pairs by 1933. Soon demand exceeded production, and by 1939 the Red Cross shoe had become the most popular brand in the United States. The firm grew, and no employees were laid off during the Depression. Joseph S. Stern, Sr., and soon his son, Joseph S. Stern, Jr., would lead the company to greater growth. Employees benefited from the prosperity—in 1940 a profit-sharing plan was introduced at a time when other industries were barely recovering from economic hard times, and in 1952 an employee pension plan was offered.

Red Cross shoes were doing well at home and abroad, where, in English-speaking countries as distant as South Africa and Australia, they were marketed as Gold Cross shoes. To keep up with demand, two factories were purchased, one in Chillicothe, Ohio, in 1936, and the shoe factory of Plaut-Butler, Inc., in Harrison, Ohio, in 1941. U.S. Shoe bid for and won the right to design the official Women's Army Corps shoe during World War II, which heightened the company's prestige. At the onset of the war, the American National Red Cross objected to the commercial use of the name Red Cross, and a ban on the use of the name was proposed by the House Foreign Affairs Committee in 1942. The board of directors of U.S. Shoe voluntarily suspended use of the name; the Federal Trade Commission allowed the resumption of its use in 1948. After the war the demand for shoes, after years of rationing, was so great that another plant was opened—a modern factory in Crothersville, Indiana. Because of a worldwide leather shortage, however, the new plant was forced to shut down temporarily soon after it opened. Finally, production climbed and between 1946 and 1953, four additional factories were added. The Red Cross label was reinstated on the condition that the company publicly disclaim any association with the American

National Red Cross, and the energetic Joseph S. Stern, Sr., became chairman of the board in 1947, a post he would hold for the next 18 years. As president and chairman, he would oversee the company's rapid expansion in the 1950s. In 1953 a record of 435,000 pairs of shoes were manufactured. In 1955, when shoe production reached 100,000 pairs a week, more factories had to be bought. In 1956 the company was listed on the New York Stock Exchange.

While still the largest manufacturer of women's shoes in the country, U.S. Shoe began to plan ahead, its directors realizing that untrammeled growth based on one shoe brand would be impossible in the long run. Europe was recovering from the ravages of World War II, and Spanish as well as Italian shoes were beginning to compete in the United States. Broadening into other marketing areas, starting with other shoe brands, was in order.

U.S. Shoe began its diversification in 1955 with the acquisition of Joyce Inc., which produced a popular brand of women's shoe under the Joyce name. In 1957 U.S. Shoe acquired rights to the brand name Selby. The company also introduced other brands, such as Cobbies and Socialites. In 1961 the company entered the lucrative children's shoe market with the purchase of Vaisey-Bristol Shoe Company, maker of Jumping-Jacks and other children's brands. These acquisitions and accompanying expansions brought the number of factories to 12, no longer confined to Ohio but located across the Midwest and in Puerto Rico. Also in 1961 U.S. Shoe formed Imperial Adhesives, Inc., to enable the company to develop its own shoe-manufacturing materials and depend less on outside suppliers.

U.S. Shoe entered the shoe retailing business in the 1960s, acquiring Wm. Hahn & Co. in 1963, and Cutter-Karcher Shoe Company in 1964. Responding to the popularity of foreign-made shoes, in 1962 U.S. Shoe acquired Marx & Newman Company, a leading importer based in New York. In 1970 U.S. Shoe opened its Europa division with the establishment of a European liaison office in Florence, Italy, followed by the establishment of an office in Alicante, Spain, and in 1978, one in Taiwan.

In 1965 Joseph S. Stern, Sr., stepped down as chairman, to be succeeded by Nathan Stix, who had been president since 1961. Joseph S. Stern, Jr., took over as president. In 1967 U.S. Shoe was the fourth-largest manufacturer of shoes in the United States and by then was also manufacturing boots, after having acquired Texas Boot Manufacturing Company in 1965. While U.S. Shoe continued acquiring other shoe companies, in the next few years it diversified into women's and men's apparel. In 1969 U.S. Shoe purchased Casual Corner, followed in 1970 by the formation of J. Riggings, a group of specialty men's stores. This was followed by the acquisition in 1981 of a discount women's apparel retailer, T.H. Mandy.

In 1980 a new office park and complex for U.S. Shoe was dedicated in Cincinnati. It would house a corporate office building, raw materials warehouse, and a finished goods distribution center. By then Philip G. Barach was president of the company and chairman of the board. The 1980s would pose the greatest challenges to the company, which had to confront the major competition of cheap Asian and South American imports.

By the late 1980s, half of the company's income was derived from women's apparel retailing operations, whose stores numbered in the 1,800 range. In fact, the clothing division of U.S.

Shoe by 1989 was the second-largest group of women's apparel stores in the United States, almost all of them located in shopping malls. The largest number of stores belonged to Casual Corner, a highly successful national retail chain; the runner-up was Petite Sophisticate, purchased in 1983 and one of the first major U.S. chains geared to petite women. Sales of Petite Sophisticate soared from $6 million in 1983 to a $168 million in 1989. Trailing the two leading chains were Ups 'N' Downs, geared to the shrinking teen market, and August Max Woman, earmarked for larger-sized women. In 1991 U.S. Shoe decided to sell Ups 'N' Downs.

By far the biggest success for U.S. Shoe in the 1980s was the performance of its optical chain, Lens Crafters. From 1988 to 1989, sales of Lens Crafters grew 28%. The largest optical store chain in the United States and Canada, Lens Crafters was the only national chain offering one-hour service. By the early 1990s, Lens Crafters numbered more than 400 stores, located not only in malls but in strategic business locations in remote areas, with plans to open 100 more. During the recession of the early 1990s, sales of Lens Crafters stores plummeted for the first time, alarming investors, although U.S. Shoe management predicted a strong comeback. Expansion into England and other European countries, where there were no optical superstores, was expected to increase sales.

Footwear accounted for only one third of U.S. Shoe's sales by the late 1980s. Despite the presence of offices in Europe, Asia, and Brazil, sales in the foreign shoe division declined throughout the 1980s. The same held true for domestic shoe sales. In 1989 U.S. Shoe attempted to sell the entire shoe division to an investor group led by Merrill Lynch Capital Partners, which later backed out for reasons not made public. The outlook however, was far from bleak. U.S. Shoe's Easy Spirit line, women's dress shoes with support and comfort features, has grown rapidly and become the largest unit in the shoe division. In the early 1990s, U.S. Shoe was considering expanding Easy Spirit into the men's and children's shoe areas.

Still, some problems in the shoe division remained. Accounting irregularities in the company's Marx & Newman subsidiary caused much concern among investors in 1990; U.S. Shoe took a $7.4 million charge against its earnings and initiated management and policy changes in the unit. The once popular shoe brands, Joyce and Cobbie, suffered from poor style designs. A new chief executive officer, Bannus B. Hudson, elected in 1990, met with skepticism from industry observers because of his inexperience in shoe and women's apparel retailing. U.S. Shoe's knack for inventiveness and adaptability however, will most likely carry the company through these problems.

Principal Subsidiaries: Marx & Newman; Lens Crafters; Women's Specialty Retailing; Cincinnati Shoe; Hahn Shoes; Banister Factory Outlet Stores; Cobbie Shop; Joyce/Selby Shoe; Shop for Pappagallo.

Further Reading: Stern, Joseph S., Jr., and Philip G. Barach, "Address," New York, The Newcomen Society in North America, 1967.

—Sina Dubovoj

UNY CO., LTD.

2-45-19 Meieki
Nakamura-ku
Nagoya 450
Japan
(052) 585 3111
Fax: 052 585 3299

Public Company
Incorporated: 1971
Employees: 6,785
Sales: ¥738.31 billion (US$5.91 billion)
Stock Exchanges: Tokyo Nagoya Luxembourg Paris

Uny Co., Ltd. is the sixth-largest supermarket chain in Japan and a dominant force in Japan's Chubu region. Uny Co., Ltd. is the parent company of a group of more than 20 subsidiaries, including specialty clothing stores, convenience stores, food supermarkets, and the Uny superstores. Uny aims to increase its share of the lucrative but highly competitive Tokyo retail market and has opened a store in Hong Kong.

Uny was founded in 1971 through the merger of the two largest retailing chains in Nagoya, Hoteiya and Nishikawaya. Nagoya is the largest city in Chubu, a group of prefectures situated between the vast industrial cities of Osaka and Tokyo. The history of the Nishikawaya and Hoteiya chains can be traced back to the early 20th century when Choju Nishikawa opened a small footwear store in Nagoya, for which he and his wife manufactured the shoes. The business supported Nishikawa's family but did not grow significantly until he decided to sell kimono. Business flourished and in 1925 the store moved to larger premises in the center of Nagoya. It was also in this year that Nishikawa's third son and future chairman of Uny, Toshio Nishikawa, was born. The store flourished but, like most of the retail sector in Japan, was devastated by World War II; store damage, distribution network disruption, power shortages, and a lack of supplies all wreaked havoc.

After graduating from college with a degree in pharmacology, Toshio Nishikawa joined a pharmaccutical company, where, due to the small size of the organization, he was involved in every aspect of corporate life, including sales, management, and finance. In 1950 Toshio Nishikawa joined the family firm and put into practice the management skills he had gained at his previous job. Nishikawaya still consisted of a single store, and Toshio Nishikawa, along with his two elder brothers, was anxious to expand. Another floor was added,

and in 1950 a limited company, Nishikawaya Co., Ltd., was formed with the aid of ¥900,000 in capital. The family's aim was to turn the group into the number-one retailer in Nagoya in terms of sales, a goal that they were to achieve in less than 20 years. By 1952 the store employed ten people and had sales of ¥30 million. This continued growth made it possible to build a new concrete and steel—rather than the traditional wood—three-story store with floor space of 660 square meters. The store became known as one of the most prestigious in the Nagoya area.

In 1959 a typhoon struck central Japan, killing 3,200 people and causing severe damage to Nagoya. Although the Nishikawaya store provided shelter during the storm for many city dwellers, it too sustained damage. This, however, did not stop the sale that took place the following week. In 1960 a second store was opened in Nagoya, selling food and household goods as well as clothes. At 1,320 square meters, the new store was twice as large as the original one.

The late 1950s and 1960s were a time of frantic economic growth in Japan as the nation strove to compete with the West. One strategy was for Japan's business leaders to travel overseas, mainly to the United States, on information-gathering tours. Returning to Japan, they would not only apply the best of what they saw, but often improve upon it. In 1961 Toshio Nishikawa visited the United States to look for new retailing ideas. Armed with a camera and his curiosity, he visited such U.S. institutions as the Sears, Roebuck and Woolworth stores and the huge supermarkets in Los Angeles. He noted how the style of retailing was geared to the lifestyle of the local people and went back to Japan full of ideas for his business. In particular, the idea of chain store operation contributed to the growth of the company in the following years. In 1963 he launched the Nishikawaya Chain Co., Ltd. and began to open stores around Nagoya and to expand aggressively, launching the first store outside the city in 1966.

In 1971 Nishikawaya Chain Co., Ltd. became the largest retailing chain in Nagoya and merged with the second-largest chain, Hoteiya, to form Uny Co., Ltd. Hoteiya was started in 1927 by two brothers, Seijiro and Shuichi Furukawa, as a kimono retailer in the port city of Yokohama, near Tokyo. Like the Nishikawaya store, Hoteiya was damaged during World War II and the Furukawas were not able to reopen for business until 1954. Hotei is the god of longevity in Japan and is depicted as a potbellied old man, which became the store's mascot. In 1957 one of the brothers, Shuichi, left Yokohama with three employees to develop business in Nagoya. He initially opened four small stores and, like the Nishikawa family, aimed to dominate the Nagoya clothing retail market. In the first year, sales were an impressive ¥80 million, and the chain expanded to stock western goods. In 1960 Seijiro Furukawa died suddenly, leaving his brother Shuichi to concentrate on expanding in Nagoya. A food division was added, and Hoteiya became a major retailer in the Chubu region.

On a European information-gathering trip in 1964, Toshio Nishikawa and Shuichi Furukawa became friends and discussed the idea of merging their respective companies. Both men had ambitions to expand beyond Nagoya, and they realized they could achieve this more easily as a single entity. The two companies used the same primary supplier and distributor, the Takihyo Company, and both men believed that Hoteiya's largely main-street presence would complement Nishikawaya's larger suburban stores, and vice versa. Thus the two chains were joined under the single brand name Uny, which suggests English words such as unique, united, and universal. This illustrated the trend in corporate Japan towards using English-sounding names. Uny immediately became the leading retailer in Nagoya, and the company's leaders set out to expand throughout Japan, to Tokyo in particular. With Toshio Nishikawa's brother Yoshio as Uny's chairman, three regional groups were established—Uny Chubu, Uny Tokai, and Uny Kanto, the last of which was responsible for operations in Tokyo and Yokohama. By this time only a small proportion of Uny's sales came from the goods with which Nishikawaya and Hoteiya had begun: kimono. However, kimono were still highly expensive and profitable retail items. The company decided to establish the kimono retailing operation as an independent business, and so the Sagami chain was formed.

Uny's formation coincided with a time of upheaval in the Japanese economy. The oil crises of the 1970s resulted in sharp decreases in consumer spending. This, in Uny's case, was compounded by the fact that the company was undergoing a rationalization as a result of the merger; new stores were being opened at a faster pace than the lower-profit-margin older stores could be closed. As a result, sales increased by 32% in fiscal year 1975 while profits fell by 16%. In the following year sales were up 12% while profits were flat. This suggested serious problems and Toshio Nishikawa frequently stated that he could not remember a more worrying three years for his company.

In 1976 Yoshio Nishikawa was replaced as chairman by Hisatoku Takagi, and Toshio Nishikawa became president. The company closed 21 unprofitable stores while opening five superstores in Nagoya—larger stores meant a lower overhead-to-sales ratio. Uny's superstores were opened under various brand names according to atmosphere and targeted customers. The flagship Uny stores were conceived as small department stores, offering a full range of products. The Sun Terrace shopping centers targeted family shoppers. Later, Uny launched stores called Apita (1983) and Seikatsu-Soko (1985), both catering to the younger fashion-conscious customer. By 1976 there were 80 Uny stores and Nishikawa made it a point to visit all of them regularly. Emphasis was put on quality rather than quantity, and new store openings and headlong expansion into the Tokyo retail market were put on hold until the financial position of the company could be improved. In 1978 Uny was listed on the Tokyo and Nagoya stock exchanges, and although 21 stores had been closed in the previous year, sales doubled due to the efficiency of the superstores.

Nonetheless, Toshio Nishikawa was not content with success in Nagoya alone and had not forgotten his ambition to become the leading retailer in Japan. He declared that the company's expansion was just beginning and initiated the second phase of his development plan, which involved both nationwide and international expansion. The internationalization of Uny had begun in 1978 when the company entered into a joint venture with the U.S. restaurant chain Denny's to open a chain of Winchell's Donut House, which is one of the divisions of Denny's, in Japan. Then the company approached the large U.S. convenience store franchise Circle K. Under license, Circle K Japan was set up in 1982, owned entirely by Uny. From Circle K, Uny learned how to operate successfully in the high-turnover and fast-changing convenience store business. The chain flourished in the Nagoya region, and Uny set itself the goal of opening 1,000 convenience stores in the first ten years of that operation. Circle K Japan, as well as offering the usual goods associated with a convenience store, also provided parcel delivery and photo processing.

Specialty stores were a high-growth area in Japanese retailing in the 1980s. Most of the leading retail chains developed small chains of stores with exotic-sounding foreign names to take advantage of the affluent Japanese consumer's taste for expensive brand-name goods. Uny started several brand-name stores during this time. Molie and Palemo sold women's fashions, Rough Ox, Depot, and Topio Tokai offered men's and boys' clothes, and the upmarket Catiart, selling furs and jewelry, opened a boutique in Paris in 1982. These ventures were the result of careful market research and monitoring of Western fashion trends. The year 1985 was busy for Uny as the company entered numerous new business areas. Comp-U-Card Japan offered telephone and electronic shopping facilities in Uny stores. Uny Hong Kong was established, joining the growing list of Japanese department store chains opening branches in the British colony. In 1987 a superstore and boutique were opened in an international shopping center in the Taikoo Shing district of Hong Kong Island. Uny acquired a license to operate a cable television station and established Central Cable TV in 1985. Uny's forays overseas also included raising capital, which was facilitated by listings on the Luxembourg and Paris stock exchanges in 1980 and 1985, respectively.

The late 1980s and 1990s brought the longest continuous period of growth in the Japanese economy since World War II—58 consecutive months as of September 1991. In 1990 Japanese retailers, among then Uny, recorded their highest sales growth for more than a decade. In 1989 Nagoya hosted the World Design Exhibition, for which Uny provided a spectacular pavilion. Uny's effort at this exhibition was organized by Toshio Nishikawa's son Toshikazu, who was by then on the board of Uny, in charge of planning.

Long-term growth for Uny may not be easy to maintain. The Japanese economy in the early 1990s was in recession, and indeed department stores have reported that sales of high-priced items such as works of art and jewelry are no longer growing. Japan's retailers will face stiff competition as the government faces pressure from both smaller retailers and the U.S. government to open up the retail market and grant licenses to operate chains. The U.S. retailer Toys "R" Us, for instance, created a stir by announcing plans for a chain of toy stores that would compete directly with the smaller Uny-owned Tom Tom chain. Competitive pressures such as this and economic uncertainty most likely mean that Uny will proceed cautiously and not hurry its expansion into Tokyo.

Principal Subsidiaries: Sagami Co., Ltd.; U Store Co., Ltd.; Circle K Japan Co., Ltd.; Molie Co., Ltd.; Palemo Co., Ltd.; Rough Ox Co., Ltd.; H.B. Hearts Co., Ltd.; Topio Tokai Co., Ltd.; Toyama Apita Co., Ltd.; U Life Co., Ltd.; Comp-U-Card Japan Co., Ltd.; Tom Tom Co., Ltd.; Depot Co., Ltd.; Uny (HK) Co., Ltd (Hong Kong).

Further Reading: Yanai, Nobuhisa, *Uny—A Company History,* Tokyo, Keizaikai Co., Ltd., 1991.

—Dylan Tanner

W H SMITH GROUP PLC

Strand House
7 Holbein Place
London SW1W 8NR
United Kingdom
(071) 730 1200
Fax: (071) 730 1200 extension 5563

Public Company
Incorporated: 1949 as W H Smith & Son (Holdings) Ltd.
Employees: 35,131
Sales: £2.13 billion (US$3.98 billion)
Stock Exchange: London

W H Smith Group PLC is one of Britain's oldest and best-known retailing companies. The group's activities in book, newspaper and stationery distribution and retailing over two centuries have made it a familiar part of daily commercial activity for British consumers. From its base in this market, the group has diversified into a range of other activities. In addition to being the United Kingdom's largest seller of books, newspapers, magazines, and stationery, W H Smith is now a strong force in the recorded music and video markets, a leading distributor of office equipment, and has a half share in Do It All Ltd., a leading do-it-yourself chain. Along with its commanding position in U.K. markets, the group has an extensive chain of outlets in the United States.

The W H Smith group had its origins in a small "newswalk," or newspaper agency, in Little Grosvenor Street, London, opened by Henry Walton Smith and his wife, Anna, in 1792. Smith died only a few months later, and Anna ran the business by herself until her death in 1816, when her two sons, Henry Edward and William Henry, began trading as H & W Smith. In 1818 they moved to Duke Street, Mayfair, and by 1820 were in a position to open a second shop in the Strand, London. William Henry became the driving force in the business, and in 1828 the firm became known as W H Smith.

The opening of the business coincided with dramatic economic and social changes in Britain. The industrial revolution and a sharp acceleration in the growth of London changed the way the English lived; among the changes was the increase in importance of newspapers and journals. These catered to a new demand for keeping track of fast-moving economic and political developments and the turbulent international politics of the time, and provided a medium for advertising, which was becoming increasingly important as the English economic structure changed and new kinds of enterprises emerged. Another effect of the economic changes was the construction of an improved network of roads, allowing comparatively swift transport by stronger, safer horse-drawn coaches. William Henry Smith spotted the opportunities offered by these developments and changed the focus of his business from simply retailing publications to distributing them. He built up a fleet of light coaches and fast horses and began carrying papers from London along the new roads to stagecoach stops in the country, allowing rural readers access to metropolitan newspapers more quickly than ever before.

It was another product of the industrial revolution—the railway—that allowed the firm to grow dramatically into the leading newspaper seller in the United Kingdom. The railway network spread quickly across the country during the 1830s and 1840s, and William Henry Smith's son, William Henry Smith II, recognized the potential of the new system for newspaper distribution. The younger Smith had reluctantly abandoned his plans to become a clergyman and agreed to join the business in 1842, at the age of 17, and soon showed himself to be as perceptive a businessman as his father. After being made a partner in 1846, giving the company the name W H Smith & Son, he took the opportunity offered when the London & North-Western Railway (LNWR) invited tenders for the sole bookstall rights on its lines. W H Smith & Son opened its first railway bookstall at Euston station, London, in 1848, signed a similar deal with the Midland Railway two weeks later, and soon won contracts with other railway companies.

Control of a monopoly retail operation at the heart of the mass transport system gave the company a perfect position from which to benefit from the booming British economy of the late 19th century. The volume of trade was big enough by 1853 for the firm to buy its first news wholesaling warehouse in Birmingham, the first in a large network of warehouses developed over the next few years. In 1849 William Henry Smith II broadened the company's base by creating a book department, and in 1851 he signed the first contract to handle advertising rights at railway stations with the LNWR, beginning an outgrowth of the business that developed swiftly. W H Smith & Son's railway bookstalls and the advertising space they sold made the company a ubiquitous presence in Britain throughout the second half of the 19th century, and created its position as one of Britain's retailing giants.

The success of the firm allowed William Henry Smith II to enter politics. After becoming a member of parliament in 1868, he retired from active partnership in the company and became in turn Parliamentary Secretary to the Treasury, First Lord of the Admiralty, Secretary for War, Irish Secretary, First Lord of the Treasury, and Leader of the House of Commons. His public prominence and attitudes prompted the humorous magazine *Punch* to nickname him "Old Morality." On his death in 1891, his widow was made Viscountess Hambleden and his 23-year-old son, Frederick, who later became the second Viscount Hambleden, became head of the company.

The company continued to develop steadily under Viscount Hambleden—opening a shop in Paris in 1903, followed in 1920 by another in Brussels, Belgium, and a bookbinding works in 1904—until its core business was threatened by a crisis in 1905. When contracts for the 200 bookstalls on the Great Western and LNWR lines ran out at the end of that year, the railway companies demanded higher rents from W H Smith & Son. The company decided that it could not afford the new prices and decided to deal with the loss of the railway bookstall monopoly by opening new shops near the stations, on the station approaches wherever possible. The replacement program succeeded, and the company managed to retain its sales despite the loss of the business upon which it had been founded. The opening of the new shops turned W H Smith & Son's operations into a more conventional newspaper, book, and stationery retail chain, and became the basis of its activities for most of the 20th century.

Viscount Hambleden died in 1928 and was succeeded as head of the company by his son, the third Viscount Hambleden. The need to pay death duties prompted the transformation of the firm into a private limited liability company in 1929. A similar process took place after the death of the third Viscount in 1948; a public holding company, W H Smith & Son (Holdings) Ltd., was formed in 1949 to buy up all the share capital, which had been held by Viscount Hambleden, and issue shares publicly.

During the 1950s, the company began to branch out beyond its traditional business under the first chairman of the public company, David Smith, the third viscount's brother. During this decade W H Smith made its first major move into another country, opening several branches in Canada, first in Toronto and later in Ottawa and Montreal. The company also diversified within the United Kingdom by expanding into the specialty book market in 1953 with the acquisition of the Bowes and Bowes group of bookshops, which included City Centre Bookshops, Truslove & Hanson, and Sherratt & Hughes. The company also broadened its activities by adding recorded music to its shelves. The continuing growth in sales prompted the company to reorganize its retail distribution network, transferring the center from Lambeth in south London to a custom-built warehouse in Wiltshire. In the same period, one of the last vestiges of the old railway-based retail network ended when, in 1972, the company decided not to renew its contract for 23 main bookstalls and 63 kiosks in London underground stations after operating there for 70 years.

In 1973, under a new chairman, Charles Troughton, the company launched a radical departure from its core business when it joined in a consortium bidding to take over the travel agency company Thomas Cook. The bid failed, but W H Smith pushed ahead with its plans to enter the travel agency business, opening a chain of agencies operating from within its existing shops. The company undertook a more ambitious move to diversify under the next chairman, Peter Bennett, when it moved into the do-it-yourself hardware market in 1979, paying £12 million for the LCP Homecentres chain, which it renamed Do It All, and expanding the chain. This was the first significant step away from the company's traditional businesses and existing shops, and it set the tone for the wave of diversification that was to follow in the 1980s under Simon Hornby, who was appointed chairman in 1982.

Following the move into hardware retailing, W H Smith's next steps to broaden its base took it into the television industry. Aiming to take advantage of the opportunities arising from cable and satellite television in Europe, in 1983 the group established W H Smith Television, a subsidiary designed to supply the industry with programs and provide services to the program industry. The group's involvement in television deep-

ened the following year, when it bought a 15% stake in a cable television channel, Screen Sport, and paid £8.5 million for a 29.9% slice of Yorkshire Television. In 1985 the company added to these acquisitions by taking a stake in British Cable Programmes, a move that the *Financial Times* said "reinforces the company's emergence as the most significant investor in cable TV programming, after Thorn EMI." Later that year the company launched a satellite-delivered cable television channel marketed mainly toward women.

W H Smith also made a major move into the United States in 1985, paying US$65 million for Elson, a chain of gift shops with 189 outlets in hotels, airports, office blocks and railway stations throughout the country. The purchase was W H Smith's second attempt to break into the U.S. market, following the establishment in 1979 of an operation publishing and wholesaling English books, which took heavy losses. Hornby assured financial analysts that the earlier effort had been badly managed and that the latest entry would be very different.

In 1985 the company also increased its involvement in the recorded music industry, paying about £5 million for Music Market, a chain of 20 music shops. This move was a precursor to a bigger acquisition in the music market the following year, when the company paid the share equivalent of £46 million for the Our Price Music Ltd. record shop chain, bringing another 130 shops in London and southeast England into the group. A month later W H Smith expanded its stationery retailing activities by buying 75% of a greeting card and stationery business, Paperchase. The group also took the next step in its travel industry plans in 1986 by opening 100 freestanding travel agencies. The rash of acquisitions continued in 1987 with the group buying 32 retail outlets in Hawaii, bringing its total number of U.S. outlets to 308. It expanded its travel operations by paying £5.7 million for 32 travel agencies owned by the Ian Allan Group and bought a controlling interest in a television and video production company, Molinaire Visions.

However, as W H Smith diversified swiftly into new businesses, it received a serious blow to its oldest operation. When Rupert Murdoch's News International moved production of its British national newspapers into its new nonunion plant at Wapping in 1986, it appointed the Australian-based transport group TNT Ltd. as its transport contractor, ending W H Smith's 190-year-old role as distributor of *The Times* and *The Sunday Times*. With the papers delivered by road, the group's business delivering them from railway stations to shops and newsstands was redundant. In late 1987, TNT and News International signed an agreement consolidating TNT's move into the wholesale newspaper distribution market. This change cost W H Smith an estimated £40 million in annual sales. The group recovered most of these losses, however, in 1988 when it won wholesale distribution contracts from Express Newspapers, Mail Newspapers, and Mirror Group Newspapers worth an estimated £25 million. In the same year, the company changed its name from W H Smith & Son (Holdings) Ltd. to W H Smith Group PLC.

The problems in newspaper distribution did not stop W H Smith from pushing ahead with new areas of activity during 1988. In addition to its newspaper and book distribution divisions, the company created a third distribution area by moving into the commercial stationery supplies market, buying two stationery suppliers, Pentagon and Satex. It added to its recorded music operations by paying £23 million to Virgin

Group for 67 of its smaller music shops and 7 sites alloted to new shops. In a deal worth about £40 million, the group also leased two transponders—radio or radar devices which, upon receiving a signal, transmit a signal of their own—from the Luxembourg television satellite, Astra, to transmit a sports channel in which it was the major shareholder, as well as reinforcing its core business by buying a chain of 21 news agencies from Next. At the same time, the group rationalized its book operations by selling its 50% share in the U.K.'s largest book club, Book Club Associates, to joint owner Bertelsmann, the West German publishing group, for £60 million.

The breadth of the expansion during the 1980s left the group somewhat unwieldy, and in 1989 management began to dispose of a number of businesses, notably among its North American operations. The most prominent of these was the sale of the group's Canadian subsidiary, W H Smith Canada Ltd., which had been operating for nearly 40 years. The trigger for the sale was an order from Canada's government for the group to sell 49% of the Canadian subsidiary to domestic investors to ensure a high level of Canadian ownership in the book industry. The company responded by pulling out of Canada completely, selling its entire 86.5% stake in the Canadian operation for about C$50 million. The sale included 133 W H Smith bookshops, 82 Classic Bookshops, 91 card shops, and a wholesaler of foreign newspapers and magazines, Gordon & Gotch. As part of a strategy to focus on retailing operations in the United Kingdom and United States, in 1989 the group also sold its U.S. wholesale news division for US$30 million, shortly after selling its U.S. publishing interests to Penguin Books U.S.A., a subsidiary of Pearson PLC. The company reduced its activity in Hawaii by selling a string of 24 shops, and 14 of W H Smith Travel's outlets were also closed.

The company had meanwhile increased its involvement in the U.K. book retailing industry by buying the Waterstone chain of 31 bookshops, the second largest independent chain in the country. The deal raised W H Smith's share of the U.K. book market from about 17% to 20%. The company merged the newly acquired shops with its existing subsidiary of 47 bookshops, Sherratt & Hughes. The commercial stationery arm was enlarged by the purchase of Sandhurst Marketing and Cartwright Brice, while the group also bought the remaining 48.9% of Molinaire Visions, which was experiencing problems. The company reorganized its noncore operations in 1990 by merging its Do It All chain of do-it-yourself hardware shops with Payless, a similar chain owned by the pharmaceutical retailing company Boots. W H Smith owned 50% of the new operation, which retained the Do It All name, and was expected to have annual sales of £550 million to £575 million. The company also extended its involvement in the U.S. recorded music market when it paid US$23 million for a chain of 49 record shops in Pennsylvania, which it integrated with Wee Three, its existing U.S. chain of 36 music shops.

In 1991 the group's new operations in diverse markets began to appear uncertain, partly because of the impact of the recession in the United Kingdom that began toward the end of 1990. In January the company announced that profits in the previous six months had fallen by 7%, and as the year progressed, analysts predicted that profits would remain static. After spending an estimated £435 million to fund acquisitions and organic growth over the previous years, the company announced in May a major restructuring of its operations, including the sale of some of its largest noncore businesses and a refocusing on the traditional retail operations. As the U.K. financial journal *Investor's Chronicle* put it, the forays into satellite television, do-it-yourself retailing, and travel had failed. In view of the unexpectedly slow progress of the cable and satellite television market, the company announced the sale of its money-losing satellite television business, W H Smith TV, which had already absorbed £80 million of the group's money and was still believed to be two years away from breaking even. A consortium that included the French television company Canal+; the U.S. communications company Capital Cities/ABC; and the French water company Compagnie Generale des Eaux, paid £65 million for the television subsidiary. W H Smith also announced in 1991 the sale of its travel agency business and launched its first rights share issue, aimed at attracting £147 million to finance a three-year expansion program in its core businesses and help reduce a £170 million debt left over from the company's previous rash of acquisitions.

The ambitious acquisition program of the 1980s left the W H Smith Group with a number of problems. However, the company's core business of selling newspapers, books, and stationery remains healthy, as do its operations in the recorded music market. With the group selling an estimated 24% of all books and similiar proportions of records and videos in the United Kingdom, it remains in a prime position.

Principal Subsidiaries: W H Smith Ltd.; W H Smith Do It All Ltd.; Our Price Music Ltd.; Waterstone Investments Ltd. (66.8%); W H Smith Group (USA) Ltd.; Pentagon Group Ltd.; Satex Group PLC; Sandhurst Marketing PLC; Cartwright Brice Holdings Ltd.; W H Smith Amsterdam BV Netherlands; W H Smith (Belgium) SA; W H Smith SA (France).

Further Reading: Hammond, Lawrence, *W H Smith: A Story That Began in 1792*, London, W H Smith Ltd, 1979; Wilson, Charles, *First With the News: The History of W H Smith 1792-1972*, London, Jonathan Cape, 1985.

—Richard Brass

W.W. GRAINGER, INC.

5500 West Howard Street
Skokie, Illinois 60077
U.S.A.
(708) 982-9000
Fax: (708) 982-3485

Public Company
Incorporated: 1928
Employees: 8,649
Sales: $1.93 billion
Stock Exchanges: New York Midwest

W.W. Grainger, Inc., once the largest distributor of electrical equipment in the United States, is a nationwide distributor of equipment, components, and supplies to the commercial, industrial, contractor, and institutional markets. The company has increased sales and earnings nearly every year since 1927. It has accomplished steady growth, not through diversification, but by expansion of its core business in terms of geographic scope and volume of its product line. Privately held until March 1967, the company finances most growth internally. The company traditionally has served small industrial contractors and institutions but has expanded to serve specialty markets for general industrial, replacement parts, safety and sanitary products, and as a supplier to large corporations with multiple locations.

In the late 1920s, William W. Grainger—motor designer, salesman, and electrical engineer—sought to tap a segment of the market for wholesale electrical equipment sales. He set up an office in Chicago in 1927 and incorporated his business one year later. The company sold goods primarily through *MotorBook,* an eight-page catalog, which would become the backbone of the company's name recognition. It contained electrical motors that Grainger himself, his sister Margaret, and two employees would ship. In 1991 Grainger published two editions of its general catalog—the successor to *MotorBook*—offering more than 35,000 items. The catalog also includes extensive technical and application data.

The market for electric motors was so expansive in the late 1920s and 1930s that many companies developed with it. In 1926 two of the ten largest U.S. corporations were electrical companies. City utilities made the switch from direct current (DC) to alternating current (AC) for nearly every apparatus driven by electricity. Manufacturers moved away from uniform, DC-driven assembly lines and toward separate work stations, each with individually driven AC motors. This development created a vast market, and distributors like Grainger could reach segments untapped by volume-minded manufacturers.

Grainger established its first branch in Philadelphia in 1933. Atlanta, Dallas, and San Francisco branches opened in 1934. Sales in 1932 fell below the previous year's, to $163,000—the first of only four years where sales would not increase. In 1937 Grainger had 16 branches and sales of more than $1 million.

The complexity of the industry allowed Grainger to decentralize marketing efforts and strengthen its regional presence by adding an outside sales force in 1939, but the company limited it to one sales representative for every branch for the first ten years. Branches opened around the country at a brisk pace, with 24 operating by 1942.

Yet Grainger did not expand solely through the number of outlets. In 1937 it began merchandising selected products under the Dayton trademark, Grainger's first private label. In order to stimulate summer business, a line of air circulators and ventilating fans was designed, assembled, and offered for sale by the company in 1938. Assembly operations continued to be performed by the company until it got out of manufacturing in the 1980s.

Grainger acted as a distributor of electric motors for government use during World War II. With its normal market disrupted, Grainger offered furniture, toys, and watches through *MotorBook* for a brief period. Grainger continued expansion during the war as sales grew from 1941's $2.6 million to $7.8 million in 1948, and earnings increased almost tenfold to $240,000 in 1948.

The rapid growth continued immediately after the war. Sales more than doubled from 1948 to 1952, calling for organizational adjustments. A single sales representative could no longer serve an entire branch, and in 1948 Grainger expanded the sales force for the first time. The postwar transition also required renewed efficiency, and in 1949 Grainger had a branch office built to its own specifications for the first time. Most new branches since also have been built specifically for Grainger.

Beginning in 1953 the company created a regional warehousing system that replenished branch stock and filled larger orders. Called regional distribution centers, they were eventually located in Chicago; Atlanta; Oakland, California; Ft. Worth, Texas; Memphis, Tennessee; and Cranford, New Jersey. This system operated until the mid-1970s.

As alternating current became standard in the United States, Grainger's market changed. No longer processing large orders, the company intensified its focus on the secondary market that existed throughout the country—small manufacturers, servicers, and dealers who purchased with high frequency but low volume. Grainger could anticipate the needs of this market and purchase from manufacturers in high volume. Grainger's distribution system, warehousing, and accounting allowed manufacturers to produce at low cost for Grainger's customers. These customers were otherwise difficult for manufacturers to reach.

Most of the increases in sales volume since the end of World War II have been due to large-scale geographic expansion. Expansion continued through the 1950s and 1960s at a consistent pace. By 1967 Grainger operated 92 branches.

Branches built after 1949 were automated to keep administrative and personnel costs low. In 1962 sales were $43.5

million. In 1966 sales were nearly doubled to $80.2 million. Automation helped build the company's reputation as a reliable supplier and brought in accounts with bigger clients. Average branch sales grew from $596,000 in 1962 to more than $2.1 million in 1974.

In 1966 Grainger acquired those shares of Dayton Electric Manufacturing Company that it did not already own. Also in the 1960s, Grainger acquired a producer of home accessories, which was divested in the 1970s. In 1967 the company went public.

In 1969 the company purchased Doerr Electric Corporation, a manufacturer of electric motors, and three Doerr affiliates. Two thirds of Doerr's sales volume was already to Grainger. In 1972 Grainger acquired McMillan Manufacturing, another maker of electric motors. By 1974—seven years since the company had gone public—sales had more than tripled.

Brands exclusive to Grainger—Dayton, Teel, Demco, Dem-Kote, and Speedaire—accounted for about 65% of the company's 1975 sales. As Grainger's branches became larger, the need for a centralized stock diminished. The company eliminated the regional distribution centers by the mid-1970s. It discontinued its McMillan Manufacturing operations in 1975.

Grainger's prominence allowed it to count on sales increases due to population growth. In addition, the replacement market for small motors exceeded that of the repair market. Slimmed-down operations and reduced long-term debt, however, poised the company for more aggressive growth through the 1980s.

Unlike the 1960s, the company saw no need to diversify during the 1980s, recognizing that the electrical industry itself could provide enough opportunity for growth. The transition from electromechanical equipment to electronics provided long-term growth during boom and bust periods—comparable to the motor market upgrades of the 1920s and 1930s. Growth in domestic business activity led to broad-scale upgrades and system replacements—resulting in increased orders for Grainger and more disposable cash for its own expansion. In 1986 the company sold Doerr to Emerson Electric Company for $24.3 million.

A study showed that while Grainger sold products in every county in the United States, it held less than a 2% share of a $70 billion to $90 billion industry. The study also indicated that most Grainger customers had fewer than 100 employees and valued immediacy over breadth of product line or price. In response, Grainger accelerated its decades-old expansion rate of six branches a year. It opened more than 100 new branches between 1987 and 1989, trying to bring a branch to within 20 minutes of every customer.

Investment in computer automation allowed Grainger to resurrect its centrally managed regional distribution centers. In 1983 the company opened a heavily automated distribution center in Kansas City, Missouri and in 1989 opened a third such operation in Greenville County, South Carolina.

During the 1980s Grainger returned to its origins, trying to reach larger institutional customers. Although essentially the same business since its inception, Grainger has expanded the scope of its services. Starting in 1986, through acquisition and internal development, the company began building specialty distribution businesses that are intended to complement the market position held by Grainger. These businesses include replacement parts, general industrial products, safety products, and sanitary supplies. Parts distribution continues to expand under the Parts Company of America (PCA) name. PCA provides parts service for more than 550 equipment manufacturers and offers 80,000 parts. General industrial distribution has developed through a series of acquisitions under the name of Bossert Industrial Supply, Inc. Bossert, positioned in the Midwest market, provides manufacturing and repair operations products, cutting tools and abrasives, and other supplies used in manufacturing processes.

In 1990, through acquisitions combined under Allied Safety, Inc., the company entered into the safety-products distribution business. Safety products include such items as respiratory systems, protective clothing, and other equipment used by individuals in the workplace and in environmental clean-up operations. JANI-SERV Supply was created in 1990 to service the sanitary supply market. JANI-SERV offers more than 1,200 items, representing a full range of sanitary products.

Principal Subsidiaries: Bossert Industrial Supply, Inc.; Allied Safety, Inc.; Ball Industries, Inc.

Further Reading: 60 Years of Growth, Skokie, Illinois, W.W. Grainger, Inc., 1987; "How the Big Get Bigger," *Industrial Distribution,* February 1988.

—Ray Walsh

WAL-MART STORES, INC.

702 Southwest 8th Street
Bentonville, Arkansas 72716
U.S.A.
(501) 273-4000
Fax: (501) 273-8650

Public Company
Incorporated: 1969
Employees: 328,000
Sales: $32.60 billion
Stock Exchanges: New York Pacific

Wal-Mart Stores, Inc., is a national discount department store chain operating primarily in small towns throughout the United States. In 1991 the company had more than 1,700 stores. Its founder, Samuel Walton, at that time was estimated to be among the richest people in the United States.

Walton graduated from the University of Missouri in 1940 with a degree in economics and became a management trainee with J.C. Penney Company. After two years he went into the army. Upon returning to civilian life three years later, he used his savings and a loan to open a Ben Franklin variety store in Newport, Arkansas. In 1950 he lost his lease, moved to Bentonville, Arkansas, and opened another store. By the late 1950s, Sam and his brother J. L. (Bud) Walton owned nine Ben Franklin franchises.

In the early 1960s Sam Walton took what he had learned from studying mass-merchandising techniques around the country and began to make his mark in the retail market. He decided that small-town populations would welcome, and make profitable, large discount shopping stores. He approached the Ben Franklin franchise owners with his proposal to slash prices significantly and operate at a high volume, but they were not willing to let him reduce merchandise as low as he insisted it had to go. The Walton brothers decided to go into that market themselves and opened their first Wal-Mart Discount City in Rogers, Arkansas, in 1962. The brothers typically opened their department-sized stores in towns with populations of 5,000 to 25,000, and the stores tended to draw from a large radius. "We discovered people would drive to a good concept," Walton said in *Financial World* on April 4, 1989.

Wal-Mart's "good concept" involved huge stores offering customers a wide variety of name-brand goods at deep discounts that were part of an everyday-low-prices strategy.

Walton was able to keep prices low and still turn a profit through sales volume and an uncommon marketing strategy. Wal-Mart's advertising costs generally came to one third that of other discount chains; most competitors were putting on sales and running from 50 to 100 advertising circulars per year, but Wal-Mart kept its prices low and only ran 12 promotions a year.

By the end of the 1960s the brothers had opened 18 Wal-Mart stores and owned 15 Ben Franklin franchises throughout Arkansas, Missouri, Kansas, and Oklahoma. These ventures became incorporated as Wal-Mart Stores, Inc., in October 1969.

The 1970s held many milestones for the company. Early in the decade, Walton implemented his warehouse distribution strategy. The company built its own warehouses so it could buy in volume and store the merchandise, then proceeded to build stores throughout 200-square-mile areas around the distribution points. This cut Wal-Mart's costs and gave it more control over operations. It meant that merchandise could be restocked as quickly as it sold, and that advertising was specific to smaller regions and cost less to distribute.

Wal-Mart went public in 1970, initially trading over the counter; in 1972 the company was listed on the New York Stock Exchange. By 1976 the Waltons phased out their Ben Franklin stores so the company could put all of its expansion efforts into the Wal-Mart stores. In 1977 the company made its first significant acquisition when it bought 16 Mohr-Value stores in Missouri and Illinois. Also in 1977, based on data from the previous five years, *Forbes* ranked the nation's discount and variety stores, and Wal-Mart ranked first in return on equity, return on capital, sales growth, and earnings growth.

In 1978 Wal-Mart began operating its own pharmacy, auto service center, and jewelry divisions, and acquired Hutchenson Shoe Company, a shoe-department lease operation. By 1979 there were 276 Wal-Mart stores in 11 states. Sales had gone from $44 million in 1970 to $1.25 billion in 1979.

Wal-Mart sales growth continued into the 1980s. In 1983 the company opened its first three Sam's Wholesale Clubs and began its expansion into bigger-city markets. Business at the 100,000-square-foot cash-and-carry discount membership warehouses proved to be good; the company had 148 such clubs in 1991, by which time the name had been shortened to Sam's Clubs.

The company continued to grow by leaps and bounds. In 1987 Wal-Mart acquired 18 Supersaver Wholesale Clubs, which became Sam's Clubs. The most significant event of that year, and perhaps the decade, was the opening of Wal-Mart's newest merchandising concept—taken from one originated by a French entrepreneur—that Walton called Hypermart USA. Hypermart USA stores combine a grocery store, a general merchandise market, and services such as restaurants, banking, shoe shines, and videotape rentals in a space that covers more area than six football fields. Prices are reduced as much as 40% below full retail level, and sales volume averages $1 million per week, compared to $200,000 for a conventional-sized discount store. Dubbed "malls without walls," there were four of these facilities in the United States in 1991.

Making customers at home in such a large-scale shopping facility required inventiveness. The Dallas store had phone hotlines installed in the aisles for customers needing directions. Hypermart floors are made of a rubbery surface for ease in walking, and the stores offer electric shopping carts for the disabled. To entertain children, there is a playroom filled with plastic balls—an idea taken from the Swedish furniture retailer Ikea.

There have also been wrinkles to work out. Costs for air conditioning and heating the gigantic spaces have been higher than expected. Traffic congestion and parking nightmares have proven a drawback. Customers also have complained that the grocery section is not as well-stocked or maintained as it needs to be to compete against nearby grocery stores. Wal-Mart has tried addressing these problems by, for example, redesigning the grocery section of the Arlington, Texas, store. Wal-Mart has also opened five smaller "supercenters"—averaging around 150,000 square feet—featuring a large selection of merchandise and offering better-stocked grocery sections, without the outside services such as restaurants or video stores.

Wal-Mart has received some criticism for its buying practices. For instance, according to *Fortune* (January 30, 1989) sales representatives are given this treatment: "Once you are ushered into one of the spartan little buyer's rooms, expect a steely eye across the table and be prepared to cut your price." Wal-Mart has been known not only for setting the tone with its vendors for buying and selling, but often for only dealing directly with the vendor, bypassing sales representatives. In 1987, 100,000 independent manufacturers representatives initiated a public information campaign to fight Wal-Mart's effort to remove them from the selling process, claiming that their elimination jeopardized a manufacturer's right to choose how it sells its products.

Meanwhile, Wal-Mart's revenues kept going up, and the company has moved into new territory. Wal-Mart enjoyed a 12-year streak of 35% annual profit growth through 1987. In 1988 the company operated in 24 states—concentrated in the Midwest and South—1,182 stores, 90 wholesale clubs, and 2 hypermarts. President and chief executive officer David D. Glass, who had been with the company since 1976, was a key player in Wal-Mart's expansion.

In a move that was part good business and part public relations, Wal-Mart sent an open letter to U.S. manufacturers in March 1985 inviting them to take part in a buy-American program. The company offered to work with them in producing products that could compete against imports. "Our American suppliers must commit to improving their facilities and machinery, remain financially conservative and work to fill our requirements, and most importantly, strive to improve employee productivity," Walton told *Nation's Business* in April 1988. Product conversions—arranging to buy competitively priced US-made goods in place of imports—are regularly highlighted at weekly managers' meetings. William R. Fields, executive vice president of merchandise and sales, estimated

that Wal-Mart cut imports by approximately 5% between 1985 and 1989. Nonetheless, analysts estimated that Wal-Mart still purchased between 25% and 30% of their goods from overseas, about twice as much as Kmart.

Wal-Mart has also been criticized for its impact on small retail businesses. Independent store owners often went out of business when Wal-Mart came to town, unable to compete with the superstore's economies of scale. In fact, Iowa State University economist Kenneth Stone conducted a study on this phenomenon and told *The New York Times Magazine* (April 2, 1989), "If you go into towns in Illinois where Wal-Mart has been for 8 or 10 years, the downtowns are just ghost towns." He found that businesses suffering most were drug, hardware, five-and-dime, sporting goods, clothing, and fabric stores, while major appliance and furniture businesses picked up, as did restaurants and gasoline stations, due to increased traffic.

Wal-Mart has a record of community service, however. It awards a $1,000 scholarship to a high school student in each community Wal-Mart serves. But the company's refusal to stock dozens of widely circulated adult and teen magazines, including *Rolling Stone,* had some critics claiming that Wal-Mart was willfully narrowing the choices of the buying public by bowing to pressure from conservative groups.

In 1990 the company continued to grow, adding its first Wal-Mart stores in California, Nevada, North Dakota, Pennsylvania, South Dakota, and Utah. It also opened 25 Sam's Clubs, of which four were 130,000-square-foot prototypes incorporating space for produce, meats, and baked goods. Late in 1990 Wal-Mart acquired the McLane Company, Inc., a distributor of grocery and retail products. Early in 1991 The Wholesale Club, Inc., merged with Sam's Clubs, adding 28 stores that were to be integrated with Sam's by year end. Also, Wal-Mart agreed to sell its nine convenience store-gas station outlets to Conoco Inc. Wal-Mart's expansion plans in 1991 included 150 to 160 Wal-Mart stores, 35 Sam's Clubs, and 2 supercenters.

Principal Subsidiaries: Kuhn's Big K Stores Corp.; North Arkansas Wholesale Co., Inc.; Wal-Mart Properties, Inc.; Wal-Mart Realty Co.; Super Saver Warehouse Club, Inc.; McLane Company, Inc.

Further Reading: Koepp, Stephen, "Make That Sale, Mr. Sam," *Time,* May 18, 1987; "Walton's Mountain," *Nation's Business,* April 1988; "Wal-Mart: Will It Take Over the World?," *Fortune,* January 30, 1989; Bowermaster, Jon, "When Wal-Mart Comes To Town," *The New York Times Magazine,* April 2, 1989; Kelly, Kevin, "Wal-Mart Gets Lost in the Vegetable Aisle," *Business Week,* May 28, 1990; "Facts About Wal-Mart Stores, Inc.," Wal-Mart Stores, Inc., corporate typescript, 1990.

—Carole Healy

Walgreens

WALGREEN CO.

200 Wilmot Road
Deerfield, Illinois 60015
U.S.A.
(708) 940-2500
Fax: (708) 940-3566

Public Company
Incorporated: 1916
Employees: 51,000
Sales: $6.73 billion
Stock Exchanges: New York Midwest

Walgreen Co. is the largest drugstore chain in the United States in terms of sales. It operates about 1,560 drugstores in 740 communities in 29 states and Puerto Rico. As of 1990, it was the 19th-largest retailer in the United States.

The company had its origin in 1901, when Charles R. Walgreen bought the drugstore, on the South Side of Chicago, at which he had been working as a pharmacist. He bought a second store in 1909; by 1915, there were five Walgreen drugstores. He made numerous improvements and innovations in the stores, including the addition of soda fountains that also featured luncheon service.

By 1916, there were nine Walgreen stores, all on Chicago's South Side, doing a business volume of $270,000 annually. That year, the stores were consolidated as Walgreen Co. with the aim of assuring economies of scale.

By 1919 there were 20 Walgreen stores, 19 of which were on Chicago's South Side while the other was on the near north side. Also in 1919, the company opened its first photofinishing studio; it promised faster service than most commercial studios.

The 1920s were a booming decade for Walgreen stores. In 1921, the company opened a store in Chicago's downtown, its first outside a residential area. Walgreen stores introduced the milkshake at their fountain counters in 1922. To meet the demand for ice cream and to assure its quality, Walgreen established its own ice cream manufacturing plants during the 1920s. The company continued to add to its number of stores, and by mid-1925, there were 65 stores with total annual sales of $1.2 million. 59 of the stores were in Chicago and its suburbs, with others in Milwaukee, Wisconsin, and St. Louis, Missouri. Before the year was out, the company had expanded into Minneapolis and St. Paul, Minnesota.

The company opened its first East Coast store, in New York's theater district, in 1927. That year, the company went public, listing its shares on the New York Stock Exchange. By the end of 1929, there were 397 Walgreen stores in 87 cities; annual sales were $47 million with net earnings of $4 million.

At first, the company suffered little from the 1929 stock market crash and the subsequent Great Depression. Sales actually rose in 1930, to $52 million. The same year, the company opened a 224,000-square-foot warehouse and laboratory on Chicago's southwest side. Early in the 1930s, the company expanded on a project begun in 1929 setting up an agency system by which independent drugstores could sell Walgreen products.

By 1934, 600 Walgreen agency stores were functioning in 33 states, mostly in midwestern communities with populations of less than 20,000. By 1932, however, the company was feeling the Depression's pinch. Sales dipped to $47.6 million, and wage cuts were instituted; the company also set up a benefit fund to assist retirees and needy families inside and outside the company. The company continued promoting itself, however; in 1931, it had become the first drugstore chain in the United States to advertise on radio.

There were several major events for Walgreen in 1933. The company paid a dividend on its stock for the first time; its concessions at Chicago's Century of Progress exposition helped boost sales, and Charles Walgreen, Jr., became a vice president of the company. With the repeal of Prohibition late that year, Walgreen Co. acquired liquor licenses and soon was selling whisky and wine in 60% of its stores.

In 1934 the company opened its first Walgreen Super Store, in Tampa, Florida. At 4,000 square feet, the store was nearly double the size of the typical store, and it had a much larger fountain and more open displays of merchandise than an average store. Other Super Stores followed in Salt Lake City, Utah; Milwaukee, Wisconsin; Miami, Florida; and Rochester, New York.

Walgreen's business recovered in the mid-to-late 1930s; 1938 sales totaled $69 million. By 1939 the founder's health was failing; Charles Walgreen, Sr., resigned the presidency of the company in August. His son was named to succeed him, and Justin Dart, who had been with the company in various capacities since 1929, was named general manager. Dart had been married to and divorced from Ruth Walgreen, the founder's daughter. Charles Walgreen, Sr., died in December of 1939 at the age of 66.

The company began the 1940s with the opening of a super store in downtown Chicago. The store was the 489th in the chain and featured a two-way high-speed escalator to provide access between the two floors of the store, the first of its kind in any drugstore in the world. The store also contained a full-service restaurant-tea room. In April of 1940, the Marvin Drug Co., which operated eight stores and a warehouse in Dallas, merged with Walgreen Co. At year end, Walgreen Co. announced the establishment of a pension plan, with an initial contribution of more than $500,000 from the proceeds of Charles Walgreen, Sr.'s, life insurance policy.

In 1941 there was a split between Charles Walgreen, Jr., and Justin Dart. Dart's unorthodox management style made others in the company uncomfortable; he was arbitrary in determining bonuses to store managers and critical of the company's conservative approach to business. Board members considered him erratic and extravagant. They called for his resignation in July 1941. In November of that year he resigned and joined United Drugs Inc., where he built a substantial career and diversified beyond the drug business.

Walgreen Co. put continued growth and expansion on hold with the United States's entry into World War II after the Pearl Harbor attack in December 1941. The company felt the war's impact in a variety of ways; certain foods became scarce, as did film and tobacco products. More than 2,500 Walgreen employees served in the armed forces; 48 did not survive. Walgreen stores sold war bonds and stamps. In 1943, the company opened a store in the Pentagon, in Washington, D.C.

After the war, expansion was once again possible. In 1946 the company acquired a 27% interest, later increased to 44%, in a major Mexican retail and restaurant company, Sanborns. More Walgreen Super Stores were opened in the late 1940s, including one on Chicago's Michigan Avenue, a street of elegant shops and restaurants. In 1948, the company expanded its corporate headquarters in Chicago. That year, sales were up to $163.6 million, and Walgreen began advertising on television.

The 1950s ushered in the era of self-service in drug retailing, a concept Walgreen had tried on an experimental basis at three stores in the 1940s. In 1949 the company canceled plans for a merger with Thrifty Drug Co., a California chain, largely because its clerk-service style would hamper a conversion of the entire company to self-service. In the course of the merger negotiations, however, Charles Walgreen, Jr., had researched Thrifty's competitors and had been impressed by the self-service Sav-On chain, which fueled his interest in taking his stores in that direction.

The first self-service Walgreen's opened on Chicago's South Side in June 1952; the second followed in a few months at Evergreen Plaza, Chicago's first major shopping center. The self-service stores offered lower prices than traditional stores but often actually required more employees, because the stores were larger and carried more products. By the end of 1953, there were 22 self-service Walgreen outlets. Self-service continued to grow throughout the 1950s; the company built many new self-service units and converted conventional ones. It also closed some older conventional stores because they were too small or in locations that had become undesirable. While the number of stores grew to only 451 in 1960—from 410 in 1950—sales grew from $163 million to $312 million over the course of that decade, thanks largely to the increased size and wider selection of the self-service stores.

With the opening of a self-service store in Louisville, Kentucky, at the end of 1960, self-service units outnumbered traditional ones. Another major event of 1960 was the opening of the first Walgreen store in Puerto Rico.

In 1962 Walgreen Co. entered the discount department store field by paying about $3 million for the assets of United Mercantile Inc., which owned three large Globe Shopping Center stores and seven smaller Danburg department stores, all in the Houston, Texas, area. The company expanded the Globe chain throughout the South and Southwest; by 1966, there were 13 Globe stores generating annual sales of more than $120 million.

Operating Globe gave Walgreen Co. experience in running larger stores, and the company began to open ever-larger stores under the Walgreen name. The first Walgreen's Super Center, the biggest Walgreen store as of 1991, opened in 1964

in the Chicago suburb of Norridge. By 1969 there were 17 Super Centers around the country.

Walgreen Co. changed and diversified its restaurant operations in the 1960s. A detailed analysis early in the decade showed that the return on investment of Walgreen's fountains and grills was generally less than that of the rest of a store. Therefore, the company decided not to include fountains and grills in new stores and began closing them in others. Instead of getting out of food service altogether, however, the company went into full-scale restaurants; the first of these was the Villager Room, located within a Walgreen's in Oak Park, a Chicago suburb. Also added during the 1960s were the fast-food chain Corky's and the medieval-decor Robin Hood restaurants. By the decade's end, there were 287 in-store restaurants, 14 Corky's and 2 Robin Hoods.

A third generation of Walgreens ascended to the company presidency in 1969. C. R. (Cork) Walgreen III was named president, succeeding Alvin Borg, who had become president when Charles Walgreen, Jr., became chairman of the board during a 1963 corporate reorganization. This made Walgreen Co. one of the few companies headed by second- and third-generation descendants of the founder, though the Walgreen family no longer owned a controlling share of company stock. Also in 1963, the company elected its first outside directors to the board.

Several changes occurred in the mid-1970s. In 1974 the company opened its first Wag's restaurant; Wags were free-standing family restaurants, many open 24 hours a day. That year it also acquired the Liggett chain of 29 Florida drugstores. In 1975 Walgreen Co. moved into a new corporate headquarters in Deerfield, a suburb of Chicago. The previous facility had become inadequate in size and outmoded. Also in 1975, the company completed the first phase of a new drug and cosmetics laboratory in Kalamazoo, Michigan; expanded its distribution center in Berkeley, Illinois; and, in Chicago, replaced its plastic container plant and photo processing studio with new ones. The company surpassed the $1 billion mark in sales in 1975.

In 1976 C. R. Walgreen III succeeded his father as chairman of the board, and Robert L. Schmitt, who had been with the company since 1948, became president. Schmitt oversaw the liquidation of the Globe chain, which had been showing significant losses. He also was charged with forming a partnership with Schnuck's, a St. Louis grocery store operator, to establish combined supermarkets and drugstores, and with opening optical centers in Walgreen stores. Schmitt's tenure ended, however, when he died suddenly in October 1978. Fred F. Canning, a 32-year company veteran, succeeded him. In 1979, Walgreen Co. acquired 16 Stein drugstores in the Milwaukee area. It closed the 1970s with 688 drugstores, sales of $1.34 billion, and earnings of $30.2 million.

The company began the 1980s by refocusing on drugstores and eliminating certain businesses. In 1980 it ended the agency program, begun in 1929, which accounted for only 2% of sales. This step did not sit well with some former agency stores; a group of store operators in Wisconsin sued Walgreen Co., eventually winning a $431,000 judgment. The following year, Walgreen closed its 27 optical centers and ended the partnership with Schnuck's. The company also eliminated many in-store restaurants, concentrating on Wag's instead; in-store restaurants decreased in number from 231 in 1979 to 119 in 1984.

Expanding the drugstore business, Walgreen Co. brought the Rennehbohm chain, based in Madison, Wisconsin, in 1980. Rennehbohm had 17 drugstores, 2 clinic pharmacies, 2 health–and beauty–aid stores, a card shop and 6 cafeterias. In 1981 Walgreen bought 21 Kroger SuperX drugstores in Houston. In 1982 the company added additional services to its drugstores: it made next-day photofinishing available chain-wide and put grocery departments in some stores located in urban areas. In 1983 it completed chain-wide installation of its Intercom computerized pharmacy system.

Walgreen opened its 1,000th store, on the near north side of Chicago, in 1984. The company continued expanding in the drugstore area, while divesting itself of other businesses; also in 1984 it sold its interest in Sanborns, by then 46.9%, to Sanborns's other principals for about $30 million, a move spurred by Mexico's high inflation rate.

In 1986 Walgreen bought the 66 Medi Mart stores, located primarily in New England, in the company's largest single acquisition ever. That year, the company also bought 25 stores from the Indiana chain, Ribordy, and opened 102 new stores, making 1986 Walgreen's biggest year for expansion.

In 1988, continuing to trim non-drugstore businesses, Walgreen sold its 87 freestanding Wag's restaurants to Marriott Corporation. In 1988, the Haft family sought regulatory clearance to acquire a block of Walgreen stock—a move that company officials feared would lead to an unfriendly takeover bid, as the Hafts had tried to acquire other retailers. Walgreen responded with a move that was seen as an antitakeover device— the establishment of "golden parachutes," payments to be made to executives if they left the firm after a takeover. No bid came through, however.

In 1989 the company opened four mini-drugstores called RxPress, which offered a full-service pharmacy and popular non-prescription items in areas where full-sized store locations are difficult to find. In 1990 it acquired Lee Drug, a nine-unit drugstore chain in New Hampshire and Massachusetts. That year Walgreen experienced a strike by pharmacists in Chicago and northwest Indiana; the strike, however, was settled in about a week. In a major 1990 event, Fred Canning retired as president. L. Daniel Jorndt, who had been senior vice president and treasurer, succeeded him.

Further Reading: Kogan, Herman, and Rick Kogan, *Pharmacist to the Nation,* Deerfield, Illinois, Walgreen Co., 1989.

—Trudy Ring

WICKES COMPANIES, INC.

3340 Ocean Park Boulevard
Santa Monica, California 90405
U.S.A.
(310) 452-0161
Fax: (310) 452-9509

Wholly Owned Subsidiary of WCI Holdings Corporation
Incorporated: 1947 as The Wickes Corporation
Employees: 25,200
Sales: $2.36 billion

Wickes Companies, Inc., conducts business in three distinct areas—automotive and industrial products, the home improvement sector, and textiles. In the automotive and industrial sector, the company makes such products as doorpanels and floor mats for cars and parts for jet engines. With its operation of 108 Builders Emporium retail stores, Wickes is a major presence in the retail home improvement market. The company is also a leading manufacturer and marketer of wall coverings for both residential and commercial use, as well as a worldwide manufacturer of textiles that include upholstery fabrics, commercial floor coverings, and women's hosiery and related products.

The company was founded by Henry Dunn Wickes and his younger brother, Edward Noyes Wickes, in Flint, Michigan. The Wickes family came to Flint in 1854 from New York state and were soon modestly established in the area's burgeoning lumber business. At the time, Michigan possessed some of the thickest and choicest pine forests in the United States, and land could be purchased at the bargain price of only $1.25 per acre.

The Wickes brothers, along with H. W. Wood, established the Genesee Iron Works, a foundry and machine shop that specialized in repair work and the casting of odd metal parts for equipment used in the logging and lumber business. The pig iron the company used had to be hauled in from Saginaw, Michigan, by ship and wagon. Conversely, the equipment the foundry manufactured was being hauled back to Saginaw for shipment. As the company's business increased, it became obvious that the closer the foundry was to Saginaw, which at the time was a boom town, the more efficient and profitable the operation would be.

Life in Saginaw did not appeal to the Wickes brothers' partner; the landscape was composed mostly of the swampland and mosquito-infested marshes adjacent to Lake Huron. In

1864 Wood sold out to the Wickes brothers. That same year, the company's name was changed to the Wickes Bros. Iron Works.

During these boom years, Henry Wickes developed and marketed the Wickes gang saw, a steam-powered mill saw capable of ripping two or three logs into boards simultaneously. In 1869 the company made some basic improvements to the design of the gang saw that revolutionized the lumber milling business. The new design gave an oscillating motion to the saw's frame, allowing all the teeth of the machine's parallel saw blades to cut evenly. The speed of the saw was increased and blades of a thinner-gauge steel were used to cut down on the amount of waste. The new design's success created a national market for Wickes Bros. International sales of the newly designed saw enabled the company to survive as the lumber business in Michigan slowly began to dry up. By 1887 there were more than 300 of these saws in operation.

As this happened, the company had to adapt to survive. One of Wickes's moves towards diversification was to begin buying up equipment from the many troubled sawmills, reconditioning the equipment, and then reselling it to mills in other parts of the country. Wickes also expanded its repair and resale business to include all kinds of machinery. As the new business grew, the Wickes brothers noticed that one of the most frequently bought and resold items were industrial boilers. After developing the machinery necessary to manufacture new boilers, the Wickes Boiler Company was founded. Two of Henry Wickes's sons took over management of the family's enterprises. Harry Wickes headed Wickes Bros. Foundry, and William Wickes took over the boiler business. In 1901 Edward Wickes died. One month and a day later, his brother Henry died in Guadalajara, Mexico, where both brothers had traditionally gone to spend their winters. It was on a trip to Guadalajara that the third Wickes business, The United States Graphite Company (U.S. Graphite), had been born.

While vacationing in Mexico, Henry and Edward had heard of a huge graphite deposit not far from where they were staying. Upon further exploration, they discovered a huge workable vein of about 85% pure graphite in the desert mountains below La Colorada, Mexico. They passed the information on to Henry Wickes's sons, who incorporated U.S. Graphite in 1891. After acquiring an abandoned shed next to a railroad siding, back in Saginaw, and having some luck—both the Mexican government and the Southern Pacific Railroad were in the process of building rail lines that would permit easy and inexpensive shipment of the raw graphite back to Michigan—U.S. Graphite began to mine, import, and sell the black powder as paint coloring, lead substitute for pencils, and an industrial lubricant. At one point, U.S. Graphite supplied the graphite-based lead substitute for at least 90% of the world's pencils. U.S. Graphite achieved even greater success in the years preceding World War I as the demand for electricity grew. Graphite was the major component in the manufacture of carbon brushes, or contacts, that are necessary in the operation of electric motors.

In the years following World War I, Wickes introduced the straight-tube vertical boiler. These new boilers lasted longer than any boiler that had been manufactured previously and did not require a shutdown to be cleaned. The phenomenal success of the Wickes Vertical Safety Boiler propelled the company to the forefront of the institutional heating and steam-plant business. As orders for hundreds of the new boilers flowed in, the company had trouble keeping up with production.

During the Great Depression the boiler business, like most others, suffered heavy losses. There was a need for larger and more powerful boilers, but there was also little profit in producing the new, larger, bent-tube–type boilers Wickes eventually introduced. World War II and the resulting increases in production needed to equip the U.S. military helped Wickes pull out of the doldrums. The U.S. Maritime Commission purchased 360 Wickes 1,000-horsepower boiler units for use in Liberty ships. Wickes also built other types of boilers that were used in many Navy vessels. The company increased its work force to 500, built its first production line, went to three shifts, and in 1944 was awarded the Maritime Commission Award of Merit.

In 1947 the three Wickes operations, Wickes Bros. Foundry, Wickes Boiler, and U.S. Graphite, were merged to form The Wickes Corporation. Under the terms of the merger, the newly formed corporation had an authorized capitalization of $10 million, consisting of two million shares with a $5 par value. Some 770,000 of these shares were used in the exchange of stock with the companies that had been absorbed. The remaining 1,230,000 shares stayed in the company's treasury for use in future purchases of other manufacturing companies.

With the end of the war, Wickes capitalized on its newly acquired production techniques. The company upgraded its bent-tube boilers' capabilities to 350,000 pounds of steam per hour and experienced great success in selling the newly designed unit to factories, refineries, schools, hospitals, and municipal utility companies. However, the company's increased sales volume brought with it new problems. Boilers do occasionally explode; in the late 1950s and early 1960s damage suits resulting from the explosion of some of the new, more powerful units resulted in millions of dollars in damage suits against Wickes. The company chose to discontinue pushing the growth of its boiler business and began to concentrate its resources toward expanding its highly profitable lumber division. In 1959 the boiler operation was sold to Combustion Engineering Company.

The post–World War II years saw a tremendous housing shortage. The lumber business as it existed in the United States was not equipped to handle the increased demand. Lumber was sold by small, independent dealers to builders who completed construction of one dwelling at a time and purchased the materials to build these houses in small quantities, resulting in high prices, which were passed along to the home buyer. Home builders were at the mercy of the local lumberyard owner, and in many instances, lumber stock needed to complete construction was not available when the builder needed it.

Wickes took advantage of the situation. In 1952 the company took a portion of a former grain terminal in Bay City, Michigan, and under the supervision of Joseph S. McMullin opened a retail outlet for building supplies. The idea was to maintain a stock of all the types of lumber and construction products needed by builders. By always having a healthy supply of product, Wickes created a one-stop store to which the builder simply sent his truck and purchased the needed supplies with no delays and at a price lower than what he had been paying to the small independent lumber yard. The new Wickes venture was called the Bay City Cash Way Company. The idea was

such an overwhelming success that Cash Way soon found itself selling to independent lumberyards, which had found that they could buy lumber at Cash Way for less than it was costing to mill the lumber themselves. The key to Cash Way's success was volume. McMullin realized that as long as the company was willing to turn large amounts of product at relatively low profit margins, the volume of sales would take care of the company's bottom line.

The company opened additional Cash Way stores, and in 1962, the year Cash Way was renamed the Wickes Lumber Company, sales topped $66 million nationally. The division had become responsible for more than half the business of the entire Wickes organization. A year later, the lumber division was doing about two-thirds of the company's business, and its growth seemed to be out of control. The company pulled Smith Bolton in from U.S. Graphite to head the lumber division and tighten up Wickes's corporate framework.

Bolton took a very hard look at the lumber division's organization, inventory distribution method, and the process used to decide where new lumber centers were to be located. He discovered that the vast majority of Wickes Lumber profits were being generated by its more established stores in Michigan and the other midwestern states, and that many of the newer ones in the South and Southwest were losing money. The reasons for these losses were twofold. First, all the stores carried identical products, irrespective of climate and local building codes. The second problem was the haphazard method that was being used to choose new locations. Bolton found out that location choices were made without any actual market research. Bolton believed the existing management team did not realize that the company was moving into a larger, more complex business arena. The changes instituted by Bolton resulted in more than 40 resignations from the lumber division's management team. The first executive to leave was the division's president, Dick Wolohan, who struck out on his own and began a competing company. The remaining resignations were, in most cases, defections to Wolohan's new company. An aggressive internal management promotion program and recruiting from outside the company eventually filled the void created by the mass resignations. By 1966 Wickes had broken the $200 million per year sales level.

The 1970s brought with it even greater growth for Wickes. In 1971 Wickes Companies, Inc., was formed to be the parent company of The Wickes Corporation. The company expanded its business into Europe and, fueled by the profits generated by the continuing growth of the lumber division, entered into many new enterprises, including the retail furniture, consumer credit, modular housing, and commercial construction businesses. In 1974 the company surpassed $1 billion a year in sales. In 1978 Wickes purchased Builders Emporium, a home-improvement retailer.

In August 1980 Wickes acquired Gamble-Skogmo Inc., a Minneapolis, Minnesota–based retail company consisting of supermarkets, drugstores, mail-order houses, and other outlets. The acquisition, valued at more than $200 million, elevated Wickes sales figures to more than $4 billion per year. To fund the purchase, however, the company took on significant debt. The worldwide recession of that time, coupled with bad planning in its building supplies and furniture lines, put the company in a tenuous situation following the Gamble-Skogmo merger.

In April 1982 Wickes and most of its domestic subsidiaries filed for protection from creditors under Chapter 11 of the U.S. Bankruptcy Code. In June 1982 the Securities and Exchange Commission began investigating charges that some of Wickes's former officials had issued false data and omitted material information about the company's deteriorating financial condition in the year preceding the filing. The investigation was prompted by complaints filed by many former Gamble-Skogmo shareholders. The following year, however, the judge presiding over the company's Chapter 11 case ordered the court-appointed examiner to terminate his investigation, as the cost of the investigation, already more than $1.5 million, and the sheer volume of work needed to complete the inquiry did not appear to be justified.

A month before Wickes filed for Chapter 11, Sanford C. Sigoloff had been brought in as the company's new chairman and chief executive officer. Immediately following his appointment, a purge of upper-level Wickes executives occurred as the first step in the new chairman's reorganization plan. After building up enough capital to see the the company through the first stages of the Chapter 11 filing, Sigoloff began to sell off practically all of Wickes's general retailing operations in an attempt to make the company less vulnerable to regional retail sales cycles and simultaneously began a program whereby the company would embark on several major acquisitions.

In 1985 Wickes emerged from the second-largest bankruptcy proceedings in U.S. history. After divesting itself of many interests, including the company's vehicle leasing operations, Wickes Machine Tool Group, and Wickes Engineered Material Division, it acquired the Consumer and Industrial Products Group of Gulf + Western Company for approximately $1 billion. In 1986 Wickes acquired a group of retail stores from W. R. Grace & Co., which it added to its Builders Emporium operations, and spent $1.16 billion to acquire The Collins & Aikman Corporation, a manufacturer and distributor of upholstery, fabrics, and wall coverings for the home, as well as carpeting, upholstery, and seat coverings for automobiles. Also in 1986 Wickes made unsuccessful takeover bids for Owens-Corning Fiberglas Corporation and National Gypsum Company.

In 1988 Wickes sold off its lumber operations. The same year Wickes agreed to be taken private by WCI Holdings Corporation, an investment group jointly owned by Blackstone Capital Partners L.P. and Wasserstein, Perella Partners L.P. The sale was completed in 1989.

In fiscal year 1990, Wickes reported operating income of $53.3 million on sales of $2.36 billion. In 1989 and 1990, the company continued divesting certain businesses, including Orchard Supply Hardware, which had been acquired in 1986, and a European hosiery division.

Principal Subsidiaries: Collins & Aikman Textiles; Kayser-Roth Corp.; Collins & Aikman Wallcoverings; Builders Emporium; Wickes Manufacturing Co; Wickes Engineering Group.

Further Reading: Bush, George, *The Wide World of Wickes,* New York, McGraw-Hill, 1976; Sansweet, Stephen, "Salvage Operation," *The Wall Street Journal,* August 2, 1985.

—William R. Grossman

WOOLWORTH CORPORATION

Woolworth Building
233 Broadway
New York, New York 10279
U.S.A.
(212) 553-2000
Fax: (212) 553-2152

Public Company
Incorporated: 1905 as F.W. Woolworth & Co.
Employees: 142,000
Sales: $9.79 billion
Stock Exchanges: New York Toronto

Woolworth Corporation is a multinational retailer with stores and support operations in 17 countries on 4 continents. The company runs more than 7,000 specialty units and 1,600 general merchandise stores in the United States, Canada, Germany, Australia, Belgium, and the Netherlands. Woolworth also has 12 buying offices throughout Asia and Mexico and 9 manufacturing plants producing footwear and apparel.

Its founder, Frank Winfield Woolworth, parlayed the idea of the 5-and-10¢ store into an international retailing empire. Born in Rodman, New York, and raised on a farm, he moved to Watertown, New York, where he apprenticed and then clerked with Augsbury & Moore, a wholesaler and dry goods store. Wanting more money, Woolworth soon left Augsbury & Moore for A. Bushnell & Company, a local dry goods and carpet store. His new employer, however, found him a poor salesman and lowered his wages from $10 to $8 a week. In response Woolworth overworked himself, had a complete breakdown, and spent six months convalescing.

When Woolworth recovered in 1876, he returned to his former employer William Moore, whose business was now called Moore & Smith. There he concentrated on window displays. In 1878 Moore & Smith found itself with high debt and excess inventory. To raise money the store held a 5¢ sale. Smith and Woolworth laid a group of goods such as tin pans, washbasins, button-hooks, and dippers, along with surplus inventory, on a counter over which they hung a sign reading: "Any Article on This Counter, 5¢." After the sale Frank Woolworth was convinced a 5¢ strategy could work on a broader basis.

In 1879 Woolworth left Moore & Smith. On February 22 of that year he opened his first "Great 5¢ Store" in Utica, New York. At first business was good, but as the 5¢ novelty faded, the store's poor location became a handicap and he closed it. Still, he had repaid Moore & Smith's loan of $315.41, which he had used for his initial inventory, and had made $252.44 in new capital.

On June 21, 1879, Woolworth opened his second Great 5¢ Store in Lancaster, Pennsylvania. This time he had three windows on a main street and $410 worth of goods. The store was a success. The first day he sold 31% of stock. In succeeding months he changed the store's name, first to Five-and-Ten, and later to Woolworth's. The increase to 10¢ allowed him to search out further bargains.

Woolworth soon began opening new outlets. Some stores succeeded, while others failed. By the mid-1880s, there were seven Woolworth's in New York and Pennsylvania. Most were run by partner-managers. These men—Woolworth's brother Charles Sumner Woolworth, cousin Seymour Horace Knox, former employer W. H. Moore, and Fred M. Kirby—ran the stores and held a 50% interest. Frank Woolworth ran the initial store and took care of purchasing.

In succeeding years these partner-managers bought out Frank Woolworth's shares and began opening chains on their own. Woolworth continued opening stores. After 1888 he did so completely with his own capital. In these new stores he entered into a profit-sharing agreement with managers.

While Woolworth owed much of his success to low prices, his treatment of the customer was also important. In the 1870s and 1880s, patrons usually had to ask for goods held behind the counter; prices varied according to the customer; and it was considered impolite to enter a store without buying. Woolworth changed all that. His merchandise sat on counters for everyone to see. His price was the same for everyone. He encouraged people to enter the store even if they were just looking.

Another reason for Woolworth's success was the decline in wholesale prices during the first 12 years of Woolworth's existence. This led to wider availability of goods in the 5-and-10¢ price range, wider margins, and higher profits.

As operations grew, Woolworth found he needed a New York City office from which he could govern his stores. In July 1886 he took an office on Chambers Street. Soon after, he began writing a daily general letter that went out to all store managers.

In 1888 Frank Woolworth contracted typhoid. Until then he had handled everything from accounting to ordering to inspecting stores; however, after two months in bed, he realized the importance of delegating authority. With that in mind, he chose Carson C. Peck to run day-to-day operations. Peck had been a fellow clerk at A. Bushnell & Co. and a partner-manager in Woolworth's Utica, New York, store. He became Woolworth's first general manager.

Freed of day-to-day operations, Woolworth made his first European buying trip in 1890. On his return, U.S. consumers flocked to obtain pottery from England and Scotland, Christmas decorations from Germany, and other goods from the great commercial fairs of Europe.

The same year, Woolworth established the "approved list." On the approved list were goods that Woolworth would reorder for his managers. This system allowed managers the leeway to adjust stock for local preferences while at the same time benefiting from the chain's buying power.

In 1897 Woolworth opened his first Canadian store, in Toronto, Ontario. Three years later there were 59 Woolworth's with sales of $5 million.

By 1904 Woolworth was opening stores at a fantastic rate. He opened some stores from scratch. Others he converted from small chains he had bought. In 1905 he incorporated as F. W. Woolworth & Co. At this point Woolworth had $10 million in sales and 120 stores.

In 1909 Woolworth sent three associates to open the first of what was to be a hugely successful group of English stores. In 1910 he appointed the first resident buyer in Germany, and in 1911 he opened his first overseas warehouse at Fuerth, Germany.

At this point competition began to increase from such retailers as J. G. McCrory and S. S. Kresge Company. Also, many former partner-managers had chains of their own. In 1912 Woolworth saw the opportunity to create a huge new entity. He merged with five other retailers—W. H. Moore, C. S. Woolworth, F. M. Kirby, S. H. Knox, and E. P. Charlton. All were former partner-managers except for Earle Perry Charlton, who had built a chain west of the Rocky Mountains. F. W. Woolworth & Co. became F. W. Woolworth Co., a nationwide retailer with 596 stores and $52 million in sales. Frank Woolworth was chief stockholder and president.

The new retailing behemoth took residence in the 60-story neo-Gothic Woolworth building in New York City. Frank Woolworth's office, within the $13.5 million "Skyline Queen," was a replica of Napoleon Bonaparte's Empire Room.

In 1915 Carson Peck died. Peck had been supervising day-to-day operations since 1888. Woolworth assumed Peck's duties, but the strain proved to be too much. On April 8, 1919, Woolworth himself died.

To succeed him as president the board named Hubert T. Parson, Woolworth's first bookkeeper and later a company director and secretary-treasurer. The board also named Charles Sumner Woolworth, F. W. Woolworth's brother, chairman of the board.

Expansion continued under Parson. The company sent its first buyers to Japan in 1919. In 1924 it opened stores in Cuba. Woolworth inaugurated a German operating subsidiary in 1926 and in 1927 opened its first German store. By the company's 50th anniversary in 1929, there were 2,247 Woolworth stores in the United States, Canada, Cuba, England, and Germany. Sales topped $303 million.

In the United States F. W. Woolworth was far and away the biggest five-and-ten retailer. Its 2,100 U.S. stores had 1929 sales of $273 million. By comparison, J. G. McCrory had about 220 stores with $40 million in sales, and S. S. Kresge had about 500 stores with $147 million in sales.

The Great Depression caused the first decline in the company's sales since 1883, reaching a low of $250 million in 1932. In 1931 the company sold off part of its British operations, allowing that subsidiary to become a public company.

In 1932 Hubert Parsons retired and Byron D. Miller became the company's third president. Miller had worked his way up in the company and had helped start Woolworth's U.K. operations. Among Miller's first acts was to raise the 10¢ price ceiling to 20¢. Woolworth was the last five-and-ten chain to raise its prices.

After three years in office, Miller retired and Charles Deyo became president. On taking office in 1935, Deyo and the board of directors removed all arbitrary price limits.

Sales turned upward during the late 1930s, but World War II prosed new problems. Nearly half of Woolworth's men employees entered the armed forces, as did many women employees. During the war, women managed 500 stores. Demand expanded. Supplies were limited, but consumers tolerated substitutions, and because the war meant labor shortages, consumers also tolerated less service.

In 1946 Alfred Cornwell succeeded Deyo. Under Deyo and Cornwell, Woolworth had difficulties adapting to the postwar rush of discount houses, supermarkets, and shopping centers. According to a 1965 *Dun's Review* article, "Woolworth was mired in a depression mentality. It was keeping costs down and prices low at a time when customers wanted service and when prosperity made prices a secondary consideration."

The situation began to deteriorate, and in 1953 earnings hit a five-year low of $29.8 million. Concerned with what was happening, three board members—Allan P. Kirby, Seymour H. Knox, and Fremont C. Peck—forced Woolworth to create a new forward-looking finance and policy committee to combat what they saw as the management's overly conservative tendencies.

Woolworth's British operation was having similar problems. Consumers were abandoning the stores for supermarkets and rivals such as Marks & Spencer, British Home Stores, and Littlewoods. In response Woolworth increased the number of stores in England but did little to upgrade the existing outlets.

In 1954 James T. Leftwich became president. Leftwich addressed some of Woolworth's problems and spent $110 million to expand, modernize, and move stores. In 1956 Woolworth opened two stores in Mexico City and in 1957 began operations in Puerto Rico. Much was left to be done, however, under the leadership of Robert C. Kirkwood, who took over as president in 1958.

Under Kirkwood, Woolworth raised price limits and added profitable soft goods such as clothing and fabrics. Kirkwood also introduced self service, opened hundreds of new stores, enlarged or relocated hundreds of others, and pushed Woolworth into shopping centers. Further, he increased advertising, instituted formal job training, and shortened hours and improved benefits for traditionally underpaid sales people, a move that reduced costly employee turnover from 43% to 19%.

Yet while Kirkwood was rejuvenating Woolworth, competitors such as Kresge and W. T. Grant had already overhauled their stores and were moving into new lines and new locations. Each was able to surpass Woolworth in earnings growth.

In fact, while Woolworth sales surpassed $1 billion for the first time in 1960, U.S. earnings dropped from $14 million in 1960 to $12.6 million in 1963. It was only the return from British Woolworth that enabled consolidated earnings to keep moving up. British stockholders later accused the U.S. board of milking the English operation without infusing the proper amount of capital.

Woolworth and Kresge both sought new types of stores that would better fit the changing retail environment. In 1962 Woolworth opened the first Woolco, and S.S. Kresge opened the first K mart. Each offered the services of a full-line department store and was very large, in some locations more than 100,00 square feet. Woolworth had 17 Woolco stores by 1965.

As the 1960s continued, Woolworth expanded, diversified, and modernized. In 1965 it acquired the G.R. Kinney Corporation for $39 million. Founded by George Romanta Kinney in 1894, Kinney had 584 family shoe stores in 45 states.

The same year, Lester A. Burcham became president. Under Burcham, Woolworth expanded operations into Spain and established a buying office in Tokyo. Two years later, it opened the first Woolco in England.

In 1968 sales topped $2 billion, and in 1969 Woolworth acquired Williams the Shoemen, an Australian shoe store chain that has since become a dominant force in Australian shoe retailing with more than 460 stores ranging from high fashion to athletic and family footwear. Also in 1969, Woolworth acquired Richman Brothers Company, a manufacturer and retailer of men's and boys' clothing. Finally, as part of a 90th anniversary celebration, Woolworth replaced the old "Diamond W" logo with a modern looking white "W" on a light blue field.

Yet Woolworth was still not growing at the rate of its competitors. By 1970 sales at Kresge were running essentially neck and neck with Woolworth. One problem was British Woolworth. In 1965 Woolworth's 52.7%-owned subsidiary, F. W. Woolworth Ltd., had contributed 50% of the parent company's profits, but during the late 1960s it began a steep decline. The reasons included a lack of investment, a devaluation of the pound, and an increase in employment taxes. By 1969 the British subsidiary was contributing just 30% of profits. In an effort to gain market share, British management cut prices. Sales grew, but profits fell.

John S. Roberts, who became Woolworth's president in 1970, also needed to address problems at Woolco, which was performing at nowhere near the rate of K mart. His solution was to consolidate Woolworth and Woolco in one division in 1972. Rather than providing economies, however, the consolidation only blurred the identity of each chain. Woolworth's 1973 sales were $3.7 billion; Kresge's were $4.6 billion, 90% generated by K mart. A positive event occurred, however, in 1974, when the Kinney shoe division opened the first two Foot Locker stores, athletic-shoe retailers that would later prove highly profitable.

With stock prices on the wane, the board recognized the need for change and in 1975 named outsider Edward F. Gibbons president. Gibbons in turn named W. Robert Harris the first president of the U.S. Woolworth and Woolco Division. In 1978 consolidated annual sales topped $6 billion, of which Kinney, growing at a rate of 18% to 20% a year, contributed $800 million. Also in 1978, Harris became president and Gibbons became chief executive officer.

While Woolco continued its sluggish growth and Woolworth stores suffered neglect, F. W. Woolworth Co. continued diversifying. In 1979 Woolworth opened the first J. Brannam, a men's clothing store whose name stood for "just brand names." J. Brannam was a quick money-maker and often stood within or beside otherwise lackluster Woolco department stores. No matter how much the management tinkered, the problems of Woolco refused to go away. After the stores lost $19 million in 1981, Harris and Gibbons hired Bruce G. Albright to revive the ailing chain. Albright, who had come from competitor Dayton Hudson's Target stores, had a plan to revive Woolco, but company projections still saw the stores losing money well into 1984. After Woolco lost $21 million

during the first six months of 1982, Gibbons decided to shut down all 336 Woolcos in the United States, shrinking the $7.2 billion company 30% and laying off 25,000 employees. Closing costs were estimated at $325 million.

In the fall of 1982, Woolworth disclosed plans to sell its interest in British Woolworth to a syndicate of English investors, for $279 million. One analyst, quoted in *Business Week*, October 11, 1982, blamed British Woolworth's failure on the U.S. parent, saying, "The American Woolworth has been milking the British unit for years, insisting on high dividend payout that has forced it to scrimp on investment and to take on more and more debt."

Analysts, however, were pleased with the company that remained. Left were the profitable, but shaky, 1,300 variety stores, Richman Brothers, Kinney Shoe Corporation—a $1.1 billion division that had done well with Kinney, Foot Locker, a women's clothing store known as Susie's Casuals, and the newly created and profitable J. Brannam. Woolco's closing, however, left 28 of the 41 J. Brannam outlets homeless.

Edward F. Gibbons died suddenly in October 1982. Contrary to expectations and much to the chagrin of younger talent, the board named company veteran John W. (Bud) Lynn chief executive officer. As a variety-store man, Lynn paid close attention to Woolworth's. He changed merchandise, reducing the number of high-priced items such as appliances and dresses and expanding basic lines like candy, and health and beauty aids. He arranged stores in arrow patterns to cut down on unprofitable corners.

Lynn pushed the company to adopt a set of strategic priorities that angled Woolworth away from money-losing businesses and toward specialty retailing. Kinney's Canadian operation had started the remarkably successful Lady Foot Locker in 1982, and in 1983 Woolworth paid $27 million for Holtzman's Little Folk Shop, a full-price children's clothing merchandiser and its subsidiary, Kids Mart, a discount operation.

Lynn retired in 1987, and the board named Harold Sells as the new chief executive officer. Sells continued to push Woolworth's profitable mall-based specialty operations. Managers sought out new ideas for stores and those that the company liked were tried. If the stores were profitable, it opened more. If they were not profitable, the company tried another idea at the same location.

In 1990 Woolworth opened 896 stores and closed 351. Many of the new ventures were specialty stores, such as Kinneys, Kids Marts, Foot Lockers, and Lady Foot Lockers. The latter two sold a full 20% of all brand-name athletic footwear in the United States in the late 1980s. The 40 types of specialty stores included Afterthoughts, which sells costume jewelry and handbags; Champs, which sells athletic goods and apparel; and Woolworth Express, which sells the fastest-moving goods of a traditional Woolworth. In 1990 Woolworth opened a store in what had been East Germany, in the city of Halle, where a Woolworth store had been located before World War II. Woolworth was the first U.S. retailer to return to the former East Germany.

Principal Subsidiaries: Holtzman's Little Folk Shop, Inc.; Little Folk Shop Inc.; Kinney Shoe Corp.; Retail Company of Germany, Inc.; The Richman Brothers Company; Rx Place, Inc.; F.W. Woolworth Co.; F.W. Woolworth Co. Limited,

Canada; Woolworth Overseas Corp.; Woolworth Mexicana, S.A. de C.V. (Mexico, 49%); Kids Mart Inc.; Randy River, Inc.; Northern Reflections Inc.; Team Edition Apparel, Inc.; Foot Locker Belgium N.V.; Foot Locker Europe B.V. (Netherlands); Foot Locker U.K. Limited; Woolworth World Trade Corp.

Further Reading: Woolworth's First 75 Years: The Story of Everybody's Store, New York, F.W. Woolworth Company, 1954; Nichols, John P., *Skyline Queen and the Merchant Prince,* New York, Pocket Books, 1973.

—Jordan Wankoff

RUBBER & TIRE

The BFGoodrich Company
Bridgestone Corporation
Compagnie Générale des Établissements Michelin
Continental Aktiengesellschaft
The Goodyear Tire & Rubber Company
Pirelli S.p.A.
Sumitomo Rubber Industries, Ltd.
The Yokohama Rubber Co., Ltd.

BFGoodrich

THE BFGOODRICH COMPANY

3925 Embassy Parkway
Akron, Ohio 44333
U.S.A.
(216) 374-2000
Fax: (216) 374-3338

Public Company
Incorporated: 1870 as Goodrich, Tew and Company
Employees: 14,700
Sales: $2.43 billion
Stock Exchange: New York

The BFGoodrich Company manufactures and markets a variety of chemical, plastic, and aerospace products. Throughout most of its history Goodrich built its business on rubber production, gaining a reputation among U.S. tire makers as a leader in product development and innovation. In the early 20th century Goodrich used its experience in the rubber industry to diversify into chemicals and plastics, and it spearheaded the development of synthetic rubber technology during World War II. The company prospered during the postwar era but faced difficulties when the U.S. auto industry's decline in the 1970s curtailed the demand for tires. Convinced that its future lay in chemicals and plastics, the company's directors embarked on a long and often difficult restructuring plan. Goodrich finally divested itself of its tire business in 1987, emerging as a much leaner and more profitable company.

Benjamin Franklin Goodrich followed a circuitous route into the rubber industry. Born in Ripley, New York, in 1841, Goodrich pursued an education in medicine and served as an assistant surgeon in the Union Army during the U.S. Civil War. After the war Goodrich pursued a career in business and entered into a real estate partnership with John P. Morris of New York City. In 1869 the partners found themselves investors in a small operation called the Hudson River Rubber Company. They soon acquired full ownership of the company, and Goodrich took over as its president.

Goodrich was not impressed with the company's prospects in New York, and he considered moving it west, where a growing population and economy offered plenty of opportunities for expansion. After listening to a stranger praise a canal town in Ohio called Akron, he investigated it for himself. Akron's citizens were as anxious to attract business as Goodrich was to develop it. After his visit a group of 19 potential investors sent George T. Perkins back to New York with Goodrich

to examine his operations there. The group received a favorable report, and it loaned Goodrich the money he needed to move west. On December 31, 1870, Goodrich formed the partnership of Goodrich, Tew and Company, with his brother-in-law Harvey W. Tew and the Akron investors. After completing a two-story factory on the banks of the Ohio Canal, Goodrich was in business as the first rubber company west of the Allegheny Mountains.

Goodrich experienced a shaky start during its first decade. The company's first product was a cotton-covered firehose designed to withstand the high pressures and low temperatures that often caused leather hoses to burst. While the firehose was a welcome innovation among the nation's firefighters, poor financing led to several reorganizations within the company. George W. Crouse, one of the original Akron investors, finally stabilized the company's finances with an additional loan in 1880, and it was incorporated in the state of Ohio as The B.F. Goodrich Company.

Goodrich died in 1888, just a few years before the bicycle craze of the 1890s revolutionized his company and the rubber industry. Among the company's early products had been the solid-band tire used on bicycles of the 1880s. The invention of the pneumatic tire in 1890 greatly increased the comfort of bicycle riding, and Goodrich began turning out bicycle tires to keep pace with the popularity of this recreation. The introduction of cord tires, which increased the speed of bicycles, and the adaptation of pneumatic tires to horse-drawn buggies expanded the nation's rubber markets further. Goodrich increased its capacity with each addition to its tire demand, and company engineers cooperated with independent inventors to find new applications for company products.

The most important of these joint efforts was a contribution Goodrich made to the nation's infant automobile industry. In 1897 Alexander Winton of Cleveland, Ohio, organized the Winton Motor Car Company to market his horseless carriages. He asked Goodrich to develop a pneumatic tire strong enough to handle its high speeds and heavier loads. Goodrich responded with the first pneumatic tires for automobiles, beginning a long partnership with the auto industry that became the foundation for the company's profits for the next 70 years.

From very early in its history Goodrich committed itself to research and development in rubber technology. Under the aegis of Goodrich's son Charles Cross Goodrich, the company opened the rubber industry's first experimental research laboratory in 1895. Arthur H. Marks, one of Goodrich's engineers, was responsible for several breakthroughs in the processing of crude rubber. In its natural form, crude rubber is very sensitive to changes in temperature, becoming hard and brittle when cooled, and soft and tacky when heated. Vulcanization, a process first discovered by Charles Goodyear in 1839, mixes crude rubber with sulfur and heat to convert it to a durable material unaffected by changes in climate. At the turn of the century, Arthur Marks pioneered a procedure for devulcanizing vulcanized rubber, thus enabling producers to reclaim crude rubber from manufactured goods for re-use. Marks also developed methods for speeding vulcanization by adding certain organic chemical accelerators to the process. The use of such compounds reduced the time necessary for vulcanization by as much as 75%.

Goodrich continued to apply the latest technology to its tire production. In 1910 it introduced the first cord tire for use on

U.S. automobiles. This tire, which reduced fuel consumption and increased the comfort of the ride, was developed in Silvertown, England, and marketed there as the Palmer Cord. Goodrich purchased the patent rights for it in the United States and sold it to U.S. consumers as the Silvertown Cord. Other innovations in Goodrich's tire manufacturing included the use of other organic compounds to resist deterioration by heat, oxidation, and flexing; and carbon black, a coloring pigment that improved the tires' resistance to abrasion.

Goodrich's success in its tire business led it into product diversifications. By the time of World War I, it was producing rubber for consumer goods such as shoes, boots, tennis balls, and waterproof clothing, and for industrial goods such as belting for power transmission and for mechanical conveyors. Goodrich also expanded into chemical production. One of its first products in this field was Vulcalock, an adhesive capable of bonding rubber to metal and used to protect pipes and storage tanks from the corrosive materials they often contained. In 1926 a Goodrich engineer developed a method for plasticizing polyvinyl chloride (PVC), turning this waste chemical compound into the material recognized today as vinyl. Goodrich marketed its PVC products under the brand names Geon and Koroseal, applying them to such varied uses as floor tiles, garden hoses, and electrical insulation. Goodrich also grew with the nation's aviation industry, producing airplane tires and the first airplane de-icers, important devices used in the achievement of all-weather flying.

The automobile and aviation industries, along with the rubber demand created by World War I, powered Goodrich's expansion through the first 30 years of the 20th century. In 1912 Goodrich re-incorporated as a New York company and increased its production capacity by acquiring the Diamond Rubber Company, which owned plants adjacent to Goodrich's in Akron. On the eve of the Great Depression, Goodrich acquired two more rubber companies, the Hood Rubber Company of Watertown, Massachusetts, and the Miller Rubber Company of Akron. The Depression, however, brought the company its first setbacks since the 1870s. The slowed U.S. economy reduced rubber demand, and Goodrich incurred over $24 million in net losses between 1930 and 1933. The depression also affected the company's labor relations with its 15,000 employees in Akron. The United Rubber Workers union (URW) formed in 1934, and in 1936 national labor leader John Lewis came to Akron to rally union support. His visit sparked a five-week strike at the plants of Goodrich, Goodyear, and Firestone, temporarily shutting down the nation's three largest rubber producers.

Recovery for Goodrich came with the nation's preparations for World War II. At the time of the war's outbreak in Europe, the United States was importing 97% of its crude rubber from Southeast Asia. Japanese expansion in the Pacific threatened this supply, while German advances in Europe and Africa interrupted supply routes through the Suez Canal and the Mediterranean Sea. In cooperation with the nation's rubber companies, the U.S. government began an intensive stockpiling and conservation effort. It also committed itself to developing synthetic rubber technology.

The rubber industry had known how to make synthetic rubber since the late 1930s. In 1937 Goodrich opened a pilot plant for producing butadiene-copolymer synthetic rubber, and within two years it was using synthetic rubber in some of its commercial products. As long as crude rubber supplies were cheap and plentiful, however, synthetic rubber remained an expensive alternative. In 1939 John L. Collyer took over as Goodrich's president after having spent ten years working for a British rubber company. Collyer returned to the United States convinced of its need to develop synthetic rubber production before it was drawn into the European conflict. Under his direction Goodrich introduced in June 1940 the first passenger-car tire in the United States to contain synthetic rubber. Called Ameripol—for its use of a polymer of American materials—this tire was more expensive than one made of natural rubber, but it gained rapid consumer acceptance because it outlasted conventional tires. After Collyer's appearance before a Senate Military Affairs Committee hearing on national preparedness, the federal government announced plans to build its own synthetic rubber plants. Goodrich cooperated with this effort, building and operating three such plants for wartime production in Port Neches and Borger, Texas, and in Louisville, Kentucky. These plants had a combined capacity of 165,000 tons per year, making Goodrich the nation's leading synthetic rubber manufacturer by the war's end.

Goodrich avoided any postwar interruptions in its growth by quickly converting to meet consumer demand. The U.S. auto industry's return to peacetime production kept the demand for tires high, and Goodrich met this demand by introducing the first 100% synthetic rubber tire in 1945. Two years later it developed the tubeless puncture-sealing tire that increased motorists' protection from blow-outs. The company's LifeSaver and Safetyliner tubeless tires gained wide popularity in the early 1950s, and by 1955 tubeless tires became standard equipment on new cars. Ten years later Goodrich brought another innovation to U.S. drivers, the first radial tires for passenger cars. The radial dramatically changed the U.S. tire industry by increasing tire life by up to 50%, and like its tubeless predecessor it ultimately became standard equipment on U.S. cars.

Goodrich further diversified its production in the postwar era. Continuing a long tradition of research and development, it opened a new research center in Brecksville, Ohio, in 1948. B.F. Goodrich Chemical Company, a subsidiary founded in 1943, took over the company's wartime plants and built new ones in Marietta and Avon Lake, Ohio, and in Calvert City, Kentucky. Production of Goodrich's Geon and Koroseal plastic products expanded into overseas markets with joint ventures in Britain and Japan. By 1955 Goodrich was manufacturing goods in five different areas, including tires, chemicals and plastics, footwear and flooring, industrial products, and sponge rubber goods. It had operations in 21 nations on 6 continents, and in 1966 its sales reached a record $1 billion.

Goodrich's fortunes declined, however, when a 1967 strike began a decade of rocky labor relations and interrupted production. In April 1967 the URW walked off of jobs at Goodrich, Firestone, and Uniroyal, and the resulting strike stalled rubber production in Akron for 86 days. That strike, along with a six-month work stoppage at one of the company's chemical plants, cost Goodrich a 27.6% decrease in its profits from the previous year. Three years later Goodrich was once again facing serious losses because of strikes in the rubber and related industries. The URW walked out on Goodrich plants for five weeks, while strikes by the Teamsters Union and General Motors workers also hurt the nation's tire markets. Goodrich's net income in 1970 dropped by $22 million. Continued hard times in the nation's auto and rubber industries brought Goodrich back to the bargaining table in 1976. A 141-day URW strike stopped production in all of Goodrich's domestic tire plants and finally required the intercession of U.S. Labor Secretary W. J. Usery Jr. to settle it.

These crippling experiences with labor disputes and the stagnation of the U.S. auto industry convinced Goodrich that its future was not in tires. In 1971 Goodrich's net income had fallen to $1.7 million from a high of $48.6 million in 1966. Ready for a drastic change, the company handed its reins to a rubber industry outsider in 1972. O. Pendleton Thomas, a former oil executive with the Atlantic Richfield Company, shook up Goodrich by having chemicals and plastics replace tires as the foundation of the company's business. At the time Thomas took over, Goodrich's position among U.S. tiremakers had fallen to a weak fourth, and the industry showed no signs of improving. The success of radials had cut consumer demand for replacement tires while the oil crisis had lessened the U.S. taste for new cars. Thomas streamlined Goodrich's tire operations by closing unprofitable plants and retail outlets and concentrating on certain product niches, such as high-performance replacement tires. By maximizing profits in its tire business, he developed the capital necessary to increase the capacity of Goodrich's chemical and plastics production. In 1976 Thomas changed The B.F. Goodrich Company's name, to The BFGoodrich Company.

Thomas's program of retrenchment and redeployment allowed his successor, John D. Ong, to develop Goodrich's chemicals business in the 1980s. Goodrich had long been the nation's number-one producer of PVC, the versatile plastic used primarily in the construction industry, as well as a producer of specialty chemicals used in products ranging from cosmetics to floor polishes. Like its tire division, Goodrich's chemical production had been hurt by the petroleum shortages and sluggish national economy of the 1970s, but when Ong took over in 1979 he maintained the course set by Thomas. The acquisition of Tremco Inc., in 1979, a producer of roofing products and construction sealants, strengthened Goodrich's position in specialty chemicals markets. Ong also announced plans to double Goodrich's PVC production by the mid-1980s, and he sunk millions into the development of a plant in Convent, Louisiana. This project backfired, however, when the nation's housing industry went into its worst slump in 36 years and PVC demand plummeted. Goodrich suddenly found itself plagued by an overcapacity in its chemical production, and the company ended 1982 with a $32.8 million loss.

Goodrich's tailspin in the early 1980s led to the most dramatic changes in its history. Taking a record loss of $354.6 million in 1985, the company sold off the Louisiana plant into which it had sunk so much capital. In 1986 Ong merged Goodrich's tire division with Uniroyal, which had just fought a costly takeover battle with corporate raider Carl Icahn. The jointly owned Uniroyal-Goodrich Tire Company looked good on paper for both companies, combining Goodrich's replacement tire business with Uniroyal's original equipment market to make it the nation's second largest tire producer. Unfortunately the relationship faltered, and in December 1987 Goodrich sold its interest in the venture for $225 million to an investment group that had already bought out Uniroyal. Shortly thereafter, Goodrich sold off its 38-acre factory complex in Akron, ending its nearly century-long association with the U.S. tire industry.

With the full divestiture of its tire business, Goodrich became a company devoted solely to the production of chemicals, plastics, and aerospace goods. The recovery of its PVC business and the wise investment of capital gained from its tire division sale had in the early 1990s stabilized the company. Its biggest growth area since 1987 had been its aerospace division. Goodrich manufactures and markets aircraft brakes, wheels, and electronics, and in 1988 it acquired Tramco Incorporated, a provider of maintenance and repair services for commercial aircraft. In the absence of its tire business, the company's chemicals and plastics production had also expanded, to account for 80% of its sales.

John N. Lauer, who joined the company from Hoechst Celanese in January 1989, was elected company president in September 1990, making him the heir apparent to Ong and cementing Goodrich's commitment to its chemicals and plastics business. After years of rocky performance, Goodrich faces the future a much leaner and more competitive company than it had been in its past.

Principal Divisions: BFGoodrich Aerospace; BFGoodrich Geon Vinyl; BFGoodrich Specialty Polymers and Chemicals; Tremco, Inc.

Further Reading: Collyer, John Lyon, *The B.F. Goodrich Story of Creative Enterprise: 1870–1952,* New York, The Newcomen Society in North America, 1952; "Goodrich's cash cow starts to deliver," *Business Week,* November 14, 1977; Deutsch, Claudia H., "Goodrich Finally Gets It Right," *The New York Times,* March 12, 1989.

—Timothy J. Shannon

⫶BRIDGESTONE

BRIDGESTONE CORPORATION

10-1 Kyobashi 1-chome
Chuo-ku
Tokyo 104
Japan
(81 3) 567 0111
Fax: (81 3) 535 2553

Public Company
Incorporated: 1931 as Bridgestone Ltd.
Employees: 100,000
Sales: ¥1.78 trillion (US$14.29 billion)
Stock Exchange: Tokyo Osaka Nagoya Fukuoka

A Japanese manufacturer of tires and related products, Bridgestone Corporation ranks among the top three companies in the world in this sector. The company's product range includes vehicle tires, industrial materials, marine products, civil engineering and agricultural products, construction and building materials, vibration and noise isolating materials, and sporting goods. Products are manufactured on six continents and marketed and sold in almost every country in the world.

Bridgestone was founded by Shojiro Ishibashi, whose name means 'stone bridge'. The company originally made *tabi*—Japanese workers' footwear—and Shojiro Ishibashi made a fortune by adding rubber soles. Deciding that his future lay in the rubber business, he began intensive research and development in 1929, founding the company, Bridgestone Ltd., two years later in Kurume, Japan. In 1942 the company changed its name to the Nippon Tire Co., Ltd. but was renamed Bridgestone Tire Co., Ltd. in 1951, and became Bridgestone Corporation (Bridgestone) in 1984. Ishibashi was an aggressive businessman with strong marketing skills whose main business principle was to expand during recessionary periods. He also thrived on business connections made through his children's marriages. It was said in Japan that his relationship by marriage to government officials allowed Bridgestone to secure orders during the Korean War of the 1950s, helping the company to gain its strong position in the domestic market.

Despite enormous growth in the years since 1931, the company remains something of a family concern with Kanichiro Ishibashi, the son of the founder, retaining the post of director and honorary chairman. The current president is Akira Yeiri. Kanichiro Ishibashi holds 6% of the voting shares in the corporation. The Ishibashi Foundation and another member of the family, Hiroshi Ishibashi, own a further 13% of the company between them. Other major shareholders are the large Japanese banks, corporations, and insurance companies, who hold around 44% of the shares. Private investors own about 32% of the company's issued stock. Before World War II, Bridgestone's business—like that of other major Japanese industrial concerns—was focused on supplying military requirements; at the same time, Bridgestone tires also supplied the growing Japanese automobile industry. Production was based at two plants, one in Kurume, the other in Yokohama. Growth after the war was rapid, with the establishment of 4 new production facilities in the 1960s and 6 during the 1970s. Bridgestone's first overseas factory was established in Singapore in 1963, with further factories built in Thailand in 1967 and Indonesia in 1973. Bridgestone Singapore ceased operations in 1980 following the Singapore government's lifting of tariff protection for locally made tires. In 1976 Bridgestone set up a sales company in Hamburg, Germany, in partnership with Mitsui. This new company, named Bridgestone Reifen G.m.b.H., was intended to increase tire sales in the important West German market. In 1990 Bridgestone set up a new subsidiary in London, Bridgestone Industrial, to handle industrial rubber products throughout Europe. Since the 1980s Bridgestone's most significant expansion has been by acquisition, acquiring majority interests in Uniroyal Holdings Ltd. (UHL), the South Australian tire manufacturer, in 1980 and a Taiwanese company in 1986. In 1982 the purchase of a plant in Nashville, Tennessee, belonging to The Firestone Tire & Rubber Company (Firestone) was the first step toward Bridgestone's acquisition of that United States company in 1988, for a total of US$2.65 billion.

Before acquiring Firestone, Bridgestone had first approached Goodyear in 1987, with proposals for a merger which would have created the world's largest tire manufacturer. However, talks in Hawaii failed to reach agreement as Bridgestone would not accept the high value that Goodyear had placed on its loss-making Trans-American oil pipeline. Bridgestone then turned to Firestone as a United States production base for the manufacture of heavy-duty radial truck tires. They were encouraged in this by the acquisition of an ailing Firestone plant in Tennessee in 1982, which Bridgestone had turned into a success. Bridgestone originally agreed to buy Firestone's tire operations for US$1.25 billion, but Pirelli, the Italian manufacturer, intervened with a rival bid, forcing the Japanese company to increase the offer. Bridgestone finally paid US$2.65 billion for the whole company, with 54,000 employees and two headquarters, in 1988.

The Firestone deal gave Bridgestone its sought-after foothold in the United States and strengthened its position in Europe, as Firestone also owned plants in Portugal, Spain, France, and Italy. In addition, it gave Bridgestone instant access to high-quality manufacturing facilities, with an extensive national marketing system for replacement tires, as well as large research and development laboratories. The Firestone name and sales network gave the Japanese company access to Detroit car makers for original equipment sales, and the sale of Firestone brand tires for the two million cars a year produced by Japanese automobile firms. In North America, Bridgestone's sales in the replacement market are through independent dealers and through their MasterCare network of over 1,500 tire and service centers. These independent dealers have also strengthened sales in the United States and Canada, and the company's marketing strategy has widened further in the past few years through mass merchandisers such as Sears and K mart. Another highlight of its international sales network is the chain of Cockpit retail outlets, which offer car audio equipment and accessories such as wheels, as well as tires. The 200th Cockpit shop opened in the spring of 1990. Within 6 months of the Firestone purchase, Bridgestone announced a US$1.5 billion modernization program. Firestone's auxiliary head office in Chicago and Bridgestone's own United States base in Nashville were closed in order to concentrate operations in Akron, and Firestone's management was reduced through a voluntary early retirement scheme. However, the investment in Firestone coincided with a slowdown in North American and European car production heralding a period of much tougher competition in tire markets. The renovation of Firestone turned out to be more expensive and time-consuming than expected. Other problems included weak markets in Latin America and the Middle East and intense competition in European markets. Fortunately for Bridgestone, not all of the massive investment came from borrowings but in part from Bridgestone's hidden assets, including land, buildings, and securities, purchases made decades ago. The company founder Shojiro Ishibashi had also invested heavily in art, mostly western, opening the Bridgestone Museum of Art in 1952.

Bridgestone continued to retain its position in Asia, where Bridgestone and Firestone brands still maintain the largest share of the market. This region promises to display rapid growth in the world's tire markets over the next decade, and Bridgestone should remain in a strong position to capitalize on this with local production operations and large market shares, particularly in Thailand, Indonesia, and Taiwan.

Bridgestone's production, however, is not limited to tires. Its technical research and development laboratories work on the development of rubber and non-rubber items. Rubber technology features prominently with such items as conveyor belts, inflatable rubber dams, and marine fenders. Multi-rubber bearings are produced for use in the construction of buildings in areas prone to earthquakes as the rubber element in the construction enables the buildings to vibrate with the earth's movement. Bridgestone's other innovative ideas include rubber "muscles" for robots and grease-free conveyor belts. Bridgestone is a Japanese leader in vibration isolating components for automobiles and through Bridgestone/Firestone, Inc. has a large share of the North American market for rubberized roofing materials. It is also a major supplier in the United States of air springs for trucks, automobiles, trailers, and other vehicles.

In 1988 Bridgestone Cycle Co., Ltd. gave cyclists the first opportunity to design their own machines. Cyclists were able to choose, from a list of standard parts, the shape, color, and materials for the frame, brakes, handlebars, and seat, to make their own unique "mix and match" bicycle. Bridgestone's advance in metallurgy has made it possible to produce bicycles that are lighter than ever in weight. The Radac line of racing, touring, and recreational bicycles was introduced in 1990, with a model that features the world's lightest frame, due to an aluminum-ceramic composite, the first ceramic material ever to be used on a bicycle. Non-rubber products include items from special batteries for electronic equipment to weighing systems for aircraft. Bridgestone is also a leading supplier of golf balls and clubs, tennis rackets, and other sporting goods. The Bridgestone Sports Co., Ltd. was established in 1972 and has won many awards, including one from the Japanese Ministry for International Trade and Industry for a new line of windsurfing boards. In 1987 the company introduced the Science Eye system which gives a high-speed photographic analysis of a golfer's swing for use in department stores and professional shops. Bridgestone also operates swimming schools and health clubs as a growing venture.

Although the Bridgestone Corporation is now competing on equal terms with the industry's two other giants, Goodyear of the United States and Michelin of France, its international expansion came late. Bridgestone concentrated on the domestic market while other Japanese companies were developing production plants and overseas markets. Japanese customers bought whatever Bridgestone sold, which did little to encourage Bridgestone to develop new products and their production of radial tires came late by Western standards. In addition, Japanese manufacturers were reluctant to import European or American tires in the 1960s and 1970s, even though foreign tires were considered superior to Bridgestone's. These factors conspired to give the company a commanding share of the Japanese market, 46% in 1990, while exports were 50%.

Since 1989 the company has taken measures to heighten the efficiency of its international tire operations. North American production and marketing have been streamlined by integrating operations at Firestone, renamed Bridgestone/Firestone, Inc., and Bridgestone (U.S.A.), Inc. Their high performance tires have been selected as original equipment on Porsche and Ferrari sports cars. Tire sales are growing steadily in the U.S. market and sales of chemical products and sporting goods are also rising. Although Firestone (U.S.) made a loss after the acquisition, 1991 was emerging as the final period for large-scale restructuring and investment, leaving Bridgestone in a position to realize its ambition of becoming the world's leading tire manufacturer.

Principal Subsidiaries: Bridgestone Cycle Company Ltd.; Bridgestone Bekaert Steel Cord Co. Ltd.; Bridgestone Sports Co. Ltd.; Bridgestone Boushingomu Co. Ltd.; Bridgestone Flowtech Corporation; Bridgestone Kaseihin Seizo Co. Ltd.; Bridgestone Machinery Co. Ltd.; Bridgestone/Firestone, Inc. (USA); Bridgestone Australia Ltd.; Thai Bridgestone Co., Ltd.; Bridgestone Taiwan Co., Ltd.; Bridgestone/Firestone Canada Inc.; Bridgestone/Firestone (Schweiz) AG (Switzerland); Bridgestone France S.A.R.L.; Bridgestone Reifen G.m.b.H. (Germany); Bridgestone Tire Co. A/S (Denmark); Bridgestone Tyre UK Ltd.; Bridgestone Earthmover Tyres Pty. Ltd. (Australia); Bridgestone Sweden AB.

—Lois Glass

COMPAGNIE GÉNÉRALE DES ÉTABLISSEMENTS MICHELIN

12 cours Sablon
63040 Clermont-Ferrand
France
(73) 92 41 95
Fax: (73) 90 28 94

Public Company
Incorporated: 1889 as Michelin et Compagnie
Employees: 130,000
Sales: FFr62.74 billion (US$12.11 billion)
Stock Exchange: Paris

Compagnie Générale des Établissements Michelin (Michelin) is the world's leading tire company, and one of the largest auto wheel manufacturers. Still controlled by the founding Michelin family from French headquarters, it is an international operation with outlets in 140 countries. French sales account for only about 15% of its tire output. It owns about 70 manufacturing plants across four continents. Michelin is also a notable publisher of maps and guides, of which it sells 18 million per year. Although they account for only a small proportion of its revenue, these items have immense promotional value. The rosettes awarded to restaurants by Michelin *Guide Rouge* inspectors are among the most coveted accolades of European haute cuisine.

Apart from its publishing, Michelin has eschewed diversification, preferring to concentrate on the quest for the perfect tire. Here Michelin exhibits a high degree of vertical integration. It produces its own materials, including steel wire and natural and synthetic rubber, and designs and manufactures much of its own industrial equipment and tooling. All this helps ensure that Michelin tires, wherever made, conform to the same high standard. The company invests heavily in research and development—its firsts include the radial tire—and guards the secrecy of its manufacturing processes. Even General de Gaulle, visiting in 1944, was denied entry to the inner sanctum and Michelin's own employees are permitted to know details of only those processes that immediately concern them. Although secretive about its methods, Michelin has always had a flair for marketing. It has an instantly recognizable symbol in Monsieur Bibendum, the chubby character made of tires who adorns its publications and products.

As a tire company, Michelin dates back to the 1880s, when the original Michelin brothers, André and Edouard, took over a rubber products business created by their grandfather, Aris-

tide Barbier, and his cousin, Edouard Daubrée. This firm's premises were in Clermont-Ferrand, in the Auvergne. Set up in 1830 to manufacture sugar, the Daubrée-Barbier enterprise had diversified into rubber a couple of years later at the instigation of Daubrée's Scottish wife, Elizabeth. As a child, Elizabeth had played with rubber balls made by her uncle, Charles Macintosh, an inventor who pioneered the use of rubber in waterproofing clothes, and gave his name to rubberised raincoats. A rubber workshop was opened at Clermont-Ferrand, and was soon making not only these balls, but also other rubber products, including hoses and drive belts.

After the death of the original partners, the business, then also manufacturing agricultural equipment, was run for a few years by a manager. Business had declined by 1886, when the 33-year-old André Michelin stepped in. He was already a businessman in his own right, making picture frames and locks in Paris, and under his management, the Clermont-Ferrand enterprise took a turn for the better. However, André sometimes had to attend to his Paris shops at the expense of Clermont-Ferrand. In 1888, André's brother Edouard, six years his junior, was prevailed upon by the family to abandon his fine art studies and come to Clermont-Ferrand. The following year, the firm, whose most successful line was then rubber brake pads for horse-drawn vehicles, was incorporated as Michelin et Compagnie. It was in this same year, 1889, that a cyclist arrived at the workshop asking to have a punctured Dunlop tire repaired. Pneumatic tires, first patented in 1845 but not commercially exploited at the time, had been reintroduced in 1888 by Scotsman John Boyd Dunlop, but were still rare enough to be a curiosity as solid ones were the norm. Edouard Michelin found the repair a major undertaking, involving three hours' worth of work followed by an all night drying session. The repair did not hold, but Edouard, struck by the comfortable ride that the troublesome tires gave, set to work on a design that would retain the comfort without the trouble. In 1891 the workshop patented a detachable tire, repairable in minutes rather than hours. That fall the brothers persuaded a cyclist to demonstrate their tires in a 1,200-kilometer race. Michelin's rider sustained five punctures on the first day. Even so, he won the race, with an eight-hour lead over the favourite. The earliest Michelin tire took 15 minutes to change, but by June 1892 the time was down to two minutes. Michelin organized another race. Nails surreptitiously planted in the road caused 244 punctures, affording ample opportunity to prove how easy repairs were. By 1893, 10,000 cyclists had fitted Michelin tires.

The following year, Michelin launched a pneumatic tire for horse-drawn hackney carriages. The fleet of five Paris cabs that test drove the tires gained such an advantage in terms of quietness and comfort that the other cabbies were driven to sabotage. Soon even the saboteurs were converted and by 1903, 600 Paris cabs were running on Michelin tires. In 1895 Michelin announced the world's first pneumatic tire for automobiles. Three cars, specially built to test the tire, were entered for a race in June 1895. One, the *Eclair,* meaning forked lightning, was driven by the Michelin brothers themselves. Despite frequent punctures, engine fires and gearbox failures, the *Eclair* was a success. Only 9 out of 19 competitors finished within the time allowed, of 100 hours for 1,209 kilometers. The *Eclair* was the ninth. This was the first of many races in which Michelin tires distinguished themselves.

Around the turn of the century, pneumatic tires were becoming the norm for the automobile industry, as well as for bicycles, carriages, and cabs. Competition was intense, with 150 tire companies in France alone by 1903. Overseas, Pirelli, Dunlop, Goodyear, Goodrich, and Firestone were all coming along fast. A strong brand image was crucial in this climate, and Michelin had come up with a brilliant one. The Michelin man, a rotund figure composed of tires, was born around 1898. His nickname of Monsieur Bibendum came from the caption of an early poster that read *Nunc est bibendum,* a phrase from Horace meaning something like "Time for a drink." The glass flourished by the convivial Michelin man contained not alcohol but nails and sharp pebbles. Michelin tires, it was implied, would gobble up such objects with no lasting ill effects. Today, Monsieur Bibendum has become one of the most widely recognized logos in the world. Apart from promoting tires, Monsieur Bibendum embellishes Michelin guides and maps. The first such publication, the *Guide Rouge* to France, appeared in 1900. Initially distributed free, it contained tire information together with journey planning advice, including hotel listings. Guides to Europe, North Africa, and Egypt followed as, in 1909, did an English-language edition of the guide to France. Michelin also furnished motorists with itineraries, via an information bureau.

About the same time as its foreign guides appeared, the company was opening its first foreign subsidiaries. The United Kingdom operation was launched in 1905, the Italian the following year. In 1905 came the acquisition of rubber plantations in Indo-China. Meanwhile, tire technology was advancing rapidly. In 1903 Michelin introduced a tire with a sole of leather and studs of steel. Three years later came the detachable wheel rim, allowing a car to carry spare Michelin tires, as did the victor of the first ever Grand Prix, at the La Sarthe circuit. By 1913 Michelin had simplified the way wheels were attached to the vehicle, giving a neater solution to the problem of punctures. Motorists could then carry a spare wheel.

Michelin was on the lookout for new applications for its tires. Around 1908 they were starting to be fitted to trucks, using twin wheels to take the heavy weight, a system tested on Clermont-Ferrand buses. Michelin linked its name to the aeronautical industry by instituting a flying competition, offering Ffr100,000 for the first pilot to complete a difficult course culminating in a landing on the peak of the Puy de Dôme mountain, near Clermont-Ferrand. Cynics said the brothers were getting free publicity by setting an impossible task, but in fact the prize was won in 1911, on the third anniversary of its creation.

When World War I came in 1914, Michelin showed a more serious side of its commitment to aeronautics by adapting its workshops to the production of bombers for the French air force. It supplied 100 free and the remaining 1,800 at cost. After the war Michelin's technological developments continued apace. In 1917 it had introduced the Roulement Universel, or all-purpose, tire with moulded treads. Two years later the woven canvas infrastructure of previous tires was replaced by parallel cord plies. During the interwar period, advances in low-pressure tires dramatically extended tire life expectancy. The first hackney carriage tire had been capable of about 129 kilometers, with pressure of 4.3 kilograms per square centimeter. Thirty years later, in 1923, there was a car tire with pressure of 2.5 kilograms per square centimeter, able to cover

15,000 kilometers. The 1932 figures were 1.5 kilograms and 24,195 kilometers or more. Improvements to durability and road holding continued throughout the 1930s.

By 1930 Michelin was the 17th-largest tire vendor in the world. Throughout the 1920s and 1930s it continued to expand overseas, with tire plants at Karlsruhe, Germany, and in Belgium, Spain, and Holland. The opening of a wire factory in Trento, Italy, illustrates that Michelin was aware of the advantages of controlling the manufacture of components of the tire making process, as well as that process itself.

To all parts of the developed world, the interwar years brought a surge in the amount of motorized traffic. Michelin eased the motorist's lot not only by its reliable tires but also through its guides and maps. As early as 1910 the company had started to publish road maps, the first maps of France especially designed for motorists. Now Michelin extended coverage to more European countries, and to Africa and the United States. It published a series of detailed regional guides, the forerunners of today's *Guides Verts*. Michelin's Information Bureau continued to offer free advice and itineraries, and Michelin campaigned for road numbering and signposting.

The technical advances of the 1930s included the *Pilote*, a car tire giving superior road holding by increasing the ratio of width to depth. In year of the *Pilote*, 1937, appeared the *Metallic*, an innovative design reinforcing rubber with steel cords to support heavier truckloads. Similar technology is still used on truck tires. United States competitors were experimenting with synthetic rubber. Michelin, too, was researching this technology in the late 1930s, although it was not until after the war that the company began to manufacture butyl for making inner tubes.

In 1935 Michelin, initially in the person of Edouard's son Pierre, went to the rescue of automobile manufacturer Citroën, then bankrupt. For almost 40 years, until Peugeot took it over in 1974, Michelin effectively ran Citroën and together the two companies made up the largest industrial group in France. Assisted by other family members, André and Edouard Michelin remained at Michelin's helm until they died, André in 1931 and Edouard in 1940. On Edouard's death his son-in-law Robert Puiseux took charge. Puiseux led the company through the war and on to a fertile period of expansion and innovation. The family was closely involved with the resistance movement during World War II, and several Michelins were interned in concentration camps. André's son Marcel died in Buchenwald, and Marcel's son Jean-Pierre was shot in action in Corsica. Despite these tragedies, Michelin kept going, although its German, Italian, and Czech plants were confiscated, and the factory at Cataroux, France, was crippled by Allied bombardments in 1944. Michelin had a long established policy of admitting only employees to its factories. Remarkably, although its French factories were obliged to produce tires for the Nazis, it managed to keep even the Germans off the premises. Inside, the patriotic Michelin workers were "customizing" their products for the occupying forces. Encountering the subzero temperatures of the Russian front, Michelin tires mysteriously disintegrated—but only the ones that were fitted to German vehicles.

Michelin maps were an invaluable weapon in the Allied armory. Michelin provided official maps for the French army at the outbreak of war, and more than two million were distributed to the liberating forces in 1944. The U.S. War Department reprinted the *Guide Rouge* for use during the Normandy landings. After the war Michelin, unlike some French companies, was free of any suggestion of Nazi collaboration. It swiftly regained its Italian and German property and reconstructed its bombed-out Cataroux plant. It declared a policy of expansion in both the industrialized and the developing world, which would be energetically pursued in the following decades. In France, many new factories would open, making not only tires but also wire, wheels, and tooling. In Italy, Germany, the United Kingdom, and other parts of Europe, existing plants would be modernized and new ones added.

In 1946 came what is arguably Michelin's most important single contribution to tire technology, the radial tire. Instead of a crisscross or cross ply casing of fabric or steel cords, the radial tire casing was a single ply of cords placed across the tire, perpendicular to the direction of travel. This technology vastly improved road holding, flexibility, and durability. The radial tire, developed in secret during the German occupation, was commercially launched in 1949 as the X-tire, and Michelin had to expand its capacity rapidly to keep pace with the public demand for these tires. By 1969, 30 million X-tires per year were racing off the production lines. Today, 75% of all tires manufactured worldwide are radial tires, but Michelin has always blazed the trail. It built on its early lead by quickly making radial tires available for more and more vehicle types. During the 1950s X-tires for trucks and earthmovers were launched. In common with other manufacturers, Michelin also began to make tubeless tires. It had patented such a tire in 1930, but had encountered some practical problems. During the middle to late 1950s, however, tubeless tires caught on, and by the early 1960s, there were tubeless X-tires.

Meanwhile, there were changes at the top of the company. In 1955 François Michelin, the 29-year-old grandson of Edouard the co-founder, became *gérant,* or joint managing partner, alongside head partner Robert Puiseux. On Puiseux's retirement in 1960, François became head partner, and over the next 30 years, led Michelin to the number-one position in the world tire market. Unlike many of its European competitors, which set up agreements with U.S. manufacturers, Michelin had continued to undertake the vast majority of its research and development activities itself. François maintained this policy, and 1963 marked the opening of a new Michelin test centre at Ladoux, not far from Clermont-Ferrand.

The company had been expanding steadily in Europe. Now it was time to look further afield. During the 1960s factories opened in Nigeria, Algeria, and Vietnam. Michelin also had an eye on the United States, where it had started a sales office in 1948, targeting owners of foreign cars. In 1965, however, Michelin entered into a contract with Sears, Roebuck to supply replacement tires for U.S. cars. So successful did this venture prove that by 1970 Michelin was selling 2.5 million tires per year through its own U.S. outlets. Overcapacity was felt in the European tire market during the 1970s, but Michelin pursued its expansion elsewhere. In the United States it constructed its first manufacturing plants in South Carolina and also built plants in Canada and Brazil. Much research continued to go toward perfecting radial technology. During the mid-1960s the XAS tire made the radial concept available to the fastest cars. Radial tires would achieve the ultimate cachet in 1979 when they helped Jody Scheckter drive his Ferrari to victory as Formula 1 World Champion. In the 1970s, Michelin

targeted several new product lines at the long distance road haulage market. With the introduction of radial tires for aircraft in 1981, and motorcycles in 1987, Michelin could offer radial technology for virtually all types of vehicle. The basic technology continued to improve, with new ranges being launched almost every year. The M series, which appeared in 1985, offered a completely new range of state-of-the-art radial tires. Among these, the MXL became Europe's best selling tire by 1990, when its replacement, the MXT, was introduced.

In 1960 Michelin had been the 10th largest tire manufacturer in the world, but by 1980, it was second only to Goodyear. In 1990 came a major acquisition, that of the U.S. tire company Uniroyal Goodrich, which made Michelin indisputably the market leader. Unfortunately, the Uniroyal deal was concluded just as a major recession hit the automobile and tire market. Faced with a Ffr5.27 billion loss for 1990 to 1991, in April 1991 Michelin had to cut costs with layoffs affecting 15% of its workforce. This, not the first but the largest round of job cuts of recent years, was an especially painful step for an employer that has encouraged its workers to see themselves as participants in the enterprise. François Michelin told the press that the main problem was not the acquisition of Uniroyal, but pressure from the automobile industry which in the past decade had forced tire prices down by 50% in real terms. In 1991, despite the pessimism expressed by some analysts about Michelin's prospects, the company itself was looking forward to reaping the benefits of the Uniroyal acquisition when the economy emerges from recession. The strengths of the two companies in the U.S. replacement tire market were complementary, and North America represented more than one-third of the total tire market. Michelin also plans to build on its footholds in Japan, Thailand and South America.

Michelin has more than 4,000 scientists and engineers engaged in research and development. Its Ladoux test center, with 32 kilometers of roadway, is the largest in Europe, and there are others in Spain and in South Carolina. Michelin has been quick to harness computer technology for simulations and design, since 1988 using a giant Cray supercomputer. The firm's share capital is structured in a way that ensures the Michelin family retains control, and French law protects it from takeovers. In 1991, 28-year-old Edouard Michelin joined his father François Michelin and René Zingraff as *gérant.* In its first century, Michelin had grown with, and often ahead of, the tire industry, by a process of unremitting innovation and improvement. In the early 1990s Michelin tires were to be found on motor vehicles of all kinds, on the trains of the Paris and other metro systems, and on aircraft. Worldwide, one in five tires was made by Michelin. The firm knows better than any the tough and fast changing nature of its chosen market. Having reached the top, Michelin showed every intention of staying there.

Principal Subsidiaries: Manufacture Française des Pneumatiques Michelin (29.99%); Société d'Exportation Michelin (99.80); Participation et Développement Industriels S.A. (99.99%); Compagnie Financière Michelin (Switzerland, 91.25%); Spika S.A. (99.99%).

Further Reading: The Michelin Magic, Blue Ridge Summit, Pennsylvania, Tab Books Inc., Modern Automotive Series, 1982; Jemain, Alain, *MICHELIN, Un Siècle de Secrets,* France, Calmann-Lévy, 1982; *Short History of Michelin,* Clermont-Ferrand, Michelin, [n.d.]; *Les Services de Tourisme MICHELIN, Une Histoire Passionnante,* Clermont-Ferrand, Michelin, [n.d.]; *Il y a 100 Ans . . . ,* Clermont-Ferrand, Michelin, 1991; *Les Brevets Michelin ont Cent Ans,* Clermont-Ferrand, Michelin, 1991; Dawkins, Will, "Michelin's man aims to ride out the bumps," *Financial Times,* April 15, 1991.

—Alison Classe

CONTINENTAL AKTIENGESELLSCHAFT

169 Postfach
Königsworther Platz 1
D-3000 Hanover 1
Germany
(0511) 765-0
Fax: (0511) 765-27-66

Public Company
Incorporated: 1871 as Continental-Caoutchouc und Gutta-Percha Compagnie
Employees: 51,064
Sales: DM8.55 billion (US$5.64 billion)
Stock Exchanges: Berlin Bremen Düsseldorf Frankfurt Hamburg Hanover Munich Stuttgart Zürich Vienna New York

Long established as the leading German tire producer, Continental Aktiengesellschaft attained international prominence through a series of major acquisitions in Europe and in the United States starting in 1979. By 1991 Continental was the fourth-largest tire producer in the world. In the second half of 1991, Continental and Pirelli, the fifth-largest tire manufacturer, were engaged in discussions of a cooperative relationship and conceivably a merger of their tire businesses, although by November 1991 these talks had proved unsuccessful.

The Continental-Caoutchouc und Gutta-Percha Compagnie (Continental) was established in Hanover in 1871, and the city remained the center of the firm's operations. It was by no means the first German rubber company; several small firms had been active in Hanover in the previous decade. Continental was promoted by a group of financiers and industrialists with established interests in the rubber business. The initial capital was 900,000 marks. The firm's product range consisted of waterproofed fabrics, footwear, and solid tires, but soon a general line of industrial rubber goods, medical supplies, and sundry consumer goods, such as balls and toys, was added.

During the 1870s Continental developed slowly; dividends were first paid in 1875 when additional capital was raised. In the following decade, however, the firm became highly prosperous and dividends increased from 7% of nominal ordinary share values in 1880 to a constant 27% between 1884 and 1892.

An expanding demand for industrial rubber goods was accompanied by the introduction of cushion tires under a patent from the British firm Macintosh. More significantly, in 1892 Continental commenced the manufacture of pneumatic tires for bicycles to cater to the growing interest in cycling. Although less innovative than Dunlop or Michelin, in the 1890s Continental was the first German producer of pneumatic tires. The 1890s proved more profitable than the previous decade. Continental's gross profit rose from 485,821 marks in 1891 to 1.8 million marks by 1898, and dividends were 55% annually between 1896 and 1898. The firm's capitalization was increased in 1897, doubled again two years later, and totaled 3 million marks by 1901. The work force expanded from 600 to 2,200 between 1893 and 1903. This growth was primarily domestic and was supported by the development of agencies throughout Germany. Continental's leading position is suggested by its 65% share of a market-sharing agreement for cycle tires with Hannoverische Gummi-Kamm in 1894. The establishment of a German factory by Dunlop in 1892, however, provided a potent rival.

The next phase was the development of the automobile tire business. During the late 19th century the prominence of German engineers in the early car industry created an additional market for solid tires, and there was also a growing demand for motorcycle tires. In 1898 Continental designed and began to manufacture a pneumatic tire, a significant technical accomplishment given the larger tires and greater weight and forces involved in automobiles. In 1904 a patterned tread was added to the previously smooth tires, an innovation in which Continental was slightly ahead of the U.S. tire industry. Four years later the detachable rim was adopted to simplify the mounting of tires. This sequence of product innovations completed the fundamental advances in motor tire design, although Continental continued to refine and improve its tires to 1914.

The effectiveness of Continental's response to the demand for car tires confirmed its leading status in Germany, particularly as Dunlop's German subsidiary failed to move into the new sector. Continental's work force expanded to 12,000 by 1913. In the same year capitalization was raised to 12 million marks while dividends averaged 43% from 1900 to 1913. Such profitable growth also encouraged regular extensions of the factory and new investment. An export trade was built up with the establishment of marketing subsidiaries in Britain, Denmark, Sweden, Romania, Italy, Norway, and Australia between 1905 and 1913. Nonetheless the firm lagged behind Dunlop, Michelin, Pirelli, and U.S. Rubber in the establishment of overseas factories and, in some cases, rubber plantations. The outbreak of World War I forced a concentration on supplying military requirements and led to the dissipation of the overseas sales network. At the same time shortages of natural rubber compelled rationing of supplies, use of reclaimed rubber, and experiments with synthetic rubber. In 1909 Continental had produced a few tires using synthetic rubber supplied by the Bayer laboratories. Overall the war severely disrupted the firm's prewar expansion and prosperity.

Civilian production began again in 1919, but despite the underlying civilian demand for tires Continental faced difficulties. Although exports resumed, the earlier momentum had been lost. Moreover, the German car industry grew relatively slowly in the 1920s, and the general economic instability was a further constraint. Continental's response was imaginative. Goodrich, then the fourth-ranking U.S. tire firm, seeking overseas connections, took a 25% financial stake in the German firm in 1920. Bertram G. Work, a prominent Goodrich executive, was a director of Continental in the mid-1920s. The relationship provided access to superior technology for tire designs, rubber chemistry, and manufacturing.

In 1921 Continental introduced the cord tire, a lower pressure tire already coming into vogue in America, and three years later added the balloon cord tire, a design adopted first in France. The Goodrich connection may also explain Continental's use of carbon black—a filler used to improve the durability of tires, especially aging, and a standard additive in the United States—in its tires from 1924. In addition, Continental endeavored to modernize its production processes, adopting U.S. tire-making machinery, with a subsequent rise in productivity. Generally the relationship with Goodrich appears to have been highly valuable for Continental. Nonetheless, the unfavorable business environment ensured that the firm's work force barely increased during the 1920s. Returns were poor compared to the heady prewar levels, and no dividends were paid in 1922, 1923, or 1926. The resulting competitive and financial pressures led to the amalgamation of several German rubber firms to create a new and larger Continental company.

In 1928 Continental took effective control of the neighboring Hannoverische Gummiwerke "Excelsior," and the Goodrich shareholding was terminated at this point. In the following year, four further companies were added to the amalgamation: Peters Union of Frankfurt, Gummiwerke Titan B. Polack of Waltershausen, Liga-Gummiwerke of Frankfurt, and Mitelland-Gummiwerke of Hanover. Negotiations to add the Phoenix Gummiwerke AG company failed, but the expanded Continental firm was by far the largest German tire company. In April 1929 it became known as Continental Gummi-Werke Aktiengesellschaft. During the amalgamation, the Opel family, which had recently sold its car business to General Motors, acquired a substantial shareholding in Continental. Fritz Opel was a director between 1932 and 1938, and the family representation on the supervisory board continued with Wilhelm von Opel from 1939 to 1946 and Georg Opel from 1939 to 1971.

At first the new combine had to retrench in the face of the depression: Continental's work force declined from 16,765 to 10,602 between 1929 and 1932 as demand, prices, and profits all slumped. From 1932 the economic upturn and, in particular, the impact of the Nazi government's program to motorize the German economy and use the construction proceeds as a contribution to reducing unemployment produced a new phase of rapid expansion in car-tire demand. Total German tire output doubled between 1934 and 1938, and Continental's work force rose to 15,254 by 1937. Output and sales expanded rapidly, although dividends rose rather modestly. At the same time the strengthening of state controls resulted in trade agreements covering rubber products so that production and pricing decisions were subject to central direction. In 1938 a new factory was opened at Stocken, Hanover. Buoyant domestic demand made Germany the principal market, but there was a revival of exports within the framework of Nazi trade policies, including expansion in Spain, where Continental established a sales subsidiary in 1934.

The rearmament program of the late 1930s increased state influence, especially given the interest in synthetic rubber development. In World War II tire and rubber output was regulated closely to meet military requirements, especially for truck and aircraft tires and the manufacture of clothing, footwear, and other supplies. With the severe shortage of natural rubber, Continental cooperated with the major German chemical firms in the development and, especially, the utilization of new synthetic rubbers. Overall, with the reduction of civilian business and conscription, sales and employment actually declined during the war.

In the immediate postwar years Continental struggled to resume civilian production amid the physical damage of war and the uncertainties of occupation and reconstruction. Factory employment, down to 6,733 in 1945, rose gradually to 11,891 four years later and dividends resumed in 1948. In a strategy reminiscent of the 1920s, Continental turned to the United States. From 1948 to 1954 Continental had a technical assistance agreement with General Tire. More indirect technical guidance was obtained through a contract to manufacture Goodyear tires for the leading U.S. firm's German marketing operation. Again, the U.S. link provided advice on modern machinery and manufacturing methods, but the necessary new investment was financed by Continental itself.

Deutsche Bank had a major influence on the company's affairs, with representatives on the board from 1953; the Opel family remained the largest single shareholder, with Georg Opel serving as chairman of the supervisory board between 1946 and 1969. The Deutsche Bank was the major financial institution involved with Continental.

Continental, like tire producers everywhere, undertook considerable product innovation. A line of mud tires and snow tires was introduced in 1951, tubeless tires in 1955, and radial tires appeared in 1960. These products kept the firm abreast of general developments, although it lagged behind Michelin and Pirelli with radials. Over the same period, there were successive changes in the materials used in tire construction with the advent of synthetic fibers. The technical challenges and the increasing sophistication of rubber and tire science required the development of research facilities, including in 1967 the opening of the Contidrom tire testing track. Continental remained the largest German tire producer and competed primarily with the subsidiaries of multinational companies.

Between 1950 and 1965 Continental enjoyed a rapid expansion due to the strong growth of the German car industry. The firm supplied original equipment tires—tires installed on new cars—to leading German carmakers and also benefited from the spread of motoring in the increasingly prosperous domestic economy. By 1965 employment totaled 27,447, more than double its 1950 level, and capitalization stood at DM210 million. Dividends averaged 14% of nominal ordinary share values in the decade to 1965.

The firm also followed the car makers, notably Volkswagen, overseas with increased export sales. This expansion was supported by investment in a tire factory in northeastern France in 1964 and the acquisition of marketing subsidiaries in Italy, Portugal, and the United Kingdom. Foreign subsidiaries were also acquired in Spain, South Africa, and Brazil. The firm promoted its tires, often on German cars, in various forms of motor sport in the 1950s. The industrial rubber goods business, much of it also related to the automotive sector, also expanded.

In the early 1960s Continental opened a new plant to produce plastic components for cars and established a new industrial-goods plant. Acquisitions of smaller, specialist rubber firms in Germany achieved further expansion of the nontire sector, including footwear, foam, rubber boats, and plastics. Continental usually purchased a full shareholding or a majority stake; later this domestic strategy of acquisitions was to be transferred to a global stage.

Continental's sales and profits remained good in the late 1960s, but as the rate of growth slackened competition increased. In the 1970s these tendencies were aggravated by the effects of recessions and higher oil prices in the car sector. There was a swift transition to radial tires, whose greater durability further dampened sales, while new investment was required to produce radials. Similar influences and the resulting financial problems affected all European and U.S. tire markets. The leading international tire companies now competed aggressively in all markets, with the Japanese industry emerging as a potent force. The consequence was a restructuring of the global industry through companies leaving the industry, acquisitions, and new foreign investments. Continental experienced financial difficulties; there were no profits between 1972 and 1974 and no dividends between 1971 and 1979.

Chairman Carl Hahn directed Continental's initial retrenchment, and reports of merger negotiations with Phoenix came to nothing. There was a degree of diversification with the expansion of the automotive products division including the addition of fan belt manufacture in 1975 and investment in a massive facility for conveyor belt production. Nonetheless, tires remained the principal product and the intensifying oligopolistic rivalries resulted in more potent competition from subsidiaries, notably Michelin, in Germany.

By world standards Continental was relatively small and exposed to the threats of takeover, isolation in a few markets, and inability to sustain investment in new technology and research. In this context Hahn settled on a bold strategy of international expansion through acquisition. Continental's approach was not unique. Pirelli, Bridgestone, and Sumitomo all pursued a similar course and many smaller firms merged defensively. By contrast, Michelin invested directly in its own foreign factories, notably in the United States. In 1979 Continental purchased the European tire factories of Uniroyal, the U.S. firm that was beginning its retreat from the tire business. As a result Continental obtained a second French factory and another German plant plus factories in Belgium and Scotland. The other gain was the established marketing position of the Uniroyal brand. The acquisition of Kleber-Colombes, a financially troubled French firm in which Michelin held a major stake, was discussed, but not pursued in 1980.

The firm's penetration of two important markets was increased by production contracts. In 1981 a contract was signed for Toyo Rubber Industry Co., Ltd. to manufacture Continental tires in Japan, and there was a similar agreement with General Tire in the United States in the following year. In 1982 Hahn was succeeded by Helmut Werner who had been with Englebert, Uniroyal's Belgian subsidiary.

In 1985 Continental purchased the tire division of Semperit, the largest Austrian rubber firm, for DM47 million. The expansion and diversification coupled with an economic upturn contributed to an improvement in the firm's finances. Dividends were resumed in 1983, and in 1986 Continental's profits totalled DM114.4 million on a total turnover of DM4.97 billion. The most remarkable step in Continental's transition, via acquisition, to major international producer came in 1987 with the purchase of General Tire for US$650 million from GenCorp. Continental obtained the four factories, the brands, the original equipment contracts, and the marketing network of

the fifth-largest U.S. tire manufacturer. In addition General Tire had owned Mexican and Canadian factories. As a result, Continental then accounted for 6.6% of the world tire market in 1988 and 8.1% in 1989, making it the fourth-largest producer, with more than double its market share at the beginning of the decade. Even so, Continental's market share remained less than half those of Michelin, Goodyear, and Bridgestone. The expansion raised Continental's market share and its profile in the business, but also substantially raised its managerial tasks in directing a large, global, and diverse business, particularly one in which the various national units often had their own traditions.

In 1990 Continental purchased a 49% stake in Nivis, a tire firm created by the earlier merger of the two leading domestic tire firms in Sweden and Norway; a share in Mabor of Portugal, and a British tire distribution business. Continental also entered several technical agreements with overseas producers. The political changes in Eastern Europe prompted further developments in the form of cooperative relationships and continuing discussions of other possible ventures as Continental followed the German car manufacturers' lead.

In 1987 the firm's name was shortened to Continental Aktiengesellschaft. During the 1980s Continental appeared in a strong position with solid finances, persistent expansion in the passenger tire and truck tire markets, and innovative tire development and research. The earlier dependence on the German market had been successfully reduced; foreign markets accounted for 62% of the group's sales in 1990 compared to 38% a decade earlier. Nonetheless, tires accounted for around three-quarters of company sales, and the competitive forces that had inspired Continental's acquisition policy remained powerful as tire capacity outstripped demand once again in 1989 and the early 1990s. The tire business, notably the General Tire subsidiaries in North America, recorded substantial losses in 1990: DM48.63 million in the United States and DM36.15 million in Canada. Despite increasing total sales, Continental's net income declined from DM227.8 million in 1989 to DM93.4 million a year later. Further restructuring plus the effort to implement improvements in quality posed new challenges.

Werner, a leading figure in the achievements of the 1980s, resigned to move to Daimler-Benz in 1987. In September 1990 Pirelli, fifth in the world tire industry and also experiencing losses on its tire business, proposed that Continental purchase Pirelli's tire division to form a combined business, in which Pirelli would hold the controlling interest and thus managerial control. Such a merged business would be virtually on a par with the largest producers in terms of market share. After negotiations Continental rejected the scheme, but Pirelli and several supporters bought a stake in Continental and claimed the backing of a majority of shareholders. In May 1991 Horst Urban, Continental's chairman and an opponent of the Pirelli proposal, resigned—an apparent indication of a softening in Continental's attitude.

Apart from Deutsche Bank, other important German shareholders were Bayer, Volkswagen, Daimler-Benz, and BMW. Discussions of possible forms of cooperation, such as research-and-development work, continued, although an immediate merger appeared less probable. The persistent trend toward the domination by Goodyear, Michelin, and Bridgestone of the world tire industry suggested that Continental would move into some form of merger sooner or later, but would seek to maintain its independence.

Principal Subsidiaries: Uniroyal Englebert Reifen; Uniroyal Englebert Tyre Trading; Göppinger Kaliko; Bamberger Kaliko; Techno-Chemie Kessler; Deutsche Semperit; Deutsche Schlauchbootfabrik Hans Scheibert; KA-RI-FIX Transportband-Technik; Clouth Gummiwerke (98.3%); SICUP SARL (France); Société de Flexibles Anoflex (France); Semperit Reifen AG (Austria); Pneu Uniroyal Englebert (Belgium); Uniroyal Englebert Textilecord (Luxembourg); Continental Industrias del Caucho (Spain); Continental Mabor Industria de Pneus (Portugal, 60%); Semperit (Ireland); Uniroyal Englebert Tyres (U.K.); General Tire (U.S.A.); General Tire Canada; General Tire and Rubber Company of Morocco (53.1%); General Tire de Mexico (99.1%); C.U.P. SNC (France); C.U.P. (U.K.); Semperit (U.K.); Continental Caoutchouc (Suisse); Pneu Uniroyal-Englebert (Switzerland); Semperit (Schweiz) (Switzerland); Continental Italia (Italy); ContiTech AGES (Italy); Hycop AB (Sweden); Continental Coordination Center (Belgium); KG Deutsche Gasrusswerke (32.1%); Deutsche Gasrusswerke GmbH (35%); Drahtcord Saar (50%); Drahtcord Saar Geschaftsfuhrung (50%); SAVA-Semperit (Yugoslavia, 27.8%); Compañia Ecuatoriana del Caucho (Ecuador, 35.8%); Nivis Tyre (Sweden, 49%).

Further Reading: Schmidt, H. Th., *Continental: Ein Jahrhundert Fortschritt und Leistung,* Hanover, Continental Aktiengesellschaft, 1971; Overy, R.J., "Cars, Roads, and Economic Recovery in Germany, 1932–8," *Economic History Review,* August 1975; West, Peter J., *Foreign Investment and Technology Transfer: The Tire Industry in Latin America,* Greenwich, Connecticut, Jai Press, 1984; Jones, Geoffrey, ed., *British Multinationals: Origins, Management, and Performance,* Aldershot, England, Gower, 1986; Chandler, Alfred D., *Scale and Scope: The Dynamics of Industrial Capitalism,* Cambridge, Massachusetts, Harvard University Press/Belknap, 1990; French, Michael J., *The US Tire Industry: A History,* Boston, Massachusetts, Twayne, 1991.

—Michael John French

GOODYEAR

THE GOODYEAR TIRE & RUBBER COMPANY

1144 East Market Street
Akron, Ohio 44316
U.S.A.
(216) 796-2121
Fax: (216) 796-1237

Public Company
Incorporated: 1898
Employees: 107,671
Sales: $11.27 billion
Stock Exchanges: New York Midwest Pacific

The Goodyear Tire & Rubber Company (Goodyear) is a major manufacturer, distributor, and seller of tires worldwide. It manufactures and sells other rubber products, and chemicals and plastics, to a number of industrial and consumer markets. It operates approximately 85 plants, of which about half are in the United States, the balance being in 25 other countries.

Without the discovery by U.S. inventor Charles Goodyear of vulcanization—the process by which extreme heat renders rubber flexible and strong—the modern rubber industry would not exist. Goodyear had nothing to do with the company that bears his name. He died insolvent in 1860, 38 years before Frank A. Seiberling founded Goodyear in Akron, Ohio, destined to be the world's first rubber concern to post $1 million in sales. It reigned as the world's largest tiremaker for seven decades.

Bicycle and carriage tires were the company's major products until the start of automobile-tire production in 1901. Seiberling's 1899 application to make carriage tires under Consolidated Tire Company's patent was refused, so he started manufacturing a similar tire without a license, claiming it was monopolistic for Consolidated to grant patent licenses selectively. The ensuing legal battle meant that Goodyear's first- and second-year profits from the sale of carriage tires were held in escrow until the court decided, in Goodyear's favor, in 1902.

Goodyear introduced its straight-side tire under the Wingfoot trademark adopted in 1900, with a full-scale national magazine advertising campaign in 1905. The tire was quickly detachable from its rim, and this popular tire made Goodyear a household name.

Seiberling followed David Hill to the presidency in 1906, with Paul W. Litchfield, George M. Stadelman, and Frank Seiberling's brother Charles Seiberling composing the formative management team. In 1907 Goodyear opened its Detroit shop, providing 1,200 tires to equip Henry Ford's new Model T. By 1909 auto tire production jumped to 36,000, and Goodyear's sales reached $4.25 million, double that of the previous year. By 1910 Goodyear provided one-third of all original tires on U.S. cars. In 1909 Goodyear started production of airplane tires.

In 1910 Litchfield acquired a method for bonding rubber over fabric from North British Rubber Company in Edinburgh, Scotland. Goodyear's rubberized fabric, soon used for planes, including the Wright brothers', also formed the shell of early dirigibles, the production of which commenced in 1910.

Goodyear's tire production rose from 250 per day in 1916 to nearly 4,000 per day by the end of the World War I. The company made 1,000 balloons and 60 airships during the war, as well as 715,000 gas masks and some 4.75 million other military supply parts, such as tire valves. It also provided many of the tires used on aircraft. Wages rose, and both the company and its employees ended the war years in prosperity. Sales had jumped from $110 million in 1916–1917 to $172 million in 1918–1919, and to $223 million in 1920.

Only two days after the November 1918 armistice, the government cancelled its contracts and decontrolled prices. The economy swelled as industry rushed to meet postwar demand, but sales fell in late 1920 as unemployment and bankruptcy soared. Goodyear felt the squeeze as early as 1918, when it made its first attempt to recapitalize by a direct sale of stock to customers and employees.

As the recession deepened, Goodyear was forced to turn to bankers, a position Frank Seiberling in particular was loathe to assume. In 1920, nonetheless, the company accepted temporary refinancing of $18 million from a banking syndicate headed by Goldman, Sachs & Co. of New York, and A.G. Becker of Chicago. The effort was not sufficient, and bankruptcy loomed imminent as the book value of its common stock, at $75 million in early 1920, was reduced to zero. By 1921 sales had fallen to $105 million with a $5 million loss.

In early 1921 the New York law firm of Cravath, Henderson, Liffingwell & De Gersdorff connected Goodyear with an investment bank, Dillon, Read, & Co., that agreed to manage Goodyear's refinancing and reorganization. Of the original officers, only Litchfield and Stadelman remained with the company. Frank Seiberling left to soon incorporate Seiberling Rubber Company, later acquired by Firestone. President E. G. Wilmer and a new management team were brought in. Wilmer focused on creating financial vigor at Goodyear, making few changes, if any, in the production and sales realms. One month after his appointment, in June 1921, he had reduced debt from $66 million to $26.5 million. Of 469 creditor claims in 1921, all but 7 were settled. Sales picked up to $123 million in 1923, from $103.5 million in 1921. In 1923 Stadelman moved into the presidency, Wilmer to board chairmanship, and Litchfield to the first vice presidency. Wilmer would resign from Goodyear to head up Dodge Brothers, the forerunner of the Dodge Motor Company, in 1926.

The world's largest tire producer since 1916, Goodyear became the world's largest rubber producer by 1926. By 1928 the company operated in 145 countries, and sales reached $250 million. Stadelman did not live to see the company reach that point, as he died in January 1926. Litchfield assumed the presidency, commencing a 30-year tenure as chief executive officer. He spent his first year resolving litigation begun in 1922 by Goodyear common stock holders to increase their power and improve the position of common and preferred stock. The battle was concluded in 1927, on terms satisfactory to the stock holders.

Goodyear had produced all the significant U.S. dirigibles since 1911, and was commissioned in 1928 to build two huge dirigibles for the U.S. Navy. The enormous Goodyear airdock, then the world's largest building without internal supports, was erected to accommodate the project. Despite Litchfield's personal interest in the field of lighter-than-air craft, the industry came to an end in 1937 with the crash of the *Hindenburg.* Goodyear's famous fleet of smaller, nonrigid blimps continued to enjoy recognition at outdoor events since they were first floated as a friendly company trademark in the 1930s.

Goodyear was the defendant in one of the most famous antitrust cases of all time beginning in 1933 when the Federal Trade Commission (FTC) charged that its cost-plus-6% purchasing contract with Sears discriminated against independent dealers in violation of the Clayton Act, a U.S. antitrust law. The FTC issued a cease-and-desist order March 1936, and Goodyear appealed to the courts, but later that year the Clayton Act was stringently amended, in large part due to the Goodyear case. In light of the stricter law, Goodyear voluntarily terminated its Sears contract. The federal Circuit Court of Appeals planned to drop the case, but Goodyear wanted its name cleared, and the commission wanted a precedent set for other cases, so the court was pushed to make a firm decision. In 1939 it came out for Goodyear, relieving any threat of future damage claims by dealers. Goodyear's one-time loyal buyer, Sears, became a serious competitor as it took its business to manufacturers selling only to mass distributors.

Prior to the 1930s Goodyear's labor conflicts had been limited. In 1913 some Goodyear workers joined 15,000 other rubber workers in a strike against Akron's other rubber companies organized by the Industrial Workers of the World (IWW). The strike was terminated after 48 days by worker vote, but it did mark the beginning of employee-initiated gains in Akron. The following year Goodyear instituted the eight-hour work day and a paid vacation plan for workers of five to nine years' tenure. A number of employee benefit programs were established, including an in-factory hospital, a worker-oriented company newspaper called *Wingfoot Clan,* and athletic leagues that attracted many a sports-minded employee. In 1915 Litchfield donated an amount equal to his first 15 years' salary, about $100,000, to the factory workers to be used at their discretion. In the early 1990s the fund provided scholarships to children of Goodyear employees or retirees.

In 1919 under Litchfield's direction, Goodyear formed the industrial assembly, a representative body of 60 employees that voiced worker interests to management. The assembly existed for 16 years, until its place was challenged by newly organized chapters of the American Federation of Labor (AFL). Coleman Claherty, a major force in the AFL, began organizing in Akron in 1933, and within the year won 20,000 members throughout the city, 1,000 of whom formed Goodyear's Local 2. The first international convention of the United Rubber Workers (URW) was held in September 1935.

In 1935 the local union chapters demanded that the companies recognize them as bargaining representatives for all employees. The companies refused, and the unions threatened to strike. At Goodyear a company-wide vote carried out by the industrial assembly voted down a strike 11,516 to 891. The unions threatened to strike based solely on member vote, and the federal government resolved tensions by establishing the Perkins agreement, which essentially required management to consult the unions on all wage and scheduling issues.

Goodyear had established a six-hour work day in 1932 to lessen the effects of the Great Depression among workers, by reducing layoffs and distributing work as evenly as possible among remaining employees. When national price controls were removed in 1935, however, Goodyear re-established the eight-hour work day to increase productivity, decrease its prices, and make its products more competitive. The industrial assembly requested a return to the six-hour shift, and when this was denied it appealed to the board of directors. Local 2, encouraged by the industrial assembly's tenacity, appealed to the secretary of labor, who ruled in January 1936 that Goodyear was unjustified in its reversion to the eight-hour shift because it had voluntarily established a shorter day. The government also charged Goodyear with discriminating between industrial assembly and union workers. At the time, union membership was at 10%.

Goodyear returned to the six-hour day as suggested, but layoffs became necessary as tire sales decreased, and the union struck in February 1936. Goodyear's strikers were supported by union sympathizers from other rubber companies and by Ohio and West Virginia coal miners from John L. Lewis's Committee for Industrial Organization (CIO). Within two days, thousands were picketing Goodyear's three major Akron plants. More than 1,000 employees, including Litchfield, moved into the factories to maintain as much production as possible. The union strategy was to break Goodyear, the largest rubber factory, so that the other companies would be more compliant. After 34 days the strike was settled by direct negotiations.

With a three-month stock of goods, Goodyear did not suffer financially from the strike, but the show of union muscle upped URW membership throughout Akron, and increased Goodyear union members to 5,000. The Wagner Act, or National Labor Relations Act, was affirmed by the U.S. Supreme Court in April 1937. The industrial assembly was categorized as a company union, and had to be disbanded. Workers supported the move to URW representation by a ratio of more than two to one.

Sitdowns and inter-worker violence frequently disrupted production after the 1935 strike, culminating in a May 1938 sitdown that attracted picketers although none were formally requested. Police were summoned to disperse the demonstrators, and in an ensuing riot 100 people were injured. The company and union negotiated three days later and sitdowns decreased. Goodyear had decreased employees in Akron from 58,316 in 1929 to 33,285 in 1939. In 1941 after three years of cooperation, Goodyear signed its first formal contract with Local 2.

Despite labor and litigation difficulties during the 1930s, Goodyear continued its expansion. An Alabama plant and two textile mills were built in 1929, followed by another textile mill in 1933. In 1935 the company acquired a bankrupted company, Kelly-Springfield Tire. Another plant was acquired in Akron in 1936, and a Vermont factory was purchased to centralize shoe sole-and-heel production.

Goodyear's foreign expansion, begun in 1910 with its first of two Canadian plants, continued during the 1930s. In addition to its London and Australian plants, operative since 1912, Goodyear had distributors located throughout northern Europe, Russia, Central and South America, and the Caribbean. In 1931 a tire plant was opened just outside Buenos Aires, Argentina. The sixth foreign factory went up in Bogor, on Java in Indonesia in 1935, and the seventh in 1938 in Sao Paolo, Brazil. A Swedish plant was opened in 1939. Rubber plantations were established during the 1930s in Indonesia, Costa Rica, and the Philippines. Goodyear Foreign Operations was created to manage the company's 18 foreign subsidiaries, 7 factories, 7 plantations, 37 branches, 28 depots, and hundreds of distributors located outside of the United States.

Goodyear patented its first synthetic rubber—Chemigum—in 1927. It was first mass produced in 1935, and tires were made of it in 1937. In 1934 the company introduced Pliolite, a compound that cemented rubber to metal, and Pliofilm, a packaging material. Other popular Goodyear products were rubber floor tiles; many new models of tires; Airfoam, a cushioning material for seats and matresses; and Neolite, a synthetic heel-and-sole material.

Goodyear began producing 200,000 gas masks a month for the U.S. Army after Adolf Hitler's April 1939 invasion of Poland. The same year, Goodyear Aircraft (GAC) was established, and the Goodyear airdock, unused since the demise of the giant airships, housed war-time airplane and parts production, as well as the construction of 132 blimps for coastal submarine defense. In 1941 Goodyear joined other manufacturers to produce parts for 100 B-26 bombers a month. In 1943 some of GAC's 32,000 employees worked on the plane that dropped A-bombs on Hiroshima and Nagasaki in 1945, a B-29 Superfortress. GAC also produced 4,008 Vought Corsair FG1 fighter planes, beginning in 1943.

In 1940 Edwin J. Thomas, who began as Litchfield's secretary and assistant in the 1920s, ascended to the presidency as Litchfield continued as chairman of the board. The company took on management of a government-owned factory producing propellant charges for 600 types of artillery shells in 1940. In 1941 the U.S. government required each of the "big four" rubber producers—Goodyear, General Tire, Firestone, and Goodrich—to construct plants that would produce 400,000 tons a year of GRS, or goverment rubber, a synthetic compound including styrene and butadiene. Goodyear supervised the construction of three synthetic rubber plants for the government. Two of the plants became owned and operated by the company. Goodyear sales increased 52% over 1940.

Goodyear also produced the top-secret phantom fleet, used to confuse Nazi reconnaissance before the D-Day invasion of Normandy. The "fleet" was made of rubberized material, from which Goodyear constructed life-size inflatable replicas of amphibious invasion craft, PT boats, tanks, combat vehicles, and heavy artillery. These imposters were blown up and set in one coastal English base, then rapidly deflated and moved by night to another. To Axis surveillance, the apparent serial establishment and abandonment of fighting bases was inexplicable, and may have contributed to their unstable coastal defense.

When the war concluded, the government cancelled $432 million in Goodyear contracts. GAC released almost 27,000 employees, reducing its payroll to 2,000 by 1946. Demobiliza-

tion increased demand for consumer tires, and sales increased to 25 million in 1946–1947. Goodyear established factories in Colombia and Venezuela in 1945, in Cuba in 1946, and in South Africa in 1947. A Japanese-occupied factory in Indonesia was regained in 1945, and a rubber plantation in 1949. In its 50th year, 1948, Goodyear reached a peacetime sales record of $705 million. It employed 72,000 workers worldwide and was poised to expand its international presence.

In its first 50 years, Goodyear total sales had been $9 billion; in the decade from 1949 to 1958, they would top $11.5 billion. In 1951 Goodyear became the first rubber company to exceed $1 billion in sales in one year. Goodyear's World War II production record garnered it several government contracts associated with the Korean War in 1950. A subsidiary, Goodyear Atomic Corp., was founded in 1952 when the government selected the company to operate a $1.2 billion atomic plant under construction in Pike County, Ohio. The facility opened in 1954.

In 1954 Goodyear acquired its first new plantation in 20 years in Belem, Brazil. In 1955 it acquired two government-owned rubber factories it had operated during the war. In 1955 at Goodyear's Gadsden, Alabama, plant, an $11.5 million investment elevated it to the largest tire-making facility in the United States. In 1957 it also built a 7,200-acre tire testing site with 18.5 miles of multisurface roads.

Rubber consumption after World War II was double prewar production. Much of the increase was due to new rubber products such as foam rubber, film, and plastics, and growth was fueled by newly developing synthetic rubbers such as polyisoprene, introduced by Goodyear in 1955 and called Natsyn, for commercial purposes. In 1960 Goodyear built a $20 million synthetic rubber plant in Beaumont, Texas; its annual production of 40,000 tons of Natsyn equaled the annual generation of 15,000 acres of rubber trees.

In 1958 Thomas became chairman of the board, and Litchfield honorary chairman. Russell DeYoung became Goodyear's ninth president; his first full-time Goodyear position had been that of a tire inspector. DeYoung appointed Robert H. Lane as public relations director in 1958. Lane was largely responsible for the makeover of Goodyear's public profile from a somewhat stodgy, though quality, tire maker, to a contemporary innovator. The key to this image update was Goodyear's reentry into racing. Once it overcame Firestone's domination of the field, Goodyear was able to equip winning cars in the Daytona 500 and other popular U.S. and European races. Lane also clearly defined the role of the Goodyear blimp as a corporate goodwill ambassador, capitalizing on the company's historic association with airships.

Foreign operations were consolidated in February 1957 under Goodyear International Corporation (GIC). In 1959 GIC initiated its European expansion program with construction of a plant in Amiens, France. Tire plants were built in 1965 at Cisterna di Latina, Italy, and in 1967 in Phillipsburg, Germany, giving Goodyear production sites in Europe's three major markets within ten years.

In the United States, Goodyear's expansion was partly by acquisition. In 1959 the company added a $3 million aeronautics research and development laboratory in Litchfield Park, Arizona, to supplement GAC's activities. The subsidiary received a $65 million contract in 1958 to produce Subroc, an antisubmarine missile. Goodyear would continue to derive much of its business from U.S. military and space program contracts, including production of equipment for several of the Apollo moon missions. In 1961 the company bought Geneva Metal Wheel Company, a maker of specialty wheels, and in 1964 acquired Motor Wheel Corporation, the world's largest maker of styled auto wheels. That same year, it was the first rubber corporation to exceed $2 billion in annual sales. Its profits were in excess of $100 million, with foreign subsidiaries contributing more than one-third.

In 1966, two years after Victor Holt assumed the presidency, Goodyear opened its tenth U.S. tire plant, in Danville, Virginia. This was followed in 1967 by a $73 million facility at its 593-acre site in Union City, Tennessee. Goodyear's sales doubled during the 1960s, topping $3 million in 1969. Net income rose from $71 million to $155 million. In 1969 it became the first rubber company to exceed $3 million in annual sales.

Goodyear's biggest challenge in the 1970s was overhauling its factories to produce radial tires. The radial, with its excellent reinforcement system and extra belt of steel, was introduced by France's Michelin in 1948, and by 1972 it equipped 8% of U.S. cars. Recognizing the superiority of the radial, Goodyear introduced a transitional fiberglass reinforced tire in 1967, and by 1972, 50% of U.S. cars rode on them. When Charles J. Pilliod assumed the presidency in 1972, he insisted that Goodyear bear the expense of adapting to full radial technology. The radial tire equipped 45% of U.S. cars by 1976, and Goodyear was the world's largest radial producer. In 1977 with a media blitz extolling its all-season tread, Goodyear introduced its Tiempo radial, the company's most successful tire to that time.

Goodyear's 75th anniversary year—1973—was marred by the debilitating Middle East oil crisis. In 1974, Pilliod became chairman and chief executive officer and John H. Gerstenmaier assumed the presidency, and Goodyear, prompted by the government, formed a joint project to stimulate domestic propagation of guayale, a native North American bush that provided 50% of U.S. rubber until 1910. As oil prices declined, however, the project slowed. In 1975 Mark Donohue, a well-known car racer, was killed when a tire blew out during pre-race preparations. In 1984 his estate was awarded a $9.6 million settlement from Goodyear, one of the largest wrongful-death payments in history.

In 1976 Goodyear suffered its longest strike ever when URW workers walked out on Goodyear, Goodrich, Uniroyal, and Firestone after talks at Firestone, the target company, failed. Goodyear's 22,000 strikers and their cohorts at the other companies returned to work some 130 days later having obtained an agreement that wages and benefits would be increased 36% over the following three years.

In 1979 Goodyear fought hard and succeeded in avoiding the "neutrality" clause accepted by the other three rubber companies, which guaranteed that companies would not interfere with URW organizing. This was motivated by its desire to create a nonunion shop at its newly built Lawton, Oklahoma, facility. Pilliod's new labor relations policies required individual workers, rather than supervisors, to be responsible for quality control. The new policies also provided regular and ongoing communications between management and laborers, and worker involvement in problem solving. The factory was considered 50% more efficient than older facilities, and by 1983, factory worker turnover was down to less one-third of 1%.

In 1977 the Securities and Exchange Commission (SEC) accused Goodyear of maintaining a clandestine fund of $1.5 million to make foreign and domestic political contributions and government and labor bribes. The SEC charged that the company had made $500,000 in dubious payments since 1970 in 20 foreign countries. Goodyear agreed, without admitting guilt, to a permanent court injunction against violations of federal securities laws, providing a report of its activities in the countries in question. Two years prior, in 1975, Goodyear said it made political contributions of at least $242,000 between 1964 and 1972.

Robert E. Mercer assumed the presidency in 1978, when Gerstenmaier retired. That year Goodyear tire production was terminated in Akron, but the company began building Goodyear Technical Center, a $750 million research and design complex located on 3,000 acres in Akron. By 1980 despite national and global recession, Goodyear had record earnings of $264.8 million and had reduced debt to its lowest level in 17 years. By 1984 it supplied one-third of the U.S. tire market, and one-fifth of the world tire market. In 1983 Pilliod retired, Mercer became chief executive officer, and Tom H. Barrett was voted president.

Having won the ten-year battle to remain leader of the tire market, Goodyear entered the 1980s planning to scale some other peaks. Its diversification goal was to reduce tire revenues to one-half of corporate earnings and generate the other half through its GAC subsidiary and Celeron, a Louisiana oil and gas concern purchased in 1983. GAC had expanded at a compound annual rate of 17% from 1973 to 1983, providing a 20% return on investment. In 1983 its annual sales were $617 million, despite a questionable $50 million investment in the production of centrifuges to enrich uranium for nuclear powerplants. Celeron, although its sales slipped the year after it was purchased, began construction of the then-promising $750 million All-American Pipeline, a 1,200-mile tube used to transport 300,000 barrels per day of off-shore California crude oil to Texas refineries.

The diversification came to an abrupt end in 1986, when takeover specialist Sir James Goldsmith made a bid for Goodyear. The company was able to beat off this takeover, but only by selling most of its nontire concerns, including GAC, which went to Loral Company for $588 million, and parts of Celeron, which went to Exxon for $650 million. Barrett became chief executive officer in 1988 and remained president. Hoyt M. Wells was voted president in 1991. In 1989 the company divested its South African operations, which it had maintained despite the social protest against apartheid during the 1980s.

In 1990 Goodyear took its first loss since 1932, and surrendered its position as the world's largest tire maker to Michelin, when the French company bought out Goodrich's tire business, which had been merged with Uniroyal's. Firestone and General, weakened by Goodyear's dominance in the radial market, were absorbed, respectively, by Japan's Bridgestone and Germany's Continental, forcing upon Goodyear competition of its own size. Its All-American Pipeline, prevented from operating at full capacity by environmental restrictions, continued to produce losses; the company's $3.3 billion long-term debt, largely incurred by the Goldsmith battle, was also a weakness. Analysts pointed to Goodyear's sluggish internal efficiency as a major problem. For the first time since 1921, Goodyear went outside company ranks to choose a chairman and chief executive officer, as Stanley C. Gault succeeded Barrett in June 1991. Gault had been chairman and chief executive of Rubbermaid, Incorporated, while serving on Goodyear's board.

Between 1989 and 1991, Goodyear eliminated 12,000 jobs—10% of its work force—with more than one-half of that coming from the salaried sector. In combination with the $1.4 billion investment in modernization and consolidation of factories, these cuts added up to an estimated savings of $250 million annually. Yet Goodyear remained committed to its annual research and development budget of more than $300 million a year, confident in this as a source of quality tires, such as 1990's Eagle GA and Eagle GT+4, successful luxury car models. By restructuring its U.S. marketing tactics, the company regained its lost market share and was holding its own in the tougher international market. While still somewhat vulnerable to takeover because of its relatively low stock price, Goodyear entered the 1990s with its major capital outlays completed and anticipating rising profits.

Principal Subsidiaries: Celeron Corp.; Goodyear Aerospace Corp.; Hose Couplings Manufacturing Inc.; Kelly-Springfield Tire Co.; Lee Tire & Rubber Co.; Ohio Poly Corp.; Reneer Films Corp.

Further Reading: O'Reilly, Maurice, *The Goodyear Story,* Elmsford, New York, The Benjamin Company, 1983; Labich, Kenneth, "The King of Tires is Discontented," *Fortune,* May 28, 1984; Schiller, Zachary, "After a Year of Spinning its Wheels, Goodyear Gets a Retread," *Business Week,* March 26, 1990.

—Elaine Belsito

PIRELLI S.P.A.

Piazzale Cadorna, 5
20123 Milan
Italy
2 85351
Fax: 2 85351

Incorporated: 1872 as Pirelli & C.
Employees: 68,703
Sales: L10.14 trillion (US$8.83 billion)
Stock Exchanges: Milan Amsterdam Antwerp Brussels
    Frankfurt Paris

Pirelli S.p.A. is one of the four largest companies in Italy, with 125 factories throughout the world. Its founder, Giovanni Battista Pirelli, a 24-year-old engineering graduate from the Milano Politecnico, formed the company Pirelli & C. with an initial share capital of L215,000. By 1990 its annual sales exceeded L10 trillion and its share of the worldwide market for rubber-based products was about 6.5%.

Pirelli had astutely realized that rubber was to become one of the most important commodities in the rapidly industrializing Italy. Less than a year after its inception, Pirelli's company built its first factory in Milan. There were 45 people employed in the small, 1,000-meter-square building as demand for the company's rubber sheets, belts, slabs, and vulcanized products increased. The rapid growth in the popularity of the motor car, which was now seen as more than a fashionable plaything for the rich, led to contracts to supply pneumatic tubes and transmission belts.

From its earliest years Pirelli demonstrated a willingness to diversify its product range and to produce overseas in order to satisfy its desire for ambitious, yet controlled, expansion. The company began the manufacture of insulated telegraph cables in 1879 and within seven years had developed the technology to produce underwater telegraph cables. In 1890 pneumatic bicycle tires rolled off the production line and were followed in 1900 by the company's first car tires.

Pirelli established a trend that many Italian companies were to follow when it began to expand abroad as early as 1902. The new cable and electrical lead factory set up near Barcelona in Spain was followed by a similar venture in Britain in 1914, and by 1920 factories had also been set up in Brazil, Greece, Argentina, Turkey, and Germany. Product diversification at home was encouraged by the firm's long-term commitment to investing in research and development. Giovanni

brought his two sons into the business and they helped to run the new motorcycle tire production plant built at Bicocca in 1908. Forever at the forefront of new technology, the company began to produce rubberized fabrics as early as 1909.

Two major factors were to account for Pirelli's growth in the years immediately preceding World War I. Firstly, between 1900 and 1914, Italy saw increased social reforms and political stability, which created more favorable conditions for trade and industry. Pirelli, which derived much of its demand from newly established ventures, was well placed to benefit from these changes by producing fluid control devices, transmission belts, and fuel distribution machinery. Secondly, the invention of the internal combustion engine in 1910 made the mass production of cars economically viable. The so-called "rubber boom" of 1911 marked the acceptance of the material as a worldwide commodity and ensured the continued success of the company.

New factories were opened in Spain in 1917 and Argentina in 1919, but the first major event to affect the company after the end of the war was a change in its organizational structure, implemented in 1920. Pirelli & C., the original company founded by Giovanni Pirelli, changed its status and became an investment rather than a production company. Società Italiana Pirelli, later to become Pirelli S.p.A., was incorporated to act as a holding company to control the group's varied industrial operations based in Italy. Compagnie Internationale Pirelli S.A., incorporated in Brussels, was set up to manage the group's rapidly increasing overseas operations.

In 1924 Luigi Emanueli, an employee of the company, developed the first commercially viable oil-filled cable. The world's first crossply tire—the Superflex Stella Bianca—was successfully launched in 1927 and within two years a new cable production unit was opened in Brazil and a new tire factory was opened at Burton-on-Trent in England. Initiatives were also made in India and Malaysia to guarantee the supply of natural rubber to Milan and Pirelli's overseas subsidiaries.

This was a period when Pirelli's products, fitted to the Ferraris and Alfa Romeos of Nuvolari and Ascari, became synonymous with success in international Grand Prix racing. However, the rise of Mussolini's fascists and Italy's increasingly disastrous foreign policy in the mid-1930s led to a further period of economic and political turbulence. To counteract the impending threat of international boycotts, Compagnie Internationale Pirelli S.A. was transferred into Pirelli Holdings S.A., a holding company incorporated in neutral Switzerland.

World War II left Italy politically and economically crippled. A weak leadership was unable to cope with the severe poverty, rampant inflation, and high unemployment that affected the whole country. However, Alcide de Gasperi, the Christian Democrat leader, was able to bring both inflation and the budget deficit under some degree of control and by 1948 a large-scale public investment program was instigated.

Italian industry had been situated in the north of the country for a number of reasons. Milan, Turin, and Genoa became business centers because of the availability of both capital and raw materials—steel for machinery and railways, coal for power—and again Pirelli, which derived much of its success from the success of others, was well placed to take advantage of the new boom in the north. Pirelli responded to this opportunity by producing the first fabric-belted tire, the Cinturato CF67, which revolutionized the tire industry.

In the 1950s and 1960s Italy enjoyed the same kind of economic miracle experienced by many European countries as postwar depression gave way to years of growth and prosperity. An influx of new talent, often from comparatively humble backgrounds, suffused the established upper crust of Italian society and led to an improvement in the quality of management. Pirelli set new records for expansion overseas, opening a further cable factory in Canada in 1953, a latex foam plant in France in 1957, and new tire plants in Greece and Turkey in 1960. The company reinforced its position in both South America and Australasia when it opened further cable manufacturing operations in Peru in 1968 and Australia in 1975. Pirelli was also involved in establishing several turnkey plants during the 1960s to provide tires for Eastern European companies.

Throughout this period of expansion Pirelli followed the strategy, common to most of the Italian multinationals, of eschewing joint ventures and the purchase of minority and majority shares in established companies. Instead, product ranges that had already proved successful in the Italian domestic market were transferred for production and sale overseas. In this way the company has been able to retain complete control over its operations abroad while being able to overcome barriers preventing Italian exports.

In the late 1960s Pirelli's reputation for being at the forefront of innovation was usurped by Michelin when the latter introduced steel-belted radial tires. Michelin also entered the U.S. cable market seven years before Pirelli. Some commentators suggested that the management of the company was more concerned with producing glossy calendars than tires. The company responded by embarking on a long-term research and development agreement with the British Dunlop group. This surprising move did not lead to a full merger and neither party seemed to be too disappointed when the agreement was terminated in 1981. Despite successes in the development of low-profile tires and in revolutionary fiber optics, the joint venture now appears, with the benefit of hindsight, to be have been too much of a defensive measure designed to counter the perceived threat of Michelin.

A personal tragedy hit the firm in the early 1970s when Giovanni Pirelli, a direct descendant of the original founder, was killed in a car crash. This natural leader of the firm was replaced by his younger brother, Leopoldo, who was also severely injured in the accident. Leopoldo led the company through a period of protracted change.

The oil crises of the 1970s brought about a change in attitude towards the role of the motor car. Sales of new cars slumped as the price of petrol soared, and as a consequence the worldwide demand for tires fell dramatically. Italy, far more dependent on imported sources of energy than most of its European partners, was particularly badly hit by the 1974 crisis, which saw the return of rampant inflation and a massive drop in the value of the lire. The second oil crisis of 1979 followed the withdrawal of the Communists from the "historic compromise" coalition government that had done so much to stabilize Italian political life. The Naples earthquake of November 1980 and the public exposure of P2, the secret Masonic lodge, six months later further damaged the morale of the country.

After the ending of the agreement with Dunlop, Pirelli benefited from the upturn in the European economy of the early 1980s. The Italian and Swiss parent companies were responsible for an extensive reorganization of the group in 1982, which saw an equalization of the shares each company held in the group's many and varied subsidiary companies. A new management company, Pirelli Société Générale S.A., was created in Basel to ensure that unified policies and centralized objectives were put in place in Pirelli companies throughout the world.

In 1985 Pirelli acquired the share capital of Metzeler Kautschuk, a German company with many interests in the rubber industry. The acquisition of Metzeler led to a 13% increase in consolidated turnover and reinforced Pirelli's position in the market for motorcycle tires and automobile components. Just as important, the move provided Pirelli with a well-established distribution chain which dealt with manufacturing activities. This apparent change in strategy—favoring growth through acquisition at the expense of traditional organic growth—was also demonstrated in 1988 when the group acquired Armstrong Tire Co., the sixth-largest U.S. tire manufacturer. In the same year Pirelli bought Filergie S.A., a cable manufacturer with 13 plants in France and Portugal. Although the pace of technical development appeared to be slowing down and no further radically different tires were introduced, the company did benefit from the increased margins offered by a shift in demand in favor of low-profile and premium radial tires.

A further share restructuring was undertaken in 1988 when Pirelli S.p.A. acquired Société Internationale Pirelli S.A.'s holding in Pirelli Société Générale S.A., thereby accepting direct responsibility for the day-to-day management of the operating companies. In turn, these operating companies were restructured into self-contained divisions in order to facilitate faster responses to financial, production, and employment problems. The three divisions—Pirelli Tire, Pirelli Cavi, and Pirelli Prodotti Diversificati—were each given separate holding companies.

The worldwide tire industry has been as badly hit by the recession of the late 1980s and early 1990s as any other manufacturing sector. Worldwide sales of tires stagnated, and producers were unable to pass on increases in the cost of raw materials—especially oil—to the final consumer. Car makers, suffering from reduced demand, cut their costs by forcing tire manufacturers to accept lower prices. A spate of ill-conceived takeovers in the early 1980s and an increasing market dominance by a decreasing number of companies led to pressure on margins in the struggle to gain market share. Excess capacity and oversupply exacerbated the situation.

Pirelli's reaction to these market forces was to engage in two major merger and acquisition exercises. Firstly, the company became involved in an acrimonious battle with Bridgestone to take control of the U.S. company Firestone in 1988 and 1989. With the benefit of hindsight, Pirelli should be content to have lost the battle and thereby have avoided what has proved to be a costly and largely unsuccessful acquisition for Bridgestone.

Pirelli's second attempt to increase its market share by entering the world of mergers and acquisitions has led to a long series of merger discussions with the German company Continental. The plan to merge the fourth- and fifth-largest tire producers in the world was designed to produce a force powerful enough to achieve critical mass in a fairly stagnant market. Damaging price competition would be avoided and overcapacity would be reduced. This deal seemed a far more attractive proposition than the opportunity to acquire Firestone two years earlier.

The proposed merger, however, proved to be problematic from the very first time the two parties met. The board of Continental, led by chief executive Horst Urban, angered the Pirelli leadership by publicly revealing details of secret meetings. Pirelli believed that its attempts to follow traditional German merger practice, in which friendly approaches are made to willing partners in order to achieve mutual benefit, was the best way to act in the early stages of the deal. Continental's belligerent defensive strategy, inspired by the aggressive tactics employed by the City of London and Wall Street in the mid-1980s, may well prove to be to the long-term detriment of both companies.

The year 1990 was not particularly good for the Pirelli group, with only the diversified products division achieving an increase in sales. The cables sector suffered from a marked decrease in turnover in the South Americas, where confusion over the privatization of the various state telephone companies was coupled with weakening domestic economies. The drop in demand for new tires was, in some cases, offset by an increase in the demand for replacements, but, in overall terms, sales were in decline. Continued uncertainty over the proposed Continental merger only served to detract top management from implementing their strategies.

Despite the stagnation in sales, Pirelli remained committed to investing in its long-term future. Research and development remained a priority for the company and an extensive program to improve global quality was instigated. As the fourth-largest company of its kind in the world, Pirelli was an attractive company for takeover, but the complexity of its financial structure, and the apparent unity of its major shareholders, suggests that any bid for the equity of the company would be vigorously resisted. The future of the Pirelli name is not in doubt: the question is what form the company will take as it approaches the demands of the 21st century.

Principal Subsidiaries: Industrie Pirelli S.p.A.—Divisione Prodotti Diversificati; Pirelli Coordinamento Pneumatici S.p.A.; Società Cavi Pirelli S.p.A.; Societá Pneumatici S.p.A.: Société Internationale Pirelli S.A. (Switzerland); Pirelli Société Générale S.A. (Switzerland); Pirelli Argentina S.A.; Pirelli Canada Inc. (Canada); Pirelli France S.A.; Pirelli Deutschland AG (Germany); Pirelli UK PLC (United Kingdom); Productos Pirelli S.A. (Spain); Pirelli Enterprises Corporation (U.S.A.); Pirelli Cable Corporation (U.S.A.).

Further Reading: Pirelli, Alberto, *Economia e guerra,* Milan, Istituto per gli Studi di Politica Internazionale, 1940; *La Pirelli: Vita di una azienda industriale,* Milan, Industrie Grafiche A. Nicola, 1946; King, Russel, *Italy,* London, Harper & Row, 1987; Pirelli, *Pirelli,* Milan, 1987; Onida, Fabrizio and Gianfranco Viesti, *The Italian Multinationals,* Beckenham, Croom Helm, 1988; *Italy: Country Profile,* London, Economist Intelligence Unit, 1990.

—Andreas Loizou

❖ SUMITOMO RUBBER INDUSTRIES, LTD.

SUMITOMO RUBBER INDUSTRIES, LTD.

1-1, Tsutsui-cho 1-chome
Chuo-ku, Kobe 651
Japan
(078) 231-4141
Fax: (078) 232-0264

Public Company
Incorporated: 1917
Employees: 4,856
Sales: ¥546.03 billion (US$4.38 billion)
Stock Exchanges: Tokyo Osaka Nagoya

Sumitomo Rubber Industries, Ltd., Japan's third-largest automobile tire producer, manufactures tires under the Dunlop name in the United Kingdom, Germany, France, and the United States, as well as in its home country. It is also a significant producer of golf and other sporting goods, and imports high-performance car tires from Europe and golf clubs from the United States.

The company is part of the Sumitomo group, one of Japan's largest *keiretsu,* or conglomerates. The Sumitomo group originated in a 17th-century book and medicine shop founded by Masatomo Sumitomo, a former samurai. Another Sumitomo family member perfected a method of extracting silver from crude copper by using lead, and by the late 17th century, the family ran a prominent copper mine and refinery. By the time of the Meiji Restoration in 1868, which initiated Japan's industrialization, Sumitomo's investment and development of copper mines made it one of Japan's largest companies.

The Sumitomo group owned an interest in Dunlop Japan, a unit of the British company Dunlop, when it was established in Kobe in 1909. Dunlop produced its first tires in Japan in 1913, and Sumitomo Rubber was established shortly thereafter, in 1917. A close relationship developed and continued between the two companies.

By the early 1940s, the Sumitomo group had matured into one of Japan's leading *zaibatsu,* huge industrial concerns tightly controlled by a central board. When Japan went to war against the United States in 1941, all Sumitomo enterprises were pressed into military production. By the end of World War II in 1945, Sumitomo's industrial facilities had been substantially damaged by air raids, but the company was slated for rehabilitation during the postwar occupation and restoration period.

All *zaibatsu* were disbanded at that time under antimonopoly laws, so each Sumitomo unit became an independent company. When antitrust legislation was eased in the early 1950s, Sumitomo associates began re-establishing former business ties. Like other former *zaibatsu,* Sumitomo gathered its former companies together again through its family-owned bank, which facilitated cross-ownership of shares between the companies. These looser, but still powerful, industrial groups were called *keiretsu,* with Sumitomo ranking third among them, after Mitsubishi and Mitsui.

Sumitomo Electric Industries, another member of the Sumitomo group, bought a majority share of Dunlop Japan in 1963, and changed Dunlop's name to Sumitomo Rubber Industries (SRI). The rubber concern remained one of Sumitomo's smaller ventures, selling mostly within Japan, and ranking 12th in the world market as of 1985. By 1987 however, SRI ranked sixth in the global tire market, with tire-manufacturing bases in Europe, the United States, and Japan, the world's three centers of automobile production. With a 6% share of the market, it was creeping up on fourth-place Firestone and fifth-place Uniroyal, while the pack was led by Goodyear with 20%, followed by Michelin with 17% and Japan's Bridgestone with 8%.

SRI's change in status came about through the company's acquisition of additional Dunlop operations. During the early 1980s, a growing number of Japanese companies realized that to compete in the world market, they must buy into foreign companies, thus obviating a static home economy and trade barriers abroad. SRI became a trendsetter when it purchased a 98% interest in Dunlop's tire production in France, Germany, and the United Kingdom for $240 million in 1984.

Dunlop was on the verge of bankruptcy when the friendly takeover was initiated. The British company had made a critical error in the early 1960s when it deemed steel-belted radial tires a passing fad. Instead of developing a steel-belted radial like pioneer Michelin, the company opted to produce cheaper textile radial tires. These wore longer than traditional cross-ply tires, but could not perform like steel-belted radials. By the 1970s, when it was clear that steel-belted radial had superseded conventional tires, Dunlop did not have the capital to initiate steel-belted radial production.

Another of Dunlop's miscues was its acquisition of an interest in the Italian tire maker Pirelli in 1971. Pirelli had significant losses that year, and Dunlop had to write off its £40 million investment in the Italian company. The highly inflationary period of 1974–1975 dealt a blow to Dunlop's borrowing power precisely when it should have been stepping up radial production. Although 1978 was one of its most profitable years ever, Dunlop's debt soon absorbed all its profits, and by 1983 the company was losing money. The company opted to reduce its product range, a mistake in the highly specialized tire market. Lack of cash meant that production facilities were in disrepair and design and development programs were canceled. Several factories were shut down as employees were cut from 5,000 to less than 3,500 in the United Kingdom. Morale was abysmal and even top executives quit. Finally in 1984, the British company found itself unable to refinance its French subsidiary's losses, and had to let it go into receivership.

SRI had maintained close technical and commercial links with Dunlop. Its investment in the operation was massive, so the Japanese company did not want Dunlop to fall into competitors' hands. Also, SRI saw that the Dunlop operations could be highly profitable if given the proper financial and managerial backing; so, at Dunlop's behest, it acquired most of the company's tire business in 1984. Dunlop's U.S. tire business was bought out by its management in 1984, but was acquired by SRI two years later.

SRI changed the U.K. company's name to SP Tyres, and the German one to SP Reifenwerke, but retained the Dunlop brand name. SRI officials predicted that the heavily loss-making U.K. operations would be profitable within three years. That appeared to be an audacious claim, but by 1986 SP Tyres achieved an operating profit, and by 1987 made after-tax profits, which increased the following year.

SRI renovated its newly acquired plants and cut the work force by about 20%. The company established a ten-point recovery plan focusing on communication, training, employee participation in company goal-setting, equality among workers, cleanliness, job security, capital expenditure, staff flexibility, improved production methods, and compensation. The Japanese company, believing that local people would know their plants better than the new parent company personnel, allowed each of its newly acquired factories to maintain its own management, with Japanese advisors standing by as consultants. A massive capital investment was directed at improving quality and production efficiency, and, by 1989, SP Tyres

was making 40% more tires than before the acquisition with 30% fewer workers.

Sumitomo Rubber Industries headed into the 1990s with growth in all three of its divisions—tires, sports equipment, and allied goods. Total sales climbed 14% in 1990, although a depressed market for automobile tires contributed to an 81% decrease in profits. The drop also reflected heavy capital investment in its overseas plants. SRI looked to new technologies and improved coordination of its operations. In December 1990, it incorporated Sumitomo Rubber Europe B.V. in the Netherlands to oversee its European operations and help prepare for the integration of the European market in 1992.

Principal Subsidiaries: Sumitomo Rubber Europe B.V. (Netherlands); SP Tyres UK Ltd.; SP Reifenwerke GmbH (Germany); Dunlop France S.A.; Dunlop Tire Corporation (U.S.A.).

Further Reading: Arbose, Jules, "What's Behind the Rebirth of Dunlop in Europe? The Japanese," *International Management,* July-August 1987; Radford, G.D., "How Sumitomo Transformed Dunlop Tyres," *Long Range Planning,* June 1989.

—Elaine Belsito

THE YOKOHAMA RUBBER CO., LTD.

36-11, Shimbashi 5-chome
Minato-ku, Tokyo 105
Japan
(03) 3432-7111
Fax: (03) 3431-4386

Public Company
Incorporated: 1917
Employees: 12,722
Sales: ¥425.16 billion (US$3.41 billion)
Stock Exchange: Tokyo

The Yokohama Rubber Co., Ltd. is one of the world's largest producers of rubber products. From its main base in vehicle tires made of natural rubber, it has developed products across the range of both natural and synthetic rubber applications, and provides a wide array of products for vehicles, aircraft, industrial systems, and other areas.

Although for most of its history the company focused on its domestic Japanese business, changes in the nature of the global rubber industry and the global economy in general have prompted it to diversify geographically in the late 20th century. The company has opened sales offices around the world, formed marketing relationships with companies in other countries and, more recently, begun buying into rubber companies outside Japan. These international moves, combined with an emphasis on research and development which is turning out a steady stream of new products, have strengthened the company's position in a worldwide industry that has encountered dramatic changes as large companies have combined and the market for rubber has changed. A diverse product range and a global reach have ensured that Yokohama Rubber will continue to be a leading force in the world rubber industry.

Formed in 1917, one of a number of Japanese industrial companies that emerged as a result of the opening of Japan to the outside world in the late 19th century, Yokohama Rubber developed during the 1920s by finding openings for innovation in Japan's growing industrial infrastructure. The company's most successful product during this period, providing the main basis for its growth, was the cord tire, which it began marketing in 1921. Until then, tires used in Japan were usually made of fabric, primarily canvas. Yokohama's Hamatown Cord, the first cord tire sold in Japan, was three times more durable than fabric tires and soon became popular on Japan's roads. At this

time the company also developed products in the area of industrial systems, using rubber to improve the efficiency of transmission belts used in spinning and other industries. In 1921 the company began marketing rubber cut-edged transmission belts, which soon replaced leather transmission belts in a number of industries, and continued to improve on belt technology in 1929 when it produced Japan's first V-type belt which offered improved flexibility and transmission.

These early moves provided the basis for expansion in the 1930s, when accelerating economic activity in Japan created strong demand for rubber products both for vehicles and industrial applications. Yokohama developed balloon tires, tires designed specifically to prevent heat problems, giant tires for trucks, Y-shaped tread tires and, following a fashion started in the United States, tires with colored sidewalls. In 1930 the company developed a soft rubber lining designed for the chemical industry, to protect metals against corrosion and leaking, and also produced a hard rubber bearing to protect ships' propeller shafts. A crucial step in the company's growth occurred in 1935, when it began supplying tires to the major Japanese car producers, Nissan and Toyota, turning Yokohama Rubber into one of Japan's key rubber companies. Its growing reputation prompted the Department of the Imperial Household to ask the company to develop a set of tires for the Japanese Emperor's car, a contract that involved a year and a half of research and development and resulted in the production of 24 tires. The company stepped into the international market in 1934 when it patented, in Japan and the United States, a bandless hose for use in loading oil, followed in 1936 by Japan's first domestically produced hydraulic brake hose for cars. In 1939, the company made its strongest move to date in the growing synthetic rubber industry by developing its first synthetic rubber material.

The outbreak of World War II prompted Yokohama Rubber to begin producing aircraft components, an area previously unexplored and, in 1941, fuel cells, flexible pipes, and tires for the Japanese army and navy's Zero and Hayabusa fighter aircraft. The strong wartime demand for these products led Yokohama, in 1944, to open a new plant at Mie to increase tire production for military aircraft. The desperate need for vehicle and industrial components in Japan's shattered postwar economy prompted the opening of another new plant at Mishima in 1946. Both of these plants remained crucial to Yokohama's production network in the early 1990s.

Like many areas of the Japanese economy, the rubber industry received a boost in the 1950s in the aftermath of the Korean War, from the U.S. Army's demand for military components. This allowed Yokohama Rubber, which was listed on the Tokyo Stock Exchange in 1950, to increase its involvement in the aircraft products market, in 1955 by beginning production of nylon cord aircraft tires and, over the next two years, aircraft fuel cells, hoses, and self-sealing couplings to meet U.S. military specifications. In 1957 the company began manufacturing and marketing tires for jet aircraft. Along with the expansion of aircraft components manufacturing, the company continued to develop and market new kinds of vehicle tires including, during the 1950s, rayon cord tires, Japan's first tubeless tires, butyl tires, snow tires, and nylon cord tires, as well as developing Hamaking all-weather tires, a basic design widely used in the early 1990s on buses and trucks in Japan. The company also began marketing its first synthetic rubber tires. On the industrial side, the 1950s saw production of a rapidly growing range of components, including Japan's first cord conveyor belts using rubber insulated cord instead of canvas, material for use as rollers in iron works, an air spring for the Japanese National Railways Technical Research Institute, pneumatic rubber fenders for use by ships at docks, nuts resistant to loosening by vibrations, and rubber based adhesives for brake linings. The growth in the range and quantity of items being produced was helped by the increase in the company's productive capacity at two new large Yokohama Rubber plants, one at Ageo in 1950 and one at Hiratsuka in 1952.

Despite diversification into the areas of industrial products and aircraft components, vehicle tires remained the biggest part of Yokohama Rubber's activities and, during the 1960s, the company pushed ahead with a number of developments that ensured its position as one of the top tire manufacturers in the dynamic Japanese economy, which was growing at an average of 10% a year. The company began marketing all-steel radial tires for trucks and buses, studded tires, car racing tires, passenger car radials, and tubeless radials. In the aircraft area, Yokohama won a contract to supply tires to All Nippon Airways Co. Ltd.'s fleet of Boeing 727 jets. U.S. military contracts continued to provide important business, prompting the company to develop aircraft sealants and Teflon aircraft hoses and duct tubes. The company also developed a stream of fuel cells, tires, hose and tube assemblies, ferry tanks, insulation blankets, and de-icers for newly developing jet aircraft and, in 1970, honeycomb core and structural adhesives for aircraft.

Yokohama's diversification into innovative industrial products continued during the 1960s, as it developed more conveyor belt systems, including nylon and fire resistant belts, rubber highway joints to replace existing metal joints, rubber lining for atomic energy equipment, and a rubber fence for sports stadiums. The company also made shockproof pipe couplings for submarines, underwater soundproof materials for warships, dredging sleeves, high pressure hoses, liquid transportation tanks, and sheets for waterproofing roads, as well as developing new materials for use as sealants and lubricants. These continuing research based developments in all three of Yokohama Rubber's main areas of activity ensured that the company benefited from Japan's continued industrial growth. Far from remaining simply a tire company Yokohama had, by 1970, established itself as a major industrial group, with products to offer across the economy. The establishment of a new factory at Shinshiro in 1964 increased the company's productive capacity, enabling it to consolidate this versatility, while the opening of a Yokohama Rubber office in the United States in 1969, followed by a Canadian branch in 1970, marked the first move by the company to expand geographically as well as industrially.

Increasing sales in all of Yokohama's main product lines prompted it to undertake a major investment program in the early 1970s, including the establishment of two new factories designed for specific purposes. The Ibaraki plant, opened in 1973, was built to produce hydraulic hose, while the Onomichi plant, which began operating in 1974, specialized in making large off-road tires. Consolidation in all three product areas continued, with the company pushing ahead with new developments in the tire industry, producing steel belted radials for passenger cars, mud and snow radials and other off-road tires, aluminum wheels, and improving the kind of rub-

ber used in its tires. During the 1970s Yokohama Rubber continued to extend its range of industrial goods, producing a rubber guard rail for highways, a rubber sheet to prevent adhesion of barnacles to ships, honeycomb sandwich structural material, new types of hose, rubber bags for oil spills at sea, all-weather paving material for tennis courts and athletic tracks, hot-melt type adhesives, soundproof rooms, sound- and vibration-proof materials for pianos, watertight floor assemblies, for ships' cargo holds, and many other products. Activity in the aircraft division also increased during this period, with the continued production of fuel cells, tube assemblies and other items developed over the previous two decades, as well as improving on the older designs and introducing new products. In 1972, the company developed an electric anti-icing device for helicopter rotor blades, and crash resistant fuel cells for aircraft, followed in later years by further developments in the areas of insulation blankets, honeycomb panels, and prepregs—semi-solid materials consisting of resin-impregnated reinforcing fibers, used in the manufacture of aircraft primary structures, which need to be light and strong. Yokohama also began producing equipment for rockets, including heat exchangers and bellows. The company continued with its industrial diversification in 1983 when it moved into the sports products business in cooperation with ten specialist sports equipment manufacturers.

In the mid-1980s, with the international rubber industry becoming increasingly dominated by large, multinational groups, Yokohama Rubber expanded its sales and production bases beyond Japan, aiming to increase its reach in terms of distribution and supplies. In 1984 the company separated its Canadian branch from its U.S. operation and, the following year, bought a 26% stake in a Malaysian tire company, IT International, in a deal involving the supply of Yokohama's technical assistance to the Malaysian company. In 1986 the company launched an automotive equipment manufacturing and marketing venture, Aeroquip Automotive, in the United States, in partnership with Yokohama Aeroquip Co., and Aeroquip Co. of the United States. Later the same year, the company bought a 10% stake in South Korea's largest tire maker, Hankook Tyre Manufacturing Company and, the following year, began cooperating with the Rubber Research Institute of Malaysia to develop extraction and pulverization technology for use in obtaining useful substances from natural rubber residue.

In 1987 Yokohama launched an expansion project for its aircraft parts plant at Hiratsuka, introducing the production of large motor parts for the H-11 rocket; bought a 40% stake in a maker of printed circuit boards for industrial machinery, Togoshi Co.; and signed a deal with a U.S. company, Technical Wire Products Inc., to produce and market its electromagnetic wave shielding materials in Japan. It also established a joint venture with another U.S. company, Morton Thiokol Inc., to manufacture and market polyurethane based automotive windscreen sealants in the United States. In the same year, Yokohama demonstrated its level of technical achievement by ending its agreements with a number of U.S. and European tire makers who had been supplying the company with technical expertise.

In 1988 following a share swap with another Japanese rubber company, Toyo Tyre and Rubber Co., Yokohama established a joint venture to sell passenger car tires and truck and bus steel radials in Germany with Marubeni Corp. Later that year, the company made its biggest move to date into the huge U.S. tire market when, in a joint venture with Toyo Tyre and Rubber and the German industrial group Continental Aktiengesellschaft, Yokohama began construction of a plant to produce radial truck and bus tires in the United States. The plant, at Mount Vernon, Illinois, was designed to produce 880,000 tires per year at full capacity. Yokohama made another significant move into the U.S. market in 1989, when it bought a U.S. rubber company, Mohawk Rubber Co. Ltd., with a tire plant in Virginia, an industrial rubber products plant in Ohio, and retread shops in Alabama and California, for about US$150 million. It announced soon afterward that it intended to spend US$200 million over the next five to six years to raise production capacity at the plant. In the same year, Yokohama strengthened its assault on the U.S. market by launching its first television advertising campaign, and began a joint venture with Hankook in South Korea to produce tire tubes and flaps. The company's president, Kazuo Motoyama, summed up the direction of Yokohama's activity in 1989, when he said "We have no intention whatsoever of remaining a local Japanese tire maker."

International expansion accelerated in 1990, when Yokohama bought 49% of a Taiwanese rubber hose maker, Shien Chi Industrial Co.; launched its products in Portugal; signed a five-year technical agreement with another South Korean company, Bukdoo Chemical; and made moves to begin exporting radial motorcycle tires to Brazil. Along with this energetic international diversification, bolstered by steady exports to southeast Asia and North America, Yokohama continued to inject funds into its research and development program. This resulted in new products in a number of areas, including the development of electroconductive, anti-static flooring material, a printed wiring board that dissipates heat more efficiently than conventional ones, new prepregs for use as primary structural components for aircraft, new car window adhesives, and a radio-wave isolation room with smooth flat walls, which satisfy a strong demand from electronics and appliance manufacturers.

Despite a slower start in the international rubber industry than some of its competitors, Yokohama Rubber's energetic global expansion program appears to have ensured that the company will remain a major rubber group, rather than being swamped by the tide of amalgamations that swept through the industry in the 1980s. With a strong base in the United States and heavy involvement in southeast Asia, the company already has a broad international profile, and plans to increase its involvement in Europe by setting up subsidiaries and distribution centers in Italy, France, Switzerland, Belgium, and the Netherlands by 1993, complementing its existing sales subsidiaries in Germany and the United Kingdom. In 1991 Yokohama was also planning moves into the emerging Eastern European market which, following the collapse of the communist regimes, is likely to prove a dynamic one for vehicle tires and other products during the 1990s. This should enable Yokohama and other rubber companies to compensate for the increasingly saturated markets of the United States and Western Europe. The emergence of this market, combined with the company's productive program of research and development, should ensure that Yokohama Rubber remains one of the world's largest rubber groups.

Principal Subsidiaries: Yokohama Tire Corporation (U.S.A.); Yokohama Tire (Canada) Inc.; Yokohama Tyre Australia Pty. Ltd.; Yokohama Reifen GmbH (Germany); The Mohawk Rubber Company (U.S.A.).

Further Reading: "This is Yokohama," Tokyo, The Yokohama Rubber Company, 1980; Key Note Report, *Rubber Manufacturing and Processing,* Middlesex, England, Key Note Publications Ltd., 1990.

—Richard Brass

TELECOMMUNICATIONS

American Telephone and Telegraph Company
Ameritech
BCE Inc.
Bell Atlantic Corporation
BellSouth Corporation
British Telecommunications plc
Cable and Wireless plc
Deutsche Bundespost TELEKOM
France Télécom Group
GTE Corporation
Koninklijke PTT Nederland NV
MCI Communications Corporation
Nippon Telegraph and Telephone Corporation

Northern Telecom Limited
NYNEX Corporation
Österreichische Post- und Telegraphenverwaltung
Pacific Telesis Group
Schweizerische Post-, Telefon- und Telegrafen-
    Betriebe
Società Finanziaria Telefonica per Azioni
Southwestern Bell Corporation
Swedish Telecom
Telefonaktiebolaget LM Ericsson
Telefónica de España, S.A.
U S West, Inc.
United Telecommunications, Inc.

AMERICAN TELEPHONE AND TELEGRAPH COMPANY

550 Madison Avenue
New York, New York 10022
U.S.A.
(212) 605-5500

Public Company
Incorporated: 1885
Employees: 274,000
Sales: $37.29 billion
Stock Exchanges: New York Philadelphia Boston Midwest
Pacific Tokyo London.

American Telephone and Telegraph Company (AT&T) was the largest corporation in the world for much of the 20th century. A government-regulated monopoly for most of its existence, it built most of the U.S. telephone system and was the standard of the worldwide telecommunications industry. It was dismembered in 1984 as a consequence of an action by the U.S. Department of Justice (DOJ) and through a consent decree signed that year. Its local operating companies became separate entities, leaving AT&T with the long-distance segment of the business, the only remaining government-regulated aspect of the company. AT&T also manufactures telecommunications equipment, computers, communications cable, and runs one of the world's foremost research centers, Bell Telephone Laboratories, Inc. (Bell Labs).

AT&T had its origin in the invention of the telephone in 1876 by Alexander Graham Bell. In 1877 Bell and several financial partners formed the Bell Telephone Company, and in 1878 they formed the New England Telephone Company to license telephone exchanges in New England. The two companies licensed local operating companies in Chicago, New York, and Boston. Over the next year Bell and his backers sold a controlling interest in the companies to a group of Boston financiers.

The companies were soon embroiled in patent disputes with Western Union Telegraph Company, the world's largest telegraph company. During the dispute, the two Bell companies were consolidated into the National Bell Telephone Company, and Theodore J. Vail was named general manager. In November 1879, the patent suit was settled out of court. Western Union left the telephone business and sold its system of 56,000 telephones in 55 cities to Bell. Bell agreed to stay out of the telegraph business, and paid Western Union a 20% royalty on telephone equipment leases for the next 17 years. Between 1877 and 1881, Bell licensed numerous local operating companies as a way to promote the telephone without having to raise capital. The companies signed five- to ten-year contracts, under which Bell got $20 per telephone per year and the right to buy the licensee's property when the contract expired.

National became the American Bell Telephone Company in 1880 and obtained more capital at that time. Starting in 1881 Bell urged the locals to make the contracts permanent, rescinding Bell's right to buy the respective properties, but giving Bell variously 30% to 50% ownership of the operating companies. The companies could build long-distance lines to connect exchanges in their territories, but they were prohibited from connecting them with those of other operating companies or independent phone companies. Bell thus became a partner in the local telephone business, allowing Bell to influence the locals and conserve capital for long-distance operations. American Bell needed large amounts of equipment, and in 1881 it acquired Western Electric, the major supplier of Western Union's telegraphic equipment, to manufacture its equipment. Bell then consolidated into Western Electric several other manufacturers it had licensed to make telephones.

More long-distance lines were being built as telephone technology improved. In 1884 Bell built an experimental line between Boston and New York. The next year it added a Philadelphia—New York line. To construct, finance, and operate its long-distance system, Bell established the American Telephone and Telegraph Company in 1885 to operate as its long-distance subsidiary. At that time the nascent U.S. telephone system was primarily a series of unconnected local networks. Vail, who was named AT&T president, wanted to get a long-distance network in place before Bell's basic patents expired in 1894. By the time it established AT&T, Bell was in firm control of the telephone business. It regulated the operating companies' long-distance lines and Western Electric, their major supplier. It also had the right to take over their property if they violated their contracts.

In 1888 a huge blizzard in New England knocked most telephones out of service. The company responded by pushing to put more cables underground. Later that year it became clear that a long-distance network would cost more than planned, and AT&T floated $2 million in bonds to raise capital. The company returned to public investors frequently throughout its history to finance its ever-expanding enterprises. For decades AT&T stock was the most widely held in the world. To attract investors so often, AT&T was forced to be efficient, even though it lacked real competition for much of its history.

Technical advances came regularly. The first coin-operated public telephone was installed in 1889. During 1891 two-party and four-party service was introduced, and the first automatic dial system was patented. A New York—Chicago long-distance line opened in 1892, and Boston—Chicago and New York—Cincinnati lines were initiated in 1893.

Bell initially had a monopoly on the telephone because of its patents, but in 1894 its patent expired. Rather than compete by providing better and less expensive service, Bell often took the growing independent phone companies to court, claiming patent infringements. As Western Electric would not sell equipment to the independents, new manufacturers sprung up to accommodate them. The independents were particularly successful in rural areas in the West and Midwest where Bell did not provide service. By 1898 some cities had two unconnected phone systems, one Bell and one independent. This competition forced Bell to expand faster than it otherwise would have. It jumped from 240,000 phones in 1892 to 800,000 in 1899.

The company needed capital to keep up with this expansion, and Massachusetts, where American Bell was based, presented far more regulatory interference than New York, where AT&T was based. As a result, AT&T in 1899 became the parent company of the Bell System until the breakup in 1984. AT&T's capital jumped from $20 million to more than $70 million. By 1900 AT&T was organizing itself into the vertical structure that characterized it for decades thereafter. It had assets of $120 million compared with a total of $55 million for the independents, but its finances were run overly conservatively and its service was often poor.

Meanwhile, the telephone was having a dramatic impact on the United States, where large numbers of people still lived in the relative isolation of farms or small towns. The telephone lessened their isolation, and the response to the new invention was enthusiastic. The number of rural telephones shot from 267,000 in 1902 to 1.4 million in 1907. The telephone was coming to be viewed as indispensable by virtually all businesses and most private homes.

Competition from independents continued to mount. Their rates were sometimes half of Bell's, and the United States was in an antimonopoly mood. Many rural communities started their own not-for-profit phone companies that were later sold to independents or Bell. By 1907 the independents operated 51% of all phones. AT&T was fighting back, having made the decision to take on the independents when it moved and changed its name. The company's first and most effective move was to slash rates. The arrogance of early company officials was replaced by a desire to please customers. AT&T also bought out independents, set up its own "independents" and used its political and financial clout to strangle competitors. AT&T's greatest advantage was its virtual monopoly of long-distance service—which it refused to let independents use.

The invention of a certain electric device, the loading coil, in 1899 gave long-distance service a push by allowing smaller-diameter wires to be used, which made underground long-distance cables feasible. They were implemented for an underground New York—Philadelphia line in 1906, but long-distance signals remained weak and difficult to hear until the invention of the vacuum-tube repeater in 1912.

Competition had given AT&T a necessary push, forcing it to expand and grow, but it also weakened its finances. Between 1902 and 1906 debt grew from $60 million to $200 million. Through a series of bond purchases starting in 1903, financier J.P. Morgan tried to wrest control of the company from the Boston capitalists, beginning a free-for-all that lasted several years. When the dust cleared in 1907, Morgan and his New York and London backers had won, and they brought back Vail as president. Vail had left in 1887 because of differences with the Bostonians, whose view was focused narrowly on short-term profit. Vail and his backers had a wider vision than the Bostonians, believing they should create a comprehensive, nationwide communications system.

In 1907 AT&T boasted 3.12 million telephones in service, but had a terrible public image, low staff morale, poor service, serious debts, and a bevy of technological problems. Within a decade Vail turned the company around, making it a model of corporate success. He soon sold millions of dollars in bonds by offering them at a discount to shareholders, which re-established confidence in the company. He also dramatically increased research and development, hiring talented young scientists and laying the foundation for what would, in 1925, become Bell Labs. Vail concentrated the company's visionaries into central management and left day-to-day network decisions to workers more interested in practical questions. For its first two decades AT&T had put profits for its shareholders above service for its customers; Vail was one of the first U.S. business leaders to balance profit with customer satisfaction.

At the same time, Vail was a monopolist, believing competition had no place in the telephone industry. He and Morgan set out to make AT&T the sole supplier of U.S. telecommunications services. In 1910 Vail became president of Western Union after AT&T bought 30% of Western's stock. For the first time telegrams could be sent and delivered by phone. Telephone and telegraph lines could back each other up in emergencies. AT&T gobbled up independent phone companies at an ever-increasing rate. When Morgan found an independent in financial trouble, he used his power as a leading banker to squeeze its credit, often forcing it to sell to AT&T. By 1911 AT&T had bought so many small independents that Vail consolidated them into a smaller number of state and regional companies. AT&T's ownership was motivated partly by profit, but also by the desire to ensure good service.

Antimonopoly pressures from consumers and government began to mount on AT&T well before then. A crucial turning point came in 1913, after Morgan's death, when Vail decided to sell Western Union and allow independents access to AT&T's long-distance lines. The move cost $10 million and ended AT&T's dream of a national telecommunications monopoly, but it won AT&T respect and ended growing pressure to dismember it.

By that time AT&T was working on the first coast-to-coast telephone line, using loading coils and repeaters. On January 25, 1915, Alexander Graham Bell, in New York, and former collaborator, Thomas Watson, in San Francisco, engaged in a coast-to-coast repeat of the first-ever telephone conversation 39 years earlier. AT&T was also making important progress in automatic switching systems and sent the first transatlantic radio message in 1915. As the telephone became a matter of national interest, pressure for federal regulation mounted, and Vail welcomed it as long as regulators were independent.

During World War I the AT&T network was used for domestic military communications. AT&T also set up extensive radio and telephone communications lines in France. The war pushed AT&T's resources to the limit, with a $118 million construction budget for 1917. In 1918 a year in which AT&T had 10 million phones in service, the U.S. government took over the telephone system. The government set rates and put AT&T under a branch of the post office, although the company continued to be run by its board of directors. One of the government's first decisions was to start a service connection charge. It then raised both local and long distance rates. Lower rates had been touted as a major benefit of public ownership. When the rates went up, support for government ownership collapsed, and in August 1919 the government gave up its control of AT&T. Vail retired in the same year, leaving the presidency to Harry Bates Thayer, and died in 1920.

AT&T grew rapidly as a regulated monopoly during the laissez-faire 1920s. The Graham Act of 1921 exempted telephony from the Sherman Antitrust Act. Of almost 14 million telephones in the United States in 1921, the Bell System controlled 64%; and 32%, although owned by independents, were plugged into the AT&T network. Commercial radio boomed, and AT&T entered cross-licensing patent agreements with General Electric, Westinghouse, and Radio Corporation of America, with which it was soon embroiled in legal disputes. By the end of 1925, AT&T had a national network of 17 radio stations. AT&T put its first submarine cable into service between Key West, Florida, and Havana, Cuba, in 1921. In 1925 Bell Labs became a separate company, jointly funded by AT&T and Western Electric. The same year, Thayer retired and was succeeded by Walter S. Gifford, who served for the next 23 years. His influence on the U.S. telephone industry was second only to Vail's.

Gifford quickly got AT&T out of radio and other side ventures, although it tried to establish a controlling interest in motion picture sound technology in the late 1920s. He reduced the fee licensees paid from the 4.5% of gross revenue established in 1902, to 4% in 1926, and 2% in 1928. AT&T stockholders grew from 250,000 in 1922 to nearly 500,000 in 1929. In 1929 Bell Labs gave the first U.S. demonstration of color television. By 1932 AT&T had the second-largest financial interest in the film industry, but sold it in 1936.

The first years of the Great Depression badly hurt AT&T. Many subscribers could no longer afford telephones. AT&T sales for 1929 were $1.05 billion; by 1933 they were $853 million. Western Electric sales in 1929 were $411 million; 1933 sales were $70 million. Western Electric laid off 80% of its employees, and AT&T laid off 20%.

By 1933 telephone use began growing again, and by 1937 it exceeded pre-Depression levels. During the late 1930s the newly formed Federal Communications Commission (FCC) conducted a long, damaging investigation of AT&T's competitive practices that reopened the battle over AT&T as a monopoly. In 1939 AT&T had assets of $5 billion, by far the largest amount of capital ever controlled by a corporation up to that time. It controlled 83% of all U.S. telephones and 98% of long-distance wires. Subsidiary Western Electric manufactured 90% of all U.S. telephone equipment. The FCC's final report was initially ignored due to the outbreak of World War II but had significant impact later.

Telephone use, particularly long distance, grew tremendously during World War II, with 1.4 million new telephones installed in 1941 alone. Western Electric and Bell Labs devoted themselves primarily to military work from 1942 to 1945, filling thousands of government contracts and making technological innovations. The most important work was in radar, the experience in which gave AT&T a huge lead when microwave radio relay became the principal means of transmitting long-distance telephone and television signals in the postwar period.

The FCC forced AT&T to lower rates during the war, and its plants and infrastructure were worn out by wartime production. AT&T's business boomed after the war, as population and prosperity increased, and the habit of long-distance telephoning acquired during the war continued. The company installed more than three million telephones in 1946. Benefits of wartime technology were many. Moving vehicles were brought into the telephone system by radio in 1946. Coaxial cable was first used to take television signals over long distances in 1946. Microwave radio began transmitting long-distance calls in 1947. Bell Labs brought out the transistor, a replacement for the vacuum tube and one of the important inventions of the 20th century, in 1948; its inventors won the Nobel prize in 1956.

The end of the war brought serious labor trouble. AT&T and the National Federation of Telephone Workers faced off over wages, working conditions, and benefits, producing a nationwide strike in 1947. Public opinion went against the strikers, and the eventual compromise favored AT&T.

Gifford retired in 1948 and Leroy A. Wilson became president. His first task was to push a rate increase past government regulators. He got one in 1949 that helped AT&T sell more stock to raise needed capital. As an outgrowth of the 1930s FCC investigation, the U.S. Department of Justice filed suit in 1949, seeking to split Western Electric from AT&T. AT&T succeeded in delaying the case until the Eisenhower administration, which was not as interested in regulation, took power. In the meantime the government talked Western Electric into taking over the management of an advanced weapons research laboratory. It formed Sandia Corp. in 1949 to do so. In the 1950s Western Electric worked on the Nike antiaircraft missiles, making $112.5 million on the venture. Western and Bell Labs worked with others on a huge air-defense radar system. These defense projects gave AT&T a powerful lever against the antitrust suit. In a consent decree in 1956 AT&T agreed to limit its business to providing common-carrier services and to limit Western Electric's to providing equipment for the Bell System, except for government contracts. The antitrust case was settled on this basis.

In 1951 Wilson died and Cleo Craig became president. In the next few years AT&T made it possible to dial directly to other cities without using an operator. This and ensuing developments enabled long-distance charges to be repeatedly reduced. In 1955 AT&T laid the first transatlantic telephone cable, jointly owned with the British Post Office and the Canadian Overseas Telecommunications Corporation. Craig retired in 1956, and Frederick R. Kappel became president.

AT&T was in enviable financial shape by the late 1950s, although some accused it of getting there by overcharging subscribers. The booming U.S. economy led to unprecedented calling volumes—particularly from teenagers, many of whom were getting their own telephones. Telephones moved from shared party lines to private lines, and telephone services like weather and time announcements became widespread, adding further revenue. AT&T split its stock three-for-one in 1959 and two-for-one in 1964. By 1966 AT&T had three million stockholders and nearly one million employees. In 1954 AT&T began offering telephones in colors other than black. In 1961 it developed Centrex, a system in which an office maintained its own automatic switching exchange; in 1963 it offered the first Touch-Tone service; in 1968 it brought out the Trimline phone, with the dial built into the handset. By 1965 the Bell System served 85% of all households in the areas in which it operated, compared with 50% in 1945. And it was providing a vast array of services at a vast array of rates.

AT&T formed Bellcom to supply most of the communications and guidance systems for the U.S. space program from 1958 to 1969. Bell Labs worked intensively on satellite communications, and the first AT&T satellite, Telstar, was launched in 1962. Comsat, a half-public, half-private company handling the United States's satellite communications, was founded in 1962, with AT&T owning 27.5% at a cost of $58 million.

AT&T worked on an electronic switching system throughout the 1950s and 1960s. The project was more complicated than expected, and by the time the first electronic equipment was installed in 1965, AT&T had spent about $500 million on the project. The speed and automation that electronic switches gave the phone system, however, made possible the vast increases in traffic volume in the 1970s and 1980s, as the United States moved to an information-based society.

In the 1950s and 1960s other companies began trying to capture specific portions of AT&T's business. The Hush-a-Phone Company marketed a plastic telephone attachment that reduced background noise. Microwave Communications Inc. (MCI) tried to establish private-line service between Chicago and St. Louis. Carter Electronics Corporation marketed a device that connected two-way radios with the telephone system. AT&T responded by forbidding the connection of competitors' equipment to the Bell System. Several FCC investigations followed, with decisions that created competition for terminal equipment and intercity private-line service. AT&T began to face serious competition for the first time in 50 years.

Kappel retired in 1967 and was replaced by H.I. Romnes, a former president of Western Electric. AT&T's earnings were leveling off after tremendous growth in the early 1960s. There also were service problems in 1969 and 1970, with numerous consumer complaints in New York. Similar predicaments followed in Boston, Denver, and Houston. AT&T borrowed money and raised rates to pay for repairs.

More serious problems were beginning for AT&T. In the early 1970s sales by the interconnect industry were growing, and businesses were buying telephone equipment from AT&T competitors. The U.S. Equal Employment Opportunity Commission accused AT&T of discriminating against women and minorities. AT&T, without admitting it had done so, signed consent decrees under which it agreed to increase the hiring, promotion, and salaries of women and minorities.

MCI claimed AT&T was still preventing it from competing and filed an antitrust lawsuit in 1974. The situation became disastrous when the DOJ filed another antitrust suit later in 1974, this time asking for the dismemberment of AT&T. The DOJ charged that AT&T had used its dominant position to supress competition. The suit dragged on for years.

During the years of the suit, AT&T continued to grow. Both 1980 and 1981 were years of record profits. The $6.9 billion AT&T made in 1981 was the highest profit for any company to that time.

The DOJ suit finally came to trial in 1981. By then AT&T and the government both wanted to settle the case. AT&T wanted to get into computers and information services, but was prevented by its 1956 agreement. In 1982 the FCC required AT&T to set up a separate, unregulated subsidiary called American Bell to sell equipment and enhanced services. In January 1982 AT&T and the DOJ jointly announced a deal to break up the Bell System, while freeing the remainder of AT&T to compete in non-long-distance areas like computers.

Federal Judge Harold Greene gave final approval for the AT&T breakup in August 1983. At that time AT&T was the largest corporation in the world; its $155 billion in assets made it larger than General Motors, Mobil, and Exxon combined. After the breakup, on January 1, 1984, AT&T had $34 billion in assets. Its net income dropped from $7.1 billion to $2.1 billion, and its work force from 1.09 million to 385,000. Its 22 regional operating companies were split off into seven regional holding companies, and AT&T lost the right to use the Bell name. AT&T stockholders received one share in each of the regional companies for every ten AT&T shares they owned. AT&T also lost the highly profitable Yellow Pages, which went to the regional companies.

The new AT&T consisted of two primary parts: AT&T Communications, the long-distance business, and AT&T Technologies, a group of other businesses that mainly involved the manufacture and sale of telecommunications equipment for consumers and businesses. Western Electric was broken up and folded into AT&T Technologies. Long distance was expected to provide the bulk of short-term revenue for the new AT&T, but the unregulated technologies group, backed by Bell Labs, was expected to quickly blossom. AT&T technologies initially concentrated on switching and transmissions systems for telephone companies. AT&T was losing ground to competitors in that sector and wanted to fight back. The company also worked on telephone-equipment sales, sold through AT&T phone centers and retailers like Sears. American Bell changed its name to AT&T Information Systems and began pushing computers. AT&T International quickly signed a deal with the Dutch company N.V. Philips to sell switching equipment throughout the world, setting up AT&T Network Systems International.

To help pay for the breakup, AT&T took a fourth-quarter charge of $5.2 billion in 1984, the largest to that time. AT&T, however, was now free to go into computers, a field it had longed to get into since the 1956 consent decree, and the company began spending hundreds of millions of dollars to develop and market a line of computers. James E. Olson became president of AT&T in 1985, cutting 24,000 jobs from the information division later that year to improve its profits. In 1986 Olson became chairman, and Robert E. Allen became president. Olson concentrated on centralizing management and refocusing company strategy around the idea of managing the flow of information.

The company chose Brussels, Belgium, as the site for its regional headquarters serving Europe, the Middle East, and Africa. It also began joint ventures with companies in Spain, Italy, Ireland, Denmark, South Korea, and Taiwan to get its telecommunications products into foreign markets. Still, foreign revenues accounted for only 10% of company earnings, compared with 40% for many other U.S.-based multinationals. Company earnings declined because of a slumping business-equipment market and greater-than-expected reorganization costs. Earnings also suffered from a drop in rental revenues as more AT&T customers decided to buy their telecommunications equipment outright.

Meanwhile AT&T's computer operations were in trouble. The company had developed a new operating system, Unix, for its computers. Unix had some advantages; but the users of personal computers were not familiar with it, manufacturers of larger computers were committed to their own proprietary systems, and buyers stayed away. AT&T computer operations lost $1.2 billion in 1986 alone. At the end of the year the company restructured its computer operations to concentrate on telecommunications-based computers and computer systems. It custom designed a system for American Express that automatically phoned customers while putting customer information on a terminal screen. At the end of 1986 AT&T cut another 27,400 jobs and took a $3.2 billion charge. Income for the year was only $139 million.

In 1987 the Justice Department recommended that the regional operating companies be allowed to compete with AT&T in long distance and telecommunications equipment manufacturing—its two core businesses. The idea was unacceptable to Judge Harold Greene, overseer of the AT&T breakup. Because of fierce competition from MCI and other companies, AT&T retained 76% of the long-distance market, down from 91% in 1983.

Unix made some gains in 1986 and 1987, and AT&T formed the Archer Group, a consortium of computer makers manufacturing Unix systems. It included Unisys and Sun Microsystems. After nearly $2 billion in losses in computers, the data systems group finally signed a major contract with the U.S Air Force in 1988. The $929 million contract for minicomputers provided only a slim profit margin, but AT&T hoped that the deal would push its computers over the top, make Unix an industry standard, and lead to further government sales. Olson died in 1988, and Allen became chairman.

MCI and others continued to erode AT&T's share of the $50 billion long-distance market, which stood at 68% at the end of 1988. To fight back, AT&T redeployed 2,500 employees to sales positions and aggressively tackled the business-communications market. AT&T also took a $6.7 billion charge to modernize its telephone network and cut 16,000 positions. As a result, the company lost $1.7 billion in 1988, its first-ever loss for the year. Some industry analysts, however, felt the company was finally turning around after four years of confusion and drift. It won two major government contracts that year. One, expected to earn AT&T $15 billion by 1989, was to build a new government telephone system. Competitor US Sprint Communications won a $10 billion contract for a second part of the same system. Regulators finally gave AT&T the right to match the low prices of MCI and US Sprint, leading to the end of the long-distance price wars waged since the AT&T breakup. AT&T showed a $2.7 billion profit for 1989, its largest since the breakup.

In mid-1990 AT&T raised its long-distance rates after low second-quarter earnings. It had been hurt by declining long-distance revenue and slow equipment sales. The company, however, soon made several important sales. It received an extension of a $100 million personal computer sale to American Airlines's Sabre Travel Information Network and signed an agreement to upgrade China's international communications system. AT&T made its first entry into Mexico's communications market, winning a $130 million contract from Mexico's national telephone company, Teléfonos de Mexico. It signed a $157 million contract to build an undersea fiber-optic cable between Hawaii and the U.S. mainland, and announced that it planned to build a high-capacity undersea cable between Germany and the United States, with Deutsche Bundespost Telekom. It also won a $600 million contract from GTE Corporation to build cellular network equipment.

Hoping to make money from its financial and information resources, AT&T launched a credit card, Universal Card, in

early 1990. By late 1990 it was the eighth leading credit card in the United States, with revenue of $750 million. Wall Street analysts, however, expected the credit card's startup costs to hold back AT&T earnings until at least 1992. Bell Labs announced important breakthroughs in computer technology in 1990, including the world's first computer using light. Products based on the new technologies were years off, but AT&T continued to manufacture computers. AT&T signed an agreement with Japan's Mitsubishi Electric Corporation to share memory-chip technology, and licensed technology from Japan's NEC Corporation to make semiconductors. Late in the year, Philips, under financial pressure, sold back its 15% stake in AT&T Network Systems International.

In the early 1990s AT&T overseas ventures began bearing fruit. About 15% of its revenue, more than $5 billion yearly, came from international calling and sales to foreign buyers of equipment and services. In 1991 AT&T made a major acquisition in the computer industry, buying NCR Corporation through an exchange of stock valued at $7.4 million. AT&T officials said the purchase of NCR, which accounts for about 60% of its sales in international markets, put AT&T on the path to becoming a truly global company and a leader in networked computing. NCR had put out more new products than any other computer company in the preceding year. NCR officials saw advantages of the merger to be an increased customer base, access to the research and development capabilities of Bell Labs, and the addition of AT&T's technical, marketing, and sales resources.

Principal Subsidiaries: AT&T Capitol Corporations; AT&T Communications, Inc.; AT&T Communications of California, Inc.; AT&T Communications of Delaware, Inc.; AT&T Communications of Illinois, Inc.; AT&T Communications of Indiana, Inc.; AT&T Communications of Maryland, Inc.; AT&T Communications of Michigan, Inc.; AT&T Communications of the Midwest, Inc.; AT&T Communications of the Mountain States, Inc.; AT&T Communications of Nevada, Inc.; AT&T Communications of New England, Inc.; AT&T Communications of New Hampshire, Inc.; AT&T Communications of New Jersey, Inc.; AT&T Communications of New York, Inc.; AT&T Communications of Ohio, Inc.; AT&T Communications of the Pacific Northwest, Inc.; AT&T Communications of Pennsylvania, Inc.; AT&T Communications of the South Central States, Inc.; AT&T Communications of the Southern States, Inc.; AT&T Communications of the Southwest, Inc.; AT&T Communications of Virginia, Inc.; AT&T Communications of Washington, D.C., Inc.; AT&T Communications of West Virginia, Inc.; AT&T Communications of Wisconsin, Inc.; AT&T Credit Corporation; AT&T International Inc.; AT&T Microelectronica de España S.A. (Spain); AT&T Nassau Metals Corporation; AT&T Network Systems International B.V. (Netherlands); AT&T Paradyne Corporation; AT&T of Puerto Rico, Inc.; AT&T Resource Management Corporation; AT&T Universal Card Services Corp.; AT&T of the Virgin Islands, Inc.; Actuarial Sciences Associates, Inc.; American Transtech Inc.; Istel Group, Ltd. (United Kingdom); NCR Corporation.

Further Reading: Brooks, John, *Telephone: The First Hundred Years*, New York, Harper and Row, 1976; Evans, David S., ed., *Breaking Up Bell: Essays on Industrial Organization and Regulation,* New York, Elsevier Science Publishing Co., 1983; Sims, Calvin, "AT&T's New Call to Arms," *The New York Times,* January 22, 1989.

—Scott M. Lewis

AMERITECH

30 South Wacker Drive
Chicago, Illinois 60606
U.S.A.
(312) 750-5000
Fax: (312) 207-1601

Public Company
Incorporated: 1983 as American Information Technologies
   Corporation
Employees: 75,780
Sales: $10.66 billion
Stock Exchanges: New York Boston Midwest Pacific
   Philadelphia London Tokyo Amsterdam Basel Geneva Zürich

Ameritech is one of the largest telecommunications companies in the United States. The Ameritech Bell Group is made up of Illinois Bell, Indiana Bell, Michigan Bell, Ohio Bell, and Wisconsin Bell; Ameritech Services; and Ameritech Information Systems. The Bell Group provides exchange telecommunications and local exchange access service for business and residential customers in the Midwest. Other Ameritech subsidiaries, offering communications-related products and services, are Ameritech Mobile Communications, Inc., Ameritech Credit Corp., Ameritech Publishing Inc., Ameritech Audiotex Services, Ameritech Development, the Tigon Corporation, and Ameritech International.

In January 1982 the U.S. Department of Justice (DOJ) ended a 13-year antitrust suit against the world's largest corporation, American Telephone and Telegraph Company (AT&T). AT&T was required, under the landmark court-ordered consent decree, to divest itself of 22 local telephone operating companies. The key issue of the divestiture was to demonopolize the telecommunications industry and ensure equal access to the local exchange facilities by all long-distance carriers.

AT&T retained its Western Electric Manufacturing subsidiary, Bell Laboratories research facilities, as well as its long distance operations, while the 22 local companies were divided into seven regional holding companies (RHCs). The midwest regional Bell operating companies (BOCs), including Illinois Bell, Indiana Bell, Michigan Bell, Ohio Bell, and Wisconsin Bell, were assigned to the RHC American Information Technologies Corporation, called Ameritech for short. In 1991 the company formally changed its name to Ameritech.

Some felt that Judge Harold Greene imposed a stiff sentence upon the new RHCs. According to the modified final judg-

ment, all RHCs were limited upon the initial breakup to providing only basic phone service, the strictly regulated arm of the U.S. telecommunications industry. Any new ventures had to be presented to the Federal Communications Commission (FCC) and Judge Greene. If approved these unregulated businesses had to be operated through separate subsidiaries.

Ameritech, with its six sibling RHCs, shared $147 billion in assets. The RHCs, however, were also ordered to share with AT&T any company debt as well as the costs of antitrust suits initiated prior to January 1, 1984, the official date of divestiture.

William L. Weiss, named president and CEO of Illinois Bell in 1981, was preceded in that position by both John DeButts, late chairman of AT&T, and Charles Brown, president and CEO of AT&T during divestiture. While the Illinois Bell CEO position appeared a stepping stone to the CEO position at AT&T, Weiss actively chose to take his chances at running an RHC rather than remain with what had been the parent company.

Anticipating its solo operation, Weiss diversified Ameritech operations into unregulated businesses that were allowed by the court. In September 1983 Ameritech incorporated several subsidiaries. One was Ameritech Services, Inc., a support company owned equally by all the midwest BOCs and designed to provide marketing, technical, and regulatory planning as well as new product development, purchasing, and national management services. The same year brought the formation of the Ameritech Development Corp., designed to target, research, and develop business-growth areas for all the Ameritech BOCs. In November Ameritech moved into publishing telephone directories through its subsidiary, Ameritech Publishing, Inc. In October 1983 Ameritech Mobile Communications, Inc., a provider of wire-free cellular telephones, was first in North America to offer cellular phone service.

Within six months Ameritech's cellular phone test markets were a model for many competitors. Under previous mobile telephone systems, operating areas could use only 12 channels, working from a single antenna; busy lines for up to 30 minutes were the norm. In contrast, by April 1984, under the cellular system, regions were divided into small areas called cells, and because each cell had its own antenna, Ameritech's Chicago-based system could accommodate up to 50,000 calls per hour. Company researchers forecasted that the total cellular service market could reach $3 billion by 1990, with equipment sales reaching $600 million. It came as no surprise that companies such as Motorola, General Electric, and Panasonic were jockeying for the chance to set up cellular systems. Ameritech Mobile Communications planned a Detroit cellular start-up by September 1984.

By summer 1984 Ameritech led the RHCs in first-quarter earnings. While Wall Street analysts did not expect the trend to continue, Weiss did. The Ameritech region, referred to disparagingly as the Rust Belt, had an image not so much to uphold as to dispel; and dispel it, it did. *Barron's* November 12, 1984, issue listed Ameritech as recording the highest return on equity of all the RHCs, after nine months of operation. Weiss was credited for all the positive numbers; he kept operating expenses low by trimming his work force by 20% prior to divestiture. Ameritech concentrated on the telephone business, investing nearly $2 billion in new technology.

Ameritech ran into some stumbling blocks on the road to independence. Modernization of Centrex, the company's central exchange switching system that linked local and long-distance carriers, was a must. Increased competition and new game rules following deregulation, however, allowed any company to buy a switchboard and thereby sidestep having to use Ameritech's Centrex system. In addition the FCC consent decree ordered Ameritech to charge access fees to users of its Centrex system, a point Weiss argued against with state regulators. Ameritech was losing money due to the bypass and enforced access fees.

To step out of the tangle, Weiss launched the corporation into converting its central offices to electronic digital switching, which used the best available technology and was a cheaper system to maintain. In the meantime Ameritech's unregulated subsidiaries, less constrained by FCC and state restrictions, surged ahead. Ameritech Mobile expanded its cellular systems, moving into the retail sector. Following a February 1985 agreement with Tandy Corporation, Tandy's Radio Shack stores marketed Ameritech cellular phones.

In March 1985 Ameritech ventured into office automation systems with Real Com, an IBM Satellite Business Systems subsidiary. With Aetna Telecommunications Laboratories, Ameritech worked on simultaneous transmission of voice, video, and data via fiber-optic cables. Despite growing potential, Weiss did not see Ameritech putting more than one-fifth of its resources into these newer ventures. Following Springer's lead, in March 1985, Ameritech Development purchased a minority interest in Davox Corporation, a producer of integrated voice and data communication systems.

Ameritech Publishing, also on the upswing, acquired Cleveland-based Purchasing Directories, Inc., in 1985 and began publishing telephone directories in Ohio, Illinois, Indiana, and Michigan. As a marketing consultant, Ameritech assisted AT&T in publishing a directory in Thailand in July 1985.

Barely through the second year of operations, the RHCs were still legally bound to seek permission from U.S. District Court Judge Greene before starting up businesses. In August 1985 an Ameritech attorney faced the FCC, asking the board to waive such restrictions. Earlier rulings outlined under the FCC's decisions known as Computer I and II established these distinctions: basic, or regulated, services comprised of local telephone hook-up and related maintenance; enhanced, or non-regulated, services, which included the development and manufacture of telephone equipment.

Computer III, announced in January 1986, ruled that the RHCs could provide enhanced communications and computer generated data and storage, through existing corporations. Accountability requirements included safeguards known as comparably efficient interconnection, open network architecture, and stringent cost accounting methods. These measures were designed by the FCC to assure competing telecommunications companies fair access to local exchange facilities currently controlled by the RHCs. The equal access was necessary for non-Bell companies to offer comprehensive information packages.

Ameritech, following competitor Bell Atlantic's lead, began diversifying to the extent it was able. In January 1986 the corporation bought Applied Data Research Inc., a database management software producer for IBM mainframe computers. Ameritech also purchased Speech Plus, Inc., a developer of speech-synthesis technology.

Ameritech Publishing extended its holdings with the May 1986 acquisition of Old Heritage Advertising & Publishing. Within two years the subsidiary expanded its coverage to 90 telephone directories in 15 states.

By June 1986 the FCC loosened its reins further. Ameritech was the first RHC authorized to enter international telecommunications as well as foreign manufacturing and nontelecommunications businesses. Ameritech's movement was limited, however. It was required to establish a subsidiary to manufacture telecommunications products, provided that the subsidiary had no financial interest in the U.S. telecommunications industry; products were not to be sold in the United States, Canada, or the U.S. Virgin Islands. In addition, Ameritech had two other restrictions. It could not buy, sell, or patent technology manufactured by, or enter joint research projects with its foreign subsidiary. Finally Ameritech had to make available any software or technology from its foreign manufacturer to any U.S. companies that requested such information. Satisfied with the ruling, Ameritech indicated that it was likely to move cautiously, via a joint venture with a foreign company.

Ameritech's presence in foreign countries was not new; through Applied Data Research, by summer 1986, Ameritech reached 40 nations. In August Ameritech Publishing bought a portion of AT&T's international telephone directory businesses. Ameritech Development, always investigating opportunities, consulted in Japan on several projects.

On the home front the company gradually expanded as well, with Ameritech Development joining David Systems of California in ongoing research and development into local network setups. Ameritech Mobile commissioned Motorola to develop a multi-feature cellular telephone. By November 1986 Ameritech Mobile was providing cellular service in Chicago-area commuter trains.

In September 1986 Ameritech Services and Siemens Communications Systems, Inc. sealed a three-year contract, the first of its kind to be made with a company other than AT&T or Northern Telecom, the RHCs' usual suppliers. Under the agreement, Siemens agreed to supply to all Ameritech Bell companies a mobile switching unit featuring business applications of the integrated services digital network (ISDN) for Ameritech's central offices.

Ameritech ended its third year as a strong competitor in the telecommunications industry. Conditions supporting Ameritech's position varied. A new price flexibility because of state deregulation allowed Illinois Bell to project service fees based on cost without consulting regulator approval, thus speeding up local service. Ameritech's moderate moves into publishing and foreign manufacturing ventures kept the company on solid financial footing. CEO Weiss also decided to buy back some of Ameritech's stock, a wise decision according to industry analysts.

Ameritech chief financial officer William Springer projected 33% of 1987 earnings to come from nontelephone operations. Ameritech put its energies into fiber-optic and digital technologies, spending nearly 10% more than it had the previous year. The corporation planned to have nearly 150,000 miles of fiber-optic cable installed by year-end 1987, to serve one-fourth of its customers on digital switching lines. Through the newly established Ameritech Business Network, the company stepped up marketing of digital products designed to provide integrated information systems.

In January 1987 Ameritech once again faced a DOJ proposal, which considered lifting the current restrictions on BOCs' manufacturing and information services. In preparation for such a policy change, Weiss announced plans to develop databases for electronic telephone directories. Other possibilities considered were joint ventures in foreign manufacturing, which would lessen Ameritech's dependence on AT&T, its major supplier.

As reported in *Telephony,* February 23, 1987, Weiss criticized the DOJ restrictions on interexchange services. Under the current rules, the large companies continued to bypass local exchange carriers run by the RHCs, while the small business and residential customers continued to have no choice of providers of local service. On the other hand, Weiss said, "The network architecture now serving large business customers reduces to insignificance any influence a BOC could leverage in related markets. . . . The MFJ [modified final court judgment] order has kept the BOCs out of the interexchange market." Weiss said Ameritech's goal—to be a provider of integrated systems to major customers—could be realized only if restrictions were lifted and if Ameritech were to be allowed to enter data transmission and private line services. Competition would be fostered as well.

Notwithstanding the pending but as yet unresolved DOJ decision, in August 1987 Ameritech paid $5 million for the option to gain a 15% equity in a Canadian-based electronic messaging company. The purchase was Ameritech's effort to enter information database markets. MCI opposed the venture, charging that it violated the MFJ. Successfully securing DOJ approval by October, Ameritech, together with Bell Canada Enterprises and Telenet Communications, announced iNet, the first computer-based information management service to be offered in the United States. The service was available through data terminals, personal computers, and word processors equipped with a telephone line and modem.

In September 1987 Ameritech's Wisconsin Bell proposed two experimental ventures with Warner Cable Communications of Milwaukee, and a six-month trial of pay-per-view cable television began. Using existing networks, Wisconsin Bell also planned to monitor gas, electric, and water meters in homes and offices. By October Ameritech Publishing was producing telephone directories in western Pennsylvania and in New York state. In response to the year's significant changes, in December 1987 Ameritech set up a midwestern regional committee to review the company's regulated and unregulated subsidiaries.

One unpredictable challenge Ameritech faced in its fifth year of operation was a fire at the Hinsdale, Illinois, switching center, which interrupted service for 35,000 customers in the greater Chicago area for more than two days. The fire began when damaged cables began arcing. The fuses, not designed to recognize arcing, did not open. As a result, by 1989, many new safety guidelines were implemented, including a variety of fire detector types, together with posted instructions for manual power-down procedures.

On the corporate level, Ameritech initiated large-scale reorganization. In March 1988 Ameritech Applied Technologies, Inc., a fully owned subsidiary, was formed. Its goal was to integrate and update computers at all Ameritech Bell locations to one standardized system. Existing differences in administration, billing, and software would be eliminated.

Although Ameritech diversified, it streamlined into ventures closely connected, both geographically and technologically, to its bread-and-butter business, the Bell telephone systems. While the company's restructuring was a reaction to the gradual loosening of government enforced regulations, there was another significant factor. Ameritech lost more of its 1987 revenue to bypass technology than any other RHC. With the iNet system as a base, the company began modernization of all its exchange networks, developing electronic digital switching and fiber-optic transmission systems. Ameritech planned to have 300,000 miles of fiber-optic cable in place to serve all of its customer lines. The company used fiber optics to speed up long-distance carriers' local access capabilities. Through the system FiberHub, for example, Ameritech routed long-distance calls from AT&T, US Sprint, or MCI to their respective customer destinations via an electronic expressway interchange.

In step with these changes, Ameritech unloaded its 17% interest in the Canadian cellular service, Cantel, for $85 million. While Weiss saw the cellular business as profitable, he did not want to sink too much money in a venture far from his midwestern business base. Ameritech Mobile, on the upswing, increased cellular service by 68% and covered 17% more territory. In September 1988 Ameritech Mobile Communications acquired the paging assets of both Multicom, Inc., from sibling Pacific Telesis, and A Beeper Company, from Bell Atlantic. Through the acquisitions, Ameritech strengthened its midwestern holdings.

Ameritech Development kept pace, buying the midwest operations of Telephone Announcement Systems, Inc., in September 1988. Through the purchase the company also acquired Telephone Announcement's audiotex network, a voice-response system that gives information to callers via touch-tone telephones. Then in Chicago and in Grand Rapids, Michigan, Ameritech planned to extend the service to Cleveland, Ohio; Detroit, Michigan; Indianapolis, Indiana; and Milwaukee, Wisconsin. With the October acquisition of The Tigon Corporation, a Dallas voice-mail company, Ameritech gained 200 corporate clients, a two-year jump on voice messaging technology, as well as a leadership position in the industry. Ameritech planned to add messaging services as an option to midwest customers.

In the largest single transaction of the busy year, Ameritech sold its software subsidiary, Applied Data Research, for $170 million, incurring an after-tax loss of $8.1 million. Two other major changes in December 1988 included the formation of Ameritech Enterprise Holdings, a holding company for Ameritech Audiotex Services, Inc., and the Tigon Corporation. By this time Tigon had reached Japan and the United Kingdom with its voice mail services. In January 1989 Ameritech Information Systems was formed to install business systems as well as to provide marketing and product and technical design support to large business customers in the Ameritech region.

Facing its sixth year, Ameritech and its representatives continued asking the FCC to remove all restrictions on information services. The previous year's gain had been the lift on information transmission—yet Ameritech, bound to transmit information generated by another company, was still unable to transmit its own information. Regardless of the 1987 pay-per-view cable trial in Wisconsin, the linkage of cable to existing networks was still forbidden. In a minor, perhaps unrelated, concession in February 1989, Ameritech was granted a waiver, allowing the company to offer directory assisted customer-name-and-address (CNA) service, provided that CNA revenues subsidized local telephone rates. As reported in the October 1989 issue of *Communications News,* Ameritech vice chairman Ormand Wade said the court-imposed limitations not only inhibited competition, it weakened U.S. potential in the international telecommunications market.

Ameritech continued research and development in information transmission, testing an electronic digital loop carrier system designed to allow transmission of large amounts of data. Fiber-optic rings linked customer locations to central offices or long-distance carriers. Ameritech targeted investment through 1994 of more than $200 million in a database, Signaling System 7 (SS7), intended to support a new software-based intelligence system.

Ameritech pushed further into retail markets. Ameritech Mobile offered cellular service through appliance centers and retail locations, including Sears and Silo, in Chicago, Detroit, Milwaukee, and Columbus and Cincinnati, Ohio. Ameritech Mobile also increased its Michigan-area paging operations, acquiring T-Com Inc., from Rochester Telephone Company. In February 1989 the Tigon subsidiary negotiated a multimillion dollar deal to supply Texas Instruments with voice-mail capability reaching 140 national and international locations.

Ameritech, with CEO Weiss's prodding, increased marketing in several areas. With US Sprint and Telesphere, Ameritech's audiotex services agreed to process "900" calls; with Teleline of Los Angeles, it entered negotiations to resell the VoiceQuest system. Ameritech Publishing announced a talking telephone directories service in the midwest Bell regions, to be accessed through a number listed in Ameritech Pages Plus directories. In 1989 Ameritech was publishing directories in 30 states as well as English-language directories in Japan.

Together with several other RHCs, Ameritech faced employee strikes in 1989. By August Ameritech union workers walked out, displeased with current wage-increase structures and health benefits. After several weeks Ameritech and the union reached agreements on the issues.

To strengthen its position, in November 1989 Ameritech restructured slightly, eliminating its subsidiary boards. The corporation also continued bidding with other RHCs in an effort to gain new national and international business. By December Illinois Bell took part in the first installation of ISDN service, linking the Andersen Consulting offices of Chicago and Tokyo.

In early 1990, with manufacturer Northern Telecom, American Information Systems worked directly with end users to test telephone audio deficiencies. Their tests resulted in new design standards to improve the transmission quality of telephones. Advancing in fiber optics, in September 1990 Ameritech initiated the nation's first passive optic network. Also in 1990 Ameritech pursued additional international ventures. With Bell Atlantic and two New Zealand companies, it bought Telecom New Zealand from that country's government. The U.S. companies planned to offer a portion of their shares to the public. Another 1990 purchase was Wer Leifert Was? (Who Supplies What?), a publisher of industrial directories in Germany and Austria.

Ameritech's greatest challenge in 1990 was centralizing. Glen Arnold, Ameritech Applied Technologies CEO, proposed a five-year data center consolidation to reduce costs resulting from duplication of work; its intent was to install company-wide information systems, trimming the number of working data centers from 21 to 4. As Glen Arnold stated in *Computerworld,* April 30, 1990: "We've got to do for Ameritech what Ameritech can do for other customers." Based on its past record, Ameritech is clearly up to the job.

Principal Subsidiaries: Ameritech Bell Group: Ameritech Services, Inc.; Ameritech Information Systems, Inc.; Illinois Bell; Indiana Bell; Michigan Bell; Ohio Bell; Wisconsin Bell; Ameritech Mobile Communications, Inc.; Ameritech Publishing Inc.; Ameritech Credit Corp.; Tigon Corporation; Ameritech Audiotex Services, Inc.; Ameritech Development Corp.; Ameritech International.

Further Reading: Pauly, David, et. al., "Ma Bell's Big Breakup," *Newsweek,* January 18, 1982; Kuttner, Bob, "Ma Bell's Broken Home," *The New Republic,* March 17, 1982; Militzer, Kenneth, and Martin Wolf, "Deregulation in Telecommunications," *Business Economics,* July, 1985; Leopold, George, "Will the FCC Free 'The Bell Operating Company Seven?,'" *Electronics,* January 20, 1986; Mikolas, Mark, "Still Yearning to Be Free at Divestiture + 3½," *Telephone Engineer and Management,* September 15, 1987.

—Frances E. Norton

BCE INC.

2000 McGill College Avenue
Suite 2100
Montreal, Quebec H3A 3H7
Canada
(514) 499-7000
Fax: (514) 499-7098

Public Company
Incorporated: 1880 as Bell Telephone Company of Canada
Employees: 62,850
Sales: C$18.37 billion (US$15.89 billion)
Stock Exchanges: Montreal Toronto Vancouver Brussels Paris Frankfurt Düsseldorf Tokyo Basel Geneva Zürich Amsterdam London New York

The history of BCE Inc. can be traced to Canada native Alexander Graham Bell's early communications experiments, which eventually led to the formation of Bell Telephone Company of Canada. Chartered by the Canadian Parliament on April 29, 1880, the company, known informally as Bell Canada, would spend the next 100-plus years growing and diversifying into one of Canada's largest and most successful organizations; in fact, by 1983, Bell Canada could be described as both a telecommunications company and a holding company, with controlling interests in more than 80 other organizations. A move to create a new parent company, Bell Canada Enterprises Inc. (BCE), in 1983, left Bell Canada and its other businesses as subsidiaries of a new holding company. The move also changed the course of history for BCE Inc.

The Canadian phone company's history began in the late 1870s, when Canada's first telephone exchange opened in 1878 in Hamilton, Ontario. Toronto's came second, in 1879. In 1881 the company had exchanges in 40 cities. By 1890 the firm was offering long-distance service over 3,670 miles. From early on, the firm used the slogan, "A telephone business run by Canadians for Canadians."

Still in its infancy, the telephone industry differed greatly from that which most countries know today. Initially telephone service was offered only during business hours to about 2,100 telephones. Business owners could use the service by buying pairs of instruments to communicate from home to office, from office to factory, or between other pairs of locations. In 1890 the company began to offer evening and Sunday service.

Although United States-based American Telephone and Telegraph Company (AT&T) owned 48% of Bell Canada's stock

in 1890, Canadians began buying more of that stock as the company grew. In 1895 Bell Canada incorporated its manufacturing arm, Northern Electric & Manufacturing Company Limited, which was partly owned by AT&T's Western Electric.

Early telephone operators were also different from those known today. In *Telephony*, April 28, 1986, one of those early employees recalled her first days as an operator in 1924. They were times characterized by hard, fast, manual work, usually lasting six days a week. The operators worked on Christmas, all summer long, and without paid sick days. For this, starting pay was C$11.50 per week. In 1924 Bell Canada introduced the dial exchange, so users could dial a party directly without waiting for an operator to come on the line.

By 1925 the company was well on its way to living up to its motto, as Canadians owned 94.5% of its stock. The late 1920s saw several advances, including a phone service that linked Canada to Britain via the United States; a carrier system; and, in 1931, the formation of the TransCanada Telephone System. The following year the system made possible the first long distance call from Montreal to Vancouver via an all-Canadian route. In 1933 the U.S. federal securities act ended AT&T's right to purchase new shares.

During the Great Depression, the need for telephone service dropped substantially. Operators worked only three days per week—about half the hours they had put in previously. When World War II began all operators were summoned back to work. Following the war, in 1945, Bell Canada installed its one millionth phone. In 1954 Bell Canada merged two subsidiaries, Eastern Townships Telephone Company and Chapleau Telephone System. In 1956 the company merged with Kamouraska Telephone Company and expanded once again in 1957, when it acquired Mount Albert Telephone Company Ltd. Also in 1957, Bell Canada acquired most of Western Electric's share of Northern Electric, which Western held through a subsidiary, Weco Corporation. In 1964 it bought the remainder. By 1958 customers in Canada and the United States could dial other telephone users directly, without going through an operator.

Bell Canada acquired Madawaska Telephone Company in 1960. It gained control in 1962 of Avalon Telephone Company Ltd., which would later be known as Newfoundland Telephone Company Ltd. The following year, Bell Canada bought Monk Rural Telephone Company, changing its name to Capital Telephone Company Ltd. in 1966. Also in 1966, Bell Canada gained a new general counsel, A. Jean de Grandpre, who would soon become a major leader in the company's growth and diversification. A Montreal native, de Grandpre graduated from McGill University in 1943, with a degree in law. He brought two decades of experience gained in his own law practice. Under his leadership, the firm grew rapidly through capital expansion and acquisition. In 1970, for example, the firm acquired control of Oxford Telephone Company Ltd. and Caradoc Ekfrid Telephone Company Ltd., as well as an interest in Telesat Canada, a communications satellite operation. The following year saw the founding of Bell-Northern Research Ltd. (BNR) to consolidate the research and development efforts of Northern Electric and Bell Canada. By 1973 de Grandpre had risen to the post of president of Bell Canada. Three years later, de Grandpre became chairman and chief executive officer.

In 1973 Bell Canada sold a portion of Northern Electric to the public, and in 1976 Northern Electric changed its name to

Northern Telecom Limited. Also in 1976, Bell Canada created Bell Canada International Management, Research and Consulting Ltd. (BCI). The firm, which succeeded Bell's Consulting Services Group founded in the mid-1960s, was designed to offer expertise in telecommunications management and technical planning. Based in Ottawa, BCI's clients included common carriers, private corporations, defense companies, contractors, manufacturers, other consultants, and Northern Telecom. In addition, the firm had business dealings across the globe, including in Africa, the Middle East, Europe, the Caribbean, South America, Saudi Arabia, and the United States. According to *Telecommunications,* October 1980, BCI "could serve as a case study of transfer of North American technology to other nations, be they underdeveloped, developing, or fully developed." In addition Northern Telecom and Bell Canada formed B-N Software Research Inc. for the research and development of new software. Late in 1978 Bell Canada introduced a fiber-optic system developed by Northern Telecom Ltd. Designed to simultaneously transmit telephony, data, and video, the company introduced the revolutionary new system during a video telephone conference call between Toronto and London. In 1981 the software firm was merged into Bell-Northern Research.

By 1982 Bell Canada controlled nearly 80 other companies. Switching control of the organizations, including Bell Canada, to a new parent company would simplify the business, de Grandpre believed. Consequently in 1983 Bell Canada Enterprises Inc., known since 1988 as BCE Inc., was created to act as a holding company for a corporate family whose assets amounted to $15 billion and included Bell Canada itself. By designating most of the company's businesses as separate BCE subsidiaries, Bell Canada was the only company that remained under the regulatory control of the Canadian Radio-Television and Telecommunications Commission (CRTC). This benefit led many critics to believe that avoiding CRTC supervision was the sole reason for the restructure. Such criticism was well founded, as relations between the phone company and the CRTC were not always smooth. In 1978, for instance, Bell Canada signed a C$1.1 billion contract to improve Saudi Arabia's telecommunications network. Although the contract did not involve any telephone service to Canadians, the CRTC ruled that profits from the venture must be considered when determining Canadian phone rates, which meant smaller rate hikes for Bell Canada. Still, de Grandpre argued that the purpose of the restructure "was to provide the flexibility necessary for Bell to take on major competitors in telecommunications and microelectronics around the world," reported *Maclean's,* February 14, 1983.

In addition to leadership and coordination, BCE provides equity investments to further the development of its various businesses and to finance their growth via new products, markets, internal growth, or acquisitions. Also in 1983, BCE acquired a sizeable percentage of TransCanada PipeLines Ltd. (TCPL), a move described in BCE's 1983 annual report as "a significant commitment by BCE to western Canada and to the resource sector of the Canadian economy." Although Radcliffe Latimer, president of TCPL and a personal friend of de Grandpre, cautioned shareholders to ignore BCE's offer of $31.50 per share, BCE still managed to swiftly take over 42% of the company. Following the feud, Latimer admitted defeat and commented in *Maclean's,* January 2, 1984, "We look at Bell as a first class major shareholder."

BCE's operations then included Bell Canada and several other locally regulated telecommunications operations: Northern Telecom Limited, a telecommunications manufacturer; Bell-Northern Research Ltd., owned by Bell Canada and Northern Telecom Ltd.; Bell Canada International Inc., a consulting firm; Bell Communications Systems Inc.; TransCanada PipeLines Ltd.; Tele-Direct (Publications) Inc., owned by Bell Canada; and Tele-Direct (Canada) Inc.

BCE's growth spurt continued through the 1980s. In fact its assets jumped from C$14.8 billion in 1983 to C$39.3 billion in 1989. There were investments in energy, real estate, printing and packaging, mobile and cellular communications, and financial services. BCE also became the first Canadian corporation to earn a net income of more than C$1 billion. Despite that success, however, other aspects of BCE's business did not fare as well. One such failure was the firm's venture into real estate in 1985, through BCE Development Corporation (BCED), a new subsidiary. The company's experiments with printing and with oil and gas investments also brought poor reviews from shareholders.

BCE managed to succeed, despite these setbacks and several conflicts with CRTC. In 1986 the CRTC held a six-week hearing to examine Bell Canada's profits from 1985 through 1987. As a result, the CRTC ordered Bell Canada to refund to consumers C$206 million worth of excess payments made earlier that year as well as in 1985. In addition the commission forced the company to decrease its predicted profits for 1987 by C$234 million by lowering long distance rates in Ontario and Quebec by nearly 20%.

In 1989 de Grandpre retired as chairman, but remained on the board of directors as founding director and chairman emeritus. J.V. Raymond Cyr, who had been chief executive officer of BCE since May 1988, took the additional post of chairman in August 1989. Bell Canada gained a new president, Jean C. Monty. Cyr faced the monumental task of restoring the faith of BCE's shareholders, who once considered buying stock in the phone company "as safe as Canada Savings Bonds," reported *Maclean's,* July 30, 1990. To do this, the company decided to take a closer look at the types of businesses best suited to its corporate strategy. It was determined that telecommunications would naturally remain as BCE's core business, but the firm's involvement in real estate was dissolved. It chose to concentrate on financial services and acquired Montreal Trustco Inc., an established firm in that field. It was, however, Bell Canada that brought the most revenue to the parent company. With a record year, Bell Canada contributed C$2.75 per share to BCE's 1989 earnings. In addition, BCE stock continued to be the most widely held stock in Canada.

Six years after taking control of TransCanada PipeLines Ltd., which BCE viewed as a solid, long-term investment, the company decided to sell its stake in the energy business. Owning TransCanada PipeLines was simply not consistent with BCE's core businesses in telecommunications and financial services.

In the early 1990s the holding company BCE Inc. owned subsidiaries in three primary areas: telecommunications services, telecommunications equipment manufacturing, and financial services. Although these subsidiaries make crucial contributions to the success of their parent company, many of them are successful enough to warrant widely recognized reputations of their own. While Bell Canada, the country's largest telecommunications company, provides most of the firm's services in that area, for example, Northern Telecom Limited is responsible for the manufacturing end of the business and is the second-largest such company in North America. Bell-Northern Research, the largest private industrial research and development organization in the country, plays a vital role in BCE's research and development activities, while financial services are provided by Montreal Trust.

It seems BCE has already hurdled a major challenge in its 1983 restructuring. As a holding company, BCE must continue to adapt to industry changes.

Principal Subsidiaries: Bell Canada; Northern Telecom Limited (53.1%); Bell-Northern Research Ltd. (30%); Bell Canada International Inc.; BCE Mobile Communications Inc. (69.7%); Montreal Trustco Inc.

Further Reading: Hardin, Helen, "Bell Canada marks its 100th year by helping others," *Telephony,* April 28, 1980; Wickens, Barbara, "Tough times for Ma Bell," *Maclean's,* July 30, 1990.

—Kim M. Magon

⊕ Bell Atlantic

BELL ATLANTIC CORPORATION

1600 Market Street
Philadelphia, Pennsylvania 19103
U.S.A.
(215) 963-6000
Fax: (215) 466-2416

Public Company
Incorporated: 1983
Employees: 81,6000
Sales: $11.53 billion
Stock Exchanges: New York Boston Midwest Pacific
  Philadelphia London Geneva Zürich Frankfurt Tokyo Basel

Bell Atlantic Corporation is prominent in U.S. and international telecommunications. The company's network services division is made up of seven telephone subsidiaries, which provide telephone service, billing services for various interexchange carriers, and printed directory advertising, and Bell Atlanticom, which sells, installs, and maintains communications systems and equipment for large business customers. Other Bell Atlantic divisions include wireless communications, which markets cellular and paging equipment; business systems, which provides integrated computer hardware, software, and support systems; diversified financial services, engaged in lease financing of commercial, industrial, medical, and high-technology equipment; and Bell Atlantic International, a consultant in systems integration services and software development.

In January 1982 the U.S. Department of Justice (DOJ) ended a 13-year antitrust suit against the world's largest corporation, the American Telephone and Telegraph Company (AT&T). Pursuant to a consent decree, AT&T maintained its manufacturing and research facilities, as well as its long-distance operations. On January 1, 1984, AT&T divested itself of 22 local operating companies, which were divided among seven regional holding companies (RHCs). Bell Atlantic serves the northern Atlantic states, and owns seven telephone subsidiaries: New Jersey Bell Telephone Company, The Bell Telephone Company of Pennsylvania, The Diamond State Telephone Company, The Chesapeake and Potomac Telephone Company, The Chesapeake and Potomac Telephone Company of Maryland, The Chesapeake and Potomac Telephone Company of West Virginia, and the Chesapeake and Potomac Telephone Company of Virginia.

Tackling AT&T as a tough competitor rather than a parent company was an immediate and ever-present challenge for Bell Atlantic. On January 2, 1984, federal Justice Harold Greene ordered Bell Atlantic to transfer a $30 million contract with the federal government to AT&T, ruling that AT&T was granted the contract pre-divestiture. Bell Atlantic claimed that many terms of the contract—which included the sale of 200,000 telephones, a year-long maintenance contract worth $6 million, and involved approximately 275 employees—were made directly with Bell Atlantic, not AT&T. Bell Atlantic argued, also unsuccessfully, that the transfer of employees would give AT&T knowledge of Bell Atlantic's advanced voice and data communications Centrex system, so that AT&T could conceivably design and market a system to underprice Bell Atlantic.

Bell Atlantic bounced back from its court loss, acquiring a 40% interest in A Beeper Company Associates in January 1984. The following month the company announced the formation of Bell Atlanticom Systems, a systems and equipment subsidiary, to market traditional, cordless, and decorator telephones, wiring components, and home-security and healthcare systems. Bell Atlantic Mobile Systems took off early from the starting gate: in March 1984 the company announced Alex, a cellular telephone service to commence April 2 in the Washington, D.C., and Baltimore, Maryland, markets. Bell Atlantic Mobile Systems invested $15.1 million in the fledgling cellular service.

Skirmishes continued between the RHCs, AT&T, and Justice Harold Greene. Greene asserted that the RHCs were more concerned with entering new business markets than in improving the local networks. In an effort to restrain RHCs from using regulated business profits to finance nontelephone ventures, the consent decree ruled that new endeavors may comprise no more than 10% of the RHCs' yearly revenues and that there be a strict financial separation between regulated telephone business and new ventures. Justice Greene set a March 23, 1984, deadline for all RHCs to submit specific requests for waivers or further explanation of the original consent decree.

In April Bell Atlantic went to court over the Federal Communications Commission's (FCC) delay in charging tariffs for customers accessing the local network. Delaying implementation of the access fee not only violated the consent decree, Bell Atlantic charged, it caused Bell Atlantic and its sibling RHCs to cover some of AT&T's service costs in the interim. To make matters worse, because Bell Atlantic was the lowest-cost provider of all the RHC's, it was losing the most money. (The FCC system was one of allocation, with access-fee funds collected first, then distributed to RHCs based on the company's cost.)

Bell Atlantic planned to succeed in spite of the access fee tangle. The corporation allotted more than half of its construction budget for improvment of the network. Bell Atlantic became the first RHC to employ the use of digital termination systems, a microwave technology for local electronic message distribution. The company experimented with a local area data transport system, and planned to install 50,000 miles of optical fiber within a year.

Bell Atlantic made several major acquisitions in its first year of operation. The purchase of Telecommunications Specialists, Inc. (TSI), a Houston, Texas, interconnect firm with offices in Dallas, San Antonio, and Austin, was completed in October 1984. Bell Atlantic planned to let TSI retain its marketing and sales staff and continue operations. TSI, a marketer of private branch exchange (PBX) and key systems, also offered financing for equipment-leasing customers.

In December 1984 Bell Atlantic bought New Jersey's Tri-Continental Leasing Corporation (Tri-Con), a computer and telecommunications equipment provider. As Tri-Con supplied TSI with financing, Bell Atlantic seemed to be vertically integrating its acquisitions. Another big Tri-Con customer was Basic Four Information Systems, owned by Management Assistance Inc. (MAI). Early in 1985 Bell Atlantic completed the purchase of MAI's Sorbus Inc. division, the second-largest U.S. computer service firm, with 187 locations and 2,200 employees, for $180 million. Bell Atlantic also bought a related company, MAI Canada Ltd. With the Sorbus acquisition Bell Atlantic hoped to strengthen its position with the federal government; as the company's largest customer, the federal government provided 3% of total company revenues in the first year of operation.

With the most aggressive diversification of all the RHCs, Bell Atlantic planned to be a full-service company in the inceasingly related merging telecommunications and computer sectors. As a struggle for large customers was inevitable, and because the larger customers could potentially set up their own information systems, the company decided to target medium-sized customers. Bell Atlantic offered this customer base everything from information services equipment and data processing to computer maintenance.

Because the original consent decree was drawn to strictly regulate RHC activity and allow long-distance carriers equal access to local networks, fledglings such as Bell Atlantic faced competition on all levels. On the national level, the FCC approved a $2 end-user fee for all subscribers to basic telephone service, another tactic to give the RHCs a cushion in large-business markets. The institution of this fee coincided with the availability of rapidly evolving technology; thus the fee merely encouraged larger customers to create their own information networks, a process termed "bypass." To help keep Bell Atlantic competitive in the large-customer markets—those most vulnerable to bypass—several states in its region granted the company considerable flexibility in pricing.

In the unregulated businesses Bell Atlantic was just entering, competition threatened to be even stiffer in the PBX market. By early 1985 IBM and Digital Equipment were offering maintenance for their mainframe users, a large portion of Bell Atlantic's recently acquired Sorbus customer base.

Larger than many competing companies nonetheless, Bell Atlantic took advantage of the buyer's market that the tough competition created: in June 1985 it acquired CompuShop Inc., a retail computer company with $75 million in sales annually, for $21 million. With the acquisition, Bell Atlantic joined siblings NYNEX, the New England and New York RHC, and Pacific Telesis, the west coast RHC, as surprise competitors in a market that, in spite of a recent surge in sales, was in decline. The retail computer slump was marked by smaller companies' rapid entry into, and exit from, a market with high overhead costs. The entrance of big names such as Bell Atlantic could, retail computer experts argued, provide just the shot in the arm that the market needed to take off.

A year and a half after divestiture, Bell Atlantic, along with its sibling RHCs and other companies, realized that convergence of telephone hardware and computer data processing

was a huge business. Over the next several years the RHCs repeatedly petitioned the DOJ for business waivers in an attempt to become more competitive in not only the national but the international telecommunications market. By July 1984 Bell Atlantic requested that the government waive a body of rules that prohibited the RHCs from supplying their own telephone hardware. Unable to provide equipment for its own Centrex system, Bell Atlantic stood to lose a huge federal government contract to competitors—nearly 370,000 Centrex lines that were coming up for bid. Having already lost 48,000 Centrex lines due to restrictions of the past year, Bell Atlantic officials thought it was time to confront the issue.

Since divestiture, the FCC allowed AT&T to resell basic services, and it was considering letting the company provide customer premise equipment as well. IBM, strengthened by its recently acquired Rolm Corporation and Satellite Business Systems, was not restricted in its marketing efforts, but Bell Atlantic was.

By the end of 1985 Bell Atlantic earnings were $1.1 billion on revenues of $9.1 billion. Rated against its competitors, Bell Atlantic was the only RHC close to turning a profit on its unregulated businesses, worth $600 million in revenues. While profits remained strong in Bell Atlantic's local phone service, its Yellow Pages directory publishing division, due to a disagreement, would be competing with Reuben H. Donneley Corporation, its previous publisher.

In the meantime, the long-distance market moved uncomfortably close to the RHCs' local turf. AT&T and other carriers began competing to carry toll calls in local areas. While this would seem to benefit the residential consumer, it did not; outside competitors cutting into RHC profits merely threatened the very profit margin that helped subsidize the cost of local service.

Ending its second year in operation, Bell Atlantic's chairman and chief executive officer, Thomas Bolger, quoted in *Telephone Engineer & Management*'s December 15, 1985, issue, described the restrictions on RHCs as "the most significant problem in the telecommunications industry." He requested that the Justice Department come to a decision before the scheduled January 1, 1987, date. If the purpose of the breakup was to promote maximum competition in the industry, the RHCs reasoned that they, the most likely competitors of industry leaders AT&T and IBM, should not be prohibited from fully competing.

Continuing to expand its unregulated businesses in spite of, or perhaps because of, line-of-business restrictions as outlined in the consent decree, in September 1986 Bell Atlantic acquired the real estate assets of Pitcairn Properties, Inc. In October the company followed with the $140 million purchase of Greyhound Capital Corporation, since renamed Bell Atlantic Systems Leasing International, Inc. Bell Atlantic then had a firm position in the financial and real estate markets.

In late November 1986, Bell Atlantic became the first RHC to propose to the FCC a new cost allocation plan under recently outlined requirements. The corporation also opted, if allowed, to begin planning its comparably efficient interconnection (CEI) system. By March 1987 Bell Atlantic filed its CEI plan asking for the provision of message storage, hoping to get a jump on offering enhanced services. Due to several regulatory restrictions, development of the service was halted. Continuing operations as usual, in June 1987 Bell Atlantic acquired Pacific Computer Corp., and within several months, the company purchased Jolynne Service Corp.

On July 2, 1987, Bell Atlantic announced a restructuring plan, combining operations of basic telephone service and unregulated businesses under one newly created position, chief operating officer (COO). The plan also called for all staff of separate Bell Atlantic telephone companies to report to their respective presidents. Raymond Smith, a Bell employee since 1959, was named COO, and would report to Bolger.

On September 10, 1987, Federal Judge Harold Greene ruled to uphold the manufacturing and long-distance restrictions on RHCs, while allowing only limited information services. The RHCs all objected, but none as strongly as Bell Atlantic. The corporation alleged that the judge alluded to information discussed during the original consent decree settlement, which claimed that the Bell operating companies, pre-divestiture, had been accused of engaging in anticompetitive practices—remarks not relevant to the case at hand.

The tables turned rather quickly for Bell Atlantic. In January 1988 the company found itself, along with BellSouth, accused of misconduct in bidding attempts to win government contracts. Senator John Glenn of Ohio led the accusations that the two RHCs had been given confidential price information by a General Services Administration chief. Bell Atlantic disputed the charges entirely, claiming that the senator's report was inaccurate.

Business transpiring as usual, that same month Bell Atlantic sold MAI Canada Ltd., and some of the assets of Sorbus Inc., for $146 million. Following that divestiture, in February the company purchased the European computer maintenance operations of Bell Canada Enterprises, Inc. Later that year, Bell Atlantic's Sorbus subsidiary acquired Computer Maintenance Co., Inc.

In 1988, following Judge Greene's approval of its CEI plans, Bell Atlantic announced it would introduce four new information services: an electronic message storage system, which would allow the subscriber to record a message for comsumers to play back; a telephone-answering service; a voice-mail service; and a videotex gateway service, through which data bases and customers could communicate. All services involved monthly surcharges for customers, as well as an hourly fee for videotex and a one-time users fee for message storage.

Juggling its assets a bit more, in June Bell Atlantic completed the sale of its retail computer CompuShop, to Compu-Com Systems, Inc., and acquired in July the assets of CPX Inc., a company specializing in Control Data Corporation equipment, through subsidiary Camex CPX, Inc. Bell Atlantic also acquired the assets of Dyn Service Network.

Thomas E. Bolger announced his retirement as CEO, effective January 1, 1989; Raymond W. Smith, chief operating officer since 1987, would become the new chief executive officer. Bolger, formerly a vice president of AT&T in business services and marketing, led Bell Atlantic through divestiture into a leading position in telecommunications, real estate and leasing finance, and computer maintenance. A strong critic of consent decree restrictions on RHCs, by January 1989, Bell Atlantic also was active in helping establish international standards for telecommunications.

On the national level, however, Judge Greene kept his eye on RHC activities. A January 1989 Bell Atlantic proposal to conduct a trial involving interstate phone traffic was rejected on the basis that the service was not a necessary, but an advanced, competitive service. Bell Atlantic wanted to cut costs by using a central processor for state-to-state traffic rather than having separate facilities perform the same tasks. Bell Atlantic held that the judge's decision was against the public interest.

Bell Atlantic implemented another reorganization in 1989, trimming its management staff by 1,700 through voluntary retirement and other incentive plans. Significant parts of the restructuring included closing the Washington, D.C., Chesapeake and Potomac Telephone Company headquarters and merging employees into other locations; refinancing various debts; reassessing computer holdings; and outlining a plan to cover future retirement of nonmanagement staff. Negotiations with its union employees resulted in Bell Atlantic's initiating a trust to cover nonmanagement union employees' future medical and dental fees.

Bell Atlantic invested $2.3 billion in network services to upgrade telephone facilities. Signaling System 7 (SS7), a high-speed information exchange system, was operating on more than 60% of Bell Atlantic telephone lines. To compete in mobile communications, the company marketed an extremely lightweight cellular telephone. Bell Atlantic Paging customers increased by 16%. In partnership with GTE, Bell Atlantic Yellow Pages increased its customer base through a new subsidiary, the Chesapeake Directory Sales Company. In October 1989 Tri-Con Leasing bought the assets and operations of Minneapolis-based Dougherty Dawkins Lease Corporation, Inc., a public lease financing group. Bell Atlantic also formed Bell Atlantic Systems Integration in 1989 to research and explore marketing capabilities in voice and data communications and in artificial intelligence.

Perhaps the biggest opportunity for Bell Atlantic came at year-end 1989, when it stepped up activity in the international arena. Economic changes in the Soviet Union and eastern Europe opened up entirely new possibilities in global telecommunications. Slowly exploring opportunities abroad since divestiture, Bell Atlantic was, by 1989, assisting in the installation of telephone software systems for the Dutch national telephone company, PTT Telecom, B.V., as well as for the national telephone company in Spain. A Bell Atlantic German subsidiary was awarded a contract to install microcomputers and related equipment at U.S. Army locations in Germany, Belgium, and the United Kingdom. With consultants located in Austria, France, Italy, and Switzerland, Bell Atlantic planned a European headquarters, Bell Atlantic Europe, S.A., to be located in Brussels, Belgium.

No matter how well the company was doing overseas, Bell Atlantic kept running into walls in the United States. In April 1990 the company's Chesapeake and Potomac Telephone Company was charged with fraud and was prohibited from seeking federal contracts by the U.S. Department of the Treasury. The dispute was over a long-running federal contract competition that AT&T had won twice; AT&T's contract award was withdrawn a third time because Bell Atlantic argued that the equipment necessary to fulfill the contract was not in current production. That was the same basis the Treasury used to charge Bell Atlantic with misrepresentation, claiming Bell Atlantic did not have the Northern Telecom integrated-services-digital network (ISDN) handset necessary to fulfill contract terms. (An ISDN combines telephone and computer transmissions on a single line.) AT&T, however, was not suspended from the bidding process; thereafter Bell Atlantic claimed the Treasury Department was operating on a double standard and abusing its authority. The contract was valued at $100 million and could be worth twice that after a two-year period.

Undaunted by its squabbles with the government, Bell Atlantic, by 1990, boasted the world's largest independent computer maintenance organization. Through its business systems division, the company was capable of servicing 500 brands of computers. With the January 1990 purchase of Control Data Corporation's third-party maintenance business, Bell Atlantic sealed its position as the leader in maintenance of both IBM and Digital Equipment Corporation systems.

Several other Bell Atlantic acquisitions of 1990 included Northern Telecom's regional PBX operations and Simborg Systems Corporation. Through the latter purchase, renamed Bell Atlantic Healthcare Systems, the company could offer hospital computer network software.

Aggressive as ever, in June 1990 Bell Atlantic, along with sibling U S West, upgraded to use synchronous optical fiber via Sonet-based equipment. These were the first two RHCs to use the systems; others waited for the technological standards to be established. In network services, Bell Atlantic invested more than $2 billion. SS7 was available in 80% of its customer lines, and ISDN was already operational in several universities and federal agencies. In sum, Bell Atlantic offered more choices by year-end 1990 than any information transmission competitor.

Bell Atlantic's biggest strides after six years in operation were in its international division. In May 1990 the corporation teamed up with the Korean Telecommunications Authority in a variety of research, marketing, and information exchanges. In June Bell Atlantic joined U S West and signed with the Czechoslovakian Ministry of Posts and Telecommunications to modernize the country's telecommunications network, which included both the construction and operation of a mobile cellular communications system. Bell Atlantic's investment of $105 million, to be paid over ten years, would give Bell Atlantic 24.5% of both the cellular and public data network.

That same month Bell Atlantic, with Ameritech and two New Zealand companies, acquired the Telecom Corporation of New Zealand. The purchase was a boon for all companies involved, as the New Zealand network was already digitally advanced and in a relaxed regulatory environment. The RHCs each paid an initial investment of $1.2 billion.

In October 1990, Bell Atlantic and NORVANS, a Norwegian telecommunications company, jointly applied for a license to develop and operate an independent cellular network in Norway. In November, with the Directorate General of Telecommunications of the Republic of China, Bell Atlantic signed an agreement to consult in marketing, research, and information exchanges. Continuing international expansion, Bell Atlantic early in 1991 joined the Belle Meade International Telephone, Inc., in a joint venture to set up a communication system in the Soviet Union. Bell Atlantic was keeping on its course of becoming an international telecommunications leader.

Principal Subsidiaries: Bell Atlantic Network Services, Inc.; New Jersey Bell Telephone Company; The Bell Telephone Company of Pennsylvania; The Diamond State Telephone Company; The Chesapeake and Potomac Telephone Company; The Chesapeake and Potomac Telephone Company of Maryland; The Chesapeake and Potomac Telephone Company of Virginia; The Chesapeake and Potomac Telephone Company of West Virginia; Bell Atlanticom Systems, Inc.; Bell Atlantic Capital Corporation; Bell Atlantic Customer Services, Inc.; Bell Atlantic Mobile Systems, Inc.; Bell Atlantic Systems Integration Corp.; Bell Atlantic Directory Graphics, Inc. (81%); Bell Atlantic Education Services, Inc.; Bell Atlantic International, Inc.; Chesapeake Directory Sales Co. (51%); Technology Concepts, Inc.; Telecommunications Specialists, Inc.; Bell Atlantic Capital Advisors, Inc.; Bell Atlantic Financial Services, Inc.; Bell Atlantic Properties, Inc.

Further Reading: Tell, Lawrence J., "Footloose and Fancy Free," *Barron's,* November 12, 1984; Gold, Howard, "Tom Bolger's one-stop-shop," *Forbes,* March 25, 1985; Lannon, Larry, "Bell Atlantic's Bolger Demands His Freedom," *Telephony,* July 14, 1986; Mason, Charles, "RHC barred from federal contracts," *Telephony,* April 16, 1990.

—Frances E. Norton

BELLSOUTH CORPORATION

1155 Peachtree Street, Northeast
Atlanta, Georgia 30367
U.S.A.
(404) 249-2000

Public Company
Incorporated: 1983
Employees: 102,000
Sales: $14.35 billion
Stock Exchanges: New York Boston Midwest Pacific
   Philadelphia London Zürich Basel Geneva Frankfurt
   Amsterdam Tokyo

BellSouth Corporation is one of seven regional telephone hold-ing companies in the United States, each with a virtual monop-oly on local telephone service in its region. BellSouth is the largest and fastest growing of the seven. In addition to local telephone service it also is engaged in cellular telephone ser-vices, telephone directories, data telecommunications, and long-distance telephone services outside the United States.

BellSouth was formed in 1983 as part of the court-ordered breakup of the American Telephone and Telegraph Company (AT&T), at that time the world's largest corporation. AT&T had built most of the U.S. phone system but was frequently accused of suppressing competition through unfair trade prac-tices. It was broken up in keeping with a consent decree to settle a lawsuit brought by the U.S. Department of Justice. AT&T had left the operation of local telephone service in the United States to 22 local telephone companies, all operating under AT&T's umbrella. The breakup divided the 22 locals among seven regional holding companies (RHCs). BellSouth was formed from the combination of Southern Bell Telephone and Telegraph Co. and South Central Bell Telephone Co. Its territory is composed of Florida, Georgia, South Carolina, North Carolina, Kentucky, Tennessee, Alabama, Mississippi, and Louisiana. BellSouth and the other RHCs were not free to enter any business they chose. The consent decree prohibited them from using their monopoly power to their advantage and from entering certain businesses, including long-distance tele-phone service. At that time the new corporation named John L. Clendenin chairman.

BellSouth began as the 12th-largest corporation in the United States, with $11 billion in assets, 13.4 million tele-phone lines, and 131,500 employees. It was also the most profitable of the seven regionals, with a promising future be-cause it was located in one of the fastest-growing areas of the country. Six of the ten fastest-growing counties in the United States were in BellSouth's territory. Southern and South Cen-tral already were prospering, their combined assets having grown 47% and their combined net income having grown 65% in the four years before the AT&T breakup. Collectively they had spent $15 billion on plant modernization and new facilities in the five years before BellSouth's creation.

AT&T had often used the South as the testing ground for new technologies, which gave BellSouth a lead in high-technology services, such as using telephone lines to monitor gas meters. Shortly before the breakup, Southern Bell began a joint videotex project, which enables subscribers to use home computers for banking and shopping. BellSouth continued that push into new technologies, starting a mobile phone subsidi-ary, BellSouth Mobility Inc., in its first year of business. In March 1984 BellSouth Mobility started a cellular telephone system in Chattanooga, Tennessee, in a joint venture with Cel-lular Radio of Chattanooga, Inc. and Chattanooga-Northwest Georgia Cellular Radio Inc. It then began a $5.2 million cellu-lar system in Memphis, Tennessee. In May 1984 it agreed to develop a $3.3 million cellular network in Baton Rouge, Loui-siana, with East Ascension Telephone Co. and Star Telephone Co., and a $4.8 million cellular system in Orlando, Florida. Plans were laid to expand many of these cellular networks even as they were being built. South Central Bell offered fiber-optic lines, completing the first direct customer hookup for Amsouth Bancorp late in 1984. Also in 1984 South Central began offering WatchAlert, a system that allowed a security-alarm signal to be transmitted even if a phone line was busy or cut. To promote these technologies to multitenant business of-fices, BellSouth Enterprises, Inc. formed BellSouth Systems Technology in 1984. The subsidiary focused on directory pub-lishing and advertising, mobile communications, and com-puter systems. BellSouth made $1.26 billion in 1984.

BellSouth, along with five other RHCs, began trading on the London Stock Exchange within its first few months of business, to gain access to European capital. In the rapidly changing telecommunications market, BellSouth could not count on all of its large customers continuing to use it for long-distance access. Advances in technology meant that large com-panies could bypass the local network and tie directly into the long-distance system through microwave antennas. BellSouth hired market researchers to develop profiles of the company's major customers. It then established special teams to work with the top 200 customers and to encourage them to continue using the BellSouth network for long-distance access. The res-idential market was split into groups based on income and phone-use patterns, with services pitched to the customer groups that would be most interested in them.

In 1984 South Central put a rate increase into effect before it was approved. The Mississippi Public Service Commission subsequently denied the rate increase. In 1985 South Central paid back—by order of the Mississippi Supreme Court—$199 million to Mississippi customers. In 1985 BellSouth signed a four-year contract to buy telecommunications equipment from Canada's Northern Telecom Inc. In the same year the Georgia Public Service Commission approved a $27 million rate in-crease for Southern Bell. The FCC ended its requirement that all Bell operating companies sell cellular telephones through a separate subsidiary. BellSouth earned $1.42 billion in 1985.

In February 1986 BellSouth Enterprises increased its presence in the lucrative cellular telephone market when it bought 15% of Mobile Communications Corp. of America for $107.5 million. The following year BellSouth Enterprises bought almost all the assets of Universal Communications Systems Inc. for $79.1 million.

By 1986 the national Yellow Pages market reached $6.8 billion, and BellSouth was expanding its Yellow Pages services out of its area of operation in search of greater profits. In February 1986 the company bought L.M. Berry & Co., a large, independent Yellow Pages publisher whose 1985 revenues topped $780 million. That made BellSouth a world leader in the profitable directory publishing business and the largest Yellow Pages publisher in the United States. The company, however, faced stiff competition for the Yellow Pages market from other companies, particularly Southwestern Bell, which was also trying to expand Yellow Pages services.

In 1987 BellSouth began offering an information gateway service that let customers access data bases using a personal computer. By dialing a number in the Atlanta area, customers could get stock quotes and make airline reservations. Customers with cellular phones could also dial a number to get local traffic reports. BellSouth continued foreign expansion by buying an Australian phone-answering machine company.

BellSouth and the other regional holding companies were dealt a major legal setback in 1987 when Justice Harold Greene, who was overseeing the breakup of AT&T, ruled that the companies still could not enter the long-distance telephone business in the United States, offer advanced information services, or manufacture phone equipment. Greene ruled that removing the restrictions would impede competition and violate antitrust laws. BellSouth and the other regionals appealed. Greene's ruling, however, prevented the regionals from transmitting only information they collected themselves. The regionals could not own or develop their own databases, but they were allowed to transmit third parties' databases. BellSouth was, therefore, able to sign an agreement with Telenet Corporation to link some of its local and national communications networks.

BellSouth hoped to increase the use of on-line information services and increase the revenue from its local network. In 1987 BellSouth's government systems division won a $25 million contract from the U.S. Army to modernize telecommunications systems at six installations in Alaska, Arizona, Colorado, and Texas.

By 1988 BellSouth was the fastest growing regional holding company, with an impressive use of new technologies and services and the addition of 600,000 new telephone lines to the network every year. That growth allowed BellSouth to install new switches and fiber-optic cables without having to tear out old equipment before it was fully depreciated. BellSouth had the largest sales, $13.6 billion; most assets, $28.5 billion; and highest profits, $1.7 billion, of all the regional holding companies in 1988. Part of the growth came from the Southeast's rapid expansion. The area's population had grown 4.3% since 1984, adding 4.5% to annual phone-line growth. The growth also came partly because BellSouth's network was the most technologically advanced in the United States, with 95.3% of its switching offices using electronic controls and nearly 98% of its major trunk lines using high-capacity fiber-optic cable. Profits were helped because BellSouth had avoided the ill-fated diversification pursued by most other RHCs, sticking instead to telephone-related businesses. While most other RHCs suffered demoralizing strikes over health care costs in 1988, BellSouth had kept down health care costs and avoided confrontation. In 1989 *Fortune* magazine labeled the company "the most admired utility" for these reasons.

In 1988 BellSouth spent $3.2 billion on advanced digital switching and transmissions systems to improve communications and lay the groundwork for new telecommunications services. Clendenin wanted to use BellSouth's advanced network to transmit a great variety of voice, data, and television programs into millions of homes for far less money than the cost of using conventional copper lines. It was the first RHC to bring fiber-optic cables directly to homes, hoping to use them to transmit security and energy-management information and cable television, in addition to voices.

BellSouth won a $55 million telephone-switch contract from the U.S. government in late 1987. In 1988, however, amid accusations that it had improperly obtained information from a government employee in the process of bidding on the contract, BellSouth withdrew its bid, and the government awarded the contract to AT&T.

Despite its early entry into cellular systems, BellSouth lost several cellular phone deals to rival RHCs. Cellular service was an area in which the regionals were allowed to compete outside of their local territory, and the lost deals meant lost opportunities to expand BellSouth's reach in a rapidly growing telecommunications market. In 1988 BellSouth reversed the trend, buying Mobile Communications Corp. for $710 million in stock. The acquisition made BellSouth the third-largest U.S. cellular telephone company, with 345,000 subscribers. It also got BellSouth into paging services. The Republican and Democratic conventions of 1988 were both held in BellSouth's market area. The company displayed its latest technology at both conventions, hoping to influence government officials to ease restrictions. Profits in 1988 were $1.67 billion.

The year 1989 began with a disappointment when Bell Atlantic beat out BellSouth in the competition for a $220 million, ten-year contract to build an advanced phone system to link government agencies in the Washington, D.C., area. Nevertheless, business was flourishing for BellSouth and for telecommunications in general. Telecommunications was a bigger business than computers or aerospace in 1989, and telephone use was growing three times faster than the population. Industry observers agreed that BellSouth, along with the other regionals, was running and selling basic local phone service better than it had been doing as part of AT&T.

In 1989 BellSouth bought the 60% of Air Call Communications that it did not already own for $34.5 million. BellSouth wanted to offer electronic Yellow Pages, but the idea was rejected in 1989 by Justice Greene, who ruled it would violate the consent decree that broke up AT&T. BellSouth moved toward further expansion of its cellular network when it formed a consortium with two British companies, The General Electric Company, PLC, and The Plessey Company, PLC, to bid on one of the mobile-telephone network licenses being offered by the British government. BellSouth then agreed to merge its cellular properties with LIN Broadcasting Corp., which would have created the second-largest cellular network in the United States. Rival McCaw Cellular Communications Inc., the largest cellular firm in the United States, however, raised its offer for LIN and ended up buying the company after a long battle. McCaw paid BellSouth $66.5 million in merger termination fees and other expenses.

BellSouth's local phone earnings, along with those of the other regional holding companies, were regulated by state commissions that allowed only a certain rate of return, about 12% to 15% by 1989. When earnings exceeded those rates, BellSouth had to give refunds. BellSouth pushed for incentive-based rate plans that would allow the company to keep a percentage of profits it earned above the allowed rate of return. It argued that the incentives would make the company more efficient and lead to better service. Three BellSouth states, Alabama, Florida, and Kentucky, passed such laws, but regulatory commissions then cut the rates BellSouth could earn. The rate cuts were expected to cost BellSouth $690 million in the early 1990s.

Continuing its interest in advancing technology, in 1990 BellSouth won FCC permission to test a wireless telephone system at the University of Georgia in Athens with the Sony Corporation. As part of a cost-cutting program, the company offered an early retirement incentive to nearly 3,000 executives.

By 1990 BellSouth had invested $550 million in overseas operations and was the only regional offering mobile communications on four continents. Telephone services that had been nationalized in many countries were being privatized, present-ing huge business opportunities. BellSouth pushed its services in the Caribbean and Latin America. It had cellular telephone interests in Argentina, Uruguay, France, Britain, Switzerland, and Mexico; paging interests in Australia, Britain, and Switzerland; and it started a joint venture in India to create telecommunications software products and services. The Australian company, Link Telecommunications, boasted that country's largest independent paging and telephone-answering services. In August 1990 BellSouth announced plans to develop a digital cellular phone system in New Zealand by mid-1992. BellSouth executives scrambled to learn foreign business practices. In Argentina they billed customers every ten days to keep pace with that country's steep inflation.

Principal Subsidiaries: BellSouth Enterprises, Inc.; BellSouth Services Inc.; South Central Bell Telephone Company; Southern Bell Telephone and Telegraph Company.

Further Reading: Schmidt, William E., "BellSouth Eager for Kickoff," *The New York Times,* November 15, 1983; Gannes, Stuart, "BellSouth Is On A Ringing Streak," *Fortune,* October 9, 1989.

—Scott M. Lewis

BRITISH
TELECOMMUNICATIONS PLC

BT Centre
81 Newgate Street
London EC1A 7AJ
United Kingdom
(071) 356 5000
Fax: (071) 356 5520

Public Company
Incorporated: 1984
Employees: 220,000
Sales: £12.32 billion (US$23.03 billion)
Stock Exchanges: London New York Toronto Tokyo

British Telecommunications plc, commonly known as BT, was born under the sign of change. In the early 1990s the largest investor-owned company in Europe in terms of sales, it came into being in spring 1984, through the transformation of a former state utility, at a turning point in the development of U.K. and European telecommunications. Like its competitors, it has seen its history largely molded by two factors—rapid technological advance, including the convergence of telecommunications and computing; and, with early moves toward the deregulation of the European Community telecommunications services market, the increasing pressure of national and international market forces.

In its first few years of existence the company had to confront the consequences of two major changes in its United Kingdom environment. The first of these is the ongoing liberalization of the U.K. telecommunications market, a process responsible for the creation of BT. The second factor is the privatization of the company itself. The public utility aspect of communications, earlier institutionalized in the U.K. Post Office, had then to hold its own in double harness, or as some critics maintain, with the interests of shareholders. BT's main activity is supplying telecommunication services in the U.K. market of 55 million people in accordance with the obligation imposed on the company by its 25-year operating license from the Department of Trade and Industry. As well as providing a vital infrastructural facility, BT plays a significant role in the national economy. It has 95% of the U.K. telecommunications market and is the United Kingdom's largest private-sector employer, employing 220,000 people in its home country. In the early 1990s it was the largest civilian purchaser of U.K. goods and services. In fiscal year 1990–1991 it spent £4 billion on

procurement. Led by its energetic chairman, Iain Vallance, and Mike Bett, deputy chairman, however, BT operates on a global scale. The company's acquisition and joint venture policy reflects an ambition to lead the world telecommunication services market.

The company's administrative and technological roots are mingled with those of the U.K. Post Office and reach back into the second half of the 19th century, when inventors at home and abroad, such as Alexander Graham Bell, Thomas Edison, and Guglielmo Marconi, were applying electromagnetic principles to the development of practicable forms of telecommunications. Out of this the modern telegraph, followed by the telephone, was born. In 1850 the first submarine telegraph cable was laid across the English Channel. In 1878 Bell demonstrated his newly patented telephone to Queen Victoria, and in 1879 England's first telephone exchange opened in London. It was in the United Kingdom, too, that the first international telephone call was made, in 1891, between England and France. The telegraph and telephone were at first exploited by private enterprises, but they were gradually taken over by a U.K. government department, the General Post Office. The reversal of that nationalization process is nearly complete.

In 1869 the Postmaster General was granted the exclusive right to transmit telegrams within the United Kingdom. At first the telephone was slow to catch on and was not regarded by the Post Office as a serious threat to its telegraphic network. The first independent U.K. telephone service provider, Telephone Company Ltd., was set up in 1879 and in 1880 merged with its competitor, Edison Telephone Company, to form United Telephone Company. Seeing that the telephone was beginning to take customers away from its telegraph service, the Post Office embarked on a series of protective measures, and in 1880 the government brought an action against the recently formed United Telephone Company, claiming that it was operating in contravention of the Telegraph Act of 1869. The High Court subsequently decided that the telephone was a form of telegraph. The merger was revoked, and telephone companies were required to be licensed by the telegraph monopoly holder, the Post Office.

The next stage in the process of squeezing out competition and establishing a state telephone monopoly was the building up of the Post Office's own system. In 1896 the Post Office completed its improved telephone network by taking over the trunk lines of National Telephone Company, the largest of its licensees, and started to set up its own local telephone exchanges. It was then decided that more national licenses would be granted. National Telephone Company continued to operate a local service until its license expired in 1911, but in 1912 the Post Office was granted a monopoly on the supply of telephone services throughout the United Kingdom. It took over all of National Telephone Company's exchanges and opened an automatic exchange in Epsom, south of London.

Since 1899 several of the larger towns and cities, including Glasgow, Brighton, Swansea, Portsmouth, and Kingston upon Hull (Hull), had each been operating an independent local telephone service, but their number gradually dwindled as they were bought out by National Telephone Company or the Post Office. In 1913 only Hull was left. By cooperating with successive competitors—National Telephone Company, the Post Office, and it has survived, first as the Hull Corporation Telephone Department, a municipal enterprise run by the Hull

City Council, and since 1987, as a limited company, Kingston Communications (Hull) PLC, wholly owned by Hull City Council. It is a licensed public telecommunications operator, with interconnection agreements with BT and BT's competitor, Mercury Telecommunications Limited.

A landmark in the prehistory of BT was the Post Office Act of 1969, which changed the status of the Post Office. This former government department became a state public corporation under the Secretary of State for Industry. The telecommunications services remained in the Post Office but were divided from the postal services into Post Office Telecommunications.

Three further events marked the telephone industry's move toward an environment of free competition. First came the passage of the 1981 British Telecommunications Act, which took Post Office Telecommunications out of the Post Office, turning it into an autonomous, though still state-owned, body known as British Telecommunications Corporation or, more familiarily, British Telecom. Second was the 1984 Telecommunications Act, by which BT was privatized, the telecommunications market was further liberalized, and a regulatory body was set up. Third, the Duopoly Review in 1990 resulted in the government's 1991 decision to further increase telecommunications competition. The government also decided to sell off its remaining shares in BT, although this decision was not influenced by the Duopoly Review.

In July 1981 the British Telecommunications Act that separated telecommunications from the Post Office and set up a new state public corporation to supply them also gave the government powers to license competitors in the operation of the domestic telephone network. As well as modifying the state company's statutory monopoly of the telephone network, this act took away its monopoly in the provision of telecommunication equipment, leaving it only with the right to supply and install a subscriber's first telephone. The act not only opened the market to competition in value-added services, such as data processing and storage, but allowed other providers to use BT's lines.

In October 1981 Mercury Communications Limited (Mercury) was chosen to receive a 25-year renewable license to operate a national and international digital network—a system that encodes information as a series of on-off signals—to compete with BT's trunk traffic. Mercury had been set up early in 1981 by British Petroleum, Barclay's Merchant Bank, and Cable and Wireless plc to enter the business of long-distance communications, offering a customized service to companies. The license allowed it to interconnect with the BT network and to enter the European and U.S. sectors. In 1983 the government undertook for seven years not to license any company but BT and Mercury to carry telecommunication services over fixed links. Under this duopoly policy, Mercury, which began operating in 1986, was to be BT's single serious network competitor until at least 1990. Mercury's market share in the early 1990s was variously estimated between 3.7% and 5%, but was increasing markedly. An efficiency and investment effort was BT management's response to this new competition and to growing demands and service expectations from its customers. Waiting times for connections and repairs were reduced, and new digital equipment was introduced into the network, including exchanges that use microchip technology to integrate the switching and transmission elements of the network, re-

sulting in a higher quality of service and improved voice transmission. In addition, new products, such as microwave radio transmission in the City of London, were offered. Less than a year after the 1981 Act, the government announced its intention of privatizing the British Telecommunications Corporation.

At the end of 1982 the first telecommunications bill had reached the committee stage, when the general election of May 1983 was called. The bill immediately died, but was presented again in the new Parliament and finally became law in its second form, the Telecommunications Act of April 12, 1984. It had undergone 320 hours of debate and discussion, during which BT itself had briefed members of Parliament on its views and interests. By the act, BT lost its exclusive right to run telecommunications systems, and all PTOs had to be licensed. The new company was to be sold as an integrated organization. Fragmentation, following the breakup of American Telephone and Telegraph Company (AT&T) in the United States, would leave the resultant entities too small to defend the home market from foreign competition, to stand up to multinationals in the world markets, and to command the technology and the financial strength for adequate research and development. The possibility of a breakup is still sometimes held over BT's head when conflict arises with the government. In November 1984, 3.01 billion ordinary shares of 25 pence were offered for sale at 130 pence per share, the first figure being the nominal or face value of the share, and the second its sale price, or market value, at the time of sale. The government retained a 48.6% stake in the new company, valued at the time of sale at £7.8 billion. All the offered shares were bought.

BT's performance and development have been conditioned since the 1984 act by an official regulatory body, the semi-independent Office of Telecommunications (Oftel), set up in August 1984 under the Secretary of State for Trade and Industry and headed by the Director General of Telecommunications, Sir Bryan Carsberg. A major role of this body has been, by simulating the effects of real competition, to prevent BT from abusing its inherited dominance of the U.K. telecommunications market during the process of deregulation. However, the fairness of the competition is often disputed by interested parties. In its severely regulated environment, BT has lost the security of being a state monopoly, without gaining the freedom of action of a wholly autonomous business. Oftel monitors BT's pricing, accounting, investment policies, and quality of services; issues licenses to further competitors; and continues to facilitate the interconnection of rival services to the BT network. Competitors, for their part, tend to feel that it is BT that is favored by the regulator. The new British Telecommunications plc created by the 1984 act then shared its monopoly in telecommunication systems with Mercury as well as Kingston Communications (Hull) PLC, plus some general licensees. For all intents and purposes, U.K. telecommunications were to be supplied by the BT and Mercury duopoly until 1991.

When BT became a separate state corporation in 1981, before its rebirth in 1984 as a privatized company, it inherited from its Post Office days an evolved network. This network had to be brought up to date at the same time BT was taking on competition from operators starting from scratch. These competitors were using the latest technology, without public service obligations and were able, for example, to go straight to digital systems and cheaper and more efficient optic fiber cable, while BT still had copper wire circuits to be amortized. BT's technology, however, is in the forefront, and the company spends 2% of its turnover on research and development to keep it there. The domestic telephone services sector is by far BT's largest operating division in terms of assets, revenue, and number of employees. In 1990 it accounted for nearly 75% of turnover. Its core business is the public switched telephone network (PSTN). The 20-millionth U.K. telephone was installed in 1975, the system became fully automatic in 1976, and in the early 1990s BT, with more than 25 million lines, operated the world's sixth-largest telephone network, with nearly 100,000 public payphones. In 1990 BTUK—the product of the 1987 merger of BT's local communications services and national networks divisions—was operating more than 7,000 local exchange units, of which nearly half were already digital. All trunk exchange units have been digital since June 1990. By 1986 there were 65,000 PABX's—private automatic branch exchanges, or private switchboards. The aim is a fully digital network by the year 2000. There are nearly a million kilometers of optic fiber in the network. However, even at more than 90% telephone penetration in the United Kingdom, BT and its competitors have some way to go before they catch up with France and the United States, which have already close to 100% telephone penetration. BT also sells, installs, and maintains a wide range of telecommunications equipment and products, from handsets to branch exchanges. British Telecom's profitable and expanding Worldwide Networks Division has a work force of 38,000 and offices in about 20 countries and on every continent, providing services, products, and expertise. Among its overseas activities are subsidiaries in the United States, Canada, Australia, Hong Kong, and Japan. In 1991 BT was preparing for the single European market that will exist after 1992 and was looking for opportunities in the newly opened East European markets, where it already provides expertise to several telecommunications companies.

Since 1981 BT has faced the most competition from Mercury for the U.K. business customer, and since 1984, from new providers. The capricious mobile communications market constitutes one of the most disputed areas. BT's Mobile Telephone System 4, a noncellular service introduced in 1981, with 7,000 subscribers at the beginning of 1990, had capacity problems at peak periods and was being replaced by a cellular network, Cellnet, shared by BT—60%—and Securicor Communications. Its rival, using another network, is Racal-Vodafone. In February 1989 BT bought, for £907 million, a 20% interest in its most important associated company, McCaw Cellular Communications, Inc., a U.S. mobile cellular telephone and broadcasting systems provider and operator.

In data communications, BT is striving to bring the U.K. market up to a volume comparable with that in other European countries and, like Mercury, is installing advanced networks for this purpose. BT offers a wide range of switched—telephone services that pass through an exchange—and nonswitched data transmission facilities. Its public data network provides nationwide data transmission; Datel provides higher-speed transmission; and International Datel offers transmission to 65 countries. The U.K. telex market has, like those of other West European providers, largely given way to fax, which BT supplies through a national and international bureau service, Bureaufax. BT, however, still provides an inland telex

service as well as an international one to more than 170 countries. Prestel, BT's public, computer-based information and communications service, launched in 1979, was the first in the world to be fully operational and is by far the largest in the United Kingdom. By 1990 there were more than 95,000 terminals installed, 45% of them for financial institutions, travel agents, hotels, and other business users. While still a state monopoly, BT had introduced a videoconferencing service in 1972. It now has videoconferencing—two-way sound and vision—links with the United States and Canada, as well as with France, Germany, Belgium, and the Netherlands.

BT offers a wide range of VANS—value-added network services, including such electronic mailbox services as Telecom Gold and Message Handling Service—in the U.K. VANS market, of which Mercury as yet enjoys only a small share. In November 1989, in order to further its strategies in the home and international VANS market, BT bought, for £231 million, the U.S. company Tymnet, one of the largest VANS companies in the world, and consolidated some of its own international services under a new company, BT Tymnet Inc. BT started setting up an ISDN—integrated services digital network—that could eventually replace the other networks by offering all data, voice, text, and image network services at high speed, with circuit-switched digital connections from a single access point. However, although ISDN is of primary importance in BT's plans for the future, the need to await definition of international standards and to raise the consciousness of potential customers, obliges the company, like others, to advance slowly in this area. A pilot service was launched by BT in June 1985 that by the end of 1989 was available to 75% of business users. In 1989 BT changed its ISDN to international CCITT—Commitée Consultatif International Télégraphe et Téléphone—standards. To assess its best uses, in the spring and summer of 1990, BT put its ISDN into a market development phase with customers and suppliers. Some of the technical drawbacks inherent in ISDN were targeted by the development of integrated broadband communications.

BT is an active participant in three satellite consortia—Eutelsat, European Telecommunications Satellite Organisation; Inmarsat, International Maritime Satellite Organisation; and Intelsat, International Telecommunications Satellite Organisation. A familiar landmark in the West End of London, the Telecom Tower, formerly the Post Office Tower, is the heart of BT's microwave transmission circuit. This is a high frequency radio link for transmission over line-of-sight routes. It provides broadcasting links with BT earth stations, allowing international transfer of television and radio material. BT also has 140,000 kilometers of sound circuits and 39,000 kilometers of vision circuits between studios and transmitters in the U.K.

In the early 1990s there were major changes. The duopoly policy was reviewed in 1990, and a report issued in January 1991 was followed two months later by a government recommendation that both BT and Mercury should face greater competition in both local, trunk, and international services. BT is still barred from offering entertainment services on cable TV, but after some hard bargaining, Sir Bryan Carsberg, director of telecommunications; Peter Lilley, secretary of state for trade and industry; and Iain Vallance, BT's chairman, agreed on amendments to BT's 25-year license. BT was then allowed to proceed with further rebalancing between telephone rentals and call charges and with customized tariffs. It was announced that the sale of a slice of the government's residual share in BT would take place in November 1991.

BT's preliminary results for the year ending March 31, 1991, showed a 14.2% increase in pretax profits and a 6.8% increase in turnover. The dividend per ordinary share at the time of the sale announcement was up from 10.5 pence in the previous year to 11.8 pence. In August 1991, in spite of poor growth in demand for services and the announcement of a 5% average increase in telephone charges, Iain Vallance declared an 11.3% rise in pretax profits, to £825 million, for the first quarter of the year. It appeared to many as if BT was being fattened up for market. BT had been engaged in a rationalizing and restructuring operation. In the year ending March 31, 1990, a slimming-down and cost-control operation had begun, covered by an exceptional charge of £390 million. In the following year, 18,800 jobs were shed and overtime work was cut, while another 10,000 terminations were planned for the year 1991 to 1992. In April 1991 the reshaped company announced that the former three operating divisions, BTUK, comprising Local Communications Services and National Networks; BTI, British Telecom International; and CSD, Communication Services Division, would be replaced. There are now two major divisions that deal directly with customers: Personal Communications and Business Communications, both supported by a Products and Services Division. BT's international and U.K. networks have been brought together into a new Worldwide Networks Division, and some business activities best managed separately, such as mobile communications and operator services, now comprise a Special Business Division.

Other European countries as well as Britain have opened to competition telecommunications equipment supply and some advanced services, but the United Kingdom is the only nation to have freed the provision of basic network infrastructure, such as the telephone services. In 1991 BT held the major portion of residential telephone connections, although Mercury had mounted a large publicity campaign to wrest customers away from BT. New competition could come from British utilities, such as British Rail, which had their own telephone networks already in place, but also from foreign private telecommunications operators or computer firms and from mobile and satellite network operators. Mercury is likely to protect itself against the giant BT by alliances with some of these newcomers.

Early in 1991 BT's intensified drive to consolidate its image as a smart, market-oriented world organization with a human face was signaled by its integration of the current BT acronym into a new blue and red logo, representing a dancing piper apparently delivering a sound message. A new designer image was commissioned for the group and was widely publicized; public telephones were replaced by newly designed models; and the bright yellow of BT vehicles began to be replaced, in a notoriously expensive replace-or-respray operation, by a stylish grey. Even if the future holds difficulties for BT in the form of growing competition, the possibility of a Labor government with a stern regulatory approach to privatized utilities, and the conjectured slowdown in a European market saturated with business services, BT patently has the muscle and the will to contend with such challenges. Technological resources multiply with magic speed, political and economic change is everywhere, and new paths are being cleared. BT, like the enthusiastic figure in its logo, is bounding forward.

Principal Subsidiaries: BT Property Ltd; BT (Marine) Limited; BT North America Inc. (USA); BT Repair Services Ltd; BT (Worldwide) Limited; British Telecom (CBP) Limited; International Aeradio plc; Manx Telecom Limited; Mitel Corporation (51%, Canada); Sharelink Limited (65%); Telecom Securicor Cellular Radio Limited (60%); Telecom Security Limited (90%); Yellow Page Sales Limited; BT & D Technologies Limited (40%); Belize Telecommunications Limited (25%); Gibraltar Telecommunications International Limited (50%); McCaw Cellular Communications, Inc. (20%); Marshalls Finance Limited (30% Ordinary, 94% Preference); Phonepoint Limited (45%).

Further Reading: Newman, Karin, *The Selling of British Telecom,* London, Holt, Rinehart and Winston, 1986; *The History & Development of Kingston Communications (Hull) PLC 1904 to Present Day,* Kingston-upon-Hull, Kingston Communications, 1988; "Major Telecommunications Companies in Europe," *Profile of the Worldwide Telecommunications Industry,* Oxford, Elsevier Advanced Technology, 1990; *Competition and Choice: Telecommunications Policy for the 1990s,* London, HMSO, March 1991; "Europe" and "The United Kingdom," *DATAPRO Reports on International Telecommunications 1990–91,* Delran, New Jersey, McGraw-Hill, 1990–1991.

—Olive Classe

CABLE & WIRELESS

CABLE AND WIRELESS PLC

New Mercury House
26 Red Lion Square
London WC1R 4UQ
United Kingdom
(071) 315 4000
Fax: (071) 315 5000

Public Company
Incorporated: 1929 as Imperial and International
  Communications Company Limited
Employees: 37,681
Sales: £2.32 billion (US$4.34 billion)
Stock Exchanges: London New York Tokyo Hong Kong
  Frankfurt Geneva Basel Zürich

As a provider of telecommunications services in some 50 territories around the globe, Cable and Wireless plc is a leading player in an industry that is growing at more than twice the average growth rate of those countries which it services. The company, whose fortunes once depended on telegraphic connections between the various parts of the British Empire, now operates all over the world, using equipment that even Guglielmo Marconi, the inventor of the wireless and one of the company's first directors, could not have dreamed of.

The history of the companies that became Cable and Wireless plc began in 1852, when a Manchester cotton merchant named John Pender joined other businessmen from the north of England on the board of the English and Irish Magnetic Telegraph Company, set up to run a telegraph cable service between London and Dublin. This was only two years after the first submarine cable had been laid, between England and France, and coincided with the first laying of cables in India, then Britain's largest overseas possession. Pender next became a director of the Atlantic Telegraph Company, whose first cable to the United States was laid in 1858 but failed to function properly. Six years later, when it became clear that the company could not afford to make a second attempt with its own resources, he was instrumental in creating the Telegraph Construction and Maintenance Company (Telcon) through a merger of the two leading cable-making companies, under Pender's chairmanship. However, the second cable broke and fell into the Atlantic during the laying stage in 1865. Pender and his colleagues had to set up a successor to the Atlantic Telegraph Company, the Anglo-American Telegraph Company Ltd, on

behalf of which Telcon not only retrieved the 1865 cable but successfully constructed and laid a transatlantic cable in 1866.

In 1868 the British government decided to buy up all the inland telegraph companies, including English and Irish Magnetic, a process completed in 1870, but left overseas telegraphy in private hands. In 1869 John Pender created three more companies. The British-Indian Submarine Telegraph Company and the Falmouth, Gibraltar and Malta Telegraph Company completed the cable system between London and Bombay in 1870, while the China Submarine Telegraph company set about connecting Singapore and Hong Kong, Britain's main possessions in East Asia. Pender's other company, Telcon, supplied cable not only for these ventures but also for a cable from Marseilles to Malta, which provided France with a link to its colonies in North Africa and Asia. When the governments of South Australia and Queensland, Australia, decided that the monthly steamships between Australia and Britain were too slow a means of communication, it was John Pender whom they invited to fill the telegraphic gap between Bombay and Adelaide, Australia. The All-Sea Australia to England Telegraph, supplied by Telcon, was opened in 1872. It was operated in two sections, Bombay to Singapore by the British India Extension Telegraph Company and Singapore to Adelaide by the British Australian Telegraph Company, both under Pender's control.

Pender now set about reorganizing his cable interests. First, in 1872, came the amalgamation of British Indian Submarine, Falmouth, Gibraltar and Malta, and the Marseilles, Algiers, and Malta companies with the Anglo-Mediterranean, which had been created in 1868 to link Malta, Alexandria, and the new Suez Canal. Pender became chairman of the Eastern Telegraph Company that resulted from their merger. Next, in 1873, he presided over the merger of his Australian, Chinese, and British India Extension companies into the Eastern Extension Australasia and China Telegraph Company. It was also in 1873 that Pender created a holding company, the Globe Telegraph and Trust Company, investors in which received portions of shares in the operating companies, chiefly the Eastern Telegraph and the Anglo-American. All the companies so far named remained within the Eastern Telegraph group, except Anglo-American, which was taken over in 1910 by a U.S. firm, Western Union. Finally, 1873 also saw the creation of the Brazilian Submarine Telegraph Company, which had several directors and shareholders in common with Eastern Telegraph and opened a cable from Lisbon, Portugal, to Pernambuco, Brazil, in 1874.

Between 1879 and 1889 Pender's group added Africa to its list of cable routes through three companies, African Direct, a joint venture with Brazilian Submarine; West African, incorporated into Eastern Telegraph; and Eastern and South African. In 1892, following the expiration of the telegraph concession operated by Brazilian Submarine, that company and its main rival, Western and Brazilian, formed a new venture, the Pacific and European Telegraph Company, to renew the concession and link Brazil with Chile and Argentina. Having helped to arrange this operation Pender became chairman of Brazilian Submarine in 1893, further reinforcing his position as the leading figure in the worldwide cable business. John Pender died in 1896; his successor as chairman of Eastern Telegraph and Eastern Extension was Lord Tweeddale, while Pender's son John Denison-Pender, later Sir John, continued as managing director. The last stage in restructuring the set of companies Pender had been so instrumental in creating came in 1899, when Brazilian Submarine, having absorbed two other London-based telegraph companies operating in South America, was renamed the Western Telegraph Company.

The first confrontation between cable and the new medium of wireless ended in acrimony. Guglielmo Marconi's success in sending a signal from Cornwall to Newfoundland, in 1901, was soured when the Anglo-American Telegraph Company, part of the Pender group, forbade any further experiments, since they would infringe on the Pender group's monopoly of communications in Newfoundland. Marconi moved his work to Nova Scotia, and found Americans and Canadians generally more receptive to his achievement than Europeans. Certainly the Eastern Telegraph group remained unimpressed, citing lack of privacy, lack of speed, interruptions, and mixing of messages as decisive disadvantages of wireless compared with cable. Even so, the management was cautious enough to have a mast secretly installed at its Cornwall station with which to listen in on Marconi's experiments and, on at least one occasion, to disrupt a demonstration of wireless transmission.

In 1900 the governments of Britain, Australia, New Zealand, and Canada had agreed on the joint financing of a Pacific Cable, for which the construction contract was won by Telcon. The project began 21 years after it had first been proposed by Sandford Fleming, the chief engineer of the Canadian Pacific Railway. It eventually involved the laying of the largest single piece of cable so far—4,000 miles, out of a total Pacific Cable length of 7,836 miles—but was completed ahead of schedule, in October 1902. Alarmed by this competition from public enterprise, the Eastern Telegraph group reduced rates on its cables in 1900, and laid a cable across the Indian Ocean to serve the three Australian states—South Australia, Western Australia, and Tasmania—which had refused to join the Pacific project.

Throughout World War I all cable services out of Britain were controlled by the government. The Eastern Telegraph group profited enormously from the diversion of business to India and East Asia away from the German-owned overland routes and from the general use of telegrams in preference to letters, which were delayed by lack of civilian shipping. For the first time cables became targets of warfare in themselves. Eastern Telegraph, the British Royal Navy, and the British General Post Office collaborated on cutting all cable links between Germany and North America. The Germans temporarily disabled both the Pacific Cable and the cable across the Indian Ocean, by attacking island stations in each ocean. However, the most spectacular event of the first "cable war" came in 1917, when, following the United States's entry into the war, the German cable that had been cut three years before was lifted out of its position between New York and Emden, Germany, moved to a new position between Nova Scotia and Cornwall, and taken over by the British government as a prize of war, to be operated by the General Post Office. In 1920 the government decided to keep this cable, despite U.S. protests, and to purchase a second line, the two together being renamed Imperial Cable.

The wartime boom in Eastern Telegraph group's business gave way to slack trading in the early 1920s, as government telegrams declined in number and length, overland rivals got back to work, and the Pacific and Imperial Cables became direct competitors for communications with North America and Australia. However, the biggest blow to the whole cable business was struck once again by Marconi when he succeeded, in 1924, in telephoning Australia from England on short-wave radio equipment. This latest kind of wireless worked faster, cost less, and used less energy than either long-wave radio transmission or cable, and offered a flexibility its rivals did not then have, since it transmitted both telephony and telegraphy. Five years later the Marconi-Wright facsimile system added picture transmission to wireless's advantages. Within six months of its establishment, the General Post Office's system of short-wave stations had taken 65% of the Eastern Telegraph group's business, as well as more than 50% of Pacific Cable's, and its service cost a fraction of the price of cabling. In the meantime, however, the cable systems were given a new lease on life, from 1925 onwards, as manual re-transmission of messages, at points where the signals weakened with distance, gave way to far less time- and labor-intensive automatic regeneration, using a system devised by Telcon.

At the suggestion of the private Marconi company, which operated separately from the G.P.O. but under a G.P.O. license, Sir John Denison-Pender met its chairman, Lord Inverforth, in December 1927, to decide on a joint response to the Imperial Wireless and Cable Conference called for the following month. In March 1928 they both signed a letter to the conference proposing a merged holding company, owned 56.25% by the Eastern Telegraph group's shareholders and 43.75% by Marconi's. This was against the wishes of the father of wireless himself, who had lost the chairmanship of his own company the year before. The conference accepted this plan. On April 8, 1929, two new companies began trading. One, Cable and Wireless Limited, had two functions, first, to control all the nontraffic interests, such as patent rights and manufacturing, and secondly to hold all the shares in the cable companies and Marconi. They, in turn, were exclusive owners of the second company, Imperial and International Communications Limited, which owned and operated the actual cable and radio stations, cables, ships, and other assets of Eastern Telegraph and Marconi, as well as the U.K. government's Imperial and Pacific Cables and, on lease, the Post Office transmitting stations. In 1934 the companies were renamed, respectively, Cable and Wireless (Holding) Limited and Cable and Wireless Limited. From the outset they were controlled by a single board, known, on the model of the Bank of England, as the Court of Directors, as Cable and Wireless's board still was in the early 1990s. Since Sir John Denison-Pender had died one month before the companies started up, it was his son John Cuthbert who became governor, and Lord Inverforth sole president of the Court.

The Great Depression hit the new companies badly. Between 1929 and 1935 the number of chargeable words carried fell by more than half, and net profits, just over £1 million in 1929, declined to £75,000 in 1931 and reached only £625,000 in 1934. By 1933 the work force had been reduced by about a third and the introduction of telex in 1932 helped to cut operating costs. Competition was intensifying, as U.S.-owned International Telephone and Telegraph Corporation (ITT) expanded worldwide and Imperial Airways built up its inexpensive air mail service with subsidies from the same governments whose 1928 conference had led to the creation of Imperial and

International. Some expansion of the cable and wireless businesses did occur, however, with the acquisition of wireless concessions in Southern Rhodesia—(now Zimbabwe), Singapore (replacing the old Bombay-Rangoon cable), Turkey, and Peru, as well as domestic telephone services in Turkey, Cyprus, and Hong Kong. The structure agreed for Cable and Wireless in 1928 was altered slightly ten years later. In return for giving the company ownership, rather than rental, of the short-wave radio system created by the General Post Office, the British government took shares in the company for the first time, although for the time being it waived its right to appoint a director to the Court. At the same time an empire flat rate scheme was introduced, cutting the company's prices to the public and improving its finances.

World War II revived the cable war of 1914–1918. In 1939 German-owned cables across the Atlantic were cut once again, and in 1940 Italian cables to South America and Spain were cut in retaliation for Italian action against two of the five British cables linking Gibraltar and Malta. Electra House, the company's head office and central cable station, was damaged by German bombing in 1941. However, the company made a considerable contribution to the Allied war effort, supplying, for instance, the wireless equipment with which the North African campaign was conducted in 1942, and sending staff, in army uniforms marked with Telcom flashes, into several campaigns, starting in Italy in 1943. In Britain the end of the European war was followed by the election of a Labour government on a program that included expanding state ownership of leading industries. With the consent of the governments of the other independent countries in the Commonwealth—as the former British Empire was then to be known—Cable and Wireless was put on the shopping list, although the holding company and the main assets—cables, ships, and wireless stations—were not. All shares in Cable and Wireless were transferred to the government on January 1, 1947, while Cable and Wireless (Holding) became an investment trust. In 1948 the company made an agreement with the government of Hong Kong to provide external telecommunications for the colony.

In 1950, following another agreement among the Commonwealth governments, most of Cable and Wireless's U.K. assets and staff were transferred to the General Post Office, just as parts of its assets overseas were acquired by governmental bodies in the other countries involved. Even so, Cable and Wireless remained the largest single international telegraphy enterprise in the world, with 186,000 miles of submarine cable still converging on a station at Porthcurno in Cornwall, England, that had been opened in 1870. By the time the station closed in 1970, the company's business had been transformed. As telegraphy became obsolete in the 1950s the development of coaxial voice transmission offered the chance to switch over to telephone cables. The company's first venture into this new field was its participation, with American Telephone and Telegraph Company and the Canadian Overseas Telecommunications Corporation, in the laying of TAT-1, the first telephone cable across the Atlantic, completed in 1956. The transmission of the high frequencies needed for telephone links under the sea had been technically possible for 30 years, but plans to lay such a cable in 1928 had been aborted by the Depression. TAT-1 was followed by the opening, in 1961, of CANTAT, a telephone cable between Scotland and Canada which, in a departure from its own traditions,

Cable and Wireless helped to lay and owned half of but took no part in operating. CANTAT was a single cable, capable of transmitting communication simultaneously in both directions. The completion of the projected Commonwealth round-the-world cable continued in stages, with COMPAC, a system that could provide capacity of at least 60 channels over distances of several hundred miles, linking Canada to Australia, New Zealand, and Fiji, being finished in 1963; and SEACOM, linking Singapore to Australia, in 1967. Cable and Wireless retained its participation in COMPAC and SEACOM, but sold its half of CANTAT to the British Post Office in 1971.

Throughout the 1960s more and more U.K. overseas possessions became independent states. In many cases their external telecommunications systems had been operated by Cable and Wireless, which then became junior partner, with the various new governments, in East African External Communications Limited (1964), Sierra Leone External Telegraph Limited (1964), Trinidad and Tobago External Telecommunications Company (1970), and other such joint ventures. Nigeria's decision, in 1966, to take 100% ownership was thus unusual.

By 1972 Cable and Wireless's largest operation was in Hong Kong, where the international telephone service it operated provided 88% of its profits, and it was here that it launched Cable and Wireless Systems Limited as a subsidiary offering specialized services. In its first few years these included microwave systems—high frequency radio links for transmission over line-of-sight routes—for customers in Hong Kong, Brunei, and Thailand, a satellite earth station in Nauru, an island in the Pacific Ocean near the equator, and airline communications in the Persian Gulf. Diversification was made even more imperative in 1973, when the Brazilian government withdrew the concession first granted 100 years earlier. Another subsidiary, Eurotech BV, was set up that year as a holding company for projects in the European community, and through participation in supplying the communications network for the U.K. sector of the North Sea oil fields. By 1978 Cable and Wireless's specialized projects included electronic systems for hotels, security systems, marine telex, and, under the largest contract in its history, communications systems for the Saudi Arabian National Guard. Cable and Wireless's reconstruction as an international telecommunications company had been entirely self-financed. While it received no assistance at all from U.K. taxpayers, its profits went to its sole shareholder, the U.K. government. However, a new administration came into office in 1979, determined to privatize as much of the state-owned sector as possible, and in 1981 it decided to sell just less than half of the shares in Cable and Wireless. By 1985 all of the shares in the company had been sold to the private sector apart from a single "golden share" retained by the government. The company's franchise to provide Hong Kong's international telecommunications was renewed in 1981, when Cable and Wireless (Hong Kong) was formed. The acquisition of Hong Kong Telephone in 1984 added the domestic services to the company's portfolio. These two companies were restructured in 1988 with the formation of Hong Kong Telecom which, by 1990, still provided half of Cable and Wireless's profits.

The 1980s saw a further transformation in the company's business, from dependence on service concessions from governments to a more varied range of governmental and commercial ventures. To take just one example, in 1981 it launched its subsidiary Mercury Communications Ltd.—initially a joint venture with Barclays Bank and British Petroleum—to compete against British Telecom, which then held a monopoly in providing telephone services in the United Kingdom. By 1990 Cable and Wireless had invested more than £1 billion in Mercury, which was estimated to have taken 3% of the U.K. telephone market from British Telecom. This was a more impressive result than it may sound; a great deal of Mercury's business was in the more profitable areas of long-distance and business communications, so that it was able to generate about 25% of Cable and Wireless's turnover. In 1991, with the entry of new competitors into the industry looking more and more likely, Cable and Wireless decided to continue Mercury's specialization in business and international services and to develop further its mobile telephone venture, Mercury PCN. Lord Young, the erstwhile trade and industry secretary, became chairman of Cable and Wireless in October 1990.

Between April 1989 and March 1990, Cable and Wireless formed new companies in Yemen and the Seychelles to continue telecommunications services. In Pakistan, a subsidiary set up a mobile telephone network, while in the Caribbean the company extended the list of countries where it provided both domestic and international services. The company's presence in the Caribbean was enhanced in 1990 by its further purchase of shares in Telecommunications of Jamaica Ltd. from the Jamaican government and raising its holding from 59% to 79%. Cable and Wireless also owns 70% of Grenada Telecommunications. In spite of diversification the company's Hong Kong businesses remain central to its profitability. Since Hong Kong will revert to Chinese sovereignty in 1997, it is obviously very important for Cable and Wireless to work closely with the regime in Beijing, whatever unease there may have been following the massacre in Tienanmen Square in 1989.

Cooperation has taken various forms. First, in March 1990 the China International Trust and Investment Corp. (CITIC), the Chinese Government's international investment body, bought 20% of the shares in Hong Kong Telecom from Cable and Wireless, having already invested in Cable and Wireless's subsidiary in Macao. Cable and Wireless's own holding in Hong Kong Telecom was subsequently increased from 55.1 to 58.5%. Secondly, April 1990 saw the launch of AsiaSat, the first privately financed domestic telecommunications satellite in Asia, from a site in China into an orbit covering half the population of the planet from the China Sea to the Mediterranean. Ownership of the satellite is shared equally by Cable and Wireless, the Hong Kong company Hutchison Whampoa, and CITIC. Thirdly, in June 1990 the Chinese government decided to make Guangzhou its third point of entry for telecommunications, after Beijing and Shanghai, thus further boosting the importance of Hong Kong Telecom to the Chinese economy. Hong Kong Telecom then began to construct fiber optic cable links to southern China. When opened in March 1991, these doubled the telecommunications capacity between the crown colony and the People's Republic of China.

The company's main objective for the 1990s is the completion of what it calls the global digital "highway," linking the centers of the world economy through fiber optic cables. The highway will include the private transatlantic telecommunications cable, which came into operation in the autumn of 1989 to link customers of Cable and Wireless and of its U.S. partner, US Sprint, in the United Kingdom, and the United States and, via connections to Ireland, the European mainland, and Bermuda, and many other Atlantic countries too. The highway also includes the North Pacific Cable, which opened one year later as a joint venture between Cable and Wireless, U.S. company Pacific Telecom, and Japanese company IDC, of which Cable and Wireless owns more than 16%. The fortunes of Cable and Wireless and its predecessors have depended, above all, on the political situation in the areas in which they have operated. The company's business could not have been built up without the approval and cooperation of governments, first in the British Empire and the Commonwealth, then all over the world, and their interest in communications has made them Cable and Wireless's main customers, although less overwhelmingly so now than in the imperial past. However, if the company can maintain its long-established tradition of adaptability, and if the former Soviet bloc and at least some countries in the Third World enter onto paths of steady development, the next 140 years of Cable and Wireless may well be as busy and successful as most of the last 140 were.

Principal Subsidiaries: Mercury Communications Ltd.; Hong Kong Telecommunications Ltd. (58.5%); Hong Kong Telephone Company Ltd.; Hong Kong Telecom International Ltd.; Telecommunications of Jamaica Ltd. (79%); Cable & Wireless North America Inc. (U.S.A.); Companhia de Telecomunicacoes de Macau SARL (51%, Macao); Barbados External Telecommunications Ltd. (85%).

Further Reading: Barty-King, Hugh, *Girdle Around the Earth,* London, Heinemann, 1979.

—Patrick Heenan

DEUTSCHE BUNDESPOST TELEKOM

Godesberger Allee 117,
5300, Bonn 2
Federal Republic of Germany
(228) 1-81-0
Fax: (228) 18188

State-Owned Company
Incorporated: 1989
Employees: 260,000
Sales: DM40.59 billion (US$26.79 billion)

Deutsche Bundespost Telekom (DBP TELEKOM), the German state near-monopoly responsible for telecommunications, was formed in 1989 when Germany's post and telecommunications company, Deutsche Bundespost, was divided into three separate companies, each with its own board of management and separate accounts. Chancellor Kohl's Christian Democrat-dominated government had begun to explore the possibility of privatization in the late 1980s, but had encountered strong opposition and had had to settle for a reform law that split the company into three separate companies: DBP Postdienst (postal services), DBP Postbank (bank services), and DBP TELEKOM (telecommunications).

Some observers noted that the reform, aimed at making the companies more independent and efficient, would make any future privatization easier. By late 1991 the enormous financial costs of updating the former East German telephone system and absorbing it into the Bundespost caused many opposition politicians to drop their objections. Privatization legislation of all or part of the business began to look likely.

Although the 1989 legislation had opened the door to some competition and limited DBP TELEKOM's monopoly to some key areas, DBP TELEKOM remained the dominant force in German telecommunications. Even with privatization, it would take some years to diminish the influence of Deutsche Bundespost's companies.

The former Bundespost's single postal and telecommunications monopoly, increasingly anachronistic in today's competition-oriented European Community, is somewhat surprising because Germany's postal system has historically been run on a more profit-oriented, and less of a public service, model than that found in other state systems. This emphasis on profits can be traced back to the Bundespost's 15th century origins in the international private enterprises of the Thurn

und Taxis family and the revenue-producing post offices of the German princely states.

The Thurn und Taxis postal system lasted for 400 years, almost until the proclamation of the German Empire in January 1871. The family not only started one of the world's first postal systems, but also provided a basis for German unification in 1871. Heinrich von Stephan, the first Postmaster of the German Empire, emphasized this fact at a tribute delivered in Frankfurt in 1895: "The House of Taxis should be praised because for a long time it formed a unity in the midst of a mosaic-like state complex; it understood how to maintain old Germany in the course of frequently trying situations and even when there was great chaos in state and legal relationships."

Roger de Tassis—the original, Italian form of the name Taxis—began a service delivering baronial correspondence in 1440 in the central part of the Holy Roman Empire—present-day Bavaria, Austria, and Northern Italy. History has it that Maximilian I, the Holy Roman Emperor, commissioned Janetto and Francesco de Tassis to operate an imperial dispatch service in 1490. Francesco changed his name to the more German-sounding Franz Taxis and used his excellent relations with Emperor Charles V to secure postal privileges to Aragon and Naples in 1516.

This monopoly was restricted to official letters and documents, but the Taxis family began to ignore this restriction and carry letters on behalf of the private merchants of Germany. Soon the restriction was modified to allow the general public to use the Taxis postal system, but at higher rates than those charged to royalty. The Taxis family insisted on a high level of profitability. Its networks extended throughout the German states, the Netherlands, Austria, and France. Relay stations were set up for the fast changing of horses and the reduction of carrying times.

The Thurn und Taxis system slowly declined with the decay of the authority of the Holy Roman Emperor and the rise of Prussia and the other independent German states in the 18th century. The Treaty of Luneville in 1801 gave France postal rights in the Netherlands and on the left bank of the Rhine, but the Thurn und Taxis family secured an agreement with France, giving the family the right to handle all German mail destined for France or Spain. Prussia chose to ignore this agreement and operated its own postal system.

Wurtemburg, Bavaria, Baden, Brunswick, Hanover, Saxony, Oldenburg, and Mecklenburg also developed their own systems but still depended on the Thurn und Taxis system for international services. Thurn und Taxis had handled the postal affairs for allied armies involved in the crusade against Napoleon's Grande Armée in 1815, and continued to rely upon the networks established during that period.

Although the Thurn und Taxis system originated as an imperial monopoly, it remained efficient and profitable, even in its last years. In May 1851, Thurn und Taxis had little choice but to enter the German-Austrian postal unions founded a year earlier. By 1866, Prussian territorial annexations following the Austro-Prussian War of 1866 had, in effect, put almost all of the German lands served by the system under Prussian control. The last "postal" Prince of the House of Thurn und Taxis, Maximilian Karl, negotiated the sale of the family business assets to Prussia and the last of its 500 post offices disappeared.

The penny post stamp originated in England in 1839. The idea behind it was to streamline post office administration by charging a single unified rate for the entire country, rather than a series of rates based on distances. However, the first German postal authority to use the penny post, Bavaria, did not follow suit until 1849. It was followed by Saxony, Prussia, and finally Thurn und Taxis on January 1, 1852. The concept worried German officials because it was feared that the penny post would not be profitable.

The German states had followed Thurn und Taxis in viewing the post office as a profit-making endeavor. For Prussia and other states, high postal rates were an important source of government revenue. Disagreements about lower rate scheduling became the principal non-political barrier to German postal unification after Austria began the process with a series of proposals to Bavaria, Baden, Saxony, and Thurn und Taxis. The process of postal unification began in April 1847, when the Prussian Postal Chief Schaper and the Austrian Hofkammer-President—president of the Imperial Chamber of the Austrian Empire—Baron von Kuebeck jointly called for a postal union and announced a conference of all German postal systems. The conference was held at Dresden in October 1847 but the delegates failed to agree.

On April 6, 1850 Austria, Prussia, and Bavaria formed the German-Austrian postal union. With few exceptions, all German states had joined by the time of the first postal union conference in Berlin on October 15, 1851. Five more conferences gradually reduced the differences in stamp pricing and revenue distribution between the states.

In 1866 a unified postal system, the North German Postal Confederation, was formed after Prussian victories in the war against Austria. Essentially, Prussia's large and efficient system absorbed those of the smaller states and formed the basis of the Deutsche Reichspost that came into being shortly after the proclamation of the unified German Empire in January 1871. The new national post office quickly absorbed the post offices of Baden, Hesse-Darmstadt, and newly-conquered Alsace-Lorraine. Bavaria and Wurtemburg, by special arrangement, retained their own separate post offices and stamps within the empire, right up to the formation of the Weimar Republic in 1919.

The first postmaster of the German Empire, Heinrich von Stephan, modernized and unified the new national system. He also introduced the newly-invented telephone to Germany and put it under Bundespost regulation and control. By 1880 Germany had 16,000 subscribers. Von Stephan was also a founder of the Universal Postal Union in 1874.

After World War I, the Bundespost had to adjust to the difficult economic circumstances engendered by the Treaty of Versailles. The famous "wheelbarrow" inflation of that period, in which raging daily price increases supposedly required a wheelbarrow full of German marks to pay for a loaf of bread, also affected postage rates badly. In 1913 one U.S. dollar was equal to about four marks. By November 1923, it took 4.2 trillion marks to buy one U.S. dollar. High denomination stamps of the period are now valued by collectors as "the inflation issue." During the inflation period of 1922–1924, about 125 different values of stamps had to be brought into use, with the highest being an amazing 50 billion marks. Prior to 1919, the German Empire had had no stamp of a value higher than 5 marks.

The Weimar government began the first of a series of attempts that have continued to this day, to find a structure that would allow the Bundespost a measure of independence as a profit-making organization. In 1924, laws were passed allowing the Bundespost a considerable degree of financial autonomy from government control. The Bundespost was specifically asked to conduct its business in a semicommercial manner, but the success of this reform was restricted, as always, by interference from politicians and trade unions.

After Adolf Hitler came to power in January 1933, the Post Office became, like other German government bodies, an instrument of the Nazi totalitarian state. Officials were forced to cooperate with the demands of Heinrich Himmler's Gestapo and the minister of propaganda, Joseph Goebbels. Letters and telephone calls were routinely intercepted and used to identify Jews and dissidents. On the positive side, the Bundespost helped pioneer air mail services during the 1920s and 1930s. Limited airmail services were available from 1909 and the first air mail stamps were sold from 1919.

Up to the famous Hindenburg disaster in 1937, the Bundespost cooperated with the Zeppelin company in experiments to develop a transatlantic air service to both North and South America. Special stamps were issued by German and foreign post offices, but international services were limited to a relative few per year and were irregular.

At the same time Lufthansa, the German propeller aircraft airline, and the Bundespost began to develop a regular airmail service to South America. Mail from Germany and seven other European countries was flown from Berlin via Stuttgart, Marseilles, Barcelona, Seville, and the Canary Islands to Gambia on the West Coast of Africa. A seaplane than carried the post to a catapult ship out at sea, where it was refuelled and sent on across the South Atlantic to Natal, Brazil. Total transit time was reduced from an original three weeks to four days. By 1939, a weekly service was carrying 90,000 items of mail per flight before the outbreak of World War II brought it to an end.

Although Bundespost services continued to function right up to Allied occupation in all areas of Germany, the service was in chaos by the time of Germany's surrender on May 7, 1945. Of the 3,420 buildings the Bundespost had owned before the war, 1,483 had been completely destroyed or damaged. Many of its former personnel were dead, wounded, or had been conscripted into the German armed services. Those who had survived were likely to be detained by the Allies as prisoners of war. Local services had been maintained by using women, old men, and young boys as carriers. Telephone lines were cut. Rail and road networks and mail vehicles had been destroyed by bombing between 1940 and 1945, and during the fighting within Germany before its surrender.

As U.S., British, and Soviet forces assumed control, they also took over postal and telephone services. Wherever possible, they used existing facilities and personnel. They used their own stamps printed in their home countries. By February 1946, special stamps marked "Deutsche Post" were issued, valid for use in these three now officially demarcated zones of occupation. Within the French occupation zone, letters were simply handstamped until 1947, when the French administration began to issue its own postage stamps.

Between 1945 and 1947, political rifts and eventually the Cold War broke out between the Western allies and the Soviet Union. In 1947 the British and American occupation zones were merged for economic purposes, and administration began to be handed back to the Germans. The Soviets' refusal to participate in the currency reforms of June 1948 and the Berlin blockade meant that a unified postal structure for all occupation zones was doomed. Postal services in the eastern part of Germany were turned over to the new East German state established by the Soviets in 1949, and not integrated into the German communications system until reunification in 1990.

An elected Parliamentary council from all three western zones met at Bonn on September 1, 1948 to draw up the West German constitution or "Basic Law." In April 1949, United States, British, and French governments published a new occupation statute guaranteeing full powers of self-government to the new West German state. The Bundespost was reborn as a state body under the control of a cabinet ministry and assumed control over posts, telephones, and telegraphs in the new Federal Republic of Germany. The new constitution specifically forbade the privatization of posts and telecommunications.

During the 1950s the Bundespost had to rebuild its communications network. Much of prewar Germany's communications had centered on east-west communication networks between Berlin and western industrial cities. The new West Germany was a long, narrow country in which many lines of communication now ran north-south. West Berlin had become an isolated city in an alien country. After the war, the division into different occupation zones had also fragmented communications and delayed the formation of an integrated network.

Hundreds of post office buildings had to be built or rebuilt. The reconstruction of the telephone service was accomplished by the end of 1951, but installation of new private telephones was slow. By 1952, there were still only 5 telephones per 100 inhabitants in Germany, compared to 28 and 11 per 100 inhabitants in the United States and Britain respectively. All German subscribers could be listed in just three volumes. By the 1960s, however, German telephone subscribership was on a par with other industrial countries. In 1947 a teletype network was put into operation and began to replace telegraphs. By the mid-1950s, Germany already had more teletype subscribers than any country in Europe.

As postwar Germany's prosperity rose, the demand for other post office services grew. A Post Office Savings Bank had been started before World War II on January 1, 1939, but public confidence was badly shaken because the system formerly had been located in Vienna, and Austria was separated from Germany after the war. Records were scattered and lost, and many were shocked when savings were lost through currency reform. But soon deposits soared as the economy boomed, and Germans regained their reputation as savers.

By the 1960s, Germany's communications network had been fully restored. Air mail services had been resumed by 1961. In 1965 the Bundespost announced that all letters would be sent by air without extra charge if they could reach their destinations more quickly than by land. The Bundespost invested in satellite communications, and new transatlantic self-dialing facilities from Bonn, Frankfurt, and Munich became available in 1970. Bundespost described itself as "Europe's largest service company".

Nevertheless, many business and consumer groups continued to criticize the post office monopoly for inefficiency. A 1970 law formally stated that the monopoly had been effectively superseded by a reservation that prevented the establishment of a rival undertaking, but little changed.

In 1973 a further reform, the Postal Organization Act, limited government intervention in the Bundespost "only to what is politically necessary and to facilitate post office management." Under the new structure, the Bundespost would be headed by an executive committee assisted by a supervisory council. The committee would, however, remain responsible to the government.

German business continued to complain that the Bundespost's telecommunications system was relatively unsophisticated and expensive. With telecommunications products expected to constitute more than 7% of the European Community's gross national product by the year 2000, these critics alleged that German manufacturers would be disadvantaged by a backward home market. Claiming that the 1970 and 1973 reforms had been failures, they urged the break-up and privatization of the Bundespost.

However, several powerful interest groups opposed change: the Social Democratic Party, a left-wing postal union, the Deutsche Postgewerkschaft, the Bavarian State Government, and large contract suppliers to the Bundespost, including the German electronic giant Siemens. All feared the loss of jobs and disappearance of preferential treatment under a more competitive system. As civil servants, the Bundespost's employees have considerable job security.

Pressures from both the European Community (EC) and the United States, however, finally forced Bonn to establish the Witte Commission in 1985 to make recommendations about the future of the Bundespost. When the report finally appeared in September 1987, four of the twelve people on the commission condemned it for not going far enough, while two others claimed it went too far. The proposals, slightly altered, became the basis of the latest legal changes to the Bundespost and became law in July 1989. The Witte Commission recommended the opening of the telecommunications equipment and services market to outside bidders. This change was likely, in any event, to be required by EC competition law. The Bundespost was, however, allowed to continue operating in all its present fields. The basic telephone monopoly, which earns 90% of the Bundespost's telecommunications income, would be retained, but some competition would be allowed in radio paging, mobile telephones, modems, videotext, and some satellite systems.

The commission also recommended that the Bundespost be divided into three businesses: Telekom, Postdienst, and Postbank, with a minimal level of political interference above the level of their respective management boards. But when it passed the reform legislation the Bundestag added a common directorate between the three businesses and limited a proposal for incentive-based pay.

Critics, including several businesses and economists, were not completely happy with the new law, but there was a belief that the organization's entrepreneurial tasks had been freed from direct political control of the Ministry of Posts and Telecommunications. The Ministry still has ultimate supervisory and regulatory authority. It is supposed to identify the public interest and prepare ordinances based on this interest.

The reformers, however, did not foresee the collapse of East Germany's hardline Communist regime in late 1989 and Germany's eventual reunification in October 1990. German reunification brought with it the unexpectedly large problem of integrating East Germany's Deutsche Post, its own telecommunications monopoly, into the Bundespost. The Bundespost and the government soon realized that the required infrastructure investment would be greater than had previously been supposed. Only 10% of East Germany's households had a telephone, compared to 98% of West Germans. Much of the existing East German telephone equipment predated World War II.

There could be no rapid improvement in East German living conditions and economic performance without a thorough modernization of telecommunications, without which the business of a market economy simply could not be transacted. A seven–year investment plan of DM55 billion was announced, with 500,000 new telephones introduced in 1991.

Privatization to provide finance and increase efficiency was increasingly seen as a solution. Chancellor Kohl publicly said that he favored privatization, but constitutional change required the support of the opposition party, the Social Democrats (SPD), to achieve the required two-thirds majority in the Bundestag. Largely because of union fears about job security, the SPD had vigorously opposed privatization. But in a surprise move in September 1991, the SPD said it would put forward its own amendment in support of privatization. It now looks likely that TELEKOM, at least, will be privatized before the next German general elections in 1994.

Unlike the old British Post Office, which it formerly resembled, Deutsche Bundespost managed to survive into the 1990s as a huge state communications semi-monopoly.

Deutsche Bundespost Telekom, like the hived-off and partly privatized British Telecom, is profitable. As long as this profit criterion—a tradition in Germany that dates back to the time of the Thurn und Taxis family—was met, the company was, until recently, unlikely to be sold off. The rapid advance of modern communications, EC competition, and the needs of a unified Germany are leading to the return of communications to private hands. But these are more likely to be those of a modern structure like British Telecom than like that of the old Thurn und Taxis family.

Principal Subsidiaries: Deutsche Postreklame GmbH; Deutsche Telepost Consulting GmbH (30%); Telepost Kabel Servicegesellschaft mbH (54%); Deutsche Fernkabelgesellschaft mbH; EUCOM (50%); INFONET Services Corporation (15%); DANET (30%); KABELCOM (24%).

Further Reading: Davis, Bernard, ed., *Federal Republic of Germany,* Philadelphia, National Philatelic Museum, 1952; Goerth, Charles L., *The Postal System of Germany,* Valparaiso, The Germany Philatelic Society, 1968.

—Clark Siewert

FRANCE TÉLÉCOM GROUP

Head Office
6 place d'Alleray
75740 Paris Cedex 15
France
(1) 44 44 22 22
Fax: (1) 45 31 53 32

State-Owned Company
Incorporated: 1889
Employees: 165,000
Sales: FFr103 billion (US$19.88 billion)

The French legal act passed on July 2, 1990, on the organization of public posts and telecommunications services, transformed France Télécom (formerly Direction Générale des Télécommunications) into a public service carrier with corporate legal status. This legal reform substantially changed the contractual relations between France's national operator and its partners; from January 1, 1991 these relations have been governed by the French concept of "private law." Thus France Télécom now has budgetary, management, and organizational independence, like most of its European competitors, but remains under the guardianship of the Ministry of Posts and Telecommunications.

The history of French telecommunications is largely that of political intervention in scientific progress. As early as 1837, five years after Samuel Morse conceived his system of electromagnetic telegraphy, the Morse Code, and when Carl von Steinheil had devised an electromagnetic machine through which messages were recorded by a needle, political control over telegraphic services was sought. The French king, Louis Philippe, perhaps saw this as a logical extension of the control of the press which Charles X had initiated as part of the July Ordinances of 1830. State monopoly of telegraphic services, for military and political reasons, was finally established in 1851.

Telegraphic communication was made practicable in the mid-19th century, after scientific experiments by Andre Ampère, Karl Freidrich Gauss, Wilhelm Eduard Weber, Michael Faraday, and Steinheil in Europe, and Morse in America, concerning the relationship between light waves and electromagnetic waves. The most celebrated technical advance in telegraphy was achieved by Emile Baudot, whose system of Rapid Telegraphy was patented in 1874. Others of Baudot's telegraphic inventions were contemporaneous with the development of the typewriter and by 1890 telegrams began to be transmitted in page form. The French Post Office gradually absorbed the telegraph service, one minister becoming responsible for both early in 1879.

From the last quarter of the 19th century the expansion of telephony in France was equally rapid. In 1880 the three private companies that the French government had licensed merged to form the Societé Générale du Telephones (SGT). The year 1883 saw the first telephone exchange installed in Rheims and 1887 the first international circuits connecting Paris to Brussels. SGT's telephone network was nationalized in September 1889, the state reserving the monopoly of telephonic developments and addressing itself to the problems of technical development with the assistance of scientists Ader and Berthon. In addition to the development of transmission equipment, work progressed on the refinement of switching equipment which automatically made the connections between the lines. In the United States, Strowger's automatic switchgear, patented in 1889, allowed subscriber connection without the interposition of a human operator. This new type of equipment became famous for its durability. The first automated exchange in France was installed in Nice in October 1913, the last being dismantled only in 1979.

Between 1890 and 1915 the number of telephones in France more than doubled every 5 years, from 15,432 to 357,515. However, the distribution of instruments in proportion to the population was modest. In 1911 there were 0.6 telephones per 100 people in France while in the United States there were 8.1, in Canada 3.7, in Denmark 3.5, in Sweden 3.4, and in Germany 1.6. One of the main reasons for this slow growth was the method of financing networks. The cities that wished to acquire a telephone system had to provide the administration with the initial finance. The administration later reimbursed the locality in proportion to the receipts from subscribers to the new network. Unequal distribution of telephone networks across the country, and lack of inter-regional connections, resulted from this approach.

Between the two world wars French government policy ensured that the telephone service was geared more closely to the needs of the commercial and industrial sectors, and that modern services were provided to all at the same price across the country. Originally there were many varieties of telephone sets available but a standard model was introduced in 1924. The setting of more, and better quality, lines was also begun, using underground cables. Long distance connections, already improved by the invention between 1904 and 1915 of the diode and the triode, the audion, and the hard valve lamps, were refined. Arteries of lines radiating from Paris to many regional telephone exchanges were constructed between 1924 and 1938. Finally, the replacement of manual by automatic exchanges was gradually achieved, using the rotary system.

Paris, its environs, and eventually the main provincial centers saw their exchanges automated from the 1930s. In the countryside, however, the problem of modernizing 25,000 exchanges, half of which supported less than 5 subscribers, had to be approached differently and a semi-automatic system resulted. Nevertheless, France still had one of the lowest ratios of telephones to people in 1938 with 3.79% whereas the United States had 15.27%, Sweden 12.47%, and the United Kingdom 6.74%. Most French telephones were used for business purposes and in the home the instrument barely penetrated below the upper middle classes. Most telephones were to be found in urban areas of northern France; elsewhere, only the exclusive resorts, such as Biarritz, Nice, and Cannes, were as well equipped.

French telephonic, telegraphic, and radiocommunications services suffered greatly from World War II, the German occupation, and the fight for liberation. Out of 140 automatic exchanges, 39 were unusable as were 104 of the 228 manual exchanges. The cable network suffered similarly, with equipment and buildings destroyed or badly damaged. A quarter of the 105 main telegraph nodes were out of commission. Submarine lines connecting France with the United Kingdom, the United States, and Africa were destroyed, as was the huge Bordeaux-Croix d'Hins radio station.

Of the several postwar economic plans, the telecommunications sector was not given priority and between 1947 and 1966 only 0.2% of the country's gross national product was spent on telecommunications. However, the creation of the Centre National d'Etudes des Télécommunications—CNET, now France Télécom's research and development organization—in 1944 was all-important in encouraging further experimentation. From the mid-1940s new technical advances were made as a result of this official collaboration with the French telecommunications and electronics industry. The first coaxial links connected Paris and Toulouse in 1947 and coaxial cable gradually replaced the old paired wire. Shortly after this date, NATO finance ensured the development of transatlantic coaxial connections.

Terrestial telecommunications technology moved apace. The old Rotary switching system was replaced by the crossbar system in around 1960, the new equipment being sufficiently versatile to meet the needs of all types of telecommunication, from urban to international. In the mid-1960s digital switching experiments had begun in France and by 1970 fiber optic cable began to be used to support signal transmission. This research was paralleled by work at CNET into the problems of electronic connection which resulted in the Aristote, Socrate, Péricles, and Platon systems of the 1960s and 1970s. These programs of scientific experiment investigated the problems of electronic connection. With hindsight France Télécom of the pre-1970s appears to have had an under-equipped infrastructure, due to delayed technological development which represented around 2% of France's gross national product. However, at that time the system began to be modernized in a long-term strategy to digitalize it. During the same period interest in space-borne telecommunications was growing and in 1962 the United States launched the Telstar satellite. Franco-American experiments resulted in the capture and broadcast of the first television signals from the United States in July 1962. The development of geostationary satellites—whose orbits keep them constantly above the same point on the earth's surface—led to the establishment of the Intelsat II fleet, which achieved full planetary coverage from 1971. France Télécom is the third largest user of these services. In 1977 Eutelsat, the European satellite organization, worked to achieve the ECS (European Communications Satellite) system. In 1979 France inaugurated a national system of space telecommunications via the Telecom I satellite which serves the domestic market. The mission sought to establish links with French overseas territories, commercial satellite links, and videocommunications. ECS was eventually inaugurated in 1983. In 1991 France Télé-

com was the fifth largest shareholder in Inmarsat, the international maritime satellite, which is the culmination of over 60 years of development in intercontinental radio-electronic telephone traffic.

By 1986 France Télécom had 25 million main lines which supported the connection of 96% of French homes, as well as the development of many innovative products and services, such as the Teletel videotex system. From 1983 Teletel began to replace paper telephone directories and its Minitel terminals were purchased by the DGT in substantial quantities to create a largely captive market. In 1989 the Teletel system boasted a total of 85 million connection hours through 5 million terminals. The connection of Teletel to Transpac, the French national packet switching network, which handles data in the form of units or "packets" routed individually through the network, now means that subscribers throughout the country can use other services, regardless of distance. National and international business connections combining voice and text distribution via the "Numeris" ISDN system are now possible, though full utilization is still some years away. Such successes are attributable to a consistent and monopolistic government policy and efficient investment in telecommunications equipment and in the supplier companies, such as the E10 digital exchanges, a way of encoding information as a series of "on" or "off" signals, made by Alcatel.

Demands for deregulation of the telecommunications industry resulted from the Commission of the European Communities (CEC) Green Paper in 1987. In part, the inability of monopoly organizations to cope with rapid technological change, and also the need for the competition essential to support an economy driven more by information rather than production informed these moves. Once again, arguments about the provision of a universal telephone service prevailed over exclusive concentration on technological progress. However, various countries have evolved different solutions to the problems of reorganization. Whereas in the United Kingdom British Telecom opted for full privatization, France Télécom resisted this and technological advance has taken place within a monopoly environment. France Télécom will lose its monopoly in some areas of telecommunication after 1993, under the terms of the European Community's Open Network Provision of 1989, which guarantees to all value-added network service (VANs) providers equal access to its country's telecommunications infrastructure. The supply of terminal equipment such as telefax machines and telephone handsets, and VANs services such as home banking, will be open to competition, although strictly licensed. Competition in the provision of computer data transfer will also be allowed, provided that private firms do not undercut France Télécom.

A frenzy of alliances and mergers has typified the French telecommunications industry since the late 1980s, as it has tried to achieve the international scale necessary to compete in new markets such as car telephones and radio telephone paging equipment. France Télécom and Matra, the recently privatized defense and electronics group, now face competition from France's largest private water distributor, the Compagnie Générale des Eaux, which has formed a partnership with Alcatel and Nokia of Finland to offer a second national car telephone network. Again, Alcatel, the telecommunications division of the Compagnie Generale d'Electricité (CGE), has absorbed ITT to form the world's second largest telecommunications venture after that of American Telephone and Telegraph. Matra, which in 1987 successfully bid with Ericsson of Sweden for control of CGCT, France's other major supplier of public switching equipment, later acquired a 15% stake in Société Anonyme de Télécommunications (SAT). Nevertheless, despite these incursions into its traditional market areas, France Télécom has emerged as one of the world's top public telecommunications carriers. It recently ranked 11th out of 20 with a 1.9% share of the world market and a total of almost 90 billion outgoing minutes of telecom traffic carried by public voice circuits. Thirty million subscribers are served by a network of 1,700 switching centers, of which 80% are digitalized, and there are 300,000 transmission lines through which 67% of calls are handled by cables and 33% by microwave relays.

Principal Subsidiaries: Transpac; Télédiffusion de France; Télésystèmes; Télécom Systèmes Mobiles; Compagnie Auxiliaire de Télécommunications; France Cables et Radio; Entreprise Générale de Télécommunications; VTCOM.

Further Reading: Tussau, G., "Les Industries Electriques et Electroniques, Notes et Etudes Documentaires," *La Documentation Française,* 1980; Haquet, C., [On Telepoints], *Le Figaro,* September 14, 1983; Garric, D., "Minitel," *Le Point,* April 15, 1985; Arvonny, M., "La Nouvelle Numérotation Téléphonique," *Le Monde,* October 28–29, 1985; Carré, P.A., "Histoire des Télécommunications," *CNET/DGT,* 1989; European High Technology and European Telecommunications Surveys, *Financial Times,* 1988–1990; Carré, P.A., "France Télécom," *Revue France Télécom,* December 1990.

—Patrick Keeley

GTE CORPORATION

One Stamford Forum
Stamford, Connecticut 06904
U.S.A.
(203) 965-2000
Fax: (203) 965-2277

Public Company
Incorporated: 1920 as Commonwealth Telephone Company
Employees: 175,000
Sales: $21.40 billion
Stock Exchanges: New York Midwest Pacific London
  Amsterdam Basel Geneva Lausanne Paris Zürich Tokyo

In March 1990 the largest merger in the history of the telecommunications industry was completed, and two former U.S. competitors, GTE Corporation and Contel Corporation, were combined under the GTE name. With a market value of $28 billion, the merged company became a telecommunications powerhouse operating as the largest U.S. local telephone company and the second-largest U.S. cellular-service provider. GTE paid $6.6 billion in stock to merge Contel. Designed to take advantage of the two companies' complementary businesses, the merger strengthened GTE's assets in two of its three major areas of operations: telephone service and telecommunications products. In its other core area of operations, electrical products, GTE remained the world's third-largest producer of lighting products. As a result of the merger with Contel, both GTE's size and scope of operations have grown, and its operating area in 1990 included 48 U.S. states and more than 40 countries. While the two companies were united under one name, each has a rich history of its own.

GTE CORPORATION

GTE's founding can be traced to 1918, when three Wisconsin public utility accountants pooled $33,500 to purchase the Richland Center Telephone Company, serving 1,466 telephones in the dairy belt of southern Wisconsin. From the outset, John F. O'Connell, Sigurd L. Odegard, and John A. Pratt worked under the guiding principle that better telephone service could be rendered to small communities if a number of exchanges were operated under one managing body.

In 1920 that principle was put into action, and the three accountants formed a corporation, Commonwealth Telephone Company, with Odegard as president, Pratt as vice president,

and O'Connell as secretary. Richland Center Telephone became part of Commonwealth Telephone, which quickly purchased telephone companies in three nearby communities. In 1922 Pratt resigned as vice president and was replaced by Clarence R. Brown, a former Bell System employee.

By the mid-1920s Commonwealth had extended beyond Wisconsin borders and purchased the Belvidere Telephone Company in Illinois. It also diversified into other utilities by acquiring two small Wisconsin electrical companies. Expansion was stepped up in 1926, when Odegard secured an option to purchase Associated Telephone Company of Long Beach, California. Odegard, with the assistance of Marshall E. Sampsell, president of Wisconsin Power and Light Company, and Morris F. LaCroix, a partner in Paine, Webber & Company in Boston, proceeded to devise a plan for a holding company, to be named Associated Telephone Utilities Company.

That company was formed in 1926 to acquire Associated Telephone Company and assume the assets of Commonwealth Telephone. Sampsell was elected president of the new company, and Odegard and LaCroix were named vice presidents. An aggressive acquisition program was quickly launched in eastern, midwestern, and western states, with the company using its own common stock to complete transactions.

During its first six years, Associated Telephone Utilities acquired 340 telephone companies, which were consolidated into 45 companies operating more than 437,000 telephones in 25 states. By the time the stock market bottomed out in October 1929, Associated Telephone Utilities was operating about 500,000 telephones with revenues approaching $17 million.

In January 1930 a new subsidiary, Associated Telephone Investment Company, was established. Designed to support its parent's acquisition program, the new company's primary business was buying company stock in order to bolster its market value. Within two years the investment company had incurred major losses, and a $1 million loan had to be negotiated. Associated Telephone Investment was dissolved but not before its parent's financial plight had become irreversible, and in 1933 Associated Telephone Utilities went into receivership.

The company was reorganized that same year and resurfaced in 1935 as General Telephone Corporation, operating 12 newly consolidated companies. John Winn, a 26-year veteran of the Bell System, was named president. In 1936 General Telephone created a new subsidiary, General Telephone Directory Company, to publish directories for the parent's entire service area.

In 1940 LaCroix was elected General Telephone's first chairman, and Harold Bozell, a former banker for Associated Telephone Utilities, was named president. Like other businesses, the telephone industry was under government restrictions during World War II, and General Telephone was called upon to increase services at military bases and war-production factories.

Following the war, General Telephone reactivated an acquisitions program that had been dormant for more than a decade and purchased 118,000 telephone lines between 1946 and 1950. In 1950 General Telephone purchased its first telephone-equipment manufacturing subsidiary, Leich Electric Company, along with the related Leich Sales Corporation.

Bozell retired in 1951 and Donald Power, a former executive secretary for Ohio Governor John Bricker, was named president. By the time Power took over, General Telephone's assets included 15 telephone companies operating in 20 states. During the 1950s Power guided the company in a steady, aggressive acquisition campaign punctuated by two major mergers.

In 1955 Theodore Gary & Company, the second-largest independent telephone company, which had 600,000 telephone lines, was merged into General Telephone, which had grown into the largest independent outside the Bell System. The merger gave the company 2.5 million lines. Theodore Gary's assets included telephone operations in the Dominican Republic, British Columbia, and the Philippines, as well as Automatic Electric, the second-largest telephone equipment manufacturer in the U.S. LaCroix and Power were to retain their positions in the merged company, but a month before the deal was closed, LaCroix died, and Power assumed the additional title of chairman.

In 1959 General Telephone and Sylvania Electric Products merged, and the parent's name was changed to General Telephone & Electronics Corporation (GT&E). The merger gave Sylvania—a leader in such industries as lighting, television and radio, and chemistry and metallurgy—the needed capital to expand. For General Telephone, the merger meant the added benefit of Sylvania's extensive research and development capabilities in the field of electronics. Power also orchestrated other acquisitions in the late 1950s, including Peninsular Telephone Company in Florida, with 300,000 lines, and Lenkurt Electric Company, Inc., a leading producer of microwave and data transmissions system.

In 1960 the subsidiary GT&E International Incorporated was formed to consolidate manufacturing and marketing activities of Sylvania, Automatic Electric, and Lenkurt, outside the United States. The following year, Leslie H. Warner, a former Theodore Gary executive, was named president. Another former Theodore Gary executive, Don Mitchell, was named to the new position of vice chairman, while Power remained chief executive officer and chairman.

During the early 1960s the scope of GT&E's research, development, and marketing activities was broadened. In 1963 Sylvania began full-scale production of color television picture tubes, and within two years it was supplying color tubes for 18 of the 23 domestic U.S. television manufacturers. About the same time, Automatic Electric began supplying electronic switching equipment for the U.S. defense department's global communications systems, and GT&E International began producing earth-based stations for both foreign and domestic markets. GT&E's telephone subsidiaries, meanwhile, began acquiring community-antenna television systems (CATV) franchises in their operating areas.

In 1964 Warner orchestrated a deal that merged Western Utilities Corporation, the nation's second-largest independent telephone company, with 635,000 telephones, into GT&E. The following year Sylvania introduced the revolutionary four-sided flashcube, enhancing its position as the world's largest flashbulb producer.

Warner assumed the additional title of chief executive officer in 1966, while Power remained chairman. Acquisitions in telephone service continued under Warner during the mid-1960s. Purchases included Quebec Telephone in Canada, Hawaiian Telephone Company, and Northern Ohio Telephone Company and added a total of 622,000 telephone lines to GT&E operations. By 1969 GT&E was serving ten million telephones.

In March 1970 GT&E's New York City headquarters was bombed by a radical antiwar group in protest of the company's participation in defense work. In December of that year the GT&E board agreed to move the company's headquarters to Stamford, Connecticut. Power retired in 1971, and Warner was named chairman and chief executive officer. The following year Theodore F. Brophy was named president.

After initially proposing to build separate satellite systems, GT&E and its telecommunications rival, AT&T, announced in 1974 joint venture plans for the construction and operation of seven earth-based stations interconnected by two satellites. That same year Sylvania acquired name and distribution rights for Philco television and stereo products. GTE International expanded its activities during the same period, acquiring television manufacturers in Canada and Israel and a telephone manufacturer in Germany.

Warner retired in 1976 and Brophy was named to the additional post of chairman. Brophy, soon after assuming his new position, reorganized the company along five global product lines: communications, lighting, consumer electronics, precision materials, and electrical equipment. GTE International was phased out during the reorganization, and GTE Products Corporation was formed to encompass both domestic and foreign manufacturing and marketing operations. At the same time, GTE Communications Products was formed to oversee operations of Automatic Electric, Lenkurt, Sylvania, and GTE Information Systems.

Thomas A. Vanderslice was elected president and chief operating officer in 1979, and another reorganization soon followed. GTE Products Group was eliminated as an organizational unit and GTE Electrical Products, consisting of lighting, precision materials, and electrical equipment, was formed. Vanderslice also revitalized the GT&E Telephone Operating Group in order to develop competitive strategies for anticipated regulatory changes in the telecommunications industry.

GT&E sold its consumer electronics businesses, including the accompanying brand names of Philco and Sylvania in 1980, after watching revenues from television and radio operations decrease precipitously with the success of foreign manufacturers. Following AT&T's 1982 announcement that it would divest 22 telephone operating companies, GT&E made a number of reorganizational and consolidation moves.

In 1982 the company adopted the name GTE Corporation and formed GTE Mobilnet Incorporated, to handle the company's entrance into the new cellular telephone business. In 1983 GTE sold its electrical equipment, brokerage information services, and cable television equipment businesses. That same year, Automatic Electric and Lenkurt were combined as GTE Network Systems.

GTE became the third-largest long-distance telephone company in 1983 through the acquisition of Southern Pacific Communications Company. At the same time, Southern Pacific Satellite Company was acquired, and the two firms were renamed GTE Sprint Communications Corporation and GTE Spacenet Corporation, respectively. Through an agreement with the Department of Justice, GTE conceded to keep Sprint Communications separate from its other telephone companies and limit other GTE telephone subsidiaries in certain markets. In December 1983 Vanderslice resigned as president and chief operating officer.

In 1984 GTE formalized its decision to concentrate on three core businesses: telecommunications, lighting, and precision metals. That same year, the company's first satellite was launched, and GTE's cellular telephone service went into operation; GTE's earnings exceeded $1 billion for the first time.

James (Rocky) L. Johnson, a former senior vice president, was named president and chief operating officer in 1986. That same year, GTE acquired Airfone Inc., a telephone service provider for commercial aircraft and railroads, and Rotaflex p.l.c., a United Kingdom-based manufacturer of lighting fixtures.

Beginning in 1986 GTE spun off several operations to form joint ventures. In 1986 GTE Sprint and United Telecommunications's long-distance subsidiary, U.S. Telecom, agreed to merge and form US Sprint Communications Company, with each parent retaining a 50% interest in the new firm. That same year, GTE transferred its international transmission, overseas central-office switching, and business-systems operations to a joint venture with Siemens AG of Germany, which took 80% ownership of the new firm. The following year, GTE transferred its business systems operations in the United States to a new joint venture, Fujitsu GTE Business Sytems, Inc., formed with Fujitsu Limited, which retained 80% ownership.

Johnson succeeded Brophy as chairman and chief executive officer in 1987 and then relinquished his president's title the following year to Charles R. Lee, a former senior vice president. Johnson continued to streamline and consolidate operations, organizing telephone companies around a single national organization headquartered in the Dallas, Texas area.

In 1988 GTE divested its consumer communications products unit as part of a telecommunications strategy to place increasing emphasis on the services sector. The following year GTE sold the majority of its interest in US Sprint to United Telecommunications and its interest in Fujitsu GTE Business Systems to Fujitsu.

In 1989 GTE and AT&T formed the joint-venture company AG Communication Systems Corporation, designed to bring advanced digital technology to GTE's switching systems. GTE retained 51% control over the joint venture, with AT&T pledging to take complete control of the new firm in 15 years.

With an increasing emphasis on telecommunications, in 1989 GTE launched a program to become the first cellular provider offering nationwide service and introduced the nation's first rural service area, providing cellular service on the Hawaiian island of Kauai. The following year GTE acquired the Providence Journal Company's cellular properties in five southern states for $710 million and became the second largest cellular-service provider in the United States.

In 1990 GTE reorganized its activities around three business groups: telecommunications products and services, telephone operations, and electrical products. That same year, GTE and Contel Corporation announced merger plans that would strengthen GTE's telecommunications and telephone sectors.

Following action or review by more than 20 governmental bodies, in March 1991 the merger of GTE and Contel was approved. Johnson and Lee maintained their positions as chairman and president, respectively, while Contel's Chairman Charles Wohlstetter became vice chairman of GTE. Contel's former president, Donald Weber, agreed to remain with the company during a six-month transition period, before leaving the merged company.

CONTEL CORPORATION

Contel Corporation's earliest predecessor, Telephone Communications Corporation, was founded by Charles Wohlstetter. After working as a Wall Street runner in the 1920s and as a Hollywood screenwriter in the 1930s, Wohlstetter returned to Wall Street in the 1940s and became a financier. In 1960 he made what he would later call a bad investment in an Alaskan oil company that would become the impetus for Contel.

To help turn that investment around, Wohlstetter recruited the services of Jack Maguire and Phillip Lucier from a telephone supply company and then raised $1.5 million to form a holding company, Telephone Communications Corporation. Wohlstetter was named chairman of the new corporation, Lucier was named president, and Maguire was named vice president. Some 30 years later, Wohlstetter's $1.5 million investment had grown into a company that had acquired and consolidated more than 750 smaller companies with total corporate assets hovering around $6 billion.

One of the company's first acquisitions was Central Western Company, which merged with Telephone Communications in 1961 to form the new parent Continental Telephone Company. The acquisition of Central Western, along with Harfil, Inc., provided the company with customer billing, general accounting, and toll separation services.

Continental based its early acquisition strategy on *Kreigspiel,* a historical war game German generals played at Prussian war colleges. Wohlstetter applied the tenets of the game to telephone company operations and amassed detailed information on each independent telephone company in the United States. When those companies came up for sale, Wohlstetter and Maguire, who were pilots, and Lucier, whose wife was a pilot, would promptly fly off to meet the owners and negotiate purchase agreements.

Many of the early acquisitions were made through exchanges of stock, including the 1964 merger with Independent Telephone Company that doubled the company's size and changed its name in the process to Continental Independent Telephone Corporation. By the close of 1964, Continental had acquired more than 100 companies operating in 30 states.

The company adopted another new name, Continental Telephone Corporation, in 1965. Also during 1965 Continental acquired 65 more telephone companies and again doubled its size. By 1966 Continental had acquired more than 500 independent companies, had become the third-largest independent telephone company in the United States, and was one of the youngest companies ever listed on the New York Stock Exchange.

By 1970 Continental's assets had topped $1 billion, and sales volume had risen to $120 million. Lucier died that year and was succeeded as president by Maguire, who moved up from a vice presidency. Aside from its dominating telephone business, the company's activities by that time had grown to include cable television systems, directory publishing, equipment leasing, and data services.

With the number of small independents having diminished considerably by 1970, Continental's pace in acquiring telephone operating companies was reduced. Continental sold its cable television business in 1971, and after a sluggish economy had taken its toll on Continental's manufacturing and supply subsidiaries, those, too, were sold in 1976.

Maguire resigned in 1976 because of health problems and was succeeded as president by James V. Napier, a former executive vice president. That same year, Continental became the first telephone company outside the Bell system to install a digital telephone switching system, a move that provided improved network operating efficiency, allowed the introduction of new calling features, and started the transition away from operations dominated by rural service areas.

In response to the changing regulatory climate of the telephone industry, in 1978 Continental mapped out a diversification strategy into nonregulated businesses. Continental's first diversification move came in 1979, with the acquisition of Executone, Inc., a New York-based communications equipment maker.

By 1980 Continental had two million telephone access lines in service and had established its first fiber-optic cable, a high-speed, high-capacity telecommunications transmission mode. While Continental continued the process of upgrading its telephone operations, during the early 1980s the company's focus turned to greater diversification.

In July 1980 Continental entered the satellite business through a joint venture with Fairchild Industries, and a communications partnership firm, American Satellite Company, was formed to operate a network of earth-based stations that provided voice and data services. To provide technology services to accommodate its expanding needs, Continental then acquired two consulting and research firms, Network Analysis Corporation and International Computing Company.

In 1981 Continental acquired Page Communications Engineers Inc., later renamed Contel Page, which gave Continental expertise in the engineering, installation, and maintenance of satellite-to-earth stations. One year later, Continental hooked up with Fairchild Industries in a second joint venture called Space Communications Company, a provider of tracking and relay data services for such clients as the National Aeronautics and Space Administration.

After the Federal Communications Commission opened the door to licenses for 30 cellular phone markets in 1981, Continental plunged into that field as well, acquiring sizable shares of cellular markets in Los Angeles, California; Washington, D.C.; and Minneapolis, Minnesota. Continental also entered the credit card authorization business in 1981, with the purchase of National Bancard Corporation. Two years later, Continental bolstered its interest in that business segment with the purchase of the Chase Merchants Services division of Chase Manhattan Bank.

In 1982 the corporation changed its name to Continental Telecom Incorporated, adopted a new corporate logo, and inaugurated an advertising campaign around the theme "architects of telecommunications." Continental's expansion into the information services sector continued in 1982 with the purchase of STSC Inc., a computer services supplier, and Cado Systems Corporation, a maker of small business computers. That same year company revenues surpassed the $2 billion mark for the first time.

In 1984 Continental formed the subsidiary Contel Cellular Inc. to handle the corporation's growing cellular operations. A year later, Continental culminated its diversification moves and reorganized into four business sectors: telephone and cellular operations; business systems, offering voice and data processing products and services; federal systems, handling

various facets of communication and information systems for government agencies; and information systems, offering telecommunications systems and services to large corporations, institutions, and government entities.

As a result of the company's growing interest in the information services marketplace, in 1985 Continental acquired several computer system and software companies, including Northern Data Systems, Data Equipment Systems Corporation, and Sooner Enterprises, Inc. Continental also purchased Fairchild Industries's interests in American Satellite Co., later renamed Contel ASC, and Space Communications Company.

That same year, Continental sold its directory publishing division, its time-share services business, and its credit card authorization business. In the midst of reorganization in 1985, Napier resigned, and John N. Lemasters, former American Satellite Company president, was named president and chief executive officer.

Continental's telephone operations were repositioned during the mid-1980s through numerous sales and exchanges. Subsidiaries in Nebraska, Colorado, Alaska, the Bahamas, and Barbados were sold, and operations in Michigan were exchanged for similar operations in Indiana and three southern states.

The name Contel Corporation was adopted in 1986. That same year, Contel's new tenant services division set the stage for future growth by acquiring tenant service operations in Atlanta and Seattle. The tenant services division installed and managed customized communications systems in commercial buildings and marketed those systems to the buildings' tenants. Contel also enhanced its information services division with the acquisition of IPC Communications, Inc., a supplier of a special-purpose telephone system used by financial traders, and expanded its federal systems operations with the purchase of Western Union Corporation's government systems division, a provider of information handling systems.

In September 1986 Contel announced it had agreed to merge with Communications Satellite Corporation (Comsat), but by mid-1987 Contel had called off the deal, citing Comsat's unstable financial picture. The failed merger sparked the resignation of Lemasters. Donald W. Weber, former executive vice president and head of telephone operations, was named Lemasters's successor as president and chief executive officer.

Contel acquired Comsat's international private-line business and its very-small-aperture terminal (VSAT) satellite business in 1987, as well as Equatorial Communications Company, a provider of private satellite data networks. That same year, Contel agreed to sell Executone, its troubled telephone interconnect business, and Texocom, Contel's equipment supply business.

In the late 1980s Contel continued to narrow its focus in the information systems sectors. In 1988 it sold its computer-based business, Contel Business Systems, and a year later disposed of Contel Credit Corporation. Contel Federal Systems continued to grow during that same period, and in 1988 it acquired two Eaton Corporation subsidiaries: Information Management Systems and Data Systems Services. Two years later Contel purchased Telos Corporation, with expertise in government-preferred computer software.

Contel's tenant services and cellular businesses also got a boost in 1988 with the acquisition of RealCom Communications Corporation, an IBM tenant services subsidiary, and Southland Mobilcom Inc.'s interests in the Mobile, Alabama, and the Pensacola, Florida, cellular markets.

In 1990 Contel completed the biggest acquisition in its history, a $1.3 billion purchase of McCaw Cellular Communications, Inc.'s controlling interests in 13 cellular markets, which added more than six million potential customers and doubled Contel's cellular market base.

Contel's biggest move of 1990, however, was its merger with GTE. Through that transition, the two former competitors were expected to integrate telephone and mobile-cellular operations and capitalize on business unit similarities in the field of satellite-communications as well as in communications systems and services targeting government entities.

Principal Subsidiaries: GTE Products of Connecticut Corporation; GTE Communications Services Incorporated; GTE Valenite Corporation; Anglo-Canadian Telephone Company (Canada, 86.39%); GTE Holdings (Canada) Limited; GTE California Incorporated (99.6%); GTE Florida Incorporated; GTE North Incorporated; GTE Northwest Incorporated; GTE South Incorporated; GTE Southwest Incorporated; GTE Hawaiian Telephone Company Incorporated; GTE Directories Corporation; GTE Data Services Incorporated; GTE Finance Corporation; GTE Global Corporation (U.S. Virgin Islands); GTE Information Services Incorporated; GTE Investment Management Corporation; GTE Mobile Communications Incorporated; GTE Mobilnet Incorporated; GTE Realty Corporation; GTE Reinsurance Company Limited (Bermuda); GTE Service Corporation; GTE Shareholder Services Incorporated; GTE Telecom Incorporated; GTE Telecom Marketing Corporation; GTE Vantage Incorporated.

Further Reading: Mikolas, Mark, "What Makes Charles Run," *TE&M,* April 1, 1987; Meeks, Fleming, " 'Fail' is not a four-letter word," *Forbes,* April 30, 1990; McCarthy, Thomas E., *The History of GTE: The Evolution of One of America's Great Corporations,* Stamford, Connecticut, GTE Corporation, 1990; "Background Information," GTE corporate typescript, 1991.

—Roger W. Rouland

KONINKLIJKE PTT NEDERLAND NV

P.O. Box 15000
9700 CD Groningen
The Netherlands
(70) 343 4343
Fax: (70) 343 4321

State-Owned Company
Incorporated: 1989
Employees: 96,254
Sales: Dfl 13.56 billion (US$7.94 billion)

Koninklijke PTT Nederland NV (NVPTT) is wholly owned by the Dutch government. It offers a complete range of products and services used to transmit data, goods, and various forms of currency within the Netherlands and abroad to large companies and to individuals, both as an exclusive license holder and on the open market. As exclusive license holder, it is answerable to the Ministry of Transport and Public Works concerning its obligations to provide a basic telephone and postal service nationwide. It also leases and sells the technical equipment and additional services needed to send and transform data. To achieve these ends it uses technology from fiber optics to satellite links. NVPTT is the holding company for two independent subsidiaries that share the above-mentioned tasks between them. PTT Telecom BV conveys electronic and optical data based on telephone, telex, and data networks, while PTT Post BV handles material goods.

The story of NVPTT can be read as that of a large establishment struggling to become a company, or as the triumph of commerce over politics. More than adapting to new technology and expanding public services, NVPTT's greatest struggle has been coping with growing demand while being run on the budget of a government department.

National postal management dates from 1803, during the Napoleonic era. Even after the departure of the French in 1813, it was run as an independent service by the Commissarissen der Bataafse Posterijen, until annexed in 1819 by the Ministry of Finance. A single administrator from the relevant department ran the postal service part time until it began to grow more rapidly beginning in the 1850s. In 1852 telegraph services, a luxury used primarily by wealthy people, became an operation independent of the postal services and was managed by the Ministry of the Interior. The telephone first made its entry in 1881 with the Netherlands Bell Telephone Company, operating under license in Amsterdam. Other private companies followed suit, and it was not until the German occupation in 1941 that these were all brought under the single management of the already-formed Staats Bedrijf der Posterijen, Telegraphie & Telephony (PTT), whereas postal and telegraph services had been unified on January 1, 1886 in order to share premises and an administration. In 1877 they ended up under the control of the newly formed Ministry for Water, Commerce, and Industry (WCI).

The first move toward the creation of a PTT came under the management of J.P. Hofstede when the section of the WCI responsible for postal services became the independent Administration of Postal Services and Telegraphy (P&T) in 1893. Its *Hoofdbestuur*, or central management, was in The Hague and run by a director general, not unlike the postmaster general of Great Britain or the United States. From the start, executive independence was not matched by financial autonomy. P&T made large investments in telephony following the introduction of a central exchange soon after 1900. The WCI realized P&T could best serve the national interest when run on a purely independent commercial basis. At the same time, however, many felt that important financial decisions concerning that national interest could not be allowed to pass from the hands of the States General, the Dutch parliament. These competing views of how the P&T should be run influenced the company until its 1989 restructuring.

A temporary compromise was effected in January 1915, during World War I, when the P&T became the State Company of Post and Telegraphy; its most lucrative component, telephony, was still not reflected in the name. It was a company in name only. Moreover, the state did not hesitate to finance part of its war expenditure by raising rates for mail, telegraphy, and telephony independent of commercial considerations. A spate of complaints followed in the 1920s when tariffs kept rising at the same time as the government forced the P&T to cut back on many services due to adverse economic conditions. Problems were compounded by the fact that P&T continued to run at a yearly loss of Dfl 8 million. This led to staff cuts and to labor disputes, which in turn resulted in further deterioration of service.

On the whole, investment, especially in telephony, kept rising. The first local exchange went up in 1911, and ten years later automation of telephone traffic handling was begun. In 1928 telephony was incorporated into the name of the company, which became the State Company of PTT. A great success during both the 1920s and 1930s was the design of a corporate image. The architect H.P. Berlage and the proponent of the De Stijl movement Gerrit Rietveld became involved with buildings and furniture, while the PTT General Secretary J.F. van Royen, who was to lose his life during the German occupation of 1941, ensured that the corporate identity was carried out and evident in every aspect of the business, from typography to office cutlery and stamps.

In 1925 the new director general, M.H. Damme, led an efficiency drive that made the PTT profitable, offering more services while decreasing its work force. Expanded postal traffic led to new branch postal facilities in remote areas, an idea that has returned to popularity. A night service was established in 1929, and the airplane improved international delivery in 1930. That same year a decision was taken to automate the whole telephone network, local as well as trunk traffic, and the country was divided into 13 districts and smaller sectors, each with its own exchange.

The PTT did not escape the consequences of the Great Depression. Demand for services fell and the government, whose main task was to finance the growing budget deficit, extracted maximum profit by setting a minimum percentage in its budget. The PTT, forced to economize, cut down on building programs and personnel. Between 1932 and 1936 it lowered salaries and introduced part-time work. The PTT moved to the Ministry of the Interior in 1933, but its request to build a reserve fund from surplus profit to preserve continuity of investment in lean years was refused because the States General felt its budget rights would be affected. M.H. Damme continued to strive for financial independence and in 1940 pressed for the whole PTT to become a corporate body with corporate rights. He wanted the director general to have the authority to set tariffs independent of the Ministry of the Interior, while profit accruing to the state was no longer to vary according to fiscal needs. It was the high command of the German occupying forces who approved the scheme, and the PTT was incorporated on March 31, 1941.

Independence, however, remained a dream. The occupying forces used the PTT for their own ends and maintained total control. After liberation, the government reharnessed the PTT in the drive for national reconstruction. As reconstruction involved thorough industrialization, the PTT expanded rapidly on the basis of generous government investments.

Although the government did not oppose retaining the PTT as a corporation, the Second Chamber of the States General still would not surrender control. The government withdrew its initial proposal in the face of Second Chamber criticism, and when the PTT was made a state company for the second time, in 1955, it had gained only a marginal amount of room to maneuver. The old *Hoofdbestuur* was rebaptized as the Central Directorate.

A telex network was introduced in 1956 and became one of the most used networks in the world, but other plans hit the wall of new governmental spending restrictions and shrinking investment, which led to complaints from manufacturers when the PTT canceled some orders. Management still believed the only solution lay in access to loans on the capital market and formulated yet another proposal for incorporation as a public company attempting to accommodate the expected complaints from the States General. The PTT wanted the ability to draw up investment plans covering more than a single year; instead, it received permission to finance investment partly from its own profits. New tariffs reflected this.

Boom years followed, beginning in the late 1950s. The PTT achieved a fully automated telephone network on May 22, 1962, second only to the United Kingdom. New problems arose at the same time; the PTT began losing personnel to the growing and better-paid private sector, and its investment plans were thwarted by the government's "conjuncture politics," in which levels of investment stood in inverse proportion to growth in other sectors in the economy so that a spread might be achieved. Thus a brake has put on growth at the moment of greatest demand.

These problems provoked the formation of the Goedhart Commission, the first of a series of government commissions. It advised in 1963 that the PTT might be allowed to make decisions autonomously on large-scale investments, although

independent company status was still deemed to infringe on the right of the Second Chamber to control the PTT. The proposals resulted in great confusion as several cabinet members disagreed with the Second Chamber and with each other. This stalemate had serious consequences in the early 1970s. Rising prices and high wages dented the PTT's profitability, and in 1971 profits were halved. In 1973 the Minister of Finance extracted Dfl 87 million from the PTT to finance his budget and was less willing than ever to contribute to the PTT's investment needs. Rates rose steeply, and by 1974 everybody was tired of the fruitless debates over autonomy. Even though the state siphoned off increasing amounts from the PTT, exceeding Dfl 1 billion in 1982, the PTT managed to fund its investments internally, while continuing to grow. The PTT started Viditel in 1981, a videotex system supplied by Britain's General Electric Company, using Prestel (U.K.) standards. In March 1982 the new backbone of data transport, a packet switched data network (PSDN), Datanet 1, was introduced and was fully connected to other PSDNs and the Dutch network by 1984. The PTT's activities extended further, into the installation of broadcasting stations for Dutch television. The PTT set up a subsidiary, Casema, to install and maintain cable television systems. Another subsidiary, Nepostel, acts as a consultant to Third World countries. The PTT was one of the tightest monopolies in the European Economic Community (EEC) and could not escape criticism, which became increasingly loud during the 1980s. Users complained about the deficient supply of leased lines, the prices of available terminal equipment, the high tariffs, and the uncertainty of the PTT's long-term policy. In 1986, in response to violent criticism over congestion, the PTT had to embark on a crash Dfl 12 billion program to install digital switches between Rotterdam and Amsterdam. The postal division had been running at a loss for a while—its losses reached Dfl 14 million in 1984—and only two-thirds of 400 technical posts could be filled in 1984.

The government knew, too, that change was inevitable, and two influential commissions, the Swarttouw Commission in 1981 and the Steenbergen Commission in 1984, helped the government accept that the PTT would be privatized. The Steenbergen Commission laid down the conditions for the PTT's privatization of 1989. Many factors made a new structure imperative. The immense advances in technology affected the whole infrastructure of the telecommunications industry and required unheard-of levels of investment, which the state did not want to take upon itself given the prevailing high interest rates. At the same time demand was higher than ever. In addition, a new ideological climate favored rolling back the power of the state while favoring free competition, and the need to attract skilled personnel required market-based salaries.

The main structures of the new PTT were approved by a Cabinet decision on November 22, 1985. Prime Minister Ruud Lubbers justified the 100% government stake in the limited liability company by pointing out that it was not a question of privatization so much as giving more flexibility to the PTT. The new holding company would contain two main subsidiaries, PTT Telecom BV, to deal with electronic and optical data transmission, and PTT Post BV, to transport physical data. This split reflected the fact that telegraphy had virtually disappeared, and postal and telephone services no longer shared the same physical location. They also differed completely in character, telecommunications being capital-intensive and postal services being labor-intensive. Another service, the Rijkspost Spaarbank (Statepost Savings Bank) and the Giro Bank were hived off in 1986. The third main function of the old PTT, the regulatory and franchise functions, would be transferred to a new office in the Ministry of Transport and Public Works, as Regelgeving and Vergunning voor PTT (Regulations and Licenses of PTT). Both PTT Telecom and PTT Post would be run by one five-member executive committee, itself supervised by a board of at least seven directors, of which three are directly nominated by the Ministry of Transport and Public Works. Further restrictions comprise a rates structure linked to indices of the Central Planning Office and several conditions attached to the running of basic telephone and postal services under exclusive license. The PTT would now be required to pay the government corporate tax as well as shareholder dividends.

A further split recommended by the Steenbergen Commission provoked a lot of argument: to separate the licensed monopoly functions—the provision of telephone lines—from the services open to competition—selling telephone equipment—by creating two telecommunications companies. There were two reasons: to protect the public interest from the commercial risks of the open market with respect to rates and to prevent the PTT from cross-subsidizing its private and public ventures and thus prejudicing fair competition. The PTT was vigorously opposed to this, on the grounds that it would prevent the company from exploiting economies of scale between the provision of basic and extra services. The final result was a strict separation between the money flow and accounting systems of each activity rather than a split, although there is a proviso for such a separation to occur by 1994.

On January 1, 1989, after a century and a half of struggle, NVPTT was incorporated. Every household in the Netherlands received a letter from Director General W. Dik promising better service. NVPTT did not escape censure in the press when it allegedly saturated the private automatic branch exchange market, a large and very restricted one until then, with price reductions of 30% to 50% a month before privatization.

The new status of the PTT coincided with an EEC paper on liberalization in the telecommunications industry suggesting a very different market. As Ben Verwaayen, president of PTT Telecom BV since 1988, said in January 1990: "There is no single market anymore. There is no consumer and business market. There is only a services market in which business clients and consumers, basing themselves on their own logic, decide to consumer or not. . . . Market decisions are even more difficult than the new technology."

The PTT's way of redefining the nature of its business during the 1980s has been a policy of total client responsiveness, achieved by renewing and expanding processes and capacity in two areas: first, connecting the client to the infrastructure, and second, enhancing his user capacity. Hence there was a strategy of relentless modernization; digitalization was on course for completion in the year 2000. A five-year plan, started in 1988, aimed to standardize language and procedures within the company. Staff, no longer civil servants, yet still working for the nation's largest employer, were encouraged to take responsibility at the lowest level and work as small independent units, a modular approach that is more market responsive. Research, on which NVPTT spends on average more than Dfl 100 million per annum, is still carried out by a wholly owned subsidiary with a staff of 480, the Dr. Neher Laboratories at Leidschendam.

PTT Telecom BV is well positioned for the largest-growth telecommunications industry, mobile telephones, where the differences between cellular and cordless varieties are becoming ever smaller. It already had an effective monopoly on car phones since 1988. There were 100,000 such customers in 1990, and numbers were expected to rise to 500,000 by the end of the 20th century. The most important task, however, was the completion of an integrated services digital network (ISDN), which would allow users to transmit speech, text, data, and images simultaneously. Trials with a link-up to Germany were started in 1989 in Rotterdam, and ISDN had to be more widely available after 1991. With national borders becoming less relevant, European and worldwide standards for the new technology were to be consolidated with the utmost urgency before greater exploitation. NVPTT has realized, however, that the field needs a market leader, even if in research only. PTT Telecom BV aims to offer complete "tele-information" packages, both at home and abroad. All these are open to competition, yet were so highly restricted prior to 1989 that they were poorly developed. Viditel does not have many users. One new facility, electronic data interchange, standardized by the United Nations, is widely advertised by PTT Telecom BV and used by customs, ports, banks, and doctors.

PTT Post BV has benefited from a similar drive toward rationalization and product diversification. New services like guaranteed 48-hour delivery for large users and extended business hours have proven effective. The most important step forward was the creation in September 1990 of a new entity in the fast-mail market: express mail service (EMS), or PTT POST EMS, which uses advanced computer techniques for the tracking and tracing of items. Both companies are being groomed for a more challenging race in the international market. With some of the lowest tariffs and highest standards in Europe, despite the relatively easy run in the past, NVPTT is off to a good start in the new market for individualized services.

Principal Subsidiaries: PTT Telecom BV; PTT Post BV.

Further Reading: Foreman-Peck, J., & J. Muller, eds., *European Telecommunication Organisations,* Baden Baden, 1988; "Regulatory Situation of Telecommunications in the EEC," *TRC Review,* 1990.

—Marc Du Ry

MCI COMMUNICATIONS CORPORATION

1133 Nineteenth Street, Northwest
Washington, D.C. 20036
U.S.A.
(202) 872-1600
Fax: (202) 887-2154

Public Company
Incorporated: 1968 as Microwave Communications, Inc.
Employees: 24,509
Sales: $7.68 billion
Stock Exchange: NASDAQ

MCI Communications Corporation is the second-largest U.S. provider of long-distance telecommunications services. The company led the charge in introducing competition in the telecommunications industry and precipitated the breakup of AT&T's Bell System. In the post-divestiture era, MCI quickly became a multibillion-dollar global enterprise. MCI serves a large and diverse clientele, including large corporations; local, state, and federal government agencies; small businesses; and individual residential customers. The company underwent explosive growth in the 1980s, but may confront slower times as the already fiercely competitive market intensifies, with rivals AT&T, US Sprint, and the approximately 450 other long-distance carriers.

Founded in 1968 as Microwave Communications, Inc. by John Goeken, owner of a mobile-radio business, MCI's regulatory history began in 1963, when Goeken filed an application with the Federal Communications Commission (FCC) for permission to construct a private-line microwave radio system between Chicago and St. Louis, Missouri. Goeken proposed to erect a series of microwave towers between the two cities that would carry calls on a microwave beam. AT&T had actually developed the technology and used microwaves on many of its long-distance routes. Unlike the Bell System, which had to expend enormous sums to maintain and operate the basic wire-and-cable network, however, Goeken proposed to offer a much cheaper alternative by employing microwave technology exclusively. As *Fortune*, April 1970, noted, Goeken contended that he would provide a service not offered by any of the existing telephone companies: "wider choice of bandwidths, greater speed, greater flexibility . . . and prices as much as 94 percent cheaper than A.T.&T.'s." In addition to carrying voice transmissions, the company stated that its greatest appeal would be to those who wanted to send data or a combination of data and voice messages.

Goeken's application set the stage for one of the great corporate battles in U.S. history by challenging the prevailing public-service principle that had been developed and applied to telephony during the 19th and 20th centuries. The public-service principle was the philosophy that universal availability of telephone service could be achieved only through one independent and interconnecting network. It was believed by those who built the system and those who came to regulate it that the communications industry was a natural monopoly, in which quality and service were best achieved through one integrated system rather than through the play of competing interests. At the time when Goeken filed his application, AT&T saw him as a small but important threat to its position as the nation's basic provider of phone services.

In 1964 several corporations, including AT&T, its Illinois Bell subsidiary, Western Union, and GTE's Illinois-based subsidiary, petitioned the FCC to deny Goeken's application. The corporations argued that Goeken's proposed service would be redundant. More important, AT&T charged that Goeken's service would skim the most profitable segment of the communications market at the expense of universal service provided by Bell. AT&T depended on charging high rates for some of its intercity services—such as private line, WATS, and regular long distance—to subsidize the vast expense of constructing and maintaining the nation's communications network. AT&T also used the revenue derived from these services to subsidize the price of local service, making the cost of basic phone service affordable to the average customer. If Goeken and others were allowed to compete openly in the market, this delicate system of rate averaging would be disrupted. Although it was in the interest of AT&T and the others to stall proceedings as long as possible in the hope that Goeken would not pursue his plan, most of the delays stemmed from Goeken himself. Filing deficiencies caused endless delays.

The seeds of change in the regulatory climate were sown in the revolution of new technologies that arose during and after World War II. Rapid technological advances in the fields of microwave relay, satellites, computers, and coaxial cable, in addition to other technologies such as mobile radio, recording devices, and answering machines, gave rise to a number of small, aggressive firms seeking to enter the telecommunications field. As these firms, armed with the new technologies, demanded increasingly more access to the telecommunications market, the FCC was compelled to respond. In a string of rulings, the FCC first in 1956 decided that under certain conditions non-Bell terminal equipment could be attached to the Bell System network. In 1959 the FCC permitted firms to operate private microwave communications systems for internal use.

With these two decisions, the FCC paved the way for entry of competitive firms into certain markets. The FCC opened completely the terminal-equipment market in 1968. Almost immediately dozens of small firms entered the market seeking to sell equipment in competition with Bell products.

In this changing regulatory climate of the early 1960s, Goeken arrived on the scene proposing a supplemental service that he claimed was not being provided by any company. Goeken claimed that he was seeking only a peripheral submarket much too small to disrupt AT&T's system of rate averaging. AT&T,

however, opposed the entry, claiming that the ostensibly new and innovative service was merely a variation of a service already offered.

In 1968, as the FCC was still considering the newly incorporated Microwave Communications, Inc.'s application, the fortunes of the small company took a dramatic turn when William McGowan joined the company as chairman and chief executive officer. McGowan saw promise in the company, put his money behind it, and soon devised a strategy that would lead Microwave Communications, Inc. (MCI) to phenomenal success. When McGowan joined the firm, MCI's major asset was a five-year-old application to provide point-to-point private-line service by microwave between Chicago and St. Louis.

Almost immediately, McGowan set up a new company, Microwave Communications of America, to attract private investors to finance MCI-affiliated companies around the country. At the same time, the company announced plans for an 11,000-mile system that would run through 40 states and be operated by 16 affiliates. Most importantly, McGowan began to orchestrate a legal-political strategy that would serve MCI extraordinarily well in later years when the company lobbied the FCC and Congress to grant its license.

On August 13, 1969, in a four-to-three decision, the FCC authorized MCI's Chicago–St. Louis application. The decision also assured MCI that it could interconnect with the Bell System network to enable MCI to provide its proposed services. Instead of settling the AT&T-MCI dispute, however, the FCC's MCI decision set the stage for a major battle over telecommunications policy as a result of the commission's failure to clearly delineate the boundaries of competition. The market threatened by MCI's entry was considerably larger than the market opened by the FCC's 1959 decision, which had allowed individual firms to set up their own in-house microwave communications systems. AT&T repeatedly charged that MCI would not be providing any new technologies or services but only skimming the most profitable routes, which AT&T needed to support unprofitable rural routes and basic local phone service.

It was clear to McGowan that to build MCI into a major national telecommunications network, AT&T's monopoly would have to be dismantled. McGowan launched a three-pronged offensive, lobbying Congress, the FCC, and the courts. The company hired Kenneth Cox in 1971 as a senior vice president who was assigned to lobby the FCC. Cox was a former FCC commissioner who had voted for approval of MCI's application in 1969.

AT&T responded aggressively to the FCC's MCI decision and was joined by Western Union and GTE in petitioning the FCC to reconsider MCI's application. Since other firms were then seeking entry to provide similar microwave private-line services, the companies argued that MCI could no longer be considered an isolated experiment, and that increased competition would lead to higher prices, interfere with universal service, and undermine the basic system of rate averaging. MCI countered that these concerns were unfounded. The FCC denied the petitions, and in 1971 MCI received final approval to build its Chicago-St. Louis route.

Ultimately the 1971 FCC decision led to open entry into the private-line market. The FCC's 1971 deregulatory move, however, was narrow in scope and intent, designed to open only a specialized segment of the market. It was not the initial inten-

tion of the FCC to encourage full-scale competition with AT&T. The goal was to allow other firms to provide services not available from AT&T.

On June 22, 1972, MCI issued public stock, raising more than $100 million, and, assisted by a $72 million line of bank credit, it began construction of the Chicago–St. Louis route. The company also laid plans for its national microwave network that would run from coast to coast. MCI soon ran into trouble with AT&T, however, over the issue of interconnection with Bell's basic phone network. The FCC ruling had assured MCI that it could use Bell's local phone network to provide its service, but it did not stipulate at what cost or how quickly AT&T should install MCI's lines. At the same time, AT&T announced that it was instituting a new pricing system called HI/LOW to compete directly with MCI and others on private line routes. By 1973 MCI was in financial trouble. Just months away from opening its nationwide microwave network, the company defaulted on its line of bank credit and was on the verge of collapse. Also in 1973 Microwave Communications, Inc. reorganized as MCI Communications Corporation.

Because the FCC's rulings—especially the decision on MCI—had spawned such competition, the commission had a political stake in MCI's success. McGowan understood the FCC's commitment to the survival of competition. To ensure MCI's preservation he worked quickly to enter the more profitable markets, capitalizing on the FCC's support. In the fall of 1973, McGowan, badly in need of cash, urged the FCC to authorize MCI to enlarge its services to include FX lines. Such lines connect a single customer in one city to another city, in which any number can be reached. The service, however, required the use of Bell's switched network, which AT&T saw as a violation of the intent of previous FCC rulings. In the protracted legal battle that ensued, MCI won a major victory that served as a prelude to the company becoming a full-scale long-distance competitor of AT&T.

In 1973 MCI also began lobbying the antitrust division of the Justice Department to file a suit against AT&T to break apart the Bell System. On March 6, 1974, MCI filed a civil antitrust suit of its own, seeking damages from AT&T. Shortly thereafter, the Justice Department filed an antitrust case against AT&T to break up the Bell System.

Even though MCI had succeeded in enlarging its markets by winning approval to provide FX services, the company had yet to make a profit. Between March 1973 and March 1975, the company lost working capital at the rate of $1 million a month. It needed new markets and, in a risky gamble, began to offer Execunet, a service nearly identical to AT&T's regular, very profitable long-distance service. If the company was successful it could become a wealthy corporation, but if it failed, MCI faced the possibility of bankruptcy.

In 1975 V. Orville Wright joined MCI. Wright soon became president. Also in 1975, AT&T protested to the FCC that by providing Execunet, MCI had flagrantly exceeded its mandate. The FCC concurred, and MCI was directed to cease providing Execunet service. MCI won an appeal, and in 1978 the Supreme Court refused to review the appeal court's ruling that overturned the FCC ban on Execunet and ordered Bell to offer interconnection service to MCI. The breakthrough Execunet victory saved MCI from possible financial collapse. The company, in opposition to both AT&T and the FCC, had won the right to provide long-distance service. In effect, MCI had cracked the Bell System monopoly. MCI soon began offering its long-distance service to residential as well as business customers. Then a full-scale competitor in the lucrative long distance market, MCI saw its revenues increase sharply. By 1981 MCI's annual revenues approached $1 billion. The Execunet victory also opened the long-distance market to other small firms. Few, however, could afford to expend the enormous sums needed to build and maintain their own network facilities.

By the early 1980s it was clear that the government was winning its antitrust suit against AT&T. On January 8, 1982, the Justice Department and AT&T announced agreement in the seven-year-old case, providing for the divestiture of the 22 wholly owned local Bell operating companies. MCI's successful crusade for deregulation and divestiture, however, placed the company under financial strain in the immediate aftermath of the Bell System's breakup in 1984. AT&T, responding to the competitive inroads made by MCI and others, began drastically reducing its rates. MCI's profit margins collapsed as it was compelled to reduce rates. Higher access charges also squeezed the company. In 1985 MCI's stock plunged from over $20 per share to under $7 per share, and in 1986 the company, despite having the second-largest share of the long-distance market, posted a loss of $448.4 million. From the beginning, MCI's profits derived not from superior technology or innovative processes, but from its cost advantage over AT&T, which it passed on to customers. Once the local Bell operating companies were divested, MCI's artificial cost advantage disappeared.

In 1985 MCI was awarded a disappointing $113.3 million in its civil antitrust suit against AT&T. Also in 1985, in need of capital to expand MCI's national network and to finance an aggressive marketing campaign to win new long-distance customers, McGowan struck a deal with IBM, which bought 18% of MCI for cash with the option to later expand its holdings up to 30%.

McGowan continued to argue the need to regulate AT&T for several years before open competition could be considered viable. Whereas McGowan had led the charge for deregulation throughout the 1970s, he now argued that only vigorous regulation could guarantee that MCI and other competitors would be able to compete effectively with AT&T. The following year, MCI called for the removal of all remaining regulatory restraints. The odd alliance was created by the companies' shared perception that deregulation would enable both to improve their financial outlook by increasing rates. The two companies also had a shared interest in opposing proposals advanced by the FCC and the Justice Department to relax regulation of the former Bell operating companies, which had become competitors of MCI and AT&T.

In 1985 V. Orville Wright retired as president of MCI, but continued to serve as vice chairman until 1990. He was replaced as president by Bert C. Roberts Jr.

MCI weathered the wake of AT&T's divestiture and had expanded rapidly into providing a wide range of domestic and international voice and data communications services. The company's communications services include domestic and international long-distance telephone service; international record communications services between the United States and more than 200 countries; and a domestic and international time-sensitive electronic mail service. Long-distance telephone service accounted for 90% of MCI's total revenue in 1989. The company had bolstered its position in domestic and international markets through a series of investments, including acquisition of Satellite Business Systems; RCA Global Communications, Inc.; and certain assets and contracts of Western Union's Advanced Transmission Systems division. In 1990 MCI also purchased a 25% interest in INFONET Services Corporation, a provider of international data services, and acquired for $1.25 billion Telecom USA, then the nation's fourth-largest long-distance company. With the acquisitions, MCI had approximately a 16% share of the domestic long-distance market. In another move, the company announced it acquired Overseas Telecommunications, Inc., which provides international digital satellite services to 27 countries worldwide, in March 1991.

Since its incorporation in 1968, MCI had profited from its successes in the regulatory arena. The company is well positioned to continue to capitalize on its strategic investments and its expanding digital transmission and switching facilities to further extend its reach worldwide.

Principal Subsidiaries: MCI Telecommunications Corporation; MCI International, Inc.; Western Union International, Inc.

Further Reading: Simon, Samuel A., *After Divestiture: What the AT&T Settlement Means for Business and Residential Telephone Service,* White Plains, New York, Knowledge Industry Publications, Inc., 1985; Tunstall, Brooke W., *Disconnecting Parties, Managing the Bell System Breakup: An Inside View,* New York, McGraw-Hill Book Co., 1985; Coll, Steve, *The Deal of the Century: The Breakup of AT&T,* New York, Atheneum, 1986; Kahaner, Larry, *On the Line: The Men of MCI—Who Took On AT&T, Risked Everything and Won,* New York, Warner Books, 1986; Faulhaber, Gerald R., *Telecommunications in Turmoil: Technology and Public Policy,* Cambridge, Ballinger Publishing Co., 1987; Stone, Alan, *Wrong Number: The Breakup of AT&T,* New York, Basic Books, 1989.

—Bruce P. Montgomery

NIPPON TELEGRAPH AND TELEPHONE CORPORATION

1-1-6 Uchi-Saiwaicho
Chiyoda-ku
Tokyo 100
Japan
(03) 3509 3051
Fax: (03) 3503 9990

Public Company
Incorporated: 1985
Employees: 261,621
Sales: ¥6.02 trillion (US$48.24 billion)
Stock Exchanges: Tokyo Osaka Nagoya

Nippon Telegraph and Telephone Corporation (NTT) is the largest investor-owned company in Japan, with an annual turnover equivalent to 10% of the Japanese national budget. Until 1986 NTT was the sole telecommunications organization in Japan, but after privatization NTT not only had to cope with fierce competition from newly legalized common carriers but also had to go about reforming itself from a large overstaffed monopoly to a new streamlined organization. NTT's role is separate from that of Kokusai Denshin Denwa Co. Ltd. (KDD), the International Telegraph and Telephone Company, as NTT is limited to active trading in the domestic market only. This strict separation is required by Japanese law. Since privatization, however, NTT has managed to extend its business abroad through the formation of subsidiaries such as NTT International Corporation (NTTI) and the International Affairs Department of NTT. The company has been quick to respond to the need for more technically advanced services. Diversifying from conventional network services, NTT has devoted its energies to developing in many different areas, including providing digital data transmission and digital data exchange services. Recent advances have been made in areas such as videotex, facsimile, and video conference services. Terminal equipment sales and telecommunications consulting are also part of NTT's varied range of services. Traditional telephone sales, however, remain NTT's largest business area. In 1990 they provided 78.4% of the total operating revenue. A series of subsidiaries and affiliates extend NTT's business into different areas, such as real estate, construction engineering, and advertising. In addition, NTT owns an extremely valuable asset, 33 million square meters of land.

In 1877, one year after its invention by Alexander Graham Bell, the telephone became available in Japan. At first its use was reserved for the government, public affairs organizations such as the police, and a few businesses. It was not until 1890 that telephone services became available to the general public. Lines were laid between Tokyo and Yokohama, connecting 155 Tokyo subscribers to 42 in Yokohama. The first long-distance service became available in 1899 between Tokyo and Osaka, and discussions began as to how the telephone industry could best be developed. In 1889 the government approved a state-run telephone system. Although there were calls for a privately run company to be established, the Sino-Japanese War of 1894 to 1895 and the Depression of the 1930s meant that calls for privatization went unheeded. In the 1930s the Ministry of Communications created the special telegraph and telephone system research committee, which discussed the establishment of a half-government, half-private company. Initial plans were made for the formation of Nippon Telegraph and Telephone Corporation, but were abandoned again due to an economic downturn and a sudden decline in the number of telephone subscribers. The outbreak of World War II led to another drop in telephone subscribers, to 468,000. It was not until 1952, after a bill for a public telephone company was passed, that the Nippon Telegraph and Telephone Public Corporation (NTTPC) was formed, based on recommendations issued in a report by the government-run Telegraph and Telephone Restoration Council. In 1953 KDD Ltd. was established to facilitate international telecommunications, and international telegraph and telephone business was transferred to this company.

As Japan began to recover after World War II, the demand for telecommunication services increased. In 1953 NTTPC's first five-year expansion project of telegraph and telephone started, leading to an increase in the number of subscribers from 1.55 million to 2.64 million. Fueled by consumers' needs and advances in telecommunications technology, by 1963 the number of subscribers had increased to 9.89 million. As NTTPC's domestic market grew rapidly, NTTPC began to expand into the international market, although at this time technical cooperation was the extent of NTTPC's international involvement.

Within Japan the demand for telecommunication services continued to grow. By 1972 the number of telephone subscribers had reached 20 million, and despite the demand caused by such enormous growth, NTTPC saw two of its aims realized in 1977: telephone services became available nationwide, and the company was able to install services as soon as they were required. Automatic dialing also became nationally available, and with the goal of international involvement, an international office was opened in 1979.

Moves towards privatization came slowly. Meanwhile, NTTPC began to examine its infrastructure. The second ad hoc commission on privatization in 1981 examined the "public" corporate side of NTTPC and saw privatization as a way of improving efficiency. A third report detailed plans for privatization, reorganizing the company's structure and making independent the data communications systems sector; in May to July 1988, the latter was established as NTT Data Communication Systems Corporation (NTT Data), a wholly owned NTT subsidiary. NTT's corporation law went into effect on December 20, 1984. Nippon Telegraph and Telephone Corporation was newly launched as a privatized joint stock corporation on April 1, 1985, with the provision that the Nippon Telegraph and Telephone Law be subject to revision within five years. On an international level, similar events were taking place in the United States and the United Kingdom. In 1984 the British Telecommunications Bill came into force, allowing the privatization of British Telecom and liberalizing the British telecommunications industry, as competitors such as Mercury were issued licenses to operate. The United States followed a similar pattern in 1984, when American Telephone & Telegraph Company's Bell System was broken up and restructured into seven regional holding companies.

After privatization, the market opened to new carriers to start operations in competition with NTT. In April 1985 three carriers, Daini-Denden, Nippon Telecom, and Teleway Japan, applied for approval to operate as telecommunications companies. One effect of direct competition was that NTT was obliged to make a reduction in long-distance rates and upgrade its services. In July 1985, several new services were launched. A further measure to enhance performance was the restructuring of NTT's business into divisional organizations and the reorganization of the research and development headquarters from four to nine laboratories. NTT's first subsidiary company was launched in April 1985 and marked the opening of a chapter in NTT's history that would lead to the establishment of over 80 subsidiaries. The first was NTT Lease Co. Ltd.; its activities included the leasing and installment sales of terminal equipment.

In terms of international activities, privatization allowed NTT slightly more room to maneuver, through the creation of subsidiaries that had greater powers abroad. Prior to privatization, NTTPC's overseas operations on the whole had been restricted to participating in international exchanges, sending experts abroad and forming agreements with a number of countries. As early as 1954 NTTPC had accepted trainees from Taiwan, and up to the early 1990s accepted approximately 160 trainees from 60 countries a year. The expert dispatch scheme that started in 1960 has resulted in more than 500 specialists being sent to 54 countries. During the 1960s and 1970s a whole series of technical assistance programs were arranged between participating countries and NTTPC. Projects as diverse as assisting with the establishment of a training center in Thailand in 1961 or setting up a microwave radio system in Paraguay characterized NTTPC's activities abroad at this time. Kuwait, in particular, was involved in a whole series of projects. A contract was signed in June 1965 between Kuwait's Minister of Communications and NTTPC, and led to the launch of a ten-year project.

The setting up of representative offices was another method whereby NTTPC extended its operations overseas. NTTPC's first overseas office opened in Bangkok in 1958, offering technical assistance, and a European base was established in 1965 with the opening of the Geneva representative office. This was followed in 1973 with the opening of NTTPC's London representative office. Prior to NTTPC's privatization, the London office had concentrated on issuing bonds and collecting information. NTT Europe Ltd. was formally incorporated in the United Kingdom in 1989 to encourage cooperation with the United Kingdom's own telecommunications industry and to help extend global networks for Japanese business users. In similar fashion, the representative office in Brasilia, Brazil, became an officially registered overseas subsidiary company

in November 1987. NTT do Brasil Comercio e Representacoes Lomita provides technical assistance and supports international exchange programs to countries in South America, in particular Brazil and Argentina, and also to Mexico. Representative offices also opened in Jakarta, Indonesia, in 1972; in Kuala Lumpur, the Malaysian capital, in 1986; and in Singapore in 1990. After the restoring of diplomatic relations between China and Japan in 1972, NTTPC made a technical exchange agreement with China in 1980, leading to the opening of an office in Beijing in 1985.

NTT has had a presence in the United States as early as 1966 when NTTPC employees were sent to New York. In 1970 a branch office was established, with the primary objective of forming connections with U.S. carriers, and that went on to play an important role in international procurement. Due to an increase in business, NTT's California representative office was established, and after privatization NTT expanded its U.S. operations, incorporating the two U.S. offices into NTT America Inc. NTT also established exchange programs with several U.S. companies, including NYNEX and Pacific Bell, and a number of equipment purchase agreements were made. In May 1986 a purchase agreement was set up with Northern Telecom in a $250 million deal.

NTT International Corporation was established in the year of NTT's privatization. Starting with ¥3 billion and 150 employees, it has become one of NTT's largest subsidiaries. Originally established with the aim of providing consulting services related to the telecommunications industry and providing products to overseas buyers, NTTI is able to carry out a number of functions overseas that the NTT Corporation is unable to do because of Japanese regulations. Marketing NTT's products overseas and carrying out market research to see which products would be profitable are two important functions of NTTI. A third is to provide services related to the establishment of telecommunications infrastructures. An example of such work was a development project funded through NTTI by the World Bank in Indonesia. Australia is another country in which NTTI has been active, helping to develop a facsimile mail service in 1987. In Finland, NTTI sold large numbers of hand-held computer terminals to a Finnish bank.

NTT's fluctuating fortunes since privatization have tended to be reflected in the company's share price. In October 1986 the minister of finance invited tender for the initial price of NTT stock before flotation. The initial price decided on was ¥1.97 million after NTT's original price was ¥50,000. By February 9, 1987, NTT was listed on the Tokyo, Nagoya, and Osaka stock exchanges and was soon to be extended to other Japanese stock exchanges. After shares were floated, they reached a high of ¥3.18 million in 1987 but then collapsed to ¥1 million by the end of 1990. Another contributing factor was the infamous Recruit scandal that hit Japan in 1988, when a number of senior officials were accused of accepting bribes. Scandal hit NTT when its former chairman Hisashi Shinto received a heavy fine and a suspended jail sentence for his part in the Recruit scandal. The post of NTT chairman was left open until Haruo Yamaguchi was appointed to the post in the middle of 1990. Although NTT corporation law originally obliged the government to hold one-third or more of the total number of outstanding shares at all times and stated that "no foreign nationals or foreign judicial persons" were allowed to possess NTT shares, after some deliberation in October 1990 NTT announced a plan overturning this law. In December 1990 the Japanese government announced that it would start selling 500,000 shares a year beginning in April 1991.

Privatization has also forced NTT to examine its operational efficiency and to provide better customer services. On May 23, 1988, NTT Data Communications Systems Corporations was established as a wholly owned subsidiary. Aimed at designing data communications that link hardware with software for financial institutions, private companies, and government organizations, NTT Data also provides training seminars and consultation facilities. It has proved to be a profitable part of the NTT group. In 1990 operating revenues from NTT Data increased to ¥306.1 billion. One of NTT Data's major achievements was helping to set up the Tokyo International Financial Futures Exchange System in June 1989. Further recognition came to NTT Data when its IC Card, a card that allows Nissan car owners to store car history information, won the 1989 Nikkei Annual Products Award. Another significant move was the introduction in April 1988 of INS-NET 64, described as the world's first wide-area commercial integrated services digital network (ISDN). NTT, KDD, and AT&T put together a three-day presentation simultaneously at sites in Japan and New York. Following this, NTT sponsored a global ISDN exhibition, NTT Collection '90. Approximately 40,000 visitors attended this exhibition, that demonstrated the capability of ISDN and featured an actual ISDN link-up between NTT, AT&T, British Telecom, France Telecom, and Singapore Telecom.

In the area of international equipment procurement NTT has begun to play a greater role. In accordance with the general agreement on tariffs and trade (GATT), by 1990 orders had grown by 9% to $352 million and included purchases as diverse as digital transmission equipment from AT&T, digital switching systems from Northern Telecom, and pocket bell pagers and cellular telephone equipment from Motorola. Procurement seminars were held at various European sites to encourage European suppliers, as well as in various cities in the United States.

By March 1989, NTT's performance was suffering because of increased competition from other common carriers, the cost of launching NTT Data, and the enforced reduction in long-distance telephone rates. In order to bring about recovery, NTT re-examined its administrative structure and in April 1989 reduced its four-tiered administrative structure to three levels. Another cost-cutting reform has been the reduction in staff numbers. At its peak in 1979, NTT had 330,000 staff, but by 1989 the company had managed to reduce this number to 276,000. Not satisfied with this, however, there were fur-

ther plans for greater reductions in staff, the target being 230,000 by the year 1994.

In an interview with the *Financial Times* in January 1991, the president of NTT, Masashi Kojima, spoke of some of the problems NTT was facing. Enforced cuts in rates, because of increased competition from other carriers, and a scheme whereby competitors are connected to the network at a rate that reduces NTT's profitability, have led to some resentment. President Kojima favored the introduction of a new kind of access charge or fee system to create a fairer market. In terms of long-term international strategy, Kojima does not have ambitious plans for NTT to play a full international role yet, but favored a specific international strategy that might mean installing a network in a country with less developed telecommunication systems. In March 1991, however, discussions were under way for a joint venture between three of the most powerful telephone companies: NTT; the British telecommunications group; and Deutsche Bundespost Telecom, the German telecommunications group. This joint venture, called Pathfinder, promises to offer a telecommunications network to large international companies. This presents NTT with the problem of operating internationally within NTT corporation law. In an effort to exploit the potential of the European market as it moves towards greater unity, and the markets of Eastern Europe and the countries of the former Soviet Union as they become more accessible, NTT announced in June 1991 the establishment of a new subsidiary in Düsseldorf, Germany: NTT Deutschland GmbH.

NTT's plans for the future center around streamlining its operations in a cost-effective fashion and offering high-quality service to its customers. In an attempt to promote a fair and open market, NTT opened the Fair Competition Promotion Office in 1990. In the long term, NTT stresses the need to develop ISDN technology and to realize the importance of the cellular mobile market. NTT's future remains far from certain. In 1995 discussions reopen on the future of NTT and the threat of the huge NTT empire being broken up into smaller components still lingers.

Principal Subsidiaries: NTT Data Communications Systems Corporation; NTT Chuo Mobile Communications Corporation (43.4%); NTT Urban Development Co., Ltd.

Further Reading: "Think Global, Challenge Global (International Activities of NTT)," Tokyo, Nippon Telegraph and Telephone Corporation, 1990.

—Clare Doran

NORTHERN TELECOM LIMITED

3 Robert Speck Parkway
Mississauga, Ontario L4Z 3C8
Canada
(416) 897-9000
Fax: (416) 275-1143

Public Company
Incorporated: 1914 as Northern Electric Company Limited
Employees: 49,039
Sales: US$6.77 billion
Stock Exchanges: New York Toronto Montreal Vancouver
London Tokyo

From its base in Canada, Northern Telecom Limited has grown steadily during its long history to become a leading global supplier of telecommunications systems. In the United States, for example, Northern Telecom was in the early 1990s the second-largest manufacturer of telecommunications equipment after American Telephone and Telegraph (AT&T). Northern Telecom sells its products in more than 80 countries and operates 42 manufacturing plants in the United States, Canada, France, Australia, Thailand, Malaysia, the Republic of Ireland, and the People's Republic of China. Its products include telephones, networks, wire and cable, telecommunications and transmissions systems, fiber-optic cable and equipment, and other equipment for both public and private communications networks.

To reach such a position, Northern Telecom implemented bold and aggressive economic strategies throughout its history. During four years alone, from 1981 to 1985, the telecommunications giant's net profit margin jumped by 30%, and its sales doubled. In 1985 sales were US$4.3 billion.

Northern Telecom's origins can be traced back to 1880, four years after Alexander Graham Bell invented the telephone in 1876. In that year Bell Telephone Company of Canada (Bell Canada) was founded. To develop adequate telephone equipment for the fledgling company, Bell established its mechanical department on July 24, 1882, in Montreal, Canada, with a staff of 3 that soon expanded to 11. Success came early to the company, and five years later the mechanical department moved to a larger facility to accommodate a staff that had increased to 54.

The growth led to Bell Canada taking out a charter in 1895 for a separate company to take over the mechanical department's work. On December 7 of that year, Northern Electric

& Manufacturing Company Limited was incorporated under the dominion charter. With C.F. Sise as president, the company called its first general meeting of stockholders on March 24, 1896. By 1902 Northern Electric employed 250 people and occupied a 48,000-square-foot plant, which it leased from Bell Canada. That plant had expanded to 241,000 square feet in 1912, the year Northern Electric and Bell Canada worked out a deal whereby Northern would become the storekeeper and purchasing agent for Bell.

In 1895 C.F. Sise had bought a small plant from Alexander Barrie that was involved in manufacturing rubber-coated wire for the fast-growing electrical industry. In turn, Sise offered the company to Bell Canada for what it had cost him. Bell Canada accepted the offer, and on December 19, 1899, the Wire & Cable Company, as the enterprise became known, was granted a province of Quebec charter. Sise was appointed president and Barrie superintendent. A big success, the Wire & Cable Company replaced its provincial charter with a dominion charter in 1911 and changed its name to Imperial Wire & Cable Company.

By then both Northern Electric and Imperial Wire & Cable were playing vital roles as Canada's major suppliers of telephone equipment. In many operational areas, however, their needs and interests overlapped. The management of both companies realized that to increase efficiency and to reduce overhead, the two enterprises should amalgamate. On July 5, 1914, they consolidated under the laws of Canada into Northern Electric Company Limited. While the general sales division continued to be located in Montreal, the company established supply and repair divisions for western Canada in 1929 and for the Maritime region in 1944. Despite the Great Depression, which forced Northern to cut back production, the company still managed to grow. It established the electronics division in 1931 and expanded its base of operations by purchasing a majority interest in Amalgamated Electric Company Ltd. in 1932 and, in 1935, by launching Dominion Sound Equipment Ltd., a wholly owned subsidiary that supplied Canada with electric sound equipment, acoustic and sound proofing supplies, radio and broadcasting sound equipment, and other lines of electrical equipment.

When the Depression ended, Northern became involved in Canada's World War II effort, converting 95% of its operation to war production. By 1944 most of the company's 9,325 employees were engaged in this activity. Soon after the war's end in 1945, Northern immediately began a flurry of construction to meet the expanding communications needs of Canada's growing communities. As a measure of its continuing growth, Northern's work force expanded to 12,775 by 1948.

The company was gradually losing its independence. By 1956 the U.S. company Western Electric, the manufacturing arm of AT&T, owned 40% of Northern Electric, an economic situation that forced Northern to operate much like a "branch plant." During this period, the company had a small research and development staff, and its sales efforts were confined to Canada. As its main function was to manufacture Western Electric products for Bell Canada, Northern Electric's product line generally lagged behind Western Electric's by two to three years.

Northern Electric ceased operating like a branch plant in 1956 when Western Electric signed a consent decree with the U.S. Department of Justice in which it agreed to relinquish its interest in Northern Electric. Bell Canada acquired most of Western Electric's interest in Northern Electric in 1957 and the remainder in 1964. With no product line of its own, and with management knowing that it must start one to remain competitive, Northern Electric stepped up its research and development efforts, establishing Northern Electric Laboratories—with a staff of 30 to 40 people—in 1958. In 1965 the company made a commitment to develop a switching device known as SP-1, stored program switch system, which it believed would meet the needs of the Canadian market and spur economic growth. From 12 researchers in 1965, the product development team working on SP-1 grew to more than 100 by the end of the decade. The commitment paid off when Northern put its product on the market. By 1975 not only had every major telephone company in Canada bought the switch, but 25% of all sales were being made in the United States.

Northern Electric's research and development division had become a conglomerate itself, mushrooming to more than 2,000 employees, and eventually incorporating as a separate entity. On January 1, 1971, Northern Electric's subsidiary, Bell-Northern Research Ltd. (BNR) was formed. In the early 1990s, BNR operated research and development facilities in ten cities: four in Canada, five in the United States, and one in the United Kingdom. In 1973 Bell Canada sold a portion of Northern Electric's shares to the public, while retaining a majority holding.

During the 1970s the company established many new subsidiaries, such as Northern Telecom (International) B.V. in Amsterdam, and Northern Telecom (Asia) Limited in Singapore and Hong Kong, both established in 1974. These subsidiaries reflected its increasingly strong presence in the international marketplace. In 1976 the company's name was changed to Northern Telecom Limited (Northern) to reflect the great advances it had made in manufacturing modern telecommunications equipment.

The same year Northern introduced the first fully digital switch. Although AT&T did not immediately authorize its affiliates to buy the switches, independent U.S. telephone companies quickly did, and by 1978 Northern sales had jumped by 130% from the previous year. The demand for the company's digital switches received a big boost in 1981 when AT&T approved the purchase of the switches for its affiliates. In 1984 the U.S. government broke up AT&T, and sales of Northern's digital switches skyrocketed, and volume increased by 1,200% over that of 1976.

Northern had ignored conventional business wisdom and taken chances to get where it had arrived. As one company official said, "When we started to work on the digital central office switches in the 1970s, we were advised to follow AT&T and continue making old analog switches since digital switches would be too expensive." Fortunately for Northern, it did not, and the introduction and marketing of the switch proved to be a major milestone in its history. By 1990 one research firm estimated that the company held close to one-third of the U.S. market for the digital switches.

Northern's fortunes, however, began to change by the mid-1980s. While AT&T was making a comeback with its own switch, Northern made a technological blunder. It began selling new software to provide its phone company subscribers with advanced service capabilities based on new technology. Poor marketing, bugs in the software, and the fact that the

processor in Northern's switch could not keep up with all the new tasks the expanded software had to do alienated many company customers. One disgruntled business executive told *Business Week* in 1987, "Their software and capacity problems are still driving us wild. We're giving our orders to AT&T."

Northern launched a public relations campaign to reassure its customers that it had solved the software problems. It also announced the availability of Supercore, a new processor that cost $50 million to develop. "[Supercore] will double the capacity of our switches and eventually increase it to whatever we want," maintained Northern President David G. Vice.

Many in the telecommunications market remained skeptical, however, and rival telecommunications companies like Japan's NEC, Sweden's Ericsson, and Germany's Siemens began to make a move for Northern's markets. Despite the setbacks, Northern had become one of the giants in the telecommunications industry. Consolidated revenues for 1989 were US$5.41 billion, up from US$4.44 billion in 1986.

Northern repositioned in 1988 because of concerns that the intense global competition combined with the money it had invested in product and market development had affected its financial performance. Under the newly elected chairman, chief executive officer, and president, Paul G. Stern, who took over in March 1989, Northern embarked on a program to restructure the corporation.

Stern's association with Northern began in April of 1988 when the company elected him to its board of directors and to membership on the executive committee. He brought to the job a strong background in advanced-technology company management and a reputation for making tough cost-cutting decisions at large corporations. He had previously served as an executive for Burroughs, Unisys, IBM, and Rockwell. Within nine months after Stern assumed the helm, Northern had reshuffled management, cutting 2,500 jobs; closed 4 of its 41 plants, selling one-fifth of the plants to employees; and changed its bonus system, tying employee incentives in each business unit to company performance.

The dramatic changes caused a stir in Canada. Northern's plans to move its research and development operations from Toronto to Texas and California made Canadians wonder if the company would move its headquarters as well. As of 1991, however, it was still a Canada-based company.

Northern, however, quickly saw positive results from the tough measures it took. In 1989 company expenses fell 18.5% from the year before, while profits jumped 18% on a 13% increase in sales. The company was making a push to garner a bigger share of the market outside the United States, not only by increasing sales of its switches, but by marketing a line of fiber-optic transmission systems and a network design concept called Fibre World. "Invariably, [customers] buy a product because a supplier has an uniqueness," Stern said. "When you're first, the perception lingers." Introduced in February 1989, the concept and its systems are based on a set of international standards established in 1988 called synchronous optical network, or Sonet, which, Northern officials said, would assure compatibility among equipment from different manufacturers, thus permitting the establishment of extensive networks and improving the speed and volume of information that telecommunications systems could carry.

To maintain its position in the highly competitive world of communications technology, Northern continued to invest heavily in research and development. Northern was spending more on research and development than any other company in Canada, and through its subsidiary, Bell-Northern Research Ltd., it had become the biggest employer of telecommunications research professionals in the country; it hired each year between one-quarter and one-third of all available electrical engineering doctoral graduates of Canadian schools. In total, Northern was employing more than 6,100 research and development staff. "For us, there is no question that the major opportunity before the telecommunications industry today is to develop innovative solutions that can link different manufacturers' equipment in public, private and hybrid networks," said Greg Sakes, president of Bell-Northern Research Ltd.

Northern's pioneering work in telecommunications during the 1980s was illustrated by the development of the international services digital network (ISDN), the company's control switching system. Two years after using the technology to make the first ISDN telephone call in North America in November 1986, Northern introduced the technology commercially throughout the continent.

By 1990 Northern was the world's sixth-largest telecommunications company, but corporate management publicly stated that it was preparing for an even more ambitious goal—to become the world's leading supplier of telecommunications equipment by the year 2000. Soon after, it took a major step in that direction when it purchased STC PLC, a large British telecommunications company in January 1991 for about US$2.6 billion. The acquisition put Northern in third place behind Alcatel NW of Belgium and the United States-based AT&T. Northern had already owned 27% of STC PLC when it made the deal.

The purchase increased Northern's total debt to C$4.3 billion, 50% of its equity, compared to 29% before the buyout. Northern said, however, that it planned to help relieve the debt using the C$1.6billion from the sale of STC's computer's division, ICL Ltd., to Fujitsu Ltd. of Japan.

In February 1991 Northern and Motorola, the world's largest supplier of cellular transmission gear, formed a cellular equipment alliance. Observers saw the alliance as the first step in a joint venture to market and develop equipment in the United States and overseas. In preparation for its international push, Northern also announced at the same time that it had undertaken a significant reorganization of its operations.

Among other changes, the marketing, sales, and service activities of Northern were divided into four geographical areas: the United States; Canada, including activities in Mexico, the Caribbean, and Central and South America; Europe, including Africa and the Middle East; and Asia and the Pacific Rim.

Northern dubbed its globalization campaign to become the world's leading supplier of telecommunications equipment Vision 2000. President Stern said the company wanted to increase annual revenues to C$30 billion by the year 2000, a figure that is about five times its 1990 sales. Some observers saw Northern's goal as overly ambitious, as the company would need more than phone switches to improve its international performance.

The skeptics have not deterred Northern Telecom, which has built a strong foundation to take on future challenges. Past performance has shown that it has every intention of following Stern's words: "For us, history is just the beginning."

Principal Subsidiaries: Northern Telecom Inc. (U.S.A.); Northern Telecom Canada Limited; Northern Telecom World Trade Corporation; Northern Telecom Electronics Limited; Bell-Northern Research Ltd. (70%); STC PLC (U.K.); Northern Telecom PLC (U.K.); BNR INC (U.S.A.); BNR Limited (U.K.); Brock Telecom Limited; Netas-Northern Electric Telekomunikasyon A.Ş. (Turkey, 31%); NorTel Australia Pty. Limited; Northern Telecom (Asia) Limited (Hong Kong); Northern Telecom International Finance B.V. (Netherlands); Northern Telecom (CALA) Corporation (U.S.A.); Northern Telecom Europe Limited (U.K.); Northern Telecom Finance Corporation (U.S.A.); Northern Telecom GmbH (Germany); Northern Telecom Industries Sdn. Bhd. (Malaysia); Northern Telecom (Ireland) Limited; Northern Telecom Japan Inc.; NT Meridian S.A. (France, 69.5%); Prism Systems Inc. (51%); Tong Guang-Nortel Limited Liability Company (China, 55%); STC Properties Limited (U.K.); STC Technology Limited (U.K.); STC (Northern Ireland) Limited; Computer Consoles Inc. (U.S.A.); STC Submarine Systems Inc. (U.S.A.).

Further Reading: Wickens, Barbara, "Becoming a Global Giant," *Maclean's*, January 14, 1991.

—Ron Chepesiuk

NYNEX

NYNEX CORPORATION

335 Madison Avenue
New York, New York 10071
U.S.A.
(212) 370-7400

Public Company
Incorporated: 1984
Employees: 95,400
Sales: $13.21 billion
Stock Exchanges: New York Boston Philadelphia Midwest
    Pacific London Tokyo Amsterdam Zürich Geneva Basel

NYNEX Corporation is one of seven regional telephone holding companies in the United States, each handling local telephone service in its region. NYNEX also publishes telephone directories, sells computers, and offers cellular telephone and other communications services. The company had been one of the more troubled of the seven, emeshed in several scandals and facing frequent criticism about its lack of speed in modernizing its infrastructure.

NYNEX was formed in 1984 as part of the breakup of the American Telephone and Telegraph Company (AT&T). AT&T was broken up in keeping with the terms of a consent decree following an antitrust suit by the U.S. Department of Justice. AT&T agreed to divest itself of 22 local telephone companies that were then grouped into seven regional holding companies (RHCs).

NYNEX was formed from New York Telephone Company and New England Telephone and Telegraph Company, two of the oldest telephone companies in the United States. The new company operated in New York, Rhode Island, Massachusetts, Vermont, New Hampshire, Maine, and in part of Connecticut. NYNEX split revenues from long-distance calls between northern New Jersey and the New York City area with Bell Atlantic, another of the seven holding companies. NYNEX began with nearly 12.6 million telephones and $10 billion in assets, making it one of the largest corporations in the United States on its first day of business. It was forbidden, however, from expanding into new information services by the terms of the consent decree and by U.S. Justice Harold Greene, who was overseeing the AT&T breakup.

NYNEX's territory included a higher-than-average income base and many information-age companies that make heavy use of telecommunications. The NYNEX region contained ten million business telephone lines, the largest number of the seven regionals. Business lines are more profitable than residential lines because they are used heavily during the day, when maximum rates are in effect. The Northeast, however, had an aging population and an older-than-average telephone infrastructure. New York Telephone was the first to use fiber-optic cables, laying a ring around Manhattan, but other parts of the NYNEX system badly needed modernization. New York Telephone derived 25% of its revenue from 1% of its customers, leaving it vulnerable to sudden economic shifts. The New York and New England companies were not the highest earners in the Bell System, yet amassed a combined profit of $973 million in 1982, on sales of $9.7 billion.

NYNEX, along with five other RHCs, began trading on the London Stock Exchange within its first few months of business. This provided access to European capital. NYNEX quickly began pushing for permission to enter new businesses relating to local telephone service. It frequently faced opposition from the Federal Communications Commission (FCC), the U.S. Department of Justice, and Justice Greene. In August 1984 the Justice Department came down against several NYNEX proposals, asserting that they would lessen telecommunications competition. In 1984 NYNEX earned $986 million.

In March 1985 NYNEX Business Information Systems, a subsidiary, signed a three-year contract to sell Wang computers and information processing products to business in the Northeast. It continued its push into foreign markets, announcing an agreement with Nippon Telephone and Telegraph to exchange information and resources. It also signed an agreement with an NEC Corporation subsidiary to market an information management service. To aid sales of telecommunications equipment and computer services, the company formed NYNEX Credit Company, providing financial services to other NYNEX companies. Profits reached $1.1 billion in 1985.

Despite the fact that it spent $1.9 billion in 1985 on network construction, frequent criticism was leveled at the company for modernizing its equipment more slowly than any of the other RHCs. While other regionals modernized equipment, NYNEX led in nonphone acquisitions. In 1986 NYNEX bought LIN Broadcasting Corporation's New York City radio-paging operations for $118 million, and the company also bought IBM's chain of 80 computer stores in 33 states, gaining some top IBM executives in the deal. Industry observers estimated the price to be around $150 million. Combined with the 16 Datago computer stores that NYNEX was operating, the new NYNEX Business Centers Co. represented the third-largest chain of company-owned—not franchised—computer stores in the United States. IBM had never made money from the stores, and some criticized NYNEX's move, saying it also would lose money on the chain. Pacific Telesis, another RHC, announced a major expansion of its computer retail stores in southern California to compete with NYNEX's growing presence in that region. In 1985 NYNEX announced a joint agreement with Citicorp and RCA Corporation to form a videotex company, a field several other RHCs also were entering. Videotex is one or more data bases, such as airline schedules and reservation services, that can be entered by means of a personal computer.

New York Telephone received a $155.6 million rate increase from the New York State Public Service Commission in 1986. The previous year New England Telephone had a $35 million rate increase turned down in Massachusetts. NYNEX faced its first significant strike when 37,600 members of the Communications Workers of America walked off the job for eight days over a three-year contract. Profits in 1986 were $1.22 billion.

In 1986 NYNEX began a serious push to enter the international long-distance market by seeking to form a $300 million to $400 million joint venture to lay a transatlantic fiber-optic cable. NYNEX wanted to enter the deal by buying British Tel-Optik Ltd. for $10 million. In 1987 with U.S. President Ronald Reagan's administration calling for expansion of competition in the telecommunications industry, the Justice Department asked Justice Greene to lift the restrictions on the RHCs. In May 1987 the FCC approved NYNEX's plan, but Greene said he feared that the NYNEX plan would cause antitrust problems. The case dragged on, and in July 1988, NYNEX's partner, Britain's Cable and Wireless PLC, scrapped the agreement because of the delay.

In 1987 NYNEX bought Business Intelligence Services Ltd., a London-based banking software, consulting, and financial services company with branches in 13 countries, for $107 million. It also signed a three-year, $400 million contract with Northern Telecom to supply equipment to New England and New York Telephone. In November 1987 the company announced plans to begin selling its white pages telephone directories on computer discs. Net income for 1987 was $1.27 billion.

NYNEX's image was tarnished in 1988 when it had to dismiss or suspend ten mid-level managers for engaging in unfair hiring and promotion and for taking bribes from contractors. In 1988, as other RHCs pulled back from nonphone investments, NYNEX poured more money into computer operations, in an effort to make its stores profitable. In May 1988 NYNEX bought the professional services and software products operations of AGS Computers Inc. for $275 million. With an eye on increasing cellular telephone revenue, NYNEX started an experiment in Boston in which it installed credit-card-operated cellular telephones in taxis. New York Telephone won a contract to build a private fiber-optic network connecting thousands of traders at major securities firms in Manhattan. In November 1988 the FCC issued a long-awaited ruling allowing RHCs to restructure their phone networks to help spread computerized services.

By 1988 New York, the state that generates by far the largest amount of NYNEX's revenue, instituted a program in which it split excess profits with consumers, which meant state regulators would allow the company to earn higher profits. NYNEX had the second-highest profit growth of the RHCs and the highest total return to stockholders. Company profits reached $1.3 billion in 1988.

In February 1989 Delbert Staley retired. He had been NYNEX's chairman and chief executive officer since the company began operating. William C. Ferguson succeeded him. Later that year Ferguson faced a divisive four-month strike by 60,000 union employees over company plans to cut health-care spending. The strike severely damaged the morale of workers and management at a time when the company needed to improve the efficiency of its work force. In 1989 NYNEX had the highest revenue per phone line of any of the seven RHCs, but also the highest costs and lowest profit margins. For 1989 NYNEX had a 13% return on equity versus a 17.5% return for Pacific Telesis. The economy was slowing in New York

and New England, and the antiquated New York Telephone network badly needed modernization. Partly because the NYNEX system was outdated, small companies sprang up in Manhattan with their own loops that bypassed the NYNEX system. In 1989 NYNEX won a bid for a 50% interest in a new company to own, operate, and modernize the phone system of Gibraltar. The other 50% was owned by the Gibraltar government, and NYNEX beat Spanish, British, and Japanese phone companies to get the contract.

The State of New York and the U.S. government launched investigations of NYNEX's unregulated purchasing subsidiary, NYNEX Materiel Enterprises Co., to see if it had overcharged New York Telephone and New England Telephone for a variety of products and services, with the telephone companies then passing the higher charges on to subscribers. The subsidiary bought equipment in bulk to save money, but former employees testified that it also routinely marked up prices. NYNEX refunded $45 million to subscribers at the end of 1988, but New York state regulators claimed that was not enough. New York Telephone hoped for a $440 million rate increase for 1991. At the same time it hoped for rate increases with a cap on its prices rather a cap on its profits, so its profits could increase as it became more efficient. The investigation threatened those goals. Asset write-offs in the fourth quarter of 1989 created the first quarterly loss for a regional holding company, and profits for the year fell to $808 million. Leading business publications pronounced the company the most disappointing of the regional holding companies. Ferguson tried to rebuild NYNEX by cutting costs, earning customers' trust and providing top products and services.

In 1989 regulators told New York Telephone to provide limited types of connections to competitors in exchange for the lifting of some pricing restrictions on its private-line services. NYNEX agreed to design a private fiber-optic network for IBM, connecting 12 of its Westchester County, New York, offices. NYNEX Mobile Communications sold its New York radio paging operations to PageAmerica for $37.5 million in November 1989 in order to focus its energy on cellular telephone service.

Cellular phone service represented an area of tremendous growth for NYNEX as such service was no longer considered an expensive toy but was reckoned instead to be a not-so-expensive necessity. NYNEX Mobile Communications increased its cellular customer base by 68% in 1989. NYNEX had grown from 36,000 cellular subscribers in 1985 to 213,000 in 1989, and its system was becoming overloaded. In August 1990 NYNEX Mobile Communications announced plans to build an ambitious new cellular system that would service 10 to 20 times as many subscribers as the system then in place. The system, using technology invented by San Diego–based Qualcomm, allowed cellular phone conversations to share radio waves by combining them with special codes. The decision was controversial because the Qualcomm system, also chosen by Ameritech Mobile Communications, was incompatible with another system chosen by the Cellular Telecommunications Industry Association to be the next cellular technology. AT&T agreed to manufacture a switch for NYNEX system-Qualcomm. NYNEX also introduced a cellular telephone with voice recognition—a user pressed a button, announced the name of the party to be called, and the phone dialed that party.

NYNEX continued to sell its expertise overseas. By 1990 it had signed telecommunications consulting contracts in the United Kingdom, France, Taiwan, Australia, South Korea, and Singapore. It was also working on the British cable television system. With local phone service growing only at about 5% a year, Eugene A. Sekulow, president of subsidiary NYNEX International, said NYNEX aimed to earn 20% of its revenue abroad by the year 2000. Many foreign telecommunications markets were growing faster than that of the United States, and Justice Greene had limited jurisdiction over what RHCs did outside of the United States. At the same time, many foreign governments were privatizing what had been nationalized telephone systems, presenting unprecedented opportunity for U.S. telecommunications companies. NYNEX had brought in Sekulow, a former president of RCA International, to build a management team specifically designed to take advantage of those opportunities.

NYNEX Information Resources Company produced more than 300 white pages directories and Yellow Pages directories every year, with total circulation topping 30 million. This subsidiary had sales of $818 million in 1989.

NYNEX profits declined to $808 million in 1989, from $1.3 billion in 1988, partly because of a worsening economy in the Northeast, particularly in New York. It began cutting the work force at its telephone operations. New York Telephone proposed an $831 million rate increase for 1991, but the New York state attorney general instead told the company to cut costs and reform its business practices. Late in 1990 New York regulators approved a $250 million rate increase.

NYNEX had been involved in another scandal in 1990 when it was alleged that NYNEX purchasing officials held a series of parties with prostitutes for about 20 NYNEX suppliers, hurting the company's image at a time when it was trying to push through large rate increases. Because of this incident and the Materiel Enterprises problems, some New York regulators considered forcing NYNEX to divest itself of New York Tele-

phone. In September 1990 NYNEX merged Materiel Enterprises with NYNEX Service Company to form Telesector Resources and split its ownership between New York Telephone and New England Telephone. Then in November 1990 NYNEX fired 28 employees of New York Telephone's Buildings Department and disciplined 28 more during an investigation into alleged kickbacks, bribery, and bid-rigging for building maintenance contracts. At the same time, New York authorities were calling for the FCC to reopen the investigation of NYNEX it had launched after reports of overcharges.

NYNEX continued to modernize its phone system, spending about $4.5 billion in 1989 and 1990 combined. By the end of 1990 more than 50% of its customers used quick and efficient digital switches. It had about 480,000 miles of fiber-optic cable in place, compared with 207,000 in 1987.

Principal Subsidiaries: New England Telephone and Telegraph Company; New York Telephone Company; NYNEX Business Information Systems Company; NYNEX Credit Company; NYNEX Information Resources Company; NYNEX Information Solutions Group, Inc.; NYNEX Mobile Communications Company; NYNEX Properties Company; NYNEX Service Company; NYNEX Systems Marketing Company; AGS Computers Inc.; The BIS Group Limited; The Data Group Corporation; Telco Research Corporation; Vista Concepts Inc.; NYNEX International Company; NYNEX Government Affairs; Telesector Resources.

Further Reading: Arenson, Karen W., "At NYNEX, X Is the Unknown," *The New York Times,* October 27, 1983; Coy, Peter, and Mark Lewyn, "The Tangle of Problems Hanging Up NYNEX," *Business Week,* February 19, 1988.

—Scott M. Lewis

ÖSTERREICHISCHE POST- UND TELEGRAPHENVERWALTUNG

Generaldirektion
Postgasse 8
A-1011 Vienna
Austria
(43) 1 515 510
Fax: (43) 1 512 8414

State-Owned Company
Incorporated: 1866
Employees: 55,044
Sales: Sch47.90 billion (US$4.49 billion)

The title of the Austrian Postal and Telegraph Department, Österreichische Post- und Telegraphenverwaltung (PTV), understates the range of this company's services. As well as providing postal and telegraphic communications for a population of 7.5 million in a territory of 84,000 square kilometers, PTV holds a monopoly in the country's basic telephone network, is the main supplier in the rapidly expanding area of telecommunications, and maintains, in cooperation with Austrian Railways, its own bus service that in 1990 represented sales of Sch1.32 billion and 111.8 million passenger journeys. PTV, the largest service industry in Austria, employs more than 57,000 people—including trainees and apprentices—and, via its suppliers, pays further large sums into the national economy. The modern identity of Austria's postal services has emerged from a long and much interrupted process.

Österreichische Post- und Telegraphenverwaltung dates from 1866, when a special department for post and telegraph was set up under a director general, within the Ministry of Trade of what from 1867 to 1918 was to be the dual monarchy of Austria-Hungary. Service in the early 1990s constitutes section III of the Federal Ministry of Public Economy and Transport. Its director general since 1985, Josef Sindelka, is responsible to the federal minister, Rudolf Streicher. The directorate, in Vienna, comprises three divisions: post and postal car services, telecommunications, and organization and personnel. Telecommunications is divided into six branches—transmission, satellite, power supply, and radio technology; switching systems; cabling; operations; legal and executive; and text and data communications. There are five regional directorates, an inspectorate based in Salzburg, and a central telecommunications engineering establishment, the Fernmeldetechnisches Zentralamt (FZA). The PTV cooperates in some telecommunications services with Radio Austria A.G., a state-owned private operating agency, as distinct from a PTO, or public telecommunications operator. PTV is responsible for radio and television transmitters and for collecting license fees, while Radio Austria is licensed by PTV to supply international telex, teletext, and public fax services to countries other than Germany, Switzerland, and Luxembourg. The PTV also cooperates with the legally separate Postsparkasse (Post Office Savings Bank), which offers counter and computerized services in post offices. There is also the Austrian Telecommunications Development Company (ÖFEG) that was set up in 1978 to develop a fully electronic switching system for the country. The state owns 51% of this company, and the rest is divided equally between the four major Austrian manufacturers: Alcatel Austria (formerly ITT), Kapsch AG, Schrack Electronic AG, and Siemens AG.

Although three-quarters of its territory consists of mountains and forests, Austria, like neighboring Switzerland, has always been at the hub of Europe's messenger routes. The history of Austria's postal communications have, in general, followed the usual European pattern, although affected by Austria's eventful history and frequently altered identity. An overall view shows a postal system of imperial splendor and Byzantine complexity eventually replaced by an efficient, logically organized industry, small by international standards and tending to follow in areas that it once led. Postal systems began in Europe before the Christian era, in the form of an official Roman messenger service, the *cursus publicus,* which disappeared in the Dark Ages. In the late 15th century, organized services, as distinct from ad hoc personal arrangements, reemerged, owned by rulers and institutions and gradually extended to the carrying of passengers as well as of private mail. State and commercial systems began to compete with one another, and by the late 18th century, this fragmentation had produced high charges and complicated, unstandardized procedures. With a marked increase in the political, social, and economic significance of postal and allied communications as well as the size of the investment required, there has been a tendency in different countries and at different times for postal services to be taken under varying degrees of state control.

In the 19th century, the harnessing of electricity and the new inventions of telegraph and telephone, together with developments in road, rail, and water transport, changed the traditional notion of the message as an object transmitted bodily from sender to receiver without change of form, by a human intermediary, and telecommunications was born. With the electronic and aeronautics revolutions that followed the two world wars, post and telecommunications technology took off again and continued to gather momentum. In the 20th century, as well as being an essential part of every country's infrastructure, telecommunications is in itself an important sector of the economy it supports. Domestic and international cooperation becomes increasingly indispensable, and the general European movement, led by the European Community Green Paper of 1987, which outlined proposals tending toward Europe-wide competition, is now moving away from state monopoly and toward deregulation.

In 1866, the year in which Austria's postal history became allied with PTV, the country was still the heartland of the vast, though by then diminished, territories ruled by the Hapsburg dynasty. These lands extended beyond Austria and Hungary to the Balkans and the Levant. Although Austria is now land-locked, from 1833 to 1914 it had its own mailboats sailing to its own post offices along the Adriatic and the eastern Mediterranean coasts.

A state postal service had existed in Austria since 1722, when Emperor Charles VI retrieved the day-to-day operating functions that had been delegated, since 1624, to the von Paar family, one of the family businesses that ran the commercial postal services that preceded the modern state systems in various European countries. Empress Maria Theresa, daughter of Charles VI, and her son, Emperor Joseph II, had continued Charles's structural and organization reforms. A central postal administration was set up in Vienna, which was to be renamed and reformed several times, and there was state supervision of charges as well as tighter timetable discipline. From 1749 new services were introduced, such as regular mailcoach and mounted messenger links between the main cities of the empire, a parcel post in 1750, hand-stamping of letters with date of origin in 1751, and, from 1788, a registered post; the system, however, was still far from perfect. The piecemeal reforms brought about by Empress Maria Theresa and her son left some private operators. In the first decades of the 19th century the organization of posts within the Empire was disrupted by the detachment and fragmentation of the German part of the system, lost to the Hapsburgs at the end of the Holy Roman Empire in 1806. Censorship and interception of the mail, especially during Metternich's chancellorship of Austria from 1809 to 1848, had become frequent, and there was a tendency for the state monopoly to be used for the benefit of the state, with high charges imposed to maximize revenues. However, between 1829 and 1848 the chief postal administrator, Maximilian Otto von Ottenfeld, had modernized the Austrian posts by coordinating regional services and establishing an inspectorate. In 1839 he began the practice of issuing printed guideline documents to employees and set up a post office library that was to evolve into the present Section 03 of PTV administration, information, and documentation. In 1847 the telegraph service came into being and in 1850 soon after von Ottenfeld's retirement, Austria followed Britain's 1840 example and introduced the adhesive prepaid uniform rate postage stamp, becoming the 16th nation in the world to do so. The year 1866, however, was a turning point, and when in 1975 PTV abandoned the official eagle and chose for its modern logo a simple stylized posthorn, the new symbol completed a transformation of the postal service. An unwieldy arm of state, conceived and organized over centuries to serve a vast imperial power, had become a streamlined, high technology, market-oriented service owned and run by, and for, the country's citizens.

By 1866 the era of post and telecommunications supported by electricity, fast transport, and international cooperation was already underway. The Austrian telegraph service was nineteen years old and a series of bilateral treaties for postal cooperation with other European countries was preparing the ground for Austria's participation in the Universal Postal Union, the Austro-German organization of 1850. Another progressive step was taken in 1869, when women were admitted to employment in rural post offices. In 1991 they constituted 23% of PTV's work force.

In 1881 five years after Bell's first public demonstration of his invention, the telephone came to Vienna, but the idea was slow to catch on. The first telephone exchange was run by a private company, the Privat-Telegraphengesellschaft, under government license for a total of 154 subscribers, and the first public telephones appeared in 1882 in the Vienna Stock Exchange. The new device was soon used in other Austrian cities, with various private companies joining in its exploitation. However, these services were not keeping up with developments abroad. In addition to being expensive, they were also ill-equipped, unreliable, and confined to cities, and PTV began to move toward a takeover. In 1886 it inaugurated the first Austrian interurban telephone link, between Vienna and Brünn, and followed it with others. The government started buying in the concessions it had granted, and in 1895 the telephone service was nationalized. The Post and Telegraphy Department was able to keep its name unchanged since it had decided to classify telephony as telegraphy using acoustic apparatus.

New technology was also affecting traditional mail service. In 1875 a pneumatic tube post started in Vienna; it lasted until 1956 when it was overtaken by high costs and competition from the telephone. Many of the developments that followed up to the end of World War I were necessary extensions of, or improvements to, existing postal, telegraph, and telephone services. One new departure, however, came in 1883, when PTV's cooperation with the P.S.K. (Post Office Savings Bank) began. Money orders had been available from post offices since 1850. In 1903 coin-operated telephones appeared. In 1907 General Director Friedrich Wagner von Jauregg embarked on the motorization of PTV with the inauguration of the post office's automobile passenger service, for which the lead had been assumed by Bavaria in 1905 and Switzerland in 1906. Another step forward was taken in 1910, when PTV began the long process of automating its telephone exchanges. This was completed in 1972 and led, in 1978, to plans for digitalization. Austria's digital network, in which speech is converted to electrical pulses, initiated in the 1980s, is scheduled to be completed by the end of the century.

World War I and its aftermath naturally set back the economics of the defeated powers, and the progress of PTV was limited until the early 1920s. Nevertheless, from 1918 PTV operated in the service of a republic. Early that year PTV gave Austria the world's first civilian airmail service. Suspended almost at once by the end of the war, it was resumed in 1921. It began as an inland service, but was extended overseas in 1928. From early in the 19th century the Austrian postal service had operated in neighboring Liechtenstein, but the link was severed in 1921 when the principality entered into a postal union with Switzerland. In 1922 PTV introduced franking machines for automatic mail handling. A new field of activity opened in 1923 with the start of the ongoing partnership between PTV and Radio Austria A.G. Initially, PTV owned 30% of Radio Austria's shares, but in 1956 the republic became the sole shareholder. In 1991 Radio Austria belonged effectively to PTV, was able to use the latter's cable and satellite installations, and was licensed by it to operate some international public telecommunications services.

The 1930s saw a series of growth-inhibiting disasters for PTV, beginning with the years of the Great Depression. More significant for PTV was the seven-year break in its identity that followed Germany's annexation of Austria in 1938, when the Austrian postal services were simply absorbed into the

Deutsche Reichspost until 1945 and the end of World War II. Not only did the war almost eradicate Austria's postal and telecommunications infrastructure, but under the Allied occupation that followed, the country was divided into four administratively separate zones, in which the remnants of the mail, telegraph, and telephone systems had to reckon with control and censorship imposed by the occupiers. Under Karl Dworschak, PTV's general director from 1945 until 1955, the resuscitated company began to recover. Postal operations covering the whole country were resumed in October 1945. The next objective was to begin catching up with the technological progress made in the outside world during Austria's troubles. The task was formidable, but was undertaken against a new background of economic growth and political stability. Great strides were taken in technology, and work was immediately resumed on the gradual mechanization of telephone exchanges.

By 1957 Austria was making use of international satellites for radio, although it was not to get its own earth station until 1980. In 1966 PTV introduced postal codes. These had previously been used in Austria under the German Reichspost. Mobile communications were launched with precellular carphones in 1974, and a radio paging service followed in 1975. In 1979 experiments began on optic cables, and these have been part of PTV's wire transmission infrastructure since 1986. Optical fibers offer greatly increased capacity; systems under trial in 1991 could transmit as many as 8,000 calls in both directions at once on a single fiber. In 1971 Austria entered the expanding satellite communications field in its own right, deciding to build an earth station to connect with the existing international information satellite systems. The location chosen was Aflenz in the Alps, and construction, which in the first 10 years cost Sch650 million, began in October 1977 under PTV general director Alfred Schlegel. Aflenz came into service on May 30, 1980, providing domestic and international links for telephone, radio, television, and data transmission, together with increased possibilities for development. By 1988 there were four antennae at Aflenz. Antenna 1 links in to the Intelsat Atlantic region, and Antenna 3 to the Intelsat Indian Ocean region. Antenna 2 operates within the framework of the Eutelsat systems covering Europe, and Antenna 4 is used for high-speed transatlantic data transmissions, including videoconferencing, within the Intelsat (International Telecommunications Satellite Organization) Business Service System. A new antenna was planned for 1992. From 1989 the Aflenz Intelsat antennae have been progressively digitalized in preparation for completion of the ongoing digitalization of the Austrian telecommunications network. By 1990 Aflenz was providing satellite links to 52 countries.

The range of telecommunications services offered by PTV mushroomed in the 1980s with a major drive to modernize the network starting in the middle of the decade. However, there was still some catching up to be done, and limiting technological idiosyncrasies were still waiting to be removed from the system. Videotex (Bildschirmtext or BTX), based on and named after a German version of Britain's Prestel, went on trial in 1981, and in the same year, Telefax and Telepost, a facsimile service, began. Packet switched data network services (PSDN) became available in 1982. In July 1985 Telebox was launched by PTV with RadioAustria A.G., as a joint public electronic mail and gateway service, providing easy multilingual access to public data banks worldwide. Telebox can also translate documents into a number of languages.

Since 1945 PTV has foregone considerable amounts of revenue through concessions on fares, charges, and license fees made to students, the handicapped, and the elderly. However, its finances are generally in good shape. In 1990 postal services accounted for 28.6% of PTV sales, 41.9% of expenditure, and 55.4% of employees. Telecommunications services accounted for 68.4% of sales, 52.2% of expenditure, and 32.1% of staff, while the bus service took 5.9% of expenditure and produced 3% of sales, using 7.9% of total personnel, of which management represented 4.6%.

The telegraph has inevitably been largely superseded by telex, private fax machines, and other more modern forms of data transmission. On the other hand, at the end of 1990 there were 3.22 million exchange telephone lines in Austria, representing a penetration of 41.8%, compared with 30.7% in 1981. In neighboring Switzerland, neighboring penetration in 1990 was 88%. Nearly 18% of PTV's telephone subscribers were linked to digital switching systems, and it is expected that by 1992 there will be 211 digital telephone exchanges serving 1.3 million subscribers. By the turn of the century PTV plans to have 4.5 million telephones in use, a penetration of 60%.

Mobile communications have become more sophisticated with three mobile telephone systems in use. By the end of 1984, the original 1974 pre-cellular Network B was fully subscribed, boasting 1,800 users, and was supplemented by a cellular system for portable telephones—Autotelefonnetz C (Network C)—which by the end of 1990 had 63,244 subscribers and is used to provide a public telephone service on some Austrian trains. An interim cellular system, Network D, employed to bridge the gap before PTV's mobile communications go digital starting in 1993, had 9,163 subscribers at the end of 1990. By then there were 79,650 subscribers to the expanding public paging system, which in 1991 the PTV plans to develop to the tune of Sch160 million.

In the early 1990s, data transmission services were sometimes hampered by technical anomalies in PTV's PSTN (public switched telephone network), but the PSDN (packet switched data network), introduced in 1983 and called Datex-P, has links to most European PSDNs. Datex-L, a circuit-switched data network, was introduced in 1983. Subscribers to these and other high-speed Datex networks totaled just under 14,000 in 1990. Affected by an increase in the use of fax machines, the fully automatic inland telex service showed a drop of nearly 25% in 1990, while use of the only partly automatic foreign Telex, operated by Radio Austria, fell by 17.3%. Teletex, a telex service with high data rates and graphics, launched in October 1983 and connected with the German system, also saw a decline in subscription, while PTV's videotex service, Bildschirmtext, started in 1981 and the object of a current sales drive involving relaxation of PTV's monopoly on terminals, saw the number of its subscribers rise to 11,668 from 9,717 in the previous year. The United Kingdom's Prestel, on which it is based, had 110,000 subscribers at the end of 1990. PTV is piloting an ISDN (integrated services digital network) along German lines in order to develop broadband ISDN for broadcast distribution, videoconferencing—two-way sound and vision link—and video telephony.

The FZA is responsible for PTV's research and development. A sum of Sch70.3 billion, 90.1% of total PTV investment in Austria, will be spent on telecommunications development between 1991 and 1995. FZA also performs a regulatory function, and its approval must be sought for telecommunications equipment supplied to subscribers or attached to the network. This function, like the PTV's monopoly on services other than basic telephony and the network infrastructure, is likely to be modified in view of Austria's hope of becoming a full member of the European Community, where telecoms policy is moving toward liberalization, with markets being opened to domestic and international competition, and separation of operative and regulatory functions. PTV maintains a close relationship with the German PTT, particularly in technical matters, through the DBT (Deutsche Bundespost Telekom). The two networks interconnect, and PTV's text services provision often follows the German lead. On telecommunications reform policy, too, PTV is likely to go along with the German move to liberalization. PTV already admits it has requested approval of terminals equipment from foreign-based companies, although it still favors suppliers who manufacture in Austria and buys its public exchange systems and much of its other equipment from the Austrian subsidiaries of the Alcatel group—Alcatel Austria—and of Siemens as well as from Kapsch and Schrack, both Austrian-owned.

In addition to being a flourishing national business and a popular public service, PTV is clearly mindful of further obligations. It serves philately and art by issuing around 35 beautiful new stamps a year and by taking measures to reduce air and noise pollution—using lead-free fuel in its fleet of vehicles, piloting the introduction of electrically powered vans, providing transport facilities for passengers' bicycles—it meets its responsibilities to a wider environment.

Further Reading: Die Post auf dem Weg ins Informationszeitalter, Vienna, Generaldirektion für die Post- und Telegraphenverwaltung, 1988; *Aus Österreichische Postgeschichte—500 Jahre Europäische Postverbindungen,* Vienna, Generaldirektion für die Post- und Telegraphenverwaltung, 1990.

—Olive Classe

PACIFIC TELESIS GROUP

130 Kearny Street
San Francisco, California 94108
U.S.A.
(415) 394-3000
Fax: (415) 362-8628

Public Company
Incorporated: 1983
Employees: 65,829
Sales: $9.72 billion
Stock Exchanges: New York Pacific Midwest London Geneva
  Zürich Basel

Pacific Telesis Group (PacTel) was incorporated in Nevada in 1983 following the U.S. District Court-ordered divestiture of American Telephone and Telegraph Company (AT&T), effective January 1, 1984. Pacific Telesis Group, established as the western holding company of the massive Bell telephone network, assumed ownership of Pacific Bell and its fully owned subsidiary Nevada Bell. PacTel's business includes providing local, long-distance, and cellular telephone services, and electronic voice, video, and data communications for residential and business customers, as well as for interexchange companies. At divestiture, the company formed PacTel Publishing to handle directory publishing and PacTel Communications Systems to expand nontelephone operations.

Like all other regional holding companies (RHCs), PacTel faced a competitive marketplace with severe restrictions, to be monitored by the Federal Communications Commission (FCC). New ventures for RHCs had to be established under separate subsidiaries, and sales from any startups could not exceed 10% of total company revenues.

Fortunately for PacTel, Pacific and Nevada Bell had been managed as one company since 1913; unifying its systems was not a problem. PacTel, however, faced other disadvantages that were formidable, though not insurmountable. Due to rapid growth in the 1960s and 1970s, Pacific Bell, then known as Pacific Telephone & Telegraph Co., faced entanglements with consumer groups, the California court system, and the California Public Utilities Commission (CPUC). From 1968 through the early 1980s, Pacific Bell sparred with the CPUC over rate regulation, causing a rift in the company's relations with AT&T. AT&T significantly curtailed investment in Pacific Telephone, which then borrowed heavily. With company debt and the number of employees high, Pacific Telephone had a reputation that was faltering.

In 1980 AT&T organized a management team to help Pacific Telephone. Donald E. Guinn, head of network services at AT&T, became chairman of Pacific Telephone. Guinn chose John Hulse, a former executive with Northwestern Bell Telephone Company, as chief financial officer. By 1983 Guinn had smoothed Pacific Telephone's relations with the CPUC and obtained a record $610 million rate increase. Hulse trimmed staff by more than 30,000 and cut capital spending and borrowing. The team also planned to update lagging technology; Pacific Telephone placed sixth out of seven in the Bell pecking order, with only half of its switching systems converted to digital by September 1983.

Within weeks of divestiture, PacTel solicited federal Judge Harold Greene's permission to sell telecommunications products and services abroad. The request was granted, and the company formed a subsidiary, Pacific Telesis International, to market the company's know-how in the design, construction, and operation of telephone systems. Sales were aimed primarily at China and Asia. The subsidiary began operations late in 1984.

By April 1984 PacTel offered domestic telecommunications packages to medium and large businesses, including data transmission, facsimile, electronic voice mail, and teleconferencing. As some states relaxed regulations, industry analysts forecast increased competition within local calling areas. The FCC's solution was to fix monthly access charges paid by long-distance companies to the local carriers. Some states raised rates in residential and rural areas, where service had previously been subsidized by the Bell system's more active business and urban markets.

The gravest problem for the RHCs was known as bypass—larger businesses could develop their own microwave or satellite-based systems, thus avoiding access charges. One large business seeking FCC permission to connect long-distance calls without accessing the local network was AT&T.

To combat the competition, Pacific Bell lost no time developing its integrated services digital network (ISDN) capabilities as well as increasing installation of fiber optic loops in the San Francisco and Los Angeles areas. The goal of such technologies was to link a range of telecommunication services to customers via computers. With such systems fully operational, Pacific Bell would be able to offer both business and residential subscribers the fastest, most efficient, and least expensive service. All this was contingent, however, on the loosening of federal restrictions. PacTel and Pacific Bell were prohibited from offering enhanced or nonregulated services under FCC rules issued in 1980. Through the granting of waivers in April 1985, however, the FCC effectively overrode its own prohibitions. Although competitors were not very pleased with the decisions, the RHCs certainly were.

Wasting no time, PacTel stepped up its nonregulated operations. In February 1985 the company established an information systems division to offer integrated telecommunications products—word processors and microcomputers—as well as the wiring, cabling, and service necessary to maintain the systems. Acquisitions made in 1985 included the Byte Shops, an eight-store, California-based computer chain; JWJ Publishing, which published tour guides; and Kensington Datacom, a private British network. PacTel initiated the purchase of Communications

Industries, Inc., a cellular and paging company, in the summer of 1985 and completed the acquisition early in 1986. At $431 million, it was the largest purchase to date by any RHC. Having established a presence in Asia the previous year, in December 1985 PacTel announced the formation of Pacific Telesis Japan K.K.

In mid-December 1985 Pacific Bell was involved in a skirmish with AT&T and MCI Communications Corporation over long-distance customers. AT&T allegedly sent thank-you notes to customers who had in fact chosen MCI as their long-distance carrier, and notified Pacific Bell to assign those customers to AT&T. AT&T blamed the mistake on a computer error. MCI asked Pacific Bell to refund customers the $5 changeover fee and the difference between MCI and AT&T long-distance service costs.

In September 1986 PacTel became the first RHC to reach a contract agreement with the Communications Workers of America. The contract, criticized by some as overly generous, included a no-layoff provision and incentive bonuses, a benefit previously reserved for executives. Chairman Donald Guinn, attempting to positively affect management morale as well, hired outside consultants to prod PacTel staff into more active roles. The company ran into trouble with sales pitches, however. The CPUC claimed PacTel deceptively marketed packages of optional services, without telling subscribers they could buy basic services for less. Twenty-five employees sued PacTel, claiming the company forced them to use deceptive sales tactics or lose their jobs. Although PacTel denied the charges, at least two senior marketing executives left, and the company scheduled the retraining of thousands of salespeople in more moderate tactics. In November 1986 PacTel acquired Northern Telecom's western regional direct-sales operation.

Although credited with smoothing Pacific Bell's rocky relations with the CPUC, by the end of 1986 Guinn still had some work to do. The CPUC finally responded—negatively—to Pacific Bell's 1984 request for a $1.4 billion rate increase. In fact Pacific Bell was ordered to plan a refund of $121 million. Guinn offered to freeze residential rates until 1990 in exchange for options in pricing other services. Pacific Bell could then lower interexchange access fees in order to reduce bypass, which was costing PacTel $400 million to $500 million. The CPUC order stood, however. Continuing the effort to diversify, by late 1986 PacTel International operated offices in England, China, Japan, Spain, South Korea, and Thailand, primarily on a consulting basis.

In 1987 Donald Guinn, who had been president, chairman, and chief executive officer of Pacific Telesis, relinquished the presidency to Samuel Ginn. Philip Quigley became the new president and CEO of Pacific Bell, succeeding Theodore Saenger. Both Ginn and Quigley, experienced in nonregulated businesses, were expected to increase diversification efforts.

To this end, PacTel sought and gained approval to offer voice mail services in July of 1987, a decision further eroding the FCC enhanced-services restrictions and leading to a more open national telecommunications policy. Continuing its efforts with ISDN technology, in September PacTel initiated its first 16-month trial in the Silicon Valley area of California. The company anticipated gathering data on the practical means of applying ISDN technology in larger markets.

In September 1987 PacTel added a cellular and personal paging system in Ohio and Michigan. By year-end 1987, Pacific Bell Directory was the largest producer of printed directories in California. By 1988 Pacific Bell was operating six bilingual service centers and offered directories in four languages. Publishing revenues, $521 million in 1989, reached $789 million by 1988.

In the cellular market, PacTel kept apace. In 1984 its cellular division served 15,000 customers; by 1988 the number jumped to 262,000. Revenues climbed from $14 million to $308 million in the same period.

PacTel entered the cable television market in 1988, acquiring a majority interest in East London Telecommunications (Holdings) Ltd. Because the United Kingdom had only four television stations at the time, the market was a favorable one.

The news was not good for PacTel, however. After spending two years and $26 million on a voice and data transmission system called Project Victoria, Pacific Bell abandoned the effort to develop Project Victoria further in mid-1988. Rather than wait for an already delayed FCC decision on whether Pacific Bell would have to market Project Victoria through a separate subsidiary, the company decided to license the technology. PacTel moved ahead in August 1988, reaching an agreement to buy American Businessphones Inc. (ABI).

As telecommunications markets became more closely connected, Pacific Telesis entered significant agreements necessary to maintain the smooth transmission of information. In a pact with the state of California, in late August 1988 Pacific Bell upgraded its central-office Centrex system to digital networks.

On the international level PacTel found itself in a skirmish with the Department of Justice (DOJ) and AT&T. PacTel, investigating opportunities in Japan since divestiture, requested a waiver allowing the company to buy an interest of less than 10% in the Japanese company International Digital Communications, Inc. (IDC). Because IDC would neither own nor operate facilities in the United States, the purchase was allowed by the FCC. While PacTel pushed for DOJ approval, AT&T refused to do business with IDC until the waiver issue was resolved. IDC could not afford to start operations without AT&T's business, because AT&T would be responsible for connecting a large number of customers to IDC. Thus AT&T's refusal to do business was, in effect, preventing PacTel from doing business with the Japanese company.

Pacific Telesis ended its fifth year of operations as a decided leader of the RHCs in the electronic voice-mail business and was competitive in cellular telephone and ISDN-related services. PacTel's chances to move ahead in telecommunications came in 1989 in a variety of ventures. PacTel International joined British Aerospace, the United Kingdom's largest manufacturer; Millikom U.K. Ltd., a cellular service provider; and Matra Communications S.A., a leading French telecommunications equipment provider, in operating a personal communications network in the United Kingdom. PacTel held a 20% interest in the group. PacTel International also gained a cellular license in Germany, through a similar joint venture. Also in 1989, PacTel gained approval of its request to do business with Japan's International Digital Communications, Inc.

Domestically, through Pacific and Nevada Bell, PacTel was operating 98% of its switches digitally. Optical fiber, a high-quality information transmission medium, made up 30% of PacTel's interoffice systems by the end of 1989. When an earthquake struck the San Francisco area in October 1989, PacTel's systems functioned well as the quake's extra pull was absorbed by reinforced floors, mechanically braced equipment, and 25 extra feet of fiber-optic cables, previously installed underground in the event of emergency.

Following an October 1989 agreement with the CPUC, Pacific Bell came under an incentive-based regulatory system. Effective in 1990, rates took into account the U.S. rate of inflation as well as Pacific Bell's productivity. The company was to share profits falling within a 13% to 16.5% rate of return range with its customers. Long-term advantages to Pacific Bell would include improved relations with the CPUC as well as the company's chance to offer customers affordable enhanced services. Accordingly, Pacific Bell announced the availability of ISDN service in all its major cities in December 1989.

In August 1990 Pacific Telesis restructured, dividing Pacific Bell into four sections. The first group, with regionally appointed vice presidents, was to oversee markets organized geographically into the Sacramento–North Valley, Los Angeles–Ventura County, and Orange-Riverside–San Bernardino County territories. A second group was to direct statewide operations; the third, product and technology support; and the fourth, corporate affairs.

In November 1990, Pacific Bell, along with Southwestern Bell, New York Telephone, and New England Telephone, was fined by the FCC on a charge of supplying incorrect data during 1988 to the National Exchange Carrier Association, an FCC accounting institution responsible for collecting and distributing access fees paid by long-distance carriers for local hook-ups.

The four companies were fined a total of $1 million. Also during 1990, PacTel decided to divest itself of its real estate holdings, setting aside a $60 million reserve to cover expected losses. Other PacTel actions in 1990 included increased investments in its overseas ventures and in upgrading its domestic telephone operations.

As Pacific Telesis entered the 1990s, competition in the telecommunications markets was likely to increase. On one point all telecommunication companies agreed: technological innovations, capably handled, could boost both national and international economies. Pacific Telesis is undeniably in the right place at the right time: the California telecommunications market is projected to be the fourth largest in the world by the year 2000.

Principal *Subsidiaries:* Pacific Bell; Pacific Bell Directory; Nevada Bell; PacTel Corporation; Pacific Telesis International; PacTel Cable; PacTel Cellular; PacTel Paging; PacTel Teletrac.

Further Reading: "How One Baby Bell Struggled to its Feet," *Business Week,* September 2, 1983; Levine, Jonathan B., "The Baby Bells' Weak Sister is Growing into a Bruiser," *Business Week,* September 8, 1986; Booker, Ellis, "PacTel's Bright Prospects," *Telephony,* December 19, 1988.

—Frances E. Norton

SCHWEIZERISCHE POST-, TELEFON- UND TELEGRAFEN-BETRIEBE

General Directorate Swiss PTT
Viktoriastrasse 21
CH-3030 Bern
Switzerland
(41) 31 62 11 11
Fax: (41) 31 62 25 49

State-Owned Company
Incorporated: 1849 as Die Schweizer Eidgenössische Post
Employees: 61,703
Sales: SFr9.91 billion (US$7.31 billion)

With its ubiquitous bright yellow post-buses and award-winning issues of elegant stamps, Schweizerische Post-, Telefon- und Telegrafen-Betriebe (Swiss PTT) presents a colorful image in Switzerland and abroad. In one of the world's most mountainous yet most densely populated countries, the PTT supplies postal and telecommunications services for a population of 6.5 million speaking four different mother tongues—German, French, Italian, and Romanche—and for over 300 international institutions within Switzerland's borders. It serves the 23 Swiss cantons and since 1921 the neighboring principality of Liechtenstein. This operating area is divided into 11 postal districts and 17 telecommunications districts. For an economy dominated by industry, banking, and tourism, good communications are essential. The PTT ranked eighth in 1989 out of Switzerland's top 50 companies and is the country's largest employer. After payments to reserves, its profits—SFr150 million in 1989—go to the state. The PTT is part of the Ministry of Energy, Transportation, and Communication. Its activities are monitored, and its policy determined, by a government-appointed administrative council. Management responsibilities are shared by three directors general, one for postal services, another for telecommunications, and the third, who is also chairman of the board, in charge of legal, marketing, and other services for the first two.

Although the Swiss PTT itself can trace an unbroken line of origin back only to 1848 or 1849, Swiss communications in the form of a state-organized, long-distance postal service go back to Roman times. From the end of the first century B.C., the area that is now Switzerland was part of the ancient Roman Empire and benefited from the *cursus publicus,* a military

and administrative postal system with mounted messengers traveling between the center of the empire and its colonies and outposts. Traces of an organized messenger service in Switzerland disappeared after the barbarian invasions and the fall of Rome in the 5th century A.D., until the 14th century. From then until the 17th century, the governments, legal and religious institutions, merchant houses, and guilds of the early confederation of 13 cantons had individual systems of official message delivery by uniformed foot messengers in the main towns and communities. Switzerland was also served by foreign-run message services, like those operating between France and Italy and between Italy and the Holy Roman Empire. Toward the beginning of the 17th century, with a surge in economic growth and international trade, runners were replaced for longer distances by teams of mounted couriers, employed by commercial postal services, some foreign-owned. By the last quarter of the 17th century, horse-drawn post coaches were operating out of all Switzerland's big towns. One famous Swiss master of posts was Beat Fischer of Berne who, in 1675, started in his own canton a service based on the one being run in the Holy Roman Empire by the German princely family von Thurn und Taxis. The Fischer post, like that of the von Thurn und Taxis, grew and spread to rival, and in many cases eclipse, those in other cantons. The Fischer posts lasted until 1832. The von Thurn und Taxis service in Schaffhausen was among those absorbed by the new federal system in 1849.

Progress in industry, commerce, and transport brought further sophistication to the Swiss postal services in the 18th and early 19th centuries. In most of the cantons they were in time taken over by local government. In 1798, during the French occupation, the Swiss postal services were nationalized by decree, but in 1803, with the end of Napoleon's Helvetic Republic, they fell back into their old anarchy. When Switzerland as a federal state came into being in 1848, a new constitution united the 22 cantons under a bicameral central government in Berne. The confederation proceeded to unify its diverse systems of coinage, weights and measures, customs duties, and posts. By 1849, when the postal laws enacted in 1848 by the new federation took effect, it was high time for order to be introduced into the system. There were by then 17 separate cantonal postal services, plus the one in Schaffhausen still run by the von Thurn und Taxis family. Each was organized with a view to its own maximum profit rather than to cooperation with neighboring postal services or to customer satisfaction. Most services were irregular, and in remoter areas, infrequent. Different cantons leveled different, often high, charges in differing currencies and weights, with resultant delays for letters and packets in transit. It could be cheaper to direct one's mail out of Switzerland and back in again, rather than via one of the internal routes.

In 1849 the 18 formerly independent postal services were amalgamated into one organization enjoying a state monopoly. Administered from Bern, the Post had 11 regional directorates. The state was to pay annual compensation for loss of earnings to cantons or private individuals whose postal services had been taken over. Services already available to the public were not to be reduced, charges were to be made as low as possible, and secrecy of the mail was guaranteed. From the beginning, the federal post office conveyed letters, newspapers, parcels, and passengers. Under the leadership of Wilhelm Matthias Naeff and Benedikt Laroche-Stehelin, who occupied various high offices in the post office department, a process of streamlining and development began immediately.

The first Swiss federal adhesive prepaid postage stamps appeared in 1850. Zürich and Geneva in 1843, followed by Basel in 1845, had already been first in the world to respond to the 1840 British lead by issuing their own cantonal paper stamps. The first railway traveling post office, operating between Zürich and Brugg, went into service in 1857. In its early days, the Swiss postal administration was quite a modestly sized affair. According to its 1850 annual report to Parliament, its entire staff numbered 2,803, including 1,528 counter and office staff, 1,004 postmen, and 166 coachdrivers. In that year its profits, duly paid into the state coffers, amounted to SFr758,213, representing 14.6% of its turnover. Comparable figures for 1989 were as follows: employees, 61,703; and profit paid to the state, SFr150 million (i.e., still roughly 14.6% of sales, which were SFr9,909 million). The range of postal services available expanded to include domestic money orders in 1862 and express delivery of mail in 1868. The year 1870 saw the introduction of the postcard. For a while, horse-drawn post coaches were used on the new Alpine and Jura pass roads, but on the main intercity routes, mail traffic was progressively transferred from the roads to the developing railways.

Electricity, meanwhile, had opened up new fields of communication. In the mid-19th century, Switzerland was one of the world's most heavily industrialized countries, as well as one of the most mountainous. The physical difficulties of conveying the post had combined with the pressing communications needs of a flourishing business community to bring about a rapid adoption of telecommunications technology. Seeing their competitors in adjacent countries gaining the advantages of communication by electric telegraph, Swiss business executives were quick to demand the same. Following a federal act of 1851, providing for a state monopoly on telegraphy, the first telegraph network opened in 1852, using the Morse system of telegraphy, in which letters of the alphabet are composed of dots and dashes. The following year telegraphic communication with neighboring countries was possible, and by 1857 all the Swiss cantons were served by an extended network.

The year 1874 was a double landmark in the history of the Swiss PTT. The Universal Postal Union was founded, and Bern was chosen for its headquarters. In the same year, with a revision of the federal constitution, new state postal regulations came into force that released the Swiss Post from its compensation payments to the cantons. Even more important, the new regulations also brought the electric telegraph network under the 1848 to 1849 provisions concerning the post, with regard to state control and monopoly, use of profits, establishment of cheap tariffs, and inviolable secrecy. From then on, Swiss postal services and the telegraph, with successive forms of what would later be called telecommunications, would be gathered under the same administration.

Switzerland was quick to see the potential of the telephone. Swiss experiments with telephony started almost as soon as Alexander Graham Bell had patented his invention in 1876. In 1878 the government announced that telephone systems came under its monopoly on communications and that would be providers of telephone networks must be licensed by the state. Two years later, the first private exchange was opened by the Zürich Telephone Company. In the 1880s the Swiss government installed its own systems in several other Swiss towns,

starting with Basel, where the exchange was inaugurated in 1881 with a grand total of 55 subscribers. The private system in Zürich was bought out in 1886, and thereafter all telephony services were state-run in PTT. Postal services were being expanded and modernized. In 1889 the army postal service was established. The year 1906 saw the introduction of the postal giro—electronic money transfer—service and the experimental motorization of two Bern post-coach routes, leading to the first Alpine post-bus service—Nesslau-Buchs—in 1918. Postage stamp vending machines appeared in 1911, followed the next year by the first canceling machines. A Swiss internal airmail service began in 1913 between Basel and Liestal. In 1919 another linked Zürich, Bern, and Lausanne, and airmail stamps were issued for the first time. In 1900 the telephone networks in Ticino Canton were connected with the rest of Switzerland by the St. Gotthard cable. Public coinbox telephones were introduced in towns in 1904. Switzerland's first transnational telephone service had begun as early as 1886, between Basel and the town of St. Louis in Alsace. After this, the international service grew rapidly until, on the eve of World War I, there were 81 separate circuits linking Switzerland to the outside world.

Motivated by the need to accommodate exceptionally heavy telephone traffic, Switzerland pioneered the automatic switching of telephone calls, and in 1917 the first semi-automatic exchange was installed at Zürich-Hottingen. The local systems were being rationalized and integrated, the links between them being laid underground for improved transmission and longevity. This work, continuing over the next four decades, was to entitle Switzerland to claim in 1959 that it had the world's first fully automatic national telephone system. In 1919 telegraph traffic reached a record 8.31 million messages. During the 1920s, radio telegraphy, provided by Radio Suisse Limited, offered an alternative transmission medium to the international network of land lines. At first radio telegraphy focused on European countries, but beginning in 1932 there was a short-wave radio telegraph service to New York. With the increasing availability of alternative means of communication, starting with the telephone, however, the number of telegrams declined steadily after its 1919 peak. The legal, organizational, and management basis of the postal services continued to be adjusted from time to time to developing circumstances. The director of posts became head of posts and telegraphs in 1920 and in 1928 was given the title of director-general of the PTT. Since 1961 PTT has appointed three directors-general to manage its services.

The 1930s were a decade of rapid expansion. In 1930 subscriber trunk dialing was introduced between Bern and Biel, and in 1931, PTT undertook an additional major area of responsibility, broadcasting. Switzerland's first radio transmitter had appeared in 1922, and various local broadcasting organizations had sprung up. Then there was a reorganization and the Swiss Broadcasting Corporation, founded in 1931 and almost entirely government-owned, assumed charge of programming while PTT undertook the engineering side. PTT duly inaugurated three national transmitters, at Sottens, Beromünster, and Monte Ceneri, in the early 1930s. In addition, it introduced a telewire-broadcasting service. This took advantage of the telephone network to transmit to users whose reception would otherwise have been inadequate, either because the Alps got in the way of the signal or because, in towns, they experienced interference from electrical equipment. In 1931 low-frequency wire broadcasting over telephone lines was introduced. The national broadcast transmitters of Sottens and Beromünster were commissioned in 1931, with ones at Monte Ceneri appearing in 1933. In 1939 radio telephone connections using VHF were made available for Swiss Alpine Club huts, and the next year the Swiss shortwave broadcasting service was equipped with its own transmitter station at Schwarzenburg.

The availability of teleprinters in the early 1930s made it possible for telegrams to be sent directly from one subscriber to another rather than via two telegraphy offices. The first teleprinters started operating in 1931. Telex services in Switzerland began in 1934; automatic switching facilities and subscriber dialing in the national telex service came along two years later. Telecommunications developed rapidly after World War II. In 1946 the Swiss PTT installed its first microwave telephone links, using high-frequency radio for transmission over line-of-sight routes, and the Zürich telegraph office was provided with picture transmission equipment. The 1950s saw many new developments, including the provision of VHF car phones and a nationwide car radio-paging service, the first stages of a national VHF radio broadcasting network, and an experimental television service. In 1954 the telegraph network was automated using the Gentex system, a post-manual telegraph message transmission and reception system that preceded the current computerized system; in 1957 subscriber dialing was extended to parts of the international telex service; and in 1958 a television service was introduced in Switzerland.

In the 1960s, a period of increasing economic success for Switzerland, there was an upsurge in telex traffic, and several improvements were made to accommodate it. By 1966 telex subscriber dialing was available between Switzerland and any other European country; by the following year telex subscriber dialing to countries outside Europe was also made possible. International telephone subscriber dialing began in 1964 and was completed in 1982. The 1960s saw the updating of some other PTT services. In 1964 a 4-digit postal code system was introduced into the mail services, and in 1968 the first fully automatic letter sorting system came into use in Bern. The first color television broadcast had been seen in 1967. Data transmission began in 1960 and by 1966 there was a service—Datex—to the United States. In 1965 telephone links were set up with the United States via Early Bird, the first communications satellite. 1974 would find Switzerland opening its own satellite earth station at Leuk, which was able to take over the major part of international telephone traffic.

In 1970 the new executive regulations for PTT came into force. PTT was given a board of directors, and another decade of expansion began. Competition from telephone, telex, and other newer services had steadily eroded the volume of telegram traffic. To make the system as cost-effective as possible, the Gentex network, which had been in use for telegrams since 1954, was replaced in 1971 by a computerized switching system called ATECO. The ATECO system was also available to private telex subscribers. In 1976 a public facsimile service—Bureaufax—was opened on an experimental basis, and work began on a national automatic carphone network. Mobile radiophones became available for Swiss motorists early in the 1950s, but these were limited as to the area in which they could be used. In the late 1970s, however, a nationwide system

was set up using the public telephone network. The first of the five areas, covering Zürich, opened in 1978; the last appeared in 1980. The country's first two fully electronic, processor-controlled telex and data exchanges came into operation at Zürich and Geneva in 1979. The same year brought the opening of a public automatic message switching service and the start of the videotex pilot trial. In 1980 the second antenna was commissioned at the Leuk satellite earth station, and an experimental telefax service, offering facsimile communication between subscribers with machines rented from PTT, began. Switzerland was linked up with the European Communities' Euronet DIANE (Direct Information Access Network for Europe). The first two motorway tunnel radio supply systems were also put into operation.

The high cost of keeping abreast of competition and rapid technological change in the telecommunications field was felt when, in 1983, PTT had to abandon its 15-year attempt to develop a national electronic switch system—Integriertes Fernmeldesystem, or IFS—and change to Swissnet, the Swiss name for ISDN, or integrated services digital network, which makes use of foreign designs but requires manufacture and installation to be carried out by Swiss companies. PTT spent SFr8.2 million and employed 330 people on research and development in 1989. In 1991 telecommunications, costly in research and equipment, dominated PTT's activities, accounting for 65% of sales in 1989. PTT continued throughout the 1980s to keep up with developments in the fields of microwave transmission, fiber-optic cables, satellite projects, and computerized systems.

The liberalizing of the telecommunications market had already begun in Switzerland in the mid–1980s, anticipating the European Economic Community green paper of 1987, which made proposals toward Europe-wide competition in telecommunications. In 1988 the Swiss telephone market was opened to competition, but PTT retained its monopoly on the supply of first handsets, which are rented to subscribers, and the right to approve equipment, including the already liberalized teletex services and modems, supplied by third parties. In answer to criticism from competitors, PTT separated its approvals department from its purchasing department. The government has plans for further deregulation of the supply and approval of telecommunications equipment, but these are likely to stop short of affecting PTT's monopoly of network provision.

Until 1986, Swiss telecommunications manufacturers depended on PTT for two-thirds of their sales. In 1989 PTT contributed SFr5.25 billion to the private sector of the Swiss economy, chiefly by way of payments to the telecommunications and construction industries. In 1987 three of PTT's main suppliers, Hasler AG, Gfeller AG, and Autophon Telecom AG, merged with Ascom AG and others to form the Ascom Group, which in 1991 was remedying this dependency by turning to foreign markets. PTT's outlook, even with increased competition, is fixed on further expansion. The demand for PTT services continues to rise in all sectors—by 5.3% overall in 1989, 3% in postal services, and 7.2% in telecommunications. With 4 million subscribers, Switzerland already has one of the highest telephone penetration levels in the world, and the telephone service accounts for more than half of PTT's sales. The digitalization of PTT networks switches—Swissnet—begun in 1987, is due to be completed before the end of the twentieth century. The NATEL system, introduced in 1978 and subsequently improved and extended, provides mobile services not limited to automobile communication and with a potential capacity of 450,000 users. The PTT Citycall radio-paging service covers Switzerland, West Germany, and France. Special coaxial cables are used along the walls of the road tunnels through mountain passes for radiophone, radio-paging, and VHF broadcasts. For data transmission, analog, the traditional telecommunications signal, and digital, information encoded as a series of on or off switches contained in circuits of 3 types—telegraph, standard analog telephone type, and broadband—are offered, and over 8,000 are in operation. Telepac, the Swiss PSDN, in the early 1990s had 19 national and 3 international gateway exchanges. The text services available in 1991 included Telex, with over 20,000 connections, giving way in popularity to fax, which has approximately 200,000 users; Videotex, with over 80,000 subscribers and 332 information providers; and Teletex, offering memory-to-memory text transmission, which had 191 lines in service in 1988 and is expected to be another growth area.

A traditional note is struck by PTT's post-buses. They still tootle on their horn the first notes of the "Overture of William Tell" and, in the mailcoach tradition, carry not only letters but also goods and passengers, traveling more than 8,000 kilometers of road. In 1989, 81.2 million passenger journeys were made in this way. In the early 1990s the Swiss PTT had some problems to solve, including increased competition and the need to fund expensive investment and recruitment. However, with growth in the telecommunications sector standing at its highest rate in 20 years, PTT, under its chairman Rudolf Trachsel, could approach the millennium in a positive mood.

Further Reading: Wyss, Arthur, "Die Schweizer Post von ihren Anfängen bis zur Gegenwart," *Archiv für Deutsche Postgeschichte,* Frankfurt, 1978; *Telecommunications in Switzerland,* Bern, General Directorate of Swiss Posts, Telephones and Telegraphs, 1983; *Our Post,* Bern, General Directorate of Swiss Posts, Telephones and Telegraphs, [n.d.]; Dabbs, P.H., F. Cassidy, and D., Long, "Swiss Bank on Peak Performance," *British Telecom Journal,* Volume 5, Number 2, Summer 1984; Lee, Alma, "An Outline of the Problems of the Postal History of Switzerland," *The London Philatelist,* Volume 94, Number 1115–16, November–December 1985.

—Olive Classe

SOCIETÀ FINANZIARIA TELEFONICA PER AZIONI

Via Bertola 28
I-10122 Torino
Italy
(11) 55951
Fax: (6) 8589434

State-Owned Company
Incorporated: 1933
Employees: 125,958
Sales: L19.96 trillion (US$17.39 billion)
Stock Exchanges: Milan London Munich Frankfurt Düsseldorf

In 1991 telecommunications underwent a renaissance in Italy, in which the state-owned holding company Società Finanziaria Telefonica per Azioni (STET) has a key role to play. STET is partially privatized, but the state controls its operations. A major modernization program has been combined with a greater awareness of the international telecommunications scene.

Società Finanziaria Telefonica per Azioni, itself a part of the Instituto per la Riccostruzione Industriale, operates through its various telecommunications companies. The most important of these is Società Italiana per L'Esercizio delle Telecomunicazioni p.A. (SIP), the main domestic telephone operator. Others include the international operator Italcable and the satellite communications operator Telespazio. Telecommunications equipment manufacturing is undertaken by Italtel, while cable wiring, engineering, and installation services are provided by Société Internationale pour les Réseaux de Télécommunications et les Installations (Sirti). Two other subsidiaries—SGS-Thomson and Selenia-Elsag—have recently been transferred to another IRI holding company, Finmeccanica. Despite its importance, STET does not have a total monopoly in Italy. Azienda di Stato per i Servizi Telefonici (ASST), a department of the Ministry of Posts and Telecommunications, is responsible for domestic intercity and some continental trunk communications, though not for switching—calls which pass through an exchange. Attempts to merge SIP and Italcable with ASST have foundered because of political opposition.

The history of STET is strongly tied to that of Gruppo IRI. This state holding company, Europe's second largest company in terms of turnover in 1989, was created as a result of the nationalization of three of the largest commercial banks in 1933 and the acquisition of their equity portfolios. IRI then decided to create a series of *finanziaria,* or semiautonomous

financial holding companies, to manage all its interests in specific industrial sectors that were a byproduct of the nationalizations. STET was the first of these and was created in 1933 to operate IRI's telephone interests. In 1925 five private companies had been given concessions to operate local telephone services, while ASST was established to run the trunk interurban and international services. Three of these concessionary companies, STIPEL, TELVE and TIMO, became part of IRI in 1933. The other two concessionary companies were TETI and SET, and for the moment they remained independent.

World War II devastated large parts of Italian industry. The telephone facilities, however, came out of the war relatively unscathed. Only 15% of the telephone exchanges and 17% of the interurban telephone network were destroyed. In addition Società Italiana Telecommunicazioni Siemens (SIT-Siemens) and the Italian subsidiaries of some other foreign telecommunications equipment manufacturers were taken over by the TETI group after the war as a result of a reparations agreement. This group was nationalized by IRI in 1957 together with the SET group. Control was transferred to STET the following year, thus enabling telecommunications in Italy to expand considerably. All nontrunk telephone operations were now under IRI's control, simplifying the introduction of subscriber trunk dialing when it was introduced. The acquisition of TETI also allowed STET's telecommunications equipment manufacturing activities to develop.

In 1961 STET established a satellite telecommunications system company, Telespazio, as a joint venture with Italcable and with RAI, the state radio and television monopoly. In the following year it was granted an exclusive concession to operate commercial satellite services. IRI's various assets included businesses in the electrical power sector that were sold to the newly nationalized electricity industry in 1964, providing additional funds for STET to develop its telecommunications activities. At the same time, the five concessionary companies were merged into SIP, previously a hydroelectric company formed by STIPEL and RAI.

Servici Cablographici Radiotelegrafici e Radioelettrici (Italcable), one of STET's partners in Telespazio, was acquired in 1965. An agreement with the Ministry of Postal Services and Telecommunications three years later extended Italcable's scope. Until then, intercontinental telecommunications links had been its sole function. Its responsibilities were now expanded to include telephone, telegram, telex, and data transmission services to all foreign countries except those physically bordering Italy and Albania, Greece and Egypt. ASST's domestic role was modified, restricting it to calls between specified central exchanges, and the rest of the domestic network was handled by SIP. STET was also given responsibility for IRI's electronics interests. The electronics activities that were in Finmeccanica were reorganized and placed within STET in 1970. STET had already taken over Raytheon's subsidiary the previous year. It then established a joint venture with Siemens and SIT-Siemens, named Siemens Data, to distribute computers in the Italian market. A ten-year plan introduced in 1970 emphasized the potential that extensive research in the electronics and computer industry could have on its telecommunications activities. IRI was in the forefront of the desire to integrate computers and communications.

State ownership of SIP appears to have been detrimental to Italy's telephone services. Not only was there considerable fragmentation with SIP, Italcable, and ASST all operating independently, but there was also serious neglect of the telephone network during the 1970s, resulting in a significant decline in the quality of service. Rates were kept down to help fight inflation, and investment was curtailed. Rate increases from 1980 improved SIP's finances and laid the groundwork for the other changes that were to come.

STET and its constituent companies were transformed in the 1980s, especially after Romano Prodi became president of IRI in 1982. One element of his policies was the partial privatization of selected state-owned enterprises to raise funds, although maintaining state control over these operations was regarded as essential. There were changes in the ownership structure of STET and several of its companies, of which Sirti was the first. Once IRI had obtained the return of Pirelli's 30% holding in 1985, in exchange for holdings in STET and in SIP, more than 40% of Sirti's shares were privatized. IRI then reduced the state's holding in SIP from 85% in 1985 to 65% in early 1986 to 51% in 1991. IRI reduced its holding in STET from the 88% it held in 1985. IRI in the early 1990s owned 69% of the ordinary shares and 52% of the savings, or nonvoting shares. There were plans to reduce the state holding to as low as 30% of the savings shares, although these plans appear unlikely to be implemented.

These changes were followed by a major modernization program, as STET sought to overcome years of neglect of the telephone network and to upgrade its quality. The Itapac packet switching network, handling data in the form of units that are routed individually through the network, was introduced in 1986. SIP then introduced its five-year *Piano Europa* modernization program, with a budget of more than L36,000 billion, part of which came from the privatization of SIP. The installation of new digital public switching systems and telephone lines was aimed at a rapid increase in the number of telephone subscribers, from 33% of the population in 1987 to 42% by the end of 1992. The ability to achieve this was heavily dependent on the extent to which Italtel, as SIT-Siemens had been renamed, could develop adequate equipment. It traditionally supplied about 60% of SIP's requirements.

Italtel, too, was transformed under Marisa Bellisario, who took over as managing director and chief executive officer in 1981. She reduced the work force by more than 35% between 1980 and 1985, replacing almost half the management, and increased its research spending to a level of 11% of turnover. She was eager to obtain foreign technology, especially digital switching equipment. To this end she entered into a joint development project with GTE Corporation of the United States and the Fiat Group's Telettra subsidiary in 1982. The outcome was the Linea UT public switching system, first installed in Italy in 1984 and since then becoming the dominant system. GTE's interest in continuing the cooperation disappeared in 1986 when it sold 80% of its manufacturing operations in Italy, Belgium, and Taiwan to Siemens. This presented STET with a dilemma. Developing a new telephone switching system required enormous resources. At the same time, an increase in domestic competition was expected as the European Commission's measures to liberalize telecommunications markets intensified. By the early 1990s this had only a limited impact. Noncentralized parts of Europe's telecommunications equipment markets have been opened to competition. The ability of telecommunications operators to use type approval as a way of

eliminating competition in the supply of telephones and facsimile equipment was reduced, and mobile telephone services were being liberalized. The result of these twin pressures was a considerable restructuring in the European telecommunications equipment sector. Italtel was too small to finance these enormous research and development costs and to compete internationally. The company made less than 10% of its sales overseas, and its exports were concentrated in the peripheral markets of East Africa, Latin America, and the Middle East.

Italtel had long recognized its need for a major foreign tie-up to provide new technology and access to foreign markets. In order to strengthen its domestic base prior to any foreign link, it proposed merging its activities with those of Fiat's Telettra into a company to be called Telit. After two years of discussions and negotiations, Fiat broke off the talks in 1987, claiming political interference. The problem was the unwillingness of either side to give up management control over a joint venture. IRI had announced that Marisa Bellisario would be managing director of Telit two months after Gianni Agnelli and Cesare Romiti of Fiat had apparently agreed with STET's chairman that the director-general of STET, Salvatore Randi, would take that position. Randi had previously worked for Telettra, while Bellisario's close connections with the Socialist party were inimical to a Fiat involvement. In any case, this initial emphasis on establishing Telit may have been misplaced. Telettra, which was about half Italtel's size, was much weaker than Italtel in all areas apart from the transmission sector. The two companies combined would not have made much of an impact internationally, even though half of Telettra's sales were overseas. There were sporadic attempts to reactivate the discussions, especially after Bellisario's sudden death in August 1988. These talks came to nothing, and in June 1989 Italtel chose American Telephone and Telegraph (AT&T) as its international partner in preference to Alcatel, L.M. Ericsson of Sweden, or Siemens, the other applicants. Italtel took a 20% share in the Dutch-based AT&T Network International, and AT&T took a similar share in Italtel, contributing US$150 million to the company. This was followed soon afterwards by major changes in the ownership structure of AT&T Network International. Philips withdrew, and Telefonica of Spain took a 6% share. AT&T and Italtel set up an export marketing joint venture to promote sales of Italtel equipment to Greece, Portugal, and Spain, among other countries, and Italtel agreed to market AT&T's System 75 and Definity private switching systems and other products in Italy. STET still coveted Telettra, wanting to buy it and merge it with Italtel. Instead Fiat established closer links with the French Compagnie Générale d'Electricité (CGE) in October 1990. Part of this agreement involved an asset swap, with Telettra going to CGE's subsidiary Alcatel.

Italtel had been developing its business links with the Soviet Union and Eastern Europe independently of its new relationship with AT&T. A distribution and technical agreement with a Polish telecommunications company was announced in November 1990. Much more significant was the announcement in the same month of the formation of a new company, Telezaria, to produce its Linea UT digital exchange in the Soviet Union. It will hold 40% of the company; the remainder will be held by the Soviet telecommunications company Krasnaja Zarja. The choice of AT&T should strengthen the group considerably, though AT&T has so far been notably unsuccessful in European equipment markets, with overseas equipment sales in 1987 estimated at only US$300 million. In the early 1990s Telezaria was aiming to supply a quarter of the Soviet Union's requirements for telephone lines, with sales expected to be more than US$3 billion during the next 20 years, 15% from exports. This may make it as important to Italtel as the AT&T link was.

Changes had also been taking place in the electronics sector. In 1987 SGS merged its semiconductor activities with Thomson Microelectronics of France. Both companies had been undergoing major changes, internationalizing their activities extensively. In 1980, 80% of SGS's production was in Italy and France. At the time of the merger only about 5% of production was in these countries, with the main production sites in Malta, Malaysia, and Singapore. Thomson had acquired Mostek's assets from United Technologies in 1985, and it had other production facilities in Morocco, Singapore, and Malaysia. At the time of the merger of the semiconductor operations of these state-owned groups, the French and Italian governments agreed to provide funding for half of SGS-Thomson's research costs and for the continuing losses of the group. The joint venture was based in Italy, with English the business language of the group. Following the merger, SGS-Thomson's 23 plants were rationalized. In 1989 the British semiconductor producer Inmos was acquired from Thorn-EMI, which itself took a 10% share in SGS-Thomson. Marketing of Inmos's products has been integrated with that of SGS-Thomson's products. In 1990 SGS-Thomson set up a joint venture with the Hong Kong-based Astec to address microelectronics applications for power conversion equipment. The opportunity for SGS-Thomson to develop further will require expansion of the group. It wants to enter the digital random access memory sector, difficult though this will be, but cannot afford to do so independently. As political priorities give preference to a European solution, rather than the choice of a Japanese partner, and with both Siemens and Philips seemingly uninterested, the options for SGS-Thomson are limited.

Most of STET's other operations are within Italy. This is largely a reflection of the fragmentation of the group's activities and the limited scope of each part. SIP's role, for example, is strictly domestic, but this emphasis is beginning to change slowly. Initially STET was interested in taking part in the lucrative mobile telephone licenses that were being offered in some European countries, was a member of a consortium that in 1989 was unsuccessful in obtaining a license for Germany, and withdrew at the same time from another consortium for the United Kingdom. In the following year, the consortium of which STET was a member acquired the northern opera-

tions of the privatized Argentinian telephone company Empresa Nacional de Telecomunicaciones (ENTel). STET has slightly less than one-third of the holding company Nortel, which will own 60% of the northern operating company Telecom Argentina. STET is thought to have taken part in the consortium because of Italian governmental pressure to support the Argentinian government's privatization program. The aim of the program was to exchange the Argentinian government's enormous debts for shares in selected state-owned corporations, with foreign banks playing a key role in the consortia formed. The international links of Italcable are also developing. It is active in an international consortium building a Mediterranean and transatlantic optical fiber cable that uses special glass fibers to transmit laser light pulses giving on and off signals of digital information. It has also been expanding its North American operations. In 1986 it acquired 20% of Voice Mail International, a company involved in recorded voice communications services in the United States, and in 1991 it acquired a similar share in the long-distance telecommunications operator LCI Communications, entering into a research and development collaboration with the company.

With IRI once again under firm political control, Romano Prodi having stepped down as president in 1989, the policies of the 1980s may not be continued. The electronics activities have been transferred to Finmeccanica to enable STET to concentrate on telecommunications. The proposal to transfer ASST to STET foundered because of the need for parliamentary approval, something that was not, as of the early 1990s, forthcoming. The possibility of integrating the disparate parts of Italy's telephone network will have to wait.

Principal Subsidiaries: Società Italiana per L'Esercizio delle Telecomunicazioni p.A. (51%); Italtel (80%); Société Internationale pour les Réseaux de Télécommunications et les Installations; (60%); Servizi Cablographici Radiotelegrafici e Radioelettrici (54%); Telespazio.

Further Reading: Despicht, Nigel, "Diversification and Expansion: The Creation of Modern Services" in *The State as Entrepreneur: New Dimensions for Public Enterprise: The IRI State,* edited by Stuart Holland, London, Weidenfeld and Nicolson, 1972; Forsyth, Douglas J., "The Rise and Fall of German-Inspired Mixed Banking in Italy, 1894–1936" in *The Role of Banks in the Interwar Economy,* edited by Harold James, Hakan Lindgren, and Alice Teichova, Cambridge, Cambridge University Press, 1991.

—Martin Bloom

🔔 **Southwestern Bell** Corporation

SOUTHWESTERN BELL CORPORATION

One Bell Center
St. Louis, Missouri 63101
U.S.A.
(314) 235-9800
Fax: (314) 331-0840

Public Company
Incorporated: 1920 as Southwestern Bell Telephone Company
Employees: 62,700
Sales: $9.11 billion
Stock Exchanges: New York Midwest Pacific London Zürich
   Geneva Basel

Southwestern Bell Corporation (SBC) is one of the seven regional holding companies formed after the breakup of American Telephone & Telegraph Corporation's (AT&T) Bell System in 1983. Its principal subsidiary, Southwestern Bell Telephone Company, provides local telephone service to more than nine million customers in Missouri, Arkansas, Kansas, Texas, and Oklahoma. Most of the regional holding companies took over several Bell System operating companies after the breakup, but Southwestern Bell Telephone was big enough to be the only operating company assigned to its new parent. Other SBC subsidiaries are in such industries as directory publishing, mobile communications, and cable television. One subsidiary owns part of the national telephone system of Mexico.

Southwestern Bell Telephone Company, formed in 1920, has about 20 predecessor companies. The four largest of these were American District Telegraph Company, formed in St. Louis, Missouri, in 1878; the Kansas City Telephone Exchange, formed in Kansas City, Missouri, in 1879; Southwestern Telegraph & Telephone Company, which began serving Texas and Arkansas in 1881; and Pioneer Telephone & Telegraph Company, which provided telephone service beginning in 1904 in Oklahoma—not then a state, but known as Indian Territory—and in parts of Kansas. During their early years these four companies became affiliated with the Bell System, acquired other companies, and went through a number of name changes. In 1912 they consolidated various operating functions and became the Southwestern Bell Telephone System.

In 1917 the four companies began moving toward a more formal merger, with the Missouri & Kansas Telephone Company—the new name of the Kansas City Telephone Exchange—acquiring Bell Telephone Company of Missouri, successor to American District Telegraph. The resulting company was named Southwestern Bell Telephone Company (Missouri). In 1920 this company bought Southwestern Telephone & Telegraph and Southwestern Bell Telephone Company (Oklahoma), the successor to Pioneer Telephone & Telegraph, establishing the new Southwestern Bell Telephone Company, which was a subsidiary of AT&T. The new company had headquarters in Kansas City, Missouri, but moved to St. Louis the following year. Its president was Eugene D. Nims, a veteran executive at several other companies.

During the 1920s Southwestern Bell absorbed several other companies. In 1923 it bought the Kinloch Telephone System, which had been a competitor in St. Louis. Southwestern Bell and Kinloch had been two of the last telephone companies to compete in a major U.S. city. In 1925 Southwestern Bell bought back from the Dallas Telephone Company the Dallas-based telephone business that Southwestern Telephone & Telegraph had sold in 1918. In 1927 Southwestern Bell Telephone made another reacquisition, this time of the Kansas City phone business, which the Southwestern system had sold to a non-Bell company in 1919. Southwestern Bell did divest itself of a few operations, selling 23 Missouri telephone exchanges to Southeastern Missouri Telephone Company in 1929.

In 1926, the year Southwestern Bell installed its one millionth telephone, the company completed its new operations center in St. Louis. At 31 stories, the building was the tallest in Missouri at that time. New or renovated administrative offices followed in Dallas, Kansas City, and Oklahoma City in 1929.

During the Great Depression that followed the 1929 stock market crash, Southwestern Bell bought up numerous small telephone companies in its region. Often these companies were on the brink of insolvency. The largest Depression-era purchase was United Telephone Company of Kansas, bought in 1938. In the Depression years, Southwestern Bell took on some employees from its parent company, AT&T, which did not want to lay them off; the Bell System operating companies were not hit as hard by the Depression as AT&T's Western Electric manufacturing arm. Southwestern Bell felt the effects of the Depression sufficiently, however, to give employees incentives to bring in new customers or to persuade existing customers not to have their phone service shut off. During the Depression, unionization of Southwestern Bell's work force was heightened. Several of U.S. President Franklin D. Roosevelt's New Deal programs, such as the Wagner Act of 1935, encouraged the formation of labor unions and protected workers from being penalized for joining unions. Southwestern Bell and its unionized employees had relatively cordial relations during this period.

More than 3,000 Southwestern Bell workers served in the armed forces in World War II. The company took steps to conserve materials, such as copper and rubber, that were in short supply during the war. Telephone sets also were scarce, but Southwestern Bell's territory held a position of priority in their allocation, because the five-state area contained many defense plants and military training facilities. Other Bell operating companies transferred parts of their inventory to Southwestern Bell. The number and length of telephone calls, particularly long-distance calls, increased greatly during the war, often resulting in long delays for callers. Southwestern Bell launched an advertising campaign encouraging customers to hold their calls to five minutes each, and operators interrupted conversations that went past this limit.

After the war ended, Southwestern Bell expanded its engineering operations to meet pent-up demand for phone service; at one point in 1945 the company had a waiting list of 205,000. The number of phones the company operated had reached two million in 1944 and soared to three million by 1948. Southwestern Bell also stepped up the marketing of enhanced telephone equipment and services, such as extensions; this effort had begun in the late 1930s but was pushed aside by more pressing matters during the war.

The late 1940s brought a break in the company's peaceful labor relations. The National Federation of Telephone Workers, the union that later became the Communications Workers of America, organized the first nationwide strike against telephone companies in 1947. The strike lasted more than 40 days. In 1953 Missouri governor Phil Donnelly signed the King-Thompson Act that outlawed utility strikes in the state, but unions and their supporters subsequently won a repeal of the act.

In 1951 Southwestern Bell acquired Southeastern Missouri Telephone Company, the company that had bought some of Southwestern Bell's exchanges in 1929. In 1952 it added Southwest Telephone Company of Kansas. The number of phones operated by Southwestern Bell reached four million in 1952, five million in 1956, and six million in 1960. The figure was ten million by 1969.

The 1950s and 1960s brought a wave of new products and services from Western Electric and Bell Laboratories, two other AT&T companies. These innovations included phones in various colors and styles, the ability to interrupt or forward calls, and push-button service. To sell all these products, Southwestern Bell Telephone created its first marketing department in 1967.

The 1950s and 1960s also were a time of social change. During the 1950s Southwestern Bell shut down a St. Louis customer service office that had been staffed entirely by blacks since the 1940s. The company had set up this office so that black customers dealt with only black employees; the growing civil rights movement, however, led the company to integrate its work force. In 1966 Southwestern Bell named its first woman manager of a business unit.

Promotion of minorities and women in Bell System companies was not moving fast enough to please the U.S. Equal Employment Opportunity Commission (EEOC), however. In 1970 the EEOC accused AT&T and its Bell System of discrimination on the basis of race and sex. The companies responded that they were moving minorities and women gradually into parity with white males. In 1973 and 1974, AT&T and the Bell companies agreed to provide millions of dollars in back pay and salary increases to thousands of minority and women employees, although the companies did not admit to having discriminated in the past.

In the late 1960s the first challenges to the Bell System's monopoly appeared. In 1968 came the Federal Communications Commission's (FCC) Carterfone decision, which struck down prohibitions on connections of other companies' equipment or systems with the Bell telephone system. Then, in 1969, the FCC decided to allow Microwave Communications,

Inc. (MCI) to build a long-distance line between St. Louis and Chicago. In 1974 the U.S. Department of Justice filed an antitrust suit against AT&T—the suit that broke up the Bell System a decade later.

In the meantime, many of the Bell companies were having labor problems. A 1968 strike lasted 18 days at Southwestern Bell, although it stretched to five months in some other parts of the system. Another strike followed in 1971; workers at Southwestern Bell and most other system companies settled within six days.

A crisis of 1974 involved management-level employees. T.O. Gravitt, who ran Southwestern Bell's Texas operations, committed suicide that year, leaving behind papers that alleged bribery of regulators and other offenses by the company. In civil litigation, Gravitt's widow won substantial compensation from Southwestern Bell, but the court's decisions were reversed on appeal. The allegations prompted an audit by AT&T of all Bell operating companies; the audit found questionable practices only in Texas and North Carolina. The situation also prompted the state of Texas, which heretofore had left telephone regulation to its cities, to establish the Public Utility Commission of Texas in 1976. It had been the last state in the union without such a commission. In one of its first actions, the commission granted Southwestern Bell less than 20% of a $298 million rate increase the company had requested.

In 1978 Southwestern Bell installed its 15 millionth telephone; it was the first company in the Bell System to reach this level. By 1982, 70% of Southwestern Bell's customers were served by electronic switching systems, a percentage that also was the highest among Bell companies. In 1982 the company made another acquisition, of the El Paso, Texas, telephone business that had been operated by Mountain States Telephone Company.

In 1982 AT&T and the Justice Department approved the consent decree that broke up the Bell System. AT&T agreed to divest itself of the Bell operating companies, and the department agreed to drop its antitrust suit. In 1983 Southwestern Bell Corporation was formed as the regional holding company for Southwestern Bell Telephone Company.

Before the breakup was effected, there was another nationwide telephone strike, that lasted for 21 days in 1983. Workers won improved benefits as well as provisions for additional severance pay or retraining if they lost their jobs—a particular concern at the time of the divestiture.

Ownership of Southwestern Bell Telephone Company was officially transferred to Southwestern Bell Corporation on January 1, 1984. SBC had three other subsidiaries: Southwestern Bell Publications, Inc., a directory publisher; Southwestern Bell Mobile Systems, Inc., in the business of mobile telephone service; and Southwestern Bell Telecommunications, Inc., focusing on marketing phone equipment to business customers. The new holding company's president, chairman, and chief executive officer was Zane Edison Barnes, who had been president of the telephone company since 1973. SBC moved its headquarters into a new 44-story building in St. Louis.

Unlike some other regional Bell holding companies, which diversified into such fields as real estate and computer sales, SBC stuck with businesses closely related to telephone service. Through several acquisitions, it solidified its position as the largest directory publisher in the United States. It purchased Mast Advertising & Publishing, Inc., from Continental

Telecom for $120 million in 1985. Mast was the 12th-largest U.S. directory publisher and brought SBC a national sales force and an entrance into the publication of directories for independent telephone companies. SBC took its publishing ventures to the international market when its publications subsidiary in 1984 won a contract to be the Yellow Pages sales and collection agent for Telecom Australia.

SBC's customers were hurt by the recession in the oil business in the mid-1980s, and this in turn affected SBC. By 1986 the company's sales growth was the slowest of any regional telephone holding company, and its earnings growth was next to last. The situation began to turn around, however, after SBC bought Metromedia Inc.'s cellular and paging business in 1987. This purchase made SBC the third-largest cellular-communications company in the United States, behind McCaw Cellular and Pacific Telesis. In 1989 SBC's cellular business began to be profitable, while its larger competitors were still showing losses. In overall profitability, SBC ranked second only to Pacific Telesis among regional telephone holding companies in 1989.

In January 1990 Edward Whitacre succeeded Barnes. Whitacre had been with SBC and Southwestern Bell Telephone for 27 years. During 1990 SBC increased its international focus. Its subsidiary, Southwestern Bell International Holdings Corporation (SBIHC), joined a consortium that bought 20.4% of the total equity and 51% of the shares with full voting rights in Télefonos de México, S.A. de C.V., Mexico's national telephone company. SBIHC's partners in the consortium were France Cables et Radio, S.A.—a subsidiary of France Telecom—and Mexican company Grupo Carso. The total purchase price was $1.76 billion; SBIHC's share of this was $486 million. Participation gave SBC a chance to sell services, such as long-distance telephone communications, that it was prohibited from offering in the United States. Mexico had an antiquated telephone system, but potential for significant growth; only 1 in 17 households had a telephone. Another international move in 1990 was SBC's agreement to purchase West Midlands Cable Communications in the United Kingdom; this system included the largest cable television franchise in that country.

In the early 1990s, SBC, like other regional holding companies, was seeking changes in the regulations that arose from the AT&T breakup. These regulations restricted the businesses that regional holding companies could enter; among those prohibited were video programming production and various other communications products. As it awaited the outcome of its fight to lift these constraints, SBC continued to focus on its core businesses, as it had done ever since the divestiture.

Principal Subsidiaries: Southwestern Bell Telephone Company; Southwestern Bell Telecommunications, Inc.; Southwestern Bell Yellow Pages, Inc.; Southwestern Bell Mobile Systems, Inc.; Southwestern Bell International Holdings Corporation; Metromedia Paging Services, Inc.; Gulf Printing Company; Mast Advertising & Publishing, Inc.

Further Reading: Park, David G., Jr., *Good Connections: A Century of Service by the Men & Women of Southwestern Bell,* St. Louis, Missouri, Southwestern Bell Telephone Company, 1984; "The Baby Bells Take Giant Steps," *Business Week,* December 2, 1985.

—Jim Bowman and Trudy Ring

SWEDISH TELECOM

S-123 86 Farsta
Sweden
(0) 8-713 10 00
Fax: (0) 8-713 3333

State-Owned Company
Incorporated: 1853 as Kongl. Elektriska Telegraf-Verket
Employees: 47,971
Sales: SKr31.42 billion (US$5.67 billion)

Swedish Telecom is a state-owned public utility, responsible for Sweden's telecommunications system, providing a national and international telephone service as well as telex, telegraph, data, and radio communications services. Swedish Telecom is considered to be one of the most successful and efficient telecommunications organizations in the world, due to its highly saturated market. No country has a higher telephone penetration than Sweden. The company is one of the largest employers in the country, with approximately 1% of Sweden's work force employed by Swedish Telecom or its subsidiaries.

Swedish Telecom began in 1853, established by the Swedish government as Kongl. Elektriska Telegraf-Verket when an electric telegraph line using the Morse system was opened between Stockholm and Uppsala. Since then the company has operated under a variety of names, including Telegrafverket after 1860 and Televerket since 1953. The opening of the initial electric telegraph line was followed by the rapid development of a widespread telegraph network, consisting initially of single-wire telegraph lines. By 1854 the first telegraph line to the continent via a submarine cable was opened, and by 1857 a telegraph line was completed between Ystad and Haparanda, linking Sweden from north to south. In 1877 the first telephone line was installed, only one year after Alexander Graham Bell's invention. At the beginning of that year it was demonstrated in Sweden to King Oscar at the Royal Castle in Stockholm. By the 1880s private telephone societies were founded in most of Sweden's large towns. By 1885 Stockholm had more telephones than any other city in the world. By the turn of the century, Telegrafverket had installed 62,000 telephones, plus several exchanges of varying sizes. In 1918 there was a major change in the company's status when it purchased the telecommunications firm Stockholms Allmänna Telefon AB, which was responsible for the largest telephone exchange in Sweden. Telegrafverket had for some time challenged this company's dominance in taking over telephone subscriptions

and long-distance calls. Although the market was still formally open, the buy-out resulted in a national *de facto* monopoly, as no other competitor seemed to have the financial means or technical resources to mount a challenge.

Swedish Telecom has always placed a high value on research and development and, from the late 1800s, manufactured its own telephone exchanges and instruments, in competition with private industry. This provided about one-third of the company's needs. At the 1900 World Fair in Paris, one of Swedish Telecom's engineers, G.A. Betulander, jointly won a gold medal for his design for an automatic exchange. In 1910 Telegrafverket collaborated with the privately owned Swedish company LM Ericsson to develop the 500-line selector system. The most exciting technical milestone, however, came when Betulander, in collaboration with another engineer, Nils Palmgren, designed the crossbar switch, and the country's first exchange using the crossbar switching system opened in 1926.

The switch was a revolution in telecommunications, not only providing the impetus for the automation of the Swedish telephone system, but also attracting wide interest from around the world. The 1926 experimental installation resulted in 1931 in the crossbar switch being used to automate small rural exchanges. In 1921 Swedish Telecom began laying the first of its long-distance cables, which has since developed into an extensive network. Until 1935 these cables were used exclusively for the transfer of regular low-frequency signals but in that year Swedish Telecom began to apply carrier frequency systems to long-distance cables. Initially, loaded circuits with single channel operation that provided one additional facility were used, but from 1939 an unloaded circuits with multichannel system operation (Westcoast cable) came into use, which allowed 18 simultaneous conversations.

During the first few years after World War II, Swedish Telecom enjoyed a marked increase in investment, compensating for the lack of such cash injections during the war. The money invested, however, did not keep pace with the rise in the number of subscribers connected or the increase in telegraph or telephone traffic, which had accelerated sharply after the war. In 1947 alone, 111,000 new telephone users were connected. Although the government increased the connection fee threefold to limit applications, this inevitably reduced investment. Shortages of material and labor during the war limited the amount of cable laid, a problem that was rectified during the three following years, when the company extended its network by implementing circuits that would have measured to the moon and back.

In 1938 the number of overseas calls to the United States was only 320, but by 1947 the number had risen to 4,800, due mainly to the reduction in rates when the direct radio telephone route to North America, via New York, was opened that year. During the mid-1940s a fully automatic Telex service was introduced. By 1948, 60% of all telephones in Sweden were fully automated, with the remaining percentage due for automation over the next 24 years, using the crossbar switch or the 500-line selector system. This automation not only gave subscribers a more efficient and reliable service but meant lower operating costs, since the cost of staffing manual exchanges had risen faster than the cost of maintaining, operating, and investing in the automatic exchanges.

The 1960s and 1970s were a period of strong growth for the company. Beginning in the mid-1960s the automatic network grew at a rate of more than 160 new exchanges each year, and new trunk exchanges were installed in the Stockholm area to deal with trunk and transit traffic. In 1965 the data communications service was introduced in Sweden. In April 1970 Swedish Telecom consolidated its strong relationship with LM Ericsson by signing agreements to set up a jointly owned research and development company, Ellemtel, which would develop advanced electronic communications systems and products. One of the first such projects was the development of electronic switching systems—the AXE system—together with equipment for data networks, electronic private exchanges, telephone systems based on the integrated system technique, and advanced electronic telephone instruments. The last manual exchange was taken out of service in 1972.

In 1971 a satellite earth station was installed near Goteburg in the western province of Bohuslan, as part of Intelsat (International Telecommunications Satellite Organisation), which owns and operates satellites used for public international telecommunications. The Nordic earth station, as it was known, was a joint undertaking between Sweden, Norway, Finland, and Denmark to provide themselves with an international network. In early 1979, Swedish Telecom established its own videotext trial service. The establishment of a joint public data network, Nordic Data Network, and the introduction of the Database-300 service in the United States in March 1980 enabled Swedish users to gain access to a large number of host computers in the U.S. Tymnet and GTE Telenet networks. By 1980 nearly 98% of domestic calls were dialed directly by Swedish telephone subscribers, and the proportion of international long-distance direct dialing was increasing steadily. More than 58% of such calls were handled automatically during the fiscal year 1969–1970, compared to 39% the previous year. In addition, this period saw domestic long-distance and international calls increasing faster than local traffic.

The 1980s saw great changes for Swedish Telecom, the most significant being the gradual removal of its monopoly. The deregulation of the Swedish telecommunications market was virtually completed in 1989, with the abolition of Swedish Telecom's monopoly on large and medium-sized PABXs (private automatic branch exchanges), resulting in one of the most open telecommunications markets in the world. In response to the need for further competition, Televerket sought permission from the government to set up a holding company called Teleinvest that would own and administer the share capital of Televerket's subsidiary companies. Permission for this was granted.

Deregulation, however, has had a devastating effect on Swedish Telecom's production market. Teli, the company's subsidiary responsible for the production of telephones, was forced to lay off almost 780 workers at the end of 1988 when it decided to cease production after showing a series of annual losses of almost SKr100 million. No longer part of a monopoly, the company found itself unable to compete with countries where wages were only one-tenth of those in Sweden. The company had stressed, however, that its other products, particularly technically advanced ones, were then profitable.

In 1984 Swedish Telecom was further challenged when it was separated from the national budget and forced to seek funding on the open market. In 1991 Swedish Telecom financed most of its investments from profits and for the fiscal year 1984–1985, Televerket was empowered by the Swedish

Parliament to take out loans on the open market. The company invests over SKr5 billion a year on the expansion and modernization of its telecommunications network, which began in the early 1980s. The computerized AXE system is gradually replacing Sweden's electromechanical telephone exchanges. In addition, optical fiber cable is making a major contribution to network quality and capacity enhancement. The company had consequently become one of the largest borrowers on the Swedish credit market, financing loans by issuing TeleCertificates and TeleBonds. It also incorporated a central finance unit that is responsible for raising loan capital and redistributing surplus funds.

Swedish Telecom International AB was formed in October 1991 as a wholly owned subsidiary of Teleinvest AB, which will market the company's international network services.

In the early 1990s however, the biggest change for the company may yet lie ahead. In 1990 the director general of Swedish Telecom, Tony Hagstrom, called for the telecommunications company to be opened up to private ownership, via a stock market flotation. This will enable it to have sufficient risk capital to meet growing competition from a deregulated European market. Hagstrom believes that there will only be three or four telecommunications companies in Europe after 1992 and that Swedish Telecom needs more risk capital if it is to persist, extending its business into world markets through cooperation and alliances with other companies as well as direct acquisitions. He has proposed selling up to 45% of the company, which could yield the government as much as US$3.5 billion, or about half the groups' value. Before proceeding, however, the company has to secure the backing of both the Swedish government and Parliament. Under existing proposals, Swedish Telecom would retain 55% of the company, with the rest being sold to the public, pension funds, private insurance companies, and other investors. The sale is, however, unlikely to take place in the near future.

Hagstrom also wants Swedish Telecom to become an international company in the 1990s through the acquisition of shares in foreign telecommunications companies. In an open letter to the company's employees, he described telecommunications as one of the most dynamic and strategic areas of European industrial growth, shaped by the emerging internal market of the European Community. "Old national monopolies and national boundaries are disappearing," he wrote. "We must follow our customers out into the world and Europe." Recognizing that Swedish Telecom is handicapped by its small size, he emphasized that the company must compensate for this by being more flexible by building up strategic alliances and consortiums with overseas companies. Swedish Telecom faces the toughest time in its more-than-100-year history. The company's earlier success, however, should provide a solid basis for future prosperity.

Principal Subsidiaries: Teleinvest AB; Teli AB; Telefinans AB; TeleLarm AB; Telemedia AB; Tele Control Communications AB; Swedtel AB; TeleDelta AB; TeleNova AB; Diab Data AB; Infologics AB; Infivix AB; Mimer Software AB; Scandinavian Telecom Trading AB; Swedish Telecom International AB; Televerket Data AB.

Further Reading: The Swedish Telephone and Telegraph Administration and Telecommunication Service in Sweden up to the 1940s (English edition), Swedish Telecom, 1950; *World Telecommunications, volume 3,* New York, Arthur Little, Inc., 1971; "Success—Swedish Style," *British Telecom Journal,* London, Summer 1981; *Telemuseum,* Stockholm, Telecommunication Museum, 1982.

—Rachel Loos

ERICSSON ≦

TELEFONAKTIEBOLAGET LM ERICSSON

S-126 25 Stockholm
Sweden
(08) 719 00 00
Fax: (08) 18 40 85

Public Company
Incorporated: 1918 as Allmänna Telefonaktiebolaget L.M.
　Ericsson
Employees: 70,238
Sales: SKr45.70 billion (US$8.25 billion)
Stock Exchanges: Stockholm NASDAQ Basel Düsseldorf
　Frankfurt Geneva Hamburg London Oslo Paris Zürich

Telefonaktiebolaget LM Ericsson (LME) is one of the world's largest telecommunications concerns. The core of its operations has almost always been the manufacture of telephones, cables, and switching equipment. During World War II LME also began manufacturing products for the Swedish military, and it later continued to produce radar equipment.

The company bears the name of Lars Magnus Ericsson, an engineer who founded a workshop to repair telegraph machines in Stockholm in 1876. At first, Ericsson only worked with telegraph equipment, but that changed in 1877 when the newly invented telephone reached Sweden. LM Ericsson began producing telephones the next year, but sales were disappointing because the American Telephone and Telegraph Company (AT&T) had a virtual monopoly on telephone service in Sweden and used its own equipment. AT&T's Bell subsidiaries faced no serious competition in Sweden until 1883, when engineer Henrik Tore Cedergren founded Stockholms Allmänna Telefonaktiebolag (SAT) to provide telephone service and purchased his equipment from LM Ericsson.

Another boost to LM Ericsson's fortunes appeared in the 1880s in the form of an expanding export market. In 1881 the company's international business was very small and limited to other Nordic countries. By the end of the decade, however, its telephones were appearing in western Europe, Great Britain, and Russia. If LM Ericsson's export business expanded in the 1880s, it exploded in the 1890s. The company began selling telephones in Australia and New Zealand. Late in the decade it sold telephone exchanges that switch calls, as well as telephones in South Africa. During the Boer War, LM Ericsson supplied field telephones to the British armed forces. In 1899 LM Ericsson opened its first foreign factory, in St. Petersburg,

Russia; and by the turn of the century it had begun selling telephones in China and the South Pacific.

In 1900 exports accounted for about 90% of LM Ericsson's total sales. Contraction of demand in the domestic market and rapidly expanding foreign markets were partly responsible for this dominance of exports. Telegrafverket, the state-run telephone company, and SAT had been Ericsson's principal customers in Sweden, but both decided to set up their own manufacturing subsidiaries. Telegrafverket did so in 1891 and SAT in 1896. Nonetheless, LME's annual sales went from SKr500,000 in 1890 to SKr4 million in 1900.

Ericsson incorporated in 1896 as Aktiebolaget LM Ericsson & Company, with Ericsson serving as chairman, president, and sole shareholder. He retired as president in 1900 and was succeeded by Axel Boström, his former office manager. Ericsson stepped down as chairman the next year and died in 1926.

Even without the guiding hand of its founder, Ericsson continued to conquer international markets in the years leading up to World War I. It began selling equipment in Egypt and set up manufacturing subsidiaries in Great Britain, the United States, France, and Austria-Hungary. It also began installing telephone exchanges, joining with SAT to set up a network in Mexico in 1905. Relations with SAT, all but severed in 1896 when it began manufacturing its own equipment, were repaired in 1901 after SAT acquired telephone concessions in Moscow and Warsaw. Realizing that his production capacity was inadequate to supply these new markets, Henrik Cedergren agreed to merge his manufacturing operations with Ericsson's. SAT sold its subsidiary, AB Telefonfabriken, to Ericsson in exchange for LME stock.

Ericsson suffered during World War I as hostilities cut off most of its foreign markets. Exports were limited to Russia and neutral countries. The Russian market dissolved in 1918 when the new Bolshevik government nationalized Ericsson's Soviet operations, seizing about SKr20 million worth of assets. Despite these setbacks, the company's sales continued to rise, from about SKr9 million in 1913 to SKr14 million in 1920.

The most important event of the World War I years was Ericsson's merger with SAT in 1918. The two companies had been allied for decades, with a short separation after the establishment of AB Telefonfabriken. The companies decided to pool their assets in the uncertain war years. The new entity was called Allmänna Telefonaktiebolaget L.M. Ericsson. Arvid Lindman of Ericsson was appointed chairman, with Hemming Johansson of Ericsson and Gottlieb Piltz of SAT serving as co-presidents.

In 1921 an attempt to hammer out a worldwide telephone cartel agreement between Allmänna Telefonaktiebolaget L.M. Ericsson, AT&T's Western Electric subsidiary, and a German engineering firm, Siemens & Halske, fell through, and the three giants of the telephone business spent the rest of the decade battling with each other along with a U.S. firm, International Telephone and Telegraph Corporation (ITT), in the world's markets. In 1926 the company dropped Allmänna (general) from its name and became known by its present name. LME had become one of the most important players in its chosen arena, but by 1930 the company would find its survival in doubt as it was caught in the machinations of Ivar Kreuger, the notorious Swedish financier and confidence man. Kreuger rose to prominence in the 1920s, trying to forge an international monopoly in the production and sale of matches. He acquired the necessary financing, however, through fraud; he lied about the extent of his assets and the profitability of his previous ventures to gain credit. For years his deceits went undetected, and his empire grew. In the late 1920s he began to diversify, and he purchased LME stock in 1926 and 1927. By 1930 Kreuger controlled LME. Kreuger's takeover had little effect on LME's operations, but the company's assets became another token in his pyramid financing scheme.

By 1931 the Great Depression had made it all but impossible to raise capital through the securities markets, so Kreuger was forced to take desperate measures to meet his debt obligations and keep his gossamer empire from disintegrating. In one last effort, he approached ITT chairman Sosthenes Behn and proposed to sell his LME stock to ITT. He would sell ITT a controlling interest in LME for US$11 million, which he needed to make interest payments on his own bonds. Early in 1932, however, ITT backed out of the deal as doubts about Kreuger's solvency began to emerge. ITT demanded its money back, but Kreuger had already spent it. Kreuger killed himself in March 1932.

After Kreuger's death, an independent audit revealed that he had also embezzled US$5 million in cash from LME by replacing the money with illiquid French telephone bonds. His looting had bankrupted the company, and furthermore, he had delivered it into the hands of ITT, one of LME's major foreign competitors. Sweden's three major banks—Skandinaviska Kredit, Stockholms Enskilda Bank, and Svenska Handelsbanken—moved quickly to restore LME's liquidity and restructure the company. They also negotiated with ITT over its share of LME, a process made delicate by the fact that Swedish law forbade foreign interests from exercising a voting majority in Swedish companies. Under agreements reached later that year, ITT was allowed a large, but not a majority, share of re-issued LME stock, and Behn was given a directorship. The new LME board met for the first time in May 1933, with former National Power Administration official Waldemar Borgquist as chairman. Marcus Wallenberg Jr. of Stockholms Enskilda Bank was also appointed to head a special committee overseeing LME's finances. This marked the beginning of Wallenberg's long association with the company—he became chairman in 1953—and effectively added LME to the Wallenberg family business empire.

The so-called Kreuger crash made the Depression doubly hard for LME. Abroad, the company secured its market share by entering into cartel agreements with its competitors. At home, it cut back its work force and did not pay a dividend from 1932 until 1936. The outbreak of World War II did not make things any easier. The German invasion of Poland eliminated a foreign market that had been an important source of revenue, and LME once again omitted its dividend in 1939. The company lost about a third of its export sales during the war as well as foreign assets that were destroyed or nationalized. On the other hand, LME did benefit from Sweden's military buildup and manufacturing of telephones, aircraft instruments, machine-guns, and ammunition for the military.

Only after World War II ended was LME able to put the troubles of the 1930s behind it. Once again, LME concentrated on its core telephone manufacturing business, and export markets played their traditional leading roles. During the war, domestic orders had accounted for a peak 80% of all sales, but this began to decrease steadily in 1946. By 1973 the ratio would be reversed; exports would account for about 75% of LME's sales, just as they had during the early 1920s. Despite the nationalization of its Mexican subsidiary in 1958, sales in Latin America and Australia boomed in the 1950s. Profits grew, and the company expanded steadily throughout the postwar years.

In 1951 LME expanded its manufacturing capacity in the United States by acquiring a majority interest in North Electric Company of Ohio for $1.7 million. In the early 1960s, however, North Electric's orders from General Telephone Corporation and the U.S. Air Force fell off sharply and the company began to lose money. In 1966 LME sold a 52% interest in the subsidiary to United Utilities, a telephone and utilities concern that had become North Electric's main customer. LME sold its remaining interest to United Utilities in 1968.

In 1960 LME finally rid itself of Ivar Kreuger's legacy. After several years of negotiation, Marcus Wallenberg, Jr., purchased an option on ITT's entire stake in the company, which consisted of almost 1.1 million shares of preferred and common stock worth a total of $22.7 million. All of the common shares were subsequently sold through underwriting syndicates, and 200,000 of the preferred shares were sold on the open market, with the remaining 438,000 divided between Providentia, a Swedish trust company, Svenska Handelsbanken, Skandinaviska Enskilda Banken, and LME itself.

LME pared back its nontelephone business in the 1960s. In 1963 it sold off ERMEX AB, a subsidiary that produced electric cattle fences and locks. In 1968 it divested its electricity-meter operations when it sold another subsidiary, Ericsson Mätinstrument, to the Swiss engineering concern Landis & Gyr. At the same time, it savored its reputation as the world's premier non-U.S. telecommunications company. The crossbar switching system, which it had pioneered in the early 1950s, formed the basis of telephone networks in many countries. In 1973 LME attempted to expand its share of the British market by entering into a joint venture with electrical manufacturer Thorn Electrical Industries to produce telephone exchanges.

LME fell behind competitors like ITT, GTE, and Siemens in technological development in the late 1960s and early 1970s. That changed in 1976, however, when LME introduced its AXE switching system. The AXE was the first fully digital switching system, converting speech into the binary language used by computers. Its competitors still used the slower and less-reliable analog system, in which electric currents conveyed the vibrations of the human voice. The AXE's modular software and hardware gave it another edge over its rivals, making it easier to manufacture and test and easier for customers to repair and modernize. The system was an immediate success, winning virtually every major international telecommunications contract for two years after its introduction. Björn Svedberg, the young engineer who led the AXE development team, was appointed president of the company in 1978.

In 1980 LME purchased a controlling interest in Datasaab, a struggling computer manufacturer that had been jointly owned by Saab-Scania and the Swedish government. LME used this acquisition as the starting point of a major effort to enter the U.S. office automation market. LME also modified its powerful MD-110 PBX switch, a central-office switch, to suit the needs of U.S. customers, and in 1983 it entered into a joint venture with Honeywell to market the MD-110 in the United

States and to develop other telecommunications products. Previously a bit player in the United States, LME realized that it needed to play a major role there to ensure its prosperity.

In 1985, however, LME discontinued the sale of personal computers in the United States after selling only 3,000 units, or one-fifth of its goal for the year, and technical problems with the MD-110 suggested that it had been brought to market too quickly. LME laid off 500 employees—one-quarter of its work force—from its money-losing U.S. operations.

At the same time, however, the AXE system continued to prove a tremendous success; in 1985 LME won its first AXE contract from British Telecom, worth US$140 million. Also in 1987, LME gained 16% of the French telephone-switching market when the French government accepted its bid for Compagnie Générale Constructions Téléphoniques, an ailing switch-maker. This coup was especially prestigious because LME bested its two largest international competitors, AT&T and Siemens.

Faced with the vitality of its core switching business and the relative torpor in its data-processing business, LME decided to divest the latter and refocus on the former in 1988, abandoning its vision of producing its own automated office system. It sold its computer and terminal operations to Nokia Corporation, a Finnish concern, for US$217 million. With this sale, LME prospered. It laid the groundwork for future profits by winning contracts for switching equipment from the U.S. regional Bell companies that were formed when AT&T was broken up. LME also benefited from a surge in the demand for cellular phone service, and the quality of its products enabled LME to capture 40% of the world's cellular systems market. The company's position solidified in 1989 when an LME-backed design for digital mobile radio transmission was selected over entries from AT&T and Motorola as the U.S. standard by the Cellular Telecommunications Industry Association.

In 1988 LME amassed gross profits of SKr1.2 billion, a 60% increase over the previous year. Profits continued to grow throughout the end of the decade, and the company continued to expand its position in overseas markets. In 1990 telecommunications giant Nippon Telephone and Telegraph chose LME, Motorola, and AT&T to be its partners in a plan to jointly develop a digital mobile telephone system. The move was expected to give LME valuable access to Japan's burgeoning mobile phone market. In 1991 the company strengthened its position in Europe's cellular phone market when it acquired 50% of Orbitel Mobile Communications, the manufacturing subsidiary of British concern Racal Telecom PLC.

LME has risen a long way from the nadir of the Kreuger crash. As a large corporation with a small domestic market, it has almost always relied heavily on export markets for most of its revenues. Despite its size disadvantage relative to international competitors, LME made it back to the top of the telecommunications industry. With its renewed focus on its core businesses giving it strength, it seems poised to remain at the top.

Principal Subsidiaries: ELLEMTEL Utvecklings AB (50%); Ericsson Business Communications AB; Ericsson Cables AB; Ericsson Components AB; Ericsson Radar Electronics AB; Ericsson Radio Systems AB; Ericsson Network Engineering AB; Ericsson Telecom AB; Radiosystem Sweden AB; Ericsson Treasury Services (Ireland); Ericsson Treasury Ireland Ltd.; LM Ericsson Holdings Ltd. (Ireland); Ericsson SETE-MER S.p.A. (Italy, 71%); Ericsson Holding International B.V. (Netherlands); Swedish Ericsson Company Ltd. (U.K.); Ericsson Eurolab Deutschland GmbH (Germany); Ericsson Communications Inc. (Canada); Ericsson North America Inc. (U.S.A.); Ericsson GE Mobile Communications Holding Inc. (U.S.A., 60%); Cia Argentina de Telefonos S.A. (78%); Cia Ericsson S.A.C.I. (Argentina); Fios e Cabos Plasticos do Brasil S.A. (Brazil, 21%); Ericsson de Colombia S.A. (92%); Teleindustria Ericsson S.A. (Mexico, 72%); Cia Anonima Ericsson (Venezuela).

Further Reading: Shaplen, Robert, *Kreuger: Genius & Swindler,* New York, Alfred A. Knopf, 1960; Attman, Artur, Jan Kuuse, and Ulf Olsson, *LM Ericsson 100 Years,* 2 vols., Stockholm, Telefonaktiebolaget LM Ericsson, 1976.

—Douglas Sun

TELEFÓNICA DE ESPAÑA, S.A.

Gran Via 28
E-28013 Madrid
Spain
(1) 531 7634
Fax: (1) 531 5825

Public Company
Incorporated: 1924 as Compañía Telefónica Nacional de
España S.A.
Employees: 71,155
Sales: Pta710.90 billion (US$7.36 billion)
Stock Exchanges: Madrid Barcelona Bilbao Valencia London
Paris Frankfurt Tokyo New York

The Spanish telecommunications industry has grown from telegraphy between cities in the early 1850s and the first local telephone conversations in 1877 into a huge, high-technology international system. For the latter half of the industry's history, the government-controlled public company known since May 1988 as Telefónica de España, S.A. (Telefónica), has been the dominant element.

Telefónica holds official concessions for the supply and operation of most of Spain's domestic and international telecommunications services. Through its subsidiaries it also designs and manufactures telephone terminal apparatus. The Spanish telephone network, the company's original *raison d'être*, is now the ninth-largest in the world. Telefónica's activities, however, extend beyond its responsibility for the public service telephone system, which is now fully automated. It has moved into wider technological fields, integrated business communications, computer systems, semiconductors, and satellite communications, making many innovations. The company shares the provision of Spanish telecommunication services with the Dirección General de Correos y Telecomunicaciónes (CyT), which is responsible for postal services, telegrams, and telex, using lines leased where possible from Telefónica. By far the largest company in Spain, Telefónica owns 4% of the country's gross capital stock. Its turnover represents 1.5% of the total annual value of the economy, and it employs 1.5% of Spain's industrial work force. It also has extensive interests in Europe, North and South America, and the former Soviet Union.

Compañía Telefónica Nacional de España S.A. (CTNE), as it was officially called until 1988, was founded in Madrid on April 19, 1924, with capital of Pta1 million, divided into 2,000 ordinary shares. Until then, the Spanish telephone ser-

vice had been a muddle, supplied since its inception in 1877 by private individuals and small French and Spanish companies holding government concessions. These companies operated incompatible and inefficient manual systems under severe government restrictions, paying heavy royalties to the state. In the first decade of the 20th century, Barcelona, with 3,000 telephones, possessed the largest of such systems. Successive royal decrees from 1882 onward had failed to bring order out of the chaos created by these concession holders, so the Spanish government decided that the responsibility for Spain's telephones should be entrusted to a single body. On August 25, 1924, the government was empowered by another royal decree to sign a contract with the new Compañia Telefónica Nacional de España, conferring upon it the monopoly for operating the national telephone service. CTNE's task was to acquire the telephone operations and premises belonging to the existing private companies, or those that had reverted to the state, and to organize, integrate, develop, and modernize—in particular by a drive toward automation—Spain's urban and trunk telephone networks. One condition of the contract was that at least 80% of CTNE's employees must be Spanish nationals.

CTNE came into being as a result of a takeover by the International Telephone & Telegraph Corporation (ITT) of one of the existing Spanish telephone companies, created in 1899. The brothers Sosthenes and Hernand Behn, who had previously operated telephone companies in Puerto Rico and Cuba, set up ITT in 1920 as a U.S. holding company for their current and future enterprises. The companies were destined to become an international telephone system with corporate headquarters in New York. When in 1924 Spain was chosen for ITT's entry into Europe, local investors came forward, influential Spaniards were invited to serve on the board of the new subsidiary, and the goodwill of Miguel Primo de Rivera's authoritarian government was secured. As a private-sector company providing a public service, CTNE would be subject to tensions between nationally and shareholder-oriented strategies. Telefónica is still accountable to the Ministry of Transport, Tourism and Telecommunications, and a nonvoting government delegate sits on the Telefónica board. Although it is government controlled, Telefónica has benefited from a high degree of autonomy. The Spanish telephone service was never hampered by being linked, as in some countries, with postal services, or by being administered directly by the state civil service.

In CTNE's early years, its efforts were concentrated on the arduous task of extending and improving the existing telephone service. It was operating in a largely agricultural, undercapitalized economy, and its geographical context was a vast mountainous central region, sparsely populated and difficult to access, bordered by coastal strips and plains containing most of the population. Prosperity varied sharply between regions and classes. The political background was unstable and would eventually erupt into the Spanish civil war of 1936 to 1939. The new company set to work briskly in September 1924 and by the end of 1925 had 1,135 exchanges and "centers," nearly twice as many as it originally had. Some that were very small were operated by a family or individual, and some village centers consisted of a single pay phone in a private house. In 1925 CTNE's first underground cable was laid in the Escorial Palace near Madrid, and the site of the company's imposing headquarters in Madrid's Gran Via was purchased. In 1926 new manual exchanges were built in 48 cities, and in 37 other cities existing exchanges were refurbished. When King Alfonso XIII opened the new Spanish intercity telephone network in December, its 3,800-kilometer circuit constituted a European long-distance telephone record. By then the number of manual exchanges in operation had risen to 1,397.

In 1926 the company's long-term drive toward the full automation of Spain's telephone system was under way. The automation process, which had actually begun just before CTNE's time, in 1923, with an automatic exchange in Balaguer, would be finally completed in 1988. Between 1926 and 1929 automated rotary switching systems were installed first in San Sebastián—an L.M. Ericsson AGF type with 5,300 lines—and then in 19 other city exchanges. Rotary switching systems are electromechanical devices—first semi-automatic, later automatic—using rotating shafts to effect telephone connections. They superseded manual operators. At the same time the company was extending the basic network by opening hundreds of large and small manual exchanges. In Madrid one manual exchange and two automatic Rotary 7-A exchanges with 10,000 lines came into use at the opening of the CTNE main offices in July 1929.

In 1928 Madrid had acquired its first prepaid call token-operated telephones. In the same year, telephone communication had been established between Spain and Cuba, and the telephone link was made with Argentina and Uruguay in 1929. In 1930 the two main islands of the Canaries, Tenerife and Gran Canaria, were telephonically linked by underwater cable, while the next year a radiotelephone service was established between the Canaries and the Iberian Peninsula. Mallorca's telephone link with the mainland was also established in 1931. Between 1936 and the early 1950s, CTNE's development suffered severely, first from the upheaval and destruction of the civil war and then from Spain's political and economic isolation, both during World War II and after the defeat of the Axis powers, which had been favored by the government of General Francisco Franco. Until 1945 most of CTNE's capital was held by ITT. At that point, Franco's government of 1939 to 1975 nationalized the company, taking over its stock from ITT and retaining 41% of the share capital, the rest going to more than 700,000 shareholders. In 1946 the state renewed CTNE's contract. The company kept its monopoly over all civil domestic telephone services in Spain and was obligated to develop and extend them according to certain state requirements. This state contract remains in force, although it was extended and varied subsequently by governmental decrees and orders.

Under the chairmanship—from 1945 to 1956—of José Navarro Reverter y Gomis, the Compañía Telefónica expanded its facilities and continued the modernization of its equipment. In 1952 Madrid and Barcelona saw their first in-city radio car phones. Next year the company installed its first pulse code modulation (PCM) radiolink, between Madrid and the Escurial and in 1955 connected its millionth telephone. In 1957 a coaxial cable carrying 432 telephone circuits went into service, linking Madrid, Saragossa, and Barcelona, and the following year it became possible for Spaniards to telephone to ships at sea and planes in flight. The company's installations—telephone sets, lines and cables, switchboards, and exchanges—were meanwhile keeping pace with, and often pioneering, the industry's rapid technological advances. The company was no longer concerned only with telephones. Telecommunications

technology was proliferating all over the world, permitting the transmission, emission, and reception not only of voice messages, but also of other sound signals, visual data, texts, and images via optical and other electromagnetic systems, including satellites, beginning in 1960. Noise and other interference with transmission of signals could be reduced by digital communications systems—PCMs—in which voice, picture, and other data were coded in binary form. International standard-setting and regulatory bodies had by this stage been set up.

From the early 1960s until the first oil crisis in 1973, Spain and CTNE enjoyed the *años de desarrollo,* or years of development. During most of this period, Telefónica was headed by Antonio Barrera, who was chairman from 1965 to 1973. There was a rise in the national standard of living. During the years from 1963 to 1964, the country passed the US$500 annual per capita income mark and was no longer to be counted as a developing nation according to the United Nations definition. Industrialization gathered speed, and there was a shift of population from the country to the towns. The demand for telephone services rose steeply and with it, especially in rural areas, the large backlog of would-be customers waiting to be connected or put within reach of a public phone. The crossbar automatic switching system was introduced into the company's telephone exchanges in 1962. Crossbar systems are much faster than rotary ones and involve less friction and therefore less wear.

In 1964 CTNE took another pioneering step when it inaugurated Spain's first experimental earth station, designed to work in conjunction with international communication satellites Relay and Telstar. This was followed by other such ventures, notably in 1970 the company's earth station at Buitrago, to be used for telephone communication, data transmission, telegraphy, and black-and-white and color television, via the INTELSAT satellites (International Organization for Telecommunications via Satellites), or a combination of satellite and submarine cable. The goal of total automation was close to being accomplished. Automatic trunk dialing was introduced in 1960, and international trunk dialing appeared in 1972. In July 1971 a telephone service to the former Soviet Union was established, routed manually via Paris, and later the same year the company opened Europe's first dedicated public packet-switched data transmission network. Toward the end of 1978 the first computer-controlled electromagnetic network exchange was installed in Madrid. In 1980 the first digital exchange systems were installed, and in the early 1990s the digitalization of lines and exchanges continued to advance rapidly. By 1985 Telefónica was providing a network for the transmission of national and international television.

As the range of products and services grew and competition increased, there was a tendency for European countries to deregulate their telecommunications industries. Spain began planning to depart from its protectionist tradition at the end of the 1950s. Events contributing to this liberalizing tendency and paving the way for a more outward looking policy for the Compañía Telefónica included the election of the first Socialist government in 1982, the entry of Spain into the European Economic Community (EEC) in 1986, the 1987 EEC Green Paper proposing the deregulation of the newer parts of the European telecommunications market, and Spain's 1988 telecommunications law, the Ley de Ordenación de las Telecomunicaciónes (LOT). The LOT implemented some of the EEC proposals, but the Spanish government contested some of the Green Paper's provisions, being particularly reluctant to see inroads made on its revenue from data transmission services.

At the end of 1982, the new Socialist government brought in the energetic Luis Solana as president of the Telefónica board. His objectives were to float the company on world markets, reduce the formidable backlog of telephone customers waiting to be connected, and make the company profitable, after the recession of the late 1970s and early 1980s. In 1983 net profits were up 11% over the previous year, and by 1985 Luis Solana could claim that Telefónica was recovering. By adopting a 4-year purchasing plan aimed at procuring over 90% of hardware from Spanish suppliers, he helped save jobs in Telefónica's subsidiaries. He announced various projects for research and development and promotion of exports, as well as for cooperative agreements and joint ventures, Spanish and international, involving both industrial production and technology transfers. In 1984 Telefónica celebrated its 60th anniversary by adopting a new logo, ten dots arranged in the shape of a T within a circle. When in June 1985 the Compañía Telefónica became the first Spanish company to be listed on the London Stock Exchange, it was able to state that in the previous 20 years it had increased the number of telephone lines in service more than sixfold and the telephone penetration per capita more than fivefold. Spain, with 13 million telephones— 35 per hundred inhabitants—and 8 million lines installed, had the ninth-largest network in the world.

In 1986 Luis Solana reaffirmed the company's international orientation, announcing initiatives that included strategic agreements and joint ventures with American Telephone and Telegraph (AT&T) Technologies Inc. of the United States for ATT Microelectrica España—application-specific integrated circuits, 70% to 80% for export; SysScan of Norway for Maptel—digital mapping; British Aerospace, Olivetti, Brown Boveri, Philips, Saab-Scania, and Telfin for European Silicon Structures ES2—integrated circuits; and Fujitsu of Japan for Fujitsu España—DP hardware and software. Through the late 1980s, profits and development continued their upward trend. World financial markets were opening up to Telefónica, which has shares quoted in Europe, the United States, and Japan. In 1988 Telefónica increased the number of seasonal telephone booths—booths installed at resorts and in population centers during tourist seasons to meet increased telephone traffic—and prepared for the introduction of cardphones. In that same year, steps were taken to reverse the decline in the quality and efficiency of the telephone service arising from failure to keep pace with the surge in demand—there was 2% average growth in demand in the 1970s, rising to 12% in 1989. Telefónica invested in new ventures, including the pan-European company Locstar and Geostar (U.S.), set up to develop radiopaging via satellite in their respective continents. The first Spanish-Soviet enterprise was set up to produce telephones of Spanish design. International cooperation agreements were signed with other public networks operators, including France Telecom, British Telecom, STET of Italy, and, in the United States, NYNEX, Bell Atlantic, Ameritech, and Southwestern Bell.

The year 1989, under the chairmanship of Cándido Velazquez, formerly head of the Spanish state-owned tobacco industry and the successor of Luis Solana in January, brought improved service quality, management restructuring (decentralization), and investment in the urgently needed expansion of the network infrastructure. The company set Pta582 billion aside for investment, 62.7% more than in 1988. Telefónica Servicios (TS-1) was created to provide VANS (value-added network services), including radiopaging, electronic mail, voice mail, electronic data interchange, videotext, and international corporate communications. Telefónica installed nearly 1.5 million telephone lines in 1989, more than 87% of them digital. Spain now had over 15 million telephones. The waiting list had been reduced under Cándido Velazquez, but it still stood at 600,000 at the end of 1989. At 30 lines per 100 inhabitants, Spain had a lower level of telephone service penetration than any other European Economic Community member. Telefónica's good financial performance culminated in 1989 in a 16% increase in annual revenue to Pta703 billion (US$5.1 billion) and an 8% increase in profits to Pta68.5 billion.

Telefónica has ensured a strong hold over its supplies of telecommunications equipment, with an interest in Spain's largest manufacturers of telecoms hardware, a 21.14% share in Alcatel Standard Electrica S.A. and 12% in Amper S.A., the main Spanish manufacturer of telecommunications terminals. Telefónica's Plan Industrial de Compras (PIC) puts a severe limit on imports, thus protecting its native suppliers, which are largely its own subsidiaries.

Because of the government's controlling interest, Telefónica's policies have always been closely linked with those of the state, and its strategies have been influenced by national unemployment and inflation figures. Government restrictions have been evident in staffing policy—the company is obliged to maintain a larger work force than it otherwise would—and in the fixing of telephone tariffs where, until recently, there was a constant cross-subsidy from international calls to local ones. The latter were traditionally very cheap by European standards, with some private domestic subscribers never exceeding their allowance of free calls and paying only the rental charge. Local tariffs have been raised over recent years, by 14% in 1990, but such increases require government approval. Governmental trends have also had an effect on the company's funding, investment, and marketing policy. Telefónica has traditionally been able to rely on the Spanish Bourses for a large part of its funding, but until LOT it was inhibited from raising capital abroad by government policy, which also constrained exports. Telefónica's tax liabilities are met by a government levy, based on its net profits and is usually a set minimum of 6% of total revenue.

Until the late 1960s the company had left most of its research to its main supplier, SESA. Once properly started, however, Telefónica's research and development took off, and by 1971 was employing about 100 people in this area. In 1989 Telefónica, with the participation of Pacific Telesis and AT&T's Bell Communications Research, opened its new US$53 million research and development center. This center, occupying 21,000 square meters and employing, at the end of 1989, a staff of 500, had developed a second-generation packet-switching system and is engaged in projects on optical communication, speech technology, and various European Economic Community and European Space Agency projects. Throughout its history the company has been attentive to the quality and concerned for the welfare of its employees. In August 1924, the same month that its first contract with the government was authorized by royal decree, a company training department was set up. In 1989 over 43,000 of the 71,155 employees were given training or refresher courses, and over 55% of 1,930 new recruits were university graduates. Since 1925, employees have been offered the opportunity of becoming shareholders in the company.

As well as maintenance and extension of the basic telephone services, Telefónica's activities in the 1990s cover data transmission; VANS (value-added network services), including radiopaging, electronic mail, electronic data interchange, videotext, and international corporate communications; and satellite communications. There is also development of the supporting infrastructures—digitalization of transmission services, installation of optical fiber cables, extension of ISDN (integrated services digital network), and maintenance of Telefónica's position among world leaders for submarine cable networks. In the early 1990s Telefónica was aimed at expansion into European and Latin American markets by acquisition. The telephone network will benefit from a program, due to be completed in 1992, to build three Hispasat satellites linking Spain, the United States, and Latin America. In Spain, Telefónica was making large-scale preparations to meet the extra calls on its telephone and telecommunications services that will be made in 1992. In that year Barcelona will host the Olympic Games, EXPO 92 will take place in Seville, and Madrid will be cultural capital of Europe.

In the early 1990s Telefónica's future looked promising. The growth of the Spanish economy should continue to attract foreign investors and partners. Because it is still developing its basic network, Telefónica has the opportunity to adopt the lat-est technology and stands a good chance of leading the telecommunications field.

Principal Subsidiaries: Sistemas e Instalaciones de Telecomunicación S.A. (SINTEL); Telefónia y Finanzas S.A. (TELFISA); Telecomunicaciones Marinas S.A. (TEMASA); Compañía Española de Tecnología S.A. (COMET); Compañia Publicitaria Exclusivas Telefónicas S.A. (CETESA) (97.33%); Seguros de Vida y Pensiones Antares S.A.; Cabinas Telefónicas S.A. (CABITEL); Control Electrónico Integrado S.A. (THM) (80.25%); Teleinformática y Comunicaciones S.A. (TELYCO); Telefónica North America Inc. (USA); Casiopeia Reaseguradora S.A.; TS-1 Telefónica de Servicios S.A.; Telefónica Investigación y Desarrollo S.A. (TIDSA); Telefónica Internacional de España S.A.; Servicios de Teledistribución S.A. (99.14%); ENTEL S.A.; Playa de Madrid S.A.; Fujitsu España S.A. (40%); Alcatel Standard Electrica S.A. (21.14%); Hispasat S.A. (25%); Telettra S.p.A. (Italy, 10%).

Further Reading: "Télécommunications" in *Grand Larousse encyclopédique,* Vol. 10, Paris, Librarie Larousse, 1964; "Telecommunications" in *The New Encyclopedia Britannica,* Vol. 28, Chicago, 1985; Hooper, John, *The Spaniards,* Harmondsworth, Viking, Penguin Books Ltd., 1986; *Automización integral de España,* Madrid, Servicio de Publicaciones de Telefónica, 1989; Lalaguna, Juan, *Spain,* Gloucestershire, Windrush Press, 1990.

—Olive Classe

U S WEST, INC.

7800 East Orchard Road
Englewood, Colorado 80111
U.S.A.
(303) 793-6500
Fax: (303) 793-6654

Public Company
Incorporated: 1983
Employees: 65,469
Sales: $9.96 billion
Stock Exchanges: New York Pacific Midwest Boston
    Philadelphia London Zürich Basel Geneva Amsterdam Tokyo

U S West, Inc. is one of seven regional holding companies (RHCs) providing local telephone service in the United States. U S West has the largest area of operation, covering 14 western states. In addition to local telephone service, it is engaged in cellular telephone services, publishing telephone directories, paging, personal communications networks, business communications systems, and financial services.

U S West was formed in 1983 as part of a consent decree between the U.S. Department of Justice (DOJ) and American Telephone and Telegraph Company (AT&T), at that time the world's largest corporation. AT&T had built most of the U.S. phone system, but suffered frequent criticism for allegedly suppressing competition through unfair trade practices. The decree followed a lengthy court battle with the DOJ. AT&T had left the operation of local telephone service in the United States to 22 companies, all under AT&T's umbrella. The breakup divided the 22 locals among seven regional holding companies. U S West was formed from the combination of Mountain States Telephone & Telegraph Co., Northwestern Bell Telephone Co., and Pacific Northwest Bell Telephone Co. Its territory comprised Arizona, Colorado, Idaho, Iowa, Minnesota, Montana, New Mexico, Nebraska, North and South Dakota, Oregon, Utah, Washington, and Wyoming. U S West and the other RHCs were not free to enter any business they chose. The consent decree forbade them to use their monopoly power to their advantage and from entering certain businesses, including long-distance telephone service and telephone equipment design and manufacture. Incorporated in 1983, U S West officially began operation January 1, 1984.

From the day of its formation, U S West had built-in disadvantages compared to its sister RHCs. It had the largest territory of any, covering about 45% of the area of the lower 48

states, but much of its territory was sparsely populated and growing slowly, which limited the return on equipment and services. Many miles of wire were needed to reach fewer people than in the other RHCs, although U S West managed to earn a higher income per line than other RHCs' average at a lower than average cost. Only 4% of AT&T's pre-breakup stock was owned by people who lived in U S West's territory, and the company feared investment might dry up. Because of these disadvantages, the new company reacted swiftly and aggressively to the AT&T breakup. It chose a name faster than any of the other Bell operating companies, dropping the "Bell" name to remove associations with the past, and calling itself U S West to symbolize its desire to take on new frontiers. To get its name recognized by the public and investors, the company spent $2.5 million on a showy advertising campaign featuring cowboys and the company slogan, "If you don't make dust, you eat dust." U S West appointed Jack A. MacAllister president and chief executive officer. He gave the company a decentralized structure. Its three local phone companies and new subsidiaries were run as separate companies, and staff at U S West headquarters was kept below 200.

MacAllister quickly moved the company into new business ventures and pushed for relaxed regulation from the states in U S West's territory and from the consent decree governing AT&T's breakup. U S West began investing millions of dollars in commercial real estate, owning a $70 million portfolio by the end of 1985. U S West also moved into financial services, buying a commercial funding company for $10 million and the Kansas City operations of Control Data Corporation's Commercial Credit Company for $65 million. Like most of the other regional holding companies, U S West began investing in cellular telephone services and directory publishing, two businesses in which they were not restricted to their own territories. U S West bought directory publisher Trans Western Publishing, with operations in Florida and California. The company formed U S West New Vector Group Inc. to manage its cellular operations and U S West Financial Services to offer leasing and sales financing to its customers. In 1984 profits amounted to $887 million.

By late 1985 U S West had won pricing flexibility for some services from regulators in eight states. The company formed subsidiary U S West Information Systems to direct its computer operations. The company's New Vector Communications bought the San Diego cellular operations of Communications Industries Inc. Justice Harold Greene, overseeing the AT&T breakup, turned down the first request by the RHCs to ease restrictions on diversification into nonregulated areas. In 1985 profits were $925.6 million.

In 1986 U S West bought Applied Communications Inc. for nearly $120 million. In 1986 the company formed a commercial real estate subsidiary, Beta West Properties; its first move was to buy the 54-story office building in Denver, in which Mountain States headquarters was located, for $235 million. A strike by 18,000 members of the Communications Workers of America at Mountain States ended after one day. Decentralization led to the formation of two U S West equipment-marketing subsidiaries, FirstTel Information Systems and Interline Communication Services. The two subsidiaries competed with each other and with the sales forces of U S West's three local phone companies. In late 1986 both companies were dissolved into a single new subsidiary, US Information

Systems. U S West took a $52 million loan to pay for the restructuring and dismissed more than 1,000 employees. The two subsidiaries had marketed telecommunications equipment nationwide. The restructuring narrowed the focus to selling equipment within U S West's territory, where the company was best known. U S West's profits for 1986 were $924 million on revenue of $8.31 billion.

Acknowledged as the most aggressive of the RHCs, U S West in 1986 told Bell Communications Research (Bellcore), the research consortium jointly owned by the seven RHCs, that it was going to sell its share when its funding commitment ran out in 1990. U S West wanted greater control of the kind of research that the lab did and over who was aware of it. At a result of U S West pressure, Bellcore changed the rules governing its research to allow it to do research for a single RHC and keep it secret from the others for two years. The changes satisfied U S West, and it stayed in Bellcore. U S West established its own 400-engineer laboratory in Colorado, however, to focus on its own research and development. The decree governing the AT&T breakup forbade any regional Bell from designing or manufacturing its own equipment, but U S West worked on artificial intelligence and voice recognition and response systems with the goal of creating a system to give repairpersons instructions from a talking computer via telephone.

By mid-1988 U S West had invested $192 million in New Vector. It had entered 22 cellular markets and had 51,000 subscribers, but it was losing money. In 1988 U S West sold 17% of New Vector on the stock market to recoup its initial investment. The stock promptly began falling, losing 28% of its value in two months. U S West's growth was falling behind that of the other RHCs, largely because the population and economy of its region was stagnant, while that of most other RHCs was growing. Telephone profits for 1987 fell 1%, although total profits rose to $1 billion.

U S West pushed for deregulation harder than any of the other regionals, often angering state regulators in the process. By the end of 1987, 11 of the 14 states the company served had loosened regulation, allowing the company to freely price new services such as central phone switching, cellular phones, and private lines. Idaho, Nebraska, and North Dakota had the least restrictive telecommunications policies in the United States. In 1988 U S West, along with the other regionals, finally won court permission to enter new information services like voice mail and database transmission as long as they did not create or manipulate data themselves. The relaxed restrictions meant more local telephone traffic and increased profits. U S West promptly announced a deal to test market Minitel, a French videotex system, in its region. The company also bought 10% of French cable company Lyonnaise Communications and announced plans to offer an information-gateway service in Omaha, Nebraska.

In 1988 U S West decided to entirely do away with the Bell name, announcing plans to restructure its three local phone companies into one subsidiary, U S West Communications. The company hoped the restructuring would cut costs by centralizing marketing and distribution. The restructuring replaced a geographic approach to sales with one organized around market segments and put new emphasis on customer service. U S West hoped the name change would increase customer awareness of it, although some analysts feared the move

could create resentment among customers already frustrated by the chaos following the AT&T breakup.

By 1988 U S West Financial Services, which bought and then leased out expensive items like airplanes and medical equipment and engaged in mortgage banking and leveraged buyouts, had grown to nearly $105 million in revenue and nearly $2 billion in assets by 1988. In May 1988 it bought two reinsurance companies for $50 million. Profits for 1988 reached $1.13 billion.

Critics accused U S West—and other RHCs—of diversifying too far too quickly reducing the quality of local phone service in its region. In rebutting its pundits, U S West pointed to its large investments in phone equipment for the local networks, $1.6 billion in 1987 alone.

In 1989 U S West introduced miniature Yellow Pages, less than two inches thick and about seven inches long, hoping they would find a niche among car-phone users and people with limited shelf space. The company's cable division invested in two British cable companies, London South Partnership and Cable London. It then joined British telephone giant STC PLC in bidding on a British cellular-communications license. The company bought Financial Security Assurance Inc. for $345 million to strengthen U S West Financial Services. Profits for 1989 were $1.1 billion.

In early 1990 U S West announced it would sell the $1.4 billion in commercial real estate owned by BetaWest Properties and instead focus on real estate financing. The company said it would sell the properties over the next five to seven years as market conditions permitted. It hoped real estate financing would bring sustained profits rather than incur the debt the company had taken on to buy property.

In 1990 U S West and its sister RHCs launched a major push to escape from federal restrictions dating from the AT&T breakup. They pooled nearly $21 million for a lobbying effort designed to shift regulation of their activities from Justice Greene to Congress and the Federal Communications Commission (FCC), where they expected a more sympathetic ear. The RHCs warned of the dire consequences of letting the U.S. telecommunications system fall behind that of other countries— a message that found a receptive audience among those fearing a decline in U.S. economic strength. Opponents, including long-distance telephone companies, cable television companies, and newspaper publishers, said the RHCs would use regulatory freedom to raise local rates and use the increased profits to subsidize their entry into new businesses.

The telecommunications market was growing faster in most of the rest of the world than it was in the United States. Partly because of that and partly because of the limits put on its U.S. activities, U S West invested $1.05 billion overseas by 1990, the second highest amount among the RHCs. U S West was the first "RHC" in Eastern Europe, with a 49% stake in a Hungarian cellular telephone project, begun in 1989. U S West had become one of the largest cable-television competitors in the world, with franchises in Hong Kong, Britain, and France. U S West's 25% stake in the Hong Kong franchise, the world's largest, required it to pay $125 million of the cost of building the cable network. In return, the consortium was to get six years of exclusive access to the market. The deal, however, soured when a Hong Kong company announced plans to beam programming into the country via satellite. In 1990 U S

West pulled out of the consortium after the Hong Kong government refused to stop the satellite system.

U S West was involved in a $500 million plan to lay fiber-optic cable across the former Soviet Union, although the U.S. government rejected the plan, citing national security concerns. A few months later U S West announced plans to build the first cellular telephone networks in the Soviet Union in Moscow and Leningrad. It also revealed plans to build Czechoslovakia's first cellular network in a joint venture with Bell Atlantic Corporation. Even if successful, the financial rewards from the company's ambitious foreign projects were expected to be years in coming because of the huge capital outlays needed to build them.

In 1990 U S West announced it was investing $35 million to develop self-healing telephone networks in five cities. The networks used loops of fiber-optic cable to prevent disruption of service by earthquakes, fires, or other disasters. If a section of the loop broke, signals could be sent the other way around the loop to the telephone switching station. The service was aimed at large businesses, government offices, long-distance carriers, and others that needed to move large amounts of information without interruption. The loops were to serve about 200 large office buildings in Denver, Minneapolis-St.Paul, Phoenix, Portland, Oregon, and Seattle.

After 40 years in the telephone business, MacAllister retired in 1990, and Richard D. McCormick took his place as president and chief executive officer. U S West's directory publishing group established an international headquarters in Brussels, Belgium. The company also bought Cable Management Advertising Control System, a personal-computer-based system that tracked local cable television advertising. It spent a record $2 billion in 1990 to modernize its telephone system. As part of a drive to develop new telephone services, U S West set up an experimental telephone system in Bellingham, Washington, allowing customers to use touch-tone telephones to turn on, turn off, and change various telephone services themselves. New product revenues almost doubled from 1989, jumping to $54 million. Cellular subscribers rose 56% to 210,000, while paging subscribers hit 161,000. Income for 1990 was $1.2 billion on sales of $9.96 billion.

Principal Subsidiaries: U S West Advanced Technologies; U S West Capital Corporation; U S West Communications Group Inc.; U S West International; U S West Marketing Resources Group; U S West New Vector Group Inc.; U S West Real Estate.

Further Reading: Arenson, Karen W., "U S West: Building an Image," *The New York Times,* November 11, 1983; Ivey, Mark, "U S West: A Trailblazer That's Getting Left Behind," *Business Week,* June 6, 1988.

—Scott M. Lewis

UNITED TELECOMMUNICATIONS, INC.

2330 Shawnee Mission Parkway
Westwood, Kansas 66205
U.S.A.
(913) 624-3000
Fax: (913) 676-3281

Public Company
Incorporated: 1925 as United Telephone & Electric Company
Employees: 43,100
Sales: $8.35 billion
Stock Exchanges: New York Midwest Pacific

United Telecommunications, Inc., (United Telecom) provides voice, data, and videoconferencing transmission and related products for the global market. It is the only large U.S. company offering both local and long-distance services.

The company history extends back to 1892 when Cleysen Brown connected a generator to his father's grist mill, supplying electric power for Abilene, Kansas. In 1898 Brown hung telephone wire on his electric poles and quickly extended the business to other towns. The fledgling company was incorporated in Delaware on September 25, 1925, as the United Telephone & Electric Company. Diversification into other businesses was ended by the Great Depression. With utility operations remaining stable, United acquired several independent telephone companies. Upon Brown's death in 1935, United Telephone & Electric fell into receivership.

In November 1938 the company was incorporated in Kansas as United Utilities, Inc., along with seven telephone companies and Central Kansas Power. The Public Utility Holding Company Act caused the company to sell gas, light, and water properties outside of the northwest Kansas area.

During the 1940s, through integrations and mergers, United Utilities grew as a holding company for independent telephone systems. By 1953 United was ranked fifth among U.S. independents. During the mid-1950s United entered the liquid petroleum gas business through acquisitions in Illinois. By the late 1950s a trend of telephone company mergers was evident; independent telephone companies had declined in number over a ten-year period by 35%.

By 1960 United Utilities was the third-largest telephone holding company in the United States, with 467,000 telephones operating. In contrast, number-two General Telephone & Electronics (GT&E) had 1.1 million telephones.

By 1963, when United Utilities was listed on the New York Stock Exchange, it had $200 million in assets and owned 14 telephone companies, a gas and electric company, and a utility merchandising firm. With local telephone exchanges in 15 states, telephone service provided roughly 90% of company revenues. United became the first major telephone system to offer dial service—the state of the art at the time—to all its customers by year-end 1963. Another industry advance was made in a North Carolina subsidiary: United completed the United States's first private electronic branch exchange, an advance over conventional switchboard systems and a predecessor of automatic dialing, call-waiting, and caller identification systems. United set up aggressive sales programs to market such innovations.

United's growth spurt was attributed to many factors: acquisitions of telephone companies; increases in suburban populations, a United stronghold as opposed to American Telephone & Telegraph (AT&T)-controlled urban centers; successful pressure for rate increases; and the relative ease with which technical innovation could be introduced, because of United's manageable size. Another positive development for United Utilities in 1963 was the increase in long-distance calling. To transmit such calls, AT&T required the use of United's facilities, for which it agreed to pay $1.25 million for the 12-month period ending June 1, 1963.

In the 1960s United benefited from the burgeoning market for farm and home intercommunications systems, including security devices, telephone extensions, answering machines, mobile service, leased wire services, and key and dial switching equipment. Acquisitions continued at a great pace. The 1964 purchase from AT&T of a 45% interest in Inter-Mountain Telephone Company, servicing Virginia and eastern Tennessee, made United a major contender in the telephone industry.

United Transmission Inc. was a new venture developed in 1965 to design and operate community antenna television systems (CATV). Through United subsidiaries, communications systems were beginning to merge. With expertise in electronic telephone service transmission, United moved into the transmission of high-quality multi-channeled television reception. It investigated CATV service and purchase opportunities throughout the United system. The same year United added eight independent telephone companies to its roster, with service extending east from Kansas, Iowa, Indiana, Ohio, and Pennsylvania, to South Carolina; and northwest to the state of Oregon.

Paul H. Henson was named president of United Utilities in 1964, succeeding Carl A. Scupin. Henson joined United Utilities in 1959, with a master's degree in electrical engineering, doctoral work in mathematics and physics, and experience as chief engineer for Lincoln Telephone Company. United's sales of $14 million were not quite 1% of AT&T's, and about 5% of GT&E's. United's hopes were pinned on a pending U.S. Department of Justice (DOJ) case. The DOJ was suing to dissolve the recent merger of GT&E and Western Utilities, the latter owning 635,000 telephones.

Prior to 1960, United's concerns were in internal organization, not acquisitions. As most large independent telephone companies had already been bought, Henson said of United Utilities, in *Forbes,* November 1, 1965: "We'll have to nickel-and-dime our way up." By the mid-1960s, however, United was paying high prices for telephone company acquisitions, prices the company claimed were justified in light of the expected growth in the telephone business.

In January 1967 United combined various operating companies in Ohio into one, Telephone Service Company of Ohio. Within several months United added more regional telephone companies in Iowa and Ohio, as well as the Gulf States Telephone Company of Texas. By the end of 1967, United merged Inter-County Telephone & Telegraph with United Telephone Company of Florida. It also streamlined utility operations, acquiring the remaining stock of Central Kansas Power (8.4%), and North Electric Company (48%).

By far the most forward-looking venture United engaged in at the time was the December 1967 acquisition of Automated Data Services Company, Inc., renamed United Computing Systems, Inc. Through the subsidiary, United entered the computer time-sharing business, with Boeing as one of its early customers. United had seen early on the need to develop high-speed data transmission capabilities. Quoted in the November 1968 issue of *Finance,* President Henson predicted: "At United we are bending every effort in this direction because we are certain data volume will surpass voice volume by 1975."

Over the next two years, United stepped up acquisitions, adding three telephone companies in Kansas, two in Missouri, and one each in Iowa, Texas, and North Dakota. The company consolidated a newly acquired electrical supply company with United Telephone Company of Indiana as well as eight telephone companies under United Telephone Company of Ohio. A significant merger at this time was Carolina Telephone and Telegraph Company, completed in March 1969. The company also delved into cable television, but sold its holdings quickly due to a Federal Communications Commission (FCC) ruling banning companies from operating cable in the same areas telephone lines.

As United grew, its telephone profits fell under rate regulation, monitored by the FCC. United initiated a rate entitlement program with the FCC, designed to increase service rates to cover higher operating costs. The company was also negotiating with AT&T's Bell System over toll calls. Other growth areas in United Utilities included its manufacturing subsidiary, North Electric. By late 1968 North sold three-quarters of its services to the Bell System, other independents, industrial companies, and computer manufacturers. By mid-1969 United picked up Rixon Electronics, Inc.

Jockeying for a leading position in the communications industry, United planned to use its increased size to diversify. More opportunities for expansion in business telephone equipment manufacturing came early in 1970 when the FCC changed some of its regulations. The company requested and was granted permission to interconnect a device called the Carterfone to the existing telephone network. The FCC then ruled that all telephone companies remove restrictions on non-Bell attachments from their tariff regulations. Accordingly, all telephone companies and equipment suppliers, together with the FCC, began negotiating new standards for the connection of outside equipment to the existing network. United Utilities, as well as foreign manufacturers like Nippon Electric of Japan and Siemens of Germany, stood to gain from the new rulings.

In step with the changes, United launched subsidiary United Business Communications, Inc., offering private voice and data communications systems, to compete with AT&T and GT&E. United Computing Systems bought the time-sharing

services, software packages, and facilities of Academy Computing Corporation in early 1971. One-third of revenues came from United's unregulated businesses—North Electric Company, United Computing Systems, and United Business Communications.

The unregulated businesses needed more attention, however; United Business Communications was not profitable in its second year, while United Computing barely edged into profitability by 1972. In contrast, at the end of 1971 United's basic telephone operations accounted for 90% of company profits. Consistent in its independent telephone company acquisitions, United added one company to its Ohio division and expanded to Minnesota and the state of Washington.

In June of 1972 United Utilities, Inc., became United Telecommunications Inc. (United Telecom). United Telecom anticipated getting into "everything in the transmission of intelligence by electronic means." Accordingly, United Telecom's Rixon Electronics subsidiary, a computer modem and terminal equipment supplier, entered a joint venture with Sangamo Electric.

While earlier FCC rulings helped United Telecom in the business of supplying telecommunications equipment, later FCC rulings threatened to limit United's capacities. An antitrust suit against United's independent competitor, GT&E, appeared likely to compel GT&E to divest itself of some equipment manufacturing companies as well as telephone companies. CEO Henson, however, saw the situations positively, reasoning that United would not be susceptible to the same rulings, as it was a small company and pursued a different acquisition and purchasing policy. United was safe from that jeopardy at the time, but the case foreshadowed the imposition of more and more FCC regulations upon the telecommunications industry.

Toll calling boomed in the early 1970s. United again benefited from revenues gained from Bell System companies required to pay independents an increasing share of toll charges. At this time United decided to finance an anticipated construction program through the sale of bonds and common stock. Total company revenues doubled over the years 1966 to 1971, and net income rose 48%.

Overall, the 1970s were an unpredictable time for United Telecom. In 1974 United picked up more independent telephone companies in Michigan, Pennsylvania, and Florida. Competition in the unregulated areas, however, caused the company to sell 100% of United Business Communications to a subsidiary of General Dynamics Corporation. After letting go of United Business Communications, United set out to expand the business of United Computing Systems. The computing systems subsidiary stepped up acquisitions; in 1975 it added International Timesharing & Foresight Systems, Inc.; and in late 1976, it acquired Infonational, Inc., a California-based software company, and Standard Computer Corporation. By 1977 United Computing acquired London University Computing Services, Ltd.

The same year United Telecom, through a tax-free exchange of stock, acquired Norfolk Carolina Telephone Company, adding 53,324 telephones to its holdings. The company sold the manufacturing divisions of North Electric Company. United retained supply operations, renaming the remaining operations North Supply Company. In a further move to position itself as a major competitor in telecommunications, United sold

Central Kansas Power for an undisclosed amount in November 1977. This sale marked the end of an era; United had made its start in the business of generating electricity 40 years earlier.

Juggling assets a bit more, the following year United added Calma Company of California, a supplier of computer-aided systems for mechanical and integrated circuit design. In November 1979 the company acquired Pittsburgh-based On-Line Systems, a $29.2 million company offering database management for defense, manufacturing, and energy-related applications. The company continued small telephone company acquisitions.

United Telecom entered the 1980s with a reorganization plan designed to aid future diversification. Effective February 15, 1980, the company was divided into three operating groups: United Communications Systems, Inc., responsible for telecommunications services and the operations of North Supply Company; United Information Systems, Inc., to tackle all facets of computing and time-sharing businesses; and United Telephone System, Inc., to oversee regulated telephone activities and corporate operations. Many executive positions were rearranged, the most significant being the election of William T. Esrey to executive vice president of corporate planning.

The 1980s were the most challenging time for the independent telephone companies yet. The debate over separations and settlements, that is, toll charge reimbursements; nationwide average pricing, the true determiner of telephone rates; and local access tariffs kept all telephone companies, independent or otherwise, at attention.

United's strength in unregulated businesses was its information systems division. Sales rose from $96 million in 1979 to $115 million in 1980. In March 1980 the company launched Uninet Inc., the third-largest packet network to compete with similar services of GT&E's Telenet. United Telecom's computer-aided design equipment business, helped by the Calma acquisition of 1978, was to be in 1980 the fastest growing part of the industry.

Later, in 1981, United Telecom sold Calma to General Electric Company. In August the company acquired Megatek Corporation of San Diego, another producer of computer-aided design and manufacturing equipment, and Insurance Systems of America, a computer software company. Because of recent acquisitions and increased competition from new players in computer-aided design, including IBM, United Information Systems lost $1.4 million in 1981.

In a further shuffle, in January 1983 United moved into the business of industrial and marine distribution with the purchase of Aeroflow Dynamics and its subsidiary Argo International. United sold some assets of Argo International the following year. A more notable divestment was United's sale of United Information Services, Inc., in December 1983. United entered the computing business when it was clear that consolidation of data was necessary. Once mini- and microcomputing became available, businesses began to do their own computing, resulting in United's decision to exit the processing arena.

With the landmark breakup of AT&T in January 1984 and the consequent regulatory changes in the telephone industry, United Telecom decided to enter the intercity carrier business. The June 1984 purchase of Dallas-based U.S. Telephone Communications, Inc., also paved the way for United Telecom to offer broad-based service to business customers as well as long distance services. Although the Department of Justice and MCI Corporation voiced objections to United's U.S. Telephone acquisition, the FCC approved the move, requiring only that United provide equal access to its network as did other common carriers. Because of the plethora of former Bell operating companies in the telecommunications marketplace following AT&T's divestment, United Telecom's move was seen as a risk, albeit a timely and positive one.

As the national marketplace became more competitive, United Telecom negotiated with more and more companies. With Continental Telecommunications, Inc. (Contel), United agreed to exchange properties in the mid-Atlantic states, merging 7,000 customers into its United Telephone-Eastern Group, based in Carlisle, Pennsylvania.

In August 1984 United Telecom teamed up with Consolidated Rail Corporation (Conrail) to install a fiber-optic network. Fiber optics, the transmitting of digital codes via pulses of light that are converted into voice at the end of the line, became the new technological standard for accuracy and efficiency. With Conrail granting the right of way, United Telecom sketched routes across Massachusetts and New York, over the mid-Atlantic states, to Indiana and Illinois. United engineering and construction crews were laying fiber for the largest planned network yet built.

William T. Esrey, named to the presidency of United Telecom in 1984, with Henson becoming chairman, addressed Congress in September of that year. Along with other industry executives, Esrey contended the concept of equal access was still just that—a concept, not a practice or law. The former Bell operating companies had not hurried to install access points allowing long-distance carriers to reach customers; as a result, AT&T had widespread access to choice interconnections, thereby dominating the long-distance market.

United Telecom's $2 billion investment in its fiber-optic network was part of its plan to become a major competitor in long-distance service. A big opportunity came on July 1, 1986, when United Telecom and GTE Corporation, formerly GT&E, United's competitor for 50 years, entered into a joint venture. GTE contributed Sprint and Telenet to United Telecom's fiber-optic network and data communications arm. The new long-distance company, named US Sprint, doubled its market, adding three million customers within the first nine months.

For two years the partnership of United Telecom and GTE poured money into US Sprint, spending—like competitor MCI—more than $2 billion on the endeavor. With AT&T investing $2.5 billion in long-distance services, these companies reached an all-time high in spending. While United Telecom hoped to convince customers they needed its all-digital network, more had to be done. By March 1987 US Sprint's losses forced GTE into a corner; Canada's Belzberg family bought much of GTE Sprint stock, hoping to make GTE sell its shares. United Telecom saw profits in the future for its long-distance arm, especially with sales of voice and electronic mail growing.

Within a year, a change was imminent. By June 1988 United Telecom calculated it had spent $1.5 billion on US Sprint. On July 18 United Telecom bought 30.1% of US Sprint from GTE. The corporation decided to unload some of its assets to further fund Sprint. In October 1988 United Telecom sold

Telespectrum to Contel for $772 million. A partner of its stable telephone business, Telespectrum had been providing cellular radio and paging for more than three years, and was definitely part of a growth industry. United Telecom was determined to stick with Sprint, and the costs were high.

US Sprint President Robert Snedaker, although credited with installing a new billing system and lowering costs by 15%, nevertheless lost some marketing chiefs in the process. Snedaker opted for early retirement while United Telecom president and CEO Esrey stepped in as CEO of Sprint as well.

Sprint's situation was improving by early 1989 for several reasons. United Telecom officially took over as Sprint's parent company, effective January 3, 1989, and completed the first nationwide fiber-optic network for coast-to-coast transmission. The company also became the first long-distance company to use Signaling System 7, the most efficient call-routing system.

Effective July 1, 1989, the company traded properties with Contel Corporation, exchanging its access lines in Iowa, Missouri, and Arkansas for 52,000 lines in Kansas. In the early 1990s United was also filing its own common carrier line tariffs with the FCC, ending its membership in the National Exchange Carrier Association. For United Telecom, being responsible for its own tariff policies would give the company more pricing flexibility.

In August 1989 US Sprint acquired full ownership of Private Transatlantic Telecommunications Systems, Inc. (PTAT), including a 50% interest in the PTAT fiber-optic cable system. The 100% fiber system, according to *Telephone Engineer & Management,* December 15, 1989, could transport "as much traffic as all previous transatlantic cables combined." With the United Kingdom's Cable and Wireless as its partner, United Telecom anticipated European business opportunities. To initiate possible entrance into the trans-Pacific market, the company followed up the purchase with a Hawaii-based firm, Long Distance/USA, in October 1989. The acquisition gave United Telecom nearly one-half of Hawaii's outgoing traffic as well as the opportunity to increase its one-fifth share of the U.S.-Japan long-distance market.

All the effort began to pay off; Sprint's fourth-quarter revenues in 1989 showed a 28% increase over the previous year. The recent streamlining of Sprint operations was paralleled in United Telecom's telephone business as well. Fiber-optic systems, in the United Telecom view, were intended for local networks as well as long-distance. In December 1989, US Sprint landed 40% of the Federal Telecommunications System ten-year contract, the largest civilian contract ever awarded.

In 1989 United Telecom consolidated operations between the parent company and US Sprint. Telenet was merged into US Sprint, and the company formed Sprint International to oversee business in electronic messaging, corporate data networks, and international voice and private line services. At this time Sprint reached twelve nations: Australia, Belgium, Canada, Chile, Finland, Hong Kong, Italy, Japan, Malaysia, Sweden, Taiwan, and the United Kingdom.

In 1990 United Telecom, together with North Supply, its equipment distribution company, initiated a standardization plan for all products to reduce construction and supply inventories. DirectoriesAmerica, formed in May 1986, remained the tenth-largest publisher of telephone directories after four years of operation, with a circulation of ten million. Local telephone service, reaching four million customers in 17 states, accounted for a solid 27% of revenues.

The firm considered changing its name to US Sprint Corporation should it choose to exercise its option to purchase the remaining 19.9% interest in Sprint from GTE. That option was delayed until Sprint's performance stabilizes. Engaging in joint ventures with the governments of the former Soviet Union, Mexico, and South Korea, Sprint International in the early 1990s was researching the eastern European markets for telecommunications infrastructure construction contracts. Paul Henson, after 31 years with United Telecom, announced his retirement as chairman in April of 1990. William Esrey succeeded Henson.

Principal Subsidiaries: Carolina Telephone & Telegraph Co.; Florida Telephone Corp.; United Inter-Mountain Telephone Co.; United Telephone Co. of Arkansas; United Telephone Co. of the Carolinas; United Telephone Co. of Florida (95%); United Telephone Co. of Indiana, Inc.; United Telephone Co. of Iowa; United Telephone Co. of Kansas; United Telephone Co. of Minnesota; United Telephone Co. of Missouri; United Telephone Co. of New Jersey; United Telephone Co. of the Northwest; United Telephone Co. of Ohio; The United Telephone Co. of Pennsylvania; United Telephone Co. of Texas, Inc.; United Telephone Co. of the West; Information Systems of America, Inc.; Megatek Corp.; North Supply Co.; Sprint/United Management Co.; UCOM, Inc.; United Business Information, Inc.; United TeleDirect Group, Inc.; United Telephone System, Inc.; US Telecom, Inc.

Further Reading: "United Utilities, Sprawling, Diversified, But Always United," *Finance,* November 1968; "Dial UT for Growth," *Investor's Reader,* November 15, 1972.

—Frances E. Norton

TEXTILES & APPAREL

Brown Group, Inc.
Burlington Industries, Inc.
Coats Viyella Plc
Courtaulds plc
Levi Strauss & Co.
Milliken & Co.
Mitsubishi Rayon Co., Ltd.
Nike, Inc.
Reebok International Ltd.
Springs Industries, Inc.
Teijin Limited
Toray Industries, Inc.
Unitika Ltd.
VF Corporation

BROWN GROUP, INC.

BROWN GROUP, INC.

8400 Maryland Avenue
St. Louis, Missouri 63166
U.S.A.
(314) 854-4000
Fax: (314) 854-4091

Public Company
Incorporated: 1881 as Bryan Brown Shoe Company
Employees: 27,500
Sales: $1.76 billion
Stock Exchanges: New York Midwest

Brown Group, Inc. was known through most of its 100-plus years as The Brown Shoe Company. The company is the largest manufacturer of name-brand shoes in the United States and has significant shoe retailing operations. The Brown Group markets many popular brands of women's, men's, and children's shoes such as Connie, Naturalizer, Roblee, and Buster Brown. The company operates hundreds of retail shoe stores in the United States and Canada, and also sells Brown brands through leased shoe departments in leading U.S. department stores. The Brown Group imports approximately 75 million pairs of shoes annually, and manufactures another 24 million pairs at 19 shoe factories in the United States and Canada. Most of the company's importing is handled by two subsidiaries, Brown Group International and the Pagoda Trading Company. The Brown Group was involved in retailing a variety of products in the 1970s and 1980s, including children's furniture and play equipment, rubber balls, women's clothing, rifle sights, and equestrian accessories, but in the early 1990s the only major nonshoe product marketed by Brown was fabric, through the company's Cloth World stores.

The company began as a shoe manufacturing concern. George Warren Brown moved to St. Louis from New York in 1873 to work in his older brother's wholesale shoe business. While working as a traveling salesman, George Brown came to see great potential in the St. Louis area for shoe manufacturing. At that time, shoes were primarily manufactured on the East Coast. Skilled workers in New England factories made shoes that were then shipped to jobbers at points west. George Warren Brown believed that shoes could be made more cheaply in St. Louis than in the established East Coast factories. After working for four years in his brother's wholesale business, Brown had accumulated enough capital to test his idea. With two other investors, Alvin L. Bryan and Jerome

Desnoyers, Brown founded Bryan, Brown and Company to make women's shoes. Brown paid five skilled shoemakers from Rochester, New York, to come to St. Louis and start the factory. The company grew rapidly. In its first year, 1878, the company had sales of $110,000. By 1885 sales were up to $500,000 and growing. In 1881 the company incorporated as the Bryan Brown Shoe Company. In 1885 when Bryan sold his interest, the name was changed to Brown-Desnoyers Shoe Company. In 1893 Desnoyers retired, and the name was changed to The Brown Shoe Company. Brown shoes were sold all over the Midwest, at prices lower than those of the older New England shoe firms. By 1900 the company was growing at a rate of $1 million a year, and St. Louis was becoming known as a major shoe manufacturing center.

In 1900 Brown Shoe contributed $10,000 to the St. Louis World's Fair, a gala event that put a spotlight on the Missouri town. The company put up a model shoe plant at the fair, and this exhibit won Brown a grand prize. Another exhibitor at the fair was the cartoonist R. Fenton Outcault, creator of popular comics "The Yellow Kid" and "Buster Brown." A young Brown executive, John A. Bush, made a lasting contribution to his company by buying the rights to the Buster Brown character. The little blond boy and his dog Tige became the emblem of the Brown Shoe Company children's line. In addition to printing the Buster logo on its shoe boxes, the company hired 20 midgets to dress as Buster Brown and tour the country. Buster and Tige played in theaters, shoe stores, and department stores across the country, to much popular acclaim.

While some youngsters were applauding the Buster Brown midgets, others were at work in Brown Shoe factories under deplorable conditions for extremely low pay. Because the cost of plant equipment and materials was relatively fixed, Brown Shoe had to make its profits by keeping its labor costs as low as possible. As manufacturing became more mechanized, shoe factory jobs became less skilled. Increasingly, shoe manufacturing jobs were filled by women and children, who could be paid less than men. For example, a 1911 survey of St. Louis shoe workers found more than half to be between the ages of 14 and 19. Some 84% of the women and close to 70% of the men were under age 24. An average wage for a girl under 16 was less than $10 per week. More shoe manufacturers had followed George Warren Brown's example and set up shoe factories in St. Louis, making the industry extremely competitive. Under these conditions, the wage paid to shoe workers spiraled down.

By 1902 Brown Shoe was operating five factories in St. Louis. In 1907 the company started its first "out of town" plant, in nearby Moberly, Missouri. Several St. Louis shoe companies began manufacturing in surrounding rural towns because of the cheaper labor available in those areas.

In response to the poor working conditions at Brown and in other St. Louis-area shoe factories, workers formed unions. The first was the moderate Boot and Shoe Workers Union; the second was the more radical United Shoe Workers of America, associated with the International Workers of the World. Bitter strikes led to increasing militancy among St. Louis shoe workers. George Warren Brown responded by becoming a local leader of the Citizens Industrial Association, a nationwide anti-union propaganda organization that maintained blacklists against union sympathizers. The best way to fight the unions, however, proved to be to leave St. Louis.

The small towns around St. Louis offered many advantages to the Brown Shoe Company. It was standard at that time for a town that wanted a shoe factory to offer to build one for a company, and exempt the company from paying taxes. In return, the company would agree to pay out a certain amount of money in wages over a five or ten year period. After the stipulated amount of wages had been paid, the company had no more obligation to the town. There were always more towns willing to subsidize a new shoe factory. While Brown's management remained headquartered in St. Louis, the company opened factories in many rural towns in Missouri and Illinois. Each town's economy became dependent on the shoe factory, and pro-company sentiments within the factory towns created a hostile climate for union organizers. The distance between the factories also made union organization more difficult than it had been in the condensed St. Louis shoe district.

Regardless of worker discontent, the Brown Shoe Company grew. In 1907 the company moved its headquarters to a stately building in downtown St. Louis. In 1913 Brown was listed on the New York Stock Exchange. With the entrance of the United States into World War I in 1917, Brown Shoe won large, profitable army contracts.

The company stumbled in 1920, however, when a sudden change in women's fashions caught Brown by surprise. Hemlines went up, and Brown was left with an overstock of sturdy high-topped shoes that did not go with the new look at all. John Bush, who had bought the Buster Brown logo rights and then worked his way up to president in 1915, when George Warren Brown became chairman of the board, had to go to Boston before he found a bank that would give the company credit. After this crisis, however, Brown Shoe boomed, until the stock market crashed in 1929, and the Great Depression set in.

During the Depression, Brown Shoe struggled to keep its costs down, which meant that workers' wages suffered. A National Labor Relations Board investigation at Brown's Salem, Illinois, plant found that workers were sometimes drawing checks for as low as $2.50 and $3.00 for a 60-hour week. Workers protested worsening conditions in Brown's factories, but the company's management grew more abusive. U.S. President Franklin D. Roosevelt drafted the National Industrial Recovery Act in 1933 to force industries to standardize wages and prices and thus alleviate the workers' downward wage spiral. Two years later, the Wagner Act guaranteed all U.S. workers the right to organize into unions and to strike. Brown's management, however, remained adamantly anti-union. When workers at the Vincennes, Indiana, factory struck for recognition of their union in 1933, Brown closed the plant. William Kaut, the company's general manager in St. Louis, declared that "The intention of the Brown Shoe Company is to do as much for their help as any shoe industry in the United States . . . and when Brown Shoe Company does its part and even more and if the help are then not satisfied, there is only one thing left to do and that is to close the mill." What the Brown Shoe Company was doing for its help, however, reportedly included physical intimidation of union organizers, spying on and infiltrating workers' organizations, and hiring a notorious strike-breaking agency, in addition to its policy of closing down "troublesome" plants.

Eventually, Brown attracted national attention when a union representative in Sullivan, Illinois, narrowly escaped being tarred and feathered in September 1935, and the Illinois Federation of Labor forced a grand-jury investigation. No indictments resulted, but the Regional Labor Board in St. Louis later issued a complaint, citing Brown for unfair labor practices and for using officers and agents of the company to intimidate employees. The hearing that followed revealed that John A. Bush had hired the A.A. Ahner detective agency in 1934. Bush testified that he did not know that Ahner was a strikebreaking agency, but Ahner was in fact known as such in St. Louis. In 1929 he had been implicated in an attempted bombing connected with anti-union work. Although Ahner himself claimed he was not hired to break unions, a report in *The Nation* on January 29, 1936, noted that termination of Ahner's connection with the shoe company coincided with the dissolution of most of the locals of the Boot and Shoe Workers' Union in Brown plants.

It was not only physical threats and the economic threat of plant shut-down that led many union locals to disband. The Labor Board hearings revealed that Brown had kept a paid spy in its Sullivan factory. The spy turned out to be the former head of the union local. After urging workers into an ill-timed strike, he then incited his union's members to burn the union charter and disband. He was later overheard telephoning Brown headquarters to report his success. Attacked from within and without, most of the Boot and Shoe Workers Union locals at Brown plants folded, because workers were desperate to hang on to their jobs. Brown sometimes closed its plants temporarily, later to rehire only workers who had had no union involvement.

The National Labor Relations Board cited Brown in 1936 for violating the Wagner Act in connection with the dissolution of the Salem local, but the company refused to reinstate strikers and workers who had been fired for union activity. The workers who had not lost their jobs at Brown were finally given some help in their struggle for decent wages when the Fair Labor Standards Act of 1938 established a minimum wage in the United States. The labor shortage during World War II finally gave a boost to union organization, although unrest continued to some degree.

In 1941 Brown opened a new plant in Dyer, Tennessee. A Brown executive, Monte Shomaker, who was later to serve as Brown's fourth president, urged the move south. Shomaker worked to modernize Brown's factories after the war, and to relocate many of them in the traditionally nonunion South. At the same time, Brown's third president, Clark Gamble, was taking steps to move the company into retailing.

Gamble assumed the presidency from John Bush in 1948, and in 1950 he initiated a merger with Wohl Shoes. Wohl was a 35-year-old wholesale and retail shoe business with headquarters in St. Louis. Wohl had annual sales of $33 million, 90% of which came from women's shoes. Brown had provided only 10% of Wohl's shoes before the merger, and the merger provided a large new market for Brown. Wohl wholesaled shoes through 2,500 stores throughout the United States, Canada, Mexico, and Cuba, and operated several hundred retail stores and leased department store shoe salons. With this first major acquisition, Brown took a giant step toward integrating its operations into both manufacturing and retailing.

The Wohl merger was followed by Brown's acquisition of another large retail chain in 1953, Regal Shoes. When Brown acquired G.R. Kinney Corporation in 1956, the company had gone far toward assuring itself of both manufacturing and retailing capabilities. Brown was then the fourth-largest shoe manufacturer in the United States, and Kinney the largest operator of family shoe stores. A U.S. District Court in St. Louis, however, found Brown guilty of antitrust violations in 1959, and ordered the company to divest itself of Kinney. The judge in the case concluded that the Brown-Kinney merger seriously limited the ability of independent retailers to compete with company-owned retail outlets, as well as limiting the market for independent manufacturers. In 1962 the Supreme Court upheld the lower court's ruling. By that year Brown had taken the number-one spot in the shoe industry. Brown subsequently sold Kinney to F.W. Woolworth.

Monte Shomaker took over the presidency of Brown from Clark Gamble in 1962. Despite the setback of the Kinney ruling, Shomaker was able to continue Brown's expansion. In 1959 the company had acquired Perth Shoe Company, a Canadian firm with wholesale, retail, and manufacturing operations. In 1965 Brown bought the Samuels Shoe Company, a high-fashion women's shoe company, and in 1970 Brown acquired a men's shoe importer, Italia Bootwear, Ltd.

Brown's earnings rose each year in the 1960s, until a flood of imports swamped the U.S. shoe industry in 1968. The company's earnings plunged 25% in 1969. A new president, W. L. Hadley Griffin, took over that year. Griffin decided to do what other large shoe companies had been doing for years, that is, to diversity into nonshoe areas. Brown quickly acquired retail fabric chains, the Eagle Rubber Company, Kent Sporting Goods, and a luggage sales company, among others. In 1972 The Brown Shoe Company changed its name to Brown Group, Inc., to reflect the company's diversification. By 1973 close to 20% of Brown's sales were coming from its nonfootwear subsidiaries. The Brown Group continued to diversify through the 1970s, buying up companies in two main areas: children's products, and sports and recreation.

In 1979 W. L. Hadley Griffin moved up to chairman, and B. A. Bridgewater became the new president. Bridgewater had worked in U.S. President Richard Nixon's Office of Management and Budget, where he set fiscal priorities for the State Department, the Defense Department, and the Central Intelligence Agency. Bridgewater introduced cost-cutting measures at Brown, including reductions in the work force and cutbacks in executive perquisites. Bridgewater's first year was a record year for the Brown Group, with sales up 16% and earnings up 25%, and with net income of $41 million. Increased costs, and foreign competition, however, led Brown to close its St. Louis warehouse in 1980.

Pressure from cheap imports led to more competitive conditions in the U.S. shoe market throughout the 1980s, and President Bridgewater had to constantly adjust the Brown Group's business strategy. In the 1970s diversification into nonshoe areas had proved essential, but in the 1980s, slimming down the company and concentrating on shoe retailing seemed to be the right thing. In 1982 Brown's recreational products division sagged, and Bridgewater ordered a restructuring, which included plant closings and changes in marketing and management. In 1985 after a very poor third quarter, the company announced it would divest itself of all its recreational products operations. The divestiture left Brown with about 75% of its business concentrated in shoe manufacture and retailing. The other 25% represented various other retail operations, such as Brown's line of fabric stores, specialty women's clothing stores, and the Meis chain of department stores.

In the mid-1980s, Brown bid to keep its shoe business competitive by moving more strongly into shoe importing. Brown acquired Arnold Dunn, Inc., a women's shoe importer, in 1984. That year Brown established an importing division, Brown Group International, and in 1986 it acquired the Pagoda Trading Company, a Far-East importing firm. Importing proved far more profitable than manufacturing. The company closed several U.S. shoe plants, but at the same time improved the efficiency of its remaining factories. By 1988 Brown was able to produce almost as many shoes as in 1980, in spite of a 40% reduction in the number of plants it operated. The company also opted to concentrate on marketing its well-known brands such as Connie, Naturalizer, and Buster Brown, and discontinue its marginal lines.

Although the 1980s saw many changes in the U.S. shoe industry, including the rise in imports, the increased popularity of athletic shoes, and the hostile takeovers and leveraged buyouts that threatened many other industries as well, Brown remained a profitable company with relatively stable growth. The Brown Group of the early 1990s was a retailer, wholesaler, importer, and manufacturer, so the company had the ability to respond quickly to changing market conditions. Because shoes are a basic item that consumers always need, even drastic economic changes are unlikely to threaten the Brown Group's core business.

Principal Subsidiaries: Brown Shoe Company; Wohl Shoe Company; Pagoda Trading Company; Cloth World.

Further Reading: Brown Group: The First Hundred Years, St. Louis, Missouri, Brown Group, Inc., 1978; Feurer, Rosemary, "Shoe City, Factory Towns: St. Louis Shoe Companies and the Turbulent Drive for Cheap Rural Labor, 1900-1940," *Gateway Heritage,* Fall 1988.

—Angela Woodward

BURLINGTON INDUSTRIES, INC.

3330 West Friendly Avenue
Greensboro, North Carolina 27420
U.S.A.
(919) 379-2000
Fax: (919) 379-4504

Private Company
Incorporated: 1937 as Burlington Hills
Employees: 24,000
Sales: $2.50 billion

Burlington Industries, Inc. is one of the world's leading producers of textiles and related items. Its products include fabrics for home furnishings and apparel, carpeting and rugs, draperies and window shades, and upholstery fabrics. It operates 44 plants in the United States and Mexico.

J. Spencer Love founded the company after he returned from military service during World War I. He initially went to work in his uncle's Gastonia, North Carolina, spinning mill, and, after gaining some experience between 1919 and 1923, Love decided to branch off on his own. He purchased a controlling interest in his uncle's mill, then convinced the Chamber of Commerce of Burlington, North Carolina, to help him finance the construction of a new plant in that city. Love shut down the original Gastonia mill, moved the equipment to Burlington, and formed Burlington Mills on November 6, 1923. The newly formed company consisted of 200 employees and one building, in the middle of a cornfield, which began textile production even before the construction had been completed.

Initially, Love's firm manufactured several cotton products, including flag cloth, bunting, cotton scrims, curtain and dress fabrics, and a type of diaper cloth called birdseye. Unfortunately for the company, many of these products were already becoming obsolete by the time manufacturing had started. Business faltered until, out of desperation, Love began producing bedspreads out of an experimental fabric called rayon. Consumers responded positively to this shiny new material, and, within a few years, Burlington became a leader in rayon textile manufacture. This success led to the opening of a second mill in 1926 and a New York sales office by 1929. In 1927 sales had reached $1 million.

During the Depression, Burlington continued to expand even as many competitors closed their doors. The company had a sizable advantage over comparable New England-based firms due to lower costs in the southern United States. Using its competitive strength during this period, Burlington acquired several mills that had closed as a result of the poor economic times and subsequently reopened them under the Burlington name.

In 1935 the company moved its headquarters from Burlington to Greensboro, North Carolina, in order to have railway access to its operations in New York. In 1937 Burlington consolidated its various operating units and was listed on the New York Stock Exchange. Company revenues were up to $25 million.

When World War II broke out, the company began producing items for the U.S. government. Its research laboratories also were employed on various government projects, including one that investigated the use of a new fiber, nylon, in making parachute cloth. This initial work provided the foundation upon which the company developed several other uses for nylon-based textiles when the war ended.

Growth continued rapidly into the 1950s. Plants often were built with one wooden wall that could be taken down, moved, and erected again to expand available floor space. Burlington also acquired several competitors during this time, including Pacific Mills and Klopman Mills. As its diversification strategy began taking the firm beyond its original spinning and weaving businesses, the company changed its name in 1955 to Burlington Industries.

In 1960 Burlington purchased James Lees & Sons, a Philadelphia-based carpet manufacturer. In 1962 Burlington became the first textile firm to exceed $1 billion in sales. To this point, the company's growth had been directed primarily by its founder, J. Spencer Love, who died in 1962. He was succeeded as president by Charles F. Myers. When Myers took over, he changed the company's strategy to more effectively manage increasing labor costs and foreign competition. Under Love, Burlington had provided fabric to other apparel and home furnishings manufacturers. Myers undertook a new approach that directly targeted consumers as the company's customers. In 1972 Burlington introduced several products under its own name, including towels, blankets, men's socks, women's hosiery, sheets, and draperies.

This activity was accompanied by other changes, including acquisitions of non-textile businesses, development of a consumer advertising campaign, and a major corporate reorganization. One of the acquisitions made during this time, that of the Globe Furniture Company in 1966, furthered the company's goals of getting closer to consumers and of finding new avenues of growth. This became particularly important three years later when a Federal Trade Commission (FTC) decree prohibited Burlington from purchasing any United States textile firms for ten years without prior FTC approval.

During his tenure, Myers, who moved up to chairman in 1968, engineered a controversial internal restructuring that altered traditional organizational functions, such as marketing and research, and redeployed them into vertically integrated businesses. The company's New York–based executives—along with Ely R. Callaway, who became president in 1968—desired a more centralized operation, while Greensboro-based executives favored the decentralized, divisional structure. In 1973 those who preferred the divisional structure forced Callaway to resign. Callaway had been charged with running the day-to-day operations of the company while Myers tended to finances. He had been held largely responsible for the company's belated entry into double-knit fabrics. The popularity of knitwear had seriously reduced the company's sales volume in traditional woven fabrics before Burlington made a major move into knit fabrics in 1971.

Callaway was succeeded as president by Horace C. Jones, the former president of the company's Lees Carpets division. Although faced with rising costs for raw materials that were in short supply, Burlington quickly retooled its worsted fabric production facilities to take advantage of the growing trend toward knit and stretch fabrics. This move resulted in a significant turnaround. Contributing to the company's recovery were U.S. trade agreements with four Asian countries that had been signed in 1971 and served to reduce import volume. The devaluation of the dollar abroad also helped by giving U.S. goods a price advantage. During this time, the company increased its emphasis on the home furnishings line, which was now being marketed under the Burlington House name. In 1973 Burlington ventured into the lighting area with its acquisition of Westwood Industries.

Internally the struggle for power continued. Jones was appointed chairman and CEO in 1974 following Myers's retirement, and four executive vice presidents competed to succeed Jones as president.

The company's recovery was short-lived. By the beginning of 1974, Burlington faced deepening shortages of raw material, fuel, and labor, combined with an inflationary economy, which threatened consumer spending for apparel and home furnishings. Demand for double-knit fabrics weakened because the material tended to snag. Strong overseas sales, however, enabled the company to finally realize a positive return on its ten-year-old investment in its European operations.

Domestic sales rebounded in 1977, due largely to gains in the home furnishings and industrial products area. Burlington succeeded in making necessary adaptations in its apparel products to meet changing fashion styles. For example, the company shifted production away from heavyweight woven fabrics into more lightweight textured products, introduced a new washable polyester and wool blend called Burlana, and expanded the manufacture of denim apparel fabrics, which were growing in popularity.

In 1976 William A. Klopman was appointed chairman and CEO of Burlington Industries. He had joined the company when it had acquired his father's firm in 1956, and had risen through the ranks, to president of the influential yarn and apparel-fabric divisions from 1963 to 1971, and then to president in 1974. Under Klopman's leadership, Burlington entered the 1980s with a critical eye on its foreign operations. It gradually strengthened its financial position overseas by restructuring its French businesses and by selling its German worsted apparel fabric subsidiary.

The company's continued emphasis on capital spending since 1977, however, met with mixed reviews. Analysts argued that Burlington's object of becoming a low-cost producer supported by technologically superior plants and long manufacturing runs prevented the company from making necessary changes flexibly and quickly enough to keep pace with trends in fashion and consumer demand. Klopman also was criticized for having an impersonal and aggressive management style, for having made incorrect product line decisions, and for cre-

ating trade friction between the United States and the Peoples' Republic of China, as he lobbied hard for limits on Chinese imports. Nevertheless, Burlington in 1981 became the first textile firm to surpass $3 billion in sales.

In 1984 Burlington, acknowledging the necessity of broadening its product mix and targeting specialized, high-margin market niches, introduced a lighter-weight crinkled denim fabric to be marketed under designer brand names. In 1986, however, Burlington decided to place greater emphasis upon its industrial textiles area, and sold the designer bed-linen lines, along with the rest of its bedding and bath textiles division, to J.P. Stevens & Company.

Frank S. Greenberg became chief executive officer and chairman in 1986 upon Klopman's retirement. Greenberg had joined the company in 1959 when Burlington had purchased Charm Tred Mills, a firm owned by his father. Like his predecessors, Greenberg rose through divisional ranks into the executive suite, beginning as the president of the rug division and, most recently, serving as company president. As chairman, Greenberg found himself and the company fighting a takeover attempt by Dominion Textile Inc., Canada's largest textile producer, and Asher Edelman, a corporate raider. Many analysts felt that Burlington's prior reluctance to exit the apparel-fabrics business when lower-priced imports began flooding the market had reduced company profits and made Burlington vulnerable to such an attack from outside the firm. Dominion, looking for a way to rejuvenate its own sales in a stagnant Canadian market, viewed Burlington's denim fabric unit as particularly attractive.

Burlington was able to thwart the Dominion-Edelman takeover through a leveraged buyout that took the company private. Through an employee stock ownership plan, Burlington's employees became its primary owners. To reduce the significant amount of debt incurred, the company began selling key assets, such as its industrial products segment, terminated 1,200 employees, and sliced operating expenses to the bare bone. Within one year, Burlington had retired 45% of its buyout debt through severe reductions in overhead spending, capitalizing on a favorable market for its divested assets, and strong apparel fabric sales.

Operating in the early 1990s as a much leaner organization than in the past, Burlington Industries faces continuing challenges in matching market demand with its manufacturing capabilities and expertise. Burlington's newly streamlined operation and ability to get out from under a massive debt load have given the firm increased flexibility to assess future economic and industry changes and then to make effective decisions designed to manage the impact of these changes on the company's strategies and goals.

Further Reading: "Charles F. Myers of Burlington Industries," *Nation's Business,* November 1972; "Giant Burlington Faces Trying Times for Textiles," *Business Week,* March 2, 1974; "Burlington Industries: A Brief History," Burlington Industries corporate typescript, 1990.

—Sandy Schusteff

COATS VIYELLA PLC

Bank House
Charlotte Street
Manchester M1 4ET
United Kingdom
(061) 236-3272
Fax: (061) 236-5837

Public Company
Incorporated: 1909 as Spirella Company of Great Britain Ltd.
Employees: 70,723
Sales: £1.82 billion (US $3.40 billion)
Stock Exchanges: London Dublin

Coats Viyella Plc functions as a holding company for a group engaged in the manufacture, processing, and distribution of knitwear and garments, housewares, woven and knitted fabrics, sewing thread for industrial and domestic use, hand-knit products, fashionwear, and precision engineering products. It is Europe's largest textile group, employing more than 70,000 people and manufacturing in 35 countries.

As an entity Coats Viyella comprehends both the history of much of the United Kingdom's industry and the business career of one man, Sir David Alliance. Alliance came from a Tehran, Iran, family already involved in textiles, arriving in Britain in 1951, at the age of 19. He stayed and eventually presided as chairman over a group that is largely his own creation.

At the beginning of the 1980s there were four large British textile companies—Carrington Viyella, Coats Patons, Courtaulds, and Tootal Group. By the end of the decade two of them had fallen into Alliance's hands and a third was firmly in his sights.

The foundations for such growth were laid in the 1950s and 1960s. Alliance's first acquisition, in 1956, was Thomas Hoghton (Oswaldtwistle) Ltd., a firm of cotton goods manufacturers. Many such companies still existed in the so-called junior league of Lancashire textile firms and their acquisition, reconstruction, and turnaround was the substance of Alliance's activities for some years. By the end of the 1960s he operated through three vehicles—Alliance Brothers, a mail-order and textiles firm, R Greg & Company Ltd., a spinning and fashion fabric firm, and Northern Counties Securities, a finance group.

The pace of growth accelerated in 1968 when Alliance took control of publicly traded Spirella Company of Great Britain Ltd. through a reverse takeover involving R Greg. Spirella was to form the nucleus of what was to become Coats Viyella. In

1969 it became a holding company as Spirella Group Ltd. into which the textile interests of Alliance Brothers were absorbed. Together with his partner Jack Menaged, Alliance reorganized Spirella into three groups—foundation garment manufacture (the business of the original company), textile merchanting and spinning (based on Greg), and household textiles (based on Alliance Brothers).

Spirella soon set off down the road of further acquisition. The foundation garment side of the business was strengthened by the purchase of Richard Cooper & Company (Ashbourne) Ltd. and Leethems (Twilfit) Ltd. A more significant growth area was that of household textiles, particularly towels, where several takeovers were made. John Ainscow & Company Ltd. of Bolton was purchased in 1970, as was WT Taylor and Company Ltd. of Horwich. These two companies were merged with Stott & Smith Ltd., toweling and cotton goods manufacturers, to form the Stott & Smith Group Ltd. Other acquisitions at this time included the Barber Textile Corporation Ltd., Horrockses Ltd., and Dorcas Ltd.

By 1973 Alliance was already contemplating the takeover of another household textiles firm, Vantona Ltd. For Vantona the takeover of 1975 represented a reversal of fortunes, since Spirella had previously been seen as a possible target for Vantona to acquire. The £5 million offer for Vantona was widely seen as shrewdly judged rather than generous and the Vantona board was very publicly split. The industrial logic, however, was undisputed for while both companies were involved in household textiles, Spirella's strength in towels complemented Vantona's own strengths. The merger, misleadingly billed as the marriage of whalebone and sheets, led to the disappearance of the Spirella name, it being felt that it was too closely connected with corsetry ever to outlive the association. In 1976 the merged company changed its name to Vantona Group Ltd.

Vantona was then the third-largest producer of household textiles in the United Kingdom but still a relatively minor player within the industry as a whole. It was all the more remarkable, therefore, that in 1978 Vantona was able to beat off the challenge of both Carrington Viyella and Courtaulds in order to acquire uniform manufacturers J Compton, Sons & Webb Ltd.

The next takeover, in 1982, was breathtaking in its scale for it involved a bid by Vantona for Carrington Viyella, a company eight times its size. Carrington Viyella, a manufacturer of garments, home furnishings, carpets, and fabrics, was a troubled giant, considered by many to be too debt-laden to be an attractive acquisition. It did, however, come with an attractive dowry of brand names including Dorma, Van Heusen, and Viyella itself.

The branded cloth was merely the most famous of a number produced by William Hollins & Company Ltd. (established 1784), the Nottingham-based yarn spinners. The name had been registered as a trade mark in 1894 and was derived from the Via Gellia, the road linking the Derbyshire villages of Cromford, where Hollins had a mill, and Bonsall. It had become synonymous with quality so that when, in 1961, Hollins became the core of a larger group, it adopted the name Viyella International Ltd. Viyella was to make numerous acquisitions throughout the 1960s before being taken over by ICI Ltd. in 1969 and merged with Carrington & Dewhurst Ltd. the following year.

Skepticism over the wisdom of the Carrington Viyella takeover was perhaps behind Alliance's difficulty in raising the required £50 million, a sum that would soon be made to seem modest. The importance of the Viyella name was again acknowledged when the group became Vantona Viyella PLC in February 1983.

The year 1985 saw another significant merger, with the Nottingham Manufacturing Company PLC, established 1805, after a friendly deal between Alliance and Harry Djanogly of Nottingham Manufacturing. The company was as cash-rich as Carrington Viyella had been debt-laden and brought with it strong links with the retailer Marks & Spencer, to whom Nottingham Manufacturers supplied hosiery and knitwear. This acquisition bolstered the group prior to the climactic merger in the following year with Coats Patons PLC.

Coats Patons was itself the result of a 1960 merger between J & P Coats Ltd. and Patons & Baldwins Ltd., J & P Coats had its origins in Paisley, near Glasgow, commencing thread manufacture in 1825. The business was especially successful in the North American market, and its growth culminated in a highly successful public offering in 1890. By the turn of the century, by amalgamation with other thread producers including its Paisley rivals, Clark & Company, Coats had become the largest textile firm in Britain, with factories worldwide.

Patons & Baldwins derived from two separate concerns—JJ Baldwin & Partners Ltd., established at Halifax in 1785, and John Paton, Son & Company Ltd. of Alloa, established 1813, that merged in 1920. The merged company was a woolen and worsted spinner, specializing in knitting wools, with factories throughout Britain, as well as in Canada, China, and Tasmania.

Early in 1986 Coats Patons was the subject of an agreed takeover bid by a knitwear group, Dawson International PLC. Coats had already been identified as a possible long-term target for Vantona Viyella but the proposed Dawson deal precipitated action by them. Dawson was successfully outbid by an offer worth £715 million. In March 1986 Vantona, like Spirella before it, was dropped from the company's name that then reflected its largest components in its new name, Coats Viyella Plc.

By 1989 it began to look as if another famous name would have to be accommodated. Tootal Group PLC was the descendant of the English Sewing Cotton Company Ltd., incorporated 1897, a sewing thread and yarn producer whose Sylko domestic sewing thread became a household name. As part of the trend towards larger groupings in the textile industry English Sewing Cotton expanded, acquiring the Manchester-based business of Tootal Broadhurst Lee & Company Ltd., incorporated 1888, in 1963. Five years later the company changed its name to English Calico Ltd. following the acquisition of the Calico Printers Association Ltd. The change of name was short-lived, and in 1973 the company became Tootal Ltd.

Although one of the "big four" of British textile firms, Tootal's disappointing performance during the 1980s had left it vulnerable to a takeover bid. This duly emerged in the shape of Australian entrepreneur Abe Goldberg, who acquired a 29.9% stake in the company. When he was rebuffed by the Tootal board Coats Viyella stepped in to acquire Goldberg's shareholding and to agree to terms for a £395 million takeover. The bid lapsed, however, after it was referred to the Monopolies and Mergers Commission (MMC).

Prospects revived after the MMC recommended that Coats divest itself of its U.K. and German sewing thread businesses, a condition with which it was relatively easy to comply. However, when it became clear that Coats was to renew its offer at a much lower valuation, Tootal's resistance grew. Reluctance to be taken over on the cheap, as they saw it, was accompanied by references to differing management cultures by the Tootal board. The *Daily Telegraph,* January 15, 1991, compared Tootal's behavior to " . . . a dowdy Jane Austen heroine: desperate to wed but equally desperate not to look too keen."

Finally, Alliance was persuaded to do what he had never done in all his deals up to this point—launch a hostile takeover bid. An initial offer worth £194 million was raised to £241 million in April and this was sufficient to win the day. Like many previous deals its appeal lay in its industrial logic rather than mere corporate aggrandizement, for while the two groups dominated the international thread market their businesses were largely complementary.

However, the takeover met with reservations on three counts. First, it had been said that the expansion of Coats Viyella has done little more than gather most of the surviving elements of a declining industry under the control of one company. The bid for Tootal succeeded, in this view, not because of Coats Viyella's own performance, which was judged disappointing, but because Tootal's results were even poorer. Second, fears had been expressed that the integration of the Tootal businesses might prove difficult and that Coats Viyella's record in this area had not been good; and third, that in achieving a dominant position in the industry, Coats Viyella might alienate customers fearful of becoming dependent on such a large supplier, and that they might now be inclined to seek alternatives.

Early indications were that Coats Viyella had appreciated the dangers of imbalance in this area and that through disposals excessive market share in certain areas would be voluntarily relinquished. The appointment of Neville Bain as chief executive in 1990 also increased business confidence. Formerly with Cadbury Schweppes PLC, his recognized skills in integrating businesses were matched by the £65 million set aside for integration costs following the Tootal takeover.

In the progression from private company to public company, to group, and finally to multinational status, certain features of the Alliance business style remained constant. Good relations at boardroom and shop-floor level generally prevailed, and management was decentralized with a small head office but tight financial control. Vertical integration was the goal, and the assistance of merchant bankers NM Rothschild & Sons Ltd. remained constant. The astonishing growth of the 1980s was arguably not matched in pace by the restructuring of the various elements of Coats Viyella into a coherent group, but the mergers themselves were a hard act to follow. Moreover, the U.K. textile industry remains particularly vulnerable to economic cycles, exchange rate fluctuations, and foreign competition in spite of all efforts to allow for these. The sheer size, diversity, and international character of Coats Viyella give it the ability to survive in a very tough marketplace. The coming years will show whether it can prosper and grow.

Principal Subsidiaries: Albert Hartley Ltd.; The British Van Heusen Company Ltd.; Thomas Burnley & Sons Ltd.; D Byford & Company Ltd.; Carrington Viyella Exports Ltd.; Carrington Viyella Garments Ltd.; CV Apparel Ltd.; Heydemann Shaw Ltd.; CV Home Furnishings Ltd.; CV Woven Fabrics

Ltd.; Youghal Carpets (Holdings) PLC (Republic of Ireland, 72%); Dynacast Ltd.; Ewart Liddell Ltd.; J Compton, Sons & Webb Ltd.; Jaeger Holdings Ltd.; Vantona Ltd.; William Hollins & Company Ltd.; CV Carpets Ltd.; Priest (Lindley) Ltd.; Patons & Baldwins Ltd.; Mansfield Knitwear Ltd.; The Nottingham Manufacturing Company PLC; Coats Patons PLC; Vantona Viyella PLC; VV Household Textiles Ltd.; West Riding Worsted & Woollen Mills Ltd.; J & P Coats Ltd.; J & P Coats (UK) Ltd.; Pasolds Ltd.; Harlander Coats GmbH (Austria); Dynacast France SA; Schachenmayr, Mann & Cie, GmbH (Germany); Cia de Linha Coats & Clark Lda (Portugal); Coats Patons (North America) Inc. (U.S.A.); Coats & Clark Inc. (U.S.A.); J & P Coats (Canada) Inc.; Dynacast do Brasil Lda (Brazil); Linhas Corrente Lda (Brazil); Coats Patons (Pty) Ltd (Australia); Coats Viyella Finance NV (Netherlands Antilles); Cia Ind Hilos Cadena SA (Chile, 93%); Hilos Cadena SACel (Argentina, 90%); Consoltex Canada Inc. (80.8%); Dynacast Deutschland GmbH (Germany, 75%); Mez AG (Germany, 97%); Opti-Werk GmbH & Co KG (Germany); Cucirini Cantoni Coats SpA (Italy, 66.7%); Cia Anon Hilaturas de Fabra Y Coats (Spain, 76.6%); Santral Dikis Sanayii AS (Turkey, 75%); Dynacast Inc. (U.S.A.); J & P Coats (South Africa) (Pty) Ltd.; Patons & Baldwins Canada Inc.; Gelvenor Textiles (Pty) Ltd. (South Africa, 50%); Coats Patons (Hong Kong) Ltd.; PT Coats Rejo (Indonesia, 60%); J & P Coats (Manufacturing) Sdn Bhd (Malaysia, 51%).

Further Reading: Wells, Frederick Arthur, *Hollins and Viyella: A Study in Business History,* Newton Abbot, David & Charles, 1968.

—Lionel Alexander Ritchie

COURTAULDS PLC

18 Hanover Square
London W1A 2BB
United Kingdom
(071) 629 9080
Fax: (071) 629 2586

Public Company
Incorporated: 1913 as Courtaulds Ltd.
Employees: 22,700
Sales: £1.91 billion (US$3.57 billion)

Courtaulds plc and Courtaulds Textiles plc existed as one entity, with a history going back to 1816, until the demerger that went into effect on January 1, 1990. As a single company Courtaulds was one of the world leaders in textiles, manmade fibers, and associated chemicals. These continue to be the dominant fields of the demerged companies.

The Courtauld family migrated to England from France at the end of the 17th century and became successful gold- and silversmiths in London. Its first link with textiles was forged in 1775 when George Courtauld was apprenticed to a silk throwster—"throwing" is the equivalent in silk manufacture of spinning in cotton or wool—in Spitalfields. In 1816, George Courtauld's eldest son, Samuel, set up independently, and the family textile firm was first established, in Essex. Vigorous, impatient, and autocratic, Samuel Courtauld moved from silk throwing to the mechanized manufacture of a textile fabric popular in Victorian Britain: silk mourning crêpe. By the 1870s, when it employed about 3,000 workers, Samuel Courtauld & Company had become one of the biggest firms in the British silk industry. It had become so profitable that the partners were then earning an average of more than 30% on their capital, and Samuel Courtauld himself was drawing an income of about £46,000 a year from his investment in the business.

Fashions began to change, however. Crêpe prices fell, and after Samuel Courtauld's death in 1881 the firm's leadership faltered. In the 1890s losses were made. The partnership was turned into a private limited liability company, and new men were brought in to modernize the business. H. G. Tetley was made a director in 1895, as was T. P.—later Sir Paul—Latham, in 1898. These two men, outsiders to the family business, virtually controlled the company for the next quarter-century and in the process created the new multinational Courtaulds Ltd. in 1913 as the world's largest producer of the first of the manmade fibers, rayon. Under the new man-

agement some modernization and diversification was achieved, but by the turn of the century a plateau had been reached. As Tetley told his fellow directors in April 1904, Samuel Courtauld & Company (Courtaulds) needed "a new source of profit to replace crêpe profits—which are leaving us." It was the adoption of his proposed remedy for this problem that put the firm on a wholly new course.

Three independent lines of enquiry—none of which involved Courtaulds—led to the discovery of rayon, which is technically a regenerated cellulosic fiber. One line of enquiry was pursued in France by Count Hilaire de Chardonnet, who set up the first factory to make artificial silk in 1892. Another, by a different process, led to a factory in Germany in 1899. The third, in Britain, was potentially the simplest and cheapest route. This "viscose" process—consisting basically of treating wood pulp with caustic soda and other chemicals and spinning the resultant substance into fibers—was developed and patented by three inventors working in a laboratory-cum-pilot plant near London. Most of the various national patent rights had been sold off when Tetley visited the plant early in 1904. He reported back enthusiastically. After successful flotation as a public company in July 1904, Samuel Courtauld & Company Ltd. bought the British rights to the patents for approximately £25,000.

A factory was built on the outskirts of Coventry. It started work in July 1905 but was still making losses in 1907. By 1913, however, it was turning out over three million pounds of rayon per annum, and Courtaulds had emerged as easily the largest and strongest of all the firms that had bought the viscose rights. It had been able to buy out the holders of the U.S. rights in 1909, set up a wholly owned subsidiary in the United States, and float Courtaulds Ltd. as a new £2 million company on the basis of a ten-for-one bonus issue.

It soon became evident that the process that Tetley had bought was unreliable. A small group of chemists and engineers at Coventry, operating largely by hit-or-miss methods, made the technical breakthrough in making the process reliable and capable of producing a fiber of consistent quality. Technical cooperation with the purchasers of the French rights and a favorable legal judgment in a patent action helped. An important reason for the company's success lay in the fact that of all the purchasers of the viscose patent rights, only Courtaulds was a textile manufacturing firm. Those directing the efforts of the chemists and engineers knew what technical qualities were needed to make a yarn useful and salable; the textile machinery and the dye house at the Essex mills were available for experimentation; and the whole range of commercial contacts made by the company in its textile business, skillfully exploited by Latham, were used for the marketing of the new product. The real architect of the achievement was Tetley. Not only did he drive the company forward in Britain but his purchase of the U.S. rights led to the foundation of the American Viscose Corporation (AVC). Starting production in 1911 and operating inside a tariff barrier, by 1915 AVC's output surpassed that of its parent, and it was soon contributing massively to profits. The combined profitability of the U.K. and U.S. sides of the business allowed not only the payment to Courtauld's shareholders of substantial dividends but also the making of further bonus issues in 1919 and 1920, thus bringing the ordinary share capital to £12 million.

Tetley had become chairman of Courtaulds in 1917. On his death in 1921 the leadership of Courtaulds passed into the hands of a very different man. For the next quarter of a century the chairman was another Samuel Courtauld, great-nephew of the Samuel who had founded the family business. Under his leadership Courtaulds became a highly respected multinational company, and its great financial strength was not matched by any comparable enterprise in technical innovation. The second Samuel Courtauld became known to a wider public as a patron of the arts. His collection of Impressionist paintings became the basis of the Courtauld Institute of Art, which he set up and endowed in 1931. As the leadership of Courtaulds changed, so also did the circumstances in which the firm operated. The end of World War I approximately coincided with the expiration of the basic patents. New firms moved into the rayon industry all over the world. New rayons, notably that made by the cellulose acetate process, were developed. Filament yarn, seen as a substitute—though rather a poor one—for silk, was joined by staple fiber, used as a substitute for cotton or even wool. The result was a gigantic boom in the output of rayon. From 1920 to 1941, world output rose from 32 million pounds to over 2.8 billion pounds. Moreover, as competition grew fiercer and as costs were cut, rayon prices fell sharply, much more than those of silk, cotton, or wool. Cheap woven or knitted fabrics and hosiery in rayon or rayon blends made cheaper stockings, underwear, furnishing fabrics, and dress materials.

Courtaulds participated in the boom in sundry ways. New plants were built—in the Midlands, North Wales, and Lancashire—for yarn production and processing. To the existing textile mills in Essex were added others in Lancashire and Yorkshire to demonstrate the uses of staple fiber. Across the Atlantic, AVC built more yarn mills, and a new subsidiary, Courtaulds (Canada), was established in Canada. In Europe a French company—La Soie Artificielle de Calais, renamed Les Filés de Calais in 1934—began production in 1927, and a joint enterprise, Glanzstoff-Courtaulds, started in Germany. Processing mills were set up in India, Denmark, and Spain, and a major investment was made in the biggest of the Italian rayon companies, Soria Viscosa. By 1928 Courtaulds's total issued capital had risen to £32 million, and nearly half of the company's gross income came in the form of dividends from AVC, about whose profits and performance Courtaulds remained secretive.

The 1929 stock market crash and the Depression of the 1930s did not afflict Courtaulds in Britain with anything like the hardships felt in older industries or by some other firms. Profits, however, were lower than in the heyday of the 1920s; the dividends from AVC came tumbling down, and in 1938 there were none. Overseas difficulties increased. The financial results of the French, German, and Canadian yarn factories were poor, and the yarn-processing mills were all sold. The value of many investments had to be written down drastically. AVC's performance was particularly worrying. The quality of its output was questioned, and a thoroughgoing enquiry into its technical and managerial shortcomings was instituted. In 1937 AVC's British boss was replaced by an American, and a substantial modernization program launched. At home, output rose substantially, especially in staple fiber. High-tenacity yarn, used in tire manufacture, was successfully developed. In 1935 a new venture, British Cellophane, was started for the manufacture of transparent film. However, the relative backwardness of the company in research was brought home to

Samuel Courtauld by du Pont's development of nylon in the United States in 1938. Although Courtaulds's laboratories proved their practical value in a variety of ways, the money spent on basic research remained very small. The need for directed research work was just dawning when war came again.

World War II brought to Courtaulds, as to other firms, sundry domestic problems, including shortages of raw materials and of labor, wartime controls, higher taxation, and damage from air raids. Such troubles were, however, minor compared with one event: the enforced sale in 1941 of AVC. Dictated by the U.S. government, it reduced Courtaulds to about half its former size. In 1942 a tribunal awarded Courtaulds some £27 million in compensation.

These substantial cash reserves helped to shape the course of postwar recovery. This proceeded, from 1947 to 1962, under the chairmanship of J. C. (later Sir John) Hanbury-Williams, who succeeded Samuel Courtauld. The first tasks—the requisite renewals and replacements postponed by war—were joined to efforts to implement those greater changes that belatedly had been seen to be necessary just before the war. New appointments were made to the board; expenditure on directed research was increased substantially; modernization programs were begun; but financial policy continued to be conservative. New rayon plants were built, mainly for staple fiber and industrial yarns. Research on the acrylic fiber Courtelle was pushed ahead. Just before the war Courtaulds had secured an interest in nylon by entering into an agreement with Imperial Chemical Industries (ICI), which had obtained the British rights to this du Pont invention. A jointly owned company, British Nylon Spinners (BNS), was set up and output grew rapidly from the 1950s. Overseas, a yarn plant was built in Australia, and the U.S. market was re-entered by the setting up of a large rayon staple fiber plant in Alabama. Fears of a world shortage of the wood pulp used in rayon manufacture led to the formation of the South African Industrial Cellulose Corporation (SAICCOR) to produce pulp from eucalyptus trees.

For a time these recovery and expansion measures seemed to be working, and profits rose during the decade 1944–1954. Soon after, they started to slip and, as the full impact of nylon and other new synthetic fibers began to be felt, the whole future of rayon was in question. New policies were contrived, owing much to Frank (later Lord) Kearton, who joined the board in 1952. Expansion and diversification were the main themes. Between 1957 and 1963 British Celanese—the main producer of acetate fibers—and five other rayon companies were bought; Courtaulds's existing interest in packaging, through British Cellophane, led to the acquisition of firms making various sorts of containers. Its chemical interests, reinforced by the acquisition of British Celanese, pointed the way to a move into paints, especially with the purchase of Pinchin, Johnson Ltd. in 1960.

The process was interrupted by a takeover bid from ICI, launched in December 1961. This resulted in a three-month wonder, at that date the biggest takeover battle in Britain, causing much public debate. In March 1962 ICI conceded defeat, having secured only about 38% of Courtaulds's equity. In 1964 Courtaulds's share in BNS was exchanged for ICI's holdings in Courtaulds's equity. Meanwhile, the bid battle had caused some upheaval on the Courtaulds board. Kearton, who had played a major part in opposing the bid, took over the chairmanship in 1962. The last two members of the Courtauld family to sit on the board retired in 1965 and 1966. Under Kearton's aegis the company then embarked on a massive series of acquisitions in the cotton and hosiery industries. This was dictated primarily by the fear that the Lancashire cotton industry, weak and decaying in the face of inexpensive imported Asian textiles, would disappear and with it Courtaulds's biggest market for staple fiber. The hosiery industry, expanding on a growing enthusiasm for knitted fabrics, was seen as a profitable outlet for acetate and nylon yarns. It was hoped that the creation of a vertically integrated fibers-textiles group would solve the company's excessive reliance on rayon. By 1968 Courtaulds controlled about 30% of U.K. cotton-type spinning capacity as well as 35% of warp-knitting production and smaller but significant shares in weaving and finishing.

In the short term the policy paid off. Profits rose to a high in 1975. Despite much reorganization carried out by Kearton—who left Courtaulds in 1975—and his immediate successor from 1975 to 1979, A. W. (later Sir Arthur) Knight, Courtaulds was not in good shape to cope with the recession of the late 1970s and especially with the crisis affecting the European manmade fiber and textile industries. Profits fell sharply in 1976 and, after some recovery, dropped in 1981 to the lowest point since World War II.

Sir Arthur Knight's successor as chairman in 1979 was C. A. (later Sir Christopher) Hogg, who began a gradual and total reorganization of the company. In the course of the ensuing decade, much of the edifice created by Kearton's move into spinning, weaving, and the mass production of textiles was dismantled. Despite investment in new machinery, yarns and fabrics had made losses or very small profits in the face of cheaper imports and falling markets overseas. Substantial closures of spinning and weaving mills followed. Restructuring overseas included the sale of the South African pulp interests. Employee numbers fell: the 1975 work force of well over 100,000 in the United Kingdom alone had contracted by 1988 to 46,000 in the United Kingdom and 22,000 overseas. In contrast, the other part of Kearton's diversification, into paints, chemicals, and packaging, fared much better and provided the basis for Hogg's achievements in expanding these and related aspects of the company's activities on a worldwide basis. The final logic of the textile-chemical mix created by the original success with the 1904 purchase of the viscose patents came with the demerger of 1990.

Courtaulds plc now exists as a specialty materials industrial manufacturing company producing paints and coatings—accounting for 33% of profits in 1990—manmade fibers and films—30%—acetates and other chemicals—23%—packaging materials, and sundry specialized products. It operates in 37 countries. Courtaulds Textiles plc, with 28,000 employees and annual sales of £983.8, is primarily a U.K.-based operation with nearly 80% of its work force in that country. Its chief activities are the making of apparel and furnishing fabrics, the manufacture of garments under various brand names, and a much-reduced spinning section.

Further Reading: Coleman, D. C., *Courtaulds. An Economic and Social History,* 3 vols., Oxford, Oxford University Press, 1969–1980; Knight, Arthur, *Private Enterprise and Public Intervention: the Courtaulds Experience,* London, Allen & Unwin, 1974; "Samuel Courtauld III," "Samuel Courtauld IV," "Henry Dreyfus," "Sir John Hanbury-Williams," "Henry Johnson," "Lord Kearton," "Sir Arthur Knight," "Sir Thomas Latham," and "Henry Tetley," in *Dictionary of Business Biography: A Biographical Dictionary of Business Leaders Active in Britain in the Period 1860–1980,* Vols. I–III, edited by David Jeremy, London, Butterworth & Co., Ltd., 1984–1986; Singleton, John, *Lancashire on the Scrap Heap,* Oxford, Oxford University Press, 1991.

—D. C. Coleman

LEVI STRAUSS & CO.

1155 Battery Street
San Francisco, California 94111
U.S.A.
(415) 544-6000
Fax: (415) 544-1693

Wholly Owned Subsidiary of Levi Strauss Associates Inc.
Incorporated: 1890
Employees: 31,000
Sales: $4.25 billion

Levi Strauss & Co., the world's largest brand-name apparel manufacturer, gave the world blue jeans and grew enormously rich on this piece of U.S. culture. Indeed, around the world the name of the company's founder has grown to be synonymous with the pants he invented: Levi's.

Levi Strauss, born in Bavaria in 1829, emigrated to the United States with his family in 1847, at the age of 18. In New York, he was met by his two half-brothers, who had already established a dry-goods business. A year later, he was dispatched to Kentucky to live with relatives and walk the countryside peddling his brothers' goods.

While Levi Strauss was still traveling about the hills of the South, his older sister's husband, David Stern, established a dry-goods store in San Francisco, California, in the wake of the 1849 California gold rush, and the company that would come to bear Levi Strauss's name dates its beginning to this 1850 founding. Three years later, Strauss made the arduous sea journey around Cape Horn to join his brother-in-law. San Francisco at the time was a booming frontier town, and the opportunity was ripe for a well-run business to flourish. Strauss and Stern set up their small store near the waterfront, where they could easily receive shipments of goods from the Strauss brothers back east.

Jeans, which would become the staple of the family business, were invented when Levi Strauss, noting the need for rugged pants for miners, had a tailor sew pants from some sturdy brown canvas he had brought with him on his journey. Once the supply of canvas was exhausted, Strauss turned to a thick fabric made in the French town of Nimes, known as *serge de Nimes,* which would be shortened to denim. The denim pants, dyed with indigo to make them blue, sold quickly, and the business of Levi Strauss & Co. expanded rapidly, moving three times to new and expanded quarters in the next 13 years. In 1866 the company moved to a luxurious new location on Battery Street, only to have the building cracked from roof to foundation in an earthquake two years later.

In 1872 the proprietors of Levi Strauss & Co. received a letter from Jacob Davis, a tailor in Nevada, offering them a half interest in the patent on a technique he had invented for strengthening the seams of pants by fastening them with rivets. In return, they would pay the cost of obtaining the patent. The cost was negligible, and Strauss and his brother-in-law quickly took the tailor up on his offer. The following year, the company was granted a patent on the use of rivets to secure pocket seams, and also on the double-arc stitching found on the back pockets of its pants.

At first, the company had the pants sewn by tailors working individually at home, in the same way that the Strauss brothers in New York manufactured goods. Soon, however, the demand for the new pants became too great, despite the economic depression that had struck California in 1873, and the company collected its stitchers under one roof, in a small factory on Fremont Street, which was managed by Davis, the tailor from Nevada. Such remarkable success brought envious competitors, and Levi Strauss & Co. filed its first lawsuit for patent infringement against two other makers of riveted clothing in January 1874. On the second day of that month, the founder of the San Francisco concern, David Stern, died. About two years later, Strauss's two oldest nephews, Jacob and Louis Stern, entered the firm with their uncle.

In 1877, in a climate of dire economic conditions, mobs attacked San Francisco's Chinatown, sacking and burning shops and homes in a three-day riot. White men, unable to find work, took out their frustrations on the Chinese, who had been willing to work for lower wages. In the wake of this event, Levi Strauss & Co. solidified its policy of courting its customers' goodwill by relying exclusively on white women as seamstresses. Because this entailed paying higher wages, the company had to charge higher prices for its products, and thus find ways to deliver higher-quality goods.

In 1877 the Levi Strauss & Co. factory expanded, and the notable features of Levi's pants—the dark blue denim, the rivets, the stitching, the guarantee of quality—became further standardized. By 1879 the pants were selling for $1.46, and they had become widely worn in the rough-and-tumble mines and ranches of the West. The firm also continued to sell other dry goods, chalking up sales of $2.4 million in 1880, and it prospered throughout the 1880s.

In 1886 the "Two Horse Brand" leather tag, showing a team of horses trying to pull apart a pair of pants, began to be sewn into the back of the company's "waist-high overalls," the term Levi Strauss preferred to "jeans." In 1890 the firm assigned its first lot numbers to its products, and the famous number "501" was assigned to the riveted pants. In that year as well, Levi Strauss & Co. was formally incorporated and issued 18,000 shares of stock in the company to family members and employees.

In September 1902, the patriarch of the company died. In his later years, Levi Strauss had entrusted the business more to his four Stern nephews, who inherited the firm, in order to devote his energy to charitable and civic causes. Four years after Strauss's death the company endured another shock, when the Great San Francisco Earthquake and Fire of 1906 struck. Both the company's headquarters building on Battery Street and the factory on Fremont Street were destroyed.

Along with the rest of the city, Levi Strauss & Co. rebuilt, but the ensuing years were difficult. In 1907 a financial panic, which started in New York and crept westward, caused a slowdown in business, and the company began to streamline the merchandise it sold, relying more and more on its own products. Overall, however, sales were flat, and the four Stern brothers had drifted into a pattern of hands-off management.

In 1912 the company introduced its first innovative product in decades, Koveralls, playsuits for children designed by Simon Davis, the son of tailor Jacob Davis, who had followed his father into the business. Advertised widely, Koveralls became the first Levi Strauss & Co. product to be sold nationwide, helping the company to eventually break out of its regional market. The coming of World War I, and the boom in production for the war, had little or no impact on Levi Strauss & Co., since the company held no government contracts. Its riveted denim goods were sold only to the western workmen for whom they had originally been manufactured, and resale of eastern goods accounted for twice the sales of goods made at the San Francisco factory. Slowly, under the hands of the aging Stern brothers, who were resistant to change, Levi Strauss & Co.'s enterprise was losing ground.

In 1919 Sigmund Stern, who would take over the presidency of the company from his brother, Jacob, in 1921, brought aboard his son-in-law, Walter Haas, to give new blood to the leadership of Levi Strauss & Co. The Haas family, part of the Stern and Strauss clans by marriage, would continue to lead the company into the early 1990s. Walter Haas had little background in the family business, but one of the first changes he made was to update the company's inefficient system of keeping financial records. Despite Haas's attempts at efficiency, the company was battered in the early 1920s by a steep drop in the cost of cotton, the primary raw material for its products, that allowed competitors from other parts of the nation to undercut its prices. Company profits fell by one-third in 1920. In addition, Haas discovered that Levi Strauss & Co. was losing $1 on every dozen Koveralls sold. After a brief internal struggle, the price of Koveralls was adjusted, and steps to increase overall productivity, including the implementation, at this late date, of the assembly-line system, were taken.

The company began attaching belt loops to its basic denim pants in 1922, in addition to the traditional suspender buttons. Throughout the 1920s, Levi Strauss & Co. did business at a profit under the direction of Haas and his brother-in-law Daniel Koshland, a banker, whom he had brought into the firm to assist him. The firm found itself relying increasingly on the pants it manufactured, rather than the other dry goods it wholesaled, for the bulk of its profits. By 1929, 70% of the firm's profit derived from its sale of jeans.

With the stock market crash in 1929, and the subsequent Great Depression, Levi Strauss & Co. fell on hard times. The widespread unemployment that swept the country throughout the 1930s hit the manual laborers who bought the company's pants particularly hard. By 1930 the company's profits had vanished, and it posted a loss on sales that had fallen one-sixth. Unwilling to cut back production by firing workers, the company amassed a large backlog of unsold products, and then put its employees on a three-day work week. By 1932 company sales had dropped to half their 1929 level. With the coming of the next year, however, the Depression had started to lessen, and sales of Levi's pants slowly began to pick up.

In the economic turmoil of the 1930s, the growing U.S. union movement gained a new stronghold in San Francisco. Although workers in the Levi Strauss & Co. factory had not joined a union, organized labor's insistence that union workers wear union-made clothes sharply limited the company's sales in the heavily unionized San Francisco area. In 1935 Levi Strauss & Co. employees joined the United Garment Workers with management's acquiescence, thereby averting a strike and ending the virtual union boycott of Levi Strauss & Co.'s products.

The Depression and subsequent farm failures of the 1930s eventually worked in the company's favor, enabling it to break out of the relatively small market it had served since its inception. Western ranchers, unable to support themselves through agriculture, turned in the mid-1930s to tourism, inviting easterners to visit "dude ranches," where they were introduced to the cowboy's habitual garb, Levi's jeans. In addition, the advent and growth in popularity of Hollywood western movies further spread the word about Levi's jeans. In its advertising the company had always emphasized durability, but now it also stressed a certain western mystique. To capitalize on its growing brand identification, the company added the trademarked red "Levi's" tab to the back pocket of its pants in 1936, the first label to be placed on the outside of a piece of clothing. As demand increased, the vast stockpile of denim pants accumulated during the early years of the 1930s became depleted, and the factory returned to normal operation.

By 1939 the Levi Strauss & Co. blue denim "waist overall" had just begun to be popular outside the world of blue-collar workers. College students in California and Oregon adopted them as a fad, and slowly this humble item of clothing began to take on a status all its own. After the United States entered World War II, the government declared the jeans an essential commodity for the war effort, available only to defense workers. This restricted distribution made them an even more coveted item, and contributed, in the long run, to the brand's success. In the short run, however, wartime price restrictions cut into the company's profits.

With the war's end, the company was well-situated to prosper. Demographic shifts had brought a large number of potential new customers to the West Coast, and Levi Strauss & Co. now operated five jeans factories, in a futile effort to keep up with demand. The immediate postwar years brought a significant production shortage, and the company instituted a strict program of allocation, favoring retailers that were long-time customers. By 1948 company profits for the first time topped $1 million on sales of four million pairs of pants.

In the booming postwar economy of the 1950s, Levi Strauss & Co. underwent the most significant transition in the company's history. Taking advantage of demographic trends, the company began to focus its marketing efforts on young people, members of the "baby boom," who would wear its pants, now known colloquially as "Levi's," for play, not work. Targeting this new market involved widening the company's sales force to a truly nationwide scope, and shifting its emphasis from rural to more urban areas. As a sign of the company's future, Levi Strauss & Co. closed down its business wholesaling others' merchandise in the early 1950s.

Once again, in the 1950s Hollywood gave the company a large boost in its efforts to sell jeans to young people, when actors such as Marlon Brando and James Dean appeared in

The Wild One and *Rebel Without a Cause,* personifying youthful rebellion, and wearing jeans. The pants were losing their status as a symbol of the rugged frontier, and becoming instead a symbol of defiance toward the adult world. Levi's were on their way to becoming the uniform of an entire generation.

In 1954 the company branched out from denim to the sportswear business, launching Lighter Blues, a line of casual slacks for men. The following year the company added jeans with zipper flies, as opposed to the traditional five-button fly, in an attempt to woo customers in the East, where the pants, relegated to department store bargain basements, lagged in popularity. By the end of the decade, Levi Strauss & Co. was selling 20 million pieces of clothing a year, half of them jeans. The company was growing fast, and profits were robust.

In the late 1950s and early 1960s, Levi Strauss & Co. experimented with different products and lines of clothing in an effort to build on its reputation and diversify its offerings. In 1959 the company introduced "Orange, Lemon and Lime," pants in six bold colors, which were a short-lived hit. The following year, white Levi's were introduced, a duplicate of traditional jeans, but made in beige twill. Also in 1960, the company introduced pre-shrunk denim jeans, in an effort to overcome the objections of eastern customers, who were uncomfortable with shrinking pants. In 1963 stretch denim and corduroy Levi's joined the fold.

In 1964, after an arduous and expensive process of development, Levi Strauss & Co. introduced Sta-Prest permanent-press pants. Although the product was an initial sales success, problems with the chemical process that created a crease resulted in a large number of defective pants, and it was only later that the pants were perfected. The following year, the company expanded its international division to cover Europe, relying on Europeans to manage company operations in their home countries.

Throughout the 1960s, the company profited from movements in U.S. society, such as campus rebellions and the counter-culture, in which jeans became a uniform. The company's growth was mindboggling. New manufacturing facilities were added steadily, but demand for jeans still outstripped supply. In the mid-1960s, sales doubled in just three years to $152 million in 1966. That year, the company negotiated a $20 million loan to finance further expansion. Two years later, the company reorganized, establishing a division to produce and market women's clothing. By 1968 the company had grown to become one of the six largest clothing manufacturers in the United States, with sales nearing $200 million.

In 1971 Levi Strauss & Co.'s long-standing status as a wholly family- and employee-owned enterprise came to an end, when the company sold stock to the public for the first time. Denim jeans, Levi's in particular, had transcended the status of a mere product to become a worldwide social and cultural phenomenon, and the company could no longer raise enough capital privately to pay for needed expansion. The craze for jeans continued to grow, with seemingly no end in sight. The company coped with a constant shortage of denim. Levi Strauss & Co.'s existing, heavily centralized structure became inadequate, and operations were broken into four divisions: jeans, Levi's for women, boys' wear, and men's sportswear.

The company's phenomenal growth caught up with it in 1973, when its European division found itself with huge supplies of jeans in an outmoded style—straight-legged, as opposed to flared, or bell-bottomed—with more of the same on order. The problem was the culmination of years of undermanagement, and cost the company $12 million as it tried to unload the overstock. For the first time since the Depression, Levi Strauss & Co. announced a losing quarter, and the company's stock price fell dramatically. The following year, European operations were reorganized, and the company moved its headquarters from the site it had occupied on Battery Street for 108 years to new quarters. Seven years later, the company would move again to Levi's Plaza, a newly built complex.

Despite the sobering demonstration in Europe of the company's fallibility, by 1974 sales of Levi Strauss & Co. products had reached $1 billion. The following year the company was once again reminded of the hazards of operating in the murky waters of international business when it was revealed that Levi Strauss & Co. employees in international locations had bribed foreign officials on four separate occasions. When the incidents were discovered by the home office in San Francisco, the practice was immediately terminated. In addition, the company ran into trouble domestically in 1976 when the Federal Trade Commission accused it of price-fixing and restraint of trade because it prohibited retailers from discounting its products. The company reached an agreement with the government in 1977 in which it did not admit wrongdoing, but gave up suggested pricing, retaining the freedom not to sell to certain retailers. In the next several years, the company settled several suits, brought in nine states that charged illegal price-setting practices. The 1970s also saw the formation of the company's community-affairs department, which is Levi Strauss & Co.'s philanthropic arm, and of community-involvement teams, which are company-funded employee groups that participate in projects in communities in which Levi Strauss & Co. does business.

By 1977 Levi Strauss & Co. had become the largest clothing maker in the world. In addition to its original products, the company had grown through acquisitions, and also licensed its name to be used on other products, such as shoes and socks. Sales doubled in just four years, to hit $2 billion in 1979. Purchases such as Koracorp Industries Inc., a large maker of men's and women's sportswear, in 1979, and Santone Industries Inc., a menswear manufacturer, in 1981, prepared the ground for further growth.

The company, now an industry behemoth, ran into difficulties in the early 1980s, however, as the demand for denim stabilized, and its profits flattened. Attempting to increase its distribution, the company reached agreements with several mass merchandisers, including J.C. Penney and Sears, to market its products. Nonetheless, earnings dropped by nearly 25% in 1981, and the company undertook another reorganization, which included the elimination of one level of corporate management. Profits continued to plummet in 1982, and the company shut down nine plants, eliminating 2,000 jobs.

Levi Strauss & Co.'s fortunes made a short recovery in 1983, and the company planned a $40 million promotional tie-in with the 1984 Olympics to promote its relatively new active-wear division. Nevertheless, the year of the Olympics, in which the firm dressed more than 60,000 participants in the games, profits were down again, and the company undertook a major retrenching, closing many factories and eliminating thousands of more jobs. Faced with a demographic trend that showed the baby boomers outgrowing jeans, the company began heavy advertising campaigns, allied itself with designer Perry Ellis in an attempt to move into the high-fashion market, and continued its plans to retrench, as profits dropped by 50%.

In 1985, as Levi Strauss & Co. continued to restructure and cut back, the company was taken private in a leveraged buyout for $1.45 billion by the Haas family, descendants of its founders and long-time company leaders. Several other officers and directors also were members of the buyout group, Levi Strauss Associates Inc. The following year the company introduced a successful upscale men's pants line, Dockers, and, with increasing demand around the world for U.S. jeans, and with the addition of innovative finishes, such as bleaching or stonewashing, 1990 sales reached $4 billion.

As it entered the 1990s, Levi Strauss & Co. brought its greatest asset, its name and the reputation for quality it con-fers, into a turbulent and risky worldwide apparel market. It seemed unlikely that the company would experience another period of growth as meteoric as that which it experienced in the 1960s and 1970s. Instead, the company can look to its already formidable size and strength, which it built up over more than a century, as the custodian of the original blue jeans, uniform of a generation, symbol of a way of life.

Further Reading: Cray, Ed, *Levi's: The "Shrink to Fit" Business That Stretched to Cover the Whole World,* Boston, Houghton Mifflin Company, 1978; *Everyone Knows His First Name,* San Francisco, Levi Strauss & Co., [1985].

—Elizabeth Rourke

MILLIKEN & CO.

920 Milliken Road
Spartanburg, South Carolina 29308
U.S.A.
(803) 573-2020
Fax: (803) 573-2100

Private Company
Incorporated: 1890 as Deering-Milliken & Co.
Employees: 15,000
Sales: $2.00 billion

Milliken & Co. is one of the largest privately held textile companies and one of the largest privately owned companies of any kind in the United States, although the precise rank of this closely held company is difficult to ascertain; Milliken has never released sales statistics. For decades Milliken & Co. has been the clear industry leader in technology and research and, to many observers, in quality and services as well. Chairman Roger Milliken, grandson of company founder Seth Milliken, has been recognized as a giant of the textile industry since his ascension to the company's chairmanship in 1947. The two characteristics that have defined Roger Milliken's reign are his commitment to research and technological innovation and his commitment to secrecy regarding company matters. The former is best illustrated by the 1,200 or so patents held by Milliken & Co. on inventions ranging from computerized dyeing equipment to color-enhancing chemicals; the latter is reflected by the fact that most of the company's shareholders, largely Milliken family members and friends, do not have access to financial information. Milliken & Co. controls about 30% of the U.S. stretch-fabric market; about 40% of the market for acetate and acetate blends used in linings for coats and outerwear; and around 25% of the market for automotive fabrics.

Milliken & Co. first appeared as Deering-Milliken, a general store and selling agent for textile mills, in 1865. Deering-Milliken was a Portland, Maine-based partnership formed by Seth Milliken and William Deering. The company moved its base of operations from Maine to New York a few years later. Soon after that, Deering left the company for Chicago, where he formed the Deering Harvesting Machinery Company. Seth Milliken continued to operate under the Deering-Milliken name as a selling agent for woolen mills in New England. In the 1860s, he was selling for 16 different mills. Deering-Milliken made its first southern contact in 1884, when it be-

gan its long-standing and successful connection with Pacolet Manufacturing Company, headed by Captain John Montgomery of Spartanburg, South Carolina.

From his vantage point as part owner, sales agent, and factor—purchasing and procurement aide—for textile mills in both New England and the South, Milliken was able to determine when a mill was struggling financially, and much of Deering-Milliken's early growth sprang from the acquisition of these concerns. In 1890 Deering-Milliken & Co. was incorporated. Under Seth Milliken, the company eventually acquired interests in at least 42 mills, helping develop the textile industry in the southern United States by financing local manufacturing firms. Seth Milliken died in 1920, and was succeeded by his son Gerrish Milliken, who had joined the company in 1916. During Gerrish Milliken's tenure as head of Deering-Milliken, the company's primary role was that of sales agent and factor for southern mills.

The company's lasting tendencies toward free-flowing cash investment and technological foresightedness were already evident during the Gerrish Milliken era. For example, by keeping debt low and capital liquid during the Great Depression, Deering-Milliken was able to acquire controlling interest in several mills that faced bankruptcy while heavily indebted to Deering-Milliken. In addition, Gerrish Milliken recognized early on the potential importance of man-made fibers. He acquired the gigantic Judson mill in Greenville, South Carolina, and tested rayon, a new fiber, there.

The onset of World War II created great demand for new, more durable textiles. Deering-Milliken was among a handful of companies that led the industry in the development of synthetics for military use. Mills that sold their goods through Deering-Milliken were commissioned by the War Production Board to produce a variety of fabrics and yarns to meet government specifications. In 1944 Deering-Milliken was designated to build a mill that would process a new man-made fiber for military tire cord. The DeFore mill, built on the Seneca River near Clemson, South Carolina, was the first windowless textile mill equipped with complete air-clearing and -cooling systems, and therefore set the plant standard for years to come. Throughout the war years, demand also continued to grow for the company's New England–produced worsteds and woolens, and more existing southern mills were purchased.

Gerrish Milliken died in 1947, and his son Roger Milliken took charge of the company. Gerrish Milliken Jr. and Minot Milliken, two other grandsons of Seth Milliken, were also given official positions in the company. Roger Milliken began to shift the company's emphasis away from commission selling toward its own manufacturing. Eight new mills were built between 1940 and 1953. The first mill Roger Milliken built was the Gerrish Milliken Mill, in Pendleton, South Carolina. In addition to weaving Orlon and nylon, this plant, along with two others, doubled as a cattle farm.

By the mid-1950s, Deering-Milliken & Co. was third-largest textile chain in the United States. About 19,000 workers were employed by the company, ranging geographically from New England through the South.

In 1956 the company became entangled in one of the ugliest and most drawn-out affairs in the history of labor relations, a case which continues to be studied by experts in labor law. On September 6, 1956, workers in Darlington, South Carolina, ignoring Roger Milliken's threats of a plant shutdown, voted to bring in the Textile Workers Union of America to represent them. The textile industry historically had been hostile to organized labor—15% to 20% of the industry had union representation by the mid-1970s—and Roger Milliken had been among the most vocal of union opponents. Milliken made good his threat, and the Darlington plant was closed. In 1962 the National Labor Relations Board ruled that the closing constituted an unfair labor practice, but this decision was reversed by a federal appeals court. The case was ultimately decided by the Supreme Court, which ruled that a plant could not be closed in order to discourage union activity at other company locations. It was not until 1980, after 24 years of litigation and negotiation over a formula for calculating back pay, that the case was finally settled. The company agreed to pay a total of $5 million to the 427 workers still alive and the survivors of the 126 workers who had died since 1956.

Originally, the mills controlled by Deering-Milliken were separate corporations, some of which had outside shareholders. By the end of the 1950s, Roger Milliken had succeeded in buying out all of them, integrating them into a single corporate entity. The year 1958 marked the opening of Deering-Milliken's gigantic research facility in Spartanburg, located on a 600-acre complex that became the company's headquarters. From this facility, the most sophisticated in the textile industry, flowed a steady stream of new fabrics and processing techniques. It was here that "durable press" and "soil release," important advancements in polyester treatment, were developed through irradiation.

Under Roger Milliken's leadership, Deering-Milliken continued in its role as industry ground-breaker into the 1960s. In the early 1960s Milliken began to question the conventional thinking of most textile executives regarding inventories. Traditionally, manufacturing and marketing were treated as separate functions, often resulting in excessive inventories. Milliken commissioned a study that indicated an inverse relationship between inventory size and profits. This led Milliken to keep tighter control of inventory by adjusting the rate of production. Deering-Milliken began its European operations in 1965, opening mills and offices in England, France, and Belgium.

In 1967 Deering-Milliken eliminated 600 mid-level management jobs in a consolidation to cut overhead. Deering-Milliken was among the trail-blazing companies in the 1960s, however, in producing double-knit fabrics. Toward the end of the decade, the company unveiled one of its most important inventions, Visa. Visa is a fabric finish that resists stains, and is used on a wide variety of products, including clothing and tablecloths. The original irradiation process for making Visa has been replaced by a chemical process. The development of Visa strongly reaffirmed the company's position as a leader in developing patented fabric finishes. It also produced huge profits.

For decades, Roger Milliken has been an active force in conservative politics. Milliken demonstrated the depth of his right-wing convictions in 1967, when, after viewing a television documentary on UNICEF aid to communist-governed countries sponsored by Xerox, he quickly had all Xerox copiers removed from company offices. Company executives routinely receive subscriptions to conservative publications. By the late 1980s, however, the company began using Xerox machinery again, and Xerox was its major copier supplier in 1991.

In 1978 the name Deering was finally removed from the company, more than a century after company founder Deering's departure. The year also marked the 25th anniversary of Milliken & Co. tradition known as the breakfast show. Each year, retail store buyers and other industry professionals are invited to a Broadway-style musical revue featuring big-name performers and staged at a major New York venue. The breakfast show has a run of 13 performances, 9 actually at breakfast and 4 at cocktail hour, and is seen by over 30,000 people annually. The show was essentially a glamourous advertisement for Milliken products, and has featured Phyllis Diller, Cyd Charisse, Ray Bolger, and Bert Parks, among others.

The first half of the 1980s was difficult for the textile industry. One reason was the doubling of textile imports between 1980 and 1985. During that period, Milliken & Co. closed 7 plants, reducing its total to 55 in North Carolina, South Carolina, and Georgia, and a quarter of its work force was laid off. These circumstances led Roger Milliken to depart from his general policy of avoiding the press. He began speaking out in favor of protectionist policies, recommending limiting the growth rate of imports to the growth rate of the U.S. market. In 1991 58% of the fabric and apparel sold at retail in the United States was imported. Milliken & Co. was also hurt during this period by Milliken's refusal to adjust to the trend among U.S. consumers toward wearing natural fibers. He believed that because synthetics required less labor, a shift in emphasis was not practical.

In 1984 Roger Milliken survived a helicopter crash. Some who knew him believe that this event brought about a new willingness to deal with the public. He began assuming leadership roles in a number of industry organizations, most notably the Crafted with Pride in U.S.A. Council. Milliken's increased public involvement resulted in his being named Textile Leader of the Year in 1986, the first such honor awarded by *Textile World,* an industrial magazine.

Despite Milliken's objections to textile imports, between 1985 and 1989 Milliken & Co. purchased 1,500 modern Japanese looms, and in 1989 the company bought 500 more from Belgium, because U.S. weaving machinery manufacturers no longer existed. These looms are able to detect defects, stop themselves, and then start up again on their own.

During the late 1980s Milliken & Co. began to show signs of moving toward diversification. The company opened a second chemical plant in 1988 in Blacksburg, South Carolina. The plant makes Millad, a clarifying agent for polypropylene products. The company's first chemical plant had been opened in Inman, South Carolina, in 1963. It makes chemical products used in the textile manufacturing process, as well as chemical additives for paint and other products.

Roger Milliken named Thomas Malone president in 1984. A struggle over future control of the company developed during the late 1980s as Roger Milliken entered his mid-70s. The family of Joan Milliken Stroud, Roger Milliken's late sister, owns about 15% of the company and has indicated it resents its lack of input on company decisions. The Stroud family had sued Milliken and his board of directors at least three times by 1989 in attempts to win shareholders' information and input. When the Strouds threatened to sell their stock, Milliken countered by making new rules that require approval by 75% of the voting power before the company can be sold, and hand-picking a new, self-perpetuating board dominated by outside directors and managers. Roger Milliken, Gerrish Milliken Jr., and Minot Milliken control about 50% of the company common stock. It has been suggested that they have stymied the Stroud family's attempts to sell their stock because it is their wish to keep the company private.

Milliken & Co. was a winner of the 1989 Malcolm Baldrige National Quality Award, an award established by Congress and administered by the U.S. Department of Commerce. Two companies were chosen as winners for the year out of 40 competing companies. Milliken & Co. was singled out for its team approach to management. The other winner was Xerox, the company that Roger Milliken had shunned more than 20 years earlier because of his rigid political beliefs.

Among textile-industry insiders Milliken & Co. has for generations been associated with quality products and services—quality usually achieved through foresight and innovation. Roger Milliken has arguably been among the most important individuals in the textile industry during the 20th century. The success of Milliken & Co. in the future will depend largely on the company's ability to continue with its steady technological and organizational advancement in the absence of the management leadership the Millikens have provided for so long. This will be the case whether the company becomes publicly owned or remains firmly in Milliken family hands.

Further Reading: "How Roger Milliken Runs Textiles' Premier Performer," *Business Week,* January 19, 1981; Andrews, Mildred Gwin, *The Men and The Mills,* Macon, Georgia, Mercer University Press, 1987; Lappen, Alyssa A., "Can Roger Milliken Emulate William Randolph Hearst?" *Forbes,* May 29, 1989.

—Robert R. Jacobson

MITSUBISHI RAYON CO., LTD.

3-19, Kyobashi
2-chome, Chuo-ku
Tokyo 104
Japan
(03) 3272-4981
Fax: (03) 3246-8781

Public Company
Incorporated: 1933 as Shinko Rayon Company Ltd.
Employees: 5,145
Sales: ¥275.41 billion (US$2.21 billion)
Stock Exchanges: Tokyo Osaka Nagoya

Mitsubishi Rayon Co., Ltd., originally a major Japanese producer of rayon, is now an important manufacturer of acrylics, plastics, polyesters, and optical fibers. The company, part of the huge Mitsubishi trading network, reflects the general trends in Japan's textile industry, which has undergone a drastic restructuring in recent years. In 1961 natural and synthetic textiles provided Japan's largest export earnings and employed 1.2 million workers. Over the last three decades, low-wage competition from textile industries in neighboring Asian countries and increasing U.S. protectionism have greatly reduced the importance of Japanese textiles and have caused Mitsubishi Rayon and its Japanese competitors to look for new products and markets.

Textiles became important early in the history of Japanese industry. Cotton and wool spinning existed before the Meiji restoration in 1868, but afterwards the Japanese government provided spurs to industrialization by buying foreign plant and equipment abroad. Inflation fears during the 1880s caused the government to sell the plant to private investors. Close links between these investors and the government allowed many of these enterprises to develop into the powerful *zaibatsu* or giant trading enterprises. Much of the textile industry, however, remained in the hands of small-scale producers. They became increasingly dependent on *zaibatsu* like Mitsubishi for the distribution and international marketing of their products.

Japan has always been famous for its silk. After Commodore Perry opened Japan to international trade in 1853, foreign demand rose and provided an important source of foreign exchange that allowed the Japanese government to purchase industrial plant and equipment abroad.

The textile industry is often cited as a textbook example of an ideal industry for an industrializing country because it is a low-wage, labor-intensive business in which countries like turn-of-the-century Japan enjoyed a strong advantage over more developed countries like Britain. Later Japan would discover that this was an advantage it could also lose, but by the 1920s Japan had become successful at cotton and wool spinning and weaving. In the early 1930s textiles accounted for about one-third of the country's industrial product and provided employment to half the country's industrial workers.

Rayon, the first universally popular man-made fiber, was taken up eagerly by Japanese industry in 1929. The plant-cellulose-derived material was first known as "artificial silk" or "wood silk" until the term "rayon" was coined in 1924. Rayon was inspired by the need to reproduce chemically what a silkworm does in creating silk from its own body fluids. In the industrial process, cellulose is converted to a liquid compound and then back to cellulose in the form of fiber. The cellulose is usually derived from soft woods or the short fibers adhering to cotton seeds.

In 1892 rayon was first commercially produced in France, but it was discontinued because of its high flammability. A year later, viscous rayon was developed in Britain and remains the most popular form. Its ability to absorb moisture has made it a popular clothing material. It is also used in carpets, home furnishings, and tires.

Mitsubishi Rayon was one of a number of rayon companies set up in the 1930s. Historically, the industry has been characterized by fragmentation and a large number of small-scale producers. Producers like Shinko Rayon Ltd., as the company was first known when it was incorporated in 1933, were and are dependent on the *zaibatsu*. The trading giant Mitsubishi controlled Shinko Rayon when it began producing rayon in 1934. By 1937 the Japanese rayon industry was already the largest in the world. Production had risen to 326 million pounds (lb) from 27 million lb in 1929. The government had encouraged production for strategic reasons, and the textile industry as a whole employed nearly half the country's industrial work force, bringing in more foreign exchange than any other export industry.

Shortages of cotton, wool, and other raw materials led the government to encourage the production of man-made and synthetic fibers, and these shortages became worse as World War II began. A 1938 law required the use of a percentage of man-made or synthetic fibers in the manufacture of woolen and cotton goods. Japan claimed to have invented a new manufacturing process for nylon—invented in the United States in the late 1930s—during the war, but soon afterward Japanese companies had to buy licensing rights for this same process from U.S. companies.

War production reorganization led to a series of reintegrations and mergers within the Mitsubishi empire. In 1942 Shinko Rayon was merged with Japan Chemical Industries and began the production of acrylics. Two years later, a further merger created the giant Mitsubishi Chemical.

After Japan's defeat in 1945, the Allied—overwhelmingly American—occupation authorities were determined to break up the huge *zaibatsu* as part of a program that purged 50,000 businessmen and politicians and reformed land tenure, education, government, and the legal and financial systems. They hoped to destroy the business and bureaucratic combinations that had been powerful engines for Japan's prewar conquests in Asia.

As one of the largest *zaibatsu,* Mitsubishi was a prominent target for the Allied restructuring of Japanese industry. In 1950 Mitsubishi Chemical was split into its original constituents: Shinko Rayon, Japan Chemical Industries, and Mitsubishi Chemical. Although Shinko Rayon was renamed Mitsubishi Rayon Company on December 1, 1952, Mitsubishi decreased its equity interest in the company through a listing on the Japanese stock exchanges in the same month.

Mitsubishi's equity interest in Mitsubishi Rayon decreased from the 1950s onward—by the 1990s it was about 14%—but the company has remained part of the Mitsubishi empire in a way that is typical of the cooperative company structures that have replaced the prewar *zaibatsu.* With interlocking directorates and shared ownerships and projects, Mitsubishi Rayon and other Mitsubishi-affiliated companies are able to buy and sell to each other at favorable rates and use the formidable international trading and financing facilities of the parent company.

Allied occupation authorities may have destroyed the power of the prewar *zaibatsu* but, fearing chaos, they left the other partner in Japan's industrial machine, the bureaucracy, largely intact. Japanese officials soon proved themselves to be just as capable of coordinating a state industrial policy with Mitsubishi and the other new, interlocking empires. This powerful combination has allowed Japan to restructure its industries to anticipate changes in the international marketplace and avoid some of the pains of industrial obsolescence and unemployment familiar to many Western industries. The textile industry is often cited as an illustration of the ability of the Japanese Ministry of Trade and Industry (MITI) to provide central "administrative guidance"—not legal but virtually compulsory rules—to force Japanese industry to respond to changing world markets.

By 1949, under encouragement from MITI, the Japanese textile industry started to manufacture synthetics on a large scale. In the 1950s Japan's role as a supply base for the Korean War led to an economic boom. MITI virtually shut down the uneconomic Japanese coal industry. It could force mergers or directly import foreign technology. Some companies and industries received favorable treatment and advice from MITI. When the textiles industry first fell into a slump in 1952, MITI circumvented the anti-monopoly law and formed an effective cartel, which included Mitsubishi Rayon, to discourage overcapacity. In 1953 the anti-monopoly law was significantly weakened by new legislation.

The textile industry quickly found its feet again. Textile workers' wages remained low, the yen was undervalued, and the United States had not yet demanded trade protection from Japanese goods. Today's Asian competitors—South Korea, Taiwan, Hong Kong, Singapore, and Malaysia—were still recovering from war. China was consolidating its Communist revolution and its huge supply of cheap labor was barely a factor in the international marketplace.

In the 1957–58 recession the cotton-spinning and rayon industries experienced a slump that caused them to reassess their position. As Mitsubishi Rayon and other large textile concerns accelerated diversification into synthetic fibers in 1959, MITI began to take a closer look at textiles, which had once again become the country's largest industry.

Mitsubishi had begun to manufacture acetate, a synthetic textile fiber made from cellulose, in the mid-1950s. By 1962 acetates were used in Japanese cigarette filters. The company increasingly specialized in acrylic fibers and set up a separate subsidiary, Shinko Acrylic Fibres, in 1957, though this was remerged into the main company in 1968. Manufacture of polypropylene, used for upholstery and carpets, began in 1962 and triacetates were added to the product list in 1967.

National production of cotton fabrics and yarns reached a high of 3.38 billion square meters in 1961 and fell into steady decline, while production of synthetics grew rapidly from 116 million square meters in 1957 to 2,397 million square meters in 1969. Much of this output was exported to the United States, where the domestic industry began to complain loudly to Congress and the Johnson and Nixon administrations.

At the same time, MITI had become worried about overcapacity. Installation of synthetics-manufacturing equipment was made subject to prior government approval in 1960. By the mid-1960s, MITI was strictly rationing facilities that could be built for the production of synthetic fibers. The fact that firms like Mitsubishi that had obtained early approval retained a competitive edge over firms that failed to get approval later was criticized.

Nevertheless, Japanese manufacturers continued to be successful in selling to the United States. After long, drawn-out negotiations failed to yield results, the Japanese Textile Federation—including Mitsubishi Rayon—and MITI decided to try to diffuse growing U.S. political opposition by adopting voluntary curbs on textile exports to the United States for three years after July 1, 1971.

The increase in exports was to be kept to 5% in the first year and 6% in the following two years, with actual exports in 1970 serving as a base, but President Richard Nixon and the U.S. textile industry quickly denounced the agreement. Nixon had received large campaign donations from the U.S. industry. He also wanted the votes of textile workers concentrated in the Southern states, where he focused his "southern strategy" for his reelection.

The president's 1971 action to discontinue the convertibility of the dollar—the "Nixon Shock"—did far more to shake up the Japanese textile industry. The yen lost its favorable fixed rate position and drifted upward. As the 1973 oil price hikes by OPEC increased synthetic production costs, Mitsubishi Rayon faced new challenges from low-wage Asian competitors who began a steady assault on the Japanese home market. By 1986 Japan was a net textile importer.

All these factors created a slump that hit the industry hard in 1974 and lasted into the early 1990s. Mitsubishi Rayon retrenched by cutting its work force by 25% in 1975–1976 and then by selling its head office building in 1977. Prices for fibers continued to drop. An attempt by the Japanese Chemical Fibers Association to form a cartel failed in early 1977. After a forum of company presidents failed to cope with domestic prices, by October 1977 MITI decided to intervene with the first "production curtailments based on MITI advice" since 1965–1966.

By the late 1970s it became clear to the company's management that changes in Japan's world market position in textile fibers were permanent. Mitsubishi Rayon decided to withdraw from rayon staple production and reduce its dependence on the production of textile fibers in favor of plastics and other synthetics.

In November 1977 Toyobo, another major textile firm, and Mitsubishi Rayon rejected a widely expected merger in favor of a joint venture to develop a joint acrylics marketing firm. In early 1978 Mitsubishi Rayon closed its rayon staple production facilities.

In 1979 MITI and the government discouraged further expansion of the synthetic fiber industry. Synthetic fiber manufacturers were required to dispose of 18% of their manufacturing facilities. MITI encouraged synthetic textile makers to diversify.

Despite efforts by Mitsubishi Rayon and other companies to cope with these changes, domestic and export textile sales continued to slump and by 1980 Japanese textiles had acquired a reputation as a "sunset industry." By this time, however, the company was well on the way to diversification into non-textile synthetic materials, especially optical fibers and engineering plastics like methyl methacrylate resin (MMA). The company soon had one of the world's largest production capacities for MMA. In the year to March 1985, non-fiber products already accounted for more than half of Mitsubishi Rayon's sales.

By the beginning of the 1990s, the name "Mitsubishi Rayon" seemed a misnomer. The company had ceased production of its original product, rayon staple, in 1978. Non-textile synthetics, rather than man-made cellulose textiles, now dominate its diversified production. The main cellulose product is now acetate: the company is the largest acetate producer in Japan and had about 50% of the cigarette filter market in 1990. Plastics and resins accounted for 41% of total sales, acrylic fibers accounted for 18%, polyester filaments for 15%, and acetate fibers for 15%. In effect, only one-third of the company's gross sales are now derived from fibers.

Mitsubishi Rayon has expanded its facilities from its original Otake Production Center near Hiroshima, where it makes acrylic fibers and MMA resins, to additional large centers at Toyohashi, near Nagoya, producing polyester, polypropylene, and carbon fiber, and Toyama, on the west coast of Honshu, producing acetates.

New high-performance fibers are expected to show significant growth in the 1990s, but for Mitsubishi Rayon diversification into non-textile activities has already paid off. Operating profits have shown a steady increase over the period 1988–1991 but even in its new diversified activities the company faces difficulties similar to those of other Japanese firms: a highly valued yen and intense competition from Taiwan and South Korea. Like all its rivals, it looks to technological efficiency and research into promising fields like biotechnology to guarantee continued success.

Principal Subsidiaries: Mitsubishi Rayon Engineering Company Ltd; Mitsubishi-Burlington; Ryoko Company Ltd (68%); Ryoko Electronics Company; Nitto Chemical Industry (53%); Dupont-Mitsubishi Rayon Company Ltd (50%); P.T. Vonex Indonesia (45%); Mitsubishi Rayon America Inc; Metco North America Inc; Pan Pacific Yarn.

—Clark Siewert

NIKE, INC.

One Bowerman Drive
Beaverton, Oregon 97005
U.S.A.
(503) 671-6453
Fax: (503) 671-6339

Public Company
Incorporated: 1964 as Blue Ribbon Sports
Employees: 4,500
Sales: $3.00 billion
Stock Exchanges: New York Pacific

Founded as an importer of Japanese shoes, Nike, Inc. has grown to be one of the world's largest makers of athletic footwear and apparel. The company has relied on consistent innovation in the design of its products and steady promotion to fuel its growth in both U.S. and foreign markets.

Nike's precursor originated in 1962, a product of the imagination of Phillip Knight, a Stanford University business graduate who had been a member of the track team as an undergraduate at the University of Oregon. Traveling in Japan after finishing up business school, Knight got in touch with a Japanese firm that made athletic shoes, the Onitsuka Tiger Company, and arranged to import some of its products to the United States on a small scale. Knight was convinced that Japanese running shoes could become significant competitors for the German products that then dominated the American market. In the course of setting up his agreement with Onitsuka Tiger, Knight invented Blue Ribbon Sports to satisfy his Japanese partner's expectations that he represented an actual company, and this hypothetical firm eventually grew to become Nike.

At the end of 1963, Knight's arrangements in Japan came to fruition when he took delivery of 200 pairs of Tiger athletic shoes, which he stored in his father's basement and peddled at various track meets in the area. Knight's one-man venture became a partnership in the following year, when his former track coach, William Bowerman, chipped in $500 to equal Knight's investment. Bowerman had long been experimenting with modified running shoes for his team, and he worked with runners to improve the designs of prototype Blue Ribbon Sports (BRS) shoes. Innovation in running shoe design eventually would become a cornerstone of the company's continued expansion and success. Bowerman's efforts first paid off in

1966, when a shoe known as the Cortez, which he had designed, became a big seller.

BRS sold 1,300 pairs of Japanese running shoes in 1964, its first year, to gross $8,000. By 1965 the fledgling company had acquired a full-time employee, and sales had reached $20,000. The following year, the company rented its first retail space, next to a beauty salon in Santa Monica, California, so that its few employees could stop selling shoes out of their cars. In 1967 with fast-growing sales, BRS expanded operations to the East Coast, opening a distribution office in Wellesley, Massachusetts.

Bowerman's innovations in running shoe technology continued throughout this time. A shoe whose upper portion was made of nylon went into development in 1967, and the following year, Bowerman and another employee came up with the Boston shoe, which incorporated the first cushioned mid-sole throughout the entire length of an athletic shoe.

By the end of the decade, Knight's venture had expanded to include several stores and 20 employees, and sales were nearing $300,000. The company was poised for greater growth, but Knight was frustrated by a lack of capital to pay for expansion. In 1971 using financing from the Japanese trading company Nissho Iwai, BRS was able to manufacture its own line of products overseas, for import to the United States. At this time, the company introduced its Swoosh trademark, and the brand name Nike, the Greek goddess of victory. These new symbols were first affixed to a soccer shoe, the first Nike product to be sold.

A year later, BRS broke with its old Japanese partner, Onitsuka Tiger, after a disagreement over distribution, and kicked off promotion of its own products at the 1972 U.S. Olympic Trials, the first of many marketing campaigns that would seek to attach Nike's name and fortunes to the careers of well-known athletes. Nike shoes were geared to the serious athlete, and their high performance carried with it a high price.

In their first year of distribution, the company's new products grossed $1.96 million, and its staff swelled to 45. In addition, operations were expanded to Canada, the company's first foreign market, which would be followed by Australia, in 1974.

Bowerman continued his innovations in running-shoe design with the introduction of the Moon shoe in 1972, which had a waffle-like sole that had first been formed by molding rubber on a household waffle iron. This sole increased the traction of the shoe without adding weight.

In 1974 BRS opened its first U.S. plant, in Exeter, New Hampshire. The company's payroll swelled to 250, and worldwide sales neared $5 million by the end of 1974.

This growth was fueled in part by aggressive promotion of the Nike brand name. The company sought to expand its visibility by having its shoes worn by prominent athletes, including tennis players Ilie Nastase and Jimmy Connors. At the 1976 Olympic Trials these efforts began to pay off as Nike shoes were worn by rising athletic stars.

The company's growth had truly begun to take off by this time, riding the boom in popularity of jogging that took place in the United States in the late 1970s. BRS revenues tripled in two years to $14 million in 1976, and then doubled in just one year to $28 million in 1977. To keep up with demand, the company opened new factories, adding a stitching plant in Maine and additional overseas production facilities in Taiwan and Korea. International sales were expanded when markets in

Asia were opened in 1977 and in South America the following year. European distributorships were lined up in 1978.

Nike continued its promotional activities with the opening of Athletics West, a training club for Olympic hopefuls in track and field, and by signing tennis player John McEnroe to an endorsement contract. In 1978 the company changed its name to Nike, Inc. The company expanded its line of products that year, adding athletic shoes for children.

By 1979 Nike sold almost half the running shoes bought in the United States, and the company moved into a new world headquarters building in Beaverton, Oregon. In addition to its shoe business, the company began to make and market a line of sports clothing, and the Nike-Air shoe cushioning device was introduced.

By the start of the 1980s, Nike's combination of groundbreaking design and savvy and aggressive marketing had allowed it to surpass the German athletic shoe company Adidas, formerly the leader in U.S. sales. In December of that year, Nike went public, offering two million shares of stock. With the revenues generated by the stock sale, the company planned continued expansion, particularly in the European market. In the United States, plans for a new headquarters on a large, rural campus were inaugurated, and an east coast distribution center in Greenland, New Hampshire, was brought on line. In addition, the company bought a large plant in Exeter, New Hampshire, to house the Nike Sport Research and Development Lab and also to provide for more domestic manufacturing capacity. The company had shifted its overseas production away from Japan at this point, manufacturing nearly four-fifths of its shoes in South Korea and Taiwan. It established factories in mainland China in 1981.

By the following year, when the jogging craze in the United States had started to wane, half of the running shoes bought in the United States bore the Nike trademark. The company was well insulated from the effects of a stagnating demand for running shoes, however, since it gained a substantial share of its sales from other types of athletic shoes, notably basketball shoes and tennis shoes. In addition, Nike benefited from strong sales of its other product lines, which included apparel, work and leisure shoes, and children's shoes.

Given the slowing of growth in the U.S. market, however, the company turned its attention to growth in foreign markets, inaugurating Nike International, Ltd., in 1981 to spearhead the company's push into Europe and Japan, as well as into Asia, Latin America, and Africa. In Europe, Nike faced stiff competition from Adidas and Puma, which had a strong hold on the soccer market, Europe's largest athletic-shoe category. The company opened a factory in Ireland to enable it to distribute its shoes without paying high import tariffs, and in 1981, bought out its distributors in England and Austria, to strengthen its control over marketing and distribution of its products. In 1982 the company outfitted Aston Villa, the winning team in the English and European Cup soccer championships, giving a boost to promotion of its new soccer shoe.

In Japan, Nike allied itself with Nissho Iwai Corp., the sixth-largest Japanese trading company, to form Nike-Japan Corporation. Because Nike already held a part of the low-priced athletic shoe market, the company set its sights on the high-priced end of the scale in Japan.

By 1982 the company's line of products included more than 200 different kinds of shoes, including the Air Force I, a basketball shoe, and its companion shoe for racquet sports, the Air Ace, the latest models in the long line of innovative shoe designs that had pushed Nike's earnings to an average annual increase of almost 100%. In addition, the company marketed more than 200 different items of clothing. By 1983 when the company posted its first-ever quarterly drop in earnings as the running boom peaked and went into a decline, resulting in slowing shoe sales, Nike's leaders were looking to the apparel division, as well as overseas markets, for further expansion. In foreign sales, the company had mixed results. Its operations in Japan were almost immediately profitable, and the company quickly jumped to second place in the Japanese market, but in Europe, Nike fared less well, losing money on its five European subsidiaries.

Faced with an 11.5% drop in domestic sales of its shoes in the 1984 fiscal year, Nike moved away from its traditional marketing strategy of support for sporting events and athlete endorsements to a wider-reaching approach, investing more than $10 million in its first national television and magazine advertising campaign. This followed the "Cities Campaign," which used billboards and murals in nine American cities to publicize Nike products in the period before the 1984 Olympics. Despite the strong showing of athletes wearing Nike shoes in the 1984 Los Angeles Olympic games, Nike profits were down almost 30% for the fiscal year ending in May 1984, although international sales were robust and overall sales rose slightly. This decline was a result of aggressive price discounting on Nike products and the increased costs associated with the company's push into foreign markets and attempts to build up its sales of apparel.

Earnings continued to fall in the next three quarters, as the company lost market share, posting profits of only $7.8 million at the end of August 1984, a loss of $2.2 million three months later, and another loss of $2.1 million at the end of February 1985. In response, Nike adopted a series of measures to change its sliding course. The company cut back on the number of shoes it had sitting in warehouses, and also attempted to fine-tune its corporate mission by cutting back on the number of products it marketed. It made plans to reduce the line of Nike shoes by 30% within a year and a half. In addition, leadership at the top of the company was streamlined, as founder Knight resumed the post of president, which he had relinquished in 1983, in addition to his duties as chairman and chief executive officer, and overall administrative costs were reduced. As part of this effort, Nike also consolidated its research and marketing branches, closing its facility in Exeter, New Hampshire, and cutting 75 of the plant's 125 employees. Overall, the company laid off about 400 workers during 1984.

Faced with shifting consumer interests, as, for instance, the U.S. market moved from jogging to aerobics, the company created a new products division in 1985 to help keep up with changing market demands. In addition, Nike purchased Proform, a small maker of weight-lifting equipment, as part of its plan to profit from all aspects of the fitness movement. The company was restructured further at the end of 1985 when its last two U.S. factories were closed and its previous divisions of apparel and athletic shoes were rearranged by sport. In a move that would prove to be the key to the company's recovery, in 1985 the company signed up basketball player Michael Jordan to endorse a new version of its Air shoe, introduced four years earlier.

In early 1986 Nike announced expansion into a number of new lines, including casual apparel for women, a less-expensive line of athletic shoes called Street Socks, golf shoes, and tennis gear marketed under the name "Wimbledon." By mid-1986 Nike was reporting that its earnings had begun to increase again, and that year sales topped $1 billion for the first time. At that time, the company sold its 51% stake in Nike-Japan to its Japanese partner, and six months later, at year's end, laid off 10% of its U.S. employees at all levels in a cost-cutting move.

Following these moves, Nike announced a drop in revenues and earnings in 1987, and another round of restructuring and cost-cutting ensued, as the company attempted to come to grips with the continuing evolution of the U.S. fitness market from jogging to walking, from aerobics to cross-training—diversified physical workout. Only Nike's innovative Air athletic shoes provided a bright spot in the company's otherwise erratic progress, allowing the company to regain market share from rival Reebok in several areas, including basketball and cross-training.

The following year, Nike branched out from athletic shoes, purchasing Cole Haan, a maker of casual and dress shoes, for $80 million. Advertising heavily, the company took a commanding lead in sales to young people to claim 23% of the overall athletic shoe market. Profits rebounded to reach $100 million dollars in 1988, as sales rose 37% to $1.2 billion. Later that year, Nike launched a $10 million dollar television campaign around the theme "Just Do It," and announced that its 1989 advertising budget would reach $45 million.

In 1989 Nike marketed several new lines of shoes, and led its market with $1.7 billion in sales, yielding profits of $167 million. The company's product innovation continued, as a basketball shoe with an inflatable collar around the ankle was introduced under the brand name Air Pressure. In addition, Nike continued its aggressive marketing, using ads featuring Michael Jordan and the Mars Blackmon character played by actor-director Spike Lee, the ongoing "Just Do It" campaign, and "Bo Knows" television spots featuring athlete Bo Jackson. At the end of 1989, the company began relocation to its newly constructed headquarters campus in Beaverton, Oregon.

In 1990 the company sued two competitors for copying the patented designs of its shoes, and found itself engaged in a dispute with the U.S. Customs Service over import duties on its Air Jordan basketball shoes. In 1990 the company's revenues hit $2 billion. The company acquired Tetra Plastics Inc., producers of plastic film for shoe soles. That year, the company opened Nike Town, a prototype store selling the full range of Nike products, in Portland, Oregon. Additional stores based on this model in other large cities are planned for 1992.

By 1991 Nike's Visible Air shoes had enabled it to surpass its rival Reebok in the U.S. market. Its efforts to conquer Europe had begun to show fruit as the company gained a second-place market share, behind only the leading German company, Adidas. Unlike the U.S. market, which had largely matured, Nike predicted ample room to grow on foreign soil.

As Nike enters the 1990s, this young company can look back on an extraordinary record of growth over a relatively short period of time. Blessed with good timing, the company rode the U.S. fitness and jogging boom to unprecedented profits, only to suffer the pangs of adjustment as the market matured and changed. Given the company's record of innovative design and savvy promotion, however, it appears unlikely that Nike will stumble again badly as it runs, jogs, walks, dances, jumps, and plays its way into the future.

Principal Subsidiaries: Cole Haan Holdings, Inc.; Tetra Plastics Inc.

Further Reading: "Fitting the World in Sport Shoes," *Business Week,* January 25, 1982; "Nike Pins Hopes for Growth on Foreign Sales and Apparel," *The New York Times,* March 24, 1983; Tharp, Mike, "Easy-Going Nike Adopts Stricter Controls To Pump Up Its Athletic-Apparel Business," *The Wall Street Journal,* November 6, 1984; *Nike Timeline,* Beaverton, Oregon, Nike, Inc., 1990; "Where Nike and Reebok Have Plenty of Running Room," *Business Week,* March 11, 1991.

—Elizabeth Rourke

Reebok®

REEBOK INTERNATIONAL LTD.

100 Technology Center Drive
Stoughton, Massachusetts 02072
U.S.A.
(617) 341-5000
Fax: (617) 341-5087

Public Company
Incorporated: 1979 as Reebok U.S.A.
Employees: 3,800
Sales: $2.16 billion
Stock Exchange: New York

Reebok International is one of the world's leading athletic footwear and apparel makers. The company first leapt to prominence by opening up a new market for athletic shoes—aerobic exercise shoes for women interested in fashion as well as function—and subsequently built upon that success by expanding into other sports and products and by seeking business around the world.

Reebok began its growth into a worldwide enterprise in 1979 when Paul B. Fireman, a marketer of camping and fishing supplies, noticed the products of a small British athletic shoe maker, Reebok International, at a Chicago sporting goods show. Looking for a business opportunity, Fireman acquired the North American license for the company's products, founding Reebok U.S.A. The British parent company, the oldest manufacturer of athletic shoes in the world, had gotten its start in the 1890s in Bolton, England, when Joseph William Foster began handcrafting shoes with spiked soles for runners. By 1895 he was the head of J.W. Foster and Sons, Inc., providing shoes to world-class athletes, including the 1924 British Olympic running team. In 1958 two of Foster's grandsons founded Reebok, named after an African gazelle, to manufacture running shoes in Bolton, and this company eventually took over the older firm.

After Fireman acquired the right to sell Reebok products made in Britain in the United States, he introduced three top-of-the-line models of running shoes, with price tags of $60, the highest on the market. Sales topped $1.5 million in 1981, but after two years in the extremely competitive U.S. market, Fireman's enterprise was out of money, and he sold 56% of his fledgling company to Pentland Industries PLC, another British shoe company, for $77,500. Reebok used this infusion of cash to open a factory in Korea, thereby significantly lowering production costs.

The company's fortunes began to change dramatically, however, in 1982 with the introduction of a shoe designed especially for aerobic exercise. Unlike traditional athletic shoes, which were made of unglamorous materials in drab colors, Reebok aerobics shoes were constructed of soft, pliable leather, and came in a rainbow of bold, fashionable colors. Reebok's Freestyle aerobics shoe was the first athletic shoe designed and marketed specifically for women, and it quickly became hugely popular. By selling its shoes to women, Reebok had opened up a new market for athletic shoe sales. This market would continue to expand as women began to wear their comfortable athletic shoes on the street, for daily life. In addition, the company both contributed to and profited from the boom in popularity of aerobics in the early 1980s, sponsoring clinics to promote the sport and its shoes.

In 1983, the year following the introduction of the shoe for aerobics, Reebok sales shot to $13 million. The company had become the beneficiary of a full-fledged fad. By the following year, sales of Reebok shoes had reached $66 million, and Reebok U.S.A. and its corporate sponsor, Pentland Industries, made arrangements to buy out Reebok International, the company's British parent, for $700,000. In addition, the company expanded its offerings to include tennis shoes, but shoes for aerobics continued to make up more than half of Reebok's sales in 1984.

By 1985 Reeboks had gained a large following of trendy young consumers, and the shoe's standing as a fashion item was solidified by the appearance on the Emmy Awards of actress Cybill Shepherd wearing a bright orange pair of Reeboks under her formal black gown. Celebrity endorsements such as this, in addition to an advertising budget of $5 million, helped to push the company's 1985 sales to more than $300 million, with profits of nearly $90 million. Fireman, Reebok's founder, set up an office in California to help the company stay on top of trends and maintain its shoe's popularity.

In July 1985 Reebok International stock was offered publicly for the first time, selling over the counter at $17 a share. By this time international sales of Reebok shoes were contributing 10% of revenues. By September the company was unable to meet the continuing high demand for its products, and was forced to restrict the number of shoes available to individual stores until it could expand production at its South Korean factories.

Consumers who were able to get their hands on a pair of Reeboks were finding that the high price tag on the shoes did not guarantee high quality, as the shoes' soft leather uppers sometimes fell apart within months, and Reebok launched an attempt to improve quality control in 1986, increasing its number of on-site factory inspectors from 7 to 27. Although the company's production reached four million pairs a month by mid-1986 there was a $400 million backlog of orders for Reebok shoes, and plans were made for further expansion of production capacity. In keeping with this gain, Reebok's advertising budget grew to $11 million, and the company began advertising on television for the first time.

Anticipating an inevitable decline in the popularity of its aerobics shoes—which contributed 42% of the company's sales in 1985—as the aerobics trend peaked and slacked off, Reebok moved to further protect its sales position in 1986 by diversifying its product offering. The company began by introducing sports clothing and accessories, limiting sales to $20 million so that growth could be controlled. In addition, the company inaugurated a line of children's athletic shoes, called Weeboks, at the end of 1986. Perhaps the most significant innovation was the introduction of a basketball shoe. In entering this market, Reebok was stepping up its competition with rival athletic shoe makers Nike and Converse, which controlled a large part of the lucrative basketball shoe market. By the end of 1986, revenues from basketball shoes totaled $72 million and made up 8.6% of Reebok's total sales.

In June 1986, Reebok was rebuffed in its first attempt to expand through the acquisition of other companies, when Stride Rite Corp. another shoe manufacturer, rejected the Reebok offer to buy it. However, Reebok was successful in its negotiations for the purchase of Rockport Company, a leading maker of walking shoes with sales of around $100 million that had gotten its start in the early 1970s. Rather than integrate the new company's operations closely with its own, Reebok maintained the separation between the two, even to the extent of allowing competition.

Later that year, the company restructured itself into three areas: footwear, apparel, and international, in an effort to better manage its growth. Sales tripled in 1986 to reach $919 million, and the company's stock began trading on the New York Stock Exchange at the end of the year.

By the start of 1987, Reebok's backlog of orders for all its lines of shoes had grown to $445 million, indicating that demand for its products continued to be strong. With Fireman, as chairman, receiving record compensation tied to the company's profits, Reebok's growth continued unabated, and the company embarked on a string of purchases of other shoe companies. In March 1987, Reebok made arrangements to buy Avia Group International, Inc., another maker of aerobic shoes, for $180 million. Following this move, the company sold $6 million worth of stock to raise money to help offset the cost of its acquisition, reducing Pentland Industries' interest in the company from 41% to 37%. The company's pace in buying other footwear manufacturers did not slow, however, as Reebok-owned Rockport acquired a boot-maker, the John A. Frye Company, in May 1987. This 125-year old company, which also marketed hand-sewn shoes, had yearly sales of about $20 million. One month later, after forming a Canadian subsidiary, Reebok Canada Inc., Reebok moved through it to purchase the ESE Sports Company, Ltd. Reebok closed out 1987 by finalizing plans to acquire the U.S. division and the U.S. and Canadian rights to the trademark of an Italian apparel company, Ellesse International S.p.A., for $25 million, a more modest version of an earlier plan to acquire the entire company.

In addition to its purchases of other shoemakers and apparel companies, Reebok continued to expand its own offerings in 1987, as part of its effort to maintain and protect its market share by providing a wide variety of products. The company introduced shoes designed specifically for walking, in hopes of establishing a presence in a field that Reebok chairman Fireman believed would be the next hot fad in fitness, and also began offering volleyball shoes and dressier styles for women. This trend continued in the next year with the introduction of shoes for golf.

In an attempt to shed its reputation as a company noted for fashion products, as opposed to serious high-performance athletic shoes, Reebok entered the fray of high-tech design innovations, an area previously dominated by its competitor Nike, with the introduction of energy return system shoes. At the end of 1987, Reebok held a quarter of the market for basketball shoes, and dominated the field in aerobics, its traditional strength, tennis shoes, and in walking shoes, its new entry.

In 1988 Reebok's long and meteoric rise began to show signs of flagging, however, as the company's historically high profit margins went into a slump. Reebok's strength in the youth market, focused primarily on basketball shoes, was shaken by a massive advertising campaign by competitor Nike, which outspent Reebok by $7 million to $1.7 million in the first quarter of 1988.

In an effort to regain lost ground, Reebok went on the offensive, publicizing its products in several ways, both usual and unusual. The company gave away shoes to young people it considered style-makers, and also renovated inner-city playgrounds. In addition, it sponsored a series of rock concerts to raise money for human rights groups, and in conjunction with this, inaugurated a Reebok Human Rights Award. Starting in August 1988, Reebok also devoted a portion of its $80 million advertising budget to an innovative and esoteric television and print campaign built around the theme, "Reeboks let U.B.U.," which featured idiosyncratic people doing bizarre things while wearing Reeboks. The campaign was a failure. By the end of 1988, earnings had fallen by one-fifth, on sales of $1.79 billion.

Trying again, the company unveiled a completely new $30 million advertising campaign, titled "The Physics Behind the Physique" half a year later, in March 1989. This push was focused on women, traditionally Reebok's strongest customer base, and connected sweaty physical exertion with sex and narcissism. These relatively rapid shifts in emphasis from performance to fashion and back again began to muddle the consumer's idea of what the company stood for, and Reebok continued to see its portion of the market slip as its sales growth waned. The company appeared to have lost its focus.

Perhaps as an expression of that blurring of purpose, Reebok underwent a period of turmoil in its administrative and executive structure during this time. In August 1989 the company's head of marketing, Mark Goldston, left after less than a year with the company, and two months later, its president, C. Joseph LaBonte, brought in by Fireman only two years earlier, resigned as well. In addition to these changes at home, Reebok moved to strengthen its foreign management team at this time.

Reebok sold its Frye boot subsidiary in 1989. It then made its only purchase outside the footwear and sportswear industries, buying a manufacturer of recreational boats, Boston Whaler, Inc. for $42 million in 1989.

Although Reebok's market share had fallen behind Nike's, to 22% by the end of 1989, the seeds of Reebok's resurgence were sown in mid-November with the introduction of "The Pump," a basketball shoe with an inflatable collar around the ankle to provide extra support. Although the expensive shoes made up only a small portion of Reebok's overall sales, the popularity of the new technology lent a sorely missed air of excitement to the company's brand name.

Reacting to its previous difficulties, and continuing challenges in both the fashion and performance shoe markets, Reebok rearranged its corporate structure at the beginning of 1990, splitting its domestic division into two areas, one focusing on performance and the other on fashion products. A month later, the company further restructured by merging its international and U.S. units into one global business. This caused the defection of Frank O'Connell, U.S. division president.

At this time there was also a shake-up in the company's marketing department, and Reebok split with its ad agency, Chiat/Day/Mojo, in an effort to regain lost market share. To do so, the company built on its recent success with The Pump technology by expanding The Pump to other lines of footwear, including aerobics, cross-training, running, tennis, walking, and children's shoes. In addition, facing a relatively mature and highly competitive U.S. market for athletic shoes, Reebok looked to foreign markets, which made up a quarter of the company's sales, for further growth. By 1990 the company's shoes were sold in 45 different countries, with the bulk of sales coming from Europe, Australia, and Japan. Overall European sales rose significantly to reach nearly $600 million in 1990, while U.S. sales of Reebok products remained flat, growing by only 2%. This pattern continued into the first quarter of 1991, as international sales grew by 86%, and growth in the recession-bound domestic market was less than 10%. Early in 1991 Reebok bought back more than 24 million of its shares from Pentland, reducing Pentland's share of Reebok to about 13%.

Heir to a corporate history of remarkable success, Reebok faces a challenging market in athletic shoes and apparel as it seeks to maintain its standing as one of the world's leading footwear companies. After an initial period of astronomical growth, followed by a slight loss of direction, the company in the early 1990s appeared strong overall, and poised for continuing progress.

Principal Subsidiaries: Highland Import Corp.; Avia Group International, Inc.; Reebok Canada Inc.; Ellesse U.S.A., Inc.; The Rockport Company; Boston Whaler, Inc.

Further Reading: Therrien, Lois, "Reeboks: How Far Can A Fad Run?" *Business Week,* February 24, 1986; Watkins, Linda M., "Reebok: Keeping a Name Hot Requires More Than Aerobics," *The Wall Street Journal,* August 21, 1986; Pereira, Joseph, "Reebok Trails Nike in Fight For Teens' Hearts and Feet," *The Wall Street Journal,* September 23, 1988; "Where Nike and Reebok Have Plenty of Running Room," *Business Week,* March 11, 1991.

—Elizabeth Rourke

SPRINGS INDUSTRIES, INC.

205 North White Street
Fort Mill, South Carolina 29716
U.S.A.
(803) 547-1500
Fax: (803) 547-3805

Public Company
Incorporated: 1887 as Fort Mill Manufacturing Company
Employees: 22,000
Sales: $1.88 billion
Stock Exchange: New York

Springs Industries, Inc. is one of the world's largest producers of home furnishings, finished fabrics, and industrial textiles. It has 44 manufacturing facilities in ten U.S. states, Belgium, and England, and a minority interest in a joint venture in Japan. Of its U.S. plants, 23 are in South Carolina. Its major brand names include Springmaid, Wamsutta, Custom Designs, Bali, Graber, Ultrasuede, and Ultraleather.

The company started in April 1887, when a group of 16 men organized Fort Mill Manufacturing Company to produce cotton cloth. The Northeast and Midwest were booming, and cotton manufacturing was seen as a way to industrialize and revive the depressed South. Samuel Elliott White, a local planter and Civil War veteran, was elected the company's first president. Among the investors was Leroy Springs, a merchant who would become White's son-in-law and a key force in the company's development. The company produced its first yard of cotton cloth in February 1888. Its first annual report, in May 1888, stated that the plant had 200 looms and was producing 8,000 yard of cloth daily.

In 1892 many of the same investors started a second plant in Fort Mill. In 1895 Leroy Springs and others established another company, Lancaster Cotton Mills, of Lancaster, South Carolina. Toward the end of the century, with the Lancaster mills flourishing, Springs acquired control of the Fort Mill plants, which were experiencing difficulties, and other troubled cotton mills in Chester, South Carolina. The Lancaster operation expanded in 1901 and again in 1913 and 1914, when it was said to be the largest cotton mill in the world under one roof. In 1914 Leroy Springs led the establishment of Kershaw Cotton Mills in Kershaw, South Carolina.

Leroy's son, Elliott White Springs, joined the company in 1919 after distinguished service as an aviator in World War I. According to the younger Springs's biographer, Burke Davis,

Leroy Springs ordered Elliott to learn the business without pay. It took Elliott Springs a while to settle into the business; several times he quit and came back. In these early years, Elliott Springs was more interested in both writing—his best-known work is *War Birds, Diary of an Unknown Aviator*—and social life than in textile manufacturing.

Leroy Springs seemed to lose interest in the business himself during the 1920s. He ran up debt and let the equipment run down; he also speculated in the stock market. In 1928 a disgruntled cotton buyer shot Leroy Springs in the head on a street in Charlotte, North Carolina. Springs recovered physically, but became emotionally withdrawn. Shortly before Leroy Springs's death in 1931, Elliott Springs took over management of the company.

At this time, the family's textile operations consisted of six plants with 5,000 employees. Elliott Springs—until then considered a playboy and a dilettante—led a dramatic revitalization of the business, which was suffering from the Great Depression as well as from Leroy Springs's neglect. He negotiated with creditors to save the mills from foreclosure, went without salary for a period, and bought used but useful machinery at bargain prices to upgrade operations. In the fall of 1933, he bought a former J.P. Stevens plant in Chester, South Carolina. Also in 1933, Springs consolidated the various mill properties into a single company, Springs Cotton Mills.

In 1934 the United Textile Workers of America attempted to organize workers at the Springs mills. Elliott Springs allowed the union to address the workers at a company-owned baseball field in Chester. After the organizers had spoken, Springs mounted the platform and told the workers that if they went on strike, he would close the plants and take his family to Europe. The workers later voted unanimously against union representation.

During the 1930s the Springs facilities had been expanded and modernized, despite the Depression. With the arrival of World War II, Elliott Springs turned over the company's entire production capacity to the military. Early in 1942 the company began manufacturing fabrics for a variety of military uses, including uniforms, tents, gas masks, and gun covers. All the Springs plants won awards from the U.S. Army and Navy for superior production.

The mills ran overtime, sometimes seven days a week, to keep up with wartime production. Elliott Springs feared this schedule would wear out the mills' machinery, so he instructed one of his plant managers to buy and store every replacement part available—an effort that paid off when the mills resumed normal operations in 1945. At the close of the war, Springs began construction of a bleaching plant and moved the company into the production of finished fabrics and consumer products, such as sheets and pillowcases. Also in 1945, the company established Springs Mills, Inc. in New York as the sales organization for its products.

The company's launch of the Springmaid brand of sheets and apparel fabrics in the late 1940s included a popular advertising campaign designed by Elliott Springs himself. Early ads included drawings of sexy, half-dressed young women and double-entendre copy. The best-remembered ad featured an American Indian brave lying exhausted in a hammock made of a sheet, with an Indian woman apparently rising from the same hammock. The caption read "A buck well spent on a Springmaid sheet." Some called the ads tasteless, but the campaign did focus attention on the Springmaid brand.

Elliott Springs remained president of the company until his death in 1959. During his tenure, the assets of Springs Cotton Mills had grown to $138.5 million from $13 million. Sales had increased more than 19-fold, to $163 million, and the work force had nearly tripled, to $13,000. The company was the seventh-largest in the U.S. textile industry, but was the most profitable. H. William Close, Elliott Springs's son-in-law, succeeded him as president. Close expanded and modernized many Springs facilities and built a new headquarters for the sales organization in New York in 1962. In 1965 the company inaugurated carpet production with a plant in York, South Carolina.

In 1966 the sales group merged with the manufacturing company, with the resulting entity named Springs Mills, Inc. The same year, the merged company went public, selling 675,000 shares at $17 each. Late that year, Springs Mills shares were listed on the New York Stock Exchange.

In 1967 Springs considered a merger with another textile firm, Collins & Aikman Corporation, but abandoned the plan because of what the companies termed "operational difficulties." In 1968 Springs formed a new division to make and market knit fabrics; indeed, the 1960s and 1970s were a time of much diversification in Springs product lines. The company made a major conversion to production of cotton-synthetic blended fabrics, which had begun to outstrip cotton in popularity—in 1969, two major facilities were converted to blend production.

Springs hired its first nonfamily president, Peter G. Scotese, in 1969, with Close moving into the newly created post of chairman, which he held until he died in 1983. Scotese had been a vice president of Federated Department Stores and, before that, a vice president of another textile company, Indian Head, Inc. During Scotese's tenure, Springs expanded via numerous acquisitions, including, early in 1970, the finished-goods division of Indian Head.

Late in 1970 the Justice Department sued Springs and four other textile makers, charging that the manufacturers conspired with wholesalers and retailers to stabilize the prices of their prime lines of sheets and pillowcases, in violation of antitrust laws. Springs agreed to a consent decree in which the company agreed not to engage in such practices, without admitting that it ever had. Fifteen years later, the Justice Department agreed to terminate the decree, citing a 1977 Supreme Court ruling that price-fixing is illegal only when intended to curb competition and legal in other circumstances.

In 1972 Springs became a partner in a joint venture to start a textile plant in Indonesia, P.T. Daralon Manufacturing Co. Early in 1973 it entered the frozen foods business, acquiring Seabrook Foods Inc. of Great Neck, New York, for about $34.5 million. In 1974 Springs sold its three terry-cloth-production plants to J.P. Stevens Inc. and discontinued operation of its carpet division at York, which had been unprofitable since its inception in 1965. Springs sold the facility to Cannon Mills Company in 1975. The Indonesian plant went into operation in 1975, but failed to generate enough revenue to maintain working capital; the unit's creditors had to defer interest

and other payments. The following year, Springs sold its interest in the venture. Springs continued updating and modernizing its plants closer to home in the late 1970s, but also got out of another unprofitable business by closing the knit division in 1978. In 1979 Springs acquired Lawtex Industries, a maker of textile home furnishing products, for $15.4 million plus the assumption of $13.5 million in liabilities, and Graber Industries, Inc., a manufacturer of blinds, shades, and other window decorating products, for $38.5 million.

Walter Y. Elisha succeeded Peter Scotese as president of Springs in 1981; like Scotese, Elisha came from the retail sector. After Close's death in 1983, Elisha became chairman of the company. In 1981 and 1982, Springs closed several Seabrook units and sold others. Also in 1982, the company adopted its present name, Springs Industries, Inc.

Springs made a major acquisition in 1985—M. Lowenstein Corporation, a New York textile maker that, like Springs, had been in business since the 19th century. The acquisition brought Springs the Wamsutta brand of household goods and an entry into the premium-priced bedding market and the industrial fabrics business through Lowenstein's Clark-Schwebel unit. The cost of the acquisition was about $265 million.

During the late 1980s Springs intensified its diversification away from the apparel-fabrics business, where foreign competition was strong. It refocused on industrial fabrics and home furnishings. In the former category, it purchased the fiberglass-weaving and -finishing operations of United Merchants & Manufacturers Inc. for about $60 million in 1988, and in the latter, it acquired Carey-McFall Corporation, a maker of window shades and blinds, for about $35 million in 1989. Springs's finished nonindustrial fabrics business declined to 26% from 52% of total sales from 1980 to 1990; about half of those sales were to U.S. apparel manufacturers.

Company officials said they would continue to serve domestic apparel markets that provided adequate returns, but predicted that growth would come from the industrial fabrics and home furnishings businesses. In 1990 provisions for restructuring of operations—such as converting or closing finished fabrics plants—resulted in Springs reporting its first loss, 39¢ per share, in its 25 years as a public company. Springs officials noted, however, that earnings before restructuring charges were $2.07 per share, reflecting strength in certain areas of the business.

Principal Subsidiaries: Graber Industries, Inc.; Clark-Schwebel Fiber Glass Corp.; Carey-McFall Corp.

Further Reading: Davis, Burke, *War Bird: The Life and Times of Elliott White Springs,* Chapel Hill, University of North Carolina Press, 1987; Andrews, Mildred Gwin, *The Men and the Mills,* Macon, Georgia, Mercer University Press, 1987; Pettus, Louise, *The Springs Story, Our First Hundred Years,* Fort Mill, South Carolina, Springs Industries, 1987.

—Trudy Ring

TEIJIN LIMITED

TEIJIN LIMITED

6-7, 1-chome, Minami Honmachi
Chuo-ku, Osaka
Japan
(06) 268-3201
Fax: (06) 268-3210

Public Company
Incorporated: 1918 as Teikoku Jinzo Kenshi Co., Ltd.
Employees: 6,511
Sales: ¥325.73 billion (US$2.61 billion)
Stock Exchanges: Tokyo Osaka Nagoya Kyoto Hiroshima Fukuoka Niigata Sapporo Hong Kong

Teijin Limited is one of the leading Japanese synthetic fiber companies, ranking second to Toray Industries, Inc. in the textile fiber industry. Textiles accounted for 64.5% of Teijin's total sales in 1990, the remainder coming from chemicals, pharmaceuticals, and other products.

Rayon yarn was produced commercially in Japan for the first time by Yonezawa Rayon Yarn Manufacturing Plant, a branch factory of Azuma Industries Ltd. Twenty-three years earlier, Count Chardonnet had established the first rayon manufacturing plant in France. The Japanese rayon industry developed rapidly despite its late start, and in 1936 attained the highest production level of rayon yarn in the world, only 22 years after it had begun commercial production. The rapid development of the Japanese rayon industry was led by Teikoku Jinzo Kenshi (Imperial Manmade Raw Silk) Company Ltd.

Naokichi Kaneko, head clerk of Suzuki Shoten Co., the second largest general trading company after Mitsui Bussan, played an important role in Teijin's establishment. Kaneko first became interested in rayon yarn in 1892. An English merchant showed him rayon yarn produced by Chardonnet's factory, demonstrating that an imitation of raw silk could be produced artificially. Kaneko established the Nihon Celluloid Jinzokenshi Kabushiki Kaisha (Japan Celluloid Rayon Yarn Co. Ltd.) jointly with Mitsubishi and Iwai Shoten in 1908, and planned to produce rayon yarn after the company had succeeded in producing celluloid. He instructed Hirotaro Nishida, the head of the engineering department, to explore possibilities for importing technology or to bring in engineers from foreign rayon manufacturing companies. Kaneko also delegated Taketaro Matsuda, former head of the Monopoly Department in the Formosa Government-General, to Europe to undertake research on celluloid and rayon yarn between June 1905 and

October 1906, and asked an engineer of the Monopoly Department to research rayon yarn when he went to Europe a little later.

Seita Kumura, a graduate of the Department of Chemicals at the Imperial Technical University of Tokyo, had been researching leather at the Taiyo Leather Manufacturing Plant, which employed 30 to 40 employees, and acquired a patent for frosted leather. Kaneko became aware of Kumura's research and established Tokyo Leather Ltd. in partnership with the owner of Taiyo Leather and Kumura in 1907. The next year this partnership was merged with Azuma Leather Co. Ltd., a subsidiary of Suzuki Shoten. Kumura became the chief engineer of Azuma Leather Co. Ltd., and began research on rayon while he continued to research and improve artificial leather production methods. Itsuzo Hata, a friend of Kumura's, became a lecturer at Yonezawa Engineering College in 1912 and dedicated himself to research on rayon yarn in close cooperation with Kumura. In 1914 Azuma Leather Co. Ltd. gave the researchers ¥1,200 to support their project. Kaneko visited Hata's laboratory the following year, was convinced of the future potential of rayon manufacturing, and decided to continue to support the research.

In October 1915 Kaneko established the Yonezawa Jinzokenshi Seizosho (Yonezawa Rayon Yarn Manufacturing Plant) as Azuma Kogyo Bunkojo, a branch factory of Azuma Leather Co. Ltd. At the end of 1915, Azuma Leather Co. Ltd. was renamed Azuma Industries Ltd. In July 1916 the plant supplied rayon yarn to Nishida Kahei Shoten, a prominent rayon yarn dealer in Japan, for the first time. However, Kahei Nishida severely criticized the yarn's quality, saying that it was no better than the foreign yarn of ten years earlier. Kumura and Hata tried to improve their yarn's quality, and the halt of imports of rayon yarn from abroad gave them a chance to acquire market share. In April 1917 they produced 100 pounds of rayon yarn per day. This was the same level at which Count Chardonnet had begun to produce rayon yarn commercially for the first time in the world. Production of rayon yarn increased steadily during World War I, and Suzuki Shoten separated the Yonezawa Rayon Yarn Manufacturing Plant from Azuma Industries Ltd. to establish Teikoku Jinzo Kenshi (Imperial Rayon Yarn) Co., Ltd., a subsidiary of Azuma Industries Ltd., whose capital amounted to ¥1 million. The executive board members consisted of persons related to Suzuki Shoten and Azuma Industries, and included Kumura and Hata.

Teikoku Jinzo Kenshi's fortunes were mixed in the early years. Many rayon yarn manufacturing companies which started up in the boom during and just after World War I went bankrupt during the Reactionary Crisis in 1920, and Teikoku Jinzo Kenshi almost went bankrupt. Its financial difficulties arose because the crisis coincided with Teikoku Jinzo Kenshi's beginning construction of a new factory in Hiroshima. Suzuki Shoten, its parent company, offered sufficient credit to enable Teikoku Jinzo Kenshi to overcome its problems and to continue the construction of the new factory. After 1923 the company entered a phase of high profits and maintained this level despite the entry into the industry of Mitsui Bussan and the three largest cotton spinning companies. Suzuki Shoten went bankrupt in the Japanese financial crisis of 1927, and Teikoku Jinzo Kenshi bore the liabilities, which amounted to ¥10 million, in place of Suzuki Shoten. Teikoku Jinzo Kenshi managed to repay the debts within four years, however, far earlier than originally scheduled, and continued to earn high profits as well. The company constructed the Iwakuni plant in 1927 and the Mihara plant in 1932. Its production volume of rayon yarn amounted to 60 million pounds in 1937, far exceeding the volume produced by Toyo Rayon Ltd., its closest competitor. By 1937, although it ranked third in the production of rayon staple, short fibers which have to be spun to make yarn, it came first in total production of rayon yarn and rayon staple. Teikoku Jinzo Kenshi was the oldest and the largest rayon producer in Japan when the Sino-Japanese War broke out.

During World War II the company's rayon production capacity decreased significantly as a result of the compulsory mergers of enterprises by the government, five of which occurred after October 1941, and the removal and destruction of equipment, the aim of which was to utilize scrapped iron as raw materials for weapons. Moreover, Teikoku Jinzo Kenshi was forced to convert to production of fuel for airplanes at the end of the war. Production of rayon staple ceased at the Mihara plant in March 1945 and production of rayon staple at the Iwakuni plant in April 1945. By the end of the war, the company was producing neither rayon yarn nor rayon staple. Immediately after World War II, the company experienced shortages of raw materials and chemicals. It produced a variety of goods such as salt, the sweeteners saccharin and dulcin, goggles, shoe cream, cosmetics, buckets, and handcarts in order to support its employees, and earned tens of millions of yen in cash by disposing of poison gas at an army plant. However, its production of rayon increased rapidly after April 1947, when the GHQ agreed that Japan could return to a rayon production capacity of 150,000 tons per year. Teikoku Jinzo Kenshi's production volume increased rapidly; rayon yarn production rose from 2.026 million pounds in 1946 to 42.5 million pounds in 1955 and rayon staple from 1.3 million pounds to 37.75 million pounds during the same period. The company began to produce rayon yarn and rayon staple at the Iwakuni and Mihara plants, and constructed the Komatsu plant in 1949 and the Nagoya plant in 1951. Moreover, it earned large profits during the Korean War boom period. Its sales amounted to ¥8.1 billion, and profits before tax were ¥3.7 billion.

After World War II, however, Teikoku Jinzo Kenshi's position in the chemical fiber industry declined. Staple production in Japan rapidly increased and in 1953 its volume surpassed 1938 levels, its previous pre- and postwar peak, whereas filament production was slow to recover and failed to reach prewar peak levels. After the war, Teikoku Jinzo Kenshi ranked first in filament production but ranked between seventh and tenth in staple production. Moreover, it lagged behind other chemical-fiber companies in entering newly developing synthetic-fiber industries. Toyo Rayon began to produce nylon and Kurashiki Rayon—known as Kuraray after 1970—produced vinylon, a synthetic fiber made from poly-vinyl-alcohol, in the early 1950s. Toyo Rayon, Teikoku Jinzo Kenshi's rival, earned high profits by succeeding in nylon production. Teikoku Jinzo Kenshi staked its existence upon importing polyester technology from Imperial Chemical Industries Ltd. (ICI) of the United Kingdom. Shinzo Ohya, a former leader of the company now active in the political world, returned to become Teikoku Jinzo Kenshi's president in 1956. Teijin succeeded in importing polyester technology from ICI jointly with Toyo Rayon, and began to produce polyester fiber at the Matsuyama plant in 1958. Its polyester fiber divi-

sion began to produce profits in the latter half of 1959, and by the latter half of 1960 contributed 82% of profits. Teikoku Jinzo Kenshi monopolized the market for polyester jointly with Toyo Rayon. It started a prize-contest for product brand names with Toyo Rayon, resulting in the name "Tetoron," which it advertised actively. Teikoku Jinzo Kenshi spent more on advertising than other companies, and in the early 1960s the company's ratio of advertisement cost to sales was higher than for any other chemical fiber producing company. Teikoku Jinzo Kenshi organized a production team in the Hokuriku district, where the largest consumers of polyester fiber were located, and assisted weavers both technically and financially. These were the main reasons for its success in the polyester business.

President Ohya developed aggressive strategies, backed by the company's good business record and the rapid growth of the Japanese economy. Teikoku Jinzo Kenshi entered other fields in the synthetic fiber industry, establishing Teijin Acrylic Ltd., which produced acrylic fiber, jointly with other two chemical companies and one wool company in 1959. Teikoku Jinzo Kenshi began to produce nylon at the Mihara plant in 1963. It thus became a general synthetic-fiber-producing company, and was renamed Teijin Ltd. in 1962. However, it withdrew from rayon staple production in 1967, from strengthened rayon yarn production in 1969, and from rayon yarn production in 1971, as they were no longer profitable. The content of Teijin's business changed significantly after 1958 when it began to produce polyester fiber. By the latter half of 1959, rayon accounted for less than half of total sales, and by the first half of 1960 synthetic fiber accounted for more than half of total sales. After that, synthetic fiber's share of sales increased rapidly to reach 75.1% in the latter half of 1973, of which polyester represented 56.6% and nylon 14.1%.

Teijin also moved upstream to the production of raw materials for synthetic fibers. In 1963 Teijin began to produce telephtalic acid, which was necessary for polyester fiber production. In 1964 it established Teijin Hercules Ltd., which produced dimethyl-telephtalate (DMT) jointly with Hercules Inc. in the United States and in 1968 established Teijin Petro Chemicals Ltd., which produced paraxylene and orthoxylene, raw materials of polyester. In 1966 it invested in Japan Soda Ltd. and participated in its management. Nisso Petro Chemical Ltd., Japan Soda's subsidiary, produced ethylene oxide and ethylene glycol. Teijin thus became able to supply its own intermediate and raw materials for polyester fiber production. In 1963 Teijin established Japan Lactam Ltd., which produced caprolactam, jointly with Sumitomo Chemicals and Kureha Chemicals.

Teijin also began an aggressive diversification strategy, establishing a Future Business Department in 1968 and setting up many subsidiary companies in the fields of pharmaceuticals, construction materials, foods, cosmetics, and leisure. It also established an Oil Development Department in 1970 and began to develop oil resources in Iran, Nigeria, and the Straits of Malacca. Its investment in and loans to related companies increased rapidly from ¥30.6 billion at the end of March 1968 to ¥169.1 billion at the end of March 1978. On the eve of the first oil crisis in 1973, oil development and future businesses constituted two of Teijin's three main pillars—the third was textiles, its traditional business.

Under Ohya's guidance, Teijin began active expansion abroad. In 1961 it established a joint venture with a local company in Sri Lanka and subsequently entered Formosa, Korea, Thailand, Vietnam, the Philippines, Brazil, and Australia. In 1973 its foreign subsidiaries consisted of 5 in textiles and yarn manufacturing and 14 in spinning, weaving, dyeing, and printing. Teijin planned to increase its overseas production of polyester textiles and yarn to more than three times the level of 1973, to exceed domestic production within five years. However, the plan was not realized.

After the first oil shock, Teijin's business performance deteriorated and its operating profits were in the red for the first time at the first half of 1977. President Ohya circulated a memorandum entitled "A State of Emergency" to all directors of departments. He ordered them to reduce manufacturing costs drastically, develop high value-added merchandise, improve non-profitable businesses, decrease administrative costs at headquarters, and develop new businesses in textiles-related fields. He emphasized the importance of adaptability if the company was to keep ahead in the 1980s. Teijin reduced its number of employees drastically, from 10,346 at the end of 1977 to 7,446 at the end of 1978, and thoroughly reexamined its related companies, including those overseas. Investment and loans in related companies decreased from ¥169 billion at the end of 1978 to ¥120 billion at the end of 1983, and its ratio to the amount of total assets decreased from 38.6% to 26.8% during this period. Teijin retreated from the oil development and polyester businesses in Spain and Brazil and from many other fields.

The liquidation of non-profitable businesses almost came to an end in 1982 and profits before tax increased from ¥11.8 billion in 1982 to ¥18.5–¥28.5 billion in 1983–1987 and to ¥31.9–¥37.6 billion in 1988–1990. In 1982 polyester continued to occupy the most important position in terms of sales. Polyester film was the most profitable item among chemicals, with various uses such as photograph films; magnetic tape for VTR, audio, and computer; and wrapping materials. Especially in the field of base film for magnetic tape, Teijin shared a monopoly with Toray. Its sales structure changed somewhat in 1990, and polyester's and nylon's share of sales decreased to 51.1% and 10.1% respectively, with pharmaceuticals accounting for 12.3%. Chemicals' share remained almost stable, accounting for 23.3% of sales. Teijin established Teijin Medi-

cine Manufacturing Ltd. in 1978 as a 100%-owned subsidiary and amalgamated it in 1983. Gamma-globulin was the most successful product of its Medicine Manufacturing Department. Non-fiber products contributed more than half of Teijin's net profits as polyester film and pharmaceuticals were far more profitable than textiles.

According to Teijin's long-term management plan, launched in 1989, the company aims to raise annual sales to ¥500 billion (from ¥310 billion in 1988) and also to raise recurring profits to ¥55 billion (from ¥35.5 billion in 1988) within the coming five or ten years. As for its business fields, it plans to expand its chemicals, pharmaceuticals, and medical equipment divisions and its compound materials division, which combines new fibers with other materials such as metals for strengthening, as the three main pillars of its business besides textiles. Teijin also plans to invest ¥25 billion per year in plant and equipment and to develop its Medicine Department to enable it to compete with specialized pharmaceuticals companies and capable of ranking among the top ten companies in this industry. It will invest aggressively in the Iwakuni plant to establish facilities to produce pharmaceuticals from raw materials to finished products. Having started as a rayon manufacturing company and became a synthetic fiber manufacturing company, Teijin now aims to become a general chemical company focusing on high-technology textiles and compound chemical materials.

Principal Subsidiaries: P.T. Teijin Indonesia Fiber Corporation (65.8%); Teijin Kakoshi; Teijin Kasei (66%); Teijin Associa; Teijin Engineering; Teijin Shoji (94.7%); Teijin Memory Media; Sankyo Keori; Teijin Butsuryu; Kokka Sangyo (58.2%); Teijin Cordley; Teijin Wow; Teijin Finance; Teijin Shokusan; Teijin Reizo (73.9%); Union Tire Code (65%); Teijin System Technology; Teijin Sagamihara Film; Kure Kogyo; Kitasen; Teisan Seiyaku (95.6%).

Further Reading: Yamazaki, Hiroaki, *Nihon Kasensangyo Hattatsushi Ron*, Tokyo, University of Tokyo Press, 1975; Teijin Limited, *Teijin no Ayumi*, vols. 1–11, Tokyo, Teijin Ltd., 1968–1977.

—Hiroaki Yamazaki

'TORAY'

TORAY INDUSTRIES, INC.

2-1 Marunouchi 2-chome
Nihonbashi, Chuo-ku
Tokyo
Japan
(03) 3245-5111
Fax: (03) 3245-5555

Public Company
Incorporated: 1926 as Toyo Rayon Company Ltd.
Employees: 10,047
Sales: ¥585.43 billion (US$4.69 billion)
Stock Exchanges: Tokyo Osaka Nagoya Kyoto Hiroshima Fukuoka Niigata Sapporo London Luxembourg Frankfurt Düsseldorf Paris

Toray Industries, Inc.'s main fields of operations are general materials, consisting of textiles and compound materials; advanced end products, consisting of pharmaceuticals, medical equipment and electronics; and services relating to fashion and information. The company is focusing on pharmaceuticals, medical equipment, and electronics as businesses that will support its growth in the medium to long term, investing more than 5% of sales in research and development.

Toray began as a fiber manufacturer. In the first half of the 1920s, two large rayon manufacturing companies—Teikoku Jinzo Kenshi Ltd. (Teikoku Jinken) and Asahi Kenshoku Ltd.—and two smaller companies occupied almost half of the Japanese rayon market, with the other half filled by imported products, mostly from Britain. Courtaulds Limited was the largest British supplier, and the Japanese trading house Mitsui Bussan Ltd. had been an exclusive agent for Courtaulds since 1919.

Rayon yarn was a substitute for raw silk, one of the most important goods Mitsui Bussan handled at that time. Mitsui Bussan was very interested in the future potential of rayon yarn and became aware of Courtaulds's good business record. In addition, the Japanese government was planning a tariff revision, and a rise in the import tariff for rayon yarn was anticipated. In 1923 Mitsui Bussan began to examine the world rayon industry with a view to importing technology, but attempts to contract licensing with Courtaulds and Du Pont were unsuccessful. In 1925 a director of Mitsui Bussan in London reported to headquarters that Mitsui Bussan should buy equipment from a rayon machine manufacturer that would send chemical and machine engineers to Japan. Mitsui Bussan decided to adopt this method of importing technology and estab-

lished Toyo Rayon Company Ltd. (Toyo Rayon) in 1926. A wholly owned subsidiary, its capital amounted to ¥10 million. In August 1927 Toyo Rayon began to produce rayon yarn at its Shiga plant. Mitsui Bussan asked the German company Oskar Kohorn & Company to establish the plant, teach Toyo Rayon employees to operate the equipment, and send engineers and skilled workers to Mitsui Bussan. Moreover, Mitsui Bussan sent a chemical engineer, who had carried out research on viscose at the University of Tokyo and had joined Mitsui Bussan, to Oskar Kohorn & Co. in order to learn the technology on the shop floor.

Toyo Rayon made profits in the first half of 1928 but retained all the profit inside the company until the latter half of 1931. Toyo Rayon began to pay dividends in the first half of 1932 and from 1933 to 1935 its profits grew rapidly. The profit to sales ratio amounted to about 20% during this period. Toyo Rayon thus became one of Japan's largest rayon manufacturing companies, next to Teikoku Jinken, by the outbreak of the Sino-Japanese War.

During World War II, Toyo Rayon's rayon production capacity decreased significantly as a result of mergers in the rayon industry, which occurred five times at the insistence of the government after October 1941, and as a result of the removal and destruction of equipment, to allow scrapped iron to be used as raw material for weapons. Toyo Rayon's rayon filament production decreased from a peak of 18,200 tons in 1937 to only 345 tons in 1945, and its rayon staple production from a peak of 12,422 tons in 1941 to 1,840 tons in 1945. After 1943 the company was forced to convert to wartime production. Part of the Shiga plant produced torpedoes and torpedo heads for the Japanese Navy, and part of the Aichi plant produced tanks for airplanes. Toyo Rayon established Sanyo Yushi (Oils and Fats) Ltd. as a joint venture with Mitsui Bussan and produced a high-grade lubricating oil for airplanes. It bought the Rakuto plant from Kyoto Sarashi Senko, which bleached and dyed textiles, mainly silks, and named it Yamashina Denki Kojo (Electric Machinery Plant). This plant produced electric and communication machinery for the Japanese Navy.

Nevertheless, Toyo Rayon developed a new product during this period that would be responsible for much of World War II. Asahiko Karashima, a president of Toyo Rayon, realized the importance of innovation in the industry and thought that Toyo Rayon should enter the field of new textiles. When Du Pont succeeded in the development of nylon 66 in 1938, he ordered branches of Mitsui Bussan in the United States to collect information on nylon and to send it, together with samples of nylon stockings, to Toyo Rayon's research institute in Japan. In 1939 Toyo Rayon succeeded in analyzing and synthesizing nylon 66 and in spinning it into yarn in both dry and molten form. It also succeeded in developing nylon 6 independently and in spinning multifilament yarn from nylon in 1941. Toyo Rayon established experimental equipment for industrial use that produced 10 kilograms of nylon per day by the end of 1942 and sold its product, named Amilan, as fishing yarn. This plant too was converted to wartime production. Toyo Rayon produced nylon chips in the plant and supplied them to the navy as raw material for electrical insulation in airplanes.

After World War II, war production stopped and employees who had been enlisted in the army returned to the company. Materials and chemicals for rayon production were in short supply, however, and, restoration of equipment was forbidden immediately after the war by the Allied powers. Toyo Rayon therefore had to undertake conversion work of wartime production facilities for civilian industries other than the rayon industry. It conducted many kinds of business, including manufacturing and repairing railroad passenger and freight wagons, and pot motors and spinning pumps for rayon manufacture. It also produced penicillin, and made ice, salt, and fertilizers and insecticides, utilizing byproducts of nylon production for the latter.

Toyo Rayon's rayon production increased rapidly after the General Headquarters of the Allied Powers permitted Japan to raise its rayon production capacity to 150,000 tons per year on April 4, 1947. Its production volume of rayon yarn increased rapidly from 570 tons in 1946 to 17,305 tons in 1957, and its production of rayon staple, fibers which are spun to make yarn, rose from 1,159 tons in 1946 to 28,560 tons in 1956. The level of rayon yarn production in 1957, the company's postwar peak, was a little lower than the peak level before and during the war, 18,200 tons, while the production level for rayon staple in 1953 already surpassed its 1942 wartime peak of 12,422 tons. The rayon staple production level in 1956, a postwar peak, was more than twice as high as the 1942 level. Profitability was high during this period of recovery, particularly during the Korean War boom period. These profits enabled Toyo Rayon to begin nylon production.

Toyo Rayon planned to change from equipment that produced 1.05 tons of nylon resin, a raw material of rayon yarn, and 0.06 tons of nylon filament for fishing line per day, to equipment which produced one ton of nylon filament per day in the Shiga plant in June 1949, and it established a new plan to construct both equipment which produced five tons of nylon filament per day and equipment which produced caprolactam, a raw material of nylon, corresponding to the volume of nylon in October 1949. This plan was launched in response to the government's promotion of a synthetic fiber industry in Japan, and came into effect in 1949. Needless to say, Toyo Rayon's experience of nylon production during World War II enabled it to respond actively to government policy. It was, however, necessary for Toyo Rayon to tie up with Du Pont, which had a nylon patent network all over the world. Shigeki Tashiro, who had become the president of Toyo Rayon in 1945 but had retired because of the Allied powers' purging of leading Japanese industrialists and had later negotiated with the Allied occupation authorities as a spokesman for the Japanese chemical fiber industry, pointed out to Toyo Rayon's management that Toyo Rayon risked accusations of infringing Du Pont's patent rights if the Japanese company exported nylon products in the future. He advised Toyo Rayon to tie up with Du Pont in order to avoid such a possibility. Toyo Rayon's production method differed from Du Pont's as the Allies knew, but Tashiro's fears were based on the fact that Du Pont had a worldwide patent network not only for the nylon production method but for nylon and nylon product manufacturing equipment. In autumn 1948 Toyo Rayon approached a representative of Du Pont's Far East Section to enquire about the possibility of importing nylon production technology, but received no response.

Toyo Rayon had to import the necessary technology in time for the implementation of a full-scale industrial production plan for nylon in the latter half of 1949. Tashiro therefore asked a manager of Mitsui Bussan's New York branch, where Tashiro himself had once worked, to contact Du Pont. This time, Du Pont replied, demanding that Toyo Rayon pay 3% of nylon sales as a royalty for use of the patent for 15 years, with $3 million payable in advance. This sum was equivalent to ¥108 billion, which far exceeded Toyo Rayon's capital, ¥759 million yen at that time. Tashiro had become chairman of Toyo Rayon's board of directors in March 1950 and was very much surprised by Du Pont's terms at first, but calculated that if the advance payment became ¥500 million yen per year, Toyo Rayon could pay it in two years without great difficulty. He succeeded in persuading Du Pont to agree to these conditions. The technology import contract for nylon was formally signed in June 1951.

At first Toyo Rayon experienced difficulties in its nylon business, even after it had overcome the problems of the nylon production process, as it had no experience in spinning, weaving, knitting, dyeing, or printing nylon. However, these problems were largely resolved by 1953. Toyo Rayon monopolized the nylon market until Nihon Rayon began full operation of its nylon production facilities in December 1956. Even after that, the Japanese nylon industry consisted of only two companies until 1963 when a few latecomers entered the industry. At first, nylon was mainly used for fishing nets, but its uses were extended to women's blouses, knitted underwear, seamless stockings, and tire-cord for use in car tires. In 1959, Toyo Rayon organized spinners, knitters, weavers, dyers, and printers into production teams, and also organized manufacturers of secondary products, trading companies, and wholesalers into sales teams, assisting them technically and financially. In 1951 it organized retailers who stocked clothing made from Toyo Rayon's nylon into the Toray Circle, assisting their research in shop management, educating employees about Toray products, advertisement of new merchandise, and the display of goods. Toyo Rayon's nylon business was highly profitable, and its profits exceeded the combined profits of the other six Japanese chemical fiber manufacturing companies between the first half of 1958 and the first half of 1962—at that time the company adopted the half-yearly accounting system.

In January 1957 Toyo Rayon imported polyester production technology from the United Kingdom's Imperial Chemical Industries (I.C.I.) together with rival company Teikoku Jinken, a pioneer in the Japanese chemical fiber industry. I.C.I. sold Toyo Rayon and Teikoku Jinken the exclusive rights to use its patent in Japan, in return for £1.15 million payable in advance by installments. Until September 16, 1968 5.25% of sales was payable for production less than 10 million pounds (lb) per year, and 3% of sales for production that surpassed 10 million lb per year in the case of products other than photograph films. Toyo Rayon and Teikoku Jinken monopolized the polyester market until 1964, when several latecomers entered the market. Toyo Rayon started a prize-contest for product brand names jointly with Teikoku Jinken, which resulted in the name of "Tetoron" for polyester fiber. The two companies advertised Tetoron jointly. Previous experience in dealing with synthetic fibers and in joint technology import and successful joint marketing with Teikoku Jinken enabled Toyo Rayon to minimize difficulties in starting up its Tetoron business. Tetoron made a significant contribution to Toyo Rayon's profits during this period.

In September 1958 Toyo Rayon established a pilot plant for acrylic fibers at its central research institute and constructed equipment which produced 3 tons of acrylic fibers per day at its Nagoya plant. In 1954 it constructed equipment which produced 15 tons of acrylic fibers at the Ehime plant. Acrylic fibers found a market in sweaters, undershirts, stockings, and fabrics. Toyo Rayon's acrylic fiber production was based on its own technology. In the middle of the 1960s the company grew to become the third largest general synthetic fiber manufacturer in the world, next to Du Pont and Monsanto Chemical Co. in the United States.

Rayon was the most important product in terms of sales up to 1954, when it contributed 54.7% and nylon contributed 45.2%. In 1955 nylon sales surpassed those of rayon, contributing 60.0% while rayon contributed 40%. In 1960 Tetoron sales surpassed rayon sales when nylon contributed 57.3% of sales, Tetoron 24.3%, and rayon 18.5%. Tetoron sales surpassed nylon and became Toyo Rayon's largest-selling product in 1965, when Tetoron's share was 43.8%, nylon's 43.6%, and rayon's only 2.3%, with Toraylon (an acrylic fiber)'s share at 4.3%, plastics' at 4.1%, and Piren (a polypropylene textile)'s at 2.0%. In 1973, when the first oil crisis occurred, Toray's sales breakdown was as follows: Tetoron 39.5%, nylon 27.9%, plastics 10.9%, Toraylon 8.5%, rayon 0.9% and others 2.4%. In the first half of 1973, Toray still ranked first in terms of profit after tax among the seven Japanese chemical fiber manufacturing companies, although the difference in profits diminished between Toray and Teijin (as Teikoku Jinken became known in 1962), which ranked second. Tetoron sales grew faster than nylon, and competition, especially in the nylon and Tetoron businesses, intensified after latecomers entered these industries aggressively. These factors caused Toray's comparative decline in the synthetic fiber industry, especially in comparison with Teijin.

Toray made several important changes in the 1960s and 1970s. Firstly, it ceased rayon production, withdrawing from rayon yarn production in 1963 and decreasing the scale of its rayon staple production from 102.6 tons to 40 tons per day in 1968. Rayon staple was used for mixed spinning with Tetoron. Toray ceased rayon staple production in May 1975.

Secondly, Toyo Rayon resumed production of raw materials for synthetic fibers. In 1969 it established the Kawasaki plant which produced 135,000 tons of cyclohexane, a raw material for nylon; 73,000 tons of paraxylene, and 100,000 tons of orthoxylene—the raw materials for polyester—per year. It cooperated with Nihon Sekiyu Kagaku (Japan Petro-Chemical Ltd.), which produced BTX (benzene, toluene, and xylene) from naphtha and supplied it to Toyo Rayon. Toyo Rayon in turn produced raw materials for nylon and Tetoron from BTX. In 1971 Toray established the Tokai branch factory of the Nagoya plant, which produced 125 tons of lactam and 50 tons of terephthalic acid—the raw materials for nylon and Tetoron— per day. In 1970, it established a joint venture with Mitsui Toatsu Kagaku Ltd., named Toyo Chemics, which produced acrylonitrile. Toray thus established a system whereby it could supply its own raw materials for the three major synthetic fibers it produced, and moved toward becoming a general chemical manufacturing company.

Thirdly, it developed new high value-added products and diversified into the non-textile field. In the former category, it established in April 1971 a department to explore possible ventures outside the textiles industry, and successfully marketed an artificial suede named Ecsaine and a carbon fiber

named Torayca in 1970 and 1971 respectively. In the non-textiles field Toray established a plastics department, and nylon resin, polyester film, ABS resin, and polypropylene film sold well. In particular, Toray's polyester film became popular for use in magnetic tape for tape recorders, chips for Fuji Shashin Film Ltd. (photographic film), and wrapping materials. In January 1970 Toyo Rayon renamed itself Toray Industries, Inc., as a result of these changes.

After the 1973 oil crisis, Toray's business performance deteriorated and its operating profits fell into the red for the second half of 1974, and at its financial year end in 1975 and 1977. Toray endeavored to rationalize production, and reduced its work force from 19,108 in 1975 to 10,000 after 1987. It continued to develop and sell new high value-added products outside the textile fields. The ratio of non-textiles to total sales increased from 22.4% in 1975 to 44.7% in 1990. Among non-textiles, the ratio of chemicals, including plastics, increased from 20% to 34.1% and the ratio of new businesses and others not elsewhere classified, including carbon fiber, increased from 2.4% to 10.6% during the same period. It also reexamined investment in and loans to related companies, and the ratio of investment and loans to total assets decreased from 26.1% in 1977 to around 20% after 1986. As a result of these efforts, Toray's post-tax profits to sales ratio returned to almost the same level as during Japan's rapid economic growth period from 1966 to 1974.

Toray's global network includes nearly 60 overseas subsidiaries and affiliates, notably in Southeast Asia, where its first overseas fiber production facilities were established, and in the United States, where Toray Plastics (America), Inc. (TPA) produces polyester and polypropylene films. In France, Toray received the active support of the French government when it formed Société des Fibres de Carbone S.A. for the transfer of PAN-based carbon fiber technology to France. In April 1991 Toray formulated a long-term business plan: to increase its consolidated sales to ¥2 trillion by the year 2000 and to become a general chemicals group.

Principal Subsidiaries: Toray Monofilament; Toyo Tire Cord; Ogaki Boseki (98.24%); Toyo Seisen; Marusa (61.85%); Toray Textile; Inami Textile; Ichimura Sangyo (85%); Maruwa Orimono; Toray Ireeve; Toray Kimono Hanmbai; Doray Diplo-mode; Sun-rich Mode (66.67%); Toray PEF Products; Toyo Plastic Seiko (66.67%); Toyo Metallizing (66.67%); Toray Gosei Film; Toray Thiokol (85%); Showa Kogyo; Toray Living (86.8%); Toray Kensetsu; Toray Engineering (99.9%); Toray Precision; Toray Medical; Eastern Viva; Toray Enterprise; Toray Research Center; Toyo Unyu; Toray System Center; Toray Sports Center; Toray International; P.T. Indonesia Toray Synthetics (64.65%); Penfibre Sdn. Berhad (Malaysia); Penfabric Sdn. Berhad (Malaysia); Woodard Textile Mills Sdn. Berhad (Malaysia); Pentley Sdn. Berhad (Malaysia); Pentex Sdn. Berhad (Malaysia); TAL Knits Limited (Hong Kong, 70%); Taltex Limited (Hong Kong); Taltex (Singapore) Pte. Ltd. (Singapore); Nan Sing Dyeing Works Ltd. (Hong Kong); Union Fabric Ltd. (Hong Kong); P.T. Easterntex (Indonesia, 80%); P.T. Acryl Textile Mills (Indonesia, 57.5%); Toray Textiles Europe Ltd. (U.K.); Toray Plastics (Malaysia) Sdn. Berhad (Malaysia); Toray Plastics (America), Inc. (U.S.A.); Filk S.A. (France, 70%); Société des Fibres de Carbone S.A. (France); Toray Industries (Singapore) Pt. Ltd. (Singapore);

Toray Industries (H.K.) Ltd. (Hong Kong); Toray Europe Ltd. (U.K.); Toray Industries (America), Inc. (U.S.A.).

Further Reading: Yamazaki, Hiroaki, *Nihon Kasensangyo Hattatsushi Ron*, Tokyo, University of Tokyo Press, 1975; Toray Industries, Inc., *Toray 50 Nenshi 1926–1976*, Tokyo, Toray Industries, 1977.

—Hiroaki Yamazaki

UNITIKA LTD.

Osaka Headquarters
1-3, Kyutaro-cho 4-chome, Chuo-ku
Osaka 541
Japan
(06) 281 5712
Fax: (06) 281 5563

Incorporated: 1889 as Amagasaki Spinners Ltd.
Employees: 5,596
Sales: ¥350.19 billion (US$2.81 billion)
Stock Exchanges: Tokyo Osaka

Unitika is one of the half dozen or so giants that dominate the Japanese natural and synthetic fibers industry. A characteristic of these companies over the last two decades has been their rapid diversification into non-fiber operations, and Unitika's activities now embrace construction and housing, pollution prevention, and plastics and glass fiber development.

Unitika was created in 1969 out of the merger of the Nichibo and Nippon Rayon companies. Until 1964 the former was known as the Dainippon Spinning Company, which formed, along with Toyobo and Kanegafuchi, the dominant triumvirate in Japan's interwar spinning industry. Dainippon itself emerged at the end of World War I out of the amalgamation of five separate concerns initiated by Amagasaki Spinners Ltd., and it is this last company which is therefore regarded as the founder of the present company.

Cotton-spinning was the chosen vehicle for Japan's industrialization in the last quarter of the 19th century, remaining until World War II the nation's most important single industry and the spearhead of its successful attempt to create a modern industrialized economy capable of competing with those of the West. Although spinning mills had existed in Japan since the 1860s, it is generally agreed that it was the establishment in 1882 of the famous Osaka Spinning Company which began the spectacular growth of Japan's indigenous cotton-spinning industry.

The Osaka mill was both sufficiently large-scale and powerful—driven by steam, and with 10,000 spindles—to be able to compete with the mills of Britain and the United States, and its success set a pattern for mill development in the ensuing two decades. The reorganization of the nation's capital in the 1880s and the emergence of a powerful merchant-banking class, especially in the Osaka area, were the other necessary ingredients for the expansion of the industry. Among the numerous spinning companies established in this period was Amagasaki Spinners Ltd., set up in 1889 in Hyogo province by a group of Osaka merchants and bankers.

By 1895 the company was ranked as one of the dozen largest spinning concerns in the country, with over 27,000 spindles. During this decade the company discarded mule frames in favor of the more efficient ring frames to enhance its productive capacity of coarse-grade cotton yarn. Amagasaki's factory workers were typical of those of the cotton-spinning industry of the day—young women recruited from the provinces who lived in the company's own dormitories. Their relative docility and—by Western standards—meager pay helped provide the company with a distinct cost advantage over foreign competitors. However, the extremely rapid expansion of the industry produced severe shortages of skilled labor and led to the phenomenon of labor piracy among competing firms. In order to combat this, the industry set up the Japan Cotton Spinners' Association in 1882, and this body remained for the next 50 years the governing body of the industry as a whole and the vehicle for governmental intervention in it. The Association's effectiveness in the latter respect was soon displayed when over-production in the final years of the 1890s led to an enforced cut-back in production, the first of many such cut-backs to affect the spinning industry in the decades to come.

By the early years of the 20th century, the industry had become characterized by an excessive number of competing companies. Although the Sino-Japanese War of 1895-1896, the Russo-Japanese War of 1904-1905, and especially World War I stimulated the industry by opening up new opportunities in China, Korea, and Formosa, it was clear that rationalization was necessary. A series of mergers was initiated in the industry, in which Amagasaki figured prominently. The company absorbed the Toyo Textile Company in 1908, the Tokyo Spinning Company in 1914, the Nihon Spinning Company in 1916, and finally in 1918 the Settu Spinning Company. The new giant composite, now with mills all over the country, was named the Dainippon Spinning Company. The merger process appears to have had the effect of bringing to an end what one industry historian, S. Yonekawa, has called "a period of trial and error" in the company's management and operational spheres.

The financial crisis of 1920 affected Dainippon severely but the management cooperated with the other large spinning firms in a far-sighted policy of using financial reserves built up in the profitable war years to avert a total breakdown in the yarn and fiber markets. From this experience Dainippon learned the importance of guarding itself against price fluctuations in raw cotton, and during the 1920s and 1930s adopted a number of measures—such as "hedge-selling," whereby the company sold raw cotton on a cotton exchange in amounts equal to cotton holdings to offset any losses on the purchases—to lessen such risks. Dainippon further protected itself from the notorious vagaries of the cotton market by diversifying into synthetic fiber production, and to this end set up the Nippon Rayon Company in 1926.

As a result of the amalgamation process of the previous decade, Dainippon in the 1920s had a somewhat complex management structure composed of departments based on its various products. A modern divisional system did not emerge until after 1945. Dainippon was, however, notable for its innovative work on production processes. A company engineer,

Kasuo Imamura, who had joined the new Dainippon after the absorption of the Settu Spinning Company in 1918, developed the new, efficient ECO-type high-draft spindle which was to become the most favored type of spindle in the industry as a whole. Dainippon was quick to take advantage of Toyota's revolutionary automatic looms after 1926 to increase efficiency in production and thereby enable it to reduce the size of its work force. The company's Sekigahara plant was the first in the country to employ the more efficient unit drive, whereby each unit had its own power source, for all of its operations in 1932. Innovations such as these enabled Dainippon to maintain its position in the inter-war decades as one of the industry's leading operations despite such setbacks as the enforcement in 1929 of the Revised Factory Law (1923) which ended the profitable all-night work system known as "midnight labor," and the great Depression which followed, during which the company had to discharge half of its labor force.

In the mid-1930s the Japanese textile industry replaced that of Britain as world leader. The threat from Japan was felt to be so grave that protectionist measures were taken by Britain and its Empire and by the United States against the Japanese, severely affecting export-dependent companies such as Dainippon. The position of the firm and of the industry as a whole was further aggravated in the second half of the decade when the imposition of sanctions against Japan by the Western democracies checked the supply of raw cotton from India and the United States, thereby forcing reductions in cotton-yarn production. The year 1937 saw the first government-imposed controls on prices, and for the next eight years virtually every aspect of the company's operations came under increasing governmental scrutiny and control. During 1940–1941 the spinning industry was reorganized into 14 so-called units in an attempt to place it on a strengthened war-footing. Dainippon managed to remain intact, constituting one of the 14 units. A further series of amalgamations took place in 1943, culminating in the emergence of a grouping known as the "Big Ten" spinners, but again Dainippon emerged unscathed as one of the Ten. For the industry the war years were harsh ones, bringing government-imposed ceiling prices, the rationing of increasingly scant supplies of raw cotton, the turning over of mills to munitions production, and their subjection to Allied aerial attack in the latter stages of the conflict. By the time of Japan's surrender in 1945, the industry was a shadow of its former self.

After the surrender, Dainippon found itself subject to the ordinances of the Supreme Commander for the Allied Powers (SCAP), some of which were designed to force the break-up of large multi-product firms such as Dainippon by stripping away their non-spinning activities. Fortunately for Dainippon and the other members of the "Big Ten", SCAP revised these plans. In 1949 the industry was allowed to return to private trade, although SCAP maintained a close supervisory control in some areas—for example, production controls were not lifted until 1951.

With the return of Japanese sovereignty, the Ministry of Trade and Industry (MITI) embarked on a series of plans to resuscitate the industry, deciding that textile manufacturing should shift its emphasis from cotton to synthetic and chemical products in view of the latter's greater foreign earnings potential. Thus it was that this decade saw Dainippon and the other majors expand their synthetic yarn production.

The Korean War gave the Japanese economy a very significant boost, stimulating recovery in the fibers industry as in many others. From the mid-1950s, Dainippon and the other majors entered upon a 15-year period of high growth. Symptomatic of the company's restored fortunes was its 1965 establishment of Nippon Ester Co., Ltd. in a joint venture.

However, the 1969–1972 Japan-U.S. textile negotiations, and even more the oil shock which followed in 1973, brought an abrupt end to this prosperity. Steep rises in raw materials, labor, and fuel costs, plus growing competition from the newly industrializing countries of Northeast and Southeast Asia, combined to present a serious threat to Unitika's competitiveness abroad and its home market in Japan. Dainippon had renamed itself Nichibo in 1964 and Unitika in 1969 on the merging of the Nichibo and Nippon Rayon Companies.

The recession forced Unitika to close down two of its cotton staple mills in 1975 and reduce synthetic fiber production. In the same year the company announced plans to work in concert with Toyobo (Toyo Boseki Kaisha) and Kanebo (Kanegafuchi Boseki Kaisha) to help pull the industry out of the recession. The one bright spot was polyester filament, for the production of which Unitika received permission to open a plant at Sabae in a joint venture with Kanebo.

Nevertheless it was clear the company had to diversify away from fibers production, and from this period dates the company's movement into non-fiber activities. However, the fruit of this diversification was at least a decade away, and in the later years of the decade the company experienced a continued decline in the profitability of its business. Consequently it withdrew in 1977 from a joint cotton-spinning venture in Singapore. In the next year it was the first of the industry's large firms to cut its work force by making 650 employees redundant—declining profitability meant there was little to invest in increasing productive capacity, so cost-reduction by this method was the company's chosen response to the recession. Further measures to bolster the fiber business were the voluntary production cutbacks in which the company took part in the late 1970s and early to mid-1980s, designed to raise low product prices, and mutual inter-company mill inspections to enforce the cutbacks.

Unitika saw that if it was to survive it had to develop new value-added high-technology products. An example of this kind of development was the commercialization in 1979 of a special type of nylon filament designed to reduce static electricity in work garments. The company also embarked on the internationalization of its operations by involvement in technology licensing agreements and a new round of joint ventures abroad, in Hong Kong, Italy, and the United States.

In 1981, in a further bid to improve production efficiency in the fibers business, Unitika announced plans to replace some 1,000 of its looms with 400 of the most up-to-date machines. Two years later the company joined with seven other leading firms in forming a Research and Development Association to speed up and reduce the cost of development of more efficient production methods. One project was the design of a new cotton-spinning machine up to 17 times as productive as existing models.

These and other moves could not prevent the post-1985 rise in the value of the yen causing further decline in the profitability of the important export sector. In 1986 Unitika announced plans to shed some 800 employees in an effort to reduce the size of its work force by the end of the decade. The impact of a strong yen on export competitiveness again underlined the necessity of rapidly expanding the non-fibers business—in 1991 amounting to about 33% of total sales—while simultaneously concentrating on the equally rapid development and commercialization of high-value high-technology products in the mainstay yarns sector. Unitika's future fortunes rest on the success with which the company manages to achieve these dual objectives.

Principal Subsidiaries: Unitika Chemical Co., Ltd. (70%); Unitika Tsusho Ltd.; Unitika U.M. Glass Co., Ltd.; Unitika Estate Co., Ltd; Unitika Sanko Co., Ltd. (98%); Unitika Building Co., Ltd.; Unitika Berkshire Co., Ltd; Sakai Shoji Co., Ltd. (95%); Unitika Service Co., Ltd; Akoh Kasei Co., Ltd. (70%).

—D. H. O'Leary

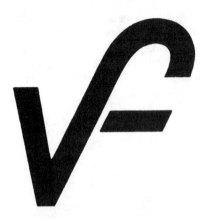

VF CORPORATION

1047 North Park Road
Wyomissing, Pennsylvania 19610
U.S.A.
(215) 378-1151
Fax: (215) 375-9371

Public Company
Incorporated: 1899 as Reading Glove & Mitten Manufacturing
    Company
Employees: 45,100
Sales: $2.61 billion
Stock Exchanges: New York Pacific

VF Corporation, one of the world's largest publicly owned fashion apparel manufacturers, designs and produces jeans, sportswear, intimate apparel, and occupational clothing for both the U.S. and international markets. The company consists of several operating units, each of which is responsible for a different set of product lines. The Lee Company, the firm's largest unit, and Blue Bell, Inc. manufacture denim and other casual apparel for adults and children under the Lee, Wrangler, and Rustler brand names. Bassett-Walker Inc. specializes in activewear, such as sweatshirts, jogging suits, and jackets. Jantzen Inc. manufactures the company's line of swimwear and related sportswear, while the Red Kap division markets a variety of apparel for industrial use. Vanity Fair Mills, Inc., produces lingerie and loungewear items under the Vanity Fair brand name.

The company was formed in 1899 in Reading, Pennsylvania, by a group of six men, including two hosiery manufacturing executives and a banker, John Barbey. They selected the name Reading Glove & Mitten Manufacturing Company for their new venture, and began producing gloves of both knitted materials and silk.

After more than ten years of slow growth, John Barbey purchased the interests of his partners in the company in 1911 and changed its name to Schuylkill Silk Mills. His son, J. E. Barbey, joined the firm as its general manager the following year. In 1914 the company expanded into the manufacture of silk lingerie. After three years of successful sales, the Barbeys decided to conduct a contest to determine the brand name for the lingerie line. The winner received a $25 prize for the name "Vanity Fair."

To establish a national reputation for the company's merchandise, the Barbeys launched an extensive advertising campaign that emphasized the superior quality and style of Vanity Fair lingerie. This direct-to-the consumer approach was considered innovative for its time since most lingerie was of mediocre quality and was sold without brand names primarily through jobbers.

The company changed its name in 1919 to Vanity Fair Silk Mills, Inc. By the early 1920s and driven by the continuing success of its lingerie product line, Vanity Fair discontinued its glove manufacturing operation to devote itself exclusively to the lingerie business. In 1937 it moved its manufacturing operation from Reading to Monroeville, Alabama.

J. E. Barbey assumed the presidency of the company upon his father's death in 1939, and held that position until he died in 1956. In 1941 the company began using rayon in its lingerie manufacturing process because of an embargo on silk during World War II. Throughout the rest of the 1940s, Vanity Fair perfected the use of other new types of lingerie fabrics and subsequently introduced products made from a nylon tricot material in 1948.

This innovation changed the course of the lingerie industry. Nylon tricot was considered to be an ideal lingerie fabric due to its strength, wearing power, elasticity, and easy-care features. It also enabled the company to produce lingerie with a variety of fashionable features and in popular colors. As a result, Vanity Fair became the first lingerie manufacturer to receive the Coty Award for Design, in 1950.

Vanity Fair achieved steady growth through its production of lingerie and foundation garments throughout the next decade. In 1969 it expanded into the robe and loungewear market, a move that helped offset softness in lingerie sales during this period.

Vanity Fair made several acquisitions in 1969, including H. D. Lee, a manufacturer of men's and boys' jeans and casual pants, and Berkshire International, a hosiery manufacturer. H. D. Lee was established in the midwestern United States in 1860 as H. D. Lee Mercantile Company, a wholesaler. In the early 1900s, the firm began selling overalls, which it obtained from an eastern U.S. supplier. Because deliveries were often unreliable, Lee began manufacturing its own overalls, jackets, and dungarees in a factory in Salina, Kansas. It also introduced the Lee Union-All, a garment designed to protect an entire suit or uniform. The Union-All became the official doughboy fatigue uniform during World War I.

Beginning in the 1920s, Lee launched a series of innovative fabrics and apparel, including heavy-duty denim and Lee Rider cowboy pants. In the 1940s, Lee improved its cowboy pants with a tighter fit and the Tighter Rider brand became the best fitting cowboy pants available.

In 1943 Lee Mercantile changed its name to the H. D. Lee Company, Inc. It established its International Division in 1959 and was rewarded a Presidential "E" citation in 1964 for making an outstanding contribution to the export expansion program of the United States.

Founded as Berkshire Knitting Mills, Berkshire International traced its roots back to the early 1900s when it was a manufacturer of cotton stockings. The company's production process applied paraffin wax to the cotton thread to give the woven stockings the luster of silk. Berkshire developed into the world's largest manufacturer of women's hosiery, thanks to the popularity of motion pictures featuring beautiful actresses in short skirts and stockings, as well as the outbreak of World War I, which fueled domestic production.

To reflect its expansion into these new areas, the name of the parent company was changed from Vanity Fair to VF Corporation in 1969. A new subsidiary was formed under the Vanity Fair name for the intimate apparel business. In 1971 VF acquired Kay Windsor, Inc., a manufacturer of budget-priced, ready-to-wear women's dresses and sportswear. This business encountered difficulties during the 1970s due to the growing popularity of women's pantsuits and was discontinued in 1982.

In 1979 VF established an International Division to manage its growing operations overseas. This area had grown from the initial export of Vanity Fair intimate apparel to Europe and the Far East to include several manufacturing and sales facilities acquired from Berkshire International and Lee Company. At the same time, several of the company's other Berkshire operations were sold or converted to jeans manufacturing facilities. This process continued throughout the rest of the 1970s and over the next two decades.

VF entered the 1980s as a more profitable producer than either of the other two major jeans makers, Levi Strauss and Blue Bell, Inc., in a jeans market experiencing diminished demand. This growth was attributed to less dependence on foreign markets; earnings from other areas, such as lingerie; million-dollar-investments in capital improvements; and tighter inventory controls. The company also benefited from Levi Strauss's decision to expand the distribution of its products to mass-merchandise outlets. Independent retailers that had previously carried the Levi's brand angrily responded to this development by stocking the Lee brand instead.

In 1982 Lawrence Pugh joined the company as president and became chairman the following year. Robert Gregory, the president of the Lee division, succeeded Pugh as president of the corporation. In an effort to inject new life into the sluggish jeans market, Pugh and Gregory embarked upon a marketing strategy to set Lee apart from other jeans industry leaders by segmenting production into men's and women's lines. VF became one of the first producers to manufacture stretch jeans for women and dressier, more expensive jeans, competing with the designer lines that had become popular. It developed the Ms. Lee brand, which became the best-selling line of women's jeans in the United States. The company also segmented and upgraded its Vanity Fair lingerie lines with more fashionable items to appeal to younger women. In addition to introducing new products, Pugh increased spending for advertising, expanded the company's retail distribution channels, and increased the size of the VF sales force.

In 1984 continuing to diversify, VF acquired Modern Globe, Inc., a manufacturer of men's and women's cotton undergarments. Modern Globe dated back to 1917. VF also purchased Troutman Industries, Inc., a manufacturer of men's casual slacks that was subsequently closed in 1986, and Bassett-Walker, Inc., a producer of fleece activewear.

Bassett-Walker was started in 1936 as the Bassett Knitting Corporation. In 1941, after a reorganization, the company was named Bassett-Walker Knitting Company. Led first by S. S. (Sam) Walker and then by his son, Dudley Walker, after Sam's death in 1960, the firm became one of the largest manufacturers of knitted outerwear in the United States. It assumed the name Bassett-Walker, Inc. in 1980.

In 1986 VF became the United States's largest apparel manufacturer and domestic jeans supplier through its acquisition of Blue Bell Holding Company, maker of Wrangler jeans. Blue Bell was founded under the name of the Jellico Clothing Manufacturing Company in 1916. Three years later, after a move from Jellico, Tennessee, to a larger plant in Middlesboro, Kentucky, the firm changed its name to the Big Ben Manufacturing Company. It merged with the Blue Bell Overall Company of Greensboro, North Carolina, in 1926 and operated under this name until 1936 when it became the Blue Bell-Globe Manufacturing Company to reflect its subsequent merger with the Globe Superior Corporation. In 1943 the name was shortened to Blue Bell, Inc.

Blue Bell was a major manufacturer of work clothes, and after acquiring H.D. Bob Company in 1940 and Casey Jones in 1943, Blue Bell began manufacturing garments needed by the military in World War II. After the war, the company applied production methods used in making military garments to the manufacture of casual clothing and western-style wear. In 1947, the brand name Wrangler was developed for this rapidly growing product line.

VF's friendly purchase of Blue Bell was viewed as an ideal marriage between two companies with similar manufacturing cultures. It offered VF an opportunity to expand more deeply into menswear and to broaden its distribution capabilities beyond existing specialty and department store channels into mass merchants and discounters. This acquisition followed an unfriendly takeover attempt of Blue Bell by buyout specialist Carl Icahn. Blue Bell averted that takeover through a leveraged buyout that took the company private. When VF acquired Blue Bell, it purchased not only the Wrangler product line, but also the Rustler jeans product line, Jantzen and JanSport swimwear and sportswear, Red Kap occupational apparel, and licenses to the Marithé and François Girbaud upscale sportswear collections.

Jantzen Inc. was established in 1910 as the Portland Knitting Company, a combination retail store and knitting operation. The company originally manufactured heavy sweaters, woolen hosiery, and other knit goods. In 1913, the firm began producing rib-stitched, wool swimsuits. Renamed Jantzen Knitting Mills in 1918, the company successfully sold swimwear during the 1920s in both the United States and overseas. With swimwear as its primary product, Jantzen broadened its product line to include sweaters, foundations, and casual sportswear. Jantzen became part of Blue Bell in 1980.

Red Kap was formed in 1923 as a wholesaler of bib overalls. During its first ten years of operation, the company expanded into the production of chambray shirts and industrial work pants. During the 1960s, the firm added coveralls to its product line. It became a division of Blue Bell, Inc. in 1964. During the 1970s, Red Kap added a line of career apparel under the Wrangler Uniforms label. This was followed by the introduction of the Big Ben brand of retail work clothes in the early 1980s.

By 1989 declining jeans sales finally caught up to VF. In the past, whenever one division's sales had slowed, VF had managed to survive the slump by relying on strong sales in its other divisions. This time, however, the company paid the price for an error in marketing strategy it had made three years earlier. At that time, management had decided to sell its main brand of Lee jeans to mass merchandisers, in addition to its department and specialty store customers, to boost sales volume. This decision alienated department store buyers who had been selling the same line at higher prices. They refused to carry the Lee line due to the lower-quality image it now possessed. This strategy also threw VF into a marketplace already dominated by low-cost importers with widely recognized brand names and large consumer advertising budgets. The Lee division traditionally had not given retail stores significant advertising support and found itself at a sizable disadvantage. As a result, both sales and profits in the jeans area fell significantly.

Compounding the company's problems was the growing popularity of a new line of casual men's apparel called Dockers, which had recently been introduced by competitor Levi Strauss. The Dockers brand cut severely into VF's sales of jeans. VF had not changed its basic Lee Rider style and had been so involved in rejuvenating its jeans business that it had neglected to notice that other jeans manufacturers had expanded into different trouser lines that took advantage of new apparel trends.

In 1990 VF purchased the Vassarette brand and Form-O-Uth manufacturing operations for intimate apparel from Munsingwear. This was followed, one year later, by the acquisition of Health-tex Inc. a leading manufacturer of children's wear. Health-tex had been formed in 1921 as the Standard Romper Company, Inc. to produce and market children's clothing. It changed its brand name in 1937 to Health-tex, although Standard Romper remained the corporate name until 1971. In 1973, Health-tex was acquired by Chesebrough-Pond's Inc., a marketer of consumer products. Health-tex was sold in 1985 in a leveraged buyout to a group of investors who subsequently sold the firm to VF six years later.

In the early 1990s, VF was responding to consumer research results by returning to basic jeans manufacture, particularly for its primary market segment of women aged 25 to 44. It is working toward strengthening relationships with its retailers through increased advertising and merchandising support. In other areas, such as its sportswear and activewear busi-

nesses, VF is improving manufacturing efficiencies and restructuring operations to achieve better financial performance. Its intimate and occupational apparel lines continue to show healthy sales. VF International serves more than 150 countries with the company's jeanswear products and expects significant growth to occur with the creation of the single European market in 1992, as well as in the North American market.

Despite this positive outlook, VF Corporation faces a mature market for its denim jeans business, which will require major strategic initiatives to sustain growth in the future. The company is focusing on a combination of new product development, cost reduction, and inventory management measures to strengthen relationships with retailers and enable the firm to respond more effectively to market needs. VF's goal is to provide the right styles and quantities of products at the right prices on the retail shelf at all times. The company's ability to meet this goal will be a key determinant in the success of VF's future activities as it strives to maintain its leadership position, build market share, and increase shareholder value.

Principal Subsidiaries: Bassett-Walker Inc.; JanSport Incorporated; Jantzen Inc.; The Lee Company; Modern Globe Inc.; Red Kap; VF International; Vanity Fair; Wrangler; Health-tex Inc.

Further Reading: Eklund, Christopher S., and Christine Dugas, "Lee + Wrangler + Rustler = A New Blue-Jeans King." *Business Week,* August 11, 1986; Agins, Teri, "Bottom Line: Once-Hot Lee Jeans Lost Their Allure In a Hipper Market," *The Wall Street Journal,* March 7, 1991; "People, Product, Pride . . . The History and Heritage of VF Corporation and Its Divisions," VF corporate typescript [1991].

—Sandy Schusteff

TOBACCO

American Brands, Inc.
Gallaher Limited
Imasco Limited
Japan Tobacco Incorporated
Philip Morris Companies Inc.
RJR Nabisco Holdings Corp.
Rothmans International p.l.c.
Tabacalera, S.A.
Universal Corporation

AMERICAN BRANDS, INC.

1700 East Putnam Avenue
Old Greenwich, Connecticut 06870
U.S.A.
(203) 698-5000
Fax: (203) 698-0706

Public Company
Incorporated: 1904 as The American Tobacco Company
Employees: 23,000
Sales: $13.78 billion
Stock Exchanges: New York Amsterdam Antwerp Basel
    Brussels Düsseldorf Frankfurt Geneva London Paris
    Tokyo Zürich

Once the dominant tobacco company in the world, American Brands, Inc. is a widely diversified conglomerate still dependent on tobacco for the bulk of its income. With interests in everything from computer accessories to life insurance, American has skillfully shifted its activities away from the embattled domestic tobacco market, which faces increasing health concerns and decreasing consumption. Domestic tobacco nevertheless remains an extremely profitable business, and American continues to derive about 30% of its earnings from the lucrative U.S. market.

American Brands traces its origin to the remarkable career of James Buchanan (Buck) Duke, founder of The American Tobacco Company. Duke was born in 1856 on a small farm outside Durham, North Carolina, where his father, Washington Duke, raised crops and livestock. The Duke farm was ravaged by armies of both North and South at the end of the Civil War, and upon his release from a military prison Washington Duke found that his sole remaining asset was a small barn full of bright leaf tobacco. Bright leaf, so called because of its golden color, had only recently been introduced, but its smooth smoking characteristics were already making it a favorite, and its fame was soon spread by the returning soldiers. Duke set out to peddle what leaf he had, and, pleased with the response, he quickly converted his land to tobacco culture, selling his wares under the name Pro Bono Publico, meaning "for the public good" in Latin. In its first year of operation, W. Duke & Sons sold 15,000 pounds of tobacco and netted a very handsome $5,000.

Along with his father, his brother Benjamin, and half-brother Brodie, Buck Duke labored to make the family business succeed, working long hours from childhood and learning every aspect of the tobacco business from crop to smoke. Duke's timing was fortuitous—bright leaf tobacco became the most prized of all U.S. varieties, and Durham was the epicenter of bright leaf country. By far the best-known brand of bright leaf was Bull Durham, the label of William T. Blackwell & Company. Blackwell gained a long lead on the rest of the Durham tobacco merchants, including the Dukes, who did not establish their first true factory in Durham until 1873. The Dukes chose to concentrate their energies on the manufacture and sale of tobacco rather than on raising the crop, which was notoriously erratic in quality and quantity. Buying their leaf from local farmers, the Dukes would cure and then shred or compress the tobacco to form, respectively, smoking or chewing tobacco. As cigarettes were yet hardly known, tobacco smoking was accomplished with a pipe or in cigars, the latter not being made by the Dukes.

Buck Duke attended a business school for six months in 1874, when he was 18, and became an increasingly dominant figure in the family business. Intensely ambitious, single-minded, and aggressive, Duke had no interest in anything less than mastery of the tobacco business. In 1878 Buck, Washington, and Ben Duke formed a partnership with businessman George Watts of Baltimore, Maryland, each contributing equally to the capital base of $70,000. Richard H. Wright joined the partnership two years later. The company was profitable and expanding, but Buck Duke was dissatisfied with its role in second place to Blackwell's Bull Durham, and in 1881 he decided to enter the new and relatively small field of cigarettes. At the time, there were only four major producers of cigarettes in the United States, and none of them had yet understood the potential importance of mechanized rolling machines and widespread advertising. Duke appreciated the power of both, and set out to catch the four leaders.

Duke located and leased two of the new automatic rollers invented by James Bonsack of Virginia, who agreed to give Duke a permanent discount in exchange for taking a chance on the untested machines. After some adjustments, the machine proved capable of rolling about 200 cigarettes per minute, or 50 times the production of the best hand-rollers. Duke next revamped his packaging, devising the slide and shell box to offer better protection against crushing; and he then marketed his Duke of Durham cigarettes at ten for 5¢, or half of the usual price. This combination of excellent bright leaf tobacco, smart packaging, and discount price was an immediate success, and to these tangible virtues Duke soon added the intangible power of advertising. He very early recognized that advertising would determine success in the cigarette business, and throughout the 1880s spent unprecedented amounts of money on promotional gimmicks of every stripe, much to the astonishment, ridicule, and—later—regret of his rivals.

While Richard Wright handled marketing overseas and Edward F. Small built up the western U.S. trade, Duke himself decided in 1884 to meet his competitors head on in New York City, the largest market and manufacturing center of the cigarette business. He moved to the city, established a local factory, and commenced an all-out war against the four leading companies—Allen & Ginter, Kinney Brothers, and Goodwin, all of New York City, and Kimball of Rochester, New York. The Big Four sold 80% of the nation's 409 million cigarettes in 1880; after a few years of Duke's relentless campaign, the total market had swollen to 2.2 billion, and W. Duke & Sons owned 38% of it. The Duke name appeared on billboards, storefront windows, and the sides of barns around the country, as well as on some 380,000 chairs Duke distributed free of charge to tobacconists, and by 1889 company sales reached $4.25 million and net income one-tenth of that. Duke had grown to dominance of the cigarette business in a single decade, and was shortly to duplicate the feat worldwide.

Though triumphant, Duke was faced with the prospect of continuing bitter competition and restricted profits. The 32-year-old veteran thereupon proposed a solution that was startling in scope: to merge all five of the competitors, and by joining forces bring to an end the wasteful price warfare. His fellow manufacturers at first balked at the initiative, but they eventually agreed and in January 1890 formed The American Tobacco Company, its $25 million in capital divided among ten incorporators, with J. B. Duke named president. The new company, one of the first true combinations in the history of U.S. business, controlled 80% of the nation's cigarette business and showed a net profit of $3 million in its first year.

While American Tobacco was a large concern, it was by no means the entire tobacco industry, and having once captured the cigarette business Duke set to work on the rest of the tobacco world. In 1891 American bought out 80% of the relatively minor snuff business; and four years later Duke launched what has come to be known as the "plug wars." Between 1895 and 1898 American Tobacco waged a prolonged struggle to enter the field of plug, or chewing, tobacco, the largest of the various tobacco markets. With this move Duke made clear the extent of his ambitions, and a number of the original American Tobacco incorporators saw fit to sell their stock rather than join him in what they saw as a foolhardy battle against superior odds. Duke's ambition proved to be realistic, however, and after three short years of price wars and buyouts he had secured more than 60% of the vast plug market, including such later giants as Lorillard, Liggett & Meyers, and Drummond. Duke's methods in doing so were much like those he used in the snuff, smoking tobacco, and cigar segments of the industry. Selective price wars were followed by acquisitions, followed by the return of prices to a more profitable and unchallenged level. Many of these practices were in violation of the Sherman Antitrust Act, one of whose more spectacular victims would later be J. B. Duke. For a long time the extent of American Tobacco's holdings was not obvious, as many of Duke's 250 acquisitions managed to maintain secrecy about their new affiliation; and neither Congress nor the executive branch of government became interested in taking on the combinations until the first decade of the next century.

At the conclusion of the plug wars in 1898, Duke united his various plug companies into a new holding company called Continental Tobacco Company, most of whose stock was in turn owned by American Tobacco. In 1901 American Tobacco bought itself the largest share of the cigar industry, which however frustrated all efforts at monopoly due to the difficulty and variety of cigar manufacture; and in the same year American Tobacco acquired a controlling interest in what would become the dominant retailer of tobacco in the country, United Cigar Stores Company. Having thus finished off nearly the entire domestic tobacco industry, Duke tightened his grip on his family of holdings, in 1901 forming and retaining the largest shareholding in Consolidated Tobacco Company, which in turn bought up the assets of the former American and Continental companies in a transaction that netted him a tidy profit while also providing more direct corporate control. Finally, Duke began to expand internationally. After a nationwide price war in England against a coalition of the leading British tobacco men, the two sides agreed not to compete in each others' countries and to pursue jointly the rest of the world's markets through a company called British-American Tobacco Company, two-thirds of which was won by James Duke and his allies. Even at this early date the overseas retail trade was significant, British-American soon employing some 25,000 salesmen in Asia alone, all of them working under Duke's director of foreign sales, James A. Thomas.

Duke's control of United Cigar Stores' more than 500 outlets gave the public a clearer picture of the extent of Duke's domain, and his company soon faced rising criticism and opposition, some of it violent. Those in both the industry and the public had reason to dislike Duke and his cartel; Kentucky tobacco growers, for example, their prices repeatedly lowered by the single large buyer in town, banded together in 1906 to burn down a number of the trust's large tobacco warehouses. More serious was the increasing pressure brought to bear by the U.S. Department of Justice, which took heart under the administration of President Theodore Roosevelt and began a series of antitrust actions against the industrial combines. In 1907 the department filed suit against Duke's creation, now once again called American Tobacco Company, and in 1911 the Supreme Court agreed that the trust must be dissolved to restore competition to the tobacco industry. Total corporate assets were estimated at more than $500 million.

From the complex dissolution of American Tobacco, designed and overseen by James Duke himself, came the elements of the modern tobacco industry. Spun off as new corporate entities were Liggett & Meyers, Lorillard, R.J. Reynolds, and a new, smaller American Tobacco Company. Each of these four except Reynolds was given assets in all phases of the tobacco business, and Reynolds, the youngest and most aggressive of the companies, soon acquired what it lacked. Control of British-American Tobacco was lost to the British, where it has remained. Duke turned over direction of American Tobacco to Percival S. Hill, one of his veteran lieutenants, and himself went with British-American as chairman and one of its directors. The founder retained large holdings of stock in each of the newly formed spin-offs, and upon his death left a great deal of money to the eponymous Duke University and a score of other charitable causes.

At the time of dissolution, the tobacco industry still exhibited two characteristics soon to be swept aside by modern advertising and changing tastes. The business continued to be dominated by chewing tobacco, and it featured a plethora of brands. In 1903, for example, no fewer than 12,600 brands of chewing tobacco were listed by an industry catalog, along with 2,124 types of cigarettes. In 1913 Joshua Reynolds, founder of R.J. Reynolds, introduced the era of nationally known cigarette brands with his new Camel, a blend of bright leaf and sweet burley tobacco that took the country by storm. Camel was probably the most successful cigarette ever launched, and in 1916 American Tobacco answered with Lucky Strike, while Liggett & Meyers pushed its Chesterfield, and together the blitz of advertising caused an enormous upsurge in national consumption, from 25 billion cigarettes in 1916 to 53 billion three years later. By 1923 cigarettes had passed chewing tobacco as America's favorite form of nicotine, an evolution helped immeasurably by the growing acceptance of women smokers, for whom the cigarette was the only fashionable smoke.

Under the leadership of Percival Hill and, after 1926, his son George Washington Hill, American Tobacco battled Reynolds for decades in the race for cigarette dominance. Each of the Big Four manufacturers settled on one or, at most, a few brands and spent inordinate amounts of money on advertising in both print and radio formats. The Great Depression years were not as bad for the tobacco companies as they were for many industries; but consumption in 1940 was nevertheless no higher than it had been ten years before, Lucky Strike sales hovering at around 40 billion cigarettes annually. World War II and its attendant anxieties provided an instant sales boost, however, pushing Lucky Strike totals to 60 billion by 1945 and 100 billion a few years later. American Tobacco also found a winner in Pall Mall, which ushered in the "king size," 85-millimeter, era in 1939 and was soon challenging Lucky Strike and Camel for the top spot. So complete was the triumph of the cigarette that when American Tobacco's sales reached $764 million in 1946, fully 95% of it was generated by cigarettes.

The immediate postwar years were good for American Tobacco, which upped its overall share of the domestic tobacco market to 32.6% in 1953; but that would prove to be the high-water mark for the company's cigarette business. The year before, R.J. Reynolds introduced Winston, the first filtered cigarette, and inaugurated the trend toward lighter and less-harmful smokes. American Tobacco replied with its Herbert Tareyton Filters in 1954, but with both Lucky and Pall Mall among the top three sellers overall it felt no urgency about the filter business and did not spend the money and effort needed to establish its brands in the new category. This failure would be crucial in determining the subsequent development of American Tobacco, which never did catch up to its competitors and eventually assumed a minor role in the cigarette world. While Reynolds and later Philip Morris reaped fortunes with Winston and Marlboro, American Tobacco belatedly pushed losers such as Hit Parade, a cigarette so unpopular that the company was reportedly unable to give away free samples.

In the long run, however, American Tobacco's relative failure in cigarettes may have been a blessing. Beginning in the mid-1960s, the company used the steady cash flow from its remaining tobacco business to make a number of promising acquisitions. Chief among these were Gallaher Limited, one of the United Kingdom's largest tobacco companies; James B. Beam Distilling Company; Sunshine Biscuits; Duffy-Mott; and several makers of office products. In recognition of the company's changing profile it was renamed American Brands

in 1969, by which date its share of the domestic tobacco market had slipped to 20% and continued to decline. After a handful of other minor acquisitions, American Brands made its largest purchase in 1979, buying The Franklin Life Insurance Company, the tenth-largest life insurer in the United States. By that time nontobacco assets were generating one-third of American Brand's operating income of $364 million, and the company's diversification program was generally regarded as a modest success.

American Brands, however, was weakest in the most lucrative of its markets, domestic tobacco. The increasing stigma attached to tobacco sales and the threat of government restrictions have ensured immense profits for those few companies still in the U.S. tobacco business, as no new potential competitors are both willing and able to venture into such troubled waters. Even as the cigarette makers diversify, therefore, domestic tobacco continues to pay up to 35% on every sales dollar, providing cash needed to diversify further out of tobacco. In domestic tobacco, American Brands' share of the market eventually fell to the neighborhood of 10%. The $1.6 billion in sales generated there in 1990, however, returned more operating income than did the company's $6.4 billion in overseas tobacco business, where margins are much tighter, and equaled the return of all of the nontobacco divisions taken together.

American Brands fought off a takeover bid by E-II Holdings in the late 1980s, and significantly strengthened its position in liquor and office products. Its liquor division is the United States' third-largest seller of spirits, its office-products division is billed as the world's largest, and Gallaher Limited had grown into the leading U.K. tobacco company, far outstripping its parent company's tobacco sales. Earnings growth had been steady for years at American Brands, whose balanced revenue structure renders the company relatively immune to sudden downturns in any one area.

Principal Subsidiaries: ACCO World Corporation; Acushnet Company; The American Tobacco Company; Jim Beam Brands Company; The Franklin Life Insurance Company; Gallaher Limited (U.K.); Golden Belt Manufacturing Company; Master-Brand Industries, Inc.

Further Reading: Winkler, John K., *Tobacco Tycoon: The Story of James Buchanan Duke,* New York, Random House, 1942; *"Sold American!"—The First Fifty Years,* New York, The American Tobacco Company, 1954.

—Jonathan Martin

GALLAHER LIMITED

GALLAHER LIMITED

Members Hill, Brooklands Road
Weybridge, Surrey
KT13 OQU
United Kingdom
(0932) 859777
Fax: (0932) 849119

Wholly Owned Subsidiary of American Brands, Inc.
Incorporated: 1896
Employees: 28,000
Sales: £4.73 billion (US$8.84 billion)

Gallaher Limited is an international company whose interests include tobacco, distilled spirits, optical services and products, retail distribution, and housewares. Its employees are spread throughout the world, with the majority in the United Kingdom. It is a wholly owned subsidiary of American Brands, Inc., of Old Greenwich, Connecticut, in the United States. American Brands is itself a diversified group of companies and its core businesses are in tobacco, distilled spirits, life insurance, office products, hardware, and home improvement products.

Gallaher was founded by Tom Gallaher, who by 1857 had started his own business in Londonderry, making and selling pipe tobaccos. Within sixteen years he had prospered enough to move to larger premises in Belfast. Toward the end of the 1870s, Tom Gallaher crossed the Atlantic for the first time in order to supervise personally the buying of his leaf. He visited Kentucky, North Carolina, Virginia, and Missouri; the trip soon became an annual event, and Gallaher a notable figure in the trade on both sides of the Atlantic.

Smoking fashions in Britain had been undergoing a change that corresponded in its development with Gallaher's working life, and it was one which he was astute enough to exploit. During the first half of the 19th century, the pipe had gradually given way in popularity to the cigar. The military were largely credited with this, as British soldiers returning from the Crimea campaign of 1854–1856 introduced an item they had adopted from their French and Turkish allies—the cigarette. Tobacco manufacturers began to cater to this change in tastes, Tom Gallaher among them. By 1888 he was producing flake tobaccos and cigarettes, which, included in the full range of Gallaher products, were displayed at the Irish exhibition in London during that same year, which also saw the opening of Gallaher's first London premises, just inside the famous

"square mile" of the City, at 60 Holborn Viaduct. The first London factory was opened in the following year at Clerkenwell Road to increase production and in 1896 the Belfast factory moved into larger quarters. An important development two years later was the discovery of yellow and white burley leaf. Gallaher started to use it immediately, and in 1908 completed a transaction unique in the history of the industry by purchasing the entire Irish tobacco crop.

The social history of smoking in the late Victorian and Edwardian ages was marked by the triumph of the cigarette. Hitherto, tobacco manufacturers had employed manual labor to make up cigarettes as required, but soon cigarette-making machinery speeded production and in turn satisfied the rising demand. It became acceptable for women to smoke and new types of cigarettes were devised to meet that market. By the outbreak of World War I in 1914, the cigarette had established its dominance over all other forms of smoking; it was considered vital to the welfare and morale of the armed forces and a valuable means of exchange. Production increased hugely, and Tom Gallaher was the master of a thriving business when he died in 1927 at the age of 87. He had maintained an active interest in the company until the time of his death, and had achieved great civic respectability as a governor of the Royal Victoria Hospital in Belfast. He was also credited with being the first person in the tobacco industry to introduce a 47-hour working week and annual paid holiday. Smoking, and cigarette smoking in particular, enjoyed a continuous popularity throughout the 1930s and 1940s. The anxieties of World War II were a further stimulus to tobacco consumption. In the 1950s, however, evidence was produced that linked smoking to lung cancer and heart disease, and suggested that long-term cigarette smokers might be more susceptible to lung cancer than pipe or cigar users, or nonsmokers. This seems to have done no harm to Gallaher Limited, which was looking to expand in 1955 and succeeded in acquiring the U.K. and Irish interests of the prestigious Benson & Hedges company.

Benson & Hedges had enjoyed parallel development and success to Gallaher Limited, though in more elevated style. Richard Benson and William Hedges began their business at 13, Old Bond Street, in 1873. Their choice of address was a shrewd one, for the area was beginning to enjoy favor—as it still does—with a stratum of society plentifully leisured and funded. Moreover, Benson & Hedges shared number 13 to great advantage with Truefitt's, the court hairdresser. While women had their coiffure attended to, men passed the time by investigating the new tobacco shop. Benson & Hedges notably departed from the custom of dispensing tobacco by weight. Their tobacco was prepared as a blend or mixture and packed in a sealed tin. This assured the customer that his goods would reach him in the freshest possible condition, and that they had not been tampered with. The business also benefited from the patronage of the *bon vivant* Prince of Wales, later King Edward VII, who asked Benson & Hedges to prepare and make into cigarettes a parcel of Egyptian tobacco leaf that he had acquired. This they did, and adapted the style to market "Cairo Citadel," one of the first Egyptian-type cigarettes to be made in Britain. Edward's princely appetites were a blessing to the tobacco industry. It was he who introduced the habit of smoking while the port went round, and so fond was he of tobacco, that he went so far as to resign from White's club when the committee refused to accommodate its use. When smoking became popular with women during Edward's reign, Benson & Hedges produced variations of the cigarette designed to appeal to women, tipped with rose leaves or violets for example, or on a miniature scale. Increasing demand led to the establishment of a separate factory, although the shop remained in Old Bond Street. During World War II the shop was bombed and practically destroyed, but was rebuilt with the return of peace. When Benson & Hedges joined Gallaher, it brought not only its best-selling cigarettes, but also its Royal Warrant—bestowed first by Queen Victoria "to purvey cigarettes and cigars for use in her household," and renewed by subsequent monarchs.

In 1962 Gallaher acquired J. Wix and Sons Ltd. of London, the makers of Kensitas, a well-known cigarette. The vendor was The American Tobacco Company, which made the transaction in exchange for 13% of Gallaher's shares. By 1968 American Tobacco had increased its holdings in Gallaher shares to 67%. American Tobacco had been of late a relative failure in its native tobacco market, but was now using a steady cash flow wisely to buy and diversify. In 1969, in recognition of its changing profile, it was renamed American Brands, Inc. Meanwhile, Gallaher itself began to broaden its scope. A substantial acquisition in 1970 was the Dollond & Aitchison Group. Its main specialty is the supply of optical services and advice, spectacles, contact lenses, and accessories, with an extensive branch network throughout the United Kingdom. There is also a small opthalmic instruments manufacturing and distributing operation, Keeler Limited. Gallaher continued this phase by making its first foray into retail distribution. In 1971 it established Marshell Group, a retail franchise operation that sells mainly tobacco products and confectionery through concessions within major retail stores across the United Kingdom. In the early 1990s the concessions numbered around 635, and the company also had over 50 of its own retail outlets. Two similar acquisitions followed in 1973. The TM Group, previously Mayfair, is a company operating vending machines that dispense cigarettes, drinks, and snacks in licensed and industrial catering outlets—perhaps its best known manifestation in the United Kingdom is the ubiquitous Vendepac machine. Forbuoys Plc is a chain of shops selling tobacco, confectionery, newspapers, and magazines, again with branches throughout the United Kingdom. Dollond & Aitchison's expansion overseas began in 1974 with the acquisition of the Italian company Salmoiraghi Vigano, which added the retailing of optical and medical instruments to the group's interests. In February 1975 American Brands finally controlled 100% of Gallaher's shares. Under the present arrangement, the chairman and chief executive of Gallaher Limited, A.D. Househam, sits on the board of American Brands, while American Brands has nonexecutive directors on the Gallaher board.

Gallaher continued to make acquisitions. In 1984 it acquired Prestige Group plc. Under this brand name, the company produces stainless steel cookware, pressure cookers, bakeware, and kitchen tools and accessories. Under the Ewbank brand, it also markets carpet sweepers. Established in 1937, Prestige is the leading nonelectrical housewares manufacturer in the United Kingdom. While the company was adversely affected by the recession at the beginning of the 1990s, major investment was made in its production facilities, which are centered at Burnley, Lancashire, to enable it to exploit its brand leadership position

when market conditions improve. Meanwhile in 1984 Dollond & Aitchison opened the first fast-service optical department store in Europe at Yardley near Birmingham, England, and further Eyeland Express stores have followed since then.

Since its inception, Gallaher has maintained considerable plant in Northern Ireland, and is now one of the largest manufacturing employers there. There is a warehouse complex for tobacco leaf at Connswater, East Belfast, and a sales distribution center on the outskirts of the city. Production takes place at Lisnafillan, near Ballymena, County Antrim, in a modern, factory complex handling cigarettes, pipe tobacco, and handrolling tobacco. Also at Lisnafillan is the company's research and development division. This is a particularly vital establishment as Gallaher is much exercised to keep its position as market leader in low-tar cigarettes. In 1988, along with other companies in Northern Ireland, Gallaher was approached by the former Fair Employment Agency for Northern Ireland, which sought cooperation in a study to ascertain to what degree equality of opportunity was being afforded to Protestants and Roman Catholics. The agency had been advised of Gallaher's long-standing interest in the question, and the report concluded: "The efforts made by the company and the local Trade Union officials to introduce locally meaningful equal opportunity measures are positive and encouraging and the Agency is satisfied that the action taken is indicative of real commitment to provide equality of opportunity."

Gallaher also operates in the Republic of Ireland, where it is the second largest tobacco company. Cigarettes, pipe tobacco, and hand-rolling tobacco are manufactured in a factory just outside Dublin. On the British mainland, three top-selling cigarette brands and a wide range of smaller brands are made at the famous Senior Service factory at Hyde, east of Manchester, and cigars are produced at Cardiff and Port Talbot in South Wales.

In 1989 that section of Gallaher Limited's business represented by Dollond & Aitchison suffered a setback when the British government abolished free vision tests for the majority of people, and spectacles and contact lenses for retail became liable for value-added tax. In fact, this severely affected the entire industry in the United Kingdom, but Gallaher remained confident, and continued as planned with the expansion of the Eyeland Express chain of stores. Dollond & Aitchison had by 1991 virtually completed a major restructuring of its retail and service facilities. It is the largest optical group in Europe, with more than 500 outlets in the United Kingdom alone and with strong and profitable overseas business.

Further strategic development of the group's nontobacco interests continued with the acquisition of Whyte & Mackay Distillers Ltd. in February 1990. This is a company which, as well as its three Scottish distilleries, has headquarters in Glasgow and a bottling company, William Muir (Bond 9) Limited, based in Leith, near Edinburgh. Its products are the blended whiskies Whyte & Mackay Special Reserve and The Claymore; and the single malts The Dalmore, Tomintoul-Glenlivet and Old Fettercairn. In April 1990 Whyte & Mackay reinforced its branded business and acquired the worldwide trademark rights to Vladivar vodka, the United Kingdom's second-largest vodka brand. After scotch whisky, vodka is the most popular distilled spirit in the United Kingdom, with some 14% of the total spirits market.

Gallaher Limited began the 1990s with a strategy confidently based in diversification. The tobacco business, managed by Gallaher Tobacco, remains a strong performer. In the declining U.K. cigarette market, Gallaher has increased its volume of sales and makes the three leading brands: Benson and Hedges Special Filter, the leading cigarette; Silk Cut, which is the leading low-tar cigarette; and Berkeley Superkings, the best-selling lower-priced brand. Benson and Hedges and Silk Cut in particular are powerfully supported by enigmatic and adventurous advertising devised by Collett, Dickinson & Pearce and Saatchi & Saatchi. Gallaher also manufactures the leading U.K. pipe tobacco, the leading cigar, and the second largest brand of hand-rolling tobacco in the United Kingdom. Gallaher International, the export arm, has been increasingly developed and is well placed to take advantage of the trend toward low-tar cigarettes, pushing for markets in France, Spain, and Greece.

Gallaher continues to invest in sponsorship of various kinds, although it withdrew patronage of the Silk Cut Tennis Championship in 1990. The Benson & Hedges Cup at Lord's, a cricket competition, will exist at least until 1995, as an arrangement has been concluded that guarantees the Test and County Cricket Board £3 million over a five year period. Other sponsorships within the Benson & Hedges portfolio are the International Open Golf Championship at St. Mellion, Cornwall; the Masters Snooker Tournament at Wembley; the Silk Cut Showjumping Derby; and the Silk Cut Nautical Awards. In Northern Ireland, small business development is encouraged by the Gallaher Business Challenge Award Scheme, and the company is the major private sponsor of the Ulster Orchestra.

Principal Subsidiaries: Benson & Hedges, Ltd.; Cope Brothers & Co. Ltd.; Cope & Lloyd (Overseas) Ltd.; John Cotton Ltd.; J.R. Freeman & Son Ltd.; Gallaher International Ltd.; Gallaher Tobacco Ltd.; Gallaher Tobacco (UK) Ltd.; Old Holborn Ltd.; Senior Service Tobacco Ltd.; Silk Cut Ltd.; Sobranie Ltd.; Sullivan Powell & Co. Ltd.; Benson & Hedges (Dublin) Ltd.; Gallaher (Dublin) Ltd.; Silk Cut (Dublin) Ltd.; Gallaher Canarias SA (Spain); Gallaher España SA (Spain); Silk Cut France SARL; Silk Cut Hellas Epe. (Greece); Dollond & Aitchison Group Plc; Dollond & Aitchison Ltd.; Theodore Hamblin Ltd.; First Sight; Keeler Ltd.; Filotecnica Salmoiraghi SpA (Italy, 99.9%); Istituto Ottico Vigano SpA (Italy); General Optica SA (Spain, 92.5%); Donal MacNally Opticians Ltd. (80%); Forbuoys Plc; NSS Newsagents Plc; TM Group Plc; Hargreaves Vending Ltd.; UBM Wittenborg Ltd.; Marshell Group Ltd.; The Prestige Group plc.; Prestige Group UK Plc; Bonny Products Ltd.; Prestige Medical Ltd.; Prestige Industrial Ltd.; Prestige Group (Australia) Pty. Ltd.; Prestige Housewares (NZ) Pty. Ltd. (New Zealand); Prestige Benelux SA (Belgium); Prestige France SA (France): Prestige Haushaltswaren GmbH (Germany); Prestige Italiana SpA; Fabricados Inoxidables SA (Spain); The Galleon Insurance Co. Ltd.; The Schooner Insurance Co. Ltd.; Whyte & Mackay Distillers Ltd.; Dalmore Distillers Ltd.; Fettercairn Distillery Ltd.; The Tomintoul-Glenlivet Distillery Ltd.; William Muir (Bond 9) Ltd.; The Scotch Whiskey Heritage Centre Ltd. (54.9%).

—Paul Stevens

IMASCO LIMITED

600 de Maisonneuve Boulevard West
Montreal, Quebec H3A 3K7
Canada
(514) 982-9111
Fax: (514) 982 9369

Public Company
Incorporated: 1912 as Imperial Tobacco Company of Canada
    Limited
Employees: 100,000
Sales: C$5.23 billion (US$4.53 billion)
Stock Exchanges: Montreal Toronto Vancouver

Imasco Limited dominates the Canadian cigarette market; its Imperial Tobacco Limited subsidiary had a 60% market share in 1990. It produces Canada's two most popular brands of cigarettes, Player's and du Maurier. Imasco, however, has interests in a broad range of other businesses. Subsidiary CT Financial Services Inc., popularly known as Canada Trust, is a leader in retail financial services. Imasco also operates fast-food restaurants, through Hardee's Food Systems; drugstores, through Shoppers Drug Mart/Pharmaprix; and specialty retailing, through The UCS Group.

The British-American Tobacco Co., Ltd. owned a controlling share in Imperial Tobacco at its founding and as of the early 1990s its successor, BAT Industries, still owned 40% of Imasco. One month after Imperial Tobacco's establishment in 1908, it subsumed the businesses of two other companies controlled by British-American Tobacco, American Tobacco Co. of Canada Ltd. and the Empire Tobacco Co., Ltd., founded in 1895 and 1898, respectively. American Tobacco of Canada was the largest tobacco manufacturer in Canada. Its holdings included D. Ritchie & Co. and the American Cigarette Co. Empire Tobacco had been 80%-owned by American Tobacco of Canada, and produced plug tobacco from Canadian-grown leaf in its Quebec factory. Imperial also obtained about 80% of cigarette-maker B. Houde Co. and 50% of the National Snuff Company, both of which had been controlled by American Tobacco of Canada. Imperial grew through acquisition as well as by increasing brand recognition. In 1930 Imperial acquired Tuckett Tobacco Co., followed in 1949 by Imperial Tobacco Company Limited, of Newfoundland, and in 1950 by Brown & Williamson Tobacco Corporation (Export) Ltd. By the late 1950s Imperial controlled slightly more than 50% of the Canadian cigarette market. Imperial's only venture outside the

manufacture of tobacco products was its United Cigar Stores, Ltd., a wholly owned subsidiary operating 200 tobacco stores.

The impetus for Imperial's diversification, begun in 1964 under President John Keith, was the increasing evidence that smoking caused disease, which was expected to affect the industry's future growth. Health concerns about the habit had increased during the 1950s, but the real end of care-free smoking was the U.S. surgeon general's 1964 report linking cigarettes with lung cancer. The report sparked an initially sharp decline in cigarette sales, which leveled off after several months. Imperial slated layoffs in anticipation of a drop in smoking, converted some factories to cigar production, and most significantly, acquired nontobacco interests—a foil packaging company and two winemakers—within a year of the report's publication. By 1967 the diversification plan was stepped up, and two vice presidents left, reportedly because of disagreements over company strategy.

In the late 1960s Imperial introduced an array of new cigarettes—some smaller, others equipped with the new filters. None of these was especially successful, and the company's market share shrank. In another effort to increase sales, Imperial included a gambling game in its 1969 Casino brand. Sales rose, but only because the game was so easy to crack that buyers won more than US$250,000 before the company took the brand off retail shelves. Among other tactics, Imperial introduced an unsuccessful cellulose-based tobacco substitute in the early 1970s. In a more successful venture, Imperial was the first company to introduce low-tar cigarettes; its four new brands, brought out in 1976, were a hit with the public and helped the company's market share rebound from 35% in 1980 to 47% in 1981.

Under Paul Paré, who became Imperial's president and chief executive officer in 1969, expansion accelerated. Paré formed Imasco Limited in 1970 as a holding company for potential diversifications as government sanctions began to curtail the tobacco industry. Canadian regulators in 1972 persuaded the industry to put warnings on cigarette packages and restricted advertising spending.

Imasco was also busy developing its other ventures. By 1976 Imasco had completely disposed of its wine businesses. A ten-year stint in sporting goods retailing began with the purchase of the Collegiate Sports Ltd. chain in 1973 and ended with its sale in 1983. In the late 1960s and early 1970s, Imasco made a concerted effort to establish a presence in the prepared-foods industry. Forming the triangular hub of this enterprise were Piñata Foods, Progresso Quality Foods, and S&W Fine Foods. Although the companies were regional successes when acquired, none had the strength to go national as Imasco intended.

Progresso, for example, when it joined Imasco in 1969, was the top Italian-food producer in the United States. Progresso's success, however, came substantially from the entrepreneurial spirit of its founder and president, Frank Paormina, who retired a year after the acquisition. Ragu soon overtook Progresso in sales. Similarly disappointing experiences with Piñata and S&W resulted in the sale of all three by 1979.

Imasco's difficulties were typical of Canadian companies attempting to break into the tough U.S. market. Although it may have preferred to expand in Canada, Imasco's Canadian activities were curtailed by the Canadian government's limits on foreign investment, which applied to Imasco since it is substantially owned by BAT. These restrictions were lifted in 1985 when Imasco was granted "deemed Canadian status " by the government.

Imasco began to land better investments in the mid-1970s and early 1980s. The company set criteria for new ventures by the late 1970s: acquisitions had to be consumer-oriented businesses with good management teams and excellent growth potential, and of sufficient size and profitability to immediately increase corporate earnings. Acquisitions also had to be in North America, Canada preferred. Among the industries that fit this profile were fast food, drugstores and financial services.

Expansion into fast food came with Hardee's restaurants. Wilbur Hardee opened his first drive-in hamburger restaurant in 1960 in Greenville, North Carolina. It eventually grew into a chain. By 1976, however, Hardee's had gotten into financial trouble while expanding to about 1,000 restaurants. That year Hardee's sold Imasco a 28% interest in the chain for US$15 million. In 1980 Imasco increased its holding to 44% and placed a member on the Hardee's board. In 1981, by which time Hardee's had 1,300 restaurants, Imasco bought out the remaining shareholders for US$85 million. With new financial resources, Hardee's remodeled, expanded its menu, and increased sales per store 47% from 1977 to 1981. In 1982 Hardee's purchased and converted 650 Burger Chefs, intensifying Hardee's already strong presence in the midwestern United States. Expanding via regional strength there and in the Southeast, Hardee's was the third-largest fast-food sandwich restaurant group in the United States in 1990, with 4,022 outlets—1,352 company-operated and 2,670 licensed to other operators. Over the years, Imasco acquired two other restaurant chains, Grisanti's Italian restaurants and Casa Lupita Mexican restaurants, but these were both disposed of by 1989 in order to concentrate resources on Hardee's.

Imasco acquired its first Canadian drugstores in 1973. Pharmaprix Stores and others were added in 1974, and Shoppers Drug Mart in 1978. The Shoppers Drug Mart/Pharmaprix group has become Canada's largest retail drug chain, claiming 30% of the market with 645 stores as of 1990. Encouraged by Canadian success, Imasco moved Shoppers into Florida in the early 1980s. Due to the troubled U.S. economy and glutted Florida market, by 1983 the company had lost $3 million on this operation. Imasco was prepared to try again and in April 1984 bought Peoples Drug Stores, Inc. Peoples, however, did not generate the returns Imasco desired, and was sold to Melville Corporation for US$325 million in 1990.

Imasco's 1986 C$2 billion takeover of Genstar Corporation brought Canada Trustco Mortgage Company, the country's trust company, into the Imasco family. The mortgage company and the Canada Trust Company are the principal operating companies of CT Financial Services Inc. CT derives most of its earnings from intermediary services. Its funds are provided mostly by depositors in personal savings accounts, term deposits, or specialized accounts like retirement savings plans. For the most part, the funds are invested in residential mortgages.

Because Imasco made its bid during a lengthy controversy over Canadian laws governing the ownership of trust companies, the deal was of concern to the federal government. These concerns were resolved when Imasco made a series of assurances to the government. Principal among these was Imasco's agreement that the government could require whole or partial divestment of CT pending a legislative review. Legislation was subsequently introduced that would require Imasco to reduce its voting stake in CT to 65% over a five-year period. The law was expected to be enacted in 1992.

The UCS Group is the progeny of United Cigar Stores. This division operates sundry retail stores in five divisions: Woolco/Woolworth Specialty Stores, Hotel Airport Shops, Den for Men/Au Masculin, and Tax and Duty Free Shops. Because of product mix—confections, reading materials, tobacco, and gifts and souvenirs—these stores face stiff competition from supermarkets, drugstores and other vendors. UCS relies on prime airport and resort location for its advantage, and gains 56% of its sales from tobacco products and accessories. UCS outlets placed in Woolco and Woolworth stores led UCS's record sales increases during the late 1980s, but the group entered the 1990s with the highest growth prospects in the tax and duty free shops in airports.

Imasco encountered further difficulties in its tobacco business in the late 1980s. In 1988 the Canadian government enacted the Tobacco Products Control Act, which required further health warnings on cigarette packages and severely limited the tobacco industry's advertising and promotional options. Imperial and other Canadian tobacco makers challenged the constitutionality of the act in court. In 1991 the Quebec Superior Court upheld the companies' challenge, but the government appealed the case to Canada's Supreme Court, where it was pending in the early 1990s.

Also in the early 1990s, Imasco made further investments in the restaurant business, as Hardee's acquired the Roy Rogers chain of 600 restaurants. Plans called for converting the Roy Rogers restaurants, located primarily in the eastern United States, to Hardee's by 1992.

Despite its difficulties, Imasco's diversification during the 1970s and 1980s was successful, and was duly noted by the financial community in the early 1990s. BAT, Imasco's substantial stockholder, deflected a takeover attempt during the early 1990s. Although the bid lapsed, it generated heretofore unseen international investor attention for Imasco. In any case, with its particularly strong positions in the financial and fast-food markets, Imasco headed into the 1990s with potential to expand lucratively under the stewardship of Purdy Crawford, who assumed the presidency in 1986 and the chairmanship in 1987.

Principal Subsidiaries: Imperial Tobacco Limited CT Financial Services Inc.; The UCS Group; Hardee's Food Systems, Inc.; Shoppers Drug Mart/Pharmaprix.

Further Reading: Thompson, Tony, "Imasco Gaining Experience in U.S. Retailing," *Advertising Age,* November 30, 1981; Bott, Robert, "Anatomy of a Bloodless Coup," *Canadian Business,* June 1986.

—Elaine Belsito

JAPAN TOBACCO INCORPORATED

12-62 Higashi Shinagawa
4-chome, Shinagawa-ku
Tokyo 140
Japan
(03) 3474 3111
Fax: (03) 5479 0386

State-Owned Company
Incorporated: 1949 as Japan Tobacco and Salt Public Corporation
Employees: 24,300
Sales: ¥2.70 trillion (US$21.63 billion)

The government-owned monopoly Japan Tobacco Incorporated (Japan Tobacco) manufactures tobacco and salt and is one of the largest tobacco companies in the world by sales volume. It also has one of the highest capitalizations of any company in Japan, with paid-in capital of ¥100 billion. In April 1985 the company was privatized as a joint stock company with the Japanese government as sole shareholder. This paved the way for more aggressive marketing of the company's products and also diversification into non-tobacco businesses. In the past few years these have included pharmaceuticals, foods, engineering, and real estate. Tobacco sales in Japan, however, will remain at the heart of the company's operations for the foreseeable future.

Japan Tobacco's origins date back to 1898 when a government bureau was established within the Ministry of Finance to operate a monopoly on tobacco production within Japan. The tobacco industry in Japan can, however, be traced back to 1869, when Yasugoro Tsuchida, a Tokyo merchant, began the production of rolled cigarettes on a small scale. This represented the introduction of locally produced cigarettes and came less than 20 years after the first introduction of cigarettes to Japan as imports from Britain and the United States. In 1883 Iwatani Co. Ltd., a trading company, began the production and sale of Japan's first popular cigarette brand, Tengu. In 1888 the government responded to the increase in tobacco smoking by placing a special tax on the products, with varying rates for rolled tobacco and cigarettes. Around this time the Murai Brothers Company began producing and selling Sunrise cigarettes and importing Hero cigarettes from the United States. In 1896 the company expanded into the Tokyo market, thus prompting a price war with Iwatani Co. Ltd.

At the time Japan was undergoing an accelerated period of industrialization. The Tokyo Stock Exchange opened in 1878, the Bank of Japan began operations in 1882, and the state-owned Yamato Iron and Steel Works began operation in 1901. In 1895 Japan established itself as a military power with the defeat of China in the Sino-Japanese War. Operations such as these needed funding and the government realized that a tobacco monopoly such as existed in several European countries could be a lucrative source of revenue. In 1898 a tobacco bureau was established within the Ministry of Finance to operate this monopoly. In 1905 a salt monopoly was added to the bureau's responsibilities. The bureau began marketing the Cherry brand of cigarettes in 1904, a brand still sold in Japan. In 1906 it began producing and selling its most popular brand at the time, Golden Bat. In 1900 Japan became one of the world's first countries to pass a law forbidding the consumption of cigarettes by minors—those under the age of 18. For the next 30 years tobacco and salt production in Japan continued to be administered by this bureau within the Ministry of Finance. Profits went directly into state coffers and were regarded as a kind of tax by the authorities. The prices charged by the government on tobacco were relatively low while those on salt were minimal, and the monopoly was in some ways used as a means of controlling the nation's economy, providing a regular source of income for the government.

By 1940 Japan was heading towards war with the Allied Powers. The supplies of raw tobacco leaves from the West, notably from North and South America, were becoming less and less reliable. The government was forced to implement rationing of cigarettes in 1943. Following Japan's defeat and subsequent occupation, the country's economy was restructured by the Allied Powers. They felt it reasonable to keep the monopoly in place as a source of income for the cash-starved Japanese government. In 1949 the government bureau traditionally responsible for tobacco production became a public company, known as the Japan Tobacco and Salt Public Corporation. Although still a wholly government-owned concern, tobacco production and sales in Japan were now to be operated on a commercial basis and as a self-accountable business concern. The company began afresh and in 1949 commenced the retailing of two brands—Peace and Corona, the former of which is still a top seller in Japan. In 1950 rationing of tobacco products was halted, and in 1952 finished tobacco products were exported from Japan for the first time, mostly to other Southeast Asian nations. In 1954 a new consumption tax was established on sales of cigarettes with the proceeds going directly to the government rather than the Japan Tobacco Corporation. In 1957 the company introduced its most popular brand, Hope, and also set up a research center to study the effects of cigarette smoking on health. This came at a time when scientists in the United States were beginning to publicize the link between smoking and lung cancer. Japan, with its lower incidence of cancer, was more concerned with its very high rate of stroke- and stress-related deaths, and the research center studied the causes of these illnesses. The Japanese population continued to take up smoking at a prodigious rate and by 1967 Japan Tobacco's best selling cigarette brand, Hope, was also the world's best selling brand. In the following year the company established a factory for producing cigarette paper and filters to cater for increased demand in Japan. Following reports of the health risks of smoking from both the West and to a lesser extent within Japan, Japan Tobacco began to issue health warnings on its cigarette boxes. The warnings were fairly low-key, however, and only advised the smoker not to overindulge in the habit.

Since the salt monopoly was established in 1905, Japan Tobacco in its various forms has been entrusted by the Japanese government with full responsibility for the country's salt supply. The salt business has traditionally been conducted with the aim of maintaining stable salt supplies and prices. As Japan does not have any salt mines, Japan Tobacco has had to import most of its salt, mainly from China and Korea. In 1972 Japan Tobacco introduced a new method of producing salt, in which sea water is separated from fresh water by membranes and the salt allowed to permeate across the membrane. This method was introduced into all Japan Tobacco salt-making facilities.

In 1973 Japan Tobacco began the sale of Marlboro cigarettes under license from Philip Morris Co. Ltd. of the United States. As the largest tobacco company in the world, the latter was determined to make inroads into the lucrative Japanese market, but was bewildered by Japan's complex distribution system. Most of Japan Tobacco's products were sold in small kiosks and vending machines, presenting an importer of cigarettes with a difficult and arduous task in cracking the market—a competitor would require a huge capital investment to set up such a network, and supply staff and maintenance staff would be required. Japan Tobacco at the time controlled almost 100% of Japan's cigarette market. In 1974 the company began its paradoxical "smoking clean" advertising campaign. The advertisement featured models in outdoor surroundings, smoking Japan Tobacco cigarettes. The irony of the suggestion that smoking is a clean habit and results in good health was obvious, but it was nonetheless built into a national campaign. In 1977 Japan Tobacco introduced its current best-selling brand, Mild Seven.

In the 1980s Japan Tobacco faced increasing pressure from foreign cigarette manufacturers to allow them to sell their products more freely on the Japanese market. The Japanese government was under pressure to cut its huge trade surplus with the United States and therefore exerted pressure on Japan Tobacco to cooperate with foreign importers and allow them the use of distribution channels, notably Japan Tobacco's large network of automatic vending machines. Philip Morris and R.J. Reynolds were the first to make inroads, with Lark, a Philip Morris brand especially designed for the Japanese market, becoming a best-seller. In 1985 Japan Tobacco underwent a fundamental restructuring. The government reorganized the company by privatizing it and re-establishing it as Japan Tobacco Incorporated, a joint stock company with its shares fully owned by the Japanese government. In the face of increasing competition from foreign imports, the move was intended to make the company more competitive, while still giving the government a monopoly on cigarette manufacture in Japan. In 1987 import tariffs on cigarettes were lifted, making it possible for importers to sell cigarettes at approximately the same price as Japan Tobacco. Since 1987, as a consequence, both Japan Tobacco's total sales and its share of the Japanese mar-

ket have been declining. The company's management realized that the new Japan Tobacco would have to diversify in order to sustain growth. Japan Tobacco International Corporation (JATICO) was established in 1985 to export cigarettes. First year sales were 7.5 billion cigarettes, which compared with the 270 billion sold domestically. The United States and Southeast Asia were the chief targets of JATICO's products. Japan Tobacco entered the pharmaceutical business in 1986 with the formation of JT Pharmaceutical Co. Ltd. This subsidiary took advantage of its parent company's extensive research and development facilities. The main areas of the pharmaceuticals business on which the company has focused so far have been over-the-counter (OTC) cough remedies and nutritional supplement drinks. One of the company's successes is Kakimaro, marketed as a hangover remedy. Through international strategic alliances, JT Pharmaceutical has also entered the field of OTC ethical drugs. Through other subsidiaries formed between 1985 and 1990, Japan Tobacco entered the food, fertilizer and agribusiness, and real estate businesses. The latter make use of Japan Tobacco's real estate holdings which, like many Japanese companies in the real estate boom years of the late 1980s, it used to its full financial advantage, through office letting, land sales, and renting.

To sustain its growth Japan Tobacco must continue to diversify and expand its overseas operations, as no significant expansion seems likely in the maturing Japanese cigarette market. Domestic cigarette sales are still the driving force behind the company which is determined, through marketing, to hold onto its market share.

Principal Subsidiaries: J.T. Agris Co., Ltd.; J.T. Canning Co., Ltd.; J.T. Drinks Co., Ltd.; J.T. Foods Co., Ltd.; Chicago Foods Co., Ltd.; Lifix Co., Ltd.; My Circle Co., Ltd.; J.T. Real Estate Co., Ltd.; Sports Club Trim Co., Ltd.; Your Factory Co., Ltd.; J.T. Enoshima Prince Hotel Co., Ltd.; J.T. Engineering Co., Ltd.; Tokyo Clinical Testing Co., Ltd.; Tokyo Establishment Enterprises Co., Ltd.; Murajo Production Centre; Enkai Enterprises Co., Ltd.; G-Tech Co., Ltd.; J.T. Anlits Co., Ltd.; Japan Tobacco International Co., Ltd.; Japan Tobacco I-Mex Co., Ltd.; Hokkaido Tobacco Services Co., Ltd.; Tokyo Tobacco Services Co., Ltd.; Chubu Tobacco Services Co., Ltd.; Kansai Tobacco Services Co., Ltd.; Kyushu Tobacco Services Co., Ltd.; Uny-Tobacco Services Co., Ltd.; Tohoku Filter Enterprises Co., Ltd.; Japan Filter Enterprises Co., Ltd.; Osaka Filter Enterprises Co., Ltd.; Neo-Filter Enterprises Co., Ltd.; J.T. CMK Co., Ltd.; J.T. Okamura Co., Ltd.; J.T.S. Electric Co., Ltd.; J.T. Nifco Co., Ltd.; Napps Co., Ltd.; J.T. Soft Services Co., Ltd.; J.T. Fashions Co., Ltd.; J.T. Kokubu Co., Ltd.; J.T. Act Co., Ltd.; J.T. Creative Co., Ltd.; J.T. Travel Co., Ltd.; S.K. Services Co., Ltd.; Planzart Co., Ltd.; C B One Co., Ltd.; Fuji Flavour Co., Ltd.; Japan Metallising Industries Co., Ltd.; Alpack Services Co., Ltd.; Nitto Industries Co., Ltd.; Tohoku Plant Services Co., Ltd.; Kanto Plant Services Co., Ltd.; Tokai Plant Services Co., Ltd.; Hachisendai Production Co., Ltd.; Kyushu Factory Services Co., Ltd.; Tobacco Benefit Association.

—Dylan Tanner

PHILIP MORRIS COMPANIES INC.

120 Park Avenue
New York, New York, 10017
U.S.A.
(212) 880-5000
Fax: (212) 907-5502

Public Company
Incorporated: 1919 as Philip Morris & Co. Ltd., Inc.
Employees: 168,000
Sales: $51.17 billion
Stock Exchanges: New York Amsterdam Antwerp Basel
    Brussels Frankfurt Geneva Lausanne London Luxembourg
    Paris Tokyo Zürich

In an industry dogged by health concerns, a shrinking domestic market, and widespread investor fears about its future, Philip Morris Companies Inc. (Morris) continues year after year to achieve record-breaking sales and profits, most of them thanks to the enduring appeal of the Marlboro Man. From a position of relative obscurity in the cigarette business in the early 1960s Philip Morris has ridden Marlboro's success to leadership of the tobacco world, and in the process accumulated enough cash to finance a series of enormous acquisitions in the food industry. The company most recently annexed both Kraft and General Foods Corporation, and is now the world's second-largest food concern as well as the largest cigarette maker; and there is little doubt that Morris will continue to wean itself of dependence on the profitable but increasingly embattled tobacco trade.

In 1847 an Englishman named Philip Morris opened a tobacco shop in London's fashionable Bond Street. When British soldiers returning from the Crimean War made fashionable the smoking of Turkish-style cigarettes, until then exclusively a habit of the poor, Morris was soon busy as a manufacturer as well as merchant of the newly popular product. He brought out a number of successful cigarette brands, including English Ovals, Cambridge, and Oxford Blues, and continued as one of the leading British tobacconists for many years. Morris's company eventually built a small but stable business in the United States, where its brands sold primarily on the strength of their British cachet. The U.S. market, however, was until 1911 all but owned by the American Tobacco trust, which enjoyed a monopoly in cigarettes comparable to that of John D. Rockefeller's Standard Oil in the oil business.

When the tobacco cartel was dissolved by court order in 1911, a U.S. financier named George J. Whelan formed Tobacco Products Corporation to absorb a few of the splinter companies not already organized into the new Big Four of tobacco—American Tobacco, R.J. Reynolds, Lorillard, and Liggett & Meyers. His first manufacturing acquisition was the maker of Melachrino cigarettes, a company at which Reuben M. Ellis and Leonard B. McKitterick had made names for themselves as outstanding salesmen. Ellis and McKitterick became vice presidents and stockholders of Tobacco Products Corporation as George Whelan considered their personal knowledge of the many thousand tobacco retailers in the New York area an invaluable asset. When Whelan picked up the U.S. business of Philip Morris Company in 1919 he formed a new company to manage its assets, Philip Morris & Company Ltd., Inc., owned by the shareholders of Tobacco Products Corporation. Ellis and McKitterick thus became part owners and managers of the new Philip Morris brands.

While George Whelan wheeled and dealed his way toward a collapse in 1929, Reuben Ellis ran Morris as its president after 1923, at which time the company had a net income of about $100,000. Ellis's first important move at Morris was the 1925 introduction of a new premium—20¢—cigarette called Marlboro, which did well from the beginning and leveled off at a steady 500 million cigarettes a year. Industry leaders such as Camel and Lucky Strike sold more than 25 billion a year. Marlboro originally was sold as a cigarette primarily for women, the wealthy, and the sophisticated, in complete contrast to its 1955 cowboy-image reincarnation. Leonard McKitterick rejoined Ellis in 1930 after a seven-year absence, and the two men set about buying Morris's stock from their former employer Whelan, now in retreat from the tobacco business. Whelan sold off all of his tobacco interests, allowing Ellis and McKitterick to gain control of Morris by 1931. The company marketed cigarettes mainly under the names of English Ovals, Marlboro, and Paul Jones; handled a modest amount of pipe tobacco as well; and owned one manufacturing facility in Richmond, Virginia. By any measure, it was a minor competitor in an industry dominated by the remaining pieces of the former American Tobacco trust.

Ellis and McKitterick were both veteran salesmen in the tobacco business, however, which in the 1930s meant that they personally had done business with many thousands of the tobacco jobbers and retailers up and down the East Coast. In a field not yet controlled by the rising mass marketers, such as supermarket chains, those years of handshaking had built for Ellis and McKitterick a powerful store of goodwill among the men who determined which cigarettes were moved expeditiously and pushed at the retail level and those that were allowed to languish. When Ellis and McKitterick launched a new mid-priced cigarette called Philip Morris English Blend in 1933, they could count on the strong support of the jobber network to help them through the difficult introductory period. To further cement their alliance with the jobbers, Morris executives let it be known that they would refrain from selling to the new mass marketers directly, preventing the latter from retailing English Blend at less than the price of 15¢ set by the jobbers and dealers. The jobbers already were beginning to suffer from price competition with the big chains and readily agreed to Morris's plan—the jobbers would push English Blend at 15¢ while Morris guaranteed that the same package would not end up on supermarket shelves at 10¢.

As experienced marketers, Ellis and McKitterick came up with several advertising gambits as additional support for their new product. Morris introduced the use of diethylene glycol as a moisture retentive in its cigarettes, adducing as proof of glycol's milder effect on the human throat a host of more or less scientific evidence gathered by bona fide researchers who were, however, paid for their work by the company. Ellis and McKitterick circulated results of the research among physicians, while settling in their advertisements for the general claim that "scientific tests have proven Philip Morris a milder cigarette." The company kept up this advertising slant for many years despite skepticism voiced by the Federal Trade Commission, among others. Morris's second advertising strategy was the revival of an earlier campaign in which a bellhop was told to fetch a pack of Morris cigarettes. The "call for Philip Morris," slogan used on posters as early as 1919, was updated for radio in 1933 with the recruitment of a bellhop named John Roventini to serve as a living representation of the ad. Roventini, under the name of Johnnie Morris, enjoyed many prosperous years putting in countless appearances in New York and other major cities, while his strident call could be heard every week on radio broadcasts.

John Roventini soon earned himself a large fortune, by bellhop standards, and Morris began its long climb to the top of the cigarette world. Sales of English Blend were strong from its introduction in January of 1933, helping Morris to triple its net income, to $1.5 million, in a single year and by 1935 to challenge Lorillard as the fourth-largest cigarette maker in the United States. Ellis and McKitterick were both dead by 1936, but under Alfred Lyon the company continued its rise, in that year selling 7.5 billion cigarettes and laying firm hold on the industry's fourth position. Morris was viewed as something of a phenomenon, its combination of marketing expertise and jobber loyalty enabling it to take market share from the much larger and wealthier cigarette leaders such as American Tobacco and Reynolds. Alfred Lyon directed the construction of the industry's largest and most effective sales force, and though Morris's special relationship with the jobbers did not last long—supermarkets proving to be the wave of the future—Morris remained a company fueled by its expertise in sales and marketing.

By 1939 sales had reached $64 million, and World War II soon put even more pressure on cigarette production. When Morris sales doubled by 1942, Chairman Lyon and President Otway Chalkey began casting about for some means to expand capacity, especially difficult given the need for large amounts of tobacco cured several years before its use. When Axton-Fisher Tobacco Company of Louisville, Kentucky, was put up for sale in 1945, Morris paid a premium price—$20 million—to win its large stores of tobacco and a second manufacturing plant. The move looked good until the war's end in August of that year precipitated a huge drop in cigarette consumption, a cut in sales made more painful by Morris's overestimate of peacetime demand. Many of the company's biggest orders in the fall of 1945 were left to grow stale on retail racks, and Morris's net income plummeted just as it floated a new bond issue at the end of the year. Morris withdrew the offering and suffered a certain amount of embarrassment, but the company's underlying business was sound and it soon bounced back. A massive 1948 advertising campaign claiming that English Blend did not cause "cigarette hangover," a previously unknown disorder, led to a fresh gain in market share and profit.

Despite Morris's success with such advertising claims, the company somehow failed to foresee the most important new development in the cigarette business in many years, the introduction of the milder and less harmful filtered cigarettes. Unlike Morris's version of mildness, filtered cigarettes were indisputably less damaging to the throat, and increased public awareness of smoking's real health dangers spurred a rapid shift to filters in the 1950s. Morris was evidently slow to recognize the importance of this innovation, and it was not until 1955 that the company repositioned its old filter entry Marlboro as a cigarette for everyone who responds to the myth of the American cowboy. It took time, however, for the new Marlboro image to take hold, and by 1960 Morris had slipped to sixth and last place among major U.S. tobacco companies, its best-selling entry able to do no better than tenth among the leading brands. It appeared that changing consumer preference had left Morris well out of the new era in tobacco.

Morris had at least three cards yet to play, however. One was the emergence in 1957 of a marketing tactician capable of resurrecting the glory days of Alfred Lyon. Joseph Cullman III took over management of the company in 1957 and guided its amazing growth over the course of the following two decades, much of it earned in the international market. Morris was perhaps the earliest, and certainly became the most successful, of U.S. tobacco companies in foreseeing the potential sales growth in the worldwide cigarette business. In 1960 Cullman appointed George Weissman as director of international operations, and he is generally credited with making Morris the United States' leading exporter of tobacco products. The company's third great resource was the Marlboro Man, who would prove in the long run to be likely the most successful advertising image ever created. For whatever combination of reasons—nostalgia for the Old West, clever packaging, tobacco taste—Marlboro almost by itself raised Morris from also-ran to industrial leader during the next quarter century.

While Joseph Cullman attended to Morris's resurgence in the tobacco business, he also began the first of many attempts to diversify the company's assets and thereby render it less dependent on a product that was gradually becoming known as a serious health hazard. In the mid-1950s Morris had bought into the flexible packaging and paper manufacturing trades, and in the early 1990s it added American Safety Razor, Burma Shave, and Clark chewing gum, hoping in each case to use Morris's existing distributor network and marketing experience to sell a wider variety of consumer products. None of these early acquisitions proved to be of great value, with the possible exception of its packaging division, not sold until the mid-1980s, but in 1970 the company added Miller Brewing to its holdings. Miller was then only the seventh-largest brewer in the United States, but the combination of a repositioned High Life beer and the introduction of the United States' first low-calorie beer, Miller Lite, brought the company all the way up to number two by 1980. On the other hand, Morris's 1978 purchase of the Seven-Up Company for $520 million was little more than a disaster, and after several failed advertising campaigns the soft drink manufacturer was sold in the mid-1980s.

In the meantime, the Marlboro Man was running wild, carrying Morris up the ranks of cigarette makers with astonishing speed. Throughout the 1960s Marlboro registered yearly leaps in popularity, especially among the growing segment of young people, and by 1973 it was the second most popular cigarette brand in the United States and accounted for roughly two-thirds of Morris's tobacco business. In 1976 it moved past Reynolds's Winston as the leader with 94 billion cigarettes sold that year, helping Morris to become the United States' and the world's second-largest seller of tobacco. In 1961, Morris had controlled 9.4% of the market; in 1976 that figure topped 25% and continued to rise. All other competitors except Reynolds declined—between the two of them, Morris and Reynolds owned well more than half the market. The two leaders thus found themselves in a very comfortable position, as growing health concerns about smoking made it unlikely that any new competitor would join the tobacco business, while the need for massive, effective advertising made it difficult for the current players to maintain their positions. The net result was abnormally large profits for the two leaders, especially as their dominance of the market really took hold in the 1980s, and they were able to raise prices frequently without fear of being undercut.

Complementing Marlboro's success was the emergence of two new fields for Morris. The 1975 introduction of Merit brand signaled Morris's entry into the new low-tar market, a category that would mushroom into ever larger numbers as U.S. smokers became more concerned with the deleterious effects of smoking. Second, under the guidance of George Weissman, the company's international business had greatly expanded. While the U.S. cigarette market was flat in the 1970s and retreating by the mid-1980s, the international business continued to grow rapidly, and Morris's Marlboro was soon the world's best selling cigarette. Thus, two of Morris's responses to the increased controversy in the United States about smoking were to sell cigarettes with lower tar and to push its brands overseas, where generally less affluent people cared less about the health risks involved. Neither strategy went to the heart of Morris's fundamental problem, the association of tobacco with disease, and the resultant product liability lawsuits. To ensure its own safety, Morris would eventually have to make a major diversification away from the tobacco business.

To that end, even as Morris passed Reynolds as the largest U.S. cigarette manufacturer it paid $5.75 billion in 1985 to acquire General Foods Corporation, the diversified food products giant. General Foods was large enough to offer Morris a significant source of revenue apart from the tobacco industry, and its reliance on advertising and an intricate distribution system was similar to Morris's business; but General Foods was a rather lackluster company in a mature industry, and the acquisition did not kindle great enthusiasm among business analysts. They compared it unfavorably to Reynolds's purchase of Nabisco Brands at about the same time, and predicted that the move would not be sufficient to free Morris of its tobacco habit. In 1987, for example, two years after the General Foods purchase, Morris's total revenue had reached $27.7 billion and its operating income $4.1 billion. The lion's share of that income—$2.7 billion—was earned by the domestic tobacco division, where the slackening of competition allowed a luxurious rate of return on its $7.6 billion in sales. By contrast, General Foods's $10 billion contribution to revenue netted only $700 million in operating income, meaning that it was fully five times as profitable to sell a pack of Marlboros as a box of Jell-O or jar of coffee from General Foods. Indeed, 60% of Morris's total profit for the year was generated by Marlboro's popularity at home and abroad.

In 1988 Morris took a more decisive step toward reshaping its corporate profile. For $12.9 billion it acquired Kraft, Inc., an even larger and more dynamic food products corporation. Morris Chairman Hamish Maxwell merged his two food divisions into Kraft General Foods, Inc., the world's second-largest food company with $24 billion in sales and more than 2,500 different products. Under its chief executive officer Michael Miles, Kraft General underwent a program of labor cuts and efficiency measures designed to raise its earnings level to something approaching that of the tobacco division, and his efforts improved the division's performance considerably. Along with Miller Brewing's $3.5 billion in sales—it too is the second-largest competitor in its field—in the early 1990s far more than half of Morris's revenue was derived from non-tobacco products. It appears likely that Morris will continue to use the extraordinary cash flow generated by its domestic tobacco sales to finance further moves into the food industry, where the relatively low rate of return can be eventually compensated by means of sheer size. It made one such move in 1990, buying Jacobs Suchard, a Swiss maker of coffee and chocolate for $4.1 billion.

Principal Subsidiaries: Philip Morris Incorporated; Philip Morris International Inc.; Kraft General Foods, Inc.; Miller Brewing Company; Philip Morris Capital Corporation.

Further Reading: "Philip Morris & Co.," *Fortune,* March 1936; "Philip Morris Comeback," *Fortune,* October 1949; Nulty, Peter, "Living with the Limits of Marlboro Magic," *Fortune,* March 18, 1985.

—Jonathan Martin

RJR NABISCO HOLDINGS CORP.

1301 Avenue of the Americas
New York, New York 10019
U.S.A.
(212) 258-5600
Fax: (212) 969-9004

Public Company
Incorporated: 1879 as R.J. Reynolds Tobacco Company
Employees: 55,000
Sales: $13.88 billion
Stock Exchange: New York

RJR Nabisco Holdings Corp., despite a major diversification into food and other consumer products, still derives the majority of its sales and profits from its original business, tobacco. The company, one of the largest tobacco manufacturers in the United States, paid $4.9 billion for Nabisco Brands in 1985. It went private in 1988 in the heretofore largest leveraged buyout in the United States, by Kohlberg Kravis Roberts & Co. at a price of $24.88 billion. With a 1991 stock offering, the company became public once again.

The company's founder, Richard Joshua Reynolds, son of prosperous tobacco manufacturer Hardin W. Reynolds of Patrick County, Virginia, sold his part interest in a tobacco business he had with his father and in 1874 moved 60 miles south to Winston, North Carolina, in the heart of the bright leaf, or flue-cured, tobacco area. Reynolds invested $7,500 in land and built and equipped a small factory there to manufacture flat plug chewing tobacco. During the first year of operation Reynolds produced 150,000 pounds of tobacco that sold primarily in the Carolinas and Virginia. In 1879 the R.J. Reynolds Tobacco Company was incorporated in North Carolina. Reynolds faced stiff competition from manufacturers in Winston and its neighboring city of Salem. Reynolds, along with his brother William Neal Reynolds, who joined the firm in 1884, controlled the company. Initially Reynolds sold his products to jobbers who distributed chewing tobacco for him under their own brand names. In 1885 he introduced his own brand, Schnapps, which became popular.

In the 1890s there were several significant changes in the Reynolds Tobacco Company. In 1890 the company issued its first stock, with R.J. Reynolds owning nearly 90% of the company. He was elected president, with his brother serving as vice president. In 1892 a sales department was created along with a systematic national advertising program.

Reynolds was one of the first companies to introduce saccharin as a sweetening agent in chewing tobacco. The company also adopted many labor-saving devices and had a 400% production increase between 1892 and 1898. In 1894 Reynolds began to experiment with smoking tobacco to compete with James Buchanan Duke's profitable brands and also because of his desire to turn scrap tobacco into a paying product. In 1895 the company introduced its first smoking tobacco brand, Naturally Sweet Cut Plug. In 1898 the company's assets were valued at more than $1 million.

Due to considerable expansion in the late 1890s, Reynolds was in need of large amounts of capital. Reluctantly, he turned to his rival Duke for help. In 1898 Duke's American Tobacco Company established a subsidiary, Continental Tobacco Company, in an effort to monopolize the nation's chewing tobacco business. In April 1899 Reynolds sold two-thirds of his stock to Continental, but retained his position as president of the R.J. Reynolds Tobacco Company. Reynolds tried to maintain his independence in Duke's tobacco trust and reportedly told friends that "if Buck Duke tries to swallow me, he will get the bellyache of his life." Duke let Reynolds have his independence as long as he acquired chewing tobacco companies in the Virginia and Carolina area for the trust. Reynolds gobbled up ten companies, but by 1905 he demonstrated his independence from the trust by producing five brands of smoking tobacco. In late 1907 he introduced Prince Albert smoking tobacco, a unique mixture of burley and flue-cured tobacco. Prince Albert achieved instant success with the slogan "it can't bite your tongue."

The tobacco trust, like most trusts during the first decade of the 20th century, proved to be unpopular. In 1911 a U.S. Circuit Court ordered the dissolution of the American Tobacco Company. American was forced to divest itself of all Reynolds stock. R.J. Reynolds and members of his family reacquired some of the company's stock. In actuality the trust years were good to Reynolds. He expanded facilities, hired aggressive new managers, and increased production and sales almost five-fold during the trust period. By the time he reacquired control of the company in 1912, the R.J. Reynolds Tobacco Company was the smallest of the big four tobacco manufactures, but it was quick to expand.

Soon after achieving independence from the trust, Reynolds instituted a plan to get the company's stock into the hands of friendly investors. A company bylaw encouraged Reynolds's employees to buy company stock, and the board of directors approved lending of surplus funds and profits to employees for the purchase of "A," or voting, stock. By 1924 the majority of the company's voting stock was in the hands of people who worked for the company. Soon all tobacco businesses began to emulate the Reynolds stock purchase plan.

As early as 1912 R.J. Reynolds considered the production of cigarettes because of the great success that the Prince Albert brand had experienced. By July 1913 Reynolds had manufactured the company's first cigarette. Reynolds decided to produce three different cigarette brands simultaneously to see which one had the greatest public demand. He personally selected the blend—Turkish tobacco, burley, flue-cured—and the name of the brand that proved most popular, Camel. The Camel brand became an instant success because of its blend, pricing, and advertising. Camels sold for 10¢ a pack, which undersold Liggett & Myers's popular Fatima. Reynolds spent more than $2 million in 1915 in an aggressive national advertising campaign. In 1919 the famous slogan "I'd walk a mile for a Camel" appeared. Reynolds also instituted the idea of selling cigarettes by the carton. Profits soared from $2.75 million in 1912 to nearly $24 million in 1924, largely because of the phenomenal sale of Camels. By 1924 the R.J. Reynolds Tobacco Company's net profits surpassed the nation's largest manufacturer, the American Tobacco Company.

The company prospered under R.J. Reynolds's paternalistic leadership and continued to do so for decades after his death in 1918. William Neal Reynolds assumed the presidency after his brother's death and remained in that position until 1924 when he was elected chairman of the board of directors, with Bowman Gray Sr. appointed president. This ensured the perpetuation of R.J. Reynolds's management philosophy and provided a continuity of leadership from people inside the company. Before R.J. Reynolds's death he had begun the process that led to the company's listing on the New York Stock Exchange—preferred stock in 1922 and common in 1927.

William Neal Reynolds retired as chairman in 1931 to be replaced by Bowman Gray, Sr. Under Gray's direction the company in 1931 introduced moisture-proof cellophane as a wrapper to preserve freshness in cigarettes—an innovation that other companies soon adopted; began to manufacture its own tinfoil and paper from factories in North Carolina to reduce dependence on foreign supplies; and developed a new sales policy that concentrated on mass sales based on brand name recognition and customer loyalty. Reynolds during the 1930s invested heavily in a series of advertising campaigns that emphasized the pleasure derived from smoking. By 1938 the company produced 84 brands of chewing tobacco, 12 brands of smoking tobacco, and 1 primary brand of cigarette, Camel.

After Gray's accidental death in 1935, S. Clay Williams directed the company until 1949. During the 1940s R.J. Reynolds faced shortages of materials and personnel because of World War II, and immediately after the war there were labor problems that included accusations of communist sympathies against certain union leaders. Labor relations improved by the early 1950s, however, as the company became agreeable to many union-advocated reforms, including the desegregation of its work force.

In 1948 a major antitrust suit against the tobacco industry went to trial. Several R.J. Reynolds officers were convicted and fined on charges of monopolistic practices, although they strongly asserted their innocence. The company itself also was convicted. The company's misfortunes continued. In 1949 Reynolds introduced of a major new cigarette brand, Cavalier. The public did not accept the brand, which lost $30 million in five years.

The innovative John C. Whitaker assumed the presidency in 1949. During his tenure Reynolds rebounded and prospered. Technical advances increased the amount of tobacco suitable for cigarette manufacturing, which helped the company's output double from 1944 to 1958. Reynolds instituted an active merchandising campaign by using display racks of cigarettes in supermarkets. In addition, company bylaws that had resulted in concentration of stock in the hands of employees were gradually eliminated, making the shares available more widely.

A major factor in Reynolds's growth during the 1950s was the introduction of Winston and Salem cigarettes, from which the company received huge profits. Winston, the company's first filter-tipped cigarette, appeared in March 1954 to compete directly with Brown & Williamson's Viceroy. With catchy advertising phrases such as "Winston tastes good like a cigarette should" and "It's what's up front that counts," the cigarette was quickly accepted, with 40 billion sold in 1954. By 1956 Reynolds began marketing Salem, the industry's first king-size filter-tipped menthol cigarette. It too made tremendous profits. Nevertheless, Camel retained its leadership as the industry's best-selling cigarette until the early 1960s. All cigarette manufacturing was centralized in 1961, when a massive modern factory opened in Winston-Salem.

During the 1950s the tobacco industry experienced for the first time critical attacks centering on the issue of smoking and health. In 1952 an article entitled "Cancer by the Carton" appeared in *Reader's Digest*, and the next year the Sloan-Kettering Cancer Institute announced that its research showed a relationship between cancer and tobacco. The development of filter-tipped cigarettes was in part a response to health concerns. The board of directors also responded by appointing a diversification committee in 1957 to study possible investment in nontobacco areas and to consider expansion of tobacco operations overseas.

Alexander H. Galloway became president in 1960 and, along with Chairman Bowman Gray Jr., led the company into a period of unparalleled growth and diversification. The corporate diversification strategy initially focused on acquisitions in food-related industries. Reynolds bought Pacific Hawaiian Products in 1963 and spent $63 million for Chun King in 1966. All nontobacco companies were placed under the direction of a subsidiary—R.J. Reynolds Foods—that was created in 1966. By the late 1960s, diversification had expanded into nonfood areas. In 1969 the company bought Sea-Land Industries, a containerized shipping business, and adopted a new corporate name—R.J. Reynolds Industries. Aminoil, a domestic crude oil and natural gas exploration firm was purchased for $600 million in 1970. Businesses later added to the R.J. Reynolds Industries portfolio were Del Monte in 1979 and Heublein in 1983.

Tobacco, however, continued to be the mainstay of Reynolds. In 1968 R.J. Reynolds International was established to develop foreign tobacco markets. Two years later all tobacco operations became a subsidiary of R.J. Reynolds Industries. In the 1960s the smoking and health controversy had intensified. In 1964 the U.S. surgeon general issued a report linking smoking with lung cancer and heart disease. The U.S. Congress in 1965 passed the Cigarette Advertising and Labeling Act, which required tobacco companies to place health warnings on cigarette packs. Cigarette advertising was banned from radio and television after 1971. The federal cigarette tax was doubled in 1983.

In addition to governmental pressure, Reynolds faced intense competition, primarily from Philip Morris, as marketing strategy focused on luring customers away from competitors instead of attracting new smokers. By 1976 Philip Morris's Marlboro surpassed Winston in domestic sales. In 1977 Reynolds introduced the Real brand cigarette to appeal to the back-to-nature movement, but its sales were disastrous, and by 1980 the so-called "Edsel of cigarettes" was discontinued. Reynolds actively engaged in the domestic tar wars of the late 1970s. Several promising new low-tar brands, such as Doral and Vantage, were marketed in an effort to improve tobacco's health image. In 1983 Reynolds began manufacturing the novel 25-cigarette-per-pack Century. Most consumers, however, preferred the traditional 20-per-pack cigarettes. By 1983 Philip Morris had replaced Reynolds as the leader in domestic sales.

Reynolds's strategy in the 1980s centered on developing new foreign markets for tobacco products to offset lower domestic demand and sales. In 1980 Reynolds was the first U.S. company to reach an agreement with the People's Republic of China to manufacture and sell cigarettes there. In September 1980 the company announced an ambitious $2 billion, ten-year construction and plant modernization plan. By 1986 the ultramodern Tobaccoville factory just north of Winston-Salem began production.

Leadership at Reynolds underwent significant changes during the diversification period. For the first time in the company's history several persons from outside the corporation were brought into major management positions. J. Paul Sticht, originally an executive from Federated Department Stores, who joined Reynolds in 1972 and his protege J. Tylee Wilson led Reynolds into a period of extensive growth. By 1980 Sticht and Wilson had developed a new direction for the company. Reynolds began to divest itself of noncomplementary companies and concentrate efforts on strengthening existing subsidiaries through acquisition of tobacco and food-related businesses. In 1984 Reynolds sold Aminoil to Phillips Petroleum for $1.7 billion. In one of the largest acquisitions ever, Reynolds purchased Nabisco Brands, Inc. in 1985 for $4.9 billion, which raised the corporation's nontobacco earnings to 40% of its total. The next year the conglomerate officially changed its name to RJR Nabisco, Inc.

Tumultuous changes followed. F. Ross Johnson, who came over from Nabisco in 1985, was appointed president and chief operations officer. By 1986 he had forced Wilson out and assumed the position of chief executive officer. He continued Wilson's policy of returning the company to its core business by selling off more than half the corporation's subsidiaries. Johnson also moved corporate headquarters from Winston-Salem to Atlanta. In 1987 Reynolds began to test-market a smokeless cigarette, Premier, in response to mounting pressure to make smoking more acceptable. Premier was a colossal failure.

At a meeting of the board of directors on October 19, 1988, Johnson proposed a massive leveraged buyout. Johnson headed a group of company executives who wanted to buy Reynolds stock for $17 billion by borrowing against the corporation's assets through bank loans and the issuance of high-yield junk bonds. Once the new company became private, unprofitable parts would be sold. Ultimately, the new and leaner company would issue stock and became public, with the Johnson group to realize huge profits. The directors, alienated by Johnson's

proposal, opened the door to other bidders. In November 1988 they accepted the $24.88 billion offered by Kohlberg Kravis Roberts & Co. (KKR), an investment firm specializing in leveraged buyouts, instead of a higher bid from the Johnson group. This was the biggest leveraged buyout in U.S. history. RJR Nabisco Holdings Corp. was set up at this time as the parent company of RJR Nabisco, Inc.

Johnson resigned in February 1989. A month later KKR selected Louis Gerstner Jr., former president of American Express, as chief executive of RJR Nabisco Holdings. He immediately began cutting costs to reduce the massive buyout debt. There was an 11.5% personnel cutback in tobacco operations; the practice of overstocking retailers with cigarettes was eliminated; corporate headquarters were moved to New York; and Del Monte and parts of Nabisco were divested in 1990. Attempts to target selected groups with new cigarette brands, such as Uptown for blacks and Dakota for blue-collar urban women, failed in 1990. RJR, however, did penetrate the Soviet market that year.

Under Gerstner, in the early 1990s, RJR Nabisco had focused on increasing the efficiency of its existing operations, rather than on making acquisitions. By 1991 it had reduced its debt to about $17 billion from $25 billion at the time of the buyout. Early in 1991 the company went public once again with a new issue of stock, although KKR continued to own a majority of shares.

Principal Subsidiaries: RJR Nabisco, Inc.; R.J. Reynolds Tobacco Company; Nabisco Brands, Inc.; Planters LifeSavers Company; R.J. Reynolds Tobacco International, Inc.

Further Reading: Sloane, Leonard, "Durable Tobacco King: Reynolds Still Faces Marketing Challenge," *The New York Times,* May 20, 1973; Salmans, Sandra, "Reynolds: Smoking Still Pays," *The New York Times,* April 12, 1981; Purdum, Todd S., "Filling the Pantry at Reynolds," *The New York Times,* June 16, 1985; Tilley, Nannie M., *The R.J. Reynolds Tobacco Company,* Chapel Hill, North Carolina, University of North Carolina Press, 1985; Dobrzynski, Judith H., "Running the Biggest LBO," *Business Week,* Oct 2, 1989; Burrough, Bryan, and John Helyar, *Barbarians at the Gate: The Fall of RJR Nabisco,* New York, Harper & Row, 1990; "Nabisco Brands, Inc.," in *International Directory of Company Histories,* Volume II, edited by Lisa Mirabile, Chicago, St. James Press, 1990; Anders, George, "Back to Biscuits: Old Flamboyance Is Out as Louis Gerstner Remakes RJR Nabisco," *The Wall Street Journal,* March 21, 1991.

—Charles C. Hay III

ROTHMANS INTERNATIONAL P.L.C.

15 Hill Street
London W1X7FB
(071) 491-4366
Fax (071) 493-8404

Public Company
Incorporated: 1903 as Carreras, Limited
Employees: 29,600
Sales: £2.22 billion (US$4.15 billion)
Stock Exchange: London

Rothmans International p.l.c. is a huge conglomerate, combining such famous names as Rothmans and Carreras, as well as substantial holdings in Dunhill Holdings and Cartier Monde, whose main interests are the manufacture and sale of tobacco and luxury products worldwide. It is among the top five tobacco companies in the world, operating 52 factories, and is active in over 30 countries.

Rothmans International was established in 1972 under the direction of Dr. Anton Rupert, a South African who headed the Rembrandt Group, one of South Africa's largest enterprises, with interests in mining, textiles, and brewing as well as tobacco. Rembrandt expanded its activities outside South Africa by buying into Rothmans Limited in 1954 and Carreras in 1958. It was Rupert's philosophy to allow these companies to operate independently, but with the companies beginning to duplicate resources and compete against each other, the formation of Rothmans International seemed preferable.

By 1972 Rothmans Limited had been in existence, in one form or another, for more than 80 years. Its founder, Louis Rothman, was born into the tobacco industry. His family owned a large tobacco factory in the Ukraine and he became an apprentice there. He emigrated to London in 1887, at the age of 18, and easily found work in the British tobacco industry. At that time there was a demand for handmade cigarettes using the blends of Balkan, Crimean, Turkish, and Oriental tobaccos which Rothman had learned how to make during his apprenticeship.

In 1890, he opened his own business, a small kiosk on Fleet Street, selling to the reporters and printers of the area by day and making his cigarettes by night. He also built his reputation by supplying to wealthy businessmen and aristocrats. This enabled him to open two more shops, but it was not until 1900

that he had a proper showroom on Pall Mall, from which he launched his Pall Mall brand of cigarettes.

The success of Rothman's Pall Mall, Royal Favourites, and other brands in the United Kingdom allowed him to extend the business into overseas markets. By 1902 he was exporting to South Africa, the Netherlands, India, and Australia. In 1903 his company was incorporated under the name of Rothmans of Pall Mall in order to distinguish it from his brother Marx's tobacco business. In 1906 Louis created the menthol cigarette, by inserting menthol crystals into the ends of the cigarettes. He also developed a better filter for his Russian cigarettes, known as the "Barber's Neck," which did not leave loose pieces of tobacco touching the lips as earlier filters had. By 1905 Rothmans of Pall Mall was supplying tobacco products to the British royal family, and extended its services to the royal family of Spain in 1910. When Louis went on to open a new store in Regent Street, his brother Marx joined the business, but by 1913 the partnership broke up, with Marx controlling the Regent Street operations and Louis the Pall Mall business. Later that year, Louis acquired a new factory in London and entered into partnership with his friend Markus Weinberg as the Yenidje Tobacco Company Limited.

The early stages of World War I were difficult for the new company. The markets for special blends of Turkish tobacco and handmade cigarettes were in decline, while demand for the cheaper, mass-produced Virginia brands and cigarettes was increasing. Weinberg did not agree with Louis Rothman's proposal to move into this market and the business folded in 1916, after a court case which ended with Louis reviving Rothmans of Pall Mall. Like other tobacco companies, Rothmans contributed to the war effort by supplying duty-free cigarettes to British troops. Louis also concentrated on reorganizing his factory to incorporate new methods of producing Virginia cigarettes.

After the war, in 1919, Louis Rothman brought his son Sidney into the business as an apprentice. Sidney became a partner in 1923, initially concentrating on expanding the company's advertising. The company had advertised in tobacco journals since 1908 but now began to use the national newspapers and leading periodicals. By 1921 such new Rothmans brands as the Marksman and Rhodesian Virginia were reaching a large market through the Rothman Diary Service, which offered customers lower prices for large orders. The use of Rhodesian tobacco was a reflection of a change in government policy. In response to the growing popularity of American tobacco, the British government was trying to encourage the import of Empire tobacco from Nyasaland, Rhodesia, India, and Canada by cutting the tariff on unmanufactured tobacco from these countries. The opening of six more shops in the heart of London between 1923 and 1926 indicates Rothmans's increasing commercial impact. In 1926, a new subsidiary, Rothmans (India) Limited, was established in Bombay. Louis Rothman died in 1926, at the age of 57, but his company's record of success continued under his son's management.

The company opened new premises in Liverpool in 1927. It was the first of many shops to open outside London. Meanwhile its mail order service was doing well, and in 1928 it introduced a new scheme of coupons for the Rothmans Direct Supply Association, which supplied many items, ranging from gardening tools to furniture, at discount prices, including a service inscribing customers' initials in gold leaf. Many manufacturers were reducing their prices at this time, forcing Rothmans to follow suit. Though the company experienced heavy competition at home, its exports were increasing with sales to China, South America, and particularly the territories of the British Empire. In 1929 Rothmans Limited, a public company, was formed, with Sidney Rothman as its first chairman and managing director. With the capital from the new shareholders, shops were established in Glasgow, Manchester, and Bristol, selling the new brands of cigarettes White Horse and Dance Time, as well as Louis D'or and Tuya tobaccos. Throughout the 1930s the company continued to develop new methods of filtration for cigarettes.

Rothmans was persuaded to drop its coupons scheme in 1933, with compensation from one of the larger tobacco companies, as restrictive practices were introduced by the Tobacco Trade Association of which Rothmans was not a member. However, expansion continued. By 1935 Rothmans had additional branches in Hull, Manchester, Birmingham, and Cambridge. Overseas, it had an office in Cuba and had established a factory in Ceylon (now Sri Lanka), though this closed after only two years because of a shortage of staff. The introduction of the famous Consulate Menthol Filter-Tipped Virginia brand secured the company's reputation, while the acquisition of Martins of Piccadilly and its associates, in 1937, secured its supplies of leaf tobacco for the duration of the international crisis of the late 1930s and World War II which followed it. During the war Rothmans supplied parcels to British troops and prisoners of war. Its tins became famous for their adaptation to various uses, for example as material for wireless sets in the prison-camps.

After the war Rothmans Limited made the important decision to look overseas for funds to finance expansion. It had started discussions with the newly founded Rembrandt Tobacco Company, part of Dr. Anton Rupert's Rembrandt Group, on making Rothmans cigarettes in South Africa and production began in 1951. The decision to associate with this South African company significantly changed Rothmans's position within the tobacco industry: by 1954 Rembrandt was in effective control.

Rothmans' association with Carreras, a significantly older company, began four years later. Don Jose Carreras-y-Ferrer, its founder, came from a family of tobacco producers in Spain whose business dated back to the 18th century. He came to London in 1843, after seeking political asylum, and soon gained a reputation as a maker of the fine cigars which were just starting to become popular. His son Don Jose Joaquin concentrated on blending tobacco and snuff and opened a shop off Leicester Square in 1852. By 1874, Carreras was producing one thousand brands of tobacco products.

The company remained a family business until it was taken over by W.J. Yapp in 1894. Yapp had been involved in the shoe leather industry but saw the economic potential of tobacco. Like Louis Rothman he saw the importance of marketing and achieved great success with the Carreras pipe tobacco Craven Mixture. In 1897 he managed to get the novelist and playwright J.M. Barrie to endorse the product. Barrie confirmed that the fictional Arcadia Mixture featured in his book *My Lady Nicotine* was in fact Craven Mixture. Carreras continued to use the endorsement for another 40 years. Yapp ran the company until 1903 when Bernhard Baron joined as director of what now became a public company. Baron had come from

the United States with his cigarette-making machine looking for a company to use it. He had been turned down by the larger companies but Carreras offered him his opportunity in 1904 by setting up Carreras and Marcianus Limited, an associated company concentrating on the production of machine-made cigarettes. Baron and his family gained a controlling interest in Carreras, which introduced new brands such as Black Cat, Carreras Ovals, and Seven Up. In 1904 Carreras was the first tobacco firm to introduce coupons for customers to redeem for gifts, in the packets of the new Black Cat cigarettes. This innovation was such a success that new premises were needed to cope with the demand. Many other companies, including Rothmans, took up the idea. In 1909, the Baron automatic pipe filler cartridges brought Carreras new custom among pipe smokers.

During World War I, Carreras supplied cigarettes to the troops but, unlike Rothmans, it added to the containers such items as French dictionaries and grammar books. In 1921 Carreras produced the first machine-made cork tip cigarette, Craven A. The demand for cigarettes grew and a new factory was needed. The Arcadia Works, which opened in 1928 in London, was unique in its design and organization. It was the first cigarette factory in Britain to have air conditioning, a dust extraction plant, and a welfare service for its workers.

In 1931 Carreras introduced Clubs, a smaller than standard cigarette sold with redeemable coupons for gifts, which was such a success that 14 factories were needed to meet demand. The "coupons war" which followed led some of the tobacco companies to approach the government and seek to have the coupons banned as detrimental to the public interest. An official report issued in 1933 concluded that there was no real problem, since cigarettes with coupons accounted for only 1% of total retail sales. The coupons war came to an end when the major tobacco companies formed the Tobacco Trade Association: Carreras was a founding member.

During World War II, the allocation of leaf tobacco to the various companies was rationed by the government. Some of the small companies felt that the system favored the majors, but Carreras enjoyed good relations with such large companies as Imperial and Gallaher. Tobacco consumption increased sharply during the war, and with import restrictions maintained until the early 1950s it became difficult for the industry to meet the demands of consumers. In 1953 Carreras acquired Murray, Sons & Company of Belfast, which still manufactures today. Carreras also moved to a new plant in Essex at that time. The new plant overstretched the resources of the company and in 1958 the Baron family sold its shares to the Rembrandt Tobacco Corporation (S.A.) Limited, which merged the company with Rothmans to create Carreras Rothmans Limited. By the 1960s the tobacco companies were spending heavily on television commercials, but in 1965 commercials for cigarettes were banned, though commercials for cigars continued until December 1991. Carreras Rothmans and its rivals reverted to using coupons schemes and began to sponsor sports and the arts.

The Third World offered new markets and resources and in 1966 Carreras Rothmans was one of the first tobacco companies to operate in Brazil, though its venture there was subsequently sold. The beginning of the 1970s saw a series of takeovers in the tobacco industry, to which Rembrandt responded with the creation of Rothmans International in 1972, bringing together Carreras Rothmans of the United Kingdom, Martin Brinkmann of West Germany, the Belgian company Tabacofina, and Turmac of the Netherlands. Rupert controlled Rothmans International through his Luxembourg-based company, the Rupert Foundation, which in turn controlled Rothmans Tobacco (Holdings), the owner of 44% of the equity and 50% of the votes and convertible stock at that time.

Rothmans International began to diversify away from tobacco products in 1978 when it acquired Rothmans of Pall Mall Canada with its holdings in the Carling O'Keefe brewery. In 1967 Carreras acquired 51% of Alfred Dunhill Limited, a rival tobacco firm that was well established in the Netherlands, Denmark, Switzerland, Germany, and France. Alfred Dunhill Limited later widened its range to include toiletries, men's wear, and other luxury items.

By the mid-1970s, cigarette sales were dropping as the issue of smokers' health came to the fore. Less than half of the world's cigarette market was, and still is, controlled by half a dozen multinationals, including Rothmans International. Markets in the United States and Europe were saturated and it was the markets of the Third World in which Rothmans now sought to build its presence, discussing the formation of a joint venture with the American firm R.J. Reynolds, the world's third largest cigarette producer. Rothmans by this time was an attractive associate for any large company, holding more than 40% of the markets in Ireland, the Netherlands, and Belgium, 18% in West Germany, 13% in the United Kingdom, 75% in New Zealand, 36% in Australia, and 26% in Canada. R.J. Reynolds, makers of cigarettes such as Camel and Winston, saw great potential in the proposal but it was abandoned when Rupert decided to sell 25% of the company to Reynolds's main competitor, Philip Morris, noted for its Marlboro cigarettes, and the second largest tobacco company in the world.

In 1983 Rothmans acquired an interest in Cartier Monde, which specializes in jewelry, watches, and other luxury accessories. In the United Kingdom, Carreras Rothmans Limited changed its operating name to Rothmans (UK) Limited in 1984, then to Rothmans International Tobacco (UK) Limited in 1986. In 1987 Rothmans decided to sell its 50% share in the Carling O'Keefe brewery in Canada, which was not meeting expectations. In 1988 the Rembrandt Group decided to restructure its international activities with the formation of a new holding company based in Switzerland, Compagnie Financière Richemont (CFR), which has only 39 shareholders. Rembrandt wanted to separate its international operations and its South African activities to concentrate on developing its interests in Europe during the development of the single European market. This reorganization meant that Richemont held 33% of Rothmans International p.l.c. This rose to 63.2% in 1990 when Richemont bought back Philip Morris's shares. Rothmans International then acquired the Dutch company Theodorus Niemeyer, makers of fine cut and pipe tobaccos such as Samson and Sail, increased its holding in Dunhill to 56.9%, and in 1991 signed an agreement with the China Tobacco Corporation to produce Rothmans and Dunhill brands in China.

Principal Subsidiaries: Tabacofina-Vander Elst N.V. (Belgium); Tabacco Exporters International Limited (United Kingdom); Martin Brinkmann AG (Germany); Turmac Tobacco Company B.V. (Netherlands); Murray, Sons and Company Limited (United Kingdom); Alfred Dunhill Limited (United Kingdom, 57%); Chloé S.A. (France, 57%); Cartier Monde S.A. (Luxembourg, 47%); Carreras of Cyprus Limited (Cyprus).

Further Reading: Corina, Maurice, *Trust in Tobacco,* London, Michael Joseph, 1975; Finger, William, ed., *The Tobacco Industry in Transition,* Lexington, Mass., Lexington Books, 1981; Taylor, Peter, *Smoke Ring,* London, The Bodley Head, 1984; *Rothmans Company History,* London, Rothmans International p.l.c., 1986.

—Monique Lamontagne

TABACALERA, S. A.

TABACALERA, S.A.

Barquillo 5
28004 Madrid
Spain
(1) 532 7600
Fax: (1) 522-7586

State-Owned Company
Incorporated: 1887 as Compañia Arrendataria de Tabacos
Employees: 8,510
Sales: Pta 593.45 billion (US$6.14 billion)

Tabacalera, S.A. is one of Spain's largest and oldest companies, and is the dominant force in its principal area of activity, tobacco manufacture and distribution. Protected for more than 300 years by a government-enforced monopoly, the company has been able to build a practically unassailable position in this market, one that looks likely to remain solid despite the recent dismantling of the monopoly.

From its base in the tobacco industry, Tabacalera has begun to diversify into a number of different areas, primarily the food industry, as a result of changes brought by Spain's membership of the European Economic Community (EEC) and the worldwide decline in tobacco consumption. Although this diversification process has been accompanied by a number of problems, the company's widespread manufacturing operations and well-developed distribution network, complete with a large fleet of trucks, provide it with a good base on which to expand operations.

Tabacalera is one of the oldest companies in the world, having its roots in the period of Spanish colonization of Central and South America. Tobacco was one of many substances unknown in Europe which the *conquistadores* discovered as they pushed the boundaries of Spanish domination south from their first settlements in Mexico during the 16th century. Regarded initially as a curiosity with supposedly medicinal properties when ground and inhaled, tobacco was used only in small quantities during the 16th century.

One of the main features of Spanish colonial expansion was the government's determination to retain tight control of the economic traffic between the colonies and Spain itself. Aimed mainly at ensuring a steady flow of mineral wealth from American mines, this policy limited the number of ports in the colonies that could ship goods to Spain and the number of ports in Spain that could receive them. At the Spanish end, the government designated Seville as the central port for trade with the colonies, controlled by the Casa de Contratacion—the hiring house for seafarers—established in 1504.

Seville thus became the center of tobacco imports from the Americas and was one of the first places in Europe where the tobacco plant was cultivated. In the early 17th century, a factory for processing tobacco was built on the banks of the Guadalquivir river near Seville to cater for the growing popularity of snuff—powdered tobacco—among Sevillans.

In 1636 the Spanish government moved to ensure its control of the growing tobacco trade within Spain as well as with the colonies by establishing a monopoly of tobacco production and sales in the kingdoms of Castille and Leon. The government decreed that the trade would be controlled by a new body, the Estanco del Tabaco. Despite considerable changes to its structure and powers in the following three and a half centuries, the Estanco del Tabaco formed the foundation of today's Tabacalera S.A.

The use of tobacco grew steadily during the late 17th and early 18th centuries, and in 1725 the Estanco del Tabaco decided to build a new factory in Seville to provide for the increasing demand. Although work began in 1728, disputes over the plans and other problems delayed completion of the new factory until 1770. The size of the new Royal Tobacco Factory of Seville and its proximity to the tobacco port made it the most important tobacco manufacturing plant in the world at the time.

As popular tobacco tastes changed in the early 19th century, the Royal Tobacco Factory restructured its operations to stop producing exclusively powdered tobacco, which was being overtaken by smoking tobacco, particularly cigars. The shift to cigar manufacture, a highly labor-intensive process, demanded a large, cheap work force to hand-roll the tobacco leaves. This demand was satisfied by using large numbers of women in the factory, one of the first instances of large-scale involvement of women in industry in Spain, which provided the inspiration for the main character in Merimée's novella, *Carmen*, which in turn inspired Bizet's opera of the same name.

The demand created by the emergence of cigars as a popular form of tobacco prompted the Estanco del Tabaco to invest heavily in expanding its productive capacity during the 19th century. With a second factory already established at Cadiz, the Estanco opened nine new factories across the country during the 19th century, creating one of Spain's biggest and most productive industrial enterprises.

In the mid-19th century, the Spanish government began looking for ways to change the managerial structure of the company to take account of the more sophisticated economic environment, in which the existing structure of direct state control appeared outdated and hampered the delivery of the highest possible profit to the state. Various proposals were put forward from 1844 onwards, and in 1887 the operations were placed under the control of a strictly corporate entity, when the state transferred its monopoly to the central bank, the Bank of Spain, which formed a company, the Compañia Arrendataria de Tabacos, which in turn leased the management of the monopoly from the bank. The new corporate structure was aimed at achieving the greatest efficiency from the operation by distancing it from the government, while ensuring the continuing supply of revenue to the state from the tobacco operations.

The leasing company controlled the tobacco monopoly for the next 60 years, during the tumultuous Spanish Civil War of the 1930s and the final victory of the fascists in 1938. When the contract between the company and the bank came up for its regular review in the early 1940s, the government changed the legal structure of the company once again, opting this time to turn it into a conventional limited company, wholly owned by the state. In March 1945 the limited company Tabacalera, Sociedad Anonima, Compañia Gestora del Monopolio de Tabacos y Servicios Anejos was formed, setting in place the corporate structure that the company retains today.

After three and a half centuries operating in the comfortable environment of a state-enforced monopoly, the company was presented with its greatest challenge in January 1986, when Spain joined the EEC. As part of the requirements for joining the community, the government was obliged to relinquish its monopoly of tobacco production and sales.

This process involved partial privatization, with the state transferring all its assets and acquired rights in the tobacco monopoly to Tabacalera, in exchange for shares issued by the company in November 1986, leaving the state with a controlling stake of 53% of the company's capital.

Under the new laws, wholesale import and tobacco trading activities for tobacco produced in the EEC—the key to Tabacalera's monopoly—were liberalized, giving anybody the right to carry out these activities. Although the company continued to manage the monopoly for tobacco products manufactured outside the EEC, and although the state retained control of the retail sales monopoly through its concessionaires, the breaking of the local production monopoly struck at the heart of Tabacalera's operations. With this fundamental change and the impending single European market due by 1993, it was clear that the company had to do more than simply continue making and selling tobacco products if it was to survive. The urgency of change was made more pressing by signs that tobacco sales could no longer be counted on to rise as anti-smoking sentiment increased worldwide.

In 1987, under the presidency of Candido Velazquez Gaztelu, Tabacalera launched a wide-ranging diversification plan aimed at ensuring the company's future in the less secure post-monopoly commercial environment. Velazquez pushed the company into two new areas—food manufacturing and retail distribution—on the basis that these two sectors were best suited to Tabacalera's existing operational structure.

After taking a first tentative step into the food industry in 1986 by setting up a snack foods operation, Nabisco Brands España y Portugal, as a joint venture with RJR Nabisco, Tabacalera bought the company completely after Kohlberg Kravis Roberts took over RJR Nabisco in 1988. In the same period, Tabacalera bought a group of companies controlled by the food group Instituto Nacional de Industria. These companies gave the group access to a range of food markets, comprising Spain's leading milk concentrate and liquid milk producer, Lactaria Española (LESA), meat and preserves company Carnes y Conservas Españolas SA (CARCESA), deep-frozen foods producer Frioalimentos (FRIDARAGO), and Congelados Ibericos SA (COISA). Tabacalera also bought a controlling share in a pulses company, Comercial Industrial Fernandez (COIFER SA), and a stake in a marine cultivation company, Acuicultura.

The company also moved strongly into retail distribution, buying 75% of retailing business Distribuciones Reus SA (DIRSA)—a company with 325 supermarkets and over 500

franchised shops, which in turn owned another company with a chain of more than a hundred supermarkets. The diversification program made Tabacalera one of Spain's leading producers of biscuits, powdered and concentrated desserts, and milk packaging, as well as giving it a leading position in the tomato sauces, pulps, conserves, juices, and pulses markets and control of one of the largest networks of retail outlets in the country.

But rather than assure Tabacalera a secure hold on a broader range of operations, the swift diversification program brought with it a number of serious problems. The main one was that, in the rush to acquire new businesses, the company had bought a number of operations which were heavy loss-makers. Tabacalera planned to use the economies of scale provided by such a large group to turn the troubled subsidiaries around, but after two years it became clear that the worst of them were largely unsalvageable and would only hamper the group's efforts to become more flexible.

Velazquez's successor as chairman, Miguel Angel del Valle Inclan, who took office in 1989, began a process of rationalizing the group's food and distribution activities, describing Velazquez's diversification program as "too ambitious", as reported by Reuter News Service on June 21, 1990. His aim was to keep only the profitable food subsidiaries, and to acquire businesses in other sectors, so that by 1992 the company's revenue from non-tobacco activities would match its tobacco revenue.

After owning it for only two years, Tabacalera sold the Dirsa retail chain to the French Promodes group for Pta 12 billion in 1990. In the same year, the company sold its interest in Fridarago and gave up its management of the Tabacos de Filipinas company, which it had entered as part of the diversification plan, but which had incurred losses of Pta 1.4 billion in 1989 and 1990.

The main problem of the diversification was the milk company Lesa, which continued to lose money despite Tabacalera's injection of large sums to try to improve it. The group provided more than Pta 8 billion to Lesa in the two years after buying it, but in 1990 the milk producer still showed a huge loss of Pta 5.2 billion. Tabacalera offered Lesa for sale, and by April 1991 was holding advanced talks with the French group Union Laitière Normande over the sale of the subsidiary.

After cleaning out the bulk of its unprofitable food operations, Tabacalera moved to consolidate the more lucrative new businesses by merging its Nabisco subsidiary with the Carcesa operation to create a leaner, more efficient food division. Under del Valle, the company also began to diversify into other areas, particularly real estate and tourism. In 1990 Tabacalera took a 33% stake in a joint venture to build a Pta 10 billion tourist complex in the Canary Islands. The company also began to take advantage of its widespread real estate holdings by leasing them out, as well as beginning to use its distribution network to deliver other companies' products. The most lucrative of these contracts was concluded in 1990, when the West German company Quelle, Europe's biggest mail-order house, chose to use Tabacalera's trucks for its Spanish deliveries.

As well as these moves into different markets, the company updated its core tobacco operations during the 1980s to take account of changes in the market. Spanish smokers began to give up their traditional preference for black tobacco in favor of blond Virginian tobacco. By 1985 Virginian tobacco sales in Spain had already risen to 44% of the total and were clearly about to eclipse black tobacco. Tabacalera responded by reorganizing its cultivation and processing to produce more Virginian, which provided a higher profit margin. The company took consideration of this consumption change when it began building a new factory at Cadiz in 1984, much bigger and more efficient than the company's existing plants.

In preparation for the challenges likely to emerge from the coming of the single European market in 1993, the company signed an agreement with Tabaqueira de Portugal in 1989 to allow cross-marketing of the two companies' brands in their respective countries. In December 1990 Tabacalera also announced a modernization plan, which would involve the loss of 1,500 jobs, to produce a leaner company in time for the advent of the single market.

The changes brought about by Spain joining the EEC and the challenges posed by the single market have caused the question of Tabacalera's relationship with the state to be raised once again. In August 1990 del Valle said that the arrival of the single market was a good time to consider whether the state should continue to be the company's major shareholder (*Cinco Dias*, August 31, 1990). The question was sharpened by the threat posed to Tabacalera by legislation passed in 1990 banning almost all forms of tobacco advertising. In December 1990 Spanish newspapers reported that Tabacalera was aiming to see a reduction in the state's stake, allowing the company to be quoted on Spanish stock exchanges by the end of 1992. It is not yet known what proportion of the company's shares will be quoted.

The growing debate reached its peak in April 1991, when del Valle was forced out of office in what the *Financial Times* described on April 10, 1991 as "what appears to be the climax of a political confrontation with the Finance Ministry." He was replaced by German Calvillo Urabayen, president of another government-controlled body, Fomento de Comercio Exterior.

Despite the initial difficulties caused by the loss of its monopoly and the problems created by an over-zealous diversification program, Tabacalera appears to have emerged in a good position to face the more competitive environment of a single European market. Its profits are healthy, its core tobacco business has been reorganized to take account of a changing market, and its expansion into other sectors has become more focused and disciplined after the initial problems. If the question of the company's relationship with the state can be resolved smoothly and the modernization program implemented without problems, Tabacalera will be well-positioned to become a powerful industrial group in post-1992 Europe.

Principal Subsidiaries: Tabacanaria, SA (Canary Islands); Cigarros de Canarias, SA (Canary Islands); Carnes y Conservas Españoles, SA (Spain); Nabisco Brands España, SA (Spain, 97%); Servicio de Venta Automatica, SA (Spain); Philip Morris España, SA (Canary Islands, 50%); BAT España, SA (Spain, 50%).

Further Reading: Torres Mulas, R. & D. Hortas, *Tabacalera: 350 Años Despues,* Tabacalera, Madrid, 1987.

—Richard Brass

UNIVERSAL CORPORATION

Hamilton Street at Broad
Richmond Virginia 23230
U.S.A.
(804) 359-9311
Fax: (804) 254-3583

Public Company
Incorporated: 1918 as Universal Leaf Tobacco Company,
   Incorporated
Employees: 25,000
Sales: $2.90 billion
Stock Exchange: New York

Universal Corporation was known until the 1980s as Universal Leaf Tobacco Company, Incorporated, and it remains the world's largest independent leaf tobacco dealer. Universal buys, processes, stores, and sells tobacco in all of the world's tobacco-growing regions. For many years, Universal's most important customer has been Philip Morris, the world's leading cigarette manufacturer. During the course of its long career in international markets, the company also has built a thriving trade in other commodities such as tea, rubber, and peanuts, and has amassed sizable European interests in timber and building supplies.

Tobacco buying in the United States has long been conducted at auctions held throughout the prime growing areas in North Carolina, Kentucky, Virginia, and other states. As intermediaries between growers and manufacturers of tobacco products, leaf dealers achieved a position of some power prior to the formation in 1889 of The American Tobacco Company, the so-called tobacco trust of James B. Duke. Duke's trust controlled all of the large U.S. tobacco manufacturers, and it was not long before American Tobacco took steps to circumvent the tobacco leaf dealers by buying its product directly from farmers at auction. Under the pressure of American Tobacco's overwhelming presence in the market, the number of independent leaf dealers dwindled until the dissolution of the trust in 1911. By that time, what dealers remained had combined into larger and more effective organizations that were able to capitalize on the sharp rise in demand for tobacco then beginning. Although the successor companies to the tobacco trust—R.J. Reynolds, Liggett & Myers, Lorillard, and a smaller American Tobacco Company—continued to dominate the leaf markets, the overall growth in tobacco consumption in the United States left room for a limited number of independent dealers to prosper throughout the 1910s.

This renewed vigor among the leaf dealers culminated in the 1916 establishment of the International Planters Corporation, a nationwide organization of dealers that was apparently powerful enough to maintain somewhat firmer prices to its large manufacturing customers. One of International Planters' largest clients was the new American Tobacco, whose president, Percival S. Hill, was instrumental in the creation of a second, competing organization of leaf dealers, Universal Leaf Tobacco Company. The company's nucleus had been formed in 1916, when Hill's vice president of leaf purchasing, Thomas B. Yuille, resigned from American Tobacco and gained control of J.P. Taylor Company, a prosperous dealer in the rich tobacco lands of Virginia and North Carolina. To this foundation, Yuille and Hill added 13 other local dealers, 6 from other states, and storage and shipping facilities in New York City. Together, Universal Leaf's subsidiaries and affiliates bought 100 million pounds of tobacco in the company's first year of existence, or nearly 10% of national production—an extraordinary figure for any industrial newcomer. Within eight years, Universal became the largest independent tobacco dealer in the world, a status it has maintained.

Percival Hill died in 1925, and by 1930 American Tobacco was again doing all of its own leaf purchasing, while Universal Leaf had forged a new alliance with Philip Morris that would prove to be of long duration. Philip Morris was late in joining the ranks of the major tobacco manufacturers, and as its business expanded dramatically in the middle decades of the 20th century Philip Morris found it simpler to leave most of its leaf buying in the hands of Universal, rather than take the time to create its own staff of buyers and warehousers. The relationship thus established between the two companies was intimate and durable, even including the financing by Universal of some of Philip Morris's tobacco purchases in the 1930s, and in effect Universal served as Philip Morris's tobacco purchasing department for many years. Philip Morris grew into the world's leading maker of cigarettes, and its leaf requirements increased, strengthening the relationship between Philip Morris and Universal Leaf.

A second important customer for Universal during its early years was Export Leaf Tobacco Company, the purchasing arm of British tobacco giant, British American Tobacco (BAT). Export Leaf did not buy its burley tobacco directly, relying instead on Universal Leaf's network of experienced burley dealers for its requirements. Leaf tobacco may broadly be divided between burley and flue-cured varieties; burley became a key ingredient of the increasingly popular "American blend" cigarette. Export Leaf shipped its burley purchases to BAT, which in turn used the bulk of it for the manufacture of Brown & Williamson brands, such as Raleigh and Viceroy. Universal bought all of its burley via a subsidiary of its own called Southwestern Tobacco Company, which by the end of the 1930s was buying about 20% of the entire U.S. crop. Some 60% of Southwestern's burley went to Export Leaf making that company one of the two pillars, with Philip Morris, of Universal Leaf's prosperity at that time. Universal Leaf was able to carve out a place for itself in the international markets by offering large manufacturers the expertise they could not otherwise obtain. In the case of Export Leaf, it was probably also helpful that the presidents of Export and of Universal were brothers.

Universal's numerous foreign affiliates and offices were important to its growth. As early as the 1930s, Universal was both exporting and importing large quantities of tobacco leaf. In addition to its sales to Export Leaf, destined for markets in the British Commonwealth, Universal shipped U.S. cigarette tobacco to manufacturers around the world, including those in Scandinavia, Turkey, and Japan. Universal Leaf not only established trading offices around the world but also built processing plants for local threshing and storage, and in some cases provided training and financial help to individual farmers. Its international business eventually included plants in Brazil, Italy, Korea, and the African nations of Malawi and Zimbabwe, as well as a network of dealers and brokers who slowly began to handle other commodities such as cocoa, tea, peanuts, and rubber. The trade in commodities was a natural outgrowth of Universal Leaf's foreign tobacco business; it developed slowly and was dispersed among a large number of non-consolidated subsidiaries and affiliates whose contribution to Universal Leaf's growth was rarely noted by financial analysts. Similarly, Universal Leaf quietly put together a large timber and building supplies distribution business in Europe, primarily in the Netherlands, which along with the commodities business grew to provide approximately 33% of the company's revenue.

In 1940 Universal Leaf was one of eight tobacco companies charged with violations of the Sherman Antitrust Act. The federal government brought suit in a Kentucky court, charging the industry leaders with price manipulation in both the purchasing and sales aspects of the business, including an alleged conspiracy to limit prices paid for leaf tobacco at auction. The three largest defendants, American Tobacco, R.J. Reynolds, and Liggett & Myers, stood trial on behalf of all eight, with Universal Leaf and the other four companies agreeing to abide by the court's decision. Like most antitrust cases, the outcome of this struggle was less than definitive. After years of argument the eight defendants were found guilty as charged, although no evidence of actual collusion was found or even asserted; and after paying the insignificant sum of $255,000 the eight companies returned to business as usual, the court offering no suggestions as to how the market might be made more competitive. The trial's message seemed to be that the tobacco market's domination by three or four manufacturers rendered it inherently monopolistic—or at least not ideally competitive—regardless of whether the parties involved were engaged in literal collusion, but no changes in the market were effected or recommended by the court. Universal Leaf was barely affected by the case, as its costs were largely borne by the three lead defendants.

The post-World War II decade saw a remarkable surge in the popularity of cigarette smoking in the United States, and in particular the rise of Philip Morris to national leadership. As Morris's unofficial leaf buyer, Universal Leaf benefited from the growing international success of such Philip Morris brands as Marlboro, which rose from obscurity to become the world's leading seller in the 1980s. Universal Leaf's sales reached $215 million in 1961, on which the company earned a low but very steady 2% to 3% profit. With commission work representing the bulk of Universal Leaf's business, its revenue was fixed to a cost-plus-fee basis, limiting net income but offering exceptionally stable growth from year to year. Still, the gradually accumulating evidence of tobacco's health hazards prompted

Universal Leaf to diversify its asset base. The company's first significant acquisition outside the tobacco leaf business was its 1968 purchase of Inta Roto Company, makers of packaging equipment, and of Overton Container Corporation, suppliers of boxes to the tobacco industry. This was followed closely by the purchase of Unitized Systems Company, the beginning of Universal's interest in the building supplies industry, and the creation of a land development subsidiary called Universal Land Use Corporation. None of these early efforts at diversification was of great importance, however, when compared to Universal's holdings in the early 1990s in commodities and European building materials.

By the mid-1970s Universal Leaf's steady growth and valuable ties with Philip Morris attracted the attention of Congoleum Corporation, a Milwaukee-based maker of linoleum and furniture that was looking for acquisitions. In October 1976 Congoleum made an unsolicited bid of $32.50 per share for all of Universal's common stock, surprising Wall Street and enraging the directors of Universal. Universal's chairman and chief executive officer, Gordon Crenshaw, led a complex strategy of resistance to the takeover, filing suits in Virginia and Chicago, and amending the corporate charter. When Crenshaw and other top Universal officials made it clear that if the company were bought they would take their customers with them to some new and competing venture, Congoleum withdrew its offer.

In 1984 with sales at around $1.3 billion, Universal made a second and more serious attempt at diversification when it purchased two of the leading title insurance companies in the United States, Lawyers Title Insurance Company and Continental Land Title. At first the insurers produced an excellent return on their $200 million in sales. The late 1980s saw a severe recession in real estate, however, which coincided with an increase in claims. In September 1991, with no end in sight for the real estate downturn, Universal spun off its title insurance companies as an independent corporation called Lawyers Title Corporation, with Universal shareholders becoming the initial owners of Lawyers Title's stock.

In the early 1990s, Universal Corporation—the company's name was changed in the mid-1980s following the adoption of a holding company structure—was sailing on much as it had for the past 60 years, the core of its business generated by tobacco. As a result of further diversification moves in the mid-1980s, its overseas subsidiaries in commodities and housing supplies have flourished to such an extent that they supply a significant amount of revenues and earnings. Universal operated in the early 1990s under the guidance of new chief executive Henry Harrell, who replaced Gordon Crenshaw in October 1988 after the latter had served nearly 25 years in that position.

Principal Subsidiaries: Universal Leaf Tobacco Company, Incorporated.

Further Reading: Nicholls, William H., *Price Policies in the Cigarette Industry,* Nashville, Tennessee, The Vanderbilt University Press, 1951.

—Jonathan Martin

TRANSPORT SERVICES

British Railways Board
Burlington Northern Inc.
Canadian Pacific Limited
Consolidated Freightways, Inc.
Consolidated Rail Corporation
CSX Corporation
Danzas Group
Deutsche Bundesbahn
East Japan Railway Company
Federal Express Corporation
Hankyu Corporation
Kawasaki Kisen Kaisha, Ltd.
Keio Teito Electric Railway Company
Kinki Nippon Railway Company Ltd.
Kühne & Nagel International AG
La Poste
Mitsui O.S.K. Lines, Ltd.
Nippon Express Co., Ltd.
Nippon Yusen Kabushiki Kaisha
Norfolk Southern Corporation

Odakyu Electric Railway Company Limited
The Peninsular and Oriental Steam Navigation Company
Penske Corporation
PHH Corporation
Post Office Group
Roadway Services, Inc.
Ryder System, Inc.
Santa Fe Pacific Corporation
Seibu Railway Co. Ltd.
Société Nationale des Chemins de Fer Français
Southern Pacific Transportation Company
The Swiss Federal Railways (Schweizerische Bundesbahnen)
TNT Limited
Tokyu Corporation
Union Pacific Corporation
United Parcel Service of America Inc.
Yamato Transport Co. Ltd.
Yellow Freight System, Inc. of Delaware

BRITISH RAILWAYS BOARD

Euston House
24 Eversholt Street
Post Office Box 100
London NW1 1DZ
United Kingdom
(071) 928-5151
Fax: (071) 922-6994

State-Owned Company
Incorporated: 1963 as British Railways Board
Employees: 136,200
Sales: £3.08 billion (US$5.76 billion)

British Railways Board administers British Rail (BR), which maintains a rail network of about 10,300 route miles, over which it operates passenger and freight train services. This comprises the entire rail network within the United Kingdom, apart from some urban transport systems—the largest of which is London Underground—and a number of small privately owned railways, many supported by preservation societies. The BR network consists of very slightly more than half the route-miles formerly owned by the private railway companies nationalized by the Transport Act of 1947.

It was not because of bankruptcy that the railways were nationalized; in their first year of public ownership, they had net receipts of £22 million and surpluses rose to a peak of £37 million in 1952. However, they disappeared by 1955, to be followed by deficits. The Labour government of 1945 to 1951 nationalized the railways as part of a plan to integrate all public inland transport under a British Transport Commission owning the railways. London Transport, the ports and canals, and public road transport whether by bus or by haulage companies. Each of these forms of transport was to be managed by an Executive responsible to the commission.

Under the central, and centralized, management of the Railway Executive, British Railways took the form of six regions, largely based on the systems of the former private railway companies, although Scotland was a single unified region. There was no general management at regional level—functional lines of authority came directly from the executive, which concentrated upon the subordination of former company loyalties to enable new standard practices to be introduced. In this it met appreciable opposition.

The lifetime of the Railway Executive, though not one of serious financial difficulty, was marked by friction between the British Transport Commission and the Executive partly due to a clash of temperaments between their respective chairmen, Sir Cyril Hurcomb, a former civil servant, who became Lord Hurcomb in 1950, and Sir Eustace Missenden, a career railwayman. Missenden's retirement in 1951 and his replacement by John Elliot—Sir John Elliot from 1953—eased the tension, but the awareness of disharmony between the Executive and both the regions below it and the commission above it was a factor in the decision by the Conservative government, which came to office in 1951, to abolish the Executive.

The Transport Act of 1953 retained the commission but removed the duty of integration. It abolished the Railway Executive, and British Railways now came directly under the British Transport Commission (BTC), which acquired new members and a formidable new chairman, General Sir Brian Robertson. The BTC considered that the past had been marked by overemphasis on standardization and a lack of innovation. Area boards were set up, as was required by the 1953 act, and regional general managers were given significant authority.

For a time, under the policy of decentralization enjoined on the BTC by the government, the regions had greater autonomy. Planning from headquarters was less decisive, and the area boards shared to some extent in policy-making. However, the BTC still had very large non-railway interests and was organized by its new chairman in a complex web of coordinating bodies. Meanwhile, the financial situation was deteriorating as the postwar recovery from austerity enabled competing private road transport to expand. In 1955 the railway deficit was £39 million. Government anxiety about the position was temporarily allayed by the announcement in that year of a modernization plan designed both to attract new rail traffic through better service and to reduce working costs. The plan proposed expenditure of £1.24 billion, soon revised to £1.5 billion, spread over a 15-year period.

The plan's most striking feature was the complete replacement of steam by diesel and electric traction. Its weakness lay in a failure to assess the market correctly, in respect of either the "container revolution" impending on the freight side or the explosion in private car ownership on the passenger side.

The continuing rise in the deficit, despite the temporary euphoria created by the plan, caused two major inquiries to be launched—a public inquiry by the House of Commons Select Committee on the Nationalised Industries, chaired by Sir Toby Low (later Lord Aldington), and a private inquiry by a group chaired by the industrialist Sir Ivan Stedeford, reporting direct to the Conservative minister of transport, Ernest Marples. Both bodies reached broadly the same conclusion: that the headquarters organization of the BTC was too cumbersome for effective management of the railways and that commercial and social objectives had become confused.

Marples accepted this general conclusion and the Transport Act of 1962 broke up the BTC into several component boards directly responsible to the minister. The railways from 1963 came under a British Railways Board (BRB) with its own capital structure and statutory objectives. Part of the BTC's capital liabilities were allocated to the new BRB as a commencing capital debt to the minister of £1.562 billion, of which only £857 million was interest-bearing, the remainder being suspended debt—that is, debt upon which payment of interest and repayment of principal were indefinitely suspended.

The first chairman of the BRB, Richard Beeching, had been a member of the Stedeford Special Advisory Group—appointed by Marples to "examine the structure, finance, and working of the organizations at present controlled by the Commission"—where he had impressed the minister. Marples and Beeching had agreed that the BRB's immediate task was to eliminate the deficit and in the process bring in new blood from the business world to stimulate the performance of the professional railway managers.

Beeching rapidly set in motion studies designed to identify loss-making activities. Data collected from the regions were analyzed by a team at headquarters and presented to Beeching. The conclusions he drew were published in a 1963 report "The Re-Shaping of British Railways," which caused a furor. While it made Beeching a celebrity overnight, it created widespread alarm and controversy. To carry out all the suggested closures and service withdrawals was politically impracticable, yet publishing lists of this kind accelerated a flight of traffic away from the railway, even on lines that in the event were to remain open.

The re-shaping report was, however, followed by another, "The Development of the Major Trunk Routes," in which Beeching called for rationalization through elimination of duplicate routes and substantial investment in the survivors. It also foreshadowed the Freightliner Company network of fast trainload container services and the bulk trainload services to coal-fired power stations.

Neither report was to be implemented in full. Marples, in any case, was succeeded by a Labour minister of transport in October 1964, Tom Fraser, with whom Beeching could not have such a continuing understanding. Beeching, therefore, left in June 1965. He was followed by Stanley Raymond, knighted in 1967, who had been one of his chief lieutenants in formulating the closures policy. Raymond was energetic, abrasive, and not good at delegating. During his short tenure of office it became clear that line closures and withdrawals alone were not going to solve BR's financial problem. In any case, even under Marples, ministerial consent to closure had been refused in politically sensitive areas.

The next (Labour) minister of transport, Barbara Castle, was determined to implement a new transport policy incorporating a modified form of integration and also to improve the structure and performance of the BRB. A joint steering group was set up, comprising ministry, BR, and outside experts, which met many times and reported at length. Raymond clashed with Castle on several issues, including charges and industrial relations, and she dismissed him at the end of 1967. He was succeeded by H.C. Johnson, a career railwayman who had been a successful regional general manager and a board vice-chairman and who received a knighthood in 1972.

Johnson, a shrewd affable man, had built his career on his ability to be in the right place at the right time. His three-and-three-quarter years as chairman were marked by several factors that worked to his advantage. Castle's Transport Act of 1968 had removed the loss-making "Sundries"—small consignments by freight train—business from BR and placed it under a new National Freight Corporation (NFC). The act also created passenger transport authorities and executives in the major conurbations, ultimately seven, which were empowered to pay British Rail to provide otherwise loss-making services in their areas. Furthermore, the government took power to make grants to BR for the maintenance of individual socially necessary train services. BR's "suspended debt" was extinguished and the "live" or interest-bearing debt was reduced to £365 million.

As a consequence, BR showed overall surpluses both on railway operating accounts and in the corporate field, allowing for interest and net income from other activities, both in 1969 and 1970.

The line closures and service withdrawals that had begun before the re-shaping report but that had been greatly accelerated by it, then were shrinking, partly because the most obvious cases had been dealt with, partly because of ministerial refusals to approve politically sensitive proposals.

One legacy of the Beeching era, the concept of fast container-carrying trains in fixed formation running on a schedule between major roadrail transhipment centers, had been realized in the setting up of the Freightliner Company, though to BR's chagrin a majority share had been vested by the 1968 act in the NFC—a decision reversed in 1978.

By 1970 many fruits of the 1955 modernization plan had been realized, despite some miscalculations such as the proliferation of diesel locomotive types and overinvestment in freight facilities that quickly became redundant. The last steam train ran in 1968, which was also the year in which the busiest main line, from London to Birmingham, Manchester, and Liverpool came into full electric operation. Electric traction had reached Dover in 1959 and Bournemouth in 1967.

There were other forces at work not apparent to the public. Inside the BRB long debates raged, fueled by reports from the joint steering group and by consultants, regarding the correct form of organization both at headquarters and in the regions. Changes followed—such as the appointment of a chief executive—only to be reversed in many cases. In the regions, geographical districts gave way to larger geographical divisions though system-based lines had existed for some years in the eastern and southern regions, and partially elsewhere.

The eastern and northeastern regions were amalgamated as an economy move in 1967. In 1971, consultants McKinsey & Co., working with a team of BR officers, produced a scheme for replacing the regions with eight territories having revised powers and responsibilities. After much open trade union, and covert managerial, opposition, this Field organization proposal, as it had been called, was abandoned in 1975.

Changes that took firm shape and were ultimately to assist privatization, were embodied in the progressive detachment of the non-railway businesses such as shipping, ultimately to become Sealink U.K.; the workshops, eventually British Rail Engineering Ltd.; and the hotels, which became British Transport Hotels Ltd. The road collection and delivery vehicles had passed to the NFC under the 1968 act. On the advice of consultants, the role of the BRB was defined as corporate, as distinct from the businesses, of which the railway was by far the most important. A BR corporate image, with the double-arrow logo and the trading name British Rail, was adopted.

Although the Beeching philosophy had sought withdrawal from nonprofit-making activities, it had increasingly become evident that this was not a final answer. Greater productivity in most aspects of the railway was essential. Single-manning of diesel and electric locomotives and withdrawal of guards from power-braked freight trains were obvious examples of the scope for economy that existed also in profitable activities.

An experienced industrial negotiator, Leonard Neal, was recruited from Esso in 1967 and his skill and patience eventually turned the railway trade unions' opposition into a modicum of cooperation, starting in 1968 with the so-called Windsor and Penzance agreements, which were concerned with pay awards, regrading of staff, new working practices, and other matters. He was knighted in 1974.

Johnson retired in September 1971 on what may be considered the crest of the wave. His successor was Richard (Sir Richard after 1976 and Lord after 1981) Marsh, who had been minister of transport in the Wilson Labour government but had left politics for private consultancy. It was a surprising appointment by a Conservative government.

Marsh's term of office was marked by difficulties. The brief financial honeymoon following the 1968 act ended, due mainly to the inexorable effects of the expansion in motor vehicles coupled with the motorway building program.

Under the Railways Act of 1974 the individual grants for unremunerative rail services were replaced by a consolidated Public Service Obligation payment. Increasing deficits, however, caused the imposition of tighter controls over investment, about which Marsh complained publicly. Unlike his predecessors, he was a strong supporter of the channel tunnel and was disappointed when in January 1975 the Labour government abruptly cancelled the project, upon which much planning had been carried out. He openly expressed regret that the British government's attitude to railways was so different from that in, for instance, France and Germany.

Marsh was succeeded in 1976 by Peter Parker, an industrialist of liberal views who had been approached to take on the chairmanship by Castle in 1967 but then had declined as the Cabinet refused to approve the salary he required. Parker, who was knighted in 1978, had a gift for public and personal relationships, though disclaiming special expertise in railway matters.

The 1970s saw a decline in rail traffic. Despite much-reduced staff numbers, railway costs remained high in relation to receipts, yet attempts to obtain authority to raise charges in 1973 were rebuffed by the Labour government. Investment was restricted; at constant 1948 prices it averaged £71.1 million annually from 1954 to 1962, but only £37.7 million from 1963 to 1973. Two electrification schemes of importance were carried out—northwards to Glasgow, and on the King's Cross suburban services—but some other projects were set aside.

The BRB was exercised over the problem of making rail services more competitive through higher speed. In Japan, France, and elsewhere, governments were investing heavily in infrastructure for new high-speed railways. There was no prospect of this in Britain, and BR put much money and effort into developing the so-called advanced passenger train with high speed capacity, using existing infrastructure through a body-tilting mechanism. After years of testing, the project was abandoned on account of mechanical unreliability; a commercial disaster was averted by exploiting a more conventional diesel high-speed train, brand-named IC125, introduced in the mid-1970s, for Inter-City, changed to InterCity in 1984, expresses.

The arrival of a Conservative government in 1979 put pressure on the BRB to eliminate or at least reduce drastically the public service obligation payment. A rapid succession of ministers of transport, later secretaries of state, began to forecast the eventual privatization of BR. This would, it was hoped,

conclude a process that was initiated with the enforced disposal by the BRB of its hotels, Sealink U.K., and the construction workshops of British Rail Engineering Ltd., the latter by a partial management-staff buy-out. A second Beeching era appeared to dawn when in 1983 Sir Peter Parker was followed as chairman by Robert Reid, a professional railwayman who nevertheless found no great difficulty in cooperating with the Conservative government's ideology as applied to transport. Reid was knighted in 1985.

The period of Reid's chairmanship was marked by two factors. Externally the tide changed, and rail traffic increased both in line with the general economic recovery and because of the perceived effects of road congestion. The revival of the channel tunnel project, with opening scheduled for 1993, was another encouraging commercial prospect. Internally, a process of identifying separate businesses within the structure of the railway itself—as opposed to the non-railway activities already dealt with—which had begun in the 1960s with the appointment of executive directors, was pushed further. Decentralization had been by function from 1948 to 1953; since 1953 it had been chiefly by territory, or regions; then it was to be by product. The phrase "the business-led railway" was used to promote the emergence of sector directors for InterCity, Freight, Parcels, London and South-East (later Network SouthEast), and Other Provincial Services (later Regional Railway).

Starting as marketing concepts after 1982, the sectors rapidly acquired the status of financial entities with separate receipts, costs, and end-results. There had, however, to be certain accounting conventions regarding in particular the apportionment of infrastructure costs. For a time the organization provided that sector directors set standards of service, pricing, and revenue budgets, while regional general managers were responsible for meeting these requirements. Overlapping, however, was inherent in this system and before long sector directors were given powers to control resources directly in order to discharge their responsibilities. The dedication of rolling stock and locomotives to sectors followed and the eventual disappearance of regions could be planned, with staff controlled by either the sectors or the engineering services used by the sectors in common.

This process identified the Freight, Parcels, and InterCity businesses as inherently profitable, while Network SouthEast and the Provincial (Regional Railways) sector needed substantial subsidy. Investment had to be provided largely from internal sources since an external financing limit was imposed by the treasury. Cash flowed from property sales and development, which expanded greatly in the 1980s. Electrification revived with the opening of the St. Pancras-Bedford line in 1983, lines to Hastings in 1986 and Norwich in 1987, and the full opening of the East Coast Main Line in 1991.

By the end of 1989 the then secretary of state for transport Cecil Parkinson was able to write to Reid giving specific financial targets for each sector business—for instance, InterCity was to earn £95 million profit in 1992–1993. Rail Freight's surplus target was to be 4.5% return on assets employed, and Parcels was to earn £9 million surplus. Network SouthEast was to provide a "commercial rate of return by 1995–1996."

Such targets involved a continued severe downward pressure on costs, particularly on staff numbers, which could not easily be reconciled with an injunction in the same letter to observe high standards of service and safety.

When Reid was succeeded early in 1991 by his namesake, Sir Bob Reid, recession was setting in and the worsened financial result for 1990 and 1991 made the Parkinson financial targets and dates appear unrealistic. While InterCity broke even, Rail Freight lost £70 million. The final loss, after allowing for interest payments and income from extraordinary activities, was £11 million. This cast serious doubt on the government's expectation that before long British Rail could be privatized, at least in part.

In any case, the method of privatization was still the subject of debate. As a starting point, the reorganization phasing out the regions had eliminated the option of breaking up the system into something resembling the former railway companies. The chief remaining options were floating the profitable sectors as companies, with the state retaining the infrastructure and the unprofitable sectors, or disposing of the infrastructure to a separate body. This body could charge for usage by the sectors, themselves reorganized as companies, some of which would be assisted by grants—centrally or locally—for a certain period. However, the imminence of a general election not later than 1992 gave BR management a breathing-space within which to cope with yet another of the many internal reorganizations since 1948.

In the 43 years following nationalization of the railways, there have been ten chairmen. Their short terms of office have, however, been nearly twice as long on average as those of ministers or secretaries of state for transport. The history of British Rail shows the effects of frequently changing objectives, especially when politically motivated.

Further Reading: Allen, G.F., *British Rail After Beeching,* London, Ian Allan, 1966; Bonavia, M.R., *The Organisation of British Railways,* London, Ian Allan, 1971; Barker, T.C., and C.I. Savage, *An Economic History of Transport In Britain,* London, Hutchison, 1974; Marsh, R. (Lord), *Off the Rails,* London, Weidenfeld & Nicolson, 1978; Bonavia, M.R., *The Birth of British Rail,* London, George Allen & Unwin, 1979; Bonavia, M.R., *British Rail: The First 25 Years,* Newton Abbot, David & Charles, 1981; Johnson, J., and R.A. Long, *British Railways Engineering 1948-80,* London, Mechanical Engineering Publications, 1981; Bagwell, P.S., *The Railwaymen Vol II,* London, George Allen & Unwin, 1982; Gourvish, T.R., *British Railways 1948-73,* Cambridge, Cambridge University Press, 1986; Bonavia, M.R., *The Nationalisation of British Transport,* London, Macmillan, 1987.

—Michael Robert Bonavia

BURLINGTON NORTHERN INC.

3800 Continental Plaza
777 Main Street
Fort Worth, Texas 76102
U.S.A.
(817) 878-2000
Fax: (817) 897-7997

Public Company
Incorporated: 1849 as Aurora Branch Railroad
Employees: 32,000
Sales: $4.67 billion
Stock Exchanges: New York Midwest Pacific

Burlington Northern Inc. is one of the largest transportation firms in the United States. Specializing in rail transportation, in the early 1990s it operated more than 25,000 miles of track in 25 states and 2 Canadian provinces, more than any other U.S. railroad company. Founded in the mid-19th century on the wave of the pioneer movement, Burlington played a central role in settling the central and western United States. Despite efforts to diversify, in the 1990s the firm still gained most of its revenues from transporting agricultural and manufactured products, especially coal and grain, to markets and to export terminals throughout the eastern and western United States.

Burlington was founded in 1849 in the small town of Aurora, Illinois, and its early fortunes were linked with the burgeoning midwestern railway industry and the growing nearby city of Chicago. In the years from 1845 to 1848, swarms of settlers began to push west, lured by vast tracts of arable land and the promise of gold in California. By 1848 Illinois had already become the largest grain producer in the nation, requiring links with established eastern markets as well as with developing western settlements. The state's promise was reflected most clearly in Chicago's explosive growth as a railroad center. In 1847 Chicago had not even a single mile of railroad, but by 1854 it had become the railway capital of the United States.

Astutely anticipating Chicago's ascendancy, Aurora businessmen in 1848 proposed the construction of a railroad to connect with the Galena and Chicago Union Railroad, thus linking Aurora not only to the hub of the Midwest but also to the markets of the East. The State of Illinois charter for the Aurora Branch Railroad was signed into law on February 12, 1849, by Governor Augustus French. It authorized 12 miles of track to connect with the Galena Railroad. The Aurora com-

missioners immediately issued stock, selling more than a quarter of the total issue in nine days, and elected five members to its board of directors with Stephen F. Gale as its president.

Construction of the Aurora Branch progressed swiftly. By August 27, 1850, six miles of rail were laid; by October 21 of the same year the fledgling railroad began regular service to Chicago. The company encountered stiff competition from the beginning. In 1850 the U.S. Congress ceded 2.5 million acres of public land in Illinois for the construction of a railroad throughout the length of the state. Eager to promote the railroad industry, the Illinois legislature in turn granted numerous charters to new rail firms during its first session of 1851. Potential routes then crisscrossed the state, some quickly materializing and threatening to cut off or supersede the Aurora Branch.

To safeguard their young firm, Aurora directors moved to consolidate with three other new lines: the Central Military Tract Railroad, Peoria and Oquawka Railroad, and Northern Cross Railroad. The move was financed by eastern interests bent on profiting from the developing Illinois railroad industry. In January 1852 Boston financiers bought enough stock to elect John W. Brooks, who represented Boston interests, to the Aurora board.

Chauncey Colton, a promoter of the Central Military Track, met with Elisha Wadsworth, an Aurora director, and James Grimes, a Peoria and Oquawka director, proposing to consolidate their three lines into one through-route between Chicago and the Mississippi River. John Brooks in turn persuaded John Murray Forbes, the leader of the Boston group, to fund the consolidation. In 1852 the respective charters were amended to accommodate the territorial changes, and the Aurora Branch officially changed its name to Chicago and Aurora Railroad Company. Eventually, Northern Cross, which extended southwest from Galesburg, Illinois, joined the group. The original 12-mile Aurora branch now reached from Chicago through Aurora and Galesburg to Burlington, Iowa, and Quincy, Illinois, two small towns on the Mississippi River, thus fulfilling the intent of Colton's original plan. In 1855 the Chicago and Aurora again changed its name, this time to The Chicago, Burlington and Quincy Railroad Company (CB&Q). By 1864 the various segments of the system had been united into a single corporate entity under the control of the Chicago, Burlington and Quincy, which became the parent company.

CB&Q received its impetus from the urgent expansion and stiff competition of the young railroad industry rather than from a single visionary leader. In the first few years, presidents rapidly succeeded one another. In 1851 director Elisha Wadsworth followed Gale as president, but exactly a year later, Gale was re-elected to succeed Wadsworth. In 1853 an easterner, James F. Joy, was elected president, reflecting the enlarging interests of the Boston financial group in the future of the company. In 1857 John Van Nortwick became president, holding the post until 1865, the longest term of any president to date. For each of these men, running the railroad was only one of many responsibilities; CB&Q was not to have a full-time president until 1876.

Van Nortwick guided the firm through the financially rocky years of the late 1850s. With Boston capital supplementing local dollars, the railroad had established a solid financial footing by 1852. The panic of 1857, however, wiped out earlier successes. Wheat and corn crops were abnormally small in 1858 and 1859, providing little for railroads to haul. In the company's fiscal year 1858–1859, tonnage moved by CB&Q amounted to only three-quarters of the previous year's haul, and the number of passengers carried was 20% less than the preceding year. Revenues in 1858 were only 60% of what they had been in 1857. Bonds and a mortgage were issued to cover outstanding bills. A portion of the income from these sources, however, was earmarked to repay old bonds. One million dollars was set aside to cover the cost of a new entry into Chicago, and a sinking fund was established to liquidate the debt on or before its maturity, bespeaking a prudent approach to financial management that guaranteed CB&Q's future. By fiscal year 1860–1861, total revenues were up 38%.

The Civil War closely followed the lean years of the late 1850s, and the wartime economy launched CB&Q's full economic recovery. The company's primary wartime challenge was to manage the increased traffic in goods and people. The railroad's physical plant and facilities were enlarged and adapted to meet this demand. During the war years, the company doubled its supply of freight cars and improved its roadbed, track, and terminal facilities in Chicago, Aurora, and Galesburg. Revenues and profits increased with the traffic. For the fiscal year ending April 30, 1863, CB&Q experienced a 90% rise in net income.

Expansion and improvement continued in the postwar years. From 1864 to 1873, CB&Q track and traffic increased fourfold. Technical improvements kept pace. In 1867 the firm laid its first steel rails, replacing iron ones. During the 1870s and 1880s the route was expanded in Iowa, Nebraska, and Illinois, and preparations were made to reach farther toward the Pacific. The push west generated intense competition among railroad companies. Although revenues increased 2.5 times in the first postwar decade, traffic climbed more quickly. After guiding CB&Q through the financial panic of the late 1850s and the Civil War, Van Nortwick resigned as president in 1865, and James Joy was re-elected. Following him, James Walker was elected president in 1871 and Robert Harris in 1876.

As the railroad industry expanded in the 1870s, it also experienced increased government regulation and labor unrest. In the early 1870s most of the states on the Burlington route, as CB&Q's network was called, passed stiff regulatory measures known collectively as the Granger Laws. Such laws fixed passenger fares and freight rates, providing that the latter be based on distance rather than the quantity or nature of the commodity shipped. In 1874 under Walker's leadership, CB&Q challenged the constitutionality of Iowa's Granger Laws. In 1877 the Supreme Court ruled in favor of Iowa. This suit was only one of many of the Granger cases. Together, these cases established the precedent of government intervention in and regulation of businesses that provided public services.

In 1877 in solidarity with railroad workers nationwide, CB&Q workers struck in Chicago, Galesburg, and Iowa. In Chicago, President Harris discontinued freight service but kept passenger lines open. Charles Perkins, vice president of CB&Q, refused to do the same in Iowa; acting independently, he completely shut down the Iowa leg. His disagreement with Harris over labor relations provoked corporate struggles that eventually moved Harris to resign. John Forbes, the eastern financier who had funded the original Aurora Branch, took over as president in 1878. Remaining in Boston, he joined forces with Perkins, who became the western partner in this two-man leadership team.

Together, Forbes and Perkins developed a highly efficient corporation. In 1881 Forbes resigned and let Perkins take over as president. Under Perkins, leadership was consolidated in the president's hands, ending the power shifts between board and president that had characterized the first 30 years of CB&Q's existence. Perkins's 20-year presidency was marked by periods of financial success in the 1880s and financial downturn in the 1890s. These years were punctuated by ongoing contests with both the government and with labor.

The early and middle 1880s were years of general economic improvement with small fluctuations. Because CB&Q's freight was largely agricultural, it was vulnerable to changing crop yields, and in 1881, for example, net income declined after a poor season. The 1883 crop was excellent, however, and net income rose to $8.7 million, the highest company income in the 19th century. In that year CB&Q was among 17 railroads serving Chicago, yet it carried 41% of all corn received in the city, 34% of all rye, 33% of all wheat, and 21% of the oats, and delivered more livestock than any other company. The year 1887 was the firm's best to that time in terms of traffic hauled and gross earnings.

Technical improvements also contributed to CB&Q's success in the 1880s. In 1886 and 1887 company engineers improved the air brake, previously devised by Westinghouse for use on heavy freight trains. The better brake allowed higher train speeds and the railroad instituted its fast mail coach in 1884. In general technical developments permitted rapid expansion. In 1882 Burlington completed a through line to Denver, and in 1886, to St. Paul–Minneapolis, Minnesota. All told, from December 31, 1880, to December 31, 1890, CB&Q track increased in length from 2,771 miles to 5,160 miles.

In the late 1880s another episode of labor unrest compromised some of the early successes of Perkins's tenure. On February 27, 1888, CB&Q engineers struck, beginning a walkout that lasted until January 4, 1889. Labor finally capitulated to management, but not without damage to the company. After the hugely successful 1887, fiscal year 1888 was disastrous. Freight revenue dropped by more than 17% from the previous year, while operating expenses increased by the same percentage. By year's end there was a net loss of almost $250,000.

Perkins was concerned about increasing government regulation. In 1887 President Cleveland signed the Interstate Commerce Act, a measure that Perkins strongly opposed as a restraint to the continued viability of the railroad industry. Along with the Chicago and Northwestern and the Union Pacific railroads, CB&Q tested the constitutionality of Nebraska's Newberry Law, passed in 1893, which established maximum rates on all freight transported in the state. This time, the U.S. Supreme Court decided in favor of the railroads.

In the 1890s circumstances coincided that reversed the financial successes of the 1880s. Increasing competition and regulation, economic depression following the panic of 1893, and rising taxes combined to decrease net income for the eight years following 1888; during those years it was only 60% of what it had been from 1881 to 1887. Improvements in physical plant were kept to a minimum, reflecting CB&Q's usual conservative fiscal policy. From 1889 to 1896 new acquisitions fell well behind the national average. In 1898 John Forbes died, closing the founding era.

By the mid-1890s CB&Q's corporate structure had become large and unwieldy. Most of the smaller railroads it had acquired were independently owned and operated, affiliated with CB&Q only through lease arrangements or stock ownership. In 1899 Perkins financed the purchase of most of the companies, greatly simplifying the corporate structure of the Burlington system. Meanwhile, E.H. Harriman, chairman of the Union Pacific Railroad, and James J. Hill, chairman of the Great Northern Railroad and a controlling voice of the Northern Pacific, were both looking longingly at the entire Burlington network. CB&Q still controlled the Chicago traffic, the major prize that had eluded both of these men. For their part, Perkins and other CB&Q executives recognized the need for a link to the Pacific Northwest with its rich supplies of lumber. In April 1901 Hill agreed to purchase two-thirds of CB&Q stock, and CB&Q became a subsidiary of the Great Northern and Northern Pacific Railroads. Although Perkins completed the negotiations for sale, he resigned from his post in January 1901. George Harris, second vice president of CB&Q, succeeded Perkins as president.

The period preceding World War I was a time of smooth and regular expansion for CB&Q. Because Hill made few changes in management and operation, CB&Q was largely unaffected by the purchase. Harris continued as president, and the entire firm simply became one efficiently functioning unit of a larger system. In 1910 Harris resigned and was followed by Darius Miller. When Miller died suddenly in 1914, Hale Holden, general counsel for CB&Q, became president. CB&Q's primary challenge after 1901 was to fill in the gaps in its rail network. From 1901 to 1915, trackage increased by 1,373 miles, 17.2%, to a total of 9,366 miles. These years made up the last great period of expansion; in 1916 the firm reached its peak mileage.

Financial performance during this period reflected smooth and steady development. Both freight and passenger revenues climbed during the prewar period but more steeply in the earlier than in the later years. By 1908 total revenues were up 56.8% over 1901, but by 1915 were only 82.2% over 1901. In the same period, operating expenses also increased. Because Hill had modernized track and physical plant after the acquisition, 1908 expenses showed a 72.5% increase over 1901. After 1908, however, the effect of modernization was reflected in reduced operating expenses. By 1915 the increase over 1901 was only 86.4%.

CB&Q began to feel the effects of World War I before the United States was directly involved. In 1916 traffic, revenues, and operating expenses all increased. When the United States declared war in 1917, the U.S. government authorized the formation of the Railroads' War Board, a committee of five top railroad executives, including Hale Holden. The board monitored the flow of rail traffic and managed railroad personnel to maximize efficiency for the war effort. In late 1917, however, the government took complete control, regulating compensation rates as well as traffic flow. Each railroad was guaranteed an annual compensation equal to its average annual operating income for the three years ending June 30, 1917. For CB&Q this amounted to $33.3 million.

During these years, the company's haulage of livestock and agricultural products increased substantially, and it set all-time records for transporting coal. The U.S. government relinquished control of the railroads on March 1, 1920, one day after passage of the Transportation Act. The act modified what had been a policy of encouraging competition among railroads; passage of the new plan permitted any mergers or acquisitions that met Interstate Commerce Commission (ICC) standards for approval and exempted railroads from antitrust laws to the extent necessary to permit these combinations. The law gave railroads broad leeway in devising policies generally, although the ICC had the final say in how the companies carried out these policies.

During the 1920s CB&Q focused on two broad tasks: testing the new industry-wide regulatory policy and reorganizing its prewar plant and traffic. In response to the new Transportation Act, Holden urged the railroad industry to follow the act's mandate and initiate policy. Hill and Holden and other officials were themselves formulating a new financial arrangement between the CB&Q, the Great Northern, and the Northern Pacific. In 1930 the ICC rejected the proposal, and the group remained in its original 1901 configuration.

Physical plant improvements and technical innovations characterized CB&Q's internal development during the 1920s. For the first time in the firm's history, there was no net growth in railroad mileage. The number of locomotives and cars actually decreased. Carrying capacity increased, however, because of technical improvements. Throughout this decade, CB&Q consistently made money; although passenger revenues declined, operating expenses also declined, and income remained steady.

Early in 1929 Holden resigned to become chairman of the Southern Pacific. Frederick E. Williamson was chosen to replace him as president. Soon afterward, the stock market crashed. CB&Q felt the effects immediately. By March 1930, as the Great Depression engulfed the economy, gross revenue was less than in any comparable month since 1919. Overall in 1930, business decreased more than 12% compared to 1929. By June 1932 the number of employees had dropped to 23,135, a decrease of more than 7,000 since June 1931. In the first quarter of 1933 CB&Q fell short in meeting fixed expenses by $1.5 million. In the second quarter of that year, however, stimulated in part by New Deal legislation, the firm began a slow recovery. In May it not only met its expenses but also showed the first increase in gross revenue over the corresponding month in the previous four years. In 1931 Williamson resigned to become president of the New York Central, and Ralph Budd, president of the Great Northern, was chosen to replace Williamson as president of the CB&Q.

New Deal legislation that aided the railroad industry included 1933's Emergency Transportation Act, which sought to eliminate duplication of services and promote financial reorganization of railroads. New Deal legislation, however, also helped labor, and in 1934 the National Railroad Board of Adjustment was established to settle labor disputes over rates of pay, work rules, and working conditions. Two other measures passed in 1935, the Railroad Retirement Act and an accompanying pension act, cost CB&Q $1.44 million in addition to the funds already paid into the company's existing pension plan.

The railroad industry also suffered during the 1930s from the effects of stiffening competition as the number of passenger cars, trucks, and airplanes increased. CB&Q met that competition with technological advancements, especially in the area of passenger service. In 1934 it introduced the *Zephyr,* the first diesel-electric locomotive, which often cut travel times in half.

In 1940 even before the United States entered World War II, the government began to mobilize resources for a wartime economy. Rather than follow World War I practice and nationalize the railroads, the Roosevelt administration worked through such existing organizations as the Interstate Commerce Commission and the Association of American Railroads. The government did appoint an advisory commission to the revived Council of National Defense; Ralph Budd was appointed commissioner of transportation to this board.

By 1941 CB&Q had emerged fully from the Depression. Net income in that year was $10.4 million—in excess of $10 million for the first time since 1931. Wartime traffic and income continued to soar. Although miles of track were actually reduced during the war, CB&Q improved its traffic control and communications, and modernized many of its facilities, rising to the demands of a wartime economy. From 1940 through 1945 CB&Q increased the amount of freight and passengers by 88% and 179%, respectively, over the previous six-year period. Net income for the years 1942 through 1945 was 98% of total net income for the years 1929 through 1941.

In the immediate postwar period, the U.S. economy continued its prosperous trend. The railroad industry, however, was faced with stiffening competition from the airline and automobile industries, its wartime successes curtailed by rising operating and compensation costs. Although CB&Q's total operating revenues did not decrease in the years 1945 to 1949, total operating expenses increased nearly 14.5% during the same period. The company met these challenges primarily by concentrating on passenger rail improvements.

In 1949 Ralph Budd resigned as president to become chairman of the Chicago Transit Authority. Harry C. Murphy was appointed as his successor. During Murphy's tenure, which lasted until 1965, CB&Q continued to face rising wage costs and competition from other forms of transportation. To counter these challenges, the firm ceased operating 343 miles of underused track between 1950 and 1963. In addition from 1949 through 1963, CB&Q spent more than $430 million to improve plant and equipment, resulting in higher efficiency for handling freight and passengers. During these years, the firm maintained its reputation for innovations in passenger service. From 1949 to 1963, a period when the number of passengers declined on other railroads, the number of passengers on CB&Q increased 10.2%. Net income during these years ranged from a high of $33.8 million in 1950 to a low of $12.5 million in 1960.

In the 1960s CB&Q, the Great Northern, and the Northern Pacific proposed to merge into one corporate entity. Murphy resigned in 1965, before the ICC could rule on the proposal. L.W. Menk succeeded him as president and chairman. In 1966 Menk resigned to become president of Northern Pacific and was succeeded by William J. Quinn.

In 1968 the ICC approved the merger plan under the name Burlington Northern Inc. In March 1970 the three firms and two smaller railroads formally consolidated, and Menk became president and chief operating officer of the new company. Burlington Northern in 1970 sought to acquire the Missouri-Kansas-Texas (Katy) Railroad but subsequently dropped its bid without comment. Industry observers speculated that the Katy's debt load may have discouraged Burling-

ton Northern or that the ICC would have been unlikely to approve the merger.

In the early 1970s Burlington Northern diversified into natural resources management, focusing especially on coal development. It also added an air freight subsidiary. Management structure changed in the 1970s; Menk became chairman and chief executive officer, with Robert Downing, Norman M. Lorentzsen, and Richard Bressler, serially, filling the dual posts of president and chief operating officer.

In 1972 Burlington Northern and Union Pacific sought joint control of Peninsula Terminal Co., a switching line in Portland, Oregon, but the U.S. Supreme Court reversed the ICC's approval of the plan. The following year brought merger negotiations between Burlington Northern and Chicago, Milwaukee, St. Paul & Pacific Railroad. The ICC rejected this merger plan. In 1980, however, Burlington Northern succeeded in acquiring the St. Louis–San Francisco Railway.

By 1978 the company had record profits, still largely from the railroad division. In 1982 Bressler became chairman, president, and chief operating officer. He streamlined existing operations by selling the air freight unit and unsuccessful segments of the railroad, and by continuing efforts to develop the company's coal, timber, and gas reserves. In 1983 Burlington Northern acquired El Paso Natural Gas Company, a diversified energy concern that specialized in producing natural gas, and in 1985 bought Southland Royal Company, producer of oil and gas. Initially these moves profitably supplemented Burlington's development of resources on its own railroad land. In June 1988, however, the company suddenly reversed its diversification trend and announced the spinoff of the energy resources operation as Burlington Resources Inc., an independent public company. The spinoff enabled Burlington Northern to avoid pending legal claims that remained against the former El Paso Natural Gas Company, which had been sued for breach of contract, and to recover from falling energy prices. Burlington Northern also sold its trucking subsidiary, Burlington Motor Carriers Inc., in 1988. The buyer was an investor group that included the subsidiary's top management.

Bressler continued as chairman of Burlington Northern and Burlington Resources, while Gerald Grinstein, who had been vice chairman of both companies, became Burlington Northern's president and chief executive officer in 1989. Bressler retired in 1990, and Grinstein assumed the additional post of chairman. In the early 1990s Burlington Northern was focused on its railroad business, the company's historic strength. It was seeking increased flexibility in its labor contracts in an effort to improve efficiency and was investing in track improvements and new rolling stock.

Principal Subsidiary: Burlington Northern Railroad Co.

Further Reading: Overton, Richard C., *Milepost 100: The Story of the Development of the Burlington Lines, 1849–1949,* Chicago, [n.p.], 1949; Overton, Richard C., *Burlington Route: A History of the Burlington Lines,* New York, Alfred A. Knopf, 1965.

—Lynn M. Voskuil

CANADIAN PACIFIC LIMITED

910 Pearl Street
Montreal, Quebec H3C 3EA
Canada
(514) 395-5151
Fax: (514) 395-7959

Public Company
Incorporated: 1881 as Canadian Pacific Railway
   Company
Employees: 72,200
Sales: C$10.50 billion (US$9.09 billion)
Stock Exchanges: Montreal Toronto Alberta Vancouver
   New York London

A Canadian-based conglomerate, Canadian Pacific Limited (CP) has interests in transportation, forest products, natural gas and oil, hotels, and waste management. As Canada's largest company, CP's operations are diverse and international in scope. The company operates a rail system of more than 13,000 miles spanning eight Canadian provinces; the Soo Line, a 5,800-mile rail network in the midwestern United States; and a service company providing container shipping between Canada and Europe. CP is engaged in the trucking business in North America. It produces oil and gas from its properties, which were reported in the early 1990s to have reserves of 152 billion barrels of petroleum and 2.2 trillion cubic feet of natural gas. It has coal mining operations with estimated coal reserves in excess of 1.5 billion tons. In addition, the company's forest products division is a major producer of wood and related products. CP also owns 27 million square feet of industrial and residential properties and owns or manages 25 hotels.

The building of the Canadian Pacific Railway was a demanding battle, both physically and politically. After negative reports from both explorers and surveyors, a long and sometimes bitter parliamentary dispute, and threats of refusal by British Columbia to become part of the Canadian dominion, a contract to build the rail line was finally approved by royal assent on February 15, 1881. The following day, the Canadian Pacific Railway Company was incorporated. A group of railroad professionals, known as The Syndicate, who had come to Canada from Scotland as fur traders, headed up the railroad's first management team. The Syndicate chose George Stephen, a former president of the Bank of Montreal and one of the principals involved in the organization of the

St. Paul, Minneapolis and Manitoba Railway as CP's first president. Stephen was assisted by CP vice president Duncan McIntyre, who left his post as president of the Canada Central Railway to help build the country's first and only transcontinental railroad.

Under the terms of the government contract, CP received C$25 million in investor-subscribed funds and 25 million acres of timberland, which eventually included the land's subsurface resources. These important assets provided the basis for the company to raise more capital. Several stock issues were floated, and large loans were made to further finance the project. In 1882 the company issued C$30 million worth of CP stock to various New York investment syndicates, followed by the sale of 200,000 shares of common stock the following year. To complete the project, CP floated a C$15 million bond issue through a London-based investment house. Although the company's contract allowed CP ten years to complete the railroad's construction, the project took less than half that time. Construction of the main line was completed in 1885. At the time the Canadian Pacific Railway was the longest and costliest railroad line ever built.

The completion of the line had many effects on both the company and the Canadian economy. The subsurface resources acquired in the land deal with the Canadian Parliament put the company into the coal, zinc, lead, gold, silver, and—later—gas businesses. The railway opened the western Canadian prairie for settlement, and CP was involved in agricultural development, including irrigation and wheat farming. A rail connection from the more industrialized eastern regions to the Pacific Coast enabled the company to expand into the export shipping business and opened up many opportunities in the Far East. It was also believed that the railway's consolidating effect on the Canadian provinces stifled further northern expansion by the United States. The company, then known to most Canadians as the CPR, continued its steady growth well into the mid-1900s.

The company in its early years added to its already rich natural resource holdings. In 1898 it acquired British Columbia Smelting and Refining Company, and in 1906 merged this and other properties into The Consolidated Mining and Smelting Company of Canada Limited, later known as Cominco Limited. In 1905 CP purchased the Esquimalt and Namaimo Railway and 1.5 million acres of timber on Vancouver Island.

As early as 1920 CP began using all-steel railroad cars. In many instances these units weighed nearly 60 tons, which limited the number of cars that could be pulled by a steam-powered locomotive. The Great Depression and then World War II slowed the introduction of diesel-powered engines to the railroad industry. By 1954, however, CP completed the conversion of its locomotives to diesel-power. Because of the ruggedness of much of the terrain over which CP operates, the company uses some of the largest diesel-powered trains in the world. Capable of hauling 10,000 tons of cargo, these units are powered by as many as 11 diesel engines.

Throughout its first 75 years in business, CP's explosive growth resulted in poor record-keeping, and only in 1956 did the company institute a comprehensive inventory of its assets. The inventory took seven years. It quickly became apparent that the CP's vast holdings warranted further exploitation and development. CP formed a wholly owned subsidiary, Canadian Pacific Oil and Gas Limited, in 1958 to develop and explore its mineral rights on more than 11 million acres of company-held western Canada land. With the completion of the CP's forest and real estate surveys, two more subsidiaries were formed. Marathon Realty Company Limited was incorporated to manage and develop the company's vast, nationwide real estate holdings. Pacific Logging Company Limited was to be responsible for reforestation and the development of tree farming on CP's timberlands.

As the survey of company holdings reached completion, it became clear that the development of the CP's nonrailroad assets needed to be centralized under a separate holding company. CP formed Canadian Pacific Investments Limited in 1962 to administer the development of CP's natural resources and real estate holdings and to operate as an investment holding company. In 1971 the parent company adopted the name Canadian Pacific Limited.

During most of CP's first 80 years, the company was owned by foreign interests, primarily by English, French, and U.S. investors. The transition to a majority of Canadian ownership began after the end of World War II and was completed in 1965. In that year, Ian Sinclair, CP's chairman, assumed control of the company's burgeoning enterprises. Sinclair brought to bear his influence and power to finally reverse the flow of foreign investment into the company.

In November 1967 the company offered to the public C$100 million in convertible preferred shares of CP stock. At the time, it was the largest single stock issue in Canadian history and provided an opportunity for Canadians to share more directly in the resource development of their country. In 1980 Canadian Pacific Investments Limited changed its name to Canadian Pacific Enterprises Limited (CP Enterprises).

Sinclair took the company into the hotel business in the United States and to locations as distant as Jerusalem. An airline catering business in Mexico City was purchased and Canadian Pacific Airlines Limited (CP Air), which for a time was Canada's second-largest airline, was formed. Sinclair's railroading focused on the transportation of goods and raw materials rather than people. At the close of Sinclair's tenure in 1981, CP's railroad inventory comprised 69,000 freight cars, 1,300 locomotives, 3,600 maintenance and equipment cars, and only 57 passenger cars.

Sinclair was succeeded by Frederic Burbidge in 1981. Burbidge acquired leadership of a company that was about to have the worst decade in its history. A worldwide recession coupled with extremely poor crop years in the early 1980s in both Canada and the midwestern United States resulted in thousands of empty Canadian Pacific and Soo Line boxcars. Many of CP's nonrailroad businesses were highly cyclical. CP's subsidiary PanCanadian Petroleum Limited, one of Canada's largest gas and oil companies, helped compensate for the rail operations' poor performance for a time, but with the collapse of oil prices in 1986, the company was faced with profound difficulties.

William Stinson replaced Burbidge as CP's chairman in 1985. Stinson, who had been with the company for 30 years, starting with CP as a management trainee in 1955, was the youngest chairman in the company's history. He set out to streamline the company's operations.

Stinson oversaw the sale of CP's 52% interest in Cominco Limited, which had become one of the world's largest zinc producers. By selling off what had been a money-loser since 1981, Stinson raised C$472 million and removed an expensive liability. On the heels of the Cominco sell-off, the company divested itself of CP Air in a C$300 million deal with Pacific Western Airlines. CP Air had not shown any profits since 1980; the sale also eliminated nearly C$600 million in long-term debt. On December 6, 1985, with the consent of both companies' stockholders, CP and CP Enterprises merged into one company. Under the terms of the merger, CP Enterprises became a wholly owned subsidiary of CP.

After the sale of Cominco and CP Air, Stinson worked to turn around three of CP's other subsidiaries, AMCA International Limited, a producer of structural steel; the Soo Line; and Algoma Steel Corporation, an Ontario-based steel manufacturer. Stinson's plan was to focus CP in four major core businesses: freight transportation, natural resources, real estate, and manufacturing. Stinson's cutbacks, sales, and restructuring had a positive effect, and the company showed a profit of a little more than C$58 million in 1987. One project that Stinson did not attempt to curtail was the construction of the longest railway tunnel in North America. The Macdonald Tunnel, located in British Columbia's Selkirk Mountains and more than nine miles in length, is named after Sir John Macdonald, a former Canadian prime minister and early supporter of the Canadian transcontinental railroad. The tunnel was completed in 1988.

The years 1988 and 1989 showed little improvement for CP's financial outlook. The Canadian economy was in a weakened condition. The company's forest products division reported a net operating loss of more than C$190 million in 1989 because of the depressed market for paper products. Marathon Realty showed a net operating loss that same year of more than C$17 million. The company's rail division held its own in 1989, however, and CP's waste services enterprises had a record-breaking year.

As CP entered the 1990s, the company's restructuring efforts suffered a major setback in a ruling by the Supreme Court of Ontario. Under the court's decision, CP was prohibited from spinning off Marathon Realty as a separate public company. CP had planned to distribute 80% of the shares of Marathon Realty to its common stock holders while retaining a 20% interest itself. The court ruled that the transaction would penalize CP's preferred stock holders. At the same time, it appeared that CP's performance would be further hindered by the lingering weakness in the company's forest products division.

The company's rail business increased in 1990, largely because of a resurgence in grain shipments. That year CP acquired the 44% of Soo Line that it did not already own. CP officials expected the transaction to make possible greater integration of the rail systems. Early in 1991 CP bought another rail company, the Delaware and Hudson Railway, operating in the northeastern United States. CP also added to its hotel operations in 1990 with the purchase of an 80% interest in the U.S.-based Doubletree/Compri hotel management group.

Principal Subsidiaries: CP Rail System; Canadian Pacific Steamships, Limited (U.K.); Centennial Shipping Limited (Bermuda); Soo Line Corporation (U.S.A.); Canadian Pacific Express & Transport Ltd.; CanPac International Freight Services Inc; PanCanadian Petroleum Limited (87.1%); Foding

Coal Limited; NYCO Minerals, Inc. (U.S.A.); Canadian Pacific Forest Products Limited (79.7%); Marathon Realty Company Limited; Canadian Pacific Hotels Corporation; United Communications Inc.; United Dominion Industries Limited (55.4%); Reserve de la Petite Nation; Canadian Pacific Enterprises Limited; Canadian Pacific Securities Limited; Canadian Pacific Securities (Ontario) Limited; Canadian Pacific (U.S.) Holdings Inc.; ConPac Car Inc. (U.S.A.).

Further Reading: Eliot, Jane, *The History of the Western Railroads,* New York, Bison Books, 1985; Ryans, Leo, "CP Undergoing Major Restructuring," *The Journal of Commerce,* February 27, 1987; Berton, Pierre, *The Last Spike: The Great Railway, 1881–1885,* New York, Penguin Books, 1989.

—William R. Grossman

CONSOLIDATED FREIGHTWAYS, INC.

3240 Hillview Avenue
Palo Alto, California 94304
U.S.A.
(415) 494-2900
Fax: (415) 813-0158

Public Company
Incorporated: 1929
Employees: 39,000
Sales: $4.21 billion
Stock Exchanges: New York Pacific London

Consolidated Freightways, Inc. has operated the largest long-haul trucking company in the United States since the late 1950s. Long-haul, less-than-truckload (LTL) freight accounts for more than half of Consolidated's overall revenue, but the company has also moved heavily into the overnight trucking and air freight businesses, with mixed results. Consolidated built a solid, truck-based overnight system in the 1980s, creating four regional subsidiaries to take advantage of this latest trend in the freight industry.

Little has been recorded of Consolidated Freightways' beginnings in Portland, Oregon. The company was created in 1929 by Leland James, a 36-year-old entrepreneur, who merged four Portland short-haul trucking companies into a single firm and began expanding the range of its operations. The trucking industry at that time was far from the dominating force it has since become; particularly in the West, a shortage of well-paved roads had retarded its growth until after World War I. The long-haul trucking business would require the eventual construction of a national system of interstate highways. Leland James's new trucking firm, therefore, concentrated on establishing its presence in Portland and the immediate surroundings, but meeting with considerable success it lengthened its routes and was soon carrying freight between many of the widely scattered cities of Oregon and Washington.

The onset of the Great Depression sparked a series of ferocious rate wars among truckers across the country. With a drop-off in tonnage and sharp downward pressure on rates, competition stiffened among the scores of trucking companies in the Pacific Northwest, many of which consisted of little more than a single vehicle and its hard-pressed owner. It was on these marginal competitors that the downturn weighed most

heavily, while more substantial firms such as Consolidated were able to wait out the lean times and in some cases pick up additional business from customers in need of more predictable and efficient delivery than was offered by the railroads. Indeed the real struggle shaping up in transportation was between the older railroads, whose strength lay in the long distance shipment of bulk goods to a limited number of destinations, and the nascent trucking companies, which could provide pinpoint delivery of smaller items wherever permitted by paved roads. As the latter were rapidly filling in to accommodate the United States's growing love of the automobile, truckers such as Consolidated had time on their side in the protracted battle with the railroads.

In 1935 the federal government stepped into the rather chaotic competition among truckers, placing interstate carriers under the general jurisdiction of the Interstate Commerce Commission (ICC), which for years had regulated the railroads. The Motor Carrier Act was indicative of the trucking industry's rapid growth, as the major firms now regularly transported goods across state lines and soon would be taking them across the entire country. Consolidated had already established itself as one of the leading truckers in the Northwest, with routes crisscrossing Washington, Oregon, and reaching down to the prosperous cities of California as well. It was not until the advent of World War II, however, that Consolidated enjoyed the remarkable growth that would characterize its history for the coming decades. With the major railroads overburdened by the demand for war materiel and personnel, truckers became a more vital part of the country's freight systems. Consolidated added dozens of new terminals throughout much of the western United States and by war's end had extended its service as far east as Chicago, the nation's transport hub.

On the eve of the greatest expansion in the history of U.S. trucking, Consolidated's 1950 revenue stood at $24 million, its net income at $700,000, and the company operated 1,600 pieces of freight equipment. Leland James remained chairman of the company he had created, then one of the largest trucking firms in the western United States. True to its name, Consolidated had achieved much of its growth by means of acquisitions and mergers, a trend that would greatly accelerate as the trucking industry matured during the 1950s. In one respect, at least, the business was already mature—as the figures for Consolidated's 1950 income indicate; trucking is a highly competitive, service-oriented industry, where despite the general rate regulation of the ICC, margins tend to remain very thin, and net income stays low. The resulting premium on efficiency tended to encourage the kind of horizontal combination that Consolidated pursued during the 1950s, by the end of which time the company had annexed 53 of its former competitors.

The majority of those acquisitions were made after 1955, when Leland James named Jack Snead president of Consolidated. Snead oversaw the rise of Consolidated from regional power to national leadership, not only extending the company's reach to the Atlantic Ocean but intensively building local service networks in each of the cities along Consolidated's routes. In addition Consolidated adopted the trucking industry's more cooperative attitude toward the railroads, as the two modes of transport each specialized in those areas of the freight business for which they were best suited. Increasingly during the 1950s, truckers and railroads joined forces by means of the piggyback system, in which a standard-sized container was moved from truck to rail and back to truck for final delivery. Jack Snead led Consolidated into the piggyback business, and less successfully, into fishyback, or truck-ship combinations. A sizable investment in Hawaiian Marine Freightways was abandoned within 24 months, but Consolidated nevertheless succeeded in establishing the beginnings of a sea link to complement its growing truck and truck-rail service.

Consolidated also enjoyed the security of operating as its own builder of trucks and related equipment. Immediately after World War II, Leland James started Freightliner Corporation in Portland to supply Consolidated with the larger, lighter, and more sophisticated trucks and trailers increasingly needed to complete in the maturing freight industry. Freightliner originally built only for its parent company, but in 1951 it signed an agreement with White Motor Corporation (Ohio) under which White would retail Freightliner trucks through its chain of dealerships across the country. The partnership proved successful for the next 25 years, sales made at White dealerships returning a profit to Freightliner while allowing it to operate at a volume large enough to provide the economies of scale. Consolidated still had ready access to new trucks at the lowest possible cost.

To the established business at Freightliner, Jack Snead added other manufacturing concerns: Transicold Corporation, railway components; and Techni-Glas Corporation, glass-fiber products. Between its expanded truck lines and the newly acquired manufacturing subsidiaries, Consolidated sales more than doubled during Snead's five-year tenure, hitting $146 million in 1959 and making Consolidated easily the largest common carrier in the United States. In order to oversee this suddenly complex organization, Snead in 1956 had moved corporate headquarters from Portland to Menlo Park, California, a San Francisco suburb, where company executives were close to Consolidated's bankers and underwriters. The company then employed nearly 11,000 people, operated 13,800 pieces of equipment in 34 states and Canada, and had made a name for itself as one of the most aggressive young firms in the transportation industry. It was also, as later developments revealed, in serious trouble.

In 1960 a combination of recession and the inadequate integration of Consolidated's many businesses led to a $2.7 million year-end loss and the suspension of dividend payments. Jack Snead was asked to resign, and in his place William G. White was named president and also chairman of Consolidated. White found that Consolidated's many acquisitions had been only rudimentarily integrated, with as many as five different terminals serving a single city, and that several of the nontrucking businesses were performing poorly. The new chief executive began a drastic program aimed at correcting both problems, beginning with a new emphasis on coordinated control from the Menlo Park headquarters—no small feat for a nationwide company in the precomputer age. Traffic routes were better defined, terminals consolidated, and new financial controls elaborated for the far-flung enterprise. Most decisive of all, White committed his company to becoming a specialist in LTL shipment. LTL is generally more difficult than truckload shipping, requiring a higher level of coordination and efficiency from both staff and equipment, but Consolidated had already established a reputation in the field, and White decided to make LTL the company's own niche. In the early 1990s, Consolidated remained an LTL specialist, with 90% of its trucking revenue generated by LTL orders.

Along with these changes in the trucking business, White sold off a number of Consolidated's manufacturing and peripheral companies. Transicold and Youngstown Steel Car were both eventually sold, along with a household moving service, a piggyback leasing company, and a fledgling package division unable to sustain direct competition from United Parcel Service. The combined effect of these steps was outstanding: Consolidated's revenue increased about 15% per year during the 1960s, and operating profits remained consistently above industry norm. Sales for 1969 reached $451 million, Freightliner maintained its tradition of manufacturing excellence, and White added two new wrinkles to the company's generally solid core in trucking. In 1969 Consolidated again ventured into the sea-borne container business, this time paying $25 million for 51% of Pacific Far East Line Inc., one of the pioneers in Pacific container shipping; and in the following year it entered the new field of air freight, forming CF Air-Freight with initial service between three cities. Consolidated thus became one of the first companies to offer the beginnings of a true intermodal system, able to transport containers by truck, rail, air, or sea.

The Pacific Far East Line investment was short-lived, however. A scant five years after buying into the company, Consolidated wrote off its investment, taking a $14 million charge at the bottom line for 1973. By that time the trucking industry was plunged into the turmoil created by the Middle East oil embargo, when soaring gas and diesel prices threatened to ruin the large trucking firms. Fortunately the ICC responded with quick rate relief and the only net effect was to swell Consolidated's revenues to $800 million in 1974 and inaugurate a trend toward lighter, more fuel-efficient tractors and trucks at Freightliner. The latter was about to enter a tumultuous period in its own history. Not only did it have to contend with the new emphasis on fuel efficiency, the truck manufacturer also endured a roller-coaster sales cycle in 1974 and 1975, when a new federal law mandating an expensive brake system set off a rush of orders in 1974 and a near drought the following year. Freightliner became increasingly dissatisfied with the sales effort it was receiving from the White Motor dealerships, and in 1977 it severed the 25-year-old relationship and began to build a network of its own dealers and agents. With about 10% of the U.S. market, Freightliner was known as a builder of relatively expensive, premium trucks, and apparently could not handle competition from the likes of International Harvester and Mack. In 1981 Consolidated announced the sale of Freightliner and its few other remaining manufacturing subsidiaries to Daimler-Benz for about $300 million. Daimler-Benz was already the number-one truck maker in the world and viewed the purchase of Freightliner as the easiest means of entry into the big U.S. market.

There may well have been other considerations behind Consolidated's decision to sell its manufacturing assets. In 1980 the trucking industry was largely deregulated by U.S. president Jimmy Carter's administration; for the first time since 1935, truckers were free to set rates as they pleased, and most analysts predicted another round of frantic mergers and takeovers as the price competition took its toll. Ray O'Brien, new chief executive at Consolidated, took seriously the prospect of renewed rate wars and made a decision to strengthen his hand in trucking while abandoning the manufacturing business, in which Consolidated would never become a leader. The air freight business had grown; CF AirFreight by 1980 had developed from a small forwarder into the number-three heavy air freight carrier in North America, with $100 million in annual revenues and an expanding service network.

Consolidated was able to create four regional trucking companies to specialize in overnight delivery. These Con-Way companies were in the early 1990s doing $600 million in sales and appeared to be well positioned in regional markets, as did CF Motor Freight in its long-haul trucking business. Deregulation did indeed usher in an era of bitter competition in trucking, with some 54% of the players out of business within eight years, but Consolidated prospered mightily, due in part to its size and in part to the decision to concentrate most of its energies on trucking. Although freight rates were lower at decade's end than at the time of deregulation in 1980, Consolidated had doubled its long-haul business and firmed its hold on the trucking industry's top position.

Perhaps unnerved by such prosperity, in April of 1989 Consolidated made an acquisition that has performed poorly. New chief executive Lary Scott decided to catapult his company to the top of the air freight ranks by buying Emery Air Freight Corporation, an industry leader doing about $1.2 billion in revenue, much of it overseas where CF AirFreight was weak. Consolidated paid $458 million for Emery and was confident that it could reverse Emery's recent slide after its own big takeover of Purolator Courier Corporation. When losses at Emery hit $100 million in the first six months of 1990, pulling Consolidated as a whole into the red, Scott was asked to leave and Ray O'Brien hustled back to his former position. O'Brien also brought back Donald E. Moffitt, a former Consolidated executive, as chief financial officer. He eventually succeeded O'Brien as president and chief executive. Between them, they managed to slow Emery's losses to a steady trickle, but Consolidated lost $41 million for the year, suspended its common stock dividend payments, and had to secure new banking arrangements. Emery's losses continued to hamper the profitability of an otherwise sound corporation. In the early 1990s it was not yet clear whether Consolidated would be able to return its air freight business to regular profits, but in the ground freight arena it remained unexcelled among national and regional carriers of LTL freight.

Principal Subsidiaries: CF Motor Freight; Canadian Freightways; Milne & Craighead Customs Brokers; Emery Worldwide; Emery Worldwide Airlines; Emery Worldwide Custom Brokers; Con-Way Transportation Services; Con-Way Western Express; Con-Way Central Express; Con-Way Southern Express; Con-Way Southwest Express; Con-Way Intermodal; Road Systems; Willamette Sales; Menlo Logistics.

Further Reading: "Transportation," *Business Week,* June 11, 1960.

—Jonathan Martin

CONSOLIDATED RAIL CORPORATION

Six Penn Center Plaza
Philadelphia, Pennsylvania 19103
U.S.A.
(215) 977-4000
Fax: (215) 977-4582

Public Company
Incorporated: 1976
Employees: 27,787
Sales: $3.37 billion
Stock Exchanges: New York Philadelphia

Consolidated Rail Corporation—best known as Conrail—was formed by the U.S. government out of six bankrupt railroads serving the northeastern United States. Conrail began operations in 1976. It was returned to the private sector through a public stock offering in 1987, after establishing a record of steady profits.

Between the 1930s and the 1960s, U.S. railroads, once the country's primary source of freight transportation, were undermined by the growth of air and road transportation. Trucking had usurped so much of the freight transportation business that many railroads merged or went under in the 1960s and 1970s. The eastern railroads were hit additionally with the collapse of coal traffic during the 1960s, as emphasis shifted to oil as an energy source. Between 1967 and 1972, six significant northeastern railroads went bankrupt: Central Railroad of New Jersey; Penn Central Transportation Company—created from the 1968 merger of Pennsylvania Railroad and New York Central Railroad; Lehigh Valley Railroad Company; Reading Company; Lehigh & Hudson River Railway Company; and Erie Lackawanna Railway Company. The roots of these companies stretched back as far as 1826.

By 1975 railroads had lost so much business to the trucking industry—which could offer door-to-door service and was not subject to the same price restrictions—that railroads handled only 36% of the nation's freight. As a result, bankruptcies and mergers left the country with only six major freight railroads. The government reacted with the 1974 Regional Rail Reorganization Act, which in turn gave birth to the United States Railway Association (USRA). A plan was devised by USRA for the consolidation of the six bankrupt lines into a single system, with the backing of federal funds. The initial investment was $2.1 billion. Conrail officially began operations in 1976, with

Edward G. Jordan as chairman and CEO, and Richard C. Spence as president. The company's mandate was to revitalize rail service in the Northeast and Midwest and to operate as a for-profit company. Conrail at its inception had about 17,700 track miles, 100,000 employees, and operated in 16 states and in Washington, D.C., and Canada. It handled both freight and passenger services. The government held 85% of the stock, with employees holding the remainder.

The first years of operation focused on rehabilitation. Deterioration of track and properties was advanced because of deferred maintenance during the years Conrail's bankrupted predecessors struggled. Severe winter storms during 1977 and 1978 increased deterioration while thwarting rehabilitation. In 1978 $1.2 billion more in federal funds was authorized. Nearly all of the money went to upkeep and modernization. In 1979 Stuart M. Reed became president. From its inception through 1980, Conrail had a cumulative net loss of about $1.5 billion. The USRA system plan for the company had predicted it would be making a profit by 1979. In 1981, however, Conrail was still losing money on 20% to 30% of its traffic, and the government continued to support its operations as the industrial economy of the Northeast depended on the line. Auto, steel, and coal industries were especially dependent upon the railroad.

In 1980 the Staggers Rail Act was signed, with huge repercussions for the industry. This act essentially deregulated the railroads, whose pricings had been fixed since the turn of the century when railroads represented virtually the only mode of transcontinental transportation. The Staggers Act made railroads more competitive with trucks by allowing them to reprice services, adjust rail rates, react to market conditions, and provide special contracts. This marked the start of Conrail's recovery.

The Staggers Act permitted Conrail to cancel and reassess joint rates with connecting railroads. It was losing money on many of these arrangements as revenues were divided according to distance not costs. As much of Conrail's lines included old terminals and yard operations—with costly upkeep and overhead—it was losing money on crucial business. The chance to offer contract rates to shippers who could guarantee a certain volume of traffic enabled Conrail to plan ahead, spending the assured revenues on equipment and maintenance. Above all, the Staggers Act allowed railroads to regain business lost to the trucking industry.

In 1981 L. Stanley Crane succeeded Jordan as chairman and CEO. Crane had been with Southern Railway Company for more than four decades when he retired as chairman in 1980, the same time the company joined Norfolk and Western Railway Company to become Norfolk Southern Corporation. Under Crane, Conrail began drastic cost-cutting measures, shaving marginal jobs, lines, and services. Another boost to Conrail's competitiveness came in 1981 with the passage of the Northeast Rail Service Act, which enabled Conrail to shed the commuter services it had been required to operate and that represented a loss to the company of $70 million annually. The main transit agencies served by Conrail—which accounted for 215,000 daily passengers—were the New York Metropolitan Transportation Authority, New Jersey Transit Corporation, and Southeastern Pennsylvania Transportation Authority. Conrail concluded its first year of profitability in 1981, with a net income of $39.2 million. An assist toward profitability was the deferral of wage increases agreed upon by Conrail workers, which saved about $150 million in 1981. By 1984 these deferrals would amount to $300 million.

Conrail again made a modest profit in 1982—$174 million—doubly notable as the recession was rocking Conrail's major customers in Pittsburgh and Detroit. Crane's streamlining continued. The work force, once at 100,000, was cut to 60,000 by 1982, and route miles were reduced from 17,700 to 15,000 as excess track was torn up to save maintenance costs. Money-losing branch lines were abandoned. Taking advantage of the Staggers Act, Conrail went after piggyback business—carrying trailers on flatbed rail cars. In 1982 Conrail was profitable despite a 20% decline in car loadings.

By 1983 Conrail was the fourth largest freight hauler in the United States, and making money even though 40% of its revenues came from industries hardest hit by the recession—steel, autos, and coal. A severance arrangement financed by the government allowed the work force to be cut further, to 42,000. By year's end, the company reported a $31.3 million profit, and suitors began to gather. Courtships would prove stormy.

By 1985 the government had spent more than $7 billion to restore Conrail's profitability. The sale of Conrail to an undercapitalized or poorly managed company would be catastrophic to the Northeast's economy and unpopular with taxpayers. Among the strong suitors were Norfolk Southern, CSX Corporation (formed by the merger of Chessie System, Inc., and Seaboard Coast Line Railroad), and Alleghany Corporation. Conrail employees submitted a $500 million bid for acquisition. The selling price range was set between $1 billion and $1.5 billion. A deadline for formal purchase offers was set in 1984, and 14 potential buyers submitted. Within a few months, these bidders were narrowed to three. Favored was Norfolk Southern, because of its financial strength and solid railroading background. Conrail finished 1984 with a net income of $500 million. The company's profits were misleading because of wage concessions granted by unions and tax advantages, but its cash balance and sustained profits were reassuring to buyers.

In 1985 Conrail management proposed a plan for public offering of Conrail stock. The company, and others in the industry, feared that sale of Conrail to Norfolk Southern would create a monopoly, as the two railroads served many of the same markets. An Interstate Commerce Commission study confirmed this possibility. The sale would also create the country's largest railroad, and would have threatened CSX. Early in 1985, Conrail reached a new agreement with labor unions and resumed paying industry scale wages, retroactive to July 1984. At year's end, Conrail earnings dipped to about $416 million.

In 1986 Norfolk withdrew its bid, citing changes in tax laws that made the purchase less appealing. In the fall, the Conrail Privatization Act was signed, authorizing a public stock offering to return Conrail to the private sector. To prevent possible mergers and takeovers, restrictions were made: no other major railroad would acquire more than 10% of Conrail for one year, and any railroad would need Interstate Commerce Commission permission for a merger after that; any nonrailroad company was prevented from making more than a 10% purchase for three years. The company concluded its sixth straight year of profitability, with a net income of $431 million.

In 1987 Conrail was returned to the private sector in the largest initial public offering to date in U.S. history, raising $1.6 billion. With the $300 million in funds that Conrail had already returned to the government, the sale generated nearly $1.9 billion. The company faced immediate challenges—an Amtrak-Conrail train collision that killed 16 people and injured more than 170 others added lawsuits to the mounting liabilities incurred by employees exposed to asbestos. Then came the October stock market crash, shaking investors confidence and further wounding the economy. Conrail concluded the year, however, with a more than 7% increase in freight traffic and purchased 30 new high-horsepower locomotives. Helping to boost its traffic despite still sagging auto sales was Conrail's commodity diversity: company revenues toward the end of 1987 were coming from chemicals, 17%; autos, 16%; truck trailers, 17%; and coal, 17%. Also a help was the fact that Conrail's average crew was 25% smaller than other major freight carriers' crews, giving it a competitive advantage.

Early in 1988, Conrail's board of directors elected Richard D. Sanborn as president. He came aboard from CSX Corporation and succeeded Crane upon his retirement as chairman and CEO in early 1989. Following Sanborn's untimely death in February 1989, however, the company again was in search of a new CEO. The board of directors elected James A. Hagen as chairman, president, and CEO in April 1989. Hagan, who had been Conrail's senior vice president of marketing and sales between 1977 and 1985, most recently had been president of CSX Distribution Services, Inc. During its first years as a private company, Conrail had proven itself enough of a moneymaker to generate takeover attention, with eyes on the 1989 expiration of takeover protection legislation. The company began instituting takeover defenses, including a poison-pill provision. Revenues for 1988 were about $3.5 billion.

Because of the still declining shipments of autos and steel in 1989, all major railroads suffered a slowdown. By year's end, Conrail reduced its nonunion work force by 12% and took a fourth-quarter pretax charge of about $234 million to cover reductions, consolidation of certain functions, and an increase in casualty reserves. Still seeking to thwart takeover early in 1990, Conrail announced a $1.3 billion plan to buy back more than a third of its outstanding shares. It also established a $300 million employee stock ownership plan. These actions helped to reduce the cash surplus that was tempting takeovers. There also were suits pending concerning safety and environmental issues, including the Amtrak collision case from 1987, which had cost Conrail more than $81 million in claims by late 1989. In addition, there was an ongoing antitrust suit for $10 million brought by the bankrupt Delaware & Hudson Railway.

While industrial freight shipments remained weak in 1990, coal and grain traffic picked up, but these were lower revenue commodities for Conrail and did not make up for the slump. Late in 1990, Conrail settled a trackage rights dispute with Canadian Pacific Ltd. (CP), based in Montreal. CP acquired Delaware & Hudson and thus revived competition against Conrail in the Northeast.

By the close of 1990, Conrail operated about 13,000 miles of track, 2,400 locomotives, and 69,000 freight cars with major ports including Philadelphia, New York, Baltimore, Boston, and Cleveland. During that year, revenues declined 1.1% to about $3.37 billion. The revenue-producing commodities were 18% chemicals and related products; 17% intermodal—trailers or containers on flatbed cars; 16% coal; 14% autos; 12% metals and related products; 10% food and grain; 9%

forest products. The continuing recession kept high-revenue products such as autos and intermodal in weak demand, accounting for Conrail's lower revenues for the year. There was a 9% decline in traffic volume early in 1991 due to the recession. Conrail was able to institute cost controls, however. As a result, although revenues were down 4.9% in the first nine months of 1990, operating expenses fell 6.6% and operating income rose 7.3%. While the company's future is connected to the economy, Conrail performed well in its first major recession since going public.

Further Reading: Williams, Winston, "Turning a Railroad Around," *The New York Times Magazine,* January 13, 1985.

—Carol I. Keeley

CSX CORPORATION

One James Center
901 East Cary Street
Richmond, Virginia 23219
U.S.A.
(804) 782-1400
Fax: (804) 782-1409

Public Company
Incorporated: 1978
Employees: 51,437
Sales: $8.21 billion
Stock Exchanges: New York London Zürich Midwest Boston
   Cincinnati Pacific Philadelphia

CSX Corporation is a large transportation-based holding company that operates one of the United States's largest rail systems. The system covers about 18,800 miles in 20 southeastern, eastern, and midwest states and the Canadian province of Ontario. CSX also owns and operates the largest U.S.-flag containership line, Sea-Land Services, Inc.; and the largest U.S. barge carrier, American Commercial Lines, Inc. In addition, CSX manages extensive real estate development activities and operates several large resorts, including the Greenbrier Hotel at White Sulphur Springs, West Virginia. Oil and gas businesses acquired in the early 1980s were sold during a restructuring between 1988 and 1990, as were interests in a telecommunications network and a chain of resort properties. CSX in the early 1990s was attempting to manage its transportation business more efficiently with special attention to improving profitable rail traffic growth. In placing greater reliance on rail traffic, the company is looking back to its distant origins. CSX's railroad, the major part of its business over the years, is the end result of a long series of consolidations involving three historic railroad systems: the Seaboard Coast Line, the Chesapeake and Ohio Railway, and the Baltimore and Ohio Railroad, which together span nearly the entire history of railroading in the United States.

The Baltimore and Ohio Railroad (B&O) was chartered in February 1827 by a group of leading Baltimore businessmen with one of their number, Philip E. Thomas, as the first president. Its purpose was twofold: to challenge major canals, especially the Erie Canal, for the trade to the West and to provide more efficient and cheaper freight and passenger service than was available. In Baltimore's case this traffic passed over the National Road, which ran from Cumberland, Maryland, to

Wheeling, West Virginia, on the Ohio River, with an eastward extension to Baltimore. The railroad's construction on July 4, 1828, at a historic celebration presided over by Charles Carroll, the last surviving signer of the Declaration of Independence. The B&O's planners intended to use horses for motive power, but Peter Cooper's first locomotive used on the line, the diminutive *Tom Thumb,* made its first successful run in 1830, ending the railroad's need for horsepower.

Construction progress was slow, however, and the rail line from Baltimore to Wheeling was finally completed in December 1852. A second western extension was completed to Parkersburg, West Virginia, in 1857, with connections to local railroads providing service to Columbus and Cincinnati, Ohio; and St. Louis, Missouri. The Ohio and West Virginia connections fostered a great increase in coal traffic from midwestern mines to the east. By 1860 revenues from coal were about one-third of total rail freight revenue, a ratio that has changed little over the years. In 1990 coal provided 32% of CSX's rail revenue.

The B&O played a key role in the Civil War, as did many other railroads, and the line suffered accordingly with substantial damage to track and equipment. Progress continued after the war under the presidency of John W. Garrett, who served from 1858 to 1884, providing a basis of sound management in an era when railroad mismanagement was all too common. Track mileage increased from 521 in 1865 to nearly 1,700 by 1885. In subsequent years as the B&O continued to expand through construction and acquisition of smaller railroads, mileage grew to 3,200 in 1900; 5,100 in 1920; and reached a peak of about 6,350 in 1935.

After Garrett's presidency, increasing debt and an over-generous dividend policy weakened the B&O financially while speculation in the company's stock hampered its fund-raising ability. The financial panic of 1893 proved disastrous for the line, and in 1896 the B&O was placed in receivership. In the following decade and a half the reorganized railroad's mileage and revenues increased satisfactorily, but the B&O came under the control of the Pennsylvania Railroad, which had purchased a majority of its stock after the bankruptcy. The Pennsylvania involved itself briefly in the B&O's management, but sold its stock position in 1906 for fear of U.S. government antitrust action. Under the long presidency of Daniel Willard from 1910 to 1941, the B&O's physical plant and service were considerably improved, and the line, which now spread through western Pennsylvania, Ohio, West Virginia, Indiana, and Illinois, enjoyed increasing prosperity until the onset of the Great Depression in the 1930s.

The 1930s saw declining revenues, layoffs, and wage reductions. In 1932 dividends on the common stock were discontinued, not to be restored until 1952. Track mileage and locomotive and equipment rosters began a long decline that would continue until the B&O came under control of the Chesapeake and Ohio Railway (C&O) in 1963. Roy B. White, however, who served as president from 1941 to 1953, inherited from Willard a first-class railroad that offered excellent service. World War II provided renewed prosperity, but the B&O faced problems during the postwar years from inflation, debt for new equipment, declines in passenger traffic, and chronic labor controversies. U.S. President Harry Truman temporarily seized the nation's railroads in 1946 to offset a threatened nationwide strike, and similar crises occurred in 1948 and 1950.

During the B&O's last decade as an independent company, Howard E. Simpson served as president from 1953 to 1961, and Jervis Langdon, Jr., served from 1961 to 1964. Operating revenues and net income generally declined during the 1950s as did track mileage and employment. Labor costs grew because of constant union demands for raises, to which the railroad gave in. In the late 1950s as the B&O's traffic and revenue position worsened, the railroad began to consider the idea of a merger with a stronger partner. The C&O and the New York Central Railroad vied briefly for dominance, but in February 1961 the C&O announced that it controlled 61% of the B&O's stock. In 1962 the Interstate Commerce Commission (ICC) approved the C&O's request to take over the B&O, and on February 4, 1963, the C&O finally took control. The affiliation produced an 11,000-mile rail system, stretching from the Atlantic to the Mississippi River and from the Great Lakes to the southern edges of Virginia, West Virginia, and Kentucky, and brought to the B&O's rescue a smaller but significantly stronger railroad, not quite as old as the B&O, but with origins that also went back to the early years of railroading.

The C&O had its beginning in a short line railroad built to provide rail traffic to farmers and merchants in central Virginia. Chartered in 1836 as the Louisa Railroad, it originally covered 21 miles from Taylorsville to Frederick Hall, Virginia. In 1850 the line's name was changed to the Virginia Central Railroad, and by 1851 it extended eastward to Richmond, Virginia. A plan to extend westward to the Ohio River was delayed by the Civil War, during which the railroad served the Southern cause effectively but was heavily damaged. In 1867 the reorganized company changed its name to the Chesapeake and Ohio Railway Company and with financial backing from Collis P. Huntington, who subsequently became president from 1869 to 1888, the line was open from Richmond to Huntington, West Virginia, by 1873. The panic of 1873 ended in receivership for the C&O in 1875. In 1888 Huntington lost control to J.P. Morgan, who improved the railroad's situation to the extent that by 1900 the C&O was a solvent, well-managed 1,445-mile line connecting Newport News, Virginia, with Cincinnati, Ohio, and Louisville, Kentucky.

The C&O's history during the 20th century was characterized by conservative financial management supported by strong coal revenues. In 1947 the C&O made a major acquisition of the Pere Marquette Railroad with nearly 2,000 miles of track in the Midwest, New York, and Canada, and a sound base of merchandise traffic. The Pennsylvania and New York Central Railroads controlled C&O's stock from 1900 and 1909. During the 1920s and early 1930s control was exercised by Martis P. Van Sweringen and his brother, Oris P. Van Sweringen. From the mid-1930s, noted financier Robert R. Young owned a majority stock position, which he sold in 1954 to Cleveland investment banker Cyrus S. Eaton. By this time the C&O was a prosperous 5,000-mile line with $350 million in annual revenues and an exceptionally competent leader, Walter J. Tuohy, who had assumed the presidency in 1948. After completing the line's dieselization in the mid-1950s, Tuohy moved aggressively to expand the C&O by acquisition, leading to the 1963 combination with the B&O.

The unification of the two railroads proceeded slowly and deliberately with a common annual report appearing in 1964 and senior administrative positions being gradually combined during the 1960s and 1970s. The continued separate opera-tions of the lines avoided the confusion and errors that led to the failure of the Penn Central combination during the same period. It also avoided a downgrading of C&O debt securities because of the weaker financial position of the B&O before the merger, and maximized the benefits of operating two railroads whose traffic was, for the most part, complementary.

Hays T. Watkins became chairman and chief executive officer of the combined C&O and B&O in 1971. He was a strong administrator, firing president John Hanifin in 1975 for spending $2 million on tennis courts at the railroad's resort, the Greenbrier Hotel. Watkins adopted the name Chessie System, Inc., in 1972 for the combined railroads and formally became CEO of Chessie System in 1973. By the late 1970s only 3% of Chessie's $1.5 billion revenues were from nonrail sources, and Watkins was considering diversification and expansion. In 1978 Chessie proposed to the ICC a possible merger with the slightly larger southeastern railroad system, Seaboard Coast Line Industries, Inc. Like the B&O and the C&O, the Seaboard was a consolidation of several railroads whose history also reached back into the 19th century.

The Seaboard's key component, the Atlantic Coast Line Railroad (ACL), began as a series of small railroads running along a northeast-southwest line parallel to the Atlantic coast and connecting communities along the "fall line," the imaginary line joining towns at the heads of navigation of the coastal rivers. The oldest part of the ACL was the Petersburg Railroad, chartered in 1830 to run from Petersburg, Virginia, south to the North Carolina border. The corporate parent of the ACL however, was the Richmond and Petersburg Railroad chartered in 1836. These and similar, small independent railroads running along the fall line through Virginia, North Carolina, South Carolina, Georgia, Alabama, and Florida were joined after the Civil War in a holding company at first called the American Improvement and Construction Company, formed in 1889. In 1893 the name was changed to the Atlantic Coast Line Company. In 1902 the ACL bought a controlling share of the Louisville and Nashville Railroad (L&N) and, following a 1914 reorganization, the name was changed again to the Atlantic Coast Line Railroad Company.

In 1958 the ACL, by then a 5,300-mile railroad with revenues of about $163 million, proposed a merger with one of its southeastern competitors, the Seaboard Air Line Railroad with 4,100 miles and roughly similar revenues. The ACL, with its affiliates, the 5,700-mile L&N and the smaller Clinchfield Railroad, tapping the coal and merchandise markets of the midwest, was the stronger of the two companies. The plan however, was to merge the ACL into the Seaboard to take advantage of the Seaboard's more modern corporate charter. The consolidation plan was filed with the ICC in 1960 but progress was slow, partly because of antitrust issues, with final approval not coming until 1967. The new company, eventually called Seaboard Coast Line Industries, Inc., was the eighth-largest railroad in the United States, with revenues of about $1.2 billion.

The merger proposed in 1978 between the $1.5 billion Chessie and the $1.8 billion Seaboard offered benefits to both sides. It would give the Chessie a relatively inexpensive expansion into the booming southeast and would provide a useful capital infusion for the Seaboard, especially for its maintenance- and equipment-starved L&N subsidiary. The ICC approved the merger in September 1980 and the two systems were consolidated into CSX Corporation on November 1, 1980. The Seaboard's Prime F. Osborn III became chairman and the Chessie's Hays T. Watkins became president. Watkins was clearly the dominant figure, becoming chairman in 1982 on Osborn's retirement.

As in the case of the B&O and C&O, the operational consolidation of the two railroad systems proceeded gradually, again to avoid the internal stresses that had marred the Penn Central merger. In the 1980s diversification was in the air. In 1983 CSX made a deal with Southern New England Telephone Company to place a fiber optics telecommunication system along the CSX rights-of-way. A more significant diversification move in 1983 was CSX's "white-knight" $1 billion purchase of Texas Gas Resources Corporation, with $2.9 billion in revenues, one of the United States's largest natural gas pipeline companies with substantial gas and petroleum reserves. For CSX with revenues of $5 billion this was a major expansion into natural resources, adding oil and gas to its already large coal holdings. Texas Gas had as a subsidiary the American Commercial Lines, Inc., a large barge operator. On July 24, 1984, the ICC voted to allow CSX to keep and operate this shipping firm, a reversal of longstanding government policy against letting railroads own steamship or barge lines.

Continuing this precedent, the ICC in 1987 voted to approve CSX's 1986 $800 million acquisition of Sea-Land Corporation, the largest U.S. ocean container-ship line. This purchase was a continuation of Watkins's somewhat controversial policy of structuring CSX as an intermodal transportation company capable of serving both national and international markets. CSX became heavily involved in resort operations following its 1986 purchase of Rockresorts, Inc., owner and manager of several luxury resorts, which CSX bought from Laurance Rockefeller.

These acquisitions were the last engineered by Watkins. The company's directors became disenchanted with CSX's low profits, declining return on investment, and stagnant stock price. Lagging rail profits, partially due to labor contracts and problems with the company's new acquisitions, resulted in major changes in management and direction for CSX. A comprehensive restructuring program was announced by Watkins in 1988, but in April 1989 John W. Snow was appointed president and chief executive officer. Watkins continued as chairman until his retirement on January 31, 1991, when that position, too, was assumed by Snow.

CSX underwent a significant change in direction between 1988 and 1990. CSX's oil and gas businesses were sold in 1988 and 1989, resulting in a net gain of more than $200 million. Most of its resort properties and the telecommunications system were also sold, although CSX kept the Greenbrier Hotel and one smaller resort. A crew-reduction agreement was signed by the railroad with the United Transportation Union in 1989. This was a key step in Snow's plan to downsize the railroad, as well as other CSX operations, to be more profitable. CSX also improved its share earnings by using money from the gas and oil sale to buy back about 39% of its outstanding common stock.

In his first years as chief executive, Snow has installed a new management team determined to improve shipping and real estate profits and to especially focus on CSX's traditionally strong rail operations in order to earn a better return on the company's $12 billion asset base. Recovering from inappropriate decisions during the 1980s, CSX seemed poised to reassert its historic role as a successful transportation company.

Principal Subsidiaries: American Commercial Lines, Inc.; CSX Transportation, Inc.; Sea-Land Services, Inc.; CSX Intermodal.

Further Reading: Dozier, Howard Douglas, *A History of the Atlantic Coast Line Railroad,* Boston, Houghton Mifflin Company, 1920; Turner, Charles Wilson, *Chessie's Road,* Richmond, Virginia, Garrett and Massie Incorporated, 1956; Stover, John F., *History of the Baltimore and Ohio Railroad,* West Lafayatte, Purdue University Press, 1987.

—Bernard A. Block

DANZAS

DANZAS GROUP

Post Office Box 2680
Leimenstrasse 1
CH-4002 Basel
Switzerland
(61) 315 9191
Fax: (61) 261 5847

Public Company
Incorporated: 1903 as Danzas & Co. AG
Employees: 15,449
Sales: SFr8.80 billion (US$6.49 billion)
Stock Exchanges: Basel Zürich Geneva

Danzas Group, one of Europe's largest transportation companies, with travel activities in Switzerland and France, celebrated its 175th anniversary in 1990. The company has grown from a small, family-run firm to a diversified transportation multinational with interests in air-, road-, rail-, and water-borne cargo transportation as well as travel and warehousing.

Danzas in the early 1990s was building links throughout Europe to take advantage of the single market, but it traces its history back to the European conflict that culminated in the battle of Waterloo in 1815. For much of the company's history, Danzas, first French, then Swiss, struggled to maintain its communication and transportation links against a background of European wars and political troubles.

After the resounding defeat of Napoleon's Grande Armée at Waterloo, a demobilized young French lieutenant named Marie Matthias Nicholas Louis Danzas, or Louis Danzas for short, joined a small freight forwarding company, Michel l'Evêque, Etablissement de Commission et d'Expédition, in St. Louis, France, just across the border from Basel, Switzerland. Within a very short time he was appointed the company's *procureur général et spécial.* Louis Danzas was an Alsatian, but his family traced its origins to Gascony and Spain; the name was originally spelt D'Anzas.

In 1840 Danzas and his brother-in-law Edouard l'Evêque formed the Maison de Commission et d'Expédition Danzas & l'Evêque a St. Louis. Seven years later Danzas and l'Evêque took their first step toward expansion by opening a branch in the nearby city of Mulhouse, France.

The company was well placed to take advantage of the new technology and the rapidly expanding rail and steamship routes in this part of Europe. Danzas began to build up a worldwide network of agents. In order to handle the regular groupage—

the organization of combined freight units for joint transportation—traffic between Zürich and Basel, they merged with the transport companies Favier-Gervais Vonier and Ouzelet & Cie to form a new general partnership, Danzas, Ouzelet & Cie, in 1855. The firm then had Ouzelet's former offices in Basel as a Swiss branch. The new *service acéléré* may have been the world's first rail groupage service. In 1859, the firm was renamed Danzas, l'Evêque & Minet—the latter was a partner in the former Ouzelet firm—but the company remained French, headquartered in St. Louis, and Louis Danzas remained the undisputed senior partner of the rapidly expanding company until he died in 1862.

His son, Emile Jules Danzas, succeeded him. Initially he had favored a military career, but his father wanted to found a Danzas business dynasty and sent Emile to work and train in the ports of Hamburg and Le Havre. When Emile received draft papers from the French army during the Crimean War in 1855, Louis Danzas found a young bricklayer to take his son's place in the military for Ffr 900 and used his influence to persuade the local authorities to accept the substitution. Edouard l'Evêque retired in 1865, and the company's name was changed to Danzas & Minet, Commissionaires, Expéditeurs, Correspondence avec les Chemins de fer, Agence en Douane, à Bâle & St. Louis.

Alsace became German at the end of the Franco-Prussian war in 1871. As a consequence, the Danzas company would eventually become Swiss. Jules Danzas was a French patriot and could not live under the new German Empire. He moved his family and business, first across the new border to Belfort, France, and then to a more geographically advantageous base at Basel, where he signed a declaration of French citizenship before the French consul. He began to expand his branch network in Switzerland.

Rising Swiss prosperity, new mountain tunnels, and rail links enhanced Basel's role as a trade center on the Rhine River at the point where Germany, France, and Switzerland meet. The Danzas company took advantage of this geographic position to forward freight between these countries and to the larger continent beyond. In 1884 Danzas obtained a subcontract from the Swiss post office for international post deliveries. Even at this time, the company was able to guarantee 24-hour Switzerland-to-London postal service.

In 1878 Jules Danzas had converted Danzas & Minet into a sole proprietorship, but he had no son. By 1884 he had made his colleague Laurent Werzinger a partner; by 1886 Danzas sold most of his interest to Werzinger and retired to Paris, where he died in 1917. Alsace reverted to France a year later after the German defeat in World War I, but by that time the company had established firm roots in the major Swiss commercial city of Basel.

Under Laurent Werzinger the company expanded its branch network and acquired an interest in a Rhine steamship company, Basel Rheinschiffahrt AG. High priority was given to the development of branch offices and international groupage services. As Danzas had become a national household name and was also known internationally, Werzinger decided to retain the name when he incorporated the company as Danzas & Co. AG on January 1, 1903 with a share capital of SFr2 million, divided into 400 registered shares with a nominal value of SFr5,000 each. He also diversified into the travel agency business, opening offices in all regions of Switzerland and also in

France. The firm retained a family character when Albert Werzinger, who had joined Danzas in 1883, succeeded his father as chairman in 1911. He remained chairman for 37 years and saw the company through the difficult political problems posed by Switzerland's neutrality in World War I and World War II. At the end of World War I, the company's international operations were threatened by French government reprisals for supposed disloyalty by the legally neutral Danzas company. Werzinger's negotiating skills and tact in putting French notables on the Danzas board were credited with the ending of the crisis and restoration of normal Danzas business in France, the company's most lucrative market. By 1908 the Paris office had a staff of 80, engaged in—among other things—the import of Swiss fabrics for Paris fashion houses, but Danzas also was able to incorporate a separate German subsidiary, Danzas GmbH, in 1919. The company became increasingly involved in seagoing traffic out of the northern European ports.

Danzas incurred substantial losses in the aftermath of the stock market crash of 1929 and found the going rough in the generally depressed world trade scene of the 1930s. A brief upswing in its fortunes was brought to an abrupt end with the outbreak of World War II. Branches in France and Germany were largely shut down in 1939 and those in Italy were closed in 1940. Danzas concentrated its efforts on Switzerland's supply line via neutral Portugal. Hans Hatt, a future Danzas chairman, spent the war years in Lisbon helping maintain this traffic.

Danzas suffered great material and personnel losses during World War II, but its base in neutral Switzerland remained intact, allowing the company to make a speedy postwar recovery. In 1948 Hans Hatt's 73-year-old father, Fritz, succeeded Albert Werzinger as chairman. Under his leadership the network of branches was expanded in Switzerland, France, Germany, and Italy. The company's name was changed to Danzas AG in 1960.

After Hans Hatt became chairman in 1963, the company began to expand outside, as well as within, Europe. New branches were established in Greece, Spain, and Portugal. Representative offices were set up in Latin America and New York and other commercial centers. Many of these were to become the basis for future subsidiary companies. Danzas Travel, concentrating on business and custom-tailored travel, continued to grow.

In 1979 David Linder, a lawyer and member of the Swiss Parliament, was appointed to the dual position of chairman of the board and president. Danzas's registered shares began to be traded on the Basel Stock Exchange in 1985, after shareholders' approval of increased capitalization to SFr10 million at an annual general meeting. Two years later, at another annual general meeting, the creation of participation certificate capital shares to be traded on the Basel, Zurich, and Geneva exchanges was approved.

International expansion continued throughout the 1980s with the takeover of the British Gentransco Group and the founding of new subsidiaries in Belgium and the Netherlands. By 1984, the Danzas office in Australia became a full-fledged subsidiary. In the following year, Danzas took over several important distribution companies including SATEM S.A. in France and S.A.D. S.A. in Spain, and to cover the United States founded Danzas Tuya S.A.—a Panamanian-registered company—in Miami, Florida.

In 1987, Danzas took over SBT NV in Belgium. New affiliate companies were established in Japan, Taiwan, and Hungary. With the purchase of Northern Air Freight of Bellevue, Washington, in 1989, Danzas had established representative offices in 36 countries and 41 U.S states. By 1991 the company was entering a period of restructuring and consolidation to absorb these new acquisitions.

Capital assets also increased as Danzas developed a policy of providing its own in-house facilities and resources. Investment in real estate, vehicles, and telecommunications assets grew throughout the 1980s. Danzas also sells its organizational expertise in storage and transportation. In a notable agreement, Jacobs Suchard, the chocolate maker, hired Danzas to set up an automated warehouse system.

On April 1, 1989, David Linder was appointed president of the board of directors. He was succeeded as delegate of the board and chairman of the executive committee by Bernd Menzinger.

The European Community (EC) made a significant step toward deregulation of transportation in the EC on July 1, 1990, when it ended national restrictions that had prohibited trucks based in one country from carrying goods within the borders of another member state. The move, along with the opening of East European borders and markets, was widely seen as starting a process that would transform the goods transportation industry.

Some observers predicted an industry shake-out with the removal of protectionist measures. Small- and medium-sized trucking firms were faced with selling out to larger rivals or allying themselves to the majors as subcontractors. In addition, new overseas competitors have appeared on the scene, including Mitsui from Japan, TNT from Australia, and Federal Express from the United States.

Danzas and other big freight transport companies were meeting this challenge not just with acquisitions but by diversification and by expanding their European networks with new routes and methods. For example, the company's new, computer-controlled Cargovia system organizes large, full-load shipments for industrial firms across Europe. Its Danznet information system allows the company to coordinate warehousing and distribution.

Danzas GmbH, the German subsidiary that contributes 20% of the company's turnover, spearheaded a move into eastern Germany. A new terminal in Halle will enable the firm to offer exporters and importers regular groupage services to East Germany. An Eastern Europe coordination department was set up to maintain contacts, evaluate opportunities, and set priorities. Danzas is negotiating with many Eastern European countries on possible new companies and joint ventures. Elsewhere in Europe, Danzas created a "flexible pipeline" to allow Bosch, a German electronics manufacturer, to supply the British car-manufacturing industry through the Danzas terminal in Colehill, West Midlands.

The Wall Street Journal of July 23, 1990, predicted that only 10 to 15 European companies would survive deregulation of the freight transportation industry. Danzas was expected to be one of these firms. Along with two other major Swiss contenders, Kühne & Nagel and Panalpina, it suffered the disadvantage of not having headquarters in a European Community member state, but emphasis on an international identity and the importance of its subsidiaries, particularly its powerful

French company, with a staff of more than 5,000, minimalized the problems.

Switzerland began to consider dropping its traditional neutrality for the advantages of the European Community's single market. Danzas, a Swiss company that traces its origins back to the battle of a divided Europe at Waterloo, is determined to prosper from the growing process of European integration.

Principal Subsidiaries: Danmar Lines AG; Danzas Reisen AG; Imadel AG (95%); Danzas Pty Ltd. (Australia); Danzas AG (Austria); Danzas NV (Belgium); SBT NV (Belgium); Danzas GmbH (Germany); Danzas & Dittes GmbH (Germany, 50%); Danzas HP (France); O.G.T. SA (France), Transvet SA (France, 50%); Danzas AE (Greece); Danzas (UK) Ltd.; Overall Transport (UK) Ltd.; C.A.T. Nationwide Carriers Ltd (U.K.); Baker Britt & Co Ltd (U.K.); Chemoldanzas KFT (Hungary, 50%); Delta Transport S.p.A. (Italy); Italdanzas S.p.A. (Italy); Samec S.p.A. (Italy); Danzas K.K. (Japan); Danzas BV (Netherlands); Danzas (Singapore) Pte Ltd.; Danzas (Southern Africa) Transport (Pty) Ltd.; Danzas SAE (Spain); Danzas Corporation (U.S.A.).

Further Reading: Danzas From 1815–1990, Basel, Danzas AG, 1990.

—Clark Siewert

DEUTSCHE BUNDESBAHN

Zentrale Hauptverwaltung
Friedrich-Ebert-Anlage 43-45
D-6000 Frankfurt am Main 1
Federal Republic of Germany
(69) 2 65-1
Fax: (69) 2 65-6480

State-Owned Company
Incorporated: 1951
Employees: 245,960
Sales: DM30.00 billion (US$19.80 billion)

The Deutsche Bundesbahn (DB) is the largest transport company in the Federal Republic of Germany. DB operates passenger and freight transport services, by rail and by road. The bulk of its business, however, is rail transport. In 1990 DB carried 1.072 billion passengers. Of those 1.043 billion were carried by rail, 18 million by bus, and 11 million by ship. Passenger traffic measured in passenger-kilometers amounted to 44.2 billion passenger kilometers, of which 43.6 billion were carried by rail. Freight traffic amounted to 66.8 billion ton-kilometers, of which 62.5 billion were carried by rail and 4.3 billion by road. The volume of freight carried amounted to 299.5 million tons in 1990.

In 1990 DB's revenue of DM30.00 billion included federal subsidies of DM4.1 billion. In addition the company's owner, the state, once again made financial subsidies of around DM9.6 billion. These figures reflect the particular political conditions under which DB operates and reveal its financial difficulties. For many years DB has seen declining demand for its transport services and decreasing profitability.

DB has experienced financial difficulties since its foundation. DB's predecessor was the Deutsche Reichsbahn, which was split up in 1945 when Germany was divided into four occupied zones, each with an independent railroad network. Beginning October 1, 1946, the Reichsbahn railroad lines in the American and British zones were placed under the control of a common central administration, based in Bielefeld. By September 7, 1949, the name "Deutsche Reichsbahn" was changed in the American and British occupied zones to "Deutsche Bundesbahn." On January 1, 1951, according to the company report for that year, the railroad in the French occupied zone was merged with the DB to form "a financial and economic community with a common economic, financial, and accounting management." The formal merger of the

DB took place when the Federal Railroad Act came into effect on December 18, 1951. The integration of the railroads of the Saar began in 1957 and was concluded in 1959 with the ending of the Saarland's economic transitional period—the Saarland joined the Federal Republic of Germany at a later date than the other states. Because of war damage, DB began operating under extremely adverse conditions. Buildings, permanent ways—tracks, points, bridges, and signal boxes—and fleets had suffered badly during the war. DB had to carry out repairs and reconstruction predominantly by itself. In addition to the material damage of the war, DB had postwar costs which also hindered the company's development. DB had to bear the costs of paying maintenance and interim payments—grants to cover refugees' losses and help them to resettle—to railway workers expelled from central and eastern Germany and to their surviving dependants, as well as to those entitled to war maintenance. These and similar non-operating overheads were later transferred to the state budget. Furthermore, the alignment of the network, which before the war had run predominantly in an east-westerly direction, no longer corresponded to the traffic flows and now ran mainly in a north-southerly direction. The re-alignment of the network through building new stretches of track required much time and expenditure.

In the 1950s and 1960s DB's freight volume and freight train services, as measured in ton-kilometers, grew considerably. The volume of freight carried rose, albeit with fluctuations, from 203.2 million tons in 1950 to reach a historic peak of 351.8 million tons in 1974. Since then, the amount of freight transported has generally declined. In 1990 freight volume totaled 275.1 million tons. The growth in freight train services operated was similar. In 1950 they stood at 38.9 billion ton-kilometers, reached 70.5 billion ton-kilometers in 1970, an all-time high, and since then have generally been in decline. In 1990 train services operated totaled 61.5 billion ton-kilometers.

The picture is somewhat different for passenger transport. While the number of rail passengers, including those using the suburban lines, grew less dramatically and while there was a downward trend in the number of rail passengers from the 1960s, passenger train services operated, including suburban lines, rose from 30.2 billion passenger-kilometers in 1950 to 38.5 billion in 1970 and reached 42.7 billion in 1985. In 1990 ridership still amounted to 43.6 billion. The number of passengers rose from 1.28 billion in 1950 to a high of 1.47 billion in 1957 and since then has tended to decline. In 1990, 1.04 billion people traveled by rail. DB has developed increasingly into a long-distance carrier, while being less attractive for short distances. The situation is different for the so-called S-Bahn rapid transit suburban services. Here passenger volume has risen sharply; ridership has quintupled since the early 1970s.

DB also declined in relative importance in the transport markets. The company has seen its share of the markets decline continuously since 1950, largely owing to the increasing popularity of road transport. While in 1950 DB had a 64.8% share of the total volume of freight carried by the German domestic long-distance transport industry—that is, excluding short-distance road haulage and maritime shipping—by 1970 this share stood at around 40% and in 1989 was only 27.2%. DB's market share of freight transport declined from 61.6% in

1950 to 39.3% in 1970 and 24.7% in 1990. In passenger business, DB had 2.6% of the total ridership in 1989 as compared with 15.2% in 1950. The situation was similar for traffic results; DB's market share fell from 35.5% in 1950 to 6.0% in 1989. In passenger transport, the motor car dominates the market and has a market share of around 82% both in traffic volume and results.

DB has tried in many ways to make its services more attractive in order to withstand competition from road transport. One of the most significant investments to enhance the competitiveness of the railroads was the increased electrification of the network. In 1950 it was envisaged that the electrified lines taken over from the Deutsche Reichsbahn be extended by 4,500 kilometers to a total of 6,000 kilometers. By the mid-1980s, this target projection was exceeded. The electrified network comprised around 11,700 kilometers in 1990. More than 80% of DB's transport services operate on the electrified lines, which make up around 40% of the total network. Diesel trains run on the non-electrified lines, while steam locomotives ceased to operate in spring 1977.

In its competition with the motor car for ridership, DB concentrated from the beginning of the 1970s on speed and regularity of long-distance services. The Intercity (IC) system linked densely populated areas with high ridership volumes. IC trains began operation in winter 1971–1972 on four lines, with trains leaving at two-hour intervals. In 1979 the interval for IC services was reduced to one hour, and in 1985 a further line was added. In freight business too, DB reoriented its services to concentrate increasingly on the transporting of goods between industrial centers, where the high volume of traffic permitted the use of through trains. DB also reduced the number of part-load stations—terminals where freight trains carrying less than full wagonloads are handled—reorganized the marshalling—or shunting—system, and in 1984 established the InterCargo overnight service. Since then, the eleven most important industrial centers have been connected by overnight services. For regional freight distribution DB uses trucks, of which it has between 3,000 to 4,000 under contract.

DB's involvement in intermodal transport has also helped to improve local collection and delivery services. The first trials with piggyback transport—the transporting of articulated trucks or trailers on special railway wagons—began in 1954. The technology of piggyback transport and container transport, where only the transport vessel is changed, superseded the Culemeyer Strassenroller (wagon-carrying road trailer), the so-called private siding, a line leading off a main line to an industrial plant for collection and deliveries of freight. The container business is operated by DB's subsidiary Transfracht Deutsche Transportgesellschaft, founded in 1969. DB is also an associate shareholder in Kombiverkehr, dealing with piggyback transport and founded in 1968. Despite the considerable growth rate in the volumes carried by intermodal services, in 1989 piggyback and container traffic represented only around 8% of DB's total rail freight business.

In parallel with its decreasing economic importance and declining market shares, DB experienced increasingly poor financial results. In 1974 Hans-Otto Lenel wrote in volume 25 of the ORDO-Jahrbuch that "the Deutsche Bundesbahn has been one of the biggest headaches in transport policy for more than one and a half decades." This statement has lost none of its relevance. According to its financial statements, since its

incorporation DB has only made a profit once, in 1951, when profits amounted to DM71.7 million. With the exception of 1955, the company's losses increased year by year. From 1958 these deficits could be attributed to changes brought about by the consumer boom that began in autumn 1959. In 1960 and 1961 the deficit stood at DM13.5 million and DM29.8 million respectively. By 1965, however, the deficit had exceeded DM1 billion deutschmarks. In addition, in the same year DB received equalization payments from the state of more than DM1 billion deutschmarks. DB's deficits and the state's subsidies to date add up to almost DM14 billion annually. It is not surprising, therefore, that DB came to be described as a drain on the budget.

Apart from a few smaller stretches of new line—the first new line built after the war went from Salzgitter-Drütte to Salzgitter-Lichtenberg, and was opened in November 1954—DB's major new line construction program began as late as August 1973 with the commencement of work on the new line between Hanover and Würzburg. This line and the link between Mannheim and Stuttgart were to replace the winding and heavily-used stretches through the mountain ranges of central western Germany. Work was delayed due to protracted planning and approval procedures and numerous legal proceedings. The two lines did not go into full service until timetable changes were made at the beginning of June 1991. The new Hanover-Würzburg line permits the operation of freight traffic at maximum speeds of up to 160 kilometers per hour and InterCargoExpress services are able to cover the Hamburg to Munich corridor on night runs.

The company's ability to compete on equal terms with other carriers and its adjustment to economic developments and changes in structure were considerably restricted by its relationship with the state. The 1951 Federal Railroad Act stipulated that DB be run in accordance with commercial principles and in the interests of Germany's national economy. Within the scope of this relationship, with its tensions resulting from DB's contradictory status as a public service undertaking and a commercial enterprise, DB's commitments toward public service duties have, until the present, been dominant, although the 1961 amendment to the transport laws formally reduced its public service obligations. The Federal Railroad Act specifically states that DB is to carry out its public service duties within the framework of a commercially run company.

In general, the duties of operation, transportation, and fares are included under the generic term of public services. DB is obliged to provide rail transport, even on unprofitable sections of its network. The closure of lines requires formal procedures in which various political bodies are involved.

The first closure of certain branch lines occurred at the end of the 1950s, but the network was not greatly reduced. In 1990, the total length of lines was 27,000 kilometers, only slightly less than the total length in 1950 of 30,500 kilometers. DB is also obliged to adjust its capacities to take account of transport demand at peak times. DB's fares were set by the minister for transport until the amendment of the transport laws—the so-called minor transport policy reform—in 1961, giving DB greater freedom to set prices. However, fare changes still required the approval of the minister for transport. Until this change in the law, DB's freight rates had to be in line with those for long-distance road haulage and inland shipping. DB's freight rates were governed by the *Reichskraftwagentarif*, from 1989 known as the long-distance road haulage tariff, which hindered DB's competitiveness in the road haulage market.

Apart from these political reasons, there were two further processes that were significant in the development of DB's transport business. Firstly, the motor car boom which had begun in the 1950s took away a great deal of DB's market share in passenger transport. Secondly, the evolution of freight structures had an adverse effect upon the railroads, as changes in Germany's industrial structure led to a dramatic increase in the proportion of goods better suited to road transport.

The deterioration in DB's financial situation could not be prevented even by various plans for reform and restructuring. As early as 1958 the DB board of directors presented its ideas for DB's financial recovery. It requested that DB be given more leeway to adapt to commercial market requirements. Prerequisites for this were equality in conditions at the outset after reform and restructuring in the transport field and the relaxation of the legal and financial relations between the state and the federal railroad. In 1960 the Brand Commission, established to examine the state of affairs at DB, presented its report.

The Brand Commission advocated a stronger commercial orientation in the field of transport. DB's businesses should be run according to independent commercial market principles. Furthermore, the Brand Commission also advocated the discontinuation of the policy whereby only civil servants could be board members, managers of the business divisions at the DB headquarters, or president of the regional headquarters, as well as clarifying the financial relations between the railroad and the state.

In 1967 the government put forward the Leber Plan, its transport program for 1968 to 1972 which gave special attention to road haulage, planned line closures, and reductions in staffing. In 1969 the advisory committee to the minister for transport proposed that financial responsibility for the public service sector be imposed on the regional administrations requiring the provision of DB services. In the 1970s the minister for transport set various objectives, the government commissioned projects, and the DB board put forward its conception for an optimum commercial network. These plans envisaged, amongst other things, the closure of lines leading to a halving of the network, DB's concentration on long-distance traffic, and staff reductions. In 1983 the government agreed to the guidelines presented by the minister for transport for DB's consolidation, according to which increases in productivity, investments, the closure of lines, and reductions in personnel were to lead to a 40% reduction in overall expenditure by 1990. In addition, a ceiling was set on government grants which were already authorized and running.

From the beginning of the 1980s DB's statement of accounts made a distinction between the commercial sector, the public sector, and the state-financed sector. The commercial sector included in particular long-distance passenger and freight services. The public sector, subsidized by the government, included those services operated by DB which are unprofitable to run but must be provided in the interest of the general public. This sector included short-distance passenger services. The state-financed sector included the provision of the infrastructure—that is, the track.

Of the various proposals for reform to bring about DB's financial recovery, three measures in particular have been put into practice already: the reduction in personnel, the discon-tinuation of insistence on civil service status for board members, and, although only to a limited extent, suitable definition of the financial relations between the government and DB.

DB has received financial resources from the federal government since the beginning of the 1950s. According to the federal minister for transport, grants allocated to the DB between 1952 and 1960 amounted to DM5.9 billion. This sum includes loans and support for banking, liquidity, and financing, as well as the waiving of transport tax. From the beginning of the 1960s financial aid from the federal government has been increasingly determined by both national and European Community (EC) legislation. This includes equalization payments for the public sector, in particular to cover losses due to the imposition of cheap fares for commuter and school traffic, equalization payments to offset losses due to the disadvantages suffered by DB in the competitive field—in particular, the enormous increases in social security payments, as DB runs its own superannuation scheme—as well as government ownership obligations such as interest payments and repayments for loans taken on by DB. Transferring these obligations from DB to the state could, in itself, hardly be conducive to DB's longterm redevelopment.

The reduction in the work force is intended to cut the company's costs: expenditure on personnel represents around 60% of DB's total outlay. The workforce reached a historic peak in 1948 at 602,000. Soon afterward, some major redundancy schemes reduced DB's average annual work force to 530,000 in 1950, after which the number of employees diminished further. Between 1960 and 1969, the number of employees fell from 498,000 to 398,000. The beginning of the 1980s brought an accelerated reduction in staff to 246,000 by the end of 1990. Since the beginning of the 1980s, managers from the private sector have been appointed to DB's board. This discontinuation of adherence to civil service status for the company's management was designed to lead to greater commercial orientation for DB. This objective has only been attained to a limited degree since government policy has still not allowed DB the necessary freedom of action. It therefore comes as no surprise that Heinz Dürr, chairman of DB's board since 1991, is pressing for a constitutional amendment to end the bureaucratic status of the railroad, thus permitting it to operate more fully as a commercial entity.

The obligation toward modification of the government's railroad policy and the economic redevelopment of DB arises not only from the company's difficult financial situation but also from the reunification of Germany, the accompanying takeover of the Deutsche Reichsbahn (DR) by the federal government, and the development of the EC transport policy. The unification treaty calls for the ultimate technical and organizational merging of the two railways.

Principal Subsidiaries: Deutsche Bundesbahn Holding GmbH; Nuclear Cargo + Service GmbH; Transfracht GmbH (79.5%); Schenker & Co. GmbH (77.5%); Rhenus AG (4.4%); Bahnbus-Holding GmbH; Deutsche Service Gesellschaft der Bahn mbH; Reisebüro Rominger (90%); Amtliches Bayerisches Reisebüro GmbH (55%); Vereinigte Bundesverkehrsbetriebe (52.9%); Bayern Express (51.7%); DER Deutsches Reisebüro (50.1%); Deutsche Touring (50.1%); BRG Bahnreinigungs-Realisierungsgesellschaft; RBRG Hannover (51%);

RBRG Nürnberg (51%); RBRG Stuttgart (51%); RBRG Frankfurt/Main (51%); RBRG Hamburg (51%); RBRG München (51%); RBRG Köln (51%); Planungsgesellschaft Airport Express; Deutsche Eisenbahn Reklame (60%); PFA Partner für Fahrzeug-Ausstattung (51%); Planungsgesellschaft Schnellbahnbau Hannover-Berlin (51%); Marbeton; Kombiwaggonprojekt GmbH (50%); MVP Versuchs- und Planungsgesellschaft für Magnetbahnsysteme (33.3%); Deutsche Gesellschaft für Kombinierten Güterverkehr (20.5%); Münchner Verkehrs- und Tarifverbund (50%); Frankfurter Verkehrs- und Tarifverbund (49%); Verkehrs- und Tarifverbund Stuttgart (50%); Eurofirma Europäische Gesellschaft für die Finanzierung von Eisenbahnmaterial (25%); START-Holding GmbH (30%); Deutsche Umschlaggesellschaft Schiene/Strasse (DUSS) (40%); Deutsche Eisenbahn-Consulting GmbH (49%); TLC Transport-, Informatik- und Logistik-Consulting (45%); Autotransportgesellschaft mbH (25%); BTT BahnTank-Transport GmbH (25%).

—Berthold Busch

EAST JAPAN RAILWAY COMPANY

1-6-5 Maranouchi
Chiyoda-ku, Tokyo 100
Japan
(03) 3212-3772

State-Owned Company
Incorporated: 1987
Employees: 80,000
Sales: ¥1.85 trillion (US$14.82 billion)

East Japan Railway Company is the largest of the six regional passenger companies into which Japan's state-owned railroad company, Japan National Railway, was divided in April 1987. Japan's railroad first began as a national railroad, since at the beginning of the Meiji Restoration no other organization could finance such a large project. The first railroad, opened in September 1872, ran from Shimbashi, west of Tokyo, to Yokohama in Kanagawa Prefecture, the main port near Tokyo. It was 23.8 kilometers long, with a gauge of 1,067 millimeters. To finance its construction, the Japanese government raised £1 million in London by issuing bonds through the Oriental Bank.

British engineers such as Edmund Morel, John Diack, and John England supervised the line's construction, giving advice to the Japanese government on railroad management and technology. Most of the materials and machines were brought from Britain as well. The British engineers were paid high salaries; for instance, the foreign general manager in the railroad office earned ¥2,000 per month, whereas the highest-ranking minister in the Japanese government earned only ¥800 per month. Most of the foreign railroad engineers left Japan by the end of the 1880s. The Japanese had learned enough about railroad construction and management from the British, and Japanese government-sponsored students of modern railroad technology had returned home from Britain to apply their expertise to domestic railroad construction.

One of these students was Masaru Inoue, who had studied civil engineering and mining at University College in London. He was invited to participate in the construction of the first Japanese railroad, and as head of the ministry of transport took the lead in railroad construction and in forming Japanese railroad policy. He was responsible for the government's decision to build all the railroads itself, but soon realized the difficulty of funding the project. Economic problems and a shortage of government funds meant that the construction of private railroads had to be permitted, though the government provided subsidies and other assistance.

The first and largest private railroad was the Nippon Railroad, operating between Ueno, Tokyo, and Aomori, the largest city in the north of Japan's main island. The Nippon Railroad was financed mainly by the *daimyo,* or nobles, who had received compensation from the government for losing their former status at the time of the Meiji Restoration. The first stretch of the railroad opened in 1883, and its success induced the railroad boom from the end of the 1880s. As a result of the boom in railroad construction, the total length of the private railroad soon came to exceed that of the national railroad by a considerable margin: in 1905, the mileage of the private railroads attained 5,282 kilometers, compared with the national railroad's 2,414 kilometers.

There was a lobby in the Japanese government for the nationalization of the private railroads. After the Russo-Japanese War, the military powers were especially anxious to nationalize major private railroad companies to facilitate through-traffic on all trunk lines, particularly in the event of an emergency such as war. Much discussion took place in the Diet, and there was strong opposition from the private railroad shareholders.

In 1906, 17 private railroad companies were nationalized as Kokuyo Tetsudo or Japan National Railway (JNR). The financial compensation paid to the private shareholders was equal to approximately double the paid capital. From the national economic viewpoint, the nationalization of the railroads made it possible to mobilize assets into other heavy industries. About ¥450 million—equal to about two-thirds of Japan's industrial, mining, and transport assets in 1907—were paid in the form of national debt to shareholders, who converted it into cash and invested it in other key industries. As the result of the nationalization, the government controlled 4,833 kilometers including unopened lines, 1,118 locomotives, 3,067 passenger carriages, 20,884 freight carriages, and 8,409 employees. The national railroad's share of transport increased drastically from the prenationalization level of 32% to 90.9%, in terms of lines in operation. In terms of passengers per kilometer and tons per kilometer, the national railroads had 83.8% and 91.4% of the total respectively, compared with 37.7% and 29.4% before nationalization. The national railroad had gained a monopoly in land transportation.

Accordingly, the management structure had to be changed. In 1907 *Tetsudosagyo-kyoku* (the Railroad Bureau) was reorganized to become *Teikoku Tetsudo-cho* (the Imperial Railroad Department), and in 1908 the latter was placed under the direct control of the Cabinet, changing its name to *Tetsudo-in* (the Railroad Ministry). *Tetsudo-in* was composed of five Control Divisions: Hokkaido, Tobu, Chubu, Seibu, and Kyushu. These divisions had a certain degree of autonomy.

The first president of *Tetsudo-in* was Shimpei Goto, who had been president of the South Manchuria Railroad for about three years. He established *Kokutetsu Dai Kazokushugi* (JNR familism), an ideology designed to unify a staff of about 90,000 into a kind of family, bringing together numerous employees who had belonged to various private railroad companies.

Goto also made efforts to change from narrow gauge—10.67 centimeters—to standard gauge—14.35 centimeters—though almost all the private and national railroads had adopted the former. It is not clear why the Meiji government had originally adopted narrow gauge, but Shigenobu Okuma, who had negotiated with the British over the introduction of the railroad system into Japan, remarked that the government had not forseen the kind of problems that would be incurred as a result of its choice of gauge. The British engineers' recommendation of narrow gauge had been based on Japan's economic climate at that time. Goto wished to increase traffic capacity by widening the gauge. However, there was strong opposition to the change from the military powers. In the end, the government chose to extend the railroads rather than widen the gauge. Japan National Railway had to wait until the introduction of the Shinkansen (Bullet Train) in 1964 for its conversion to standard gauge.

In 1910 Japan had 7,838 kilometers of railroad; by 1930 it had increased to 14,574 kilometers. The national railroad was, however, easily affected by the politicians who promoted the construction of lines in certain regions in order to win local support, regardless of profitability.

Japan National Railway increased the amount of passenger and freight traffic from the mid-1910s to the 1920s. Forty-five million tons of freight were transported in 1916, as opposed to eighty-one million tons in 1926. In 1916 the number of freight carriages was about 43,000, increasing to about 60,000 in 1926. However, from the latter part of the 1920s, especially during the Great Depression from 1929, JNR's freight transport growth was slow, with a 17% increase from 12.5 billion tons per kilometer in 1926 to 14.5 billion tons per kilometer in 1935, a sharp contrast to the freight traffic growth rate of 79% in the 11 years from 1916 to 1926. Passenger traffic was similarly affected. In the 1910s and 1920s, passenger numbers had increased rapidly, especially season ticket holders, as workers tended to commute by train from the expanding suburbs. In the latter part of the 1920s JNR faced increasing competition from motor vehicles. In 1930 JNR's freight traffic revenue in the 50-kilometer range fell by 41% owing to competition from trucks. As for passenger transport, JNR faced competition from bus services for short-distance journeys of between 5 and 20 kilometers. Urban transport was gradually taken over by private and municipal electric trams and private electric railroads, and by the subway system, which first opened in 1927. However, JNR still held a strong position and its business flourished, especially long-distance transportation. It also launched bus services, connecting with railroad stations, in 1930. Bus services acted as feeders for the railroads as well as replacing railroads in areas where the demand for transport was not strong, but some form of transport was essential.

The development of civil and mechanical engineering is an important part of JNR's history, culminating in high-technology systems such as the Shinkansen. The construction of early railroad lines was undertaken by Japanese civil engineers, though initially under the guidance of British engineers. By 1880, however, the time of the Kyoto-Otsu project, Japanese engineers were able to carry out all types of construction, including a tunnel of 18 kilometers.

JNR was also able to manufacture rolling stock at an early stage, first by importing the main parts and later obtaining them from Japanese suppliers. Passenger and freight carriages were relatively easy to manufacture, compared to locomotives. At the beginning of the 1880s, almost 100% of passenger carriages and freight cars were manufactured in Japan. By con-

trast, most of the locomotives were initially imported from Britain, but from the 1890s American locomotives were introduced, mainly in Hokkaido, in the north of Japan's main island, and German locomotives in Kyushu, south of the main island. The dominance of British locomotives was gradually eroded by these newcomers.

It took some time for Japanese engineers to master locomotive manufacturing. The first domestic-built locomotive was made in 1893 under the guidance of Richard Trevithic, a grandson of Richard Trevithic, one of the pioneers of British railroad engineering. As the length of lines and volume of transport increased, the number of Japanese-produced locomotives grew as Japanese familiarity with Western technology increased, especially through maintenance and repair. The nationalization of the railroads promoted the growth of the indigenous locomotive industry, because at the time of nationalization 147 types of locomotives from different countries and different manufacturers came under government control. It proved difficult for the government to combine these in one system. By 1912, Japanese factories had produced 162 locomotives and JNR ceased to import locomotives. At that time, 6.7% of the total locomotives available at that time were Japanese-made. Between the wars, Japanese factories gradually increased the locomotive manufacturing capacity. Japanese locomotives performed well, even in comparison with western locomotives.

The early introduction of electricity to the railroads indicates the formation of a technocratic element in JNR. Electrification was urgently needed to increase speed and capacity. Around the end of the 1910s, high coal prices became another reason for accelerating electrification. The electrification of the lines was largely restricted to urban areas and some hilly areas such as Yokokawa. By 1935 JNR had electrified 579 kilometers of its lines, but this was only about 4% of its total track length. The private railroad companies were more active in converting from steam to electricity because they were more innovative, operating in urban areas over relatively short distances. Generally speaking, JNR's profitability increased along with freight volume.

In World War II, JNR buildings and lines sustained heavy damage and JNR was under strong pressure from the government to cooperate in military transportation. During the war JNR lost 10% of its rolling stock, including 891 locomotives, about 14% of JNR's total. About 20% of JNR's buildings, including stations and warehouses, were destroyed, and 1,600 kilometers of track were damaged, about 5% of the total. 65% of the tonnage of ships owned by JNR was lost. About ¥1.8 billion was estimated lost as the result of war damage.

Following the war, JNR had to rebuild its transport facilities and begin to reform its management structure, including its relations with the government. During the occupation period, JNR was under the control of the Railway Transportation Office of the 3rd Transportation Military Railway Service of the U.S. army, but was left to operate by itself. In 1949 JNR was reorganized as a public corporation, as were the Nippon Telegraph and Telephone Public Corporation and the Japan Tobacco Monopoly Corporation, though they were still owned and heavily supervised by the government. JNR was to be run as an independent profit-making unit outside the government budget, though considerable subsidization was needed, especially for investment in new lines. JNR's management was regulated and supervised by the Ministry of Transport. Increases in fares, freight rates, and employees' wages had to be approved by the Diet.

Freight and passenger volumes increased particularly rapidly during the period of strong economic growth which began in the 1960s. Freight volume in 1955 was 81.8 trillion tons/km, rising to 341.9 billion tons/km in 1970, an increase of 4.2 times. Over the same period, passenger traffic rose 3.5 times from 165.8 billion persons/km to 587.2 persons/km. Modernization of JNR can be measured by the rate of electrification of the lines and the growth in the percentage of double tracks among JNR lines. Only 9.8% of the lines were electrified in 1955, but by 1984 it had risen to 43.4%. Only 12.7% of JNR lines were double tracks in 1960, against 27.1% in 1984. The number of steam locomotives decreased from 3,974 in 1960 to 1,601 in 1970, in contrast to the dramatic increase in electric locomotives from 4,534 in 1960 to 12,582 in 1970. In provincial areas single track was laid, as it was cheaper and adequate for low levels of traffic. The conversion from steam to electricity and the introduction of diesel engines were the preferred ways of increasing capacity rather than the conversion of lines from single to double track.

The most significant event in the postwar development of JNR was the introduction of the Shinkansen (Bullet train) in 1964, for a distance of 515 kilometers between Tokyo and Osaka. The maximum speed attained was 200 kilometers per hour, which made it possible to shorten the time of the journey from six and a half hours by the earlier trains to four hours by Shinkansen. The Shinkansen reached peak performance in time for the increase in passenger demand for the Tokyo Olympic Games, which opened in 1964. The sum of $80 million, estimated to cover total construction costs for the Shinkansen, was borrowed from the World Bank. The total cost when it was completed in 1961 was nearly double the original estimate. The Shinkansen line was extended westward to Okayama in 1972 and then to Hakata, the largest city in Kyushu, in 1975. In 1982 the Shinkansen line was extended further, northward from Ueno, Tokyo to Morioka in Iwate prefecture, and to Niigata.

As a result of heavy investment in the Shinkansen and modernization of old lines, JNR's accounts were in the red from the latter part of the 1960s. The deficit was exacerbated by the comparative decline of freight transportation by rail as against other forms of land transport, and the costs of maintaining a work force of 400,000 employees. JNR's performance was particularly poor in provincial areas which were responsible for 94% of the total deficit in 1970, although they represented only 8% of JNR's total traffic. The railroads' share of freight and passenger transport was decreasing dramatically. In 1950 the railroads had a 51% share of all freight traffic compared with 9% for road transport and 39% for coastal shipping, but in 1980 the railroads' share was only 8%, compared with 41% for road transport and 51% for coastal shipping.

JNR's deficit grew rapidly in spite of huge subsidies from the government, and was a major political problem. JNR's total accumulated debt in 1987 was ¥37.5 trillion, the result of employees' pension financing, retirement payments, and the construction of new Shinkansen lines. The Diet, the government, and JNR made several attempts to resolve the problem. However, none of these plans were successful. Eventually, in 1982, the government's Second Special Committee for the Rationalization of Administration *(Daini Rincho)* proposed the privatization of JNR as a solution to its deficit. This occurred during the course of discussions on the simplification of public sector administration in general. Following the recommendation of the committee, a new committee, *Kokutetsu Kanri Jinkai,* was established to carry out the privitization of JNR.

At this time JNR was operating more than 20,000 kilometers of railroads nationwide, with about 200 railroad lines, 500 stations, and 600 kiosks. JNR's assets also included 45,500 railroad cars and ¥41.5 billion of capital investment in 155 related businesses with 58,500 hectares of land. The biggest problem was to reduce the number of personnel, which totaled 276,000.

In April 1987, ending its 115-year-old history as the state railroad firm, the Japanese National Railway was divided into six regional passenger companies—Hokkaido Railway Co., East Japan Railway Co., Tokai Japan Railway Co., West Japan Railway Co., Shikoku Railway Co., and Kyushu Railway Co.—and one freight company, Japan Railway Cargo, with four other companies, including JNR Accounts Settlement Corp., charged with custody of JNR's assets and the clearing of debt through real estate sales and public share offerings. The total work force was reduced by 61,000 to 215,000.

In April 1988, the company's first anniversary, the six regional passenger companies and one freight company reported total pretax profits of ¥151.6 billion, four times greater than the initial target. In 1989 the seven Japan Railway group companies posted total current profits of ¥211.8 billion, which represented a 39.8% jump from the previous year, over 70% greater than projected in their business plan. The following fiscal year, the seven companies announced a 26.7% increase in total profits from the previous year, and in the fourth year the total profits of the seven companies reached ¥387.6 billion, a 44.4% increase from 1989. Following these good results, the individual companies' shares will be publicly quoted in the near future, though they are now owned by the government.

Further Reading: Nippon Tetsudoshi, 3 vols., Tokyo, JNR, 1919–1921; Minami, R., *Railroads and Electric Utilities,* Tokyo, Toyo Keizai Shimposha, 1965; *Nippon Kokuyu Tetsudo Hyakunenshi,* 17 vols., Tokyo, JNR, 1969–1972; Harada, K., *Nippon no Kokutetsu,* Tokyo, Iwanamishoten, 1984; Noda, M. et al., *Nippon no Tetsudo,* Tokyo, Nippon Keizai Hyoronsha, 1986.

—Takeshi Yuzawa

FEDERAL EXPRESS CORPORATION

2005 Corporate Avenue
Memphis, Tennessee 38132
U.S.A.
(901) 369-3600
Fax: (901) 346-1013

Public Company
Incorporated: 1971
Employees: 81,711
Sales: $7.69 billion
Stock Exchanges: New York Toronto Boston Midwest Pacific

Federal Express Corporation specializes in overnight delivery of high-priority packages, documents, and heavy freight. The company created the overnight air-express industry virtually singlehandedly in the 1970s, although it now faces increasing competition. Federal's mastery of logistics enables it to act as a moving warehouse for many corporate customers and to track packages during the shipping process. It operates in 147 countries, and serves all of the United States.

Federal Express was founded in Memphis, Tennessee, by 28-year-old Frederick W. Smith in 1971. Smith originally outlined his idea for an overnight delivery service in a term paper he wrote for a Yale University economics class. Smith felt that air freight had different needs than air passenger service and that a company that specialized in air freight, rather than making it an add-on to passenger service, would find an unfilled niche. He thought speed was more important than cost and that it was essential for a company to reach smaller cities. His strategy was to ship all packages through a single hub, and to own his own aircraft. Aircraft ownership freed Federal from commercial-airline schedules and shipping regulations. The single hub allowed the tight control that got packages to their destinations overnight. He chose Memphis as his hub because of its central location and its modern airport that bad weather rarely closed.

Smith used a $4 million inheritance from his father, and raised $91 million in venture capital to get his idea off the ground. In 1973 Federal Express began service in 25 cities with a fleet of 14 Dassault Falcon—relatively small—aircraft and 389 employees. The planes collected packages from airports every night, and brought them to Memphis where they were immediately sorted. They were then flown to another airport and delivered to their destination by Federal Express trucks by the next morning.

Smith's idea was costly because it required creating an entire system before the company's first day of business. Federal Express began advertising and direct-mail campaigns in 1975, which were also expensive. The company lost $29 million in its first 26 months of operation. It had $43.5 million in sales in 1975 but lost $11.5 million. Smith's investors considered removing him from control of the company, but company president Arthur Bass backed Smith. Bass improved delivery schedules and Federal's volume climbed, making it profitable. By late 1976 Federal was carrying an average of 19,000 packages a night, and at the end of the year the company was $3.6 million in the black.

In 1977 company profits hit $8 million on sales of $110 million. The company had 31,000 regular customers, including IBM and the U.S. Air Force, which used it to ship spare parts. It also shipped blood, organs for transplant, drugs, and other items needing swift transport. Federal serviced 75 airports and 130 cities. The major airlines gave Federal stiff competition on heavily traveled passenger routes, but there was virtually no competition on routes between smaller cities. Its principal competitor, Emery Air Freight, used commercial airlines to ship its packages, giving Federal an important time advantage.

Deregulation of the airline industry in 1977 gave the still-struggling company an important boost. At the time of Federal's startup, the U.S. airline industry was tightly regulated by the government. Federal Express had only managed to get into business through an exemption that allowed any company to enter the common carrier business if its payloads were under 7,500 pounds. The regulations, written in 1938 to protect passenger airlines, were holding back Federal's growth. The company was forced to fly up to eight small Falcon jets side-by-side to bigger markets, when it could have used one larger jet and saved money. Smith led a legislative fight to end regulation, and a bill doing so was passed in 1977. Deregulation meant the company could fly anywhere in the United States anytime, and use larger aircraft like 727s, and later, DC-10s. Federal bought a fleet of used 727-100Cs. The Falcons were used to expand into small- and medium-sized markets.

In 1978 with its prospects looking solid, Federal went public, selling its first shares on the New York Stock Exchange. The move raised needed capital and gave the company's backers a chance to make some of their investment back. Profits for 1979 were $21.4 million on sales of $258.5 million. By late 1980 Federal was well established and growing at about 40% a year. It had 6,700 employees and flew 65,000 packages a night to 89 cities. Its fleet included thirty-two Falcons, fifteen 727s, and five 737s. Explosive growth continued as a tidal wave of businesses switched to overnight service. Miniaturization of consumer electronics and scientific instruments meant ever-more small, valuable packages needing express shipment. Many U.S. companies were shifting to just-in-time inventories to keep prices down, lessen quality-control problems, and save money. As a result, companies more often needed emergency shipment of goods and parts, and Federal began billing itself as a "500-mile-an-hour warehouse."

A decline in the reliability of the U.S. Postal Service caused many companies to switch to Federal Express for important packages. Courier-Paks were the fastest growing part of

Federal's business and accounted for about 40% of revenue. Courier-Paks, which are envelopes, boxes, or tubes used for important documents, photographs, blueprints, and other items cost $17 in 1980 for guaranteed overnight delivery. By mid-1980 the company had eight $24 million DC-10s on order or option from Continental Airlines, each capable of carrying 100,000 pounds of small packages. It had bought 23 more used 727s, and operated 2,000 delivery vans.

In mid-1981 Federal announced a new product that brought it into direct competition with the U.S. Postal Service for the first time: the overnight letter. The document-size cardboard envelope, containing up to two ounces, would be delivered overnight for $9.50 at that time.

By 1981 Federal Express had the largest sales of any U.S. air freight company, unseating competitors like Emery Air Freight, Airborne Freight, and Purolator Courier that had gone into business about 20 years before it. Federal's competitors had shipped any size of package using regularly scheduled airlines, and had not stressed speed. Federal's narrowly focused, speed-oriented service had won many of their customers. To compete Emery copied Federal's strategy, buying its own planes, opening a small-package sorting center, and pushing overnight delivery. Airborne Freight also pushed into the small-package air express business. United Parcel Service of America (UPS), the leading package-shipper by truck, moved into the air-express business in 1981. The U.S. Postal Service began heavily marketing its own overnight-mail service when Federal's Courier-Pak began eating into its revenues. The Postal Service's overnight mail was about half the price of Federal's but not as accessible in many locations. While Federal was the leader in the U.S. overnight package-delivery industry, DHL Worldwide Courier Express Network built a similar service overseas. DHL became a major competitor when Federal started building its own overseas network.

The increased competition put pressure on Federal's niche, but its lead was large and its reputation excellent. In 1983 the company reached $1 billion in annual revenues—the first company in the United States to do so within ten years of its start-up without mergers or acquisitions. In 1984 Federal made its first acquisition, Gelco Express, a Minneapolis, Minesota, package courier that served 84 countries. Federal, hoping to recreate its U.S. market dominance overseas, made further acquisitions in Britain, the Netherlands, and the United Arab Emirates. UPS also began building an overseas system.

By the late 1970s Smith realized that up to 15% of Courier-Pak business was information that eventually might be digitally transmitted as telephone and computer technology improved. He began developing an electronic-mail system, spending $100 million. In 1984 Federal launched ZapMail, a system for sending letters by fax machine and couriers. Federal promised ZapMail delivery within two hours. ZapMail had technology problems from its beginning. Fax machines broke down frequently, light-toned originals would not transmit, and minor telephone-line disturbances interrupted transmissions. High-volume customers discovered it was less expensive to install their own fax machines. ZapMail cost $35 for documents up to five pages, plus $1.00 for each additional page. It also faced competition from the electronic-mail system of MCI Communications. ZapMail was still losing money in 1986 when Federal abandoned the system, taking a $340 million charge

against earnings. The 1,300 employees working on the Zap-Mail system were absorbed into the rest of the company.

In 1985 Federal took a major step in its attempt to expand its services to Europe, opening a European hub at the Brussels airport. Revenue reached $2 billion in 1985. In 1986 Federal opened sorting centers in Oakland, California, and in Newark, New Jersey, to more quickly handle shipments with nearby destinations. Federal's hubs were becoming warehouses for its clients, storing parts until customers needed them, then shipping the parts overnight. IBM used Federal to store mainframe parts and get them quickly to malfunctioning computer systems. This trend coincided with a drop-off of Federal's overnight mail volume, which was hurt by the spread of fax machines and the lower rates charged by competitors. Revenue for 1987 was $3.2 billion, while rival UPS collected about $1.7 billion from overnight delivery.

By 1988 Federal provided service to about 90 countries, claimed to ship about 50% of U.S. overnight packages, and had 54,000 employees. Increasing competition, however, led to a price war that lowered company profits from 16.9% of revenue in 1981 to 11% in 1987. Profits in 1988 were $188 million on revenue of $3.9 billion.

Expanding overseas proved tougher than Federal had anticipated, and the company's international business lost $74 million between 1985 and 1989. In February 1989, hoping to build a global delivery system instantly, Federal bought Tiger International, Inc., particularly for its heavy-cargo airline, Flying Tiger Line, for $883 million. Before the acquisition, Federal had landing rights in five airports outside the United States: Montreal, Toronto, Brussels, London, and limited rights in Tokyo. Federal wanted the delivery routes Tiger had built over its 40-year history. They included landing rights in Paris and Frankfurt, three Japanese airports, and cities through east Asia and South America. Federal could use its own planes on these routes, not subcontract to other carriers, which the company had been doing in many countries. Tiger's large fleet of long-range aircraft also gave Federal an important foothold in the heavy-freight business. In 1988 Tiger had twenty-two 747s, eleven 727s, and six DC-8s; 6,500 employees, and revenue of $1.4 billion. Many of Tiger's planes needed quick repairs to meet U.S. government safety deadlines, however, leading to lower profits.

The purchase also increased Federal's debt by nearly 250% to $2.1 billion, and put the company into a market that was more capital-intensive and cyclical than the small-package market. Owning Tiger put Federal into an awkward position—many of Tiger's best customers were Federal's competitors, and Federal feared it might lose many of them. The fears proved unfounded, although Tiger's on-time record temporarily fell to 80% after the takeover, climbing to 96% by early 1990.

At the same time price wars continued with competitors, some of which made inroads into the overnight market. Earnings from UPS's overnight service rose 63% between 1984 and 1988, and its revenues tripled. Federal had a 55% share of the U.S. overnight letter market and shipped 33% of U.S. overnight packages. It was clearly the leader in the express-delivery business, but its growth was slowing. Federal's U.S. shipment volume grew 58% in 1984; 25% in 1988. The company compensated by pushing its higher-margin package service, which grew 53% from 1987 to 1989. Analysts estimated that packages provided 80% of Federal's revenues and about 90% of its profits.

In April 1990 Federal raised its domestic prices, ending the seven-year price war. The U.S. air-freight industry was consolidating, and rival UPS had heavy capital expenses from its own overnight air service, giving Federal room to raise its prices. The company needed the extra profits, estimated at between $50 million and $75 million a year, to help pay for losses in its international business. Federal's foreign operations lost $194 million in 1989 as it struggled to integrate Tiger and build a delivery system in Europe. Tiger was unionized but unstructured; Federal was non-union but bureaucratic. Several uneasy months passed while the two systems were unified and a pilot-seniority list was drawn up. Many industry analysts said that Federal had paid too much for Tiger. To help increase overseas tonnage, Federal began a one-, two-, and three-day service to large shippers between 25 cities worldwide and 85 cities in the United States.

Federal entered the 1990s with increasing competition in the U.S. market, but was maintaining its leading market share. UPS slowly was winning some of its customers by introducing volume discounts, which it had resisted for years. Federal's foreign operations were troubled, and their losses dragged down Federal's earnings. Federal's sales rose from $5.2 billion in 1989 to $7.69 billion in fiscal 1991, but its operating income fell from $424 million in 1989 to $279 million in 1991. Industry analysts were divided over whether or how soon Federal would be able to make its foreign operations profitable. Smith argued that when Federal's international volume increased, international service would become profitable. Some analysts, however, questioned how long Federal could accept international losses with $2.15 billion in long-term debt.

Principal Subsidiaries: Federal Express Aviation Services; Federal Express International; Flying Tiger Line Inc.; Tiger Inter Modal Inc.; Tiger Trucking Subsidiary Inc.; Warren Transport Inc.

Further Reading: Flaherty, Robert J., "Breathing Under Water," *Forbes,* March 1, 1977; "Transportation," *Business Week,* March 31, 1980; "Federal Express Background," Federal Express corporate typescript, [1988]; Foust, Dean, et al, "Mr. Smith Goes Global: He's Putting Federal Express' Future on The Line To Expand Overseas," *Business Week,* February 13, 1989.

—Scott M. Lewis

HANKYU CORPORATION

8-8, Kakuta-cho
Kita-ku
Osaka 530
Japan
(06) 373 5088
Fax: (06) 373 5669

Public Company
Incorporated: 1907 as Minōō Arima Electric Railway
    Company
Employees: 5,443
Sales: ¥311.53 billion (US$2.49 billion)
Stock Exchanges: Tokyo Osaka

Hankyu Corporation is Kansai's third-largest railway company. The Kansai region of Japan is the country's second largest metropolitan area and contains the industrial cities of Osaka and Kobe and the historic towns of Kyoto and Nara. The railway business forms the core of Hankyu Corporation, which consists of more than 155 companies in many areas of business including retail, entertainment, and tourism. Hankyu is primarily engaged in transportation, which contributes about 60% of sales, and operates six rail and seven bus and taxi companies covering the major cities in the Kansai region. Hankyu's nontransport businesses consist of urban development and the operation of leisure resorts and hotels.

Hankyu Corporation was founded in 1907 by Ichizo Kobayashi as Minōō Arima Electric Railway Company. Kobayashi obtained government permission to operate electric railways between Takarazuka and Osaka. In 1909 a railway bridge was completed, spanning the Yodo River in Osaka and thus allowing a 25-kilometer stretch of railway to be built in the following year between Umeda in central Osaka and Takarazuka. A smaller four-kilometer line was also built, branching off the main line to reach Minōō. Railway companies were major users of electric power at the time in Japan, and they tended to generate their own power. Minōō Arima Electric Railway Company began the generation of its own power via a thermal station built in 1910. Both lines began operation following a ceremony at the train depot at Ikeda station in March 1910. In 1911 the lines began to provide freight as well as passenger transport, and in 1912 the nearby Arima Electric Railway was acquired. Kobayashi's hometown of Takarazuka was then the company's base. Kobayashi opened a hot spring resort in Takarazuka in 1912, hoping the attraction would encourage Osaka city dwellers to use his railway line. The hot spring continued to flourish and was the predecessor of Takarazuka Familyland, Japan's first amusement park. In addition to being an astute businessman, Ichizo Kobayashi was a lover of the arts. In 1913 he formed the Takarazuka Revue Company, an all-female theater group that gained an international reputation. Although its contribution to the railway company's profits was minimal, it provided invaluable publicity.

In 1917 Kobayashi changed the name of his company to Hanshin Kyuko Railway Company, which came to be known simply as Hankyu from the 1920s. The next five years were a period of great expansion for the company with the establishment of the main Kobe line in 1920. This line joined the cities of Osaka and Kobe and spanned 30 kilometers. North Osaka Electric Railway was also formed, operating two lines within the city. Hankyu was not only the leading private railway company in Kansai but was one of the largest in Japan as well. In 1921, in response to increased demand for electric power, Hankyu merged with Inagawa Hydroelectric Power. In the following year, the company formed the New Keihan Electric Railway, which absorbed the lines run by North Osaka Railway, and in the following five years opened four new railway lines within the city of Osaka. In 1924, in response to the success of the Takarazuka Revue Company, a new theater was built for the group. A hotel was added in 1926, adding to the town's attraction as a tourist resort.

Although Hankyu Department Store Company is now an independent entity and one of the major chains in the country, it has its roots within Hankyu Corporation. Kobayashi formed Hankyu's first proper store in 1928 by renovating and expanding the existing Hankyu store located in the vicinity of Hankyu's main Umeda station in Osaka. The Hankyu group entered the real estate business at this time with the completion of the New Hankyu Umeda buildings in the central Osaka district of Umeda. Hankyu had in the past entered areas of business that were not necessarily very profitable but were of interest to the company's leaders. The theater venture was one example. In 1936 Hankyu formed a professional baseball team to compete with the ten or so existing teams in the country. Imported from the United States, the sport had grown to become Japan's number-one spectator sport. Most of the teams were named after the companies that sponsored them, the most famous and successful at the time being the Tokyo Yomiuri Giants.

In 1943 the company merged its railway operations with those of the next largest private railway operator in Kansai, Keihan Electric Railway. The resulting company was called Keihan Shinkyu Electric Railway. This trend toward mergers was spreading throughout Japanese industry, and the closest Tokyo equivalent of the Keihan Shinkyu Electric Railway at the time was the Tokyu group, which was swallowing up large portions of Tokyo's electric railways. These mergers were reversed upon Japan's defeat in World War II when occupation forces began to split up the huge Japanese industrial combines. Hankyu was no exception. Its department store division was made into a separate company in 1947 and in 1949 the railway operations of the group were split up, with Keihan Electric Railway becoming an independent company again. This still left Hankyu with a fairly extensive rail network, however, and the company's management decided to concentrate immediate investment on upgrading and repairing routes damaged in the war. Construction work was completed on Hankyu's main station in Osaka, Umeda, to allow the New Keihan Line's trains to utilize the station. In 1948 Hankyu opened an office at Osaka Airport and acted as agent for Pan American Airlines. In the 1950s Hankyu's rail business began to grow fairly quickly in terms of the number of passengers served. Freight service was stopped as the more lucrative passenger service increased.

In 1957, on the 50th anniversary of Hankyu's founding, Ichizo Kobayashi died. He had become renowned throughout the country not only as a leading figure in the development of the railway in Japan, but also a patron of the arts. In 1959 his son, Yonezo Kobayashi, became president of Hankyu. Under Yonezo Kobayashi, the company embarked on an expansionary program concentrating on the development of the areas around the company's major railway stations. The Umeda underground complex was completed in 1958 with similar work completed in the Omiya area of Kyoto in 1963. A new station was completed in Takarazuka in 1961 and a new hotel constructed nearby. New rolling stock was introduced on all lines—the so-called 2000 and 3000 series cars—and the Senriyama line was extended by two kilometers northwards with a further five kilometers to be added four years later. To cope with an increasingly complex railway network, an IBM 1440 computer was introduced in the operations department at the company's headquarters in Umeda station. In 1967 Hankyu became the first railway company in Japan to install automatic ticket vending machines at its stations, and the company is probably the leader in Japan in introducing safety- and efficiency-enhancing technology into its railway operations. Most of Hankyu's track within the center of Osaka was elevated to avoid traffic congestion, and in 1967 an automatic-train-stopping system was introduced on the Kyoto line. Hankyu's various real estate companies were busy developing and constructing the choice central Osaka real estate that the group owned, and a series of new buildings were completed in the Umeda station vicinity. In 1967 following a severe typhoon, many Hankyu lines sustained damage as the embankments upon which the lines were raised collapsed. Although the damage was not serious, valuable lessons were learned about railway line construction; elevated embankments were subsequently strengthened to withstand severe weather.

In 1967 the baseball team, known as the Hankyu Braves, won its first league title. As founder of the team, the late Ichizo Kobayashi was voted into Japan's version of the Baseball Hall of Fame in 1969. Hankyu's founder was further honored when the Itsuo Art Museum was constructed on the site of his birthplace in Takarazuka. It has grown to become the city's premier museum with more than 5,000 works from all over the world. Japan's first amusement park was being developed in the city and was known as Familyland. This, along with city's hot springs and cultural activities, made it a popular place to visit for the residents of nearby Kobe and Osaka. The year 1969 also marked the death of Yonezo Kobayashi and the appointment of Kaoru Mori as chairman of Hankyu Corporation. The introduction of the total-traffic-control system in 1969 allowed Hankyu's headquarters to maintain absolute control over the network's trains, and resulted in one of the best safety records of any railway company in the world. There has not been an accident on a Hankyu railway since 1979. By 1969 Hankyu operated 141 kilometers of track, only slightly less than today's total of 147 kilometers. Expansion of Hankyu from the 1970s onward was thus largely in the nonrail areas of

urban development and leasing and sales of real estate. Other transport-related ventures were started, however, such as Japan Car Rental in 1970 and the expansion of the existing bus routes. In 1973 the company officially changed its name to Hankyu Corporation. The group took advantage of the continuing golf boom in Japan by opening Kanzaki River Golf Club and a number of smaller practice ranges. The company's expertise in sophisticated computer control systems was marketed by the formation of Hankyu Computer Services in 1974. The Hankyu Braves continued their success as a professional baseball team by taking the Japan Series from Tokyo archrivals Yomiuri Giants in 1975. Two more consecutive titles followed, and to some people the name Hankyu became synonymous with baseball rather than railways.

Takarazuka Familyland was undergoing continual improvement and was becoming one of the most popular attractions in the Kansai region. New theme sub-parks such as Machine Land were added. One of Ichizo Kobayashi's goals for Hankyu had been that the company should invest and help in the development of the local community. Hankyu Swimming School was opened in 1977, operating several pools in the Kansai region. The Ikeda Library, founded by Kobayashi, contained one of Japan's largest collections of works on the theater and entertainment. The 1970s saw the expansion of Hankyu's hotel business with new hotels in Kobe and Kyoto and several more planned. To finance these capital investment projects, Hankyu looked to the foreign as well as domestic bond market and raised Sfr50 million in 1985. Although Hankyu was not actively increasing its total rail network mileage to any great extent, money was invested in passenger comfort and safety as competition in the marketplace heightened with the dismantling of the enormous government-owned railway combine in 1987. Air conditioning was installed on underground platforms as well as on all railway cars. Ticket and rail pass payment was facilitated by the introduction of Hankyu credit cards acceptable by the vending machines at Umeda station in 1986. For the benefit of handicapped commuters, braille ticket vending machines were installed and special restrooms added to all the major stations.

In 1990 following a reorganization, the company decided to focus on three main business areas—transport, urban development, and leisure. It divided its 155 companies into these three separate management groups, whereas formerly they had been loosely controlled by the railway sector. The six railway companies operated by the group contribute almost 60% of revenue and half of the operating profits. The group's sports and leisure facilities are growing, but their contribution to Hankyu's overall profit is negligible. Property rental and sales accounted for a third of the group's profits, with the remainder coming from so-called *zaitech* or speculation on Japan's stock and real estate markets. Urban development projects in the pipeline include the Chiyamachi area near Umeda station, the construction of a new Hankyu headquarters building in the same area, and a plan to develop an international culture park in Ibaraki City north of Osaka. In the core business of railway operation the emphasis is—as in the past—on progress through technological advances. Hankyu operates the most efficient network in the Kansai region, earning more revenue per kilometer of track than its major competitors Keihan and Hinshin Electric Railways. The major construction work being undertaken is on the elevation of track, to be completed on all above-ground lines.

Kohei Kobayashi became president of Hankyu in 1982, representing the third generation of Kobayashis at the head of the firm. He is looking at areas of international involvement, and pinpointing Hankyu's areas of weakness.

Principal Subsidiaries: Nose Electric Railway Co., Ltd; Kobe Electric Railway Co., Ltd; Kita-Osaka Railway Co., Ltd; Hokushin Kyuko Electric Railway Co., Ltd; Kobe Rapid Transport Railway Co., Ltd; Hankyu Bus Co., Ltd; Hankyu Realty Co., Ltd. (50%); Hankyu Sangyo Co., Ltd; Arima Kogyo Co., Ltd; HOTEL new HANKYU Co., Ltd; Hankyu Taxi Co., Ltd.

—Dylan Tanner

KAWASAKI KISEN KAISHA, LTD.

Hibiya Central Building
2-9 Nishi-Shinbashi
1-chome, Minato-ku
Tokyo 105
Japan
(3) 595-5000
Fax: (3) 595-6111

Public Company
Incorporated: 1919
Employees: 1,190
Sales: ¥363.94 billion (US$2.92 billion)
Stock Exchanges: Tokyo Osaka Nagoya Kyoto Niigata Frankfurt Brussels Antwerp

Kawasaki Kisen Kaisha, Ltd. ("K" Line) is the third largest shipping company in Japan, operating a fleet of 218 vessels totaling 10.37 million deadweight tons, including 35 Japanese flag vessels of 2.33 million deadweight tons owned by the company itself. More than 95% of sales come from shipping activities. These activities include bulk-carrier, car-carrier, and tanker services in addition to the liner services offered by ships covering the Japan-North and South America, the Japan-Europe, and the Japan-Australia routes.

"K" Line was established on April 10, 1919, in Kobe, a major shipping center in Japan. After World War I, the world maritime industries were hit by a severe depression, which was felt strongly by the Japanese shipping and shipbuilding industries. This situation was in contrast to their enormous expansion during World War I, when they had taken advantage of their favorable geographical position far away from the main battlefield in Europe, although Japan was a member of the Allied Forces.

Kawasaki Zosenjo (Kawasaki Shipbuilding Co., established in 1886), the second largest and oldest shipbuilder in Japan after Mitsubishi Zosen, was left after World War I with a large fleet of unsold ships. This fleet continued to increase for some time after the war because Kawasaki Zosenjo was forced to go on building ships due to the continued supply of steel plates from America under the Ship-Steel Exchange Agreement (Sen-Tetsu Kokan Keiyaku). The agreement had been concluded in 1918 between the U.S. government and individual Japanese shipbuilders, as well as several shipowners.

In order to deal with these unwanted stock boats, Kawasaki Zosenjo invested 11 ships of a total 100 thousand deadweight tons in setting up Kawasaki Kisen ("K" Line) in Kobe in 1919. The remainder of the unsold stock boats—16 ships totaling 139 thousand deadweight tons—was kept under the management of the Sempaku-bu, created in 1918 as a ship operation division within Kawasaki Zosenjo. The actual operation of these ships was, however, entrusted to "K" Line on a commission basis. Thus "K" Line entered the shipping business with a total of 27 ships of 239 thousand deadweight tons. The ships were initially chartered out to NYK (Nippon Yusen Kaisha), the biggest liner company in Japan, Suzuki Shoten, and other shipping companies. Among these, the most closely connected customer was Suzuki Shoten, a trading corporation that had achieved rapid growth during the war and was almost as large as Mitsui Bussan, the largest trading corporation at the time. In the latter half of 1920, however, "K" Line started to carry cargoes on its own account, due to the depressed chartering market.

In the meantime, an independent shipping company named Kokusai Kisen was established in Kobe in 1919, with an investment-in-kind of ships amounting to some 500 thousand deadweight tons, mainly from the shipbuilders and their subsidiary shipping companies. Although the process of establishment was complicated, the aim was to form, with some financial assistance from the government, a shipping company to operate unsold stock boats on a larger scale. Here again the majority of the investment, ships of 275 thousand deadweight tons, came from the Kawasaki group—Kawasaki Zosenjo and "K" Line. This meant that Kokusai Kisen became part of the Kawasaki group, although Suzuki Shoten and others also contributed some tonnage. Kokusai Kisen's ships sailed under A1 flags which demonstrated that they were of superior quality, qualified as A1 class by Lloyd's Register, and were deployed mainly on cross trades in order to reduce competition among Japanese shipping firms on the routes to and from Japan. Kokusai Kisen's business, however, was not particularly successful.

In August 1920, several months after the formation of Kokusai Kisen, Kojiro Matsukata was nominated as president of Kokusai Kisen and as a result assumed three presidential positions, including those of Kawasaki Zosenjo and "K" Line, which he already possessed. He planned to incorporate the tonnage owned by the three companies into a single operation to achieve efficiency, and in 1921 organized a joint service named K Line, with its head office in Kobe.

K Line must be distinguished from "K" Line. It took the initial letter K, common to the names of the three participants. Nominating Suzuki Shoten as its sole agent, K Line started tramp shipping—taking cargo as the opportunity arose—largely on the cross trades in the Atlantic region. It entered the liner trade as the tramp market became depressed, and gradually expanded the business to include Japan Australia Line (JAL), a joint liner service with Yamashita Kisen between Japan and Australia. In 1923 a pooling agreement on revenue, cargo, and chartering was concluded among the participants to rationalize operations to meet the depressed market. Thus K Line came to operate 103 ships of 7.91 million deadweight tons in 1926, its peak year. With the establishment of K Line, "K" Line transferred most of the trade in the distant sea region to K Line, and mainly concentrated on trade in the near sea region.

The Great Kanto Earthquake of 1923 resulted in an enormous demand for tonnage to carry relief and reconstruction goods. Taking advantage of this opportunity, "K" Line entered into near-sea liner services and opened new services successively: Japan-Korea and Japan-Taiwan in 1924, Japan-Vladivostok in 1925, and Japan-Shanghai and Japan-Sakhalin in 1926. These services developed further after around 1931 when Japan invaded China.

In 1927 the Japanese economy was hit by the so-called *Kinyu Kyoko*—financial crisis—and entered a severe depression, which was to be aggravated by the impending worldwide Depression that started in 1929. Under the direct impact of the crisis, Suzuki Shoten went bankrupt in 1927 and was no longer able to act as sole agent for K Line. Kawasaki Zosenjo was also a victim of the crisis and went into liquidation in the same year. As a result, Kojiro Matsukata was forced to resign as president and relinquished his position as president of "K" Line. Kokusai Kisen could not remain untouched by the crisis and soon experienced difficulties of its own.

These events had completely changed the situation for "K" Line. With the liquidation of Kawasaki Zosenjo and the resignation of President Matsukata, Kokusai Kisen broke away from the Kawasaki group and entered the control of the banks which had lent it money. The movement led to the withdrawal of Kokusai Kisen from K Line. This meant that K Line virtually disappeared and "K" Line had to carry on its shipping business in distant seas independently, operating in 1928 a fleet of 41 ships totaling 265 thousand tons, probably including the tonnage of Kawasaki Zosenjo, which "K" Line had undertaken to operate. At this time "K" Line was a fully-owned subsidiary of Kawasaki Zosenjo, and does not seem to have achieved complete independence until 1934 when "K" Line bought 11 ships from Kawasaki Zosenjo.

During the period from "K" Line's fresh start to the end of World War II, world shipping as well as Japanese shipping experienced frequent changes: a severe depression until around 1935, then a brief period of prosperity due to increasing international political tension which led to increased shipping of war supplies, and finally chaos with the outbreak of World War II. "K" Line was, as a matter of course, exposed to these changes.

For some time after its fresh start, "K" Line concentrated, in the liner sector, on the Japan-North American Pacific Coast route in addition to the JAL, giving up the other businesses shared with Kokusai Kisen due to the shortage of tonnage. The main cargo on this trade was silk. In 1932 the company opened the Japan-New York service, following the change in silk transport from the Pacific Coast route to the direct service to New York.

From the middle of the 1930s new services were opened, assisted by favorable trade conditions and various government schemes to promote new shipbuilding, such as the Yushu-sempaku Kenzo Josei Shisetsu (the Superior Ship Building Promotion Scheme) in 1937, and the Interest Subsidy to Shipbuilding Finance in 1940. This marked the "K" Line's entry to genuine liner trade on the distant sea routes. Prior to this change, "K" Line provided a semi-liner service (*han-teiki*), whereby it carried tramp cargoes at least on return voyages. Thus "K" Line opened the Japan-African East Coast service in 1934, reopened the Japan-Bombay service in 1935—it had been closed owing to the overall shortage of ships in 1928—the Japan-Middle and South American West Coast service in 1936, and the Round the World westbound service in 1937. "K" Line also strengthened services on the existing routes such as the New York route, the North American Pacific Coast

route, and the JAL. However, it was forced to terminate these new and strengthened services with the approaching Pacific War in 1941.

"K" Line was active in the liner business, but its main business line had originally been tramp shipping, following the K Line tradition, and continued to be so until 1941. Moreover, even when liner services began, the ships took tramp cargoes as return cargoes. Tramp activities were carried out with changes to routes and cargoes according to circumstances. This procedure differed from the K Line period when the main field was in cross trades. In 1935 Malaysian iron ore was added to the main cargoes. Most important for "K" Line in the nonliner sector was the entry into tanker trade in 1933, with two chartered British tankers. This was a very early attempt among the common carriers in Japan to venture into tanker trade, and was motivated by the increased oil consumption and the change in fuel transportation policy of the Japanese Navy in 1929, which up to that time had used its own tankers but thereafter relied on commercial tankers. "K" Line acquired a newly built tanker in 1935. Thereafter, "K" Line's tanker fleet grew to include 14 tankers in operation, totaling 193 thousand deadweight tons in 1937, the peak year in terms of fleet size.

To achieve the increase in the tonnage required due to expansion, "K" Line started to charter foreign ships in addition to domestic ships. Chartered tonnage continued to increase year after year up to 1938, when it amounted to 444 thousand deadweight tons and accounted for 65% of the total operating tonnage. In that year chartered foreign tonnage accounted for 60% of total chartered tonnage.

Emphasis on tramp shipping, gradual expansion in liner trade, which accelerated after 1932, and reliance on chartered tonnage, which led to comparatively good business performance even in the depressed market, were the characteristics common to the so-called *Shagaisen* to which "K" Line belonged. The *Shagaisen,* which were originally tramp ship operators, together with the *Shasen,* the two large long-established liner companies, formed the Japanese shipping industry between the wars.

In December 1941 the Pacific War began. As early as May 1942, all merchant ships above 100 gross tonnage and seamen were requisitioned by the state, and were put under the unified control of a body called the *Sempaku Uneikai.* The war ended in August 1945, with heavy damage to the merchant fleet. "K" Line also suffered severely. At the start of the war it owned 36 ships with a total of 260 thousand deadweight tons, but only 12 ships totaling 31 thousand deadweight tons survived, notwithstanding additions during the war. Indeed, "K" Line's war loss amounted to 60 ships of 271 thousand deadweight tons, for which no compensation was made under the policy of the Allied Powers.

Commercial ocean-going shipping was not permitted by the Allied Powers until 1950 and free activity was permitted only after 1952, when the Peace treaty came into effect. From then onward, the Japanese shipping industry grew rapidly along with the Japanese economy as a whole, partly as a result of the 1947 state shipbuilding policy, the *Keikaku Zosen* (Programmed Shipbuilding Scheme). "K" Line resumed oceangoing shipping business based on expertise accumulated in the interwar period and began technological improvement of its ships. The first oceangoing ship was contracted in 1950 to transport rice from Thailand. In the following year the first liner service was launched on the Japan-Bangkok route. "K" Line continued to open new liner services, following its pre-war policy of placing more emphasis upon liner trade. By 1957, all of "K" Line's major liner services had been opened. By this time "K" Line succeeded in setting up a liner service network that extended over North and South America, Africa, Australia, and Asia, leaving the Japan-Europe and the Japan-India, Pakistan routes, among major ones, untouched. The Japan-India, Pakistan route was to be opened in 1964 when "K" Line merged the liner department of Iino Kaiun together with its sailing rights on this service. In the period between 1957 and 1964, existing services were developed while several new but minor services were added.

In the non-liner sector development also took place, extending the service area and carrying a greater variety of cargoes. Most important among these was the re-entry into the tanker trade in 1953 with a chartered foreign tanker, followed in 1957 by a tanker built for "K" Line. Another important development was the introduction of ore carrier trade in 1960. The tanker and ore-carrier trades were to expand year after year as the size of the respective ships increased.

In the period between 1957 and 1964 the Japanese shipping industry underwent remarkable expansion in terms of fleet size, but its performance deteriorated steadily. This decline was partly due to the worldwide shipping depression, but was largely due to the negative effect of the Programmed Ship-building Scheme, which caused excessive competition among Japanese firms, particularly in the liner sector. Finally in 1964 a major reorganization took place—involving about 90% of Japan's deep sea fleet and with strong guidance from the government—in order to reduce excessive competition within the industry. This resulted in the formation of six groups. "K" Line formed one of these groups as a core company with 15 subsidiaries. This necessitated "K" Line's merger with the liner department of Iino Line.

A few years after the reorganization, "K" Line, along with the Japanese deep sea shipping industry as a whole, made a rapid recovery from the depression and thereafter enjoyed nearly ten years of prosperity for the first time in its history. During this period "K" Line expanded its tonnage from 735 thousand gross tonnage in September 1964 to 2.5 million gross tonnage in March 1973, while greatly diversifying its business into the operation of specialized ships to meet the enormous increase in Japan's foreign trade. As a result, "K" Line's fleet composition by ship type underwent a fundamental change between 1964 and 1973, with cargo ships declining from 44.4% to 16% of the fleet, specialized ships increasing from 12.7% to 34.6%, and tankers from 42.5% to 49.6%.

The specialized ships introduced in this period included coal carriers, reefers, timber carriers, and LPG tankers. Most important among them was the introduction of a car-bulker in 1968 to carry Toyota cars to the United States. In 1970 a PCC (Pure Car Carrier—a ship which carried only cars) was built, the first ship of this type in Japan. Since then, particularly after the oil crisis in 1973, the car carrier trade experienced remarkable growth, and "K" Line ranked among the four big-gest car carriers in the world.

In the liner sector, "K" Line ventured into container ser-vices, starting with the Japan-North American California route in 1967 and forming a consortium on a space charter basis with three other Japanese firms. Thereafter "K" Line ex-tended its container services and by 1979 had established a container network which included the main routes. In 1975 "K" Line opened a container service on the Far East–Europe route by organizing a container consortium, the ACE group, with several Scandinavian shipowners. Prior to this, "K" Line had been admitted to the Far Eastern Conference in 1968 through its participation in Kawasaki Maersk Line (KML), a joint ser-vice with the Danish shipowners Maersk Line. In 1973, when "K" Line was contemplating opening a container service on this route, the company succeeded in gaining membership inde-pendently and therefore dissolved KML. On the Japan-Australia route "K" Line organized a container consortium, the Eastern Seaboard Service (ESS), with the Australian National Line (ANL) and started a container service in 1969 with roll-on/roll-off (RORO) container ships. As a result the Japan Austra-lian Line (JAL), a long-established joint service with Yamashita Kisen, was dissolved. Another development in the liner sector was carriage of industrial equipment using ships with derricks of increasing capacity. The trade increased sharply after the oil crisis, but declined in importance toward the mid-1980s.

The Oil Crisis of 1973 brought dramatic changes. The world shipping industry entered a depression which affected Japa-nese shipping particularly severely due to the sharp rise in the value of the yen. The depression, with only a brief intermis-sion, lasted until 1988. Under these circumstances "K" Line switched from an expansion policy to reduction in tonnage. Its main goal was to sell a large tonnage of its redundant large-size tankers and the smaller ships that had become uneconomi-cal due to the high yen value and high labor costs. At the same time, "K" Line tried to rationalize its operations. This in-cluded an increasing use of flag of convenience (FOC) ships, often in the form of *Shikumisen* or "tie-in" ships, and reduc-tion in the manning of Japanese flag ships.

"K" Line also tried to enter or develop a number of busi-nesses that looked promising. In 1981 "K" Line launched its LNG tanker operation, building a new ship jointly with several other Japanese firms. The business has continued to grow. Car-carrier business was another of the few sectors that flour-ished after the oil crisis.

In the liner sector, while extending or consolidating its net-work with container or conventional ships, "K" Line has been attaching more importance to the Far East–North America route on which the company was a pioneer among Japanese firms. To develop the intermodal service on this route and to gain advantage over competitors, in 1986 "K" Line began operation of its Double Stack Train (DST), originated by "K" Line for its own use, in the United States. This was followed by a door-to-door delivery service for small cargoes on this route in 1988. In 1990 "K" Line ventured into cruise business via a subsidiary, Seven Seas Cruise Line.

Principal Subsidiaries: Daito Unyu Co. Ltd. (98%); Kawasaki Kinkai Kisen Kaisha (88.8%); "K" Line Air Service, Ltd. (90%); Kobe Kisen Kaisha, Ltd. (50%); Nitto Unyu Co., Ltd. (90%).

Further Reading: Kawasaki Kisen, *50-nen Shi,* Tokyo, 1969; Nakagawa, Keiichiro, *Ryo-Taisen kan no Nippon Kaiun Gyo,*

Tokyo, Nippon Keizai Shinbun Sha, 1980; Chida, T. and P. N. Davies, *The Japanese Shipping and Shipbuilding Industries,* London, The Athlone Press, 1990.

—Tomohei Chida

KEIO TEITO ELECTRIC RAILWAY COMPANY

1-9-1 Sekido, Tama City
Tokyo 206
Japan
(0423) 37 3112
Fax: (0423) 74 9810

Public Company
Incorporated: 1948 as Keio Teito Electric Railway
Employees: 15,400
Sales: ¥504.00 billion (US$3.49 billion)
Stock Exchange: Tokyo

Keio Teito Electric Railway Company (KTR) is one of the eight private railway operators in the Kanto region of Japan, which encompasses the cities of Tokyo, Kawasaki, and Chiba, with a population of almost 40 million. KTR operates the Inokashira and Keio Lines from the center to the densely populated western suburbs of Tokyo. The company also operates 650 buses on routes around Tokyo. Like the other big private railway groups, KTR has taken advantage of Japan's postwar economic boom and has diversified into such areas as real estate development and the hotel business.

Keio Teito Electric Railway was formed in 1948 when the huge Tokyu Railway group was split up on the orders of the General Headquarters of the Allied Powers. The history of the actual railway lines concerned can, however, be traced back to two companies—Keio Electric Railway and Teito Electric Railway. Keio was founded first in 1906 under a different name, Musashi Electric Railway. The government at the time was encouraging the formation and construction of railway companies, and had designated and developed certain areas of the city as future railway stations. It then invited interested companies to apply for permission to build and operate electric railways in the city. Musashi Electric Railway applied to operate in several areas around Tokyo but received permission to run an 18-kilometer stretch between the western Tokyo districts of Chofu and Tama and central Tokyo. Due to confusion with a similarly named railway company, Musashi Electric Railway changed its name to Keio Electric Railway. Like the other railway operators at the time, Keio produced its own electricity to power the trains. Thus, before commencement of the tracks began in earnest, a 55-kilowatt thermal generating station was completed in 1910. Construction was then begun on a 12-kilometer stretch of track between Chofu and central

Tokyo. In addition, an electric power company was formed to sell any excess capacity, and became a major supplier to the area. In 1913 a passenger service began on the line and following successive extensions to it during the following five years the line extended 15 kilometers between Chofu and Shinjuku. Branches were also added at the Chofu end to reach the rapidly growing residential population in the area. By 1923 the company operated 22 kilometers of track, with a further 16 kilometers planned. The Great Kanto Earthquake of 1923 put a temporary halt to these plans and the company's equipment sustained major damage. At the request of the government, Keio Electric Railway donated its power generating facilities, by now 150 kilowatts, to the relief and rebuilding effort.

The company, and Tokyo in general, recovered relatively quickly from the disaster. In 1924 all Keio's lines were reopened, with the delayed Gyakunan Railway line opening between Fuchu and Hachioji in western Tokyo. The next ten years brought rapid expansion for the company. Headquarters were moved to central Tokyo and in 1932 a new company, Takao Railway Company, was formed. This year also saw diversification with the operation of the "Blue Bus" service. Under the company's policy of aggressive expansion through takeovers, three bus companies, Fujisawa, Nakano, and Musashi, became part of the group and helped make Keio a major transportation force in the region. In 1942 the company joined forces with the Tokyu Railway Company, which had previously swallowed up the Odakyu, Keihin, and Teito companies to create a giant private railway conglomerate.

Teito Electric Railway, as part of the Tokyu group, was operating a railway line in close proximity to Keio Electric Railway and the combination of the two was an obvious choice in the dismantling of Tokyu after World War II. Teito was founded in 1927 when a railway entrepreneur, Ippei Ohta, obtained government permission to operate a railway in central Tokyo. With start-up capital of ¥3.4 million he founded the Tokyo Yamate Express Railway, which became Teito Electric Railway in 1933. In 1928 the Inokashira line between Shibuya and Inokashira Park opened to the public, and in the following year bus routes were added. In 1940 Teito Electric Railway was bought up and merged with the Tokyu group.

Following the dismantling of the Tokyu group, Keio Teito Electric Railway was left with the Keio lines, the Inokashira line, and three bus regions. An initial ¥50 million was injected into the new company, whose first president was Shiro Sannomiya. He began by recovering some of the bus routes lost after the dismantling, and also by acquiring new ones. In the second year of business, in an economically devastated Japan, KTR started a taxi firm and introduced the first Shinjuku-Chofu express on the Keio line. Like the other remaining private railway companies, KTR realized that the key to rapid growth did not lie in the relatively mature electric railway market but in diversification into related businesses that would make use of the company's real estate resources. In the next five years KTR entered the cinema, tourist, construction supply, and leisure industries. The main business, however, remained the electric railways, and in the early postwar years KTR stressed the modernization of the network. The journey between Hachioji and Shinjuku was cut down to 53 minutes and the company's own railway car manufacturer produced the first all-stainless steel so-called 3000 series cars for the Inokashira line. KTR also emphasized the expansion of the bus network, with sightseeing tours to other parts of Japan being offered and the facilities at Shinjuku station being improved. In 1959 KTR started two new ventures: Keio Shokuhin, which was involved in the food distribution and retail business, and Sakuragaoka Golf, which developed golf courses in the area. In the following year, Keio Construction and Keio Department Store were founded. The same year saw reorganization within the railway group, with the railway operations department becoming simply one of many business departments within the company structure. This reflected the growing diversification of the group. A logistics division was formed to coordinate the technical aspects of the rail operations, which were becoming more and more automated. In 1960 the Keio line began the running of one-driver trains for the first time.

The areas around the Keio line—Hachioji, Chofu, and Hashimoto—were becoming very densely populated with residents who used the line daily to commute to work in the Tokyo business districts of Shinjuku and Marunouchi. The Keio line gained a reputation as one of the most crowded lines in Tokyo during rush hour. KTR responded to this problem by increasing the number of cars on each train, improving the speed and frequency of the express services to Shinjuku, and introducing the new 20-meter-long 6000 series cars in 1972. To combat the sweltering heat of midsummer Tokyo, air conditioning was installed in all of KTR's trains on the Inokashira line by 1969. Air conditioning is now considered to be essential on all Japanese trains.

In 1969 Koshiro Kobayashi became president of KTR and the group entered the hotel business with the formation of the Keio Plaza Hotel Company. Subsequently the first luxury Keio Plaza Hotel was opened in Tokyo in Shinjuku, and regional hotels were opened in Takamatsu and Sapporo. Aside from the railway and bus concerns, the hotel business is the largest source of revenue within the KTR group of companies. KTR was one of the first Japanese companies to introduce a five-day work week for all employees from 1972, the year of Keio's 60th and Inokashira's 40th anniversaries as railway lines. By 1974 all stations within the group had automatic ticket machines, and the Keio line was extended south to Sagamihara. The company also spent money on the bus operations, with new routes added and modern air-conditioned buses put into service. Like the trains, the buses could be operated completely by the driver, cutting down on labor costs.

The first Keio restaurants were opened in KTR's many station premises. The company's management regarded these stations as lucrative development sites, and constructed shopping complexes and hotels in Shinjuku and Tama to take advantage of the spending power of the thousands of commuters passing through the stations daily. Shinjuku by then had become one of the busiest stations in the world. The length of the trains on the Keio line had risen to ten cars and the trains traveled at speeds of up to 105 kilometers per hour, reaching Shinjuku from Ha-

chioji in 35 minutes. The year 1978 saw the 30th anniversary of KTR as a company and the continued expansion of the bus network, which now extended throughout the whole of western Tokyo as well as in Japan's provinces. A computerized tracking system was introduced to improve efficiency. KTR's safety record was excellent, and at its many railroad crossings there was not a single accident in 1980. To cope with increased demand for railway cars, the group's railway car manufacturing facilities were expanded. In 1986 the construction of KTR's stations continued with the development of an underground complex around Hachioji station, the terminus of the Keio line. Between 1979 and 1989, sales of the KTR group of companies approximately doubled to ¥510 billion, and to cope with this expansion the headquarters moved from crowded and expensive Shinjuku to Sakuragaoka, a Keio line station midway between Shinjuku and Hachioji. Along with the new headquarters building, an extensive shopping complex was constructed.

The late 1980s saw an economic boom in Japan, with consumer spending soaring and stock and real estate prices reaching dizzying heights. This meant big profits for all the large private railway companies, many of which possessed sites in the most expensive areas of central Tokyo. Increases in KTR's overall profits have been due to real estate leasing and effective fund management. In the early 1990s transportation accounted for only 26% of the group's revenues, with property 7%, leisure and services 25%, and the remaining 42% being made up by the retail operations of its department stores and restaurants. Unlike its rival railway groups Tokyu and Seibu, KTR did not seem intent on expansion overseas. Investment plans largely centered on the core areas of transport, retail, and hotels. On the Sagamihara branch of the Keio line, a major extension project was underway, as was the construction of two Keio Plaza Hotels in Tama and Hachioji. Responding to the rapid increase in the elderly population of Japan, KTR formed the Keio Senior Club, offering the group's services at a discount to the over-60s market. KTR was a fairly mature, well-run company that looked set for slow but steady growth in the 1990s.

Principal Subsidiaries and Affiliates: Keio Agency K.K.; Nishi Tokyo Bus K.K.; Keio Automobile K.K.; Keio Stores K.K.; Keio Department Stores K.K.; Elite K.K.; Keio Atman K.K.; Keio Plaza Hotels K.K.; South Shinjuku Parking K.K.; Restaurant Keio K.K.; Keio Travel Agency K.K.; Keio Recreation K.K.; Keio Construction K.K.; Keio Service K.K.; Keio Diesel Industry K.K.; Keio Plaza Hotel K.K.

Further Reading: Livingstone, J., J. Moore, F. Oldfather, *Postwar Japan: 1945 to Present,* London, Random House, 1973.

—Dylan Tanner

KINKI NIPPON RAILWAY COMPANY LTD.

6-1-55 Ue-Hommachi
Tennoji-ku
Osaka 543
Japan
(06) 775 3444
Fax: (06) 773 0588

Public Company
Incorporated: 1944
Employees: 11,873
Sales: ¥791.71 billion (US$6.34 billion)
Stock Exchanges: Tokyo Osaka Nagoya Kyoto

The Kinki Nippon Railway Company is the largest and oldest private railway company in Japan, with daily traffic of 2.1 million passsengers over 595 kilometers of track. It is also the parent company of the Kinki Nippon Tetsudo Kabushiki group (Kintetsu), which has 170 subsidiaries employing 81,000 people worldwide, total assets of ¥180 billion and annual sales nearing ¥2.7 trillion. The business interests of Kintetsu range from tourism to real estate, air freight, hotels, and cable television, among others.

The Kinki Nippon Railway Company Ltd. began life with two main corporate predecessors, the Osaka Electric Tramway and the Sangu Express Company (Sankyu). The Osaka Electric Tramway was a modest concern, founded in 1907, whose first project was to build a standard gauge interurban tramway between Osaka and Nara. As Japan's ancient former capital, Nara had a rich heritage of important historical sites, including the Todaiji temple, renowned for its great statue of the Buddha. The 17-mile stretch between the two cities took seven years to complete and involved blasting a two-mile tunnel through the Ikoma mountains, east of Osaka. The unhurried pace of railway development was quite typical of the times and in striking contrast to modern Japanese efficiency.

Through the 1920s Osaka Electric Tramway added two further lines, one south from the Nara area to the shrine at Kashihara and the second providing a link from Fuse, just east of Osaka, to Sakurai, an area of great natural beauty. In the 1920s it also acquired a number of smaller railways, the Tenri Light Railway, the Ikoma Cable Railway, the Hase Railway, the Yoshino Railway, and the Iga Electric Railway, which improved its coverage of the region. Much of the 1930s was spent upgrading the tramways to railway standards.

The second corporate predecessor of the Kinki Nippon Railway, Sangu—or "Pilgrimage"—Express Electric Railway (Sankyu) was founded in 1927. Its main holding was a line from Sakurai in the middle of the peninsula across the mountains to the shrines at Ise. This link, which was completed in 1931, allowed passage directly from Osaka in the west to the Grand Shrines at Ise on the Shima peninsula in the east of Japan. Since the early 1900s there had been a series of plans to provide better transportation to this region. The shrines attracted a great deal of pilgrimage traffic, but state-run Japan National Railways services from Osaka and Nagoya were indirect and slow. From 1915 the Ise Railway began a line which by its completion in 1930 ran from Kuwana in the north to Ise in the south. In 1938, Kankyu forged the last link between Kuwana and the northern city of Nagoya, which did much to unite the area as a whole.

In 1936 Sankyu took over the Ise Electric Railway, as the Ise Railway had become in 1926. In 1940 it absorbed the Kansai Express Electric Railway (Kankyu) and a year later added the important Osaka Electric Tramway, renaming itself the Kansai Express Railway. Government-prompted wartime railway mergers brought four smaller companies into the fold—Osaka Railway, an interurban railway out of Osaka; the Yoro Electric Railway, a line in the Kuwana region; the Mt. Shigi Express Electric Railway; and the Nanwa Electric Railway. Kansai Express Railway merged with the Nakai Railway and renamed itself the Kinki Nippon Railway on January 6, 1944. In the postwar untangling of wartime railway mergers, the Nankai Railway, with its lines running south of Osaka and out along the bay, was split off in 1947. Although small, it still remained a going concern in the early 1990s.

The history of the Kinki Nippon Railway Company Ltd. in post-war Japan is closely linked with the phenomenal economic developments in that country as a whole. The end of the war in August 1945 revealed an economy in tatters, with food prices rising ten times in the first six months and an outbreak of strikes and sit-ins across the country. The railway systems were not immune. In one railway company, workers took over the running of the trains themselves in sheer frustration. Nevertheless, by the end of the Allied occupation in 1952, the tide had begun to turn. Substantial U.S. investment had begun to stimulate Japanese economic growth, and by the mid-1950s Japan had taken matters into its own hands. Carefully laid five-year plans aimed at achieving economic independence and an end to U.S. subsidies through modernization of production, boosting exports, and encouraging household savings.

As Japan's economy grew, so did the importance of its rail and transport services. The railways, culturally regarded as one of the most convenient and popular modes of land transportation, brought the people to work in the newly industrialized areas around Tokyo and Osaka, and allowed them to escape on brief holidays and day trips. With a scarcity of motor cars, the railways had been popular and profitable in the 1930s, so much so that the state-owned Japan National Railways had developed plans to standardize the Tokyo-Nagoya-Kyoto-Osaka line to relieve congestion. Furthermore, many of the railway companies in Japan, both private and state-run, owned considerable land banks that dated back to the companies' beginnings and which would provide rich sources of revenue in the future.

The succession of prewar and wartime mergers and acquisitions put the Kinki Nippon Railway in a strong position as it began to establish itself under its new name. It covered much of the region in a network of mainline, branch, and suburban lines, and was operating bus services, tourism, and freight transport services through its Kintetsu subsidiaries, Kintetsu being the group name of the developing corporation. However, the capital investment required on the lines, which used a wide range of gauges and were in various states of repair, was immense, and the permanent presence of Japan National Railways in the area could not be overlooked.

On August 10, 1947, Kinki Nippon began its first Limited Express service. Two daily round trips ran from Osaka to Nagoya, but the lack of gauge standardization meant passengers had to change trains at Nakagawa to continue their journey in either direction. Plans were made for standardization on this route in 1959 when one of Japan's record-breaking storms, the Ise Bay typhoon, struck the area in September 1959. The Nagoya line was put out of service, but in the subsequent reconstruction the lines to both Nagoya and Ise from Nakagawa were standardized and a Vista car service began running on these lines from 1959. Meanwhile, standardization of the Nara line was in progress, including modernization of the pre-1920s Ikoma tunnel in 1964, and the service was generally speeded up. In 1962 Kinki Nippon founded a Research and Development Institute, the first of its kind for a private railway, which was designed to keep the railway at the forefront of technological and engineering advances.

The early 1960s brought new acquisitions. The Nara Electric Railway, which provided a link between Nara and Kyoto, was added in 1963; the Shigi Ikoma Electric Railway, acquired by Kintetsu in 1964, brought a north-south line from Oji to Ikoma on the main Kinki Nippon line; and the important Mie Electric Railway, with its lines in the Ise-Shima peninsula, was added in the same year. Mie was the railway division of Kintetsu subsidiary Mie Transport until it was merged into the corporation in 1964. In 1964, Kinki Nippon Railway announced profits of ¥2.04 billion which were to rise steadily at a rate of 10% a year.

In the late 1960s an automatic train stop was installed on the main lines and subsequently on branch lines through the early 1970s. Branch lines were also brought up to standard on voltage, which was increased from 600 to 1500 on the Nara, Kyoto, Kashihara, Tenri, Ikoma, and Tawaramoto lines in 1969. The Shima line was standardized in 1969 and thereby linked to the rest of the system.

Railways formed the hub of the Kintetsu empire, but were not its only interests. Like many private interurban railways, it had a range of interests that had developed over the years in assorted areas. One of the first subsidiaries was the Kinki Nippon Tourist Co. Ltd (KNT), which dated back to 1941 and was acquired by the Kinki Nippon Railway in 1947. As well as being one of the oldest subsidiaries of Kintetsu, KNT was the first travel agency to be quoted on the Tokyo Stock Exchange.

Until the Tokyo Olympic Games in 1964, the Japanese people were not free to travel overseas as they wished, and KNT operated mainly in the domestic market, cooperating with the Kinki Nippon Railway to develop the tourist potential of the shrines, national parks, and resorts of the Kansai region. KNT also developed links with other railway lines and with hotel chains in Japan for the development of tourism on a nation-wide scale and began the building of its Miyako hotel chain in Japan's major cities.

The 1960s were also important for Kintetsu on the international stage. In February 1968 the newly-formed Kintetsu Enterprises Company of America opened its five-acre Japan Culture and Trade Center in the heart of San Francisco. The center was designed to provide a cultural bridge between Japan and the United States, introducing a U.S. audience to Japanese food, products, art, and artifacts, and the complex included a 218-room luxury hotel, the San Francisco Miyako. The center caught the world's attention and the project was the first of a series of property and hotel enterprises in San Francisco and Los Angeles. A return export from the United States to Japan was baseball. Kintetsu put forward a team, the Kintetsu Buffaloes, which won the championships in 1979, 1980, and 1989, boosting railway income considerably in the traffic of fans to the Kintetsu Fujidera Stadium, the team's home ground.

The 1970s brought both setbacks and successes to the group. The oil crisis of 1973 triggered recession in Japan, and Kintetsu—particularly the railway and bus services—suffered a big decline in 1974 and 1975. Nevertheless, by 1976 profits across the board had recovered to 1973 levels and the group was looking for new directions for growth and development.

Real estate development, including hotels, shopping malls, and residential development for leasing purposes, was the direction chosen. In 1978 Kintetsu began developing a shopping area under the overhead railway line in Osaka. In the same year, construction was begun on another Miyako hotel, this time in Tokyo. By 1982 there were plans to redevelop the areas around two terminal stations in Osaka, the Uehommachi, whose development would include the Miyako Hotel and Kintetsu Theater, and the Abenobashi, including the new and extended Kintetsu Department Store, at a combined cost of ¥50 billion. Meanwhile, Kintetsu was adding office buildings, flats, and land for inner-city development in Tokyo, Nagoya, and Osaka to its portfolio, and becoming increasingly interested in residential housing in the Kansai region. As land prices soared in and around Tokyo and Osaka in the 1980s, Kintetsu found itself with a reputation as one of the leading private residential developers in Japan.

Enthusiastic dabbling in real estate contrasted with great difficulties in the railway business at the beginning of the 1980s. Installation of a new automatic wicket gate system brought the railways' equipment up to date, but interest payments following capital investment were high. The cost of the electricity supply to the railways rose dramatically, and Kinki Nippon Railway was committed to laying a new line in eastern Osaka, the Higashi-Osaka line, scheduled for completion in 1983 but not actually ready for operation until November 1986. By 1983 profits had slumped to ¥6.06 billion due to the slow growth in the number of passengers and depreciation costs.

The late 1980s marked a recovery for the railway. Fare increases of 12.5% in 1987 brought an increase in operating revenue, and in 1988 the Silk Road Exposition in Nara and the popularity of Urban Liner express trains led to an increase in the number of rail users.

The privatization of Japan National Railways in 1987 and heavy marketing by the new local company Japan Railways West (JR West), part of the privatized Japan Railways, brought unwelcome competition, as a fit and lean JR West began building up its commuter services into Osaka, Kobe, and Kyoto. In response, Kinki Nippon introduced a discount system for passengers who bought their tickets in bulk, as well as a plan allowing passengers unlimited travel for a three-day period.

The 1980s brought tremendous opportunities for KNT. The Japanese government aimed to double the number of people who went abroad in 1986—5.52 million—over the next five years. The intention was to familiarize the Japanese people with other cultures and also improve Japan's trade imbalance. In 1990, one year short of target, the number of Japanese travelers overseas reached 10 million. KNT's business mirrored the government's aspirations. In 1987, 29,000 Japanese tourists used KNT to visit the United Kingdom alone; by 1990 this figure had increased to 50,891. In 1989 KNT organized overseas travel arrangements for 815,939 Japanese visitors, which represented 35% of its business, the remaining 65% being concentrated in the domestic market. KNT offered luxury tours both at home and abroad, with the honeymoon business viewed as a growth area for the 1990s. Through the 1980s KNT built up a network of 19 overseas offices to add to its 252 domestic branches and 174 sub-agencies. It also negotiated agreements with United Airlines and the Westin, Sheraton, and Hilton hotels in the United States, and formed a business arrangement with Berlitz to strengthen the travel publications.

Meanwhile Kintetsu Enterprises Company of America had developed the 125-room Miyako Inn San Francisco and the 40-lane Japantown Bowl in California, and in 1987 started to construct a 432-room Los Angeles Miyako Hotel, due to open in 1992. The move into hotels in the United States in the 1980s followed the Japanese government's relaxation in 1980 of foreign exchange controls that had prohibited large-scale investment outside Japan.

The profile of Kintetsu as it entered the final decade of the 20th century was impressive. Turnover in 1990 for the group was ¥2.46 trillion. The railway was responsible for 10% of this, with an unrivaled network of rail systems in Western Japan. High speed limited express rails linked Osaka, Kyoto, Nagoya, Nara, Yoshin, and the shrines and resorts of the Shima Peninsula. In addition, commuter trains provided an important service to and from the major cities, and branch lines gave access to the rural areas of the Kinki and Tokai districts. Kintetsu's bus services provided a nationwide service through a fleet of 4,300 buses and combined routes of 14,000 kilometers. Through 28 subsidiaries, Kintetsu operated 3,200 taxicabs in western Japan. Trucking companies, aerial trams, cable cars, ferry boats, hydrofoils, and coach operations were all part of a transport empire.

Kintetsu's interests did not stop there. A shopping mall in San Francisco, large Kintetsu department stores in 15 major Japanese cities, boutiques, supermarkets, and the development of shopping areas at railway terminals demonstrated the company's strong commitment to retail. The funding of museums, theaters, and cultural and educational centers represented a move toward subliminal marketing and advertising, and as the Japanese government urged its people to make more of their leisure time, Kintetsu's hotels, golf courses, nightclubs, and resort facilities under development at Shima were set to benefit.

However, on the railway side, the tight government regulation of fares left Kinki Nippon Railway with its hands tied, at a time when the company faced stiff competition from JR West. On the real estate side, land prices were stagnant or falling in the Osaka area, and Kintetsu could no longer rely on quick returns to offset lean years on the railway. Finally, Kintetsu faced the challenge of many large companies with an extended family of subsidiaries—achievement of greater synergies between the business areas.

—Catriona Luke

KÜHNE & NAGEL INTERNATIONAL AG

Churerstrasse 135
CH-8808 Pfäffikon
Switzerland
(55) 484212
Fax: (55) 483623

Private Company
Incorporated: 1890 as Kühne & Nagel, Bremen
Employees: 10,000
Sales: SFr4.62 billion (US$3.41 billion)

The Kühne & Nagel Group (KN) ranks as Europe's third-largest freight-forwarding business in terms of turnover and staff, moving cargoes by land, sea, river, and air. It has offices in more than 60 countries, and a work force of about 10,000 worldwide. The cargoes carried under the Kühne & Nagel (KN) logo, the anchor and wheel, vary from Beaujolais Nouveau, which is air freighted around the world from France, to exotic fruits and flowers, which are air freighted to Europe from Africa. At the other end of the scale, huge pieces of machinery and equipment for oil refineries in the Middle East and hydroelectric projects in the Third World have been transported by KN.

The Kühne & Nagel Group is headed by two holding companies: Kühne & Nagel International AG, based in Switzerland, the holding company for all businesses except the companies in Canada and the United States, with a share capital of SFr80 million, and Kuehne & Nagel Holding, Inc., the holding company for businesses in Canada and the United States, with a share capital of US$3.3 million.

Although freight forwarding remains the core of the company's business, KN has diversified into insurance through the Nacora Group; shipbroking through the Unimar Group; port handling at Rotterdam and Hamburg, and travel agencies in Germany, Canada, South Africa, and Turkey. On July 1, 1990, KN celebrated its 100th anniversary. The company was started on July 1, 1890, from a small office in Bremen, by August Kühne and Friedrich Nagel.

August Kühne, the son of a forester, was born in 1855. He had intended to study law, but when his father could not afford to fund his studies, he began an apprenticeship with L.G. Dyes & Co., a Bremen import and export company. He completed his apprenticeship but was laid off during the economic slump of the mid-1870s. After a while he began work as a

shipping clerk with Fr. Naumann, a forwarding company in Bremen. He rose to be a partner in the firm and became engaged to Naumann's daughter. She died before the wedding and August later fell out with Naumann. In 1890 he left Naumann's company to set up his own business.

Friedrich Nagel, who was born in 1864, was a shipping agent at Fr. Naumann. August Kühne persuaded Nagel to join him as a business partner. They scraped together their working capital of just 30,000 marks, and placed an advertisement in the *Bremen Nachrichten,* the local newspaper, on July 1, 1890. The advertisement announced that "a forwarding and commissioning agency under the name of Kühne & Nagel has been established here and in Bremerhaven."

Initially KN went into business as a forwarder of glassware and cotton. An essential part of the activities of a forwarding agent is pooling services, the grouping together of consignments from several customers to form one full load, to be transported to the same destination. The risk is that railway cars must sometimes travel half full to meet deadlines. KN kept to schedules, absorbing extra costs itself, and the clients' confidence was won. At the same time, the firm established warehouses for brand-name merchandise.

During the final years of the 19th century, sugar was a main German export commodity. When the Weser River, along which much sugar was shipped to England, froze up, August Kühne sensed an opportunity for more business. He convinced the managers of large sugar refineries in Hamburg that the problem could be solved by his forwarding firm. KN routed the sugar during the winter months by rail to Bremen, where it was transferred to ocean-going ships.

Before long the firm's activities comprised general export and import shipping, and specialization in expert handling, sampling and testing of cotton, grain, lumber, feedstuff, and sugar. Added to this were pooling services or consolidations, general warehousing, and distribution warehouses for the ever-increasing volume of brand-name merchandise.

When it became apparent the firm needed a branch in Hamburg, its foundation was entrusted to Adolf Maass, a former apprentice with the firm who had become manager of the glass transport department. Maass founded the Hamburg office at Groningerstrasse in February 1902. The branch developed rapidly, and transport by water along the Elbe River began to flourish. In 1910 Adolf Maass became a partner in KN.

In 1907 Friedrich Nagel died, and August Kühne took over his shares in the business. Although no member of the Nagel family has been involved with the firm since Friedrich's death, Kühne & Nagel had already become an established name among freight forwarders, and so Nagel's name has been retained in the company's title.

August Kühne's thoughts turned to a successor. His eldest son had died, and two other sons had expressed no interest in joining the business. One son, Alfred, however, decided to forego training as an artist, and in 1910 began an apprenticeship in the Hamburg branch. After two years, Alfred Kühne continued his apprenticeship in Bremen, working in all the main departments, under the supervision of his father.

In 1909 August Kühne acquired the von Kapff Mansion near the Weser Bridge in Bremen, where he had worked as an apprentice. He converted the building into his company's headquarters, and it was still the site of KN's German head office in the early 1990s.

In the years before World War I the business flourished. Both the Bremen and Hamburg branches were efficient and profitable, employing 50 people between them. Bremerhaven had warehousing facilities, just like Bremen; there were representatives of the firm in Lübeck and Leipzig, and in 1913 an office was opened in Berlin, the capital of imperial Germany.

The outbreak of World War I in August 1914 brought business to a near-standstill, however. Most overseas connections were cut immediately. Many employees were called up for military service, while others volunteered, including Alfred Kühne, his younger brother Werner, and Adolf Maass. August Kühne tried to keep the business going, but the total naval blockade of 1915 put an end to the last ocean connections that had been sustained with a few neutral states. By the end of the war in 1918, German merchant ships had all but disappeared from the seas. All cargo ships had to be surrendered to the victorious powers and operated under foreign flags. German offices, warehouses, and seaports were undamaged, however. Whereas before the war KN had engaged mainly in transporting imported merchandise, now the firm handled increasing amounts of exports.

Alfred Kühne, who had spent some time arranging sea freight forwarding in Rotterdam, returned to his father's company in 1921. At the same time, his brother Werner also joined the Bremen office. In the autumn of 1921 they both moved to Hamburg.

In the early 1920s KN took over another company, Johs. Weber & Freund, which brought in more business in the field of imports as well as in the pooling service. A joint venture with a Prague forwarding agent, the Europäische Transportgesellschaft, increased dealings with Czechoslovakia.

The rapid devaluation of the German mark in 1923 brought havoc to German businesses. The Hamburg branch of KN was weakened by the departure of five head clerks who set up in business on their own and persuaded other clerks to join them. Even Adolf Maass, manager of the Hamburg branch, thought of leaving. Alfred and Werner Kühne, aged 28 and 25 respectively, persuaded their father to let them run the Hamburg office. Alfred took over the import department, Werner the export department, and Adolf Maass remained, running the bulk cargo and grain departments as well as the business with Czechoslovakia.

Alfred Kühne wanted to extend the existing special services handling raw materials. He established services for cocoa and leather products, and developed the firm's business with Switzerland and Austria, also venturing into the Balkan countries. Werner Kühne expanded the export department, setting up services to England, South America, the United States, and Canada. He traveled abroad a great deal, creating a network of foreign representatives.

In 1924 a branch was opened in Lübeck to handle traffic in the Baltic sea. Additional domestic representative offices were opened in Cottbus, Magdeburg, Gera, Erfurt, Frankfurt, Braunschweig, Hanover, and Stuttgart. In 1928 August Kühne made both sons his partners.

The later 1920s were a time of rampant inflation and mass unemployment in Germany. Like nearly all German firms, KN was struck by a serious downturn in business.

On May 20, 1932, the founder and senior partner, August Kühne, died at the age of 77. Alfred and Werner Kühne became joint partners, Werner in Bremen, and Alfred in Ham-

burg, the main offices in the two most important German seaports. When Adolf Maass left in April 1933 to become a partner with his relatives in another business, Alfred and Werner Kühne were left as sole owners.

Cartage and barge operations were added to the Hamburg business, while Bremen expanded the pooling service, lumber shipments, and dealings with England, and had great success handling cotton. In 1932 a bonded warehouse was set up in Leipzig, and in 1934 a KN branch was opened in Stettin, which specialized in handling fibers.

The outbreak of World War II in September 1939 brought overseas traffic to a standstill. A restricted pooling service within Germany operated throughout the war. Highway and traffic routes were opened up, establishing a link to both the Middle East and the Far East, via Russia.

Alfred Kühne suffered from a foot disability, which meant he could not serve in the army. He continued to run the company, helped by Ludwig Rössinger who had joined KN in 1924 as representative in Frankfurt. KN was reorganized in 1942 and was run from the central office in Berlin. In the same year, a branch was established at Königsberg and another at Regensburg in 1943.

The war left much of Germany's industry in ruins, and its seaports had been destroyed by bombing. KN's headquarters in Bremen, including the archives, were completely destroyed during an air raid in 1944. By 1945 there were few docks left in Germany, and large areas of industrial hinterland had been lost. Germany was divided into four occupation zones, while the Allies decided the shape of the future Germany.

When the first ocean-going vessels, mostly carrying food parcels from the United States, tied up in Germany, KN established emergency offices and converted its damaged facilities into makeshift work places. Without hope for the resumption of worldwide shipping activities, KN concentrated its efforts on providing transport in the three remaining German occupation zones. In 1946 a branch was established in Düsseldorf, followed by one in Braunschweig in 1947.

Gradually the German economy recovered, helped by a massive amount of aid from the United States, known as the Marshall Plan. Sugar, cocoa, coffee, and cotton imports increased. Ruined quays were rebuilt. Alfred Kühne took the opportunity to erect a modern warehousing and cargo-handling facility in Hamburg Free Port. It was opened in September 1950, and had a storage capacity initially of 6,000 square meters, which was later expanded to 25,000 square meters.

During the period of postwar reconstruction, political leaders and industrialists came increasingly to realize that the future lay in a tightly interlinked Europe. With this in mind, KN swiftly expanded its German organization, linking the seaports by means of rail and trucks. Branches were opened in Frankfurt in 1949; Bonn—the new capital, Passau, and Hanover in 1950; Mannheim in 1953; Cologne in 1954; Munich and Stuttgart in 1955; Bielefeld in 1960; Wuppertal in 1961; and Hagen and Nuremberg in 1963. Altogether the 19 German branches had 1.6 million square feet of storage area.

Changes took place in top management. Werner Kühne emigrated to South Africa at the end of 1951, and Dieter Liesenfeld, junior partner since 1945, left the company at the end of 1953. Ludwig Rössinger became Alfred Kühne's partner on January 1, 1954.

In the postwar economic boom of the 1950s and 1960s, worldwide cargo traffic assumed great proportions. KN realized that to benefit from the new trade routes it was necessary to have employees on the spot, and therefore began to establish a worldwide network of operating bases. As well as road, rail, and sea freighting, the air freighting business began to grow in importance.

The formation of the European Economic Community (EEC) produced an increase in traffic; in response KN instituted an express service by rail to and from all EEC countries. KN needed to find suitable forwarding agents in European countries; where this was not possible, KN set up subsidiaries. Consequently, in 1954 establishments were set up in Antwerp and Rotterdam, followed by the foundation of Kühne & Nagel AG, Switzerland, with offices in Basel and Zürich in 1959. In 1963 KN became the majority shareholder in Proodos S.A., of Athens. Special pooling services from Italy were incorporated in 1964, and the Kühne & Nagel S.a.r.l., Milan, was founded. This completed the European organization for the time being.

In 1953 a KN subsidiary was founded in Canada, with branches in Toronto and Montreal. At the time Alfred Kühne said, "We want to create an organization paralleling that in Germany and Western Europe. We have chosen Canada because we consider her a country of great potential, and because she is a nation of dynamic progress." The basis of the Canadian expansion was the tremendous growth in German imports. A licensed customs house broker, J.W. Mills & Son, Ltd., of Montreal and Toronto, was incorporated into KN, thus making it possible to combine shipping operations with customs clearance.

In the winter, when Montreal and Toronto were cut off from the Atlantic by the freezing up of the St. Lawrence River, KN used the ice-free ports of Halifax and St. John. Consignments from Europe were loaded into boxcars and sent by rail to Montreal and Toronto. KN also established bonded warehouses and eventually built up a total storage area of 329,000 square meters in Canada.

A branch was opened in Vancouver in 1957 to handle incoming goods from Japan and Hong Kong, and to reship them to eastern Canada. To complete the chain, additional branches were opened in Quebec City, Hamilton, Ontario, and Winnipeg. KN is the biggest freight forwarder in Canada.

In the early 1990s KN was run by a third-generation member of the Kühne family, Klaus-Michael Kühne, Alfred Kühne's son. Klaus-Michael Kühne joined his father and Ludwig Rössinger as a junior partner in 1963, having completed an apprenticeship in banking. In 1966, at the age of 30, he joined the top management as chairman of the executive board. He initiated the further growth of KN's activities with particular emphasis on Europe and the Far East. The KN organization has 400 offices in 60 countries around the world.

Alfred Kühne died in 1981. In July of that year, the British conglomerate Lonrho Plc acquired 50% of KN's shares at a cost of DM90 million. Since then, Klaus-Michael Kühne and Lonrho's head, Roland W. (Tiny) Rowland have been joint chief executives of the entire organization. The main reason for the sale of half of KN to Lonrho was because of losses sustained by the Kühne family in attempting to expand its shipping fleet.

Although KN Germany remains the biggest KN company worldwide, its senior management is based in Switzerland at Pfäffikon. In 1989 the prestigious German business publication *Manager Magazin* voted Klaus-Michael Kühne "Mr. Europe," reflecting the farsighted approach KN took in the increasing economic integration of Europe and the removal of internal trading barriers, scheduled for 1993.

In 1985 KN's management devised a pan-European strategy to prepare the company for the single European market. The company's top priority was to expand its transport, warehousing, and distribution network in Europe. This concept is called "KN Euro Logistics."

To prepare for the single market, KN has bought into leading freight companies in Italy—Domenichelli SpA, the Netherlands—Van Vliet BV, the United Kingdom—Hollis Transport Group Ltd., and Spain—Transportes TresH. Further capacity has been acquired in Denmark, Norway, and Sweden. KN is also looking to acquire a stake in a suitable company in France. These acquisitions have been masterminded by a special corporate development department.

Without doubt, German reunification was the outstanding event of the 1990 business year. In May 1990 KN founded, via a joint venture contract with the former state-owned forwarder VEB Deutrans, the KN Speditions-GmbH in East Berlin. Later, KN having bought out the Deutrans share, it became a wholly owned KN company. It consists of a network of a dozen branches, field offices, logistics depots, and air freight stations in the five states of the former German Democratic Republic.

KN is the second-largest freight forwarding firm in Germany, behind Schenker-Rhenus, but reunification has provided the impetus to KN to expand its "KN Euro Logistics" service across Germany. KN holds the contract to distribute branded goods across Germany for three major manufacturers—Philip Morris, maker of Marlboro cigarettes; Tchibo coffee, and Thomson Consumer Electronics Group.

The 1990 annual report stated that the company's future strategy would "continue to center on the consolidation and integration of KN's activities in Europe." KN's involvement in Eastern Europe began in the 1950s, when imports of timber, paper, and furniture were forwarded from Romania, Poland, and Hungary. Political and economic liberalization in the former communist-bloc countries presents many business opportunities for KN. KN formed joint ventures or signed contracts of cooperation with local freight forwarders in Soviet Russia, Romania, Bulgaria, Albania, Hungary, Poland, Czechoslovakia, and Yugoslavia. KN aims to provide the full range of freight forwarding services, as well as special container, trade fair, seaworthy packaging and distribution services.

The year 1990 saw a reduction in KN's net operating profits to SFr34.2 million from SFr37.5 million in 1989. The decline was partly due to the general economic downturn, and to unavoidable losses in connection with the development of new products ("KN Euro Logistics"). The weakening of the U.S. dollar, high interest rates, the Persian Gulf War, and overdemand in some European countries leading to higher costs all contributed to the decline in profitability. Substantial additional costs for freight purchasing were necessary—KN's own transport capacities are limited. Therefore, in the future, KN will acquire further vehicles to fulfill this demand, particularly in Germany. Canada, the Far East and several European countries were the main contributors to net profits.

Principal Subsidiaries: Kühne & Nagel Beteiligungs-AG; Kühne & Nagel Speditions-Aktiengesellschaft; Kühne & Nagel (AG & Co); Kühne & Nagel Luftfracht GmbH; Cargopack Verpackungsges für Industriegüter mbH; Kühne & Nagel Speditions-AG (Austria); Kühne & Nagel Ges.m.b.H (Austria); Kühne & Nagel N.V. (Belgium); Kuehne & Nagel A/S Padborg (Denmark); OY Nakutrans Ltd. (Finland); Kühne & Nagel S.A. (France); Delta-Trans S.A. (France); Kuehne & Nagel (UK) Ltd.; Kuehne & Nagel Ltd. (United Kingdom); Kuehne & Nagel Air Cargo Ltd. (United Kingdom); Kühne & Nagel Holding SpA (Italy); Kühne & Nagel Spedition G.m.b.H. (Luxembourg); Kuehne & Nagel Malta Ltd.; Kühne & Nagel N.V. (Netherlands); Kühne & Nagel S.A. (Spain); Kühne & Nagel Airfreight A/B (Sweden); Kühne & Nagel International AG (Switzerland); Kühne & Nagel Management AG (Switzerland); Kühne & Nagel Internationale Transporte AG (Switzerland); Kühne & Nagel Aktiengesellschaft (Switzerland); H.W. Feustel Nakliyat ve Seyahat A.S. (Turkey); Kühne & Nagel Nakliyat, STI (Turkey); Kuehne & Nagel (Far East) Ltd. (Hong Kong); Kuehne & Nagel (Hong Kong) Ltd.; Kuehne & Nagel (Japan) Ltd.; Nakufreight (Malaysia) Sdn. Bhd.; Kuehne & Nagel (Philippines) Inc.; Kuehne & Nagel (Singapore) Private Ltd.; Kuehne & Nagel (Taiwan) Ltd.; Kuehne & Nagel (Australia) Pty. Ltd.; Kuehne & Nagel (New Zealand) Ltd.; Kuehne & Nagel (Kenya) Ltd.; Kuehne & Nagel (Pty) Ltd. (Namibia); Kuehne & Nagel (Pty) Ltd. (South Africa); Nakutrans S.A. (Argentina); Kühne & Nagel do Brazil Transportes Internacionais Ltda.; Kühne & Nagel de Colombia Ltda.; Kühne & Nagel de México S. de R.L.; Kuehne & Nagel Canada Holding Inc. (Canada); Kuehne & Nagel International Ltd. (Canada); Kuehne & Nagel Holding Inc. (U.S.A.); Kuehne & Nagel, Inc. (U.S.A.); Kuehne & Nagel Airfreight, Inc. (U.S.A.); Kuehne & Nagel Distribution Services, Inc. (U.S.A.).

Further Reading: Kühne & Nagel, *75 Years Kühne & Nagel,* Bremen, Carl Schünemann, 1965.

—Caroline Hinton

LA POSTE

20, avenue de Ségur
75700 Paris
France
(1) 45 64 22 22
Fax: (1) 45 64 33 48

State-Owned Company
Incorporated: 1990
Employees: 300,000
Sales: FFr69.1 billion (US$13.34 billion)

France's postal service has a very long history. Dating back to the Roman empire, it developed into a public service as early as the 17th century, and is still partly a state monopoly. The postal service has also played a major role in the development of transportation in France, and, since the 19th century, in the history of the French financial system. The 20th century has been a time of institutional and technological modernization.

The history of the postal service in France goes back to the time of Julius Caesar, who mentions in his *De Bello Gallico* a mail service running along the Rhone valley in Gaul. The province then benefited from Emperor Augustus's creation of the *cursus publicus,* which was at first restricted to carrying administrative mail. Private messages were carried by *tabellarii,* personal slaves or freedmen in the service of patrician families. During the Middle Ages, the state postal service disappeared, giving way to various private mail services. Messages were carried between abbeys by monks; the messengers of the University of Paris carried letters between the University's numerous foreign students and their families in Europe, and aristocrats and rich merchants such as Jacques Coeur employed messengers for their private correspondence. Messengers were appointed by municipalities, initially restricted to carrying mail between municipal officials, but by the 14th and 15th centuries they were also entrusted with private letters. The royal postal service remained one of many postal services for a long time. King Louis XI, who reigned from 1461 to 1483, reintroduced the Roman post house system, a relay system whereby horses could be changed along the route. King Louis XII, who reigned from 1498 to 1515, established such relays every seven leagues along royal roads. In 1533 permanent postal routes were created between France, England, and Switzerland.

On May 8, 1597, a royal edict created *relais de louage,* a stagecoach service intended for private use. This system was merged with the *poste aux cheveux* in 1602. The *controleur général* of the posts, Guillaume Fouquet de la Varane, appointed in 1595, played a major part in establishing a royal monopoly on the collection, carriage, and delivery of mail, with varying rates according to weight and destination. However, Louis XIII, who reigned from 1610 to 1643, gradually contracted the service to individuals in an attempt to raise funds for the royal treasury. During the reign of Louis XVI—from 1643 to 1715—various post-related positions were sold as special offices. Later, however, under the influence of minister Jean-Baptiste Colbert, the superintendent of the posts, Jérôme de Nouveau, sought to abolish postmasters' offices. This took place in 1662. In 1668 the *secrétaire de la guerre* (minister of war), François-Michel Letellier, marquis of Louvois, took the role of superintendent of the posts, left vacant after the death of de Nouveau in 1665.

Louvois entirely reorganized the postal service, placing it under two authorities. The superintendent, a government minister, was to set postage rates, while the *fermier général* was contracted by the royal treasury to administer the postal service. The first contract for the latter function was drawn up between the state and the Pajot and Rouillé families, who occupied this position for more than 50 years. The *ferme générale* included more than 800 post offices in France as well as offices in Rome, Genoa, Turin, and Geneva. There were six postal routes, covering the six major French highways, along which mail was carried by postcoaches. In 1738 the Grimod and Thiroux families took on the role of *fermier général,* which they retained until the 1789 revolution. During this period post was delivered between towns but not within them. The *poste aux chevaux* (horse post) was operated by postmasters who ran posthouses—these were often inns—and were responsible for carrying mail, while there were around 1,000 post offices in France, headed by salaried directors, which were responsible for collecting and dispatching correspondence. In 1759 C. H. Piarron de Chamousset obtained from the king the right to undertake local postal delivery in Paris. The service proved so profitable that the crown soon decided to recover the rights and to extend local delivery throughout France. The so-called *Petite Poste* (intra-town post) was extended by royal decree in 1786 throughout France, eventually covering all French municipalities. The 1789 revolution did not affect the mail service until 1793, when it became a state-owned agency. Financial difficulties prompted the government to revert to the contract system several years later. State control of the posts was established definitively in 1804 with the creation of a directorate general under the Ministry of Finance. Antoine-Marie Chamans, count of La Valette, remained in charge of the posts from this date until the fall of the First Empire in 1815, when he gained a place in history by escaping from prison, disguised in his wife's clothes, the day before he was due to be executed.

The Restoration period brought several major changes in the postal service. A royal decree of February 24, 1817, made possible the introduction of the money order, which allowed funds to be delivered at one post office upon receipt of an order transmitted from another. From April 1, 1830, postal collections and deliveries were made every second day from and to homes in every municipality in France. This was the first appearance in France of the modern postman, and brought the end of rural isolation. During the reign of Louis-Philippe, mail transport was accelerated by the introduction of the railway. In 1842 mail was carried on the Strasbourg-Basel line. In 1845 mail began to be sorted in designated wagons during the train journey from city to city. Soon this method of transport replaced the horse post, which officially ended in 1873. A major improvement was due to Etienne Arago, a famous scientist and director of the posts under the Second Republic, who was responsible for the introduction of the fixed postage rate and the postage stamp, based on the English innovation of the penny post. On August 24, 1848, the National Assembly decreed that a single postage rate should be charged regardless of distance, though varying with the weight of the letter. In December 1848 another decree marked the introduction of the first three French postage stamps. In the first year after the reform, postal traffic jumped from 122 million to 158 million letters per year. During the Second Empire, rapid improvements were made in postal services abroad, especially by boat, when regular postal links were established with Indochina in 1861; the United States, Mexico, and the West Indies in 1864; and South America and West Africa in 1866.

After a short period during the seige of Paris by the German army in 1870 when a pigeon post operated, the postal service extended its role during the Third Republic. The postal service, controlled by the Ministry of Finance, and the telegraph service, controlled by the Ministry of the Interior, were combined under a single administration, the Ministry of Posts and Telegraph, headed by Adolphe Cochery. Later, however, the postal and telegraph services were attached to several other ministries until 1906, when an undersecretariat of posts and telegraph services (P&T) was reestablished as a single ministry within the government. On April 9, 1881, a new state institution was created, the Caisse Nationale d'Epargne (National Savings and Loans), with a separate budget, which was supervised by the posts and telegraphs undersecretariat. Savers could use any post office in the country as a savings bank. At the same time, this gave the state vast sums of money to finance large social and housing programs. In 1900 deposit accounts at the Caisse Nationale d'Epargne totaled FFr3.5 billion. Following the example of Austria (1883), Switzerland (1906), Germany (1909), and Belgium (1913), under the law of January 7, 1918, the French posts and telegraphs undersecretariat was allowed to operate a current account service. In the face of violent opposition from the French banks, the undersecretariat was not allowed to offer interest-bearing accounts. The funds accumulated by postal current accounts were placed in the custody of the Public Treasury.

In the 20th century, an airmail service was introduced. The first attempt to transport mail by air took place in July 1912, near Nancy in Lorraine. The airplane, carrying 40 kilograms of mail, flew for 17 minutes. On October 15, 1913, the same pilot, Lieutenant Ronin, flew from Paris to Bordeaux carrying an urgent letter to the steamship *Peru*, bound for the West Indies. During World War I the development of airmail services was suspended. In 1918 the Paris–Le Mans–St. Nazaire route began to be exploited for the use of the U.S. army. Several state-subsidized private firms carrying airmail, such as the Compagnie Aéropostale and the Compagnie Farman, appeared in 1919. At the end of the year, the pilot and airplane-builder Pierre Latécoère made the first international airmail delivery, to Barcelona, Spain. The service was soon extended to Rabat, Morocco, by way of Alicante and Malaga. In 1922 the pilot

Maurice Nogues established the first commercial Paris-Bucharest-Constantinople-Ankara airlink, and in February 1930 the first postal airlink between France and Indochina. Jean Mermoz made the first direct mail-carrying flight between France and South America on May 12, 1930. On September 2, 1930, Dieudonné Costes and Maurice Bellonte flew from New York to Paris without stopping. In 1939 the airmail service consisted of four routes covering eleven French municipalities with daily flights.

The French P&T was affected severely by World War II: by the end of the war, 25% of post offices, 50% of mailwagons, and 75% of Paris's post vans had been lost, destroyed, or stolen. Old German warplanes were used to start up airmail services again. During the 1950s and 1960s the P&T concentrated on improving existing services, introducing motorized postal delivery and mechanical sorting. Postal codes, included in addresses to facilitate sorting, were introduced in 1964. In 1973 the first automatic sorting center opened in Orléans. In 1961 a helicopter service was introduced to deliver mail to the islands off Brittany. At the same time, postal services began to be rationalized; first Sunday and then Saturday afternoon deliveries were withdrawn.

It is only since the 1970s that national P&Ts have begun to experience competition from new communication techniques. Between 1976 and 1985, international mail traffic decreased by 10% because of growing recourse to telecommunications. Meanwhile European Economic Community (EEC) regulations were introduced to control competition between data and written material transmission services. This led to the French government's decision to separate telecommunication and postal services. The reform law of 1971 separated the Direction Générale des Télécommunications (DGT) from the Direction Générale de la Poste (DGP). In 1990 the two entities adopted new names—La Poste and France Télécom respectively—in recognition of their new legal status. La Poste and France Télécom are now *exploitants autonomes de droit public*, state-owned firms which are largely autonomous. The powers of the ministry in charge of these are now clearly defined: general regulation of the sector, planning contracts between La Poste and the state, and protection of employees' status as civil servants. Postal and telephone rates are no longer set by the ministries of finance and posts and telecommunications. The financial status of La Poste is markedly different from that of the DGP. In 1923 a law had been passed that separated the budget of the postal services from that of the state. This, however, allowed the state to levy large sums of money from the mail service's profits in order to subsidize government electronic and space programs. The 1990 reform law granted La Poste a totally independent budget. The question of reduced postal rates for the press, which represent half the public subsidies given in total to that sector, has also been solved by the reform, which obliged the state to contribute to press rates subsidies.

Other subsidies have to be found to finance loss-making post offices in rural areas; in 1990 there were 17,000 post offices, 12,000 of which were based in areas with fewer than 10,000 inhabitants.

The 1990 reform aimed to support the structurally loss-making postal services by developing La Poste's expertise in financial services. La Poste's share of current account funds has been diminishing steadily for 40 years; it fell from 30% of total current account funds in 1950 to 12% in 1988. Traditional savings products are also facing serious competition from new stock-exchange-oriented savings products. The 1990 reform authorized La Poste to act as an insurance company in offering all types of personal insurance. A major difference remains between La Poste and the French banks, however; the first cannot make real estate loans unless the borrower has previous savings, nor consumer loans, the two types of loans for which there is growing demand. Meanwhile, the P&T began to develop a marketing policy, since it was allowed to establish individualized contracts for mail services with major private clients, generally corporate. The 1980s were characterized by the development of new services: telecopy (facsimile, or fax) services were launched in 1981. Chronopost, a rapid-delivery service for delivery of correspondence and goods with guaranteed time limits began in 1986. The P&T started to explore services such as gift or advertisement delivery or company mail, whereby special prices could be negotiated for large mailings. In 1990 computerized scanners were installed for post-code sorting.

Although its international financial services are not extensive, La Poste plays a major part in solving international mail problems through its participation in the Universal Postal Union, created in 1878 after the Bern Convention of 1874 signed by 22 states including France. La Poste is also an active member of the European Posts and Telecommunications Conference, the EEC Posts working groups, and the UNIPOST Agency, while its specialized subsidiaries contribute to assisting with third-world postal problems.

Principal Subsidiaries: SOFIPOST; SFMI CHRONOPOST (66%); SECURIPOST SA; SOMEPOST; MEDIAPOST SA (70%); POLYMEDIAS (85%); SOGEPOSTE (49%); AEROPOSTALE (40%).

Further Reading: Histoire d'une Réforme, Paris, Ministry of Posts, Telecommunications and Space, Paris, 1990; Vaille, *Histoire Générale de la Poste de Louis XI à 1789,* 5 volumes, Paris, Presses Universitaires de France, 1950; *Vingt Siècles d'Histoire de la Poste,* Paris, Ministère des PTT, 1954; *Encyclopédie des PTT,* 2 volumes, Paris, Rombaldi, 1957; Rolland, *Chronologie de l'Histoire des Postes,* Paris, SNSL, 1975; Chauvigny, *Les Grands Moments de La Poste,* Paris, France-Empire, 1988; Fourre, Jean-Pierre, *Rapport à l'Assemblée Nationale Relatif à L'Organization du Service Public des Postes et des Telecommunications,* no 1323, Imprimerie Nationale, Paris, 1990.

—William Baranès

MITSUI O.S.K. LINES, LTD.

1-1,Toranomon, 2-chome
Minato-ku
Tokyo 105-91
Japan
(03) 3587-7111
Fax: (03) 3587-7702

Public Company
Incorporated: 1964
Employees: 1,610
Sales: ¥455.8 billion (US$3.65 billion)
Stock Exchanges: Tokyo Osaka Nagoya Kyoto Hiroshima
  Fukuoka Niigata Sapporo Brussels Antwerp Frankfurt

Mitsui O.S.K. Lines, Ltd. (MOL) was founded in 1964 following the merger of Osaka Shosen Kaisha (OSK) and Mitsui Steamship Co., Ltd., formerly Mitsui Line, under the Law Concerning the Reconstruction and Reorganization of the Shipping Industry. At that time the company was the largest shipping company in Japan, capitalized at ¥13.1 billion, with 83 vessels aggregating 1,237 thousand pennyweight (dwt).

OSK was founded in 1884 when 55 shipowners, each of whom had only a small number of vessels, combined their operations. The chief representative of these shipowners was Hirose Saihei, senior manager of the Sumitomo *zaibatsu*, or conglomerate, and a prominent figure in Osaka financial circles. OSK was capitalized at ¥1.2 million, with 93 vessels totaling 15,400 gross registered tonnage (grt). In the first few years its routes were limited to coastal services in the western area of Japan. In 1890 OSK inaugurated an Osaka/Pusan run followed in 1893 by the operation of an Osaka/Inchon route and Korean coastal services. The company was recapitalized at ¥1.8 million in 1893, rising to ¥2.5 million in 1894, to ¥5 million in 1896, when the government of Taiwan granted OSK subsidies for Osaka/Taiwan liner services, and to ¥10 million in 1898 when the company started to operate on the Yangtze River.

In 1898 Tokugoro Nakahashi became the company's fourth president. He made a great effort to rationalize the internal organization of OSK, to penetrate the Chinese market, and also to inaugurate the first OSK ocean route, a Hong Kong to Tacoma, Washington service, in 1908. In 1911 OSK started a Kobe to Bombay service. The route was under the monopoly of the Far Eastern Freight Conference (FEFC) of which Nippon Yusen K.K. (NYK) was the only Japanese member. OSK fought against the FEFC and was admitted to the conference in

1913. In 1918 the company opened a Bombay to Marseilles route and was admitted to full membership of the Far Eastern Freight Conference (FEFC). Meanwhile, it opened a San Francisco route, an Australia route, and a South America route, offering a worldwide liner service. It began a New York service in 1920 but operated at a deficit. In 1930 OSK made a huge investment in five new high-speed motor ships in order to start a New York express service. This service entirely transformed raw-silk transportation from Asia to America; raw silk began to be carried by water all the way to New York instead of going by land. OSK's share of cargo shipped on this route grew, and its business performance improved in spite of unfavorable business conditions. During the Depression, OSK and NYK made a cooperative agreement in 1931 whereby OSK abolished its Puget Sound route, which had called at Tacoma and Seattle, and in turn acquired a monopoly on the South American east coast route. OSK quickly recovered from the deficits of 1930 and 1931, and resumed paying dividends in 1932. The company's profits peaked in 1941, when OSK was capitalized at ¥87 million and had 112 vessels aggregating 557,126 grt.

During the war OSK, like other Japanese shipping companies, was forced to be a mere shipowner. When the war ended it had only 55 vessels left, totaling 143,976 grt, most of which were so-called wartime standard ships, of poor quality. All ships were under control of the Allied powers through the Civilian Merchant Marine Committee. In 1950, however, OSK returned to global service. By the end of 1957 the company had almost recovered the sailing rights it had been given by the FEFC before the war, and was making 18 voyages per month on 13 overseas liner routes. Competition was far more intense than before the war, as anyone who had money could construct ships under the government-sponsored shipbuilding program, started in 1947. Before the war, conference members had sought to exclude newcomers. OSK constructed 38 ships under the program. In 1953 OSK established an eastbound route to South America to transport emigrants from Japan. At first the service was profitable, but the number of emigrants fell to below 2,000 per year in 1962. In 1963 OSK established the Japan Emigration Ship Co., Ltd. (JES) to hive off this lossmaking business. Later, JES was reorganized into Mitsui OSK Passenger Co., Ltd. In this period most of OSK's businesses were lossmaking. In 1964 it owned 41 vessels totaling 376,539 grt. The company was capitalized at ¥7.6 billion and its debts totaled approximately ¥34.9 billion.

Mitsui Line was originally the shipping department of the trading company Mitsui Bussan Kaisha. Mitsui Bussan was established in 1876 and obtained exclusive rights to export and market the coal mined at the state-run Miike mines. It chartered boats and transported coal on its own account. In 1878 it bought a steamship, and in 1888 it bought the mines. Mitsui Bussan became an industrial carrier and the shipping section was established in 1898. The section expanded to become the Shipping Department and moved to Kobe in 1904. The company then owned 9 ships aggregating 36,752 dwt, and on the eve of World War I the fleet totaled 15 ships with 74,635 dwt, increasing to 30 ships totaling 127,141 dwt in 1919. The third general manager, Teijiro Kawamura, expanded the business of the department during World War I; in 1914 it began a tramp service carrying the company's own cargo and that of other companies. In 1917 it constructed a shipyard and set up the shipbuilding department and in 1920 it opened a semi-liner service from Dalien via Kobe to Seattle, whereby a liner service operated on outbound voyages but on the return voyage, owing to insufficient cargo at Seattle, ships had to stop and collect cargo at other ports.

Mitsui Bussan's Shipping Department built two sister ships in 1924. One was equipped with reciprocal oil-burners, the other had diesel engines and was the first oceangoing diesel ship in Japan. The department put these ships on the North American route and compared their performance. *Akagisan Maru*, the diesel ship, proved superior, and Mitsui concluded a manufacturing and marketing license agreement with Burmeister and Wain Co. (B&W), who had manufactured the engine, in 1926. In 1928 Mitsui opened a Bangkok route, in 1931 a Philippines route, in 1932 a Dalien to New York route, and in 1935 a Persian Gulf route. From 1933 the Shipping Department became known as Mitsui Line. In 1937 it owned 35 ships aggregating 227,044 dwt. The shipbuilding department was separated off as the Mitsui Tama Shipyard in 1937, and in 1942 the former Shipping Department too became a separate company, Mitsui Steamship Co., Ltd. (MS). It was capitalized at ¥50 million, and Takaharu Mitsui was elected chairman.

During World War II, and after the war, all MS ships were under the control of the government. When Japan lost the war in 1945, only 17 of MS's vessels were left, increasing to 22 vessels totaling 77,459 dwt when MS re-acquired operations that had previously been chartered out to the Civilian Merchant Marine Committee (CMMC). MS then began a vigorous expansion of its fleet and routes to re-establish its prewar network, and went so far as to apply to the FEFC. When its application was rejected, MS placed outsider—non-conference-member—ships on this route in 1953. After a long struggle, the conference attempted to resolve the issue politically and the British ambassador openly criticized Japan's shipping policies in 1955. Japan joined the General Agreement on Tariffs and Trade (GATT) the same year, and Japan's minister of transport was anxious to settle the issue without dispute. The final proposal of the conference, through the mediation of the minister of transport, contained extremely harsh conditions which MS had to accept, one of which was that MS could only join the FEFC if it operated under the management of NYK for several years. The 39-month battle was over, and MS began placing ships under the auspice of NYK in 1956. Five years later, MS at last joined the conference.

MS constructed 38 vessels between 1950 and its merger with OSK in 1964, and its operating tonnage was the largest in Japan. One of its ships, *Kinkasan Maru*, was the first bridge-controlled ship in the world. MS planned to rationalize its crews and at the same time improve the working conditions of engineers. It cooperated with Mitsui Shipbuilding & Engineering Co., a direct successor of Mitsui Tama Shipyard, and designed innovatory bridge-controlled ships. The *Kinkasan Maru* was delivered in 1961 and MS placed it, along with another bridge-controlled ship, on the New York route, which was re-opened in 1951. Besides the New York route, MS operated westbound and eastbound routes around the world, a Central and South America route, a west Africa route, and a Great Lakes route. In 1964 MS owned 45 vessels aggregating 737,098 dwt. However, MS's performance was disappointing from 1950 until the OSK merger in 1964, when it was capitalized at ¥5.5 billion and had debts of ¥26.7 billion.

Soon after the shipping industry reorganization of 1964, in which Japanese shipping companies were restructured into six groups, world shipping moved toward containerization. Mitsui O.S.K. Lines, Ltd. (MOL), formed by the merger of OSK and MS, began container services on the California route, joining a space-charter consortium of four Japanese operators. The first container ship, MOL's *America Maru*, sailed from Kobe to San Francisco in October 1969. Containerization spread to other routes, including the Australia route, with NYK and Yamashita-Shinnihon Steamship Co., in 1970; the north Pacific route, with five other Japanese companies, in 1971; and the Europe route, as part of the TRIO Group consisting of MOL, Nippon Yusen Kaisha, Overseas Container Lines, Ben Line, and Hapag-Lloyd, in 1971. On the New York route and Mediterranean routes a container service began in 1972.

The other trend was toward specialization. Both OSK and MS had ore carriers, and after the merger MOL held the largest share of the Japanese ore market. The *Yachiyosan Maru*, at 123,800 dwt, built in 1970 under a cargo guarantee from Nippon Steel Corporation, was the largest ore carrier in Japan at that time. MOL built *Oppama Maru*, the first car carrier in Japan, in 1965 under cargo guarantee from Nissan Motor Company. MOL could not carry cars at a low freight rate because it had to stick to the conference rate. Nissan therefore established the Nissan Motor Car Carrier Co. in 1970 to operate the *Oppama Maru* and transport its cars. Based on this model, MOL and Honda Motor Co. established the Act Maritime Co. in 1973 to carry Honda cars to the United States.

Business results improved after the merger, and the loss brought forward was written off in 1966. The company was recapitalized at ¥20 billion in 1968, and at ¥30 billion in 1972. The owned fleet increased to 152 vessels, totaling 6.6 million dwt in 1974, and the operating fleet—owned vessels and time-chartered vessels—numbered 291 vessels, totaling 10 million dwt.

The U.S. gold embargo in 1971 and the advent of a floating world monetary system was a severe blow for MOL. It changed its financial strategy, keeping more funds in U.S. dollars and in other currencies. More serious was the 1973 oil crisis. MOL immediately canceled tankers under construction and recorded its best business performance since the merger; freight revenue topped ¥327.5 billion. Soon afterward, however, results deteriorated rapidly and the downslide continued until 1978. MOL made great efforts to curtail costs, and simultaneously increased the size and number of container ships. Containerization increased on routes between industrially advanced and developing countries, and huge investment was needed to finance this expansion. The development of intermodal transportation on the North America route also began, and MOL introduced a Mini Land Bridge (MLB) service in 1972, using rail transport as well as shipping to reduce transit time, to compete with the U.S. shipping company Sea-Land, extending the service to IPI (Interior Point Intermodal) service in 1980. Around the time that the MLB service started, the world trade structure began to change and in 1979 about 60% of general cargo from Asia to the United States came to be loaded at newly industrialized countries (NICs). MOL reorganized its routes, changing its starting ports for U.S. voyages from Japan to Hong Kong, Taiwan, and other NICs, while shipping companies in the newly industrialized countries captured this new demand and branched out into the

Pacific routes. The competition in sea transportation increased and MOL began a direct container service between the Far East and the west coast of North America in 1982. MOL invested huge capital to consolidate these services and to establish a service network in the United States.

As a countermeasure against rising oil costs MOL built energy-efficient ships, cooperating with Mitsui Engineering & Shipbuilding. *Awobasan Maru*, delivered in 1981, was the first ship incorporating innovations that reduced fuel consumption by 30%. In 1974 MOL established the Saudi Arabian Shipping Co., Ltd. (SASCO) and Arabian Marine Operation Co. Ltd. (AMOCO) as joint ventures with the prince of Saudi Arabia in Jeddah. SASCO is the shipowner, while AMOCO manages tanker operations. MOL hoped that this joint venture would give it an advantageous status in any future nationalization of oil, but at first the performance of these companies was not good, and AMOCO acquired the rights to bunker supply in 1977. Two years later the second oil crisis occurred and MOL was able to get a stable bunker supply.

Personnel expenses increased after the first oil crisis, and the yen was revalued. These changes hit MOL heavily as a large part of its income was in U.S. dollars. To make itself more competitive, MOL reduced the number of its own vessels and increased the number of flag of convenience (FOC) ships; its own ships fell in number from 127 in 1975 to 82 in 1982, and the number of employees at sea from 3,127 to 2,233, while freight revenue increased from ¥282 billion to ¥476 billion over the same period. MOL also built highly rationalized ships in cooperation with MES, which would require a crew of only 18, the minimum number accepted by the Seamen's Act, while other ships required 22 or 24. The first super-advanced ship was the *Canberra Maru*, delivered in 1979, which was put on the Australia route.

In 1970 MOL established Mitsui OSK Passenger Co., Ltd. (MOP), with the reorganization of JES. MOP has three passenger ships. The company was the only one in Japan to operate an oceangoing passenger service at that time, but later in the 1990s a few Japanese shipping companies entered this market to cope with the boom in traveling by sea.

In 1984 the Maritime Act of the United States was revised and the mandatory independent action clause was introduced. This gave shipping companies the right to introduce a discount tariff if registered at the Federal Maritime Commission. The conferences on North American routes became extremely weak and freight rates on the routes dropped sharply. Every route between the Far East and the United States made losses and MOL's business performance deteriorated again. Once more, MOL worked hard to curtail expenses and establish greater competitiveness on these routes. In the same year it decided to enlarge its container terminal facilities at Los Angeles, and also installed its own container terminals at Asian ports, including Kaohsiung.

MOL also made great efforts to reorganize operations on the Pacific routes, dissolving the consortium of six Japanese companies. In 1985 it began a two-company consortium with Kawasaki Steamship's K Line service (KL) on the Japan/Pacific southwest route, and with East Asiatic Co. (EAC) on the Far East/Pacific southwest route. It also decided to start a three-company consortium with KL and EAC on the Pacific northwest route. On each route it began a weekly service with newly built large container ships. The first such ship, *Asian Venture*, was an FOC ship at 1,960 20 feet equivalent unit (TEU), indicating the number of containers loaded, and the main ships placed on this route became FOC ships after they were launched in 1984. Moreover, MOL began operating a double stack train service between Los Angeles, Chicago, and Columbus, Ohio in 1985 and extended it to New York in the following year.

The New York route became the most competitive because of this trend toward intermodal forms of transport. NYK, Yamashita-Shinnihon Steamship Co.—later merged with Japan Line to establish Nippon Liner Systems for liner business and Navix Lines for tramp business—and MOL began a joint operation service in 1986 and put on it six high-speed large vessels including MOL's Alligator series ships. To improve services, MOL introduced a computer booking system in 1984 and enlarged its online system to cover the United States and the Far East in 1986. This route, however, became lossmaking after 1986, seriously affecting the company's performance; MOL did not pay dividends between 1987 and 1989.

In 1983 the import of liquefied natural gas (LNG) on Free on Board (FOB) conditions began as part of the diversification of Japan's energy resources, and MOL, NYK, Kawasaki Steamship, Chubu Electric Power Company, Incorporated and other Japanese electricity and gas companies jointly established two specialized companies, Badak LNG Transport Inc. and Arun, to transport LNG from Indonesia. These two companies operated seven LNG ships, constructed by MOL and other shipping companies. MOL also took delivery in 1983 of the *Kohzan Maru*, Japan's first large-sized methanol carrier, and transported methanol from Saudi Arabia to Japan. Japan's exports of industrial plant grew at that time and modularization began. MOL was interested in the transportation of massive plants and took delivery of five specialized ships, including the *Atlas Maru*, equipped with a 600-ton capacity derrick, one of the largest in the world. Plant exports began to decline in the late 1980s and these special ships were mostly sold or changed their flags.

MOL's financial activities became more international after the first oil crisis. The company issued corporate debentures and warrant bonds on the Swiss capital market. Shareholders' equity was ¥57.36 billion, and net income ¥5.94 billion in 1991. In the same year, the number of directly owned vessels was 54, aggregating 4.15 million dwt, and there were 296 operating vessels, aggregating 13.43 million dwt.

Principal Subsidiaries: International Energy Transport Co., Ltd. (45%); International Marine Transport Co., Ltd. (58%); Mitsui OSK Passenger Line Co., Ltd. (51%); M.O. Seaways, Ltd. (99%); International Container Terminal (92%); The Shosen Koun (62%); Trans Pacific Container Service (90%); Japan Express Co., Ltd. (Kobe) (86%); Japan Express Co., Ltd. (Yokohama) (81%); Blue Highway Line (25.4%); Kusakabe Steamship Co., Ltd. (80%); Mitsui OSK Kogyo Kaisha, Ltd. (79%); Euromol B.V. (100%); MOL International S.A. (100%); Orange Finance Ltd. (100%); Arabian Marine Bunker Sales Co., Ltd. (90%).

Further Reading: Tatsuki, Mariko and Goshi Yamamoto, *The First Century of Mitsui O.S.K. Lines, Ltd.*, Tokyo, Mitsui O.S.K.

Lines, 1985; Nakagawa, Keiichiro, Tomohei Chida et. al., *Sogyo Hyakunen-shi*, Tokyo, Mitsui O.S.K. Lines, 1985.

—Mariko Tatsuki

⊕ **NIPPON EXPRESS**

NIPPON EXPRESS CO., LTD.

12-9, Sotokanda 3-chome
Chiyoda-ku
Tokyo 101
Japan
(03) 3253 1111
Fax: (03) 3257 1648

Public Company
Incorporated: 1937
Employees: 50,377
Sales: ¥1.52 trillion (US$12.18 billion)
Stock Exchanges: Tokyo Osaka Nagoya

Nippon Express Co., Ltd. is Japan's leading general transportation company. It is also one of the largest and most diverse operations of its kind in the world.

Nittsu, as it is familiarly called, is best known as a freight forwarder, an agent that arranges the shipment of goods, using the optimal combination of road, rail, air, and sea, and that takes care of all administration, including customs clearance. The company assumes full responsibility for the door-to-door, worldwide delivery of all types of goods, from electronic components, through fine art and household effects, to plant for oil refineries.

As well as subcontracting the services of other carriers, Nippon Express undertakes freight carriage, especially trucking and marine transportation, on its own account. Nippon Express is familiar to Japanese householders for the "Pelican" parcel delivery service, its vans and personnel instantly recognizable by the logo of a white pelican on a yellow background. Aside from its distribution business, the company has diversified into related fields including warehousing, tourism, plant installation, and packaging.

The name "Nippon Express" was first used in 1937, but the company's immediate antecedents date from the 19th century, and it can trace the origins of its express courier business back centuries before that. Several other strands of business, such as tourism and marine transportation, figured in the company's distant past, then disappeared, only to reappear in the late 20th century.

Messenger services existed in Japan from the seventh century A.D. onward, but the service evolved greatly during the period when, for two and a half centuries, from the year 1600 onward, Japan was ruled by shoguns of the house of Tokugawa. The shogun, officially the emperor's deputy, effectively governed with the aid of a handful of counselors and a quasi-feudal network of samurai. After many centuries of civil war, the relative peace of the first years of Tokugawa rule encouraged a surge of economic growth. Because the country's ruling class was centered on the shogun's capital of Edo (now Tokyo), whereas the commercial center was Osaka, more than two hundred miles away, the growth of commerce stimulated the rapid development of transportation systems.

The first Tokugawa shogun, Ieyasu, set up a system of staged or relay courier services: men and horses were kept on hand at staging posts, or occasionally requisitioned from convenient villages, for the use of noble travelers and those carrying their property and mail. A number of commercial horseback express messenger services flourished. These services multiplied between about 1800 and 1868, the last years of the Tokugawa regime, which were, like its first years, associated with a resurgence of commercial growth.

The shoguns kept Japan isolated from the outside world, but the country was becoming irresistible to the West, both as a trading partner and as a port of call where ships could take on fuel and provisions. In 1854 Commodore Matthew Perry of the United States secured the first of a series of treaties which were to open up Japan to international commerce. Contact with the outside world contributed to the destabilization of the Tokugawa regime, which fell in 1868, when the Meiji Restoration assigned to the emperor the administrative power that the shoguns had appropriated.

The Meiji government undertook a radical modernization of the Japanese economy. The Postal Service Law of 1871 inaugurated a national mail system. The messenger services found themselves unable to compete with the government's 3,000 offices, which soon offered a telegraph service alongside the conventional post.

Sosuke Sasaki was the manager of Izumiya, the most powerful of the express messenger companies; Sasaki also acted as a trade representative. Aware of the nature of modern postal services, he bowed to the inevitable. After consultation between Sasaki and Hisoka Maejima, the minister for the postal service, it was agreed that the express messenger services would cede their business to the official mail and would switch instead to bulk freight transportation. They would be rewarded with an exclusive contract for the government's own haulage requirements.

Accordingly, in 1872 the former courier suppliers joined to form the Riku-un Moto Kaisha, or General Land Transportation Company, under the presidency of former Izumiya head Jinbei Yoshimura and the vice presidency of Sosuke Sasaki. The new enterprise, launched with capital of ¥50,000, was Japan's first joint-stock transportation company. It was to form the backbone of the company later known as Nippon Express. Riku-un Moto Kaisha operated through a number of small Riku-un Kaisha (Land Transportation) companies, each corresponding with one of the old relay stages. This organizational structure was overhauled in 1875, when the small Riku-un Kaisha companies were abolished and the parent company, with its 2,000 employees, was renamed Naikoku Tsu-un Kabushiki Kaisha, the Domestic Express Company.

As Riku-un Moto Kaisha, the company had started a horse-drawn freight carting service between Tokyo and Odawara in 1874. Shortly afterwards the route was extended to Kyoto and Atsuta. At the end of the 1870s the service started to carry passengers as well as freight. Although the road service was temporarily supplanted by the coming of railways in the late 19th century, in the late 20th century road freight was once again the most important component of Nippon Express's business.

The year of the company's inauguration, 1872, had also seen the opening of Japan's first railway service. In 1873, the trains began to accept freight, and by 1875 Naikoku Tsu-un Kaisha was handling rail freight, transporting it between sender and station at one end and between station and recipient at the other. With the expansion of the railway network over the following two decades, railway cargo became a major source of revenue.

As Naikoku Tsu-un Kaisha, the company began to operate river freight transport services in 1876. A paddle steamer was acquired the following year, the first to be put to civil use in Japan. River transportation declined in importance with the appearance of motorized road transport and the expansion of the railways. But once again, the wheel has come full circle: in 1990 containerized shipping and other marine transport earned Nippon Express almost ¥120 billion.

Naikoku Tsu-un Kaisha entered the motorized road transport business in 1911 with the purchase of four trucks for the carriage of imperial mail. Their white-liveried drivers confined their activities to the driving of the trucks; loading and unloading them was too menial a task.

The spread of railways and motor vehicles at a time of rapid growth in industrialization and trade attracted new entrants into the express transportation business. By 1910 there were 5,000 competitors; by 1919 the number had almost doubled. This made for an overcrowded market at a time when Japan, in common with most of the developed world, was suffering from the severe economic slump that followed World War I. In 1923 an earthquake devastated Tokyo, after which scarce funds had to go into reconstruction, with further adverse economic effects. The Japanese economy's response to the doldrums of the 1920s was to rationalize. In harmony with this tendency, the government decided to reduce the number of competitors in the transportation business. In 1928 Naikoku Tsu-un Kaisha merged with its two main competitors, Nihon Un-so Kaisha and Meiji Un-so Kaisha.

The resultant joint-stock company, named Kokusai Tsu-un (International Express), engaged in both domestic and international freighting, and was the immediate predecessor of Nippon Express. At war with China during the late 1930s, the Japanese government was actively managing the economy in the national interest; under the new Express Business Law and the Nippon Express Co. Ltd. Law, Kokusai Tsu-un was dissolved and its business taken over by Nippon Express, which came into being on October 1, 1937, and was 53% government-owned.

After World War II the Allied forces occupying Japan considered that too much of the country's economic power was concentrated in too few hands. Among other initiatives, they threatened to break up Nippon Express, whose market strength was contrary to the provisions of the Law for Decentralization of Excessive Economic Power. In the end, however, the company was not abolished but was privatized; in February 1950 it began to operate as a private enterprise.

During the postwar years Nippon Express embarked on a series of measures that equipped it to share in and to contrib-

ute to Japan's economic boom. These measures changed both the way the company was run and the nature of its business. Nippon Express was among the earliest companies to adopt a decentralized management structure, delegating a high degree of financial autonomy to its divisions. It also gradually reduced its focus on the handling of rail freight, hitherto its most important activity, and diversified into other forms of transport and into completely new business areas.

One of the earliest diversifications came in 1949, when the company began to engage in international air freight forwarding, acting as cargo sales agent for various international airlines. This new enterprise received the stamp of International Air Transport Association approval in 1953. Air transportation proved a profitable area. In 1990 the magazine *Business Japan* interviewed Nippon Express's vice president Kiyosumi Hosokawa, who was also chairman of the International Air Express Association of Japan and the International Airfreight Forwarders' Association of Japan. He said that the air freight business could look back on three decades of steady growth, interrupted only by the two oil crises. He added that "the air freight growth rate is far higher than Japan's economic growth rate."

Another landmark was 1955, the year Nippon Express became an authorized travel agent. In doing so, it was returning to a business in which it had dabbled 80 years before, as a sideline to its horse-drawn haulage service: Sosuke Sasaki had founded an association of inns approved for use by his messengers, and soon the company had begun to act as a travel agency, offering a room-booking service to the public. This side of the business had atrophied with the coming of the railways. This time the emphasis was on arranging package tours of Japan, and also on assisting the Japanese with foreign travel. In the two decades from their launch in 1968, more than three million people would buy the "Look" packages catering to Japanese tourists abroad.

The late 1950s and the 1960s were a time of phenomenal expansion for the Japanese economy. Between 1960 and 1970, a year-on-year growth rate of about 13% was sustained. Foreign trade, too, was increasing dramatically: during the same years, imports multiplied in value by a factor of four, and exports by a factor of five. In order to be able to play its part in the internationalization of Japanese industry, Nippon Express embarked on the construction of a network of overseas offices that eventually spanned five continents. The process began in 1958 with the inauguration of a representative office in New York. The year 1962 saw the establishment of a New York subsidiary, which by 1991 had a chain of 97 U.S. offices with 1,808 employees.

During the 1960s the marine transportation industry was revolutionized by the advent of containerization. Since the early years of the 20th century, road and rail freight had been packed in large, tough boxes, which rendered loading and unloading more efficient and reduced the risk of loss or damage. In the 1960s container ships, able to use the same type of boxes, began to be built. The adoption of standard-size containers, which can be loaded on ship, truck, or train, facilitates intermodal transport, where the forwarder is able to combine different modes of transport to get the most cost-effective package. For example, in shipping to Brazil from Japan, Nippon Express sends containers by sea to Seattle, then trucks the containers to Miami, before transferring the goods to airplanes for the last stage of the journey.

Nippon Express was quick to see the advantages of containerization. As well as using the scheduled services of other shipping companies to carry its containers around the coasts of Japan, Nippon Express acquired ships of its own. In 1973 it bought its first container vessel, the *Acacia Maru,* and launched a cargo service between Tokyo and Tomakomai.

International container services, too, became an important source of business for Nippon Express, attracting both Japanese and overseas customers. Germany is one of the most important markets for Far Eastern container traffic; in 1991 Nippon Express (Deutschland) reported that it obtained only half its revenue from Japanese companies; the rest came from German companies buying from and selling into Japan. In the 1990s sea transportation by container vessel will have become one of Nippon Express's most rapidly growing services.

During the 1970s Nippon Express became a highly diversified business. Plant transportation and installation was one new venture. As early as 1966, the company had become involved with the transportation and installation of petrochemical equipment, which had begun in 1966 with its participation in the construction of a Peru oil refinery. The year 1977 marked the start of Nippon Express's involvement in a major petrochemical construction project in Iran. This project was cut short by Iran's internal upheavals a couple of years later.

The 1970s and 1980s were a period of continued expansion for Nippon Express's overseas activities. Subsidiaries opened in Singapore in 1973; the Netherlands in 1977; Hong Kong and Brazil in 1979; the United Kingdom and West Germany in 1981; Saudi Arabia, Belgium, and Canada in 1983; Malaysia in 1984; Australia and France in 1985; and Italy in 1986.

Also during the 1970s and 1980s a new market known as *takuhaibin,* the parcel delivery service, was opening up in Japan. Domestic or international door-to-door delivery of documents and small packages was provided, with a guaranteed delivery deadline. This service was originally a U.S. import, introduced by DHL Corporation, which established DHL Japan in 1979. Once launched in Japan, it was a runaway success, both with consumers and with the business community that needed to exchange items such as contracts and product samples with minimal delay. The profile of Japan's industrial output was changing to include less heavy industry and more high-technology products; for carrying such fragile, relatively low-volume loads, the express parcel service was ideal.

Nippon Express was soon a leader in the parcel delivery market, with its Pelican services, aimed at deliveries to the private individual, and Arrow services for company-to-company deliveries. In 1990 Nippon Express was second only to Yamato in the Japanese parcel delivery market, and whereas this was 41% of Yamato's business, it represented only 28% of Nippon Express's.

Nippon Express had one massive advantage, both in parcel deliveries and other types of international transportation. Whereas other carriers set up links with foreign companies, Nippon Express had its own overseas representation. This consisted in 1990 of 31 overseas affiliates and 16 representative offices. It had 366,000 square meters of overseas warehouse space in addition to its 2 million square meters inside Japan.

To manage this vast network in the most efficient way possible, and speed the decision-making process, in 1990 the company grouped its overseas branches and affiliates under three regional supervisory bodies. Nippon Express U.S.A., Inc.

was responsible for North and South America, Nippon Express (U.K.) Ltd. took charge of Europe, and Nippon Express (H.K.) Co., Ltd. covered Southeast Asia and Oceania.

Nippon Express looks set to maintain the competitive edge that its extensive international network gives it. September 1990 saw it entering the Mexican freight market ahead of its Japanese competitors with the launch of Nippon Express de Mexico. In April 1991 it opened a new trucking service between Singapore and Malaysia.

A key component of Nippon Express's integration is the efficient communication of information. Through the late 1980s the company was engaged in establishing an on-line data network to connect all its offices, enabling it to track individual cargo items across the world. Its communications expertise enabled it to engage in several new specializations, for example just-in-time (JIT) deliveries. JIT is a manufacturing method whereby parts are brought to the shop floor from a remote warehouse at the moment they are needed, in order to minimize on-site stock holding. In 1989 Nippon Express's U.S. information networks enabled it to start NEX Transport Inc., to supply JIT services to Japanese automobile manufacturers operating in Ohio.

The company is continuing to invest in new ventures, at home and overseas. In December 1990 it announced that it was about to set up an air cargo company, the Japan Universal System Transport Co. Ltd., as a joint venture with Japan Airlines Co. Ltd. and the Yamato Transport Co. Ltd. In March 1991 Nippon Express made public another new venture, the Dalian Nittsu Container Manufacturing Company, which would manufacture shipping containers in Dalian, China.

In an economy that is a byword for dynamism, Nippon Express is one of the most successful and fastest growing companies of all; in June 1991, *Tokyo Business Today* ranked it Japan's 127th most profitable company, a position to which it had climbed from 164th the year before, with a 50% growth in declared income.

Even the Japanese economy had its difficulties, however. A labor shortage was pushing up costs, and in August 1990 Nippon Express and other leaders of the transportation industry applied to the Japanese Ministry of Transport for permission to raise tariffs for regular delivery routes for the first time in five years. At the same time chartered delivery prices were raised. Such price adjustments enabled the company to sustain its profitability despite the rising costs.

Automation was one response to a labor shortage, and in March 1991 the company announced that it was about to install a new information network to manage its two million railway containers. Also in 1991 it announced plans to invest ¥540 million in modernizing its international telecommunications network.

In June 1991 Shoichiro Hamanaka succeeded Takeshi Nagaoka as president. Hamanaka, who has been with the company since 1954, had previously been in charge of the Sendai branch and of the general affairs and labor management divisions.

Nippon Express approaches the millenium under the threat of increased competition in its domestic distribution business, which the Japanese government is taking steps to deregulate. To deal with this competition it plans to rely on accurate market research and an ever-improving quality of service to its customers. Overseas, it is preparing for the single European market and the opening up of Eastern Europe, developing its

European trucking network and improving its warehousing facilities. By increasing its representation in China and building a Chinese transport network, it is preparing for the increased trade that is expected to ensue from the reversion of Hong Kong to Chinese rule in 1997. Adept at anticipating the wishes of its customers, actual and potential, Nippon Express is the last company to miss such opportunities.

Principal Subsidiaries: Nittsu Shoji Co., Ltd.; Nippon Truck Co., Ltd.; Nittsu Real Estate Co., Ltd., Nippon Shipping Co., Ltd., Bingo Express Co., Ltd.; Nittsu Driving School; Sakai Minato Kairiku Unso Co., Ltd.; Tokushima Express Co., Ltd.; Niigata Chuo Unso Co., Ltd.; Tohoku Truck Co., Ltd.; Shiogamako Unso Co., Ltd.; Sendai Port Silo Co., Ltd.; Nittsu Kicoh Co., Ltd.; North Nippon Shipping Co., Ltd.; Hokuo Unyu Co., Ltd.; Izu Fujimiland Co., Ltd.; Taiyo Nissan Motor Co., Ltd.; Nippon Express U.S.A., Inc.; Nippon Express Travel U.S.A., Inc.; Nippon Express U.S.A. (Ill.), Inc.; Nittsu New York, Inc. (U.S.A.); NEX Transport Inc. (U.S.A.); Nippon Express Hawaii, Inc. (U.S.A.); Nippon Express do Brasil Transportes Internacionais Ltda.; Nippon Express Canada, Ltd.; Nippon Express (U.K.) Ltd.; Nippon Express Tours (Europe) Ltd. (U.K.); Nippon Express (Nederland) B.V.; Nippon Express Euro Cargo B.V. (Netherlands); Nippon Express (Deutschland) GmbH (Germany); Nippon Express (Belgium) N.V./S.A.; Nippon Express Tours (Belgium) S.A.; Nippon Express France, S.A.; Nippon Express Tours France S.A.R.L.; Nippon Express (Italia), S.R.L.; Nippon Express (Schweiz) AG. (Switzerland); Nippon Express de España, S.A. (Spain); Nippon Express (H.K.) Co., Ltd. (Hong Kong); Nippon Express Travel (H.K.) Ltd. (Hong Kong); Nippon Express (Singapore) Pte., Ltd.; Nippon Express (Malaysia) Sdn, Bhd.; Nippon Express (Australia) Pty., Ltd.; Nittsu-Nantai Express Co., Ltd. (Taiwan); Nippon Express (Thailand) Co., Ltd.; Nippon Express (New Zealand) Ltd.

Further Reading: "Historical Materials of Japan's Old-Time Transportation," Tokyo, Nippon Express Co. Ltd. [n.d.]; "General Information on Nippon Express," Tokyo, Nippon Express Co. Ltd, 1987; "Here Come the Just-in-Time Japanese Truckers," *The Economist,* December 5, 1987; "Courier/Small Package Service in the Spotlight," *Quarterly Survey, Japanese Finance and Industry,* Industrial Bank of Japan, No. 71 (1987 III); Eller, David, "Resolved: The Nittsu Enigma," *Containerisation International,* January 1988; Mino, Hokaji, "Courier, Shipping Services Meet the Needs of the Times," *Business Japan,* June 1988; Fujimura, Masanori, "Int'l Air Deliveries Continue Sharp Growth," *Business Japan,* June 1990.

—Alison Classe

NIPPON YUSEN KABUSHIKI KAISHA

Yusen Building
3-2 Marunouchi 2-chome
Chiyoda-ku, Tokyo 100
Japan
(3) 3284-5151
Fax: (3) 3284-6371

Public Company
Incorporated: 1885 as Nippon Yusen Kaisha
Employees: 2,525
Sales: ¥532.71 billion (US$4.27 billion)
Stock Exchanges: Tokyo Osaka Frankfurt

For most of the 20th century Nippon Yusen Kabushiki Kaisha (NYK) was the largest shipping company in Japan. Today, based on a composite index of tonnage owned and operated as well as income from shipping business, it is the world's leading shipping enterprise. NYK provides a full range of shipping services, including regular liners, trampers, tankers, and specialized vessels such as automobile carriers. Historically, its most distinctive characteristic, still strong, has been its leading role in freight conferences or shipping cartels.

The history of NYK's business operations can be divided into four periods. The first marks the company's establishment in 1885 and consolidation over the next decade. In the second, from the mid-1890s to around 1908, the company carried out an initial and rapid expansion of overseas lines. In the third, after the Russo-Japanese War of 1904 to 1905, NYK began to concentrate more exclusively on regular lines within conferences. This was a conservative strategy that lasted until the late 1950s, when the company started a comprehensive series of services, a move which led to the fourth period, one of diversification, that has continued to the present day.

NYK was formed in 1885 through a merger between the shipping assets of Mitsubishi and the Kyodo Unyu Kaisha (KUK) or Union Transport Company. The Mitsubishi firm had been subsidized by the new Meiji government since 1875, while KUK was an amalgam of trading firms, local shipping enterprises, and government investment that had been motivated by Mitsubishi's increasing neglect of shipping in favor of outside investments, mostly in mining. NYK was initially a joint-stock company, with more than three-quarters of the steamships in Japan. It spent its first decade consolidating its finances and fleet under government subsidization and regula-

tion. At first most of its routes were domestic. These became less profitable by the early 1890s because of competition from railways and another shipping firm with regional strength in western Japan, the Osaka Shosen Kaisha (OSK).

There were two main forces behind NYK's expansion in the 1890s. One was the support of the cotton-spinning industry, which enabled NYK to start a line to Bombay in 1893 to import raw cotton. This trade entailed a series of mutual guarantees among the cotton spinners, NYK, and trading firms such as Mitsui Bussan Kaisha, as well as credit to shippers from government-affiliated banks. The second impetus came from greatly increased subsidization made possible by the indemnity Japan received from China after the Sino-Japanese War. This encouraged NYK to establish lines to Australia and Europe, and to Seattle in the United States in 1896. The subsidies were particularly efficacious on the European line, where they gave the company bargaining power to overcome initial opposition from British firms to NYK's entrance into the Far Eastern Freight Conference, which operated between Europe and East Asia. Generally, lines to India could operate with little or no subsidization, whereas the Seattle line was more dependent. In contrast to the plentiful cargo of the outward-bound silk trade, the inward-bound trans-Pacific route was much less profitable because many manufactured goods from the eastern and southern United States went to Japan via the Suez Canal before the Panama Canal was opened. The European line generated about 40% of the company's revenue, and was strong on its eastward run because Japan imported much of its machinery. On the westward run, however, Japanese export freight was insufficient, and NYK came to depend on Chinese goods, which it loaded through feeder services in China, with transshipment at Shanghai.

This pattern of expansion changed after the Russo-Japanese War. Domestic business was hurt by recession and the emergence of many new shipowners that had sprung up with the government's wartime ship purchasing policy. Also, government colonial policy overseas, and hence closer supervision, made feeder lines more problematic, and stricter subsidy legislation encouraged withdrawal from many domestic services and concentration on regular transoceanic lines. This change in strategy occurred in the third period of NYK business. In the years prior to World War I, the company was reluctant to initiate new lines without subsidization unless it had a strong shippers' network. This it had on the Calcutta line, opened in 1911, but it lacked one on a proposed line through Panama, and the silk export trade remained on the northern route through Seattle. For this reason it held back until subsidies were received early in World War I.

Although NYK earned huge profits during World War I, with government controls over freight rates on subsidized lines, the company exploited the war less effectively than many independent Japanese operators, who carried on tramp services outside of government restrictions. The war and its aftermath opened up new lines for the company, to New York via Panama, to Liverpool, and to Hamburg. The central problem of the interwar years was how to operate this more geographically extensive network with steady growth in the face of increased competition from Japanese firms and the emergence of a much larger U.S. fleet.

The most famous strategic response of NYK during these years was its substantial investment in passenger services. In

1926 it purchased the Pacific operations of the Toyo Kisen Kaisha, which ran mostly to San Francisco, and proceeded to build a series of world-class passenger ships. Decades later, long after NYK had withdrawn from the passenger business, the company's popular identity was still associated with these vessels. Despite their popularity, the passenger business did represent a specialized version of the already cautious liner strategy and NYK fell behind OSK in introducing express ships on the New York line in the late 1920s. These ships were fast enough to effect a change in the silk trade, from the rail route via northern Pacific ports to the Panama route. NYK was slow to enter the tramp business also, remaining instead primarily within the conference systems. This presented two additional problems linked to the United States. One was U.S. antitrust law, which forbids exclusionary practices of cartels like the Far Eastern Freight Conference. The second was economic, and emerged through the restructuring of many shipping routes in response to changing demand from U.S. trade and industry. With its cautious strategy NYK had difficulty responding to these changes, and by the eve of World War II it was being seriously challenged by OSK for pre-eminence among Japanese shipping firms.

During World War II NYK lost virtually all of its large oceangoing vessels, and its fleet fell from a peak of 866,000 gross tons in 1941 to 155,000 at the end of the war. Under the restrictive economic policies of the early U.S. occupation of Japan, large shipping firms like NYK had three strikes against them: severe limits on the size of ships—6,000 tons, threats of dissolution under corporate deconcentration programs, and prohibitions against private trade. Nevertheless, in the most general sense, the war and occupation had a leveling effect on all shipping firms, and in the long run allowed NYK to recapture the strategic initiative that had been passing to OSK and others, like Mitsui Bussan's shipping division, before the war.

In the late occupation, the United States began some subsidization through its aid programs, the Korean War effected shipping recovery, and occupation authorities helped Japanese firms re-enter overseas lines and conferences. The event that triggered a transformation in NYK strategy, leading to the fourth period, was known as the "Mitsui Fight." This was a three-year unsuccessful attempt in the mid-1950s by NYK and OSK, in cooperation with European firms, to keep Mitsui Senpaku KK—Mitsui Bussan's former division—out of the Far Eastern Freight Conference. All firms suffered in this struggle, but Mitsui survived because of its strength in the tanker business which had supported it during the competition. This realization led NYK to undertake its strategy of diversification, a move accompanied by a restructuring of its business division into three major services—liners, trampers, and tankers.

It was some time, however, before NYK enjoyed the fruits of this strategic change. The 1950s were a difficult time for all Japanese shipping companies, and NYK operated without profit from 1956 to 1965. Two forms of financial consolidation emerged in the 1960s. First, the government encouraged consolidation in the industry, linking a policy of merger with a commitment to increased subsidization. Under this process, six groups emerged to constitute the core of the industry. NYK merged with Mitsubishi Kaiun KK, a former division within Mitsubishi Corporation, while rivals OSK and Mitsui Senpaku joined to form Mitsui O.S.K. Lines, Ltd. The second form of consolidation was technological. The government aided the

shift to containerization by aiding firms that formed cooperative container groupings known as the space charter system. This was particularly effective on the Pacific. Earlier, NYK had worked with the Matson Navigation Company of San Francisco to introduce containers, and on the European line, along with Mitsui O.S.K., it established a container consortium with British and German firms called the Trio Group.

NYK also pursued its diversification by building tankers for both oil and ores and developing a fleet of car carriers. These promising beginnings, however, were partially offset by a series of shocks in the early 1970s. These included a revaluation of the Japanese yen and a major strike, both of which increased the cost of Japanese shipping. In addition, the oil crisis entailed both a short-term boom and long-term risk; freight conferences were threatened by flag-preference policies of developing countries—the latter shipped goods on the ships of their own countries wherever possible—supported by the United Nations Conference on Trade and Development (UNCTAD); and rate-cutting wars on the Pacific undermined profitability there. During this era of crisis for the shipping industry, NYK displayed remarkable strategic adaptability. Its most decisive move was a partial withdrawal in 1975 from the tanker business, to the point of canceling contracts on some ships already under construction, even though this business was still very profitable. The wisdom of this decision was borne out in the 1980s when several Japanese firms that had continued to pursue the oil tanker boom went bankrupt. Meanwhile, NYK continued to diversify, ordering liquefied natural gas (LNG) tankers and a larger fleet of car carriers to service the growing exports of automobiles to North America. With its still profitable base in conferences systems, these moves gave NYK a balanced business profile that enabled it to remain the largest and generally most profitable Japanese shipping firm into the early 1990s.

During its first half-century, NYK's largest stockholders were the Mitsubishi *zaibatsu*—family-owned enterprise group—and the Imperial Household Ministry, whose shares had been transferred from the Finance Ministry in the late 1880s. Most of the leading managers in the early NYK came from Mitsubishi. During its era of expansion, however, because most of its shippers were outside the Mitsubishi *zaibatsu*, NYK was able to conduct a relatively autonomous management. As a ship purchaser, it also played an important role in the development of Mitsubishi Heavy Industries, Ltd. During the occupation, all *zaibatsu*-related shareholding was broken up and NYK stock became widely dispersed for the next decade. Following the reorganization of the industry in 1964, Mitsubishi firms quickly began to purchase NYK shares so that by the 1970s they controlled about 30%. Likewise, NYK holds substantial shares in numerous Mitsubishi companies and is a full member of the present Mitsubishi Group.

Through its earlier era of expansion NYK had been led by its president, Rempei Kondo. During World War I, however, he began to lose control of the firm as internal disputes arose over capital stock increases and dividend policy, and several executives resigned. After his death in 1921 the company suffered labor problems involving a split between shore and sea employees, and many more executives left. Consequently, over the next decade NYK presidents came from outside the company to restore order. The most important of these was Kenkichi Kagami, the chairman of The Tokio Marine and Fire

Insurance Company, another member of the Mitsubishi *zaibatsu.* Serving from 1929 to 1935, Kagami was known as an economizer and was reluctant to invest in the new express ships for the New York line. Managerially, his key contribution was to promote NYK career managers from within. Since then, all NYK presidents have risen from within the company.

In the postwar period, perhaps the most effective of these presidents was Shojiro Kikuchi—president from 1971 to 1978 and chairman from 1978 to 1984. As a junior executive in the 1950s he played a key role in company strategy, particularly in the era of changes that followed the Mitsui Fight and in the container arrangement with the Matson Line. Something of an intellectual, Kikuchi worked closely with the company's Research Chamber in anticipating long-term changes in the country's industrial structure. This vision gave him the courage in 1975 to override the almost unanimous opposition of his executives and cut back on tanker operations.

NYK has been able to finance some of its new investments from its own capital. This marks a shift from its heavy reliance on subsidies and loans in the 25 years after the occupation. In the early years of its expansion, up to about 1910, NYK's main source of financing was subsidies. Thereafter reserves grew rapidly and they became a key source of funds until the 1920s. After World War I, however, the company allowed money to flow out of the firm in excessive dividends. For the remainder of the interwar years it relied on bonds and loans.

Financially, the major shock to the Japanese shipping industry in the 1980s was the doubling of the value of the yen against the U.S. dollar between 1985 and 1987. Since so much freight is denominated in dollars, this meant a substantial reduction in income. NYK responded to this crisis in three ways: retrenchment, diversification, and broadening of its base in shipping, in which it still holds a comparative advantage. Perhaps the key measure under the retrenchment strategy was to spin off internal functions such as accounting and information systems as new subsidiaries. Between 1987 and 1991 this helped to reduce the number of company employees by 30%. The wide range of the company's diversification is best typified by two firms that began operations in the 1980s. One, Nippon Cargo Airlines, is a joint venture of NYK, several shipping firms, and an airline, and was established to preserve market share in what is increasingly miniaturized cargo. The other, Crystal Cruises, Inc. a wholly owned subsidiary registered in Los Angeles, is NYK's entry into the luxury cruise market.

What profits NYK earned in the first few years after the 1985 to 1987 yen shock came from another form of diversification, financial subsidiaries and other financial investments, not from shipping operations themselves. In the late 1980s, however, increases in freight rates sparked a business recovery in the shipping industry, a trend that NYK itself was well prepared for with its expanded investments in transportation infrastructure. Since its 100th anniversary in 1985, the company

has taken to calling itself a "mega-carrier," a term that symbolizes its global network of multi-modal transport and the broad logistical capability to integrate shippers and cargo movement. Much of this effort has concentrated on new computerized information systems. Business of this sort also is being spun off in the form of new subsidiaries.

One trend that has emerged in 1991, perhaps only in embryonic form, is that the presidents of some of these new subsidiaries, who are themselves former NYK career employees, have been appointed to the company's board of directors. This is a department from the pattern of most of the postwar period, when the board was composed almost exclusively of executives from within NYK itself. These strategies, therefore, may change the company's structure to reflect the broadening base of company operations. Most of these subsidiaries, however, still support shipping itself. This suggests that, in contrast to the pattern of diversification followed by British shipping firms, where shipping operations have shrunk to a small portion of their overall business, NYK is not moving far from its core business of shipping.

Principal Subsidiaries: Shinwa Kaiun (27%); Tokyo Senpaku (37%); Taiheiyo Kaiun (25%); Kyoei Tanker (30%); Yusen Real Estate Corporation; Hikawa Shoji Kaisha (67%); Yusen Air & Sea Service (77%); Yusen Accounting & Finance; NYK Systems Research Institute; NYK International Luxemburg S.A. (Luxembourg); Nippon Cargo Airlines (11%); Crystal Cruises, Inc. (U.S.A.).

Further Reading: Wray, William D., *Mitsubishi and the N.Y.K., 1870-1914: Business Strategy in the Japanese Shipping Industry*, Cambridge, Harvard University Press, 1984; Wray, William D., "NYK and the Commercial Diplomacy of the Far Eastern Freight Conference, 1896-1956," in Yui, Tsunehiko and Keiichiro Nakagawa, eds; *Business History of Shipping: Strategy and Structure,* Tokyo, Tokyo University Press, 1985; *Nippon Yusen Kabushiki Kaisha Hyakunen Shi,* Tokyo, NYK, 1988; Wray, William D., "Kagami Kenkichi and the N.Y.K., 1929-1935: Vertical Control, Horizontal Strategy, and Company Autonomy," in Wray, William D., ed., *Managing Industrial Enterprise: Cases From Japan's Prewar Experience,* Cambridge, Harvard University Press, 1989; Tomohei, Chida, and Peter N. Davies, *The Japanese Shipping and Shipbuilding Industries: A History of Their Modern Growth*, London, The Athlone Press, 1990; Wray, William D., " 'The Mitsui Fight,' 1953-1956: Japan and the Far Eastern Freight Conference," in Fischer, Lewis, and Helge Nordvik, eds, *Shipping and Trade, 1750-1950: Essays in International Maritime Economic History*, Pontefract, Lofthouse Publications, 1990.

—William D. Wray

NORFOLK SOUTHERN CORPORATION

Three Commercial Place
Norfolk, Virginia 23510
U.S.A.
(804) 629-2600
Fax: (804) 629-2822

Public Company
Incorporated: 1980
Employees: 31,968
Sales: $4.62 billion
Stock Exchange: New York

Norfolk Southern Corporation (NS) is a transportation holding company created in 1982 by the merger of Norfolk and Western Railway Company with Southern Railway Company. It operates a rail subsidiary, Norfolk Southern Railway Company, and a motor transportation business, North American Van Lines, Inc., acquired in 1985. The railway company covers 14,000 miles of track in 20 states, making it the fourth largest U.S. rail system. Most of its revenues come from the transportation of coal, coke, and iron ore. The railway's predecessors date back to the 1830s.

Norfolk and Western Railway Company was the result of numerous mergers. It started as a ten-mile line, City Point Railroad, which served two small Virginia towns beginning in 1838. William Mahone orchestrated the company's first mergers. He was elected president of a successor, the Norfolk and Petersburg Railroad (N&P) in 1860. He joined the company in 1853 as chief engineer, and was the innovator of a roadbed through swampland that continues to hold up under the huge tonnages of coal traffic. After the Civil War, N&P linked up with South Side Railroad and Virginia & Tennessee Railroad, forming Atlantic, Mississippi & Ohio Railroad (AM&O). In 1870 this line extended from Norfolk to Bristol, Virginia. The combined railroads were damaged during the war and reconstruction was slow and expensive. One-half of the railroads in the South failed between 1873 and 1880. Mahone borrowed heavily and three years after the crash and financial panic of 1873, the company was put into receivership by its creditors. A private Philadelphia banking firm—E.W. Clark and Company—purchased the AM&O in 1881, changing its name to Norfolk and Western Railroad Company.

A partner in the firm, Frederick Kimball, took charge of Norfolk and Western, merging it with the Shenandoah Valley

Railroad. Kimball's interest in minerals led to lines being built with access to coal deposits, although at this time, the railroad was mainly an agricultural line, cotton being its primary freight. Four years later, the coal handled by Norfolk passed the one-million-ton mark. Within a decade, coal would account for the line's greatest traffic.

Henry Fink became president when the company emerged from bankruptcy in 1896 as Norfolk and Western Railway Company (NW). For the next three decades, NW expanded aggressively. Building through West Virginia, north to Ohio and south to North Carolina, NW established its trademark route. Between 1895 and 1905 railroads across the nation consolidated and improved operations. In 1904 Lucius Johnson became president of NW.

During World War I, traffic was heavy, and equipment condition and upkeep suffered from material shortages. Government control of the railroads took place in 1917, and was relinquished in 1920. For the next ten years, NW consolidated its strength as a coal carrier. The early 1920s saw increased Interstate Commerce Commission (ICC) involvement in the industry and increased union activity. The drive for greater efficiency and reduced costs, as well as the company's coal revenues, helped NW through the Great Depression, but unprofitable branch lines were abandoned, and equipment purchases were delayed.

With the start of World War II, NW rebounded. Traffic volume reached a peak in 1944. Robert H. Smith assumed the presidency in 1946. Between 1945 and 1950, $14 million was spent on improvements. During this same time, diesel locomotives were becoming an indelible presence in the industry. Although NW had great investments in coal burning power and steam engines, the greater economy and efficiency of diesel were decisive; the company ordered its first diesel engines in 1955.

The 1950s were marked by union battles, the abandonment of steam power, and a decline in coal traffic, but growth nonetheless. Stuart Saunders became president in 1958. A lawyer, he stepped up the company's mergers through complicated transactions, beginning with Virginian Railway in 1959. In 1964 NW acquired two rail-ways: Wabash, Nickel Plate, Pittsburgh & West Virginia and Akron, Canton & Youngstown. With this, NW became a Midwestern presence, providing service between the Atlantic, the Great Lakes, and the Mississippi River. Saunders expected expansion to reduce the company's reliance on coal as a revenue source.

Following the flurry of merger activity in the 1960s, the ICC authorized rights to NW in 1971 for portions of the tracks of the Atchison, Topeka & Santa Fe Railway. NW began merger talks with Southern Railway in 1979. The year before the consummation of the NW-Southern merger in 1982, NW acquired the Illinois Terminal Railroad.

Like NW, Southern Railway was the result of many railroad lines combined and reorganized—nearly 150 lines. The earliest of these lines was the South Carolina Canal & Rail Road Company, a nine-mile line chartered in 1827. It was the first regularly scheduled passenger train in the United States in 1830. It was also the first to carry U.S. troops and mail. Within three years, it was 136 miles long, the longest in the world.

Prior to the Civil War, rail expansion crossed the South. By 1857 Charleston, South Carolina, and Memphis, Tennessee, were linked by rail, but growth was stopped by the Civil War. With the devastation of the southern economy and railroads by the war, rebuilding of the industry was slow. Repairs and reorganization took place during the postwar period, and new railroads were built along the Ohio and Mississippi rivers.

Southern Railway (SR) was formed in 1894, when the Richmond & Danville merged with the East Tennessee, Virginia & Georgia Railroad. The company's first president was Samuel Spencer. Its line spread over 4,400 miles, two-thirds of which SR owned. The Alabama Great Southern Railway, and the Georgia Southern and Florida were also under SR's control. Over the span of Spencer's 12-year presidency, SR acquired many more lines and equipment, and revenues went from $17 million to more than $153 million. The company shifted from dependency on tobacco and cotton to more involvement with the South's industrial development. By 1916 SR had an 8,000-mile line over 13 states, establishing its territory for the next half century.

Fairfax Harrison became president in 1913. World War I traffic was substantial but was offset by inflation, and the postwar boom period helped pay for repairs and equipment replacement delayed by the war. In 1922 SR invested $77 million in improvements. The stock market crash of 1929 came two months after SR moved into lavish new headquarters. Many U.S. railroads were forced into bankruptcy in the early 1930s. SR operated at a loss for the first time in 1931, and began amassing debts. The company did not show a profit again until 1936.

Under Ernest Norris, SR recovered, paying its debts to the Reconstruction Finance Corporation in 1941. That same year, SR purchased its first diesel equipment, and World War II began. Wartime traffic led to increased efficiency and safety. By 1951 SR owned a fleet of almost 850 diesel-electric units that drove nearly 92% of its freight service and 86% of its passenger service. SR became the first U.S. railroad to convert entirely to diesel-powered locomotives in 1953, closing the era of the steam locomotive.

SR prospered as a result of dieselization. The southern economy led the nation in growth in the late 1950s. SR took advantage of this growth by acquiring railroads and gaining access to developing industrial areas beginning with the 1952 purchase of the Louisiana-Southern Railway. In 1957 it acquired the Atlantic & North Carolina Railroad and in 1961 the Interstate Railroad, which brought SR to new coal fields in southwest Virginia. In 1963 the Central of Georgia merged with SR.

W. Graham Claytor became president in 1967, instituting the streamlined management and tough budgets that saw the company through the 1974 recession. An unrelated company called Norfolk Southern Railway was acquired in 1974, adding 622 miles of line in an area marked for economic growth. At this time, SR was thriving. There was a 70% increase in revenue between 1974 and 1978. In 1979 Harold Hall became president and later ushered the company through its merger with Norfolk and Western. SR was considered one of the best-managed railroads in the industry. In 1980 the company enjoyed its fifth consecutive year of record profits.

At the time of their merger, both NW and SR were among the most profitable firms in the industry. Between 1971 and 1981, net income at NW had increased fivefold. At SR it had tripled. Prior to merging, both railroads had added many

miles and much time to their transportation routes in order to avoid using each other's tracks; the amount of overlap was small but affected operations significantly. In some cases three days of transportation time was added just to circumvent 10 miles of track operated by the other system. SR operated a 10,000-mile line between Washington D.C.; New Orleans, Louisiana; Cincinnati, Ohio; and St. Louis, Missouri. NW had a 7,000 mile line between Norfolk and Kansas City.

In 1980 Chessie System Inc. and Seaboard Coast Line Industries, Inc. merged forming CSX Corporation. This provided some impetus for the Norfolk Southern merger. Equally compelling was the complementary territories and corporate objectives of NW and SR. Norfolk Southern, incorporated in 1980 and completing its acquisition of the railroads in 1982, became the lowest cost, highest profit corporation in the industry. Merging also made NS the nation's fourth-largest system in terms of track line. Robert Claytor, who had been president of NW, became the first chairman of Norfolk Southern Corporation. Huge assets and conservative investments kept NS sound in 1982, when the steel and coal businesses slowed, but NW's revenues dipped as a result. It was expected that SR's merchandise traffic would help offset NW's coal business if it slowed, and vice versa. Both slumped, however, in the early 1980s.

With an eye toward becoming the country's first integrated transportation company, NS moved to purchase North American Van Lines, Inc., (NAVL) in 1984. The acquisition was completed in 1985. NAVL was known mostly for its household moving, which, however constituted only one-third of its revenues. Other services offered include commercial transport, moving general commodities from manufacturer to distributor; and transporting high-value products such as computers. NAVL was founded in Ohio in 1933, moved to Indiana in 1947, and was purchased by Pepsico in 1968. The purchase of NAVL by NS for $369 million put the recent industry deregulation policy of the ICC to the test. NS became the dominant railroad in trucking, developing a transportation system that provided both motor carrier and rail service.

In the mid-1980s, NS aggressively pursued the purchase of Consolidated Rail Corporation (Conrail) from the U.S. government. Conrail was founded in 1976 from six bankrupt northwestern railroads and subsequently became profitable. The purchase would have made NS the nation's largest railroad, but after several years of negotiations, it fell through. The unsuccessful bid to take over Conrail, however, resulted in 1986 in a profitable cooperation between the two companies, including an interchange agreement that allowed by NS and Conrail to offer competitive services over the same areas.

In the mid-1980s, NS's principal revenue-producing commodities, besides fuel, were paper, chemicals, and automobiles. In 1985 NS had revenues of $3.8 billion and was the most profitable railroad in the nation. In 1987 Arnold McKinnon succeeded Robert Claytor as CEO and chairman, and Harold Hall became vice chairman.

The company further profited from its investments in Santa Fe Southern Pacific and Piedmont Aviation, both of which it sold later at huge profits. By 1988 coal and merchandise traffic began to increase after a long slump. McKinnon worked on cutting costs and smoothing the way for increased intermodal traffic, traffic that shifts easily between railroad and highway. Only 6% of NS's business in 1988, intermodal traffic posed great growth potential.

With the recession in 1989, automobile and steel industries suffered, as did housing, and therefore lumber shipments and coal. The decline in industrial freight shipments hit railroads hard. NS's revenues were down by about 3% because of traffic declines early in 1989. At the same time fuel prices and insurance costs rose.

While heavy freight and merchandise revenues remained lower in 1990, increased shipments of coal, coke, and iron ore helped the company offset losses. Profits dipped in 1990, the result of higher fuel costs and the expense of employee layoffs and early retirements. At the end of 1990, NS restructured its rail operations, changing Southern Railway's name to Norfolk Southern Railway Company, and transferring ownership of Norfolk and Western to it.

Principal Subsidiaries: Atlantic Investment Co.; Lamberts Point Barge Co.; Norfolk Southern Railway Company; Norfolk Southern Properties, Inc.; North American Van Lines, Inc.; NS Fiber Optics Inc.; NS Transportation Brokerage Corp.; NW Equipment Corp.; Pocahontas Development Corp.; Pocahontas Land Corp.; Triple Crown Services, Inc.

Further Reading: Striplin, E.F. Pat, *The Norfolk & Western: A History,* Norfolk, Virginia, The Norfolk & Western Railway Company, 1981; Davis, Burke, *The Southern Railway: Road of the Innovators,* Chapel Hill, University of North Carolina Press, 1985; "Our Corporate History," Norfolk, Virginia, Norfolk Southern Corporation, [n.d.].

—Carol I. Keeley

ODAKYU ELECTRIC RAILWAY COMPANY LIMITED

1-8-3 Nishishinjuku
Shinjuku-ku
Tokyo 160
Japan
(03) 3349-2291
Fax: (03) 3349-2140

Public Company
Incorporated: 1922 as Odawara Express Railway Co., Ltd.
Employees: 3,967
Sales: ¥135 billion (US$1.08 million)
Stock Exchange: Tokyo

Odakyu Electric Railway Company Limited (Odakyu) is one of the major private railroad companies in Japan. The core of the company's operations is the Odakyu Line which connects Shinjuku Station—the busiest station in Japan, with approximately three million passengers per day—with Fuji-Hakone National Park, which lies at the foot of Mount Fuji, and also with Shonan, Japan's most famous seaside resort. Odakyu is at the core of a group of 107 subsidiaries and affiliates with 27,354 employees.

Japanese society is increasingly concentrated in large cities and centered around railroad stations. The rapid growth of the Japanese economy has accelerated the trend, and there is continuing demand for space in or within easy access of a city, for residential and business purposes.

As Tsutomu Shimizu, one of Odakyu's top executives, puts it, "Just as the ancient civilizations flourished in the basins of big rivers, modern civilization develops alongside railways." Private railroad companies in Japan usually build their railroads on undeveloped and unused sites with easy access to city centers, and construct supermarkets and department stores in the station buildings, thus establishing their stations as centers for distribution and commercial activities. Railroad companies acquire massive amounts of land around their stations, and diversify into businesses such as real estate, construction, leisure and tourism, and information services.

Tsurumatsu Toshimitsu, the founder of Odakyu, was a lawyer and then a member of the National Diet before he became involved in the management of the railroad business. He founded the Kinugawa Hydro-Electric Co., Ltd. in 1911, which was eventually to develop into Odakyu Railway Company Limited. In 1921 Toshimitsu applied on behalf of Tokyo High Speed Railway Co., Ltd. for a license to build a railroad linking the southwestern part of Tokyo with the central region of Kanagawa Prefecture. The license was granted in 1922 and the company was renamed Odawara Express Railway Co., Ltd. after Odawara City, which lies at the foot of Mount Fuji. The official inauguration of the company took place on May 1, 1923. Nearly four months after Toshimitsu had embarked on this difficult project, which required enormous initial investment, the Great Kanto Earthquake struck, reducing Tokyo and Yokohama to ashes. However, it worked to the advantage of the newly established Odakyu, because many people whose homes had been destroyed began to want to move into the less-affected suburbs, boosting new land development and construction work. As the development of suburban Tokyo was an important social issue at that time and a great number of investors were willing to invest in this project, there was no difficulty in securing funding for the construction of the railroad. In 1925 government permission was given for the execution of the whole project and an 82-kilometer-long railroad between Shinjuku and Odawara was built in one and a half years, the fastest completion period recorded in the history of Japan's railroads. Business went well until Japan was hit by the Depression.

Odakyu's business started to recover again in the mid-1930s, but in 1937 the Sino-Japanese War broke out and there was every sign that it would be long and hard. As part of the wartime emergency measures, the Japanese government decided that the power industry should come under the control of the state. As a result, Kinugawa Hydro-Electricity Company, the parent company of Odawara, had to close down and merge with its subsidiary to form Odakyu Electric Railway Company (Odakyu) in 1941. As the war continued and its ferocity intensified, the government took further steps to establish the land transport infrastructure. In 1944 Odakyu was merged with three other railroad companies, now known as Keio Electric Co., Ltd., Keihin Express Electric Railway Co., Ltd., and Tokyu Corporation. The new company, Tokyo Express Electric Railway Co., Ltd., was headed by Keita Grotoh, previously the third president of Odawara Express Electric Railway Company, who had had experience in many other electric railroad companies and was to become Minister of Transport and Communications. The unification of private railways in the southwestern suburbs of Tokyo was thus completed by the newly named Tokyo Express Electric Railway Co., Ltd.

The end of World War II made it possible for those railroad companies that had been forced to amalgamate during the state of emergency to become independent again, and in June 1948 they started to go their separate ways. In October 1948 the newly born Odakyu introduced a non-stop special express between Shinjuku and Odawara, and in 1950 it fulfilled its long-cherished dream by opening a new direct line to Hakone-Yumoto, one of Japan's best-known hot spa resorts. In 1957 it launched the epoch-making Romance Car SE, which set the world speed record on the narrow-gauge track. In 1960 it completed the Golden Course, a round-trip route around the Hakone area. In order to strengthen the company's grip on tourist transport, it put new strategies into practice.

Until the mid-1960s, Odakyu's main strategic task was to expand its flagship line connecting the western gateway of Tokyo with Japan's most famous tourist resort, Hakone. However, since the mid-1960s the strategy of Odakyu has developed into a second phase, directed toward enhancing the quality of life of the residents along its lines. Odakyu's strategy in the second phase was, as is the case in other major private railway companies, to further promote affiliated divisions and subsidiaries through diversification, and thereby to reinforce the overall strength of the Odakyu Group. The Odakyu Group comprises many diversified divisions and subsidiaries, with Odakyu Electric Railway Company as its core. Their business activities are classified into six fields: public transport, leisure, distribution, real estate/construction, information services, and overseas business.

In 1967 Odakyu completed the rebuilding of Shinjuku Terminal Building and in 1975 it opened a branch line, the Tama Line, to Tama New Town for the commuters among the town's 300,000 inhabitants. In 1978 a direct route into all areas of Tokyo was opened by way of the agreement with the Underground Chiyoda Line, enabling trains of both companies to use the same track, dramatically enhancing the function of Odakyu in providing urban transport networks.

However, as the population of the areas along its lines has been growing rapidly, Odakyu's transport capability is increasingly unable to cope with the growing number of passengers. During the rush hours Odakyu runs one ten-carriage train every two minutes or so, yet the trains are filled to more than twice their capacity, so that the passengers often find it difficult to read even magazines on their journey.

With an increasing number of high-tech industries and universities either newly set up or moving out from the city center, and with population expected to increase further in the areas along the Odakyu Line, the consensus of management is that the only way to solve the problem is to build a four-track line as soon as possible. Odakyu attempted to raise finance for this project; for example, obtaining government grants, issuing warrant and convertible bonds, and issuing foreign bonds in 1978, the first such attempt made by a Japanese railroad company. Having successfully secured such financing, Odakyu began to build a four-track line in the early 1990s. In 1991 Odakyu achieved the extension of its operations to Nishi-Izu, a fashionable seaside resort particularly popular among young people, and developed its business activities into the new area.

In the leisure industry Odakyu has always had the advantage of running a railroad between Shinjuku and Fuji-Hakone. In spite of this, Odakyu was rather late in establishing a comprehensive leisure business. However, since it started its operations in the field of international travel services as an authorized International Air Transport Association (IATA) agent in 1972, and especially since it set up Odakyu Service Co., Ltd. in 1976, it has begun to develop a complete range of travel services.

In the early stages of its entry into hotel-related business Odakyu ran mainly resort hotels. However, since it opened the Hotel Century Hyatt, in conjunction with Hyatt International of the United States in 1980, it has been progressing into the urban hotel business, and has built chain hotels in many local cities. It also runs approximately 220 restaurants and coffee shops in these hotels and around the Odakyu line. Moreover, it has recently entered the field of sport and leisure facilities and the health industry. In 1979 it opened Seijo Tennis Garden, and since then it has added a great number of swimming pools, skating rinks, bowling alleys, and athletic clubs in the Tokyo and Kanagawa areas. Furthermore, it has stepped up its operations by opening Nishi-Fuji Golf Club in 1989, and Naka-Izu Club in 1990.

Odakyu's involvement in the retail business dates back to 1962, when the Odakyu Department Store was opened at the west exit of Shinjuku Station. Since the reconstruction of Odakyu Station building in 1967, it has become the jewel in the company's crown. At present the task of the Shinjuku Odakyu Department Store is to respond to changes in the type and increasing number of customers resulting from the move of the municipal government offices into this area. It is estimated that the daytime population has increased by 25,000. Odakyu Shoji Co., Ltd, which is another significant part of the group, has moved into variety stores, supermarkets, and convenience stores. The first store was opened in Sagami-Ohno in 1963, and in the early 1990s the company had more than 38 stores. In the face of intense competition Odakyu has achieved good results, making full use of its prime locations by stocking high-quality goods and thoroughly training employees in customer service. In 1976 the Odakyu Department Store opened a branch in Machida, Tokyo's most rapidly developing satellite town, has also expanded its operations in Fujisawa, and has since recorded steady growth.

The real estate department of a railroad company tends to focus only on the land close to its lines. In order to overcome this tendency, Odakyu Real Estate Co., Ltd. was established in 1964 with the aim of providing general real estate services and developing related businesses. Its operations cover the sale and leasing of land and properties as well as other intermediary services throughout the Kanto area.

The redevelopment plan for the area along the Odakyu Line is already under discussion by the interested parties, including local authorities, looking ahead to the 21st century. The real test of the company's ability will be how effectively it can play its part in the long-term plan. Odakyu has concentrated its energies on renting out office buildings. Its leasing business has shown steady growth since its reorganization in 1975. It has utilized the open spaces in unused railroad land, station buildings, and hotels by letting them to tenants. In this field Odakyu has shown remarkable growth, and its future prospects are highly promising.

Since about 1982, the phrase "the Era of New Media" has been frequently used in Japanese mass media. Cable television has become very popular and its future is promising, but it requires major investment in plant and equipment as well as in software development. Odakyu's management was initially cautious, but eventually decided to enter into this business.

First, Odakyu set up a subsidiary, Odakyu Cable Vision Co., Ltd, in 1987, and then in 1988 it joined in the management of International Cable Network Co., Ltd. The viewers' chief motives for subscribing were the desire for clearer TV pictures, satellite transmission, and special local programs. Technical research is under way to establish a service network through which the customers can make payments automatically to participating shops from their own homes. In its effort to enhance its services, Odakyu Computer System Co., Ltd. and Odakyu CAP Agency Co, Ltd.—CAP stands for Communication And Promotion—were set up in 1989 and in 1990 respectively.

Approaching the 21st century, the most important project in the company's third phase is the enhancement of cooperation within the Group in its search for new business both in Japan and abroad.

Since the second half of the 1980s, Odakyu has seen overseas markets as fertile ground for new business opportunities. In 1989 the Odakyu Group opened its representative office in London, and it also established Odakyu Hawaii Corp. through the acquisition of Outrigger Hobron, Condominium Hotel, in Hawaii, which has 600 rooms. In 1990 the Odakyu Department Paris Office was renamed Odakyu France S.A.R.L., and Odakyu Tours U.S.A. Inc. was established to provide better services for overseas tourists.

Principal Subsidiaries: Hakone Tozan Railway Co., Ltd. (58.8%); Kanagawa Chuo Kotsu Co., Ltd. (44.2%); Odakyu Bus Co., Ltd. (97%); Tachikawa Bus Co., Ltd. (38%); Tokai Jidosha Co., Ltd. (33.1%); Odakyu Kotsu Co., Ltd.; Odakyu Hotels Co., Ltd. (30%); The International Tourist Corporation (94.2%); Odakyu Restaurant System Co., Ltd.; Odakyu Department Store Co., Ltd. (58.5%); Fujisawa Odakyu Co., Ltd. (30%); Odakyu Real Estate Co., Ltd. (47.8%); Odakyu Construction Co., Ltd. (45.9%); Odakyu Building Service Co., Ltd. (100%).

—Norimasa Satoh

THE PENINSULAR AND ORIENTAL STEAM NAVIGATION COMPANY

79 Pall Mall
London SW1Y 5EJ
United Kingdom
(071) 930 4343
Fax: (071) 925 0384

Public Company
Incorporated: 1840
Employees: 75,000
Sales: £5.03 billion (US$9.40 billion)
Stock Exchanges: London Paris Amsterdam Frankfurt
Hong Kong Sydney Tokyo New York

The Peninsular and Oriental Steam Navigation Company (P&O) began as a shipping company. It was founded at the crucial period for the shipping industry of transition from sail to steam. Many companies were founded at this time, only to fail quickly in the early days of steam. P&O, along with Cunard, is one of the few survivors of the steamship pioneers and has outlasted its competitors through a mixture of caution, shrewdness, ruthlessness, and good luck.

P&O remained primarily a shipping company for the first 140 years of its existence. In the mid-1970s it began to diversify to become a major international group of over 250 companies, involved not only in freight and passenger shipping but also in housebuilding, large construction projects, property, and numerous service activities. Despite this diversification, P&O continues to consolidate its position as the United Kingdom's dominant shipping company and as a major player on the world's shipping market.

The founding of P&O traditionally dates from the awarding of the contract by the Admiralty for the carriage of the mail between England and the Iberian Peninsula in August 1837.

In 1815 Brodie McGhie Willcox opened a shipping agency and brokers' office in Lime Street, London, and employed Arthur Anderson as clerk. Anderson was made a partner in 1822. In 1826 Willcox and Anderson were appointed London agents for the Dublin and London Steam Packet Company, an aggressive and highly successful steam-packet company that ran between the two cities in its name. This connection brought together the three founders of P&O—Willcox, Anderson, and Richard Bourne, a man of great financial acumen.

In the early days, Willcox and Anderson ran small sailing vessels to Spain and Portugal. This trade forced them to take sides in the 1833 civil war in Portugal and shortly afterward in the Carlist uprising in Spain. In both cases they chose the winners and the fledgling company was granted trading facilities and official favors from the grateful Spanish and Portuguese royal families. They attempted in 1834 to float the Peninsular Steam Navigation Company but were soon in financial difficulties.

It was the contract to carry the mails to the Iberian Peninsula, awarded to Bourne rather than to Willcox and Anderson, that enabled the company to survive and develop into a giant. Mail contracts guaranteed a regular income and provided P&O with steady income for decades. The existing mail packet ships were inefficient and corrupt. P&O undertook to reach Lisbon in 84 hours, compared to up to three weeks for the mail packets, for the sum of £30,000 a year—significantly less than the packets. The first run ended in disaster when the *Don Juan* was wrecked off the Spanish coast, but the company's reputation was enhanced by the daring rescue of the mails and £21,000 in cash.

In 1840 the company was awarded a contract to take the mails to Alexandria, the key staging post in the carriage of mails to India. This contract heralded the start of rapid company growth, beginning with the purchase of two large ships, the *Great Liverpool* and the *Oriental*.

In December 1840 the company was incorporated by royal charter under its present name of the Peninsular & Oriental Steam Navigation Company, with authorized capital of £1 million, and Willcox and Anderson as joint managing directors. Despite the absence of a mail contract at this stage and the East India Company's monopolistic hold on this trade, P&O was obliged to set up a regular steamship service to India within two years.

Prevented by the East India monopoly from operating out of Bombay, the most convenient port of call, P&O set about organizing a service between Suez, Aden, Point de Galle, and Calcutta to link up with its service between England and Egypt. Before the opening of the Suez Canal, passengers to India had to disembark at Alexandria and endure an arduous and often unsafe journey by carriage across the desert to the Red Sea where they joined another ship. P&O actively encouraged the construction of a railway across Egypt and, in order to secure supplies, ran farms and repair yards en route.

P&O's first voyage to India was carried out in 1842 by the *Hindostan*, its largest ship to date. This ambitious undertaking necessitated the setting up of coal and supply stations at intermediate points along the route and of arrangements for the overland part of the journey. The greater speed and reliability of P&O's service in comparison with that of its rival, the East India Company, eventually won P&O access to Bombay.

In 1844 Anderson introduced the novel concept of leisure cruising to Victorian Britain. The first cruises took place in the Mediterranean Sea and involved shore excursions to Malta, Smyrna, Constantinople, Jaffa, and Egypt. The Crimean War of the mid-1850s put a stop to cruising until the 1880s, when it was taken up by other companies. P&O only re-entered this business in 1904 with the conversion of a liner, the *Rome*, into a cruise ship, the *Vectis*.

Meanwhile, P&O pressed further east and built more ships. In 1845 the *Lady Mary Wood*, the first P&O steamship to travel to Singapore, completed the journey in 41 days—sailing ships could take up to a year to complete this journey—before opening a service between Ceylon and Hong Kong. The company's steamers took silk out of and opium into China. Its first connection with Australia was made in 1852 and with Japan in 1859.

Problems were looming on the horizon, however. Substantial increases in coal prices played havoc with operating costs. The Crimean War brought great disruption to services; in 1855 one-third of P&O tonnage was in the Black Sea transporting men, horses, supplies, and equipment. The 1869 opening of the Suez Canal was also a mixed blessing. P&O's ships' draft and breadth were inappropriate for the canal, and the company's regional offices and dockyards became redundant after the canal opened, as it became more economical to send ships back to England for repairs. Passengers still had to be transferred overland across Egypt for a decade or more after ships that could use the canal had been built, because the Post Office took years to be convinced it was safe for the mails. Other companies were not thus restricted, and within a couple of years the company's income was falling by £100,000 a year.

It was at this stage that a new regime took the helm. In 1854 Willcox resigned as managing director but remained on the board and became chairman from 1858 until his death in 1862. He was succeeded by Anderson, who remained chairman until his death in 1868. Thomas Sutherland became chairman in 1872 at the relatively young age of 38. At the age of 18, Sutherland had become a P&O office boy. He had spent a dozen years of impressive service in Hong Kong and upon taking charge of the company was faced with the burden of cutting expenditure and of rebuilding the fleet.

Sutherland gradually turned P&O's fortunes around. By 1884 P&O's fleet contained 50 ships, only 6 more than in 1870, but the ships of 1884 had almost double the gross tonnage of 1870. The end of the 19th century was a period of calm for British shipping generally. Consolidation of the empire was underway and ships were increasing in size, speed, and comfort to the extent that Bombay could be reached from England within 15 days.

In 1910 P&O bought the Blue Anchor Line, a company that specialized in the carriage of emigrants and general cargo from the United Kingdom to Australia and of Australian wool on the return journey. Until this point, P&O had concentrated on first-class passenger trade. This purchase gave P&O an interest in all classes of passenger traffic.

The process of expansion by acquisition accelerated. In 1914 Sutherland masterminded secret negotiations leading to the merger of P&O and British India (BI). BI was Britain's largest shipping company, with 131 vessels totaling 598,203 gross registered tons (grt), compared to P&O's 70 ships of 548,654 grt. BI's routes complemented those of P&O; it was strong in the Indian Ocean, the Persian Gulf, and Southeast Asia, but rarely ventured west of Suez. There was no change of company name following the merger, but until the 1950s P&O and BI shared the same board of directors.

At this point, after leading P&O for over 40 years, 78-year-old Thomas Sutherland retired and handed over the reins to James Lyle Mackay, Lord Inchcape, chairman of BI. The change at the top coincided with the outbreak of World War I during which the merchant fleet had to contend with torpe-does, submarines, airstrikes, and mines. By the end of 1914, 100 ships of the enlarged P&O fleet had been requisitioned.

At the outbreak of war, the tonnage of the P&O fleet was over 1.1 million grt. Over 500,000 grt were lost during hostilities, but by the war's end the P&O fleet stood at over 1.5 million grt. This expansion was achieved by an aggressive program of acquisition to prepare P&O for the postwar era. In 1916 P&O acquired the New Zealand Shipping Company and Federal Steam Navigation Company, prominent in the frozen food trade from New Zealand to the United Kingdom. In 1917 it acquired interests in the Union Steamship Company of New Zealand; the Hain Steamship Company, which had worldwide tramping interests; and James Nourse Ltd., which operated between India and the West Indies. P&O bought the Orient Line in 1918 and the Khedivial Mail Line in 1919. In 1920 P&O bought Britain's oldest steamship company, the General Steamship Navigation Company, founded in 1824. By 1923, when P&O bought the Strick Line, the P&O fleet was composed of 500 vessels.

The first ten postwar years were prosperous for P&O: the war had created a backlog of trade; passenger traffic picked up briskly; and emigration from Britain, Australia, and New Zealand reached new highs. The growth of foreign competition was loosening the hold of British ships in many markets, however. Building and operating costs were rising rapidly, and there was a ship surplus. These problems were exacerbated by the civil war in China, which badly hurt P&O's trade, and the Wall Street crash of 1929, which heralded the start of the Depression of the 1930s. P&O encountered severe financial difficulties, necessitating salary cuts of 10% in 1931. By 1932 P&O was unable to pay a dividend to its shareholders.

Alexander Shaw, Lord Inchcape's son-in-law, became chairman in 1932. He inherited a modern fleet with which to combat the crisis. This fleet included the most successful vessel of the decade, the 20,000-ton *Viceroy of India,* which was completed in 1929. This ship was quieter than its predecessors, traveled at 19 knots, and brought a new level of luxury to sea travel, including the first onboard indoor swimming pool.

As the 1930s progressed, international politics again disrupted the merchant shipping market. In 1935, following Mussolini's invasion of Ethiopia, nine BI ships were requisitioned to support League of Nations sanctions. In 1937 Japan began eight years of undeclared war on China. These events, plus growing uncertainty in Europe, disordered supplies and routes. Nevertheless, business improved and Alexander Shaw—now Lord Craigmyle—retired in 1938, two years after restoration of the company's dividend.

Shaw was succeeded by Sir William Crawford Currie, who remained as chairman until 1960. World War II began. The *Rawalpindi* was requisitioned in August 1939, only to be lost three months later. The pace of requisitioning accelerated, and by Easter 1940 all of BI's 103 ships, composed of 55 passenger ships and 48 cargo ships, were under official direction. P&O contributed 16 troop carriers, which transported over one million troops during the conflict.

In 1939 the fleet of the P&O group contained 371 vessels totaling 2.2 million grt. During the course of the conflict, 182 vessels, equivalent to 1.2 million grt, were destroyed. P&O itself lost over 40% of its fleet in tonnage terms. Elsewhere within the group, Hain lost all 24 of its cargo vessels; Nourse lost 7 vessels; BI lost 45; and one quarter of Union Line and 85% of Strick Line were destroyed.

A steep rise in shipbuilding prices and increased foreign competition, particularly from developing countries, characterized the immediate postwar period. The postwar era also saw the end of the British Empire; India regained its independence in 1947, causing a rapid decline in the number of steady passengers, such as soldiers, civil servants, and their families.

P&O responded to the new situation by refocusing its activities on cargo. By 1949 P&O's cargo fleet had been rebuilt to its prewar levels, whereas the passenger fleet was only at 60% of its 1939 strength. P&O also began its involvement with the tanker market in the late 1950s and by the mid-1960s P&O was the main independent tanker operator in the United Kingdom.

International politics intervened briefly again in 1956 with the Suez Canal crisis and the closure of the canal. The canal was crucial to the company's U.K./Far East and U.K./Australian routes. Longer voyages and the fear of war, however, led to higher returns and a short-term stimulus for P&O.

Despite the threat to passenger shipping from the growth of civil aviation, the passenger business was not neglected, and in the mid-1950s two new prestigious passenger ships were ordered—the 2,050-berth *Oriana* for the Orient Line, launched in 1959, and the 2,250-berth *Canberra,* launched in 1960. In May 1960 P&O bought the remainder of Orient Line, and briefly renamed its passenger operation P&O Orient Lines.

The 1960s were difficult years for shipping. P&O suffered from the general shipping slump and competition from the growth of flags of convenience—ships were usually registered or flagged in the country of ownership, but certain flags attracted ships by offering financial or legal advantages and became known as "flags of convenience." The company also entered new areas of business during this decade. In 1961 the abolition of national service marked the end of BI ships as troop carriers and the beginning of a program of educational cruises. In 1963 P&O, now chaired by Sir Donald Anderson, concluded a long-term agreement with Anglo-Norness Shipping Company, the world's major tanker and bulk shipping operator, to market its fleet of bulk and combination carriers. In 1965, through Ranger Fishing, which was sold in 1974, P&O entered the freezer trawler business. Through North Sea Ferries, P&O bought and operated its first roll-on roll-off vessels—cargo ships or ferries on or off which cars, lorries, and trailers drive directly.

The most important development of all, however, was P&O's pioneering role in containerization, one of the most important changes in shipping this century. P&O was at the forefront of the containerization revolution through the creation of Overseas Containers Ltd. (OCL), which was formed by four British shipping companies—P&O, Alfred Holt, British and Commonwealth, and Furness Withy. Sir Andrew Crichton was seconded from the P&O board as OCL chairman.

In March 1969 OCL's first fully cellular container service began between the United Kingdom and Australia. Initially a lossmaker, OCL gradually became a success, and in 1986 P&O bought that part of OCL which it did not already own, changing the name to P&O Containers Ltd. Development of the container business continues; in 1991 P&O acquired the bulk of the Ellerman cargo shipping business from Cunard, giving it over a quarter of the British share of container trades

between Australasia and Europe, 100% of the United Kingdom–Australasia run, and 15% of Europe–South Africa trade.

In 1971 Ford Geddes became P&O chairman. He took charge of a group composed of 127 companies whose profits had fallen to £4.9 million, from £12.6 million in 1969. Geddes immediately set about a thorough overhaul of P&O's structure. The company was divided into five divisions: bulk cargo, passenger, general cargo, a general holding company, and European and air transport. This rationalization led to the disappearance of old names such as Hain and Nourse, BI, General Steam, and many others.

The effects of the rationalization were slow to filter through, and P&O increasingly cast around for opportunities in other sectors. In the early 1970s the property market was booming, encouraging P&O to make a bid for the construction company Bovis. The bid stirred up serious opposition within P&O, based partly on resistance to diversification but mostly a belief that the bid was pitched too high. This led to the resignation of Geddes in November 1972. He was replaced by the third Lord Inchcape as non-executive chairman, with Alexander Marshall as managing director. P&O's purchase of Bovis went through in 1974 at about half the price of the original offer.

Competition from air travel caused the withdrawal of regular liner passenger services with the final scheduled trip to the Far East taking place in 1969. Passenger business now consisted of the ferry service and cruises. In 1974 P&O bought Princess Cruises which today forms the cornerstone of P&O's extensive U.S. cruise business, augmented by the 1988 purchase of Sitmer Cruises.

Lord Inchcape became chief executive in 1978 and initiated another reorganization. This entailed the sale of all interests in the North Sea and the U.S. oil and gas industry acquired in the 1960s; the dismantling of the energy division; and a reduced role for general cargo and the bulk division. During the period 1974–1980, the number of ships in the P&O fleet fell from 178 to 89. Because of the introduction of much larger ships, however, total tonnage fell only by 3%–4%, standing at 2.45 million grt in 1981.

By the late 1970s Lord Inchcape was searching for younger talent for the board. His eye alighted on Jeffrey Sterling, a City financier who had built up his own group of companies based on the Sterling Guarantee Trust. Sterling joined the board in 1980.

Shortly afterward a hostile bid for the company was received from Trafalgar House, the owner of Cunard and also a competitor in the construction business. The bid was referred to the Monopolies and Mergers Commission, which allowed it to proceed in early 1984. This interlude gave Jeffrey Sterling, who became chairman in November 1983, time to organize P&O's defense, however, and the bid was not renewed.

In 1985 P&O merged with Sterling's Sterling Guarantee Trust. This deal brought the group numerous non-shipping interests, including Town and Country Properties; the ownership and management of the Earls Court and Olympia exhibition centers; the catering company Sutcliffes; a security company; and various other service-related concerns. In 1986 P&O bought Stock Conversion, a major property company, and in 1991 a half share in Laing Properties, another major property concern.

P&O enters the 1990s as by far the largest British shipping company and as one of the United Kingdom's biggest property, investment, and development groups, not necessarily a desirable position in the depressed property market of the early 1990s. The trend in shipping is away from small, family businesses toward large international conglomerates. P&O is in a good position to survive in this highly competitive market, although its dominant position on English Channel routes faces a major challenge from 1993 with the opening of the channel tunnel between Britain and France.

Principal Subsidiaries: P&O Cruises Ltd.; Canberra Cruises Ltd.; Swan Hellenic Ltd.; P&O Lines Ltd.; Princess Cruises Inc.; Sitmar International Inc. (Panama); P&O European Ferries Ltd.; North Sea Ferries Ltd.; P&O Scottish Ferries Ltd.; P&O Bulk Shipping Ltd.; P&O Bulk Carriers Ltd. (Bermuda); Rowbotham Tankships Ltd. (50%); P&O Containers Ltd.; Earls Court and Olympia Ltd.; Sutcliffe Services Group; Sutcliffe Catering Group Ltd.; Spring Grove Services Group Ltd.; Plantation Group Ltd.; Sterling Security Services Ltd.; P&O Vending Services Ltd.; Buck and Hickman Ltd.; Sea Oil Homco Ltd.; Three Quays International Ltd.; Mackinnon Mackenzie and Co. of Pakistan; P&O European Transport Services Ltd.; P&O Roadways Ltd.; P&O Roadtanks Ltd.; H&S Transport BV (Netherlands); Rhenania Schiffahrts und Speditions GmbH; Pandoro Ltd.; Northern Ireland Trailers (Scotland) Ltd.; P&O Distribution Ltd.; P&O Harbours Ltd.; Larne Harbour Ltd. (Northern Ireland); P&O Australia Ltd; P&O New Zealand Ltd; Bovis Ltd.; Ashby & Horner Ltd.; Wyseplant Ltd.; Yeomans & Partners Ltd.; McDevitt & Street Company Inc.; P&O Developments Ltd.; Crowngap Ltd.; Pall Mall Properties Plc (50%); P&O Properties Inc.; P&O Property Holdings Ltd.; P&O Properties Ltd.; P&O Shopping Centres Ltd.; Arndale Communications Ltd.; Chelsea Harbour Ltd.

Further Reading: Cable, Boyd, *A Hundred Year History of the P&O,* London, Ivor Nicholson and Watson, 1937; Divine, David, *These Splendid Ships—The Story of the Peninsular and Oriental Line,* London, Frederick Muller Limited, 1960; Haws, Duncan, *The Ships of the P&O, Orient and Blue Anchor Lines,* Cambridge, Stephens, 1978; Padfield, Peter, *Beneath The House Flag of the P&O,* London, Hutchinson, 1981; Apthorp, Brian, *Surgeon P&O: A Personal Account of Three Voyages in the Light White Ships of the P&O Steam Navigation Company,* Hong Kong, Joplin Trading Company, 1985; McCart, Neil, *Twentieth Century Passenger Ships of the P&O,* Wellingborough, Stephens, 1985; Howarth, David and Stephen, *The Story of P&O,* London, Weidenfeld and Nicholson, 1986; Kirk, R., *The Postal History of the P&O Service to the Peninsula,* London Royal Philatelic Society, 1987; Rabson, Stephen and O'Donoghue, Kevin, *P&O: A Fleet History,* World Ship Society, 1988; McCart, Neil, *P&O's Canberra,* Kingfisher Railway Publications, 1989.

—Debra Johnson

PENSKE CORPORATION

13400 Outer Drive West
Detroit, Michigan 48239
U.S.A.
(313) 592-5000
Fax: (313) 592-5256

Private Company
Incorporated: 1969
Employees: 10,000
Sales: $2.80 billion

Penske Corporation is a transportation services company with major interests as diverse as truck leasing, diesel engine manufacture, auto racing, and retail automobile sales. Founded by former Indianapolis 500 racer Roger Penske, the company has revenues approaching $3 billion. Principal owner and CEO Penske has earned a reputation for building contenders on and off the racetrack. His company's stunning turnaround of ailing companies like General Motors's Detroit Diesel Allison and Hertz's Truck Leasing is at least as impressive as his racing team's record eight Indianapolis 500 wins and seven national IndyCar championships.

The corporation operates three distinct groups: transportation services, retail automotive, and automotive performance. The transportation services group includes the nation's second largest full service truck leasing and renting business, Penske Truck Leasing Co., L.P., and the diesel engine manufacturing company Detroit Diesel Corporation. The retail automotive group includes Longo Toyota, Penske Cadillac, and Penske Honda in California. The dealerships collectively sell more than 35,000 Cadillacs, Chevrolets, Hondas, Lexus, and Toyotas a year. The automotive performance group is built upon the highly successful Penske racing team, and also runs the Michigan International Speedway and the Pennsylvania International Raceway. The group also participates in a joint venture, Ilmor Engineering of Great Britain, with Chevrolet, to build the V-8 engine used in the vast majority of winning Indianapolis race cars in the late 1980s and early 1990s.

In the early 1960s, while still a sales representative for the Aluminum Company of America, Roger Penske became one of the most successful race car drivers around, competing in sports car, endurance, and Formula One races on weekends. In 1962 Penske was voted Sports Car Driver of the Year by *Sports Illustrated, The New York Times,* and *The Los Angeles Times.* Penske's love of cars convinced him to leave the aluminum company, and in 1963 he became general manager of a Chevrolet dealership in Philadelphia. Two years later, Penske bought the dealership and gave up racing to pursue his business interests, but he soon returned to the sport as the owner of a racing team that became the most successful in history.

In the middle and late 1960s, Roger Penske's Chevy dealership prospered. Penske acquired a pair of specialty tire distributorships, Competition Tire East and Competition Tire West, and a small truck leasing operation. The truck leasing business soon enjoyed spectacular growth as private fleet owners discovered the benefits of leasing versus buying their trucks—purchasing, fuel supply, scheduled maintenance, and repair were left in the hands of the lessor, allowing the fleet operator to focus on the distribution and routing of their products. By 1969 Penske Leasing had 33 locations in the northeastern United States. The Penske Corporation was set up that year as a holding company for Roger Penske's automotive-related enterprises.

By 1971 Roger Penske had auto dealerships in Philadelphia and Allentown, Pennsylvania, and in Detroit. His nearly legendary attention to detail set the pace at the dealerships. Sales climbed, helping to fuel expansion into other ventures.

Started as a business, Team Penske in many ways revolutionized motor sports. One of Penske's racing competitors conceded to *Forbes,* May 28, 1979, "He markets his car and sets up sponsorship programs more effectively than anyone else." The exposure on televised broadcasts of major racing events, including the Indianapolis 500, provided enormous value when compared to the cost of a 30-second commercial spot.

Penske's businesses, too, benefited from the publicity generated by the racing team. Renowned drivers like Mark Donohue, Mario Andretti, Bobby Unser, and Tom Sneva in the 1970s; Danny Sullivan, Rick Mears, and Al Unser Sr. in the 1980s; and Emerson Fittipaldi and Paul Tracy in the 1990s helped make Team Penske the most successful organization in the history of racing's greatest event—the Indianapolis 500—with a record eight wins by 1991. Penske's winning image was clearly valuable to the corporation's nonracing businesses—buying a new car from auto racing's most successful team seems just a little flashier than buying it from just an average dealer.

While Penske's businesses enjoyed growth throughout the 1970s, that growth accelerated in the 1980s. Sales were $254 million in 1981, but by 1988, they had topped $2 billion. The first business segment to swell was truck leasing. The unit had enjoyed excellent growth throughout the 1970s, but in 1982, Penske entered a joint venture with the ailing giant Hertz Truck Leasing. The Hertz unit had lost $40 million in 1981, and the company considered unloading it altogether. Roger Penske was invited to tour Hertz's operations, and soon agreed to merge Penske Leasing with Hertz's truck operations. Penske trimmed 500 jobs and 30 locations from Hertz. After one year, the new Hertz-Penske Leasing made $1.2 million. Penske's initial stake in the company was 35%. By 1986 the share was upped to 50%, and Hertz-Penske acquired the heavy-duty truck leasing business of another major company, Leaseway Transportation, for $94 million. Hertz-Penske was then the second-largest truck leasing company in the United States behind Ryder System, Inc., although a distant second—Ryder's sales quadrupled those of Hertz-Penske.

In June 1988 Penske Corporation bought Hertz's half of Hertz-Penske Leasing. Two months later, in August, Penske

Corporation's truck leasing operations merged with General Electric Credit Corporation's Gelco Truck Services. The resulting company was a limited partnership named Penske Truck Leasing Co., L.P., with a Penske Corporation subsidiary as the general partner, responsible for operation of the firm. Penske initially owned 69% of the partnership and GE purchased another 3% in January 1989. The joint venture operated 365 locations and 55,000 vehicles, but remained second to Ryder System in market share.

Penske Corporation's retail automotive group also made large acquisitions in the 1980s. In 1985 the nation's largest Toyota dealership, Longo Toyota of suburban Los Angeles, came up for sale. Founded by Dominic Longo in 1967, the dealership had been the number-one Toyota dealership in the United States since 1969. After Dominic Longo died in 1985, Penske agreed to buy it.

In 1988, Longo Toyota moved into a brand new facility in El Monte, California. The new facility covered 23 acres, employed more than 360 people, and boasted 104 service bays and 54 body-shop stalls. Penske's continued emphasis on service was crucial to Longo's exceptional rate of repeat and referral business. The dealership carefully targeted its market. For example, it employed special teams of salespeople who were collectively fluent in Mandarin and Cantonese Chinese, Japanese, Korean, Vietnamese, and Thai, as well as Spanish and English—making it easy and comfortable for L.A. residents originating from the Pacific Rim to do business at Longo. Roger Penske's son Greg serves as general manager of the dealership. In 1989 Penske started Longo Lexus; for both 1990 and 1991 this dealership was the Lexus retail sales leader in the U.S.

In December 1987 Penske Corporation made its biggest acquisition ever, and leapt into the large-scale manufacturing sector at the same time with the purchase of 60% of General Motors' $900-million-in-sales Detroit Diesel Allison division. Penske was approached in late 1987 by GM's investment banking firm, Salomon Brothers, with the possibility of a deal. General Motors hoped an entrepreneurial infusion could save the troubled engine-maker. Detroit Diesel had reportedly lost $70 million in 1987. Its North American market share had declined from nearly 30% in 1979 to 3%. Product and consumer service problems were the root of the trouble. GM lost its diesel customers to Cummins and Caterpillar, and despite sinking $100 million into upgraded plant during the 1980s the automotive giant seemed incapable of turning the unit around by itself.

Penske Corporation's experience with fleet truck purchasing, and earlier operation of Detroit Diesel Allison distributorships in the East, made the company an excellent choice as a partner. Penske took control of operations and quickly began streamlining the new Detroit Diesel Corporation. The operating budget was slashed by more than $70 million by cutting jobs, consolidating facilities, and cutting unnecessary computer costs.

GM's poor management of the unit throughout the 1980s and uncertainty about the immediate future had depressed the morale of Detroit Diesel workers. Roger Penske set out to convince his new employees that their company would be competitive once again. In August 1988, several months after he began running Detroit Diesel, Roger Penske invited his 3,000 Detroit Diesel employees to the Michigan International Speedway for the Marlboro 500. After watching Team Penske drivers Rick Mears win the pole position, Al Unser Sr. in the Detroit Diesel-sponsored car lead for a time, and Danny Sullivan win the race, the Detroit Diesel employees were elated.

Revitalizing Detroit Diesel's work force was key to improving the company's fortunes. Also essential was bringing a better product to market. General Motors had invested a good deal of research and development into a new engine—the Series 60. The six-cylinder, four-stroke diesel featured integral electronic controls, improved fuel efficiency, durability, and was relatively low-cost. The new engine was well received in the marketplace, helping Detroit Diesel turn a profit.

In September 1988 Penske Transportation bought the diesel electronic unit injector line from GM's Rochester Products Division. Penske's transportation services group also expanded Detroit Diesel's product range through an operating agreement with Perkins Engines, a British subsidiary of the Canadian machinery maker Varity, formerly Massey-Ferguson, to market Detroit Diesel engines overseas, and to provide smaller diesel engines for Penske to sell in North America. The arrangement gave Detroit Diesel a wide range of diesel engines, from 5 horsepower to 2,000 horsepower.

Penske's leaner Detroit Diesel was able to offer significant savings, and began to win back market share. Confident of the subsidiary's future, Penske Corporation bought another 20% in 1988, and by 1990 the subsidiary was 80% owned by Penske Transportation, with GM owning 20%.

Penske Corporation's three groups, retail automotive, transportation services, and automotive performance, operate under Roger Penske's philosophy of maximizing performance while minimizing expenses. Undoubtedly, the 1990s will offer new challenges to transportation companies, but Penske Corporation's play-to-win philosophy likely will serve the company well across its varied business segments.

Principal Subsidiaries: Detroit Diesel Corporation; Penske Truck Leasing Co.; Diesel Technology Co.; Longo Toyota; Longo Lexus; Penske Honda; Penske Racing; Penske Cars, Ltd.; Michigan International Speedway; Pennsylvania International Speedway; Indy Car Grand Prix Corporation.

Further Reading: Finch, Peter, "Roger Penske: Running On 16 Cylinders," *Business Week,* June 1, 1987; DeLorenzo, Matt, "Roger Penske: Multi-talented entrepreneur just keeps on growing," *Automotive News,* January 18, 1988; Moses, Sam, "His Time is Money," *Sports Illustrated,* November 21, 1988; Lowell, Jon, "Roger roars ahead: Penske fires up GM's dying diesels; profits replace problems," *Ward's Auto World,* November 1988.

—Thomas M. Tucker

PHH

PHH CORPORATION

11333 McCormick Road
Hunt Valley, Maryland 21031
U.S.A.
(410) 771-3600
Fax: (410) 771-2841

Public Company
Incorporated: 1953 as Peterson, Howell & Heather, Inc.
Employees: 4,589
Sales: $2.03 billion
Stock Exchanges: New York London Toronto

PHH Corporation is the world's largest provider of vehicle fleet management services, with operations in the United States, Canada, and Europe. It has retained all of its major fleet management clients since its founding. PHH's other services are employee relocation and real estate management.

The company originated in 1946, when Duane Peterson, Harley Howell, and Dick Heather formed a partnership to manage corporate automobile fleets. They signed management agreements with two companies in their first year: Gibson Art Company and Johnson & Johnson. The assumption was that corporations would save money by hiring a group that specialized in running car fleets, rather than supervising the car rentals and management themselves. The idea was advanced at the time when postwar cars were just beginning to be produced, and the firm prospered. It was incorporated in 1953 as Peterson, Howell & Heather. By 1955 a Canadian branch had been formed. The first public offering of stock took place three years later. The client list grew to include Honeywell and Du Pont.

After a decade of steady growth, the company was ready to expand and diversify its services. PHH acquired National Truckers Service (NTS) of Texas in 1969 and acquired Homequity, Inc., of Connecticut in 1971. This latter marked PHH's entry into relocation and real estate management services.

Homequity was then the nation's largest provider of such services, which include the appraisal and purchase of homes from workers being transferred, with the homes' subsequent resale. The building of company headquarters in Hunt Valley, Maryland, began in 1972. In 1978 the company name was changed to PHH Group, Inc.

During the 1980s, PHH continued its expansion, especially in European markets. In 1980 the company purchased AllStar Petrol Card Ltd. of London. That same year, Jerome W.

Geckle, then president and CEO, succeeded John Lalley as chairman. Geckle oversaw a decade of explosive growth. In 1981 PHH International was formed to manage the company's European operations. The following year, business services grew to include aviation management, and over the next several years, PHH acquired Aviation Information Services; Aviation Consulting, Inc.; Beckett Flight Management; and Ryan Aviation Corporation. Despite the recession of the early 1980s, PHH had 2,000 corporate clients in 1982 and a record of 24 consecutive years of increased earnings.

Relocation services were expanded in 1984 with the purchase of Transamerica Corporation's relocation service, which was then ranked as the United States's fourth-largest relocater of corporate personnel. PHH also acquired US Mortgage Corporation that year, adding the related service of mortgage lending to the relocation segment. Fleet management thrived in the United Kingdom, where the country's tax structure encouraged such corporate perquisites as company-provided cars. PHH was listed on the London Stock Exchange in 1984 and the Toronto Stock Exchange in 1986.

PHH signed about 100 new fleet clients in 1984, involving almost 50,000 vehicles. The following year, 78 more clients signed on. At this time, just more than half the company's profits came from fleet services. Aviation management was showing a slight return on investment by 1985. The company orchestrated 29,000 corporate relocations in 1985.

While PHH's major competitor—Gelco Corporation—branched out into containers and truck leasing, PHH broadened only into closely related services, such as credit cards for fuel, tire, and battery purchases, and vehicle expense and maintenance control. In addition to scale economies, PHH offered clients the advantages of its close attention to vehicle prices and values, while handling all the tax, title, and insurance paperwork. In 1985 PHH still ranked among the 100 fastest-growing and most profitable major U.S. companies, despite the fact that falling interest rates had reduced its earnings growth rate in 1983.

In 1986 PHH acquired the Avis Leasing domestic fleet operations from Wesray Capital Corporation for about $136 million. Avis added 35,000 cars to PHH's 281,000 cars in the United States and Canada. More than three-quarters of Avis's business was within 200 miles of New York City, but PHH soon widened the range. Also in 1986, PHH formed an office resources management business segment. These services were to include choosing design, construction, and telecommunications firms and sites for new offices and overseeing the purchase and resale of office equipment. To this new segment were added the 1986 acquisitions of Avenue Group, Inc., of Chicago, and Philadelphia's Interspace, Inc.—both office design firms.

PHH continued expansion in Europe in the late 1980s. It acquired CashCard GmbH in 1987, thus moving into fuel management services in Germany. The company also opened offices in Dublin and Paris. The company's name was changed to PHH Corporation in 1988. The following year, profits rose again, despite hard economic times for both the auto and housing industries. PHH sold its aviation management services business this same year.

Company growth slowed considerably during 1988 and 1989, but profits were steady. Longtime chairman Geckle retired in 1990 and was succeeded by Robert D. Kunisch. The company picked up important new fleet management clients in 1990, including Coca Cola Enterprises and Smith Kline Beecham. PHH Relocation and Real Estate Management Services USA was formed the same year to oversee the PHH businesses in that area. Also formed were the used vehicle service and card service divisions, to complement fleet management services. Profits dipped slightly in the fiscal year that ended in April 1991, largely due to the worldwide recession. PHH put off geographic expansion of its fleet services in Europe until the economy recovered.

PHH officials decided in 1990 to exit the facilities management services operations because the required investments of assets and time were too great. PHH seemed to know and build on its strengths as a streamlined provider of certain management services.

Principal Subsidiaries: PHH Fleet America; PHH Financial Services, Inc.; NTS, Inc.; PHH Vehicle Management Services, Canada; PHH Deutschland, Inc.; PHH AllStar, Ltd. (U.K.); PHH Homequity Corp.; PHH Fantus; Homequity Canada, Inc.; PHH Homequity Ltd. (U.K.); PHH US Mortgage Corporation; PHH France S.A.R.L.; PHH Network Services; PHH Destination Services.

Further Reading: Cook, James, "The PHH Factor," *Forbes,* November 4, 1985; "Forty-Five Years of PHH Quality," Hunt Valley, Maryland, PHH Corporation, [1990].

—Carol I. Keeley

THE POST OFFICE

POST OFFICE GROUP

30 St. James's Square
London SW1Y 4PY
United Kingdom
(071) 490 2888

State-Owned Company
Incorporated: 1969
Employees: 207,438
Sales: £4.72 billion (US$9.11 billion)

The Post Office, the largest carrier of mail and parcels in the United Kingdom, is organized as a group with three separate business divisions. Royal Mail, with its monopoly of the letter service, is profitable; Parcelforce, which competes with private firms in the delivery of parcels, makes a loss; and Post Office Counters makes a modest profit both from selling the group's own services to the public and from acting as an agent to the government in paying state pensions, licensing motor vehicles, and so on. For most of its existence, the Post Office was a civil service department headed by a politician, the Postmaster General, but since 1969 it has been a public corporation on the lines of other nationalized industries such as British Railways.

The Post Office developed from the needs of the crown to carry messages and dispatches. Although the service was intended for the use of the crown, it was unofficially used by private individuals, and in 1635 the situation was clarified by the creation of a public service under the control of Thomas Witherings. Witherings lost his monopoly in 1637, however, and a period of confusion followed as rivals vied for the profitable privilege. In 1653 the crown decided to sell the postal monopoly to the highest bidder, who could then derive profit from the various fees and perquisites within a framework of rates laid down by the government. The practice of delegating the service to a contractor for a fixed sum under government control was continued for some time after the Restoration; the rates were fixed by an act of 1660, and the contractor paid £21,500. Charles II retained part of the income to pay pensions to his mistresses, and assigned the remainder to his brother, the Duke of York. When the latter succeeded Charles as James II in 1685, the revenue of the Post Office reverted to the crown, and it remained an important element in royal finances until 1760 when George III surrendered it to the government as part of his financial settlement with Parliament.

The Post Office at first only provided a service along the main routes out of London, and it was left to the private initiative of a merchant, William Dockwra, to establish a penny post within the metropolis in 1680. This threatened the monopoly of the Post Office, and in 1682 the courts ruled against Dockwra. Shortly afterwards, the Post Office itself created a postal service for London at a rate of one penny (1d) which was extended to the suburbs in 1794 for the payment of a further 1d. London was for a long time the only city with an internal postal service, and it was not until 1765 that penny posts were permitted elsewhere in Britain. During the 18th century, the importance of the main post roads which radiated from London was complemented by a growing traffic within the provinces. The traffic was difficult to control from London, and much of the revenue was lost. In 1720, the management of this business was given to Ralph Allen, the Postmaster of Bath and the owner of the quarries used to supply stone to the growing city. He acted as contractor for postal services between provincial centers until his death in 1764, and was largely responsible for improving the national coverage of the mail service.

Further improvements were made from 1784 by John Palmer, who owned theaters in Bath and Bristol. Allen relied upon horse posts, and Palmer argued that a better service could be supplied by fast mail coaches on the improved turnpike roads. The coaches were owned by a firm in London which was paid a mileage rate by both the Post Office and the operator; the operator, who supplied horses and drivers, was paid a mileage rate by the Post Office, took the revenue from passengers, and was exempt from tolls on the roads. The new system was introduced between London and Bristol in 1784, and in 1786 Palmer was appointed Surveyor and Comptroller General of the Mails at a salary of £1,500 with a commission of $2^1/2$% of any increase in the net revenue. The mail services had been improved, yet their administration was complex. There were separate offices for inland and London district letters; there was a host of private interests within the service, with individuals receiving salaries and taking profits from office; and the revenue was charged with a large number of pensions.

The government saw the Post Office as a source of revenue to finance the wars with France during the 18th century, and William Pitt had welcomed Palmer's improvement to the service as a justification for raising postage rates. In 1711 rates were fixed at 3d for a single sheet up to 80 miles, and 4d for longer distances; by 1815, the rates were 4d for distances up to 15 miles, rising to 14d for up to 500 miles. In London, the 1d rate was replaced by a 2d rate in 1801. These higher rates proved counterproductive. The net revenue of the Post Office increased from about £200,000 in 1784 to £1.6 million in 1815, and then stagnated; it was only £1.5 million in 1835. There was a widespread evasion of postage. The privilege of Members of Parliament to frank mail for free transmission was widely abused, and a large number of letters ignored the Post Office monopoly. An expanding network of stage coaches and common carriers handled "contraband" mail, which was perhaps greater in volume than the mail carried by the Post Office.

In the 1830s the Post Office faced demands for reform, associated in particular with Rowland Hill's pamphlet *Post Office Reform* of 1837 which argued for a reduction in the postage rate to 1d, regardless of distance. Hill was reflecting a general sentiment. There was already a select committee considering Post Office matters, and Henry Parnell had commented in *On Financial Reform* in 1830 that "when a tax has been carried to an excessively high point, the reducing of it is not necessarily followed by a reduction of revenue." The experience of cuts in duties on tea, coffee, and sugar had suggested that demand increased, and the revenue was not affected. Hill believed that high rates of postage were similarly reducing demand for the mail services, and that lower rates would lead to an increase in traffic by five and a quarter times. He argued that the cost of conveying a letter was minimal, so that the postage rate could be the same regardless of distance. Most of the cost arose from administrative charges, which resulted from the need to inspect each letter to determine the distance it was traveling and the number of sheets of paper it contained, and to calculate the charge. The payment of the postage was usually made by the recipient, which meant that the delivery of letters was a time-consuming business. Costs were further inflated because there were separate offices and staffs for inland letters, foreign letters, and the London district service. Hill proposed a sweeping change in administration in order to reduce costs: letters should be prepaid by the use of postage stamps, and the offices amalgamated. Greater economy of administration, and an increased volume of mail, would allow the net revenue of the Post Office to be maintained.

Hill's program had the backing of a number of groups, including City merchants who would benefit from cheaper postage, and the radical publisher Charles Knight who saw the usefulness of the Post Office in creating a wider market for his literature. Knight published Hill's pamphlet, and they were both involved in the Society for the Diffusion of Useful Knowledge. Hill was on the fringes of the utilitarian reform movement, and his allies mounted an impressive campaign which succeeded in 1839 when an act was passed to introduce a penny post throughout the country in 1840. Many remained skeptical of Hill's logic. They wondered whether the price elasticity of letter writing was as great as Hill assumed, and argued that distance was the key to the value of the service to the consumer. Above all, the fiscal situation around 1840 made a reduction in postage rates problematic. Income tax had been abolished at the end of the Napoleonic wars, and the highly regressive tax regime that followed was threatening social unrest. There was a fear that a reduction in postage rates would be at the expense of other tax reductions with greater popular support. The result was much as the skeptics warned. Although the number of letters did rise from 75.9 million in 1839 to 168.8 million in 1840, the net revenue fell from £1.63 million to £500,789. The government's budget slid into deficit, which contributed to the fall of the Whig administration in 1841.

Hill was, like Allen and Palmer, an outsider who forced the Post Office to reconsider its entrenched attitudes, and the circumstances of his appointment to oversee the new penny post did not help him to gain acceptance. He was given a two-year appointment at the Treasury, and had to work with the Secretary of the Post Office, W.L. Maberly, who felt that Hill's scheme was misconceived. The budget crisis weakened Hill's position at the Treasury, and in 1842 he left the service of the government. It was only in 1846, with the return of the Whigs to power, that he obtained a position in the Post Office, as

Secretary to the Postmaster General. He started to enforce strict controls over costs and in 1854 he at last obtained the position he wanted: Secretary to the Post Office as the sole permanent head of its administration. The introduction of income tax had solved the budget crisis, and the net revenue of the Post Office was increasing; Hill was transformed into a national benefactor. Until his retirement in 1864 he ran the Post Office in a high-handed and autocratic manner, with scant regard for the fact that he was in theory answerable to the Postmaster General who was the political head of the department.

By the early 1860s Hill was becoming an unpopular figure within the Post Office, increasingly reliant upon his brother Frederic as his only dependable ally. The need to reduce expenditure obsessed him, which led him into conflict with railway companies, shipowners, and the work force. When Hill argued for a reduction of the postage rate to one penny, he was adamant that uniformity of charge be justified by uniformity of cost; he argued that the actual cost of carriage of letters was so insignificant that it need not influence the charge. However, this argument was applied only to the main distribution between towns, and he felt that delivery to other areas should be paid for by the local authority. Although Hill abandoned this distinction between the primary and secondary distribution in order to secure the introduction of penny post, he firmly opposed any further concession. He was deeply hostile to any cross-subsidization between services, and was, indeed, opposed to the postal monopoly for he felt that the Post Office should be competitive with any rival. Increasingly, his colleagues in the Post Office felt that he was jeopardizing the operation of the mail services in his blind pursuit of economy. His younger colleagues such as John Tilley and Frank Scudamore wished to move into new directions. To them, the Post Office was more of a social service, and they were willing to utilize the profit from the letter service in order to cover loss-making ventures. In the later 19th century, Hill's emphasis upon strict economy was overturned.

The penny post was gradually extended to wider areas, with the introduction of an imperial penny post in 1898 and its extension to the United States in 1908. These services made a loss, and the principle of uniformity could not be justified by cost. Hill had been willing to accept the introduction of a parcel post operated in conjunction with the railway companies, and this was finally introduced in 1883. What would have horrified him was that the service made a loss. The railway companies received 55% of the postage on rail-borne items, which did not leave sufficient revenue for the Post Office to cover its costs. There was no monopoly on the parcel service and the Post Office insisted on charging a uniform national rate, with the result that competitors were able to cream off the profitable local traffic.

The Post Office also moved into financial services. Money orders had been provided as a private venture by employees of the Post Office in 1792, with official sanction, as a means to remove the need to send bank notes through the post. The money order business was taken over by the Post Office in 1838, and made a loss. The problem was the low commission on smaller orders, and Hill's solution was to develop the more profitable larger orders with a higher commission. Here he ran foul of the Treasury, which was wary of competing with commercial banks, and Scudamore, who argued that the Post Office had a moral duty to assist workers in transmitting small sums. In 1881 the solution was the introduction of postal orders, a cheaper means of sending small sums. In 1861 the financial services were again extended to provide the Post Office Savings Bank. Hill was skeptical, but the opportunity was seized by Scudamore. The supporters of the POSB hoped that it would encourage thrift amongst the working classes, while at the same time solving two pressing political problems. The existing Trustee Savings Banks which were provided by the middle class imposed a financial drain on the state, and were outside the scope of government regulation; Gladstone hoped that they would gradually be replaced by a government system of banks with a national coverage. He also hoped that the deposits of small savers in the Post Office Savings Bank (POSB) would be directed to the reduction of the national debt. Gladstone believed that the POSB would encourage both private morality through thrift and self-help, and public morality by reducing the burden of the state on enterprise. Unfortunately, these expectations were not realized. Most depositors were not working class, and in the late 19th century the Bank started to make a loss. The rate paid to depositors was fixed at $2^{1}/_{2}\%$, and the POSB was obliged to purchase government stock which paid a lower rate at the end of the century. There was some discussion of extending the Post Office's interest in remittance services and savings banks into a giro bank such as that developed in Austria. However, it was felt that the state should not enter into competition with the commercial banks, and the introduction of a giro bank was delayed until 1968. These financial services have subsequently been removed from the Post Office.

The financial services were important additions to the services of the Post Office; even more significant was the movement into telecommunications. The nationalization of the telegraph system was approved by Parliament in 1868, and the private companies were transferred to the Post Office in 1870 when a program of rapid expansion was started under Scudamore. His eagerness to expand the public sector led him into serious error. He diverted funds from the POSB for use in the telegraph service, in order to circumvent the control of Parliament and the Treasury. There was some virtue in his argument that he could not have undertaken the task if he had waited for approval, and many other Post Office officials were to be frustrated by the obfuscations of the Treasury. Unfortunately, Scudamore had misjudged the economics of the telegraph service, and the telegraph service was overcapitalized and unprofitable. The Post Office was given a monopoly of the telegraph service, and in 1879 the courts ruled that this also covered telephones. The Postmaster General consequently had control over the new technology, and licenses for 31 years expiring in 1911 were awarded to the telephone companies in return for a royalty of 10% of gross receipts. The Post Office had the right to purchase at fixed intervals, and in 1892 decided to purchase the trunk lines and leave the local exchanges to the private companies. In 1898 this policy of cooperation between private and public enterprise was abandoned, and the Post Office decided to move into direct competition or to grant licenses to local authorities in order to force the private company into selling its plant on reasonable terms when the licenses expired. In 1912 the Post Office acquired the telephone system whose development had been distorted and frustrated by the previous 30 years of policy. There was little improvement after national-

ization. Telecommunications were the poor relations of the Post Office. In 1930–1931, for example, the postal services had a surplus of £9.85 million, whereas the telegraphs had a deficit of £1.01 million which was only partly covered by a surplus of £340,000 on telephones.

By 1914 the Post Office had become a huge organization and was facing problems. It was conservative, a creature of habit and routine; its ethos was largely that of a mail service, with a lack of sympathy for telephones. It was the largest single employer in the country, and the negotiations with unions, which were recognized in 1906, took up ever more time and energy. The administration was highly centralized in London, with a lack of initiative and a stultifying grip of routine. Not surprisingly, it was suggested in 1928 by the Lever Committee—appointed by the Postmaster General "to inquire into the Inland Telegraph Service"—that telegraphs and telephones should be removed from the Post Office and civil service traditions in order to permit more active development, but no action was taken. A large part of the effort of the administration was devoted to persuading the Treasury of the justice of any expenditure, however minor. The entire surplus was handed over to the Exchequer, which made it difficult to formulate an investment program, especially for telephones. Clement Attlee in 1931 drew a conclusion from his experience as Postmaster General in the Labour government: Treasury control "is wholly incompatible with the flexibility necessary in the conduct of a business concern," and he argued that "long ago, a bargain should have been made definitely limiting the amount of the contribution to be made to the State by the Post Office." The 1932 Bridgeman report, the outcome of an enquiry on the Post Office under the chairmanship of Lord Bridgeman, accepted the force of these criticisms, and in 1933 it was agreed that the Post Office should pay a fixed contribution of £10.75 million to the Exchequer, with a degree of autonomy in decision making. The triumph of this "self-contained finance" was short-lived, for it was suspended during World War II and was only reintroduced in 1956. The administrative structure of the Post Office also underwent considerable revision, with an attempt to create a regional structure to break down the excessive over-centralization of power. The revision was not complete until 1940, when the Post Office was overtaken by other issues.

After World War II the postal services barely broke even, and there was a serious crisis for this labor-intensive business during an era of full employment and wage inflation. By the late 1960s there was a deficit on the postal services and attention increasingly turned to attempts to reduce labor costs. Traditionally, the Post Office had been able to cover its peaks in sorting and delivery by the employment of part-timers who did not receive the full benefits of established civil servants. However, the union had secured the abolition of casual labor, and the solution was to spread the workload over the day. In the 1950s and 1960s the Post Office moved towards the mechanization of sorting in a few large offices, which required the introduction of post codes in 1965 and a two-tier service in 1968 which allowed second-class mail to be handled during the slack period of the day. In many ways the program was mishandled. Public acceptance of postal codes was poor, and the relations with the unions broke down. It seemed to many that the Post Office had lost the will to manage, and was trapped into a circle of consultation with the unions which had led to a dead-end. The unions were not willing to cooperate in improving productivity, with the result that wages lagged, and labor relations deteriorated with a national postal strike in 1971. There was a vicious circle of increasing postage rates, declining traffic, and deteriorating productivity, which was at last addressed in the 1980s by more aggressive marketing to increase mail volumes and to improve productivity by tackling entrenched work practices. The result was a considerable improvement in the performance of the Post Office in the 1980s. It proved possible to produce a surplus and to finance a large investment program.

Meanwhile the reforms of the 1930s were extended. In 1960 Post Office finances were treated in a similar way to a nationalized industry, with the creation of a Post Office Fund into which all revenue was paid and from which expenditure was met. The conclusion was drawn in 1966, when the Labor government decided to shift the Post Office from the civil service and to make it a public corporation like other nationalized industries. In 1981 the recommendation of the Lever Committee was finally implemented, when the Post Office was split into two separate corporations with the formation of British Telecommunications. The result was closer to the ideal laid down by Rowland Hill: an organization that was concerned about profit and productivity, concentrating upon the mail services and competing with its rivals in a more aggressive way, free of direct political and Treasury control. The mail monopoly, which Hill felt was an unnecessary interference with free competition, still remains; whether it will continue is one of the crucial issues facing the Post Office in the 1990s.

Further Reading: Robinson, H., *The British Post Office: A History,* Cambridge, Mass., 1948; Daunton, M.J., *Royal Mail: The Post Office since 1840,* London, The Athlone Press, 1985.

—Martin James Daunton

ROADWAY SERVICES, INC.

1077 Gorge Boulevard
Akron, Ohio 44039
U.S.A.
(216) 384-8184
Fax: (216) 258-6599

Public Company
Incorporated: 1930 as Roadway Express, Inc.
Employees: 40,000
Sales: $2.97 billion
Stock Exchange: NASDAQ

Roadway Services, Inc. is the second-largest motor freight carrier company in the United States. The company's principal operating group, Roadway Express, has specialized in less-than-truckload (LTL) shipments across North America for many years, and until the mid-1980s was the industry leader. After being surpassed at that time by rival Yellow Freight, Roadway has taken significant steps to make itself more competitive and was once again in the early 1990s gaining ground.

Roadway Express was founded in 1930 by brothers Galen and Carroll Roush in Akron, Ohio. Although trucking had made great strides during the 1920s, the motor carrier industry was still in its infancy. Railroads provided the primary transportation for goods from point of manufacture to point of sale. Trucks were used for less than full-load shipments, still Roadway's primary market. In 1930 Roadway entered the business it would come to lead with a load of tires shipped from Akron to St. Louis, Missouri.

Roadway Express started with ten owner-operators, and moved shipments to Chicago; Houston, Texas; and Kansas City. Within several months terminals were opened in Atlanta, Georgia; Baltimore, Maryland; Birmingham, Alabama; Charlotte, North Carolina; Indianapolis, Indiana; Knoxville, Memphis, and Nashville, Tennessee; New York; and Philadelphia, Pennsylvania. Roadway's rapid expansion reflected the growth of interstate trucking in general.

Before long, railroaders, fearful of unrestrained competition, began to clamor for regulation. In 1935 Congress passed the Motor Carrier Act, limiting the right to operate in interstate commerce to those carriers already in operation and to new ones that could prove "necessity and convenience." The Interstate Commerce Commission would oversee standard rates, preventing particular customers from receiving preferential rates.

While regulation had its disadvantages, founder Galen Roush, originally trained as a lawyer, saw great potential in the new regulated business climate. Roadway had kept detailed records of its shipments over the years. These records became the basis of Roush's claim to some of the busiest freight routes in the country. Regulation helped limit competition, and at the same time elevated the status of the trucking industry to the equivalent of a public utility. Although it took 16 years of court battles before Roadway's routes were finally secured, the company held exclusive rights to its most lucrative routes.

The Roush brothers recognized the significance of hiring good managers, and instituted tight financial controls early on. Roadway was conservatively run, and kept a very low profile. It maintained this approach for decades.

In the 1940s demand for truck transportation increased as the defense economy of World War II eliminated the last effects of the Great Depression. At the same time, new trucks were not being built as the necessary materials were being diverted for war goods. In 1945 Roadway Express began replacing owner-operators with hired drivers to run its own fleet. After the war, trucking gained significant ground from the railroad industry. By 1950 the ratio of truck to train ton-miles was 20%, twice that of two years earlier. Roadway began to stress its less-than-truckload service in the early 1950s. The price charged per pound shipped was sometimes three or more times the cost of a full load, and the flexibility of the service improved the chances of a return load.

Business boomed, and Roadway needed to establish a broader terminal network. The company's excellent financial record helped Galen Roush convince Chase Manhattan Bank to loan Roadway millions of dollars for expansion. Trucking companies were previously poorly regarded by most financiers. By 1956 Roadway's fleet and terminal expansion program had progressed to the point where Roadway no longer used owner-operators at all.

In 1956 Carroll Roush, the younger of the two founding brothers, decided to sell his interest in Roadway. He was barely speaking with his brother, Galen, and in a move designed at least in part to annoy him, Carroll sold his shares to the public for about $5 million. Traveling west, he bought ONC Fast Freight, which later became a part of ROCOR International.

In the late 1950s and in the 1960s, Galen Roush set out to expand the terminal network. Population centers were spreading out, and trucking needed to be less centered around big cities. The greater number of terminals allowed decentralized service. Roadway Express expanded its network from 60 terminals in 1958 to 135 in 1968.

At the same time, Roadway instituted the most sophisticated accounting procedures in the industry—the brainchild of cost accountant John L. Tormey. The company could identify profit and loss by route, commodity, weight bracket, and individual customer. As the company expanded rapidly, it was able to focus on profitable business and easily control costs. Roadway truckers continued to haul less-than-truckload shipments and produce higher profit margins. Each terminal was a profit-and-loss center; aggressive managers were enriched with hefty bonuses.

Roadway's expansion during the 1960s required heavy borrowing, but the decision to risk the debt paid off later. The loans were paid off by the 1970s, and cash flow was high. Meanwhile Roadway's competitors were still heavily burdened. When the recession hit in 1974–1975, this financial strength kept Roadway the number-one trucker despite hard times. Roadway's return on investment averaged 20% a year in the early 1970s. Direct coverage grew to 40 states in the mid-1970s, and the company became a transcontinental carrier in 1977.

In 1980 deregulation of rates and services opened new avenues for motor carriers. This gave Roadway Express the opportunity to expand into new areas of business, but at the same time it faced new challenges from competitors. While other trucking companies slashed prices to attract customers, Roadway marketed itself as the high-quality carrier with the widest geographic coverage, and clung to its high margins. By 1982, however, with revenues slipping, Roadway chose to discount its prices. The company had fallen to third in market share, surpassed by Yellow Freight and Consolidated Freightways. Realizing the need to step out of the shadows and reassert its position, Roadway launched its first advertising campaign in history.

After the initial shock of deregulation settled, Roadway embarked on a campaign of acquisition and new services. In 1982 a holding company, Roadway Services, Inc., was set up with Roadway Express as its chief operating subsidiary. In 1984 Roadway Services acquired Spartan Express, Inc.; Nationwide Carriers, Inc.; and Roberts Express, Inc. Spartan Express, Roadway's first acquisition, operated as a short-haul carrier in the South. Unlike Roadway Express, Spartan handled shipments with 24- and 48-hour service requirements. Nationwide Carriers specialized in irregular route truckload shipments throughout the continental United States. Nationwide hauled dry freight, temperature-controlled freight, and freight requiring flatbed transport. Roberts Express specialized in critical or fragile shipments needing special handling or speedy delivery.

In 1985 Roadway's earnings dipped for the first time in 32 years. Conversion of Roadway's truck fleet to twin trailers and start-up costs of a new unit were the chief reasons. The new subsidiary, Roadway Package System (RPS), got a slow start, but became a transportation success story in the 1980s.

RPS set out to take a piece of the $12 billion small-package surface delivery business, then dominated by United Parcel Service (UPS). RPS concentrated on business-to-business delivery of packages up to 100 pounds, and implemented some innovative procedures to keep costs down. By selling or leasing RPS trucks to independent owner-operators, the company cut labor costs to 60% of UPS's while giving each driver a personal stake in efficient service.

It took three years and $103 million in investments before RPS showed a profit, but considering the scale of the start-up, it was an impressive accomplishment. By 1988 the subsidiary boasted 130 terminals, and geographic coverage of 70% of the United States. By 1990, 147 terminal facilities served 42 states. While UPS had 20 times the revenue of RPS, Roadway's subsidiary had carved a healthy niche out of a growing business segment. RPS contributed one-fourth of Roadway Services's profits in 1989. Growth prospects looked excellent.

Roadway Services, meanwhile, continued to seek less-than-truckload carriers that would complement its existing geographic coverage. In 1988 Roadway acquired Viking Freight, the largest regional carrier in the western United States. Viking had two operating subsidiaries: Viking Freight System, a regional LTL carrier, and VFS Transportation, an irregular-route truckload carrier. Viking was almost alone among carriers in being nonunion.

In 1989 Roadway closed its Nationwide Carriers subsidiary. Nationwide had been unprofitable despite reorganization. The Roadway Express unit struggled with discounted rates in the later 1980s, but successfully held its position against smaller carriers. In 1987 a New York City trucking firm, Lifschultz Fast Freight Inc., filed suit against trucking's big three—Yellow Freight, Roadway Services, and Consolidated Freightways—charging predatory pricing and conspiracy to restrain trade and free competition in certain segments of the industry. The suit was still pending four years after it was filed, and was expected to go to trial. The suit sought $598 million in damages.

Competition from the railroad industry also grew fierce as the 1980s closed. Threatened by the prospect of bigger double and triple trailers hauling freight on highways, railroad lobbyists launched campaigns painting a grim picture of motor carriers' safety standards. When one such group, the Coalition for Reliable and Safer Highways (CRASH), used a photo of a Roadway Express truck accident at government hearings in California, Roadway's chairman Joseph Clapp objected, citing Roadway's top safety record. Competition between railroaders and truckers promised to become increasingly heated in the 1990s.

In March 1990 Roadway's Roberts Express unit launched a European subsidiary, Roberts Express, B.V., headquartered in Maastricht, the Netherlands. The subsidiary offered Roberts's traditional services in Belgium, France, Luxembourg, the Netherlands, and Germany. Roadway Express in 1990 set up a Mexican subsidiary, Roadway Bodegas y Consolidación, and expanded operations in Canada.

As Roadway Services entered the 1990s, its various units showed mixed results, although as a whole the company continued to expand. Roadway Express increased revenues and profits. Spartan Express was divided into two geographic divisions in 1988 but remained unprofitable; in 1990 it became a subsidiary of Viking Freight. Roberts Express's growth was good, but less than expected. RPS and Viking Freight both performed well, but the latter's VFS Transportation subsidiary did not, and was closed down in 1990. The surface transportation industry was in for some turmoil, as railroads promised to fight for their space, and as air transport became more competitive. Roadway had dropped its image as a stodgy company, and no longer hesitated to step into the public eye as had been characteristic of the company from its founding through the 1970s. The change at Roadway Services was characteristic of the industry as a whole, illustrated by the fact that in 1991 the Dow Jones transportation averages added Roadway Services as one of the key indicators of the industry's overall performance.

Principal Subsidiaries: Roadway Express, Inc.; Roberts Transportation Services, Inc.; Roadway Logistics System, Inc.; Roadway Package System, Inc.; Viking Freight, Inc.

Further Reading: "Doing It the Hard Way," *Forbes,* December 1, 1975; Briggs, Jean A., "Easing into High Gear," *Forbes,* August 31, 1981; "The No. 1 Trucker Joins a Price-Cutting Convoy," *Business Week,* February 8, 1982; Hannon, Kerry, "Shifting Gears," *Forbes,* December 11, 1989.

—Thomas M. Tucker

RYDER SYSTEM, INC.

3600 Northwest 82nd Avenue
Miami, Florida 33166
U.S.A.
(305) 593-3726

Public Company
Incorporated: 1955
Employees: 40,362
Sales: $5.16 billion
Stock Exchanges: New York Pacific Midwest

Ryder System, Inc. is a major transportation services provider with annual revenues in excess of $5 billion. Ryder operates the world's largest full-service truck leasing and short-term rental company; North America's largest new-automobile transport company; the largest independent jet-aircraft engine maintenance and overhaul company; a leading aircraft leasing and parts distribution company; and a leading provider of mass transit and school bus services throughout the United States. Ryder is the market leader in most of its operating areas.

In 1932 James A. Ryder gave up his job as a straw boss in a construction firm, and bought a Model A pickup truck with a down payment of $125. Ryder hauled trash from Miami beaches and delivered construction materials to Palm Beach. In 1934 he entered the truck-leasing business through a contract with a local beer distributor. At the age of 21, Ryder was the owner of the first truck-leasing firm in the United States, Ryder Truck Rental System, Inc.

In 1939 Ryder took on a partner, Roy N. Reedy, and the two men set out to build a trucking empire. Truck leasing was novel, and the company broke new ground. Highway trucking began to rival rail as a means of overland shipping, based partly on the vast network of better highways constructed during the 1930s. World War II boosted demand for trucking, as the war economy stretched the existing transportation system to capacity, and Ryder's trucking and leasing operations grew.

The postwar era brought continued growth to the trucking industry as the interstate highway program further improved the efficiency of trucking. By 1952 Ryder was bringing in $3 million annually by renting 1,300 trucks. In the summer of that year news came that the Southeast's largest, most profitable trucking outfit, the Great Southern Trucking Company, was up for sale. Ryder was familiar with Great Southern; his company leased its pickup and delivery trucks. Founded in 1933 by L.A. Raulerson, it had grown into the Southeast's

largest freight carrier with some routes as long as 1,100 miles. Ryder raised the $2 million asking price by December. His company's revenues were then quadruple what they had been, and Ryder was a huge motor carrier, as well as a major truck-leasing concern.

The Great Southern acquisition put Ryder on the map. Ryder System, Inc., was created in 1955 to absorb Ryder Truck Rental and Great Southern, and the new company offered shares to the public. Shortly thereafter Ryder System bought more than 25 companies in five years. The larger companies included Baker Truck Rental, Inc., of Denver, Colorado; Barrett Truck Leasing Co. of Detroit; T.S.C. Motor Freight Lines, Inc.; the truck leasing business of Columbia Terminals Co.; Dixie Drive-It-Yourself System, of Alabama; the truck leasing business of Barrett Garages, Inc., of San Francisco; Morrison International Corporation; and International Railway Car Leasing Corporation.

This growth resulted in certain problems. The company had neglected proper financial controls. By 1960 Ryder System was forced to write off $2 million in bad debt, and profits dipped from $2.7 million in 1959 to about $1 million in 1960. A central accounting system was implemented to remedy the problems, and steady growth returned in the early 1960s.

In 1965 Ryder System sold the motor carrier division to International Utilities (IU), a diversified holding company. The trucking division grew under IU's direction until its spin-off in 1982, keeping the Ryder name. Ryder System focused on the fast-growing truck-leasing business, and despite common misperceptions had not operated as a freight carrier since 1965.

The late 1960s saw the development of new services in truck leasing and rental. In 1967 Ryder began offering one-way truck rental service. This service had been introduced and popularized by the U-Haul Company several years earlier. Ryder started with 1,000 trucks and expanded the one-way fleet to 7,630 the first year. Competition in this field grew rapidly; Hertz Corporation and E-Z Haul, division of National Car Rental System, Inc., entered the field at the same time. As a result, the one-way market was oversupplied, and Ryder's one-way unit got off to a slow start. Ryder was intent on capturing this market, however. In 1968 the company offered to buy U-Haul International Co., a subsidiary of Americo, Inc., but no deal was ever worked out. Ryder expanded its one-way dealership network through an agreement with Budget Rent-A-Car. While many competitors dropped out in the early 1970s, Ryder did not, selling surplus vehicles when necessary, and eventually surpassed U-Haul's one-way rental in 1987.

In 1968 Ryder entered the new-automotive carriage business when it acquired M & G Convoy, Inc., and expanded it with the purchase of Complete Auto Transit, Inc., in January 1970. Ryder's automotive carriage services were used by General Motors Corporation and Chrysler Corporation for the transport of new automobiles to dealerships. Also around this time, Ryder entered the dedicated contract carriage business, in which it provides transportation and distribution services customized for its clients.

In the late 1960s Ryder System diversified into services unrelated to transport leasing. In late 1969 Ryder made a foray into the growing temporary help industry, initially placing office and industrial personnel, later technical help. Ryder also acquired several trade schools in 1969 and 1970, offering courses in auto mechanics, truck driving, and a number of other technical fields. In 1970 Ryder purchased Mobile World Inc., a distributor of mobile homes and a mobile-home-park operator and franchiser. Also in 1970 an insurance firm, Southern Underwriters, Inc., was acquired, and later that year, a joint venture, Ryd-Air Inc., was formed to provide pickup and delivery service for 27 airlines in New York.

Ryder's main line—full service truck leasing—remained strong in the early 1970s, but the company's management was spread thin over a growing number of new service fields. In 1973 the oil crisis enticed Ryder to purchase Toro Petroleum Corporation of Louisiana to insure a steady fuel supply for its trucks, but the acquisition proved a somewhat rash move. The value of Toro's oil reserves dropped as oil prices fell a few months after the purchase. Ryder had bought high and ended up with a $7 million operating loss.

Other problems caused a 13¢ per share adjustment after the company's 1973 audit. They were adjustments in the calculation of receivables from the education unit, tax assessments on the mobile home subsidiary, and reserve assessments on the insurance subsidiary. The truck leasing and rental businesses continued to borrow in order to finance an expanded fleet. Ryder's debts were more than $400 million, four times shareholders' equity. Moody's Investors Service downgraded Ryder's rating on commercial paper in late 1974. Ryder System lost $20 million, and the company's investors were deeply concerned. The board of directors began to question James Ryder's ability to guide the future of the growing concern.

The recession of 1973–1974 had taken a heavy toll on Ryder's vast contract carriage and automotive carriage operations, which were heavily dependent upon the welfare of the automotive industry. Although Ryder's core business of truck leasing and rental was holding its own despite the hard times, company borrowing had gotten out of control. Stockholders displeased with the company's troublesome acquisitions from the early 1970s demanded a refocusing of attention to Ryder's basic businesses. In 1975 James Ryder, under pressure from the boardroom and his bankers, announced that he was seeking a "more professional manager" to run the still growing company. In the summer of 1975, after disposing of unprofitable subsidiaries like Toro Petroleum; Miller Trailers, Inc.; and the major portion of the technical schools, James Ryder stepped down as head of the company he had founded.

Ryder's successor was Leslie O. Barnes, former head of Allegheny Airlines. Barnes inherited a company that was tattered after weathering a great storm, and the 59-year-old CEO was intent on whipping Ryder System back into shape. The debt-to-equity ratio was quickly pared from four-to-one to three-to-one. Ryder Liftlease Inc., a small but troublesome subsidiary was sold, as well as the remainder of the technical schools. Refocused on its primary businesses, Ryder rebounded. In 1977 the company acquired a major automobile carrier, Janesville Auto Transport Company, for $10 million in common stock. Ryder's automotive carriage operations were profitable as a result of the industry's rebound and tighter financial controls. During the 1979 downturn in the automotive markets, Ryder's automotive contract carriage unit, representing 16% of Ryder System's turnover, made a profit.

In the late 1970s Ryder continued to grow internally and through acquisitions in the full-service truck-leasing business, the company continued to lead the market, which continued to expand. According to Barnes, only 38% of the U.S. private truck fleets were wholly owned by 1980, down from 60% in 1970. The vast majority of fleets were at least partially leased. Encouraged by the basic business's performance during the latter half of the 1970s, Ryder System once again began to seek acquisitions in new areas. Barnes, however, unlike James Ryder, was inclined to test out new ventures on a small scale before fully committing to them. In 1978 a parcel delivery service, Jack Rabbit Express, was acquired. A small property and casualty reinsurance company, Federal Assurance Co., was added to existing insurance operations.

By the late 1970s the one-way rental market was well-established. Ryder trailed U-Haul in this field, and in 1978, a third major competitor, Jartran Inc., joined the field. Jartran was an acronym for James A. Ryder Transportation. James Ryder gave up a $100,000 annual stipend to get out of his noncompetition agreement with Ryder System. The upstart company established by Ryder System's founder and former head made a smashing entry into the field, building a 30,000 vehicle fleet in less than 18 months. James Ryder's new company became a thorn in the side of his former company. The feisty Ryder appeared in Jartran ads as "the man who invented truck rental," and his new vehicles resembled Ryder System's enough to spark a lawsuit.

Nevertheless, Jartran had trouble making a profit. Once again, it appeared that James Ryder had grown too big too fast. A downturn in the economy in 1979 killed the short-term rental market. Jartran cumulatively lost $30 million in 1979 and 1980. In July 1981 Jartran dumped its commercial leasing division, and the company was foundering.

Ryder System, on the other hand, grew under the balanced leadership of Barnes and his new executive vice president, M. Anthony Burns. In the early 1980s, new tax laws encouraged diversification into new areas. Ryder began shopping for a financial services company in order to take full advantage of available tax credits. Insurance was the obvious choice because of Ryder's existing insurance business. In September 1981 Ryder System announced its desire to purchase the third largest insurance broker in the United States, Frank B. Hall and Co. Hall, however, was not interested in being acquired, and maneuvered to avert a takeover. In October 1981 Hall announced its intentions to purchase Jartran, Ryder System's troubled competitor, opening up potential antitrust obstacles for a takeover. Hall also filed a number of suits against Ryder.

Ryder System's pursuit of Hall continued through 1982. By August Ryder System had boosted its holdings in Hall to 9.5%. Jartran was on its way to bankruptcy, but Hall had bought enough time to discourage Ryder System from acquiring any more Hall stock. In 1983 Ryder sold its interest in the insurance broker for $33 million.

In 1982 a severe recession shook the North American economy. Ryder System was well prepared with a $70 million cash surplus, and a very low debt-to-equity ratio. While the majority of transportation companies were devastated, Ryder System's profits increased. Burns moved up to CEO, and soon proclaimed Ryder's intention to "be more forward-thinking, more risk-taking." By slashing prices in half on one-way rentals, Ryder usurped a huge chunk of the market. By acquiring two new strategically located automobile carriage firms, Ryder improved its efficiency by reducing the number of trailers sent back empty.

Ryder System's long-standing desire to enter financial services was satisfied in 1983 when the company became an 80% partner in a pension fund specialist, Forstmann, Leff, Kimberly. The joint venture set up long-term trusts for pension fund investors. Ryder also decided to revise its in-house business information systems and offer them for sale to other transportation companies, and contemplated a computer-services company acquisition to assist.

In its core transportation businesses, Ryder continued to make strides. Deregulation had been the industry trend since 1980. In 1983 new rules concerning single-source leasing allowed private fleet operators to get drivers through Ryder as a part of the leasing agreement. Private shippers were also allowed to solicit outside freight business, effectively allowing direct competition with independent truckers. Ryder set up a new division to handle single-source leasing, and bought three new freight packaging companies to book return loads for private shippers leasing from Ryder. In 1984, Ryder sold its Truckstops Corporation of America unit for $85 million to free managerial resources for more profitable businesses.

In the early 1980s Ryder System began to delve into another expanding transportation field—aviation leasing. In 1983 the Aviation Sales Co. Inc. and its subsidiary General Hydraulics Corporation, of Florida, an aircraft leasing and spare parts firm was acquired. In 1985 Ryder bought Aviall, Inc., a turbine engine repair and overhaul firm located in Dallas. Aviall was also a parts distributor. A number of smaller leasing and repair companies were acquired. By late 1986 aviation services made up about one-fifth of Ryder System's revenues, and in 1987 the division branched out overseas with the purchase of Caledonian Airmotive, Ltd. The Scottish subsidiary serviced the big engines on British Caledonian Airways' DC-10s and 747s, among others. Caledonian Airmotive complemented Aviall's operation both geographically and in services offered.

By 1988 just six years after entering the field, Ryder System was the world's largest jet engine overhaul and rebuilding company, the largest aviation parts distributor, and one of the largest aircraft and jet-engine leasing companies. Ryder's aviation division counted 300 commercial airlines among its clients, and dozens of private operators. In 1988 revenues from aviation neared $1 billion.

Ryder's truck leasing continued to surge ahead. In 1986 a major federal tax law revision made it desirable for private fleet operators to lease their fleets rather than buy. Ryder had been determinedly expanding its truck fleet; between 1984 and 1988 it nearly doubled. More and more fleet operators turned over the hassles of fleet purchase, maintenance, and insurance to Ryder, allowing them to concentrate on manufacture and sale of their products.

In one-way rental, Ryder excelled. The longtime leader in the field—U-Haul—was distracted as family members battled amongst themselves for control of the business. U-Haul started renting all kinds of equipment, from rototillers to hoists, and its truck fleet quietly grew old. In 1987 the average age of a U-Haul truck was ten years. Ryder's, on the other hand, averaged two years, and had all kinds of features not found at U-Haul, like power steering, air-conditioning, AM-FM radios, fuel efficient engines, and radial tires. Ryder's market share was 45%, equal to U-Haul's in 1987, and surging forward.

Between 1983 and 1987 Ryder System spent $1.1 billion on 65 acquisitions. This time the company's rapid expansion was readily digested. In 1985 Ryder entered the school-bus leasing business, and quickly grew to be the second-largest private student-transport company in the United States. Ryder also entered into public transportation system consulting and leasing at about the same time. Dedicated contract carriage received greater attention in the late 1980s. Ryder provided trucks, drivers, and management system design to specialty freight companies like Emery Air Freight, retailers like Montgomery Ward, Sears, and J.C. Penney, and newspaper publishers like Dow Jones and the Miami Herald.

In 1989 Ryder's growth flattened out, but its potential in its existing areas of operation remained strong. Late in the year the company sold its insurance operations, and, anticipating the coming recession, trimmed its fleet to better match demand. Ryder had proven its ability to manage well in tough times during the 1982 recession. As the automotive carriage and commercial truck operations were in the downside of the cycle, Ryder focused on improving market share while awaiting a general economic recovery. Its success was demonstrated in 1990 when Ryder moved 39% of the automobiles shipped in the United States and Canada.

As Ryder System entered the 1990s, its full-service truck leasing, contract carriage, jet turbine aircraft overhaul and maintenance, and new aviation parts-distribution were performing well; and other units would eventually rebound alongside the manufacturing economy. Ryder had grown from a one-truck outfit to a massive concern leasing or renting more than 130,000 trucks and nearly 50 jet airplanes. It remained the leader in most of its business segments, and was well-positioned to take advantage of further sophistication of the transportation industry in the future.

Principal Subsidiaries: Ryder Truck Rental, Inc.; Ryder Truck Rental Canada Ltd.; Ryder Truck Rental, Ltd. (U.K.); Ryder Transport Services, GmbH (Germany); Ryder Distribution Resources, Inc.; Ryder Driver Leasing, Inc.; Ryder Student Transportation Services, Inc.; ATE Management and Service Company, Inc.; Ryder Temperature Controlled Carriage, Inc.; A.T.G. Automotive Transport Group Ltd. (Canada); Blazer Truck Lines, Inc.; Commercial Carriers, Inc.; Complete Auto Transit Inc.; Convoy Company; Delavan Industries, Inc.; Fleet Carrier Corporation; Janesville Auto Transport Co.; M&G Convoy Inc.; Aviall, Inc.; Caledonian Airmotive Ltd. (U.K.); Aviation Sales Company, Inc.; General Hydraulics Corporation; Inventory Locator Services, Inc.

Further Reading: Ryder, James A., "Shooting for the Big Time—and Making It," *Nation's Business,* January 1970; Wax, Alan, "Institutions Grill Ryder over Earnings Change," *The Commercial and Financial Chronicle,* April 8, 1974; "From Wings To Wheels," *Forbes,* September 18, 1978; Engardio, Pete, "Tony Burns Has Ryder's Rivals Eating Dust," *Business Week,* April 6, 1987; Cook, James, "Repetition Compulsion," *Forbes,* March 21, 1988.

—Thomas M. Tucker

SANTA FE PACIFIC CORPORATION

1700 East Golf Road
Schaumburg, Illinois 60173
U.S.A.
(708) 995-6000
Fax: (708) 995-6219

Public Company
Incorporated: 1983 as Santa Fe Southern Pacific Corporation
Employees: 14,944
Sales: $2.30 billion
Stock Exchanges: New York Midwest Pacific

Santa Fe Pacific Corporation (SFP) is a holding company for subsidiaries engaged in transportation, mining, and petroleum products transmission. One of its wholly owned subsidiaries is the Atchison, Topeka and Santa Fe Railway Company, one of the nation's major freight railroads, serving 12 states. Another subsidiary, Santa Fe Pacific Minerals Corporation, has significant coal mining operations and is a large producer of precious metals. Santa Fe Pacific Pipelines, Inc., the third subsidiary, transports gasoline, diesel, and jet fuel.

The history of SFP begins with a railroad. In 1859 Cyrus K. Holliday founded the Atchison and Topeka Railroad Company. The Kansas drought hit immediately thereafter and the company foundered. Through the early 1860s the company searched for funding and land grants. The company name became Atchison, Topeka and Santa Fe Railroad (ATSF) in 1863, but the first train movement did not take place until 1869, on a line of about 26 miles from Topeka to Burlingame, Kansas. The ATSF became the pioneering railroad of the southwest portion of the United States. The East had fairly reliable railroad service by 1860, but the West was still largely untouched. The ATSF started in eastern Kansas and ultimately reached Santa Fe, New Mexico, paving the way for the growth of towns and commerce. The company was built upon faith in the prospects of the West and Southwest.

By 1873 the company had more than 130 miles of track. In 1875 the road expanded eastward toward Kansas City. The first train entered Las Vegas, Nevada, in 1879, and Albuquerque, New Mexico, was entered in 1880. ATSF acquired the Sonora Railway in 1882. Hardships in the southwestern United States were crippling the Gulf, Colorado and Santa Fe Railroad in 1885. ATSF absorbed that company, thus stretching to Houston, Texas, and the Gulf of Mexico. Other smaller additions to the ATSF were being transacted through the company's subsidiary—the Chicago, Kansas and Western Railroad Company. Many of these branches were not completed until 1887.

The company also worked to protect its presence in California. In 1886 ATSF purchased from the fading Chicago and St. Louis Railway a right of way into Chicago. After rusted tracks were replaced and bridges built, train service began in 1888. In 1890 the company purchased the St. Louis and San Francisco Railway and the Colorado Midland Railway. In 24 years, the ATSF had grown from the Topeka groundbreaking to a system of 9,300 miles, linking Lake Michigan, the Gulf of Mexico, and the Pacific Ocean. It served Chicago, Dallas, Denver, St. Louis, Los Angeles, Kansas City, and San Francisco.

During this time, the company's growth was characterized by quality construction. It was the creation of railroad men, not financiers, and lines were often built ahead of traffic, leading the way for trade and settlement. ATSF absorbed and repaired dozens of bankrupt lines along the way.

The company suffered some setbacks around the turn of the century. In 1889 the California boom stalled, and passenger business dropped. During the financial panic of 1893, banks and rail empires crashed. Crop failures and dropping rates due to competition between 1889 and 1895 had weakened the company. Its troubles compounded by purchases and upkeep, the ATSF was pinched financially. The company went into receivership and in 1895 the financially troubled system was sold to Edward King, representing a reorganization committee, for $60 million. The company was reincorporated as the Atchison, Topeka and Santa Fe Railway Company, and reorganization began with the sale of the two lines acquired in 1890. Other unprofitable lines were sold and business picked up. By 1898 the company's line had been trimmed to about 7,000 miles. The new president of the reorganized company was Edward P. Ripley.

Pruning continued, but the company revitalized enough to purchase the unfinished San Francisco and San Joaquin Valley Railway in 1899. The line was operative by 1900. Numerous short lines were also acquired. In 1901 the Santa Fe, Prescott and Phoenix Railroad was purchased, giving ATSF exclusive presence in Arizona, then a promising area. By 1902 the company had added almost 1,000 miles to its reorganized line. Careful purchase and expansion continued as ATSF extended through Arizona, New Mexico, northern California, and Texas.

Between the company's inception and 1917, passenger travel rose 600%. The railway was operated by the U.S. government between 1917 and 1920, because of its strategic importance during World War I. Between 1920 and 1929, the ATSF concentrated on maintenance and improvement of equipment and lines. There were ups and downs in operating revenue as the postwar economy surged and faltered in the regions serviced by ATSF, but the decade overall was a good one. The company in 1928 purchased the Orient Line, a system that included about 300 miles of line in Mexico.

During the Great Depression the company's business suffered. In 1935 the company started a track-improvement program between Chicago and California in order to institute a new fast schedule. At the same time, the first diesel-electric locomotive was being built. By 1938 ATSF was running two of the new diesel-electric trains between Chicago and the West Coast. The trains were much faster and more economical than their predecessors, a boon to both passenger and freight services. While the number of passengers dropped, travel distances had increased. Freight traffic was hit hard by the Depression. To offset this, the company reduced operating costs by increasing efficiency, primarily by equipment replacements. ATSF also began branching into other forms of transportation. It bought bus operations and acquired a system of truck lines. In 1935 it purchased the Southern Kansas Stage bus lines. The motor-carrier companies that ATSF acquired were consolidated into the Santa Fe Trail Transportation Company in 1937. By the decade's end, ATSF owned 15 diesels and 44 motor coaches. By 1940 a freight-handling system was coordinated between the company's truck operations. Just as ATSF was enjoying economic recovery, World War II broke out.

With the war came a surge in traffic, both passenger and freight. War halted the delivery of needed new locomotives, but availability was resumed right after the war. Despite the strain, the line and equipment survived the record-breaking traffic. The result was the development of an automated system of centralized control. In 1946 the company established the Santa Fe Skyway, Inc., offering air freight service to round out its business with shippers. Complete transportation integration was prevented by the Civil Aeronautics Board and the Interstate Commerce Commission (ICC). The skyway was discontinued in 1947. Truck and bus operations continued, covering 12,000 and 9,400 miles, respectively, by 1949.

In another postwar development, the ATSF returned its attentions to improving equipment and methods. Streamlined train use was expanded. The 1950s were marked by the complete phasing out of steam locomotives; by 1954, ATSF was entirely dieselized. During the 1950s, many railroads began de-emphasizing passenger service as a result of the growth of air travel and the improvement of highways due to U.S. President Dwight Eisenhower's Interstate Highway Act. In contrast, ATSF, whose reputation had been built on passenger service, applied itself to upgrading passenger travel, buying passenger rail cars and developing high-quality, high-speed service.

In the late 1950s and early 1960s, the company pursued greater diversification that led to the creation of separate companies involved in pipelines, energy resources, and trucking. In 1968 Santa Fe Industries Inc. (SFI), a new parent company, was established as the holding company for these separate enterprises. Also in 1968 SFI inaugurated the fastest freight train in the world. During this time, ATSF began to enter a new market segment—the intermodal truck-train-container business—which allowed freight to be shifted from ships to trucks to trains more fluidly. In the early 1990s 60% of its trains were intermodal, and 40% of the railroad's revenues came from intermodal operations.

The shift in emphasis was auspicious; by the late 1960s, railroads lost mail contracts to jets and thus lost the main revenue subsidizing passenger service. In 1968 ATSF's losses on passenger service necessitated the sale of trains. It was a prelude to turning passenger service over to Amtrak in 1971. This marked the end of an era for ATSF, and the start of a new focus on freight service.

In 1972 SFI sought and found resources in its underused acreage in New Mexico and Arizona: tons of coal. Diversification made sense, and the company committed to mining the coal itself in 1982. The following year, John Schmidt took over as chairman and CEO, and Southern Pacific Company (SPC) agreed to merge with SFI, creating an umbrella holding

company—Santa Fe Southern Pacific Corporation (SFSP), with $11 billion in assets. The merger application was filed with the ICC in 1984. At the time of the merger, SPC was not performing well. The company had diversified into industrial parks and office complexes. SFI had diversified into transportation, natural resources, and real estate. The ATSF and SPC were then the two least profitable of the major U.S. railroads. Joining forces would shorten routes, create economies by cutting overlaps, and eliminate competition with each other. Other major railroads were moving to merge in the early 1980s, making the ATSF and SPC merger necessary for survival.

While awaiting ICC approval, SPC's rail business could not be operated by SFI, so SFI looked to SPC's real estate to generate income. In 1983 real estate income supplied nearly a third of SFSP's revenue. Development projects became a new source of income. Its natural resource division also contributed significantly to operating profits.

ICC hearings continued through 1985 and into 1986. SFSP suffered from being unable to run 40% of its business—the Southern Pacific Railroad. Placed in trust, the railroad deteriorated. Then the ICC ordered divestiture of either the Santa Fe or Southern Pacific rail operations, claiming the merger would create a monopoly on some important routes. By 1986 SFSP's major businesses—transportation and fuel—were suffering, and real estate earnings were also down. In 1985 SPC contributed one-third of SFSP's real estate earnings, which accounted for nearly half of the company's operating profit that year. In 1987 the ICC refused to reconsider its rejection of the merger. SFSP reported a net loss of $138 million for 1986. Schmidt resigned as CEO, and the company underwent drastic restructuring, beginning with the sale of unprofitable businesses. Robert Krebs filled the CEO seat.

Six subsidiaries were put on the block, including three pipeline companies, a leasing company, a building contractor, and the Santa Fe Pacific Timber Company. Raiders circled the troubled company, aided by the October 1987 stock market crash. By the year's end, SFSP announced the sale of SPC's rail business to Rio Grande Industries, for $1 billion. SFSP's net income was $373.5 million for 1987.

To discourage takeover, the company underwent a $4.7 billion leveraged recapitalization. Despite restructuring and the sale of subsidiaries, the company remained highly diversified: in addition to being the seventh-largest U.S. railroad, it held the second-largest petroleum products pipeline, remained one of the largest real estate operations, and oversaw the sixth-largest domestic oil and gas company. In 1988 ATSF had 12,000 miles of track. Undeveloped holdings included urban and agricultural land in 15 states, and oil and mineral holdings. Income from continuing operations for 1988 was $146 million. After accounting for discontinued operations, however, the company showed a net loss of $46.5 million.

Further setbacks came in 1989. In addition to slowed shipments because of the recession, the company received a $1.04 billion verdict in a federal antitrust case brought by Energy Transportation Systems, Inc. (ETSI) in Texas. ETSI was a coal-slurry pipeline company that accused SFSP of blocking a project. The settlement was adjusted to $350 million in 1990.

The company name was changed to Santa Fe Pacific Corporation in 1989. Hard times in the industry produced greater cooperation between companies; SFP reached agreements with Burlington Northern Inc., including sharing a rail terminal.

Early in 1990 SFP sold a 20% stake in its real estate subsidiary. Selling assets continued to reduce the company's debt. SFP made public a portion of its Santa Fe Energy Resources, Inc. unit in 1990, and spun it off completely by year's end. SFP Realty changed its name to Catellus Development Corporation, which also was spun off as an independent company in 1990.

Principal Subsidiaries: Atchison, Topeka and Santa Fe Railway Company; Santa Fe Pacific Minerals Corporation; Santa Fe Pacific Pipelines, Inc.

Further Reading: Marshall, James, *Santa Fe: The Railroad That Built an Empire,* New York, Random House, 1945; Waters, L.L., *Steel Trails to Santa Fe,* Lawrence, University of Kansas Press, 1950.

—Carol I. Keeley

SEIBU RAILWAY CO. LTD.

1-11-1 Kusunokidai
Tokorozawa City
Saitama Prefecture
Japan
(0429) 26 2035
Fax: (0429) 26 2237

Public Company
Incorporated: 1912 as Musashino Railway Company
Employees: 5,239
Sales: ¥493.66 billion (US$3.96 billion)
Stock Exchange: Tokyo

Seibu Railway Co. Ltd. (Seibu Railway) is one of Japan's leading railway operators and the nucleus of the Seibu Railway Group of companies, whose interests range from railways to real estate development and hotel operation to the ownership of one of Japan's leading baseball teams. The company operates several of the busiest commuter railway lines in Tokyo, originating from the downtown stations of Shinjuku and Ikebukuro and stretching into the commuter belt suburbs. The company's revenue from the railway is gradually increasing, while its real estate ventures both in Japan and overseas are a high-growth area.

The origins of Seibu Railway lie in a railway company called Musashino Railway Company, founded in 1912 by one of Japan's most famous entrepreneurs, Yasujido Tsutsumi. He was a Tokyo-based businessman who was seeking to profit from Japan's fast-growing economy. In 1872 Japan's first railway was opened, providing transport between the cities of Yokohama and Tokyo. The ensuing 40 years saw Japan industrialize at a fast pace. The government's policy was to encourage private investors to develop the infrastructure, and it became apparent that the electric railway would be the dominant form of public transport in the Tokyo area. The government began awarding licenses to investors who wished to develop and build track along major routes. Tsutsumi obtained a license for the construction and operation of an electric railway between Ikebukuro in cental Tokyo and the outlying town of Tokorozawa. The government, as it had done with all the private railways, issued guidelines on the fares that could be charged. Tsutsumi succeeded in raising ¥1 million in capital for the company, Musashino Railway Company (Musashino). Construction began in 1912 and was completed three years later, when passenger services between Ikebukuro and Hanno, on

route to Tokorozawa, commenced. The initial trains were steam-driven, as the 44-kilometer route was not electrified. Electrification took place in 1922, and the track was extended to Tokorozawa. In the following year, however, the Tokyo area experienced a catastrophic earthquake, with devastating consequences for the infrastructure. Large portions of the Musashino track were ruined, and reconstruction took over a year. Musashino, and the city of Tokyo in general, recovered quickly, however, and by 1927 the company was able to open a new service between the city of Nerima, near Tokorozawa, and Ikebukuro. The service was double-track, permittting trains to run more frequently.

By 1930 Tokyo was one of the largest metropolitan areas in the world, with a population of over three million. The agricultural areas surrounding the city gradually became residential as the city grew. To a large extent the growth was most pronounced in the vicinity of major rail routes, and Musashino saw steady housing development along its two routes. This meant a growth in passenger volume and revenue. The company continued to invest in track, converting all to double by 1930. Branch lines were built from the main lines to cater to local residential areas. Musashino's main rival at this time was the Tokyo Express Railway Company (Tokyu), under the leadership of Keita Gotoh. Gotoh and Tsutsumi became fierce rivals, as Gotoh's strategy was to take over smaller railway companies and thus expand his empire. Indeed, by the late 1930s Gotoh's company had swallowed up almost all the private railways in the Tokyo area, one of the exceptions being Musashino. The two companies were also faced with competition from the nationally owned railway network covering the whole of Tokyo. Musashino flourished, however, and in 1940 acquired Tamako Railway Company, which had also escaped takeover by Gotoh, and with it an additional service in the vicinity of its network.

In the early 1940s Japan was preparing for full-scale war with the Allies. All major companies were ordered by the military government to play their part in this effort, and Musashino contributed by supplying railway freight cars. In 1944 Musashino's tracks were severely damaged by the bombing raids carried out by the U.S. Air Force and at the time of Japan's surrender in August 1945 its infrastructure was in need of rebuilding. Following the occupation, the U.S. command began the process of dismantling the huge Japanese industrial conglomerates that had emerged before the war. Tokyu was split up but Musashino, being smaller, was left with its routes intact. With Tsutsumi still in charge, the company became known as Seibu Railway Co. Ltd. (Seibu Railway) in 1946.

Seibu Railway began the rebuilding of its track, aided by grants from the government, which was in turn subsidized by the U.S. government. As well as rebuilding the old lines, Seibu Railway began the development of routes from Shinjuku, another major central Tokyo station, to suburban regions. The company also bought a baseball team, the Seibu Lions, in 1949. A stadium was built in the vicinity of Tokorozawa and the team soon came to dominate its league. Seibu Railway also began to develop the real estate it owned in the vicinity of its track. This became a lucrative source of income for the company, in addition to its core railway business. The company continued to invest in its infrastructure, with the 1950s being a time of extensive track expansion. The station platforms were expanded to accommodate longer trains, and the frequency of services along the major Shinjuku and Ikebukuro routes increased. In 1963 a ten-car express train service between Ikebukuro and Tokorozawa was inaugurated. In the following year the company built a large railway car depot at Koteshi, along the route, to service its rapidly growing fleet of railway cars. At that time the emphasis for Seibu Railway was on speed of service. Tokyo's population was growing rapidly, with the residential regions around Seibu's lines forming a continuous metropolitan region. The majority of the residents commuted to work in the center of Tokyo, and the morning rush-hour on Seibu Railway's lines was becoming increasingly congested. While expanding its services, Seibu Railway was aware of the safety risks of transporting hundreds of thousands of passengers daily. In 1968 Seibu Railway's train tracking system was computerized and television monitors were placed along the lines. Tokyo's many level-crossings had long been a source of accidents, so Seibu Railway installed automatic safety systems at its crossings in 1969; as a result, fatalities fell dramatically.

Seibu continued to develop its real estate and in 1973 completed a huge underground complex in Ikebukuro Station. This complex included shops and restaurants as well as Seibu Railway's terminals. The development of Shinjuku Station followed in 1974. In 1976 Seibu Railway completed the building of the Seibu Shinjuku Building, its first major piece of real estate near Shinjuku Station. Toward the end of the 1970s Seibu Railway installed a computerized switching system. The company also invested heavily in station improvement, building new stations, including Tamako Station in 1961, and renovating others.

With a large stake in the ownership of the company, Yasujido Tsutsumi's family was one of the wealthiest in Japan. Although the ailing Yasujido died in 1989, he had passed control of the company over to his son Yoshiaki in the 1970s. Seibu Railway's traditional rivalry with Tokyu had diminished as both companies grew into diversified conglomerates. The 1980s saw Seibu Railway diversify into resort development, beginning with a project on the Hawaiian island of Maui in 1987. The company continued to develop family homes along its railway lines. In the late 1980s, with the boom in Japanese real estate prices, the leasing of Seibu Railway property in central Tokyo became lucrative.

In the early 1990s Seibu Railway ranked fourth behind the Tobu, Tokyu, and Odakyu Railway Companies in terms of passenger volume among private railway firms in the Tokyo area. Seibu Railway's railway business continues to be the core of the business, although in percentage revenue terms it is on a par with the company's resort and tourism businesses. The latter account for around 40% of revenue each, with the remaining 20% coming from real estate. The company's baseball team has been extremely successful, winning the Japan Series three years in succession in the late 1980s. Yoshiaki Tsutsumi, who became chairman in 1989, intends to continue to diversify his company, having opened two large hotels in Hawaii and Yokohama in 1990. The core business of railway operations will provide the base from which Seibu will expand.

Principal Subsidiaries: Seibu Bus Co., Ltd.; Seibu Hire Co., Ltd.; Seibu Transport Co., Ltd.; Izu Hakone Railroad Co., Ltd.; Omi Railroad Co., Ltd.; Seibu Travel Co., Ltd.; Seibu Lions Co., Ltd.; Seibu Golf Co., Ltd.; Prince Hotel Co., Ltd.; Kokudo Planning Co., Ltd.; Seibu Construction Co., Ltd.; Seibu Materials Co., Ltd.; Seibu Real Estate Co., Ltd.; Seibu Amusement Parks Co., Ltd.; Seibu Trading Co., Ltd.

—Dylan Tanner

SOCIÉTÉ NATIONALE DES CHEMINS DE FER FRANÇAIS

88 Rue Saint-Lazare
75436 Paris, Cedex 09
France
(1) 42 85 60 00

State-Owned Company
Incorporated: 1938
Employees: 218,000
Sales: FFr51.78 billion (US$10.00 billion)

From the earliest days of steam to the modern era of the super-speed passenger train, France has played a leading role in the development of rail transportation, and the Société Nationale des Chemins de Fer Français (SNCF) occupies an enduring place at the heart of the country's economic and social life.

The first railway line in France opened in 1827, carrying coal from Saint-Etienne to Andrezieux, a small port on the Loire. The primitive carriages were drawn by horses, but in 1831 the first steam locomotives and the first passenger service came into operation between Saint-Etienne and Lyon, initially using the former coal trucks as passenger compartments. The value of effective rail links was quickly apparent; within ten years, coal output in Saint-Etienne more than doubled, and industry boomed across the region.

Railways arrived in the capital on August 26, 1837, with a new passenger service from Paris to Le Pecq, near Saint-Germain-en-Laye. The line was inaugurated by Queen Marie-Amélie—King Louise Philippe was advised against boarding the new-fangled "steel monster"—and was an immediate success with Parisians; some 400,000 traveled the line within the first few weeks, at the then-wondrous speed of 60 kilometers per hour (km/h). In 1841 a major rail link was built from Strasbourg to Basel, and by 1846 three more important routes had been laid between Paris and the provincial centers of Orléans, Rouen, and Lille.

Unlike roads or canals, the early railways were not state-owned, but built and operated by private speculators. The government, however, kept ultimate control over the expanding network by requiring each new line to seek an official license or concession, and it also assumed the right to veto or amend fares and tariffs. In 1839, for example, the fares on the Paris to Versailles line were set by the prefect of police.

Successive governments took an even closer interest in the railways. Napoleon III saw railway building as the mainspring of an ambitious program of economic and industrial expansion. His Second Empire of 1852 to 1870 encouraged a host of new lines; efficient rail links stretched from Paris to all important towns and cities, which simultaneously galvanized the regional economies and tightened the capital's hold on national life. The length of the network grew from 3,000 kilometers to 17,430 kilometers, and by the time of Napoleon III's downfall in 1870 all of the major routes that exist in the 1990s had been laid.

Napoleon III's work was enthusiastically continued by the new republic. In 1878 the minister of public works, Charles de Freycinet, set up the first state-owned network by buying several ailing small lines in the west of the country. A year later he implemented the Freycinet Plan, which established a further 9,000 kilometers of track.

There followed a period of further expansion—between 1870 and 1914 the national network grew to a total length of 39,400 kilometers—and of increasing public and commercial popularity. The era of international prestige trains arrived in 1880, with the launch of the Orient Express, and France took its place at the center of a European rail network. Travel times improved; through the 1880s, the highly competitive Orléans line offered a Paris to Saint-Pierre-des-Corps service at slightly more than three and a half hours. During this period there were further developments in the relationship between the state and the railways. Another Freycinet Plan, agreed upon between the government and railway companies in 1883, reversed the system under which the state financed new rail services. Hitherto, public funds had been used to cover estimated costs of fresh projects, with any surpluses being met by the private backers. Under the revised plan, the government would only meet the surpluses, handing responsibility for the main costs back to individual companies. The prestige of the railways was reflected in magnificent new stations across the country, including the remarkable terminus at the Quai d'Orsay in Paris, built at the turn of the century like a sunken cathedral at the end of a 3,100-meter tunnel beneath the left bank of the Seine. From the outset, the station used exclusively electric traction to ferry about 200 trains a day through a tunnel from the nearby Austerlitz station. In 1909 the state-owned network was considerably increased by the acquisition of a collection of lines in Normandy and Brittany previously run by the Compagnie de l'Quest. Between 1910 and 1914 the first electrified rail services in France were introduced by the Midi network, on the mountainous secondary lines of the Pyrenees.

Rail development was disrupted by World War I, although the French network played a major role in the conflict. As well as ferrying troops and supplies to the front and keeping the civilian population mobile, the railways proved vital to defense industries. Those in the northern and eastern sections of the country, however, suffered extensive damage, particularly in German-occupied territory. After the armistice, the railways faced a crippling backlog of repairs and improvements, made virtually impossible by spiraling costs and inflation. In 1920 all networks showed considerable losses; a 1921 agreement between individual lines to pool technology and resources was fatally undermined by world recession and mounting road competition. Against the odds there were some advances, notably in international traffic. The first nonstop express from Paris to Brussels started in 1923, traveling at 100 km/h on rebuilt track through the devastated battlefields of the recent war, and in 1932 a direct service was launched between Paris and Liège. The first 239–kilometer stretch of the Liège line, as far as Jeumont, carried trains traveling at an average speed of 106.3 km/h, much the fastest sustained run in Europe. However, these achievements were scored against a background of seemingly inexorable decline. By 1936 the railways' total deficit stood at FFr37 billion. The network was in crisis, and turned to the state for rescue.

On August 31, 1937, the state reached an agreement with the five largest railway companies to establish a unified French railway system, the Société Nationale des Chemins de Fer Français, or SNCF. The deal was given a lifespan of 45 years, and came into effect on January 1, 1938. The SNCF embraced all of the big five rail systems—Compagnie du Nord, Compagnie de l'Est, Compagnie du Paris-Lyon-Mediterranée, Compagnie du Paris-Orléans, and Compagnie du Midi—and the two existing state services. The agreement specified that the newly integrated network be managed on a commercial basis, in that it was to increase fares and operate efficiently so as to cover its costs. However, the company was required to recognize its public service responsibilities and undertake to uphold standards and services. These sometimes irreconcilable requirements, to operate both profitably and in the public interest, were to dog the company for four decades. The state reserved the right to block fare increases, on the understanding that it would compensate for the lost revenue. The new SNCF was under the ultimate control of the state, which owned 51% of capital; the remainder was held by the big five, newly formed into financial companies.

The onset of World War II predictably threw rail services into chaos. Despite German occupation from May 1940, however, some development was possible; for instance, seven large express locomotives were built to a new design and successfully introduced to the northern region. The railways in occupied France played a pivotal role in the logistics of the Nazi war effort, and were put to use as a vital channel of troops, armaments, fortifications, and supplies. They quickly became priority war targets, particularly after the Normandy landings of 1944 when practically every main route in France was severely damaged by Allied bombers—and French resistance fighters—intent on disrupting enemy lines of communication.

After the war France set about rebuilding its railways for the second time in 30 years. Reconstruction was carried out with the full backing of the newly liberated state. As well as replacing and renovating damaged facilities, engineers used the opportunity to improve the network; in particular, major junctions such as those at Laroche and Melun were skillfully realigned so that trains could run through them without any loss of speed. Unfettered by government interference, the SNCF was left to embark on an aggressive period of promotion and improvement. Passenger services were improved by new rolling stock, modernized stations, and yet more new lines; the freight sector benefited from upgraded services and forceful marketing. The postwar reconstruction work force reached a peak of 500,000 in 1947 and 1948.

Although there were detailed plans for a new generation of steam locomotives, an early decision was made to electrify the entire mainline network as soon as possible. Beginning in 1950 the SNCF made a series of technological advances in electric traction, which were subsequently exported around the globe. Instead of the 1,500-volt direct-current traction system, in use around the world and in France itself, French engineers developed a system using 20,000 volts of alternating current at the commercial frequency, adopted by all commercial Swiss traffic, of 50 cycles per second. This reduced the need for trackside substations, allowed for much lighter ancillary equipment, and brought installation costs down by a third. The scheme was successfully introduced in the French Alps, and then extended to the northern region and beyond. Furthermore, new French locomotives were designed so they could switch smoothly to differing power systems as they crossed international borders. Other innovations involved widespread automation, including luminous blocks for track spacing, and automated signal boxes and level crossings. The electrification program continued at such a pace that by 1964 France had 7,600 kilometers of powered mainline track, compared with 2,700 kilometers in Britain and 2,900 kilometers in the United States. By 1983 more than 80% of SNCF traffic was powered by domestically produced electricity, thus allowing the railways to claim the environmental high ground with "almost zero-level atmospheric pollution."

In 1955 two French electric engines traveled at a world record 331 km/h on the Landes line, which led to a wave of lucrative export orders and confirmed the company's resolve to remain at the forefront of high-speed technology. Railway systems throughout the developed world were suffering from the preeminence of the bus and the automobile as a means of transport over short journeys. From the 1950s the airplane posed a new threat to the railway's supremacy in the business of long-distance travel. Squeezed in this way between road and air rivals, the SNCF committed itself to meeting the dual challenge by means of speed, combined with comfort, reliability, and unrivaled safety standards. To this end French engineers studied every detail of railway design, from the locomotives to the track and signaling, to find ways of improving performance. Their achievements in this field would earn French railways a worldwide reputation for speed and efficiency.

In the 1960s the SNCF developed an aeronautical-type gas turbine to power a railway engine, thus paving the way for Europe's first turbotrains. In 1972 a prototype gas turbine train achieved speeds of 318 km/h in time trials. Turbotrains were scheduled for use on the new Paris to Lyon service, approved in 1974, but the government cancelled the plan following the oil crisis.

By the late 1960s it was clear that the 1937 formation agreement had placed the SNCF in permanent financial difficulties, preventing it from responding effectively to the competition from road and air transport and new oil pipelines; the railway had to operate under the public service obligations imposed by the original agreement, while its rivals enjoyed commercial and technical freedom. To even the odds, the government revised the 1937 agreement in the codicil of January 27, 1971, which allowed a fundamental overhaul of the SNCF. In return for its new freedom, however, the railway took responsibility for balancing its books, leaving the state to make contributions to specified areas only, such as public service charges and social insurance contributions.

The SNCF entered a new period of steady development. In the early 1970s France established some 25 regional councils, with significant powers delegated by central government. The SNCF set up close dialogue with the new councils, to discuss detailed ways of improving local rail services. Although central government retained responsibility for basic transport support, the regions were given the right and resources to make local improvements. Some councils funded new rolling stock; others secured improvements or extensions to the local network, or reached agreement on fares policy. The relationship between the regions and SNCF blossomed through the 1980s and into the 1990s, and the railway company furnished the councils with regular computer bulletins on trends and developments.

By the end of the 1970s, however, the national railway company's progress was again undermined by financial imbalance. In particular, the network complained bitterly of its constant reliance on debt; since its inception, the SNCF had capital of just 0.03% of its operating budget, meaning that all investment had to be raised through loans. This placed a massive financial burden on the company. Furthermore, despite the codicil of 1971, the company still felt it was being forced to compete on unequal terms with other haulers. These problems were tackled in another overhaul of the SNCF, introduced from December 31, 1982, the expiration date of the 1937 agreement that established the company. All assets of the SNCF passed over to the state, in accordance with the original 45-year deal, and the company became a permanently state-owned concern. The SNCF was also brought into a national program aimed at improving and integrating the various transport systems, and placing them under corporate legislative control. The new law also clarified and reconciled the SNCF's dual role as both public servant and competitive commercial enterprise. Of more immediate importance, the reorganization helped resolve the company's financial difficulties; the state reaffirmed its commitment to its national railways, the largest in western Europe with double the traffic of, for instance, British Rail. It stepped up contributions to pension and infrastructure costs, and innovatively made capital grants toward railway projects of national value. It also continued to subsidize fares and less profitable regional services. The SNCF diversified, through a range of subsidiaries, into a wide range of transport-related fields, from hotel management to haulage and tourism.

The changes in the SNCF coincided with spectacular success in the development of the Train à Grande Vitesse (TGV), the world's fastest train. The French described the TGV, run on electric traction, as a synthesis of technological progress, combining an aerodynamic profile, stability, and cabin signalling. On February 26, 1981, the TGV set a track speed world record, clocking 380 km/h on the Paris to Lyon line. The train entered commercial service in September of the same year, with a normal operating speed limit of 270 km/h. The first TGV service followed a southeast route embracing Lyon, Saint-Etienne, Dijon, Besançon, and Geneva in Switzerland. In 1982 the service was extended to the population centers of the Rhône Valley and the south of France, and other important routes were added at the rate of more than one a year; to Lausanne and Toulon in 1984, to Lille, Lyon, and Grenoble that winter, to Rouen in 1986, and to Nice, Neuchatel, and Bern in 1987. By that time 43 cities were connected to Paris by TGV, with a further 9 destinations during the winter sports season. The 300 km/h Atlantic TGV was opened in two phases during 1989 and 1990; the west branch served Le Mans, Rennes, Britanny, and Nantes, and the southwest branch took in the Bordeaux region up to the Spanish border, and Toulouse. In 1989 the pioneering Southeast service car-

ried its 100 millionth passenger, and the line recorded a 15% return on its investment, 3% more than planned. The TGV reduced travel times dramatically, bringing Marseilles, for example, to within five hours of Paris; over medium intercity distances the railway suddenly rivaled aircraft as the fastest travel option. Moreover, the railways were cheaper and claimed clear advantages in comfort, reliability, and convenience. Trains were able to arrive in the heart of cities, rather than remote, isolated airports.

The French saw the TGV as the future of high-speed travel within a uniting Europe; in the early 1990s some airlines were investing in rail links rather than in short-haul air trips. The shift from air to rail travel for medium distances also has the backing of the European Community, which in the late 1980s commissioned an exhaustive study into the potential of a high-speed, pan-European network. The SNCF was anxious for the system to use French trains, and was confident its TGV would beat off fierce competition from Japan, Germany, and Scandinavia. The government was backing a FFr210 billion scheme to more than double the size of the TGV network over 20 years. The north European TGV system was planned for 1993, to coincide with the opening of the Channel Tunnel; it will cover northern France—Paris to Lille in one hour—and extend to Brussels, Cologne, and Amsterdam. The proposed TGV East would serve the eastern edge of France and southern Germany. A TGV hub was planned for Roissy, near Paris, creating the first high-speed rail network in the world. There are domestic plans for a direct TGV link from Paris to Marseilles, to bring the travel time down from four hours and forty minutes to just three hours. Meanwhile the TGV continued to break records, reaching speeds of 500 km/h during 1990.

By recognizing before any of its competitors the possibility of a second rail revolution based on speed, the SNCF bucked an international trend and reversed falling passenger figures. It also adopted a leading role in transport technology which, it was hoped, had laid the foundations of a prosperous future. In the late 1980s the network focused its efforts on improving its freight business, having witness a 30% drop in goods volume over the previous 15 years. The decline was further hastened at the end of 1986 by a bitter rail strike, the longest in French history. At the end of the decade the SNCF relaunched its freight sector under the brandname Fret, and promoted it aggressively. The service claimed sweeping improvements in performance, based on the use of computers to improve customer communications and to process consignments more quickly and effectively. It also entered into partnership with road companies for intermodal traffic, using giant containers adapted for both railway and lorry haulage. The SNCF hoped that intermodal traffic would account for at least 30% of its goods business. Meanwhile electrification continued apace, with many new schemes such as those on the Paris-Massif Central main line, and in Brittany.

In 1990 the SNCF announced a major reorganization of its top management structure, after consultants found the development of divisive "empires" within the company. The new structure strengthened the top-level directorate, and regrouped the company into five separate businesses, each with its own budget, covering passenger, freight, Ile-de-France region, regional, and Sernam, the intermodal subsidiary.

Principal Subsidiaries: SCETA Holding (85%); France Rail Publicité; Société de Gérance de Wagons de grande capacité (80%); Société Hydro-Eléctrique du Midi (99%); Société Française d'Etudes et de Réalisations Ferroviaires (61%); Les Editions La Vie du Rail (65%); French Rail Incorporated (U.K.); French Railways Ltd. (U.K.); Continental Shipping and Travel Limited (U.K.).

Further Reading: Nock, O.S., *Railways of Western Europe,* London, Adam & Charles Black, 1977; "The SNCF, Historical Background, Status, Recent Developments," Paris, SNCF, 1984.

—Linda Anderson

SOUTHERN PACIFIC TRANSPORTATION COMPANY

Southern Pacific Building
One Market Plaza
San Francisco, California 94105
U.S.A.
(415) 541-1000
Fax: (415) 541-1256

*Wholly Owned Subsidiary of Rio Grande Industries, Inc.,
　through SPTC Holding, Inc.*
Incorporated: 1884 as Southern Pacific Company of Kentucky
Employees: 21,477
Sales: $2.47 billion

The venerable Southern Pacific railroad operates a core route of 7,500 miles of railway in 14 of the western United States, its territory forming a broad crescent from Portland, Oregon, to New Orleans, Louisiana, and up through the Midwest. Faced with new and overwhelming competition in the 1980s, Southern Pacific first attempted a merger with the Santa Fe Railroad, and, when that was struck down by the Interstate Commerce Commission, joined Philip Anschutz's growing stable of transportation companies known as Rio Grande Industries, Inc. It then enjoyed integrated operations with Rio Grande's other railroad holdings, principally the Denver and Rio Grande Western Railroad Company, and expected thereby to prosper in the new era of consolidated railway systems; but Southern also retained its corporate identity and a relative degree of functional independence. The nature of its business remained much as it had been since the company's inception—bulk transport of manufactured goods, timber, and agricultural products between the far West and the more densely populated regions of the eastern United States.

The history of Southern Pacific begins with the efforts of Theodore D. Judah to build an earlier railroad, the Central Pacific. Judah was a Connecticut engineer experienced in railroad construction who moved to California in 1854 and immediately became absorbed by the possibility of a rail link between that state and the East. Not a financier, Judah lobbied Congress for help with his grand project, and around 1860 became acquainted with four ambitious businessmen from Sacramento. This quartet, whose members would go on to build and own the Southern Pacific, were Collis P. Huntington, proprietor of a large hardware store; Leland Stanford, lawyer and in 1861 governor of California; Charles Crocker,

dry goods merchant; and Mark Hopkins, partner to Huntington. Along with Judah and a few other investors, the four promoters created the Central Pacific Railroad of California on June 28, 1861, and then set about finding the cash infusions that would be needed even to begin the mammoth construction project from Sacramento, California, to the East.

The bulk of these funds were eventually provided by the U.S. government, which under the terms of the railroad acts of 1862 and 1864 agreed to loan to Central Pacific a varying amount of government bonds for every mile of road built, depending on the difficulty of terrain traversed, and to grant it a checkerboard pattern of land on alternate sides of the railroad that would eventually total millions of acres of urban and range property. An important caveat deprived the railroad of most mineral rights to this land, a category generally interpreted by the courts to include oil. In addition to this federal aid, Central Pacific was empowered to sell stocks and bonds of its own, but in the early years few buyers for these could be found. The four original promoters were therefore continually scrambling for enough money to support the road's construction, which began in January 1863. To ease its chronic financial burden, Central Pacific persuaded municipalities to buy its bonds, threatening bluntly that if such support were not forthcoming the railroad would simply be built around the town in question, destroying its economic viability. In this way, Central managed to raise a substantial amount of money to complement its federal funds, but by revealing the threat inherent in its monopoly status also earned the resentment of the people of California. As it became clear that the partners would succeed in their project, public optimism about the benefits thus gained was tempered by the realization that there would be one and only one major rail system in northern California.

Further blackening the reputation of the Central Pacific was the widespread belief that the promoters of the road were skimming profits. They awarded lucrative contracts to construction companies owned by themselves, contracts calling for payments in the form of both cash and Central Pacific stock and so liberal in terms that by the time the road was completed in 1869 the construction company was, in effect, its owner. The net result was that a railroad had been built over the Sierra mountains to Ogden, Utah, with government funds, but was now owned by four individuals.

Once the road was finished the promoters decided to remain in the railroad business, foreseeing that with a modicum of effort they could establish a virtual monopoly over the state of California. They began an intensive campaign of acquisition and expansion, rapidly solidifying their hold on rail transport throughout the state's midsection. In particular, Central Pacific's attention was drawn to a new government railroad venture known as the Southern Pacific, chartered by Congress in 1866 to build rail lines from the San Francisco Bay area to San Diego, California, thence eastward to California's eastern boundary. The Central Pacific promoters gained control of this new road in 1868, recognizing that such a project would allow them to duplicate their construction profits and also grow to be the dominant railroad in the far West. In the following 15 years the Southern Pacific spread its myriad lines from Sacramento all the way to New Orleans, having effected a number of mergers in the process, and as early as 1877 the Central Pacific–Southern Pacific combination controlled 85% of all rail traffic in the state of California as well. In that year the combined companies had sales of $22.2 million and a capital of $225 million, soon greatly enlarged by the additional tracks reaching out to Texas and New Orleans.

In 1884 the three remaining promoters—Hopkins having died in 1878—took steps to ensure their control of the rapidly expanding Southern Pacific. Having sold the bulk of their holdings in Central Pacific, which by then was clearly of secondary value, they formed a new corporation, Southern Pacific Company of Kentucky, with which they acquired all of the stock of the old Southern Pacific and its subsidiaries while agreeing to lease the use of Central Pacific's roads. This arrangement not only further concentrated their hold upon Southern Pacific, it also distanced the promoters from California's laws of incorporation, under which stockholders' liability was unlimited.

Southern Pacific and its owners remained extremely unpopular for many years. The railroad's early bullying of municipalities, its discriminatory pricing, suspected trafficking in legislative votes by means of bribery, and monopoly power fueled popular resentment. Various legal remedies were attempted by the state of California, including the creation of a state Railroad Commission in 1876, but all were undermined by the Southern Pacific. In the 1890s the federal government also became increasingly involved in the regulation of railroads. The source of its concern was not only the public welfare but the more tangible fact that the transcontinental railroads owed the U.S. government a great deal of money, in the form of the 30-year bonds they had borrowed for construction and due to mature in the mid-1890s.

None of the roads, including Southern Pacific, had made provision for the repayment of these huge debts, operating income instead ending up in the hands of promoters. Partly in response to this crisis the Interstate Commerce Commission (ICC) was created in 1887 as a federal agency charged with general regulation of the railroads; more specifically, by the mid-1890s it was clear that Southern Pacific was unable to pay its debts and would require refinancing. So unpopular was the company in its home state of California that a San Francisco newspaper gathered 195,000 signatures—more than 10% of the state population—on a petition asking the government to foreclose on the railway and to run it as a public service. This the government was disinclined to do, preferring to get its money back rather than enter the railroad business, and after long negotiations the debt was re-funded until 1909 and Southern Pacific was instructed to have it paid off by that date. As the Southern Pacific was by then already the largest railroad in the United States, with 7,300 miles of track, and a profitable company when managed properly, it was able to meet the new debt schedule and was by 1909 financially independent of the government.

In 1901, shortly after the death of the last of Southern Pacific's founders had left the company vulnerable, the rival Union Pacific bought a controlling interest in the road and in effect merged the two great western rail systems. The railroad monopoly of California thus became part of an even larger corporate giant, stretching from Portland to New Orleans and Los Angeles to St. Louis, Missouri, and including a fleet of steamships traveling between California and the Far East and between New Orleans and New York. E.H. Harriman, Union Pacific's chairman, was a far more prudent administrator than the previous generation of rail magnates, and under his direc-

tion both the Union Pacific and Southern Pacific were run according to a conservative philosophy of low dividends, the reinvestment of income in capital improvements, and a tight lid on debt accumulation. As a result, Southern Pacific was able to pay off the federal government while strengthening its physical assets and generally to grow into a mature, efficient corporation.

Congress and the U.S. populace were less interested in Harriman's skills than in the monopolistic status of his railroads. As two monopolies do not make a market, an ICC investigation was followed in 1911 by a federal antitrust suit against the Union Pacific-Southern Pacific combination. The Supreme Court agreed that the combine inhibited competition and in 1913 ordered the sale of Southern Pacific stock, much of which ended up in the hands of the Pennsylvania Railroad. As of that date, then, the Southern Pacific Railroad was restored to the general configuration it had had before the 1901 merger, its three principal routes being those between San Francisco and Portland, San Francisco and Ogden, Utah, and San Francisco and New Orleans. A second antitrust action deprived Southern Pacific of its Ogden lines for a number of years, but these were eventually restored. Other litigation forced Southern Pacific to give up most of the oil-producing land included in its original grants, oil falling under the rubric of mineral rights, as well as its timberland.

Southern Pacific survived, however, and enjoyed a decade of unbroken prosperity in the 1920s. Buoyed by a strong national economy and the rapid growth of its two main markets, California and Texas, Southern's net income steadily rose to its 1929 peak of $48 million, despite having lost to the ICC the right to fix its own freight rates. These results were misleading, however, for in the meantime the nature of U.S. transportation had undergone a fundamental change as great as that of the railroad itself. Truck and auto traffic trebled during the 1920s, and along with the airplane would soon wrest from the railroads most long-distance passenger service and many types of freight, except those bulk items for which rail transport is ideal. The impact of these changes was not really felt by Southern Pacific until the Great Depression brought to an end the era of plentiful business for all; reeling from these double blows, Southern Pacific watched its net decline to $4 million in 1931 and then disappear altogether for the next four years.

The age of railroads had come to an end, and under new president Angus McDonald the Southern Pacific began the long evolution needed if it were to survive in a truly competitive marketplace. The former monopoly became far more responsive to the needs of its customers, offering a much more flexible schedule of service and the use of the railroad's own short-haul trucking company, Pacific Motor Trucking Company. Although the latter was barred by law from competing with full-service truck lines it became an integral adjunct to Southern Pacific's rail system, transporting goods between the rail depots and customer warehouses. Southern Pacific also fought a well-publicized if losing battle for passenger business, offering low-priced tickets on a number of famous routes between California and the East. These efforts may well have kept the Southern Pacific name before the public eye, but it proved simply impossible to move passengers by rail as cheaply and directly as by car and airplane, and for many years passenger travel was a money-losing burden on all railroads.

Despite these generally gloomy developments, Southern Pacific remained a true giant among U.S. corporations. Its 1936 assets of $1.95 billion were exceeded by only two other U.S. industrial corporations; it retained ownership of millions of acres of land that would some day become extremely valuable; and with 16,000 miles of track and $200 million in annual sales, Southern Pacific was among the three largest U.S. railroads by any measure chosen. Although the industry as a whole faced new competition, Southern Pacific itself continued to enjoy the benefits of its relatively uncrowded western territory, where only Union Pacific and Santa Fe offered any challenge to its supremacy. The company was thus well positioned to take advantage of the enormous upsurge in heavy freight caused by the outbreak of war in 1939. With every segment of the industrial economy straining to meet the requirements of war, the railroad entered a period of unprecedented prosperity. Southern Pacific's net income reached an all-time high of $80 million in 1942 and remained strong for several years, despite a vigorous program of debt reduction and capital outlays for new rolling stock and track.

Following the war, Southern Pacific settled into a long period of sedate good fortune. Business lost to the truckers and airlines was more than compensated by the overall economic growth of its western home. Passenger revenue continued to decline, except for commuter service, but under the regulatory regime of the ICC the railroads were ensured a living wage in the bulk freight business, and since neither mergers nor rate wars were permitted the competitive environment was stable and modestly profitable. Under Donald J. Russell, Southern Pacific's chief from 1952 through the mid-1960s, revenue rose from $650 million to $840 million, and the company expanded its trucking service as well as added a profitable oil pipeline along a segment of its track in the Southwest. Russell spent liberally on maintenance of track and rolling stock, and Southern Pacific generally built a reputation as one of the country's soundest railroads, although the sheer size of its operations forced the company to incur debt for capital expenditures at a level higher than Wall Street thought prudent. The tremendous growth of California's population and agricultural production kept Southern Pacific healthy, along with the rapid increase in intermodal—rail-to-truck and truck-to-rail—transport and a booming oil business in Texas and Louisiana. The latter portion of the Southern Pacific system had been solidified years before by the acquisition in 1932 of the "cotton belt" lines extending northward to St. Louis from Dallas, Texas.

While Southern Pacific's market area and rate structure were both fixed, it could and did increase efficiency by means of technological innovation and consequent labor cuts. By 1969 the entire railroad was under the guidance of a computerized information system that helped to cut down on idle cars and switching delays. By means of such changes Southern Pacific was able to reduce its labor force from 76,000 in the mid-1950s to 45,000 by 1970, while substantially increasing its volume of rail traffic. This trend continued; in 1990 Southern Pacific employed about 21,000 workers.

In 1972 Southern Pacific diversified into telecommunications. Using its existing network of microwave transmitters, the company became a carrier of long-distance telephone and data communications, first to large corporate users and later to the general public under the Sprint name. In 1979 it also bought Ticor, the largest title insurer in the United States. Neither venture was particularly successful, however. Telecommunications was a world all its own, one that demanded expertise and more capital than Southern Pacific could spare from its own vast physical plant; and the Ticor purchase had barely been signed when a severe recession all but killed the residential real estate market on which the title business depends. As a result, both companies were eventually sold off. In 1982 two of Southern Pacific's chief rivals announced a potentially devastating merger—Union Pacific and Missouri Pacific would soon form the largest rail combine since the days of E.H. Harriman.

The merger of Union Pacific and Missouri Pacific was made possible by U.S. President Ronald Reagan's deregulation of the railroad industry and presented Southern Pacific with grave problems. The new Union Pacific would be able to offer longer through service and lower rates than Southern Pacific in nearly every market area, and Southern Pacific immediately began casting about for a merger partner of its own. Southern Pacific and Santa Fe Industries agreed to merge in 1983, but four years later the ICC declared this conglomerate anticompetitive. In October 1988 Southern Pacific found a new home among the holdings of Denver businessman Philip Anschutz, whose Rio Grande Industries already owned the Denver and Rio Grande Western Railroad. Anschutz paid $1 billion for Southern Pacific, which thus became a part of Rio Grande Industries, a group of railroads that function as cooperating but distinct rail systems. Rio Grande in 1989 secured access to the important Chicago rail hub, acquiring 282 miles of track between that city and St. Louis. In 1990 it acquired the right to use Burlington Northern tracks between Chicago and Kansas City, Missouri; and in the early 1990s initial reports from the combined companies indicated renewed vigor and enthusiasm for Chairman Anschutz. On the other hand, Southern Pacific continued to show operating losses after the merger and was profiting mainly from the proceeds of real estate sales, which left open the question of the railroad's long-term viability.

Principal Subsidiaries: Southern Pacific Telecommunications Company; Southern Pacific Environmental Systems, Inc.; Pacific Pipelines, Inc.

Further Reading: "Southern Pacific," *Fortune,* November 1937; Daggett, Stuart, *Chapters on the History of the Southern Pacific,* New York, Kelley, 1966.

—Jonathan Martin

THE SWISS FEDERAL RAILWAYS (SCHWEIZERISCHE BUNDESBAHNEN)

Hochschulstrasse 6
CH-3030 Bern
Switzerland
(31) 602403
Fax: (31) 604358

State-Owned Company
Incorporated: 1902
Employees: 37,700
Sales: SFr2.70 billion (US$1.99 billion)

The Swiss Federal Railways has developed from unpromising beginnings into one of the most advanced passenger and freight networks in the world. As well as playing a pivotal role in the nation's economic and social life, it stands at the hub of the central European transportation system.

The need for a comprehensive rail system in Switzerland was apparent by the early 1830s. However, early projects were dogged by lack of investment, the mountainous nature of the country, and a fragmented political system that imposed some 400 internal customs barriers within the national boundaries. The first railway built in Swiss territory was the two-kilometer St. Louis to Basel section of the Strasbourg to Basel line, no more than a small extension of the French network, and not opened until June 15, 1844. The first real Swiss railway came into operation on August 9, 1847, connecting Zürich with Baden. This was opened some 22 years after England's pioneering Stockton-Darlington line, and at a time when England already had 3,928 kilometers and the United States 7,454 kilometers of track under steam. The 23-kilometer Zürich to Baden line was nicknamed the "Spanisch-Brötli-Bahn" (the "Spanish Bun Railway"); Spanish buns were a specialty of Baden patisseries and with the new train service they arrived in Zürich fresher than before. SBB has survived as the German-language title for Swiss Federal Railways, although nowadays the initials officially stand for Schweizerische Bundesbahnen. In French, the railways are known as Chemins de Fer Fédéraux (CFF).

The breakthrough for Swiss railways came with the country's new constitution of 1848, when Switzerland was transformed from a loose collection of cantons or small states into a united confederation with a central government in Bern. This change swept away cumbersome internal tariffs and border restrictions. Moreover, while leaving detailed legislation to individual cantons, the federal government committed itself to the development of rail transport as a vital component of the new confederation's commercial strategy. In 1850 the government invited Robert Stephenson, son of the inventor of the Rocket, a locomotive that could run at 58 kilometers per hour, to help devise a railway system following the main valleys. The same year the Swiss parliament passed the Federal Act of Compulsory Expropriation of Private Property, handing the cantons crucial powers of compulsory purchase for rail building. Hitherto, expansion of the network had been frustrated by landowners and by vested interests who supported the road transport monopoly and viewed the railways as a threat.

There followed a period of intense development and construction. By 1872 five major rail projects linked all the Swiss population centers from the west to the east. In 1883 the north and south of the country were linked by the opening of the Gotthard Railway. This route, the first to cross the Alps, was of immense importance to international trade and was built as the result of a trilateral agreement between Switzerland, Germany, and Italy. Almost 5,500 workers constructed the tunnel over 12 years. Some 307 lost their lives, 177 of them in the tunnel itself. Although the railway was constructed privately, Switzerland and Germany made subsidies of SFr20 million, and Italy contributed SFr45 million. The Swiss money was collected by the cantons, still responsible for railway construction, in partnership with private enterprise. However, political debate mounted over the question of private versus public ownership. The early rail companies were, to a great extent, foreign-owned and created by foreign investment. This effectively left the newly united Switzerland with little control over it own transport policy. Often the individual companies were on the brink of collapse, seeking financial rescue from the cantons in times of crisis. What profits there were went to the shareholders, rather than toward reinvestment in new rolling stock or improved services. Furthermore, dishonest share dealings, particularly in the Paris stock exchange, infected the nascent rail industry with a permanent atmosphere of near panic. Public anxiety grew into open resentment which, fired by a new mood of national consciousness, expressed itself in the popular slogan: "Swiss Railways for Swiss people." With a new Federal Railway Act, central government wrested control of railway legislation away from the cantons. From then onward, rail concessions, company statutes, and building plans had to be approved from Bern, with federal engineers supervising construction work and safety levels. Timetables and fares were made subject to the approval of the Federal Traffic Office.

The trend toward nationalization was clear, and the struggle for state ownership of the railways raged for a decade. In 1891 the federal government made its first attempt to buy the Central Swiss Railway, but the move was defeated in a referendum. Seven years later, on February 20, 1898, the nationalization of the country's main lines was again put to the popular vote, and on this occasion accepted by a majority of 200,000. The philosophy behind nationalization, and the birth of the Swiss Federal Railways, was enshrined in statute by the Rück-kaufgesetz, or Redemption Law, which stated: "The Swiss Confederation is rightfully empowered and commissioned to purchase any railway which, in their opinion, serves from a military defense or economic point of view the interests of the Confederation or a major part of it, and to operate it under the name of Swiss Federal Railways."

The Swiss Federal Railways came into being on January 1, 1902, when the state nationalized the Central Swiss Railway, the Swiss North-Eastern, the Wohlen-Bremgarten line, the Aargaulische Südbahn, and the Bötzbergbahn. Three further services, the United Swiss Railways, the Toggenburg Railway, and the Wald-Rütibahn, were absorbed that July. They were followed by the Jura-Simplon Railway in 1903, and the Gotthard Railway on May 1, 1909. Altogether some 2,730 kilometers of track were purchased, at a cost of SFr160.49 million. Perhaps because of the political controversy, the government paid shareholders SFr114 million more than the original capital invested, a gesture historically viewed as overgenerous, and one that placed a heavy financial burden on the new Swiss Federal Railways.

Railway construction continued during the nationalization period. The Simplon Tunnel through the Alps opened on January 25, 1906, born of western Switzerland's desire for a direct link with Italy, and to place Berne on an important international route from France. Aside from its commercial importance, the tunnel ushered in the era of prestigious international trains, such as the Simplon-Orient Express. The tunnel was electrified from its beginning, but the rest of the network remained under steam, and during World War I was nearly paralyzed by desperate shortages of coal. Having learned a bitter lesson, the Swiss Federal Railways introduced a systematic electrification program from 1919 onward. The Saint Gotthard route came live between 1920 and 1922, and the entire network, except for 16 kilometers, was electrified by 1960.

Despite the fuel shortages of World War I, the network managed to enlarge many stations and build new links from Wilerfeld to Kiesen, and from Nottwil to Rothenbourg. Further improvements were made to track and crossings, train announcement facilities, and bridges.

The interwar period witnessed consolidation and steady improvement. Passenger and freight figures rose in line with the ambitious electrification program, and the system earned a reputation for efficiency, innovation, and safety. The second gallery of the Simplon tunnel was built in 1922, and the next five years saw the completion of a second tunnel from Monte Ceneri on the Giubiasco-Rivera to Bironico line, and a replacement line on the left bank of Lake Zürich.

In 1929, when half the network had been electrified, colored light signals were installed because of the greater speeds and stopping distances of the modern services. For a number of years the colored lights functioned beside the traditional semaphore system, until the entire network was converted to the new signals. Automatic barriers were also developed. In addition, many bridges were upgraded to accommodate the bigger, faster new trains; most notably, major improvements were made to the Grandfey and the Saint-Ursanne viaducts.

The years up to World War II also saw the development of a crucial safety innovation in Switzerland. Increasing speeds had led to a number of accidents, caused by drivers who had either missed or misunderstood warning signals. Under the new Signum system, electromagnetic sensors were sunk into the track itself, and communicated with similar sensors installed in the locomotives. The electromagnets in the track would warn each train electronically whether the line was clear; if it

was not, a horn would be activated in the driver's cab. The driver was then required to take instant action. If the horn was ignored, emergency brakes would automatically cut in and halt the train. The system was a great success, and from 1934 was installed in all electric and multiple-unit trains in the Swiss network. An originator of automatic braking systems, Signum was subsequently used and adapted internationally. In 1935 the green electric warning signals were replaced by orange.

During World War II private road traffic was virtually paralyzed by fuel rationing; the railways kept the nation moving, insulated as the system was from fuel shortages by the far-sighted electrification program. A wartime timetable was introduced, and fares were kept to a minimum. New season tickets offered discounts of 32% to 38%, and similar concessions were made to goods traffic. Passenger figures more than doubled and, although international traffic slumped dramatically, domestic freight exceeded its prewar volume. Learning from the shortages of the previous war, care was taken to stockpile building materials, in particular iron.

Some rolling stock was loaned to the French, primarily for the transportation of casualties. Although Switzerland was a non-belligerent nation, Swiss railway stations and track were bombed during the conflict, mainly by the British. The imposition of strict blackout regulations added to the network's organizational problems. In 1941 both the Renens station and the Zurich viaduct suffered considerable damage. Similar strikes on the Swiss network continued until 1945, when 40 bombs and several incendiaries hit the marshaling yards for the Wolf to Basel line.

Rebuilding began after the war, coupled with further expansion. When the conversion to electric traction was nearly complete, the Swiss railways made advances in the field of power signaling. The control consoles of new installations were now often built up of individual units, rather than stamped as a whole on steel sheeting. The adapted "domino" system allowed for constant changes to be made, simply by adding or removing the constituent units. Previously a whole new sheeting console would have to be made if, for example, a new siding was introduced.

Even in the age of the automobile, the Swiss did not qualify their commitment to rail development; major improvements were made to leading lines, as part of immense projects authorized in the years 1956 and 1965. In 1956 The Swiss Federal Railways agreed upon massive plans with the city and canton of Bern to rebuild and upgrade the capital's main station, the Hauptbahnhof. The scheme was endorsed by public vote and work began in 1957. It required the demolition of the former terminal, and the construction of a new station with six island platforms, two new tunnels, and a vast post office block. The first new platform came into operation in 1961, and the last five years later. In the 1950s and 1960s underpasses and bridges replaced many level crossings on the Geneva to Zürich line, probably the most important in the country. By 1967 this brought the traveling time for the fast Geneva to Lausanne stretch from 50 minutes down to 32 minutes. Further improvements were made to the Basel-Zürich-Chur line, including costly and laborious track-doubling beyond Ziegelbrücke, along the tortuous contours beside Lake Zürich. The work, which involved building the double-line Kerenzerberg tunnel, was completed in 1970. As part of the same program, flyover lines were built at Brugg and Thalwil. The Olten to Zürich section of the Bern-Zürich line was completely remodeled with the construction of the vast Limmattal marshaling yards. On other major lines, steady advances in efficiency and safety lowered traveling times of both domestic and, most notably, international services. For example, the 508–mile Milan to Paris journey was brought down to a total traveling time of 7 hours, 44 minutes. Advances were further aided by the development in Switzerland of lightweight rolling stock.

By 1972 railway author Cecil J. Allen observed in his book *Swiss Travel Wonderland* that the Swiss had complete faith in their railways, and that the closure of lines or stations was "practically unknown." "Indeed," he added, "the railways are regarded as so essential a part of the nation's life and well-being that the necessary finance is never withheld from any economically justifiable plans for their improvement."

The policy of energy self-sufficiency carried over into the electric age, with one-third of the traction current produced by The Swiss Federal Railways' own power stations. About half comes from jointly-owned power stations, with only the remainder supplied by outside contractors. Simultaneously, the railway fostered new breakthroughs in energy efficiency. Latter-day electric train motors are so advanced that the railways consume nine times less energy, per ton-kilometer, than road traffic, and research continues into further improvement. With regenerative braking, the trains produce as well as use power; three freight trains running downhill on, for example, the Gotthard line, produce enough energy to pull a fourth train uphill. The company accounts for only 1.1% of all electricity consumed in Switzerland, further enhancing its new image as an environment-friendly service.

Of necessity, The Swiss Federal Railways has led the world in tunnel technology. More than 200 kilometers of the system's track are in 243 tunnels; joined together, they would provide an underground line from Basel to Lugano. In addition, the company is responsible for some 4,000 rail bridges and about 1,000 road bridges. The Saint Gotthard remains the principal transit route between northern and southern Europe, transporting some six million people and 13.5 million tons of goods per year. The Simplon is the second most important transalpine route between Italy and the rest of the continent, and each year some three million passengers and three million tons of cargo travel through this international tunnel system.

In the early 1990s a second golden era of tunnel building was an immediate prospect, with ambitious federal government plans to update and expand the Alpine rail axis to meet the increased transport demands of the single European market. As a first phase, piggyback rail services will be modernized to ferry up to 2,000 lorries through the Alps per day. By 1994 the piggyback capacity of the Saint Gotthard route alone will have been more than doubled, to 365,000 consignments per year. There are further proposals for a pan-European New Trans-Alpine Railway (NEAT), centering on a 49-kilometer tunnel between Amsteg and Bodio, which should be open by the year 2015. The Simplon line would be refined to speed traffic between Paris, Geneva, Lausanne, and Italy, thus reducing the traveling time from Basel to Milan from 5 hours and 17 minutes to an initial 3 hours and 10 minutes, and just 2 hours 45 minutes when all the work is complete. Paris would then be less than six hours from Milan. Shorter traveling times would improve employment and production opportunities in many regions, and the new railways would balance traffic

and economic activity, thus softening the impact on the environment.

To encourage motorists to travel longer distances by train, The Swiss Federal Railways, in cooperation with federal, cantonal, and communal authorities, has launched a major car park building scheme around all main stations, offering preferential rates for rail users. Furthermore, the railway shuttles cars and lorries through the Alpine tunnels, and sleeper trains transport road vehicles many hundreds of kilometers, from Zürich to Naples and Narbonne.

The policy of transport integration has also led to close links between Switzerland's rail and air networks. Passengers flying by Swissair can check in and collect their boarding passes when they begin their journey at selected rail stations. Hourly trains connect the nation with the two principal international airports of Zürich and Geneva, with platforms directly under the runways. Zürich airport station, opened in 1980, is served daily by 172 trains of the Zürich-Winterthur line, and is used by some 6.6 million passengers each year. The new Geneva airport station was opened in 1987, and is used by some 2.6 million travelers each year.

After eight years of the regular interval timetable, which replaced the old empiric timetable in 1982, passenger traffic has risen by 23%. Business was also boosted by a range of attractive fare incentives, such as the half-fare travel card, government-subsidized from 1987 to 1991. The Swiss take more train journeys per person—an average of 39 per year—than any other people except the Japanese.

The company enjoys a status defined in recent legislation as an "autonomous federal enterprise." It publishes its accounts separately from the state and, in common with stock companies, has a board of directors and its own capital stock. However, the Federal Assembly retains ultimate authority over the network; it approves its accounts and annual reports, and decides on grants, subsidies, and track acquisition or closure. Each of the assembly's two chambers appoints permanent transport committees. The Federal Council, the federal executive body, oversees the company's business and finances, and nominates the board of directors, the three general managers, and the three regional managers. The supervisory powers are in turn delegated to the Federal Department of Transport, Communications and Energy.

The Swiss Federal Railways was beset from its formation by an apparent contradiction in the requirements placed upon it by the country. The federal law of June 23, 1944, charged the network with operating its fares and services in line with the national interest, while at the same time running on strict business lines which would produce enough surplus for reinvestment, technological advance, and capital works. The government sought to reconcile these principles in the Performance Contract 1987–1994, which separates the network's activities into two areas: the commercial sector (including long-haul passenger traffic, wagonload, container and part-load traffic), and the public service sector (regional passenger traffic, the regular interval timetable, and piggyback traffic.) The company kept responsibility for the operating costs of the commercial sector, but the government agreed to subsidize the expenses of the public service sector. This sum is set in advance, and reached SFr592 million in 1990. In addition, the Confederation has been paying the SBB's infrastructure costs since 1987, encompassing depreciation, interest charges, and maintenance of specified fixed assets. In return, the network pays the government a "user's tax" against infrastructure expenses, in the amount of SFr37 million in 1990. The company has shareholdings in transport companies—Swissair, 1.5%; Interfreigo, 10%; Intercontainer, 5.7%—as well as in cooling houses, power plants, and car parking.

Further Reading: "The Railways of Switzerland," Railway Gazette Publication, 1947; "Aperçu des 50 Ans d'Activité des Chemins de Fer Fédéraux 1902–1952," SBB pamphlet, 1952; "Bulletin du Personnel des CFF," Direction Générale des CFF, 1970 and 1976; Allen, Cecil J., *Swiss Travel Wonderland,* London, Ian Allen, 1972; "Chemins de Fer Fédéraux Suisses—Rapport de Gestion," Direction Générale des CFF, 1976; Nock, O.S., *Railways of Western Europe,* London, Adam & Charles Black, 1977; "Simplon 75 ans," Direction Générale des CFF, 1981; "Les CFF Aujourd'hui," Direction Générale des CFF, 1982; "Saint-Gotthard 1882–1982," Direction Générale des CFF, 1982; "A l'Avenir, Le Train!," Direction Générale des CFF, 1984; "Railway Springtime," SBB General Secretariat, 1990.

—Linda Anderson

TNT LIMITED

9th Floor, TNT Plaza
Tower One, Lawson Square
Redfern New South Wales 2016
Australia
(02) 699 2222
Fax: (02) 699 9238

Public Company
Incorporated: 1962 as Thomas Nationwide Transport Limited
Employees: 52,000
Sales: A$4.83 billion (US$3.67 billion)
Stock Exchanges: Sydney London Wellington

TNT Limited is the world's largest diversified transport group in terms of sales, a huge conglomerate providing air, land, and sea freight transport for anything from a single envelope to a crate of machinery. Although based in Australia, which was the limit of its activities for its first 20 years, the company is now a major carrier in Europe, North and South America, South East Asia, and New Zealand, following an energetic international expansion program begun in the late 1960s. This expansion, driven by TNT's managing director, Sir Peter Abeles, has transformed the company's structure to the point where international operations have begun to displace Australian business as the heart of the company's activities.

TNT began in 1946 when Ken W. Thomas started operating a one-man trucking business in Sydney, Australia. After several years of steady growth, he incorporated the business as a private company in 1951. Continuing growth over the next decade, with the expansion of the company's fleet and extension of its routes across Australia, led to its incorporation as a public company in 1962, under the name Thomas Nationwide Transport Limited (TNT), and listing on the Sydney Stock Exchange the following year. Access to public funds allowed the company to continue expanding until, as the end of the decade approached, the limits of the Australian trucking market became apparent and TNT began to look for opportunities to extend its business beyond Australia. The chance came in 1967, a key year in TNT's history, when the company merged with another growing Australian transport enterprise, the Alltrans Group. Like TNT, Alltrans was another company that began in a small way in the optimistic environment of postwar Australia. One of Alltrans's two principal shareholders, Peter Abeles, was a refugee from war-torn Hungary. Abeles stepped off a ship in Sydney in the late 1940s with £4,000. With a

partner, George Rockey, he bought two trucks on time payment, named them *Samson* and *Delilah* and, like Thomas, set about building up his business. Abeles would spend weeks driving his car through the Australian bush, drumming up contracts for the fledgling business. Although the merger with TNT involved discarding the Alltrans name and Thomas remaining head of the merged group, Abeles soon emerged as the driving force in the company, its key strategist and its public face.

The merger gave TNT its first international operations via Alltrans's activities in New Zealand, which had begun in 1964. The size of the new group gave it the base required to begin expanding internationally. TNT began an ambitious international acquisition program, starting with its entry into the tough U.S. trucking industry through the purchase of a California truck line, Walkup's Merchant Express Inc., in 1969. In 1970 TNT bought Gill Interprovincial Lines in Canada, and acquired one-third of a shipping company, Bulkships. Over the next two years, the expansion continued with the purchase of another Canadian operator, Scott Transport, one-sixth of the Union Steamship Co. of New Zealand Ltd., and TNT's entry into the U.S. air transport business through a joint venture with Shulman Transport Enterprises Inc. In 1972 the company also opened a small office in the United Kingdom, its first European presence. These swift moves were not without problems, however. The U.S. trucking industry is a very difficult market for a newcomer. TNT's efforts to move into this market were accompanied by a series of wildcat strikes, mysterious bombings, and arson attacks. The damage caused by this interference was the first in a number of problems that would affect TNT's U.S. operations for years.

The company continued with its acquisition plans, aimed at attaining Abeles's vision of an integrated global transport operation. In 1973 TNT went into partnership with two West German companies to form an international ship brokering company, Montan TNT Pty Ltd. It also formed Kwikasair Ltd., an express delivery service between the United Kingdom and continental Europe. TNT's U.S. base was also expanded, through the purchase in the same year of Overland Western Ltd., a trucking company operating in Ontario and New York and Michigan; and Acme Fast Freight Inc. The company also began developing a strong South American presence in 1973 when it bought 70% of the Brazilian transport group Pampa OTT and established Kwikasair Brazil.

It was TNT's activities within Australia, however, that suddenly brought the company to international attention in 1972. TNT had continued to grow steadily since the 1967 merger, and it was well on its way to becoming the country's dominant transport group. In 1972 the company tried to accelerate the process by launching a hostile takeover bid for Ansett Transport Industries Limited (Ansett), the operator of one of Australia's two major domestic airlines. Protected from free competition by a government-endorsed airline duopoly, Ansett was a highly profitable company that would have secured TNT's position as Australia's leading carrier. Ansett's chairman and founder, Sir Reginald Ansett, was a tough adversary. At the height of the battle he called on the Victorian state government, headed by his personal friend Sir Henry Bolte, for assistance. The government ruled that it was unacceptable for a company based in Victoria to be taken over by a company from New South Wales, and stopped the takeover. TNT withdrew with 23% of Ansett's shares, but kept a close eye on Ansett.

The failed bid for Ansett did not stop TNT's international growth program, which continued through the mid-1970s with a series of acquisitions—particularly in the United Kingdom and Canada—which the company was using as launchpads for later growth in Europe and United States respectively. In 1975 Abeles foreshadowed the company's next international step when he launched an attack on international shipping conferences and the effect these cartels had on the global transport industry and trade prospects. The following year, TNT directly challenged one of the most powerful of these cartels, the North Atlantic Freight Conference, comprising some of the world's largest shipping companies, by operating a non-conference container shipping service, Trans Freight Lines, on the Atlantic run.

Ten years after the merger between TNT and Alltrans, TNT had become Australia's major transport group, despite its failure to take over Ansett, and was a growing presence internationally. The group's annual revenue had increased tenfold from A$46 million in 1967 to A$462.7 million by 1977, while its after-tax profits had risen over the same period from A$956,000 to A$15.3 million. Such a swift expansion, however, had left the group exposed to a wide range of fluctuating markets and economies. TNT had bought heavily, was a relative newcomer in many of its markets, and was losing money from some of its operations in the difficult U.S. market. In 1977 to 1978, for the first time since its public incorporation in 1961, TNT's profits fell.

The company responded with a recovery strategy aimed at rationalizing its international activities to cut out the weaker activities and build up other operations to the point where they were more prominent than the Australian operations. The program began in 1979 with the sale of the U.S. trucking company Acme Fast Freight, which had lost money every year since being acquired in 1973. The group also cut a loss-making stake in Nigerian Shipping Operations from 100% to 25%. By 1980, the company projected, more than half of its profits would for the first time be earned outside Australia. These projections were overshadowed later in 1979, when a new takeover battle for Ansett Transport Industries Limited began. With Sir Henry Bolte gone and a more liberalized corporate climate in Australia, two groups, Ampol Petroleum and Bell Resources, began buying Ansett shares heavily. TNT entered the battle, which also involved Rupert Murdoch's The News Corporation Limited. Just as the latter emerged as the likely victor, it suddenly became clear that TNT's stake was large enough to prevent Murdoch's company from taking control. The two companies agreed to share control of Ansett, with 50% each. Ansett's operations included a major Australian domestic airline—Ansett Australia, freight services, and tourist resort operations.

The cash flow provided by its share of Ansett gave TNT renewed strength to pursue its international expansion plans. The company changed its international focus to concentrate on the United Kingdom and Europe as its most important growth area. This focus became clear in October 1980 when, sponsored by the British merchant bank Hambros, TNT was listed on the London Stock Exchange, after removing itself from the Toronto and Vancouver exchanges earlier in the year. TNT was now well placed to expand into Europe, although it continued to look for openings in the United States, buying another trucking and warehousing company, Pilot Freight Carriers, while Trans Freight Lines doubled its size by buying another container line, Seatrain International.

The impact TNT's services were having in its new markets was indicated in 1982 in a confidential U.K. Post Office report that stated that a new TNT private parcel delivery service, Homefast, would pose a serious threat to the Royal Mail parcels network. TNT took a significant step toward building a European freight network in 1983 when it bought Skypak, IPEC Holdings Ltd.'s international courier operations, which operated in 26 countries. Combined with TNT's existing courier networks, this gave the group bases in 49 countries and provided access to Middle and Far East markets. Four months after the Skypak acquisition, TNT bought IPEC Europe, the leader in the European international express freight market, complete with more than 60 purpose-built terminals and 600 radio-equipped vehicles.

With its Ansett stake and its growing international business, TNT itself became a prime candidate for takeover in the early 1980s. One of Australia's most skilled take-over operators, Robert Holmes à Court, stalked TNT through 1981 and 1982 but was held off, although at one stage Ansett and another of TNT's associates, McIlwraith McEachern Limited, were called upon to pay more than A$60 million for a strategic stake in TNT to protect it from predators.

The vulnerability of a widespread transport group to the cyclical movements of economies became clear again when the company's profits plunged by half in 1982 to 1983. A recession in Australia had severely cut freight volumes, while in other markets competition had forced TNT to reduce its rates and thus its profit margin. TNT continued to pour money into expansion, however, opening a steady stream of operations and services in the United Kingdom, where it was a pioneer in the area of overnight delivery service, as it had been in Australia, and constantly looking out for new acquisition or expansion opportunities in Europe. In view of its international emphasis, the company changed its name in 1985 from Thomas Nationwide Transport Limited to simply TNT Limited (TNT).

A key event for TNT's European operation occurred in 1986 and came largely by virtue of the close relationship that had developed between Abeles and Rupert Murdoch since the Ansett takeover. When Murdoch planned to move his British national newspapers in London from Fleet Street to a new plant in Wapping, in the face of fierce resistance from the printing unions, he also anticipated problems from the unions at British Rail, which distributed all of his publications nationwide. Murdoch therefore worked closely with TNT, whose U.K. manager, Alan Jones, built up a fleet of trucks in the weeks leading up to the transfer to Wapping. The weekend before the move, Jones hired 550 drivers, and when Wapping began operating, TNT's trucks rolled through the gates and the picket lines. For TNT the effort paid off, as the company was awarded the contract to distribute all of Murdoch's British papers, providing a massive boost to the company's U.K. operation. The plan also marked the end of British Rail's dominance of the newspaper distribution market, as more publishers followed Murdoch's lead and switched to road distribution.

In the late 1980s, TNT emerged from a period that could have damaged a company with a different approach. Faced with a recession and exposed in a number of geographical areas, TNT under Abeles spent heavily on expansion and outlasted the problems. The company was particularly well positioned in the £500 million-a-year European express-delivery market, which was growing at 50% a year. The emphasis on Europe was shown by the fact that the company's European turnover grew by an average of almost 50% a year from when the U.K. office was opened in 1972 to 1987. By 1987 TNT had become the world's largest diversified transportation group, with operations in 105 countries. Abeles indicated that the company was moving into a new phase when he said in the *Sunday Times*, June 28, 1987, "The growing pains of setting up and consolidating into a truly worldwide transportation group are coming to an end."

From its wider base, TNT began a new series of developments aimed at furthering its reach in its existing markets, particularly in Europe. In 1987 the company sold its last shares in the U.S. shipping company Trans Freight Lines, which had been unsuccessful in its attempt to penetrate the tight North Atlantic shipping business and had lost a net A$80 million since 1976. TNT also unloaded another big loss-making U.S. operation, the trucking business TNT Pilot, which had lost more than A$60 million since 1980. In 1987 TNT made one of its biggest investments when it negotiated a right of first refusal of five years' production of British Aerospace's new BAe 146 Quiet Trader freight aircraft, worth an estimated total of about £1 billion, and used the first 18 planes to establish a transEuropean air express freight network servicing 17 countries.

TNT also pushed toward the goal of running a new freight airline in Europe. In 1988 it merged its European express freight division with that of its biggest competitor, Scandinavian Airline System's Air de Cologne and bought a 75% stake in the leading Spanish domestic freight carrier, Unitransa. It also bought KLM Airlines' parcel express business, XP, and linked its air freight business in Europe with its road operations, creating a formidable new network, TNT Express Europe. By mid-1989 the European operations accounted for 35% of TNT's total worldwide assets, double the proportion of just two years before. Abeles's eyes were clearly fixed on the coming of the single European market in 1992 and his strategy of dominating the highly segmented European freight industry by offering a comprehensive range of services between and within all European countries appeared to be working.

The late 1980s also marked TNT's extension into Eastern Europe, just in time for the collapse of the Eastern Bloc in 1989 and 1990. The company formed a joint venture with the Hungarian airline Malev in 1988, created TNT Aeroflot—a joint venture with Russia's Aeroflot—in 1989 and started a joint venture with Yugoslavia's airline JAT in 1990. As other countries in the region became liberalized, TNT moved toward similar operations throughout Eastern Europe. It also expanded in South East Asia, investing in joint ventures with the Philippine Aerospace Development Corporation to develop the Philippines as a regional hub.

From late 1989, however, TNT encountered a series of serious problems. The problems began in August 1989 when Aus-

tralia's domestic airline pilots resigned en masse as part of a campaign to secure a 29.7% salary increase which was outside the government's 6% wages accord and centralized system. Accordingly, the pilots' union's industrial awards were cancelled by the Industrial Relations Commission. The four airlines, namely Ansett Airlines, East-West Airlines, government-owned Australian Airlines, and IPEC Aviation slowly rebuilt their airlines by employing pilots on individual contracts. This took several months and was completed by March 1990. The number of pilots reemployed was significantly lower than prior to the dispute. The dispute, which lasted for months, ended in favor of the airlines, but caused serious damage to the airlines' revenue. At the height of the dispute, Ansett was estimated to be losing A$10 million a week. TNT's profits for the September quarter of 1989 were 70% lower than for the same period a year before.

The damage subsided after the dispute, but hopes for a return to profit growth disappeared in 1990, when Australia, the United Kingdom, and North America fell into recession. As usual, the economic downturn hit the transport industry hard, and TNT's broad exposure in these regions left it open to a severe drop in revenue. This problem was compounded in Australia in November 1990, when the federal government deregulated the domestic airline industry and ended the two-airline agreement which had protected Ansett's share of the air market for so long. Compass Airlines, a new company headed by a former Ansett employee, entered the market and began offering big fare reductions, forcing Ansett Australia, East-West Airlines, and Australian Airlines to introduce fare discounts of up to 61%, further slashing revenue.

These problems caused a surge of concern in financial markets about TNT's capacity to generate liquidity in tough times. In January 1991 the company's share price on the Australian Stock Exchange fell to a record low of A75¢. Due to the unfavorable market conditions, the company decided not to issue A$200 million of preference shares, issuing later, in April 1991, 50 million new ordinary shares of A50¢ at a premium of A$1.00 to ease its liquidity problems. The hardest blow came in May 1991, when TNT revealed that it had lost nearly A$90 million in the nine months to the end of March 1991.

In July 1991 the company announced the establishment of a joint venture (50/50) between its own TNT Express Worldwide and five major post offices incorporated under the entity GD Net BV, comprising the postal organizations of Germany, France, The Netherlands, Sweden, and Canada to effect high-quality time-certain delivery services with global coverage. All regulatory approvals have been given for this joint venture and the aim was to close it in the first quarter of 1992; the effective date was October 1, 1991.

Principal Subsidiaries: TNT Australia Pty. Ltd.; TNT Express Europe B.V. (The Netherlands); TNT Transport Group Inc.; TNT Shipping & Development Limited; TNT (U.K.) Ltd.; TNT Canada Inc.; TNT Brasil S.A. (85%).

—Richard Brass

TOKYU CORPORATION

26-20, Sakuragaoka-cho
Shibuya-ku, Tokyo 150
Japan
(03) 3477-6111
Fax: (03) 3496-2965

Public Company
Incorporated: 1922 as Tokyu Kyuko Electric Railway
   Company Ltd.
Employees: 92,600
Sales: ¥373.33 billion (US$2.99 billion)
Stock Exchange: Tokyo

The Tokyu Corporation, operating railways and bus routes in Tokyo, is the nucleus and parent company of a group of more than 300 companies. Tokyu is one of Japan's relatively new conglomerates, unlike the long-established, finance-oriented groups such as Mitsubishi and Mitsui. The subsidiaries' activities include real estate development, hotels, department stores, distribution, tourism, and the manufacture of railway cars. Like the other railway companies, such as Seibu, Tokyu used its railway lines as a base from which to exploit the densely populated surrounding areas. In the 1980s Tokyu fulfilled its ambitions to expand overseas, notably in the tourism industry in the Asia Pacific region.

The story of Tokyu began in the rural town of Aoki in Nagano Prefecture in western Japan, where founder Keita Kobayashi was born in 1883. After completing primary school in his native village he attended high school in the nearby city of Matsumoto, where he spent a year before moving to Tokyo to attend what is now the law department of Tokyo University, the country's most prestigious university. He graduated in 1907 at the age of 24. While at the university Keita Kobayashi made the acquaintance of a politician, Takaaki Katoh, who would later become prime minister of Japan. Katoh was an inspiration to the young Kobayashi and provided him with a prestigious position upon graduation with the civil service in the Agricultural Ministry. The following year Kobayashi took the name of his wife's family, Gotoh, which means "raider" in Japanese. The pun has been used by countless journalists alluding to Keita Gotoh's style of doing business.

By 1921 Gotoh was employed by the Ministry of Transport. He was involved in supervising Japan's national railway system, and was given a post as director of the newly privatized and ailing Musashi Railway. At the time Musashi Railway was a so-called paper company because it did not actually own or operate any trains, but possessed real estate and planning permission to do so. Gotoh not only turned the company around but in 1922 also bought a controlling interest in it for ¥50,000. This was to be the first of the many corporate buyouts that characterized Keita Gotoh's rise. In the same year, he founded Tokyo Kyuko Electric Railway Company Ltd., which absorbed Musashi Railway.

The following year Eichi Shibusawa, a leading Japanese industrialist and founder of Denenchofu Corporation, one of Japan's first electric railway companies, was looking for help in building and developing the railway arm of his company, Mekata Railway. He approached Ichizo Kobayashi, founder of Hankyu Corporation, who promptly recommended Gotoh. Gotoh not only accepted the offer, but following the Great Kanto Earthquake of 1923 he took control of its railway interests.

The next five years saw ambitious construction projects realized, including a 13.2-kilometer line through the southwest section of Tokyo. The late 1920s and the 1930s in Japan were a time of rapid industrialization, and Gotoh realized that the key to a modern and industrialized Japan was an efficient infrastructure. In densely populated Tokyo and in Kawasaki and Yokohama, rail transport was becoming increasingly important. Gotoh's aggressive expansion policy continued as the Tokyu Corporation—as it was then named, "Tokyu" being an abbreviation of "Tokyo Kyuko," or "Tokyo Express"—came to include the Ikejoh and Tamagawa lines and Tokyo Underground line. Gotoh became a pioneer in what became the most efficient underground railway system in the world by building in 1937 an underground link from Shibuya to Shinbashi, both districts of Tokyo. Other acquisitions made around this time were Enoshima Electric Railways and Shizuoka Electric Railways companies, both outside Tokyo; Sotetsu Transport Company; and Kanto United Cars, a railway car manufacturer. In the decade before the end of World War II, Gotoh continued his policy of buying weak companies and turning them around. He also began exploiting the extensive lands his company owned around its railway lines. One of the first areas to be developed—which became one of Tokyo's most exclusive residential areas—was Denenchofu. During its first two decades, leading up to World War II, Tokyu was not only providing the crucial transport links to this area but also developing and constructing real estate.

About this time, another railway and real estate group was flourishing in Tokyo, the Seibu Group. The two companies became bitter rivals.

The years 1935 to 1945 were prosperous years. The Japanese war machine was in full gear and provided the various group companies with contracts in such areas as cargo, construction, and the manufacture of railway cars for the Japanese army. The saturation bombing of Tokyo during 1944 and 1945, however, proved disastrous for the company, severely disrupting the railway lines. The U.S. occupation proved equally disastrous. Like the other huge industrial and financial combines, or *zaibatsu*, Tokyu was dismantled under the Economic Decentralization Law imposed by General Douglas MacArthur. Rail and bus transportation networks were broken up and transferred to other companies. With its operations reduced, Tokyu Corporation attempted a new beginning as did the remnants of other Japanese companies. Although much of the infrastructure had been damaged or destroyed, Gotoh used this as an opportunity to modernize the company's enterprises and make inroads into new businesses to meet the various needs of consumers. Gotoh made the remaining businesses into subsidiaries, thus encouraging them to develop and prosper independently. In 1949, in order to raise capital for continued expansion, Gotoh floated Tokyu on the Tokyo stock exchange. In the early 1950s Gotoh's son Noboru, born in 1920, began to rise through the ranks within the company. As his father was still the largest single shareholder in Tokyu, it was natural that Noboru Gotoh should succeed him at the helm of the company. Indeed, it was the young and dynamic Noboru who was encouraging his father to lead Tokyu into new markets. In 1934 Tokyu opened its first department store with the innovative idea of locating it in one of its Tokyo railway stations. In 1948 the Tokyu Department Store Company was formed to expand the chain nationwide and eventually overseas. Tokyu Tourist Corporation was established in 1956 to provide travel services both in Japan and overseas, and in 1960 Tokyu added the hotel business to its activities. Noboru Gotoh became president of Tokyu in 1958 at the age of 38. Keita Gotoh died in 1962, leaving his son clearly in charge of the group. Although Noboru was a less aggressive businessman than his father, he was perhaps more of a visionary and made ambitious plans for Tokyu both in Japan and overseas. He even healed the rift between Tokyu and Seibu by attending the opening of a new Seibu department store.

In 1953 Tokyu began the development of the real estate it owned around its Denentoshi line in Tokyo. The project spanned three decades and involved the development of a relatively sparsely populated suburb called Tama Denentoshi. As Tokyo grew as a center of business and government, and as residential real estate in centrally located areas became more expensive, the new development provided thousands of Japanese with the opportunity to own decent homes within commuting distance of their workplaces. Tokyu would later apply this domestically acquired experience on overseas projects in Seattle, Washington, in the United States and in Perth in Australia.

In 1961 Tokyu, under the leadership of Noboru Gotoh, branched out into two new areas of business: air travel, through the formation of Toa Domestic Airlines, later Japan Air System, and information services, through the formation of Tokyu Agency, which became one of the largest advertising agencies in Japan and, later, overseas. Tokyu also began manufacturing automobile parts in 1964 with the formation of Shiroki Corporation.

While the company branched out into these new areas, Tokyu's mainstay remained its railways, and although the latter did not experience growth as rapid as for some of the newer businesses, it provided steady growth along with a financially stable backbone for the group. In 1961 Tokyu established Izukyu Corporation, a railway line carrying tourists to the National park of Fuji-Hakone-Izu. In 1966 the opening of a new Tokyu railway in the Tama Denentoshi area brought the number of Tokyu lines in the Tokyo area to seven, totaling more than 100 kilometers. The Ueda Kotsu Company, operating a line in Nagano Prefecture, completed Tokyu's national railway network.

In the 1970s Noboru Gotoh led Tokyu into the car rental business through Nippon Rent a Car Tokyu and also dramatically expanded Tokyu's hotel network by forming two companies: Tokyu Hotel Chain, which operates luxury hotels such as the Tokyu Capitol Hotel in the heart of Tokyo, and Tokyu Inn Chain, which was set up in 1958 to cater to the economizing business traveler. In 1972 with the opening of the Hawaiian Regent Hotel in Honolulu, Tokyu Hotels International was established. By the mid-1970s Tokyu was once again a huge conglomerate and like many large companies used its financial clout for charitable as well as investment purposes. Tokyu Foundation for Better Environment was established in 1974 and, as its name suggests, is concerned with environmental issues, one of the first such organizations in Japan. This, along with the Tokyu Foundation for Inbound Students, provides scholarships for postgraduate and research students. The Gotoh Museum contains a fine Japanese and Chinese art collection, including the original manuscript of what is recognized as the world's first novel, *The Tale of Genji.*

The 1980s were years of accelerated overseas expansion for the Tokyu Corporation. In 1980 Tokyu established Tokyu Zurich AG and in 1982 launched a large-scale residential development project in Jakarta, Indonesia. In 1983 Tokyu opened the Mauna Lani Bay Hotel and in the following year the Palau Pacific Resort, both in Hawaii. Tokyu was one of the leading developers in Hawaii. Early in 1986 Tokyu completed construction of a prestigious hotel/office complex in Vancouver. Again, Tokyu was one of the pioneer Japanese developers in a city that was to become one of the world's most lucrative real estate investment areas. In 1987 Tokyu branched out into television broadcasting with the formation of Tokyu Cable Television. As his father had done before him, Noboru Gotoh relied on the infrastructure base of Tokyu's railway lines to move into a new area of business. Cables were laid initially to span the Tama Denentoshi region, covering 600,000 households. A broadcasting center and studios were constructed in Tama Denentoshi, and to launch their activities a two-way Tokyu Cable Computer was developed. The system, which links the center's host computer to each subscriber's home terminal, is designed to provide subscribers with diversified two-way information services.

Although Tokyu's railway and bus transportation business now contributes only one-tenth of the group's annual revenues, it has always been the nucleus of the group. In 1987 Japan National Railways (JNR), carrying 86% of Japan's passenger traffic, was privatized and split up into regional companies which were organized to be more cost-effective and profit-oriented. This in the late 1980s meant increased competition for Tokyu and the other private railway companies such as Seibu and Hankyu, and heralded a turbulent time both financially and politically for the usually steady Japanese railway industry. A goal of Tokyu is therefore to increase its competitiveness through better service. This means alleviation of overcrowding, greater passenger comfort, and greater speed and frequency of service. An example of investment toward these ends by Tokyu is the construction of triple tracks and station improvement along the heavily used Toyoko line between Tokyo and Yokohama.

The profit potential of the railway business is to some extent limited by government-imposed caps on fare increases. Tokyu also operates 17 bus companies, which serve regular as well as tourist routes. Tokyu owns three air transport companies including Japan Air System, Japan's third-largest carrier, which in 1988 completed its maiden international flight, to Seoul. It also flies to Singapore and Hawaii, and operates a fleet of 70 aircraft. Tokyu's various manufacturing companies provide the technology to ensure safety in its transport activities, while also exporting to the United States and Southeast Asia.

By the mid-1980s Noboru Gotoh was approaching retirement. Like his father before him, his eldest son was rapidly rising within the Tokyu organization. Konsuke Gotoh was born in 1949, and by 1987 was a senior manager in Tokyu Construction. In an interview with the *Yomiuri Newspaper* shortly before his death in 1989, Noboru Gotoh stated that Tokyu was no longer a Gotoh family concern and that although he would give his son Konsuke the chance to take over the reins, he would like to see his son work his way up competitively. Although Noboru Gotoh became president at age 38, the Tokyu Corporation has grown and diversified tremendously since then. The president is Jiro Yokota, but Konsuke Gotoh is fairly powerful within Tokyu, and it remains to be seen whether he will lead the company that his grandfather founded into the 21st century.

Principal Subsidiaries: Tokyu Car Corporation; Izukyu Corporation; Japan Air System Co., Ltd.; Taiyo Aviation Co., Ltd.; Ueda Kotsu Corporation; Gumma Bus Corporation; Nippon Kotsu Co., Ltd.; Tokyu Land Corporation; Tokyu Construction Co., Ltd.; Tokyu U.S.A. Inc.; Tokyu Land Development (Hawaii), Inc.; Tokyu Department Store Co., Ltd.; Tokyu Store Chain Co., Ltd.; Tokyu Agency, Inc.; Tokyu Agency International, Inc.; Tokyu Trading Corporation; Tokyu Air Cargo Co. Ltd.; Tokyu Freight Service Co., Ltd.; Tokyu Hotel Chain Co., Ltd.; Tokyu Inn Chain; Tokyu Hotels International Co., Ltd.; Nippon Rent a Car Tokyu Co., Ltd.; Tokyu Cable Television Co., Ltd.; Tokyu Bunkamura, Inc.

Further Reading: Tsushi, Kazunari, *Tokyu and Noburu Gotoh*, Tokyo, Pal Publishing, 1984.

—Dylan Tanner

UNION PACIFIC CORPORATION

Martin Tower
Eighth and Eaton Avenues
Bethlehem, Pennsylvania 18018
U.S.A.
(215) 861-3200
Fax: (215) 861-3111

Public Company
Incorporated: 1897 as Union Pacific Railroad Company
Employees: 48,300
Sales: $6.96 billion
Stock Exchange: New York

The Union Pacific railroad covers much of the western and midwestern United States and comprises the nation's second-largest rail system. Famed for its role in building a significant part of the country's first transcontinental railroad in 1869, Union Pacific (UP) survived early years of scandal and financial uncertainty to emerge as perhaps the most respected U.S. railroad. Blessed with valuable land and mineral rights along its many miles of track, UP has built a substantial business in natural resources. At one time in the 1970s it appeared that its energy holdings might eventually overshadow UP's rail business, and some day they may well do so; but in the early 1990s the heart and soul of Union Pacific Corporation remained its railroad.

Union Pacific came into existence in response to the widely held belief, fully formed by the 1850s, that the United States needed a rail link between its older, eastern states and the distant but rapidly growing states of the far West. Various proposals were made for northern, southern, and central routes, but the U.S. Congress could not agree on a plan. Following the southern states' secession from the United States in 1861 the remaining congressmen from the North quickly agreed upon a route, and U.S. President Abraham Lincoln finally signed the Pacific Railroad Act of 1862, urged on by military considerations as much as by those of economics. The act called for the creation of a public corporation, called Union Pacific Railroad Company, to build a railroad from Nebraska to the California-Nevada border and there to meet the Central Pacific, building east from Sacramento, California, and later linked with San Francisco. Later, the meeting place of the two railroads was set at Promontory Summit, Utah Territory. As amended by a second piece of legislation, the act specified that the company would be supported by a loan from the federal government of U.S. bonds, to be paid back in 30 years, and by the issuance of its own bonds and capital stock. Further, the company would receive land grants in the amount of 6,400 acres on alternating sides of every mile of track laid, a checkerboard swath of land across the middle of the country that would eventually total around 12 million acres of valuable minerals, grazing land, and metropolitan real estate. The government retained the right to inspect each section of track laid before releasing the allotted number of bonds, and it would keep two directors on UP's board, but the company was to be otherwise a venture of the private sector.

While the logic and value of a railroad across the western United States is obvious in the late 20th century, it was much less so in 1864. The men who became involved in the leadership of the UP—chiefly Thomas C. Durant and the Ames brothers, Oliver and Oakes—did so largely in order to make handsome profits off the railroad's hurried construction. Durant was the vice president and dominant figure in the company's early years, and it was he and a handful of others who formed a construction company called Credit Mobilier of America (CMA) to receive contracts from UP for the building of its vast railroad. Estimates vary as to precisely how inflated these contracts were, but later congressional investigations left no doubt that the backers of CMA intentionally siphoned off far more of the UP's capital than was fair to its investors or good for its future financial health. The investigations of the early 1870s also revealed that the CMA principals bribed members of Congress with company stock.

Still, the railroad they built was a splendid success, and so vast a project might never have been undertaken without the promise of equally vast profits to be made. In five years the UP crews laid more than 1,000 miles of rail between Omaha, Nebraska, and Promontory Summit, Utah Territory, where on May 10, 1869, a golden spike completed the first transcontinental rail line. The railroad's completion supplied a critical impetus to the development of the U.S. West, which to that time had been settled only on the Pacific Coast and in areas of unusual mineral wealth, such as Colorado. With the coming of the railroad, farmers, ranchers, and manufacturers were able to transport their goods to the great eastern metropolitan markets cheaply and quickly, and the West began to fill with pioneers. As the area's most significant railroad for almost 15 years, UP enjoyed rapid growth and excellent earnings for its scandal-ridden promoters, who were dominated from 1873 to the mid-1880s by financier Jay Gould.

Gould's direction of UP was notable for two things. First, the railroad expanded considerably during the decade of the 1870s. Its main route from Omaha, Nebraska, to Ogden, Utah, was soon joined by a host of feeder lines extending into the neighboring territory, some of them of substantial length; and from its Ogden terminus the company acquired control of two new branches, the Utah and Northern running to Montana, and the Utah Central progressing in the general direction of Los Angeles, which it reached in 1901. More immediately significant was the 1880 annexation by the UP of one of its rivals, the Kansas Pacific. The Kansas line ran from Kansas City, Kansas, to Cheyenne, Wyoming, via Denver, Colorado, and although its finances were in even worse condition than UP's it added an important link to the company's midwestern network. Finally, UP defended its transcontinental business by building a bridge to the Pacific Ocean through Idaho and

Oregon, a system of new and existing lines that eventually fell under the aegis of UP's Oregon Short Line Railway Company. UP's original link to the ocean, the Central Pacific line to San Francisco, became a part of its most formidable rival, Southern Pacific, and was therefore lost to UP's purposes until late in the 20th century.

The second legacy of Jay Gould's years at UP was less beneficial. Beginning about 1875, Gould used the railroad's considerable income to pay an extremely high dividend on its common stock, of which he happened to own about two-thirds. As a result of Credit Mobilier's excessive construction contracts, UP was already badly overcapitalized and faced stiff periodic interest payments on its own bonds as well as an eventual lump sum reimbursement to the federal government of about $76 million of principal and interest on the latter's bond loan. Instead of taking prudent steps to provide for these liabilities, Gould bled UP of its cash flow, drove up the company's stock price by means of the huge dividends, and then sold the bulk of his shares in 1878 for a bulging profit. UP staggered on until 1884 with Gould and others of like persuasion in charge of its failing finances, at which time the company tried to make a fresh start under its newly elected president, Charles Francis Adams Jr., a Bostonian of impeccable credentials and a scholar's grasp of the railroad business.

Adams faced a doubly difficult situation. UP's actual and reputed past sins made it nearly impossible to convince Congress and the public that the new president was in fact taking commendable steps toward reducing the company's debt and improving its efficiency. As a result, Adams's efforts were often thwarted, and UP continued to struggle under the burden laid upon it by its founders. At the same time, UP was by then no longer the sole provider of transcontinental rail service. Competition from three rival lines had cut severely into UP's operating income by the mid-1880s, further complicating Adams's task. The combination of looming government debt—due to mature in 1895—fresh competition in the market, and a skeptical legislative climate proved too much for the company when the financial panic of 1893 strained the U.S. economy to the utmost. In October of that year UP went into government receivership.

It was not until the end of 1895 that a satisfactory resolution of UP's debt was accomplished, during which interval the railroad lost many of its most important branch lines to local receiverships. In 1895 a reorganization committee representing UP's first-mortgage bondholders and backed by the New York investment banking house of Kuhn, Loeb and Company came up with a plan to foreclose on the railroad and sell its assets to a new company of the same name. The foreclosure sale was held in November 1897, and Kuhn, Loeb was able to raise the capital needed to pay off most of the government's $71 million in remaining debt and launch the new corporation on a solid financial basis. Quickly asserting himself on the UP's board of directors was an astute New York financier, Edward H. Harriman, who used his chairmanship of UP as the centerpiece of a remarkable railroad empire. Harriman was as brilliant a dealmaker as Jay Gould, but he also represented a new class of industrial magnate, one who was more interested in the construction of vast and durable business combines than in the clever manipulation of capital for immediate profit. Under Harriman's leadership, UP became one of the best run as well as one of the largest of U.S. railroads.

Harriman first set about retrieving the various pieces of UP lost during the receivership and soon reassembled the company's three basic networks: those running between Omaha and Ogden, Ogden and the Pacific Northwest, and Ogden and Los Angeles. Between 1898 and Harriman's death in 1909, the UP increased its track miles from 2,000 to 6,000, and when the chairman became frustrated by UP's failure to gain control of the old Central Pacific run between Ogden and San Francisco's bay area, he wasted no time in buying up Central's owner, Southern Pacific (SP). SP was UP's chief rival and equal, the owner of three main routes between San Francisco and Portland, Oregon; San Francisco and Ogden; and San Francisco and the entire southwest to New Orleans. SP also owned a series of steamship lines extending from California to Japan and Panama, and from New Orleans to New York. UP's purchase of 45% of SP's stock in 1901 for $90 million virtually merged the two giants of western rail transport into a single, monopolistic entity dominating the markets from Kansas City to San Francisco and Denver to New Orleans, Louisiana.

E.H. Harriman was a man of unlimited ambition. Shortly after sealing the Southern Pacific merger, he entered into a complicated series of maneuvers that resulted in the purchase by UP of a strong minority position in Northern Pacific, owner of vital Chicago connections operated by the Chicago, Burlington and Quincy Railroad. In turn, Northern Pacific and Great Northern Railroad became a part of a holding company known as Northern Securities Corporation, which was ordered dissolved by the U.S. Supreme Court in 1904. When the pieces of this gigantic, short-lived combination were sorted out, UP emerged as the owner of 20% of both Northern Pacific and Great Northern and a substantial amount of cash profit as well. With the proceeds of this wrangling, Harriman bought sizable shares of many of the other important railroads in the western United States, in particular the Illinois Central and the Atchison, Topeka and Santa Fe, the latter providing the UP-SP's sole competition in the Southwest. The empire of E.H. Harriman and UP-SP thus comprised large numbers of railroads, railroad stocks, steamship lines, increasingly valuable real estate holdings, and uncounted tons of coal, iron, and other minerals.

Harriman was a prudent administrator of his roads, reinvesting the bulk of their net income in extensive renovation and new rolling stock. In 1906, however, he began paying an unusually large dividend of 10%, raising widespread accusations that Harriman was another profiteer out to gouge the public for his own benefit. The Interstate Commerce Commission (ICC) initiated an investigation into Harriman and UP that resulted in a 1913 decision by the U.S. Supreme Court that the company was inhibiting competition and must divest itself of its Southern Pacific holdings. Harriman did not live to see the UP thus reduced roughly to the size and shape it had been in 1900, the company's lines once again restricted to the three main routes between Omaha and Ogden, Ogden and the northwest port cities, and Ogden and Los Angeles. Lost was the prized route between Ogden and San Francisco, but in the meantime UP had beefed up its branch system and added new lines between Portland and Seattle.

Although Harriman died in 1909, his family retained a powerful influence at the UP, Harriman's sons W. Averell Harriman and E. Roland Harriman sitting on the company's board for many years and both serving as chairmen. Furthermore, so successful was the elder Harriman that the company he left behind became a model for the railroad industry of financial strength and unexcelled performance. From 1916's gross revenue of slightly more than $100 million, UP more than doubled sales to $211 million by 1923, where they remained for much of that prosperous decade. Earnings were steadily excellent in the 1930s and 1940s, an increasing portion of them in the 1930s generated by UP's oil and gas holdings and industrial real estate. A long-term problem for the railroad industry had by then made itself felt, however; truck and automobile traffic was eroding the railroads' share of both freight and passenger miles. This trend, which would intensify during much of the 20th century, was especially painful when the Great Depression of the 1930s curtailed the heavy industrial transport upon which the railroads had come to depend. UP revenues did not approach their former heights until World War II recharged the industrial economy after 1940, and in the early 1930s they barely topped $125 million annually.

Averell Harriman was chairman of UP for most of the 1930s, and did an excellent job of keeping expenses down during the lean years while also investing needed capital in technological developments such as the diesel locomotive. With the outbreak of World War II the Harrimans had little to worry about in the financial realm. The need to shuttle huge amounts of personnel and heavy equipment around the United States gave UP all the business it could handle, company employment nearly doubling to 60,000 and revenue pushing to more than $500 million by war's end. Between 1914 and 1944 alone, UP purchased 2,270 new locomotives, including a number of Big Boys, the world's largest steam locomotive designed for the most taxing Rocky Mountain routes. The end of the war in 1945 caused only a temporary drop in sales for UP, and by the early 1950s revenue was again exceeding $500 million annually and the company remained in generally excellent financial health.

The next few years were not as kind, however. UP faltered in the late 1950s, its income, dividend, and stock price all falling between 1956 and 1961. Part of the problem lay in the rapid depletion of the company's best oil well, outside Los Angeles, and part in the continuing loss of railroad freight sales to the trucking industry. In response, UP restructured its holdings into three divisions—transportation, land development, and natural resources—and in the mid-1960s began a concentrated program of mineral, oil, and gas exploration. The reorganization into divisions helped UP pursue what had grown into three very distinct businesses, each one with the potential to add significant dollars to the company's bottom line. Only a small percentage of the railroad's 7.8 million acres of remaining land had been fully explored and utilized, but even so by 1967 the firm operated five oil and gas fields and was the owner of the world's largest known deposit of trona soda ash ore; vast reserves of coal; and sizable holdings of iron, titanium, and uranium. In a further step toward the exploitation of these resources, in 1969 UP acquired Champlin Petroleum Company and Pontiac Refineries from Celanese Corporation for $240 million, thus completing the formation of a fully integrated oil and gas business. Champlin would eventually operate three refineries, in Texas, Oklahoma, and California, and to ensure that its plants were kept busy UP also signed a joint-venture agreement allowing a subsidiary of Standard Oil Company of Indiana to drill for oil on its acreage,

with UP getting royalties and retaining a quarter interest in whatever oil was found.

Overseeing this diversification at UP was chief executive officer Frank Barnett, the first CEO without intimate ties to the Harriman family to run the company in the 20th century. Barnett, who became CEO in 1967, had as his goal to develop equally strong transportation and nontransport divisions at UP, which in 1969 became a holding company called Union Pacific Corporation. With oil prices soaring after the oil crisis of 1973–1974, UP's revenue quadrupled during the 1970s to $4 billion, more than half of which was provided in the late 1970s by the nontransportation businesses. The company's coal reserves also became more valuable during the energy-conscious 1970s, when UP upped its production tenfold. Less successful was the company's 13-year effort, begun in 1962, to win ICC approval of a merger with Chicago, Rock Island & Pacific Railroad and thereby secure a valuable link between UP's Omaha terminus and both Chicago and St. Louis, Missouri. The merger was opposed by rivals of UP who feared the impact of its entry into Chicago, the nation's busiest rail center. In 1982 UP solved the problem in another way. In a move reminiscent of E.H. Harriman's reign, the company took advantage of U.S. President Ronald Reagan's deregulation of the railroads to accomplish an important merger with the Missouri Pacific and Western Pacific railroads. Missouri Pacific operated some 11,500 miles of track in Texas, Oklahoma, and Missouri, and also provided the crucial bridge between Chicago and Omaha long sought by UP, along with three key gateways to Mexico; while the addition of Western Pacific united the two builders of the original transcontinental road of 1869, Western Pacific operating a route between Ogden, Utah, and the bay area of San Francisco.

The merger was a major undertaking, and it signaled a new era of consolidation in the U.S. railroad industry. While the move would benefit all three partners in the long run, it also presented UP with a massive organizational problem. With suddenly bloated employee and management ranks and a doubling of track mileage, UP slipped to dead last in operating profitability among U.S. railroads in 1984, although profits were up nearly 30%. The company's problems were not helped by the steadily falling price of oil, which was especially hard on domestic producers trying to squeeze the last drop out of older oil wells; but its basic need was for a drastic pruning of its labor force. This has been accomplished by Drew Lewis, UP chairman since 1987, and his railroad president, Michael Walsh, who together cut nearly 12,000 employees from UP's ranks. The cuts had resulted in far greater productivity from line workers as well as a more responsive management, whose ranks were thinned from nine administrative levels to only three. Walsh resigned in 1991 to become CEO of Tenneco. He was succeeded by Richard K. Davidson.

In 1986 UP gave up trying to beat the truckers and instead joined them, buying Overnite Transportation Company, a national trucking company, and stepping up its capacity for intermodal services. The company in the early 1990s seemed to be balanced between a streamlined, comprehensive rail and truck carrier and a natural resources division capable of considerable expansion or contraction depending on the market price of commodities.

Principal Subsidiaries: Union Pacific Railroad Company; Union Pacific Resources Company; Overnite Transportation Company; USPCI, Inc.; Union Pacific Technologies.

Further Reading: Trottman, Nelson, *History of Union Pacific,* New York, The Ronald Press Company, 1923; "Back to Railroading for a New Era," *Business Week,* July 14, 1980; Klein, Maurice, *Union Pacific, Volume I: Birth of a Railroad,* New York, Doubleday, 1987; Willoughby, Jack, "The Rebuilding of Uncle Pete," *Forbes,* November 14, 1988; Klein, Maurice, *Union Pacific: The Rebirth 1894–1969,* New York, Doubleday, 1990.

—Jonathan Martin

UNITED PARCEL SERVICE OF AMERICA INC.

400 Perimeter Center Terraces North
Atlanta, Georgia 30346
U.S.A.
(404) 913-6000
Fax: (404) 913-6593

Private Company
Incorporated: 1907
Employees: 252,000
Sales: $13.60 billion

United Parcel Service of America Inc. (UPS) is the world's largest package-delivery company, in terms of sales. It began overnight air-express service in the 1980s. A conservatively run, management-owned company, it provides highly rated service by running its operations like clockwork down to the smallest details. Its insular corporate culture is spartan and egalitarian.

UPS was founded in 1907 in Seattle, Washington, by 19-year-old Jim Casey as a six-bicycle messenger service. He set the future tone of the company by mandating that it be employee-owned. Casey delivered telegraph messages and hot lunches, and sometimes took odd jobs to keep his struggling business going. By 1913 UPS consisted of seven motorcycles. With Casey's tacit approval, UPS drivers joined the International Brotherhood of Teamsters in 1916. In 1918 three Seattle department stores hired the service to deliver merchandise to purchasers on the day of the purchase. Department store deliveries remained the center of UPS's business until the late 1940s.

In 1929 UPS began air delivery through a new division, United Air Express, which put packages onto passenger planes. The Great Depression ended plans for an overnight air service, and UPS terminated United Air Express in 1931, with resumption of air service not coming until the 1950s. In the late 1940s the urban department stores that UPS serviced began following their clients to the new suburbs. More people owned cars and picked up their own parcels. UPS's revenue declined.

Casey decided to change direction and expand the common-carrier parcel business, picking up parcels from anyone and taking them to anyone else, charging a fixed rate per parcel. The company's initial customers were primarily industrial and commercial shippers, although the firm also serviced consu-

mers. The company had offered common-carrier service in Los Angeles since 1922, and in 1953 UPS extended it to San Francisco, Chicago, and New York. UPS delivered any package meeting weight and size requirements to any location within 150 miles of these bases. After this initial expansion, UPS frequently appeared before the Interstate Commerce Commission (ICC) to expand its operating rights.

UPS scaled its operations to fit its market niche, refusing packages weighing more than 50 pounds or with a combined length and width of more than 108 inches. These limits since have been raised to 70 pounds and 130 inches. Its average package weighed about ten pounds and was roughly the size of a briefcase, making sorting and carrying easy. UPS competed with scores of regional firms but most had not limited the size and weight of their packages. They ended up with the heavier packages, higher overheads, and lower volumes.

Casey resigned as chief executive officer in 1962 and was replaced by George D. Smith. UPS more than doubled its sales and profits between 1964 and 1969, when the company made $31.9 million on sales of about $548 million. The company remained privately owned, its stock held by several hundred of its executives. UPS in 1969 served 31 states on the East and West coasts. It had just gotten ICC approval to add nine Midwestern states, and soon got approval for three more states. Only the lightly populated states of Arizona, Alaska, Hawaii, Idaho, Montana, Nevada, and Utah were without UPS service. The firm kept a low profile, avoiding publicity, and refusing interviews of its chief executives. UPS officials believed only one parcel shipping company could exist in the United States, and hoped keeping a low profile would prevent anyone from copying its methods.

The firm's secrecy policy was possible because it was closely held. Its 3,700 stockholders—a number raised to 23,000 by 1991—were its own top and middle managers and their families. Stockholders wanting to sell, sold their stock back to the company. Because management owned UPS, the company could make long-range plans without the pressure for instant profits faced by many publicly owned firms. Most managers started as UPS drivers or sorters and came up through the ranks, creating great loyalty. The company's management structure was relatively informal, stressing partnership and the involvement of management at all levels.

In 1970 Congress considered a reform of the U.S. Postal Service that would allow it to subsidize its parcel post operations with profits from its first-class mail. This would allow it to lower prices and compete more directly with UPS. UPS hired a public relations firm and for the first time officially announced its earnings, trying to build a case that it was an integral part of the U.S. economy and that the postal reform would be disruptive. UPS handled 500 million packages in 1969, for 165,000 regular customers. The company said 95% of all deliveries within 150 miles were delivered overnight. The company centered operations around a five-day-a-week cycle. Drivers made deliveries in the morning, made pickups in the afternoon, and returned to operations centers around 6 PM. Their packages were immediately sorted and transferred for delivery.

UPS trucks are painted brown to avoid showing soil and are cleaned every night. Trucks are assigned to specific drivers, who the company treats as future managers and owners. The company had 22,000 drivers in 1969, and most were kept on the same route to develop a relationship with customers. Some drivers, however, found UPS management inflexible, resulting in occasional local strikes.

In 1976 UPS tried to gradually replace all of its full-time employees who sorted and handled packages at warehouses with part-time workers. Teamsters locals in the South, Midwest, and West accepted the idea, but 17,000 UPS employees from Maine to South Carolina went on strike. The strike caused chaos for east coast retailers as their suppliers were forced to send Christmas goods through the overburdened U.S. Postal Service. UPS eventually reached agreement with the Teamsters, but its labor relations continued to be spotty. Because management owned the business, it tended to drive its employees hard, and many drivers complained of the long hours and hard work. To maximize driver performance, the company kept records of the production of every driver and sorter and compared them to its performance projections. Drivers' routes were timed in great detail.

In 1976 UPS launched service in Germany with 120 delivery vans. It quickly ran into trouble because of cultural and language differences. UPS eventually adapted by hiring some German managers and accepting the German dislike of working overtime. George C. Lamb Jr. succeeded Harold Oberkotter as UPS chairman in 1980.

UPS continued to grow rapidly, aided by trucking deregulation in 1980. By 1980 UPS earned $189 million on revenues of $4 billion, shipping 1.5 billion packages. Federal Express Corporation, however, which began operations in 1973, was siphoning off a growing amount of UPS's business. Federal shipped packages overnight by air, and many businesses began shipping high-priority packages with Federal. UPS had the resources to challenge Federal, but it meant taking on significant debt, something the conservatively run UPS was reluctant to do. In 1981 it had only $7 million in long-term debt and a net worth of $750 million. To compete with Federal, UPS bought nine used 727 airplanes in 1981 from Braniff Airlines for $28 million. It opened an air hub in Louisville, Kentucky, but was hesitant about directly challenging Federal because of the huge cost of building an air fleet. It decided to stick with two-day delivery rather than overnight delivery, hoping that many businesses would be willing to let packages take an extra day if it meant savings of up to 70%. It called its two-day delivery Blue Label Air, and spent $1 million in 1981 to promote it—a large sum for UPS, which had rarely advertised. In 1982 UPS ran its first-ever television ads, trying to convince executives that two-day service was fast enough for most packages.

The recession of the early 1980s helped UPS because many companies shifted to smaller inventories, shipping smaller lots more frequently and demanding greater reliability. Package volume grew 6% in 1981. Because of the recession, the Teamsters accepted a contract in 1982 that limited wage increases to a cost-of-living adjustment, which then was diverted to pay the increased cost of medical benefits. When UPS then released information showing its net income rose 74% in 1981, labor relations worsened. Bitterness continued between UPS management and drivers as company profits swelled 48% to $490 million in 1983. UPS and the Teamsters secretly negotiated for two months in 1984 and reached a three-year agreement providing for bonuses and increased wages. The move averted a probable strike by 90,000 employees. Despite this labor ten-

sion, UPS's employee turnover remained remarkably low at 4%. Many workers were recruited as part-time employees while college students and were offered full-time positions after graduation.

In 1982 UPS decided to offer overnight air service, charging about half of Federal's rate. By 1983 its second-day and next-day services were shipping a combined 140,000 packages a day. In 1982 UPS earned $332 million on $5.2 billion in sales. It had a fleet of more than 62,000 trucks. Mail-order firms and catalog houses were the fastest-growing part of UPS's business. Jack Rogers became UPS chairman in 1984.

Despite labor troubles, a *Fortune* survey found UPS's reputation the highest in its industry every year from 1984 to 1991. It was by far the most profitable U.S. transportation company, making more than $700 million in 1987 on revenue of $10 billion. Federal Express, however, had 57% of the rapidly growing overnight package business; UPS had only 15%. Federal was highly automated and used electronics to track packages en route and perform other services. UPS still did most jobs manually, but was rapidly switching to the use of electronic scanners at its sorting centers and to computers on its trucks. UPS introduced technology methodically, buying a software firm and a computer design shop to create the necessary equipment. It then field-tested its new gear at a 35-car messenger service it owned in Los Angeles. It launched a $1.5 billion five-year computerization project, trying to create a system that tracked packages door-to-door—which Federal already did. UPS's healthy river of cash flow enabled it to pay $1.8 billion for 110 aircraft in 1987. The purchase made it the tenth-largest U.S. airline. The company launched its first wide-range television advertising campaign in 1988, spending $35 million to publicize the slogan, "We run the tightest ship in the shipping business." Despite these expenses, the company still had only $114 million in long-term debt, and continued to finance large projects out of its cash flow.

By 1988 UPS's ground service was growing 7% to 8% a year, while air service was growing by 30% a year. UPS handled 2.3 billion packages a year, compared with 1.4 billion for the U.S. Postal Service. The 300-plane fleet of the UPS overnight service handled 600,000 parcels and documents per day; making $350 million on $2.2 billion in sales in 1988. UPS continued building an overseas air network, but in West Germany, where it had 6,000 employees it delivered only on the ground. The company shipped eight million packages overseas in 1988, losing $20 million in the process. UPS bought its Italian partner, Alimondo in 1988, hoping to use it and its German base to expand through Europe. The company also bought nine small European courier companies to expand air service. Its overseas acquisitions cost UPS less than $100 million. UPS and rival Federal Express both were losing money on overseas operations, but UPS had an advantage: Federal could not match its $6.5 billion in assets and $480 million in cash with minimal debt. UPS hoped this would give it greater staying power as the two companies struggled to build global delivery networks. Meanwhile UPS slowly won some Federal customers by giving volume discounts, which it previously had refused to do. In 1990 UPS bought 17% of the shipping-related retail outlet Mail Boxes Etc. Inc. for $11.3 million.

The overseas shipping war escalated as Federal bought Tiger International, Inc., a major international shipper that UPS used for some of its foreign deliveries. UPS's overseas losses reached $200 million in a 15-month period as it struggled to stay in the game. The company's overall profit margin fell to 5.6% in 1989 from 8% in 1987, although it still made $693 million on sales of $12.4 billion. In 1985, UPS operated in Canada and in a few European countries. During 1989 and 1990 the company added 145 countries to its shipping routes expanding vigorously into Eastern Europe as political changes allowed it freedom to do so. Its foreign market share went to 6% in 1989 from 2% in 1988. Additional European acquisitions included domestic delivery services in France and Spain, and a ground delivery service, Seaborne Express Parcels, that operated all over the Continent. UPS handled more than 500,000 packages a day in Europe by 1991. To further its plans for a worldwide delivery network, the company finished a $80 million communications center in Mahwah, New Jersey, in 1991. Its continually growing fleet included 55 757s, 47 727s, 49 DC-8s, and 11 747s, as well as it 119,000 ground vehicles.

In the early 1990s UPS operated or had under construction regional air hubs in Philadelphia, Pennsylvania; Dallas, Texas; Ontario, California; a Miami hub for service to Latin America and South America; Pacific Rim hubs in Singapore and Hong Kong; and a European hub near Cologne, Germany. UPS's air volume grew to 800,000 packages daily by 1991. It was gaining market share in overnight delivery; according to one study, UPS's share had risen to 30% by the early 1990s, while Federal Express had 50%.

Principal Subsidiaries: II Morrow Inc.; Road Net Technologies Inc.; Red Arrow Messenger Service Inc.; UPS Properties Inc.; UPS Truck Leasing Inc.

Further Reading: "The Quiet Giant of Shipping," *Forbes,* January 15, 1970; "Why United Parcel Admits Its Size," *Business Week,* July 18, 1970; "Behind the UPS Mystique: Puritanism and Productivity," *Business Week,* June 6, 1983; Madden, Stephen J., "Big Changes at Big Brown," *Fortune,* January 18, 1988.

—Scott M. Lewis

YAMATO TRANSPORT CO., LTD.

YAMATO TRANSPORT CO. LTD.

2-12-16 Ginza
Chuo-ku
Tokyo 104
Japan
(03) 3541 3411
Fax: (03) 3541 7579

Public Company
Incorporated: 1929 as Yamato Transport Co. Ltd.
Employees: 39,951
Sales: ¥426.21 billion (US$3.15 billion)
Stock Exchange: Tokyo

Yamato Transport Co. Ltd. (Yamato) is the founder of the private parcel delivery service industry in Japan, and with a 41% market share it is by far the largest player in the market today. The company delivered 450 million parcels in Japan in 1990. Links with United Parcel International of the United States allow Yamato to deliver in 175 countries. A strong domestic service includes home moving, delivery of refrigerated goods, and facsimile transmission. The large size of Yamato has made information technology an important consideration for management in the control of the vast range of activities in which the company is involved.

Yamato was founded in 1919 in the Chuo ward of Tokyo, although it was not incorporated as a company until ten years later. The company's founder was a young entrepreneur, Koshin Kogura, who began with ¥100,000 in capital and four new trucks. The establishment of the company came at a time when Tokyo and the rest of Japan, to a lesser extent, were rapidly building the transport and industrial infrastructure necessary to sustain Japan's growing economic power. Kogura's business, delivering business documents and parcels throughout the Tokyo area, boomed. It was, in effect, the city's first courier service. By 1923 the range of delivery was extended to the adjacent city of Yokohama, and in the same year Yamato was contracted by Tokyo's most prestigious department store, Mitsukoshi, to deliver purchases to customers. Mitsukoshi generally catered to upper-class clientele and the items to be delivered were usually expensive Western imported goods. Yamato obtained its second prestigious client in 1925 when it was appointed by the Imperial household as its official courier and delivery service. The ministry of communications also used Yamato for the speedy delivery of important documents.

By 1929, with Kogura as its first president, the Yamato Transport Co. Ltd. was officially incorporated. A regular Tokyo to Yokohama delivery service was initiated, running several times a day. Customers could rely on Yamato, as opposed to the postal service, for swift delivery of mail within the Tokyo-Yokohama area. In the 1930s Yamato concentrated on expanding its network in the city of Tokyo and surrounding suburbs, and by 1940 claimed that it could deliver anywhere within the Kanto region within one day. Yamato bought a controlling interest in Kawase Cars Co. Ltd., a Tokyo-based operator of taxis and rental cars, to add to its network in the city. This was followed by the purchase of Sanwa Transport Co. Ltd., a competitor in the courier business, in 1944. Like many essential infrastructure-related businesses in wartime Japan, Yamato was forced by the military government to aid in the war effort. This in effect meant that the company's resources were directed mainly at supplying goods for military use. The company played a role in the military's communication network within the city of Tokyo.

The U.S. air force's bombing campaign during the summer of 1945 left Tokyo in ruins and much of its transport infrastructure in disarray. Yamato was asked by the city authorities and the U.S. occupation forces to assist in the transport of vital goods within the city. Yamato's fleet of trucks was used extensively in the rebuilding of certain areas of Tokyo. Yamato thrived in the immediate postwar period and in 1949 obtained a listing on the Tokyo Stock Exchange for the first time. New branch offices were opened in Tokyo near the main stations of Akihabara and Idabashi in 1950. In the same year Yamato signed an agreement with the Tokyo municipal authorities which allowed the company to act as clearing agents at customs. By acting as such, Yamato was in a position to deliver parcels efficiently overseas. The company did this in 1951 by setting up a liaison office in Haneda Airport, Tokyo and forming an agreement with CAT Airlines Co. Ltd. to transport parcels. An overseas freight service from Haneda followed in 1952, allowing Yamato to ship large-scale items for customers. An agreement with the port authorities in nearby Yokohama allowed Yamato to clear goods through customs in this important port. In 1954 Yamato bought a controlling stake in one of its competitors in Tokyo, Teito Transport Co. Ltd. Three years later Yamato made another acquisition, the Tokyo-based Chiyoda Konpo Kogyo Co. Ltd., a packaging and moving company.

Yamato's plans for developing an international delivery service received a boost in 1954 when the International Association of Transport Airlines (IATA) certified the company as fit to handle packages and goods transported by its member air-cargo companies. Yamato was now in a position to set up representative offices at all of Japan's major airports. Japan's largest airline, Japan Airlines Co. Ltd., named Yamato as the internal distributor of its cargo goods in 1958, and in 1960 Yamato began handling freight to New York in conjunction with Japan Airlines and others. The now-familiar logo, visible on thousands of trucks all over Japan, was introduced in 1957. It depicts a mother cat carrying a kitten between its teeth, symbolizing the careful and efficient handling of goods. Yamato's history of assisting governmental agencies continued in 1965, when the company was involved in helping the post office to ensure that its year-end rush of post was delivered on time. This was to be repeated in the ensuing years.

During this period, Yamato was increasingly expanding its main business—the delivery of parcels within Japan. One of the goals of the company, with founder Kogura still at the helm, was to develop the capacity to deliver goods nationwide. This was achieved by the establishment of subsidiaries throughout Japan and by strategic alliances and acquisitions of regional delivery companies. In 1967 Yamato took advantage of its growing network by diversifying into the travel business and offering package tours. Due to the increasing complexity of its network, Yamato began computerizing all of its operations in 1969. The company was, however, slow to realize the need for this and lagged behind other business sectors, such as retailing, in the introduction of computers. Yamato soon realized that information technology would play a major role in the company's operations and established a subsidiary, Yamato Computer Systems Development Co. Ltd., in 1973. This company was primarily set up to offer systems support to Yamato but would later also work for other organizations. In 1974 the company succeeded in establishing an on-line system for the control of a package to its destination. This system greatly reduced instances of delayed or lost goods and improved overall efficiency.

Since 1958, when it arranged the safe transport of a Van Gogh exhibition to Tokyo from Europe, Yamato prided itself on being able to handle almost any goods for transport. In 1970, when Japan hosted the World Expo, Yamato was responsible for the shipment of works of art and expensive machinery from all over the world to the exhibition site. In 1972 Yamato was asked to aid in the transport of the Chinese National Theater's set during the group's tour of Japan. In the same year, founding president Koshin Kogura received the Third Order of Merit from the emperor for his achievements in the Japanese business world. At this time Japan was becoming one of the major exporting nations in the world. Many Japanese companies were setting up subsidiaries overseas, notably in the United States. Mainly to serve this market, Yamato opened a representative office in New York in 1971, which dealt with the delivery of business packages between the United States and Japan. On the domestic front, Yamato established freight train operations between Osaka and the southern island of Kyushu, in conjunction with the regional railway company Shimabara Railroad Co. Ltd.

In 1975 Yamato underwent a reorganization and six divisions were formed, representing the major regional areas of Japan: Hokkaido, Kanto, Tohoku, Chubu, Kansai, and Kyushu. The vast majority of Japan's population is concentrated within these regions and Yamato planned to develop the capability to reach all of these regions with its delivery services. The year 1976 marked the establishment of the now well-known Takkyubin parcel delivery service aimed at both the business and consumer markets. Initially the service offered to deliver a parcel anywhere in the Kanto area within one working day. This was soon extended to cover most of Japan, with the delivery time varying according to distance and accessibility. The Takkyubin, which means literally "home express post," is now the cornerstone of Yamato's business. During the late 1970s the company focused on the expansion of the Takkyubin service, which extended to Niigata on the west coast of Japan, in 1978. The year 1979 marked the delivery of the 10 millionth Takkyubin parcel. In the same year Yamato's founder and president, Koshin Kogura, died.

At the start of the 1980s, with a comprehensive Japanese domestic network in place, Yamato embarked on a program to establish an international delivery service network. A subsidiary, Yamato Transport USA Inc., was established and based in New York. In the same year representative offices were set up in Singapore and Frankfurt. Yamato used these offices to market its services and coordinate operations with Japan Airlines, and in 1983 the Takkyubin service was extended to include overseas destinations. Yamato's 1981 upgrade to the First Section of the Tokyo Stock Exchange from the Second Section in 1981 was followed by domestic and overseas fund-raising activities on the world's money markets. The company raised SFr50 million and US$40 million in two separate bond issues in 1982. An agreement with United Parcel Service (UPS), a leading U.S. courier company with its own fleet of planes, marked the beginning of the realization of Yamato's worldwide delivery service network. Yamato's Takkyubin could now deliver to 175 countries around the globe. In the same year Yamato established overseas subsidiaries in the United Kingdom, Germany, the Netherlands, and France. In 1987 Yamato added Cool Takkyubin to its list of services. This offered the delivery of refrigerated goods within Japan. Fresh fruit is transported at 5 degrees centigrade, fish at zero degrees, and frozen goods at minus 18 degrees. The service is served by a fleet of refrigerated trucks.

Yamato is concentrating on improving the efficiency of its operations. Its position as the leading delivery company in Japan is assured, with 448 million parcels delivered in 1991 alone—about four parcels for every man, woman, and child in the country. A major challenge for Yamato, and other labor-intensive companies in Japan, is the availability of semi-skilled and unskilled labor. The company is trying to overcome this potentially serious problem by the use of shift work and the increased recruitment of women and middle-aged persons. In 1990 Yamato solidified its link with UPS by the formation of a joint-venture company, UPS Yamato Co. Ltd. Virtually all of Yamato's air forwarding operations were transferred to this company, and it manages every step of the shipment process, from receipt to delivery. In the near future, Yamato plans to increase the efficiency of its operations through the use of computers and continue its diversification into such areas as telecommunications. The company is currently headed by Koji Miyauchi as president and Mikihiko Tsuzuki as chairman.

Principal Subsidiaries: Yamato System Development Co., Ltd.; Chiyoda Packaging Industry Ltd.; Konan Industry Co., Ltd.; Kyushu Yamato Transport Co., Ltd.; Kyoto Yamato Transport Co., Ltd.; Shikoku Yamato Transport Co., Ltd.; Kobe Yamato Transport Co., Ltd.; Okinawa Yamato Transport Co., Ltd.; Yamato Shoji Co., Ltd.; Far East Lease Co., Ltd.; Yamato Home Service Co., Ltd.; Chubu Yamato Home Service Co., Ltd.; Kansai Yamato Home Service Co., Ltd.; Chugoku Yamato Home Service Co., Ltd.; Kyushu Yamato Home Service Co., Ltd.; Tohoku Yamato Home Service Co., Ltd.; Book Service Co., Ltd.; Yamato Collect Service Co., Ltd.; Yamato Parcel Service Co., Ltd.; Food Systems Co., Ltd.; UPS Yamato Co., Ltd. (50%); Yamato Transport U.S.A., Inc. (50%); Yamato Customs Brokers U.S.A., Inc. (50%); Yamato International Forwarding, Inc. (50%); UPS Yamato Partnership USA; Yamato Shoji U.S.A., Inc.; Yamato Systems

U.S.A., Inc.; Yamato Transport (Canada) Inc.; Yamato Transport (U.K.) Ltd.; Yamato Transport (Deutschland) GmbH.; Yamato Transport (France) S.A.; Yamato Transport (Nederland) B.V.; Yamato Transport (Hong Kong) Ltd.; Yamato Travel (Hong Kong) Ltd.; Yamato Transport (S) Pte. Ltd.; Yamato Transport (M) Sdn. Bhd.; Yamato Transport Taiwan Ltd.; Yamato Unyu (Thailand) Co., Ltd.

—Dylan Tanner

YELLOW FREIGHT SYSTEM, INC. OF DELAWARE

10990 Roe Avenue
Overland Park, Kansas 66207
U.S.A.
(913) 345-1020
Fax: (913) 344-3523

Public Company
Incorporated: 1983
Employees: 29,000
Sales: $2.30 billion
Stock Exchange: NASDAQ

Yellow Freight System, Inc. of Delaware is one of the largest long-haul common carriers in the United States. Since the company's rescue from bankruptcy in 1952, Yellow had been skillfully directed by three generations of men named George E. Powell, father, son, and grandson, each contributing to the Powell family's record of unbroken success. In the early 1990s, George E. Powell III presided as chief executive over a company determined to continue its tradition of outstanding less-than-truckload (LTL) service and unusually healthy bottom line performance. Yellow Freight has not only survived but prospered through decades of mergers and the competition unleashed by the industry's deregulation in 1980.

Yellow Freight was originally a franchise of the Yellow Cab Company in Oklahoma City, Oklahoma. Encouraged by the growing use of motor trucks for carrying freight after World War I, Yellow Cab's owners decided that more money could be made hauling boxes than people, and in 1924 they exchanged the company's cabs for a small fleet of trucks. Since there were as yet few dependable highways of any length in Oklahoma, Yellow Freight at first confined its business to Oklahoma City and its environs. Another handicap faced by early truckers such as Yellow was the dominance of the railroads, upon whom generations of business people had come to depend for their long-distance freight requirements. Conversely, since there had been as yet no real alternative to the railroads' bulk transport system, manufacturers of smaller, fragile, or perishable items had not had an opportunity to develop the long-distance business that would support a large trucking industry. Yellow Freight was thus kept busy with primarily local and short-run business until the onset of the Great Depression in 1929.

The Depression subtly altered the relative competitiveness of the railroads and truckers. With money too scarce to leave tied up in inventory, shippers began to appreciate the flexibility of motor trucks, which could deliver as little as a single package to a specific locale at the precise time desired. The trucking industry enjoyed tremendous growth during the 1930s, when thousands of people started their own truck lines with little more than a single vehicle and their own labor. The upsurge in trucking resulted in intense price competition, but it was an important leap forward for the industry and signaled the beginning of the end of the railroads' dominance in the transportation field.

For Yellow Freight, the 1930s saw the company expand its operations across state borders. By the middle of the decade, Yellow was shipping as far south as Houston, Texas, and north to Kansas City, Missouri, already displaying an orientation to north-south routes that would stand the company in good stead during the coming years. Most of the great railroad systems in the United States run east-west across the great plains; by expanding north and south, Yellow was able to serve the growing Texas economy without undue competitive pressure from the railroads. Yellow had also begun a policy of leasing both vehicles and terminals, an economical method of rapid expansion in times of low interest rates such as the 1930s, but always vulnerable to sudden inflation or a sharp drop in revenue.

Yellow prospered continuously through World War II and by 1950 was operating 51 small subsidiary companies, most of them using leased equipment. Its routes then covered many of the middle southern states, with special strength in Texas, and company revenue had reached the neighborhood of $7 million. Yellow's heavy reliance on leased equipment, however, had so strapped corporate finances that after a quick change of ownership the company tumbled into Chapter 11 bankruptcy in 1951. Its troubles attracted the attention of George E. Powell, a Kansas City banker who was also vice chairman of a larger Midwest trucking line, Riss & Company. Powell surveyed the wreckage of Yellow Freight, and with the help of Michigan and Kansas City investors organized a purchase of Yellow's stock in 1952. From Riss & Company the elder Powell brought along his son, 26-year-old George Powell Jr., and a number of other young managers, including Donald McMorris and Mark D. Robeson.

The combination of talents represented by the new owners would prove well adapted to the postwar era of U.S. trucking. Formerly composed of myriad small, independent operators, trucking was rapidly maturing into a more typical modern industry, with the need for efficiency and tight controls outweighing the importance of individual initiative. Many of the smaller operators were shortly to lose their businesses to the new giants, but Yellow Freight's team of bankers and young managers was not wedded to the traditional strategies of the trucking industry. The Powells were primarily business people, and with insight into the need for organization and efficiency they put Yellow at the forefront of trucking innovation, with a new emphasis on customer service, information flow, and cost accounting.

Within five months Yellow climbed out of Chapter 11 and began making money. The expanding postwar economy provided a constantly increasing volume of freight, of which a greater percentage went to the truckers than ever before. From its bases in Oklahoma City and Kansas City, Yellow was able to serve as a bridge between the older industrial states in the Midwest and the growing population centers of Texas. The Powells pursued an expansion policy that took Yellow farther to the north and east, marked especially by the 1957 purchase of Michigan Motor Freight Lines, a company doing about two-thirds of Yellow's $15 million in revenue. Although the largest of Yellow's acquisitions to date, Michigan Motor required extensive pruning and realignment before melding successfully with the rest of Yellow's operations. Yellow dropped many of the new company's short-haul routes, having decided to concentrate its energies on the long-haul, primarily LTL freight market.

It was a time of rapid advance in tractor-trailer design, and Yellow maintained a policy of turning over its equipment inventory as quickly as possible. Here was another key difference between the early days of trucking and the postwar era. Since highway weight limits were largely fixed, and the Interstate Commerce Commission (ICC) regulated the rates charged by common carriers such as Yellow, one of the few ways to cut costs and increase income was by carrying more freight per pound of truck. New designs in both tractors and trailers made it possible to pull more cargo more efficiently than ever before, which gave an advantage to those companies large enough and smart enough to invest heavily in new equipment. Yellow's policy of rapid turnover allowed it to capitalize on the latest trucking improvements, which in turn kept Yellow's cost lower and its service faster than the older, smaller operators. As the latter continued to fall behind the industry standard, aggressive young companies like Yellow were able to buy them out and add hundreds of new routes to their systems—a much easier method of expansion than petitioning the ICC for permission to create new routes.

It was roughly in this way that Yellow developed into one of the superstars of the trucking industry during the next two decades. By the mid-1960s, its annual revenues had climbed past $40 million, making it the 13th-largest trucker in the country. In 1965 Yellow announced a merger that would radically alter the scope of its operations. Its new partner was Watson-Wilson Transportation System, an east-west carrier that was larger than Yellow, with annual revenues of $66 million, but had fallen on hard times for precisely the reason Yellow had thrived, the ability of management to cope with change in the industry. The larger part of Watson-Wilson was the former Watson Brothers Transportation Company, with routes westward from Chicago through Kansas City and St. Louis, Missouri, to the West Coast. Only one of the Watson brothers really knew the transportation business, and he ran the company with an autocratic style of management that served quite well. When he died in 1958, however, Watson-Wilson drifted through several ownership changes until it was sold as a money-losing venture to Yellow for about $13 million.

The purchase of Watson-Wilson was a risky move by the Powells, but by more than doubling Yellow's size and opening up an entirely new axis of travel the acquisition was decisive in the company's growth. Bringing the sprawling Watson-Wilson routes under the more disciplined aegis of Yellow, the Powells entered a 15-year period in which their company would emerge as the most efficient trucker in the United States. Yellow's operating ratio—expenses as percentage of revenue—was consistently among the industry's lowest. A fully computer-

ized command center in Kansas City allowed Yellow to monitor shipments with a high degree of accuracy, improving customer service and refining operations at the crucial "break-bulk" centers. As of 1970, Yellow had nine of these large transport hubs, where shipments were broken down and repacked on new trucks for the next leg of their journey. Break-bulk centers require large amounts of labor and depend on precise coordination between the chain of trucks involved; by implementing a computer network earlier than many of its rivals, Yellow was able to hone its break-bulk operations to the point where freight rarely touched the ground on its way from truck to truck. In addition, Yellow was among the earliest of the truckers to experiment with automated handling systems, beginning in 1971.

By that time, Yellow's revenue had shot up to $230 million, making it the third-largest trucker in the country. Its operations then stretched from the Atlantic to the Pacific coasts, an east coast firm having been acquired in 1969, and net income was rising at the very healthy rate of 24% per year. George Powell Jr. had taken over from his father as chairman of Yellow, in which the Powells retained a 22% family stock holding, and it would not be long before George Powell III began his tenure with the firm. The 1970s were perhaps the apex of Yellow's success. Between 1972 and 1977 the company averaged a 32% return on equity—the best in the industry—doubled its revenue, and extended its operations to 44 states via 223 terminals, all during a time of unprecedented rises in the cost of fuel and widespread talk of industry deregulation. Yellow had never suffered a losing year under the Powells.

They were less successful in the oil and gas industry, into which they plunged in 1976, with the creation of Overland Energy Company. Although Overland never became a dangerous liability, it did soak up about $60 million before its dissolution in the early 1980s, when Yellow needed every penny to wage war on another front—deregulation. Yellow's top management failed to predict the congressional approval of Ronald Reagan's 1980 deregulation of the trucking industry. As a result, Yellow was forced to write off some $34 million in operating rights fees rendered obsolete by the advent of unrestricted route competition, a charge that pushed the company into the red for 1980. Of potentially greater significance was Yellow's failure to keep up with its main rivals in the LTL market, which, because of the need for sophisticated break-bulk handling and widespread route systems, would become the specialty of the largest, wealthiest truckers after deregulation. Yellow found that it was not in a position to compete with Consolidated Freightways and Roadway Express for the valuable LTL freight and had to lay off 20% of its work force in 1981.

Powell Jr. and Powell III responded with a program of "hub and spoke" upgrading of the Yellow system, in which 17 terminals were converted into full-scale break-bulk centers in three years. Yellow's LTL freight, as a percentage of its total tonnage, rose from 45% in 1979 to 1982's 61.4%, and over the next four years the company increased its number of terminals to more than 600, a rate of expansion greater than that of any other trucker. In an era of unprecedented competition, which between 1980 and 1986 forced out of business a group of truckers with aggregate sales of $3 billion, Yellow enjoyed a revenue leap that solidified its hold on the number-three spot among U.S. trucking lines. By the end of the decade, sales were regularly over the $2 billion mark, and Yellow had largely completed the heavy expenditures needed to build its hub-and-spoke system.

In the early 1990s, under the direction of George Powell III, Yellow seemed well prepared to prosper in the mature trucking industry, which featured a small number of large, multifaceted organizations operating across the country. Perhaps mindful of Consolidated Freightways' disastrous detour into the Emery Air Freight business, Yellow maintained a strict trucking-only principle in its investment decisions, more than happy to stay in the business it had mastered for many years. Indeed, the management philosophy of Powell III seemed remarkably like that of his grandfather; for both men, success in trucking had required strict quality control, accountability, and conservative investments.

Principal Subsidiaries: Adley Canada Ltd.; Mission Supply Company; Overland Energy, Inc.; Yellow Freight System, Inc.; Yellow Freight System of British Columbia, Inc.; Yellow Freight System of Ontario, Inc.; Yellow Redevelopment Corporation.

Further Reading: "Yellow Transit—Trucker in a Hurry," *Business Week,* August 28, 1965.

—Jonathan Martin

UTILITIES

Allegheny Power System, Inc.
American Electric Power Company, Inc.
Arkla, Inc.
Baltimore Gas and Electric Company
Bayernwerk AG
British Gas plc
Carolina Power & Light Company
Centerior Energy Corporation
Central and South West Corporation
Chubu Electric Power Company, Incorporated
Chugoku Electric Power Company Inc.
CMS Energy Corporation
The Columbia Gas System, Inc.
Commonwealth Edison Company
Consolidated Edison Company of New York, Inc.
Consolidated Natural Gas Company
The Detroit Edison Company
Dominion Resources, Inc.
Duke Power Company
Electricité de France
ENDESA Group
Enron Corp.
Enserch Corporation
Ente Nazionale per L'Energia Elettrica
Entergy Corporation
Florida Progress Corporation
FPL Group, Inc.
Gaz de France
General Public Utilities Corporation
Générale des Eaux Group
Hokkaido Electric Power Company Inc.
Hokuriku Electric Power Company
Houston Industries Incorporated
The Kansai Electric Power Co., Inc.

Kyushu Electric Power Company Inc.
Long Island Lighting Company
Lyonnaise des Eaux-Dumez
N.V. Nederlandse Gasunie
New England Electric System
Niagara Mohawk Power Corporation
Northeast Utilities
Northern States Power Company
Nova Corporation of Alberta
Ohio Edison Company
Osaka Gas Co., Ltd.
Pacific Enterprises
Pacific Gas and Electric Company
PacifiCorp
Panhandle Eastern Corporation
Pennsylvania Power & Light Company
Philadelphia Electric Company
PreussenElektra Aktiengesellschaft
Public Service Enterprise Group Incorporated
Ruhrgas AG
RWE Group
San Diego Gas & Electric Company
SCEcorp
Shikoku Electric Power Company, Inc.
The Southern Company
Texas Utilities Company
Tohoku Electric Power Company, Inc.
The Tokyo Electric Power Company,
Incorporated
Tokyo Gas Co., Ltd.
TransCanada PipeLines Limited
Transco Energy Company
Union Electric Company
Vereinigte Elektrizitätswerke Westfalen AG

ALLEGHENY POWER SYSTEM, INC.

12 East 49th Street
New York, New York 10017
U.S.A.
(212) 752-2121
Fax: (212) 836-4340

Public Company
Incorporated: 1925 as West Penn Electric Company
Employees: 6,048
Sales: $2.30 billion
Stock Exchanges: New York   Midwest   Pacific   Amsterdam

Allegheny Power System, Inc. provides electrical power to a 29,100-square-mile area in the United States, centered over the border shared by Pennsylvania and West Virginia and including parts of Maryland, Ohio, and Virginia. The greater part of its service area is rural, with the exception of the counties around Pittsburgh, where the declining steel industry has changed the revenue mix at Allegheny significantly. To supplement its shrinking base of industrial customers, Allegheny has increased sales to the residential and commercial sectors while also taking advantage of its low-cost, coal-fired generators to sell large amounts of electricity to other utilities. The latter source of revenue was, however, threatened by the 1990 Clean Air Act Amendments, which will force Allegheny to spend in the neighborhood of $2 billion for new pollution control devices, mainly scrubbers for its high-sulfur coal plants.

The history of Allegheny Power is interleaved with the controversial history of utility holding companies in the United States. From the beginnings of centralized power generation in the 1880s, ownership of the nation's electric companies was concentrated increasingly in the hands of financiers such as J.P. Morgan and Samuel Insull. The power industry required more capital per dollar of operating revenue than any other business and thus became controlled largely by a small number of men with intimate connections on Wall Street and in the banking community. The early power magnates found it useful to unite many small generating companies under the umbrella of a single holding company. Such a holding company, with a far larger asset base than any of its constituents, was more likely to impress investors as a reasonable gamble than were the individual companies, thus providing a means of generating the immense capital needed to expand in the power industry.

One of these holding companies was the New York–based American Water Works & Electric Company, which in the first decades of this century began to acquire control of both water facilities and power plants in the northeastern part of the United States. Among the companies it controlled were the 53 Pennsylvania light and power companies that in 1916 had been united to form the West Penn Power Company. Included in the purchase of these small power companies was their former parent, West Penn Traction Company—later known as West Penn Railways—a minor operator of electric railways. West Penn Power served much of Pennsylvania's southwest corner, with the important exception of Pittsburgh proper, as well as a chunk of the state's north-central region and most of its border with Maryland. The company's generators were a mix of water turbines and coal-fired steam, the percentage of the latter growing rapidly as the area's electrical needs outstripped its limited hydroelectric capacity. Much of West Penn Power's revenue was derived from industrial sales, primarily to the region's iron, steel, and coal mining operations.

Another of American Water Works' major investments was Washington County Light & Power Company, based in Marietta, Ohio, but with most of its customers in neighboring West Virginia. Washington County served a predominately rural area that, like West Penn's, was rich in both coal and in rivers suitable for hydroelectric damming. Farther to the east lay a number of electric companies amalgamated in 1923 into The Potomac Edison Company, doing most of its business in western Maryland along the Potomac River. Potomac Edison, like Washington County Light & Power, was a relatively small, rural electric system that also controlled several local bus lines and electric railways.

By assembling these three regional companies, American Water Works had succeeded in gaining control of the power generation in a sizable portion of land in five states. Nearly all of the plants involved were tiny, pioneering outfits that, given the economic and engineering realities of the utility industry, were certain one day to be unified in one form or another. In 1925 American Water Works took a second step toward doing so by consolidating all of its electrical, bus, rail, and natural gas companies under the name of West Penn Electric Company. West Penn Electric, a Maryland corporation, took charge of the three operating companies—West Penn Power, Washington County Light & Power, and Potomac Edison—and began the gradual integration of the system's complex array of power plants, transformers, and transmission lines. The area served by West Penn Electric's companies in 1925 was very nearly identical to that served by the Allegheny Power System in 1991; further expansion evidently was blocked by other, more powerful utilities busy consolidating their own holdings. West Penn Electric officially incorporated in 1925.

In the 1920s the formation of public utility holding companies reached its zenith. Amid growing public concern, people such as Samuel Insull put together enormous pyramids of interlocking corporations, many of them widely overcapitalized and all difficult to police with the existing regulatory resources. When the stock market crash of 1929 brought many of these holding companies to bankruptcy, thousands of stock and bond holders were ruined and the outcry prompted a series of congressional investigations of the power industry. In 1935 Congress enacted the Public Utility Holding Company Act, a comprehensive piece of legislation designed to restrict the concentration of ownership in the power industry to those instances where it clearly resulted in greater efficiency and lower consumer costs. In particular, power companies serving noncontiguous areas were not to be held in common ownership unless such benefits could be shown, which was not likely; hence, under the aegis of the Securities and Exchange Commission (SEC), a long series of dissolution proceedings was instituted against the leading utility holding companies.

Among the targets of the SEC was American Water Works & Electric Company. Although the latter's electric holdings under the direction of West Penn Electric were all within a single geographic area, American Water Works also owned water works in other parts of the country. The SEC objected to this arrangement and ordered American Water Works to propose a plan for segregation of its water and electric holdings, which was forwarded and accepted in January 1948. Under the American Water Works plan, equity in West Penn Electric owned by American Water Works would be distributed to American Water Works shareholders, the water works firms would be similarly spun off, and American Water Works itself would cease to exist. Accordingly, as of January 1948, West Penn Electric became the independent owner of its three operating companies, whose territories and facilities were not otherwise affected. West Penn Electric's headquarters remained in New York City.

The newly independent power company faced an ambiguous economic situation. Use of electricity was growing as never before, the U.S. postwar boom adding daily to the applications of electricity in the home and in the factory. Yet, the steel industry was moving away from Pittsburgh. Within a scant ten years the Pittsburgh area would lose its position as the world's leading steel center, and steel production provided West Penn Electric with the largest portion of its industrial sales. A third, even more crucial factor was the price of fuel. In this respect, West Penn Electric was extremely fortunate. Since the earliest years of power generation, utilities in the eastern part of the country had been shifting from hydroelectric energy to coal-fired steam turbines, whose capacity was far greater than that offered by Appalachian rivers. West Penn Electric was located in the midst of one of the richest coal regions in the United States, which meant that its fuel costs would remain low as long as coal remained its primary fuel. West Penn Electric always had owned a number of minor coal deposits as an emergency reserve but for the most part had relied on long-term contracts with the region's large mining companies for its supply.

Guaranteed a secure and inexpensive source of fuel, West Penn Electric was able to compile an admirable record of unbroken growth in the postwar decades. With the exception of 1958, the company increased its dividend payments every year from 1948 to 1990. By the mid-1950s West Penn Electric had divested itself of all interests outside the utility business, selling off the various minor bus and rail lines inherited from the company's early years. The company also became interested in the newly emerging field of nuclear power, which it considered as an alternative energy source for the coming years despite its ready access to coal. West Penn Electric joined a number of other utilities in forming the East Central Nuclear Group to study further the possibilities of nuclear power, but in the end decided that the expense and risk inherent in nuclear generation could not be justified given the company's coal resources. West Penn Electric was thus spared the in-

creasingly severe problems faced by the nuclear power industry. The company's total reliance on coal-fired plants, however, had left it vulnerable to national concern about acid rain and air pollution in general.

In 1960 West Penn Electric adopted its present name of Allegheny Power System, Inc. Its three principal subsidiaries, then as in the early 1990s, were West Penn Power, Potomac Edison, and Monongahela Power, the latter formerly Washington County Light & Power. The 1960s continued the postwar trend toward a decreasing industrial revenue offset by general population growth and by increased per capita use of electricity. With the U.S. economy generally in robust health, Allegheny Power System faced few problems more serious than the occasional wind storm or system overload. This pleasant scenario changed abruptly in 1973, when the OPEC oil embargo changed forever the economics of energy. Almost overnight the price of coal tripled, a jump that would have spelled disaster for Allegheny if it had been forced to rely on the usual laborious procedure for rate adjustments. State and federal regulatory agencies, however, agreed to let Allegheny and most other utilities establish a special fuel index as part of their rate structure, passing on to the consumer such wholesale leaps in the cost of doing business. Despite the turmoil, Allegheny did not suffer any significant reverses.

In the early 1980s, Allegheny agreed to purchase 40% of the output of Virginia Electric and Power Company's pumped storage project, forming Allegheny Generating Company to act as its representative in the partnership. Pumped storage is a type of hydroelectric generation that adds to output capacity. The pumped storage project provided about 10% of Allegheny's 1990 total of 7,991 megawatts of power, with the remainder generated almost entirely by coal.

In 1985 Klaus Bergman assumed the titles of president and chief executive at Allegheny, from which vantage he prepared for the difficulties awaiting the company in the 1990s, in particular the cost of compliance with the Clean Air Act Amendments of 1990. The new amendments were aimed squarely at owners of coal-fired generators such as Allegheny's operating companies, setting new, more stringent limits on sulfur dioxide emissions that were to become fully effective in the year 2000. Thus, Allegheny faced the downside of its decision in the 1950s not to pursue nuclear power; with 90% of its electricity from coal, the company estimated that compliance with the new standards would cost as much as $2 billion. Allegheny planned to lower emissions by installing scrubbers—equipment that cleans up the emissions from smoke stacks—at its coal plants, rather than abandoning its local suppliers of high-sulfur coal in favor of more distant sources of low-sulfur coal. The company has concluded that scrubbers are more cost-effective in the long run and will obviate the need for fuel purchasing changes that would hurt the local economy. In either case, residents and industry are likely to see higher electricity bills. Still, the Allegheny operating companies' rates have remained below the national average.

Principal Subsidiaries: Monongahela Power Company; The Potomac Edison Company; West Penn Power Company; Allegheny Generating Company.

Further Reading: Bauer, John, and Peter Costello, *Public Organization of Electric Power: Conditions, Policies, and Program,* New York, Harper, 1949.

—Jonathan Martin

AMERICAN ELECTRIC POWER COMPANY, INC.

1 Riverside Plaza
Columbus, Ohio 43215
U.S.A.
(614) 223-1000
Fax: (614) 223-1667

Public Company
Incorporated: 1906 as American Gas & Electric Company
Employees: 22,798
Sales: $5.17 billion
Stock Exchange: New York

American Electric Power Company (AEP) is a public utility holding company that—through eight subsidiary operating companies—generates, purchases, transmits, and distributes electric power. Seven million people in Michigan, Indiana, Ohio, Kentucky, Virginia, West Virginia, and Tennessee are serviced by AEP's interconnected power grid delivering electricity from coal-fired, nuclear, and hydroelectric generating facilities. AEP also has two service subsidiaries: American Electric Power Service Corporation, a nonprofit organization providing management and technological services to affiliated companies, and AEP Energy Services, Inc., which provides the same services to nonaffiliated companies for profit. AEP Energy Services' customers include foreign companies, most notably the Water & Power Development Authority of Pakistan. AEP has always served a multistate area, emphasizing consolidation of its subsidiaries, integration of its system, and technological leadership. It has become one of the largest electric utilities in the United States.

The company was incorporated as American Gas & Electric Company in 1906, when the structure of the electric utility industry in the United States was changing from small, individually owned generator plants to consolidated single systems serving a large area. This change was seen in other industries as well. As president of the United States from 1901 to 1907, Theodore Roosevelt denounced such business combinations. By 1906, however, Roosevelt had come to believe that, with proper government regulation, the consolidation of businesses could be beneficial to the public interest. Thus, when Richard E. Breed, Harrison Williams, and Sidney Z. Mitchell met in 1906 to consider forming a holding company to buy the 23 small companies held by Electric Company of America, they were in the right place at the right time.

Electric Company of America was itself a holding company founded in 1899 that, because of its directors' failure to grasp the economics of the newly developed industry, was in financial difficulty. Breed, a glass manufacturer in Marion, Indiana, was a major stockholder. Williams, Breed's brother-in-law, was a prominent financial entrepreneur. Mitchell was president of Electric Bond & Share Company, a subsidiary of General Electric Company. Electric Bond & Share was a utilities holding company. After some negotiation, Electric Company of America agreed to sell its assets for $6.28 million to American Gas & Electric Company (AG&E). The sale was completed in January of 1907, with Breed and Williams as board directors of AG&E, Mitchell as chairman, and Henry L. Doherty—later to begin his own chain of electric companies—as president until 1910, when Breed stepped in.

The acquired companies were a varied lot, including nine utilities in Pennsylvania; four in New Jersey; and two each in New York, West Virginia, Illinois, Indiana, and Ohio. They supplied services including electricity, gas, water, steam, and ice. For the most part, the companies' service was poor, their rates high, and their equipment faulty. Customers desiring service often had to invest in the company since the operating company lacked financing to extend its lines.

Sidney Z. Mitchell had the experience and financial expertise to remedy this situation. An 1883 graduate of the U.S. Naval Academy, Mitchell had installed the first incandescent electric lighting system on a U.S. naval vessel while stationed aboard the U.S.S. *Trenton*. After leaving the navy in 1885, Mitchell had met Thomas Edison and started working for him in New York City. That same year he left for the Pacific Northwest, where he ran Edison's operations for the next 20 years. He returned to New York in 1905 to help organize Electric Bond & Share Company (EB&S) of which he was soon president and chairman, with the responsibility of making the small operating companies turn a profit.

AG&E, while not owned by EB&S, did benefit from its financial services and was influenced by EB&S, because Mitchell simultaneously held the top positions in both companies. Under Mitchell's direction, the operating companies of AG&E established 24-hour service, gave away electric irons to new customers, and presented free toasters to households using the most electricity. In addition, the company rented vacuum cleaners to customers and ran cooking schools using electric ranges. As new plants came on line, rates were lowered and put on a sliding-scale basis, continuing to decrease as consumption increased.

Mitchell's business acumen went beyond sales promotion and rate juggling; he also restructured AG&E. By 1910 Mitchell had sold all of the gas properties included in the original acquisitions, a policy the company consistently followed in later years. He also sold some electric companies that could not be merged readily into a unified system. The largest of these isolated AG&E operations was in Rockford, Illinois. Retaining the companies in Marion and Muncie, Indiana; Bridgeport, Ohio; Atlantic City, New Jersey; and Scranton, Pennsylvania, Mitchell began acquiring smaller, adjoining companies consolidating their operations and extending their lines into neighboring communities.

Having created several core markets in which to expand, AG&E began to construct long-range transmission lines to tie its properties together. An early step in consolidation was the construction of a 32-mile-long tie-line between Muncie and Marion. AG&E replaced existing equipment in this region with more powerful generators, and the Indiana properties became an interconnected system. This process was repeated in the area between Canton, Ohio, and Wheeling, West Virginia. George N. Tidd managed the ongoing consolidation and became president of AG&E in 1923 and chairman in 1924. By 1926 Mitchell had acquired additional properties in Virginia, West Virginia, and Kentucky, and the area that the company serves had been shaped.

The greatest cost of producing electricity was financing charges for new equipment. As cash flowed into AG&E from sales of unwanted properties, the company purchased more common stock in its partially owned subsidiaries. This in turn supported further issues of common stock and bonds to the public to raise more money for capital improvements.

Mitchell's corporate strategy was guided by a few basic principles. First, sales were to increase by 6% to 8% each year. Second, small generating stations were to be replaced by larger, more efficient plants strategically located to allow for future growth and interconnection. Third, small operating companies located close together in one state were to be consolidated into one company. Fourth, the sales of preferred and common stock would provide for increased capital investment. Mitchell understood that utilities had inherent qualities that would force out competition and favor large holding companies. The cost of equipment was quite high and could be recouped only by companies with large customers bases. Quoted by his son, S.A. Mitchell, in *S.Z. Mitchell and the Electrical Industry,* Mitchell stated, "The only way that I know to make money in the public-utility business today, is by following the large volume of business, low cost of operation, low cost of money, low rates to the customers, and small margin of profit idea." In following this idea, AG&E had increased the number of kilowatt-hours it provided from 53 million in 1907 to 427 million in 1917.

In 1914 the United States had opened to commercial shipping the Panama Canal, and World War I had begun in Europe. Following a period of strained neutrality, the United States entered the war in 1917, and the increased demands of wartime industries caused a 40% increase in the demand for electricity. At this time, Mitchell served on a committee of the War Industries Board overseeing electrical supply to defense plants. By interconnecting all generating plants, regardless of ownership, the committee achieved more balanced loads in order to meet war needs. This pooling system became popular in the postwar period. Implemented on a more limited basis than first conceived, it lowered production costs, created more reliable service, and contributed to company savings.

In the United States, the decade of the 1920s was characterized by a tremendous increase in industrial expansion and financial speculation. Mitchell was instrumental in establishing the principles upon which was based the first piece of federal legislation specifically aimed at regulating electric power, the Federal Power Act of 1920.

For power utilities, this was a golden age of growth, and AG&E flourished with the times. After reincorporating in 1925 upon merging with Appalachian Securities Corporation, the company paid special stock dividends of 50% in 1925, 40% in 1927, and 50% in 1929. By 1926 AG&E had three primary electric power centers in place, one near Atlantic City,

New Jersey; one in the Scranton area of Pennsylvania; and the third, known as the Central System, stretching from Virginia to Michigan. In building these systems, the company had constructed four "superplants," which went into operation from 1924 to 1930; each was built outside the areas it would serve but near to fuel sources. This large-scale technology decreased unit costs.

During the Great Depression with its monopoly shielded by regulation, AG&E and other utilities fared comparatively well. In 1933 revenues fell by 11%, the decline in industrial use being offset by residential customers, whose rate of use actually increased 20% between 1929 and 1933. U.S. President Herbert Hoover requested that electric utilities begin construction of facilities to meet future need to ease unemployment. Mitchell responded by directing companies controlled by Electric Bond & Share Company to spend $97 million on construction in 1930. Associated holding companies advanced more than $330 million to help the operating companies between 1930 and 1934. Mitchell retired in 1933, however. He died in 1944. One of the last of the giants of the early era of electrical utilities, his greatest contribution was the financial management that had supported rapid growth.

The Public Utility Holding Company Act of 1935, which established the Securities and Exchange Commission to enforce its provisions, was designed to demolish pyramid holding companies such as AG&E, which had been built on a mountain of debt. The value of large interconnected systems serving a single area was widely accepted by this time, however, and while AG&E was forced to dispose of two noncontiguous companies—Atlantic City Electric and Scranton Electric—the Central System was left intact.

In 1939 the start of World War II in Europe led to increased production of war supplies, which lessened the effects of the Depression. When the United States entered the war in 1941, there was a rise in power demand by wartime industries, which the utilities were able to meet. In addition, as construction priorities shifted to defense materiel, new generating equipment could not be built. After the war, demand dropped and industrial production returned to normal. While consumers rushed to buy the new appliances then available, the utility industry had to wait for the delivery of new equipment before it could resume growth.

By 1949, Philip Sporn, a one-time assistant to Tidd who had become AG&E's president in 1947, announced that the worst of the power shortage was over. With comfortable margins of reserve, AG&E picked up 82,000 customers in 1948, representing 250,000 kilowatts of demand. Load expansion was bolstered by AG&E's sale of 45,000 electric ranges and 30,000 water heaters. To Sporn, the most significant problems of the decade ahead would be developing technology that could handle an expected doubling of demand and raising capital for new facilities costing an anticipated $500 million.

With Sporn in charge, AG&E increased the number of kilowatt-hours provided to 23.3 billion in 1959, achieving growth through acquisitions, technological breakthroughs, and sales promotions. In 1948 the company bought Indiana Service Corporation in Fort Wayne and consolidated it with an AG&E subsidiary, Indiana & Michigan Electric Company. This was only one of six acquisitions during the years between 1945 and 1956.

Sporn had been an engineer with AG&E since 1920, and he was interested in the technical aspects of the power industry.

As president of the company until 1961, Sporn's approach was to take risks with new equipment that was untested in the field in order to surpass competition. In the 1950s Sporn worked with General Electric Company on the design of a new 225-megawatt generator. After achieving favorable results with a prototype, he ordered another six units. AG&E became widely known for its technological leadership.

Sporn did not neglect the sales side of the business, however, and he structured it to mesh with the growth of the system. Sales of room air conditioners went up from 43,000 in 1947 to 1.67 million in 1958 and while this meant consumption, it also created a new problem: summer peaking of load demand. In 1955 Sporn began promoting heat pumps and home electrical heating as a way to achieve balanced seasonal loads. By creating demand, Sporn hoped to project more accurately future generating needs.

The development of nuclear power was also a major concern of the utility industry in the 1950s. To raise the enormous capital required for such development, Sporn urged that the Public Utility Holding Company Act be revised to allow private companies to develop facilities jointly. In 1954 U.S. President Dwight D. Eisenhower signed the Atomic Energy Act, making possible the private development of nuclear energy in the United States.

In 1958 AG&E changed its name to American Electric Power Company. During the 1960s the electric utility industry was a success story in which new equipment and business techniques encouraged growth and profits. This success was reflected in rising stock prices, with averages doubling between 1958 and 1965, and while the growth rate of demand advanced at an annual pace of 7% on average between 1920 and 1973, rates continued to drop.

The power failure in the northeast United States that prompted a power blackout in New York City in 1965 led to threats of federal intervention to guarantee reliability. Donald C. Cook, who had succeeded Sporn as president of AEP in 1961, argued that a proposed national power grid system was unworkable and that such federal intervention was not needed. As proof he pointed to the role of private industries in alleviating the blackout crisis by sending power to New York through their transmission lines. Nevertheless, regional power pool arrangements were worked out through the North American Electrical Reliability Council, a new industrial body.

Cook continued to address the problem of the national power supply when, in 1967, he told a National Power Conference in Washington, D.C., that most of the electrical systems in the United States were outmoded and inefficient. Cook called for their replacement. Within 25 years, he speculated, the country would be served by approximately 15 electric mega-systems. Indeed, in the late 1960s an industry-wide trend toward corporate consolidation did emerge. As part of this, AEP absorbed Michigan Gas & Electric Company and proposed taking over Southern Ohio Electric.

Another trend in the late 1960s was a growth in the annual rate for electrical consumption to an unforeseen level. The need to increase capacity set off a race among utilities to buy new equipment, causing high prices and delays in delivery. To avoid these problems, AEP bought 2,200 megawatts of power equipment overseas in 1967, an unusual procedure for a U.S. utility.

The climate of expansion ended abruptly in the 1970s, largely because of three factors: a general market decline set off by the OPEC oil embargo; rising costs that could not be offset; and a technological standstill, in which existing technologies could no longer provide higher levels of efficiency at lower costs. In 1973, the year the oil embargo began, 17% of power generation nationwide depended on oil. In the Northeast, the figure was 60%. As oil prices rose eightfold, the price of electricity shot up almost 50%. In 1974 power demand went down for the first time since 1970, partly due to exports to Japan; Cook suggested export restrictions.

Another problem for utilities in the 1970s was a series of federal regulatory acts spurred on by an increase in public awareness of the environmental movement. Jimmy Carter became U.S. president in 1977, and the National Energy Act of 1978 soon followed. For AEP, which used coal produced by subsidiary-controlled mines, the regulatory environment had become stifling. W.S. (Pete) White, who had become chairman of the board of AEP in 1976, predicted in 1979 that projected construction costs would be 40% higher for the company because of Clean Air Act amendments.

In the midst of declining demand and increased regulatory restrictions, AEP had opened its 2.13 million-kilowatt Cook nuclear plant in Michigan. For a time, the company was sheltered by its sales to other utilities, which could purchase electricity from AEP at a cost lower than they could produce it themselves. In 1980 AEP acquired Columbus and Southern Ohio Electric Company, located in the middle of its operating system, and moved its headquarters to Columbus, then the largest city it served. By 1982, however, a recession severely affecting industry in AEP's territories caused a drop in industrial sales of 18%. Sales to other utilities declined by 20%. In response, White cut salaries, froze wages, and laid off workers.

Recovery, however, came as early as 1984. In that year, increased auto sales led to the recovery of the aluminum and steel industries, which were AEP's largest industrial customers. As industrial sales rose 22% in the year's first quarter over the year before, sales to other utilities meeting the increased demand rose 40%. Residential and commercial demand rose 10% and 8%, respectively. For AEP, which had been granted a rate increase of $260 million in 1983, the corner had been turned. Although revenues would decline in both 1985 and 1990, AEP's financial situation generally improved from its 1983 low. In 1986 a project 19 years in duration, a 2,022-mile-long, 765,000-volt transmission network stretching from Virginia to Michigan, began operation. At a cost of $800 million, AEP established an electrical grid expected to serve into the 21st century.

AEP still faced three major problems in the late 1980s and early 1990s: completion of the Zimmer nuclear plant in Ohio, amendments to the Clean Air Act, and proposed deregulation of the utility industry. Begun in 1971 as a joint-project of AEP and two other utilities, Zimmer was planned as an 810-megawatt nuclear facility, but the national controversy over the development of such plants, especially after the nuclear accident that occurred in 1979 at the Three Mile Island plant in Pennsylvania, helped to bring a halt to Zimmer in 1982. With the facility almost completed with an investment of $1.7 billion, the project was stalled. Then in 1984, despite industry skepticism, the company decided to convert Zimmer to a coal-fired plant. AEP's subsidiary, AEP Service Corporation, using modular construction methods, completed the conversion three months ahead of schedule and below budget by almost $300 million.

The history of American Electric Power Company shows that under the leadership of Sidney Z. Mitchell it had the financial stability to support the technological leadership most apparent when Philip Sporn was president. Starting out with a collection of unconnected operating companies, the holding company managed its consolidation into a vast, interconnected power system that could take advantage of opportunities during good economic periods and ride out economic decline. With the completion of its Zimmer facility, AEP, for the first time since World War II, was not constructing any more generating capacity, but was planning carefully during a time when the very structure of the industry might change. While W.S. White in 1991 delegated chief executive duties to Richard E. Disbrow, AEP's president, White remained chairman.

Principal Subsidiaries: AEP Energy Services, Inc.; American Electric Power Service Corporation; Appalachian Power Company; Columbus Southern Power Company; Indiana Michigan Power Company; Kentucky Power Company; Kingsport Power Company; Michigan Power Company; Ohio Power Company; Wheeling Power Company.

Further Reading: Mitchell, Sidney Alexander, *S.Z. Mitchell and the Electrical Industry,* New York, Farrar, Straus & Cudahy, 1960; White, W.S., Jr., *American Electric Power Company: 75 Years of Meeting the Challenge,* New York, The Newcomen Society in North America, 1982; *Where the future is now. . . . ,* Columbus, Ohio, American Electric Power Company, Inc., [n.d.].

—Wilson B. Lindauer

ARKLA▮

ARKLA, INC.

Arkla Building
525 Milam
Shreveport, Louisiana 71101
U.S.A.
(318) 429-2700
Fax: (318) 429-2793

Public Company
Incorporated: 1928 as Southern Cities Distributing Company
Employees: 10,000
Sales: $2.44 billion
Stock Exchange: New York

Arkla, Inc. is an integrated natural gas company with three primary business segments—natural gas transmission, distribution, and production and exploration. Arkla serves key markets in the central United States. It operates more than 14,000 miles of pipelines; distributes gas to 2.6 million customers; and has interests in 186 gas and oil fields.

Arkla's predecessor, Southern Cities Distributing Company (SC), was incorporated in 1928, with headquarters in Shreveport, Louisiana. In an era of acquisitions and mergers, Southern Cities was established to acquire and operate natural gas production and distribution systems. In 1934 Southern Cities merged with Arkansas Louisiana Pipeline Company, Reserve Natural Gas Company, Arkansas Natural Gas Company, and Public Utilities Company of Arkansas to form the Arkansas Louisiana Gas Company, (ALG), a subsidiary of Cities Service Company. The earliest predecessor of these companies dated back to 1905, when significant natural gas discoveries were first made in Louisiana. During the Great Depression, ALG expanded slowly. In 1936 it bought Little Rock Gas & Fuel.

In 1944 the Securities and Exchange Commission (SEC), under the Public Utility Holding Company Act, required the divestiture of ALG from Cities Service. Full reorganization did not occur until 1952 because of litigation and hearings. That year ALG became a publicly owned corporation, separate from Cities Service, and its stock was listed on the American Stock Exchange.

Wilton R. Stephens acquired a controlling stock interest in 1954 and became a director in 1956, board chairman in 1957, and president in 1958. Stephens owned a large investment bank, Stephens Inc., and was a dominant figure in Arkansas business and politics. Through the next decade, the company diversified. In 1957 it formed the subsidiary, Arkla Air Conditioning, to purchase a manufacturer of air conditioning equipment. Soon to follow were Arkansas Louisiana Finance Corporation, which financed appliances and construction; Arkla Chemical Corporation, a fertilizer and plywood manufacturer; and Arkansas Cement Corporation. There was even an amusement park called Arkla Village.

In 1960 and 1961 ALG expanded its gas operations and acquired three other distribution utilities—Consolidated Gas Utilities Corporation, with operations in Oklahoma and Kansas; Mid-South Gas Company of east Arkansas; and Southwest Natural Gas Company, which served parts of Louisiana, Oklahoma, and Texas. Also acquired was Southwest Natural Gas Company's gas production company, which was renamed Arkla Exploration Company. Given these expansions, the ALG gas sources in northwestern Louisiana and east Texas were not sufficient. Drilling and gas acquisition activities reached into Oklahoma and the Texas panhandle. In 1963 ALG built a new pipeline between its central gas system in Arkansas and new gas fields in Oklahoma. ALG's earnings were volatile during this decade of experimentation and expansion; from $15.5 million in 1960, they rose to $25 million in the mid-1960s, and dipped to $21 million by the decade's end. In the late 1970s Stephens cut dividends.

The 1970s ushered in a recession, oil embargoes, and energy shortages. There was also increased energy regulation. In 1973, the year ALG's stock listing moved to the New York Stock Exchange, Stephens relinquished the reins to Don W. Weir and Sheffield Nelson, who served as chairman and president of the company, respectively, and became co-chief executives. Under the unusual arrangement, Weir oversaw the subsidiaries, finances, and exploration, and Nelson handled pipeline operations and politics as well as relations with customers and regulations. ALG sold its unprofitable fertilizer and plywood operations and concentrated on finding new sources of gas. There were also dedicated efforts to work with regulators. In a highly regulated industry, the company was answerable to six different state agencies and the Federal Energy Regulatory Commission.

During the energy crunch of the mid-1970s, ALG had difficulty competing for gas because intrastate companies could pay more, as they were free of federal price controls. Stepping up its own-source supplies was vital, and ALG, between 1975 and the early 1980s, found more gas than it produced. Also in 1975 Nelson persuaded the Arkansas Public Service Commission—regulator of more than half of ALG's gas sales—to institute a new state gas-pricing formula, which allowed ALG to charge higher prices in return for promising better supplies. The company's expanded supply allowed it to win additional industrial customers. By 1976 the company's financial health had significantly improved. It successfully renegotiated contracts at bargain prices with gas producers before the 1978 Natural Gas Policy Act, which marked the start of gas decontrol. In the early 1980s, these contracts accounted for more than 60% of ALG's supplies and allowed the company to offer competitive prices to customer. ALG surpassed $1 billion dollars in total assets by 1979, when Weir retired as chairman and passed that title to Nelson. Earnings were up to $73 million in 1980.

In 1981 the company name was changed to Arkla, Inc. Around the same time, Arkla signed a 15-year contract with Central Louisiana Electric Company, agreeing to sell the company more than 100 million cubic feet of gas daily. After federal regulators approved the contract in 1982, it reduced the oversupply that had resulted from Arkla's abundant discoveries of its own and favorable contracts with other suppliers, to the large industrial gas market in southern Louisiana. Arkla was on track. The company's bond rating had been upgraded four times in three years, granting it a reputation for high growth and solid earnings. In 1983 Thomas F. McLarty III was elected president and in 1985 became chairman and CEO, succeeding Nelson. In 1985 McLarty initiated reorganization of the company into independent business units—natural gas distribution, transmission, and exploration and production. Arkla sold its Arkansas Cement Corporation in 1985. In 1986 Arkla's exploration division expanded with the purchase of Arkoma Production Company. Arkla acquired Mississippi River Transmission Corporation for $305 million in 1986, providing access to new service territories in western Illinois and St. Louis, Missouri.

In 1988 Arkla acquired Entex, Inc. through a $500 million stock swap. It was Arkla's largest merger to date, Entex serving about 1.2 million customers in the Houston metropolitan area and more than 500 other markets in the Gulf of Mexico region. In 1989 Arkla bought Louisiana Intrastate Gas for about $170 million, adding 1,900 miles of pipeline—the largest intrastate system in Louisiana. Also in 1989, Arkla sold 18% of Arkla Exploration Company to the public. The explo-

ration subsidiary's shares traded on the New York Stock Exchange.

Late in 1990, Arkla acquired Diversified Energies, Inc., whose main unit is Minnegasco, which distributes natural gas in Minnesota, Nebraska, and South Dakota, and brought with it some 650,000 customers. The stock transaction was valued at $630 million. Between 1984 and 1990 Arkla more than doubled its size through acquisitions and reached new markets in Houston, Texas; Minneapolis, Minnesota; and St. Louis, Missouri. In the early 1990s it operated the sixth-largest pipeline system in the United States and was among the ten largest operators of natural gas reserves.

Principal Subsidiaries: Arkla Energy Marketing Company; Mississippi River Transmission Corporation; Louisiana Intrastate Gas Corporation; Arkla Exploration Company (82%); Diversified Energies, Inc.

Further Reading: Nulty, Peter, "Little Rock's Hot-Cookin' Gas Company," *Fortune,* October 5, 1981; *The History of Arkla, Inc.: 1905–Today,* Shreveport, Louisiana, Arkla, Inc., [n.d.].

—Carol I. Keeley

BALTIMORE GAS AND ELECTRIC COMPANY

Gas and Electric Building
Charles Center
Baltimore, Maryland 21201
U.S.A.
(301) 234-5000
Fax: (301) 685-0665

Public Company
Incorporated: 1906 as Consolidated Gas Electric Light and
Power Company of Baltimore
Employees: 9,149
Sales: $2.16 billion
Stock Exchanges: New York Midwest Pacific Boston
Cincinnati Philadelphia

Baltimore Gas and Electric Company (BG&E) began lighting the streets and homes of Baltimore in 1816. It is an investor-owned utility with diversified operations in energy and environmental projects, real estate, and investments. BG&E's principal business remains the purchase, production, and sale of electricity and gas. The company's performance was undermined by problems in the late 1980s at its Calvert Cliffs nuclear plant.

Baltimore Gas and Electric Company dates back to 1816, when Rembrandt Peale, William Gwynn, and three other partners formed the Gas Light Company of Baltimore. Peale was the son of the painter Charles Willson Peale, and was himself a well-known painter of portraits and historical scenes. Gwynn was a local businessman. Another of the partners was a wealthy merchant, William Lorman. Within a week of a successful demonstration of gas lighting in what is now the Peale Museum, the new company secured a franchise to light the streets and homes of Baltimore, Maryland, with gas. The Gas Light Company was the first gas utility in the United States. Lorman was the company's first president, serving from 1816 to 1832. The Gas Light Company set to work laying pipes throughout Baltimore, bringing the new method of lighting to more neighborhoods. The company's first seven years were hard, producing no profit. The new company faced several problems of a technical nature. The method of gas manufacturing it had adopted proved inadequate for large-scale production; there were no means of measuring the quality of the gas produced; and gas meters, although they existed in England, were not available in the United States, so there was no method for measurement of gas used, and the company had to charge a flat annual rate.

The Gas Light Company continued to lose money, and by 1818 the company had exhausted its capital. To raise the money necessary to continue operating, the company made an initial public stock offering in 1818. The capital raised by the offering was to be used to buy equipment to expand the number of customers Gas Light Company served. By increasing its customer base the company could sell more gas and thus increase profit. Between 1818 and 1821, Baltimore, in common with other U.S. cities, was rocked by financial panic. The company's new influx of capital saw it through this period. In 1822, using a process already established in England, the company began manufacturing gas from coal. Previously tar was the raw material used. Coke, the by-product of this process, was a salable commodity. The company paid its first dividends in 1826.

In 1832 Columbus O'Donnell became president of the company and served until 1871. By 1830 the company was again running low on capital and was unable to continue to grow as quickly as the city of Baltimore. Much of the capital raised in 1818 had been spent on pipes and equipment of unsatisfactory quality and on experimentation. In 1833 the company issued new stock to raise capital.

The use of gas meters was under way in some homes by 1834, despite widespread opposition by members of the public, who did not trust the accuracy of gas meters. In fact, the meters lowered rates for most consumers.

Meanwhile, the city was still inadequately lit due to the cost of laying pipes, and by 1850 critics of the company, including Baltimore's mayor, were vocal. In 1860 Gas Light's first local competitor, Peoples' Gas Light Company, was formed. The organizers of Peoples' capitalized on Gas Light Company's unpopularity in persuading members of the Maryland state legislature to charter their company. Peoples' did not begin to operate until 1871, however, due first to internal disagreements among its founders, then to the Civil War.

In 1861 the Civil War broke out, imposing difficulties and setbacks, especially in railroad traffic. The war ended in 1865, but the higher cost of living, and thus of doing business, that it produced continued. Peoples' Gas Light Company began to operate in 1871, after reaching an agreement with Gas Light Company to divide the city. Also in 1871, William Sinclair assumed the presidency of Gas Light Company, serving until 1880. In 1876 another contender in the increasingly profitable industry was formed—Consumers Mutual Gas Light Company of Baltimore. Fierce price wars between the three gas companies were waged until 1880 when the companies merged to become Consolidated Gas Company of Baltimore City. John W. Hall served as president for the next 20 years.

During the mid-1880s Consolidated Gas faced competition in some areas from the Chesapeake Company, another provider of gas for lighting. In areas where both companies provided service, prices were slashed. In 1886 the Maryland legislature restricted competition among gas companies by making it more difficult to establish a new company. In 1881 two electric light companies, Brush Electric Light Company and The United States Electric Light and Power Company, had appeared in the city. Consolidated Gas was not yet involved in electric light, which was still fairly experimental at this time. When Thomas Edison's incandescent light bulb came into common use during the late 19th century, however, electric light became the standard. Electricity became the new competitor to gas.

In 1904 the city was devastated by the Great Baltimore Fire. Company employees labored to protect exposed mains from exploding. Despite the loss of property and the disruption of commerce, the company emerged prosperous and on solid ground and began to attract New York financiers.

By 1906 it had become clear to the leaders of Consolidated Gas that most homes and businesses favored electricity over gas for lighting. It was also clear that both gas and electric companies could operate more cheaply and efficiently if they did not duplicate services. In 1906, therefore, Consolidated Gas Company of Baltimore City merged with Consolidated Gas Electric Light and Power Company to form Consolidated Gas Electric Light and Power Company of Baltimore. The new company provided fully integrated gas and electric service in Baltimore. Chairman S. Davies Warfield made good use of New York investors' capital and thus launched the direct predecessor of BGE. General Ferdinand C. Latrobe became president, serving until 1910. Its capital shortages behind it, Consolidated grew at a healthy pace. During the financial panic and depression of 1907-1908, the new company managed a small increase in sales.

The Public Service Commission of Maryland was created in 1910 to regulate utilities. Also during this time, natural gas was becoming a popular substitute for manufactured gas. Warfield wanted to bring natural gas to Baltimore but did not succeed in doing so. Between 1906 and 1910, gross income increased by 31%, and in 1910 Warfield resigned and was succeeded by J.E. Aldred as chairman. Aldred embarked upon vigorous expansion. Much of the company's electricity was supplied by hydroelectric plants on the Susquehanna River, and Consolidated owned several gas generating plants. With production in place, the company could offer more competitive rates.

The domestic economy, especially manufacturing, was boosted when World War I started in Europe. After the United States entered the war in 1917, demand for fuel rose, and a coal shortage that coincided with a severe cold wave developed. This period of strain and high prices did not end after the war. Two rate increases were granted and cost-cutting measures enforced to make up for the increased cost of labor, coal, oil, and gas manufacture. In 1921 a contract was formed between Consolidated, United Railways & Electric Company and Pennsylvania Water & Power Company, under which all of Baltimore's electric power was organized under one management. It was another year of depressed earnings, but Consolidated began to recover in 1922 and 1923.

Due to several years of low water levels in the Susquehanna, the company began relying more heavily on its Baltimore steam plants in 1923, and Consolidated ordered two large turbine generators. By 1924 electric refrigerators and other appliances had become increasingly popular. The company was expanding to the north for power supplies. It entered an entirely new field in 1925, with the establishment of WBAL, a radio station that was sold to the American Radio News Corporation in 1935. In 1926, the use of gas was still growing. The company's Gould Street generating station began service in 1927, and was the first of the city's power plants to burn pulverized coal. In 1928 the company further diversified with the purchase of the Terminal Freezing & Heating Company. Steam heating was related to Consolidated's gas and electric interests, but the purchased system still had to be overhauled.

In 1928, to simplify its corporate structure, a number of companies held by Consolidated were dissolved and absorbed. The company contracted to buy two-thirds of the energy generated by the Safe Harbor Water Power Company in 1931. Safe Harbor produced hydroelectricity at a plant on the Susquehanna River. In the early 1930s there was a boom in air conditioning, and population and industry increased in Baltimore; but these factors did not entirely offset the effects of the Depression.

By 1936 the company's lean years were abating. A long-term contract for electricity supply was signed with Bethlehem Steel Company. Between 1929 and 1936 the company's operating revenue increased by more than 18%. In 1939 Consolidated benefited from a number of newly established, large industrial plants in Baltimore. Within two years World War II began to have an impact on the U.S. economy. War and the defense industry stimulated production, and Consolidated was called upon to meet higher demands. Charles M. Cohn became president of Consolidated in 1942, serving four years. During the war, the company had to use lower quality fuels to meet the demands of increased production. Electric and gas sales soared.

In 1946, the year after the war's end, William Schmidt, Jr., was elected president and chairman. At this time, gas use was still in steady decline nationwide, while the cost of manufacturing gas had risen nearly 300% in two decades. Consolidated was still expanding its capacity to provide service to new customers. In 1948 its third 60,000-kilowatt generating unit was completed and a fourth was ordered. Another, larger plant was under way at the company's Westport, Maryland site. The company set a record for new property expenditures in 1948—more than $21 million.

With revenues and energy demands on the rise, net earnings declined. The company had been working to discontinue the production and sale of manufactured gas and to convert to natural gas, and the conversion was completed in 1950. It was an enormous undertaking that involved changes in equipment from pipelines to appliances; the total cost of the conversion to the company was $9 million. The benefits were many: natural gas is less expensive, more efficient, and cleaner burning than manufactured gas. The lower cost of natural gas led to increased consumption. Also in 1950, Charles P. Crane became president, with Schmidt continuing as chairman. In 1951 the 20-year effort to convert Baltimore's electric system from direct current (DC) to alternating current (AC) was completed.

In 1955 the company's name was changed to Baltimore Gas and Electric Company. The following year, BG&E formed one of the world's largest fully integrated power pools when it signed a contract with seven other electricity distributors to inaugurate the Pennsylvania-New Jersey-Maryland Interconnection.

The 1960s saw more steady growth, marked by construction of a new BG&E headquarters in 1964 and the announcement in 1967 that BG&E would build Maryland's first nuclear-powered generating plant. The two-unit facility was built at Calvert Cliffs, about 60 miles south of Baltimore and represented an enormous investment. The first of these units was in operation by 1975. In its first year, it produced more than a third of the company's generation and reduced customer fuel rate adjustment charges by more than $50 million. The second unit began operation in 1977.

Demand had continued to grow and, in 1981 expansion of the Safe Harbor Hydroelectric Project started a four-year expansion project. In an effort to improve profitability, BG&E trimmed its operating budget in 1982 and 1983, and sought diversification into other businesses. In 1983, however, the Maryland Public Service Commission turned down BG&E's application to form a holding company, stating that Maryland law forbids such a structure for utilities. The holding-company reorganization would have enabled BG&E to diversify freely.

The Brandon Shores Unit Number 1—a coal-burning electricity-generating plant—opened in 1984, helping to eliminate the company's dependence on foreign oil. A second Brandon Shores unit started up in 1991. In 1983 about 60% of the company's operating revenues were in electric power sales, and around the same time gas sales began to slump. In 1986 BG&E formed Constellation Holdings, Inc., a subsidiary through which it planned to expand its nonutility interests, despite being denied the right to form a holding company.

By the mid-1980s, problems with the Calvert Cliffs nuclear power plant began to emerge. The Nuclear Regulatory Commission (NRC) fined the company for procedural and equipment violations at the plant in 1985. The NRC proposed further fines for alleged violations at the Calvert Cliffs plant in 1988. By year's end, the NRC placed Calvert Cliffs on its watch list of plants "warranting close agency monitoring" because of "declining performance." In 1988 these units were providing 40% of BG&E's fuel mix and were the company's lowest-cost producers of power.

Calvert Cliffs' second unit was shut down in 1989, after stress and erosion cracks were discovered. The NRC identified a number of equipmental and managerial problems at the plant, and the first unit was also closed for inspection.

The shutdown of Calvert Cliffs forced BG&E to purchase more expensive electricity from other utilities. The cost incurred by the idled plant ran to $300,000 a day, and BG&E sought numerous rate increases that were held up by debate. In addition, the NRC has fined BG&E for safety-related violations, one of which involved a worker's death. Startup of Calvert Cliffs' first unit eased somewhat the expense of purchased—rather than produced—electricity, but the facility's second unit was closed until May 1991.

BG&E's credit ratings were lowered in 1990, the result of financial deterioration brought on by the extended Calvert Cliffs outage, cost of energy replacements, and uncertainty about approval of rate increases. In December 1990 Maryland regulators approved base rate increases totaling $201 million annually and authorized BG&E to apply for surcharges to recover a portion of it purchased power costs.

With the startup of Calvert Cliffs' second unit in 1991, BG&E's prospects improved. A second coal-fired unit at Brandon Shores also went into operation early in 1991. Debate was ongoing among regulatory officials regarding how much of the costs of the Calvert Cliffs failure could be passed on to customers. The company estimates total replacement power costs run to $415 million.

Principal Subsidiaries: Constellation Holdings. Inc.; Safe Harbor Water Power Corporation (50%); BNG, Inc.

Further Reading: King, Thomson, *Consolidated of Baltimore: 1816-1950,* Baltimore, Maryland, Consolidated Gas Electric Light and Power Company of Baltimore.

—Carol I. Keeley

BAYERNWERK AG

Nymphenburger Strasse 39
D-8000 Munich 2
Federal Republic of Germany
(89) 12 54-1
Fax: (89) 12 54-39 06

Public Company
Incorporated: 1921
Employees: 9,570 (Group)
Sales: DM6.01 billion (US$4.02 billion) (Group)

Bayernwerk AG (Bayernwerk) is the largest electricity supplier in Bavaria and one of the largest in Germany. It provides about two-thirds of the electricity requirement for the Free State of Bavaria. Bayernwerk's purpose is to guarantee electricity supply through electricity generation, electricity distribution, and cooperative business ventures at home and abroad. As a national electricity supplier Bayernwerk builds and runs power stations that use nuclear and conventional sources of energy. In 1991 the company's power station capacity stood at approximately 8,000 megawatts (MW). The most important concerns serviced by the company are the regional energy supply companies within the greater Bayernwerk group, the German state-owned railway company, Deutsche Bundesbahn (DB), and large chemical companies. In 1991 the company supplied about 43.9 billion kilowatt hours (kwh) of electricity. The company's activities do not center exclusively around supplying energy, however. Bayernwerk has shareholdings not only in gas supply companies but also in paper manufacturing and glass manufacturing companies, which enable it to put the surplus profits from its electricity supply business to good use in other areas, including the management of nuclear waste. In 1991 around 60% of Bayernwerk was owned by the state of Bavaria and its governing regions and around 40% by Vereinigte Industrie-Unternehmungen AG (VIAG).

Since the beginning of the industrial age, which in Germany dated from 1795, every German state endeavoured to build up a good energy supply of its own. Bavaria was handicapped in this respect. It did not possess large deposits of fossil fuels such as coal; it did not have cheap transport facilities; and because it was not densely populated, the transport routes were long and transport costs high. Bavaria was well provided, however, with rapid mountain streams and powerful rivers. The development of energy supply in Bavaria therefore began with "white coal": hydroelectric power.

Visitors to the International Electricity Exhibition in Munich in 1882 were offered an unusual attraction—an artificial waterfall powered by electricity. The electrical current had been carried over 57 kilometers from Miesbach to Munich, the royal seat and capital. With this demonstration, the organizer of the exhibition company, the Bavarian pioneer in electrical engineering, Oskar von Miller, proved that with the help of electric current, the production and application of energy could be divided from each other by large distances. Oskar von Miller had recognized the possibilities offered by the use of the great hydroelectric power on hand in Bavaria, especially the Alpine rivers. As technical director of the Frankfurt Electricity Exhibition in 1891, he succeeded in carrying an appreciably greater capacity over a distance of 175 kilometers. This achievement created the breakthrough for the first high-tension transmission lines; electric power stations could be constructed in locations where energy sources could be supplied cheaply. In 1894 Isarwerke GmbH, the first German long-distance supply station, began to operate. It ran a large hydroelectric power plant near Höllriegelskreuth, south of Munich on the Isar River. Oskar von Miller contributed to the design for the mechanical and electrical installation.

Oskar von Miller, son of the brass founder Ferdinand von Miller, was a civil engineer by training. When he visited the Paris Electricity Exhibition in 1881, he was so impressed by what he saw that he began to study the relatively new subject of electrical engineering. In 1884 von Miller went to Berlin with Emil Rathenau to set up the Deutsche Edison-Gesellschaft, later to become the Allgemeine Elektrizitäts-Gesellschaft (AEG). In 1890 he opened an office in Munich and soon made a name for himself as a power transmission expert. Together with his achievements in the field of electrical engineering, his name is inseparably associated with the Deutsches Museum in Munich. Oskar von Miller was always in search of new sources of money for this collection, which consisted of masterpieces of science and technology.

In the early 20th century, public electricity supply made huge strides forward. Power stations and overhead power works were established all over Bavaria, but there was no comprehensive, unified plan for supplying the whole state. In 1911 von Miller proposed devising a general plan for the conversion of Bavaria's hydroelectric power. A thorough estimate of requirements was projected, as was the registration of existing power stations and the building of additional installations. Furthermore, a unified electricity grid was to be created to deliver energy from large state-owned hydroelectric power stations to overhead electricity works. Oskar von Miller was also responsible for naming this project: Bayernwerk.

He was unable initially to put his ideas into practice, since it was not settled as to whether and under which form the Walchensee power station should be established. The particular geographical location of the Walchensee and the Kochelsee, separated from each other by a height of 200 meters, had already been thought of in 1897 for use in producing energy. There were lengthy discussions, but it was ten years before a design could be drawn up, after it became clear that the Bavarian state railroad's electrification would depend upon the energy produced by the Walchensee power station. When it was revealed how high the costs would be for construction and electrification, the Bavarian transport ministry shied away from the project. A motion was even proposed in the Bavarian state parliament that the Bavarian state should give up completely its plans for constructing the Walchensee power station. However, Oskar von Miller's proposal to use the huge volume of energy from the Walchensee power station for his planned Bayernwerk finally won the day.

Before the planning could begin, World War I started. In September 1914 Oskar von Miller declared himself willing to take on the preparatory work for the building of the Walchensee power station and the planning for Bayernwerk at his own expense. Hindered by the war, Oskar von Miller was only able to table his plans as state government commissioner. On June 21, 1918, the founding of Bayernwerk as well as that of the Walchensee power station was voted through.

The socialist revolution of November 1918 in Bavaria and the attendant radical political changes posed new problems for Oskar von Miller. He succeeded, however, in winning the approval he needed from the socialist government for his plans by drawing attention to the jobs that would be created for the soldiers demobilized after World War I. The construction work advanced rapidly despite the difficulties caused by Germany's losing the war. However, the project's financing became increasingly difficult to guarantee due to rising inflation, and both companies had to be changed into public limited companies. On April 5, 1921, Oskar von Miller went to the offices of a Munich solicitor, accompanied by several representatives of the Finance Ministry and Ministry of the Interior, to register Bayernwerk AG. The company was capitalized at Papiermarks 100 million. Forty-nine per cent of the shares were intended to be distributed among the future electricity purchasers—cities and long-distance electricity companies—but the Bavarian state took up all the shares. The board of directors of the new company was also nominated: Rudolf Decker, assistant head of the Ministry of Trade and Industry, and Ernst Obpacher, chief planning officer in the Bavarian Ministry of the Interior. The founding of Walchenseewerk AG, with capital of Papiermarks 50 million, had taken place a few months earlier on January 5, 1921. The Bavarian state had taken up eight-ninths of the shares, and the Deutsche Reichsbahn took the other ninth. Oskar von Miller acted as chairman of both companies until the end of June 1921, when he stepped down to turn to other tasks.

Alongside Walchenseewerk AG, another large hydroelectric power company, the Mittlere Isar AG, fed into Bayernwerk's network. A private consortium had created the Mittlere Isar GmbH toward the end of World War I to exploit the Munich-Landshut stretch of the Isar. Dr. Theodor Rümelin, a hydraulic engineer was commissioned to draw up a design. When the Bavarian government was faced with the problem of finding jobs for soldiers returning from military service after the war, the conversion of the Isar's water power became part of its emergency program. The Bavarian parliament approved the project on March 25, 1919, and took over the shares of the company as well as the incomplete plans. The assistant secretary to the government, Franz Krieger, was appointed state commissioner and the senior civil servant, Dr. Siegfried Kurzmann, his deputy. The construction works close to Munich began immediately, and the founding of the Mittlere Isar AG followed on January 5, 1921, with a capital of Papiermarks 75 million. The Bavarian state took eight-ninths of the shares and the Deutsche Reichsbahn one-ninth. Like Walchenseewerk

AG, Mittlere Isar AG was to contribute to the electrification of the railway lines in southern Germany.

In the statutes of the three companies, which were adapted to work in close cooperation, the responsibilities of a public utility were brought to the fore. They were to be run according to commercial principles, but the interest return to the shareholders was limited. In accordance with the general plan drawn up, Bayernwerk gave up the right to supply the end user with electricity, in contrast to other big supply companies in other German states. Its role, rather, was to supply the electricity distribution companies with energy if they could not meet their electricity needs through their own power stations. The first 25-year contracts to deliver electricity, which Bayernwerk concluded between June 23 and June 30, 1923 with nine large electricity distributors in Bavaria, were based on this principle. Contracts with firms outside Bavaria were also concluded in the same year, the first being a contract to deliver electricity to the electricity supply company of the town of Stuttgart. Despite rising inflation, the two power stations on the Walchensee and the Middle Isar were able to start providing electricity as early as 1924. The growing demand for electricity and a water level which was at the mercy of the seasons led the company to look for new sources of energy. In 1928 Bayernwerk acquired the Wackersdorf mine from the Bayerische Braunkohlenindustrie AG and built its own steam power station in Schwandorf, which began operating in 1930. Although Bayernwerk had not escaped the effects of the worldwide Depression, there was a considerable upturn in business with the general armaments boom. For example, the Vereinigte Aluminiumwerke AG (VAW) agreed on a contract with Bayernwerk for the supply of steam, electricity, and briquettes to its aluminum oxide factory in Schwandorf. In view of the strong demand for electricity that came with the economic revival, Bayernwerk was once again forced to develop additional sources of potential energy. The brown coal power stations in central Germany presented an obvious choice, situated close to the coal supplies. A contract with AG Sächsische Werke and Elektrowerke AG, the latter owned by the Reich, to deliver electricity followed in 1939.

Furthermore, Bayernwerk set about extending the electricity grid to guarantee the electricity supply for the chemical works situated in Innviertel, to the southeast of Bavaria, which were important in the arms build-up. In the course of the National Socialists' policy of forcibly placing enterprises under state control, the Reich also strove to ensure its influence over energy supplies. Bayernwerk's share capital was taken over by the Reich's Vereinigte Industrie-Unternehmungen AG (VIAG) on April 1, 1939. Since 1933, Bayernwerk had carried out the business for the Walchenseewerk AG and Mittlere Isar power stations, but in 1942 the latter companies were formally merged with Bayernwerk. The Reichsbahn, which had held one-ninth of Bayernwerk's shares up until then, relinquished its holdings. 60% of the capital went to the Bavarian state, and 40% was taken over by VIAG. In the business year 1943 to 1944, Bayernwerk's electricity sales peaked, only to decline considerably in fiscal year 1944 to 1945. In the air attacks by the Allied Forces, industrial works, railway installations, and towns were increasingly bombarded. When the Americans marched into Bavaria in April 1945, there was virtually no electricity supply.

Like many other Bavarian companies, at the end of the war, Bayernwerk found itself in extreme difficulties. Its own electricity plants had remained intact to a large degree, but division of Germany into zones and the dismantling of both the brown coal power stations in central Germany and the electricity grids linked with power and distribution stations in Bavaria meant that Bayernwerk lost its most important suppliers of thermal energy. As building materials were in short supply in Bavaria after the war, it was not possible to redevelop the electricity grid. In addition, the Allied Control Council had forbidden the building of new power station plants. Bayernwerk was therefore obliged to extend its already existing sources of power. Thanks to a seven-kilometer-long tunnel, the fast-flowing Rissbach river on the Tyrolean border was diverted into the Walchensee. Furthermore, Bayernwerk made efforts to link up with the West German thermal power station network, building a 220 kilovolt (kv) grid from Ludersheim near Nuremberg to its own transformer station in Aschaffenburg. In 1949 Bayernwerk concluded a contract with Rheinisch-Westfälisches Elektrizitätswerk AG (RWE), Essen.

Once the Allied ban on building had been lifted in 1947, Bayernwerk embarked upon the construction of power stations on the Alpine rivers and on the great rivers of the Danube and the Main in Bavaria with increased vigor. The company was aware, however, that there were natural limits to the further expansion of hydroelectric power, and that the reserves of brown coal in the Upper Palatinate would one day be exhausted. It decided to supplement the energy supply from hydroelectric power and brown coal with hard coal from the Ruhr area. In 1952 the first engines of a thermal energy power station built on the Main near Aschaffenburg went into operation. Both DB and the Preussische Elektrizitäts-AG had shareholdings in this power station. As Bayernwerk's oldest coal-fired power station, it has been equipped with the most up-to-date flue-gas treating installations and is drawn on at times of peak demand.

For Bayernwerk, the 1950s brought economic and political challenges in the field of energy. Bavaria's position, both politically and geographically on the edge of the western European economic sphere, brought high energy prices and hampered its economic growth. At the same time, Bavarian industry was dependent upon a dynamically growing energy supply. The state had to find new and cheaper sources of energy. The "Bavarian economic miracle" took place with the introduction of atomic energy and the use of petroleum, and Bayernwerk bore this development in mind from an early stage. As early as 1957 an internal nuclear energy department had been created and employees were being sent to train in England, Sweden, and the United States. Bayernwerk took part in the research into a new type of reactor using heavy water and carbon dioxide cooling via the Gesellschaft für die Entwicklung der Atomkraft in Bayern mbH.

The atomic age for Bavaria's electricity supply industry dawned on June 17, 1961, when the 15MW experimental nuclear power station of Kahl am Main fed the first nuclear-generated electricity into the grid system integrated with the Bavarian network. Bayernwerk had a 20% holding in the operating company, the Versuchsatomkraftwerk Kahl GmbH (VAK). In 1966 the first large German nuclear power station, in Gundremmingen on the Danube, was connected to the grid. Bayernwerk took a 25% share in the construction of this 250MW nuclear power station.

Bavaria owes its efficient oil industry today to the initiative of the Bavarian economic minister Dr. Otto Schedl. His plan to lay oil lines to the Mediterranean ports of Genoa and Trieste was initially viewed with skepticism. At the end of 1963, however, work began on this project with the construction of the first two refineries located at Ingolstadt. Bayernwerk constructed a power station in the heart of the new refinery center of Ingolstadt, which came into operation in 1965 with a 150MW engine. Further down the Danube, near Pleinting, another 300MW oil-fired power station was built in 1968. By the end of the 1960s, thermal energy had overtaken hydroelectric power, the former supplying more than 60% of Bavaria's electricity requirement. Therefore, Bayernwerk concluded a long-term contract with Tiroler Wasserkraftwerke AG, and RWE for the financing of the Kaunertal power station in the Tyrol and for the supply of electricity from the Prutz power staion to the upper Inntal.

Oil became the driving force behind Bavaria's economic development in the 1960s. It was possible to reduce substantially the oil prices between the port of Hamburg and the Bavarian city of Munich. However, the massive use of oil also meant that Bavaria was particularly affected by the oil crises of 1973/1974 and 1979. Bayernwerk learned its lesson from the oil shocks of the 1970s, with the enormous increases in the price of oil. A secure and inexpensive electricity supply meant that the company had to free itself from dependence on unstable imports. Bayernwerk's decision to expand its activities in nuclear energy proved crucial for the future. As early as 1977 the 907MW nuclear power station Isar I, close to Landshut, came into operation and Bayernwerk had a 50% share in the enterprise. The first electricity generation from the nuclear power station of Grafenrheinfeld followed in 1981. With a capacity of 1,300MW it was Bayernwerk's biggest power station to date. In 1984 Bayernwerk took a share in the addition to the network of two new blocks at the Gundremmingen nuclear power station. Each block has a capacity of 1,300MW. Growing energy demand made it necessary to build a new installation, the 1,400MW nuclear power station Isar II, 50% owned by the Bayernwerk group. From a technical point of view this power station counts among the most modern in the world. With an electricity production of 10.3 billion kwh each, the nuclear power stations Grafenrheinfeld and Isar II are among the leaders in the 21 nuclear power stations in operation in Germany.

In 1991 more than half of Bavaria's electricity needs were generated by nuclear power stations. While the price of electricity in Bavaria was clearly above the German average in the 1960s and 1970s, Bayernwerk's expansion into nuclear power contributed to the fact that Bavaria, although poor in raw materials, had cheap electricity at its disposal by the beginning of the 1990s. Furthermore, the preservation of the environment plays an important part in Bayernwerk's policies. With electricity generated by nuclear power and hydroelectric power, harmful substances such as carbon dioxide are not released. In 1991 almost one quarter of the electricity Bayernwerk generated came from coal-fired power stations, while oil and gas power stations only served as reserve generators, thus conserving precious fossil fuel reserves. Moerover, as part of Bayernwerk's environment program, the removal of nitrogen and desulfurization of the coal and oil were made in modern flue-gas treating installations to reduce emissions of harmful substances to a minimum.

Along with good value electricity and care for the environment, the reliability of supply is one of Bayernwerk's stated aims. As a national electricity supply company, Bayernwerk runs a network of high voltage and maximum voltage lines totaling 5,500 kilometers in length and is linked to the Western European grid system. The provision to this grid as well as the use of the power stations is regulated from Bayernwerk's distribution center in Karlsfeld near Munich. This center ensures that the balance between electricity demand and electricity production is maintained with its high-technology computer installations.

The constantly growing demand for energy and the limited quantity of natural resources make the development of new technologies and research into possible energy sources for the future indispensable. Bayernwerk has a 60% shareholding in the Solar-Wasserkraft-Bayern GmbH in Neunburg vorm Wald in the Upper Palatinate. Hydrogen—perhaps the energy source of the future—is derived from the fission of water in electrolysis plants in this research center. The electricity for this process is derived from solar cells. The hydrogen produced in this manner can be stored and employed according to requirements. Furthermore, Bayernwerk has put into operation a trial model for providing solar energy in Flanitzhütte, a remote area it supplies with current in the natural park of the Bayerischer Wald. The aim is to supply five estates there, totally independently from the public network, with electricity derived from solar power from a photovoltaic plant.

The reunification of Germany has provided Bayernwerk with another task for the future. The construction of a highly efficient and environmentally friendly energy supply in the former German Democratic Republic has been undertaken in conjunction with other West German companies in the energy sector. Three new subsidiary companies, Energieversorgung Nordthüringen AG, Ostthüringer Energieversorgung AG, and Südthüringer Engergieversorgung AG were founded at the beginning of 1991, Bayernwerk holding a 51% majority share in them. These subsidiaries, provided with a great deal of investment and specialist technical support, are to bring about the reorganization of the supply of electricity and long-distance heating in the eastern German state of Thuringia. In 1991 Bayernwerk had already built a 380-kilovolt grid from Redwitz in Bavaria to Remptendorf in Thuringia.

The opening of the Iron Curtain has also enabled closer cooperation with the states of eastern Europe. Thanks to the direct current network coupling in the border region near Etzenricht in the Upper Palatinate, it will become possible in the future to exchange current between the two maximum voltage networks in Bavaria and Czechoslovakia. This will make mutual help possible in the case of power station breakdowns or if power stations have to be closed down temporarily owing to a danger of smog.

Principal Subsidiaries: Energieversorgung Oberfranken AG (EVO) (70.7%); CONTIGAS Deutsche Energie AG (Contigas) (81.3%); Energieversorgung Ostbayern AG (OBAG) (92.8%); Uberlandwerk Unterfranken AG (54.4%); Grosskraftwerk Franken AG (98.3%); Ostbayerische Energieanlagen GmbH & Co. KG; Ilse-Bayernwerk Energieanlagen GmbH (50%); Fränkische Gas-Lieferungs-Gesellschaft mbH (FGL) (65%); Energiebeteiligungsgesellschaft mbH (EBG); Untere Iller AG (UIAG) (60%); Solar-Wasserstoff-Bayern GmbH (SWB) (60%); WBG-Wohnen, Bauen, Grund, Gesellschaft für Wohn- u. Gewerbeimmobilien GmbH (WBG) (54%); Kernkraftwerk Isar GmbH (KKI) (50%); Gemeinschaftskernkraftwerk Isar 2 GmbH (KK12) (40%).

Further Reading: Bayernwerk AG, *25 Jahre Bayernwerk,* Munich, 1946; Bayernwerk AG, *30 Jahre Bayernwerk AG Bayerische Landeselektrizitätsversorgung. 1921–1951,* Munich, 1952; von Miller, Walther, *Oskar von Miller,* Munich, Bruckmann Verlag, 1932, 2nd edition, Munich, 1955; Kristl, Wilhelm Lukas, *Der weißblaue Despot. Oskar von Miller in seiner Zeit,* Munich, Richard Pflaum Verlag, 1965; "Fünfzig Jahre Bayernwerk 1921–1971," in *Bayerischer Braunkohlen Bergbau,* No. 81, June 1971; Zorn, Wolfgang, "Bayerns Gewerbe, Handel und Verkehr (1806–1970)", in Max Spindler, *Handbuch der bayerischen Geschichte,* vol. IV, Das neue Bayern 1800–1970, verbesserter Nachdruck, Munich, 1979.

—Eva Moser
Translated from the German by Philippe A. Barbour

BRITISH GAS PLC

Rivermill House
152 Grosvenor Road
London SW1V 3JL
United Kingdom
(071) 821-1444
Fax: (071) 821-1870

Public Company
Incorporated: 1986
Employees: 79,900
Sales: £9.49 billion (US$17.74 billion)
Stock Exchanges: London Tokyo New York Toronto

The history of British Gas plc is the history of the whole British gas industry. British Gas plc was incorporated in 1986 when the state-owned British Gas Corporation was privatized, and more than 4,025 million shares were issued by the British government. This privatization of the gas industry reversed the nationalization of 1949, when more than 1,000 separate private or municipally-owned companies were taken into state ownership. During nearly 40 years of public ownership, the technical basis of the industry underwent two profound changes. In 1949 the gas industry manufactured almost all its gas from coal. During the 1950s and 1960s coal became too expensive, and processes were developed to convert cheap oil feedstocks into a coal-gas equivalent. When natural gas—methane—became available in quantity, the industry undertook the enormous ten-year task of converting the 35 million appliances of its 13 million customers so that they could use natural gas. The business in the early 1990s served 17.3 million households—that is, more than 88% of homes where a gas supply is available—and is currently the largest integrated gas supply business in the world. Its profit after tax in 1991 was £916 million.

Experiments using coal gas for lighting were made in the late 18th century. William Murdock lit his home in Redruth, Cornwall with gas in 1792, and in the early years of the 19th century, when Britain was the world's first industrial nation, several factories made their own gas for lighting. The first gas company in the world to provide a public supply was the Gas Light and Coke Company of London, which received its charter in 1812. Gas for lighting proved both popular and profitable; by 1829, around 200 gas companies had been set up. Almost all of these companies relied on private capital, but the first municipal gas department was set up in Manchester in 1817 by the police commissioners and was taken over by Manchester Corporation in 1843.

The first gas companies were established in a competitive climate; there were no restrictions on where a company might set up in business if it could raise the capital and thought it could make a profit. In the early days it was by no means unknown for two companies to serve the same street; in one notable case in South London no less than four competing companies had mains in the same street. It was soon recognized that unbridled competition served neither the interests of gas companies nor their customers. Within London, where the problem was most severe, the Metropolis Gas Act of 1860 allocated each company its own district within which it had a monopoly. To prevent exploitation of captive customers, a statutory limit of 10% on dividends had been imposed by the Gasworks Clauses Act of 1847. This limitation did not satisfy customers. Companies were enjoying monopoly powers and already earning the maximum dividend; there was little incentive for them to cut prices despite increasing sales and improved technology. This form of statutory regulation proved to be ineffective in protecting the interests of the public.

From the mid-1870s competition began to offer customers the prospects of a better deal. At first the competition came from lighting oil. Persistent overproduction in the Pennsylvania oil fields in the United States meant there was a surplus over U.S. needs, which would then be shipped out and dumped cheaply on world markets, especially in the early 1870s. Oil lamps proved a popular alternative to gas. By the late 1870s, electricity was also beginning to emerge as a competitor for the gas lighting business. A practical arc lamp was produced in 1876, and Edison in the United States and Swan in Britain independently produced the first incandescent light bulbs in 1879–1880. The gas industry responded in three ways; it attempted to improve the efficiency of its lamps, it looked for alternative markets, and it looked to its pricing structure.

At the suggestion of George Livesey, chief engineer of the British South Metropolitan Gas Company and the foremost gas engineer of his generation, the sliding scale was introduced from 1875; dividends and prices were linked inversely, that is, increased dividends could be paid if the price of gas came down but if the price of gas rose, dividends had to be cut. Individual companies sought private legislation to permit them to introduce the sliding scale; by the year 1900, two-thirds of all gas sold was covered by this arrangement. Its fairness to customers depended crucially on the datum price, that is, the price from which variations would be calculated. It was the good fortune of the gas companies that many technical improvements to cut costs were made after they adopted the sliding scale. Shares in the major gas companies were regarded as a very sound investment. Livesey also introduced a profit-sharing scheme for his workers in 1889; the bonus was linked to reductions in the price of gas. Similar co-partnership schemes were set up by several of the larger gas companies, but few outside the industry adopted the concept.

When gas companies were looking for alternative uses for gas, they began to consider its use for cooking and heating in the home. The first geyser water heater was invented in 1868 and gas fires to heat individual rooms were developed in the 1880s; but gas companies were more interested in persuading customers to use gas for cooking. Experimental gas stoves had been shown at the Great Exhibition of 1851, but these made no headway against the popular coal-fired kitchen ranges that provided heat and hot water as well as facilities for cooking. By the 1870s there were gas stoves recognizably similar in layout to most modern stoves, with an oven below and burners above. As far as the gas managers of the time were concerned, the special advantage of the stove was that it was likely to be used more during the day than at night; it would therefore use *off-peak* gas. Lighting, of course, was still the predominant load. For rational, promotional, and financial reasons, the installation of stoves could be subsidized from the profits on gas sales. As customers were disinclined to buy, they were supplied with basic, robust cast-iron stoves on cheap rental terms. By contrast, in the United States stoves were offered for sale, not rent, and were of lighter construction, well-finished, and with attractive trim. This policy of supplying subsidized stoves was developed more extensively in Britain between 1890 and the 1920s than anywhere else in the world, and British companies sold more gas than the rest of Europe put together.

Despite the excitement engendered by the first incandescent electric light bulbs, customers soon found they were costly and unreliable. Gas saw a strong return to popularity in the 1890s, following the invention by an Austrian chemist of the Welsbach incandescent mantle, which increased fivefold the efficiency of gas for lighting. Gas was still very much a middle-class fuel; poorer people living in rented homes used coal, oil, and candles. They could not afford to have gas installed, even if they wanted to use it. This situation was about to change dramatically. The change is usually attributed to the invention in 1888 of the prepayment, penny-in-the-slot meter. This alone would not have brought about the spread of gas into working-class homes. The manager of the municipal Ramsgate gas undertaking, W.A. Valon, noted that half the houses in the town had no gas supply. He decided that instead of offering to provide just the stove on easy terms, he would provide the whole gas installation—pipes, stove, and lights. As his new customers would pay for their gas in advance through a prepayment meter, there was no need to ask for a deposit as security. The profit on gas sales to poor homes was unlikely to be sufficient to pay for the installation costs, so there was a surcharge on the gas price for such customers, typically 25%— the prepayment supplement. The scheme spread like wildfire. In the words of George Livesey, "this extension of gas supply to weekly tenants is the most extraordinary and remarkable development of the business that has ever been known." Between 1892 and 1912 the number of gas customers increased from 2 1/2 million to 7 million and sales doubled. The use of gas for cooking became more important than gas for lighting, as virtually all new customers were supplied with a stove.

This expansion of the industry was not accompanied by any structural change; it was still extremely fragmented. In 1914 there were some 1,500 suppliers of gas, two-thirds of whom had statutory monopoly powers within their areas of gas supply. There was little pressure toward amalgamation, in part because of high legal and consultancy fees, and also because of geography since supply networks could not easily be linked to achieve economies of scale. Another major factor was the split between the municipal and privately owned companies; about one-third of the industry was municipally owned. Each company could set its own technical standards and, because

subsidized rental of appliances was almost universal, there was no independent appliance retailing network that might have encouraged harmonization of standards and appliance innovation.

The interwar period was a difficult time for the gas industry. At the outbreak of World War I in 1914, ten times more homes had a gas supply than electricity. Although the number of gas customers continued to rise until 1939, the increase in gas sales slowed, while electricity sales grew sharply. The prepayment supplement had paid for so many homes to be equipped with gas lighting that the defense of the lighting business was a major preoccupation; it was feared that if electricity displaced gas for lighting, it would soon displace gas stoves and heaters. As a consequence, the industry was distracted and could not concentrate its efforts fully on displacing the huge stock of obsolete rented appliances and selling modern stoves, heaters, and water heaters in their place. The real value of the prepayment supplement—fixed in cash terms before 1914—fell, and cost increases meant there was no surplus for upgrading appliances.

Electric stoves were attractive and modern by contrast with the traditional rented gas stoves. The gas industry had no answer to new types of electric appliances—vacuum cleaners, irons, and radios—which were sold aggressively through retailers and by door-to-door salesmen. These and the convenience and cleanliness of electric lighting ensured that householders came to regard electricity as a necessity. Many builders and customers, attracted by the idea of the all-electric house, saw no need to install gas; some councils with their own municipal electricity undertakings even sought to ban their tenants from using gas. In the right market, however, gas could hold its own. The Ascot instantaneous water heater, developed in Germany by Junkers, was efficient and stylish; it provided a service where electricity could not compete. Its makers targeted their main promotional efforts at architects and builders rather than at gas companies and achieved conspicuous success. The Ascot became synonymous with gas water heating in Britain as the Hoover did with vacuum cleaning.

The Electricity (Supply) Act of 1926 brought about the restructuring of the electrical industry, which until then had been as fragmented as gas. The government-appointed Central Electricity Board was charged with building a national grid. This initiative during the worst years of the Great Depression might suggest that electricity was the key to a prosperous national future, and politicians of all parties were keen to jump on the electrical bandwagon. Nothing comparable was planned for gas. Under the leadership of David Milne-Watson of the Gas Light & Coke Company, the gas industry lobbied strongly for a "level playing field" but its pleas fell on deaf ears. By the late 1930s, people both within and outside the industry realized the existing structure could not survive without radical change. There was a need for some form of national framework for gas; those in the industry hoped that this would not mean state control.

These rumblings were muted during World War II, but thoughts on the future of the industry continued. A government committee under Geoffrey Heyworth proposed the compulsory purchase of all gas companies and the establishment of ten regions; regulation would be undertaken by commissioners, following the analogy of the electricity industry. His report was published in 1945, but by then a Labour government committed to the nationalization of the industry had been elected. There was little public concern or controversy, unlike the debates on the nationalization of coal, transport, electricity, or steel. Few may have given the industry much chance of survival, let alone expansion. Opposition came more from Conservative members of Parliament than from the industry, whose senior leaders gave an undertaking to cooperate with the government's plans "to maintain an efficient gas service to the public," in the words of the British Gas Council.

Under the Gas Act of 1948, the industry passed into public ownership on May 1, 1949. Some £220 million of British Gas 3% stock—3% annual interest was payable on the face value of the stock—was issued as compensation to the former owners; 1,037 separate undertakings, previously under private or municipal ownership, were amalgamated into 12 area gas boards. Scotland and Wales each had their own board; Northern Ireland was outside the scope of the act. The Gas Council, a small central coordinating body, was established. Apart from its chairman and vice-chairman, this comprised the 12 area board chairmen. Most had held senior positions in the industry although other interests were presented; for example, one had a trade union and one a local government background. The duties of the Gas Council were to advise the minister on gas matters and to promote the efficient exercise of their functions by the area boards; the central body had a small secretariat, of 159 members, one-third of whom dealt with publicity and another third with purchase of coal and the sale of coke. The main executive power rested with the boards, though capital investment programs had to be submitted through the council to the minister for approval. There were national arrangements for wage-bargaining; close cooperation soon brought a measure of voluntary harmonization between the various boards over technical standards, commercial policy, and other areas of common interest. The industry was legally bound to take account of the interests of both work force and customers through consultative arrangements.

The new area boards settled down quickly but faced two long-term problems. Their public image was still that of an old-fashioned if not immediately moribund industry, and they were losing the battle for the domestic load to electricity. In the ten years from 1948, sales of gas increased by 20%; over the same period, sales of electricity more than doubled. Old rented stoves, heaters, and water heaters were not being replaced quickly with modern equipment, and the sales efforts of the boards were hindered at first by postwar material shortages and the export drive, and also by government purchase tax and restrictions on renting. The other problem was the price of gas, which no longer enjoyed its traditional advantage over electricity. While the price of electricity rose by 17% between 1950 and 1957, gas rose by 51%. The cost of high-grade coal for gas-making doubled between 1947 and 1957, whereas power stations could use cheaper grades.

Efforts to rebuild the market for gas appliances were urgently needed but less important than the need to reduce the relative price of gas, and the industry began to search for alternative methods of gas production. One path explored was the total gasification of coal, a process developed in Germany before the war. Another alternative which seemed to offer better prospects was the use of oil feedstocks for gas-making, either as an enricher of gas made by other processes or later by direct catalytic conversion of oil into gas. Britain, and nota-

bly the Gas Council's own scientists, were pioneers in the intense research efforts that resulted in a number of processes that could take any oil feedstock available in large quantity at low cost, especially naphtha and refinery waste gas, and convert it direct into usable gas. Major contracts were signed with oil companies to secure long-term supplies. For the first time in its history, the gas industry's fortunes were unshackled from coal, during the 1960s.

This technical breakthrough was matched by a change, of course, in marketing. Market research showed that gas still had a negative image by contrast with the strong modern image of electricity. W.K. Hutchison, the deputy chairman of the Gas Council, put himself at the head of the campaign to change the image of gas. In the words of the advertising agents, "The amiable, innocuous figure of 'Mr. Therm' around which the Gas Council's advertising had for many a year revolved, seemed too bland, too typecast to take up the challenge . . . And so it was that 'High Speed Gas, Heat That Obeys You' . . . invited newspaper readers to realize how 'with it' they were to be using gas." This coincided with the arrival on the market of a new generation of stoves with timers and automatic ignition, and stylish and efficient gas heaters that quickly took over from coal the main task of heating living rooms. Showrooms were modernized and moved to prime high-street locations. The next stage was to attack the domestic central heating market, which was at the time being vigorously promoted by the oil companies. Gas was helped both by the arrival of natural gas and the OPEC oil price rises from 1973. It was also helped by the introduction of the Clean Air Act in 1956, which aimed to reduce the air pollution caused by coal-burning domestic fires. Natural gas enabled a significant reduction of smoke in the atmosphere. By 1989 more than 70% of all gas customers had gas central heating, a clear indication of the success of this campaign.

The 1960s saw other momentous changes that were to have even more far-reaching effects. Natural gas arrived in quantity for the first time in Britain. In its early days the Gas Council commissioned British Petroleum to act as operator to prospect for natural gas onshore; this search proved unsuccessful. The Gas Council was therefore particularly interested to hear of U.S. plans to ship liquefied natural gas (LNG) by tanker; cooling to very low temperatures reduces methane to a liquid, the volume of which is $1/600$th of its gaseous state. The British government gave its approval to a trial to assess the practicality of the scheme, and the first experimental shipment arrived at Canvey Island in the Thames estuary in 1959. Gas Council proposals to proceed with import of LNG on a large scale ran into fierce opposition in government, predictably from the coal and oil lobbies. Approval was finally given by the British cabinet to a 15-year contract to buy gas from Algeria; two tankers shuttling to and fro would carry the equivalent of 10% of British gas output at that time. The two vessels came into service in 1964. To enable all parts of the country to take advantage of these supplies of natural gas, a high-pressure national grid was constructed, at first linking eight boards to Canvey Island. The grid network was 320 miles long in 1966-1967; by 1976-1977 the network extended 2,915 miles, and all boards were connected.

The liquefied methane project was running in parallel with another natural gas project. A huge discovery of natural gas in Holland in 1959 led to speculation that more might be discovered under the North Sea. The Gas Council was very keen to participate in the search and joined in partnership with experienced U.S. operators to explore, drill, and subsequently to produce gas and oil. The necessity for Gas Council involvement was questioned at the time as, under British law, all gas found and landed in the United Kingdom had to be offered for sale to the council. The election of a Labour government in 1964 strengthened the hand of the Gas Council; it was positively encouraged to participate in North Sea activities.

It was fortunate that some of the early acreage allotted contained the huge Leman gas field. The council thus had invaluable information on the actual costs of finding and producing gas; it was able to negotiate prices based more on the costs of production (then 2 pence per therm; 240 pence = £1) than on average revenue (16.5 pence) or the cost of seaborne gas from Algeria (6.5 pence). A whole series of discoveries soon proved that supplies of natural gas from the North Sea would meet British needs for a few decades at least. This raised the question of how best to use it. Up until then, natural gas had been converted into a coal-gas equivalent of only half the heat value of methane, volume for volume. There were enormous advantages of distributing methane without dilution; processing costs would be minimal, and the capacity of gas mains would be effectively doubled. Against this had to be set the cost of converting every appliance so that it could burn methane instead of coal gas. A survey of several thousand customers round the Canvey Island terminal in 1966 showed the great variety of equipment to be converted, three or four appliances per home on average. A large proportion were 15 years old or more. Ways had to be found to convert all these old appliances or to persuade customers, by offering generous terms, to buy new ones.

Despite the cost and potential problems, the advantages of complete conversion were overwhelming, This was an enormous technical, marketing, and public relations exercise. There was undoubted inconvenience, but considering the opportunities for error and complaint, most customers accepted the conversion with good will; it gave them a direct and personal opportunity to share in the excitement of the North Sea discoveries. Conversion was free and, for many, it gave an opportunity for old appliances to be brought up to scratch or replaced cheaply; besides, North Sea gas was cheaper. The conversion exercise was, in the words of Sir Denis Rooke, chairman of British Gas from 1976 until 1989, "perhaps the greatest peacetime operation in the nation's history." The main conversion program began in 1967 and, 13 million customers later, the last home was converted in 1977. From 1912 until nationalization in 1940, sales had more than doubled. Between 1949 and the end of the conversion program they increased sixfold.

Until the early 1960s, the gas industry had managed to avoid the relentless tinkering by politicians that had bedeviled the other nationalized industries: coal, steel, transport, and electricity. It had not been perceived as having any long-term significance and had neither failed nor succeeded dramatically. With its involvement in North Sea exploration and consequently higher public profile, this situation changed. Now the government thought seriously about establishing a production board along the lines of the Central Electricity Generating Board. The Gas Council persuaded the government that the existing arrangements were working harmoniously and suited

the needs of the industry. As a consequence the 1965 Gas Act, essential to clarify the powers of the Council to buy gas in bulk and sell to its area board customers, left the basic structure untouched. It was clear, however, that strong central leadership was necessary to enable the company to cope with the changes brought by natural gas; new headquarters departments were set up covering production and supply, marketing, and economic planning. Rooke, who had been a member of the team working on the import of LNG from its inception in 1957, became development engineer, responsible for new production processes and planning an integrated supply system. Later, as member for production and supply, he played a crucial role in the technical changes in gas manufacture and distribution in the 1960s and 1970s. The arrangements under the 1965 Act were temporary; a restructuring was necessary to place overall responsibility at the center. In 1973 the Gas Council was replaced by the British Gas Corporation (BGC), still state-owned, and the area boards set up in 1949 became regions under direct control of the BGC.

One outcome of the success of the North Sea search for gas was that the BGC became a producer of oil and thus became involved in international fuel markets. This situation did not survive the election of the Conservatives to power in 1979. BGC was required to sell its oil assets, spun off as Enterprise Oil; the proceeds went not to the industry but to the government. At this time the government also became concerned at the dominant position enjoyed by BGC in the business of retail sale of appliances. The matter was referred to the Monopolies and Mergers Commission, which ruled that BGC's position in the market was against the public interest. The government drew back from enforcing a withdrawal from appliance trading; gas showrooms served to deal with accounts and service queries as well as selling. Independent retailers now play a larger part in appliance retailing than ever before in the history of the industry; even so, British Gas today has a turnover of £300 million from appliance trading.

When the privatization of the industry was under consideration, some ministers were keen to introduce an element of competition and to break up the unified structure of the industry that had evolved since nationalization, largely in response to the availability of natural gas. Any breakup was opposed by Rooke, who lobbied strongly for the retention of the unified structure that had served the nation so well; his views ultimately prevailed, although the nationalized electricity industry was to be split up in its subsequent privatization. The BGC was privatized as a whole by the Gas Act of 1986 and returned to private ownership in what was then the largest company flotation ever undertaken. After a vigorous TV advertising campaign to "Tell Sid" to buy shares, 3 million people became owners of British Gas plc shares. The advertising alone cost £25 million, much of it paid by the government; the total cost of the privatization, including fees, underwriting, and value-added tax, was £347 million.

As a private company, British Gas is no longer geographically restricted to the United Kingdom and U.K. offshore waters. The government, however still prefers it to purchase its supplies from the U.K. sector of the North Sea for strategic and balance of payments reasons. Rooke retired in 1989 and was succeeded as chairman and chief executive by Robert Evans. The company has made substantial investments in foreign oil and gas assets to strengthen its business worldwide.

Since its privatization, British Gas has acquired interests in four exploration and production companies: Acre Oil and part of Texas Eastern North Sea were acquired to strengthen the company's oil and gas holdings in the North Sea's U.K. sector; some of Tenneco's subsidiaries were purchased, with exploration and production interests in a number of countries around the world; a 51% stake in Canada's Bow Valley Industries gave exposure to the North American energy market; and British Gas also bought Consumers Gas, Canada's largest natural gas distributor. It also continues to offer a consultancy service so that others may benefit from its expertise.

With privatization came the need to reinstate a regulatory organization to safeguard the public from the misuse of British Gas's monopoly position. The Office of Gas Supply (OFGAS), under a director general, monitors tariffs and commercial practices. In 1989 British Gas was obliged to formalize its charging structure for large non-domestic customers. It was also obliged to make its transmission network available to carry gas not sold directly; this allows producers of gas to contract directly with customers for the sale of large quantities of gas. This regulatory change removed the monopoly of gas distribution that had been enjoyed by gas undertakings since the middle of the 19th century.

In the postwar years the position of the gas industry in the British fuel market was totally transformed. From its per-ceived role as a minor player, it has emerged to become a major force in not only the U.K. but also world energy markets. In the early 1990s it supplied more than half the energy used in British homes. It has made enormous technical and commercial strides and demonstrates that the question of state ownership of the business for much of the period has been irrelevant to its record of dynamism and success. Entrepreneurship is not the exclusive prerogative of the private sector.

Further Reading: Chantler, Philip, *The British Gas Industry: An Economic Study,* Manchester, Manchester University Press, 1938; *Report on the Gas Industry in Great Britain,* London, Political and Economic Planning, 1939; Everard, Stirling, *The History of the Gas Light and Coke Company 1812–1949,* London, Benn, 1949; Elliott, Charles, *The History of Natural Gas Conversion in Great Britain,* Royston, Cambridge Info. & Research Services with BGC, 1980; Williams, Trevor I., *A History of the British Gas Industry,* Oxford, Oxford University Press, 1981; Barty-King, Hugh, *New Flame,* Tavistock, Graphmitre, 1984; Hutchison, Sir Kenneth, *High-Speed Gas: An Autobiography,* London, Duckworth, 1987; Falkus, Malcolm, *Always under Pressure: A History of North Thames Gas since 1949,* London, Macmillan, 1988.

—Francis Goodall

CAROLINA POWER & LIGHT COMPANY

411 Fayetteville Street
Raleigh, North Carolina 27602
U.S.A.
(919) 546-6111
Fax: (919) 546-7678

Public Company
Incorporated: 1926
Employees: 8,100
Sales: $2.62 billion
Stock Exchanges: New York Pacific

Carolina Power & Light Company (CPL) has supplied electricity to parts of North Carolina and South Carolina since the early years of the 20th century. In 1990 it served approximately one million customers with a balanced array of coal-fired steam, nuclear, and hydroelectric plants. Having planned in the 1970s to increase greatly the proportion of its nuclear generators, CPL, like many other utilities, ran into severe regulatory and cost problems and abandoned many of its nuclear projects. CPL continued to use nuclear and coal-fired plants for the bulk of its electricity in the 1990s, but the company had decided to meet new demands for power with a cautious program of inexpensive, flexible combustion turbines.

Carolina Power & Light was one of the many utilities created and nurtured by General Electric (GE). The latter was formed in 1889 by a group of investors led by J.P. Morgan, with the purpose of amalgamating a number of the manufacturing facilities associated with Thomas Edison's early work in light and power transmission. GE supplied the nation's new power industry with much of its equipment and technical leadership, often receiving as payment shares of stock in the young, undercapitalized utilities.

Some of GE's client companies grew into thriving businesses, but many others—most of them small utilities in rural areas—had trouble attracting the vast amounts of capital needed to build a system of electrical distribution. In order to help these smaller utilities raise capital—and in turn become good customers for GE equipment as well as increase the value of GE's equity holdings—GE created in 1905 a wholly owned subsidiary called Electric Bond & Share Company (EBS). EBS was given GE's stock portfolio and told to arrange financing, provide technical aid, and advise the management of these struggling utilities, including a number of companies

in England and France. EBS generally owned but a small percentage of stock in each of its client firms. It was not a holding company, but the recommendations of EBS were followed by its much-smaller partners.

Among the many U.S. cities in which EBS became active was Raleigh, North Carolina, where electric lights were first provided in 1886 by the Thomson-Houston Electric Light Company. In 1892 Thomson-Houston was merged with GE, which thereby acquired a position in a number of the small power plants then beginning to harness the hydroelectric potential of the Appalachian river systems. When GE had formed EBS in 1905, it transferred its interest in these local plants to EBS, which quickly arranged for a merger of three of them in 1908. In that year, Carolina Power & Light Company was established in Raleigh by the merger of Raleigh Electric Company, Central Carolina Power Company, and Consumer Light and Power Company. Unlike many of EBS's ventures, CPL was controlled directly by EBS and its president, S.Z. Mitchell, who for many years was a leader of the electrical industry in the United States. As EBS was wholly owned by GE, Carolina Power was controlled indirectly by the company from which it bought all of its equipment, a situation that was common in the electrical industry and that later would prompt charges of conflict of interest leading to the dissolution of the great U.S. electrical holding companies.

The chief obstacle faced by Mitchell was the fragmentation of power generation in the Raleigh area, compounded by the difficulty of raising enough capital to consolidate and expand CPL's system. The early electric power companies generally did not foresee the enormous growth in demand for electricity; they operated generators of limited capacity and charged customers a relatively high price for power. Mitchell and other early leaders of the electrical business recognized that electricity was unlike any other commodity; it was destined to become universally and intensively utilized, it was a fungible product, and its generation and distribution required so much capital that competing firms could not survive in the same geographical area. It was thought that electric power was a natural monopoly, with a large central power station serving many square miles of customers. It was the chief goal of men like Mitchell to develop the electrical industry according to these principles: Mitchell encouraged mergers and expansion among EBS's many affiliates, and arranged the funding for same; he stressed the advantages of large central power stations; and he urged his colleagues to sell more electricity at a lower rate rather than less at a higher rate. That all of these rationalizations of the industry would benefit GE was, of course, understood from the beginning, but they were also to a large degree dictated by the nature of electric power.

CPL accordingly set about expanding its facilities, which originally consisted of two hydroelectric plants and one steam plant generating a total of 3,900 kilowatts of power. CPL's capacity in 1991 was slightly less than 10 million kilowatts. In 1911 the company acquired the assets of two struggling power companies in nearby Henderson and Oxford, North Carolina, and the following year opened a western branch with the purchase of Asheville Power & Light Company. To help finance the construction of main transmission lines between CPL's growing network of stations, EBS in 1911 created a second subsidiary to handle construction projects. North State Hydro Electric Company built and maintained power lines that it then leased to CPL, obviating the need for CPL to raise the cash needed for such large undertakings.

After battling the local gas company for several years, CPL bought out its rival in 1911, becoming the sole supplier of both gas and electricity for the city of Raleigh. Its next milestone was a 1913 agreement to sell electricity wholesale to the city of Smithfield, North Carolina, which would handle its distribution to the customer. Such rapid expansion on the part of power companies raised the concerns of local legislators, who saw the threat of onerous rates by utilities given such monopolies. In 1913 North Carolina accordingly placed all power companies under the jurisdiction of its Corporation Commission, which would eventually be granted power to regulate all utility business, including rate schedules. A similar commision had already been formed in South Carolina, where another EBS subsidiary, Yadkin River Power Company, was operated by CPL management. CPL thus became a regulated monopoly, one of a great many around the country affiliated with EBS and ultimately with General Electric.

As the economies of North Carolina and South Carolina grew following World War I, an increasing number of manufacturing plants and residential customers alike switched to electricity for a growing number of applications. Most important among industrial users were the textile and tobacco manufacturers. Residential customers were encouraged to use electricity for a plethora of new gadgets and tools, often sold directly by CPL's representatives. As with many technical evolutions, electrical customers often had to be shown the possibilities of electric power, and CPL was eager to push the sale of GE appliances. It was the dawn of a new era for rural Carolinians, and electricity was soon in great demand; but, as always, there remained a shortage of capital required to meet such demands. Through its wide experience in the industry, EBS had learned that the best method for smaller utilities such as CPL to raise large amounts of capital was to form a holding company in charge of many such small firms. The holding company's larger asset base would attract investors more readily than could the individual utilities. One such holding company was National Power and Light, formed by EBS in 1921. Carolina Power & Light was made a part of National in 1927, and for the next 20 years would satisfy its capital requirements via its new parent company.

On April 6, 1926, CPL was itself reconstituted into a new and larger corporation. Along with the former CPL, the new company included Yadkin River Power Company, Asheville Power and Light, Pigeon River Power Company, and Carolina Power Company. Together, the utilities served 130 communities throughout the central parts of North Carolina and South Carolina, providing up to 59,000 kilowatts of power to about 20,000 customers. It was not long before the Great Depression slowed CPL's growth, however, as the region's big textile mills reduced operations and the economy generally crumbled. To replace the lost industrial revenue, new CPL president Louis V. Sutton initiated a sales program designed once again to increase the amount of electricity used in the home. CPL published an "electric cookbook" and encouraged the adoption of the latest home conveniences, cut its rates, and halted all new construction until the economy showed signs of reviving.

In the meantime, the electrical industry's highly concentrated organization continued to attract criticism. The power trust, as its opponents labeled the GE-based network of utilities, responded by pointing out that the cost of electricity per kilowatt hour had fallen steadily since the industry's beginning; but the persistent allegations of monopoly caused GE to distribute its EBS stock to GE's shareholders in 1924. Of equal concern, however, was the number of electrical holding companies across the country whose often-precarious financing was underscored in 1932 by the collapse of Samuel Insull's midwestern power conglomerate. In response, Congress passed the Public Utility Holding Company Act in 1935, setting restrictions on such organizations and placing them under the jurisdiction of the Securities and Exchange Commission (SEC). As part of a general campaign, the SEC began dissolution proceedings against National Power and Light in 1940, and the holding company's stock was finally given over in 1946 to its parent, EBS. Two years later, EBS in turn sold most of its stock in CPL to the public, at which time CPL became a wholly independent, investor-owned utility with its stock traded on the New York Stock Exchange.

The robust postwar economy of the 1950s was accompanied by a huge increase in the demand for electricity among both residential and industrial consumers. To provide the needed power, CPL began constucting a series of new plants of unprecedented size. Major plants were added at a rate of about one every two years during the 1950s, the majority of them using coal-fired steam generators in place of the earlier hydroelectric units. In 1956 CPL began experimenting with the third great source of electric power, nuclear reaction. It formed the Carolinas-Virginia Nuclear Power Association with three other regional utilities to study the details of nuclear power generation. The group built a prototype reactor at Parr Shoals, South Carolina, where electricity was first obtained from nuclear fission in 1963. Encouraged by the results, CPL applied for and received approval from the Atomic Energy Commission to build its own full-scale nuclear plant, upon which it began work at Hartsville, South Carolina, in 1966. When it came on-line several years later, the Robinson number 2 reactor was the first commercial nuclear reactor in the Carolinas, and, with energy sales tripling during the hectic 1960s, CPL planned a second unit at Southport, North Carolina. Along with its growing confidence in nuclear power, CPL increased its electrical capacity by joining a power pool formed by utilities in the Carolinas-Virginia area. This 1964 agreement, and its 1970 revision, provided for a flexible sale and purchase of power among the participating utilities as needed.

With the death of Sutton in 1970, CPL entered a new era, in several ways. Shearon Harris became the company's chief executive, only the third to date, but more fundamental were the changes wrought by the 1973–1974 oil crisis and subsequent, prolonged "stagflation." CPL was hit by a double blow of rocketing fuel costs and a contracting economy, at a time when its ambitious construction projects were well under way and soaking up great amounts of cash. When Consolidated Edison of New York, the nation's largest public utility, failed to pay a dividend in the first quarter of 1974, Wall Street's faith in utilities was shaken, and CPL found that it could not obtain financing at reasonable rates. Thus, although the company escaped immediate damage during the energy crunch by passing along to the customer its higher fuel costs, CPL was forced in 1975 to postpone plans for two steam and three nuclear generators, the first in a series of delays and cancellations that would continue to trouble CPL.

To cope with the company's difficult conditions, CPL shook up its management. Harris remained chairman but handed the presidency to Sherwood H. Smith Jr., who remained the company's chief executive in 1991. Under Smith, CPL abandoned uncontrolled growth for a more conservative strategy. With the financial, construction, and fuel costs of new plants rising faster than consumers would agree to higher rates, most utilities began to advocate energy conservation in the 1970s to relieve themselves of the need to raise ever more capital. In the aftermath of the Three Mile Island, Pennsylvania, nuclear accident of 1979, nuclear construction came to a virtual standstill for the next decade. CPL canceled the nuclear units it had postponed in 1975, and, during the 1980s, slowly gave up hope of completing more than one of the four nuclear units originally planned for its Shearon Harris Plant in New Hill, North Carolina. In the atmosphere of tighter inspections following Three Mile Island, CPL had not won for itself a particularly distinguished reputation. The Nuclear Regulatory Commission levied a number of fines against the company for poor performance, including a 1983 levy of $600,000 that was then the largest civil penalty ever assessed for nuclear mismanagement.

CPL planned no new coal or nuclear construction projects through the end of the century. With electrical demand slowing and the company's problems with nuclear plants still fresh in the minds of management, CPL decided to supply its next 2,000 megawatts of capacity by means of smaller, combustion turbine generators. These provide, in the words of CPL chairman and president Smith, "reasonably short construction schedules, relatively low cost, and quick start-up when needed"—three qualities lacking in the average coal- or nuclear-fired steam plant. The company also planned to continue purchasing significant amounts of electricity from its sister utilities in the region, and had even resorted to selling four of its units to a state agency and then buying back electricity as needed.

Principal Subsidiaries: Capitan Corporation; Carolina Power & Light Finance, N.V. (Netherlands Antilles).

Further Reading: Mitchell, Sidney A., *S.Z. Mitchell and the Electrical Industry*, New York, Farrar Strauss & Cudahy, 1960; *A Brief History of Carolina Power & Light Company*, Raleigh, North Carolina, Carolina Power & Light Company, 1984.

—Jonathan Martin

CENTERIOR ENERGY CORPORATION

6200 Oak Tree Boulevard
Independence, Ohio 44131
U.S.A.
(216) 447-3100

Public Company
Incorporated: 1985
Employees: 8,517
Sales: $2.37 billion
Stock Exchanges: New York Midwest Pacific

Centerior Energy Corporation is a public utilities holding company operating in Ohio through two electrical subsidiaries, The Toledo Edison Company and The Cleveland Electric Illuminating Company. Both subsidiaries operate in highly industrialized regions; principal industries include automotive, steel, chemical, and glass. The business climate remains attractive for heavy manufacturers and service alike.

Centerior was created in 1985, when Toledo Edison and Cleveland Electric Illuminating agreed to combine forces. The two companies officially came under the Centerior banner on April 29, 1986. The Securities and Exchange Commission approved the combination just ten months after it was applied for, a rapid pace for utilities merger approval. Each company retained its separate identity, while taking advantage of cost savings, initially estimated at $53 million annually.

Toledo Edison, the smaller partner, operates in northwestern Ohio, principally around the city of Toledo. Toledo is a major rail center, and an important Great Lakes port. Toledo Edison sells electrical energy at wholesale to 13 municipally owned power companies and one rural cooperative. The company has about 283,000 customers in its 2,500-square-mile operating region.

Toledo Edison was initially incorporated in 1901 as Toledo Railways & Light Company after absorbing Toledo Traction Company and Toledo Consolidated Electric Company. It added Toledo Gas, Electric & Heating Company in 1907.

In 1921 the company sold its street railway properties to Community Traction Company, and changed its name to Toledo Edison. In 1928 the company sold most of its natural gas operations to Columbia Gas System, Inc.

It acquired small power companies in the 1920s and 1930s, including Acme Power Company; Defiance Gas & Electric; Swanton Light & Power Company; Holgate Light & Power

Company; Northwestern Light & Power Company; Dixie Light & Power Company; Toledo Suburban Electric Company; the electric properties of the Toledo, Ottawa Beach & Northern Railway; Apex Service Company; Lake Shore Power Company; and Ohio Utilities Finance Company.

In 1950 Toledo Edison's parent company, Cities Service Company, was forced to divest itself of Toledo Edison to comply with the Public Utility Holding Company Act. Cities transferred the bulk of Toledo Edison's stock to its own shareholders and sold the remainder to the public. Management remained the same, as did shareholder identity, for the most part. Toledo Edison was the last utility to be divested by Cities Service, which had once held 49 utility companies.

In the 1950s many regions suffered from power shortages. The postwar industrial boom demanded greatly increased capacity from electric companies; Toledo Edison, however, had no problems keeping up with the demand. In 1949 it added a 100,000-kilowatt generating unit to its Acme plant. Originally built in 1917, Acme was upgraded once more in 1951, and remained a central part of Toledo Edison's power generation system. In 1955 the Bay Shore facility came into service, expanding greatly over the years. In 1965 the Richland Plant in Defiance started generating electricity via its combustion turbines; it was expanded in 1966. The Stryker Station, completed in 1968, produced combustion power also using turbines.

The late 1960s and 1970s saw a great deal of cooperation between regional electrical utility companies in the north central Ohio industrial corridor. In 1967 Cleveland Electric Illuminating Company, Duquesne Light Company, Ohio Edison Company, Pennsylvania Power Company, and Toledo Edison organized into the Central Area Power Coordination (CAPCO) group. CAPCO was to pool interests to build power generating facilities and transmission facilities. Limiting excess generating capacity is key to efficient operation of an electrical utility. Several CAPCO plants were built during the 1970s and 1980s, and the cooperative effects of the joint venture proved gainful to all of the companies participating.

CAPCO was successful in organizing regional bulk power distribution. It also forged Cleveland Electric Illuminating–Toledo Edison cooperative ties. The Davis-Besse nuclear plant, begun in 1970 and completed seven years later, was co-owned by Toledo Edison and Cleveland Electric; the project proved the two companies could work well together. Cleveland Electric's business was very similar to Toledo Edison's: they had similar corporate structures and similar mixes of residential, industrial, and commercial customers, and their service territories were nearly adjacent.

Cleveland Electric Illuminating Company had a long history like Toledo Edison and had experienced a nearly identical pattern of industrial development. The city of Cleveland was highly industrialized; its port handled coal and iron shipments and its rail lines served the city's various steel, automotive, electrical and mechanical businesses, chemicals—including plastics and paints—and nonferrous metal fabrication. Since its incorporation in 1892 as Cleveland General Electric Company from the merger of the Brush Electric Light & Power Company and the Cleveland Electric Light Company, Cleveland Electric Illuminating had grown to meet the power requirements of a heavily industrialized region. Like Toledo Edison, it had been part of a holding company, in this case

North American Company, which divested Cleveland Electric in 1947. After the divestiture and into the 1960s and 1970s, the utility enjoyed steady sales and earnings growth.

Cleveland Electric's plants were mostly fossil-fuel powered. Coal, being readily available and popular in Ohio's industrialized districts, made up the majority of the fuel requirements. Diversification of fuel began in the early 1970s. In 1970 two plants were converted to low-sulfur oil, and in 1972 the Seneca hydro-pumped plant was completed. Cleveland Electric also made strong commitments to nuclear power development through its CAPCO affiliation. In addition to Davis-Besse, Cleveland Electric participated in two other nuclear plants, Perry Unit 1 and Beaver Valley Unit 2, both of which went online in late 1987.

In 1985 Toledo Edison proposed an affiliation between that company and Cleveland Electric Illuminating. The merger would cut costs for both companies and provide the security of pooled power reserves for peak surges in either operating area.

Initial opposition to the proposed merger from competitors, local governments, and antinuclear groups was short-lived. By the end of April 1986, Centerior Energy was in the electricity business as the parent of Toledo Edison and Cleveland Electric Illuminating. Assets came to $11 billion; customers totaled 2.6 million. The name Centerior combined the words center and interior, which described the company's location in the United States.

In 1986 Centerior's construction expenditures totaled $1.1 billion. With the completion of Perry Unit 1 and Beaver Valley 2, the system's power needs appear to be met through the 1990s, without major additions.

In November 1987 Beaver Valley 2 and Perry Unit 1 began providing power commercially. Meanwhile, the Davis-Besse plant was productive 84% of the year, a new high. By 1988 the company generated 27% of its power via nuclear facilities. In September 1987, the company transacted a $1.7 billion sale and leaseback deal that allowed Centerior to retire $860 million in high-cost debt and preferred stock. Also in 1987 the company reduced its work force by about 6% through a voluntary early retirement program.

In 1988, after finding it impossible to have its costs covered by current and future rate increases, Centerior wrote off $349 million of its investment in its nuclear construction program. The write-off resulted in the first loss, $74 million, in the history of Centerior, Toledo Edison, or Cleveland Electric Illuminating, but also ended the uncertainty surrounding the issue and reduced the possibility of litigation. The loss also led the company to reduce its common stock dividend. The utility began the 1990s with a focus on cutting costs along with an expectation of continued sales growth in the increasingly diversified northern Ohio market.

Principal Subsidiaries: The Toledo Edison Company; The Cleveland Electric Illuminating Company; Centerior Service Company.

Further Reading: Maugans, Edward H., "The Cleveland Electric–Toledo Edison Affiliation: Stars in the Right Places," *Public Utilities Fortnightly,* July 24, 1986.

—Thomas M. Tucker

CENTRAL AND SOUTH WEST CORPORATION

1616 Woodall Rodgers Freeway
Dallas, Texas 75266
U.S.A.
(214) 754-1000
Fax: (214) 754-1033

Public Company
Incorporated: 1925 as Central & South West Utilities Company
Employees: 8,377
Sales: $2.74 billion
Stock Exchanges: New York Midwest

Central and South West Corporation is a holding company for four electric utilities and six other subsidiaries involved in such businesses as the gathering and transmission of natural gas and various financial services. Its utility subsidiaries are Central Power and Light Company, serving south Texas; Public Service Company of Oklahoma, operating in the eastern and southwestern portions of that state; Southwestern Electric Power Company, whose service area includes northwestern Louisiana, northeastern Texas, and western Arkansas; and West Texas Utilities Company, operating in western and central Texas. More than half of Central and South West's electricity sales come from Texas, and electric operations contribute about 95% of the company's profits. The company's operating area has enjoyed growth in both the residential and industrial sectors. After a brief downturn in the mid-1980s, the petrochemical, metal fabrication, and tourism industries in the region were booming in the early 1990s. In 1991 the company's service area spanned 152,000 square miles and had a population of four million.

In 1925 Central & South West Utilities Company was formed to hold the following subsidiaries: American Public Service Company, Public Service Company of Oklahoma, Central Power and Light Company, and Chickasha Gas and Electric Company. Central & South West's parent was Middle West Corporation. In 1935 the Public Utility Holding Company Act was passed, subjecting Central & South West to federal supervision, in addition to regulation by the states in which the company operated its subsidiaries. In 1947 Central & South West Utilities merged with its American Public Service Company and changed its name to Central and South West Corporation. The same year, to comply with the Public

Utility Holding Company Act, Middle West divested itself of Central and South West, distributing its interest to shareholders.

In the 1950s the popularity of natural gas as an energy source proved a bonus to the region's economy. Rich in oil and natural gas, Texas, Oklahoma, and western Louisiana enjoyed cheap energy prices. In 1961 Central and South West purchased the Transok Pipe Line Company. Transok operated throughout Oklahoma, piping natural gas from suppliers to Public Service Company of Oklahoma over its 720 miles of pipeline. In 1962 Transok was transferred to Public Service Company of Oklahoma and operated as a unit of that company for 20 years, adding an additional 200 miles of pipeline over time. In September 1982, Transok, Inc. was formed as a separate subsidiary of Central and South West, although it continued to serve Public Service Company of Oklahoma. In the early 1990s Transok began serving other utilities in the Central and South West system and delivering gas to outside companies as well.

In the late 1960s, increasing awareness of air pollution brought a number of utilities much criticism. Many burned coal or oil to generate electricity. Central and South West avoided this problem because its plants were all gas-powered, and most were located away from population centers. Growing opposition to nuclear-powered generators was also moot in the company's operating region at this time. Central and South West enjoyed uninterrupted growth into the early 1970s, when the energy crisis brought into question the single fuel dependency of the system.

Ten new generating plants, which would boost capacity by 45% were planned between 1972 and 1976. Flattened earnings in 1974, a result of high natural gas prices and the subsequent need to burn oil, resulted in plans to diversify its fuels. Plans for new generating plants focused on coal, lignite, and nuclear facilities. The cost of generating electricity from oil and natural gas had risen 40% in 1976, justifying Central and South West's program. In 1977 the company's first coal-powered plant went on-line.

By the late 1970s, cheap natural gas was no longer available to Central and South West's subsidiaries. The company laid down plans in 1976 to interconnect all of its subsidiaries' power output into one grid, and link that to the Texas power grid. This would enable Central and South West to buy power from Texas Utilities and from Houston Lighting & Power, two companies that paid half the cost of power that Central and South West did because they had already converted to inexpensive lignite-fueled generators and had long-term contracts for cheap natural gas in force. Texas Utilities and Houston Lighting & Power, however, had no desire to send their power across state lines and subject themselves to federal regulation. They cut ties with Central and South West, which resulted in a flurry of litigation.

In 1981 Central and South West, the Federal Energy Regulatory Commission, and the Texas companies reached a settlement—the power shipped across Texas borders was sent as direct current rather than as alternating current. This was interpreted to mean that the other Texas utilities were not technically connected to the alternating-current power grid and thus were not subject to federal regulation. Although Central and South West had to build stations to reconvert the direct current back to alternating current, the savings were still substantial. By 1985 the lines and plants were in operation.

CSW Credit Incorporated was launched in the mid-1980s to buy and collect the accounts receivable of Central and South West's subsidiaries and other utilities. The subsidiary borrowed money to purchase accounts receivable at significantly less than face value, then collected the bills, receiving nearly the full amount. This business, known as factoring, promised to add millions to Central and South West's bottom line.

Central and South West's revenues had risen steadily in the early 1980s, peaked in 1984, and decreased for the next four years. Annual dividend increases, however, continued as they had since 1950. The regional economy faltered as a result of plummeting oil prices worldwide. The earnings decline was also a result of Central Power and Light Company's 25% participation in the South Texas Project, a nuclear plant. Central Power and Light had operated for several years with increased costs but without a rate increase. By 1989 the subsidiary's investment was $2.3 billion, and annual costs related to the project were about $140 million. In 1988 Unit 1 of the South Texas Project began generating electricity, at five times the cost and eight years later than originally planned. A year later, Unit 2 came on-line. This completed Central and South West's expansion program, and the company was able to reduce capital spending. In 1990 the Public Utility Commission of Texas granted Central Power and Light a $264 million rate increase so the utility could begin to earn a return on its $2.7 billion investment in the nuclear plant. Central Power and Light agreed not to seek further rate increases until 1994.

As of the early 1990s, Central and South West had invested $4.5 billion on eight new coal plants, two lignite plants, and the two nuclear generators since the early 1970s, when gas had provided 99.9% of the systems' power needs. In 1991 coal provided 44% and natural gas provided 41% of Central and South West's electricity, lignite provided 9%, and nuclear contributed 6%. Refurbishing of seven old gas-powered generators was planned for the 1990s, and one small gas generator was scheduled to come on-line in 1999. With major expansion behind them the operating subsidiaries of Central and South West were poised to profit from the economic boom that appeared to be heading in the direction of the region.

Principal Subsidiaries: Central Power and Light Company; Public Service Company of Oklahoma; Southwestern Electric Power Company; West Texas Utility Company; Transok, Inc.; Central and South West Services, Inc.; CSW Financial, Inc.; CSW Leasing, Inc.; CSW Energy, Inc.; CSW Credit, Inc.

Further Reading: "Uptrend at Central and South West," *Financial World,* November 29, 1972; "Texas Vs. Si Phillips," *Forbes,* October 16, 1978.

—Thomas M. Tucker

CHUBU ELECTRIC POWER COMPANY, INCORPORATED

1 Toshin-cho
Higashi-ku
Nagoya 461-91
Japan
(052) 951-8211
Fax: (06) 441 8598

Public Company
Incorporated: 1951
Employees: 20,359
Sales: ¥1.70 trillion (US$13.62 billion)
Stock Exchanges: Tokyo Osaka Nagoya

Chubu Electric Power Company, Incorporated (Chubu Electric) ranks third among the nine major Japanese electric power companies in terms of generating capacity, kilowatt-hour sales, revenues, and total assets. The company serves over 8 million consumers in a 39,000 square kilometer area in the center of Japan ("Chubu" means "central"). The Chubu region is located on the main island of Honshu, between Tokyo and Osaka, and consists of a prosperous coastal plain with excellent harbors and rich farmland. Inland are the mountain ranges known as the Japanese Alps which rise to 3,000 meters above sea level. The rivers cascading down these mountains provide an abundant and steady source of hydroelectric power. Today the Chubu region accounts for 20% of Japan's industrial output.

Chubu Electric was established in May 1951, a few months before the Japanese Constitution was promulgated, and the year before the U.S. occupation ended. It was one of nine companies formed at the same time as part of the restructuring of Japan's energy industry after World War II. In addition to these nine companies, with a total generating capacity of 164 million kilowatts (kw) and annual sales of 599 billion kilowatt-hours (kwh), Okinawa Electric Power acts as a regional supplier to Okinawa prefecture. Except for Okinawa, the power systems of these companies are interconnected to ensure stable and efficient service for the entire country. In recognition of the public nature of electric power utilities, rates and other important factors are under the supervision of the Ministry of International Trade and Industry (MITI), although the industry itself is private.

At the time of its formation, Chubu Electric was given responsibility for supplying electricity to Aichi, Gifu, Mie, and Nagano prefectures, as well as that portion of Shizuoka prefec-ture west of the Fuji River. Its shareholders' equity was ¥29.4 billion, and its generating capacity was 1.03 million kw. It soon emerged, however, that this capacity was inadequate. Because of the age of the company's equipment, which it had inherited from the restructuring, its actual generating capacity was in fact only 600,000–700,000kw. To make matters worse, the Korean War created a sudden surge in demand for electric power as Japan became a rear-base for the U.S. Army. In order to tackle this problem the company adopted a dual approach, conducting a publicity campaign for energy savings and constructing new power plants, both hydroelectric and coal-fired. Construction of the Hiraoka hydroelectric plant in 1952 was followed by the construction of the Oigawa hydro-electric plant and the Mie and Shin-Nagoya coal-fired plants. By the latter half of the 1950s, supply and demand finally balanced out. This expansion of Chubu Electric's generating power required spending ¥210 billion over ten years, which was mainly covered with financing from the Japan Development Bank and with foreign capital.

In September 1959 a typhoon struck Chubu Electric's operating region, badly damaging one of the company's plants and flooding another on the coast for several months. Using the slogan "Electric power is the generator of recovery," the company responded with an all-out restoration effort. The efforts of the company to cope with this disaster earned it an award from the Disaster Committee Headquarters—it was the only award of this kind given to a private-sector company—and formed the basis of its approach to future disasters.

The 1960s were a period of marked economic growth in Japan, highlighted by the 1964 Tokyo Olympics and the improvement of the country's infrastructure, with the opening of the Tokaido bullet train and the Tomei and Meishin highways which linked up major industrial areas in central Japan with Tokyo. Because it occupies part of the Pacific coast belt, the Chubu region attracted the heavy chemicals industry and demand for electric power increased by more than 10% per annum. For several years, the growth rate in this area was one of the highest in Japan.

To meet the increasing demand, the company introduced a large volume of new oil-fired generating capacity. In 1960 fossil-fuel-fired plants contributed more than half of the company's electricity output for the first time, and subsequently new coal-fired plants with capacities of over 4 million kw were built around the Ise Bay, in Yokkaichi, Owashi, Chita, Nishi Nagoya, and Atsumi. At the same time this base was supplemented with hydroelectric plants—Hatanagi Unit 1 and Takane Unit 1—to meet peak demand.

In addition to developing new electricity sources, the company expanded its grid, constructing a 270,000 volt (V) transmission line around Ise Bay and strengthening its links with other utilities. Because oil prices remained stable during this period of rapid economic growth, the company did not need to revise its rates between 1954 and 1964.

In the 1970s, problems stemming from the period of high economic growth began to emerge. Environmental pollution had been a growing problem in Japan since the late 1950s when people began to suffer from mysterious and horrific diseases. Because the symptoms of those affected became so widespread, developing "Citizens' Movements" (Shimin-Undo) were able to coerce the government and industry into tackling the problem. In response to the pollution problem,

Chubu Electric promoted dual measures—for fuel and plant—concerning atmospheric pollution, noise, and waste water. These included reducing the sulfur content of its fuel. As with the later oil crises, Japan managed to turn adversity to advantage with the pollution problem, and was to become one of the worlds' leading nations in terms of pollution control.

The first oil crisis hit in October 1973, a product of the fourth Middle East War. The price of crude oil—oil-generated electricity accounts for about 30% of Chubu's generation—rose above $10 a barrel, and after the second oil crisis in 1979 above $30. Chubu Electric revised its rates three times—in 1974, 1976, and in 1980—and largely managed to overcome the difficult times. A three-tiered rate system was introduced for household use, and a special rate for industrial users was introduced as the company promoted the concept of energy saving.

The oil crises proved a major turning point in Japan's economic development. The industrial emphasis moved from heavy chemicals to manufacturing, assembly, and knowledge-intensive industries. The rate of growth in demand for electric power, which had been almost 10% per annum anyway, steadily increased. In response, Chubu Electric adopted what was called a "positive management" policy aimed at restructuring its business. Subsequent stabilization and decline in oil prices and the appreciation of the yen, reducing fuel costs further, meant that with little pressure on its balance of revenues and expenditures the company was able to reduce its rates four times up until April 1989, following the recommendations of MITI's Electricity Utility Industry Council.

In the early 1970s the company began promoting diversification of its energy sources, mainly into nuclear power and Liquefied Natural Gas (LNG). The promotion of these power generation methods is perceived by the company to reduce environmental pollution, especially carbon dioxide emissions. Its first nuclear power plant, Hamaoka Unit 1, started operation in March 1976, five years after construction began. Construction of Units 2, 3, and 4 followed. In December 1973, at the height of the oil crisis, Chubu Electric entered into a contract with Indonesia for long-term supplies of LNG, and in March 1978 it commenced operation of two exclusively LNG-fired plants, Chita Units 5 and 6. It also promoted switches to LNG at Chita Units 1 to 4, Yokkaichi and Kawagoe. As a result, LNG's share of power generation reached 33% in 1989.

During the 1970s and 1980s, customer needs grew more sophisticated. Chubu Electric met the demand with various measures to introduce new technology and reduce costs. Measures included construction of a second 500,000 kilovolt (kv) transmission line, the introduction of super-high voltage lines for urban areas, enhancement of protection against lightning, the introduction of optical communications, enhancement of information capabilities, and automation of facilities. In addition, the thermal efficiency of Yokkaichi Unit 4 and Kawagoe Unit 1, which started in 1989 using the latest technology, was raised to over 40%, compared with an industry average for the nine companies of 38.8%, within a year.

To meet increasingly varying customer needs, Chubu Electric promoted equipment for late-night consumption of electricity, heat pumps, 200-volt household appliances, office building air conditioning, area heating and cooling—the leveling-off of demand over peak and trough times in a particular area—and electric heat for industrial use and institutional kitchens.

In conjunction with these measures, Chubu Electric inaugurated a Challenge program in 1984 aimed at rationalization and quality control, and supported by Action Challenge Circles—information- and finance-gathering organizations set up abroad to facilitate these two functions. It established offices in Washington D.C. in 1982 and London in 1985, and diversified its activities, principally into telecommunications and heat supply. In 1988 the company embarked on a program to update its corporate image and prepare itself for the 21st century.

Chubu Electric continues to implement anti-pollution measures at its thermal power plants. Greater use of low-sulfur fuel oils, flue-gas desulfurizers, and LNG has reduced sulfur-oxide pollution. Flue-gas denitrification, use of low-nitrogen fuels, and boiler modification have greatly suppressed generation of nitrogen oxides. Also, all company power plants are equipped with electrostatic precipitators which remove soot from flue gases with a high collection efficiency of 90% or more. Measures being adopted to prevent water pollution by power plants include the purification of discharge water by such methods as coagulating sediment, neutralization, and filtration.

To deal with noise and vibration problems, consideration is given to the use of low noise apparatus and the installation of noise suppression devices. Also, where necessary, installation of machinery is confined to indoor or underground sites. In addition, the grounds of power plant sites are landscaped with greenery. The amount spent on thermal power protection in fiscal year 1990 came to ¥40.8 billion ($258.2 million). However, Chubu Electric's overall policy on environmental protection considers that a rational balance must be kept between environmental protection and the stable supply of energy necessary for sustained economic growth.

Chubu Electric also continues to diversify power sources, improve overall energy efficiency, and develop carbon dioxide removal techniques. Due to rising crude oil prices and the recent depreciation of the yen, power generation costs are rising. To maintain the current level of rates charged to consumers, the company is implementing radical cost reduction measures by upgrading operations.

Between the years 1991–2000 Chubu Electric is planning to reach a capacity of 10.86 million kw. Of this, 10.3 million kw are to come from sources developed by Chubu Electric—2.24 million kw from nuclear power, 6.1 million kw from coal, 700,000kw from LNG, and 1.26 million kw from hydroelectric sources.

Chubu Electric believes that nuclear power generation is needed to ensure adequate power supplies and a sufficient diversity of sources. In addition to the 1.137 million kw Unit 4 reactor under construction at Hamaoka, the Units 1 and 2 at Ashihama (each with a planned output capacity of 1.1 million kw) are expected to provide power for the early 21st century.

Active development of thermal power, also considered necessary, centered primarily on coal. In addition to the Unit 1 to 3 generators now under construction at Hekinan, each with an output of 700,000kw, plans for the Unit 1 and 2 generators at Shimizu, each with a capacity of one million kw, are being implemented.

With a view to fully exploiting indigenous Japanese energy resources, construction work on hydroelectric plants is proceeding at six sites with a combined total capacity of 1.095 million kw. As for existing hydroelectric plants, remodeling or improvement plans are presently in operation.

Power supply is to be stabilized in relation to demand over the next ten years, with the prospect of maintaining an additional 8–9% of demand in reserve capacity. The proportion of power supplied by nuclear power plants is expected to increase from 18% recorded in 1990, to 22% by the year 2000, while oil-fired power is expected to decrease from 40% to 24% during the same period, in accordance with an accelerated trend toward reduced dependence on petroleum.

Chubu Electric also plans to make improvements to supply reliability. At present, the Chubu trunk transmission line system is composed primarily of 500kv lines, and electricity is distributed around the load centers, or high-consumption areas, of Nagoya. Power transmission facilities are to be expanded to cope with factors such as increasing power demand, progress in development of new power sources, and growing urbanization.

Future developments include the installation of a second 500kv outer loop line. In addition, the 275kv system within the city of Nagoya is being expanded. Specific measures to improve reliability include further lightning protection for transmission lines and reinforcement of lines linking substations, as well as automation of troubleshooting and service restoration procedures. The funds required for the implementation of the above-mentioned projects were set to total ¥618 billion during the fiscal year 1991 and ¥649 billion in 1992.

—Julian James Kinsley

CHUGOKU ELECTRIC POWER COMPANY INC.

4-33, Komachi
Naka-ku, Hiroshima 730-91
Japan
(082) 241 0211
Fax: (082) 244 3753

Public Company
Incorporated: 1951
Employees: 10,851
Sales: ¥897.5 billion (US$7.19 billion)
Stock Exchanges: Tokyo Osaka

The Chugoku Electric Power Company (CEPCO) generates and supplies electricity to the Chugoku region of Japan, the most westerly part of Japan's main island, Honshu. The region is made up of the prefectures of Yamaguchi, Hiroshima, Shimane, Tottori, and Okayama, which with local heavy industry and a total population of 7.75 million provides the sixth-largest customer base of the nine electric power companies in Japan. Its electricity-generating capacity is dominated by oil- and coal-burning thermal power stations, though many oil-burning stations are currently being converted to run on imported coal. The company also utilizes hydroelectric power to a great extent and is diversifying its generating capacity into liquefied natural gas (LNG)-powered plants. In February 1989, 15 years after opening its first nuclear power station, the company began operating its second, both located in the Shimane prefecture. Both coal and LNG are becoming more important as CEPCO seeks to further diversify its generating base.

CEPCO was incorporated along with the other eight regional electric power companies in May 1951, but the story of its foundation goes back to the start of the Allied occupation of Japan in 1945. Japan's energy-intensive, military industrial complex, centered around the production of steel, ships, and munitions, had been largely destroyed at the beginning of the occupation. Although the nuclear bomb dropped on Hiroshima in August 1945 had all but destroyed the main industrial city of the Chugoku region, and enormous damage had been caused by conventional bombing of other industrial sites in the region, Chugoku's electricity-generating facilities had survived the war relatively unscathed. The first year of the Allied occupation saw an energy surplus in the region due to the wartime depletion of industrial demand. This pattern was mirrored

throughout the country. As the process of postwar reconstruction gathered pace, however, demand for electricity increased dramatically and soon exceeded supply. The General Headquarters of the Allied Powers (GHQ) feared that an expansion of electricity production under the surviving and highly centralized wartime structure of the Japan Electricity Generation and Transmission Company (JEGTCO) and the nine local distribution companies could be a step in the direction of rearmament. The wartime structure itself had played a key role in Japan's military expansion in the first place. In 1948 GHQ decided to dismantle the centralized JEGTCO structure and replace it with nine regionally-based, vertically-integrated electricity generation and distribution companies. After a certain amount of disagreement between GHQ and the fledgling Japanese government about the precise structure, status, and organization of the new companies, the government acted to establish the nine electric power companies by implementing the Electricity Utility Industry Reorganization Order and the Public Utilities Order.

On May 1, 1951 operating rights and facilities of the state-run Chugoku branch of the Japan Electricity Generation and Transmission Company and the Chugoku Electric Power Distribution Company were taken over by the newly created Chugoku Electric Power Company. Under government decree, the new company was given the task of generating and supplying electric power to the entire Chugoku district.

While the demand for electricity had already caught up with supply in the late 1940s as a result of rapid reconstruction, the manufacturing economy of Chugoku was given a further boost in the 1950s by the need for components and material support for the war raging on the Korean peninsula. The resulting surge in demand for electricity from local industry stimulated CEPCO to seek the immediate stabilization and expansion of its generating capabilities. The company turned to the United States for technical assistance toward expanding generating capacity through the construction of new coal- and oil-fired thermal power stations.

By the early 1960s the Japanese economy had entered a period of unprecedented growth, and demand for electricity in Chugoku was increasing by over 10% per year. This need was fueled by industrial demand from the chemicals, metals, steel, shipbuilding, and automobile industries which were growing up along the region's southern coastal corridor. New demand also came from the rapidly expanding small-business sector and from private consumers. The latter were beginning to see the fruits of Japan's rapid postwar growth as an increasing number of electric household goods came on the market. The additional electricity necessary for lighting and heating, and in the summer months for air-conditioning, contributed substantially to the company's business.

The surge in demand for electric power required the progressive modernization and expansion of CEPCO's electricity generation and transmission facilities. In 1962 the company completed the 81-kilometer, 220,000-volt Chugoku-West trunk line and substations, resulting in a super-high-voltage transmission system linking the Chugoku region with Kansai to the east and Kyushu to the west. By the mid-1960s the annual rate of growth in electricity demand and production was dramatic.

From the early 1960s new generating facilities developed by CEPCO were predominantly thermal plants using imported oil and coal rather than the more traditional hydroelectric power.

These included a total of five coal-fired plants commissioned at Mizushima and Shin Ube between 1958 and 1964 and oil-powered facilities opened at Kudamatsu and Iwakuni in 1964 and 1966 respectively. In terms of generating volume, hydroelectric power exceeded that of thermal electric power in 1963, but a decade later the balance had changed to 88% thermal, 10% hydroelectric, and 2% nuclear. This was due not only to the new availability of cheap oil from overseas as an alternative source of energy, but also to technological advancements which had brought the cost of building thermal power stations substantially below that of hydroelectric equivalents.

By 1971, after more than 15 years of uninterrupted growth in demand for electricity in the region accompanied by the continued availability of cheap oil, the first signs of a slowdown in CEPCO's performance began to appear. In that year the Organization of Petroleum Exporting Countries (OPEC) managed to secure the first substantial increase in the price it was charging for oil. This did not cause immediate problems for CEPCO other than necessitating a slight revision of revenue projections, though this was more than offset by continued strong demand from the industrial and domestic sectors. On the expenditure side of the company's finances, rising personnel and repair costs were starting to undermine the company's annual financial performance, though not drastically. The company's investment plans were also influenced by government regulations aimed at reducing atmospheric pollution levels which required the installation of expensive flue gas scrubbers in thermal power stations. CEPCO responded to these changing and challenging conditions by bringing forward the completion dates for a number of its new power-generating projects. These included the company's first nuclear power plant at Shimane and two oil-burning plants at Tamashima and Iwakuni.

In early 1971, with Kansaku Yamane as president and Kimio Sakurauchi as chairman, CEPCO was anticipating further steady—and by international standards, spectacular—growth in the forseeable future. However, the outbreak of war in the Middle East in mid-1973 and the subsequent quadrupling of oil prices by OPEC hit Japan harder than any other country in the Organization for Economic Co-operation and Development (OECD) because of the country's heavy dependence on Middle-Eastern oil. The immediate effect on CEPCO was an increase in the price of fuel for its oil-powered thermal generating plants. This resulted in financial difficulties in the short term because the company, like Japan's eight other electric power companies, was not free to pass on the higher fuel rates to its industrial and domestic consumers without approval from the Ministry of International Trade and Industry (MITI). In December 1973 the Japanese government introduced measures to enforce conservation of electric power, but it was not until later the following year that MITI finally consented to allowing a 60% electricity rate increase for CEPCO and the other electric power companies. The first sharp rise in the electricity rate for 20 years, though alleviating short-term financial pressures on the industry as a whole, failed to ultimately benefit the power companies because the price of oil continued to rise. Furthermore, as higher charges were passed on to the large energy-intensive manufacturing sector, output fell, inflation rose, and the economy moved into its first real post-war recession.

The oil-price hikes which continued throughout the 1970s stimulated a major reappraisal of Japan's resource security. While individual power and oil companies were able to meet their requirements for oil by paying inflated prices at spot markets around the world, it soon became apparent that Japan needed to diversify its supply of energy away from the Middle East and its oil.

Although a number of projects had been in the planning phase for some time, the events of 1973–1974 added urgency to strategic decision-making in Tokyo and at CEPCO's head office in Hiroshima.

The commissioning in 1974 of the Shimane Boiling Water Reactor (BWR) as CEPCO's first nuclear power unit, with a capacity of 460 megawatts, contributed substantially to oil-saving measures. In 1976 the diversification policy was pursued actively through a large financial commitment towards construction of the 620-megawatt pumped-storage-type hydroelectric power complex at Nabara.

By 1976 both local and national economies were recovering, and CEPCO's sales for that year increased by 21% over the previous year after much lower sales in the 1974–1975 period.

In spite of the strenuous efforts made by CEPCO after the first oil shock in 1973–1974, by the time of the second oil crisis, following the Iranian revolution in 1979, CEPCO was still heavily dependent on imported oil for electricity generation. Its vulnerability to rising oil prices was such that in 1980 CEPCO was forced to raise its rates again, this time by 67%, the highest rate rise of the nine electric power companies. In the same year, in order to accelerate the diversifiation policy, it was decided that three existing oil-burning power stations at Shin Ube would be converted to coal power.

In 1981 CEPCO was still dependent on oil for 52% of its generating capacity, the highest dependency of the nine electric power companies. To reduce further the destabilizing effects of this dependency, in 1980 plans were launched by CEPCO to import coal from China and Australia, and since 1989 liquefied natural gas has been imported from Australia.

The Three Mile Island nuclear accident in the United States in 1979 led to a suspension of nuclear-plant construction plans in Japan for one year, and resulted in a general distrust of all nuclear-related matters by the Japanese population, especially in the Hiroshima region. Nevertheless, the building of Shimane No. 2 started in July 1984. The plant began operations less than five years later, in February 1989, adding a further 820 megawatts of capacity to the existing output of 460 megawatts from the Shimane No. 1 reactor. Also in 1989, plans were completed to build a third nuclear reactor in Yamaguchi Prefecture to provide electric power for the early 21st century.

In 1991 CEPCO's chairman, Kenichiro Matsutani, headed a company with a much-reduced dependency on imported oil and a generating capacity well diversified between imported LNG, coal, and oil, and locally-produced hydroelectric and nuclear power. As the leader of the Chugoku business community, with a regional monopoly in the supply and distribution of electricity to domestic and industrial customers, CEPCO is now better prepared for fluctuations in the price of energy resources and demand for electricity than it has been for many years.

Further Reading: Thomas, Steve and Chris Cragg, *Japan Power Station Fuel Demand to 2000,* London, Financial Times Business Information, 1986; *History of Electric Power Industry in Japan,* Tokyo, Japan Electric Power Information Centre, 1988.

—Stephen Christopher Kremer

CMS ENERGY CORPORATION

330 Town Center Drive
Dearborn, Michigan 48126
U.S.A.
(313) 436-9200
Fax: (313) 436-9225

Public Company
Incorporated: 1910 as Consumers Power Company
Employees: 9,624
Sales: $2.98 billion
Stock Exchange: New York

CMS Energy Corporation is a diversified energy concern with utility and nonutility operations. Its principal subsidiary, Consumers Power, provides electricity and natural gas for much of Michigan's lower peninsula, excluding Detroit. Non-utility assets include an exploration and production firm, NOMECO Oil & Gas; holdings in independent power production facilities such as the Midland Cogeneration Venture; and companies involved in natural gas transportation, storage, and marketing.

CMS was established in 1987 as a holding company for Consumers Power, but its roots can be traced to independent Michigan gas and electric companies in the late 1800s. In the 1850s, 1860s, and 1870s groups of merchants in Kalamazoo, Pontiac, Jackson, and four other Michigan towns created the state's first gas-lighting companies. In the 1880s Michigan's electric lighting businesses began taking shape. First was the Grand Rapids Electric Light and Power Company. Organized by William Powers, it completed one of the world's first hydroelectric systems in July 1880.

By the late 1880s gas and electric lighting operations were ripe for rationalization and consolidation. The man who brought order to the situation was W.A. Foote. Foote, a young miller from Adrian, Michigan, saw the earliest hydroelectric plants and observed the potential of electricity for lighting streets and houses. With his younger brother J.B. Foote, an engineer, W.A. Foote built hydroelectric companies first in Adrian and then in Jackson, Michigan.

In Jackson, he and his partner Samuel Jarvis, who ran an iron works and built the machines Foote needed, organized Jackson Electrical Light Works and beat the already ensconced competition by installing the town's first street lights. Foote and Jarvis soon repeated their success in Battle Creek, Albion, and other Michigan towns. Capital was often short but W.A.

Foote had a knack for convincing wealthy people to invest in his company.

Among his projects was a series of dams on the Kalamazoo River. In 1896 Foote visited the Kalamazoo River and saw its potential for hydroelectric energy, but whether the electricity would travel 24 miles from the dam to the town was questionable. Consulting with his brother J.B. and engineer George Stecker, Foote decided to build. The completion of the first of these dams, the Trowbridge, coincided with one of Foote's many takeovers. This time it was Kalamazoo Electric Company, the name of which he soon changed to Kalamazoo Valley Electric.

Foote often made competitors his allies. In the late 1890s, George Erwin, a Michigan real estate broker, bought up the dam-building rights to the Muskegon River and tried to get J.B. Foote to build a dam there. W.A. Foote squelched that deal but then bought a third of Erwin's partnership, and in 1906 built the Rogers Dam for Erwin and his associates. Foote sold the electricity to the Grand Rapids–Muskegon Water Power Electric Company, of which he had lately become a director.

During these years, the demand for electricity was exploding, especially due to the electric streetcar, which appeared on the scene in the early 1890s. Foote not only sold electricity for streetcars, he and his companies often held substantial shares of them.

Foote also controlled interurbans, electric train lines that ran between cities. Although Foote's first interurban from Jackson to Ann Arbor, Michigan, was a failure, he eventually controlled circuits from Jackson to Battle Creek and Battle Creek to Kalamazoo.

In 1904 Foote consolidated his properties into Commonwealth Power Company, headquartered in Jackson. In total, he had 2,472 electric and gas customers.

In 1905, while seeking financing for dams on the Au Sable River in Michigan, Foote met representatives of an investment banking firm, Hodenpyl-Walbridge & Company, with whom he decided to establish a large utility holding company. Because of regulatory difficulties, the merger could not be consummated in the state of Michigan. Instead, in 1910 they incorporated a new Maine company, Commonwealth Power Railway & Light Company. It would act as an umbrella company for Foote's Consumers Power—itself organized to be a holding company for his electric concerns in Michigan—as well as Hodenpyl-Walbridge's Michigan Light Company and a number of smaller concerns.

The merger enabled Foote to build six dams on the Au Sable. The new dams and their power transmission lines allowed Foote to establish an integrated power system for Michigan. Previously, power had been directed to a specific community. Now, with the aid of a young innovator named Timothy A. Kenney, Foote was able to effect an essentially modern system of central switching.

The merger also brought two important new players into the picture. George Hardy became Anton G. Hodenpyl's partner after Hodenpyl and Henry D. Walbridge parted ways, and Bernard Capen Cobb, Walbridge's protege, became chairman of Hodenpyl-Hardy's electric, gas, and transportation properties. After Foote's death in 1915, Cobb became president of both Commonwealth Power Railway & Light and Consumers Power and another Hodenpyl-Walbridge man, C.W. Tippy, became Consumers Power's general manager.

World War I expanded demand for electricity while severely depleting capital and personnel. At Michigan Light new, automated gas processes increased output. At Consumers the war's credit squeeze meant the company had to be rescued by loans from the War Finance Corporation. After the war, Consumers abandoned flat rates in favor of metering, or charges based on the number of rooms, motors, or lights. Rates also standardized statewide.

In the early 1920s capital remained tight. Hodenpyl-Hardy had Consumers Power workers sell preferred shares of Consumers Power to customers. At $95 a share, the stock would pay a $7 dividend. After a brief postwar recession and a devastating 1922 ice storm, business rebounded. Michigan's industry grew and a new gas-powered water heater buoyed consumer demand. Between 1921 and 1929 the number of gas customers rose from 60,291 to 162,590 while electric customers increased from 130,421 to 296,030.

The 1920s were also a period of consolidation and acquisition. In 1922 Consumers Power and Michigan Light merged under a single management. In succeeding years Consumers bought a variety of large and small utilities around Michigan. Among these were Thornapple Gas and Electric, Southern Michigan Light and Power, Lansing Fuel and Gas, Charlotte Gas, and Citizens Electric Company of Battle Creek.

The company's passenger rail business was losing customers to automobiles and buses. In 1924 Cobb divided Commonwealth Power Railway and Light into two companies, Commonwealth Power Corporation and Electric Railway Securities Company. The latter was set up to liquidate the railway properties.

In the late 1920s Commonwealth Power went through several corporate reorganizations which were preceded by a giant acquisition. In 1928 Cobb gained control of Southeastern Power & Light Company, which did business in Alabama, Mississippi, Georgia, and part of Florida. In the same year Hodenpyl-Hardy & Company joined with Stevens & Wood, an engineering and construction firm that controlled Penn-Ohio Edison Company, to create Allied Power & Light Corporation as a holding company for Commonwealth Power & Light and Penn-Ohio Edison. In the process of creating Allied, Hodenpyl-Hardy went out of business, and Cobb became chairman of Allied. This new structure was covered by yet another corporate shell, The Commonwealth & Southern Corporation (C&S), which in 1929 joined Commonwealth Power, Southeastern Power & Light, and Penn-Ohio Edison. This time Cobb became president and chairman of Commonwealth & Southern and several other companies.

The early 1930s brought management changes both at Consumers Power and at Commonwealth & Southern. In 1932 B.C. Cobb resigned from the presidency of Consumers Power and was replaced by Timothy A. Kenney, who had earlier designed the company's dispatching system. In October 1933 Charles Tippy, the company's general manager, died in a car accident. Dan E. Karn, Tippy's assistant, took his place. In January 1933 B.C. Cobb resigned from the presidency of Commonwealth & Southern and was replaced by future Republican presidential candidate Wendell Willkie.

Through the 1930s Willkie sold the public on electric power, fought the drive for government-owned utilities, and worked to rid Commonwealth & Southern's board of super-holding-company representatives who were trying to join all of the United States's electric companies under a giant holding company. Willkie boosted consumption by selling electric appliances. As an incentive, he pioneered the "objective" rate, which lowered the kilowatt-hour price to customers who used more energy.

During Willkie's tenure, the Tennessee Valley Authority (TVA) encroached on Commonwealth & Southern's territories, and the Public Utility Holding Company Act of 1935 pronounced what was ultimately Commonwealth & Southern's death sentence by prohibiting utility holding companies whose systems were not contiguous and interconnected. Because the TVA and C&S competed head to head in the South, Willkie challenged the TVA in court and on the speaking platform, but C&S eventually had to sell some of its properties to the TVA.

The TVA issue propelled Willkie into national politics and in 1940 he left Commonwealth & Southern to run for U.S. president. His replacement was Justin R. Whiting, a lawyer who had helped liquidate Consumers Power's streetcar business and later worked for some of Commonwealth & Southern's backers. Whiting was to preside over the breakup of Commonwealth & Southern but before this could be effected, World War II intervened. In Michigan, even before the war, the demand for electricity was tremendous. Dan Karn and his assistant general manager, Wilson Arthur, did their best to meet requirements but personnel and capital were too scarce to add any capacity.

When the war ended, the C&S breakup again became an issue. After wrangling for years about the exact method to use, on July 15, 1949, each share of C&S preferred was exchanged for 2.8 shares of Consumers Power common, 0.55 of a share of Central Illinois Light, common, and $1 in cash. The remaining assets went to C&S's common shareholders. Consumers Power was now an independent entity with Whiting as its president.

After the war, Michigan experienced a huge boom both in population and industry. Dan E. Karn became president of Consumers Power in 1951, and by 1955 the company had again doubled its customer base—788,00 electric and 427,000 gas—and was stretching its capacity.

To meet the electric demand, Consumers Power built three new steam plants. Michigan was not self-sufficient in natural gas supplies, so Consumers Power bought from Panhandle Eastern Pipe Line Company and stored supplies for peak demand in disused underground shafts. For this purpose, in 1946 Consumers Power established Michigan Gas Storage Company.

The availability of cheap natural gas and the expansion of new homes made gas Consumers's biggest product. In 1955, however, the price of gas went up, and Consumers was not allowed to pass costs on to the customer. By the end of the 1950s it had 858,000 electric and 559,000 gas customers.

In 1960 Alphonse H. Aymond became chief executive officer of Consumers Power, and J.H. Campbell became president. Aymond, a financing expert, had seen the breakup of Commonwealth & Southern. Campbell, an engineer, had spent his life with utilities and was interested in nuclear power.

Although 1960 profits declined in proportion to revenue, Consumers was essentially in good shape. Aided by expansion in the residential and industrial belt around Detroit, gas revenues increased nearly fourfold between 1950 and 1961 to $100.8 million. Its electric business showed a 110% gain to $180 million.

Much of the 1960s was devoted to securing reliable sources of gas and electricity. In 1962 Consumers opened an experimental nuclear facility at Big Rock, Michigan. In 1963 it acquired underground storage facilities and ten oil and gas fields from Panhandle Eastern. In 1966 it announced plans for a $93 million nuclear power plant called Palisades, on Lake Michigan. The same year a power pool with four other utilities was formed to ensure reliability during peak demand.

In 1967 the company began a two-unit nuclear plant at Midland, Michigan. Scheduled to be completed in 1975 at an estimated cost of $267 million, the nuclear plant was plagued by cost overruns, opposition by environmentalists, quality problems, and capital shortages. An early critic of the plant was Midland resident Mary Sinclair. Over the years, Sinclair intervened in licensing hearings on the project, alleging many safety problems and instances of shoddy workmanship, and causing Consumers Power to make many expensive alterations.

Also in 1967 Consumers Power formed Northern Michigan Exploration Company (NOMECO) to prospect for natural gas and other hydrocarbons in the northern part of Michigan's lower peninsula. This subsidiary would prove increasingly important as it branched out into offshore and foreign exploration.

As it neared completion, the Palisades nuclear power plant began having problems. The Sierra Club and fishing groups charged that the plant would pollute the neighboring lake, and Consumers had to install $15 million of pollution control equipment before the Atomic Energy Commission (AEC) would license it. After its completion in December 1971, at a cost of $188 million—double the original price—the plant was plagued by breakdowns. In the mid-1970s, Consumers Power filed a $300 million suit charging Bechtel Power Cooperation and several other contractors on the project with various abuses.

In the 1970s Consumers was beset by additional regulatory difficulties and cost overruns. In 1973 the company suspended construction at Midland because of what the AEC saw as inadequate welding inspection procedures. The same year a synthetic gas plant at Marysville, Michigan, was completed $70 million over budget. The gas and oil Marysville produced cost $2 more per gallon than gas and oil from the pipeline.

As Midland costs mounted, Consumers sought rate increases. State regulators blamed the company for cost overruns and refused to raise rates. Earnings became depressed, and the company could not raise money in the capital markets. The utility had to abandon plans for two additional nuclear units, cut almost $850 million from its construction spending plans for the next five years, and cut 540 employees from its work force of 11,500.

In 1977 John D. Selby, a nuclear engineer, replaced A.H. Aymond as chief executive officer. Aymond remained as chairman. The management change, however, did not reverse the nuclear situation. In 1977 it was discovered that portions of the Midland plant were sinking. In 1979 the Nuclear Regulatory Commission fined Consumers Power $450,000 for safety violations at the Pallisades reactor. In 1980 Bechtel, the main contractor at Midland, submitted a new estimate boosting the total price from $1.67 billion to $3.1 billion. In 1983 Dow Chemical Co., which was to be Midland's prime customer, canceled its contract to buy steam from the plant and sued Consumers Power for negligence.

Consumers Power finally abandoned Midland in 1984, after investing $4.1 billion on the project. Selby who had risen to chairman, had also become a lightning rod for critics, and that summer Roger Fischer, chief of staff of the Michigan Public Service Commission, called for Selby's resignation.

The Midland situation had destroyed the company's credit standing. Strapped for cash and with no rate increase in sight, it could not pay its bills. Some banks claimed Consumers was in default on loans but the utility disputed the claims.

In March 1985 Selby retired. In reaction, the Michigan Public Service Commission agreed to give Consumers higher rates if it would pledge not to resume Midland construction, restructure its debt, promise not to declare bankruptcy, and agree not to pay more than token dividends.

In November 1985, Consumers Power named William T. McCormick Jr. as its new chief executive officer. In 1987 he strengthened the company's financial integrity by reincorporating it as CMS Energy Corporation, a holding company with utility (Consumers Power) and nonutility (NOMECO Oil & Gas) assets. The same year, he banded together with six other partners, including Dow Chemical, to form the Midland Cogeneration Venture (MCV). MCV, in which CMS has a 49% stake, used some of Midland's abandoned nuclear assets to create a 1,300-megawatt gas and electricity plant.

In October of 1987 McCormick agreed to place the Palisades nuclear plant into a joint venture with Bechtel Power and Westinghouse Electric. The transaction, if ever consummated, would yield CMS at least $450 million, much more than the plant's $311 million book value. The transaction still awaited regulatory approval in the early 1990s. In addition, he set up CMS Gas Marketing to take advantage of CMS's extensive experience with natural gas.

By 1989 McCormick's efforts began to pay off. Upon the cogeneration plant's completion, CMS gained $1.5 billion in a sale and leaseback of the Midland site to the cogeneration venture. In the wake of the cogeneration venture's success—the first conversion of its kind—CMS set up CMS Generation Company to convert other abandoned nuclear power plants into conventional fuel-powered facilities.

In November 1989, CMS reestablished its common stock dividend. Under McCormick, Consumers Power had become the leanest major utility in the United States, with an average of 283 customers served per employee. At its fossil-fueled plants, efficiency was among the top in the nation and the National Safety Council named it the safest major electric and gas utility.

In 1990 CMS finally wrote off the losses from the Midland plant taking a pretax charge of $657.2 million, giving it a fourth-quarter loss of $604.2 million, or $7.42 a share. For the entire year the net loss was $493.4 million, or $6.07 a share. Company officials expected no further significant losses from the plant. On the positive side, CMS's nonutility operations grew in 1990, although utility operations continued to make up the bulk of sales.

Principal Subsidiaries: Consumers Power Company; CMS Enterprises Company; CMS Gas Company.

Further Reading: Bush, George, *Future Builders: The Story of Michigan's Consumers Power Company,* New York, McGraw-Hill Book Company, 1973; Ernshwiller, John, "Losing Power: How a Thriving Utility Became a Sagging One After Its Giant Step," *The Wall Street Journal,* October 8, 1974.

—Jordan Wankoff

COLUMBIA GAS
System

THE COLUMBIA GAS SYSTEM, INC.

20 Montchanin Road
Wilmington, Delaware 19807
U.S.A.
(302) 429-5000
Fax: (302) 429-5461

Public Company
Incorporated: 1926 as Columbia Gas & Electric Corporation
Employees: 10,379
Sales: $2.17 billion
Stock Exchanges: New York Philadelphia Toronto

The Columbia Gas System, Inc. (Columbia) is one of the largest integrated natural gas systems in the United States. Columbia has two production subsidiaries that explore for and produce natural gas at numerous sites throughout North America. The company also operates five distribution subsidiaries that serve 1.8 million customers—residential, commercial, and industrial—in Ohio, Kentucky, Pennsylvania, Virginia, and Maryland. Columbia also provides wholesale service to other gas distributors. Gas transmission for other producers throughout its 23,000 miles of pipeline makes up the largest segment of the company's revenues.

Columbia Corporation, formed in 1906 in Huntington, West Virginia, produced natural gas in that state and eastern Kentucky for delivery to Cincinnati, Ohio. Later renamed Columbia Gas & Electric Company, it doubled in size with the acquisition of Ohio Fuel Corporation in 1926. The resulting company was incorporated in Delaware as Columbia Gas & Electric Corporation.

The addition of Ohio Fuel greatly increased the volume of gas that the company sold. Natural gas had rapidly decreased in price as gathering and transmission systems improved and usage increased. Columbia's electricity sales, although still significant, were flattening. By the late 1920s it was clear that natural gas held the key to the company's growth. Oil was a companion product that Columbia Gas & Electric exploited.

The arrival of high-pressure pipelines in the late 1920s broadened the company's growth potential; natural gas then could be transported vast distances from the fields where it originated. Columbia pushed its lines eastward throughout Pennsylvania, and into New Jersey and New York state. In 1930 the acquisition of a 50% interest in Panhandle Eastern Pipe Line Company allowed Columbia to connect its eastern lines with natural gas fields in Texas. Meanwhile, Columbia Gas & Electric had gained control of virtually all the important reserves in northern Appalachia.

The greater availability of natural gas during the 1930s resulted in an increase in its utilization by industry. Natural gas burns almost twice as hot as manufactured gas and burns more cleanly. As its price fell, demand rose. At the same time that industry was discovering natural gas, however, industrial output was being curtailed due to the Great Depression. As a result, Columbia's earnings declined steadily from 1929 until 1935. In 1935, however, rebounding earnings doubled those of the previous year.

In 1935 the Public Utility Holding Company Act brought Columbia Gas & Electric under federal regulation. Antitrust litigation forced the company to divest Columbia Oil & Gasoline, the subsidiary that controlled Panhandle Eastern Pipe Line Company. In 1936 Detroit, Michigan, was linked with the Columbia system, and natural gas was transmitted directly from Columbia's Texas fields. The connection helped Columbia reach new heights in sales and earnings for 1936.

In 1938 the Justice Department filed an antitrust suit against Columbia Gas & Electric citing restraint of trade in the natural gas industry. Antitrust suits plagued Columbia for the next few years. In 1946 the company was forced to sell off the last of its electrical subsidiaries, a process that had been underway for several years. The company changed its name to The Columbia Gas System, Inc. in 1948 to reflect this change. Columbia was now almost exclusively in the natural gas business, although oil remained a part of these operations because the two resources were usually found together. During World War II demand for fuel was such that many turned to natural gas. The popularity of natural gas as a fuel was so great by the end of World War II, that suppliers simply could not keep up with demand, and Columbia had to turn down new requests for service. Gas shortages continued until the early 1950s, when pipelines connected Columbia with gas fields in the Southwest and the Gulf of Mexico.

The Columbia Gas System grew in the 1950s through acquisitions in and around the company's chief operating region—northern Appalachia. In 1956 the company began a corporate simplification process aimed at reducing the number of subsidiaries subject to both federal and state regulation. The consolidation was completed in 1971.

Throughout the 1960s Columbia performed very well. Revenues increased an average of 5.9% each year between 1961 and 1971. By 1967 Columbia was the largest integrated natural gas system in the United States. Demand for natural gas had doubled between 1956 and 1970, and throughout the 1970s demand for natural gas heavily outweighed supply. Columbia blamed U.S. regulation of interstate gas prices for this situation.

Columbia reacted to shortages by broadening its search for gas. Drilling efforts increased in Appalachia, offshore Louisiana, and in Alaska. Columbia looked to liquefied natural gas (LNG) imports to help fill the gap between supply and demand. LNG was shipped from Algeria to a new regasification plant in Maryland. Although the price of natural gas was climbing, it still remained a relatively cheap form of energy in the early 1970s. In Columbus, Ohio, for example, the cost of heating a home by gas was about half that of using heating oil. Columbia's gas sales reached a new peak in 1972. The relative economy of natural gas continued to grow in 1973 and 1974, when the OPEC oil embargo sent the price of oil to new heights.

By 1974 the natural gas shortage was becoming critical. Regulators were reluctant to grant rate increases, causing Columbia's funds earmarked for new exploration to remain limited. Columbia curtailed delivery of gas, and no new customers were accepted.

In April 1974 Columbia began producing synthetic natural gas from oil at high cost. The company was capable of synthesizing 4% of its needs from a single plant. Natural gas supplies continued to fall far short of demand, and in 1976 25% less gas was sold than in the company's peak in 1972.

The severe winter of 1976–1977 was devastating for Columbia. Caught without adequate reserves after selling gas it projected would be in excess of demand, the company cut service. Factories and schools closed for weeks in some of the company's operating areas, and public outrage focused on Columbia. Columbia Gas System, then selling 7% of all natural gas sold in the United States, attempted to remedy the situation by signing long-term contracts to buy gas from producers.

Utility regulators tried to remedy the shortage problem in the late 1970s by allowing rate increases that afforded Columbia improved earnings despite the low volume. Earnings in 1978 were up sharply over 1977.

Legislation was passed in 1978 that effectively deregulated the prices gas producers could charge at the wellhead. Intended to give incentive to producers to drill new wells, it resulted in very rich, long-term deals at guaranteed rates for producers. Hoping to ensure that it would never again experience shortages like those of 1976–1977, Columbia Gas System entered into long-term contracts with producers at fixed rates during the late 1970s. It was a seller's market, and producers required pipelines like Columbia to accept take-or-pay clauses, which ensured that any gas the producers tapped would be purchased no matter what the market conditions were.

Columbia then had assured supply. The company's higher prices were more easily passed on to customers since regulation had become less stringent. Problems arose, however, because regulatory approval was required on rate increases or decreases. Once Columbia's price went up, it stayed up until regulatory commissions allowed it to drop. Columbia's gas was actually priced 28% above the national average in 1980. In response, Columbia's industrial customers, already annoyed by the interrupted service of the 1970s, defected to cheaper energy sources. In 1982 Columbia's largest single industrial customer, the Sohio Chemical anhydrous-ammonia plant in Lima, Ohio, quit Columbia altogether. The plant had previously bought nearly 2% of Columbia's total output. By the time rate reductions came through, many of Columbia's industrial customers had deserted the company.

The recession of the early 1980s hit Columbia's remaining industrial users hard, causing demand to fall. At the same time, energy prices worldwide collapsed. Columbia still had long-term contracts with producers to buy natural gas at the high prices of the late 1970s—gas it had to buy whether or not it could be sold.

In 1982 the company tried to cancel all its contracts, claiming that the catastrophic effects of the recession on Columbia's customers constituted a *force majeure*, nullifying the contracts. Producers and other pipelines serving Columbia refused, offering only to renegotiate. Major lawsuits followed in 1983, and, although gas producers eventually did renegotiate with other pipelines and distributors owing to the difficult economic times, Columbia was dealt with less cordially.

In 1985 Columbia faced possible bankruptcy. Still bound to long-term contracts, the company offered its major suppliers $800 million to settle the take-or-pay contracts. Faced with little choice, the producers took the deal. Columbia reduced prices and sold its gas at a total of $1 billion below cost over the next two years.

In the mid-1980s, new Federal Energy Regulatory Commission rules required pipelines to ship other distributors' gas. Columbia entered this business heavily. By 1989 only 30% of the natural gas moving through Columbia's pipelines was owned by the company, compared with 90% a decade earlier. By 1990 Columbia's share was down to 6%. In the late 1980s Columbia announced it intended to resume shipping its own gas—an activity that was riskier but also more profitable.

Losses plagued the company throughout the later 1980s, as it continued to fulfill its long-term contracts. Columbia continued to write off millions of dollars each year, and expected to continue to do so through 1995. Up to $40 million in losses would be recovered annually through rate increases, but the rest was a certain loss.

In 1990 unusually warm weather caused gas prices on the spot—short-term—market to remain much lower than expected. Columbia suspended its dividend payment in June 1991, and the company was again in serious financial straits. Columbia and a subsidiary, Columbia Gas Transmission, filed for protection from creditors under Chapter 11 of the U.S. Bankruptcy Code in July.

While the future of Columbia was uncertain, several factors caused optimism. Clean air legislation refocused attention on natural gas as a clean fuel source, and successful horizontal drilling techniques promised to improve efficiency in Columbia's gas production. Cogeneration, the process of generating heat and electricity simultaneously, has been initiated by Columbia facilities in New York and New Jersey.

Whether or not these factors will put The Columbia Gas System back in good health remains to be seen. The company's sheer size makes it a difficult ship to sink. The prospects for natural gas as a fuel source are excellent, however, and as a major supplier, Columbia Gas System might profit from the fuel's bright future.

Principal Subsidiaries: Columbia Gas Development Corporation; Columbia Natural Resources, Inc.; Columbia Gas Transmission Corporation; Columbia Gulf Transmission Company; Columbia LNG Corporation; Columbia Gas of Kentucky, Inc.; Columbia Gas of Ohio, Inc.; Columbia Gas of Maryland, Inc.; Columbia Gas of Pennsylvania, Inc.; Commonwealth Gas Services, Inc.; Columbia Atlantic Trading Corporation; Columbia Coal Gasification Corporation; Columbia Propane Corporation; Commonwealth Propane, Inc.; The Inland Gas Company, Inc.; TriStar Capital Corporation; TriStar Ventures Corporation.

Further Reading: Pomroy, John, "Recent Merger Aids Earning Power of Columbia Gas & Electric," *The Magazine of Wall*

Street, January 29, 1927; "Columbia Gas—Sound Income Issue," *Financial World*, August 23, 1972; Baldwin, WIlliam, "Paying the Piper," *Forbes*, November 22, 1982.

—Thomas M. Tucker

COMMONWEALTH EDISON COMPANY

One First National Plaza
Chicago, Illinois 60690
U.S.A.
(312) 294-4321
Fax: (312) 294-2995

Public Company
Incorporated: 1907
Employees: 18,910
Sales: $5.26 billion
Stock Exchanges: New York Midwest Pacific

Commonwealth Edison (Com Ed) is responsible for the production, transmission, and distribution of electricity to more than three million wholesale and retail customers in northern Illinois. This company serves 70% of the population of Illinois, including Chicago and its greater metropolitan area. Commonwealth Edison uses nuclear-generated power to supply 80% of its electricity, more than any other investor-owned electric company in the United States.

Samuel Insull helped make Commonwealth Edison the giant company it is today. In fact, he laid the foundations of the electrical power industry. Insull popularized mass production and selling at the lowest possible cost, developed modern public relations, and devised methods for marketing securities in a way that led to the large public corporations of today.

At the age of 21 Insull possessed outstanding financial acumen and unwavering ambition to succeed in business. In the early 1880s, he traveled from his home in London to the United States to take his position as Thomas Edison's personal secretary. Insull gained from his employer vast financial responsibilities and decision-making power, while quadrupling sales at Edison Electric Light Company's main factory and selling central power plants to cities across the country.

Edison's company was renamed Edison General Electric Company in 1889. In 1892 the company merged with Thomson-Houston Electric Company, forming General Electric Company. Insull was offered a $36,000-a-year executive position at General Electric (GE). Instead he took a $12,000-a-year position as president of Chicago Edison Company. The 32-year-old Insull borrowed $250,000 from the newspaper tycoon Marshall Field, purchased a large share of the company's stock, and then went to work selling electricity.

There were almost four dozen electric companies competing for Chicago's electricity business when Insull came on the scene. At the time, less than 1% of Chicago's homes used electric lamps. Insull's goal was to grow—exponentially. Expansion spelled greater volume, which meant lower unit costs of production, which meant greater profit. More income meant more investment, and more growth, and so on.

Insull formed a 25-person sales department and, according to Forrest McDonald in *Insull*, told them to "sell at the lowest possible price." Insull was not lowering prices to compete. Insull thought competition was "economically wrong," and was, in fact, lowering prices in an attempt to wipe out competition. Insull quietly bought exclusive rights to electric equipment manufactured by General Electric and most other U.S. manufacturers to thwart competition. In his first 42 months in Chicago, Insull increased Chicago Edison's sales almost five times. He also expanded Chicago Edison by buying out competitors.

Local politicians soon caught wind of Edison's success. Accustomed to receiving kickbacks from companies doing business in Chicago, a group of politicians devised a plan to extort $1 million from Chicago Edison. They formed a dummy company, called Commonwealth Electric Company and gave it a 50-year franchise to provide the city's electricity. The founders of Commonwealth planned to force Insull to buy their company for $1 million or be frozen out of the market. They did not realize, however, that Insull owned the rights to the equipment it would take to run this company. Insull therefore was able to buy Commonwealth with its 50-year electricity franchise for the city of Chicago for just $50,000. In 1907 Insull merged Commonwealth Electric Company and Chicago Edison Company to form Commonwealth Edison, a company whose sales exceeded the combined sales of New York Edison, Brooklyn Edison, and Boston Edison. After the merger, Insull formed a holding company called Middle West Utilities (MWU) to own small interests in Com Ed and other investor-owned utilities. MWU itself was also a publicly traded company. Insull controlled MWU, and by 1912 MWU, in turn, controlled utilities in 13 states through relatively small shareholdings.

Insull wanted nothing less than a monopoly wherever he operated. In order to get monopolies, he was willing to sacrifice a degree of control. Therefore, Insull agreed that his exclusive franchises with municipalities, should be regulated by a state commission.

In 1906 Insull's customers numbered 50,000; in 1909, the number was up to 100,000. Com Ed's growth was both rapid and smart. Insull diversified customers, spreading the demand for power as much as possible. For instance, he obtained major contracts with Chicago electric streetcar companies, which drew the most power when residential customers were at work and not at home using electric lamps and appliances. He went after industry, offering huge subsidies to induce these daytime users away from using small, private power stations. Insull termed this approach to business "massing production," and was succeeding at it before Henry Ford gained fame as a mass producer of the automobile.

Taking an idea he learned from the English electricity business, Insull charged a dual rate for power; a higher rate for the first several hours of electrical usage, and a progressively lower rate thereafter. This covered the costs of adding equipment for new customers and encouraged greater use. He also kept cutting rates. The company, from early on, regularly paid out an 8¢ dividend to shareholders.

Insull approached generating electricity with the same zeal he showed for selling electricity. He ignored the apparent limits of the day's technology, pushing his engineers to build generators that were several times larger than any other generators in existence. Insull was progressive in his dealings with workers not because of personal conviction, but to ensure the smooth operation of Com Ed's facilities. Insull hired women and minorities, gave his employees relatively generous benefits, and maintained a cooperative relationship with labor leaders.

Insull was ahead of his time in yet another significant way—he was a master at public relations. He established an advertising department as early as 1901. His rate cuts were well timed and well publicized. He published and distributed a free tabloid, *Electric City*, which shaped a positive public opinion of electricity, and, of course, the electric company itself. Insull began publishing annual reports 15 years before they became standard.

During World War I Insull was a fervent supporter of England. He personally spent $250,000 attempting to sway public opinion in favor of the U.S. entry into the war, after which Insull worked to raise money for the war effort. After World War I, Insull was able to capitalize on the high profile he had cultivated during the war, to promote the interests of Com Ed.

The post-World War I period was a time of immense growth in demand for the electric industry. In 1923, the year the electric refrigerator became available to residential customers, Commonwealth Edison added over 75,000 new customers to its service area, its largest annual increase up to that time. Commonwealth Edison proved to be the only major steam-power electric company in the nation that neither raised its rates nor cut its dividends during the postwar period, though money for expansion was scarce. Insull exploited an idea he got from Pacific Gas & Electric, and launched a hugely successful customer ownership drive. From 1919 to 1921 the number of Com Ed shareholders who lived in Illinois grew from 50,000 to 500,000. Insull's name was equated with trust by small investors.

The phenomenal control Insull had been able to exercise over his empire's destiny began to crumble around 1926. Insull made several less-than-wise, if not illegal, financial moves in the next few years. After the October 1929 stock market crash, Insull, who believed the Great Depression would be short, continued to spend great sums of money—on the company and on his many philanthropic endeavors. He was perhaps most recognized for his contribution to the Chicago Civic Opera. Com Ed continued to grow and its stock continued to rise.

Much of this growth, however, was artificial. Assets and earnings were inflated, and in 1931 utility stock prices plunged. MWU's stock dropped from $570 to $1.25 per share. Insull had financed much of MWU's growth by using other utility properties as collateral. In 1932 banks took over MWU. Insull was forced to resign, and claimed a personal loss of nearly $15 million. Eventually he was tried for fraud and embezzlement. Though Insull was not found guilty, he was out of the picture for good.

Commonwealth Edison itself, however, weathered the Depression relatively well, and business carried on. Modern conveniences like the air conditioner and the electric water heater

came on the scene in the 1930s and continued to stimulate increased demand for electricity.

During World War II reserve capacity attracted war industries to the Chicago area; and in 1943 about 40% of the company's yearly output was tied to war production. In 1947 the city of Chicago conducted a study of Commonwealth Edison's service and found the company was significantly overcharging, especially residential and commercial customers. The utility's initial franchise with the city was soon to expire, and a battle involving politicians, the utility, and customers ensued.

As a utility overseen by a regulatory commission, Commonwealth Edison was allowed a "reasonable rate of return." There was a great deal of debate over what "reasonable" meant. In comparing utilities in the nation's 23 largest cities, Commonwealth Edison was found to spend twice as much on advertising as any other utility. Should customers pay high rates to support advertising of a monopoly? If the city took Commonwealth Edison to court, would legal fees be passed on to customers? Although these and other criticisms were addressed in the report, in the media, and by members of the city council, a powerful faction in the city council supported Commonwealth Edison, and the city ultimately signed a 42-year franchise that did little to address these criticisms. Some observers believed that neither the franchise agreement nor the state regulatory body, the Illinois Commerce Commission (ICC), clearly defined "reasonable rate of return"—it was left up to Commonwealth Edison, although the ICC did set a maximum rate.

Com Ed's customers did not feel the sting of this arrangement until many years down the road, when Edison's nuclear program ran into decades of cost overruns. In the short term the company flourished and customers benefited. By 1951 Commonwealth Edison had assets of $1 billion. In 1953 the Public Service Company of Northern Illinois—which had been created in 1950 by the merger of Western United Gas & Electric Company and Illinois Northern Utilities Company—merged with Com Ed. In 1954 Com Ed created the Northern Illinois Gas Company to own and operate its gas properties. In 1955 the company began using an electronic computer for billing. In 1959 Com Ed reached two million customers.

Rate reductions averaged more than $36 million a year between 1962 and 1967; the utility's operating revenues rose from $492 million in 1962 to $658.7 million in 1966. In 1966 Com Ed absorbed the Central Illinois Electric and Gas Company, basically establishing an integrated electric system for all of northern Illinois, and further capitalizing on economies of scale.

In 1960 Commonwealth Edison began operating the nation's first privately financed commercial nuclear power station, a 200,000-kilowatt facility called Dresden I near Morris, Illinois. Commonwealth Edison was leading the national charge toward nuclear power. J. Harris Ward became Com Ed's chairman the next year. He linked the company's growth to nuclear power, and committed large sums of capital investment to this program.

The utility's ambitious plans called for 40% of its entire generating capacity to be supplied by seven nuclear-fueled plants by 1973. By 1969, however, the company's nuclear program was experiencing technical difficulties, falling behind schedule, and suffering rapidly escalating costs. Commonwealth Edison was forced to begin building a $160 million coal-fired unit at its Powerton plant in Pekin, Illinois. "The delays forced us to double-build," Ward told *Forbes*, September 15, 1969. This adjustment in Com Ed's nuclear program was only one in a long line of costly setbacks.

The company's commitment to nuclear-generated power was due, in part, to nuclear power's promise as a cleaner fuel. The problems associated with burning fossil fuels came to a head in 1970 when the Chicago Department of Environmental Control named Commonwealth Edison the worst polluter in Chicago, accusing the electric company's fossil-fuel plants of causing more sulfur pollution than all other companies in the city combined. Thomas G. Ayers, president of Com Ed, began bringing in low-sulfur coal from Montana, cutting sulfur emissions by 60% by 1973. In 1973 he was elected chairman and CEO of Commonwealth Edison. By 1972 Commonwealth Edison was using nuclear power to generate 22% of its capacity, more than any other investor-owned utility in the nation. In the interest of assuring a uranium supply, Com Ed acquired Cotter Corporation, a uranium mining and milling company in 1974.

In 1971 planning began on a joint proposal with the Tennessee Valley Authority to build and operate the United States' first commercial fast breeder reactor. This kind of power plant would produce more fuel than it used. It would also produce more highly radioactive waste than its predecessors. The project was approved by the Atomic Energy Commission in 1972, and though that breeder reactor was completed and more followed, the problems of disposing of the high-level nuclear waste continued. In 1973 the company, for the third time in its history, received the industry's Edison award for its leadership in the development of the breeder reactor.

During the 1970s the company faced soaring operating and expansion costs, exacerbated by problems of getting rate increases and plant construction clearances. The widely publicized nuclear accident at Three Mile Island, Pennsylvania, in 1979 heightened attention of both the public and regulators. Commonwealth Edison sent teams of nuclear experts to assist and study the situation.

In 1980, in the middle of Com Ed's $4.5 billion construction of six new nuclear plants, earnings per share sank to their lowest level since 1965. As heavy industry in the area stopped growing, Edison's sales slowed drastically.

Into this bleak picture stepped Commonwealth Edison's newly appointed CEO, James O'Connor. Beginning in 1980, the ICC granted the utility a series of large rate increases. Com Ed began to rebound, and by December 1984, O'Connor was predicting that rates would increase about 2.5% a year for three years, level off in 1988, and then stabilize.

In 1986, as Edison struggled to finance the $7.1 billion building program for the last 3 of 12 nuclear plants, problems with the company's Braidwood nuclear plant increased its construction cost more than 40%. This meant Edison would need a 4.8% annual increase for 11 years to cover the cost. Many observers felt that Com Ed should have canceled or postponed some of its plants in the early 1980s, due to underestimated construction costs and overestimated demand.

As a result of overbuilding in its nuclear program, Commonwealth Edison's generating capacity exceeded average peak demand by 33% in 1990—most utilities maintain a 15% surplus. Thus, while many major utilities around the nation were found to be spending $15 to $51 on conservation per customer, Commonwealth Edison was spending 39¢ per customer, according to a study by a committee of the Chicago City Council.

In 1990 the company's net income fell to $128 million, or 22¢ per share, from the previous year's $693 million, or $2.83 per share, largely because of court-ordered refunds and rate rollbacks. Also in 1990, at a time when customers were growing increasingly unhappy with paying some of the nation's highest rates, the utility's franchise term with the city of Chicago was due to expire. A coalition of community and environmental groups formed in 1988 to pressure the city to stir up public debate over the city's electricity options. These amounted to a renegotiated franchise or municipal acquisition. Meanwhile, Commonwealth Edison waged an advertising campaign to tout the quality of its service.

In the summer of 1990, two major substation fires caused 60,000 customers to lose power for up to three days. The city postponed its decision on the franchise to allow more time to study the utility's reliability. Negotiations on a new franchise concluded in 1991, and Commonwealth Edison was granted a 29-year contract.

Principal Subsidiaries: Commonwealth Edison of Indiana; Edison Development Company; Commonwealth Research Corporation; Cotter Corporation; Edison Development of Canada; Concomber Ltd.

Further Reading: McDonald, Forrest, *Insull*, Chicago, The University of Chicago Press, 1962; Munson, Richard, *The Power Makers*, Emmaus, Pennsylvania, Rodale Press, 1985.

—Carole Healy

CONSOLIDATED EDISON COMPANY OF NEW YORK, INC.

4 Irving Place
New York, New York 10003
U.S.A.
(212) 460-4600
Fax: (212) 674-6470

Public Company
Incorporated: 1936
Employees: 19,500
Sales: $5.74 billion
Stock Exchanges: New York Midwest Pacific Amsterdam

Consolidated Edison (Con Ed) supplies various forms of power to the greater New York City area. The company's earliest predecessors illuminated New York streets with gas in the 1820s, Thomas Edison's original electrical distribution system formed the basis of the modern Consolidated Edison in the 1880s, and the company built the world's first privately funded atomic power plant in the middle decades of the 20th century. As the chief power source for a vital metropolitan area, Consolidated Edison was for many years the undisputed leader among utilities. Since about 1970 Con Ed has improved both its services and financial performance, and its customers have come to better appreciate the complexities of power generation in an age of oil politics and environmental stewardship.

Con Ed began as New York Gas Light Company, founded in 1823 to provide gas for New York's street lamps and homes. Gas illumination had only recently been introduced in the United States and, at first, met widespread resistance due to concerns about safety, but its economy and efficiency soon made gas the standard light source for much of the 19th century. By the last quarter of the century, New York Gas Light and five rival companies supplied gas to the great majority of New York's already vast population, much of which could not imagine a time when the city had been without gas light.

An alternative source of illumination was under intense scrutiny by the 1870s, however; this was electricity. After years of experimentation, the first electric arc lights began appearing in U.S. cities in that decade, and it was soon obvious that electricity would one day become the standard illuminant. The arc light was, nevertheless, a crude and dangerous innovation, suitable only for outdoor lighting of public space, and a host of inventors around the world continued searching for an acceptable alternative.

Among the men who became interested in the future of electric light was Thomas Alva Edison, already famous for his invention of the phonograph and a series of improvements in telegraphy. It was clear to Edison that electricity was destined to light the world, and in 1878 he focused his energies on solving the problems remaining in its development. To make electric light truly universal, two things were needed: a sturdy and economical form of incandescent illumination, and a power grid able to distribute safe, reliable electric current from its source of generation into distant apartments and homes, something which had not yet been attempted on a large scale. Incandescence was a well-known method of illumination, but no one had yet found a material able to withstand long hours of operation without burning up. The inventor shelved his other projects and devoted himself and his considerable staff to experiments in electric light.

The scope of Edison's ambition in these ventures can hardly be overestimated. In essence, he was proposing to design and build the system of electric power distribution upon which the entire world remains dependent. Literally everything had to be created—generators, transmission lines, switching equipment, and protective devices; and, within the home or office, internal wiring, outlets, lamps, meters, and even the light source, the bulb, itself. Such an immense project naturally would require capital, and in October 1878 Edison's group joined forces with Wall Street financiers in forming the Edison Electric Light Company. Edison's backers included J.P. Morgan and the Vanderbilt interests, both of whom saw the potential of the new system. With his financing in place, Edison redoubled his experiments, and by the end of 1879, working furiously to best the efforts of Joseph Swan in England, he had devised a workable incandescent light using a filament of high-heat-and-electric-resistant "thread" in an evacuated glass globe.

Edison simultaneously had solved most of the generation and transmission problems, and by 1880 was ready to apply to the city of New York for permission to build the nation's first commercial electric power station. At that point a legal technicality forced the creation of a subsidiary corporation, Edison Electric Illuminating Company, to act as an operating company on behalf of Edison Electric Light, which would remain only a holding company and in control of all patents. The newly formed Edison Electric Illuminating applied for and received its license—apparently with the help of liberal payments to New York's open-handed city government—and at 3:00 PM on September 4, 1881, current began to flow from the generators at 255-57 Pearl Street in lower Manhattan. London's Holborn Viaduct Station had gone on-line nine months earlier; it too was an Edison project. The Pearl Street Station, like all of Edison's later generating plants, could supply power only a mile or two in any direction from the plant before its direct-current electricity began to lose voltage, but for several years its design was unchallenged and imitations sprang up everywhere. By the spring of 1883 there were some 334 Edison plants in operation, most of them considerably smaller than the one at Pearl Street.

The success of Edison's power system was an event of the first order; the advent of electricity changed every aspect of modern life. Locally, Edison found himself quickly enmeshed in the struggles and strategies generated by any such leap in technology. The inventor and his associates incorporated many subsidiary manufacturing companies in order to build power stations wherever they were wanted, and by 1884, greatly assisted by a young financial wizard, Samuel Insull, Edison had even gained control of Edison Light as well as Edison Illuminating. As an innovator in electricity, however, Edison's day was past; in the great debate that shortly arose as to the relative merits of alternating current (AC) and direct current (DC), Edison stuck with his original conception of DC generators long after the rest of the industry had recognized AC as the wave of the future. By the late 1880s George Westinghouse had won the battle of the currents, and Edison had long since dropped active participation in his electrical holdings.

Given this situation, Edison was more than happy to listen when a group of German financiers led by Henry Villard proposed the formation of a new electrical combination, to include all of Edison's manufacturing companies and the valuable stock of Edison Electric Light, the holding company. Although the latter had come under the managing direction of Edison's group in an 1884 proxy fight, its largest block was controlled by the interests of J.P. Morgan. In the complex negotiations leading to the creation of Villard's new company—later to be known as General Electric—Morgan used his stock position and financial muscle to demand and win 40% of General Electric's stock, while Edison settled for 10% and enough cash to make his fortune. Meanwhile, the creation of General Electric led to Edison Illuminating being spun off on its own in a utility market increasingly crowded with efficient AC competitors and the newly roused gas companies.

New York's gas companies were hardly pleased by the success of electric lighting. Edison's earliest announcements on the subject had sent gas stocks reeling, and in 1884 the city's six largest gas concerns joined forces in a new utility giant called Consolidated Gas Company of New York. This merger initiated a long process whereby the scores of small electricity, gas, and steam companies operating in the greater New York area would be melded into the single and far more efficient entity known since 1936 as Consolidated Edison Company of New York. At first, the electric and gas concerns faced each other as rivals, each side augmenting its forces by annexation or combination with neighboring firms.

The gas companies united in Consolidated Gas, while the bulk of Manhattan's electricity supply was collected in 1898 under the umbrella of The New York Gas & Electric Light, Heat & Power Company (NYG&ELH&P). NYG&ELH&P also gained a controlling share of Edison Electric Illuminating. Consolidated Gas bought NYG&ELH&P in 1899, when Consolidated Gas decided to use its superior financial might to overcome a growing technological gap by buying up as many electricity companies as it could. In 1901 Consolidated Gas merged the electric companies it controlled, including Edison Electric Illuminating, NYG&ELH&P, and others into a single subsidiary known as The New York Edison Company. The gas companies thus themselves became providers of electricity, and by 1910 controlled, under the name of New York Edison, most of the electricity generated in Manhattan and the western portion of the Bronx.

By that time, of course, electricity had become the standard source of power not only for illumination but for a widening variety of household gadgets and industrial tools. Alternating current had won the day, allowing the construction of very large central generators capable of serving vast numbers of customers at long distances. New York Edison gradually replaced its last few small DC-generating stations, and the city's power network began to assume its modern structure. In particular, as it became apparent that large-scale power distribution was by nature a type of monopoly, utility companies came under the regulatory control of the state legislature in Albany, New York. The power of the legislature to fix rates of return for utilities was tested in a landmark court case arising out of its 1906 attempt to limit Consolidated Gas's price for its gas to 80¢ per 1,000 cubic feet. The United States Supreme Court eventually ruled that while governmental bodies had a clear right to oversee the operation of utilities, they could not set rates so low as to prevent the utilities from earning a reasonable rate of return on investment; in the case of Consolidated Gas, however, the rate of 80¢ was not found to be excessively low. In the course of its analysis, the Court estimated Consolidated Gas's asset value at $56 million.

For many years Consolidated Gas and its subsidiary New York Edison grew quietly. The long process of unifying New York's various power companies continued apace, and by 1932 Consolidated Gas was the largest company in the world providing electrical service. The final step occurred in 1936 when Consolidated Gas became Consolidated Edison Company of New York. Under the direction of Hudson R. Searing, the previously cool relations between Edison's gas and electric divisions were quietly improved, and the gigantic combine took on its present configuration as New York City's sole power company.

As the single purveyor of light and electricity to New York's millions of inhabitants and workers, Con Ed attracted the suspicions and criticism that accompany a monopoly. When Mayor Fiorello La Guardia threatened to create a municipal power utility to compete with Con Ed during the Great Depression, company executives worked to develop closer relationships with other members of the city's government. Con Ed was the city's largest employer of construction workers and paid more taxes than any other single organization in the city, and, largely through the efforts of Charles Eble—later Con Ed's chief executive—was able to stave off La Guardia's threat. The interests of New York City and Con Ed meshed from the mid-1930s on.

In 1955 Con Ed was among the first utilities to apply for permission from the Atomic Energy Commission to build and operate a private atomic power plant. Permission granted, Con Ed built its reactor at Indian Point, New York, some miles up the Hudson River from New York City, inaugurating what it hoped would be a new era of clean, cheap power for New York. Con Ed's path-breaking project took far longer and much more money to build than anyone had expected. When it was completed in the early 1960s, Indian Point's cost per kilowatt of capacity was 2.5 times that of a conventional generator, adding to a general growing perception among New Yorkers that Con Ed was an inefficient utility. The origins of this reputation seem to be split between the unavoidable difficulties of supplying power in so complex an environment as New York City and Con Ed's failure to meet that challenge.

The burdens of a New York City utility are severe. Since the 19th century, most utility lines and pipes have been required by law to be laid underground, vastly increasing Con Ed's expense for upkeep and expansion of its system. Con Ed has more miles of underground wire than the rest of the nation's utilities combined. New York's extremely dense population creates additional problems, and the high percentage of residential users necessitates the metering, billing, and servicing of thousands of relatively small accounts, in contrast to a utility with a higher proportion of industrial customers. The preponderance of office workers in Manhattan means that Con Ed must be prepared to supply a midday peak of electricity far greater than its 24-hour average, forcing the construction and maintenance of a generating capacity larger than would otherwise be needed. Such underutilized capacity is highly inefficient for power companies, whose single greatest burden is the cost of construction and upkeep. Con Ed also pays extremely high taxes which it passes on to customers. Thus Con Ed, in effect, collects taxes on behalf of the various city, state, and federal agencies that through taxes have helped make Con Ed the nation's most expensive utility for many years. Finally, space restrictions in New York made it much easier for Con Ed to repair old power stations than to build new ones, which meant that by the 1950s much of its physical plant was antiquated and inefficient. Despite that handicap, Con Ed was the subject of some of the earliest restrictions on air pollution adopted in the United States, further increasing its already excessive costs.

The upshot of these unique drawbacks was to make Con Ed an expensive and erratic provider of gas, electricity, and steam; but some of its problems lay with management as well. By the 1960s, Chairman Charles Eble and his team of top advisors had all been with the company for a number of years, and many felt that they had developed an aloof, isolated mentality that angered New Yorkers, irate over poor service, high bills, and a series of famous blackouts beginning in 1959. Typical of the company's poor handling of public relations was its 1962 effort to build a second atomic power plant in the middle of the borough of Queens; such judgment helped make Con Ed notorious. Equally damaging was Con Ed's poor financial performance. While 1965 revenues of $840 million made Con Ed the nation's largest utility, its revenue growth was very slow, net earnings were low, and earnings per share were moving up at only 4% per year, or half the pace of a typical competitor such as Commonwealth Edison in Chicago.

The man chosen to lead Con Ed out of this trough was Charles F. Luce. Appointed chairman in mid-1967, Luce was formerly an under-secretary with the Department of the Interior. He was chosen both for his abilities and because he was an outsider to New York power politics. The new chief executive took a number of decisive steps toward the renewal of Con Ed: a virtual makeover of top management; division of the company into six operating divisions, one for each city borough plus one for suburban Westchester County; the addition of several new plants; plans to replace aging equipment; and a new emphasis on customer service.

Con Ed's stock price continued to drop, however, and it soon found itself in the worst crisis of the company's history. After agreeing in 1972 to halt the use of coal for environmental reasons, Con Ed was dependent on oil for 85% of its generating capacity when the OPEC oil embargo doubled the price of crude in the fall of 1973. As fuel price increases could not be passed along to customers for about four months, and Con Ed was in the midst of yet more construction projects to increase capacity, the company was suddenly faced with a critical shortage of cash. Luce took the unprecedented step of withholding dividends in the first quarter of 1974, unleashing an avalanche of criticism from stockholders, Wall Street, and other utilities, who watched their own stocks follow Con Ed on a sharp decline.

Luce had a second, far more important strategy. Knowing that the state government had no interest in seeing New York's power supply disrupted by financial collapse, Luce persuaded it to buy two of Con Ed's generating plants which were still under construction. At one stroke, Con Ed received $612 million in cash and was relieved of the heavy cost burden associated with new-plant construction. What additional power Con Ed required was bought back from the state; but 1973 and 1974 also marked the beginning of a long decline in the expansion rate of New York's energy usage, partly in response to the high price of oil and partly as a result of vigorous conservation campaigns promoted by Con Ed, which realized that nothing could be better from a financial perspective than an end to the cycle of borrowing required for new generating equipment and plants.

By 1978 Con Ed was regarded as one of the most efficient and profitable utilities in the country, and Chairman Luce was credited with a remarkable turnaround of the once-hated institution. Customer complaints dropped off dramatically, earnings per share and the price of stock rose, and Con Ed gradually eased itself back into a more balanced pattern of fuel usage, much of it natural gas and nuclear. Since the late 1970s Con Ed has operated smoothly and quietly. The generally conservative pattern of energy usage in New York has allowed Con Ed to avoid the costly construction projects that once threatened to sink it, keeping earnings high. During the late 1980s, Con Ed even began posting the lowest rates of customer interruption for any utility in the country, which, in light of its long tradition of sub-par performance, may be its most impressive achievement. Charles Luce's decision to sell off two of the company's plants in 1974 made possible a renaissance at Con Ed.

Luce retired in September 1982 and was succeeded by Arthur Haupsburg. By this time Con Ed had begun an era of stability in its electric rates. A rate increase requested in April 1982 and granted the following year was its last for a decade; in April 1990 the utility extended its current electric rates until 1992. Haupsburg retired in September 1990 without having had to request a single electric rate increase. During his tenure, electric sales rose, fuel prices generally declined, and dividends were increased annually. Con Ed had ample capacity to meet the demand generated by the healthy local economy.

Eugene R. McGrath became chairman, president, and chief executive officer upon Haupsburg's retirement. He faced a somewhat different situation than did his predecessor. Con Ed remained financially strong, but the New York City area's economy had weakened. Con Ed launched a major energy conservation program in 1990, with the goal of reducing customers' electric energy usage by 15% by 2008, as compared to expected consumption without the program. Con Ed planned to spend about $4.2 billion on the program during that period. To maintain its power supply, Con Ed continued modernizing its existing plants and signed contracts with several prospective independent power producers. These measures will help ensure Con Ed continues to prosper through the 1990s and into the next century.

Further Reading: O'Hanlon, Thomas, "Con Edison: The Company You Love to Hate," *Fortune,* March 1966; Silverberg, Robert, *Light for the World: Edison and the Power Industry,* Princeton, New Jersey, Van Nostrand, 1967.

—Jonathan Martin

**CONSOLIDATED
NATURAL GAS
COMPANY**

CONSOLIDATED NATURAL GAS COMPANY

CNG Tower
625 Liberty Avenue
Pittsburgh, Pennsylvania 15222
U.S.A.
(412) 227-1000
Fax: (412) 227-1304

Public Company
Incorporated: 1942
Employees: 7,753
Sales: $2.71 billion
Stock Exchange: New York

Consolidated Natural Gas Company (CNG) operates one of the largest natural gas systems in the United States. It explores for, produces, and buys natural gas, which it transports to utilities and consumers in the East and Midwest. It owns the largest group of underground gas-storage fields in the nation, and is involved in subsidiary businesses including gas by-products and oil production.

In the late 1870s, when the companies that later became CNG were being formed, western Pennsylvania held the same promise of profit that the Middle East oil fields were to have 100 years later. The company was founded by the merger of five individual businesses that were formed, merged, or acquired by John D. Rockefeller as a part of his Standard Oil Company, then consolidated to form one of the largest fully integrated producers and distributors of natural gas in the United States. Based on its early history of growth through mergers and reliance on its skills in exploring and developing new gas wells and properties, CNG has been able to expand as a service and distribution company as well as a producer of natural gas.

The companies that became CNG were born of an important by-product of the Standard Oil Company's search for oil. Standard Oil's original mission was to find and develop oil in the Appalachian mountains of western Pennsylvania, and early in Standard Oil's history, Rockefeller saw that natural gas, the discovery of which goes hand-in-hand with oil, was a valuable commodity. Within the first 30 years after Standard Oil's founding in 1870, Rockefeller had formed and acquired companies that explored for gas throughout the Appalachian basin and piped it to Pittsburgh, Pennsylvania; Cleveland and Akron, Ohio; and other growing industrial centers in the region.

Natural gas fueled the nascent iron, steel, rubber, and glass industries. It also provided home heating and, in the early portion of this period, municipal street lighting.

In 1911 the network of natural gas production, transmission, and distribution companies assembled by Standard Oil came under the umbrella of the Standard Oil Company (New Jersey), one of the 34 companies that resulted from the dissolution of Standard Oil that was ordered by the U.S. Supreme Court under the Sherman Antitrust Act. At that time, Standard Oil Company (New Jersey) held four of the five companies that were to form the Consolidated Natural Gas system: The Peoples Natural Gas Company, of Pittsburgh, Pennsylvania, which had been founded in 1885; The River Gas Company, of Marietta, Ohio, which had been founded in 1894; The Hope Natural Gas Company, now known as Hope Gas Inc., of Clarksburg, West Virginia, which had been founded in 1898; and The East Ohio Gas Company, of Cleveland, Ohio, also originating in 1898. Each of these companies remained in the early 1900s as operating units of CNG. They were augmented in 1930 by a pipeline that supplied nonaffiliated utilities in New York state. In 1942 Standard Oil (New Jersey) organized Consolidated Natural Gas Company as a subsidiary and transferred to CNG its natural gas gathering and transmission assets. CNG was spun off as a privately held, independent company from Standard Oil (New Jersey) in 1943 because Standard did not want to be declared a public utility holding company falling under the Public Utility Holding Company Act of 1935.

CNG began its independent corporate history with assets of more than $211 million and with 750,000 retail customers in Ohio, western Pennsylvania, and West Virginia. In its first year as an independent company, it sold 127 billion cubic feet of gas. During World War II defense production created such a demand for natural gas that CNG contracted for the first time to purchase gas, piped from the southwestern United States, to supplement the gas it produced in the Appalachian basin.

In 1947 to cope with the postwar surge in demand, CNG made its first public stock offering, totaling $8.2 million. CNG's first debenture issue, which totaled $30 million, came in 1948. Postwar growth forced the company into occasional restrictions on gas sales, and proceeds from the equity and debt issues were used to finance the construction of additional pipelines and storage fields.

By the early 1960s CNG had extended its market saturation in northeastern Ohio from Cleveland to the Pennsylvania border with the purchase of Lake Shore Gas Company of Ashtabula, Ohio, and had reached a market share of 92% for space heating and 96% for water heating. At the same time, in pursuing additional supplies of natural gas, CNG in 1957 became one of the first companies to explore and drill in the Gulf of Mexico, and was a lease owner in the gulf by 1962. With a group of partners, CNG purchased 168,000 acres of developable drilling sites in the gulf that year, and in 1966 established a full-scale exploration and production staff in New Orleans, Louisiana, to become the operator on many of its leases. By 1972 the New Orleans office was made into a subsidiary, CNG Producing Company.

CNG formed Consolidated Natural Gas Service Company, Inc. in 1961 to centralize accounting, data processing, employee relations, marketing, and rate and tax administration functions. In 1965 CNG merged its Hope and New York State

Natural Gas interstate pipeline companies to form Consolidated Gas Supply Corporation, now known as CNG Transmission Corporation. CNG Transmission Corporation continues to supply gas to CNG's six distribution companies and sells gas at wholesale to utilities throughout the northeastern United States. In 1969 CNG acquired the West Ohio Gas Company, of Lima, Ohio, along with its 50,000 customers.

In the early 1970s CNG and its competitors were faced with shortages of natural gas supplied from the southwestern United States. The company established CNG Producing Company to pursue new production sources and Consolidated System LNG Company to import liquefied natural gas (LNG) from Algeria and convert the LNG back to gas.

The record cold winter of 1976–1977 led the U.S. Congress to pass the Natural Gas Policy Act of 1978. CNG, which by then had plentiful gas supplies, expected the act to encourage conservation. At the same time, the steel industry, an important GNG customer, was undergoing an historic contraction. This prompted CNG to develop nontraditional markets for gas and its other services. In 1979 CNG became the first gas utility company to sell significant amounts of gas and associated storage to neighboring pipelines and utilities, and later sold independent storage services.

CNG, like the United States in general, developed an oversupply of natural gas by the mid-1980s. That oversupply, worsened by a string of unusually warm winters, led to declining gas and oil prices, and produced a trying time for CNG. Profits remained flat or fell off while corporate revenues reached peak levels, cresting at $3.5 billion in 1984. Despite this difficulty, CNG continued its exploration and development activities, taking advantage of low costs to build reserves and to increase its drilling prospects. CNG made a major find of oil at Cottonwood Creek in Carter County, Oklahoma, in 1988. It was the second-largest oil- and gas-producing well in the history of Oklahoma, with production levels of 3,700 barrels of crude oil per day and 2.9 billion cubic feet of gas per day. The company centralized all of its drilling in the Appalachian region under the CNG Development Company, a non-utility subsidiary established in 1982 and, in 1990, merged CNG Development with CNG Producing, which then oversaw all of the company's drilling programs in the Appalachian basin, in the Gulf of Mexico, and in other areas.

In 1983 CNG negotiated agreements with a group of utilities in New England, New Jersey, and the New York City metropolitan area, under which CNG would sell gas at wholesale prices to the utilities. Those negotiations produced contracts to supply 20 utilities with a total of up to 39 billion cubic feet of gas annually. Deliveries began in 1984. In 1988 CNG expanded its market again, beginning deliveries of gas under 20–year contracts to utilities in Washington, D.C.; New York City; and Baltimore, Maryland.

Although CNG's year-to-year profitability was volatile, the company provided a 24% average annual return to investors during the 1980s and by January 1990 had a 98% saturation of its traditional distribution area. At that point, it moved to expand this area by acquiring Virginia Natural Gas, Inc., of Norfolk, Virginia, from Dominion Resources Inc. for $160 million. This gave CNG access to a fast-growing and economically diversified region. It also required a 162–mile pipeline extension, construction of which began in early 1990.

CNG has always depended on the discovery and successful exploitation of supplies of natural gas. To cope with peaks and valleys in natural gas demand, CNG has developed a system of storage for the gas it produces throughout the year. Since 1937 CNG has led the United States in natural gas storage capacity. The capacity was developed through conversion of depleted Appalachian gas fields into 26 underground storage pools. CNG also has used its storage capacity as a new source of revenue. It provided 128 billion cubic feet of storage service to other companies in 1990.

Gas distribution, historically the company's core business, accounted for $102.1 million of CNG's 1990 operating income, a 16% decline from the previous year, due to abnormally warm weather in its service areas. The income came on sales of 125.2 billion cubic feet of gas to industrial customers and 185.9 billion cubic feet of gas to residential customers, both down slightly from 1989, while sales to commercial customers were 80.8 billion cubic feet, about the same as in 1989.

Gas transmission activities contributed $74 million to the company's operating income in 1990, compared with $64.9 million in 1989. The increase resulted from the positive impact of a rate settlement case, higher transportation rates, and higher prices for by-products and lower income taxes, all of which combined to offset reduced demand.

To enhance its position in this area of service, CNG embarked on a five-year, $900 million capital improvement program in 1990 aimed at adding transportation and storage facilities. This program was the largest single investment in the company's history and was financed partly through the company's first stock offering since the 1950s. CNG has won praise from the investment community for its conservative finances, including a generally low amount of debt.

Throughout its history, CNG has grown by providing a basic utility service to its residential, industrial, and commercial customers under the direction of its conservative management. Through considered acquisitions, measured capital expansion, and the exploration and development of oil and gas resources, the company won a high ranking in the industry. With its transmission and storage facilities expansion under way, and with the wellhead price of natural gas expected to rise through the 1990s as resources become depleted, CNG seems to be headed for increasing profits.

Principal Subsidiaries: CNG Transmission Corporation; The East Ohio Gas Company; The Peoples Natural Gas Company; Virginia Natural Gas, Inc.; Hope Gas, Inc.; West Ohio Gas Company; The River Gas Company; CNG Producing Company; CNG Energy Company; CNG Trading Company.

—Bruce Vernyi

Detroit Edison

THE DETROIT EDISON COMPANY

2000 Second Avenue
Detroit, Michigan 48226
U.S.A.
(313) 237-8000
Fax: (313) 237-7098

Public Company
Incorporated: 1903
Employees: 9,699
Sales: $3.31 billion
Stock Exchanges: New York Midwest

The Detroit Edison Company serves roughly 1.9 million electrical customers in southeastern Michigan. While the company's market territory only covers 13% of Michigan's total area, it accounts for half of Michigan's total population, energy consumption, and industrial capacity. Electricity accounts for almost all the company's revenues, but Detroit Edison also sells a small amount of steam.

Electric companies sprang up throughout the United States after Thomas Edison's development of electric lighting in 1879. In Detroit alone Brush Electric Light Company, Fort Wayne Electric Company, Commercial Electric Light Company, Detroit Electric Light and Power Company, Edison Illuminating Company of Detroit, and Peninsular Electric Light Company all simultaneously existed. Edison Illuminating had been formed on April 15, 1886, to supply alternating current to homes and businesses; and Peninsular Electric Light Company had been formed on June 16, 1891, to operate Detroit's street lights. It was not long before competition became so fierce that the less successful companies were swallowed up, and Peninsular Electric Light Company and Edison Illuminating were all that remained.

On January 1, 1903, Detroit Edison's founders purchased the securities of the Edison Illuminating Company and the Peninsular Electric Light Company and on January 17 The Detroit Edison Company was incorporated with Edison Illuminating as a subsidiary. For financial reasons, incorporation took place in New York rather than Michigan. Charles W. Wetmore became the company's first president and remained in that position until 1912. Detroit Edison's first general manager, Alex Dow, came to the company from its predecessor Edison Illuminating.

At that time the customer base it had acquired through Edison Illuminating had already outgrown its power supply, so one of the company's first objectives was to create additional generating capacity. In 1903 Detroit Edison began to construct the Delray power house. By 1904 this plant's two turbine generators were producing 3,000 kilowatts of electricity each, yet the city of Detroit was growing so rapidly that in 1905 another two turbine generators had to be added to the plant, and one more the next year.

In 1905 Detroit Edison began to expand through acquisition, in addition to construction. Among its purchases were Washtenaw Light and Power Company, Michigan Milling Company, and Ann Arbor Agricultural Company, making Detroit Edison the owner of the Argo, Barton, Geddes, and Superior generating dams on the Huron River. On July 24, 1906, the company formed a wholly owned subsidiary, Eastern Michigan Edison Company and transferred all the Huron River companies to it as subsidiaries.

By 1907 it had become obvious that the company had to add more turbines, and construction began on a second power station at Delray to house a turbine capable of generating station/house 14,000 kilowatts of energy. In 1910 and 1911 two more 14,000-kilowatt turbines were put on-line.

In 1912 Alex Dow became president of Detroit Edison. During his tenure Detroit Edison grew substantially. In 1913 a 15,000-kilowatt turbine was added to the new power house at Delray, and Detroit Edison began to construct a power plant at Conners Creek.

For roughly the first decade of The Detroit Edison Company's existence—the period ranging from 1903 until 1915—the company's subsidiary Edison Illuminating Company distributed, sold, billed for, and collected on, the energy produced by its parent, Detroit Edison. In 1915 under Dow, Detroit Edison began to serve its customers directly. Edison Illuminating survived as a company handling Detroit Edison's real estate. Also in 1915, the company put two of the Conners Creek facility's three 20,000-kilowatt units into service, with the third becoming operational in 1917.

The Detroit Edison Company's generating capacity continued to grow under Dow, and in 1919, Detroit Edison bought Port Huron Gas and Electric Company. In 1920 a 30,000-kilowatt generator was added to the plant at Delray. In 1922 Detroit Edison completed its first in suburban Marysville. Detroit Edison put its second at Trenton Channel in Trenton in July 1924. The Trenton Channel plant burned powdered coal, a technical innovation at the time, but also a process that tended to pollute the air because powdered coal is burned while suspended. Detroit Edison was aware of this fact and consequently equipped the plant—the first of its kind to use these pollution control devices—with electrostatic precipitators.

In addition to expanding its generating capacity, Detroit Edison expanded its service area. By 1929 the company supplied more than 4,582 square miles. In 1936 Detroit Edison purchased the Michigan Electric Power Company and acquired the entire "thumb" territory of southeastern Michigan, to increase its service area to 7,587 square miles.

In 1940 Alex Dow retired as company president. Two years later, he withdrew from the company's board of directors. Under Dow's leadership, not only had generating capacity and service area expanded, but Detroit Edison had developed its own engineering research department, founded in 1913, and improved customer service. This included instituting free light bulb service, financing the connection of electricity to customers previously using gas, and lending electrical motors.

From 1944 to 1954 former U.S. Senator Prentiss M. Brown held the post of first chairman of the board, while James W. Parker served as president and general manager. Walker Cisler, who joined Detroit Edison in 1943, became the company's first executive vice president in 1948 and, in addition, worked with the U.S. government on the Marshall Plan, developing the economic and electric power of other nations.

In 1951 when Parker retired, Cisler took over as president and general manager. Cisler's primary objectives for the company involved expanding generating capacity and improving transmission to the farthest reaches of Detroit Edison's service area, as well as exploring research opportunities. By 1954 the St. Clair Power Plant was completely operational, with a total capacity of 624,000 kilowatts. That year Cisler became senior officer of Detroit Edison, which by then was looking into nuclear energy.

In 1952 Cisler assumed the leadership responsibilites for organizing electric utilites to explore the possibilities of nuclear energy, a development he named the Enrico Fermi Breeder Reactor Project. Among the companies he persuaded to join the project was the Public Service Electric and Gas Co. of Newark, New Jersey, and he convinced that company to assign one of its nuclear engineers, Walter J. McCarthy, to join the project as head of the nuclear and analytical division in October 1952. The project was headquartered at Detroit Edison. It was formally organized in 1955, with 34 companies participating, as the Power Reactor Development Company (PRDC), which owned and operated the Enrico Fermi Power Plant. Ground was broken on Fermi's first unit that year with Cisler as president and principal organizer of PRDC.

As the possibilities of atomic energy were explored, Cisler continued to build conventional generating capacity. The River Rouge plant was completed in 1956, and by 1958 it had a capacity of 841,500 kilowatts. In 1961 St. Clair's capacity was upped to 1.35 million kilowatts when its sixth turbine generator went into operation. With its assets growing so rapidly, Detroit Edison authorized a two-for-one common stock split in December 1962.

In 1963 Walter McCarthy became general manager of PRDC, with Cisler continuing as president. McCarthy also formally joined the Detroit Edison staff at this time, while continuing on loan to PRDC. On August 23 of that year, Fermi 1, the first commercial-sized fast breeder nuclear reactor went into operation and began its first self-sustaining chain reaction. The plant used uranium to generate steam to produce electricity, and as part of the reaction process it produced plutonium, which was also an atomic fuel. In October 1966 a metal device that had been attached to the reactor's inside wall after it was built, broke away. The device, whose purpose was to direct the flow of liquid sodium—used to transfer heat—through the nuclear core, ended up blocking the flow and caused the fuel to overheat and begin melting, damaging both the reactor and the fuel assemblies.

In spite of Walker Cisler's campaign for constant generating plant growth, demand still threatened to outstrip supply, and so, in 1966, peaking units were introduced into the generating system. Peaking generators burn gas and oil, are mobile, and

can be brought on-line in ten minutes. The first peaking units were installed at the company's generating facility near Monroe, Michigan.

In the midst of repairs at Fermi 1 and its efforts to continue building generating capacity, The Detroit Edison Company was reincorporated in Michigan on April 17, 1967. By the time Detroit Edison's Harbor Beach Power Plant went on-line in 1968, nine peaking units were being used.

In that same year Detroit Edison requested its first electric rate increase in 20 years from the Michigan Public Service Commission (MPSC). The company sought the increase to help meet the expenses of building generating capacity.

In 1970 the first of the Monroe power plant's coal-fired units went on-line. At the time, the four-unit Monroe plant was the largest in the world, and the company planned to add five more units: the two-unit Belle River coal-burning plant, the Greenwood Energy Center with its oil-burning plant, and two nuclear reactors, Fermi 2 and 3.

In November 1971 William G. Meese took over Cisler's position as chief executive officer while Cisler remained chairman. It had taken four years to repair the reactor and fuel assemblies at Fermi 1, and when the repairs were completed the plant was only operated on and off for several months, with its last operation being September 22, 1972. In November of that year the PRDC executive committee decided to decommission the plant as of December 31, 1975. By 1973 the Monroe power plant's four units had a total capacity of 3 million kilowatts. In 1973 the Ludington pumped storage plant began to operate commercially, supplying 49% of its generating capacity to Detroit Edison, with the remainder going to Consumers Power. Then the Middle East oil embargo hit, striking the southeastern Michigan auto industry hard, and the demand for energy dropped as automobile production slumped and inflation and environmental protection costs continued to rise.

William Meese began to look for ways to cut Detroit Edison's costs. The energy-efficient Ludington plant was part of this effort. In 1974 Meese began to implement other important practices, such as the increased hiring of minorities and women, as well as establishing a strategic planning procedure designed to help management anticipate future conditions. To deal with the new difficulties brought about by southeastern Michigan's economic recession, during 1974 Meese temporarily suspended all power plant construction and environmental modifications.

In 1975 Cisler retired and Meese assumed Cisler's position as chairman of the board. The company reorganized, setting up six divisions within Detroit Edison's service area, each headed by managers responsible for their division's business. That year, Walter McCarthy became executive vice president of operations.

In 1976 another Meese cost-efficient measure was implemented when the Superior Midwest Energy Terminal was opened by a subsidiary of Detroit Edison. All of The Detroit Edison Company's major power plants consumed coal, but the company did not mine or transport the coal itself. Realizing the company's dependence on reliable transport and supply of coal, Meese created the energy terminal at Superior, Wisconsin, to provide rail and water shipment of western low-sulfur coal. He also negotiated a 26-year contract for the purchase of coal from Montana, and had the company purchase its own coal cars to ensure shipment.

In 1977 Walter McCarthy became executive vice president of divisions. That year the temporary suspension on power plant construction was lifted, the Greenwood power plant was set into operation, and construction was started on the Belle River power plant.

In 1979, McCarthy became president and chief operating officer of Detroit Edison and John R. Hamann was elected to the newly created position of vice chairman of the board. That was also the year that the company's Greenwood Power Plant became fully operational.

In 1979, as Fermi 2 was in the midst of construction, the disaster at Three Mile Island hit. Two weeks later Detroit Edison had formed a 24-member safety review task force to review Fermi 2 again and recheck all its operating systems and safety features. Although the task force found everything to be entirely operational at Fermi 2, it took Detroit Edison several years of readjustments before Fermi 2 could meet the new regulations that arose in response to the Three Mile Island incident. In fact, the added cost of meeting these new standards spun Detroit Edison into financial crisis.

The company began taking steps to help revive southeastern Michigan's economy. In 1979 it began the Energy Plus advertising campaign on a national and international level to interest companies in bringing their manufacturing facilities to Michigan. With the Greater Detroit Chamber of Commerce, Michigan's Department of Commerce, and the Southeastern Michigan Council of Governments, Detroit Edison founded the Greater Detroit–Southeastern Michigan Business Attraction and Expansion Council. Detroit Edison also helped develop the Economic Alliance for Business, an organization aimed at improving Michigan's business climate. In September 1981 Meese retired and was succeeded by McCarthy as chairman and chief executive officer.

In April of 1983, in order to consolidate the company, which was operating under dual incorporation in the states of New York and Michigan, Detroit Edison stockholders agreed to a merger plan. This plan was put into effect on June 30, 1983, when both the New York and the Michigan corporations merged with Detroit Edison's wholly owned inoperative subsidiary, Peninsular Electric Light Company. The Detroit Edison Company was the merger's sole surviving company, and retained only its Michigan incorporation. All liabilities, capital, assets, and operations remained unchanged.

In 1985 Fermi 2 was completed, and low-power testing began. McCarthy, having been general manager of Fermi 1 during its early stages, felt experienced operating management was needed. With the delays involved in bringing in new plant management and in receiving approval of the Nuclear Regulatory Commission, Fermi 2 resumed low-power testing in July 1986.

In 1987 Detroit Edison's wholly owned subsidiary, Washtenaw Energy Corporation, was merged into the company. Later that year, Detroit Edison bought the electric business and properties serving the city of Pontiac from Consumers Power and began to supply the people of Pontiac directly, increasing the company's total service area to 7,598 square miles. Consumers Power had served Pontiac with electricity bought from Detroit Edison.

On January 15, 1988, Fermi 2 began full-power operation. By November 1988 Fermi 2 had passed its warranty run and was on its way to long-term operation. However, after-tax write-offs of $968 million resulting partially from the MPSC's dissallowances of costs connected with the unit, dating from a 1986 rate case, caused Detroit Edison to post a net loss of $378.8 million in 1988.

McCarthy began to implement programs designed to increase sales and cut costs, keeping close watch on operating and maintenance expenses, capital expenditures, and the size of the company's staff, reducing it to its smallest size in 12 years—9,669 at the end of 1990. Perhaps most important was the resolution of rate-making issues involving Fermi 2. In December 1988 the MPSC increased Detroit Edison's base rates by adding $29.5 million to a previously authorized $404.2 million—for a total of $433.7 million—to partly cover the cost of building Fermi 2. This increase was to be phased in over five years beginning January 1, 1989. That year Fermi 2 was taken off the Nuclear Regulatory Commission's list of plants requiring special attention. It completed its first scheduled shutdown for refueling in December 1989, and it produced more than 5 billion kilowatt-hours of electricity during the year. By June 1989 The Detroit Edison Company stock had risen to its highest price in 17 years, positioning Detroit Edison as one of the top-performing U.S. utilities.

In 1989 Fermi 2 had represented 31% of Detroit Edison's assets. In 1990 this grew to 33% as the company purchased the minority share of Fermi 2 from Wolverine Power Supply Cooperative, Inc. for $539.6 million, giving Detroit Edison total ownership of the plant. On May 1, 1990, McCarthy retired as chairman and cheif executive officer of Detroit Edison and John E. Lobbia was elected to replace him. As a result of strong lobbying in Washington, Detroit Edison was already in compliance with the first phase of the requirements of the 1990 Clean Air Act amendments, scheduled to take effect in 1995.

In 1990 Detroit Edison achieved record revenues as well as record earnings for common stock. Detroit Edison's common stock hit its highest point in 23 years, when it reached $30.25, closing at $28.25, a full 11% higher than 1989's close.

Although the recession of the early 1990s had hit southeastern Michigan hard, slowing production at many automotive and steel plants and reducing demand from these industries, Detroit Edison had aggressively marketed its services to other industries, so much so that it had record sales to the commercial segment in 1990. In 1991 Detroit Edison received the "Electric Utility of the Year" award from the trade magazine *Electric Light & Power.* The company had record revenues and earnings, and in mid-December 1991 its common stock reached $35 per share, the highest price in 25 years. Michigan's economy and state policy continued to be uncertain as its basic industries struggled to compete with foreign manufacturers and its governor was defining state goals. All this will affect Detroit Edison's future. For these reasons Detroit Edison has chosen to minimize staff levels, reduce its use of foreign crude, and cut its dependence on industrial sales, thereby maximizing the company's flexibility.

Principal Subsidiaries: Midwest Energy Resources Company; St. Clair Energy Corporation; Edison Illuminating Company; SYNDECO, Incorporated.

Further Reading: McCarthy, Walter J. Jr., *Detroit Edison Generates More Than Electricity*, New York, The Newcomen Society in North America, 1983; "A Short History of Detroit Edison," Detroit Edison corporate typescript, 1990.

—Maya Sahafi

DOMINION RESOURCES, INC.

Riverfront Plaza, West Tower
901 East Byrd Street
Richmond, Virginia 23219
U.S.A.
(804) 775-5700
Fax: (804) 775-5819

Public Company
Incorporated: 1909 as Virginia Railway and Power Company
Employees: 13,000
Sales: $3.53 billion
Stock Exchange: New York

Dominion Resources, Inc. (DRI) is a holding company whose largest subsidiary, Virginia Electric and Power Company (Vepco), accounted in the early 1990s for $3.46 billion of DRI's $3.53 billion operating revenues. Vepco, a regulated public utility, supplies electric power to more than 1.7 million customers in Virginia and the northeast portion of North Carolina, where it is known as North Carolina Power. Other subsidiaries are involved in real estate and investment. Vepco is a leader among U.S. electric utilities in the use of nuclear power and is able to sell power to other utilities.

Vepco was founded in 1909, but its corporate roots date to the Appomattox Trustees, established in 1781 by the Virginia General Assembly to foster navigation on the Appomattox River for hauling rum and tobacco. The trustees, who included George Washington and James Madison, founded the Upper Appomattox Company, a canal company, in 1795.

In 1888 Upper Appomattox, which possessed water rights in the area, took over some hydroelectric plants, adding a steam generating plant in 1889. In 1901 control of the water rights passed to the Virginia Passenger and Power Company, a transit and electric utility owned by George Fisher & Associates, which went into receivership in 1904. Virginia Passenger and Power was bought in 1909 by the newly formed Virginia Railway and Power Company, (VR&P) owned chiefly by Frank Jay Gould, son of financial speculator Jay Gould.

A Gould cousin, William Northrop, the new company's first president, died in 1912. Northrop's successor, Thomas S. Wheelwright, impatient with delays in reaching company objectives, once put his men to work chopping down trees on a main thoroughfare to make way for trolley tracks, precipitating a rush of protesters on city hall.

VR&P bought three more transit and power companies in Richmond, whose street railways had been the nation's first successful electrified trolley system—Richmond Passenger & Power, Richmond Traction Company, and Richmond & Petersburg Electric Railway Company. As was typical of the day, the new company's earnings came overwhelmingly from transit, $1.4 million compared to $614,000 for business and consumer electricity in 1910.

There followed a series of acquisitions by VR&P—Norfolk & Portsmouth Traction Company in 1911; Richmond Railway & Viaduct Company in 1916; and Norfolk & Ocean View Railway Company in 1917. In 1911 the company also acquired gas properties in Norfolk, Virginia and entered the natural gas distribution business. The Norfolk acquisitions provided access to a fast-growing market during World War I, since Norfolk was a major U.S. Navy port. Indeed, a naval officer was assigned to direct the use of electricity during the war, and trolley cars were halted when the military needed extra power. Disappointed passengers nicknamed the company "The Virginia Railway and Powerless Company." The electric-transit business was in decline.

In 1925 VR&P was purchased by a syndicate headed by Stone & Webster, Inc., a New York engineering and consulting company. A holding company, Engineers Public Service, was formed to own and manage the company, whose name was changed to Virginia Electric and Power Company, the better to reflect the changing electrical industry. Luke C. Bradley, former president of a Texas utility company, became president, succeeding Wheelwright. In the same year, Vepco acquired Petersburg Power Company and expanded electrical service north into the Fredericksburg-Ashland areas of Virginia and south into eastern North Carolina.

Vepco's new Petersburg, Virginia office building, fronting on a new bridge over the Appomattox River, was dedicated in October 1925. Its second floor opened onto the bridge and served as a waiting room for passengers on Vepco's interurban trolley between Richmond and Petersburg, 20 miles south. Vepco's goal was to put public transportation within four blocks of every Richmond resident. It spent more than $3.8 million on extensions and improvements in 1924 and 1925.

Because the auto had begun to challenge the streetcar, Vepco provided more comfortable trolley cars, including 15 with mahogany interiors and deep-cushioned leather seats. These were unveiled with fanfare and the offer of free rides for several days. Other cars were refurbished with seats of woven rattan over cushions. On the outside over the windows was painted the slogan, "Why not ride with us and save the difference?"

In 1926 Vepco received a 30-year public-transit franchise from the city of Richmond, over the mayor's veto; he objected to provisions governing tax revenues. The agreement was generally well received, however, and an era of good feeling ensued, demonstrated in part by the stationing of police officers to help streetcars manage busy intersections during rush hours. William E. Wood, Vepco's vice president, succeeded Bradley in 1927 when Bradley left to head another utility company.

Vepco made two acquisitions in the next few years—the Norfolk Railway & Light Company in 1927 and the City Gas Company of Norfolk in 1930. The former added territory in the southern part of Virginia. In 1930 Vepco also made its last major track expansion, the Broad Street extension to the Richmond city limits. The company acquired new leadership in

1929, when Jack G. Holtzclaw became president a few months after Wood left for New York to become executive vice president of the holding company, Engineers Public Service. Vepco had 100,000 customers and annual revenues of $11 million.

Vepco's transit business suffered in the 1920s as the automobile grew in popularity. Annual revenues dropped from $290,000 in 1923 to $85,000 in 1931, and the company cut back service. The 40-mile round trip between Richmond and Petersburg was reduced from 70 to 58 minutes by making an earlier turnaround in Richmond, and baggage service was dropped. A more significant change was the substitution of motor buses for electric streetcars on this route in September 1936. The streetcars were on their way out; the last was to run in September 1949. During World War II, as in World War I, several Vepco-area cities in Virginia were central to the war effort, Norfolk as Atlantic Fleet headquarters, Newport News as site of a major shipyard, and Yorktown as site of the Naval Mine Depot.

Meanwhile, Vepco ownership was challenged by the Securities and Exchange Commission (SEC) in its widespread dissolution of utility holding companies. Sued by the SEC in 1940, the Vepco owner, Engineers Public Service, had to divest itself of everything but Vepco. It sold the Richmond and Norfolk transit systems, which became the Virginia Transit Company. The Portsmouth and Petersburg lines were sold a few months later.

Vepco merged in the same year with the Virginia Public Service Company, a series of systems in northern and western Virginia and in the Hampton Roads area near Norfolk. The merger more than doubled the Vepco service area, making Vepco one of the largest U.S. electric utilities. Rather than keep Vepco and divest its gas operations, as was required, Engineers Public Service dissolved itself. Vepco became independent in 1947, with 450,000 gas and electric customers. Vepco was ready to face the postwar rise in demand. In 1949 it acquired the East Coast Electric Company, operating in Virginia's Tidewater section; in 1952 it added the territory of the Hydro-Electric Corporation of Virginia, and in 1957 it acquired Roanoke Utilities Company, Inc.

In 1955 the Roanoke Rapids (North Carolina) dam, a remotely controlled hydroelectric operation on the Roanoke River, was completed after a long, hard court fight with the U.S. Department of the Interior. Vepco had received a license in 1929 from the Federal Power Commission to build the dam, but had not carried out construction during the Depression. When the company reapplied for a license after World War II, the Interior Department claimed responsibility for hydroelectric power development, and opposed the license grant. Ultimately, after hearings before the Federal Power Commission and the courts, the commission granted Vepco the license. The decision was upheld by the U.S. Supreme Court in 1953, and the project was begun. It was dedicated in April 1956, in honor of Jack Holtzclaw, who had died of a heart attack in 1955. In Holtzclaw's 26 years as president, Vepco had grown from a local power company to one serving two-thirds of the counties in Virginia and parts of North Carolina and West Virginia.

During these years, Vepco's general counsel was T. Justin Moore, whom Erwin H. Will described in his Newcomen Society lecture in 1965 as "probably the most outstanding utility lawyer in the United States." Its chief guide in financial matters was Donald C. Barnes, president of Engineers Public Service in the 1930s and 1940s and chairman of Vepco's board from 1947 to 1960.

Erwin Will succeeded Holtzclaw as president in 1956. He led Vepco into the nuclear power field as one of four utilities that formed a nonprofit corporation, Carolinas-Virginia Nuclear Power Association, to research and develop a prototype, experimental reactor. This was built in the early 1960s at Parr Shoals, South Carolina. Vepco thus became on of the nation's front-runners in nuclear energy.

Alfred H. (Pete) McDowell Jr. succeeded Will in 1958, Will remaining as board chairman. In 1959 McDowell and Will observed that Vepco, unlike some utilities, did not depend on large customers in any one industry and had thus been insulated somewhat from economic hard times. Another factor was the population growth of its service area at about twice the rate of the United States as a whole, while the number of electric customers grew 47%, to 704,000 from 1950 through 1957.

In the realm of technical innovation, Vepco installed, in the 1960s, probably the first underground residential distribution system, using buried cables, of lighter weight than the lead cables used in major cities but permitting higher voltage than previously carried by such cables. The approach became standard for newly developed residential communities, where overhead cables became obsolete.

Another innovation of the 1960s was the world's first extra-high-voltage system, at Mount Storm, West Virginia, where Vepco built its Mine Mouth coal-fired steam station, which opened in 1965, virtually on top of West Virginia's estimated 100 million tons of unmined coal. Vepco also built the first 500,000-volt transmission system in the country and started one of the largest hydroelectric facilities in the world, in Bath County, in the mountainous western part of Virginia. The company developed it during the very difficult years of the 1970s, opening it in the mid-1980s. The Bath County system pumped water at night to a high elevation, and then used the energy of the falling water during the day to run turbines.

In 1965 Vepco's annual revenues were $215 million, compared to $11 million in 1929. Its property and plant had more than doubled in 10 years. Will stated "while some still don't seem to believe it," rates had dropped for each of the previous four years.

The 1970s brought great changes, caused by the oil embargo and the subsequent shortages and rising costs. Vepco had begun converting coal stations to oil-fired ones in the 1960s, because oil was priced low. It reversed the process in the 1970s, and by the 1980s most of its stations were coal-fired. The ill-timed switch to oil did not set well with some. The resulting image problems became one reason that Vepco, or Virginia Power as it is also known, is called North Carolina Power when it serves North Carolina.

The 1970s changed the industry because rising fuel bills, inflation, and high interest rates did away with the economies of scale that had in part justified the monopoly system for public utilities. Demand had been predictable, growing at 7% a year before the embargo, and technology had once lowered the price of electricity. Neither was the case in the 1970s. The industry faced new challenges.

Vepco's president in the late 1970s, Stanley Ragone, died in May 1980. In his short time as president, Ragone had promoted nuclear power and had worked to bring Vepco into nuclear prominence. It had been thought at one time that Vepco would have an all-nuclear system; a difficult regulatory climate put an end to such speculation. Ragone's successor, William W. Berry, was an electrical engineer with 24 years of experience with Vepco.

Reversals had been such during the difficult 1970s that Vepco was financially hard-pressed, nearly bankrupt in 1980, according to *Forbes* magazine, May 2, 1988. Berry pulled back from the nuclear commitment, canceling two units under construction. He made considerable managerial changes, and started a push to recovery with the help of his first assistant, Jack Ferguson. He persuaded state regulators to allow competitive bidding on cogenerated power, produced by one source for both industrial use and sale. Then he sold cogenerated power to utilities in states whose regulators did not allow competitive bidding. It was a strategy that less venturesome utilities shrank from, because of the risks involved, among them the problem of identifying reliable cogenerators and the possibility of adverse regulatory changes. Berry also promised that rate increases in the 1980s would be less than the rate of inflation, a promise he kept.

Early in his time as CEO, Berry was recognized as unique among electric utility executives for his advocacy of deregulation and competition. He proposed dividing electric utilities into three components: generation, transmission, and retail distribution. Only the latter should be considered a natural monopoly, he said. Into the process he wanted to insert regional energy brokers, owners of transmission equipment, who would act like stock exchange specialists making markets. Vepco was buying cheap coal-fired power from adjacent utilities near midwestern coal fields at the time, in mid-1982, and was taking advantage of a freer market in bulk power.

In 1983 Berry took a greater step towards competition, leading to the formation of a holding company, Dominion Resources, Inc., which would make use of Vepco's expertise in unregulated areas. Dominion Resources formed its first subsidiary, an investment and investment management company, Dominion Capital, in 1985. Its involvement in real estate led it to form a real estate development and management subsidiary, Dominion Lands, in 1987. Nonutility earnings were to exceed 20% annually in the next five years.

Meanwhile, Berry called a halt to almost all plant construction. Vepco, now DRI's chief subsidiary, was operating four nuclear reactors but had canceled three others for lack of demand and a fourth because of high construction cost estimates. It was trying to sell part interest in two of the remaining four. The new emphasis was on transmission rather than generation, on being energy managers as one utility executive called it.

Vepco's nuclear capability meant much to the company. In 1984 it was one of the few utilities to reduce its rates, mainly due to its reliance on nuclear energy. Its four reactors were supplying 40% of its needs and were inexpensive to operate. Its fuel bill had dropped from more than $1 billion in 1980 to $725 million in 1983. Its customers were paying 2% less on average than a year earlier. Vepco had gotten out of nuclear construction, an expensive proposition, just in time. The strategy now was to rely on coal; Vepco embarked on the largest oil-to-coal conversion in the United States. By early 1987, it had only two oil units supplying just 3% of its power. Since the coal was a low-sulfur variety, acid rain was not a worry, and scrubbers were needed on only 1 of 11 units.

Demand was up 5%, but Berry was expecting no great upsurge, because, he argued, customers had learned to do with less. This situation was good for business, because it ruled out expensive new construction.

As cited in *Electric Light & Power,* November 1986, Berry argued for a "level playing field," or a chance to compete on equal terms. Economic efficiency demanded more than the "piecemeal changes" urged by regulators, he told a meeting of large industrial users, predicting an end to the "chummy fraternity" among electric utilities as those with excess capacity entered the open power market.

DRI entered northern Virginia in 1986, acquiring the retail territory of the Potomac Electric Power Company. The company formed a third subsidiary in 1987, Dominion Energy, a developer of power plants to perform in this open market. DRI sold its retail territory in West Virginia that year, to UtiliCorp United, Inc.

At Berry's side during these years was Jack Ferguson, president of Vepco since DRI was formed in 1983. Berry was the financial expert; Ferguson handled operations. Thomas E. Capps, executive vice president of Vepco, who succeeded Berry as DRI's president and CEO in 1990, was responsible for external social, legal, and political tasks.

In 1987 Berry's response to industry changes was called "cagey and controversial" by *Forbes,* May 2, 1988. DRI had taken a "regulatory sidestep," was engaged in "regulatory arbitrage," buying power at the low price that prevailed in Virginia and selling power at higher prices elsewhere. DRI was investing in 13 new plants out of state to produce power for other, nearby utilities. It was earning 20% to 25% return on its equity in these new units, in contrast to 13.25% on its Virginia plants.

DRI was thus expanding its unregulated business, which contributed only 4.4% of net earnings in fiscal 1987, while putting limits on its regulated business. Percentages of net earnings from unregulated business rose to 6% in 1988, 7% in 1989, and 8% in 1990.

Federal law had forced utilities to buy at a high fixed price from cogenerators, with a view to encouraging cogeneration, an energy-saving tactic, but Berry had pushed successfully for a bidding process in Virginia, and the idea began to gain momentum nationwide. It was a privatizing of generation sources, with investors building stations so as to sell power to the local utility. DRI through its Dominion Energy subsidiary went to West Virginia, California, and even South America for power.

In 1988 DRI bought half of Enron Cogeneration from Enron Corp. of Houston. It sold its natural gas operation in 1990, while its subsidiary Dominion Energy became involved in joint ventures to acquire and develop natural gas reserves.

In 1990 DRI prepared to make better use of its generating facilities. Nuclear units reached more than 80% of capacity compared to 67% of capacity that was average for U.S. nuclear plants. Every change in the economy showed in business volume. During the Gulf War, for instance, when fewer naval vessels docked in Virginia ports, business suffered, because an aircraft carrier in port uses a great deal of electricity. DRI was serving fast-growing areas, and plans for the 1990s were to increase capacity to meet rising demand, but with less construction, less borrowing, and more cash on hand.

Principal Subsidiaries: Virginia Electric and Power Company; Dominion Capital; Dominion Energy; Dominion Lands.

Further Reading: A Half Century of Progress: A picture history of the Virginia Electric and Power Company, Richmond, Virginia, Virginia Electric and Power Company, 1959; Will, Erwin H., *The Past—Interesting; The Present—Intriguing; The Future—Bright: A Story of Virginia Electric and Power Company,* New York, Newcomen Society in North America, 1965; Sherrid, Pamela, "Live wire," *Forbes,* September 27, 1982; McKenney, Carlton Norris, *Rails in Richmond,* Glendale, California, Interurban Press, 1986; Novack, Janet, "The regulatory sidestep," *Forbes,* May 2, 1988.

—Jim Bowman

DUKE POWER COMPANY

422 South Church Street
Charlotte, North Carolina 28242
U.S.A.
(704) 373-4011
Fax: (704) 382-8375

Public Company
Incorporated: 1905 as The Southern Power Company
Employees: 19,400
Sales: $3.68 billion
Stock Exchange: New York

Duke Power Company is one of the premier public utilities in the United States. Its system of nuclear, coal-fired, and hydroelectric power plants is among the most efficient in the country, and the company has performed well financially in recent years. Long noted for the large number of engineers in its top administrative ranks, Duke built a reputation as the country's top nuclear utility before that industry ran into significant opposition in the 1980s, at which point Duke resumed its role as expert builder of coal-fired plants. To capitalize further on its coal plant expertise, Duke in 1989 formed a joint venture with Fluor Corporation, the nation's largest construction firm, to design, build, and service coal facilities worldwide.

Duke Power owes its name and origin to James Buchanan (Buck) Duke, the hugely successful founder of The American Tobacco Company. In the tradition of Rockefeller and Carnegie, Duke turned his family's modest business into a vast cartel wielding monopolistic control over the entire tobacco industry, until, like Rockefeller's, his organization was formally dissolved through antitrust action in 1911.

Duke was born in 1856 to a farming family outside Durham, North Carolina. His father's small farm and livestock holdings were ruined during the Civil War, leaving the family no choice but to peddle a barn of tobacco unnoticed by the looting soldiers. The tobacco was of the variety now known as bright leaf, a then-recently developed, mild, golden leaf grown in the Durham area and soon to become widely popular under the Bull Durham label. Young James Duke began selling tobacco with his father at age nine and never stopped; the family's bright leaf sold well, and the Duke business grew rapidly. Along with his father, Washington Duke, brother Benjamin, and half-brother Brodie, Buck Duke worked day and night to make the family's Pro Bono Publico brand of tobacco competi-

tive with the Bull Durham leader, but as late as 1880 the Dukes remained a profitable also-ran in the booming bright leaf business.

James Duke was an ambitious young man, and in 1881 he shifted to the manufacture of cigarettes, a new and not yet fashionable form of tobacco use. Armed with a number of efficient automatic rolling machines and the excellent tobacco of his native area, Duke became a national power in the cigarette business within a few years. Relocating to New York City, Duke gained some 38% of the nation's cigarette sales by 1889, and in the following year engineered the formation of The American Tobacco Company, merging W. Duke Sons & Company with the four leading cigarette makers in the country. During the following two decades Duke made American Tobacco the core of what came to be known as the tobacco trust, a network of interlocking corporations controlling about three-fourths of the U.S. tobacco business. Duke became an extremely wealthy, powerful, and well-known figure in U.S. business.

Among his myriad other ventures, Duke became interested in the 1890s in the future of North Carolina hydroelectric power. Electrification was slow in coming to the rural Piedmont, an area of central North Carolina and western South Carolina, but several early investors, including W. Gill Wylie of South Carolina, had begun harnessing the power generated by the many Appalachian mountain rivers coursing through the area. Duke saw the potential value of electricity to the local textile industry, in which he and his brother Ben already had extensive interests, and in 1898 the brothers began buying Piedmont river properties for later development. Duke also met Wylie and agreed to back his existing electric projects, but it was not until 1904 that the tobacco tycoon took a serious interest in the business of power.

In that year Duke, Wylie, and Wylie's chief engineer, William States Lee, met in New York to discuss the future of electric power in the Piedmont. Impressed by Lee's detailed plans for a series of hydroelectric plants along the Catawba and Yadkin rivers, Duke matched a $50,000 investment of Wylie's, and the two men formed The Southern Power Company in June of 1905. Southern Power, incorporated in New Jersey and capitalized at $7.5 million, would be the holding company for Duke and Wylie's power assets, which at that time included extensive tracts of land, several power stations, and manufacturing facilities. By 1907 Southern Power was operating two full-fledged electric plants, one at India Hook Shoals and the other at Great Falls, both in South Carolina. Three years later the company created a subsidiary, Mill Power Supply Company, to purchase, manufacture, and sell various types of electrical equipment.

Duke's investment in Piedmont power was not limited to the millions he poured into Southern Power, however. As he had in the tobacco business, Duke went into power expecting to change the face of the industry. Not only would he bring electricity to the Piedmont, he and his brother Ben would also bring the textile factories that would buy the electricity, in that way beginning an industrial revolution in the area with Duke power as its indispensable base. He and Ben made countless investments in new and existing textile mills, offering the financial backing of the mighty American Tobacco Company to any mill owner who would buy power from the Dukes. Many of them did, their mills prospering with the efficiencies made possible by electrified spindles. The Dukes would then sell their stock to buy into another mill and thus keep the expansionary cycle rolling. By this method the Dukes were largely responsible for a surge in Piedmont textiles, where, by the early 1920s, fully one-sixth of all U.S. spindles were powered by Duke generators. Duke Power Company, as the firm was known after the mid-1920s, supplied electricity to about 300 cotton mills, in many of which it held large shares of stock, and the Carolinas' textile industry rivaled that of Massachusetts for national leadership.

In 1911 Duke's tobacco trust was broken up by the U.S. Supreme Court, coincidentally, also the year in which Rockefeller's Standard Oil was dissolved, but the change had little impact on either Duke's fortune or the growing success of his power company. Along with its many textile industry customers, Duke Power began supplying electricity to private residences in the area, a source of revenue soon to be considerably expanded by the increasing number of electric appliances in the home. Mill-Power Supply Company, Duke's equipment subsidiary, took a leading role in the appliance revolution in the Piedmont, introducing electric irons, water heaters, and other inventions to the largely rural, conservative homeowners. Together with the universal shift to electric lighting, the growth in appliance use would eventually make residential service one of Duke's three main sources of revenue, the others being industrial and commercial. Once the electrical household was firmly established and most of the modern conveniences introduced, residential sales remained at the level of about 25% of total company revenue.

In 1923, W. Gill Wylie died, followed two years later by James Duke, leaving W.S. Lee as the company's leader. At about the same time, Duke Power began adding to its hydroelectric generating stations a series of larger and more powerful steam plants. The company had previously used steam generators only as auxiliaries, but with the increasing demand for electricity in the Piedmont, W.S. Lee decided to embark on a comprehensive program of steam construction. The Buck Steam Station, named after the company's late founder, went on line in 1927, the first of many steam plants that were later to dwarf the original hydroelectric network. In 1989, the latter consisted of 26 units that together generated only 2% of Duke's 13-million-kilowatt capacity.

The Great Depression years were difficult for many utilities, especially those which depend heavily on industrial users for their revenue. W.S. Lee's career as one of the country's top power plant engineers came to an abrupt halt in October of 1929, the crash and ensuing lean years ending all plans for future construction in the Piedmont. With industrial usage down, Duke Power sought to increase its residential sales by once more pushing the acceptance of household appliances and several times cutting its rates. In the midst of these hard times, Lee died in 1934 at the age of 63, bringing to an end the first generation of leaders at Duke Power. Lee's grandson, also called William S. Lee, later became chairman and president of the company. It was not until 1938 that Duke built another power plant, and not until after World War II that it regained its earlier rapid pace of expansion.

The postwar years brought a resurgence of business and consumer activity in the Piedmont, as it did elsewhere in the United States. Duke immediately began revamping and repairing its system of plants, and was soon to spend $200 million developing a number of new and highly efficient steam facilities. The two largest of these, Dan River and Plant Lee, were in service by 1952 and together added 320,000 kilowatts to the Duke Power grid, and both plants were praised as being unusually well engineered. Duke always excelled at the construction of power stations, doing all of its own design, building, and maintenance. The company attributed to the experience thus gained, the consistently high marks its plants have earned from industry analysts. In 1982, for example, six of the eight most efficient generating plants in the United States were owned by Duke Power; as of 1989, Duke's team of coal-fired stations had been ranked number one nationally for 15 straight years.

It was no doubt this tradition of engineering excellence that encouraged Duke to join with three other utilities in a 1956 venture called Carolinas-Virginia Nuclear Power Association. Even as they continued adding ever-larger steam plants, more than doubling the company's capacity during the 1950s, Duke engineers had become much interested in the long-term potential of nuclear energy as an alternative source of electricity. Carolinas-Virginia was formed to build a small, experimental nuclear generator as a first step toward the eventual construction of complete nuclear stations. Its Parr Shoals, South Carolina plant opened in 1962, the first nuclear facility in the southeastern United States and a generally successful conclusion to the years of planning required. Duke officials decided that, despite the evident environmental dangers inherent in the use of nuclear energy, its engineering abilities would allow it to shift its entire power grid over a number of years, from coal and water to nuclear without an unacceptable diminution of safety. Duke, like all other nuclear power utilities, was often faced with formidable opposition to its nuclear program. Scientists and the general public were alarmed by the possibility of radiation leaks and the more remote chance of explosion.

Steam construction continued apace, including the world's largest such plant located at Lake Norman, North Carolina, but in 1967 Duke received a permit from the Atomic Energy Commission to build the first of its full-scale nuclear units, the Oconee Nuclear Station. The proportion of electricity generated by nuclear energy at Duke rose rapidly, reaching 31% as early as 1975, and Duke's overall capacity approximately doubled during the same short span. To feed its massive coal system, in 1970 Duke bought four coal mines in Harlan County, Kentucky, creating a new subsidiary called Eastover Mining to operate the mines. Eastover soon became embroiled in a prolonged and bitter dispute with the United Mine Workers (UMW) union, which claimed that the Duke subsidiary was preventing its workers from joining their ranks. The union took out full-page ads in leading national financial newspapers urging investors to boycott Duke stock for the company's anti-union stance and an assortment of other alleged corporate misdeeds, including pollution and poor worker housing. To make matters worse, the economy was rocked by the OPEC oil embargo of 1973, inducing a recession just as Duke began the most intensive campaign of capital expenditures in its history, a 10-year, $6.6 billion program to run until 1982. In 1974 a belated rate hike approval from the North Carolina Utilities Commission buoyed the company, sales in that year hitting $823 million and net income $103 million. The dispute with the UMW was eventually settled, and Duke later divested itself of the mines.

By 1977 sales had again jumped, to $1.3 billion, but Duke had already begun scaling back its plans for a wholesale shift to nuclear power. The 1979 accident at Three Mile Island further darkened the nuclear horizon; although Duke continued to bring on line the nuclear plants it had under construction, by 1985 it had cancelled or postponed a total of six new units. The rising tide of opposition to nuclear power was especially painful for Duke, which had already gained a reputation for outstanding work in the nuclear field and whose chairman, William S. Lee, had been called the leading expert on nuclear power in the utility industry. The company did not initiate new construction on any nuclear units after the early 1980s, confining development to a massive hydroelectric pumped-storage station in South Carolina. Duke nevertheless remained an ardent supporter of nuclear power, which in 1989 supplied 63% of its total kilowatts. That year Lee was elected president of the new World Association of Nuclear Operators (WANO), an organization he was instrumental in creating. WANO provides a forum in which owner-operators of the world's more than 400 commercial nuclear reactors can meet to discuss safety and related technical issues.

Further evidence of Duke's continued commitment to nuclear power was its 1989 formation, with four other companies, of Louisiana Energy Services, a joint venture to build the nation's first privately owned uranium enrichment facility, capable of supplying 15% of the U.S. nuclear industry's uranium needs. Also that year, Hurricane Hugo swept through the Carolinas, interrupting service to 700,000 of Duke's customers and causing extensive damage to transmission lines and other company equipment. Repairs took up to two weeks of nonstop work by a crew of 9,000, but Duke's response to the crisis seemed to have been generally well received and the effect on its financial performance was negligible. In 1990 construction proceeded—ahead of schedule—on Duke's $1.1 billion Bad Creek Hydroelectric Station. Also that year, Duke split its common stock two-for-one to make the shares more accessible to individual investors, and sold Mill-Power Supply, whose business was too small to have a significant impact on corporate earnings.

Ranked in 1990 as the country's seventh-largest public utility, Duke Power appeared to be situated to prosper in any future energy environment. An acknowledged leader in both nuclear and coal-fired technology, Duke, in the early 1990s, was prepared to build power plants for itself or on contract for other utilities, and its highly efficient designs result in fuel conservation as well as profits.

Principal Subsidiaries: Nantahala Power and Light Company; Church Street Capital Corp.; Crescent Resources, Inc.; Duke Energy Corp.; Duke Engineering & Services, Inc.; Duke/ Fluor Daniel.

Further Reading: Winkler, John K., *Tobacco Tycoon,* New York, Random House, 1942; Maynor, Joe, *Duke Power: The First 75 Years,* Charlotte, North Carolina, Duke Power Company, 1979.

—Jonathan Martin

ELECTRICITÉ DE FRANCE

2 rue Louis Murat
75384 Paris
Cedex 08
France
(1) 4042 2222
Fax: (1) 4042 3183

State-Owned Company
Incorporated: 1946
Employees: 119,900
Sales: FFr156.46 billion (US$30.20 billion)

Electricité de France, France's state-owned electric utility, has a greater cash flow than any other company in France. In 1991, its immense generating system produced more than 406 billion kilowatt hours of electricity, the bulk of it in nuclear power stations built in the world's largest nuclear power program. In addition to providing France's electricity, Electricité de France (EDF) is selling an increasing amount of power to neighboring countries.

EDF was formed in 1946 when the French government decided to nationalize the production and distribution of electricity. This was part of a general wave of nationalizations of key industries in France and elsewhere in Europe following the end of World War II.

Before 1946, the French electrical industry was in the hands of a large number of private companies, providing production, distribution, and other services connected with the industry under a variety of agreements with local authorities and regional administrations. The system had developed without any kind of centralized planning following the appearance of the first distribution networks in 1884. By the outbreak of the Second World War, electricity was provided by about 200 companies engaged in production, another 100 in transport, and about 1,150 involved in distribution. An estimated 20,000 concession-holders provided equipment and other services to these companies. The system was irrational and inefficient, and its absurdity even went as far as having two companies providing electricity to the same place, such as in the Lyon region, where two companies competed directly, one selling alternating current from its hydroelectric plant, the other offering direct current produced at a coal-fired thermal station.

The main reason for the government's decision to consolidate the electrical industry into a single nationalized utility was its determination to speed up industrialization and urban-

ization after World War II. Defeat by the German forces had revealed the weaknesses of the French economy, and there was a widespread agreement on the need to modernize what was still a largely rural, agricultural society. The electric industry was central to these plans for industrialization, and a single utility was regarded as the best way of providing the resources for the swift increase in productive capacity that would be needed, as well as overcoming the inefficiencies of the old system.

The decision to establish a nationalized utility, rather than a private one, was largely due to the influence of Marcel Paul, a Communist who, in November 1945, seven months after being freed from the Nazi concentration camp at Buchenwald, was appointed Minister for Industrial Production by the head of the government, Charles De Gaulle. Besides strong technical arguments for nationalization as the most efficient means of rationalizing the industry, Paul brought a firm ideological commitment to nationalization, as well as the bitter enmity of the French political left toward the private electricity owners, who had often funded right-wing political organizations and were widely suspected of collaborating with the Nazi occupiers during the war. Paul's work toward nationalization paid off on April 8, 1946, when the National Assembly voted almost unanimously in favor of the law nationalizing electricity and gas.

Given the task of dramatically increasing France's output of electricity, the new organization immediately began work on a massive program of hydroelectric plant construction, which was the method favored by Marcel Paul and by Pierre Simon, whom Paul appointed as first president and director general of EDF. Simon was the former director of hydroelectric energy at the Ministry of Public Works. The dam-building program dominated EDF's activities throughout the late 1940s and 1950s. Although generally well-received by the public, the program gave the utility its first encounter with public opposition, when its first dam, which required the flooding of the village of Tignes in the Alps, met strong local resistance, including the bombing of a crane at the building site in 1946. Nevertheless EDF pressed on with the program.

Seven new hydroelectric installations were delivered in 1949, ten more in 1950, eight in 1951, and another eight in 1952. By 1957 a further 15 hydroelectric facilities were brought into service, turning the French Alps into the heart of the French electrical industry. The dam-building program culminated in the largest project, the redirection of the Durance river inland from Marseille, a project which created one of the largest lakes in France when it began operating in 1960.

This vast hydroelectric expansion increased EDF's production by two-and-a-half times, and made water power the most important part of the French electrical system. Until 1961 hydroelectric installations provided at least half of EDF's total production every year except in two years of drought. In 1960 the dams and their associated plants produced over 37.1 billion kilowatt hours of electricity, representing 71.5% of EDF's total production, compared with 18% provided by coal-fired thermal stations and only 3% by oil-burning stations.

The hydroelectric program had succeeded in providing France with a solid electrical supply. In the 1960s, however, as demand for electricity continued to increase in response to the rapid growth of the French economy, EDF turned away from its hydroelectric policy in the search for more highly productive capacity. Urbanization and general prosperity had caused a sharp increase in the use of domestic electrical appliances, creating much greater variation in the seasonal and daily demand for electricity. To cater for these changes, EDF turned to oil-fired thermal power stations, which burned a cheap fuel and were capable of providing a flexible output of current in accordance with the demand for energy. By 1973, EDF's oil-fired power stations were producing 59.7 billion kilowatt hours of power, providing 43% of EDF's total output compared with only 3% 13 years before. Over the same period, hydroelectricity had dropped to only 32% of EDF's output compared with 71.5% in 1960.

While oil had come to dominate EDF's activities, the company had also begun relatively small-scale developments in producing electricity from nuclear fission. Closely connected with the French military's development of its own arsenal of nuclear weapons, a civil nuclear project was begun in the late 1940s. In 1957 EDF decided to build its first nuclear power station at Chinon in the Loire valley, using technology developed by the French Atomic Energy Commissariat (CEA). Compared with later projects the Chinon plant was fairly small, using natural uranium as fuel, graphite as a moderator, and carbon gas as a refrigerant. The first phase of the project, with a capacity of just 68 megawatts (MW), came into service in 1962; the second 200MW stage in 1965; and the third in 1967, with capacity of 500MW. Research and development programs were launched on Heavy Water Reactors and Pressurized Water Reactors (PWR). It was determined that PWR was the more efficient technology and a 1300MW system was undertaken. As nuclear power gradually increased in importance within EDF during the 1960s, the utility commissioned more plants, turning from gas-graphite technology to the more efficient PWR. By 1973, nuclear stations were producing 14 million kilowatt hours of electricity a year, representing 8% of EDF's output.

Despite this development, nuclear power remained the poor relation of the French electrical family, dominated by oil and hydroelectricity, until oil was delivered a devastating blow in 1973. When the Organization of Petroleum Exporting Countries (OPEC) decided to increase oil prices sharply in that year, the importance of oil to the industrialized west was crudely illustrated. In France, the prospect of a huge increase in the oil bill for the electrical industry prompted the government to swing strongly in favor of rapid nuclear development, which had previously been considered too expensive compared to the use of oil. Now, as oil prices rocketed, the slogan of French independence, which had prompted the postwar hydroelectric projects, reemerged as the rationale for a massive nuclear power project to ensure that France would never again depend on other countries' whims for its energy.

The French prime minister, Pierre Messmer, outlined the pro-nuclear case in a speech on national television on March 6, 1974: "France has not been favored by nature in energy resources. There is almost no petrol on our territory, we have less coal than England and Germany and much less gas than Holland. . .our great chance is electrical energy of nuclear origin because we have had good experience with it since the end of World War II. . . In this effort that we will make to acquire a certain independence, or at least reduced dependence in energy, we will give priority to electricity and in electricity to nuclear electricity." The Messmer Plan, as it became known, involved a huge and sudden swing toward nu-

clear dependence, foreseeing the launch of 13 nuclear power plants, each with a capacity of 1,000MW, within two years.

In 1974 alone, three new plants—Tricastin, Gravelines, and Dampierre, with a combined capacity of nearly 11,000MW—were begun. By 1977 work had begun on another five stations, all using PWR, with a total capacity of 13,000MW. As part of a consortium of Euopean utilities, in which it holds a 51% stake, EDF also began building the most ambitious of all its nuclear installations—the FFr27 billion Superphenix fast-breeder reactor at Creys-Malville on the banks of the Rhone, the world's only commercial fast-breeder reactor, using enriched uranium and plutonium and capable of generating 12,000MW.

The Messmer plan succeeded in turning France into a nuclear-powered country. In the six years to 1979, nuclear energy's share of EDF's total output rose from 8% to 20%. By 1983 it had jumped to 49%, and by 1990 nuclear plants were providing 75% of EDF's electricity. By contrast, the share produced by stations burning oil or coal fell from 53% in 1973 to 24% in 1983, and down to just 11% in 1990. The importance of hydroelectricity also continued to decline, although less sharply, dropping from 32% in 1973 to 14% in 1990. EDF's total nuclear capacity had reached 54,000MW by the end of 1990, with another 6,800MW under construction, giving France a nuclear capacity greater than those of West Germany, the United Kingdom, Spain, and Sweden combined.

EDF's nuclear buildup faced opposition from anti-nuclear groups, but the utility and the government refused to yield to any pressure to moderate their ambitious nuclear plans, or even to accept a public debate on the issue. When huge demonstrations took place at the building site for the Superphenix plant in 1977, the authorities relied on firm police action to disperse the protesters. One demonstrator was killed in the violent clashes that followed. The unimpeded nuclear program finally slowed in 1981, when the newly elected Socialist government of François Mitterrand froze reactor construction. However, the government soon changed its position and allowed construction to continue, but at a greatly reduced rate.

In the mid-1980s it gradually became clear that the frenzied rush towards nuclear dependence had been overambitious. The construction program had compelled EDF to borrow heavily and, although building a standardized reactor had allowed EDF to streamline the construction process and thus cut costs, this saving would only be realized if the plants were operating at full capacity. The sheer size of the nuclear build-up, caused by incorrect energy demand forecasts made in the late 1970s and by the obsession with energy independence, had, however, left EDF with an immense overcapacity. By 1988, EDF's nuclear units were operating at an average load factor of 61%, compared with West Germany's 74%, and the much more efficient systems of smaller nuclear operators like Switzerland, at 84%, and Finland, at 92%.

During this period EDF began to sell its expertise and its product in foreign markets. The utility became closely involved in power projects in francophone countries in Africa and in 1985 began a series of projects in China, working on thermal, hydroelectric, and nuclear generation, distribution networks, maintenance, and training. By 1990, EDF had signed 20 contracts in China, had become project consultant for a controversial 1,800MW sea-water-cooled nuclear plant at Daya Bay and on the construction of a 1,200MW pumped storage power station.

EDF also began a concerted campaign to export its electricity to neighboring countries. In 1986, after six years of building, an undersea electrical cable was completed between France and Britain. Although this was theoretically to allow each country to draw on the other's power grid in times of shortage, it effectively became a one-way cable for the export of electricity from France to Britain. By 1990, France was exporting 11.9 billion kilowatt hours (kWh) of power a year to Britain, close behind its two biggest customers: Italy, with 12.9 billion kWh, and Switzerland, with 13.6 billion kWh. EDF also exported large bands of power to Germany, the Netherlands, Belgium, and Luxembourg and in 1990 signed an agreement worth $4 million to supply the Spanish electrical grid with 1,000MW of capacity beginning in the mid-1990s.

The utility was also quick to take advantage of the dramatic changes in eastern Europe following the collapse of Communism in 1989 and 1990. In 1991, EDF was on the verge of joining a German-led consortium to modernize eastern Germany's power network, and was leading an international team providing technical and management advice to Bulgaria's troubled nuclear industry. EDF was also broadening its activities in more developed markets. In July 1991, the utility became a key part of a consortium with Britain's East Midlands Electricity and several other companies to build a £400 million, 800 MW gas-fired power station in Lincolnshire, in a direct challenge to the two main British power companies, National Power and PowerGen, on their own territory. The consortium, Independent Power Generators, planned to invest in private power projects around the world.

While these foreign moves went ahead, EDF was also trying to stimulate demand for electricity within France to soak up its spare capacity. EDF also set out to encourage industrial companies to build power-consuming plants in France. However, large companies would only do this if EDF offered them power at a heavily subsidized rate, which the utility agreed to do when the aluminum producer Pechiney threatened to move its production to Venezuela because French power was too expensive. Instead, Pechiney, in partnership with EDF, built a new plant at Dunkirk in 1988, to which EDF agreed to provide electricity at half the production cost per kilowatt hour for the first six years, with the price rising gradually over subsequent years. The European Commission (EC) regarded the deal as nothing less than anti-competitive electricity dumping, and forced EDF to renegotiate it on more competitive grounds, but EDF received EC approval in 1990 for similar cheap power deals with the Exxon Chemicals and Allied Signal, two U.S. companies.

The problems confronting EDF crystallized in 1989, when the utility reported an annual loss of FFr4 billion, a result which EDF's president, Pierre Delaporte, described in the *Financial Times* of January 31, 1990, as "catastrophic, though mainly due to unforeseen problems, such as the mild winter, drought, and reduced availability of the PWR 1300MW series." In 1990, it received a further blow when the overseer of nuclear technology in France, EDF's former partner, the CEA, released a report sharply criticizing EDF's overinvestment in nuclear capacity and calling for urgent solutions to unresolved problems of nuclear waste disposal. By 1990, EDF had begun looking for ways to diversify its power sources.

Although EDF returned a small profit in 1990, a nuclear program costing FFr800 billion had left the utility with long-term debt of FFr226 billion. The long-term problems of waste disposal needed to be dealt with, while many of EDF's older reactors would soon be due for decommissioning, an operation whose cost, although unknown, was expected to be very high and would provide no financial return. However, the problem of overcapacity had been reduced, owing to the development of exports and increasing demand from French heavy industries. EDF ordered a new nuclear plant in 1991 and anticipated further investment in peak facilities and nuclear plants. From 1990 onward, debt was also decreasing. By 1990 repayment exceeded borrowing by FFr 3 billion, with a provisional figure of FFr 13 billion for 1991. EDF's rates, meanwhile, though already among the lowest in Europe, continued to decrease at 1.5% per year in real terms. In the coming European single market, utilities may be obliged to allow others to sell power into their grids, exposing the French system to direct competition. However, EDF is confident that its nuclear plants will give its generating arm a competitive edge in electricity production.

Principal Subsidiaries: Gérance Générale Foncière; Régie Foncière (60%); Société Immobilière de la Région Parisienne (97%); Centrale Nucléaire Européenne à Neutrons Rapides SA (51%); Société de Developpement et Services; Société Belgo-Française d'Energie Nucléaire Mosane (Belgium, 50%); FRAMATOME (10%); Compagnie Nationale du Rhone (16%).

Further Reading: Picard, J.-F., A. Beltran, and M. Bungener, *Histoires de l'EDF,* Paris, Dunod, 1985; Holmes, A., *Electricity in Europe: Power and Profit,* London, Financial Times Business Information Ltd., 1990.

—Richard Brass

ENDESA GROUP

Principe de Vergara 187
28002 Madrid
Spain
(91) 563 0923
Fax: (91) 563 8181

State-Owned Company
Incorporated: 1944
Employees: 15,700
Sales: Pta348.77 billion (US$3.61 billion)
Stock Exchanges: Madrid   New York

The ENDESA Group, one of Spain's largest electricity producers, has enjoyed phenomenal growth since its reorganization in 1983. The reorganization changed its relationship with its state parent company, Instituto Nacional de Industria (INI), by transferring all power companies under INI control, to ENDESA's authority. Prior to 1983, Endesa was one of a number of power companies controlled by the Spanish government through INI. At present, 33% of INI's holding in ENDESA has been privatized. The Spanish government hopes that ENDESA will become a private but Spanish-controlled utility giant that will be able to hold its own in the competitive post-1992 European single market.

If ENDESA's history was undistinguished from the time of its founding in 1944 to its reorganization in 1983, it was because it was a small, bureaucratic state organization without much policy- or decision-making power of its own. ENDESA was run by a succession of state appointees, often military or political figures close to the Spanish dictator Francisco Franco, but real power rested with INI which, in turn, had to refer all major decisions to central government.

Actually, much of the power company's pre-1983 history is INI's history. INI had its origins in the Law of Protection and Development of National Industry of October 1939. It was designed to help the nation rebuild an economic infrastructure that had been, at best, weak before the devastation of three years of civil war.

The law, drafted by Juan Antonio Suanez, a close childhood friend of Franco, continued the protectionist traditions found in Spain and typically in economically weak countries that find they must compete with powerful neighbors. Every investment decision required government approval, and no industrial facility could be constructed without official sanction.

As stark and bureaucratic as this law sounds, it made sense to the new dictator Francisco Franco and his government. No foreign money and very few domestic resources were available to develop the economy. Many of these had to be diverted to national defense. Franco had won the Spanish Civil War, but the country was politically isolated. Under pressure from his German Nazi and Italian Fascist civil war backers to join their side in World War II, which had engulfed Europe by the time of Franco's victory, he announced a policy of "non-belligerency." In effect, non-belligerency meant sympathetic gestures to the Axis powers, the most dramatic of which was the dispatch of the Spanish Blue Division to aid Hitler's troops on the Russian Front, while maintaining relations with Britain and the United States on the basis of Spain's neutrality. Franco had to have strong military forces to bolster this policy, and he had to quell nascent Republican support for the war. Spain was in an effective state of siege that seemed to justify strict government controls on all areas of life, including the economy.

A state economic apparatus was necessary to control the major sectors of the economy. It is no surprise that the chosen model for INI was Italy's Instituto per la Riconstruzione Industriale (IRI), created to reconstruct Italy's economy under the direct control of its dictator Benito Mussolini. Like its Italian counterpart, INI had a strong initial defense production orientation, but it was also directed to invest in enterprises that were unlikely to attract private capital and, at government request, INI had to take over failing private companies. This last requirement, the nursing of "lame duck" companies, has been a burden on INI for most of its history.

Electricity generation was one of the early major non-military sectors to receive special attention and investment from INI. By 1944, Franco's government was able to look toward the end of World War II and began to take more economic initiatives. Spain remained a backward country. There was little electricity available outside major industrial areas, and even there, it was not sufficient enough to supply the industries.

ENDESA was created as a public limited company, 98%-owned by INI, to construct badly needed power stations. Unlike most other INI companies, ENDESA was not an industrial monopoly. Two years later, in 1946, INI formed the Empresa Nacional Hidro-electrica del Ribagorzana (ENHER) to develop power generated from the River Noguera-Ribagorzana and its tributaries. Other state and private power companies were allowed to sell in local markets. Prior to the 1983 reorganization, ENDESA was responsible for less than one-third of the country's electricity output, but it was the largest generator in the sector.

INI poured investment into dams and power stations, but blackouts and electric power shortages persisted in Spain throughout the 1950s. The electricity industry, like others under INI's control, suffered from all the usual problems found in businesses run by massive state organizations. The two most prominent problems were bureaucratic inefficiency and inability to raise private and foreign capital for new investment projects. By 1948, Spanish industrial production only matched 1929 levels.

INI's empire had expanded into most of Spain's major industries, including petroleum, aviation, transportation, engineering, and manufacturing. Much of the rest of the economy was composed of small companies lacking in modern methods, equipment, and facilities, and with low production levels. Spain's industrial production expanded but failed to reach the boom levels of growth in Germany, Italy, France, and other European countries that, unlike Franco's Spain, had agreed to participate in the Marshall Plan.

In the late 1950s Spain suffered an economic crisis involving high inflation, low export levels, and insufficient growth. In 1958 the government cut off budgetary support for INI, but INI and its constituent companies borrowed heavily from private sector banks.

The government began to realize its mistake and in 1958–1960 adopted a "cold bath" stabilization plan similar to that typically favored by conservative economists today. The plan imposed ceilings on borrowing and forced ENDESA and other INI companies to become self-financing. The liberalization of business restrictions that had begun in the 1950s was speeded up to attract long-term and foreign investment.

However, little privatization was allowed. There was still a widespread fear that privatization would mean foreign domination. The fear has persisted to the present time. It was a major reason why Spain remained behind a protectionist wall until it moved to join the European Community (EC) in the early 1980s.

Initially, the impact was inflationary and electricity prices were allowed to rise by up to 50%, but by 1960 the groundwork was laid for what has been referred to as the Spanish miracle. The so-called miracle did not extend much beyond the major metropolitan areas. Concerns about "the two Spains" caused the government to once again rely on a centralized approach to national development.

Three national development plans aimed to develop regional industry. INI's role was limited in the first two, but it was crucial to the third of these plans, which were generally successful in creating new industrialization. The government made a number of attempts to reform INI during the 1960s and 1970s in an effort to make it and INI's constituent companies more businesslike. In 1968, INI was placed under the jurisdiction of the Ministry of Industry. Claudio Boada, appointed INI president in 1970, set up a three-year reorganization plan designed to make the company more profitable and less dependent on government subsidies.

ENDESA and other subsidiaries were expected to operate more like regular companies that operated on a profit-and-loss basis. A steel crisis hit INI in the early 1970s. The oil shocks of 1973 and 1979 hit Spain badly because the government continued to subsidize oil price levels until the death of Franco in 1975. INI nevertheless continued to expand and absorb lossmaking companies in rescue operations.

In 1978 a new INI president, Jose Miguel de la Rica, set significant reforms in place when he won the right not to be required by the government to take over failing companies, except by parliamentary order. From the beginning of the 1980s, this development and the general world trends that favored free market solutions and privatization encouraged INI to act more like a public sector company. INI sold all or part of its interest in a number of unprofitable companies.

The ENDESA reorganization of 1983 was part of the government's general plan to make INI more efficient and modernize Spain's institutions in preparation for full Spanish membership in the European Community. INI transferred all its power companies, Empresa Nacional Hidro-Electrica del Ribagorzana (ENHER), General Europea S.A. (GESA), Union Electrica de Canarias S.A. (UNELCO), and Empresa Nacional Electrica de Cordoba (ENECO) to ENDESA. The reorganization did not create a monopoly, however; at least seven major power companies remained in private hands. After reorganization, however, ENDESA became the country's largest electricity producer.

Ownership of several of the private companies was heavily concentrated in the hands of Spain's traditional elite and families who were close to General Franco. Unused to competitive pressures, these companies made some disastrous overinvestments in nuclear power during the 1970s. In 1983, a government moratorium was imposed on further investment in nuclear plants.

The government called on ENDESA to bail out these companies. As a result of a 1985 asset swap, ENDESA was further strengthened. The Spanish government required heavily indebted private and public companies like ENHER, Union Fenosa, and Fuerzas Electricas de Cataluna (FECSA) to sell large parts of their power stations and market share to ENDESA. This asset swap added more than Pta5 billion to the consolidated balance sheet and caused ENDESA to double in size.

In 1988 ENDESA followed Repsol as the second of three Spanish companies to be floated in New York, which, in effect, privatized 20% of the company for $670 million. Telefonica was the third. ENDESA quickly became acknowledged as an appreciating stock. INI's stake in ENDESA—then 75%—was now one of INI's most important assets because ENDESA accounted for most of the INI group's profits.

As a result of these reorganizations, ENDESA changed from being solely a power-generating company wholesaling electricity, to a more diversified—but integrated—energy production company with interests in coal, oil, nuclear, and hydroelectric-generated power.

In 1990 the company expanded into coal production with the acquisition of another INI company, ENCASUR. Traditionally, ENDESA was a wholesaler of power from generating stations. It continues in this role, but its subsidiaries are full-cycle companies that can produce and sell their own products.

In 1983, however, the government also created Red Eléctrica de España or REDESA, with ENDESA as the majority shareholder, to regulate the distribution system by deciding which plants will cover the country's electric power demands. This decision is calculated according to the cost at which certain companies can produce electricity regardless of who owns the plant. The basis is strict optimization of the costs. REDESA may buy power from other ENDESA companies or it may buy from smaller, privately owned electricity companies. There is a complicated payment system. This in effect puts ENDESA in a role sometimes played by regulatory bodies and electricity-generating boards in other countries. It must not be forgotten, however, that despite a degree of privatization, ENDESA remains a government institution in an industry in which market forces do not fully dictate its moves.

In another important way, ENDESA has continued to function through the late 1980s to the early 1990s as a government instrument. ENDESA has recently embarked on a campaign of buying interests in private companies dictated not so much by economic self-interest as by the dictates of Spanish government policy. In early 1991, ENDESA took over the small

Electra de Viesgo private utility in northern Spain and increased its stakes in other small private generators and distributors.

The Spanish Socialist Economy Minister Carlos Solchaga has stated his intention to use ENDESA as his main weapon to restructure the Spanish energy sector dramatically. The government knows that its ability to intervene in the energy sector will be curtailed severely when EC rules on liberalizing the entire European energy network come onstream at the end of 1992.

In 1990, the government warned foreign power utilities not to try to buy into their Spanish counterparts. The government fears that French utility companies will sell their cheap nuclear power in Spain after 1992, severely undercutting Spanish companies, threatening Spanish jobs, and making Spain dependent on France for her power needs.

Critics claim that ENDESA has high costs and low productivity and has been kept alive by the government to buy coal from loss-making, state-owned pits. The government claims that ENDESA would severely undermine private utilities' profits if it were allowed to compete directly in the retail market, but it also hopes that its rationalization plan for the power industry will cure any real inefficiencies before it has to compete with stronger EC firms.

Solchaga wants the power industry—including ENDESA, seven large private-sector generating and distributing companies, and several small local suppliers—to merge into, at most, three large conglomerates which would be the sole generators of electricity in the sector. The three would then supply a central network that would sell electricity to four or five distribution companies.

The mergers would also be aimed at putting Spain in a position to supply a projected 5% increase in annual demand. The government estimates that Spain must spend an estimated Pta600 billion to add the further 7,500 megawatts of electricity required by the end of the decade.

In April 1991, two major private utilities, Hidroelectrica España S.A. and Iberduero, announced that they would merge to form Iberdrola. The new company would control most of Spain's low-cost electricity generated from hydroelectric plants and challenge ENDESA's market position. The merger thwarted a possible bid by ENDESA, which then mounted a July bid to gain management control for Seville-based Compañia Sevillana de Electricidad S.A.

After a legal wrangle in which Sevillana's lawyers threatened to bring ENDESA before the European Commission on grounds of unfair competition, a compromise formula was found, enabling ENDESA to raise its stake above 20% without assuming management control. The deal also allowed Sevillana to buy a 2% interest in ENDESA and a further 6% will be sold on the market. INI's stake in ENDESA will be reduced to 67%.

The highly profitable ENDESA has been put in a privileged position by a Spanish government that is determined to build up Spanish bulwarks against foreign domination in the post-1992 single market. Prospects for further privatization of the company's shares are uncertain.

More partial privatizations of ENDESA are likely to take place. Solchaga has said the government intends to privatize ENDESA once its rationalization plans are in place. In the short term, however, it seems unlikely that the government would want INI to give up control and risk foreign domination over ENDESA, one of Spain's largest electricity producers and the most influential player in the power sector.

Principal Subsidiaries: Empresa Nacional Hidro-Electrica del Ribagorzana (91%); General Europa S.A. (55%); Union Electrica de Canarias SA (99%); Empresa Nacional Electrica de Cordoba (99%); Union Fabricantes Electrodomesticos S.A. (99%); Empresa Nacional Carbonifera del Sur S.A. (86%); Red Eléctrica de España (50%).

Further Reading: Donaghy, Peter and Michael Newton, *Spain: A Guide To Political and Economic Institutions*, Cambridge, Cambridge University Press, 1989.

—Noel Peter Byde and Clark Siewert

ENRON CORP.

1400 Smith Street
Houston, Texas 77002
U.S.A.
(713) 853-6161
Fax: (713) 853-6790

Public Company
Incorporated: 1930 as Northern Natural Gas Company
Employees: 7,000
Sales: $13.17 billion
Stock Exchanges: New York Pacific Midwest London
    Frankfurt

Enron Corp. is the largest integrated natural gas company in the United States. It operates a 38,000-mile pipeline network that supplies nearly 18% of U.S. natural gas consumption. In addition to natural gas transmission and marketing, it is involved in oil and gas exploration and production, liquid fuels processing and marketing, electricity development and production, and nonregulated purchasing and marketing of long-term natural gas commitments.

Enron began as Northern Natural Gas Company, organized in Omaha, Nebraska, in 1930 by three other companies. North American Light & Power Company and United Light & Railways Company each held a 35% stake in the new enterprise, while Lone Star Gas Corporation owned the remaining 30%. The company's founding came just a few months after the stock market crash of 1929, an inauspicious time to launch a new company. Several aspects of the Great Depression actually worked in Northern's favor, however. Consumers initially were not enthused about natural gas as a heating fuel, but its low cost led to its acceptance during tough economic times. High unemployment brought the new company a ready supply of cheap labor to build its pipeline system. In addition, the 24-inch steel pipe, which could transport six times the amount of gas carried by 12-inch cast iron pipe, had just been developed. Northern grew rapidly in the 1930s, doubling its system capacity within two years of its incorporation and bringing the first natural gas supply to the state of Minnesota.

In the 1940s there were changes in Northern's regulation and ownership. The Federal Power Commission, created as a result of the Natural Gas Act of 1938, regulated the natural gas industry's rates and expansion. In 1941 United Light & Railways sold its share of Northern to the public, and in 1942 Lone Star Gas distributed its holdings to its stockholders.

North American Light & Power would hold on to its stake until 1947, when it sold its shares to underwriters who then offered the stock to the public. Northern was listed on the New York Stock Exchange that year.

In 1944 Northern acquired the gas-gathering and transmission lines of Argus Natural Gas Company. The following year, the Argus properties were consolidated into Peoples Natural Gas Company, a subsidiary of Northern. In 1952 Peoples was dissolved as a subsidiary, its operations henceforth becoming a division of the parent company. Also in 1952, the company set up another subsidiary, Northern Natural Gas Producing Company, to operate its gas leases and wells. Another subsidiary, Northern Plains Natural Gas Company, was established in 1954 and eventually would bring Canadian gas reserves to the continental United States.

Through its Peoples division, the parent company acquired a natural gas system in Dubuque, Iowa, from North Central Public Service Company in 1957. In 1964 Council Bluffs Gas Company of Iowa was acquired and merged into the Peoples division.

Northern created two more subsidiaries in 1960: Northern Gas Products Company, now Enron Gas Processing Company, for the purpose of building and operating a natural gas extraction plant in Bushton, Kansas; and Northern Propane Gas Company, for retail sales of propane. Northern Natural Gas Producing Company was sold to Mobil Corporation in 1964, but the parent company continued expanding on other fronts. In 1966 it formed Hydrocarbon Transportation Inc., now Enron Liquids Pipeline Company, to own and operate a pipeline system carrying liquid fuels. Eventually, this system would bring natural gas liquids from plants in the Midwest and Rocky Mountains to upper-midwest markets, with connections for eastern markets as well.

Northern made several acquisitions in 1967: Protane Corporation, a distributor of propane gas in the eastern United States and the Caribbean; Mineral Industries Inc., a marketer of automobile antifreeze; National Poly Products Inc.; and Viking Plastics of Minnesota. Also in 1967, Northern created Northern Petrochemical Company to manufacture and market industrial and consumer chemical products. The petrochemical company acquired Monsanto Corporation's polyethylene marketing business in 1969.

Northern continued expanding during the 1970s. In February 1970 it acquired Plateau Natural Gas Company, which became part of the Peoples division. In 1971 it bought Olin Corporation's antifreeze production and marketing business. It set up UPG Inc., now Enron Oil Trading & Transportation, in 1973 to transport and market the fuels produced by Northern Gas Products. UPG eventually would handle oil and liquid gas products for other companies as well.

In 1976 Northern formed Northern Arctic Gas Company, a partner in the proposed Alaskan arctic gas pipeline, and Northern Liquid Fuels International Ltd., a supply and marketing company. Northern Border Pipeline Company, a partnership of four energy companies with Northern Plains Natural Gas as managing partner, began construction of the eastern segment of the Alaskan pipeline in 1980. This segment, stretching from Ventura, Iowa, to Monchy, Saskatchewan, was completed in 1982. About that time, it became apparent that transporting Alaskan gas to the lower 48 U.S. states would be prohibitively expensive. Nevertheless, the pipeline provided an important link between Canadian gas reserves and the continental United States.

Northern changed its name to InterNorth, Inc. in 1980. That same year, while attempting to grow through acquisitions, InterNorth became involved in a takeover battle with Cooper Industries Inc. to acquire Crouse-Hinds Company, an electrical-products manufacturer. Cooper rescued Crouse-Hinds from InterNorth's hostile bid and bought Crouse-Hinds in January 1981. The takeover fight brought a flurry of lawsuits between InterNorth and Cooper. The suits were dropped after the acquisition was finalized.

While InterNorth grew through acquisitions, it also expanded from within. In 1980 it set up Northern Overthrust Pipeline Company and Northern Trailblazer Pipeline Company to participate in the Trailblazer pipeline, which runs from southeastern Nebraska to western Wyoming. Also that year, it created two exploration and production companies, Nortex Gas & Oil Company and Consolidex Gas and Oil Limited. The latter company was a Canadian operation. In 1981 InterNorth set up Northern Engineering International Company to provide professional engineering services. In 1982 it formed Northern Intrastate Pipeline Company and Northern Coal Pipeline Company as well as InterNorth International Inc., now Enron International, to oversee non-U.S. operations.

InterNorth significantly expanded its oil and gas exploration and production activity in 1983 with the purchase of Belco Petroleum Corporation for about $770 million. Belco quadrupled InterNorth's gas reserves and added greatly to its crude oil reserves. Exploration efforts focused on the United States, Canada, and Peru.

Other acquisitions of the early 1980s included the fuel trading companies P & O Falco Inc. and P & O Falco Ltd.; their operations joined with UPG—renamed UPC Falco—in 1984; and Chemplex Company, a polyethylene and adhesive manufacturer, also acquired in 1984. InterNorth had sold Northern Propane Gas in 1983.

InterNorth made an acquisition of enormous proportions in 1985, when it bid to purchase Houston Natural Gas Corporation for about $2.26 billion. The offer was received enthusiastically, and the merger created the largest gas pipeline system in the United States—about 37,000 miles at the time. Houston Natural Gas brought pipelines from the Southeast and Southwest to join with InterNorth's substantial system in the Great Plains area. Valero Energy Corporation of San Antonio, Texas, sued to block the merger. InterNorth had entered into joint ventures with Valero early in 1985 to transport and sell gas to industrial users in Texas and Louisiana. Because these ventures competed with Houston Natural Gas, InterNorth withdrew from them when it agreed to the merger. Valero alleged that InterNorth had breached its fiduciary obligations, but the Valero lawsuit failed to stop the acquisition.

Although still officially named InterNorth, the merged company initially was known as HNG/InterNorth, with dual headquarters in Omaha, Nebraska, and Houston, Texas. In 1986 the company's name was changed to Enron Corp., and headquarters were consolidated in Houston.

After some shuffling in top management, Kenneth L. Lay, HNG's chairman, emerged as chairman of the combined company. HNG/InterNorth began divesting itself of businesses that did not fit in with its long-term goals. The $400 million in assets sold off in 1985 included the Peoples division, which sold for $250 million. Also in 1985, Peru's government nationalized Enron's assets there, and Enron began negotiating for payment, taking a $218 million charge against earnings in the meantime. In 1986 Enron's chemical subsidiary was sold for $603 million. Also in 1986, Enron sold 50% of its interest in Citrus Corporation to Sonat Inc. for $360 million, but continued to operate Citrus's pipeline system, Florida Gas Transmission Company. Citrus originally was part of Houston Natural Gas.

In 1987 Enron centralized its gas pipeline operations under Enron Gas Pipeline Operating Company. Also that year, Enron Oil & Gas Company, with responsibility for exploration and production, was formed out of previous InterNorth and HNG operations, including Nortex Oil & Gas, Belco Petroleum, HNG Oil Company, and Florida Petroleum Company. In 1989 Enron Corp. sold 16% of Enron Oil & Gas's common stock to the public for about $200 million. That year Enron received $162 million from its insurers for the Peruvian operations, and it continued to negotiate with the government for additional compensation.

Enron made significant moves into electrical power, in both independent production and cogeneration facilities, in the late 1980s. Cogeneration plants produce electricity and thermal energy from one source. It added major cogeneration units in Texas and New Jersey in 1988; in 1989 it signed a 15-year contract to supply natural gas to a cogeneration plant on Long Island. Also in 1989, Enron reached an agreement with Coastal Corporation that allowed Enron to increase the natural gas production from its Big Piney field in Wyoming; under the accord, Coastal agreed to extend a pipeline to the field, since the line already going to it could not handle increased volume. The same year, Enron and El Paso Natural Gas company received regulatory approval for a joint venture, Mojave Pipeline Company. The pipeline transports natural gas for use in oil drilling. In 1990 Enron made significant progress on its plans for a gas-fired electrical power plant in Teesside, England, as well as one in Milford, Massachusetts.

In the early 1990s, Enron appeared to be reaping the benefits of the InterNorth–Houston Natural Gas merger. Its revenues, at $16.3 billion in 1985, fell to less than $10 billion in each of the next four years, but recovered to $13.1 billion in 1990. Low natural gas prices had been a major cause of the decline. Enron, however, had been able to increase its market share, from 14% in 1985 to 18% in 1990, with help from efficiencies that resulted from the integration of the two predecessor companies' operations. Enron also showed significant growth in its liquid fuels business as well as in oil and gas exploration.

Principal Subsidiaries: Florida Gas Transmission Company (50%); Houston Pipe Line Company; Northern Border Pipeline Company (35%); Northern Natural Gas Company; Transwestern Pipeline Company; Enron Finance Corp.; Enron Gas Marketing Inc.; Enron Power Corp.; Enron Europe Ltd.; Enron Oil & Gas Company (84%); Enron Exploration Company; Enron Oil Canada Ltd.; Enron Gas Processing Company; Enron Gas Liquids Inc.; Enron Liquids Pipeline Company; Enron Oil Trading & Transportation Company, Enron Americas, Inc.

—Trudy Ring

ENSERCH CORPORATION

Enserch Center
300 South St. Paul Street
Dallas, Texas 75201
U.S.A.
(214) 651-8700
Fax: (214) 573-3351

Public Company
Incorporated: 1909 as Lone Star Gas Company
Employees: 11,200

Sales: $2.82 billion
Stock Exchanges: New York Midwest London

Enserch Corporation operates in the field of energy, engineering, and construction. Since its formation in 1909 as a Texas-based natural gas utility, the company has grown to include some 28,000 miles of pipeline serving 1.25 million customers in nearly 600 Texas and Oklahoma communities. During the 1970s Enserch diversified into petroleum exploration and production conducted primarily onshore in Texas and Oklahoma and offshore in the Gulf of Mexico; as well as into engineering and construction services.

Enserch's beginnings date back to 1909 when the Lone Star Gas Company was chartered as a gas production and transmission company to take advantage of the Petrolia gas field, discovered a year earlier in Clay County, Texas. Lone Star's headquarters were established in Fort Worth, with Henry Clay Edrington serving as president. Lone Star acquired a pipeline extending from Petrolia field to the communities of Byers, Wichita Falls, and Henrietta, and constructed a 130-mile pipeline running from Petrolia field to the Dallas–Fort Worth area.

For several years Lone Star operated as an independent pipeline company, selling natural gas wholesale in towns it served through distribution companies. By 1910 Petrolia field oil was being sold to the Fort Worth Gas Company, the Dallas Gas Company, and the North Texas Gas Company.

When Edington died in 1915, Lee B. Denning, an attorney instrumental in Lone Star's incorporation, became president. By the time the United States entered World War I in 1917, the Petrolia field was nearly played out, and the company was in serious financial trouble. In 1918 Lone Star turned to new sources of gas, removing old pipelines to build an extension to the newly discovered Fox field in southern Oklahoma. Two

years later Lone Star began removing gas from both southern Oklahoma and the newly discovered Ranger field in west Texas.

By the mid-1920s transmission lines had been extended to Lone Star's new gas sources, and the threat of bankruptcy had passed. In 1926 Lone Star Gas Corporation was organized as a holding company to acquire Lone Star Gas Company. Headquarters were established in Dallas, and the new corporation immediately began to expand its producing, transmission, and distribution holdings through acquisition of numerous companies and construction of town distribution plants. Between 1926 and 1927 Lone Star acquired several Texas distribution companies that were former customers, including the Fort Worth Gas Company and several companies serving numerous smaller north and west Texas communities.

In 1927 Lone Star began serving several Oklahoma communities after acquiring pipeline, gas wells, gas rights, and leases in southern Oklahoma. That same year Lone Star began serving Abilene, Texas, after purchasing a pipeline running to the city. In 1929 it bought Texas Cities Gas Company with distribution operations in both Texas and Juarez, Mexico, and expanded into the Midwest and Pacific Northwest, acquiring the Council Bluffs Gas Company in Iowa, Coos Bay Gas Company in Oregon, and Northwest Cities Gas Company, with gas manufacturing plants in Washington, Idaho, and Oregon.

George W. Crawford, part owner of Lone Star's original Petrolia well, was named the company's first chairman in 1929. That same year the company laid a transmission line tying the southwestern Oklahoma panhandle and north Texas gas fields to Lone Star's central system, marking the end of the company's early field transmission line construction.

Throughout the 1920s Lone Star extended service to Oklahoma and Texas communities; by the end of the decade more than 200 communities were included in the company's distribution system. Despite the onset of the Great Depression in late 1929, expansion continued into the 1930s, largely through acquisitions and the creation of new subsidiaries. In 1930 the subsidiary Lone Star Gasoline Company was organized to acquire several natural gas production properties and gasoline plants in west Texas. Lone Star also acquired Stamford and Western Gas Company, with town gas plants in 21 west Texas communities. Two years later Lone Star acquired Northwest Texas Gas Company, with distribution and transportation properties serving the former Stamford and Western area. In 1931 the Abilene gas distribution system was added to the Lone Star system.

In 1935 Crawford died, and T.B. Gregory was elected chairman. That same year Lone Star began tapping new sources of gas and resumed pipeline construction, which continued at an active pace through the remainder of the decade. In 1938 it disposed of Northwest Cities Gas Company and acquired the gas production, transportation, and distribution properties serving San Angelo in west Texas.

Denning died in 1940, and Dechard Anderson Hulcy was elected president. That same year the Securities and Exchange Commission (SEC) ordered Lone Star to comply with the 1935 Public Utility Holding Company Act and divest itself of specified properties in order to have a system of interconnected pipelines; Lone Star carried out the divestment restructuring process between 1942 and 1944, selling all of its remaining assets outside of Texas and southern Oklahoma.

The company also complied with an order to divest its Texas Cities Gas Company and the distribution systems at El Paso and Gavelston.

The Delaware-chartered Lone Star Gas Corporation ceased to exist in 1943, replaced by the Lone Star Gas Company with operations revolving around the Dallas-Fort Worth area, extending into southern Oklahoma. Lone Star's only remaining affiliate was a gas supply subsidiary, Lone Star Producing Company, an outgrowth of the former Lone Star Gas Corporation.

Following the United States's entrance in World War II in 1941, Lone Star undertook a construction program to bring gas service to new defense projects, including an airplane bomber plant. In 1946 Lone Star initiated a postwar construction program. Before the decade was over, more than 2,200 miles of new transmission, gathering, and distribution lines connected numerous Texas and Oklahoma communities to the Lone Star system. In the first three years of the 1950s an additional 3,400 miles of pipeline was constructed or acquired, giving Lone Star over 15,000 miles of pipeline.

In 1951 Gregory died, and the following year President Hulcy assumed the additional duties of chairman. In 1952 Lone Star resumed acquisition activities and acquired the Abilene distribution division of United Gas System in north Texas with gas distribution, production, and transmission properties in ten communities. Three years later Lone Star purchased the distribution properties in Cisco, Texas, near Abilene.

During the mid-1950s Lone Star launched an expansion program in west Texas. In 1953 Lone Star constructed a major gasoline plant in west Texas to produce gas and an underground storage reservoir to safeguard its gas supply for the area. In 1954 a new production office was opened in San Antonio, and three years later a new west Texas district and regional headquarters building was opened in Abilene.

By 1959 Lone Star was providing gas to 838,000 customers, an increase of nearly 500,000 customers since the end of World War II. Through acquisitions of small companies and extension of its distribution and transmission system, Lone Star closed the decade serving more than 425 communities.

In 1961 Lone Star Gas organized the subsidiary Lone Star Gathering Company to purchase, gather, and market natural gas in south Texas. The company diversified in 1964 when a division of Lone Star Producing Company built a fertilizer complex near Kerens, Texas.

In 1966 Lone Star Gas acquired an interest in the Katy Gas Field near Houston, described at the time as the largest untapped reservoir of natural gas in the United States. By 1967 Lone Star had constructed a 200-mile pipeline from the field to an area just east of Dallas.

L.T. Potter was named chairman in 1967, and Louis G. James was promoted from vice president to president. James retired in 1970, giving way to William Charles McCord, a former senior vice president of operations. In 1971 Potter retired as chairman and was replaced by Roy E. Pitts. Under McCord and Pitts the size and nature of the company began to change quickly during a period of accelerated growth. In 1970 Lone Star purchased the Amarillo-based City Gas Company with distribution systems in seven surrounding north and west Texas towns, pushing the total number of Lone Star system communities to over 560. The following year Lone Star entered the oil field services business with the purchase of Mobile Well Service, Inc., an east Texas oil well maintenance and

service provider. In 1972 Lone Star acquired Pool Company, the nation's largest gas and oil well production service firm, and established the subsidiary LSG Transtexas Gas Company, to engage in intrastate gathering and transmission of natural gas.

During 1972 and 1973 Lone Star expanded its business to include foreign gas and oil exploration and development subsidiaries in Australia, Malaysia, Canada, Bolivia, the Netherlands, and Greece. In 1973 Lone Star discontinued the majority of its gas appliance sales. That same year the company purchased recently discovered gas reserves in Galveston Bay, and in 1974 Lone Star acquired the Gulf Offshore Company of Texas, a petroleum productions services concern.

During the early and middle 1970s pipeline construction was again accelerated. Major products included a pipeline running through the Kiamichi Mountains of Oklahoma and a line running from far western Texas to the Dallas–Fort Worth area.

In 1975 the parent corporation's name was changed to Enserch to distinguish utility operations from growing nonutility operations and to reflect the company's diversified energy-related activities. With the name change, Lone Star Gas became a division of the new parent. That same year Louis B. Hulcy was promoted from senior vice president of operations to president of Lone Star Gas, while McCord was named president of Enserch. Pitts remained chairman of Lone Star Gas and also became chairman of Enserch.

In 1976 Enserch acquired Ebasco Service Inc., a major engineering, construction, and consulting service company specializing in energy and environmental markets. Through the remainder of the decade, Enserch concentrated on expansion of its oil field services business and acquired several oil well service firms providing oil rigs and other well-producing services both onshore in Texas and Oklahoma and offshore in the Gulf of Mexico. It also purchased the Louisiana-based Livingston Corporation, an oil service firm specializing in the marine tubing market, and the Boston-based Samson Ocean System Inc., a producer of cordage and other marine-related products and systems.

In 1977 McCord became president and chairman of Enserch and remained chairman of Lone Star Gas. Carol Neaves became president of Lone Star Gas in 1979.

By the late 1970s more than half of Enserch's revenues were coming from nonpipeline, energy-related services. Enserch entered the 1980s with a fully developed oil field services business; a gas and oil development and exploration business operating worldwide; and goals of expanding its established construction and engineering business. Those plans took shape between 1981 and 1983 when Enserch acquired Alaska International Industries, an engineering and construction company; Humphreys & Glasgow Ltd., a London-based process, design and engineering firm; a 50% interest in Losinger AG, a Swiss construction and engineering firm specializing in the intrastructure market; and a 49% interest in Dorsch Consult, a German engineering and consulting firm. During the early 1980s Enserch posted record gains, including sales of $3.7 billion in 1982.

Reduced domestic exploration activity led Enserch to cut its rig-making work force in 1982. By 1983 oil and gas prices were dropping. With losses mounting in its oil services division, in 1984 Enserch began selling marine-related oil services assets and the following year wrote down $225 million on its assets.

To reduce debt and raise money for petroleum exploration and production, in 1985 Enserch transferred substantially all of its development and exploration assets to the newly formed master limited partnership, Enserch Exploration Partners, Ltd. Fifteen percent of the new partnership was sold to the public to finance company activities. Enserch closed its 1985 books with a $62.3 million loss.

Neaves became chairman of Lone Star in 1985, and David W. Biegler was named president. In response to a changing regulatory and pricing climate in the natural gas industry, in 1986 Lone Star Gas formed two subsidiaries, Enserch Gas Company and Enserch Gas Transmission Company. Enserch Gas was created to supply gas for the growing short-term or spot market, and Enserch Gas Transmission was formed to target the industrial and electric-generation markets along the Texas gulf coast with a gas supply separate from Lone Star. In other moves to boost business, in 1986 the umbrella subsidiary Enserch Development Corporation was formed to seek, develop, and manage project opportunities in which multiple Enserch companies could be involved. In early 1988 Enserch Development landed its first major project, a cogeneration plant near Sweetwater, Texas, to coproduce electricity and process heat with end products being purchased by an electric utility and a local factory.

In 1988 Enserch discontinued its remaining oil field services. That same year Lone Star elected to participate in the new open access plan, which allowed the company to utilize nonaffiliated interstate pipelines for interstate gas and off-system marketing sales.

The company's troubles in construction and engineering and its losses due to discontinued oil field services led to a net loss in 1988 of $181 million. Enserch bounced back into the black the following year, accompanying an upturn in gas prices and profits in all three business segments.

Spurred by low oil prices, in 1989 Enserch Corporation traded its shares for those of Enserch Exploration Partners in a public exchange, resulting in the corporation gaining control of more than 99% of the partnership. With renewed interest in natural gas as an environmentally sound fuel, in 1989 Lone Star Gas constructed a compressed natural gas (CNG) fueling station at its Dallas service center to provide fuel for the Dallas transit system and local school district fleets, which had converted vehicles to run on CNG. That same year, Biegler assumed the additional duties of Lone Star Gas chairman.

In 1990 Enserch sold its 50% interest in the A.G. Losinger and the Pool Company, comprising all of Enserch's remaining interest in oil field services. The next year Lone Star reached an agreement to sell all of its Oklahoma transmission and distribution properties. Also in 1991 Biegler was named president of Enserch, succeeding McCord, who remained chairman, and J. Michael Talbert was named president of Lone Star, succeeding Biegler, who remained chairman. Enserch's goals in the early 1990s called for its natural gas division to capitalize on anticipated growth in environmental and energy-related markets and to expand third-party transportation sales, short-term sales, and sales stemming from additional uses of natural gas for such purposes as vehicle fuel.

Principal Subsidiaries: Lone Star Gas Company; Lone Star Energy Company; Enserch Gas Company; Enserch Gas Transmission Company; Enserch Exploration, Inc.; Enserch Exploration Partners Ltd. (99.2%); Ebasco Services Incorporated; Humphreys & Glasgow International (U.K.); Dorsch Consult (Germany, 49%); Enserch Development Corporation.

Further Reading: The First Seventy-five Years: A Pictorial History of Lone Star Gas Company, 1909–1984, Dallas, Texas, Lone Star Gas Company, 1984.

—Roger W. Rouland

ENTE NAZIONALE PER L'ENERGIA ELETTRICA

via G.B. Martini, 3
00198 Rome
Italy
(06) 85091
Fax: (06) 8509-3771

State-Owned Company
Incorporated: 1962
Employees: 112,329
Sales: L16.46 trillion (US$14.34 billion)

Ente Nazionale per l'Energia Elettrica (ENEL) is the National Electricity Authority of Italy. It distributes 84% of Italy's electricity demand, the bulk of the remainder being generated by industrial self-producers and municipal electricity undertakings. Among similar national boards in the world, ENEL is the fourth largest after Electricité de France, the Central Electricity Generation Board in the United Kingdom (before its privatization), and Tokyo Electric Power Company in Japan.

ENEL was established on December 6, 1962 by a special nationalization law after a long and complex debate. With a few exceptions, the law defines ENEL's task as the implementation of "all activities of production, import and export, transmission, transformation, distribution and sale of electricity from whatever source, on national territory." The exceptions include production and distribution of electricity by local authorities ("municipalities"), by smaller companies with annual production of less than 15 Megawatts/hour (MWh), and by industrial self-producers (subject to authorization). In addition to the production, transport, and distribution of electricity, ENEL performs a number of complementary activities: it operates as an electricity "bank" for the whole country, buying electricity from all producers in the country and reallocating it to its customers; it attends to all stages of plant engineering and construction; it carries out research and development on electricity and related fields; it undertakes consulting activity and technical assistance for foreign electric power companies and Italian companies operating abroad; and it undertakes exploration and development of geothermic sources. While remaining a unified national body, ENEL is operationally divided into a number of specialized departments. In order to ensure greater overall efficiency, this structure is complemented by regional organizations for the distribution of electricity at the Italian administrative levels of compartment, zone, and district.

The production and distribution of electricity remain ENEL's major activities, and the nationalization law requires ENEL to attend to the coordinated operation and enlargement of all its generating plants "in order to ensure—at minimum operating costs—a supply of electricity which is adequate, both in volume and price, for the balanced economic growth of the country." ENEL's activities are undertaken under the supervision of the Ministry of Industry and Commerce and in accordance with the directives of the Interministerial Committee for Economic Planning (CIPE).

Many of ENEL's past and current features cannot be fully understood without considering the political and historical circumstances that led to its formation. After World War II the debate on energy issues in Italy was essentially limited to the desirable nature—private or public—of firms that might operate in this area. At the time, electricity was generated by a large number of private companies, a few municipal plants, and a few generating companies controlled by IRI (Instituto per la Ricostruzione Industriale), a public holding company founded in 1933 to save the substantial portion of Italy's industry that was involved in a major banking collapse. The combined output of the public sector—IRI's public utilities, municipal plants, and the railways—accounted for about 30% of Italy's total electricity supply. In the Constitutional debate, the parties of the political left were in favor of the complete nationalization of the electricity industry, but these demands were blunted by a compromise: while the Constitution retained the principle of nationalizing entire sectors ("when related to essential public services, or energy sources, or situations of monopoly"), any implementation in the electricity industry was deferred. The government formally regulated electricity rates, but the influence of the private sector utilities was strong; they subsidized political parties and newspapers in order to influence political decisions and public opinion, and the rates they charged their largest industrial customers were not fully revealed so that the administrative bodies charged with the determination of rates lacked much of the information necessary to perform the function.

Many felt that full nationalization was the only possible solution, as the decentralization of decision-making was an obstacle to the integration of thermoelectric and hydroelectric power production as well as to the construction of the national power grid. Lobbying was strong, however, in favor of maintaining the status quo, and the anti-nationalization lobby also advocated the privatization of Agip—the national hydrocarbons corporation that was perceived as a remnant of the Benito Mussolini years. While the privatization of Agip was averted by the initiative and determination of Enrico Mattei, who strongly believed in the importance of an autonomous Italian presence in the world oil and gas scene, the utilities succeeded in stalling any nationalization plans for a considerable time.

The vested interests against nationalization were so strong that until 1962 no reform plan was brought to Parliament for discussion. In the meantime, in the absence of any explicit commitment toward a national energy policy from the government, a leading role was assumed by Ente Nazionale Idrocarburi (ENI), the national hydrocarbon corporation created in 1953 under the forceful management of Enrico Mattei. Not surprisingly, most of Italy's industry and its political referents were hostile to ENI, whose dynamism and ambitions served to highlight the stagnation of the electricity industry.

In the 1950s three main factors contributed to the acceleration of the drive toward nationalization: the development of nuclear technology in the production of electricity, which called for a substantial public intervention because of the massive investments involved; the long lead times—time necessary for project design, planning, and implementation—needed before reaching commercial generation; and the economic boom of the 1950s, which emphasized the risks and limits of thriving economic growth when not adequately supported by the necessary infrastructure. The issue of a national energy policy was put back onto the agenda, and three main bodies of opinion formed: a defensive position, championed by the private electricity companies, supporters of the status quo; the concentration in ENI of all activities related to the production of energy, including electricity from all sources; and the creation of a separate national electricity board. The third lobby prevailed, and this was probably the most important and longlasting achievement of the first center-left government in Italy's republican history. The Parliamentary debate was intense, but the decision was reached comparatively quickly, as the powerful *avant-garde* of Italy's industry—led by FIAT—had come to the conclusion that defending the status quo in electricity was no longer a primary concern.

As for the choice of the legal status of the new body, the possible options included: an IRI-type formula (a holding company of which the majority of shares would be held by the State); an ENI-type formula (a state-owned holding company with its own equity, which would carry out its statutory tasks via the creation of companies fully or partially controlled by the state); a full integration of the electricity sector in the public sector; or an autonomous public body that would finance itself by issuing bonds but could not create affiliated companies or hold shares in any other company. The latter option prevailed, and 1,189 electricity companies of different sizes and with different structures were merged into a unified and integrated body for the production, transmission, and distribution of electricity throughout Italy. It was an operation of unprecedented complexity compared with electricity nationalizations in France (1946) and Britain (1947), which were effected in considerably simpler conditions. In 1963, 73 companies were consolidated, representing about 85% of the total assets being nationalized; the companies consolidated in ENEL rose to 221 at the end of 1964, representing around 92% of the industry's asset value, and to 905 at the end of 1966. This year marked the de facto completion of the nationalization process, as the 284 companies transferred to ENEL in the following years were of relatively minor importance.

The nationalization law decreed that ENEL's original assets were to be obtained through the transfer of assets from the former generating companies. Unlike ENI, ENEL was not endowed by the state with any initial capital, and the nationalization law established that funds for the compensation of shareholders and for future investments were to be raised by issues of special ENEL bonds guaranteed by the state, within the limits set on a case-by-case basis by an interministerial committee.

The weight of social and political considerations on ENEL's management has been very heavy from its inception. First, the law established that ENEL paid compensation not to the individual shareholders, but rather to the nationalized companies as such, so as to encourage them to carry out activities in other strategic sectors. The favorable terms adopted for compensation were intended to encourage this transition. ENEL was to pay the former electricity companies stock market prices for their shares, which led to a flurry of speculation on the stock market such that ENEL actually paid inflated prices. In addition, all compensation was to be completed in a comparatively short period with a number of credit and fiscal allowances made in favor of the nationalized companies; the agreed amounts were to be credited in cash every six months over a total period of ten years, with an annual interest of 5.50%. The total principal and interest paid amounted to L2.3 trillion. These conditions had the effect of imposing a heavy financial burden on ENEL, given that ENEL had to finance itself by external borrowing and bond issues. For several years the debt incurred for compensations to ex-producers severely affected ENEL's balance sheet. Another burden for the newly-created body was that nationalization, while creating some efficiency gains in transport and distribution, also generated pressure for an increased work force and higher levels of wages and salaries: the total number of ENEL's employees grew from nearly 68,000 in 1963 to an all-time high of nearly 118,000 in 1981.

On the technical front, the crucial challenge for the electricity industry was to undertake the transition from a structure predominantly based on hydroelectric generation to a system that was better equipped to meet the needs of fast industrial growth. In 1960 hydroelectric power was still the predominant source—about 75% of the total—while electricity from petroleum products (fuel oil), natural gas, and solid fuels represented 15%, 3%, and 7% respectively. This structure was bound to change rapidly. In order to meet the fast growth in electricity demand, ENEL started a massive investment program focused on the construction of new thermoelectric plants. At the end of the 1960s thermoelectric production had come to represent 60% of the total, thus becoming the axis of the whole system. Within this share, electricity from fuel oil represented 80%. The policy of diversification of sources also embraced nuclear power generation, and three nuclear plants were built.

However, ENEL's overall efficiency and productivity of labor in its first decade of activity was very low, largely because of two factors: the difficulties inherent in the nationalization process itself and the constraints imposed on personnel management by politicians and unions. As for the former, ENEL had incorporated a large number of heterogeneous plants not adequately interconnected, and the rationalization and restructuring of plants and grids required massive investments in the first few years. As for the latter, it was soon clear that for political reasons the creation of ENEL was not to be allowed to result in any redundancies, and this led to a rapid expansion of the work force. In short, in the first decade of nationalization, the dramatic expansion in the work force and the rise in labor costs counterbalanced the advantages of nationalization in terms of scale and grid economies. Furthermore, for many years ENEL had to suffer the consequences of a political ceiling imposed by government on the rates it could set and other allowances in favor of household users, which created distortions in the patterns of consumption and investment.

The first oil crisis of 1973 transformed the underlying premise of Italy's electricity industry, an abundant availability of cheap imported oil. At the time Italy was already in a position of strong dependency on hydrocarbons for electricity generation, which made the need for a change of direction in national energy policy even more pressing. The approach chosen, in the Italian tradition, was to widen the scope of central planning in defining broad aims and policy lines, thus imposing a further layer of bureaucracy on the existing powers of guidance of the national energy boards (ENI and ENEL). Furthermore, since the time involved in the preparation and discussion of these programs tended to be very long, it often happened that by the time definitive approval was given many of the key elements of the picture had become obsolete.

The 1975 and 1977 National Energy Plans (PENs) recommended a major shift toward coal and nuclear power stations, together with fuller exploitation of domestic energy sources, increased imports of natural gas, and the encouragement of energy conservation. In the Italian institutional system the planning stage is only the initial phase of a complex procedure to be completed before reaching the implementation stage; very soon obstacles were put in the way of the implementation of these programs and the construction of planned capacity. Electricity generation from fuel oil, which was to be phased out in the context of the proposed diversification of energy sources, remained the cornerstone of Italy's electricity generation. During the period 1970–1974, the consumption of Italian thermoelectric power stations, essentially petroleum products, increased from 15.7 million tons oil equivalent (Mtoe) to 22.8 Mtoe.

The debate over the future of energy policy became more intense in the wake of the second oil shock of 1979, which had grave consequences for domestic inflation rates. But the seriousness of the situation did not stimulate a more decisive approach, and the 1981 and 1986 PENs essentially reiterate most of the previous documents' recommendations. The commitment to the nuclear sector remained, together with major emphases on coal, increased imports of natural gas, and the development of domestic sources of gas. During the period 1980–1987, the consumption of thermoelectric power stations increased to 33.3 Mtoe, of which 19.3 Mtoe was oil products. The only concession to diversification was the start-up of the Caorso nuclear station and the conversion of some power stations from fuel oil to coal. On the demand side, the transition from a model of economic development based on heavy industry—highly energy-intensive—to a lower energy intensity manufacturing industry caused a decline in industrial energy demand from 41.5 Mtoe in 1974 to 31.5 Mtoe in 1985. This was more than offset by an increase of electricity consumption in the household and service sectors.

On the whole, there is no doubt that ENEL's efficiency has been heavily constrained by bureaucratic delays and the failure of government and parliament to devise and implement a workable energy policy. The major problem for ENEL lies in the bureaucratic procedures for the authorization of new plants. Attempts have been made to simplify and speed up procedures, but in essence the government lacks the power to authorize the construction of a plant against the wishes of local authorities. Local opposition to the setting-up of electricity plants has also had the effect of preventing ENEL from optimizing the choice of plant-types on the basis of their expected economic merit.

ENEL is also heavily dependent on the political authorities for investment financing, both because electricity rates are im-

posed by CIP for all users and because any recourse to external borrowing by ENEL is subject to government authorization. The control of electricity rates is a sensitive political issue, as they have been used as an instrument for attaining more general policy objectives, such as the battle against inflation and the subsidization of particular consumer groups or areas. This contributed to ENEL's serious financial difficulties in the first part of the 1980s, when soaring production costs added to the burden of interest repayments. These difficulties were eased in the second part of the decade after a substantial increase in rates and an injection of funds from the government; between 1986 and 1990 the ratio of overall financial charges on ENEL's total assets declined from 65.4% to 58.6%. Another substantial rates increase was granted by CIP in December 1990 after some years of steady or declining electricity prices. In the 1980s ENEL also began an overdue rationalization of its work force. The total number of employees declined to 112,000 in 1988 and has remained fairly stable since. At the same time, electricity sales have increased substantially; in 1990, 4.7 times as many kWh were sold as in 1963, with an associated growth of productivity measured in terms of sales of electricity per employee.

The major problems for ENEL in recent years have been the veto imposed on the operation and construction of nuclear power plants and the growing hostility—for environmental reasons—toward thermoelectric plants, with the exception of natural gas. The consolidated features of Italy's energy policy were put into serious question by the Chernobyl accident in the former Soviet Union in April 1986. The ensuing debate culminated in a National Energy Conference in February 1987 that embraced all themes of the economic, technical, and institutional viability of a series of energy options and took on a number of environmental concerns neglected in previous decades. However, the fundamental problem of Italy's energy policy—the wealth of programs contrasted with the lack of implementation and choice—was not solved as the conference could not provide a definitive answer to the question of how to reconcile economic viability, environmental concerns, and safety.

Together with other factors, the failure of the political parties in the government coalition to find an agreement on these issues led in April 1987 to the fall of the government that had convened the conference and to an early general election. A referendum was held in November 1987 that revealed strong public hostility toward nuclear power. This referendum effectively marked the end of nuclear electricity in Italy, and ENEL was forced to interrupt the operation of all existing plants and to convert plants under construction—at a huge overall cost—to coal-fired or oil-fired power stations.

The major effect of this development was a dramatic rise in Italy's net electricity imports, which reached almost 35 billion kWh in 1990, equivalent to nearly 15% of all electricity consumed. Imports of electricity have always found their economic rationale in the fact that the unit cost of imports can be lower than domestic production costs, due to overcapacity in neighboring countries, in particular France, with its excess of nuclear power. But to a very large extent this increase in imports has become a necessity in recent years. While the domestic supply/demand ratio improved between 1980 and 1985—because electricity demand slowed down and approximately 9,000 MW of capacity was brought into use—in the second part of the decade the situation deteriorated considerably. Despite sustained demand growth and the closure of the existing nuclear plants, with capacity totaling approximately 1,300 MW, only a modest increase in capacity has been possible in hydroelectric, geothermic, and thermoelectric plants. The growth of electricity imports is responsible for a fall in productivity over the last few years; given that the production process is very rigid in the short term, a rise in imports does not translate into a proportional reduction in the use of other production factors, and the result is an efficiency loss. ENEL's strategy in the early 1990s was to sign more long-term supply contracts with different suppliers: in addition to traditional imports from France, Switzerland, and Germany, ENEL import contracts were being negotiated with Tunisia and the former Soviet Union. In short, despite having achieved many of the objectives it had originally set, ENEL has not quite succeeded in fully providing for Italy's electricity requirements. This failure, however, cannot be blamed exclusively on the board's management, but rather on the influence of social and political factors. The increase in imports is a direct consequence of the block imposed on nuclear power, while the excess of regulation that has burdened ENEL throughout its history has made it nearly impossible to construct large thermoelectric power stations, which are also those with lower unit costs. On a few occasions, attempts have been made to initiate a reform of ENEL. The first of such reform commissions was set up by the Italian government at the end of 1984, with the task of advancing proposals for restructuring ENEL's organization and changing its ownership structure. The commission's conclusions, however, were that the organization of ENEL had to be left unchanged, while the question of ownership was left for the government to decide. In February 1990 a second commission was appointed by the Ministry for Industry to study the reform of ENEL, and it had three objectives: to analyze the relationship with other Italian producers, to analyze possible ENEL-private sector joint ventures for the production of electricity, and to consider amendments to the law that might allow the entry of private capital into ENEL. As of mid-1991, however, the commission's conclusions were not yet known.

Considering that the debate over privatization has been going on for some time and is gaining support, the possibility cannot be excluded that a decision in favor of full or, more likely, partial privatization will eventually be made, but it will require delicate political mediations. In the meantime, the emerging supply constraint led to the approval of a new law (January 1991) intended to relaunch self-production of electricity and to liberalize—within certain limits—the production of electricity. ENEL is obliged to transport electricity produced by the new undertakings, but at the same time they remain committed to selling any surplus production only to ENEL. The law also introduced partial decontrol of electricity sales, whereas before the self-producers of electricity were forced to sell any surplus only to ENEL, now they can sell this surplus to other end-users, provided the electricity is produced from renewable resources or from combined heat and power plants (cogeneration).

Further Reading: Zanetti, G., and G. Fraquelli, *Una nazionalizzazione al buio,* Bologna, Il Mulino, 1979; Zorzoli, G.B., "La politica energetica in Italia dalla Ricostruzione al boom economico," in *Energia,* no.4, Bologna, *Nomisma,* 1987; Pazzi, C., "L'Elettricita," in G. Stefani, ed., *Gli investimenti delle Imprese pubbliche in Italia,* Milan, Ciriec, Collana di Studi e Monografie no. 77, 1988; Balduzzi, F., "Effetti delle tariffe elettriche sull'autoproduzione industriale in Italia," in *Energia,* no.3, Bologna, *Nomisma,* 1988; Fraquelli, G., "Investimenti e politica finanziaria dell'ENEL dalla nazionalizzazione ad oggi," in *Economia Pubblica* no. 1/2; Zorzoli, G.B., "Se manca l'energia (ma soprattutto la potenza)," in *Energia,* no.1, Bologna, *Nomisma,* 1989; D'Ermo, V., "Linee evolutive del sistema energetico italiano: 1950–1989," in *Energia,* no.2, Bologna, *Nomisma,* 1990; De Paoli, L., "Organization and Regulation of the Italian Electric System," in *ENER Bulletin,* Milan, IEFE, Universita' Bocconi, 1991.

—Cristina Caffarra

ENTERGY CORPORATION

225 Baronne Street
New Orleans, Louisiana 70112
(504) 529-5262
Fax: (504) 569-4269

Public Company
Incorporated: 1949 as Middle South Utilities
Employees: 13,373
Sales: $3.98 billion
Stock Exchanges: New York Midwest Pacific

Entergy is a holding company for utilities that supply electric energy to the middle south of the United States, including Arkansas, Louisiana, Mississippi, and southeastern Missouri. Its subsidiaries also provide gas service in New Orleans and parts of Arkansas and Missouri. At the end of 1990, the company provided 1.7 million customers with electricity.

Although Entergy was incorporated as a public company called Middle South Utilities (MSU) in 1949, its four constituent power companies had operated as an interdependent system for 25 years. These companies were Arkansas Power & Light, Louisiana Power & Light, Mississippi Power & Light, and New Orleans Public Service, Inc. In 1981 Arkansas-Missouri Power was merged into Arkansas Power & Light after having been owned by MSU since the early 1970s.

During the 1950s, the company was one of the fastest-growing utility systems in the United States, largely because of the industrialization of its territory and the ensuing rise in the standard of living. Much of this expansion sprung from industrial development programs inititated by MSU-supplied companies. Among the more significant and economically resilient industries founded were oil, natural gas, and chemicals. Large manufacturers, including General Motors, built plants in the region. Reynolds Metals brought the area the electricity-intensive aluminum industry. In addition, from 1945 to 1955, use of electricity per residential customer in the middle south region rose faster than the national average. Three of the four constituent companies did not have a rate increase from the end of World War II until the early 1960s. From 1947 through 1951, MSU and its predecessor companies spent $236 million on plant expansions, financed by common stock sales in 1950, 1951, and 1952.

In 1953 MSU became involved in a dispute with the U.S. government. Edgar H. Dixon, head of MSU, and Eugene A. Yates, head of the Southern Company, proposed a plant to supply power to the Tennessee Valley Authority (TVA), which would make this power available to the Atomic Energy Commission. The plan stirred up a battle in Congress between those favoring government ownership of utilities and those favoring investor ownership, eventually causing U.S. President Dwight Eisenhower to void the contract. Although the government claimed that the contract's cancellation was based on a conflict of interest by an investment banker, Adolphe Wenzell, who was advising both the utilities and the government, the utilities sued the government in 1955. The U.S. Court of Claims found no conflict of interest and granted the utilities $1.8 million in damages in 1959.

Despite the legal battle, the 1950s were prosperous for Middle South, as the next decade would be. In 1961 MSU was one of 11 private power firms, headed by Robert Welch of Southwestern Electric Power Company, to offer to exchange energy with the TVA, whose surplus summer power would be exchanged for the companies' surplus power in the winter, effecting considerable savings for both parties.

In a similar agreement in October 1967, Middle South united with Southern Company to coordinate planning and operation of their facilities for ten years. Such partnerships were part of a general trend among utilities to foster joint ventures and cooperation. The plan included mutual assistance in case of emergencies that would reduce probability of large-scale power failures. The firms also planned to coordinate building of plants and long-distance power lines. The two systems were already directly connected with each other through transmission facilities in Mississippi and Louisiana and indirectly connected through neighboring systems.

The increasing need for electricity in MSU's region called for $1.12 billion worth of construction during the 1960s, or about $118 million per year during the decade. During the 1960s, total electric energy sales almost tripled, going from 10.4 billion kilowatt-hours in 1959 to 31 billion kilowatt-hours in 1969. Although annual electricity use per household increased more than two and a half times, and revenue per customer nearly doubled, increased efficiency meant that the average cost to the customer per kilowatt-hour decreased 28.6% during the decade.

When founded, MSU assumed unlimited availability of natural gas as its major fuel source. During the 1960s, however, gas became increasingly scarce, and MSU had to consider other fuel options. In 1967 the company began construction of its first nuclear plant, built by its Arkansas Power & Light subsidiary. The $140 million plant was erected in Russellville, Arkansas, at the Dardanelle Reservoir on a 1,110-acre parcel of land. It began producing energy in 1974. Beginning in 1969, due to the Federal Power Commission's heightened restriction of interstate natural gas delivery, MSU founded its System Fuels, Inc. subsidiary to provide fuel for utility operations. By 1974 the subsidiary had located six natural gas wells. It also purchased fuel oil. By 1974 MSU was building four 700-megawatt coal-fired units, the first to go into operation in 1978. MSU bought the coal for these units from Kerr-McGee Oil Company and Peabody Coal Company.

MSU was a leader in the trend toward nuclear energy. In the 1970s it planned to derive 43% of its new capacity—2,965 megawatts—from nuclear power plants. Among the company's most significant research projects were those under way at the Southwest Nuclear Research Center near Fayetteville, Arkansas. Installed there was the Southwest Experimental Fast

Oxide Reactor, which at the time was the only reactor in the United States fueled with plutonium oxide. Its purpose was to verify the safety and desirability of breeder reactors. To back the project MSU joined with 13 other investor-owned companies, called Southwest Atomic Energy Associates, as well as General Electric, the U.S. Atomic Energy Commission, and the Karlsruhe Nuclear Research Center of Germany.

In 1974, with the company's Arkansas nuclear plant in operation, two MSU subsidiaries, Mississippi Power & Light and Middle South Energy, Inc., began construction of two more nuclear plants at the Grand Gulf station in Mississippi. During the early 1970s, however, the system continued to rely on natural gas. In 1974 oil provided 27% of total fuel requirements, gas 68%, and nuclear and hydroelectric production about 5%.

In 1975, to secure a steady fuel supply until its nuclear and coal-based facilities would be in full operation in the 1980s, MSU entered a joint project with Northeast Petroleum and Ingram Corp. The companies founded Energy Corporation of Louisiana to build a $300 million refinery in Garyville, Louisiana, producing low-sulfur fuel oil. Floyd Lewis, who began as a lawyer with New Orleans Public Service, became president of MSU in 1970. He led the company through a decade of growth despite mounting economic stress. Debilitating outside factors included the Middle East oil embargo and the attendant rise in fuel costs; environmental and other controls on construction; inflation and interest rates that increased building costs; and the nuclear accident at Three Mile Island that strengthened the resolve of the U.S. antinuclear movement. In 1977 sales topped $1 billion, a 23% increase from 1976.

By 1977 MSU was involved in its most ambitious construction program ever. From 1970 through 1976, it had spent $2.67 billion on plant expansion. Expenditures of $2.37 billion were anticipated for 1977 through 1979. However, while new production sites formerly lowered utility rates, the opposite became true: new plants, whether coal or nuclear, were time-consuming and expensive to build—six to eight years for a coal-run facility and ten to fourteen years for a nuclear plant, with a cost of $1,000 to $2,000 per kilowatt. MSU sought numerous rate increases to cover its costs, but regulators would not allow the construction costs to be reflected in rates until the plants were operational. MSU continued to build, tying up capital in plants under construction that it was unable to invest to generate income for most of the decade. From 1974 through 1985, MSU sank $6.1 billion into construction of its Grand Gulf and Waterford nuclear plants. During construction, MSU was able to disguise its financial weakness through the allowance for funds used during construction, which allowed it to register the profits it would make on its construction assets if the plants were in fact producing. In 1985 such noncash credit constituted 91% of MSU's earnings.

Reality set in, however, after production began at Grand Gulf in mid-1985. The facility, owned by MSU subsidiary System Energy Resources, Inc., sold power wholesale to MSU's four operating companies according to an allocation established by the Federal Energy Regulatory Commission. The commission also set the wholesale cost of Grand Gulf's power. The rate increases needed to cover these costs were so high—up to 20%—that state regulatory commissions initially refused any increase at all.

The company absorbed more than $330 million in Grand Gulf construction costs, planning to recover the rest through gradual rate increases over the next decade. It also took a substantial loss on its $950 million investment in the rudiments of the second Grand Gulf plant, whose construction was halted by the Mississippi Public Service Commission (MPSC). MSU stopped paying its common stock dividends in order to save money. Mississippi regulators finally granted a $326 million interstate wholesale rate increase to Mississippi Power & Light in September 1985.

In 1986 President and Chairman Floyd Lewis was hospitalized, and Edwin Lupberger assumed Lewis's duties as MSU's difficulties continued. The interest rate the company had to pay on its debt rose, and common stock sold for 50% to 75% of book value, as contrasted with the 110% to 120% typical of a healthy utility stock. Lupberger, in an interview with *Forbes,* July 28, 1986, characterized the company's situation as "more uncertain than it's been since the Depression."

In 1987 the Mississippi Supreme Court rescinded the MPSC's 1985 rate increase. Mississippi Power & Light appealed to the U.S. Supreme Court, saying that cancellation of the increase would bankrupt it. At the same time, Louisiana regulators reduced by $28 million a $76 million increase granted to another subsidiary. Standard & Poor's lowered its ratings on $7 billion worth of MSU debt and preferred stock. On June 28, 1988, the U.S. Supreme Court ruled that the 1985 Mississippi rate increase was valid, and as a result MSU's security ratings were upgraded. More than $200 million that had been collected, but held in escrow pending the court's decision, was released on August 11, 1988. Although earnings continued to be lower than the previous year, overall financial stability of the organization was on the upswing, as evidenced by the reinstitution on September 10 of its quarterly common stock dividend for the first time since its 1985 suspension. By the end of 1988, the company's financial recovery was basically complete, although its stock continued to sell at 75% of book value, nearly 39% less than the industry average. In late 1988, MSU consolidated the management of all four of its nuclear plants at System Energy Resources, a move expected to lower costs by $23 million.

Lawsuits questioning other nuclear investments continued to plague MSU. Lupberger, fearing the uncertainty and strain of more drawn-out litigation, negotiated a compromise agreement called Project Olive Branch, settling the suits out of court. This hoisted the company's return on capital nearer to the industry average of 8.6%. Its stock price rebounded as well.

At the annual meeting on May 19, 1989, shareholders approved changing MSU's name to Entergy Corporation. Heading into the 1990s, the company had largely regained financial stability. In 1991 its New Orleans Public Service subsidiary reached an agreement with the New Orleans City Council that let the utility recover a portion of its investment in Grand Gulf. Late in 1991 Entergy increased its common stock dividend.

Principal Subsidiaries: Arkansas Power & Light Company; Louisiana Power & Light Company; Mississippi Power & Light Company; New Orleans Public Service Operations, Inc.; System Energy Resources, Inc.; Entergy Power, Inc.; Entergy Operations, Inc.; Electec, Inc.

Further Reading: Gray, Robert T., "The Timeless Skills of a Modern Manager," *Nation's Business,* December 1983; Cook, James, "A Nuclear Survivor," *Forbes,* July 28, 1986.

—Elaine Belsito

FLORIDA PROGRESS CORPORATION

Barnett Tower
One Progress Plaza
St. Petersburg, Florida 33701
U.S.A.
(813) 824-6400

Public Company
Incorporated: 1899 as St. Petersburg Electric Light & Power
  Company
Employees: 7,879
Sales: $2.01 billion
Stock Exchanges: New York Pacific

Florida Progress Corporation is a diversified holding company with more than 40 subsidiaries. Its primary subsidiary, Florida Power Corporation, is Florida's second-largest utility, supplying electricity in 32 counties with 375 municipalities. Its service area has a population of more than four million and is primarily in northern and central Florida, including the cities of Clearwater, St. Petersburg, and Winter Park. While the electric utility provides the bulk of Florida Progress's revenues, the company has become involved in a broad range of other businesses, including energy resources and transportation, real estate development, and financial services.

Florida Progress was formed in 1982 as a holding company for Florida Power, for the purpose of diversifying beyond utility operations. Florida Power originated in 1899 as St. Petersburg Electric Light & Power Company. Its name was changed to St. Petersburg Lighting Company in 1915, to Pinellas County Power Company in 1923, and to Florida Power Corporation in 1927. Florida Power's parent company was General Gas & Electric Corporation, part of the Associated Gas & Electric System, one of the large utility holding companies prominent in the early 20th century.

In the 1920s and the 1930s the utility expanded through acquisitions of both investor-owned electric companies and municipal systems in Florida. Among the former purchases were Clearwater Lighting Company in 1923 and both Oklawaha Power Company and West Florida Power Company in 1935. Florida Power acquired several municipal electric systems in 1930, in New Port Richey, Dunnellon, and Branford, and in 1934 added the operations of four other small Florida communities.

The Public Utility Holding Company Act of 1935 eventually broke up the Associated Gas & Electric System, which included utilities in Georgia, New Jersey, New York, and Pennsylvania, as well as Florida. The act limited each holding company's operations to a single contiguous system, rather than the far-flung empires that many such companies had. The Securities and Exchange Commission, which administered the holding companies' divestiture, organized Associated Gas & Electric's Florida and Georgia operations into a single system. Florida Power became an independent, publicly-held company in 1945, with Georgia Power & Light Company as a subsidiary.

In 1951 Florida Power acquired electrical operations in Madison, Monticello, and Perry, Florida, from Florida Power & Light Company. In 1957 it sold Georgia Power & Light to Georgia Power Company for about $11.8 million.

Florida Power's sales and earnings grew steadily during the 1960s, and the company gained a reputation for good management. *Electric Light & Power*, a trade magazine, named the company electric utility of the year in 1970. The utility, however, had a potential problem in its heavy dependence on imported oil to run its generating plants. Florida Power had researched nuclear energy for several years during the 1960s, and in 1968 it began construction of a nuclear unit at its Crystal River plant, which already had two fossil-fuel units.

The nuclear unit was scheduled for completion in 1972 but cost far more than expected and also had construction problems that delayed its completion. Meanwhile, the soaring cost of oil after the Middle East oil embargo of the early 1970s plunged Florida Power into financial difficulties, as imported oil accounted for about 80% of its fuel consumption. In 1974, when Florida Power's earnings fell 35% from the previous year, it temporarily suspended construction of the nuclear unit to conserve cash.

During this period, to reduce its use of foreign oil, Florida Power looked to coal as well as nuclear power. It began converting two oil-burning plants to coal in 1975. In 1976 it formed Electric Fuels Corporation, a company involved in coal mining and the transportation of coal and other commodities via rail and barge, with customers including Florida Power and other utility and industrial companies.

The nuclear unit finally went into operation in March 1977, and saved the utility $46.7 million in fuel costs during the remainder of the year. Florida Power's 1977 earnings were up 38% from their 1976 level.

However, problems soon developed. In March 1978, the utility was forced to shut down the nuclear unit after a coolant leakage was detected. Company officials subsequently discovered that a latch had given way, shattering a reactor assembly and flushing pieces through the coolant system. Broken tubes then caused the leaks. The unit was shut down for repairs for seven months in 1978. Florida Power wanted Babcock & Wilcox Company, the firm that had built the unit, to perform the repairs at its own expense, but Babcock & Wilcox refused, citing a limited warranty clause in its contract. It then did the repairs for an additional fee.

In 1981 Florida Power sued Babcock & Wilcox in an effort in recover its costs. The utility contended that the unit's design and construction had been inadequate in the first place; therefore, Babcock & Wilcox was responsible for the accident. In 1984 Florida Power reached a settlement with Babcock & Wilcox, in which the utility received $11.8 million—about $7.2

million from insurers and $4.6 million directly from the construction firm. The latter was mainly in the form of credits against future bills for equipment and services.

During this period, diversification became a priority for Florida Power. Taking advantage of Florida's rapid population growth, in 1981 it formed Talquin Corporation, a real estate developer and building-products manufacturer. Stepping up its move beyond utility operations, it formed Florida Progress Corporation in 1982, and Florida Power became its principal subsidiary. Florida Power's stockholders received one Florida Progress common share for each common share of Florida Power they held. Florida Power's subsidiaries, Electric Fuels and Talquin, became subsidiaries of Florida Progress.

In 1983 Florida Progress formed Progress Credit Corporation, an equipment-leasing and -financing business concentrating on aircraft. In 1985 the holding company formed Progress Technologies Corporation to develop and market technology-based products and processes for use in a variety of industries. Florida Progress bought Mid-Continent Life Insurance Company, which specializes in low-premium life insurance marketed through independent agents, in 1986. The insurer, based in Oklahoma City, Oklahoma, dated back to 1909. These diversifications, along with the diversification of Florida Power's fuel sources, produced improvements in Florida Progress's sales, earnings, and stock price. Florida's population growth was a factor as well; in 1987 the company's utility customer base increased 4.4%, double the U.S. average.

In 1988 Florida Progress formed Progress Capital Holdings, Inc. to handle financing for its nonutility operations. Progress Capital subsequently became the parent of all the nonutility subsidiaries except Electric Fuels. Also formed that year was Progress Energy Corporation, whose purpose was to invest in cogeneration projects and small power plants outside Florida, but Florida Progress discontinued this business just two years later.

Another venture begun in 1988 was Talquin's formation of partnerships to construct luxury apartment buildings in Florida cities, including Tampa, Orlando, and Fort Myers. The real estate company was seeking projects that would provide a quick return on investment, but the recession in Florida's real estate market and the national economy hurt results in 1989 and 1990. In 1990 Florida Progress decided to sell Talquin's building-products operations, because they did not fit in with the company's future direction. The establishment of a $14 million reserve to cover the expected loss on sales of these businesses was the principal reason for a 12.5% drop in Florida Progress's earnings in 1990.

In 1990 Talquin sold 3,200 acres of south Florida citrus groves it had acquired as an investment six years earlier, for an after-tax profit of about $10 million. That same year Talquin completed and sold its first luxury apartment complex, in Orlando, and finished other projects including Barnett Tower, a 26-story building in downtown St. Petersburg that became the new headquarters for Florida Progress, with portions occupied by several other companies.

Florida Progress's insurance and coal operations both grew in the late 1980s and early 1990s. From 1986, when it was acquired, through 1990, Mid-Continent had a 19% annual increase in its insurance in force, topping $8.5 billion in 1990. Its earnings increased an average of 26.5% annually during those five years. It added more than 4,000 agents, putting the total at more than 6,000, and doubled its number of regional offices, to 26. Electric Fuels bought a rail-car repair company, Kustom Karr, in 1990. It also added to its coal reserves that year, buying Kentucky mines with a capacity of producing about two million tons of coal annually. During 1990 it sold five million tons of coal to companies other than Florida Power. Its operations also reduced the cost of coal used by Florida Power by 14% from 1985 to 1990.

Florida Power by 1990 had greatly decreased its use of oil. Its fuel mix was 54% coal, 22% oil, 13% nuclear energy, 10% purchased power, and 1% natural gas. In 1990 Florida Power signed a 20-year contract to purchase power from The Southern Company and made plans to build a transmission line to connect it with Southern's operations in south Georgia. The nuclear unit at Crystal River, despite experiencing a variety of outages in 1988 and 1989, received its highest performance rating ever from the Nuclear Regulatory Commission in 1990. The nuclear unit was one of five electricity-generating units at the Crystal River site, the others being fossil-fueled; Florida Power explored sites for another complex of a similar size.

As it entered the 1990s, Florida Power was a relatively energy-efficient utility, able to offer its customers low rates. About 90% of its customers were residential, leaving Florida Power less vulnerable to the vagaries of the economy than are utilities that depend more on industrial and commercial customers. Its customer base had grown 3.8% annually from 1985 to 1990, almost twice the national average, thanks to the influx of people into Florida. The outlook for other Florida Progress subsidiaries was mixed. Electric Fuels expected to maintain a constant level of coal sales to Florida Power, while increasing sales to other companies, and Mid-Continent was growing and healthy. Talquin was facing a weak real estate market, and planned to sell certain properties after conditions improved. Overall, however, Florida Progress was an example of a company that had successfully diversified beyond its original utility operations, while continuing to improve those operations' performance.

Principal Subsidiaries: Florida Power Corporation; Electric Fuels Corporation; Progress Capital Holdings, Inc.

Further Reading: "Today A Hero. But Tomorrow?" *Forbes,* December 15, 1974; Hannon, Kerry, "Lights, action, prudence," *Forbes,* September 19, 1988.

—Donald R. Stabile and Trudy Ring

FPL GROUP, INC.

700 Universe Boulevard
Juno Beach, Florida 33408
U.S.A.
(407) 694-6300
Fax (407) 694-6230

Public Company
Incorporated: 1925 as Florida Power & Light Company
Employees: 19,138
Sales: $6.29 billion
Stock Exchanges: New York Tokyo London

FPL Group, Inc. was formed in 1984 as a holding company for Florida Power & Light Company, which was planning to diversify beyond utility operations. Florida Power & Light, as the holding company's principal subsidiary, provides electrical power to Miami, most of the eastern coast of Florida, and large parts of the state's southwest coast. FPL Group's other primary businesses are nonutility energy production, conducted by ESI Energy, Inc., and quality consulting by Qualtec, Inc. In the 1980s the holding company had diversified into businesses not related to energy, but in the late 1990s decided to leave these areas.

Florida Power & Light Company (FP&L) was formed in 1925 when a number of local electric and gas companies were consolidated by American Power & Light Company, a large utility holding company. FP&L included properties formerly owned and operated by Miami Electric Light & Power Company, Miami Gas Company, Miami Beach Electric Company, Southern Utilities Company, Daytona Public Service Company, Ormond Supply Company, Lakeland Gas Company, St. Johns Electric Company, and Southern Holding Company. By 1930 company profits were $2.7 million on revenue of $11.4 million.

In 1941 the city of Miami bought the company's water operations for $5.1 million, and FP&L sold its Miami Beach bus transportation system. In 1946 FP&L sold its water distribution system in Coral Gables, Florida. In 1950 American Power & Light, carrying out the provisions of a Congressional act limiting utility holding companies, spun off FP&L as an independent company. In 1951 FP&L sold its electric properties in the Florida towns of Perry, Madison, and Monticello to Florida Power Corporation.

FP&L was able the weather the Great Depression with the help of increasing demand for home electricity. During World War II, the U.S. economy recovered, and industrial demand for electricity increased sharply. Southern Florida's population and economy grew quickly after World War II, as soldiers who had been stationed in the area returned with their families to live there or to vacation. From 1949 to 1954 the customers in FP&L's territory increased from 295,000 to 463,000, while company revenue doubled from $38.7 million to $77.5 million. In 1952 FP&L announced a ten-year, $332 million construction program designed to triple the firm's electricity production capacity. The plan included construction of ten major power stations throughout FP&L's territory. Florida was growing so fast that in 1954 FP&L increased its ten-year plan to $410 million. By 1955 FP&L supplied electric power to 1.54 million people in 448 communities in the central and northern parts of Florida. Its gas system included 300 miles of gas mains, and gas plants in Miami, Daytona Beach, Lakeland, and Palatka, Florida. In 1958 the company sold its three gas plants and distribution systems to the Houston Corporation.

Florida continued to grow, and FP&L along with it. By 1964 FP&L served 2.7 million people in 555 communities, its revenue reaching $235 million in 1964. In 1965 the company signed 20-year contracts to buy natural gas from Pan-American Petroleum Corporation and Florida Gas Transmission Company. FP&L also decided to develop the use of nuclear power. Its two nuclear plants, south of Miami at Turkey Point, however, did not come on line until 1973, and did so at a cost of $120 million each.

FP&L has suffered many power shortages due in part to the heat, humidity, and salt from the ocean, which make generating and delivery equipment difficult to maintain. On August 5, 1969, an explosion and fire at the firm's Cutler Ridge power plant caused a blackout along 50 miles of Florida's east coast, including Miami and Fort Lauderdale. Much of the power returned within 90 minutes for the nearly two million people affected. In April 1973 power failed twice in two days, affecting three million residents, some for as long as seven hours. The cause was defective equipment at the Turkey Point nuclear plants and at the oil-fueled plant at Port Everglades. The failures hurt the company's image, especially since they occurred the day after the company was awarded a $40 million rate increase.

Despite problems at Turkey Point, FP&L's fuel diversification proved important when the energy crisis hit in 1973 and oil prices skyrocketed. Natural gas and nuclear energy supplied about half of the firm's fuel needs, but the remainder of FP&L's fuel needs were filled by oil. Thus, FP&L was granted a rate increase to offset the large increase in oil prices. The rate increases angered consumers.

In 1973 the company formed Fuel Supply Service, Inc. to secure fuel supplies. In 1974 Florida's attorney general ruled that utilities could not automatically pass along rises in fuel costs to customers. The ruling came just as FP&L was preparing a large stock and bond offering, which had to be canceled. The incident caused a lowering of the company's bond rating that management estimated would cost $300 million in higher interest rates. FP&L also was hurt in a recession that caught Florida with rows of unsold condominiums, and the state's growth slowed for the first time since World War II. Within a few years, however, Florida again was growing rapidly, and FP&L launched a massive building program to keep up, building seven new generating plants.

Another blackout left three million customers without electricity for several hours in 1977. It was FP&L's seventh major blackout in eight years, giving the company the worst power-failure record of U.S. electric utilities. The company was particularly vulnerable to power failures because it was isolated from the rest of the U.S. power grid. FP&L could draw some power from other Florida utilities when failures hit, but not enough to meet demand. The other utilities often did not have enough surplus power to offer, and FP&L's connections with them were inadequate. In 1979 FP&L began a $335 million transmission expansion project, building two high-capacity power lines from Miami to the Georgia border to increase its access to other utilities. In 1981 FP&L won a major rate increase of $256 million, followed by increases of $101 million in 1982 and $238 million in 1983.

By 1977, the company's two Turkey Point nuclear power plants, damaged by corrosion, needed to be rebuilt, at a cost of about $500 million each. The Nuclear Regulatory Commission fined the company on several occasions for safety violations at the plants. FP&L also had to make extensive repairs to its nuclear plant at St. Lucie, north of Palm Beach. Nonetheless, FP&L pushed ahead with a second nuclear power plant at St. Lucie. FP&L finished the plant nearly on time in 1983, a rarity in nuclear-power-plant construction.

Partly because of the problems with power failures and its nuclear power plants, FP&L moved to a Japanese-inspired style of management during the early 1980s. FP&L began stressing quality control, creating special quality-control teams, and keeping detailed records of the causes of power failures and other problems. The new management style initially faced opposition from middle managers. By 1989 the company had 1,900 quality-control teams, with most of its work force participating. Each team worked to solve specific problems that prevented the company from achieving its goals. Results were impressive. Service outages dropped from 100 minutes per customer per year to 43 minutes per year, far below the U.S. average of 90 minutes per year. Employee injuries decreased, as did customer complaints. The company was adding 130,000 customers a year, but requested no rate increases to pay for additional equipment. Government officials and managers from other U.S. companies attended FP&L seminars on adapting these management techniques, and FP&L was widely praised as one of the best-managed U.S. corporations.

In 1984 FPL Group, Inc. was formed as a holding company with FP&L as the primary subsidiary. Through a stock offering, the company raised $75 million for diversification. In 1985 John J. Hudiburg became chairman and CEO of FPL Group's Florida Power & Light subsidiary. He and FPL Group Chairman Marshall McDonald pushed quality control even harder. FPL Group made its first major move to diversify in 1985 when it bought the Philadelphia, Pennsylvania-based Colonial Penn Life Insurance Company for $565 million. The same year FPL Group also set up ESI Energy Inc. to participate in nonutility energy projects, such as converting waste to energy and finding other alternative energy sources. Additional FPL Group ventures included cable television, commercial and industrial real estate, and the maintainence of citrus groves.

By 1985 FP&L was the fourth-largest electric utility in the United States, and one of the fastest growing. It supplied service to 700 communities in 35 counties of Florida, including most of the territory along the east and lower west coasts of the state. With the addition of the second nuclear plant at St. Lucie, only 13% of the company's power was oil-generated. FP&L was working on ways to increase off-peak sales and reduce peak demand. In 1987 the utility raised the price of electricity during peak hours and lowered it during off-peak hours.

In 1989 James Broadhead replaced McDonald as chairman of FPL Group. Also that year, FPL Group became the first non-Japanese company to receive the Deming Prize, the prestigious Japanese quality-control award. However, Hudiburg, who, with McDonald, led the company's drive to win the award, had resigned several months earlier in the wake of Broadhead's appointment. Broadhead had made clear his intention of discontinuing FPL Group's new direction in management. In 1990 Broadhead moved the company back toward decentralized U.S. management. The Japanese-based system had become unpopular among large segments of the company's work force because of the long hours and paperwork involved. A subsidiary, Qualtec, Inc., continued to advise outside clients on certain aspects of quality improvement. Broadhead also was displeased with continuing maintenance problems at Turkey Point. Broadhead felt Hudiburg had not adequately addressed operating deficiencies at Turkey Point.

Meanwhile, FPL Group's diversification efforts had proven disastrous. Colonial Penn Life Insurance was losing money, as was FPL's Telesat cable-television service. FPL Group took a $72 million write-off in 1986 when it discontinued several unprofitable insurance lines. In 1989, with the U.S. insurance industry in recession, FPL Group took a $689 million write-off for Colonial Penn's losses and a $62 million write-off related to its cable television and real estate businesses. Because of the write-offs, income for 1990 came to only $6 million on sales of $6.3 billion.

FPL Group decided to sell its troubled insurer, as well as its real estate and cable television businesses, and to focus its attention on energy-related businesses. It sold Colonial Penn in August 1991, while the real estate and cable television businesses remained on the market. In addition, predictions that Florida's population growth would slow in the 1980s proved wrong. A cold spell in late 1989 led to rotating blackouts. When two plants failed in July 1990, FP&L asked customers to use less air conditioning to prevent brownouts. In 1990 the company announced a plan to spend $6.6 billion by 1999 to increase its capacity by 5,400 megawatts, or about 36%. FPL Group raised $677 million for the project in 1990 through two stock offerings. To ease its power squeeze, the utility bought its first out-of-state property, purchasing 76% of Georgia Power Company's 846-megawatt, modern, coal-fired plant near Atlanta for $614 million. The company also planned to build a 100-mile transmission line, further connecting its electrical grid with that of Florida Power Corporation.

In 1990 nuclear power made up 24% of FP&L's energy mix, oil 23%, natural gas 17%, coal 3%, and purchased power 33%. In late 1990 the company had to shut down its Turkey Point nuclear plant for 11 months to refuel it and install a backup generator, cutting FP&L's generating capacity by 10%. The Turkey Point plant had run at only 49% capacity since 1987, suffering from poor maintenance and equipment failures that lead to $700 million in repair bills between 1983 and 1990.

FPL Group faced a difficult rebuilding program in the 1990s, following its largely failed diversification program. It faced a profitable future, however, supplying electricity to one of the fastest-growing regions of the United States. Its primary task in the 1990s was to keep up with that growth.

Principal Subsidiaries: Florida Power & Light Company; ESI Energy, Inc.; Qualtec, Inc.

Further Reading: Jacobson, Gary, and John Hillkirk, "Crazy About Quality," *Business Month,* June 1989; Fins, Antonio N., "Feeling the Heat at a Florida Utility," *Business Week,* November 12, 1990.

—Scott M. Lewis

GAZ DE FRANCE

23 rue Philibert-Delorme
75840 Paris, Cedex 17
France
(1) 47 54 20 20
Fax: (1) 47 54 31 79

State-Owned Company
Incorporated: 1946
Employees: 27,649
Sales: FFr41.80 billion (US$8.07 billion)

Gaz de France, one of the largest gas utilities in the world, is chiefly responsible for the import, transmission, storage, distribution, and marketing of natural gas. Gaz de France (GDF) is managed by an 18-member board of directors which includes 6 representatives of the French government, 6 consumer and/or industry representatives, and 6 representatives of the work force. The chairman, chosen from the board members, and the chief executive officer are appointed by the French cabinet.

When it was established the role of GDF was to concentrate the production and distribution of gas in France. Before 1946 gas was mainly manufactured from coal, in more than 500 gas works, located throughout the country, which were owned by companies of various sizes: large companies supplied the areas around major cities, whereas subsidiaries of coal companies, such as Les Houillères Nationales, now Charbonnages de France (CDF), delivered gas to mining areas. For economical, political, and social reasons, the energy industries were nationalized soon after World War II by the *Gouvernement provisoire,* a tripartite government consisting of Mouvement Republicain Populaire, Socialist, and Communist parties.

Nationalization took place on the recommendation of Général de Gaulle, the former head of government, and Marcel Paul, the Communist Minister of Industry. On April 8, 1946, the Nationalization Act was effected, nationalizing the production, transport, distribution, import, and export of electricity and combustible gas; and establishing two new public corporations—Gaz de France and Electricité de France (EDF). Several gas producers remained exempt from nationalization, particularly those whose main activity was not gas production, transmission, or distribution including the producers of natural gas and gas manufacturing companies with an annual production of less than six million cubic meters. Gas distributors supplying less than this quantity were also exempt from na-

tionalization. These included local authorities and in 1991, 21 municipal utilities remained as independent companies.

Eventually the mixed enterprises, those companies providing both gas and electricity, were absorbed by EDF, including the gas activity which was later to be allocated to GDF. Under the Nationalization Act, these companies were financially autonomous and consequently commercially and technically independent. Initially, to simplify and unify the organization, EDF was in charge of the management of GDF whose first chairman, George Reclus, was under the authority of EDF's chief executive officer, Roger Gaspard. On January 4, 1949, however, GDF was partially separated from EDF when a law came into force giving it financial autonomy, with a credit of FFr6 billion and the order to separate its management from EDF within 6 months.

On February 23, 1949, Jean Le Guellec, former General Inspector of Industry and Commerce, was elected first chairman of Gaz de France, with George Combet, former chairman of Société de Gas et d'Electricité de Nice, as chief executive officer. Their first task was to modernize and concentrate gas manufacturing facilities and to develop the local transmission networks. The first long-distance pipeline was established in 1953, from the Nancy area to Paris, to open up a new market for the Lorraine coal gas. In southwest France, meanwhile, several small natural gas fields remained unexploited. A new law, the *Loi Armengaud,* came into force on August 2, 1949, excluding natural gas transmission from GDF's monopoly. This was in opposition to the Nationalization Act, which excluded only natural gas production from GDF's monopoly.

In 1951, the Lacq gas field in southwest France, then one of the largest in the world, was discovered by Elf Aquitaine and launched in 1957. The first transmission system, 4,000 kilometers long, was built to supply gas to southwest France, Brittany, and the Paris area. As a result, sales of natural gas increased threefold over the following five years from 1957 to 1962. Cities connected to the mains switched progressively to natural gas and by 1965 approximately half of France was supplied with natural gas. This was known as the natural gas revolution. The period was marked by the birth of the Fifth Republic and the arrival in 1959 of Général de Gaulle as head of state. It was also the period of the Algerian War and the loss of this colony was to be significant for French energy resources. In 1958, a special regime was established for the transmission and sale of natural gas in France. The Société Nationale des Gaz du Sud Ouest (SGNSO), owned by GDF, retained a monopoly within its area and the Compagnie Française du Méthane (CFM), owned 50% by GDF, 40% by TOTAL Compagnie Française des Pétroles and 10% by Elf, was established to carry out all operations relating to transmission and sale outside southwest France. With these subsidiaries GDF had a virtual monopoly of gas transport and distribution in France.

By the end of the 1960s, 70% of gas supplied to customers by gas utilities was natural gas, as opposed to 99.5% in 1991. Supplies from Lacq were insufficient and it was necessary to import gas. The French tradition of strong government intervention and involvement in the energy sector influenced negotiations for contracts. The purchase of gas was a useful diplomatic ploy, as confirmed by the first contract with Algeria, which procured gas from the Hassi R'Mel gas field. Signed in 1965 with the Algerian company Sonatrach, this initiated GDF's international involvement. The second gas import contract was signed with the Netherlands in 1967, linking GDF with the Dutch company Gasunie until 2005. Gas from the Groningen field was carried by pipeline via Belgium to northern and eastern France, leading to the extension of the transport network in Europe as well as in France, where the network reached a length of 13,000 kilometers in 1970.

Aware of its important role in the national program, and international energy markets, GDF extended its research and development program, particularly in the field of high-pressure pipelines and gas liquefaction, to improve transmission and storage facilities. GDF participated in the construction of the first natural gas liquefaction plant, GL4Z, in Algeria; designed and built the LNG (liquefied natural gas) receiving terminal at Le Havre; and ordered its first LNG carrier, the *Jules Verne*. Later, the Fos-sur Mer, Provence and Montoir de Bretagne, Brittany, terminals were designed and built, the latter being larger and more efficient. Underground storage facilities had been in operation since 1956 and GDF had pioneered the development of storage engineering. From a strategic and load-matching viewpoint, these needed to be developed to allow GDF to cope with winter's peak demand. The largest unit, 2,760 million cubic meters, was put into service in 1968 at Chémery in central France and in 1991 was still the world's largest underground storage facility.

In 1969 Robert Hirsh, a former state representative at Commissariat à l'Energie Atomique (CEA) and a member of the board of Electricité de France, replaced Jean Le Guellec as chairman of Gaz de France. Hirsch's nomination was particularly significant for the French energy policy. The period leading to the 1973 oil shock was characterized by cheap oil which boosted France's industrial development and more than doubled energy consumption. The use of oil greatly increased, demand for gas and electricity grew substantially, and the French nuclear power program was started. The period of the two main oil price rises, 1973 to 1979, boosted natural gas consumption in France and throughout the world.

In response to the first oil price shocks, French government policy was to adopt a far-reaching nuclear power strategy, enabling France to rely more on nuclear power for energy production. This resulted in significant diversification of primary energy suppliers. The idea was to avoid a situation where one supplier accounted for more than 5% of France's total energy supply and this remained the case in 1991. To follow this policy, GDF looked for alternative suppliers of natural gas, resulting in the purchase of Soviet and Norwegian North Sea gas in addition to the former Algerian and Dutch contracts. With the most important natural gas reserves in the world, Russia became its largest producer. Three contracts were signed between GDF and Soyouzgazexport, one from 1976 to 2000 for 2.5 billion cubic meters per year, one from 1980 to 2000, and the third, from 1984 to 2009, for 8 billion cubic meters per year. The Norwegian contracts were signed with four separate producers—Ekofisk in 1977, Statfjord in 1985, Heimdal in 1986, and Gullfaks in 1987 In 2003 other deliveries are planned to come from Norway—Troll and Sleipner—after contracts agreed with Norway's Statoil. Two more contracts were signed with Algeria, one in 1973 for 3.5 billion cubic meters per year, and one in 1982 for 5 billion cubic meters. Both were long-term contracts, 25 years and 20 years long respectively, and have been renegotiated.

In 1976 Robert Hirsch left Gaz de France and Jean Blancard became chairman after a long career in the energy sector. In 1979 Blancard was in turn replaced by Pierre Alby, former chief executive manager of GDF. The nomination of such distinguished representatives of the energy industry demonstrated the government's concern with the gas industry. Furthermore, by 1979 Paris was relying soley upon natural gas. Production of manufactured gas had ceased and GDF was importing huge quantities of natural gas to meet increasing French consumption. GDF had been induced to liaise with other gas companies in managing the transmission of purchased gases and in supplying security clauses. The 1970s, marked by the energy crisis, saw the total transformation of Gaz de France into an active member of the international energy market and network.

Natural gas consumption's share of primary energy, which was 7.9% in 1973, increased to 12.7% in 1979, while the electricity share increased from 9.2% to a mere 11.7%. The competition between the two sources was strong, and GDF, aware of changing times ahead for the enterprises, whether private or public, developed a new attitude toward its friendly rival Electricité de France (EDF). GDF was divided into a number of operating divisions which dealt only with GDF. At a local distribution level, GDF and EDF shared a joint role. Distribution regions were divided into a number of distribution areas. Each distribution area had a budget for each type of energy, but for the general public EDF and GDF were closely connected with private consumers of both gas and electricity generally invoiced on the same bill. This was still the case in 1991.

To differentiate between gas and electricity as energy sources was a daunting task for GDF. GDF programs and rates were regulated by the Minister of Industry and the Minister of Economy and Finance. Despite this close link with the government, GDF was ostensibly run as a commercial enterprise, financially independent and taxed in the same way as a private firm. In the early 1980s GDF recorded severe losses which it was necessary to restrict.

GDF has had a difficult position in the national economy compared to EDF. France exports electrical energy and EDF has had to face overcapacity of electricity, whereas huge quantities of gas are imported. In 1985 Pierre Alby, then chairman of GDF, summed up the problem in a speech on the competition between natural gas and nuclear power during the Fifteenth World Conference of the International Gas Union when he said that in France, a country lacking major national gas resources, "the gas industry is a factor which cannot be neglected by a policy striving to establish a balance between imports and exports." He added, however, that the gas industry could not isolate itself from balance of trade concerns. His analysis of the position of gas as opposed to nuclear energy revealed the new policy GDF decided to adopt. After major technical achievements at national and international levels, GDF must, he said, accept the laws of competition on the energy market and, above all, nuclear competition.

Once again GDF was ready to accept a new commercial challenge. GDF could not compete with lower prices as the government controlled these closely. Initially GDF continued to implement its strategy of promoting the export of French gas expertise by becoming involved in several trans-European pipeline companies and obtaining part ownership of two tankers used to transport LNG from Algeria. In this respect, GDF has developed its industrial activity, and this has made it possible to reduce the import bill.

The next stage was to promote a modern image of the gas industry to the general public as well as domestic, commercial, and industrial users, in order to compete with electricity. To this end natural gas was promoted as a plentiful, flexible, powerful, and clean source of energy. The environmental safety of the product, particularly important in the industrial sector, helped GDF to increase its market share significantly. The promotion of clean energy was also welcomed by the increasingly vocal ecology movement, which was strongly against nuclear energy. Fondation du Gaz de France was established to promote protection of the environment.

To tackle the domestic and commercial market was, however, more difficult. GDF was in fierce competition with EDF for the domestic market, the new housing sector being one of the main targets. EDF had an advantage with the public authorities who were concerned about the excess of electric energy and tended to favor electrical installations. GDF therefore had to develop efficient marketing methods as well as new communication skills and the company structure was modified to cope equally with government control and with the competitive energy market. The new logo, a single flame designed in 1987, was a sign of this change.

Since the mid-1980s, the European gas market has become considerably more international in character and there have been significant developments regulating competition, the establishment of a European Economic Community internal market program, and environmental issues. Jacques Fournier, who, before his appointment as GDF chairman in 1986, was secretary general of the former Socialist government, was at the same time chairman of the CEEP, European Center of Public Enterprises, and was thus aware of the importance of an internal European market. During a meeting organized by the Fondation Europe et Société early in 1988, he said that GDF would have to adapt itself to the changing situation in Europe concerning standardization, markets, and the fiscal system, at the same time declaring that public services and the spirit of enterprise were not in opposition. State control, he said, was necessary in order to preserve GDF's autonomy. Francis Gutmann, former French ambassador in Madrid, appointed GDF chairman in August 1988, continued the battle for the autonomy of his company while the monopoly of imports and distribution began to be contested at national and European levels.

GDF showed a loss of FFr96 million in 1990 on a turnover of FFr41.8 billion—more than twice the loss of 1989. Despite these losses, the company had by 1991 proven an ability to cope with technological changes and marketing adaptations. With its industrial assests, research facilities, and expertise, GDF's active part in worldwide gas development made the company a major factor in French economic growth. The need to make a profit was recognized.

A contract signed with the government in February 1991 enabled GDF to make a profit. Based on discussions under way since fall 1989, the contract covered objectives and management during the period 1991 to 1993. At the press conference held soon after its signing, Francis Gutmann declared: "At a time when natural gas is recognized as a major source of energy and when GDF continues to increase its strategic weight in France and abroad, the new contract provides the responsibility and the autonomy necessary to accomplish a continually improved public service." The tariff policy was also covered in the contract allowing GDF, among other things, to follow the fluctuations of supply costs. This enabled GDF to stand up to international competition and protect its distribution monopoly from challenges by the French parliament and the European commission.

In France, as Elf Aquitaine and Total threatened GDF's gas market shares, a parliamentary amendment was signed which changed the statute of 1946. According to the *Financial Times* of April 20–21, 1991, the new amendment gave *communes*, the basic units of French local government, freedom in organizing their own gas distribution. This amendment, known as the Desrosiers amendment, was later revoked. At the same time, the European commission continued efforts to break up national energy policies.

In its history so far, Gaz de France has overcome all opposition. In 1991 SGNSO and Société Nationale Elf Aquitaine Production (SNEA-P), Elf's French oil and gas subsidiary, continued to transport and sell natural gas from fields in southwest France to public distribution companies, including GDF, and to large industrial customers. The establishment of the European market will allow the company to hold its own.

Principal Subsidiaries: Gaz Marine (99.98%); Société Mulhousienne du Gaz (SMG) (99.97%); Compagnie Industrielle d'Activités Immobilières et Industrielles (COGAC) (99.34%); Société pour le Développement de l'Industrie du Gaz en France (SDIG) (98.80%); Société Financière de l'Industrie du Gaz (SFIG) (68.78%); S.A.R.L. Gaz Transport (51.00%); Société Française d'Etudes et de Réalisations d'Equipements Gaziers (SOFREGAZ) (49.99%); Compagnie Française du Méthane (CeFeM) (49.97%); Société Nationale des Gaz du Sud-Ouest (SGNSO) (29.98%); MEGAL GmbH (Germany, 43%); Baumgarten Oberkappel Gasleitung GmbH (BOG) (Austria, 44%).

Further Reading: Mougin, Pierre, *Mémoires,* Paris, Imprimerie Barneoud, 1966; Picard, Bertrand, Bungener, *Histoire de l'EDF,* Paris, Dunod, 1985; *Environmental Pressures and the Response of the European Gas Industry,* Report of the Institution of Gas Engineers of the 10th W.H. Bennett Traveling Fellowship, 1988; EDF-GDF, *Mémoire Ecrite de L'Electricité et du Gaz,* Paris, 1990; Lyle, C.D., and R.O. Marshall, *Gas Regulation in Western Europe,* London, Financial Times Business Information, 1990.

—Florence Protat

**GENERAL
PUBLIC
UTILITIES
CORPORATION**

GENERAL PUBLIC UTILITIES CORPORATION

100 Interpace Parkway
Parsippany, New Jersey 07054
U.S.A.
(201) 263-6500
Fax: (201) 263-6822

Public Company
Incorporated: 1906 as Associated Gas & Electric Company
Employees: 12,516
Sales: $3.00 billion
Stock Exchange: New York

General Public Utilities Corporation (GPU), a public utility holding company, holds all the stock of three electric operating subsidiaries that provide about 1.9 million customers with 39 billion kilowatt-hours of electricity in a service territory covering about half the land area of New Jersey and Pennsylvania. Jersey Central Power & Light Company accounts for about half of the GPU system's revenue, and supplies about 43% of New Jersey with power. Pennsylvania Electric Company serves a largely rural 17,000-square-mile area that includes many mining, manufacturing, and agribusiness customers. Metropolitan Edison Company's 3,274-square-mile service area in Pennsylvania contains a wide range of manufacturing, agricultural, recreational, and tourist facilities. Another key subsidiary is GPU Nuclear Corporation, which operates the system's nuclear facilities. The Oyster Creek generating station at Forked River, New Jersey, and the Three Mile Island nuclear generating station near Harrisburg, Pennsylvania, generated about 22% of GPU's total energy needs in 1990. GPU also owns GPU Service Corporation, which performs various services for the operating utilities, and General Portfolios Corporation, which makes nonutility investments.

GPU was originally incorporated as Associated Gas & Electric Company (Ageco) in 1906. A group of small-town promoters around Ithaca, New York, created Ageco as a holding company for 12 small gas and electric properties: 10 in south central New York and one each in Pennsylvania and Ohio. The total value of the properties was $1.2 million. In spite of some minor acquisitions over the next several years, Ageco remained a group of small, rural New York companies as late as 1921, with assets under $7 million. In 1922, however, Ageco entered a period of almost two decades of dramatic growth tied

in with incredibly convoluted and often illicit financial manipulations.

In 1908 at the age of 26, Howard C. Hopson had been hired by the New York State Public Service Commission as chief of its division of capitalization. In this position, Hopson was a central figure in New York state public utility regulation from 1908 to 1915. Here he met John I. Mange, general manager of Ageco and president of several of its operating subsidiaries. Hopson and Mange became close friends. In 1915 Hopson left the commission to become an independent consultant. In 1922, through an amazing series of transactions involving dummy companies, Hopson and Mange bought all the stock in Ageco. With the pair now firmly in power, Mange became president of Ageco, and Hopson became treasurer and vice president. The expansion that followed turned Ageco into a utilities giant, including about 180 intricately connected subsidiaries and service companies, possessing properties in 26 states and in the Philippines.

By 1924 Ageco's assets were up to $65 million, and more than tripled to $217 million in 1925. The most significant acquisitions of this period were the Pennsylvania Electric Corporation and the Manila Electric Company. Hopson funded these purchases by issuing the first of several unusual types of convertible securities that were to become his standard operating method. Hopson's method involved complex juggling of assets between holding companies and sub-holding companies. The process was so complicated that accountants, lawyers, and shareholders could not follow it, enabling Hopson to derive huge sums from the system by way of his personally held service companies, which performed various tasks for the operating companies and charged them outrageous rates. In the three years preceding the stock market crash of 1929, Hopson sold nearly $500 million worth of Ageco debentures convertible to stock. Because stock prices were rising so fast during this time, people were anxious to exercise these conversion rights and bought up the bonds quickly. Ageco ended 1929 as one of the five largest holding-companies in the nation. With the collapse of the stock market, however, Hopson was no longer able to support Ageco's pyramid-like structure through the sale of new securities.

By 1932 Ageco was in a desperate situation. The Depression had slowed revenue growth of the operating companies, and Ageco had difficulty raising money to pay off maturing bonds. In an effort to save his empire, Hopson announced in early 1932 that over the last few years all of Ageco's income-producing assets had been shifted into a subsidiary, Associated Gas & Electric Corporation (Agecorp), formerly called Associated Utilities Investment Corporation. Ageco security holders suddenly discovered that their stock was subornate to any debt that Agecorp might create.

Then, in a further attempt to avoid bankruptcy, Hopson unveiled his plan for recapitalization, in 1933. Under the plan, investors were given the option of exchanging their Ageco debentures for Agecorp securities. The catch was that they would have to take either a 50% reduction in their principal amount, or retain their principal and accept a significant cut in interest rate.

Although the recapitalization plan was somewhat successful as a stalling tactic, a group of security holders attempted to force Ageco into receivership. This litigation and similar legal attacks lasted until 1937, when a compromise was struck. The compromise required Hopson to appoint three independent directors to his board to help work out a more equitable reorganization plan and to protect the shareholders' interests. At the same time as this battle raged, the Treasury Department was trying to collect $54 million in back taxes from Ageco. Throughout these attacks Hopson personally continued to fare very well financially. He and his family collected at least $3.6 million between 1934 and 1938 from the service companies alone.

Meanwhile, Congress had begun its work on the Public Utility Holding Company Act, passed in 1935. Hopson's furious lobbying against the act helped to make him a target for investigation by the Securities and Exchange Commission (SEC) and other federal agencies. In the course of its investigation, the SEC put a halt to certain illegal accounting practices used by Ageco and Agecorp, and both companies filed for bankruptcy in January 1940. Hopson himself eventually was convicted of mail fraud and sentenced to five years in prison.

The reorganization that followed bankruptcy was a success. The reorganization staff included Albert F. Tegen, who had served on the SEC investigation team and then became president of Ageco, and Willard Thorp, a leading economist, who became chairman of the board. During this period of trusteeship, creditors received Ageco stock, claims were settled, reduced power rates improved customer relations, the tangle of securities and holdings was simplified, and $14 million a year in interest savings was filtered back into previously delayed maintenance and new construction projects. By 1945 Ageco stock was six times as high as it had been in 1942, and the new streamlined Ageco was the pride of the SEC. The company's name was changed in 1946 to General Public Utilities Corporation.

The end of World War II led to increased growth for utility companies throughout the country. Although GPU's growth in territory was about average, its gains in earnings were considerably higher than the industry average during these postwar years. In the decade after the war, GPU's operating revenues more than doubled, surpassing $174 million in 1955. A major reason for this exceptional growth in earnings was tremendous progress in operating efficiency. In 1948 1.35 pounds of coal was required to generate one kilowatt-hour of electricity. By 1955, 36% less coal was needed. The new Shawville station of the Pennsylvania Electric subsidiary was highly efficient, requiring less than 0.75 of a pound of coal to produce one kilowatt-hour. By 1955, even after divesting several properties by order of earlier SEC rulings, the GPU system was making electricity for 1.2 million customers in New Jersey, Pennsylvania, and the Philippines. Of these customers 43% were residential, 29% industrial, 21% commercial, and 7% in other categories. The variety of industries that comprised the industrial sector was extremely wide, with the metals industry making up 10% of this segment.

In the 1960s GPU began turning to nuclear power. In 1963 the Jersey Central Power & Light subsidiary signed a $68 million contract with General Electric for construction of a nuclear facility at Oyster Creek, New Jersey, making it the first U.S. company to lay out money for a nonexperimental nuclear generator. The Oyster Creek station was scheduled to begin producing in mid-1967, but did not actually go into service until December 1969—the kind of delay that would come

to be expected in the construction of nuclear facilities. Because of this delay, GPU was forced to spend $79 million in these two years on power from other sources in order to meet its expanding electricity demands. Despite the fact that the Oyster Creek generator cost $60 million more than expected, and GPU's capital outlays had tripled in the latter half of the 1960s—largely due to nuclear projects—GPU President William Kuhns remained committed to a growing emphasis on nuclear energy, including construction of two generators at the now-notorious Three Mile Island site in Pennsylvania. Throughout the decade, operating revenues rose slowly but steadily, from $205 million in 1960 to $384 million in 1970. By 1970 the combined service area of GPU's three utility subsidiaries was approaching its early 1990 size.

Nuclear power remained GPU's great hope for the future into the mid-1970s. With oil prices skyrocketing, nuclear generation was increasingly seen as the method of choice. The cost of nuclear fuel to generate one kilowatt-hour in 1974 was less than one-third that of coal and about one-eleventh that of oil. That year, the fuel used by GPU for generating was 58% coal, 22% nuclear, and 20% oil. This was also the year that the first Three Mile Island unit went into commercial operation.

GPU entered 1979 as the 17th-largest utility in the United States, with assets of $4.6 billion. In the previous year, GPU had earned $139 million on $1.3 billion of operating revenues. On March 28, 1979, an accident occurred at the new, second nuclear generator at Three Mile Island, which had been producing electricity for only a few months. A valve at the unit failed to close, allowing cooling water to escape from the reactor. The plant, run by a Metropolitan Edison subsidiary, was operating at 97% of capacity at the time, and the absence of the cooling water caused the plant's core to overheat, damaging fuel rods and releasing radioactive particles, thereby contaminating the building.

The costs of the accident were enormous. GPU estimated the cost of cleaning up Three Mile Island at $1 billion. In addition, it would cost GPU $2.3 billion to maintain electrical service to all of its customers, including $24 million per month to purchase power to replace that which was no longer being produced at Three Mile Island. At this time, $400 million came due on maturing securities. With net earnings drastically reduced, investors wary, and the Pennsylvania Public Utility Commission threatening to cancel Metropolitan Edison's franchise, it appeared that GPU could become the first public utility to go bankrupt since the Depression.

GPU's recovery from the devastation of the Three Mile Island accident was slow. Profits were much lower through the first half of the 1980s. A major obstacle to GPU's return to stability was the length of time it took for the Nuclear Regulatory Commission (NRC) to determine whether the undamaged Three Mile Island unit could be returned to operation, and if so, whether it could be operated by GPU. The company's competency to run a nuclear facility was questioned, by the NRC and by many other critics. Members of Congress urged that GPU Chairman and Chief Executive Kuhns and President Herman Dieckamp be replaced. Criminal charges were filed against Metropolitan Edison alleging that records regarding the leakage of coolant had been falsified.

The turning point finally came in November 1985, when the NRC ruled that GPU could return Three Mile Island to operation, ending more than six years of inactivity. The ruling almost instantly added $1 per share to company earnings and allowed rates to be lowered in both New Jersey and Pennsylvania, since the need to purchase power from outside sources was dramatically reduced. In May 1987, GPU reinstated dividends to shareholders for the first time since 1980. In 1988 earnings rose to $284 million, from $259 million the previous year, and dividends were increased twice. These results were achieved partly due to record-setting operation by the company's generating units, particularly those fueled by coal. GPU-owned generators produced 31 million megawatt-hours in 1988.

In 1989 Kuhns retired as president, chairman, and CEO, and was replaced by Standley H. Hoch. Kuhns, who had been chief executive for 20 years, had first retired two years earlier, but that initial retirement was short lived, as he returned to active duty upon the death of his successor, John O'Leary. Hoch, who had been executive vice-president and chief financial officer of General Dynamics Corporation, continued to reshape GPU into a more streamlined and cohesive system, focusing on improved communication networks among the parent company and operating subsidiaries; on eliminating unnecessary work and positions; and on maximizing production efficiency. GPU increased its dividends twice in 1989 and once each in 1990 and 1991.

The year 1990 brought the completion of the Three Mile Island cleanup, a project that drained GPU financially and made consideration of further construction projects much more difficult. Also in 1990, a 6.1% rate increase was ap-proved for Jersey Central, the first such hike since 1986, meaning an additional $95.5 million in revenue. The company's operating and maintenance expenses were lower than in 1989, and when 24 officers retired in a 15-month period, only 8 were replaced, reflecting the stated commitment to streamlining. In addition, an agreement was reached with DQE, a western Pennsylvania utility, which agreed to produce and transmit electricity from western Pennsylvania, where demand was lower, to the eastern part of the state over 240 miles of transmission line.

GPU's status as a regulated public utility has helped to prevent its demise, in spite of regulations that sometimes hinder profits and require spending on safety and environmental control. GPU's continued success will be greatly influenced by society's verdict on nuclear energy.

Principal Subsidiaries: Jersey Central Power & Light Company; Metropolitan Edison Company; Pennsylvania Electric Company; GPU Service Corporation; GPU Nuclear Corporation; General Portfolios Corporation.

Further Reading: "An End to Hopson's Labyrinth," *Business Week,* December 8, 1945; "Through the Wringer With A.G.&E.," *Fortune,* December 1945.

—Robert R. Jacobson

GÉNÉRALE DES EAUX GROUP

52 rue d'Anjou
75384 Paris Cedex 08
France
(1) 42 66 91 50
Fax: (1) 42 66 22 69

Public Company
Incorporated: 1853 as Compagnie Générale des Eaux
Employees: 173,105
Sales: FFr116.82 billion (US$22.55 billion)
Stock Exchange: Paris

The Générale des Eaux Group is the world's foremost supplier of drinking water, with over 22 million users in France and sizeable shares of the markets in Spain, the United Kingdom, and the United States. It also ranks as the world's most important public services organization and has 1,200 subsidiaries operating worldwide in areas of thermal and electrical power, waste, real estate, leisure, healthcare, and communications.

Compagnie Générale des Eaux was founded in 1852 during the reign of Napoleon III and is often described as France's first capitalist venture. The company was authorized by imperial decree on December 14, 1853, and from the start benefited enormously from the emperor's personal interest, as well as from support and investment from the international business community in Paris, London, and Lyons, which had studied the water supply companies of the United States and the United Kingdom and realized rich pickings could be had. The list of founders included the Rothschild family, a Fould, a Lafitte, the Duc de Morny—the Emperor's half brother—and a large proportion of the imperial nobility. Shareholders included James de Rothschild, who had the largest single subscription of 5,000 shares, and a cross-section of members of the nobility, stockbrokers, and bankers. The initial capital was FFr20 million which was raised from an 80,000 share subscription.

The political and financial influence of its founders and shareholders gave the new company a high profile from the start, but the company also caught the mood of the day with its declared objective of providing "assistance for municipal authorities in implementing schemes of fundamental importance to public health." Not only was the notion of water-for-all part of a new municipal socialism which had already taken root in the United Kingdom and Germany, but also France's growing industries were becoming insatiable in their need for water and

power. Without an industrial base, France could not compete with its neighbors, the United Kingdom and Germany. If the foundation of Compagnie Générale des Eaux was a calculated political move, it was also an astute financial one. "We shall be opening up a mine, the wealth of which has not been explored," reported the first board of management to the shareholders, continuing, "as the first occupants of this mine, it will be our privilege to select and exploit the best seams." The shareholders were not disappointed.

Projected returns of 4% were realized at 25% from the first year of business. Lyons and Nantes headed the list of municipal authorities anxious to receive Générale des Eaux water. Within months, a 99-year agreement had been concluded with Lyons to provide water for domestic and industrial consumption. For an initial investment of FFr6 million and operating costs of FFr80,000 per year, Générale des Eaux guaranteed a gross annual income of FFr381,500 before a drop of water had even flowed through the pipes. A contract with Nantes followed in 1854, with Générale des Eaux undercutting the haphazard services of current suppliers, but still managing to make a healthy 20% profit.

Securing the contract for the Paris water supply took a little longer. Initially turned down for the bid to supply the capital's water, Générale des Eaux began buying into small local water companies in the suburbs. When in 1860 the suburbs were annexed to the city, the company was in a strong position to negotiate with the prefecture of the Seine and the city of Paris authorities. Slow penetration into and around the desired market was a clever strategy, and became something of a hallmark of Générale des Eaux's acquisition policies thereafter. The seven-year wait was worth it. Générale des Eaux won a 50-year contract to supply Paris and the suburbs. The city of Paris, for its part, took possession of all water machinery and installations which had previously belonged to the company. Générale des Eaux guaranteed a supply of water which they charged back to the authorities. As the population of Paris grew and the demand for both domestic and industrial water increased, the water supplier saw its profits grow.

The character of Générale des Eaux was beginning to emerge. The company preferred to deal with large municipal authorities which would contract agreements for long periods of time and sought out projects which would bring high profits to enable greater investment. It also displayed a strong speculative and entrepreneurial streak, the latter of which is particularly remarkable. Générale des Eaux anticipated the growth of the Côte d'Azur and the so-called Emerald Coast of Brittany some 20 to 30 years before the resorts became fashionable, installing water supplies and drainage systems in Nice and the surrounding areas from the 1860s and subsequently supplying Antibes, Menton, Hyères, and Monaco in the 1870s and 1880s. Towards the end of the century, the coastal towns and large cities of Brittany and Normandy were supplied by Générale des Eaux.

Despite heady successes in the company's first 50 years, the end of the century brought an unforeseen problem. In 1892 there was a major typhoid epidemic in Paris. The authorities acted by ordering a systematic sampling of water for laboratory analysis, and in 1902 the Public Hygiene Act laid down standards for public health in relation to the water supply. The connection between water supply and cholera and typhoid was finally understood. From now on municipal authorities demanded not just efficiency but guarantees that the water being delivered for domestic consumption was clean and disease-free. For Générale des Eaux, the Public Hygiene Act meant hefty investment in research and new machinery. Treating waste water before it ran back into the clean water supplies also became a priority.

There was, too, a new competitor in the field. Société Lyonnaise des Eaux et de L'Eclairage was founded in 1880 and by the start of the 20th century had established itself as a force to be reckoned with. From then on, something of a race developed between the two companies to acquire market shares in the supplying of water to unserviced municipalities. Between 1900 and 1940 the rate at which water supply networks spread through France accelerated with each decade. Both companies expanded their areas of influence by buying up local water companies and overhauling their operations, so that by the outbreak of World War II Compagnie Générale des Eaux and Société Lyonnaise des Eaux et de L'Eclairage supplied 50% of all town dwellers.

Dominating the fortunes of Compagnie Générale des Eaux in the postwar years was the personality of Guy Dejouany. An engineer by profession, he was educated at the Ecole Polytechnique and, after appointments in Metz and Paris, joined Générale des Eaux in 1950. His rise through the company was swift. A director in 1960, he became deputy director general in 1965, director general in 1972, and president and director general in 1976. In the 1960s he was instrumental in the development of a thermal energy program, showing himself to be a strong advocate of diversification beyond the traditional water concerns. Moreover, he turned the company from a fairly institutional concern into a dynamic, highly diversified group which, in 1991, was one of the most successful companies on the Paris Stock Exchange. Dejouany has remained a decidedly unpublic figure, declining to give interviews and running an unusually small headquarters with only 15 managers. Dejouany was involved in the first tentative moves, in the 1970s, into urban cleaning and maintenance, waste, electrical contracting, house building, and construction.

By 1981 Compagnie Générale des Eaux was beginning to make the headlines with its profits of FFr331 million. Ironically, its attractiveness nearly brought about its downfall. At the start of the 1980s, 75% of shares were held by small investors, headed by Dejouany. In March 1981 Compagnie Générale d'Electricité announced a 15% stake, a significant interest held by a large company. Two years later Saint-Gobain, the glass and pipe manufacturer, which had already bought enthusiastically into Olivetti and Bull CH Honeywell only to have the government insist that it pull out, announced a 33% holding in Compagnie Générale des Eaux. Months of complicated manouvers on the Paris Stock Exchange had been necessary, but Générale des Eaux had exposed itself to the risk of a buy-in by a large company when it issued new shares at the start of 1983 to raise capital for investment. The announcement brought crises within the water company and within the government. Dejouany and a number of government critics complained that Saint-Gobain, one of France's six major companies nationalized in 1982, was attempting a creeping nationalization of the water company. Saint-Gobain replied that it was merely seeking to expand its business by ordinary means, but was soon requested by the government to cut its stake to 20.7%. Dejouany further redressed the balance by asking Schlumberger,

the Franco-American service and electronics group, to buy a 10% share at a cost of FFr550 million to offset Saint-Gobain's interest.

This share purchase ended the crisis and signaled the end, too, of the growing pains of Générale des Eaux. From this moment on, the company went from strength to strength, multiplying its interests abroad and buying into some of France's leading companies at home. The results were dramatic. The 1980s, as a whole, saw sales at home increase seven and a half times, from FFr11.5 billion to FFr76.5 billion, and sales abroad multiply 35 times, from FFr630 million to FFr22 billion. Net profits rose from FFr331 million in 1981 to FFr766 million in 1986 and then took off sharply to finish at FFr1.8 billion in 1989.

The weighty program of investment and activity abroad produced both admiration and controversy in countries targeted for Générale des Eaux treatment. In 1991 Générale des Eaux was now the second largest water distributor in Spain and the third largest distributor of bottled water in the United States, and also supplied water in Portugal, Malta, and Italy. It collected waste in Bogota and Prague, cleaned the streets and underground system of Madrid, supplied cable television in Montreal, and managed industrial waste and thermal power from California to Benelux.

Générale des Eaux also moved across the English Channel. Britain in the late 1980s, with a water industry heading for privatization and local authorities beginning to put many of their service contracts out for tender, was ripe for investment. Lyonnaise des Eaux and Société d'Aménagement Urbain et Rural (SAUR) made large tenders for the ten regional water companies, Lyonnaise paying £47.6 million for Essex Water in June 1988, and SAUR paying £58.6 million for Mid Southern Water in January 1989. Générale des Eaux, in contrast, focused on buying shares in a number of smaller companies, including Three Valleys, Folkestone & District, Mid-Kent, Severn and Trent, and Bristol, and looked to the wider areas of energy, waste, healthcare, construction, and cable television to establish a foothold in Britain. The foothold was designed to be flexible. When British electricity companies were privatized in 1990, Générale des Eaux dropped some of its water interests and bought into Associated Electricity. Similarly, when television franchises were put up for bids in 1991, Générale des Eaux bought shares in a number of cable television operations. Less expected was the purchase of American Medical International's chain of private hospitals in Britain in March 1990 and an 83% stake in Norwest Holst. In June 1991, Générale des Eaux's U.K. waste company Onyx announced a seven-year rubbish collection contract with the city of Liverpool, the latest of twenty such contracts with municipalities all over Britain.

The progress of Générale des Eaux in Britain mirrors the development of the company in France during its early days in the 19th century. The profits have been just as rich—in 1990 the company made £900 million in Britain, which now represents almost one-tenth of total group sales revenue worldwide. In the general spread of its international and home operations there are similarities, too, in company behavior in the previous century and in the present day. Générale des Eaux is responsive to current environment issues. In May 1990 it paid US$100 million for a 16% stake in Air and Water Technologies, a major pollution-control company based in New Jersey in the United States. Air, water, and soil pollution prevention is high on the list of priorities for Générale des Eaux in the 1990s and its activities have already earned it attention from Europe's press for its environmental concerns.

Générale des Eaux's interests in cable television and cellular car phones include a 21.6% share in Canal Plus, 90% of Générale d'Images, and 80% of Compagnie Générale de Vidéo-communications, making Générale des Eaux the leading operator of cable networks in France. Although the 1991 Gulf War boosted viewing figures, cable television has yet to take off in a big way, but it is thought that the mid-1990s will see a large increase in the subscription base. The launch of cellular carphones showed quicker returns. Between the inception of the service in March 1989 and the end of the year, there were 10,000 subscribers. At a European level, the carphone subsidiary, Compagnie Financière pour le Radio Téléphone, works with BMW and Veba in Germany to install telephones directly.

In addition to entering the communications sector, Générale des Eaux had bought into a number of French blue chip companies including, since 1986, Saint-Gobain. Saint-Gobain's major subsidiary, Société Générale d'Entreprise, which had in turn been acquired from Compagnie Générale d'Electricité, was bought out by Générale des Eaux in 1988, thereby giving it a major position in France's construction industry. Phenix, Seeri, and Sari have added to Générale des Eaux's command in this area, with projects such as the La Défense building in Paris. In Paris, the company cleans the Louvre, the Métro, the Ministry of Finance, and the Musée d'Orsay art gallery, and collects waste for Peugeot, Air France, the SNCF (Société Nationale des Chemins de Fer Français), and Nestlé. The company plans to move into health care and leisure in the 1990s. What remains to be seen is how the company will fare when Guy Dejouany eventually retires, and how it intends to consolidate the tremendous advances of the 1980s.

Principal Subsidiaries: Compagnie des Eaux et de l'Ozone (84.9%); Société Française de Distribution d'Eau (84.9%); Compagnie Fermière de Services Publics (78.1%); Compagnie Méditerranéenne des Services d'Eau (96.4%); Société des Eaux de Melun (85.8%); Compagnie des Eaux de Paris (99.8%); Société des Eaux du Nord (49.5%); Société des Eaux de Marseille (48.6%); Société des Eaux de Versailles et de Saint-Cloud (50%); General Utilities (United Kingdom); Sogesur (Spain, 75%); Sade-Compagnie Générale de Travaux d'Hydraulique (92.9%); Société des Tuyaux Bonna (91.7%); Omnium de Traitements et de Valorisation (97.9%); SEPEREF-TMP; Compagnie Générale de Chauffe (90.8%); Compagnie Financière Montenay (99.8%); Compagnie Générale de Travaux et d'Installations Electriques (95.8%); Santerne (88.6%); Groupe Energies (99.9%); Sofitam (83%); Société Lyonnaise d'Exploitation de Chauffage (98.5%); Société Prodith (96.8%); Cofima (95.2%); Compagnie Générale d'Entreprises Automobiles (CGEA) (83.9%); Société d'Assainissement Rationnel et de Pompage (SARP) (95.5%); SARP Industries (95.1%); Union de Services Publics (83.2%); Start Barla (76.4%); Société d'Equipments Manutentions et Transport (Semat) (98.6%); Comatec (44.8%); Traitement des Résidus Urbains (44.7%); SMA (Spain); Rénosol (50%); SGE (74.6%); Compagnie Générale de Bâtiment et de Construction (CBC) (80%); Sari (54.9%); Seeri (64.6%); Immobilière du Parvis (58.5%); Défense Nord (60%); Compagnie Générale de Vidéocommunication (86.1%); Générale d'Images (99.9%); Société Française de Radiotéléphone (SFR) (41.1%); General Cable; Antennes Tonna (48.9%); Compagnie Générale de Santé (90.9%); Générale de Santé Internationale; Locapark (88.7%); Setex (98.7%); Sappel (94.9%); Aqualand (66.5%); Angibaud (72.5%); Société d'Applications Hydrauliques, d'Investissements et d'Entreprises (95.7%); Anjou International (U.S.A.); Société Nouvelle d'Investissements et de Gestions (93.7%); IOS (59.1%);

—Catriona Luke

HOKKAIDO ELECTRIC POWER COMPANY INC.

2, Ohdori Higashi 1-chome
Chuo-ku, Sapporo
Hokkaido 060-91
Japan
(011) 251 1111
Fax: (011) 221 0192

Public Company
Incorporated: 1951
Employees: 6,364
Sales: ¥450.42 billion (US$3.61 billion)
Stock Exchanges: Tokyo Osaka Sapporo

Hokkaido Electric Power Company Inc. (HEPCO) supplies electricity to the whole of Hokkaido, the second largest and least densely populated of Japan's main islands. Of the nine regional electric power companies in Japan, HEPCO is the smallest in terms of capitalization (¥113 billion) and the second smallest in terms of generating capacity, with 4,876 megawatts (MW). Local environmental, demographic, and economic conditions contribute to factors which set the company apart from the other regional electric power companies (EPCs) in other parts of Japan. With the exception of the island's administrative and economic capital, Sapporo, HEPCO's industrial and residential customers are thinly spread over a large area. Transmission costs are therefore higher than elsewhere in the archipelago and the average unit cost of electricity is the highest in Japan. Many of HEPCO's thermal power stations run on locally produced coal—virtually unique in Japan—and while purchase cost is higher than for imported coal, the local supply is secure and does not suffer from price instability as a result of fluctuating exchange rates. In addition to the core activity of electricity generation and distribution, HEPCO is currently involved in research and development into renewable energy sources like solar power and fuel cells. In the northernmost part of Japan with its notoriously cold winter weather, the company is undertaking research into heat insulation and energy conservation for domestic, industrial, and agricultural application. HEPCO is also diversifying into telecommunications following that sector's progressive liberalization from 1985 onward.

Although HEPCO was incorporated along with the other eight regional Electric Power Companies (EPCs) in May 1951, the history of its foundation goes back to the beginning of the Allied occupation of Japan in 1945. Japan's energy-intensive munitions industry had been eliminated by the start of the occupation, leading immediately to an electricity surplus in the first year of occupation. As the process of reconstruction gathered momentum, demand soon caught up with and exceeded supply. The General Headquarters of the Allied Powers (GHQ) feared that an expansion of electricity production under the surviving and highly centralized wartime structure of the Japan Electricity Generation and Transmission Company (JEGTCO) and the nine distribution companies could be a step in the direction of rearmament. In 1948 it was decided by GHQ to dismantle the JEGTCO structure and replace it with nine regionally-based and vertically-integrated electricity generation and distribution companies. After a number of disagreements between GHQ and the government of Japan about the precise structure, status, and organization of the new companies, the government acted to establish the nine EPCs by implementing the Electricity Utility Industry Reorganization Order and the Public Utilities Order.

Until the end of April 1951 generation and distribution of electricity in Hokkaido had been the responsibility of the centrally controlled Hokkaido branch of the Nippon Hasso Electric Company Ltd. (NHEC) and the locally based and only semi-autonomous Hokkaido Haiden Company Ltd. (HHC). On May 1, 1951, following the promulgation of the Public Utilities Order, the two companies were merged and the independent Hokkaido Electric Power Co. Inc. (HEPCO) was established to manage the generation and supply of electric power in Hokkaido. At that time, capitalization of HEPCO was £330 million and generating capacity 312,000 MW.

The early 1950s saw electricity demand increase rapidly throughout Japan as the process of economic and industrial regeneration got under way. In Hokkaido, as in other parts of Japan, demand for electricity in this period of growth exceeded supply and HEPCO was forced to restrict electric power consumption. Supplies were also affected by industrial action taken by members of the Council of All Japan Electric Workers Union from September to December 1952. The widespread and disruptive blackouts, which were particularly unsettling for industry during these early years, were finally outlawed by the Law for the Regulation of Strike Activity in the Electric Utility and Coal Industries, in 1953. The company actively developed hydroelectric and coal power sources to expand its generating capacity further in the face of the immediate problems. As a result HEPCO was able to remove restrictions on supply in 1953.

As Japan entered the prolonged period of rapid economic growth, industrial output and living standards rose. Demand for electricity from industry and from private consumers expanded by an average of 10% per annum throughout Japan as a whole, and to meet this demand locally HEPCO had to develop further power sources. For hydroelectric power (HEP) resources, HEPCO promoted the Hidaka Development of Power Resources scheme. This led to the construction of the 13,500 kilowatt (kW) Iwachishi Power Station and in 1963 HEPCO completed the 44,000 kW Okunikappu Power Station, the first "Arch-Dam" type—a concrete structure across a valley which is arch-shaped and faces up the valley, when seen in plan—to be built in Hokkaido.

In the field of thermoelectric resources, following the governmental policy of protection and promotion of coal mining industrial areas, HEPCO promoted the construction of coal-powered generating stations, Takigawa Power Station (225,000kW) and Ebetsu Power Station (375,000kW). In 1962 HEPCO thermal electric generation capacity overtook its HEP generating capacity for the first time and in 1964 total electricity generation broke through the one million kW barrier for the first time.

Although the nine EPCs had been established at the same time from the components of the previously centralized JEGTCO, HEPCO had always remained a "semi-detached" part of the Japanese electricity generating industry—even before 1965, there were no transmission links between HEPCO and the rest of Japan, while the other EPCs traded electricity between their areas of supply. This detachment became more apparent when in October 1965 the 300MW Sakuma Frequency Converter Station started operations in central Honshu, Japan's main island, effectively connecting the 50 Herz and 60 Herz systems used in Japan. As a result, the other eight EPCs were connected up into a national grid, while Hokkaido remained on the outside.

The year 1973 was the 100th anniversary of the Hokkaido government. This was heralded by the Winter Olympics held in 1972 in and around Sapporo and by the completion of the Sapporo underground railway system and underground shopping center. HEPCO had been actively involved in supporting these projects as they represented a boost to demand for electric power and provided a useful showcase for HEPCO's involvement in Hokkaido's rapid reconstruction and development. By the end of the year, however, HEPCO's fourth president, Iwamoto Tsunetsugu, found himself in charge of a company that was about to receive the biggest shock of its short history.

The outbreak of war in the Middle East in 1973 and subsequent quadrupling of the crude oil price imposed by the Organization of Petroleum Exporting Countries (OPEC) affected Japan more than most industrially advanced countries because the country received about 70% of its oil from the region. The Japanese EPCs were hit in two ways by the oil crisis and its aftermath. Firstly, the price of oil for oil-powered thermal power stations skyrocketed, adversely affecting the companies' daily financial position. Secondly, in the longer term, higher energy costs stimulated a dramatic restructuring of Japan's economy away from energy-intensive industry. HEPCO's ability to deal with these changes in conditions was greater than the other EPCs because imported oil accounted for only a small fraction of electricity-generating capacity, while HEP and locally-mined coal provided a secure energy source. Nevertheless, such was the impact of the oil price rise on the company's oil-powered thermal power stations that in April 1974 HEPCO sought government approval for a 48% raise in charges. This was in fact the lowest raise of those requested by the nine EPCs.

As a result of the oil shocks, electricity rates throughout Japan were raised on a number of occasions and in 1981 HEPCO raised its rates once again, thereby becoming the most expensive electricity supplier in Japan and reflecting the company's poor financial structure. The company's deteriorating financial position could not be blamed entirely on international pressures. The late 1970s had witnessed further OPEC price rises, the second oil crisis following the Iranian revolution, economic stagnation throughout Japan, and a dramatic depreciation of the value of the yen against the dollar. The

other eight EPCs had weathered the storm after suffering their worst losses in financial year 1979–1980. For the eight, salvation came in the form of an agreement from the Ministry of International Trade and Industry (MITI) to allow the companies to raise their electricity rates by an average of 50% which, combined with windfall profits from currency fluctuations and a fall in demand for expensive oil-generated electricity, led to a spectacular recovery the following year. HEPCO, on the other hand, had been offered a lower rate increase by MITI because at the time it was considered to be less dependent on imported oil. Unfortunately, the price of locally-produced coal was also escalating, but because of a long-term commitment on the part of MITI to promote the development of Japan's domestic coal reserves, HEPCO had not been in a position to develop oil, as the cheap and flexible power source, to anything like the degree of the other EPCs. HEPCO thus suffered the consequences of its own close relationship with the local coal industry until the company was able to develop a more diverse electricity generating capacity.

Regarding development of new power resources, HEPCO started construction of the crude oil-powered thermoelectric Date Power Station (700,000kW) in 1979, and announced the selection of the site for the Tomari Power Station, which was to be Hokkaido's first nuclear plant. In 1980 Date Power Station was completed, as was the construction of Tomatoatsuma Power Station (960,000kW) which was the first facility designed to use imported coal. In the nuclear sector, construction eventually started on the Tomari Power Station (1,158,000kW), progress on which had been suspended for one year in the wake of the Three Mile Island nuclear accident in the United States.

The demand for electricity did not increase in the latter half of this period, though it could be recognized as an era in which the "best mix" of resources was promoted between hydroelectric power, oil, coal, and nuclear-powered electricity generation under the company's fifth president, Yotsuyanagi Takashige. In order to stimulate demand for electricity in the region, HEPCO embarked upon a variety of public relations and electricity promotion schemes, and in January 1988 HEPCO cut its electricity rates. This was beneficial to local consumers but resulted in a steep drop in profits the following year.

In March 1989 HEPCO's first nuclear facility, its 579MW Tomari No.1 generating plant, began full-power testing. In June of the same year it went into commercial operation. Tomari No.2 Nuclear Power Plant was scheduled to start operations in June 1991. Together, the nuclear generating plants became HEPCO's largest generation facilities. HEPCO lagged behind the other EPCs in diversifying generating capacity but generating costs were expected to fall as the current phase of nuclear power development was completed.

HEPCO is instituting a number of measures to lower the cost of producing electricity at coal-fired power stations. Its aim is to reduce reliance on higher priced domestic coal in the years ahead as part of the diversification strategy. At Tomatoatsuma No.2 HECPO is now using low-cost coal imported from Australia and Canada. The interim aim is to reduce the coal content of the total electricity generation equation from 64.1% in 1988 to about 29.3% by 1993.

Faced with structural disadvantages in the provision of electricity in Hokkaido, namely higher generating and transmission costs than in other parts of Japan, HEPCO has been keen to diversify its activities. Following the start of the liberalizing of Japan's telecommunications business in 1985, the company paid great attention to opportunities within the telecommunications market. Telecommunications was identified as a potential market because the company had already obtained a wealth of experience in developing and maintaining an expansive electricity transmission network. It was felt that this experience, combined with the latest technological innovations, would enable the company to run a parallel telecommunications network to challenge the Nippon Telegraph and Telephone Corporation (NTT) monopoly. In October 1987 HEPCO became involved in setting up Hokkaido Telemessage Inc. to market paging systems. In July 1988, together with Daini Denden, it set up Hokkaido Cellular Telephone Co. to market automobile telephones, and in April 1989, in conjunction with Mitsui Co. and Mitsubishi Co., it established Hokkaido Telecommunications Network Co. Inc. This new company uses a portion of the optical fiber cable system installed by HEPCO to provide low-cost data transmission and specialized telephone services.

In recent years the company has successfully introduced a number of new technologies and products developed specifically for the climate of Hokkaido, which is characterized by cold winters and abundant snowfall. These products include a range of electric heaters which incorporate heat storage devices utilizing cheap offpeak electricity. The company has also developed new snow melting equipment.

As part of the company effort to promote the use of electricity, HEPCO constructed an experimental, all-electric cold weather research house in 1988. Similarly, with an eye to the local agricultural producer, HEPCO has been conducting research, in an experimental greenhouse, into the possibility of growing vegetables in cold climates. In line with strict national regulations on emissions of pollutants from power stations, work has been carried out on a new system of dry desulfurization using coal ash. The results of this work are expected to be incorporated in the huge Tomatoatsuma No.1 coal fired generating plant.

In spite of these encouraging developments, HEPCO is still faced with a number of longer-term structural problems which need to be resolved. Dependency on expensive local coal is still high in relation to the other EPCs, and full diversification into oil, nuclear power, and imported coal has yet to be achieved. But as sole supplier of electricity to Hokkaido, HEPCO's operational base is stable.

Further Reading: Thomas, Steve and Chris Cragg, *Japan Power Station Fuel Demand to 2000,* London Financial Times Business Information, 1987; *History of the Electric Power Industry in Japan,* Tokyo, Japan Electric Power Information Center Inc., March 1988.

—Stephen Christopher Kremer

╫ Hokuriku Electric Power Company

HOKURIKU ELECTRIC POWER COMPANY

15-1 Ushijima-cho
Toyama City 930
Japan
(0764) 41 2511
Fax: (0764) 32 4975

Public Company
Incorporated: 1951
Employees: 5,543
Sales: ¥394.3 billion (US$3.16 billion)
Stock Exchanges: Tokyo Osaka

Hokuriku Electric Power Company is one of the nine regional power companies that generate, transmit, and distribute electricity throughout Japan. The Hokuriku district consists of three prefectures in the middle of Japan's main island of Honshu. The three prefectures—Toyama, Ishikawa, and Fukui—border the Sea of Japan on the north and are separated from Japan's industrial centers of Kanto and Kansai by the Japan Alps. The numerous rivers running toward the sea from these mountains have provided Hokuriku with abundant electric power since the early 1900s and today Hokuriku Electric Power relies on its rivers for 40% of its power. With its rich cultural heritage and majestic scenery, the Hokuriku district of Japan is a favorite tourist attraction. Recently it has also become important as a regional center of high-technology industry.

Hokuriku Electric Power was formed as a company on May 1, 1951 when the General Headquarters of the Allied Powers (GHQ) under General Douglas MacArthur approved a plan submitted by the Japanese government to reorganize and rationalize the electrical power industry. Although as a corporate entity Hokuriku Electric Power is relatively young, its roots can be traced back to the end of the 19th century when electricity was first introduced into the region. The history of electric power in Japan as a whole goes back to 1878 when Professor W.E. Aryton of the Institute of Technology in Tokyo unveiled an arc lamp to celebrate the opening of the Central Telegraph Office. Japan's first electric utility company, Tokyo Electric Lighting Company, was established in 1887, four years after Thomas Edison had invented the incandescent lamp in the United States. Its first electric power plant was completed in 1887 as a 25 kilowatt (kW) facility in Nihonbashi, Tokyo. Japan has always been able to effectively assimilate and improve upon outside technology and ideas, and electric power was no exception.

The introduction of electricity to the Hokuriku region was initiated by an industrial exposition in the city of Toyama in 1894. A merchant named Kokichi Mitsuda displayed an electric lamp powered by a portable generator he had brought from Tokyo. A young Toyama businessman named Matazacman Kanaoka was impressed by the lamp and generator, and realized the implications of electricity. Kanaoka also heard about the development in Kyoto in 1891 of Japan's first hydroelectric power plant and saw Hokuriku's abundant rivers as a future energy source. Technical information on the subject was scarce and he had to rely on translations of papers he had obtained from General Electric of the United States. Even scarcer were Japanese engineers in Japan who had worked with electricity, so Kanaoka's workers in the early days proceeded by trial and error. Nevertheless, a site for the first hydroelectric facility 12 kilometers south of Toyama was chosen and in 1897 the Toyama Electric Light Company was formed with an initial capitalization of ¥100,000. Using technology imported from General Electric, a 150kW generating facility capable of providing lighting for 1,500 homes was built.

The people of Toyama loved the new electric lamps and were happy to dispense with their clumsy and dangerous oil lamps. Kanaoka could not keep up with demand with only a single generator, and he had ambitious expansion plans. However, disaster struck in 1899 when a fire destroyed a large portion of Toyama City and with it the electricity distribution network. Kanaoka started again, and by 1903 had brought the company up to its previous level. Electric lighting had been introduced into Fukui prefecture by Kyoto Electric Lighting Company with the construction of the 80kW Shikununo hydroelectric power station in 1899. In 1900 the city of Kanazawa in Ishikawa prefecture set up a publicly owned company, Takaoka Electric Lighting, to provide 250 kW of hydroelectric power for the city.

As a consequence of its victory over Russia in the 1904–1905 Russo-Japanese War, Japan's status in the world improved dramatically and trade with Southeast Asian markets increased. Hokuriku's position on the west coast of Japan, close to Korea and China, made it an important trade route with railway being the most important form of transport. A good proportion of the early railway in the region was electric-powered and, as in Japan as a whole, the growth of electric power was enhanced by the proliferation of rail transport. In 1911 the government established the Electric Utility Industry Law. The law made it necessary to obtain permission for the production and distribution of electric power and was an attempt by the government to control the hundreds of small electric power companies springing up all over Japan. In Toyama, Kanaoka's company was flourishing but was under increasing competition from smaller competitors.

The combined effects of World War I, the Great Kanto Earthquake in 1923, and the collapse of silk prices sent the Japanese economy into depression in the 1920s, and this caused the stagnation of demand for electric power. The power companies competed fiercely for customers and there occurred cases of up to three power companies supplying one user. The smaller utilities began to go out of business and were acquired by a group of large electric utilities known as the "Big Five."

They were dominated by Tokyo Electric Lighting and Daido Power in particular. Japan's economic boom of the 1930s substantially improved the position of the industry. The government was gearing up for war at the time and thought it essential to have control over Japan's power generation industry. It regulated the industry by passing four laws in 1938 that ensured state control over price, plant development, transmission, and all other aspects of the industry. In effect it had formed one of the largest electric companies in the world, with the establishment of JEGTCO (Japan Electric Generation and Transmission Company).

The Allied bombing of Japan between 1943 and 1945 seriously damaged 44% of Japan's thermal power stations and devastated its industry. Although the Hokuriku cities of Toyama and Kanazawa were targeted along with Japan's other major cities, the region was not strategically important and hence was not systematically destroyed as were Tokyo and Osaka. The GHQ, which was effectively in charge of Japan from 1945 to 1952, made sweeping changes in Japan's electric power industry. The Council for Reorganization of Electric Utility Industry was formed in 1949 and chaired by Yasuzaemon Matsunaga, former president of Toho Electric Power Company. After much negotiation a plan was produced that divided the country into nine areas, each with its own privately owned electric power company.

Thus Hokuriku Electric Power was formed in May 1951 and Shosaku Yamada chosen by the council as its first president. His first task was similar to that of the presidents of the other regional electric utilities—the unification of Hokuriku's power generation capacity as a single company. The company's initial capitalization of ¥370 million was dwarfed by the total for the nine companies of ¥100 billion, which made it the smallest. In the past, for very large-scale projects, Hokuriku had entered into joint venture arrangements with other regional utilities, such as nearby Kansai, and these would continue. In the first half of the 1950s, Japan's economy was experiencing rapid growth, and in order to meet increased capital expenditure needs Hokuriku Electric Power issued ¥740 million worth of shares and was listed on the Tokyo Stock Exchange. Along with the other utility companies in Japan, Hokuriku embarked on a promotional campaign to encourage both the general public and industry to use electricity. The opening of a customer service center in Toyama was a step toward this goal. Yamada organized the company by setting up branch offices in the three prefectures which would be responsible for customer support in their respective regions. The head office remained in Toyama, in a separate location from the Toyama prefectural office. At the time in Japan the most common method of distributing electricity in the cities was via a network of cables suspended on concrete poles running along the roadside. Hokuriku Electric Power's demand for these poles made it financially viable for the company to set up a subsidiary to supply them, called Nihankai Concrete Industry. In 1954 two new hydroelectric power stations were completed on the Jinzu River in Toyama to give a combined output of 120,000kW. At this time there was an ongoing operation to close down the company's redundant, small-scale plant and replace it with larger modernized facilities. The company was aided financially by grants from the central government and loans from the World Bank, including a $25 million loan obtained in 1958 after negotiations in Washington.

In the 1950s Japan was desperate to modernize and rebuild its economy, and technology and information were absorbed in large quantities from the West, mainly the United States. With help from the latter, the Japan Atomic Energy Research Institute was established in 1955 and a year later Hokuriku Electric Power set up its own nuclear power committee. Its original function was simply to gather data on the peaceful use of nuclear power with a long term view. Following a visit to several electric power companies in the United States by several senior company executives, a radio communication system was set up to connect all generating and servicing centers and an IBM mainframe computer was installed at the Toyama headquarters. Technology was also imported from Europe, with Siemens of West Germany supplying Hokuriku Electric Power with a hydroelectric station installed on Wada River in Toyama prefecture in 1957.

In 1960 a management shake-up occurred in the company with most of the main board replaced by younger managers, and Mr. Kanai became the second president of the company. The new management sought to accelerate the expansion program and ambitious construction schemes were begun, including work on the company's 33rd power station in Toyama. By this time Hokuriku Electric Power was the leader of the business community in the region.

The 1960s were a dynamic time for Japanese industry and it was a challenge for the electric utilities to keep up with demand. The average annual growth rate during the ten years leading up to the first oil shock in 1973 was 11%. The figure for Hokuriku Electric Power was slightly lower, but still represented a significant increase in generating capacity. The widespread use of air-conditioning during the summer had shifted the time and season of peak use from winter evenings to summer days. The period also marked the increased use of oil as a source of fuel. The halving of the crude oil price between 1961 and 1971 caused its use to more than quadruple between these years in Japan as a whole. While a similar trend was seen in Hokuriku, hydroelectric power remained the single most significant energy source. In 1968 Hokuriku Electric Power's internal nuclear power development program was boosted with the formation of a nuclear power development committee and the participation by several board members in a conference on the peaceful use of nuclear power in the United States. However, the company's nuclear program lagged behind most of the other regional utilities, many of whom had construction under way.

Japan's reliance on Middle Eastern oil fired thermal power stations caused the country to be badly hit by the oil shock of 1973 and profoundly changed the electric power industry. The utility companies had to cope with slumping demand and fuel conservation by the public. Furthermore they found it necessary to develop serious alternatives to oil as a fuel—mainly nuclear, gas, and coal power. A 25% decrease in net income due to drastically increased expenses, especially fuel costs, for Hokuriku Electric Power between 1973 and 1974 made it necessary for the company to seek a series of substantial loans form foreign as well as domestic banks. However, major rate revision allowances in 1974, 1976, and 1980 ensured that the company had sufficient revenues to survive. By increasing its use of coal and hydroelectric power, the company managed to reduce its dependence on oil as a fuel. Hokuriku Electric Power also procured power from Japan Atomic Power Company's

Tsuruga nuclear power station in southern Fukui prefecture. Growth in the Japanese economy slowed in the 1980s and there was an increasing shift away from the traditional heavy chemical industries to the service and high technology sectors which tend to use less power. Hokuriku Electric Power responded to these changes by increasing marketing aimed at public consumers and increasing efficiency through improved technology. Personnel costs were cut significantly by the automation of the distribution of electricity. So-called ELEAM houses, all-electric model homes, were exhibited at the regional sales offices.

In terms of diversification, the main feature of Hokuriku Electric Power's immediate plans is the completion of the 540,000kW Shika Nuclear Power Station in northern Ishikawa. It will be, according to the company, one of the safest and most environmentally friendly stations in the world. On the management side, the company stated its "Fundamental Business Policy" in 1988, targeting the pursuit of cost reduction, community revitalization, increased marketing efforts, and establishment of better relations with customers.

Further Reading: Hokuriku Denki no Sunju-nen, Toyama, Hokuriku Electric Power, 1981; *Story of Tohoku Electric Power,* Sendai, Tohoku Electric Power, 1990; *History of Electric Power In Japan,* Tokyo, Japan Electric Power Information Center, 1990/1991.

—Dylan Tanner

HOUSTON INDUSTRIES INCORPORATED

Five Post Oak Park
4300 Post Oak Parkway
Houston, Texas 77027
U.S.A.
(713) 629-3000
Fax: (713) 629-3129

Public Company
Incorporated: 1906 as Houston Lighting & Power Company 1905
Employees: 13,084
Sales: $4.18 billion
Stock Exchanges: New York Midwest London

Houston Industries Incorporated (HI) is a holding company historically recognized for its electric utility business in Houston and the surrounding Gulf Coast region and is the eighth-largest investor-owned electric utility in the United States based on kilowatt-hour sales. HI's second principal business segment is cable television, with a cable system that has become one of the 20 largest in the United States.

Houston Industries' earliest predecessor, Houston Electric Light & Power Company (HEL&P), was chartered in 1882 by Emanuel Raphael, a cashier at the Houston Savings Bank and one of several prominent Houston businessmen bent on bringing electric lights to their city. Other investors included Houston Mayor William R. Baker, who ushered the new utility through a franchise agreement with the city, which allowed HEL&P to construct and operate a power plant and electric lines.

HEL&P's policy of charging flat rates, coupled with low electrical usage, spelled early financial problems for the company, and by 1886 the firm had entered receivership. The following year a bankrupt HEL&P was sold to a competing Houston utility, Houston Gas Light Company. In 1889 Citizens' Electric Light & Power Company entered the Houston utility arena and two years later bought out Houston Gas Light's interest in HEL&P.

In late 1897 Citizens' Electric defaulted on bank loans, and in January 1898 the utility was placed under control of another receiver, Houston attorney Blake Dupree. William H. Chapman, a Boston businessman, was soon brought in as general manager of the company and became a stabilizing force, initi-ating a power line rebuilding program and advocating use of residential lighting.

Shortly after Chapman arrived in Houston, a boiler exploded at the utility's Gable Street power plant during the evening of March 26, killing four men and leaving the city in total darkness. Early the following morning, a fire started in the damaged plant and destroyed everything of value. Vowing to continue operations, Dupree promptly signed a contract with General Electric Corporation for new power plant equipment, and by 1900 a new Gable Street plant was operational.

Citizens' Electric continued to have financial troubles, and in 1901 its assets were transferred to United Electric Securities Company, the investment arm of General Electric and the Houston utility's major creditor at that time. That same year Citizens' Electric was reorganized as Houston Lighting and Power Company (1901) (HL&P).

Under United Electric Securities, HL&P established a fully metered system for keeping track of electrical use, and abandoned a flat-rate fee system for one that offered rate incentives for increased usage. Following the discovery of oil in the Houston area during the year of its incorporation, HL&P changed its boiler fuel from coal to oil.

The discovery of oil also changed Houston, spawning a period of growth and industrialization along the Gulf Coast. General Electric's infusion of cash and electrical generators helped HL&P keep pace, and by 1902 the company's electrical lines were serving nearly all of Houston.

On January 9, 1906, a day after the company declared its first dividend, HL&P was purchased by Isadore Newman & Sons, a holding company based in New York and New Orleans that operated under the name of American Cities Railway and Light Company. That same year the Houston utility was reorganized as Houston Lighting & Power Company 1905, and became part of an electric utility holding company structure that operated a string of southern U.S. properties.

During the first decade of the 20th century HL&P's sales grew with the area's oil industry. Power lines were extended to oil fields as they sprouted up, as well as the growing number of refiners locating along the Houston Ship Channel. In 1910 the company also began supplying electricity to pipeline firms.

In 1911 American Cities Railway & Light Company, renamed American Cities Company, was sold to Bertron Griscom & Company, a holding company with offices in New York, Philadelphia, and Paris. That same year the Bertron Griscom board of directors promoted general manager William H. Chapman to company president.

In 1913 Houston voters approved city charter amendments that empowered Houston to regulate public utilities and establish its own electric utility in the event it was unhappy with HL&P's service. The amendments set in motion a year-long series of negotiations between HL&P and the city, culminating in a profit-sharing agreement, which guaranteed the company a 12% rate of return and the city any profits above that return.

Shortly after the profit-sharing agreement was reached in 1914, Chapman retired and the Bertron Griscom board named Edwin B. Parker, an attorney with the firm that represented the company in negotiations with the city, to replace Chapman. Unlike Chapman, Parker served mostly as a figurehead president, who left the day-to-day operations in the hands of Sam Bertron, who was named general manager a year after Parker's appointment.

By 1914 HL&P was showing a profit for the first time in its history. That same year HL&P began expanding into suburban Houston, acquiring electrical assets in Houston Heights and establishing a franchise agreement to serve the city of Magnolia Park. During the next four years electrical systems were acquired in Sunset Heights, Brunner, and Park Place, with all of the suburbs eventually becoming part of Houston.

After the United States entered World War I in 1917, HL&P was called on to extend its power lines to Camp Logan, a U.S. Army barracks in Houston. The war helped prolong Houston's industrial boom, but during the conflict, company finances took a turn for the worse, as HL&P struggled to fund additional generating capacity needed to serve the growing area.

Financial problems continued for HL&P after the war, and Bertron Griscom, close to receivership itself by 1921, was in no position to help. In 1922 financial help came, as it did 21 years earlier, from a company affiliated with General Electric. In 1922 the Electric Bond & Share Company through its subsidiary National Power & Light Company, acquired HL&P. Electric Bond & Share had been spun off by General Electric as a holding company for public utilities. With the change in ownership, HL&P once again became part of a healthy holding company structure, with operations in 33 states.

Electric Bond & Share put a quick infusion of capital into HL&P's operations, part of which came from an aggressive program of local stock sales beginning in 1922. Among the modernization and construction projects laid out by Electric Bond & Share was a sorely needed modern power plant. In 1923 construction began on the $5 million Deepwater plant along the Houston Shipping Channel, which would more than double the company's generating capacity with the ability to serve two million residents.

By 1924 Deepwater's first two generating units were operational. While the company continued to improve its service system throughout the 1920s with additional generating units; transmission; and distribution line improvements, after Deepwater went on line HL&P turned its focus toward marketing and expansion efforts.

In 1924 HL&P moved from its three-story headquarters into the ten-story downtown Electric Building, where a seven-story lighted sign was hung. HL&P began using the widely visible first floor of the Electric Building to display the variety of electrical appliances it marketed. HL&P also organized sales crews to canvass residential neighborhoods, and demonstrate and sell appliances. With expansion that followed, within a few years HL&P canceled its exclusive merchandise franchises and began encouraging residents to buy appliances from area dealers.

Deepwater's construction allowed HL&P to seek out new industrial as well as residential customers. Rate reductions were offered to attract new business to the area and to bring on line existing industries that had constructed their own generating facilities during the American Cities Railway era of low-generating capacity.

On the residential side, with its increased capacity HL&P entered nearly 70 Houston-area communities during the 1920s, acquiring existing electrical properties while extending lines into nonserviced areas for the first time. During the second half of the 1920s HL&P also began building a backup power supply, entering into electric system interconnection agreements with neighboring Texas utilities.

Following the death of Edwin Parker in 1930, Sam Bertron Jr. was promoted to president and Hiram O. Clarke was named vice president. Despite the Great Depression that began in 1929, HL&P continued expansion efforts through 1931, when it acquired its largest service system to date by purchasing the assets of the Galveston Electric Company.

While the Great Depression never hit Houston as hard as it struck other areas, in 1931 company revenues began to slide and by 1932 workers were forced to take wage reductions to keep their jobs. Revenues bottomed out in 1933, and three years later a financially stable HL&P began a series of rate reductions that stretched through the end of the 1930s. By 1937 the company had resumed construction programs halted earlier in the decade, including a submarine cable to Galveston Island and the addition of a generating unit at the Gable Street plant, which had not been updated since Bertron Griscom controlled the utility.

HL&P entered the 1940s with a 5,000-square-mile service area, which included 150,000 customers in 140 communities. In 1942 HL&P also entered a new era, becoming an independent company after National Power & Light Company was forced to sell its interests in the Houston utility in order to comply with the provisions of the 1935 Public Utility Holding Company Act.

After the United States entered World War II, HL&P was called on to construct additional power plants to meet wartime construction needs. In 1943 the first unit of HL&P's third power plant, West Junction, went on line. With concern for power failures, the company also accelerated its interconnection activities during the war and became part of a power-pool arrangement that tied investor-owned utilities in Texas to dams along the state's major rivers.

Following the war, the demands of a petroleum-related industrial boom in the Houston area replaced the war as a motivating factor, and spurred HL&P to increase its generating capacity. Between 1946 and the end of the decade the company placed additional generating units at West Junction, and built a fourth plant, Greens Bayou.

During the first half of the 1950s power plant construction continued at a rapid clip. The company built a fifth power facility, the Webster plant, and added generating units at West Junction and Greens Bayou. In 1950 Hiram Clarke died, and the West Junction plant that Clarke had designed was renamed in his honor. In late 1953 Bertron died, and the following year Walter Alvis Parish, a former company attorney, was tapped to succeed Bertron.

Between 1956 and the end of the decade the company continued to increase its generating capacity, constructing the Sam Bertron plant, the Smithers Lake plant—later renamed the W.A. Parish plant—and the North Houston plant. In 1957 the Houston City Council granted the company a new 50-year franchise, and HL&P promptly turned to the other 37 incorporated communities it served for similar 50-year franchise agreements.

W.A. Parish was named the company's first chairman in 1958, and Tom H. Wharton, a former executive vice president, was promoted to president. The following year Parish died, and Wharton assumed the additional post of chairman.

After decades of rate reductions, in 1960 HL&P requested the first rate increase in its history in order to offset the financial effects of its building program and a recession in the Texas economy. The company was granted a $4.1 million increase, half of its $8.2 million request. A year later HL&P faced another setback when Hurricane Carla ripped through its service area, causing $1.6 million worth of electrical system damages.

Despite a slow start, HL&P continued to witness explosive growth in its service area during the 1960s. In response to that growth, three generating units were added to existing plants during the first half of the decade. During the same period HL&P continued building its "power highway," a network of interconnected transmission systems with other electric utilities that would stretch from the Gulf of Mexico to the Red River.

In 1963 P. H. Robinson, an executive vice president, was promoted to president while Wharton continued to serve as chairman for the next two years. In 1964 Robinson announced the start of a five-year, $939 million growth and expansion plan dubbed Project Enterprise, aimed at doubling the company's generating capacity with the addition of four new generating units, including construction of what would become the P. H. Robinson plant. Project Enterprise's construction projects also included a fully-computerized energy control center, seven new service centers, and a new 27-story corporate headquarters, named the Electric Tower.

In 1970 Robinson was named to fill the five-year vacancy in the chairman's seat, and Carl Sherman, a former executive vice president, was promoted to president. By 1971 the company began serious study of nuclear power plants, but those plans as well as other proposals for increased generating capacity during the decade became subject to increasing federal regulations.

HL&P first felt the effects of the changing regulatory environment in 1971, when the U.S. Environmental Protection Agency challenged the location of the company's gas-fired Cedar Bayou generating station, less than a month after the plant had been dedicated. The EPA alleged that Cedar Bayou's discharge of water into Trinity Bay would damage marine life, while HL&P maintained it would improve it. After a two-year legal battle the EPA agreed to end its opposition. In return, the company agreed to reduce its planned number of generating units from six to three, and expand its water-quality monitoring programs.

In 1972 HL&P announced plans for two Austin County, Texas, nuclear power plants, one to be located on Allens Creek and a second plant on the lower Mill Creek. In 1973 Mill Creek plans were scuttled in response to public opposition, and nine years later a series of regulatory hearing delays and escalating construction costs led HL&P to kill the Allens Creek project.

In 1973 HL&P formed a joint venture with the cities of San Antonio and Austin and neighboring Central Power and Light Company to construct a nuclear power plant southwest of Houston along the Gulf Coast. HL&P became managing partner of the venture, owning a 30.8% interest in what became known as the South Texas Project (STP). While HL&P was making plans for nuclear plants, during the first half of the 1970s HL&P finished construction of seven gas-fired units at existing plants.

Following the Organization of Petroleum Exporting Countries (OPEC) oil embargo of 1973 HL&P began promoting conservation of electricity. The increasing complexities surrounding fuel supplies also led HL&P to form two wholly owned subsidiaries, Primary Fuels, Inc. (PFI) and Utility Fuels, Inc. (UFI). PFI was created in 1973 to explore for and develop oil and gas reserves along the Texas Gulf Coast. In 1974 UFI was formed to acquire and deliver power plant fuels, with activities initially limited to HL&P fuels and later expanded to serve other companies.

In 1974 Robinson retired as chairman and was replaced by Sherman. Before the year was over Sherman died and in the ensuing corporate reshuffle two former executive vice presidents took over, with J.G. Reese elected chairman and Don Jordan, at the age of 42, elected the youngest president in the company's history.

Following a corporate restructuring process in 1976, the holding company Houston Industries Incorporated (HI) was formed to give HL&P and its affiliates greater financial and organizational flexibility. In 1977 HI became the owner of all HL&P, UFI, and PFI assets. Reese was named chairman of the new holding company and Jordan president. After exactly 50 years of service to HL&P and affiliates, in April 1978 Reese retired, leaving his two chairmen seats vacant.

With increased federal government pressure to abandon oil and natural gas as boiler fuels, during the late 1970s HL&P began converting its generators to coal. UFI played a major role in the gradual transition to coal, negotiating long-term coal-supply contracts and purchasing more than 1,000 railroad cars for coal transportation, which during the following decade led to expansion of UFI's business activities outside of HL&P operations. In 1979 HL&P announced it would construct a power plant in Limestone County, Texas, that would burn lignite, a soft form of coal. Six years later, after escalating costs delayed construction, the Limestone plant began operations.

The South Texas Project also experienced considerable construction delays, and by 1979, three years after building had started, serious questions were being raised about quality control at the construction site. During 1979 and 1980 the company issued several stop-work orders at STP in response to governmental concerns.

With STP just one-third finished, in late 1981 HL&P dismissed Brown & Root, Inc. as construction manager and architect, but asked the firm to retain its assignment to do the actual construction. Brown & Root, however, resigned that post. In moves unprecedented in the construction of nuclear power plants, HL&P changed both its architect and builder, naming Bechtel Corporation as architect-engineer and Ebasco Constructors Inc. as builder. In 1982 HL&P filed suit against Brown & Root charging the firm with breach of contract, and three years later HL&P received a $750 million settlement from its former contractor. Facing the inflationary conditions of 1982, a backlogged construction schedule and heightened public dissent over company rate increases and HL&P's handling of STP, Don Jordan was named chairman and chief executive officer of HL&P, and Don Sykora, a former executive vice president, was elevated to president and chief operating officer of the utility.

To ease the strain on its generating capacity caused by construction delays, in 1983 HL&P tapped three of its industrial customers and began purchasing power produced through cogeneration, the simultaneous production of electricity and thermal energy from the same fuel source. In a move to improve public relations that same year, Jordan created a community services division to provide bill-paying assistance to low-income, elderly, and handicapped customers. In 1983 Hurricane Alicia ripped through Houston, leaving a path of devastation that knocked out 8,000 miles of power lines and left an unprecedented 750,000 customers without electricity, with some customers waiting more than two weeks for power to be restored.

In 1985 HI began a three-year series of diversification moves and formed the subsidiary Innovative Controls, Inc., to develop and market lightweight security lights. In 1986 HI and Time Inc.'s cable television unit formed Paragon Communications, a 50-50 joint venture to purchase 22 cable television systems serving 550,000 customers, primarily in Texas, Florida, and the Northeast. That same year HI formed the subsidiary KBLCOM Incorporated to manage its cable operations.

In 1987 HL&P formed two other subsidiaries. Development Ventures, Inc., a venture capital organization, was formed to provide start-up financing for small businesses; while Houston Industries Finance, Inc., an unconsolidated subsidiary, was created to purchase accounts receivables of HL&P and other HI subsidiaries to reduce the utility's capital requirements.

In 1988 the South Texas Project was cleared by government bodies of all safety concerns and granted a full operating license, more than 15 years after plans for the plant had begun and after construction costs had risen by nearly 500% to $5.5 billion. HL&P also won the first round in a lawsuit brought by the city of Austin, which alleged HL&P had mismanaged the project, leading to the cost overrun. HL&P argued that regulatory changes, not poor management, were responsible, and a state district court agreed. The city of Austin appealed the ruling; its appeal was pending in the early 1990s. The project's co-owners, the city of San Antonio and Central Power & Light, also alleged HL&P had breached its duties as project manager; these claims were also in arbitration in the early 1990s.

In 1989 HI made the strategic decision to limit its diversified operations, and concentrate immediate expansion efforts on cable television. That same year it sold PFI and acquired the U.S. cable television system of Rogers Communications, Inc. KBLCOM spent more than $1.3 billion on the Rogers Communications purchase, which included more than 550,000 customers in the metropolitan areas of San Antonio and Laredo, Texas; Minneapolis, Minnesota; Portland, Oregon; and Orange County, California.

In 1990 KBLCOM formed KBL-TV to sell advertising on cable channels. The same year HI sold the assets of Innovative Controls, and Development Ventures stopped funding new businesses.

Houston Industries entered the 1990s projecting improved earnings, with its cable subsidiary expected to shave losses and begin to show a profit, and its principal subsidiary, HL&P, expecting to manage the growth of Houston's electrical needs in a less-transitory regulatory environment. HI's plans for the near future did not include major acquisitions, although KBLCOM continued to be interested in expansion of its cable system and services.

Principal Subsidiaries: Houston Lighting & Power Company; KBLCOM Incorporated; Utility Fuels, Inc.; Houston Industries Finance, Inc.; Development Ventures, Inc.

Further Reading: Beck, Bill, *At Your Service: An Illustrated History of Houston Lighting & Power Company*, Houston, Texas, Houston Lighting & Power Company, 1990.

—Roger W. Rouland

THE KANSAI ELECTRIC POWER CO., INC.

3-22 Nakanoshima 3-chome
Kita-ku
Osaka 530
Japan
(06) 441-8821
Fax: (06) 441-8598

Public Company
Incorporated: 1951
Employees: 24,825
Sales: ¥2.25 trillion (US$18.03 billion)
Stock Exchanges: Tokyo Osaka Nagoya

The Kansai Electric Power Co., Inc. (Kansai Electric) is the second largest Japanese electricity utility and accounts for 19% of utility electricity sales in Japan. The company is one of the nine Japanese electric power companies established on May 1, 1951, as a result of a nationwide reorganization of the electric utility industry under the Law for the Elimination of Excessive Concentration of Economic Power, which was directed at breaking up monopolistic enterprises.

Kansai Electric services the central part of the main island of the Japanese archipelago, covering an area of 28,643 square kilometers—about 8% of the nation's total land area. This area includes the three major cities of Osaka, Kyoto, and Kobe as well as the industrial region along the coast of Osaka. Thus the region served by Kansai Electric is highly urbanized and industrialized and constitutes an economic area of prime importance for Japan, ranking second to the Tokyo metropolitan area. The electricity consumption in the area therefore amounts to 19% of the nation's total, while the service area accounts for only 8% of Japan's total land area.

Although immediately after World War II there was a sharp decrease in demand for electricity, since the bulk of electricity prior to this had been allocated to munitions production, the speed of reconstruction gathered pace so quickly that by the time of its inauguration the most pressing need for Kansai Electric was to build up its generating capacity to meet a critical power shortage. Despite booming demand, however, national pricing policies kept electricity rates so low that even costs could not be covered. Over the next three years, therefore, three rates reviews were allowed. In 1951 the average rates of the electric power companies (EPCs) rose by 30%; in 1952 they rose by 28%; and in 1954 they rose by 11%. In July 1952 the Electric Power Development Promotion Law was enacted, to further the construction of generating plants and transmission and transformation facilities. The law created the Electric Power Development Coordination Council under the Prime Minister's Office, which enabled the Electric Power Development Co. Ltd. (EPDC)—a government-owned corporation which could use government funds to promote power generation and transmission development—to begin operations in September 1952 using authorized capital totaling ¥100 billion.

With its share of this money, and with its financial situation improved by the three rates reviews, Kansai Electric was able to commence construction of the 125MW Maruyama hydroelectric power plant, which was then the largest in Japan and which pioneered large-scale hydroelectric power development. In 1954, with the completion of the Maruyama hydroelectric power plant, the power supply situation began to stabilize, and the shortage was gradually met.

In 1956 the company began the Kurobegawa No. 4 hydroelectric power project, an unprecedentedly arduous and large-scale civil engineering undertaking. Kurobegawa No. 4 was finally completed in 1963. However, from the mid-1950s, hydroelectric power had begun to take a back seat to thermal power in Japan. This was due to several factors: firstly, most of the good sites for hydroelectric power generation had already been developed; secondly, rapid progress in thermal power technology had improved efficiency and made large-scale plants possible; thirdly, thermal construction costs per kilowatt (KW) had fallen; and fourthly, fossil fuel costs were lower. Following this trend, in the mid-1950s Kansai Electric began replacing its worn-out fossil-fired generating capacity by constructing new high-performance plants using the latest technology from the United States. The first such plant was Tanagawa, with two units of 75MW. With the completion of Osaka Unit No. 1, by 1959 the system's total fossil-fired generating capacity had exceeded its total hydro-generating capacity.

Although all through the period of high economic growth in Japan—1961–1973—oil remained the principal source of electrical energy, accounting for 43% of fuels used for generation by the EPCs in 1963 and 87% in 1973, it was in 1954 that the first inroads into research and development on nuclear power were made. Albeit not without hindrances, this was a trend which was to develop substantially over the next four decades.

The 1950s had seen a general settling into the new system for the EPCs in Japan. This had been encouraged in part by the establishment of various regulatory bodies. The Public Utility Bureau, established in 1952, took the place of the abolished Public Utilities Commission as part of the Ministry of International Trade and Industry (MITI). The Federation of Electric Power Workers Unions was formed in May 1954 in response to labor disputes that had led to blackouts and serious disruptions of industry in the early 1950s. It was also part of an attempt to reconcile labor with the Law for the Regulation of Strike Activities in Electric Utility and Coal Industries, enacted in August 1953, which prohibited strikes that interrupted service. The Research Committee on Electricity Rate System was created in December 1957 in order to examine the existing rates and adjust them, through MITI, to a level more in line with actual conditions. The Japan Electric Power Information Center, Inc. was created in May 1958 to encourage the free flow of information within the industry on an international basis.

The 1960s saw the development of the electric power industry in Japan on an impressive scale. With many of its initial problems ironed out in the 1950s, flourishing industry and rising living standards led to an ever-booming market for the EPCs during the 1960s and a chance to build on the foundations they had already laid.

During the years 1961–1973, Japan's EPCs experienced an average annual increase in demand of 10.7%. This was due not only to Japan's booming economy but also to technological advances made by the industry during the period. Fossil fuel was the chief generator of energy in this period, and technological advancement in this area was impressive. Innovation in this area was also encouraged by the low price of oil. Crude oil, which cost $2.30 per barrel in 1960, went down to as little as $1.80 in 1971. Conversely, with improved technology, steam pressure increased from $60kg/cm^2$ to $246kg/cm^2$. Steam temperature went from 450°C to 566°C, and unit generating capacity from 53MW to 600MW. Heat efficiency also went up from 32% to 38%. As experience was gained in constructing these new superplants, costs were cut and capacity per unit was increased. Also, the introduction of computers made possible the rationalization of personnel.

Fuel was also switched, initially from coal to heavy oil, and then from heavy to crude oil, which was more cost-efficient as well as more environmentally friendly. Also with a view to pollution problems, LNG-fired plants began to be introduced in an effort to reduce sulfur emissions as well as to remove dependence on oil, all of which had to be imported. Tokyo Electric took the lead in this area from 1963–1973, and from 1964–1971 Kansai Electric commissioned two LNG/oil-fired plants, one at Himeji 2 and one at Sakaiko.

In December 1966 the company started to construct its first nuclear power plant, Mihama Unit No. 1—rated at 340MW—which employed a pressurized water reactor imported from the United States. In August 1970 the first nuclear-generated power from the unit was sent to the site of the EXPO '70 exhibition of industry, technology, and commerce held in Osaka. The unit itself was completed in November 1970.

Technological advances in transmission and distribution were also made during this period. Building on foundations laid in the mid-1950s, in 1960 Kansai Electric and Chubu Electric linked up utilities with Tokyo and Tohoku Electric Power companies. In 1962 Kansai Electric commissioned an Economic Load Dispatching System. This led to the starting of an automatic load dispatching operation in 1968, which made possible centralized control of unmanned hydroelectric power plants and substations. In 1964 Kansai Electric launched a campaign to provide a more reliable service to customers. In 1967 a Technical Research Center was established to strengthen the organization's research and development.

Thicker cables, adoption of multiconductors, allowing pylons to carry more than one transmission line, and improved pylons helped with the linking of systems. In addition, after Tokyo Electric boosted its Boso line in Chiba prefecture to 500kV, Kansai Electric completed its first 500kV trunkline, the Wakasa Line, in 1969. In 1970 the company's first large-scale pumped storage hydro plant, Kisenyama (466MW), was completed.

However, industrial development was to take its toll on the Japanese environment. The problem was particularly severe in comparison to other countries, and the electric power industry was involved. As the use of oil increased in the effort to meet demand for electricity, sulfur oxide emissions rose, causing bronchial problems and noise pollution. In the face of mounting public anger in the second half of the 1960s, the EPCs, along with other industrial sectors, began to take steps toward pollution control. These included the desulfurization of crude oil, a shift to the use of crude oil and LNG, using higher chimneys, and efforts to reduce particle emissions.

After years of hedging the issue owing to its links with the industrial sector, the government was eventually moved to tackle the problem and a number of pollution control laws were finally forced through the Diet. These included in 1967 the Basic Law for Environmental Pollution Control, and in 1968 the Air Pollution Control Law and Noise Control Law. In 1970 the Diet made these laws more stringent and added the Water Pollution Control Law so that now the electric power stations acted under a strict set of pollution regulations. The result of this was that by the mid-1970s Japan had begun to lead the world in terms of pollution control.

Also during this period, in 1966, owing to the rapid increase of the use of air-conditioning units, system peak demand changed from winter to summer.

In the 1970s, after enjoying a boom for many years, the electric power industry in Japan was plunged into an acute slump. The major reason for this was the fourth Middle East conflict, which broke out in autumn 1973, upsetting the world oil market. Two sharp increases in the price of oil ensued, in 1973–1974, and in 1978–1979, which profoundly changed the shape of the Japanese economy. Since oil was the prime source of fuel for electricity generation up until the first oil shock, accounting for 87% of fuels used, the electric power industry was hit particularly hard by the steep price increases. Kansai Electric was forced to revise its electricity rates in 1974 for the first time in 19 years, so that between 1970 and 1980 the price per unit of electric power for Kansai rose from ¥4.74 to ¥19.58 per kilowatt-hour.

The oil crises led to two main changes in the Japanese economy which affected the electricity industry directly. Firstly, demand for electricity within the industrial sector nosedived as higher energy costs forced smokestack industries out of business and encouraged a shift to high technology and service sectors. Energy conservation measures also contributed to declining demand.

Secondly, owing to increases in the price of oil, the EPCs were forced to seek alternative fuels for generation. Between 1973 and 1975, the percentage of oil-fired thermal generation was virtually halved in terms of total generation. The shortfall was made up largely by nuclear generation and liquefied natural gas (LNG).

In 1974, 1976, and 1980, the EPCs sought major rate increases to counteract the soaring price of oil. After the third increase in 1980, the cost of electricity was 3.5 times higher than it had been before the first oil shock. The average rise on each occasion was 56.8% in 1974, 23.1% in 1976, and 52% in 1980.

By 1977, because of these hikes, and also because of the rising value of the yen, the EPCs' profits began to improve again. In 1977 Kansai Electric's sales were 23.2% higher than in the previous year, and post-tax profits were 21.3% higher. Originally the EPCs had marked out new rate increase margins far in excess of those actually enforced, in anticipation of a 5% increase in the price of crude oil and fuel oil in 1976.

Judging that no oil markup would take place, however, MITI cut down the original proposals. In approving the increases, MITI also set the value of the yen against the dollar at $1.00: ¥299, which was important to the EPCs as they procured all of their oil supplies from abroad. The yen subsequently continued to rise, reaching ¥272 against the dollar in the second half of 1977. In six months, the foreign exchange gains of Kansai Electric rose by ¥10 billion. Operation costs during the same period increased by ¥5 billion.

Thus, despite further oil price hikes by OPEC in 1979, leading to the 1980 rate hike, the EPCs did not fare as badly as they might have done, or indeed as they seem to have expected, partly due to the rising value of the yen. With decreases in the price of oil beginning in late 1985, the companies temporarily and tentatively cut their rates, in 1986 for seven months and in 1987 for one year. In 1988 MITI approved a further cut, bringing the average reduction in rates for the industrial and residential sectors of the EPCs to about 17%.

Because of its heavy dependence on imported oil, and because of the two oil shocks, Japan developed nuclear and other alternative energy sources. Nuclear power has assumed an important position in Japan's energy policy.

Kansai Electric started its research and study of nuclear power in the 1950s and completed its first nuclear reactor in 1970. The company owns and operates nine reactors, with nuclear plant making up just over a quarter of its capacity and about 45% of its power needs. The development of nuclear power, however, has not been without obstacles.

A total of 36 legislations and 66 different legal procedures are required before construction of a nuclear-power plant can proceed. The process may take 7 to 15 years from the announcement of construction to the start of operation. Approval for construction is granted by the Electric Power Development Adjustment Council, which is chaired by the prime minister. After approval, the plan is then subjected to strict safety examinations by the Nuclear Safety Commission. After the government procedure, two public hearings must be held to reflect the interests of local residents. These hearings are sponsored by MITI. The system was established in 1978.

Another problem with nuclear power generation has been the non-nuclear proliferation policy followed by the United States. Following this policy, nations buying nuclear fuel from the United States need to get case-by-case U.S. permission to reprocess spent uranium. In 1988 the U.S. Congress refused to ratify a Japan–U.S. nuclear cooperation agreement signed by Tokyo and Washington in November 1987, which would have allowed Japan to reprocess spent fuel for a 30-year period.

Especially in the early 1980s, in the light of President Ronald Reagan's massive arms build-up, demonstrations against the use of nuclear power have been widespread in Japan. In 1980, the venue for the public hearings regarding Kansai Electric's plans to build the No. 3 and No. 4 reactors at Takahama was surrounded by demonstrators.

Public outcry was exacerbated and construction of nuclear reactors further set back by a number of accidents around the world in the late 1970s, the 1980s, and the early 1990s. Repercussions of the Three Mile Island accident in the United States in March 1979 were keenly felt in Japan, resulting in the suspension for one year of all plans to build nuclear power plant. This delayed the construction of Kansai's 3 and 4 reac-

tors at Takahama for a year, and partly accounted for the public demonstrations when the hearings eventually began. Public confidence in nuclear power was not improved by the leaking of nuclear waste at Tsuruga nuclear plant, which was intentionally left unannounced by the Japan Atomic Power Co. The Chernobyl accident in the Soviet Union again shook public confidence. However, it must be noted that Japan has developed technology to prevent accidents due to tubing stress corrosion and steam generator tubing pit holing. Although accident prevention is extremely expensive, the EPCs have had no alternative but to follow a safety-first nuclear program because of public concern.

Accidents do still happen in Japan, however, and in February 1991 Unit No. 2 at Kansai Electric's Mihama plant had to be closed down after a problem with a steam generator. Although there was no radioactive leakage, this incident indicates that despite a waning of public opposition to nuclear fuel in the light of global warming, and despite the safety measures followed by the EPCs, nuclear power generation is still unlikely to be free of problems for the foreseeable future.

Partly as a response to environmental pollution, several non-nuclear alternatives to oil have been developed by the EPCs since 1970, when Tokyo Electric opened the world's first LNG-fired plant at Minami-Yokohama. A little less than one-fifth of Kansai Electric's capacity is LNG-fired, or LPG (Liquid Petroleum Gas)-fired, accounting for about 25% of thermal power generation.

In 1984, partly due to an industrial move into a high-technology environment and partly in order to exploit their utilities more fully, the EPCs began diversifying into the telecommunications business. While this is to remain a peripheral aspect of the industry, the EPCs have become major rivals of NTT (Nippon Telegraph and Telephone Ltd.). Kansai Electric plans to continue its exploitation of the telecommunications industry, as well as launching into cogeneration and other local heat supply business.

Continuing its diversification, as well as contributing to various regional projects such as the construction of the 24-hour Kansai International Airport in Osaka Bay and the Kansai Science and Research Park, Kansai Electric is producing new businesses that are being incorporated as the company's subsidiaries and affiliates. As of March 1991, the company had a direct equity participation of 20% or more in 40 corporations.

In 1984 Kansai Electric was awarded the prestigious Demming Prize by the Association of Quality Control in the United States and Japan for the performance of its Total (company-wide) Quality Control program. Kansai Electric was the first EPC ever to be awarded the prize and the company intends to develop its quality improvement activities further.

Since the first oil crisis the EPCs have been developing power-saving electrical devices. Paradoxically, this development has led to a boost in demand for power. Kansai Electric expects a continued rise in demand for electricity, and so continues to construct generating plants.

Kansai Electric continues to take an interest in environmental issues, and in April 1991 organized a Global Environment Project Development Conference, chaired by the president of the company. The conference adopted a four-point plan to continue tackling the environmental issue, and also has recently made some headway in the field of reducing emissions from thermal-fired plants.

The present breakdown of the company's energy sources is as follows: nuclear—7,408MW (24%); oil-fired—11,519MW (37%); LNG-fired—6,062MW (19%); combustion turbines—360MW (1%); conventional hydro—3,109MW (10%); and pumped storage hydro—2,920MW (9%). Its long-range plan, *Kansai Electric Power in the Year 2030,* released in 1988, envisages a generating capacity mix of 40% nuclear, 33% oil and LNG, 18% hydro, and 9% coal.

—Julian Kinsley

KYUSHU ELECTRIC POWER COMPANY INC.

1-82 Watenabe-dori 2-chome
Chuo-ku, Fukuoka 810
Japan
(092) 761 3031
Fax: (092) 713 8449

Public Company
Incorporated: 1951
Employees: 14,503
Sales: ¥1.06 trillion (US$8.49 billion)
Stock Exchanges: Tokyo Osaka Fukuoka

The Kyushu Electric Power Company (KEPCO) supplies electricity and other services to the most southerly of Japan's four main islands, Kyushu, and to a large number of much smaller islands within the jurisdiction of Kyushu's prefectural governments. Its electricity-generating capacity is well diversified between hydroelectric power (HEP), nuclear power, coal, oil, and gas. In addition KEPCO runs the largest geothermal electricity-generating program in Japan. Of the company's thermal electricity-generating capacity, about 60% is conventionally generated, with oil-powered plants accounting for the majority of production, and liquid natural gas (LNG) and coal accounting for the rest. Both coal and LNG are becoming more important as KEPCO seeks to diversify its generating base further. The company now receives LNG on long-term contract from Indonesia and Australia, and coal from the People's Republic of China and Australia. In terms of nuclear generating capacity, KEPCO is the third largest producer out of Japan's ten electric power companies (EPCs) and has consistently performed better than the sector average in terms of both reliability and in terms of nuclear energy's share of total electricity output. Forty-one percent of the electricity in Kyushu is nuclear generated, against the Japanese average of twenty-one percent. In addition to the company's mainstream activities, it is conducting research and development into a number of electricity-related fields aimed at raising demand for electricity by making it a cheaper and more flexible alternative to other power sources. These activities include research into domestic cookers, and heat pumps for the agricultural sector. The company is also developing generating systems that combine solar panels and diesel generators for use on Kyushu's remote islands. In 1987, in an effort to diversify business operations and to make the best use of available

technology and equipment within the company, KEPCO established a car telephone business and expanded its optical fiber communications network for possible commercial use.

KEPCO was incorporated along with the other eight regional EPCs in May 1951, but the story of its foundation goes back to the start of the Allied occupation of Japan in 1945. Japan's energy-intensive military-industrial complex, centered around the production of steel, ships, and munitions, had been largely eradicated by the start of the occupation. Although the nuclear bomb aimed at one of Kyushu's major shipyards, Nagasaki, had failed to destroy the industrial target, enormous damage had been caused by conventional bombing of other industrial sites in northern Kyushu. Because part of Kyushu's electricity-generating facilities had survived the war relatively unscathed, the first year of occupation saw an energy surplus in the region. This pattern was mirrored throughout the country. As the process of reconstruction gathered pace, demand for electricity increased dramatically and soon exceeded supply. The General Headquarters of the Allied Powers (GHQ) feared that an expansion of electricity production under the surviving and highly centralized wartime structure of the Japan Electricity Generation and Transmission Company (JEGTCO) and the local distribution companies could be a step in the direction of rearmament because the structure itself had been an integral factor in Japan's military expansion in the first place. In 1948 CHQ decided to dismantle the centralized JEGTCO structure and replace it with regionally-based, vertically-integrated electricity generation and distribution companies. After a certain amount of disagreement between GHQ and the fledgling Japanese government regarding the precise structure, status, and organization of the new companies, the government acted to establish the EPCs by implementing the Electricity Utility Industry Reorganization Order and the Public Utilities Order.

On May 1, 1951, operating rights and facilities of the state-run Kyushu branch of the Japan Electricity Generation and Transmission Company and the Kyushu Electric Power Distribution Company were taken over by the newly-created Kyushu Electric Power Company. KEPCO's first president was Tokujiro Sato, and under government decree the new company was given the task of generating and supplying electric power to the entire Kyushu district including outlying islands. The company's start-up capital was ¥760 million.

While the demand for electricity had already caught up with supply in the late 1940s thanks to rapid reconstruction, the manufacturing economy of Kyushu was given a second boost by demand for components and material support for the war raging on the Korean peninsula. The resulting surge in demand for electricity from local industry stimulated KEPCO to seek the immediate stabilization and expansion of its generating capabilities and the company turned to the United States for assistance. The latest technology was imported for Kyushu's first Arch-Type dam—an arch-shaped concrete structure across a valley, which faces up the valley when seen in plan—at the Kamishiba HEP station. In addition, the company imported a model plant—bought off-the-shelf, and of a tried and tested design—from the United States, which was built at Karita, and work was undertaken to expand and strengthen the high-voltage distribution trunk lines and other installations in the central and northern parts of Kyushu.

In April 1957 a new 220,000-volt trunk line was inaugurated in order to enhance distribution of electricity to the industrial centers of Kyushu where demand was already starting to outstrip KEPCO's ability to distribute electricity, and to allow further expansion of electricity consumption in the future. By the end of the 1950s, as a result of the incorporation of new technology and plant, KEPCO had managed to double its generating capacity while increasing its thermal efficiency—a measure of the conversion rate from thermal energy to electrical energy in a generating system—from 20% to over 30%.

By the early 1960s demand for electricity in Kyushu was increasing by over 10% per year, fueled by industrial demand from heavy industry in the north of the island, from the rapidly-expanding small business sector, and from private consumers. The latter were using more electricity for lighting and heating, and in the summer months for air conditioning. By the mid-1960s the annual peak demand for electricity in Kyushu, with its warm climate, had switched from winter to summer as a direct result of the growing use of air conditioning.

In the past KEPCO and its predecessor had relied on local coal production to generate electricity, but by the late 1950s oil had started to appear a far cheaper and more flexible alternative. In 1955 Kyushu had produced 23 million tons of coal or 43% of Japan's coal output, much of it for the energy industry. But as the switch to oil-fired power stations proceeded, local coal production was progressively cut back. By 1988 Kyushu produced slightly more than 4 million tons of coal.

In the meantime, new generating facilities were tending to use imported oil and coal. While hydroelectric power (HEP) had accounted for a large proportion of generating capacity in the first half of the century in Kyushu, its relative importance had started to decline by the early 1960s. This was due not only to the availability of cheaper alternative sources of energy, but because technological advancements had brought the cost of building thermal power stations substantially below that of HEP equivalents.

In August 1968 KEPCO achieved 3,000 megawatts of electricity production for the first time and, with demand still rising year by year, further oil- and coal-powered facilities were inaugurated. In July 1969 a large crude-oil-powered thermal power station opened at Oita. In the same year KEPCO strengthened its international standing by establishing a technical exchange agreement with the Korea Electric Power Co.

In early 1973, with Kiyoshi Kawarabayashi in the position of president, KEPCO was looking towards further steady—and by international standards, spectacular—growth in the foreseeable future. The outbreak of war in the Middle East in mid-1973 and the subsequent quadrupling of oil prices imposed by the Organization of Petroleum Exporting Countries (OPEC) hit Japan harder than any other Organization for Economic Cooperation and Development (OECD) country because of the country's heavy dependence on Middle Eastern oil. The immediate effect on KEPCO was to raise the price of fuel for its oil-powered thermal generating plants. This resulted in financial difficulties in the short term because the company, like the rest of Japan's EPCs, was not free to pass the higher fuel rates on to its industrial and domestic consumers without approval from the Ministry of International Trade and Industry (MITI). In December 1973 the Japanese government introduced measures to enforce conservation of electric power, but it was not until later the following year that MITI finally consented to allowing a 48% electricity rate rise for KEPCO and the other EPCs. Although it alleviated short-term financial pressures on

the generation industry as a whole, the first sharp rise in the price of electricity in 20 years failed to benefit the power companies in the medium term because the price of oil continued to rise. Furthermore, as higher charges were passed on to the large energy-intensive manufacturing sector in Kyushu, a chain of events was set under way leading to a wholesale restructuring of the Kyushu economy away from energy-intensive industrial production. This in turn stimulated KEPCO to reappraise its customer base and eventually concentrate on the non-manufacturing sector—consumption by offices and the retail and service sectors—to make up the shortfall in demand from heavy industry.

The oil price hikes which continued throughout the 1970s stimulated a major reappraisal of resource security at the national level. While individual power companies and oil companies were able to meet their requirements for oil by paying inflated prices in spot markets around the world, it soon became apparent that Japan needed to diversify its supply of energy away from the Middle East and away from oil. Although a number of projects had been in the planning phase for some time, the events of 1973–1974 added urgency to strategic decision-making in Tokyo and at KEPCO's head office in Fukuoka. In July 1974 the Electric Power Resource Development Adjustment Council in Tokyo approved construction of a second nuclear plant at Genkai in northwest Kyushu with a planned capacity of 559,000kW. In October 1975 Genkai No.1 Nuclear Power Station was inaugurated and in December 1975 the Taihei thermal power station started operations.

While the Japanese economy languished in recession in the mid-1970s, KEPCO was achieving encouraging results at its Genkai No.1 Nuclear Power Station. The pressurized water reactor (PWR) set a Japanese record for trouble-free running by operating for 367 days without an unscheduled break, much to the pleasure of the then president of KEPCO, Saburo Nagakura. In addition to the nuclear development program, liquid natural gas (LNG)-fired thermal energy was actively pursued as an efficient and clean alternative to oil. In 1977 KEPCO entered into a long-term contract to the year 2000 for the supply of LNG from North Sumatra.

The island of Kyushu is noted for its geothermal resources and by the end of the 1970s these were also being utilized by KEPCO to complement its conventional generating facilities. In June 1977 Hachobaru geothermal power station opened, and in April 1980 it achieved an output of 55,000kW, making it the largest of its type in the country. The company is actively developing its geothermal sites on the Hakusan and Kirishima volcanic plateaus. Together, KEPCO's geothermal facilities account for half of Japan's geothermal energy production.

Although there had been some easing of electricity prices in 1978, in 1980 KEPCO was forced to raise its rates again by a further 46%. This was a result of further steep rises in the price of oil in the aftermath of the Iranian revolution. But by this stage KEPCO's prospects of a secure and stable energy supply were looking better than they had for a number of years. Despite the widespread alarm in Japan caused by the Three Mile Island nuclear accident in 1979, KEPCO took several steps toward becoming one of Japan's major generators of nuclear power. In 1980 the Nuclear Safety Commission (NSC) held public hearings concerning the construction of No.2 Sendai nuclear plant and in the same year MITI started hearings about the construction of Genkai No.3 and No.4 PWR projects. These new nuclear plants will be the first of their type in Japan and are designed so that they can quickly adjust their generation to changes in demand in the daytime and at night. Their planned generation capacity is 1,180MW each and they are due to start operation in the mid-1990s.

Electric Power Development Company (EPDC) was founded jointly by the Japanese government and the power companies immediately after the end of World War II for the purpose of propelling the nation's power resource development. KEPCO is now working with EPDC to build a large coal-powered power station at Matsuura, Nagasaki Prefecture. Due for completion in 1994, and with a planned capacity of 2000MW, the Matsuura No. 2 coal-fired generating plant is currently under construction, also in collaboration with EPDC. KEPCO is also building two coal-powered units at Reihoku with a planned combined output of 1400MW.

KEPCO's current chairman, Tetsuya Watenabe, is now heading a company with better future prospects than it had for many years. The leader of the Kyushu business community is also leading Japan's other EPCs in the development of new energy resources. Despite opposition from the anti-nuclear lobby, particularly after nuclear accidents at Three Mile Island and Chernobyl, the company has managed to commission a nuclear program which accounts for 41% of its electricity production, twice the national average. With an electricity monopoly in Kyushu and a highly diversified generation base, the company's future looks secure.

Further Reading: Thomas, Steve and Chris Cragg, *Japan Power Station Fuel Demand to 2000,* London, Financial Times Business Information, 1987; *History of the Electric Power Industry in Japan,* Tokyo, Japan Electric Power Information Center, March 1988.

—Stephen Christopher Kremer

LONG ISLAND LIGHTING COMPANY

175 Old Country Road
Hicksville, New York 11801
U.S.A.
(516) 933-4590
Fax: (516) 935-1729

Public Company
Incorporated: 1910
Employees: 6,600
Sales: $2.45 billion
Stock Exchanges: New York Pacific

Long Island Lighting Company (LILCO) supplies electric and gas service in Nassau and Suffolk counties and the Rockaway Peninsula in Queens County, all on Long Island, New York. The company serves approximately 2.8 million people in an area of 1,230 square miles. As a utility, LILCO has played an indispensable part in the economic growth of Long Island. At the same time, this investor-owned company has been embroiled throughout much of its history in a succession of disputes over rate increases, environmental issues, and other concerns that have buffeted its fortunes and threatened its stability. With the settlement in 1989 of a protracted controversy over a nuclear power plant, LILCO sees itself headed for new financial health.

Long Island Lighting Company traces its genealogy back to the offices of E.L. Phillips and Company, located in 1910 on the 16th floor of a new skyscraper at 50 Church Street, New York City. Ellis Phillips, born in 1873 in western New York, held degrees in both mechanical and electrical engineering. He had worked for Westinghouse, Church & Kerr, one of the largest engineering and construction firms in the United States, and advanced to become head of design and construction for the company, but in 1904 he left to set up his own engineering consulting and contracting firm. Under the patronage of J.P. Morgan, Phillips also served the New York Stock Exchange as a utilities analyst.

As Phillips worked throughout New York, New Jersey, and Pennsylvania, he noticed many small electric light companies in need of more transmission lines and greater operational efficiency. Seizing an opportunity near his boyhood home, Phillips linked four communities together by forming the Genessee Valley Electric Company. Part of the capital for this endeavor was supplied by George W. Olmsted of the J.C. Curtis Leather

Company in Ludlow, Pennsylvania. Olmsted and Phillips were business acquaintances, and as partners they soon sold Genessee to a larger adjacent company.

In similar fashion, the partners purchased small electric companies in Percy and Warsaw, New York, and sought to develop them into a larger enterprise. Over two decades they made many other acquisitions, creating the New York State Electric Corporation. Further growth transformed this firm into the Rochester Central Power Corporation. Simultaneously, Phillips and Olmsted sought like opportunities on Long Island, where Clarence R. Dean, a supplier of generating equipment, became a valued source of information on many local electric companies.

On the last day of 1910, the Long Island Lighting Company was organized. The new company merged four small Suffolk County utilities: the Amityville Electric Light Company, the Islip Electric Light Company, the Northport Electric Light Company, and the Sayville Electric Company. On June 1, 1911, the New York Public Service Commission (PSC) allowed Long Island Lighting to begin to function. Five directors—including Phillips, Olmsted, and Dean—were authorized to issue $300,000 of common stock and sell $295,000 in bonds. Phillips became general manager at a salary of $200 per month. By the end of 1911, LILCO had grossed $70,000 serving 1,048 accounts. The company's business was conducted by four officers, four general office workers, and 34 other employees.

As revenues grew steadily, LILCO made rapid improvements to its system for generating and delivering electric power. New turbines were constructed and older ones relegated to standby or emergency status. In 1915 the company acquired the Babylon Electric Light Company. Two years later it added the Suffolk Gas & Electric Light company and the South Shore Gas Company to its holdings. The company charter was amended in 1917 to provide coverage for all villages and towns in Suffolk County plus parts of adjacent Nassau County.

During World War I, LILCO made a special effort to supply electric service to the U.S. Army's Camp Upton in Yaphank. By the time of the arrival of the first draftees in September 1917, the company had installed four transmission lines, a main distribution ring, and a substation to provide the new soldiers with the electrical comforts of the day.

In 1918 LILCO established a centralized billing service from an office in Bay Shore, and meter reading became a continuous task, with two readers working six days a week. Further acquisitions immediately followed the war: The Huntington Light & Power Company, the Huntington Gas Company, and the North Shore Electric Light & Power Company were all bought in 1919.

A major gas explosion at the Bay Shore works in 1919 interrupted service for three days. The accident pointed to the need for upgrading facilities and improvements followed. Major acquisitions continued through the 1920s and so did projects to buy land and build gas works and power plants. The company set as its goal the accumulation of all its holdings into one company, simplifying rates, and standardizing operations, but also creating a monopoly. By 1925, with Long Island experiencing a real estate boom, LILCO was in a very favorable position. Loans were readily available, and 97% of all stockholders regularly attended meetings.

Still, the public was not entirely satisfied with LILCO's performance. A group of consumers who had first organized to oppose a rate increase by the Long Island Railroad moved against LILCO in 1927. They presented a petition for a rate decrease to the Public Service Commission. The petition failed, but the PSC initiated comprehensive audits of LILCO and all other utilities in New York. Simultaneously, the state legislature established a committee to investigate the utility business.

Over the next decade, LILCO officers spent a good deal of time in hearings, confronting new regulations, and opposing rate cuts. In 1930 a series of hearings began that subjected the company to intense scrutiny. Nearly every aspect of LILCO's business was examined, including salaries, dividends, legal fees, contracts with E.L. Phillips and Company, and construction costs.

In response to this negative publicity, the company inaugurated a community responsibility program in 1932. The company developed display models of its electric system, produced a movie about itself, and promoted tours of its facilities by school groups and clubs. Employees were encouraged to participate in a variety of activities such as cooking schools, light demonstrations, and an employee orchestra.

In 1938 and 1944, hurricanes tested LILCO's ability to cope with severe natural disasters. On September 21, 1938, a hurricane, preceded by ten days of rain that softened the ground considerably, caused damage estimated at $500,000 to LILCO's equipment. Most service in Nassau County and 85% of service in Suffolk County was restored within four days. In September 1944 another hurricane knocked out 91% of LILCO's system. Most power was restored in about 12 days, aided considerably by LILCO's use of Nassau County's police radio network.

In the wake of this storm LILCO installed its own radio system. There were other changes in the 1940s, too. During World War II the company was forced to abandon its policy of not employing married women, as many single women resigned to marry men in military service. As restaurants closed during the war, the company also decided to open its own cafeterias. The first one, in the Mineola office, served lunch at cost.

Ellis Phillips retired as chairman of the board in 1945. His position was not immediately filled, but Edward F. Barrett, later to serve as chairman, was named chief executive officer.

As World War II came to a close, LILCO's service area was still not much more than a conglomeration of small towns, large estates, and vacation retreats amidst miles of farmland. Long Island's greatest period of growth, spurred by the migration of thousands of returning veterans and their new families to hundreds of bedroom communities such as Levittown, was just about to begin. LILCO positioned itself to meet this challenge by building new facilities, constructing new main lines, and establishing a connection to Consolidated Edison, its corporate neighbor to the west. All New York State power systems, in fact, were interconnected by 1948, a cooperative arrangement that played a key role in the great blackout of 1965.

In 1945 the company sought permission from the Securities and Exchange Commission (SEC) and the PSC to effect a corporate reorganization by bringing most of its subsidiaries into a consolidated Long Island Lighting Company. It was not until 1950, following many negotiations and preliminary decisions, that the reorganization gained final approval.

LILCO's managers continued to look ahead. In 1952 a 60-acre tract in Hicksville became the site of a new central headquarters housing facilities for system gas and electric controls, line crews, warehouses, repair shops, automotive maintenance, training classes, and, later, administrative offices. The company also established an equity annuity plan to supplement the fixed benefits paid retirees since 1937. In 1953 the state granted LILCO a 3.5% rate increase, the first general electric rate boost in the company's history. At the close of 1954 LILCO joined Atomic Power Development Associates, composed of 43 companies looking for practical ways to use atomic materials to generate electricity.

While safe and inexpensive nuclear power remained a goal, the company continued to cope with other aspects of its business. Three hurricanes in 1954 caused severe damage and added $1.4 million to the year's operating expenses. In 1957 plans were made to purchase land in Northport for what would become the largest power station in the country. By 1959, when Ellis Phillips died at 85, LILCO's residential customers numbered more than half a million and annual revenues topped $100 million. Peak load electric use passed one million kilowatts in 1960, the same year that saw the number of customers using gas heat jump to six times what it had been just a decade before.

President John J. Tuohy announced LILCO's intention to build a nuclear power plant on Long Island at a stockholders' meeting in April 1965. A year later the company bought 450 acres in the north shore village of Shoreham for a 540-megawatt plant estimated to cost between $65 million and $75 million. A proposal to construct a second nuclear facility in Lloyd Harbor led to the creation of a citizens' group in opposition. Their study, completed in 1969, branded both plants uneconomical and unsafe.

The Lloyd Harbor proposal was withdrawn, but LILCO pressed on with Shoreham. In fact, when the demand for electricity increased in the summer of 1968 at twice the anticipated rate, the company redrew its plan and proposed an 820-megawatt plant. By September 1970, when federal construction permit hearings began before the Atomic Energy Commission—precursor of the Nuclear Regulatory Commission (NRC)—citizen awareness of environmental hazards had grown considerably. In addition, the federal Environmental Policy Act of 1970 forced developers to guarantee that their projects would do no ecological harm.

The hearings set records for length and complexity: 100 witnesses were heard in 70 sessions, 401 legal briefs were filed, and 20,000 pages of transcripts resulted. Three issues became paramount: the environmental impact of the plant's construction, safety measures in case of an accident, and the effects of radiation. The opposition also raised a new concern—how Long Island would be evacuated in the event of an emergency. The Atomic Energy Commission ruled that this issue need not be addressed until Shoreham applied for an operating license, and on April 12, 1973, the commission granted LILCO a construction permit.

Before construction began, however, the Organization of Petroleum Exporting Countries (OPEC) oil embargo drove petroleum prices skyward, and consumers conceded the need for alternative energy sources. LILCO had converted most of its plants from coal to oil in the 1960s and, due to the fast-rising price of oil, raised its rates 13 times in 12 years to offset rising costs. Every time rates were increased, however, demand dropped, and the company's fiscal woes deepened.

The price tag for completing the Shoreham plant, which ran well behind schedule, jumped to $1.2 billion by 1977. LILCO blamed most of the cost overruns on increased federal regulations, but outside studies pointed to poor supervision and abusive labor practices as well. The company took over design and construction responsibilities from an outside firm, but costs continued to rise.

The March 1979 accident at the Three Mile Island nuclear reactor in Pennsylvania delayed the NRC's consideration of an operating license for Shoreham. It also stimulated the anti-Shoreham faction and crystallized the debate around the evacuation issue. With the threat of a nuclear accident now a demonstrated possibility, the fate of Shoreham was thrown into mainstream politics on Long Island and throughout New York state. Governor Hugh Carey and Nassau County Executive Francis T. Purcell continued to support the project, as did *The New York Times* and Long Island's *Newsday.* The estimated cost of completing the plant continued to rise, to $4.6 billion by 1986, an increase of more than $1 million a day between 1981 and 1986.

After Three Mile Island, the NRC required all nuclear plant operators to develop an evacuation plan in conjunction with local and state government. Suffolk County officials clashed with LILCO over virtually every aspect of the proposed plan, and eventually the county ended attempts to come to an agreement. One by one, county leaders dropped their support of the plant. County Executive Peter Cohalan, once in favor, changed his mind when he attempted to visit the plant site and found the gates locked. In February 1983 the county's legislature voted 15 to 1 that it believed Suffolk County could not safely be evacuated, a position bolstered by the support of Governor Mario Cuomo. In office only a month, he ordered state officials not to sanction any emergency response plan sponsored by LILCO.

The company's general financial health declined gravely during this crisis. Bond-rating agencies downgraded LILCO's bonds, and bankruptcy became a possibility. Critics accused the company of pushing ahead for an operating license for Shoreham simply to begin charging customers for the construction. Nevertheless, the plant neared completion. In August 1983, however, LILCO discovered cracks in the crankshafts of all three back-up diesel generators, two of which would be needed to shut the plant down in an emergency. The following January, the company's directors voted to withhold payment of $26.2 million in county and local property taxes to protest opposition to the plant. With the crisis at its height, LILCO's president, Wilfred O. Uhl, retired, and its chairman, Charles Pierce, was replaced by board member William J. Catacosinos, a computer-industry entrepreneur with little experience in utilities. Catacosinos commenced a massive austerity program, including cutting 1,000 jobs from a 5,900-member work force, but stood by Shoreham resolutely.

The fight dragged on, and LILCO persisted against considerable opposition from government, the public, and the local business community. The company completed construction in 1984 without fanfare and repaired the generators, even installing a second back-up set. The NRC in July 1985 approved operation at 5% of capacity, a low-level test prior to final licensing. LILCO's position got a sudden and unexpected boost

when Peter Cohalan, fearful of financial ruin for Suffolk County, dropped his opposition in exchange for receipt of the company's back taxes.

The public rejected Cohalan's reversal and paid little heed as LILCO employees simulated a successful evacuation of the area within a 10-mile radius of the plant. Whatever credibility this drill might have engendered, however, had been lost in September 1985, when Hurricane Gloria knocked out electricity to 750,000 customers. LILCO took more than a week to restore power during which time Catacosinos absented himself from Long Island.

Support grew slowly in New York state for a bill to create the Long Island Power Authority (LIPA) to take over LILCO and close Shoreham. Some legislators backed the bill because of LILCO's increasingly high rates; others were convinced by the Soviet nuclear disaster at Chernobyl that nuclear power could never be safe. The bill passed the New York General Assembly on July 3, 1986, and Governor Cuomo signed it.

LILCO placed its hopes for survival as an investor-owned company with the NRC, which decided in 1987 to relax its rule that government had to participate in formulation of a disaster plan. A week later, the state PSC exerted its fiscal leverage for the first time. It denied LILCO's request for an $83 million rate hike and ordered the company and the state to end their deadlock.

After more than a year of intense negotiations, the disputing parties did just that. The PSC endorsed a wide-ranging settlement in April 1989, and LILCO stockholders approved it that June. Under its terms, Shoreham was fully licensed to operate, transferred to LIPA for $1, and closed. LILCO was granted permission for a series of annual rate increases, targeted at 5% per year, for a ten-year period. The company also settled a lawsuit that Suffolk County had brought under the Racketeer Influenced and Corrupt Organizations (RICO) Act, resumed dividend payments, and refinanced its long-term debt. The fuel rods were removed from Shoreham's reactor vessel in August 1989, and the plant stood idle. The cost of absorbing the Shoreham debt pushed LILCO's rates to the highest of any utility in the country.

LILCO seemed to recover some fiscal stability in the wake of the settlement. The price of its common stock rose, and it sold a $1.1 billion offering of debentures. Events in 1990, however, threw the company's future into doubt. Oil prices and inflation rose at rates higher than anticipated, threatening the adequacy of the proposed 5% annual rate increases. As the international situation in the Persian Gulf deteriorated in late 1990 and early 1991, LILCO requested rate hikes for the next three years with certain adjustments that would keep the 5% ceiling intact, thereby forestalling what would likely be another long and divisive controversy.

Further Reading: Marks, Peter, "Shoreham: the History," *Newsday,* May 15, 1988; "Cuomo and LILCO Sign a New Accord to Shut Shoreham," *New York Times,* March 1, 1989; Carpenter, James W., *Lighting Long Island,* Hicksville, New York, Long Island Lighting Company, [n.d.].

—Steven P. Gietschier

LYONNAISE DES EAUX-DUMEZ

72 avenue de la Liberté
92022 Nanterre
France
(1) 46 95 50 00
Fax: (1) 46 95 51 86

Public Company
Incorporated: 1880 as Lyonnaise des Eaux et de l'Eclairage
Employees: 110,000
Sales: FFr75.51 billion (US$14.58 billion)
Stock Exchange: Paris

The Lyonnaise des Eaux-Dumez group was formed in 1990 by the full merger of the groups Lyonnaise des Eaux and Dumez, and now ranks among the 15 largest industrial groups in France. Lyonnaise des Eaux-Dumez offers a range of services in national and regional development of local industries and public services, particularly in urban planning and in the protection of the environment, to local communities, industrial companies, and individuals. The newly-formed group is active in the construction, real estate, environmental protection, and services sectors.

The group's services activities are a direct inheritance of the activities of Lyonnaise des Eaux et de l'Eclairage. This company was founded in 1880 by the Crédit Lyonnais, one of France's largest banks, to manage the public services of water and gas distribution which municipalities entrusted to private companies by concessionary contracts. In this, it was following the example of the Compagnie Générale des Eaux, created in 1853, which would remain its main rival.

The Second Empire in France (1852–1870) and the years immediately after it were a period of considerable growth in large urban public works. Large parts of Paris were rebuilt according to the plan designed by Baron Georges Eugène Haussmann. Urban planning grew in popularity and spread to France's main cities and towns which, at the same time, created or improved upon their water distribution equipment. Cannes, for example, was developed thanks to Lord Brougham, Lord Chancellor of England and Wales, and the French writer Prosper Mérimée, whose influence with the emperor Napoleon III allowed them to secure the concession for the Canal de Siagne ensuring Cannes's water supply. One of Lyonnaise des Eaux's first actions after its foundation was to buy up the rights for this canal.

From the first years of its existence the company was not satisfied with the management alone of water and gas distribution activities, so it acquired some of the capital of companies already involved in this sector. Lyonnaise des Eaux also secured a foothold in Spain from that time, with the acquisition of two-thirds of the company Les Eaux de Barcelone.

During the company's first 30 years it grew at a moderate but steady pace. Lyonnaise des Eaux concentrated on establishing its activities in the suburbs of big towns that lacked equipment. Its activities were evenly divided among water, gas, and lighting. Often, in the same town, it would go from providing one service to adding another, for example moving on from water to lighting or from gas to electricity. Its activities were mainly based in France, although it also had interests in Spain and North Africa, the latter then a part of France's colonial empire.

World War I halted the group's development just as it was beginning to accelerate. The installations in North Africa were destroyed. Public lighting was reduced for security reasons and to economize on the use of coal. Social security contributions rose, as did the prices of raw materials, whereas the rates set down in the concessionary contracts were fixed. This discrepancy inevitably caused the company financial difficulties. In 1917, for the only time in its history, Lyonnaise des Eaux was not able to pay dividends to its shareholders.

Immediately after the war Lyonnaise des Eaux embarked upon the production of electricity, thus becoming a fully-integrated industrial group. The instigator of this policy was Albert Pestche, an engineer and lawyer. He joined Lyonnaise des Eaux in 1896, having left the service of the state, where he was employed in public works. He was president of the company from 1922 to 1933. During his early years with the group he acquired technical expertise in electricity production and became convinced that it was necessary to centralize and unify production facilities throughout France. He also attached great importance to the role to be played by hydraulically produced energy.

In 1919 Pestche created the Union d'Electricité in association with the other companies that supplied electricity to the networks of the Parisian suburbs and to the public transport services, both metros and trains. The Union d'Electricité's aim was to centralize production—each regional distribution sector had until then been supplied by a different production center, often with different frequencies. The Union d'Electricité undertook the building of hydroelectric dams, thermal power stations, transmission lines, and converter stations. In this manner the centers supplying the Parisian suburbs and then those across the whole of France were gradually unified. To release the capital needed for these investments, Lyonnaise des Eaux sold off certain companies and raised its capital six times in ten years. Lyonnaise des Eaux became one of the main electricity suppliers in France and took over the management of the Union d'Electricité at the beginning of the 1930s.

At the same time, Lyonnaise des Eaux increased its shareholdings in electricity companies without neglecting water and gas distribution. The company extended its water distribution network in France and also in Africa, especially in Morocco. Lyonnaise des Eaux broke new ground when it created a laboratory in a suburb of Paris for water monitoring and analysis. In the gas sector it continued its policy of grouping together companies and, as in the water sector, looked to develop innovative techniques in the areas of pipe manufacturing, pressurized gas, and long-distance transport.

The Depression of the 1930s affected the group badly. Industrial production and industrial electricity consumption slowed down. The French state reduced subsidies to municipalities for public lighting and exerted pressure on the concessionary companies to keep their rates moderate.

A coalition of left-wing parties came to power in 1936, provoking a social explosion in France. Violent strikes took place. The cost to companies of new social legislation—including a 40-hour maximum working week and the introduction of compulsory paid holidays for all workers—along with the devaluation of the franc disturbed economic activity generally and Lyonnaise des Eaux in particular. However, its constant development and its investments in francophone Africa and Latin America helped the company compensate for the difficulties it was experiencing in France and enabled it to figure among the top French industrial enterprises.

Lyonnaise des Eaux's success during this period was due to the work of Albert Pestche and his second-in-command for many years, Ernest Mercier, who succeeded him as president. Mercier was an engineer who had acquired his expertise in electricity production in the service of the state. Invited by Pestche to join Lyonnaise des Eaux, he continued to use his skills in the field of energy before becoming president of the company from 1933 to 1954. He therefore took on the heavy responsibility of leading Lyonnaise des Eaux through World War II and the period of nationalization that followed.

During World War II, Lyonnaise des Eaux, like other companies, had to overcome the difficulties created by the lack of personnel, the disruption in transport services, and the coal shortages. In addition, installations were destroyed by air raids, and the company faced financial difficulties.

Immediately after the war Lyonnaise des Eaux received a further blow: the nationalization of a large part of its activities. The government of liberation, under Général Charles de Gaulle, decided that all electrical production activity should be transferred to the state. This program of nationalization was in perfect accord with the spirit of the time; it satisfied both the collectivist ideology of the socialist and communist parties, whose influence then was considerable, and Général de Gaulle's conception of the role of the state. "From now on, the role of the state is to ensure the development of the important energy sources," he announced to the Consultative Assembly on March 2, 1946. The vote was passed for the nationalization of the electrical and gas industries on April 8, 1946. The transfer of activities to Electricité de France and Gaz de France took place in the same year. The only production facilities to escape nationalization were those in which local communities already held a majority interest. Lyonnaise des Eaux thus kept its interests in a gas distribution company in Strasbourg, in the east of France. The nationalization law did not establish terms of indemnity payments; these would only be made five years after the transfer of the property to state control and after the introduction of several contentious procedures. La Lyonnaise sued the French state for nationalization compensation.

Lyonnaise des Eaux therefore was forced to restructure the range of its activities. At first it fell back on its traditional activities; it then tried to diversify into other sectors. Lyonnaise des Eaux intensified its involvement in the energy and water sectors both in France and in francophone Africa. The group did not totally abandon the electricity sector. Outside France, it continued its production activities. Within France, it became involved in sectors connected with electricity production, such as electrical systems and equipment for industrial purposes and for building.

The company was also very active in water distribution, an industry that was being radically transformed. Most of the distribution networks had been damaged during the war and had to be replaced. The installations required modernization, and new technology, notably in water purification, had to be incorporated. Throughout this period Lyonnaise des Eaux accelerated its expansion into francophone Africa, providing water, gas, and electricity to towns.

The group also began to diversify. The nationalization indemnity payments enabled it to invest in industries more or less linked with its traditional activities. It decided to exploit its expertise in electricity by increasing the room allocated in its portfolio to technical research companies.

Lyonnaise des Eaux took advantage of the boom in the construction industry in the immediate postwar period to increase its shareholdings in the public works and construction sectors. It strengthened its links with companies involved in road construction and in building prefabricated houses. Its technical expertise in generators led the company to embark on engineering equipment production. In the energy sector it took an active interest in drilling and exploration for oil. Lastly, the group entered the electronics sector.

Lyonnaise des Eaux's development was hindered by the worldwide process of decolonization, which affected the majority of the company's activities in French overseas territories. Until the 1950s Lyonnaise des Eaux was established in numerous African countries: Algeria, Morocco, Tunisia, Madagascar, Guinea, Congo, Central Africa, Senegal, and Togo. All these countries were to become independent. In certain cases, for example in Morocco, the state would wait for the end of the concessionary contract before transferring management to wholly state-owned companies. In other cases, the contracts were revoked abruptly. Negotiations over indemnity payments for these nationalizations were protracted, and compensation was hard to obtain. In some cases, however, Lyonnaise des Eaux managed to maintain its presence by working in a technical capacity for the new managing companies.

Faced with this reduction in its activities, Lyonnaise des Eaux underwent some restructuring. It abandoned its shareholdings in certain sectors, such as mechanical construction, electronics, and oil exploration. It then set about changing its strategy. Whereas before it had only held shares for investment purposes, Lyonnaise des Eaux decided to strengthen its direct involvement in activities connected with the protection of the environment. The end of the 1960s marked the beginning of the period when western countries began to become conscious of the problem of industrial and domestic pollution and of the necessity for environmental protection. Lyonnaise des Eaux already had experience in the treatment and purification of water. It moved from the treatment of liquid waste to solid waste and became involved in the collection and treatment of household refuse and industrial waste. The company also entered the heating sector, producing equipment for hot and cold air distribution, district heating, air-conditioning, incinerators for waste management, and flame-retardant materials.

Jérome Monod's appointment as president of the company in 1980 led to further restructuring of the company's activities. Monod was a high-ranking civil servant who started his career working for the state. He worked notably for the Ministry of Public Works, where he was principally concerned with dealing with problems in national and regional development of local industries and public services. Appointed director of the cabinet of prime minister Jacques Chirac, he followed the latter in 1976 to create the political party Rassemblement pour la République, for which he would serve as general secretary. He joined Lyonnaise des Eaux in 1979. Monod soon decided to refocus Lyonnaise des Eaux's activities on the provision of services to local communities. New divestments of subsidiaries took place as a result, in particular in public works, construction, and oil drilling, and the group ceased its manufacturing activities proper. The provision of local services was strongly encouraged by the laws of decentralization passed from 1982 onward, involving the transfer of power from the centralized state to the local communities. All Lyonnaise des Eaux's activities benefited—the distribution of water and energy, the collection of refuse, and the servicing and maintenance of public buildings.

To compensate for the slowing down of growth in the French market for water and energy distribution, Jérome Monod decided to expand the range of services the group offered, and at the same time to improve Lyonnaise des Eaux's international position. The group therefore embarked on new activities in the services sector. It took over Pompes Funèbres Générales, the European leader in funeral services. It also entered the television sector. The modification in the laws on audiovisual communications in France brought about by the privatization of several public channels allowed Lyonnaise des Eaux to participate in the creation of the private channel M6, of which it owns 25%. The company also took part in the creation of local cable television, managing several networks, notably in the Paris region.

Lyonnaise des Eaux also moved into the health sector. The change in the structure of the population and, in particular, the increase in the number of old people dependent on help led the group to build retirement homes offering medical services. Lyonnaise des Eaux also became active in the leisure sector and managed the construction of several golf courses.

Meanwhile Lyonnaise des Eaux embarked on a course of international expansion, targeting countries other than the francophone ones in which it had traditionally operated. This policy was favored by the growing privatization of public services that began to occur in various countries. Within Europe, Lyonnaise established itself, or continued to develop, in Spain, the United Kingdom, Belgium, Italy, and Portugal. It was also active in the United States. In Asia, from 1980 onward, it developed its activities in Japan, China, and numerous southeast Asian countries, as well as in Australia and Polynesia.

In the meantime it became increasingly obvious to Jérome Monod that a synergy existed between the provision of services to the towns and urban development, including the construction, maintenance, and servicing of houses and other buildings. The synergy was commercial, as in both cases the clients—local, municipal, regional, and government authorities—were of the same kind. It was also functional; with regard to water or heat distribution, improvement of the services offered often depended upon the improvement of urban infrastructure, even upon technical assistance at the time of construction of the facilities.

Monod also wished to enlarge Lyonnaise des Eaux's financial base and to reinforce its international development, and therefore envisaged forming ties with a construction group of international standing. This was the Dumez group, which merged with Lyonnaise des Eaux in July 1990.

Dumez is one of the largest French industrial groups, established in 1891, operating both in France and across the world, with over 50% of its activities in the United States. Its core activities are construction and large-scale—long-term contract—works, both directly and via Grands Travaux de Marseille, a 59.7%-owned subsidiary. The group is also involved in related areas, such as road works, real estate, electrical works and equipment, industrial installations, and the management of car parks and concessions on motorways. In 1987 the Dumez group also embarked upon an important diversification into distribution, when it acquired United Westbourne, the leading Canadian distributor of electrical material and plumbing equipment. The newly formed group, combining Dumez's construction activities and Lyonnaise des Eaux's service activities, has become "a leading force in construction, urban development, and environmental services," according to Monod.

In 1990 the group's turnover was FFr75.5 billion, compared with Lyonnaise des Eaux's turnover of FFr21 billion in 1989, before the merger, and the group is capitalized at FFr30 billion. The merger's success depends upon the new group's ability to exploit the synergies and complementary nature of the two former groups' activities, both in France and abroad, where almost half of the group's activities now take place.

Principal Subsidiaries: Dumez SA; GTM Entrepose SA; United Westbourne (Canada); Degrémont (76.4%); Ufiner (92.1%); Sita (76.5%); Pompes Funèbres Générales.

Further Reading: La Lyonnaise des Eaux a cent ans, Paris, Lyonnaise des Eaux, 1979; *Les Nationalizations de la Libération,* Andrieu, 1987; *Lyonnaise des Eaux-Dumez,* PF Publications, 1991; "La Naissance d'un nouveau grand de l'equipement," *Le Figaro,* July 12, 1990; "Les Secrets d'une fusion à froid," *Le Nouvel Observateur,* July 12, 1990; "La Lyonnaise des Eaux-Dumez sur les fonds baptismaux," *Les Echos,* September 24, 1990.

—Anne-Laure Gaudillat

N.V. NEDERLANDSE GASUNIE

Laan Corpus den Hoorn 102
P.O. Box 19
9700 MA Groningen
The Netherlands
(50) 219111
Fax: (50) 267248

Private Company
Incorporated: 1963
Employees: 1,984
Sales: Dfl15.4 billion (US$9.02 billion)

N.V. Nederlandse Gasunie (referred to hereafter as Gasunie) was formed to purchase, transmit, and market natural gas. The company fulfills its brief of ensuring a continuous supply of gas under all circumstances and marketing it on a commercial basis by operating a transmission network of 10,685 kilometers, 1,098 supply stations, 17 export stations, 8 compressor stations, and 7 blending stations, worth, together with other capital investment, Dfl4.5 billion in 1991. Gasunie serves 138 gas boards, 30 power stations, 370 large industries, and 5 other countries. It submits an annual sales and marketing plan, projecting 25 years, for approval by the minister of economic affairs. Its wholly owned subsidiary Gasunie Engineering B.V. sells its technical expertise all over the world, and its research center, Gasunie Research, has made widely recognized contributions to the study of natural gas.

The history of Gasunie began with the introduction of natural gas as a fossil fuel in the first half of the 20th century. As early as 1923 it was already evident that Dutch soil contained bituminous minerals and the first gas in Holland flowed on February 21, 1924. The most important Netherlands find occurred during World War II, near Coevorden, and in 1947 the Bataafsche Petroleum Maatschappij—BPM, a subsidiary of Shell Nederland BV (Shell) and the Standard Oil Company of New Jersey (ESSO)—jointly founded the Nederlandse Aardolie Maatschappij (Dutch Crude Oil Company; NAM) to explore more extensively. The Napoleonic mining law of 1810, modified in the 1970s for North Sea operations, ensured that concessions awarded by the crown were subject to many conditions. In 1956 NAM had to pay 10% of its profits to the state as royalties and sell its gas at a reasonable price. In 1957 the state handled the sale and transmission of gas by means of the State Gas Company (SGB) but operated only in the eastern provinces, while other regions had their own plants for coke

gas, such as State Mines (SM) in Limburg. SGB purchased gas from NAM at an absurdly low price of 2 to 4 Guilder cents per cubic meter but had committed itself to buying a fixed percentage of gas produced, irrespective of demand, for a period of 20 years. This contract could be ruinous for SGB if production were to increase dramatically. Production did in fact increase, to such an extent that NAM could have bankrupted the Netherlands.

The story of the Slochteren gas field, from the first discovery in 1959 to the first concession in 1963, with its initial silence and secrecy, is well documented. When Belgian senator Victor Leeman broke the news of the find unofficially at Strasbourg in 1960, NAM and the current minister for economic affairs, Jan Willem de Pous, had to open negotiations for exploitation of the field earlier than either had planned. Ironically, initial reports from NAM to New York had been filed away routinely, and it was only when Leeman's revelations appeared in the *New York Times* that the managers became aware of the enormous size of the Groningen find. The two representatives sent to Holland, D. Stewart and M. Orlean, were, together with two Dutch colleagues, C.P.M. van der Post and J.P. van den Berg, known collectively as the "Esso four" and were responsible for Gasunie's success, indeed its very existence. They saw the enormous commercial and social potential of natural gas, and worked day and night in the basement of the Esso building in The Hague to produce a revolutionary report for its sale and application. The plan aimed at meeting all the domestic and space heating needs of domestic consumers, industrial users, and exports. They worked out the necessary investment, covering the conversion of appliances designed for gas of a different calorific value, the distribution network, and everything else needed to achieve total market penetration of gas as an alternative to domestic fuel oil and coal.

After initial skepticism and the help of an accurate model provided by the town of Hilversum, the natural gas plan was finally accepted by Shell in 1961 and submitted by NAM to Minister de Pous. Since SM was a commercial concern handling its own finances, de Pous decided to use SM to negotiate the state's share. As it was coal that gas would replace, SM seemed better placed than SGB to effect the transition without too great a loss. The oil companies, for their part, wanted to avoid setting a precedent of state intervention which the sheiks of oil-producing countries, recently strengthened by the formation of OPEC, could seize upon to justify a greater share in the oil concessions in their own countries. Shell's legal division played down the greater state participation demanded by de Pous by suggesting that the concession be granted to NAM, which would then bring in SM independently as a partner. Shell and Esso would have a 30% controlling interest each with SM at 40%. In conjunction with 10% royalties, this would bring de Pous 50%, which he accepted. The plan was to form a limited liability company which would buy and distribute the gas, taking over the old SGB and the pipelines of SM's distribution company. Discussion stalled as de Pous insisted on 50% rather than 40%, since the state had formerly had total control over gas sales, and NAM in turn was adamant. A great national debate broke out. A. Vondeling of the Labour party even pressed for nationalization. His party chief, Joop den Uyl, was satisfied with the 10% of direct state participation that de Pous finally agreed on with Shell director Schepers. Shell and Esso had 25% each while SM had its 40%.

The ensuing Gas Bill of de Pous was a lucid account of what to do with gas and how to do it. There was to be vigorous exploitation as the envisaged lifetime of the entire field was set at 30 years. A commercial sales policy to provide the nation with the highest yield was to be implemented and a balanced approach was to be taken as regards competing energy supplies, with the expectation that nuclear energy would cater to most needs by the year 2000. Ministerial approval for long-term strategy was to be submitted annually, as well as approval for rates and conditions of delivery. Two years of enormous preparatory effort by managers and specialists from the three partners, Shell, Esso, and SM, was crowned with success when, on April 6, 1963, N.V. Nederlandse Gasunie was incorporated. Its share capital was purposefully low and its profits, which mainly pay dividends, were also meant to be low in order that the bulk of return on capital might go to the state and to NAM. Uniquely, the producer from whom it buys the gas—the state and NAM—is also the shareholder to whom it pays dividends. From the beginning no single personality imposed his vision on the company and the first director, P.A. Zoetmulder, had to work hard to create a team from staff who brought with them their own working methods. The company has continued to be run as a team, supervised by three managers—technical, commercial, and financial—themselves accountable to a general managing director and a board of supervisors. Gasunie has built up a formidable pool of expertise and more than a fifth of its employees have been with the company for more than 21 years.

Upon its establishment, Gasunie employed 97 people. The company's first order of business was setting a price for gas, and the Esso four had the novel idea that the market value of gas to the large consumer should be taken from the nearest alternative, fuel oil, while taking account of export revenue and its advantages over oil—for example, the lack of a need for storage—without undercutting oil altogether. For domestic consumers too, household fuel provided a comparable basis for setting a price. Finally, the commission of Regional Gas Services (SROG), formed at the insistence of the government after long bargaining with Gasunie, set a sliding rate that benefited those who used large quantities of gas for space heating. This price stayed the same for ten years, despite fluctuations in the price of oil.

In 1963 Gasunie contacted Bechtel Group of San Francisco, which possessed the building expertise lacking in Holland. As a result the most ambitious construction project ever seen in Holland was established, lasting from 1963 to 1968, with a second phase to 1972. Thousands of kilometers of pipeline were laid all over the country. As even the pipes had to be imported, technical director A.H. Kloosterman overcame foreign suppliers' attempts to fix prices and negotiated his way among the contractors. No expense was spared in winning over recalcitrant landowners and stubborn local authorities, but these were few in number due to good public relations, generous compensation, and generally high standards of land restoration. The 1966 crossing of the stormy Schelde River to Belgium was a feat in itself, with constructors working partly under water to avoid disturbing the ship traffic to Antwerp. This extensive transmission network was still increasing in 1991 and is safeguarded by regular helicopter flights. Simultaneously, a five-year national gas appliance conversion program was launched, aiming at one million conversions a year.

Again, Gasunie and SROG cooperated, enlisting a special company, Gascon N.V., which in turn enlisted U.S. support. Shriver Gas Conversions of Virginia sent 24 technicians to pave the way. Natural gas had to be made available as soon as household conversions were complete, to ensure an uninterrupted supply. Gasunie worked with great dedication, often at night, to lay pipes and install equipment, bearing the main cost of the conversion by paying the municipality Dfl50 for each conversion. On December 7, 1968 there was a ministerial celebration when, after four and a half years, conversion was formally complete and more than 90% of the Netherlands was switched on to natural gas, the highest percentage in the world.

Two more important projects were completed in 1968. With the aid of further U.S. expertise, the world's largest compressor station was started at Ommen, built to the highest-known standards of safety and automation, while Gasunie moved to prestigious new headquarters in Groningen. During the 1960s the hard work and heavy investment program followed the pattern of economic growth in postwar Holland as a whole, with low inflation, low unemployment, and a high level of exports contributing to this growth. Unlike some sectors of the economy, Gasunie was not, however, a victim of its own success nor of the higher demand and wage increases that followed. The success of the export contracts with Belgium, Germany, and France greatly increased in the 1970s following upward revision of proven gas reserves. This was a factor in the establishment of the hard guilder currency that was to prove so punishing to some smaller export companies.

During this time, SM, now renamed Dutch State Mines (DSM), had to close the mines but saw a chance to turn to chemicals and retrain thousands of workers. Such was the effectiveness of Gasunie's Dfl3.4 billion investment that the share of gas in Dutch energy needs stood at 14% more than the initial estimate of 30%, and would climb to 54% in 1976. Space heating was a spectacular success and annual per capita consumption increased from 300 to 3,300 cubic meters in 9 years. The Dutch standard of living improved, directly because of heated homes and indirectly through social security payments such as unemployment benefits, funded by state revenue from gas. Confidence was at its peak at the beginning of the 1970s and supplies seemed endless. This mood soon changed, however, when NAM realized that production capacity could not keep pace with growing demand, and it seemed that too much gas was being squandered at too low a price. Confirming this caution, the Rome Report published in 1972 changed official thinking about natural resources. As nuclear energy could no longer be expected to fulfill all energy needs by the year 2000, owing to its costliness and public opposition, Gasunie had to change its long-term policy completely. It was time for vigorous conservation rather than exploitation. The Groningen gas field would therefore be considered a strategic reserve, not to be tapped, except to supplement production from smaller fields, which were being developed and included those on the recently partitioned North Sea. This policy was maintained, and in 1987 Groningen gas accounted for only 55% of total sales.

Despite a bomb attack in 1972 by Black September terrorists on the compressor stations of Ommen and Ravenstein, Gasunie continued to ensure the maximum long-term security of Holland's energy supply and to invest unstintingly in equipment that guaranteed uninterrupted supply even on the coldest days. In 1974 the minister for economic affairs, Ruud Lubbers, renegotiated the state's share of revenue from domestic consumption of Groningen gas from 85% above a certain agreed price level, an agreement reached in the early 1970s, to 95%. He reopened foreign contracts made at a time when gas was a novelty and had lower market value, because it took too long for increased value to be reflected in increased price. There was a freeze on new contracts and a law against selling gas to wasteful power stations. More importantly, a law on minimum prices was passed and used in the Energy Bill of 1974 to set a price that would encourage saving and investment in insulation. Meanwhile Gasunie had already begun buying gas from abroad at market prices. In 1973 domestic fuel oil was double the price of gas but the minister, Gasunie, and VEGIN—the association of gas distributors—agreed to phase in the price increases over a number of years. In the 1970s, for the first time, Gasunie was in a position to sell its engineering expertise which had been built up in the 1960s. Success in the Netherlands, mainly on offshore projects, led to demands from abroad. These were finally established with the creation of Gasunie Engineering in 1975, established as a limited company on May 4, 1983 and owned by Gasunie. It has worked all over the world since, to the advantage of many other Dutch companies. Gasunie has also invested heavily in research into the transmission, application, and quality of gas. Since 1978 Gasunie Research has been based at the Bernoulli laboratory at Westerbork. It works in association with VEGIN and with several universities to improve appliances and has gained recognition for its work with condensation problems.

During the 1970s negotiations for the import of gas in highly explosive liquid form from Algeria came to nothing, and Norway emerged as the major new supplier. The higher price paid for Norwegian gas was traded off against greater security of delivery. The challenge of supplying the same quality gas as Groningen has been met successfully. The first mixing station was set up at Ommen, and a more advanced station opened at Wietringermeer in 1984. Other plants, including one to add nitrogen extracted from the air, were added over the years following the discovery of new types of gas, some eight varieties by 1991. This added to the complexity of the Central Command Post (CCP) in Groningen, a constantly updated computer system to monitor and direct all operations including financial ones, to calculate daily supplies, and to regulate pressure throughout the network.

Following the start of the Gulf War in 1979, the oil price doubled in two years. Minister Van Aardenne again hoped to renegotiate foreign contracts to improve their price responsiveness, even though an oil price index had been built into contracts in the 1970s. To do this he employed an ex-diplomat, D.P. Spierenburg. Several factors were employed as arguments, namely Holland's strategic position on the continent, its network, Gasunie's history of helping troubled clients, and Groningen's stabilization of supply and demand fluctuations. Acceptable agreements were reached in 1981.

Setting a rate for the large greenhouse industry, which had been revolutionized by gas in the 1970s, provoked a conflict with the European Commission. Despite Gasunie's agreement with VEGIN and the agricultural board to implement annual increases from 1981, the Dutch government was accused of protectionism. The maximum price, which gardeners needed to estimate the current price of their own products and which

had been agreed to the end of 1985, was declared null and void. Just when the gardeners were considering switching to coal, the oil prices fell in two successive years. Gas fell with it, from 45 Guilder cents per cubic meter to 15.7 Guilder cents per cubic meter in 1986. In 1991 the problem resurfaced. Gasunie is waiting with some concern for the European Commission's verdict on a new contract signed by the same parties in 1989.

Restrictive policies and enthusiastic economizing by domestic consumers resulted in a decline in demand in the early 1980s. Gasunie aimed to preserve its market share in Europe and ease sales restrictions by extending existing contracts at their current levels. Customer flexibility. however, was restricted further. The option of buying between 70% and 170% of contracted volume to meet peaks and troughs was reduced to 90–110%. Gasunie further indexed the price of gas to domestic heating oil rather than fuel oil. New contracts were opened with power stations, as the 1975 ban became obsolete, because new gas turbine stations were more efficient than the coal-fired ones and 20% cheaper to run. The massive price drop after 1985 curtailed some price wars but also signaled a drop in income for the state. In 1987, Gasunie was on the side of VEGIN when applying to the minister for a drop of 18 rather than 12 cents per cubic meter to keep in line with the price of oil. The minister refused, promising instead not to apply an environmental levy, which has since come into force and was condemned by managing director A.H.P. Grotens. The Hague has always used gas profits to finance the budget deficit and government pressure on Gasunie's policies is part of the company's structure. To balance the books further, the government privatized DSM in 1989 and incorporated its holding stake in Gasunie as Energiebeheer Nederland BV (Netherlands Energy Management—EBN).

After average sales growth of 1.3% between 1980 and 1989, compared to 9% in the 1970s, Gasunie has entered the 1990s by securing contracts of 200 billion cubic meters into the next century, thereby contributing 5% of state revenue after the year 2000. Reserves, including new finds, have recently increased to 2,500 billion cubic meters, equal to 1975 levels, leaving Gasunie well positioned for the dramatic increase in demand of 23% over 20 years, forecast for both western and eastern Europe and due mainly to its ecological advantage over other fuels. This confidence is reflected in a number of investments, such as the new head office, due for completion in 1993, costing Dfl70 million, the combined heat and power installations (CHPs) on which it cooperates with VEGIN, and the Northern offshore gas transmission pipeline project (NOGAT) coming onshore near Den Helder, which will deliver North Sea gas by the end of 1991. Most important for its own task of matching supply and demand is dealing again with the expected decline in production speed once the pressure in the Groningen field becomes too low. Just as transport and blending were the dominant issues in previous decades, now volume flexibility, the fine tuning of supply and demand, needs attention. A detailed study undertaken with NAM shows that underground storage facilities, including salt caverns, are the best solution, and the depleted Norg field southwest of Groningen is planned to take 3 billion cubic meters.

Gasunie is affiliated with the western European gas lobby, Eurogas, to state its case with the new supranational authorities. If the position of gas is well assured far into the next century, there is growing uncertainty about who can do what in this market. Gas provides 16% of European energy needs as opposed to 25% in the United States. Although Europe has more reserves than the United States, its gas is three times as expensive. Most of the move to end state monopolies, initiated by European commissioner Sir Leon Brittan, is aimed at those who own both transmission and distribution facilities, such as British Gas and Gaz de France, and aims to allow producers to sell directly to big consumers. Gasunie's only real monopoly is Groningen gas, but in practice, as the producers of most gas fields, NAM and EBN, also own Gasunie, it has effectively monopolized the sale of gas in Holland. Gasunie's conflict has been with the distributors represented by VEGIN which claims that price transparency has always been lacking at production level and represents an opaque spot in the company structure, with producers selling to themselves. Gasunie in turn advocates secrecy at the export level, where years of hard bargaining are at stake.

The tide has turned against Gasunie. On June 5, 1991 the European Commission approved the so-called principle of common carriage or third-party access, which will oblige Gasunie to transport other producers' gas through its network at a fixed tariff. A.H.P. Grotens has always been against this new competition and had indicated the need for security of supply and proper investment. Dfl350 billion is needed by 1995 to prevent European supply problems. Both supply and investment are endangered by too much competition, as illustrated by the fragmentation experienced in the United States. And pricing methods may change once again. Foreign competitors, aiming at the electricity generation market may fix prices with coal rather than oil in mind. Gas might even start competing with gas and cease altogether to shadow oil. Even when the Groningen field is depleted next century, Gasunie will probably play a leading role in supplying its European customers with gas purchased from abroad.

Principal Subsidiaries: Gasunie Engineering B.V.; Computercentrum Groningen bv.

Further Reading: Lubbers, R.F.M. and C. Lemckert, "The Influence of Natural Gas on the Dutch Economy," in Griffiths, R.T., ed., *Economy and Politics of the Netherlands since 1945*, The Hague, [n.p.], 1980; *Natural Gas in Holland*, Groningen, Gasunie, 1987; Kielich, Wolf, *Subterranean Commonwealth, 25 years of Gasunie and Natural Gas,* Amsterdam, Uniepers, 1988.

—Marc Du Ry

New England Electric System

NEW ENGLAND ELECTRIC SYSTEM

25 Research Drive
Westborough, Massachusetts 01582
U.S.A.
(508) 366-9011
Fax: (508) 366-9011, extension 2698

Public Company
Incorporated: 1926 as New England Power Association
Employees: 5,666
Sales: $1.86 billion
Stock Exchanges: New York Boston Pacific Cincinnati
   Philadelphia

New England Electric System (NEES) is a public utility holding company that derives its revenues from electric power that its generating company subsidiary, New England Power Company, sells to its retail subsidiaries. These, in turn, sell electricity directly to residential and industrial customers. The retail subsidiaries are Massachusetts Electric Company, Narragansett Electric Company in Rhode Island, and Granite State Electric Company in New Hampshire. NEES's market share of state electricity sales is 73.2% in Rhode Island, 35% in Massachusetts, and 6.1% in New Hampshire; in terms of the six-state New England region, NEES's market share is about 20%. Other NEES subsidiaries include a second wholesale generating company, three transmission companies, a service company, and an oil and gas exploration and fuels company.

The company traces its origins back to 1906, when Malcolm Chace and Henry Harriman obtained charters from Vermont and New Hampshire to construct a dam and hydroelectric generating plant at Vernon, Vermont. Even in 1910, when the Vernon plant began to transmit electric power to industries in central Massachusetts, the structure of the Chace-Harriman operations was complex. There was a company formed under the more liberal corporation laws of Maine, the Connecticut River Power Company of Maine, and a holding company, the Massachusetts Company, as well as two operating companies, the Connecticut River Power Company of New Hampshire and the Connecticut River Transmission Company. The Massachusetts Company, not subject to the regulations on public utilities, was able to issue and hold securities and therefore had greater flexibility in financing. Within a few years Chace and Harriman expanded their hydroelectric operations to include one plant on the Connecticut River at Bellows Falls, Vermont,

and several plants along the Deerfield River in Massachusetts. The New England Power Company was established to develop the Deerfield projects and to manage the electricity transmission lines in Massachusetts. The combined operations of the companies became known as New England Power System during this period.

As neither the Connecticut River nor the Deerfield River had a sufficiently large flow of water, especially during the summer months, to serve as a single, reliable source of electricity, Chace and Harriman decided to secure additional sources from thermal units, in which steam-driven turbines, rather than falling water, produced electricity. In the early years, they did this through sharing arrangements with the thermal plants of local lighting companies in Massachusetts and Rhode Island. Later, they purchased or constructed their own steam-generating plants.

In 1926 the New England Power System, the Northeastern Power Corporation, Stone & Webster, and International Paper Company formed New England Power Association (NEPA). This Massachusetts voluntary association had sufficient funds to purchase a number of smaller electric and gas companies in New England. By the 1930s, NEPA controlled 26 hydroelectric stations, 17 steam-generating plants, and more than 2,000 miles of transmission lines.

The Great Depression and the World War II years were difficult for NEPA financially. Annual earnings from 1933 through 1937 were lower than those of 1932, although sales rose, and full preferred dividend amounts were paid only three times between 1935 and 1946. Part of the problem lay in the fact that state authorities would not allow the retail companies to increase their charges for electricity, and the complicated network of holding companies prevented operating company mergers that could have resulted in economies of scale in production and distribution.

In 1942, the Securities and Exchange Commission (SEC) ordered NEPA to simplify its corporate structure. An acceptable reorganization was not worked out until 1947, when NEPA emerged as New England Electric System, a new holding company that replaced five former holding companies and reduced 18 different classes of securities to 2. NEES at this time was the largest electric utility system in New England, with 10,000 employees serving a population of 2.5 million.

The postwar years, and especially the 1960s, were a period of prosperity and reorganization for NEES. Electricity demand increased at an annual average of 7.7% in New England, and NEES revenues from electricity sales, and from the distribution and sale of manufactured and natural gas in Massachusetts, rose from $160 million in 1961 to $251 million in 1969. During this period the company gradually sold off a number of its generating units. In 1960, it operated 22 hydroelectric plants and 13 steam-generating plants, and in 1970, only 13 hydroelectric plants and 8 steam-generating plants. The number of employees in 1970 had fallen to 7,000. The main change in its retail operations involved the merger of a number of small electric companies to form the Massachusetts Electric Company in 1961. Some of this reorganization resulted from federal regulation. In 1957 the SEC ordered NEES to divest its minority interest in a number of small electricity subsidiaries and, in 1958, opened hearings regarding the company's natural gas distribution and sales outlets. NEES appealed the commission's 1964 order that it dispose of these up to the U.S. Supreme Court, which upheld the SEC ruling in 1968. The company subsequently sold off its eight gas companies gradually over the next few years.

In 1967 the three major electric utilities in New England, NEES, Boston Edison Company, and Northeast Utilities, began merger talks; Northeast Utilities later withdrew from these negotiations and was replaced by Eastern Utilities Associates. A corporate affiliation plan was drawn up in mid-1968 and presented to the SEC. The Justice Department opposed the merger, but an SEC hearing officer approved it in 1972, subject to certain conditions; the three utilities objected to these and the proposal was referred to the full SEC, which denied the application early in 1975.

In the 1960s electricity generating plants burning oil were fairly inexpensive to build and run and had cleaner emissions than those burning coal. By 1969 all NEES steam-generating plants were burning oil, including several that had previously burned coal, and, in 1971, the company announced the construction of a new large oil-fired power plant in Salem, Massachusetts. By the mid-1970s, oil was providing 78% of NEES's energy requirements, and the company ranked third among U.S. electric utilities in its dependence on oil. It was therefore very vulnerable to the effects of the oil price and supply crises of this period and concerned about government proposals to levy import fees on foreign oil.

In 1979 to counter this threat, NEES President Guy Nichols, later credited with building NEES into one of the region's strongest utilities, announced a 15-year plan to reduce the company's use of foreign oil and to keep customers' electricity costs to a minimum through conservation measures and load growth management. To lower the share of oil in its energy requirements to less than 10% by 1996, the company decided to convert some of its oil-fired generating plants to coal burning. The Environmental Protection Agency (EPA) granted a temporary waiver of pollution-control rules in 1979 to permit the conversion of NEES's biggest generating station at Brayton Point in Somerset, Massachusetts. The conversion of three of its Brayton Point units to coal burning, which was completed in the early 1980s, was the first large-scale conversion of an oil-burning generating plant by a U.S. electric utility. NEES then proceeded with a second major conversion of three of its oil-burning units at Salem. To ensure coal supplies for its plants, NEES contracted for the construction of its own coal-carrying ship in 1980. *Energy Independence,* the first coal-fired ship built in the United States since 1929, began carrying coal up the eastern seaboard to Brayton Point in 1983.

NEES also reduced its dependency on oil by using, on a small scale, alternative energy sources for electricity generation, such as wood, windmills, solid waste, and small hydroelectric projects. To secure oil for the steam-generating units it could not convert to coal burning, NEES established a partnership with Noble Affiliates, an independent oil producer, to drill and develop domestic oil wells. By 1984 the percentage of oil used for NEES energy requirements had fallen to around 25%, and by 1990, the company's fuel mix was 22% oil, 42% coal, 19% nuclear, 8% hydroelectricity, 3% natural gas, and 6% alternative energy sources. The latter included 32 low-head hydroelectric plants, 79 wind or solar generators, 4 trash-burning plants, and 24 cogenerators—facilities producing thermal energy and electricity from the same source.

To meet the second goal of keeping customers' electricity bills to a minimum, NEES focused on slow growth. Peak load capacity—the amount of generating capacity that an electric utility needs to satisfy residential and commercial demand at its highest point in the day—determines the amount of generating capacity that the utility must have. The NEES slow-growth strategy involved an extensive conservation and load management (C&LM) program designed to reduce the annual peak load growth for the mid-1990s from the previous forecast of 3.1% to 1.9%. Achieving this would reduce the need for constructing additional generating capacity by the 1990s; it would also eliminate the need for rate increases for customers to pay for plant construction. The C&LM program included rate discounts to large industrial, commercial, and residential users for off-peak—9 PM to 8 AM—use of electricity; the dispatch of energy audit teams to customers to give them free energy-saving tips; the promotion, through rate incentives, of the installation of heat and/or cooling storage systems; the holding of large public programs on energy conservation; and the initiation of a solar project.

For additional generating capacity to meet the lower peak load growth, NEES intended to rely on nuclear power, hydroelectric projects, and natural gas–burning plants. Nuclear power was a significant source of energy in New England in the 1970s, and its seven nuclear power plants supplied about 28% of the region's power, more than double the national figure of 12%. New England Power, the NEES generating company subsidiary, was a stockholder in the Massachusetts-based Yankee Rowe, Vermont Yankee, Connecticut Yankee, and Maine Yankee nuclear power plants completed between 1961 and 1972. Its ownership in these varied between 30% and 15%, and it purchased electricity in accordance with these ownership percentages.

In 1974 NEES announced plans to build a nuclear power station in Charlestown, Rhode Island. The Three Mile Island accident in March 1979, however, resulted in new safety requirements for nuclear plants, making them much more expensive to build and operate. Late in 1979, NEES canceled plans for the Charlestown plant. At the time, it still had a stake in three nuclear projects scheduled for completion in the 1980s: the Millstone 3 plant in Waterford, Connecticut; the Pilgrim II plant in Plymouth, Massachusetts; and the two Seabrook plants in New Hampshire. Construction of Pilgrim II was canceled in 1981, but Millstone 3, in which NEES had a 12.2% share, became operational in 1986. The Seabrook project, however, had serious problems, with estimates of construction costs for Seabrook 2, some 17% complete, having risen from $900 million in 1972 to $5.24 billion by the early 1980s.

In 1983 NEES announced that it wanted to sell its 10% interest in Seabrook 2 but to retain its interest in Seabrook 1, then 70% complete. If it could not sell its share of Seabrook 2, it proposed that the project be canceled, and eventually it was. In 1985 the Federal Energy Regulatory Commission (FERC) ruled that NEES could charge its customers for construction costs on Pilgrim II and, in 1986, for the construction costs of Seabrook 2. The main investor in Seabrook 2, Public Service Company of New Hampshire (PSNH), however, did not fall under FERC jurisdiction, and its rates were regulated entirely by the state public utility commission. PSNH filed for bankruptcy in 1988 after the courts barred it from passing along the

Seabrook 2 costs to its customers. NEES then submitted a bid to buy PSNH, exclusive of its shares in Seabrook 2, but dropped its offer when other utilities submitted higher bids.

The Seabrook 1 nuclear plant was completed in late 1986, but the Chernobyl accident in April of that year led the Nuclear Regulatory Commission to refuse to license the plant for commercial operation until emergency response measures were in place. These measures were subject to review by the states. Seabrook is located two miles from the Massachusetts border, and for four years Massachusetts refused to submit the evacuation plan the commission required. Seabrook 1 finally started commercial operations in June 1990.

NEES continued to follow its slow-growth program through the 1980s even though growth in electricity demand in New England between 1982 and 1988 generally was more than 5% per year, considerably higher than the NEES forecast. In 1985 Samuel Huntington, who had succeeded Guy Nichols as chief executive officer, announced further measures to provide an adequate supply of electricity at the lowest possible cost and to encourage customers to use electricity efficiently and economically. The company's subsidiary, NEES Energy, began to provide energy conservation services under contracts that provided for sharing of resultant energy savings between the company and customers. In 1989, the SEC approved the application of NEES Energy to expand its business and to participate in cogeneration projects.

When high electricity demand in New England resulted in voltage reductions during the summers of 1987 and 1988, the wisdom of a slow-growth program was questioned by a rival utility, Northeast Utilities, which noted that NEES then had no spare generating capacity. The recession, however, lessened the pressure on NEES as the annual increase in electricity demand in the region fell to 2.0% in 1989, down from 5.4% in 1988.

In July 1988 CEO Samuel Huntington was killed during a lightning storm. A successor, John Rowe, was not selected until December of that year. In the interim, Chairman Joan T. Bok, long the highest woman executive in the electric utility industry, assumed CEO responsibility.

In the late 1980s, NEES decided to include natural gas as a fuel source and announced plans to expand and convert its Providence, Rhode Island, oil-fired plant to natural gas by 1995. It also planned to add the capability of burning natural gas at its oil-fired Brayton unit in Somerset, Massachusetts. In addition, in 1988 it formed the Narragansett Energy Re-

sources Company to take a 20% interest in Ocean State Power, a general partnership established to build, own, and operate a gas-fired electric power plant in Burrillville, Rhode Island. The first unit of the Ocean State Power plant was operational in late 1990; the second was scheduled for completion in 1991.

For additional hydroelectric power, NEES tapped Canadian sources through arrangements with the New England Power Pool (NEPOOL), a consortium of New England utilities that coordinates the generation and transmission facilities of its members. In 1983 NEPOOL had made an agreement with Hydro-Quebec, the electric utility owned by the province of Quebec, to purchase sufficient surplus power generated by hydroelectric stations in the James Bay region to meet 3% to 4% of the region's energy needs. NEES has been heavily involved in the building of many of the direct-current transmission lines and terminals required to link the Canadian and New England electric systems. The first stage in the Hydro-Quebec project went into operation in 1987; the second in late 1990.

At the start of the 1990s, NEES was doing well. The two new nuclear plants in which it had a share, Millstone Unit 3 and Seabrook 1, the Hydro-Quebec hydroelectric project, and the Ocean State Power gas plant were all in operation. Its oil and gas exploration subsidiary, which had been operating at a loss, was being wound down, and the coal-carrying ship, which it owned, had been sold to Keystone Shipping Co., which would continue to transport coal to NEES's generating stations. Revenues were up. Whether the company would be able to continue its slow-growth policy once the recession of the early 1990s lifted in New England, however, was not certain. It also had to reduce its power plants' emissions because of the 1990 Clean Air Act.

Principal Subsidiaries: New England Power Company; Massachusetts Electric Company; The Narragansett Electric Company; Granite State Electric Company; Narragansett Energy Resources Company; New England Energy Incorporated; New England Electric Transmission Corporation; New England Hydro-Transmission Corporation; New England Hydro-Transmission Electric Company, Inc.; New England Power Service Company.

Further Reading: "New England Electric System thrives on slower growth," *Electric Light and Power,* November 1979.

—Judith Gurney

N ▼ NIAGARA
N ◣ MOHAWK

NIAGARA MOHAWK POWER CORPORATION

300 Erie Boulevard West
Syracuse, New York 13202
U.S.A.
(315) 474-1511
Fax: (315) 428-6678

Public Company
Incorporated: 1929 as Niagara Hudson Power Corporation
Employees: 11,800
Sales: $3.15 billion
Stock Exchanges: New York Boston Cincinnati
　Midwest Pacific Philadelphia

Niagara Mohawk Power Corporation is a utility company with a long history of providing electricity and gas to the upstate–New York region through a wide variety of means, from hydroelectricity, through fossil fuels, to nuclear power. The company takes its names from two rivers in the region it serves. The Niagara and Mohawk rivers powered the company's first generators, as the Industrial Revolution led industry and settlement north up the Hudson River valley, and west to the Great Lakes to form the backbone of Niagara Mohawk's area of service.

The company did not assume its present configuration nor take its present name until 1950. As early as the late 1870s, however, the great natural resource of Niagara Falls had been tapped to provide energy in the form of water that turned a wheel, which in turn generated electricity that operated several mills. In addition, water power from the Niagara River was used to operate a primitive electric light machine, and thus the hydroelectric era at Niagara was inaugurated in the years before 1880. By the early 1890s advances in the design of power plants resulted in the Niagara producing more energy than could be used in the immediate surroundings. In the wake of this success, other hydroelectric stations, which would one day become part of the Niagara Mohawk network, were set up in the late 1890s and early years of the 20th century to exploit the power of the many rivers of upstate New York.

Within a few years, the problem of how to transmit power from its source to the places where it was needed had been solved with the use of transformers and high wires carrying alternating current. In 1896 the streets of the nearby city of Buffalo, New York, were lighted for the first time by energy from Niagara Falls. Slowly, power lines were extended from

water-powered generating plants into other urban areas. By 1917 steam-generated electricity had come to play a significant role in providing power to upstate New York.

By the end of the 1920s, three separate holding companies encompassing 59 different companies served the energy needs of northern New York State. One holding company used the waters of the Hudson River to generate electricity for the area around Albany, New York; another was centered primarily on the Mohawk River and its tributaries; and a third drew from the resources of Niagara Falls and a large steam-generating plant near Buffalo, New York. Each company within these groupings provided for the needs of its area with its own generating plant and bought and sold excess power as it was needed or became available. In 1929 all 59 companies were brought together under the aegis of the Niagara Hudson Power Corporation, which had been formed specifically for this purpose. Although this united the companies under one owner, their corporate structure and operations remained much the same as before.

In 1932 Niagara Hudson completed a large Art Deco–style headquarters building in Syracuse, New York, whose architecture, incorporated many different kinds of decorative illumination, illustrating the wonders of electric power. In this same year, Niagara Hudson also first mixed natural gas into the manufactured gas that it supplied to its customers for use in furnaces, water heaters, and household appliances such as stoves and ovens.

Although lighting powered by gas manufactured from coal or oil had been seen as a competitor for electric illumination in the late 19th century, it soon gave way before the superior qualities of Thomas Edison's incandescent light bulb, and purveyors of gas were forced to fall back on the market for household conveniences. In order to finance the construction of larger generating plants and pipelines to residential areas, gas companies allied themselves with electric companies, and pipelines were subsequently constructed under power-line rights-of-way by these new, dual-purpose companies.

In 1937 in the midst of the Great Depression, Niagara Hudson's two-fold electric and gas businesses were reorganized. The 59 separate companies within its structure were reduced to 20, and these companies were separated into three wholly owned principal operating subsidiaries corresponding to their old geographical groupings. These three subsidiaries were Central New York Power Corporation, New York Power and Light Corporation, and Buffalo Niagara Electric Corporation. The entire company was incorporated under the name of Central New York Power Corporation.

With the arrival of the 1940s and the entry of the United States into World War II, the country converted to a wartime economy, and as a symbol of the new austerity the elaborate external decorative lighting of the Niagara Hudson headquarters building was removed. By the end of the 1940s, it had become clear that the geographic administrative divisions that remained within the company were not appropriate for the production of electricity and distribution of natural gas, and a final level of consolidation was undertaken. In 1950 the three operating divisions and the 20 companies within them were combined to form a single operating company, Niagara Mohawk Power Company.

In this new entity, power distribution for the entire area was brought under central control. All energy produced was pooled, and then allotted to users depending on need and supply. The new company was investor-owned, as its predecessors had been. As a utility, with a monopoly to provide an essential service to a particular area, the company operated under the scrutiny of the New York State Public Services Commission, and other such entities. The company was required to submit to this commission requests for periodic increases in rates to cover costs.

Throughout the 1950s Niagara Mohawk acquired a number of power companies and power-generating facilities in its region. By 1958 the Niagara Mohawk system covered more than 21,000 square miles in New York state, and encompassed 83 hydroelectric plants and 7 steam-driven plants, as well as several thousand miles of gas mains.

In 1963 Niagara Mohawk announced plans to construct an atomic power plant at Nine Mile Point, New York, near the town of Oswego on Lake Ontario. Two years later, the company received permission from the Atomic Energy Commission to build the plant. That same year Niagara Mohawk's service area was affected by a blackout that originated with a power surge in a Canadian company's plant on the Canadian side of the Niagara River. This led Niagara Mohawk, along with other utilities, to improve plant design and construction.

Niagara Mohawk's Nine Mile Point Nuclear Unit One went into commercial operation in December 1969. Six months later, in June 1970, the utility announced plans to construct a second nuclear power plant at the site. In addition to expanding its nuclear capabilities, Niagara Mohawk modernized and enlarged its conventional power-generating plants at this time in anticipation of increased demand for electricity in the coming years. The company converted four coal-burning plants at its Oswego steam station to oil and constructed an additional oil-burning facility. Two years later, in 1972, the company announced plans to add a sixth oil-burning unit at Oswego, to begin operation in 1976.

Niagara Mohawk, like the rest of the utility industry, was taken by surprise and heavily affected by the OPEC oil embargo of late 1973, which touched off an energy crisis. The price of petroleum, a major raw material for power plants, skyrocketed, and the company duly passed on this increase to its customers, winning permission to increase rates in February 1974, and then again seven months later. An indicator of customer dissatisfaction with rising utility costs came in May 1974, when the town of Massena, New York, voted to take over the company's facilities on municipal land and operate them itself.

With earnings squeezed by the energy crisis, the company scaled back its construction budget for 1975 and halted work on its sixth generating plant at the Oswego site, delaying its operation for two years. Nine months later, the company announced that it had sold a 24% stake in the plant to Rochester Gas & Electric Corporation, a nearby utility. In early 1975 the company cut costs further by eliminating 1,000 jobs.

To strengthen its construction program, Niagara Mohawk sought alliances with other power companies. The company set up Empire State Power Resources, Inc., a joint venture with six other New York utilities to build and operate power plants. Niagara Mohawk also purchased an interest in a nuclear plant being planned for Sterling, New York, and brought in four additional partners to help it construct its Nine Mile Point Two nuclear reactor. These arrangements allowed the

company to reduce its budgets for the rest of the 1970s and to begin work in June 1975 on the Nine Mile Point Two facility.

By 1977 Niagara Mohawk earnings had come out of a mid-1970s slump. By the following year, however, demand for electricity had begun to fall, and the company announced the first delay of the opening of its second nuclear plant under construction at Nine Mile Point. In addition in 1979 General Electric Company accepted responsibility for damages to Niagara Mohawk's first nuclear generator at that site, incurred during a routine shutdown for refueling and maintenance, which kept the plant out of operation for a costly month.

Public opposition to nuclear power and skepticism of projected increases in energy needs resulted in hostility toward the nuclear power industry in the 1980s. Niagara Mohawk was further plagued by its Nine Mile Point facilities in 1980, when it was announced that cost projections for Nine Mile Point Two, only one-third completed, had been increased by 78% to reach $2.4 billion. Citing concerns about technical and environmental issues, as well as regulatory difficulties, the company postponed the plant's operating date until late 1986. In addition, plans for the nuclear plant in Sterling, New York, in which Niagara Mohawk had acquired a partial interest, were scrapped by a regulatory commission in 1981.

In March 1982 the utility closed its Nine Mile Point One unit when leaks from cracked pipes were discovered during routine testing. The plant was scheduled to be closed for a year, and Niagara Mohawk purchased energy from Ontario Hydro, its Canadian neighbor, to make up for the loss in supply. In October 1982 the plant closure was extended for six months, when additional flaws in the reactor cooling-system were discovered, necessitating repairs totaling $50 million.

In February 1984 progress toward completion of Nine Mile Point Two was jeopardized when one of Niagara Mohawk's partners, Long Island Lighting Company, temporarily withdrew from the consortium financing construction of the plant, and Niagara Mohawk had to take on its share of the costs. Critics continued to maintain that the project was unnecessary and uneconomical. Niagara Mohawk received a further blow later that month when the New York State Public Service Commission accused the company of "widespread mismanagement" in operating some of its conventional power plants, and recommended an $83.2 million rebate of fuel adjustment charges to customers. The following month, the commission ordered a $100 million rebate relating to charges for nuclear waste disposal.

In the same month, Niagara Mohawk suffered another rebuke at the hands of a different regulatory agency when the Nuclear Regulatory Commission levied its seventh fine against the utility since its Nine Mile Point One nuclear generating unit had opened, ordering the company to pay $180,000 for failing to test equipment and failing to follow quality-control procedures. By April 1984 when the Nine Mile Point Two plant was 75% completed, its estimated cost was raised again by one-fifth, to $5.1 billion. Since the company was forbidden by regulations to pass on more than 80% of cost overruns on the project to its customers, this meant that Niagara Mohawk shareholders would absorb a total loss of $100 million.

Niagara Mohawk's regulatory troubles continued in 1985. In January the company was ordered to refund an additional $20 million to its customers after an investigation of its management of plants burning fossil fuels, and two months later a further $32.5 million refund was added.

Construction of the Nine Mile Point Two reactor finally came to an end in March 1988, and the facility went into commercial operation in April. The total cost of building the plant was $6.4 billion. This was offset by the closing of Nine Mile Point One in December 1987 for repairs and inspections that would ultimately take 31 months to complete, depressing the company's earnings. The closing came after the plant had set a U.S. record for continuous operation by a boiling-water reactor, with 415 consecutive days. In August 1988 Niagara Mohawk sued three of its subcontractors on Nine Mile Point Two in an attempt to win back some of the money it had lost on the project. The company eventually settled with the subcontractors out of court. In October 1988 the newly operational Nine Mile Point Two plant was also forced to close temporarily, and the utility had to buy power from other sources to meet demand.

In August 1989 Niagara Mohawk completed an extensive agreement with its regulators in the hope of having Nine Mile Point removed from a list of problem plants and returned to profitable operation. Nine Mile Point was removed from this list in 1991 and received its best-ever rating from the Nuclear Regulatory Commission. Despite lowered income and the failure to pay dividends on its common stock throughout 1990, the company was able to conclude agreements closing out the era of construction on Nine Mile Point Two and instituted a cost-reduction plan that included eliminating 1,100 jobs.

In August 1991 Niagara Mohawk experienced further difficulties with Nine Mile Point Two when a failure in the plant's monitoring system automatically shut down the reactor and sent out an alert at the second-highest level of emergency. Regulatory officials closed the plant until an investigation into the causes of the incident was completed, resulting in yet further loss of revenue for Niagara Mohawk. The reactor returned to service six weeks later. Niagara Mohawk must overcome the obstacles of operation in a strict regulatory environment in order to balance economic and environmental concerns as well as the needs of its customers for power and its shareholders for profit. The company's financial picture, however, improved somewhat in 1991, as its credit ratings were upgraded and it was able to resume dividend payments.

Principal Subsidiaries: Opinac Energy Corporation (Canada); HYDRA-CO Enterprises, Inc. (66%); N M Uranium, Inc.

Further Reading: Piper, Fred W., *Niagara Mohawk: The People and the Land It Serves*, New York, Niagara Mohawk Power Corporation, 1958.

—Elizabeth Rourke

THE CONNECTICUT LIGHT AND POWER COMPANY
WESTERN MASSACHUSETTS ELECTRIC COMPANY
HOLYOKE WATER POWER COMPANY
NORTHEAST UTILITIES SERVICE COMPANY
NORTHEAST NUCLEAR ENERGY COMPANY

NORTHEAST UTILITIES

107 Selden Street
Berlin, Connecticut 06037
U.S.A.
(203) 665-5000
Fax: (203) 665-5262

Public Company
Incorporated: 1927 as Western Massachusetts Companies
Employees: 8,000
Sales: $2.62 billion
Stock Exchange: New York

Northeast Utilities (NU) is New England's largest utility company and ranks among the 30 largest in the United States. With the expected addition of Public Service Company of New Hampshire in 1992, NU would serve 1.6 million electricity customers in Connecticut, western Massachusetts, and New Hampshire.

In 1966 Northeast Utilities was formed by combining Western Massachusetts Electric Company with Connecticut Light and Power Company and Hartford Electric Light Company. Western Massachusetts Companies, a voluntary association, had been organized in 1927 to acquire 11 utility companies in western Massachusetts. These were subsequently consolidated into Western Massachusetts Electric Company (WMECO), based in Springfield, Massachusetts. The company added Huntington Electric Light Company to its holdings in 1959.

An early NU project, begun in 1968, was the construction of a million-kilowatt, $72 million pumped-storage hydroelectric power project on the Connecticut River in Franklin County, Massachusetts. In a pumped-storage system, power is produced from high-elevation lakes during high demand periods; during less busy times, the water is pumped back to the high elevation.

Lelan F. Sillin, Jr., became president of NU in April 1968. Sillin was committed to developing New England's use of nuclear power. The region's electricity prices were higher than the national average, and Sillin viewed nuclear power as the least expensive, most efficient, and cleanest energy option. In 1973, NU generated 24% of its energy from nuclear units. By 1974, it was 33%, and by 1980 nuclear energy supplied almost half the company's requirements. As of 1992 nuclear power accounted for 60% of NU's energy needs.

Before joining the holding company, the individual utilities had invested together in four nuclear plants in New England

known as the Yankee Rowe, Vermont Yankee, Maine Yankee, and Connecticut Yankee plants. NU added its Millstone Point nuclear power station whose first unit went into commercial operation in 1970. Its second unit was completed in 1975. Millstone Point Company was established to construct and operate these two units. The company in 1972 launched a new program for nuclear fuel financing in which the fuel itself served as security on long-term debt. Plans for a third Millstone unit were set in 1975, and two more installations were planned for Montague, Massachusetts.

During the 1970s, the Middle East oil embargo, escalating inflation, and rising construction cost and time requirements began eroding NU's financial viability. The Montague units, originally set for 1981 and 1983, were rescheduled to start up in 1988 and 1992, and the third Millstone unit's in-service date was first pushed up from 1978 to 1980, to 1982, then to 1986, to reduce the company's financial burden. The delay in the Millstone unit, along with inflation and regulatory requirements, increased its cost from $400 million to $2.49 billion. The company decreased its overall building budget by $2.5 billion from 1974 to 1982.

The 1970s were punctuated by annual tussles with the regulatory boards in Connecticut and Massachusetts. In all, the company filed eight rate increase requests in Connecticut and six in Massachusetts. Never successful in obtaining its full request, NU averaged about 51% of the total amount applied for. In 1976, for instance, the Connecticut regulatory commission answered the company's request for a $56 million increase with a rate reduction of $22 million.

The company had borrowed all that it could under federal laws by 1976 but still did not have enough money to remain financially stable. NU stock fell from 120% of book value in 1970 to 65% in 1981, and bond ratings deteriorated from AA to BAA standing in the same period.

By the early 1980s, NU had revamped its demand outlook considerably. In 1970 it had anticipated a decade of growth at 9% per year and intended to build 6,238 megawatts of capacity, but the company actually experienced cumulative growth of only 25% during the entire decade and added only 2,813 megawatts of capacity. By 1980 its projected annual growth rate was reduced to just 1.7% with a target zone of no more than 1.5% annually.

NU would change its direction during the 1980s, largely due to its new chief executive officer, William B. Ellis. At Sillin's behest, Ellis left the consulting firm of McKinsey & Co. in 1976 to become NU's chief financial officer. In that year, total income was $85 million on revenues of $830 million. Two years later he was named president, and in 1983 he became chief executive officer. By 1982 revenues were up to $1.8 billion, but income had risen only to $151 million; by 1986, however, margins had improved, with sales of $2 billion and income of $300.9 million.

Ellis was able to create a more friendly relationship with regulators, one of his most successful negotiations being the Connecticut rate case settlement of 1986, the year Millstone's third unit came into full production. NU initially requested a $155.5 million increase, $133 million of which would go toward the Millstone unit's expenses. The request was denied, and the state ordered NU to put $46.5 million in a fund to offset rate increases in 1987. NU sued to protest the state's demand for this fund; eventually, in an out-of-court settlement, the state agreed to restore this amount, as well as to allow a rate increase phased in over five years, beginning in 1988, to cover Millstone. Also, NU's Connecticut Light and Power subsidiary agreed not to ask for any more rate increases until 1988.

NU's financial recovery strategy also included a massive conservation effort. The utility planned to reduce all energy consumption, especially oil-generated energy. Oil-based production, already reduced from 74% in 1973 to 47% in 1980, was to be 10% by 1987. The Massachusetts legislature and the regulatory commissions of both Connecticut and Massachusetts allowed the company to use two-thirds of the fuel cost savings to fund the conversion of facilities from oil- to coal-burning. The other third was passed on to customers immediately. The Mt. Tom plant was converted to coal in 1981 at a cost of about $35 million, recovered through oil-cost savings in about three years. The company planned to convert seven more plants, which originally had been oil-burning units but were switched to coal in 1971 in order to meet more stringent air pollution-control standards.

Other conservation efforts included ongoing research on fuel cells, modular plants that cleanly and efficiently convert various fuels directly into electricity without burning them. NU also gave conservation tips to customers and gave school districts rebates for switching to energy-efficient equipment, such as fluorescent rather than incandescent lighting.

Despite these efforts, Connecticut regulators ruled during a 1988 rate-increase hearing that NU must greatly expand its conservation efforts. The company therefore put up $250,000 to fund a collaborative project between itself and the Conservation Law Foundation of New England, attorneys general, consumer counsels, and other agencies in Massachusetts and Connecticut. The first project began in Connecticut in February 1988 and a multiutility process followed in Massachusetts, with WMECO as a participant. This effort identified new areas for conservation by bringing the company into closer contact with the communities it served; for example, a conservation program for public housing projects was a result of the process.

In April 1990 NU took over management of Public Service Company of New Hampshire (PSNH), which had filed for bankruptcy in 1988, substantially because of its investment in the Seabrook nuclear power plant. NU offered to buy PSNH outright, and PSNH accepted pending regulatory approval. In late 1991 the companies were awaiting approval from the Nuclear Regulatory Commission, the Federal Energy Regulatory Commission, and the Connecticut Department of Public Utility Control. With NU's purchase of PSNH's stock, valued at $750 million, and assumption of its liabilities, the deal's total price was $2.36 billion. The company would have enough capacity to sell over $100 million worth of excess electricity to other utilities each year. NU projected $516 million in savings from its management and operation of PSNH and Seabrook. The addition of Seabrook would eliminate the need for significant construction during the next decade.

Principal Subsidiaries: The Connecticut Light and Power Company; Holyoke Water Power Company; Western Massachusetts Electric Company.

Further Reading: Sillin, Lelan F. Jr., "Managing Utilities in an Inflationary Economy," *Public Utilities Fortnightly,* April 1, 1982; Christie, Claudia M., "Businessperson of the Year. William B. Ellis: An Expectation of Excellence," *New England Business,* December 7, 1987; Geehern, Christopher, "Regional Power," *New England Business,* January 1991.

—Elaine Belsito

Northern States Power Company

NORTHERN STATES POWER COMPANY

414 Nicollet Mall
Minneapolis, Minnesota 55401
U.S.A.
(612) 330-5500
Fax: (612) 330-2900

Public Company
Incorporated: 1909 as Washington County Light & Power
   Company
Employees: 7,471
Sales: $2.06 billion
Stock Exchanges: New York Midwest Pacific

Northern States Power Company (NSP) provides electricity
and gas to customers in Minnesota, Wisconsin, North Dakota,
South Dakota, and the upper peninsula of Michigan. In 1990 it
had 1.3 million electricity customers and 358,000 natural gas
customers. The bulk of its sales is direct to consumers, but it
provides a small amount of energy for resale by other utilities.

NSP's roots go back to 1881 when Henry Marison Byllesby,
NSP's founder—then a 22-year-old dropout from engineering
school—joined Thomas Edison as a draftsman to build a
power plant in New York City. Byllesby went on to design
plants for Edison in Chile and Montreal. In 1885 Edison's
rival George Westinghouse offered Byllesby $10,000 a year to
become vice president and general manager of Westinghouse
Electric, and Byllesby accepted.

In his four years with Westinghouse, Byllesby invented and
designed more than 40 electric lighting devices. In 1891 he
received a job offer from another competitor, Charles A. Coffin, president of Thomson-Houston Electric Company. Coffin
sent Byllesby to St. Paul, Minnesota, to run a subsidiary there.
In St. Paul, Byllesby noted that most midwestern electric companies had inadequate finances and other resources to meet
customer demand. The weakest companies quickly went bankrupt or were swallowed by their competitors. Byllesby spent
four years in St. Paul, until Thomson-Houston merged with
Edison's General Electric Company. Unwilling to work for
Edison again, Byllesby went to Oregon and became vice president of the Portland General Electric Company, where he designed, financed, and built four hydroelectric developments in
four years.

In 1902 he put his years in St. Paul to use and organized his
own engineering and operating firm in Chicago, with Samuel

Insull and other backers, to buy and upgrade struggling midwestern utilities. Insull was a leading financier and acquirer of
utilities. Financially troubled electric companies would approach Insull, and Insull would bail them out in exchange for
stock in the company and an executive position. Byllesby
bought companies in Illinois, Ohio, and Oklahoma, then in
1909 returned to Minnesota, where he organized the Washington County Light & Power Company in June 1909. In December 1909, the company's name was changed to Consumers
Power Company. Byllesby and Insull also organized two utility
holding companies: Northern States Power Company of Delaware in 1909 and Standard Gas and Electric in 1910.

Byllesby, like Insull, ended up acquiring many of the companies he helped. The companies for which Byllesby built
steam and hydroelectric plants became insolvent. Byllesby's
company would take over these troubled companies and provide engineering, management, and financial assistance. In
1912 Byllesby made his most important acquisition when he
bought Minneapolis General Electric of Minnesota. That company was destined to become NSP's flagship company. Also in
1912 Byllesby and Insull parted ways.

On February 5, 1916, Byllesby changed his company's
name to Northern States Power Company. The United States's
entry into World War I in 1917 put a great strain on NSP's
generating capabilities as wartime production and industrial
customers' demands grew. After the war, the country experienced a brief depression followed by a business boom that saw
increased demand for electricity and encouragement of merger
activity.

In the company's first 20 years, NSP bought 25 more upper-
midwest utility companies. It acquired the Northwest Light &
Power Company in 1917 and the Brainerd Gas & Electric
Company, St. Cloud Water Power Company, Hutchinson Light
& Manufacturing Company, and Ottumwa Railway & Light
Company in 1920. Ottumwa's electric and steam heating busi-
ness was reorganized in 1923 as the Northern States Power
Company (New Jersey), while its railway business became the
Ottumwa Traction Company. All of the old Ottumwa proper-
ties were sold in 1925, except transmission lines in northern
Iowa. NSP acquired the Wisconsin-Minnesota Light and
Power Company in 1923; the Minnesota Valley Electric Com-
pany, Renville County Electric Company, and St. Cloud Pub-
lic Service Company in 1924; Glenwood Electric Light, Heat
& Power Company, Farmers Light & Power Company, and the
St. Cloud Electric Power Company in 1926; and the St. Paul
Gas Light Company, Sauk Rapids Water Power Company,
South St. Paul Gas & Electric Company, St. Croix Power
Company, and the Minnesota Power Company in 1927.

As NSP expanded its network of operating companies, it
interconnected them. Interconnection allowed massive power
production and brought customers lower rates and more reliable service. NSP also replaced old plants with newer, more
efficient ones, constructing major hydroelectric units at Rapi-
dan, Cannon Falls, and Coon Rapids, Minnesota, in addition
to many smaller installations all over the Midwest. The company put a great deal of effort into improving its steam generating plants, focusing attention on the Riverside plant in
Minneapolis. Riverside was huge by standards of the day, and
its expansion illustrated Byllesby's belief that it was less expensive to generate power at a favorable site and transmit it
than to generate power at the site where it is used. Byllesby

died in 1924, but numerous associates carried on his work, especially Robert F. Pack, general manager and later president of NSP.

Between 1921 and 1929, 3,744 U.S. public utility companies were absorbed in mergers and acquisitions. This meant that 84% of all U.S. utility assets were in the hands of slightly more than 1% of all utility corporations. During the Great Depression, large holding companies such as NSP became the subjects of much scrutiny.

The scrutiny resulted in the Public Utility Holding Company Act of 1935, under which utilities had to simplify their structures. As a result of this law, NSP had to dissolve Standard Gas and Electric, and NSP's Chicago-based financial backers had to sell their stock back to the company.

During this period, NSP experienced major financial problems. The Securities and Exchange Commission (SEC) forced the company to reevaluate assets it had overvalued for stock issuing purposes in 1924, and NSP lost $75 million through this readjustment. The SEC also ordered NSP to eliminate its Class B voting stock, which had been created by Byllesby to guarantee him control of NSP, since the company could no longer pay dividends.

Another part of U.S. President Franklin D. Roosevelt's New Deal that affected NSP was the agency he developed to help finance electrical lines for impoverished farmers, the Rural Electrification Administration (REA). The REA encouraged farmers to form electric cooperatives in order to borrow federal funds for line extensions. These cooperatives competed directly with private utilities.

The third blow the New Deal dealt power companies was government sponsorship of municipal power company ownership. The government agreed to pay 45% of the cost for any community willing to build, generate, and distribute its own power. After an extensive battle and many town hall debates, most communities ended up choosing NSP's service anyway, for NSP had made voluntary rate reductions consistently since it started operating.

Roosevelt's final implementation that affected NSP was his National Recovery Act, which guaranteed employees the right to organize, bargain collectively, and strike. This act, and the safer working conditions encouraged by a union, was welcomed by NSP linemen, who had lost nearly half their workers to electrical accidents. On February 23, 1937, NSP suffered its first labor strike. By the eighth day of the strike, Robert Pack decided to cut his loses and agreed to recognize the workers' union International Brotherhood of Electrical Workers. NSP was one of the first utility companies in the United States to become unionized.

In 1939 the company continued to expand in Wisconsin. On August 29, 1941, NSP merged the wholly owned subsidiaries Minneapolis General Electric Company, St. Croix Falls Minnesota Improvement Company, and Minnesota Brush Electric Company into NSP. On December 27 NSP dissolved Northern States Power Company (New Jersey) after selling certain assets to South Dakota Public Service Company and transferring the remainder to itself.

After the United States entered World War II in 1941, demand for electricity rose rapidly, as industry contributed to the war effort. NSP responded by adding a 50,000-kilowatt steam turbine to its St. Paul High Bridge plant. NSP employees were fingerprinted, as a precaution against sabotage and theft. Most

of NSP's advertising during the war focused on conservation and salvage programs. The electric-utility industry's cartoon-character spokesperson, Reddy Kilowatt, regularly promoted victory gardens. More than 600 NSP employees served in the war. In 1942 NSP's president, Robert Pack, retired, turning over his office to his assistant, Ted Crocker.

While many utility companies saw demand slow after the war, NSP reported a record load on December 17, 1945, almost 10% higher than in 1944. Sales for 1945 were a record $53 million. NSP became heavily involved in a postwar planning program that helped businesses expand and convert their wartime production to peacetime needs. While NSP helped these businesses, the businesses' growth often helped NSP enlarge its customer base.

NSP's customer base grew so rapidly that when President Ted Crocker died unexpectedly on June 29, 1947, and B.F. Braheney took over, he was faced with a power shortage. Braheney quickly developed a demand-control system and called on customers to conserve. NSP also built new plants, many of them diesel-powered. During the 1950s the company launched its largest-ever construction program, investing nearly $400 million. After 1947 NSP's daily kilowatt-hour output surpassed that of the entire year 1916. Operating revenues doubled from 1941 to 1951.

In 1950 NSP sold the utility properties of its Illinois-based subsidiary, Interstate Light & Power Company, and dissolved it. In 1955 NSP ranked among the top ten utilities in the United States. In 1956 NSP consolidated three of its subsidiaries—St. Croix Falls Wisconsin Improvement Company, St. Croix Power Company, and Interstate Light & Power Company—into its already existing principal subsidiary, Northern States Power Company (Wisconsin) (NSP-Wisconsin). In October 1956 NSP sold its gas property in Brainerd, Minnesota, to Minnesota Valley Natural Gas Company and bought electrical distribution properties that served 13 Minnesota communities and surrounding rural areas, from Interstate Power Company.

In March 1957 NSP continued to consolidate, acquiring hydroelectric developments at St. Anthony Falls on the Mississippi River in Minneapolis from its wholly owned subsidiaries, St. Anthony Falls Water Power Company and the Minneapolis Mill Company. In August of that year NSP acquired an electrical distribution system in Farmington, Minnesota, from Central Electric & Gas Company. The following month NSP added more electrical distribution facilities in Delhi and North Redwood, Minnesota, from the city of Redwood Falls. In October of 1957, NSP-Wisconsin acquired properties from Wisconsin Hydro Electric Company.

NSP had been interested in nuclear energy since 1945, and in the early 1950s it became one of the first utilities to receive access to information from the Atomic Energy Commission. In 1957 the company announced plans for its first full-scale atomic power plant, the Pathfinder, and chose a site on the Big Sioux River. Pathfinder began operating in 1964, but operating and safety costs were so high that in 1967, NSP substituted a gas-fired steam boiler for the nuclear reactor.

In January 1960 NSP acquired NSP-Wisconsin's Minnesota properties, as well as the Wisconsin properties of Mississippi Valley Public Service Company. Later that year, NSP acquired NSP-Wisconsin's Minnesota gas properties, which were in the Winona and Red Wing areas. In May 1961 NSP acquired

Western Power and Gas Company's eastern business, which served the southeastern portion of South Dakota. In 1962 NSP sold its Tracy, Minnesota, water utility to the city of Tracy.

In March 1964 NSP acquired the properties and assets of Deichen Power, Inc. that had supplied southern Minnesota. In 1964 NSP began construction of the Allen S. King steam electric plant in Wisconsin on the St. Croix River and stirred up an environmental confrontation. The public outcry raised by the construction of this plant, which was perceived as a threat to the area's wildlife, was NSP's next real experience with public opposition and foreshadowed the controversy NSP's nuclear plant would raise. Despite an injunction—later lifted—brought by the Wisconsin attorney general, the company went ahead with the plant, which began production in 1968.

Around that time Allen King, NSP president until 1965, and his successor, Earl Ewald, created Mid-Continent Area Power Planners (MAPP), which brought 22 upper midwest power suppliers together to coordinate the planning, construction, and operation of new electrical plants throughout the region, in hopes of maximizing efficiency and minimizing duplication and waste. Through interconnection and coordination these companies were able to help each other supply the area.

All went smoothly for NSP through 1965. In June 1965 NSP acquired distribution facilities in Grand Forks, North Dakota, from the Nodak Rural Electric Cooperative. The tide turned in 1966, however, when NSP announced its plans for the Monticello nuclear plant. Demonstrators rose up in opposition. Although ground for the plant was broken in 1966, it took five years and $20 million in losses before the plant became operational. The controversy led NSP to create an environmental affairs department in 1969.

NSP continued expanding; in 1967 it acquired distribution facilities from Wright-Hennepin Cooperative Electric Association, as well as the electric distribution facilities of the village of Bayport, Minnesota. In 1968 NSP acquired the electric generating, transmission, and distribution facilities of the village of Mazeppa, Minnesota, and sold the electric distribution system of the village of Fischer, Minnesota, to the Otter Tail Power Company. In December 1969 NSP acquired several electric distribution facilities from Interstate Power Company.

In 1971 NSP donated land skirting the Upper St. Croix River to the states of Minnesota and Wisconsin and to the National Park Service to be managed cooperatively. In 1973 as the OPEC oil embargo drove home the importance of conservation, NSP began researching solar energy, wind power, burning garbage as fuel, and even enormous underwater sea turbines. However, 94% of NSP's power still came from nuclear and coal-fired plants in 1978. It had added a second nuclear plant, Prairie Island, in 1973.

The 1970s were tough for NSP; as taxes and interest rates went up, NSP's earnings dropped, although revenues reached record highs. NSP, which had cut rates in earlier years, sought rate increases, but not all were approved by regulators. Near the end of the 1970s, NSP began to explore the possibilities of another nuclear power plant to produce low-cost energy. The company planned to participate in a plant called Tyrone, located in western Wisconsin. In early 1979, however, in the middle of NSP's battle with the Wisconsin Public Service Commission, came the nuclear accident at Three Mile Island, Pennsylvania. Soon after, NSP and other Tyrone owners voted to cancel the project.

NSP spent nearly $1 billion on pollution control from 1977 to 1987. The company also continued consolidating its principal subsidiary. In 1987 NSP merged its subsidiary, Lake Superior District Power Company, into NSP-Wisconsin.

From 1980 to 1990, both NSP's sales and profits nearly doubled. It increased dividends for the 16th consecutive year in 1990. The company, however, contended that many of its costs, such as property taxes, were beyond its control and in 1989 had sought a $120 million electric rate increase from the Minnesota Public Utilities Commission. The commission rejected the request in 1990, and the Minnesota Court of Appeals upheld the commission's decision. In December 1991 the commission granted a smaller increase, $53.5 million. Also in 1991, NSP won rate increases in South Dakota and Wisconsin, although these, too, were smaller than initially requested. In North Dakota, a court case over a rate increase was pending. NSP also reported that its pollution control efforts of the 1970s and 1980s meant the company would not face great setbacks as a result of the restrictions of the Clean Air Act amendments passed in 1990.

Principal Subsidiaries: Northern States Power Company (Wisconsin); NRG Group, Inc.; Chippewa & Flambeau Improvement Company; United Power and Land Company; Cormorant Corporation; First Midwest Auto Park, Inc.

Further Reading: Pine, Carol, *NSP. Northern States People: the past 70 years,* Minneapolis, Minnesota, North Central Publishing, 1979.

—Maya Sahafi

NOVA CORPORATION OF ALBERTA

801 Seventh Avenue Southwest
Calgary, Alberta T2P 3P7
Canada
(403) 290-6000
Fax: (403) 290-6379

Public Company
Incorporated: 1954 as The Alberta Gas Trunk Line Company
   Ltd.
Employees: 8,500
Sales: C$4.74 billion (US$4.10 billion)
Stock Exchanges: Toronto Montreal Alberta New York London
   Geneva Zürich Basel

Nova Corporation of Alberta is the primary natural gas transporter in the Alberta region. In addition, it markets and manufactures petrochemicals and plastics, with divisions that handle consulting, research, and product development. It is one of the largest ethylene producers in North America; one of the largest North American producers and marketers of polyethylene; and it owns the only facility in North America that produces and markets methyl-methacrylate resins (SMMA resins), from which housewares, appliances, and faucet handles are made.

Nova's beginnings can be traced to 1954, when it was incorporated as The Alberta Gas Trunk Line Company Ltd. (AGTL) by the premier of Alberta, Ernest Manning. Initially it was involved in gas gathering within the province of Alberta. By the mid-1960s, several Canadian gas companies were vying for the attention of the National Energy Board to secure permission to compete in the gas export market. In 1967 the United States approved a pipeline that would stretch from the north central United States to eastern Canada, with the potential of bringing billions of dollars in revenue to the gas industry in Alberta.

In an effort to assert itself in this growing marketplace, AGTL announced in 1970 its plans to build a C$1.5 billion Alaskan pipeline. This was the brainstorm of S. Robert Blair, who came on board as executive vice president of AGTL in 1970 and was appointed president and chief executive officer later that year. Blair, a Canadian nationalist, foresaw a pipeline that stretched from Prudhoe Bay, Alaska, to Alberta, covering AGTL's existing transmission system, and then on to the rest of Canada and the United States, ultimately drawing from and including the gas fields in the mostly untapped Canadian

Northwest Territories. Eventually, AGTL joined forces with other interested parties to form a study group to research the feasibility of the plan. Economic restrictions, protests by environmental groups, and logistical concerns slowed down the plan's momentum, and by the time the pipeline's proposed completion date drew near in 1974, AGTL had withdrawn from the consortium that had grown to 26 companies. Instead, perhaps in reaction to the rerouting of the pipeline solely through the United States, AGTL proposed to develop its own all-Canadian pipeline stemming largely from the Northwest Territories. Ultimately, this project, the Alaska Natural Gas Transportation System, received approval from the Canadian and U.S. governments. As of 1991, it had not been built, but was expected to be constructed when demand for Alaskan gas increased in the lower 48 states.

During the 1970s AGTL began to form and incorporate several subsidiary companies related to the gas and oil industry. AGTL formed Alberta Gas Chemicals Ltd.; Algas Resources Ltd., now Noval Enterprises; Algas Engineering Services Ltd., now Novacorp Engineering Services Ltd.; and Novacorp International Consulting Inc. The company also acquired a 50.001% interest in Pan-Alberta Gas Ltd., which AGTL had used previously to supply gas to companies outside of Alberta. In 1974 AGTL incorporated The Alberta Gas Ethylene Company Ltd. and Algas Mineral Enterprises Ltd., now Novalta Resources Ltd. The latter was formed to carry out gas exploration and development. Later that year, AGTL formed Foothills Pipe Lines Ltd. with Westcoast Transmission Company Ltd. to continue its work on the Arctic pipeline project. By the end of 1974, AGTL's net income was C$17.8 million, almost triple its earnings a decade earlier.

In 1975 AGTL began to explore possibilities for producing ethylene, a derivative of natural gas used in plastics. At this time, Dow Chemical Company of Canada and Dome Petroleum Ltd. were also exploring petrochemical possibilities in Alberta, and Dow had plans to build such a plant. After resistance both from industry officials, about the need for two plants, and from the Alberta government, which had already given AGTL the go-ahead, the three companies decided to merge their plans. AGTL would build the plant near Red Deer, Alberta, supply Dow with the ethylene the plant produced, and allow Dome to build the pipeline that would transport the surplus chemicals to eastern Canada and the United States.

AGTL continued to acquire companies in 1975 and 1976, including Grove Valve and Regulator Company through its U.S. subsidiary, A.G. Industries International Inc., and WAGI International S.p.A., now Grove Italia S.p.A. In 1977 Q & M Pipe Lines Ltd., which formed a joint venture with Trans-Canada Pipe Lines Limited, was incorporated. The pipeline joint venture, Trans Quebec & Maritimes Pipeline Inc., was created to build a pipeline connecting Montreal to Nova Scotia. AGTL's net income in 1977 had grown to nearly US$58 million, and Blair was ready for his biggest move to date—a 35% share purchase in Husky Oil Ltd.

Husky Oil was a prominant oil and gas producer and marketer in Canada. Blair had watched Husky as a possible acquisition, but when another Canadian oil company, Petro-Canada, placed its bid, AGTL was forced to act. In the meantime, Husky called on U.S.-based Occidental Petroleum to counter the Petro-Canada bid. While officials of Occidental and Petro-Canada fought over the legalities of the takeover, AGTL, in what is known as a "creeping takeover," was buying shares in Husky openly, confounding both the Toronto Stock Exchange and the Ontario Securities Commission, which held that AGTL should have made its acquisition intentions public. AGTL had made its purchases in the New York market, however, outside of these bodies' jurisdiction. The Husky coup was a much-discussed incident in the industry, and once again, it was speculated that nationalism provided extra incentive for Blair, who wanted to rescue Husky from Occidental. By the following year, AGTL had purchased 69% of the Husky stock.

In 1980 AGTL changed its name to Nova, an Alberta Corporation, a name that better reflected the company's growing activities. Nova continued to assert itself in the marketplace, acquiring Western Star Trucks, Inc., a truck manufacturer, and forming a joint venture with the Alberta government for NovAtel Communications, a cellular telephone company. It also dissolved some joint ventures it had owned with Shell Canada Ltd. and built a polyethylene plant in Joffre, Alberta, in addition to the new plant it was planning to build with Dome Petroleum Ltd. at Empress, Alberta, for liquefied natural gas extraction. With its increased interests in petrochemicals, Nova formed Novacor Chemicals Ltd. in 1981 to manage and operate the plants.

These changes, however, could not deter such problems as a declining petrochemical industry and subsidiaries that were losing money. By 1982 a recession, coupled with severe price restrictions and higher taxes from Canada's national energy program, threatened the profitability of Nova's Husky Oil and Alberta Gas Chemicals. By the end of 1983, stockholders saw stock prices that had peaked at C$14.38 two years earlier plummet to C$6. The year 1984 was better for the company. Husky was able to sell off some of its assets, earning Nova a US$505 million profit, and Nova put its valve companies up for sale. Net income for that year quintupled 1983 income at C$203.4 million.

The year 1985 brought the deregulation in crude oil pricing, as well as a positive shift in taxes and other charges. Blair became chairman of Nova, in addition to his titles as president and CEO.

The company was also dealing with the scandal surrounding Husky Oil and its US$5 million lawsuit against John A. Grambling Jr. for breach of contract. Grambling had conspired with another businessman, Robert H. Libman, to illegally borrow US$100 million from several banks to buy Husky's Denver, Colorado–based refining and marketing unit. Eventually, the complex network of loans began to unravel, and both businessmen were caught. Grambling was indicted on 32 counts of bank fraud and Libman was indicted on 2 counts of conspiracy, among other charges. The year 1985 had been a difficult one in the oil industry overall, with a fall in crude oil prices and a large decrease in net income. Blair and other Nova officers took a 15% pay cut, and the company reported its first annual loss, of C$192 million.

Blair had to do some quick restructuring to rescue the company; in 1986, after much discussion, Nova took Husky private, retaining a 43% share and transferring 43% to a Hong Kong investment group led by Li Ka-shing, for C$855 million. A Canadian bank also retained some shares. The company name changed to Nova Corporation of Alberta, and shareholders' rights were reorganized so that class B shareholders, primarily gas companies, would no longer be allowed to elect members of Nova's board. Class A shareholders received full voting rights through the conversion of their shares into ordinary common shares. Blair also replaced Nova's president, Robert Pierce, with James Butler, chairman of Novacor Chemicals Ltd., Nova's petrochemicals subsidiary, and consolidated Novacor into Nova.

In 1988 Nova took over Polysar Energy & Chemical Corporation of Toronto, a petrochemicals company, for nearly C$1.92 billion. The takeover was hostile. The drawn-out battle ended when Nova agreed to pay Polysar its asking price. Blair ultimately felt the battle was worth it because it allowed Nova to expand its role in the global marketplace and achieve prominence as one of two of the largest ethylene producers in North America. At the same time, Husky bought Polysar's subsidiary, Canterra Energy Ltd., for C$400 million. Later that year, Husky was given permission through government financial backing to upgrade its Lloydminster plant, and Nova was guaranteed by the government a sustained supply of ethane, a necessary material for the production of ethylene, so that it could move ahead with plans to expand its petrochemicals output. The Canadian government, eager to build its Canadian resources, was very supportive of the growth of Nova Corporation. By the end of 1988, Nova reported net income of C$424 million.

The following year, import tariffs between Canada and the United States were eliminated, and the National Energy Board, which previously had placed certain controls on the export of natural gas, loosened its restrictions. In addition, Canada gained access to U.S. oil from the north slope of Alaska. Such changes encouraged an increase in natural gas trade between the two countries.

Conditions conspired to undercut Nova, however. The petrochemicals industry languished the following year, with tremendous financial repercussions on Nova. Coupled with the debt it took on to purchase Polysar, Nova's cash flow as well as its earnings shrunk to half that of the year before, and it was forced to put subsidiaries Novalta Resources, Grove Italia, Western Star Trucks, and Trans Quebec & Maritimes Pipelines up for sale. Nova also sold NovAtel Communications Ltd. to Alberta Government Telephones. Nova was restructured internally into autonomous divisions of petrochemicals, plastics, and rubber. Stock prices languished, and rumors circulated that the company might put its remaining interest in Husky up for sale.

By 1990 the oil industry was caught in the Persian Gulf crisis, which boosted oil prices temporarily. That year Nova President James Butler resigned, his position was left vacant, and all division presidents reported directly to Blair. Nova sold Grove Italia for approximately C$114 million to an Italian bank subsidiary and its Polysar rubber operations to Bayer AG of Germany for C$1.25 billion, in order to increase its earnings. It also began a program to ensure Nova's practices were environmentally sensitive. Nova's net income in 1990 was C$185 million, considerably lower than projected, due to volatile prices in the petrochemicals and plastics industries and due to the continuing debt caused by the acquisition of Polysar.

Along with several other Canadian energy companies, Nova rode the wave of the oil boom in the late 1970s and 1980s and was struggling to pick up the pieces in the 1990s. In addition, both Canada and the United States continued to suffer a recession in 1991. Subject to the disappointing profits of the heavy oil and gas industry and the fluctuating prices of the petro-chemical industry, in early 1991 Nova entered discussions with securities analysts to decide whether to sell off its interests in Husky Oil and whether to split its company into two separate entities, a pipeline concern and a petrochemical concern. Later that year, Nova decided to sell Husky for $325 million, after determining that a split was not feasible at the time. Blair retired September 1, 1991, and was succeeded as president and chief executive officer by J. E. (Ted) Newall, formerly chairman and chief executive officer of DuPont Canada Inc. Nova's natural gas transportation system through Alberta continued to be its stabilizing force.

Principal Subsidiaries: Pan-Alberta Gas Ltd. (50.005%); Foothills Pipe Lines Ltd. (50%); Novacorp International Consulting Inc.; Novalta Resources Inc.; Novacor Chemicals Ltd.

Further Reading: Carlisle, Tamsin, "Blair driven to rekindle Nova. Vindicating corporate 'child' a personal quest," *Financial Post,* March 22, 1990.

—Susan Telingator

OHIO EDISON COMPANY

76 South Main Street
Akron, Ohio 44308
U.S.A.
(216) 384-5100
Fax: (216) 384-5791

Public Company
Incorporated: 1930
Employees: 6,792
Sales: $2.23 billion
Stock Exchanges: New York Midwest

Ohio Edison Company is the 17th-largest investor-owned electric company in the United States in terms of kilowatt-hour sales. The company and a subsidiary, Pennsylvania Power Company, serve more than one million customers in a 9,000-square-mile region of central and northeastern Ohio and western Pennsylvania.

Ohio Edison Company was formed in the early months of the Great Depression and incorporated in June 1930 by The Commonwealth and Southern Corporation to consolidate five Ohio public utility companies. Those companies were Northern Ohio Power & Light Company of Akron, The Pennsylvania-Ohio Power & Light Company of Youngstown, The Ohio Edison Company of Springfield, The London (Ohio) Light & Power Company, and The Akron Steam Heating Company. The oldest of the five dates back to 1883, while predecessor companies, which include more than 300 already consolidated companies, date back to the Civil War.

The new Ohio Edison Company was a subsidiary of The Commonwealth & Southern Corporation, a New York–based holding company that bought all 600,000 shares of Ohio Edison's stock for $15 million in cash. Headquarters were established in Akron, Ohio, and A.C. Blinn was named vice president and general manager to lead the company, which began operations without a president.

Through consolidation, the parent company planned to improve the financial picture of the five companies by pooling resources. Upon incorporation of Ohio Edison, transportation assets belonging to the five former companies were transferred to three transportation companies, which for the first few years were operated under Ohio Edison's control before being spun off as separate entities.

During its first full year of operation Ohio Edison grew despite the Depression. A new office building was constructed

in Youngstown; and electric distribution systems were acquired through a trade, which brought Ohio Edison properties in Ravenna, Medina, Doylestown, and Seville, Ohio, in exchange for less-profitable assets north of Springfield, Ohio. In 1931 Ohio Edison also began construction of an East Akron power transmission line, which replaced power purchased from a Cleveland utility company.

The company's finances remained strained during the Depression, however, affecting personnel from top to bottom. Both lower level and senior management workers took pay cuts to keep their jobs, and stockholder dividends were suspended. The company often had to wait for customers to pay their bills, but it met its payrolls.

As a means of boosting electric sales, from its outset Ohio Edison promoted and marketed electric appliances, an aspect of operations that endured for more than four decades. During the early 1930s division offices established small appliance service departments and sales departments, which expanded their inventory as new products entered the marketplace.

Blinn was named Ohio Edison's first president in 1938 and continued to guide the company through most of World War II. After the United States entered the war in 1941, Ohio Edison and other utilities were placed under supervision of the War Production Board and were temporarily restricted from selling appliances and constructing new power lines.

Industrial electricity sales skyrocketed with wartime production. In response to increased need for power generation during the war, Ohio Edison constructed the new R.E. Burger plant in Belmont County, Ohio, and expanded plants in Akron, Marion, and Warren, Ohio.

In 1944 Blinn was replaced as president by the expansion-minded Walter Sammis, who had been instrumental in forming the company 14 years earlier. In 1944 in one of his first moves as president, Sammis orchestrated the acquisition of Pennsylvania Power Company (Penn Power) from Commonwealth & Southern. Penn Power had been incorporated through a consolidation move the same year Ohio Edison was formed, and as a new wholly owned subsidiary, it gave the Ohio Edison system more than 1,500 square miles of service area in western Pennsylvania.

Following the war, restrictions on utilities were lifted. Postwar prosperity made it easier to obtain credit, and Ohio Edison sales of new appliances boomed. At the same time, industrial expansion gave rise to increased residential and nonresidential electric sales and left the company in need of increased power generation. Ohio Edison responded to that need in the first few years following the war with additions to the Burger Plant and facilities in Springfield and Akron.

In its first postwar acquisition, in 1946 Ohio Edison acquired an electric distribution system serving McDonald, Ohio. Ohio Edison became an independent company in 1949 after the Securities and Exchange Commission (SEC) forced Commonwealth & Southern to divest its interests in Ohio Edison.

As a result of another SEC divestiture order, in 1949 Ohio Edison's competitor, Ohio Public Service Company (OPS), also became an independent company, and in 1950 Ohio Edison acquired OPS. The OPS merger added the Ohio communities of Sandusky, Marion, Mansfield, Massillon, Lorain, and Warren to the Ohio Edison system, pushing the company's customer base to more than 500,000 and making Ohio Edison the tenth-largest electric utility in the United States in terms of operating revenues.

To offset rising operating costs, in 1950 Ohio Edison initiated its first rate increase, which added about 22¢ a month to the average residential bill. During the mid-1950s Ohio Edison continued to add to its system and acquired distribution systems in the Ohio communities of Leroy, Huron, and Plain City.

To keep pace with those acquisitions and increased electrical use, postwar power plant expansion followed; and in 1954 the company added a new plant in Niles, Ohio. Additions to the Burger plant and the Edgewater plant in Lorain, Ohio, followed, and in 1959 the W.H. Sammis plant in Stratton was opened.

By the early 1960s Ohio Edison's service area had grown to within five miles of Cleveland's city limits, and Penn Power was within three miles of Pittsburgh. In 1962 Penn Power expanded its service area northward from Pittsburgh and acquired a 121-square-mile distribution system in Crawford County, Pennsylvania, abutting the parent company's Ohio network.

After 20 years at the helm, in 1964 Sammis retired and was replaced as president by D. Bruce Mansfield, who quickly moved Ohio Edison into an era of electric utility power pools formed through joint plant ownership. In 1965 Ohio Edison acquired the municipally owned distribution system of Lowellville, Ohio, just southeast of Youngstown. That same year Ohio Edison made its first move toward forming a power pool and joined with Cleveland Electric Illuminating Company (CEIC) to construct and operate a power plant addition for their common areas of service.

In 1967 Ohio Edison and Penn Power joined with CEIC, Duquesne Light Company, and Toledo Edison Company to form a power pool known as Central Area Power Coordination Group (CAPCO). Designed to share the burden of constructing and operating power plants, the CAPCO members initially committed to the installation of six large generating units.

In 1970 Ohio Edison, through a CAPCO project, began construction in Shippingport, Pennsylvania, on the firm's first nuclear-powered facility, Beaver Valley Power Station. Three years later the company discontinued its appliance sales operations, which had been declining since the 1950s.

Service area expansion continued. In 1972 Ohio Edison acquired the 5,700-customer municipal electric system of Norwalk, Ohio. It added the Hiram, Ohio, municipal system serving 271 customers and the former East Palatine, Ohio, municipal systems with its 2,653 customers in 1975.

John R. White, a former executive vice president and 22-year veteran of the company, succeeded Mansfield as president in 1975. That same year CAPCO's first new facility, the Bruce Mansfield plant in Shippingport, Pennsylvania, began operation under control of Penn Power, and in 1976 the first unit of the Beaver Valley nuclear plant began operation under the control of Duquesne Light Company; Ohio Edison owned a 35% share.

Despite the company's increased power capacity, White's five-year tenure as president was marred by weather, labor, and environmental complications. A long period of sub-zero days in January 1977, resulted in record electricity demand and made the Ohio River impassible for barges bringing coal to company plants. One year later, the worst blizzard in Ohio's history, on January 26 and 27, resulted in major power outages, with high winds and frigid temperatures stalling repairs for a time.

In 1978 a 109-day coal miners' strike depleted the company's fuel reserves at its coal-fired generating plants, forcing Ohio Edison to turn to backup generating sources and to purchase power from other utilities. That same year, 2,000 members of the Utility Workers Union of America went on strike for two months at five of Ohio Edison's nine plants and its two largest power-line operations. Foremen, supervisory personnel, and technicians ran the utility's operations. The strike was resolved only after the utility threatened to hire permanent replacement workers.

During the miners' strike the U.S. Environmental Protection Agency (EPA) filed suit against Ohio Edison to push the company into compliance with the Clean Air Act standards and install pollution-control devices. In a settlement reached three years later, Ohio Edison agreed to pay the government more than $1.5 million for past emission violations and install more than $500 million in antipollution devices, with the bulk earmarked for the company's Sammis Plant.

Mansfield retired in 1980 and was replaced by Justin T. Rogers, Jr., an executive vice president and 22-year veteran of the company. Rogers took over a company that officials conceded was suffering from inflation, a bulging construction budget, high fuel prices, and a low bond rating.

In one of his first moves as president, Rogers took Ohio Edison out of what had become its unprofitable steam power operations; in addition, steam systems in Akron and Youngstown were sold and a similar operation in Springfield abandoned. Citing the political and regulatory problems facing nuclear plants following the 1979 accident at Three Mile Island power plant, in 1980 CAPCO agreed to cancel four nuclear power plants scheduled for construction.

Including the 1981 settlement with the EPA over emission controls at the Sammis plant, during his first two years in office Rogers led the company over four major legal hurdles. In February 1980 Ohio Edison was one of four utilities that agreed to settle an antitrust suit filed by the city of Cleveland five years earlier. Ohio Edison denied charges of conspiring to force the city's municipal electric light plant out of business, but agreed to pay $500,000 to the city to avoid future litigation. It also was to provide technical assistance to the city's plant.

In March 1980 Ohio Edison dropped a one-year-old suit against Exxon Corporation over delivery of nuclear fuel, after Exxon agreed to renegotiate its contract. One year later North American Coal Co. consented to dropping a breach-of-contract suit it had filed against Ohio Edison, after the fuel supplier agreed to a contract giving the utility more favorable options for the purchase and delivery of coal.

With the help of new contracts, by 1982 Ohio Edison's average fuel costs were the lowest in the state for an investor-owned electric company. That same year Rogers began streamlining operations and cutting staff.

The company also began marketing its increased electric generating capacity in 1982 and during the next two years landed long-term bulk-sales contracts with utilities in New Jersey, Ohio, and Washington, D.C. To increase industrial sales in its own service area, in 1984 the company initiated a price incentive program for new or expanding industries.

In 1985 Ohio Edison suspended construction of the second unit of a nuclear power plant at North Perry, Ohio, but continued work on its Perry 1 and Beaver Valley 2 nuclear units, which became operational in November 1987. To reduce the revenue required to provide a profit on the two nuclear units, upon their completion Ohio Edison agreed to sell and then lease back portions of the units, while retaining a 41% interest in Beaver Valley 2 and 35% of Perry 1.

With the opening of the two nuclear units, Ohio Edison's credit rating received a boost in 1987. That same year, the company negotiated a 13-year coal contract with North American Coal. Ohio Edison also renegotiated a power sale agreement with Potomac Electric Power Company of Washington, D.C., in 1987, with an 18-year agreement expected to give Ohio Edison $150 million in annual sales.

With bulk sales on the rise and Ohio Edison's service area seeing an influx of diverse business and industry, in 1988 Ohio Edison's total sales surpassed the $2 billion mark for the first time. That same year the company formed two wholly owned finance-related subsidiaries, OES Capital, Incorporated and OES Fuel, Incorporated. Both subsidiaries began doing business in 1989, with OES Capital financing customer accounts receivable and OES Fuel financing the purchase of nuclear fuel.

During the late 1980s Ohio Edison began to actively change its image on environmental matters. In 1989 a coal technology project that reduced emissions at its Lorain, Ohio, plant received the Ohio Governor's Award for Outstanding Achievement in Waste Management and Pollution Control. In 1990 Ohio Edison began studying the feasibility of burning treated municipal waste at coal-fired generating plants and became the first Ohio utility to test-burn waste tires. The following year Ohio Edison was one of a group of utilities that won a $33 million government contract to build a system at the company's Niles plant to reduce pollutants associated with acid rain.

In line with its ongoing plans to trim payroll costs, in 1990 Ohio Edison initiated an employee stock ownership program to help the company reduce costs of matching contributions to employee savings plans. That same year Ohio Edison's bonus program for senior management was suspended. Ohio Edison began 1991 with 1,100 fewer employees than it had a decade earlier and was committed to further work force reductions.

The company's future plans call for delaying costly plant construction by encouraging off-peak hour use through rate incentives, maintaining its customer base through a public image of a utility with staying power and reasonable rates and broadening its sales through further incentives to new and expanding businesses. The company appears well positioned with enough generating capacity to carry it through the 20th century and to accommodate anticipated sales growth both in its service area and through power sale agreements. Ohio Edison seems poised to meet the 1996 compliance deadline established for the 1990 Clean Air Act amendments, with almost half of the company's generating capacity coming from nuclear or other units that will not need major additions of sulfur-dioxide control equipment.

Principal Subsidiaries: Pennsylvania Power Company; OES Capital, Incorporated; OES Fuel, Incorporated.

Further Reading: The Fiftieth Anniversary Issue: Ohio Edisonian, Akron, Ohio, Ohio Edison Company, 1980.

—Roger W. Rouland

OSAKA GAS CO., LTD.

4-1-2 Hiranomachi
Chuo-ku
Osaka 541
Japan
(06) 202 2221
Fax: (06) 226 1681

Public Company
Incorporated: 1897
Employees: 9,323
Sales: ¥559.39 billion (US$4.48 billion)
Stock Exchanges: Tokyo Osaka Nagoya

Osaka Gas Co., Ltd. (Osaka Gas) is Japan's second largest supplier of city gas, after Tokyo Gas. It supplies gas to over 15 million people in the Kansai area's major cities of Osaka, Kobe, and Kyoto, and surrounding suburban areas. Traditionally the company was involved only in the distribution of gas for lighting, heating, and power, but it has diversified into areas related to its engineering expertise. Today the Osaka Gas Group of companies, of which Osaka Gas is the nucleus, numbers more than 60 companies which engage in activities ranging from engineering services to information processing.

Osaka's gas industry originated in 1871 when Japan's first gas-powered lamp was unveiled, providing lighting for the city mint. This came just 18 years after the United States navy, under Admiral Perry, had forced Japan to open up her doors to the Western world and restore the power of the emperor for the first time since the 17th century. What followed was a remarkable and rapid period of industrial development, originating from the major cities of Tokyo and Osaka. The introduction of gas lighting to Osaka was soon repeated in Japan's other major cities. At the same time, kerosene lamps were also imported from the West. For a time the latter became more popular than gas, being easy to use, but widespread fires caused by these lamps convinced authorities that gas was the best source of city lighting. Consequently Osaka Gas was formed in 1897 with capital provided by the municipal authorities and also by overseas investors. Osaka Gas's foreign patron was the Edison power company in the United States. An Osaka businessman, Taro Asano, had met the president of Edison, Anthony Brady, while in New York, and the two became friends. Brady was impressed with Asano and sent an Edison representative, Alexander Chizon, to Osaka to arrange financing and aid the fledgling operation in technical matters. Along with Asano, in

1902 the Edison Company became a large shareholder in Osaka Gas, with a 50% stake, which it later sold to Japanese investors. Asano and other Japanese investors held the remaining 50%. Masagi Kataoka was chosen as the company's first president, and his first task was to prepare the infrastructure for the production and distribution of gas in Osaka. In the 19th century all city gas was produced using coal as the raw material; the technology required to tap and transport natural gas had yet to be developed. In the Iwazaki area of Osaka, a factory was constructed consisting of eight gas-producing retorts imported from the United States. Using coal, this factory could produce 4,000 cubic meters of gas per day. Underground piping was installed to transport this gas to various parts of the city. In the relatively short space of two years, from 1902 to 1904, 80 kilometers of piping were laid by manual laborers and animal power. A steel gas storage tank was constructed with a capacity of 10,000 cubic meters of gas. At the time it was hailed as the largest gas tank east of the Suez canal. In 1905, after Kataoka had traveled to New York to finalize arrangements for financing from the United States, gas supplies finally commenced. Initially 3,350 homes were connected and supplied with gas, which was monitored with installed meters. The price was, ¥0.08 per square meter, which meant that only the affluent could afford this new source of lighting.

Byproducts of the gas production process included coke, tar, and benzene, and were sold to industry. An agreement was signed with Sakamitsu Industries, a local metal-casting firm, to supply coke for Sakamitsu's metal reduction needs. Osaka Gas also began refining and selling coal tar that was, among other things, used to pave roads. By 1908 the success and expansion of the company seemed assured, with four branch offices opening throughout the city. By now the factory was operating at full capacity. Due to the comparatively high price and unreliability of electricity, the alternative source of power to city gas, demand for gas was high. In the rapidly expanding Japanese economy, gas-powered engines became popular. This trend began to change during the early 1900s, however, with the advent of hydroelectric power and the tungsten lamp replacing gas as a source of lighting energy. From this time onward, gas would be used for the more high-power function of heat production. For consumers, this meant the use of gas for heating and cooking and for industry in furnaces and engines.

Japan's victory in the Sino-Japanese War of 1897 and the Russo-Japanese War of 1904 made the country a major world power in both industrial and military terms, and the following 20 years were a period of intense economic growth. Although this growth brought rapid inflation, the price of gas rose by only 50% between 1905 and 1925. This compares with a rise of 250% in coal and rice prices and shows how heavily the industry was subsidized and regulated by the government. After World War I and the ensuing depression in Japan, Osaka Gas was allowed to regulate its prices. The management of the company under Kataoka set the long-term strategy of dropping gas prices during the Depression of the late 1920s. This had the twofold effect of preventing customers from being forced to give up their gas supply and winning the company new customers, as firewood became scarcer and more expensive as a source of heating. The results were dramatic; in 1927 the number of households supplied by Osaka Gas doubled to

110,000 and rose to 300,000 by 1933. During the late 1920s and early 1930s, the company conducted market research, sending employees out on door-to-door surveys of households in Osaka. A campaign was initiated to promote gas use in Osaka, utilizing billboards and exhibitions. In 1928 Kataoka and 20 of his executives traveled to the United States and Europe to witness the applications of city gas in the West. At an exhibition of gas appliances in Europe they saw gas-powered refrigerators manufactured by Electrolux of Sweden. The result of the visit was the promotion in Osaka of an array of gas-powered appliances, including refrigerators, irons, and rice cookers. The ensuing demand for gas prompted the construction of a second factory unit at the Iwazaki site in 1928, followed by a third in 1935.

In the 1930s the use of gas for home cooking spread throughout the major cities in Japan, including Osaka. In 1937 Osaka Gas decided to invest heavily in a major new project— the construction of a huge gas works on Yujima island in Osaka Bay. The facility, completed in 1940, was capable of producing 35,000 tons of gas per day and also manufactured tar, pitch, naphthalene, and benzene as byproducts for industrial use. A second coke burner was added in 1942. During this time the Japanese government was steering the economy toward war-related production, and Osaka Gas, as a key industry, was in close contact with the military government regarding its production plans. The Japanese invasion of Manchuria and China in 1931 gave Japan a plentiful and virtually free source of coal, that greatly aided the war machine. Consumer and industrial demand for gas soared during the war years.

During 1944, however, the tide turned against Japan, and its cities were increasingly the targets of bomber attacks by the B-29s of the United States Air Force. Although less publicized than the atomic bomb attacks, these raids resulted in far greater damage and casualties. Indeed, on August 14, 1945, the day Nagasaki was destroyed by an atomic bomb, Osaka was attacked by 180 B-29s resulting in widespread fires in the city, the destruction of 40,000 homes, and more than 80,000 casualties. This and similar raids caused severe damage to Osaka Gas's production and pipeline distribution facilities. All the major city gas companies in the region were similarly affected, and in December 1944 they merged to help ensure their survival. The main companies in this merger were Osaka Gas Co., Ltd., Kobe Gas Co., Ltd., and Kyoto Gas Co., Ltd. Following Japan's surrender, the Allied powers—led by the United States—took temporary control of the country. Gas supply in Osaka was sporadic at best and explosions, due to damaged pipelines, were frequent. The years 1945–1950 were spent identifying and repairing pipeline and reconnecting as many households as possible. Like most essential items in Japan immediately after the war, gas was rationed; its use by the public was limited to two hours a day.

In 1949, under the Law for the Elimination of Excessive Concentration of Economic Power, implemented by the Allies to break up the big Japanese industrial groups, the merged gas companies were split up, and Osaka Gas became a separate entity again. The year 1949 also saw the death of Kataoka, who had led the company since its founding. He was replaced by Jiro Iiguchi, a former vice-president of the company. During the years 1950 to 1955 Japan underwent a remarkable period of reconstruction that involved the united efforts of the entire Japanese population. Using manual labor when necessary, Osaka Gas began a full-scale rebuilding of its Yujima facility, which had returned to its prewar production level by 1952. A gas appliance research center was opened in the same year, and in 1953 the Yujima factory produced its first oil-based gas. Using German technology, high-pressure storage and gas transport mechanisms were added. A combination of U.S. aid and cheap educated labor fueled Japan's growth during the 1950s, and toward the end of the decade, the Japanese began to see the fruits of their hard work in the form of consumer goods such as televisions and cookers. The government promoted the use of gas in all areas of Japan as an alternative to firewood for cooking and heating. Osaka Gas stepped up its own promotional campaign, hailing gas as being four times as cheap and twice as quick as electricity, for equivalent costs, for heating and cooking purposes. Customer service was made a priority, with a fleet of three-wheeled motorized bicycles providing emergency cover and a Univac computer introduced at the company's Osaka headquarters.

In 1960 the capacity of the Yujima factory was increased. In 1962 the production capacity at Iwazaki was closed, the site being demoted to a storage facility. Osaka Gas's high-pressure storage and supply network was expanded in 1961 into what became known as the 370 kilometer network, in reference to the length of high-pressure gas piping installed throughout the city. In 1964 the company announced a "calorie-up" program in which the energy content of its city gas was upgraded from 3,600 kilocalories per cubic meter to 4,500. This necessitated the inspection of 6.5 million appliances in 1.7 million homes being supplied by Osaka Gas. The company also began to sell gas to customers who were not connected by the pipe network, in the form of liquid propane gas (LPG) steel canisters. Company representatives delivered filled canisters to customers and took away the empty ones for refilling.

By 1965 Osaka Gas was a major corporation with several thousand employees and staff training facilities. A 5-day 40-hour working week was introduced. A 160-strong research and development center was opened in 1966, adjacent to the production site on Yujima. By 1968 the Japanese economy ranked second only to the United States in terms of gross national product (GNP), which continued to grow uninterrupted between 1966 and 1973. This period, known as the Izanagi Boom, ended abruptly with the oil shock of 1973. Japan had come to rely on cheap plentiful Middle Eastern oil for more than 70% of its energy needs, and when OPEC trebled its oil prices overnight the effects on the economy were profound. In 1974, for the first time since World War II, the Japanese economy registered a negative year-on-year growth figure of -0.5%, and the Japanese government set about reducing its dependency on oil. There were three major alternatives: nuclear power, coal, and natural gas. At that stage Osaka Gas produced all of its gas from relatively cheap oil and coal, the import of natural gas being uneconomical. Technological advances in the storing and transport of natural gas as a liquid, coupled with the sharp increase in the price of oil, now made the import of natural gas feasible. Osaka Gas began to amass a supply of gas in 1980, with huge refrigeration ships transporting the liquid natural gas (LNG) at -160°C from fields throughout Southeast Asia and Australia. This achievement required the rapid development of refrigeration technology by the company, which it undertook with other Japanese users, notably Tokyo Gas. Beginning in 1980 Osaka Gas relied increasingly on LNG for the bulk of its gas supply, and by 1990 it used LNG exclusively.

During the 1980s Osaka Gas used its considerable engineering expertise to diversify into other areas. This process began with the sale of coal-related byproducts such as coke, benzene, and coal-tar products, which have been supplied by the company since its founding. In 1987 a subsidiary, Donac Company, was formed to produce the Donacarbo carbon fibers used in a range of products, including golf clubs, that are sold throughout the world. Another subsidiary, Harman Company, develops and manufactures gas-run appliances and has relied heavily on Osaka Gas's research and development facilities. Osaka Gas imports three million tons of LNG, about 10% of Japan's total. It has used the low temperature of the gas while being shipped to collaborate with the food industry, forming Kinki Cryogenics as a supplier of frozen foods. This subsidiary also became the first company in the world to utilize LNG to produce liquid carbon dioxide.

In 1978 Osaka Gas Engineering was formed, providing technological assistance to outside clients. Offices were established in California, U.S.A., and London, England, in the late 1980s to market this expertise. Like many Japanese utility and transportation companies, Osaka Gas has taken advantage of rapidly rising city land prices between 1984 and 1990. As a major land owner in Osaka, it formed Urbanex Company in 1989 to develop surplus company land for commercial and private use. Other diversified businesses include retail and restaurant operations and business consulting services.

The supply of gas remains the core business of the Osaka Gas Group, accounting for almost 75% of revenue. The group is organized into five main business divisions: gas-related, refrigeration, engineering services, computer services, and consumer services. The last division, which includes real estate, is the fastest-growing. The group has recently announced a restructuring whereby these divisions will be given more independence. Masafumi Ohnishi, president since 1981, has stated his desire to increase the international activities of Osaka Gas in many of the group's business areas. This policy, along with continued diversification and investment in new technology, will ensure that Osaka Gas inclusion among the most successful and interesting of the Japanese utilities during the 1990s.

Principal Subsidiaries: AD'ALL Co., Ltd.; DONAC Co., Ltd.; Harman Co., Ltd.; Kansai Tar & Chemical Products Co., Ltd.; Kinki Coke Sales Co., Ltd.; Kinki Piping Co., Ltd.; Osaka Gas Europe plc. (U.K.); Rinku Energy Center Corporation; Cold Air Products Co., Ltd.; Kinki Cryogenics Co., Ltd.; KRI International, Inc. (U.S.A.); Kyoto Research Park Corporation; Planet Pacific, Inc. (U.S.A.); Osaka Gas Information System Co., Ltd; Active Life, Inc.; OG Auto Service Co., Ltd.; OG Credit Co., Ltd.; OG Industries Co., Ltd; Osaka Gas Housing Equipment Co., Ltd.; Rinku Energy Center Building Corporation; Urbanex Co., Ltd.

Further Reading: Livingstone, J., J. Moore, and F. Oldfather, *Postwar Japan, 1945 to Present,* London, Random House, 1973.

—Dylan Tanner

PACIFIC ENTERPRISES

633 West Fifth Street
Los Angeles, California 90071
U.S.A.
(213) 895-5000
Fax: (213) 629-1225

Public Company
Incorporated: 1907 as Pacific Lighting Corporation
Employees: 42,000
Sales: $6.92 billion
Stock Exchanges: New York Pacific

Pacific Enterprises was formed in 1988, two years after Pacific Lighting Corporation bought Thrifty Corporation, which owned drug, discount, and sporting-goods stores. Pacific Lighting's main business had been Southern California Gas Company, the largest gas utility in the United States, supplying about 15 million people in a 23,000-square-mile territory that includes the Los Angeles area. Pacific Enterprises also engages in oil and gas exploration and drilling.

Pacific Lighting Corporation was founded in San Francisco in 1886 as Pacific Lighting Company by C.O.G. Miller and Walter B. Cline. Both men, who had worked for Pacific Gas Improvement Company—owned by Miller's father—saw an opportunity to start their own business when their employer decided not to use the newly invented Siemens gas lamp. Miller and Cline began buying Siemens lamps in San Francisco and soon expanded into the southern California utility business, buying a half interest in a gas manufacturing plant in San Bernardino, California. Their business flourished, and in 1889 Pacific Lighting Company bought three Los Angeles-area gas and electric firms with combined assets of more than $1 million. Miller and Cline created a subsidiary, Los Angeles Lighting Company, to consolidate the three formerly competing firms. Pacific Lighting's attention remained focused on the Los Angeles area for most of the next century.

Pacific Lighting supplied the gas and lighting for the small but rapidly growing city of Los Angeles. Los Angeles Lighting immediately began to make needed improvements in the Los Angeles gas system, also dropping its prices. The company faced stiff competition from numerous small utilities during the 1890s, however, that retarded its growth. To help increase profits, Los Angeles Lighting began importing and selling coal and selling gas-powered appliances, hoping to stimulate the demand for gas. Pacific Lighting then bought a controlling interest in Los Angeles Electric Company in 1890, and in 1904 it combined all of its Los Angeles lighting and electric operations to form Los Angeles Gas and Electric Company (LAG&E). In 1907 Pacific Lighting Company was incorporated and changed its name to Pacific Lighting Corporation.

Pacific Lighting's gas sales increased tenfold between 1896 and 1906 as Los Angeles expanded. Sales grew further, after the San Francisco earthquake of 1906 caused many to move from northern California to Los Angeles. The city grew so fast that LAG&E could not meet demand, and some parts of the city went without gas for days during cold spells in the winter of 1906 to 1907. Seeing an opportunity, a group of Los Angeles businessmen created the City Gas Company in an effort to win LAG&E's disaffected customers. The City Gas Company could not match the resources of the older LAG&E, however, and in 1910 it sold out to Pacific Light and Power, which owned Southern California Gas Company, one of LAG&E's largest competitors. A conservatively run company, LAG&E concentrated on supplying its service area and collecting its rates while rivals Southern Gas and Southern Counties Gas Company of California worked on new gas technology.

By 1915 the Los Angeles utility industry was dominated by LAG&E and three other firms. These utilities were extremely unpopular with the public and had to continually fight off the threat of municipal ownership and government regulation. LAG&E and the other utilities fought Los Angeles's attempts to build a municipal electric system by trying to block the financing and by launching time-consuming lawsuits. In 1917 the utilities came under the jurisdiction of the newly formed California Public Utilities Commission (CPUC).

Because LAG&E supplied Los Angeles's densely populated downtown area, where operating costs were low, a municipal utility would not be able to match LAG&E's rates. This situation slowed the momentum of the municipal ownership movement, and the battle remained stalemated throughout the 1920s. Meanwhile, southern California continued to grow rapidly, and LAG&E put its resources into expanding its services, spending $10 million to build a new electric plant and enlarge its substations. To fight off municipal ownership, LAG&E began a public relations campaign and sold stock.

After the Great Depression began in 1929, the tide shifted toward municipal ownership of utilities, partly because cash-starved citizens hoped municipal ownership would lower their bills, and partly because of the anti-corporation political climate. In 1929 the city of Los Angeles announced it was going to buy LAG&E electrical properties. The city had contracted to buy a share of the hydroelectric power produced by the new Hoover Dam and wanted to use LAG&E's power grid to deliver it. The company's electric properties provided one-sixth of its revenue, so it fought the move as long as it could. LAG&E, however, needed to renew its gas franchise, and the city would do that only if LAG&E agreed to sell its electric properties. LAG&E sold the properties in 1937 for $46 million.

Though stung by the loss of LAG&E's electric operations, Pacific Lighting continued to grow as a gas utility. Pacific Lighting ran its operations conservatively, initially expanding its services only to regions that could be served by existing gas generating plants. As natural gas became more widely available in California, Pacific Lighting's gas operations expanded.

Pacific Lighting acquired control of the gas distribution systems of Southern Counties Gas in 1925, Santa Maria Gas

Company in 1928, and Southern California Gas in 1929. These companies had expanded more aggressively than Pacific Lighting, particularly around Los Angeles, in some cases quadrupling output during the 1920s. Part of this expansion came from the rapid growth of Los Angeles, and part from new uses for gas, such as space heating and water heating. By 1930 Los Angeles led the United States in natural gas consumption, and Pacific provided gas to half the population of California by 1930. It was the largest gas utility in the United States, serving nearly two million people. Pacific Lighting made broad policy decisions for its new subsidiaries, leaving the day-to-day operating decisions to the management of those firms.

Natural gas was a more efficient and less expensive fuel than manufactured gas. Because Pacific Lighting and its subsidiaries had switched to natural gas during the 1920s, both gas rates and gas consumption dropped. To compensate for the loss in volume, Pacific Lighting successfully promoted gas for industrial use. Industrial customers were attracted to the low rates and ease of handling associated with natural gas as well as to the fact that natural gas did not require storage facilities. Industries used natural gas primarily during the summer to absorb Pacific Lighting's excess capacity, while during the winter Pacific Lighting required industries to use more energy from other sources. To maintain natural gas sources as the fuel became more scarce in the Los Angeles area, Pacific Lighting built longer pipelines, aided by improvements in technology.

Pacific Lighting worked on advertising campaigns with other gas utilities during the Great Depression to counter the belief that gas supplies would soon run out and to push the sales of gas-fueled appliances. This successful campaign helped the company weather the Depression, despite decreased use of its gas by industry.

In 1933 an earthquake caused extensive damage to Pacific Lighting's gas pipeline system, as did torrential rains in 1938. In an attempt to help recoup some of the losses suffered during the 1930s, Pacific attempted to combine Southern Counties Gas and Southern California Gas. The request was denied by California regulators, however, on the grounds that two companies, even if owned by the same holding company, would produce more competition than would one company.

During World War II Pacific Lighting diverted energy to defense manufacturers and converted an old gas plant to the manufacture of war-related chemicals. The demand for natural gas increased dramatically during and after the war, and Pacific Lighting sought new means of keeping pace. Because new defense industries drew yet more people to southern California, conditions for the company during the late 1940s and 1950s were similar to those during the 1920s, requiring large capital outlays for new construction.

In 1947 Pacific Lighting spent $25 million to build the Biggest Inch pipeline, which brought large amounts of natural gas to California from southern Texas. Demand grew so quickly that an extension to the large gas fields of the Texas panhandle was built in 1949. The company also built vast underground storage areas in southern California. Over the next ten years Pacific Lighting greatly increased the volume of its interstate delivery system, and out-of-state gas made up 90% of the company's supply. In addition, the company had promoted gas-powered appliances so effectively that 90% of all cooking ranges and 98% of water heaters and home heating systems in

southern California used natural gas. To meet demand, Pacific Lighting offered industries low rates in exchange for using other energy sources when demand peaked on cold winter days.

By 1950 the cost of bringing gas to customers had doubled since the years before World War II, but rates had risen only 15%. Pacific Lighting repeatedly sought unpopular rate hikes during the 1950s, and it increased its public relations efforts to help improve its image. Prices stabilized in the early 1960s as a result of regulatory changes that gave Pacific Lighting and its suppliers greater pricing flexibility. By the mid-1960s Pacific Lighting had become the largest gas supplier in the world, and its prices were among the lowest in the United States. C.O.G. Miller died in 1952, and his son Robert Miller became chairman.

In 1965 Pacific Lighting restructured its pipeline subsidiary, Pacific Lighting Gas Supply Company changing its name to Pacific Lighting Service and Supply. In 1967 the firm moved its headquarters from San Francisco to Los Angeles.

In 1970 Pacific Lighting received regulatory permission to merge Southern California and Southern Gas into one company, called Southern California Gas Company. Pacific Lighting created another subsidiary in 1972, Pacific Lighting Coal Gasification Company, to build a coal gasification plant.

Despite the new pipelines, by the late 1960s gas supplies were dwindling again. Paul Miller, who became president of Pacific Lighting in 1968, sought additional supplies across an increasingly wider area, including Alaska, the Canadian Arctic, and the Rocky Mountains. In 1970 the company created a subsidiary, Pacific Lighting Gas Development Company, to find new gas sources. It soon signed a contract with Gulf Oil Canada to purchase large amounts of gas from a new pipeline that the company was building in Canada's Northwest Territories. Pacific Lighting also got involved in the Alaska Natural Gas Transportation System approved by the U.S. government in 1976, although more than a decade passed before any gas from the project was transported to southern California.

The 1970s energy crisis presented grave problems. Energy needs were increasing while Pacific Lighting's gas suppliers began cutting back the company's supplies. Pacific Lighting considered bringing in liquid gas from overseas, working with Pacific Gas & Electric, another California utility. The two firms began construction of a liquid natural gas plant at Little Cojo Bay, California, in 1979, although construction was halted in 1984 because the natural gas shortage had eased. The shortage ended because of conservation efforts and because of a federal law passed in 1978 that partially deregulated prices for new gas finds. The deregulation led to higher prices that in turn caused widespread complaints, however, and the company launched another public relations campaign on radio and television to explain why prices were rising.

The price increases, fuel shortages, and slowing population growth in southern California convinced Pacific Lighting executives to begin diversifying. At first Pacific Lighting's new affiliates were gas-related, but soon the company branched into real estate, air conditioning, agriculture, alternative energy, and retailing. In the early 1970s Southern California Gas began two major solar energy research projects. More importantly, the company moved into gas and oil exploration and development. In 1975 Pacific Lighting Exploration Company invested in drilling in the Dutch sector of the North Sea. The ventures into agriculture and air conditioning were sold off in the late 1970s and early 1980s. In 1987 the firm sold its real estate operations for $325 million, believing the money could be more profitably invested elsewhere.

In 1983 Pacific Lighting bought Terra Resources, which owned oil and gas property in 18 states. In 1988 it bought Sabine Corporation, a Dallas, Texas–based exploration firm. By the late 1980s oil and gas exploration provided 11% of Pacific Lighting's revenue. Pacific Lighting still wanted to move into areas unrelated to the utility business, however, and in 1986 it bought Thrifty Corporation, a chain of Los Angeles–based retail stores. The purchase brought Pacific Lighting 500 Thrifty Drug Stores, 27 Thrifty Jr. drugstores, and 89 Big 5 sporting goods stores. Pacific acquired Thrifty in a stock swap valued at $886 million, or 25 times Thrifty's annual earnings.

Thrifty had been founded in 1919 by two brothers, Harry and Robert Borun, with their brother-in-law, Norman Levin. Initially the firm sold drugs and sundries wholesale. After the stock market crash in 1929, the firm opened its own cut-rate drugstores. By World War II the firm operated 17 stores in the Los Angeles area. In the 1950s, with strip malls appearing and Thrifty's sales dropping, the firm switched to larger stores with a broader selection. In the 1970s, with competition increasing, Thrifty adopted a more aggressive marketing strategy, switching from low-end promotions to a policy of total discounts. By the mid-1980s the firm feared a hostile takeover. When Pacific Lighting offered to buy Thrifty, the company reluctantly accepted, partly because Pacific Lighting had a reputation for allowing its subsidiaries great freedom.

Pacific Lighting moved further into retailing in the next two years, buying more sporting-goods retailers in the Midwest and in Colorado, more than 100 Pay'n Save drugstores, and 37 Bi-Mart general merchandise stores. These purchases made Pacific Lighting the second-largest sporting-goods retailer in the United States and the largest drugstore chain in the western United States.

To reflect its increasing diversity, Pacific Lighting changed its name to Pacific Enterprises in 1988. Paul Miller retired in 1989, and James R. Ukropina became chairman and CEO, ending 103 years of leadership by the Miller family.

In buying Thrifty, Pacific Enterprises had decided to trade short-term profits for long-term growth. The purchase left Pacific Enterprises short of funds, however, while its retail operations suffered from price wars, shoplifting, increased competition from supermarkets, and changing economics. The company also failed to find any large oil or gas deposits. To pay its stock dividends, Pacific Enterprises borrowed money or raised it by issuing stock, worrying some Wall Street analysts. To deal with the situation, Ukropina restructured management and temporarily cut back on oil and gas drilling. Revenue for 1990 was $6.92 billion, though the firm suffered a net loss of $43 million because of write-offs relating to its retail and gas and oil exploring operations.

Principal Subsidiaries: Southern California Gas Company; Pacific Enterprises Oil Company; Thrifty Corporation.

Further Reading: Littlefield, Douglas R., and Thanis C. Thorne, *The Spirit of Enterprise,* Los Angeles, Pacific Enterprises, 1990.

—Scott M. Lewis

PACIFIC GAS AND ELECTRIC COMPANY

77 Beale Street
San Francisco, California 94106
U.S.A.
(415) 972-7000
Fax: (415) 973-0956

Public Company
Incorporated: 1905
Employees: 26,200
Sales: $9.47 billion
Stock Exchanges: New York Pacific London Basel Zürich
    Amsterdam

Pacific Gas and Electric Company is the largest investor-owned gas and electric utility in the United States in terms of sales. It has a service area covering about 94,000 square miles—most of northern and central California—and a population of more than ten million people. The company is regulated by one of the toughest state regulatory bodies in the United States, the California Public Utility Commission.

Pacific Gas and Electric Company (PG&E) was formed in 1905 by John Martin and Eugene de Sabla, Jr., to acquire and merge power companies in central California. Martin and de Sabla, who had earlier been involved with gold mines in the Yuba River region north of Sacramento, California, began in the 1890s to use hydroelectric power to operate their mines. De Sabla located customers and raised the capital for their first hydroelectric plant in Nevada City, California, in 1895; Martin handled the engineering with help from William Stanley, developer of the Westinghouse alternating-current electrical system. The plant proved successful and convinced them there was a market for electrical power in Sacramento and San Francisco. They built another plant in 1898 and in 1899 formed Yuba Power Company to build a third, more powerful facility.

In 1900 the three plants were consolidated into Bay Counties Power Company, with de Sabla as president and general manager. In 1901 the company built a 140-mile transmission line, the world's longest at that time, to power an electric railway in Oakland, California. The line, suspended across the San Francisco Bay, carried 60,000 volts—a very high voltage for the time—and attracted great publicity. The company then joined its three plants into a single power grid, although it remained primarily a power-generating company, not a distribution-based utility.

In 1903 de Sabla and Martin formed California Gas & Electric Company (CG&E) to buy power companies and merge them into a large electric grid that could use economies of scale to its advantage. In the next few years CG&E bought many power companies, backed by capital from New York financiers. CG&E's acquisitions included long-established utilities like Oakland Gas Light & Heat Company, serving Oakland and Berkeley, and United Gas & Electric Company, serving communities south of San Francisco. In 1905 de Sabla and Martin bought San Francisco Gas & Electric Company (SFG&E), the dominant utility in San Francisco, giving the company a power grid in the most important city in central California. They merged SFG&E with CG&E to form Pacific Gas and Electric Company, capitalized at about $45 million. The San Francisco company had steam power plants, which complemented PG&E's hydroelectric plants by carrying peak loads when demand was high or when freezes or droughts cut hydroelectric output.

PG&E continued buying power companies and merging electric grids. By 1914 it owned the largest integrated regional system on the Pacific Coast and was one of the five largest utilities in the United States. It supplied 1.3 million people in a 37,000-square-mile area and had 36% of California's electric and gas business. During most of this period the company's steam-power capacity was growing faster than its hydroelectric capacity, partly because of the falling price of California crude oil. In 1912 PG&E began to increase its hydroelectric capacity. Using water from the South Yuba and Bear Rivers, it built a series of six plants with a projected capacity of 190,750 horsepower. A 110-mile transmission line strung across steel towers carried 100,000 volts to PG&E's switching station at Cordelia, California.

PG&E also continued to grow through mergers. In 1927 it bought the Sierra and San Francisco Power Company, and in 1930 it bought its only major competitor, the Great Western Power Company. In 1935 PG&E consolidated the operations of the companies it had bought.

PG&E and most other electric utilities were not greatly affected by the Great Depression because of their status as monopolies. Most sales that were lost to declining industry were made up by increasing residential sales.

In 1948 Pacific signed an interchange agreement with Southern California Edison Company that stated that either company would sell the other excess electricity when needed until 1962. PG&E continued to expand, buying Vallejo Electric Light & Power Company in 1949 and Pacific Public Service Company in 1954. By 1955 PG&E's network extended into 46 counties in northern and central California. It supplied electricity to 168 cities and towns and gas to 146 cities and towns. Pacific operated 57 hydroelectric plants and 12 steam plants generating about 84% of its total electric output, but bought 68% of its gas from El Paso Natural Gas Company. The company had 18,000 employees. Total revenue for 1954 was $386 million.

In 1957 PG&E and the General Electric Company constructed the small Vallecitos atomic power plant. Plans for a large nuclear power plant at Bodega Bay, north of San Francisco, were scrapped in the early 1960s because of public opposition. The company constructed a 63,000-kilowatt nuclear power plant at Humboldt Bay near Eureka, California, in 1963. From 1968 to 1970, Pacific participated in a design study of a 350,000-kilowatt sodium-cooled nuclear power plant. The company contributed $10 million over the following ten years to a joint U.S. government-industry project to build the first large sodium-cooled reactor. It also began construction of two pressurized-water nuclear power plants at Diablo Canyon, expected to total one million kilowatts. The plants were scheduled to be finished in 1975 and 1976.

By 1973 PG&E was the second-largest utility in the United States, with 65 hydroelectric plants and 12 steam electric plants and total revenue of $494 million. The Diablo Canyon nuclear power plants, however, were running years behind schedule. PG&E entered the 1970s expecting demand to increase by 6% to 7% annually, as it had for years; but California was growing rapidly, and demand grew faster than PG&E had projected. In addition, natural gas, which fueled the steam electric plants, was in short supply in California. The energy crisis of the early 1970s sent the price of gas skyrocketing, and the company's natural gas business shriveled. Between 1975 and 1984 PG&E lost 60% of its industrial gas sales.

PG&E announced the urgent need to convert its plants to oil, which was also in short supply. At a cost of $100 million, the conversion involved building moorings for oil supertankers at 7 of PG&E's 12 steam electric plants. To pay for the conversion, the company asked for a $233 million rate increase by 1975, the largest in California history.

The California Public Utilities Commission (CPUC), the state body that regulates PG&E, traditionally had been one of the toughest in the United States. From 1966 to 1974, however, when Ronald Reagan was governor of California, the CPUC became more sympathetic to utilities. One decision by the Reagan-appointed commission allowed utilities to increase rates without public hearings as the price of oil increased. By early 1974, with the price of oil soaring, rate increases were enacted almost monthly. As a result, PG&E's $233 million rate increase received wide news coverage and was opposed vigorously by consumer groups, which used public outrage to push for utility reform. Jerry Brown, Reagan's successor, appointed reform-oriented commissioners to the CPUC. In 1975 the CPUC ordered PG&E to offer a minimal amount of electricity at subsidized rates to all residential customers. The move was opposed by PG&E and its largest customers, whose electric rates would pay for the subsidy.

PG&E also faced opposition from environmentalists. The Environmental Defense Fund (EDF) confronted the utility, claiming PG&E would not need to build more power plants if it used its existing capacity more wisely. Both sides ran television commercials to push their viewpoints. The EDF eventually helped pressure PG&E into using alternative energy suppliers such as windmill farms, and use-strategies such as redirecting customer demand to stretch generating capacity further. By the late 1970s PG&E was offering incentives to customers who fulfilled their energy requirements at nonpeak hours.

In 1979 the CPUC granted PG&E a $269 million annual rate increase, but it also pushed the company to buy more power from alternative energy sources. In 1980 the CPUC granted a $530 million gas- and electric-rate increase, but over the next few years it ordered the company to give several refunds. Net income for 1980 was $525 million. In 1981 the CPUC authorized the company to begin a six-year, interest-free home loan program for customers who installed insulation or energy-saving devices.

One of the two Diablo Canyon nuclear plants was finished in 1981, but PG&E did not receive permission to begin testing because of concerns that the plant, located just two miles from an earthquake fault, was not safe. Questions were also raised about quality control during the plant's construction. Protesters blockaded the plant for two days while the U.S. Nuclear Regulatory Commission considered approving its start-up. Permission was granted in late 1981, and in 1982 the company hired Bechtel Power Corporation to manage the project while it was completed and licensed. In late 1983 uranium fuel was finally loaded into the Diablo Canyon reactor, and testing began in 1984. The company then requested rate increases to pay for the plant, which cost $5.8 billion, 18 times initial projections.

At the same time the company continued buying electricity from alternative sources. Under the 1978 Public Utility Regulatory Policies Act, U.S. electric utilities were required to buy power offered by independent producers at prices set by state utility commissions. In 1982 PG&E signed a contract to buy most of the wind-generated power from a wind farm in Solano County, California. In 1983 it agreed to buy all the electricity from a solar-energy power plant being built by a subsidiary of Atlantic Richfield Company. By mid-1986 PG&E had signed 695 contracts to buy 20% of alternative capacity planned for the United States, more than half of PG&E's own capacity. The company had so many alternative generating contracts that it had excess capacity.

In 1982 PG&E appointed Richard Clarke as head of utility operations. Clarke won CPUC approval to overhaul the structure of natural gas rates for PG&E's industrial customers. That move helped reverse a long decline in gas sales and doubled the utility's net income to $1 billion during the next four years. Also in 1982 the CPUC ordered PG&E to suspend its large fuel-oil contract with Chevron USA Inc. PG&E had signed a long-term contract with Chevron during the early 1970s, when natural gas prices and power-demand projections were high. In 1981, however, capacity increased due to alternative electric sources, and natural gas prices dropped. In part because PG&E had contracted to buy more expensive fuel oil, residential electric rates rose 6% in 1981. The CPUC used contingency provisions in PG&E's oil contract that allowed for suspension of deliveries if a government agency ordered it.

In 1984 the CPUC granted the company $697 million in rate increases, a 1.7% hike. Net income for 1984 was $975 million. In 1985 the CPUC ordered PG&E to lower its natural gas rates by $316.9 million per year. The following year the company acquired the 48.9% of Pacific Gas Transmission Company that it did not already own in a stock swap valued at $164 million, and in 1986 Pacific Gas Transmission became a wholly owned subsidiary of PG&E.

In 1986 Richard Clarke became chairman and chief executive officer of PG&E, and George Maneatis became president. While PG&E's managers had traditionally begun as engineers, Clarke was an attorney-turned-manager, and his experience as an attorney served his company's interest in the ensuing years.

California had become the most competitive power market in the United States, partly because of high rates the CPUC had mandated for independent power generators. Because PG&E had to buy relatively high-priced power from independents, the company's electricity rates were forced up. To protect residential customers from the rising costs, the CPUC raised industrial power rates and used them to subsidize residential rates. As a result, many large industrial customers devised plans to build their own power stations, or to import power from other states where electricity was 15% to 30% cheaper. To be more competitive, Clarke pressed the CPUC to make changes that would allow his company to offer better rates to large customers and to set up a major accounts program that would give individual attention to PG&E's biggest customers.

In 1988 PG&E reorganized into five new business divisions. Four of the divisions focused on primary markets: electric supply, gas supply, distribution, and nonutility business. The electric supply division generated, transported, bought, and sold electricity for the distribution division and for other wholesale customers throughout the western United States. The gas supply division acquired natural gas for the distribution and electric supply divisions and for large customers outside PG&E's service area; it operated about 5,000 miles of pipeline from southern California to Alberta, Canada, as well as underground storage tanks. The distribution division provided gas, electric, and steam service to customers and was responsible for maintaining the customer base. The nonutility operations included natural gas exploration and production, enhanced oil recovery, real estate development, and power plant operations. The company formed a subsidiary, PG&E Enterprises, to manage the nonutility businesses. The fifth division, engineering and construction, provided services to the other divisions and was responsible for designing and building most of the company's dams, power plants, and other transmission and distribution systems. The new structure was designed to help managers identify costs, know their customers, understand their competition, and respond quickly to technological and regulatory changes.

In 1988 the company took a $576 million charge to pay for cost overruns during the construction of the Diablo Canyon nuclear plant. The charge reduced net income for 1988 to $62.1 million.

Also in 1988 PG&E–Bechtel Generating Company, a joint venture of PG&E and Bechtel Power, began construction of its first power plant, in Montana. The joint venture was formed to build and operate plants outside of PG&E's territory. By 1990 the venture had completed the Montana plant, had one under way in Pennsylvania, and was planning another in New Jersey.

PG&E was well prepared for the major earthquake that hit the San Francisco area in 1989. Although power was cut off from 1.4 million customers, it was restored to 1 million of them within 12 hours. The company sustained $100 million in damage, mostly to transmission and generating equipment, with distribution and communications barely disrupted.

PG&E has one of the United States's most far-reaching affirmative-action policies. While few women or minority employees had reached the company's top echelon of 49 officers, by the early 1990s they comprised 20% of the 1,800 upper- and middle-level managers.

In 1990 the company added a sixth division, nuclear power generation, which was responsible for the Diablo Canyon nuclear power plants and the support services they required. Earnings were strong in 1990, with an increase of 10.5% from 1989. PG&E had held the operating costs of its utility business at 1986 levels, while utility revenues had increased 20% during the years 1986 to 1990. The utility business accounted for about 70% of PG&E's earnings in 1990, but the company, through PG&E Enterprises, continued to pursue nonutility ventures that offered a potentially higher return than the strictly regulated utility operations.

Principal Subsidiaries: Pacific Gas Transmission Company; Alberta and Southern Gas Company Limited (Canada); Pacific Gas Properties Co.; Standard Pacific Gas Line Inc. (85.71%); Pacific Conservation Services Co.; PG&E Enterprises; Mission Trail Insurance (Cayman) Ltd.; Pacific Energy Fuels Co.; Pacific Northwest Gas Systems Inc.; Pacific California Gas System, Incorporated; Magnesium Company of Canada Ltd.

Further Reading: Hughes, Thomas P., *Networks of Power,* Baltimore, Johns Hopkins University Press, 1983.

—Scott M. Lewis

▰◆ PACIFICORP

PACIFICORP

700 Northeast Multnomah
Portland, Oregon 97232
U.S.A.
(503) 731-2000
Fax: (503) 233-0508

Public Company
Incorporated: 1910 as Pacific Power & Light Company
Employees: 16,426
Sales: $3.78 billion
Stock Exchanges: New York Pacific Boston Midwest
   Philadelphia

The most diversified electric utility in the United States and the nation's 14th-largest, PacifiCorp owns Pacific Telecom, a telecommunications company, and NERCO, a mining company, in addition to its electric properties. After a merger with Utah Power & Light Company in 1989, PacifiCorp provided electric power to more than one million customers in parts of seven states, including Washington, Oregon, Utah, Wyoming, California, Montana, and Idaho.

PacifiCorp began in 1910 as Pacific Power & Light Company, which was formed through the merger of several financially troubled electric utilities in the Pacific Northwest. Pacific included utilities in Astoria, Pendleton, and The Dalles, Oregon; Yakima, Walla Walla, and Pasco, Washington; and Lewiston, Idaho. It had a total of 14,344 electric, gas, and water customers and first-year revenues of $832,200.

The electric industry was in its infancy in 1910. Most large towns had their own electric companies, which often provided gas, steam, or water service as well. Because it was difficult for these small firms to raise enough capital to expand or improve service, holding companies sprang up across the United States, buying smaller companies and integrating them into regional electric utilities. Holding companies like Electric Bond & Share, which owned Pacific, provided capital and expertise.

Customers in Pacific's mostly rural area wanted the electricity-powered conveniences: lights, electric ranges, toasters, vacuum cleaners, washing machines, and water pumps. Pacific successfully marketed and sold electric appliances to help increase electricity sales, although the Great Depression slowed Pacific's sales until 1941. During the Depression employees were forced to take pay cuts, and stockholders' dividends were cut.

Except for the worst years of the Great Depression, rural electrification was an important source of company growth. By 1938 Pacific's system included 10,000 farms. In addition to lighting, farmers used electric power to run irrigation pumps, which created more farm land and more demand for electricity. Pacific often wired the houses and sheds of its new customers and supplied the power.

By 1941 Pacific was in a solid financial position, with income of $740,000 on sales of $6.7 million. It had 73,000 customers, including 4,400 electrified farms. In 1942 it joined the newly formed Northwest Power Pool, formed with several other regional power companies to coordinate resources when capacity was stretched.

One of the biggest of U.S. President Franklin D. Roosevelt's New Deal projects was the development of regional hydroelectric systems, such as the Pacific Northwest system, which included the Bonneville dam and the Grand Coulee dam. Paul B. McKee, president of Pacific starting in 1933, realized that the massive government projects presented Pacific with tremendous opportunities for growth—partly because the projects would stimulate the regional economy, but also because the company could buy a share of the low-cost hydroelectric power that the dams would produce. McKee also dealt with a strong government-ownership movement in Washington and northern Oregon from the Depression through the mid-1950s. More than 100 votes were held on establishing public utility districts or municipal ownership, and Pacific won most of them. It had fairly strong support from the public because of its good service record and its efforts to stimulate economic growth in the regions it served.

In 1950 Electric Bond & Share spun off Pacific as an independent, publicly traded company. Pacific pushed aggressively to build itself into a self-sufficient organization, moving to secure its power supply. The Pacific Northwest area was booming, and Pacific was unsure it would be able to renew its contract to buy cheap government power, so it began building its own hydroelectric generating stations. It completed Yale dam in southwest Washington in 1953, but the company still generated only 50% of its power. That generating dearth lead to Pacific's first major merger, with Mountain States Power Company.

Mountain States, founded in 1917, served western Oregon, northern Idaho, western Montana, and Wyoming. In 1940 the company reorganized because the lingering effects of the Depression left it unable to meet its bond debts. It became an independent company that year, when its holding company spun it off as a result of the Public Utility Holding Company Act of 1935. Throughout the 1940s Mountain States acquired nearby systems and built lines into rural areas that had no service. It pushed electric appliances hard, increasing demand. From 1941 to 1953 the company's customer load nearly doubled, leaving it unable to meet demand for electricity. Mountain States had no hydroelectric sites it could develop economically, did not have the capital to build new generating plants, and worried it might fold.

In 1954 Mountain States merged into Pacific, creating a company twice as large as it had been, with service territory spread over five states. The merger also brought Pacific two small telephone companies, one in Oregon and one in Montana. Pacific immediately began building generating plants in Wyoming, where Mountain States had been unable to meet demand. Large coal veins nearby fueled the new plants near Glenrock, Wyoming. Pacific also built a third hydroelectric plant on the Lewis River in Washington and a large coal-fired steam plant near Centralia, Washington.

In the late 1950s and early 1960s Pacific bought coal leases that gave it more than one billion tons of reserves. In 1961 the company merged with California Oregon Power Company (COPCO). COPCO, which served southern Oregon and northern California, was formed in 1911 and acquired by Standard Gas & Electric in 1925. In 1947 COPCO became independent again, partly as the result of the 1935 holding company act. With the COPCO acquisition, Pacific jumped to 411,000 customers from 318,000, and reached annual revenues of $90 million.

During the 1960s Pacific struggled to integrate the COPCO system and meet demand, which was growing at 7% a year. The region's hydroelectric potential was already tapped, so the company added thermal generating plants.

In the early 1970s Pacific decided to build up its small but profitable phone operations. In 1973 the company bought a majority interest in Telephone Utilities, a company in rural Washington that had assembled a network by buying small local telephone companies that had been ignored by the Bell System. In 1979 Pacific bought Alascom from RCA Corporation for $210 million. Alascom, which provides long-distance and local telephone service in Alaska, proved to be a good investment, as Alaskan toll calls grew 23% to 25% annually for the next several years. In 1981 Pacific bought about 48% of the second-largest independent phone equipment manufacturer in the United States, when it bought General Dynamics's phone manufacturing operations for nearly $50 million. In 1982 Pacific changed the name of Telephone Utilities to Pacific Telecom and its own name to PacifiCorp, of which Pacific Power became a subsidiary. By 1983 Pacific Telecom had revenues of $341 million.

Pacific also continued expanding its coal mining and energy exploring operations. In 1976 it formed Northern Energy Resources Company (NERCO) to manage its coal properties and mining operations. Because Pacific already had bought so many coal and mineral properties, NERCO was one of the biggest producers of coal, silver, and gold in North America at the time it was formed. It continued to grow through acquisitions, spending $15.2 million in 1981 for a Fairbanks, Alaska, exploration company that owned mineral rights to 5.5 million acres of Alaska. NERCO had become the sixth-largest U.S. coal miner. In 1982 NERCO acquired Clements Energy Incorporated, an oil and gas exploration company.

Pacific ran into trouble in the late 1970s and early 1980s because of inflation, runaway construction costs, shifts in energy supplies and costs, and then a recession. However, a collapse in energy demand left Pacific Power with excess capacity and investments in several nuclear power plants under construction that were no longer needed. The collapse of the Washington Public Power Supply System (WPPSS), financed by Pacific Power and three other utilities, attracted nationwide attention. PacifiCorp's diversification helped it weather a $292 million write-off in 1983 for investments in WPPSS and another $260 million write-off on three other nuclear plants.

By 1982, 46% of PacifiCorp's revenue came from nonutility operations, which offered a rate of return two to three times greater than the company's electric unit. At the same time, the company decided to push electricity sales to make use of its huge excess generating capacity. It took out ads touting electric home heating, tried to increase economic development in its territory by helping communities form industrial-development groups, and sold surplus power to industry and neighboring utilities at wholesale rates. To reduce expenses PacifCorp cut 600 positions from electricity operations between 1982 and 1984. NERCO launched a drive in 1983 to sign industrial customers to long-term coal contracts to make up for declining sales to utilities. Its earnings also were helped by the 1982 purchase of two gold and silver mines in Nevada. In 1984 PacifiCorp formed Inner PacifiCorp, Inc., to hold NERCO, Pacific Telecom, and other nonelectric businesses.

By 1985 conditions had improved for PacifiCorp's electric business. Electrical income was up nearly 85% since 1981, compared with 34% for Pacific Telecom and 29% for NERCO, which was hurt by declining coal prices. That year PacifiCorp formed a financial services arm, buying Northwest Acceptance Corporation for $53 million and changing its name to PacifiCorp Financial Services. It then bought Hyster Credit for $120 million. It lost, however, $44 million in an oil and gas exploration venture and $78 million in various venture capital and telecommunication manufacturing investments. In 1987 NERCO bought 42 oil and gas wells in southern Louisiana, and PacifiCorp bought Thomas Nationwide Computer Corporation for $25 million. Net income for 1987 was $266 million.

In 1987 PacifiCorp agreed to merge with Utah Power & Light Company, which ran along Pacific's southern flank, in a $1.85 billion stock swap, but the merger did not actually occur until 1989 because of regulatory hurdles. To get regulatory approval for the merger, PacifiCorp accepted conditions imposed by the Federal Energy Regulatory Commission, agreeing to open its transmission system to outside producers under certain circumstances. The company received criticism within the utility industry for the move, which other companies feared would set a harmful precedent. For PacifiCorp the agreement was worth a small amount of competition from independent producers. Utah Power's transmission system was connected to the southwestern and California markets, and the merger allowed PacifiCorp to move surplus power out of Wyoming and into those markets. The companies also fit together well because PacifiCorp's demand peaked in winter, while Utah Power's peaked in summer.

PacifiCorp operated Utah Power as a separate subsidiary, with about 535,000 customers in a 90,000-square-mile area in Utah and parts of Idaho and Wyoming. Pacific Power serves about 682,000 customers in a 63,000-square-mile area in parts of Oregon, Wyoming, Washington, Idaho, Montana, and California. Utah and Oregon provided most of the company's electric revenue, with 37.2% and 29.6%, respectively, in 1989.

In 1989 PacifiCorp offered to buy the troubled Arizona Public Service Company for nearly $2 billion in cash and stock. When the plan faltered, PacifiCorp offered to buy Arizona Public's parent company, Pinnacle West Capital Corporation, which rejected PacifiCorp's $1.87 billion bid as inadequate. The purchase would have given PacifiCorp an electric grid stretching from the Canadian to the Mexican border. Arizona Public eventually agreed to seasonal power swaps with PacifiCorp, so both companies could take advantage of differences in their peak demand times. Also in 1989 Pacific Telecom agreed to buy Wisconsin's North West Telecommunications Incorporated for $250 million in cash and securities, completing the purchase in mid-1990. Net income for 1989 was $466 million on sales of $3.6 billion.

By 1990 PacifiCorp provided electricity to 1.2 million customers. Its generating capacity was 86% coal-powered and 13% hydroelectric. NERCO was one of the top ten U.S. coal producers, with most of its coal sold to electric utilities under long-term contracts. Pacific Telecom provided local telephone service for 352,000 access lines in parts of ten states. In 1991 NERCO bought Union Texas Petroleum's oil and gas operations in the Gulf of Mexico, dramatically increasing its petroleum reserves.

Principal Subsidiaries: Inner PacifiCorp, Inc.; Pacific Power & Light Company; Utah Power & Light Company.

Further Reading: Frisbee, Don C., "The PacifiCorp Story," New York, The Newcomen Society of the United States, 1985.

—Scott M. Lewis

PANHANDLE EASTERN CORPORATION

PANHANDLE EASTERN CORPORATION

5400 Westheimer Court
Houston, Texas 77056
U.S.A.
(713) 627-5400
Fax: (713) 627-4145

Public Company
Incorporated: 1929 as Interstate Pipe Line Company
Employees: 5,400
Sales: $2.99 billion
Stock Exchanges: New York Pacific Toronto
   Boston Cincinnati Midwest Philadelphia

Panhandle Eastern Corporation is one of the largest natural-gas pipeline companies in the United States. Due to its 1989 merger with Texas Eastern, another pipeline firm, Panhandle Eastern controls 27,500 miles of pipeline connecting customers in the Northeast and Midwest with the gas-producing areas of Texas, Kansas, Oklahoma, and the Louisiana-Texas gulf coast. In addition, the company operates a helium-extraction plant in Kansas through its National Helium subsidiary.

Panhandle Eastern was founded in 1929 under the name Interstate Pipe Line Company. It began as a subsidiary of a gas pipeline company, Missouri-Kansas Pipe Line Company (Mo-Kan). Interstate's original network consisted of an 860–mile line that supplied the Midwest with gas from the southwest Kansas and Texas panhandle. The next year, its name was changed to Panhandle Eastern Pipe Line Company at the suggestion of William G. Maguire, then a consultant to Mo-Kan. The network's route was also altered based on a Maguire proposal; originally, it was supposed to terminate at Minneapolis, Minnesota, but Maguire reasoned that it should feed into the more populous Midwestern states that bordered Lake Michigan. Thus began Maguire's long association with running Panhandle Eastern's affairs.

Soon, however, the company found itself embroiled in a protracted legal struggle. In 1930 Mo-Kan had sold a 50% stake in Panhandle Eastern to a direct competitor, Columbia Oil and Gasoline Corporation, an affiliate of Columbia Gas and Electric Corporation. Two years later, Mo-Kan went bankrupt and was placed in receivership. In 1935 its trustees filed an antitrust lawsuit against Columbia, charging that Columbia had wrested control of Panhandle Eastern from Mo-Kan through bad-faith bargaining and in so doing, had driven Mo-Kan to its ruin. According to the suit, Mo-Kan had transferred most of its pipeline and gas reserves to Panhandle Eastern on the understanding that the subsidiary would then use them to secure a public bond issue that would finance the construction of more pipeline. Columbia, however, bought the entire issue from the underwriter and gained control of Panhandle Eastern.

The proceedings dragged on until 1943, when U.S. Circuit Court and Securities and Exchange Commission rulings forced Columbia to sign over its entire stake in Panhandle Eastern to a third party designated by Mo-Kan, Phillips Petroleum Company. Phillips then sold half of the shares to Mo-Kan, on whose behalf it had been acting. This again gave Mo-Kan, which had emerged from receivership in 1937, a controlling interest in Panhandle Eastern. Maguire, by then president of Mo-Kan, became chairman and CEO of Panhandle Eastern.

With the legal wrangling over, Mo-Kan emerged as a holding company for Panhandle Eastern, controlling stock and cash, but little else in the way of assets; Panhandle Eastern still held the gas and pipeline assets. An effort was made to merge Mo-Kan and Panhandle Eastern in 1943, but it failed. The next year, a liquidation scheme for Mo-Kan was conceived, under which shareholders would have the right to convert their Mo-Kan stock into Panhandle Eastern stock. Enough shareholders took advantage of the plan, and Panhandle Eastern eventually gained independence from Mo-Kan, which was merged into Panhandle Eastern and dissolved in 1971.

In 1951 Panhandle Eastern founded its Trunkline Gas Company subsidiary to ship gas from fields on the gulf coast to its markets in the Midwest. Thanks to Maguire's conservative approach to business, Panhandle remained throughout the 1950s a company that grew slowly, but kept its debt burden low and its profit margins healthy in an industry where how much a company could charge for its product was closely regulated by the government. Maguire also believed in the importance of maintaining a high level of gas reserves in order to meet growing demand, reasoning that although one could lay down pipe relatively quickly, exploring for gas was troublesome and time-consuming. True to this philosophy, Panhandle Eastern founded Andarko Production in 1959, to develop leases on more than 500,000 acres of land in the gas-laden Andarko basin, which is spread over portions of Texas, Oklahoma, and Kansas.

In 1960 Panhandle Eastern formed National Helium Corporation in a joint venture with National Distillers & Chemical Corporation, a company in which Panhandle Eastern owned a minority stake. Three years later, National Helium opened what was then the world's largest helium extraction plant, in Kansas.

Maguire died in 1965. He was succeeded by W.K. Sanders, who had been president of Trunkline Gas. Sanders retired as CEO in 1970 and was succeeded by Richard O'Shields. Under O'Shields, Panhandle Eastern, like most of its competitors, began to anticipate a shortfall in natural gas supplies. The shortfall was expected because governmental price controls on natural gas discouraged producers from exploring for new sources, and rising demand would soon catch up with shrinking supply, driving the price upward and making alternative sources of fuel both economically feasible and necessary. By the middle of the 1970s, there was indeed a gas shortage. Synthetic fuels, coal gasification, and liquefied natural gas

(LNG) were seen as expensive solutions, but necessary and cost effective because of short supply and because the cost of these products was expected to remain competitive with rapidly rising oil prices. In connection with its coal gasification plans, Panhandle Eastern in 1976 acquired Youghioheny and Ohio Coal Company. In 1979 Panhandle Eastern joined with ten other pipeline companies in proposing a giant pipeline project that would bring natural gas down from the fields in Alaska's Prudhoe Bay.

The U.S. government began deregulating natural gas prices in 1978, however, and conventional sources of natural gas became worthwhile to exploit once again. Supply rebounded and the price fell, aided in part by the fact that higher natural gas prices had made residual fuel oil an affordable option for customers with furnaces that could use either. Unconventional sources of gas soon became expensive and unnecessary, and for that reason Panhandle Eastern came to regret its biggest foray into alternative fuel sources. In 1977 it had entered into an agreement to buy Algerian liquefied natural gas from Entreprise Nationale Sonatrach (Sonatrach), the Algerian national energy company. The agreement involved substantial capital outlays for Panhandle Eastern—$508 million for a new receiving and regasification facility in Louisiana and $36 million for a stake in two tankers—and was to last into the 21st century. Delivery was scheduled to begin in 1981. As consumers began to discover the economic benefits of using fuel oil and downward pressure on gas prices accumulated, however, the deal became a liability. Matters worsened when Sonatrach postponed the date at which it would begin supplying the LNG. Ostensibly, Sonatrach was having technical problems, but, in fact, it had reconsidered the selling price to which it had originally agreed. New prices were negotiated before delivery began in 1982.

In 1981 Panhandle Eastern Corporation was formed to hold Panhandle Eastern Pipe Line Company as a subsidiary. O'Shields was succeeded by Robert D. Hunsucker in 1982. In 1983, caught between upward cost pressure from Sonatrach and downward price pressure from customers, Panhandle Eastern unilaterally suspended its contract with Sonatrach. Immediately, Panhandle Eastern was sued by Sonatrach and by Lachmar, Panhandle Eastern's shipping partner. In 1986, after the initiation of arbitration proceedings, Panhandle Eastern agreed to purchase the interests of its partners in Lachmar for $32 million.

The Algerian LNG deal did not affect Panhandle Eastern right away. The company had the highest return on equity of any gas producer-pipeliner between 1977 and 1982. Panhandle Eastern, however, perhaps distracted by its misadventure with imported LNG, was slow to adapt to its increasingly deregulated market environment. Nevertheless, the 1.5 trillion cubic feet of reserves that Panhandle Eastern owned through its Andarko subsidiary made it an attractive takeover target. In 1986 Wagner & Brown, an oil and gas firm owned by Texas wildcatters Cyril Wagner Jr. and Jack E. Brown, offered $2.3 billion,

60% in cash and the remainder in preferred stock for Panhandle Eastern, only to be turned down. Takeover speculation continued to surround the company after the brief battle, which occurred amidst the spate of oil and gas industry leveraged buyouts in the mid–1980s, but no further action occurred. Several months afterward, Panhandle Eastern spun off Andarko. Rumors also circulated that Hunsucker had intentionally slowed resolution of the company's Algerian liabilities so that they would act as repellents against further hostile bids. Hunsucker actually had tried to expedite the settlements, a prerequisite to spinning off Andarko as an independent company, which was accomplished in October 1986.

The problem of how to grow in a business environment that had suddenly become more competitive remained unsolved. The company lost market share, a trend that halted in 1988 only after Panhandle Eastern began discounting transportation fees. In 1989, however, Panhandle Eastern acquired 81% of Texas Eastern Corporation stock for a total of $2.61 billion in cash. The merger was completed by the issuance of 27.1 million shares of Panhandle Eastern stock for the remaining shares of Texas Eastern. Texas Eastern operated a pipeline network that ran from Texas to Pennsylvania, New York, New Jersey, and southern New England; its geographical strength thus complemented Panhandle Eastern's presence in the Midwest.

Hunsucker retired in 1990 and was succeeded by Philip Burguieres. Burguieres stepped down later that year because of ill health. Former Texas Eastern CEO Dennis Hendrix then became the top executive. The merger was not working out as planned at least initially, because of intense competition in the interstate pipeline industry, which depressed profit margins for all participants. This competition was engendered by a combination of regulatory changes and market forces, including a lingering oversupply of gas and reduced U.S. economic activity. Panhandle Eastern took several steps to improve the situation, including decentralizing management for its pipeline operations. These steps led to a resumption of earnings growth and reaffirmation of investment-grade status for the company's senior debt in 1991. The company also planned increased service to the northeastern United States, thus achieving the synergies originally envisioned in combining Panhandle Eastern and Texas Eastern. While the merger may not have solved Panhandle Eastern's problems immediately, in the long run it may have positioned the company to compete effectively as a bigger entity in an increasingly competitive business environment.

Principal Subsidiaries: Panhandle Eastern Pipe Line Company; Trunkline Gas Company; Texas Eastern Transmission Corporation; Algonquin Gas Transmission Company; Trunkline LNG Company; Centana Energy Corporation; Panhandle Trading Company.

—Douglas Sun

PENNSYLVANIA POWER & LIGHT COMPANY

Two North Ninth Street
Allentown, Pennsylvania 18101
U.S.A.
(215) 774-5151
Fax: (215) 774-5281

Public Company
Incorporated: 1920
Employees: 8,149
Sales: $2.39 billion
Stock Exchanges: New York   Philadelphia

Pennsylvania Power & Light Company (PP&L) provides electricity to more than 2.5 million people living in a 10,000-square-mile area in eastern Pennsylvania. It is also involved in coal mining, refined-petroleum pipelines, and commercial and industrial building.

PP&L grew out of the consolidation of numerous small Pennsylvania electric utilities in the first two decades of the 20th century. The utilities included several small electric lighting companies formed in the 1880s in eastern Pennsylvania and the Edison Electric Illuminating Company of Sunbury, used by Thomas Edison to perfect central-station incandescent lighting in small cities and towns in Pennsylvania. Small electric companies proliferated at this time, and by 1900, 64 companies served 88 communities in the area PP&L later would serve.

In the 1910s a complicated series of mergers began consolidating the electric utilities into small regional companies. Pennsylvania Power & Light Company was formed in 1920 as a holding company for five territorially contiguous regional companies. PP&L, itself backed by another holding company called the Lehigh Power Securities Corporation, sold stocks and bonds to the public, but kept control of voting common stock of the utilities.

Like many other U.S. utilities, PP&L went through an important consolidation period in the 1920s, buying out other utilities, which in turn already had bought smaller utilities. It continued to expand its territory in this way, acquiring 5 utilities in 1923, 34 in 1928, and 21 in 1930, including the Edison Electric Company of Lancaster, Pennsylvania, one of the earliest U.S. electric companies. The early PP&L primarily supplied power for industry in Pennsylvania's coal-mining and steel-producing region, concentrated in the Lehigh River val-

ley. By 1930, 70% of its power was used by industrial customers, and 45% of that went to coal-mining operations. PP&L also supplied small industry and agriculture in the Susquehanna River valley north of Harrisburg, capital of Pennsylvania. Allentown and Bethlehem were the largest cities in its territory, with populations of 90,000 and 60,000, respectively, in 1930. At this time PP&L's system consisted of a large territory with widely dispersed power plants, each with a relatively small network of transmission lines, and interconnections between the various systems.

PP&L and most other electric utilities were not greatly hurt by the Depression because of their status as protected, regulated monopolies. Most sales that were lost to declining industry were made up by increasing residential sales.

PP&L added hundreds of miles of high-voltage transmission lines to its system in the 1920s and 1930s, also building a 220,000-volt interconnection with two urban utilities, Philadelphia Electric Company and Public Service Electric & Gas Company of New Jersey. PP&L's industrial customers caused the company's load to peak in the morning, while the urban utilities' loads peaked in the late afternoon, when workers returned home. This led to an ideal power-sharing arrangement, although it required complex contracts to spell out which company would supply how much power under what circumstances.

PP&L took other steps to spread risks in its service area, shifting its emphasis from regions that had mined out their coal to regions with fresh coal seams. To encourage industrial use of power, the company charged industrial customers far lower rates than it charged residential and farm customers. Some political pressure was put on PP&L to change this practice, but it resisted, pointing out that it already encouraged rural electrification in other ways. PP&L had begun hooking up farmers rapidly in 1936, the year the U.S. government established the Rural Electrification Administration to make loans to farmers to create their own electric cooperatives. By 1939 57% of farms in PP&L territory had electricity, compared with a U.S. average of 28%.

In 1947 PP&L acquired two electric utilities and the Allentown, Pennsylvania, operations of another. By the following year the company had 487,000 customers, and revenue of $62 million. In 1949 and 1951, PP&L sold all its gas operations. It also sold its steam heating operations in Wilkes-Barre, Pennsylvania, in 1951, leaving it with steam operations in Harrisburg and Scranton, Pennsylvania. In 1953 it acquired Scranton Electric Company, and in 1955 Pennsylvania Water & Power Company. By 1955 it had about 7,000 employees, and operated in about 10,000 square miles of east central Pennsylvania. It supplied a population of 2.1 million people in a large number of communities including Allentown, Wilkes-Barre, Harrisburg, Lancaster, Bethlehem, Williamsport, Hazelton, Pottsville, Shenandoah, Shamokin, Mt. Carmel, Sunbury, and Scranton. The company owned one hydroelectric and eight steam power-generating stations and had 29,000 miles of transmission lines. Its principal fuel supply was purchased under 50-year contracts with coal companies based in Philadelphia and Reading, Pennsylvania.

PP&L spent about $142 million on new construction between 1954 and 1959, including the building of two new power-generating stations. It also spent about $4 million between 1958 and 1962 as its share of a joint project with

Philadelphia Electric Company to develop a prototype nuclear power station. In 1961 the company built a new conventionally fueled power station at Brunner Island, Pennsylvania, with a capacity of 302,000 kilowatts. Between 1961 and 1965 the company reduced rates seven times. By 1964 29% of company electric revenue came from industrial customers. The company had begun pooling power with other companies in Pennsylvania, New Jersey, and Maryland. This interconnection had grown into one of the world's largest power pools, including many other electric utilities in a 48,700-square-mile area with a population of 18.4 million. In addition, PP&L planned $315 million in construction between 1965 and 1969, including two new power plants.

By 1972 PP&L owned seven steam, two hydroelectric, eleven combustion turbine, and five diesel-engine generating stations with a total capacity of about four million kilowatts. It announced plans to build a 2.2-million kilowatt nuclear generating station on the Susquehanna River between Wilkes-Barre and Bloomsburg, Pennsylvania, in the late 1970s.

PP&L began operating its own coal mines when commercial coal companies proved unable to meet the terms of PP&L's contracts. PP&L's ownership of mines protected the company from runaway fuel costs as well as interruptions in fuel supplies.

The power-sharing arrangement with Pennsylvania, New Jersey, and Maryland companies also was proving financially beneficial since PP&L was putting more electricity into the pool than it took out. In 1973 it sold 6.5 billion kilowatt-hours to other companies in the pool, and earned $67 million on revenue of $385 million. Escalating fuel prices and an economic recession following the oil embargo in 1973 and 1974 sharply cut the growth of power utilities. PP&L used coal for 96% of its fossil fuel needs. Much of that coal came from PP&L's own mines at below-market costs, helping to insulate the company from oil price increases. Even so, PP&L's sales growth dropped to 3% in 1974 from 7% in 1973. Power conservation was briefly in vogue, which further cut the demand for electric power.

In 1977 PP&L appointed an outsider as president when it named Robert K. Campbell, formerly with Western Electric, to the position. PP&L was considered one of the best-managed utilities in the United States, with a profit margin of 17%, compared to a U.S. industry average of 12%. Net income for 1978 was $149 million. In 1980 Standard Oil Company of Ohio signed an agreement with a PP&L subsidiary under which Standard mined coal on certain PP&L properties. In 1981 the Pennsylvania Public Utility Commission (PUC) approved a $101 million annual rate increase for PP&L that went into effect in 1982.

The company's Susquehanna nuclear power plant, delayed for years, was finally completed at a cost of more than $4 billion in 1982. In 1983 PP&L began the first of a series of incentive rates designed to increase usage and attract new in-

dustry. The central effort focused on pricing schemes that would sell more power during off-peak hours, increasing company revenue without requiring the construction of new power plants. The company also began consulting with industrial customers to enhance their uses for electricity. Encouraged by the initial response, PP&L expanded the program in 1987. PP&L also began testing new lighting systems designed to use light more efficiently. In the mid-1980s PP&L developed a lightweight steel transmission pole to replace its wooden poles, which were becoming expensive and scarce. In 1985 the Pennsylvania PUC approved only $121 million of a $330 million rate increase requested by the utility, boosting electricity prices about 8%. PP&L spent about $850 million on construction between 1987 and 1989.

The late 1980s were a good time for PP&L, with record sales and earnings in 1989, despite rate decreases and a softening economy in the northeastern United States. The company was following a strategy that stressed aggressive marketing, cost management, and increased sensitivity to customers. By 1990 PP&L's total generating capacity was 7.9 million kilowatts.

In 1990 the company decided to phase out its affiliated mining companies beginning in 1991, instead buying its coal through contract and on the open market. Mining its own coal had become more expensive than buying it on the open market and many of the company's mines were depleted. PP&L began working on plans to reduce its sulfur dioxide emissions by about 50% by 2000 because of pollution provisions in the 1990 Clean Air Act amendments. Also in 1990, PP&L began the $22 million renovation of two of the four coal-fired generating units at its Sunbury power plant. In addition, the company discovered that fuel oil was leaking into groundwater at its Brunner Island generating station, and that filters from that plant contained enough cadmium to be considered hazardous waste. Cleaning up these problems was expected to cost over $100 million during the next several years.

PP&L opened a new customer service office in Allentown as the beginning of a process of consolidating its customer service operations in a single location. Robert Campbell died in 1990 and John T. Kauffman became company president.

Principal Subsidiaries: CEP Group Inc.; Interstate Energy Company; Pennsylvania Mines Corporation; Rushton Mining Company; Tunnelton Mining Company; Realty Company of Pennsylvania; BDW Corporation; Green Hill Coal Company; Green Manor Coal Company; Lady Jane Collieries Incorporated; Safe Harbor Water Power Corporation (33%).

Further Reading: Hughes, Thomas P., *Networks of Power: Electrification in Western Society, 1880–1930,* Baltimore, Johns Hopkins University Press, 1983.

—Scott M. Lewis

PHILADELPHIA ELECTRIC COMPANY

2301 Market Street
Philadelphia, PA 19101
U.S.A.
(215) 841-4000
Fax: (215) 841-4188

Public Company:
Incorporated: 1902 as The Philadelphia Electric Company
Sales: $3.71 billion
Employees: 9,600
Stock Exchanges: New York Philadelphia

Philadelphia Electric Company (PECO) is one of the oldest and largest utility companies in the United States, and a leading producer of nuclear power. A total of 65% of its power output is generated by its three nuclear power plants at Limerick and Peach Bottom, Pennsylvania, and Salem, New Jersey, compared to 20% for the United States as a whole.

PECO has its origins in the work of Thomas Edison. Between 1876 and 1900, Edison applied for over 1,000 patents for inventions produced by him and his team of research assistants. It was Edison's idea that a single fiber charged with an electric current could glow indefinitely in a vacuum. Edison perfected his invention in 1879, and in a few years electric lighting supplanted gas light.

In 1836, the first gas plant in Philadelphia had been built, and shortly thereafter most of the city was lighted by gas. In 1881 the first electric arc lamps, predecessor to Edison's incandescent light bulb, were installed on Chestnut Street, by Brush Electric Light Company. Brush Electric Light Company manufactured the most advanced form of electric light prior to Edison's bulb. By 1881 numerous individuals sensed that considerable profits could be made from electric lighting, as well as from other applications of electricity. In 1882 two Philadelphia high school teachers, Edwin J. Houston and Elihu Thomson, established The Philadelphia Electric Lighting Company, a predecessor of General Electric Company, although it did not begin to do business until 1886. This company sold the electrical equipment invented and tested by Houston and Thomson to utilities. The Thomson-Houston electric lighting system was widely used by the many companies providing electric service in Philadelphia. With the city's wealth, huge coal supplies, and a population in 1880 of 847,500, second in

the United States only to New York City, Philadelphia became a lucrative field for entrepreneurs of electricity.

Throughout the 1880s and 1890s, intense competition faced the purveyors of electrical street lighting. A leader among these companies was Edison Electric Light Company of Philadelphia. It was not uncommon for several rival electric companies to set up wiring on the same street, using entirely different systems and leading to extremes in the quality of service. Many Philadelphians, however, objected to what they saw as dangerous and unsightly overhead wires strung up on every street, and put pressure on electric companies to come up with an effective means of burying cable underground. Ultimately, it was determined that the various electric companies should be consolidated, to provide uniformity and economy of service. The task of consolidating the approximately 20 electric companies into one company, with sole authority to produce electricity in the city, fell to Martin Maloney, a Philadelphia entrepreneur, and The Philadelphia Electric Company was formed in 1902. The Philadelphia Electric Company was the principal operating subsidiary of the nearly identically named Philadelphia Electric Company, a holding company.

Joseph McCall was president of the holding company and was responsible for consolidating and modernizing The Philadelphia Electric Company. In 1902 the company had 853 employees and 12,090 customers. In 1903 the company built its largest power station to date, Schuylkill station, using coal that was hauled from the company's own wharf. No sooner was Schuylkill completed than electricity demand exceeded supply, and plans by 1913 were made for another generating station at Schuylkill. In 1917 the corporate structure was simplified, as Philadelphia Electric Company was dissolved, and its shares in The Philadelphia Electric Company distributed to stockholders. The Philadelphia Electric Company then consolidated its operations.

At first World War I had little effect on PECO, but as it became apparent that the war would last longer than had been expected, the strain on PECO increased. The U.S. war industries supplying the Allied effort in Europe began to make heavy demands on PECO, and when the United States entered the war in April 1917, the Philadelphia area quickly became a major industrial center geared to war production, necessitating the start-up of PECO's Chester generating station. Labor and material, especially coal, became scarce and very expensive, culminating in a severe coal shortage in the winter of 1917-1918. In the end, supply simply could not keep up with demand, and electricity had to be strictly rationed with the backing of the federal government.

On the heels of Armistice Day of 1918 came a deadly influenza epidemic that struck the company's work force. At the same time, PECO faced strikes and labor disturbances, as the recession following the war dampened returning soldiers' hopes of employment. In 1919 a miners' strike erupted, followed in 1920 by major walkouts in the steel, railroad, and coal industries. Nevertheless, growth in demand for electricity continued.

By 1923 PECO had 306,000 customers, up from 103,000 in 1918. PECO had made the mistake of adopting Edison's direct current (DC) system over George Westinghouse's alternating current (AC) system. The AC system prevailed, and PECO was rapidly switching from DC to AC. AC offered much greater electrical capacity, and demand kept growing. In the 1920s a new era in electricity began with a change of emphasis from traditional electric lighting to consumer products, in the form of washing machines, radios, cooking ranges, and refrigerators. The demand for electricity was so high that in 1928 the second-largest hydroelectric dam in the United States was constructed at Conowingo, Maryland, on the Susquehanna River.

At this time, three suburban gas and electric companies served areas bordering PECO's own region. The three companies, American Gas Company, Philadelphia Suburban Gas & Electric Company, and Counties Gas and Electric Company, were controlled by a holding company known as United Gas Improvement (UGI). The advantages of a merger between UGI and PECO were clear; economies of scale and increased financial leverage were chief among them. Thus, in 1928, UGI acquired control of The Philadelphia Electric Company. The following year, UGI merged with The Philadelphia Electric Company. "The" was dropped from PECO's name, and Philadelphia Electric Company became an operating subsidiary of UGI. This was the biggest merger of any two utility companies in the United States up to that point. From the perspective of PECO's management, the merger offered the prospect of a significant increase in business. With its merger in 1929 with UGI, PECO entered the gas business for the first time, and in this way added 112,000 gas customers and 88,000 new electric customers, and increased its service territory by 1,380 square miles.

The stock market crash of 1929 and the ensuing Great Depression stopped growth of demand for electricity in PECO's service area, although demand did not shrink. The slowdown or closure of businesses decreased the number of PECO's commercial customers, but this loss was offset by the growth in private consumption. In the 1930s an aggressive campaign was launched to bring electricity to rural areas, and the retail sales department continued to market consumer products successfully, holding its first air conditioning sales campaign in 1934.

With growth halted, PECO canceled Christmas bonuses as well as pay raises, and froze hiring. In 1931 PECO became one of the first utility companies in the nation to establish a customer-service department. In the following year the largest generator in the world at that time, Richmond 12, was constructed, marking the transition to a new era of pulverized-coal–fired plants. Richmond 12 was ahead of its time in that it was equipped with the technology to control stack emissions, long before the emergence of widespread ecological awareness.

By the late 1930s the economy had entered an upswing. Schuylkill's third generating station was constructed, and 1938 saw the inauguration of a new PECO president, Horace P. Liveridge, who would guide PECO for nine years, spanning World War II and the postwar boom.

World War II brought a shortage of labor and material, but the strain on PECO was less pronounced than during World War I. The labor shortage was resolved by inaugurating longer working hours, while many workers postponed retirement; in some cases, chauffeurs became machinists, and janitors found themselves learning to fit pipe. The company thus managed to maintain services. As early as 1944, the company had passed through the worst electrical and employment shortages of the war.

In 1943 the Securities and Exchange Commission, enforcing the Public Utility Holding Company Act of 1935, ordered UGI to divest itself of PECO. UGI and PECO had never operated harmoniously, mainly because PECO was in the electric business, and UGI in the competing gas business. Following PECO, PECO still carried on its gas business, but this fared poorly compared to its electricity business.

The postwar era was marked by increasing government regulation, by the advent of computers and nuclear energy, and by growing ecological concerns. R. George Rincliffe, president of PECO from 1952 to 1962, guided the company through this period of transition. Demand rose for both electricity and gas. Between 1939 and 1958, 13 new generating stations were built. Much of this demand arose from the growing popularity of television. The number of gas customers also expanded steadily, many converting from oil because of effective advertising of natural gas as a lower-cost fuel. Eddystone 1, then the world's largest and most efficient coal-fired generator, was completed in 1960.

In the late 1950s PECO, along with several other electric utilities, began studying the feasibility of nuclear power. In 1967 PECO's first nuclear unit, a small prototype reactor at Peach Bottom, Pennsylvania, went into operation. That unit produced power until 1974, when two full-size nuclear units went into commercial operation at Peach Bottom. The company expanded its nuclear program in the 1980s, with the first unit of the Limerick generating station in Montomery County, Pennsylvania, going into service in 1986.

In March 1987 the U.S. Nuclear Regulatory Commission (NRC) ordered both units at Peach Bottom shut down because of management problems and operator inattention. During the subsequent overhaul of plant operations, PECO's chairman at the time, James Everett, and its president, John H. Austin Jr., took early retirement. All other supervisory personnel with responsibility for the Peach Bottom Plant either resigned, retired, or were transferred. A group of shareholders sued Everett and Austin, alleging the two men failed to address the problems at the plant. Insurers for Everett and Austin settled the suit out of court with a $34.5 million payment, minus $6.5 million for attorneys' fees and expenses, to PECO in 1990. The payment went to the company rather than the shareholders because the shareholders filed the suit on behalf of the company.

Joseph F. Paquette, Jr., a 30-year PECO veteran who had moved to Consumers Power in Dearborn, Michigan, returned to PECO in 1988 as chairman and chief executive officer. Corbin A. McNeill, Jr., came to PECO from Public Service Electric and Gas (PSEG) to be executive vice president–nuclear, with responsibility for revitalizing PECO's nuclear operations and restarting Peach Bottom. Peach Bottom went back into operation in 1989, after the company incurred maintenance and replacement power costs totaling $225 million, which were not passed on to customers. McNeill was named president and chief operating officer of PECO in 1990.

Although PECO's use of nuclear power met strong opposition from activists, the company continued developing this source of energy. A second nuclear unit at the Limerick plant went into service in 1990. To recover the unit's cost, PECO sought a base rate increase of $549 million. The Pennsylvania Public Utility Commission (PUC) ruled that PECO had excess generating capacity and allowed only $242 million of the increase. As a result, PECO reduced its common stock dividend from $2.20 to $1.20 per share, froze salaries, and cut operating expenses by $100 million annually. This cut was achieved largely through an early retirement program accepted by 1,900 employees.

In April 1991 the PUC agreed to let PECO market its excess capacity to utilities outside its service territory, while PECO agreed not to file for a base rate increase until at least 1994. In May of that year the PUC released an report lauding PECO for its recovery from Peach Bottom's troubles and from the austerity measures that resulted from the rate ruling. PECO was generating more than 65% of its electricity from its nuclear plants, which in addition to Peach Bottom and Limerick included the Salem Generating Station in New Jersey, whose ownership, like Peach Bottom's, PECO shared with other utilities. Late in 1991 PECO increased its common stock dividend by 10¢ per share. Under the continuing leadership of Paquette and McNeill, the company appeared poised for further financial improvement.

Principal Subsidiaries: Susquehanna Electric Company; Conowingo Power Company; Adwin Companies.

Further Reading: Wainwright, Nicholas B., *History of the Philadelphia Electric Company: 1881–1961,* Philadelphia, Philadelphia Electric Company, 1961; *Milestones: Philadelphia Electric Company, 1881–1981,* Philadelphia, Philadelphia Electric Company, 1981.

—Sina Dubovoj

PREUSSENELEKTRA AKTIENGESELLSCHAFT

Postfach 48 49
Tresckowstrasse 5
3000 Hanover 91
Germany
(05 11) 4 3-90
Fax: (05 11) 4 39-23-75

Wholly Owned Subsidiary of Veba AG
Incorporated: 1927
Sales: DM9.10 billion (US$6.01 billion)
Employees: 17,245

PreussenElektra Aktiengesellschaft (PreussenElektra) is Germany's second largest electricity utility behind RWE. In 1990, PreussenElektra delivered 53.6 billion kilowatt hours (kWh) of electricity to 15 million customers in an area extending from the Danish border to Frankfurt am Main and incorporating Schleswig-Holstein, Lower Saxony, and parts of Northrhine-Westphalia and Hesse. PreussenElektra also trades electricity with utilities in Denmark, France, the Netherlands, and, more recently, in Switzerland. Following the unification of Germany in 1990, PreussenElektra, along with RWE and Bayernwerk, became a partner in the modernization of the electricity supply industry of east Germany.

PreussenElektra is a key member of the VEBA group. In 1929 the Prussian state founded the Vereinigte Elektrizitäts-und Bergwerks Aktiengesellschaft, today known as VEBA A.G., to act as a holding company for its industrial shareholdings which included PreussenElektra. VEBA remained wholly in the hands of the Prussian state until 1965 when it was partially privatized. In 1987 the state's remaining 25.5% stake in the VEBA group and its member companies was sold. VEBA retained its role as a holding company and has interests in four sectors: electricity, oil, chemical, and transport and related services.

PreussenElektra itself was founded two years before VEBA. In 1927 three electricity suppliers, Grosskraftwerk Hannover AG, Preussische Kraftwerke Oberweser AG, and the Gewerkschaft Grosskraftwerk Main-Weser, joined together to form the Preussische Elektrizitäts-Aktiengesellschaft (PreussenElektra). The new company had its headquarters in Berlin and operated two thermal power stations, Borken in Hesse and Ahlem in Hanover, and eight hydroelectric stations—Hemfurth I and II, Krotzenburg, Kesselstadt, Mainkur, Werrawerk, Helminghausen, and Dörverden.

PreussenElektra was established on the basis of a law governing the participation of the state in electricity companies. According to this law, the newly formed company was to oversee the electricity interests of the Prussian state which, in addition to its stake in the founding companies of PreussenElektra, included the Nordwestdeutsche Kraftwerke AG (NWK). NWK was founded by Siemens and Halske at the turn of the century, under the name Siemens Elektrische Betriebe, in order to create markets both at home and abroad for electrical equipment manufactured by Siemens. In 1925 the Prussian state acquired the majority shareholding and the company became known as the Nordwestdeutsche Kraftwerke Aktiengesellschaft. Until their formal merger in 1985, PreussenElektra and NWK cooperated very closely in all aspects of electricity supply.

At the time of the foundation of PreussenElektra, the Prussian state participation in the electricity sector also extended to Ostpreussenwerke AG and the Überlandwerke and Strassenbahnen Hannover AG. The addition of the electricity assets of the Prussian state to its portfolio gave PreussenElektra extensive influence over the power stations of Herrenwyk, Harburg-Wilhelmsburg, Farge, and Wiesmoor.

From 1928 to 1931, through a series of joint ventures and acquisitions, PreussenElektra laid the foundations of its current production and supply network. In common with other major German electricity utilities, PreussenElektra worked closely with local municipal authorities and during this period founded several regional electricity supply undertakings in partnership with these authorities. These new ventures included the Schleswig-Holsteinische Stromversorgungs-AG, today known as the SCHLESWAG AG Rendsburg; the Stromsversorgungs-AG Oldenburg-Friedland, now known as the Energieversorgung Weser-Ems AG/EWE, Oldenburg; the Elektrizitäts-Aktiengesellschaft Mitteldeutschland (EAM), Kassel; and the Hannover-Braunschweigische Stromversorgungs-AG (HASTRA).

During the same period, PreussenElektra also took stakes in the Braunschweigische Kohlen-Bergwerke AG (Helmstedt), the Westpreussische Überlandwerke Marienwerder GmbH (Marienwerder), and Thüringer Gasgesellschaft, originally based in Leipzig but which moved its headquarters to Munich. In 1929 NWK took over the power station at Oldenburg, and in 1932 the pump storage station Waldeck 1 was commissioned.

The result of this extensive activity and expansion was that by 1937 the annual electricity output of PreussenElektra exceeded one billion kWh. From the point of view of acquisitions, the following decades were much quieter but expansion continued through organic growth—that is, through the development of existing facilities and the construction of new ones.

World War II caused severe disruption to the German electricity industry which was a strategic target for Allied bombers. The construction of the hard coal station Lahde, for example, which began in 1941, was interrupted several times by the war and was finally stopped by it. It was not until 1951 that the Lahde power station—renamed Heyden in 1953—entered the PreussenElektra supply network. This station was still in operation at the beginning of the 1990s with an installed capacity of 740MW.

The war did not inhibit all construction work. In 1942–1943, the first expansion of NWK's Lübeck Siems works was completed—a further 50MW expansion took place in 1950–1951—and PreussenElektra's first 110 kilovolt (kV) line went into operation, connecting Lübeck, Lüneberg, Harburg, and Farge.

After the war, electricity production and distribution in the part of PreussenElektra's supply area that was located in the new state of East Germany came under state control and the headquarters of PreussenElektra were moved from Berlin to Hanover in 1947.

The next decade was primarily one of unspectacular but steady expansion. In 1947 NWK leased the power station Süd from the former naval dockyard in Wilhelmshaven. The expansion of the power station at Farge by a further 70MW was begun in the winter of 1948–1949 and completed in 1950–1951. In 1953 the brown coal power station Hessen-Frankfurt A.G. was integrated into the PreussenElektra network and renamed Wölfersheim. In 1954 NWK set up its central command offices in Harburg. At NWK's hard coal power station Lübeck-Herrenwyk a new 25MW unit produced its first electricity in 1955. In the same year, the first 70MW unit at Emden came into operation and the Kraftwerk Kassel GmbH was founded: PreussenElektra had a 60% stake in the new venture and the Städtische Werke AG Kassel owned the remaining 40%. In 1956 the hydroelectric power stations Schlusselburg and Drakenburg (Mittelweser) were commissioned.

In retrospect, 1957 was an important year for Preussen-Elektra. Together with other electricity utilities, Preussen-Elektra and NWK founded the Studiengesellschaft für Kernkrafte GmbH, a research company dedicated to the study of the utilization of nuclear power in electricity production. By 1990 nuclear power was to account for over 60% of PreussenElektra's electricity production, the largest nuclear share of any of the major German electricity utilities.

It was some years before PreussenElektra's first nuclear power station came into operation, however, and in the interim PreussenElektra continued to build up its conventional generating capacity. The hydroelectric power station at Langwedel an der Weser was commissioned in 1958. In 1959–1960, the first 125MW unit of the power station Stade went into operation and the construction of the power station at Schilling, the first big oil-fired station in West Germany, began. In 1960 the hydroelectric power station Landesbergen began operation and in 1962 PreussenElektra acquired a stake in the Paderborner Elektrizitätswerk und Strassenbahn AG.

It was during the early 1960s that NWK began its cooperation with electric utilities from neighboring countries. In 1961–1962 NWK collaborated with the Danish utility Det Jyskfynske Elsamarbedje (ELSAM) in the completion of the 220kV link from Flensburg to Apenrade: a further link between the power station at Schilling and Audorf was also under construction. Shortly afterwards, Danish electricity suppliers Vattenfall and ELSAM and NWK agreed to link Sweden, Denmark (Jutland and Funen), and northwest Germany through the building of a direct connection, known as Konti-Scan, from Gothenburg to Aalborg. This link, which was to be jointly managed, went into operation in 1964.

The Danish connection grew stronger over the coming years. In 1974 NWK decided to build a 600MW power station in cooperation with ELSAM and Snderjyllands Hjspaendingsvaerk An/S in Apenrade, Denmark. In order to smooth supply peaks and troughs, PreussenElektra engages in supply exchanges with utilities in Denmark, the Netherlands, and France, and from 1990 with Switzerland.

Domestic production was not neglected during the forging of these overseas links. In 1963 PreussenElektra took over the management of the power station Robert Frank at Landesbergen (Mittelweser), Germany's first large power station based on natural gas. In 1965 the 52MW gas turbine at Emden was completed and the 620MW Staudinger power station was commissioned. A 25MW gas turbine was commissioned at Wiesmoor in 1968. In 1966 PreussenElektra acquired the majority shareholding in the Paderborner Elektrizitätswerk und Strassenbahn A.G., which is today known as PESAG A.G.

The fiscal year 1967–1968 marked the beginning of a major phase of nuclear power station construction as work commenced on PreussenElektra's station at Würgassen and the Stade plant, which was two-thirds owned by NWK and one-third owned by HEW. These plants, the first nuclear plants in West Germany to be operated on a purely commercial basis, began to deliver electricity in 1971–1972. In 1969 NWK and HEW founded Kernkrafts Brunsbüttel GmbH, with stakes of one-third and two-thirds respectively, for the later joint construction of a nuclear power plant at Brunsbüttel.

PreussenElektra's investment decisions in the early 1970s were greatly influenced by the oil crisis of 1973 and the fears of the industrialized world about possible future energy shortages. In 1971 PreussenElektra decided to build a nuclear power station at Unterweser which was completed in 1976. In 1973 PreussenElektra and Interargem, a consortium composed of Stadtwerke Bielefeld GmbH, the Elektrizitätswerke Wesertal GmbH, and the Elektrizitätswerk Minden-Ravensberg GmbH, decided to build a nuclear power station at Grohnde. This power station produced its first commercial power in 1985, a year before the start-up of NWK's nuclear power plant at Brokdorf, which took ten years to build.

By 1990 PreussenElektra had the largest nuclear generating capacity in Germany, slightly ahead of its much bigger rival RWE. Altogether the company had a stake in 7182MW of nuclear power plant, of which 4898MW was wholly owned by the company.

A major lesson of the oil crisis was that over-reliance on one form of energy was to be avoided. PreussenElektra heeded this message and continued to bolster its existing conventional supply network. In 1970 the 380kV line from Landesbergen to Dollem Bei Stade came into operation and the hard coal station at Kiel began its deliveries to NWK's 220kV network. In 1970–1971 NWK began to operate the 88MW gas turbine power station at Itzehoe. Shortly afterwards NWK's 450MW natural gas-fired unit at Emden was opened.

In 1972–1973 construction work began on the 705MW hard coal/oil power station at Wilhelmshaven which started production in 1976. In 1973 88MW and 57MW gas turbines commenced operations at Audorf and Wilhelmshaven respectively. NWK started construction of the 290MW gas turbine unit at Huntorf in 1975. In the following year the pump storage station Waldeck II was commissioned, 42 years after Waldeck I. The coal-fired 642MW Mehrum power station, in which PreussenElektra and Hannover-Braunschweig GmbH had equal shares, was completed in 1979.

West Germany was one of the first European countries in which environmental concerns became a serious issue. Such concerns will continue during the 1990s and will affect investment costs and patterns. PreussenElektra was quick to tackle the environmental problems caused by its plants. As early as

1977, PreussenElektra had arranged for the partial removal of sulfur, one of the main causes of acid rain, from the chimney gases of the hard coal power station at Wilhelmshaven. Complete desulfurization was completed by 1986. Desulfurization was also completed at the Mehrum power station by 1986, and work continues on other plants.

Concern for the environment and energy conservation also manifests itself in a number of district heating projects and in combined heat and power plants. In 1983, for example, NWK's plant at Glückstadt began production and simultaneously delivered processed steam to a nearby industrial undertaking. Shortly afterwards, PreussenElektra embarked upon a number of schemes with Volkswagen which involved the delivery of heat as well as electricity to the Volkswagen works at Wolfsburg.

After decades of close cooperation, PreussenElektra and NWK finally merged into a single company in 1985. The merged company was subsequently fully integrated into VEBA, which was fully privatized in 1987. In 1986, the first full year of the enlarged company's operation, the 740MW hard coal station Heyden IV at Petershagen-an-der-Weser was completed and the hydroelectric units at Kesselstadt-am-Main began operations.

Three factors will preoccupy PreussenElektra during the 1990s. The first, the environment, has already been incorporated into the planning process. However, the prolonged closures of two nuclear power stations in 1990 to bring them into line with more stringent federal requirements could be a harbinger of stronger regulations to follow.

The second is the creation of the single European market. Given its central location in Europe, PreussenElektra is well placed to take advantage of greater integration of the European electricity network. The gathering support for the idea of a European energy charter, which covers not only the countries of the European Community but also those of EFTA and Central and Eastern Europe, including Russia, will only benefit PreussenElektra.

The third and major challenge for PreussenElektra in the 1990s, however, will come from its involvement in the modernization of the electricity industry of the new postunification German states, especially as PreussenElektra's traditional supply area is conveniently adjacent to east Germany.

PreussenElektra had already agreed in 1987 to construct a 380kV line from Helmstedt to Berlin via Magdeburg, the initial stages of which were completed and operating by late 1989. The 1987 acquisition by PreussenElektra of VIAG's stake in the Braunschweigischen Kohlen Bergwerke (BKB) was an important element of this plan as BKB's plant at Offleben was designated to supply power to this line. PreussenElektra will also be instrumental in the Krümmel-Lübeck-Görries link between Schleswig-Holstein and Mecklenburg-Vorpommerania and the Mecklar-Vieselbach link between Hesse and Thuringia, both of which are to be built during the early 1990s.

Plans for reconstruction of the East German electricity network were set out in the German Electricity Agreement of August 22, 1990. According to this agreement PreussenElektra, Bayernwerk, and RWE hold joint responsibility for overhauling the antiquated, inefficient, and environmentally harmful electricity supply industry in east Germany. PreussenElektra and RWE hold 35% and Bayernwerk 30% of the agent company, which is responsible for Vereinigte Kraftwerks A.G. Peitz (lignite-power stations) and Verbundnetz Elektroenergie A.G., the high tension network.

At the beginning of 1991 these two companies were merged to form the company VEAG Vereinigte Energiewerke A.G. Once the initial assessment of the modernization needs of the East German network is completed, PreussenElektra, RWE, and Bayernwerk will together hold 75% of the shares in company with the remaining shares going to other German utilities and to Electricité de France (EDF), provided there is scope for equivalent investment by the German company in EDF.

On a regional level, the 15 former energy *Kombinate* of the DDR have been converted into distribution companies: 51% of the shares will be open to West German companies and the municipal and regional authorities will be eligible for a maximum of 49%. PreussenElektra plans to become involved in Rostock, Neubrandenburg, Magdeburg, Potsdam, and Frankfurt/Oder, in which RWE will also have a 5% stake. PreussenElektra also plans a 17% holding in the region of Erfurt where Bayernwerk will be the major shareholder.

Principal Subsidiaries: Braunschweigische Kohlen-Bergwerke (99.9%); Energiewerke Frankfurt/Oder AG (90%); Energiewerke Magdeburg AG; Energiewerke Neubrandenburg AG; Energiewerke Potsdam AG; Energiewerke Rostock AG; Fränkische Licht- und Kraftversorgung AG (96.7%); Gasbetriebe GmbH; Gasversorgung für den Landkreis Helmstedt GmbH; Hannover-Braunschweigische Stromversorgung AG (57.5%); HKWG Heizkraftwerk Glückstadt GmbH (70%); Interkohle Beteiligungsgesellschaft mbH (75%); Kernkraftwerk Brokdorf GmbH (80%); Kernkraftwerk Stade GmbH (66.7%); Kernkraftwerk Unterweser GmbH; Kraftwerk Kassel GmbH (60%); Landesgasversorgung Niedersachsen AG (52.8%); Norddeutsche Gesellschaft zur Beratung und Durchführung von Entsorgungsaufgaben bei Kernkraftwerken mbH (88.3%); PESAG Aktiengesellschaft (54.7%); PreussenElektra Telekom GmbH; PreussenElektra Windkraft Niedersachsen GmbH; PreussenElektra Windkraft Schleswig-Holstein GmbH; SCHLESWAG Aktiengesellschaft (58.3%); SCHLESWAG Entsorgung GmbH; Thüga AG (52.8%); Thüga-Konsortium Beteiligungs-GmbH (75.7%); Überlandwerk Schäftersheim GmbH (75%); Überland-Zentrale Helmstedt AG.

Further Reading: Kitchen, Martin, *The Political Economy of Germany 1815–1914*, London, Croom Helm, 1978; Hardach, Kevin, *The Political Economy of Germany in the Twentieth Century*, Berkeley, University of California Press, [n.d.]; Fischer, Wolfram, *Germany in the World Economy during the Nineteenth Century*, German Historical Institute, Annual Lecture, 1983; Berghahn, V.R., *Modern Germany—Society, Economy and Politics in the Twentieth Century*, Cambridge, Cambridge University Press, 1987.

—Debra Johnson

PUBLIC SERVICE ENTERPRISE GROUP INCORPORATED

80 Park Plaza
Newark, New Jersey 07101
U.S.A.
(201) 430-7000
Fax: (201) 430-5983

Public Company
Incorporated: 1903 as Public Service Corporation of New
   Jersey
Employees: 13,500
Sales: $4.80 billion
Stock Exchanges: New York Philadelphia London

Public Service Enterprise Group Incorporated (Enterprise) is a diversified New Jersey holding company whose principal wholly owned subsidiary is Public Service Electric and Gas Company (PSEG). PSEG is a regulated public utility company that provides electric and gas service to more than 5.5 million residents of New Jersey, about 70% of the state's population. PSEG is New Jersey's largest utility; its service area covers about 2,600 square miles in northeast and central New Jersey, and includes the metropolitan areas of Jersey City, Newark, and Trenton.

A smaller wholly owned subsidiary, Enterprise Diversified Holdings, Inc., functions as the parent of Enterprise's nonutility businesses, which include power cogeneration, oil and gas exploration and development, commercial real estate investment and development, and other financial investments. The nonutility businesses, representing about 17% of Enterprise's assets, contributed 6.2% of the holding company's earnings in 1990 with a target goal of contributing 10%.

Enterprise's profits depend primarily on PSEG's sale of electricity, which provides about 73% of utility revenues, and gas, which accounts for about 27% of utility revenues. This is a far different outcome than was anticipated by the company's founder in 1903 when the corporation's main activity and hope for future growth involved the business of transportation, especially the operation of trolley cars.

At the beginning of the 20th century New Jersey's utilities were primarily operators of streetcars; secondarily manufacturers and distributors of gas; and minimally producers of electricity, most of which was used to power trolley cars. Streets, homes, and businesses were, for the most part, lighted by gas, and the industrial use of electricity was in its infancy.

The utility operators were fragmented into hundreds of small companies, many of which were owned by out-of-state interests, inefficiently run, and poorly maintained. On February 19, 1903, in Newark a streetcar full of high school students skidded down an icy hill onto a railroad crossing and was struck by a train, killing and injuring more than 30 people. A subsequent investigation into the affairs of the car operator, the North Jersey Street Railway Company, revealed shoddy management and extreme financial instability, not only of North Jersey but of many other New Jersey streetcar, electric, and gas companies.

Reform was called for by the public, and by the insurance companies and banks whose utility investments were at risk. One of the largest of these banks, the Fidelity Trust Company of Newark, was managed by a member of a prominent New Jersey family, Uzal McCarter. Uzal's brother, 35-year-old lawyer Thomas Nesbitt McCarter, was the youngest attorney general in the state's history, a director of Prudential Insurance Company, and a director and general counsel of Fidelity Trust. Thomas McCarter saw the opportunity offered by the utility crisis and proposed the creation of a single company that would provide transportation, gas, and electricity services for the entire state. The New Jersey, New York, and Pennsylvania financial and political establishments, with which he was well connected, agreed to McCarter's plan; and he resigned his public office to become president of the new corporation.

With an initial $10 million capitalization to begin its acquisition program, Public Service Corporation of New Jersey (PSC) was incorporated in May 1903. The original shareholders were Thomas Dolan, president of Philadelphia's United Gas Improvement Company; John I. Waterbury, president of New York's Manhattan Trust Company; and Thomas McCarter, who in effect represented Prudential Insurance Company and Fidelity Trust. The company clearly originated in the desire of these institutions to secure and re-establish the value of their New Jersey utility investments. Their plan was successful largely thanks to McCarter, who proved to be a strong, skillful manager, especially capable in the financial and political affairs so critical to a growing regulated utility. McCarter served as president for 36 years and as chairman of the board for an additional 6 years, until his retirement in 1945. During this long period he dominated the company's affairs.

PSC began by acquiring the securities of four street railway companies and one electric generating company, the beginning of an acquisition program that eventually brought more than 500 gas, electric, and traction businesses under the control of PSC and its successor companies. Revenues for 1904, the first year of operation, were $8.4 million from street railways, $5.4 million from gas manufacturing and sale, and $3.5 million from electricity.

Along with growth in operations and revenues over time came changes in corporate structure. Until 1907 PSC was a straightforward operating company, acquiring and leasing properties and improving and managing them. State regulation of utilities was institutionalized in 1907, by the creation of the State Railroad Commission, which expanded in 1910 to become the New Jersey State Board of Public Utility Commissioners. In August 1907 PSC was obliged to incorporate the Public Service Railway Company as a wholly owned subsidiary to operate its traction lines. In 1909 PSC formed Public Service Gas Company, also wholly owned, and in 1910 created Public Service Electric Company to generate and distribute electricity. PSC therefore became a holding company for the operating companies. There were further changes for the operating companies. In 1924 the gas and electric businesses were merged to form Public Service Electric and Gas Company, and in 1948 PSC was dissolved and PSEG became the parent company with the transportation company as a subsidiary.

McCarter's original belief that PSC's future lay primarily in the transportation business proved to be erroneous. This business did grow and prosper in the early years, culminating in the opening in 1916 of a magnificent new street railway terminal and office building in Newark. PSC's transportation system grew to carry over 450 million passengers a year. It included street and interurban railways centered around Newark and reaching south to Camden and Trenton, as well as the ownership of amusement parks, ferry lines, cab companies in Newark and Camden, and eventually jitney and bus lines.

The company pioneered the development and use of gas-electric streetcars and buses, and in 1937 began operating the world's first diesel-electric bus fleet. The subsidiary Public Service Transportation Company was formed in 1924 to operate buses, and in 1928 this company and Public Service Railway Company were merged to form Public Service Coordinated Transport Company. The spread of suburban residential areas coupled with the rise of the automobile led to the gradual replacement of the streetcar and the interurban rail by the bus, however, and eventually to declining profitability for all forms of public transportation. The 1960s and 1970s saw a continuation of rising fares and increasing dependence on state subsidies. In 1971 Public Service Coordinated Transport became Transport of New Jersey, largely an operator of buses owned by the state and leased to the company. In 1979 legislation was passed to permit New Jersey to acquire and operate private bus lines, and PSEG negotiated the sale of its transport subsidiary to the state.

Unlike the traction companies it acquired, PSC's early gas acquisitions tended to be relatively sound physically and financially, and PSC's goal was to consolidate and expand these properties. In the early years gas was manufactured from coal or oil—natural gas pipelines were in the future—and sold mainly for lighting, cooking, and heating water; electricity use by the public was still minimal. PSC increased its gas sales by aggressively marketing gas stoves and water heaters as well as by increasing its distribution areas. Gas sales grew from 5 billion cubic feet in 1904 to about 20 billion cubic feet by the mid-1920s, then slowed during the 1930s and early 1940s. After World War II the use of gas for home heating expanded enormously, outstripping the company's gas manufacturing capacity. In 1949 PSEG began purchasing natural gas from Texas Eastern Gas Corporation and in 1950 from Transcontinental Gas Pipe Line Corporation.

Customers gradually were switched over from manufactured gas to natural gas, a process completed by 1965. During the energy shortages of the early 1970s PSEG experimented with plans to purchase liquefied natural gas from Algeria and to produce synthetic natural gas from naphtha. Both projects proved to be impractical because of cost, but gas sales continued to increase, reaching 200 billion cubic feet annually by the late 1970s. In 1972 PSEG established a subsidiary, Energy Development Corporation, to engage in gas exploration and development. EDC continued to explore for oil and gas for Public Service Enterprise Group as a subsidiary of its Enterprise Diversified Holdings Company. PSEG also continued to expand its gas sales by encouraging home heating conversions from oil, selling gas for electric cogeneration, and experimenting with natural-gas-fueled vehicles. PSEG also enlarged its gas supply by initiating purchases of natural gas from Canada in 1990.

Electric generating machinery at the turn of the century was still primitive and unreliable, with little residential or industrial use of electricity. When PSC began operations, its 14 generating stations had a capacity of about 40,000 kilowatts, most of which went to power street railways, realizing $3.5 million in electric revenues in 1904. Generator technology improved and electrical use increased tremendously over time. By 1978 PSEG operated 13 generating plants with a capacity of 9 million kilowatts and achieved electric revenues of more than $1.5 billion. In 1990 the company's generating capability was 10.1 million kilowatts, and electric revenues were $3.3 billion.

The character of PSEG's electrical history was shaped by its role as an innovator and pioneer of advanced techniques in power generation. PSEG began early in this role by installing then-new rotating steam turbines in its Newark and Jersey City plants in 1905 and 1906. These two formerly separate plants acquired by PSC were linked into a single network, increasing the reliability and efficiency of the power system. The idea of linkage was enlarged in 1927 by agreements with Philadelphia Electric Company and Pennsylvania Power & Light Company for the interconnection and exchange of power. This led to the operation of a 230,000-volt transmission ring that was the world's first integrated power pool and that has expanded over the years to become the Pennsylvania–New Jersey–Maryland interconnection.

In 1933 PSEG experimented with a 20,000-kilowatt mercury boiler-turbine, the largest unit of its type in the world, but mercury technology proved unsatisfactory. The company was also one of the first utilities to experiment with wind-power generation, financing pilot wind-power stations in Burlington, New Jersey, during the early 1930s. Slowing service growth during the Great Depression put an end to this project, however.

PSEG pioneered the use of airplane-type jet engines to drive electric generators for periods of peak power requirements. Generating units at the mouths of coal mines and pumped-storage generating plants were also built as part of the company's continued search for low-cost power. Tests of solar generating systems were carried out during the late 1970s but proved not to be cost-effective.

PSEG joined with Philadelphia Electric Company, Atlantic City Electric Company, and Delmarva Power & Light Company during the 1960s to plan and build nuclear generating facilities. The first plant, owned jointly with Philadelphia Electric Company, was put in service at Peach Bottom, Pennsylvania, in 1974. Another nuclear plant began operation in 1977 at Salem, New Jersey, and a third went on line at Hope Creek, New Jersey, both in the southern part of the state.

Along with construction cost overruns, PSEG has had other problems with nuclear power, including the temporary closing of the Peach Bottom units in 1987 by the U.S. Nuclear Regulatory Commission because of mismanagement. Among the infractions were workers sleeping on duty. This incident led to financial losses, although Philadelphia Electric, as the operator, was generally held responsible. PSEG was also criticized in 1988 because of below-average performance of its Salem and Hope Creek facilities. In 1989, PSEG was required to pay customers a $32 million rebate as compensation for the Peach Bottom shutdown. PSEG made a determined effort to improve its nuclear operations, and in 1990 reported that its nuclear plants had their most productive year ever. The company held a 95% interest in the Hope Creek plant, and a 42.5% interest in the Peach Bottom and Salem units. In 1990 about 47% of PSEG's electricity supplied to customers was provided by nuclear generation.

The period since the mid-1980s has seen a corporate restructuring and a gradual move to diversify. On May 1, 1986, PSEG became a subsidiary of Enterprise, which also serves as a parent of the company's nonutility subsidiaries. In 1989, the nonutility businesses were gathered together into a nonutility subholding company subsidiary, Enterprise Diversified Holdings, Inc. (Holdings). In 1989 Enterprise agreed to buy Pelto Oil Corporation from the Southdown Company for about $320 million. Pelto, with substantial oil and gas reserves, operated as a subsidiary of Holdings. Enterprise's other nonutility investments include aircraft and utility plant leasing, alternative energy projects, cogeneration, real estate, venture capital, and leveraged buyout funds.

The central motive for this diversification is that the state of New Jersey limits PSEG's earnings to 13% of equity. Thus Enterprise, like many utilities, feels it must diversify to grow. E. James Ferland, chairman, president, and CEO since 1986, has stated that Enterprise's future diversification will be focused on businesses relating to the energy industry. The announcement in November 1990 of a joint venture with Brooklyn Union Gas Company to build and operate a $250 million cogeneration plant to produce electricity for Kennedy International Airport in New York City is a step in that direction. Meanwhile Enterprise will continue for the foreseeable future primarily to serve the people of New Jersey through its ownership of the state's largest utility.

Principal Subsidiaries: Public Service Electric and Gas Company; Enterprise Diversified Holdings, Inc.

Further Reading: Conniff, James C.G., and Richard Conniff, *The Energy People: A History of PSE&G,* Newark, New Jersey, Public Service Electric and Gas Company, 1978; Smith, Robert I., *A Cycle of Service: The Story of Public Service Electric and Gas Company,* New York, The Newcomen Society in North America, 1980.

—Bernard A. Block

RUHRGAS AG

Huttropstrasse 60
W-4300 Essen 1
Federal Republic of Germany
(201) 184-1
Fax: (201) 184–3766

Private Company
Incorporated: 1926 as AG für Kohleverwertung
Employees: 9,235
Sales: DM12.19 billion (US$8.05 billion)

Ruhrgas AG, Germany's largest natural gas distribution company, plays a prominent role in international business and politics. Germany is the world's leading natural gas importer. As recently as the early 1960s, however, Ruhrgas was an internationally insignificant private German utility company, supplying coke-derived gas from German coal. The rise in its fortunes has paralleled the massive growth in the use of natural gas in Europe since World War II.

Natural gas is a hydrocarbon mixture largely consisting of methane. Although natural gas has been used for fuel in China for at least 3,000 years, it was unknown in Europe before its discovery in England in 1659. Natural gas is used primarily for space heating, manufacturing processes, and power generation. Until the early 1960s, natural gas tended to be seen as an unwelcome byproduct of oil production. Since long-distance transportation was difficult or expensive, many producing companies did not bother to separate the gas and sell it commercially. They simply burned or "flared" it off near the wellhead. Many of the world's oil fields were lit at night by these natural gas waste flares.

Most of the early advances in natural gas technology occurred in the United States, where natural gas is produced in abundance. The invention of leakproof pipe-coupling in 1890 is regarded as the beginning of modern long-distance pipeline transportation of natural gas. From the late 1920s, further developments in pipeline technology and the construction of ten major transmission systems eventually made natural gas cheaper to transport and affordable to U.S. consumers. By the 1930s, natural gas was rapidly replacing other energy sources as a home-heating material in the United States.

The development of the natural gas industry in Europe was much slower. The economic dislocations of the 1930s and World War II also slowed the development of the European industry. As late as 1965, only 1% of German energy needs were met by natural gas and few residential customers heated their homes with it. Coal-derived artificial gases and other materials dominated the industrial market, and oil and coal dominated home heating.

Ruhrgas has its earliest antecedents in a number of artificial-gas-producing and selling firms in the Ruhr, Germany's most important industrial area, that today encompasses Essen, Dortmund, and several other cities. Coal-derived gases predominated; the area is at the center of a rich coal deposit.

The first German gasworks, for street lighting, was built in Hanover in 1825, but Ruhrgas's home city of Essen did not have its own gasworks, Essener Gas A.G., until 1856. Although artificial gas became popular for manufacturing processes and municipal street lighting, it was less competitive with oil and petroleum products for heating purposes throughout most of the 19th century. The abundant coal of the Ruhr made artificial gas especially attractive to businesses. By 1900, the German gas industry was producing 1.2 billion cubic meters annually.

The first commercial German natural gas deposits were discovered in bore holes at Neuengamme in 1910. Between 1911 and 1919, when the source failed, small quantities from these deposits were used industrially in Hamburg. Coal-derived gases would continue to dominate the German market for another 50 years.

In 1926 Vereinigte Stahlwerke A.G. and Stinnes-Zechen set up a new gas transportation company, the A.G. für Kohleverwertung, in Essen in 1926. The directors envisaged a system for selling surplus gas to customers throughout the entire country. The following year, the company signed a contract to transport gas to the city of Hanover. On May 30th, 1928 the company was renamed Ruhrgas AG.

By 1929 Ruhrgas had secured a supply contract with the city of Cologne, had built a 180-kilometer pipeline from Hamm to Hanover, and had planned a pipeline to Frankfurt. During the early 1930s gas supply contracts were concluded with Düsseldorf and with a number of industrial concerns, including the Adam Opel motorworks. By 1936 Ruhrgas was delivering 2 billion cubic meters of coke-derived gas along a 1,128-kilometer-long network.

In 1938 the Deilmann company found natural gas near Bentheim in north Germany. The well was large and the flow took weeks to control, but it was another 6 years before a 75-kilometer pipeline was built to carry this gas to chemical works in Hüls.

In 1942 Ruhrgas was prospering, with deliveries of more than 3 billion cubic meters over a pipeline network of 1,644 kilometers. Although crews worked to repair frequent bomb damage, Allied bombing took a heavy toll, and gas deliveries fell drastically. At times only 3 out of 51 cokeries on the pipeline network were capable of supplying gas.

After the war Ruhrgas recovered more quickly than many German concerns. By 1946, 98% of its pipeline network was restored but deliveries were only 1 billion cubic meters, one-third of the volume reached during wartime peak levels. Two years later, Ruhrgas and Thyssengas were exporting gas to the Netherlands. In 1951, with demand greater than supply, Ruhrgas was delivering gas at well over its 1942 record levels. The company's pipeline network had reached 2,000 kilometers and the company employed 1,043 workers.

In 1954 Ruhrgas began to take natural gas from the Bentheim field and began to demonstrate to its customers that this fuel, with estimated reserves of 20 to 30 billion cubic meters in West Germany alone, could be of the same quality as coal-derived gas.

In 1956 a new company, Erdgasverkaufs-Gesellschaft of Münster, was organized to market the newly discovered natural gas of north Germany. Within four years the Dutch firm NAM discovered the Slochteren field in the Netherlands, then the largest natural gas find in Europe.

From 1965 onward, even larger offshore discoveries in the North Sea in Dutch, British, Norwegian, and Danish sectors made it clear that Europe had large reserves of commercially exploitable natural gas. Europeans began to adapt American pipeline technology to bring it ashore and distribute it over long distances. Cheap natural gas won many new industrial and municipal customers.

During the same period, Soviet technicians found huge natural gas reserves in Siberia. The Soviet government realized that new technology made its gas exportable to Europe as a lucrative hard-currency earner.

Natural gas looked like the fuel of the future, but through most of the 1960s coke-derived gas transport remained the primary business of Ruhrgas as it extended its pipeline network through the most populous regions of West Germany. Although in 1965 natural gas supplied only a small portion of the country's energy, it already represented 10% of Ruhrgas's total deliveries of 7 billion cubic meters. The company entered into large-scale supply contracts with Dutch and other gas production companies to ensure that it would be able to meet the booming demand. Supply contracts of 20 or 25 years' duration are normal in the industry.

From 1965 to 1968, 371 kilometers of extensive new pipelines were built in cooperation with Thyssen and other companies to transport north German and Dutch natural gas, first to Mannheim and then to south Germany.

In 1969 Ruhrgas and the Soviet agency Soyuzneftexport negotiated the sale of Soviet gas. The talks coincided with Chancellor Brandt's new *Ostpolitik* or initiative to improve West Germany's relations with the Soviet Union and other Communist neighbors to its east, but worried the country's American allies. On February 1, 1970 an agreement was reached, providing for the yearly sale of 3 billion cubic meters of Soviet natural gas to Ruhrgas. The deal also provided for the export of badly-needed pipe to the Soviet Union by the German industrial firm Mannesmann and financing by a consortium of German banks.

By 1970 natural gas already represented 70% of Ruhrgas's deliveries of 18 billion cubic meters along its 4,991-kilometer pipeline network. In February 1971 it reached an agreement with the Italian company SNAM to deliver gas from Aachen to the Swiss border along a pipeline now known as the Trans Europe Natural Gas Pipeline.

Increased quantities of natural gas were purchased under agreements with the Soviet Union. A 1974 contract provided for an annual delivery of 9.5 billion cubic meters until the year 2000. Ruhrgas, however, knew that it needed to diversify its supply sources. In 1973 it headed a buying consortium that negotiated a contract with Phillips Petroleum of the United States to buy an annual 5 billion cubic meters of Norwegian natural gas from the Ekofisk field in the North Sea.

By 1975, natural gas represented 89% of Ruhrgas's annual delivery of 27 billion cubic meters. The company entered fur-

ther consortiums to buy Norwegian gas. French companies also wanted access to Soviet natural gas. In June 1976 Gaz de France joined with Ruhrgas to form Mittel-Europäische-Gasleitungsgesellschaft (MEGAL GmbH), a pipeline company, to transport Soviet gas from the German-Czech border to the French border.

In September 1977 gas from the Norwegian Ekofisk field began to flow through a new subsea pipeline to the German port of Emden in fulfillment of a contract between Phillips Petroleum and a consortium led by Ruhrgas, which included Gasunie of the Netherlands and Gaz de France. Ruhrgas's share of the gas was 50%.

In November 1981 Ruhrgas took the controversial step of signing an agreement with the Soviet Gas export agency Soyuzgaz export to help build and finance a huge new gas pipeline from the Soviet Union. For the obvious needs of diversification, Ruhrgas sought and contracted with a number of other countries to supply its needs. Ruhrgas has continued to exercise options for increased deliveries from the Netherlands. In 1991 the company signed an agreement with the Dutch company Gasunie for the supply of an additional 100 billion cubic meters up to the year 2013.

Ruhrgas is developing facilities at the German port of Wilhelmshaven for the import of liquefied natural gas (LNG) from Algeria, Nigeria, and other far-flung sources.

In September 1982 Ruhrgas had joined a consortium including Thyssen, Gasunie, Gaz de France, and the Norwegian companies to buy natural gas through an 850-mile undersea pipeline from the Norwegian Statfjord field. The line connected with the Ekofisk pipeline that had been delivering gas to the North German port of Emden since 1977. In 1985 this pipeline became operational.

The company announced in August 1990 that it intended to make Norway a more important supply source. The same year, Ruhrgas and the other German importers exercised their option under the 1986 Troll Agreement with Norway and seven Norwegian North Sea gas producers to increase their imports from 8.5 billion cubic meters a year to 13.5 billion cubic meters per year beginning in 1993. Ruhrgas will take about 80% of this annual increase. Two new undersea pipelines are planned.

In the early 1990s 24% of Germany's natural gas came from domestic sources, 32% from the Soviet Union, 28% from the Netherlands, and only 15% from Norway. Denmark provides just 1% of the total. By the year 2000, however, it is envisaged that Norway will furnish about 25% of Germany's supplies and much of this will be bought by Ruhrgas. In recognition of Norway's importance, Ruhrgas is making a major public relations effort in Norway, sponsoring scholarships for Norwegian students in Germany and German-Norwegian history conferences.

Through the 1980s the German gas industry was able to expand its residential market steadily at an annual rate of 300,000 households per year as more German household consumers switched from oil- and coal-based heating systems to natural gas. By 1990 about 33% of West Germany's households had gas-fired central heating. In 1990 gas demand in West Germany reached an all-time high of 68.6 million tons of coal equivalent (tce).

The unification process that began in November 1989 connected the western German gas industry with the markets in the former East Germany, where gas demand was 9.5 million tce unit and represented only 8.7% of East German energy consumption. A large gas supply infrastructure was already in place but 40% of deliveries were to power plants and 35% to industry. Only 4% went to private households.

This market opportunity was enhanced greatly by the realization that much of East German industry was an ecological disaster area. Heavy dependence on brown lignite coal and coal-derived gas meant that pollution levels were far above the levels considered acceptable in West Germany and other European Community countries.

Concern about the environment has given a huge boost to Ruhrgas and other natural gas companies as they stress the environmental advantages of their product. Studies by the German Environmental Protection Agency show that natural gas is the cleanest fossil fuel and interferes less with the environment than any other source of energy. It is moved by buried pipelines. Almost no pollution or waste heat is produced by its conversion into a secondary energy source. Natural gas-fired plants emit hardly any uncombusted matter such as soot.

In the past, the German government has had to balance this advantage against the fact that Germany's coal reserves remain vast. In the former West Germany alone, they are estimated at 25,000 million tons and unified Germany is second in the world after the Soviet Union in the production of lignite brown coal. In the past, government policy has provided subsidies to keep seams in working order in the event of an energy crisis, but the "green" vote and the environmental crisis are compelling an increased emphasis on natural gas.

By December 1989 Ruhrgas had signed an extensive cooperation agreement with Schwarze Pumpe (Black Pump), the East German energy group. The agreement provided for contracts at all levels and envisaged the connection of the two countries' gas supply grids.

By the middle of 1990, the Erdgasversorgungsgesellschaft (EVG), a subsidiary of Ruhrgas and Verbundnetz Gas AG (VNG), a company originally under Schwarze Pumpe's authority and responsible for the country's gas supply network, began to build a 300-mile connecting pipeline through Thuringia and Saxony at a cost of DM600 million. Ruhrgas agreed to supply VNG with 2 billion cubic meters of natural gas when the pipeline was completed in 1992.

In June 1990 Ruhrgas purchased 35% of VNG from Treuhandanstalt, the East German privatization agency. Another 10% was purchased by the West German company BEB.

In September 1991 the remaining tranches of shares in VNG were divided up among the East German cities and several European energy companies, giving them access to the East German gas network. Wintershall AG, a subsidiary of BASF with 15% of VNG, and British Gas, with 5% of VNG and an interest in several former municipal and local networks, announced plans for aggressive new investment and competition. Wintershall said it would challenge Ruhrgas's traditional market dominance with new pipelines.

Ruhrgas's growth has been phenomenal and it believes there is great potential for further expansion in a unified Germany. In 1951 it delivered 3 billion cubic meters of artificial gases. In 1990 it sold 510 billion kilowatt hours of gas, 98% of which was natural. With a commanding position in the German gas industry and ownership of its own highly complex transmission system of pipelines, compressor stations, underground storage, and other facilities, Ruhrgas is a national institution.

Ruhrgas is not afraid of market competition. Governmental intervention in the natural gas industry is unlikely because the changing European political situation seems to have eased previous economic and strategic worries about natural gas supplies. Of all gas used in the European Community member states, 53% is now transmitted across borders. As the end of 1992 and the European single market draws nearer, Ruhrgas is arguing for a Community-wide, market-oriented non-regulatory energy policy. Ruhrgas believes this philosophy, which has guided German energy policy, is responsible for the company's success.

Principal Subsidiaries: Elster AG; Elster Produktion GmbH; Loi Essen Industrieofenlagen GmbH; Pipeline Engineering Gesellschaft für Planung, Bau- und Betriebsüberwachung von Fernleitungen mbH; diga-die gasheizung; Erdgas-Energiesysteme GmbH; Mittelrheinische Erdgastransport Gesellschaft mbH (67%); Ferngas Nordbayern GmbH (54%); Trans Europa Naturgas Pipeline GmbH (51%); Trans European Natural Gas Pipeline Finance Company Limited (50%); Erdgasversorgungsgesellschaft mbH (50%); Süddeutsche Erdgas Transport Gesellschaft mbH (50%); MEGAL GmbH (50%); MEGAL Finance Company Ltd. (50%).

Further Reading: Gas Today and Tomorrow, Essen, Ruhrgas, 1991.

—Clark Siewert

RWE GROUP

Kruppstrasse 5
4300 Essen
Federal Republic of Germany
(201) 185-0
Fax: (201) 185 51 99

Public Company
Incorporated: 1898 as Rheinisch-Westfälisches Elektrizi-
   tätswerk Aktiengesellschaft
Employees: 102,190
Sales: DM49.8 billion (US$32.87 billion)
Stock Exchanges: Berlin Bremen Düsseldorf Frankfurt
   Hamburg Hanover Munich Stuttgart Zürich
   Basel Amsterdam Geneva

RWE AG is the dominant electricity producer in Germany, supplying 34% of the country's electricity in 1990 via a distribution and transmission network that extends over 139,000 kilometers—that is, a distance over three times around the world. The company was founded at the end of the 19th century to supply electricity to the city of Essen. Originally known as Rheinisch-Westfälisches Elektrizitätswerk AG, the company's name was officially changed to RWE AG in February 1990 as part of a major restructuring exercise. Since then, RWE AG has been the holding company for the RWE Group, which has six independently operating divisions. The entire field of mains-borne energy and water supply was taken over by RWE Energie AG, a subsidiary company of RWE AG. Electricity production remains its core business but there has been some diversification in recent years into other energy sectors, namely oil, natural gas, and petrochemicals.

The timing of RWE's foundation was fortuitous. At the end of the 19th century, Germany underwent the most rapid industrialization to date. In the decades before World War I, Germany moved into second place behind the United States among the world's industrial nations. Between 1880 and 1913 German coal output increased fourfold and production of steel tenfold. Chemicals manufacturing and heavy engineering were other strengths. Given its location at the heart of Germany's coal and steel industry and the presence of factories owned by Krupp, Thyssen, Siemens, and other German industrial giants, Essen was an appropriate base for the company that would come to dominate Germany's electricity supply. Even today, following the relative decline of heavy industry, Essen's state of North Rhine Westphalia still produces over one-quarter of German gross domestic product. Essen itself remains the energy center of Germany, playing host also to Ruhrgas and Ruhrkohle.

Such a dynamic economy, with its predominance of energy-intensive industries, needed power. Towards the end of the 19th century, only Friedrich Krupp AG generated electricity in Essen; this power was consumed primarily by Krupp plants. However, the municipal authorities were debating the desirability of establishing electricity supplies for electric trams and street lighting; small-scale electric street lighting was introduced in 1888 and the debate about power for trams was well under way in 1890.

In 1896, Elektrizitäts AG vorm W. Lahmeyer & Company of Frankfurt am Main applied to the authorities of Essen for approval to build and manage a small power station. Despite heavy competition from Allgemeine Elektrizitäts-Gesellschaft (AEG) and Siemens & Halske, in 1898 Lahmeyer signed a 40-year contract to supply Essen with electricity. On April 25, 1898, Lahmeyer, together with banks from Frankfurt, founded the Rheinisch-Westfälisches Elektrizitätswerk Aktiengesellschaft (RWE). The company began operating with a steam generator to supply a few thousand consumers in the immediate environs of Essen. The first RWE-generated electricity was supplied on April 1, 1900.

From the beginning, RWE's leaders were conscious of the key role electricity would play in the industrial economy. Hugo Stinnes, a leading industrialist in the region, became chairman of the board. He was convinced the electricity industry would grow into an industrial giant and that an integrated supply industry able to take advantage of economies of scale was the best way forward. RWE throughout its history has been heavily involved in the development of larger-scale generating units and high voltage transmission and distribution networks.

Stinnes also believed the task of developing this new industry was too important to be left solely to private enterprise. He concluded that the way forward lay in the coming together of private business and public authorities in a synthesis of the principles of private enterprise and public service. The city fathers of Essen, Mülheim an der Ruhr, and Gelsenkirchen, persuaded by Stinnes of the advantages of this approach, bought shares in RWE. By the beginning of World War I, a majority of the seats on the RWE board—17 out of 29—were occupied by public representatives. The mixed economy of RWE was established from an early stage. Private entrepreneurs managed the daily affairs of the company but the public authorities retained an influence on all fundamental policy questions.

It was in the first decade of the 20th century that the basic structure of Germany's industry took shape. In 1908, RWE and Vereinigte Elektrizitätswerke Westfalen AG (VEW) signed the first demarcation contract—a contract which remains in force to this day. Demarcation contracts mark out the supply areas of a utility and enable the larger companies to carve up the country by agreeing to keep out of each other's territory. Demarcation contracts are bolstered by concession contracts which grant utilities exclusive rights to public land for cables in return for concession payments to public authorities. In view of its growing contracts with a number of municipal authorities, RWE was rapidly able to build up its business and extend its supply area.

The system of concession contracts has persisted until the present day. However, attempts are being made to open up electricity supply to competition again. In 1980 a 20-year limit was placed on the duration of a concession contract, and by the end of 1994 local authorities will be free to chose alternative electricity suppliers. Large amounts of money are at stake; Essen, for example, receives 20% of RWE's non-industrial tariff income, an arrangement the city may wish to leave intact. However, other utilities are known to wish to expand their activities into RWE's area and competition could become more intensive as the 1990s unfold.

In 1899 Stinnes took on the young engineer Bernhard Goldenberg as technical adviser. By 1902 Goldenberg had become chairman of the technical board and was deciding company policy. Goldenberg shared Stinnes's belief that it was necessary to take advantage of scale economies if electricity supply was to be cost-effective. This strategy of maximizing sales needed a secure and plentiful supply of cheap fuel and technological advances in generation and distribution.

From the beginning, coal has been central to the growth of the German industrial economy and to the development of RWE in particular. Coal retains its importance today. In 1990-1991, brown coal and hard coal accounted for 48.1% and 23% respectively of electricity generated by RWE. Nuclear power was responsible for a further 21%, with water accounting for almost 4%. Gas and oil accounted for RWE's remaining primary energy consumption.

Hugo Stinnes, the driving force behind the creation of RWE, was originally a coal merchant and was most conscious of the direct connection between coal and electricity. In the early days of RWE, brown coal was not at first considered for use in electricity generation. The Reisholz power station built by Goldenberg to the south of Düsseldorf in 1908-1909, for example, was designed for hard coal. Goldenberg was, however, aware of the potential of brown coal, which is mined from open-cast mines and hence is much easier and cheaper to mine than hard coal, which is mined from deep pits, and knew that Europe's largest reserve of this fuel was to be found west of the Rhine between Cologne and Aachen.

The end of World War I brought serious coal shortages as two million tons of hard coal had to be exported monthly as part of Germany's war reparations. This situation precipitated the use of brown coal in Germany and RWE set about securing its brown coal supplies. In 1920, a "common interest" contract involving an exchange of shares was signed between RWE and Roddergrube AG according to which Roddergrube, the first company commercially to exploit brown coal back in the 1870s, undertook to supply brown coal to RWE. Shortly afterwards, RWE acquired a majority holding in Roddergrube. Similar "common interest" contracts were signed with other coal producers in 1921.

In 1932 RWE developed its relationships with coal producers a stage further and acquired a majority shareholding in Rheinische Aktiengesellschaft für Braunkohlenbergbau (Rheinbraun). RWE's participation helped Rheinbraun, which owned the Fortuna power station, one of the largest power stations at that time and the subject of expansion plans, to extend its contract to supply electricity to the city of Cologne. Over the years, the Rheinbraun family of companies has been fully integrated into the RWE group. RWE's relationship with Rheinbraun is typical of the complex cooperation and ownership network which RWE gradually developed with coal producers and other electricity suppliers.

German military requirements of the late 1930s and World War II made big demands on German heavy industry, including electricity. The end of the war brought with it the need for massive reconstruction, not only for the German economy but also for RWE. The Goldenberg works were destroyed, other plants were severely damaged, and coal mines, pipelines, and distribution networks were devastated. Massive external financial assistance was required as much as technical rebuilding.

The RWE leadership was more convinced than ever that the future of the electricity industry lay in the development of a fully integrated network of electricity producers, and was instrumental in the 1948 formation of the Deutsche Verbundgesellschaft (DVG). The membership of this organization, which provides a forum for national electricity cooperation, is composed of Germany's largest electricity utilities.

Reconstruction brought technical opportunities. Plant was not merely rebuilt or repaired; obsolete equipment was replaced by the most modern high pressure boilers and turbines.

In 1952 RWE and its subsidiaries were finally released from the postwar control of the Allies. At this time Franz Hellberg, an internationally recognized expert on brown coal, joined the RWE board. He was charged with the task of building up the production of electricity from brown coal, a comparatively cheap source of fuel.

In the postwar years, brown coal was increasingly mined from new deep-lying open-cast mines. These mines, which could reach a depth of 300 meters, were part of a transition to bigger management units and required new mining technology. Excavators and diggers were developed which could move 100,000 cubic meters of coal a day.

By 1957, 45% of RWE's brown coal supply originated from the new open-cast mines. This transition made big investment demands. An extraordinary general meeting in October 1959 increased authorized capital by DM147 million to DM575 million. These funds were used to acquire 85% of the brown coal company Neurath AG.

Increasing electricity demand necessitated productivity increases. RWE chose to bring these about through a major rationalization of Rhine brown coal. In December 1959 it transferred its shareholding in Neurath AG to Rheinbraun. In the same month, several other brown coal subsidiaries of RWE were brought under the umbrella of Rheinbraun. The assets so transferred included those of the Braunkohlen- und Brikettwerke Roddergrube AG, the Rheinische AG für Braunkohlenbergbau und Brikettfabrikation and the Braunkohlen-Industrie AG (Biag).

As the German economic miracle got into its stride in the early 1960s, electricity demand surged ahead and a new phase of power station construction orders began. Brown coal provided the basis for this expansion, but it was also in the early 1960s that RWE became involved in the development of nuclear power. By 1990 nuclear power was responsible for over 20% of RWE-generated electricity. However, questions have been raised in Germany about the safety of nuclear power, which will limit the contribution of this source of electricity in the foreseeable future.

The development of secure and cheap fuel supplies was only one factor in RWE's growth. Bernhard Goldenberg initiated the policy of the development of coal and the technology of larger generating units, but Arthur Koepchen, Goldenberg's successor in 1917 as chairman of the technical board, was responsible for implementing the distribution of electricity over much longer distances than had hitherto been possible.

Koepchen was firmly anchored in the RWE tradition of optimizing economies of scale. He believed electricity production was justified on economic grounds only through the generation of electricity in favorable locations and through the supply of large districts, and envisaged increasing cooperation between neighboring utility companies. In short, he had a vision of a fully integrated national electricity supply industry with cooperation between power stations regardless of fuel basis.

In order to achieve this, Koepchen had to connect RWE with the south where, since World War I, utilities in Prussia, Bavaria and Baden had developed rapidly, with a particular reliance on hydroelectric power. Koepchen's goal was to connect the Alpine hydroelectric plants with the stations on the Rhine and the Ruhr. This brought legal, technical and economic challenges.

Koepchen drew on the experience of the South Californian Edison Company which, since 1921, had demonstrated the possibility of transmitting electricity over high tension cables of 220 kilovolts, rather than the previous technical limit of 110 kilovolts. This breakthrough made possible a more extensive distribution network possible and in 1924 RWE began the construction of a north-south network with the assistance of Germany's biggest electrical engineering companies, Siemens and AEG.

By April 1930, Germany's first "electric highway" was completed, linking the densely populated areas of the Rhineland and Westphalia with the South. It was only within such a union that the development of the water power of Bavaria made economic sense, as Bavaria was sparsely populated in comparison to RWE's main supply area and by itself could not justify the construction of large production units. With work on the distribution network underway, RWE became involved in the construction of power stations in the southern part of the country. For example, in 1924 RWE participated, along with Grosskraftwerk Würtemberg, in the founding of the Voralpberge Illwerke and in 1928 work on the massive Schluchseewerk in the southern Black Forest began.

Electricity production has always been and remains one of the main sectors of RWE's activities. In 1988 RWE took a major step towards diversification with the acquisition of Deutsche Texaco. This deal prompted a reorganization of RWE's activities into the following six divisions: energy, mining and raw materials; petroleum and chemicals; waste management; mechanical and plant engineering, and construction. All divisions operate independently. RWE AG fulfils the role of a holding company and serves to steer and coordinate Group interests in all strategically important matters.

The two main revenue-generating divisions were energy, organized under RWE Energie AG, and petroleum and petrochemicals, organized under RWE-DEA AG für Mineralöl und Chemie (RWE-DEA). In the financial year 1990–1991 RWE Energie contributed 37% of the total earnings of the RWE group and RWE-DEA 41% (including petroleum tax).

The formation of RWE-DEA signals the fact that, although electricity remains the core business of the RWE group, diversification within the energy field is an important theme of the future. RWE-DEA has its roots in the 19th century. It was established in 1899 as the Deutsche Tiefbohr AG. In 1911 its name was changed to Deutcesh Erdöl AG. In 1966 the Texaco

Group acquired over 97% of the capital and altered the name to Deutsche Texaco in 1970. On June 29, 1988, Texaco sold its share in the company to RWE, giving rise to the reorganization is RWE and the creation of RWE-DEA. This new division of RWE was responsible for sales of DM20.2 billion in 1990–1991. RWE-DEA is involved in exploration for and processing and marketing of crude oil and natural gas, and the production of chemicals of petrochemicals.

The petroleum business of RWE-DEA's dominant source of income and is likely to remain so. The company has rationalized its retail network. It is engaged in some expansion in eastern Germany and is examining the possibility of involvement in other European countries. Interest in the former East Germany is not confined to petroleum products. In June 1991 an international consortium led by RWE and VEBA, with shares of 37.5% each, was reportedly poised to take over east Germany's largest oil refinery, Schwedt, which has an annual capacity of 11 million tons and a pipeline link to the USSR. RWE-DEA also intends to build up its chemical business and with a view to this it made a bid for Vista Chemicals of the United States in December 1990. The bid was ultimately successful. RWE-DEA finalized the acquisition in June 1991.

By taking over RWE's core business of electricity production, RWE Energie represents the greatest continuity with the past. The 1990s hold out exciting possibilities for this division as a result of the unification of Germany in 1990. The east German electricity supply industry was unmodernized, inefficient, and polluting. The joint venture Vereinigte Energiewerke AG (VEAG) was formed in 1991 to rectify the situation. In return for investment in the supply of electricity to eastern Germany of DM30-40 billion, VEAG has been accorded a major slice of the market. The main participants in the venture are RWE Energie and PreussenElektra, with 35% each, and Bayernwerk, with 30%. Electricité de France is expected to exercise its option to participate in VEAG and further foreign participation cannot be ruled out. Eastern Germany will preoccupy the electricity arm of RWE for some years. However, the demands of European integration and continuing environmental vigilance will also provide major challenges in the 1990s.

Principal Subsidiaries: RWE Energie Aktiengesellschaft; Kernkraftwerke Gundremmingen Betriebsgesellschaft mbH (75%); Koblenzer Elektrizitätswerk und Verkehrs-AG (57%); Kraftwerk Aftwürttemberg AG (92%); Lech-Elektrizitätswerke AG (75%); Main-Kraftwerke AG (70%); Moselkraftwerke GmbH; Rhenag Rheinische Energie AG (54%); Rheinbraun Aktiengesellschaft; Maria Theresia Bergbaugesellschaft mbH; Reederei und Spedition "Braunkohle" GmbH; Rheinbraun Australia Pty Ltd; Rheinbraun US Corporation; Rheinbraun Verkaufsgesellschaft mbH; RWE-DEA Aktiengesellschaft für Mineraloel und Chemie (99%); Condea Chemia GmbH; DEA MINERALOEL AKTIENGESELLSCHAFT; Vista Chemical Company (USA); RWE Entsorgung Aktiengesellschaft; American NuKEM Corp; R + T Entsorgung GmbH (51%); Lahmeyer Aktiengesellschaft für Energie-wirtschaft (64%); Rheinelektra AG (62%); Heidelberger Druckmaschinen AG (57%); Heidelberg Harris GmbH; Lahmeyer International GmbH (55%); NUKEM GmbH; Starkstrom-Anlagen-Gesellschaft mbH; Starkstrom-Gerätebau GmbH; Stierlen-

Maquet AG; HOCHTIEF AKTIENGESELLSCHAFT vorm.
Gebr. Helfmann (56%); D & M Partner, Inc (USA); MIT
Gesellschaft für Management-Beratung, Informationssysteme
und Technologie mbH (MIT-Beratung).

Further Reading: Kitchen, Martin, *The Political Economy of Germany 1815-1914,* London, Croom Helm, 1978; Hardach, Kevin, *The Political Economy of Germany in the Twentieth Century,* Berkeley, Berkeley University of California Press; Fisher, Wolfram, *Germany in the World Economy during the Nineteenth Century*, German Historical Institute, Annual Lecture, 1983; Berghahn, V.R., *Modern Germany—Society, Economy and Politics in the Twentieth Century,* Cambridge, Cambridge University Press, 1987.

—Debra Johnson

SAN DIEGO GAS & ELECTRIC COMPANY

101 Ash Street
San Diego, California 92112
U.S.A.
(619) 696-2000
Fax: (619) 239-0015

Public Company
Incorporated: 1905 as San Diego Consolidated Gas & Electric Company
Employees: 4,175
Sales $1.77 billion
Stock Exchanges: New York Pacific

San Diego Gas & Electric Company (SDG&E), a west coast energy management company, derives 75% of its revenues from its utility businesses. The company provides electric service to San Diego County, California, and part of Orange County, and gas service to San Diego County. SDG&E owns two power plants, part of a nuclear generating station, a transmission line, and a natural-gas pipeline. The company also owns two subsidiaries: Pacific Diversified Capital Company, which owns various companies that serve utility and real estate markets, and Califia Company, used for general corporate needs, such as holding real estate.

SDG&E was founded in 1881 as the San Diego Gas Company and incorporated as San Diego Consolidated Gas & Electric Company in April 1905. Standard Gas and Electric Co. owned the bulk of the utility's common stock. In 1910 San Diego Consolidated acquired the United Light, Fuel & Power Co. of San Diego. The utility also built its first principal electric generating plant, Station B, that year. It had a monopoly on the gas and electric business for San Diego and its suburbs. The utility grew rapidly. Its number of electricity customers increased from 2,212 in 1906 to 14,321 in 1912; gas customers multiplied from 4,594 in 1906 to 17,864 in 1912. Sales topped $1 million for the first time in 1912, and surpassed $2 million in 1918.

In November 1923 the company, headed by President Robert J. Graf and Chairman John J. O'Brien, contracted to connect its transmission lines with those owned by Southern Sierras Power Company of Pincon, California. Through this agreement, the company assured Southern Sierras of an uninterrupted power supply in the Imperial Valley of southern California should Southern Sierras experience shortages or power failures. By 1927 the company's system included two steam electric generating stations, and it had signed an electric power interchange agreement with Southern California Edison Company (SoCal Edison). SoCal Edison was based in Rosemead, California, and served parts of the Los Angeles area. The 1920s were a time of booming business throughout the United States and growth in California especially, and this showed in San Diego Consolidated's sales, which grew from $2.6 million in 1920 to $7.3 million in 1929.

In May 1932, under Graf's successor as president, W.F. Raber, the company applied to the California Railroad Commission, its regulating body, to replace manufactured gas with natural gas in its service area. The application was approved and the company contracted with a subsidiary of Pacific Lighting Company, the Southern Counties Gas Co., to provide 24 million cubic feet of natural gas daily. The necessary pipeline, covering 120 miles from Long Beach to La Jolla, California, was estimated to cost $1.7 million. At the time, the utility was serving a population of 222,000. The company began supplying natural gas in September 1932. Two years later San Diego Consolidated bought a small share of the power produced by the Boulder Dam. The dam was erected by the U.S. government beginning in 1931 on the Colorado River. States, cities, and utilities bought or leased the output of the dam.

The utility's sales dipped somewhat during the Great Depression, dropping to $6.8 million in 1934, but growth resumed the following year. The company remained profitable even in the Depression's worst years.

In June 1939 the company entered a new agreement to increase the amount of power it exported to its wholesale customers in Tecate, Mexico. San Diego Consolidated was authorized to export 3.6 million kilowatt hours per year. Previously, the Federal Power Commission had set its export limit at 700,000 kilowatt hours per year. Mexico figured prominently in SDG&E's long-term strategic plan.

In 1940 as a result of the Public Utility Holding Company Act of 1935, the Securities and Exchange Commission ordered Standard Gas & Electric to sell all its utility holdings, including San Diego Consolidated, which changed its name to San Diego Gas & Electric Company and became publicly owned. In 1941 the last unit of the company's generating Station B was installed. During the 1940s, agriculture, mining, fishing, and aircraft manufacturing were important industries in San Diego. The population of the area had decreased slightly since the 1930s to 219,000. In 1942 Hance H. Cleland succeeded W.F. Raber as president. During World War II, army and navy bases became important to San Diego's economy, and the navy continued to influence the company's fortunes. In 1943 the Silver Gate steam electric generating station was completed. Operation began on January 27.

The population of SDG&E's service area had grown to 620,000 by 1949, and its sales were up to $23.3 million. In view of this growth, the company had installed another unit at the Silver Gate plant in 1948, and planned to add a fourth turbogenerating unit to the plant by 1952. Work also had begun on a generating station in Encino, California. SDG&E's first turbogenerator came into service in 1954. That year, SDG&E requested and received a rate increase. Unit 2 of the Encino station came online on July 26, 1956, and Unit 3 became operational in July 1958. The company also bid on 144 acres of land as the site of a possible future steam-generating plant.

SDG&E began research into nuclear power in the late 1950s. In 1961 it agreed to participate in a 350,000-kilowatt nuclear power plant with Southern California Edison. SDG&E owned 20% of the plant, located in San Onofre, California; SoCal Edison owned 80%. The plant went into operation in 1967.

SDG&E's new steam South Bay generating station was in operation by July 1960. H.G. Dillon became president in 1961, succeeding E.D. Sherwin, who remained on the board. Two years later, Dillon was chairman of the executive committee and J.F. Sinnott became president. The second South Bay unit began operation in June 1962. Unit 3 was put in service in September 1964.

SDG&E enjoyed the best earnings growth rate among California's four largest utilities from 1963 through 1968, averaging 9% annually. By 1970, its ninth consecutive year of record earnings, it was one of the fastest growing utilities in the United States. That year, San Diego became the nation's 15th-largest city. San Diego County's economy was diversifying from a dependence on the aerospace industry and military installations to include recreation, electronics, oceanography, and education.

By the late 1960s antismog ordinances were hindering the company's efforts to build plants to supply the booming population. Fuel oil costs increased in 1970 due to local regulations that required the utility to burn higher-priced low-sulfur crude. The company began to look elsewhere for its power needs.

Between 1971 and 1976, SDG&E began three plants that would use cheaper fuels: a coal-fired plant at Kaiparowits, an oil-burning plant at Sycamore Canyon, and a nuclear plant at Sundesert, all in California. Stringent environmental regulations, however, made construction of the new plants prohibitively expensive, and SDG&E eventually canceled them all. From 1973 to 1978, SDG&E's cost of producing electricity increased by 250% while the rates it was permitted to charge increased only 145%. The company was in poor financial shape, its bond rating was lowered from AA to BBB, and $55 million it spent on Sundesert before canceling the project was a complete loss. In December 1978 SDG&E resorted to buying power, signing a ten-year contract with Tucson Gas & Electric Co. for up to 500 megawatts of power annually. In March 1979, needing cash, it sold a generating unit to a group of banks to raise $132 million, then leased back the unit since it needed the output.

In 1980 inflation, a time lag between application for a rate increase, action by the California Public Utilities Commission (CPUC), and weather both warmer in winter and cooler in summer contributed to a disastrous year. Although sales rose to $960 million, 29% more then the previous year, net income fell 26% to $52 million. SDG&E's customers paid some of the highest rates in the United States because of the utility's dependence on high-priced oil, the cost of its canceled plants, and repairs at its nuclear plant. As 1981 began SDG&E focused on the future: the CPUC had suggested annual rate adjustments, instead of bi-annual, to more accurately reflect prevailing economic conditions; and a new fuel mix would be utilized in the 1980s, consisting of nuclear, purchased, and geothermal power. Nuclear power from San Onofre Unit 1 was already available to SDG&E customers. Units 2 and 3 were nearing completion. The company was negotiating for the purchase of coal-generated power, with Public Service Company of New Mexico. It already had several contracts for the purchase of geothermal power from companies in the United States and from Mexico's national utility, Comision Federal de Electricidad. The proximity of San Diego to Tijuana, Mexico, encouraged cooperation between the two utilities. The experimental Heber binary geothermal plant was another avenue explored to reduce the use of oil. The binary cycle process used the hot brine that lies just beneath the surface in the Imperial Valley to produce high-pressure gas. The gas, in turn, ran a turbine that generated electricity. In June 1983, work began on the plant. At completion in 1985, energy produced at Heber would serve 45,000 residential customers. SDG&E was the majority owner of the plant. The U.S. Department of Energy paid for half of the project but was not an owner.

SDG&E had another disappointing year in 1981. In April Robert Morris, president since 1975, was elected chairman of the board of directors, and Thomas A. Page, formerly executive vice president and chief operating officer, was elected president. On October 1, Page also assumed the position of chief executive officer, and continued to emphasize SDG&E's goal of reducing its dependence on oil. Almost every part of the company suffered adverse affects during 1981. The San Onofre nuclear plant's Unit 1 was out of service for 14 months in 1980 and 1981 due to equipment failure and retrofitting required in the wake of the Three Mile Island disaster. In addition, SDG&E ran into problems with a fuel oil exchange. In the late 1970s the utility had excess oil and, rather than sell it at a loss, agreed to an oil exchange with United Petroleum Distributors Inc. of Houston, Texas, which later failed to deliver the oil it owed SDG&E when the utility needed it. SDG&E lost $31 million and was ordered to refund $4.4 million on the transaction in 1980–1981, representing the price of the replacement oil it had to buy, to its customers by the CPUC in 1982. There was a positive development in December 1981, when the company received CPUC approval to construct the eastern interconnection transmission line, later named the Southwest Powerlink, that connected SDG&E with less expensive, coal-fired power generated in Arizona and New Mexico. The transmission line would extend 280 miles from the Palo Verde switchyard near Phoenix, Arizona, to SDG&E's Miguel substation southeast of San Diego. Cost of the Powerlink was estimated at $320 million.

By 1982 San Diego had grown into the eighth-largest city in the country. Energy demand, however, had leveled off due to lower industrial energy consumption and energy conservation measures. SDG&E reaffirmed its decision to purchase more of its power. Utility networks were one way to mitigate the effects of variations in energy consumption. Work on the Southwest Powerlink began in mid-1982 with anticipated completion in 1984. At the same time, two new transmission lines to Mexico were under construction, with completion anticipated in 1983 and 1934. Power production would be boosted by San Onofre Units 2 and 3. Both units were scheduled to begin full power production by the end of 1983. SDG&E hoped to sell a portion of both units' output to help cover the costs of construction and keep rates down. Unit 1 was again out of service as questions about the plant's ability to withstand earthquakes had been raised.

After several difficult years, 1983 held the promise of improvement in SDG&E's financial health. The utility's bond rating was upgraded to A, making the cost of borrowing money much lower. San Onofre Unit 2 was put in operation while full power testing went on in Unit 3. Average fuel costs declined for the first time in ten years, and natural gas prices were stabilized. SDG&E closed its 60-year old Station B generating plant and temporarily shut down its Silver Gate plant. Three-quarters of the Southwest Powerlink was completed. At this point, 44% of the company's electric energy was purchased from other utilities, and SDG&E began to define itself as an energy management company.

In 1984 both Moody's and Standard & Poor's upgraded SDG&E's bond ratings again. The company's short-term debt was eliminated, and common stock was trading at a ten-year high. The Southwest Powerlink became operational in May. San Onofre Unit 1 returned to operation in November for the first time since closing down for engineering modifications in 1982. A second transmission link with Mexico also was completed that month.

In 1985 the company had record earnings of $3.25 per share, and San Diego itself continued to enjoy record residential growth. The business community expanded to include information services companies, biomedical research, and other scientific industries. SDG&E's Heber geothermal plant was completed on schedule in May. Page sought approval from the CPUC to establish a holding company that would allow SDG&E to venture into unregulated industries. Stockholders approved the plan on November 1. In March 1986 SDG&E received conditional approval from the CPUC to diversify into real estate, utility services, and energy products. Pacific Diversified Capital Company, an SDG&E subsidiary since 1982, was activated to manage all nonutility operations. The subsidiary quickly acquired Phase One Development, Inc., a commercial real estate development company; Computer Solutions, Inc., a software company; and a majority holding in Mock Resources, Inc., a natural gas and petroleum products distributor.

Early in 1986 SDG&E's final single-fuel power plant, Encino, was converted to burn either gas or oil, allowing the company to purchase the least expensive of the two fuels. SDG&E signed a ten-year power purchase contract with Mexico's national electric utility. The U.S. Navy, SDG&E's largest single customer, announced in 1986 that it planned to withdraw from SDG&E's system and contract for a cogeneration plant to meet its power needs. SDG&E quickly began negotiations with the navy to prevent this from happening. In October, the CPUC decided to disallow $329.9 million in San Onofre Units 2 and 3 costs, about half of the original figure. The decision included $69.1 million in costs for SDG&E, owner of 20% of the plant. SDG&E vowed to appeal the ruling. In spite of this, SDG&E posted record profits while reducing customer rates in 1986.

Dividends went up for the 11th consecutive year in 1987. An employee incentive program begun in 1986 to encourage money-saving ideas helped the company save $2 million. The experimental Heber geothermal plant was shut down in 1987 because its production costs were too high. SDG&E established an environmental department to respond to concerns including the removal of polychlorinated biphenyls (PCBs) in it system.

In June 1988 SDG&E agreed in principle to merge with Tucson Electric Power Company (TEP), a company with which it had a long-term power sale agreement made possible by the Southwest Powerlink. TEP had excess capacity and SDG&E sought the merger as a way of assuring its access to low-cost coal-fired power. Just a month after the merger was announced, SoCal Edison's parent company, SCEcorp, made an unsolicited $2.3 billion bid for SDG&E. If approved, the merger would join California's second- and third-largest utilities to create the largest investor-owned utility in the United States, with approximately $17 billion in assets. By August the city of San Diego called for hearings on the legality of a merger with SoCal Edison. SDG&E had not yet decided whether to accept the second merger offer. SCEcorp promised to reduce residential power rates by 10% within six months of completing the merger. On September 1, the day SDG&E's board was to consider its previous offer, SCEcorp increased its bid to $2.36 billion. SDG&E's board voted unanimously to decline SCEcorp's new offer and merge with TEP. If SCEcorp's bid were successful, between 800 and 1,000 SDG&E employees would lose their jobs. In light of the vote, SCEcorp's Chairman and Chief Executive Officer Howard P. Allen did not rule out a hostile takeover. Any deal would have to be approved by the CPUC. Allen said he was willing to wait years for a merger to go through.

In November 1988 SDG&E ended its agreement to merge with TEP. The two utilities had disagreed over the best way to counter SCEcorp's efforts to stop their merger. SCEcorp continued to pursue SDG&E, raising its offer to $2.53 billion and offering Tom Page the position of vice chairman of SCEcorp and president of the San Diego division. On November 30, by a vote of six to two, SDG&E accepted SCEcorp's offer. The two directors who voted against the merger resigned from the board.

Apart from merger negotiations, 1988 was an active year for SDG&E. The U.S. Navy dropped plans to generate its own power and signed a ten-year contract with SDG&E. SDG&E applied for a rate decrease, which CPUC approved effective in January 1989. The company hooked up its one millionth customer, and revenues rose to $2.1 billion from $1.9 billion in 1987.

SDG&E's merger into SoCal Edison was contingent on approval by the CPUC, the Federal Energy Regulatory Commission (FERC), and shareholders of both companies. The companies were sensitive to the politics of the approval process and promised rate reductions for commercial, industrial, and agricultural customers, in documents filed with the CPUC in April 1989. This pledge was in addition to the 10% rate cuts promised residential customers before the merger vote.

In December 1989 SDG&E approached the CPUC to begin the licensing process for a new two-unit, 460-megawatt, combined-cycle power plant. The plant would combine a natural gas turbine generator and a steam-producing unit to produce more cost-efficient power. If the merger did not take place, this plant would put SDG&E in a better position to generate more of the energy it needed in the future. In another move to augment its power resources, SDG&E anticipated returning its Silver Gate plant to service in 1992 due to a growing customer base.

In February 1990 California state Attorney General John Van de Kamp and an advocacy division of the CPUC stated their opposition to the merger. In November George P. Lewnes, an administrative law judge for the FERC, also opposed it on the basis that it was anticompetitive, but his decision was not binding on the FERC board, which was still considering the merger. SCEcorp Chairman Allen retired at the end of 1990 with a decision still pending. On February 1, 1991, two judges with the CPUC had not yet voted. SCEcorp and SDG&E both claimed they would rather cancel the merger than be forced to sell unregulated subsidiaries, which the CPUC judges had recommended should the merger go through. The CPUC began its final hearings on the merger in March 1991. In May the five-member board handed down a unanimous decision rejecting the merger, citing a lack of long-term benefits and the lessening of competition. The two companies agreed not to appeal the CPUC's ruling and withdrew the application before the FERC. The decision meant that SDG&E needed to line up new sources for purchased power almost immediately. SoCal Edison was one of those sources.

Principal Subsidiaries: Pacific Diversified Capital Company; Califia Company.

—Lynn M. Kalanik

SCECORP

2244 Walnut Grove Avenue
Rosemead, California 91770
U.S.A.
(818) 302-2222
Fax: (818) 302-7827

Public Company
Incorporated: 1909 as Southern California Edison
    Company
Employees: 16,604
Sales: $7.20 billion
Stock Exchanges: New York Pacific London Tokyo

SCEcorp is a large holding company whose combined assets from its subsidiaries total more than $16 billion. SCEcorp's primary subsidiary, Southern California Edison Company (Edison), is the second-largest electric utility in the United States, and it accounts for nearly 90% of SCEcorp's earnings. Edison serves an area covering 50,000 square miles in central and southern California and containing more than four million electricity customers. About 15% of the electricity used in 1990 by Edison's customers was generated by the three units at the San Onofre nuclear generating station, which Edison operates and in which it owns a 75% interest. Edison also owns a small share of the Palo Verde nuclear generating station near Phoenix, Arizona. Renewable and alternative energy sources, such as biomass, solar, wind, hydroelectric, and geothermal, accounted for about one-third of the power used by customers in 1990.

SCEcorp's other principal subsidiary is The Mission Group, which controls several nonutility subsidiaries, including Mission Energy Company, Mission First Financial, and Mission Land Company. Mission Energy, the largest, develops independent power-generating projects. Mission First Financial invests mostly in energy-related projects, while Mission Land invests in real estate in southern California, where it owns several industrial parks.

In the first three decades of the 20th century, the population of California grew four-and-a-half times as quickly as the total population of the United States. This growth meant a giant leap in the area's need for power, a need that was reflected in the expansion of public utilities there. By 1909 Edison Electric Company of Los Angeles was already a sizable utility concern. Over several years, Los Angeles Edison had acquired and consolidated the generating and distributing capabilities of 13 pioneer utility companies in and around Los Angeles. Southern California Edison was organized in August 1909 to acquire all of Edison's properties. In the next several years, Edison made only one minor acquisition, the Downey Light, Power and Water Company in 1914, and rather than expanding, it concentrated primarily on developing the existing electric properties and eliminating its gas properties, which were bringing in only about 6% of the company's gross revenues.

The most important expansion in Edison's early years occurred in 1917, when the company acquired all of the assets and business of Pacific Light & Power Corporation and a controlling interest in Mount Whitney Power & Electric Company. Pacific was a rapidly growing power company controlled by H.E. Huntington and Los Angeles Railway Company and operating in the same service area as Edison. Mount Whitney was operating in the nearby agricultural area of Tulare County and had no competitors there. These acquisitions left Edison firmly in control of the electricity business in the region. Also in 1917, the city of Los Angeles purchased Edison's distribution system inside the city, and began to buy power wholesale from Edison for its municipal plant.

By adding the facilities formerly belonging to Pacific, Edison more than doubled its generating capacity. Shortly after the acquisition, Edison embarked on a decade-long construction project in the area of Pacific's Big Creek hydroelectric station, transforming it from a plant capable of generating about 63,700 kilowatts of power to a huge system that included 3 reservoirs, 8 concrete dams, and 41 miles of tunnels, and that could generate more than 373,000 kilowatts of power. Through 1928, the area's population was growing so rapidly that Edison had no problem using this greatly increased capacity. Because overall use of electricity was accelerating, especially in industry and agriculture, Edison found no need to seek new business.

Edison's gross revenues grew each year during the 1920s, and as the 1930s began the company continued to do well in spite of a general downturn in industry. By the end of 1930, revenues had reached $41 million, and the balance Edison had achieved between hydroelectric and steam generation helped protect the company against fluctuating earnings due to weather problems or fuel-price hikes. For instance, when low-water conditions hindered hydroelectric generation, emphasis could be shifted to steam. In addition, Edison's steam plants were capable or running on either oil or natural gas, so costs could be minimized by taking advantage of price fluctuations between the two types of fuel. The drop in industrial power use was largely offset by great increases in residential use. More households during this period were beginning to use electric appliances such as washers, refrigerators, space heaters, and water heaters. Agricultural use of electricity also was rising quickly. Pumping plants for irrigation, previously powered by other means, were converted to electricity, and by 1930 these irrigation plants accounted for roughly one-eighth of Edison's total connected load. In 1930 the company changed its name to Southern California Edison Company Ltd. The "Ltd." was dropped in 1947.

Edison's output, revenues, and service area continued to expand through the 1930s. In 1930 construction began on the Boulder Dam—later renamed Hoover Dam—project. Built on the Colorado River about 300 miles northeast of Los Angeles, the dam's power stations initially were capable of generating nearly 750,000 kilowatts of electricity. The dam was constructed and run by the U.S. government, and contractual agreements were made with several power companies and municipal systems concerning the use of the power it generated. Edison's share of the power was to be 7.2% of the total output, although the company was obligated to absorb up to 14.4% more of the total if the states of Nevada and Arizona did not use their shares. The company spent more to purchase Boulder Dam power than it did to generate power at its most efficient steam plant.

Population growth of Edison's service area continued to outpace by far that of the United States as a whole in the 1940s, increasing by 80% compared to the national rate of 15%. This statistic was reflected in the growth of company revenues. While the national average during this decade for privately owned electric utilities was an 83% increase in gross operating revenues, Edison's figure was 135%. While Edison's rates continued to be significantly lower than the national average through the first half of the decade, this situation began to change over the next several years as the national average began to drop rapidly. One reason for the company's increase in electric rates relative to the national average was an increasing emphasis in the post–World War II years on steam-generated power, which cost the company up to twice as much to produce as hydroelectric.

By the early 1950s Edison was the fifth-largest investor-owned power company in the United States. Its service area covered 18,500 square miles and contained about 225 communities with a combined population of almost three million. The company's customers numbered more than one million by 1952, twice the count for 1940, and were very diverse in nature. Of the power sales in its territory, 25% was to industrial concerns, 34% to residential, 10% to agricultural, and 21% to commercial. The region had proven in many ways to be nearly ideal for a utility company: the climate was excellent, agriculture was widespread and booming, and industries were thriving and greatly varied. The only major drawback of the area seemed to be the competition provided by cheap and readily available natural gas, which could be used for many appliances.

From the end of World War II through 1953, Edison spent about $500 million on construction, and by 1954 the company's 24 hydroelectric plants and 5 steam stations had a capacity of 1.6 million kilowatts. Most of the postwar expansion went toward steam generating which, while more expensive than hydroelectricity, was not hampered by water shortages. The largest cost increases the company experienced during this period were due to jumps in the prices of gas and oil—required to run the steam plants—that occurred during the Korean War. Still, Edison's sources of power were both diverse and geographically separated, thereby spreading the risk of property damage and offering protection from droughts. Half of the company power came from its steam plants in the Los Angeles area; 35% came from its own hydroelectric properties fed by the western slopes of the Sierra Nevadas; and 15% was purchased, mainly from the Hoover Dam.

Edison's revenues nearly doubled during the 1960s, rising gradually from $369 million in 1960 to $721 million in 1970. The company continued to stay ahead of most others within its industry in such statistics as net income, revenues, and kilowatt-hour sales, largely due to the fact that California's population continued to grow faster than any other state's. Jack K. Horton, an important figure at Edison during this decade, became president in 1959, chief executive officer in 1965, and chairman of the board in 1968.

The period from 1960 to 1968 was defined by three trends: the acquisition of several smaller utilities, a shift from oil to natural gas to fuel the steam plants, and a gradual decrease of electricity rates. All three of these trends ceased after 1968. Edison's minor burst of expansion during the period included the 1962 acquisition of all the utilities—gas, electric, and fresh-water services—on Santa Catalina, an island about 25 miles off the coast of southern California; the 1963 acquisition of California Electric Power Company; the purchase in 1965 of Desert Electric Cooperative, Inc., which involved 2,600 customers and 600 miles of distribution line near Twentynine Palms, California; and the 1966 purchase of most of the physical assets belonging to Valley Power Company, which served a small number of Nevada customers.

The shift from oil to natural gas is reflected in the following fuel-mix statistics. In 1960 almost half of Edison's power output was fueled by natural gas, more than one-third by oil, and the rest primarily hydroelectric. By 1968 the balance was 74% gas and only 12% oil. This trend began to reverse itself in the next couple of years, however, as the availability of natural gas decreased. By 1970 when the share fueled by natural gas was down to 56%, the company began to enter long-term oil supply contracts in anticipation of this reversal continuing.

Utility costs per unit of power generally declined well into the 1960s, and accordingly Edison's rates dropped by 16% from 1960 to 1968. In the late 1960s and early 1970s, however, the company saw huge jumps in the costs of fuel, construction, and interest. Also, around this time both public and government agencies started to become more concerned about the environment, and utility companies faced greater difficulties getting approval for the construction of new power plants. This was especially true for Edison because of its location in the southern California "smog belt." By the early 1970s approval from roughly 30 different agencies was required before a new plant could be built; and in 1972 a referendum was overwhelmingly passed requiring any who wanted to undertake major development along the California coastline to first seek approval from the California Coastal Zone Construction Commission. One way in which Edison dealt with California's environmental regulation was to build out of state. Two coal-burning plants were started in joint ventures with other companies. The two plants, located in New Mexico and southern Nevada, accounted for 12% of the company's total capacity in 1973. By 1973 Edison ranked behind only New York's Consolidated Edison, Chicago's Commonwealth Edison, and the Southern Company of Atlanta, Georgia in gross revenues for electric companies, bringing in nearly $1 billion. The company had 7.5 million customers in a 50,000 square-mile area, and more than $3 billion in assets.

The oil embargo of 1973 created difficulties for many utility companies, including Edison, and the price of electricity increased throughout the United States. Excluding increases in the cost of fuel, however, Edison's rates rose more slowly than the industry average through the remainder of the 1970s. Edison's electricity prices went up about 6.7% annually, while prices nationally grew at the rate of about 9% per year.

In 1980 William R. Gould became chairman and chief executive officer of Edison, marking an important change in approach for the company. Gould had joined Edison in 1948 as a mechanical engineer, working his way up to vice president in 1963, senior vice president in 1973, and president in 1978. Within a few months of being named chairman in 1980, Gould unveiled a plan calling for a major commitment to alternative and renewable energy sources in the coming years. In 1981 oil, gas, and coal supplied the fuel for 70% of the company's 15.5-million kilowatt capacity. Under Gould's plan, however, one-third of the company's new power needs during the 1980s would come from nontraditional sources such as solar, geothermal, and wind power. The plan also entailed increasing the purchase of alternative forms of power from third-party sources, thereby decreasing the company's reliance on power from large, centralized generating stations, which were no longer as economical to run as they once were. In 1980 Edison began generating 3,000 kilowatts with a wind-powered turbine at San Gorgino Pass near Palm Springs, California. In 1981 it purchased the steam required to produce about 10,000 kilowatts of power from a geothermal well operated by Union Oil Company of California. Construction on a pilot solar facility was begun in the Mojave Desert that year as well.

In 1984 Howard P. Allen became chief executive officer of Edison, inheriting Gould's expansive network of energy suppliers, which together represented nine different sources of power. Although not all of these sources were as cost-efficient as oil, this diversified approach made the company less vulnerable to the volatile world oil market. By 1985 oil accounted for only 2% of the company's fuel needs, down from 60% ten years earlier. In the mid-1980s, the emergence of cogeneration by nonutility companies began to erode the earnings of some electric utilities, including Edison.

One way that Allen and Edison battled this trend was by reducing the rates charged to large industry, which accounted for about one-fifth of Edison's revenues, in order to encourage them to stay within Edison's system. Another strategy employed by the company was to start its own cogenerating subsidiary, Mission Energy.

By 1987 Edison was the second-largest electric-generating company in the United States, earning a company record $789 million that year. One-tenth of its power came from cogeneration and alternative sources, and 20% came from the San Onofre nuclear facility.

In 1988 SCEcorp was formed as the holding company for Edison, and a newly formed subsidary called The Mission Group. The Mission Group in turn became a holding company for SCEcorp's nonutility subsidiaries. Edison stockholders received shares of SCEcorp stock, and operations continued essentially as before. Also in 1988 a merger was proposed between SCEcorp and San Diego Gas & Electric Company. The merger was approved by the shareholders of both companies the following year, but after two years of review it was rejected by the California Public Utilities Commission (CPUC).

Howard Allen retired in 1990, and was replaced as chairman and chief executive of both SCEcorp and Edison by John Bryson. Bryson, a former head of the CPUC, had joined Edison in 1984 as chief financial officer. Company records were set in 1990 in both earnings and revenue. Two trends that had begun in the 1980s had continued into the 1990s: the movement toward cogeneration has continued to the degree that 57% of the new generating capacity built in the United States in 1990 was built by nonutility companies; and the trend toward zero consumption of oil as a generating fuel has reduced SCEcorp's oil use to 3 million barrels in 1990 from a peak of 58 million barrels in 1977.

SCEcorp and Southern California Edison have benefited from the advantages of their location; advantages that are grounded in demographic, economic, and environmental factors. Although California's rate of growth will not assure the health of its utility companies forever, SCEcorp's willingness to adapt to the demands of the global economy and the global environment would seem to put in in a position to thrive for some time to come.

Principal Subsidiaries: Southern California Edison Company; The Mission Group.

Further Reading: "One of California's Leading Utilities," *Barron's,* May 23, 1932; "Southern California's Edison," *Barron's,* March 10, 1952.

—Robert R. Jacobson

SHIKOKU ELECTRIC POWER COMPANY, INC.

2-5, Marunouchi
Takamatsu 760-91
Shikoku
Japan
(0878) 21-5061
Fax: (0878) 21-0497

Public Company
Incorporated: 1951
Employees: 5,947
Sales: ¥410 billion (US$3.2 billion)
Stock Exchanges: Tokyo Osaka

Shikoku Electric Power Company, Inc. (Shikoku Electric) is one of the nine major regional power companies that generate, transmit, and distribute electricity throughout Japan. The company supplies electricity to all four of Shikoku's prefectures: Tokushima, Kochi, Ehime, and Kagawa. Shikoku, with an area of 19,000 square kilometers and 4.25 million people, has an industrial output of ¥7 trillion. This is small compared with Japan's total, but makes Shikoku Electric one of the business leaders in Shikoku, the least industrialized of Japan's four main islands.

Shikoku Electric was formed as a company on May 1, 1951, when the General Headquarters of the Allied Powers (GHQ) under General MacArthur approved a plan submitted by the Japanese government to reorganize and rationalize the electrical power industry. Under the scheme, the nation was divided into nine blocks, each with its own privately owned electric power company (EPC). At the time of inauguration the nine companies served 16 million customers with a combined capacity of 8,500 megawatts (MW). Of this, Shikoku Electric's portion was a relatively small 290MW or just over 3%. Shikoku is the smallest and least developed of Japan's four main islands, but since ancient times has maintained close ties with the old capital cities in Honshu such as nearby Kyoto and Nara and more recently Tokyo. It has played an important role as a transit island in shipping between Japan and its trading partners through ports such as Kochi on the south Pacific Coast. Although the chief industries in the region have traditionally been low-technology, such as forestry and handicrafts, there has been a recent boom in the Ehime and Kagawa prefectures in the high-technology sector, prompted in part by the government's "Technopolis" scheme to promote high-technology in-

dustry in Shikoku. There has also been a recent boom in tourism on the island, peaking in 1989. Thus the history of electric power on a large scale in Shikoku starts fairly recently.

The history of electric power in Japan as a whole, however, goes back to 1878 when Professor W.E. Aryton of the Institute of Technology in Tokyo unveiled an arc lamp to celebrate the opening of the Central Telegraph Office. Japan's first electric utility company was established in 1886, seven years after Thomas Edison invented the incandescent lamp in the United States. The company was Tokyo Electric Lighting Company, and its first electric power plant—the first in Japan also—was completed in 1887 as a 25 kilowatt (kW) facility in Nihonbashi, Tokyo. Throughout its history Japan has always been able to assimilate and improve upon outside technology and ideas, and electric power was no exception. After the opening of the Tokyo Electric Lighting plant, many electric utilities started up in main cities. Although demand had increased rapidly—electricity was a great improvement over the troublesome oil lamps then in use—service was generally limited to government and commercial offices and factories. Most of the first plants in Japan were thermal, powered by coal, but in 1891 the first hydroelectric power station was completed in Kyoto. A large part of the demand for electricity came from the electric railways that were springing up all over the country. Spurred on by these developments, electricity in the form of electric lighting was first introduced to Shikoku in 1896 by the Tokushima Electric Lighting Company in Tokushima City. The next seven years saw the spread of electric lighting into Shikoku's four prefectures by Takamatsu Lighting, Tosa Lighting, and Iyo Hydroelectric Power, which pioneered hydroelectricity in Shikoku by building the first plant in Ehime prefecture in 1903. The years 1896 to 1912 saw the rapid development of these four power companies. The turnover of Tokushima Electric, for example, increased a thousandfold between 1900 and 1912. The most common initial usage of electricity was in the lighting of streets and public areas, but increasingly the upper-class town dwellers had electric lights installed in their homes.

In 1911 the government enacted the Electric Utility Industry Law. The law necessitated government permission for the production and distribution of electric power. By 1920 there were 3,000 power companies in Japan, riding on Japan's economic boom, and the number operating in the towns of Shikoku numbered about 50. The depression of the 1920s in Japan, following its defeat in World War I, was exacerbated by the Great Kanto Earthquake in 1923 and the worldwide market crash in 1929; it did not have an excessive effect on the economy of Shikoku but it did prevent growth during this period. The period between 1926 and 1937 can be characterized as the era of the "Big Five" in the history of electric power in Japan. It was dominated by Tokyo Electric Lighting and Daido Power in particular. The government regulated the industry by passing four laws in 1938 which ensured state control over prices, plant development, transmission, and all other aspects of the industry. In effect it had formed one of the largest electric companies in the world with the establishment of JEGTCO (Japan Electric Generation and Transmission Company). The Allied bombing of Japan from 1943 to 1945 seriously damaged 44% of Japan's power stations and devastated Japanese industry. Shikoku, however, not being a strategic target, was largely untouched. The GHQ, which was effectively in charge of Japan from 1945 to 1952, made sweeping changes in Japan's electric power industry.

The Council for Reorganization of Electric Utility Industry was formed in 1949 and chaired by Yasuzaemon Matsunaga, former president of Toho Electric Power Company. After much negotiation, a plan was produced that divided the country into nine areas, each with its own privately owned electric power company. Thus the Shikoku Electric Power Company was formed, with initial capitalization of ¥400 million or US$1.1 million.

The first chairman was Yoichi Takeoka, who was formally in charge of Takamatsu Electric Light Company. Takeoka began a consolidation of Shikoku Electric's facilities and the company embarked on an immediate expansion program. Just two months after the company's establishment, work began on a hydroelectric facility on the Kuro River. Like the rest of Japan, much of the center of Shikoku is mountainous and thus a good source of hydroelectric power, on which most of Shikoku's power facilities at this time operated. The company began to promote the use of electric power in the more rural areas that had previously been uneconomical markets for the smaller utilities in Shikoku. The central headquarters were rationalized and divisions between the regional offices abolished. Pensions, health care, and insurance were offered on an equal basis to all company employees. Some of the less modern generating facilities were closed and replaced with more efficient plants, with more thermal facilities being built. A listing on the Osaka stock exchange in October 1952 was followed by a Tokyo listing in May 1953. By the end of 1953 customer service branches were established in all the major towns of Shikoku, and the capitalization of the company had trebled to ¥1.19 billion. Also in this year a pioneering automatic combustion control system was installed on all Shikoku Electric's transmission and generating equipment to regulate the amount of fuel burnt and hence save energy. This was followed in the 1950s and early 1960s with a series of technological upgradings. Emphasis was also placed on the training of staff and customers in the safe use of electrical equipment. As a result Shikoku had the lowest electricity-related accident rate in the country.

In 1956 company president Chikuma Miyagawa initiated research into the use of nuclear power by the company. Shikoku Electric was at this time the most advanced of Japan's nine regional electric utility companies with regards to nuclear power. By 1985 nuclear energy had become the dominant source of power in Shikoku, accounting for 39% of the total, and was expected to rise to 50% by the year 2000. Realizing that the potential of hydroelectric power in the region was ultimately limited, a section was created within the company in 1956 devoted to the development of coal, gas, and oil-fired power. In order to keep abreast of the latest technology in electric power generation, Shikoku Electric sent its chief engineers and planning officers to Europe and the United States on conferences, training courses, and exchange programs. In this, it was typical of Japanese industry at the time, desperate for technological knowledge which it saw as the key to success. At this time the company began in earnest the process of closing down redundant transformer substations and replacing them with a smaller number of higher voltage, more efficient units. Also in 1956, by boosting the existing capacity of Hirayama Power Station by 470kW to 2900kW, Shikoku Electric came to

own the largest hydroelectric facility in the country and in 1959 began operating the country's first reverse wheel hydroelectric plant, the 11,800kW facility on Omori River. The year 1958 saw changes in the organization of the company, with increasing centralization of planning, engineering, and sales operations. In 1960 Miyazawa took over as chairman of the company, which by this time was the largest company in Shikoku with a capitalization of US$19 million. For the next decade, like the other EPCs in Japan, Shikoku Electric concentrated on the building of oil-fired generating stations such as the 125MW plant completed in Tokushima in 1963. Cheap and plentiful Middle Eastern oil and lax environmental controls at the time made this form of generation the most economically attractive. The oil shocks of 1973 and 1978 and increasing emission control quotas changed all this, and Shikoku Electric's main priority following these events was the development and construction of a nuclear power station. With technological help from and cooperation with France's nuclear power program as well as the other domestic companies, Ikata Nuclear Plant was completed in 1978 with two initial pressurized water reactors and a combined output of almost 1,200MW, with an additional 890MW planned for 1995. Japan's nuclear program has long been a sensitive public issue and therefore extremely stringent safety controls were laid down. Japan's nuclear energy safety record is one of the world's best, and Shikoku Electric has the additional distinction of operating the world's most efficient reactor.

During the 1970s Shikoku Electric's sales trebled and although the company's work force remained fairly steady at about 5,000, its revenues and profits increased dramatically. These profits were spent almost entirely on capital investment and research. In the early 1980s, plans for the largest bridge in the world, to link Shikoku with the main island of Honshu, were drawn up. The impressive Seto bridge was completed in 1988 at a cost of about ¥1.13 trillion and had the important effect of creating a tourist boom and urban renewal in the area. For Shikoku Electric, not only did this mean more business, but the bridge was also used to carry a major trunkline connecting it with Kansai Electric Power's grid. The late 1980s saw a slowdown of the growth seen from the 1970s as Shikoku Electric's market matured. To some extent the company has diversified into new areas such as telecommunications with the formation of Shikoku Information & Telecommunication Network and the production of electric power equipment with Techno-Success Company. It is unlikely that these ventures will contribute significantly to profits in the near future, however, and emphasis is placed on the continued development of the electric power market. Schemes such as the all-electric house, increased customer service, and the application of the hourly rate fluctuation system are some examples. On the international scene, the company continues to exchange information with similar companies worldwide, and was a founding member of the World Association of Nuclear Operators formed in 1989. As most of the company's crucial raw materials come from abroad, a tight check is kept on commodity prices, and long-term purchase agreements such as those for uranium from France and Australia have been entered into. Financially, the company is in an excellent position, with a AAA rating with regard to raising money on the domestic bond market. Overseas, the company conducted two bond issues in Europe in 1989.

To mark the 40th year of business as Shikoku Electric, the company in 1991 planned to launch a new corporate profile containing plans for the 21st century. Although the plans have not yet been made public, it is likely that they will be based on the environmentally safe and efficient generation of power along with increased provision for the development of customer services related to the core business of power generation.

Principal Subsidiaries: Shikoku Information & Telecommunication Network Co. Inc. (45%); Shikoku General Research Centre; Shikoku Electrical Engineering (20%); Shikoku Tech (16%); Shiden Engineering (87%); Shikoku Engineering (80%); Shikoku Industries (90%); Shikoku Technical Consultants (72%); Shikoku Research (50%); Shikoku Sales Service (64%); Aizen General Business (80%); Kochi General Business (71%); Shikoku Cellular Phone (20%); Techno-Success (18%).

Further Reading: History of the Electric Power Industry in Japan, Tokyo, Japan Electric Power Information Center, 1989.

—Dylan Tanner

THE SOUTHERN COMPANY

64 Perimeter Center East
Atlanta, Georgia 30346
U.S.A.
(404) 393-0650
Fax: (404) 668-2672

Public Company
Incorporated: 1945
Employees: 30,263
Sales: $7.98 billion
Stock Exchanges: New York Pacific Cincinnati Philadelphia
    Boston Midwest

The Southern Company is a utility holding company whose
principal subsidiaries provide power in Alabama, Georgia,
Florida, and Mississippi. Nonutility assets include Southern
Electric International, which markets technical services, and
The Southern Investment Group, which seeks new business
opportunities.

The Southern Company traces its roots to a group of entrepreneurs in Alabama and Georgia. Alabama's early power industry was led by James Mitchell and Thomas Martin.
Mitchell worked for the Thomson-Houston Company, a predecessor of General Electric, and later built power plants and
railroads in Brazil. After leaving Brazil he met with the United
Kingdom's financial community and then came to the southern
United States, where he scouted sights for hydroelectric installations. Eventually he decided to build a dam on Cherokee
Bluffs along Alabama's Tallapoosa River.

Seeking to acquire the necessary land, in November 1911
Mitchell met Thomas Martin of Tyson, Wilson & Martin, a
law firm handling the title work for hydroelectric developers
along the Tallapoosa. Mitchell's technical expertise and access
to U.K. capital meshed with Martin's legal training and local
knowledge, and the two decided to join forces.

After the Cherokee Bluffs site became embroiled in a lawsuit brought by the owner of a waterwheel plant nearby, Mitchell and Martin turned to a site on the Coosa River at Gadsden,
Alabama. The Gadsden site was owned by William P. Lay who
in 1906 had organized the Alabama Power Company to dam
the river. Lay had been unable to secure capital and readily
agreed to join with Mitchell and Martin on the project.

Others were also planning hydroelectric projects along the
Coosa and Tallapoosa Rivers. To prevent ruinous competition,
Mitchell and 14 investor groups joined in the Alabama Trac-

tion, Light and Power Company, Ltd., a holding company organized in Canada to attract U.K. investment.

Through Alabama Traction, Light and Power Mitchell
raised British capital for Lay's dam. Built by engineer Eugene
Adams Yates, Lay Dam was completed in 1914.

At this time Alabama Traction, Light and Power was also
acquiring small hydroelectric power companies already in existence. During 1912 and 1913 it bought a 10,000-kilowatt
steam electric plant in Gadsden, Alabama, and a 2,000-kilowatt
hydroelectric plant at Jackson Shoals, Alabama. By 1913 the
company was supplying electricity to Talladega and Gadsden.

Alabama Power Company, the operating subsidiary of Alabama Traction, Light and Power, expanded rapidly, but World
War I depleted British capital and left Alabama Power overextended. Unable to meet his obligations Mitchell went to the
U.K. and convinced bondholders to defer interest payments
and authorize the sale of new bonds and preferred stock.

James Mitchell died in 1920 and was replaced as president
by his lawyer partner Tom Martin. Martin helped Alabama
Power grow by buying up small electric systems, sponsoring
industrial development, and pushing rural electrification. He
remained a force in the southern power industry through the
1950s.

Georgia's first hydroelectric project was built by S. Morgan
Smith. In the 1870s Smith had invented a water turbine that
won wide acceptance in Pennsylvania grist mills. Later he
adapted his turbine to hydroelectric purposes and built a facility for clients at Appleton, Wisconsin. Around 1900 he began
looking for a major city where he could build his own facility.
Eventually he organized the Atlanta Water & Electric Power
Company and dammed up the Chattahoochee River 17 miles
north of Atlanta.

Smith died in 1903, so his sons Elmer and Fahs finished the
dam, ran the S. Morgan Smith Company, and took over the
Atlanta Water & Electric Power Company. They expanded the
operation, built new plants and sold turbines to other power
projects, often taking an equity share in the new ventures as
payment for their product.

Another person working on hydroelectric power in Georgia
was A.J. Warner. Warner and investors formed the North
Georgia Electric Company and built a dam, transmission
lines, and an office building in the Atlanta area.

Soon after completing the dam the company fell on economic hard times. To strengthen cash flow, Warner worked
out a deal with Elmer Smith in which Smith would buy Warner's
electricity and sell it in Atlanta through the newly organized
Atlanta Power Company. Despite the new business Warner's
situation continued to worsen, and in 1910 Fahs Smith bought
North Georgia Electric at a foreclosure sale.

Harry Atkinson, a young banker, also was active in the electric power industry in Georgia. In 1883 the Georgia Electric
Light Company of Atlanta had received a franchise to supply
the city. Georgia Electric Light of Atlanta got off to a poor
start and became heavily in debt to the Thomson-Houston
Company. In 1891 Atkinson and a group of Boston financiers
gained control of the company and reorganized as the Georgia
Electric Light Company.

Despite Atkinson's failures in sidelines such as shipping and
railroads, Georgia Electric Light grew. With attorney Jack
Spalding, Atkinson conducted a series of acquisitions, mergers, and consolidations. In 1912 he gathered a variety of

Georgia utilities, including the Smith brother's North Georgia Electric, into the Georgia Railway and Power Company. Most of the leading lights of the Georgia power industry sat on Georgia Railway and Power's board, and the company was the natural predecessor of Atkinson's Georgia Power Company, which in 1927 consolidated most of the state's remaining electric power companies.

Steps toward the union of Alabama and Georgia Power began in 1924 when Tom Martin and Eugene Yates created Southeastern Power & Light Company, a holding company whose purpose was to amalgamate and integrate utilities throughout the state. Southeastern's first acquisition was Alabama Power, then owned by Alabama Traction, Light and Power of Canada. In 1925 Martin began negotiations with Georgia Railway and Power. A union seemed advantageous for both companies. The Georgia company needed new capital and supplementary power for dry seasons when rivers ran low. Southeastern was seeking new markets. In 1926 Southeastern acquired all the common stock of Georgia Railway and Power, which subsequently became Georgia Power Company.

Southeastern also acquired smaller utilities. In 1926 it bought properties in Augusta, Columbus, Macon, and Rome, Georgia, and amalgamated them into Georgia Power. The same year it acquired disparate electric properties in South Carolina, northwest Florida, and eastern Mississippi. The South Carolina properties became the South Carolina Power Company, the Florida operations became the Gulf Power Company, and the Mississippi properties became the Mississippi Power Company.

Martin's general manager, Yates, led the move toward technical interconnection. Southeastern also set up a wholesale power division to help convert factories from steam to electric power. Among early industrial converts were textile mills and coal mines.

The late 1920s saw electrical consolidation on a national scale. In 1929 a New York holding company called Commonwealth & Southern acquired all of Southeastern Power and Light's utilities.

Commonwealth & Southern's chairman was a merger-and-acquisitions man named B.C. Cobb. In addition to the Southeastern properties, Commonwealth & Southern had a variety of midwestern utilities and one other southern one, the Tennessee Electric Power Company, whose service area was contiguous with Southeastern's.

With the acquisition, Southeastern's president, Tom Martin, became president of Commonwealth & Southern. Cobb and Martin did not get along, nor at least initially did the northern and southern subsidiaries of Commonwealth & Southern. Within two years, Martin returned to the presidency of Alabama Power.

In 1932 Cobb retired and was replaced by Wendell Willkie. Willkie had been the company's general counsel and would later run for president of the United States. The Great Depression had caused a drop in industrial production and thus a drop in industrial consumption of electricity. Willkie needed to increase consumption and cut costs. To increase consumption, he pushed the sale of electric appliances. To reduce costs, he made draconian cuts in wages and personnel. Despite his efforts, the company lost money in the mid-1930s.

Willkie also had to face the Tennessee Valley Authority (TVA) and the Public Utility Holding Company Act of 1935,

both of which threatened Commonwealth & Southern. In 1933 Congress created the TVA, chartered to develop surplus power from navigation and flood control dams. The TVA competed directly with the southern subsidiaries of Commonwealth & Southern. These subsidiaries and other utilities sued to question the TVA's constitutionality, but lost. Commonwealth & Southern sold Tennessee Electric Power to the TVA for $78 million in 1939, and in 1940 it sold sections of Alabama Power, Georgia Power, and Mississippi Power to the authority.

The Public Utility Holding Company Act of 1935 was written in response to the abuses of utility financiers such as Samuel Insull and Howard Hopson. The act permitted only contiguous and integrated systems and thus called for divestiture of some of Commonwealth & Southern's subsidiaries. Court challenges, negotiations, and World War II delayed dissolution until 1947 when the Securities and Exchange Commission (SEC) approved the creation of The Southern Company, comprising Alabama Power, Georgia Power, Mississippi Power, and Gulf Power. The company had to sell South Carolina Power to South Carolina Electric & Gas Company.

The Southern Company's first president was Eugene A. Yates, former general manager of Southeastern Power & Light. Tom Martin, still a power in the organization, backed him.

The Southern Company lacked certain facilities. Among Yates's first acts was the creation of Southern Company Services, which ran power pooling operations, provided engineering for major projects, furnished pension and insurance services, and contributed staff services such as accounting and internal auditing. First owned jointly by the four operating subsidiaries, Southern Company Services became a directly owned subsidiary in 1963. Other housekeeping chores Yates was faced with included the sale of gas and transportation businesses, as required by the SEC.

The postwar years saw an increase in demand for power and a consequent increase in the need for capital. Southern made its first sale of common stock—1.5 million shares—in December 1949.

In 1950 The Southern Company acquired the Birmingham Electric Company (BECO). Long pursued by Tom Martin, BECO's owner, the Electric Bond & Share Company of New York, put it up for sale in 1950 after the SEC ordered Electric Bond & Share to divest its holdings.

Also in 1950 Yates became chairman of The Southern Company, and Eugene McManus, president of Georgia Power, was promoted to president of the holding company. McManus gained nationwide attention for taking a new, friendlier approach in government-utility relations. He offered to supply municipalities and rural electric cooperatives at cost and he ended opposition to government hydroelectric projects.

In the mid-1950s The Southern Company became involved in a conflict-of-interest controversy. The Eisenhower administration had challenged industry to provide 600,000 kilowatts for the Atomic Energy Commission's (AEC) southern installation. The Southern Company and Middle South Utilities proposed a plant that would sell electricity to the TVA, which in turn would sell it to the AEC. The Southern Company–Middle South venture won the contract but was dropped after it was discovered that a First Boston Corporation investment banker, working temporarily with the Bureau of the Budget, also had advised the utilities. In the end, the city of Memphis, Tennessee, built a municipal power plant to take up the load.

The late 1950s marked the beginning of a dramatic period of capital construction. In 1956 the company organized the Southern Electric Generating Company (SEGCO), as a cooperative venture between Georgia Power and Alabama Power. With no coal deposits of its own, Georgia Power wanted a power plant in Alabama where it could be close to the source of energy and not pay rail costs; Alabama Power was attracted by economies of scale. Built on the Coosa River near Wilsonville, Alabama, and completed in 1962, the plant consisted of four 250,000-kilowatt units as well as two fully mechanized coal mines.

At the same time that SEGCO was gearing up, Tom Martin of Alabama Power was pushing for a series of dams on Alabama's Coosa and Warrior Rivers. The extensive project, which eventually provided 852,525 kilowatts of energy, took ten years and $245 million to build.

In January 1957 McManus left the presidency and was elected vice chairman. Harllee Branch, president of Georgia Power, became president of The Southern Company. When Yates died in October 1957, McManus became chairman of the board.

Branch's tenure was a long and satisfying one. As president and later chairman he served until June 1971. In Branch's first year, Georgia Power paid $11 million to acquire Georgia Power and Light, which served 38,000 customers in southern Georgia.

The 1960s were a time of construction, expansion, and profits. Sales, income, and dividends all increased yearly. Between 1960 and 1969 sales rose from $317 million to $666 million, net income went from $46 million to $94 million, and dividends rose from 70¢ to $1.15 per share.

By the late 1960s The Southern Company was showing the fruits of its huge building campaign. In 1969 it had 21 steam-electric plants and 30 hydroelectric power projects. Of the system's capacity, 81% came from steam-electric plants and 19% from hydroelectric dams. Overall, 31% of capacity had been constructed in the previous five years. The late 1960s also marked the beginning of a nuclear construction program.

In 1969 Harllee Branch, who had been president and chairman, retired as president in favor of Alvin W. Vogtle Jr. The following year Vogtle became chief executive officer in anticipation of Branch's retirement as chairman.

The energy crisis of the early 1970s left The Southern Company virtually unscathed. At that point 84% of its electricity was generated by coal-fueled steam-electric plants and only 7.5% of the system's energy came from oil or natural gas.

Two concerns the company did have at this point were cleanliness of coal in an increasingly environmentally conscious nation and the availability of capital at a time when the company was spending more than $1 billion annually on construction. In the late 1970s a series of rate disputes between Southern's subsidiary Alabama Power and the Alabama Public Service Commission depressed earnings and caused the subsidiary to leave some jobs vacant and the parent to freeze its dividend payment.

The early 1980s saw a return to growth. In January 1982 The Southern Company formed Southern Electric International Inc. to market The Southern Company's technical expertise to utilities and industrial concerns. Large building programs were also continued. In 1984 The Southern Company announced it would spend $7.1 billion over three years to complete seven generating plants including two nuclear units at the Vogtle site near Augusta, Georgia.

As the decade came to a close, Southern, like many utilities, found that its nuclear building program was over budget. In 1985 Southern had pledged not to pass through to ratepayers any more than $3.56 billion, which was then its share of the $8.35 billion estimated total cost of the Vogtle plant, which also had several smaller utilities as investors. Southern said any amount above that cap would be charged to its shareholders. When the estimated price of the project increased by $522 million in 1986, Southern posted a charge of $229 million against 1987 earnings. Problems with construction costs and regulators led to a series of disappointing earnings years and stagnant dividends.

In March 1988 The Southern Company acquired Savannah Electric & Power Company of Savannah, Georgia, for approximately 11 million common shares, exchanging 1.05 Southern shares for each Savannah Electric common share, a stock transaction valued at $239.3 million. Later that year the U.S. Attorney General's office in Atlanta began investigating Southern's tax accounting practices for spare parts. In 1989 it also began investigating whether executives at Gulf Power had made illegal political contributions. In 1989 Gulf Power pleaded guilty to conspiring to make political contributions in violation of the Public Utility Holding Company Act and impeding the Internal Revenue Service in its collection of income taxes. In accordance with the plea agreement, Gulf Power paid a fine of $500,000.

The year 1990 brought another disappointment as Georgia regulators refused to allow Southern to charge customers for a portion of its investment in the Vogtle nuclear plant. On a positive note, Southern agreed to sell a unit of Georgia Power's Plant Scherer to two Florida utilities for $810 million and formed the Southern Nuclear Operating Company to provide services for nuclear power plants. Also in 1990, the Attorney General's office dropped its investigation of Southern's spare parts accounting practices.

Principal Subsidiaries: Alabama Power Company; Georgia Power Company; Gulf Power Company; Mississippi Power Company; Savannah Electric and Power Company; Southern Company Services Inc.; Southern Electric International, Inc.; The Southern Investment Group; Southern Nuclear Operating Company.

Further Reading: Crist, James F., *They Electrified the South,* Atlanta, Georgia, The Southern Company, 1981.

—Jordan Wankoff

TEXAS UTILITIES COMPANY

2001 Bryan Tower
Dallas, Texas 75201
U.S.A.
(214) 812-4600
Fax: (214) 812-4079

Public Company
Incorporated: 1945
Employees: 15,216
Sales: $4.54 billion
Stock Exchanges: New York Midwest Pacific

Texas Utilities Company is a holding company with six wholly owned subsidiaries, the largest of which is Texas Utilities Electric Company (TU Electric). TU Electric produces and distributes electricity in the eastern, north central, and western sections of Texas, including the Dallas–Forth Worth metropolitan area. This region has about one-third of Texas's population and is highly diversified economically, with such industries as aerospace manufacturing, oil and gas development, banking, insurance, and agriculture. As of the early 1990s, TU Electric had more than two million electricity customers. Other Texas Utilities subsidiaries are involved in the acquisition and transportation of fuels, and various other services for the electric utility.

Texas Utilities was formed in 1945 as a holding company for three utilities: Dallas Power & Light Company (DP&L), Texas Electric Service Company (TESCO), and Texas Power & Light Company (TP&L). DP&L had been formed in 1917, TESCO in 1929, and TP&L in 1912, while predecessors of these companies dated back as far as the 1880s. Each company had its own electricity generation and distribution system.

Before the formation of Texas Utilities, DP&L had been a subsidiary of Electric Power & Light Company, while TESCO and TP&L had been subsidiaries of American Power & Light Company. Both parent companies, in turn, were subsidiaries of Electric Bond & Share Company, which had been set up by General Electric Company in 1905 to finance electrical power systems and form operating companies.

These holding companies were required to divest themselves of their utility operations under the Public Utility Holding Company Act of 1935. To that end, under an order of the Securities and Exchange Commission, Texas Utilities was formed in 1945 to acquire and run DP&L, TESCO, and

TP&L. At the time, the utilities had combined revenues of $40.4 million, with about 427,000 electricity customers.

As Texas's population and industry grew, so did the utilities. Sales surpassed $100 million in the mid–1950s, $200 million by 1960, and $400 million by 1969. During the 1960s, the number of customers grew to more than one million.

While D&L, TESCO, and TP&L each retained their own identity, they often combined their efforts for acquisition of fuel and construction of power plants. Their parent company formed other subsidiaries to meet these needs, such as Texas Utilities Fuel Company, established in 1970 to provide natural gas to the utilities. Other subsidiaries formed during the 1970s included Chaco Energy Company, focusing on the production and delivery of coal and other fuels to the utilities, and Basic Resources Inc., with the purpose of developing additional energy sources and technology.

At the beginning of the 1970s, Texas Utilities, like other utility operators in Texas, depended almost wholly on natural gas to run its electricity generating plants. During the decade, as natural gas became increasingly scarce in Texas, the company turned to lignite, an inexpensive type of coal it already had in reserve. By 1975 Texas Utilities was meeting 25% of its fuel needs with lignite, and was continuing to acquire lignite reserves. Texas Utilities won praise for its foresight in turning to this fuel; its chairman and chief executive officer, T.L. Austin Jr., was named top utility executive for 1978 by *Financial World*. Even environmentalists liked Austin and his company; Howard Saxton, chairman of the Lone Star Sierra Club, told *Financial World* in June 1979 that Austin represented "the good side of an industry that has been under continuous attack."

Texas Utilities also looked to nuclear power to reduce its use of natural gas. Its Comanche Peak nuclear plant, about 35 miles southwest of Fort Worth, originally was scheduled to begin operation in 1980. As was the case with many other utilities' nuclear plants, however, Comanche Peak had numerous delays and cost escalations, which Austin blamed on design changes ordered by the Nuclear Regulatory Commission (NRC). By 1983 the plant was still not in operation, and its cost had risen from $787 million to $3.4 billion.

On the positive side, by 1983 Texas Utilities was using natural gas for only 45% of its fuel needs, with lignite supplying almost all of the remainder. Texas Utilities's sales had surpassed $3 billion, its earnings were rising steadily, and its credit rating was the highest possible. In 1984 the company reorganized internally, with each of the operating utilities becoming a division of a new sub-holding company, TU Electric. At that time Texas Utilities Mining Company, another subsidiary, took on the job of providing lignite to TU Electric's plants.

Comanche Peak continued to encounter rising costs and extended delays. In 1985 its estimated total cost was revised to $5.46 billion. Because of studies and inspections mandated by the NRC and the Atomic Safety Licensing Board, Comanche Peak's first unit was expected to go into operation in mid–1987 and the second about six months later. These dates passed without startup of the units, however.

In addition to regulatory hurdles, the plant had come up against opposition by antinuclear activists. One such group, Citizens Association for Sound Energy (CASE), had questioned the plant's safety numerous times during its construction. Juanita Ellis, a leader of the group, found that TU

Electric employees who had made safety complaints had been fired. A total of 50 such employees sued the company.

TU Electric then took an unusual approach, deciding to negotiate with Ellis and the whistle-blowing employees. William G. Counsil, an executive vice president of TU Electric, began meeting with Ellis in 1986 and providing her with information she requested. The NRC had certified CASE as an intervenor, with legal authority to raise questions and introduce evidence pertaining to the licensing of Comanche Peak. Until Counsil had begun meeting with Ellis, however, it had been difficult for CASE to obtain any TU Electric documents or to be taken seriously by the utility. In 1988 Ellis agreed to end her opposition to the licensing of Comanche Peak, and the utility made her a member of the plant's independent safety review committee. TU Electric also acknowledged the plant's past safety problems, and paid $4.5 million to reimburse CASE for its expenses and $5.5 million to settle with the employees who had sued.

Comanche Peak's first unit finally went into operation in August 1990, with a capability of producing 1,150 megawatts of electricity. The second unit was scheduled for startup in 1993. Overall, Texas Utilities had put more than $9 billion into the nuclear plant. TU Electric's use of lignite and nuclear energy had greatly reduced its dependence on natural gas. In 1990 TU Electric generated 44.4% of its power with lignite; 37.7% with natural gas; 3.9% with the nuclear unit, which was in use only part of the year; and 0.2% with oil. The remaining 13.8% was power purchased from other utilities.

In 1990 the utility had record electricity sales of 84 billion kilowatt hours, up 2.2% from 1989. It also had record hourly peak demand of 18 million kilowatts on August 30, 1990. This also was 2.2% more than the previous record, set in August 1988.

Texas Utilities Mining reached a milestone in 1990, mining its 400 millionth ton of lignite. The fifth-largest coal-mining company in the United States, it produced 30.6 million tons in 1990, a single-year record. The company won praise for its effort to reclaim mined land, with an award from the U.S. Department of the Interior in 1990.

In the early 1990s the economy in Texas Utilities's service area was hurt somewhat by cutbacks in U.S. defense spending, but the area was attracting diversified businesses that made up for this to some degree. A total of 101 companies located in the area in 1990, bringing with them 9,600 jobs, and another 69 companies expanded, adding 7,800 jobs.

Texas Utilities's earnings per share decreased slightly, from $4.44 to $4.40 from 1989 to 1990. Contributing factors were the discontinuance of the allowance for funds used during construction of Comanche Peak's first unit, and the unit's operating expenses. Still, the company increased its common stock dividend for the 44th consecutive year.

In January 1990 TU Electric requested a 10.2% rate increase, its first since 1984, from the Public Utility Commission (PUC) of Texas. The PUC allowed the utility to begin collecting this amount in August of that year. Late in 1991 the PUC ordered the utility to write off $1.38 billion of its investment in Comanche Peak. PUC staff members had questioned some of the expenditures on the nuclear plant. The ordered write-off meant that, after accounting and tax adjustments, Texas Utilities would have to subtract $1 billion from a year's net income. This almost produced a net loss for 1991. The posting of such a loss rendered the company unable to raise capital through debt issues or preferred stock for at least a year.

Texas Utilities promptly filed a motion with the PUC, asking to have the order overturned. Company officials planned to go through the courts if their appeal to the PUC did not succeed; the entire process was likely to take up to 18 months. In the meantime, Texas Utilities instituted a hiring freeze and cut spending on such items as employee travel and company vehicles. The company expected to delay completion of certain power plants under construction, including two lignite-fueled units that originally had been scheduled to begin operation in 1995 and 1996. Texas Utilities also planned to review and reconsider several other plants that had been set to open later in the 1990s.

Principal Subsidiaries: Texas Utilities Electric Company; Texas Utilities Fuel Company; Texas Utilities Mining Company; Texas Utilities Services Inc.; Basic Resources Inc.; Chaco Energy Company.

Further Reading: Levy, Robert, "Texas' Triple-A Utility," *Dun's Business Month,* June 1983; Mason, Todd, and Corie Brown, "Juanita Ellis: Antinuke Saint or Sellout?" *Business Week,* October 24, 1988.

—Trudy Ring and Donald R. Stabile

TOHOKU ELECTRIC POWER COMPANY, INC.

3-7-1 Ichibancho
Aoba-ku
Sendai 980
Japan
(022) 225 2111
Fax: (022) 221 1917

Public Company
Incorporated: 1951
Employees: 13,745
Sales: ¥1.16 trillion (US$9.29 billion)
Stock Exchanges: Tokyo Osaka

Tohoku Electric Power Company, Inc. (Tohoku Electric Power) serves nearly five million residences and one million commercial and industrial customers in the Tohoku region, which comprises the seven northernmost prefectures of Japan's main island of Honshu. The region contains 20% of Japan's land and 10% of its population, but accounts for only 6% of its GNP. With its mountainous landscape and heavy winter snow, Tohoku has lagged behind the rest of Japan in terms of industrial development. The region is still largely rural and is known as Japan's *furusato* or country home. However, the city of Sendai in Miyagi prefecture has boomed in recent years to rival the southern Japanese centers. Tohoku's climate and the inaccessibility of many parts of the region has presented Tohoku Electric Power with special problems.

Tohoku Electric Power was formed as a company on May 1, 1951 when the General Headquarters of the Allied Powers (GHQ) under General MacArthur approved a plan submitted by the Japanese government to reorganize and rationalize the electrical power industry. Under the scheme the nation was divided into nine blocks, each with its own privately-owned electric power company. At the time of inauguration, the nine companies served 16 million customers with a combined capacity of 8,500 megawatts (MW).

The history of electric power in Japan as a whole, however, goes back to 1878 when Professor W.E. Aryton of the Institute of Technology in Tokyo unveiled an arc lamp to celebrate the opening of the Central Telegraph Office. Japan's first electric utility company was established in 1886, seven years after Thomas Edison had invented the incandescent lamp in the United States. The company was Tokyo Electric Lighting Company and its and Japan's first electric power plant was completed in 1887 as a 25 kilowatt (KW) facility in Nihonbashi, Tokyo. Throughout its history Japan has always assimilated and improved upon outside technology and ideas, and electric power was no exception. After the opening of Tokyo Electric Lighting many electric utilities started up in main cities. One of the first hydroelectric plants to open in Japan was Sankyozawa Power Station, operated by Fukushima Electric Lighting, in 1899. This facility was the first of numerous generating sites to be constructed in Tohoku, thus providing the foundation of what was eventually to become Tohoku Electric Power. Coming only 17 years after the world's first hydroelectric facility in Wisconsin in the United States and transmitting electric power at 11 thousand volts over a distance of 25 kilometers, this was a remarkable achievement. As in the West, the very early Japanese power stations were constructed close to where the power was required due to the primitive transmission techniques available at that time. An example of this was the hydroelectric power plant built in the Kosaka mine works in the northern Tohoku prefecture of Akita in 1903. The plant was the brainchild of the chief electrical engineer at the mine, Namihei Odaira. Odaira was later to found Hitachi Co. Ltd. and remained the dominant figure in the development of Japan's electrical industry.

Although demand had increased rapidly, the use of electricity was generally limited to government and commercial offices and factories. In Tohoku, where hydroelectric power was the main source of electricity, it was not until about 1910 that technological advances allowed the output of hydroelectric stations to be as efficient and effective as conventional thermal coal- and oil-powered stations. In 1915 the Iwamuro station in Fukushima, Tohoku accomplished the long-distance transmission of 115,000 voltage power to Tokyo 220 kilometers away. The significance of the event was not only that the transmission line was the third longest in the world at the time, but also that the turbines were produced in Japan by Odaira who by then had started manufacturing under the name of Hitachi.

The relatively high price of electricity also held growth in check. A large proportion of the demand for electricity came from the electric railways that were springing up all over the country. Japan fought three wars between the years 1894 and 1918: the Sino-Japanese War, won by Japan in 1894; the Russo-Japanese War, won by Japan in 1905; and World War I, where Japan was on the losing side. These wars had the effect of spurring industrial development. In 1911 the government promulgated the Electric Utility Industry Law. It provided government permission for the production and distribution of electric power. By 1920 there were 3,000 power companies in Japan riding on Japan's economic boom. The period 1926 to 1937 can be characterized as the era of the "Big Five" in the history of electric power in Japan. It was dominated by Tokyo Electric Lighting and Daido Power in particular. Many of the companies in operation in Tohoku, such as Inawashiro Hydroelectric Power Company, were subsidiaries of the Big Five. The government regulated the industry by passing four laws in 1938 which ensured state control over price, plant development, transmission, and all other aspects of the industry. In effect it had formed one of the largest electric companies in the world with the establishment of JEGTCO (Japan Electric Generation and Transmission Company). The Allied bombing of Japan in 1943 to 1945 seriously damaged 44% of Japan's power stations and devastated its industry. The GHQ, which effectively was in charge of Japan from 1945 to 1952, made sweeping changes in Japan's electric power industry. The Council for Reorganization of Electric Utility Industry was formed in 1949 and chaired by Yasuzaemon Matsunaga, former president of Toho Electric Power Company. After much negotiation a plan was produced that divided the country into nine areas, each with its own privately owned electric power company.

One of these nine companies was Tohoku Electric Power, which was formed to consolidate the existing power generating concerns in the seven northernmost prefectures of Honshu. With start-up capital of ¥900 million, equivalent to US$2.5 million at the time, and under the leadership of President Uchiyama, the company was launched. With the area's abundance of snowcapped mountains and rivers, the vast majority of the region's electricity-generating facilities were hydroelectric-powered and hence located in sometimes inaccessible regions. Traditionally, the supply of electric power in the region had been somewhat unreliable. In 1945 Tohoku and all the electric power distribution systems on Honshu were standardized onto a 50 Hertz (Hz) system which helped alleviate the problem. Along with chairman Jiro Shirasu, Uchiyama had three priorities in running the company. The first was to ensure that the customer's needs were satisfied. He also stressed the need to accommodate the 16,000 employees for whom he was now responsible, and to ensure their wellbeing. As a private concern, he strove to make Tohoku Electric Power attractive to both its existing and prospective shareholders. To achieve the first of these objectives, the management set about reorganizing the company and developing a corporate identity. Localized sales offices were developed and the number and quality of maintenance staff increased. Ambitious construction work began on hydroelectric facilities surrounding Tadami River in Fukushima Prefecture to modernize and expand on the region's existing facilities. At the same time priority was given to the development of thermal stations within the Tohoku region. The reliability of hydroelectric power depends to some extent on precipitation levels, and less-than-average precipitation can result in power shortages. This, coupled with falling costs of thermal power generation, resulted in the latter's increased use. By the early 1990s Tohoku Electric Power had 12 thermal installations, responsible for more than 70% of output.

In 1959, in order to coordinate the nine electric power companies, the Central Electric Power Council was established. Its first task was to facilitate the exchange of power by linking all the systems together. Its first link joined Tohoku Electric Power's generating capability with that of Tokyo Electric Power via the Tadami Line. The 1960s in Japan were a time of double-digit economic growth and all of the EPCs, including Tohoku, experienced annual growth in demand of more than 10%. Large-scale oil-fired power stations were central to meeting Japan's energy needs during this expansionary period, and Tohoku Electric Power invested heavily in facilities such as the Shinsendai Thermal Unit. By 1973 oil-fired thermal power accounted for over half the company's output. A law passed in 1965 by the Japanese parliament, the Electric Utility Industry Law, was concerned with safety aspects of new facilities. A further law, passed in 1967, was concerned with pollution control. Tohoku Electric Power responded to these by drawing up strict environmental guidelines, and today is known as one of the most environmentally conscious compan-

ies in Japan. The oil shocks of 1973 and 1978 profoundly affected Japan's economy. As a direct buyer of large amounts of Middle Eastern oil, Tohoku Electric Power had to cope with the higher price of fuel as well as the corresponding sharp drop in consumer and industrial demand for electricity. A government campaign urging energy conservation in 1973 had been very successful, and resulted in a sharp drop in the EPCs' profits. In the short term this affected the growth of Tohoku Electric Power, and the company was forced to develop alternatives to oil-based energy sources. One possible solution lay in increased development of hydroelectric power, but the majority of efficient sources had been tapped. Tohoku and the other electric utilities began the development of Japan's nuclear energy program. Via this and the increased use of LNG (liquid natural gas), Tohoku Electric Power halved its dependence on oil between 1973 and 1985. A 524,000 kilowatt (kW) nuclear facility was commissioned in the 1980s in Onagawa, north of Sendai, and in the early 1990s this plant alone provided 5% of the region's electricity. There were plans to build an adjacent facility by 1996 with a capacity of almost a million kilowatts.

In 1987 the management, under current president Terayuki Akema, launched the Basic Business Development Strategy for the 21st Century. The first year was spent restructuring the main office and sales force, which had become bureaucratic and inefficient. Akema felt that the main challenge facing the company was to remain at the leading edge of technology in the industry, and that a highly efficient work force was necessary. In 1990 a research and development facility was opened in Sendai dealing with new energy sources and environmentally-oriented innovations. Students from developing countries in Asia came to Tohoku in 1989 for the first Electric Power Development Planning Course, and exchange programs were initiated with power companies in the United States. Another feature of Akema's plan was to develop business in new areas. In 1990 Tohoku Cellular Telephone began selling cellular telephones and ELTAS Tohoku, established in 1989, offered real estate services and advertising. The success of Tohoku Electric Power in these non-core activities remains to be seen.

In terms of technological advances, Tohoku Electric Power is a leader among the Japanese utilities and in 1989 introduced an automated transmission monitoring system to iron out peaks and troughs in demand, thus making substantial savings. A fleet of helicopters constantly monitors transmission lines in the rugged Tohoku mountains, ensuring speedy repair. The booming regional economy of Tohoku in the 1990s has meant that its electricity utility is experiencing higher-than-average growth as a utility company. The challenge now for Tohoku Electric Power is to develop the necessary non-oil energy sources for electricity in order to achieve long-term stability.

Principal Subsidiaries: Yuatech Company (33%); North Japan Electric Transmission (60%); United Insulation (91%); East Japan Heavy Industries; Tohoku Cement (67%); Towa Kyodo Thermal Power (49%); Todo Heavy Industry; Tsukyu Electrical Engineering (82%); Tohoku Electrical Products (50%); Ryukawa Hydroelectric Power (50%); Tohoku Electrical Development; Tohoku Electrical Goods (69%); Tohoku Transmission (30%); Shuda Kyodo Thermal Power; Japan Sea LNG

(41%); Tohoku Port Service (60%); Tohoku Land Development; Gunma Kyodo Thermal Power (50%); Indonesia LNG (60%); Tohoku Development Consultants (20%); Electric Power Life Create Company; Tohoku Information Network Services (38%); Tohoku Cellular Phone (20%); Eltas Tohoku (89%); Tohoku Air Service; Tohoku Electrical Appliance Centre; Tohoku OE Services (90%).

Further Reading: Muramatsu, Teijiro, *Industrial Technology in Japan: A Historical Review,* Hitachi Ltd., 1968; *History of Electric Power Industry in Japan,* Tokyo, Japan Electric Power Information Center, March 1988; *Story of Tohoku Electric Power,* Sendai, Tohoku Electric Power, 1990.

—Dylan Tanner

THE TOKYO ELECTRIC POWER COMPANY, INCORPORATED

1-3, Uchisaiwai-cho, 1-chome
Chiyoda-ku, Tokyo 100
Japan
(03) 3501-8111
Fax: (03) 3591-4609

Public Company
Incorporated: 1951
Employees: 39,640
Sales: ¥4.25 trillion (US$34.05 billion)
Stock Exchanges: Tokyo Osaka Nagoya Niigata

The Tokyo Electric Power Company (TEPCO) is the world's largest privately-owned electric utility company. Japan has eight other major regional power companies—as well as the power company for the island of Okinawa, which the United States returned to Japan in 1973—but TEPCO alone supplies approximately one-third of Japan's electricity. In fiscal year 1990, the company distributed 219.9 billion kilowatt-hours (kWh) of electricity to 22.7 million industrial, commercial, and individual customers over a service area of 39,500 square kilometers. The service area includes Tokyo, its suburbs, and eight surrounding prefectures, among them Kanagawa prefecture, which includes the city of Yokohama.

In the ongoing conversion to low-polluting fuels, TEPCO is the world's largest importer of liquefied natural gas (LNG), and accounts for approximately one-fourth of the global LNG trade. The company also orchestrates the import of nuclear fuels, their international processing, and their disposal, as a major component of the national program to make nuclear power the leading form of energy by the 21st century.

The company has its roots in Japan's first electric utility, Tokyo Electric Lighting Company, which emerged in the mid-1880s, although TEPCO only dates its incorporation from 1951, the year in which the Japanese electric power industry returned to private ownership after government monopoly control during World War II.

Even as the world's first public power stations were being established in London and New York in 1882, the Meiji government, in its effort to modernize Japan, formed an Institute of Technology. English and other foreign experts were invited to Tokyo to train the Japanese in the technology. In November 1885, Tokyo Electric Lighting Company used a Japanese-made portable generator to light 40 incandescent lamps in the

Bank of Tokyo. Regular service began the following year when the company, capitalized at ¥200,000, was granted a charter to generate and distribute electricity and sell lighting accessories. A coal-fired thermal station, generating 25 kilowatts (kW), began operating in November 1887. By 1892, 14,100 lamps had been installed in post offices, banks, ministries, and Japan's first modern factories.

Tokyo Electric Lighting Company used thermal plants because coal was plentiful; the only other domestic energy resource, major river systems, was beyond the range of its primitive transmission technology. Hydroelectric power generation, introduced by the city of Kyoto in 1891, would become Japan's leading prewar electricity source, but was available to Tokyo only over long-distance trunk lines.

The company began to consolidate neighborhood thermal plants and by 1897 had ten units in Asakusa Kuramae power station, aggregating a capacity of 2,390kW. Distribution efficiency improved in 1907 with 55 kilovolts (kV) transmission. By 1911 the company was also making tungsten bulbs.

In the same year the government consolidated ad hoc legislation over the rapidly growing industry with an Electric Utility Industry Law. From then on, power plants had to be licensed, and regulation began providing for common use of transmission lines. War, too, had become a spur to growth. The Sino-Japanese war of 1894–1895 boosted Japanese industry with its procurement demands. At the same time tramcar systems proliferated in Tokyo and other Japanese cities.

Following the 1904–1905 Russo-Japanese War, the government promoted heavy industry and the electric power industry also grew rapidly, becoming second only to banks in terms of capital. Tokyo Electric Lighting Company, now able to draw power from hydroelectric stations in the hinterland, remained the largest utility in the country even as the number of generating and distribution companies rose from 11 in 1892 to 1,752 by 1915. Its service region encompassed the political capital, a major university center, and a burgeoning of satellite heavy- and light-industrial complexes and their international trading ports.

Japan was allied to Britain and France in World War I. While British and French industries were occupied in war production, exports of Japanese light-industrial goods to Europe soared, notably raw silk, but also tea, toys, household utensils, and machine parts. In 1925, the total number of companies in the electricity utility field peaked at around 3,000.

In September 1923, however, there came a huge setback, the Great Kanto Earthquake, accompanied by fires which destroyed much of Tokyo and Yokohama. International aid poured in and the restoring of utilities was given the highest priority. By 1924 the company was again moving forward in the development of a national grid. It had been among Japanese companies importing American equipment which produced current at 50 Herz (Hz). Companies in western Japan, including Osaka, had opted for German equipment, delivering 60Hz. New transmission technology could now deliver and convert hydroelectric power from the hinterland mountain regions. This began the wide area electric power exchange system, which continues to overcome power shortages in the Tokyo region.

In the 1920s Europe was again producing light-industrial goods, and the Japanese economy slid into severe depression. Japan's leading export, raw silk, slumped by more than half.

There was fierce competition in the electric power industry. In some cases, three power companies supplied a single customer at different times of the day. Tokyo Electric Lighting Company began absorbing bankrupt competitors during an industry shake-out.

By 1928 it was the largest of the Big Five utilities operating the self-regulating Electric Power Control Council. In general, Japan's industries were adopting the cartel system in an effort to stabilize the marketplace. At the same time, militarist factions were turning the nation toward war in mainland China; by 1932 the government began enforcing a revised Electric Utility Industry Law. This gave the bureaucrats the final say on rates, company mergers, and even expropriation of utilities for military production.

By 1937 governments increasingly dominated by personalities wanting to emulate the German and Italian imperial example had led Japan into full-scale war against China. Tokyo Electric Lighting Company, along with the rest of the industry, came under state control in 1938. The core legislation established the Japan Electric Generation and Transmission Company (JEGTCO) or *Nippon Hasso Den*. The Electric Utility Bureau of the Ministry of Communications supervised the industry. The Japanese government wanted to ensure an abundant supply of cheap electricity for military production. Government permission was required for rate levels, building new power stations, or installing transmission lines. Tokyo Electric Lighting Company was at that time a component of what was, in effect, one of the largest electricity companies in the world.

By 1942 the framework for exerting state control over the electric power industry was firmly in place. In 1943 the task of supervision passed to the Electric Power Office of the Ministry of Munitions. The industry thus became part of the mobilization for global war. Hydroelectric power development took priority, and 17 new plants were built on river systems across the country. The Tokyo region could use only coal-fired thermal plants locally. The military planning brought a national grid closer to reality, however; Tokyo and most of eastern Japan were standardized on 50Hz current while all western Japan now used 60Hz. Military intervention, however, had in fact slowed down development. In the four years before World War II, electricity production capacity had been increasing at an annual rate of 600MW. During the war years, annual growth in capacity declined to an average 170MW.

When Japan surrendered in 1945, Tokyo had been bombed and burned to rubble. Facilities of the former Tokyo Electric Lighting Company represented a large proportion of the 44% of thermal power plant capacity that had been destroyed nationwide. The JEGTCO monopoly was transferred to the Ministry of Commerce and Industry, forerunner of the Ministry of International Trade and Industry (MITI). The American-led military occupation authorities of Japan initially intended to return the nation to the level of an agricultural economy. By August 1946, surviving equipment in some 20 war-damaged thermal power plants had been included among factory machinery which was to be shipped to Asian countries invaded by Japan, in part payment of war reparations.

The national industrial base had been almost halved by air-raid destruction, and with the munitions factories closed, Japan started out anew in 1945 with a surplus of electric power capacity to demand. With their legendary energy, however, the Japanese began to reconstruct factories from whatever machinery was available. As early as 1946, electric power demand increased by 25% and rose by an average of 10% for the next several years.

The Allied occupation at first refused to allow new capacity to be added, fearing that this might be a first step toward rearmament. By 1948, the JEGTCO monopoly was targeted for breakup, along with other industrial and financial concentrations, like the *zaibatsu*. Just how this was to be accomplished became an issue of heated debate among the Japanese leaders and the Allied occupation planners over whether centralized state control should continue, or whether utilities should return to private ownership. The situation was complicated by the rising power of unions encouraged by occupation policies. Paradoxically, unions in the electric power industry tended to favor state control for job security, and from 1946 often-violent strikes began, with the aim of ensuring a future for domestic coal fuel, among other issues.

The Cold War began to change U.S. priorities for Japan; for the strategy of containing Stalinist communism, it was becoming more desirable to have an industrially strong Japan with at least a military capability for self-defense. One of the most influential Japanese voices regarding electricity utility reform proved to be that of Yasuzaemon Matsunaga. This Meiji Era entrepreneur was an important link between the prewar Tokyo Electric Lighting Company and the TEPCO that emerged in 1951. He had no direct business ties to the Tokyo utility, but was a role model for Kazutaka Kikawada, who became TEPCO president during the high-growth economic breakthrough of the 1960s.

Matsunaga had prospered in western Japanese electric utilities and electric railways early in the century. By 1924 he was president of the Japan Electric Association. He opposed the military takeover, and when the JEGTCO monopoly was imposed in 1938 retired to private life. In the postwar debate over future policy, he championed the private enterprise solution and his views prevailed.

While the debate continued, in May 1949 the MITI was established and its Agency of Natural Resources assumed control of utilities. Finally, on November 24, 1950, the government invoked occupation powers to force reform legislation through parliament. From December 1950 a Public Utilities Commission, comprising businessmen and academics, free of political control, divided the nation into nine regions, each with a privately-owned electric power company, to begin operating in May 1951. TEPCO assumed the assets and liabilities of JEGTCO in the Tokyo region, including a subsidiary, the Kanto Power Distribution Company.

The Korean War had been underway since June 1950 and from its inception TEPCO played a leading role in supplying power to a still-occupied and capital-starved Japan. TEPCO relied on power transferred from distant hydroelectric stations for 80% of the supply for the Tokyo region.

The Korean War was the first of a succession of unforeseen circumstances fostering the Japanese economic miracle. It stimulated the first postwar boom because Japan was the main rear-base for American-led United Nations forces turning back the invasion of South Korea by the communist North Korea. The extent to which U.S. policy toward Japan had been reversed is indicated by the fact that in April 1952 MITI was permitted to exclude thermal power station equipment from the list of machinery earmarked, in principle at least, for shipment abroad as war reparations.

TEPCO began increasing rates to profitable levels and cashflow was helped further by an easing of the tax structure, allowing more generous depreciation write-offs. What was emerging was the uniquely Japanese modification of classic free-enterprise capitalism based on competition but also due consideration for overriding national goals. State planning continued to have a role, especially for ensuring stability of supply for something as crucial as energy.

At an early stage TEPCO management gave priority to developing a new generation of managerial talent. In-house training courses have now reached the level of university education.

While TEPCO and the other regional companies were evolving as private enterprises, as early as 1951 Matsunaga succeeded in establishing a Central Research Institute for the Electric Power Industry. By 1952, the Prime Minister's Office had added an administrative Electric Power Development Coordination Council. A government-financed Electric Power Development Company, Ltd. (EPDC), capitalized at ¥100 billion, took on the job of developing major new hydroelectric power stations.

The Allied occupation ended in April 1952. By November, a Federation of Electric Power Companies had been organized and numerous symposiums and study groups debated whether the country should limit itself to the domestically available coal and hydroelectric energy resources. External events were to influence the outcome once more; in particular, technology became available from the United States and Europe, and oil became increasingly cheaper.

Studies began on the potential of nuclear power as early as 1954, although Japan was as barren of uranium ores as it was of oil. TEPCO research laboratories began exploring nuclear power in 1955, ahead of the promulgation in December of that year of an Atomic Energy Basic Law to guide the industry. In January 1956 the Prime Minister's Office added an Atomic Energy Commission to its roster of administrative bodies. The Japan Atomic Energy Research Institute (JAERI), funded by both the government and the industry, opened in the same year. A separate entity, the Japan Atomic Power Company, followed in November 1957. TEPCO could coordinate its nuclear future through these and other supplementary organizations.

In 1958 the company became a founding member of the Japan Electric Power Information Center (JEPIC), whose major purpose was to promote technological exchanges with American and European utilities. High-voltage transmission and bridging the disparate frequencies in the two halves of the country became priorities. In 1959 a new Central Electric Power Council supervised the opening of the Tadami Line, linking the 50Hz system of TEPCO and the hydroelectric plants of the Tohoku Electric Power Company far to the northeast of Tokyo.

In 1961 Kazutaka Kikawada became president of TEPCO. Kikawada had joined the Tokyo Electric Lighting Company in 1926 during the depression. He had studied economics at Tokyo Imperial University, and had developed an interest in the problems of unemployment and social welfare. He took the TEPCO helm just as Prime Minister Hayato Ikeda was launching a program to double the national income within a decade, boosting public spending, reducing taxes, and lowering interest

rates. Ikeda, who had become prime minister in 1960, was disabled by cancer in 1964, but by then Japan had joined the Organization for Economic Cooperation and Development (OECD) and had developed a domestic market whose prospering consumers would underpin manufacturing growth in the decades ahead.

Matsunaga, who had headed yet another commission planning the way forward for utilities in 1960, had been Kikawada's entrepreneurial model. As TEPCO president, in 1963 Kikawada also became chairman of the *Keizai Doyukai*, the Japan Association of Corporate Executives. This business association, formed in 1946, focused mainly on the appropriate role of private enterprise in improving the quality of life in general; today it is affiliated with six similar business organizations in Europe, the United States, and Australia, involved in developing a private-sector role for easing global economic problems. Kikawada also became chairman of an advisory Economic Council of the Economic Planning Agency during 1966 and 1967.

The prosperity of the 1960s brought a proliferation of electric home appliances and air-conditioning. TEPCO's peak demand season shifted from winter to summer, and the Tokyo region needed more and more supplementary power. In October 1965, the 50Hz system of eastern Japan was able for the first time to exchange power easily with the 60Hz system of western Japan through a sophisticated frequency converter station in central Japan. From 1963, thermal power generation had taken the lead over hydroelectric sources nationwide. By 1973 TEPCO's long-term development plan, applying large-scale thermal power generation technology, had quadrupled the company's capacity of eight years earlier.

Increasing American involvement in Vietnam throughout the 1960s accounted in part for orders flooding into Japan; heavy and chemical industries developed rapidly. As in the Korean War, Japan provided a major Asian support base, repairing air, land, and sea-battle equipment and supplying many materials and services. While U.S. industry met wartime priorities, new export markets opened for Japan, notably in consumer electronics. TEPCO, teamed with Japan's general trading houses (*sogo shosha*), began to diversify its overseas sources of fuel; Japan was following the rest of the industrial world into an era of oil-fired thermal power generation.

Air pollution reached critical levels, and in 1967 TEPCO turned to Indonesia for low-sulfur Minas crude oil. In 1970 its Minami-Yokohama Thermal Power Station became the first in the world to use liquefied natural gas (LNG), from Alaska. By 1973, coal-firing had been discontinued. Pilot nuclear power plants had begun operating in 1966; in 1971 TEPCO began operating Japan's third boiling-water reactor (BWR). The main supplier of the reactor and technology was General Electric of the United States.

TEPCO located its nuclear-power plants far from the crowded capital region, on the coast of Fukushima prefecture to the north, the service region of its longtime partner, the Tohoku Electric Power Company. By 1979, five further BWR reactors had been added to the Fukushima No. 1 complex. The company now used its own technology, and contracted construction to other Japanese corporations that were experts in the field. Despite potential earthquake hazards, nuclear power began gaining ascendancy, mainly to reduce air pollution. In 1970 the government legislated severe controls on air, land, and water pollution. An Environmental Agency on the American model emerged in 1971. The oil crisis of 1973–1974 reinforced commitment to a nuclear future.

TEPCO declared a state of emergency and began shifting away from oil, a process accelerated by the second oil crisis at the end of the 1970s. Between 1973 and 1981, the share of nuclear fuel in the overall fuel mix increased from 3% to 21%. LNG consumption rose from 1.4 million tons annually to 6.9 million tons. The share of oil in thermal power generation declined from 90% to 56%. The company also researched new coal-burning technologies, from Coal-Oil-Mixture to the gassification of raw coal. By 1984 one major thermal power station had been converted back to improved coal fuel, and another is planned for 1993 in a joint-venture with Tohoku Electric Power Company.

The company entered the 1990s under the leadership of Gaishi Hiraiwa. Hiraiwa was elevated to chairman and chief executive officer in 1984. After graduating from Tokyo Imperial University Faculty of Law, and after briefly joining Tokyo Electric Lighting Company in 1939, he was drafted into the army and sent to war in China. After the war, he rose to become TEPCO's president in 1976. Hiraiwa was chairman of the Economic Council advising the government, and in December 1990 was elevated from vice president to chairman of the powerful Federation of Economic Organizations (*Keidanren*).

Under Hiraiwa's leadership in the 1980s, TEPCO moved into the realm of high technology applied far beyond the boundaries of the electric power industry. In 1980 Japan adopted a Law for Promoting Development and Introduction of Alternative Energies to Oil. By 1991, TEPCO was operating 13 of the 17 nuclear reactors installed in operating power stations; two more were under construction and another was in the advanced planning stage. The Three Mile Island and Chernobyl nuclear accidents revived popular opposition to nuclear technology in Japan. This has delayed but not halted the development of nuclear power; TEPCO and the government emphasized a net gain in combating conventional pollution, at least, which was still severe in Japan. A need for more generating capacity became evident in the 1991 summer peak demand season when Tokyo was close to requiring rationing.

TEPCO imports uranium ores from the United States, Canada, Australia, and Niger. Specialized processing has been carried out in the United States, Canada, the United Kingdom, and France, and spent nuclear fuel sent to the United Kingdom and France for reprocessing. Both uranium enrichment and spent-fuel reprocessing have begun to be carried out in Japan, however, and nuclear power stations are adding repositories for low-level wastes. In 1991 nuclear power accounted for 28% of TEPCO's total generation; this is projected to reach 39% by the year 2000.

TEPCO fully considers national policy needs in its business decisions. Since the 1970s, the main contractors for its nuclear power plants have been Toshiba and Hitachi. To ease trade friction, equipment orders for two new plants were switched to the General Electric Company (GEC) of the United States. TEPCO also turned to GEC for advanced gas turbines and generators to enhance the efficiency of thermal plants fired by LNG. In 1991 TEPCO was the world's largest user of LNG (along with LPG). The LNG share in TEPCO's thermal power fuel mix increased from 10% in 1973 to 56% in 1991.

TEPCO buys from suppliers as far afield as Alaska, Brunei, Abu Dhabi (Das Island), Malaysia, Indonesia, and Australia. Through trading houses such as Mitsubishi Corporation and Mitsui & Company, it seemed likely that TEPCO would have access to Russian LNG resources on Sakhalin Island, and possibly on the Siberian mainland if Russia followed through on invitations for shared development with Japan.

Oil had dwindled from 47% of TEPCO's total generating facilities in 1970 to 21% in 1990, and was projected to shrink to 15% by 2000 even before the Gulf War provoked new concern about supply stability. Hydroelectric power, representing 88% of supply in 1952, the company's first full year of operation, has leveled off at around 9%; it survives for peak load demand fluctuations in a strategy of nuclear power for "base load" and LNG for "middle load". Coal has been returned to the list of fuels in less-polluting guises, partly because the new technologies should make it possible to begin buying American and other coals as well as Australian as a trade-balancing measure.

TEPCO is heavily involved, domestically and internationally, in research and development (R&D). In 1991 the central Engineering R&D Administration alone had 400 staff. Already TEPCO is using new types of chemical fuel cells for local electricity supplies and electric power storage cells to help during peak demand, harbingers of future alternatives. Like many Japanese corporations, TEPCO maximizes the application of its technology and expertise wherever opportunity beckons.

In 1986, for example, when the Japanese government began to liberalize the telecommunications market, previously monopolized by Nippon Telegraph and Telephone Corp. (NTT), TEPCO used its expertise in computerized power grid communications in joining with two *sogo shosha* to form Tokyo Telecommunications Network Company, Inc. (TTNet) to develop an optical fiber digital network for facsimile, data, and public telephone services. This led to mobile communications and, in 1989, a TEPCO cable television system. The founding president of TTNet was Kazuo Fujimori, who had joined TEPCO in 1951 as an engineer and had become executive vice-president.

Research into nuclear power plant safety under earthquake conditions is also being applied to prototype high-rise buildings which can adjust to withstand earthquake vibrations. This is a contribution to Tokyo's major waterfront urban redevelopment projects. In seeking to reduce peak demand, TEPCO technologies have given Tokyo its first district air-conditioning system using waste heat on the heat-pump principle; in some cases the heat is extracted from river waters warmed by factory discharge, in others heat is recovered from sewage beneath high-rise "new towns". TEPCO recycles 60% of the copper used in power lines. TEPCO's laboratories are researching high-temperature industrial ceramics, superconductivity, and artificial intelligence for computers.

TEPCO is involved with major international research projects in the United States and Europe while encouraging visits from overseas students and scientists. TEPCO technology has enabled the company to achieve the world's lowest levels of sulfur dioxide and carbon dioxide emissions; research has revealed the photosynthesis potential of seaweed for absorbing carbon dioxide. At the 1991 Tokyo Auto Show, TEPCO displayed an electric car prototype that can reach 170 kilometers per hour and can drive the 500 kilometers to Osaka without a battery recharge. Because of these wide-ranging activities, the company has begun to refer to itself as the TEPCO Group. It has entered international capital markets with the issue of corporate bonds.

Principal Subsidiaries: Kandenko Company, Ltd. (46%); Tokyo Telecommunication Network Company, Inc. (33%); The Japan Atomic Power Company (28%).

Further Reading: Japan Electric Power Information Center, *History of the Electric Power Industry in Japan*, Tokyo, JEPIC, 1988; Hein, Laura E., *Fueling Growth*: *The Energy Revolution and Economic Policy in Postwar Japan*, London, Harvard University Press, 1990; Ozaki, Robert S., *Human Capitalism: the Japanese Enterprise System as World Model*, Tokyo, Kodansha International, 1991.

—Rowland G. Gould

T TOKYO GAS

TOKYO GAS CO., LTD.

1-5-20 Kaigan
Minato-ku
Tokyo 105
Japan
(03) 3433 2111
Fax: (03) 3432 4574

Public Company
Incorporated: 1885
Employees: 12,519
Sales: ¥782.00 billion (US$6.27 billion)
Stock Exchanges: Tokyo Osaka Nagoya

Tokyo Gas Co., Ltd. (Tokyo Gas) is Japan's largest city gas supplier, distributing gas to the Kanto region, encompassing the cities of Tokyo, Yokohama, and Kawasaki, as well as to eight other prefectures. With around 7.5 million customers and a vast, highly developed supply infrastructure, Tokyo Gas is one of Japan's leading energy companies. Encouraged by the government energy policy of reducing the nation's dependence on crude oil, Tokyo Gas has developed the use of liquefied natural gas (LNG) as its primary raw material and has forged close links with several supplier nations such as Malaysia and Australia. Recently the company has sought to diversify, moving into business areas such as appliances and home security systems.

The use of city gas in Japan began in 1871, when a gas-powered street lamp was unveiled in Osaka. Tokyo's first gas lamps appeared three years later when 85 street lamps were installed as lighting in the vicinity of the Diet (Japan's governmental national assembly) building. One of the main proponents of city gas in Tokyo was Eichi Shibusawa, Japan's leading industrialist at that time. Shibusawa was a central figure in Japan's extremely rapid economic growth following Commodore Perry's mission of 1853 to 1854. Perry threatened to use the fire-power of the U.S. navy unless Japan opened its doors to the West. This event initiated a rapid assimilation of the best of Western culture and technology into Japan via young scholars sent abroad by the newly unified Japanese government. Shibusawa and the national authorities saw gas as a safe replacement for oil lamps common in Japanese cities. These had traditionally been a source of countless blazes. Gas lighting was spectacularly displayed at a technology exhibition in Ueno, Tokyo, in 1887, when a giant

chrysanthemum—a symbol of imperial Japan—made of numerous gas power lights was unveiled.

Shibusawa was named head of the City of Tokyo's gas board in 1879, and in 1885, when the government sold the business and licenses to supply gas, he became the first chairman of Tokyo Gas. With only 343 customers and 61 employees, Tokyo Gas was very small, but Shibusawa had ambitious plans for the company. The number of users was increasing daily and the company could not meet the demand for gas in northern areas of Tokyo. The initial priority was the installation of gas pipeline and the construction of a gas production plant. A new factory containing a coal-operated retort began operation in 1889 in what is now the Kogawa part of Tokyo. By 1893 the facility was capable of producing 30,000 cubic feet of city gas per day.

The business was growing to such an extent that in 1895 city authorities set up a gas tax office. Initially Tokyo Gas was taxed according to the number of gas lamps it operated, and the yearly tax per lamp was set at ¥0.06. Accompanying the increase in the number of customers, the company's tax bill was mushrooming. Shibusawa persuaded the city tax authorities to adopt the more sensible policy of taxing the company on its profits.

Part of Tokyo Gas's strategy was to exploit gas for as many uses as possible. Shibusawa formed Tokyo Gas Railway Company in the hope of building a network of gas-powered trains in the city. The advent of electric power as a far safer and more convenient source of power for trains dashed these plans before they were seriously underway. Shibusawa was, however, instrumental in the spread of electricity into Japan and set up one of the first electric train companies.

Victory over China in the 1897 Sino-Japanese War was a key factor in the economic and military development of Japan. The nation joined the Western powers as a major force on the world stage. The war spurred even faster industrial development, and Tokyo Gas was likewise expanding. Company headquarters were moved to a new building in Kanda in central Tokyo. In 1898 a third gas factory was completed in Fukagawa, capable of producing 250,000 cubic feet of gas per day.

During the late 1890s and early 1900s, electricity was gradually replacing gas as a source of power for lighting. The fastest growing use of gas was as a fuel for cooking and home heating. The company's head of technology, Goro Nakagawa, returned from a fact-finding tour of the United States to report on a range of new cooking devices powered by gas. The decision was made to concentrate marketing efforts in this area. In 1900 the company stated its four main business areas as gas production and supply, gas by-product supply, production and sales of gas appliances, and the development of business related to the gas industry.

In 1906 Japan again experienced victory in a war, this time over Russia, which once more boosted the economy. The demand for gas in Tokyo was booming, and Tokyo Gas opened nine new sales offices around the town. By 1908, 23 years after its founding, the company supplied 100,000 homes with gas, operated 825 kilometers of pipeline, and supplied 1.2 billion cubic feet of gas per year. Of this total, 80% was consumed by household customers, with the remainder supplied to industry.

Indeed business was so good that a rival Tokyo-based gas company, Chiyoda Gas, was started up in 1908. The two companies, in an attempt to attract the same base of customers, began a price war. This price war was a major headache for the management of Tokyo Gas and in 1911 both companies signed a pricing agreement in order to avoid financial disaster. Chiyoda Gas was so weakened financially that it eventually went bankrupt, and its assets were taken over by Tokyo Gas. By 1913 Tokyo Gas had emerged as the major supplier of city gas in the Kanto region and in that year began supplying gas to the outlying suburbs of the cities of Kawasaki and Saitama.

Japan experienced an economic depression from 1918 until the late 1920s. Inflation ensued, and Tokyo Gas was forced to raise the price of gas as the price of coal increased. In 1919 the union representing the 560 workers at Tokyo Gas's three production sites in Tokyo demanded higher wages. The number of new customers was no longer increasing, and indeed a fair number could no longer afford to be connected to the gas supply network. To add to this situation, in 1923 the Kanto region of Japan experienced a catastrophic earthquake. Forty-five percent of houses using gas were destroyed, leaving only 130,000 connected. The pipeline network was severely damaged, with many leaks and resultant fires. The city of Tokyo was quick to rebuild, however, and with frantic around-the-clock repair work underway, gas supplies were resumed after two months.

By 1926 the demand for city gas began to increase as Japan emerged from depression, and in that year Tokyo Gas began to expand its marketing activities. A questionnaire was sent to each customer, seeking to ascertain the public's impression of the service offered by the company's representatives. Sixty-five percent of those asked responded by saying the service was excellent. Rival gas companies were emerging, taking advantage of the devastation of Tokyo Gas's supply network in the 1923 earthquake. The company responded by aiming to attract 100,000 new customers within six years. In fact, it achieved double this figure. The new president, Shoshichi Iwazaki, stressed the importance of service to the company's large customer base, and 200 adding machines from the United States were incorporated into the headquarters and sales offices to make the company's accounting more efficient. Furthermore, after a long safety campaign in the company's three production sites, a 100% safety record was achieved in 1935.

During the late 1930s Japan was again moving toward war and the increasingly powerful military government began to take control of the vital industries, of which gas production was one. By 1938 Tokyo Gas had one million users but on orders from the military was urging its customers to conserve gas and use gas appliances only when necessary. The military were interested in the by-products of coal gas production—coal tar, benzene, and ammonia for industrial use—as well as in using gas to power armaments factories. Coal was also in shorter supply as the nation's steel industry consumed increasing amounts. By 1944, at the height of Japan's war efforts, two of Tokyo Gas's three production facilities were designated military suppliers, and were in effect run by a representative of the Imperial Japanese Army. To control Tokyo's gas industry the military authorities merged all the companies within the Kanto region into a single concern. A similar exercise was carried out in other regions of Japan, and eight main gas companies were formed. On March 10, 1945, the U.S. airforce sent wave after wave of B-29 bombers to destroy Tokyo, spar-

ing only the Imperial Palace. The result was devastating, with 120,000 dead and 260,000 houses destroyed. Tokyo Gas's headquarters building was saved by the work force, who prevented it from being burnt to the ground.

Only 22 years after the Great Kanto Earthquake Tokyo had succumbed to the military might of the United States. Tokyo Gas's infrastructure was a shambles, with fewer than 1,500 houses receiving gas in August 1945. Once again the city's inhabitants rebuilt Tokyo with amazing speed. This time they were greatly aided by the U.S. occupation forces, eager to rebuild Japan as a democratic state. By November 1945 the number of houses supplied with gas had risen to 340,000 and was rising daily. In the year following the devastation, work began in earnest to reconnect and resupply the city with gas. By early 1946, 55% of the prewar level had been achieved. During this time both the government and industry of Japan was managed by the American occupation forces. General MacArthur formulated the Law for the Elimination of Excessive Concentration of Economic Power to break up the huge Japanese industrial conglomerates that had dominated Japan economically before and during the war. Tokyo Gas came under the management of the occupying powers, with representatives of the U.S. armed forces giving guidance in the early postwar years. In 1949 the gas rationing in place since 1945 came to an end, and Tokyo Gas was free to operate as an independent company.

The Japanese economy recovered swiftly, and by the early 1950s was experiencing rapid growth. Before the war Japan had relied on Manchuria in China, which she occupied, for a large proportion of her coal. This source became more unreliable and expensive in the postwar years, and the Japanese power companies looked increasingly to crude oil to supply industry needs. Tokyo Gas began a conversion of its Omori coal gas facility to produce gas from oil. In 1954 construction began of a new oil-gas production facility in Toyosu, a project involving the reclamation of land in Tokyo Bay. The huge complex was completed in 1956 and began producing two million cubic meters of gas per day. By 1955 the company was once again supplying one million households. Univac punchcard computers were procured and installed in the headquarters building to monitor customers' consumption. Gas service stations were opened in and around Tokyo, including nine in Yokohama, to cater for customer enquiries. In 1959 a gas promotion exhibition, entitled Gas in Life, took place to demonstrate how the company produced gas and to display new uses of gas. With the aim of diversifying its sources of raw materials, Tokyo Gas began the purchase of liquid propane gas (LPG) from Saudi Arabia in 1962. In the same year a 329-kilometer pipeline was constructed to transport 500,000 cubic meters of natural gas daily from a field off Niigata on the west coast of Japan. Unfortunately the pipeline was severely damaged in an earthquake which hit Niigata two years later.

Japan emerged as an economic superstate in the 1960s. In 1969 Japan's gross national product was second only to that of the United States. A visible contribution made by Tokyo Gas to this success was the completion in 1968 of the world's largest steel gas-storage tank. With a capacity of 200,000 cubic meters and constructed from steel plates 35 millimeters thick, the tank was designed to hold high-pressure gas.

Around this time the company was developing a technology that would come to dominate Japan's gas industry—the import of natural gas as a liquid, known as liquefied natural gas (LNG). Natural gas had several major advantages over gas manufactured from oil or coal; for instance, once the transport technology was perfected it became the cheaper alternative; natural gas is also more environmentally friendly than oil- or coal-manufactured gas, both to produce and to burn. The most important factor in its adoption, however, was that both Tokyo Gas and the Japanese government wanted to reduce the nation's dependence on Middle Eastern oil, which had risen to supply almost 70% of the nation's energy needs by 1970.

Motivated by these factors, Tokyo Gas, along with Tokyo Electric Power Company, began negotiations with Phillips Petroleum and Marathon Oil of the United States to procure 96,000 tons of LNG per year from fields off Alaska. Supply began in 1969 with the LNG refrigerator ship *Polar Alaska* docking at the world's first LNG terminal in Negishi in Yokohama. The Sodegaura works on the opposite side of Tokyo Bay began operation as an LNG terminal four years later. Today these two terminals remain Tokyo Gas's two most important LNG terminals. Because of the lower energy value of natural gas as compared to manufactured gas (2,000 as opposed to 4,800 kilocalories per cubic meter), it was necessary to convert and inspect the company's network as well as customers' appliances to cater for the new gas. This was done by Tokyo Gas engineers in the early 1970s, and the exercise gave the company the chance to promote and sell its new range of natural gas appliances as well as to inspect its own network.

The oil shock of 1974, which sent the Japanese economy into negative growth, reinforced Tokyo Gas's decision to concentrate on LNG. Sourcing of LNG was expanded to Indonesia, Brunei, and Malaysia and a computerized loading system was developed for transferring the minus 160 degrees centigrade liquefied gas from ship to storage tank. In 1976 the manufacture of gas from coal at the Toyosu facility was abandoned after 20 years of production.

During the late 1970s and early 1980s Tokyo Gas sought to present itself as a company that was environmentally aware and concerned with the safety of its factories. In a statement in 1982 it took great pride in the fact that no major accident associated with the transport of the volatile LNG had occurred since the company had started using it. The conversion to a 100% natural gas supply was completed in 1988. The supply and distribution of LNG is controlled today by what the company describes as an "intelligent service system"; it monitors the gas as it travels from the supply ship to the consumer's home appliance. Any malfunction is corrected by emergency stations operating around the clock.

Like most other Japanese utility companies, Tokyo Gas has diversified, and the group of companies with Tokyo Gas as the nucleus is informally known as the Tokyo Gas Group. In 1991 75% of the group's sales came from the supply of gas to 7.5 million households in the Kanto region as well as to industrial users. The group's other major business area is gas appliances, which have been manufactured and sold by the company since the early 1900s. In a field related to the refrigeration technology associated with LNG transport, the Tokyo Gas Group is involved in the production of low-temperature chemicals such as liquid oxygen and dry ice, as well as providing a food refrigeration service. Recently the group's profits have been reduced by an increase in the price of LNG and rising interest rates. The Tokyo Gas Group is, however, a mainstay of industrial Japan. Tokyo Gas will continue to compete with Tokyo Electric Power as a supplier of energy to the region's population. Tokyo Gas currently supplies about a third of Tokyo's residential energy and will be seeking to increase its share through technological developments and the marketing of gas as a source of all home energy needs.

Principal Subsidiaries: Tokyo Coke Co., Ltd.; Kanto Tar Products Co., Ltd.; Tokyo Cryogenic Industries Co., Ltd.; Tokyo Gas Urban Development Co., Ltd.; Tokyo Gas Building Service Co., Ltd.; KANPAI Co., Ltd.; Tokyo Gas Engineering Co., Ltd.; TG Information Network Co., Ltd.; Tosetz Co., Ltd.; Gasstar Co., Ltd.; Tokyo Gas Housing Co., Ltd.; TG Credit Service Co., Ltd.; TG Finance Co., Ltd.; Tokyo LPG Co., Ltd.; Chiba Gas Co., Ltd.

Further Reading: *The Story of Tokyo Gas 1885–1985*, Tokyo, Tokyo Gas, 1985.

—Dylan Tanner

TRANSCANADA PIPELINES LIMITED

111 5th Avenue Southwest
Calgary, Alberta T2P 3Y6
Canada
(403) 267-6100
Fax: (403) 267-8993

Public Company
Incorporated: 1951
Employees: 1,757
Sales: C$3.03 billion (US$2.62 billion)
Stock Exchanges: Toronto Montreal Vancouver Alberta
  Winnipeg New York

TransCanada PipeLines Limited (TCPL) is a major North American natural gas transportation and marketing corporation with 35 years' experience delivering western Canadian natural gas to markets in Canada and the United States. The core of the company is its mainline gas transmission system—more than 11,000 kilometers of pipeline—which runs from the Alberta-Saskatchewan border to the Quebec-Vermont border. A wholly owned subsidiary, Western Gas Marketing Limited, is the leading Canadian gas marketer and has the largest supply pool in North America. TransCanada has investments in five pipelines that link to its mainline system: Foothills Pipe Lines (Sask.) Ltd. (44%) and Trans Quebec & Maritimes Pipeline (50%), in Canada, and Great Lakes Gas Transmission System (50%), Northern Border Pipeline Company (30%) and Iroquois Gas Transmission System (29%) in the United States. Since 1989, the company has undertaken a major expansion of its mainline system to meet the increased demands of markets in eastern Canada and the northeastern United States. Applied-for and approved facilities total C$4 billion to 1993.

The company also has investments in electric power generation projects, including a 40% interest in the 500-megawatt Ocean State Power Plant in Rhode Island and a 100% ownership of the 36-megawatt Nipigon Power Plant, which will use waste heat from TransCanada's adjacent compressor station. Another subsidiary, Cancarb Limited, is the leading international manufacturer of high-quality, thermal carbon black.

The company overcame engineering and financial hurdles in its early years. Building a gas pipeline across Canada was a project equal in scale to the building of the cross-country railway and was one of the most contentious chapters in Canada's economic and political history.

Although a trans-Canadian natural gas pipeline had been proposed as early as 1931, the coming of the pipeline to Canada was linked to events that took place in an atmosphere peculiar to 1950s Canada. For one, the country's population was booming, especially in the cities. Montreal's population grew from 1.83 million in 1956 to 2.57 million in 1966. The 1950s also witnessed the greatest economic boom in Canada's history, and the energy shortage was real. At no period of history was this more apparent than during the World War II years, when Canadians learned that they could not depend on energy from the United States, as the United States put its own energy needs first. The young generation of the 1950s was self-consciously Canadian and deeply suspicious of its U.S. neighbor. While economic prosperity increased, so did U.S. ownership of most of Canada's wealth: approximately 70% of Canada's oil industry, 56% of its manufacturing industry, and 52% of Canadian mines were owned by U.S. businesses, and these percentages would grow. Growing national sentiment called for railways and a trans-Canadian pipeline to be built completely within Canada, even if this was not necessarily the best route.

Economic boom times, the looming energy shortage, and the election of a new government in 1957, which brought to the helm Prime Minister John Diefenbaker, renowned for his Canadian nationalism, all set the stage for the adoption of a plan to harvest Alberta's rich deposits of natural gas. At the same time, the St. Lawrence Seaway, which would enable Canadian agricultural and industrial products to be shipped worldwide, was under construction.

As it turned out, it took an almost epic struggle to build the trans-Canadian pipeline. L.D.M. Baxter, a Canadian financier, was the first to advocate a trans-Canadian pipeline to bring Alberta natural gas to eastern Canada, although even he had doubts about the plan's feasibility. The obstacle, as he saw it, was the Laurentian Shield of northern Ontario, a vast rocky area that is the chief geographical barrier separating eastern from western Canada. Canadians were not alone, however, in perceiving the value of a pipeline. On the U.S. side, the prospect of natural gas from Canada also tempted some businessmen to invest in such a venture. Clint Murchison, a Texan and head of Canadian Delhi Oil Company, believed the pipeline could be run through the Laurentian Shield. By 1954 both Canadian and U.S. interests had agreed on the usefulness of a pipeline through Canada that also would export gas to the United States. The difficulty, however, was in reaching agreement on the financing of the scheme. Since it was to be an all-Canadian route, the U.S. participants—who had formed a company called TransCanada PipeLines—insisted that financing should be split evenly, while the Canadian interest group, Western Pipe Lines Limited, opposed this 50–50 proposal because the United States had far greater financial resources at its disposal than did Canada. The Canadian group wanted the United States to take on 90% of the cost. In the end the Canadian investors agreed to the 50–50 split and sought to persuade their government to finance the pipeline. The person sponsoring the pipeline bill in Parliament was Minister of Transport C.D. Howe. An engineer by training, he would come to view the pipeline as the crowning achievement of his life.

TransCanada PipeLines was incorporated in 1951 to undertake the pipeline project. The first president of the new company was Nathan Eldon Tanner, who remained at the helm until the pipeline was completed. While other members of the board of directors had greater influence and experience, Tanner was a mediator. The major problem to be negotiated in 1955 was convincing the government of the financial viability of the company. After prolonged negotiations, the Royal Bank of Canada loaned TCPL C$25.5 million, and a Montreal financier successfully negotiated large loans from the Canada Bank of Commerce as well as from the Royal Bank, thus enabling the company to win crucial government backing. The pipeline bill reached the floor of Parliament in 1956, and engendered months of rancorous debate and fears of a tighter U.S. hold, despite the strenuous efforts of Transport Minister Howe to convince doubters of the wholly Canadian nature of the enterprise. By then, Canadian interests lobbying against the pipeline bill regarded it as a sellout to U.S. interests. Opponents felt that the pipeline would only provide the United States with cheap Canadian gas. Even in the United States opposition was beginning to mount. In the coal industry in particular fears were voiced that Canadian natural gas would displace coal and lead to layoffs, while only Canadians would benefit. Howe was not a smooth negotiator, but his expertise and influence ultimately combined to steer the bill successfully through Parliament. The pipeline was finally approved in June 1956.

Building commenced on a monumental scale in 1957. By December 1, the Toronto-Montreal segment had been completed. The entire project was finished in October 1958, as originally scheduled. More than 2,200 miles long, it was the longest pipeline in the world, and was expanded almost continuously.

In 1958 Tanner resigned as chief executive officer and president; his replacement was James Kerr. Kerr was new to the pipeline business. He had worked for Canadian Westinghouse since 1937, becoming a divisional vice president of Westinghouse in 1956; like others on the board of directors of TCPL, Kerr was a Canadian nationalist, who accepted the offer to become head of TCPL out of patriotism. At this time, TCPL's deficit was the company's biggest problem, one which it would not overcome until 1961.

In the 1960s the company entered the computer age, developing a highly sophisticated computer system that could measure and control the flow of gas precisely, the first such system devised for pipelines. In the 1960s the company diversified into the chemical industry, establishing the first of numerous gas-extraction plants in Empress, Alberta. In 1967 TCPL was permitted to extend its pipeline along the Great Lakes in the United States, an extension that was completed in 1967. One year later, TCPL celebrated the tenth anniversary of its pipeline operations. Between 1958 and 1968, operating revenue had shot up from C$30 million to C$200 million, and net income had risen from a deficit of C$8.5 million to a surplus

of C$17.5 million, while the proportion of Canadian shareholders had grown to 94%.

By the 1970s TCPL already was a world leader in pipeline technology. Vast subterranean natural gas pockets lay untouched in northern and western Canada, and exploiting this natural wealth was the goal of the company in the 1970s. Since the mid-1980s, expansion rather than diversification was TCPL's motto, as natural gas became Canada's most important fuel and energy source. Altogether, TCPL's capital investments in 1990 alone totaled C$682 million, with 69% of this amount invested in the TCPL mainline system.

In the beginning of the 1990s regulatory decisions were extremely beneficial to TCPL's long-range prospects. The most favorable decision, made by the U.S. Federal Energy Regulatory Commission (FERC), allowed TCPL to deliver western Canadian gas to the northeastern United States; other FERC and Canadian National Energy Board rulings gave TCPL permission to expand its Great Lakes gas transmission system and mainline systems respectively, which allowed Canadian natural gas to be carried through TCPL's mainline system to Iroquois, Ontario, across the St. Lawrence River to the U.S. states of New York, Connecticut, and New Jersey; it meant an important breakthrough for TCPL into the competitive U.S. natural gas market. In 1990 the company also obtained a contract to sell to the California market and received a license to export natural gas to Michigan. The company appears to have been unaffected by the recession of the early 1990s, with the president and chief executive officer, Gerald Maier, expecting an annual earnings growth rate of from 10% to 15% in the 1990s. To raise money to carry on its expansion, TCPL has been issuing new stock and selling debentures, while the cost of the Iroquois pipeline to the northeastern United States will be borne by all shareholders, a decision vigorously contested by major Canadian gas users in Ontario, Quebec, and Manitoba, but approved by the Canadian National Energy Board.

Despite the enormous cost, the company not only projects a handsome return but has been running profitably despite recessionary trends. Net income for the company in 1990 was up 14.9% from 1989, while the company pursues streamlining, divesting itself of unprofitable businesses, such as its interests in Les Mines Selbaie and the Montreal Pipeline Ltd. in Quebec province.

Principal Subsidiaries: Western Gas Marketing Limited; Cancarb Limited.

Further Reading: Kilbourn, William, *Pipeline: TransCanada and the Great Debate, A History of Business and Politics,* Toronto, Clarke, Irwin & Co. Ltd., 1970.

—Sina Dubovoj

TE Transco Energy Company

TRANSCO ENERGY COMPANY

2800 Post Oak Boulevard
Houston, Texas 77056
U.S.A.
(713) 439-2000
Fax: (713) 439-4154

Public Company
Incorporated: 1948 as Transcontinental Gas Pipe Line
  Corporation
Employees: 5,400
Sales: $3.08 billion
Stock Exchange: New York

Transco Energy Company's primary business is the transportation and sale of natural gas, largely to markets in the eastern and midwestern United States. It runs the largest gas-gathering system in the Gulf of Mexico and operates a huge pipeline network, including a line that extends 10,000 miles, from the gulf to New York City. In 1990 Transco's total pipeline system deliveries provided more than 10% of natural gas used in the United States, including the gas that lights the eternal flame at the grave of the late U.S. President John F. Kennedy. Transco also has interest in oil and gas exploration and production, electric power generation, and coal mining and marketing, although in 1991 the company decided to exit the coal and oil and gas production businesses.

The company was organized in October 1948, as Transcontinental Gas Pipe Line Corporation, to build what would be, at the time, the world's longest pipeline, stretching 1,832 miles from Hidalgo County, Texas, to New York City. Claude Williams, the company's first president, broke ground for the pipeline in May 1949. More than 540,000 tons of steel were used to build the line, and 40 rivers were crossed during its construction. The pipeline made its first delivery of gas in December 1950, to Danville, Virginia, and began serving New York a month later. In 1952 the company engineered another coup, laying a pipeline 100 feet deep to connect the New York boroughs of Brooklyn and Staten Island. The line crossed under the Narrows, the body of water where the Atlantic Ocean and the Hudson River meet.

Transcontinental Gas Pipe Line built the first offshore pipeline in the Gulf of Mexico in 1957, a 21-mile line off the coast of Louisiana. The following year, it bought a natural gas storage field in north central Pennsylvania. In December 1958 the company's daily deliveries of gas exceeded one billion cubic feet for the first time; seven years earlier, the largest daily demand had been less than 350 million cubic feet.

In 1963 the company began development of an underground storage field in Pennsylvania and started construction on an above-ground storage tank for liquefied natural gas in New Jersey. In 1968 corporate assets reached $1 billion for the first time, up from $54.8 million at the company's inception 20 years earlier.

In 1973 Transco Companies Inc. was incorporated as a holding company, and Transcontinental Gas Pipe Line Corporation became its subsidiary. The latter's common stock was converted share-for-share into the common stock of the new parent company. Creation of the holding company was designed to allow greater breadth and flexibility in financing of construction and other ventures.

Later in 1973, Transco prepared to launch a joint venture with National Iranian Oil Company, in which natural gas products would be processed in Iran and transported to the United States for conversion into pipeline-quality gas. The agreement called for the two companies to be equal partners in a $650 million facility. The project was canceled the following year, however, because the Iranian company needed the gas to repressure Iranian oil fields. In 1974 Transco discontinued its participation in various oil and gas exploration projects in Canada. Company officials said programs in Canada had been disappointing.

In 1975 Transco was listed on the New York Stock Exchange. Later that year, it entered into a joint venture with McMoRan Exploration Company for gas exploration along the gulf coast of Texas and Louisiana. Also that year, Transco and United Gas Pipeline Company applied for Federal Power Commission (FPC) approval to build an offshore pipeline to transport natural gas produced in the High Island area in the gulf, off the Texas coast.

Transco's exploration ventures were in part a response to the energy crisis of the 1970s. Unlike many other pipeline operators, Transco had only small gas supplies of its own, and the FPC strictly limited the price it could pay for gas producers' output. With energy prices rising across the board, producers were not eager to sell to Transco. In 1974 the FPC raised price limits for newly discovered gas, and the producers became more interested in Transco, which in turn was willing to finance exploration. Leading Transco's efforts in this area was Jack Bowen, who became chairman and president late in 1974. Bowen came to Transco from Florida Gas Company, a pipeline operator that had significant gas exploration experience as well.

During the winter of 1974–1975, Transcontinental Gas Pipe Line cut back on gas deliveries, leading to an FPC investigation. In 1977 an FPC administrative law judge found the company innocent of improperly withholding gas supplies, noting the decline in natural gas supplies. The parent company, Transco, had already begun aggressively seeking new sources.

This aggressiveness was apparent in several events that occurred during 1977. Transcontinental Gas Pipe Line applied for FPC approval for additional offshore pipelines. Another Transco unit, Transco Exploration Company, reported discovery of three natural gas reservoirs in the Gulf of Mexico, in an area Transco was exploring along with McMoRan and Mesa Petroleum Company. Transco Exploration and Texaco Inc. teamed up to produce oil and gas from another tract in the gulf. Transco Exploration, on its own, drilled two exploratory wells in yet another part of the gulf. Late in the year, the exploration company entered into another joint venture with McMoRan and three other companies to seek oil and gas in federal waters in the gulf.

The success of the exploration work buoyed the parent company's bottom line. Earnings per share were $2.84 in 1977, up 30% from the previous year and more than 400% since 1974.

The search for new supplies continued; Transco Exploration found commercial quantities of gas off the Texas coast in 1979. The parent company also ventured into other energy businesses, including coal; it bought three coal companies from General Energy Corporation of Lexington, Kentucky, in 1982, for about $70 million. The same year, the parent company's name was changed to Transco Energy Company.

During the early 1980s Transco's gas supply situation was the reverse of what it had been during the 1970s. Large increases in Transco's own gas-production capacity, and that of its outside suppliers, had left the company with a great deal of gas it could not sell. Oil prices had fallen, so many of Transco's industrial customers had begun to use inexpensive fuel oil instead of natural gas. Transco responded by renegotiating contracts with its suppliers, often arriving at a lower price, and also reduced the prices it charged industrial customers by tying its gas price to that of fuel oil. Also, Transco converted its exploration operations into a limited partnership, Transco Exploration Partners, Ltd. (TXP), and sold 12% of the partnership to the public in 1983 generating $120 million in cash.

In 1985 Transco Energy gave up on a North Dakota coal-gasification plant it had operated with four other energy companies. The project, in which Transco held a 20% share, had been viewed a decade earlier as a means to secure U.S. energy supplies into the future. Although subsidized by the U.S. government, the project was hurt by slumping energy prices and had to be terminated after the Department of Energy rejected a last-minute bailout plan. Transco took a $91 million charge against its third-quarter 1985 earnings for the shutdown. Also in 1985, the company expanded further into coal with the $233 million purchase of Interstate Coal Company.

The natural gas transmission industry underwent significant regulatory changes in the 1980s. Beginning in 1984, the Federal Energy Regulatory Commission (FERC)—successor to the FPC created in 1977—issued orders that freed pipeline customers from their obligations to buy minimum amounts of gas from their pipeline suppliers, instead allowing the customers to buy their gas from other companies and have it transported via the pipeline. There was a resulting decrease in natural gas prices and an increase in competition; responding to this, Transco's pipeline subsidiaries became permanent open access pipelines in 1988, transporting gas that customers had purchased from other companies. Still, Transco's financial performance suffered; it reported a loss of $61 million, or $3.52 per share, for 1987, followed by a net loss of $91 million, or $3.1 per share, in 1988.

Transco enlarged its pipeline network in 1989 with the purchase of Texas Gas Transmission Corporation and two related companies for about $600 million from CSX Corporation. Texas Gas Transmission had about 6,000 miles of pipeline extending from the Louisiana gulf coast to Ohio and Indiana.

Transco's financial performance improved in 1989, with net income of $89 million. Also, to improve cash flow, it decided to liquidate TXP, while continuing some exploration projects through Transco Exploration and Production Company, formed in 1989 to develop sources in the gulf.

Transco Exploration and Production made 11 gas discoveries in 1990. Also in 1990, the FERC gave preliminary approval to a project by which Transco's two major pipeline systems—Transcontinental Gas Pipe Line and Texas Gas Transmission—would be expanded and connected with other companies' systems, creating the first major new route for domestic gas to the northeastern United States since the 1970s.

Early in 1991 Transcontinental Gas Pipe Line and five other companies joined to launch onshore and offshore pipeline systems to transport natural gas from the Mobile Bay area in the gulf off Alabama. The year also was marked by the abrupt resignation of George S. Slocum, Transco's president since 1984. Observers speculated that Slocum had become frustrated by the company's legal and regulatory problems. These included a lawsuit by the state of Alabama that alleged archaeological and environmental damage from a pipeline project and an FERC order that Transco make refunds to certain customers as reparation for improperly billing for certain costs. Transco took a $6.3 million charge against its second-quarter 1991 earnings to reflect the settlement of these matters. In 1991 Transco and Duke Power Company completed financing for their joint venture in a cogeneration facility.

Having posted a modest profit in 1990, Transco showed a net loss of $47.2 million in the first nine months of 1991. Some of this was due to the establishment of a reserve to cover the outcome of a rate case pending before the FERC. Also, however, Transco's nonpipeline businesses were performing poorly. Late in 1991, John P. DesBarres, who had succeeded Slocum as president with Bowen remaining chairman, announced Transco would get out of its oil and gas production businesses and coal operations, while focusing on its pipeline, gas marketing, and power generation segments. He also planned to reduce capital spending by 40% in 1992, while cutting common stock dividends and 500 jobs.

Principal Subsidiaries: Transcontinental Gas Pipe Line Corporation; Texas Gas Transmission Corporation; Transco Energy Marketing Company; Transco Gas Gathering Company; Transco Energy Ventures Company; Transco Exploration and Production Company; Transco Coal Company.

Further Reading: "Transcontinental Gas Pipe Line Corporation: 1948–1988," Houston, Transco Energy Company, 1988.

—Trudy Ring

ᵫ *UnionElectric*

UNION ELECTRIC COMPANY

1901 Chouteau Avenue
St. Louis, Missouri 63166
U.S.A.
(314) 621-3222
Fax: (314) 621-2888

Public Company
Incorporated: 1922 as Union Electric Light and Power Company
Employees: 6,950
Sales: $2.02 billion
Stock Exchange: New York

Union Electric Company is the largest electric utility in the state of Missouri. Also serving parts of Illinois and Iowa, the company supplies electricity to roughly one million customers and is a distributor of natural gas, steam, and water. Union Electric's territory is strong in the metal, chemical, and petroleum-refining industries. A major member of regional power pools and electric reliability councils, the company participates in planning, operating, and maintaining reserve supplies of energy for the states of Missouri, Illinois, and Wisconsin. Through its 100% ownership of Union Colliery Company, the company owns coal reserves and industrial properties in Illinois. Coal is Union Electric's major fuel, but at a number of sites, many constructed during the late 1960s and early 1970s, it has various hydroelectric, steam, and diesel plants. In late 1984 the Callaway nuclear plant came on line, contributing one-fourth of the company's energy supply.

Union Electric was incorporated in Missouri in 1922 as Union Electric Light and Power Company, a successor to a company of the same name incorporated in May 1902 as a result of the merger of Imperial Electric Light, Heat and Power Company; Citizens Electric Lighting and Power Company; and Missouri Edison Electric Company. An early task for Union Electric Light and Power was providing power for the St. Louis World's Fair of 1904. Through its Ashley Street Plant, the company controlled 12 megawatts of power, enough to light the fair and make clear that electricity was readily available.

As more individuals and businesses began to rely on electricity, Union Electric Light and Power sought out additional generating sources. In 1913 the company began buying power from the Keokuk dam, 150 miles north of St. Louis. Union Electric later bought the dam, providing power carried over a longer distance than had ever been achieved before.

During World War I the company expanded to serve rural areas. With the addition of a plant in Cahokia, Illinois, Union Electric Light and Power progressed through the 1920s, acquiring smaller light and power companies in Missouri and Illinois.

In the early 1930s, the Great Depression notwithstanding, Union Electric Light and Power completed construction of Bagnell dam in Missouri's Ozark mountains and organized Lakeside Light & Power Company in 1931 for residents in the surrounding area. In 1937 the company changed its name to Union Electric Company of Missouri. Its Illinois operations became a subsidiary, Union Electric Company of Illinois, with subsidiaries in Iowa renamed Iowa Union Electric Company. In 1940 the company proceeded with further corporate simplification, merging several Missouri subsidiaries into the parent. By 1945 surrounding Illinois and Iowa properties were merged into one subsidiary, Union Electric Power Company. In March 1945 Union Electric made the significant acquisition of Laclede Power & Light Company, a former competitor controlling 15% of the electric business in St. Louis.

With some delay in construction due to World War II, the company completed a new plant in Venice, Illinois, in 1950, bringing the total company capacity to 1,000 megawatts. Acquisitions continued. The company acquired Missouri Power & Light Company in 1950, following up with the 1954 addition of Missouri Edison Company to its roster. In February 1955 the company absorbed its holding company, North American Company, and in August 1955 purchased all properties and on-going businesses in Illinois and Iowa of the subsidiary Union Electric Power Company. Following this consolidation, Union Electric Company of Missouri became simply Union Electric Company in 1956. The company made one more electric company acquisition in southeastern Iowa in 1958.

Reacting to such growth, Union Electric recognized the need to organize the generation and storage of power at its various plants. In a program begun in the early 1950s the company built intercompany transmission lines, establishing power pools that any unit connected to the system could access. Soon outside companies joined the power pool; the total number of utilities reached 17.

Union Electric constructed the Merramec plant, with a capacity of 900 megawatts, in 1961, while launching construction for a plant at Taum Sauk, 90 miles southwest of St. Louis. The Taum Sauk plant was the world's first and largest pumped storage facility, more powerful than any yet built. The system was designed to pump up to five million tons of unused water from a lower to an upper reservoir. The water would then flow downhill during peak periods, funneled into two water wheels that would in turn drive turbines and other equipment to produce electricity. Major advantages of the plant were its automation—it requiring only 15 maintenance employees and its cost, $50 million, in contrast to $67 million for a comparable steam facility. Completed in 1963, the plant drew visiting engineers from the United States and Europe.

Approximately 75% of Union's business was providing electricity to St. Louis. The company benefited from the modernization of the metropolitian area; in the 1960s the city was adding a new expressway, civic center, sports stadium, riverfront memorial park, and a number of office and apartment complexes as well as industrial plants. In the early 1960s the company negotiated a contract with the city to redesign the street lighting. Using all mercury vapor fixtures, Union Electric in 1964 installed in St. Louis the brightest business district lighting of any city in the United States.

Another boon to the electric utility business in general came with the reduction of natural gas rates in 1964. The U.S. Supreme Court ordered the Federal Power Commission to extend the benefits of lower wholesale costs to the customers in the form of rate reductions, but due to the difference in federal and state regulations, not all rate cuts were mandatory. For those utilities whose earnings were below the allowed rate of return—and Union Electric was one of these—savings did not have to be passed along to the customers.

In 1965 Union Electric extended its reach in generation, transmission, and interconnection by joining six other utilities in Mid-Continent Area Power Planners to pool resources. Member area reached from St. Louis north to St. Paul, Minnesota. The company enlarged its scope further when it joined with a group of 12 utility companies to form the largest power pool in the United States, the Mid-America Interpool Network. Connecting ten states, from Michigan and Missouri east to Virginia, the group would increase its number of high voltage power lines to nearly 4,000 within six years. The interconnection would further reduce costs through the coordinated planning of power plants.

Union Electric continued building its own plants as well as joining power pools. The first section of its Sioux Plant in St. Charles County, near St. Louis, went into operation in 1967 and the second in 1968. The two units' combined capacity was 1,000 megawatts. The company added three smaller plants in Missouri in 1967. The Venice, Kirksville, and Viaduct combustion-turbine plants had a combined net capability of 62,000 kilowatts. The four-unit Labadie plant was launched in 1970, with one unit added each year. Labadie was by far the company's largest generating plant, with a total capacity of 2.22 million kilowatts. In July 1973 Union Electric announced its intention to build Missouri's first nuclear plant in Callaway County, approximately 100 miles west of St. Louis.

The 1970s brought environmental issues to the focus of U.S. civic and business organizations in a number of ways. In February 1977 the company announced its withdrawal from plans to generate electricity from solid waste, a scheme that had been in the works since 1972. The Environmental Protection Agency (EPA) had contributed $800,000 and Union Electric $600,000, to build a prototype waste-processing plant. By 1974 Union Electric was ready to set the station in motion, collecting trash from four sites in St. Louis and processing up to 2.5 million tons of garbage at the Labadie plant. One of the four sites was not approved by community residents, forcing Union Electric to buy another site, which also was not approved. The issue then went to court, at which time Union Electric decided to cancel the entire project.

The decision to discontinue the trash recycling plan coincided with Union Electric's plan to delay construction on its nuclear plant. Charles Dougherty, president, attributed the delay of its nuclear plant to a reaction to a 1976 referendum prohibiting Union Electric from including anticipated construction costs in its current utility rates.

Another event contributing to a delay in Union Electric's nuclear plant plans was the March 1979 accident at the Three Mile Island nuclear plant near Harrisburg, Pennsylvania. Due to failure of valves in the water cooling system, water levels in the reactor temporarily fell, unshielding nuclear radiation. The accident spurred public opposition to the construction and operation of nuclear plants. Union Electric waited for further information to apply to its own design and personnel training for the Callaway plant.

In August 1979 the Missouri Public Service Commission advised suspension of the company's nuclear plant construction permit. As a condition of a rate increase granted in 1978, the commission had been investigating Union Electric's generation-facility expansion program and found the company's load forecasts beyond peak demand levels. Union Electric held that its generation amounts had been leveling off, but the company also anticipated demand for electric power to increase, since other sources such as oil and natural gas were less available.

By November 1979 Union Electric made final arrangements for fuel financing sources including commercial paper and letters of credit, for its Callaway plant. The following December the company reached a settlement with Westinghouse Electric, which Union Electric had sued, charging failure to fulfill a 1975 uranium-supply contract. Union Electric stood to gain from the settlement $200 million in cash, uranium, and various other goods and services over a 20-year period.

In April 1980 Union Electric named president Charles Dougherty chairman, a position unoccupied since 1973. W.E. Cornelius, former director of corporate planning and more recently executive vice-president, was elected president at age 48. Company stockholders agreed to increase the number of common shares available to 100 million, up 25%.

In November the company increased the estimated costs of the first unit of the Callaway plant to $1.58 billion, $260 million more than previous estimates, while the second unit was priced at $1.72 billion, an increase of $54 million. The company cited inflation, financing, costs of meeting regulatory requirements, and two spring 1980 labor strikes as causes.

A respite for the company came with the July 1981 approval of a $50 million rate increase. September, however, brought announcement of further delays and higher estimates for the Callaway plant. Union Electric stated that complex testing and installation procedures postponed start-up of the first Callaway unit, and would raise costs, although by how much was unknown. The company also was considering canceling the second unit at a possible loss of $7 million, which it would seek to regain via rate increases.

By October Union Electric canceled the second unit, increased projected costs of the first unit to $2.1 billion, and consulted with state regulators regarding a time plan to write off the investment expenses. The company considered other means of power generation to replace, if necessary, the more than one million kilowatts lost in the second unit cancellation.

Investment-rating services lowered ratings on Union Electric bonds and preferred stock as a result of the utility's August 1982 announcment of a further delay in the Callaway nuclear plant. Originally scheduled for completion in April 1983, the plant operation was set for late 1984 or early 1985. The estimated cost increased to $2.85 billion. Union Electric cited continuing design changes required by the Nuclear Regulatory Commission and additional skilled labor costs as the major factors for the increase. Union Electric received a rate increase of 9% from Missouri regulators to help defray expenses, but the amount was not enough to keep industry investors from considering the company financially weakened. Union Electric requested a 16.8% rate increase for its 70,000 Illinois customers, a proposal that the Illinois attorney general opposed. The company offered 6.5 million common shares of stock in December 1982, and sold a total of $220 million in various bond issues to help offset the short-term debt caused by the nuclear plant construction delay.

In October 1984 the Callaway nuclear plant finally went on-line, producing enough power for one million customers. In November the company was granted a full-power operating license from the Nuclear Regulatory Commission. Full commercial operation commenced at the Callaway plant on December 19, 1984. The plant produced more electricity in its first year of operation than any other U.S. nuclear power plant.

In the spring of 1985 the Missouri commission significantly cut the amount that Union Electric attempted to charge its customers in rate increases to pay for Callaway-related expenses. The commission called the rate increase request a result of inefficiency and unreasonable or unexplained costs. The commission okayed a six-year phased-in rate increase designed to gain Union Electric a total of $455 million. Union Electric denied the commission's charges, commenting that the Callaway plant cost one-fifth less than nuclear plants under construction during the same time period. The company planned to appeal the Missouri decision and pursue further rate increases in Iowa and Illinois to recover costs.

By the end of April it was clear that the Missouri commission opposed Union Electric's appeal to include all Callaway-related construction costs in rate increases. Outstanding costs amounted to $384 million; after taxes, the amount was $250 million, which the company would post as a one-time loss. Utilities, formerly able to list construction costs expected to be regained in rate increases as profit, were under review by the financial accounting standards boards. Union Electric stated, however, that its 1985 net income would be reduced by only $50 million. Also during 1985, Illinois and Iowa granted phased-in rate increases, similar to the Missouri plan.

The year 1986 provided good news; sales of electricity to commercial and residential customers increased, while Union Electric's fuel costs decreased as a result of reduced generation. During 1987 and 1988, Moody's Investors Service and Standard & Poor's Corporation upgraded Union Electric's credit ratings, as the company regained its solid financial footing. The unusually hot summer of 1988 prompted extra use of electricity for air conditioning, boosting Union Electric sales to double the normal level.

Following a 15-month review of the Callaway nuclear plant, in mid-1988 the Nuclear Regulatory Commission concluded that Union Electric management was aggressive in responding to safety concerns, and granted the company a license to in-

crease power generation at the plant. By the end of 1988, Callaway generated one-fourth of total electricity for Union Electric.

While much attention had been centered on the company's Callaway nuclear plant, coal continued to be Union Electric's chief source of fuel. Burning coal transforms water to steam, the steam powers generators, which in turn produce more than 70% of the utility's electric energy needs. The advantage of using coal is that the supply is plentiful and relatively inexpensive; a disadvantage is that the use of coal causes noxious emissions. Union Electric, however, reduced emissions by 33% from the mid-1970s to 1989. The company's Keokuk and Osage hydroelectric plants, while dependent on weather conditions, continued to provide power dependably and at low cost.

At the close of the 1980s Union Electric concentrated on increasing productivity and reducing its work force; by 1989 staff decreased by 16% in fossil-fuel and hydroelectric operations. To stay competitive in customer services the company introduced a new electronic telephone system, Braille billing, and home-weatherizing programs. Other projects stressing energy efficiency included an all-electric apartment complex designed jointly with residential developers.

In 1990 the U.S. Congress approved amendments to the Clean Air Act. The amendments require a two-thirds reduction, by 2000, of sulfur dioxide emissions as well as a decrease in nitrogen oxide output. The amendments do allow utility companies flexible means of compliance. In 1990 the company was also named a potentially responsible party for five hazardous waste sites. Costs for cleaning up the sites, however, were not expected to reduce earnings significantly.

Union Electric faces the 1990s a streamlined company. The work force in the early 1990s was decreasing at the rate of 100 people per year. The Callaway nuclear plant's performance had been consistently superior. Production costs were half that of the company's coal-based plants, and refueling took half the time comparable nuclear plants need. An agreement with the Missouri Public Service Commission to reduce rates and not seek an increase until 1993 freed both parties from rate-related disputes. The ensuing rate reductions, while reducing company revenue by $30 million a year, will likely spur commercial and industrial development. While implementation of the requirements of the Clean Air Act may cost up to $300 million through the 1990s, fuel prices likely will decrease by a similar amount. Union Electric, with no apparent need for new construction necessary, seemed financially fit for the future.

Principal Subsidiary: Union Colliery Company.

Further Reading: Union Electric Company: Service to People, St. Louis, Missouri, Union Electric Company, 1986.

—Frances E. Norton

VEREINIGTE ELEKTRIZITÄTS-WERKE WESTFALEN AG

Rheinlanddamm 24
4600 Dortmund 1
Federal Republic of Germany
(0231) 438-1
Fax: (0231) 438-2147

Public Company
Incorporated: 1925 as Vereinigte Elektrizitätswerke Westfalen
   GmbH
Employees: 8,004
Sales: DM6.33 billion (US$4.24 billion)
Stock Exchanges: Basel Berlin Bremen Düsseldorf Frankfurt
   Geneva Hamburg Hanover Munich Stuttgart Zurich

The Vereinigte Elektrizitätswerke Westfalen AG (VEW) is
Germany's third largest energy supplier. Its supply zone in the
federal states of North Rhine–Westphalia and Lower Saxony in
northwestern Germany covers an area of some 13,200 square
kilometers with a population of around five million people.
Within this area, VEW provides electricity and natural gas as
well as district heating and water either directly or via other
companies. In 1990, the company had a generating plant capacity of 6,569 megawatts, 74,000 kilometers of electricity
transmission lines, and a gas distribution network of some
8,800 kilometers in length. In that year, the company provided
its customers with 38.2 billion kilowatt hours of electricity and
30.1 billion kilowatt hours of gas.

VEW was created in 1925, when several municipal electricity companies from the eastern, Westphalian part of the
Ruhr—Europe's largest industrial conglomeration—merged
voluntarily. Its roots go back in part to the 19th century. The
oldest company in the merger, the Städtische Elektrizitätswerk
Dortmund, was founded in 1897. Prior to its foundation there
had been bitter disputes in Dortmund over the provision of
electricity for the town. The local gas company, which had the
sole rights to provide gas lighting for the town, had objected
several times to the introduction of electricity. The town administration, on the other hand, was in favor of it. With the
construction of the port of Dortmund at the end of the new
canal to the North Sea, the town resolved to break the dead-
lock, and in 1895 decided to establish a new electric power
station to supply energy to the docks and the town. The engineer Carl Döpke was commissioned to construct the power
station, which went into operation in 1897. Designed to pro-

vide industry and commerce with the new three-phase current,
its 2,000-kilowatt generating capacity made it one of the biggest power stations in Imperial Germany.

Now that the transmission of three-phase current was technically feasible, it was possible to supply large areas from central power stations. In the Ruhr, this development caused
considerable political strife. The two other companies later
involved in the merger to form VEW—the Elektrizitätswerk
Westfalen AG (EWW), established in Bochum in 1906, and
the Westfälische Verbands-Elektrizitätswerk (WVE), created
in 1908—were the product of municipal political disputes
triggered by the introduction of the new long-distance power
supply.

The industrialist Hugo Stinnes's Rheinisch-Westfälische
Elektrizitätswerk (RWE), based in Essen and operating in the
western Ruhr area, invited the Ruhr municipalities to join the
grid connected to its high-powered station, and within just a
few years of the turn of the century many municipalities had
done so, attracted by the favorable rates. In 1905 Stinnes built
a second power station in Kruckel near Dortmund in order to
supply the eastern Ruhr area, but his plans for expansion met
with resistance from Westphalian town councillors. Their
spokesman, Karl Gerstein, the chief administrative officer for
the Bochum district, saw Stinnes's plans as an attempt to create
a private electricity monopoly. Gerstein believed electricity
supply to be a municipal matter and, together with a number
of town and district administrations, founded EWW as a coun-
terbalance to RWE. EWW did not intend to build its own
power stations but to use the electricity-generating capacity of
the power stations at the many mines in the area. The 1906
report of the Bochum district's administrative council stated
that: "It is with great pleasure and satisfaction that the administrative council can look back on the founding of the company
after overcoming untold difficulties. The significance of the
founding is that it has prevented the creation of a monopoly
which threatened to take a hold on the entire industrial region." In the years that followed, EWW extended its grid well
beyond the Ruhr area. Between 1911 and 1914 it began the
systematic electrification of the rural regions in northern
Westphalia (Münsterland). As the demand for energy grew, the
company built two new large power stations of its own, the
Gemeinschaftswerk Hattingen in 1912, and the Gersteinwerk
in 1914, which were to form the nucleus of the company's
electricity-generating capacity.

WVE in Kruckel also came into being as a result of the
conflict between Stinnes and the municipalities of the eastern
Ruhr. RWE, with its new power station in Kruckel, had already signed power supply agreements with several Westphalian communities by 1905 when Gerstein managed to persuade
the municipal authorities to deny the company the right to use
the public highways for its power lines and cable. After years
of bitter disputes and reciprocal blockades, agreement was finally reached in 1908. RWE transferred its power station in
Kruckel to a new company, the Westfälische Verbands-
Elektrizitätswerk (WVE). The municipalities were the majority share holders with 73%, while the mining companies held
18% and RWE 9%. At the same time, a demarcation agreement between the powerful RWE on the one hand and the
municipal electricity companies in the Westphalian part of the
Ruhr on the other brought a temporary respite from the battles
between the two sides, without permanently resolving the issue.

Because of rapidly increasing demand in the region, the three Westphalian electricity companies expanded quickly in the years before World War I. From 1909 all the companies were involved in the gas supply industry as well, initially restricted to small, local distribution systems. During the war the companies experienced considerable difficulties in obtaining coal for the power stations. These difficulties were dramatically intensified by the reparations demands on German coal at the end of the war. Against the background of these coal shortages and the Reich's government's efforts to nationalize the industry, a number of Westphalian electricity companies formed a loose association—the Kommunaler Elektrizitätswerks-Verband Westfalen-Rheinland GmbH (KEV)—at the beginning of the 1920s to protect their interests. They particularly wanted to protect themselves from being taken over by RWE. The latter was in a powerful position, as it used brown coal predominantly as opposed to hard coal, and brown coal was not affected by reparations demands. The municipal companies, previously heavily reliant on hard coal, had to ask RWE to help them supply electricity, but RWE would only do so in exchange for shareholdings. Among KEV's main aims were the careful distribution of hard coal reserves and mutual support. In the mid-1920s the hard coal shortages ended and the government dropped its plans to nationalize the electricity industry. KEV was consequently disbanded. Only the Städtische Elektrizitätswerk Dortmund and WVE intensified their relationship and under Carl Döpke's leadership created a joint holding company, the Dortmunder und Verbands-Elektrizitätswerk GmbH, in 1923. On January 1, 1925, EWW also joined this company, which was renamed the Vereinigte Elektrizitätswerke Westfalen GmbH (VEW) and became the nucleus of the present VEW. The private shareholders sold their shares during 1925 and VEW became wholly owned by the Westphalian municipalities. The merged companies' supply areas proved complementary to each other, containing as they did different types of electricity consumer, and the merger allowed the power stations to be used more efficiently. The new overall management board, based in Dortmund, was headed by Döpke, VEW's founding father. Regional centers were set up in Bochum, Dortmund and Münster. At the time of its foundation VEW had a generating plant capacity of 176,000 kilowatts of steam-generated and hydroelectric power. The company had 9,300 kilometers of electrical transmission lines and supplied 270 million kilowatt hours of electricity and 6.8 million cubic meters of gas a year. These figures placed VEW in fifth position among Germany's electricity supply companies.

Over the next few years the new management presided over a period of considerable expansion. Two factors were of particular significance. First, in the mid-1920s, the political and economic situation in the Weimar Republic stabilized, bringing sustained economic recovery. Second, the rationalization then underway in industry and commerce coupled with the electrification of Westphalia's agricultural areas produced a rapidly growing demand for electricity. In VEW's heavily industrialized supply area, electricity demand doubled between 1924 and 1929 to 520 million kilowatt hours. The result was substantial expansion of the power stations and a corresponding increase in the capacity of the supply network. By 1930, the company's generating plant capacity had risen to 267,000 kilowatts and the network now encompassed some 17,000 ki-

lometers of lines. In 1925–1926 VEW acquired three coal mines in order to guarantee continued coal supplies for its power stations. In addition, the company invested large sums in extending its grid, particularly in the region of southern Westphalia, the Sauerland. Here the town of Arnsberg became the seat of a new regional division of the company. With this step, the company's supply area attained virtually its current extent. As far as gas supply was concerned, this period saw the construction of the first long-distance gas pipelines, opening up new areas and creating new business opportunities for the company. From 1925 to 1929, VEW's gas output quadrupled to 24.4 million cubic meters.

VEW had some RM60 million in share capital, yet during this five-year period it funded investments totalling RM130 million. VEW's municipal partners, with financial worries of their own, were unable to provide the company with the additional capital it needed. As long-term loans were not available from a German capital market that had been severely hit by the inflation of the early 1920s and as VEW was able to obtain dollar loans, secured against property from the United States, only in 1925 and 1928, the investments were financed almost exclusively by short-term loans. Between 1925 and 1930, the company's obligations rose ten-fold, and this form of raising finance led to a worrying imbalance between equity and borrowed capital.

By the beginning of the 1930s, the combination of rapid expansion, management mistakes, and the unbalanced capital structure had put the company in a precarious financial situation. On top of this the Depression had already led to a dramatic fall in demand for electricity and gas. The company was on the verge of bankruptcy. An attempt to reschedule its debt failed due to the worsening situation in the U.S. capital market. Instead, a German-American banking consortium made available a medium-term loan. The loan was secured by a borrower's note providing for a share option if the loan were not repaid. One result of this rescue package was the restructuring of VEW GmbH into a joint stock company. VEW AG was founded on January 1, 1930, with a share capital of RM60 million. The capital was then increased by a further RM60 million of preferential shares which provided the security on the loan. Together with the departure of the company's former management, the rescue package ensured the company's survival at least for a while, especially as an attempt by RWE to take over VEW was foiled by the resistance of the U.S. creditor banks.

As a result of the world Depression, the producer goods industries which formed some of VEW's most important customers suffered a massive contraction in output and employment. This in turn led to a sharp reduction in the demand for electricity, gas and water. Mass unemployment and growing poverty led to reductions in the energy consumption of private consumers as well. The summer of 1932 marked the absolute low point in energy demand. VEW was forced to undertake drastic economy measures. All construction work was halted and around a quarter of the work force dismissed. However, these measures brought no improvement in the company's financial situation. VEW had continued to run at a loss since 1930 and found it difficult to maintain repayments on its loan. It was only at the end of 1933 that assistance from the Reich's Economic Ministry allowed the company to carry out a thorough rescheduling and restructuring of its debt. When the loan secured by borrower's note was replaced by securer forms of debt, the preferential shares option was rendered invalid, thus removing the risk of a takeover by another company. At the end of its restructuring VEW was able to emerge once more as a financially stable and technically advanced company.

The Nazi seizure of power in January 1933 had far-reaching consequences for companies such as VEW that were in municipal hands. Almost all VEW's top management was dismissed and replaced by figures close to the Nazi party. At the same time, the economic situation improved as the recovery that had begun in autumn 1932 was strengthened from 1933 onwards by the Nazis' job creation schemes and armaments programs as part of their Four Year Plan. The increase in economic activity brought with it a growing demand for electricity, gas and water. In 1934 VEW supplied 541 million kilowatt hours of electricity, surpassing the previous record of 1929.

During the 1930s the political situation continued to exert a considerable influence on VEW's development. The energy demands of the Four Year Plan forced the company to expand its power stations and supply grid. For example, the Reich's government pressed VEW to provide the power for a new aluminum works in Lünen. Considerable expansion of the Gersteinwerk power station was required before the aluminum works could be connected to the grid, a step taken in 1938. Supplying the Lünen works was in some ways a special case, but it was characteristic of the growing demand for energy within the dynamic economy of the rearmament era. Whereas industrial electricity consumption trebled between 1932 and 1939, demand as a whole increased only twofold. Within the industrial sector, it was the iron and steel industry, with a four-fold increase in electricity consumption, the mines, with a five-fold increase, and the cement industry, whose commitments to help build motorways and the defensive Siegfried line caused a seven-fold increase, that led the field in electricity demand.

Because the Ruhr mining industry was interested in ensuring a guaranteed demand for coal even in times of economic downturn, it pressed to provide a larger share of public electricity supply. Between 1935 and 1939, VEW signed agreements with 12 large mining companies, several more smaller ones, and Steinkohle-Elektrizitäts AG (STEAG)—an electricity-generating company founded in 1937 by mining companies in the Ruhr and selling its electricity to the public supply companies—with the result that the mines came to provide 20% of VEW's generating plant capacity. The growing demand for energy substantially improved VEW's own financial position and in 1936 the company resumed paying dividends.

World War II initially had relatively little effect on VEW's activities. By the end of the war, however, substantial sections of VEW's power stations and grid had been destroyed. The company's Dortmund power station and the hydroelectric power station on the Möhnetal barrier were almost completely destroyed. The Hattingen municipal station and the Kruckel power station suffered only minor damage while the Gerstein power station remained intact. The high tension networks across the whole supply area as well as the electricity and gas networks in the larger cities suffered the worst damage.

The collapse of the Third Reich in May 1945 brought about far-reaching changes in VEW's structure. The company came under the control of Allied powers, its mines were expropriated and management subjected to denazification. In the period up to the end of 1945, all the members of the management and supervisory boards were replaced. Efforts to rebuild the grid began at an early stage and by early summer 1945 some parts of Westphalia were already being supplied with energy.

The West German currency reform of June 1948 stabilized the economic situation and allowed the company once again to restore its position as a technically advanced energy company. A large loan from Marshall Plan funds helped it to modernize its power stations. The remaining investment was largely self-financed. Between 1948 and 1955 VEW, a company with DM91 million equity capital, was able to finance a construction program of DM500 million. As the company celebrated its 25th anniversary in 1950, it had a generating capacity of 611 megawatts, 21,600 kilometers of electricity transmission lines, and a gas distribution network some 1,300 kilometers in length. In that year it supplied 1.9 billion kilowatt hours of electricity and 160 million cubic meters of gas.

If the company was to keep pace with West Germany's rapidly growing energy demand, further expansion was vital and this would require outside sources of finance. The company's equity was increased in two stages to DM280 million. Because of the lack of liquidity of the company's shareholders, the municipalities, this increase was made possible only by retaining dividends. In the long term, however, this was not a satisfactory way to meet VEW's financial needs, and during the 1960s there were protracted discussions over what would be politically and economically the most expedient way to increase the company's equity. Bringing in private capital came to seem the best option. In 1966 VEW's partial privatization was carried out with the issue of DM75 million of bearer shares. The shares were initially placed on all the German exchanges and later on the Swiss exchanges as well. This was a turning point in the company's history, since VEW changed from being wholly in municipal hands to being a mixed public service and private company. The company's equity, which rose to DM1 billion in 1985, divides up as follows: 31.5% is held by the municipalities in the form of registered shares with restricted transferability—these shares have treble voting rights and thus the municipalities control a majority of the votes; the remaining shares, bearer shares with single voting rights, are in both municipal and private hands, and are owned by some 41,000 shareholders both in Germany and abroad. Two holding companies have more than 25% of the equity, namely the Kommunale Energie-Beteiligungsgesellschaft mbH, Dortmund, and the Energie-Verwaltungs-Gesellschaft mbH, Düsseldorf.

Among VEW's most important technical developments was the company's adoption of nuclear energy during the 1960s. A nuclear plant was built in Lingen and began supplying the VEW grid in 1968 (the plant was closed in 1977 because of technical defects). VEW's supply network, too, had to be modernized extensively. Before the war, high voltage lines carrying 50 and 110 kilovolts had been erected. In the mid-1950s these were replaced by 220 kilovolt lines and from 1975 380 kilovolt lines had been adopted in the European supply grid. For gas supply, it was the 1960s that saw key innovations, most notably the progressive replacement of coking plant gas by cheaper natural gas. VEW began the changeover in 1965 and took about ten years to complete the process. In addition, the 1960s and 1970s also saw the expansion of the district heating schemes that VEW had begun in Dortmund back in 1951. Large industrial enterprises and dense urban areas were the chief beneficiaries. At its 50th anniversary in 1975, VEW had a generating capacity of 6,062 megawatts of electricity in steam turbine and hydroelectric power stations, 62,000 kilometers of power lines, and a gas supply network of 4,000 kilometers. With a turnover of DM2.5 billion, the company supplied 17 billion kilowatt hours of electricity and 3 billion kilowatt hours of gas.

Electricity generation from hard coal had always played a predominant role for VEW. The coal crisis in the 1960s and 1970s, brought about by industry's extensive switching to oil, forced the company to close its own mines, but VEW continued to use hard coal to produce most of its electrical power—85% in 1986. This had two consequences. First, the company has been extensively involved in research projects to achieve optimum use of coal in electricity generation. Second, it acquired a larger share of Ruhrkohle AG, the largest German mining company, between 1984 and 1987. As VEW's annual report for 1984 explained, "The electricity industry has become Ruhrkohle's biggest consumer. As one of the biggest consumers of German hard coal, VEW is especially interested in intensifying cooperation in the area of energy technology, in particular in the further development of new coal technology and environmental protection." Since the oil crises of the 1970s, and with the growing debate about the world climate, protecting the environment and saving resources have become top priorities in all VEW's energy policy decisions. This is manifest in innovations to prevent harmful chemical emissions, in the company's use of renewable energy sources, and in the energy-saving advice it offers customers and partners.

The end of the 1980s saw a number of significant changes whose importance for VEW's development will become fully apparent only later in the 1990s. In a major expansion of its existing areas of activity, VEW decided in 1987 to make use of its long years of experience in waste disposal to offer waste and refuse disposal as a commercial service.

April 1988 saw the completion of VEW's biggest investment project to date when the DM5 billion nuclear power station Emsland, belonging to the VEW subsidiary Kernkraftwerke Lippe-Ems GmbH, supplied electricity to the public grid for the first time.

At the end of 1989 VEW acquired part of Steinmüller Verwaltungsgesellschaft mbH, a leading player in construction of steam power generators and in tool technology. This was VEW's first acquisition outside the energy sector and forms part of its strategy of developing and converting to new tech-

nology both for environmental protection and for advanced electricity generation.

The unification of East and West Germany in October 1990, after more than 40 years of division, represented a major challenge for Germany's energy industry. The power stations and systems in East Germany were completely outdated and desperately in need of renovation. The building of a reliable and environmentally friendly energy supply network on a commercial basis in the new German federal states will require the efforts of companies from Germany and other European countries. VEW has become involved in both the electricity and gas supply sectors in eastern Germany. Alongside other German electricity companies, it has acquired a share in the Mitteldeutsche Energieversorgung AG (MEAG) in Halle (Saale). Together with British Gas, Gaz de France, and Westfälische Ferngas AG, it has also acquired shares in several regional gas companies in Sachsen-Anhalt, Saxony, and Brandenburg. Further activities and acquisitions in the new German federal states are under consideration.

VEW's shareholdings in industrial companies, its search for new and fruitful areas of operation, and its involvement in developing the new German federal states will ensure VEW's secure place in the German and European energy markets of the future.

Principal Subsidiaries: Kernkraftwerke Lippe-Ems GmbH (75%); MEAG Geschäftsbesorgungs-AG (67.2%); Abfallverwertungsgesellschaft Westfalen mbH (51%); VEW-Harpen Kraftwerk Werne oHG (51%); AVU Aktiengesellschaft für Versorgungs-Unternehmen (50%); ORFA Organ-Faser Aufbereitungsgesellschaft mbH & Co KG (30%); Ruhrkohle AG (30.2%); Gelsenwasser AG (27%); Steinmüller Verwaltungsgesellschaft mbH (25.1%); Gasversorgung Leipzig GmbH (25.5%); Gasversorgung Sachsen-Anhalt GmbH (17%); Märkische Gasversorgung GmbH (12.8%).

Further Reading: Vereinigte Elektrizitätswerke Westfalen Aktiengesellschaft, Köln, Mueller & Co., 1930; *25 Jahre VEW 1925-1950,* Dortmund, 1950; Horstmann, Th., ed., *Elektrifizierung in Westfalen. Fotodokumente aus dem Archiv der VEW,* Hagen, v. d. Linnepe, 1990.

—Theo Horstmann
Translated from the German by Mark Roseman

WASTE SERVICES

Browning-Ferris Industries, Inc.
Waste Management, Inc.

BROWNING-FERRIS INDUSTRIES, INC.

757 North Eldridge
Houston, Texas 77079
U.S.A.
(713) 870-8100
Fax: (713) 870-7844

Public Company
Incorporated: 1970
Employees: 26,000
Sales: $3.25 billion
Stock Exchanges: New York Midwest Pacific London

Browning-Ferris Industries, Inc. (BFI) is one of a small group of U.S. garbage collectors that during the 1970s and 1980s grew to become a provider of waste disposal services. From a one-truck operation established in Houston, Texas, in 1966, Browning-Ferris grew with phenomenal speed into the waste industry's second-largest corporation, active throughout the United States and in international markets as well. Like its bigger rival, Waste Management, BFI offers a full range of waste, recycling, and sanitation services, with the notable exception of hazardous-waste treatment. After a series of legal and financial reversals Browning-Ferris withdrew from the hazardous-waste business in 1990.

Browning-Ferris's extremely rapid growth was made possible by the wholesale change that overtook the waste-disposal industry in the 1960s. Prior to that time, waste was known as garbage, and usually was transported by municipalities or small local collection firms to a distant plot of land and there dumped or incinerated. Regulations were few and the industry was completely fragmented, a typical company consisting of no more than a few trucks and the family that owned them.

This was the situation in Houston in 1964 when a young accountant named Tom Fatjo Jr. began keeping financial records for a number of local garbage collectors. Fatjo became intrigued with the wide-open business, and in 1966 bought a truck and opened his own garbage collection company, one of the 17 small firms at that time working in the Houston area. At the time, national legislation designed to tighten regulation of both collection and disposal services had recently been enacted. This legislation would change radically the nature of garbage treatment in the United States. Henceforth, collection trucks would have to meet higher standards of sanitation, while for reasons of air pollution the incineration of garbage

would give way increasingly to landfill burial. Both changes would require large capital investments on the part of waste operators, most of whom were in no position to raise the sums involved. The situation was ripe for the creation of a large, multicity company capable of spending the money needed to establish the garbage business as a modern, sanitary, technologically competent industry. The days of one-horse garbage hauling were over.

Tom Fatjo accordingly began looking for ways to expand his Houston company. After beginning with residential waste collection, he added accounts in the commercial and industrial sectors such as shopping malls and small factories. In 1968 he branched into the disposal end of the business, winning a large landfill contract from the city of Houston. At about this time Fatjo, his eyes trained on a much larger, regional organization, became partners with Louis A. Waters, then a vice president of corporate finance for a New York securities brokerage. The two of them decided to embark on a program of acquisitions designed to weld together scores of the tiny collection and disposal companies operating across Texas and the South. To help raise the capital needed for so ambitious an undertaking, Fatjo and Waters in 1969 gained control of Browning-Ferris Machinery Company, a publicly traded manufacturer of garbage trucks and landfill equipment, among other things. Not only did Browning-Ferris offer an obvious match for the two partners' collection business, it also allowed them to issue stock for the purposes of working capital and equity swaps.

Thus fortified, Fatjo and Waters went to work over the next three years buying up small operators at the rate of one a week. By consolidating its acquisitions, most of which were in Houston; Memphis, Tennessee; and Puerto Rico, Browning-Ferris, renamed Browning-Ferris Industries, Inc., was able to take advantage of the basic axiom of the collection business: the more adjacent stops made by each truck, the greater the return on equity. It is much more profitable to collect waste, for example, from ten large apartment complexes in a row than to collect from the first, fifth, and tenth buildings and then be forced to move elsewhere for the next pickup. Therefore, as BFI bought up the businesses of rival collectors in Houston or Memphis, its costs per customer dropped sharply and profits accordingly rose, paving the way for further acquisitions. In the meantime, growing public pressure for environmental protection prompted a continuing flurry of new regulations affecting every aspect of the waste industry. Compliance with such legislation is expensive, in terms of either equipment or know-how, which in turn made it easier for BFI to buy out financially strapped, smaller competitors. BFI bought out competitors as fast as the contracts could be written. Most owners of the acquired companies stayed on as managers.

By 1975 BFI's revenues had climbed to $256 million. The company operated 2,800 trucks in 131 different cities, employed 7,700 workers, and had accumulated 60 landfills. The latter would prove critically important, as further regulation and public anxiety made it nearly impossible to create new landfills and raised the costs of operating those already in existence. Dumping charges skyrocketed, adding a new source of bottom-line funds to BFI's resources; more importantly, the scarcity of landfill sites discouraged new competitors from jumping into the business. Those companies such as BFI and Waste Management that got into garbage early, stayed in and grew at prodigious rates; those that came later found the industry nearly locked up. BFI expanded its landfill holdings whenever possible, and also began handling a new form of waste variously labeled as chemical, toxic, or hazardous. Although toxic waste would later play an important role in BFI's history, in the mid-1970s the company had just begun to explore the complex and notoriously litigious field, chiefly in the form of waste-oil treatment.

In 1976 Tom Fatjo withdrew from BFI to run an investment company of his own, leaving Louis Waters in charge of the firm's finances and Harry Phillips Sr. as its chief operating officer. Phillips had owned a number of the garbage collection companies in Memphis acquired by BFI, and his hands-on experience made him invaluable to the company's founders, neither of whom knew intimately the day-to-day problems of the garbage business. Phillips remained chief operating officer and served as chairman from 1979 until the appointment of William D. Ruckelshaus in 1988, and even then continued as chairman of the executive committee.

Aside from its core business in solid waste, by the mid-1970s BFI had developed a number of peripheral interests. It was one of the earliest companies to experiment with the recycling of paper waste, using its own collection supply and also buying paper from thousands of users that could then be treated, shredded, and sold to papermakers. A sharp recession in the paper markets in 1975 threw BFI's paper division into the red, however, and in the following year its paper recycling assets were spun off to shareholders in the form of a separate company. Of greater importance was BFI's first foreign contract, a 1973 agreement to provide sanitation services in parts of Spain. The business of international waste services grew rapidly during the 1970s, particularly after rival Waste Management signed a contract in 1975 to clean the city of Riyadh, Saudi Arabia, for five years, and it seems that despite its early success in Spain, BFI was generally slow to pursue the many opportunities overseas. As a result, Waste Management won most of the lucrative international contracts, while BFI only established its presence in Europe and the Far East markets in later years, winning the Riyadh contract back from Waste Management in the next round.

Harry Phillips proved to be an outstanding leader for BFI. His background in operations enabled him to keep a tight lid on costs even as the company continued to expand at breakneck speed through the early years of the 1980s. Thus, not only did BFI's revenue double between 1978 and 1983 to $843 million, its operating margin also increased dramatically, from just under 31% to 35.8%. The latter was due to BFI's economies of scale, by which a greater number of pick-ups translate into a larger bottom line; to a large and highly motivated sales force expected to bring in scores of new customers every year; and to Phillips's ability to coordinate the day-to-day complexities of a rapidly growing corporation.

It was also during this period that chemical and toxic waste became a more important factor at BFI. In 1976 Congress passed the Resource Conservation and Recovery Act, a piece of legislation designed to tighten control of all forms of potentially dangerous landfills. By the time the law was fully implemented in 1980 it had sharply increased the difficulty and cost of chemical and toxic disposal, giving much additional business to companies like BFI with some experience in the field. By 1983 chemical waste provided 10% of BFI's revenue and was projected to be a mainstay of the company's future, as it

became more difficult to find opportunities for expansion in the solid-waste sector. About half of the company's toxic-waste business was the result of the 1983 purchase of CECOS International Inc., one of the industry's leaders, along with the smaller Newco Waste Systems. The CECOS acquisition brought with it two toxic disposal sites—giving BFI a total of eight—and opened up the important New York and Ohio markets. With the Environmental Protection Agency (EPA) about to begin distributing billions of dollars from its Superfund to clean up toxic waste, and BFI's 400-person sales force aggressively on the march, the company had every reason to expect hazardous disposal to become a second major revenue stream.

As it turned out, however, it was primarily those two elements that caused BFI much grief during the next five years. BFI's sales force was not only large and aggressive, rival firms and a number of grand juries alleged, it also engaged in predatory pricing. As of 1984 the company was under investigation in seven states for suspected monopolistic practices such as price-fixing, charges that it denied but often settled out of court for amounts totaling $15 million by 1989. The monetary damages were relatively minor, but such publicity hurt the company's image with customers and with the increasing group of governmental, environmental, and industrial parties involved. The problem was intensified in 1985, when a BFI toxic dump in Williamsburg, Ohio, was repeatedly closed by both state and federal environmental authorities. A grand jury also brought criminal charges against BFI, claiming the company had contaminated a nearby creek. Amid the attendant turmoil, BFI's hazardous division as a whole dropped into the red for the first half of the year.

While the company's solid-waste business continued to grow profitably and its first few waste-to-energy plants opened in New York and New Jersey, the comparatively minor hazardous-waste division became a major liability. Company-owned toxic landfills in New York, Ohio, and Louisiana were found wanting when BFI applied for permit extensions near the end of the 1980s.

Concerned that the company might be permanently shut out of these three sites, and generally in need of a face-lift, BFI in October 1988 announced that it had hired William D. Ruckelshaus as its new chairman and chief executive. Ruckelshaus brought with him a reputation for integrity, first established during the Watergate scandal when as deputy attorney general he refused President Richard Nixon's order to fire special prosecutor Archibald Cox and later burnished by his second term as head of the EPA following the scandalous reign of Anne Gorsuch Burford in the early 1980s. Ruckelshaus was respected by the business community, environmentalists, and public servants, and it was thought that he could salvage BFI's hazardous-waste contracts.

Ruckelshaus was very much an outsider at BFI, however, and his arrival as the company's chairman struck observers as a public relations ploy. The company's relationship with the federal and state environmental agencies was strained beyond the point of immediate repair, and despite the presence of Ruckelshaus, BFI was unable to win approval for any of the three dumps in question. BFI announced in the spring of 1990 that it was withdrawing from the toxic-waste business, citing poor profit margins as the source of its decision. The company took a $452 million pre-tax charge against earnings to cover the cost of devalued assets, pushing fiscal 1990 into the red and sending a clear signal that in the battle between BFI and Waste Management for the industry's top spot, BFI would at least temporarily settle for second. Despite the legal liabilities inherent in toxic waste, the field is extremely profitable and is certain to grow indefinitely; in the year of BFI's withdrawal, for example, Waste Management earned $176 million in that segment of its business.

A wave of resignations followed Ruckelhaus's appointment, including that of President John Drury in January 1991. A short time later former chairman Harry Phillips returned to top management in an attempt to restore morale at BFI.

The company remains, for all its setbacks, a formidable competitor in an industry whose eventual boundaries will be as large and varied as those of the environmental movement itself. Aside from its primary solid-waste business, BFI has positioned itself to take advantage of the burgeoning market for curb-side recycling services; is the nation's top supplier of medical waste services, a field that is growing at a rapid pace; and has established a solid base in the European market. The company operates three of its big waste-to-energy plants, via its 50%-owned American Ref-Fuel joint venture with Air Products and Chemicals, Inc., and leases out some 60,000 portable toilets to the construction industry. In the long run it is possible that the company will be better off without carrying the massive liability inherent in the toxic-waste business.

Principal Subsidiaries: A.B.C. Disposal, Inc.; Atkinson Enterprises, Inc.; CECOS International, Inc.; Cotecnica, C.A.; Dave Systems, Inc.; Dooley Equipment Corp.; Eastern Disposal Inc.; Empire Sweeping Co.; Empresa Nacional de Residuos Ltd.; Environmental Equipment Corp.; ESI, Inc.; Geneva Waste Services, Inc.; Heavy Equipment Leasing Services Co., Inc.; Hennepin Transfer, Inc.; HL-NIW, Inc.; Indoco, Inc.; International Disposal Corp.; Joe Ball Sanitation Service, Inc.; Land Reclamation, Inc.; Landfill, Inc.; Lanham Waste Control, Inc.; Louis Kmito & Son, Inc.; Lyon Development Co.; Multi-Packer Inc.; National Disposal Service, Inc.; Newco Waste Systems, Inc.; Pine Bend Landfill, Inc.; Prince William Trash Service, Inc.; Removal, Inc.; Residential Service, Inc.; Risk Services, Inc.; Rot's Disposal Service, Inc.; Servicos Metropolitanos, C.A.; Waste Disposal, Inc.; West Roxbury Crushed Stone Co.; Westowns Disposal Systems, Inc.; Woodlake Sanitary Service, Inc.

Further Reading: Miller, William H., "Cashing in on Trash," *Industry Week,* February 16, 1976; Bailey, Jeff, "Trash Troubles: Browning-Ferris Fails To Boost Its Business By Hiring 'Mr. Clean'," *The Wall Street Journal,* May 14, 1991.

—Jonathan Martin

Waste Management, Inc.

WASTE MANAGEMENT, INC.

3003 Butterfield Road
Oak Brook, Illinois 60521
U.S.A.
(708) 572-8800
Fax (708) 572-9857

Public Company
Incorporated: 1968
Employees: 62,000
Sales: $6.03 billion
Stock Exchanges: New York Midwest London Tokyo
   Toronto Frankfurt Australian Geneva Zürich Basel

Waste Management, Inc. has made a fortune taking care of what the rest of the world prefers not to think about. Waste Management is the undisputed world leader in nearly all facets of waste treatment, including low-level nuclear, chemical, and asbestos cleanup; and daily garbage removal, waste reduction, and recycling. Waste Management has expanded its operations both technically and geographically, acquiring a host of sophisticated suppliers of trash-to-energy plants, pollution control equipment, and recycling services, while signing contracts with municipalities from Buenos Aires to Hong Kong. The company has frequently been attacked by governmental agencies and environmental groups for a variety of alleged failings, but its phenomenal growth and strenuous efforts in the recycling and pollution-control areas make it likely that in the future Waste Management will be perceived as a hero rather than villain by the world's increasingly polluted cities. Waste Management, it seems, is well on the way to becoming the planet's garbage collector.

Sensitivity to the problems of waste disposal is a comparatively recent development. When the predecessors of Waste Management, Inc. (WMI) were hauling trash in the 1950s, neither they nor their customers gave much thought to the complexities of garbage. Garbage generally was collected by municipalities or small private haulers such as Ace Scavenger, WMI's immediate forerunner, a Chicago-area company with 12 trucks and 1956 revenue of about $750,000. In that year, Ace Scavenger's founder died, and management of the company was turned over to his 24-year-old son-in-law, Dean L. Buntrock. Buntrock already had experience running a family farm-implement business in his native South Dakota, and his in-laws felt that although young he was the best family member to take over their refuse company. Ace was a prosperous, well-established firm, and Buntrock was able to take command with little difficulty.

It was an exceedingly good time to join the waste-treatment industry. Not only was the national economy at the peak of its postwar prosperity, the U.S. consumer was just then beginning to be inundated with a wave of new packaging and convenience items designed to be used once and thrown away. The nation's production of garbage was growing much faster even than its population, and companies such as Ace Scavenger found themselves in great demand. Dean Buntrock moved aggressively to expand his business, buying up and creating a number of similar companies in Chicago and Wisconsin during the early 1960s. In getting to know the waste-treatment industry, Buntrock met his father-in-law's nephew, H. Wayne Huizenga, then running a small collection company of his own in Pompano Beach, Florida. The two men compared notes and talked about the possibility of someday joining forces, although at the time few if any waste-collection companies operated in more than one state.

That situation changed shortly after Congress passed the Solid Waste Disposal Act of 1965. The act, in response to a growing awareness of the need for safe, efficient waste removal, required collection companies to meet new standards of hygiene and effectively forced out of business many of the oldest and least sophisticated companies. The Solid Waste Disposal Act also mandated higher safety levels at disposal sites, again increasing the costs of doing business and encouraging the formation of larger, better capitalized companies able to afford the necessary investments. Buntrock and Huizenga correctly interpreted the 1965 act as the beginning of a new era in U.S. waste management, in which increasing population pressures and pollution awareness would render inadequate the industry's former standards of competence and organization. Belatedly, the garbage business was about to take on the characteristics of modern industrial efficiency, and in 1968 Buntrock and Huizenga accordingly agreed to unite their various collection firms as Waste Management, Inc.

In its first year of operation, WMI companies in Illinois, Wisconsin, and Florida totaled a modest $5.5 million in revenue, but its founders recognized that the waste industry had a nearly unlimited future. To create a nationwide organization, Buntrock and Huizenga took WMI public in 1971 with an initial offering of 320,000 shares. WMI's founders used the proceeds of that stock sale to launch one of the most spectacular success stories in the history of U.S. business. From 1971 to 1980, WMI revenue grew at a rate of 48% per year. In 1979 earnings were almost 10% of sales.

Most of this phenomenal growth was achieved by means of acquisition—WMI bought 75 companies in the 18 months following its stock offering—but some of the growth reflected increasing concern for the long-term health and appearance of the planet. The oil crisis of 1973–1974 impressed upon the U.S. public the need for conservation of resources and the potentially disastrous effects of unrestrained energy use. A result of these shifts in public awareness was a new emphasis on the professional, safe, and environmentally responsible handling of all forms of waste, which was no longer perceived simply as whatever was unwanted. A company such as WMI offered the appearance of professional service and provided fiscally troubled municipalities with garbage collection at up to 30% less than what it cost them to collect trash on their own.

From the beginning, Buntrock and Huizenga made provision for a large corporation of national scope. During the hectic expansion of the early 1970s WMI hired Arthur Andersen & Company to design and install a centralized information network and system of managerial controls that assured the company of uniform procedures among its suddenly numerous subsidiaries. The control system funneled to company headquarters in Oak Brook, Illinois, detailed information on everything from the monthly volume of garbage hauled by each of the company trucks to billing and payment patterns. This powerful system was an example of the kind of prescient thinking that within a few years effected a revolution in the entire waste industry.

Also of significance at this time was WMI's decision to enter the newly recognized field of chemical- and toxic-waste treatment. The proliferation of oil-based plastics and other industrial chemicals had burdened the country with a growing mass of dangerous materials in need of secure final disposal. Neither the companies that generated these substances nor the average disposal service was equipped to handle such problems, which posed dangers of both a physical and legal nature. WMI recognized the extent of the problem—and the profits likely to be generated by its solution—and cautiously purchased a few of the as-yet rare and little-known toxic-waste dumps around the country.

Toxic-waste control remained a relatively minor part of WMI's business, however, until Congress passed the Resource Conservation and Recovery Act in 1976. The act was the first significant piece of legislation to address the issue of toxic and chemical waste, setting minimum standards for disposal and greatly increasing public awareness of the dangers involved. The resulting tightening of controls and heightened scrutiny scared off most of the companies capable of handling toxic waste; but for those like WMI that chose to pursue the business, the rewards proved to be very large. Under a three-quarter-owned subsidiary, Chemical Waste Management, Inc., WMI rapidly enlarged its presence in the toxic field, acquiring a number of the largest toxic landfills and by 1980 emerging as the industry leader.

As they had demonstrated in founding WMI in 1968, Buntrock and Huizenga displayed remarkable foresight in thus plunging into the hazardous-waste business. Rapidly increasing public fears about all forms of toxic waste soon made it extremely difficult to gain approval for new landfills, which in turn drove up the market value of existing sites, many of them in the hands of Chemical Waste Management by the early 1980s. In 1980, the year in which the last phases of the Resource Conservation and Recovery Act became law, WMI stock rose from $36 to $123.

In 1975 yet another rich opportunity presented itself to the company's founders. The royal city of Riyadh, Saudi Arabia, made it known that it sought help in handling its mounting garbage and sanitation problems. The Saudis wanted unusually comprehensive services—including daily garbage pick-up from every home, street cleaning, and the disposal of dead animals—and WMI formed a 60–40 joint venture with a British-Saudi partner to pursue the lucrative business. Management came up with a slightly curtailed package of services at a cost of US$242 million over five years and was awarded the contract beginning in 1977.

For WMI, a company in existence for only nine years, the deal was audacious in the extreme; it required the assembly of 2,500 workers, many of them recruited in India, and all of whom needed housing, medical services, and extensive training to meet the Saudis's fastidious standards. As Huizenga told *Fortune,* April 7, 1980, "We had to succeed. We couldn't afford to fail." Succeed WMI did, becoming in effect the world's first international supplier of sanitation services, and paving the way for a plethora of subsequent contracts.

Soon the city of Buenos Aires turned to WMI for help with its waste program, in 1980 giving the firm a contract for the disposal of garbage generated by two million residents and a substantial portion of the city's commercial and industrial concerns. In rapid succession followed agreements with Jeddah, Saudi Arabia; Caracas, Venezuela; Brisbane, Australia; and, in the late 1980s, a number of European cities as well as Hong Kong. As in toxic waste, WMI no sooner entered the international field than it became the dominant player.

In 1979 WMI sales stood at $382 million; three years later that figure was close to $1 billion, and net income remained comfortably above the 10% level. In the space of a decade, WMI had shot ahead of its rivals to become the world's largest disposal company and a favorite investment of many securities analysts. WMI had also become the favorite target of innumerable governmental and environmental groups outraged by what they perceived as WMI's slipshod and even criminal mishandling of its responsibilities. Most widely publicized of the many lawsuits brought against the company were those arising from the discovery in March 1983 that WMI's oil-waste landfill in Vickery, Ohio, contained 135,000 gallons of material contaminated with polychlorinated biphenyls (PCBs). A former employee at Vickery charged that he was fired for refusing to falsify test results, while both the state of Ohio and the Environmental Protection Agency (EPA) brought suit against WMI, the former asking $480 million in damages and the latter $6.8 million. Though the suits were settled for a fraction of those amounts, the incident was only one of a raft of similar controversies. In the two years following the Ohio incident, WMI faced suits alleging illegal dumping in at least six states, and several competitors brought actions complaining of monopolistic practices.

The company responded with characteristic energy. At each of its nine chemical dumps, WMI installed environmental-compliance officers with power to override the decisions of local plant managers. These watchdog foremen reported to WMI's new environmental-management head, Walter C. Barber, a former acting chief of the EPA. In addition, the Chemical Waste subsidiary in charge of most of the troubled sites was provided with a new president, Jerry E. Dempsey, former president of Borg-Warner Corporation. To smooth relations with Congress, WMI hired Frank B. Moore as its chief lobbyist. Moore had previously served as President Jimmy Carter's liaison officer with Congress. Finally, WMI adopted new advertising campaigns stressing the company's services on behalf of the environment and customers alike.

While such moves had not satisfied critics such as Greenpeace International, it appeared that WMI learned a lesson from its legal battles and took some pains to adopt more safety measures. As proof of its progress in these areas, WMI can point to the long-term contracts it won in the late 1980s to handle much of the waste from Portland, Oregon; and Seattle,

Washington; two cities known for their strong environmental commitment. In both cases, the municipalities found that WMI's experience and resources made it the best choice for waste problems of great magnitude.

Despite its shaky image in the mid-1980s, WMI's revenue and net income continued to grow at an impressive pace. Most significant among its many acquisitions was the 1984 purchase of 60% of SCA Services, Inc., a Boston-based company ranking third in the waste-treatment industry. The purchase added about $200 million to WMI's $1 billion revenue, opening up 43 markets for the parent company and increasing its total number of landfills to 89; but the move also brought its share of controversy. SCA Services was widely rumored to have ties with organized crime in New York and New Jersey, and the company had endured its own spate of lawsuits in the late 1970s over the resignation and alleged improprieties of its president, Christopher Recklitis. Once integrated into the WMI network, however, the SCA units dropped from the headlines, becoming only one more piece of WMI's highly profitable and constantly expanding business empire. WMI was perfectly positioned to take advantage of the public's hardening attitude of not-in-my-back-yard toward any proposed new toxic-waste dump sites. Existing dumps continued to grow in value, and as of 1986 WMI owned eight of the twenty largest hazardous dumps in the country. A similar public concern about the safety and extent of conventional landfills also strengthened WMI's hand in that field, where its 100-odd sites and its international experience gave it a prestige hard to match. Sales continued to spiral, approaching $2 billion by 1985.

Since that time, WMI has added a number of secondary businesses to its threefold core of solid-waste collection, chemical-waste treatment, and international waste services. Most important of these developments are the group of companies known collectively as Wheelabrator Technologies, Inc. and WMI's increasing involvement in all phases of the recycling business. Wheelabrator Technologies includes a number of companies involved in the waste-to-energy business, in which solid waste is burned and a certain amount of energy recaptured in the form of electricity that can be sold to local utilities. In 1988 when Wheelabrator sold 20% of its stock to WMI, it was the second-leading builder and operator of such systems, with sales of about $1 billion. WMI acquired controlling interest in Wheelabrator in 1990 and restructured its assets into a number of divisions including waste-to-energy companies, makers of air-pollution control systems, and waste-water treatment facilities. Another part of Wheelabrator, Rust International, is the world's leading engineer of waste-to-energy incinerators, which WMI believes will play an increasingly important role in the disposal of urban solid wastes. By combining with WMI, Wheelabrator solved what had been its most serious problem, the difficulty of finding land on which to situate its plants. Such facilities are generally less objectionable to the public when built on land already zoned as a garbage dump. If the cost of electricity and the burden of excess garbage continue to mount, Wheelabrator's systems may well become a far more common sight in many cities.

In recycling, which enjoyed a tremendous boom starting in the late 1980s, WMI repeated its pattern of entering an industry as its leader, in 1987. By 1991 WMI, the largest collector of recyclable materials in the United States and Canada, served some four million households. WMI and Stone Container created Paper Recycling International, L.P., to market recycled paper products back to Stone as well as to other manufacturers. Similarly, the company has substantial footholds in the areas of aluminum recycling, waste sorting centers, and tire shredding. In 1990 WMI's residential recycling service grew 150%.

In every facet of waste treatment, in fact, WMI continued to expand quickly. Since the company's creation, WMI had yet to overlook a development of any significance in its exploding industry. In solid waste, hazardous, chemical, recycling, and waste-to-energy, WMI in the early 1990s enjoyed a position of undisputed leadership. Its international division had developed significant accounts in Europe; its chemical division was the country's largest operator of asbestos-abatement programs; and WMI was also the leading disposer of low-level radioactive wastes in the United States. WMI was doubling its revenue every two years, which is even faster than the world can pile up new garbage.

Principal Subsidiaries: Waste Management of North America, Inc.; Chemical Waste Management, Inc. (77%); Wheelabrator Technologies Inc. (56%); Waste Management International, Inc.

Further Reading: Burck, Charles G., "There's Big Business in All That Garbage," *Fortune,* April 7, 1980; "Waste Management, Inc.: Company History," Waste Management, Inc. corporate typescript, 1988.

—Jonathan Martin

INDEX TO COMPANIES AND PERSONS ——

Listings are arranged in alphabetical order under the company name; thus Eli Lilly & Company will be found under the letter E. Company names appearing in bold type have historical essays on the page numbers appearing in bold. The index is cumulative, with volume numbers printed in bold type.

Goldwyn Picture Corp., **II** 148
Goldwyn, Samuel, **II** 146, 147, 148, 154
Golhan, Mehmet, **IV** 563
Gomez, Alain, **II** 116, 117
Gómez, Juan Vicente (Gen.), **IV** 507, 565
Gompertz, Benjamin, **III** 373
Gonda, Keiji, **III** 638
Good Foods, Inc., **II** 497
Good Weather International Inc., **III** 221
Goodbody & Co., **II** 425
Goodenough, Frederick Crauford, **II** 235, 236
Goodenough, William Macnamara, **II** 236
Gooderham and Worts, **I** 216, 263–64
Goodheart, William, **II** 143
Goodlass, Wall & Co., **III** 680, 681
Goodlass Wall & Lead Industries, **III** 680–81
Goodman, Benny, **II** 543; **III** 443
Goodman, Ed, **IV** 620
Goodman Fielder Wattie Ltd., **II** 565
Goodrich, **V** 240, 241
Goodrich, Benjamin Franklin, **V** 231
Goodrich, Charles Cross, **V** 231
Goodrich, M. Keith, **IV** 646
Goodrich Oil Co., **IV** 365
Goodrich, Tew and Company, **V** 231
Goodwin, Jacob, **I** 60
Goodwin, James, **III** 236, 237
Goodwin, W. Richard, **III** 707, 708
Goodyear, Charles, **V** 244
Goodyear Tire & Rubber Company, V 244–48
Goodyear Tire and Rubber Corp., **I** 21; **II** 304; **III** 452
Gookin, R. Burt, **II** 508
Göransson, Anders Henrik, **IV** 202
Göransson family, **IV** 203
Göransson, Göran Fredrik, **IV** 202
Göransson, Karl Fredrik, **IV** 202, 203
Gorden, Maynard M., **I** 145
Gordon A. Freisen, International, **III** 73
Gordon Capital Corp., **II** 245
Gordon Investment Corp., **II** 245
Gordon, Peter, **IV** 209
Gordon Publications, **IV** 610
Gore Newspapers Co., **IV** 683
Göring, Hermann, **IV** 200
Gorman, Paul A., **IV** 287
Gorman, Willis A., **III** 355
Gormully & Jeffrey, **IV** 660
Gorst, Vernon, **I** 47, 128
Gorton's, **II** 502
Goschen, G.J., **III** 278
Gosho Co., Ltd., **IV** 442
Gosho Corp., **IV** 442
Gosho Trading Co., Ltd., **IV** 442
Goss, Dick, **I** 288
Gosse, Henry, **IV** 476
Gossett, William T., **II** 170
Götabanken, **II** 303, 353
Göteborgs Handelsbank, **II** 351
Göteborgs Handelskompani, **III** 425
Göth, Elis, **I** 665
Gothenburg Tramways Co., **II** 1
Goto, Shimpei, **V** 448
Goto, Yasuo, **III** 406
Gotoh, Keita, **V** 199, 510, 526–27
Gotoh, Konsuke, **V** 528
Gotoh, Noboru, **V** 527–28
Gotoh, Shinpei, **III** 454
Gott Corp., **III** 614
Gott, Edwin H., **IV** 574
Götte, Klaus, **III** 563

Gottstein, Kurt (Dr.), **III** 693
Gottstein, L., **III** 692
Gottwald, Floyd, **I** 334
Gottwald, Floyd, Jr., **I** 334
Goudefroy, Hans, **III** 184, 185
Goulard and Olena, **I** 412
Goulart, Jo-o, **IV** 55
Gould, Bruce, **I** 56
Gould, Charles N., **IV** 391
Gould Inc., **III** 745
Gould, Jay, **II** 329; **V** 529–30
Gould, William R., **V** 716, 716
Goulding Industries Ltd., **IV** 295
Gourmet Foods, **II** 528
Gousseland, Pierre, **IV** 19
Government Employee Insurance Co., **II** 448
Government Employees Life Insurance Co., **III** 273
Government National Mortgage Assoc., **II** 410
Gower, Bob, **IV** 456–57
GPU. *See* General Public Utilities Corporation
Graber Industries, Inc., **V** 379
Grable, Errett M., **III** 613
Grace. *See* W.R. Grace & Co.
Grace, Eugene G., **IV** 35, 36
Grace, J. Peter, **I** 547–49
Grace, James, **I** 547
Grace, Joseph, **I** 547
Grace, Michael P., **I** 547; **III** 525
Grace, Robert, **I** 584
Grace, William R., **I** 170, 547; **III** 525
Grade, Lew (Sir), **I** 531
Gradmann & Holler, **III** 283
Graebner, Wolfgang, **II** 242
Graef & Schmidt, **IV** 54
Graf, Robert J., **V** 711
Gräff, Leo, **I** 542
Gragg, Williford, **III** 397
Graham, Ann, **I** 575
Graham, D.M., **II** 261
Graham, Donald, **IV** 690
Graham family, **IV** 688, 690
Graham, Katharine Meyer, **IV** 689, 690
Graham Page, **III** 568
Graham, Peter, **II** 358
Graham, Philip, **IV** 689, 690
Graham, William B., **I** 627–28
Grahams Builders Merchants, **I** 429
Grainger, Isaac, **II** 251
Grainger, William W., **V** 214
Gralla, **IV** 687
Grambling, John A., Jr., **V** 674
Granada Computer Services, **II** 139
Granada Computer Services International, **II** 139
Granada Group Limited, **II** 138
Granada Group PLC, II 70, **138–40**
Granada Group Services, **II** 139
Granada Hospital Group, **II** 139
Granada Microcomputer Services, **II** 139
Granada Motorway Services, **II** 138
Granada Overseas Holdings, **II** 139
Granada Overseas Limited, **II** 138
Granada Television, **II** 138, 139
Granada Television International, **II** 138
Granada Theatres Limited, **II** 138
Grand Metropolitan plc, I 247–49, 259, 261; **II** 555–57, 565, 608, 613–15
Grand Union, **II** 637, 662
Grand-sons of Francois de Wendel, **IV** 226
Granda Cable and Satellite, **II** 139

Grandell, Leonard (Lt. Gen.), **III** 647
Grandi, Alberto, **IV** 422
Grandmet USA, **I** 248
Grands Magasins L. Tietz, **V** 103
Granger, William, Jr., **II** 468
Gränges, **III** 480
Granica, Pablo, **II** 198
Granier de Lilliac, René, **IV** 560
Grant, Alexander, **II** 592–93
Grant, Alistair, **II** 609–10
Grant, Allen (Sir), **I** 574
Grant, Margaret, **II** 593
Grant, Norman, **III** 738
Grant Oil Tool Co., **III** 569
Grant, Robert McVitie, **II** 592–93
Grant Street National Bank, **II** 317
Grant, Ulysses S., **III** 247; **IV** 604
Graphic Controls Corp., **IV** 678
Graphic Services, **III** 166
Graphic Systems, **III** 169
Graphite Oil Product Co., **I** 360
Grass, Alex, **V** 174, 176
Grasselli Dyestuffs Corp., **I** 337
Grasset, **IV** 618
Grasset-Fasquelle, **IV** 617
Grattan, **V** 160
Grava, Alfred, **I** 202
Graves, Bob, **IV** 492
Gray, A.A. **I** 715
Gray, Bowman, **V** 409
Gray, Bowman, Jr., **V** 409
Gray, Byron A., **III** 529
Gray Dawes & Co., **III** 522, 523
Gray Dawes Bank, **III** 523
Gray Dawes Travel, **III** 523
Gray Drug Stores, **III** 745
Gray Dunn and Co., **II** 569
Gray, Elisha (Bud), **II**, **III** 653, 654
Gray, George, **III** 359
Gray, Harold, **I** 452
Gray, Harry, **I** 68, 85–86, 143; **III** 74
Gray, Jim, **II** 167
Gray, John S., **I** 164
Gray, Latimer W., **II** 208
Gray Mackenzie & Co., **III** 522, 523
Gray, R.F., **II** 505
Grayarc, **III** 157
Grayburn, Vandeleur, **II** 297
Grayrock Capital, **I** 275
Great American Corp., **III** 191
Great American First Savings Bank of San Diego, **II** 420
Great American Holding Corp., **III** 191
Great American Indemnity Co., **III** 191
Great American Insurance Co., **III** 190–92
Great American Life Insurance Co., **III** 190, 191, 192
Great American Reserve Insurance Co., **IV** 343
Great American Tea Co., **II** 636, 666
Great Atlantic & Pacific Tea Company, Inc., II 636–38, 629, 655–56, 666
Great Beam Co., **III** 690
Great 5¢ Store, **V** 224
Great Halviggan, **III** 690
Great Lakes Bankgroup, **II** 457
Great Lakes Chemical Corp., I 341–42
Great Lakes Corp., **IV** 136
Great Lakes Pipe Line Co., **IV** 400, 575
Great Lakes Steel Corp., **IV** 236
Great Land Seafoods, Inc., **II** 553
Great Northern, **III** 282
Great Northern Import Co., **I** 292

Gulliver, James, **II** 609–10, 628
Gummi Werke, **I** 208
Gumucio, Marcelo, **III** 131
Gund, John, **I** 253
Gunda, John, **III** 323
Gunfred Group, **I** 387
Gunns Ltd., **II** 482
Gunpowder Trust, **I** 379
Gunter Wulff Automaten, **III** 430
Gunther, Hans, **I** 349
Gunther, John, **I** 15
Gurneys, Birkbeck, Barclay & Buxton, **II** 235
Gusswerk Paul Saalmann & Sohne, **I** 582
Gustav V, King (Sweden), **I** 448; **III** 28
Gustav Schickendanz KG, **V** 165
Gustavus A. Pfeiffer & Co., **I** 710
Gut, Rainer, **II** 268
Gutehoffnungshütte Aktienverein AG, **III** 561, 563; **IV** 104, 201
Gutfreund, John, **II** 448, 449
Guth, Charles G., **I** 276–77
Guth, W., **IV** 141
Guthrie Balfour, **II** 499, 500
Guthrie, Giles, **I** 93
Gutman, Eugene, **II** 281
Gutta Percha Co., **I** 428
Gutzeit. *See* AB W. Gutzeit & Co. *and* W. Gutzeit & Co.
Gutzeit, Hans, **IV** 274
Guy Carpenter & Co., **III** 282
GW Utilities Ltd., **I** 264
Gwathmey & Co., **II** 424
Gwilt, George, **III** 361
Gwinn, W.P., **I** 85
Gwynn, William, **V** 552
Gyllenhammar, Pehr G., **I** 210–11
Gypsum, Lime, & Alabastine Canada Ltd., **IV** 271
Gysler, Friedrich, **III** 402

H.A. Job, **II** 587
H.B. Claflin Company, **V** 139
H.B. Reese Candy Co., **II** 511
H.C. Christians, **II** 536
H.C. Frick Coke Co., **IV** 573
H.C. Petersen & Co., **III** 417
H.D. Pochin & Co., **III** 690
H.F. Ahmanson & Company, II 181–82
H.F. Ahmanson Co., **II** 181
H. Fairweather and Co., **I** 592
H. Hackfeld & Co., **I** 417
H. Hamilton Pty, Ltd., **III** 420
H.I. Rowntree and Co., **II** 568
H.J. Green, **II** 556
H.J. Heinz Co., Ltd., **II** 508; **III** 21
H.J. Heinz Company, I 30–31, 605, 612; **II** 414, 480, 450, **507–09,** 547
H.L. Judd Co., **III** 628
H.M. Gousha Co., **IV** 677, 678
H.P. Foods, **II** 475
H.P. Smith Paper Co., **IV** 290
H.R. MacMillan Export Co., **IV** 306, 307, 308
H. Reeve Angel & Co., **IV** 300
H.V. McKay Proprietary, **III** 651
H.W. Heidmann, **I** 542
H.W. Johns Manufacturing Co., **III** 706
H.W. Johns-Manville Corp., **III** 663, 706–08
H. Williams and Co., Ltd., **II** 678
Haack, Robert, **I** 66
Haagen Dazs, **II** 556, 557, 631
Haagn, Ernst (Dr.), **IV** 99

Haas, Carl, **IV** 323
Haas Corp., **I** 481
Haas, James, **V** 152
Haas, John, **I** 392–93
Haas, Otto, **I** 391–92
Haas, Rudolf Christian, **IV** 323
Haas, Walter, **V** 363
Haase, Alfred, **III** 185
Haber, Fritz, **I** 349
Haber, Ludwig F., **I** 369
Haberer, Jean Yves, **II** 260
Habib, Philip, **I** 559
Habirshaw Cable and Wire Corp., **IV** 177
Hachette, George, **IV** 617
Hachette, IV 614, 615, **617–19,** 675
Hachette, Louis, **IV** 617, 618
Hachette Première, **IV** 619
Hachette-Littérature, **IV** 617
Hachirobei, Takatoshi, **II** 325
Hachisuka, Mochiaki, **III** 383
Hachmeister, Inc., **II** 508
Hackblock, W.H., **I** 287
Hacker-Pschorr Brau, **II** 242
Hackfeld, Heinrich, **I** 417
Hadden, Briton, **IV** 673
Hadleigh-Crowther, **I** 715
Hafez Insurance Co., **III** 242
Haffner, Charles C. (Gen.), Jr., **IV** 661
Haft family, **II** 656
Hagan, Ward S., **I** 711–12
Hagen, James A., **V** 436
Häggert, Carl Erick, **I** 664
Haggerty, Patrick E., **II** 112, 113, 114
Haggie, **IV** 91
Haggin, James Ben Ali, **I** 527
Haglund, Wilhelm, **IV** 203
Hagstrom, Tony, **V** 332
Hagura, Nobuya, **II** 274
Hahn, Carl C., **I** 207–08
Hahn, T. Marshall, Jr., **IV** 282, 283
Hahnemann, Paul, **I** 139
Haid, Paul, **III** 241
Haig, Alexander, **I** 86, 559
Hain Pure Food Co., **I** 514
Hainaut-Sambre, **IV** 52
Hait, James M., **I** 442–43
Hakkarainen, Niilo, **IV** 349, 350
A.B. Hakon Swenson, **II** 639
Halaby, Najeeb, **I** 116
Halbou, Alphonse, **IV** 52
Halcon International, **IV** 456
Haldeman, H.R., **I** 20
Hale, Charles, **I** 314
Hale, Prentis, **V** 29, 30
Halfords, **V** 17, 19
Halfords Ltd., **IV** 382, 383
Halifax Banking Co., **II** 220
Halifax (Lord), **I** 107
Halifax, **III** 309
Halifax Timber, **I** 335
Hall, A. Rupert, **I** 715
Hall and Co., **III** 737
Hall and Ham River, **III** 739
Hall & Levine Agency, **I** 14
Hall, Arnold (Sir), **I** 51; **III** 509
Hall, Arthur Fletcher, **III** 274–75
Hall Bros. Co., **IV** 620, 621
Hall, Charles Martin, **IV** 14
Hall Containers, **III** 739
Hall, Donald, **IV** 620, 621
Hall, Edward Smith, **II** 388
Hall, Floyd, **I** 102
Hall, Harold, **V** 485
Hall, John, **III** 285

Hall, John R., **IV** 374
Hall, Joseph, **II** 644
Hall, Joyce C., **IV** 620–21
Hall, Perry, **II** 431
Hall, Rollie, **IV** 620
Hall, Ronald E., **IV** 392, 393
Hall, Wilfred, **IV** 271–72
Hall, William, **IV** 620
Hallamore Manufacturing Co., **I** 481
Hallas-Moller, Gudrun, **I** 658
Hallas-Moller, Knud, **I** 658–59
Halle, Pentti, **IV** 276
Haller, Raymond & Brown, Inc., **II** 10
Halliburton Company, II 112; **III** 473, **497–500,** 617
Halliburton, Erle Palmer, **III** 497, 498
Halliburton Oil Well Cementing Co., **III** 497–98
Halliburton, Vida, **III** 497
Hallivet China Clay Co., **III** 690
Hallmark Cards, Inc., IV 620–21
Hallstein, D. Wayne, **III** 526
Haloid Co., **II** 159; **III** 171
Haloid Xerox, **III** 171–72
Halpern, Ralph, **V** 2
Halsey, Brenton S., **IV** 289, 290
Halsey, Stuart & Co., **II** 431; **III** 276
Halske, J.G., **II** 97
Halstead, Ronald (Sir), **III** 66
Halsted, G.A. (Capt.), **III** 278
Ham, Arthur, **IV** 418
Hamada, Hiroshi, **III** 160
Hamada Printing Press, **IV** 326
Hamanaka, Shoichiro, **V** 479
Hamashbir Lata'asiya, **II** 47
Hambro Life Assurance, **I** 426
Hambros, **II** 422
Hamburg Banco, **II** 351
Hamburg-Amerika, **I** 542
Hamburger Flugzeubau GmbH., **I** 74
Hamersley Holdings, **IV** 59–60, 61
Hamersley Iron, **IV** 59, 60
Hamilton Aero Manufacturing, **I** 47, 84
Hamilton, Alex D., **IV** 272
Hamilton, Alexander, **II** 207, 216
Hamilton Blast Furnace Co., **IV** 208
Hamilton Brown Shoe Co., **III** 528
Hamilton, David, **III** 522
Hamilton, George (Lord), **IV** 217
Hamilton, Lloyd N., **IV** 536
Hamilton Malleable Iron Co., **IV** 73
Hamilton Oil Corp., **IV** 47
Hamilton, Richard W., **IV** 645
Hamilton Steel and Iron Co., **IV** 208
Hamilton, William, **III** 369
Hamish Hamilton, **IV** 659
Hamlet, Kenneth, **III** 94, 95
Hamlyn, Paul, **IV** 667
Hammamatsu Commerce Bank, **II** 291
Hammarforsens Kraft, **IV** 339
Hammer, Armand, **IV** 392, 480–82
Hammer, Frances, **IV** 480
Hammerich & Lesser, **IV** 589
Hammermill Paper Co., **IV** 287
Hammerson, Lew, **IV** 696
Hammerson Property and Investment Trust, **IV** 696–97
Hammerson Property Investment and Development Corporation PLC, IV 696–98
Hammerstein, Oscar, II, **IV** 671
Hammond Corp., **IV** 136
Hammond, John Hays, **IV** 95
Hammond Lumber Co., **IV** 281

Ricard, Patrick, **I** 280–81
Ricard, Paul, **I** 280
Riccardo, John J., **I** 145
Rice Broadcasting Co., Inc., **II** 166
Rice, Caleb, **III** 285
Rice, George W., **III** 285
Rice, Isaac L.; **I** 57
Rice-Stix Dry Goods, **II** 414
Rice, Victor A., **III** 650, 652
Rich, Lee, **II** 149
Rich, Marc, **II** 170, 171
Richard D. Irwin Inc., **IV** 602, 603, 678
Richard Hellman Co., **II** 497
Richard Manufacturing Co., **I** 667
Richard Shops, **III** 502
Richard Thomas & Baldwins, **IV** 42
Richards Bay Minerals, **IV** 91
Richards, Benjamin Wood, **II** 315
Richards, J. T., **IV** 408, 409
Richards, Michael, **I** 592–93
Richardson, Frank H., **IV** 541
Richardson, J. Ernest, **IV** 308
Richardson, Kenneth, **I** 196
Richardson-Vicks Co., **III** 53
Richdale, Gordon, **IV** 79
Richetti, Edmondo, **III** 207
Richfield Oil Corp., **IV** 375, 376, 456
Richie, Lionel, **I** 278
Richman, John M., **II** 533–34
Richmond Corp., **I** 600
Richter, Hermann, **IV** 141
Ricils, **III** 47
Rickel Home Centers, **II** 673
Rickenbacker, Eddie, **I** 78, 99, 101–02, 475
Ricker, John B., Jr., **III** 243
Rickover, Hyman, **I** 59
Ricoh Company, Ltd., III 121, 157, **159–61**, 172, 454
Ricoh Corp. (Canada), **III** 160
Ricoh Electronics, **III** 159, 160
Ricoh Espana, **III** 160
Ricoh Finance, **III** 160
Ricoh France, **III** 160
Ricoh Industrie France, **III** 160
Ricoh Industries USA, **III** 159
Ricoh Nederlands, **III** 160
Ricoh of America, **III** 159
Ricoh UK Products Ltd., **III** 160
Ridder, Bernard, **IV** 582, 629
Ridder, Bernard H., Jr., **IV** 612–13, 629, 630
Ridder, Herman, **IV** 628, 629
Ridder, Joseph, **IV** 582, 629
Ridder Publications, **IV** 612–13, 629
Ridder, Tony, **IV** 630
Ridder, Victor, **IV** 582, 629
Ridge Tool Co., **II** 19
Ridgely, Henry, **II** 315
Rieck-McJunkin Dairy Co., **II** 533
Riedy, John K., **III** 530
Riegel Bag & Paper Co., **IV** 344
Riegel, John S., **IV** 344
Rieke Corp., **III** 569
Riemsdijk, Henk van, **II** 79
Rieter, Heinrich (Col.), **III** 402
Rieter Machine Works, **III** 638
Riggio, Vincent, **I** 13
Riggs, Gus, **II** 34
Rijkens, Paul, **II** 589
Riken Corp., **IV** 160
Riken Kankoshi Co. Ltd., **III** 159
Riken Optical Co., **III** 159
Riku-un Moto Kaisha, **V** 477

Riley, Richard, **III** 440
Riley, W.P., **III** 261
Riney, Hal, **I** 26
Ringköpkedjan, **II** 640
Ringoen, Richard M., **I** 597–98
Rinker Materials Corp., **III** 688
Rio Grande Oil Co., **IV** 375, 456
Rio Grande Valley Gas Co., **IV** 394
Rio Tinto Co., **IV** 58, 189–91
Rio Tinto Mining Co. of Australia, **IV** 59
Rio Tinto-Zinc Corp., **II** 628; **IV** 56, 58, 59, 60, 61, 380
Rioblanco, **II** 477
Riordan Holdings Ltd., **I** 457
Ris, Victor, **III** 697
Rising, Adolf, **I** 625
Rising Sun Petroleum Co., **IV** 431, 460, 542
Risk Planners, **II** 669
Risse, Klaus H., **I** 654
Rit Dye Co., **II** 497
Ritchie, Cedric E., **II** 223
Ritchie, Martin, **IV** 259
Rite Aid Corporation, V 174–76
Rite-Way Department Store, **II** 649
Rittenhouse and Embree, **III** 269
Ritty, James, **III** 150
Ritty, John, **III** 150
Riunione Adriatica di Sicurtà SpA, III 185, 206, **345–48**
River-Raisin Paper Co., **IV** 345
River Steam Navigation Co., **III** 522
Rivett, Rohan, **IV** 650
Riviana Foods, **III** 24, 25
Rizzoli Publishing, **IV** 586, 588
RJR Nabisco, **I** 249, 259, 261; **II** 370, 426, 477–78, 542–44. *See also* Nabisco Brands, Inc.
RJR Nabisco Holdings Corp., V 408–10, 415
RKO. *See* Radio-Keith-Orpheum
RMC-Australia, **III** 738
RMC Group p.l.c., III 734, **737–40**
RMF Inc., **I** 412
Roach, Hal, **II** 147, 148
Roach, John, **II** 106, 107
Roadway Bodegas y Consolidación, 503
Roadway Express, **V** 502–03
Roadway Package System, (RPS), **V** 503
Roadway Services, Inc., V 502–03
Roaman's, **V** 115
Roan Consolidated Mines Ltd., **IV** 239, 240
Roan Selection Trust Ltd., **IV** 18, 239, 240
Robarts, David, **II** 334
Robbers, Jacobus George, **IV** 610
Robbins Co., **III** 546
Robbins, Harold, **IV** 672
Robbins, Joseph, **II** 666
Robbins, Julius, **II** 666
Robeco Group, **IV** 193
Robens (Lord), **IV** 39
Roberk Co., **III** 603
Robert Allen Cos., **III** 571
Robert Benson & Co. Ltd., **II** 232, 421
Robert Benson, Lonsdale & Co. Ltd., **II** 421, 422; **IV** 191
Robert Bosch GmbH., I 392–93, 411; **III** 554, 555, 591, 593
Robert Fleming & Co., **I** 471; **IV** 79
Robert Grace Contracting Co., **I** 584
Robert, Joseph C., **I** 336
Robert R. Mullen & Co., **I** 20

Robert W. Baird & Co., **III** 324
Robert Warschauer and Co., **II** 270
Robert Watson & Co. Ltd., **I** 568
Roberts Express, **V** 503
Roberts, George A., **I** 523
Roberts, John C., **III** 528
Roberts, John G., **I** 508
Roberts, Johnson & Rand Shoe Co., **III** 528, 529
Roberts, Leslie, **II** 426
Roberts, Roy, **IV** 480
Robertson, A.W., **II** 120–21
Robertson, Brian, **V** 421
Robertson, Charles, **II** 644
Robertson, Cliff, **II** 136
Robertson, Hugh, **II** 123
Robertson, Mary Ella, **III** 267
Robertson, Nelson, **III** 257
Robertson, Norman T., **III** 241
Robertson, Oran W., **V** 55
Robertson, Reuben B., **IV** 263, 264
Robertson, Reuben B., Jr., **IV** 264
Robertson, Robert M., **IV** 278
Robespierre, Maximilian, **III** 391
Robinson Clubs, **II** 163, 164
Robinson-Danforth Commission Co., **II** 561
Robinson, Edward G., **II** 175
Robinson, Henry, **IV** 569
Robinson, Henry S., **III** 238
Robinson-Humphrey, **II** 398
Robinson, James D., III., **II** 398; **IV** 637
Robinson, Morris, **III** 305
Robinson, R.G., **IV** 708
Robinson Radio Rentals, **I** 531
Robinson, W.S., **IV** 95
Robinson's Japan Co. Ltd., **V** 89
Roc, **I** 272
Rocco, Fiammetta, **III** 335
Roche Products Ltd., **I** 643
Rochereau, Denfert, **II** 232
Rochester American Insurance Co., **III** 191
Rochester German Insurance Co., **III** 191
Rock, Arthur, **II** 44
Rock, David, **IV** 577
Rock Island Oil & Refining Co., **IV** 448–49
Rock-Tenn Co., **IV** 312
Rockcor Ltd., **I** 381
Rockefeller & Andrews, **IV** 426
Rockefeller Center Properties, **IV** 714
Rockefeller, David, **II** 248
Rockefeller family, **I** 286; **III** 80, 347
Rockefeller Group, **IV** 714
Rockefeller, James, **II** 254
Rockefeller, John D., **II** 247, 397; **IV** 31, 368, 379, 426, 427, 428, 429, 463, 488, 530, 714; **V** 590
Rockefeller, William, **IV** 31, 426, 427, 463, 464
Rockefeller, William A., **IV** 426
Rockford Drilling Co., **III** 439
Rockmoor Grocery, **II** 683
Rockne, Knute, **I** 54
Rockower of Canada Ltd., **II** 649
Rockport Company, **V** 376–377
Rockwell International, I 71, **78–80,** 154–55, 186; **II** 3, 94, 379
Rockwell-Standard, **I** 79
Rockwell, Willard, **I** 79–80
Rockwell, Willard, Jr., **I** 79–80
Rocky Mountain Pipe Line Co., **IV** 400
Rodamco, **IV** 698

South Improvement Co., **IV** 427
South Manchuria Railroad Co. Ltd., **IV** 434
South Penn Oil Co., **IV** 488, 489
South Puerto Rico Sugar Co., **I** 452
South Puerto Rico Telephone Co., **I** 462
South Sea Textile, **III** 705
South Texas Stevedore Co., **IV** 81
Southco, **II** 602, 603
Southeast Banking Corp., **II** 252
Southern Biscuit Co., **II** 631
Southern California Edison Co., **II** 402; **V** 711, 713, 714, 715, 717
Southern California Gas Co., **I** 569
Southern Casualty Insurance Co., **III** 214
Southern Clay Products, **III** 691
Southern Clays Inc., **IV** 82
Southern Comfort Corp., **I** 227
Southern Company, V 721–23
Southern Connecticut Newspapers Inc., **IV** 677
Southern Cotton Co., **IV** 224
Southern Cotton Oil Co., **I** 421
Southern Extract Co., **IV** 310
Southern Gage, **III** 519
Southern Guaranty Cos., **III** 404
Southern Japan Trust Bank, **V** 114
Southern Kraft Corp., **IV** 286
Southern National Bankshares of Atlanta, **II** 337
Southern Natural Gas Co., **III** 558
Southern Nitrogen Co., **IV** 123
Southern Pacific Railroad, **I** 13; **II** 329, 381, 448; **IV** 625
Southern Pacific Transportation Company, V 516–18
Southern Peru Copper Corp., **IV** 33
Southern Pine Lumber Co., **IV** 341
Southern Railway Company, **V** 484, 485
Southern States Trust Co., **II** 336
Southern Sun Hotel Corp., **I** 288
Southern Surety Co., **III** 332
Southern Television Corp., **II** 158; **IV** 650
Southern Utah Fuel Co., **IV** 394
Southland Corporation, II 449, 660–61; **IV** 392, 508; **V** 89
Southland Ice Co., **II** 660
Southlife Holding Co., **III** 218
Southview Pulp Co., **IV** 329
Southwest Airlines Co., **I** 106
Southwest Airmotive Co., **II** 16
Southwest Forest Industries, **IV** 287, 289, 334
Southwest Potash Corp., **IV** 18
Southwestern Bell Corporation, V 328–30
Southwestern Life Insurance, **I** 527; **III** 136
Southwestern Pipe, **III** 498
Southwestern Refining Co., Inc., **IV** 446
Sovereign Corp., **III** 221
Soye, C. Van, **II** 305
SP Reifenwerke, **V** 253
SP Tyres, **V** 253
Spacemakers Inc., **IV** 287
Spackman, Walter S., **II** 479
Spang, Joseph P., Jr., **III** 28
Spanish International Communication, **IV** 621
Spanish River Pulp and Paper Mills, **IV** 246
Sparklets Ltd., **I** 315
Sparks, Jack D., **III** 654
Spartan Food Systems, Inc., **I** 127; **II** 679–80

Spater, George A., **I** 90
Spear, Lawrence, **I** 57
Spécia, **I** 388
Special Light Alloy Co., **IV** 153
Specialty Papers Co., **IV** 290
SpeeDee Marts, **II** 661
Speer, Edgar B., **IV** 574
Speer, Roy M., **V** 77
Speich, Rudolf, **II** 369
Speidel Newspaper Group, **IV** 612
Spence, Richard C., **V** 435
Spencer Beef, **II** 536
Spencer Gifts, **II** 144
Spencer, Percy, **II** 85, 86
Spencer, Tom, **V** 124
Spencer, Walter O., **III** 745
Spencer, William, **IV** 437
Spenco Medical Corp., **III** 41
Spenser, Mark, **II** 250
Spero, Joan E., **I** 464
Sperry Aerospace Group, **II** 40, 86
Sperry Corp., **I** 101, 167; **III** 165, 642
Sperry Milling Co., **II** 501
Sperry Rand Corp., **II** 63, 73; **III** 126, 129, 149, 166, 329, 642
Spethmann, Dieter, **IV** 222
Spicer, Clarence, **I** 152
Spicer Manufacturing Co., **I** 152; **III** 568
Spie-Batignolles, **I** 563; **II** 93, 94
Spiegel, **III** 598; **V** 160
Spielberg, Steven, **II** 144
Spielvogel, Carl, **I** 18, 27
Spillers, **II** 500
Spin Physics, **III** 475, 476
Spirella Company of Great Britain Ltd., **V** 356
Spizzico, Giacinto, **IV** 588
Spock, Benjamin (Dr.), **IV** 671
Spokane Gas and Fuel, **IV** 391
Spom Japan, **IV** 600
Spoor Behrins Campbell and Young, **II** 289
Spoor, William H., **II** 556, 557
Sporck, Charles L., **II** 63, 64
Sporn, Philip, **V** 547–48
Sporting News Publishing Co., **IV** 677–78
Sports Experts Inc., **II** 652
Sprague Co., **I** 410
Sprague Electric Railway and Motor Co., **II** 27
Sprague, Frank Julian, **II** 27
Sprague, Peter, **II** 63
Sprague, Warner & Co., **II** 571
Sprayon Products, **III** 745
Spray-Rite, **I** 366
Spriggs, Frank S., **III** 508
Spring Industries, Inc., V 378–379
Spring Valley Brewery, **I** 265
Springbok Editions, **IV** 621
Springer, Axel Cäsar, **IV** 589–90, 591
Springer family, **IV** 591
Springer, Ferdinand, **IV** 641
Springer, Friede, **IV** 590, 591
Springer, Julius, **I** 410
Springer Verlag GmbH & Co., **IV** 611, 641
Springhouse Corp., **IV** 610
Springhouse Financial Corp., **III** 204
Springorum, Friedrich, **IV** 104
Springorum, Fritz, **IV** 104
Springs, Elliott White, **V** 378–379
Springs, Leroy, **V** 378
Springsteen, Bruce, **II** 134
Sprint. *See* US Sprint Communications

Sprott, J.S., **I** 201
Spruce Falls Power and Paper Co., **III** 40; **IV** 648
Squibb Beech-Nut, **I** 695–96
Squibb Corporation, I 380–81, 631, 651, 659, 675, **695–97**; **III** 17, 19, 67
Squibb, Edwin Robinson, **I** 695
SR Beteiligungen Aktiengesellschaft, **III** 377
Ssangyong Cement (Singapore), **III** 748
Ssangyong Cement Industrial Co., Ltd., **III** 747–50
Ssangyong Computer Systems Corp., **III** 749
Ssangyong Construction Co. Ltd., **III** 749
Ssangyong Corp., **III** 748
Ssangyong Engineering Co. Ltd., **III** 749
Ssangyong Heavy Industries Co., **III** 748
Ssangyong Investment & Securities Co., **III** 749
Ssangyong Motor Co., **III** 750
Ssangyong Oil Refining Co. Ltd., **III** 748, 749; **IV** 536, 537, 539
Ssangyong Paper Co., **III** 748, 749
Ssangyong Precision Industry Co., **III** 748
Ssangyong Shipping Co. Ltd., **III** 748
Ssangyong Software & Data Co., **III** 749
Ssangyong Trading Co. Ltd., **III** 748
SSC&B, **I** 17
SSC&B: Lintas Worldwide, **I** 16
SSMC Inc., **II** 10
Stadelman, George M., **V** 244
Städtische Elecktricitäts-Werke A.G., **I** 410
Stafford, John M., **II** 556
Stafford, John R., **I** 624
Stafford Old Bank, **II** 307
Stag Cañon Fuel Co., **IV** 177
Stahle, Hans, **III** 420
Stahlwerke Peine-Salzgitter AG, **IV** 201
Stahlwerke Röchling AG, **III** 694, 695
Stahlwerke Röchling-Buderus AG, **III** 695
Stahlwerke Südwestfalen AG, **IV** 89
Stal-Astra GmbH, **III** 420
STAL Refrigeration AB, **III** 420
Staley Continental, **II** 582
Stalin, Josef, **I** 166; **IV** 314, 348, 448
Stampleman, Samuel C., **III** 28
Standard Accident Co., **III** 332
Standard Aero, **III** 509
Standard Aircraft Equipment, **II** 16
Standard and Chartered Bank Ltd., **II** 358, 386
Standard and Chartered Banking Group Ltd., **II** 357–58
Standard and Chartered Leasing, **II** 357
Standard & Poor's Corp., **IV** 29, 482, 636, 637
Standard Bank, **II** 319, 357
Standard Bank of British South Africa, **II** 357
Standard Bank of Canada, **II** 244
Standard Brands, **I** 248; **II** 542, 544
Standard Chartered Bank, **II** 357
Standard Chartered PLC, II 298, 309, **357–59**
Standard Chemical Products, **III** 33
Standard Drug Co., **V** 171
Standard Electric Lorenz A.G., **II** 13, 70
Standard Electrica, **II** 13
Standard Equities Corp., **III** 98
Standard Fire Insurance Co., **III** 181, 182
Standard Fruit and Steamship Co. of New Orleans, **II** 491

NOTES ON ADVISERS AND CONTRIBUTORS

ANDERSON, Linda. Subeditor on the International Companies Newsdesk at the *Financial Times*, London.

ARIMA, Kenji. Teaching assistant at Waseda University, Tokyo.

BADARRACO, Claire. Assistant Professor, College of Communication, Marquette University, Milwaukee, Wisconsin. Author of annotated edition of *The Cuba Journal 1833-35 of Sophia Peabody Hawthorne*, 1984, and *R.R. Donnelley's "Four American Books Campaign" at The Lakeside Press 1926-1930*, 1990. Guest editor for "Publicity and American Culture" issue of *Public Relations Review*, 1990.

BARANÉS, William. Administrative Judge at the Administrative Tribunal of Versailles. Author of articles in various magazines, including *Autrement, Ça m'intéresse, Qui Vive,* and *Stratégies Télématiques.*

BARBOUR, Philippe A. Editor, St. James Press, London. Editor of *Wine '89*, 1989, and co-author of *Wine Buyers Guide: Saint Emilion*, 1991.

BARKER, T.C. Professor Emeritus of Economic History, University of London; President, International Historical Congress, 1990-95. Author of *A Merseyside Town in the Industrial Revolution*, 1954, *A History of the Worshipful Company of Carpenters*, 1968, *A History of British Pewter*, 1974, *The Economic and Social Effects of the Spread of Motor Vehicles*, 1987, *Moving Millions*, 1990, and other works in business history.

BAUERT-KEETMAN, Ingrid. Author and archivist. Author of *Deutsche Industrie-Pioniere*, 1966, *Raiffeisen. Verwirklichung einer Idee*, 1st edition 1970, 2nd edition 1987, and of numerous company monographs, including *Chronik der Kaufhof Holding AG*, as yet unpublished.

BELSITO, Elaine. Free-lance writer and editor. Assistant Managing Editor, *Archives of Physical Medicine and Rehabilitation*, 1988-90.

BLOCK, Bernard A. Documents Librarian and Assistant Professor, Ohio State University Libraries, Columbus, Ohio. Author of "Romance and High Purpose: The National Geographic," *Wilson Library Bulletin*, 1984, and "A Magazinist's View of the Encyclopedia of Associations," *The Reference Librarian*, 1990.

BLOOM, Martin. Associate Fellow, Royal Institute of International Affairs, London, and Director, Emblem Research Associates Ltd. Author of "Linking Regional Policy to Industrial and Technology Policy," *Japan Forum*, volume 2, no. 1, April 1990, *Technological Change and the Korean Electronics Industry*, 1992, and "Japan: Compounding its Component Success," *Business Technology International*, Issue 1, 1992.

BONAVIA, Michael Robert. Author and consultant. Formerly Chief Officer, British Railways Board. Author of, among others, *The Economics of Transport*, 1963, *The Orga-*

nisation of British Railways, 1971, *The Birth of British Rail*, 1979, *The Four Great Railways*, 1980, *Railway Policy Between the Wars*, 1981, *British Rail: the First 25 Years*, 1981, *The History of the London & North Eastern Railway*, 1983, *Twilight of British Rail?*, 1985, *The Nationalisation of British Transport*, 1987, *The History of Southern Railway*, 1987, *The Channel Tunnel Story*, 1987, *Historic Railway Sites in Britain*, 1987.

BOWMAN, Jim. Corporate history writer, writing teacher, Columbia College, Chicago, Illinois. Columnist, *Chicago Tribune*, 1982-85. Reporter, *Chicago Daily News*, 1968-78. Author of *Good Medicine: The First 150 Years of Rush-Presbyterian-St.Luke's Medical Center*, 1987, and *"Waste Not . . .": The Safety-Kleen Story*, 1989.

BRASS, Richard. Free-lance writer. Formerly Marketing and Media Editor and banking writer, *The Australian Financial Review*, 1988-91, and industrial reporter, *Tribune Newspaper*, Sydney, 1986-88.

BRIGGS, Asa. Historian. Formerly Provost, Worcester College, Oxford University, 1976-91; Vice-Chancellor, University of Sussex, 1967-76; Professor of History, University of Sussex, 1961-1976; Professor of Modern History, Leeds University, 1955-61. Author of *Victorian People*, 1954, *The Age of Improvement*, 1959, *History of Broadcasting in the United Kingdom*, four volumes, 1961, 1965, 1970 and 1979, *Victorian Cities*, 1963, *A Social History of England*, 1983, *Victorian Things*, 1988, and many other works on history.

BRÜNINGHAUS, Beate. Manager of the Society for Business History, Cologne; member of editorial staff of the *Zeitschrift für Unternehmensgeschichte* (ZUG) since 1983 and the *German Yearbook on Business History*, 1984-89. Co-author of "Die Daimler-Benz AG in den Jahren 1933 bis 1945," *ZUG*, 1987.

BUSCH, Berthold. Consultant, *Institut der deutschen Wirtschaft*, Cologne.

BYDE, Noel Peter. Chief sub-editor at Spain's international news agency, EFE, and free-lance journalist.

CAFFARRA, Cristina. Research Officer, Oxford Institute for Energy Studies. Co-author of *Interdipendenza e Instabilità nei Regioni Oligopolistici: Il Caso del Petrolio*, 1988, "Petroleum Stocks: Role, Perceptions and Reality," in *Oxford Energy Forum*, Volume 1, no. 3, 1990, "The Role and Behaviour of Oil Inventories," working paper, 1990, "The Search for Oil in a Low Price Environment," working paper, forthcoming.

CHANDLER, Alfred D., Jr. Straus Professor of Business History, Emeritus, Graduate School of Business Administration, Harvard University, Cambridge, Massachusetts. Author of *Strategy and Structure: Chapters in the History of the American Industrial Enterprise*, 1962, *The Visible Hand: The Managerial Revolution in American Business*, 1977, winner of the

Pulitzer Prize for History, 1978, *Managerial Hierarchies*, 1980, *The Coming of Managerial Capitalism*, 1985, *Scale and Scope: The Dynamics of Industrial Capitalism*, 1990, and other works in business history.

CHEPESIUK, Ron. Head of Special Collections, Dacus Library, Winthrop College, Rock Hill, South Carolina. Author of *Chester County: A Pictorial History*, 1985.

CHIDA, Tomohei. Professor, Aoyama Gakuin University. Co-author with P.N. Davies of *The Japanese Shipping and Shipbuilding Industries, A History of their Modern Growth*, 1990.

CLASSE, Alison. Free-lance writer and computer consultant. Contributor to *Computing, Accountancy, Banking Systems International*, and to *The Annual Obituary 1989*.

CLASSE, Olive. Free-lance writer and translator. Formerly Senior Lecturer in French, University of Glasgow, retired 1990. Author of "*En quelle situation?* Some notes on Racine's *Phèdre*," *Newsletter of the Society for Seventeenth Century French Studies*, 1982, and critical notes in J. Pradon's *Phèdre et Hippolyte*, Textes littéraires LXII, University of Exeter, 1987.

COLEMAN, D.C. Professor Emeritus of Economic History, Cambridge University. Author of *Courtaulds. An Economic and Social History*, three volumes, 1969 and 1980, and of *The British Paper Industry: 1495-1860*, 1958. Formerly joint editor, *Economic History Review*, 1967-1972, and English editor, *Scandinavian Economic History Review*, 1952-1961.

COLLINS, Lisa. Associate Editor, *Crain's Chicago Business*. Reporter, *The Des Moines Register*, 1986-89.

CROMPTON, Gerald W. Lecturer in Economic and Social History, University of Kent at Canterbury. Author of "Issues in British Trade Union Organisation 1890-1914," *Archiv für Sozialgeschichte*, XX, 1980, and "Squeezing the Pulpless Orange: Labour and Capital on the Railways in the Inter-War Years," *Business History*, XXXI, 1989. Editor of *Trade Unions in the Victorian Age—Debates on the Issue from 19th Century Critical Journals*, four volumes, 1973.

DAUNTON, Martin James. Professor of Modern History, University College, London. Author of *Coal Metropolis: Cardiff, 1870-1914*, 1977, *Royal Mail: The Post Office since 1840*, 1985, *House and Home in the Victorian City: Working-Class Housing, 1850-1914*, 1983, and *A Property Owning Democracy? Housing in Britain*, 1987.

DORAN, Clare. Assistant correspondent for the Japanese daily newspaper *Yomiuri Shimbun*. Contributor to the *The Daily Yomiuri* and to the *Kyushu Post*, magazines for the English speaking community in Japan.

DU RY, Marc. Training psychoanalyst. Editor of the journal of the Centre for Freudian Analysis and Research, London.

DUBOVOJ, Sina. History contractor and free-lance writer; Adjunct Professor of History, Montgomery College, Rockville, Maryland.

FRENCH, Michael John. Lecturer, Department of Economic History, University of Glasgow. Author of "Structural Change and Competition in the United States Tire Industry, 1920-1937," *Business History Review*, spring 1986, and of *The U.S. Tire Industry: A History*, 1991.

FUCHS, Konrad. Professor, History Department, Johannes-Gutenberg-Universität, Mainz.

GAUDILLAT, Anne-Laure. French teacher at the French Institute, London. Formerly manager at Peugeot SA, France.

GIETSCHIER, Steven P. Director of Historical Records, *The Sporting News*, St. Louis. Formerly Supervisor, Repository Services Division, South Carolina Department of Archives and History, 1978-86, and Archivist, Ohio Labor History Project, Ohio Historical Society, 1975-78. Author of "Thomas C. Cochran," *Twentieth-Century American Historians, Dictionary of Literary Biography*, 1983, and "Leading Off: The First Years of *The Sporting News* Archives," *Provenance*, spring 1989.

GLASS, Lois. Free-lance writer and researcher in art history.

GOODALL, Francis. Business History Unit, London School of Economics. Author of *Bibliography of British Business Histories*, 1987, and contributor to the *Dictionary of Business Biography*, 1984-1986.

GOULD, Rowland G. President, Gould Communications, Inc., a global service in public relations, magazine articles, books and television programs. Formerly Foreign Correspondent in Asia and the Middle East, Mutual Broadcasting System, New York, and Managing Editor, *The Importer*, Tokyo, 1973-80; Supervising Editor, *Encyclopedia Britannica*, 1974 edition, updating Asia material, 1970-73; and Foreign Correspondent, radio and television, for NBC New York, 1960-70. Author of *The Matsushita Phenomenon*, 1970, and *Those Words that Bind*, 1989.

GRIFFIN, Jessica. Editor, St. James Press, London. Japanese Investment Manager, Thornton Group, London, 1987-89.

GROSS, Daniel. Graduate student in History, Harvard University, Cambridge, Massachusetts. Reporter for *The New Republic*, 1989-90.

GROSSMAN, William R. Free-lance writer. Author of *The Dating Maze*, 1989.

GURNEY, Judith. Senior Research Analyst, Resource Planning Corporation, Washington DC. Formerly Business Information Analyst, Harvard Business School, 1984-87;

Manuscript Editor, Harvard Business Review, 1982–84; Editor, British Petroleum, 1980–81; Publications Officer, Royal Institute of International Affairs, 1974–79; Editor, DC Heath (U.K.) 1967–73. Author of "The U.S. Strategic Petroleum Reserve," *Petroleum Review*, October 1990, "The U.S. Clean Air Act," *Petroleum Review*, December 1990, and "The Yemen Oil Rush," *Petroleum Review*, January 1991.

HAWKINS, Richard. Lecturer in European Studies (Economics), Wolverhampton Polytechnic. Compiler for the "Annual List of Publications on the Economic and Social History of Great Britain and Ireland," *Economic History Review*, since 1987. Author of "The Pineapple Canning Industry during the World Depression of the 1930s," *Business History*, 1989.

HAY, Charles C. III. Archivist, Eastern Kentucky University, Richmond, Kentucky.

HEALY, Carole. Free-lance writer. Contributing editor, *Global Press*, 1986–87. Has written business and feature articles for *The Washington Post*, *The Chicago Tribune*, and the *Daily Yomiuri* in Tokyo.

HEENAN, Patrick. Course Tutor, St. Catherine's College (University of Oxford), Kobe Institute, Japan. Editor, Books Department of Euromoney Publications, 1989–90. Editor of *1992*, 1990.

HINTON, Caroline. Free-lance journalist with *International Financing Review*. Formerly researcher and assistant producer with BBC News and Current Affairs.

HORSTMANN, Theo. Press Officer for VEW, Dortmund, and visiting lecturer for Economic and Social History at the Gesamthochschule Paderborn. Author of "Die Furcht vor dem finanziellen Kollaps—Banken- und Kreditpolitik in der britischen Besatzungszone 1945-1948," in *Wirtschaftspolitik im britischen Besatzungsgebiet*, 1984, " 'The Worst Banking Practice in the World'—The Inter-Allied Discussion over American Plans to Reform the German Banking System in 1945/46," in the *German Yearbook on Business History*, volume VI, 1986, "Demonstratives Status symbol oder ökonomisch fundierter Nützlichkeitsbau?—Ein Diskussionsbeitrag zur Funktion und Baugeschichte der Maschinenhalle auf Zeche 'Zollern II' in Dortmund," in *Technikgeschichte*, 1988, "Kontinuität und Wandel im deutschen Notenbanksystem—Die Bank deutscher Länder als Ergebnis alliierter Besatzungspolitik nach dem Zweiten Weltkrieg," in *Autonomie und Kontrolle. Beiträge zur Soziologie des Finanz- und Steuerstaates*, 1989, "Die 'Zweite Industrielle Revolution' in Westfalen. Zur Elektrifizierung einer Region," in *Electrotechnik für mehr Lebensqualität*, 1990, *Die Alliierten und die deutschen Grossbanken. Bankenpolitik nach dem Zweiten Weltkrieg in Westdeutschland*, 1991, " 'Die elektrische Ausstellung wollte der Mitwirkung der Künste nicht entraten': Kunst und Kunstgewerbe auf der Internationalen Elektrotechnischen Ausstellung 1891 in Frankfurt," in *Moderne Energie für eine neue Zeit*, 1991. Contributor to *Der Weg ins Licht. Zur Geschichte der Elektrifizierung des Märkischen Sauerlands*, 1989, and editor of *Elektrifizierung in Westfalen. Fotodokumente aus dem Archiv der VEW*, 1990.

JACOBSON, Robert R. Free-lance writer and musician.

JEFFERYS, James B. General Secretary of the International Association of Department Stores, Paris, retired. Author of *The Story of the Engineers, 1800-1945*, 1946, *Labour's Formative Years, 1849-1879*, 1948, *The Distribution of Consumer Goods*, 1950, *Retail Trading in Britain, 1850-1950*, 1954, *Productivity in the Distributive Trade in Europe*, 1954, and *The Distributive Trades in the Common Market*, 1973. Co-author of *National Income and Expenditure of the United Kingdom, 1870-1952* (with Dorothy Walters), 1955, *Retailing in Europe: present structure and future trends* (with Derek Knee), 1962, and *The Policies of European Department Stores in the Past Decade* (with Derek Knee), 1988.

JOHNSON, Debra. International economist specializing in the petroleum, chemical, and shipping industries. Author of *The Future of Plastics: Applications and Markets Worldwide*, Financial Times Management Report Series, 1990.

KALANIK, Lynn M. Advertising Copywriter, Richard D. Irwin Inc., Homewood, Illinois. Creative consultant and project director, The Waterkotte Co. Inc., Pittsburgh, Pennsylvania, 1987–88.

KEELEY, Carol I. Free-lance writer and researcher; columnist in *Neon*; researcher for *Ford Times* and *Discovery*. Author of *Oxford Poetry*, 1987, and *Voices International*, 1989.

KEELEY, Patrick. Free-lance economic and social researcher, Centre for Employment, Manchester, United Kingdom. Author of "A Devon Family and their Estates: The Northcotes of Upton Pyne, 1660-1851," in *Town and Countryside: The English Landowner in the National Economy, 1660-1870*, 1989.

KINSLEY, Julian James. Teacher in Tokyo. Formerly an in-house writer for the *London Dayori* newspaper.

KREMER, Stephen Christopher. Analyst, Anglo-Japanese Economic Institute, London. Author of "Asia and the Environment" in the *Wall Street Journal*, October 24, 1990.

LAMONTAGNE, Monique. Research student, Birkbeck College, University of London. Research assistant, St. Francis Xavier University, Nova Scotia, 1988–89. Research and archival officer, National Museums of Canada, 1983–85. Co-editor of *Reminiscences of the Rebellion of 1885*, 1985.

LARKE, Roy. Assistant Professor and researcher at the University of Marketing and Distribution, Kobe, Japan. Author of "The Pride of the Scots" (in Japanese), *RIRI Ryutsu Sangyo*, September 1988, "A Consideration of Consumer Loyalty in Japan," working paper, 1988, "Issues in European Retailing" (a series of ten articles in Japanese), *Nikkei Ryutsu Shinbun*, 1989–90, and of "Consumer Perceptions of Large Stores in Japan," unpublished PhD thesis, 1991.

LEUNIS, Joseph V. Professor of Marketing and Distribution at the Catholic University of Louvain (KU. Leuven), Belgium, and President of the Belgian Committee of Distribution, Brussels. Author of "Het Huff-model en de winkelkeuze," *Tijdschrift voor Economie en Management*, volume XXIX, no.1, 1984, and *Inleiding tot de Marketing*, 1990. Co-author of "Marketing into the next Century," *Corporate Revival: Managing into the Nineties*, 1988, "The Impact of Belgian Public Policy upon Retailing: the Case of the Second Padlock Law" in *Transnational Retailing*, 1991, and "Public policy and the establishment of large stores in Belgium" in *The International Review of Retail, Distribution and Consumer Research*, volume 1, no. 4, July 1991.

LEWIS, Scott M. Free-lance editor and writer; contributing editor, *Option*. Staff editor, *Security, Distributing and Marketing*, 1989–90.

LINDAUER, Wilson B. Free-lance writer.

LLOYD-OWEN, Jonathan. Free-lance writer, Japan.

LOIZOU, Andreas. Business analyst, City of London.

LOOS, Rachel. Free-lance journalist. Formerly assistant travel editor, features writer and news reporter on *The Sun-Herald*, Australia.

LUKE, Catriona. Marketing consultant at The Bloomsbury Centre for European Study Programmes, London, and free-lance writer. Author of *A Small Book of Extravagances*, 1987.

MACKERVOY, Susan. Lecturer in German, Reading University.

MAGON, Kim M. Consultant, KGM Communications; free-lance editor, *World Facts & Maps*. Associate Editor, Technical Reporting Corp., Chicago, 1985–88.

MARTIN, Jonathan. Free-lance writer; doctoral candidate in English, University of Chicago. Screenplay, *A Life of Her Own*, in production.

MOHNKE, Mary Sue. Free-lance writer. News Bureau Manager and Instructor, Northeastern Illinois University, Chicago, 1979–86; Coordinator of Public Information, Chicago Architecture Foundation, 1976–79; and Publications Editor, Roosevelt National Investment and Life Insurance Company, Springfield, Illinois, 1974–75. Author of "Partners Against Crime," *Illinois Quarterly*, 1990, and "Invisible Neighbors," *North Shore*, 1991.

MOLLA DESCALS, Alejandro. Professor of Marketing and Director, *Instituto Universitario de Gestion Empresarial* at the University of Valencia.

MONTGOMERY, Bruce P. Curator and Head of Western Historical Collections, University of Colorado at Boulder. Formerly Historian and Archivist, Communications Workers

of America, Washington DC, 1986–91; Historical and Archival Consultant, History Associates, Inc., Rockville, Maryland, 1985–86; and Hospital Archivist and Historian, St. Mary's Hospital of Rochester, Minnesota, 1984–85.

MOORE, Betty T. Free-lance writer. Fomerly Senior Editor, Joint Commission on Accreditation of Healthcare Organizations, Oakbrook Terrace, Illinois. Author of *How to Manage Financial Systems*, 1981, *Housing for the Elderly*, 1984, and *Quality Assurance in Ambulatory Care*, 1990.

MOSER, Eva. Researcher at the Förderkreis IHK-Wirtschaftsarchiv für München und Oberbayern e.V., Munich. Author of "Bayerns Arbeitgeberverbände im Wiederaufbau. Der Verein der Bayerischen Metallindustrie 1945–1962," a supplement to the *Zeitschrift für Unternehmensgeschichte*, issue 59, 1990.

NAGASHIMA, Kota. Assistant Professor at Tokyo International University. Author of "The Lifecycle of the Shopping Centre in Tokyo," in *City and Commerce*, 1986.

NORTON, Frances E. Free-lance writer; contributor to *Evanston Arts Review* and *Helicon*.

O'LEARY, D.H. Corporate lawyer. Formerly worked in commerce in Japan and in London.

PARRY, John. Free-lance writer. Formerly journalist, *International Management*, and analyst, Anglo-Japanese Economic Institute, London.

PROTAT, Florence. Information researcher. Formerly manager of in-house users' guides for advanced software and of documentation for computer facilities, Philips, Suresnes, France.

RING, Trudy. Free-lance writer and editor. Assistant editor, St. James Press, 1991–1992.

RITCHIE, Lionel Alexander. Curatorial Officer, Royal Commission on Historical Manuscripts, London. Author of *Modern British Shipbuilding: A Guide to Historical Records*, 1980, and of *The Shipbuilding Industry: A Guide to Historical Records*, forthcoming. Part of editorial team on *Records of British Business and Industry 1760–1914: Textiles and Leather*, 1990.

ROBERTS, Julia. Copywriter, K.L.P., London. Formerly copywriter at Basten Greenhill Andrews, London, 1989–1990, and at Young & Rubicam Advertising, Sydney, Australia.

ROSEMAN, Mark. Lecturer, History Department, Keele University. Author of *Recasting the Ruhr, 1945-1958. Manpower, economic recovery and labour relations*, 1992.

ROULAND, Roger W. Free-lance writer for *Chicago Tribune*, *Chicago Sun-Times*, and other newspapers. Author of "One bank era ends, another begins," *The Genoa-Kingston-Kirkland News*, 1987, received First Place Award in business news, Northern Illinois Newspaper Association.

ROURKE, Elizabeth. Free-lance writer.

SAHAFI, Maya. Free-lance writer. Developmental Editor, Arab Bank Limited, 1988.

SATOH, Norimasa. Professor at Obirin University, Tokyo. Author of "Business Administration in the Era of Internationalization," *Annual Bulletin of the Institute for Industrial Research of Obirin University,* 1987, "Individual and Organization," *Annual Bulletin of the Institute for Industrial Research of Obirin University,* 1988, "Management Philosophy in the Era of Management Culture," 1988, "Top Interview, The Owner of WELLA Co., Ltd.," *Kokusai Shogyo,* 1988, *The Foreign Company in Japan,* 1988, and *International Society and Business Administration,* 1990.

SCHUSTEFF, Sandy. Marketing and communications consultant; Adjunct Professor, Lake Forest Graduate School of Management, Lake Forest, Illinois.

SHANNON, Timothy J. Doctoral candidate in History, Northwestern University, Evanston, Illinois. Author of "The Ohio Company and the Meaning of Opportunity in the American West, 1786–1795," *New England Quarterly,* 1991.

SIEWERT, Clark. Free-lance writer and editor. Editor of *Financial Compliance Watch,* 1990–91, and *The London Traveletter,* 1985–89. Contract lawyer in the North Sea oil industry, 1981–83. Author of *The London Traveletter Guidebook,* 1989.

SIGSWORTH, Eric Milton. Late Professor of Economic and Social History, University of York. Author of, among others, "Bradford 1830–1870," *Round About Industrial Britain 1830–70, Black Dyke Mills, A History: with introductory chapters on the History of the Worsted Industry,* 1957, "Modern York," *Victoria County History of York,* 1963, "The Distribution of Wool Textiles," *The Wool Textile Industry: an Economic Analysis,* 1965, "Leeds in the Industrial Revolution," *Leeds and its Region,* 1967, *The Brewing Trade in the Industrial Revolution: The Case of Yorkshire,* 1967, "The Woollen and Worsted Industries 1875–1914," (with J. Blankman), *The Development of British Industry and Foreign Competition 1875–1914,* 1968, "Victorian Prostitution," (with T.E. Wyke), *Suffer and Be Still,* 1976, "The Wool Textile Industry," *Studies in Victorian Entrepreneurship,* 1980, *Montague Burton: The Tailor of Taste,* 1990. Editor of *In Search of Victorian Values: Aspects of Nineteenth-Century Thought and Society,* 1988. *Number 5 Tram,* a text of memories of Leeds, forthcoming. Died 1992.

SLINN, Judy. Free-lance business historian. Associate, Business History Unit, London School of Economics. Author of *A History of May & Baker 1834–1984,* 1984, and of *Linklaters & Paines: The First 150 Years,* 1987.

STABILE, Donald R. Professor of Economics, St. Mary's College of Maryland, St. Mary's City. Author of *Prophets of Order: The Rise of the New Class, Technocracy and Socialism in America,* 1984, and "The DuPont Experiments with Scientific Management: Efficiency and Safety, 1911–1919," *Business History Review,* 1987.

STEVENS, Paul. Free-lance writer.

SUN, Douglas. Doctoral candidate in English, University of Chicago. Author of book reviews in *Los Angeles Times,* 1988–89.

SWAN, John. Free-lance writer and researcher.

SWORSKY, Mary F. Editor, American Association of Law Libraries, Chicago, Illinois; free-lance writer.

TANNER, Dylan. Research Analyst, Intermatrix Ltd., London. Formerly management consultant at W.S. Atkins Ltd. and labor consultant, TMT, Tokyo.

TATSUKI, Mariko. Research fellow, Japan Business History Institute. From April 1992, Professor, Keisen Jogakuen College. Formerly Professor, Faculty of Economics, Teikyo University. Co-author of *The First Century of Mitsui O.S.K. Lines, Ltd.,* 1988, and of "Kigyo Keiei no Kekishiteki Kenkyu," 1990.

TELINGATOR, Susan. Free-lance writer. Author of *The Chicago Arts Guide,* forthcoming.

TOGAWA, Yoko. Director of the Research Division, Research Institute of Retail Industry and Distribution System (RIRI), Tokyo. Co-author of *New Era of Home-Shopping,* 1979, and of *Reconstruction of the Retailing and Distribution System in Japan,* 1991; author of "The Progress of Japanese Department Stores after World War II," RIRI, April 1980; co-author of "International Comparison of Distribution Systems," Economic Research Institute Economic Planning Agency, Government of Japan, 1991.

TUCKER, Thomas M. Free-lance writer.

VERNYI, Bruce. Reporter, *Plastics News.* Formerly reporter, *The Toledo Blade* and *American Metal Market;* free-lance contributor to *Business Week,* the *Wall Street Journal, National Real Estate Investor,* and *American Banker.*

VOSKUIL, Lynn M. Doctoral candidate in English, University of Chicago. Director, Office of Research Administration, Illinois Institute of Technology, Chicago, 1985–89.

WALSH, Ray. Free-lance writer and broadcaster. Author of "Cracking the Genetic Code," *In These Times,* 1989, and "Stalemate in Hormone-Raised Beef Dispute," *North American Farmer,* 1989.

WANKOFF, Jordan. Free-lance writer; co-editor of *Vice Versa* literary magazine. Museum Editor, *California Art Review,* 1989.

WOLF, Gillian. Free-lance writer. Author of "The Ultimate Slingshot," *Jewish Affairs*, 1989, and "Akh, Odessa!" *Jewish Affairs*, 1990.

WOODWARD, Angela. Free-lance writer. Author of "The Hand of Odeon," *Pig Iron: Labor & the Post-Industrial Age*, 1990.

WRAY, William D. Associate Professor, History Department, University of British Columbia. Author of *Mitsubishi and the N.Y.K., 1870–1914: Business Strategy in the Japanese Shipping Industry*, 1984, reprinted 1986, "NYK and the Commercial Diplomacy of the Far Eastern Freight Conference, 1896–1956," in *Business History of Shipping: Strategy and Structure*, 1985, *Japan's Economy: A Bibliography of its Past & Present*, 1989, "Japan's Big Three Service Enterprises in China, 1896–1936," in *The Japanese Informal Empire in China, 1895–1937*, 1989, "Kagami Kenkichi and the N.Y.K., 1929–1935: Vertical Control, Horizontal Strategy, and Company Autonomy," in *Managing Industrial Enterprise: Cases from Japan's Prewar Experience* (edited by William Wray—see especially "Afterword: The Writing of Japanese Business History"), 1989, and of " 'The Mitsui Fight', 1953–1956: Japan and the Far Eastern Freight Conference," in *Shipping and Trade, 1750–1950: Essays in International Maritime Economic History*, 1990.

YAMAZAKI, Hiroaki. Professor, Institute of Social Science, University of Tokyo. Author of, among others, *Nihon Kasensangyo Hattatsushi Ron* (an essay on the history of the Japanese chemical fiber industry), 1975.

YUI, Tsunehiko. Professor of Business History, Meiji University; Executive Director of the Japan Business History Institute, Tokyo. Formerly Executive Director of the Business History Society (Japan), 1984–1989. Author of *Historical Study on the Policies of the Small Business* (in Japanese), 1964, *The Development of Japanese Business, 1600–1980* (with Johannes Hirschmeier), 1983, and editor of *Japanese Management in Historical Perspective* (with Keiichiro Nakagawa), 1989. Author and editor of other works on business and company history.

YUZAWA, Takeshi. Professor of Business History, Gakushuin University, Tokyo. Author of "The Introduction of Electric Railways in Britain and Japan" in *The Journal of Transport History*, 3rd series, vol. 6, no. 1, March 1987, *Business History of English Railway* (in Japanese), 1988, "Das japanische Transportsystem als staatliches Unternehmen," in *Wissenschaftliche Zeitschrift der Humboldt-Universität zu Berlin*, 39. Jg. 1990 Heft 1, "The Transfer of Railway Technologies from Britain to Japan, with special reference to locomotive manufacture" in *International Technology Transfer, Europe, Japan and the USA, 1700–1914*, 1991, and co-editor of *Foreign Business in Japan before World War II*, 1990.

ZARACH, Stephanie. Business Development Manager of Book Production Consultants. Research Director of Debrett Business History Research Ltd., 1984–88. Editor of *Debrett's Bibliography of Business History*, 1987.